WORLD TREATY INDEX

Volume 1

INTRODUCTION

MAIN ENTRY SECTION

League of Nations Treaty Series

Volume 2

MAIN ENTRY SECTION

United Nations Treaty Series: Series I, Numbers 1–6485

Volume 3

MAIN ENTRY SECTION

United Nations Treaty Series: Series I, Numbers 6486–10841; Series II, Numbers 1–657

National Treaty Collections

Volume 4

CHRONOLOGICAL SECTION

PARTY SECTION

INTERNATIONAL ORGANIZATION SECTION

UNTS SELF-INDEX SECTION

Volume 5

TOPIC SECTION

WORLD TREATY INDEX

MAIN ENTRY SECTION

United Nations Treaty Series: Series I, Numbers 1–6485

VOLUME 2

PETER H. ROHN

Associate Professor of Political Science
University of Washington

Santa Barbara, California
Oxford, England

Library of Congress Catalog Card Number 73-83352
ISBN Clothbound 5-Volume Set 0-87436-125-7
ISBN Clothbound 6-Volume Set 0-87436-132-X
ISBN Clothbound Volume 2 0-87436-127-3

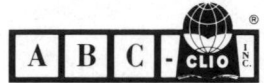

American Bibliographical Center—Clio Press, Inc.
2040 Alameda Padre Serra
Santa Barbara, California

European Bibliographical Center—Clio Press
Woodside House
Hinksey Hill
Oxford OX1 5BE, England

Designed by Barbara Monahan
Composed by Datagraphics Press
Printed and bound by Halliday Lithograph Corporation
in the United States of America

Contents

List of Abbreviations

Accept UN Charter	Unilateral declaration accepting UN Charter obligations
Admin Cooperation	Administrative Cooperation
African Coffee Org	African Coffee Organization
African Devel Bank	African Development Bank
African Insur Org	African Insurance Organization
African Tech Org	African Technical Organization
Afromalagasy Coffee	Afro-Malagasy Coffee Organization
Afromalagasy Org	Afro-Malagasy Organization
AID (Int Devel)	Agency for International Development
Allied Milit Occup	Allied Military Occupation
Anglo-Egypt Sudan	Anglo-Egyptian Sudan
Asian Devel Bank	Asian Development Bank
Asian Productivity	Asian Productivity Organization
Bel-Lux Econ Union	Belgium-Luxembourg Economic Union
BENELÜX Econ Union	Belgium-Netherlands-Luxembourg Economic Union
Bnk Int Settlement	Bank for International Settlements
British Occup Germ	British Occupied Germany
Brit Solomon Is	British Solomon Islands
Brit Virgin Is	British Virgin Islands
Central Afri Power	Central African Power Company
Central Afri Rep	Central African Republic
Central Am Bank	Central American Bank
CERN (Nuc Resrch)	European Organization for Nuclear Research
China People's Rep	People's Republic of China
Cmte Industr Devel	Committee for Industrial Development
COMECON (Econ Aid)	Council for Mutual Economic Assistance
Consul/Citizenship	Consular Matters and Citizenship
Customs Coop Coun	Customs Cooperation Council
East Afri Service	East African Common Services Organization
ECSC (Coal/Steel)	European Coal and Steel Community
EEC (Econ Commnty)	European Economic Community
EFTA (Free Trade)	European Free Trade Association
EURATOM	European Atomic Energy Commission
Eur Foot Mouth Dis	European Commission for the Control of Foot and Mouth Disease
EUROCONTROL	European Organization for the Safety of Air Navigation
Eur Plant Protect	European and Mediterranean Plant Protection Organization
Eur Space Research	European Space Research Organization
Eur Space Vehicle	European Space Vehicle Launcher Development Organization
FAO (Food Agri)	Food and Agricultural Organization of the United Nations
Fed Malay States	Federation of Malay States
Fed of Malaya	Federation of Malaya
Fed Rhod/Nyasaland	Federation of Rhodesia and Nyasaland
French Occup Germ	French Occupied Germany
Fr Equatorial Afri	French Equatorial Africa
GATT (Tariff/Trade)	General Agreement on Tariffs and Trade
Gen Communications	General Communications
General HEW	General Health, Education and Welfare

General IGO	General Intergovernmental Organizations
Hague Private IL	The Hague Conference on Private International Law
IAEA (Atom Energy)	International Atomic Energy Agency
IBRD Project	International Bank for Reconstruction and Development Project
IBRD (World Bank)	International Bank for Reconstruction and Development
ICAO (Civil Aviat)	International Civil Aviation Organization
ICJ (Int Court)	International Court of Justice
ICJ Option Clause	International Court of Justice Optional Clause
	Unilateral declaration accepting ICJ optional clause, or
	Unilateral declaration regarding UN General Assembly in connection with ICJ optional clause, or
	Unilateral limited declaration regarding ICJ optional clause
IDA (Devel Assoc)	International Development Association
IFC (Finance Corp)	International Finance Corporation
IGO Establishment	Intergovernmental Organization Establishment
IGO Multilat	Three or more IGO's and no State
IGO Operations	Intergovernmental Organization Operations
IGO Status/Immunit	Intergovernmental Organizational Privileges and Immunities
ILO Labor	International Labour Organization Labor Matters
ILO (Labor Org)	International Labour Organization
IMCO (Maritime Org)	Inter-Governmental Maritime Consultative Organization
IMF (Fund)	International Monetary Fund
Indo-Pac Fish Coun	Indo-Pacific Fisheries Council
Int Bureau Educ	International Bureau of Education
Int Coffee Org	International Coffee Organization
Int Coun Expl Sea	International Council for the Exploration of the Sea
Inter-Allied Com	Inter-Allied Commission
Inter-Am Devel Bnk	Inter-American Development Bank
Inter-Am Nuc Energ	Inter-American Nuclear Energy Commission
Int Exhibit Bureau	International Exhibition Bureau
Intgov Eur Migrat	Intergovernmental Committee for European Migration
Int Org Metrology	International Organization of Legal Metrology
Int Rail Transport	Central Office for International Railway Transport
Int Relief Union	International Relief Union
Int Rice Com	International Rice Commission
Int Sugar Council	International Sugar Council
Int Whaling Com	International Whaling Commission
Int Wheat Coun	International Wheat Council
Int Wine Office	International Vine and Wine Office
IRO (Refugee Org)	International Refugees Organization
It Aegean Colonies	Italian Colonies in the Aegean
ITU (Telecommun)	International Telecommunication Union
LAFTA (Free Trade)	Latin American Free Trade Association
Lat Am Nuclear Arm	Agency for the Prohibition of Nuclear Weapons in Latin America
Medit Fish Council	Mediterranean Fisheries Council
Micronesia (US)	Micronesia (US Trust Territories in the Pacific)
Milit Assistance	Military Assistance
Milit Installation	Military Installations
Milit Occupation	Military Occupation
Milit Servic/Citiz	Military Service and Citizenship
Mostfavored Nation	Most Favored Nation
NATO (North Atlan)	North Atlantic Treaty Organization
NE Atlantic Fish	Northeast Atlantic Fisheries Commission
Netherld Antilles	Netherlands Antilles
New Hebrides Is	New Hebrides Islands
Non-IBRD Project	Non-International Bank for Reconstruction and Development Project
Non-ILO Labor	Non-International Labour Organization Labor Matters
Northern Territ	Northern Territories
NW Atlantic Fish	International Commission for the Northwest Atlantic Fisheries
OAS (Am States)	Organization of American States
OAU (Afri Unity)	Organization of African Unity
OECD (Econ Coop)	Organization for Economic Co-operation and Development
Org Ctrl Am States	Organization of Central American States
Org Rail Collabor	Soviet Railroad Organization
Other HEW	Other Health, Education and Welfare
Other Party Combin	More than one State and more than one IGO, or
	Other combination of parties

Other Unilat Decla	Other unilateral declaration
Pan Am Health Org	Pan American Health Organization
Patents/Copyrights	Patents and Copyrights
Peace/Disarmament	Peace and Disarmament
Petrol Export Org	Organization of Petroleum Exporting Countries
Portug Colonies	Portuguese Colonies
Portug East Africa	Portuguese East Africa
Portug West Africa	Portuguese West Africa
Privil/Immunities	Privileges and Immunities
Refrigeration Inst	International Institute for Refrigeration
Rhine Navigation	Central Commission for the Navigation of the Rhine
Russ Fed Sov Rep	Russian Federation of Soviet Republics
Scientific Project	Scientific Projects
SEATO (SE Asia)	Southeast Asia Treaty Organization
Serb/Croat/Slovene	The Kingdom of the Serbs, Croats and Slovenes
South Africa	Union of South Africa
South Pacific Com	South Pacific Commission
Spanish Colonies	Spanish Colonies in Africa
Special Decla ICJ	Unilateral special declaration regarding ICJ
Specif Claim/Waive	Specific Claims and Waivers
Specif Goods/Equip	Specific Goods and Equipment
State/IGO Group	One State and mixed group of IGO-State partners, or
	One State and three or more IGO's, or
	One State and two IGO's, or
	Two or more States and one IGO
States Multilat	Three or more military governments and one State, or
	Three or more States and no IGO, or
	Three or more States under FAO auspices, or
	Three or more States under IAEA auspices, or
	Three or more States under ILO auspices, or
	Three or more States under UN auspices, or
	Three or more States under UNESCO auspices, or
	Three or more States under WHO auspices
Subsahara Tech Com	Commission for Technical Cooperation in Africa South of the Sahara
Tech Assistance	Technical Assistance
Trinidad/Tobago	Trinidad and Tobago
Turk-Caicose Is	Turk-Caicose Islands
UK Great Britain	United Kingdom of Great Britain and Northern Ireland
Ukrainian SSR	Ukrainian Soviet Socialist Republic
UN Charter	United Nations Charter
UN Emergency Fund	United Nations Emergency Fund
UNESCO (Educ/Cult)	United Nations Scientific and Cultural Organization
UN Hi Com Refugees	Office of the United Nations High Commissioner for Refugees
UNICEF (Children)	United Nations Children's Fund
UNIDO (Industrial)	United Nations Industrial Development Organization
United Arab Rep	United Arab Republic
UNKRA (Korean Rec)	United Nations Commission for the Unification and Rehabilitation of Korea
UN Mission Congo	United Nations Mission to the Congo
UN Relief Palestin	United Nations Relief and Works Agency for Palestine Refugees in the Near East
UNRRA (Relief)	United Nations Relief and Rehabilitation Association
UN Special Fund	United Nations Special Fund
UNTAB (Tech Assis)	United Nations Technical Assistance Board
UPU (Postal Union)	Universal Postal Union
US Agri Commod Aid	US Agricultural Commodity Aid
USA (United States)	United States of America
US Occup Germ	United States Occupied Germany
USSR (Soviet Union)	Union of Soviet Socialist Republics
Vatican/Holy See	The Vatican and the Holy See
WEU (West Europe)	Western European Union
WHO (World Health)	World Health Organization
WMO (Meteorology)	World Meteorological Organization
W Pacif Hi Command	West Pacific High Command

MAIN ENTRY SECTION

United Nations Treaty Series: Series I, Numbers 1–6485

United Nations Treaty Series:

Series I, Numbers 1–6485

100001 Unilateral Instrument **1 UNTS 3**
SIGNED: 13 Feb 46   FORCE: 13 Feb 46
REGISTERED: 14 Dec 46 United Nations
ARTICLES: 1 LANGUAGE: English.
HEADNOTE: DECLARATION ON ICJ
TOPIC: ICJ Option Clause
CONCEPTS: Compulsory jurisdiction.
INTL ORGS: International Court of Justice.
PROCEDURE: Duration.
PARTIES:
  UK Great Britain
          ANNEX
80 UNTS 304. UK Great Britain. Prolongation
  12 Feb 51. Force 12 Feb 51.

100002 Unilateral Instrument **1 UNTS 7**
SIGNED: 5 Aug 46   FORCE: 5 Aug 46
REGISTERED: 14 Dec 46 United Nations
ARTICLES: 1 LANGUAGE: French.
HEADNOTE: ACCEPTANCE ICJ JURISDICTION
TOPIC: ICJ Option Clause
CONCEPTS: Compulsory jurisdiction.
INTL ORGS: International Court of Justice.
PROCEDURE: Termination.
PARTIES:
  Netherlands
          ANNEX
248 UNTS 357. Netherlands. Termination
  1 Aug 56. Force 6 Aug 56.

100003 Unilateral Instrument **1 UNTS 9**
SIGNED: 14 Aug 46   FORCE: 14 Aug 46
REGISTERED: 14 Dec 46 United Nations
ARTICLES: 1 LANGUAGE: English.
HEADNOTE: ACCEPTANCE ICJ JURISDICTION
TOPIC: ICJ Option Clause
CONCEPTS: Compulsory jurisdiction.
INTL ORGS: International Court of Justice.
PROCEDURE: Duration
PARTIES:
  USA (United States)

100004 Multilateral Convention **1 UNTS 15**
SIGNED: 13 Feb 46   FORCE: 13 Feb 46
REGISTERED: 14 Dec 46 United Nations
ARTICLES: 9 LANGUAGE: English. French.
HEADNOTE: PRIVILEGES & IMMUNITIES
TOPIC: IGO Status/Immunit
CONCEPTS: Annex type material. Frontier formali-
  ties. Non-visa travel documents. Diplomatic privi-
  leges. Diplomatic missions. Inviolability. Privi-
  leges and immunities. Property. Diplomatic cor-
  respondence. Juridical personality. Mediation
  and good offices. Procedure. Customs exemp-
  tions. IGO status. Special status. Status of ex-
  perts.
INTL ORGS: United Nations.
PROCEDURE: Accession.
PARTIES:
  Multilateral

          ANNEX
1 UNTS 263. Dominican Republic. Ratification
  7 Mar 47.
1 UNTS 263. Liberia. Accession 14 Mar 47.
5 UNTS 413. Guatemala. Ratification 6 Jul 47.
5 UNTS 413. El Salvador. Accession 9 Jul 47.
5 UNTS 413. Ethiopia. Accession 22 Jul 47.
6 UNTS 433. Haiti. Accession 6 Aug 47.
7 UNTS 353. Norway. Accession 18 Aug 47.
7 UNTS 353. France. Ratification 18 Aug 47.
7 UNTS 353. Sweden. Ratification 28 Aug 47.
7 UNTS 353. Afghanistan. Accession 5 Sep 47.
11 UNTS 406. Nicaragua. Ratification 29 Nov 47.
11 UNTS 406. New Zealand. Qualified Accession
  10 Dec 47.
11 UNTS 406. Greece. Accession 29 Dec 47.
12 UNTS 416. Poland. Accession 8 Jan 48.
12 UNTS 416. Canada. Qualified Accession
  22 Jan 48.
14 UNTS 490. Iceland. Accession 10 Mar 48.
42 UNTS 354. Iraq. Accession 15 Sep 49.
42 UNTS 354. Israel. Accession 21 Sep 49.
43 UNTS 335. Costa Rica. Accession 26 Oct 49.
66 UNTS 346. Yugoslavia. Accession 30 Jun 50.
70 UNTS 266. Turkey. Qualified Accession
  22 Aug 50.
173 UNTS 369. USSR (Soviet Union). Qualified
  Accession 22 Sep 53.
173 UNTS 370. Syria. Accession 29 Sep 53.
173 UNTS 370. Paraguay. Accession 2 Oct 53.
177 UNTS 324. Byelorussia. Qualified Accession
  22 Oct 53.
180 UNTS 296. Ukrainian SSR. Qualified Accession 20 Nov 53.
202 UNTS 320. Burma. Accession 25 Jan 55.
214 UNTS 348. Czechoslovakia. Qualified Accession 7 Sep 55.
230 UNTS 454. Norway. Supplementation
  12 May 55. Force 12 May 55.
230 UNTS 454. Greece. Supplementation
  12 May 55. Force 12 May 55.
231 UNTS 347. Thailand. Qualified Accession
  30 Mar 56.
247 UNTS 384. Romania. Qualified Accession
  5 Jul 56.
248 UNTS 358. Hungary. Qualified Accession
  30 Jul 56.
252 UNTS 308. Argentina. Accession 12 Oct 56.
254 UNTS 404. Laos. Qualified Accession
  24 Nov 56.
261 UNTS 373. Morocco. Accession 18 Mar 57.
266 UNTS 363. Tunisia. Accession 7 May 57.
266 UNTS 363. Austria. Accession 10 May 57.
270 UNTS 372. Turkey. Withdrawal of Reservation 20 Jun 57.
271 UNTS 382. Albania. Qualified Accession
  2 Jul 57.
280 UNTS 346. Fed of Malaya. Acceptance
  16 Oct 57. Force 31 Aug 57.
284 UNTS 361. Jordan. Accession 3 Jan 58.
286 UNTS 329. Italy. Accession 3 Feb 58.
308 UNTS 300. Finland. Accession 31 Jul 58.
308 UNTS 300. Ghana. Accession 5 Aug 58.
316 UNTS 268. Libya. Accession 28 Nov 58.

340 UNTS 323. Cuba. Accession 9 Sep 59.
376 UNTS 402. Bulgaria. Qualified Accession
  30 Sep 60.
381 UNTS 348. New Zealand. Withdrawal of Reservation 25 Nov 60.
399 UNTS 249. Nigeria. Succession 26 Jun 61.
405 UNTS 275. Niger. Declaration 25 Aug 61.
411 UNTS 289. Cameroon. Succession
  20 Oct 61.
415 UNTS 422. Ivory Coast. Succession
  8 Dec 61.
423 UNTS 276. Togo. Succession 27 Feb 62.
423 UNTS 276. Sierra Leone. Succession
  13 Mar 62.
426 UNTS 333. Upper Volta. Accession
  27 Apr 62.
429 UNTS 246. Madagascar. Succession
  23 May 62.
429 UNTS 246. Mongolia. Qualified Accession
  31 May 62.
437 UNTS 331. Central Afri Rep. Succession
  4 Sep 62.
442 UNTS 293. Congo (Brazzaville). Succession
  15 Oct 62.
443 UNTS 310. Tanganyika. Accession
  29 Oct 62.
445 UNTS 287. Mexico. Qualified Accession
  26 Nov 62.
460 UNTS 293. Japan. Accession 18 Apr 63.
466 UNTS 374. Senegal. Succession 27 May 63.
470 UNTS 373. Somalia. Accession 9 Jul 63.
471 UNTS 294. Yemen. Accession 23 Jul 63.
471 UNTS 294. Peru. Accession 24 Jul 64.
475 UNTS 346. Jamaica. Accession 9 Sep 63.
480 UNTS 308. Algeria. Qualified Accession
  31 Oct 63.
480 UNTS 308. Cambodia. Accession 6 Nov 63.
480 UNTS 308. Cyprus. Succession 5 Nov 63.
483 UNTS 288. Kuwait. Accession 15 Dec 63.
490 UNTS 442. Gabon. Accession 13 Mar 64.
493 UNTS 304. Rwanda. Accession 15 Apr 64.
520 UNTS 421. Congo (Zaire). Accession
  8 Dec 64.
540 UNTS 329. Kenya. Accession 1 Jul 65.
547 UNTS 308. Nepal. Qualified Accession
  28 Sep 65.
547 UNTS 308. Trinidad/Tobago. Accession
  19 Oct 65.
559 UNTS 344. Singapore. Succession
  18 Mar 66.
562 UNTS 323. Malawi. Accession 17 May 66.
616 UNTS 492. Guinea. Accession 10 Jan 68.
633 UNTS 381. Mali. Accession 28 Mar 68.
639 UNTS 325. Malta. Succession 27 Jun 68.

100005 Unilateral Instrument **1 UNTS 35**
SIGNED: 26 Oct 46   FORCE: 26 Oct 46
REGISTERED: 14 Dec 46 United Nations
ARTICLES: 1 LANGUAGE: English.
HEADNOTE: ACCEPTANCE ICJ JURISDICTION
TOPIC: ICJ Option Clause
CONCEPTS: Compulsory jurisdiction.
INTL ORGS: International Court of Justice.
PROCEDURE: Duration.

PARTIES:
Taiwan

100006 Unilateral Instrument **1 UNTS 37**
SIGNED: 16 Nov 46   FORCE: 16 Nov 46
REGISTERED: 14 Dec 46 United Nations
ARTICLES: 1 LANGUAGE: English.
HEADNOTE: ACCEPTANCE ICJ JURISDICTION
TOPIC: ICJ Option Clause
CONCEPTS: Compulsory jurisdiction.
INTL ORGS: International Court of Justice.
PROCEDURE: Duration.
PARTIES:
Norway

100007 Unilateral Instrument **1 UNTS 39**
SIGNED: 19 Nov 46   FORCE: 19 Dec 46
REGISTERED: 14 Dec 46 United Nations
ARTICLES: 1 LANGUAGE: English.
HEADNOTE: ADHERENCE UN CHARTER
TOPIC: UN Charter
CONCEPTS: Acceptance of UN obligations.
INTL ORGS: United Nations.
PARTIES:
Afghanistan

100008 Unilateral Instrument **1 UNTS 41**
SIGNED: 19 Nov 46   FORCE: 19 Dec 46
REGISTERED: 14 Dec 46 United Nations
ARTICLES: 1 LANGUAGE: English.
HEADNOTE: ADHERENCE UN CHARTER
TOPIC: UN Charter
CONCEPTS: Acceptance of UN obligations.
INTL ORGS: United Nations.
PARTIES:
Iceland

100009 Unilateral Instrument **1 UNTS 43**
SIGNED: 19 Nov 46   FORCE: 19 Dec 46
REGISTERED: 14 Dec 46 United Nations
ARTICLES: 1 LANGUAGE: French.
HEADNOTE: ADHERENCE UN CHARTER
TOPIC: UN Charter
CONCEPTS: Acceptance of UN obligations.
INTL ORGS: United Nations.
PARTIES:
Sweden

100010 Unilateral Instrument **1 UNTS 45**
SIGNED: 10 Dec 46   FORCE: 10 Dec 46
REGISTERED: 14 Dec 46 United Nations
ARTICLES: 1 LANGUAGE: French.
HEADNOTE: ACCEPTANCE ICJ JURISDICTION
TOPIC: ICJ Option Clause
CONCEPTS: Compulsory jurisdiction.
INTL ORGS: International Court of Justice.
PARTIES:
Denmark

100011 Unilateral Instrument **1 UNTS 47**
SIGNED: 16 Dec 46   FORCE: 16 Dec 46
REGISTERED: 16 Dec 46 United Nations
ARTICLES: 1 LANGUAGE: English.
HEADNOTE: ADHERENCE UN CHARTER
TOPIC: UN Charter
CONCEPTS: IGO constitution. Admission.
INTL ORGS: United Nations.
PARTIES:
Thailand

100012 Unilateral Instrument **1 UNTS 49**
SIGNED: 27 Jan 47   FORCE: 27 Jan 47
REGISTERED: 10 Feb 47 United Nations
ARTICLES: 1 LANGUAGE: Spanish.
HEADNOTE: ACCEPTANCE ICJ JURISDICTION
TOPIC: ICJ Option Clause
CONCEPTS: Compulsory jurisdiction.
INTL ORGS: International Court of Justice.
PARTIES:
Guatemala

100013 Bilateral Treaty **1 UNTS 53**
SIGNED: 18 Mar 46   FORCE: 18 Mar 46
REGISTERED: 31 Mar 47 Yugoslavia
ARTICLES: 5 LANGUAGE: Polish. Serbo-Croat.

HEADNOTE: TERRITORIAL EXTENSION TREATY
    COMMERCE NAVIGATION
TOPIC: General Military
CONCEPTS: Territorial application.
INTL ORGS: United Nations.
PARTIES:
Poland
Yugoslavia

100014 Bilateral Treaty **1 UNTS 67**
SIGNED: 9 May 46   FORCE: 9 May 46
REGISTERED: 31 Mar 47 Yugoslavia
ARTICLES: 6 LANGUAGE: Czechoslovakian. Serbo-Croat.
HEADNOTE: FRIENDSHIP MUTUAL AID PEACEFUL
    COOPERATION
TOPIC: General Military
CONCEPTS: Friendship and amity. Non-prejudice to UN charter. Peaceful relations. General cooperation. Defense and security. Military assistance.
INTL ORGS: United Nations.
PROCEDURE: Duration. Future Procedures Contemplated. Ratification. Renewal or Revival. Termination.
PARTIES:
Czechoslovakia
Yugoslavia

100015 Bilateral Treaty **1 UNTS 81**
SIGNED: 23 Mar 44   FORCE: 9 Jul 46
REGISTERED: 31 Mar 47 Yugoslavia
ARTICLES: 6 LANGUAGE: Albanian. Serbo-Croat.
HEADNOTE: FRIENDSHIP
TOPIC: General Military
CONCEPTS: Friendship and amity. Peaceful relations. Defense and security.
INTL ORGS: United Nations.
PROCEDURE: Denunciation. Duration.
PARTIES:
Albania
Yugoslavia

100016 Unilateral Protocol **2 UNTS 3**
SIGNED: 5 Apr 47   FORCE: 6 Apr 47
REGISTERED: 6 Apr 47 United Nations
ARTICLES: 1 LANGUAGE: French.
HEADNOTE: ICJ OPTION CLAUSE ACCEPTANCE
TOPIC: ICJ Option Clause
CONCEPTS: Optional clause ICJ. Compulsory jurisdiction.
INTL ORGS: International Court of Justice.
PARTIES:
Sweden

100017 Bilateral Agreement **2 UNTS 5**
SIGNED: 6 Nov 45   FORCE: 6 Nov 45
REGISTERED: 25 Apr 47 Netherlands
ARTICLES: 12 LANGUAGE: English.
HEADNOTE: FINANCE
TOPIC: Finance
CONCEPTS: Detailed regulations. Territorial application. General cooperation. Accounting procedures. Banking. Currency. Monetary and gold transfers. Investments. Exchange rates and regulations. Interest rates. Payment schedules. Transportation costs. Local currency.
PROCEDURE: Amendment. Termination.
PARTIES:
Netherlands
Norway
ANNEX
76 UNTS 240. Norway. Amendment 6 Jul 50. Force 6 Jul 50.
76 UNTS 240. Netherlands. Amendment 6 Jul 50. Force 6 Jul 50.
450 UNTS 400. Netherlands. Termination 6 Dec 60. Force 6 Dec 60.
450 UNTS 400. Norway. Termination 6 Dec 60. Force 6 Dec 60.

100018 Multilateral Instrument **2 UNTS 17**
SIGNED: 7 Nov 45   FORCE: 26 Sep 46
REGISTERED: 25 Apr 47 Netherlands
ARTICLES: 6 LANGUAGE: English. French.
HEADNOTE: AMEND ILO
TOPIC: IGO Establishment
CONCEPTS: Treaty interpretation. Treaty violation. Exchange of information and documents. Do-

mestic legislation. Private contracts. Accounting procedures. Financial programs. Funding procedures. Admission. Establishment.
INTL ORGS: International Labour Organization. United Nations.
PROCEDURE: Amendment. Accession. Denunciation. Ratification. Termination.
PARTIES:
Multilateral
ANNEX
20 UNTS 306. Chile. Ratification 19 Oct 48.
191 UNTS 356. Panama. Ratification 13 May 54.

100019 Bilateral Agreement **2 UNTS 27**
SIGNED: 30 Nov 45   FORCE: 30 Nov 45
REGISTERED: 25 Apr 47 Netherlands
ARTICLES: 11 LANGUAGE: English.
HEADNOTE: FINANCE
TOPIC: Finance
CONCEPTS: Territorial application. General cooperation. Accounting procedures. Banking. Balance of payments. Monetary and gold transfers. Currency deposits. Exchange rates and regulations. Interest rates. Payment schedules.
PROCEDURE: Amendment. Duration. Termination.
PARTIES:
Netherlands
Sweden

100020 Multilateral Agreement **2 UNTS 39**
SIGNED: 27 Dec 45   FORCE: 27 Dec 45
REGISTERED: 25 Apr 47 Netherlands
ARTICLES: 31 LANGUAGE: English.
HEADNOTE: BRETTON WOODS
TOPIC: IGO Establishment
CONCEPTS: Default remedies. Definition of terms. Detailed regulations. Treaty interpretation. Annex or appendix reference. Treaty violation. Privileges and immunities. Court procedures. Standardization. General cooperation. Exchange of official publications. Exchange of information and documents. Domestic legislation. General property. Private contracts. Procedure. Export subsidies. Accounting procedures. Balance of payments. Currency. Monetary and gold transfers. Exchange rates and regulations. Financial programs. Funding procedures. Inadequacy of funds. Internal finance. Interest rates. Payment schedules. Local currency. Assets transfer. Quotas. Customs exemptions. Communications linkage. IGO constitution. Admission. Establishment. Regional offices. Internal structure. Special status. Status of experts. Inter-agency agreements.
INTL ORGS: International Bank for Reconstruction and Development. International Monetary Fund.
PROCEDURE: Amendment. Accession. Denunciation. Duration. Future Procedures Contemplated. Ratification. Renewal or Revival. Termination.
PARTIES:
Bolivia SIGNED: 27 Dec 45
Brazil SIGNED: 27 Dec 45
Canada SIGNED: 27 Dec 45
Chile SIGNED: 31 Dec 45
China SIGNED: 27 Dec 45
Colombia SIGNED: 27 Dec 45
Costa Rica SIGNED: 27 Dec 45
Cuba SIGNED: 31 Dec 45
Czechoslovakia SIGNED: 27 Dec 45
Dominican Republic SIGNED: 28 Dec 45
Ecuador SIGNED: 27 Dec 45
United Arab Rep SIGNED: 27 Dec 45
Ethiopia SIGNED: 27 Dec 45
France SIGNED: 27 Dec 45
Greece SIGNED: 27 Dec 45
Guatemala SIGNED: 27 Dec 45
Honduras SIGNED: 27 Dec 45
Iceland SIGNED: 27 Dec 45
India SIGNED: 27 Dec 45
Iran SIGNED: 28 Dec 45
Iraq SIGNED: 27 Dec 45
Luxembourg SIGNED: 27 Dec 45
Mexico SIGNED: 31 Dec 45
Netherlands SIGNED: 27 Dec 45
Norway SIGNED: 27 Dec 45
Paraguay SIGNED: 27 Dec 45
Peru SIGNED: 31 Dec 45
Philippines SIGNED: 27 Dec 45
Poland SIGNED: 27 Dec 45
South Africa SIGNED: 27 Dec 45
UK Great Britain SIGNED: 27 Dec 45
USA (United States) SIGNED: 27 Dec 45

Uruguay SIGNED: 27 Dec 45
Yugoslavia SIGNED: 27 Dec 45
ANNEX
141 UNTS 355.
141 UNTS 356.
199 UNTS 308.
199 UNTS 309.
260 UNTS 432.
287 UNTS 260.
303 UNTS 284.
303 UNTS 285.
316 UNTS 269.
316 UNTS 270.
406 UNTS 282.
406 UNTS 283.
426 UNTS 334.
426 UNTS 335.
458 UNTS 268.
458 UNTS 269.
480 UNTS 310.
480 UNTS 312.
544 UNTS 284.
547 UNTS 309.
547 UNTS 310.
606 UNTS 294.
640 UNTS 334.

100021   Bilateral Agreement   **3 UNTS 3**
SIGNED: 31 Jan 46   FORCE: 31 Jan 46
REGISTERED: 25 Apr 47 Netherlands
ARTICLES: 8 LANGUAGE: French.
HEADNOTE: PAYMENTS
TOPIC: Finance
CONCEPTS: Definition of terms. Territorial application. General cooperation. Accounting procedures. Banking. Balance of payments. Currency. Monetary and gold transfers. Exchange rates and regulations. Interest rates. Payment schedules.
PROCEDURE: Amendment. Denunciation. Termination.
PARTIES:
Denmark
Netherlands

100022   Bilateral Exchange   **3 UNTS 13**
SIGNED: 7 Feb 46   FORCE: 7 Feb 46
REGISTERED: 25 Apr 47 Netherlands
ARTICLES: 6 LANGUAGE: English. Spanish.
HEADNOTE: EXPROPRIATED OIL PROPERTY COMPENSATION
TOPIC: Specif Claim/Waive
CONCEPTS: Claims, debts and assets. Debt settlement. Specific claims or waivers.
PARTIES:
Mexico
Netherlands

100023   Bilateral Exchange   **3 UNTS 37**
SIGNED: 11 Feb 46   FORCE: 13 Feb 46
REGISTERED: 25 Apr 47 Netherlands
ARTICLES: 3 LANGUAGE: English.
HEADNOTE: RELEASE ASSETS
TOPIC: Claims and Debts
CONCEPTS: Detailed regulations. Conformity with municipal law. Licenses and permits. General property. Accounting procedures. Indemnities and reimbursements. Payment schedules. Debts. Assets transfer. Enemy financial interests.
INTL ORGS: United Nations.
PARTIES:
Netherlands
USA (United States)

100024   Bilateral Exchange   **3 UNTS 57**
SIGNED: 9 Apr 46   FORCE: 9 Apr 46
REGISTERED: 25 Apr 47 Netherlands
ARTICLES: 2 LANGUAGE: French.
HEADNOTE: MONETARY
TOPIC: Finance
CONCEPTS: Annex or appendix reference. Finances and payments.
PARTIES:
France
Netherlands

100025   Bilateral Agreement   **3 UNTS 73**
SIGNED: 24 Oct 45   FORCE: 24 Oct 45
REGISTERED: 25 Apr 47 Netherlands

ARTICLES: 12 LANGUAGE: French.
HEADNOTE: REGULATE COMMERCIAL PAYMENTS
TOPIC: Finance
CONCEPTS: Change of circumstances. Territorial application. Trade procedures. Accounting procedures. Banking. Balance of payments. Currency. Monetary and gold transfers. Exchange rates and regulations. Expense sharing formulae. Financial programs. Interest rates. Payment schedules. Transportation costs.
PROCEDURE: Denunciation. Duration. Renewal or Revival.
PARTIES:
Netherlands
Switzerland
ANNEX
134 UNTS 356.   Netherlands.   Amendment 24 Dec 46. Force 1 Jan 47.
134 UNTS 356.   Switzerland.   Amendment 24 Dec 46. Force 1 Jan 47.
134 UNTS 359.   Netherlands.   Amendment 1 Jan 52. Force 1 Jan 52.
134 UNTS 359.   Switzerland.   Amendment 1 Jan 52. Force 1 Jan 52.
293 UNTS 326.   Netherlands.   Supplementation 26 Aug 53. Force 24 Mar 54.
293 UNTS 326.   Switzerland.   Supplementation 26 Aug 53. Force 24 Mar 54.

100026   Multilateral Instrument   **3 UNTS 123**
SIGNED: 15 Nov 45   FORCE: 15 Nov 45
REGISTERED: 20 May 47 USA (United States)
ARTICLES: 9 LANGUAGE: English.
HEADNOTE: AGREED DECLARATION ATOMIC ENERGY
TOPIC: Atomic Energy
CONCEPTS: Peaceful relations. Research results. Scientific exchange. Peaceful use. Security of information.
INTL ORGS: United Nations. Special Commission.
PARTIES:
Canada SIGNED: 15 Nov 45 FORCE: 15 Nov 45
UK Great Britain SIGNED: 15 Nov 45 FORCE: 15 Nov 45
USA (United States) SIGNED: 15 Nov 45 FORCE: 15 Nov 45

100027   Bilateral Exchange   **3 UNTS 131**
SIGNED: 6 Dec 45   FORCE: 6 Dec 45
REGISTERED: 20 May 47 USA (United States)
ARTICLES: 2 LANGUAGE: English.
HEADNOTE: RESUMPTION NORMAL COMMERCIAL RELATIONS
TOPIC: General Trade
CONCEPTS: Establishment of trade relations.
TREATY REF: 204LTS384.
PROCEDURE: Future Procedures Contemplated.
PARTIES:
Italy
USA (United States)

100028   Bilateral Agreement   **3 UNTS 139**
SIGNED: 6 Dec 45   FORCE: 6 Dec 45
REGISTERED: 20 May 47 USA (United States)
ARTICLES: 11 LANGUAGE: English. Portuguese.
HEADNOTE: AIR TRANSPORT
TOPIC: Air Transport
CONCEPTS: Annex or appendix reference. Conformity with municipal law. Licenses and permits. Recognition of legal documents. Use of facilities. Fees and exemptions. National treatment. Customs exemptions. Competency certificate. Routes and logistics. Navigational conditions. Permit designation. Air transport. Airport facilities. Airworthiness certificates. Conditions of airlines operating permission. Licenses and certificates of nationality.
INTL ORGS: International Civil Aviation Organization.
PROCEDURE: Amendment. Registration. Termination.
PARTIES:
Portugal
USA (United States)
ANNEX
24 UNTS 300. USA (United States). Amendment 28 Jun 47. Force 28 Jun 47.
24 UNTS 300. Portugal. Amendment 28 Jun 47. Force 28 Jun 47.

184 UNTS 322. USA (United States). Amendment 11 Nov 52. Force 11 Nov 52.
184 UNTS 322. Portugal. Amendment 11 Nov 52. Force 11 Nov 52.

100029   Bilateral Agreement   **3 UNTS 157**
SIGNED: 10 Dec 45   FORCE: 10 Dec 45
REGISTERED: 20 May 47 USA (United States)
ARTICLES: 28 LANGUAGE: English. Spanish.
HEADNOTE: MILITARY MISSION
TOPIC: Military Mission
CONCEPTS: Definition of terms. Use of facilities. Compensation. Indemnities and reimbursements. Investments. Expense sharing formulae. Tax exemptions. Customs exemptions. Military assistance. Military training. Security of information. Airforce-army-navy personnel ratio. Ranks and privileges. Conditions for assistance missions. Third country military personnel.
PROCEDURE: Denunciation. Duration. Renewal or Revival. Termination.
PARTIES:
Costa Rica
USA (United States)
ANNEX
93 UNTS 350. USA (United States). Extension and Amendment 3 Feb 50. Force 15 Feb 50.
93 UNTS 350. Costa Rica. Extension and Amendment 15 Feb 50. Force 15 Feb 50.
393 UNTS 306. USA (United States). Prolongation 4 Mar 58. Force 10 Dec 57.
393 UNTS 306. Costa Rica. Prolongation 17 Oct 58. Force 10 Dec 57.
411 UNTS 290. USA (United States). Amendment 25 Feb 59. Force 13 May 59.
411 UNTS 290. Costa Rica. Amendment 13 May 59. Force 13 May 59.
476 UNTS 246. USA (United States). Prolongation 16 May 62. Force 17 May 62.
476 UNTS 246. Costa Rica. Prolongation 17 May 62. Force 17 May 62.

100030   Bilateral Exchange   **3 UNTS 177**
SIGNED: 10 Dec 45   FORCE: 10 Dec 45
REGISTERED: 20 May 47 USA (United States)
ARTICLES: 2 LANGUAGE: English.
HEADNOTE: COMMITTEE ON INQUIRY
TOPIC: Refugees
CONCEPTS: Border traffic and migration. Refugees and stateless persons. Refugees. Establishment of commission. Establishment. Internal structure.
INTL ORGS: Special Commission.
PARTIES:
UK Great Britain
USA (United States)

100031   Bilateral Agreement   **3 UNTS 185**
SIGNED: 28 Dec 45   FORCE: 28 Dec 45
REGISTERED: 20 May 47 USA (United States)
ARTICLES: 26 LANGUAGE: English. Spanish.
HEADNOTE: MILITARY MISSION
TOPIC: Military Mission
CONCEPTS: Definition of terms. Use of facilities. Compensation. Indemnities and reimbursements. Exchange rates and regulations. Expense sharing formulae. Tax exemptions. Customs exemptions. Military assistance. Military training. Security of information. Airforce-army-navy personnel ratio. Ranks and privileges. Conditions for assistance missions. Third country military personnel.
PROCEDURE: Denunciation. Duration. Renewal or Revival. Termination.
PARTIES:
Honduras
USA (United States)

100032   Bilateral Exchange   **3 UNTS 203**
SIGNED: 11 Jan 46   FORCE: 11 Jan 46
REGISTERED: 20 May 47 USA (United States)
ARTICLES: 2 LANGUAGE: English.
HEADNOTE: COMMERCIAL RELATIONS
TOPIC: General Trade
CONCEPTS: General provisions.
PROCEDURE: Future Procedures Contemplated.
PARTIES:
Greece
USA (United States)

100033 Bilateral Exchange **3 UNTS 209**
SIGNED: 1 Dec 43 FORCE: 1 Dec 43
REGISTERED: 20 May 47 USA (United States)
ARTICLES: 2 LANGUAGE: English.
HEADNOTE: EXCHANGE INFORMATION PENICIL-
LIN
TOPIC: Scientific Project
CONCEPTS: Definition of terms. Annex or appen-
dix reference. General cooperation. Exchange of
information and documents. Licenses and per-
mits. Research and scientific projects. Research
results. Laws and formalities. Recognition. Secu-
rity of information.
PROCEDURE: Duration.
PARTIES:
UK Great Britain
USA (United States)

100034 Bilateral Exchange **3 UNTS 239**
SIGNED: 7 Feb 46 FORCE: 7 Feb 46
REGISTERED: 20 May 47 USA (United States)
ARTICLES: 2 LANGUAGE: English. French.
HEADNOTE: NATURAL RUBBER PURCHASE
TOPIC: Commodity Trade
CONCEPTS: General cooperation. Payment sched-
ules. Non-interest rates and fees. Commodity
trade. Transport of goods. Merchant vessels.
Raw materials.
PARTIES:
France
USA (United States)

100035 Bilateral Exchange **3 UNTS 247**
SIGNED: 9 Feb 46 FORCE: 9 Feb 46
REGISTERED: 20 May 47 USA (United States)
ARTICLES: 2 LANGUAGE: English.
HEADNOTE: NATURAL RUBBER PURCHASE
TOPIC: Commodity Trade
CONCEPTS: General cooperation. Payment sched-
ules. Non-interest rates and fees. Commodity
trade. Transport of goods. Merchant vessels.
Raw materials.
PARTIES:
Netherlands
USA (United States)

100036 Bilateral Agreement **3 UNTS 253**
SIGNED: 11 Feb 46 FORCE: 11 Feb 46
REGISTERED: 20 May 47 USA (United States)
ARTICLES: 14 LANGUAGE: English.
HEADNOTE: AIR SERVICES
TOPIC: Air Transport
CONCEPTS: Definition of terms. Exceptions and
exemptions. Annex or appendix reference. Non-
prejudice to third party. Conformity with municipal law. Licenses and permits. Recognition of
legal documents. Use of facilities. Procedure. Existing tribunals. Competence of tribunal. Fees
and exemptions. Most favored nation clause. National treatment. Customs exemptions. Competency certificate. Routes and logistics. Navigational conditions. Permit designation. Airport facilities. Airworthiness certificates. Conditions of
airlines operating permission. Overflights and
technical stops. Operating authorizations and
regulations. Licenses and certificates of nationality.
INTL ORGS: International Civil Aviation Organization.
TREATY REF: EAS469.
PROCEDURE: Amendment. Future Procedures
Contemplated. Registration. Termination.
PARTIES:
UK Great Britain
USA (United States)
ANNEX
24 UNTS 312. USA (United States). Amendment
27 Jan 47. Force 27 Jan 47.
24 UNTS 312. UK Great Britain. Amendment
20 Dec 46. Force 27 Jan 47.
71 UNTS 264. UK Great Britain. Amendment
19 Jan 48. Force 14 Jan 48.
71 UNTS 264. USA (United States). Amendment
19 Jan 48. Force 14 Jan 48.
263 UNTS 392. USA (United States). Amendment
17 Oct 56. Force 30 Oct 56.
263 UNTS 392. UK Great Britain. Amendment
30 Oct 56. Force 30 Oct 56.
263 UNTS 396. USA (United States). Amendment
2 Dec 56. Force 28 Dec 56.

263 UNTS 396. UK Great Britain. Amendment
28 Dec 56. Force 28 Dec 56.
425 UNTS 296. USA (United States). Supplementation 22 Nov 61. Force 22 Nov 61.
425 UNTS 296. UK Great Britain. Supplementation 22 Nov 61. Force 22 Nov 61.
573 UNTS 274. USA (United States). Amendment
27 May 66. Force 27 May 66.
573 UNTS 274. UK Great Britain. Amendment
27 May 66. Force 27 May 66.

100037 Bilateral Exchange **3 UNTS 293**
SIGNED: 1 Mar 46 FORCE: 1 Mar 46
REGISTERED: 20 May 47 USA (United States)
ARTICLES: 2 LANGUAGE: English.
HEADNOTE: PURCHASE NATURAL RUBBER
TOPIC: Commodity Trade
CONCEPTS: General cooperation. Non-interest
rates and fees. Commodity trade. Transport of
goods. Merchant vessels. Raw materials.
PARTIES:
UK Great Britain
USA (United States)

100038 Bilateral Exchange **3 UNTS 301**
SIGNED: 21 Mar 46 FORCE: 21 Mar 46
REGISTERED: 20 May 47 USA (United States)
ARTICLES: 3 LANGUAGE: English.
HEADNOTE: AMENDING AIR TRANSPORT SER-
VICES
TOPIC: Air Transport
CONCEPTS: Annex or appendix reference. Annex
type material. Routes and logistics. Air transport.
Overflights and technical stops.
TREATY REF: US EXEC AGREE SERIES 430;
58STAT1458.
PROCEDURE: Amendment.
PARTIES:
Denmark
USA (United States)
ANNEX
222 UNTS 366. USA (United States). Amendment
6 Aug 54. Force 6 Aug 54.
222 UNTS 366. Denmark. Amendment 6 Aug 54.
Force 6 Aug 54.
312 UNTS 398. USA (United States). Amendment
8 Jul 58. Force 8 Jul 58.
312 UNTS 398. Denmark. Amendment 8 Jul 58.
Force 8 Jul 58.

100039 Bilateral Instrument **4 UNTS 2**
SIGNED: 27 Mar 46 FORCE: 27 Mar 46
REGISTERED: 20 May 47 USA (United States)
ARTICLES: 5 LANGUAGE: English.
HEADNOTE: SETTLEMENT LEND-LEASE RECIPRO-
CAL AID SURPLUS WAR PROPERTY CLAIMS
TOPIC: Milit Assistance
CONCEPTS: Definition of terms. Territorial applica-
tion. Guarantees and safeguards. Annex or ap-
pendix reference. Non-prejudice to UN charter.
General cooperation. Title and deeds. Proce-
dure. Compensation. Expense sharing formulae.
Lump sum settlements. Domestic obligation.
Surplus property. Merchant vessels. Payment for
war supplies. Lease of military property. Military
assistance. Lend lease. Naval vessels. Return of
equipment and recapture. Surplus war property.
Bases and facilities. Post-war claims settlement.
Raw materials.
PROCEDURE: Future Procedures Contemplated.
PARTIES:
UK Great Britain
USA (United States)
ANNEX
71 UNTS 270. USA (United States). Other
12 Jul 48. Force 12 Jul 48.
71 UNTS 270. UK Great Britain. Other 12 Jul 48.
Force 12 Jul 48.
71 UNTS 270. USA (United States). Other
12 Jul 48. Force 12 Jul 48.
71 UNTS 270. UK Great Britain. Other 12 Jul 48.
Force 12 Jul 48.
89 UNTS 368. USA (United States). Interpretation
19 Feb 47. Force 28 Feb 47.
89 UNTS 368. UK Great Britain. Interpretation
28 Feb 47. Force 28 Feb 47.
89 UNTS 372. UK Great Britain. Amendment
7 Jan 48. Force 7 Jan 48.
89 UNTS 372. USA (United States). Amendment
7 Jan 48. Force 7 Jan 48.

134 UNTS 366. USA (United States). Extension
and Amendment 28 Apr 52. Force 1 Jan 52.
134 UNTS 366. UK Great Britain. Extension and
Amendment 30 Apr 52. Force 1 Jan 52.
284 UNTS 362. USA (United States). Prolongation
24 Apr 57. Force 25 Apr 57.
284 UNTS 362. UK Great Britain. Prolongation
25 Apr 57. Force 25 Apr 57.

100040 Bilateral Agreement **4 UNTS 101**
SIGNED: 27 Mar 46 FORCE: 27 Mar 46
REGISTERED: 20 May 47 USA (United States)
ARTICLES: 17 LANGUAGE: English.
HEADNOTE: INTERCHANGE INFORMATION
PATENT RIGHTS INVENTIONS DESIGNS PRO-
CESSES
TOPIC: Patents/Copyrights
CONCEPTS: Definition of terms. Annex type mate-
rial. Nationality and citizenship. Conformity with
municipal law. Domestic legislation. Responsi-
bility and liability. Indemnities and reimburse-
ments. Payment schedules. Claims and settle-
ments. Patents, copyrights and trademarks. Post-
war adjustment. Lend lease. Security of
information. Exchange of defense information.
INTL ORGS: Special Commission.
PROCEDURE: Duration. Termination.
PARTIES:
UK Great Britain
USA (United States)

100041 Bilateral Agreement **4 UNTS 125**
SIGNED: 5 Apr 46 FORCE: 5 Apr 46
REGISTERED: 20 May 47 USA (United States)
ARTICLES: 12 LANGUAGE: English. French.
HEADNOTE: AIR SERVICES
TOPIC: Air Transport
CONCEPTS: Conditions. Definition of terms. Annex or appendix reference. Previous treaty replacement. Conformity with municipal law. Licenses and permits. Recognition of legal documents. Use of facilities. Procedure. Existing
tribunals. Competence of tribunal. Fees and exemptions. Most favored nation clause. National
treatment. Customs exemptions. Competency
certificate. Routes and logistics. Navigational
conditions. Permit designation. Air transport. Airport facilities. Airworthiness certificates. Conditions of airlines operating permission. Licenses
and certificates of nationality.
INTL ORGS: International Civil Aviation Organization.
TREATY REF: INT.CIVI.AVIA.CONF.,CHICAGO,7-
DEC44,FINAL ACT PP.59.
PROCEDURE: Amendment. Future Procedures
Contemplated. Registration. Termination. Application to Non-self-governing Territories.
PARTIES:
Belgium
USA (United States)

100042 Bilateral Exchange **4 UNTS 155**
SIGNED: 24 Apr 46 FORCE: 24 Apr 46
REGISTERED: 20 May 47 USA (United States)
ARTICLES: 2 LANGUAGE: English.
HEADNOTE: ECONOMIC FINANCIAL COOPER-
ATION
TOPIC: General Economic
CONCEPTS: General cooperation. Informational
records. Expropriation. Import quotas. Reciproc-
ity in trade. Trade procedures. Compensation.
Economic assistance. Surplus property. Credit
provisions. Withdrawal or relief of occupation
forces. Surplus war property.
TREATY REF: US EXEC AGREE SERIES
257;26STAT1542; 139LTS395.
PARTIES:
Poland
USA (United States)

100043 Bilateral Exchange **4 UNTS 165**
SIGNED: 4 May 46 FORCE: 4 May 46
REGISTERED: 20 May 47 USA (United States)
ARTICLES: 2 LANGUAGE: Arabic. English.
HEADNOTE: FRIENDSHIP COMMERCE
TOPIC: General Economic
CONCEPTS: Exceptions and exemptions. Territo-
rial application. General provisions. Recognition.
Diplomatic relations establishment. Diplomatic
missions. Privileges and immunities. Establish-

ment of trade relations. Most favored nation clause.
PROCEDURE: Termination.
PARTIES:
USA (United States)
Yemen

100044 Bilateral Agreement **4 UNTS 179**
SIGNED: 14 May 46 FORCE: 14 May 46
REGISTERED: 20 May 47 USA (United States)
ARTICLES: 1 LANGUAGE: English. French.
HEADNOTE: EXECUTIVE AMENDMENT AGREEMENT
TOPIC: Finance
CONCEPTS: Detailed regulations. Previous treaty amendment. Payment schedules.
TREATY REF: US EXEC AGREE SERIES 220; 55STAT1348.
PARTIES:
Haiti
USA (United States)

100045 Bilateral Agreement **4 UNTS 183**
SIGNED: 16 May 46 FORCE: 16 May 46
REGISTERED: 20 May 47 USA (United States)
ARTICLES: 11 LANGUAGE: English.
HEADNOTE: SETTLE LEND-LEASE SURPLUS PROPERTY CLAIMS
TOPIC: Milit Assistance
CONCEPTS: Definition of terms. Non-prejudice to UN charter. General cooperation. General property. Exchange. General cultural cooperation. Exchange rates and regulations. Financial programs. Transportation costs. Lump sum settlements. Payment for war supplies. Lease of military property. Lend lease. Return of equipment and recapture. Surplus war property. Restrictions on transfer. Post-war claims settlement.
INTL ORGS: United Nations.
TREATY REF: 4UNTS2;.
PROCEDURE: Future Procedures Contemplated.
PARTIES:
India
USA (United States)

100046 Bilateral Agreement **4 UNTS 201**
SIGNED: 24 May 46 FORCE: 24 May 46
REGISTERED: 20 May 47 USA (United States)
ARTICLES: 5 LANGUAGE: English. Russian.
HEADNOTE: COMMERCIAL RADIO TELETYPE COMMUNICATION CHANNELS
TOPIC: Telecommunications
CONCEPTS: Tariffs. Facilities and equipment. Money orders and postal checks. Parcel post.
PROCEDURE: Duration. Termination.
PARTIES:
USA (United States)
USSR (Soviet Union)

100047 Bilateral Agreement **4 UNTS 215**
SIGNED: 3 Jun 46 FORCE: 3 Jun 46
REGISTERED: 20 May 47 USA (United States)
ARTICLES: 31 LANGUAGE: English. Spanish.
HEADNOTE: MILITARY MISSION
TOPIC: Military Mission
CONCEPTS: Definition of terms. Use of facilities. Compensation. Indemnities and reimbursements. Exchange rates and regulations. Expense sharing formulae. Customs duties. Customs exemptions. Military assistance. Military training. Security of information. Airforce-army-navy personnel ratio. Ranks and privileges. Conditions for assistance missions. Third country military personnel. Status of forces.
PROCEDURE: Denunciation. Duration. Renewal or Revival. Termination.
PARTIES:
USA (United States)
Venezuela

100048 Bilateral Agreement **4 UNTS 237**
SIGNED: 7 Jun 46 FORCE: 7 Jun 46
REGISTERED: 20 May 47 USA (United States)
ARTICLES: 10 LANGUAGE: English.
HEADNOTE: SETTLE LEND-LEASE SURPLUS PROPERTY CLAIMS

TOPIC: Milit Assistance
CONCEPTS: Definition of terms. Guarantees and safeguards. Annex or appendix reference. General cooperation. General property. Title and deeds. Exchange. General cultural cooperation. Exchange rates and regulations. Financial programs. Lump sum settlements. Payment for war supplies. Lease of military property. Lend lease. Return of equipment and recapture. Surplus war property. Restrictions on transfer. Post-war claims settlement.
PARTIES:
Australia
USA (United States)
ANNEX
229 UNTS 262. USA (United States). Amendment 9 Jul 52. Force 25 Aug 52.
229 UNTS 262. Australia. Amendment 25 Aug 52. Force 25 Aug 52.

100049 Bilateral Agreement **4 UNTS 253**
SIGNED: 14 Jun 46 FORCE: 14 Jun 46
REGISTERED: 20 May 47 USA (United States)
ARTICLES: 7 LANGUAGE: English.
HEADNOTE: DISPOSITION LEND-LEASE SUPPLIES INVENTORY PROCUREMENT
TOPIC: Milit Assistance
CONCEPTS: Definition of terms. Detailed regulations. Guarantees and safeguards. Annex or appendix reference. General cooperation. Inspection and observation. Expense sharing formulae. Interest rates. Payment schedules. Transportation costs. Claims and settlements. Payment for war supplies. Lease of military property. Lend lease. Return of equipment and recapture.
PARTIES:
Taiwan
USA (United States)

100050 Unilateral Instrument **4 UNTS 265**
SIGNED: 22 May 47 FORCE: 22 May 47
REGISTERED: 6 Jun 47 United Nations
ARTICLES: 1 LANGUAGE: English.
HEADNOTE: ACCEPTANCE ICJ JURISDICTION
TOPIC: ICJ Option Clause
CONCEPTS: Conformity with municipal law. Compulsory jurisdiction.
INTL ORGS: International Court of Justice.
PROCEDURE: Duration.
PARTIES:
Turkey
ANNEX
191 UNTS 357. Turkey. Prolongation 22 May 52.
491 UNTS 385. Turkey. Prolongation 19 Mar 64. Force 23 May 62.
604 UNTS 349. Turkey. Renewal 31 Aug 67. Force 23 May 67.

100051 Bilateral Exchange **4 UNTS 269**
SIGNED: 24 Dec 46 FORCE: 11 Jan 47
REGISTERED: 12 Jun 47 Lebanon
ARTICLES: 2 LANGUAGE: French.
HEADNOTE: ISSUE VISAS ON DIPLOMATIC SPECIAL SERVICE PASSPORTS
TOPIC: Visas
CONCEPTS: Passports diplomatic. Passports non-diplomatic. Visas.
PARTIES:
Lebanon
Turkey

100052 Multilateral Instrument **4 UNTS 275**
SIGNED: 16 Nov 45 FORCE: 4 Nov 46

REGISTERED: 12 Jun 47 Netherlands
ARTICLES: 15 LANGUAGE: English. French.
HEADNOTE: UN EDUCATIONAL SCIENTIFIC & CULTURAL ORGANIZATION
TOPIC: IGO Establishment
CONCEPTS: Detailed regulations. Treaty interpretation. Treaty violation. Friendship and amity. Non-prejudice to UN charter. Peaceful relations. Standardization. Exchange of information and documents. Public information. Education. Commissions and foundations. Teacher and student exchange. Exchange. Financial programs. Funding procedures. Mass media exchange. Information agency. Subsidiary organ. Establishment. Liaison with other IGO's. Internal structure. Status of experts. Inter-agency agreements.
INTL ORGS: International Court of Justice. United Nations Educational, Scientific and Cultural Organization. United Nations.
PROCEDURE: Amendment.
PARTIES:
Argentina SIGNED: 16 Nov 45
Belgium SIGNED: 16 Nov 45 RATIFIED: 29 Nov 46 FORCE: 29 Nov 46
Bolivia SIGNED: 16 Nov 45 RATIFIED: 13 Nov 46 FORCE: 13 Nov 46
Brazil SIGNED: 16 Nov 45 RATIFIED: 4 Oct 46 FORCE: 4 Nov 46
Canada SIGNED: 16 Nov 45 RATIFIED: 6 Sep 46 FORCE: 4 Nov 46
Chile SIGNED: 16 Nov 45
Taiwan SIGNED: 16 Nov 45 RATIFIED: 13 Sep 46 FORCE: 4 Nov 46
Colombia SIGNED: 16 Nov 45
Cuba SIGNED: 16 Nov 45
Czechoslovakia SIGNED: 16 Nov 45 RATIFIED: 5 Oct 46 FORCE: 4 Nov 46
Denmark SIGNED: 16 Nov 45 RATIFIED: 20 Sep 46 FORCE: 4 Nov 46
Dominican Republic SIGNED: 16 Nov 45 RATIFIED: 2 Jul 46 FORCE: 4 Nov 46
Ecuador SIGNED: 16 Nov 45
United Arab Rep SIGNED: 16 Nov 45 RATIFIED: 16 Jul 46 FORCE: 4 Nov 46
Greece SIGNED: 16 Nov 45 RATIFIED: 4 Nov 46 FORCE: 4 Nov 46
Guatemala SIGNED: 16 Nov 45
Haiti SIGNED: 16 Nov 45 RATIFIED: 18 Nov 46 FORCE: 18 Nov 46
India SIGNED: 16 Nov 45 RATIFIED: 12 Jun 46 FORCE: 4 Nov 46
Iran SIGNED: 16 Nov 45
Iraq SIGNED: 16 Nov 45
Lebanon SIGNED: 16 Nov 45 RATIFIED: 28 Oct 46 FORCE: 4 Nov 46
Liberia SIGNED: 16 Nov 45
Luxembourg SIGNED: 16 Nov 45
Mexico SIGNED: 16 Nov 45 RATIFIED: 12 Jun 46 FORCE: 4 Nov 46
Netherlands SIGNED: 16 Nov 45 RATIFIED: 1 Jan 47 FORCE: 1 Jan 47
Nicaragua SIGNED: 16 Nov 45
Norway SIGNED: 16 Nov 45 RATIFIED: 8 Aug 46 FORCE: 4 Nov 46
Panama SIGNED: 16 Nov 45
Peru SIGNED: 16 Nov 45 RATIFIED: 21 Nov 46 FORCE: 21 Nov 46
Philippines SIGNED: 16 Nov 46 RATIFIED: 21 Nov 46 FORCE: 21 Nov 46
Poland SIGNED: 16 Nov 45 RATIFIED: 6 Nov 46 FORCE: 6 Nov 46
Saudi Arabia SIGNED: 16 Nov 45 RATIFIED: 30 Apr 46 FORCE: 4 Nov 46
South Africa SIGNED: 16 Nov 45 RATIFIED: 3 Jun 46 FORCE: 4 Nov 46
Syria SIGNED: 16 Nov 45 RATIFIED: 15 Nov 46 FORCE: 15 Nov 46
Turkey SIGNED: 16 Nov 45 RATIFIED: 6 Jul 46 FORCE: 4 Nov 46
UK Great Britain SIGNED: 16 Nov 45 RATIFIED: 20 Feb 46 FORCE: 4 Nov 46
Uruguay SIGNED: 16 Nov 45
Venezuela SIGNED: 16 Nov 45 RATIFIED: 25 Nov 46 FORCE: 25 Nov 46
Yugoslavia SIGNED: 16 Nov 45
ANNEX
21 UNTS 336.
34 UNTS 382.
43 UNTS 336.
45 UNTS 319.
53 UNTS 407.
68 UNTS 261.
98 UNTS 264.
126 UNTS 346.

161 UNTS 360.
166 UNTS 368.
172 UNTS 326.
190 UNTS 376.
191 UNTS 358.
213 UNTS 369.
250 UNTS 289.
253 UNTS 307.
256 UNTS 326.
257 UNTS 359.
300 UNTS 298.
307 UNTS 300.
316 UNTS 271.
353 UNTS 308.
383 UNTS 310.
387 UNTS 332.
393 UNTS 307.
415 UNTS 423.
423 UNTS 278.
425 UNTS 300.
429 UNTS 248.
444 UNTS 291.
450 UNTS 404.
503 UNTS 325.
510 UNTS 312.
522 UNTS 334.
530 UNTS 330.
561 UNTS 344.
613 UNTS 401.

100053   Bilateral Protocol   **4 UNTS 303**
SIGNED: 20 Dec 45   FORCE: 1 Jun 44
REGISTERED: 12 Jun 47 Netherlands
ARTICLES: 11 LANGUAGE: English.
HEADNOTE: CURRENCY MUTUAL AID
TOPIC: Milit Assistance
CONCEPTS: General cooperation. Indemnities and reimbursements. Currency. Exchange rates and regulations. Funding procedures. Commodities and services. General aid. Materials, equipment and services. Military assistance. Return of equipment and recapture. Procurement and logistics.
PROCEDURE: Duration.
PARTIES:
Netherlands
UK Great Britain

100054   Bilateral Agreement   **4 UNTS 317**
SIGNED: 12 Apr 46   FORCE: 12 Apr 46
REGISTERED: 12 Jun 47 Netherlands
ARTICLES: 13 LANGUAGE: Dutch. English. Portuguese.
HEADNOTE: AIR TRANSPORT
TOPIC: Air Transport
CONCEPTS: Exceptions and exemptions. Annex or appendix reference. Conformity with municipal law. Licenses and permits. Use of facilities. Arbitration. Existing tribunals. Reexport of goods, etc.. Fees and exemptions. Most favored nation clause. National treatment. Customs exemptions. Competency certificate. Routes and logistics. Navigational conditions. Permit designation. Air transport. Airport facilities. Airworthiness certificates. Conditions of airlines operating permission. Operating authorizations and regulations. Licenses and certificates of nationality.
INTL ORGS: International Civil Aviation Organization. Arbitration Commission.
PROCEDURE: Amendment. Future Procedures Contemplated. Registration. Termination.
PARTIES:
Netherlands
Portugal

100055   Bilateral Convention   **4 UNTS 351**
SIGNED: 13 Jul 46   FORCE: 13 Jul 46
REGISTERED: 12 Jun 47 Netherlands
ARTICLES: 15 LANGUAGE: French.
HEADNOTE: AIR SERVICES
TOPIC: Air Transport
CONCEPTS: Annex or appendix reference. Nonprejudice to third party. Conformity with municipal law. Exchange of information and documents. Licenses and permits. Recognition of legal documents. Use of facilities. Investigation of violations. Arbitration. Existing tribunals. Reexport of goods, etc.. Fees and exemptions. National treatment. Customs exemptions. Competency certificate. Routes and logistics. Naviga-

tional conditions. Permit designation. Airport facilities. Airworthiness certificates. Conditions of airlines operating permission. Operating authorizations and regulations. Licenses and certificates of nationality.
INTL ORGS: International Civil Aviation Organization.
PROCEDURE: Future Procedures Contemplated. Registration. Termination.
PARTIES:
Netherlands
Spain

100056   Bilateral Agreement   **4 UNTS 367**
SIGNED: 13 Aug 46   FORCE: 13 Aug 46
REGISTERED: 12 Jun 47 Netherlands
ARTICLES: 12 LANGUAGE: Dutch. English.
HEADNOTE: AIR SERVICES
TOPIC: Air Transport
CONCEPTS: Annex or appendix reference. Conformity with municipal law. Licenses and permits. Arbitration. Procedure. Existing tribunals. Reexport of goods, etc.. Fees and exemptions. Most favored nation clause. Customs exemptions. Competency certificate. Routes and logistics. Navigational conditions. Permit designation. Airport facilities. Airworthiness certificates. Conditions of airlines operating permission. Operating authorizations and regulations. Licenses and certificates of nationality.
INTL ORGS: International Civil Aviation Organization. Arbitration Commission.
PROCEDURE: Amendment. Future Procedures Contemplated. Registration. Termination. Application to Non-self-governing Territories.
PARTIES:
Netherlands
UK Great Britain
                     ANNEX
11 UNTS 407. UK Great Britain. Amendment 21 May 47. Force 21 May 47.
11 UNTS 407. Netherlands. Amendment 28 Mar 47. Force 21 May 47.
17 UNTS 358. UK Great Britain. Amendment 9 Oct 47. Force 10 Oct 47.
17 UNTS 358. Netherlands. Amendment 10 Oct 47. Force 10 Oct 47.

100057   Bilateral Exchange   **4 UNTS 401**
SIGNED: 16 Sep 46   FORCE: 16 Sep 46
REGISTERED: 12 Jun 47 Netherlands
ARTICLES: 2 LANGUAGE: English.
HEADNOTE: 1945 MONETARY AGREEMENT
TOPIC: Finance
CONCEPTS: Previous treaty amendment. Payment schedules.
TREATY REF: 2UNTS325.
PARTIES:
Netherlands
UK Great Britain

100058   Bilateral Convention   **4 UNTS 407**
SIGNED: 11 Jul 46   FORCE: 12 Sep 46
REGISTERED: 16 Jun 47 Yugoslavia
ARTICLES: 38 LANGUAGE: French.
HEADNOTE: CIVIL AVIATION
TOPIC: Air Transport
CONCEPTS: Border control. Airport facilities. Airworthiness certificates. Conditions of airlines operating permission. Overflights and technical stops. Operating authorizations and regulations. Licenses and certificates of nationality.
PROCEDURE: Denunciation. Duration. Ratification.
PARTIES:
Albania
Yugoslavia

100059   Bilateral Agreement   **4 UNTS 429**
SIGNED: 8 Apr 46   FORCE: 8 Apr 46
REGISTERED: 16 Jun 47 Denmark
ARTICLES: 7 LANGUAGE: French.
HEADNOTE: FREEING ASSETS
TOPIC: Claims and Debts
CONCEPTS: Juridical personality. Recognition of legal documents. Certificates of origin. Accounting procedures. Banking. Bonds. Exchange rates and regulations. Payment schedules. Assets. Assets transfer. Enemy financial interests.

PARTIES:
Belgium
Denmark

100060   Bilateral Agreement   **4 UNTS 435**
SIGNED: 21 May 46   FORCE: 21 May 46
REGISTERED: 16 Jun 47 Denmark
ARTICLES: 7 LANGUAGE: French.
HEADNOTE: FREEING ASSETS
TOPIC: Claims and Debts
CONCEPTS: Juridical personality. Recognition of legal documents. Certificates of origin. Accounting procedures. Banking. Bonds. Exchange rates and regulations. Assets. Assets transfer. Enemy financial interests.
PARTIES:
Denmark
Luxembourg

100061   Bilateral Agreement   **5 UNTS 3**
SIGNED: 6 Dec 45   FORCE: 6 Dec 45
REGISTERED: 28 Jul 47 Denmark
ARTICLES: 18 LANGUAGE: English.
HEADNOTE: RESTORATION MONEY PROPERTY AFTER WAR
TOPIC: Finance
CONCEPTS: Detailed regulations. Treaty implementation. Conformity with municipal law. General cooperation. Immovable property. General property. Accounting procedures. Attachment of funds. Banking. Bonds. Compensation. Monetary and gold transfers. Exchange rates and regulations. Fees and exemptions. Payment schedules. Claims and settlements.
PARTIES:
Denmark
UK Great Britain
                     ANNEX
157 UNTS 357. Denmark. Termination 21 Nov 52. Force 21 Nov 52.
157 UNTS 357. UK Great Britain. Termination 21 Nov 52. Force 21 Nov 52.

100062   Bilateral Agreement   **5 UNTS 15**
SIGNED: 1 Nov 45   FORCE: 5 Nov 45
REGISTERED: 30 Jul 47 UK Great Britain
ARTICLES: 9 LANGUAGE: English.
HEADNOTE: FINANCE
TOPIC: Finance
CONCEPTS: Definition of terms. Treaty implementation. General cooperation. Accounting procedures. Banking. Balance of payments. Currency. Monetary and gold transfers. Investments. Exchange rates and regulations. Payment schedules. Local currency.
PROCEDURE: Amendment. Termination.
PARTIES:
Czechoslovakia
UK Great Britain
                     ANNEX
11 UNTS 409. UK Great Britain. Supplementation 3 Jul 47. Force 8 Jul 47.
11 UNTS 409. Czechoslovakia. Supplementation 3 Jul 47. Force 8 Jul 47.
81 UNTS 307. UK Great Britain. Prolongation 4 Nov 48. Force 5 Nov 48.
81 UNTS 307. Czechoslovakia. Prolongation 4 Nov 48. Force 5 Nov 48.
82 UNTS 314. UK Great Britain. Prolongation 3 Jan 49. Force 5 Jan 49.
82 UNTS 314. Czechoslovakia. Prolongation 31 Dec 48. Force 5 Jan 49.
82 UNTS 316. UK Great Britain. Prolongation 28 Feb 49. Force 5 Mar 49.
82 UNTS 316. Czechoslovakia. Prolongation 2 Mar 49. Force 5 Mar 49.
82 UNTS 320. UK Great Britain. Prolongation 27 Apr 49. Force 5 May 49.
82 UNTS 320. Czechoslovakia. Prolongation 30 Apr 49. Force 5 May 49.
82 UNTS 322. UK Great Britain. Prolongation 4 Jul 49. Force 5 Jul 49.
82 UNTS 322. Czechoslovakia. Prolongation 4 Jul 49. Force 5 Jul 49.
82 UNTS 324. UK Great Britain. Prolongation 4 Aug 49. Force 5 Aug 49.
82 UNTS 324. Czechoslovakia. Prolongation 4 Aug 49. Force 5 Aug 49.

100063   Bilateral Agreement   **5 UNTS 27**
SIGNED: 8 Nov 45   FORCE: 8 Nov 45
REGISTERED: 30 Jul 47 UK Great Britain
ARTICLES: 9 LANGUAGE: English.
HEADNOTE: FINANCE
TOPIC: Finance
CONCEPTS: Definition of terms. General cooperation. Accounting procedures. Banking. Balance of payments. Currency. Monetary and gold transfers. Exchange rates and regulations. Internal finance. Payment schedules.
PROCEDURE: Amendment. Termination.
PARTIES:
Norway
UK Great Britain
ANNEX
11 UNTS 412. UK Great Britain. Supplementation 27 Jun 47. Force 1 Jul 47.
11 UNTS 412. Norway. Supplementation 27 Jun 47. Force 1 Jul 47.
11 UNTS 416. UK Great Britain. Supplementation 27 Jun 47.
11 UNTS 416. Norway. Supplementation 30 Jun 47.
34 UNTS 384. UK Great Britain. Supplementation 9 Jul 48. Force 9 Jul 48.
34 UNTS 384. Norway. Supplementation 9 Jul 48. Force 9 Jul 48.
34 UNTS 388. UK Great Britain. Supplementation 31 Mar 49. Force 31 Mar 49.
34 UNTS 388. Norway. Supplementation 31 Mar 49. Force 31 Mar 49.

100064   Bilateral Agreement   **5 UNTS 37**
SIGNED: 6 Dec 45   FORCE: 16 Jul 46
REGISTERED: 30 Jul 47 UK Great Britain
ARTICLES: 12 LANGUAGE: English. Portuguese.
HEADNOTE: AIR SERVICES
TOPIC: Air Transport
CONCEPTS: Annex or appendix reference. Conformity with municipal law. Licenses and permits. Recognition of legal documents. Arbitration. Existing tribunals. Competence of tribunal. Fees and exemptions. Most favored nation clause. Customs exemptions. Competency certificate. Routes and logistics. Navigational conditions. Permit designation. Airport facilities. Airworthiness certificates. Conditions of airlines operating permission. Operating authorizations and regulations. Licenses and certificates of nationality.
INTL ORGS: International Civil Aviation Organization. Arbitration Commission.
TREATY REF: UK MISC NO.6(1945) CMD.6614;.
PROCEDURE: Amendment. Future Procedures Contemplated. Ratification. Registration. Termination. Application to Non-self-governing Territories.
PARTIES:
Portugal
UK Great Britain
ANNEX
136 UNTS 370. UK Great Britain. Amendment 3 Apr 52. Force 3 Apr 52.
136 UNTS 370. Portugal. Amendment 3 Apr 52. Force 3 Apr 52.

100065   Bilateral Agreement   **6 UNTS 3**
SIGNED: 6 Dec 45   FORCE: 16 Aug 46
REGISTERED: 30 Jul 47 UK Great Britain
ARTICLES: 12 LANGUAGE: English. Portuguese.
HEADNOTE: AIR SERVICES
TOPIC: Air Transport
CONCEPTS: Annex or appendix reference. Conformity with municipal law. Licenses and permits. Recognition of legal documents. Use of facilities. Arbitration. Procedure. Existing tribunals. Competence of tribunal. Fees and exemptions. Most favored nation clause. National treatment. Customs exemptions. Competency certificate. Routes and logistics. Navigational conditions. Permit designation. Airport facilities. Airworthiness certificates. Conditions of airlines operating permission. Operating authorizations and regulations. Licenses and certificates of nationality.
INTL ORGS: International Civil Aviation Organization. Arbitration Commission.
TREATY REF: UK MISC NO.6(1945) CMD.6614.
PROCEDURE: Amendment. Future Procedures Contemplated. Ratification. Registration. Termi-

nation. Application to Non-self-governing Territories.
PARTIES:
Portugal
UK Great Britain
ANNEX
136 UNTS 378. UK Great Britain. Amendment 3 Apr 52. Force 3 Apr 52.
136 UNTS 378. Portugal. Amendment 3 Apr 52. Force 3 Apr 52.
211 UNTS 336. UK Great Britain. Amendment 25 Mar 55. Force 25 Mar 55.
211 UNTS 336. Portugal. Amendment 25 Mar 55. Force 25 Mar 55.

100066   Multilateral Agreement   **6 UNTS 35**
SIGNED: 4 Jan 46   FORCE: 1 Jan 46
REGISTERED: 30 Jul 47 UK Great Britain
ARTICLES: 10 LANGUAGE: English. French.
HEADNOTE: ESTABLISHMENT EUROPEAN COAL ORGANIZATION
TOPIC: IGO Establishment
CONCEPTS: Constitutional amendment. Establishment. Headquarters and facilities. Extension of functions. Internal structure. Regulation of natural resources.
INTL ORGS: European Coal and Steel Community. United Nations.
PROCEDURE: Duration.
PARTIES:
Belgium SIGNED: 4 Jan 46 FORCE: 1 Jan 46
Denmark SIGNED: 4 Jan 46 FORCE: 1 Jan 46
France SIGNED: 4 Jan 46 FORCE: 1 Jan 46
Greece SIGNED: 4 Jan 46 FORCE: 1 Jan 46
Luxembourg SIGNED: 4 Jan 46 FORCE: 1 Jan 46
Netherlands SIGNED: 4 Jan 46 FORCE: 1 Jan 46
Norway SIGNED: 4 Jan 46 FORCE: 1 Jan 46
Turkey SIGNED: 4 Jan 46 FORCE: 1 Jan 46
UK Great Britain SIGNED: 4 Jan 46 FORCE: 1 Jan 46
USA (United States) SIGNED: 4 Jan 46 FORCE: 1 Jan 46
ANNEX
10 UNTS 372. Poland. Prolongation 12 Dec 46. Force 1 Jan 47.
10 UNTS 372. Denmark. Prolongation 12 Dec 46. Force 1 Jan 47.
10 UNTS 372. Greece. Prolongation 12 Dec 46. Force 1 Jan 47.
10 UNTS 372. Luxembourg. Prolongation 12 Dec 46. Force 1 Jan 47.
10 UNTS 372. Turkey. Prolongation 12 Dec 46. Force 1 Jan 47.
10 UNTS 372. UK Great Britain. Prolongation 12 Dec 46. Force 1 Jan 47.
10 UNTS 372. USA (United States). Prolongation 12 Dec 46. Force 1 Jan 47.
10 UNTS 372. Belgium. Prolongation 12 Dec 46. Force 1 Jan 47.
10 UNTS 372. Czechoslovakia. Prolongation 12 Nov 46. Force 1 Jan 47.
91 UNTS 368. Poland. Accession 14 Mar 46.
93 UNTS 354. Czechoslovakia. Accession 17 Jun 46.

100067   Bilateral Exchange   **6 UNTS 45**
SIGNED: 24 Jan 46   FORCE: 24 Jan 46
REGISTERED: 30 Jul 47 UK Great Britain
ARTICLES: 2 LANGUAGE: English.
HEADNOTE: AID REDUCTION DEFICIT GREEK BUDGET
TOPIC: Finance
CONCEPTS: Treaty implementation. Previous treaty replacement. Informational records. Specialists exchange. Import quotas. Accounting procedures. Banking. Compensation. Currency. Currency deposits. Exchange rates and regulations. Financial programs. Internal finance. Interest rates. Non-interest rates and fees. Local currency. Commodity trade. Equitable taxes. General technical assistance. Agriculture. Agricultural commodities. Economic assistance. Materials, equipment and services. Loan and credit. Loan repayment. Terms of loan. Reparations and restrictions.
INTL ORGS: United Nations Relief and Rehabilitation Administration.
PARTIES:
Greece
UK Great Britain

100068   Bilateral Exchange   **6 UNTS 55**
SIGNED: 7 Feb 46   FORCE: 7 Feb 46
REGISTERED: 30 Jul 47 UK Great Britain
ARTICLES: 6 LANGUAGE: English. Spanish.
HEADNOTE: COMPENSATION EXPROPRIATED PETROLEUM PROPERTY
TOPIC: Claims and Debts
CONCEPTS: Time limit. Treaty implementation. General cooperation. Exchange of information and documents. Informational records. Expropriation. General property. Negotiation. Attachment of funds. Compensation. Currency. Financial programs. Interest rates. Payment schedules. Assessment procedures.
PARTIES:
Mexico
UK Great Britain

100069   Bilateral Agreement   **6 UNTS 79**
SIGNED: 12 Feb 46   FORCE: 21 Jun 46
REGISTERED: 30 Jul 47 UK Great Britain
ARTICLES: 12 LANGUAGE: English. Turkish.
HEADNOTE: AIR SERVICES
TOPIC: Air Transport
CONCEPTS: Exceptions and exemptions. Annex or appendix reference. Conformity with municipal law. Licenses and permits. Recognition of legal documents. Use of facilities. Arbitration. Procedure. Existing tribunals. Fees and exemptions. Most favored nation clause. National treatment. Customs exemptions. Competency certificate. Routes and logistics. Navigational conditions. Permit designation. Airport facilities. Airworthiness certificates. Conditions of airlines operating permission. Operating authorizations and regulations. Licenses and certificates of nationality.
INTL ORGS: International Civil Aviation Organization. Arbitration Commission.
TREATY REF: UK MISC NO.6(1945) CMD.6614;.
PROCEDURE: Amendment. Future Procedures Contemplated. Ratification. Registration. Termination.
PARTIES:
Turkey
UK Great Britain
ANNEX
35 UNTS 364. UK Great Britain. Amendment 29 Mar 48. Force 1 Apr 48.
35 UNTS 364. Turkey. Amendment 1 Apr 48. Force 1 Apr 48.
108 UNTS 310. UK Great Britain. Amendment 17 May 51. Force 17 May 51.
108 UNTS 310. Turkey. Amendment 17 May 51. Force 17 May 51.

100070   Bilateral Agreement   **6 UNTS 107**
SIGNED: 12 Mar 46   FORCE: 12 Mar 46
REGISTERED: 30 Jul 47 UK Great Britain
ARTICLES: 11 LANGUAGE: English. French.
HEADNOTE: FINANCE
TOPIC: Finance
CONCEPTS: Definition of terms. Detailed regulations. General cooperation. Accounting procedures. Banking. Balance of payments. Currency. Monetary and gold transfers. Exchange rates and regulations. Internal finance. Payment schedules. Local currency.
PROCEDURE: Amendment. Termination.
PARTIES:
Switzerland
UK Great Britain
ANNEX
86 UNTS 268. Switzerland. Extension and Amendment 4 Mar 50. Force 4 Mar 50.
86 UNTS 268. UK Great Britain. Extension and Amendment 4 Mar 50. Force 4 Mar 50.
117 UNTS 368. UK Great Britain. Amendment 10 Nov 50. Force 10 Nov 50.
117 UNTS 368. Switzerland. Amendment 10 Nov 50. Force 10 Nov 50.
117 UNTS 371. Switzerland. Prolongation 10 Mar 51. Force 11 Mar 51.
117 UNTS 371. UK Great Britain. Prolongation 10 Mar 51. Force 11 Mar 51.
117 UNTS 373. UK Great Britain. Prolongation 9 Jun 51. Force 11 Jun 51.
117 UNTS 373. Switzerland. Prolongation 9 Jun 51. Force 11 Jun 51.

117 UNTS 375.   Switzerland.   Prolongation 2 Oct 51. Force 11 Oct 51.
117 UNTS 375. UK Great Britain.   Prolongation 2 Oct 51. Force 11 Oct 51.
131 UNTS 306. UK Great Britain.   Prolongation 24 Mar 52. Force 11 Mar 52.
131 UNTS 306.   Switzerland.   Prolongation 24 May 52. Force 11 Mar 52.
135 UNTS 330. UK Great Britain.   Prolongation 16 May 52. Force 12 May 52.
135 UNTS 330.   Switzerland.   Prolongation 16 May 52. Force 12 May 52.
138 UNTS 318. UK Great Britain.   Prolongation 30 Jul 52. Force 30 Jul 52.
138 UNTS 318.   Switzerland.   Prolongation 30 Jul 52. Force 30 Jul 52.
164 UNTS 360. UK Great Britain.   Prolongation 29 Dec 52. Force 1 Jan 53.
164 UNTS 360.   Switzerland.   Prolongation 29 Dec 52. Force 1 Jan 53.
175 UNTS 337. UK Great Britain.   Prolongation 24 Jun 53. Force 1 Jul 53.
175 UNTS 337.   Switzerland.   Prolongation 24 Jun 53. Force 1 Jul 53.

100071   Bilateral Agreement   **6 UNTS 119**
SIGNED: 16 Apr 46   FORCE: 16 Apr 46
REGISTERED: 30 Jul 47 UK Great Britain
ARTICLES: 11 LANGUAGE: English.
HEADNOTE: FINANCE PAYMENTS
TOPIC: Finance
CONCEPTS: Definition of terms. Detailed regulations. General cooperation. Accounting procedures. Banking. Balance of payments. Currency. Monetary and gold transfers. Exchange rates and regulations. Internal finance. Payment schedules. Local currency.
PROCEDURE: Amendment. Termination.
PARTIES:
  Portugal
  UK Great Britain
       ANNEX
11 UNTS 418. UK Great Britain. Supplementation 26 Feb 47. Force 27 Feb 47.
11 UNTS 418.   Portugal.   Supplementation 26 Feb 47. Force 27 Feb 47.
66 UNTS 347. UK Great Britain. Prolongation 14 Apr 48. Force 16 Apr 48.
66 UNTS 347. Portugal. Prolongation 14 Apr 48. Force 16 Apr 48.
71 UNTS 282. UK Great Britain. Abrogation 9 Oct 48. Force 12 Dec 47.
71 UNTS 282. Portugal. Abrogation 9 Jan 48. Force 12 Dec 47.
97 UNTS 310. UK Great Britain. Prolongation 14 Apr 49. Force 14 Apr 49.
97 UNTS 310. Portugal. Prolongation 14 Apr 49. Force 14 Apr 49.
98 UNTS 266. UK Great Britain. Amendment 7 Feb 50. Force 22 Feb 50.
98 UNTS 266. Portugal. Amendment 22 Feb 50. Force 22 Feb 50.
98 UNTS 268. UK Great Britain. Prolongation 14 Apr 50. Force 14 Apr 50.
98 UNTS 268. Portugal. Prolongation 14 Apr 50. Force 14 Apr 50.
98 UNTS 268. Portugal. Amendment 11 Dec 50. Force 11 Dec 50.
98 UNTS 270. UK Great Britain. Amendment 30 Nov 50. Force 11 Dec 50.

100072   Bilateral Exchange   **6 UNTS 131**
SIGNED: 16 Dec 46   FORCE: 16 Dec 46
REGISTERED: 7 Aug 47 UK Great Britain
ARTICLES: 3 LANGUAGE: English. Portuguese.
HEADNOTE: RENEWAL COMMERCIAL MODUS VIVENDI
TOPIC: General Trade
CONCEPTS: Previous treaty extension.
TREATY REF: 128LTS417; 2UNTS221.
PARTIES:
  El Salvador
  UK Great Britain

100073   Bilateral Exchange   **6 UNTS 137**
SIGNED: 21 Feb 46   FORCE: 21 Feb 46
REGISTERED: 7 Aug 47 UK Great Britain
ARTICLES: 2 LANGUAGE: English.
HEADNOTE: FREE IMPORTATION GOODS LEASED BASES
TOPIC: General Trade

CONCEPTS: Annex type material. Investigation of violations. Free trade. Customs declarations.
TREATY REF: 204LTS15;.
PARTIES:
  UK Great Britain
  USA (United States)

100074   Bilateral Treaty   **6 UNTS 143**
SIGNED: 22 Mar 46   FORCE: 17 Jun 46
REGISTERED: 7 Aug 47 UK Great Britain
ARTICLES: 14 LANGUAGE: Arabic. English.
HEADNOTE: ALLIANCE
TOPIC: General Amity
CONCEPTS: Friendship and amity. Defense and security.
INTL ORGS: International Court of Justice. United Nations.
PROCEDURE: Duration. Termination.
PARTIES:
  Jordan
  UK Great Britain

100075   Bilateral Convention   **6 UNTS 177**
SIGNED: 17 Apr 46   FORCE: 23 Nov 46
REGISTERED: 7 Aug 47 UK Great Britain
ARTICLES: 16 LANGUAGE: English. French.
HEADNOTE: INTELLECTUAL ARTISTIC SCIENTIFIC ACTIVITIES
TOPIC: Health/Educ/Welfare
CONCEPTS: Territorial application. General cooperation. Establishment of commission. Recognition of degrees. Commissions and foundations. Teacher and student exchange. Scholarships and grants. Exchange. General cultural cooperation. Artists. Publications exchange.
INTL ORGS: Special Commission.
PROCEDURE: Denunciation. Duration. Ratification. Renewal or Revival. Application to Non-self-governing Territories.
PARTIES:
  Belgium
  UK Great Britain

100076   Bilateral Convention   **6 UNTS 189**
SIGNED: 16 Apr 45   FORCE: 25 Jul 46
REGISTERED: 7 Aug 47 UK Great Britain
ARTICLES: 24 LANGUAGE: English.
HEADNOTE: AVOIDANCE DOUBLE TAXATION PREVENTION FISCAL EVASION
TOPIC: Taxation
CONCEPTS: Definition of terms. Conformity with municipal law. Exchange of information and documents. Responsibility and liability. Teacher and student exchange. Wages and salaries. Non-interest rates and fees. Taxation. Equitable taxes. General. Tax exemptions.
PROCEDURE: Duration. Ratification. Termination.
PARTIES:
  UK Great Britain
  USA (United States)
       ANNEX
207 UNTS 312. UK Great Britain. Amendment 25 May 54. Force 19 Jan 55.
207 UNTS 312. USA (United States). Amendment 25 May 54. Force 19 Jan 55.
336 UNTS 330. UK Great Britain. Amendment 19 Aug 57. Force 15 Oct 58.
336 UNTS 330. USA (United States). Amendment 19 Aug 57. Force 15 Oct 58.
351 UNTS 368. UK Great Britain. St. Lucia. Force 3 Dec 58.
351 UNTS 368. UK Great Britain. St. Vincent. Force 3 Dec 58.
351 UNTS 368. UK Great Britain. Nevis. Force 3 Dec 58.
351 UNTS 368. UK Great Britain. Anguilla. Force 3 Dec 58.
351 UNTS 368. UK Great Britain. Seychelles. Force 3 Dec 58.
351 UNTS 368. UK Great Britain. Sierra Leone. Force 3 Dec 58.
351 UNTS 368. UK Great Britain. Trinidad/-Tobago. Force 3 Dec 58.
351 UNTS 368. UK Great Britain. Brit Virgin Islands. Force 3 Dec 58.
351 UNTS 368. USA (United States). Acknowledgement 3 Dec 58. Force 3 Dec 58.
351 UNTS 368. UK Great Britain. Acknowledgement 3 Dec 58. Force 3 Dec 58.
351 UNTS 368. UK Great Britain. Aden. Force 3 Dec 58.

351 UNTS 368. UK Great Britain. Antigua. Force 3 Dec 58.
351 UNTS 368. UK Great Britain. Barbados. Force 3 Dec 58.
351 UNTS 368. UK Great Britain. British Honduras. Force 3 Dec 58.
351 UNTS 368. UK Great Britain. Cyprus. Force 3 Dec 58.
351 UNTS 368. UK Great Britain. Gambia. Force 3 Dec 58.
351 UNTS 368. UK Great Britain. Grenada. Force 3 Dec 58.
351 UNTS 368. UK Great Britain. Dominican Republic. Acknowledgement 3 Dec 58. Force 3 Dec 58.
351 UNTS 368. UK Great Britain. Falkland Islands. Force 3 Dec 58.
351 UNTS 368. UK Great Britain. Jamaica. Force 3 Dec 58.
351 UNTS 368. UK Great Britain. Montserrat. Force 3 Dec 58.
351 UNTS 368. UK Great Britain. Nigeria. Force 3 Dec 58.
351 UNTS 368. UK Great Britain. Fed Rhod/-Nyasaland. Force 3 Dec 58.
351 UNTS 368. UK Great Britain. St. Christopher. Force 3 Dec 58.
505 UNTS 300. UK Great Britain. Prolongation 31 Dec 63. Force 31 Dec 63.
505 UNTS 300. USA (United States). Prolongation 31 Dec 63. Force 31 Dec 63.
571 UNTS 313. USA (United States). Termination 30 Jun 65. Force 1 Jan 66.

100077   Bilateral Agreement   **6 UNTS 223**
SIGNED: 4 Jul 46   FORCE: 4 Jul 46
REGISTERED: 7 Aug 47 UK Great Britain
ARTICLES: 9 LANGUAGE: English. Icelandic.
HEADNOTE: TRANSFER AIRFIELD
TOPIC: Specific Property
CONCEPTS: Definition of terms. Assets transfer. Airport facilities. Airport equipment. Overflights and technical stops. Facilities and property.
INTL ORGS: International Civil Aviation Organization.
PARTIES:
  Iceland
  UK Great Britain

100078   Bilateral Agreement   **6 UNTS 235**
SIGNED: 31 Aug 46   FORCE: 31 Aug 46
REGISTERED: 7 Aug 47 UK Great Britain
ARTICLES: 13 LANGUAGE: English. Norwegian.
HEADNOTE: AIR COMMUNICATIONS
TOPIC: Air Transport
CONCEPTS: Detailed regulations. Annex or appendix reference. Non-prejudice to third party. Conformity with municipal law. General cooperation. Licenses and permits. Recognition of legal documents. Use of facilities. Procedure. Existing tribunals. Competence of tribunal. Fees and exemptions. Most favored nation clause. National treatment. Customs exemptions. Competency certificate. Routes and logistics. Navigational conditions. Permit designation. Airworthiness certificates. Conditions of airlines operating permission. Operating authorizations and regulations. Licenses and certificates of nationality.
INTL ORGS: International Civil Aviation Organization. Arbitration Commission.
TREATY REF: UK MISC NO.6(1945) CMD.6614.
PROCEDURE: Amendment. Future Procedures Contemplated. Registration. Termination.
PARTIES:
  Norway
  UK Great Britain

100079   Bilateral Agreement   **6 UNTS 259**
SIGNED: 27 Sep 46   FORCE: 27 Sep 46
REGISTERED: 7 Aug 47 UK Great Britain
ARTICLES: 4 LANGUAGE: English.
HEADNOTE: SUPPLY AIRCRAFT EQUIPMENT
TOPIC: Milit Installation
CONCEPTS: Annex or appendix reference. Indemnities and reimbursements. Delivery schedules. Payment for war supplies. Surplus war property. Restrictions on transfer.
PARTIES:
  Norway
  UK Great Britain

100080   Bilateral Exchange   **6 UNTS 273**
SIGNED: 4 Dec 45   FORCE: 4 Dec 45
REGISTERED: 11 Aug 47 USA (United States)
ARTICLES: 2 LANGUAGE: English. French.
HEADNOTE: AMENDING AIR TRANSPORT AGREE-
MENT
TOPIC: Air Transport
CONCEPTS: Annex or appendix reference. Annex
type material. Passenger transport. Routes and
logistics. Transport of goods. Air transport.
Overflights and technical stops.
TREATY REF: 006UNTS397.
PROCEDURE: Amendment.
PARTIES:
Sweden
USA (United States)
              ANNEX
222 UNTS 376. USA (United States). Amendment
6 Aug 54. Force 6 Aug 54.
222 UNTS 376. Sweden. Amendment 6 Aug 54.
Force 6 Aug 54.
321 UNTS 204. USA (United States). Amendment
8 Jul 58. Force 8 Jul 58.
321 UNTS 204. Sweden. Amendment 8 Jul 58.
Force 8 Jul 58.

100081   Bilateral Exchange   **6 UNTS 279**
SIGNED: 3 Mar 46   FORCE: 3 Jan 46
REGISTERED: 11 Aug 47 USA (United States)
ARTICLES: 2 LANGUAGE: English.
HEADNOTE: DISPOSITION STORAGE LOADING
FACILITIES
TOPIC: Specific Property
CONCEPTS: Assets transfer. Surplus war property.
Facilities and property.
INTL ORGS: United States-Canadian Defense Or-
ganization.
PARTIES:
Canada
USA (United States)

100082   Bilateral Exchange   **6 UNTS 285**
SIGNED: 7 May 46   FORCE: 7 May 46
REGISTERED: 11 Aug 47 USA (United States)
ARTICLES: 2 LANGUAGE: English.
HEADNOTE: AMENDING AGREEMENT
TOPIC: Water Transport
CONCEPTS: Previous treaty extension. Legal pro-
tection and assistance. Responsibility and liabil-
ity. Financial programs. Payment schedules.
Claims and settlements. Water transport. Pay-
ment for war supplies. Specific claims or waiv-
ers.
TREATY REF: 205LTS033.
PARTIES:
UK Great Britain
USA (United States)

100083   Bilateral Agreement   **6 UNTS 293**
SIGNED: 7 May 46   FORCE: 25 May 46
REGISTERED: 11 Aug 47 USA (United States)
ARTICLES: 6 LANGUAGE: English. Turkish.
HEADNOTE: LEND-LEASE CLAIMS
TOPIC: Milit Assistance
CONCEPTS: Definition of terms. General cooper-
ation. General property. Title and deeds. Pay-
ment schedules. Lump sum settlements. Lend
lease. Return of equipment and recapture. Re-
strictions on transfer. Post-war claims settle-
ment.
INTL ORGS: International Bank for Reconstruction
and Development.
PARTIES:
Turkey
USA (United States)

100084   Bilateral Agreement   **6 UNTS 309**
SIGNED: 3 Jan 46   FORCE: 3 Jan 46
REGISTERED: 11 Aug 47 USA (United States)
ARTICLES: 10 LANGUAGE: Czechoslovakian. En-
glish.
HEADNOTE: AIR TRANSPORT
TOPIC: Air Transport
CONCEPTS: Exceptions and exemptions. Annex or
appendix reference. Conformity with municipal
law. Licenses and permits. Recognition of legal
documents. Use of facilities. Fees and exemp-

tions. Most favored nation clause. National treatment. Customs exemptions. Competency certificate. Routes and logistics. Navigational conditions. Permit designation. Air transport. Airport
facilities. Airworthiness certificates. Conditions
of airlines operating permission. Operating authorizations and regulations. Licenses and certificates of nationality.
INTL ORGS: International Civil Aviation Organization.
TREATY REF: DEPT STATE PUB 2282, CONF. SE-
RIES 64.
PROCEDURE: Amendment. Ratification. Registration. Termination.
PARTIES:
Czechoslovakia
USA (United States)

100085   Bilateral Agreement   **6 UNTS 327**
SIGNED: 28 Jun 46   FORCE: 28 Jun 46
REGISTERED: 11 Aug 47 USA (United States)
ARTICLES: 10 LANGUAGE: English.
HEADNOTE: DISPOSITION LEND-LEASE SUP-
PLIES INVENTORY PROCUREMENT US
TOPIC: Milit Assistance
CONCEPTS: General cooperation. Title and deeds.
Transportation costs. Payment for war supplies.
Lease of military property. Lend lease. Restric-
tions on transfer.
PARTIES:
Brazil
USA (United States)

100086   Bilateral Instrument   **6 UNTS 335**
SIGNED: 4 Jul 46   FORCE: 4 Jul 46
REGISTERED: 11 Aug 47 USA (United States)
ARTICLES: 5 LANGUAGE: English.
HEADNOTE: FRIENDLY RELATIONS DIPLOMATIC
CONSULAR REPRESENTATION
TOPIC: General Amity
CONCEPTS: Recognition. Diplomatic relations es-
tablishment. Privileges and immunities.
PARTIES:
Philippines
USA (United States)

100087   Bilateral Agreement   **6 UNTS 341**
SIGNED: 10 Jul 46   FORCE: 10 Jul 46
REGISTERED: 11 Aug 47 USA (United States)
ARTICLES: 11 LANGUAGE: English.
HEADNOTE: SETTLE LEND-LEASE SURPLUS
PROPERTY CLAIMS
TOPIC: Milit Assistance
CONCEPTS: Definition of terms. Guarantees and
safeguards. Treaty implementation. General co-
operation. General property. Title and deeds. Ex-
change. General cultural cooperation. Exchange
rates and regulations. Lump sum settlements.
Payment for war supplies. Lease of military prop-
erty. Lend lease. Naval vessels. Return of equip-
ment and recapture. Surplus war property. Re-
strictions on transfer. Post-war claims settlement.
PROCEDURE: Future Procedures Contemplated.
PARTIES:
New Zealand
USA (United States)

100088   Bilateral Treaty   **7 UNTS 3**
SIGNED: 4 Jul 46   FORCE: 22 Oct 46
REGISTERED: 11 Aug 47 USA (United States)
ARTICLES: 8 LANGUAGE: English.
HEADNOTE: GENERAL RELATIONS
TOPIC: General Amity
CONCEPTS: Recognition. Consular relations es-
tablishment. Diplomatic relations establishment.
Privileges and immunities. General property.
Claims and settlements. Debt settlement. De-
fense and security. Bases and facilities.
TREATY REF: 343UTS; 30STAT175; 345UTS;
31STAT1942.
PROCEDURE: Ratification.
PARTIES:
Philippines
USA (United States)

100089   Bilateral Exchange   **7 UNTS 15**
SIGNED: 30 Mar 46   FORCE: 31 Mar 46
REGISTERED: 11 Aug 47 USA (United States)

ARTICLES: 4 LANGUAGE: English.
HEADNOTE: TRANSFER DEFENSE INSTALLA-
TIONS EQUIPMENT
TOPIC: Milit Installation
CONCEPTS: Previous treaty replacement. General
property. Surplus property. Payment for war supplies. Return of equipment and recapture. Military training. Surplus war property.
INTL ORGS: United States-Canadian Defense Organization.
PARTIES:
Canada
USA (United States)
              ANNEX
200 UNTS 250. USA (United States). Extension
and Amendment 24 Jan 48. Force 2 Mar 48.
200 UNTS 250. Canada. Extension and Amendment 2 Mar 48. Force 2 Mar 48.
200 UNTS 258. USA (United States). Implementation 7 Jun 49. Force 18 Jun 49.
200 UNTS 258. Canada. Implementation
18 Jun 49. Force 18 Jun 49.

100090   Bilateral Exchange   **7 UNTS 41**
SIGNED: 30 Jul 46   FORCE: 31 Jul 46
REGISTERED: 11 Aug 47 USA (United States)
ARTICLES: 2 LANGUAGE: English. Spanish.
HEADNOTE: COMMERCIAL RELATIONS
TOPIC: General Trade
CONCEPTS: Previous treaty extension.
TREATY REF: 6UNTS409;UN EXEC AG.-
SERIES119;52STAT1479; 204LTS38.
PROCEDURE: Denunciation. Duration. Future Pro-
cedures Contemplated.
PARTIES:
Chile
USA (United States)
              ANNEX
22 UNTS 300. Chile. Prolongation 30 Jul 47.
Force 30 Jul 47.
22 UNTS 300. USA (United States). Prolongation
30 Jul 47. Force 30 Jul 47.

100091   Bilateral Exchange   **7 UNTS 49**
SIGNED: 17 Sep 46   FORCE: 17 Sep 46
REGISTERED: 11 Aug 47 USA (United States)
ARTICLES: 3 LANGUAGE: English. Portuguese.
HEADNOTE: AMENDING EXTENDING NAVAL MIS-
SION AGREEMENTS
TOPIC: Military Mission
CONCEPTS: Annex type material. Previous treaty
extension. Military assistance missions.
PARTIES:
Brazil
USA (United States)
              ANNEX
238 UNTS 258. Brazil. Extension and Amendment
9 Oct 54. Force 9 Oct 54.
238 UNTS 258. USA (United States). Extension
and Amendment 29 Jun 54. Force 9 Oct 54.

100092   Bilateral Agreement   **7 UNTS 71**
SIGNED: 7 Oct 46   FORCE: 7 Oct 46
REGISTERED: 11 Aug 47 USA (United States)
ARTICLES: 36 LANGUAGE: English. Spanish.
HEADNOTE: AIR FORCES MISSION
TOPIC: Military Mission
CONCEPTS: Definition of terms. Conformity with
municipal law. Responsibility and liability. Use of
facilities. Compensation. Indemnities and reim-
bursements. Exchange rates and regulations. Ex-
pense sharing formulae. Tax exemptions. Cus-
toms duties. Customs exemptions. Military assis-
tance. Military assistance. Military training.
Airforce-army-navy personnel ratio. Ranks and
privileges. Third country military personnel.
Status of forces.
PROCEDURE: Denunciation. Duration. Renewal or
Revival. Termination.
PARTIES:
Peru
USA (United States)
              ANNEX
152 UNTS 272. USA (United States). Prolongation
31 Oct 50. Force 31 Oct 50.
152 UNTS 272. Peru. Prolongation 29 Sep 50.
Force 31 Oct 50.
541 UNTS 291. USA (United States). Prolongation
15 Mar 61. Force 2 Jun 61.
541 UNTS 291. Peru. Prolongation 2 Jun 61.
Force 2 Jun 61.

100093 Bilateral Agreement **7 UNTS 97**
SIGNED: 14 Oct 46 FORCE: 14 Oct 46
REGISTERED: 11 Aug 47 USA (United States)
ARTICLES: 29 LANGUAGE: English. Spanish.
HEADNOTE: NAVAL MISSION
TOPIC: Military Mission
CONCEPTS: Definition of terms. Use of facilities.
Compensation. Exchange rates and regulations.
Expense sharing formulae. Financial programs.
Tax exemptions. Military assistance. Military
training. Security of information. Airforce-army-
navy personnel ratio. Ranks and privileges. Con-
ditions for assistance missions. Third country
military personnel. Status of forces.
PROCEDURE: Denunciation. Duration. Renewal or
Revival. Termination.
PARTIES:
Colombia
USA (United States)
ANNEX
237 UNTS 288. USA (United States). Prolongation
6 Oct 54. Force 4 Nov 54.
237 UNTS 288. Colombia. Prolongation
4 Nov 54. Force 4 Nov 54.
342 UNTS 342. USA (United States). Amendment
18 Feb 59. Force 31 Mar 59.
342 UNTS 342. Colombia. Amendment
31 Mar 59. Force 31 Mar 59.

100094 Bilateral Exchange **7 UNTS 119**
SIGNED: 14 Nov 46 FORCE: 14 Nov 46
REGISTERED: 11 Aug 47 USA (United States)
ARTICLES: 2 LANGUAGE: English.
HEADNOTE: COMMERCIAL POLICIES
TOPIC: General Trade
CONCEPTS: Expropriation. Licenses and permits.
General property. Export quotas. Import quotas.
Trade procedures. Balance of payments. Most
favored nation clause.
TREATY REF: US EX.AG.SERIES 261;
56STAT1562.
PROCEDURE: Future Procedures Contemplated.
PARTIES:
Czechoslovakia
USA (United States)

100095 Bilateral Exchange **7 UNTS 131**
SIGNED: 19 Sep 46 FORCE: 19 Sep 46
REGISTERED: 14 Aug 47 USA (United States)
ARTICLES: 3 LANGUAGE: English. Spanish.
HEADNOTE: SALE VEGETABLE OILS
TOPIC: Commodity Trade
CONCEPTS: Trade procedures. Currency. Ex-
change rates and regulations. Non-interest rates
and fees. Commodity trade. Quotas.
INTL ORGS: International Emergency Food Orga-
nization.
PARTIES:
Argentina
USA (United States)

100096 Bilateral Exchange **7 UNTS 141**
SIGNED: 15 Nov 46 FORCE: 15 Nov 46
REGISTERED: 14 Aug 47 USA (United States)
ARTICLES: 3 LANGUAGE: English.
HEADNOTE: WAIVER LEGAL MARITIME CLAIMS
TOPIC: Specif Claim/Waive
CONCEPTS: Definition of terms. Previous treaty re-
placement. Claims and settlements. Merchant
vessels. Naval vessels. Specific claims or waiv-
ers.
TREATY REF: 007UNTS345.
PARTIES:
Canada
USA (United States)

100097 Bilateral Agreement **7 UNTS 151**
SIGNED: 16 Nov 46 FORCE: 16 Nov 46
REGISTERED: 14 Aug 47 USA (United States)
ARTICLES: 11 LANGUAGE: English.
HEADNOTE: AIR TRANSPORT
TOPIC: Air Transport
CONCEPTS: Exceptions and exemptions. Annex or
appendix reference. Conformity with municipal
law. Licenses and permits. Recognition of legal
documents. Use of facilities. Fees and exemptions. Most favored nation clause. National treatment. Customs exemptions. Competency certificate. Routes and logistics. Navigational conditions. Permit designation. Air transport. Airport

facilities. Airworthiness certificates. Conditions
of airlines operating permission. Operating authorizations and regulations. Licenses and certificates of nationality.
INTL ORGS: International Civil Aviation Organization.
TREATY REF: INTER CIVIL AVIA.CONF.INOV1944.
PROCEDURE: Amendment. Future Procedures
Contemplated. Registration. Termination.
PARTIES:
Philippines
USA (United States)
ANNEX
44 UNTS 336. USA (United States). Amendment
27 Aug 48. Force 27 Aug 48.
44 UNTS 336. Philippines. Amendment
27 Aug 48. Force 27 Aug 48.

100098 Bilateral Instrument **7 UNTS 163**
SIGNED: 2 Dec 46 FORCE: 1 Jan 47
REGISTERED: 14 Aug 47 USA (United States)
ARTICLES: 12 LANGUAGE: English.
HEADNOTE: ECONOMIC FUSION ZONES OCCU-
PATION
TOPIC: Milit Occupation
CONCEPTS: Establishment of commission. Import
quotas. Indemnities and reimbursements. Ex-
change rates and regulations. Funding proce-
dures. Post-war reconstruction. Industrial con-
trols. Control and occupation machinery.
INTL ORGS: Allied Military Occupation. Special
Commission.
PROCEDURE: Amendment. Duration. Future Procedures Contemplated. Renewal or Revival.
PARTIES:
UK Great Britain
USA (United States)
ANNEX
34 UNTS 390. USA (United States). Amendment
17 Dec 47. Force 17 Dec 47.
34 UNTS 390. UK Great Britain. Amendment
17 Dec 47. Force 17 Dec 47.
34 UNTS 410. USA (United States). Prolongation
31 Dec 48. Force 31 Dec 48.
34 UNTS 410. UK Great Britain. Prolongation
31 Dec 48. Force 31 Dec 48.
67 UNTS 336. USA (United States). Extension and
Amendment 31 Mar 49. Force 31 Mar 49.
67 UNTS 336. UK Great Britain. Extension and
Amendment 31 Mar 49. Force 31 Mar 49.
67 UNTS 340. USA (United States). Extension and
Amendment 30 Jun 49. Force 30 Jun 49.
67 UNTS 340. UK Great Britain. Extension and
Amendment 30 Jun 49. Force 30 Jun 49.
88 UNTS 412. UK Great Britain. Amendment
28 Jun 50. Force 28 Jun 50.
88 UNTS 412. USA (United States). Amendment
28 Jun 50. Force 28 Jun 50.

100099 Bilateral Agreement **7 UNTS 175**
SIGNED: 3 Dec 46 FORCE: 3 Dec 46
REGISTERED: 14 Aug 47 USA (United States)
ARTICLES: 13 LANGUAGE: English.
HEADNOTE: AIR TRANSPORT
TOPIC: Air Transport
CONCEPTS: Conditions. Definition of terms. An-
nex or appendix reference. Conformity with municipal law. General cooperation. Informational
records. Licenses and permits. Recognition of legal documents. Use of facilities. Procedure. Existing tribunals. Fees and exemptions. Most favored nation clause. National treatment. Cus-
toms exemptions. Temporary importation.
Competency certificate. Routes and logistics.
Navigational conditions. Permit designation. Air
transport. Airport facilities. Airport equipment.
Airworthiness certificates. Conditions of airlines
operating permission. Operating authorizations
and regulations. Licenses and certificates of nationality.
INTL ORGS: International Civil Aviation Organiza-
tion.
TREATY REF: EAS469; 15UNTS295.
PROCEDURE: Amendment. Future Procedures
Contemplated. Registration. Termination.
PARTIES:
New Zealand
USA (United States)
ANNEX
401 UNTS 204. New Zealand. Supplementation
30 Dec 60. Force 30 Dec 60.

401 UNTS 204. USA (United States). Supplementation 30 Dec 60. Force 30 Dec 60.
410 UNTS 280. USA (United States). Amendment
30 Jun 61. Force 30 Jun 61.
410 UNTS 280. New Zealand. Amendment
30 Jun 61. Force 30 Jun 61.
458 UNTS 270. USA (United States). Prolongation
29 Jun 62. Force 29 Jun 62.
458 UNTS 270. New Zealand. Prolongation
29 Jun 62. Force 29 Jun 62.
479 UNTS 350. USA (United States). Amendment
28 Jun 63. Force 28 Jun 63.
479 UNTS 350. New Zealand. Amendment
28 Jun 63. Force 28 Jun 63.

100100 Bilateral Agreement **7 UNTS 201**
SIGNED: 3 Dec 46 FORCE: 3 Dec 46
REGISTERED: 14 Aug 47 USA (United States)
ARTICLES: 13 LANGUAGE: English.
HEADNOTE: AIR TRANSPORT
TOPIC: Air Transport
CONCEPTS: Definition of terms. Annex or appendix reference. Conformity with municipal law.
General cooperation. Informational records. Licenses and permits. Recognition of legal documents. Use of facilities. Procedure. Existing tribunals. Competence of tribunal. Fees and exemptions. Most favored nation clause. National
treatment. Customs exemptions. Temporary importation. Competency certificate. Routes and
logistics. Permit designation. Air transport. Airport facilities. Airport equipment. Airworthiness
certificates. Conditions of airlines operating permission. Operating authorizations and regulations. Licenses and certificates of nationality.
INTL ORGS: International Civil Aviation Organization.
TREATY REF: EAS469.
PROCEDURE: Amendment. Future Procedures
Contemplated. Registration. Termination.
PARTIES:
Australia
USA (United States)
ANNEX
290 UNTS 280. USA (United States). Amendment
12 Aug 57. Force 12 Aug 57.
290 UNTS 280. Australia. Amendment
12 Aug 57. Force 12 Aug 57.

100101 Unilateral Instrument **7 UNTS 229**
SIGNED: 12 Jul 47 FORCE: 21 Aug 47
REGISTERED: 21 Aug 47 United Nations
ARTICLES: 1 LANGUAGE: English.
HEADNOTE: ACCEPTANCE ICJ JURISDICTION
TOPIC: ICJ Option Clause
CONCEPTS: Compulsory jurisdiction.
INTL ORGS: International Court of Justice.
PROCEDURE: Duration.
PARTIES:
Philippines

100102 Bilateral Treaty **7 UNTS 233**
SIGNED: 6 Jan 46 FORCE: 19 Apr 47
REGISTERED: 28 Aug 47 Taiwan
ARTICLES: 9 LANGUAGE: Chinese. English. Por-
tuguese.
HEADNOTE: AMITY
TOPIC: General Amity
CONCEPTS: Friendship and amity. Border traffic
and migration. Alien status. Consular relations
establishment. Diplomatic relations establish-
ment. Privileges and immunities.
PROCEDURE: Future Procedures Contemplated.
Ratification.
PARTIES:
Taiwan
Ecuador

100103 Bilateral Protocol **7 UNTS 247**
SIGNED: 8 Jul 46 FORCE: 8 Jul 46
REGISTERED: 5 Sep 47 Denmark
ARTICLES: 1 LANGUAGE: Danish. Norwegian.
HEADNOTE: NOTICE DENUNCIATION
TOPIC: Territory Boundary
CONCEPTS: Annex type material.
TREATY REF: 27LTS207.
PARTIES:
Denmark
Norway

100104   Bilateral Convention   **7 UNTS 251**
SIGNED: 18 Nov 46   FORCE: 1 Jan 47
REGISTERED: 5 Sep 47 Denmark
ARTICLES: 7 LANGUAGE: Danish. Swedish.
HEADNOTE: TRANSFER LABOR
TOPIC: Non-ILO Labor
CONCEPTS: Resident permits. General cooperation. Exchange of information and documents. Domestic legislation. Establishment of commission. Non-ILO labor relations. Social security. Migrant worker.
INTL ORGS: Special Commission.
PROCEDURE: Denunciation. Ratification.
PARTIES:
   Denmark
   Sweden

100105   Bilateral Agreement   **7 UNTS 267**
SIGNED: 20 Jun 47   FORCE: 20 Jun 47
REGISTERED: 12 Sep 47 USA (United States)
ARTICLES: 12 LANGUAGE: English. Greek.
HEADNOTE: AID
TOPIC: Direct Aid
CONCEPTS: Guarantees and safeguards. Annex or appendix reference. Privileges and immunities. Conformity with municipal law. General cooperation. Exchange of information and documents. Inspection and observation. Personnel. Public information. Title and deeds. Use of facilities. Domestic obligation. General aid. Use restrictions. Aid missions. Withdrawal conditions.
INTL ORGS: United Nations.
PROCEDURE: Duration. Registration.
PARTIES:
   Greece
   USA (United States)

100106   Bilateral Agreement   **7 UNTS 299**
SIGNED: 12 Jul 47   FORCE: 12 Jul 47
REGISTERED: 12 Sep 47 USA (United States)
ARTICLES: 8 LANGUAGE: English. Turkish.
HEADNOTE: AID
TOPIC: Direct Aid
CONCEPTS: Guarantees and safeguards. Conformity with municipal law. General cooperation. Personnel. Public information. Domestic obligation. General technical assistance. General aid. Use restrictions. Aid missions.
INTL ORGS: United Nations.
PROCEDURE: Duration. Registration.
PARTIES:
   Turkey
   USA (United States)

100107   Bilateral Agreement   **7 UNTS 309**
SIGNED: 20 Dec 46   FORCE: 20 Dec 46
REGISTERED: 17 Sep 47 Denmark
ARTICLES: 16 LANGUAGE: English.
HEADNOTE: MONEY PROPERTY SUBJECTED SPECIAL MEASURES
TOPIC: Reparations
CONCEPTS: Definition of terms. Treaty implementation. General property. Accounting procedures. Currency. Assets transfer. Post-war claims settlement.
PARTIES:
   Denmark
   India

100108   Bilateral Exchange   **7 UNTS 321**
SIGNED: 9 Jul 47   FORCE: 9 Jul 47
REGISTERED: 17 Sep 47 Denmark
ARTICLES: 2 LANGUAGE: Danish. Norwegian.
HEADNOTE: SUPPLEMENTARY AGREEMENT
TOPIC: Territory Boundary
CONCEPTS: Annex type material. Fish, wildlife, and natural resources. Markers and definitions.
PARTIES:
   Denmark
   Norway

100109   Multilateral Exchange   **7 UNTS 331**
SIGNED: 3 Jun 46   FORCE: 3 Jun 46
REGISTERED: 19 Sep 47 UK Great Britain
ARTICLES: 6 LANGUAGE: English.
HEADNOTE: AMENDING WHEAT AGREEMENT
TOPIC: Commodity Trade
CONCEPTS: Annex type material. Commodity trade.

TREATY REF: US EX.AG.SERIES 384; 57STAT1382.
PROCEDURE: Amendment.
PARTIES:
   Argentina SIGNED: 9 Apr 46 RATIFIED: 9 Apr 46
     FORCE: 3 Jun 46
   Australia   SIGNED: 20 Mar 46   RATIFIED:
     20 Mar 46 FORCE: 3 Jun 46
   Canada   SIGNED: 25 Mar 46   RATIFIED:
     25 Mar 46 FORCE: 3 Jun 46
   UK Great Britain SIGNED: 3 May 46 RATIFIED:
     3 May 46 FORCE: 3 Jun 46
   USA (United States) SIGNED: 3 Jun 46 FORCE:
     3 Jun 46

100110   Bilateral Agreement   **8 UNTS 3**
SIGNED: 22 Apr 47   FORCE: 22 Apr 47
REGISTERED: 24 Sep 47 Denmark
ARTICLES: 10 LANGUAGE: Danish. English.
HEADNOTE: PARTICIPATION OCCUPATION
TOPIC: Milit Occupation
CONCEPTS: Exceptions and exemptions. Use of facilities. Indemnities and reimbursements. Joint defense. Payment for war supplies. Military training. Jurisdiction. Procurement and logistics. Control and occupation machinery.
PARTIES:
   Denmark
   UK Great Britain
             ANNEX
24 UNTS 318. Denmark. Prolongation 30 Nov 48. Force 13 Nov 48.
24 UNTS 318. UK Great Britain. Prolongation 4 Nov 48. Force 13 Nov 48.
45 UNTS 320. Denmark. Prolongation 10 Dec 48. Force 15 Dec 48.
45 UNTS 320. UK Great Britain. Prolongation 10 Dec 48. Force 15 Dec 48.
78 UNTS 362. Denmark. Prolongation 15 Feb 50. Force 15 Nov 50.
78 UNTS 362. UK Great Britain. Prolongation 14 Nov 50. Force 15 Nov 50.
81 UNTS 310. Denmark. Amendment 13 Dec 50. Force 13 Dec 50.
81 UNTS 310. UK Great Britain. Amendment 13 Dec 50. Force 13 Dec 50.

100111   Bilateral Agreement   **8 UNTS 21**
SIGNED: 30 Dec 46   FORCE: 7 Mar 47
REGISTERED: 26 Sep 47 Denmark
ARTICLES: 12 LANGUAGE: Danish. Norwegian.
HEADNOTE: PREVENTION DOUBLE TAXATION
TOPIC: Taxation
CONCEPTS: Definition of terms. Territorial application. Negotiation. Taxation. General.
PROCEDURE: Denunciation. Duration. Ratification.
PARTIES:
   Denmark
   Norway

100112   Unilateral Instrument   **8 UNTS 57**
SIGNED: 30 Sep 47   FORCE: 30 Sep 47
REGISTERED: 30 Sep 47 United Nations
ARTICLES: 1 LANGUAGE: English.
HEADNOTE: ADHERENCE UN CHARTER
TOPIC: UN Charter
CONCEPTS: Adherence to UN Charter. Acceptance of UN obligations. Acceptance of obligations upon admittance to UN.
INTL ORGS: United Nations.
PARTIES:
   Pakistan

100113   Unilateral Instrument   **8 UNTS 59**
SIGNED: 30 Sep 47   FORCE: 30 Sep 47
REGISTERED: 30 Sep 47 United Nations
ARTICLES: 1 LANGUAGE: French.
HEADNOTE: ADHERENCE UN CHARTER
TOPIC: UN Charter
CONCEPTS: Acceptance of UN obligations.
INTL ORGS: United Nations.
PARTIES:
   Yemen

100114   Bilateral Exchange   **8 UNTS 61**
SIGNED: 26 Jun 46   FORCE: 11 Dec 46
REGISTERED: 1 Oct 47 United Nations
ARTICLES: 2 LANGUAGE: French.
HEADNOTE: ICJ PRIVILEGES IMMUNITIES

TOPIC: IGO Status/Immunit
CONCEPTS: Annex or appendix reference. Diplomatic privileges. Inviolability. IGO status. Special status. Status of experts.
INTL ORGS: United Nations.
PARTIES:
   Netherlands
   ICJ (Int Court)

100115   Multilateral Agreement   **8 UNTS 71**
SIGNED: 13 Dec 46   FORCE: 13 Dec 46
REGISTERED: 1 Oct 47 United Nations
ARTICLES: 16 LANGUAGE: English. French.
HEADNOTE: TRUSTEESHIP
TOPIC: Trusteeship
CONCEPTS: Annex or appendix reference. Non-visa travel documents. Human rights. Exchange of information and documents. Arms limitations. Conformity with IGO decisions. Administering authority. Disposition of territory. Definition of territory. Socio-economic development. Respect for local customs. Regulation of natural resources.
INTL ORGS: League of Nations. International Court of Justice.
PARTIES:
   Multilateral
             ANNEX
418 UNTS 325. United Nations. Termination 18 Oct 61. Force 1 Jan 62.

100116   Multilateral Agreement   **8 UNTS 91**
SIGNED: 13 Dec 46   FORCE: 13 Dec 46
REGISTERED: 1 Oct 47 United Nations
ARTICLES: 19 LANGUAGE: English. French.
HEADNOTE: TRUSTEESHIP
TOPIC: Trusteeship
CONCEPTS: Exchange of information and documents. Procedure. Exchange. Arms limitations. Administering authority. Disposition of territory. Definition of territory. Socio-economic development. Internal travel. Regulation of natural resources.
INTL ORGS: League of Nations. International Court of Justice.
TREATY REF: 190LTS095.
PROCEDURE: Amendment.
PARTIES:
   Multilateral
             ANNEX
416 UNTS 298. United Nations. Termination 6 Nov 61. Force 9 Dec 61.

100117   Multilateral Agreement   **8 UNTS 105**
SIGNED: 13 Dec 46   FORCE: 13 Dec 46
REGISTERED: 1 Oct 47 United Nations
ARTICLES: 19 LANGUAGE: English. French.
HEADNOTE: TRUSTEESHIP
TOPIC: Trusteeship
CONCEPTS: Diplomatic missions. Existing tribunals. Exchange. Arms limitations. Administering authority. Disposition of territory. Definition of territory. Socio-economic development. Respect for local customs. Regulation of natural resources.
INTL ORGS: League of Nations. International Court of Justice.
TREATY REF: 190LTS95.
PROCEDURE: Amendment.
PARTIES:
   Multilateral
             ANNEX
431 UNTS 200. Rwanda. Termination 1 Jul 62.
431 UNTS 200. Burundi. Termination 1 Jul 62.

100118   Multilateral Agreement   **8 UNTS 119**
SIGNED: 13 Dec 46   FORCE: 13 Dec 46
REGISTERED: 1 Oct 47 United Nations
ARTICLES: 19 LANGUAGE: English. French.
HEADNOTE: TRUSTEESHIP
TOPIC: Trusteeship
CONCEPTS: Non-visa travel documents. Human rights. Exchange of information and documents. Existing tribunals. Conformity with IGO decisions. Assistance to United Nations. Administering authority. Disposition of territory. Definition of territory. Socio-economic development. Respect for local customs.
INTL ORGS: League of Nations. International Court of Justice.

PARTIES:
Multilateral
ANNEX
397 UNTS 328. United Nations. Termination
21 Apr 61. Force 1 Jun 61.
410 UNTS 284. United Nations. Termination
21 Apr 61. Force 1 Oct 61.

100119 Multilateral Agreement **8 UNTS 135**
SIGNED: 13 Dec 46 FORCE: 13 Dec 46
REGISTERED: 1 Oct 47 United Nations
ARTICLES: 15 LANGUAGE: English. French.
HEADNOTE: TRUSTEESHIP
TOPIC: Trusteeship
CONCEPTS: Previous treaty extension. Non-visa
travel documents. Human rights. Exchange of in-
formation and documents. Existing tribunals.
Customs exemptions. Administering authority.
Disposition of territory. Definition of territory.
Socio-economic development. Respect for local
customs.
INTL ORGS: International Court of Justice.
PARTIES:
Multilateral
ANNEX
348 UNTS 344. United Nations. Termination
13 Mar 59. Force 1 Jan 60.
348 UNTS 344. France. Termination 13 Mar 59.
Force 1 Jan 60.

100120 Multilateral Agreement **8 UNTS 151**
SIGNED: 13 Dec 46 FORCE: 13 Dec 46
REGISTERED: 1 Oct 47 United Nations
ARTICLES: 19 LANGUAGE: English. French.
HEADNOTE: TRUSTEESHIP
TOPIC: Trusteeship
CONCEPTS: Exchange of information and docu-
ments. Existing tribunals. Exchange. Disposition
of territory. Definition of territory. Socio-eco-
nomic development. Respect for local customs.
Internal travel.
INTL ORGS: League of Nations. International Court
of Justice.
PARTIES:
Multilateral
ANNEX
261 UNTS 374. United Nations. Termination
6 Mar 57.

100121 Multilateral Agreement **8 UNTS 165**
SIGNED: 13 Dec 46 FORCE: 13 Dec 46
REGISTERED: 1 Oct 47 United Nations
ARTICLES: 15 LANGUAGE: English. French.
HEADNOTE: TRUSTEESHIP
TOPIC: Trusteeship
CONCEPTS: Exchange of information and docu-
ments. Existing tribunals. Administering author-
ity. Disposition of territory. Definition of territory.
Socio-economic development. Respect for local
customs.
INTL ORGS: International Court of Justice.
PARTIES:
Multilateral
ANNEX
357 UNTS 333. France. Termination 5 Dec 59.
Force 27 Apr 60.
357 UNTS 333. United Nations. Termination
5 Dec 59. Force 27 Apr 60.

100122 Multilateral Agreement **8 UNTS 181**
SIGNED: 13 Dec 46 FORCE: 13 Dec 46
REGISTERED: 1 Oct 47 United Nations
ARTICLES: 8 LANGUAGE: English. French.
HEADNOTE: TRUSTEESHIP
TOPIC: Trusteeship
CONCEPTS: Administering authority. Disposition
of territory. Definition of territory. Socio-eco-
nomic development. Respect for local customs.
INTL ORGS: League of Nations.
PARTIES:
Multilateral

100123 Unilateral Agreement **8 UNTS 189**
SIGNED: 2 Apr 47 FORCE: 18 Jul 47
REGISTERED: 1 Oct 47 United Nations
ARTICLES: 16 LANGUAGE: English. French.
HEADNOTE: TRUSTEESHIP FORMER JAPANESE
MANDATED ISLANDS
TOPIC: Trusteeship

CONCEPTS: Trusteeship. Administering authority.
Disposition of territory. Definition of territory.
Socio-economic development. Internal travel.
INTL ORGS: League of Nations.
PARTIES:
Multilateral

100124 Bilateral Treaty **8 UNTS 201**
SIGNED: 17 Aug 46 FORCE: 31 Dec 46
REGISTERED: 14 Oct 47 Denmark
ARTICLES: 17 LANGUAGE: Danish. Russian.
HEADNOTE: COMMERCE NAVIGATION
TOPIC: General Economic
CONCEPTS: Exceptions and exemptions. Previous
treaty replacement. Privileges and immunities.
Free passage and transit. Legal protection and
assistance. General property. Arbitration. Proce-
dure. Negotiation. General economics. Import
quotas. Trade agencies. Most favored nation
clause. Customs duties. Transport of goods. Wa-
ter transport. Merchant vessels. Tonnage. Ports
and pilotage. Shipwreck and salvage.
TREATY REF: 18LTS15; 27LTS149; 36LTS251.
PROCEDURE: Denunciation. Duration. Ratification.
Renewal or Revival. Termination.
PARTIES:
Denmark
USSR (Soviet Union)

100125 Multilateral Protocol **9 UNTS 3**
SIGNED: 22 Jul 46 FORCE: 22 Jul 46
REGISTERED: 20 Oct 47 United Nations
ARTICLES: 7 LANGUAGE: Chinese. English.
French. Russian. Spanish.
HEADNOTE: FINAL ACT INTERNATIONAL HEALTH
CONFERENCE
TOPIC: IGO Establishment
CONCEPTS: Annex or appendix reference. Annex
type material. General health, education, culture,
welfare and labor. Admission. Establishment. UN
recommendations.
INTL ORGS: League of Nations. United Nations Re-
lief and Rehabilitation Administration. United
Nations. World Health Organization.
PROCEDURE: Ratification. Termination.
PARTIES:
Albania SIGNED: 22 Jul 46 FORCE: 22 Jul 46
Argentina SIGNED: 22 Jul 46 FORCE: 22 Jul 46
Australia SIGNED: 22 Jul 46
Austria SIGNED: 22 Jul 46 FORCE: 22 Jul 46
Belgium SIGNED: 22 Jul 46
Bolivia SIGNED: 22 Jul 46 FORCE: 22 Jul 46
Brazil SIGNED: 22 Jul 46 FORCE: 22 Jul 46
Bulgaria SIGNED: 22 Jul 46 FORCE: 22 Jul 46
Byelorussia SIGNED: 22 Jul 46 FORCE:
22 Jul 46
Canada SIGNED: 22 Jul 46 FORCE: 22 Jul 46
Chile SIGNED: 22 Jul 46 FORCE: 22 Jul 46
Taiwan SIGNED: 22 Jul 46 FORCE: 22 Jul 46
Colombia SIGNED: 22 Jul 46 FORCE: 22 Jul 46
Costa Rica SIGNED: 22 Jul 46 FORCE: 22 Jul 46
Cuba SIGNED: 22 Jul 46 FORCE: 22 Jul 46
Czechoslovakia SIGNED: 22 Jul 46 FORCE:
22 Jul 46
Denmark SIGNED: 22 Jul 46 FORCE: 22 Jul 46
Dominican Republic SIGNED: 22 Jul 46 FORCE:
22 Jul 46
Ecuador SIGNED: 22 Jul 46 FORCE: 22 Jul 46
United Arab Rep SIGNED: 22 Jul 46 FORCE:
22 Jul 46
El Salvador SIGNED: 22 Jul 46 FORCE:
22 Jul 46
Ethiopia SIGNED: 22 Jul 46 FORCE: 22 Jul 46
Finland SIGNED: 22 Jul 46 FORCE: 22 Jul 46
France SIGNED: 22 Jul 46 FORCE: 22 Jul 46
Greece SIGNED: 22 Jul 46 FORCE: 22 Jul 46
Guatemala SIGNED: 22 Jul 46 FORCE: 22 Jul 46
Haiti SIGNED: 22 Jul 46 FORCE: 22 Jul 46
Honduras SIGNED: 22 Jul 46 FORCE: 22 Jul 46
Hungary SIGNED: 19 Feb 47
India SIGNED: 22 Jul 46 FORCE: 22 Jul 46
Iran SIGNED: 22 Jul 46 FORCE: 22 Jul 46
Iraq SIGNED: 22 Jul 46 FORCE: 22 Jul 46
Ireland SIGNED: 22 Jul 46 FORCE: 22 Jul 46
Italy SIGNED: 22 Jul 46 FORCE: 22 Jul 46
Lebanon SIGNED: 22 Jul 46 FORCE: 22 Jul 46
Liberia SIGNED: 22 Jul 46 FORCE: 22 Jul 46
Luxembourg SIGNED: 22 Jul 46
Mexico SIGNED: 22 Jul 46 FORCE: 22 Jul 46
Netherlands SIGNED: 22 Jul 46 FORCE:
22 Jul 46

New Zealand SIGNED: 22 Jul 46 FORCE:
22 Jul 46
Nicaragua SIGNED: 22 Jul 46 FORCE: 22 Jul 46
Norway SIGNED: 22 Jul 46 FORCE: 22 Jul 46
Panama SIGNED: 22 Jul 46 FORCE: 22 Jul 46
Paraguay SIGNED: 22 Jul 46 FORCE: 22 Jul 46
Peru SIGNED: 22 Jul 46 FORCE: 22 Jul 46
Philippines SIGNED: 22 Jul 46 FORCE:
22 Jul 46
Poland SIGNED: 22 Jul 46 FORCE: 22 Jul 46
Portugal SIGNED: 22 Jul 46 FORCE: 22 Jul 46
Saudi Arabia SIGNED: 22 Jul 46 FORCE:
22 Jul 46
Siam SIGNED: 22 Jul 46 FORCE: 22 Jul 46
South Africa SIGNED: 22 Jul 46 FORCE:
22 Jul 46
Sweden SIGNED: 13 Jan 47 FORCE: 13 Jan 47
Switzerland SIGNED: 22 Jul 46 FORCE:
22 Jul 46
Syria SIGNED: 22 Jul 46 FORCE: 22 Jul 46
Transjordan SIGNED: 22 Jul 46 FORCE:
22 Jul 46
Turkey SIGNED: 22 Jul 46 FORCE: 22 Jul 46
UK Great Britain SIGNED: 22 Jul 46 FORCE:
22 Jul 46
USA (United States) SIGNED: 22 Jul 46 FORCE:
22 Jul 46
Ukrainian SSR SIGNED: 22 Jul 46 FORCE:
22 Jul 46
Uruguay SIGNED: 22 Jul 46 FORCE: 22 Jul 46
USSR (Soviet Union) SIGNED: 22 Jul 46 FORCE:
22 Jul 46
Venezuela SIGNED: 22 Jul 46 FORCE: 22 Jul 46
Yugoslavia SIGNED: 22 Jul 46 FORCE: 22 Jul 46
ANNEX
10 UNTS 376. Yugoslavia. Ratification
19 Nov 47.
11 UNTS 421. United Arab Rep. Ratification
16 Dec 47.
12 UNTS 417. India. Ratification 12 Jan 48.
13 UNTS 474. Czechoslovakia. Accession
1 Mar 48.
14 UNTS 491. Greece. Ratification/Acceptance
12 Mar 48.
14 UNTS 491. South Africa. Ratification/Accept-
ance 19 Mar 48.
17 UNTS 361. Portugal. Ratification 11 Aug 48.
27 UNTS 400. Honduras. Ratification 8 Apr 49.
34 UNTS 416. Guatemala. Ratification
26 Aug 49.
54 UNTS 383. Cuba. Acceptance 9 May 50.
81 UNTS 312. Panama. Acceptance 20 Feb 51.
117 UNTS 377. Japan. Acceptance 11 Dec 51.

100126 Bilateral Exchange **9 UNTS 91**
SIGNED: 3 Sep 47 FORCE: 3 Sep 47
REGISTERED: 25 Oct 47 USA (United States)
ARTICLES: 2 LANGUAGE: Chinese. English.
HEADNOTE: PRESENCE ARMED FORCES
TOPIC: Status of Forces
CONCEPTS: Airforce-army-navy personnel ratio.
Withdrawal of forces.
INTL ORGS: United Nations.
PARTIES:
Taiwan
USA (United States)

100127 Unilateral Instrument **9 UNTS 97**
SIGNED: 23 Oct 47 FORCE: 1 Mar 47
REGISTERED: 28 Oct 47 United Nations
ARTICLES: 1 LANGUAGE: Spanish.
HEADNOTE: ACCEPTANCE ICJ JURISDICTION
TOPIC: ICJ Option Clause
CONCEPTS: Conformity with municipal law. Com-
pulsory jurisdiction.
INTL ORGS: International Court of Justice.
PARTIES:
Mexico

100128 Multilateral Agreement **9 UNTS 101**
SIGNED: 4 Dec 45 FORCE: 29 Mar 46
REGISTERED: 31 Oct 47 UK Great Britain
ARTICLES: 6 LANGUAGE: English.
HEADNOTE: TELECOMMUNICATION
TOPIC: Telecommunications
CONCEPTS: General provisions. Annex or appen-
dix reference. Standardization. Tariffs. Currency.
Expense sharing formulae. Non-interest rates
and fees. Cable. Services. Radio-telephone-tele-

graphic communications. Press and wire services. Extension of functions.
INTL ORGS: International Telecommunication Union.
TREATY REF: BRETTON WOODS AGREEM.
PARTIES:
Australia SIGNED: 4 Dec 45 RATIFIED: 29 Mar 46 FORCE: 29 Mar 46
Canada SIGNED: 4 Dec 45 RATIFIED: 1 Mar 46 FORCE: 29 Mar 46
India SIGNED: 4 Dec 45 RATIFIED: 29 Mar 46 FORCE: 29 Mar 46
New Zealand SIGNED: 4 Dec 45 RATIFIED: 23 Mar 46 FORCE: 29 Mar 46
South Africa SIGNED: 4 Dec 45 RATIFIED: 27 Mar 46 FORCE: 29 Mar 46
Southern Rhodesia SIGNED: 4 Dec 45 RATIFIED: 9 Mar 46 FORCE: 29 Mar 46
UK Great Britain SIGNED: 4 Dec 45 RATIFIED: 13 Mar 46 FORCE: 29 Mar 46
USA (United States) SIGNED: 4 Dec 45 RATIFIED: 16 Mar 46 FORCE: 29 Mar 46

100129 Bilateral Exchange **9 UNTS 121**
SIGNED: 4 Dec 45 FORCE: 4 Dec 45
REGISTERED: 31 Oct 47 UK Great Britain
ARTICLES: 6 LANGUAGE: English. French.
HEADNOTE: SUPPLY AIRCRAFT
TOPIC: Milit Installation
CONCEPTS: Annex or appendix reference. Military installations and equipment.
PARTIES:
France
UK Great Britain

100130 Bilateral Agreement **9 UNTS 163**
SIGNED: 16 Aug 46 FORCE: 16 Aug 46
REGISTERED: 31 Oct 47 UK Great Britain
ARTICLES: 3 LANGUAGE: English.
HEADNOTE: SUPPLY AIRCRAFT
TOPIC: Milit Installation
CONCEPTS: Time limit. Annex or appendix reference. Inspection and observation. Responsibility and liability. Indemnities and reimbursements. Delivery schedules. Payment for war supplies. Surplus war property.
PARTIES:
Denmark
UK Great Britain

100131 Bilateral Agreement **9 UNTS 173**
SIGNED: 19 Feb 47 FORCE: 19 Feb 47
REGISTERED: 31 Oct 47 UK Great Britain
ARTICLES: 3 LANGUAGE: Czechoslovakian. English.
HEADNOTE: SUPPLY AIRCRAFT EQUIPMENT
TOPIC: Milit Installation
CONCEPTS: Military assistance. Payment for war supplies. Lend lease.
PARTIES:
Czechoslovakia
UK Great Britain

100132 Bilateral Treaty **9 UNTS 187**
SIGNED: 4 Mar 47 FORCE: 8 Sep 47
REGISTERED: 31 Oct 47 UK Great Britain
ARTICLES: 6 LANGUAGE: English. French.
HEADNOTE: ALLIANCE MUTUAL ASSISTANCE
TOPIC: General Amity
CONCEPTS: Non-prejudice to UN charter. Economic assistance. Defense and security.
INTL ORGS: United Nations.
PROCEDURE: Duration. Ratification. Termination.
PARTIES:
France
UK Great Britain

100133 Bilateral Exchange **9 UNTS 197**
SIGNED: 5 Jun 47 FORCE: 5 Jun 47
REGISTERED: 31 Oct 47 UK Great Britain
ARTICLES: 2 LANGUAGE: English.
HEADNOTE: MAINTENANCE COMMUNICATIONS FLIGHT
TOPIC: Status of Forces
CONCEPTS: Use of facilities. Airport facilities. Airforce-army-navy personnel ratio. Status of military forces.

PARTIES:
Greece
UK Great Britain

100134 Bilateral Exchange **9 UNTS 203**
SIGNED: 18 Jun 47 FORCE: 18 Jun 47
REGISTERED: 31 Oct 47 UK Great Britain
ARTICLES: 2 LANGUAGE: English. French.
HEADNOTE: APPLICATION CHICAGO AIR TRANSIT AGREEMENT
TOPIC: Air Transport
CONCEPTS: Annex type material. Air transport.
TREATY REF: CMD6614; CMD6787.
PROCEDURE: Termination.
PARTIES:
France
UK Great Britain

100135 Bilateral Agreement **9 UNTS 207**
SIGNED: 23 Jul 47 FORCE: 23 Jul 47
REGISTERED: 31 Oct 47 UK Great Britain
ARTICLES: 14 LANGUAGE: Chinese. English.
HEADNOTE: AIR TRANSPORT
TOPIC: Air Transport
CONCEPTS: Default remedies. Definition of terms. Exceptions and exemptions. Remedies. Annex or appendix reference. Conformity with municipal law. General cooperation. Licenses and permits. Recognition of legal documents. Arbitration. Procedure. Existing tribunals. Fees and exemptions. Most favored nation clause. Customs exemptions. Competency certificate. Navigational conditions. Permit designation. Air transport. Airport facilities. Airworthiness certificates. Conditions of airlines operating permission. Overflights and technical stops. Operating authorizations and regulations. Licenses and certificates of nationality.
INTL ORGS: International Civil Aviation Organization. Arbitration Commission.
TREATY REF: G.B. MISC.6(1945) CMD.6614.
PROCEDURE: Amendment. Duration. Future Procedures Contemplated. Registration. Termination.
PARTIES:
Taiwan
UK Great Britain

100136 Bilateral Agreement **9 UNTS 259**
SIGNED: 13 Aug 47 FORCE: 15 Jul 47
REGISTERED: 31 Oct 47 UK Great Britain
ARTICLES: 12 LANGUAGE: English.
HEADNOTE: FINANCE
TOPIC: Finance
CONCEPTS: Definition of terms. Exchange of information and documents. Informational records. Assets.
PROCEDURE: Duration. Renewal or Revival. Termination.
PARTIES:
Iraq
UK Great Britain
ANNEX
88 UNTS 418. UK Great Britain. Supplementation 18 Feb 51. Force 18 Feb 51.
88 UNTS 418. Iraq. Supplementation 18 Feb 51. Force 18 Feb 51.

100137 Bilateral Agreement **9 UNTS 277**
SIGNED: 19 Aug 47 FORCE: 17 Aug 47
REGISTERED: 31 Oct 47 UK Great Britain
ARTICLES: 8 LANGUAGE: English.
HEADNOTE: INDUSTRIAL PROPERTY
TOPIC: Reparations
CONCEPTS: Definition of terms. Territorial application. Time limit. Post-war adjustment. Post-war claims settlement.
PROCEDURE: Application to Non-self-governing Territories.
PARTIES:
Denmark
UK Great Britain

100138 Multilateral Agreement **10 UNTS 3**
SIGNED: 1 Nov 47 FORCE: 1 Nov 47
REGISTERED: 1 Nov 47 United Nations
ARTICLES: 7 LANGUAGE: English. French.
HEADNOTE: TRUSTEESHIP
TOPIC: Trusteeship
CONCEPTS: Administering authority. Disposition

of territory. Definition of territory. Socio-economic development. Respect for local customs.
INTL ORGS: United Nations. Special Commission.
PARTIES:
Multilateral
ANNEX
620 UNTS 253. Nauru. Termination 19 Dec 67.

100139 Bilateral Convention **10 UNTS 11**
SIGNED: 16 Mar 46 FORCE: 7 Jul 46
REGISTERED: 6 Nov 47 Poland
ARTICLES: 7 LANGUAGE: Polish. Serbo-Croat.
HEADNOTE: CULTURAL COLLABORATION
TOPIC: Culture
CONCEPTS: Detailed regulations. Friendship and amity. Conformity with municipal law. Operating agencies. Dispute settlement. Recognition of degrees. Commissions and foundations. Teacher and student exchange. Professorships. Institute establishment. Scholarships and grants. General cultural cooperation. Artists. Athletes. Meteorology. Scientific exchange. Indemnities and reimbursements. Expense sharing formulae.
INTL ORGS: Special Commission.
PROCEDURE: Denunciation. Duration. Ratification. Renewal or Revival.
PARTIES:
Poland
Yugoslavia

100140 Bilateral Exchange **10 UNTS 29**
SIGNED: 14 Oct 46 FORCE: 14 Oct 46
REGISTERED: 15 Nov 47 South Africa
ARTICLES: 7 LANGUAGE: English.
HEADNOTE: RELEASE FUNDS PROPERTY HELD CUSTODIAN ENEMY PROPERTY
TOPIC: Claims and Debts
CONCEPTS: Detailed regulations. General cooperation. Exchange of information and documents. General property. Recognition of legal documents. Responsibility and liability. Accounting procedures. Banking. Bonds. Assets. Claims and settlements. Assets transfer. Most favored nation clause. War claims and reparations. Enemy financial interests.
PARTIES:
Denmark
South Africa

100141 Bilateral Exchange **10 UNTS 39**
SIGNED: 18 Sep 46 FORCE: 13 Sep 46
REGISTERED: 17 Nov 47 Denmark
ARTICLES: 3 LANGUAGE: English.
HEADNOTE: RELEASE WARTIME DANISH OWINGS
TOPIC: Claims and Debts
CONCEPTS: Bonds. Currency deposits. Investments. Interest rates. Assets. Claims and settlements. Debts. Debt settlement. Assessment procedures. Enemy financial interests.
PARTIES:
Denmark
New Zealand

100142 Bilateral Agreement **10 UNTS 47**
SIGNED: 11 Jun 46 FORCE: 11 Jun 46
REGISTERED: 18 Nov 47 Australia
ARTICLES: 13 LANGUAGE: English.
HEADNOTE: AIR SERVICES
TOPIC: Air Transport
CONCEPTS: Annex or appendix reference. Conformity with municipal law. Exchange of information and documents. Licenses and permits. Recognition of legal documents. Use of facilities. Arbitration. Procedure. Existing tribunals. Fees and exemptions. Most favored nation clause. National treatment. Customs exemptions. Competency certificate. Navigational conditions. Airport facilities. Airworthiness certificates. Conditions of airlines operating permission. Operating authorizations and regulations. Licenses and certificates of nationality.
INTL ORGS: International Civil Aviation Organization. Arbitration Commission.
PROCEDURE: Amendment. Future Procedures Contemplated. Registration. Termination. Application to Non-self-governing Territories.
PARTIES:
Australia
Canada

127 UNTS 324. Australia. Amendment
16 Mar 51. Force 16 Mar 51.
127 UNTS 324. Canada. Amendment 16 Mar 51.
Force 16 Mar 51.

100143 Bilateral Exchange **10 UNTS 63**
SIGNED: 16 Sep 46 FORCE: 16 Sep 46
REGISTERED: 18 Nov 47 Australia
ARTICLES: 18 LANGUAGE: English.
HEADNOTE: TRADE COMMERCE
TOPIC: General Trade
CONCEPTS: Licenses and permits. Establishment
of trade relations. Trade procedures. Currency.
Financial programs. Commodity trade. Water
transport.
TREATY REF: 5UNTS241.
PARTIES:
Australia
Sweden

100144 Bilateral Exchange **10 UNTS 77**
SIGNED: 24 Jan 47 FORCE: 24 Jan 47
REGISTERED: 18 Nov 47 Australia
ARTICLES: 10 LANGUAGE: English.
HEADNOTE: FINANCIAL ARRANGEMENTS
TOPIC: Finance
CONCEPTS: Detailed regulations. Exchange of in-
formation and documents. Informational
records. General property. Responsibility and lia-
bility. Accounting procedures. Banking. Bonds.
Indemnities and reimbursements. Currency. Ex-
change rates and regulations. Funding proce-
dures. Interest rates. Payment schedules. Non-
interest rates and fees. Credit provisions. Pay-
ment for war supplies. Military assistance.
PARTIES:
Australia
Netherlands

100145 Bilateral Agreement **10 UNTS 89**
SIGNED: 10 Mar 47 FORCE: 10 Mar 47
REGISTERED: 18 Nov 47 Australia
ARTICLES: 8 LANGUAGE: English.
HEADNOTE: AERODROME FACILITIES
TOPIC: Air Transport
CONCEPTS: Personnel. Use of facilities.
Meteorology. Fees and exemptions. Routes and
logistics. Navigational conditions. Airport facili-
ties. Operating authorizations and regulations.
Bands and frequency allocation. Facilities and
equipment. Facilities and property.
INTL ORGS: International Civil Aviation Organiza-
tion.
PARTIES:
Australia
USA (United States)

100146 Bilateral Exchange **11 UNTS 3**
SIGNED: 21 Apr 47 FORCE: 21 Apr 47
REGISTERED: 25 Nov 47 Jordan
ARTICLES: 2 LANGUAGE: Arabic.
HEADNOTE: PROVISIONAL COMMERCIAL AGREE-
MENT
TOPIC: General Trade
CONCEPTS: Annex type material. Most favored na-
tion clause.
PROCEDURE: Denunciation.
PARTIES:
Jordan
United Arab Rep

100147 Bilateral Agreement **11 UNTS 11**
SIGNED: 26 Jun 47 FORCE: 21 Nov 47
REGISTERED: 21 Nov 47 United Nations
ARTICLES: 9 LANGUAGE: English. French.
HEADNOTE: UN HEADQUARTERS
TOPIC: IGO Establishment
CONCEPTS: Definition of terms. Annex or appen-
dix reference. Diplomatic privileges. Diplomatic
missions. Inviolability. Property. Diplomatic cor-
respondence. Conformity with municipal law.
Headquarters and facilities. Special status.
PROCEDURE: Denunciation.
PARTIES:
United Nations
USA (United States)

554 UNTS 308. United Nations. Implementation
9 Feb 66. Force 9 Feb 66.
554 UNTS 308. USA (United States). Implementation 9 Feb 66. Force 9 Feb 66.

100148 Multilateral Protocol **11 UNTS 43**
SIGNED: 3 Mar 47 FORCE: 3 Mar 47
REGISTERED: 26 Nov 47 UK Great Britain
ARTICLES: 9 LANGUAGE: English.
HEADNOTE: REGULATION OF WHALING
TOPIC: Humanitarian
CONCEPTS: Definition of terms. Time limit. Previ-
ous treaty extension. Exchange of information
and documents. Quotas. Merchant vessels. Fish,
wildlife, and natural resources. Ocean resources.
TREATY REF: 190LTS79; 196LTS131.
PROCEDURE: Accession. Ratification.
PARTIES:
Australia SIGNED: 26 Nov 45 RATIFIED:
23 Jul 46 FORCE: 3 Mar 47
Canada SIGNED: 26 Nov 45 FORCE: 3 Mar 47
Denmark SIGNED: 26 Nov 45 RATIFIED:
10 Apr 46 FORCE: 3 Mar 47
France SIGNED: 26 Nov 45 RATIFIED: 24 Oct 46
FORCE: 3 Mar 47
Mexico SIGNED: 26 Nov 45
Netherlands SIGNED: 26 Nov 45
New Zealand SIGNED: 26 Nov 45 RATIFIED:
7 Mar 46 FORCE: 3 Mar 47
Norway SIGNED: 26 Nov 45 RATIFIED: 4 Apr 46
FORCE: 3 Mar 47
South Africa SIGNED: 26 Nov 45 RATIFIED:
11 Dec 46 FORCE: 3 Mar 47
UK Great Britain SIGNED: 26 Nov 45 RATIFIED:
29 Mar 46 FORCE: 3 Mar 47
USA (United States) SIGNED: 26 Nov 45 RATI-
FIED: 30 Aug 46 FORCE: 3 Mar 47
USSR (Soviet Union) RATIFIED: 25 Nov 46
FORCE: 3 Mar 47
32 UNTS 396. Netherlands. Ratification 6 Mar 48.
161 UNTS 361. Australia. Prolongation 1 Dec 47.
Force 5 Feb 48.
161 UNTS 361. France. Prolongation 5 Feb 48.
Force 5 Feb 48.
161 UNTS 361. Iceland. Prolongation 21 Apr 47.
Force 5 Feb 48.
161 UNTS 361. New Zealand. Prolongation
22 Jul 47. Force 5 Feb 48.
161 UNTS 361. Norway. Prolongation 27 Aug 47.
Force 5 Feb 48.
161 UNTS 361. South Africa. Prolongation
6 Nov 47. Force 5 Feb 48.
161 UNTS 361. USSR (Soviet Union). Prolongation 11 Dec 47. Force 5 Feb 48.
161 UNTS 361. Canada. Prolongation 12 Nov 47.
Force 5 Feb 48.
161 UNTS 361. Denmark. Prolongation
25 Aug 47. Force 5 Feb 48.
161 UNTS 361. UK Great Britain. Prolongation
17 Jun 47. Force 5 Feb 48.
161 UNTS 361. USA (United States). Prolongation
18 Jul 47. Force 5 Feb 48.

100149 Bilateral Agreement **11 UNTS 59**
SIGNED: 24 Jun 46 FORCE: 19 Jun 47
REGISTERED: 26 Nov 47 UK Great Britain
ARTICLES: 7 LANGUAGE: English. Polish.
HEADNOTE: SETTLEMENT FINANCIAL QUES-
TIONS
TOPIC: Claims and Debts
CONCEPTS: Use of facilities. Accounting proce-
dures. Banking. Monetary and gold transfers.
Payment schedules. Transportation costs. Lump
sum settlements. Assets transfer. Loan repay-
ment. Payment for war supplies. Surplus war
property. Post-war claims settlement.
PROCEDURE: Future Procedures Contemplated.
Ratification.
PARTIES:
Poland
UK Great Britain
374 UNTS 370. UK Great Britain. Amendment
23 May 60. Force 23 May 60.
374 UNTS 370. Poland. Amendment 23 May 60.
Force 23 May 60.

100150 Multilateral Agreement **11 UNTS 73**
SIGNED: 15 Oct 46 FORCE: 13 Jan 47

REGISTERED: 26 Nov 47 UK Great Britain
ARTICLES: 25 LANGUAGE: English. French.
HEADNOTE: ISSUE TRAVEL DOCUMENT REF-
UGEES
TOPIC: Refugees
CONCEPTS: Detailed regulations. Time limit. An-
nex or appendix reference. Non-visa travel docu-
ments. Visas. Fees and exemptions.
INTL ORGS: Special Commission.
TREATY REF: 13LTS237; 89LTS47; 105LTS193;
159LTS199.
PROCEDURE: Denunciation. Termination.
PARTIES:
Argentina SIGNED: 15 Oct 46 FORCE:
13 Jan 47
Belgium SIGNED: 15 Oct 46 FORCE: 13 Jan 47
Brazil SIGNED: 15 Oct 46 FORCE: 13 Jan 47
Chile SIGNED: 15 Oct 46 FORCE: 13 Jan 47
Dominican Republic SIGNED: 15 Oct 46 FORCE:
13 Jan 47
Ecuador SIGNED: 15 Oct 46 FORCE: 13 Jan 47
France SIGNED: 15 Oct 46 FORCE: 13 Jan 47
Greece SIGNED: 15 Oct 46 FORCE: 13 Jan 47
India SIGNED: 15 Oct 46 FORCE: 13 Jan 47
Luxembourg SIGNED: 15 Oct 46 FORCE:
13 Jan 47
Netherlands SIGNED: 15 Oct 46 FORCE:
13 Jan 47
Sweden SIGNED: 15 Oct 46 FORCE: 13 Jan 47
Switzerland SIGNED: 15 Oct 46 FORCE:
13 Jan 47
UK Great Britain SIGNED: 15 Oct 46 FORCE:
13 Jan 47
Venezuela SIGNED: 15 Oct 46 FORCE:
13 Jan 47
76 UNTS 244. UK Great Britain. Northern
Rhodesia.
82 UNTS 328. India. Signature 8 Nov 46. Force
6 Feb 47.
82 UNTS 328. Italy. Signature 1 Oct 47. Force
31 Dec 47.
82 UNTS 328. Taiwan. Signature 23 Feb 48.
Force 24 May 48.
82 UNTS 328. South Africa. Signature 8 Mar 48.
Force 5 Jun 48.
82 UNTS 328. Norway. Signature 6 Jul 49. Force
4 Oct 49.
82 UNTS 328. Liberia. Signature 16 Aug 50.
Force 14 Nov 50.
82 UNTS 328. Denmark. Signature 30 Nov 50.
Force 28 Feb 51.
91 UNTS 369. Trinidad. Force 28 Feb 48.
91 UNTS 369. UK Great Britain. British Guiana.
91 UNTS 369. UK Great Britain. British Honduras.
91 UNTS 369. UK Great Britain. Gambia.
91 UNTS 369. UK Great Britain. Kenya.
91 UNTS 369. UK Great Britain. Nyasaland.
91 UNTS 369. UK Great Britain. Sarawak.
91 UNTS 369. UK Great Britain. Seychelles.
91 UNTS 369. UK Great Britain. Tanganyika.
91 UNTS 369. UK Great Britain. Uganda.
91 UNTS 369. UK Great Britain. Southern
Rhodesia.
91 UNTS 369. Germany, West. Signature
21 Mar 51. Force 19 Jun 51.
91 UNTS 369. UK Great Britain. Bahamas.
91 UNTS 369. UK Great Britain. Bermuda.
97 UNTS 314. UK Great Britain. St. Vincent.
267 UNTS 362. Brazil. Ratification 6 May 52.

100151 Multilateral Agreement **11 UNTS 107**
SIGNED: 30 Oct 46 FORCE: 23 Apr 47
REGISTERED: 26 Nov 47 UK Great Britain
ARTICLES: 6 LANGUAGE: English.
HEADNOTE: PROVISIONAL MARITIME COUNCIL
TOPIC: IGO Establishment
CONCEPTS: Previous treaty renunciation. Ex-
change of information and documents. Maritime
products and equipment. General technical as-
sistance. Establishment. Liaison with other
IGO's. Internal structure.
INTL ORGS: Inter-Governmental Maritime Consul-
tative Organization. United Nations.
PROCEDURE: Accession. Ratification. Termina-
tion.
PARTIES:
Australia RATIFIED: 23 Apr 47 FORCE:
23 Apr 47
Belgium RATIFIED: 3 Dec 46 FORCE: 23 Apr 47
Canada RATIFIED: 5 Dec 46 FORCE: 23 Apr 46
Chile RATIFIED: 12 Dec 46 FORCE: 23 Apr 47
Denmark RATIFIED: 4 Feb 47 FORCE: 23 Apr 47

France RATIFIED: 18 Dec 46 FORCE: 23 Apr 47
Greece RATIFIED: 29 Jan 47 FORCE: 23 Apr 47
Netherlands RATIFIED: 1 Jan 47 FORCE: 23 Apr 47
Norway RATIFIED: 14 Jan 47 FORCE: 23 Apr 47
Poland RATIFIED: 27 Feb 47 FORCE: 23 Apr 47
UK Great Britain RATIFIED: 1 Dec 46 FORCE: 23 Apr 47
USA (United States) RATIFIED: 20 Nov 46 FORCE: 23 Apr 46

100152 Bilateral Agreement **11 UNTS 115**
SIGNED: 31 Oct 46 FORCE: 30 Nov 46
REGISTERED: 26 Nov 47 UK Great Britain
ARTICLES: 14 LANGUAGE: English. Portuguese.
HEADNOTE: AIR TRANSPORT
TOPIC: Air Transport
CONCEPTS: Definition of terms. Annex or appendix reference. Previous treaty replacement. Conformity with municipal law. Licenses and permits. Recognition of legal documents. Use of facilities. Arbitration. Procedure. Existing tribunals. Fees and exemptions. Most favored nation clause. Customs exemptions. Competency certificate. Routes and logistics. Navigational conditions. Permit designation. Air transport. Airport facilities. Airport equipment. Airworthiness certificates. Conditions of airlines operating permission. Operating authorizations and regulations. Licenses and certificates of nationality.
INTL ORGS: International Civil Aviation Organization. Arbitration Commission.
TREATY REF: U.K. MISC 6(1945) CMD.6614.
PROCEDURE: Amendment. Future Procedures Contemplated. Registration. Termination.
PARTIES:
Brazil
UK Great Britain
ANNEX
160 UNTS 370. UK Great Britain. Amendment 27 Jun 52. Force 27 Jun 52.
160 UNTS 370. Brazil. Amendment 27 Jun 52. Force 27 Jun 52.

100153 Bilateral Exchange **11 UNTS 153**
SIGNED: 2 Nov 46 FORCE: 2 Nov 46
REGISTERED: 26 Nov 47 UK Great Britain
ARTICLES: 2 LANGUAGE: Arabic. English.
HEADNOTE: SETTLEMENT PENDING CASES SYRIAN MIXED COURT
TOPIC: Dispute Settlement
CONCEPTS: Definition of terms. Juridical personality. Competence of tribunal.
PARTIES:
Syria
UK Great Britain

100154 Bilateral Exchange **11 UNTS 161**
SIGNED: 2 Dec 46 FORCE: 2 Dec 46
REGISTERED: 26 Nov 47 UK Great Britain
ARTICLES: 2 LANGUAGE: English. Spanish.
HEADNOTE: RECIPROCAL NOTIFICATION IMPRISONMENT DEATH PRISON
TOPIC: Admin Cooperation
CONCEPTS: Exchange of information and documents.
PARTIES:
Cuba
UK Great Britain

100155 Bilateral Agreement **11 UNTS 167**
SIGNED: 11 Dec 46 FORCE: 11 Dec 46
REGISTERED: 26 Nov 47 UK Great Britain
ARTICLES: 17 LANGUAGE: English. French.
HEADNOTE: MONEY PROPERTY ENEMY OCCUPATION
TOPIC: Claims and Debts
CONCEPTS: Definition of terms. Detailed regulations. Treaty implementation. General cooperation. Immovable property. General property. Bonds. Fees and exemptions. Claims and settlements. Debts. Assets transfer.
PROCEDURE: Termination.
PARTIES:
Luxembourg
UK Great Britain
ANNEX
158 UNTS 480. UK Great Britain. Termination 1 Dec 52. Force 1 Dec 52.

158 UNTS 480. Luxembourg. Termination 1 Dec 52. Force 1 Dec 52.

100156 Bilateral Exchange **11 UNTS 187**
SIGNED: 15 Jan 47 FORCE: 15 Jan 47
REGISTERED: 26 Nov 47 UK Great Britain
ARTICLES: 2 LANGUAGE: English. Norwegian.
HEADNOTE: DIPLOMATIC CORRESPONDENCE
TOPIC: Consul/Citizenship
CONCEPTS: Diplomatic correspondence.
PARTIES:
Norway
UK Great Britain
ANNEX
70 UNTS 268. Norway. Supplementation 30 Oct 47. Force 1 Nov 47.
70 UNTS 268. UK Great Britain. Supplementation 30 Oct 47. Force 1 Nov 47.

100157 Bilateral Exchange **11 UNTS 195**
SIGNED: 19 Mar 47 FORCE: 1 Jan 47
REGISTERED: 26 Nov 47 UK Great Britain
ARTICLES: 2 LANGUAGE: English. Spanish.
HEADNOTE: PROLONGING COMMERCIAL AGREEMENT
TOPIC: General Trade
CONCEPTS: Annex type material. Previous treaty extension.
TREATY REF: UKTS 46(1946) CMD.6953.
PROCEDURE: Denunciation.
PARTIES:
Argentina
UK Great Britain

100158 Bilateral Exchange **11 UNTS 201**
SIGNED: 7 Apr 47 FORCE: 31 Mar 47
REGISTERED: 26 Nov 47 UK Great Britain
ARTICLES: 4 LANGUAGE: English.
HEADNOTE: ADMINISTRATION DODECANESE ISLANDS
TOPIC: Territory Boundary
CONCEPTS: Indemnities and reimbursements. Currency. Debt settlement. Definition of territory. Changes of territory.
TREATY REF. U.K. MISC.NO.1(1947) CMD.7022; NO.6(1908) CMD.4175.
PARTIES:
Greece
UK Great Britain

100159 Bilateral Exchange **11 UNTS 211**
SIGNED: 23 May 47 FORCE: 23 May 47
REGISTERED: 26 Nov 47 UK Great Britain
ARTICLES: 2 LANGUAGE: English.
HEADNOTE: USE AIRPORT
TOPIC: Specific Property
CONCEPTS: Use of facilities. Operating authorizations and regulations. Facilities and property.
PARTIES:
UK Great Britain
USA (United States)

100160 Bilateral Exchange **11 UNTS 217**
SIGNED: 10 Jun 47 FORCE: 24 Jun 47
REGISTERED: 26 Nov 47 UK Great Britain
ARTICLES: 2 LANGUAGE: English. French.
HEADNOTE: RECIPROCAL ABOLITION VISAS
TOPIC: Visas
CONCEPTS: Visa abolition. Employment regulations.
PARTIES:
Switzerland
UK Great Britain
ANNEX
71 UNTS 284. Switzerland. Confirmation 29 Oct 48. Force 10 Nov 48.
71 UNTS 284. UK Great Britain. Newfoundland. Force 10 Nov 48.
71 UNTS 284. UK Great Britain. Southern Rhodesia. Force 10 Nov 48.
71 UNTS 284. UK Great Britain. Aden. Force 10 Nov 48.
71 UNTS 284. UK Great Britain. Bahamas. Force 10 Nov 48.
71 UNTS 284. UK Great Britain. Barbados. Force 10 Nov 48.
71 UNTS 284. UK Great Britain. Basutoland. Force 10 Nov 48.

71 UNTS 284. UK Great Britain. Bechuanaland. Force 10 Nov 48.
71 UNTS 284. UK Great Britain. Bermuda. Force 10 Nov 48.
71 UNTS 284. UK Great Britain. British Guiana. Force 10 Nov 48.
71 UNTS 284. UK Great Britain. British Honduras. Force 10 Nov 48.
71 UNTS 284. UK Great Britain. Brunei. Force 10 Nov 48.
71 UNTS 284. UK Great Britain. Cyprus. Force 10 Nov 48.
71 UNTS 284. UK Great Britain. Falkland Islands. Force 10 Nov 48.
71 UNTS 284. UK Great Britain. Fed of Malaya. Force 10 Nov 48.
71 UNTS 284. UK Great Britain. Fiji Islands. Force 10 Nov 48.
71 UNTS 284. UK Great Britain. St. Christopher. Force 10 Nov 48.
71 UNTS 284. UK Great Britain. Nevis. Force 10 Nov 48.
71 UNTS 284. UK Great Britain. Jamaica. Force 10 Nov 48.
71 UNTS 284. UK Great Britain. Antigua. Force 10 Nov 48.
71 UNTS 284. UK Great Britain. Montserrat. Force 10 Nov 48.
71 UNTS 284. UK Great Britain. Virgin Islands. Force 10 Nov 48.
71 UNTS 284. UK Great Britain. St. Helena. Force 10 Nov 48.
71 UNTS 284. UK Great Britain. Northern Rhodesia. Force 10 Nov 48.
71 UNTS 284. UK Great Britain. Seychelles. Force 10 Nov 48.
71 UNTS 284. UK Great Britain. Sierra Leone. Force 10 Nov 48.
71 UNTS 284. UK Great Britain. Singapore. Force 10 Nov 48.
71 UNTS 284. UK Great Britain. Swaziland. Force 10 Nov 48.
71 UNTS 284. UK Great Britain. Tanganyika. Force 10 Nov 48.
71 UNTS 284. UK Great Britain. Trinidad. Force 10 Nov 48.
71 UNTS 284. UK Great Britain. Uganda. Force 10 Nov 48.
71 UNTS 284. UK Great Britain. Gilbert Islands. Force 10 Nov 48.
71 UNTS 284. UK Great Britain. Brit Solomon Is. Force 10 Nov 48.
71 UNTS 284. UK Great Britain. Dominican Republic. Force 10 Nov 48.
71 UNTS 284. UK Great Britain. Mauritius. Force 10 Nov 48.
71 UNTS 284. UK Great Britain. North Borneo. Force 10 Nov 48.
71 UNTS 284. UK Great Britain. Grenada. Force 10 Nov 48.
71 UNTS 284. UK Great Britain. St. Lucia. Force 10 Nov 48.
71 UNTS 284. UK Great Britain. St. Vincent. Force 10 Nov 48.
71 UNTS 284. UK Great Britain. Zanzibar. Force 10 Nov 48.
86 UNTS 272. Switzerland. Acknowledgement 11 Aug 50. Force 24 Aug 50.
86 UNTS 272. UK Great Britain. Singapore. Withdrawal 10 Aug 50. Force 24 Aug 50.
86 UNTS 272. UK Great Britain. Fed of Malaya. Withdrawal 10 Aug 50. Force 24 Aug 50.
91 UNTS 370. UK Great Britain. Newfoundland. Withdrawal 25 Apr 49. Force 25 Apr 49.
93 UNTS 355. UK Great Britain. Kenya. Force 11 Nov 49.
117 UNTS 378. UK Great Britain. North Borneo. Withdrawal 1 Oct 51. Force 15 Oct 51.
117 UNTS 378. UK Great Britain. Brunei. Withdrawal 1 Oct 51. Force 15 Oct 51.
175 UNTS 339. UK Great Britain. Singapore.
175 UNTS 339. UK Great Britain. Fed of Malaya.
175 UNTS 339. UK Great Britain. North Borneo.
218 UNTS 377. UK Great Britain. Sarawak. Force 1 Oct 55.
264 UNTS 318. UK Great Britain. Cyprus. Withdrawal 6 Nov 56. Force 12 Nov 56.
267 UNTS 363. UK Great Britain. Gibralter. Force 20 Jul 55.
349 UNTS 303. Switzerland. Acknowledgement 1 Oct 51. Force 1 Feb 58.
349 UNTS 303. Switzerland. Acknowledgement 18 Apr 58. Force 1 May 58.

349 UNTS 303. UK Great Britain. Amendment 18 Apr 58. Force 1 May 58.
349 UNTS 303. UK Great Britain. North Borneo. Force 1 Feb 58.
349 UNTS 303. UK Great Britain. Brunei. Force 1 Feb 58.
349 UNTS 304. Switzerland. Acknowledgement 3 Sep 58. Force 1 Oct 58.
349 UNTS 304. UK Great Britain. Gambia. Force 1 Oct 58.
398 UNTS 307. UK Great Britain. Cyprus. Force 22 May 59.
398 UNTS 307. UK Great Britain. British Somaliland. Force 15 Feb 59.

100161 Bilateral Exchange **11 UNTS 223**
SIGNED: 20 Jun 47 FORCE: 1 Jul 47
REGISTERED: 26 Nov 47 UK Great Britain
ARTICLES: 2 LANGUAGE: English.
HEADNOTE: RECIPROCAL ABOLITION VISAS
TOPIC: Visas
CONCEPTS: Visa abolition. Border traffic and migration.
PARTIES:
Iceland
UK Great Britain
ANNEX
71 UNTS 290. UK Great Britain. Barbados. Force 10 Nov 48.
71 UNTS 290. UK Great Britain. Antigua. Force 10 Nov 48.
71 UNTS 290. UK Great Britain. Tanganyika. Force 10 Nov 48.
71 UNTS 290. UK Great Britain. St. Christopher. Force 10 Nov 48.
71 UNTS 290. UK Great Britain. Bechuanaland. Force 10 Nov 48.
71 UNTS 290. UK Great Britain. Seychelles. Force 10 Nov 48.
71 UNTS 290. UK Great Britain. Sierra Leone. Force 10 Nov 48.
71 UNTS 290. UK Great Britain. Uganda. Force 10 Nov 48.
71 UNTS 290. UK Great Britain. Gilbert Islands. Force 10 Nov 48.
71 UNTS 290. UK Great Britain. Nevis. Force 10 Nov 48.
71 UNTS 290. UK Great Britain. Montserrat. Force 10 Nov 48.
71 UNTS 290. UK Great Britain. Bermuda. Force 10 Nov 48.
71 UNTS 290. UK Great Britain. British Guiana. Force 10 Nov 48.
71 UNTS 290. UK Great Britain. British Honduras. Force 10 Nov 48.
71 UNTS 290. UK Great Britain. Brunei. Force 10 Nov 48.
71 UNTS 290. UK Great Britain. Cyprus. Force 10 Nov 48.
71 UNTS 290. UK Great Britain. Falkland Islands. Force 10 Nov 48.
71 UNTS 290. UK Great Britain. Fed of Malaya. Force 10 Nov 48.
71 UNTS 290. UK Great Britain. Northern Rhodesia. Force 10 Nov 48.
71 UNTS 290. UK Great Britain. St. Helena. Force 10 Nov 48.
71 UNTS 290. UK Great Britain. Fiji Islands. Force 10 Nov 48.
71 UNTS 290. UK Great Britain. Jamaica. Force 10 Nov 48.
71 UNTS 290. UK Great Britain. Brit Solomon Is. Force 10 Nov 48.
71 UNTS 290. UK Great Britain. Dominican Republic. Force 10 Nov 48.
71 UNTS 290. UK Great Britain. Grenada. Force 10 Nov 48.
71 UNTS 290. UK Great Britain. St. Lucia. Force 10 Nov 48.
71 UNTS 290. UK Great Britain. St. Vincent. Force 10 Nov 48.
71 UNTS 290. UK Great Britain. Zanzibar. Force 10 Nov 48.
71 UNTS 290. UK Great Britain. Singapore. Force 10 Nov 48.
71 UNTS 290. UK Great Britain. Swaziland. Force 10 Nov 48.
71 UNTS 290. Iceland. Acknowledgement 26 Oct 48. Force 10 Nov 48.
71 UNTS 290. UK Great Britain. Newfoundland. Force 10 Nov 48.
71 UNTS 290. UK Great Britain. Southern Rhodesia. Force 10 Nov 48.

71 UNTS 290. UK Great Britain. Aden. Force 10 Nov 48.
71 UNTS 290. UK Great Britain. Bahamas. Force 10 Nov 48.
71 UNTS 290. UK Great Britain. Basutoland. Force 10 Nov 48.
86 UNTS 276. Iceland. Acknowledgement 11 Aug 50. Force 24 Aug 50.
86 UNTS 276. UK Great Britain. Fed of Malaya. Withdrawal 10 Aug 50. Force 24 Aug 50.
86 UNTS 276. UK Great Britain. Singapore. Withdrawal 10 Aug 50. Force 24 Aug 50.
91 UNTS 371. UK Great Britain. Newfoundland. Withdrawal 25 Apr 49. Force 25 Apr 49.
93 UNTS 356. UK Great Britain. Kenya. Force 11 Nov 49.
175 UNTS 340. UK Great Britain. Singapore.
175 UNTS 340. UK Great Britain. Fed of Malaya.
175 UNTS 340. UK Great Britain. North Borneo.
218 UNTS 377. UK Great Britain. Sarawak. Force 1 Oct 55.
264 UNTS 318. UK Great Britain. Cyprus. Withdrawal 6 Nov 56. Force 12 Nov 56.
267 UNTS 363. UK Great Britain. Gibralter. Force 20 Jul 55.
349 UNTS 305. Iceland. Acknowledgement 3 Sep 58. Force 1 Oct 58.
349 UNTS 305. UK Great Britain. North Borneo. Force 1 Oct 58.
349 UNTS 305. UK Great Britain. Brunei. Force 1 Oct 58.
349 UNTS 305. UK Great Britain. Gambia. Force 1 Oct 58.
398 UNTS 308. UK Great Britain. Cyprus. Force 22 May 59.
403 UNTS 360. Iceland. Supplementation 3 Sep 58. Force 3 Sep 58.
560 UNTS 232. UK Great Britain. Southern Rhodesia.

100162 Bilateral Agreement **11 UNTS 229**
SIGNED: 27 Nov 46 FORCE: 27 Nov 46
REGISTERED: 4 Dec 47 UK Great Britain
ARTICLES: 14 LANGUAGE: English. Swedish.
HEADNOTE: AIR SERVICES
TOPIC: Air Transport
CONCEPTS: Definition of terms. Annex or appendix reference. Conformity with municipal law. General cooperation. Licenses and permits. Recognition of legal documents. Use of facilities. Procedure. Existing tribunals. Fees and exemptions. Most favored nation clause. National treatment. Customs exemptions. Competency certificate. Routes and logistics. Navigational conditions. Permit designation. Air transport. Airport facilities. Airworthiness certificates. Conditions of airlines operating permission. Operating authorizations and regulations. Licenses and certificates of nationality.
INTL ORGS: International Civil Aviation Organization.
TREATY REF: U.K. MISC NO.6(1945) CMD.6614.
PROCEDURE: Amendment. Future Procedures Contemplated. Registration. Termination.
PARTIES:
Sweden
UK Great Britain
ANNEX
35 UNTS 367. UK Great Britain. Amendment 2 Dec 47. Force 19 Dec 47.
35 UNTS 367. Sweden. Amendment 19 Dec 47. Force 19 Dec 47.
53 UNTS 408. UK Great Britain. Amendment 1 Jun 48. Force 1 Jun 48.
53 UNTS 408. Sweden. Amendment 13 May 48. Force 1 Jun 48.
53 UNTS 412. Sweden. Amendment 28 Sep 49. Force 28 Sep 49.
53 UNTS 412. UK Great Britain. Amendment 20 May 49. Force 28 Sep 49.
150 UNTS 336. UK Great Britain. Amendment 23 Jun 52. Force 23 Jun 52.
150 UNTS 336. Sweden. Amendment 23 Jun 52. Force 23 Jun 52.
172 UNTS 328. UK Great Britain. Amendment 13 Mar 53. Force 13 Mar 53.
172 UNTS 328. Sweden. Amendment 13 Mar 53. Force 13 Mar 53.
229 UNTS 268. UK Great Britain. Amendment 25 Aug 55.
229 UNTS 268. Sweden. Amendment 25 Aug 55.

100163 Bilateral Exchange **11 UNTS 255**
SIGNED: 27 Dec 46 FORCE: 1 Jan 47
REGISTERED: 4 Dec 47 UK Great Britain
ARTICLES: 2 LANGUAGE: English. French.
HEADNOTE: MUTUAL ABOLITION VISAS
TOPIC: Visas
CONCEPTS: Visa abolition. Border traffic and migration.
PARTIES:
France
UK Great Britain
ANNEX
183 UNTS 342. UK Great Britain. Implementation 1 Sep 53. Force 1 Oct 53.
183 UNTS 342. France. Implementation 28 Aug 53. Force 1 Oct 53.
267 UNTS 364. UK Great Britain. Gibralter. Force 20 Jul 55.
267 UNTS 364. UK Great Britain. Mauritius. Force 24 May 54.

100164 Bilateral Exchange **11 UNTS 261**
SIGNED: 5 Feb 47 FORCE: 15 Feb 47
REGISTERED: 4 Dec 47 UK Great Britain
ARTICLES: 2 LANGUAGE: English. French.
HEADNOTE: RECIPROCAL ABOLITION VISAS
TOPIC: Visas
CONCEPTS: Territorial application. Visa abolition. Border traffic and migration. Resident permits.
PARTIES:
Belgium
UK Great Britain
ANNEX
229 UNTS 272. UK Great Britain. Implementation 20 Dec 55. Force 20 Dec 55.
229 UNTS 272. Belgium. Implementation 20 Dec 55. Force 20 Dec 55.
267 UNTS 365. UK Great Britain. Gibralter. Force 20 Jul 55.
286 UNTS 330. Belgium. Acknowledgement 10 Dec 57. Force 1 Jan 58.
286 UNTS 330. UK Great Britain. Malta. Force 1 Jan 58.
349 UNTS 306. UK Great Britain. Seychelles. Force 1 Oct 57.

100165 Bilateral Exchange **11 UNTS 267**
SIGNED: 14 Feb 47 FORCE: 15 Feb 47
REGISTERED: 4 Dec 47 UK Great Britain
ARTICLES: 2 LANGUAGE: English.
HEADNOTE: RECIPROCAL ABOLITION VISAS
TOPIC: Visas
CONCEPTS: Territorial application. Visa abolition. Border traffic and migration. Resident permits.
PARTIES:
Luxembourg
UK Great Britain
ANNEX
81 UNTS 313. UK Great Britain. Bahamas. Force 10 Nov 48.
81 UNTS 313. UK Great Britain. Southern Rhodesia. Force 10 Nov 48.
81 UNTS 313. Luxembourg. Acknowledgement 26 Oct 48. Force 10 Nov 48.
81 UNTS 313. UK Great Britain. Newfoundland. Force 10 Nov 48.
81 UNTS 313. UK Great Britain. Aden. Force 10 Nov 48.
81 UNTS 313. UK Great Britain. Barbados. Force 10 Nov 48.
81 UNTS 313. UK Great Britain. Basutoland. Force 10 Nov 48.
81 UNTS 313. UK Great Britain. Bechuanaland. Force 10 Nov 48.
81 UNTS 313. UK Great Britain. Bermuda. Force 10 Nov 48.
81 UNTS 313. UK Great Britain. British Guiana. Force 10 Nov 48.
81 UNTS 313. UK Great Britain. British Honduras. Force 10 Nov 48.
81 UNTS 313. UK Great Britain. Sierra Leone. Force 10 Nov 48.
81 UNTS 313. UK Great Britain. Singapore. Force 10 Nov 48.
81 UNTS 313. UK Great Britain. Swaziland. Force 10 Nov 48.
81 UNTS 313. UK Great Britain. Dominican Republic. Force 10 Nov 48.
81 UNTS 313. UK Great Britain. Grenada. Force 10 Nov 48.

81 UNTS 313. UK Great Britain. St. Lucia. Force 10 Nov 48.
81 UNTS 313. UK Great Britain. St. Vincent. Force 10 Nov 48.
81 UNTS 313. UK Great Britain. Tanganyika. Force 10 Nov 48.
81 UNTS 313. UK Great Britain. Trinidad. Force 10 Nov 48.
81 UNTS 313. UK Great Britain. Gilbert Islands. Force 10 Nov 48.
81 UNTS 313. UK Great Britain. Brit Solomon Is. Force 10 Nov 48.
81 UNTS 313. UK Great Britain. Brunei. Force 10 Nov 48.
81 UNTS 313. UK Great Britain. Cyprus. Force 10 Nov 48.
81 UNTS 313. UK Great Britain. Falkland Islands. Force 10 Nov 48.
81 UNTS 313. UK Great Britain. Fed of Malaya. Force 10 Nov 48.
81 UNTS 313. UK Great Britain. Fiji Islands. Force 10 Nov 48.
81 UNTS 313. UK Great Britain. Jamaica. Force 10 Nov 48.
81 UNTS 313. UK Great Britain. Antigua. Force 10 Nov 48.
81 UNTS 313. UK Great Britain. St. Christopher. Force 10 Nov 48.
81 UNTS 313. UK Great Britain. Nevis. Force 10 Nov 48.
81 UNTS 313. UK Great Britain. Montserrat. Force 10 Nov 48.
81 UNTS 313. UK Great Britain. Virgin Islands. Force 10 Nov 48.
81 UNTS 313. UK Great Britain. Mauritius. Force 10 Nov 48.
81 UNTS 313. UK Great Britain. St. Helena. Force 10 Nov 48.
81 UNTS 313. UK Great Britain. North Borneo. Force 10 Nov 48.
81 UNTS 313. UK Great Britain. Northern Rhodesia. Force 10 Nov 48.
81 UNTS 372. UK Great Britain. Newfoundland. Withdrawal 25 Apr 49. Force 25 Apr 49.
93 UNTS 357. UK Great Britain. Kenya. Force 11 Nov 49.
117 UNTS 380. UK Great Britain. North Borneo. Withdrawal 1 Oct 51. Force 15 Oct 51.
117 UNTS 380. UK Great Britain. Brunei. Withdrawal 1 Oct 51. Force 15 Oct 51.
175 UNTS 341. UK Great Britain. Singapore.
175 UNTS 341. UK Great Britain. Fed of Malaya.
175 UNTS 341. UK Great Britain. North Borneo.
218 UNTS 378. UK Great Britain. Sarawak. Force 1 Oct 55.
264 UNTS 319. UK Great Britain. Cyprus. Withdrawal 6 Nov 56. Force 12 Nov 56.
267 UNTS 366. UK Great Britain. Gibralter. Force 20 Jul 55.
349 UNTS 307. Iceland. Acknowledgement 3 Sep 58. Force 1 Oct 58.
349 UNTS 307. UK Great Britain. North Borneo. Force 1 Feb 58.
349 UNTS 307. UK Great Britain. Brunei. Force 1 Feb 58.
349 UNTS 307. UK Great Britain. Gambia. Force 1 Oct 58.
398 UNTS 308. UK Great Britain. Cyprus. Force 22 May 59.
403 UNTS 361. UK Great Britain. Supplementation 3 Dec 58. Force 13 Jan 59.
403 UNTS 361. Luxembourg. Supplementation 13 Jan 59. Force 13 Jan 59.

00166   Bilateral Exchange   **11 UNTS 273**
SIGNED: 26 Feb 47   FORCE: 1 Mar 47
REGISTERED: 4 Dec 47 UK Great Britain
ARTICLES: 2 LANGUAGE: English.
HEADNOTE: MUTUAL ABOLITION VISAS
TOPIC: Visas
CONCEPTS: Territorial application. Visa abolition. Border traffic and migration. Resident permits.
PARTIES:
Norway
UK Great Britain
ANNEX
77 UNTS 338. UK Great Britain. Aden. Force 10 Nov 48.
77 UNTS 338. Norway. Confirmation 30 Oct 48. Force 10 Nov 48.
77 UNTS 338. UK Great Britain. Newfoundland. Force 10 Nov 48.

77 UNTS 338. UK Great Britain. Southern Rhodesia. Force 10 Nov 48.
77 UNTS 338. UK Great Britain. Bahamas. Force 10 Nov 48.
77 UNTS 338. UK Great Britain. Barbados. Force 10 Nov 48.
77 UNTS 338. UK Great Britain. Basutoland. Force 10 Nov 48.
77 UNTS 338. UK Great Britain. Bechuanaland. Force 10 Nov 48.
77 UNTS 338. UK Great Britain. Bermuda. Force 10 Nov 48.
77 UNTS 338. UK Great Britain. British Guiana. Force 10 Nov 48.
77 UNTS 338. UK Great Britain. British Honduras. Force 10 Nov 48.
77 UNTS 338. UK Great Britain. Cyprus. Force 10 Nov 48.
77 UNTS 338. UK Great Britain. Falkland Islands. Force 10 Nov 48.
77 UNTS 338. UK Great Britain. Fed of Malaya. Force 10 Nov 48.
77 UNTS 338. UK Great Britain. Fiji Islands. Force 10 Nov 48.
77 UNTS 338. UK Great Britain. Jamaica. Force 10 Nov 48.
77 UNTS 338. UK Great Britain. Antigua. Force 10 Nov 48.
77 UNTS 338. UK Great Britain. St. Christopher. Force 10 Nov 48.
77 UNTS 338. UK Great Britain. Nevis. Force 10 Nov 48.
77 UNTS 338. UK Great Britain. Montserrat. Force 10 Nov 48.
77 UNTS 338. UK Great Britain. Virgin Islands. Force 10 Nov 48.
77 UNTS 338. UK Great Britain. Mauritius. Force 10 Nov 48.
77 UNTS 338. UK Great Britain. Brunei. Force 10 Nov 48.
77 UNTS 338. UK Great Britain. North Borneo. Force 10 Nov 48.
77 UNTS 338. UK Great Britain. Northern Rhodesia. Force 10 Nov 48.
77 UNTS 338. UK Great Britain. Gilbert Islands. Force 10 Nov 48.
77 UNTS 338. UK Great Britain. Brit Solomon Is. Force 10 Nov 48.
77 UNTS 338. UK Great Britain. Dominican Republic. Force 10 Nov 48.
77 UNTS 338. UK Great Britain. Grenada. Force 10 Nov 48.
77 UNTS 338. UK Great Britain. St. Lucia. Force 10 Nov 48.
77 UNTS 338. UK Great Britain. St. Vincent. Force 10 Nov 48.
77 UNTS 338. UK Great Britain. Zanzibar. Force 10 Nov 48.
77 UNTS 338. UK Great Britain. Seychelles. Force 10 Nov 48.
77 UNTS 338. UK Great Britain. Sierra Leone. Force 10 Nov 48.
77 UNTS 338. UK Great Britain. Singapore. Force 10 Nov 48.
77 UNTS 338. UK Great Britain. Swaziland. Force 10 Nov 48.
77 UNTS 338. UK Great Britain. Tanganyika. Force 10 Nov 48.
77 UNTS 338. UK Great Britain. Trinidad. Force 10 Nov 48.
77 UNTS 338. UK Great Britain. Uganda. Force 10 Nov 48.
77 UNTS 338. UK Great Britain. St. Helena. Force 10 Nov 48.
78 UNTS 317. Norway. All Territories. Force 13 Sep 48.
81 UNTS 317. UK Great Britain. Acknowledgement 6 Sep 48. Force 13 Sep 48.
81 UNTS 317. Norway. All Territories. Force 13 Sep 48.
86 UNTS 284. UK Great Britain. Singapore. Withdrawal 10 Aug 50. Force 24 Aug 50.
86 UNTS 284. UK Great Britain. Fed of Malaya. Withdrawal 10 Aug 50. Force 24 Aug 50.
91 UNTS 373. UK Great Britain. Newfoundland. Withdrawal 25 Apr 49. Force 25 Apr 49.
93 UNTS 358. UK Great Britain. Kenya. Force 11 Nov 49.
117 UNTS 381. UK Great Britain. Brunei. Withdrawal 1 Oct 51. Force 15 Oct 51.
117 UNTS 381. UK Great Britain. North Borneo. Withdrawal 1 Oct 51. Force 15 Oct 51.
175 UNTS 342. UK Great Britain. Singapore.
175 UNTS 342. UK Great Britain. Fed of Malaya.

175 UNTS 342. UK Great Britain. North Borneo.
218 UNTS 378. UK Great Britain. Sarawak. Force 1 Oct 55.
264 UNTS 319. UK Great Britain. Cyprus. Withdrawal 6 Nov 56. Force 12 Nov 56.
267 UNTS 366. UK Great Britain. Gibralter. Force 20 Jul 55.
349 UNTS 308. UK Great Britain. Gambia. Force 1 Oct 58.
349 UNTS 308. UK Great Britain. North Borneo. Force 1 Feb 58.
349 UNTS 308. UK Great Britain. Brunei. Force 1 Feb 58.
398 UNTS 308. UK Great Britain. Cyprus. Force 22 May 59.
560 UNTS 232. UK Great Britain. Southern Rhodesia.

100167   Bilateral Agreement   **11 UNTS 279**
SIGNED: 26 Feb 47   FORCE: 27 Feb 47
REGISTERED: 4 Dec 47 UK Great Britain
ARTICLES: 4 LANGUAGE: English.
HEADNOTE: EXTENDING SCOPE FINANCIAL ARRANGEMENTS
TOPIC: Finance
CONCEPTS: Previous treaty amendment. Annex type material. Banking. Monetary and gold transfers. Payment schedules.
PROCEDURE: Termination.
PARTIES:
Netherlands
UK Great Britain
ANNEX
77 UNTS 344. UK Great Britain. Abrogation 12 Mar 48. Force 12 Mar 48.
77 UNTS 344. Netherlands. Abrogation 12 Mar 48. Force 12 Mar 48.

100168   Bilateral Exchange   **11 UNTS 285**
SIGNED: 20 Mar 47   FORCE: 22 Mar 47
REGISTERED: 4 Dec 47 UK Great Britain
ARTICLES: 2 LANGUAGE: English.
HEADNOTE: RECIPROCAL ABOLITION VISAS
TOPIC: Visas
CONCEPTS: Territorial application. Visa abolition. Border traffic and migration. Resident permits.
PARTIES:
Denmark
UK Great Britain
ANNEX
71 UNTS 294. Denmark. Acknowledgement 26 Oct 48. Force 10 Nov 48.
71 UNTS 294. UK Great Britain. Newfoundland. Force 10 Nov 48.
71 UNTS 294. UK Great Britain. Southern Rhodesia. Force 10 Nov 48.
71 UNTS 294. UK Great Britain. Aden. Force 10 Nov 48.
71 UNTS 294. UK Great Britain. Bahamas. Force 10 Nov 48.
71 UNTS 294. UK Great Britain. Barbados. Force 10 Nov 48.
71 UNTS 294. UK Great Britain. Basutoland. Force 10 Nov 48.
71 UNTS 294. UK Great Britain. Bechuanaland. Force 10 Nov 48.
71 UNTS 294. UK Great Britain. Bermuda. Force 10 Nov 48.
71 UNTS 294. UK Great Britain. British Guiana. Force 10 Nov 48.
71 UNTS 294. UK Great Britain. British Honduras. Force 10 Nov 48.
71 UNTS 294. UK Great Britain. Brunei. Force 10 Nov 48.
71 UNTS 294. UK Great Britain. Cyprus. Force 10 Nov 48.
71 UNTS 294. UK Great Britain. Falkland Islands. Force 10 Nov 48.
71 UNTS 294. UK Great Britain. Fed of Malaya. Force 10 Nov 48.
71 UNTS 294. UK Great Britain. Fiji Islands. Force 10 Nov 48.
71 UNTS 294. UK Great Britain. Jamaica. Force 10 Nov 48.
71 UNTS 294. UK Great Britain. Antigua. Force 10 Nov 48.
71 UNTS 294. UK Great Britain. St. Christopher. Force 10 Nov 48.

71 UNTS 294. UK Great Britain. Nevis. Force 10 Nov 48.
71 UNTS 294. UK Great Britain. Montserrat. Force 10 Nov 48.
71 UNTS 294. UK Great Britain. Virgin Islands. Force 10 Nov 48.
71 UNTS 294. UK Great Britain. Mauritius. Force 10 Nov 48.
71 UNTS 294. UK Great Britain. North Borneo. Force 10 Nov 48.
71 UNTS 294. UK Great Britain. Northern Rhodesia. Force 10 Nov 48.
71 UNTS 294. UK Great Britain. St. Helena. Force 10 Nov 48.
71 UNTS 294. UK Great Britain. Seychelles. Force 10 Nov 48.
71 UNTS 294. UK Great Britain. Sierra Leone. Force 10 Nov 48.
71 UNTS 294. UK Great Britain. Singapore. Force 10 Nov 48.
71 UNTS 294. UK Great Britain. Swaziland. Force 10 Nov 48.
71 UNTS 294. UK Great Britain. Tanganyika. Force 10 Nov 48.
71 UNTS 294. UK Great Britain. Trinidad. Force 10 Nov 48.
71 UNTS 294. UK Great Britain. Uganda. Force 10 Nov 48.
71 UNTS 294. UK Great Britain. Gilbert Islands. Force 10 Nov 48.
71 UNTS 294. UK Great Britain. St. Vincent. Force 10 Nov 48.
71 UNTS 294. UK Great Britain. Zanzibar. Force 10 Nov 48.
71 UNTS 294. UK Great Britain. Brit Solomon Is. Force 10 Nov 48.
71 UNTS 294. UK Great Britain. Dominican Republic. Force 10 Nov 48.
71 UNTS 294. UK Great Britain. Grenada. Force 10 Nov 48.
71 UNTS 294. UK Great Britain. St. Lucia. Force 10 Nov 48.
86 UNTS 288. UK Great Britain. Singapore. Withdrawal 10 Aug 50. Force 24 Aug 50.
86 UNTS 288. Denmark. Acknowledgement 14 Aug 50. Force 24 Aug 50.
86 UNTS 288. UK Great Britain. Fed of Malaya. Withdrawal 10 Aug 50. Force 24 Aug 50.
91 UNTS 374. UK Great Britain. Newfoundland. Withdrawal 25 Apr 49. Force 25 Apr 49.
93 UNTS 359. UK Great Britain. Kenya. Force 11 Nov 49.
117 UNTS 382. UK Great Britain. North Borneo. Withdrawal 1 Oct 51. Force 15 Oct 51.
117 UNTS 382. UK Great Britain. Brunei. Withdrawal 1 Oct 51. Force 15 Oct 51.
175 UNTS 343. UK Great Britain. Singapore.
175 UNTS 343. UK Great Britain. Fed of Malaya.
175 UNTS 343. UK Great Britain. North Borneo.
218 UNTS 378. UK Great Britain. Sarawak. Force 1 Oct 55.
264 UNTS 319. UK Great Britain. Cyprus. Withdrawal 6 Nov 56. Force 12 Nov 56.
267 UNTS 367. UK Great Britain. Gibralter. Force 20 Jul 55.
349 UNTS 309. UK Great Britain. Brunei. Force 1 Feb 58.
349 UNTS 309. UK Great Britain. North Borneo. Force 1 Feb 58.
349 UNTS 309. UK Great Britain. Gambia. Force 1 Oct 58.
398 UNTS 308. UK Great Britain. Cyprus. Force 22 May 59.
560 UNTS 232. UK Great Britain. Southern Rhodesia.

100169 Bilateral Exchange **11 UNTS 291**
SIGNED: 20 Mar 47 FORCE: 1 Apr 47
REGISTERED: 4 Dec 47 UK Great Britain
ARTICLES: 2 LANGUAGE: English.
HEADNOTE: RECIPROCAL ABOLITION VISAS
TOPIC: Visas
CONCEPTS: Territorial application. Visa abolition. Border traffic and migration. Resident permits.
PARTIES:
Sweden
UK Great Britain
ANNEX
71 UNTS 300. UK Great Britain. Bahamas. Force 10 Nov 48.
71 UNTS 300. UK Great Britain. Basutoland. Force 10 Nov 48.

71 UNTS 300. UK Great Britain. Bechuanaland. Force 10 Nov 48.
71 UNTS 300. UK Great Britain. Bermuda. Force 10 Nov 48.
71 UNTS 300. UK Great Britain. British Guiana. Force 10 Nov 48.
71 UNTS 300. UK Great Britain. British Honduras. Force 10 Nov 48.
71 UNTS 300. UK Great Britain. Brunei. Force 10 Nov 48.
71 UNTS 300. UK Great Britain. Cyprus. Force 10 Nov 48.
71 UNTS 300. UK Great Britain. Falkland Islands. Force 10 Nov 48.
71 UNTS 300. UK Great Britain. Fed of Malaya. Force 10 Nov 48.
71 UNTS 300. UK Great Britain. Fiji Islands. Force 10 Nov 48.
71 UNTS 300. UK Great Britain. Jamaica. Force 10 Nov 48.
71 UNTS 300. UK Great Britain. Antigua. Force 10 Nov 48.
71 UNTS 300. UK Great Britain. St. Christopher. Force 10 Nov 48.
71 UNTS 300. UK Great Britain. Nevis. Force 10 Nov 48.
71 UNTS 300. UK Great Britain. Montserrat. Force 10 Nov 48.
71 UNTS 300. UK Great Britain. Virgin Islands. Force 10 Nov 48.
71 UNTS 300. UK Great Britain. Mauritius. Force 10 Nov 48.
71 UNTS 300. UK Great Britain. North Borneo. Force 10 Nov 48.
71 UNTS 300. UK Great Britain. Northern Rhodesia. Force 10 Nov 48.
71 UNTS 300. UK Great Britain. St. Helena. Force 10 Nov 48.
71 UNTS 300. UK Great Britain. Seychelles. Force 10 Nov 48.
71 UNTS 300. UK Great Britain. Sierra Leone. Force 10 Nov 48.
71 UNTS 300. UK Great Britain. Grenada. Force 10 Nov 48.
71 UNTS 300. UK Great Britain. St. Lucia. Force 10 Nov 48.
71 UNTS 300. UK Great Britain. St. Vincent. Force 10 Nov 48.
71 UNTS 300. UK Great Britain. Singapore. Force 10 Nov 48.
71 UNTS 300. UK Great Britain. Swaziland. Force 10 Nov 48.
71 UNTS 300. UK Great Britain. Zanzibar. Force 10 Nov 48.
71 UNTS 300. UK Great Britain. Tanganyika. Force 10 Nov 48.
71 UNTS 300. UK Great Britain. Trinidad. Force 10 Nov 48.
71 UNTS 300. UK Great Britain. Uganda. Force 10 Nov 48.
71 UNTS 300. UK Great Britain. Gilbert Islands. Force 10 Nov 48.
71 UNTS 300. UK Great Britain. Brit Solomon Is. Force 10 Nov 48.
71 UNTS 300. UK Great Britain. Dominican Republic. Force 10 Nov 48.
71 UNTS 300. UK Great Britain. Newfoundland. Force 10 Nov 48.
71 UNTS 300. Sweden. Acknowledgement 26 Oct 48. Force 10 Nov 48.
71 UNTS 300. UK Great Britain. Aden. Force 10 Nov 48.
71 UNTS 300. UK Great Britain. Southern Rhodesia. Force 10 Nov 48.
71 UNTS 300. UK Great Britain. Barbados. Force 10 Nov 48.
86 UNTS 292. Sweden. Acknowledgement 12 Aug 50. Force 24 Aug 50.
86 UNTS 292. UK Great Britain. Singapore. Withdrawal 10 Aug 50. Force 24 Aug 50.
86 UNTS 292. UK Great Britain. Fed of Malaya. Withdrawal 10 Aug 50. Force 24 Aug 50.
91 UNTS 375. UK Great Britain. Newfoundland. Withdrawal 25 Apr 49. Force 25 Apr 49.
93 UNTS 360. UK Great Britain. Kenya. Force 11 Nov 49.
117 UNTS 383. UK Great Britain. North Borneo. Withdrawal 1 Oct 51. Force 15 Oct 51.
117 UNTS 383. UK Great Britain. Brunei. Withdrawal 1 Oct 51. Force 15 Oct 51.
175 UNTS 344. UK Great Britain. Singapore.
175 UNTS 344. UK Great Britain. Fed of Malaya.
175 UNTS 344. UK Great Britain. North Borneo.

218 UNTS 379. UK Great Britain. Sarawak. Force 1 Oct 55.
264 UNTS 320. UK Great Britain. Cyprus. Withdrawal 6 Nov 56. Force 12 Nov 56.
267 UNTS 367. UK Great Britain. Gibralter. Force 20 Jul 55.
349 UNTS 310. UK Great Britain. Gambia. Force 1 Oct 58.
349 UNTS 310. UK Great Britain. North Borneo. Force 1 Feb 58.
349 UNTS 310. UK Great Britain. Brunei. Force 1 Feb 58.
398 UNTS 310. UK Great Britain. Cyprus. Force 22 May 59.
560 UNTS 232. UK Great Britain. Southern Rhodesia.

100170 Bilateral Exchange **11 UNTS 297**
SIGNED: 21 Mar 47 FORCE: 15 Apr 47
REGISTERED: 4 Dec 47 UK Great Britain
ARTICLES: 2 LANGUAGE: English.
HEADNOTE: RECIPROCAL ABOLITION VISAS
TOPIC: Visas
CONCEPTS: Territorial application. Visa abolition. Border traffic and migration. Resident permits.
PARTIES:
Netherlands
UK Great Britain
ANNEX
86 UNTS 296. UK Great Britain. Seychelles. Force 1 Jan 50.
86 UNTS 296. UK Great Britain. Seychelles. Force 1 Jan 50.
86 UNTS 296. UK Great Britain. Bahamas. Force 1 Jan 50.
86 UNTS 296. UK Great Britain. Barbados. Force 1 Jan 50.
86 UNTS 296. Netherlands. Acknowledgement 10 Dec 49. Force 1 Jan 50.
86 UNTS 296. UK Great Britain. Southern Rhodesia. Force 1 Jan 50.
86 UNTS 296. UK Great Britain. Aden. Force 1 Jan 50.
86 UNTS 296. UK Great Britain. Basutoland. Force 1 Jan 50.
86 UNTS 296. UK Great Britain. Bechuanaland. Force 1 Jan 50.
86 UNTS 296. UK Great Britain. Bermuda. Force 1 Jan 50.
86 UNTS 296. UK Great Britain. British Guiana. Force 1 Jan 50.
86 UNTS 296. UK Great Britain. British Honduras. Force 1 Jan 50.
86 UNTS 296. UK Great Britain. Brunei. Force 1 Jan 50.
86 UNTS 296. UK Great Britain. Cyprus. Force 1 Jan 50.
86 UNTS 296. UK Great Britain. Falkland Islands. Force 1 Jan 50.
86 UNTS 296. UK Great Britain. Fed of Malaya. Force 1 Jan 50.
86 UNTS 296. UK Great Britain. Fiji Islands. Force 1 Jan 50.
86 UNTS 296. UK Great Britain. Jamaica. Force 1 Jan 50.
86 UNTS 296. UK Great Britain. Kenya. Force 1 Jan 50.
86 UNTS 296. UK Great Britain. Zanzibar. Force 1 Jan 50.
86 UNTS 296. UK Great Britain. Mauritius. Force 1 Jan 50.
86 UNTS 296. UK Great Britain. North Borneo. Force 1 Jan 50.
86 UNTS 296. UK Great Britain. St. Helena. Force 1 Jan 50.
86 UNTS 296. UK Great Britain. Sierra Leone. Force 1 Jan 50.
86 UNTS 296. UK Great Britain. Singapore. Force 1 Jan 50.
86 UNTS 296. UK Great Britain. Swaziland. Force 1 Jan 50.
86 UNTS 296. UK Great Britain. Tanganyika. Force 1 Jan 50.
86 UNTS 296. UK Great Britain. Uganda. Force 1 Jan 50.
86 UNTS 296. UK Great Britain. Antigua. Force 1 Jan 50.
86 UNTS 296. UK Great Britain. St. Christopher. Force 1 Jan 50.
86 UNTS 296. UK Great Britain. Nevis. Force 1 Jan 50.
86 UNTS 296. UK Great Britain. Montserrat. Force 1 Jan 50.

36 UNTS 296. UK Great Britain. Virgin Islands. Force 1 Jan 50.

36 UNTS 296. UK Great Britain. Gilbert Islands. Force 1 Jan 50.

36 UNTS 296. UK Great Britain. Brit Solomon Is. Force 1 Jan 50.

36 UNTS 296. UK Great Britain. Dominican Republic. Force 1 Jan 50.

36 UNTS 296. UK Great Britain. Grenada. Force 1 Jan 50.

36 UNTS 296. UK Great Britain. St. Lucia. Force 1 Jan 50.

36 UNTS 296. UK Great Britain. St. Vincent. Force 1 Jan 50.

36 UNTS 296. UK Great Britain. Trinidad. Force 1 Jan 50.

36 UNTS 300. Netherlands. Acknowledgement 16 Aug 50. Force 24 Aug 50.

36 UNTS 300. UK Great Britain. Singapore. Withdrawal 10 Aug 50. Force 24 Aug 50.

36 UNTS 300. UK Great Britain. Fed of Malaya. Withdrawal 10 Aug 50. Force 24 Aug 50.

117 UNTS 384. UK Great Britain. North Borneo. Withdrawal 1 Oct 51. Force 15 Oct 51.

117 UNTS 384. UK Great Britain. Brunei. Withdrawal 1 Oct 51. Force 15 Oct 51.

75 UNTS 345. UK Great Britain. Singapore.

75 UNTS 345. UK Great Britain. Fed of Malaya.

75 UNTS 345. UK Great Britain. North Borneo.

218 UNTS 379. UK Great Britain. Sarawak. Force 1 Oct 55.

264 UNTS 320. UK Great Britain. Cyprus. Withdrawal 6 Nov 56. Force 12 Nov 56.

267 UNTS 368. UK Great Britain. Gibralter. Force 20 Jul 55.

349 UNTS 311. UK Great Britain. Brunei. Force 1 Feb 58.

349 UNTS 311. UK Great Britain. North Borneo. Force 1 Feb 58.

349 UNTS 311. UK Great Britain. Gambia. Force 1 Oct 58.

398 UNTS 310. UK Great Britain. Cyprus. Force 22 May 59.

100171 Bilateral Agreement **11 UNTS 303**
SIGNED: 6 Oct 47 FORCE: 6 Oct 47
REGISTERED: 5 Dec 47 USA (United States)
ARTICLES: 25 LANGUAGE: English. Persian.
HEADNOTE: MILITARY MISSION
TOPIC: Military Mission
CONCEPTS: Informational records. Inspection and observation. Licenses and permits. Compensation. Indemnities and reimbursements. Exchange rates and regulations. Expense sharing formulae. Tax exemptions. Dangerous goods. Military assistance. Military training. Security of information. Airforce-army-navy personnel ratio. Ranks and privileges. Conditions for assistance missions. Third country military personnel. Status of forces.
PROCEDURE: Denunciation. Duration. Renewal or Revival. Termination.
PARTIES:
Iran
USA (United States)
ANNEX
30 UNTS 339. USA (United States). Extension and Amendment 5 Jan 49. Force 5 Jan 49.
30 UNTS 339. Iran. Extension and Amendment 29 Dec 48. Force 5 Jan 49.
32 UNTS 371. USA (United States). Extension and Amendment 28 Nov 49. Force 10 Jan 50.
32 UNTS 371. Iran. Extension and Amendment 10 Jan 50. Force 10 Jan 50.
41 UNTS 357. USA (United States). Prolongation 17 Sep 50. Force 20 Mar 51.
41 UNTS 357. Iran. Prolongation 18 Sep 50. Force 20 Mar 51.
29 UNTS 278. USA (United States). Extension and Amendment 18 Apr 54.
29 UNTS 278. Iran. Extension and Amendment 18 Apr 54.
35 UNTS 353. USA (United States). Prolongation 22 Sep 54. Force 21 Mar 55.
35 UNTS 353. Iran. Prolongation 22 Nov 54. Force 21 Mar 55.
70 UNTS 373. USA (United States). Prolongation 13 Feb 56. Force 13 Feb 56.
70 UNTS 373. Iran. Prolongation 13 Feb 56. Force 13 Feb 56.

100172 Bilateral Exchange **11 UNTS 325**
SIGNED: 6 Mar 47 FORCE: 1 Mar 47
REGISTERED: 15 Dec 47 Canada
ARTICLES: 2 LANGUAGE: English.
HEADNOTE: DISPOSAL CANAL PROJECT
TOPIC: Specific Resources
CONCEPTS: Surplus property. Facilities and property.
PARTIES:
Canada
USA (United States)

100173 Bilateral Exchange **11 UNTS 341**
SIGNED: 9 Jan 47 FORCE: 9 Jan 47
REGISTERED: 15 Dec 47 Canada
ARTICLES: 2 LANGUAGE: English.
HEADNOTE: DISPOSAL SURPLUS PROPERTY
TOPIC: Specific Property
CONCEPTS: Surplus property. Facilities and property.
PARTIES:
Canada
USA (United States)

100174 Bilateral Agreement **11 UNTS 347**
SIGNED: 18 Dec 47 FORCE: 18 Dec 47
REGISTERED: 18 Dec 47 United Nations
ARTICLES: 5 LANGUAGE: English.
HEADNOTE: UN HEADQUARTERS
TOPIC: IGO Status/Immunit
CONCEPTS: Annex or appendix reference. Annex type material. Diplomatic privileges. Diplomatic missions. Inviolability. Property. Diplomatic correspondence. Headquarters and facilities.
PARTIES:
United Nations
USA (United States)

100175 Bilateral Treaty **11 UNTS 361**
SIGNED: 18 Apr 47 FORCE: 24 Oct 47
REGISTERED: 19 Dec 47 Taiwan
ARTICLES: 10 LANGUAGE: Chinese. English.
HEADNOTE: AMITY
TOPIC: General Amity
CONCEPTS: Friendship and amity. Alien status. Consular relations establishment. Diplomatic relations establishment. Privileges and immunities. General property. Procedure. Most favored nation clause.
PROCEDURE: Future Procedures Contemplated. Ratification.
PARTIES:
Taiwan
Philippines

100176 Bilateral Agreement **11 UNTS 371**
SIGNED: 14 Aug 47 FORCE: 14 Aug 47
REGISTERED: 24 Dec 47 UK Great Britain
ARTICLES: 11 LANGUAGE: English.
HEADNOTE: TEMPORARY ARRANGEMENT STERLING BALANCE
TOPIC: Finance
CONCEPTS: Definition of terms. Detailed regulations. General cooperation. Accounting procedures. Banking. Monetary and gold transfers. Funding procedures. Payment schedules. Assets. Assessment procedures.
PROCEDURE: Termination.
PARTIES:
India
UK Great Britain
ANNEX
196 UNTS 324. UK Great Britain. Prolongation 8 Feb 52. Force 8 Feb 52.
196 UNTS 324. India. Prolongation 8 Feb 52. Force 8 Feb 52.

100177 Bilateral Agreement **12 UNTS 3**
SIGNED: 16 Jul 47 FORCE: 16 Sep 47
REGISTERED: 2 Jan 48 Denmark
ARTICLES: 6 LANGUAGE: French.
HEADNOTE: PROTECTION INDUSTRIAL PROPERTY

TOPIC: Patents/Copyrights
CONCEPTS: Licenses and permits. Trademarks. Post-war adjustment.
TREATY REF: 205LTS218; 192LTS17; 204LTS469.
PARTIES:
Denmark
France

100178 Bilateral Agreement **12 UNTS 11**
SIGNED: 27 Oct 47 FORCE: 27 Oct 47
REGISTERED: 8 Jan 48 Taiwan
ARTICLES: 10 LANGUAGE: Chinese. English.
HEADNOTE: RELIEF ASSISTANCE
TOPIC: Direct Aid
CONCEPTS: Time limit. Non-visa travel documents. Diplomatic privileges. Privileges and immunities. Conformity with municipal law. General cooperation. Exchange of information and documents. Informational records. Personnel. Public information. Accounting procedures. Payment schedules. Local currency. Customs exemptions. Domestic obligation. General aid. Relief supplies. Withdrawal conditions. Procurement. Distribution. Press and wire services.
PROCEDURE: Duration. Termination.
PARTIES:
Taiwan
USA (United States)

100179 Bilateral Agreement **12 UNTS 39**
SIGNED: 30 Aug 46 FORCE: 10 Nov 47
REGISTERED: 8 Jan 48 Taiwan
ARTICLES: 14 LANGUAGE: Chinese. English.
HEADNOTE: USE FUNDS 1946 SURPLUS AGREEMENT
TOPIC: Direct Aid
CONCEPTS: Definition of terms. Detailed regulations. Annex type material. Conformity with municipal law. General cooperation. Exchange of information and documents. Exchange. Commissions and foundations. Currency deposits. Exchange rates and regulations. Funding procedures. Internal structure.
PROCEDURE: Amendment.
PARTIES:
Taiwan
USA (United States)
ANNEX
303 UNTS 286. Taiwan. Amendment 30 Nov 57. Force 30 Nov 57.
303 UNTS 286. USA (United States). Amendment 30 Nov 57. Force 30 Nov 57.
405 UNTS 276. Taiwan. Amendment 28 Feb 61. Force 28 Feb 61.
405 UNTS 276. USA (United States). Amendment 28 Feb 61. Force 28 Feb 61.

100180 Bilateral Treaty **12 UNTS 59**
SIGNED: 20 May 46 FORCE: 20 May 46
REGISTERED: 19 Jan 48 Denmark
ARTICLES: 16 LANGUAGE: Chinese. Danish. English.
HEADNOTE: RELINQUISH EXTRATERRITORIAL RIGHTS CHINA
TOPIC: Privil/Immunities
CONCEPTS: Exceptions and exemptions. General consular functions. Privileges and immunities. Protection of nationals. Expropriation. General property. Abolition of treaty ports. Abolition of extraterritorial rights. Fees and exemptions. Most favored nation clause. National treatment. Inland and territorial waters. Ports and pilotage.
TREATY REF: 91LTS207.
PROCEDURE: Future Procedures Contemplated. Ratification.
PARTIES:
Taiwan
Denmark

100181 Bilateral Convention **12 UNTS 95**
SIGNED: 19 May 47 FORCE: 13 Jun 47
REGISTERED: 23 Jan 48 Poland
ARTICLES: 11 LANGUAGE: French. Polish.
HEADNOTE: INTELLECTUAL COOPERATION
TOPIC: Education
CONCEPTS: Friendship and amity. General cooperation. Establishment of commission. Recognition of degrees. Exchange. Commissions and foundations. Teacher and student exchange.

Professorships. Scholarships and grants. Exchange. General cultural cooperation. Artists. Athletes. Scientific exchange. Indemnities and reimbursements. Publications exchange. Mass media exchange. Press and wire services.
PROCEDURE: Denunciation. Duration. Ratification. Renewal or Revival.
PARTIES:
France
Poland

100182   Bilateral Agreement   **12 UNTS 109**
SIGNED: 15 Mar 47   FORCE: 24 Jul 47
REGISTERED: 28 Jan 48 Austria
ARTICLES: 23 LANGUAGE: French. German.
HEADNOTE: CULTURAL AGREEMENT
TOPIC: Culture
CONCEPTS: Tourism. Alien status. Privileges and immunities. Standardization. Conformity with municipal law. Exchange of information and documents. Recognition of degrees. Commissions and foundations. Teacher and student exchange. Professorships. Institute establishment. Scholarships and grants. Vocational training. General cultural cooperation. Artists. Athletes. Research cooperation. Research results. Payment schedules. Tax exemptions. Customs exemptions. Mass media exchange.
PROCEDURE: Denunciation. Duration. Ratification.
PARTIES:
Austria
France

100183   Bilateral Exchange   **12 UNTS 131**
SIGNED: 5 Apr 46   FORCE: 1 Jan 46
REGISTERED: 30 Jan 48 USA (United States)
ARTICLES: 22 LANGUAGE: English. Portuguese.
HEADNOTE: VOCATIONAL INDUSTRIAL EDUCATION
TOPIC: Education
CONCEPTS: Definition of terms. Annex or appendix reference. Annex type material. Previous treaty extension. Privileges and immunities. General cooperation. Personnel. General property. Exchange. Teacher and student exchange. Scholarships and grants. Vocational training. Accounting procedures. Indemnities and reimbursements. Expense sharing formulae. Funding procedures. Tax exemptions. Customs exemptions. Assistance. Economic assistance. Materials, equipment and services. Aid missions.
PROCEDURE: Amendment. Duration. Renewal or Revival.
PARTIES:
Brazil
USA (United States)
ANNEX
162 UNTS 324. USA (United States). Prolongation 23 Jul 48. Force 30 Oct 38.
162 UNTS 324. Brazil. Prolongation 21 Oct 48. Force 30 Oct 38.
162 UNTS 331. USA (United States). Prolongation 29 Sep 49. Force 4 Oct 49.
162 UNTS 331. Brazil. Prolongation 23 Aug 49. Force 4 Oct 49.
177 UNTS 326. USA (United States). Prolongation 14 Oct 50. Force 27 Feb 51.
177 UNTS 326. Brazil. Prolongation 14 Oct 50. Force 27 Feb 51.
234 UNTS 291. USA (United States). Supplementation 18 Feb 52. Force 5 Apr 52.
234 UNTS 291. Brazil. Supplementation 18 Feb 52. Force 5 Apr 52.
264 UNTS 321. USA (United States). Prolongation 13 Jun 55. Force 16 Jun 55.
264 UNTS 321. Brazil. Prolongation 3 Jun 55. Force 16 Jun 55.
393 UNTS 308. Brazil. Extension and Amendment 29 Jun 60. Force 29 Jun 60.
393 UNTS 308. USA (United States). Extension and Amendment 29 Jun 60. Force 29 Jun 60.
401 UNTS 208. USA (United States). Extension and Amendment 31 Dec 60. Force 31 Dec 60.
401 UNTS 208. Brazil. Extension and Amendment 31 Dec 60. Force 31 Dec 60.
451 UNTS 316. USA (United States). Prolongation 29 Dec 61. Force 11 Jan 62.
451 UNTS 316. Brazil. Prolongation 11 Jan 62. Force 11 Jan 62.

100184   Bilateral Exchange   **12 UNTS 163**
SIGNED: 7 Oct 46   FORCE: 7 Oct 47
REGISTERED: 30 Jan 48 USA (United States)
ARTICLES: 12 LANGUAGE: English.
HEADNOTE: TERMINATING DEFENSE AGREEMENT PROVIDING INTERIM AIRPORT
TOPIC: Milit Installation
CONCEPTS: Annex type material.
TREATY REF: 12UNTS405;.
PARTIES:
Iceland
USA (United States)

100185   Bilateral Exchange   **12 UNTS 173**
SIGNED: 21 Nov 46   FORCE: 21 Nov 46
REGISTERED: 30 Jan 48 USA (United States)
ARTICLES: 2 LANGUAGE: English.
HEADNOTE: EXPANSION TRADE EMPLOYMENT
TOPIC: General Trade
CONCEPTS: General cooperation. Customs duties.
PARTIES:
Netherlands
USA (United States)

100186   Multilateral Protocol   **12 UNTS 179**
SIGNED: 11 Dec 46   FORCE: 11 Dec 46
REGISTERED: 3 Feb 48 United Nations
ARTICLES: 9 LANGUAGE: Chinese. English. French. Russian. Spanish.
HEADNOTE: PROTOCOL NARCOTIC DRUGS
TOPIC: Sanitation
CONCEPTS: Definition of terms. Detailed regulations. Treaty implementation. Treaty interpretation. Exchange of information and documents. Narcotic drugs. WHO used as agency. Extension of functions.
INTL ORGS: World Health Organization.
TREATY REF: 51LTS337.
PROCEDURE: Ratification.
PARTIES:
Afghanistan   SIGNED: 11 Dec 46   FORCE: 11 Dec 46
Albania RATIFIED: 23 Jun 47 FORCE: 23 Jun 47
Argentina   SIGNED: 11 Dec 46   FORCE: 11 Dec 46
Australia   SIGNED: 11 Dec 46   RATIFIED: 28 Aug 47 FORCE: 28 Aug 47
Belgium SIGNED: 11 Dec 46 FORCE: 11 Dec 46
Bolivia SIGNED: 14 Dec 46 FORCE: 14 Dec 46
Brazil SIGNED: 17 Dec 46 FORCE: 17 Dec 46
Byelorussia   SIGNED: 11 Dec 46   FORCE: 11 Dec 46
Canada SIGNED: 11 Dec 46 FORCE: 11 Dec 46
Chile SIGNED: 11 Dec 46 FORCE: 11 Dec 46
Taiwan SIGNED: 11 Dec 46 FORCE: 11 Dec 46
Colombia   SIGNED: 11 Dec 46   FORCE: 11 Dec 46
Costa Rica SIGNED: 11 Dec 46
Cuba SIGNED: 12 Dec 46
Czechoslovakia   SIGNED: 11 Dec 46   FORCE: 11 Dec 46
Denmark SIGNED: 11 Dec 46
Dominican Republic SIGNED: 11 Dec 46 FORCE: 11 Dec 46
Ecuador SIGNED: 14 Dec 46
United Arab Rep SIGNED: 11 Dec 46
Finland RATIFIED: 3 Feb 48 FORCE: 3 Feb 48
France SIGNED: 11 Dec 46 RATIFIED: 10 Oct 47 FORCE: 10 Oct 47
Greece SIGNED: 11 Dec 46
Guatemala SIGNED: 13 Dec 46
Haiti SIGNED: 14 Dec 46
Honduras   SIGNED: 11 Dec 46   FORCE: 11 Dec 46
India SIGNED: 11 Dec 46 FORCE: 11 Dec 46
Iran SIGNED: 11 Dec 46 FORCE: 11 Dec 46
Iraq SIGNED: 12 Dec 46
Italy SIGNED: 25 Mar 48
Lebanon SIGNED: 13 Dec 46 FORCE: 13 Dec 46
Liberia SIGNED: 11 Dec 46 FORCE: 11 Dec 46
Liechtenstein   RATIFIED: 25 Sep 47   FORCE: 25 Sep 47
Luxembourg SIGNED: 11 Dec 46
Mexico SIGNED: 11 Dec 46 FORCE: 11 Dec 46
Monaco SIGNED: 21 Nov 47 FORCE: 21 Nov 47
Netherlands SIGNED: 11 Dec 46
New Zealand   SIGNED: 11 Dec 46   FORCE: 11 Dec 46
Nicaragua SIGNED: 13 Dec 46
Norway SIGNED: 11 Dec 46 RATIFIED: 2 Jul 47 FORCE: 2 Jul 47

Pakistan SIGNED: 11 Dec 46 FORCE: 11 Dec 46
Panama SIGNED: 15 Dec 46 FORCE: 15 Dec 46
Paraguay SIGNED: 14 Dec 46
Peru SIGNED: 26 Nov 48
Philippines SIGNED: 11 Dec 46
Poland SIGNED: 11 Dec 46 FORCE: 11 Dec 46
Saudi Arabia SIGNED: 11 Dec 46 FORCE: 11 Dec 46
Siam SIGNED: 27 Oct 47 FORCE: 27 Oct 47
South Africa SIGNED: 15 Dec 46
Sweden SIGNED: 17 Oct 47 FORCE: 17 Oct 47
Switzerland   RATIFIED: 25 Sep 47   FORCE: 25 Sep 47
Syria SIGNED: 11 Dec 46 FORCE: 11 Dec 46
Turkey SIGNED: 11 Dec 46 FORCE: 11 Dec 46
UK Great Britain SIGNED: 11 Dec 46 FORCE: 11 Dec 46
USA (United States) SIGNED: 11 Dec 46 RATIFIED: 12 Aug 47 FORCE: 12 Aug 47
Ukrainian SSR SIGNED: 11 Dec 46 RATIFIED: 8 Jan 48 FORCE: 8 Jan 48
Uruguay SIGNED: 14 Dec 46
USSR (Soviet Union) SIGNED: 11 Dec 46 RATIFIED: 8 Jan 48 FORCE: 25 Oct 47
Venezuela SIGNED: 11 Dec 46
Yugoslavia SIGNED: 11 Dec 46
ANNEX
12 UNTS 418. Ireland. Acceptance 18 Feb 48.
12 UNTS 418. South Africa. Acceptance 24 Feb 48.
12 UNTS 419. Ethiopia. Accession 9 Sep 47.
12 UNTS 420. Ethiopia. Ratification 9 Sep 47.
14 UNTS 492. Netherlands. Acceptance 10 Mar 48.
27 UNTS 401. UK Great Britain. Gilbert Islands. Force 4 Jul 49.
42 UNTS 355. Ethiopia. Accession 28 Dec 48.
43 UNTS 338. Luxembourg. Ratification 13 Oct 49.
51 UNTS 322. UK Great Britain. New Hebrides Is. Force 15 Jun 50.
51 UNTS 322. France. New Hebrides Is. Force 15 Jun 50.
53 UNTS 418. Nicaragua. Ratification 24 Apr 50.
54 UNTS 384. Austria. Acceptance 17 May 50.
54 UNTS 384. Philippines. Acceptance 25 May 50.
71 UNTS 304. Iraq. Acceptance 14 Sep 50.
73 UNTS 244. Vietnam. Replacement 11 Aug 50.
73 UNTS 244. Laos. Replacement 7 Oct 50.
88 UNTS 426. Laos. Replacement 9 Mar 51.
88 UNTS 426. Vietnam. Replacement 28 Mar 51.
88 UNTS 427. Haiti. Acceptance 31 May 51.
90 UNTS 322. Ecuador. Ratification 8 Jun 51.
104 UNTS 342. Cambodia. Replacement 3 Oct 51.
104 UNTS 344. Cambodia. Accession 3 Oct 51.
121 UNTS 326. UK Great Britain. Basutoland. Force 14 May 52.
121 UNTS 326. UK Great Britain. Bechuanaland. Force 14 May 52.
121 UNTS 326. UK Great Britain. Swaziland. Force 14 May 52.
126 UNTS 347. Japan. Acceptance 27 Mar 52.
131 UNTS 307. Israel. Accession 16 May 52.
132 UNTS 379. Israel. Accession 12 May 52.
151 UNTS 373. Switzerland. Ratification 31 Dec 52. Force 31 Mar 53.
209 UNTS 328. Mexico. Qualified Ratification 6 May 55. Force 4 Aug 55.
211 UNTS 341. Luxembourg. Accession 28 Jun 55. Force 26 Sep 55.
214 UNTS 349. Japan. Ratification 7 Sep 55. Force 6 Dec 55.
216 UNTS 359. Spain. Signature without Reservation as to Approval 26 Sep 55.
223 UNTS 315. Hungary. Acceptance 16 Dec 55.
251 UNTS 368. Austria. Ratification 17 May 50. Force 15 Aug 50.
251 UNTS 368. Laos. Accession 13 Jul 51. Force 11 Oct 51.
251 UNTS 370. Jordan. Accession 12 Apr 54. Force 10 Aug 54.
253 UNTS 308. Morocco. Succession 7 Nov 56.
258 UNTS 381. Afghanistan. Accession 29 Jan 57.
282 UNTS 352. Ceylon (Sri Lanka). Accession 4 Dec 57. Force 4 Mar 58.
292 UNTS 358. Indonesia. Accession 3 Apr 58. Force 2 Jul 58.
292 UNTS 358. Ghana. Acceptance 7 Apr 58.
292 UNTS 358. Indonesia. Accession 3 Apr 58.
299 UNTS 407. Jordan. Accession 7 May 58. Force 5 Aug 58.

300 UNTS 300. Ghana. Acceptance 3 Apr 58.
302 UNTS 352. Dominican Republic. Accession 9 Jun 58. Force 7 Sep 58.
303 UNTS 297. Netherlands. Accession 29 May 58.
309 UNTS 352. Fed of Malaya. Replacement 21 Aug 58. Force 31 Aug 57.
327 UNTS 322. Netherlands. Qualified Ratification 19 Mar 59. Force 17 Jun 59.
327 UNTS 322. Netherlands. Surinam. Force 17 Jun 59.
327 UNTS 322. Netherlands. Dutch New Guinea. Force 17 Jun 59.
338 UNTS 325. Germany, West. Acceptance 12 Aug 59.
348 UNTS 345. Germany, West. Berlin.
371 UNTS 264. Netherlands. Netherlands Antilles. Force 2 Nov 60.
394 UNTS 251. Italy. Qualified Accession 3 Apr 61. Force 2 Jul 61.
396 UNTS 315. Liechtenstein. Accession 24 May 61. Force 22 Aug 61.
399 UNTS 250. Nigeria. Succession 26 Jun 61.
405 UNTS 286. Niger. Succession 25 Aug 61.
410 UNTS 285. Romania. Acceptance 11 Oct 61.
414 UNTS 372. Cameroon. Succession 20 Nov 61.
415 UNTS 424. Ivory Coast. Succession 8 Dec 61.
415 UNTS 424. Dahomey. Succession 5 Dec 61.
417 UNTS 348. Ivory Coast. Accession 20 Dec 61. Force 20 Mar 62.
419 UNTS 341. Cameroon. Accession 15 Jan 62. Force 15 Apr 62.
423 UNTS 280. Togo. Succession 27 Feb 62.
423 UNTS 280. Sierra Leone. Succession 13 Mar 62.
426 UNTS 336. Guinea. Succession 26 Apr 62.
429 UNTS 250. Congo (Zaire). Succession 31 May 62.
437 UNTS 332. Central Afri Rep. Succession 4 Sep 62.
442 UNTS 294. Congo (Brazzaville). Succession 15 Oct 62.
462 UNTS 326. Upper Volta. Accession 26 Apr 63. Force 25 Jul 63.
463 UNTS 312. Senegal. Succession 2 May 63.
466 UNTS 376. Cyprus. Succession 16 May 63.
480 UNTS 314. Algeria. Accession 31 Oct 63. Force 29 Jan 64.
484 UNTS 406. Jamaica. Succession 26 Dec 63.
502 UNTS 360. Tanzania. Accession 3 Jul 64. Force 1 Oct 64.
503 UNTS 326. Rwanda. Succession 5 Aug 64.
538 UNTS 329. Malawi. Accession 8 Jun 65. Force 6 Sep 65.
541 UNTS 298. Malawi. Succession 22 Jul 65.
547 UNTS 311. Uganda. Accession 20 Oct 65. Force 18 Jan 66.
550 UNTS 401. Netherlands. Denunciation 14 Dec 65.
550 UNTS 401. Netherlands. Surinam. Denunciation 14 Dec 65.
550 UNTS 401. Netherlands. Netherlands Antilles. Denunciation 14 Dec 65.
551 UNTS 264. Malta. Succession 3 Jan 66. Force 21 Sep 64.
560 UNTS 234. Trinidad/Tobago. Succession 11 Apr 66. Force 31 Aug 62.
603 UNTS 294. Cuba. Qualified Ratification 9 Aug 67.

100187 Bilateral Agreement **12 UNTS 241**
SIGNED: 4 Dec 46 FORCE: 4 Dec 46
REGISTERED: 9 Feb 48 Netherlands
ARTICLES: 3 LANGUAGE: Dutch. English.
HEADNOTE: SUPPLY AIRCRAFT EQUIPMENT
TOPIC: Milit Installation
CONCEPTS: Annex or appendix reference. Indemnities and reimbursements. Delivery schedules. Payment for war supplies. Surplus war property. Restrictions on transfer.
PARTIES:
Netherlands
UK Great Britain

100188 Bilateral Agreement **12 UNTS 257**
SIGNED: 22 Jul 47 FORCE: 22 Jul 47
REGISTERED: 9 Feb 48 Netherlands
ARTICLES: 12 LANGUAGE: Afrikaans. Dutch. English.
HEADNOTE: AIR SERVICES

TOPIC: Air Transport
CONCEPTS: Definition of terms. Annex or appendix reference. Conformity with municipal law. Licenses and permits. Recognition of legal documents. Use of facilities. Special tribunals. Reexport of goods, etc.. Fees and exemptions. Most favored nation clause. National treatment. Customs exemptions. Competency certificate. Routes and logistics. Navigational conditions. Permit designation. Airport facilities. Airworthiness certificates. Conditions of airlines operating permission. Operating authorizations and regulations. Licenses and certificates of nationality.
PROCEDURE: Amendment. Termination. Application to Non-self-governing Territories.
PARTIES:
Netherlands
South Africa

ANNEX
231 UNTS 348. Netherlands. Supplementation 17 Jun 54. Force 1 Oct 54.
231 UNTS 348. South Africa. Supplementation 17 Jun 54. Force 1 Oct 54.
335 UNTS 280. Netherlands. Amendment 13 Mar 58. Force 17 Mar 58.
335 UNTS 280. South Africa. Amendment 13 Mar 58. Force 17 Mar 58.

100189 Bilateral Convention **12 UNTS 287**
SIGNED: 11 Feb 47 FORCE: 1 Oct 47
REGISTERED: 16 Feb 48 Poland
ARTICLES: 9 LANGUAGE: French.
HEADNOTE: DEATH DISABILITY PENSIONS WAR VICTIMS
TOPIC: Reparations
CONCEPTS: Time limit. Annex or appendix reference. Conformity with municipal law. Legal protection and assistance. Service in foreign army. Loss and/or damage.
PROCEDURE: Denunciation. Ratification. Termination.
PARTIES:
France
Poland

100190 Bilateral Agreement **12 UNTS 295**
SIGNED: 18 Mar 47 FORCE: 4 Jun 47
REGISTERED: 16 Feb 48 Poland
ARTICLES: 7 LANGUAGE: French.
HEADNOTE: REGULATING COMMERCIAL EXCHANGES
TOPIC: General Economic
CONCEPTS: Annex or appendix reference. Establishment of commission. General trade. Export quotas. Import quotas. Payment schedules. Delivery schedules. Quotas.
INTL ORGS: Special Commission.
PROCEDURE: Denunciation. Duration. Renewal or Revival.
PARTIES:
Poland
Sweden

ANNEX
26 UNTS 400. Sweden. Extension and Amendment 22 Apr 48. Force 5 Jun 49.
26 UNTS 400. Poland. Extension and Amendment 22 Apr 48. Force 5 Jun 49.

100191 Bilateral Agreement **12 UNTS 323**
SIGNED: 15 Apr 47 FORCE: 15 Apr 47
REGISTERED: 16 Feb 48 Denmark
ARTICLES: 8 LANGUAGE: Danish. Norwegian.
HEADNOTE: PAYMENTS
TOPIC: Finance
CONCEPTS: Change of circumstances. Balance of payments. Currency. Monetary and gold transfers. Exchange rates and regulations. Payment schedules.
PARTIES:
Denmark
Norway

100192 Bilateral Agreement **12 UNTS 351**
SIGNED: 15 Jul 47 FORCE: 15 Jul 47
REGISTERED: 16 Feb 48 Norway
ARTICLES: 14 LANGUAGE: French.
HEADNOTE: PAYMENTS SETTLEMENT
TOPIC: Finance
CONCEPTS: Detailed regulations. Treaty imple-

mentation. General cooperation. Establishment of commission. Trade procedures. Accounting procedures. Banking. Balance of payments. Currency. Monetary and gold transfers. Exchange rates and regulations. Payment schedules. Interest rates.
INTL ORGS: Special Commission.
PROCEDURE: Amendment. Denunciation.
PARTIES:
Norway
Switzerland

100193 Bilateral Agreement **12 UNTS 363**
SIGNED: 9 Aug 47 FORCE: 25 Oct 47
REGISTERED: 16 Feb 48 Poland
ARTICLES: 11 LANGUAGE: French.
HEADNOTE: AIR SERVICES
TOPIC: Air Transport
CONCEPTS: Annex or appendix reference. Previous treaty replacement. Inspection and observation. Licenses and permits. Recognition of legal documents. Use of facilities. Arbitration. Procedure. Existing tribunals. Special tribunals. Indemnities and reimbursements. Expense sharing formulae. Fees and exemptions. Most favored nation clause. National treatment. Customs exemptions. Competency certificate. Routes and logistics. Navigational conditions. Permit designation. Airport facilities. Airworthiness certificates. Conditions of airlines operating permission. Operating authorizations and regulations. Licenses and certificates of nationality.
PROCEDURE: Amendment.
PARTIES:
Poland
Romania

100194 Bilateral Exchange **12 UNTS 377**
SIGNED: 30 Jul 47 FORCE: 30 Jul 47
REGISTERED: 25 Feb 48 Taiwan
ARTICLES: 2 LANGUAGE: English.
HEADNOTE: PAYMENT MANNER
TOPIC: Reparations
CONCEPTS: Treaty implementation. General cooperation. Exchange of information and documents. Accounting procedures. Banking. Balance of payments. Monetary and gold transfers. Exchange rates and regulations. Payment schedules. Local currency.
PARTIES:
Taiwan
Italy

100195 Bilateral Exchange **12 UNTS 383**
SIGNED: 30 Jul 47 FORCE: 30 Jul 47
REGISTERED: 25 Feb 48 Taiwan
ARTICLES: 2 LANGUAGE: English.
HEADNOTE: REGULATION CERTAIN OFFICIAL ASSETS
TOPIC: Consul/Citizenship
CONCEPTS: Property. General property. Use of facilities.
PARTIES:
Taiwan
Italy

100196 Bilateral Agreement **13 UNTS 3**
SIGNED: 12 Feb 46 FORCE: 25 May 46
REGISTERED: 3 Mar 48 USA (United States)
ARTICLES: 10 LANGUAGE: English. Turkish.
HEADNOTE: AIR TRANSPORT
TOPIC: Air Transport
CONCEPTS: Exceptions and exemptions. Annex or appendix reference. Conformity with municipal law. Licenses and permits. Recognition of legal documents. Use of facilities. Fees and exemptions. Most favored nation clause. National treatment. Customs exemptions. Competency certificate. Routes and logistics. Navigational conditions. Permit designation. Air transport. Airport facilities. Airworthiness certificates. Conditions of airlines operating permission. Operating authorizations and regulations. Licenses and certificates of nationality.
TREATY REF: DEPT.STATE PUB.2282.
PROCEDURE: Amendment. Ratification. Registration. Termination.
PARTIES:
Turkey
USA (United States)

100197 Bilateral Exchange **13 UNTS 19**
SIGNED: 10 Jun 46 FORCE: 10 Jun 46
REGISTERED: 3 Mar 48 USA (United States)
ARTICLES: 2 LANGUAGE: English.
HEADNOTE: WAIVER MOST FAVORED NATION
CLAUSE
TOPIC: Mostfavored Nation
CONCEPTS: Independence maintenance. Transi-
tion period. General trade. Tariffs. Quotas. Most
favored nation clause. Customs duties.
TREATY REF: UTS32; 12STAT1003.
PARTIES:
Bolivia
USA (United States)

100198 Bilateral Exchange **13 UNTS 27**
SIGNED: 4 Jul 46 FORCE: 4 Jul 46
REGISTERED: 3 Mar 48 USA (United States)
ARTICLES: 2 LANGUAGE: English.
HEADNOTE: WAIVER MOST FAVORED NATION
CLAUSE
TOPIC: Mostfavored Nation
CONCEPTS: Independence maintenance. Transi-
tion period. General trade. Tariffs. Quotas. Most
favored nation clause. Customs duties.
TREATY REF: UTS32; 12STAT1003.
PARTIES:
Ethiopia
USA (United States)

100199 Bilateral Exchange **13 UNTS 35**
SIGNED: 8 Jul 46 FORCE: 8 Jul 46
REGISTERED: 3 Mar 48 USA (United States)
ARTICLES: 2 LANGUAGE: English.
HEADNOTE: WAIVER MOST FAVORED NATION
CLAUSE
TOPIC: Mostfavored Nation
CONCEPTS: Independence maintenance. Transi-
tion period. General trade. Tariffs. Quotas. Most
favored nation clause. Customs duties.
TREATY REF: UTS32; 12STAT1003.
PARTIES:
Norway
USA (United States)

100200 Bilateral Exchange **13 UNTS 43**
SIGNED: 11 Jul 46 FORCE: 11 Jul 46
REGISTERED: 3 Mar 48 USA (United States)
ARTICLES: 2 LANGUAGE: English.
HEADNOTE: WAIVER MOST FAVORED NATION
CLAUSE
TOPIC: Mostfavored Nation
CONCEPTS: Independence maintenance. Transi-
tion period. General trade. Tariffs. Quotas. Most
favored nation clause. Customs duties.
TREATY REF: UTS32; 12STAT1003.
PARTIES:
Belgium
USA (United States)

100201 Bilateral Exchange **13 UNTS 51**
SIGNED: 11 Jul 46 FORCE: 11 Jul 46
REGISTERED: 3 Mar 48 USA (United States)
ARTICLES: 2 LANGUAGE: English. Spanish.
HEADNOTE: WAIVER MOST FAVORED NATION
CLAUSE
TOPIC: Mostfavored Nation
CONCEPTS: Independence maintenance. Transi-
tion period. General trade. Tariffs. Quotas. Most
favored nation clause. Customs duties.
TREATY REF: UTS32; 12STAT1003.
PARTIES:
Spain
USA (United States)

100202 Bilateral Exchange **13 UNTS 59**
SIGNED: 15 Aug 46 FORCE: 15 Aug 46
REGISTERED: 3 Mar 48 USA (United States)
ARTICLES: 2 LANGUAGE: English.
HEADNOTE: WAIVER MOST FAVORED NATION
CLAUSE
TOPIC: Mostfavored Nation
CONCEPTS: Independence maintenance. Transi-
tion period. General trade. Tariffs. Quotas. Most
favored nation clause. Customs duties.
TREATY REF: 107LTS419.
PARTIES:
United Arab Rep
USA (United States)

100203 Bilateral Exchange **13 UNTS 67**
SIGNED: 26 Aug 46 FORCE: 26 Aug 46
REGISTERED: 3 Mar 48 USA (United States)
ARTICLES: 2 LANGUAGE: English.
HEADNOTE: WAIVER MOST FAVORED NATION
CLAUSE
TOPIC: Mostfavored Nation
CONCEPTS: Independence maintenance. Transi-
tion period. General trade. Tariffs. Quotas. Most
favored nation clause. Customs duties.
TREATY REF: UTS32; 12STAT1003.
PARTIES:
Portugal
USA (United States)

100204 Bilateral Exchange **13 UNTS 75**
SIGNED: 10 Sep 46 FORCE: 10 Sep 46
REGISTERED: 3 Mar 48 USA (United States)
ARTICLES: 2 LANGUAGE: English.
HEADNOTE: WAIVER MOST FAVORED NATION
CLAUSE
TOPIC: Mostfavored Nation
CONCEPTS: Independence maintenance. Transi-
tion period. General trade. Tariffs. Quotas. Most
favored nation clause. Customs duties.
TREATY REF: UTS32; 12STAT1003.
PARTIES:
Denmark
USA (United States)

100205 Bilateral Exchange **13 UNTS 83**
SIGNED: 3 Oct 46 FORCE: 3 Oct 46
REGISTERED: 3 Mar 48 USA (United States)
ARTICLES: 2 LANGUAGE: English.
HEADNOTE: WAIVER MOST FAVORED NATION
CLAUSE
TOPIC: Mostfavored Nation
CONCEPTS: Independence maintenance. Transi-
tion period. General trade. Tariffs. Quotas. Most
favored nation clause. Customs duties.
TREATY REF: UTS32; 12STAT1003.
PARTIES:
USA (United States)
Yugoslavia

100206 Bilateral Exchange **13 UNTS 91**
SIGNED: 7 Oct 46 FORCE: 7 Oct 46
REGISTERED: 3 Mar 48 USA (United States)
ARTICLES: 2 LANGUAGE: English. Spanish.
HEADNOTE: WAIVER MOST FAVORED NATION
CLAUSE
TOPIC: Mostfavored Nation
CONCEPTS: Independence maintenance. Transi-
tion period. General trade. Tariffs. Quotas. Most
favored nation clause. Customs duties.
TREATY REF: UTS32; 12STAT1003.
PARTIES:
Dominican Republic
USA (United States)

100207 Bilateral Agreement **14 UNTS 3**
SIGNED: 23 Dec 47 FORCE: 1 Jan 48
REGISTERED: 4 Mar 48 Denmark
ARTICLES: 7 LANGUAGE: Danish. Swedish.
HEADNOTE: TRANSFER MEMBERS SICK FUNDS
TOPIC: Non-ILO Labor
CONCEPTS: Detailed regulations. Conformity with
municipal law. General cooperation. Recogni-
tion and enforcement of legal decisions. Non-ILO
labor relations. Sickness and invalidity insur-
ance. Payment schedules. Assets transfer.
PROCEDURE: Denunciation.
PARTIES:
Denmark
Sweden

100208 Bilateral Agreement **14 UNTS 21**
SIGNED: 26 Jun 46 FORCE: 24 Oct 46
REGISTERED: 9 Mar 48 Turkey
ARTICLES: 11 LANGUAGE: French.
HEADNOTE: AIR TRANSPORT
TOPIC: Air Transport
CONCEPTS: Exceptions and exemptions. Annex or
appendix reference. Conformity with municipal
law. Licenses and permits. Recognition of legal
documents. Use of facilities. Arbitration. Procedure. Existing tribunals. Negotiation. Fees and
exemptions. Most favored nation clause. National treatment. Customs exemptions. Compe-

tency certificate. Routes and logistics. Naviga-
tional conditions. Permit designation. Air trans-
port. Airport facilities. Airworthiness certificates.
Conditions of airlines operating permission. Op-
erating authorizations and regulations. Licenses
and certificates of nationality.
INTL ORGS: International Civil Aviation Organiza-
tion.
PROCEDURE: Amendment. Denunciation. Future
Procedures Contemplated. Ratification. Registra-
tion.
PARTIES:
Sweden
Turkey

100209 Bilateral Agreement **14 UNTS 33**
SIGNED: 12 Oct 46 FORCE: 30 Jun 47
REGISTERED: 9 Mar 48 Turkey
ARTICLES: 11 LANGUAGE: French. Turkish.
HEADNOTE: AIR COMMUNICATIONS
TOPIC: Air Transport
CONCEPTS: Exceptions and exemptions. Annex or
appendix reference. Conformity with municipal
law. Licenses and permits. Recognition of legal
documents. Use of facilities. Arbitration. Procedure. Existing tribunals. Negotiation. Fees and
exemptions. Most favored nation clause. National treatment. Customs exemptions. Competency certificate. Routes and logistics. Navigational conditions. Permit designation. Airport facilities. Airworthiness certificates. Conditions of
airlines operating permission. Operating authorizations and regulations. Licenses and certificates of nationality.
INTL ORGS: International Civil Aviation Organization.
PROCEDURE: Amendment. Denunciation. Future
Procedures Contemplated. Ratification. Registration.
PARTIES:
France
Turkey

100210 Bilateral Treaty **14 UNTS 49**
SIGNED: 11 Jan 47 FORCE: 31 Mar 47
REGISTERED: 9 Mar 48 Turkey
ARTICLES: 8 LANGUAGE: Arabic. Turkish.
HEADNOTE: FRIENDSHIP
TOPIC: General Amity
CONCEPTS: Friendship and amity. Diplomatic rela-
tions establishment. Privileges and immunities.
Procedure.
PROCEDURE: Duration. Future Procedures Con-
templated. Ratification.
PARTIES:
Jordan
Turkey

100211 Bilateral Agreement **14 UNTS 59**
SIGNED: 19 Mar 47 FORCE: 3 Sep 47
REGISTERED: 9 Mar 48 Turkey
ARTICLES: 11 LANGUAGE: French.
HEADNOTE: AIR COMMUNICATIONS
TOPIC: Air Transport
CONCEPTS: Exceptions and exemptions. Annex or
appendix reference. Conformity with municipal
law. Licenses and permits. Recognition of legal
documents. Use of facilities. Procedure. Existing
tribunals. Negotiation. Reexport of goods, etc..
Fees and exemptions. Most favored nation
clause. Customs exemptions. Competency cer-
tificate. Dangerous goods. Routes and logistics.
Navigational conditions. Permit designation. Air-
port facilities. Airworthiness certificates. Operating authorizations and regulations. Licenses and
certificates of nationality.
INTL ORGS: International Civil Aviation Organization.
PROCEDURE: Amendment. Denunciation. Future
Procedures Contemplated. Registration.
PARTIES:
Netherlands
Turkey

100212 Bilateral Exchange **14 UNTS 74**
SIGNED: 12 Jan 48 FORCE: 12 Jan 48
REGISTERED: 18 Mar 48 Taiwan
ARTICLES: 2 LANGUAGE: Chinese. English.
HEADNOTE: CUSTOMS
TOPIC: Customs

CONCEPTS: Customs duties.
PARTIES:
　Taiwan
　UK Great Britain

100213 Bilateral Exchange **14 UNTS 93**
SIGNED: 2 Aug 46　　　FORCE: 2 Aug 46
REGISTERED: 30 Mar 48 Iraq
ARTICLES: 2 LANGUAGE: Arabic. English.
HEADNOTE: STATUS IRAQI DIPLOMATIC MIS-
SION
TOPIC: Consul/Citizenship
CONCEPTS: Annex type material.
TREATY REF: 132LTS363.
PARTIES:
　Iraq
　UK Great Britain

100214 Bilateral Agreement **14 UNTS 101**
SIGNED: 5 Mar 47　　　FORCE: 12 Dec 47
REGISTERED: 31 Mar 48 Turkey
ARTICLES: 11 LANGUAGE: French.
HEADNOTE: RICE
TOPIC: Air Transport
CONCEPTS: Time limit. Non-interest rates and
fees. Commodity trade. Water transport.
INTL ORGS: International Civil Aviation Organiza-
tion.
PARTIES:
　Czechoslovakia
　Turkey

100215 Bilateral Treaty **14 UNTS 113**
SIGNED: 28 Feb 46　　　FORCE: 8 Jun 46
REGISTERED: 5 Apr 48 Taiwan
ARTICLES: 13 LANGUAGE: Chinese. French.
HEADNOTE: RELINQUISHMENT EXTRATER-
RITORIAL RELATED RIGHTS CHINA
TOPIC: Privil/Immunities
CONCEPTS: Definition of terms. Territorial applica-
tion. Previous treaty replacement. General con-
sular functions. General property. Abolition of
treaty ports. Abolition of diplomatic quarters.
Abolition of extraterritorial rights. Fees and ex-
emptions. National treatment. Tax exemptions.
TREATY REF: 2DEMARTEN32'94;.
PROCEDURE: Future Procedures Contemplated.
Ratification.
PARTIES:
　Taiwan
　France

100216 Bilateral Agreement **14 UNTS 137**
SIGNED: 28 Feb 46　　　FORCE: 28 Feb 46
REGISTERED: 5 Apr 48 Taiwan
ARTICLES: 4 LANGUAGE: Chinese. French.
HEADNOTE: SINO-INDOCHINESE RELATIONS
TOPIC: General Amity
CONCEPTS: General provisions. Alien status. Most
favored nation clause. Equitable taxes. Customs
declarations. Customs duties.
TREATY REF: CHINA-FRANCE, INDO-CHINA, YUN-
NAN RAILWAY; 29OCT3;.
PROCEDURE: Ratification.
PARTIES:
　Taiwan
　France

100217 Bilateral Exchange **14 UNTS 151**
SIGNED: 28 Feb 46　　　FORCE: 28 Feb 46
REGISTERED: 5 Apr 48 Taiwan
ARTICLES: 2 LANGUAGE: Chinese. French.
HEADNOTE: RELIEF OCCUPATION TROOPS
TOPIC: Milit Occupation
CONCEPTS: Prisoners of war. Withdrawal of occu-
pation.
PARTIES:
　Taiwan
　France

100218 Bilateral Exchange **14 UNTS 159**
SIGNED: 13 Mar 46　　　FORCE: 13 Mar 46
REGISTERED: 5 Apr 48 Taiwan
ARTICLES: 2 LANGUAGE: French.
HEADNOTE: RENUNCIATION SWISS CONSULAR
JURISDICTION CHINA
TOPIC: Consul/Citizenship

CONCEPTS: Annex type material. Previous treaty
replacement. Alien status. General property.
TREATY REF: 14DEMARTENS643.
PROCEDURE: Future Procedures Contemplated.
PARTIES:
　Taiwan
　Switzerland

100219 Bilateral Exchange **14 UNTS 167**
SIGNED: 26 Sep 46　　　FORCE: 26 Sep 46
REGISTERED: 5 Apr 48 Taiwan
ARTICLES: 2 LANGUAGE: Chinese. English.
HEADNOTE: COMMERCIAL MODUS VIVENDI
TOPIC: General Trade
CONCEPTS: Exceptions and exemptions. Reci-
procity in trade. Most favored nation clause. Cus-
toms duties.
PROCEDURE: Duration. Termination.
PARTIES:
　Canada
　Taiwan

100220 Bilateral Exchange **14 UNTS 177**
SIGNED: 1 Apr 47　　　FORCE: 1 Apr 47
REGISTERED: 5 Apr 48 Taiwan
ARTICLES: 2 LANGUAGE: English.
HEADNOTE: RELINQUISHMENT RIGHTS RELAT-
ING CONSULAR JURISDICTION
TOPIC: Privil/Immunities
CONCEPTS: Conformity with municipal law. Gen-
eral property. Abolition of diplomatic quarters.
National treatment.
PARTIES:
　Taiwan
　Portugal

100221 Multilateral Instrument **14 UNTS 185**
SIGNED: 22 Jul 46　　　FORCE: 7 Apr 48
REGISTERED: 7 Apr 48 United Nations
ARTICLES: 82 LANGUAGE: Chinese. English.
French. Russian. Spanish.
HEADNOTE: WORLD HEALTH ORGANIZATION
TOPIC: IGO Establishment
CONCEPTS: Default remedies. Treaty interpreta-
tion. Treaty violation. Privileges and immunities.
Information centers. Exchange of official publi-
cations. Exchange of information and docu-
ments. Quarantine. Border control. Disease con-
trol. Public health. Institute establishment. Ac-
counting procedures. Funding procedures.
Assistance. Specific technical assistance. Mate-
rials, equipment and services. Mass media ex-
change. Admission. Constitutional amendment.
Subsidiary organ. Establishment. Regional of-
fices. Headquarters and facilities. Liaison with
other IGO's. Internal structure. Special status.
Status of experts. Assistance to United Nations.
Inter-agency agreements.
INTL ORGS: World Health Organization.
PROCEDURE: Amendment. Accession. Ratifica-
tion. Registration.
PARTIES:
　Albania　　SIGNED:　　22 Jul 46　　RATIFIED:
　26 May 47 FORCE: 7 Apr 48
　Argentina SIGNED: 22 Jul 46 FORCE: 7 Apr 48
　Australia SIGNED: 22 Jul 46 RATIFIED: 2 Feb 48
　FORCE: 7 Apr 48
　Austria SIGNED: 22 Jul 46 RATIFIED: 30 Jun 47
　FORCE: 7 Apr 48
　Belgium SIGNED: 22 Jul 46
　Bolivia SIGNED: 22 Jul 46 FORCE: 7 Apr 48
　Brazil SIGNED: 22 Jul 46 FORCE: 7 Apr 48
　Bulgaria SIGNED: 22 Jul 46
　Byelorussia　SIGNED:　22 Jul 46　RATIFIED:
　7 Apr 48 FORCE: 7 Apr 48
　Canada　SIGNED:　22 Jul 46　RATIFIED:
　29 Aug 46 FORCE: 7 Apr 48
　Chile SIGNED: 22 Jul 46
　Taiwan SIGNED: 22 Jul 46 FORCE: 7 Apr 48
　Colombia SIGNED: 22 Jul 46 FORCE: 7 Apr 48
　Costa Rica SIGNED: 22 Jul 46 FORCE: 7 Apr 48
　Cuba SIGNED: 22 Jul 46 FORCE: 7 Apr 48
　Czechoslovakia　SIGNED:　22 Jul 46　RATIFIED:
　11 Mar 48 FORCE: 7 Apr 48
　Denmark SIGNED: 22 Jul 46 FORCE: 7 Apr 48
　Dominican Republic SIGNED: 22 Jul 46 FORCE:
　7 Apr 48
　Ecuador SIGNED: 22 Jul 46 FORCE: 7 Apr 48
　United Arab Rep SIGNED: 22 Jul 46 RATIFIED:
　16 Dec 47 FORCE: 7 Apr 48
　El Salvador SIGNED: 22 Jul 46 FORCE: 7 Apr 48

　Ethiopia　SIGNED:　22 Jul 46　RATIFIED:
　11 Apr 47 FORCE: 7 Apr 48
　Finland SIGNED: 22 Jul 46 RATIFIED: 7 Oct 47
　FORCE: 7 Apr 47
　France SIGNED: 22 Jul 46 FORCE: 7 Apr 48
　Greece SIGNED: 22 Jul 46 RATIFIED: 12 Mar 48
　FORCE: 7 Apr 47
　Guatemala SIGNED: 22 Jul 46 FORCE: 7 Apr 47
　Haiti SIGNED: 22 Jul 46 RATIFIED: 12 Aug 47
　FORCE: 7 Apr 47
　Honduras SIGNED: 22 Jul 46 FORCE: 7 Apr 47
　Hungary SIGNED: 22 Jul 46
　India SIGNED: 22 Jul 46 RATIFIED: 12 Jan 48
　FORCE: 7 Apr 47
　Iran　SIGNED:　22 Jul 46　RATIFIED:　23 Nov 46
　FORCE: 7 Apr 47
　Iraq SIGNED: 22 Jul 46 RATIFIED: 23 Sep 47
　FORCE: 7 Apr 47
　Ireland SIGNED: 22 Jul 46 RATIFIED: 20 Oct 47
　FORCE: 7 Apr 48
　Italy SIGNED: 22 Jul 46 RATIFIED: 11 Apr 47
　FORCE: 7 Apr 47
　Lebanon SIGNED: 22 Jul 46 FORCE: 7 Apr 47
　Liberia SIGNED: 22 Jul 46 RATIFIED: 14 Mar 47
　FORCE: 7 Apr 48
　Luxembourg SIGNED: 22 Jul 46
　Mexico SIGNED: 22 Jul 46 RATIFIED: 7 Apr 48
　FORCE: 7 Apr 48
　Netherlands　SIGNED:　22 Jul 46　RATIFIED:
　25 Apr 47 FORCE: 7 Apr 48
　New Zealand SIGNED: 22 Jul 46 RATIFIED:
　10 Dec 46 FORCE: 7 Apr 48
　Nicaragua SIGNED: 22 Jul 46
　Norway　SIGNED:　22 Jul 46　RATIFIED:
　18 Aug 47 FORCE: 7 Apr 48
　Panama SIGNED: 22 Jul 46
　Paraguay SIGNED: 22 Jul 46
　Peru SIGNED: 22 Jul 46
　Philippines SIGNED: 22 Jul 46
　Poland SIGNED: 22 Jul 46
　Portugal　SIGNED:　22 Jul 46　RATIFIED:
　13 Feb 48 FORCE: 7 Apr 47
　Saudi Arabia SIGNED: 22 Jul 46 RATIFIED:
　26 May 47 FORCE: 7 Apr 48
　Siam SIGNED: 22 Jul 46 RATIFIED: 26 Sep 47
　FORCE: 7 Apr 47
　South Africa SIGNED: 22 Jul 46 RATIFIED:
　7 Aug 47 FORCE: 7 Apr 48
　Sweden　SIGNED:　13 Jan 47　RATIFIED:
　28 Aug 47 FORCE: 7 Apr 47
　Switzerland　SIGNED:　22 Jul 46　RATIFIED:
　26 Mar 47 FORCE: 7 Apr 47
　Syria SIGNED: 22 Jul 46 RATIFIED: 18 Dec 46
　FORCE: 7 Apr 48
　Transjordan　SIGNED:　22 Jul 46　RATIFIED:
　7 Apr 47 FORCE: 7 Apr 48
　Turkey SIGNED: 22 Jul 46 RATIFIED: 2 Jan 48
　FORCE: 7 Apr 48
　UK Great Britain SIGNED: 22 Jul 46
　USA (United States) SIGNED: 22 Jul 46
　Ukrainian SSR SIGNED: 22 Jul 46 RATIFIED:
　3 Apr 48 FORCE: 7 Apr 48
　Uruguay SIGNED: 22 Jul 46
　USA (Soviet Union) SIGNED: 22 Jul 46 RATI-
　FIED: 24 Mar 48 FORCE: 7 Apr 48
　Venezuela SIGNED: 22 Jul 46
　Yugoslavia　SIGNED:　22 Jul 46　RATIFIED:
　19 Nov 47 FORCE: 7 Apr 48
　　　　　　ANNEX
24 UNTS 320.
27 UNTS 402.
29 UNTS 412.
34 UNTS 417.
44 UNTS 339.
45 UNTS 326.
53 UNTS 418.
54 UNTS 385.
81 UNTS 319.
88 UNTS 427.
131 UNTS 309.
173 UNTS 371.
180 UNTS 298.
228 UNTS 386.
264 UNTS 326.
293 UNTS 334.
328 UNTS 286.
358 UNTS 247.
375 UNTS 341.
376 UNTS 404.
377 UNTS 380.
377 UNTS 387.
380 UNTS 384.
381 UNTS 350.
383 UNTS 312.

384 UNTS 328.
385 UNTS 361.
387 UNTS 324.
389 UNTS 306.
390 UNTS 333.
391 UNTS 317.
411 UNTS 294.
419 UNTS 342.
424 UNTS 319.
425 UNTS 301.
429 UNTS 252.
442 UNTS 296.
443 UNTS 311.
450 UNTS 406.
455 UNTS 441.
456 UNTS 485.
486 UNTS 396.
489 UNTS 366.
514 UNTS 253.
523 UNTS 318.
530 UNTS 332.
548 UNTS 327.
557 UNTS 244.
573 UNTS 290.
600 UNTS 372. Lesotho. Acceptance 7 Jul 67.
635 UNTS 344.

100222 Multilateral Agreement **14 UNTS 287**
SIGNED: 8 Feb 47   FORCE: 8 Feb 47
REGISTERED: 16 Apr 48 Denmark
ARTICLES: 11 LANGUAGE: French.
HEADNOTE: RESTORATION INDUSTRIAL PROP-
ERTY RIGHTS
TOPIC: Patents/Copyrights
CONCEPTS: Territorial application. Conformity
with municipal law. Trademarks. Laws and for-
malities. Post-war adjustment.
TREATY REF: MADRID AGREEMENT.
PROCEDURE: Accession. Ratification. Registra-
tion.
PARTIES:
Belgium SIGNED: 8 Feb 47
Brazil SIGNED: 8 Feb 47
Czechoslovakia SIGNED: 8 Feb 47 RATIFIED:
31 Jul 47 FORCE: 31 Jul 47
Denmark SIGNED: 8 Feb 47 RATIFIED: 16 Jul 47
FORCE: 16 Jul 47
Dominican Republic RATIFIED: 23 May 47
FORCE: 23 May 47
Finland SIGNED: 8 Feb 47 RATIFIED: 26 Jun 47
FORCE: 26 Jun 47
France SIGNED: 8 Feb 47 RATIFIED: 4 Aug 47
FORCE: 4 Aug 47
Greece SIGNED: 8 Feb 47
Hungary SIGNED: 8 Feb 47
Ireland SIGNED: 8 Feb 47
Italy SIGNED: 8 Feb 47
Lebanon SIGNED: 8 Feb 47
Liechtenstein SIGNED: 8 Feb 47
Luxembourg SIGNED: 8 Feb 47
Morocco SIGNED: 8 Feb 47 RATIFIED: 4 Aug 47
FORCE: 4 Aug 47
Netherlands SIGNED: 8 Feb 47
New Zealand SIGNED: 8 Feb 47 RATIFIED:
22 Sep 47 FORCE: 22 Sep 47
New Zealand Western Samoa RATIFIED:
22 Sep 47 FORCE: 22 Sep 47
Norway SIGNED: 8 Feb 47 RATIFIED: 30 May 47
FORCE: 30 May 47
Poland SIGNED: 8 Feb 47
Portugal SIGNED: 8 Feb 47
Romania SIGNED: 8 Feb 47
South Africa RATIFIED: 1 Dec 47 FORCE:
1 Dec 47
Spain RATIFIED: 19 Jul 47 FORCE: 19 Jul 47
Spain Spanish Colonies RATIFIED: 15 Dec 47
FORCE: 15 Dec 47
Spain Spanish Morroco RATIFIED: 26 Jul 47
FORCE: 26 Jul 47
Sweden SIGNED: 8 Feb 47 RATIFIED: 20 Jun 47
FORCE: 20 Jun 47
Switzerland SIGNED: 8 Feb 47 RATIFIED:
23 May 47 FORCE: 23 May 47
Syria SIGNED: 8 Feb 47
Tunisia SIGNED: 8 Feb 47 RATIFIED: 4 Aug 47
FORCE: 4 Aug 47
Turkey SIGNED: 8 Feb 47 RATIFIED: 25 Aug 47
FORCE: 25 Aug 47
UK Great Britain SIGNED: 8 Feb 47 RATIFIED:
23 May 47 FORCE: 23 May 47

100223 Bilateral Agreement **14 UNTS 307**
SIGNED: 21 Jan 48   FORCE: 1 Jan 48
REGISTERED: 16 Apr 48 Denmark
ARTICLES: 7 LANGUAGE: Danish. Norwegian.
HEADNOTE: TRANSFER MEMBERS BETWEEN
SICK FUNDS
TOPIC: Non-ILO Labor
CONCEPTS: Detailed regulations. Conformity with
municipal law. General cooperation. Recogni-
tion and enforcement of legal decisions. Non-ILO
labor relations. Sickness and invalidity insur-
ance. Payment schedules. Assets transfer.
PROCEDURE: Denunciation.
PARTIES:
Denmark
Norway

100224 Bilateral Exchange **14 UNTS 321**
SIGNED: 21 Feb 48   FORCE: 21 Feb 48
REGISTERED: 16 Apr 48 Denmark
ARTICLES: 9 LANGUAGE: French.
HEADNOTE: EXCHANGE STUDENT EMPLOYEES
TOPIC: Non-ILO Labor
CONCEPTS: Definition of terms. Resident permits.
General cooperation. Employment regulations.
Wages and salaries. Non-ILO labor relations.
PROCEDURE: Denunciation. Duration. Renewal or
Revival.
PARTIES:
Denmark
Switzerland

100225 Unilateral Instrument **15 UNTS 3**
SIGNED: 17 Mar 48   FORCE: 19 Apr 48
REGISTERED: 19 Apr 48 United Nations
ARTICLES: 1 LANGUAGE: English.
HEADNOTE: ADHERENCE UN CHARTER
TOPIC: UN Charter
CONCEPTS: Acceptance of obligations upon ad-
mittance to UN.
INTL ORGS: United Nations.
PARTIES:
Burma

100226 Bilateral Agreement **15 UNTS 5**
SIGNED: 15 Jul 47   FORCE: 15 Jul 47
REGISTERED: 30 Apr 48 Norway
ARTICLES: 6 LANGUAGE: French.
HEADNOTE: POWER COMPANY
TOPIC: Specific Property
CONCEPTS: Lump sum settlements. Assets trans-
fer. Reconversion to normalcy. Post-war claims
settlement. Facilities and property.
PARTIES:
France
Norway

100227 Bilateral Agreement **15 UNTS 13**
SIGNED: 6 Mar 46   FORCE: 6 Mar 46
REGISTERED: 2 May 48 Norway
ARTICLES: 12 LANGUAGE: French.
HEADNOTE: PAYMENTS
TOPIC: Finance
CONCEPTS: Balance of payments. Currency. Mon-
etary and gold transfers. Payment schedules.
Non-interest rates and fees.
PARTIES:
France
Norway

100228 Bilateral Exchange **15 UNTS 29**
SIGNED: 22 Nov 47   FORCE: 1 Dec 47
REGISTERED: 21 May 48 New Zealand
ARTICLES: 2 LANGUAGE: English. French.
HEADNOTE: MUTUAL ABOLITION VISAS
TOPIC: Visas
CONCEPTS: Territorial application. Visa abolition.
Border traffic and migration. Resident permits.
PARTIES:
France
New Zealand

100229 Multilateral Instrument **15 UNTS 35**
SIGNED: 9 Oct 46   FORCE: 20 Apr 48
REGISTERED: 21 May 48 ILO (Labor Org)
ARTICLES: 3 LANGUAGE: English. French.
HEADNOTE: AMENDMENT ILO
TOPIC: IGO Establishment

CONCEPTS: Annex or appendix reference. Constitutional amendment. Internal structure.
INTL ORGS: International Labour Organization.
PROCEDURE: Amendment. Ratification.
PARTIES:
Multilateral
                    ANNEX
20 UNTS 307.   Luxembourg.   Ratification
29 Oct 48.
20 UNTS 307. Haiti. Ratification 5 Jul 48.
191 UNTS 359. Panama. Ratification 31 May 54.

100230 Bilateral Agreement **15 UNTS 123**
SIGNED: 28 Jun 47   FORCE: 12 Jan 48
REGISTERED: 2 Jun 48 Poland
ARTICLES: 11 LANGUAGE: Bulgarian. Polish.
HEADNOTE: CULTURAL COOPERATION
TOPIC: Culture
CONCEPTS: Previous treaty replacement. Friend-
ship and amity. Conformity with municipal law.
Personnel. Recognition of degrees. Exchange.
Commissions and foundations. Teacher and stu-
dent exchange. Professorships. Institute estab-
lishment. Scholarships and grants. Vocational
training. General cultural cooperation. Athletes.
Research cooperation. Scientific exchange. In-
demnities and reimbursements. Information
agency.
INTL ORGS: Special Commission.
PROCEDURE: Denunciation. Duration. Ratification.
Renewal or Revival.
PARTIES:
Bulgaria
Poland

100231 Bilateral Agreement **15 UNTS 145**
SIGNED: 28 Aug 47   FORCE: 13 Dec 47
REGISTERED: 2 Jun 48 Poland
ARTICLES: 19 LANGUAGE: French.
HEADNOTE: AIR COMMUNICATIONS
TOPIC: Air Transport
CONCEPTS: Definition of terms. Exceptions and
exemptions. Annex or appendix reference. Previous treaty replacement. Conformity with municipal law. General cooperation. Licenses and permits. Personnel. Recognition of legal documents. Procedure. Negotiation. Humanitarian
matters. Bonds. Fees and exemptions. Most favored nation clause. National treatment. Patents,
copyrights and trademarks. Customs exemptions. Competency certificate. Registration certificate. Routes and logistics. Navigational conditions. Permit designation. Air transport. Airport
facilities. Airworthiness certificates. Conditions
of airlines operating permission. Operating authorizations and regulations. Licenses and certificates of nationality. Postal services.
PROCEDURE: Amendment. Denunciation. Duration. Future Procedures Contemplated. Ratification. Renewal or Revival.
PARTIES:
Hungary
Poland

100232 Bilateral Agreement **15 UNTS 163**
SIGNED: 30 Aug 46   FORCE: 30 Aug 46
REGISTERED: 7 Jun 48 Norway
ARTICLES: 7 LANGUAGE: French.
HEADNOTE: PAYMENTS
TOPIC: Finance
CONCEPTS: Detailed regulations. Accounting pro-
cedures. Banking. Balance of payments. Cur-
rency. Payment schedules. Local currency.
PROCEDURE: Denunciation. Duration.
PARTIES:
Norway
Yugoslavia
                    ANNEX
33 UNTS 344. Yugoslavia. Prolongation 2 Apr 49
Force 2 Apr 49.
33 UNTS 344. Norway. Prolongation 2 Apr 49
Force 2 Apr 49.

100233 Bilateral Agreement **15 UNTS 171**
SIGNED: 22 Nov 46   FORCE: 1 Jan 47
REGISTERED: 7 Jun 48 Norway
ARTICLES: 9 LANGUAGE: Norwegian. Swedish.
HEADNOTE: PAYMENTS
TOPIC: Finance
CONCEPTS: Accounting procedures. Banking. Ba

ance of payments. Currency. Monetary and gold transfers. Exchange rates and regulations. Interest rates. Payment schedules. Local currency.
PROCEDURE: Amendment. Termination.
PARTIES:
Norway
Sweden

100234 Bilateral Agreement **15 UNTS 203**
SIGNED: 3 Dec 46   FORCE: 1 Jan 47
REGISTERED: 7 Jun 48 Norway
ARTICLES: 13 LANGUAGE: French.
HEADNOTE: PAYMENTS
TOPIC: Finance
CONCEPTS: Detailed regulations. Treaty implementation. Licenses and permits. General cooperation. Exchange of information and documents. Establishment of commission. Accounting procedures. Banking. Balance of payments. Monetary and gold transfers. Interest rates. Payment schedules. Local currency.
INTL ORGS: Special Commission.
PROCEDURE: Amendment. Denunciation. Duration. Renewal or Revival.
PARTIES:
Norway
Poland
ANNEX
25 UNTS 344. Norway. Amendment 4 Feb 48. Force 4 Feb 48.
25 UNTS 344. Poland. Amendment 4 Feb 48. Force 4 Feb 48.

100235 Bilateral Agreement **15 UNTS 211**
SIGNED: 14 Apr 47   FORCE: 14 Apr 47
REGISTERED: 7 Jun 48 Norway
ARTICLES: 6 LANGUAGE: French.
HEADNOTE: PAYMENTS
TOPIC: Finance
CONCEPTS: Payment schedules.
PARTIES:
Austria
Norway

100236 Unilateral Instrument **15 UNTS 217**
SIGNED: 2 Feb 48   FORCE: 10 Feb 48
REGISTERED: 17 Jun 48 United Nations
ARTICLES: 1 LANGUAGE: Spanish.
HEADNOTE: ICJ COMPULSORY JURISDICTION
TOPIC: ICJ Option Clause
CONCEPTS: Annex or appendix reference. Diplomatic privileges. Privileges and immunities. Materials, equipment and services. Regional offices. Special status.
INTL ORGS: International Court of Justice.
PROCEDURE: Duration.
PARTIES:
Honduras
ANNEX
190 UNTS 377. Honduras. Prolongation 19 Apr 54. Force 24 May 54.
353 UNTS 309. Honduras. Renewal 20 Feb 60.

100237 Unilateral Instrument **15 UNTS 221**
SIGNED: 12 Feb 48   FORCE: 12 Mar 48
REGISTERED: 21 Jun 48 United Nations
ARTICLES: 1 LANGUAGE: English. French.
HEADNOTE: ICJ COMPULSORY JURISDICTION
TOPIC: ICJ Option Clause
CONCEPTS: Optional clause ICJ.
INTL ORGS: International Court of Justice.
PARTIES:
Brazil

100238 Bilateral Exchange **15 UNTS 225**
SIGNED: 30 Oct 48   FORCE: 30 Oct 45
REGISTERED: 21 Jun 48 USA (United States)
ARTICLES: 2 LANGUAGE: English. Polish.
HEADNOTE: GRANTING CERTAIN RECIPROCAL CUSTOMS PRIVILEGES
TOPIC: Consul/Citizenship
CONCEPTS: Diplomatic privileges.
PARTIES:
Poland
USA (United States)

100239 Bilateral Agreement **15 UNTS 233**
SIGNED: 27 Mar 46   FORCE: 27 Mar 46

REGISTERED: 21 Jun 48 USA (United States)
ARTICLES: 12 LANGUAGE: English.
HEADNOTE: AIR TRANSPORT
TOPIC: Air Transport
CONCEPTS: Exceptions and exemptions. Annex or appendix reference. Conformity with municipal law. Licenses and permits. Recognition of legal documents. Use of facilities. Procedure. Existing tribunals. Fees and exemptions. Most favored nation clause. National treatment. Customs exemptions. Competency certificate. Routes and logistics. Navigational conditions. Permit designation. Air transport. Airport facilities. Airworthiness certificates. Conditions of airlines operating permission. Operating authorizations and regulations. Licenses and certificates of nationality.
INTL ORGS: International Civil Aviation Organization.
TREATY REF: EAS469.
PROCEDURE: Amendment. Future Procedures Contemplated. Ratification. Registration. Termination.
PARTIES:
Greece
USA (United States)

100240 Bilateral Exchange **15 UNTS 249**
SIGNED: 17 Sep 46   FORCE: 17 Sep 46
REGISTERED: 21 Jun 48 USA (United States)
ARTICLES: 2 LANGUAGE: English. French.
HEADNOTE: FINANCIAL COMMISSION MANILA
TOPIC: IGO Establishment
CONCEPTS: Accounting procedures. Banking. Financial programs. Establishment.
INTL ORGS: Special Commission.
PARTIES:
Philippines
USA (United States)

100241 Bilateral Exchange **15 UNTS 257**
SIGNED: 30 Sep 46   FORCE: 30 Sep 46
REGISTERED: 21 Jun 48 USA (United States)
ARTICLES: 2 LANGUAGE: English. French.
HEADNOTE: AMENDING FINANCES
TOPIC: Other Ad Hoc
CONCEPTS: Annex type material. Control of internal finance.
TREATY REF: US EXEC.AGREE. SERIES 220; 55STAT 1348.
PARTIES.
Haiti
USA (United States)

100242 Bilateral Exchange **15 UNTS 265**
SIGNED: 10 Dec 46   FORCE: 10 Dec 46
REGISTERED: 21 Jun 48 USA (United States)
ARTICLES: 2 LANGUAGE: English.
HEADNOTE: CULTURAL AGREEMENT
TOPIC: Visas
CONCEPTS: Annex or appendix reference. Friendship and amity. Standardization. Recognition of degrees. Exchange. Teacher and student exchange. Professorships. Scholarships and grants. Vocational training. Exchange. Artists. Scientific exchange. Accounting procedures. Fees and exemptions. Publications exchange.
PROCEDURE: Denunciation. Ratification.
PARTIES:
France
USA (United States)

100243 Bilateral Exchange **15 UNTS 273**
SIGNED: 7 Jan 47   FORCE: 7 Jan 47
REGISTERED: 21 Jun 48 USA (United States)
ARTICLES: 2 LANGUAGE: English.
HEADNOTE: RECIPROCAL EXEMPTION DOUBLE TAXATION SHIPPING PROFITS
TOPIC: Taxation
CONCEPTS: Conformity with municipal law. Taxation. Tax exemptions. Merchant vessels.
PROCEDURE: Termination.
PARTIES:
Finland
USA (United States)

100244 Bilateral Exchange **15 UNTS 281**
SIGNED: 23 Jan 47   FORCE: 23 Jan 47
REGISTERED: 21 Jun 48 USA (United States)

ARTICLES: 2 LANGUAGE: English.
HEADNOTE: MODIFYING AGREEMENT CLAIMS DAMAGES
TOPIC: Status of Forces
CONCEPTS: Annex or appendix reference. Status of military forces. Jurisdiction.
PARTIES:
UK Great Britain
USA (United States)

100245 Bilateral Agreement **16 UNTS 3**
SIGNED: 14 Feb 47   FORCE: 14 Feb 47
REGISTERED: 21 Jun 48 USA (United States)
ARTICLES: 16 LANGUAGE: English.
HEADNOTE: ROAD STREET AND BRIDGE PROGRAM
TOPIC: Non-IBRD Project
CONCEPTS: Exchange of official publications. Inspection and observation. Domestic legislation. Customs exemptions. Use restrictions. Materials, equipment and services. Plans and standards. Agricultural development/credit.
PROCEDURE: Amendment. Duration. Termination.
PARTIES:
Philippines
USA (United States)
ANNEX
174 UNTS 278. USA (United States). Amendment 16 Dec 49. Force 21 Dec 49.
174 UNTS 278. Philippines. Amendment 21 Dec 49. Force 21 Dec 49.
174 UNTS 281. USA (United States). Amendment 6 Jul 51. Force 17 Jul 51.
174 UNTS 281. Philippines. Amendment 17 Jul 51. Force 17 Jul 51.

100246 Bilateral Agreement **16 UNTS 17**
SIGNED: 26 Feb 47   FORCE: 26 Feb 47
REGISTERED: 21 Jun 48 USA (United States)
ARTICLES: 12 LANGUAGE: English.
HEADNOTE: AIR SERVICES
TOPIC: Air Transport
CONCEPTS: Exceptions and exemptions. Annex or appendix reference. Conformity with municipal law. Licenses and permits. Recognition of legal documents. Use of facilities. Procedure. Existing tribunals. Competence of tribunal. Fees and exemptions. Most favored nation clause. National treatment. Customs exemptions. Competency certificate. Routes and logistics. Navigational conditions. Permit designation. Air transport. Airport facilities. Airworthiness certificates. Conditions of airlines operating permission. Operating authorizations and regulations. Licenses and certificates of nationality.
INTL ORGS: International Civil Aviation Organization.
TREATY REF: INTER CIVIL AVIA.CONF.1NOV1944.
PROCEDURE: Amendment. Future Procedures Contemplated. Registration. Termination.
PARTIES:
Thailand
USA (United States)

100247 Bilateral Agreement **16 UNTS 31**
SIGNED: 14 Mar 47   FORCE: 14 Mar 47
REGISTERED: 21 Jun 48 USA (United States)
ARTICLES: 14 LANGUAGE: English.
HEADNOTE: FISHERIES DEVELOPMENT REHABILITATION TRAINING
TOPIC: Non-IBRD Project
CONCEPTS: Conformity with municipal law. Inspection and observation. Domestic legislation. Financial programs. Customs exemptions. Materials, equipment and services. Plans and standards. Non-bank projects. Inland and territorial waters. Ocean resources.
PROCEDURE: Amendment. Duration. Termination.
PARTIES:
Philippines
USA (United States)

100248 Bilateral Exchange **16 UNTS 47**
SIGNED: 21 Mar 47   FORCE: 21 Mar 47
REGISTERED: 21 Jun 48 USA (United States)
ARTICLES: 2 LANGUAGE: English.
HEADNOTE: SETTLEMENT LEND-LEASE RECIPROCAL AID SURPLUS WAR PROPERTY CLAIMS
TOPIC: Milit Assistance
CONCEPTS: Definition of terms. Guarantees and

safeguards. Annex or appendix reference. General cooperation. General property. Payment schedules. Claims, debts and assets. Lump sum settlements. Materials, equipment and services. Lend lease. Naval vessels. Return of equipment and recapture. Surplus war property. Restrictions on transfer. Post-war claims settlement.
PARTIES:
South Africa
USA (United States)

100249   Bilateral Exchange   **16 UNTS 65**
SIGNED: 27 Mar 47   FORCE: 27 Mar 47
REGISTERED: 21 Jun 48 USA (United States)
ARTICLES: 2 LANGUAGE: English. French.
HEADNOTE: COPYRIGHT LAWS
TOPIC: Patents/Copyrights
CONCEPTS: Conformity with municipal law. Domestic legislation. Laws and formalities. Post-war adjustment.
PARTIES:
France
USA (United States)

100250   Bilateral Exchange   **16 UNTS 79**
SIGNED: 24 Apr 47   FORCE: 24 Apr 47
REGISTERED: 21 Jun 48 USA (United States)
ARTICLES: 2 LANGUAGE: English.
HEADNOTE: COPYRIGHT LAWS
TOPIC: Patents/Copyrights
CONCEPTS: Conformity with municipal law. Domestic legislation. Laws and formalities. Post-war adjustment.
PARTIES:
New Zealand
USA (United States)

100251   Bilateral Exchange   **16 UNTS 97**
SIGNED: 25 Apr 47   FORCE: 25 Apr 47
REGISTERED: 21 Jun 48 USA (United States)
ARTICLES: 12 LANGUAGE: English.
HEADNOTE: DIPLOMATIC CONSULAR REPRESENTATION COMMERCE NAVIGATION
TOPIC: Consul/Citizenship
CONCEPTS: Exceptions and exemptions. Alien status. Diplomatic privileges. Consular relations establishment. Diplomatic relations establishment. Privileges and immunities. Most favored nation clause. Customs declarations.
INTL ORGS: United Nations.
PROCEDURE: Duration.
PARTIES:
Nepal
USA (United States)

100252   Bilateral Agreement   **16 UNTS 109**
SIGNED: 12 May 47   FORCE: 12 May 47
REGISTERED: 21 Jun 48 USA (United States)
ARTICLES: 13 LANGUAGE: English.
HEADNOTE: COAST GEODETIC SURVEY WORK
TOPIC: Scientific Project
CONCEPTS: Privileges and immunities. Operating agencies. Personnel. General property. Use of facilities. Vocational training. Research and scientific projects. Research results. Research and development. Indemnities and reimbursements. Tax exemptions. Materials, equipment and services. Inland and territorial waters. Ports and pilotage.
PROCEDURE: Duration. Termination.
PARTIES:
Philippines
USA (United States)
ANNEX
324 UNTS 342. Finland. Acceptance 9 Apr 57.
324 UNTS 342. Morocco. Acceptance 26 Aug 57.
324 UNTS 342. Ireland. Acceptance 15 Nov 57.
324 UNTS 342. Costa Rica. Acceptance 1 May 58.
324 UNTS 342. Australia. Acceptance 10 Dec 58.
324 UNTS 342. Ceylon (Sri Lanka). Succession 1 Apr 57.

100253   Bilateral Agreement   **16 UNTS 123**
SIGNED: 12 May 47   FORCE: 12 May 47
REGISTERED: 21 Jun 48 USA (United States)
ARTICLES: 12 LANGUAGE: English.
HEADNOTE: METEOROLOGICAL   FACILITIES TRAINING

TOPIC: Scientific Project
CONCEPTS: Visas. Privileges and immunities. Exchange of information and documents. Operating agencies. Personnel. Use of facilities. Programs. Vocational training. Research cooperation. Meteorology. Research results. Tax exemptions. Industry.
PROCEDURE: Amendment. Duration. Termination.
PARTIES:
Philippines
USA (United States)

100254   Bilateral Agreement   **16 UNTS 137**
SIGNED: 12 May 47   FORCE: 12 May 47
REGISTERED: 21 Jun 48 USA (United States)
ARTICLES: 12 LANGUAGE: English.
HEADNOTE: AIR NAVIGATION FACILITIES TRAINING
TOPIC: Scientific Project
CONCEPTS: Visas. Privileges and immunities. Exchange of information and documents. Operating agencies. Personnel. Use of facilities. Programs. Vocational training. Research and scientific projects. Research results. Tax exemptions. Materials, equipment and services. Airport equipment.
PROCEDURE: Amendment. Duration. Termination.
PARTIES:
Philippines
USA (United States)

100255   Bilateral Exchange   **16 UNTS 151**
SIGNED: 3 Jun 47   FORCE: 3 Jun 47
REGISTERED: 21 Jun 48 USA (United States)
ARTICLES: 2 LANGUAGE: English.
HEADNOTE: AIR TRANSPORT SERVICES
TOPIC: Air Transport
CONCEPTS: Annex or appendix reference. Annex type material. Routes and logistics. Air transport. Overflights and technical stops.
TREATY REF: US EXEC. AGREE. SERIES 460; 59STAT1402.
PARTIES:
Ireland
USA (United States)
ANNEX
303 UNTS 298. USA (United States). Amendment 4 Mar 58. Force 4 Mar 58.
303 UNTS 298. Ireland. Amendment 4 Mar 58. Force 4 Mar 58.

100256   Bilateral Agreement   **16 UNTS 157**
SIGNED: 8 Jul 47   FORCE: 8 Jul 47
REGISTERED: 21 Jun 48 USA (United States)
ARTICLES: 10 LANGUAGE: English. Greek.
HEADNOTE: RELIEF ASSISTANCE
TOPIC: Direct Aid
CONCEPTS: Non-visa travel documents. Diplomatic privileges. Privileges and immunities. Conformity with municipal law. General cooperation. Exchange of information and documents. Informational records. Personnel. Public information. Accounting procedures. Payment schedules. Local currency. Customs exemptions. Domestic obligation. General aid. Relief supplies. Withdrawal conditions. Procurement. Distribution.
PROCEDURE: Duration.
PARTIES:
Greece
USA (United States)

100257   Multilateral Protocol   **16 UNTS 179**
SIGNED: 23 Apr 46   FORCE: 30 Apr 46
REGISTERED: 23 Jun 48 USA (United States)
ARTICLES: 5 LANGUAGE: English. French.
HEADNOTE: SANITARY CONVENTION AERIAL NAVIGATION
TOPIC: Sanitation
CONCEPTS: Time limit. Treaty implementation. WHO used as agency. Funding procedures. Extension of functions.
INTL ORGS: United Nations Relief and Rehabilitation Administration. World Health Organization.
TREATY REF: 16UNTS247; 161LTS65.
PROCEDURE: Accession. Duration. Ratification. Renewal or Revival.
PARTIES:
Australia SIGNED: 30 Apr 46 FORCE: 30 Apr 46
Belgium SIGNED: 24 Apr 46
Canada SIGNED: 25 Apr 46 FORCE: 30 Apr 46

Taiwan SIGNED: 30 Apr 46 FORCE: 30 Apr 46
Dominican Republic RATIFIED: 29 May 46 FORCE: 29 May 46
Ecuador SIGNED: 30 Apr 46
France SIGNED: 30 Apr 46 FORCE: 30 Apr 46
Greece SIGNED: 30 Apr 46 FORCE: 30 Apr 46
Haiti SIGNED: 30 Apr 46 FORCE: 30 Apr 46
Honduras RATIFIED: 8 Jul 46 FORCE: 8 Jul 46
India RATIFIED: 28 Aug 47 FORCE: 28 Aug 47
Italy RATIFIED: 23 Jul 46 FORCE: 23 Jul 46
Luxembourg SIGNED: 30 Apr 46 FORCE: 30 Apr 46
Netherlands RATIFIED: 5 Mar 48 FORCE: 5 Mar 48
New Zealand SIGNED: 23 Apr 46 FORCE: 30 Apr 46
Nicaragua SIGNED: 26 Apr 46 FORCE: 30 Apr 46
Philippines RATIFIED: 13 Jan 48 FORCE: 13 Jan 48
Poland RATIFIED: 28 May 46 FORCE: 28 May 46
South Africa RATIFIED: 12 Jul 46 FORCE: 12 Jul 46
Syria RATIFIED: 31 Oct 46 FORCE: 31 Oct 46
UK Great Britain SIGNED: 29 Apr 46 FORCE: 30 Apr 46
USA (United States) SIGNED: 30 Apr 46 RATIFIED: 6 Aug 46 FORCE: 6 Aug 46

100258   Bilateral Exchange   **16 UNTS 189**
SIGNED: 3 Jun 48   FORCE: 3 Jun 48
REGISTERED: 24 Jun 48 Australia
ARTICLES: 2 LANGUAGE: English.
HEADNOTE: GIFT WOOL FOR POST-UNRRA RELIEF
TOPIC: Direct Aid
CONCEPTS: General cooperation. Operating agencies. Public information. Title and deeds. General technical assistance. General aid. Use restrictions.
INTL ORGS: United Nations Relief and Rehabilitation Administration.
PARTIES:
Australia
Poland

100259   Unilateral Instrument   **16 UNTS 197**
SIGNED: 22 Jun 48   FORCE: 9 Jul 48
REGISTERED: 9 Jul 48 United Nations
ARTICLES: 1 LANGUAGE: English.
HEADNOTE: ACCEPTANCE ICJ JURISDICTION
TOPIC: ICJ Option Clause
CONCEPTS: Compulsory jurisdiction.
INTL ORGS: International Court of Justice.
PROCEDURE: Duration.
PARTIES:
Pakistan
ANNEX
257 UNTS 360. Pakistan. Termination 21 Dec 56 Force 21 Jun 57.

100260   Unilateral Instrument   **16 UNTS 203**
SIGNED: 10 Jun 48   FORCE: 13 Jul 48
REGISTERED: 13 Jul 48 United Nations
ARTICLES: 1 LANGUAGE: French.
HEADNOTE: ACCEPTANCE ICJ JURISDICTION
TOPIC: ICJ Option Clause
CONCEPTS: Compulsory jurisdiction.
INTL ORGS: International Court of Justice.
PROCEDURE: Duration.
PARTIES:
Belgium

100261   Unilateral Instrument   **16 UNTS 207**
SIGNED: 5 Jul 48   FORCE: 16 Jul 48
REGISTERED: 16 Jul 48 United Nations
ARTICLES: 1 LANGUAGE: Spanish.
HEADNOTE: ACCEPTANCE COMPULSORY JURISDICTION ICJ
TOPIC: ICJ Option Clause
CONCEPTS: Optional clause ICJ. Compulsory jurisdiction.
INTL ORGS: International Court of Justice.
PARTIES:
Bolivia

100262   Bilateral Exchange   **16 UNTS 21**
SIGNED: 3 May 46   FORCE: 3 May 4
REGISTERED: 22 Jul 48 New Zealand

ARTICLES: 3 LANGUAGE: English.
HEADNOTE: RELEASE MONETARY ASSETS
TOPIC: Claims and Debts
CONCEPTS: Conformity with municipal law. Exchange rates and regulations. Assets transfer.
TREATY REF: 5UNTS27.
PARTIES:
New Zealand
Norway

100263 Bilateral Agreement **16 UNTS 219**
SIGNED: 2 Jul 47 FORCE: 16 Sep 47
REGISTERED: 22 Jul 48 New Zealand
ARTICLES: 6 LANGUAGE: English. French.
HEADNOTE: CREDIT GRANTING WOOL ETC. PURCHASES
TOPIC: Commodity Trade
CONCEPTS: Accounting procedures. Banking. Currency. Interest rates. Payment schedules. Commodity trade. Credit provisions. Terms of loan.
PROCEDURE: Ratification.
PARTIES:
France
New Zealand

100264 Bilateral Agreement **16 UNTS 229**
SIGNED: 22 Jan 48 FORCE: 22 Jan 48
REGISTERED: 22 Jul 48 New Zealand
ARTICLES: 6 LANGUAGE: English.
HEADNOTE: CREDIT GRANTING WORK PURCHASES
TOPIC: Commodity Trade
CONCEPTS: Accounting procedures. Banking. Currency. Interest rates. Payment schedules. Commodity trade. Credit provisions. Terms of loan.
PARTIES:
Czechoslovakia
New Zealand

100265 Multilateral Protocol **17 UNTS 3**
SIGNED: 23 Apr 46 FORCE: 30 Apr 46
REGISTERED: 26 Jul 48 USA (United States)
ARTICLES: 5 LANGUAGE: English. French.
HEADNOTE: INTERNATIONAL SANITARY CONVENTION
TOPIC: Sanitation
CONCEPTS: Conditions. Treaty implementation. Treaty interpretation. General cooperation. WHO used as agency. UN administrative tribunal.
INTL ORGS: United Nations Relief and Rehabilitation Administration.
TREATY REF: 17UNTS305; 78LTS229.
PROCEDURE: Accession. Duration. Future Procedures Contemplated. Ratification.
PARTIES:
Australia SIGNED: 30 Apr 46 FORCE: 30 Apr 46
Belgium SIGNED: 24 Apr 46
Canada SIGNED: 25 Apr 46 FORCE: 30 Apr 46
Taiwan SIGNED: 30 Apr 46 FORCE: 30 Apr 46
Denmark RATIFIED: 23 Aug 46 FORCE: 23 Aug 46
Dominican Republic RATIFIED: 29 May 46 FORCE: 29 May 46
Ecuador SIGNED: 30 Apr 46
France SIGNED: 30 Apr 46 FORCE: 30 Apr 46
Greece SIGNED: 30 Apr 46 FORCE: 30 Apr 46
Haiti SIGNED: 30 Apr 46 FORCE: 30 Apr 46
Honduras RATIFIED: 8 Jul 46 FORCE: 8 Jul 46
India SIGNED: 28 Aug 47 FORCE: 28 Aug 47
Italy RATIFIED: 23 Jul 46 FORCE: 23 Jul 46
Luxembourg SIGNED: 30 Apr 46 FORCE: 30 Apr 46
Netherlands RATIFIED: 5 Mar 48 FORCE: 5 Mar 48
New Zealand SIGNED: 23 Apr 46 FORCE: 30 Apr 46
Nicaragua SIGNED: 26 Apr 46 FORCE: 30 Apr 46
Philippines RATIFIED: 13 Jan 48 FORCE: 13 Jan 48
Poland RATIFIED: 28 May 46 FORCE: 28 May 46
South Africa RATIFIED: 12 Jul 46 FORCE: 12 Jul 46
Syria RATIFIED: 31 Oct 46 FORCE: 31 Oct 46
UK Great Britain SIGNED: 29 Apr 46 FORCE: 30 Apr 46
USA (United States) SIGNED: 30 Apr 46 RATIFIED: 6 Aug 46 FORCE: 6 Aug 46

100266 Bilateral Agreement **17 UNTS 13**
SIGNED: 16 May 46 FORCE: 22 Dec 47
REGISTERED: 27 Jul 48 Netherlands
ARTICLES: 16 LANGUAGE: Dutch. French.
HEADNOTE: CULTURAL INTELLECTUAL RELATIONS
TOPIC: Culture
CONCEPTS: Detailed regulations. Annex or appendix reference. Previous treaty replacement. Friendship and amity. Conformity with municipal law. General cooperation. Recognition of degrees. Exchange. Commissions and foundations. Teacher and student exchange. Professorships. Vocational training. General cultural cooperation. Artists. Scientific exchange. Mass media exchange.
INTL ORGS: Special Commission.
TREATY REF: 89LTS37.
PROCEDURE: Duration. Ratification. Renewal or Revival. Termination.
PARTIES:
Belgium
Netherlands
ANNEX
23 UNTS 313. Netherlands. Correction 30 Jul 47. Force 22 Dec 47.
23 UNTS 313. Belgium. Correction 30 Jul 47. Force 22 Dec 47.
303 UNTS 302. Netherlands. Supplementation 29 Mar 57. Force 21 May 58.
303 UNTS 302. Belgium. Supplementation 29 Mar 57. Force 21 May 58.
510 UNTS 313. Belgium. Amendment 22 Apr 64. Force 10 Aug 64.
510 UNTS 313. Netherlands. Amendment 22 Apr 64. Force 10 Aug 64.

100267 Bilateral Agreement **17 UNTS 29**
SIGNED: 28 May 47 FORCE: 28 May 47
REGISTERED: 27 Jul 48 Netherlands
ARTICLES: 10 LANGUAGE: English.
HEADNOTE: SETTLEMENT LEND-LEASE AID SURPLUS PROPERTY MILITARY RELIEF CLAIMS
TOPIC: General Military
CONCEPTS: Definition of terms. Emergencies. General provisions. Annex or appendix reference. Non-prejudice to UN charter. General property. Exchange rates and regulations. Expense sharing formulae. Interest rates. Payment schedules. Local currency. Lump sum settlements. Post-war adjustment. Naval vessels. Return of equipment and recapture. Surplus war property. Post-war claims settlement.
INTL ORGS: United Nations Relief and Rehabilitation Administration. United Nations.
PROCEDURE: Future Procedures Contemplated.
PARTIES:
Netherlands
USA (United States)
ANNEX
81 UNTS 320. USA (United States). Interpretation and Implementation 1 Jun 50. Force 8 Jun 50.
81 UNTS 320. Netherlands. Interpretation and Implementation 8 Jun 50. Force 8 Jun 50.
205 UNTS 324. USA (United States). Implementation 8 Apr 53. Force 8 Apr 53.
205 UNTS 324. Netherlands. Implementation 17 Sep 52. Force 8 Apr 53.
205 UNTS 324. Indonesia. Implementation 15 Oct 52. Force 8 Apr 53.

100268 Bilateral Agreement **17 UNTS 65**
SIGNED: 31 May 47 FORCE: 31 May 47
REGISTERED: 27 Jul 48 Netherlands
ARTICLES: 13 LANGUAGE: English.
HEADNOTE: AIR SERVICES
TOPIC: Air Transport
CONCEPTS: Dispute settlement. Arbitration. Procedure. Airport facilities. Airport equipment. Airworthiness certificates. Conditions of airlines operating permission. Overflights and technical stops. Operating authorizations and regulations. Licenses and certificates of nationality.
INTL ORGS: International Civil Aviation Organization.
PROCEDURE: Termination.
PARTIES:
India
Netherlands

100269 Multilateral Agreement **17 UNTS 89**
SIGNED: 18 Nov 47 FORCE: 18 Nov 47
REGISTERED: 27 Jul 48 Netherlands
ARTICLES: 9 LANGUAGE: French.
HEADNOTE: MONETARY COOPERATION
TOPIC: Finance
CONCEPTS: Treaty implementation. Annex or appendix reference. General cooperation. Exchange of information and documents. Establishment of commission. Accounting procedures. Balance of payments. Payment schedules.
PROCEDURE: Accession. Denunciation.
PARTIES:
Belgium SIGNED: 18 Nov 47 FORCE: 18 Nov 47
France SIGNED: 18 Nov 47 FORCE: 18 Nov 47
Italy SIGNED: 18 Nov 47 FORCE: 18 Nov 47
Luxembourg SIGNED: 18 Nov 47 FORCE: 18 Nov 47
Netherlands SIGNED: 18 Nov 47 FORCE: 18 Nov 47

100270 Bilateral Agreement **17 UNTS 99**
SIGNED: 22 Jan 48 FORCE: 22 Jan 48
REGISTERED: 27 Jul 48 Netherlands
ARTICLES: 11 LANGUAGE: English.
HEADNOTE: AIR TRANSPORT
TOPIC: Air Transport
CONCEPTS: Exceptions and exemptions. Annex or appendix reference. Non-prejudice to third party. Conformity with municipal law. Licenses and permits. Recognition of legal documents. Use of facilities. Arbitration. Procedure. Reexport of goods, etc.. Fees and exemptions. National treatment. Customs exemptions. Competency certificate. Routes and logistics. Navigational conditions. Permit designation. Air transport. Airport facilities. Airworthiness certificates. Conditions of airlines operating permission. Operating authorizations and regulations. Licenses and certificates of nationality.
PROCEDURE: Amendment. Termination.
PARTIES:
Austria
Netherlands
ANNEX
392 UNTS 326. Netherlands. Amendment 19 Dec 50. Force 19 Dec 50.
392 UNTS 326. Austria. Amendment 19 Dec 50. Force 19 Dec 50.
392 UNTS 326. Austria. Amendment 13 Mar 59. Force 13 Mar 59.
392 UNTS 326. Netherlands. Amendment 13 Mar 59. Force 13 Mar 59.
463 UNTS 314. Netherlands. Amendment 25 May 61. Force 25 May 61.
463 UNTS 314. Austria. Amendment 25 May 61. Force 25 May 61.

100271 Unilateral Instrument **17 UNTS 111**
SIGNED: 6 Jul 48 FORCE: 28 Jul 48
REGISTERED: 28 Jul 48 United Nations
ARTICLES: 1 LANGUAGE: French.
HEADNOTE: ACCEPTANCE ICJ JURISDICTION
TOPIC: ICJ Option Clause
CONCEPTS: Funding procedures. Optional clause ICJ.
INTL ORGS: International Court of Justice. United Nations.
PARTIES:
Switzerland

100272 Unilateral Instrument **17 UNTS 115**
SIGNED: 6 Jul 48 FORCE: 28 Jul 48
REGISTERED: 28 Jul 48 United Nations
ARTICLES: 1 LANGUAGE: French.
HEADNOTE: ACCEPTANCE ICJ JURISDICTION
TOPIC: ICJ Option Clause
CONCEPTS: Compulsory jurisdiction.
INTL ORGS: International Court of Justice.
PROCEDURE: Duration.
PARTIES:
Switzerland

100273 Bilateral Agreement **17 UNTS 119**
SIGNED: 3 Jul 48 FORCE: 3 Jul 48
REGISTERED: 2 Aug 48 Taiwan
ARTICLES: 12 LANGUAGE: Chinese. English.
HEADNOTE: ECONOMIC AID
TOPIC: Direct Aid
CONCEPTS: Annex or appendix reference. Privi-

leges and immunities. Conformity with municipal law. General cooperation. Exchange of information and documents. Personnel. Public information. Existing tribunals. Accounting procedures. Currency deposits. Local currency. Claims
and settlements. Commodities and services. Domestic obligation. Economic assistance. Aid missions. Grants. Withdrawal conditions. Procurement. Distribution. Paragraph 2, Article 36. Raw
materials.
INTL ORGS: International Court of Justice. Special
Commission.
PROCEDURE: Amendment. Duration. Future Procedures Contemplated. Registration. Termination.
PARTIES:
Taiwan
USA (United States)
ANNEX
45 UNTS 326. Taiwan. Interpretation 3 Jul 48.
45 UNTS 326. USA (United States). Interpretation
3 Jul 48.
45 UNTS 328. Taiwan. Interpretation 28 Jul 48.
45 UNTS 328. USA (United States). Interpretation
27 Jul 48.
76 UNTS 245. Taiwan. Amendment 31 Mar 49.
Force 31 Mar 49.
76 UNTS 245. USA (United States). Amendment
26 Mar 49. Force 31 Mar 49.
235 UNTS 354. Taiwan. Amendment 31 Jan 50.
Force 31 Jan 50.
235 UNTS 354. USA (United States). Amendment
21 Jan 50. Force 31 Jan 50.
573 UNTS 291. Taiwan. Amendment 11 Aug 65.
Force 11 Aug 65.
573 UNTS 291. USA (United States). Amendment
11 Aug 65. Force 11 Aug 65.

100274 Multilateral Agreement **17 UNTS 159**
SIGNED: 31 Mar 46   FORCE: 31 Mar 46
REGISTERED: 6 Aug 48 UK Great Britain
ARTICLES: 6 LANGUAGE: English.
HEADNOTE: DEFENSE INSTALLATIONS
TOPIC: Milit Installation
CONCEPTS: Change of circumstances. Conformity
with municipal law. General cooperation. Per-
sonnel. Research and scientific projects. Re-
search results. Fees and exemptions. Payment
schedules. Airport facilities. Airworthiness cer-
tificates. Overflights and technical stops. Status
of forces. Military installations and equipment.
Bases and facilities.
PROCEDURE: Amendment. Duration. Application
to Non-self-governing Territories.
PARTIES:
Canada SIGNED: 31 Mar 46 FORCE: 31 Mar 46
Newfoundland SIGNED: 31 Mar 46 FORCE:
31 Mar 46
UK Great Britain SIGNED: 31 Mar 46 FORCE:
31 Mar 46

100275 Bilateral Agreement **17 UNTS 169**
SIGNED: 29 Jul 46   FORCE: 29 Jul 45
REGISTERED: 6 Aug 48 UK Great Britain
ARTICLES: 22 LANGUAGE: English.
HEADNOTE: AIR TRANSPORT
TOPIC: Air Transport
CONCEPTS: Existing tribunals. Non-ILO labor rela-
tions. Fees and exemptions. Most favored nation
clause. Customs exemptions. Air transport. Air-
port facilities. Airport equipment. Overflights
and technical stops. Operating authorizations
and regulations. Postal services.
INTL ORGS: International Civil Aviation Organiza-
tion.
TREATY REF: 15UNTS295.
PROCEDURE: Amendment. Future Procedures
Contemplated. Registration.
PARTIES:
Canada
Newfoundland

100276 Bilateral Agreement **17 UNTS 181**
SIGNED: 29 Oct 46   FORCE: 3 Jun 47
REGISTERED: 6 Aug 48 UK Great Britain
ARTICLES: 16 LANGUAGE: English.
HEADNOTE: DOUBLE TAXATION FISCAL EVA-
SION
TOPIC: Taxation
CONCEPTS: Definition of terms. Exchange of infor-
mation and documents. Teacher and student ex-
change. Taxation. Tax exemptions

PROCEDURE: Duration. Termination.
PARTIES:
Australia
UK Great Britain

100277 Bilateral Agreement **17 UNTS 211**
SIGNED: 27 May 47   FORCE: 8 Aug 47
REGISTERED: 6 Aug 48 UK Great Britain
ARTICLES: 19 LANGUAGE: English.
HEADNOTE: PAYMENTS AGREEMENT
TOPIC: Taxation
CONCEPTS: General cooperation. Accounting pro-
cedures. Banking. Bonds. Balance of payments.
Currency. Monetary and gold transfers. Ex-
change rates and regulations. Financial pro-
grams. Interest rates. Payment schedules. Local
currency. Assets.
PROCEDURE: Amendment. Denunciation. Dura-
tion. Renewal or Revival.
PARTIES:
New Zealand
UK Great Britain

100278 Bilateral Agreement **17 UNTS 239**
SIGNED: 9 Oct 47   FORCE: 11 Feb 48
REGISTERED: 6 Aug 48 UK Great Britain
ARTICLES: 10 LANGUAGE: English.
HEADNOTE: FINANCE
TOPIC: Finance
CONCEPTS: Annex or appendix reference. Gen-
eral cooperation. General trade. Accounting pro-
cedures. Banking. Bonds. Currency. Monetary
and gold transfers. Exchange rates and regula-
tions. Interest rates. Loan and credit. Purchase
authorization.
INTL ORGS: International Monetary Fund.
PARTIES:
South Africa
UK Great Britain

100279 Bilateral Agreement **17 UNTS 247**
SIGNED: 27 Nov 45   FORCE: 27 Nov 45
REGISTERED: 19 Aug 48 Norway
ARTICLES: 12 LANGUAGE: Finnish. Norwegian.
HEADNOTE: REGULATING PAYMENTS
TOPIC: Finance
CONCEPTS: General cooperation. Import quotas.
Accounting procedures. Banking. Balance of
payments. Currency. Exchange rates and regula-
tions. Interest rates. Payment schedules. Trans-
portation costs. Local currency. Claims and set-
tlements.
PROCEDURE: Denunciation.
PARTIES:
Finland
Norway

100280 Bilateral Agreement **17 UNTS 261**
SIGNED: 13 Dec 45   FORCE: 13 Dec 45
REGISTERED: 19 Aug 48 Norway
ARTICLES: 11 LANGUAGE: English.
HEADNOTE: FINANCE
TOPIC: Finance
CONCEPTS: General cooperation. Accounting pro-
cedures. Banking. Balance of payments. Cur-
rency. Monetary and gold transfers. Currency de-
posits. Exchange rates and regulations. Payment
schedules. Local currency.
PROCEDURE: Amendment. Termination.
PARTIES:
Czechoslovakia
Norway
ANNEX
25 UNTS 346. Norway. Amendment 28 Jul 48.
Force 28 Jul 48.
25 UNTS 346. Czechoslovakia. Amendment
28 Jul 48. Force 28 Jul 48.
88 UNTS 428. Norway. Amendment 4 Nov 50.
Force 4 Nov 50.
88 UNTS 428. Czechoslovakia. Amendment
4 Nov 50. Force 4 Nov 50.

100281 Bilateral Agreement **17 UNTS 273**
SIGNED: 20 Jul 46   FORCE: 1 Aug 46
REGISTERED: 19 Aug 48 Norway
ARTICLES: 11 LANGUAGE: French.
HEADNOTE: REGULATION RECIPROCAL PAY-
MENTS
TOPIC: Finance

CONCEPTS: Detailed regulations. Treaty imple-
mentation. Licenses and permits. Import quotas.
Accounting procedures. Banking. Currency. Ex-
change rates and regulations. Interest rates. Pay-
ment schedules. Local currency. Debt settle-
ment.
PROCEDURE: Denunciation. Duration. Renewal or
Revival.
PARTIES:
Italy
Norway

100282 Bilateral Agreement **17 UNTS 283**
SIGNED: 27 Dec 46   FORCE: 27 Dec 46
REGISTERED: 19 Aug 48 Norway
ARTICLES: 13 LANGUAGE: Norwegian. Russian.
HEADNOTE: FACILITATING TRADE REGULATING
PAYMENTS
TOPIC: Finance
CONCEPTS: Detailed regulations. Treaty imple-
mentation. General cooperation. Export quotas.
Import quotas. Trade procedures. Accounting
procedures. Banking. Balance of payments. Cur-
rency. Monetary and gold transfers. Exchange
rates and regulations. Payment schedules. Local
currency. Debt settlement. Delivery schedules.
PROCEDURE: Duration. Termination.
PARTIES:
Norway
USSR (Soviet Union)

100283 Multilateral Instrument **18 UNTS 3**
SIGNED: 15 Dec 46   FORCE: 20 Aug 48
REGISTERED: 20 Aug 48 United Nations
ARTICLES: 18 LANGUAGE: Chinese. English.
French. Russian. Spanish.
HEADNOTE: CONSTITUTION INTERNATIONAL
REFUGEE ORGANIZATION
TOPIC: IGO Establishment
CONCEPTS: IGO constitution. Subsidiary organ.
Establishment. Extension of functions.
INTL ORGS: International Court of Justice. Interna-
tional Refugees Organization. United Nations.
TREATY REF: CHARTER UN.
PARTIES:
Argentina SIGNED: 10 Jun 47
Australia   SIGNED: 13 May 47   FORCE:
20 Aug 48
Belgium   SIGNED: 1 May 47   RATIFIED:
30 Mar 48 FORCE: 20 Aug 48
Bolivia SIGNED: 5 Jun 47
Brazil SIGNED: 1 Jul 47
Canada SIGNED: 16 Dec 46 RATIFIED: 7 Aug 47
FORCE: 20 Aug 48
Taiwan SIGNED: 29 Apr 47 FORCE: 20 Aug 47
Denmark   SIGNED: 20 Aug 48   FORCE:
20 Aug 48
Dominican Republic SIGNED: 17 Dec 46 RATI-
FIED: 22 Oct 47 FORCE: 20 Aug 48
France SIGNED: 17 Dec 46 RATIFIED: 3 Mar 48
FORCE: 20 Aug 48
Guatemala   SIGNED: 16 Dec 46   RATIFIED:
28 Jul 47 FORCE: 20 Aug 48
Honduras SIGNED: 18 Dec 46
Iceland SIGNED: 12 May 47 FORCE: 20 Aug 48
Italy SIGNED: 24 Mar 49
Liberia SIGNED: 31 Dec 46
Netherlands   SIGNED: 28 Jan 47   RATIFIED:
10 Aug 47 FORCE: 20 Aug 48
New Zealand SIGNED: 17 Mar 47 FORCE:
20 Aug 48
Norway SIGNED: 4 Feb 47 RATIFIED: 18 Aug 47
FORCE: 20 Aug 48
Panama SIGNED: 23 Jan 47
Peru SIGNED: 25 Jul 47
Philippines SIGNED: 18 Dec 46
UK Great Britain SIGNED: 5 Feb 47 FORCE
20 Aug 48
USA (United States) SIGNED: 16 Dec 46 RATI-
FIED: 3 Jul 47 FORCE: 20 Aug 48
Venezuela SIGNED: 4 Jun 48

100284 Bilateral Agreement **18 UNTS 139**
SIGNED: 21 Apr 48   FORCE: 1 Apr 48
REGISTERED: 20 Aug 48 Denmark
ARTICLES: 8 LANGUAGE: Danish. Norwegian.
HEADNOTE: FACILITATING PAYMENTS
TOPIC: Finance
CONCEPTS: General cooperation. Accounting pro
cedures. Banking. Balance of payments. Cur
rency. Monetary and gold transfers. Currency de

posits. Exchange rates and regulations. Interest rates. Payment schedules. Local currency. Debt settlement.
PROCEDURE: Amendment. Denunciation.
PARTIES:
 Denmark
 Norway

100285 Bilateral Exchange **18 UNTS 161**
SIGNED: 8 Aug 47 FORCE: 25 Nov 47
REGISTERED: 26 Aug 48 New Zealand
ARTICLES: 3 LANGUAGE: English.
HEADNOTE: RELEASE MONETARY ASSETS
TOPIC: Claims and Debts
CONCEPTS: Detailed regulations. Conformity with municipal law. Exchange rates and regulations. Lump sum settlements. Debts. Assessment procedures. Assets transfer.
TREATY REF: 5UNTS15.
PARTIES:
 Czechoslovakia
 New Zealand

100286 Bilateral Exchange **18 UNTS 171**
SIGNED: 4 Jun 48 FORCE: 1 Jul 48
REGISTERED: 26 Aug 48 New Zealand
ARTICLES: 2 LANGUAGE: English.
HEADNOTE: MUTUAL ABOLITION VISAS
TOPIC: Visas
CONCEPTS: Territorial application. Visa abolition. Border traffic and migration. Resident permits.
PARTIES:
 New Zealand
 Sweden

100287 Bilateral Exchange **18 UNTS 177**
SIGNED: 30 Jul 48 FORCE: 1 Aug 48
REGISTERED: 26 Aug 48 New Zealand
ARTICLES: 2 LANGUAGE: English. French.
HEADNOTE: MUTUAL ABOLITION VISAS
TOPIC: Visas
CONCEPTS: Territorial application. Visa abolition. Border traffic and migration. Resident permits. Non-visa travel documents. Employment regulations.
PARTIES:
 New Zealand
 Switzerland

100288 Bilateral Exchange **18 UNTS 185**
SIGNED: 24 Mar 47 FORCE: 24 Mar 47
REGISTERED: 8 Sep 48 Australia
ARTICLES: 2 LANGUAGE: English.
HEADNOTE: RELEASE ASSETS
TOPIC: Claims and Debts
CONCEPTS: Definition of terms. Detailed regulations. Exceptions and exemptions. Conformity with municipal law. General cooperation. Exchange of information and documents. Informational records. Legal protection and assistance. General property. Exchange rates and regulations. Expense sharing formulae. Payment schedules. Claims and settlements. Debts. Assessment procedures. Liens. Assets transfer. Enemy financial interests.
PARTIES:
 Australia
 Norway

100289 Bilateral Treaty **18 UNTS 197**
SIGNED: 15 Nov 46 FORCE: 24 Apr 48
REGISTERED: 20 Sep 48 Taiwan
ARTICLES: 7 LANGUAGE: Arabic. Chinese. English.
HEADNOTE: AMITY
TOPIC: General Amity
CONCEPTS: Friendship and amity. Consular relations establishment. Diplomatic relations establishment. Immovable property. Most favored nation clause.
PROCEDURE: Future Procedures Contemplated. Ratification.
PARTIES:
 Taiwan
 Saudi Arabia

100290 Bilateral Exchange **18 UNTS 211**
SIGNED: 16 Jun 48 FORCE: 16 Jun 48
REGISTERED: 6 Oct 48 Australia
ARTICLES: 2 LANGUAGE: English.
HEADNOTE: RELEASE PROPERTY
TOPIC: Claims and Debts
CONCEPTS: Definition of terms. Detailed regulations. Exceptions and exemptions. Exchange of information and documents. Informational records. Responsibility and liability. Compensation. Assets. Claims and settlements. Debt settlement. Assessment procedures. Assets transfer. Most favored nation clause. War claims and reparations. Loss and/or damage. Enemy financial interests.
PARTIES:
 Australia
 Greece

100291 Bilateral Treaty **18 UNTS 221**
SIGNED: 28 Jan 47 FORCE: 18 Mar 47
REGISTERED: 11 Oct 48 Belgium
ARTICLES: 3 LANGUAGE: French.
HEADNOTE: ABOLITION PASSPORT VISAS
TOPIC: Visas
CONCEPTS: Visa abolition. Resident permits.
PARTIES:
 Belgium
 Denmark
ANNEX
308 UNTS 302. Belgium. Supplementation 30 Apr 58. Force 1 May 58.
308 UNTS 302. Denmark. Supplementation 29 Apr 58. Force 1 May 58.

100292 Bilateral Exchange **18 UNTS 227**
SIGNED: 25 Mar 47 FORCE: 1 Apr 47
REGISTERED: 11 Oct 48 Belgium
ARTICLES: 2 LANGUAGE: French.
HEADNOTE: ABOLITION PASSPORT VISAS
TOPIC: Visas
CONCEPTS: Territorial application. Visa abolition. Border traffic and migration. Resident permits.
PARTIES:
 Belgium
 Ireland

100293 Bilateral Exchange **18 UNTS 237**
SIGNED: 25 Feb 48 FORCE: 3 Mar 48
REGISTERED: 11 Oct 48 Belgium
ARTICLES: 2 LANGUAGE: French.
HEADNOTE: ISSUE PASSPORT VISAS
TOPIC: Visas
CONCEPTS: Detailed regulations. Visas.
PROCEDURE: Amendment.
PARTIES:
 Belgium
 Turkey

100294 Bilateral Instrument **18 UNTS 245**
SIGNED: 5 Jun 48 FORCE: 5 Jul 48
REGISTERED: 18 Oct 48 Belgium
ARTICLES: 1 LANGUAGE: French.
HEADNOTE: RECIPROCAL ISSUE CIVIL STATUS RECORDS
TOPIC: Admin Cooperation
CONCEPTS: Previous treaty replacement. Nationality and citizenship. Informational records. Fees and exemptions.
PARTIES:
 Belgium
 Monaco

100295 Bilateral Agreement **18 UNTS 251**
SIGNED: 14 Sep 48 FORCE: 14 Sep 48
REGISTERED: 18 Oct 48 New Zealand
ARTICLES: 16 LANGUAGE: English.
HEADNOTE: SETTLEMENT LEND LEASE RECIPROCAL AID SURPLUS WAR PROPERTY CLAIMS
TOPIC: General Military
CONCEPTS: Definition of terms. Exchange. Commissions and foundations. Teacher and student exchange. Exchange rates and regulations. Lend lease. Surplus war property.
TREATY REF: 6LTS341.
PROCEDURE: Amendment.
PARTIES:
 New Zealand
 USA (United States)

ANNEX
74 UNTS 288. New Zealand. Amendment 9 Mar 49. Force 9 Mar 49.
74 UNTS 288. USA (United States). Amendment 3 Mar 49. Force 9 Mar 49.

100296 Multilateral Agreement **18 UNTS 267**
SIGNED: 14 Sep 48 FORCE: 14 Oct 48
REGISTERED: 14 Oct 48 United Nations
ARTICLES: 6 LANGUAGE: English. French.
HEADNOTE: MOST FAVORED NATION TREATMENT AREAS UNDER MILITARY OCCUPATION
TOPIC: Milit Occupation
CONCEPTS: Annex or appendix reference. Tariffs. Most favored nation clause. Control and occupation machinery.
INTL ORGS: United Nations.
PROCEDURE: Amendment. Accession. Denunciation. Duration.
PARTIES:
 Belgium SIGNED: 14 Sep 48 FORCE: 14 Oct 48
 Brazil SIGNED: 14 Sep 48
 Canada SIGNED: 14 Sep 48 FORCE: 14 Oct 48
 Ceylon (Sri Lanka) SIGNED: 14 Sep 48
 France SIGNED: 14 Sep 48 FORCE: 14 Oct 48
 India SIGNED: 14 Sep 48
 Luxembourg SIGNED: 14 Sep 48 FORCE: 14 Oct 48
 Netherlands SIGNED: 14 Sep 48 FORCE: 14 Oct 48
 Norway SIGNED: 14 Sep 48 FORCE: 14 Oct 48
 Pakistan SIGNED: 14 Sep 48 FORCE: 14 Oct 48
 South Africa SIGNED: 14 Oct 48
 UK Great Britain SIGNED: 14 Sep 48 FORCE: 14 Oct 48
 USA (United States) SIGNED: 14 Sep 48 FORCE: 14 Oct 48
ANNEX
20 UNTS 308. Ceylon (Sri Lanka). Acceptance 9 Dec 48. Force 8 Jan 49.
24 UNTS 320. Taiwan. Signature 18 Jan 49. Force 17 Feb 49.
35 UNTS 370. Dominican Republic. Signature 7 Sep 49. Force 7 Oct 49.
42 UNTS 356. India. Interpretation 13 Aug 49. Force 13 Aug 49.
42 UNTS 356. Luxembourg. Interpretation 13 Aug 49. Force 13 Aug 49.
42 UNTS 356. Belgium. Interpretation 13 Aug 49. Force 13 Aug 49.
42 UNTS 356. Syria. Signature 24 Sep 49. Force 24 Oct 49.
42 UNTS 356. Brazil. Interpretation 13 Aug 49. Force 13 Aug 49.
42 UNTS 356. Taiwan. Interpretation 13 Aug 49. Force 13 Aug 49.
42 UNTS 356. France. Interpretation 13 Aug 49. Force 13 Aug 49.
42 UNTS 356. Canada. Interpretation 13 Aug 49. Force 13 Aug 49.
42 UNTS 356. Ceylon (Sri Lanka). Interpretation 13 Aug 49. Force 13 Aug 49.
42 UNTS 356. Netherlands. Interpretation 10 Oct 49. Force 10 Oct 49.
42 UNTS 356. Norway. Interpretation 13 Aug 49. Force 13 Aug 49.
42 UNTS 356. Pakistan. Interpretation 13 Aug 49. Force 13 Aug 49.
42 UNTS 356. South Africa. Interpretation 13 Aug 49. Force 13 Aug 49.
42 UNTS 356. UK Great Britain. Interpretation 13 Aug 49. Force 13 Aug 49.
42 UNTS 356. USA (United States). Interpretation 13 Aug 49. Force 13 Aug 49.
42 UNTS 356. Syria. Interpretation 24 Sep 49. Force 24 Sep 49.
42 UNTS 356. Dominican Republic. Interpretation 5 Oct 49. Force 5 Oct 49.
43 UNTS 339. Netherlands. Signature 10 Oct 49.
44 UNTS 339. Denmark. Signature 8 Nov 49. Force 8 Dec 49.
46 UNTS 350. Greece. Signature 7 Feb 50. Force 9 Mar 50.
53 UNTS 419. Pakistan. Signature 24 Apr 50.
70 UNTS 272. South Africa. Acceptance 6 Sep 50. Force 6 Oct 50.
117 UNTS 385. Netherlands. Withdrawal 14 Dec 51. Force 15 Jun 52.
117 UNTS 385. Norway. Withdrawal 14 Dec 51. Force 15 Jun 52.
117 UNTS 385. Belgium. Withdrawal 14 Dec 51. Force 15 Jun 52.

117 UNTS 385. Ceylon (Sri Lanka). Withdrawal 14 Dec 51. Force 15 Jun 52.
117 UNTS 385. Denmark. Withdrawal 14 Dec 51. Force 15 Jun 52.
117 UNTS 385. India. Withdrawal 14 Dec 51. Force 15 Jun 52.
117 UNTS 385. Canada. Withdrawal 14 Dec 51. Force 15 Jun 52.
117 UNTS 385. Pakistan. Withdrawal 14 Dec 51. Force 15 Jun 52.
117 UNTS 385. UK Great Britain. Withdrawal 14 Dec 51. Force 15 Jun 52.
117 UNTS 385. USA (United States). Withdrawal 14 Dec 51. Force 15 Jun 52.
117 UNTS 385. Dominican Republic. Withdrawal 14 Dec 51. Force 15 Jun 52.
121 UNTS 327. Taiwan. Withdrawal 4 Feb 52. Force 4 Aug 52.
121 UNTS 327. France. Withdrawal 18 Feb 52. Force 19 Aug 52.
121 UNTS 327. Greece. Withdrawal 20 Feb 52. Force 21 Aug 52.
121 UNTS 327. Luxembourg. Withdrawal 24 Feb 52. Force 25 Aug 52.
121 UNTS 327. France. Withdrawal 18 Feb 52. Force 19 Aug 52.
121 UNTS 327. Greece. Withdrawal 20 Feb 52. Force 21 Aug 52.
128 UNTS 293. South Africa. Withdrawal 6 May 52. Force 7 Nov 52.

100297 Bilateral Agreement **18 UNTS 279**
SIGNED: 24 Mar 47   FORCE: 1 Apr 47
REGISTERED: 25 Oct 48 Belgium
ARTICLES: 5 LANGUAGE: French.
HEADNOTE: SOCIAL INSURANCE ORGANIZATIONS COOPERATION
TOPIC: Non-ILO Labor
CONCEPTS: General provisions. General cooperation. Public health. Old age and invalidity insurance. Non-ILO labor relations. Sickness and invalidity insurance. Social security. Payment schedules. Assets transfer.
PROCEDURE: Denunciation. Duration. Renewal or Revival.
PARTIES:
Belgium
Poland

100298 Bilateral Agreement **18 UNTS 299**
SIGNED: 10 Nov 47   FORCE: 10 Nov 47
REGISTERED: 27 Oct 48 Belgium
ARTICLES: 9 LANGUAGE: French. Russian.
HEADNOTE: IMPORTATION PRIVILEGES
TOPIC: Finance
CONCEPTS: Diplomatic privileges. Import quotas.
PARTIES:
Belgium
USSR (Soviet Union)

100299 Bilateral Instrument **18 UNTS 309**
SIGNED: 25 Mar 47   FORCE: 1 Apr 47
REGISTERED: 28 Oct 48 Belgium
ARTICLES: 19 LANGUAGE: Dutch.
HEADNOTE: POSTAL ADMINISTRATION
TOPIC: Postal Service
CONCEPTS: Conformity with municipal law. Conveyance in transit. Money orders and postal checks. Rates and charges.
PROCEDURE: Amendment. Termination.
PARTIES:
Belgium
Netherlands

100300 Bilateral Exchange **18 UNTS 323**
SIGNED: 25 Mar 48   FORCE: 25 Mar 48
REGISTERED: 28 Oct 48 Belgium
ARTICLES: 2 LANGUAGE: French.
HEADNOTE: STATUS DOUBLE TAXATION FRONTIER WORKERS
TOPIC: Taxation
CONCEPTS: Wages and salaries. Taxation. Markers and definitions.
PROCEDURE: Ratification. Termination.
PARTIES:
Belgium
Luxembourg
ANNEX
51 UNTS 323. Belgium. Prolongation 28 Dec 49. Force 1 Jan 50.

51 UNTS 323.   Luxembourg.   Prolongation 28 Dec 49. Force 1 Jan 50.

100301 Bilateral Exchange **19 UNTS 3**
SIGNED: 24 Jan 47   FORCE: 7 Apr 47
REGISTERED: 1 Nov 48 Belgium
ARTICLES: 2 LANGUAGE: French. Spanish.
HEADNOTE: MODIFYING 1870 CONVENTION
TOPIC: Admin Cooperation
CONCEPTS: Annex type material. Previous treaty extension.
PARTIES:
Belgium
Spain

100302 Bilateral Agreement **19 UNTS 9**
SIGNED: 28 Jun 48   FORCE: 10 Jul 48
REGISTERED: 1 Nov 48 USA (United States)
ARTICLES: 12 LANGUAGE: English. French.
HEADNOTE: ECONOMIC COOPERATION
TOPIC: Direct Aid
CONCEPTS: Definition of terms. Territorial application. General provisions. Guarantees and safeguards. Treaty implementation. Annex or appendix reference. Tourism. Privileges and immunities. Conformity with municipal law. General cooperation. Exchange of information and documents. Personnel. Public information. Existing tribunals. Accounting procedures. Exchange rates and regulations. Funding procedures. Local currency. Claims and settlements. Domestic obligation. Economic assistance. Aid missions. Relief supplies. Procurement. Access to materials. Paragraph 2, Article 36.
INTL ORGS: International Court of Justice. International Refugees Organization. Organization for Economic Co-operation and Development. United Nations.
TREATY REF: 1UNTS39.
PROCEDURE: Amendment. Duration. Ratification. Registration. Termination.
PARTIES:
France
USA (United States)
ANNEX
34 UNTS 318. France. Amendment 1 Oct 48. Force 1 Oct 48.
34 UNTS 418. USA (United States). Amendment 21 Sep 48. Force 8 Oct 48.
34 UNTS 421. USA (United States). Amendment 20 Nov 48. Force 20 Nov 48.
34 UNTS 421. France. Amendment 17 Nov 48. Force 20 Nov 48.
79 UNTS 270. USA (United States). Amendment 9 Jan 50. Force 9 Jan 50.
79 UNTS 270. France. Amendment 9 Jan 50. Force 9 Jan 50.
141 UNTS 358. USA (United States). Amendment 22 May 51. Force 22 May 51.
141 UNTS 358. France. Amendment 22 May 51. Force 22 May 51.
174 UNTS 284. USA (United States). Amendment 25 Sep 51. Force 27 Sep 51.
174 UNTS 284. France. Amendment 27 Sep 51. Force 27 Sep 51.
214 UNTS 350. USA (United States). Amendment 11 Sep 53. Force 11 Sep 53.
214 UNTS 350. France. Amendment 11 Sep 53. Force 11 Sep 53.

100303 Bilateral Agreement **19 UNTS 43**
SIGNED: 23 Mar 48   FORCE: 31 Aug 48
REGISTERED: 1 Nov 48 United Nations
ARTICLES: 7 LANGUAGE: English.
HEADNOTE: LOAN AGREEMENT
TOPIC: Loans and Credits
CONCEPTS: Detailed regulations. Operating agencies. Financial programs. Liens. Loan and credit. Loan repayment. Terms of loan.
TREATY REF: 11UNTS11.
PARTIES:
United Nations
USA (United States)

100304 Multilateral Treaty **19 UNTS 51**
SIGNED: 17 Mar 48   FORCE: 25 Aug 48
REGISTERED: 2 Nov 48 Belgium
ARTICLES: 10 LANGUAGE: English. French.
HEADNOTE: COLLABORATION ECONOMIC SO-

CIAL CULTURAL MATTERS COLLECTIVE SELF-DEFENSE
TOPIC: General Military
CONCEPTS: General provisions. Non-prejudice to third party. Friendship and amity. Non-prejudice to UN charter. Establishment of commission. Procedure. Conciliation. General cultural cooperation. General economics. Economic assistance. Defense and security. Military assistance. Paragraph 2, Article 36.
INTL ORGS: International Court of Justice. United Nations. Special Commission.
PROCEDURE: Accession. Denunciation. Duration. Future Procedures Contemplated. Ratification. Renewal or Revival.
PARTIES:
Belgium   SIGNED: 17 Mar 48   RATIFIED: 30 Apr 48 FORCE: 25 Aug 48
France   SIGNED: 17 Mar 48   RATIFIED: 25 Aug 48 FORCE: 25 Aug 48
Luxembourg SIGNED: 17 Mar 48 FORCE: 25 Aug 48 10 Jun 48 FORCE: 25 Aug 48
Netherlands SIGNED: 17 Mar 48 RATIFIED: 20 Jul 48 FORCE: 25 Aug 48
UK Great Britain SIGNED: 17 Mar 48 RATIFIED: 2 Jun 48 FORCE: 25 Aug 48
ANNEX
211 UNTS 342. Netherlands. Supplementation 1 May 55. Force 6 May 55.
211 UNTS 342. France. Supplementation 5 May 55. Force 6 May 55.
211 UNTS 342. Germany, West. Supplementation 5 May 55. Force 6 May 55.
211 UNTS 342. Italy. Supplementation 20 Apr 55. Force 6 May 55.
211 UNTS 342. Luxembourg. Supplementation 4 May 55. Force 6 May 55.
211 UNTS 342. UK Great Britain. Supplementation 5 May 55. Force 6 May 55.
211 UNTS 342. Belgium. Supplementation 22 Apr 55. Force 6 May 55.
211 UNTS 358. Luxembourg. Supplementation 4 May 55. Force 6 May 55.
211 UNTS 358. UK Great Britain. Supplementation 5 May 55. Force 6 May 55.
211 UNTS 358. Belgium. Supplementation 22 Apr 55. Force 6 May 55.
211 UNTS 358. France. Supplementation 5 May 55. Force 6 May 55.
211 UNTS 358. Netherlands. Supplementation 1 May 55. Force 6 May 55.
211 UNTS 358. Italy. Supplementation 20 Apr 55. Force 6 May 55.
211 UNTS 358. Germany, West. Supplementation 5 May 55. Force 6 May 55.
211 UNTS 364. France. Supplementation 5 May 55. Force 6 May 55.
211 UNTS 364. Italy. Supplementation 20 Apr 55. Force 6 May 55.
211 UNTS 364. Belgium. Supplementation 22 Apr 55. Force 6 May 55.
211 UNTS 364. Germany, West. Supplementation 5 May 55. Force 6 May 55.
211 UNTS 364. UK Great Britain. Supplementation 5 May 55. Force 6 May 55.
211 UNTS 364. Luxembourg. Supplementation 4 May 55. Force 6 May 55.
211 UNTS 364. Netherlands. Supplementation 1 May 55. Force 6 May 55.
211 UNTS 364. Italy. Supplementation 20 Apr 55. Force 6 May 55.
211 UNTS 364. UK Great Britain. Supplementation 5 May 55. Force 6 May 55.
211 UNTS 364. Belgium. Supplementation 5 May 55. Force 6 May 55.
211 UNTS 364. Luxembourg. Supplementation 22 Apr 55. Force 6 May 55.
211 UNTS 364. Netherlands. Supplementation 4 May 55. Force 6 May 55.
211 UNTS 364. France. Supplementation 1 May 55. Force 6 May 55.
545 UNTS 316. Germany, West. Implementation 14 Dec 57. Acceptance 13 Nov 61.
545 UNTS 316. Netherlands. Implementation 14 Dec 57. Acceptance 5 Sep 58.
545 UNTS 316. UK Great Britain. Implementation 14 Dec 57. Acceptance 20 Jun 58.
545 UNTS 316. Luxembourg. Implementation 14 Dec 57. Acceptance 8 Aug 61.
545 UNTS 316. Italy. Implementation 14 Dec 57 Acceptance 24 Mar 58.
545 UNTS 316. Belgium. Implementation 14 Dec 57. Acceptance 18 Apr 58.

545 UNTS 316.　France.　Implementation
　14 Dec 57. Acceptance 20 May 59.
545 UNTS 316. Italy. Force 13 Nov 61.
545 UNTS 316. Belgium. Force 13 Nov 61.
545 UNTS 316.　UK　Great　Britain.　Force
　13 Nov 61.
545 UNTS 316. Netherlands. Force 13 Nov 61.
545 UNTS 316. Luxembourg. Force 13 Nov 61.
545 UNTS 316. France. Force 13 Nov 61.
545 UNTS 316.　Germany,　West.　Force
　13 Nov 61.

100305　　Bilateral Protocol　　**19 UNTS 65**
SIGNED: 23 Jun 46　　　　　FORCE: 23 Jun 46
REGISTERED: 8 Nov 48 Belgium
ARTICLES: 14 LANGUAGE: French. Italian.
HEADNOTE: RECRUITING SETTLEMENT ITALIAN
　WORKERS BELGIUM
TOPIC: Non-ILO Labor
CONCEPTS: Annex or appendix reference. Pass-
　ports non-diplomatic. Visas. General cooper-
　ation. Investigation of violations. Public health.
　Labor statistics. Wages and salaries. Non-ILO la-
　bor relations. Family allowances. Migrant
　worker. Accounting procedures.
PARTIES:
　Belgium
　Italy

100306　　Bilateral Exchange　　**19 UNTS 87**
SIGNED: 30 Oct 45　　　　　FORCE: 30 Oct 45
REGISTERED: 16 Nov 48 Belgium
ARTICLES: 2 LANGUAGE: French.
HEADNOTE: SETTLEMENT CLAIMS
TOPIC: Reparations
CONCEPTS: General cooperation. Procedure. Loss
　and/or damage. Post-war claims settlement.
PROCEDURE: Future Procedures Contemplated.
PARTIES:
　Belgium
　France
　　　　　　　ANNEX
51 UNTS 326.　Belgium.　Supplementation
　10 Nov 49. Force 8 Dec 49.
51 UNTS 326.　France.　Supplementation
　8 Dec 49. Force 8 Dec 49.

100307　　Bilateral Agreement　　**19 UNTS 95**
SIGNED: 23 Apr 48　　　　　FORCE: 1 May 48
REGISTERED: 16 Nov 48 Belgium
ARTICLES: 12 LANGUAGE: French.
HEADNOTE: FRONTIER AGREEMENT
TOPIC: Territory Boundary
CONCEPTS: Annex or appendix reference. Visa
　abolition. Frontier permits. Nationality and citi-
　zenship. Establishment of commission. Markers
　and definitions. Frontier peoples and personnel.
PROCEDURE: Denunciation.
PARTIES:
　Belgium
　France

100308　　Multilateral Agreement　　**19 UNTS 113**
SIGNED: 8 Oct 48　　　　　FORCE: 8 Oct 48
REGISTERED: 16 Nov 48 Belgium
ARTICLES: 14 LANGUAGE: English. French.
HEADNOTE: USE FUNDS REGARDING SETTLE-
　MENT LEND-LEASE AID SURPLUS PROPERTY
　CLAIMS
TOPIC: Education
CONCEPTS: Definition of terms. Exchange. Com-
　missions and foundations. Teacher and student
　exchange. Exchange rates and regulations.
　Lease of military property. Lend lease. Surplus
　war property.
PROCEDURE: Amendment.
PARTIES:
　Belgium SIGNED: 8 Oct 48 FORCE: 8 Oct 48
　Luxembourg SIGNED: 8 Oct 48 FORCE: 8 Oct 48
　USA (United States) SIGNED: 8 Oct 48 FORCE:
　8 Oct 48
　　　　　　　ANNEX
147 UNTS 154. USA (United States). Amendment
　17 Mar 50. Force 29 Mar 50.
147 UNTS 154.　Luxembourg.　Amendment
　29 Mar 50. Force 29 Mar 50.
300 UNTS 301. USA (United States). Amendment
　18 Mar 49. Force 6 Apr 51.
300 UNTS 301.　Luxembourg.　Amendment
　6 Apr 51. Force 6 Apr 51.

526 UNTS 308. USA (United States). Amendment
　2 Apr 64. Force 2 Apr 64.
526 UNTS 308. Belgium. Amendment 2 Apr 64.
　Force 2 Apr 64.
526 UNTS 308.　Luxembourg.　Amendment
　2 Apr 64. Force 2 Apr 64.

100309　　Bilateral Agreement　　**19 UNTS 127**
SIGNED: 2 Jul 48　　　　　FORCE: 3 Aug 48
REGISTERED: 26 Nov 48 Belgium
ARTICLES: 12 LANGUAGE: English. French.
HEADNOTE: ECONOMIC COOPERATION
TOPIC: Direct Aid
CONCEPTS: Definition of terms. Territorial applica
　tion. General provisions. Guarantees and safe-
　guards. Treaty implementation. Annex or appen-
　dix reference. Tourism. Privileges and immuni-
　ties. Conformity with municipal law. General
　cooperation. Exchange of information and docu-
　ments. Personnel. Public information. Existing
　tribunals. Accounting procedures. Funding pro-
　cedures. Local currency. Claims and settle-
　ments. Domestic obligation. Economic assis-
　tance. Aid missions. Relief supplies. Procure-
　ment. Access to materials. Paragraph 2, Article
　36.
INTL ORGS: International Court of Justice. Orga-
　nization for Economic Co-operation and Devel-
　opment.
TREATY REF: EEC CONV. 16APR48; 1UNTS9.
PROCEDURE: Amendment. Duration. Ratification.
　Registration. Termination.
PARTIES:
　Belgium
　USA (United States)
　　　　　　　ANNEX
31 UNTS 485. Belgium. Correction 22 Nov 48.
　Force 29 Nov 48.
31 UNTS 485. USA (United States). Correction
　29 Nov 48. Force 29 Nov 48.
76 UNTS 250. Belgium. Amendment 29 Jun 50.
　Force 29 Jun 50.
76 UNTS 250. USA (United States). Amendment
　29 Jun 50. Force 29 Jun 50.
140 UNTS 428. Belgium. Amendment 10 Sep 51.
　Force 10 Sep 51.
140 UNTS 428. USA (United States). Amendment
　10 Sep 51. Force 10 Sep 51.
207 UNTS 316. USA (United States). Amendment
　11 Dec 52. Force 5 Mar 53.
207 UNTS 316. Belgium. Amendment 5 Mar 53.
　Force 5 Mar 53.

100310　　Bilateral Exchange　　**19 UNTS 159**
SIGNED: 7 Jan 46　　　　　FORCE: 7 Jan 46
REGISTERED: 30 Nov 48 Belgium
ARTICLES: 4 LANGUAGE: French. Portuguese.
HEADNOTE: ECONOMIC RELATIONS
TOPIC: Finance
CONCEPTS: Banking. Payment schedules.
PARTIES:
　Belgium
　Portugal

100311　　Bilateral Agreement　　**20 UNTS 3**
SIGNED: 6 Mar 46　　　　　FORCE: 6 Mar 46
REGISTERED: 1 Dec 48 Canada
ARTICLES: 7 LANGUAGE: English.
HEADNOTE: SETTLEMENT WAR CLAIMS
TOPIC: Reparations
CONCEPTS: Lump sum settlements. Post-war
　claims settlement.
PARTIES:
　Canada
　UK Great Britain

100312　　Bilateral Agreement　　**20 UNTS 13**
SIGNED: 6 Mar 46　　　　　FORCE: 30 May 46
REGISTERED: 1 Dec 48 Canada
ARTICLES: 9 LANGUAGE: English.
HEADNOTE: FINANCE
TOPIC: Finance
CONCEPTS: General cooperation. General trade.
　Import quotas. Balance of payments. Exchange
　rates and regulations. Fees and exemptions.
　Funding procedures. Interest rates. Payment
　schedules. Loan and credit. Credit provisions.
　Terms of loan.
INTL ORGS: International Monetary Fund.

PARTIES:
　Canada
　UK Great Britain
　　　　　　　ANNEX
316 UNTS 272. Canada. Amendment 6 Mar 57.
　Force 29 Apr 57.
316 UNTS 272. UK Great Britain. Amendment
　6 Mar 57. Force 29 Apr 57.

100313　　Bilateral Exchange　　**20 UNTS 33**
SIGNED: 7 Jun 48　　　　　FORCE: 7 Jun 48
REGISTERED: 7 Dec 48 Belgium
ARTICLES: 2 LANGUAGE: English. French.
HEADNOTE: COMPENSATION WAR DAMAGES
TOPIC: Reparations
CONCEPTS: Definition of terms. Time limit. Com-
　pensation. National treatment. Loss and/or dam-
　age. Post-war claims settlement.
PARTIES:
　Belgium
　UK Great Britain

100314　　Bilateral Agreement　　**20 UNTS 43**
SIGNED: 28 Jun 48　　　　　FORCE: 28 Jun 48
REGISTERED: 9 Dec 48 USA (United States)
ARTICLES: 12 LANGUAGE: English. Italian.
HEADNOTE: ECONOMIC COOPERATION
TOPIC: Direct Aid
CONCEPTS: Definition of terms. General provi-
　sions. Guarantees and safeguards. Treaty imple-
　mentation. Annex or appendix reference. Tour-
　ism. Privileges and immunities. Conformity with
　municipal law. General cooperation. Exchange
　of information and documents. Personnel. Public
　information. Accounting procedures. Funding
　procedures. Local currency. Claims and settle-
　ments. Commodities and services. Domestic obli-
　gation. Economic assistance. Aid missions. Re-
　lief supplies. Procurement. Access to materials.
　Paragraph 2, Article 36.
INTL ORGS: International Court of Justice. Interna-
　tional Monetary Fund. Organization for Eco-
　nomic Co-operation and Development. United
　Nations.
TREATY REF: EEC CONV. 16APR48; 1UNTS9.
PROCEDURE: Amendment. Duration. Registration.
　Termination.
PARTIES:
　Italy
　USA (United States)
　　　　　　　ANNEX
55 UNTS 318. USA (United States). Amendment
　28 Sep 48. Force 2 Oct 48.
55 UNTS 318. Italy. Amendment 2 Oct 48. Force
　2 Oct 48.
79 UNTS 274. USA (United States). Amendment
　7 Feb 50. Force 7 Feb 50.
79 UNTS 274. Italy. Amendment 7 Feb 50. Force
　7 Feb 50.
141 UNTS 362. USA (United States). Amendment
　21 May 51. Force 21 May 51.
141 UNTS 362. Italy. Amendment　21 May 51.
　Force 21 May 51.
200 UNTS 264. USA (United States). Amendment
　13 Jan 53. Force 13 Jan 53.
200 UNTS 264. Italy. Amendment　13 Jan 53.
　Force 13 Jan 53.

100315　　Bilateral Agreement　　**20 UNTS 91**
SIGNED: 2 Jul 48　　　　　FORCE: 2 Jul 48
REGISTERED: 9 Dec 48 USA (United States)
ARTICLES: 12 LANGUAGE: Dutch. English.
HEADNOTE: ECONOMIC COOPERATION
TOPIC: Direct Aid
CONCEPTS: Definition of terms. General provi-
　sions. Guarantees and safeguards. Treaty imple-
　mentation. Annex or appendix reference. Tour-
　ism. Privileges and immunities. General cooper-
　ation. Exchange of information and documents.
　Personnel. Public information. Existing tribunals.
　Accounting procedures. Funding procedures.
　Local currency. Claims and settlements. Com-
　modities and services. Domestic obligation. Eco-
　nomic assistance. Aid missions. Relief supplies.
　Procurement. Access to materials. Paragraph 2,
　Article 36.
INTL ORGS: International Court of Justice. Interna-
　tional Monetary Fund. Organization for Eco-
　nomic Co-operation and Development. United
　Nations.
TREATY REF: EEC CONV. 16APR48; 1UNTS9.

PROCEDURE: Amendment. Duration. Registration.
Termination.
PARTIES:
Netherlands
USA (United States)
ANNEX
93 UNTS 361. USA (United States). Amendment
16 Jan 50. Force 2 Feb 50.
93 UNTS 361. Netherlands. Amendment
2 Feb 50. Force 2 Feb 50.
141 UNTS 368. USA (United States). Amendment
7 Mar 51. Force 3 Apr 51.
141 UNTS 368. Netherlands. Amendment
3 Apr 51. Force 3 Apr 51.
173 UNTS 372. USA (United States). Amendment
8 Jan 52. Force 8 Jan 52.
173 UNTS 372. Netherlands. Amendment
8 Jan 52. Force 8 Jan 52.
173 UNTS 378. USA (United States). Supplementation 24 Sep 53. Force 7 Oct 52.
173 UNTS 378. Netherlands. Supplementation
7 Oct 52. Force 7 Oct 52.
173 UNTS 382. USA (United States). Amendment
28 Nov 52. Force 28 Nov 52.
173 UNTS 382. Netherlands. Amendment
28 Nov 52. Force 28 Nov 52.

100316 Bilateral Agreement **20 UNTS 141**
SIGNED: 3 Jul 48 FORCE: 3 Jul 48
REGISTERED: 9 Dec 48 USA (United States)
ARTICLES: 12 LANGUAGE: English. Icelandic.
HEADNOTE: ECONOMIC COOPERATION
TOPIC: Direct Aid
CONCEPTS: Definition of terms. General provisions. Guarantees and safeguards. Treaty implementation. Annex or appendix reference. Tourism. Privileges and immunities. Conformity with
municipal law. General cooperation. Exchange
of information and documents. Personnel. Public
information. Existing tribunals. Accounting pro-
cedures. Funding procedures. Local currency.
Claims and settlements. Domestic obligation.
Economic assistance. Aid missions. Procurement. Access to materials. Paragraph 2, Article
36.
INTL ORGS: International Court of Justice. International Monetary Fund. Organization for Economic Co-operation and Development. United
Nations.
TREATY REF: EEC CONV. 16APR48; 1UNTS9.
PROCEDURE: Amendment. Duration. Registration.
Termination.
PARTIES:
Iceland
USA (United States)
ANNEX
79 UNTS 280. Iceland. Amendment 7 Feb 50.
Force 7 Feb 50.
79 UNTS 280. USA (United States). Amendment
7 Feb 50. Force 7 Feb 50.
148 UNTS 398. Iceland. Amendment 23 Feb 51.
Force 23 Feb 51.
148 UNTS 398. USA (United States). Amendment
23 Feb 51. Force 23 Feb 51.
223 UNTS 316. USA (United States). Amendment
9 Oct 52. Force 1 Oct 53.
223 UNTS 316. Iceland. Amendment 1 Oct 53.
Force 1 Oct 53.

100317 Bilateral Agreement **20 UNTS 185**
SIGNED: 3 Jul 48 FORCE: 3 Jul 48
REGISTERED: 9 Dec 48 USA (United States)
ARTICLES: 12 LANGUAGE: English. Norwegian.
HEADNOTE: ECONOMIC COOPERATION
TOPIC: Direct Aid
CONCEPTS: Definition of terms. General provisions. Guarantees and safeguards. Treaty implementation. Annex or appendix reference. Tourism. Privileges and immunities. Conformity with
municipal law. General cooperation. Exchange
of information and documents. Personnel. Public
information. Existing tribunals. Accounting procedures. Funding procedures. Local currency.
Claims and settlements. Domestic obligation.
Economic assistance. Aid missions. Procurement. Access to materials. Paragraph 2, Article
36.
INTL ORGS: International Court of Justice. International Monetary Fund. Organization for Economic Co-operation and Development. United
Nations.
TREATY REF: EEC CONV. 16APR48; 1UNTS9.

PROCEDURE: Amendment. Duration. Registration.
Termination.
PARTIES:
Norway
USA (United States)
ANNEX
79 UNTS 284. Norway. Amendment 17 Jan 50.
Force 17 Jan 50.
79 UNTS 284. USA (United States). Amendment
17 Jan 50. Force 17 Jan 50.
148 UNTS 402. Norway. Amendment 5 Jul 51.
Force 5 Jul 51.
148 UNTS 402. USA (United States). Amendment
5 Jul 51. Force 5 Jul 51.
198 UNTS 366. Norway. Amendment 8 Jan 53.
Force 8 Jan 53.
198 UNTS 366. USA (United States). Amendment
8 Jan 53. Force 8 Jan 53.

100318 Multilateral Protocol **20 UNTS 229**
SIGNED: 9 Dec 48 FORCE: 9 Dec 48
REGISTERED: 9 Dec 48 United Nations
ARTICLES: 7 LANGUAGE: Chinese. English.
French. Russian. Spanish.
HEADNOTE: ECONOMIC STATISTICS
TOPIC: Scientific Project
CONCEPTS: Annex or appendix reference. Annex
type material. Previous treaty extension. General
cooperation. Informational records. Research
and scientific projects. Research and develop-
ment.
INTL ORGS: United Nations.
TREATY REF: 110LTS171; 117LTS330.
PROCEDURE: Amendment. Accession.
PARTIES:
Australia SIGNED: 9 Dec 48 FORCE: 9 Dec 48
Burma SIGNED: 9 Dec 48
Canada SIGNED: 9 Dec 48 FORCE: 9 Dec 48
Denmark SIGNED: 9 Dec 48
United Arab Rep SIGNED: 9 Dec 48 FORCE:
9 Dec 48
France SIGNED: 9 Dec 48
Greece SIGNED: 9 Dec 48
India SIGNED: 9 Dec 48
Netherlands SIGNED: 9 Dec 48
Norway SIGNED: 9 Dec 48
South Africa SIGNED: 10 Dec 48
Sweden SIGNED: 9 Dec 48 FORCE: 9 Dec 48
Switzerland SIGNED: 9 Oct 49
UK Great Britain SIGNED: 9 Dec 48 FORCE:
9 Dec 48
ANNEX
21 UNTS 336. South Africa. Signature without
Reservation as to Approval 10 Dec 48.
24 UNTS 321. France. Acceptance 11 Jan 49.
34 UNTS 424. Finland. Acceptance 17 Aug 49.
42 UNTS 359. Denmark. Acceptance 27 Sep 49.
44 UNTS 340. Austria. Acceptance 10 Nov 49.
51 UNTS 329. Netherlands. Acceptance
13 Apr 50.
122 UNTS 334. Pakistan. Signature without Reservation as to Approval 3 Mar 53.
122 UNTS 334. Greece. Acceptance 9 Oct 50.
122 UNTS 334. Ireland. Acceptance 28 Feb 52.
150 UNTS 355. Japan. Acceptance 2 Dec 52.

100319 Multilateral Instrument **20 UNTS 259**
SIGNED: 26 Dec 45 FORCE: 27 Dec 45
REGISTERED: 10 Dec 48 USA (United States)
ARTICLES: 7 LANGUAGE: English. Russian.
HEADNOTE: PREPARATION PEACE TREATIES
TOPIC: Peace/Disarmament
CONCEPTS: Annex or appendix reference. Gen-
eral cooperation. Armistice and peace.
INTL ORGS: United Nations. Special Commission.
PARTIES:
UK Great Britain SIGNED: 27 Dec 45 FORCE:
27 Dec 45
USA (United States) SIGNED: 27 Dec 45 FORCE:
27 Dec 45
USSR (Soviet Union) SIGNED: 27 Dec 45 FORCE:
27 Dec 45

100320 Bilateral Exchange **21 UNTS 3**
SIGNED: 27 Sep 46 FORCE: 27 Sep 46
REGISTERED: 10 Dec 48 USA (United States)
ARTICLES: 2 LANGUAGE: English.
HEADNOTE: PATENT RIGHTS
TOPIC: Patents/Copyrights
CONCEPTS: Detailed regulations. Licenses and
permits. Laws and formalities.

PARTIES:
Canada
USA (United States)

100321 Bilateral Exchange **21 UNTS 13**
SIGNED: 22 Oct 46 FORCE: 22 Oct 46
REGISTERED: 10 Dec 48 USA (United States)
ARTICLES: 2 LANGUAGE: English. Spanish.
HEADNOTE: FISHERIES MISSION
TOPIC: Non-IBRD Project
CONCEPTS: Annex type material. Previous treaty
extension. Non-bank projects. Ocean resources.
TREATY REF: USA TIAS 1624 P.1.
PARTIES:
Mexico
USA (United States)
ANNEX
80 UNTS 306. Mexico. Prolongation 6 Oct 48.
Force 6 Oct 48.
80 UNTS 306. USA (United States). Prolongation
15 Sep 48. Force 6 Oct 48.

100322 Bilateral Exchange **21 UNTS 21**
SIGNED: 29 Oct 47 FORCE: 29 Oct 47
REGISTERED: 10 Dec 48 USA (United States)
ARTICLES: 2 LANGUAGE: English. Spanish.
HEADNOTE: EXCHANGE OFFICIAL PUBLICA-
TIONS
TOPIC: Admin Cooperation
CONCEPTS: Exchange of official publications. Ex-
change of information and documents.
PARTIES:
Ecuador
USA (United States)

100323 Bilateral Agreement **21 UNTS 29**
SIGNED: 2 Jul 48 FORCE: 2 Jul 48
REGISTERED: 10 Dec 48 USA (United States)
ARTICLES: 11 LANGUAGE: English. German.
HEADNOTE: ECONOMIC COOPERATION
TOPIC: Direct Aid
CONCEPTS: Definition of terms. General provi-
sions. Guarantees and safeguards. Treaty implementation. Annex or appendix reference. Tourism. Privileges and immunities. Conformity with
municipal law. General cooperation. Exchange
of information and documents. Personnel. Public
information. Existing tribunals. Accounting pro-
cedures. Funding procedures. Local currency.
Claims and settlements. Domestic obligation.
Economic assistance. Aid missions. Relief supplies. Procurement. Paragraph 2, Article 36.
INTL ORGS: International Court of Justice. International Monetary Fund. Organization for Economic Co-operation and Development.
TREATY REF: EEC CONV. 16APR48; TAIS 1631;
TIAS 1632.
PROCEDURE: Amendment. Duration. Registration.
Termination.
PARTIES:
Austria
USA (United States)
ANNEX
79 UNTS 288. USA (United States). Amendment
30 Nov 49. Force 20 Feb 50.
79 UNTS 288. Austria. Amendment 20 Feb 50.
Force 20 Feb 50.
141 UNTS 372. USA (United States). Amendment
16 Jan 51. Force 7 Mar 51.
141 UNTS 372. Austria. Amendment 7 Mar 51.
Force 7 Mar 51.
181 UNTS 326. USA (United States). Amendment
1 Jul 52. Force 31 Jul 52.
181 UNTS 326. Austria. Amendment 31 Jul 52.
Force 31 Jul 52.
185 UNTS 322. USA (United States). Amendment
15 Oct 52. Force 6 Dec 52.
185 UNTS 322. Austria. Amendment 6 Dec 52.
Force 6 Dec 52.
336 UNTS 336. USA (United States). Amendment
23 Oct 58. Force 23 Oct 58.
336 UNTS 336. Austria. Amendment 23 Oct 58.
Force 23 Oct 58.

100324 Multilateral Treaty **21 UNTS 77**
SIGNED: 2 Sep 47 FORCE: 3 Dec 48
REGISTERED: 20 Dec 48 OAS (Am States)
ARTICLES: 26 LANGUAGE: English. French. Span-
ish. Portuguese.
HEADNOTE: RECIPROCAL ASSISTANCE

TOPIC: General Military
CONCEPTS: Definition of terms. Detailed regulations. Exceptions and exemptions. Treaty violation. Friendship and amity. Non-prejudice to UN charter. General cooperation. Procedure. Existing tribunals. Defense and security.
INTL ORGS: Organization of American States. United Nations.
PROCEDURE: Denunciation. Duration. Future Procedures Contemplated. Ratification.
PARTIES:
Argentina SIGNED: 2 Sep 47
Bolivia SIGNED: 2 Sep 47
Brazil SIGNED: 2 Sep 47 RATIFIED: 20 Mar 48 FORCE: 3 Dec 48
Chile SIGNED: 2 Sep 47
Colombia SIGNED: 2 Sep 47 RATIFIED: 3 Feb 48 FORCE: 3 Dec 48
Costa Rica SIGNED: 2 Sep 47 RATIFIED: 3 Dec 48 FORCE: 3 Dec 48
Cuba SIGNED: 2 Sep 47 RATIFIED: 9 Dec 48 FORCE: 9 Dec 48
Dominican Republic SIGNED: 2 Sep 47 RATIFIED: 21 Nov 47 FORCE: 3 Dec 48
El Salvador SIGNED: 2 Sep 47 RATIFIED: 15 Mar 48 FORCE: 3 Dec 48
Guatemala SIGNED: 2 Sep 47
Haiti SIGNED: 2 Sep 47 RATIFIED: 25 Mar 48 FORCE: 3 Dec 48
Honduras SIGNED: 2 Sep 47 RATIFIED: 5 Feb 48 FORCE: 3 Dec 48
Mexico SIGNED: 2 Sep 47 RATIFIED: 23 Nov 48 FORCE: 3 Dec 48
Nicaragua RATIFIED: 12 Nov 48 FORCE: 3 Dec 48
Panama SIGNED: 2 Sep 47 RATIFIED: 12 Jan 48 FORCE: 3 Dec 48
Paraguay SIGNED: 2 Sep 47 RATIFIED: 28 Jul 48 FORCE: 3 Dec 48
Peru SIGNED: 2 Sep 47
USA (United States) SIGNED: 2 Sep 47 RATIFIED: 30 Dec 47 FORCE: 3 Dec 48
Uruguay SIGNED: 2 Sep 47 RATIFIED: 28 Sep 48 FORCE: 3 Dec 48
Venezuela SIGNED: 2 Sep 47 RATIFIED: 4 Oct 48 FORCE: 3 Dec 48
ANNEX
82 UNTS 330. Ecuador. Signature 10 Nov 49.
82 UNTS 330. Argentina. Ratification 21 Aug 50.
82 UNTS 330. Bolivia. Ratification 26 Sep 50.
82 UNTS 330. Peru. Ratification 25 Oct 50.
82 UNTS 330. Ecuador. Ratification 7 Nov 50.
209 UNTS 330. Guatemala. Qualified Ratification 6 Apr 55.

100325 Bilateral Exchange **22 UNTS 3**
SIGNED: 1 Jul 48 FORCE: 1 Jul 48
REGISTERED: 21 Dec 48 Australia
ARTICLES: 2 LANGUAGE: English.
HEADNOTE: WOOL
TOPIC: Direct Aid
CONCEPTS: General cooperation. Public information. Title and deeds. Indemnities and reimbursements. Financial programs. Commodities and services. General aid. Use restrictions. Distribution.
PARTIES:
Australia
Hungary

100326 Bilateral Exchange **22 UNTS 11**
SIGNED: 8 Jul 48 FORCE: 8 Jul 48
REGISTERED: 21 Dec 48 Australia
ARTICLES: 2 LANGUAGE: English.
HEADNOTE: WOOL
TOPIC: Direct Aid
CONCEPTS: General cooperation. Public information. Title and deeds. Indemnities and reimbursements. Financial programs. Commodities and services. General aid. Use restrictions. Distribution.
PARTIES:
Australia
Italy

100327 Bilateral Exchange **22 UNTS 17**
SIGNED: 9 Jul 48 FORCE: 9 Jul 48
REGISTERED: 21 Dec 48 Australia
ARTICLES: 2 LANGUAGE: English.
HEADNOTE: WOOL
TOPIC: Direct Aid

CONCEPTS: General cooperation. Public information. Title and deeds. Indemnities and reimbursements. Financial programs. Commodities and services. General aid. Use restrictions. Distribution.
PARTIES:
Australia
Yugoslavia

100328 Bilateral Exchange **22 UNTS 25**
SIGNED: 19 Jul 48 FORCE: 19 Jul 48
REGISTERED: 21 Dec 48 Australia.
ARTICLES: 2 LANGUAGE: English.
HEADNOTE: WOOL
TOPIC: Direct Aid
CONCEPTS: General cooperation. Public information. Title and deeds. Indemnities and reimbursements. Financial programs. Commodities and services. General aid. Use restrictions. Distribution.
PARTIES:
Australia
Austria

100329 Bilateral Exchange **22 UNTS 33**
SIGNED: 1 Jul 48 FORCE: 1 Jul 48
REGISTERED: 21 Dec 48 Australia
ARTICLES: 2 LANGUAGE: English.
HEADNOTE: RELIEF SUPPLIES
TOPIC: Direct Aid
CONCEPTS: Annex or appendix reference. General cooperation. Public information. Title and deeds. Indemnities and reimbursements. Financial programs. Use restrictions. Relief supplies. Procurement.
PARTIES:
Australia
Greece

100330 Bilateral Exchange **22 UNTS 43**
SIGNED: 8 Oct 48 FORCE: 8 Oct 48
REGISTERED: 21 Dec 48 Australia
ARTICLES: 2 LANGUAGE: English.
HEADNOTE: RELEASE ASSETS
TOPIC: Claims and Debts
CONCEPTS: Definition of terms. Exceptions and exemptions. Conformity with municipal law. General cooperation. Legal protection and assistance. Immovable property. General property. Culture. Banking. Bonds. Currency. Fees and exemptions. Payment schedules. Assets. Liens. Assets transfer. Enemy financial interests.
PARTIES:
Australia
Denmark

100331 Bilateral Agreement **22 UNTS 55**
SIGNED: 14 Nov 46 FORCE: 14 Nov 48
REGISTERED: 23 Dec 48 USA (United States)
ARTICLES: 13 LANGUAGE: English.
HEADNOTE: AIR SERVICES
TOPIC: Air Transport
CONCEPTS: Definition of terms. Detailed regulations. Annex or appendix reference. Friendship and amity. Conformity with municipal law. General cooperation. Exchange of information and documents. Domestic legislation. Procedure. Existing tribunals. Fees and exemptions. Non-interest rates and fees. Most favored nation clause. National treatment. Customs exemptions. Routes and logistics. Permit designation. Airport facilities. Conditions of airlines operating permission. Operating authorizations and regulations.
INTL ORGS: International Civil Aviation Organization.
TREATY REF: US EXEC.AGREE.SERIES 469,487.
PROCEDURE: Amendment. Future Procedures Contemplated. Registration. Termination.
PARTIES:
India
USA (United States)

100332 Bilateral Agreement **22 UNTS 87**
SIGNED: 20 Dec 46 FORCE: 20 Dec 46
REGISTERED: 23 Dec 48 USA (United States)
ARTICLES: 13 LANGUAGE: Chinese. English.
HEADNOTE: AIR TRANSPORT
TOPIC: Air Transport

CONCEPTS: Definition of terms. Exceptions and exemptions. Annex or appendix reference. Non-prejudice to third party. Conformity with municipal law. Licenses and permits. Recognition of legal documents. Use of facilities. Procedure. Existing tribunals. Fees and exemptions. Most favored nation clause. National treatment. Customs exemptions. Competency certificate. Routes and logistics. Navigational conditions. Permit designation. Air transport. Airport facilities. Airworthiness certificates. Conditions of airlines operating permission. Operating authorizations and regulations. Licenses and certificates of nationality.
INTL ORGS: International Civil Aviation Organization.
TREATY REF: EAS469.
PROCEDURE: Duration. Registration. Renewal or Revival. Termination.
PARTIES:
Taiwan
USA (United States)
ANNEX
133 UNTS 306. USA (United States). Extension and Amendment 1 Dec 50. Force 20 Dec 50.
133 UNTS 306. Taiwan. Extension and Amendment 19 Dec 50. Force 20 Dec 50.
269 UNTS 264. USA (United States). Amendment 15 Apr 55. Force 15 Apr 55.
269 UNTS 264. Taiwan. Amendment 7 Feb 55. Force 15 Apr 55.

100333 Bilateral Agreement **22 UNTS 119**
SIGNED: 8 Jan 47 FORCE: 24 Apr 47
REGISTERED: 23 Dec 48 USA (United States)
ARTICLES: 14 LANGUAGE: English. Spanish.
HEADNOTE: COMMERCIAL AIR TRANSPORT
TOPIC: Air Transport
CONCEPTS: Definition of terms. Exceptions and exemptions. Annex or appendix reference. Non-prejudice to third party. Conformity with municipal law. Licenses and permits. Recognition of legal documents. Use of facilities. Procedure. Existing tribunals. Competence of tribunal. Fees and exemptions. Most favored nation clause. National treatment. Customs exemptions. Competency certificate. Routes and logistics. Navigational conditions. Permit designation. Air transport. Airport facilities. Airworthiness certificates. Conditions of airlines operating permission. Operating authorizations and regulations. Licenses and certificates of nationality.
INTL ORGS: International Civil Aviation Organization.
TREATY REF: INTER CIVIL AVIA.CONF.INOV1944.
PROCEDURE: Amendment. Future Procedures Contemplated. Ratification. Registration. Termination.
PARTIES:
Ecuador
USA (United States)
ANNEX
133 UNTS 312. USA (United States). Amendment 3 Jan 51. Force 10 Jan 51.
133 UNTS 312. Ecuador. Amendment 10 Jan 51. Force 10 Jan 51.

100334 Bilateral Agreement **22 UNTS 141**
SIGNED: 25 Jun 47 FORCE: 25 Jun 47
REGISTERED: 23 Dec 48 USA (United States)
ARTICLES: 10 LANGUAGE: English. German.
HEADNOTE: RELIEF ASSISTANCE
TOPIC: Direct Aid
CONCEPTS: Privileges and immunities. Conformity with municipal law. Exchange of information and documents. Inspection and observation. Public information. Accounting procedures. Funding procedures. Local currency. Tax exemptions. Customs exemptions. Domestic obligation. Aid missions. Relief supplies. Withdrawal conditions. Procurement. Distribution. Press and wire services.
PROCEDURE: Duration. Future Procedures Contemplated.
PARTIES:
Austria
USA (United States)

100335 Bilateral Exchange **22 UNTS 165**
SIGNED: 4 Jul 47 FORCE: 4 Jul 47
REGISTERED: 23 Dec 48 USA (United States)

ARTICLES: 2 LANGUAGE: English. French.
HEADNOTE: COMMERCE PAYMENTS
TOPIC: Other Ad Hoc
CONCEPTS: Detailed regulations. General cooperation. Exchange of information and documents. General trade. Accounting procedures. Banking. Interest rates. Payment schedules. Local currency.
TREATY REF: 4UNTS179; 15UNTS257.
PROCEDURE: Duration. Renewal or Revival. Termination.
PARTIES:
Haiti
USA (United States)

100336 Bilateral Agreement **22 UNTS 173**
SIGNED: 4 Jul 47　　　　FORCE: 4 Jul 47
REGISTERED: 23 Dec 48 USA (United States)
ARTICLES: 10 LANGUAGE: English. Italian.
HEADNOTE: RELIEF ASSISTANCE
TOPIC: Direct Aid
CONCEPTS: Privileges and immunities. Conformity with municipal law. Exchange of information and documents. Inspection and observation. Public information. Accounting procedures. Funding procedures. Local currency. Tax exemptions. Customs exemptions. Domestic obligation. Aid missions. Relief supplies. Withdrawal conditions. Procurement. Distribution. Press and wire services.
PARTIES:
Italy
USA (United States)

100337 Bilateral Agreement **22 UNTS 203**
SIGNED: 22 Dec 47　　　　FORCE: 1 Jan 48
REGISTERED: 23 Dec 48 Norway
ARTICLES: 7 LANGUAGE: Norwegian. Swedish.
HEADNOTE: TRANSFER MEMBERS SICK FUNDS
TOPIC: Non-ILO Labor
CONCEPTS: Detailed regulations. Conformity with municipal law. General cooperation. Recognition and enforcement of legal decisions. Non-ILO labor relations. Sickness and invalidity insurance. Payment schedules. Assets transfer.
PROCEDURE: Denunciation.
PARTIES:
Norway
Sweden

100338 Bilateral Agreement **22 UNTS 217**
SIGNED: 29 Jun 48　　　　FORCE: 2 Jul 48
REGISTERED: 24 Dec 48 USA (United States)
ARTICLES: 12 LANGUAGE: Danish. English.
HEADNOTE: ECONOMIC COOPERATION
TOPIC: Direct Aid
CONCEPTS: Definition of terms. Territorial application. General provisions. Guarantees and safeguards. Treaty implementation. Annex or appendix reference. Tourism. Privileges and immunities. Conformity with municipal law. General cooperation. Exchange of information and documents. Personnel. Public information. Existing tribunals. Accounting procedures. Funding procedures. Local currency. Claims and settlements. Commodities and services. Domestic obligation. Economic assistance. Aid missions. Procurement. Access to materials. Paragraph 2, Article 36.
INTL ORGS: International Court of Justice. International Monetary Fund. Organization for Economic Co-operation and Development.
TREATY REF: EEC CONV. 16APR48; 1UNTS9.
PROCEDURE: Amendment. Duration. Ratification. Registration. Termination.
PARTIES:
Denmark
USA (United States)
ANNEX
55 UNTS 322. Denmark. Amendment 4 Nov 48. Force 18 Nov 48.
55 UNTS 322. USA (United States). Amendment 18 Nov 48. Force 18 Nov 48.
79 UNTS 294. Denmark. Amendment 7 Feb 50. Force 7 Feb 50.
79 UNTS 294. USA (United States). Amendment 7 Feb 50. Force 7 Feb 50.
132 UNTS 380. USA (United States). Amendment 2 Feb 51. Force 9 Feb 51.
132 UNTS 380. Denmark. Amendment 9 Feb 51. Force 9 Feb 51.

184 UNTS 327. USA (United States). Amendment 24 Nov 52. Force 24 Nov 52.
184 UNTS 327. Denmark. Amendment 24 Nov 52. Force 24 Nov 52.

100339 Bilateral Agreement **22 UNTS 263**
SIGNED: 6 Jul 48　　　　FORCE: 6 Jul 48
REGISTERED: 24 Dec 48 USA (United States)
ARTICLES: 13 LANGUAGE: English.
HEADNOTE: ECONOMIC COOPERATION
TOPIC: Direct Aid
CONCEPTS: Definition of terms. Territorial application. Guarantees and safeguards. Treaty implementation. Annex or appendix reference. Tourism. Privileges and immunities. Conformity with municipal law. General cooperation. Exchange of information and documents. Personnel. Public information. Existing tribunals. Accounting procedures. Funding procedures. Local currency. Claims and settlements. Domestic obligation. Economic assistance. Aid missions. Relief supplies. Procurement. Access to materials. Paragraph 2, Article 36.
INTL ORGS: International Bank for Reconstruction and Development. International Court of Justice. International Monetary Fund. Organization for Economic Co-operation and Development.
TREATY REF: EEC CONV. 16APR48; 1UNTS9.
PROCEDURE: Amendment. Duration. Registration. Termination.
PARTIES:
UK Great Britain
USA (United States)
ANNEX
86 UNTS 304. USA (United States). Amendment 3 Jan 50. Force 3 Jan 50.
86 UNTS 304. UK Great Britain. Amendment 3 Jan 50. Force 3 Jan 50.
86 UNTS 308. UK Great Britain. Southern Rhodesia. Force 17 Feb 50.
86 UNTS 308. UK Great Britain. Aden Colony. Force 17 Feb 50.
86 UNTS 308. UK Great Britain. British Honduras. Force 17 Feb 50.
86 UNTS 308. UK Great Britain. Brunei. Force 17 Feb 50.
86 UNTS 308. UK Great Britain. Falkland Islands. Force 17 Feb 50.
86 UNTS 308. UK Great Britain. Gibralter. Force 17 Feb 50.
86 UNTS 308. UK Great Britain. Northern Rhodesia. Force 17 Feb 50.
86 UNTS 308. UK Great Britain. Sarawak. Force 17 Feb 50.
86 UNTS 308. UK Great Britain. Seychelles. Force 17 Feb 50.
86 UNTS 308. UK Great Britain. Sierra Leone. Force 17 Feb 50.
86 UNTS 308. UK Great Britain. Trinidad. Force 17 Feb 50.
86 UNTS 308. UK Great Britain. Tanganyika. Force 17 Feb 50.
86 UNTS 308. UK Great Britain. Uganda. Force 17 Feb 50.
86 UNTS 308. UK Great Britain. Windward Islands. Force 17 Feb 50.
86 UNTS 308. UK Great Britain. Cyprus. Force 17 Feb 50.
86 UNTS 308. UK Great Britain. Gold Coast. Force 17 Feb 50.
86 UNTS 308. UK Great Britain. Leeward Islands. Force 17 Feb 50.
86 UNTS 308. UK Great Britain. Mauritius. Force 17 Feb 50.
86 UNTS 308. UK Great Britain. Malta. Force 17 Feb 50.
86 UNTS 308. UK Great Britain. Nyasaland. Force 17 Feb 50.
87 UNTS 384. UK Great Britain. Leeward Islands.
87 UNTS 384. UK Great Britain. North Borneo.
87 UNTS 384. UK Great Britain. Trinidad.
87 UNTS 384. UK Great Britain. Southern Rhodesia.
87 UNTS 384. UK Great Britain. Barbados.
87 UNTS 384. UK Great Britain. Falkland Islands.
87 UNTS 384. UK Great Britain. Fed of Malaya.
87 UNTS 384. UK Great Britain. Northern Rhodesia.
87 UNTS 384. UK Great Britain. Sarawak.
87 UNTS 384. UK Great Britain. British Honduras.
87 UNTS 384. UK Great Britain. Brunei.
87 UNTS 384. UK Great Britain. British Guiana.

87 UNTS 384. UK Great Britain. British Somaliland.
87 UNTS 384. UK Great Britain. Jamaica.
87 UNTS 386. UK Great Britain. British Guiana.
87 UNTS 386. UK Great Britain. Fiji Islands.
87 UNTS 386. UK Great Britain. Gambia.
87 UNTS 386. UK Great Britain. Hong Kong.
87 UNTS 386. UK Great Britain. Fed of Malaya.
87 UNTS 386. UK Great Britain. Nigeria.
87 UNTS 386. UK Great Britain. North Borneo.
87 UNTS 386. UK Great Britain. Singapore.
87 UNTS 386. UK Great Britain. British Somaliland.
87 UNTS 386. UK Great Britain. Zanzibar.
87 UNTS 386. UK Great Britain. Bahamas.
87 UNTS 386. UK Great Britain. Barbados.
87 UNTS 386. UK Great Britain. Kenya.
87 UNTS 386. UK Great Britain. W Pacif Hi Command.
87 UNTS 386. UK Great Britain. Aden.
87 UNTS 386. UK Great Britain. Jamaica.
87 UNTS 387. UK Great Britain. St. Helena.
99 UNTS 308. USA (United States). Amendment 25 May 51. Force 25 May 51.
99 UNTS 308. UK Great Britain. Amendment 25 May 51. Force 25 May 51.
126 UNTS 348. UK Great Britain. Aden.
126 UNTS 348. UK Great Britain. British Guiana.
126 UNTS 348. UK Great Britain. British Honduras.
126 UNTS 348. UK Great Britain. Cyprus.
126 UNTS 348. UK Great Britain. Fed of Malaya.
126 UNTS 348. UK Great Britain. Nigeria.
126 UNTS 348. UK Great Britain. North Borneo.
126 UNTS 348. UK Great Britain. Sarawak.
126 UNTS 348. UK Great Britain. Singapore.
126 UNTS 348. UK Great Britain. British Somaliland.
126 UNTS 348. UK Great Britain. Tanganyika.
126 UNTS 348. UK Great Britain. Trinidad.
126 UNTS 348. UK Great Britain. Uganda.
126 UNTS 348. UK Great Britain. Zanzibar.
126 UNTS 348. UK Great Britain. Bahamas.
126 UNTS 348. UK Great Britain. Barbados.
126 UNTS 348. UK Great Britain. Brunei.
126 UNTS 348. UK Great Britain. Falkland Islands.
126 UNTS 348. UK Great Britain. Gambia.
126 UNTS 348. UK Great Britain. Jamaica.
126 UNTS 348. UK Great Britain. Malta.
126 UNTS 348. UK Great Britain. Nyasaland.
126 UNTS 348. UK Great Britain. St. Helena.
126 UNTS 348. UK Great Britain. W Pacif Hi Command.
126 UNTS 348. UK Great Britain. Windward Islands.
126 UNTS 348. UK Great Britain. Seychelles.
126 UNTS 348. UK Great Britain. Sierra Leone.
126 UNTS 348. UK Great Britain. Northern Rhodesia.
126 UNTS 348. UK Great Britain. Fiji Islands.
126 UNTS 348. UK Great Britain. Gibralter.
126 UNTS 348. UK Great Britain. Gold Coast.
126 UNTS 348. UK Great Britain. Hong Kong.
126 UNTS 348. UK Great Britain. Kenya.
126 UNTS 348. UK Great Britain. Leeward Islands.
126 UNTS 348. UK Great Britain. Mauritius.
133 UNTS 316. UK Great Britain. Southern Rhodesia. Force 23 Nov 51.
172 UNTS 332. USA (United States). Amendment 25 Feb 53. Force 25 Feb 53.
172 UNTS 332. UK Great Britain. Amendment 25 Feb 53. Force 25 Feb 53.
266 UNTS 364. USA (United States). Acknowledgement 28 Feb 55. Force 28 Feb 55.
266 UNTS 364. UK Great Britain. Channel Islands. Force 28 Feb 55.
266 UNTS 364. UK Great Britain. Isle of Man. Force 28 Feb 55.
272 UNTS 246. UK Great Britain. Fed Rhod/Nyasaland. Force 22 Jul 57.
405 UNTS 288. USA (United States). Amendment 26 Jun 59. Force 20 Aug 59.
405 UNTS 288. UK Great Britain. Amendment 20 Aug 59. Force 20 Aug 59.

100340 Multilateral Agreement **23 UNTS 3**
SIGNED: 14 Jul 48　　　　FORCE: 14 Jul 48
REGISTERED: 24 Dec 48 USA (United States)
ARTICLES: 11 LANGUAGE: English.
HEADNOTE: ECONOMIC COOPERATION
TOPIC: Direct Aid

CONCEPTS: Definition of terms. General provisions. Guarantees and safeguards. Treaty implementation. Annex or appendix reference. Tourism. Privileges and immunities. Conformity with municipal law. General cooperation. Exchange of information and documents. Personnel. Public information. Accounting procedures. Funding procedures. Local currency. Domestic obligation. Economic assistance. Aid missions. Relief supplies. Procurement. Access to materials. Occupation regime.
INTL ORGS: Organization for Economic Co-operation and Development.
TREATY REF: EEC CONV. 16APR48.
PROCEDURE: Amendment. Duration. Registration. Termination.
PARTIES:
  USA (United States) SIGNED: 14 Jul 48 FORCE: 14 Jul 48
  British Occup Germ SIGNED: 14 Jul 48 FORCE: 14 Jul 48
  US Occup Germ SIGNED: 14 Jul 48 FORCE: 14 Jul 48

100341   Bilateral Exchange   **23 UNTS 35**
SIGNED: 19 Mar 47   FORCE: 12 Oct 48
REGISTERED: 24 Dec 48 Belgium
ARTICLES: 2 LANGUAGE: French.
HEADNOTE: NATIONALIZED CONFISCATED TRANSFERRED PROPERTY CONCERNS
TOPIC: Claims and Debts
CONCEPTS: Time limit. Expropriation. General property. Compensation. Interest rates. Payment schedules. Claims and settlements. Assets transfer. Most favored nation clause. National treatment.
PARTIES:
  Belgium
  Czechoslovakia

100342   Bilateral Agreement   **23 UNTS 43**
SIGNED: 2 Jul 48   FORCE: 3 Jul 48
REGISTERED: 24 Dec 48 USA (United States)
ARTICLES: 13 LANGUAGE: English. Greek.
HEADNOTE: ECONOMIC COOPERATION
TOPIC: Direct Aid
CONCEPTS: Definition of terms. General provisions. Guarantees and safeguards. Annex or appendix reference. Annex type material. Tourism. Privileges and immunities. Conformity with municipal law. General cooperation. Exchange of information and documents. Personnel. Public information. Existing tribunals. Accounting procedures. Exchange rates and regulations. Funding procedures. Local currency. Claims and settlements. Domestic obligation. Economic assistance. Aid missions. Relief supplies. Procurement. Access to materials. Paragraph 2, Article 36.
INTL ORGS: International Bank for Reconstruction and Development. International Court of Justice. Organization for Economic Co-operation and Development. United Nations.
TREATY REF: EEC CONV. 16APR48; 1UNTS9; USA-GREECE 20JUNE47.
PROCEDURE: Amendment. Duration. Ratification. Registration. Termination.
PARTIES:
  Greece
  USA (United States)
ANNEX
79 UNTS 298. Greece. Amendment 24 Dec 49. Force 24 Dec 49.
79 UNTS 298. USA (United States). Amendment 15 Dec 49. Force 24 Dec 49.
105 UNTS 304. South Africa. Ratification 10 Oct 51. Force 8 Jan 52.
132 UNTS 384. USA (United States). Amendment 6 Mar 51. Force 30 Mar 51.
132 UNTS 384. Greece. Amendment 30 Mar 51. Force 30 Mar 51.
225 UNTS 250. USA (United States). Amendment 14 Oct 52. Force 2 Dec 53.
225 UNTS 250. Greece. Amendment 2 Dec 53. Force 2 Dec 53.
476 UNTS 250. USA (United States). Supplementation 19 Apr 63. Force 19 Apr 63.
476 UNTS 250. Greece. Supplementation 19 Apr 63. Force 19 Apr 63.

100343   Bilateral Agreement   **23 UNTS 101**
SIGNED: 3 Jul 48   FORCE: 21 Jul 48
REGISTERED: 24 Dec 48 USA (United States)
ARTICLES: 11 LANGUAGE: English. Swedish.
HEADNOTE: ECONOMIC COOPERATION
TOPIC: Direct Aid
CONCEPTS: Definition of terms. General provisions. Guarantees and safeguards. Annex or appendix reference. Tourism. Privileges and immunities. Conformity with municipal law. General cooperation. Exchange of information and documents. Personnel. Public information. Existing tribunals. Claims and settlements. Domestic obligation. Economic assistance. Aid missions. Procurement. Access to materials. Paragraph 2, Article 36.
INTL ORGS: International Court of Justice. International Refugees Organization. Organization for Economic Co-operation and Development. United Nations.
TREATY REF: EEC CONV. 16APR48; 1UNTS9.
PROCEDURE: Amendment. Duration. Ratification. Registration. Termination.
PARTIES:
  Sweden
  USA (United States)
ANNEX
76 UNTS 254. USA (United States). Amendment 5 Jan 50. Force 17 Jan 50.
76 UNTS 254. Sweden. Amendment 17 Jan 50. Force 17 Jan 50.
185 UNTS 326. USA (United States). Amendment 8 Feb 51. Force 22 Feb 51.
185 UNTS 326. Sweden. Amendment 22 Feb 51. Force 22 Feb 51.

100344   Bilateral Exchange   **23 UNTS 139**
SIGNED: 1 Sep 48   FORCE: 1 Sep 48
REGISTERED: 24 Dec 48 Belgium
ARTICLES: 2 LANGUAGE: French.
HEADNOTE: FREE TRANSIT STAFF ENGAGED AIR SERVICES
TOPIC: Visas
CONCEPTS: Non-visa travel documents. Free passage and transit.
PARTIES:
  Belgium
  Switzerland

100345   Bilateral Treaty   **23 UNTS 148**
SIGNED: 14 Apr 47   FORCE: 10 Jun 47
REGISTERED: 29 Dec 48 Iraq
ARTICLES: 12 LANGUAGE: Arabic.
HEADNOTE: BROTHERHOOD ALLIANCE
TOPIC: General Amity
CONCEPTS: Definition of terms. Non-prejudice to third party. Friendship and amity. Establishment of commission. Procedure. Military assistance.
PROCEDURE: Duration. Ratification. Termination.
PARTIES:
  Iraq
  Jordan

100346   Bilateral Agreement   **23 UNTS 163**
SIGNED: 14 May 48   FORCE: 1 Jan 49
REGISTERED: 5 Jan 49 Denmark
ARTICLES: 8 LANGUAGE: Danish.
HEADNOTE: TRANSFER MEMBERS SICK FUNDS
TOPIC: Non-ILO Labor
CONCEPTS: Detailed regulations. Conformity with municipal law. General cooperation. Recognition and enforcement of legal decisions. Non-ILO labor relations. Sickness and invalidity insurance. Payment schedules. Assets transfer.
PROCEDURE: Denunciation.
PARTIES:
  Denmark
  Iceland

100347   Bilateral Exchange   **23 UNTS 179**
SIGNED: 12 Oct 46   FORCE: 12 Oct 46
REGISTERED: 6 Jan 49 Belgium
ARTICLES: 2 LANGUAGE: French.
HEADNOTE: UNFREEZING ASSETS
TOPIC: Claims and Debts
CONCEPTS: Treaty implementation. Annex or appendix reference. Assets.
TREATY REF: 24MAY46; FINANCIAL AGREE..

PARTIES:
  Belgium
  Netherlands
ANNEX
307 UNTS 302. Belgium. Abrogation 3 Jul 56. Force 19 Jun 58.
307 UNTS 302. Netherlands. Abrogation 3 Jul 56. Force 19 Jun 58.

100348   Bilateral Exchange   **23 UNTS 197**
SIGNED: 30 Dec 46   FORCE: 30 Dec 46
REGISTERED: 6 Jan 49 Belgium
ARTICLES: 2 LANGUAGE: French.
HEADNOTE: UNFREEZING FUNDS
TOPIC: Claims and Debts
CONCEPTS: Annex or appendix reference. Assets. Debt settlement. Assets transfer.
PARTIES:
  Belgium
  Sweden

100349   Bilateral Agreement   **24 UNTS 3**
SIGNED: 28 Jun 48   FORCE: 2 Jul 48
REGISTERED: 18 Jan 49 USA (United States)
ARTICLES: 12 LANGUAGE: English.
HEADNOTE: ECONOMIC COOPERATION
TOPIC: Direct Aid
CONCEPTS: Definition of terms. General provisions. Treaty implementation. Annex or appendix reference. Tourism. Privileges and immunities. Conformity with municipal law. General cooperation. Exchange of information and documents. Personnel. Public information. Existing tribunals. Accounting procedures. Funding procedures. Local currency. Claims and settlements. Domestic obligation. Economic assistance. Aid missions. Relief supplies. Procurement. Access to materials. Paragraph 2, Article 36. Guarantees and safeguards.
INTL ORGS: International Bank for Reconstruction and Development. International Court of Justice. United Nations. World Health Organization.
TREATY REF: EEC CONV. 16APR48; 1UNTS9.
PROCEDURE: Amendment. Duration. Ratification. Registration. Termination.
PARTIES:
  Ireland
  USA (United States)
ANNEX
79 UNTS 302. Ireland. Amendment 18 Feb 50. Force 18 Feb 50.
79 UNTS 302. USA (United States). Amendment 17 Feb 50. Force 18 Feb 50.
140 UNTS 432. USA (United States). Amendment 20 Apr 51. Force 7 Jun 51.
140 UNTS 432. Ireland. Amendment 7 Jun 51. Force 7 Jun 51.

100350   Bilateral Agreement   **24 UNTS 35**
SIGNED: 3 Jul 48   FORCE: 3 Jul 48
REGISTERED: 18 Jan 49 USA (United States)
ARTICLES: 12 LANGUAGE: English. French.
HEADNOTE: ECONOMIC COOPERATION
TOPIC: Direct Aid
CONCEPTS: Definition of terms. Territorial application. General provisions. Guarantees and safeguards. Treaty implementation. Annex or appendix reference. Tourism. Privileges and immunities. Conformity with municipal law. General cooperation. Exchange of information and documents. Personnel. Public information. Existing tribunals. Accounting procedures. Funding procedures. Local currency. Claims and settlements. Domestic obligation. Economic assistance. Aid missions. Relief supplies. Procurement. Access to materials. Paragraph 2, Article 36.
INTL ORGS: International Bank for Reconstruction and Development. International Court of Justice. United Nations. World Health Organization.
TREATY REF: EEC CONV. 16APR48; 1UNTS9.
PROCEDURE: Amendment. Duration. Registration. Termination.
PARTIES:
  Luxembourg
  USA (United States)
ANNEX
55 UNTS 324. USA (United States). Amendment 17 Nov 48. Force 22 Dec 48.
55 UNTS 324. Luxembourg. Amendment 22 Dec 48. Force 22 Dec 48.

79 UNTS 306. USA (United States). Amendment 17 Jan 50. Force 19 Jan 50.

79 UNTS 306. Luxembourg. Amendment 19 Jan 50. Force 19 Jan 50.

137 UNTS 280. USA (United States). Amendment 30 Aug 51. Force 17 Oct 51.

137 UNTS 280. USA (United States). Amendment 17 Oct 51. Force 17 Oct 51.

212 UNTS 286. USA (United States). Amendment 31 Dec 52. Force 26 Feb 53.

212 UNTS 286. Luxembourg. Amendment 26 Feb 53. Force 26 Feb 53.

100351   Bilateral Agreement   **24 UNTS 67**
SIGNED: 4 Jul 48   FORCE: 13 Jul 48
REGISTERED: 18 Jan 49 USA (United States)
ARTICLES: 11 LANGUAGE: English. Turkish.
HEADNOTE: ECONOMIC COOPERATION
TOPIC: Direct Aid
CONCEPTS: Definition of terms. Territorial application. General provisions. Guarantees and safeguards. Treaty implementation. Annex or appendix reference. Tourism. Privileges and immunities. Conformity with municipal law. General cooperation. Exchange of information and documents. Personnel. Public information. Existing tribunals. Claims and settlements. Domestic obligation. Economic assistance. Aid missions. Procurement. Paragraph 2, Article 36.
INTL ORGS: International Court of Justice. International Refugees Organization. Organization for Economic Co-operation and Development. United Nations.
TREATY REF: EEC CONV. 16APR48; 1UNTS9.
PROCEDURE: Amendment. Duration. Ratification. Registration. Termination.
PARTIES:
Turkey
USA (United States)
ANNEX
76 UNTS 258. USA (United States). Amendment 31 Jan 50. Force 31 Jan 50.
76 UNTS 258. Turkey. Amendment 31 Jan 50. Force 31 Jan 50.
152 UNTS 276. USA (United States). Amendment 16 Aug 51. Force 16 Aug 51.
152 UNTS 276. Turkey. Amendment 16 Aug 51. Force 16 Aug 51.
185 UNTS 330. Turkey. Amendment 30 Dec 52. Force 30 Dec 52.
185 UNTS 330. USA (United States). Amendment 30 Dec 52. Force 30 Dec 52.

100352   Bilateral Agreement   **24 UNTS 103**
SIGNED: 9 Jul 48   FORCE: 9 Jul 48
REGISTERED: 18 Jan 49 USA (United States)
ARTICLES: 11 LANGUAGE: English. French.
HEADNOTE: ECONOMIC COOPERATION
TOPIC: Direct Aid
CONCEPTS: Definition of terms. General provisions. Guarantees and safeguards. Treaty implementation. Annex or appendix reference. Tourism. Privileges and immunities. Conformity with municipal law. General cooperation. Exchange of information and documents. Personnel. Public information. Accounting procedures. Funding procedures. Local currency. Domestic obligation. Economic assistance. Aid missions. Relief supplies. Procurement. Access to materials. Occupation regime.
INTL ORGS: International Refugees Organization. Organization for Economic Co-operation and Development. United Nations.
TREATY REF: EEC CONV. 16AP48.
PROCEDURE: Amendment. Duration. Registration. Termination.
PARTIES:
France
USA (United States)

100353   Bilateral Agreement   **24 UNTS 133**
SIGNED: 4 Apr 47   FORCE: 10 Nov 47
REGISTERED: 19 Jan 49 USA (United States)
ARTICLES: 9 LANGUAGE: English. French.
HEADNOTE: RESTORATION INDUSTRIAL PROPERTY RIGHTS
TOPIC: Patents/Copyrights
CONCEPTS: Non-prejudice to third party. Conformity with municipal law. General. Post-war adjustment.
TREATY REF: 205LTS218.

PARTIES:
France
USA (United States)
ANNEX
77 UNTS 348. USA (United States). Supplementation 28 Oct 47. Force 27 Feb 48.
77 UNTS 348. France. Supplementation 28 Oct 47. Force 27 Feb 48.

100354   Bilateral Agreement   **25 UNTS 3**
SIGNED: 8 Oct 47   FORCE: 8 Oct 47
REGISTERED: 19 Jan 49 USA (United States)
ARTICLES: 12 LANGUAGE: English. German.
HEADNOTE: EXCHANGE WAR CRIPPLES
TOPIC: Air Transport
CONCEPTS: Definition of terms. Public health. Vocational training. Humanitarian matters. Materials, equipment and services.
INTL ORGS: International Civil Aviation Organization. Arbitration Commission.
TREATY REF: 1943SDB310; 1946SDB175.
PROCEDURE: Accession. Ratification. Termination.
PARTIES:
Austria
USA (United States)

100355   Bilateral Agreement   **25 UNTS 27**
SIGNED: 28 Feb 47   FORCE: 22 Dec 47
REGISTERED: 19 Jan 49 USA (United States)
ARTICLES: 16 LANGUAGE: English.
HEADNOTE: USE FUNDS FROM SALE SURPLUS PROPERTY
TOPIC: Direct Aid
CONCEPTS: Definition of terms. Detailed regulations. Privileges and immunities. Conformity with municipal law. Exchange of information and documents. Personnel. Procedure. Negotiation. Commissions and foundations. Currency deposits. Exchange rates and regulations. Funding procedures. Local currency. Tax exemptions. Customs exemptions. Materials, equipment and services. Surplus property. Internal structure.
INTL ORGS: Special Commission.
PROCEDURE: Amendment.
PARTIES:
Burma
USA (United States)
ANNEX
80 UNTS 312. Burma. Amendment 12 May 49. Force 12 May 49.
80 UNTS 312. USA (United States). Amendment 18 Dec 48. Force 12 May 49.
418 UNTS 326. Burma. Amendment 29 Aug 61. Force 29 Aug 61.
418 UNTS 326. USA (United States). Amendment 29 Aug 61. Force 29 Aug 61.

100356   Bilateral Exchange   **25 UNTS 45**
SIGNED: 28 Jun 48   FORCE: 28 Jun 48
REGISTERED: 19 Jan 49 USA (United States)
ARTICLES: 2 LANGUAGE: English. Italian.
HEADNOTE: MOST FAVORED NATION TREATMENT AREAS UNDER MILITARY OCCUPATION
TOPIC: Milit Occupation
CONCEPTS: Tariffs. Most favored nation clause. Control and occupation machinery.
INTL ORGS: General Agreement on Tariffs and Trade.
PROCEDURE: Future Procedures Contemplated. Termination.
PARTIES:
Italy
USA (United States)

100357   Bilateral Exchange   **25 UNTS 53**
SIGNED: 2 Jul 48   FORCE: 2 Jul 48
REGISTERED: 19 Jan 49 USA (United States)
ARTICLES: 2 LANGUAGE: English.
HEADNOTE: MOST FAVORED NATION TREATMENT AREAS UNDER MILITARY OCCUPATION
TOPIC: Milit Occupation
CONCEPTS: Tariffs. Most favored nation clause. Control and occupation machinery.
INTL ORGS: General Agreement on Tariffs and Trade.
TREATY REF: 118LTS241;.
PROCEDURE: Duration. Termination.

PARTIES:
Austria
USA (United States)

100358   Bilateral Exchange   **25 UNTS 61**
SIGNED: 6 Jul 48   FORCE: 6 Jul 48
REGISTERED: 19 Jan 49 USA (United States)
ARTICLES: 2 LANGUAGE: English.
HEADNOTE: MOST FAVORED NATION TREATMENT AREAS UNDER OCCUPATION CONTROL
TOPIC: Milit Occupation
CONCEPTS: Tariffs. Most favored nation clause. Control and occupation machinery.
INTL ORGS: General Agreement on Tariffs and Trade.
TREATY REF: 118LTS241;.
PROCEDURE: Duration. Termination.
PARTIES:
UK Great Britain
USA (United States)
ANNEX
151 UNTS 374. USA (United States). Germany, West. Withdrawal 17 Sep 52. Force 17 Sep 52.
151 UNTS 374. UK Great Britain. Germany, West. Withdrawal 9 Sep 52. Force 17 Sep 52.

100359   Bilateral Treaty   **25 UNTS 69**
SIGNED: 4 Nov 46   FORCE: 30 Nov 48
REGISTERED: 21 Jan 49 Taiwan
ARTICLES: 30 LANGUAGE: Chinese. English.
HEADNOTE: FRIENDSHIP COMMERCE NAVIGATION
TOPIC: General Amity
CONCEPTS: Friendship and amity. Peaceful relations. Establishment of trade relations. Export quotas. Import quotas. Reciprocity in trade. Trade agencies. Trade procedures. Investments. Payment schedules. Debt settlement. Private investment guarantee. National treatment.
INTL ORGS: International Court of Justice. International Monetary Fund.
TREATY REF: 7DEMARTENS134,2'20DEMARTENS100,ETC,52LTS121;$.
PROCEDURE: Duration. Ratification. Termination.
PARTIES:
Taiwan
USA (United States)

100360   Bilateral Exchange   **25 UNTS 151**
SIGNED: 28 Oct 48   FORCE: 1 Jan 49
REGISTERED: 25 Jan 49 Belgium
ARTICLES: 2 LANGUAGE: French.
HEADNOTE: FREE TRANSIT AIR NAVIGATION STAFF
TOPIC: Visas
CONCEPTS: Exceptions and exemptions. Passports non-diplomatic. Non-visa travel documents. Free passage and transit. Licenses and permits. Competency certificate.
PROCEDURE: Denunciation. Duration.
PARTIES:
Belgium
France

100361   Bilateral Exchange   **25 UNTS 159**
SIGNED: 9 Dec 48   FORCE: 9 Dec 48
REGISTERED: 25 Jan 49 Australia
ARTICLES: 2 LANGUAGE: English.
HEADNOTE: RELEASE ASSETS
TOPIC: Claims and Debts
CONCEPTS: Definition of terms. Exceptions and exemptions. General cooperation. Exchange of information and documents. Informational records. Legal protection and assistance. Licenses and permits. General property. Existing tribunals. Bonds. Exchange rates and regulations. Payment schedules. Assets. Claims and settlements. Debt settlement. Assessment procedures. Liens. General. Enemy financial interests.
PARTIES:
Australia
Belgium

100362   Bilateral Exchange   **25 UNTS 173**
SIGNED: 30 Dec 48   FORCE: 1 Jan 49
REGISTERED: 26 Jan 49 Denmark
ARTICLES: 2 LANGUAGE: French.

HEADNOTE: SETTLEMENT DISPUTES OUTSIDE TERRITORIAL WATERS
TOPIC: Dispute Settlement
CONCEPTS: Inspection and observation. Establishment of commission. Procedure.
TREATY REF: 2DEMARTENS9'556:.
PARTIES:
Belgium
Denmark

100363 Bilateral Agreement **25 UNTS 181**
SIGNED: 24 Jan 46 FORCE: 13 Nov 47
REGISTERED: 28 Jan 49 Poland
ARTICLES: 11 LANGUAGE: Czechoslovakian. Polish.
HEADNOTE: AIR COMMUNICATIONS
TOPIC: Air Transport
CONCEPTS: Annex or appendix reference. Conformity with municipal law. Licenses and permits. Recognition of legal documents. Use of facilities. Arbitration. Existing tribunals. Fees and exemptions. Most favored nation clause. National treatment. Customs exemptions. Competency certificate. Routes and logistics. Navigational conditions. Permit designation. Airport facilities. Airworthiness certificates. Conditions of airlines operating permission. Operating authorizations and regulations. Licenses and certificates of nationality.
INTL ORGS: International Civil Aviation Organization. Arbitration Commission.
PROCEDURE: Amendment. Denunciation. Duration. Future Procedures Contemplated. Ratification. Renewal or Revival.
PARTIES:
Czechoslovakia
Poland

100364 Bilateral Agreement **25 UNTS 207**
SIGNED: 12 Feb 46 FORCE: 12 Feb 46
REGISTERED: 28 Jan 49 Poland
ARTICLES: 9 LANGUAGE: Czechoslovakian. Polish.
HEADNOTE: MUTUAL RETURN PROPERTY
TOPIC: Reparations
CONCEPTS: Definition of terms. General cooperation. Legal protection and assistance. General property. Establishment of commission. Indemnities and reimbursements. Assets transfer. Postwar claims settlement.
INTL ORGS: Arbitration Commission. Claims Commission.
PROCEDURE: Future Procedures Contemplated. Ratification.
PARTIES:
Czechoslovakia
Poland

100365 Bilateral Treaty **25 UNTS 231**
SIGNED: 10 Mar 47 FORCE: 10 Mar 47
REGISTERED: 28 Jan 49 Poland
ARTICLES: 6 LANGUAGE: Czechoslovakian. Polish.
HEADNOTE: FRIENDSHIP MUTUAL AID
TOPIC: General Military
CONCEPTS: Annex or appendix reference. Friendship and amity. Non-prejudice to UN charter. Peaceful relations. Alien status. General cultural cooperation. General trade. Defense and security.
INTL ORGS: United Nations.
PROCEDURE: Denunciation. Duration. Future Procedures Contemplated. Ratification.
PARTIES:
Czechoslovakia
Poland

100366 Bilateral Agreement **25 UNTS 249**
SIGNED: 4 Jul 47 FORCE: 2 Jul 48
REGISTERED: 28 Jan 49 Poland
ARTICLES: 10 LANGUAGE: Czechoslovakian. Polish.
HEADNOTE: CULTURAL COOPERATION
TOPIC: Culture
CONCEPTS: Conformity with municipal law. Exchange of information and documents. Personnel. Recognition of degrees. Exchange. Teacher and student exchange. Professorships. Institute establishment. General cultural cooperation. Artists. Athletes. Scientific exchange. Accounting

procedures. Publications exchange. Mass media exchange.
INTL ORGS: Special Commission.
PROCEDURE: Ratification.
PARTIES:
Czechoslovakia
Poland

100367 Bilateral Agreement **25 UNTS 269**
SIGNED: 14 Nov 47 FORCE: 5 Oct 47
REGISTERED: 28 Jan 49 Belgium
ARTICLES: 13 LANGUAGE: English. French.
HEADNOTE: MONETARY
TOPIC: Finance
CONCEPTS: Balance of payments. Currency. Exchange rates and regulations. Non-interest rates and fees.
INTL ORGS: International Monetary Fund.
TREATY REF: 5UNTS227.
PARTIES:
Belgium
UK Great Britain
ANNEX
83 UNTS 396. Belgium. Prolongation 30 Jun 49. Force 6 Oct 48.
83 UNTS 396. UK Great Britain. Prolongation 30 Jun 49. Force 6 Oct 48.
83 UNTS 398. UK Great Britain. Prolongation 30 Sep 49. Force 1 Oct 49.
83 UNTS 398. Belgium. Prolongation 30 Sep 49. Force 1 Oct 49.

100368 Bilateral Convention **25 UNTS 283**
SIGNED: 31 Jan 48 FORCE: 6 Oct 48
REGISTERED: 28 Jan 49 Poland
ARTICLES: 12 LANGUAGE: Czechoslovakian. Hungarian.
HEADNOTE: CULTURAL CONVENTION
TOPIC: Culture
CONCEPTS: Previous treaty replacement. Friendship and amity. Conformity with municipal law. Personnel. Exchange. Commissions and foundations. Teacher and student exchange. Professorships. Institute establishment. Scholarships and grants. General cultural cooperation. Research cooperation. Research results. Scientific exchange. Accounting procedures. Publications exchange. Mass media exchange.
INTL ORGS: Special Commission.
TREATY REF: 163LTS9.
PROCEDURE: Denunciation. Duration. Ratification. Renewal or Revival.
PARTIES:
Hungary
Poland

100369 Bilateral Convention **25 UNTS 301**
SIGNED: 13 May 48 FORCE: 6 Sep 48
REGISTERED: 28 Jan 49 Poland
ARTICLES: 7 LANGUAGE: Czechoslovakian. Hungarian.
HEADNOTE: ECONOMIC COOPERATION
TOPIC: General Economic
CONCEPTS: Conditions. Establishment of commission. Establishment of trade relations. Export quotas. Import quotas. Economic assistance. Ports and pilotage. Facilities and equipment.
INTL ORGS: Special Commission.
PROCEDURE: Duration. Future Procedures Contemplated. Ratification. Renewal or Revival.
PARTIES:
Hungary
Poland

100370 Bilateral Treaty **25 UNTS 319**
SIGNED: 18 Jun 48 FORCE: 6 Sep 48
REGISTERED: 28 Jan 49 Poland
ARTICLES: 7 LANGUAGE: Czechoslovakian. Hungarian.
HEADNOTE: SCIENTIFIC CULTURAL COOPERATION
TOPIC: Culture
CONCEPTS: Exchange of information and documents. Personnel. Establishment of commission. Specialists exchange. Exchange. Teacher and student exchange. Exchange. General cultural cooperation. Artists. Athletes. Research results. Scientific exchange. Publications exchange. Mass media exchange.
INTL ORGS: United Nations.

PROCEDURE: Duration. Termination.
PARTIES:
Hungary
Poland
ANNEX
657 UNTS 399. Poland. Termination 28 Jun 68.
657 UNTS 399. Hungary. Termination 28 Jun 68.

100371 Bilateral Exchange **25 UNTS 333**
SIGNED: 11 Nov 48 FORCE: 10 Nov 48
REGISTERED: 31 Jan 49 Denmark
ARTICLES: 6 LANGUAGE: English.
HEADNOTE: APPLICATION TO FAROE ISLANDS
TOPIC: Finance
CONCEPTS: Territorial application. Annex type material.
PARTIES:
Denmark
UK Great Britain
ANNEX
71 UNTS 306. UK Great Britain. Prolongation 18 Aug 50. Force 18 Aug 50.
71 UNTS 306. Denmark. Prolongation 14 Aug 50. Force 18 Aug 50.

100372 Bilateral Exchange **26 UNTS 3**
SIGNED: 16 Dec 48 FORCE: 1 Jan 49
REGISTERED: 2 Feb 49 Belgium
ARTICLES: 2 LANGUAGE: French.
HEADNOTE: FREE TRANSIT AIR CREWS
TOPIC: Visas
CONCEPTS: Detailed regulations. Free passage and transit. Licenses and permits. Competency certificate.
PROCEDURE: Denunciation. Duration.
PARTIES:
Belgium
Sweden

100373 **UNTS**
SIGNED:
REGISTERED:
ARTICLES:
HEADNOTE: AGREEMENT REGISTERED UNDER 100362
TOPIC:
PARTIES:

100374 Bilateral Agreement **26 UNTS 11**
SIGNED: 29 Apr 48 FORCE: 1 Jan 48
REGISTERED: 7 Feb 49 Norway
ARTICLES: 9 LANGUAGE: Norwegian. Swedish.
HEADNOTE: PAYMENT MANOR
TOPIC: Finance
CONCEPTS: General cooperation. Accounting procedures. Banking. Currency. Monetary and gold transfers. Currency deposits. Exchange rates and regulations. Interest rates. Payment schedules.
PROCEDURE: Duration. Renewal or Revival.
PARTIES:
Norway
Sweden

100375 Bilateral Agreement **26 UNTS 33**
SIGNED: 29 Apr 48 FORCE: 8 Sep 48
REGISTERED: 7 Feb 49 Norway
ARTICLES: 5 LANGUAGE: Norwegian. Swedish.
HEADNOTE: EXCHANGE COMMODITIES
TOPIC: Commodity Trade
CONCEPTS: Conformity with municipal law. Licenses and permits. General trade. Export quotas. Import quotas. Quotas.
PROCEDURE: Denunciation. Duration. Renewal or Revival.
PARTIES:
Norway
Sweden

100376 Bilateral Agreement **26 UNTS 41**
SIGNED: 29 Apr 48 FORCE: 9 Jul 48
REGISTERED: 7 Feb 49 Norway
ARTICLES: 12 LANGUAGE: Norwegian. Swedish.
HEADNOTE: FISHERIES QUESTIONS
TOPIC: Commodity Trade
CONCEPTS: Detailed regulations. Licenses and permits. General trade. Trade procedures. Non-

interest rates and fees. Commodity trade. Quotas. National treatment.
PROCEDURE: Denunciation. Duration. Renewal or Revival.
PARTIES:
Norway
Sweden

100377 Bilateral Convention **26 UNTS 55**
SIGNED: 6 May 48 FORCE: 1 Dec 48
REGISTERED: 10 Feb 49 Denmark
ARTICLES: 23 LANGUAGE: Danish. English.
HEADNOTE: DOUBLE TAXATION FISCAL EVASION
TOPIC: Taxation
CONCEPTS: Definition of terms. Privileges and immunities. Conformity with municipal law. General cooperation. Exchange of official publications. Negotiation. Teacher and student exchange. Wages and salaries. Assets. Claims and settlements. Taxation. Equitable taxes. Tax exemptions. Air transport. Merchant vessels.
PROCEDURE: Duration. Ratification. Termination.
PARTIES:
Denmark
USA (United States)

100378 Unilateral Instrument **26 UNTS 91**
SIGNED: 18 Feb 47 FORCE: 1 Mar 49
REGISTERED: 1 Mar 49 United Nations
ARTICLES: 1 LANGUAGE: French.
HEADNOTE: ACCEPTANCE ICJ JURISDICTION
TOPIC: ICJ Option Clause
CONCEPTS: Compulsory jurisdiction.
INTL ORGS: International Court of Justice.
PROCEDURE: Duration.
PARTIES:
France
ANNEX
337 UNTS 375. France. Termination 10 Jul 59.

100379 Bilateral Exchange **26 UNTS 95**
SIGNED: 11 Oct 48 FORCE: 11 Oct 48
REGISTERED: 7 Mar 49 Belgium
ARTICLES: 2 LANGUAGE: French.
HEADNOTE: FINANCE
TOPIC: Finance
CONCEPTS: Annex or appendix reference. Accounting procedures.
PARTIES:
Belgium
Netherlands

100380 Bilateral Instrument **26 UNTS 103**
SIGNED: 25 Feb 48 FORCE: 25 Feb 48
REGISTERED: 9 Mar 49 Czechoslovakia
ARTICLES: 1 LANGUAGE: French.
HEADNOTE: PRE-WAR BILATERAL TREATIES KEEP FORCE
TOPIC: Admin Cooperation
CONCEPTS: Revival of treaties.
TREATY REF: 34LTS55; 55LTS207,189,171; 126LTS185.
PARTIES:
Czechoslovakia
Italy

100381 Bilateral Instrument **26 UNTS 109**
SIGNED: 1 Mar 48 FORCE: 1 Mar 48
REGISTERED: 9 Mar 49 Czechoslovakia
ARTICLES: 1 LANGUAGE: French.
HEADNOTE: PRE-WAR BILATERAL TREATIES KEEP FORCE
TOPIC: Admin Cooperation
CONCEPTS: Revival of treaties.
TREATY REF: 54LTS17; 168LTS241,257,249; 54LTS51.
PARTIES:
Czechoslovakia
Romania

100382 Bilateral Instrument **26 UNTS 115**
SIGNED: 5 Mar 48 FORCE: 5 Mar 48
REGISTERED: 9 Mar 49 Czechoslovakia
ARTICLES: 1 LANGUAGE: Czechoslovakian.
HEADNOTE: PRE-WAR BILATERAL TREATIES KEEP FORCE
TOPIC: Admin Cooperation

CONCEPTS: Revival of treaties.
TREATY REF: 60LTS203,169; 50LTS254; 50LTS254; 60LTS203,169.
PARTIES:
Bulgaria
Czechoslovakia

100383 Bilateral Instrument **26 UNTS 119**
SIGNED: 27 Feb 49 FORCE: 27 Feb 49
REGISTERED: 9 Mar 49 Czechoslovakia
ARTICLES: 1 LANGUAGE: Czechoslovakian. Hungarian.
HEADNOTE: PRE-WAR BILATERAL TREATIES KEEP FORCE
TOPIC: Admin Cooperation
CONCEPTS: Revival of treaties.
TREATY REF: 101LTS265; 189LTS403.
PARTIES:
Czechoslovakia
Hungary

100384 Bilateral Agreement **26 UNTS 137**
SIGNED: 20 May 48 FORCE: 20 Jan 49
REGISTERED: 15 Mar 49 Turkey
ARTICLES: 11 LANGUAGE: French.
HEADNOTE: AIR TRANSPORT
TOPIC: Air Transport
CONCEPTS: Exceptions and exemptions. Annex or appendix reference. Conformity with municipal law. Licenses and permits. Recognition of legal documents. Use of facilities. Arbitration. Procedure. Existing tribunals. Fees and exemptions. Most favored nation clause. National treatment. Customs exemptions. Competency certificate. Routes and logistics. Navigational conditions. Permit designation. Airport facilities. Airworthiness certificates. Conditions of airlines operating permission. Operating authorizations and regulations. Licenses and certificates of nationality.
INTL ORGS: International Civil Aviation Organization. Arbitration Commission.
TREATY REF: 15UNTS295.
PROCEDURE: Denunciation. Future Procedures Contemplated. Registration.
PARTIES:
Norway
Turkey

100385 Bilateral Exchange **26 UNTS 151**
SIGNED: 1 Jan 49 FORCE: 1 Jan 49
REGISTERED: 16 Mar 49 Belgium
ARTICLES: 2 LANGUAGE: French. Italian.
HEADNOTE: IDENTITY DOCUMENTS AIR CREWS
TOPIC: Visas
CONCEPTS: Exceptions and exemptions. Territorial application. Free passage and transit. Licenses and permits. Competency certificate.
PARTIES:
Belgium
Italy

100386 Bilateral Exchange **26 UNTS 159**
SIGNED: 16 Apr 48 FORCE: 1 May 48
REGISTERED: 16 Mar 49 Belgium
ARTICLES: 2 LANGUAGE: French.
HEADNOTE: ABOLITION PASSPORT VISAS
TOPIC: Visas
CONCEPTS: Territorial application. Time limit. Visa abolition. Border traffic and migration. Resident permits. Conformity with municipal law.
TREATY REF: 18UNTS227.
PARTIES:
Belgium
Ireland

100387 Bilateral Treaty **26 UNTS 167**
SIGNED: 11 Mar 46 FORCE: 18 Dec 48
REGISTERED: 17 Mar 49 Belgium
ARTICLES: 24 LANGUAGE: English. French.
HEADNOTE: STATUS FORCES FACILITIES
TOPIC: Status of Forces
CONCEPTS: Annex or appendix reference. Previous treaty replacement. Conformity with municipal law. General cooperation. General property. Use of facilities. Investigation of violations. Establishment of commission. Indemnities and reimbursements. Tax exemptions. Customs exemptions. Bands and frequency allocation.

Postal services. Radio-telephone-telegraphic communications. Post-war reconstruction. Prisoners of war. Surplus war property. Procurement and logistics. Withdrawal of forces. Status of forces. Bases and facilities.
INTL ORGS: Allied Military Occupation.
PROCEDURE: Duration. Future Procedures Contemplated. Ratification. Termination.
PARTIES:
Belgium
UK Great Britain
ANNEX
183 UNTS 346. UK Great Britain. Abrogation 22 Oct 53. Force 22 Oct 53.
183 UNTS 346. Belgium. Abrogation 22 Oct 53. Force 22 Oct 53.

100388 Bilateral Convention **26 UNTS 191**
SIGNED: 8 Apr 48 FORCE: 22 Oct 48
REGISTERED: 21 Mar 49 Poland
ARTICLES: 9 LANGUAGE: Polish. Russian.
HEADNOTE: QUARANTINE AGRICULTURAL PLANTS
TOPIC: Sanitation
CONCEPTS: Non-diplomatic delegations. General cooperation. Exchange of information and documents. Domestic legislation. Programs. Specialists exchange. Quarantine. Border control. Disease control. Insect control. Research results. Agriculture.
PROCEDURE: Duration. Ratification. Renewal or Revival. Termination.
PARTIES:
Poland
USSR (Soviet Union)

100389 Bilateral Treaty **26 UNTS 213**
SIGNED: 29 May 48 FORCE: 17 Sep 48
REGISTERED: 21 Mar 49 Poland
ARTICLES: 7 LANGUAGE: Bulgarian. Polish.
HEADNOTE: FRIENDSHIP COOPERATION MUTUAL SECURITY
TOPIC: General Military
CONCEPTS: Friendship and amity. Non-prejudice to UN charter. Peaceful relations. General cultural cooperation. General trade. Defense and security.
INTL ORGS: United Nations.
PROCEDURE: Denunciation. Duration. Ratification.
PARTIES:
Bulgaria
Poland
ANNEX
636 UNTS 361. Bulgaria. Termination 6 Apr 67. Force 24 Aug 67.
638 UNTS 361. Poland. Termination 6 Apr 67. Force 24 Aug 67.

100390 Bilateral Agreement **26 UNTS 227**
SIGNED: 27 Dec 46 FORCE: 27 Dec 46
REGISTERED: 1 Apr 49 USA (United States)
ARTICLES: 12 LANGUAGE: English. Spanish.
HEADNOTE: AIR TRANSPORT
TOPIC: Air Transport
CONCEPTS: Definition of terms. Exceptions and exemptions. Annex or appendix reference. Conformity with municipal law. Licenses and permits. Procedure. Existing tribunals. Competence of tribunal. Fees and exemptions. Most favored nation clause. Customs exemptions. Competency certificate. Routes and logistics. Navigational conditions. Permit designation. Airport facilities. Airworthiness certificates. Conditions of airlines operating permission. Operating authorizations and regulations. Licenses and certificates of nationality.
INTL ORGS: International Civil Aviation Organization. Arbitration Commission.
TREATY REF: EAS469.
PROCEDURE: Amendment. Registration. Termination.
PARTIES:
Peru
USA (United States)
ANNEX
317 UNTS 312. USA (United States). Amendment 24 Apr 58. Force 28 May 58.
317 UNTS 312. Peru. Amendment 28 May 58. Force 28 May 58.
606 UNTS 296. USA (United States). Amendment 2 Mar 66. Force 2 Mar 66.

606 UNTS 296. Peru. Amendment 2 Mar 66. Force 2 Mar 66.

100391 Bilateral Exchange **26 UNTS 27**
SIGNED: 21 Jun 47 FORCE: 21 Jun 47
REGISTERED: 1 Apr 49 USA (United States)
ARTICLES: 2 LANGUAGE: English. Spanish.
HEADNOTE: HEALTH SANITATION PROGRAM
TOPIC: Sanitation
CONCEPTS: Programs. Public health. Sanitation. Accounting procedures. Expense sharing formulae. Financial programs. Funding procedures. Tax exemptions. Credit provisions
TREATY REF: 26UNTS350; 26UNTS384.
PROCEDURE: Duration. Ratification. Renewal or Revival.
PARTIES:
Ecuador
USA (United States)
ANNEX
152 UNTS 279. USA (United States). Prolongation 6 Aug 48. Force 20 Aug 48.
152 UNTS 279. Ecuador. Prolongation 18 Aug 48. Force 20 Aug 48.
152 UNTS 282. USA (United States). Prolongation 26 Jul 49. Force 26 Aug 49.
152 UNTS 282. Ecuador. Prolongation 22 Aug 49. Force 26 Aug 49.
152 UNTS 286. USA (United States). Prolongation 15 Sep 50. Force 20 Sep 50.
152 UNTS 286. Ecuador. Prolongation 15 Sep 50. Force 20 Sep 50.
152 UNTS 290. USA (United States). Supplementation 27 Sep 51. Force 27 Sep 51.
152 UNTS 290. Ecuador. Supplementation 27 Sep 51. Force 27 Sep 51.
160 UNTS 375. USA (United States). Supplementation 4 Oct 51. Force 29 Oct 51.
160 UNTS 375. Ecuador. Supplementation 24 Oct 51. Force 29 Oct 51.
177 UNTS 334. USA (United States). Supplementation 18 Mar 52. Force 31 Mar 52.
177 UNTS 334. Ecuador. Supplementation 31 Mar 52. Force 31 Mar 52.
269 UNTS 268. USA (United States). Prolongation 17 Mar 55. Force 18 Apr 55.
269 UNTS 268. Ecuador. Prolongation 12 Apr 55. Force 18 Apr 55.

100392 Bilateral Exchange **27 UNTS 3**
SIGNED: 20 Aug 47 FORCE: 20 Aug 47
REGISTERED: 1 Apr 49 USA (United States)
ARTICLES: 2 LANGUAGE: English.
HEADNOTE: MOBIL RADIO TRANSMITTING STATIONS
TOPIC: Telecommunications
CONCEPTS: Domestic legislation. Licenses and permits. Radio-telephone-telegraphic communications.
PARTIES:
Canada
USA (United States)

100393 Bilateral Exchange **27 UNTS 11**
SIGNED: 29 Aug 47 FORCE: 29 Aug 47
REGISTERED: 1 Apr 49 USA (United States)
ARTICLES: 2 LANGUAGE: English. Spanish.
HEADNOTE: STATIONING FORCES
TOPIC: Status of Forces
CONCEPTS: Defense and security. Airforce-army-navy personnel ratio. Status of forces.
INTL ORGS: United Nations.
PARTIES:
Guatemala
USA (United States)

100394 Bilateral Agreement **27 UNTS 19**
SIGNED: 30 Oct 47 FORCE: 30 Oct 47
REGISTERED: 1 Apr 49 USA (United States)
ARTICLES: 1 LANGUAGE: English.
HEADNOTE: SUPPLEMENTARY AGREEMENT TARIFFS TRADE
TOPIC: General Economic
CONCEPTS: Annex type material.
INTL ORGS: United Nations.
TREATY REF: 199LTS91; 200LTS594; 203LTS211.
PROCEDURE: Duration. Termination.

PARTIES:
Canada
USA (United States)

100395 Bilateral Exchange **27 UNTS 29**
SIGNED: 26 Dec 47 FORCE: 26 Dec 47
REGISTERED: 1 Apr 49 USA (United States)
ARTICLES: 2 LANGUAGE: English.
HEADNOTE: FUR SEALS
TOPIC: Commodity Trade
CONCEPTS: Annex type material. Incorporation of treaty provisions into national law.
TREATY REF: 26UNTS363.
PARTIES:
Canada
USA (United States)

100396 Bilateral Exchange **27 UNTS 35**
SIGNED: 29 Jun 48 FORCE: 2 Jul 48
REGISTERED: 1 Apr 49 USA (United States)
ARTICLES: 2 LANGUAGE: English.
HEADNOTE: APPLICATION MOST FAVORED NATION CLAUSE
TOPIC: Mostfavored Nation
CONCEPTS: Tariffs. Exchange rates and regulations. Most favored nation clause. Occupation regime.
INTL ORGS: General Agreement on Tariffs and Trade.
TREATY REF: 6DEMARTENS2'919; 18 PART 1P.210. 55UNTS187;.
PROCEDURE: Duration. Ratification. Termination.
PARTIES:
Denmark
USA (United States)

100397 Bilateral Exchange **27 UNTS 43**
SIGNED: 2 Jul 48 FORCE: 2 Jul 48
REGISTERED: 1 Apr 49 USA (United States)
ARTICLES: 1 LANGUAGE: English. French.
HEADNOTE: APPLICATION MOST FAVORED NATION CLAUSE
TOPIC: Mostfavored Nation
CONCEPTS: Tariffs. Fees and exemptions. Most favored nation clause. Occupation regime.
INTL ORGS: General Agreement on Tariffs and Trade.
TREATY REF: 1-6UNTS4.
PARTIES:
Belgium
USA (United States)

100398 Bilateral Exchange **27 UNTS 49**
SIGNED: 3 Jul 48 FORCE: 3 Jul 48
REGISTERED: 1 Apr 49 USA (United States)
ARTICLES: 2 LANGUAGE: English. Icelandic.
HEADNOTE: MOST FAVORED NATION TREATMENT AREAS UNDER MILITARY OCCUPATION
TOPIC: Milit Occupation
CONCEPTS: Tariffs. Most favored nation clause. Control and occupation machinery.
INTL ORGS: General Agreement on Tariffs and Trade.
PROCEDURE: Duration. Termination.
PARTIES:
Iceland
USA (United States)

100399 Bilateral Exchange **27 UNTS 59**
SIGNED: 3 Jul 48 FORCE: 3 Jul 48
REGISTERED: 1 Apr 49 USA (United States)
ARTICLES: 2 LANGUAGE: English. Norwegian.
HEADNOTE: MOST FAVORED NATION TREATMENT AREAS UNDER OCCUPATION
TOPIC: Milit Occupation
CONCEPTS: Tariffs. Most favored nation clause. Control and occupation machinery.
INTL ORGS: General Agreement on Tariffs and Trade.
PROCEDURE: Duration. Termination.
PARTIES:
Norway
USA (United States)

100400 Bilateral Exchange **27 UNTS 69**
SIGNED: 3 Jul 48 FORCE: 3 Jul 48
REGISTERED: 1 Apr 49 USA (United States)
ARTICLES: 2 LANGUAGE: English.
HEADNOTE: MOST FAVORED NATION TREATMENT AREAS UNDER OCCUPATION
TOPIC: Milit Occupation
CONCEPTS: Tariffs. Most favored nation clause. Control and occupation machinery.
INTL ORGS: General Agreement on Tariffs and Trade.
TREATY REF: 116LTS109;.
PARTIES:
Sweden
USA (United States)

100401 Multilateral Agreement **27 UNTS 77**
SIGNED: 30 Oct 46 FORCE: 6 Aug 48
REGISTERED: 8 Apr 49 USA (United States)
ARTICLES: 21 LANGUAGE: Dutch. English. French.
HEADNOTE: CARIBBEAN COMMISSION
TOPIC: IGO Establishment
CONCEPTS: Definition of terms. Treaty interpretation. Juridical personality. Sanitation. Education. Old age and invalidity insurance. General trade. Accounting procedures. Financial programs. Funding procedures. Agriculture. Land transport. Admission. Subsidiary organ. Establishment. Headquarters and facilities. Liaison with other IGO's. Internal structure. Inter-agency agreements. Fish, wildlife, and natural resources.
INTL ORGS: Caribbean Commission. United Nations.
PARTIES:
France SIGNED: 30 Oct 46 RATIFIED: 11 Dec 46 FORCE: 6 Aug 48
Netherlands SIGNED: 30 Oct 46 RATIFIED: 6 Aug 48 FORCE: 6 Aug 48
UK Great Britain SIGNED: 30 Oct 46 RATIFIED: 4 Mar 47 FORCE: 6 Aug 48
USA (United States) SIGNED: 30 Oct 46 RATIFIED: 8 Mar 48 FORCE: 6 Aug 48

100402 Multilateral Convention **27 UNTS 103**
SIGNED: 17 Apr 46 FORCE: 1 Mar 49
REGISTERED: 11 Apr 49 Luxembourg
ARTICLES: 13 LANGUAGE: French.
HEADNOTE: LUXEMBOURG RAILWAYS
TOPIC: Land Transport
CONCEPTS: Detailed regulations. Exceptions and exemptions. Continuity of rights and obligations. Procedure. Indemnities and reimbursements. Expense sharing formulae. Non-interest rates and fees. Debts. Materials, equipment and services. Loan and credit. Routes and logistics. Railways. Optional clause ICJ.
INTL ORGS: International Court of Justice.
PROCEDURE: Ratification.
PARTIES:
Belgium SIGNED: 17 Apr 46 RATIFIED: 1 Mar 47 FORCE: 1 Mar 47
France SIGNED: 17 Apr 46 RATIFIED: 1 Mar 47 FORCE: 1 Mar 47
Luxembourg SIGNED: 17 Apr 46 RATIFIED: 1 Mar 47 FORCE: 1 Mar 47

100403 Multilateral Convention **27 UNTS 117**
SIGNED: 8 Mar 48 FORCE: 22 Jul 48
REGISTERED: 11 Apr 49 Denmark
ARTICLES: 9 LANGUAGE: Danish. Norwegian. Swedish.
HEADNOTE: RECOGNITION ENFORCEMENT JUDGEMENTS CRIMINAL MATTERS
TOPIC: Admin Cooperation
CONCEPTS: Operating agencies. Recognition and enforcement of legal decisions.
PROCEDURE: Denunciation. Ratification.
PARTIES:
Denmark SIGNED: 8 Mar 48 RATIFIED: 22 Jul 48 FORCE: 22 Jul 48
Norway SIGNED: 8 Mar 48 RATIFIED: 22 Jul 48 FORCE: 22 Jul 48
Sweden SIGNED: 8 Mar 48 RATIFIED: 1 Jan 49 FORCE: 1 Jan 49

ANNEX
490 UNTS 443. Denmark. Termination 7 Jan 64.
Force 1 Jan 64.
490 UNTS 443. Norway. Termination 7 Jan 64.
Force 1 Jan 64.
490 UNTS 443. Sweden. Termination 7 Jan 64.
Force 1 Jan 64.

100404 Bilateral Agreement **27 UNTS 135**
SIGNED: 29 Dec 48 FORCE: 1 Mar 49
REGISTERED: 11 Apr 49 Belgium
ARTICLES: 11 LANGUAGE: English.
HEADNOTE: ISSUE FRONTIER PASSES
TOPIC: Visas
CONCEPTS: Annex or appendix reference. Border
traffic and migration. Frontier permits. Fees and
exemptions.
PARTIES:
Belgium
UK Great Britain
ANNEX
32 UNTS 397. British Occup Germ. Supplementation 19 May 49. Force 1 Jun 49.
32 UNTS 397. Belgium. Supplementation
19 May 49. Force 1 Jun 49.
46 UNTS 351. Belgium. Amendment 7 Sep 49.
Force 14 Sep 49.
46 UNTS 351. British Occup Germ. Amendment
11 Aug 49. Force 14 Sep 49.
55 UNTS 328. Belgium. Supplementation
15 Feb 50. Force 21 Feb 50.
55 UNTS 328. British Occup Germ. Supplementation 21 Feb 50. Force 21 Feb 50.
68 UNTS 262. British Occup Germ. Supplementation 19 May 50. Force 19 May 50.
68 UNTS 262. Belgium. Supplementation
11 May 50. Force 19 May 50.

100405 Bilateral Agreement **27 UNTS 155**
SIGNED: 21 Dec 45 FORCE: 21 Dec 45
REGISTERED: 13 Apr 49 ICAO (Civil Aviat)
ARTICLES: 13 LANGUAGE: English.
HEADNOTE: AIR SERVICES
TOPIC: Air Transport
CONCEPTS: Annex or appendix reference. Conformity with municipal law. Exchange of information and documents. Licenses and permits. Recognition of legal documents. Use of facilities. Arbitration. Existing tribunals. Fees and
exemptions. Most favored nation clause. National treatment. Customs exemptions. Competency certificate. Routes and logistics. Navigational conditions. Permit designation. Airport facilities. Airworthiness certificates. Conditions of
airlines operating permission. Operating authorizations and regulations. Licenses and certificates of nationality.
INTL ORGS: International Civil Aviation Organization. Arbitration Commission.
TREATY REF: 15UNTS295.
PROCEDURE: Amendment. Future Procedures
Contemplated. Registration. Termination.
PARTIES:
Canada
UK Great Britain

100406 Bilateral Exchange **27 UNTS 169**
SIGNED: 4 Jan 46 FORCE: 4 Jan 46
REGISTERED: 13 Apr 49 ICAO (Civil Aviat)
ARTICLES: 2 LANGUAGE: French.
HEADNOTE: OPERATION REGULAR AIRLINE
PARIS COPENHAGEN
TOPIC: Air Transport
CONCEPTS: Time limit. Routes and logistics. Air
transport.
PARTIES:
Denmark
France

100407 Bilateral Agreement **27 UNTS 173**
SIGNED: 28 Feb 46 FORCE: 28 Feb 46
REGISTERED: 13 Apr 49 ICAO (Civil Aviat)
ARTICLES: 12 LANGUAGE: English. French.
HEADNOTE: AIR TRANSPORT BRITISH FRENCH
TERRITORIES
TOPIC: Air Transport
CONCEPTS: Annex or appendix reference. Previ-
ous treaty replacement. Conformity with munici-
pal law. Licenses and permits. Personnel. Recog-
nition of legal documents. Use of facilities. Arbi-

tration. Procedure. Existing tribunals. Fees and
exemptions. Most favored nation clause. National treatment. Customs exemptions. Competency certificate. Routes and logistics. Navigational conditions. Permit designation. Air transport. Airport facilities. Airworthiness certificates.
Conditions of airlines operating permission. Licenses and certificates of nationality.
INTL ORGS: International Civil Aviation Organization. Arbitration Commission. Special Commission.
TREATY REF: 15UNTS295.
PROCEDURE: Amendment. Future Procedures
Contemplated. Registration. Termination. Application to Non-self-governing Territories.
PARTIES:
France
UK Great Britain
ANNEX
175 UNTS 346. France. Amendment 21 Jan 53.
Force 21 Jan 53.
175 UNTS 346. UK Great Britain. Amendment
21 Jan 53. Force 21 Jan 53.
420 UNTS 332. UK Great Britain. Amendment
11 Sep 61. Force 11 Sep 61.
420 UNTS 332. France. Amendment 6 Sep 61.
Force 11 Sep 61.
566 UNTS 332. France. Amendment 29 Nov 65.
Force 29 Nov 65.
566 UNTS 332. UK Great Britain. Amendment
29 Nov 65. Force 29 Nov 65.

100408 Bilateral Agreement **27 UNTS 207**
SIGNED: 5 Jun 46 FORCE: 6 Nov 46
REGISTERED: 13 Apr 49 ICAO (Civil Aviat)
ARTICLES: 18 LANGUAGE: English.
HEADNOTE: DOUBLE TAXATION FISCAL EVA-
SION
TOPIC: Taxation
CONCEPTS: Definition of terms. Territorial applica-
tion. Previous treaty replacement. Conformity
with municipal law. Exchange of official publica-
tions. Teacher and student exchange. Non-inter-
est rates and fees. Taxation. Tax credits. General.
Tax exemptions.
TREATY REF: 8MAY1930.
PROCEDURE: Termination.
PARTIES:
Canada
UK Great Britain
ANNEX
304 UNTS 336. Canada. Acknowledgement
2 Aug 56. Force 30 Sep 56.
304 UNTS 336. UK Great Britain. Kenya. Force
30 Sep 56.
304 UNTS 336. UK Great Britain. Tanganyika.
Force 30 Sep 56.
304 UNTS 336. UK Great Britain. Uganda. Force
30 Sep 56.
304 UNTS 336. UK Great Britain. Zanzibar. Acknowledgement 2 Aug 56. Force 30 Sep 56.
345 UNTS 326. Canada. Acknowledgement
14 Aug 51. Force 25 Sep 51.
345 UNTS 326. UK Great Britain. All Territories.
Force 25 Sep 51.
345 UNTS 332. UK Great Britain. British Guiana.
Force 8 Jul 52.
345 UNTS 332. UK Great Britain. St. Lucia. Force
8 Jul 52.
345 UNTS 332. Canada. Acknowledgement
22 May 52. Force 8 Jul 52.
345 UNTS 336. Canada. Acknowledgement
9 Apr 53. Force 1 May 53.
345 UNTS 336. UK Great Britain. Southern
Rhodesia. Force 1 May 53.
345 UNTS 340. Canada. Acknowledgement
21 Jul 53. Force 29 Aug 53.
345 UNTS 340. UK Great Britain. Dominican
Republic. Force 29 Aug 53.
345 UNTS 344. UK Great Britain. Fed Rhod/-
Nyasaland. Force 30 Jun 57.
345 UNTS 344. Canada. Acknowledgement
16 Jul 57. Force 30 Jun 57.
345 UNTS 348. UK Great Britain. Southern
Rhodesia. Force 2 Nov 57.
345 UNTS 348. UK Great Britain. Nyasaland.
Force 2 Nov 57.
345 UNTS 348. Canada. Acknowledgement
13 Feb 58. Force 2 Nov 57.

100409 Bilateral Agreement **27 UNTS 231**
SIGNED: 25 Jul 46 FORCE: 25 Jul 46

REGISTERED: 13 Apr 49 ICAO (Civil Aviat)
ARTICLES: 13 LANGUAGE: Czechoslovakian. Russian.
HEADNOTE: ESTABLISHING AIR SERVICES
TOPIC: Air Transport
CONCEPTS: Conformity with municipal law. General cooperation. Licenses and permits. Personnel. Recognition of legal documents. Negotiation. Humanitarian matters. Reexport of goods,
etc.. Indemnities and reimbursements. Customs
exemptions. Registration certificate. Routes and
logistics. Airport facilities. Airworthiness certificates. Overflights and technical stops. Operating
authorizations and regulations. Postal services.
PROCEDURE: Denunciation. Duration. Renewal or
Revival.
PARTIES:
Czechoslovakia
USSR (Soviet Union)

100410 Bilateral Agreement **27 UNTS 251**
SIGNED: 2 Aug 46 FORCE: 2 Aug 46
REGISTERED: 13 Apr 49 ICAO (Civil Aviat)
ARTICLES: 10 LANGUAGE: French.
HEADNOTE: AIR TRANSPORT
TOPIC: Air Transport
CONCEPTS: Annex or appendix reference. Confor-
mity with municipal law. Licenses and permits.
Recognition of legal documents. Use of facilities.
Arbitration. Procedure. Existing tribunals. Fees
and exemptions. Most favored nation clause. Na-
tional treatment. Customs exemptions. Compe-
tency certificate. Routes and logistics. Naviga-
tional conditions. Permit designation. Air trans-
port. Airport facilities. Airworthiness certificates.
Conditions of airlines operating permission. Licenses and certificates of nationality.
INTL ORGS: International Civil Aviation Organization. Arbitration Commission.
TREATY REF: 15UNTS295.
PROCEDURE: Amendment. Future Procedures
Contemplated. Termination.
PARTIES:
France
Sweden
ANNEX
94 UNTS 298. France. Supplementation
19 Mar 47. Force 19 Mar 47.
94 UNTS 298. Sweden. Supplementation
19 Mar 47. Force 19 Mar 47.
94 UNTS 302. France. Amendment 27 May 47.
Force 10 Jun 47.
94 UNTS 302. Sweden. Amendment 10 Jun 47.
Force 10 Jun 47.

100411 Bilateral Agreement **27 UNTS 267**
SIGNED: 29 Jan 47 FORCE: 29 Jan 47
REGISTERED: 13 Apr 49 ICAO (Civil Aviat)
ARTICLES: 12 LANGUAGE: Czechoslovakian. English.
HEADNOTE: AIR TRANSPORT
TOPIC: Air Transport
CONCEPTS: Annex or appendix reference. Conformity with municipal law. Licenses and permits.
Waiver of immunity. Recognition of legal documents. Arbitration. Procedure. Existing tribunals.
Fees and exemptions. Most favored nation
clause. National treatment. Customs exemp-
tions. Competency certificate. Routes and logis-
tics. Navigational conditions. Permit designation. Air transport. Airport facilities. Airworthiness certificates. Conditions of airlines
operating permission. Operating authorizations
and regulations. Licenses and certificates of nationality.
INTL ORGS: International Civil Aviation Organization. Arbitration Commission.
PROCEDURE: Amendment. Future Procedures
Contemplated. Ratification. Registration. Termination.
PARTIES:
Czechoslovakia
Ireland

100412 Bilateral Agreement **27 UNTS 287**
SIGNED: 5 Apr 47 FORCE: 5 Apr 47
REGISTERED: 13 Apr 49 ICAO (Civil Aviat)
ARTICLES: 17 LANGUAGE: English.
HEADNOTE: CIVIL AIR
TOPIC: Air Transport
CONCEPTS: Personnel. Immovable property

Bonds. Fees and exemptions. Non-interest rates and fees. Customs exemptions. Airport facilities. Airport equipment. Overflights and technical stops. Operating authorizations and regulations. Facilities and equipment.
PROCEDURE: Duration. Future Procedures Contemplated. Renewal or Revival.
PARTIES:
Muscat and Oman
UK Great Britain

100413 Bilateral Agreement **27 UNTS 297**
SIGNED: 14 May 47 FORCE: 14 May 47
REGISTERED: 13 Apr 49 ICAO (Civil Aviat)
ARTICLES: 11 LANGUAGE: French.
HEADNOTE: AIR SERVICES
TOPIC: Air Transport
CONCEPTS: Annex or appendix reference. Non-prejudice to third party. Conformity with municipal law. Licenses and permits. Recognition of legal documents. Use of facilities. Arbitration. Procedure. Existing tribunals. Fees and exemptions. Most favored nation clause. National treatment. Customs exemptions. Competency certificate. Routes and logistics. Navigational conditions. Permit designation. Airport facilities. Airworthiness certificates. Conditions of airlines operating permission. Operating authorizations and regulations. Licenses and certificates of nationality.
INTL ORGS: International Civil Aviation Organization.
PROCEDURE: Amendment. Future Procedures Contemplated. Ratification. Termination.
PARTIES:
Czechoslovakia
Denmark

100414 Bilateral Agreement **27 UNTS 313**
SIGNED: 27 Jun 47 FORCE: 27 Jun 47
REGISTERED: 13 Apr 49 ICAO (Civil Aviat)
ARTICLES: 12 LANGUAGE: English.
HEADNOTE: AIR SERVICES
TOPIC: Air Transport
CONCEPTS: Annex or appendix reference. Conformity with municipal law. Licenses and permits. Recognition of legal documents. Use of facilities. Procedure. Existing tribunals. Competence of tribunal. Fees and exemptions. Most favored nation clause. National treatment. Customs exemptions. Competency certificate. Routes and logistics. Navigational conditions. Airport facilities. Airworthiness certificates. Conditions of airlines operating permission. Operating authorizations and regulations. Licenses and certificates of nationality.
INTL ORGS: International Civil Aviation Organization. Arbitration Commission.
TREATY REF: 15UNTS295.
PROCEDURE: Amendment. Future Procedures Contemplated. Registration. Termination.
PARTIES:
Canada
Sweden
ANNEX
53 UNTS 420. Canada. Supplementation 28 Jun 48. Force 28 Jun 47.
53 UNTS 420. Sweden. Supplementation 27 Jun 47. Force 28 Jun 47.
53 UNTS 424. Canada. Supplementation 5 Jul 49. Force 5 Jul 49.
53 UNTS 424. Sweden. Supplementation 30 Jun 49. Force 5 Jul 49.
353 UNTS 312. Sweden. Amendment 16 May 58. Force 16 May 58.
353 UNTS 312. Canada. Amendment 16 May 58. Force 16 May 58.

100415 Bilateral Agreement **27 UNTS 325**
SIGNED: 16 Jul 47 FORCE: 16 Jul 47
REGISTERED: 13 Apr 49 ICAO (Civil Aviat)
ARTICLES: 13 LANGUAGE: English. French.
HEADNOTE: RELATING AIR SERVICES
TOPIC: Air Transport
CONCEPTS: Definition of terms. Detailed regulations. Annex or appendix reference. Conformity with municipal law. General cooperation. Exchange of information and documents. Use of facilities. Procedure. Existing tribunals. Reexport of goods, etc.. Non-interest rates and fees. Most favored nation clause. National treatment. Cus-

toms exemptions. Routes and logistics. Permit designation. Air transport. Airport facilities. Conditions of airlines operating permission. Operating authorizations and regulations.
INTL ORGS: International Civil Aviation Organization. Arbitration Commission.
TREATY REF: 15UNTS295.
PROCEDURE: Amendment. Future Procedures Contemplated. Registration. Termination. Application to Non-self-governing Territories.
PARTIES:
France
India
ANNEX
496 UNTS 319. India. Amendment 30 Oct 61. Force 30 Oct 61.
496 UNTS 319. France. Amendment 30 Oct 61. Force 30 Oct 61.

100416 Bilateral Agreement **28 UNTS 3**
SIGNED: 17 Jul 47 FORCE: 17 Jul 47
REGISTERED: 13 Apr 49 ICAO (Civil Aviat)
ARTICLES: 13 LANGUAGE: English.
HEADNOTE: ESTABLISHMENT AIR COMMUNICATIONS
TOPIC: Air Transport
CONCEPTS: Definition of terms. Annex or appendix reference. Conformity with municipal law. Licenses and permits. Recognition of legal documents. Use of facilities. Arbitration. Procedure. Existing tribunals. Negotiation. Fees and exemptions. Most favored nation clause. National treatment. Customs exemptions. Competency certificate. Routes and logistics. Navigational conditions. Permit designation. Airport facilities. Airworthiness certificates. Conditions of airlines operating permission. Operating authorizations and regulations. Licenses and certificates of nationality.
INTL ORGS: International Civil Aviation Organization. Arbitration Commission.
TREATY REF: 15UNTS295.
PROCEDURE: Amendment. Future Procedures Contemplated. Registration. Termination. Application to Non-self-governing Territories.
PARTIES:
Canada
UK Great Britain

100417 Bilateral Agreement **28 UNTS 27**
SIGNED: 18 Jul 47 FORCE: 18 Jul 47
REGISTERED: 13 Apr 49 ICAO (Civil Aviat)
ARTICLES: 12 LANGUAGE: English.
HEADNOTE: AIR SERVICES
TOPIC: Air Transport
CONCEPTS: Exceptions and exemptions. Annex or appendix reference. Conformity with municipal law. Licenses and permits. Recognition of legal documents. Use of facilities. Existing tribunals. Reexport of goods, etc.. Fees and exemptions. Most favored nation clause. National treatment. Customs exemptions. Competency certificate. Routes and logistics. Navigational conditions. Permit designation. Airport facilities. Airworthiness certificates. Conditions of airlines operating permission. Operating authorizations and regulations. Licenses and certificates of nationality.
INTL ORGS: International Civil Aviation Organization. Arbitration Commission.
PROCEDURE: Registration. Termination. Application to Non-self-governing Territories.
PARTIES:
Netherlands
Thailand
ANNEX
95 UNTS 336. Siam. Amendment 22 Feb 51. Force 27 Mar 51.
95 UNTS 336. Netherlands. Amendment 27 Mar 51. Force 27 Mar 51.
216 UNTS 360. Thailand. Amendment 24 Sep 54. Force 24 Sep 54.
216 UNTS 360. Netherlands. Amendment 21 Sep 54. Force 24 Sep 54.

100418 Multilateral Agreement **28 UNTS 41**
SIGNED: 4 Aug 47 FORCE: 4 Aug 47
REGISTERED: 13 Apr 49 ICAO (Civil Aviat)
ARTICLES: 6 LANGUAGE: English.
HEADNOTE: FORMATION BRITISH COMMONWEALTH PACIFIC AIRLINES

TOPIC: Air Transport
CONCEPTS: Programs. Currency. Financial programs. Air transport.
PARTIES:
Australia SIGNED: 4 Aug 47 FORCE: 4 Aug 47
New Zealand SIGNED: 4 Aug 47 FORCE: 4 Aug 47
UK Great Britain SIGNED: 4 Aug 47 FORCE: 4 Aug 47

100419 Bilateral Agreement **28 UNTS 47**
SIGNED: 8 Aug 47 FORCE: 8 Aug 47
REGISTERED: 13 Apr 49 ICAO (Civil Aviat)
ARTICLES: 10 LANGUAGE: English.
HEADNOTE: AIR SERVICES
TOPIC: Air Transport
CONCEPTS: Annex or appendix reference. Conformity with municipal law. Procedure. Existing tribunals. Negotiation. Routes and logistics. Permit designation. Conditions of airlines operating permission. Operating authorizations and regulations.
INTL ORGS: International Civil Aviation Organization. Arbitration Commission.
TREATY REF: 15UNTS295.
PROCEDURE: Amendment. Future Procedures Contemplated. Registration. Termination.
PARTIES:
Canada
Ireland
ANNEX
128 UNTS 294. Ireland. Amendment 9 Jul 51. Force 9 Jul 51.
128 UNTS 294. Canada. Amendment 9 Jul 51. Force 9 Jul 51.
335 UNTS 281. Ireland. Amendment 23 Dec 57. Force 23 Dec 57.
335 UNTS 281. Canada. Amendment 23 Dec 57. Force 23 Dec 57.

100420 Bilateral Agreement **28 UNTS 63**
SIGNED: 7 Jan 48 FORCE: 7 Jan 48
REGISTERED: 13 Apr 49 ICAO (Civil Aviat)
ARTICLES: 14 LANGUAGE: English.
HEADNOTE: AIR SERVICES
TOPIC: Air Transport
CONCEPTS: Conditions. Definition of terms. Detailed regulations. Conformity with municipal law. Exchange of information and documents. Arbitration. Procedure. Existing tribunals. Negotiation. Non-interest rates and fees. Passenger transport. Routes and logistics. Permit designation. Transport of goods. Conditions of airlines operating permission. Overflights and technical stops. Operating authorizations and regulations. Regulations.
INTL ORGS: International Civil Aviation Organization. Arbitration Commission.
TREATY REF: 15UNTS295.
PROCEDURE: Amendment. Future Procedures Contemplated. Termination. Application to Non-self-governing Territories.
PARTIES:
Philippines
UK Great Britain
ANNEX
216 UNTS 366. UK Great Britain. Termination 11 Aug 53. Force 11 Aug 54.

100421 Bilateral Agreement **28 UNTS 81**
SIGNED: 14 Mar 48 FORCE: 20 Aug 48
REGISTERED: 13 Apr 49 ICAO (Civil Aviat)
ARTICLES: 16 LANGUAGE: Czechoslovakian. Serbo-Croat.
HEADNOTE: AIR TRANSPORT
TOPIC: Air Transport
CONCEPTS: Annex or appendix reference. Previous treaty replacement. Conformity with municipal law. General cooperation. Informational records. Licenses and permits. Personnel. Recognition of legal documents. Use of facilities. Procedure. Bonds. Fees and exemptions. National treatment. Laws and formalities. Customs exemptions. Competency certificate. Registration certificate. Routes and logistics. Permit designation. Air transport. Airport facilities. Airworthiness certificates. Conditions of airlines operating permission. Overflights and technical stops. Licenses and certificates of nationality.

PARTIES:
Czechoslovakia
Yugoslavia

100422 Bilateral Agreement **28 UNTS 121**
SIGNED: 10 May 48   FORCE: 10 May 48
REGISTERED: 13 Apr 49 ICAO (Civil Aviat)
ARTICLES: 11 LANGUAGE: Dutch. English.
HEADNOTE: AIR TRANSPORT
TOPIC: Air Transport
CONCEPTS: Annex or appendix reference. Conformity with municipal law. Licenses and permits. Recognition of legal documents. Use of facilities. Arbitration. Existing tribunals. Reexport of goods, etc.. Fees and exemptions. Most favored nation clause. National treatment. Customs exemptions. Competency certificate. Routes and logistics. Navigational conditions. Permit designation. Air transport. Airport facilities. Airworthiness certificates. Conditions of airlines operating permission. Operating authorizations and regulations. Licenses and certificates of nationality.
INTL ORGS: International Civil Aviation Organization. Arbitration Commission.
TREATY REF: 15UNTS295.
PROCEDURE: Amendment. Future Procedures Contemplated. Registration. Termination.
PARTIES:
Ireland
Netherlands
ANNEX
335 UNTS 282. Netherlands. Amendment 12 Oct 57. Force 12 Oct 57.
335 UNTS 282. Ireland. Amendment 2 Oct 57. Force 12 Oct 57.

100423 Bilateral Agreement **28 UNTS 143**
SIGNED: 23 Jun 48   FORCE: 1 Jul 48
REGISTERED: 13 Apr 49 ICAO (Civil Aviat)
ARTICLES: 14 LANGUAGE: English.
HEADNOTE: AIR SERVICES
TOPIC: Air Transport
CONCEPTS: Definition of terms. Detailed regulations. Annex or appendix reference. Conformity with municipal law. General cooperation. Exchange of information and documents. Use of facilities. Procedure. Existing tribunals. Negotiation. Reexport of goods, etc.. Non-interest rates and fees. Most favored nation clause. National treatment. Customs exemptions. Routes and logistics. Permit designation. Airport facilities. Conditions of airlines operating permission. Overflights and technical stops. Operating authorizations and regulations.
INTL ORGS: International Civil Aviation Organization. Arbitration Commission.
TREATY REF: 15UNTS295.
PROCEDURE: Amendment. Future Procedures Contemplated. Registration. Termination.
PARTIES:
India
Pakistan

100424 Bilateral Exchange **28 UNTS 165**
SIGNED: 2 Aug 48   FORCE: 2 Aug 48
REGISTERED: 13 Apr 49 ICAO (Civil Aviat)
ARTICLES: 2 LANGUAGE: English. Italian.
HEADNOTE: AIRCRAFT QANTAS EMPIRE AIRWAYS FLY OVER ITALY LAND CIAMPINO (ROME)
TOPIC: Air Transport
CONCEPTS: Informational records. Routes and logistics. Air transport. Airport facilities. Overflights and technical stops.
PARTIES:
Australia
Italy

100425 Bilateral Convention **28 UNTS 173**
SIGNED: 23 Aug 48   FORCE: 23 Aug 48
REGISTERED: 13 Apr 49 ICAO (Civil Aviat)
ARTICLES: 32 LANGUAGE: French. Spanish.
HEADNOTE: CIVIL AVIATION RELATIONS
TOPIC: Air Transport
CONCEPTS: Definition of terms. Exceptions and exemptions. Previous treaty replacement. Non-prejudice to third party. Passports non-diplomatic. Visas. Conformity with municipal law. General cooperation. Exchange of informa-

tion and documents. Licenses and permits. Recognition of legal documents. Use of facilities. Arbitration. Procedure. Reexport of goods, etc.. Fees and exemptions. Non-interest rates and fees. National treatment. Customs exemptions. Competency certificate. Routes and logistics. Permit designation. Airport facilities. Airworthiness certificates. Conditions of airlines operating permission. Overflights and technical stops. Operating authorizations and regulations. Licenses and certificates of nationality. Postal services.
INTL ORGS: Arbitration Commission.
PROCEDURE: Amendment. Denunciation. Application to Non-self-governing Territories.
PARTIES:
France
Spain

100426 Bilateral Agreement **28 UNTS 209**
SIGNED: 8 Oct 48   FORCE: 1 Nov 48
REGISTERED: 13 Apr 49 ICAO (Civil Aviat)
ARTICLES: 13 LANGUAGE: French.
HEADNOTE: REGULATION CIVIL AIR LINES
TOPIC: Air Transport
CONCEPTS: Annex or appendix reference. Non-prejudice to third party. Conformity with municipal law. General cooperation. Licenses and permits. Recognition of legal documents. Responsibility and liability. Use of facilities. Investigation of violations. Arbitration. Procedure. Competence of tribunal. Reexport of goods, etc.. Fees and exemptions. National treatment. Customs exemptions. Competency certificate. Routes and logistics. Navigational conditions. Permit designation. Air transport. Airport facilities. Airworthiness certificates. Conditions of airlines operating permission. Operating authorizations and regulations. Licenses and certificates of nationality.
INTL ORGS: Arbitration Commission.
PROCEDURE: Denunciation.
PARTIES:
Netherlands
Spain

100427 Bilateral Agreement **28 UNTS 223**
SIGNED: 21 Dec 48   FORCE: 21 Dec 48
REGISTERED: 13 Apr 49 ICAO (Civil Aviat)
ARTICLES: 13 LANGUAGE: English.
HEADNOTE: AIR SERVICES
TOPIC: Air Transport
CONCEPTS: Conditions. Definition of terms. Detailed regulations. Annex or appendix reference. Conformity with municipal law. General cooperation. Exchange of information and documents. Arbitration. Procedure. Existing tribunals. Non-interest rates and fees. Routes and logistics. Permit designation. Conditions of airlines operating permission. Overflights and technical stops. Operating authorizations and regulations.
INTL ORGS: International Civil Aviation Organization. Arbitration Commission.
TREATY REF: 15UNTS295.
PROCEDURE: Amendment. Future Procedures Contemplated. Registration. Termination.
PARTIES:
Ceylon (Sri Lanka)
India

100428 Bilateral Agreement **28 UNTS 247**
SIGNED: 3 Jan 49   FORCE: 3 Jan 49
REGISTERED: 13 Apr 49 ICAO (Civil Aviat)
ARTICLES: 14 LANGUAGE: English.
HEADNOTE: AIR SERVICES
TOPIC: Air Transport
CONCEPTS: Definition of terms. Detailed regulations. Annex or appendix reference. Conformity with municipal law. General cooperation. Exchange of information and documents. Arbitration. Procedure. Existing tribunals. Negotiation. Reexport of goods, etc.. Non-interest rates and fees. Most favored nation clause. National treatment. Customs exemptions. Routes and logistics. Permit designation. Airport facilities. Conditions of airlines operating permission. Overflights and technical stops. Operating authorizations and regulations.
INTL ORGS: International Civil Aviation Organization. Arbitration Commission.
TREATY REF: 15UNTS295.

PROCEDURE: Amendment. Future Procedures Contemplated. Registration. Termination.
PARTIES:
Ceylon (Sri Lanka)
Pakistan

100429 Bilateral Agreement **28 UNTS 267**
SIGNED: 16 Sep 48   FORCE: 16 Sep 48
REGISTERED: 13 Apr 49 ICAO (Civil Aviat)
ARTICLES: 17 LANGUAGE: English. French. Spanish.
HEADNOTE: AIR NAVIGATION SERVICES
TOPIC: Air Transport
CONCEPTS: Arbitration. Payment schedules. Air transport. Airport facilities.
INTL ORGS: United Nations.
TREATY REF: 15UNTS295.
PROCEDURE: Duration. Ratification. Termination.
PARTIES:
Iceland
ICAO (Civil Aviat)

100430 Bilateral Agreement **29 UNTS 3**
SIGNED: 31 Dec 48   FORCE: 1 Jan 49
REGISTERED: 15 Apr 49 Norway
ARTICLES: 8 LANGUAGE: French.
HEADNOTE: EXCHANGE COMMODITIES
TOPIC: General Trade
CONCEPTS: Treaty implementation. Annex or appendix reference. Licenses and permits. Establishment of commission. General trade. Export quotas. Import quotas. Reciprocity in trade. Trade agencies. Quotas. Internal loans.
INTL ORGS: Special Commission.
PROCEDURE: Denunciation. Duration. Renewal or Revival.
PARTIES:
Norway
Poland
ANNEX
47 UNTS 356. Norway. Amendment 21 Dec 49. Force 1 Jan 50.
47 UNTS 356. Poland. Amendment 21 Dec 49. Force 1 Jan 50.

100431 Bilateral Protocol **29 UNTS 13**
SIGNED: 9 Feb 49   FORCE: 9 Feb 49
REGISTERED: 15 Apr 49 Norway
ARTICLES: 3 LANGUAGE: French. Norwegian.
HEADNOTE: COMMERCE FINANCE
TOPIC: General Economic
CONCEPTS: Territorial application. Annex or appendix reference. Previous treaty extension. Licenses and permits. Procedure. Export quotas. Import quotas. Reexport of goods, etc.. Balance of payments. Financial programs. Payment schedules. Commodity trade. Merchant vessels.
INTL ORGS: Organization for Economic Co-operation and Development. Special Commission.
PARTIES:
France
Norway

100432 Bilateral Protocol **29 UNTS 33**
SIGNED: 26 Feb 49   FORCE: 26 Feb 49
REGISTERED: 15 Apr 49 Norway
ARTICLES: 4 LANGUAGE: English.
HEADNOTE: FINANCIAL RELATIONS EXCHANGE GOODS
TOPIC: General Economic
CONCEPTS: Annex or appendix reference. Export quotas. Import quotas. Banking. Bonds. Currency. Monetary and gold transfers. Financial programs. Quotas. Navigational equipment.
INTL ORGS: Special Commission.
PARTIES:
Netherlands
Norway
ANNEX
42 UNTS 360. Norway. Implementation 23 Aug 49. Force 23 Aug 49.
42 UNTS 360. Netherlands. Implementation 23 Aug 49. Force 23 Aug 49.

100433 Bilateral Agreement **29 UNTS 47**
SIGNED: 24 Feb 49   FORCE: 7 Mar 49
REGISTERED: 15 Apr 49 Norway
ARTICLES: 6 LANGUAGE: French.

HEADNOTE: DEVELOPING COMMERCIAL RELA-
TIONS
TOPIC: General Trade
CONCEPTS: Annex or appendix reference. Infor-
mational records. Payment schedules.
PROCEDURE: Denunciation. Duration. Renewal or
Revival.
PARTIES:
Norway
Turkey

100434 Multilateral Agreement **29 UNTS 53**
SIGNED: 28 Feb 49   FORCE: 25 Aug 47
REGISTERED: 15 Apr 49 Norway
ARTICLES: 18 LANGUAGE: English.
HEADNOTE: JOINT OCEAN WEATHER STATION
TOPIC: Scientific Project
CONCEPTS: Treaty implementation. Annex or ap-
pendix reference. Operating agencies. Person-
nel. General property. Use of facilities. Research
and scientific projects. Research cooperation.
Meteorology. Accounting procedures. Expense
sharing formulae. Payment schedules. Facilities
and equipment. Repatriation of civilians.
PROCEDURE: Amendment. Duration. Termination.
PARTIES:
Norway SIGNED: 28 Feb 49 FORCE: 25 Aug 47
Sweden SIGNED: 28 Feb 49 FORCE: 25 Aug 47
UK Great Britain SIGNED: 28 Feb 49 FORCE:
25 Aug 47

100435 Bilateral Protocol **29 UNTS 83**
SIGNED: 8 Mar 49   FORCE: 8 Mar 49
REGISTERED: 15 Apr 49 Norway
ARTICLES: 1 LANGUAGE: French.
HEADNOTE: COMMERCE
TOPIC: General Trade
CONCEPTS: Annex or appendix reference. Annex
type material. Licenses and permits. Quotas.
INTL ORGS: Special Commission.
PARTIES:
Belgium
Norway

100436 Multilateral Protocol **29 UNTS 95**
SIGNED: 16 Mar 49   FORCE: 16 Mar 49
REGISTERED: 15 Apr 49 Norway
ARTICLES: 3 LANGUAGE: English. French.
HEADNOTE: PAYMENTS MONETARY
TOPIC: Finance
CONCEPTS: General trade. Accounting proce-
dures. Payment schedules.
PARTIES:
French Occup Germ SIGNED: 16 Mar 49 FORCE:
16 Mar 49
Norway SIGNED: 16 Mar 49 FORCE: 16 Mar 49
British Occup Germ SIGNED: 16 Mar 49 FORCE:
16 Mar 49
US Occup Germ SIGNED: 16 Mar 49 FORCE:
16 Mar 49

100437 Bilateral Instrument **29 UNTS 101**
SIGNED: 8 Mar 48   FORCE: 8 Mar 48
REGISTERED: 18 Apr 49 USA (United States)
ARTICLES: 1 LANGUAGE: English.
HEADNOTE: PRE-WAR BILATERAL TREATIES KEPT
FORCE
TOPIC: Admin Cooperation
CONCEPTS: Revival of treaties.
TREATY   REF: 93LTS337;   191LTS207;
136LTS23; 93LTS331; 26LTS27.
PARTIES:
Bulgaria
USA (United States)

100438 Bilateral Agreement **29 UNTS 163**
SIGNED: 30 Mar 46   FORCE: 1 Apr 46
REGISTERED: 20 Apr 49 Norway
ARTICLES: 7 LANGUAGE: Danish. Norwegian.
HEADNOTE: EXCHANGE COMMODITIES
TOPIC: General Trade
CONCEPTS: Time limit. Annex or appendix refer-
ence. Licenses and permits. Establishment of
commission. General trade. Export quotas. Im-
port quotas. Quotas.
INTL ORGS: Special Commission.
PARTIES:
Denmark
Norway

ANNEX
73 UNTS 246. Denmark. Supplementation
25 Mar 50. Force 25 Mar 50.
73 UNTS 246. Norway. Supplementation
25 Mar 50. Force 25 Mar 50.

100439 Bilateral Agreement **29 UNTS 179**
SIGNED: 15 Nov 47   FORCE: 1 Nov 47
REGISTERED: 20 Apr 49 Norway
ARTICLES: 5 LANGUAGE: Finnish. Norwegian.
HEADNOTE: EXCHANGE COMMODITIES
TOPIC: General Trade
CONCEPTS: General provisions. Annex or appen-
dix reference. General cooperation. Exchange of
information and documents. Licenses and per-
mits. Establishment of commission. General
trade. Export quotas. Import quotas. Quotas.
TREATY REF: 129LTS455; 161LTS211.
PROCEDURE: Duration. Denunciation. Duration.
Renewal or Revival.
PARTIES:
Finland
Norway

100440 Bilateral Protocol **29 UNTS 193**
SIGNED: 26 Jun 48   FORCE: 26 Jun 48
REGISTERED: 20 Apr 49 Norway
ARTICLES: 5 LANGUAGE: French.
HEADNOTE: COMMERCIAL EXCHANGES
TOPIC: General Trade
CONCEPTS: Territorial application. Exchange of in-
formation and documents. Licenses and permits.
Export quotas. Import quotas. Reciprocity in
trade. Payment schedules. Quotas.
PARTIES:
Norway
Switzerland

100441 Bilateral Agreement **29 UNTS 199**
SIGNED: 30 Jun 48   FORCE: 1 Jul 48
REGISTERED: 20 Apr 49 India
ARTICLES: 10 LANGUAGE: English.
HEADNOTE: FINANCE
TOPIC: Finance
CONCEPTS: Detailed regulations. Annex type ma-
terial. General cooperation. Accounting proce-
dures. Banking. Bonds. Currency. Monetary and
gold transfers. Currency deposits. Investments.
Exchange rates and regulations. Local currency.
INTL ORGS: International Monetary Fund.
PROCEDURE: Duration. Renewal or Revival. Termi-
nation.
PARTIES:
India
Pakistan
ANNEX
54 UNTS 386. India. Supplementation
10 Sep 49. Force 1 Jul 49.
54 UNTS 386. Pakistan. Supplementation
10 Sep 49. Force 1 Jul 49.
54 UNTS 394. Pakistan. Interpretation 10 Sep 49.
54 UNTS 394. India. Interpretation 10 Sep 49.

100442 Bilateral Agreement **29 UNTS 213**
SIGNED: 28 Sep 48   FORCE: 28 Sep 48
REGISTERED: 27 Apr 49 USA (United States)
ARTICLES: 11 LANGUAGE: English. Portuguese.
HEADNOTE: ECONOMIC COOPERATION
TOPIC: Direct Aid
CONCEPTS: Definition of terms. Territorial application. General provisions. Guarantees and safeguards. Treaty implementation. Annex or appendix reference. Tourism. Conformity with municipal law. General cooperation. Exchange of
information and documents. Personnel. Public
information. Existing tribunals. Claims and set-
tlements. Domestic obligation. Economic assis-
tance. Aid missions. Relief supplies. Procure-
ment. Access to materials. Paragraph 2, Article
36.
INTL ORGS: International Court of Justice. International Refugees Organization. Organization for
Economic Co-operation and Development.
United Nations.
TREATY REF: EEC CONV. 16APR48; 1UNTS9.
PROCEDURE: Amendment. Duration. Registration.
Termination.
PARTIES:
Portugal
USA (United States)

ANNEX
79 UNTS 310. USA (United States). Amendment
14 Feb 50. Force 14 Feb 50.
79 UNTS 310. Portugal. Amendment 14 Feb 50.
Force 14 Feb 50.
134 UNTS 370. USA (United States). Amendment
17 May 51. Force 17 May 51.
134 UNTS 370. Portugal. Amendment
17 May 51. Force 17 May 51.
207 UNTS 320. USA (United States). Amendment
9 Mar 53. Force 18 Mar 53.
207 UNTS 320. Portugal. Amendment 18 Mar 53.
Force 18 Mar 53.
212 UNTS 290. USA (United States). Amendment
22 May 53. Force 26 May 53.
212 UNTS 290. Portugal. Amendment
25 May 53. Force 26 May 53.

100443 Bilateral Agreement **29 UNTS 249**
SIGNED: 15 Oct 48   FORCE: 15 Oct 48
REGISTERED: 27 Apr 49 USA (United States)
ARTICLES: 10 LANGUAGE: English.
HEADNOTE: ECONOMIC COOPERATION
TOPIC: Direct Aid
CONCEPTS: Definition of terms. General provisions. Guarantees and safeguards. Annex or ap-
pendix reference. Tourism. Privileges and immu-
nities. Conformity with municipal law. General
cooperation. Exchange of information and docu-
ments. Personnel. Public information. Account-
ing procedures. Funding procedures. Local cur-
rency. Domestic obligation. Economic assis-
tance. Aid missions. Relief supplies.
Procurement. Occupation regime.
INTL ORGS: Organization for Economic Co-operation and Development. United Nations.
TREATY REF: EEC CONV. 16APR48; ITALY PEACE
TREATY 10FEB47.
PROCEDURE: Duration. Registration. Termination.
PARTIES:
Trieste
USA (United States)
ANNEX
76 UNTS 270. USA (United States). Amendment
27 Dec 49. Force 28 Dec 49.
76 UNTS 270. Trieste. Amendment 28 Dec 49.
Force 28 Dec 49.
141 UNTS 376. Trieste. Amendment 19 Apr 51.
Force 19 Apr 51.
141 UNTS 376. USA (United States). Amendment
29 Mar 51. Force 19 Apr 51.
179 UNTS 212. USA (United States). Amendment
28 Dec 51. Force 3 Jan 52.
179 UNTS 212. Trieste. Amendment 3 Jan 52.
Force 3 Jan 52.

100444 Bilateral Exchange **29 UNTS 277**
SIGNED: 3 Jul 47   FORCE: 15 Jul 47
REGISTERED: 28 Apr 49 Belgium
ARTICLES: 2 LANGUAGE: French.
HEADNOTE: ABOLITION PASSPORT VISAS
TOPIC: Visas
CONCEPTS: Territorial application. Visa abolition.
Resident permits.
PARTIES:
Belgium
Switzerland

100445 Multilateral Protocol **30 UNTS 3**
SIGNED: 4 May 49   FORCE: 4 May 49
REGISTERED: 4 May 49 United Nations
ARTICLES: 8 LANGUAGE: Chinese. English.
French. Russian. Spanish.
HEADNOTE: AMENDING 1910 OBSCENITY
AGREEMENT
TOPIC: Admin Cooperation
CONCEPTS: Annex type material. Previous treaty
extension.
INTL ORGS: United Nations.
PARTIES:
Brazil SIGNED: 4 May 49
Canada SIGNED: 4 May 49 FORCE: 4 May 49
Taiwan SIGNED: 4 May 49 FORCE: 4 May 49
Cuba SIGNED: 4 May 49
Luxembourg SIGNED: 4 May 49
Norway SIGNED: 4 May 49 FORCE: 4 May 49
Turkey SIGNED: 4 May 49
UK Great Britain SIGNED: 4 May 49 FORCE:
4 May 49
USA (United States) SIGNED: 4 May 49
Yugoslavia SIGNED: 4 May 49

32 UNTS 399. Ceylon (Sri Lanka). Signature without Reservation as to Approval 14 Jul 49.

42 UNTS 366. United Arab Rep. Ratification 16 Sep 49.

42 UNTS 366. Switzerland. Acceptance 23 Sep 49.

43 UNTS 340. Finland. Acceptance 31 Oct 49.

43 UNTS 340. Finland. Acceptance 31 Oct 49.

44 UNTS 341. Denmark. Acceptance 21 Nov 49.

44 UNTS 341. Denmark. Acceptance 21 Nov 49.

45 UNTS 330. Australia. Signature without Reservation as to Approval 8 Dec 49.

45 UNTS 330. India. Acceptance 28 Dec 49.

47 UNTS 362. Denmark. Acceptance 1 Mar 50.

68 UNTS 264. Austria. Signature without Reservation as to Approval 4 Aug 50.

68 UNTS 264. USA (United States). Ratification 14 Aug 50.

71 UNTS 310. Netherlands. Ratification 26 Sep 50.

71 UNTS 310. South Africa. Signature without Reservation as to Approval 1 Sep 50.

71 UNTS 310. Turkey. Ratification 13 Sep 50.

71 UNTS 310. Iraq. Ratification 14 Sep 50.

73 UNTS 256. New Zealand. Signature without Reservation as to Approval 14 Oct 50.

73 UNTS 256. Iceland. Acceptance 25 Oct 50.

76 UNTS 274. Romania. Signature without Reservation as to Approval 22 Nov 50.

76 UNTS 274. Romania. Signature without Reservation as to Approval 22 Nov 50.

88 UNTS 432. Pakistan. Ratification 4 May 51.

88 UNTS 433. Honduras. Ratification 7 Feb 50.

88 UNTS 433. Nicaragua. Ratification 26 Jul 50.

88 UNTS 433. El Salvador. Ratification 11 Sep 50.

92 UNTS 398. Czechoslovakia. Ratification 21 Jun 51.

92 UNTS 398. Czechoslovakia. Ratification 21 Jun 51.

122 UNTS 335. Ireland. Acceptance 28 Feb 52.

134 UNTS 375. Mexico. Acceptance 2 Jul 52.

134 UNTS 375. Mexico. Acceptance 2 Jul 52.

140 UNTS 436. Belgium. Qualified Acceptance 13 Oct 52.

149 UNTS 388. Italy. Acceptance 13 Nov 52.

164 UNTS 361. Yugoslavia. Ratification 29 Apr 53.

207 UNTS 326. Luxembourg. Acceptance 14 Mar 55.

347 UNTS 358. Iran. Acceptance 30 Dec 59.

100446   Multilateral Protocol   **30 UNTS 23**
SIGNED: 4 May 49   FORCE: 4 May 49
REGISTERED: 4 May 49 United Nations
ARTICLES: 8 LANGUAGE: Chinese. English. French. Russian. Spanish.
HEADNOTE: AMENDING 1904 WHITE SLAVE AGREEMENT
TOPIC: Admin Cooperation
CONCEPTS: Annex type material. Previous treaty extension.
INTL ORGS: United Nations.
TREATY REF: 1LTS83.
PARTIES:
Brazil SIGNED: 4 May 49
Canada SIGNED: 4 May 49 FORCE: 4 May 49
Taiwan SIGNED: 4 May 49 FORCE: 4 May 49
Cuba SIGNED: 4 May 49
Luxembourg SIGNED: 4 May 49
Norway SIGNED: 4 May 49 FORCE: 4 May 49
Turkey SIGNED: 4 May 49
UK Great Britain SIGNED: 4 May 49 FORCE: 4 May 49
USA (United States) SIGNED: 4 May 49
Yugoslavia SIGNED: 4 May 49
ANNEX
32 UNTS 400. Ceylon (Sri Lanka). Signature without Reservation as to Approval 14 Jul 49.

42 UNTS 367. United Arab Rep. Ratification 16 Sep 49.

42 UNTS 367. Switzerland. Acceptance 23 Sep 49.

43 UNTS 341. Finland. Acceptance 31 Oct 49.

44 UNTS 342. Denmark. Acceptance 21 Nov 49.

45 UNTS 331. Australia. Signature without Reservation as to Approval 8 Dec 49.

45 UNTS 331. India. Acceptance 28 Dec 49.

45 UNTS 331. Australia. All Territories.

47 UNTS 363. Denmark. Acceptance 1 Mar 50.

65 UNTS 317. Austria. Signature without Reservation as to Approval 7 Jun 50.

70 UNTS 273. USA (United States). Ratification 14 Aug 50.

71 UNTS 311. Turkey. Acceptance 13 Sep 50.

71 UNTS 311. Netherlands. Acceptance 26 Sep 50.

87 UNTS 388. Yugoslavia. Ratification 26 Apr 51.

92 UNTS 399. Czechoslovakia. Ratification 21 Jun 51.

98 UNTS 279. South Africa. Acceptance 14 Aug 51.

121 UNTS 328. Sweden. Signature without Reservation as to Approval 23 Feb 52.

133 UNTS 317. Pakistan. Acceptance 16 Jun 52.

140 UNTS 437. Belgium. Qualified Acceptance 13 Oct 52.

149 UNTS 389. Italy. Acceptance 12 Nov 52.

207 UNTS 327. Luxembourg. Acceptance 14 Mar 55.

347 UNTS 359. Iran. Acceptance 30 Dec 59.

401 UNTS 213. Ireland. Acceptance 19 Jul 61.

541 UNTS 300. Cuba. Qualified Acceptance 4 Aug 65.

100447   Bilateral Exchange   **30 UNTS 45**
SIGNED: 12 Apr 49   FORCE: 1 May 49
REGISTERED: 10 May 49 Belgium
ARTICLES: 2 LANGUAGE: French.
HEADNOTE: FACILITATE MOVEMENT PERSONS
TOPIC: Visas
CONCEPTS: Passports non-diplomatic. Non-visa travel documents.
PARTIES:
Belgium
France
ANNEX
31 UNTS 489. France. Supplementation 12 May 49. Force 1 Jun 49.

31 UNTS 489. Belgium. Supplementation 14 May 49. Force 1 Jun 49.

47 UNTS 364. France. Supplementation 6 Sep 49. Force 1 Oct 49.

47 UNTS 364. Belgium. Supplementation 6 Sep 49. Force 1 Oct 49.

48 UNTS 306. Belgium. Supplementation 24 Jan 50. Force 1 Feb 50.

48 UNTS 306. France. Supplementation 24 Jan 50. Force 1 Feb 50.

71 UNTS 312. France. Amendment 12 Jun 50. Force 16 Jun 50.

71 UNTS 312. Belgium. Amendment 16 Jun 50. Force 16 Jun 50.

277 UNTS 339. Belgium. Supplementation 1 Mar 57. Force 1 Jan 57.

277 UNTS 339. France. Supplementation 7 Mar 57. Force 1 Jan 57.

100448   Unilateral Instrument   **30 UNTS 53**
SIGNED: 29 Nov 48   FORCE: 11 May 49
REGISTERED: 11 May 49 United Nations
ARTICLES: 1 LANGUAGE: English.
HEADNOTE: ADHERENCE UN CHARTER
TOPIC: UN Charter
CONCEPTS: Acceptance of obligations upon admittance to UN.
INTL ORGS: United Nations.
PARTIES:
Israel

100449   Multilateral Treaty   **30 UNTS 55**
SIGNED: 30 Apr 48   FORCE: 6 May 49
REGISTERED: 13 May 49 OAS (Am States)
ARTICLES: 60 LANGUAGE: English. French. Portuguese. Spanish.
HEADNOTE: AMERICAN TREATY PACIFIC SETTLEMENT
TOPIC: Dispute Settlement
CONCEPTS: Exceptions and exemptions. Previous treaty replacement. Inspection and observation. Recognition and enforcement of legal decisions. Arbitration. Mediation and good offices. Procedure. Conciliation.
INTL ORGS: International Court of Justice. Organization of American States. United Nations. Special Commission.
TREATY REF: 33LTS25; 100LTS399; 130LTS135; 158LTS393.
PROCEDURE: Accession. Denunciation. Ratification. Registration.
PARTIES:
Argentina SIGNED: 13 Apr 48
Bolivia SIGNED: 10 Apr 48

Brazil SIGNED: 13 Apr 48
Chile SIGNED: 10 Apr 48
Colombia SIGNED: 13 Apr 48
Costa Rica SIGNED: 13 Apr 48 RATIFIED: 6 May 49 FORCE: 6 May 49
Cuba SIGNED: 10 Apr 48
Dominican Republic SIGNED: 10 Apr 48
Ecuador SIGNED: 13 Apr 48
El Salvador SIGNED: 10 Apr 48
Guatemala SIGNED: 10 Apr 48
Haiti SIGNED: 13 Apr 48
Honduras SIGNED: 10 Apr 48
Mexico SIGNED: 10 Apr 48 RATIFIED: 23 Nov 48 FORCE: 6 May 49
Nicaragua SIGNED: 10 Apr 48
Panama SIGNED: 10 Apr 48
Paraguay SIGNED: 10 Apr 48
Peru SIGNED: 10 Apr 48
USA (United States) SIGNED: 10 Apr 48
Uruguay SIGNED: 10 Apr 48
Venezuela SIGNED: 13 Apr 48
ANNEX
87 UNTS 389. Haiti. Ratification 28 Apr 51.

88 UNTS 433. Dominican Republic. Ratification 12 Sep 50.

88 UNTS 433. Panama. Ratification 25 Apr 51.

377 UNTS 389. Uruguay. Ratification 1 Sep 55.

552 UNTS 360. Brazil. Ratification 16 Nov 65.

100450   Bilateral Agreement   **30 UNTS 117**
SIGNED: 18 Dec 48   FORCE: 1 Jan 49
REGISTERED: 16 May 49 Norway
ARTICLES: 5 LANGUAGE: Norwegian. Swedish.
HEADNOTE: RECIPROCAL CREDITING UNEMPLOYMENT INSURANCE CONTRIBUTIONS
TOPIC: Non-ILO Labor
CONCEPTS: Annex or appendix reference. General cooperation. Incorporation of treaty provisions into national law. Non-ILO labor relations. Unemployment. Assets transfer.
PARTIES:
Norway
Sweden

100451   Bilateral Agreement   **30 UNTS 137**
SIGNED: 17 Feb 49   FORCE: 17 Feb 49
REGISTERED: 16 May 49 Norway
ARTICLES: 6 LANGUAGE: English.
HEADNOTE: TRADE DISCUSSIONS MIXED COMMISSION
TOPIC: Milit Occupation
CONCEPTS: Annex or appendix reference. Private contracts. General trade. Delivery schedules. Control and occupation machinery.
PARTIES:
Allied Milit Occup
Norway

100452   Bilateral Protocol   **30 UNTS 145**
SIGNED: 28 Jan 49   FORCE: 28 Jan 49
REGISTERED: 31 May 49 Norway
ARTICLES: 2 LANGUAGE: French.
HEADNOTE: MIXED COMMISSION TRADE PROTOCOL
TOPIC: General Trade
CONCEPTS: Annex type material. Accounting procedures. Banking. Commodity trade.
INTL ORGS: Special Commission.
PARTIES:
Austria
Norway

100453   Bilateral Agreement   **30 UNTS 151**
SIGNED: 24 Feb 49   FORCE: 7 Mar 49
REGISTERED: 31 May 49 Norway
ARTICLES: 10 LANGUAGE: French.
HEADNOTE: PAYMENTS
TOPIC: Finance
CONCEPTS: Standardization. General cooperation. Accounting procedures. Banking. Balance of payments. Currency. Exchange rates and regulations. Payment schedules. Credit provisions.
PARTIES:
Norway
Turkey

100454   Bilateral Agreement   **30 UNTS 161**
SIGNED: 12 Mar 49   FORCE: 12 Mar 49
REGISTERED: 31 May 49 Norway

ARTICLES: 9 LANGUAGE: French.
HEADNOTE: COMMERCE
TOPIC: General Trade
CONCEPTS: Annex or appendix reference. Licenses and permits. Establishment of commission. Export quotas. Import quotas. Payment schedules. Quotas. General.
INTL ORGS: Special Commission.
PROCEDURE: Denunciation. Duration.
PARTIES:
  Greece
  Norway
ANNEX
178 UNTS 384. Norway. Supplementation 21 Jun 52. Force 21 Jun 52.
178 UNTS 384. Greece. Supplementation 21 Jun 52. Force 21 Jun 52.

100455 Bilateral Exchange **30 UNTS 171**
SIGNED: 8 Dec 47   FORCE: 8 Dec 47
REGISTERED: 1 Jun 49 Norway
ARTICLES: 2 LANGUAGE: French.
HEADNOTE: GRANTING CREDIT
TOPIC: Loans and Credits
CONCEPTS: Interest rates. Loan and credit. Credit provisions. Purchase authorization. Loan repayment.
PARTIES:
  Greece
  Norway

100456 Bilateral Agreement **30 UNTS 177**
SIGNED: 20 Jul 46   FORCE: 20 Jul 46
REGISTERED: 1 Jun 49 Norway
ARTICLES: 8 LANGUAGE: French.
HEADNOTE: COMMERCE
TOPIC: General Trade
CONCEPTS: Annex or appendix reference. Licenses and permits. Establishment of trade relations. Export quotas. Import quotas. Trade agencies. Quotas.
PROCEDURE: Denunciation. Duration. Ratification. Renewal or Revival.
PARTIES:
  Italy
  Norway

100457 Bilateral Agreement **30 UNTS 187**
SIGNED: 30 Aug 46   FORCE: 30 Aug 46
REGISTERED: 1 Jun 49 Norway
ARTICLES: 7 LANGUAGE: French.
HEADNOTE: COMMERCE
TOPIC: General Trade
CONCEPTS: Annex or appendix reference. Licenses and permits. Establishment of commission. Establishment of trade relations. Export quotas. Import quotas. Payment schedules. Smuggling.
INTL ORGS: Special Commission.
TREATY REF: 15UNTS163; 26UNTS414.
PROCEDURE: Denunciation. Duration.
PARTIES:
  Norway
  Yugoslavia
ANNEX
33 UNTS 346. Norway. Prolongation 2 Apr 49. Force 2 Apr 49.
33 UNTS 346. Yugoslavia. Prolongation 2 Apr 49. Force 2 Apr 49.

100458 Bilateral Agreement **30 UNTS 205**
SIGNED: 4 Feb 48   FORCE: 4 Feb 48
REGISTERED: 1 Jun 49 Norway
ARTICLES. 9 LANGUAGE: French.
HEADNOTE: EXCHANGE GOODS
TOPIC: General Trade
CONCEPTS: Treaty implementation. Annex or appendix reference. Licenses and permits. Establishment of commission. Procedure. Establishment of trade relations. Export quotas. Import quotas. Reciprocity in trade. Quotas.
INTL ORGS: Special Commission.
TREATY REF: 29UNTS3.
PROCEDURE: Duration.
PARTIES:
  Norway
  Poland

100459 Bilateral Exchange **30 UNTS 215**
SIGNED: 16 Aug 46   FORCE: 16 Aug 46
REGISTERED: 1 Jun 49 Norway
ARTICLES: 6 LANGUAGE: French.
HEADNOTE: EXCHANGE COMMODITIES
TOPIC: Commodity Trade
CONCEPTS: Trade procedures. Commodity trade.
PROCEDURE: Denunciation.
PARTIES:
  Norway
  Portugal
ANNEX
88 UNTS 434. Portugal. Prolongation 22 Dec 50. Force 10 Feb 51.
88 UNTS 434. Norway. Prolongation 22 Dec 50. Force 10 Feb 51.

100460 Bilateral Agreement **30 UNTS 223**
SIGNED: 20 Mar 47   FORCE: 13 Feb 47
REGISTERED: 1 Jun 49 Norway
ARTICLES: 9 LANGUAGE: French.
HEADNOTE: EXCHANGE GOODS
TOPIC: General Trade
CONCEPTS: Annex or appendix reference. General cooperation. Establishment of commission. Export quotas. Import quotas. Payment schedules. Reparations and restrictions.
INTL ORGS: International Refugees Organization. Special Commission.
TREATY REF: 20LTS355.
PROCEDURE: Denunciation. Duration.
PARTIES:
  Czechoslovakia
  Norway
ANNEX
88 UNTS 438. Norway. Prolongation 4 Nov 50. Force 4 Nov 50.
88 UNTS 438. Czechoslovakia. Prolongation 4 Nov 50. Force 4 Nov 50.

100461 Multilateral Protocol **30 UNTS 249**
SIGNED: 19 Sep 47   FORCE: 19 Sep 47
REGISTERED: 1 Jun 49 Norway
ARTICLES: 6 LANGUAGE: English.
HEADNOTE: EXCHANGE GOODS
TOPIC: General Trade
CONCEPTS: Exchange of information and documents. Private contracts. Interest rates.
PROCEDURE: Duration.
PARTIES:
  Norway SIGNED: 19 Sep 47 FORCE: 19 Sep 47
  British Occup Germ SIGNED: 19 Sep 47 FORCE: 19 Sep 47
  US Occup Germ SIGNED: 19 Sep 47 FORCE: 19 Sep 47

100462 Multilateral Agreement **30 UNTS 269**
SIGNED: 19 Sep 47   FORCE: 19 Sep 47
REGISTERED: 1 Jun 49 Norway
ARTICLES: 7 LANGUAGE: English.
HEADNOTE: PAYMENTS
TOPIC: Finance
CONCEPTS: Detailed regulations. General cooperation. General trade. Accounting procedures. Banking. Balance of payments. Interest rates. Payment schedules.
TREATY REF: 29LTS95.
PROCEDURE: Duration. Termination.
PARTIES:
  Norway SIGNED: 19 Sep 47 FORCE: 19 Sep 47
  British Occup Germ SIGNED: 19 Sep 47 FORCE: 19 Sep 47
  US Occup Germ SIGNED: 19 Sep 47 FORCE: 19 Sep 47

100463 Bilateral Agreement **30 UNTS 281**
SIGNED: 5 Jul 48   FORCE: 5 Jul 48
REGISTERED: 1 Jun 49 Norway
ARTICLES: 7 LANGUAGE: French.
HEADNOTE: COMMERCE
TOPIC: General Trade
CONCEPTS: Annex or appendix reference. Licenses and permits. Private contracts. Trade agencies. Non-interest rates and fees.
PROCEDURE: Denunciation. Duration.
PARTIES:
  France
  Norway

100464 Bilateral Agreement **30 UNTS 293**
SIGNED: 19 Feb 47   FORCE: 19 Feb 47
REGISTERED: 1 Jun 49 Norway
ARTICLES: 10 LANGUAGE: English.
HEADNOTE: DEVELOPING TRADE
TOPIC: General Trade
CONCEPTS: Treaty implementation. Annex or appendix reference. Establishment of trade relations. Trade procedures. Accounting procedures. Banking. Payment schedules. Delivery schedules.
PROCEDURE: Duration.
PARTIES:
  Norway
  USSR (Soviet Union)

100465 Bilateral Agreement **31 UNTS 3**
SIGNED: 27 Aug 46   FORCE: 27 Aug 46
REGISTERED: 1 Jun 49 Norway
ARTICLES: 5 LANGUAGE: French.
HEADNOTE: COMMERCE
TOPIC: General Trade
CONCEPTS: Annex or appendix reference. Licenses and permits. Public information. Establishment of trade relations. Trade procedures.
PROCEDURE: Denunciation. Duration.
PARTIES:
  Hungary
  Norway

100466 Bilateral Agreement **31 UNTS 21**
SIGNED: 14 Apr 47   FORCE: 14 Apr 47
REGISTERED: 1 Jun 49 Norway
ARTICLES: 5 LANGUAGE: French.
HEADNOTE: COMMERCE
TOPIC: General Trade
CONCEPTS: Annex or appendix reference. Licenses and permits. Establishment of commission. Establishment of trade relations. Payment schedules.
INTL ORGS: Special Commission.
PROCEDURE: Duration. Future Procedures Contemplated.
PARTIES:
  Austria
  Norway

100467 Bilateral Agreement **31 UNTS 29**
SIGNED: 28 Jan 47   FORCE: 1 Jan 47
REGISTERED: 1 Jun 49 Norway
ARTICLES: 6 LANGUAGE: English.
HEADNOTE: TRADE
TOPIC: General Trade
CONCEPTS: Territorial application. Annex or appendix reference. Establishment of commission. Export quotas. Import quotas.
PROCEDURE: Duration. Termination.
PARTIES:
  Netherlands
  Norway

100468 Bilateral Exchange **31 UNTS 69**
SIGNED: 26 Mar 46   FORCE: 26 Mar 46
REGISTERED: 1 Jun 49 Norway
ARTICLES: 2 LANGUAGE: French.
HEADNOTE: MEASURES PREVENT REINDEER CROSSING FRONTIER
TOPIC: General Trade
CONCEPTS: Detailed regulations. General provisions. Exchange of information and documents. Investigation of violations. Procedure. Compensation. Expense sharing formulae. Payment schedules. Non-interest rates and fees. Claims and settlements. Pasturage in frontier zones. Markers and definitions. Frontier crossing points.
INTL ORGS: Special Commission.
PROCEDURE: Denunciation. Future Procedures Contemplated. Ratification.
PARTIES:
  France
  Norway

100469 Bilateral Exchange **31 UNTS 83**
SIGNED: 11 Jun 48   FORCE: 11 Jun 48
REGISTERED: 1 Jun 49 Norway
ARTICLES: 2 LANGUAGE: French.
HEADNOTE: GOODS EXCHANGE
TOPIC: General Trade

CONCEPTS: Annex or appendix reference. Ex-
change of information and documents. Licenses
and permits. Trade agencies.
INTL ORGS: Special Commission.
TREATY REF: 29LTS13.
PARTIES:
  France
  Norway

100470   Bilateral Agreement   **31 UNTS 97**
SIGNED: 2 Jan 48   FORCE: 2 Jan 48
REGISTERED: 2 Jun 49 USA (United States)
ARTICLES: 3 LANGUAGE: English. French.
HEADNOTE: RELIEF ASSISTANCE
TOPIC: Direct Aid
CONCEPTS: Annex or appendix reference. Confor-
mity with municipal law. Domestic obligation.
Relief supplies. Procurement.
PROCEDURE: Duration. Termination.
PARTIES:
  France
  USA (United States)

100471   Bilateral Agreement   **31 UNTS 105**
SIGNED: 3 Jan 48   FORCE: 3 Jan 48
REGISTERED: 2 Jun 49 USA (United States)
ARTICLES: 3 LANGUAGE: English. Italian.
HEADNOTE: RELIEF ASSISTANCE
TOPIC: Direct Aid
CONCEPTS: Annex or appendix reference. Confor-
mity with municipal law. Domestic obligation.
Relief supplies. Procurement.
PROCEDURE: Duration. Termination.
PARTIES:
  Italy
  USA (United States)
                ANNEX
80 UNTS 316. Italy. Prolongation 30 Dec 48.
Force 30 Dec 48.
80 UNTS 316. USA (United States). Prolongation
30 Dec 48. Force 30 Dec 48.

100472   Bilateral Exchange   **31 UNTS 115**
SIGNED: 28 Jun 48   FORCE: 28 Jun 48
REGISTERED: 2 Jun 49 USA (United States)
ARTICLES: 2 LANGUAGE: English. French.
HEADNOTE: APPLICATION MOST FAVORED NA-
TION CONTROLLED OCCUPIED AREAS
TOPIC: Mostfavored Nation
CONCEPTS: General trade. Tariffs. Exchange rates
and regulations. Most favored nation clause.
Customs duties. Occupation regime.
TREATY REF: UN TREATY PUB.47 2'48;.
PROCEDURE: Duration. Termination.
PARTIES:
  France
  USA (United States)

100473   Multilateral Exchange   **31 UNTS 123**
SIGNED: 14 Jul 48   FORCE: 14 Jul 48
REGISTERED: 2 Jun 49 USA (United States)
ARTICLES: 2 LANGUAGE: English.
HEADNOTE: APPLICATION MOST FAVORED NA-
TION TREATMENT
TOPIC: Mostfavored Nation
CONCEPTS: Exceptions and exemptions. General
trade. Most favored nation clause. Occupation
regime.
TREATY REF: UNTS PUB.47; GATT.
PROCEDURE: Duration. Termination.
PARTIES:
  USA (United States) SIGNED: 14 Jul 48 FORCE:
    14 Jul 48
  British Occup Germ SIGNED: 14 Jul 48 FORCE:
    14 Jul 48
  US Occup Germ SIGNED: 14 Jul 48 FORCE:
    14 Jul 48

100474   Bilateral Exchange   **31 UNTS 131**
SIGNED: 2 Jul 48   FORCE: 2 Jul 48
REGISTERED: 2 Jun 49 USA (United States)
ARTICLES: 2 LANGUAGE: English.
HEADNOTE: APPLICATION MOST FAVORED NA-
TION CONTROLLED OCCUPIED AREAS
TOPIC: Mostfavored Nation
CONCEPTS: Exceptions and exemptions. General
trade. Tariffs. Exchange rates and regulations.
Most favored nation clause. Customs duties. Oc-
cupation regime.

TREATY REF: 2UNTS10;.
PROCEDURE: Duration. Termination.
PARTIES:
  Greece
  USA (United States)

100475   Bilateral Exchange   **31 UNTS 139**
SIGNED: 28 Sep 48   FORCE: 28 Sep 48
REGISTERED: 2 Jun 49 USA (United States)
ARTICLES: 2 LANGUAGE: English. Portuguese.
HEADNOTE: APPLICATION MOST FAVORED NA-
TION CONTROLLED OCCUPIED AREAS
TOPIC: Mostfavored Nation
CONCEPTS: Exceptions and exemptions. General
trade. Tariffs. Exchange rates and regulations.
Most favored nation clause. Customs duties. Oc-
cupation regime.
PROCEDURE: Duration. Termination.
PARTIES:
  Portugal
  USA (United States)

100476   Bilateral Agreement   **31 UNTS 147**
SIGNED: 13 Jun 46   FORCE: 17 Jan 47
REGISTERED: 6 Jun 49 Afghanistan
ARTICLES: 5 LANGUAGE: Persian. Russian.
HEADNOTE: FRONTIER AGREEMENT
TOPIC: Territory Boundary
CONCEPTS: Establishment of commission. Mark-
ers and definitions.
INTL ORGS: Special Commission.
PROCEDURE: Ratification.
PARTIES:
  Afghanistan
  USSR (Soviet Union)

100477   Bilateral Agreement   **31 UNTS 169**
SIGNED: 24 May 46   FORCE: 24 May 46
REGISTERED: 6 Jun 49 Belgium
ARTICLES: 1 LANGUAGE: French.
HEADNOTE: COOPERATION PEACEFUL USES
ATOMIC ENERGY
TOPIC: Finance
CONCEPTS: Definition of terms. Non-prejudice to
third party. Conformity with municipal law. In-
spection and observation. Investigation of viola-
tions. Research cooperation. Purchase authoriza-
tion. Nuclear materials. Non-nuclear materials.
Peaceful use. Security of information.
TREATY REF: 2UNTS281.
PROCEDURE: Duration. Termination.
PARTIES:
  Belgium
  Netherlands

100478   Bilateral Convention   **31 UNTS 173**
SIGNED: 18 Feb 49   FORCE: 18 Feb 49
REGISTERED: 6 Jun 49 Belgium
ARTICLES: 5 LANGUAGE: French.
HEADNOTE: COMPENSATION   NATIONALIZED
ELECTRICITY & GAS
TOPIC: Claims and Debts
CONCEPTS: Detailed regulations. Time limit. An-
nex or appendix reference. Expropriation. Arbi-
tration. Procedure. Existing tribunals. Bonds.
Compensation. Claims and settlements. Most fa-
vored nation clause.
INTL ORGS: International Court of Justice. Arbitra-
tion Commission.
PARTIES:
  Belgium
  France
                ANNEX
73 UNTS 256. Belgium. Amendment 20 Mar 50.
Force 12 Apr 50.
73 UNTS 256. France. Amendment 12 Apr 50.
Force 12 Apr 50.

100479   Bilateral Exchange   **31 UNTS 199**
SIGNED: 21 Feb 46   FORCE: 21 Feb 46
REGISTERED: 6 Jun 49 Belgium
ARTICLES: 2 LANGUAGE: French.
HEADNOTE: SUPPLEMENTARY PAYMENTS
TOPIC: Finance
CONCEPTS: Banking. Currency. Payment sched-
ules.
TREATY REF: 16UNTS311.
PROCEDURE: Denunciation.

PARTIES:
  Belgium
  Norway
                ANNEX
47 UNTS 370.   Belgium.   Supplementation
29 Oct 46. Force 1 Oct 49.
47 UNTS 370.   Norway.   Supplementation
29 Oct 46. Force 1 Oct 49.
47 UNTS 372.   Norway.   Supplementation
29 Oct 46. Force 1 Oct 49.
47 UNTS 372.   Belgium.   Supplementation
11 Apr 47. Force 11 Apr 47.
47 UNTS 374.   Norway.   Supplementation
12 Mar 48. Force 12 Mar 48.
47 UNTS 374. Bel-Lux Econ Union. Supplementation 12 Mar 48. Force 12 Mar 48.
109 UNTS 314. Belgium. Denunciation 9 Jul 51.
Force 8 Jan 52.

100480   Bilateral Convention   **31 UNTS 205**
SIGNED: 21 Jan 49   FORCE: 10 Apr 49
REGISTERED: 8 Jun 49 Poland
ARTICLES: 89 LANGUAGE: Czechoslovakian. Polish.
HEADNOTE: LEGAL RELATIONS CIVIL CRIMINAL
CASES
TOPIC: Admin Cooperation
CONCEPTS: Court procedures. Limits of prosecu-
tion. Material evidence. General cooperation. Ex-
change of information and documents. Informa-
tional records. Inspection and observation. Ju-
ridical personality. Legal protection and
assistance. Recognition and enforcement of le-
gal decisions. Jurisdiction. Recognition of legal
documents. Investigation of violations. Penal
sanctions. Debts.
TREATY   REF:
46LTS201,177LTS139,178LTS159.
PROCEDURE: Ratification. Termination.
PARTIES:
  Czechoslovakia
  Poland

100481   Bilateral Agreement   **31 UNTS 325**
SIGNED: 5 Apr 48   FORCE: 1 Oct 48
REGISTERED: 8 Jun 49 Poland
ARTICLES: 15 LANGUAGE: Czechoslovakian. Pol-
ish.
HEADNOTE: APPLICATION MOST FAVORED NA-
TION CONTROLLED OCCUPIED AREAS
TOPIC: Admin Cooperation
CONCEPTS: Exceptions and exemptions. General
trade. Tariffs. Exchange rates and regulations.
Most favored nation clause. Customs duties. Oc-
cupation regime.
INTL ORGS: Special Commission.
PROCEDURE: Duration. Termination.
PARTIES:
  Czechoslovakia
  Poland
                ANNEX
340 UNTS 324. Czechoslovakia. Supplementa-
tion 30 Sep 55. Force 27 Feb 57.
340 UNTS 324.   Poland.   Supplementation
30 Sep 55. Force 27 Feb 57.

100482   Bilateral Agreement   **31 UNTS 355**
SIGNED: 5 Apr 48   FORCE: 1 Oct 48
REGISTERED: 8 Jun 49 Poland
ARTICLES: 24 LANGUAGE: Czechoslovakian. Pol-
ish.
HEADNOTE: SOCIAL INSURANCE
TOPIC: Non-ILO Labor
CONCEPTS: Detailed regulations. Exceptions and
exemptions. General provisions. Domestic legislation. Jurisdiction. Dispute settlement. Public
health. Old age and invalidity insurance. Non-ILO
labor relations. Family allowances. Sickness and
invalidity insurance. Social security. Unemployment. Payment schedules. National treatment.
PROCEDURE: Denunciation. Ratification.
PARTIES:
  Czechoslovakia
  Poland
                ANNEX
340 UNTS 332. Czechoslovakia. Supplementation 30 Sep 55. Force 27 Feb 57.
340 UNTS 332.   Poland.   Supplementation
30 Sep 55. Force 27 Feb 57.

100483 Bilateral Convention **31 UNTS 409**
SIGNED: 13 Apr 48 FORCE: 9 May 48
REGISTERED: 23 Jun 49 Belgium
ARTICLES: 11 LANGUAGE: French.
HEADNOTE: OPERATION INTERNATIONAL STATIONS
TOPIC: Territory Boundary
CONCEPTS: Border traffic and migration. Conformity with municipal law. Inspection and observation. Tax exemptions. Customs exemptions. Markers and definitions. Frontier crossing points.
PROCEDURE: Ratification. Termination.
PARTIES:
Belgium
France

100484 Bilateral Exchange **31 UNTS 423**
SIGNED: 8 Aug 46 FORCE: 8 Aug 46
REGISTERED: 28 Jun 49 USA (United States)
ARTICLES: 2 LANGUAGE: English. Persian.
HEADNOTE: EXTENDING AGREEMENT MILITARY MISSION
TOPIC: Military Mission
CONCEPTS: Annex type material. Previous treaty extension. Military assistance missions.
PARTIES:
Iran
USA (United States)
ANNEX
141 UNTS 380. USA (United States). Prolongation 16 Aug 50. Force 3 Oct 50.
141 UNTS 380. Iran. Prolongation 16 Aug 50. Force 3 Oct 50.
229 UNTS 279. Iran. Prolongation 18 Apr 54.
229 UNTS 279. USA (United States). Prolongation 18 Apr 54.
252 UNTS 309. USA (United States). Prolongation 15 Mar 55. Force 20 Mar 55.
252 UNTS 309. Iran. Prolongation 19 Mar 55. Force 20 Mar 55.
271 UNTS 384. USA (United States). Prolongation 13 Feb 56. Force 13 Feb 56.
271 UNTS 384. Iran. Prolongation 13 Feb 56. Force 13 Feb 56.

100485 Bilateral Agreement **31 UNTS 435**
SIGNED: 21 Feb 46 FORCE: 21 Feb 46
REGISTERED: 30 Jun 49 Belgium
ARTICLES: 5 LANGUAGE: French.
HEADNOTE: COMMERCIAL AGREEMENT
TOPIC: General Trade
CONCEPTS: Detailed regulations. Annex or appendix reference. Licenses and permits. Establishment of trade relations. Export quotas. Import quotas. Quotas.
INTL ORGS: Special Commission.
PROCEDURE: Denunciation. Duration.
PARTIES:
Belgium
Norway

100486 Bilateral Convention **32 UNTS 3**
SIGNED: 10 Sep 48 FORCE: 13 Jun 49
REGISTERED: 1 Jul 49 Norway
ARTICLES: 24 LANGUAGE: Finnish. Norwegian.
HEADNOTE: MEASURES PREVENT REINDEER CROSSING FRONTIER
TOPIC: Specific Resources
CONCEPTS: Pasturage in frontier zones. Fish, wildlife, and natural resources. Frontier crossing points.
INTL ORGS: Arbitration Commission.
TREATY REF: 16.LTS33,197LTS361.
PROCEDURE: Denunciation.
PARTIES:
Finland
Norway

100487 Bilateral Agreement **32 UNTS 39**
SIGNED: 20 Feb 48 FORCE: 10 May 49
REGISTERED: 5 Jul 49 Belgium
ARTICLES: 19 LANGUAGE: French.
HEADNOTE: CULTURAL AGREEMENT
TOPIC: Culture
CONCEPTS: Definition of terms. Annex or appendix reference. Friendship and amity. Standardization. Personnel. Recognition of degrees. Exchange. Commissions and foundations. Teacher and student exchange. Professorships. Scholar-

ships and grants. Vocational training. General cultural cooperation. Artists. Research cooperation. Scientific exchange. Publications exchange. Mass media exchange.
INTL ORGS: Special Commission.
PROCEDURE: Amendment. Denunciation. Duration. Ratification.
PARTIES:
Belgium
Norway

100488 Bilateral Agreement **32 UNTS 49**
SIGNED: 1 Mar 49 FORCE: 1 Mar 49
REGISTERED: 5 Jul 49 Belgium
ARTICLES: 14 LANGUAGE: French.
HEADNOTE: FINANCE
TOPIC: Finance
CONCEPTS: Definition of terms. Detailed regulations. Proxy diplomacy. Accounting procedures. Banking. Balance of payments. Currency. Monetary and gold transfers. Currency deposits. Investments. Exchange rates and regulations. Interest rates. Payment schedules. Transportation costs. Local currency.
PROCEDURE: Amendment. Duration. Renewal or Revival.
PARTIES:
Belgium
Portugal
ANNEX
54 UNTS 398. Belgium. Prolongation 3 Apr 50. Force 3 Apr 50.
54 UNTS 398. Portugal. Prolongation 3 Apr 50. Force 3 Apr 50.
67 UNTS 348. Belgium. Supplementation 15 Jun 50. Force 15 Jun 50.
67 UNTS 348. Portugal. Supplementation 15 Jun 50. Force 15 Jun 50.
68 UNTS 266. Belgium. Amendment 28 Feb 50. Force 11 May 50.
68 UNTS 266. Portugal. Amendment 11 Mar 50. Force 11 May 50.

100489 Bilateral Exchange **32 UNTS 69**
SIGNED: 28 Jun 48 FORCE: 28 Jun 48
REGISTERED: 7 Jul 49 USA (United States)
ARTICLES: 2 LANGUAGE: English.
HEADNOTE: MERCHANDISE TRADE OCCUPATION AREAS
TOPIC: Mostfavored Nation
CONCEPTS: Reciprocity in trade. National treatment.
PARTIES:
Ireland
USA (United States)

100490 Bilateral Exchange **32 UNTS 77**
SIGNED: 2 Jul 48 FORCE: 2 Jul 48
REGISTERED: 7 Jul 49 USA (United States)
ARTICLES: 2 LANGUAGE: English.
HEADNOTE: APPLICATION MOST FAVORED NATION CONTROLLED OCCUPIED AREAS
TOPIC: Mostfavored Nation
CONCEPTS: General trade. Tariffs. Exchange rates and regulations. Most favored nation clause. Customs duties. Occupation regime.
TREATY REF: 2UNTS10;.
PROCEDURE: Duration. Termination.
PARTIES:
Netherlands
USA (United States)

100491 Bilateral Exchange **32 UNTS 85**
SIGNED: 3 Jul 46 FORCE: 3 Jul 48
REGISTERED: 7 Jul 49 USA (United States)
ARTICLES: 2 LANGUAGE: English. French.
HEADNOTE: APPLICATION MOST FAVORED NATION CONTROLLED OCCUPIED AREAS
TOPIC: Mostfavored Nation
CONCEPTS: General trade. Tariffs. Exchange rates and regulations. Most favored nation clause. Customs duties. Occupation regime.
TREATY REF: 2UNTS10;.
PROCEDURE: Duration. Termination.
PARTIES:
Luxembourg
USA (United States)

100492 Bilateral Exchange **32 UNTS 93**
SIGNED: 9 Jul 48 FORCE: 9 Jul 48
REGISTERED: 7 Jul 49 USA (United States)
ARTICLES: 2 LANGUAGE: English. French.
HEADNOTE: APPLICATION MOST FAVORED NATION CONTROLLED OCCUPIED AREAS
TOPIC: Mostfavored Nation
CONCEPTS: Exceptions and exemptions. General trade. Most favored nation clause. Occupation regime.
TREATY REF: 2UNTS10;.
PROCEDURE: Duration. Termination.
PARTIES:
France
USA (United States)

100493 Bilateral Agreement **32 UNTS 101**
SIGNED: 19 Nov 46 FORCE: 7 Jul 48
REGISTERED: 7 Jul 49 Netherlands
ARTICLES: 17 LANGUAGE: Dutch. French.
HEADNOTE: CULTURAL AGREEMENT
TOPIC: Culture
CONCEPTS: Standardization. Conformity with municipal law. Personnel. Exchange. Commissions and foundations. Teacher and student exchange. Professorships. General cultural cooperation. Artists. Scientific exchange. Indemnities and reimbursements. Recognition. Customs exemptions. Publications exchange. Mass media exchange.
INTL ORGS: Special Commission.
PROCEDURE: Duration. Ratification. Renewal or Revival. Termination.
PARTIES:
France
Netherlands

100494 Bilateral Agreement **32 UNTS 115**
SIGNED: 17 Apr 47 FORCE: 22 Dec 48
REGISTERED: 7 Jul 49 Netherlands
ARTICLES: 13 LANGUAGE: French.
HEADNOTE: AIR TRANSPORT
TOPIC: Air Transport
CONCEPTS: Exceptions and exemptions. Annex or appendix reference. Conformity with municipal law. General cooperation. Licenses and permits. Recognition of legal documents. Use of facilities. Arbitration. Procedure. Existing tribunals. Reexport of goods, etc.. Fees and exemptions. Most favored nation clause. National treatment. Customs exemptions. Competency certificate. Routes and logistics. Permit designation. Airport facilities. Airworthiness certificates. Conditions of airlines operating permission. Operating authorizations and regulations. Licenses and certificates of nationality.
INTL ORGS: International Civil Aviation Organization.
PROCEDURE: Amendment. Denunciation. Future Procedures Contemplated. Ratification. Registration. Termination.
PARTIES:
Greece
Netherlands

100495 Bilateral Agreement **32 UNTS 129**
SIGNED: 1 Sep 47 FORCE: 5 Aug 48
REGISTERED: 7 Jul 49 Netherlands
ARTICLES: 10 LANGUAGE: French.
HEADNOTE: AIR SERVICES
TOPIC: Air Transport
CONCEPTS: Exceptions and exemptions. Annex or appendix reference. Conformity with municipal law. Licenses and permits. Recognition of legal documents. Use of facilities. Reexport of goods, etc.. Fees and exemptions. Most favored nation clause. National treatment. Customs exemptions. Competency certificate. Routes and logistics. Permit designation. Airport facilities. Airworthiness certificates. Conditions of airlines operating permission. Operating authorizations and regulations. Licenses and certificates of nationality. Postal services.
INTL ORGS: International Civil Aviation Organization.
PROCEDURE: Amendment. Denunciation. Future Procedures Contemplated. Ratification. Registration.
PARTIES:
Czechoslovakia
Netherlands

100496 Multilateral Protocol **32 UNTS 143**
SIGNED: 22 Dec 47 FORCE: 1 Jan 48
REGISTERED: 7 Jul 49 Netherlands
ARTICLES: 4 LANGUAGE: Dutch. French.
HEADNOTE: CUSTOMS
TOPIC: Customs
CONCEPTS: Annex type material. Tariffs. Customs duties. Customs exemptions.
INTL ORGS: Benelux Economic Union.
PROCEDURE: Ratification.
PARTIES:
Belgium SIGNED: 22 Dec 47 FORCE: 1 Jul 48
Luxembourg SIGNED: 22 Dec 47 FORCE: 1 Jul 48
Netherlands SIGNED: 22 Dec 47 FORCE: 1 Jul 48
ANNEX
123 UNTS 292. Belgium. Amendment 24 May 49. Force 19 Dec 51.
123 UNTS 292. Luxembourg. Amendment 24 May 49. Force 19 Dec 51.
123 UNTS 292. Netherlands. Amendment 24 May 49. Force 19 Dec 51.
123 UNTS 292. Belgium. Amendment 24 May 49. Force 19 Dec 51.
123 UNTS 292. Luxembourg. Amendment 24 May 49. Force 19 Dec 51.
123 UNTS 292. Netherlands. Amendment 24 May 49. Force 19 Dec 51.
137 UNTS 284. Belgium. Amendment 3 Jul 50. Force 19 Nov 51.
137 UNTS 284. Netherlands. Amendment 3 Jul 50. Force 19 Nov 51.
137 UNTS 284. Luxembourg. Amendment 3 Jul 50. Force 19 Nov 51.
137 UNTS 302. Belgium. Amendment 17 Nov 50. Force 19 Nov 51.
137 UNTS 302. Netherlands. Amendment 17 Nov 50. Force 19 Nov 51.
137 UNTS 302. Luxembourg. Amendment 17 Nov 50. Force 19 Nov 51.
189 UNTS 316. Belgium. Supplementation 28 Nov 51. Force 10 May 54.
189 UNTS 316. Luxembourg. Supplementation 28 Nov 51. Force 10 May 54.
189 UNTS 316. Netherlands. Supplementation 28 Nov 51. Force 10 May 54.
287 UNTS 262. Netherlands. Supplementation 29 Apr 53. Force 19 Feb 58.
287 UNTS 262. Belgium. Supplementation 29 Apr 53. Force 19 Feb 58.
287 UNTS 262. Luxembourg. Supplementation 29 Apr 53. Force 19 Feb 58.
287 UNTS 296. Netherlands. Supplementation 16 Jul 53. Force 19 Feb 58.
287 UNTS 296. Luxembourg. Supplementation 16 Jul 53. Force 19 Feb 58.
287 UNTS 296. Belgium. Supplementation 16 Jul 53. Force 19 Feb 58.
306 UNTS 256. Netherlands. Supplementation 22 Jun 54. Force 21 Jun 58.
306 UNTS 256. Belgium. Supplementation 22 Jun 54. Force 21 Jun 58.
306 UNTS 256. Luxembourg. Supplementation 22 Jun 54. Force 21 Jun 58.
306 UNTS 314. Luxembourg. Supplementation 23 Sep 54. Force 21 Jun 58.
306 UNTS 314. Belgium. Supplementation 23 Sep 54. Force 21 Jun 58.
306 UNTS 314. Netherlands. Supplementation 23 Sep 54. Force 21 Jun 58.
306 UNTS 318. Belgium. Supplementation 8 Dec 54. Force 21 Jun 58.
306 UNTS 318. Netherlands. Supplementation 8 Dec 54. Force 21 Jun 58.
306 UNTS 318. Luxembourg. Supplementation 8 Dec 54. Force 21 Jun 58.
306 UNTS 326. Netherlands. Supplementation 22 Dec 55. Force 21 Jun 58.
306 UNTS 326. Luxembourg. Supplementation 22 Dec 55. Force 21 Jun 58.
306 UNTS 326. Belgium. Supplementation 22 Dec 55. Force 21 Jun 58.
356 UNTS 318. Belgium. Supplementation 10 Jul 59. Force 15 Mar 60.
356 UNTS 318. Belgium. Supplementation 10 Jul 59. Force 15 Mar 60.
356 UNTS 318. Luxembourg. Supplementation 15 Mar 60. Force 15 Mar 60.
356 UNTS 318. Luxembourg. Supplementation 15 Mar 60. Force 15 Mar 60.
356 UNTS 318. Netherlands. Supplementation 21 Jun 58. Force 15 Mar 60.

356 UNTS 318. Netherlands. Supplementation 21 Jun 58. Force 15 Mar 60.

100497 Bilateral Convention **32 UNTS 153**
SIGNED: 13 Apr 48 FORCE: 8 May 48
REGISTERED: 7 Jul 49 Netherlands
ARTICLES: 16 LANGUAGE: Dutch. French.
HEADNOTE: CUSTOMS OPERATIONS
TOPIC: Customs
CONCEPTS: Definition of terms. Visa abolition. Conformity with municipal law. Investigation of violations. Indemnities and reimbursements. Tax exemptions. Customs duties. Customs exemptions. Subsidiary organ. Frontier crossing points.
PROCEDURE: Denunciation. Termination.
PARTIES:
Belgium
Netherlands
ANNEX
73 UNTS 264. Netherlands. Implementation 8 May 48. Force 9 May 48.
73 UNTS 264. Belgium. Implementation 8 May 48. Force 9 May 48.
73 UNTS 267. Belgium. Implementation 1 Jul 50. Force 8 Jul 50.
73 UNTS 267. Netherlands. Implementation 1 Jul 50. Force 8 Jul 50.
109 UNTS 315. Netherlands. Implementation 18 Sep 51. Force 1 Oct 51.
109 UNTS 315. Belgium. Implementation 18 Sep 51. Force 1 Oct 51.
150 UNTS 356. Belgium. Implementation 10 Sep 52. Force 16 Sep 52.
150 UNTS 356. Netherlands. Implementation 10 Sep 52. Force 16 Sep 52.
150 UNTS 360. Belgium. Implementation 22 Sep 52. Force 1 Oct 52.
150 UNTS 360. Netherlands. Implementation 22 Sep 52. Force 1 Oct 52.
171 UNTS 408. Netherlands. Supplementation 11 Jun 53. Force 1 Jul 53.
171 UNTS 408. Belgium. Supplementation 19 Jun 53. Force 1 Jul 53.
173 UNTS 386. Netherlands. Implementation 21 Aug 53. Force 1 Sep 53.
173 UNTS 386. Belgium. Implementation 21 Aug 53. Force 1 Sep 53.
173 UNTS 390. Netherlands. Implementation 1 Sep 53. Force 16 Sep 53.
173 UNTS 390. Belgium. Implementation 1 Sep 53. Force 16 Sep 53.
198 UNTS 370. Netherlands. Implementation 16 Jul 54. Force 26 Jul 54.
198 UNTS 370. Belgium. Implementation 16 Jul 54. Force 26 Jul 54.
199 UNTS 310. Netherlands. Implementation 11 Aug 54. Acceptance 14 Aug 54.
199 UNTS 310. Belgium. Implementation 11 Aug 54. Acceptance 14 Aug 54.
200 UNTS 270. Netherlands. Abrogation and Replacement 29 Sep 54. Force 3 Oct 54.
200 UNTS 270. Belgium. Abrogation and Replacement 1 Oct 54. Force 3 Oct 54.
236 UNTS 374. Netherlands. Implementation 27 Mar 56. Force 27 Mar 56.
236 UNTS 374. Belgium. Implementation 17 Mar 56. Force 27 Mar 56.
239 UNTS 335. Netherlands. Implementation 21 May 55. Force 22 May 55.
239 UNTS 335. Belgium. Implementation 21 May 55. Force 22 May 55.
261 UNTS 375. Netherlands. Implementation 22 Jan 57. Force 1 Feb 57.
261 UNTS 375. Belgium. Implementation 22 Jan 57. Force 1 Feb 57.
275 UNTS 286. Netherlands. Supplementation 17 May 57. Force 1 Jun 57.
275 UNTS 286. Belgium. Supplementation 17 Apr 57. Force 1 Jun 57.
277 UNTS 342. Netherlands. Supplementation 12 Aug 55. Force 15 Aug 55.
277 UNTS 342. Belgium. Supplementation 12 Aug 55. Force 15 Aug 55.
342 UNTS 346. Netherlands. Supplementation 14 Jul 59. Force 16 Jul 59.
342 UNTS 346. Belgium. Supplementation 14 Jul 59. Force 16 Jul 59.
346 UNTS 310. Netherlands. Supplementation 30 Sep 59. Force 1 Oct 59.
346 UNTS 310. Belgium. Supplementation 30 Sep 59. Force 1 Oct 59.
380 UNTS 386. Belgium. Implementation 10 Oct 60. Force 1 Nov 60.

380 UNTS 386. Netherlands. Implementation 10 Oct 60. Force 1 Nov 60.
387 UNTS 326. Netherlands. Implementation 29 Nov 60. Force 1 Dec 60.
387 UNTS 326. Belgium. Implementation 29 Nov 60. Force 1 Dec 60.
388 UNTS 330. Netherlands. Implementation 23 Dec 60. Force 1 Jan 61.
388 UNTS 330. Belgium. Implementation 23 Dec 60. Force 1 Jan 61.
398 UNTS 312. Netherlands. Implementation 12 May 61. Force 15 May 61.
398 UNTS 312. Belgium. Implementation 12 May 61. Force 15 May 61.
422 UNTS 314. Netherlands. Supplementation 30 Dec 61. Force 1 Jan 62.
422 UNTS 314. Belgium. Supplementation 30 Dec 61. Force 1 Jan 62.
434 UNTS 266. Belgium. Implementation 15 Jun 62. Force 1 Jul 62.
434 UNTS 266. Netherlands. Implementation 15 Jun 62. Force 1 Jul 62.
472 UNTS 386. Belgium. Implementation 26 Jun 63. Force 1 Jul 63.
472 UNTS 386. Netherlands. Implementation 26 Jun 63. Force 1 Jul 63.
502 UNTS 362. Belgium. Implementation 6 May 64. Force 11 May 64.
502 UNTS 362. Netherlands. Implementation 6 May 64. Force 11 May 64.
521 UNTS 374. Belgium. Implementation 26 Aug 64. Force 1 Oct 64.
521 UNTS 374. Netherlands. Implementation 26 Aug 64. Force 1 Oct 64.
533 UNTS 316. Netherlands. Implementation 24 Feb 65.
533 UNTS 316. Belgium. Implementation 24 Feb 65.
555 UNTS 250. Belgium. Implementation 7 Jan 66. Force 10 Jan 66.
555 UNTS 250. Netherlands. Implementation 6 Jan 66. Force 10 Jan 66.
653 UNTS 448. Netherlands. Force 18 Nov 68.
653 UNTS 448. Belgium. Force 18 Nov 68.

100498 Bilateral Convention **32 UNTS 167**
SIGNED: 29 Apr 48 FORCE: 1 Jan 47
REGISTERED: 7 Jul 49 Netherlands
ARTICLES: 28 LANGUAGE: Dutch. English.
HEADNOTE: TAXES INCOME CERTAIN OTHER TAXES
TOPIC: Taxation
CONCEPTS: Definition of terms. Treaty violation. Previous treaty renunciation. Conformity with municipal law. Exchange of official publications. Responsibility and liability. Negotiation. Teacher and student exchange. Wages and salaries. Assets. Claims and settlements. Taxation. Equitable taxes. General. Tax exemptions.
TREATY REF: 112LTS433.
PROCEDURE: Duration. Ratification. Termination.
PARTIES:
Netherlands
USA (United States)
ANNEX
239 UNTS 342. USA (United States). Supplementation 15 Jun 55. Force 10 Nov 55.
239 UNTS 342. Netherlands. Supplementation 15 Jun 55. Force 10 Nov 55.
239 UNTS 346. Netherlands. Netherlands Antilles. Force 10 Nov 55.
239 UNTS 346. USA (United States). Acknowledgement 10 Nov 55. Force 10 Nov 55.
521 UNTS 376. Netherlands. Amendment 23 Oct 63. Force 28 Sep 64.
521 UNTS 376. USA (United States). Supplementation 23 Oct 63.
521 UNTS 376. USA (United States). Amendment 23 Oct 63. Force 28 Sep 64.
521 UNTS 376. Netherlands. Supplementation 23 Oct 63.

100499 Bilateral Agreement **32 UNTS 215**
SIGNED: 2 Jun 48 FORCE: 2 Jun 48
REGISTERED: 7 Jul 49 Netherlands
ARTICLES: 12 LANGUAGE: English.
HEADNOTE: AIR SERVICES
TOPIC: Air Transport
CONCEPTS: Annex or appendix reference. Conformity with municipal law. Arbitration. Procedure. Existing tribunals. Negotiation. Routes and logistics. Permit designation. Conditions of airlines

operating permission. Operating authorizations and regulations.
INTL ORGS: International Civil Aviation Organization.
TREATY REF: 15UNTS295.
PROCEDURE: Amendment. Future Procedures Contemplated. Registration. Termination.
PARTIES:
Canada
Netherlands

100500   Bilateral Exchange   **32 UNTS 229**
SIGNED: 23 Jun 48   FORCE: 23 Jun 48
REGISTERED: 7 Jul 49 Netherlands
ARTICLES: 2 LANGUAGE: French.
HEADNOTE: FREEDOM AIR REGULAR INTERNATIONAL AIR SERVICES
TOPIC: Air Transport
CONCEPTS: Annex type material. Passenger transport. Transport of goods. Overflights and technical stops. Operating authorizations and regulations. Postal services.
TREATY REF: 15UNTS295.
PARTIES:
Luxembourg
Netherlands

100501   Bilateral Exchange   **32 UNTS 235**
SIGNED: 6 Sep 48   FORCE: 6 Sep 48
REGISTERED: 7 Jul 49 Netherlands
ARTICLES: 2 LANGUAGE: English.
HEADNOTE: EXTENSION MONETARY AGREEMENT 1945
TOPIC: Finance
CONCEPTS: Annex type material. Previous treaty extension. Post-war claims settlement.
TREATY REF: 2UNTS325.
PARTIES:
Netherlands
UK Great Britain
ANNEX
86 UNTS 310.   Netherlands.   Prolongation 6 Sep 49. Force 7 Sep 49.
86 UNTS 310. UK Great Britain. Prolongation 6 Sep 49. Force 7 Sep 49.
86 UNTS 312. UK Great Britain. Prolongation 27 Oct 49. Force 27 Oct 49.
86 UNTS 312.   Netherlands.   Prolongation 27 Oct 49. Force 27 Oct 49.

100502   Bilateral Exchange   **32 UNTS 241**
SIGNED: 17 Jan 49   FORCE: 17 Jan 49
REGISTERED: 7 Jul 49 Netherlands
ARTICLES: 2 LANGUAGE: English.
HEADNOTE: RELIEF SUPPLIES
TOPIC: Direct Aid
CONCEPTS: Definition of terms. Annex type material. Inspection and observation. Accounting procedures. Indemnities and reimbursements. Payment schedules. Transportation costs. Customs exemptions. Relief supplies.
TREATY REF: ECON COOP US-NETHER.
PROCEDURE: Amendment. Duration. Termination.
PARTIES:
Netherlands
USA (United States)
ANNEX
324 UNTS 343.   Costa   Rica.   Acceptance 1 May 58.

100503   Bilateral Convention   **32 UNTS 251**
SIGNED: 9 Jun 48   FORCE: 1 Mar 49
REGISTERED: 12 Jul 49 Poland
ARTICLES: 34 LANGUAGE: French.
HEADNOTE: SOCIAL SECURITY
TOPIC: Non-ILO Labor
CONCEPTS: Exceptions and exemptions. General provisions. Representation. Treaty implementation. Previous treaty replacement. General cooperation. Domestic legislation. Incorporation of treaty provisions into national law. Dispute settlement. Old age and invalidity insurance. Non-ILO labor relations. Old age insurance. Sickness and invalidity insurance. Social security. Exchange rates and regulations. Fees and exemptions. Payment schedules.
TREATY REF: 1LTS338; 3LTS260.
PROCEDURE: Duration. Future Procedures Contemplated. Ratification. Renewal or Revival. Termination.

PARTIES:
France
Poland
ANNEX
423 UNTS 282. Poland. Amendment 6 Mar 59. Force 1 Nov 59.
423 UNTS 282. France. Amendment 6 Mar 59. Force 10 Nov 59.

100504   Bilateral Agreement   **32 UNTS 301**
SIGNED: 30 Jun 47   FORCE: 1 Mar 48
REGISTERED: 13 Jul 49 Turkey
ARTICLES: 11 LANGUAGE: French.
HEADNOTE: AIR TRANSPORT
TOPIC: Air Transport
CONCEPTS: Exceptions and exemptions. Annex or appendix reference. Conformity with municipal law. Licenses and permits. Recognition of legal documents. Use of facilities. Arbitration. Procedure. Existing tribunals. Negotiation. Fees and exemptions. Most favored nation clause. National treatment. Customs exemptions. Competency certificate. Routes and logistics. Navigational conditions. Permit designation. Airport facilities. Airworthiness certificates. Conditions of airlines operating permission. Operating authorizations and regulations. Licenses and certificates of nationality.
INTL ORGS: International Civil Aviation Organization.
TREATY REF: 15UNTS295.
PROCEDURE: Amendment. Denunciation. Future Procedures Contemplated. Registration.
PARTIES:
Denmark
Turkey
ANNEX
308 UNTS 301. Turkey. Renewal 7 Aug 58. Force 23 May 57.

100505   Bilateral Agreement   **32 UNTS 313**
SIGNED: 7 May 48   FORCE: 23 Feb 49
REGISTERED: 13 Jul 49 Turkey
ARTICLES: 12 LANGUAGE: Arabic. Turkish.
HEADNOTE: AIR TRANSPORT
TOPIC: Air Transport
CONCEPTS: Exceptions and exemptions. Annex or appendix reference. Conformity with municipal law. Licenses and permits. Recognition of legal documents. Use of facilities. Arbitration. Procedure. Existing tribunals. Negotiation. Fees and exemptions. Most favored nation clause. National treatment. Customs exemptions. Competency certificate. Routes and logistics. Navigational conditions. Permit designation. Air transport. Airport facilities. Airworthiness certificates. Conditions of airlines operating permission. Operating authorizations and regulations. Licenses and certificates of nationality.
INTL ORGS: International Civil Aviation Organization.
TREATY REF: 15UNTS295.
PROCEDURE: Amendment. Denunciation. Future Procedures Contemplated. Ratification. Registration.
PARTIES:
Jordan
Turkey

100506   Bilateral Exchange   **32 UNTS 337**
SIGNED: 31 May 49   FORCE: 31 May 49
REGISTERED: 14 Jul 49 Belgium
ARTICLES: 2 LANGUAGE: French.
HEADNOTE: FREE TRANSIT AIRLINE CREWS
TOPIC: Visas
CONCEPTS: Exceptions and exemptions. Territorial application. Non-visa travel documents. Free passage and transit. Licenses and permits. Competency certificate.
PROCEDURE: Termination.
PARTIES:
Belgium
Denmark

100507   Bilateral Agreement   **32 UNTS 345**
SIGNED: 25 May 49   FORCE: 25 May 49
REGISTERED: 29 Jul 49 Norway
ARTICLES: 16 LANGUAGE: English. Norwegian.
HEADNOTE: USE FUNDS UNDER LETTER CREDIT AGREEMENT

TOPIC: Education
CONCEPTS: Detailed regulations. Friendship and amity. Domestic legislation. Operating agencies. Personnel. General property. Responsibility and liability. Dispute settlement. Exchange. Commissions and foundations. Institute establishment. Scholarships and grants. Accounting procedures. Currency. Fees and exemptions. Financial programs. Funding procedures. Tax exemptions. Credit provisions.
PROCEDURE: Amendment.
PARTIES:
Norway
USA (United States)
ANNEX
234 UNTS 298. Norway. Amendment 30 Oct 54. Force 30 Oct 54.
234 UNTS 298. USA (United States). Amendment 12 Aug 54. Force 30 Oct 54.
261 UNTS 380. USA (United States). Amendment 15 Jun 55. Force 15 Jun 55.
261 UNTS 380. Norway. Amendment 15 Jun 55. Force 15 Jun 55.
377 UNTS 390. Norway. Amendment 21 Jun 60. Force 21 Jun 60.
377 UNTS 390. USA (United States). Amendment 21 Jun 60. Force 21 Jun 60.
524 UNTS 294. USA (United States). Amendment 16 Mar 64. Force 16 Mar 64.
524 UNTS 294. Norway. Amendment 16 Mar 64. Force 16 Mar 64.

100508   Bilateral Exchange   **32 UNTS 369**
SIGNED: 14 Mar 49   FORCE: 1 Apr 49
REGISTERED: 29 Jul 49 New Zealand
ARTICLES: 2 LANGUAGE: English.
HEADNOTE: TRAVEL VISAS
TOPIC: Visas
CONCEPTS: Territorial application. Time limit. Passports non-diplomatic. Resident permits. Non-visa travel documents. Visas.
PARTIES:
New Zealand
USA (United States)

100509   Bilateral Treaty   **33 UNTS 3**
SIGNED: 14 Aug 48   FORCE: 5 May 49
REGISTERED: 3 Aug 49 India
ARTICLES: 9 LANGUAGE: English. French.
HEADNOTE: FRIENDSHIP ESTABLISHMENT
TOPIC: General Amity
CONCEPTS: Friendship and amity. Alien status. Consular relations establishment. Diplomatic relations establishment. Arbitration. Negotiation. Most favored nation clause.
PROCEDURE: Future Procedures Contemplated. Ratification.
PARTIES:
India
Switzerland

100510   Bilateral Agreement   **33 UNTS 13**
SIGNED: 12 Mar 49   FORCE: 12 Mar 49
REGISTERED: 8 Aug 49 Norway
ARTICLES: 10 LANGUAGE: French.
HEADNOTE: PAYMENTS
TOPIC: Finance
CONCEPTS: General cooperation. Accounting procedures. Banking. Balance of payments. Currency. Exchange rates and regulations. Payment schedules. Local currency. Credit provisions. Loan repayment.
TREATY REF: 30UNTS161.
PARTIES:
Greece
Norway

100511   Bilateral Exchange   **33 UNTS 25**
SIGNED: 15 Jul 47   FORCE: 18 Jul 47
REGISTERED: 11 Aug 49 Belgium
ARTICLES: 2 LANGUAGE: French.
HEADNOTE: ABOLITION PASSPORT VISAS
TOPIC: Visas
CONCEPTS: Territorial application. Visa abolition. Resident permits. Conformity with municipal law.
PARTIES:
Belgium
Norway

ANNEX
308 UNTS 306.   Belgium.   Supplementation
30 Apr 58. Force 1 May 58.
308 UNTS 306.   Norway.   Supplementation
29 Apr 58. Force 1 May 58.

100512   Bilateral Exchange   **33 UNTS 33**
SIGNED: 23 Jul 47   FORCE: 23 Jul 47
REGISTERED: 11 Aug 49 Belgium
ARTICLES: 2 LANGUAGE: English. French.
HEADNOTE: ESTABLISHMENT CEMETERIES
TOPIC: Other Military
CONCEPTS: Treaty implementation. Title and
deeds. Use of facilities. Sanitation. Compensa-
tion. Tax exemptions. Customs exemptions. Up-
keep of war graves. Establishment of war ceme-
teries.
PARTIES:
Belgium
USA (United States)
          ANNEX
149 UNTS 390. Belgium. Amendment 31 Jan 49.
Force 31 Jan 49.
149 UNTS 390. USA (United States). Amendment
17 Jan 49. Force 31 Jan 49.
263 UNTS 400. USA (United States). Prolongation
28 Dec 54. Force 7 Jan 55.
263 UNTS 400. Belgium. Prolongation 7 Jan 55.
Force 7 Jan 55.

100513   Bilateral Agreement   **33 UNTS 43**
SIGNED: 12 Mar 47   FORCE: 26 Mar 47
REGISTERED: 12 Aug 49 Belgium
ARTICLES: 8 LANGUAGE: French.
HEADNOTE: FACILITATE PAYMENTS
TOPIC: Finance
CONCEPTS: Definition of terms. General cooper-
ation. Banking. Currency. Monetary and gold
transfers. Payment schedules.
PARTIES:
Belgium
Turkey

100514   Bilateral Convention   **33 UNTS 49**
SIGNED: 27 Apr 47   FORCE: 24 Jul 47
REGISTERED: 12 Aug 49 Yugoslavia
ARTICLES: 17 LANGUAGE: Czechoslovakian. Ser-
bo-Croat.
HEADNOTE: CULTURAL COOPERATION
TOPIC: Culture
CONCEPTS: Friendship and amity. Tourism. Con-
formity with municipal law. Personnel. Recogni-
tion of degrees. Exchange. Commissions and
foundations. Teacher and student exchange.
Professorships. Institute establishment. Scholar-
ships and grants. General cultural cooperation.
Artists. Athletes. Scientific exchange. Publica-
tions exchange. Mass media exchange.
INTL ORGS: Special Commission.
PROCEDURE: Duration. Ratification. Renewal or
Revival. Termination.
PARTIES:
Czechoslovakia
Yugoslavia

100515   Bilateral Convention   **33 UNTS 73**
SIGNED: 15 Oct 47   FORCE: 13 Jan 48
REGISTERED: 12 Aug 49 Yugoslavia
ARTICLES: 6 LANGUAGE: Hungarian. Serbo-Croat.
HEADNOTE: CULTURAL COOPERATION
TOPIC: Culture
CONCEPTS: Friendship and amity. Conformity
with municipal law. Personnel. Recognition of
degrees. Exchange. Commissions and founda-
tions. Teacher and student exchange. Professor-
ships. Institute establishment. Scholarships and
grants. General cultural cooperation. Artists. Ath-
letes. Scientific exchange. Publications ex-
change. Mass media exchange. Press and wire
services.
INTL ORGS: United Nations. Special Commission.
PROCEDURE: Denunciation. Duration. Ratification.
Renewal or Revival.
PARTIES:
Hungary
Yugoslavia

100516   Bilateral Convention   **33 UNTS 91**
SIGNED: 9 Jul 47   FORCE: 28 Nov 47

REGISTERED: 12 Aug 49 Yugoslavia
ARTICLES: 17 LANGUAGE: French.
HEADNOTE: CULTURAL COOPERATION
TOPIC: Culture
CONCEPTS: Friendship and amity. Conformity
with municipal law. Personnel. Recognition of
degrees. Exchange. Commissions and founda-
tions. Teacher and student exchange. Professor-
ships. Institute establishment. Scholarships and
grants. General cultural cooperation. Artists. Ath-
letes. Scientific exchange. Recognition. Publica-
tions exchange. Mass media exchange.
INTL ORGS: Special Commission.
TREATY REF: 1UNTS81.
PROCEDURE: Denunciation. Duration. Ratification.
Renewal or Revival.
PARTIES:
Albania
Yugoslavia

100517   Bilateral Agreement   **33 UNTS 105**
SIGNED: 3 Feb 49   FORCE: 3 Feb 49
REGISTERED: 12 Aug 49 Yugoslavia
ARTICLES: 18 LANGUAGE: Italian. Serbo-Croat.
HEADNOTE: MINOR FRONTIER TRAFFIC
TOPIC: Visas
CONCEPTS: Emergencies. Passports non-
diplomatic. Frontier permits. Immovable prop-
erty. General property. Procedure. Veterinary.
Export quotas. Import quotas. Taxation. Pastur-
age in frontier zones. Markers and definitions.
Frontier peoples and personnel.
PROCEDURE: Denunciation. Duration. Renewal or
Revival.
PARTIES:
Italy
Yugoslavia

100518   Multilateral Convention   **33 UNTS 181**
SIGNED: 18 Aug 48   FORCE: 11 Apr 49
REGISTERED: 12 Aug 49 Yugoslavia
ARTICLES: 47 LANGUAGE: French. Russian.
HEADNOTE: REGIME NAVIGATION DANUBE
TOPIC: Water Transport
CONCEPTS: Detailed regulations. Exceptions and
exemptions. Annex or appendix reference. Inviolability. Privileges and immunities. Standardization. Conformity with municipal law. General cooperation. Informational records. Use of facilities. Investigation of violations. Establishment of
commission. Procedure. Negotiation. Conciliation. Competence of tribunal. Research and
scientific projects. Research results. Fees and exemptions. Funding procedures. Non-interest
rates and fees. Customs exemptions. Navigational conditions. Transport of goods. Operating
authorizations and regulations. Merchant vessels. Inland and territorial waters. Ports and pilotage. Facilities and equipment. Establishment.
Headquarters and facilities.
INTL ORGS: Danube Commission.
PROCEDURE: Amendment. Ratification.
PARTIES:
Bulgaria   SIGNED: 18 Aug 48   RATIFIED:
22 Feb 49 FORCE: 11 May 49
Czechoslovakia SIGNED: 18 Aug 48 RATIFIED:
23 Feb 49 FORCE: 11 May 49
Hungary   SIGNED: 18 Aug 48   RATIFIED:
14 Mar 49 FORCE: 11 May 49
Romania   SIGNED: 18 Aug 48   RATIFIED:
5 Mar 49 FORCE: 11 May 49
Ukrainian SSR SIGNED: 18 Aug 48 RATIFIED:
14 May 49 FORCE: 14 May 47
USSR (Soviet Union) SIGNED: 18 Aug 48 RATI-
FIED: 11 May 49 FORCE: 11 May 49
Yugoslavia   SIGNED: 18 Aug 48   RATIFIED:
23 Feb 49 FORCE: 11 May 49
          ANNEX
351 UNTS 378. Austria. Accession 17 Jan 60.

100519   Bilateral Agreement   **33 UNTS 227**
SIGNED: 8 Feb 49   FORCE: 1 Feb 49
REGISTERED: 15 Aug 49 Denmark
ARTICLES: 8 LANGUAGE: Danish. Swedish.
HEADNOTE: METHOD SETTLING PAYMENTS
TOPIC: Finance
CONCEPTS: General cooperation. Accounting pro-
cedures. Banking. Balance of payments. Cur-
rency. Monetary and gold transfers. Exchange
rates and regulations. Payment schedules. Local
currency. Credit provisions.

PROCEDURE: Termination.
PARTIES:
Denmark
Sweden

100520   Bilateral Agreement   **33 UNTS 247**
SIGNED: 22 Mar 49   FORCE: 22 Mar 49
REGISTERED: 15 Aug 49 Denmark
ARTICLES: 7 LANGUAGE: Danish. Finnish.
HEADNOTE: PAYMENTS
TOPIC: Finance
CONCEPTS: General cooperation. Accounting pro-
cedures. Banking. Balance of payments. Cur-
rency. Currency deposits. Exchange rates and
regulations. Interest rates. Payment schedules.
PROCEDURE: Termination.
PARTIES:
Denmark
Finland

100521   Multilateral Convention   **33 UNTS 261**
SIGNED: 21 Nov 47   FORCE: 2 Dec 48
REGISTERED: 16 Aug 49 Netherlands
ARTICLES: 11 LANGUAGE: Chinese. English.
French. Russian. Spanish.
HEADNOTE: IMMUNITIES OF AGENCIES
TOPIC: IGO Status/Immunit
CONCEPTS: Definition of terms. Annex or appendix reference. Frontier permits. Non-visa travel
documents. Diplomatic privileges. Diplomatic
missions. Inviolability. Privileges and immunities. Property. Diplomatic correspondence. Procedure. Existing tribunals. Status of experts.
INTL ORGS: United Nations.
PROCEDURE: Accession.
PARTIES:
Multilateral
          ANNEX
43 UNTS 342.
46 UNTS 355.
51 UNTS 330.
71 UNTS 316.
71 UNTS 318.
76 UNTS 274.
79 UNTS 326.
81 UNTS 332.
84 UNTS 412.
88 UNTS 446.
90 UNTS 323.
91 UNTS 376.
92 UNTS 400.
96 UNTS 322.
101 UNTS 288.
102 UNTS 322.
110 UNTS 314.
117 UNTS 386.
122 UNTS 335.
127 UNTS 328.
131 UNTS 309.
136 UNTS 386.
161 UNTS 364.
168 UNTS 322.
171 UNTS 412.
175 UNTS 364.
183 UNTS 348.
187 UNTS 415.
193 UNTS 342.
199 UNTS 314.
202 UNTS 321.
207 UNTS 328.
211 UNTS 388.
216 UNTS 367.
221 UNTS 409.
231 UNTS 350.
275 UNTS 298.
276 UNTS 352.
277 UNTS 343.
277 UNTS 344.
280 UNTS 348.
282 UNTS 354.
286 UNTS 334.
299 UNTS 408.
300 UNTS 305.
301 UNTS 439.
302 UNTS 353.
304 UNTS 342.
308 UNTS 310.
309 UNTS 354.
310 UNTS 318.
314 UNTS 308.
314 UNTS 310.
316 UNTS 276.

ARTICLES: 2 LANGUAGE: French.
HEADNOTE: ABOLITION PASSPORT VISAS
TOPIC: Visas
CONCEPTS: Territorial application. Visa abolition. Resident permits. Conformity with municipal law.
PARTIES:
 Belgium
 Sweden

100523 Bilateral Exchange **34 UNTS 9**
SIGNED: 13 Jun 49 FORCE: 13 Jun 49
REGISTERED: 17 Aug 49 Norway
ARTICLES: 2 LANGUAGE: Norwegian. Finnish. Swedish.
HEADNOTE: NEW REGULATION REGARDING FISHING TUNA RIVER
TOPIC: Commodity Trade
CONCEPTS: Annex type material. Licenses and permits. Currency. Exchange rates and regulations. Fees and exemptions.
PARTIES:
 Finland
 Norway

100524 Bilateral Exchange **34 UNTS 17**
SIGNED: 21 Mar 49 FORCE: 21 Mar 49
REGISTERED: 18 Aug 49 Belgium
ARTICLES: 2 LANGUAGE: French.
HEADNOTE: RECIPROCAL ISSUE CIVIL STATUS RECORDS
TOPIC: Admin Cooperation
CONCEPTS: Exchange of information and documents. Fees and exemptions.
PROCEDURE: Denunciation.
PARTIES:
 Belgium
 Switzerland

100525 Multilateral Agreement **34 UNTS 23**
SIGNED: 5 Oct 47 FORCE: 22 Oct 47
REGISTERED: 22 Aug 49 Denmark
ARTICLES: 7 LANGUAGE: English.
HEADNOTE: PAYMENTS
TOPIC: Finance
CONCEPTS: General cooperation. Export quotas. Import quotas. Accounting procedures. Banking. Balance of payments. Currency. Exchange rates and regulations. Interest rates. Payment schedules.
PROCEDURE: Duration. Renewal or Revival.
PARTIES:
 Denmark SIGNED: 22 Oct 47 FORCE: 22 Oct 47
 French Occup Germ
 British Occup Germ SIGNED: 22 Oct 47 FORCE: 22 Oct 47
 US Occup Germ SIGNED: 22 Oct 47 FORCE: 22 Oct 47

100526 Bilateral Convention **34 UNTS 33**
SIGNED: 19 Feb 48 FORCE: 28 Feb 49
REGISTERED: 23 Aug 49 Norway
ARTICLES: 21 LANGUAGE: English. Norwegian.
HEADNOTE: CULTURE
TOPIC: Culture
CONCEPTS: Definition of terms. Territorial application. Standardization. Personnel. Recognition of degrees. Commissions and foundations. Teacher and student exchange. Professorships. Institute establishment. Scholarships and grants. Vocational training. Exchange. General cultural cooperation. Artists. Research cooperation. Scientific exchange. Publications exchange. Mass media exchange.
INTL ORGS: Special Commission.
PROCEDURE: Amendment. Duration. Ratification. Termination.
PARTIES:
 Norway
 UK Great Britain
ANNEX
158 UNTS 482. UK Great Britain. Amendment 25 Nov 52. Force 25 Nov 52.
158 UNTS 482. Norway. Amendment 25 Nov 52. Force 25 Nov 52.

100527 Bilateral Agreement **34 UNTS 49**
SIGNED: 22 Oct 46 FORCE: 22 Oct 46
REGISTERED: 25 Aug 49 Belgium

ARTICLES: 11 LANGUAGE: French. Portuguese.
HEADNOTE: AIR TRANSPORT
TOPIC: Air Transport
CONCEPTS: Annex or appendix reference. Previous treaty replacement. Conformity with municipal law. General cooperation. Licenses and permits. Recognition of legal documents. Use of facilities. Arbitration. Procedure. Existing tribunals. Negotiation. Fees and exemptions. Most favored nation clause. National treatment. Customs exemptions. Competency certificate. Routes and logistics. Navigational conditions. Permit designation. Air transport. Airport facilities. Airworthiness certificates. Conditions of airlines operating permission. Licenses and certificates of nationality.
INTL ORGS: International Civil Aviation Organization.
TREATY REF: 15UNTS295.
PROCEDURE: Amendment. Future Procedures Contemplated. Registration. Termination. Application to Non-self-governing Territories.
PARTIES:
 Belgium
 Portugal
ANNEX
133 UNTS 318. Belgium. Amendment 5 Jul 51. Force 5 Jul 51.
133 UNTS 318. Portugal. Amendment 5 Jul 51. Force 5 Jul 51.
268 UNTS 348. Belgium. Amendment 26 Mar 56. Force 26 Mar 56.
268 UNTS 348. Belgium. Ruanda-Urundi. Force 26 Mar 57.
268 UNTS 348. Portugal. Supplementation 26 May 57. Force 26 Mar 57.
268 UNTS 348. Belgium. Supplementation 15 Dec 56. Force 26 Mar 57.
304 UNTS 343. Belgium. Supplementation 24 Feb 58. Force 29 Apr 58.
304 UNTS 343. Portugal. Supplementation 28 Feb 58. Force 29 Apr 58.

100528 Bilateral Agreement **34 UNTS 77**
SIGNED: 6 Mar 47 FORCE: 6 Mar 47
REGISTERED: 25 Aug 49 Belgium
ARTICLES: 14 LANGUAGE: Czechoslovakian. French.
HEADNOTE: CULTURAL RELATIONS
TOPIC: Culture
CONCEPTS: Detailed regulations. Annex or appendix reference. Friendship and amity. Conformity with municipal law. General cooperation. Establishment of commission. Recognition of degrees. Exchange. Teacher and student exchange. Scholarships and grants. Exchange. General cultural cooperation. Artists. Scientific exchange. Publications exchange. Mass media exchange.
INTL ORGS: Special Commission.
PROCEDURE: Denunciation. Duration. Ratification. Renewal or Revival.
PARTIES:
 Belgium
 Czechoslovakia

100529 Bilateral Agreement **34 UNTS 93**
SIGNED: 1 Jul 47 FORCE: 1 Jul 47
REGISTERED: 25 Aug 49 Belgium
ARTICLES: 11 LANGUAGE: French.
HEADNOTE: RELEASE BLOCKED ASSETS
TOPIC: Claims and Debts
CONCEPTS: Detailed regulations. Exceptions and exemptions. Nationality and citizenship. Conformity with municipal law. General cooperation. Exchange of information and documents. Informational records. General property. Responsibility and liability. Accounting procedures. Banking. Currency. Exchange rates and regulations. Payment schedules. Assets. Claims and settlements. Debts. Assessment procedures. Assets transfer. National treatment.
PROCEDURE: Future Procedures Contemplated.
PARTIES:
 Belgium
 United Arab Rep

100530 Bilateral Agreement **34 UNTS 103**
SIGNED: 26 Apr 49 FORCE: 26 Apr 49
REGISTERED: 25 Aug 49 Belgium
ARTICLES: 10 LANGUAGE: French. Spanish.

00522 Bilateral Exchange **34 UNTS 3**
SIGNED: 20 Mar 47 FORCE: 20 Mar 47
REGISTERED: 17 Aug 49 Belgium

HEADNOTE: PAYMENTS AGREEMENT INCREASE TRADE
TOPIC: Finance
CONCEPTS: Definition of terms. Detailed regulations. Proxy diplomacy. General cooperation. Accounting procedures. Banking. Balance of payments. Currency. Monetary and gold transfers. Exchange rates and regulations. Funding procedures. Interest rates. Local currency.
INTL ORGS: International Monetary Fund.
PROCEDURE: Denunciation. Duration.
PARTIES:
Belgium
Bolivia
ANNEX
423 UNTS 290. Bolivia. Termination 11 Dec 61.
423 UNTS 290. Belgium. Termination 20 Sep 62.

100531   Bilateral Agreement   **34 UNTS 117**
SIGNED: 7 Jun 49   FORCE: 1 May 49
REGISTERED: 25 Aug 49 Belgium
ARTICLES: 1 LANGUAGE: French.
HEADNOTE: ADDITION POSTAL CONVENTION CONGO
TOPIC: Postal Service
CONCEPTS: Rates and charges.
TREATY REF: 89LTS207; 130LTS450.
PARTIES:
Belgium
Luxembourg
ANNEX
303 UNTS 306. Belgian Colonies. Supplementation 29 Apr 58. Force 1 Jan 58.
303 UNTS 306. Luxembourg. Supplementation 29 Apr 58. Force 1 Jan 58.

100532   Bilateral Agreement   **34 UNTS 121**
SIGNED: 28 Jun 46   FORCE: 28 Jun 46
REGISTERED: 26 Aug 49 USA (United States)
ARTICLES: 6 LANGUAGE: English.
HEADNOTE: APPLYING MUTUAL AID PROSECUTION WAR
TOPIC: Milit Assistance
CONCEPTS: Loan and credit. Terms of loan. Defense and security. Payment for war supplies. Military assistance. Military training. Disarmament and demilitarization. Control and occupation machinery.
TREATY REF: 14UNTS343; 204LTS381.
PROCEDURE: Future Procedures Contemplated.
PARTIES:
Taiwan
USA (United States)

100533   Bilateral Exchange   **34 UNTS 129**
SIGNED: 9 Oct 47   FORCE: 9 Oct 47
REGISTERED: 26 Aug 49 USA (United States)
ARTICLES: 2 LANGUAGE: English.
HEADNOTE: FURNISHING MILITARY EQUIPMENT SUPPLIES
TOPIC: Milit Assistance
CONCEPTS: Exceptions and exemptions. General cooperation. Accounting procedures. Financial programs. Materials, equipment and services. Payment for war supplies. Military assistance. Military assistance missions. Airforce-army-navy personnel ratio.
TREATY REF: 7UNTS281.
PROCEDURE: Future Procedures Contemplated.
PARTIES:
UK Great Britain
USA (United States)

100534   Bilateral Agreement   **34 UNTS 141**
SIGNED: 2 Jan 48   FORCE: 2 Jan 48
REGISTERED: 26 Aug 49 USA (United States)
ARTICLES: 3 LANGUAGE: English. German.
HEADNOTE: RELIEF ASSISTANCE
TOPIC: Direct Aid
CONCEPTS: Annex or appendix reference. Conformity with municipal law. Inspection and observation. Title and deeds. Relief supplies. Procurement. Distribution. Loan and credit.
PROCEDURE: Duration. Termination.
PARTIES:
Austria
USA (United States)

100535   Bilateral Agreement   **34 UNTS 155**
SIGNED: 24 Feb 48   FORCE: 24 Feb 48
REGISTERED: 26 Aug 49 USA (United States)
ARTICLES: 6 LANGUAGE: English.
HEADNOTE: SETTLE LEND-LEASE MILITARY RELIEF CLAIMS
TOPIC: Milit Assistance
CONCEPTS: Time limit. Annex or appendix reference. Non-prejudice to UN charter. Exchange rates and regulations. Lump sum settlements. Payment for war supplies. Lend lease. Return of equipment and recapture. Restrictions on transfer. Post-war claims settlement.
PROCEDURE: Future Procedures Contemplated.
PARTIES:
Norway
USA (United States)

100536   Bilateral Exchange   **34 UNTS 185**
SIGNED: 4 Jul 48   FORCE: 13 Jul 48
REGISTERED: 26 Aug 49 USA (United States)
ARTICLES: 2 LANGUAGE: English. Turkish.
HEADNOTE: APPLICATION MOST FAVORED NATION CONTROLLED OCCUPIED AREAS
TOPIC: Mostfavored Nation
CONCEPTS: Exceptions and exemptions. General trade. Tariffs. Exchange rates and regulations. Most favored nation clause. Customs duties. Occupation regime.
PROCEDURE: Duration. Termination.
PARTIES:
Turkey
USA (United States)

100537   Bilateral Agreement   **34 UNTS 195**
SIGNED: 19 Jul 48   FORCE: 19 Jul 48
REGISTERED: 26 Aug 49 USA (United States)
ARTICLES: 11 LANGUAGE: English.
HEADNOTE: SETTLE LEND-LEASE MILITARY RELIEF CLAIMS
TOPIC: Milit Assistance
CONCEPTS: Definition of terms. General property. Title and deeds. Currency. Lump sum settlements. Payment for war supplies. Naval vessels. Return of equipment and recapture. Post-war claims settlement.
PARTIES:
USA (United States)
Yugoslavia

100538   Bilateral Exchange   **34 UNTS 207**
SIGNED: 3 Mar 49   FORCE: 1 Apr 49
REGISTERED: 29 Aug 49 New Zealand
ARTICLES: 2 LANGUAGE: English.
HEADNOTE: MUTUAL ABOLITION VISAS
TOPIC: Visas
CONCEPTS: Territorial application. Visa abolition. Resident permits. Conformity with municipal law.
PARTIES:
Netherlands
New Zealand

100539   Bilateral Exchange   **34 UNTS 213**
SIGNED: 12 Aug 49   FORCE: 12 Aug 49
REGISTERED: 30 Aug 49 Australia
ARTICLES: 2 LANGUAGE: English.
HEADNOTE: CLAIM SETTLEMENT NETHERLANDS INDONESIA
TOPIC: Reparations
CONCEPTS: Detailed regulations. Guarantees and safeguards. Time limit. Previous treaty replacement. Responsibility and liability. Payment schedules. Claims and settlements. Lump sum settlements. Loan repayment. Surplus war property. Loss and/or damage. Post-war claims settlement.
PARTIES:
Australia
Netherlands

100540   Bilateral Agreement   **34 UNTS 225**
SIGNED: 15 Apr 49   FORCE: 1 Jul 49
REGISTERED: 31 Aug 49 Australia
ARTICLES: 29 LANGUAGE: English.
HEADNOTE: SOCIAL SECURITY
TOPIC: Non-ILO Labor
CONCEPTS: Detailed regulations. Representation. Previous treaty replacement. General cooper-

ation. Exchange of information and documents. Old age and invalidity insurance. Non-ILO labor relations. Old age insurance. Sickness and invalidity insurance. Social security. Unemployment. Payment schedules.
PROCEDURE: Duration. Termination.
PARTIES:
Australia
New Zealand

100541   Multilateral Treaty   **34 UNTS 243**
SIGNED: 4 Apr 49   FORCE: 24 Aug 49
REGISTERED: 7 Sep 49 USA (United States)
ARTICLES: 14 LANGUAGE: English. French.
HEADNOTE: NORTH ATLANTIC TREATY
TOPIC: General Military
CONCEPTS: Definition of terms. Non-prejudice to third party. Friendship and amity. Non-prejudice to UN charter. Peaceful relations. General cultural cooperation. General trade. Joint defense. Defense and security. Subsidiary organ.
INTL ORGS: North Atlantic Treaty Organization. United Nations.
PROCEDURE: Accession. Denunciation. Ratification.
PARTIES:
Belgium SIGNED: 4 Apr 49 RATIFIED: 16 Jun 49 FORCE: 24 Aug 49
Canada SIGNED: 4 Apr 49 RATIFIED: 3 May 49 FORCE: 24 Aug 49
Denmark SIGNED: 4 Apr 49 RATIFIED: 24 Aug 49 FORCE: 24 Aug 49
France SIGNED: 4 Apr 49 RATIFIED: 24 Aug 49 FORCE: 24 Aug 49
Iceland SIGNED: 4 Apr 49 RATIFIED: 4 Aug 49 FORCE: 24 Aug 49
Italy SIGNED: 4 Apr 49 RATIFIED: 24 Aug 49 FORCE: 24 Aug 49
Luxembourg SIGNED: 4 Apr 49 RATIFIED: 27 Jun 49 FORCE: 24 Aug 49
Netherlands SIGNED: 4 Apr 49 RATIFIED: 12 Aug 49 FORCE: 24 Aug 49
Portugal SIGNED: 4 Apr 49 RATIFIED: 24 Aug 49 FORCE: 24 Aug 49
UK Great Britain SIGNED: 4 Apr 49 RATIFIED: 7 Jun 49 FORCE: 24 Aug 49
USA (United States) SIGNED: 4 Apr 49 RATIFIED: 25 Jul 49 FORCE: 24 Aug 49
ANNEX
126 UNTS 350. France. Amendment 14 Feb 52. Force 15 Feb 52.
126 UNTS 350. Belgium. Amendment 14 Feb 52. Force 15 Feb 52.
126 UNTS 350. Greece. Accession 18 Feb 52. Force 18 Feb 52.
126 UNTS 350. Turkey. Accession 18 Feb 52. Force 18 Feb 52.
126 UNTS 350. Canada. Amendment 21 Jan 52. Force 15 Feb 52.
126 UNTS 350. Denmark. Amendment 2 Feb 52. Force 15 Feb 52.
126 UNTS 350. Iceland. Amendment 29 Jan 52. Force 15 Feb 52.
126 UNTS 350. Italy. Amendment 15 Feb 52. Force 15 Feb 52.
126 UNTS 350. Luxembourg. Amendment 5 Feb 52. Force 15 Feb 52.
126 UNTS 350. Netherlands. Amendment 7 Feb 52. Force 15 Feb 52.
126 UNTS 350. Norway. Amendment 24 Jan 52. Force 15 Feb 52.
126 UNTS 350. Portugal. Amendment 8 Feb 52. Force 15 Feb 52.
126 UNTS 350. UK Great Britain. Amendment 6 Dec 51. Force 15 Feb 52.
126 UNTS 350. USA (United States). Amendment 11 Feb 52. Force 15 Feb 52.

100542   Bilateral Agreement   **34 UNTS 257**
SIGNED: 11 Nov 47   FORCE: 11 Nov 47
REGISTERED: 7 Sep 49 ICAO (Civil Aviat)
ARTICLES: 12 LANGUAGE: Norwegian. Portuguese. English.
HEADNOTE: AIR TRANSPORT
TOPIC: Air Transport
CONCEPTS: Annex or appendix reference. Conformity with municipal law. Licenses and permits. Recognition of legal documents. Use of facilities. Procedure. Existing tribunals. Fees and exemptions. Most favored nation clause. National treatment. Customs exemptions. Competency certificate. Routes and logistics. Navigational condi-

tions. Permit designation. Air transport. Airport facilities. Airworthiness certificates. Conditions of airlines operating permission. Operating authorizations and regulations. Licenses and certificates of nationality.
INTL ORGS: International Civil Aviation Organization. Arbitration Commission.
TREATY REF: 15UNTS;95.
PROCEDURE: Amendment. Future Procedures Contemplated. Registration. Termination.
PARTIES:
Norway
Portugal

100543   Bilateral Agreement   **34 UNTS 285**
SIGNED: 21 May 48   FORCE: 21 May 48
REGISTERED: 7 Sep 49 ICAO (Civil Aviat)
ARTICLES: 14 LANGUAGE: English.
HEADNOTE: AIR SERVICES
TOPIC: Air Transport
CONCEPTS: Definition of terms. Detailed regulations. Annex or appendix reference. Conformity with municipal law. General cooperation. Exchange of information and documents. Arbitration. Procedure. Existing tribunals. Negotiation. Reexport of goods, etc.. Non-interest rates and fees. Most favored nation clause. National treatment. Customs exemptions. Routes and logistics. Permit designation. Air transport. Airport facilities. Conditions of airlines operating permission. Operating authorizations and regulations.
INTL ORGS: International Civil Aviation Organization. International Court of Justice. Arbitration Commission.
TREATY REF: 15UNTS295.
PROCEDURE: Amendment. Future Procedures Contemplated. Registration. Termination.
PARTIES:
India
Sweden

100544   Bilateral Exchange   **34 UNTS 311**
SIGNED: 25 May 48   FORCE: 25 May 48
REGISTERED: 7 Sep 49 ICAO (Civil Aviat)
ARTICLES: 2 LANGUAGE: English. Portuguese.
HEADNOTE: EXTENSION TRANSIT FACILITIES
TOPIC: Milit Installation
CONCEPTS: Use of facilities. Overflights and technical stops. Status of military forces.
TREATY REF: 41UNTS21.
PROCEDURE: Termination.
PARTIES:
Portugal
UK Great Britain

100545   Bilateral Agreement   **34 UNTS 317**
SIGNED: 21 Jun 48   FORCE: 21 Jun 48
REGISTERED: 7 Sep 49 ICAO (Civil Aviat)
ARTICLES: 12 LANGUAGE: English.
HEADNOTE: AIR SERVICES
TOPIC: Air Transport
CONCEPTS: Annex or appendix reference. Conformity with municipal law. Licenses and permits. Recognition of legal documents. Use of facilities. Procedure. Existing tribunals. Fees and exemptions. Most favored nation clause. National treatment. Customs exemptions. Competency certificate. Routes and logistics. Navigational conditions. Permit designation. Airport facilities. Airworthiness certificates. Conditions of airlines operating permission. Operating authorizations and regulations. Licenses and certificates of nationality.
INTL ORGS: International Civil Aviation Organization. Arbitration Commission.
TREATY REF: 15UNTS295.
PROCEDURE: Amendment. Future Procedures Contemplated. Registration. Termination.
PARTIES:
Ireland
Norway

ANNEX
27 UNTS 328. Norway. Amendment 2 Oct 57. Force 19 Oct 57.
27 UNTS 328. Ireland. Amendment 19 Oct 57. Force 19 Oct 57.

00546   Bilateral Agreement   **34 UNTS 329**
SIGNED: 22 Oct 48   FORCE: 22 Oct 48
REGISTERED: 7 Sep 49 ICAO (Civil Aviat)

ARTICLES: 13 LANGUAGE: Portuguese. Spanish.
HEADNOTE: CIVIL AIR TRANSPORT
TOPIC: Air Transport
CONCEPTS: Exceptions and exemptions. Annex or appendix reference. Non-prejudice to third party. Conformity with municipal law. Licenses and permits. Recognition of legal documents. Use of facilities. Arbitration. Existing tribunals. Reexport of goods, etc.. Fees and exemptions. Most favored nation clause. National treatment. Customs exemptions. Competency certificate. Routes and logistics. Navigational conditions. Permit designation. Airport facilities. Airworthiness certificates. Conditions of airlines operating permission. Operating authorizations and regulations. Licenses and certificates of nationality.
INTL ORGS: International Civil Aviation Organization. Arbitration Commission.
TREATY REF: 15UNTS295.
PROCEDURE: Amendment. Future Procedures Contemplated. Registration. Termination.
PARTIES:
Mexico
Portugal

100547   Bilateral Agreement   **35 UNTS 3**
SIGNED: 1 Jan 48   FORCE: 28 Jan 49
REGISTERED: 7 Sep 49 ICAO (Civil Aviat)
ARTICLES: 1 LANGUAGE: English.
HEADNOTE: AIR SERVICES
TOPIC: Air Transport
CONCEPTS: Conformity with municipal law. Informational records. Non-interest rates and fees. Routes and logistics. Permit designation. Conditions of airlines operating permission. Overflights and technical stops. Operating authorizations and regulations.
INTL ORGS: International Civil Aviation Organization.
TREATY REF: 15UNTS295.
PROCEDURE: Amendment. Duration. Ratification. Registration.
PARTIES:
Ethiopia
Pakistan

100548   Bilateral Exchange   **35 UNTS 13**
SIGNED: 7 Jun 49   FORCE: 6 Jan 49
REGISTERED: 7 Sep 49 ICAO (Civil Aviat)
ARTICLES: 2 LANGUAGE: English.
HEADNOTE: TEMPORARY ETHIOPIAN AIR SERVICE
TOPIC: Air Transport
CONCEPTS: Conformity with municipal law. Informational records. Non-interest rates and fees. Routes and logistics. Permit designation. Airport facilities. Conditions of airlines operating permission. Overflights and technical stops. Operating authorizations and regulations.
INTL ORGS: International Civil Aviation Organization.
TREATY REF: 15UNTS295.
PROCEDURE: Duration. Registration.
PARTIES:
Ethiopia
India

100549   Bilateral Agreement   **35 UNTS 23**
SIGNED: 3 Jun 49   FORCE: 3 Jun 49
REGISTERED: 7 Sep 49 ICAO (Civil Aviat)
ARTICLES: 14 LANGUAGE: English.
HEADNOTE: AIR SERVICES
TOPIC: Air Transport
CONCEPTS: Conditions. Definition of terms. Detailed regulations. Annex or appendix reference. Conformity with municipal law. General cooperation. Exchange of information and documents. Use of facilities. Arbitration. Procedure. Existing tribunals. Negotiation. Reexport of goods, etc.. Non-interest rates and fees. National treatment. Customs exemptions. Routes and logistics. Permit designation. Airport facilities. Conditions of airlines operating permission. Overflights and technical stops. Operating authorizations and regulations.
INTL ORGS: International Civil Aviation Organization. International Court of Justice. Arbitration Commission.
TREATY REF: 15UNTS295.

PROCEDURE: Amendment. Future Procedures Contemplated. Registration. Termination.
PARTIES:
Australia
Pakistan

100550   Bilateral Agreement   **35 UNTS 49**
SIGNED: 23 Jun 49   FORCE: 23 Jun 49
REGISTERED: 7 Sep 49 ICAO (Civil Aviat)
ARTICLES: 14 LANGUAGE: English.
HEADNOTE: AIR SERVICES
TOPIC: Air Transport
CONCEPTS: Definition of terms. Detailed regulations. Annex or appendix reference. Conformity with municipal law. General cooperation. Exchange of information and documents. Use of facilities. Arbitration. Procedure. Existing tribunals. Negotiation. Reexport of goods, etc.. Non-interest rates and fees. Most favored nation clause. National treatment. Customs exemptions. Routes and logistics. Permit designation. Airport facilities. Conditions of airlines operating permission. Overflights and technical stops. Operating authorizations and regulations.
INTL ORGS: International Civil Aviation Organization. International Court of Justice. Arbitration Commission.
TREATY REF: 15UNTS295.
PROCEDURE: Amendment. Future Procedures Contemplated. Registration. Termination.
PARTIES:
Norway
Pakistan

100551   Bilateral Agreement   **35 UNTS 69**
SIGNED: 7 Mar 49   FORCE: 7 Mar 49
REGISTERED: 7 Sep 49 ICAO (Civil Aviat)
ARTICLES: 11 LANGUAGE: French.
HEADNOTE: AIR SERVICES
TOPIC: Air Transport
CONCEPTS: Detailed regulations. Annex or appendix reference. Conformity with municipal law. General cooperation. Licenses and permits. Recognition of legal documents. Use of facilities. Arbitration. Procedure. Existing tribunals. Negotiation. Reexport of goods, etc.. Fees and exemptions. Non-interest rates and fees. Most favored nation clause. National treatment. Customs exemptions. Competency certificate. Routes and logistics. Navigational conditions. Permit designation. Air transport. Airport facilities. Airworthiness certificates. Conditions of airlines operating permission. Operating authorizations and regulations. Licenses and certificates of nationality.
INTL ORGS: International Civil Aviation Organization. Arbitration Commission.
TREATY REF: 15UNTS295.
PROCEDURE: Amendment. Registration. Termination.
PARTIES:
Netherlands
Switzerland

100552   Bilateral Agreement   **35 UNTS 83**
SIGNED: 11 Jul 49   FORCE: 11 Jul 49
REGISTERED: 7 Sep 49 ICAO (Civil Aviat)
ARTICLES: 15 LANGUAGE: English.
HEADNOTE: AIR SERVICES
TOPIC: Air Transport
CONCEPTS: Conditions. Definition of terms. Detailed regulations. Time limit. Annex or appendix reference. Conformity with municipal law. General cooperation. Exchange of information and documents. Arbitration. Procedure. Existing tribunals. Negotiation. Fees and exemptions. Non-interest rates and fees. National treatment. Customs exemptions. Routes and logistics. Permit designation. Conditions of airlines operating permission. Operating authorizations and regulations.
INTL ORGS: International Civil Aviation Organization. International Court of Justice. Arbitration Commission.
TREATY REF: 15UNTS295.
PROCEDURE: Amendment. Future Procedures Contemplated. Termination.
PARTIES:
Australia
India

425 UNTS 304. India. Amendment 14 Dec 60. Force 14 Dec 60.
425 UNTS 304. Australia. Amendment 14 Dec 60. Force 14 Dec 60.
543 UNTS 334. India. Amendment 10 Jul 65. Force 10 Jul 65.
543 UNTS 334. Australia. Amendment 10 Jul 65. Force 10 Jul 65.

100553 Bilateral Agreement **35 UNTS 111**
SIGNED: 16 Jul 49 FORCE: 16 Jul 49
REGISTERED: 7 Sep 49 ICAO (Civil Aviat)
ARTICLES: 15 LANGUAGE: English.
HEADNOTE: AIR SERVICES
TOPIC: Air Transport
CONCEPTS: Conditions. Definition of terms. Detailed regulations. Exceptions and exemptions. Annex or appendix reference. Conformity with municipal law. General cooperation. Exchange of information and documents. Arbitration. Procedure. Existing tribunals. Negotiation. Reexport of goods, etc.. Non-interest rates and fees. Most favored nation clause. Customs exemptions. Temporary importation. Routes and logistics. Permit designation. Airport facilities. Conditions of airlines operating permission. Overflights and technical stops. Operating authorizations and regulations.
INTL ORGS: International Civil Aviation Organization. International Court of Justice. Arbitration Commission.
TREATY REF: 15UNTS295.
PROCEDURE: Amendment. Future Procedures Contemplated. Registration. Termination.
PARTIES:
Pakistan
Philippines

100554 Bilateral Agreement **35 UNTS 137**
SIGNED: 5 Aug 49 FORCE: 5 Aug 49
REGISTERED: 7 Sep 49 ICAO (Civil Aviat)
ARTICLES: 14 LANGUAGE: English.
HEADNOTE: AIR SERVICES
TOPIC: Air Transport
CONCEPTS: Conditions. Definition of terms. Detailed regulations. Annex or appendix reference. Non-prejudice to third party. Conformity with municipal law. General cooperation. Exchange of information and documents. Arbitration. Procedure. Existing tribunals. Special tribunals. Negotiation. Non-interest rates and fees. Most favored nation clause. National treatment. Customs exemptions. Routes and logistics. Permit designation. Conditions of airlines operating permission. Overflights and technical stops. Operating authorizations and regulations.
INTL ORGS: International Civil Aviation Organization. Arbitration Commission.
TREATY REF: 15UNTS295.
PROCEDURE: Amendment. Future Procedures Contemplated. Registration. Application to Non-self-governing Territories.
PARTIES:
Ceylon (Sri Lanka)
UK Great Britain

100555 Bilateral Agreement **35 UNTS 161**
SIGNED: 26 Nov 45 FORCE: 26 Nov 45
REGISTERED: 7 Sep 49 ICAO (Civil Aviat)
ARTICLES: 12 LANGUAGE: English. Greek.
HEADNOTE: AIR SERVICES EUROPE
TOPIC: Air Transport
CONCEPTS: Exceptions and exemptions. Annex or appendix reference. Conformity with municipal law. Licenses and permits. Recognition of legal documents. Use of facilities. Procedure. Existing tribunals. Special tribunals. Fees and exemptions. Most favored nation clause. National treatment. Customs exemptions. Competency certificate. Routes and logistics. Navigational conditions. Permit designation. Airport facilities. Airworthiness certificates. Conditions of airlines operating permission. Operating authorizations and regulations. Licenses and certificates of nationality.
INTL ORGS: International Civil Aviation Organization. Arbitration Commission.
PROCEDURE: Amendment. Future Procedures Contemplated. Ratification. Registration. Termination.

PARTIES:
Greece
UK Great Britain
77 UNTS 352. UK Great Britain. Amendment 21 Mar 49. Force 21 Mar 49.
77 UNTS 352. Greece. Amendment 21 Mar 49. Force 21 Mar 49.
77 UNTS 354. Greece. Amendment 9 May 50. Force 9 May 50.
77 UNTS 354. UK Great Britain. Amendment 9 May 50. Force 9 May 50.

100556 Bilateral Agreement **35 UNTS 197**
SIGNED: 30 Apr 46 FORCE: 30 Apr 46
REGISTERED: 7 Sep 49 ICAO (Civil Aviat)
ARTICLES: 11 LANGUAGE: French. Portuguese.
HEADNOTE: COOPERATION FIELD SOCIAL PROBLEMS
TOPIC: Air Transport
CONCEPTS: Time limit. General cooperation. Exchange of official publications. Exchange of information and documents. Old age insurance. Sickness and invalidity insurance. Social security. Unemployment. Migrant worker.
INTL ORGS: International Civil Aviation Organization. Arbitration Commission.
TREATY REF: 15UNTS295.
PROCEDURE: Denunciation. Duration. Ratification. Renewal or Revival.
PARTIES:
France
Portugal
150 UNTS 364. France. Amendment 26 May 52. Force 9 Jun 52.
150 UNTS 364. Portugal. Amendment 9 Jun 52. Force 9 Jun 52.

100557 Bilateral Exchange **35 UNTS 231**
SIGNED: 29 May 46 FORCE: 29 May 46
REGISTERED: 7 Sep 49 ICAO (Civil Aviat)
ARTICLES: 2 LANGUAGE: English.
HEADNOTE: AIR TRANSPORT
TOPIC: Air Transport
CONCEPTS: Annex or appendix reference. Conformity with municipal law. Licenses and permits. Recognition of legal documents. Use of facilities. Procedure. Existing tribunals. Special tribunals. Fees and exemptions. Most favored nation clause. National treatment. Customs exemptions. Competency certificate. Routes and logistics. Navigational conditions. Permit designation. Air transport. Airport facilities. Airworthiness certificates. Conditions of airlines operating permission. Operating authorizations and regulations. Licenses and certificates of nationality.
INTL ORGS: International Civil Aviation Organization. Arbitration Commission.
PROCEDURE: Amendment. Future Procedures Contemplated. Registration. Termination.
PARTIES:
Ireland
Sweden
327 UNTS 332. Sweden. Amendment 21 Oct 57. Force 21 Oct 57.
327 UNTS 332. Ireland. Amendment 2 Oct 57. Force 21 Oct 57.

100558 Bilateral Agreement **35 UNTS 243**
SIGNED: 6 Mar 47 FORCE: 6 Mar 47
REGISTERED: 7 Sep 49 ICAO (Civil Aviat)
ARTICLES: 13 LANGUAGE: English. Portuguese. Swedish.
HEADNOTE: AIR TRANSPORT
TOPIC: Air Transport
CONCEPTS: Annex or appendix reference. Conformity with municipal law. Licenses and permits. Recognition of legal documents. Use of facilities. Procedure. Existing tribunals. Special tribunals. Fees and exemptions. Most favored nation clause. National treatment. Customs exemptions. Competency certificate. Routes and logistics. Navigational conditions. Permit designation. Air transport. Airport facilities. Airworthiness certificates. Conditions of airlines operating permission. Operating authorizations and regulations. Licenses and certificates of nationality.

INTL ORGS: International Civil Aviation Organization.
TREATY REF: 15UNTS295.
PROCEDURE: Amendment. Future Procedures Contemplated. Registration. Termination.
PARTIES:
Portugal
Sweden
216 UNTS 368. Sweden. Supplementation 6 Mar 47. Force 6 Mar 47.
216 UNTS 368. Portugal. Supplementation 6 Mar 47. Force 6 Mar 47.
392 UNTS 328. Sweden. Supplementation 15 Jan 59. Force 25 Mar 59.
392 UNTS 328. Portugal. Supplementation 15 Jan 59. Force 25 Mar 59.

100559 Bilateral Agreement **35 UNTS 275**
SIGNED: 10 Sep 47 FORCE: 14 Apr 48
REGISTERED: 7 Sep 49 ICAO (Civil Aviat)
ARTICLES: 9 LANGUAGE: Czechoslovakian. French.
HEADNOTE: AIR SERVICES
TOPIC: Air Transport
CONCEPTS: Annex or appendix reference. Frontier formalities. Conformity with municipal law. General cooperation. Licenses and permits. Recognition of legal documents. Use of facilities. Arbitration. Procedure. Existing tribunals. Special tribunals. Negotiation. Fees and exemptions. Most favored nation clause. National treatment. Customs exemptions. Competency certificate. Routes and logistics. Navigational conditions. Permit designation. Air transport. Airport facilities. Airworthiness certificates. Conditions of airlines operating permission. Operating authorizations and regulations. Licenses and certificates of nationality.
INTL ORGS: International Civil Aviation Organization. Arbitration Commission.
TREATY REF: 15UNTS295.
PROCEDURE: Amendment. Future Procedures Contemplated. Ratification. Registration. Termination.
PARTIES:
Czechoslovakia
Switzerland

100560 Bilateral Agreement **35 UNTS 295**
SIGNED: 14 Nov 47 FORCE: 14 Nov 47
REGISTERED: 7 Sep 49 ICAO (Civil Aviat)
ARTICLES: 12 LANGUAGE: French.
HEADNOTE: OPERATION REGULAR AIR SERVICES
TOPIC: Air Transport
CONCEPTS: Annex or appendix reference. Conformity with municipal law. Licenses and permits. Recognition of legal documents. Use of facilities. Procedure. Existing tribunals. Special tribunals. Fees and exemptions. Most favored nation clause. National treatment. Customs exemptions. Competency certificate. Routes and logistics. Navigational conditions. Permit designation. Airport facilities. Airworthiness certificates. Conditions of airlines operating permission. Operating authorizations and regulations. Licenses and certificates of nationality.
INTL ORGS: International Civil Aviation Organization. Arbitration Commission.
TREATY REF: 15UNTS295.
PROCEDURE: Amendment. Future Procedures Contemplated. Ratification. Registration. Termination.
PARTIES:
Denmark
Greece

100561 Bilateral Exchange **35 UNTS 309**
SIGNED: 18 Nov 47 FORCE: 18 Nov 47
REGISTERED: 7 Sep 49 ICAO (Civil Aviat)
ARTICLES: 2 LANGUAGE: English.

HEADNOTE: AIR TRANSPORT
TOPIC: Air Transport
CONCEPTS: Annex or appendix reference. Conformity with municipal law. Licenses and permits. Recognition of legal documents. Use of facilities. Procedure. Existing tribunals. Special tribunals. Fees and exemptions. Most favored nation clause. National treatment. Customs exemptions. Competency certificate. Routes and logistics. Navigational conditions. Permit designation. Air transport. Airport facilities. Airworthiness certificates. Conditions of airlines operating permission. Operating authorizations and regulations. Licenses and certificates of nationality.
INTL ORGS: International Civil Aviation Organization. Arbitration Commission.
TREATY REF: 15UNTS295.
PROCEDURE: Amendment. Future Procedures Contemplated. Registration. Termination.
PARTIES:
Denmark
Ireland

ANNEX
327 UNTS 336. Ireland. Amendment 2 Oct 57. Force 29 Oct 57.
327 UNTS 336. Denmark. Amendment 29 Oct 57. Force 29 Oct 57.

100562   Bilateral Exchange   35 UNTS 321
SIGNED: 18 Nov 47   FORCE: 18 Nov 47
REGISTERED: 7 Sep 49 ICAO (Civil Aviat)
ARTICLES: 3 LANGUAGE: English.
HEADNOTE: OPERATION AIR SERVICES ORIENT AIRWAYS, LTD.
TOPIC: Air Transport
CONCEPTS: Change of circumstances. Registration certificate. Routes and logistics. Air transport. Airport facilities.
PARTIES:
Burma
Pakistan

100563   Bilateral Agreement   35 UNTS 329
SIGNED: 15 Dec 47   FORCE: 15 Dec 47
REGISTERED: 7 Sep 49 ICAO (Civil Aviat)
ARTICLES: 12 LANGUAGE: Danish. English. Portuguese.
HEADNOTE: AIR TRANSPORT
TOPIC: Air Transport
CONCEPTS: Annex or appendix reference. Conformity with municipal law. Licenses and permits. Recognition of legal documents. Use of facilities. Procedure. Existing tribunals. Special tribunals. Fees and exemptions. Most favored nation clause. National treatment. Customs exemptions. Competency certificate. Routes and logistics. Navigational conditions. Permit designation. Airport facilities. Airworthiness certificates. Conditions of airlines operating permission. Operating authorizations and regulations. Licenses and certificates of nationality.
INTL ORGS: International Civil Aviation Organization. Arbitration Commission.
TREATY REF: 15UNTS295.
PROCEDURE: Amendment. Future Procedures Contemplated. Registration. Termination.
PARTIES:
Denmark
Portugal

100564   Bilateral Agreement   36 UNTS 3
SIGNED: 6 May 48   FORCE: 6 May 48
REGISTERED: 7 Sep 49 ICAO (Civil Aviat)
ARTICLES: 14 LANGUAGE: English.
HEADNOTE: AIR SERVICES
TOPIC: Air Transport
CONCEPTS: Definition of terms. Detailed regulations. Annex or appendix reference. Non-prejudice to third party. Conformity with municipal law. General cooperation. Exchange of information and documents. Use of facilities. Procedure. Existing tribunals. Special tribunals. Negotiation. Reexport of goods, etc.. Non-interest rates and fees. Most favored nation clause. National treatment. Customs exemptions. Permit designation. Air transport. Airport facilities. Conditions of airlines operating permission. Overflights and technical stops. Operating authorizations and regulations.
INTL ORGS: International Civil Aviation Organiza-

tion. International Court of Justice. Arbitration Commission.
TREATY REF: 15UNTS295.
PROCEDURE: Amendment. Registration. Termination.
PARTIES:
Pakistan
Sweden

ANNEX
216 UNTS 372. Pakistan. Amendment 24 Apr 52. Force 6 May 52.
216 UNTS 372. Sweden. Amendment 6 May 52. Force 6 May 52.
216 UNTS 374. Pakistan. Supplementation 8 Jul 52. Force 8 Jul 52.
216 UNTS 374. Sweden. Supplementation 28 May 52. Force 8 Jul 52.

100565   Bilateral Exchange   36 UNTS 25
SIGNED: 24 Jun 47   FORCE: 24 Jun 47
REGISTERED: 9 Sep 49 USA (United States)
ARTICLES: 2 LANGUAGE: English.
HEADNOTE: EXCHANGE TRANSACTIONS MODIFICATION COMMERCE AGREEMENT
TOPIC: General Economic
CONCEPTS: Detailed regulations. Annex type material. General cooperation. Licenses and permits. General trade. Trade procedures. Balance of payments. Monetary and gold transfers. Financial programs. Assets. Assets transfer. Quotas. Transport of goods.
TREATY REF: 161LTS109.
PROCEDURE: Amendment.
PARTIES:
Sweden
USA (United States)

ANNEX
88 UNTS 448. Sweden. Prolongation 27 Jun 49. Force 27 Jun 49.
88 UNTS 448. USA (United States). Prolongation 27 Jun 49. Force 27 Jun 49.

100566   Bilateral Instrument   36 UNTS 53
SIGNED: 14 Aug 47   FORCE: 14 Aug 47
REGISTERED: 9 Sep 49 USA (United States)
ARTICLES: 7 LANGUAGE: English. Italian.
HEADNOTE: SETTLEMENT WARTIME CLAIMS RELATED MATTERS
TOPIC: Reparations
CONCEPTS: Definition of terms. Annex or appendix reference. Responsibility and liability. Compensation. Return of equipment and recapture. Restrictions on transfer. Post-war claims settlement.
PARTIES:
Italy
USA (United States)

ANNEX
80 UNTS 319. Italy. Interpretation 24 Feb 49. Force 24 Feb 49.
80 UNTS 319. USA (United States). Interpretation 24 Feb 49. Force 24 Feb 49.

100567   Bilateral Instrument   36 UNTS 105
SIGNED: 14 Aug 47   FORCE: 14 Aug 47
REGISTERED: 9 Sep 49 USA (United States)
ARTICLES: 5 LANGUAGE: English. Italian.
HEADNOTE: ASSETS CLAIMS
TOPIC: Claims and Debts
CONCEPTS: Definition of terms. Detailed regulations. Annex or appendix reference. Annex type material. Conformity with municipal law. General property. Currency. Payment schedules. Assets. Claims and settlements. Lump sum settlements. Assets transfer. Merchant vessels. Surplus war property. Enemy financial interests. Post-war claims settlement.
PARTIES:
Italy
USA (United States)

100568   Bilateral Convention   36 UNTS 145
SIGNED: 9 Jan 47   FORCE: 3 Aug 49
REGISTERED: 9 Sep 49 Belgium
ARTICLES: 7 LANGUAGE: French.
HEADNOTE: NATIONALITY MARRIED WOMEN
TOPIC: Admin Cooperation
CONCEPTS: Previous treaty replacement. Acquisition of nationality. Nationality and citizenship.
TREATY REF: 123LTS91.

PROCEDURE: Denunciation. Ratification.
PARTIES:
Belgium
France

100569   Bilateral Agreement   36 UNTS 151
SIGNED: 8 Jan 49   FORCE: 8 Jan 49
REGISTERED: 9 Sep 49 Belgium
ARTICLES: 39 LANGUAGE: French.
HEADNOTE: FRONTIER WORKS
TOPIC: Non-ILO Labor
CONCEPTS: Definition of terms. Detailed regulations. Annex or appendix reference. Resident permits. Frontier permits. Alien status. Legal protection and assistance. Investigation of violations. Establishment of commission. Dispute settlement. Vocational training. Safety standards. Right to organize. Wages and salaries. Non-ILO labor relations. Exchange rates and regulations. Fees and exemptions. Frontier peoples and personnel.
INTL ORGS: Special Commission.
PROCEDURE: Amendment.
PARTIES:
Belgium
France

ANNEX
187 UNTS 416. France. Supplementation 28 Nov 53. Force 28 Nov 53.
187 UNTS 416. Belgium. Supplementation 28 Nov 53. Force 28 Nov 53.
314 UNTS 313. France. Supplementation 12 Sep 58. Force 12 Sep 58.
314 UNTS 313. Belgium. Supplementation 12 Sep 58. Force 12 Sep 58.

100570   Bilateral Convention   36 UNTS 233
SIGNED: 17 Jan 48   FORCE: 1 Jul 49
REGISTERED: 9 Sep 49 Belgium
ARTICLES: 37 LANGUAGE: French.
HEADNOTE: SOCIAL SECURITY
TOPIC: Non-ILO Labor
CONCEPTS: Exceptions and exemptions. Treaty implementation. Annex type material. Previous treaty replacement. General consular functions. Conformity with municipal law. General cooperation. Domestic legislation. Old age and invalidity insurance. Non-ILO labor relations. Old age insurance. Sickness and invalidity insurance. Social security. Fees and exemptions. National treatment.
TREATY REF: 2DEMARTENS35 P.18; 95LTS293; 167LTS2.
PROCEDURE: Duration. Future Procedures Contemplated. Ratification. Renewal or Revival. Termination.
PARTIES:
Belgium
France

ANNEX
149 UNTS 396. Belgium. Correction 6 Jun 52. Force 1 Jul 49.
149 UNTS 396. France. Correction 6 Jun 52. Force 1 Jul 49.
182 UNTS 221. Belgium. Implementation 29 Jul 53. Force 1 Jul 49.
182 UNTS 221. France. Implementation 29 Jul 53. Force 1 Jul 49.

100571   Bilateral Convention   36 UNTS 305
SIGNED: 30 Apr 48   FORCE: 1 Sep 49
REGISTERED: 9 Sep 49 Belgium
ARTICLES: 41 LANGUAGE: French.
HEADNOTE: SOCIAL INSURANCE
TOPIC: Non-ILO Labor
CONCEPTS: Exceptions and exemptions. General cooperation. Exchange of information and documents. Domestic legislation. Old age and invalidity insurance. Non-ILO labor relations. Family allowances. Old age insurance. Sickness and invalidity insurance. Social security. Unemployment. Fees and exemptions. Payment schedules. National treatment.
PROCEDURE: Amendment. Duration. Ratification. Renewal or Revival. Termination.
PARTIES:
Belgium
Italy

ANNEX
202 UNTS 322. Italy. Amendment 17 Nov 54. Force 1 Jan 55.

202 UNTS 322. Belgium. Amendment 17 Nov 54. Force 1 Jan 55.
300 UNTS 306. Italy. Amendment 9 Sep 57. Force 1 Oct 57.
300 UNTS 306. Italy. Implementation 20 Oct 50. Force 20 Oct 50.
300 UNTS 306. Belgium. Amendment 9 Sep 57. Force 1 Oct 57.
300 UNTS 306. Belgium. Implementation 20 Oct 50. Force 20 Oct 50.

100572 Bilateral Exchange **36 UNTS 339**
SIGNED: 14 Jan 49　　FORCE: 14 Jan 49
REGISTERED: 9 Sep 49 Belgium
ARTICLES: 2 LANGUAGE: French.
HEADNOTE: DISTRIBUTION ASSISTANCE
TOPIC: Direct Aid
CONCEPTS: Annex type material. Non-prejudice to third party. General cooperation. Exchange of information and documents. Private contracts. Responsibility and liability. Accounting procedures. Currency deposits. Funding procedures. Payment schedules. Economic assistance. Grants. Distribution. Loan and credit.
INTL ORGS: Organization for Economic Co-operation and Development.
TREATY REF: 19UNTS129; 24UNTS35.
PARTIES:
　Belgium
　Luxembourg

100573 Bilateral Convention **36 UNTS 349**
SIGNED: 29 Aug 47　　FORCE: 1 Oct 49
REGISTERED: 9 Sep 49 Belgium
ARTICLES: 23 LANGUAGE: Dutch. French.
HEADNOTE: LEGISLATION TWO COUNTRIES AFFECTING SOCIAL INSURANCE
TOPIC: Non-ILO Labor
CONCEPTS: Detailed regulations. Previous treaty replacement. Conformity with municipal law. Incorporation of treaty provisions into national law. Dispute settlement. Public health. Old age and invalidity insurance. Non-ILO labor relations. Family allowances. Administrative cooperation. Old age insurance. Sickness and invalidity insurance. Social security. Unemployment. Payment schedules. Tax exemptions.
TREATY REF: 11LTS333; 64LTS385; 137LTS411.
PROCEDURE: Amendment. Duration. Ratification. Renewal or Revival. Termination.
PARTIES:
　Belgium
　Netherlands
　　　　　ANNEX
363 UNTS 382. Netherlands. Amendment 4 Nov 57. Force 15 Jun 60.
363 UNTS 382. Belgium. Amendment 4 Nov 57. Force 15 Jun 60.

100574 Bilateral Agreement **37 UNTS 3**
SIGNED: 30 May 48　　FORCE: 12 Jan 49
REGISTERED: 13 Sep 49 Poland
ARTICLES: 7 LANGUAGE: Bulgarian. Polish.
HEADNOTE: ECONOMIC COOPERATION GOODS EXCHANGE
TOPIC: General Trade
CONCEPTS: General provisions. Establishment of commission.
INTL ORGS: Special Commission.
PROCEDURE: Duration. Future Procedures Contemplated. Ratification. Termination.
PARTIES:
　Bulgaria
　Poland

100575 Bilateral Agreement **37 UNTS 25**
SIGNED: 8 Jul 48　　FORCE: 20 Jan 49
REGISTERED: 13 Sep 49 Poland
ARTICLES: 39 LANGUAGE: Polish. Russian.
HEADNOTE: REGIME POLISH-SOVIET STATE FRONTIER
TOPIC: Territory Boundary
CONCEPTS: Non-visa travel documents. Exchange of information and documents. Inspection and observation. Customs exemptions. Frontier waterways. Fish, wildlife, and natural resources. Markers and definitions. Frontier crossing points.
INTL ORGS: Special Commission.

TREATY REF: 10UNTS193.
PROCEDURE: Denunciation. Duration. Ratification. Renewal or Revival.
PARTIES:
　Poland
　USSR (Soviet Union)
　　　　　ANNEX
221 UNTS 410. USSR (Soviet Union). Amendment 17 Mar 52. Force 17 Mar 52.
221 UNTS 410. Poland. Amendment 9 Feb 52. Force 17 Mar 52.

100576 Bilateral Convention **37 UNTS 107**
SIGNED: 8 Jul 48　　FORCE: 15 Mar 49
REGISTERED: 13 Sep 49 Poland
ARTICLES: 20 LANGUAGE: Polish. Russian.
HEADNOTE: PROCEDURE SETTLE FRONTIER DISPUTES
TOPIC: Dispute Settlement
CONCEPTS: Visas. Frontier permits. Exchange of information and documents. Inspection and observation. Recognition and enforcement of legal decisions. Personnel. Establishment of commission. Procedure. Fees and exemptions. Frontier crossing points.
PROCEDURE: Denunciation. Ratification.
PARTIES:
　Poland
　USSR (Soviet Union)
　　　　　ANNEX
221 UNTS 410. USSR (Soviet Union). Amendment 17 Mar 52. Force 17 Mar 52.
221 UNTS 410. Poland. Amendment 9 Feb 52. Force 17 Mar 52.

100577 Bilateral Convention **37 UNTS 199**
SIGNED: 28 Apr 47　　FORCE: 24 Apr 49
REGISTERED: 14 Sep 49 Belgium
ARTICLES: 10 LANGUAGE: Dutch. French.
HEADNOTE: PRACTICE MEDICINE FRONTIER COMMUNES
TOPIC: Visas
CONCEPTS: Exchange of information and documents. Export quotas. Frontier peoples and personnel.
TREATY REF: CONV. 7DEC1868.
PROCEDURE: Denunciation. Ratification.
PARTIES:
　Belgium
　Netherlands

100578 Bilateral Agreement **37 UNTS 215**
SIGNED: 12 Mar 47　　FORCE: 26 Mar 47
REGISTERED: 14 Sep 49 Belgium
ARTICLES: 6 LANGUAGE: French.
HEADNOTE: DEVELOPING TRADE
TOPIC: General Trade
CONCEPTS: Exceptions and exemptions. Annex or appendix reference. Informational records. Establishment of commission. Establishment of trade relations. Trade procedures. Payment schedules.
INTL ORGS: Special Commission.
TREATY REF: 33UNTS43.
PROCEDURE: Duration. Future Procedures Contemplated.
PARTIES:
　Belgium
　Turkey

100579 Bilateral Instrument **37 UNTS 221**
SIGNED: 12 Mar 47　　FORCE: 26 Mar 47
REGISTERED: 14 Sep 49 Belgium
ARTICLES: 1 LANGUAGE: French.
HEADNOTE: APPLICATION MOST FAVORED NATION
TOPIC: Mostfavored Nation
CONCEPTS: Exceptions and exemptions. Reciprocity in trade. Most favored nation clause. Customs duties. Navigational conditions.
PROCEDURE: Denunciation. Termination.
PARTIES:
　Belgium
　Turkey

100580 Bilateral Treaty **37 UNTS 226**
SIGNED: 29 Mar 46　　FORCE: 10 May 48
REGISTERED: 15 Sep 49 Iraq
ARTICLES: 7 LANGUAGE: Arabic. French. Turkish.

HEADNOTE: FRIENDSHIP NEIGHBORLY RELATIONS
TOPIC: General Amity
CONCEPTS: Annex or appendix reference. Friendship and amity. Non-prejudice to UN charter. Procedure.
INTL ORGS: United Nations.
TREATY REF: 64LTS379.
PROCEDURE: Amendment. Duration. Ratification.
PARTIES:
　Iraq
　Turkey

100581 Bilateral Convention **37 UNTS 333**
SIGNED: 29 Mar 46　　FORCE: 25 May 48
REGISTERED: 15 Sep 49 Iraq
ARTICLES: 27 LANGUAGE: Arabic. French. Turkish.
HEADNOTE: LEGAL ASSISTANCE CIVIL PENAL COMMERCIAL MATTERS
TOPIC: Admin Cooperation
CONCEPTS: Extradition, deportation and repatriation. Witnesses and experts. General cooperation. Legal protection and assistance. Recognition and enforcement of legal decisions. Recognition of legal documents. Indemnities and reimbursements. National treatment.
PROCEDURE: Denunciation. Ratification.
PARTIES:
　Iraq
　Turkey

100582 Bilateral Convention **37 UNTS 369**
SIGNED: 29 Mar 46　　FORCE: 25 May 48
REGISTERED: 15 Sep 49 Iraq
ARTICLES: 17 LANGUAGE: Arabic. French. Turkish.
HEADNOTE: EXTRADITION
TOPIC: Extradition
CONCEPTS: Extradition, deportation and repatriation. Court procedures. Extraditable offenses. Special factors. Refusal of extradition.
PARTIES:
　Iraq
　Turkey

100583 Multilateral Convention **38 UNTS 3**
SIGNED: 9 Oct 46　　FORCE: 28 May 47
REGISTERED: 15 Sep 49 ILO (Labor Org)
ARTICLES: 9 LANGUAGE: English. French.
HEADNOTE: PARTIAL REVISION ILO CONVENTION
TOPIC: ILO Labor
CONCEPTS: Definition of terms. Detailed regulations. Previous treaty extension. ILO conventions.
INTL ORGS: League of Nations. International Labour Organization. United Nations.
TREATY REF: 15UNTS38.
PROCEDURE: Amendment. Ratification.
PARTIES:
　Multilateral
　　　　　ANNEX
44 UNTS 343. Chile. Ratification 3 Nov 49.
54 UNTS 400. Argentina. Ratification 14 Mar 50.
66 UNTS 349. Czechoslovakia. Ratification 12 Jun 50.
71 UNTS 322. Ceylon (Sri Lanka). Ratification 19 Sep 50.
92 UNTS 336. Australia. Nauru.
122 UNTS 336. Australia. New Guinea.
122 UNTS 336. Australia. Papua.
122 UNTS 336. Australia. Norfolk Islands
131 UNTS 310. Yugoslavia. Ratification 21 May 52.
133 UNTS 336. Greece. Ratification 13 Jun 52.
167 UNTS 262. Vietnam. Ratification 6 Jun 53.
172 UNTS 336. Cuba. Ratification 20 Jul 53.
190 UNTS 380. Panama. Ratification 13 May 54.
191 UNTS 360. Japan. Ratification 27 May 54.
222 UNTS 386. Bulgaria. Ratification 7 Nov 55.
268 UNTS 354. Morocco. Ratification 20 May 57.
304 UNTS 395. Spain. Ratification 24 Jun 58.
373 UNTS 336. United Arab Rep. Syria.
413 UNTS 344. Syria. Ratification 30 Oct 61.
429 UNTS 256. Peru. Ratification 4 Apr 62.
444 UNTS 294. Algeria. Succession 19 Jan 62. Force 19 Jan 62.

100584 Multilateral Convention **38 UNTS 17**
SIGNED: 28 Nov 19 FORCE: 28 May 47
REGISTERED: 15 Sep 49 ILO (Labor Org)
ARTICLES: 22 LANGUAGE: English. French.
HEADNOTE: LIMITING HOURS WORK INDUSTRY
TOPIC: ILO Labor
CONCEPTS: Definition of terms. Detailed regulations. Emergencies. Exceptions and exemptions. Territorial application. Previous treaty extension. Conformity with municipal law. Exchange of information and documents. Incorporation of treaty provisions into national law. ILO conventions. Holidays and rest periods. Labor statistics. Safety standards.
INTL ORGS: International Labour Organization.
TREATY REF: 38UNTS3.
PROCEDURE: Amendment. Denunciation. Duration. Ratification. Registration. Renewal or Revival.
PARTIES:
Multilateral

ANNEX
92 UNTS 401. Israel. Ratification 26 Jun 51.
127 UNTS 329. Haiti. Ratification 31 Mar 52. Force 31 Mar 53.
361 UNTS 227. United Arab Rep. Ratification 10 May 60.
410 UNTS 286. Kuwait. Ratification 21 Sep 61.
413 UNTS 346. Syria. Ratification 30 Oct 61.
545 UNTS 375. Iraq. Ratification 24 Aug 65.
560 UNTS 308. Paraguay. Ratification 21 Mar 66.

100585 Multilateral Convention **38 UNTS 41**
SIGNED: 28 Nov 19 FORCE: 28 May 47
REGISTERED: 15 Sep 49 ILO (Labor Org)
ARTICLES: 11 LANGUAGE: English. French.
HEADNOTE: UNEMPLOYMENT
TOPIC: ILO Labor
CONCEPTS: Territorial application. Previous treaty extension. General cooperation. Exchange of information and documents. ILO conventions. Old age and invalidity insurance. Labor statistics. Administrative cooperation. Unemployment.
INTL ORGS: International Labour Organization.
TREATY REF: 38UNTS3.
PROCEDURE: Amendment. Denunciation. Duration. Ratification. Registration.
PARTIES:
Multilateral

ANNEX
68 UNTS 270. Turkey. Ratification 14 Jul 50.
100 UNTS 289. Netherlands. Surinam.
100 UNTS 289. Netherlands. Netherlands Antilles.
196 UNTS 330. United Arab Rep. Ratification 3 Jul 54.
272 UNTS 247. Sudan. Ratification 18 Jun 57.
285 UNTS 368. Denmark. Faroe Islands. Withdrawal 2 Dec 57.
287 UNTS 341. Iceland. Ratification 17 Feb 58.
373 UNTS 337. United Arab Rep. Syria.
373 UNTS 337. Bulgaria. Denunciation 20 Jul 60. Force 20 Jul 61.
380 UNTS 389. Morocco. Ratification 14 Oct 60.
413 UNTS 347. Syria. Ratification 30 Oct 61.
423 UNTS 291. Ecuador. Ratification 5 Feb 62.
457 UNTS 326. UK Great Britain. Gibralter.
463 UNTS 370. UK Great Britain. Singapore.
463 UNTS 370. UK Great Britain. Bahamas.
468 UNTS 414. UK Great Britain. Declaration 8 May 63.
471 UNTS 350. UK Great Britain. Grenada.
475 UNTS 368. UK Great Britain. Fed Rhod/-Nyasaland.
479 UNTS 430. UK Great Britain. Mauritius.
479 UNTS 430. UK Great Britain. Kenya.
480 UNTS 458. UK Great Britain. British Guiana.
488 UNTS 336. Kenya. Ratification 13 Jan 64. Force 13 Jan 64.
499 UNTS 356. UK Great Britain. Malta.
499 UNTS 356. UK Great Britain. Gambia.
504 UNTS 318. Central Afri Rep. Ratification 9 Jun 64.
504 UNTS 318. UK Great Britain. Basutoland.
510 UNTS 344. UK Great Britain. Brunei. Declaration 3 Aug 64.
515 UNTS 332. UK Great Britain. Seychelles.
521 UNTS 406. UK Great Britain. British Guiana.
524 UNTS 342. Malta. Ratification 4 Jan 65.
527 UNTS 330. UK Great Britain. St. Helena. Declaration 8 Feb 65.
530 UNTS 392. UK Great Britain. Seychelles.

548 UNTS 380. Cyprus. Ratification 8 Oct 65.
567 UNTS 338. Guyana. Ratification 8 Jun 66. Force 8 Jun 66.
567 UNTS 338. Ethiopia. Ratification 11 Jun 66.

100586 Multilateral Convention **38 UNTS 53**
SIGNED: 29 Nov 19 FORCE: 28 May 47
REGISTERED: 15 Sep 49 ILO (Labor Org)
ARTICLES: 12 LANGUAGE: English. French.
HEADNOTE: EMPLOYMENT WOMEN BEFORE AFTER CHILDBIRTH
TOPIC: ILO Labor
CONCEPTS: Definition of terms. Detailed regulations. Territorial application. Previous treaty extension. ILO conventions. Employment regulations. Holidays and rest periods. Safety standards. Sickness and invalidity insurance.
INTL ORGS: International Labour Organization.
TREATY REF: 38UNTS3.
PROCEDURE: Amendment. Denunciation. Duration. Ratification. Registration.
PARTIES:
Multilateral

ANNEX
77 UNTS 360. France. Ratification 16 Dec 50.
149 UNTS 402. Italy. Ratification 22 Oct 52.
193 UNTS 343. Italy. Italian Somaliland.
212 UNTS 384. France. French Guinea.
212 UNTS 384. France. Guadeloupe.
212 UNTS 384. France. Reunion.
212 UNTS 384. France. Martinique.
222 UNTS 387. Uruguay. Denunciation 17 Oct 55. Force 17 Oct 56.
304 UNTS 396. Panama. Ratification 3 Jun 58.
399 UNTS 254. Ivory Coast. Ratification 5 May 61.
401 UNTS 215. Gabon. Ratification 13 Jun 61.
406 UNTS 285. Brazil. Denunciation 26 Jul 61. Force 26 Jul 62.
444 UNTS 296. Algeria. Succession 19 Oct 62. Force 19 Oct 62.
483 UNTS 394. Mauritania. Ratification 8 Nov 63.
504 UNTS 320. Central Afri Rep. Ratification 9 Jun 64.

100587 Multilateral Convention **38 UNTS 67**
SIGNED: 28 Nov 19 FORCE: 28 May 47
REGISTERED: 15 Sep 49 ILO (Labor Org)
ARTICLES: 15 LANGUAGE: English. French.
HEADNOTE: EMPLOYMENT WOMEN DURING NIGHT
TOPIC: ILO Labor
CONCEPTS: Definition of terms. Exceptions and exemptions. Territorial application. Previous treaty extension. Domestic legislation. ILO conventions. Employment regulations. Holidays and rest periods. Labor statistics.
INTL ORGS: International Labour Organization.
TREATY REF: 38UNTS3.
PROCEDURE: Amendment. Denunciation. Duration. Ratification. Registration.
PARTIES:
Multilateral

ANNEX
105 UNTS 298. Ceylon (Sri Lanka). Ratification 8 Oct 51.
167 UNTS 262. Vietnam. Ratification 6 Jun 53.
193 UNTS 345. Italy. Italian Somaliland.
222 UNTS 388. Uruguay. Denunciation 17 Oct 55. Force 17 Oct 56.
222 UNTS 388. France. Denunciation 8 Nov 55. Force 8 Nov 56.
249 UNTS 442. Morocco. Ratification 13 Jul 56. Force 13 Jul 56.
264 UNTS 327. Yugoslavia. Denunciation 4 Mar 57. Force 4 Mar 58.
269 UNTS 273. Tunisia. Ratification 15 May 57.
272 UNTS 248. Romania. Denunciation 28 May 57. Force 28 May 58.
323 UNTS 368. Guinea. Ratification 21 Jan 59. Force 21 Jan 59.
366 UNTS 368. Mali. Succession 21 Jun 60. Force 21 Jun 60.
366 UNTS 368. Togo. Succession 7 Jun 60. Force 7 Jun 60.
366 UNTS 368. Cameroon. Succession 7 Jun 60. Force 7 Jun 60.
373 UNTS 338. Bulgaria. Denunciation 20 Jul 60. Force 20 Jul 61.
380 UNTS 390. Gabon. Succession 14 Oct 60. Force 14 Oct 60.

380 UNTS 391. Central Afri Rep. Succession 27 Oct 60. Force 27 Oct 60.
381 UNTS 354. Congo (Zaire). Succession 20 Sep 60. Force 20 Sep 60.
381 UNTS 355. Mali. Succession 22 Sep 60. Force 22 Sep 60.
384 UNTS 330. Malagasy. Succession 1 Nov 60. Force 1 Nov 60.
384 UNTS 331. Senegal. Succession 4 Nov 60. Force 4 Nov 60.
384 UNTS 331. Chad. Succession 10 Nov 60. Force 10 Nov 60.
384 UNTS 332. Upper Volta. Succession 21 Nov 60. Force 21 Nov 60.
384 UNTS 332. Congo (Brazzaville). Succession 10 Nov 60. Force 10 Nov 60.
384 UNTS 332. Ivory Coast. Succession 21 Nov 60. Force 21 Nov 60.
386 UNTS 364. Dahomey. Succession 12 Dec 60.
390 UNTS 334. Niger. Succession 27 Feb 61.
401 UNTS 216. Mauritius. Succession 20 Jun 61.
416 UNTS 299. Burma. Denunciation 9 Nov 61. Force 9 Nov 62.
443 UNTS 314. Rwanda. Succession 18 Sep 62. Force 18 Sep 62.
444 UNTS 297. Cameroon. Succession 3 Sep 62.
457 UNTS 328. Burundi. Succession 11 Mar 63.
488 UNTS 338. Czechoslovakia. Denunciation 21 Jan 64. Force 21 Jan 65.
488 UNTS 338. Laos. Ratification 23 Jan 64. Force 23 Jan 64.
510 UNTS 345. Albania. Denunciation 11 Aug 64. Force 11 Aug 65.
545 UNTS 376. Mauritania. Denunciation 2 Aug 65. Force 2 Aug 66.
548 UNTS 381. Vietnam, South. Denunciation 26 Oct 65. Force 26 Oct 66.
638 UNTS 330. Guinea. Denunciation 28 May 68. Force 28 May 69.
660 UNTS 424. Cambodia. Ratification 24 Feb 69.

100588 Multilateral Convention **38 UNTS 81**
SIGNED: 28 Nov 19 FORCE: 28 May 47
REGISTERED: 15 Sep 49 ILO (Labor Org)
ARTICLES: 14 LANGUAGE: English. French.
HEADNOTE: MINIMUM AGE INDUSTRIAL EMPLOYMENT CHILDREN
TOPIC: ILO Labor
CONCEPTS: Definition of terms. Exceptions and exemptions. Territorial application. Previous treaty extension. Domestic legislation. ILO conventions. Employment regulations. Labor statistics.
INTL ORGS: International Labour Organization.
TREATY REF: 38UNTS3.
PROCEDURE: Amendment. Denunciation. Duration. Ratification. Registration.
PARTIES:
Multilateral

ANNEX
104 UNTS 346. Ceylon (Sri Lanka). Ratification 27 Sep 51.
167 UNTS 263. Vietnam. Ratification 6 Jun 53.
183 UNTS 349. Israel. Ratification 23 Dec 53.
196 UNTS 331. Denmark. Greenland.
198 UNTS 374. Bolivia. Ratification 19 Jul 54.
218 UNTS 380. India. Ratification 9 Sep 55.
222 UNTS 388. Uruguay. Denunciation 17 Oct 55. Force 17 Oct 56.
266 UNTS 370. Haiti. Ratification 12 Apr 57.
323 UNTS 369. Guinea. Ratification 21 Jan 59. Force 21 Jan 59.
366 UNTS 370. Cameroon. Succession 7 Jun 60. Force 7 Jun 60.
366 UNTS 370. Togo. Succession 7 Jun 60. Force 7 Jun 60.
366 UNTS 370. Mali. Succession 21 Jun 60. Force 21 Jun 60.
373 UNTS 339. Bulgaria. Denunciation 20 Jul 60. Force 20 Jul 61.
380 UNTS 392. Gabon. Succession 14 Oct 60. Force 14 Oct 60.
380 UNTS 392. Central Afri Rep. Succession 27 Oct 60. Force 27 Oct 60.
381 UNTS 356. Mali. Succession 22 Sep 60. Force 22 Sep 60.
384 UNTS 334. Malagasy. Succession 1 Nov 60. Force 1 Nov 60.
384 UNTS 334. Senegal. Succession 4 Nov 60. Force 4 Nov 60.

384 UNTS 334. Chad. Succession 10 Nov 60. Force 10 Nov 60.

384 UNTS 334. Congo (Brazzaville). Succession 10 Nov 60. Force 10 Nov 60.

384 UNTS 334. Ivory Coast. Succession 21 Nov 60. Force 21 Nov 60.

384 UNTS 334. Upper Volta. Succession 21 Nov 60. Force 21 Nov 60.

386 UNTS 365. Dahomey. Succession 12 Dec 60.

390 UNTS 335. Niger. Succession 27 Feb 61.

401 UNTS 217. Mauritius. Succession 20 Jun 61.

401 UNTS 217. Sierra Leone. Ratification 15 Jun 61.

434 UNTS 270. UK Great Britain. Hong Kong.

434 UNTS 270. UK Great Britain. Seychelles.

434 UNTS 270. UK Great Britain. Kenya.

434 UNTS 270. UK Great Britain. Brit Solomon Is.

434 UNTS 270. UK Great Britain. Zanzibar.

434 UNTS 270. UK Great Britain. Antigua.

434 UNTS 270. UK Great Britain. Bahamas.

434 UNTS 270. UK Great Britain. Montserrat.

434 UNTS 270. UK Great Britain. St. Lucia.

434 UNTS 270. UK Great Britain. Barbados.

434 UNTS 270. UK Great Britain. British Guinea.

434 UNTS 270. UK Great Britain. Mauritius.

434 UNTS 270. UK Great Britain. Uganda.

434 UNTS 270. UK Great Britain. Fiji Islands.

434 UNTS 270. UK Great Britain. Malta.

434 UNTS 270. UK Great Britain. British Honduras.

434 UNTS 270. UK Great Britain. Falkland Islands.

434 UNTS 270. UK Great Britain. Gibralter.

434 UNTS 270. UK Great Britain. Gilbert Islands.

435 UNTS 296. UK Great Britain. Singapore.

437 UNTS 334. UK Great Britain. St. Vincent.

444 UNTS 298. UK Great Britain. Brit Virgin Islands.

444 UNTS 298. UK Great Britain. Gambia.

444 UNTS 298. UK Great Britain. St. Helena.

444 UNTS 298. Cameroon. Succession 3 Sep 62.

455 UNTS 446. UK Great Britain. Northern Rhodesia.

457 UNTS 329. UK Great Britain. Swaziland.

468 UNTS 416. UK Great Britain. St. Christopher.

471 UNTS 352. UK Great Britain. Grenada.

471 UNTS 352. Uganda. Ratification 4 Jun 63.

488 UNTS 339. Kenya. Ratification 13 Jan 64. Force 13 Jan 64.

492 UNTS 373. UK Great Britain. Declaration 24 Feb 64.

495 UNTS 266. Malaysia. Singapore. Succession 3 Mar 64.

499 UNTS 358. UK Great Britain. Bechuanaland.

504 UNTS 321. Tanzania. Succession 22 Jun 64.

510 UNTS 346. UK Great Britain. Bermuda.

511 UNTS 319. UK Great Britain. Dominican Republic. Declaration 17 Sep 64.

522 UNTS 358. Zambia. Ratification 2 Dec 64. Force 2 Dec 64.

524 UNTS 344. Malta. Ratification 4 Jan 65. Force 4 Jan 65.

530 UNTS 394. UK Great Britain. Bechuanaland.

533 UNTS 390. UK Great Britain. Brunei.

541 UNTS 368. UK Great Britain. Basutoland.

548 UNTS 382. Singapore. Ratification 25 Oct 65. Force 25 Oct 65.

567 UNTS 340. Guyana. Ratification 8 Jun 66. Force 8 Jun 66.

100589 Multilateral Convention **38 UNTS 93**
SIGNED: 28 Nov 19   FORCE: 28 May 47
REGISTERED: 15 Sep 49 ILO (Labor Org)
ARTICLES: 15 LANGUAGE: English. French.
HEADNOTE: NIGHT WORK YOUNG PERSONS
TOPIC: ILO Labor
CONCEPTS: Definition of terms. Detailed regulations. Exceptions and exemptions. Territorial application. Previous treaty extension. Domestic legislation. ILO conventions. Employment regulations. Holidays and rest periods.
INTL ORGS: International Labour Organization.
TREATY REF: 38UNTS3.
PROCEDURE: Amendment. Denunciation. Duration. Ratification. Registration.
PARTIES:
    Multilateral
            ANNEX
76 UNTS 275. Ceylon (Sri Lanka). Ratification 26 Oct 50.

167 UNTS 263. Vietnam. Ratification 6 Jun 53.

184 UNTS 330. Italy. Italian Somaliland.

196 UNTS 331. Denmark. Greenland.

202 UNTS 326. Netherlands. Denunciation 22 Oct 54. Force 22 Oct 55.

222 UNTS 389. Uruguay. Denunciation 17 Oct 55. Force 17 Oct 56.

248 UNTS 395. Mexico. Denunciation 20 Jun 56. Force 20 Jun 57.

261 UNTS 386. Yugoslavia. Denunciation 20 Feb 57. Force 20 Feb 58.

323 UNTS 369. Guinea. Ratification 21 Jan 59. Force 21 Jan 59.

323 UNTS 369. Tunisia. Ratification 12 Jan 59.

366 UNTS 371. Cameroon. Succession 7 Jun 60. Force 7 Jun 60.

366 UNTS 371. Togo. Succession 7 Jun 60. Force 7 Jun 60.

366 UNTS 371. Mali. Succession 21 Jun 60. Force 21 Jun 60.

380 UNTS 393. Gabon. Succession 14 Oct 60. Force 14 Oct 60.

380 UNTS 393. Central Afri Rep. Succession 27 Oct 60. Force 27 Oct 60.

381 UNTS 357. Mali. Succession 22 Sep 60. Force 22 Sep 60.

384 UNTS 335. Malagasy. Succession 1 Nov 60. Force 1 Nov 60.

384 UNTS 335. Senegal. Succession 4 Nov 60. Force 4 Nov 60.

384 UNTS 335. Chad. Succession 10 Nov 60. Force 10 Nov 60.

384 UNTS 335. Congo (Brazzaville). Succession 10 Nov 60. Force 10 Nov 60.

384 UNTS 335. Ivory Coast. Succession 21 Nov 60. Force 21 Nov 60.

384 UNTS 335. Upper Volta. Succession 21 Nov 60. Force 21 Nov 60.

386 UNTS 366. Dahomey. Succession 12 Dec 60.

390 UNTS 336. Niger. Succession 27 Feb 61.

401 UNTS 218. Mauritius. Succession 20 Jun 61.

444 UNTS 299. Cameroon. Succession 3 Sep 62.

444 UNTS 299. Algeria. Succession 19 Oct 62. Force 19 Oct 62.

488 UNTS 340. Laos. Ratification 23 Jan 64. Force 23 Jan 64.

638 UNTS 331. Guinea. Denunciation 28 May 68.

660 UNTS 426. Cambodia. Ratification 24 Feb 69.

100590 Multilateral Convention **38 UNTS 109**
SIGNED: 9 Jul 20   FORCE: 28 May 47
REGISTERED: 15 Sep 49 ILO (Labor Org)
ARTICLES: 12 LANGUAGE: English. French.
HEADNOTE: MINIMUM AGE EMPLOYMENT CHILDREN SEA
TOPIC: ILO Labor
CONCEPTS: Definition of terms. Territorial application. Previous treaty extension. Incorporation of treaty provisions into national law. ILO conventions. Employment regulations. Holidays and rest periods. Administrative cooperation. Merchant vessels.
INTL ORGS: International Labour Organization.
TREATY REF: 38UNTS3.
PROCEDURE: Amendment. Denunciation. Duration. Ratification. Registration.
PARTIES:
    Multilateral
            ANNEX
71 UNTS 323. Ceylon (Sri Lanka). Ratification 2 Sep 50.

135 UNTS 334. Mexico. Denunciation 18 Jul 52. Force 18 Jul 53.

184 UNTS 331. Italy. Italian Somaliland.

196 UNTS 332. Denmark. Greenland.

222 UNTS 389. Uruguay. Denunciation 17 Oct 55. Force 17 Oct 56.

338 UNTS 327. Australia. New Guinea.

338 UNTS 327. Australia. Papua.

380 UNTS 395. Portugal. Ratification 24 Oct 60.

401 UNTS 219. Sierra Leone. Ratification 15 Jun 61.

434 UNTS 272. UK Great Britain. Bahamas. Force 4 Jun 62.

434 UNTS 272. UK Great Britain. Malta.

434 UNTS 272. UK Great Britain. British Honduras.

434 UNTS 272. UK Great Britain. Hong Kong.

434 UNTS 272. UK Great Britain. Falkland Islands.

434 UNTS 272. UK Great Britain. Seychelles.

434 UNTS 272. UK Great Britain. Gibralter.

434 UNTS 272. UK Great Britain. Gilbert Islands.

434 UNTS 272. UK Great Britain. Brit Solomon Is.

434 UNTS 272. UK Great Britain. Zanzibar.

434 UNTS 272. UK Great Britain. St. Lucia.

434 UNTS 272. UK Great Britain. Antigua.

434 UNTS 272. UK Great Britain. Barbados.

434 UNTS 272. UK Great Britain. Mauritius.

434 UNTS 272. UK Great Britain. British Guiana.

434 UNTS 272. UK Great Britain. Montserrat.

435 UNTS 297. UK Great Britain. Singapore.

437 UNTS 335. UK Great Britain. St. Vincent.

437 UNTS 335. UK Great Britain. Sarawak.

444 UNTS 300. UK Great Britain. Brit Virgin Islands.

444 UNTS 300. UK Great Britain. St. Helena.

444 UNTS 300. UK Great Britain. Gambia.

468 UNTS 417. UK Great Britain. St. Christopher.

471 UNTS 354. UK Great Britain. Grenada.

473 UNTS 386. Jamaica. Ratification 8 Jul 63.

479 UNTS 432. UK Great Britain. Kenya.

492 UNTS 374. UK Great Britain. Declaration 24 Feb 64.

495 UNTS 266. Malaysia. Succession 3 Mar 64.

495 UNTS 268. UK Great Britain. Fiji Islands.

495 UNTS 268. Malaysia. Sarawak. Succession 3 Mar 64.

504 UNTS 322. Tanzania. Succession 22 Jun 64.

510 UNTS 347. UK Great Britain. Bermuda.

511 UNTS 320. UK Great Britain. Dominican Republic. Declaration 17 Sep 64.

524 UNTS 345. Malta. Ratification 4 Jan 65. Force 4 Jan 65.

533 UNTS 392. UK Great Britain. Brunei.

548 UNTS 383. Singapore. Ratification 25 Oct 65. Force 25 Oct 65.

567 UNTS 340. Guyana. Ratification 8 Jun 66. Force 8 Jun 66.

100591 Multilateral Convention **38 UNTS 119**
SIGNED: 9 Jul 20   FORCE: 28 May 47
REGISTERED: 15 Sep 49 ILO (Labor Org)
ARTICLES: 11 LANGUAGE: English. French.
HEADNOTE: UNEMPLOYMENT INDEMNITY CASE LOST SHIP
TOPIC: ILO Labor
CONCEPTS: Definition of terms. Detailed regulations. Territorial application. Previous treaty extension. ILO conventions. Administrative cooperation. Social security. Merchant vessels.
INTL ORGS: International Labour Organization.
TREATY REF: 38UNTS3.
PROCEDURE: Amendment. Denunciation. Duration. Ratification. Registration.
PARTIES:
    Multilateral
            ANNEX
46 UNTS 356. Finland. Ratification 20 Jan 50.

88 UNTS 452. Ceylon (Sri Lanka). Ratification 25 Apr 51.

218 UNTS 380. Japan. Ratification 22 Aug 55.

276 UNTS 353. Netherlands. Netherlands Antilles.

358 UNTS 248. Switzerland. Ratification 21 Apr 60.

401 UNTS 220. Sierra Leone. Ratification 15 Jun 61.

401 UNTS 220. Nigeria. Ratification 16 Jun 61.

429 UNTS 257. Peru. Ratification 4 Apr 62.

434 UNTS 274. UK Great Britain. Falkland Islands.

434 UNTS 274. UK Great Britain. Barbados.

434 UNTS 274. UK Great Britain. Dominican Republic.

434 UNTS 274. UK Great Britain. Brit Solomon Is.

434 UNTS 274. UK Great Britain. Gibralter.

434 UNTS 274. UK Great Britain. St. Vincent.

434 UNTS 274. UK Great Britain. Seychelles.

434 UNTS 274. UK Great Britain. Fiji Islands.

434 UNTS 274. UK Great Britain. Malta.

434 UNTS 274. UK Great Britain. Montserrat.

434 UNTS 274. UK Great Britain. St. Lucia.

435 UNTS 298. UK Great Britain. Singapore.

437 UNTS 336. UK Great Britain. Zanzibar.

437 UNTS 336. UK Great Britain. Mauritius.

444 UNTS 301. UK Great Britain. Brit Virgin Islands.

444 UNTS 301. UK Great Britain. St. Helena.

444 UNTS 301. UK Great Britain. Gambia.

468 UNTS 418. UK Great Britain. St. Christopher.

471 UNTS 355. UK Great Britain. Grenada.

473 UNTS 387. Jamaica. Ratification 8 Jul 63.

475 UNTS 370. UK Great Britain. Hong Kong.

492 UNTS 375. UK Great Britain. Declaration 24 Feb 64.

495 UNTS 268. Malaysia. Singapore. Prolongation 3 Mar 64.

495 UNTS 270. Malaysia. Singapore. Succession 3 Mar 64.

495 UNTS 270. UK Great Britain. Declaration 3 Mar 64.

504 UNTS 322. UK Great Britain. British Honduras. Force 12 Jun 64.

524 UNTS 346. Malta. Ratification 4 Jan 65. Force 4 Jan 65.

530 UNTS 395. Ghana. Ratification 18 Mar 65.

533 UNTS 393. UK Great Britain. Brunei.

541 UNTS 369. UK Great Britain. British Guiana.

548 UNTS 384. Singapore. Ratification 25 Oct 65. Force 25 Oct 65.

561 UNTS 358. Iraq. Ratification 19 Apr 66.

561 UNTS 358. Iraq. Ratification 19 Apr 66.

100592 Multilateral Convention **38 UNTS 129**
SIGNED: 10 Jul 20   FORCE: 28 May 47
REGISTERED: 15 Sep 49 ILO (Labor Org)
ARTICLES: 18 LANGUAGE: English. French.
HEADNOTE: FINDING EMPLOYMENT SEAMEN
TOPIC: ILO Labor
CONCEPTS: Definition of terms. Detailed regulations. Exceptions and exemptions. Territorial application. Previous treaty extension. Domestic legislation. Operating agencies. Incorporation of treaty provisions into national law. Investigation of violations. ILO conventions. Employment regulations. Labor statistics. Administrative cooperation. Unemployment.
INTL ORGS: International Labour Organization.
TREATY REF: 38UNTS3.
PROCEDURE: Amendment. Denunciation. Duration. Ratification. Registration.
PARTIES:
  Multilateral

ANNEX
276 UNTS 354. Netherlands. Netherlands Antilles.
276 UNTS 354. Netherlands. Declaration 5 Aug 57.
429 UNTS 257. Peru. Ratification 4 Apr 62.

100593 Multilateral Convention **38 UNTS 143**
SIGNED: 16 Nov 21   FORCE: 28 May 47
REGISTERED: 15 Sep 49 ILO (Labor Org)
ARTICLES: 11 LANGUAGE: English. French.
HEADNOTE: AGE MINIMUM AGRICULTURAL EMPLOYMENT CHILDREN
TOPIC: ILO Labor
CONCEPTS: Detailed regulations. Exceptions and exemptions. Territorial application. Previous treaty extension. ILO conventions. Employment regulations. Holidays and rest periods.
INTL ORGS: International Labour Organization.
TREATY REF: 38UNTS3.
PROCEDURE: Ratification. Registration.
PARTIES:
  Multilateral

ANNEX
91 UNTS 377. France. Ratification 7 Jun 51.
183 UNTS 350. Israel. Ratification 23 Dec 53.
184 UNTS 332. Italy. Italian Somaliland.
212 UNTS 385. France. Reunion.
212 UNTS 385. France. French Guinea.
212 UNTS 385. France. Guadeloupe.
212 UNTS 385. France. Martinique.
249 UNTS 443. USSR (Soviet Union). Ratification 10 Aug 56.
253 UNTS 374. Ukrainian SSR. Ratification 14 Sep 56.
253 UNTS 374. Byelorussia. Ratification 6 Nov 56.
256 UNTS 328. Netherlands. Ratification 28 Nov 56.
261 UNTS 387. Norway. Ratification 28 Jan 57.
264 UNTS 328. Germany, West. Ratification 20 Mar 57.
265 UNTS 327. Netherlands. Netherlands Antilles.
272 UNTS 248. Albania. Ratification 3 Jun 57.
285 UNTS 369. Australia. Ratification 24 Dec 57.
338 UNTS 328. Australia. New Guinea.
338 UNTS 328. Australia. Papua.
338 UNTS 328. Australia. Norfolk Islands.
353 UNTS 320. Peru. Ratification 1 Feb 60. Force 1 Feb 60.
401 UNTS 221. Gabon. Ratification 13 Jun 61.
444 UNTS 302. Algeria. Succession 19 Oct 62. Force 19 Oct 62.
444 UNTS 302. Senegal. Ratification 22 Oct 62.
473 UNTS 388. UK Great Britain. Ratification 11 Jul 63.
480 UNTS 464. UK Great Britain. Isle of Man.
480 UNTS 465. UK Great Britain. Swaziland.

483 UNTS 396. UK Great Britain. Declaration 20 Nov 63.

485 UNTS 378. UK Great Britain. Declaration 18 Dec 63.

492 UNTS 376. UK Great Britain. Gilbert Islands.

492 UNTS 376. UK Great Britain. Seychelles.

492 UNTS 376. UK Great Britain. Declaration 24 Feb 64.

495 UNTS 270. UK Great Britain. Grenada.

495 UNTS 270. UK Great Britain. Malta.

499 UNTS 359. UK Great Britain. Bermuda.

504 UNTS 323. UK Great Britain. Dominican Republic.

504 UNTS 323. UK Great Britain. British Guiana.

504 UNTS 323. UK Great Britain. Jersey Island.

504 UNTS 323. Central Afri Rep. Ratification 9 Jun 64.

522 UNTS 360. UK Great Britain. St. Vincent.

524 UNTS 347. Malta. Ratification 4 Jan 65. Force 4 Jan 65.

530 UNTS 396. UK Great Britain. Brit Virgin Islands.

533 UNTS 394. UK Great Britain. Brunei.

561 UNTS 360. UK Great Britain. Antigua.

561 UNTS 360. UK Great Britain. Antigua.

567 UNTS 340. Guyana. Ratification 8 Jun 66. Force 8 Jun 66.

100594 Multilateral Convention **38 UNTS 153**
SIGNED: 12 Nov 21   FORCE: 28 May 47
REGISTERED: 15 Sep 49 ILO (Labor Org)
ARTICLES: 9 LANGUAGE: English. French.
HEADNOTE: RIGHT ORGANIZED AGRICULTURAL WORKERS
TOPIC: ILO Labor
CONCEPTS: Territorial application. Previous treaty extension. Informational records. Incorporation of treaty provisions into national law. ILO conventions. Right to organize.
INTL ORGS: International Labour Organization.
TREATY REF: 38UNTS3.
PROCEDURE: Amendment. Denunciation. Duration. Duration.
PARTIES:
  Multilateral

ANNEX
109 UNTS 320. New Zealand. Cook Islands.
133 UNTS 336. Greece. Ratification 13 Jun 52.
136 UNTS 386. Ceylon (Sri Lanka). Ratification 25 Aug 52.
196 UNTS 333. United Arab Rep. Ratification 3 Jul 54.
196 UNTS 334. Denmark. Greenland.
225 UNTS 254. Belgium. Ruanda-Urundi.
225 UNTS 254. Netherlands. Netherlands Antilles.
225 UNTS 254. Belgium. Belgian Colonies.
249 UNTS 443. Iceland. Ratification 21 Aug 56.
249 UNTS 443. USSR (Soviet Union). Ratification 10 Aug 56.
253 UNTS 375. Byelorussia. Ratification 6 Nov 56.
253 UNTS 375. Ukrainian SSR. Ratification 14 Sep 56.
266 UNTS 371. Brazil. Ratification 25 Apr 57. Force 25 Apr 57.
268 UNTS 355. Morocco. Ratification 20 May 57.
269 UNTS 273. Tunisia. Ratification 15 May 57.
272 UNTS 249. Albania. Ratification 3 Jun 57.
276 UNTS 354. Netherlands. Surinam.
285 UNTS 370. Australia. Ratification 24 Dec 57.
312 UNTS 402. France. French West Africa.
312 UNTS 402. France. Comoro Islands.
312 UNTS 402. France. French Polynesia.
312 UNTS 402. France. French Somaliland.
312 UNTS 402. France. Madagascar.
312 UNTS 402. France. New Caledonia.
312 UNTS 402. France. St. Pierre.
312 UNTS 402. France. Miquelon.
312 UNTS 402. France. Togo.
312 UNTS 402. France. Fr Equatorial Afri.
312 UNTS 402. France. French Cameroon.
323 UNTS 370. Guinea. Ratification 21 Jan 59. Force 21 Jan 59.
338 UNTS 329. Australia. New Guinea.
338 UNTS 329. Australia. Norfolk Islands.
338 UNTS 329. Australia. Papua.
349 UNTS 313. Fed of Malaya. Ratification 11 Jan 60.
366 UNTS 372. Cameroon. Succession 7 Jun 60. Force 7 Jun 60.
366 UNTS 372. Togo. Succession 7 Jun 60. Force 7 Jun 60.
366 UNTS 372. Mali. Succession 21 Jun 60. Force 21 Jun 60.

373 UNTS 340. United Arab Rep. Syria.

380 UNTS 395. Gabon. Succession 14 Oct 60. Force 14 Oct 60.

380 UNTS 395. Central Afri Rep. Succession 27 Oct 60. Force 27 Oct 60.

381 UNTS 358. Denmark. Faroe Islands.

381 UNTS 358. Mali. Succession 22 Sep 60. Force 22 Sep 60.

381 UNTS 358. Congo (Zaire). Succession 20 Sep 60. Force 20 Sep 60.

384 UNTS 336. Malagasy. Succession 1 Nov 60. Force 1 Nov 60.

384 UNTS 336. Senegal. Succession 4 Nov 60. Force 4 Nov 60.

384 UNTS 336. Chad. Succession 10 Nov 60. Force 10 Nov 60.

384 UNTS 336. Congo (Brazzaville). Succession 10 Nov 60. Force 10 Nov 60.

384 UNTS 336. Ivory Coast. Succession 21 Nov 60. Force 21 Nov 60.

384 UNTS 336. Upper Volta. Succession 21 Nov 60. Force 21 Nov 60.

386 UNTS 367. Dahomey. Succession 12 Dec 60.

390 UNTS 337. Niger. Succession 27 Feb 61.

396 UNTS 316. Turkey. Ratification 29 Mar 61.

401 UNTS 222. Nigeria. Ratification 16 Jun 61.

401 UNTS 222. Mauritius. Succession 20 Jun 61.

413 UNTS 348. Syria. Ratification 30 Oct 61.

434 UNTS 276. UK Great Britain. Bermuda.

434 UNTS 276. UK Great Britain. Uganda.

434 UNTS 276. UK Great Britain. Montserrat.

434 UNTS 276. UK Great Britain. British Honduras.

434 UNTS 276. UK Great Britain. Falkland Islands.

434 UNTS 276. UK Great Britain. Fiji Islands.

434 UNTS 276. UK Great Britain. Gibralter.

434 UNTS 276. UK Great Britain. Gilbert Islands.

434 UNTS 276. UK Great Britain. Hong Kong.

434 UNTS 276. UK Great Britain. Kenya.

434 UNTS 276. UK Great Britain. Seychelles.

434 UNTS 276. UK Great Britain. Brit Solomon Is.

434 UNTS 276. UK Great Britain. Zanzibar.

434 UNTS 276. UK Great Britain. Antigua.

434 UNTS 276. UK Great Britain. Bahamas.

434 UNTS 276. UK Great Britain. Barbados.

434 UNTS 276. UK Great Britain. St. Vincent.

434 UNTS 276. UK Great Britain. Bermuda.

434 UNTS 276. UK Great Britain. British Guiana.

434 UNTS 276. UK Great Britain. Dominican Republic.

434 UNTS 276. UK Great Britain. Mauritius.

434 UNTS 276. UK Great Britain. St. Lucia.

434 UNTS 276. UK Great Britain. Malta.

435 UNTS 299. UK Great Britain. Singapore.

437 UNTS 337. UK Great Britain. Sarawak.

443 UNTS 316. Rwanda. Succession 18 Sep 62. Force 18 Sep 62.

444 UNTS 303. UK Great Britain. Gambia.

444 UNTS 303. UK Great Britain. Brit Virgin Islands.

444 UNTS 303. Cameroon. Succession 3 Sep 62.

444 UNTS 303. UK Great Britain. St. Helena.

444 UNTS 303. Algeria. Succession 19 Oct 62. Force 19 Oct 62.

449 UNTS 273. Tanganyika. Ratification 19 Nov 62.

449 UNTS 273. UK Great Britain. Basutoland.

452 UNTS 353. UK Great Britain. Nyasaland.

455 UNTS 449. UK Great Britain. Northern Rhodesia.

455 UNTS 449. Cameroon. Ratification 29 Jan 63.

457 UNTS 330. UK Great Britain. Swaziland.

457 UNTS 330. Burundi. Succession 11 Mar 63.

468 UNTS 419. UK Great Britain. St. Christopher.

471 UNTS 356. UK Great Britain. Grenada.

471 UNTS 356. Uganda. Ratification 4 Jun 63.

471 UNTS 356. Ethiopia. Ratification 4 Jun 63.

473 UNTS 389. Jamaica. Ratification 8 Jul 63. Force 8 Jul 64.

479 UNTS 434. Costa Rica. Ratification 16 Sep 63.

483 UNTS 397. UK Great Britain. Declaration 20 Nov 63.

488 UNTS 341. Kenya. Ratification 13 Jan 64. Force 13 Jan 64.

492 UNTS 377. UK Great Britain. Declaration 24 Feb 64.

495 UNTS 272. Malaysia. Sarawak. Succession 3 Mar 64.

495 UNTS 272. Malaysia. Malaya. Succession 3 Mar 64.

495 UNTS 272. Malaysia. Singapore. Succession 3 Mar 64.
504 UNTS 324. UK Great Britain. Bechuanaland.
522 UNTS 361. Zambia. Ratification 2 Dec 64. Force 2 Dec 64.
524 UNTS 348. Malta. Ratification 4 Jan 65. Force 4 Jan 65.
530 UNTS 397. UK Great Britain. Malawi. Ratification 22 Mar 65. Force 22 Mar 65.
533 UNTS 395. UK Great Britain. Brunei.
548 UNTS 385. Singapore. Ratification 25 Oct 65. Force 25 Oct 65.
567 UNTS 340. Guyana. Ratification 8 Jun 66. Force 8 Jun 66.
634 UNTS 473. Ghana. Ratification 14 Mar 68. Force 14 Mar 69.
638 UNTS 332. Paraguay. Ratification 16 May 68.

100595 Multilateral Convention **38 UNTS 165**
SIGNED: 12 Nov 21 FORCE: 28 May 47
REGISTERED: 15 Sep 49 ILO (Labor Org)
ARTICLES: 9 LANGUAGE: English. French.
HEADNOTE: WORKMEN COMPENSATION AGRICULTURE
TOPIC: ILO Labor
CONCEPTS: Territorial application. Previous treaty extension. Domestic legislation. Incorporation of treaty provisions into national law. ILO conventions. Old age and invalidity insurance. Unemployment.
INTL ORGS: International Labour Organization.
TREATY REF: 38UNTS3.
PROCEDURE: Amendment. Denunciation. Duration. Ratification. Registration.
PARTIES:
Multilateral
ANNEX
46 UNTS 357. Finland. Ratification 20 Jan 50.
46 UNTS 600. Finland. Ratification 20 Jan 50.
66 UNTS 349. Czechoslovakia. Ratification 12 Jun 50.
191 UNTS 361. Austria. Ratification 14 Jun 54.
210 UNTS 324. Haiti. Ratification 19 Apr 55.
219 UNTS 325. El Salvador. Ratification 11 Oct 55.
225 UNTS 255. Netherlands. Netherlands Antilles.
248 UNTS 396. Hungary. Ratification 8 Jun 56.
253 UNTS 376. Morocco. Ratification 20 Sep 56.
266 UNTS 371. Brazil. Ratification 25 Apr 57. Force 25 Apr 57.
269 UNTS 274. Tunisia. Ratification 15 May 57.
286 UNTS 335. Yugoslavia. Ratification 27 Jan 58.
304 UNTS 396. Panama. Ratification 3 Jun 58.
361 UNTS 228. Portugal. Ratification 16 May 60.
366 UNTS 373. Australia. Ratification 7 Jun 60.
381 UNTS 359. Congo (Zaire). Succession 20 Sep 60. Force 20 Sep 60.
381 UNTS 359. Denmark. Faroe Islands.
401 UNTS 223. Fed of Malaya. Ratification 5 Jun 61.
401 UNTS 223. Gabon. Ratification 13 Jun 61.
429 UNTS 258. Peru. Ratification 4 Apr 62.
434 UNTS 278. UK Great Britain. Brit Solomon Is. Force 4 Jun 62.
434 UNTS 278. UK Great Britain. British Honduras.
434 UNTS 278. UK Great Britain. Falkland Islands.
434 UNTS 278. UK Great Britain. Gibralter.
434 UNTS 278. UK Great Britain. Gilbert Islands.
434 UNTS 278. UK Great Britain. Kenya.
434 UNTS 278. UK Great Britain. Zanzibar.
434 UNTS 278. UK Great Britain. Antigua.
434 UNTS 278. UK Great Britain. Barbados.
434 UNTS 278. UK Great Britain. British Guiana.
434 UNTS 278. UK Great Britain. Dominican Republic.
434 UNTS 278. UK Great Britain. Mauritius.
434 UNTS 278. UK Great Britain. Montserrat.
434 UNTS 278. UK Great Britain. St. Lucia.
434 UNTS 278. UK Great Britain. St. Vincent.
434 UNTS 278. UK Great Britain. Malta.
434 UNTS 278. UK Great Britain. Uganda.
434 UNTS 278. UK Great Britain. Fiji Islands.
435 UNTS 300. UK Great Britain. Singapore.
437 UNTS 338. UK Great Britain. Sarawak.
437 UNTS 338. Madagascar. Ratification 10 Aug 62.
443 UNTS 317. Rwanda. Succession 18 Sep 62. Force 18 Sep 62.

444 UNTS 304. Senegal. Ratification 22 Oct 62.
444 UNTS 304. UK Great Britain. Gambia.
444 UNTS 304. UK Great Britain. St. Helena.
444 UNTS 304. UK Great Britain. Brit Virgin Islands.
449 UNTS 274. Tanganyika. Ratification 19 Nov 62.
452 UNTS 354. UK Great Britain. Nyasaland.
455 UNTS 450. UK Great Britain. Northern Rhodesia.
455 UNTS 450. Norway. Ratification 22 Jan 63.
457 UNTS 331. Burundi. Succession 11 Mar 63.
468 UNTS 420. UK Great Britain. St. Christopher.
471 UNTS 357. Uganda. Ratification 4 Jun 63.
488 UNTS 342. Kenya. Ratification 13 Jan 64. Force 13 Jan 64.
492 UNTS 378. UK Great Britain. Declaration 24 Feb 64.
495 UNTS 273. Malaysia. Singapore. Succession 3 Mar 64.
495 UNTS 273. Malaysia. Sarawak. Succession 3 Mar 64.
495 UNTS 273. Malaysia. Malaya. Succession 3 Mar 64.
521 UNTS 408. UK Great Britain. Southern Rhodesia. Declaration 24 Nov 64.
522 UNTS 362. Zambia. Ratification 2 Dec 64. Force 2 Dec 64.
524 UNTS 349. Malta. Ratification 4 Jan 65. Force 4 Jan 65.
530 UNTS 398. UK Great Britain. Malawi. Ratification 22 Mar 65. Force 22 Mar 65.
533 UNTS 396. UK Great Britain. Brunei.
548 UNTS 386. Singapore. Ratification 25 Oct 65. Force 25 Oct 65.
553 UNTS 344. Australia. Papua.
553 UNTS 344. Australia. New Guinea.
567 UNTS 342. Guyana. Ratification 8 Jun 66. Force 8 Jun 66.

100596 Multilateral Convention **38 UNTS 175**
SIGNED: 19 Nov 21 FORCE: 28 May 47
REGISTERED: 15 Sep 49 ILO (Labor Org)
ARTICLES: 15 LANGUAGE: English. French.
HEADNOTE: ILO WHITE LEAD PAINTING
TOPIC: ILO Labor
CONCEPTS: Detailed regulations. Exceptions and exemptions. Territorial application. Treaty implementation. Previous treaty extension. Domestic legislation. ILO conventions. Employment regulations. Labor statistics. Safety standards. Administrative cooperation.
INTL ORGS: International Labour Organization.
TREATY REF: 38UNTS3.
PROCEDURE: Ratification. Registration.
PARTIES:
Multilateral
ANNEX
149 UNTS 402. Italy. Ratification 22 Oct 52.
167 UNTS 263. Vietnam. Ratification 6 Jun 53.
248 UNTS 396. Hungary. Ratification 8 Jun 56.
249 UNTS 444. Tunisia. Ratification 12 Jun 56. Force 12 Jun 56.
276 UNTS 355. Netherlands. Surinam.
323 UNTS 370. Guinea. Ratification 21 Jan 59. Force 21 Jan 59.
366 UNTS 374. Cameroon. Succession 7 Jun 60. Force 7 Jun 60.
366 UNTS 374. Togo. Succession 7 Jun 60. Force 7 Jun 60.
366 UNTS 374. Mali. Succession 21 Jun 60. Force 21 Jun 60.
380 UNTS 396. Gabon. Succession 14 Oct 60. Force 14 Oct 60.
380 UNTS 396. Central Afri Rep. Succession 27 Oct 60. Force 27 Oct 60.
381 UNTS 360. Mali. Succession 22 Sep 60. Force 22 Sep 60.
384 UNTS 337. Chad. Succession 10 Nov 60. Force 10 Nov 60.
384 UNTS 337. Upper Volta. Succession 21 Nov 60. Force 21 Nov 60.
384 UNTS 337. Senegal. Succession 4 Nov 60. Force 4 Nov 60.
384 UNTS 337. Malagasy. Succession 1 Nov 60. Force 1 Nov 60.
384 UNTS 337. Congo (Brazzaville). Succession 10 Nov 60. Force 10 Nov 60.
384 UNTS 337. Ivory Coast. Succession 21 Nov 60. Force 21 Nov 60.
386 UNTS 368. Dahomey. Succession 12 Dec 60.
390 UNTS 338. Niger. Succession 27 Feb 61.

401 UNTS 224. Mauritius. Succession 20 Jun 61.
444 UNTS 305. Algeria. Succession 19 Oct 62. Force 19 Oct 62.
444 UNTS 305. Cameroon. Succession 3 Sep 62.
488 UNTS 343. Laos. Ratification 23 Jan 64. Force 23 Jan 64.
561 UNTS 362. Iraq. Ratification 19 Apr 66.
561 UNTS 596. Iraq. Ratification 19 Apr 66.
660 UNTS 426. Cambodia. Ratification 24 Feb 69.

100597 Multilateral Convention **38 UNTS 187**
SIGNED: 17 Nov 21 FORCE: 28 May 47
REGISTERED: 15 Sep 49 ILO (Labor Org)
ARTICLES: 15 LANGUAGE: English. French.
HEADNOTE: WEEKLY REST INDUSTRY
TOPIC: ILO Labor
CONCEPTS: Definition of terms. Detailed regulations. Exceptions and exemptions. Previous treaty extension. Domestic legislation. ILO conventions. Holidays and rest periods. Labor statistics. Administrative cooperation.
INTL ORGS: International Labour Organization.
TREATY REF: 38UNTS3.
PROCEDURE: Amendment. Denunciation. Duration. Ratification. Registration.
PARTIES:
Multilateral
ANNEX
92 UNTS 401. Israel. Ratification 26 Jun 51.
131 UNTS 311. Haiti. Ratification 14 May 52.
172 UNTS 337. Cuba. Ratification 20 Jul 53.
196 UNTS 334. Denmark. Greenland.
198 UNTS 374. Bolivia. Ratification 19 Jul 54.
212 UNTS 385. Vietnam. Ratification 14 Jun 55.
229 UNTS 280. Belgium. Ruanda-Urundi.
229 UNTS 280. Belgium. Belgian Colonies.
248 UNTS 397. Hungary. Ratification 8 Jun 56.
253 UNTS 376. Morocco. Ratification 20 Sep 56.
266 UNTS 372. Brazil. Ratification 25 Apr 57. Force 25 Apr 57.
269 UNTS 274. Tunisia. Ratification 15 May 57.
323 UNTS 371. Guinea. Ratification 21 Jan 59. Force 21 Jan 59.
361 UNTS 229. United Arab Rep. Ratification 10 May 60.
361 UNTS 229. Iraq. Ratification 12 May 60.
366 UNTS 375. Togo. Succession 7 Jun 60. Force 7 Jun 60.
366 UNTS 375. Cameroon. Succession 7 Jun 60. Force 7 Jun 60.
366 UNTS 375. Mali. Succession 21 Jun 60. Force 21 Jun 60.
380 UNTS 397. Central Afri Rep. Succession 27 Oct 60. Force 27 Oct 60.
380 UNTS 397. Gabon. Succession 14 Oct 60. Force 14 Oct 60.
381 UNTS 361. Congo (Zaire). Succession 20 Sep 60. Force 20 Sep 60.
381 UNTS 361. Mali. Succession 22 Sep 60. Force 22 Sep 60.
384 UNTS 338. Chad. Succession 10 Nov 60. Force 10 Nov 60.
384 UNTS 338. Malagasy. Succession 1 Nov 60. Force 1 Nov 60.
384 UNTS 338. Senegal. Succession 4 Nov 60. Force 4 Nov 60.
384 UNTS 338. Ivory Coast. Succession 21 Nov 60. Force 21 Nov 61.
384 UNTS 338. Congo (Brazzaville). Succession 10 Nov 60. Force 10 Nov 60.
384 UNTS 338. Upper Volta. Succession 21 Nov 60. Force 21 Nov 60.
386 UNTS 369. Dahomey. Succession 12 Dec 60.
390 UNTS 339. Niger. Succession 27 Feb 61.
401 UNTS 225. Mauritius. Succession 20 Jun 61.
413 UNTS 349. Syria. Ratification 30 Oct 61.
435 UNTS 301. Lebanon. Ratification 26 Jul 62.
443 UNTS 318. Rwanda. Succession 18 Sep 62. Force 18 Sep 62.
444 UNTS 306. Algeria. Succession 19 Oct 62. Force 19 Oct 62.
444 UNTS 306. Cameroon. Succession 3 Sep 62.
457 UNTS 332. Burundi. Succession 11 Mar 63.
471 UNTS 357. UK Great Britain. Grenada.
488 UNTS 344. Kenya. Ratification 13 Jan 64. Force 13 Jan 64.
495 UNTS 274. Malaysia. Sarawak. Succession 3 Mar 64.
521 UNTS 409. Honduras. Ratification 17 Nov 64.

545 UNTS 377. Netherlands. Ratification 14 Jul 65. Declaration 14 Jul 65.

545 UNTS 377. Netherlands. Netherlands Antilles. Ratification 14 Jul 65. Declaration 14 Jul 65.

545 UNTS 377. Netherlands. Surinam. Ratification 14 Jul 65. Declaration 14 Jul 65.

560 UNTS 308. Paraguay. Ratification 21 Mar 66.

607 UNTS 358. USSR (Soviet Union). Ratification 22 Sep 67.

636 UNTS 423. Thailand. Ratification 5 Apr 68.

640 UNTS 382. Ukrainian SSR. Ratification 19 Jun 68.

100598 Multilateral Convention **38 UNTS 203**
SIGNED: 11 Nov 21   FORCE: 28 May 47
REGISTERED: 15 Sep 49 ILO (Labor Org)
ARTICLES: 14 LANGUAGE: English. French.
HEADNOTE: MINIMUM AGE EMPLOYMENT CHILDREN TRIMMERS STOKERS
TOPIC: ILO Labor
CONCEPTS: Definition of terms. Exceptions and exemptions. Territorial application. Previous treaty extension. Exchange of information and documents. ILO conventions. Employment regulations. Labor statistics. Merchant vessels.
INTL ORGS: International Labour Organization.
TREATY REF: 38UNTS3.
PROCEDURE: Amendment. Denunciation. Duration. Ratification. Registration.
PARTIES:
Multilateral
ANNEX
88 UNTS 452. Ceylon (Sri Lanka). Ratification 25 Apr 51.

184 UNTS 333. Italy. Italian Somaliland.

196 UNTS 335. Denmark. Greenland.

249 UNTS 445. Iceland. Ratification 21 Aug 56.

249 UNTS 445. USSR (Soviet Union). Ratification 10 Aug 56.

253 UNTS 377. Ukrainian SSR. Ratification 14 Sep 56.

253 UNTS 377. Byelorussia. Ratification 6 Nov 56.

269 UNTS 275. Ghana. Ratification 20 May 57. Force 20 May 57.

276 UNTS 355. Netherlands. Declaration 5 Aug 57.

293 UNTS 365. Morocco. Ratification 14 Mar 58.

343 UNTS 340. Turkey. Ratification 29 Sep 59.

345 UNTS 353. New Zealand. Qualified Ratification 26 Nov 59.

358 UNTS 249. Switzerland. Ratification 21 Apr 60.

380 UNTS 398. Nigeria. Succession 17 Oct 60. Force 17 Oct 60.

381 UNTS 362. Cyprus. Succession 23 Sep 60. Force 23 Sep 60.

401 UNTS 226. Sierra Leone. Succession 13 Jun 61.

422 UNTS 316. Tanganyika. Succession 30 Jan 62. Force 30 Jan 62.

443 UNTS 319. Cameroon. Succession 3 Sep 62. Force 3 Sep 62.

452 UNTS 355. Jamaica. Succession 26 Dec 62.

468 UNTS 421. Trinidad/Tobago. Ratification 24 May 63. Force 24 May 63.

483 UNTS 395. UK Great Britain. Declaration 20 Nov 63.

483 UNTS 398. Mauritania. Ratification 8 Nov 63.

488 UNTS 345. Kenya. Ratification 13 Jan 64. Force 13 Jan 64.

495 UNTS 275. Malaysia. Sarawak. Succession 3 Mar 64.

495 UNTS 275. Malaysia. State of Sabah. Succession 3 Mar 64.

495 UNTS 275. Malaysia. Singapore. Succession 3 Mar 64.

504 UNTS 326. Tanzania. Succession 22 Jun 64.

524 UNTS 350. Malta. Ratification 4 Jan 65. Force 4 Jan 65.

548 UNTS 387. Singapore. Ratification 25 Oct 65. Force 25 Oct 65.

561 UNTS 362. Iraq. Ratification 19 Apr 66.

561 UNTS 596. Iraq. Ratification 19 Apr 66.

567 UNTS 342. Guyana. Ratification 8 Jun 66. Force 8 Jun 66.

100599 Multilateral Convention **38 UNTS 217**
SIGNED: 11 Nov 21   FORCE: 28 May 47
REGISTERED: 15 Sep 49 ILO (Labor Org)
ARTICLES: 12 LANGUAGE: English. French.

HEADNOTE: COMPULSORY MEDICAL EXAMINATION CHILDREN EMPLOYED
TOPIC: ILO Labor
CONCEPTS: Domestic legislation. Public health. ILO conventions. Employment regulations. Safety standards. Merchant vessels.
INTL ORGS: International Labour Organization.
PROCEDURE: Amendment. Denunciation. Duration. Ratification. Registration.
PARTIES:
Multilateral
ANNEX
88 UNTS 452. Ceylon (Sri Lanka). Ratification 25 Apr 51.

184 UNTS 334. Italy. Italian Somaliland.

196 UNTS 335. Denmark. Greenland.

249 UNTS 446. USSR (Soviet Union). Ratification 10 Aug 56.

253 UNTS 378. Ukrainian SSR. Ratification 14 Sep 56.

253 UNTS 378. Byelorussia. Ratification 6 Nov 56.

269 UNTS 276. Ghana. Ratification 20 May 57. Force 20 May 57.

272 UNTS 249. Albania. Ratification 3 Jun 57.

358 UNTS 250. Switzerland. Ratification 21 Apr 60.

380 UNTS 399. Nigeria. Succession 17 Oct 60. Force 17 Oct 60.

381 UNTS 363. Cyprus. Succession 23 Sep 60. Force 23 Sep 60.

384 UNTS 339. Somalia. Succession 18 Nov 60. Force 18 Nov 60.

401 UNTS 227. Sierra Leone. Succession 13 Jun 61.

420 UNTS 336. New Zealand. Ratification 5 Dec 61.

422 UNTS 317. Tanganyika. Succession 30 Jan 62. Force 30 Jan 62.

443 UNTS 320. Cameroon. Succession 3 Sep 62. Force 3 Sep 62.

452 UNTS 356. Jamaica. Succession 26 Dec 62.

468 UNTS 422. Trinidad/Tobago. Ratification 24 May 63. Force 24 May 63.

495 UNTS 276. Malaysia. Singapore. Succession 3 Mar 64.

495 UNTS 276. Malaysia. State of Sabah. Succession 3 Mar 64.

495 UNTS 276. Malaysia. Sarawak. Succession 3 Mar 64.

504 UNTS 327. Tanzania. Succession 22 Jun 64.

524 UNTS 351. Malta. Ratification 4 Jan 65. Force 4 Jan 65.

548 UNTS 388. Singapore. Ratification 25 Oct 65. Force 25 Oct 65.

561 UNTS 362. Iraq. Ratification 19 Apr 66.

561 UNTS 596. Iraq. Ratification 19 Apr 66.

100600 Multilateral Convention **38 UNTS 229**
SIGNED: 10 Jun 25   FORCE: 28 May 47
REGISTERED: 15 Sep 49 ILO (Labor Org)
ARTICLES: 19 LANGUAGE: English. French.
HEADNOTE: WORKMENS COMPENSATION ACCIDENTS
TOPIC: ILO Labor
CONCEPTS: Detailed regulations. Exceptions and exemptions. Territorial application. Previous treaty extension. Incorporation of treaty provisions into national law. Penal sanctions. Public health. ILO conventions. Old age and invalidity insurance. Debt settlement. Domestic obligation.
INTL ORGS: International Labour Organization.
TREATY REF: 38UNTS3.
PROCEDURE: Amendment. Denunciation. Duration. Ratification. Registration.
PARTIES:
Multilateral
ANNEX
54 UNTS 401. Argentina. Ratification 14 May 50.

66 UNTS 350. Czechoslovakia. Ratification 12 Jun 50.

126 UNTS 356. Italy. Italian Somaliland.

133 UNTS 336. Greece. Ratification 13 Jun 52.

210 UNTS 324. Haiti. Ratification 19 Apr 55.

212 UNTS 386. France. Guadeloupe.

212 UNTS 386. France. Martinique.

212 UNTS 386. France. French Guiana.

212 UNTS 386. France. Reunion.

212 UNTS 386. Germany, West. Ratification 14 Jun 55.

229 UNTS 281. Burma. Ratification 16 Feb 56.

253 UNTS 379. Morocco. Ratification 20 Sep 56.

269 UNTS 276. Tunisia. Ratification 15 May 57.

276 UNTS 356. Netherlands. Netherlands Antilles.

282 UNTS 355. Fed of Malaya. Ratification 11 Nov 57. Force 11 Nov 57.

300 UNTS 368. Netherlands. Surinam.

304 UNTS 397. Panama. Ratification 3 Jun 58.

361 UNTS 230. United Arab Rep. Ratification 10 May 60.

373 UNTS 341. Iraq. Ratification 5 Jul 60.

381 UNTS 364. Congo (Zaire). Succession 20 Sep 60. Force 20 Sep 60.

384 UNTS 340. Somalia. Succession 18 Nov 60. Force 18 Nov 60.

384 UNTS 340. Philippines. Ratification 17 Nov 60.

401 UNTS 228. Sierra Leone. Succession 13 Jun 61.

413 UNTS 350. Syria. Ratification 30 Oct 61.

422 UNTS 318. Tanganyika. Succession 30 Jan 62. Force 30 Jan 62.

443 UNTS 321. Rwanda. Succession 18 Sep 62. Force 18 Sep 62.

444 UNTS 307. Algeria. Succession 19 Oct 62. Force 19 Oct 62.

457 UNTS 333. Burundi. Succession 11 Mar 63.

471 UNTS 358. Uganda. Ratification 4 Jun 63.

483 UNTS 399. Mauritania. Ratification 8 Nov 63.

488 UNTS 346. Kenya. Ratification 13 Jan 64. Force 13 Jan 64.

495 UNTS 277. Malaysia. Malaya. Succession 3 Mar 64.

504 UNTS 328. Central Afri Rep. Ratification 9 Jun 64.

504 UNTS 328. Tanzania. Succession 22 Jun 64.

522 UNTS 363. Zambia. Ratification 2 Dec 64. Force 2 Dec 64.

613 UNTS 421. UK Great Britain. St. Lucia. Declaration 6 Nov 67.

642 UNTS 392. Mali. Ratification 12 Jul 68. Force 12 Jul 68.

100601 Multilateral Convention **38 UNTS 243**
SIGNED: 10 Jun 25   FORCE: 28 May 47
REGISTERED: 15 Sep 49 ILO (Labor Org)
ARTICLES: 10 LANGUAGE: English. French.
HEADNOTE: WORKMENS COMPENSATION DISEASE
TOPIC: ILO Labor
CONCEPTS: Definition of terms. Detailed regulations. Exceptions and exemptions. Territorial application. Previous treaty extension. Domestic legislation. Operating agencies. ILO conventions. Sickness and invalidity insurance. Domestic obligation.
INTL ORGS: International Labour Organization.
TREATY REF: 38UNTS3.
PROCEDURE: Amendment. Denunciation. Duration. Ratification. Registration.
PARTIES:
Multilateral
ANNEX
131 UNTS 312. Ceylon (Sri Lanka). Ratification 17 May 52.

222 UNTS 390. Uruguay. Denunciation 17 Oct 55. Force 17 Oct 56.

253 UNTS 379. Argentina. Ratification 24 Sep 56.

253 UNTS 379. Morocco. Ratification 20 Sep 56.

323 UNTS 371. Tunisia. Ratification 12 Jan 59.

323 UNTS 371. Guinea. Ratification 21 Jan 59. Force 21 Jan 59.

330 UNTS 349. Australia. Ratification 22 Apr 59.

361 UNTS 231. United Arab Rep. Ratification 10 May 60.

366 UNTS 376. Mali. Succession 21 Jun 60. Force 21 Jun 60.

381 UNTS 365. Congo (Zaire). Succession 20 Sep 60. Force 20 Sep 60.

381 UNTS 365. Mali. Succession 22 Sep 60. Force 22 Sep 60.

384 UNTS 341. Senegal. Succession 4 Nov 60. Force 4 Nov 60.

384 UNTS 341. Ivory Coast. Succession 21 Nov 60. Force 21 Nov 61.

384 UNTS 341. Upper Volta. Succession 21 Nov 60. Force 21 Nov 60.

386 UNTS 370. Dahomey. Succession 12 Dec 60.

390 UNTS 340. Australia. Nauru.

390 UNTS 340. Australia. Papua.

390 UNTS 340. Niger. Succession 27 Feb 61.

390 UNTS 340. Australia. New Guinea.

401 UNTS 229. Mauritius. Succession 20 Jun 61.
413 UNTS 351. Syria. Ratification 30 Oct 61.
443 UNTS 322. Rwanda. Succession 18 Sep 62. Force 18 Sep 62.
444 UNTS 308. Algeria. Succession 19 Oct 62. Force 19 Oct 62.
457 UNTS 334. Burundi. Succession 11 Mar 63.
504 UNTS 329. Central Afri Rep. Ratification 9 Jun 64.
527 UNTS 332. Zambia. Ratification 22 Feb 65.

100602 Multilateral Convention **38 UNTS 257**
SIGNED: 5 Jun 25   FORCE: 28 May 47
REGISTERED: 15 Sep 49 ILO (Labor Org)
ARTICLES: 12 LANGUAGE: English. French.
HEADNOTE: EQUAL TREATMENT FOREIGNERS WORKMENS COMPENSATION
TOPIC: ILO Labor
CONCEPTS: Detailed regulations. Territorial application. Previous treaty extension. Exchange of information and documents. Incorporation of treaty provisions into national law. ILO conventions. Anti-discrimination. Old age and invalidity insurance. Administrative cooperation. Domestic obligation.
INTL ORGS: International Labour Organization.
TREATY REF: 38UNTS3.
PROCEDURE: Amendment. Denunciation. Duration. Ratification. Registration.
PARTIES:
   Multilateral
                    ANNEX
54 UNTS 401. Argentina. Ratification 14 Mar 50.
104 UNTS 347. Indonesia. Succession 31 May 51.
107 UNTS 78. Netherlands. Surinam.
126 UNTS 356. Italy. Italian Somaliland.
196 UNTS 336. Denmark. Greenland.
198 UNTS 375. Bolivia. Ratification 19 Jul 54.
210 UNTS 324. Haiti. Ratification 19 Apr 55.
249 UNTS 447. Tunisia. Ratification 12 Jun 56.
249 UNTS 447. Morocco. Ratification 13 Jun 56.
256 UNTS 329. Dominican Republic. Ratification 5 Dec 56.
258 UNTS 382. Belgium. Belgian Colonies.
258 UNTS 382. Belgium. Ruanda-Urundi.
266 UNTS 372. Brazil. Ratification 25 Apr 57. Force 25 Apr 57.
269 UNTS 277. Ghana. Ratification 20 May 57. Force 20 May 57.
272 UNTS 250. Sudan. Ratification 18 Jun 57.
282 UNTS 356. Fed of Malaya. Ratification 11 Nov 57. Force 11 Nov 57.
302 UNTS 354. Israel. Ratification 5 May 58.
337 UNTS 377. Australia. Ratification 12 Jun 59.
373 UNTS 342. United Arab Rep. Syria.
380 UNTS 400. Nigeria. Succession 17 Oct 60. Force 17 Oct 60.
381 UNTS 366. Congo (Zaire). Succession 20 Sep 60. Force 20 Sep 60.
384 UNTS 342. Somalia. Succession 18 Nov 60. Force 18 Nov 60.
390 UNTS 341. Australia. Nauru.
390 UNTS 341. Australia. New Guinea.
390 UNTS 341. Australia. Papua.
399 UNTS 255. Ivory Coast. Ratification 5 May 61.
401 UNTS 230. Sierra Leone. Succession 13 Jun 61.
401 UNTS 230. Gabon. Ratification 13 Jun 61.
406 UNTS 286. Guatemala. Ratification 2 Aug 61.
413 UNTS 352. Syria. Ratification 30 Oct 61.
422 UNTS 319. Tanganyika. Succession 30 Jan 62. Force 30 Jan 62.
437 UNTS 339. Madagascar. Ratification 10 Aug 62.
443 UNTS 323. Rwanda. Succession 18 Sep 62. Force 18 Sep 62.
443 UNTS 323. Cameroon. Succession 3 Sep 62. Force 3 Sep 62.
444 UNTS 309. Senegal. Ratification 22 Oct 62.
444 UNTS 309. Algeria. Succession 19 Oct 62. Force 19 Oct 62.
452 UNTS 357. Jamaica. Succession 26 Dec 62.
455 UNTS 451. Cameroon. Ratification 29 Jan 63.
457 UNTS 335. Burundi. Succession 11 Mar 63.
468 UNTS 423. Trinidad/Tobago. Ratification 24 May 63. Force 24 May 63.
471 UNTS 359. Uganda. Ratification 4 Jun 63.
483 UNTS 400. Mauritania. Ratification 8 Nov 63.

488 UNTS 347. Kenya. Ratification 13 Jan 64. Force 13 Jan 64.
495 UNTS 278. Malaysia. Sarawak. Succession 3 Mar 64.
495 UNTS 278. Malaysia. Malaya. Succession 3 Mar 64.
495 UNTS 278. Malaysia. Singapore. Succession 3 Mar 64.
504 UNTS 330. Tanzania. Succession 22 Jun 64.
504 UNTS 330. Central Afri Rep. Ratification 9 Jun 64.
510 UNTS 348. Mali. Ratification 17 Aug 64.
522 UNTS 364. Zambia. Ratification 2 Dec 64. Force 2 Dec 64.
524 UNTS 352. Malta. Ratification 4 Jan 65. Force 4 Jan 65.
530 UNTS 399. Malawi. Ratification 22 Mar 65.
548 UNTS 389. Singapore. Ratification 25 Oct 65. Force 25 Oct 65.
567 UNTS 342. Guyana. Ratification 8 Jun 66. Force 8 Jun 66.
636 UNTS 424. Thailand. Ratification 5 Apr 6 .

100603 Multilateral Convention **38 UNTS 269**
SIGNED: 8 Jun 25   FORCE: 28 May 47
REGISTERED: 15 Sep 49 ILO (Labor Org)
ARTICLES: 13 LANGUAGE: English. French.
HEADNOTE: NIGHT WORK BAKERIES
TOPIC: ILO Labor
CONCEPTS: Definition of terms. Exceptions and exemptions. Territorial application. Previous treaty extension. Incorporation of treaty provisions into national law. ILO conventions. Holidays and rest periods. Safety standards. Administrative cooperation.
INTL ORGS: International Labour Organization.
TREATY REF: 38UNTS3.
PROCEDURE: Amendment. Denunciation. Duration. Ratification. Registration.
PARTIES:
   Multilateral
                    ANNEX
73 UNTS 270. Nicaragua. Denunciation 19 Sep 50. Force 19 Sep 51.
97 UNTS 315. Israel. Ratification 26 Jul 51.
204 UNTS 340. Argentina. Ratification 17 Feb 55. Force 17 Feb 55.
429 UNTS 258. Peru. Ratification 4 Apr 62.

100604 Multilateral Convention **38 UNTS 281**
SIGNED: 5 Jun 26   FORCE: 28 May 47
REGISTERED: 15 Sep 49 ILO (Labor Org)
ARTICLES: 15 LANGUAGE: English. French.
HEADNOTE: INSPECT IMMIGRANTS BOARD SHIP
TOPIC: ILO Labor
CONCEPTS: Definition of terms. Detailed regulations. Territorial application. Previous treaty extension. Alien registration. Alien status. Protection of nationals. Exchange of information and documents. Inspection and observation. ILO conventions.
INTL ORGS: International Labour Organization.
TREATY REF: 38UNTS3.
PROCEDURE: Amendment. Denunciation. Duration. Ratification. Registration.
PARTIES:
   Multilateral
                    ANNEX
54 UNTS 401. Argentina. Ratification 14 Mar 50.
199 UNTS 315. Cuba. Ratification 7 Sep 54. Force 7 Sep 54.
210 UNTS 326. Denmark. Ratification 18 May 55.
261 UNTS 388. Norway. Ratification 28 Jan 57.
282 UNTS 357. Sweden. Force 28 Jan 57.
541 UNTS 370. Brazil. Ratification 18 Jun 65.

100605 Multilateral Convention **38 UNTS 295**
SIGNED: 24 Jun 26   FORCE: 28 May 47
REGISTERED: 15 Sep 49 ILO (Labor Org)
ARTICLES: 23 LANGUAGE: English. French.
HEADNOTE: SEAMENS ARTICLES AGREEMENT
TOPIC: ILO Labor
CONCEPTS: Definition of terms. Detailed regulations. Exceptions and exemptions. Territorial application. Previous treaty extension. Domestic legislation. Private contracts. Investigation of violations. ILO conventions. Employment regulations. Labor statistics. Administrative cooperation. Merchant vessels.
INTL ORGS: International Labour Organization.
TREATY REF: 38UNTS3.

PROCEDURE: Amendment. Denunciation. Duration. Ratification. Registration.
PARTIES:
   Multilateral
                    ANNEX
54 UNTS 401. Argentina. Ratification 14 Mar 50.
218 UNTS 381. Japan. Ratification 22 Aug 55.
276 UNTS 356. Netherlands. Netherlands Antilles.
293 UNTS 366. Morocco. Ratification 14 Mar 58.
384 UNTS 343. Somalia. Succession 18 Nov 60. Force 18 Nov 60.
401 UNTS 231. Sierra Leone. Ratification 15 Jun 61.
429 UNTS 259. Peru. Ratification 4 Apr 62.
455 UNTS 452. UK Great Britain. Bahamas.
457 UNTS 336. UK Great Britain. Bermuda.
457 UNTS 336. UK Great Britain. Malta.
457 UNTS 336. UK Great Britain. Singapore.
468 UNTS 424. UK Great Britain. Falkland Islands.
468 UNTS 424. UK Great Britain. Nyasaland.
475 UNTS 372. UK Great Britain. Anguilla.
475 UNTS 372. UK Great Britain. Grenada.
480 UNTS 466. UK Great Britain. Dominican Republic.
483 UNTS 401. Mauritania. Ratification 8 Nov 63.
495 UNTS 279. Malaysia. Singapore. Succession 3 Mar 64.
499 UNTS 360. UK Great Britain. Gambia.
504 UNTS 331. UK Great Britain. Hong Kong.
504 UNTS 331. UK Great Britain. British Honduras.
504 UNTS 331. UK Great Britain. St. Christopher.
510 UNTS 349. UK Great Britain. Aden. Declaration 3 Aug 64.
515 UNTS 334. UK Great Britain. Seychelles.
521 UNTS 410. UK Great Britain. British Guiana. Declaration 24 Nov 64.
524 UNTS 353. Malta. Ratification 4 Jan 65. Force 4 Jan 65.
527 UNTS 333. UK Great Britain. St. Helena. Declaration 8 Feb 65.
530 UNTS 400. Ghana. Ratification 18 Mar 65.
541 UNTS 371. Brazil. Ratification 18 Jun 65.
548 UNTS 390. Singapore. Ratification 25 Oct 65. Force 25 Oct 65.
559 UNTS 376. UK Great Britain. Barbados.

100606 Multilateral Convention **38 UNTS 315**
SIGNED: 23 Jun 26   FORCE: 28 May 47
REGISTERED: 15 Sep 49 ILO (Labor Org)
ARTICLES: 14 LANGUAGE: English. French.
HEADNOTE: REPATRIATION SEAMEN
TOPIC: ILO Labor
CONCEPTS: Definition of terms. Detailed regulations. Territorial application. Previous treaty extension. Repatriation of nationals. Domestic legislation. ILO conventions. Indemnities and reimbursements. Merchant vessels.
INTL ORGS: International Labour Organization.
TREATY REF: 38UNTS3.
PROCEDURE: Amendment. Denunciation. Duration. Ratification. Registration.
PARTIES:
   Multilateral
                    ANNEX
54 UNTS 402. Argentina. Ratification 14 Mar 50.
276 UNTS 357. Netherlands. Declaration 5 Aug 57.
276 UNTS 357. Netherlands. Netherlands Antilles.
358 UNTS 250. Switzerland. Ratification 21 Apr 60.
384 UNTS 344. Somalia. Succession 18 Nov 60. Force 18 Nov 60.
384 UNTS 344. Philippines. Ratification 17 Nov 60.
429 UNTS 259. Peru. Ratification 4 Apr 62.
483 UNTS 402. Mauritania. Ratification 8 Nov 63.
530 UNTS 400. Ghana. Ratification 18 Mar 65.

100607 Multilateral Convention **38 UNTS 327**
SIGNED: 15 Jun 27   FORCE: 28 May 47
REGISTERED: 15 Sep 49 ILO (Labor Org)
ARTICLES: 18 LANGUAGE: English. French.
HEADNOTE: SICKNESS INSURANCE WORKERS
TOPIC: ILO Labor
CONCEPTS: Territorial application. Previous treaty extension. Domestic legislation. Incorporation of treaty provisions into national law. Jurisdiction. Public health. ILO conventions. Administrative

cooperation. Sickness and invalidity insurance. Bonds.
INTL ORGS: International Labour Organization.
TREATY REF: 38UNTS3.
PROCEDURE: Amendment. Denunciation. Duration. Ratification. Registration.
PARTIES:
Multilateral
ANNEX
210 UNTS 327. Haiti. Ratification 19 Apr 55. Force 19 Jul 55.
212 UNTS 386. France. Declaration 27 Apr 55.
399 UNTS 256. Norway. Ratification 29 May 61. Force 27 Aug 61.
423 UNTS 292. Ecuador. Ratification 5 Feb 62. Force 6 May 62.
444 UNTS 310. Algeria. Succession 19 Oct 62. Force 19 Oct 62.
468 UNTS 425. UK Great Britain. Declaration 8 May 62.
471 UNTS 360. UK Great Britain. Grenada.
475 UNTS 373. UK Great Britain. Fed Rhod/-Nyasaland.
480 UNTS 467. UK Great Britain. Gilbert Islands.
499 UNTS 361. UK Great Britain. Malta.
510 UNTS 350. UK Great Britain. Brunei. Declaration 3 Aug 64.
515 UNTS 335. UK Great Britain. Seychelles. Declaration 16 Oct 64.
521 UNTS 411. UK Great Britain. British Guiana. Declaration 24 Nov 64.
527 UNTS 334. UK Great Britain. St. Helena. Declaration 8 Feb 65.
549 UNTS 362. Netherlands. Ratification 15 Nov 65. Force 15 Feb 66.

100608 Multilateral Convention **38 UNTS 343**
SIGNED: 15 Jun 27　　　　FORCE: 28 May 47
REGISTERED: 15 Sep 49 ILO (Labor Org)
ARTICLES: 17 LANGUAGE: English. French.
HEADNOTE: SICKNESS INSURANCE AGRICULTURAL WORKERS
TOPIC: ILO Labor
CONCEPTS: Exceptions and exemptions. Territorial application. Previous treaty extension. Domestic legislation. Incorporation of treaty provisions into national law. Jurisdiction. Public health. ILO conventions. Administrative cooperation. Sickness and invalidity insurance. Bonds.
INTL ORGS: International Labour Organization.
TREATY REF: 38UNTS3.
PROCEDURE: Amendment. Denunciation. Duration. Ratification. Registration.
PARTIES:
Multilateral
ANNEX
131 UNTS 313. Yugoslavia. Ratification 21 May 52. Force 19 Aug 52.
210 UNTS 327. Haiti. Ratification 19 Apr 55. Force 19 Jul 55.
353 UNTS 321. Peru. Ratification 1 Feb 60. Force 1 May 60.
399 UNTS 257. Norway. Ratification 29 May 61. Force 27 Aug 61.
468 UNTS 426. UK Great Britain. Declaration 8 May 62.
471 UNTS 361. UK Great Britain. Grenada.
475 UNTS 374. UK Great Britain. Fed Rhod/-Nyasaland.
499 UNTS 362. UK Great Britain. Malta.
504 UNTS 334. UK Great Britain. Montserrat.
504 UNTS 334. Tanzania. Succession 22 Jun 64.
504 UNTS 334. Paraguay. Ratification 24 Jun 64. Force 24 Jun 65.
510 UNTS 351. UK Great Britain. Brunei. Declaration 3 Aug 64.
515 UNTS 335. UK Great Britain. Seychelles. Declaration 16 Oct 64.
521 UNTS 412. UK Great Britain. British Guiana. Declaration 24 Nov 64.
527 UNTS 335. UK Great Britain. St. Helena. Declaration 8 Feb 65.
549 UNTS 363. Netherlands. Ratification 15 Nov 65. Force 15 Feb 66.
638 UNTS 333. Netherlands. Netherlands Antilles. Declaration 30 May 68.

100609 Multilateral Convention **39 UNTS 3**
SIGNED: 16 Jun 28　　　　FORCE: 28 May 47
REGISTERED: 15 Sep 49 ILO (Labor Org)
ARTICLES: 11 LANGUAGE: English. French.

HEADNOTE: MINIMUM WAGE FIXING MACHINERY
TOPIC: ILO Labor
CONCEPTS: Definition of terms. Previous treaty extension. Exchange of information and documents. Domestic legislation. Succession. Investigation of violations. ILO conventions. Holidays and rest periods. Labor statistics.
INTL ORGS: International Labour Organization.
TREATY REF: 38UNTS3.
PROCEDURE: Denunciation. Duration. Ratification. Renewal or Revival.
PARTIES:
Multilateral
ANNEX
54 UNTS 402. Argentina. Ratification 14 Mar 51. Force 14 Mar 51.
66 UNTS 350. Czechoslovakia. Ratification 12 Jun 50. Force 12 Jun 51.
191 UNTS 362. Burma. Ratification 21 May 54. Force 21 May 55.
196 UNTS 337. Ecuador. Ratification 6 Jul 54. Force 6 Jul 55.
198 UNTS 375. Bolivia. Ratification 19 Jul 54. Force 19 Jul 55.
202 UNTS 327. India. Ratification 10 Jan 55. Force 10 Jan 56.
212 UNTS 387. Belgium. Belgian Colonies.
212 UNTS 387. Belgium. Ruanda-Urundi.
212 UNTS 387. Vietnam. Ratification 14 Jun 55. Force 14 Jun 56.
256 UNTS 330. Dominican Republic. Ratification 5 Dec 56. Force 5 Dec 57.
266 UNTS 373. Brazil. Ratification 25 Apr 57. Force 25 Apr 58.
269 UNTS 277. Tunisia. Ratification 15 May 57. Force 15 May 58.
272 UNTS 250. Sudan. Ratification 18 Jun 57. Force 18 Jun 58.
293 UNTS 366. Morocco. Ratification 14 Mar 58. Force 14 Mar 59.
293 UNTS 366. Luxembourg. Ratification 3 Mar 58. Force 3 Mar 59.
323 UNTS 372. Guinea. Ratification 21 Jan 59. Force 21 Jan 59.
338 UNTS 330. Ghana. Ratification 2 Jul 59. Force 2 Jul 60.
345 UNTS 354. Portugal. Ratification 10 Nov 59. Force 10 Nov 60.
361 UNTS 232. United Arab Rep. Ratification 10 May 60.
366 UNTS 377. Cameroon. Succession 7 Jun 60. Force 7 Jun 60.
366 UNTS 377. Togo. Succession 7 Jun 60. Force 7 Jun 60.
366 UNTS 377. Mali. Succession 21 Jun 60. Force 21 Jun 60.
380 UNTS 401. Gabon. Succession 14 Oct 60. Force 14 Oct 60.
380 UNTS 401. Central Afri Rep. Succession 27 Oct 60. Force 27 Oct 60.
381 UNTS 367. Mali. Succession 22 Sep 60. Force 22 Sep 60.
381 UNTS 367. Congo (Zaire). Succession 20 Sep 60. Force 20 Sep 60.
384 UNTS 345. Malagasy. Succession 1 Nov 60. Force 1 Nov 60.
384 UNTS 345. Senegal. Succession 4 Nov 60. Force 4 Nov 60.
384 UNTS 345. Chad. Succession 10 Nov 60. Force 10 Nov 60.
384 UNTS 345. Upper Volta. Succession 21 Nov 60. Force 21 Nov 60.
384 UNTS 345. Congo (Brazzaville). Succession 10 Nov 60. Force 10 Nov 60.
384 UNTS 345. Ivory Coast. Succession 21 Nov 60. Force 21 Nov 60.
386 UNTS 371. Dahomey. Succession 12 Dec 60.
390 UNTS 342. Niger. Succession 27 Feb 61.
399 UNTS 258. Guatemala. Ratification 4 May 61. Force 4 May 61.
401 UNTS 232. Sierra Leone. Ratification 15 Jun 61. Force 15 Jun 62.
401 UNTS 232. Nigeria. Ratification 16 Jun 61. Force 16 Jun 62.
401 UNTS 232. Mauritius. Succession 20 Jun 61.
413 UNTS 353. Syria. Ratification 30 Oct 61.
429 UNTS 260. Peru. Ratification 4 Apr 62. Force 4 Apr 63.
434 UNTS 280. UK Great Britain. Swaziland.
434 UNTS 280. UK Great Britain. Kenya.
434 UNTS 280. UK Great Britain. Seychelles.
434 UNTS 280. UK Great Britain. Fiji Islands.

434 UNTS 280. UK Great Britain. St. Lucia.
434 UNTS 280. UK Great Britain. British Honduras.
434 UNTS 280. UK Great Britain. Falkland Islands.
434 UNTS 280. UK Great Britain. St. Vincent.
434 UNTS 280. UK Great Britain. Gibralter.
434 UNTS 280. UK Great Britain. British Guiana.
434 UNTS 280. UK Great Britain. Dominican Republic.
434 UNTS 280. UK Great Britain. Mauritius.
434 UNTS 280. UK Great Britain. Uganda.
434 UNTS 280. UK Great Britain. Hong Kong.
434 UNTS 280. UK Great Britain. Brit Solomon Is.
434 UNTS 280. UK Great Britain. Zanzibar.
434 UNTS 280. UK Great Britain. Malta.
434 UNTS 280. UK Great Britain. Barbados.
435 UNTS 302. Lebanon. Ratification 26 Jul 62.
437 UNTS 340. UK Great Britain. Sarawak.
443 UNTS 324. Rwanda. Succession 18 Sep 62. Force 18 Sep 62.
444 UNTS 311. Cameroon. Succession 3 Sep 62.
444 UNTS 311. UK Great Britain. Brit Virgin Islands.
444 UNTS 311. UK Great Britain. St. Helena.
444 UNTS 311. UK Great Britain. Gambia.
449 UNTS 275. Tanganyika. Ratification 19 Nov 62.
449 UNTS 275. Iraq. Ratification 26 Nov 62. Force 26 Nov 63.
449 UNTS 275. UK Great Britain. Basutoland.
452 UNTS 358. UK Great Britain. Nyasaland.
455 UNTS 455. UK Great Britain. Northern Rhodesia.
455 UNTS 455. Cameroon. Ratification 29 Jan 63.
457 UNTS 342. Burundi. Succession 11 Mar 63.
468 UNTS 427. UK Great Britain. St. Christopher.
471 UNTS 362. Uganda. Ratification 4 Jun 63.
471 UNTS 362. UK Great Britain. Grenada.
473 UNTS 390. Jamaica. Ratification 8 Jul 63.
488 UNTS 348. Kenya. Ratification 13 Jan 64. Force 13 Jan 64.
492 UNTS 379. UK Great Britain. Declaration 24 Feb 64.
510 UNTS 352. UK Great Britain. Bahamas.
522 UNTS 365. Zambia. Ratification 2 Dec 64. Force 2 Dec 64.
524 UNTS 354. Malta. Ratification 4 Jan 65. Force 4 Jan 65.
527 UNTS 336. UK Great Britain. Bechuanaland. Declaration 8 Feb 65.
530 UNTS 401. UK Great Britain. Malawi. Ratification 22 Mar 65.
567 UNTS 342. Guyana. Ratification 8 Jun 66. Force 8 Jun 66.

100610 Multilateral Convention **39 UNTS 15**
SIGNED: 26 Jun 28　　　　FORCE: 28 May 47
REGISTERED: 15 Sep 49 ILO (Labor Org)
ARTICLES: 8 LANGUAGE: English. French.
HEADNOTE: WEIGHT HEAVY PACKAGES MARKING
TOPIC: ILO Labor
CONCEPTS: Previous treaty extension. Domestic legislation. Incorporation of treaty provisions into national law. ILO conventions. Domestic obligation.
INTL ORGS: International Labour Organization.
TREATY REF: 38UNTS3.
PROCEDURE: Denunciation. Ratification. Registration. Renewal or Revival.
PARTIES:
Multilateral
ANNEX
54 UNTS 402. Argentina. Ratification 14 Mar 51. Force 14 Mar 51.
104 UNTS 347. Indonesia. Succession 31 May 51.
167 UNTS 263. Vietnam. Ratification 6 Jun 53. Force 6 Jun 54.
199 UNTS 315. Cuba. Ratification 7 Sep 54. Force 7 Sep 55.
200 UNTS 275. Belgium. Belgian Colonies.
200 UNTS 275. Belgium. Ruanda-Urundi.
253 UNTS 380. Morocco. Ratification 20 Sep 56. Force 20 Sep 57.
276 UNTS 357. Netherlands. Surinam.
381 UNTS 368. Congo (Zaire). Succession 20 Sep 60. Force 20 Sep 60.
429 UNTS 260. Peru. Ratification 4 Apr 62. Force 4 Apr 63.
457 UNTS 343. Burundi. Succession 11 Mar 63.

100611 Multilateral Convention **39 UNTS 27**
SIGNED: 21 Jun 29   FORCE: 28 May 47
REGISTERED: 15 Sep 49 ILO (Labor Org)
ARTICLES: 24 LANGUAGE: English. French.
HEADNOTE: ACCIDENT PROTECTION WORKERS
TOPIC: ILO Labor
CONCEPTS: Definition of terms. Exceptions and
exemptions. Previous treaty extension. Incorpo-
ration of treaty provisions into national law. In-
vestigation of violations. Humanitarian matters.
Old age and invalidity insurance. Safety stan-
dards. Domestic obligation.
INTL ORGS: International Labour Organization.
TREATY REF: 38UNTS3.
PROCEDURE: Amendment. Denunciation. Dura-
tion. Ratification. Renewal or Revival.
PARTIES:
  Multilateral

100612 Multilateral Convention **39 UNTS 55**
SIGNED: 28 Jun 30   FORCE: 28 May 47
REGISTERED: 15 Sep 49 ILO (Labor Org)
ARTICLES: 33 LANGUAGE: English. French.
HEADNOTE: COMPULSORY LABOR
TOPIC: ILO Labor
CONCEPTS: Definition of terms. Territorial applica-
tion. Time limit. Previous treaty extension. Ex-
change of information and documents. Incorpo-
ration of treaty provisions into national law. In-
vestigation of violations. ILO conventions.
Employment regulations. Holidays and rest peri-
ods. Labor statistics. Safety standards.
INTL ORGS: International Labour Organization.
TREATY REF: 38UNTS3.
PROCEDURE: Amendment. Denunciation. Ratification. Registration. Renewal or Revival.
PARTIES:
  Multilateral
                    ANNEX
54 UNTS 403. Argentina. Ratification 14 Mar 51.
  Force 14 Mar 51.
54 UNTS 406. Ceylon (Sri Lanka). Ratification
  5 Apr 50. Force 5 Apr 51.
104 UNTS 347.   Indonesia.   Succession
  31 May 51.
133 UNTS 336. Greece. Ratification 13 Jun 52.
  Force 13 Jun 53.
167 UNTS 264. Vietnam. Ratification 6 Jun 53.
  Force 6 Jun 54.
172 UNTS 337. Cuba. Ratification 20 Jul 53.
  Force 20 Jul 54.
196 UNTS 337. Ecuador. Ratification 6 Jun 54.
  Force 6 Jul 55.
198 UNTS 376. France. All Territories.
202 UNTS 328. India. Ratification 30 Nov 54.
  Force 30 Nov 55.
210 UNTS 328. Burma. Ratification 4 Mar 55.
  Force 4 Mar 56.
211 UNTS 389.   Israel.   Ratification 7 Jun 55.
  Force 7 Jun 56.
225 UNTS 256. United Arab Rep. Ratification
  29 Nov 55. Force 29 Nov 56.
248 UNTS 398. USSR (Soviet Union). Ratification
  23 Jun 56. Force 23 Jun 57.
248 UNTS 398. Portugal. Ratification 26 Jun 56.
  Force 26 Jun 57.
248 UNTS 398. Hungary. Ratification 8 Jun 56.
  Force 8 Jun 57.
248 UNTS 398.   Germany,   West.   Ratification
  13 Jun 56. Force 13 Jun 57.
249 UNTS 448.   Ukrainian   SSR.   Ratification
  10 Aug 56. Force 10 Aug 57.
249 UNTS 448.   Byelorussia.   Ratification
  21 Aug 57. Force 21 Aug 57.
253 UNTS 381. Netherlands. New Guinea.
256 UNTS 331. Dominican Republic. Ratification
  5 Dec 56. Force 5 Dec 57.
261 UNTS 389. Honduras. Ratification 21 Feb 57.
  Force 21 Feb 58.
266 UNTS 373. Brazil. Ratification 25 Apr 57.
  Force 25 Apr 58.
268 UNTS 355. Morocco. Ratification 20 May 57.
  Force 20 May 58.
272 UNTS 251. Sudan. Ratification 18 Jun 57.
  Force 18 Jun 58.
272 UNTS 251. Romania. Ratification 28 May 57.
  Force 28 May 58.
272 UNTS 251. Albania. Ratification 25 Jun 57.
  Force 15 Jun 58.
272 UNTS 251.   Iran.   Ratification   10 Jun 57.
  Force 10 Jun 58.
280 UNTS 349.   Czechoslovakia.   Ratification
  30 Oct 57. Force 30 Oct 58.

282 UNTS 358.   Fed   of   Malaya.   Ratification
  11 Nov 57. Force 11 Nov 57.
285 UNTS 371. Pakistan. Ratification 23 Dec 57.
  Force 23 Dec 58.
287 UNTS 342. Iceland. Ratification 17 Feb 58.
  Force 17 Feb 59.
293 UNTS 367. Haiti. Ratification 4 Mar 58. Force
  4 Mar 59.
312 UNTS 403. Poland. Ratification 30 Jul 58.
  Force 30 Jul 59.
323 UNTS 372. Guinea. Ratification 21 Jan 59.
  Force 21 Jan 59.
353 UNTS 321. Peru. Ratification 1 Feb 60. Force
  1 Feb 61.
366 UNTS 376. Cameroon. Succession 7 Jun 60.
  Force 7 Jun 60.
366 UNTS 378.   Mali.   Succession   21 Jun 60.
  Force 21 Jun 60.
366 UNTS 378. Costa Rica. Ratification 2 Jun 60.
  Force 2 Jun 61.
366 UNTS 378.   Austria.   Ratification   7 Jun 60.
  Force 7 Jun 61.
366 UNTS 378.   Togo.   Succession   7 Jun 60.
  Force 7 Jun 60.
373 UNTS 343. United Arab Rep. Syria.
380 UNTS 402. Nigeria. Succession 17 Oct 60.
  Force 17 Oct 60.
380 UNTS 402. Gabon. Succession 14 Oct 60.
  Force 14 Oct 60.
380 UNTS 402. Central Afri Rep. Succession
  27 Oct 60. Force 27 Oct 60.
381 UNTS 369. Congo (Zaire). Succession
  20 Sep 60. Force 20 Sep 60.
381 UNTS 370. Cyprus. Succession 23 Sep 60.
  Force 23 Sep 60.
381 UNTS 370.   Mali.   Succession   22 Sep 60.
  Force 22 Sep 60.
384 UNTS 346. Senegal. Succession 4 Nov 60.
  Force 4 Nov 60.
384 UNTS 346. Malagasy. Succession 1 Nov 60.
  Force 1 Nov 60.
384 UNTS 346.   Chad.   Succession   10 Nov 60.
  Force 10 Nov 60.
384 UNTS 346. Congo (Brazzaville). Succession
  10 Nov 60. Force 10 Nov 60.
384 UNTS 347.   Ivory   Coast.   Succession
  21 Nov 60. Force 21 Nov 61.
384 UNTS 347.   Upper   Volta.   Succession
  21 Nov 60. Force 21 Nov 60.
384 UNTS 347. Somalia. Succession 18 Nov 60.
  Force 18 Nov 60.
386 UNTS 372.   Dahomey.   Succession
  12 Dec 60.
390 UNTS 343. Niger. Succession 27 Feb 61.
401 UNTS 233. Libya. Ratification 13 Jun 61.
  Force 13 Jun 62.
401 UNTS 233. Mauritius. Succession 20 Jun 61.
401 UNTS 233.   Sierra   Leone.   Succession
  13 Jun 61.
413 UNTS 354. Syria. Ratification 30 Oct 61.
422 UNTS 320.   Tanganyika.   Succession
  30 Jan 62. Force 30 Jan 62.
443 UNTS 325. Cameroon. Succession 3 Sep 62.
  Force 3 Sep 62.
444 UNTS 312. Cameroon. Succession 3 Sep 62.
444 UNTS 312. Algeria. Succession 19 Oct 62.
  Force 19 Oct 62.
449 UNTS 276.   Iraq.   Ratification   26 Nov 62.
  Force 26 Nov 63.
452 UNTS 359. Jamaica. Succession 26 Dec 62.
452 UNTS 359. Tunisia. Ratification 17 Dec 62.
  Force 17 Dec 63.
457 UNTS 344. Burundi. Succession 11 Mar 63.
468 UNTS 428. Trinidad/Tobago. Ratification
  24 May 63. Force 24 May 63.
488 UNTS 349. Kenya. Ratification 13 Jan 64.
  Force 13 Jan 64.
488 UNTS 349. Laos. Ratification 23 Jan 64.
  Force 23 Jan 64.
495 UNTS 280. Malaysia. Malaya. Succession
  3 Mar 64.
495 UNTS 280. Malaysia. Singapore. Succession
  3 Mar 64.
495 UNTS 280. Malaysia. Sarawak. Succession
  3 Mar 64.
495 UNTS 280. Malaysia. State of Sabah. Succession 3 Mar 64.
504 UNTS 336. Tanzania. Succession 22 Jun 64.
504 UNTS 336.   Luxembourg.   Ratification
  24 Jul 64. Force 24 Jul 65.
522 UNTS 366. Zambia. Ratification 2 Dec 64.
  Force 2 Dec 64.
524 UNTS 355. Malta. Ratification 4 Jan 65.
  Force 4 Jan 65.

548 UNTS 391.   Singapore.   Ratification
  25 Oct 65. Force 25 Oct 65.
567 UNTS 344.   Jordan.   Ratification   6 Jun 66.
  Force 6 Jun 67.
567 UNTS 344. Guyana. Ratification 8 Jun 66.
  Force 8 Jun 66.
607 UNTS 360. Paraguay. Ratification 23 Aug 67.
  Force 28 Aug 68.
648 UNTS 388. Kuwait. Ratification 23 Sep 68.
  Force 23 Sep 69.
660 UNTS 427.   Cambodia.   Ratification
  24 Feb 69.
660 UNTS 427. Thailand. Ratification 26 Feb 69.
  Force 26 Feb 70.

100613 Multilateral Convention **39 UNTS 85**
SIGNED: 28 Jun 30   FORCE: 28 May 47
REGISTERED: 15 Sep 49 ILO (Labor Org)
ARTICLES: 19 LANGUAGE: English. French.
HEADNOTE: HOURS WORK COMMERCE OFFICES
TOPIC: ILO Labor
CONCEPTS: Definition of terms. Emergencies. Ex-
ceptions and exemptions. Previous treaty exten-
sion. Incorporation of treaty provisions into na-
tional law. Investigation of violations. ILO con-
ventions. Employment regulations. Holidays and
rest periods. Labor statistics.
INTL ORGS: International Labour Organization.
TREATY REF: 38UNTS3.
PROCEDURE: Amendment. Duration. Ratification.
Registration. Termination.
PARTIES:
  Multilateral
                    ANNEX
54 UNTS 403. Argentina. Ratification 14 Mar 51.
  Force 14 Mar 51.
92 UNTS 402. Israel.   Ratification   26 Jun 51.
  Force 26 Jun 52.
127 UNTS 329.   Haiti.   Ratification   31 Mar 52.
  Force 31 Mar 53.
171 UNTS 413.   Norway.   Ratification   29 Jun 53.
  Force 29 Jun 54.
293 UNTS 367.   Luxembourg.   Ratification
  3 Mar 58. Force 3 Mar 59.
325 UNTS 329. Panama. Ratification 16 Feb 59.
  Force 16 Feb 60.
361 UNTS 233.   United   Arab   Rep.   Ratification
  10 May 60.
406 UNTS 287.   Guatemala.   Ratification
  4 Aug 61. Force 4 Aug 62.
410 UNTS 287. Kuwait. Ratification 21 Sep 61.
  Force 21 Sep 62.
413 UNTS 355. Syria. Ratification 30 Oct 61.
449 UNTS 277.   Iraq.   Ratification   26 Nov 62.
  Force 26 Nov 63.
560 UNTS 310. Paraguay. Ratification 21 Mar 66.
  Force 21 Mar 67.

100614 Multilateral Convention **39 UNTS 103**
SIGNED: 27 Apr 32   FORCE: 28 May 47
REGISTERED: 15 Sep 49 ILO (Labor Org)
ARTICLES: 25 LANGUAGE: English. French.
HEADNOTE: PROTECTION AGAINST ACCIDENTS
SHIP LOADERS
TOPIC: ILO Labor
CONCEPTS: Definition of terms. Previous treaty ex-
tension. Exchange of official publications. Ex-
change of information and documents. Domes-
tic legislation. Incorporation of treaty provisions
into national law. Investigation of violations. Pub-
lic health. ILO conventions. Safety standards.
Ports and pilotage.
INTL ORGS: International Labour Organization.
TREATY REF: 38UNTS3.
PROCEDURE: Amendment. Denunciation. Ratifica-
tion. Registration. Renewal or Revival.
PARTIES:
  Multilateral
                    ANNEX
46 UNTS 358. Bulgaria. Ratification 29 Dec 49.
  Force 29 Dec 50.
54 UNTS 403. Argentina. Ratification 14 Mar 51.
  Force 14 Mar 51.
122 UNTS 337. Finland. Ratification 23 Aug 49.
  Force 23 Aug 50.
134 UNTS 376. UK Great Britain. Belgian Colo-
  nies. Declaration 2 Jul 52.
134 UNTS 376. UK Great Britain. Ruanda-Urundi.
  Declaration 2 Jul 52.
134 UNTS 376. Belgium. Ratification 2 Jul 52.
  Force 2 Jul 53.

199 UNTS 316. Cuba. Ratification 7 Sep 54. Force 7 Sep 55.
211 UNTS 390. France. Ratification 27 May 55. Force 27 May 56.
248 UNTS 399. Norway. Ratification 23 Jun 56. Force 23 Jun 57.
401 UNTS 234. Sierra Leone. Ratification 15 Jun 61. Force 15 Jun 62.
401 UNTS 234. Nigeria. Ratification 16 Jun 61. Force 16 Jun 62.
429 UNTS 261. Peru. Ratification 4 Apr 62. Force 4 Apr 63.
444 UNTS 313. Algeria. Succession 19 Oct 62. Force 19 Oct 62.
449 UNTS 278. Tanganyika. Ratification 19 Nov 62. Force 19 Nov 63.
457 UNTS 346. UK Great Britain. Kenya.
457 UNTS 346. UK Great Britain. Malta.
457 UNTS 346. UK Great Britain. Singapore.
471 UNTS 364. UK Great Britain. Grenada.
475 UNTS 375. UK Great Britain. Northern Rhodesia.
475 UNTS 375. UK Great Britain. Anguilla.
479 UNTS 435. UK Great Britain. Mauritius.
488 UNTS 351. Kenya. Ratification 13 Jan 64. Force 13 Jan 64.
495 UNTS 281. Malaysia. Singapore. Succession 3 Mar 64.
499 UNTS 363. UK Great Britain. Gambia.
504 UNTS 337. UK Great Britain. Basutoland. Declaration 7 Jul 64.
504 UNTS 337. Tanzania. Succession 22 Jun 64.
504 UNTS 337. UK Great Britain. St. Christopher. Declaration 12 Jun 64.
504 UNTS 337. UK Great Britain. Aden. Declaration 12 Jun 64.
504 UNTS 337. UK Great Britain. Antigua. Declaration 12 Jun 64.
510 UNTS 353. UK Great Britain. Aden. Declaration 3 Aug 64.
510 UNTS 353. Netherlands. Ratification 25 Aug 64. Force 25 Aug 65.
515 UNTS 337. UK Great Britain. Seychelles. Declaration 16 Oct 64.
521 UNTS 413. Honduras. Ratification 17 Nov 64. Force 17 Nov 65.
522 UNTS 367. UK Great Britain. Falkland Islands.
530 UNTS 402. UK Great Britain. British Guiana.
534 UNTS 356. Malta. Ratification 4 Jan 65. Force 4 Jan 65.
548 UNTS 392. Singapore. Ratification 25 Oct 65. Force 25 Oct 65.

100615 Multilateral Convention **39 UNTS 133**
SIGNED: 30 Apr 32　　　FORCE: 28 May 47
REGISTERED: 15 Sep 49 ILO (Labor Org)
ARTICLES: 16 LANGUAGE: English. French.
HEADNOTE: AGE ADMISSION CHILDREN NONINDUSTRIAL EMPLOYMENT
TOPIC: ILO Labor
CONCEPTS: Detailed regulations. Exceptions and exemptions. Previous treaty extension. Exchange of information and documents. Domestic legislation. Incorporation of treaty provisions into national law. Investigation of violations. ILO conventions. Employment regulations. Holidays and rest periods.
INTL ORGS: International Labour Organization.
TREATY REF: 38UNTS3.
PROCEDURE: Amendment. Denunciation. Duration. Ratification. Registration. Termination.
PARTIES:
Multilateral
ANNEX
54 UNTS 404. Argentina. Ratification 14 Mar 51. Force 14 Mar 51.
276 UNTS 358. Netherlands. Netherlands Antilles.
323 UNTS 373. Guinea. Ratification 21 Jan 59. Force 21 Jan 59.
366 UNTS 379. Togo. Succession 7 Jun 60. Force 7 Jun 60.
366 UNTS 379. Cameroon. Succession 7 Jun 60. Force 7 Jun 60.
366 UNTS 379. Mali. Succession 21 Jun 60. Force 21 Jun 60.
380 UNTS 403. Gabon. Succession 14 Oct 60. Force 14 Oct 60.
380 UNTS 403. Central Afri Rep. Succession 27 Oct 60. Force 27 Oct 60.
381 UNTS 371. Mali. Succession 22 Sep 60. Force 22 Sep 60.

384 UNTS 348. Malagasy. Succession 1 Nov 60. Force 1 Nov 60.
384 UNTS 348. Senegal. Succession 4 Nov 60. Force 4 Nov 60.
384 UNTS 348. Chad. Succession 10 Nov 60. Force 10 Nov 60.
384 UNTS 348. Congo (Brazzaville). Succession 10 Nov 60. Force 10 Nov 60.
384 UNTS 348. Ivory Coast. Succession 21 Nov 60. Force 21 Nov 61.
384 UNTS 348. Upper Volta. Succession 21 Nov 60. Force 21 Nov 60.
386 UNTS 373. Dahomey. Succession 12 Dec 60.
390 UNTS 344. Niger. Succession 27 Feb 61.
401 UNTS 235. Mauritius. Succession 20 Jun 61.
444 UNTS 314. Algeria. Succession 19 Oct 62. Force 19 Oct 62.
444 UNTS 314. Cameroon. Succession 3 Sep 62.

100616 Multilateral Convention **39 UNTS 151**
SIGNED: 29 Jun 33　　　FORCE: 28 May 47
REGISTERED: 15 Sep 49 ILO (Labor Org)
ARTICLES: 14 LANGUAGE: English. French.
HEADNOTE: FEE-CHARGING EMPLOYMENT AGENCIES
TOPIC: ILO Labor
CONCEPTS: Exceptions and exemptions. Previous treaty extension. Exchange of information and documents. Domestic legislation. Incorporation of treaty provisions into national law. Investigation of violations. ILO conventions. Employment regulations.
INTL ORGS: International Labour Organization.
TREATY REF: 38UNTS3.
PROCEDURE: Amendment. Denunciation. Duration. Ratification. Registration. Renewal or Revival.
PARTIES:
Multilateral
ANNEX
46 UNTS 358. Bulgaria. Ratification 29 Dec 49. Force 29 Dec 50.
54 UNTS 404. Argentina. Ratification 14 Mar 51. Force 14 Mar 51.
66 UNTS 350. Czechoslovakia. Ratification 12 Jun 50. Force 12 Jun 51.

100617 Multilateral Convention **39 UNTS 165**
SIGNED: 29 Jun 33　　　FORCE: 28 May 47
REGISTERED: 15 Sep 49 ILO (Labor Org)
ARTICLES: 30 LANGUAGE: English. French.
HEADNOTE: OLD-AGE INSURANCE WORKERS
TOPIC: ILO Labor
CONCEPTS: Detailed regulations. Exceptions and exemptions. Previous treaty extension. Court procedures. Domestic legislation. Operating agencies. Incorporation of treaty provisions into national law. Investigation of violations. ILO conventions. Old age and invalidity insurance. Sickness and invalidity insurance. Claims and settlements.
INTL ORGS: International Labour Organization.
TREATY REF: 38UNTS3.
PROCEDURE: Amendment. Denunciation. Duration. Ratification. Registration. Renewal or Revival.
PARTIES:
Multilateral
ANNEX
46 UNTS 359. Bulgaria. Ratification 29 Dec 49. Force 29 Dec 50.
204 UNTS 340. Argentina. Ratification 17 Feb 55. Force 17 Feb 56.
423 UNTS 293. Ecuador. Ratification 5 Feb 62. Force 5 Feb 63.
495 UNTS 282. UK Great Britain. Declaration 13 Apr 64.
499 UNTS 364. UK Great Britain. Gibralter.
499 UNTS 364. UK Great Britain. Malta.
499 UNTS 364. UK Great Britain. Falkland Islands.
504 UNTS 339. UK Great Britain. St. Vincent. Declaration 12 Jun 64.
504 UNTS 339. UK Great Britain. St. Helena. Declaration 12 Jun 64.
504 UNTS 339. UK Great Britain. Brit Solomon Is. Declaration 12 Jun 64.
504 UNTS 339. UK Great Britain. Montserrat. Declaration 12 Jun 64.
504 UNTS 339. UK Great Britain. British Guiana. Declaration 7 Jul 64.

504 UNTS 339. UK Great Britain. Barbados. Declaration 7 Jul 64.
504 UNTS 339. UK Great Britain. St. Christopher. Declaration 7 Jul 64.
504 UNTS 339. UK Great Britain. Basutoland. Declaration 7 Jul 64.
510 UNTS 354. UK Great Britain. Dominican Republic. Declaration 3 Aug 64.
515 UNTS 338. UK Great Britain. Seychelles. Declaration 16 Oct 64.
521 UNTS 414. UK Great Britain. Gilbert Islands. Declaration 11 Nov 64.
521 UNTS 414. UK Great Britain. Southern Rhodesia. Declaration 24 Nov 64.
522 UNTS 368. UK Great Britain. Brunei. Declaration 11 Dec 64.
524 UNTS 357. Malta. Ratification 4 Jan 65. Force 4 Jan 65.
530 UNTS 403. UK Great Britain. Seychelles.

100618 Multilateral Convention **39 UNTS 189**
SIGNED: 29 Jun 33　　　FORCE: 28 May 47
REGISTERED: 15 Sep 49 ILO (Labor Org)
ARTICLES: 30 LANGUAGE: English. French.
HEADNOTE: OLD-AGE INSURANCE AGRICULTURAL WORKERS
TOPIC: ILO Labor
CONCEPTS: Detailed regulations. Exceptions and exemptions. Previous treaty extension. Court procedures. Domestic legislation. Operating agencies. Incorporation of treaty provisions into national law. Investigation of violations. ILO conventions. Old age and invalidity insurance. Sickness and invalidity insurance. Migrant worker. Claims and settlements.
INTL ORGS: International Labour Organization.
TREATY REF: 38UNTS3.
PROCEDURE: Amendment. Denunciation. Duration. Ratification. Registration. Renewal or Revival.
PARTIES:
Multilateral
ANNEX
46 UNTS 359. Bulgaria. Ratification 29 Dec 49. Force 29 Dec 50.
204 UNTS 341. Argentina. Ratification 17 Feb 55. Force 17 Feb 56.
353 UNTS 322. Peru. Ratification 1 Feb 60. Force 1 Feb 61.
495 UNTS 283. UK Great Britain. Declaration 13 Apr 64.
499 UNTS 366. UK Great Britain. Malta.
499 UNTS 366. UK Great Britain. Falkland Islands.
504 UNTS 340. UK Great Britain. Antigua. Declaration 12 Jun 64.
504 UNTS 340. UK Great Britain. Montserrat. Declaration 12 Jun 64.
510 UNTS 355. UK Great Britain. Dominican Republic. Declaration 3 Aug 64.
515 UNTS 339. UK Great Britain. Seychelles. Declaration 16 Oct 64.
521 UNTS 415. UK Great Britain. Gilbert Islands. Declaration 11 Nov 64.
521 UNTS 415. UK Great Britain. Southern Rhodesia. Declaration 24 Nov 64.
522 UNTS 369. UK Great Britain. Brunei. Declaration 11 Dec 64.
524 UNTS 358. Malta. Ratification 4 Jan 65. Force 4 Jan 65.
530 UNTS 404. UK Great Britain. Seychelles.

100619 Multilateral Convention **39 UNTS 211**
SIGNED: 29 Jun 33　　　FORCE: 28 May 47
REGISTERED: 15 Sep 49 ILO (Labor Org)
ARTICLES: 31 LANGUAGE: English. French.
HEADNOTE: INVALID INSURANCE WORKERS
TOPIC: ILO Labor
CONCEPTS: Detailed regulations. Exceptions and exemptions. Territorial application. Previous treaty extension. Court procedures. Domestic legislation. Operating agencies. Incorporation of treaty provisions into national law. Investigation of violations. Dispute settlement. ILO conventions. Old age and invalidity insurance. Sickness and invalidity insurance. Claims and settlements.
INTL ORGS: International Labour Organization.
TREATY REF: 38UNTS3.
PROCEDURE: Amendment. Denunciation. Duration. Ratification. Registration. Renewal or Revival.

PARTIES:
Multilateral
ANNEX
46 UNTS 360. Bulgaria. Ratification 29 Dec 49.
Force 29 Dec 50.
423 UNTS 294. Ecuador. Ratification 5 Feb 62.
Force 5 Feb 63.
495 UNTS 284. UK Great Britain. Declaration
13 Apr 64.
510 UNTS 356. UK Great Britain. Dominican
Republic. Declaration 3 Aug 64.
515 UNTS 340. UK Great Britain. St. Lucia. Declaration 16 Oct 64.
521 UNTS 416. UK Great Britain. Gilbert Islands.
Declaration 11 Nov 64.
521 UNTS 416. UK Great Britain. Southern
Rhodesia. Declaration 24 Nov 64.
522 UNTS 370. UK Great Britain. Brunei. Declaration 11 Dec 64.
530 UNTS 405. UK Great Britain. Seychelles.

100620 Multilateral Convention **39 UNTS 235**
SIGNED: 29 Jun 33   FORCE: 28 May 47
REGISTERED: 15 Sep 49 ILO (Labor Org)
ARTICLES: 31 LANGUAGE: English. French.
HEADNOTE: INVALID INSURANCE AGRICUL-
TURAL WORKERS
TOPIC: ILO Labor
CONCEPTS: Detailed regulations. Previous treaty
extension. Court procedures. Domestic legisla-
tion. Operating agencies. Incorporation of treaty
provisions into national law. Investigation of vio-
lations. ILO conventions. Old age and invalidity
insurance. Migrant worker. Sickness and invalidity insurance. Claims and settlements.
INTL ORGS: International Labour Organization.
TREATY REF: 38UNTS3.
PROCEDURE: Amendment. Denunciation. Duration. Ratification. Registration. Renewal or Revival.
PARTIES:
Multilateral
ANNEX
46 UNTS 360. Bulgaria. Ratification 29 Dec 49.
Force 29 Dec 50.
353 UNTS 322. Peru. Ratification 1 Feb 60. Force
1 Feb 61.
495 UNTS 285. UK Great Britain. Declaration
13 Apr 64.
510 UNTS 357. UK Great Britain. Dominican
Republic. Declaration 3 Aug 64.
515 UNTS 341. UK Great Britain. St. Lucia. Declaration 16 Oct 64.
521 UNTS 417. UK Great Britain. Gilbert Islands.
Declaration 11 Nov 64.
521 UNTS 417. UK Great Britain. Southern
Rhodesia. Declaration 24 Nov 64.
522 UNTS 371. UK Great Britain. Brunei. Declaration 11 Dec 64.
530 UNTS 406. UK Great Britain. Seychelles.

100621 Multilateral Convention **39 UNTS 259**
SIGNED: 29 Jun 33   FORCE: 8 Nov 46
REGISTERED: 15 Sep 49 ILO (Labor Org)
ARTICLES: 33 LANGUAGE: English. French.
HEADNOTE: WIDOWS ORPHANS INSURANCE
WORKERS
TOPIC: ILO Labor
CONCEPTS: Detailed regulations. Exceptions and
exemptions. Previous treaty extension. Privi-
leges and immunities. Domestic legislation. Op-
erating agencies. Incorporation of treaty provi-
sions into national law. ILO conventions. Old age
and invalidity insurance. Sickness and invalidity
insurance. Migrant worker. Claims and settle-
ments.
INTL ORGS: International Labour Organization.
TREATY REF: 38UNTS3.
PROCEDURE: Amendment. Denunciation. Duration. Ratification. Registration. Renewal or Revival.
PARTIES:
Multilateral
ANNEX
46 UNTS 361. Bulgaria. Ratification 29 Dec 49.
Force 29 Dec 50.
149 UNTS 403. Italy. Ratification 22 Oct 52.
Force 22 Oct 53.
423 UNTS 295. Ecuador. Ratification 5 Feb 62.
Force 5 Feb 63.
495 UNTS 286. UK Great Britain. Declaration
13 Apr 61.

499 UNTS 370. UK Great Britain. Gibralter.
499 UNTS 370. UK Great Britain. Malta.
510 UNTS 358. UK Great Britain. Dominican
Republic. Declaration 3 Aug 64.
515 UNTS 342. UK Great Britain. St. Lucia. Declaration 16 Oct 64.
521 UNTS 418. UK Great Britain. Gilbert Islands.
Declaration 11 Nov 64.
521 UNTS 418. UK Great Britain. Southern
Rhodesia. Declaration 24 Nov 64.
522 UNTS 372. UK Great Britain. Brunei. Declaration 11 Dec 64.
530 UNTS 407. UK Great Britain. Seychelles.

100622 Multilateral Convention **39 UNTS 285**
SIGNED: 29 Jun 33   FORCE: 29 Sep 49
REGISTERED: 15 Sep 49 ILO (Labor Org)
ARTICLES: 33 LANGUAGE: English. French.
HEADNOTE: WIDOWS ORPHANS INSURANCE
AGRICULTURAL WORKERS
TOPIC: ILO Labor
CONCEPTS: Detailed regulations. Exceptions and
exemptions. Previous treaty extension. Privi-
leges and immunities. Domestic legislation. Op-
erating agencies. Incorporation of treaty provi-
sions into national law. ILO conventions. Old age
and invalidity insurance. Sickness and invalidity
insurance. Migrant worker. Attachment of funds.
INTL ORGS: International Labour Organization.
TREATY REF: 38UNTS3.
PARTIES:
Multilateral
ANNEX
46 UNTS 361. Bulgaria. Ratification 29 Dec 49.
Force 29 Dec 50.
149 UNTS 403. Italy. Ratification 22 Oct 52.
Force 22 Oct 53.
353 UNTS 323. Peru. Ratification 1 Feb 60. Force
1 Feb 61.
495 UNTS 287. UK Great Britain. Declaration
13 Apr 61.
499 UNTS 372. UK Great Britain. Malta.
504 UNTS 344. UK Great Britain. Basutoland.
Declaration 7 Jul 64.
504 UNTS 344. UK Great Britain. Barbados. Declaration 7 Jul 64.
504 UNTS 344. UK Great Britain. British Guinea.
Declaration 7 Jul 64.
504 UNTS 344. UK Great Britain. St. Christopher.
Declaration 7 Jul 64.
504 UNTS 344. UK Great Britain. Montserrat. Declaration 12 Jul 64.
504 UNTS 344. UK Great Britain. St. Helena. Declaration 12 Jul 64.
504 UNTS 344. UK Great Britain. St. Vincent. Declaration 12 Jul 64.
504 UNTS 344. UK Great Britain. Brit Solomon Is.
Declaration 12 Jul 64.
504 UNTS 344. UK Great Britain. Antigua. Declaration 12 Jul 64.
510 UNTS 359. UK Great Britain. Declaration
13 Aug 64.
515 UNTS 343. UK Great Britain. St. Lucia. Declaration 16 Oct 64.
521 UNTS 419. UK Great Britain. Gilbert Islands.
Declaration 11 Nov 64.
521 UNTS 419. UK Great Britain. Southern
Rhodesia. Declaration 24 Nov 64.
522 UNTS 373. UK Great Britain. Brunei. Declaration 11 Dec 64.
530 UNTS 408. UK Great Britain. Seychelles.

100623 Multilateral Convention **40 UNTS 3**
SIGNED: 19 Jun 34   FORCE: 28 May 47
REGISTERED: 15 Sep 49 ILO (Labor Org)
ARTICLES: 15 LANGUAGE: English. French.
HEADNOTE: EMPLOYMENT WOMEN DURING
NIGHT
TOPIC: ILO Labor
CONCEPTS: Definition of terms. Exceptions and
exemptions. Previous treaty extension. ILO con-
ventions. Employment regulations. Holidays and
rest periods.
INTL ORGS: International Labour Organization.
TREATY REF: 38UNTS3.
PROCEDURE: Amendment. Denunciation. Dura-
tion. Ratification. Registration. Renewal or Re-
vival.
PARTIES:
Multilateral

ANNEX
54 UNTS 404. Argentina. Ratification 14 Mar 51.
Force 14 Mar 51.
71 UNTS 324. Ceylon (Sri Lanka). Ratification
2 Sep 50. Force 2 Sep 51.
107 UNTS 79. Netherlands. Surinam.
249 UNTS 449. Morocco. Ratification 13 Jun 56.
323 UNTS 373. Guinea. Ratification 21 Jan 59.
Force 21 Jan 59.
366 UNTS 380. Togo. Succession 7 Jun 60.
Force 7 Jun 60.
366 UNTS 380. Mali. Succession 21 Jun 60.
Force 21 Jun 60.
380 UNTS 404. Gabon. Succession 14 Oct 60.
Force 14 Oct 60.
380 UNTS 404. Central Afri Rep. Succession
27 Oct 60. Force 27 Oct 60.
381 UNTS 372. Mali. Succession 22 Sep 60.
Force 22 Sep 60.
384 UNTS 349. Chad. Succession 10 Nov 60.
Force 10 Nov 60.
384 UNTS 349. Malagasy. Succession 1 Nov 60.
Force 1 Nov 60.
384 UNTS 349. Senegal. Succession 4 Nov 60.
Force 4 Nov 60.
384 UNTS 349. Congo (Brazzaville). Succession
10 Nov 60. Force 10 Nov 60.
384 UNTS 349. Ivory Coast. Succession
21 Nov 60. Force 21 Nov 61.
384 UNTS 349. Upper Volta. Succession
21 Nov 60. Force 21 Nov 60.
386 UNTS 373. Dahomey. Succession
12 Dec 60.
390 UNTS 345. Niger. Succession 27 Feb 61.

100624 Multilateral Convention **40 UNTS 19**
SIGNED: 21 Jun 34   FORCE: 28 May 47
REGISTERED: 15 Sep 49 ILO (Labor Org)
ARTICLES: 9 LANGUAGE: English. French.
HEADNOTE: WORKMENS COMPENSATION OC-
CUPATIONAL DISEASE
TOPIC: ILO Labor
CONCEPTS: Definition of terms. Detailed regula-
tions. Previous treaty extension. Domestic legis-
lation. ILO conventions. Old age and invalidity
insurance.
INTL ORGS: International Labour Organization.
TREATY REF: 38UNTS3.
PROCEDURE: Amendment. Denunciation. Dura-
tion. Ratification. Registration. Renewal or Re-
vival.
PARTIES:
Multilateral
ANNEX
46 UNTS 362. Finland. Ratification 20 Jan 50.
Force 20 Jan 51.
46 UNTS 362. Bulgaria. Ratification 29 Dec 49.
Force 29 Dec 50.
54 UNTS 405. Argentina. Ratification 14 Mar 51.
Force 14 Mar 51.
107 UNTS 80. Netherlands. Surinam.
123 UNTS 302. South Africa. Ratification
26 Feb 52. Force 26 Feb 53.
133 UNTS 338. Greece. Ratification 13 Jun 52.
Force 13 Jun 53.
149 UNTS 404. Italy. Ratification 22 Oct 52.
Force 22 Oct 53.
193 UNTS 347. Italy. Italian Somaliland.
198 UNTS 377. Bolivia. Ratification 19 Jul 54.
Force 19 Jul 55.
210 UNTS 329. Haiti. Ratification 19 Apr 55.
Force 19 Apr 56.
212 UNTS 388. France. French Guinea.
212 UNTS 388. France. Guadeloupe.
212 UNTS 388. Germany, West. Ratification
17 Jun 55. Force 17 Jun 56.
212 UNTS 388. France. Martinique.
212 UNTS 388. France. Reunion.
225 UNTS 257. Netherlands. Netherlands Antilles.
268 UNTS 356. Burma. Ratification 17 May 57.
Force 17 May 58.
268 UNTS 356. Morocco. Ratification 20 May 57.
Force 20 May 58.
277 UNTS 345. Belgium. Belgian Colonies.
277 UNTS 345. Belgium. Ruanda-Urundi.
286 UNTS 336. South Africa. Southwest Africa.
293 UNTS 368. Luxembourg. Ratification
3 Mar 58. Force 3 Mar 59.
304 UNTS 397. Spain. Ratification 24 Jun 58.
Force 24 Jun 59.
325 UNTS 330. Panama. Ratification 16 Feb 59.
Force 16 Feb 60.

330 UNTS 350. Australia. Ratification 29 Apr 59. Force 29 Apr 60.
381 UNTS 373. Congo (Zaire). Succession 20 Sep 60. Force 20 Sep 60.
390 UNTS 346. Australia. New Guinea.
390 UNTS 346. Australia. Nauru.
390 UNTS 346. Australia. Papua.
443 UNTS 326. Rwanda. Succession 18 Sep 62. Force 18 Sep 62.
444 UNTS 315. Algeria. Succession 19 Oct 62. Force 19 Oct 62.
457 UNTS 348. Burundi. Succession 11 Mar 63.
488 UNTS 352. India. Ratification 13 Jan 64. Force 13 Jan 65.
495 UNTS 288. UK Great Britain. Declaration 13 Apr 61.
499 UNTS 374. UK Great Britain. Gibralter.
499 UNTS 374. UK Great Britain. British Honduras.
499 UNTS 374. UK Great Britain. Malta.
499 UNTS 374. UK Great Britain. Mauritania.
499 UNTS 374. UK Great Britain. Gambia.
504 UNTS 345. UK Great Britain. Swaziland.
504 UNTS 345. UK Great Britain. Barbados.
511 UNTS 321. UK Great Britain. Basutoland.
511 UNTS 321. UK Great Britain. St. Christopher.
511 UNTS 321. UK Great Britain. Nevis.
511 UNTS 321. UK Great Britain. Anguilla.
515 UNTS 344. UK Great Britain. Bechuanaland.
515 UNTS 344. UK Great Britain. Montserrat.
521 UNTS 420. UK Great Britain. St. Lucia.
521 UNTS 420. UK Great Britain. Gilbert Islands. Declaration 11 Nov 65.
521 UNTS 420. Honduras. Ratification 17 Nov 64. Force 17 Nov 65.
521 UNTS 420. UK Great Britain. Southern Rhodesia. Declaration 24 Nov 64.
521 UNTS 420. UK Great Britain. British Somaliland.
521 UNTS 420. UK Great Britain. British Guiana.
524 UNTS 359. Malta. Ratification 4 Jan 65. Force 4 Jan 65.
530 UNTS 409. UK Great Britain. Gilbert Islands. Declaration 30 Mar 65.
530 UNTS 409. UK Great Britain. Hong Kong. Declaration 30 Mar 65.
533 UNTS 397. UK Great Britain. Brunei.
545 UNTS 378. UK Great Britain. Declaration 20 Jul 65.
545 UNTS 378. UK Great Britain. Fiji Islands.
547 UNTS 365. UK Great Britain. Declaration 24 Sep 65.
559 UNTS 382. UK Great Britain. Bermuda.
560 UNTS 312. UK Great Britain. St. Lucia.
567 UNTS 345. Guyana. Ratification 8 Jun 66. Force 8 Jun 66.
600 UNTS 405. UK Great Britain. Gilbert Islands. Declaration 7 Jun 67.

100625 Multilateral Convention **40 UNTS 33**
SIGNED: 21 Jun 34   FORCE: 28 May 47
REGISTERED: 15 Sep 49 ILO (Labor Org)
ARTICLES: 11 LANGUAGE: English. French.
HEADNOTE: WORK HOURS AUTOMATIC SHEET-GLASS WORKERS
TOPIC: ILO Labor
CONCEPTS: Definition of terms. Treaty implementation. Previous treaty extension. Domestic legislation. ILO conventions. Holidays and rest periods.
INTL ORGS: International Labour Organization.
TREATY REF: 38UNTS3.
PROCEDURE: Amendment. Denunciation. Duration. Ratification. Registration. Renewal or Revival.
PARTIES:
Multilateral
ANNEX
46 UNTS 362. Bulgaria. Ratification 29 Dec 49. Force 29 Dec 50.
320 UNTS 322. UK Great Britain. Denunciation 4 Dec 58. Force 4 Dec 59.
401 UNTS 236. Mauritius. Succession 20 Jun 61.

100626 Multilateral Convention **40 UNTS 45**
SIGNED: 23 Jun 34   FORCE: 28 May 47
REGISTERED: 15 Sep 49 ILO (Labor Org)
ARTICLES: 23 LANGUAGE: English. French.
HEADNOTE: ALLOWANCES INVOLUNTARILY UNEMPLOYED WORKERS
TOPIC: ILO Labor
CONCEPTS: Detailed regulations. Exceptions and

exemptions. Previous treaty extension. Exchange of information and documents. Domestic legislation. ILO conventions. Unemployment.
INTL ORGS: International Labour Organization.
TREATY REF: 38UNTS3.
PROCEDURE: Amendment. Denunciation. Duration. Ratification. Registration. Renewal or Revival.
PARTIES:
Multilateral
ANNEX
46 UNTS 363. Bulgaria. Ratification 29 Dec 49. Force 29 Dec 50.
66 UNTS 350. Czechoslovakia. Ratification 12 Jun 50. Force 12 Jun 51.
149 UNTS 404. Italy. Ratification 22 Oct 52. Force 22 Oct 53.
212 UNTS 388. France. Martinique.
212 UNTS 388. France. French Guinea.
212 UNTS 388. France. Guadeloupe.
212 UNTS 388. France. Reunion.
268 UNTS 357. Norway. Ratification 20 May 57. Force 20 May 58.
429 UNTS 261. Peru. Ratification 4 Apr 62. Force 4 Apr 63.
444 UNTS 316. Algeria. Succession 19 Oct 62. Force 19 Oct 62.
457 UNTS 349. UK Great Britain. St. Lucia.
468 UNTS 429. UK Great Britain. Declaration 8 May 62.
471 UNTS 365. UK Great Britain. Grenada.
475 UNTS 376. UK Great Britain. Fed Rhod/-Nyasaland.
499 UNTS 376. UK Great Britain. Malta.
504 UNTS 346. UK Great Britain. Aden. Declaration 12 Jun 64.
504 UNTS 346. UK Great Britain. Basutoland. Declaration 7 Jun 64.
510 UNTS 360. UK Great Britain. Brunei. Declaration 13 Aug 64.
521 UNTS 422. UK Great Britain. Gibralter.
521 UNTS 422. UK Great Britain. Southern Rhodesia. Declaration 24 Nov 64.
527 UNTS 337. UK Great Britain. St. Helena. Declaration 8 Feb 65.
548 UNTS 292. Singapore. Ratification 25 Oct 65. Force 25 Oct 65.
553 UNTS 345. Netherlands. Ratification 17 Jan 66. Force 17 Jan 67.

100627 Multilateral Convention **40 UNTS 63**
SIGNED: 21 Jun 35   FORCE: 28 May 47
REGISTERED: 15 Sep 49 ILO (Labor Org)
ARTICLES: 10 LANGUAGE: English. French.
HEADNOTE: EMPLOYMENT WOMEN UNDERGROUND MINES
TOPIC: ILO Labor
CONCEPTS: Definition of terms. Exceptions and exemptions. Previous treaty extension. Domestic legislation. ILO conventions. Employment regulations.
INTL ORGS: International Labour Organization.
TREATY REF: 38UNTS3.
PROCEDURE: Amendment. Denunciation. Duration. Ratification. Registration. Renewal or Revival.
PARTIES:
Multilateral
ANNEX
46 UNTS 363. Bulgaria. Ratification 29 Dec 49. Force 29 Dec 50.
54 UNTS 405. Argentina. Ratification 14 Mar 51. Force 14 Mar 51.
66 UNTS 351. Czechoslovakia. Ratification 12 Jun 50. Force 12 Jun 51.
77 UNTS 361. Ceylon (Sri Lanka). Ratification 20 Dec 50. Force 20 Dec 51.
104 UNTS 348. Indonesia. Succession 31 May 51.
131 UNTS 314. Yugoslavia. Ratification 21 May 52. Force 21 May 52.
149 UNTS 404. Italy. Ratification 22 Oct 52. Force 22 Oct 53.
167 UNTS 264. Vietnam. Ratification 6 Jun 53. Force 6 Jun 54.
175 UNTS 365. Australia. Ratification 7 Oct 53. Force 7 Oct 54.
193 UNTS 349. Italy. Italian Somaliland.
196 UNTS 338. Ecuador. Ratification 6 Jul 54. Force 6 Jul 55.
201 UNTS 366. Germany, West. Ratification 15 Nov 54. Force 15 Nov 55.
202 UNTS 329. Australia. Papua.

202 UNTS 329. Australia. New Guinea.
248 UNTS 400. Japan. Ratification 11 Jun 56. Force 11 Jun 57.
253 UNTS 382. Morocco. Ratification 20 Sep 56. Force 20 Sep 57.
269 UNTS 278. Tunisia. Ratification 15 May 57. Force 15 May 58.
272 UNTS 252. Poland. Ratification 15 Jun 57. Force 15 Jun 58.
276 UNTS 359. Netherlands. Netherlands Antilles. Declaration 5 Aug 57.
276 UNTS 359. Dominican Republic. Ratification 12 Aug 57. Force 12 Aug 58.
276 UNTS 359. Netherlands. Netherlands Antilles.
282 UNTS 359. Fed of Malaya. Ratification 11 Nov 57. Force 11 Nov 58.
293 UNTS 369. Luxembourg. Ratification 3 Mar 58. Force 3 Mar 59.
304 UNTS 398. Spain. Ratification 24 Jun 58. Force 24 Jun 59.
325 UNTS 331. Panama. Ratification 16 Feb 59. Force 16 Feb 60.
356 UNTS 343. Guatemala. Ratification 7 Mar 60. Force 7 Mar 61.
356 UNTS 343. Costa Rica. Ratification 22 Mar 60. Force 22 Mar 61.
358 UNTS 251. Haiti. Ratification 5 Apr 60. Force 5 Apr 61.
366 UNTS 381. Honduras. Ratification 20 Jun 60. Force 20 Jun 61.
373 UNTS 344. United Arab Rep. Syria.
380 UNTS 405. Nigeria. Succession 17 Oct 60. Force 17 Oct 60.
381 UNTS 374. Cyprus. Succession 23 Sep 60. Force 23 Sep 60.
384 UNTS 350. Somalia. Succession 18 Nov 60. Force 18 Nov 60.
399 UNTS 259. Ivory Coast. Ratification 5 May 61.
399 UNTS 259. USSR (Soviet Union). Ratification 4 May 61. Force 4 May 62.
401 UNTS 237. Gabon. Ratification 13 Jun 61.
401 UNTS 237. Sierra Leone. Succession 13 Jun 61.
406 UNTS 288. Ukrainian SSR. Ratification 4 Aug 61. Force 4 Aug 62.
406 UNTS 288. Byelorussia. Ratification 4 Aug 61. Force 4 Aug 62.
413 UNTS 356. Syria. Ratification 30 Oct 61.
422 UNTS 321. Tanganyika. Succession 30 Jan 62. Force 30 Jan 62.
435 UNTS 303. Lebanon. Ratification 26 Jul 62. Force 26 Jul 63.
443 UNTS 327. Cameroon. Succession 3 Sep 62. Force 3 Sep 62.
455 UNTS 459. Cameroon. Ratification 29 Jan 63.
471 UNTS 366. Uganda. Ratification 4 Jun 63.
488 UNTS 353. Kenya. Ratification 13 Jan 64. Force 13 Jan 64.
495 UNTS 289. UK Great Britain. Declaration 13 Apr 61.
504 UNTS 347. Tanzania. Succession 22 Jun 64.
522 UNTS 374. Zambia. Ratification 2 Dec 64. Force 2 Dec 64.
530 UNTS 410. UK Great Britain. Malawi. Ratification 22 Mar 65.
548 UNTS 394. Singapore. Ratification 25 Oct 65. Force 25 Oct 65.
567 UNTS 345. Guyana. Ratification 8 Jun 66. Force 8 Jun 66.
600 UNTS 406. Sweden. Denunciation 15 Jun 67. Force 15 Jun 68.

100628 Multilateral Convention **40 UNTS 73**
SIGNED: 22 Jun 35   FORCE: 28 May 47
REGISTERED: 15 Sep 49 ILO (Labor Org)
ARTICLES: 29 LANGUAGE: English. French.
HEADNOTE: SCHEME MAINTAINING INVALIDITY OLD-AGE WIDOWS ORPHANS INSURANCE
TOPIC: ILO Labor
CONCEPTS: Definition of terms. Detailed regulations. Previous treaty extension. General cooperation. Exchange of information and documents. Legal protection and assistance. Domestic legislation. Establishment of commission. ILO conventions. Old age and invalidity insurance. Labor statistics. Sickness and invalidity insurance. Indemnities and reimbursements. National treatment.
INTL ORGS: International Labour Organization.
TREATY REF: 38UNTS3.

PROCEDURE: Amendment. Denunciation. Duration. Ratification. Registration. Renewal or Revival.
PARTIES:
Multilateral
ANNEX
66 UNTS 351. Czechoslovakia. Ratification 12 Jun 50. Force 12 Jun 51.
149 UNTS 404. Italy. Ratification 22 Oct 52. Force 22 Oct 53.
455 UNTS 460. Israel. Ratification 16 Jan 63. Force 16 Jan 64.
488 UNTS 354. Czechoslovakia. Denunciation 21 Jan 64. Force 21 Jan 65.

100629 Multilateral Convention **40 UNTS 97**
SIGNED: 25 Jun 35   FORCE: 28 May 47
REGISTERED: 15 Sep 49 ILO (Labor Org)
ARTICLES: 12 LANGUAGE: English. French.
HEADNOTE: HOURS WORK GLASS-BOTTLE WORKS
TOPIC: ILO Labor
CONCEPTS: Definition of terms. Detailed regulations. Exceptions and exemptions. Treaty violation. ILO conventions. Holidays and rest periods. Labor statistics.
INTL ORGS: International Labour Organization.
PROCEDURE: Amendment. Denunciation. Duration. Ratification. Registration. Renewal or Revival.
PARTIES:
Multilateral
ANNEX
46 UNTS 364. Bulgaria. Ratification 29 Dec 49. Force 29 Dec 50.

100630 Multilateral Convention **40 UNTS 109**
SIGNED: 20 Jun 36   FORCE: 28 May 47
REGISTERED: 15 Sep 49 ILO (Labor Org)
ARTICLES: 32 LANGUAGE: English. French.
HEADNOTE: REGULATION SYSTEMS RECRUITING WORKERS
TOPIC: ILO Labor
CONCEPTS: Definition of terms. Detailed regulations. Territorial application. Treaty violation. Previous treaty extension. Repatriation of nationals. Public health. ILO conventions. Employment regulations. Migrant worker. Indemnities and reimbursements. Domestic obligation. General transportation.
INTL ORGS: International Labour Organization.
TREATY REF: 38UNTS3.
PROCEDURE: Amendment. Denunciation. Duration. Ratification. Registration. Renewal or Revival.
PARTIES:
Multilateral
ANNEX
54 UNTS 405. Argentina. Ratification 14 Mar 51. Force 14 Mar 51.
269 UNTS 279. Ghana. Ratification 20 May 57. Force 20 May 57.
282 UNTS 360. Fed of Malaya. Ratification 11 Nov 57. Force 11 Nov 57.
300 UNTS 369. UK Great Britain. Basutoland.
300 UNTS 369. UK Great Britain. Swaziland.
300 UNTS 369. UK Great Britain. Bechuanaland.
380 UNTS 406. Nigeria. Succession 17 Oct 60. Force 17 Oct 60.
381 UNTS 375. Congo (Zaire). Succession 20 Sep 60. Force 20 Sep 60.
384 UNTS 351. Somalia. Succession 18 Nov 60. Force 18 Nov 60.
401 UNTS 238. Sierra Leone. Succession 13 Jun 61.
422 UNTS 322. Tanganyika. Succession 30 Jan 62. Force 30 Jan 62.
429 UNTS 262. UK Great Britain. Zanzibar.
443 UNTS 328. Rwanda. Succession 18 Sep 62. Force 18 Sep 62.
443 UNTS 328. Cameroon. Succession 3 Sep 62. Force 3 Sep 62.
452 UNTS 360. Jamaica. Succession 26 Dec 62.
457 UNTS 350. Burundi. Succession 11 Mar 63.
468 UNTS 430. Trinidad/Tobago. Ratification 24 May 63. Force 24 May 63.
471 UNTS 367. Uganda. Ratification 4 Jun 63.
488 UNTS 355. Kenya. Ratification 13 Jan 64. Force 13 Jan 64.
495 UNTS 290. Malaysia. Malaya. Succession 3 Mar 64.

495 UNTS 290. Malaysia. State of Sabah. Succession 3 Mar 64.
495 UNTS 290. Malaysia. Singapore. Succession 3 Mar 64.
495 UNTS 290. Malaysia. Sarawak. Succession 3 Mar 64.
504 UNTS 348. Tanzania. Succession 22 Jun 64.
522 UNTS 375. Zambia. Ratification 2 Dec 64. Force 2 Dec 64.
527 UNTS 338. UK Great Britain. Bechuanaland.
548 UNTS 395. Singapore. Ratification 25 Oct 65. Force 25 Oct 65.
567 UNTS 346. Malawi. Ratification 7 Jun 66. Force 7 Jun 67.
567 UNTS 346. Guyana. Ratification 8 Jun 66. Force 8 Jun 66.

100631 Multilateral Convention **40 UNTS 137**
SIGNED: 24 Jun 36   FORCE: 28 May 47
REGISTERED: 15 Sep 49 ILO (Labor Org)
ARTICLES: 16 LANGUAGE: English. French.
HEADNOTE: ANNUAL HOLIDAY WITH PAY
TOPIC: ILO Labor
CONCEPTS: Definition of terms. Detailed regulations. Exceptions and exemptions. Treaty violation. Previous treaty extension. General cooperation. ILO conventions. Employment regulations. Labor statistics.
INTL ORGS: International Labour Organization.
TREATY REF: 38UNTS3.
PROCEDURE: Amendment. Denunciation. Duration. Ratification. Registration. Renewal or Revival.
PARTIES:
Multilateral
ANNEX
46 UNTS 364. Bulgaria. Ratification 29 Dec 49. Force 29 Dec 50.
54 UNTS 406. Argentina. Ratification 14 Mar 51. Force 14 Mar 51.
66 UNTS 351. Czechoslovakia. Ratification 12 Jun 50. Force 12 Jun 51.
76 UNTS 276. New Zealand. Ratification 10 Nov 50. Force 10 Nov 51.
100 UNTS 290. Israel. Ratification 22 Aug 51. Force 22 Aug 51.
122 UNTS 338. Finland. Ratification 23 Aug 49. Force 23 Aug 50.
133 UNTS 338. Greece. Ratification 13 Jun 52. Force 13 Jun 53.
149 UNTS 405. Italy. Ratification 22 Oct 52. Force 22 Oct 53.
163 UNTS 374. Yugoslavia. Ratification 26 Mar 53. Force 26 Mar 54.
167 UNTS 264. Vietnam. Ratification 6 Jun 53. Force 6 Jun 54.
172 UNTS 337. Cuba. Ratification 20 Jul 53. Force 20 Jul 54.
191 UNTS 363. Burma. Ratification 21 May 54. Force 21 May 55.
196 UNTS 339. United Arab Rep. Ratification 3 Jul 54. Force 3 Jul 55.
248 UNTS 401. Hungary. Ratification 8 Jun 56. Force 8 Jun 57.
249 UNTS 450. USSR (Soviet Union). Ratification 10 Aug 56. Force 10 Aug 57.
253 UNTS 383. Ukrainian SSR. Ratification 14 Sep 56. Force 14 Sep 57.
253 UNTS 383. Byelorussia. Ratification 6 Nov 56. Force 6 Nov 57.
253 UNTS 383. Morocco. Ratification 20 Sep 56. Force 20 Sep 57.
256 UNTS 332. Dominican Republic. Ratification 5 Dec 56. Force 5 Dec 57.
269 UNTS 279. Tunisia. Ratification 15 May 57. Force 15 May 58.
272 UNTS 252. Albania. Ratification 3 Jun 57. Force 3 Jun 58.
304 UNTS 399. Panama. Ratification 3 Jun 58. Force 3 Jun 59.
353 UNTS 324. Peru. Ratification 1 Feb 60. Force 1 Feb 61.
361 UNTS 234. Iraq. Ratification 12 May 60. Force 12 May 61.
373 UNTS 345. United Arab Rep. Syria.
399 UNTS 260. Ivory Coast. Ratification 5 May 61.
401 UNTS 239. Chad. Ratification 8 Jun 61. Force 8 Jun 62.
401 UNTS 239. Denmark. Faroe Islands.
401 UNTS 239. Gabon. Ratification 13 Jun 61.
410 UNTS 288. Kuwait. Ratification 21 Sep 61. Force 21 Sep 62.

413 UNTS 357. Syria. Ratification 30 Oct 61.
434 UNTS 282. Libya. Ratification 20 Jun 62. Force 20 Jun 63.
435 UNTS 304. Lebanon. Ratification 26 Jul 62. Force 26 Jul 63.
437 UNTS 341. Madagascar. Ratification 10 Aug 62. Force 10 Aug 63.
444 UNTS 317. Senegal. Ratification 22 Oct 62.
471 UNTS 368. Colombia. Ratification 7 Jun 63. Force 7 Jun 64.
483 UNTS 403. Mauritania. Ratification 8 Nov 63. Force 8 Nov 64.
495 UNTS 291. Malaysia. Malaya. Succession 3 Mar 64.
495 UNTS 291. Malaysia. Sarawak. Succession 3 Mar 64.
495 UNTS 291. Malaysia. State of Sabah. Succession 3 Mar 64.
495 UNTS 291. Malaysia. Singapore. Succession 3 Mar 64.
504 UNTS 348. Central Afri Rep. Ratification 9 Jun 64. Force 9 Jun 65.
560 UNTS 314. Paraguay. Ratification 21 Mar 66. Force 21 Mar 67.
642 UNTS 393. Mali. Ratification 12 Jul 68. Force 12 Jul 68.

100632 Multilateral Convention **40 UNTS 153**
SIGNED: 24 Oct 36   FORCE: 28 May 47
REGISTERED: 15 Sep 49 ILO (Labor Org)
ARTICLES: 14 LANGUAGE: English. French.
HEADNOTE: REQUIREMENTS MASTERS OFFICERS MERCHANT SHIPS
TOPIC: ILO Labor
CONCEPTS: Definition of terms. Detailed regulations. Exceptions and exemptions. Territorial application. Treaty violation. Previous treaty extension. Standardization. General cooperation. Incorporation of treaty provisions into national law. Investigation of violations. ILO conventions. Labor statistics. Competency certificate.
INTL ORGS: International Labour Organization.
TREATY REF: 38UNTS3.
PROCEDURE: Amendment. Denunciation. Duration. Ratification. Registration. Renewal or Revival.
PARTIES:
Multilateral
ANNEX
46 UNTS 365. Bulgaria. Ratification 29 Dec 49. Force 29 Dec 50.
149 UNTS 405. Italy. Ratification 22 Oct 52. Force 22 Oct 53.
204 UNTS 341. Argentina. Ratification 17 Feb 55. Force 17 Feb 56.
212 UNTS 389. France. Guadeloupe.
212 UNTS 389. France. Martinique.
212 UNTS 389. France. French Guinea.
212 UNTS 389. France. Reunion.
361 UNTS 235. Liberia. Ratification 9 May 60. Force 9 May 61.
373 UNTS 346. United Arab Rep. Syria.
384 UNTS 352. Philippines. Ratification 17 Nov 60.
399 UNTS 261. Yugoslavia. Ratification 26 May 61. Force 26 May 62.
401 UNTS 240. USA (United States). Micronesia (US).
413 UNTS 358. Syria. Ratification 30 Oct 61.
429 UNTS 263. Peru. Ratification 4 Apr 62. Force 4 Apr 63.
483 UNTS 404. Mauritania. Ratification 8 Nov 63. Force 8 Nov 64.
522 UNTS 376. Taiwan. Ratification 10 Dec 64. Force 10 Dec 65.

100633 Multilateral Convention **40 UNTS 169**
SIGNED: 24 Oct 36   FORCE: 28 May 47
REGISTERED: 15 Sep 49 ILO (Labor Org)
ARTICLES: 20 LANGUAGE: English. French.
HEADNOTE: LIABILITY SHIPOWNER INJURY ETC. SEAMAN
TOPIC: ILO Labor
CONCEPTS: ILO conventions. Holidays and rest periods.
INTL ORGS: International Labour Organization.
TREATY REF: 38UNTS3.
PROCEDURE: Denunciation. Duration.
PARTIES:
Multilateral

ANNEX

46 UNTS 365. Bulgaria. Ratification 29 Dec 49. Force 29 Dec 50.
149 UNTS 405. Italy. Ratification 22 Oct 52. Force 22 Oct 53.
212 UNTS 389. France. Martinique.
212 UNTS 389. France. Guadeloupe.
212 UNTS 389. France. French Guinea.
212 UNTS 389. France. Reunion.
293 UNTS 370. Morocco. Ratification 14 Mar 58. Force 14 Mar 59.
361 UNTS 236. Liberia. Ratification 9 May 60. Force 9 May 61.
429 UNTS 263. Peru. Ratification 4 Apr 62. Force 4 Apr 63.
640 UNTS 383. Greece. Ratification 19 Jun 68. Force 19 Jun 69.

100634 Multilateral Convention **40 UNTS 187**
SIGNED: 24 Oct 36   FORCE: 20 May 47
REGISTERED: 15 Sep 49 ILO (Labor Org)
ARTICLES: 19 LANGUAGE: English. French.
HEADNOTE: SICKNESS INSURANCE SEAMEN
TOPIC: ILO Labor
CONCEPTS: Conditions. Definition of terms. Detailed regulations. Exceptions and exemptions. Territorial application. Non-prejudice to third party. Operating agencies. Personnel. Public health. ILO conventions. Old age and invalidity insurance. Domestic obligation.
INTL ORGS: International Labour Organization.
PROCEDURE: Amendment. Denunciation. Duration. Ratification. Registration. Renewal or Revival.
PARTIES:
Multilateral
ANNEX
46 UNTS 366. Bulgaria. Ratification 29 Dec 49. Force 29 Dec 50.
212 UNTS 390. France. Guadeloupe.
212 UNTS 390. France. Martinique.
212 UNTS 390. France. French Guinea.
212 UNTS 390. France. Reunion.
256 UNTS 333. Germany, West. Ratification 12 Dec 56. Force 12 Dec 57.
314 UNTS 324. Yugoslavia. Ratification 13 Oct 58. Force 13 Oct 59.
320 UNTS 323. UK Great Britain. Malta.
429 UNTS 264. Peru. Ratification 4 Apr 62. Force 4 Apr 63.
444 UNTS 318. Algeria. Succession 19 Oct 62. Force 19 Oct 62.
567 UNTS 347. Norway. Ratification 6 Jun 66. Force 6 Jun 67.

100635 Multilateral Convention **40 UNTS 205**
SIGNED: 24 Oct 36   FORCE: 28 May 47
REGISTERED: 15 Sep 49 ILO (Labor Org)
ARTICLES: 12 LANGUAGE: English. French.
HEADNOTE: MINIMUM AGE EMPLOYMENT CHILDREN SEA
TOPIC: ILO Labor
CONCEPTS: Conditions. Definition of terms. Exceptions and exemptions. Previous treaty extension. Domestic legislation. ILO conventions. Employment regulations. Labor statistics.
INTL ORGS: International Labour Organization.
TREATY REF: 38UNTS3.
PROCEDURE: Amendment. Denunciation. Duration. Future Procedures Contemplated. Ratification. Registration. Renewal or Revival.
PARTIES:
Multilateral
ANNEX
46 UNTS 366. Bulgaria. Ratification 29 Dec 49. Force 29 Dec 50.
102 UNTS 323. Canada. Ratification 10 Sep 51. Force 10 Sep 52.
134 UNTS 377. Mexico. Ratification 18 Jul 52. Force 18 Jul 53.
149 UNTS 405. Italy. Ratification 22 Oct 52. Force 22 Oct 53.
172 UNTS 338. Cuba. Ratification 20 Jul 53. Force 20 Jul 54.
204 UNTS 342. Argentina. Ratification 17 Feb 55. Force 17 Feb 56.
211 UNTS 391. Denmark. Ratification 4 Jun 55. Force 4 Jun 56.
212 UNTS 390. France. Martinique.
212 UNTS 390. France. French Guinea.
212 UNTS 390. France. Reunion.
212 UNTS 390. France. Guadeloupe.

218 UNTS 381. Japan. Ratification 22 Aug 55. Force 22 Aug 56.
249 UNTS 451. USSR (Soviet Union). Ratification 10 Aug 56. Force 10 Aug 57.
249 UNTS 451. Iceland. Ratification 21 Aug 56. Force 21 Aug 57.
253 UNTS 384. Byelorussia. Ratification 6 Nov 56. Force 6 Nov 57.
253 UNTS 384. Ukrainian SSR. Ratification 14 Sep 56. Force 14 Sep 57.
269 UNTS 280. Ghana. Ratification 20 May 57. Force 20 May 57.
272 UNTS 253. Albania. Ratification 3 Jun 57. Force 3 Jun 58.
276 UNTS 360. Netherlands. Netherlands Antilles.
276 UNTS 360. Netherlands. Declaration 5 Aug 57.
302 UNTS 355. Yugoslavia. Ratification 5 May 58. Force 5 May 59.
330 UNTS 351. Ceylon (Sri Lanka). Ratification 18 May 59. Force 18 May 60.
343 UNTS 341. Turkey. Ratification 29 Sep 59. Force 29 Sep 60.
358 UNTS 252. Switzerland. Ratification 21 Apr 60. Force 21 Apr 61.
361 UNTS 237. Liberia. Ratification 9 May 60. Force 9 May 61.
401 UNTS 241. Nigeria. Ratification 16 Jun 61. Force 16 Jun 62.
401 UNTS 241. Sierra Leone. Succession 13 Jun 61.
413 UNTS 359. Syria. Ratification 30 Oct 61.
429 UNTS 264. Peru. Ratification 4 Apr 62. Force 4 Apr 63.
444 UNTS 318. Algeria. Succession 19 Oct 62. Force 19 Oct 62.
452 UNTS 361. Jamaica. Succession 26 Dec 62.
480 UNTS 472. Greece. Ratification 9 Oct 63. Force 9 Oct 64.
483 UNTS 405. Mauritania. Ratification 8 Nov 63. Force 8 Nov 64.
488 UNTS 356. Kenya. Ratification 13 Jan 64. Force 13 Jan 64.
504 UNTS 349. Tanzania. Succession 22 Jun 64.
504 UNTS 349. Tanzania. Succession 22 Jun 64.
522 UNTS 377. Taiwan. Ratification 10 Dec 64. Force 10 Dec 65.

100636 Multilateral Convention **40 UNTS 217**
SIGNED: 22 Jun 37   FORCE: 28 May 47
REGISTERED: 15 Sep 49 ILO (Labor Org)
ARTICLES: 16 LANGUAGE: English. French.
HEADNOTE: MINIMUM AGE EMPLOYMENT CHILDREN INDUSTRY
TOPIC: ILO Labor
CONCEPTS: Definition of terms. Detailed regulations. Exceptions and exemptions. Previous treaty extension. Exchange of information and documents. Domestic legislation. ILO conventions. Employment regulations. Labor statistics.
INTL ORGS: International Labour Organization.
TREATY REF: 38UNTS3.
PROCEDURE: Amendment. Denunciation. Duration. Ratification. Registration. Renewal or Revival.
PARTIES:
Multilateral
ANNEX
149 UNTS 406. Italy. Ratification 22 Oct 52. Force 22 Oct 53.
199 UNTS 316. Cuba. Ratification 7 Sep 54. Force 7 Sep 55.
211 UNTS 392. Pakistan. Ratification 26 May 55. Force 26 May 56.
249 UNTS 452. USSR (Soviet Union). Ratification 10 Aug 56. Force 10 Aug 57.
253 UNTS 385. Byelorussia. Ratification 6 Nov 56. Force 6 Nov 57.
253 UNTS 385. Ukrainian SSR. Ratification 14 Sep 56. Force 14 Sep 57.
269 UNTS 280. Ghana. Ratification 20 May 57. Force 20 May 57.
272 UNTS 253. Albania. Ratification 3 Jun 57. Force 3 Jun 58.
293 UNTS 370. Luxembourg. Ratification 3 Mar 58. Force 3 Mar 59.
373 UNTS 347. Bulgaria. Ratification 22 Jul 64. Force 22 Jul 61.
374 UNTS 375. Iraq. Ratification 5 Jul 60. Force 5 Jul 61.
384 UNTS 353. Philippines. Ratification 17 Nov 60.

401 UNTS 242. Sierra Leone. Ratification 15 Jun 61. Force 15 Jun 62.
401 UNTS 242. Nigeria. Ratification 16 Jun 61. Force 16 Jun 62.
422 UNTS 323. Tanganyika. Succession 30 Jan 62. Force 30 Jan 62.
429 UNTS 265. Peru. Ratification 4 Apr 62. Force 4 Apr 63.
475 UNTS 377. UK Great Britain. Swaziland.
488 UNTS 357. Kenya. Ratification 13 Jan 64. Force 13 Jan 64.
499 UNTS 377. UK Great Britain. Bermuda.
504 UNTS 350. Tanzania. Succession 22 Jun 64.
560 UNTS 314. Paraguay. Ratification 21 Mar 66. Force 21 Mar 67.

100637 Multilateral Convention **40 UNTS 233**
SIGNED: 23 Jun 37   FORCE: 28 May 47
REGISTERED: 15 Sep 49 ILO (Labor Org)
ARTICLES: 25 LANGUAGE: English. French.
HEADNOTE: SAFETY PROVISIONS BUILDING
TOPIC: ILO Labor
CONCEPTS: Detailed regulations. Previous treaty extension. Exchange of information and documents. Incorporation of treaty provisions into national law. Public health. ILO conventions. Safety standards. Domestic obligation.
INTL ORGS: International Labour Organization.
TREATY REF: 38UNTS3.
PROCEDURE: Amendment. Denunciation. Duration. Ratification. Registration. Renewal or Revival. Termination.
PARTIES:
Multilateral
ANNEX
46 UNTS 367. Bulgaria. Ratification 29 Dec 49. Force 29 Dec 50.
54 UNTS 407. Poland. Ratification 17 Apr 50. Force 17 Apr 51.
54 UNTS 407. Netherlands. Ratification 2 May 50. Force 2 May 51.
77 UNTS 362. France. Ratification 16 Dec 50. Force 16 Dec 51.
104 UNTS 349. Belgium. Qualified Ratification 3 Oct 51. Force 3 Oct 52.
107 UNTS 81. Netherlands. Surinam.
212 UNTS 391. Germany, West. Ratification 14 Jun 55. Force 14 Jun 56.
212 UNTS 391. France. Martinique.
212 UNTS 391. France. Guadeloupe.
212 UNTS 391. France. French Guinea.
212 UNTS 391. France. Reunion.
248 UNTS 401. Hungary. Ratification 8 Jun 56. Force 8 Jun 57.
258 UNTS 383. Belgium. Belgian Colonies.
258 UNTS 383. Belgium. Ruanda-Urundi.
304 UNTS 400. Spain. Ratification 24 Jun 58. Force 24 Jun 59.
323 UNTS 374. Tunisia. Ratification 12 Jan 59. Force 12 Jan 60.
381 UNTS 376. Congo (Zaire). Succession 20 Sep 60. Force 20 Sep 60.
429 UNTS 266. Peru. Ratification 4 Apr 62. Force 4 Apr 63.
443 UNTS 329. Rwanda. Succession 18 Sep 62. Force 18 Sep 62.
444 UNTS 319. Algeria. Succession 19 Oct 62. Force 19 Oct 62.
457 UNTS 352. Burundi. Succession 11 Mar 63.
483 UNTS 406. Mauritania. Ratification 8 Nov 63. Force 8 Nov 64.
504 UNTS 350. Central Afri Rep. Ratification 9 Jun 64. Force 9 Jun 65.
521 UNTS 424. Honduras. Ratification 17 Nov 65. Force 17 Nov 65.

100638 Multilateral Convention **40 UNTS 255**
SIGNED: 20 Jun 38   FORCE: 28 May 47
REGISTERED: 15 Sep 49 ILO (Labor Org)
ARTICLES: 315 LANGUAGE: English. French.
HEADNOTE: STATISTICS WAGES HOURS
TOPIC: ILO Labor
CONCEPTS: Definition of terms. Detailed regulations. Exceptions and exemptions. Territorial application. Previous treaty extension. Exchange of official publications. Exchange of information and documents. ILO conventions. Labor statistics.
INTL ORGS: International Labour Organization.
TREATY REF: 38UNTS3.
PROCEDURE: Amendment. Denunciation. Dura-

tion. Ratification. Registration. Renewal or Revival.
PARTIES:
Multilateral

ANNEX

66 UNTS 351. Czechoslovakia. Ratification 12 Jun 50. Force 12 Jun 51.

94 UNTS 312. France. Ratification 28 Jun 51. Force 28 Jun 51.

136 UNTS 389. Ceylon (Sri Lanka). Ratification 25 Aug 52. Force 25 Aug 53.

193 UNTS 350. Germany, West. Ratification 22 Jun 54. Force 22 Jun 55.

199 UNTS 316. Cuba. Ratification 7 Sep 54. Force 7 Sep 55.

210 UNTS 330. Burma. Ratification 4 Mar 55. Force 4 Mar 56.

212 UNTS 391. France. Reunion.

212 UNTS 391. France. French Guinea.

212 UNTS 391. France. Martinique.

212 UNTS 391. France. Guadeloupe.

267 UNTS 369. Chile. Ratification 10 May 57. Force 10 May 68.

318 UNTS 418. Austria. Ratification 26 Nov 58. Force 26 Nov 59.

373 UNTS 348. United Arab Rep. Syria.

401 UNTS 243. Burma. Denunciation 20 Jun 61. Force 20 Jun 62.

406 UNTS 289. Guatemala. Ratification 4 Aug 61. Force 4 Aug 62.

413 UNTS 360. Syria. Ratification 30 Oct 61.

416 UNTS 300. Burma. Ratification 24 Nov 61. Force 24 Nov 62.

444 UNTS 320. Algeria. Succession 19 Oct 62. Force 19 Oct 62.

449 UNTS 279. Tanganyika. Ratification 19 Nov 62.

463 UNTS 376. UK Great Britain. Kenya.

468 UNTS 431. UK Great Britain. Declaration 8 May 62.

475 UNTS 378. UK Great Britain. Fed Rhod/-Nyasaland.

480 UNTS 474. UK Great Britain. Malta.

480 UNTS 474. UK Great Britain. Hong Kong.

480 UNTS 474. UK Great Britain. Zanzibar.

483 UNTS 407. UK Great Britain. Northern Rhodesia.

488 UNTS 358. Kenya. Ratification 13 Jan 64. Force 13 Jan 64.

499 UNTS 278. UK Great Britain. Gambia.

499 UNTS 278. UK Great Britain. Barbados.

499 UNTS 278. UK Great Britain. Gilbert Islands.

504 UNTS 351. UK Great Britain. Gibralter.

504 UNTS 351. UK Great Britain. Basutoland. Declaration 7 Jul 64.

504 UNTS 351. UK Great Britain. Grenada. Declaration 7 Jul 64.

510 UNTS 361. UK Great Britain. Aden. Declaration 13 Aug 64.

521 UNTS 425. UK Great Britain. British Guiana.

521 UNTS 425. UK Great Britain. Southern Rhodesia. Declaration 24 Nov 64.

524 UNTS 360. UK Great Britain. St. Lucia. Declaration 22 Jan 65.

533 UNTS 398. UK Great Britain. Brunei.

533 UNTS 398. UK Great Britain. Bechuanaland.

533 UNTS 398. UK Great Britain. Brunei.

541 UNTS 372. UK Great Britain. St. Helena.

545 UNTS 379. UK Great Britain. Declaration 20 Jul 65.

100639 Multilateral Convention **40 UNTS 281**
SIGNED: 27 Jun 39   FORCE: 8 Jul 48
REGISTERED: 15 Sep 49 ILO (Labor Org)
ARTICLES: 28 LANGUAGE: English. French.
HEADNOTE: REGULATION WRITTEN CONTRACTS EMPLOYMENT
TOPIC: ILO Labor
CONCEPTS: Definition of terms. Detailed regulations. Territorial application. Previous treaty extension. Repatriation of nationals. Domestic legislation. Incorporation of treaty provisions into national law. Public information. Private contracts. Responsibility and liability. Public health. ILO conventions. Employment regulations. Labor statistics.
INTL ORGS: International Labour Organization.
TREATY REF: 38UNTS3.
PROCEDURE: Amendment. Denunciation. Duration. Ratification. Registration. Renewal or Revival.

PARTIES:
Multilateral

ANNEX

269 UNTS 281. Ghana. Ratification 20 May 57. Force 20 May 57.

282 UNTS 361. Fed of Malaya. Ratification 11 Nov 57. Force 11 Nov 57.

356 UNTS 344. UK Great Britain. North Borneo.

380 UNTS 407. Nigeria. Succession 17 Oct 60. Force 17 Oct 60.

381 UNTS 377. Congo (Zaire). Succession 20 Sep 60. Force 20 Sep 60.

384 UNTS 354. Somalia. Succession 18 Nov 60. Force 18 Nov 60.

401 UNTS 244. Sierra Leone. Succession 13 Jun 61.

422 UNTS 324. Tanganyika. Succession 30 Jan 62. Force 30 Jan 62.

425 UNTS 312. UK Great Britain. Bahamas.

443 UNTS 330. Rwanda. Succession 18 Sep 62. Force 18 Sep 62.

443 UNTS 330. Cameroon. Succession 3 Sep 62. Force 3 Sep 62.

452 UNTS 362. Jamaica. Succession 26 Dec 62.

457 UNTS 354. Burundi. Succession 11 Mar 63.

471 UNTS 369. Uganda. Ratification 4 Jun 63.

488 UNTS 359. Kenya. Ratification 13 Jan 64. Force 13 Jan 64.

504 UNTS 352. Tanzania. Succession 22 Jun 64.

522 UNTS 378. Zambia. Ratification 2 Dec 64. Force 2 Dec 64.

548 UNTS 396. Singapore. Ratification 25 Oct 65. Force 25 Oct 65.

567 UNTS 348. Guyana. Ratification 8 Jun 66. Force 8 Jun 66.

567 UNTS 348. Malawi. Ratification 7 Jun 66. Force 7 Jun 67.

100640 Multilateral Convention **40 UNTS 311**
SIGNED: 27 Jun 39   FORCE: 8 Jul 48
REGISTERED: 15 Sep 49 ILO (Labor Org)
ARTICLES: 10 LANGUAGE: English. French.
HEADNOTE: PENAL SANCTION BREACHES CONTRACTS
TOPIC: ILO Labor
CONCEPTS: Definition of terms. Territorial application. Previous treaty extension. Private contracts. Corporations. ILO conventions.
INTL ORGS: International Labour Organization.
TREATY REF: 38UNTS3.
PROCEDURE: Amendment. Denunciation. Duration. Ratification. Registration. Renewal or Revival.
PARTIES:
Multilateral

ANNEX

126 UNTS 358. Italy. Italian Somaliland.

248 UNTS 402. New Zealand. Tokelau Islands.

269 UNTS 281. Ghana. Ratification 20 May 57. Force 20 May 57.

282 UNTS 362. Fed of Malaya. Ratification 11 Nov 57. Force 11 Nov 57.

380 UNTS 408. Nigeria. Succession 17 Oct 60. Force 17 Oct 60.

401 UNTS 245. Sierra Leone. Succession 13 Jun 61.

406 UNTS 290. Guatemala. Ratification 4 Aug 61. Force 4 Aug 62.

422 UNTS 325. Tanganyika. Succession 30 Jan 62. Force 30 Jan 62.

425 UNTS 313. Niger. Ratification 23 Mar 62. Force 23 Mar 62.

431 UNTS 201. Liberia. Ratification 25 May 62. Force 25 May 63.

443 UNTS 331. Cameroon. Succession 3 Sep 62. Force 3 Sep 62.

452 UNTS 363. Jamaica. Succession 26 Dec 62.

452 UNTS 363. Tunisia. Ratification 17 Dec 62. Force 17 Dec 63.

457 UNTS 355. Morocco. Ratification 27 Mar 63. Force 27 Mar 64.

468 UNTS 432. Trinidad/Tobago. Ratification 24 May 63. Force 24 May 63.

471 UNTS 370. Uganda. Ratification 4 Jun 63.

488 UNTS 360. Kenya. Ratification 13 Jan 64. Force 13 Jan 64.

495 UNTS 292. Malaysia. State of Sabah. Succession 3 Mar 64.

495 UNTS 292. Malaysia. Sarawak. Succession 3 Mar 64.

495 UNTS 292. Malaysia. Malaya. Succession 3 Mar 64.

495 UNTS 292. Malaysia. Singapore. Succession 3 Mar 64.

504 UNTS 352. Tanzania. Succession 22 Jun 64.

522 UNTS 379. Zambia. Ratification 2 Dec 64. Force 2 Dec 64.

530 UNTS 411. UK Great Britain. Malawi. Ratification 22 Mar 65.

548 UNTS 397. Singapore. Ratification 25 Oct 65. Force 25 Oct 65.

567 UNTS 349. Guyana. Ratification 8 Jun 66. Force 8 Jun 66.

100641 Bilateral Convention **41 UNTS 3**
SIGNED: 29 Nov 48   FORCE: 23 Jun 49
REGISTERED: 19 Sep 49 Belgium
ARTICLES: 15 LANGUAGE: French.
HEADNOTE: CULTURAL CONVENTION
TOPIC: Culture
CONCEPTS: Friendship and amity. Conformity with municipal law. Personnel. Exchange. Commissions and foundations. Teacher and student exchange. Professorships. Institute establishment. Scholarships and grants. Vocational training. Exchange. General cultural cooperation. Artists. Scientific exchange. Publications exchange. Mass media exchange.
INTL ORGS: Special Commission.
PROCEDURE: Amendment. Denunciation. Duration. Ratification. Renewal or Revival.
PARTIES:
Belgium
Italy

100642 Bilateral Exchange **41 UNTS 13**
SIGNED: 15 Jul 49   FORCE: 1 Aug 49
REGISTERED: 19 Sep 49 Belgium
ARTICLES: 2 LANGUAGE: French.
HEADNOTE: FREEDOM MOVEMENT PERSONS
TOPIC: Visas
CONCEPTS: Border traffic and migration. Non-visa travel documents. Frontier permits.
PARTIES:
Belgium
Luxembourg

100643 Multilateral Treaty **41 UNTS 21**
SIGNED: 10 Feb 47   FORCE: 15 Sep 47
REGISTERED: 21 Sep 49 USA (United States)
ARTICLES: 38 LANGUAGE: Bulgarian. English French. Russian.
HEADNOTE: TREATY PEACE
TOPIC: Peace/Disarmament
CONCEPTS: Definition of terms. Time limit. Annex or appendix reference. Repatriation of nationals. Nazi organizations. Democratic institutions. Human rights. General cooperation. Exchange of information and documents. Free passage and transit. Legal protection and assistance. General property. Revival of treaties. Use of facilities. Investigation of violations. Procedure. Conciliation. Competence of tribunal. Archives and objects. Exchange rates and regulations. Lump sum settlements. Assets transfer. Most favored nation clause. National treatment. Tax exemptions. Rearmament restrictions and controls. Armistice and peace. Reparations and restrictions. Post war claims settlement. Disarmament and demilitarization. Withdrawal of occupation. Markers and definitions.
INTL ORGS: League of Nations. International Civil Aviation Organization. United Nations. Special Commission.
TREATY REF: 26UNTS115.
PROCEDURE: Accession. Ratification.
PARTIES:
Australia SIGNED: 10 Feb 47 RATIFIED 10 Jul 48 FORCE: 10 Jul 48
Bulgaria SIGNED: 10 Feb 47 RATIFIED 15 Sep 47 FORCE: 15 Sep 47
Byelorussia SIGNED: 10 Feb 47
Czechoslovakia SIGNED: 10 Feb 47 RATIFIED 14 Oct 47 FORCE: 14 Oct 47
Greece SIGNED: 10 Feb 47 RATIFIED 14 Nov 47 FORCE: 14 Nov 47
India SIGNED: 10 Feb 47 RATIFIED: 19 Sep 47 FORCE: 19 Sep 47
New Zealand SIGNED: 10 Feb 47 RATIFIED 31 Dec 47 FORCE: 31 Dec 47
South Africa SIGNED: 10 Feb 47 RATIFIED 17 May 48 FORCE: 17 May 48

UK Great Britain SIGNED: 10 Feb 47 RATIFIED: 15 Sep 47 FORCE: 15 Sep 47
USA (United States) SIGNED: 10 Feb 47 RATIFIED: 15 Sep 47 FORCE: 15 Sep 47
Ukrainian SSR SIGNED: 10 Feb 47
USSR (Soviet Union) SIGNED: 10 Feb 47 RATIFIED: 15 Sep 47 FORCE: 15 Sep 47
Yugoslavia SIGNED: 10 Feb 47 RATIFIED: 19 Sep 47 FORCE: 19 Sep 47

100644 Multilateral Treaty **41 UNTS 135**
SIGNED: 10 Feb 47 FORCE: 15 Sep 47
REGISTERED: 21 Sep 49 USA (United States)
ARTICLES: 42 LANGUAGE: English. French. Hungarian. Russian.
HEADNOTE: TREATY PEACE
TOPIC: Peace/Disarmament
CONCEPTS: Definition of terms. Time limit. Annex or appendix reference. Repatriation of nationals. Nazi organizations. Democratic institutions. Human rights. General cooperation. Exchange of information and documents. Free passage and transit. Legal protection and assistance. General property. Revival of treaties. Use of facilities. Investigation of violations. Procedure. Competence of tribunal. Archives and objects. Exchange rates and regulations. Lump sum settlements. Assets transfer. Most favored nation clause. Rearmament restrictions and controls. Armistice and peace. Post-war claims settlement. Disarmament and demilitarization. Withdrawal of occupation. Markers and definitions.
INTL ORGS: League of Nations. International Civil Aviation Organization. United Nations. Special Commission.
PROCEDURE: Accession. Ratification.
PARTIES:
Australia SIGNED: 10 Feb 47 RATIFIED: 10 Jul 48 FORCE: 10 Jul 48
Byelorussia SIGNED: 10 Feb 47
Canada SIGNED: 10 Feb 47 RATIFIED: 19 Sep 47 FORCE: 19 Sep 47
Czechoslovakia SIGNED: 10 Feb 47 RATIFIED: 14 Oct 47 FORCE: 14 Oct 47
Hungary SIGNED: 10 Feb 47
India SIGNED: 10 Feb 47 RATIFIED: 19 Sep 47 FORCE: 19 Sep 47
New Zealand SIGNED: 10 Feb 47 RATIFIED: 31 Dec 47 FORCE: 31 Dec 47
South Africa SIGNED: 10 Feb 47 RATIFIED: 17 May 48 FORCE: 17 May 48
UK Great Britain SIGNED: 10 Feb 47 RATIFIED: 15 Sep 47 FORCE: 15 Sep 47
USA (United States) SIGNED: 10 Feb 47 RATIFIED: 15 Sep 47 FORCE: 15 Sep 47
Ukrainian SSR SIGNED: 10 Feb 47
USSR (Soviet Union) SIGNED: 10 Feb 47 RATIFIED: 15 Sep 47 FORCE: 15 Sep 47
Yugoslavia SIGNED: 10 Feb 47 RATIFIED: 19 Sep 47 FORCE: 19 Sep 47

100645 Multilateral Treaty **42 UNTS 3**
SIGNED: 10 Feb 47 FORCE: 15 Sep 47
REGISTERED: 21 Sep 49 USA (United States)
ARTICLES: 40 LANGUAGE: English. French. Russian. Romanian.
HEADNOTE: TREATY PEACE
TOPIC: Peace/Disarmament
CONCEPTS: Peaceful relations. Repatriation of nationals. Democratic institutions. Procedure. Monetary and gold transfers. Claims and settlements. Post-war reconstruction. Repatriation of combatants. Rearmament restrictions and controls. Return of equipment and recapture. Equipment and supplies. Restrictions on transfer. Foreign nationals. Reconversion to normalcy. Arms limitations. War claims and reparations. Enemy financial interests. Reparations and restrictions. Post-war claims settlement.
INTL ORGS: League of Nations. International Civil Aviation Organization. United Nations. Special Commission.
PARTIES:
Australia SIGNED: 10 Feb 47 RATIFIED: 10 Jul 48 FORCE: 10 Jul 48
Byelorussia SIGNED: 10 Feb 47
Canada SIGNED: 10 Feb 47 RATIFIED: 19 Sep 47 FORCE: 19 Sep 47
Czechoslovakia SIGNED: 10 Feb 47 RATIFIED: 14 Oct 47 FORCE: 14 Oct 47
India SIGNED: 10 Feb 47 RATIFIED: 19 Sep 47 FORCE: 19 Sep 47

New Zealand SIGNED: 10 Feb 47 RATIFIED: 31 Dec 47 FORCE: 31 Dec 47
Romania SIGNED: 10 Feb 47
Ukrainian SSR SIGNED: 10 Feb 47
USSR (Soviet Union) SIGNED: 10 Feb 47 RATIFIED: 15 Sep 47 FORCE: 15 Sep 47

100646 Bilateral Agreement **42 UNTS 125**
SIGNED: 9 Sep 49 FORCE: 24 Aug 49
REGISTERED: 3 Oct 49 Norway
ARTICLES: 42 LANGUAGE: Norwegian. Spanish.
HEADNOTE: COMMERCE FINANCE
TOPIC: Finance
CONCEPTS: Detailed regulations. General provisions. Treaty implementation. Annex or appendix reference. Previous treaty replacement. Standardization. General cooperation. Licenses and permits. Responsibility and liability. Use of facilities. Establishment of commission. General trade. Certificates of origin. Reciprocity in trade. Reexport of goods, etc.. Trade agencies. Trade procedures. Accounting procedures. Banking. Balance of payments. Monetary and gold transfers. Exchange rates and regulations. Interest rates. Payment schedules. Non-interest rates and fees. Transportation costs. Local currency. Assets. Most favored nation clause. Credit provisions. Purchase authorization. Water transport. Ports and pilotage.
INTL ORGS: International Monetary Fund. Special Commission.
PROCEDURE: Denunciation. Duration. Ratification. Renewal or Revival.
PARTIES:
Argentina
Norway

100647 Bilateral Exchange **42 UNTS 183**
SIGNED: 18 Jun 46 FORCE: 18 Jun 46
REGISTERED: 5 Oct 49 USA (United States)
ARTICLES: 2 LANGUAGE: English. French.
HEADNOTE: AIR SERVICES
TOPIC: Air Transport
CONCEPTS: Airport facilities. Airport equipment. Airworthiness certificates. Conditions of airlines operating permission. Overflights and technical stops. Operating authorizations and regulations. Licenses and certificates of nationality.
INTL ORGS: International Civil Aviation Organization.
PARTIES:
France
USA (United States)

100648 Bilateral Exchange **42 UNTS 199**
SIGNED: 31 Jul 46 FORCE: 31 Jul 46
REGISTERED: 5 Oct 49 USA (United States)
ARTICLES: 2 LANGUAGE: English.
HEADNOTE: AIR SERVICE FACILITIES TRANSFER MAINTENANCE RADIO RANGE SSC 51 EQUIPMENT
TOPIC: Air Transport
CONCEPTS: Exceptions and exemptions. Personnel. Navigational conditions. Airport facilities. Airport equipment. Operating authorizations and regulations. Facilities and equipment. Surplus war property. Bases and facilities.
INTL ORGS: International Civil Aviation Organization.
TREATY REF: 4UNTS88.
PARTIES:
UK Great Britain
USA (United States)

100649 Bilateral Agreement **42 UNTS 213**
SIGNED: 30 Sep 46 FORCE: 30 Sep 46
REGISTERED: 5 Oct 49 USA (United States)
ARTICLES: 8 LANGUAGE: English.
HEADNOTE: AIR SERVICE FACILITIES SWEDEN
TOPIC: Air Transport
CONCEPTS: Change of circumstances. General cooperation. Personnel. Meteorology. Fees and exemptions. Routes and logistics. Airport facilities. Airport equipment. Operating authorizations and regulations. Bands and frequency allocation. Facilities and equipment. Facilities and property.
INTL ORGS: International Civil Aviation Organization.
TREATY REF: USA EXEC.SERIES 469; 59STAT1516.

PARTIES:
Sweden
USA (United States)

100650 Bilateral Exchange **42 UNTS 219**
SIGNED: 1 Oct 46 FORCE: 1 Oct 46
REGISTERED: 5 Oct 49 USA (United States)
ARTICLES: 2 LANGUAGE: English.
HEADNOTE: AIR SERVICE FACILITIES KASTRUP AIRPORT DENMARK
TOPIC: Air Transport
CONCEPTS: General cooperation. Personnel. Meteorology. Non-interest rates and fees. Materials, equipment and services. Routes and logistics. Airport facilities. Operating authorizations and regulations. Facilities and equipment. Surplus war property. Bases and facilities.
INTL ORGS: International Civil Aviation Organization.
TREATY REF: USA EXEC.SERIES 469; 59STAT1516.
PARTIES:
Denmark
USA (United States)

100651 Bilateral Agreement **42 UNTS 227**
SIGNED: 12 Nov 46 FORCE: 12 Nov 46
REGISTERED: 5 Oct 49 USA (United States)
ARTICLES: 6 LANGUAGE: English.
HEADNOTE: AIR COMMUNICATIONS FACILITIES GARDERMOEN AIRFIELD NORWAY
TOPIC: Air Transport
CONCEPTS: Change of circumstances. General cooperation. Personnel. Fees and exemptions. Materials, equipment and services. Routes and logistics. Airport facilities. Airport equipment. Operating authorizations and regulations. Bands and frequency allocation. Facilities and equipment. Surplus war property. Facilities and property.
INTL ORGS: International Civil Aviation Organization.
TREATY REF: USA EXEC.SERIES 469; 59STAT1516.
PARTIES:
Norway
USA (United States)

100652 Bilateral Agreement **42 UNTS 235**
SIGNED: 30 Apr 47 FORCE: 30 Apr 47
REGISTERED: 5 Oct 49 USA (United States)
ARTICLES: 5 LANGUAGE: English.
HEADNOTE: AIRPORT EQUIPMENT
TOPIC: Specif Goods/Equip
CONCEPTS: Airport facilities. Airport equipment. Facilities and property.
INTL ORGS: International Civil Aviation Organization.
PARTIES:
Switzerland
USA (United States)

100653 Bilateral Agreement **42 UNTS 241**
SIGNED: 8 May 47 FORCE: 8 May 47
REGISTERED: 5 Oct 49 USA (United States)
ARTICLES: 10 LANGUAGE: English.
HEADNOTE: AIR SERVICE FACILITIES DON MUANG AIRPORT BANGKAAI SIAM
TOPIC: Air Transport
CONCEPTS: Change of circumstances. General cooperation. Personnel. Responsibility and liability. Meteorology. Fees and exemptions. Materials, equipment and services. Routes and logistics. Navigational conditions. Airport facilities. Airport equipment. Operating authorizations and regulations. Bands and frequency allocation. Facilities and equipment. Surplus war property. Withdrawal of forces. Bases and facilities.
INTL ORGS: International Civil Aviation Organization.
TREATY REF: USA EXEC.SERIES 469; 59STAT1516.
PARTIES:
Thailand
USA (United States)

100654 Bilateral Agreement **42 UNTS 251**
SIGNED: 24 Feb 49 FORCE: 24 Feb 49
REGISTERED: 6 Oct 49 Israel

ARTICLES: 12 LANGUAGE: English.
HEADNOTE: GENERAL ARMISTICE
TOPIC: Peace/Disarmament
CONCEPTS: Repatriation of combatants. Prisoners of war. Withdrawal of forces. Armistice and peace. Loss and/or damage.
INTL ORGS: United Nations. Special Commission.
TREATY REF: 118LTS303,122LTS367,ETC,-31UNTS497.
PROCEDURE: Ratification.
PARTIES:
Israel
United Arab Rep
ANNEX
70 UNTS 274. United Arab Rep. Supplementation 22 Feb 50. Force 22 Feb 50.
70 UNTS 274. Israel. Supplementation 22 Feb 50. Force 22 Feb 50.

100655 Bilateral Agreement **42 UNTS 287**
SIGNED: 23 Mar 49 FORCE: 23 Mar 49
REGISTERED: 6 Oct 49 Israel
ARTICLES: 8 LANGUAGE: English. French.
HEADNOTE: GENERAL ARMISTICE
TOPIC: Peace/Disarmament
CONCEPTS: Definition of terms. Detailed regulations. Annex or appendix reference. Non-prejudice to UN charter. Peaceful relations. Repatriation of nationals. Exchange of information and documents. Inspection and observation. Establishment of commission. Procedure. Indemnities and reimbursements. Claims and settlements. Self-defense. Withdrawal of forces. Armistice and peace. Markers and definitions.
INTL ORGS: United Nations. Special Commission.
TREATY REF: 31UNTS497.
PROCEDURE: Amendment. Future Procedures Contemplated.
PARTIES:
Israel
Lebanon

100656 Bilateral Agreement **42 UNTS 303**
SIGNED: 3 Apr 49 FORCE: 3 Apr 49
REGISTERED: 6 Oct 49 Israel
ARTICLES: 12 LANGUAGE: English.
HEADNOTE: GENERAL ARMISTICE
TOPIC: Peace/Disarmament
CONCEPTS: Definition of terms. Detailed regulations. Annex or appendix reference. Non-prejudice to UN charter. Peaceful relations. Repatriation of nationals. Exchange of information and documents. Inspection and observation. Establishment of commission. Procedure. Indemnities and reimbursements. Claims and settlements. Self-defense. Withdrawal of forces. Armistice and peace. Markers and definitions.
INTL ORGS: United Nations. Special Commission.
PROCEDURE: Amendment. Future Procedures Contemplated.
PARTIES:
Israel
Jordan

100657 Bilateral Agreement **42 UNTS 327**
SIGNED: 20 Jul 49 FORCE: 20 Jul 49
REGISTERED: 6 Oct 49 Israel
ARTICLES: 8 LANGUAGE: English. French.
HEADNOTE: GENERAL ARMISTICE
TOPIC: Peace/Disarmament
CONCEPTS: Definition of terms. Detailed regulations. Annex or appendix reference. Non-prejudice to UN charter. Peaceful relations. Repatriation of nationals. Exchange of information and documents. Inspection and observation. Establishment of commission. Procedure. Indemnities and reimbursements. Claims and settlements. Self-defense. Withdrawal of forces. Armistice and peace. Markers and definitions.
INTL ORGS: United Nations. Special Commission.
PARTIES:
Israel
Syria

100658 Bilateral Agreement **43 UNTS 3**
SIGNED: 5 Feb 46 FORCE: 5 Feb 46
REGISTERED: 10 Oct 49 Canada
ARTICLES: 11 LANGUAGE: English.
HEADNOTE: PAYMENTS
TOPIC: Finance

CONCEPTS: Definition of terms. Detailed regulations. Treaty interpretation. Previous treaty extension. Previous treaty replacement. General cooperation. General trade. Accounting procedures. Banking. Bonds. Currency. Monetary and gold transfers. Exchange rates and regulations. Interest rates. Payment schedules. Loan and credit. Loan repayment. Terms of loan.
TREATY REF: 1MAY45.
PARTIES:
Canada
Netherlands

100659 Bilateral Agreement **43 UNTS 23**
SIGNED: 7 Feb 46 FORCE: 7 Feb 46
REGISTERED: 10 Oct 49 Canada
ARTICLES: 10 LANGUAGE: English.
HEADNOTE: TRADE FINANCE
TOPIC: Finance
CONCEPTS: Definition of terms. General trade. Accounting procedures. Banking. Bonds. Currency. Interest rates. Payment schedules. Loan and credit. Loan repayment. Terms of loan.
PARTIES:
Canada
Taiwan

100660 Bilateral Agreement **43 UNTS 43**
SIGNED: 9 Apr 46 FORCE: 2 May 46
REGISTERED: 10 Oct 49 Canada
ARTICLES: 10 LANGUAGE: English. French.
HEADNOTE: COMMERCE FINANCE
TOPIC: Finance
CONCEPTS: Definition of terms. Territorial application. General trade. Accounting procedures. Banking. Bonds. Currency. Interest rates. Payment schedules. Loan and credit. Terms of loan.
PROCEDURE: Ratification.
PARTIES:
Canada
France

100661 Bilateral Agreement **43 UNTS 67**
SIGNED: 6 Jun 46 FORCE: 6 Jun 46
REGISTERED: 10 Oct 49 Canada
ARTICLES: 10 LANGUAGE: English.
HEADNOTE: FINANCE
TOPIC: Finance
CONCEPTS: Annex type material. Loan and credit.
TREATY REF: CTS,1945 NO-29.
PARTIES:
Canada
Norway

100662 Bilateral Agreement **43 UNTS 81**
SIGNED: 28 Jun 46 FORCE: 28 Jun 46
REGISTERED: 10 Oct 49 Canada
ARTICLES: 7 LANGUAGE: English.
HEADNOTE: FINANCE
TOPIC: Finance
CONCEPTS: Annex type material. Loan repayment.
TREATY REF: CTS,1945 NO-29.
PARTIES:
Canada
Czechoslovakia

100663 Bilateral Exchange **43 UNTS 97**
SIGNED: 19 May 47 FORCE: 19 May 47
REGISTERED: 10 Oct 49 Canada
ARTICLES: 2 LANGUAGE: English.
HEADNOTE: EXCHANGE AGRICULTURAL LABOR MACHINERY
TOPIC: Non-ILO Labor
CONCEPTS: Annex type material. Non-ILO labor relations.
TREATY REF: CANADA T.S. 1947 NO.2.
PARTIES:
Canada
USA (United States)
ANNEX
253 UNTS 310. USA (United States).
253 UNTS 310. Canada.

100664 Bilateral Exchange **43 UNTS 103**
SIGNED: 14 Jul 47 FORCE: 14 Jul 47
REGISTERED: 10 Oct 49 Canada
ARTICLES: 2 LANGUAGE: English. French.
HEADNOTE: FRIENDSHIP

TOPIC: Admin Cooperation
CONCEPTS: Previous treaty extension.
PARTIES:
Canada
Switzerland

100665 Bilateral Exchange **43 UNTS 111**
SIGNED: 28 Jul 47 FORCE: 28 Aug 47
REGISTERED: 10 Oct 49 Canada
ARTICLES: 2 LANGUAGE: English.
HEADNOTE: TRADE
TOPIC: Customs
CONCEPTS: Exceptions and exemptions. Most favored nation clause. Customs duties.
PROCEDURE: Termination.
PARTIES:
Canada
Greece

100666 Bilateral Exchange **43 UNTS 119**
SIGNED: 31 Jan 49 FORCE: 31 Jan 49
REGISTERED: 12 Oct 49 USA (United States)
ARTICLES: 2 LANGUAGE: English.
HEADNOTE: SEARCH RESCUE OPERATIONS
TOPIC: Humanitarian
CONCEPTS: Definition of terms. Visa abolition. Exchange of information and documents. Humanitarian matters. Claims, debts and assets. Claims and settlements. Overflights and technical stops. Operating authorizations and regulations.
PROCEDURE: Duration. Termination.
PARTIES:
Canada
USA (United States)

100667 Bilateral Exchange **43 UNTS 127**
SIGNED: 23 Mar 49 FORCE: 23 Mar 49
REGISTERED: 15 Oct 49 USA (United States)
ARTICLES: 2 LANGUAGE: English.
HEADNOTE: CIVIL AVIATION MISSION
TOPIC: Admin Cooperation
CONCEPTS: Personnel. Responsibility and liability. Use of facilities. Accounting procedures. Indemnities and reimbursements. Financial programs. Internal finance. Payment schedules. Tax exemptions. Customs exemptions. Special projects. Materials, equipment and services. Aid missions. Registration certificate. Air transport.
PROCEDURE: Amendment.
PARTIES:
Austria
USA (United States)

100668 Bilateral Agreement **43 UNTS 135**
SIGNED: 4 Jul 46 FORCE: 2 Jan 47
REGISTERED: 1 Nov 49 Philippines
ARTICLES: 10 LANGUAGE: English.
HEADNOTE: TRADE RELATED MATTERS TRANSITIONAL PERIOD FOLLOWING INDEPENDENCE
TOPIC: General Trade
CONCEPTS: Definition of terms. Detailed regulations. Border traffic and migration. Resident permits. Trade procedures. Currency. Monetary and gold transfers. Commodity trade. Quotas. General. Customs declarations. Temporary importation.
PARTIES:
Philippines
USA (United States)
ANNEX
234 UNTS 306. USA (United States). Supplementation 7 Jul 54. Force 7 Jul 54.
234 UNTS 306. Philippines. Supplementation 7 Jul 54. Force 7 Jul 54.
238 UNTS 264. USA (United States). Amendment 6 Sep 55. Force 1 Jan 56.
238 UNTS 264. Philippines. Amendment 6 Sep 55. Force 1 Jan 56.

100669 Bilateral Agreement **43 UNTS 185**
SIGNED: 6 Dec 47 FORCE: 6 Dec 47
REGISTERED: 1 Nov 49 Netherlands
ARTICLES: 14 LANGUAGE: Chinese. Dutch. English.
HEADNOTE: AIR TRANSPORT
TOPIC: Air Transport
CONCEPTS: Definition of terms. Exceptions and exemptions. Treaty interpretation. Annex or appendix reference. Conformity with municipal

law. Licenses and permits. Recognition of legal documents. Use of facilities. Procedure. Special tribunals. Competence of tribunal. Reexport of goods, etc.. Fees and exemptions. Most favored nation clause. National treatment. Customs exemptions. Competency certificate. Routes and logistics. Navigational conditions. Permit designation. Airport facilities. Airworthiness certificates. Conditions of airlines operating permission. Operating authorizations and regulations. Licenses and certificates of nationality.
INTL ORGS: International Civil Aviation Organization. Arbitration Commission.
TREATY REF: 15UNTS295.
PROCEDURE: Amendment. Duration. Registration. Termination.
PARTIES:
Taiwan
Netherlands

100670 Bilateral Agreement **43 UNTS 231**
SIGNED: 11 Sep 46 FORCE: 2 Sep 46
REGISTERED: 5 Nov 49 Philippines
ARTICLES: 6 LANGUAGE: English.
HEADNOTE: SALE CERTAIN SURPLUS WAR PROPERTY
TOPIC: Milit Assistance
CONCEPTS: Detailed regulations. Inspection and observation. General property. Procedure. Exchange. General cultural cooperation. Fees and exemptions. Transportation costs. General. Surplus property. Payment for war supplies. Naval vessels. Return of equipment and recapture. Surplus war property. Restrictions on transfer. Post-war claims settlement.
PROCEDURE: Ratification.
PARTIES:
Philippines
USA (United States)

100671 Bilateral Agreement **43 UNTS 247**
SIGNED: 23 Mar 48 FORCE: 23 Mar 48
REGISTERED: 5 Nov 49 Philippines
ARTICLES: 16 LANGUAGE: English.
HEADNOTE: USE FUNDS MADE AVAILABLE SALE SURPLUS WAR PROPERTY
TOPIC: Education
CONCEPTS: Definition of terms. Exceptions and exemptions. General provisions. Exchange. Commissions and foundations. Teacher and student exchange. Scholarships and grants. Exchange rates and regulations. Expense sharing formulae. Tax exemptions. Surplus war property.
PROCEDURE: Amendment.
PARTIES:
Philippines
USA (United States)
ANNEX
74 UNTS 292. Philippines. Amendment 8 Apr 48. Force 8 Apr 48.
74 UNTS 292. USA (United States). Amendment 2 Apr 48. Force 8 Apr 48.
74 UNTS 296. USA (United States). Amendment 8 Dec 48. Force 20 Dec 48.
74 UNTS 296. Philippines. Amendment 20 Dec 48. Force 20 Dec 48.
337 UNTS 378. USA (United States). Amendment 18 Sep 58. Force 3 Oct 58.
337 UNTS 378. Philippines. Amendment 3 Oct 58. Force 3 Oct 58.

100672 Bilateral Agreement **43 UNTS 263**
SIGNED: 19 Oct 46 FORCE: 19 Oct 46
REGISTERED: 5 Nov 49 Philippines
ARTICLES: 9 LANGUAGE: English.
HEADNOTE: TEMPORARY USE FACILITIES RADIO STATION KZFM
TOPIC: Telecommunications
CONCEPTS: Indemnities and reimbursements. Facilities and equipment. Radio-telephone-telegraphic communications.
PARTIES:
Philippines
USA (United States)

100673 Bilateral Agreement **43 UNTS 271**
SIGNED: 14 Mar 47 FORCE: 26 Mar 47
REGISTERED: 5 Nov 49 Philippines
ARTICLES: 29 LANGUAGE: English.
HEADNOTE: MILITARY BASES

TOPIC: Milit Installation
CONCEPTS: Treaty implementation. Annex or appendix reference. Informational records. General property. Use of facilities. Investigation of violations. Public health. Indemnities and reimbursements. Claims and settlements. National treatment. Tax exemptions. Customs exemptions. Innocent passage. Ports and pilotage. Facilities and equipment. Postal services. Joint defense. Defense and security. Military training. Security of information. Jurisdiction. Status of forces. Bases and facilities. Service in foreign army. Upkeep of war graves. Establishment of war cemeteries.
INTL ORGS: United Nations.
PROCEDURE: Duration. Renewal or Revival.
PARTIES:
Philippines
USA (United States)
ANNEX
68 UNTS 272. Philippines. Prolongation 16 May 49. Force 16 May 49.
68 UNTS 272. USA (United States). Prolongation 14 May 49. Force 16 May 49.
185 UNTS 334. Philippines. Amendment 12 Dec 47. Force 12 Dec 47.
185 UNTS 334. USA (United States). Amendment 1 Jul 47. Force 12 Dec 47.
185 UNTS 338. USA (United States). Implementation 12 Oct 47. Force 12 Oct 47.
185 UNTS 338. Philippines. Implementation 12 Oct 47. Force 12 Oct 47.
185 UNTS 348. USA (United States). Implementation 3 Oct 47. Force 14 Oct 47.
185 UNTS 348. Philippines. Implementation 14 Oct 47. Force 14 Oct 47.
185 UNTS 352. Philippines. Implementation 19 Dec 47. Force 19 Dec 47.
185 UNTS 352. USA (United States). Implementation 18 Dec 47. Force 19 Dec 47.
185 UNTS 362. USA (United States). Implementation 23 Dec 47. Force 24 Dec 47.
185 UNTS 362. Philippines. Implementation 24 Dec 47. Force 24 Dec 47.
185 UNTS 370. Philippines. Implementation 3 Jan 48. Force 3 Jan 48.
185 UNTS 370. USA (United States). Implementation 2 Jan 48. Force 3 Jan 48.
185 UNTS 374. Philippines. Implementation 29 Feb 48. Force 29 Feb 48.
185 UNTS 374. USA (United States). Implementation 19 Feb 48. Force 29 Feb 48.
185 UNTS 378. USA (United States). Amendment 31 Mar 48. Force 1 Apr 48.
185 UNTS 378. Philippines. Amendment 1 Apr 48. Force 1 Apr 48.
185 UNTS 384. Philippines. Implementation 29 Dec 52. Force 29 Dec 52.
185 UNTS 384. USA (United States). Implementation 29 Dec 52. Force 29 Dec 52.
213 UNTS 370. USA (United States). Implementation 17 Jun 53. Force 17 Jun 53.
213 UNTS 370. Philippines. Implementation 29 May 53. Force 17 Jun 53.
229 UNTS 282. Philippines. Amendment 15 Jan 53. Force 9 Feb 53.
229 UNTS 282. USA (United States). Amendment 9 Feb 53. Force 9 Feb 53.
325 UNTS 332. Philippines. Supplementation 22 Jul 53. Force 22 Jul 53.
325 UNTS 332. USA (United States). Supplementation 7 Jul 53. Force 22 Jul 53.
325 UNTS 332. USA (United States). Termination 30 Jun 54. Force 30 Jun 54.
325 UNTS 332. Philippines. Termination 30 Jun 54. Force 30 Jun 54.
649 UNTS 306. USA (United States). Force 22 Dec 65.
649 UNTS 306. Philippines. Force 22 Dec 65.

100674 Bilateral Treaty **44 UNTS 3**
SIGNED: 9 Jul 47 FORCE: 10 Dec 48
REGISTERED: 7 Nov 49 Philippines
ARTICLES: 6 LANGUAGE: English. Italian.
HEADNOTE: FRIENDSHIP GENERAL RELATIONS
TOPIC: General Amity
CONCEPTS: Friendship and amity. Alien status. Consular relations establishment. Diplomatic relations establishment. Privileges and immunities. Procedure. Negotiation. Compulsory jurisdiction.
INTL ORGS: International Court of Justice.

PROCEDURE: Future Procedures Contemplated. Ratification. Termination.
PARTIES:
Italy
Philippines

100675 Bilateral Agreement **44 UNTS 13**
SIGNED: 27 Aug 48 FORCE: 27 Aug 48
REGISTERED: 5 Nov 49 Philippines
ARTICLES: 13 LANGUAGE: English.
HEADNOTE: PAYMENT PRIVATE PUBLIC CLAIMS
TOPIC: Reparations
CONCEPTS: Detailed regulations. Treaty implementation. Visas. Privileges and immunities. Conformity with municipal law. Use of facilities. Investigation of violations. Establishment of commission. Fees and exemptions. Financial programs. Funding procedures. Claims and settlements. General. Taxation of professional services. General transportation. War claims and reparations. Post-war claims settlement. Decisions. Status of experts.
PROCEDURE: Amendment. Duration. Renewal or Revival. Termination.
PARTIES:
Philippines
USA (United States)

100676 Bilateral Agreement **44 UNTS 25**
SIGNED: 28 Feb 47 FORCE: 16 Feb 48
REGISTERED: 24 Nov 49 USA (United States)
ARTICLES: 12 LANGUAGE: English. Spanish.
HEADNOTE: AIR TRANSPORT
TOPIC: Air Transport
CONCEPTS: Exceptions and exemptions. Annex or appendix reference. Non-prejudice to third party. Conformity with municipal law. Licenses and permits. Recognition of legal documents. Use of facilities. Procedure. Existing tribunals. Special tribunals. Competence of tribunal. Fees and exemptions. Most favored nation clause. National treatment. Customs exemptions. Competency certificate. Routes and logistics. Navigational conditions. Permit designation. Airport facilities. Airworthiness certificates. Conditions of airlines operating permission. Operating authorizations and regulations. Licenses and certificates of nationality.
INTL ORGS: International Civil Aviation Organization. Arbitration Commission.
TREATY REF: INT.CIVI.AVI.CONF.; US DEPT STATE PUB 2282.
PROCEDURE: Ratification. Registration. Termination.
PARTIES:
Paraguay
USA (United States)

100677 Bilateral Exchange **44 UNTS 45**
SIGNED: 27 Oct 47 FORCE: 27 Oct 47
REGISTERED: 24 Nov 49 USA (United States)
ARTICLES: 2 LANGUAGE: English. Spanish.
HEADNOTE: CIVIL AVIATION MISSION
TOPIC: Air Transport
CONCEPTS: Assistance. Air transport. Airport equipment.
PARTIES:
Ecuador
USA (United States)

100678 Bilateral Exchange **44 UNTS 57**
SIGNED: 24 Mar 48 FORCE: 24 Mar 48
REGISTERED: 24 Nov 49 USA (United States)
ARTICLES: 2 LANGUAGE: English. Spanish.
HEADNOTE: CIVIL AVIATION MISSION
TOPIC: Air Transport
CONCEPTS: Personnel. Use of facilities. Accounting procedures. Indemnities and reimbursements. Financial programs. Payment schedules. Tax exemptions. Customs exemptions. Special projects. Materials, equipment and services. Aid missions. Registration certificate. Air transport.
PROCEDURE: Amendment. Denunciation. Duration.
PARTIES:
USA (United States)
Venezuela

100679 Bilateral Agreement **44 UNTS 69**
SIGNED: 4 Jan 49 FORCE: 4 Jan 49
REGISTERED: 24 Nov 49 USA (United States)
ARTICLES: 30 LANGUAGE: English. French.
HEADNOTE: AIR FORCE MISSION
TOPIC: Military Mission
CONCEPTS: Definition of terms. Use of facilities. Compensation. Indemnities and reimbursements. Exchange rates and regulations. Expense sharing formulae. Tax exemptions. Customs exemptions. Military assistance. Military training. Security of information. Airforce-army-navy personnel ratio. Ranks and privileges. Conditions for assistance missions. Third country military personnel. Status of forces.
PROCEDURE: Denunciation. Duration. Renewal or Revival. Termination.
PARTIES:
Haiti
USA (United States)
ANNEX
205 UNTS 330. USA (United States). Prolongation 28 Jan 53. Force 4 Jan 53.
205 UNTS 330. Haiti. Prolongation 2 Mar 53. Force 4 Jan 53.
266 UNTS 374. USA (United States). Prolongation 7 Jan 57. Force 7 Jan 57.
266 UNTS 374. Haiti. Prolongation 3 Dec 56. Force 7 Jan 57.
341 UNTS 382. USA (United States). Amendment 20 Feb 59. Force 20 Feb 59.
341 UNTS 382. Haiti. Amendment 20 Feb 59. Force 20 Feb 59.

100680 Bilateral Agreement **44 UNTS 83**
SIGNED: 21 Feb 49 FORCE: 21 Feb 49
REGISTERED: 24 Nov 49 USA (United States)
ARTICLES: 29 LANGUAGE: English. Siamese.
HEADNOTE: AIR FORCE MISSION
TOPIC: Military Mission
CONCEPTS: Definition of terms. Use of facilities. Compensation. Indemnities and reimbursements. Exchange rates and regulations. Expense sharing formulae. Tax exemptions. Customs exemptions. Military assistance. Military assistance. Military training. Airforce-army-navy personnel ratio. Ranks and privileges. Conditions for assistance missions. Third country military personnel. Status of forces.
PROCEDURE: Denunciation. Duration. Renewal or Revival. Termination.
PARTIES:
Colombia
USA (United States)
ANNEX
237 UNTS 293. USA (United States). Prolongation 6 Oct 54. Force 4 Nov 54.
237 UNTS 293. Colombia. Prolongation 4 Nov 54. Force 4 Nov 54.
342 UNTS 348. USA (United States). Amendment 18 Feb 59. Force 31 Mar 59.
342 UNTS 348. Colombia. Amendment 31 Mar 59. Force 31 Mar 59.

100681 Bilateral Agreement **44 UNTS 105**
SIGNED: 16 May 46 FORCE: 16 May 46
REGISTERED: 24 Nov 49 ICAO (Civil Aviat)
ARTICLES: 11 LANGUAGE: English. French.
HEADNOTE: AIR TRANSPORT
TOPIC: Air Transport
CONCEPTS: Annex or appendix reference. Conformity with municipal law. Licenses and permits. Recognition of legal documents. Use of facilities. Arbitration. Procedure. Existing tribunals. Special tribunals. Negotiation. Fees and exemptions. Most favored nation clause. National treatment. Customs exemptions. Competency certificate. Routes and logistics. Navigational conditions. Permit designation. Airport facilities. Airworthiness certificates. Conditions of airlines operating permission. Licenses and certificates of nationality.
INTL ORGS: International Civil Aviation Organization. Arbitration Commission.
TREATY REF: 15UNTS295.
PROCEDURE: Amendment. Future Procedures Contemplated. Registration. Termination.
PARTIES:
France
Ireland

ANNEX
192 UNTS 314. France. Amendment 14 Aug 52. Force 14 Aug 52.
192 UNTS 314. Ireland. Amendment 10 Jul 52. Force 14 Aug 52.
335 UNTS 286. Ireland. Amendment 21 Jan 58. Force 21 Jan 58.
335 UNTS 286. France. Amendment 21 Jan 58. Force 21 Jan 58.
353 UNTS 325. France. Amendment 19 Aug 58. Force 19 Aug 58.
353 UNTS 325. Ireland. Amendment 19 Aug 58. Force 19 Aug 58.

100682 Bilateral Agreement **44 UNTS 123**
SIGNED: 16 Sep 47 FORCE: 21 Mar 48
REGISTERED: 29 Nov 49 ICAO (Civil Aviat)
ARTICLES: 12 LANGUAGE: Arabic. Turkish.
HEADNOTE: AIR TRANSPORT
TOPIC: Air Transport
CONCEPTS: Exceptions and exemptions. Annex or appendix reference. Conformity with municipal law. Licenses and permits. Recognition of legal documents. Use of facilities. Arbitration. Procedure. Existing tribunals. Special tribunals. Negotiation. Narcotic drugs. Fees and exemptions. Most favored nation clause. National treatment. Customs exemptions. Competency certificate. Routes and logistics. Navigational conditions. Permit designation. Airport facilities. Airworthiness certificates. Conditions of airlines operating permission. Licenses and certificates of nationality.
INTL ORGS: International Civil Aviation Organization.
TREATY REF: 15UNTS295.
PROCEDURE: Amendment. Denunciation. Future Procedures Contemplated. Ratification. Registration.
PARTIES:
Lebanon
Turkey

100683 Bilateral Agreement **44 UNTS 149**
SIGNED: 15 Oct 47 FORCE: 5 Feb 49
REGISTERED: 29 Nov 49 ICAO (Civil Aviat)
ARTICLES: 11 LANGUAGE: French.
HEADNOTE: AIR SERVICES
TOPIC: Air Transport
CONCEPTS: Annex or appendix reference. Nonprejudice to third party. Conformity with municipal law. Licenses and permits. Recognition of legal documents. Use of facilities. Arbitration. Procedure. Existing tribunals. Special tribunals. Negotiation. Fees and exemptions. Most favored nation clause. National treatment. Customs exemptions. Competency certificate. Routes and logistics. Navigational conditions. Permit designation. Airport facilities. Airworthiness certificates. Conditions of airlines operating permission. Licenses and certificates of nationality.
INTL ORGS: International Civil Aviation Organization.
TREATY REF: 15UNTS295.
PROCEDURE: Amendment. Denunciation. Future Procedures Contemplated. Ratification. Registration.
PARTIES:
Czechoslovakia
Sweden
ANNEX
53 UNTS 428. Czechoslovakia. Supplementation 11 Mar 48. Force 11 Mar 48.
53 UNTS 428. Sweden. Supplementation 11 Feb 48. Force 11 Mar 48.
53 UNTS 428. Sweden. Supplementation 11 Mar 48. Force 11 Mar 48.
53 UNTS 432. Czechoslovakia. Supplementation 22 Dec 49. Force 22 Dec 49.
53 UNTS 432. Sweden. Supplementation 5 Nov 49. Force 22 Dec 49.
327 UNTS 340. Czechoslovakia. Amendment 25 Jan 57. Force 25 Jan 57.
327 UNTS 340. Sweden. Amendment 25 Jan 57. Force 25 Jan 57.
327 UNTS 345. Sweden. Supplementation 28 Feb 57. Force 28 Feb 57.
327 UNTS 345. Czechoslovakia. Supplementation 28 Feb 57. Force 28 Feb 57.

100684 Bilateral Agreement **44 UNTS 163**
SIGNED: 14 Nov 47 FORCE: 10 Mar 49
REGISTERED: 29 Nov 49 ICAO (Civil Aviat)
ARTICLES: 12 LANGUAGE: French. Norwegian. Portuguese.
HEADNOTE: AIR TRANSPORT
TOPIC: Air Transport
CONCEPTS: Definition of terms. Treaty interpretation. Annex or appendix reference. Previous treaty replacement. Conformity with municipal law. Use of facilities. Arbitration. Procedure. Fees and exemptions. Most favored nation clause. National treatment. Customs exemptions. Routes and logistics. Permit designation. Airport facilities. Conditions of airlines operating permission. Operating authorizations and regulations.
INTL ORGS: International Civil Aviation Organization. Arbitration Commission.
TREATY REF: 15UNTS295.
PROCEDURE: Amendment. Future Procedures Contemplated. Ratification. Registration. Termination.
PARTIES:
Brazil
Norway

100685 Bilateral Agreement **44 UNTS 199**
SIGNED: 27 Jul 49 FORCE: 27 Jul 49
REGISTERED: 29 Nov 49 ICAO (Civil Aviat)
ARTICLES: 15 LANGUAGE: English.
HEADNOTE: AIR SERVICES
TOPIC: Air Transport
CONCEPTS: Conditions. Definition of terms. Detailed regulations. Exceptions and exemptions. Annex or appendix reference. Conformity with municipal law. General cooperation. Exchange of information and documents. Arbitration. Procedure. Existing tribunals. Special tribunals. Negotiation. Reexport of goods, etc.. Non-interest rates and fees. Most favored nation clause. National treatment. Customs exemptions. Routes and logistics. Permit designation. Air transport. Airport facilities. Conditions of airlines operating permission. Overflights and technical stops. Operating authorizations and regulations.
INTL ORGS: International Civil Aviation Organization. Arbitration Commission.
TREATY REF: 15UNTS295.
PROCEDURE: Amendment. Future Procedures Contemplated. Registration. Termination. Application to Non-self-governing Territories.
PARTIES:
Pakistan
UK Great Britain
ANNEX
310 UNTS 320. Pakistan. Amendment 21 Dec 56. Force 21 Dec 56.
310 UNTS 320. UK Great Britain. Amendment 21 Dec 56. Force 21 Dec 56.

100686 Bilateral Agreement **44 UNTS 223**
SIGNED: 19 Aug 49 FORCE: 19 Aug 49
REGISTERED: 29 Nov 49 ICAO (Civil Aviat)
ARTICLES: 15 LANGUAGE: English.
HEADNOTE: AIR SERVICES
TOPIC: Air Transport
CONCEPTS: Conditions. Definition of terms. Detailed regulations. Exceptions and exemptions. Previous treaty replacement. Conformity with municipal law. General cooperation. Exchange of information and documents. Procedure. Domestic jurisdiction. Existing tribunals. Special tribunals. Non-interest rates and fees. Most favored nation clause. National treatment. Routes and logistics. Permit designation. Air transport. Conditions of airlines operating permission. Overflights and technical stops. Operating authorizations and regulations.
INTL ORGS: International Civil Aviation Organization. Arbitration Commission.
TREATY REF: 15UNTS2955; 28UNTS155; 27UNTS155.
PROCEDURE: Amendment. Future Procedures Contemplated. Registration. Termination. Application to Non-self-governing Territories.
PARTIES:
Canada
UK Great Britain
ANNEX
353 UNTS 326. UK Great Britain. Amendment 18 Aug 58. Force 18 Aug 58.

353 UNTS 326. Canada. Amendment 18 Aug 58. Force 18 Aug 58.
412 UNTS 284. UK Great Britain. Amendment 6 Sep 60. Force 6 Sep 60.
412 UNTS 284. Canada. Amendment 6 Sep 60. Force 6 Sep 60.

100687 Bilateral Agreement **44 UNTS 255**
SIGNED: 9 Nov 49 FORCE: 9 Nov 49
REGISTERED: 29 Nov 49 ICAO (Civil Aviat)
ARTICLES: 14 LANGUAGE: English.
HEADNOTE: AIR SERVICES
TOPIC: Air Transport
CONCEPTS: Definition of terms. Detailed regulations. Annex or appendix reference. Conformity with municipal law. General cooperation. Exchange of information and documents. Use of facilities. Procedure. Existing tribunals. Special tribunals. Negotiation. Reexport of goods, etc.. Non-interest rates and fees. Most favored nation clause. National treatment. Customs exemptions. Routes and logistics. Permit designation. Air transport. Airport facilities. Conditions of airlines operating permission. Operating authorizations and regulations.
INTL ORGS: International Civil Aviation Organization. Arbitration Commission.
TREATY REF: 15UNTS2955.
PROCEDURE: Amendment. Future Procedures Contemplated. Registration. Termination.
PARTIES:
Denmark
Pakistan

100688 Multilateral Protocol **44 UNTS 277**
SIGNED: 19 Nov 48 FORCE: 1 Dec 49
REGISTERED: 1 Dec 49 United Nations
ARTICLES: 11 LANGUAGE: Chinese. English. French. Russian. Spanish.
HEADNOTE: DRUGS OUTSIDE 1931 CONVENTION MANUFACTURING NARCOTIC DRUGS
TOPIC: Sanitation
CONCEPTS: Change of circumstances. Conditions. Definition of terms. Territorial application. General provisions. Treaty implementation. Treaty interpretation. Narcotic drugs. WHO used as agency. Research results.
INTL ORGS: United Nations. World Health Organization.
TREATY REF: 139LTS301; 2UNTS179.
PROCEDURE: Accession. Denunciation. Duration. Ratification.
PARTIES:
Afghanistan SIGNED: 19 Nov 48 FORCE: 1 Dec 49
Albania SIGNED: 19 Nov 48 RATIFIED: 25 Jul 49 FORCE: 1 Dec 49
Argentina SIGNED: 19 Nov 48
Australia All Territories RATIFIED: 19 Nov 48 FORCE: 1 Dec 49
Australia SIGNED: 19 Nov 48 FORCE: 1 Dec 49
Belgium SIGNED: 19 Nov 48
Bolivia SIGNED: 19 Nov 48
Brazil SIGNED: 19 Nov 48
Burma SIGNED: 19 Nov 48
Byelorussia SIGNED: 19 Nov 48 FORCE: 1 Dec 49
Canada SIGNED: 19 Nov 48 FORCE: 1 Dec 49
Ceylon (Sri Lanka) RATIFIED: 17 Jan 49 FORCE: 1 Dec 49
Chile SIGNED: 19 Nov 48
Taiwan SIGNED: 19 Nov 48 FORCE: 1 Dec 49
Colombia SIGNED: 19 Nov 48
Costa Rica SIGNED: 19 Nov 48
Czechoslovakia SIGNED: 19 Nov 48
Denmark SIGNED: 19 Nov 48 RATIFIED: 19 Oct 49 FORCE: 1 Dec 49
Dominican Republic SIGNED: 19 Nov 48
Ecuador SIGNED: 19 Nov 48
United Arab Rep SIGNED: 6 Dec 48 RATIFIED: 16 Sep 49 FORCE: 1 Dec 49
El Salvador SIGNED: 19 Nov 48
Ethiopia SIGNED: 5 May 49 FORCE: 1 Dec 49
Finland RATIFIED: 31 Oct 49 FORCE: 1 Dec 49
France Algeria RATIFIED: 15 Sep 49 FORCE: 1 Dec 49
France Cameroon RATIFIED: 15 Sep 49 FORCE: 1 Dec 49
France Comoro Islands RATIFIED: 15 Sep 49 FORCE: 1 Dec 49
France Fr Equatorial Afri RATIFIED: 15 Sep 49 FORCE: 1 Dec 49

France French India RATIFIED: 15 Sep 49 FORCE: 1 Dec 49
France French Somaliland RATIFIED: 15 Sep 49 FORCE: 1 Dec 49
France French West Africa RATIFIED: 15 Sep 49 FORCE: 1 Dec 49
France Guyana RATIFIED: 15 Sep 49 FORCE: 1 Dec 49
France New Hebrides Is RATIFIED: 15 Sep 49 FORCE: 1 Dec 49
France Madagascar RATIFIED: 15 Sep 49 FORCE: 1 Dec 49
France Martinique RATIFIED: 15 Sep 49 FORCE: 1 Dec 49
France Morocco RATIFIED: 15 Sep 49 FORCE: 1 Dec 49
France New Caledonia RATIFIED: 15 Sep 49 FORCE: 1 Dec 49
France Oceania RATIFIED: 15 Sep 49 FORCE: 1 Dec 49
France Reunion RATIFIED: 15 Sep 49 FORCE: 1 Dec 49
France SIGNED: 19 Nov 48 RATIFIED: 11 Jan 49 FORCE: 1 Dec 49
France Togo RATIFIED: 15 Sep 49 FORCE: 1 Dec 49
France Tunisia RATIFIED: 15 Sep 49 FORCE: 1 Dec 49
France Vietnam RATIFIED: 25 Nov 49 FORCE: 1 Dec 49
Greece SIGNED: 7 Dec 48
Guatemala SIGNED: 19 Nov 48
Honduras SIGNED: 19 Nov 48
India SIGNED: 19 Nov 48
Iraq SIGNED: 12 Jul 49
Italy SIGNED: 14 Mar 49 FORCE: 1 Dec 49
Lebanon SIGNED: 19 Nov 48 FORCE: 1 Dec 49
Liberia SIGNED: 19 Nov 48
Liechtenstein SIGNED: 19 Nov 48
Luxembourg SIGNED: 19 Nov 48
Mexico SIGNED: 19 Nov 48 FORCE: 1 Dec 49
Monaco SIGNED: 19 Nov 48 FORCE: 1 Dec 49
Netherlands SIGNED: 19 Nov 48
New Zealand All Territories RATIFIED: 19 Nov 48 FORCE: 1 Dec 49
New Zealand SIGNED: 19 Nov 48 FORCE: 1 Dec 49
Nicaragua SIGNED: 19 Nov 48
Norway SIGNED: 19 Nov 48 RATIFIED: 24 May 49 FORCE: 1 Dec 49
Pakistan SIGNED: 21 Nov 48
Panama SIGNED: 19 Nov 48
Paraguay SIGNED: 19 Nov 48
Peru SIGNED: 19 Nov 48
Philippines SIGNED: 10 Mar 49
Poland SIGNED: 16 Jan 49 FORCE: 1 Dec 49
Romania SIGNED: 19 Nov 48
San Marino SIGNED: 19 Nov 48
Saudi Arabia SIGNED: 19 Nov 48 FORCE: 1 Dec 49
South Africa SIGNED: 8 Dec 48 FORCE: 1 Dec 49
Sweden SIGNED: 3 Mar 49 FORCE: 1 Dec 49
Switzerland SIGNED: 19 Nov 48
Turkey SIGNED: 19 Nov 48
UK Great Britain Aden RATIFIED: 19 Nov 48 FORCE: 1 Dec 49
UK Great Britain Bahamas RATIFIED: 19 Nov 48 FORCE: 1 Dec 49
UK Great Britain Barbados RATIFIED: 19 Nov 48 FORCE: 1 Dec 49
UK Great Britain Basutoland RATIFIED: 19 Nov 48 FORCE: 1 Dec 49
UK Great Britain Bechuanaland RATIFIED: 19 Nov 48 FORCE: 1 Dec 49
UK Great Britain Bermuda RATIFIED: 19 Nov 48 FORCE: 1 Dec 49
UK Great Britain British Honduras RATIFIED: 19 Nov 48 FORCE: 1 Dec 49
UK Great Britain Brit Solomon Is RATIFIED: 19 Nov 48 FORCE: 1 Dec 49
UK Great Britain British Somaliland RATIFIED: 19 Nov 48 FORCE: 1 Dec 49
UK Great Britain Brunei RATIFIED: 19 Nov 48 FORCE: 1 Dec 49
UK Great Britain Cyprus RATIFIED: 19 Nov 48 FORCE: 1 Dec 49
UK Great Britain Falkland Islands RATIFIED: 19 Nov 48 FORCE: 1 Dec 49
UK Great Britain Fiji Islands RATIFIED: 19 Nov 48 FORCE: 1 Dec 49
UK Great Britain Fed of Malaya RATIFIED: 19 Nov 48 FORCE: 1 Dec 49

UK Great Britain Fed Rhod/Nyasaland RATIFIED: 19 Nov 48 FORCE: 1 Dec 49
UK Great Britain Gambia RATIFIED: 19 Nov 48 FORCE: 1 Dec 49
UK Great Britain Gibralter RATIFIED: 19 Nov 48 FORCE: 1 Dec 49
UK Great Britain Gilbert Islands RATIFIED: 19 Nov 48 FORCE: 1 Dec 49
UK Great Britain Gold Coast RATIFIED: 19 Nov 48 FORCE: 1 Dec 49
UK Great Britain Guyana RATIFIED: 19 Nov 48 FORCE: 1 Dec 49
UK Great Britain Hong Kong RATIFIED: 19 Nov 48 FORCE: 1 Dec 49
UK Great Britain Jamaica RATIFIED: 19 Nov 48 FORCE: 1 Dec 49
UK Great Britain Kenya RATIFIED: 19 Nov 48 FORCE: 1 Dec 49
UK Great Britain Malta RATIFIED: 19 Nov 48 FORCE: 1 Dec 49
UK Great Britain Mauritius RATIFIED: 19 Nov 48 FORCE: 1 Dec 49
UK Great Britain Newfoundland RATIFIED: 19 Nov 48 FORCE: 1 Dec 49
UK Great Britain Nigeria RATIFIED: 19 Nov 48 FORCE: 1 Dec 49
UK Great Britain North Borneo RATIFIED: 19 Nov 48 FORCE: 1 Dec 49
UK Great Britain Northern Rhodesia RATIFIED: 19 Nov 48 FORCE: 1 Dec 49
UK Great Britain SIGNED: 19 Nov 48 FORCE: 1 Dec 49
UK Great Britain Sarawak RATIFIED: 19 Nov 48 FORCE: 1 Dec 49
UK Great Britain Seychelles RATIFIED: 19 Nov 48 FORCE: 1 Dec 49
UK Great Britain Sierra Leone RATIFIED: 19 Nov 48 FORCE: 1 Dec 49
UK Great Britain Singapore RATIFIED: 19 Nov 48 FORCE: 1 Dec 49
UK Great Britain Southern Rhodesia RATIFIED: 19 Nov 48 FORCE: 1 Dec 49
UK Great Britain St. Helena RATIFIED: 19 Nov 48 FORCE: 1 Dec 49
UK Great Britain Tanganyika RATIFIED: 19 Nov 48 FORCE: 1 Dec 49
UK Great Britain Tonga RATIFIED: 19 Nov 48 FORCE: 1 Dec 49
UK Great Britain Trinidad RATIFIED: 19 Nov 48 FORCE: 1 Dec 49
UK Great Britain Uganda RATIFIED: 19 Nov 48 FORCE: 1 Dec 49
UK Great Britain Windward Islands RATIFIED: 19 Nov 48 FORCE: 1 Dec 49
UK Great Britain Zanzibar RATIFIED: 19 Nov 48 FORCE: 1 Dec 49
USA (United States) All Territories RATIFIED: 19 Nov 48 FORCE: 1 Dec 49
USA (United States) SIGNED: 19 Nov 48
Ukrainian SSR SIGNED: 19 Nov 48
Uruguay SIGNED: 22 Nov 48
USSR (Soviet Union) SIGNED: 19 Nov 48 FORCE: 1 Dec 49
Venezuela SIGNED: 19 Nov 48
Yugoslavia SIGNED: 19 Nov 48 RATIFIED: 10 Jun 49 FORCE: 1 Dec 49
ANNEX
45 UNTS 332.
46 UNTS 367.
48 UNTS 310.
54 UNTS 408.
67 UNTS 352.
68 UNTS 278.
71 UNTS 325.
73 UNTS 271.
76 UNTS 277.
81 UNTS 333.
110 UNTS 315.
128 UNTS 298.
131 UNTS 315.
135 UNTS 335.
136 UNTS 388.
141 UNTS 381.
157 UNTS 359.
161 UNTS 364.
182 UNTS 224.
187 UNTS 422.
196 UNTS 340.
199 UNTS 318.
216 UNTS 380.
253 UNTS 311.
271 UNTS 385.
292 UNTS 360.
299 UNTS 409.

302 UNTS 356.
309 UNTS 355.
328 UNTS 287.
338 UNTS 331.
347 UNTS 360.
348 UNTS 346.
384 UNTS 356.
396 UNTS 317.
399 UNTS 262.
405 UNTS 292.
410 UNTS 289.
414 UNTS 374.
415 UNTS 426.
423 UNTS 269.
435 UNTS 305.
437 UNTS 342.
442 UNTS 300.
462 UNTS 328.
463 UNTS 318.
484 UNTS 408.
494 UNTS 290.
511 UNTS 265.
531 UNTS 305.
541 UNTS 304.
560 UNTS 238.

100689 Multilateral Agreement **45 UNTS 3**
SIGNED: 10 Aug 49   FORCE: 10 Aug 49
REGISTERED: 8 Dec 49 Denmark
ARTICLES: 14 LANGUAGE: English. French.
HEADNOTE: FINANCE
TOPIC: Finance
CONCEPTS: Detailed regulations. Annex or appen-
dix reference. Previous treaty replacement. Gen-
eral cooperation. Negotiation. Import quotas. Ac-
counting procedures. Banking. Balance of pay-
ments. Currency. Exchange rates and
regulations. Interest rates. Payment schedules.
Local currency. Loan and credit. Credit provi-
sions. Purchase authorization.
INTL ORGS: International Monetary Fund.
TREATY REF: 34UNTS23.
PROCEDURE: Duration. Renewal or Revival. Termi-
nation.
PARTIES:
Denmark   SIGNED: 10 Aug 49   FORCE:
10 Aug 49
British Occup Germ SIGNED: 10 Aug 49 FORCE:
10 Aug 49
US Occup Germ SIGNED: 10 Aug 49 FORCE:
10 Aug 49

100690 Bilateral Convention **45 UNTS 23**
SIGNED: 14 Mar 47   FORCE: 18 Nov 48
REGISTERED: 13 Dec 49 Philippines
ARTICLES: 16 LANGUAGE: English.
HEADNOTE: CONSULAR
TOPIC: Consul/Citizenship
CONCEPTS: General consular functions. Diplo-
matic privileges. Consular relations establish-
ment. Privileges and immunities. Responsibil-
ity and liability. Use of facilities. Shipwreck and sal-
vage. Foreign nationals.
PROCEDURE: Duration. Ratification. Termination.
PARTIES:
Philippines
USA (United States)

100691 Bilateral Agreement **45 UNTS 47**
SIGNED: 21 Mar 47   FORCE: 21 Mar 47
REGISTERED: 13 Dec 49 Philippines
ARTICLES: 23 LANGUAGE: English.
HEADNOTE: MILITARY ASSISTANCE
TOPIC: Milit Assistance
CONCEPTS: Definition of terms. Non-prejudice to
UN charter. Privileges and immunities. General
cooperation. Public information. Expense shar-
ing formulae. Materials, equipment and services.
Lease of military property. Military assistance.
Military training. Security of information. Military
assistance missions. Airforce-army-navy person-
nel ratio. Ranks and privileges. Conditions for
assistance missions. Exchange of defense infor-
mation. Restrictions on transfer.
INTL ORGS: United Nations.
TREATY REF: 43UNTS271.
PROCEDURE: Denunciation. Duration. Termina-
tion.
PARTIES:
Philippines
USA (United States)

ANNEX
70 UNTS 280. USA (United States). Amendment
6 May 48. Force 7 Jun 48.
70 UNTS 280. Philippines. Amendment 7 Jun 48.
Force 7 Jun 48.
82 UNTS 332. USA (United States). Extension and
Amendment 13 Mar 50. Force 13 Mar 50.
82 UNTS 332. Philippines. Extension and Amendment 11 Mar 50. Force 13 Mar 50.

100692 Bilateral Agreement **45 UNTS 63**
SIGNED: 7 Jun 49   FORCE: 7 Jun 49
REGISTERED: 13 Dec 49 Philippines
ARTICLES: 28 LANGUAGE: English.
HEADNOTE: GRANTS HOSPITAL VETERANS MED-
ICAL CARE
TOPIC: Direct Aid
CONCEPTS: Definition of terms. Visas. Conformity
with municipal law. General cooperation. Exchange of information and documents. Inspection and observation. Personnel. Responsibility
and liability. Public health. Indemnities and reimbursements. Tax exemptions. Customs exemptions. Domestic obligation. Materials, equipment
and services. Grants.
PROCEDURE: Amendment. Duration. Termination.
PARTIES:
Philippines
USA (United States)
ANNEX
82 UNTS 342. USA (United States). Interpretation
5 Aug 49.
82 UNTS 342.   Philippines.   Interpretation
7 Jun 49.
235 UNTS 360.   Philippines.   Amendment
6 Oct 54. Force 6 Oct 54.
235 UNTS 360. USA (United States). Amendment
6 Oct 54. Force 6 Oct 54.

100693 Bilateral Convention **45 UNTS 81**
SIGNED: 12 Oct 48   FORCE: 1 Jul 49
REGISTERED: 15 Dec 49 Czechoslovakia
ARTICLES: 35 LANGUAGE: French.
HEADNOTE: SOCIAL SECURITY
TOPIC: Non-ILO Labor
CONCEPTS: Detailed regulations. Exceptions and
exemptions. General provisions. Conformity
with municipal law. Domestic legislation. Incor-
poration of treaty provisions into national law.
Old age and invalidity insurance. Non-ILO labor
relations. Family allowances. Administrative co-
operation. Old age insurance. Sickness and inva-
lidity insurance. Social security. Payment sched-
ules. National treatment.
PROCEDURE: Amendment. Duration. Ratification.
Renewal or Revival. Termination.
PARTIES:
Czechoslovakia
France

100694 Multilateral Protocol **45 UNTS 125**
SIGNED: 29 Sep 47   FORCE: 29 Sep 47
REGISTERED: 20 Dec 49 Canada
ARTICLES: 1 LANGUAGE: English. Russian.
HEADNOTE: SUPPLEMENT MOSCOW PROTOCOL
8 OCT 44 ARMISTICE
TOPIC: Peace/Disarmament
CONCEPTS: Exchange rates and regulations. Pay-
ment schedules. Payment for war supplies.
TREATY REF: 45UNTS311.
PARTIES:
Canada SIGNED: 29 Sep 47 FORCE: 29 Sep 47
UK Great Britain RATIFIED: 19 Nov 47
USSR (Soviet Union) SIGNED: 29 Sep 47
FORCE: 29 Sep 47

100695 Bilateral Agreement **45 UNTS 133**
SIGNED: 26 Nov 49   FORCE: 26 Nov 49
REGISTERED: 22 Dec 49 Australia
ARTICLES: 17 LANGUAGE: English.
HEADNOTE: USE FUNDS SETTLEMENT LEND-
LEASE RECIPROCAL SURPLUS PROPERTY
CLAIMS
TOPIC: Reparations
CONCEPTS: Definition of terms. Detailed regula-
tions. Conformity with municipal law. Exchange
of information and documents. Exchange. Com-
missions and foundations. Indemnities and reim-
bursements. Funding procedures. Tax exemp-
tions. Customs exemptions.

TREATY REF: 4UNTS237.
PARTIES:
Australia
USA (United States)
ANNEX
198 UNTS 378. Australia. Amendment 3 Sep 54.
Force 3 Sep 54.
198 UNTS 378. USA (United States). Amendment
3 Sep 54. Force 3 Sep 54.
229 UNTS 288. Australia. Amendment 9 Jul 52.
Force 25 Aug 52.
229 UNTS 288. USA (United States). Amendment
25 Aug 52. Force 25 Aug 52.

100696 Multilateral Agreement **45 UNTS 149**
SIGNED: 16 Jun 49   FORCE: 1 Jan 50
REGISTERED: 1 Jan 50 United Nations
ARTICLES: 7 LANGUAGE: English. French.
HEADNOTE: PROVISIONAL APPLICATION CUS-
TOMS CONVENTION COMMERCIAL VEHICLES
TOPIC: Land Transport
CONCEPTS: Territorial application. Annex or ap-
pendix reference. Transport of goods. Commer-
cial road vehicles. Roads and highways.
INTL ORGS: United Nations.
PROCEDURE: Accession. Denunciation. Duration.
Registration. Renewal or Revival. Termination.
PARTIES:
Austria SIGNED: 27 Dec 49 FORCE: 4 Jan 50
Bel-Lux Econ Union SIGNED: 16 Jun 49
Czechoslovakia SIGNED: 28 Dec 49
Denmark SIGNED: 29 Dec 49 FORCE: 4 Jan 50
France SIGNED: 16 Jun 49 FORCE: 4 Jan 50
Italy SIGNED: 16 Jun 49 FORCE: 4 Jan 50
Liechtenstein   RATIFIED: 6 Dec 49   FORCE:
1 Jan 50
Netherlands SIGNED: 16 Jun 49
Norway SIGNED: 16 Jun 49 FORCE: 4 Jan 50
Switzerland   SIGNED: 16 Jun 49   FORCE:
4 Jan 50
UK Great Britain SIGNED: 16 Jun 49 FORCE:
1 Jan 50
ANNEX
51 UNTS 331. UK Great Britain. Somalia.
51 UNTS 331. UK Great Britain. Gibralter.
51 UNTS 331. UK Great Britain. Malta.
51 UNTS 331. UK Great Britain. Mauritius.
51 UNTS 331. UK Great Britain. Nyasaland.
51 UNTS 331. UK Great Britain. Sarawak.
65 UNTS 318.   France.   Supplementation
11 Mar 50. Force 11 Mar 50.
65 UNTS 318.   Switzerland.   Supplementation
11 Mar 50. Force 11 Mar 50.
65 UNTS 318. Bel-Lux Econ Union. Supplementation 11 Mar 50.
65 UNTS 318.   Netherlands.   Supplementation
11 Mar 50. Force 11 Mar 50.
65 UNTS 318. Italy. Supplementation 11 Mar 50.
Force 11 Mar 50.
67 UNTS 353. Denmark. Signature 7 Jul 50.
68 UNTS 278. UK Great Britain. Seychelles.
68 UNTS 278. UK Great Britain. Fiji Islands.
68 UNTS 278. UK Great Britain. Aden Colony.
68 UNTS 279. UK Great Britain. Cyprus.
68 UNTS 279. UK Great Britain. St. Helena.
71 UNTS 326. Sweden. Accession 15 Sep 50.
Force 1 Jul 50.
73 UNTS 272. UK Great Britain. Sierra Leone.
73 UNTS 272. UK Great Britain. Sierra Leone.
73 UNTS 272. UK Great Britain. North Borneo.
73 UNTS 272. UK Great Britain. Singapore.
73 UNTS 272. UK Great Britain. Windward Islands.
73 UNTS 272. UK Great Britain. Leeward Islands.
73 UNTS 272. UK Great Britain. Fed of Malaya.
73 UNTS 272. UK Great Britain. British Honduras.
73 UNTS 272. UK Great Britain. Singapore.
73 UNTS 272. UK Great Britain. Trinidad.
73 UNTS 272. UK Great Britain. British Guiana.
76 UNTS 278. Sweden. Accession 7 Dec 50.
101 UNTS 289. UK Great Britain. Brunei.
101 UNTS 289. UK Great Britain. Gambia.
101 UNTS 289. UK Great Britain. Kenya.
101 UNTS 289. UK Great Britain. Jamaica.
101 UNTS 289. UK Great Britain. Tanganyika.
101 UNTS 289. UK Great Britain. Uganda.
101 UNTS 289. UK Great Britain. Zanzibar.
121 UNTS 329. UK Great Britain. Nyasaland.
121 UNTS 329. UK Great Britain. Northern
Rhodesia. Force 6 Feb 52.
127 UNTS 331.   Netherlands.   Accession
10 Apr 52.
185 UNTS 394. Italy. Ratification 26 Jan 54.

212 UNTS 296. Austria. Amendment 3 Jun 54. Force 7 Jul 55.
212 UNTS 296. Norway. Amendment 10 Feb 54. Force 7 Jul 55.
212 UNTS 296. Netherlands. Amendment 28 Nov 52. Force 7 Jul 55.
212 UNTS 296. Sweden. Amendment 28 Nov 52. Force 7 Jul 55.
212 UNTS 296. Switzerland. Amendment 28 Nov 52. Force 7 Jul 55.
212 UNTS 296. France. Amendment 28 Nov 52. Force 7 Jul 55.
212 UNTS 296. Italy. Amendment 7 Jul 55. Force 7 Jul 55.
212 UNTS 296. Denmark. Amendment 28 Nov 52. Force 7 Jul 55.
257 UNTS 361. Turkey. Accession 16 Jan 57.
304 UNTS 348. Yugoslavia. Accession 10 Jul 58.
313 UNTS 336. UK Great Britain. Denunciation 30 Sep 58. Force 1 Jan 59.
320 UNTS 324. Poland. Accession 7 Jan 59.
324 UNTS 298. Sweden. Denunciation 25 Feb 59. Force 1 Jan 60.
338 UNTS 332. UK Great Britain. Denunciation 30 Jul 59.
351 UNTS 379. Norway. Denunciation 2 Mar 60. Force 1 Jan 61.
358 UNTS 253. France. Denunciation 6 May 60. Force 1 Jan 61.
366 UNTS 382. Switzerland. Denunciation 7 Jul 60. Force 1 Jan 61.
366 UNTS 382. Liechtenstein. Denunciation 7 Jul 60. Force 1 Jan 61.
378 UNTS 370. Netherlands. Denunciation 16 Sep 60. Force 1 Jan 61.
381 UNTS 378. Yugoslavia. Denunciation 8 Dec 60. Force 1 Jan 62.
394 UNTS 254. Austria. Denunciation 25 Apr 61. Force 1 Jan 62.
407 UNTS 234. Denmark. Denunciation 15 Sep 61. Force 1 Jan 62.
411 UNTS 295. Poland. Denunciation 20 Oct 61. Force 1 Jan 63.
480 UNTS 318. Austria. Denunciation 15 Oct 63. Force 1 Jan 65.
486 UNTS 397. Yugoslavia. Denunciation 29 Jan 64. Force 1 Jan 65.
489 UNTS 366. Italy. Denunciation 20 Feb 64. Force 1 Jan 65.
505 UNTS 304. Turkey. Denunciation 10 Aug 64. Force 1 Jan 65.
523 UNTS 319. Norway. Denunciation 3 Feb 65. Force 1 Jan 66.

100697 Bilateral Agreement **46 UNTS 3**
SIGNED: 8 Dec 48 FORCE: 10 Dec 48
REGISTERED: 11 Jan 50 Afghanistan
ARTICLES: 12 LANGUAGE: French. Persian.
HEADNOTE: EDUCATIONAL MISSION
TOPIC: Education
CONCEPTS: Definition of terms. Privileges and immunities. General cooperation. Exchange of official publications. Personnel. Responsibility and liability. Exchange. Vocational training. Indemnities and reimbursements. Expense sharing formulae. Funding procedures. Aid missions.
TREATY REF: 4UNTS275; 18UNTS383.
PROCEDURE: Amendment. Duration. Future Procedures Contemplated.
PARTIES:
Afghanistan
UNESCO (Educ/Cult)

100698 Bilateral Convention **46 UNTS 15**
SIGNED: 20 Jun 47 FORCE: 23 Apr 48
REGISTERED: 16 Jan 50 Czechoslovakia
ARTICLES: 18 LANGUAGE: Bulgarian. Czechoslovakian.
HEADNOTE: CULTURAL EDUCATIONAL RELATIONS
TOPIC: Education
CONCEPTS: Tourism. Exchange of information and documents. Domestic legislation. Dispute settlement. Specialists exchange. Recognition of degrees. Exchange. Teacher and student exchange. Professorships. Institute establishment. Scholarships and grants. Vocational training. Exchange. Artists. Athletes. Research cooperation. Scientific exchange. Tax exemptions. Laws and formalities. Publications exchange. Mass media exchange. Press and wire services. Conferences.
INTL ORGS: Special Commission.

PROCEDURE: Duration. Ratification. Renewal or Revival. Termination.
PARTIES:
Bulgaria
Czechoslovakia

100699 Bilateral Convention **46 UNTS 37**
SIGNED: 5 Sep 47 FORCE: 8 Apr 48
REGISTERED: 16 Jan 50 Czechoslovakia
ARTICLES: 19 LANGUAGE: Czechoslovakian. Romanian.
HEADNOTE: CULTURAL COLLABORATION
TOPIC: Education
CONCEPTS: Tourism. General cooperation. Exchange of information and documents. Domestic legislation. Specialists exchange. Recognition of degrees. Exchange. Commissions and foundations. Teacher and student exchange. Professorships. Institute establishment. Scholarships and grants. Vocational training. Exchange. Artists. Research cooperation. Scientific exchange. Recognition. Publications exchange. Mass media exchange. Press and wire services. Conferences.
INTL ORGS: Special Commission.
PROCEDURE: Duration. Future Procedures Contemplated. Ratification. Renewal or Revival. Termination.
PARTIES:
Czechoslovakia
Romania

100700 Bilateral Convention **46 UNTS 61**
SIGNED: 16 Jun 47 FORCE: 15 Oct 47
REGISTERED: 16 Jan 50 Czechoslovakia
ARTICLES: 17 LANGUAGE: Czechoslovakian. English.
HEADNOTE: CULTURAL COOPERATION
TOPIC: Education
CONCEPTS: Definition of terms. Territorial application. Annex or appendix reference. Exchange of information and documents. Recognition of degrees. Exchange. Commissions and foundations. Teacher and student exchange. Professorships. Institute establishment. Scholarships and grants. Vocational training. Artists. Research cooperation. Scientific exchange. Mass media exchange. Conferences.
INTL ORGS: Special Commission.
PROCEDURE: Duration. Future Procedures Contemplated. Ratification. Termination.
PARTIES:
Czechoslovakia
UK Great Britain
ANNEX
70 UNTS 302. Czechoslovakia. Confirmation 16 Jun 47.
70 UNTS 302. UK Great Britain. Confirmation 16 Jun 47.

100701 Bilateral Protocol **46 UNTS 77**
SIGNED: 8 Dec 45 FORCE: 8 Dec 45
REGISTERED: 16 Jan 50 Czechoslovakia
ARTICLES: 15 LANGUAGE: Czechoslovakian. French.
HEADNOTE: SCIENTIFIC LITERARY EDUCATIONAL RELATIONS
TOPIC: Education
CONCEPTS: Nazi organizations. General cooperation. Exchange of information and documents. Exchange. Commissions and foundations. Teacher and student exchange. Professorships. Scholarships and grants. Vocational training. Exchange. Research cooperation. Research results. Scientific exchange. Indemnities and reimbursements. Publications exchange. Mass media exchange. Conferences.
INTL ORGS: Special Commission.
PROCEDURE: Future Procedures Contemplated.
PARTIES:
Czechoslovakia
France

100702 Bilateral Exchange **46 UNTS 97**
SIGNED: 14 Oct 49 FORCE: 15 Oct 49
REGISTERED: 20 Jan 50 Denmark
ARTICLES: 2 LANGUAGE: English.
HEADNOTE: MODIFYING VISA REQUIREMENTS
TOPIC: Visas
CONCEPTS: Territorial application. Time limit. De-

nial of admission. Visas. Tourism. Conformity with municipal law.
PARTIES:
Canada
Denmark
ANNEX
392 UNTS 332. Canada. Amendment 14 Jul 58. Force 14 Jul 58.
392 UNTS 332. Denmark. Amendment 14 Jul 58. Force 14 Jul 58.

100703 Bilateral Exchange **46 UNTS 103**
SIGNED: 25 Jul 49 FORCE: 25 Jul 49
REGISTERED: 24 Jan 50 Belgium
ARTICLES: 2 LANGUAGE: French. Spanish.
HEADNOTE: EXEMPTION TAXATION PROFITS SHIPPING COMPANIES
TOPIC: Taxation
CONCEPTS: Definition of terms. Taxation. Tax exemptions. Merchant vessels.
PROCEDURE: Denunciation.
PARTIES:
Argentina
Belgium

100704 Bilateral Convention **46 UNTS 111**
SIGNED: 30 Dec 49 FORCE: 29 Dec 47
REGISTERED: 24 Jan 50 Belgium
ARTICLES: 10 LANGUAGE: French.
HEADNOTE: AVOIDANCE DOUBLE TAXATION REGARD TAXES CAPITAL
TOPIC: Taxation
CONCEPTS: Nationality and citizenship. Negotiation. Assets. Taxation. General.
PROCEDURE: Ratification.
PARTIES:
Belgium
France

100705 Bilateral Exchange **46 UNTS 125**
SIGNED: 21 Dec 49 FORCE: 23 Dec 49
REGISTERED: 24 Jan 50 Denmark
ARTICLES: 2 LANGUAGE: Danish. Swedish.
HEADNOTE: ABOLITION VISA REQUIREMENTS
TOPIC: Visas
CONCEPTS: Time limit. Visa abolition. Denial of admission. Tourism.
PARTIES:
Denmark
Finland

100706 Bilateral Convention **46 UNTS 133**
SIGNED: 20 Aug 49 FORCE: 19 Sep 49
REGISTERED: 26 Jan 50 Belgium
ARTICLES: 6 LANGUAGE: Dutch. French.
HEADNOTE: VETERINARY PRACTICE FRONTIER COMMUNITIES
TOPIC: Visas
CONCEPTS: Detailed regulations. Previous treaty replacement. Exchange of information and documents. Export quotas. Frontier peoples and personnel.
TREATY REF: DECLA-5MAR1884.
PROCEDURE: Denunciation. Ratification.
PARTIES:
Belgium
Netherlands

100707 Bilateral Agreement **46 UNTS 143**
SIGNED: 27 Feb 48 FORCE: 11 Nov 48
REGISTERED: 31 Jan 50 Poland
ARTICLES: 7 LANGUAGE: Polish. Romanian.
HEADNOTE: CULTURAL COOPERATION
TOPIC: Culture
CONCEPTS: Friendship and amity. Conformity with municipal law. Operating agencies. Establishment of commission. Recognition of degrees. Exchange. Teacher and student exchange. Professorships. Institute establishment. Scholarships and grants. General cultural cooperation. Artists. Research cooperation. Scientific exchange. Publications exchange. Mass media exchange. Press and wire services.
INTL ORGS: Special Commission.
PROCEDURE: Denunciation. Duration. Ratification. Renewal or Revival.
PARTIES:
Poland
Romania

100708 Bilateral Exchange **46 UNTS 163**
SIGNED: 23 Aug 49　　FORCE: 1 Jul 49
REGISTERED: 22 Sep 49 Belgium
ARTICLES: 2 LANGUAGE: French. Spanish.
HEADNOTE: GENERAL ECONOMIC AGREEMENT
　TRADE TARIFFS
TOPIC: General Economic
CONCEPTS: Treaty implementation. General
　trade. Tariffs.
TREATY REF: GATT PUB., 1947 2-10.
PROCEDURE: Renewal or Revival.
PARTIES:
　Belgium
　Chile

100709 Multilateral Protocol **46 UNTS 169**
SIGNED: 12 Nov 47　　FORCE: 12 Nov 47
REGISTERED: 2 Feb 50 United Nations
ARTICLES: 7 LANGUAGE: Chinese. English.
　French. Russian. Spanish.
HEADNOTE: AMENDMENT
TOPIC: Admin Cooperation
CONCEPTS: Annex type material. Previous treaty
　extension.
INTL ORGS: League of Nations. United Nations.
PARTIES:
　Afghanistan　SIGNED:　12 Nov 47　FORCE:
　　12 Nov 47
　Albania RATIFIED: 25 Jul 49 FORCE: 25 Jul 49
　Argentina SIGNED: 12 Nov 47
　Australia SIGNED: 13 Nov 47 FORCE: 13 Nov 47
　Belgium SIGNED: 12 Nov 47 FORCE: 12 Nov 47
　Brazil SIGNED: 17 Mar 48
　Burma SIGNED: 13 May 49 FORCE: 13 May 49
　Canada SIGNED: 24 Nov 47 FORCE: 24 Nov 47
　Taiwan SIGNED: 12 Nov 47 FORCE: 12 Nov 47
　Czechoslovakia　SIGNED:　12 Nov 47　FORCE:
　　12 Nov 47
　Denmark　SIGNED:　12 Nov 47　RATIFIED:
　　21 Nov 49 FORCE: 21 Nov 49
　United Arab Rep SIGNED: 12 Nov 47 FORCE:
　　12 Nov 47
　Finland RATIFIED: 6 Jan 49 FORCE: 6 Jan 49
　Guatemala　SIGNED:　9 Jul 48　RATIFIED:
　　26 Aug 49 FORCE: 26 Aug 49
　Haiti SIGNED: 12 Nov 47
　Hungary SIGNED: 12 Feb 50 FORCE: 12 Feb 50
　India SIGNED: 12 Nov 47 FORCE: 12 Nov 47
　Italy SIGNED: 16 Jun 49 FORCE: 16 Jun 49
　Luxembourg SIGNED: 12 Nov 47
　Mexico SIGNED: 4 Feb 48 FORCE: 4 Feb 48
　Netherlands　SIGNED:　12 Nov 47　RATIFIED:
　　7 Mar 49 FORCE: 7 Mar 49
　New Zealand　SIGNED:　28 Oct 48　FORCE:
　　28 Oct 48
　Norway　SIGNED:　12 Nov 47　RATIFIED:
　　28 Nov 47 FORCE: 28 Nov 47
　Pakistan SIGNED: 12 Nov 47 FORCE: 12 Nov 47
　Panama SIGNED: 20 Nov 47
　South Africa　SIGNED:　12 Nov 47　FORCE:
　　12 Nov 47
　Turkey SIGNED: 12 Nov 47 FORCE: 12 Nov 47
　UK Great Britain SIGNED: 16 May 49 FORCE:
　　16 May 49
　USSR (Soviet Union) SIGNED: 18 Dec 47 FORCE:
　　18 Dec 47
　Yugoslavia　SIGNED:　12 Nov 47　FORCE:
　　12 Nov 47
ANNEX
51 UNTS 332. Brazil. Ratification 3 Apr 50.
68 UNTS 280. Austria. Signature without Reserva-
　tion as to Approval 4 Aug 50.
76 UNTS 279. Romania. Signature without Reser-
　vation as to Approval 2 Nov 50.
77 UNTS 363. Poland. Acceptance 21 Dec 50.
122 UNTS 339. Ireland. Acceptance 28 Feb 52.
207 UNTS 329.　Luxembourg.　Acceptance
　14 Mar 55.
354 UNTS 391. Greece. Acceptance 5 Apr 60.

100710 Multilateral Convention **46 UNTS 201**
SIGNED: 12 Nov 47　　FORCE: 2 Feb 50
REGISTERED: 2 Feb 50 United Nations
ARTICLES: 16 LANGUAGE: English. French.
HEADNOTE: SUPPRESS OBSCENE PUBLICA-
　TIONS
TOPIC: Admin Cooperation
CONCEPTS: Court procedures. General cooper-
　ation. Domestic legislation. Investigation of vio-
　lations. Domestic jurisdiction. Existing tribunals.
INTL ORGS: League of Nations. International Court
　of Justice. United Nations.

PROCEDURE: Accession. Denunciation. Ratifica-
　tion.
PARTIES:
　Afghanistan FORCE: 2 Feb 50
　Albania FORCE: 2 Feb 50
　Australia FORCE: 2 Feb 50
　Belgium FORCE: 2 Feb 50
　Burma FORCE: 2 Feb 50
　Canada FORCE: 2 Feb 50
　China FORCE: 2 Feb 50
　Czechoslovakia FORCE: 2 Feb 50
　Denmark FORCE: 2 Feb 50
　United Arab Rep FORCE: 2 Feb 50
　Finland FORCE: 2 Feb 50
　Guatemala FORCE: 2 Feb 50
　Hungary FORCE: 2 Feb 50
　India FORCE: 2 Feb 50
　Italy FORCE: 2 Feb 50
　Mexico FORCE: 2 Feb 50
　Netherlands FORCE: 2 Feb 50
　New Zealand FORCE: 2 Feb 50
　Norway FORCE: 2 Feb 50
　Pakistan FORCE: 2 Feb 50
　South Africa FORCE: 2 Feb 50
　Turkey FORCE: 2 Feb 50
　UK Great Britain FORCE: 2 Feb 50
　USSR (Soviet Union) FORCE: 2 Feb 50
　Yugoslavia FORCE: 2 Feb 50
ANNEX
51 UNTS 333. Brazil. Accession 3 Apr 50.
68 UNTS 280. Austria. Accession 4 Aug 50.
76 UNTS 279. Romania. Accession 2 Nov 50.
77 UNTS 363. Poland. Accession 21 Dec 50.
122 UNTS 339. Ireland. Accession 28 Feb 52.
172 UNTS 339. Haiti. Ratification 26 Aug 53.
207 UNTS 330.　Luxembourg.　Accession
　14 Mar 55.
292 UNTS 360. Ghana. Acceptance 7 Apr 58.
293 UNTS 335. Ceylon (Sri Lanka). Accession
　15 Apr 58.
309 UNTS 356. Fed of Malaya. Replacement
　21 Aug 58. Force 31 Aug 57.
327 UNTS 348. Cambodia. Accession 30 Mar 59.
328 UNTS 288. Jordan. Accession 11 May 59.
354 UNTS 392. Greece. Acceptance 5 Apr 60.
399 UNTS 263. Nigeria. Succession 26 Jun 61.
423 UNTS 297.　Sierra　Leone.　Succession
　13 Mar 62.
429 UNTS 267.　Congo　(Zaire).　Succession
　31 May 62.
445 UNTS 289.　　Tanganyika.　　Accession
　28 Nov 62.
458 UNTS 276.　　Madagascar.　　Accession
　10 Apr 63.
466 UNTS 380. Cyprus. Succession 16 May 63.
503 UNTS 327. Jamaica. Succession 30 Jul 64.
541 UNTS 305. Malawi. Accession 22 Jul 65.
560 UNTS 238.　Trinidad/Tobago.　Succession
　11 Apr 66.
603 UNTS 295.　　Denmark.　　Denunciation
　16 Aug 67. Force 16 Aug 68.

100711 Bilateral Agreement **46 UNTS 215**
SIGNED: 1 Sep 49　　FORCE: 2 Sep 49
REGISTERED: 2 Feb 50 Australia
ARTICLES: 24 LANGUAGE: English.
HEADNOTE: PARCEL POST
TOPIC: Postal Service
CONCEPTS: Customs duties. Postal services. Reg-
　ulations. Conveyance in transit. Parcel post.
　Rates and charges.
TREATY REF: UNIVERSAL POSTAL CONV.
PROCEDURE: Ratification. Termination.
PARTIES:
　Australia
　Philippines

100712 Bilateral Exchange **46 UNTS 233**
SIGNED: 22 Dec 49　　FORCE: 15 Jan 50
REGISTERED: 13 Feb 50 Belgium
ARTICLES: 2 LANGUAGE: French.
HEADNOTE: RE-ENTRY FORCE CERTAIN INSTRU-
　MENTS LEGAL ASSISTANCE
TOPIC: Admin Cooperation
CONCEPTS: Revival of treaties.
TREATY REF: 50LTS180; 112LTS43.
PARTIES:
　Austria
　Belgium

100713 Bilateral Exchange **46 UNTS 241**
SIGNED: 15 Jan 49　　FORCE: 15 Jan 49
REGISTERED: 13 Feb 50 Netherlands
ARTICLES: 2 LANGUAGE: Spanish.
HEADNOTE: DOUBLE TAXATION REVENUE SHIP-
　PING AIR TRANSPORT
TOPIC: Taxation
CONCEPTS: Taxation. Tax exemptions. Air trans-
　port. Merchant vessels.
PARTIES:
　Argentina
　Netherlands

100714 Multilateral Agreement **46 UNTS 249**
SIGNED: 6 Jun 47　　FORCE: 10 Jun 49
REGISTERED: 13 Feb 50 Netherlands
ARTICLES: 14 LANGUAGE: Danish. French.
HEADNOTE: ESTABLISHMENT INTERNATIONAL
　PATENTS BUREAU
TOPIC: Patents/Copyrights
CONCEPTS: Laws and formalities. Establishment.
　Headquarters and facilities. Liaison with other
　IGO's. Internal structure.
INTL ORGS: International Union for the Protection
　of Industrial Property. International Patent Insti-
　tute.
TREATY REF: 74LTS289.
PROCEDURE: Accession. Denunciation. Ratifica-
　tion.
PARTIES:
　Belgium SIGNED: 6 Jun 47 FORCE: 10 Jun 49
　France SIGNED: 6 Jun 47 FORCE: 10 Jun 49
　Luxembourg　SIGNED:　6 Jun 47　FORCE:
　　10 Jun 49
　Netherlands　SIGNED:　6 Jun 47　FORCE:
　　10 Jun 49
ANNEX
572 UNTS 295. Turkey. Adherence 23 Sep 55.
572 UNTS 295. Morocco. Adherence 1 Jan 56.
572 UNTS 295. Monaco. Adherence 2 Aug 56.
572 UNTS 295.　　Switzerland.　　Adherence
　1 Jan 60.
572 UNTS 295.　UK Great Britain.　Adherence
　2 Aug 65.
572 UNTS 295. Tunisia. Denunciation 8 Feb 61.
　Force 8 Mar 62.
572 UNTS 295. Tunisia. Adherence 30 Mar 55.

100715 Bilateral Exchange **46 UNTS 263**
SIGNED: 9 May 49　　FORCE: 9 May 49
REGISTERED: 13 Feb 50 Netherlands
ARTICLES: 2 LANGUAGE: English.
HEADNOTE: SETTLEMENT CLAIMS
TOPIC: Reparations
CONCEPTS: Indemnities and reimbursements.
　Currency. Payment schedules. Lump sum settle-
　ments. Loss and/or damage. Post-war claims set-
　tlement.
INTL ORGS: Allied Military Occupation.
PARTIES:
　Canada
　Netherlands

100716 Bilateral Instrument **46 UNTS 271**
SIGNED: 4 Dec 48　　FORCE: 4 Dec 48
REGISTERED: 13 Feb 50 Netherlands
ARTICLES: 14 LANGUAGE: French.
HEADNOTE: ITALIAN WORKERS NETHERLANDS
　MINES
TOPIC: Non-ILO Labor
CONCEPTS: Repatriation of nationals. Jurisdic-
　tion. Private contracts. Use of facilities. Estab-
　lishment of commission. Employment regula-
　tions. Safety standards. Wages and salaries.
　Non-ILO labor relations. Migrant worker. Pay-
　ment schedules. Transportation costs. National
　treatment.
INTL ORGS: Special Commission.
PROCEDURE: Denunciation. Duration.
PARTIES:
　Italy
　Netherlands

100717 Bilateral Agreement **46 UNTS 291**
SIGNED: 17 May 49　　FORCE: 17 May 49
REGISTERED: 13 Feb 50 Netherlands
ARTICLES: 17 LANGUAGE: Dutch. English.
HEADNOTE: SETTLEMENT LEND-LEASE AID SUR-
　PLUS PROPERTY MILITARY RELIEF CLAIMS
TOPIC: Milit Assistance

CONCEPTS: Definition of terms. Exceptions and exemptions. General provisions. Guarantees and safeguards. Procedure. Exchange. Commissions and foundations. Teacher and student exchange. Scholarships and grants. Monetary and gold transfers. Exchange rates and regulations. Expense sharing formulae. Tax exemptions. Customs exemptions. Surplus property. Lend lease.
TREATY REF: 17UNTS29.
PARTIES:
Netherlands
USA (United States)

100718 Bilateral Exchange **46 UNTS 319**
SIGNED: 14 Nov 49 FORCE: 1 Dec 49
REGISTERED: 17 Feb 50 Belgium
ARTICLES: 2 LANGUAGE: Czechoslovakian. French.
HEADNOTE: EXEMPTING CREWS AIRCRAFT TRANSIT VISA REQUIREMENTS
TOPIC: Visas
CONCEPTS: Visa abolition.
PARTIES:
Belgium
Czechoslovakia
ANNEX
73 UNTS 273. Czechoslovakia. Supplementation 28 Jun 50. Force 13 Jul 50.
73 UNTS 273. Belgium. Supplementation 3 Apr 50. Force 13 Jul 50.

100719 Bilateral Instrument **47 UNTS 3**
SIGNED: 25 Feb 49 FORCE: 6 Aug 49
REGISTERED: 17 Feb 50 Belgium
ARTICLES: 5 LANGUAGE: French.
HEADNOTE: RECIPROCAL COMMUNICATION CIVIL STATUS CERTIFICATES NATIONALITY RECORDS
TOPIC: Admin Cooperation
CONCEPTS: Previous treaty replacement. Exchange of information and documents. Fees and exemptions.
TREATY REF: 197LTS141.
PARTIES:
Belgium
Luxembourg

100720 Bilateral Exchange **47 UNTS 9**
SIGNED: 4 Jul 47 FORCE: 4 Jul 47
REGISTERED: 17 Feb 50 Belgium
ARTICLES: 12 LANGUAGE: Afrikaans. Dutch.
HEADNOTE: RELEASE ASSETS
TOPIC: Claims and Debts
CONCEPTS: Definition of terms. Territorial application. Exchange of information and documents. Informational records. General property. Responsibility and liability. Compensation. Monetary and gold transfers. Fees and exemptions. Assets. Lump sum settlements. Assessment procedures. Assets transfer. Most favored nation clause. General. War claims and reparations. Enemy financial interests.
PARTIES:
Belgium
South Africa

100721 Bilateral Agreement **47 UNTS 23**
SIGNED: 23 Jan 47 FORCE: 10 Mar 47
REGISTERED: 17 Feb 50 Belgium
ARTICLES: 12 LANGUAGE: English. French.
HEADNOTE: ADMISSION BELGIUM DISPLACED PERSONS AMERICAN ZONE GERMANY
TOPIC: Visas
CONCEPTS: Border traffic and migration. Legal status.
INTL ORGS: Intergovernmental Committee on Refugees.
PARTIES:
Belgium
USA (United States)

100722 Bilateral Agreement **47 UNTS 39**
SIGNED: 14 Nov 47 FORCE: 10 Mar 49
REGISTERED: 20 Feb 50 ICAO (Civil Aviat)
ARTICLES: 12 LANGUAGE: Dutch. French. Portuguese.

HEADNOTE: AIR TRANSPORT
TOPIC: Air Transport
CONCEPTS: Definition of terms. Treaty interpretation. Annex or appendix reference. Previous treaty replacement. Conformity with municipal law. Use of facilities. Arbitration. Procedure. Fees and exemptions. Most favored nation clause. National treatment. Customs exemptions. Routes and logistics. Air transport. Airport facilities. Conditions of airlines operating permission. Operating authorizations and regulations.
INTL ORGS: International Civil Aviation Organization. Arbitration Commission.
TREATY REF: 15UNTS295.
PROCEDURE: Amendment. Future Procedures Contemplated. Ratification. Registration. Termination.
PARTIES:
Brazil
Denmark

100723 Bilateral Agreement **47 UNTS 75**
SIGNED: 19 Nov 49 FORCE: 19 Nov 49
REGISTERED: 24 Feb 50 Norway
ARTICLES: 7 LANGUAGE: French.
HEADNOTE: COMMERCE
TOPIC: General Trade
CONCEPTS: Annex or appendix reference. Previous treaty replacement. Establishment of commission. Reciprocity in trade. Payment schedules.
INTL ORGS: Special Commission.
TREATY REF: 30UNTS177.
PROCEDURE: Denunciation. Duration. Ratification.
PARTIES:
Italy
Norway

100724 Bilateral Agreement **47 UNTS 89**
SIGNED: 19 Nov 49 FORCE: 19 Nov 49
REGISTERED: 24 Feb 50 Norway
ARTICLES: 11 LANGUAGE: French.
HEADNOTE: SETTLEMENT RECIPROCAL PAYMENTS
TOPIC: Finance
CONCEPTS: Detailed regulations. Previous treaty replacement. Governor-general functions. Accounting procedures. Banking. Balance of payments. Exchange rates and regulations. Interest rates. Payment schedules. Local currency. Debt settlement. Loan and credit. Loan repayment.
TREATY REF: 47UNTS75.
PROCEDURE: Denunciation. Duration. Renewal or Revival.
PARTIES:
Italy
Norway

100725 Bilateral Agreement **47 UNTS 107**
SIGNED: 21 Dec 49 FORCE: 21 Dec 49
REGISTERED: 24 Feb 50 Norway
ARTICLES: 13 LANGUAGE: French.
HEADNOTE: SETTLEMENT PAYMENTS
TOPIC: Finance
CONCEPTS: Detailed regulations. Previous treaty replacement. General cooperation. Licenses and permits. Establishment of commission. Negotiation. Accounting procedures. Banking. Exchange rates and regulations. Interest rates. Payment schedules. Local currency.
INTL ORGS: Special Commission.
TREATY REF: 29UNTS3 357; 15UNTS203; 25UNTS344.
PROCEDURE: Amendment. Denunciation. Duration. Renewal or Revival.
PARTIES:
Norway
Poland

100726 Bilateral Agreement **47 UNTS 117**
SIGNED: 28 Nov 49 FORCE: 28 Nov 49
REGISTERED: 24 Feb 50 Norway
ARTICLES: 11 LANGUAGE: French.
HEADNOTE: PAYMENTS
TOPIC: Finance
CONCEPTS: Detailed regulations. Previous treaty replacement. General cooperation. Accounting procedures. Banking. Balance of payments. Currency. Currency deposits. Exchange rates and

regulations. Internal finance. Payment schedules. Local currency. Assets.
PROCEDURE: Amendment. Duration. Renewal or Revival.
PARTIES:
Norway
Portugal

100727 Multilateral Convention **47 UNTS 127**
SIGNED: 27 Aug 49 FORCE: 1 Dec 49
REGISTERED: 24 Feb 50 Norway
ARTICLES: 7 LANGUAGE: Danish. Finnish. Icelandic. Swedish. Norwegian.
HEADNOTE: MUTUAL PAYMENT OLD-AGE PENSIONS
TOPIC: Non-ILO Labor
CONCEPTS: Detailed regulations. Representation. Annex type material. Non-ILO labor relations. Old age insurance. Payment schedules. National treatment.
PROCEDURE: Denunciation. Ratification.
PARTIES:
Denmark SIGNED: 27 Aug 49 RATIFIED: 30 Sep 49 FORCE: 1 Dec 49
Finland SIGNED: 27 Aug 49 RATIFIED: 30 Sep 49 FORCE: 1 Dec 49
Iceland SIGNED: 27 Aug 49 RATIFIED: 30 Sep 49 FORCE: 1 Dec 49
Norway SIGNED: 27 Aug 49 RATIFIED: 30 Sep 49 FORCE: 1 Dec 49
Sweden SIGNED: 27 Aug 49 RATIFIED: 30 Sep 49 FORCE: 1 Dec 49

100728 Multilateral Agreement **47 UNTS 159**
SIGNED: 4 May 49 FORCE: 1 Mar 50
REGISTERED: 1 Mar 50 United Nations
ARTICLES: 8 LANGUAGE: French.
HEADNOTE: SUPPRESSION CIRCULATION OBSCENE PUBLICATIONS
TOPIC: Admin Cooperation
CONCEPTS: Territorial application. General cooperation. Operating agencies.
INTL ORGS: United Nations.
TREATY REF: 11LTS438.
PROCEDURE: Accession. Denunciation. Ratification.
PARTIES:
Australia FORCE: 1 Mar 50
Canada FORCE: 1 Mar 50
Ceylon (Sri Lanka) FORCE: 1 Mar 50
Taiwan FORCE: 1 Mar 50
Denmark FORCE: 1 Mar 50
United Arab Rep FORCE: 1 Mar 50
Finland FORCE: 1 Mar 50
France FORCE: 1 Mar 50
India FORCE: 1 Mar 50
Norway FORCE: 1 Mar 50
Switzerland FORCE: 1 Mar 50
UK Great Britain FORCE: 1 Mar 50
USSR (Soviet Union) FORCE: 1 Mar 50
ANNEX
68 UNTS 281. Austria. Accession 4 Aug 50.
68 UNTS 281. USA (United States). Accession 14 Aug 50.
71 UNTS 327. South Africa. Accession 1 Sep 50.
71 UNTS 327. Netherlands. Accession 26 Sep 50.
71 UNTS 327. Turkey. Accession 13 Sep 50.
71 UNTS 327. Iraq. Accession 14 Sep 50.
73 UNTS 277. Iceland. Accession 25 Oct 50.
73 UNTS 277. New Zealand. Accession 14 Oct 50.
76 UNTS 280. Romania. Accession 2 Nov 50.
88 UNTS 453. Pakistan. Accession 4 May 51.
92 UNTS 403. Czechoslovakia. Accession 21 Jun 51.
122 UNTS 340. Ireland. Accession 28 Feb 52.
134 UNTS 378. Mexico. Accession 22 Jul 52.
140 UNTS 438. Belgium. Accession 13 Oct 52.
149 UNTS 409. Italy. Accession 13 Nov 52.
164 UNTS 361. Yugoslavia. Accession 29 Apr 53.
172 UNTS 339. Haiti. Acceptance 26 Aug 53.
207 UNTS 331. Luxembourg. Accession 14 Mar 55.
292 UNTS 360. Ghana. Acceptance 7 Apr 58.
309 UNTS 357. Fed of Malaya. Replacement 21 Aug 58. Force 31 Aug 57.
327 UNTS 349. Cambodia. Acceptance 30 Mar 59.
328 UNTS 289. Jordan. Acceptance 11 May 59.
347 UNTS 361. Iran. Acceptance 30 Dec 59.
399 UNTS 264. Nigeria. Succession 26 Jun 61.

423 UNTS 298. Sierra Leone. Succession 13 Mar 62.
429 UNTS 267. Congo (Zaire). Succession 31 May 62.
458 UNTS 277. Madagascar. Accession 10 Apr 63.
466 UNTS 380. Cyprus. Succession 16 May 63.
541 UNTS 306. Malawi. Acceptance 22 Jul 65.
560 UNTS 238. Trinidad/Tobago. Succession 11 Apr 66.

100729 Bilateral Agreement **47 UNTS 167**
SIGNED: 27 Aug 48   FORCE: 20 Dec 47
REGISTERED: 1 Mar 50 United Nations
ARTICLES: 6 LANGUAGE: English.
HEADNOTE: 1948 UN APPEAL CHILDREN
TOPIC: Humanitarian
CONCEPTS: Humanitarian matters. Aid and development.
PROCEDURE: Duration.
PARTIES:
 Canada
 United Nations

100730 Bilateral Agreement **47 UNTS 185**
SIGNED: 7 Oct 48   FORCE: 19 Jan 48
REGISTERED: 1 Mar 50 United Nations
ARTICLES: 6 LANGUAGE: English.
HEADNOTE: CAMPAIGN UN APPEAL CHILDREN
TOPIC: Humanitarian
CONCEPTS: Definition of terms. Detailed regulations. Annex or appendix reference. Conformity with municipal law. General cooperation. Inspection and observation. Juridical personality. General property. Establishment of commission. Humanitarian matters. Accounting procedures. Expense sharing formulae. Tax exemptions. Assistance to United Nations. UN recommendations.
PARTIES:
 Czechoslovakia
 United Nations

100731 Bilateral Agreement **47 UNTS 203**
SIGNED: 10 Mar 48   FORCE: 10 Dec 47
REGISTERED: 1 Mar 50 United Nations
ARTICLES: 6 LANGUAGE: French.
HEADNOTE: CAMPAIGN UN APPEAL CHILDREN
TOPIC: Humanitarian
CONCEPTS: Definition of terms. Detailed regulations. Annex or appendix reference. Conformity with municipal law. General cooperation. Inspection and observation. Juridical personality. General property. Establishment of commission. Humanitarian matters. Accounting procedures. Expense sharing formulae. Tax exemptions. Assistance to United Nations. UN recommendations.
PARTIES:
 France
 United Nations

100732 Bilateral Agreement **47 UNTS 223**
SIGNED: 12 Feb 48   FORCE: 12 Feb 48
REGISTERED: 1 Mar 50 United Nations
ARTICLES: 6 LANGUAGE: English. Greek.
HEADNOTE: CAMPAIGN UN APPEAL CHILDREN
TOPIC: Humanitarian
CONCEPTS: Definition of terms. Detailed regulations. Annex or appendix reference. Conformity with municipal law. General cooperation. Inspection and observation. Juridical personality. General property. Establishment of commission. Humanitarian matters. Accounting procedures. Expense sharing formulae. Tax exemptions. Assistance to United Nations. UN recommendations.
PARTIES:
 Greece
 United Nations

100733 Bilateral Agreement **47 UNTS 251**
SIGNED: 19 Apr 48   FORCE: 1 Feb 48
REGISTERED: 1 Mar 50 United Nations
ARTICLES: 6 LANGUAGE: English.
HEADNOTE: 1948 UN APPEAL CHILDREN
TOPIC: Humanitarian
CONCEPTS: Humanitarian matters. Aid and development.
PROCEDURE: Duration.

PARTIES:
 Iceland
 United Nations

100734 Bilateral Agreement **47 UNTS 269**
SIGNED: 27 Aug 48   FORCE: 29 Feb 48
REGISTERED: 1 Mar 50 United Nations
ARTICLES: 6 LANGUAGE: English.
HEADNOTE: CAMPAIGN UN APPEAL CHILDREN
TOPIC: Humanitarian
CONCEPTS: Definition of terms. Detailed regulations. Annex or appendix reference. Conformity with municipal law. General cooperation. Inspection and observation. Juridical personality. General property. Establishment of commission. Humanitarian matters. Accounting procedures. Expense sharing formulae. Tax exemptions. Assistance to United Nations. UN recommendations.
PARTIES:
 Pakistan
 United Nations

100735 Bilateral Agreement **47 UNTS 287**
SIGNED: 5 Oct 48   FORCE: 5 Oct 48
REGISTERED: 1 Mar 50 United Nations
ARTICLES: 6 LANGUAGE: English.
HEADNOTE: CAMPAIGN UN APPEAL CHILDREN
TOPIC: Humanitarian
CONCEPTS: Definition of terms. Detailed regulations. Annex or appendix reference. Conformity with municipal law. General cooperation. Inspection and observation. Juridical personality. General property. Establishment of commission. Humanitarian matters. Accounting procedures. Expense sharing formulae. Tax exemptions. Assistance to United Nations. UN recommendations.
PARTIES:
 United Nations
 Thailand

100736 Bilateral Agreement **47 UNTS 305**
SIGNED: 18 Mar 49   FORCE: 5 Jul 49
REGISTERED: 1 Mar 50 United Nations
ARTICLES: 9 LANGUAGE: English.
HEADNOTE: CAMPAIGN UN APPEAL CHILDREN
TOPIC: Humanitarian
CONCEPTS: Definition of terms. Detailed regulations. Annex or appendix reference. Conformity with municipal law. General cooperation. Inspection and observation. Juridical personality. General property. Establishment of commission. Humanitarian matters. Accounting procedures. Indemnities and reimbursements. Expense sharing formulae. Tax exemptions. Assistance to United Nations. UN recommendations.
INTL ORGS: United Nations Children's Fund.
PARTIES:
 United Nations
 UK Great Britain

100737 Bilateral Convention **48 UNTS 3**
SIGNED: 22 Jun 49   FORCE: 31 Oct 49
REGISTERED: 3 Mar 50 Denmark
ARTICLES: 6 LANGUAGE: English.
HEADNOTE: MILITARY SERVICE
TOPIC: Milit Servic/Citiz
CONCEPTS: Dual nationality. Certificates of service. Service in foreign army.
PROCEDURE: Denunciation.
PARTIES:
 Denmark
 France

ANNEX
605 UNTS 328. Denmark. Termination 3 Feb 65.
605 UNTS 328. France. Termination 3 Feb 65.

100738 Bilateral Instrument **48 UNTS 9**
SIGNED: 26 Feb 48   FORCE: 26 Feb 48
REGISTERED: 10 Mar 50 USA (United States)
ARTICLES: 13 LANGUAGE: English.
HEADNOTE: PRE-WAR BILATERALS REVIVE OR RETAIN
TOPIC: Admin Cooperation
CONCEPTS: Revival of treaties.
INTL ORGS: United Nations.
TREATY REF: 105LTS19;   115LTS115;   105LTS85.

PARTIES:
 Romania
 USA (United States)
ANNEX
139 UNTS 458. USA (United States). Force 27 Jul 52.
139 UNTS 458. Romania. Force 27 Jul 52.

100739 Bilateral Exchange · **48 UNTS 107**
SIGNED: 5 Nov 49   FORCE: 20 Nov 49
REGISTERED: 14 Mar 50 Belgium
ARTICLES: 2 LANGUAGE: French.
HEADNOTE: REVIVAL INTERNATIONAL INSTRUMENTS RELATING EXTRADITION
TOPIC: Extradition
CONCEPTS: Territorial application. Public information. Revival of treaties.
TREATY REF: 72BFSP539;   112LTS37; 129LTS141.
PARTIES:
 Austria
 Belgium

100740 Bilateral Agreement **48 UNTS 115**
SIGNED: 27 Jan 50   FORCE: 27 Jan 50
REGISTERED: 15 Mar 50 Denmark
ARTICLES: 7 LANGUAGE: Danish. English.
HEADNOTE: MUTUAL DEFENSE ASSISTANCE AGREEMENT
TOPIC: Milit Assistance
CONCEPTS: Annex or appendix reference. Non-prejudice to UN charter. Privileges and immunities. Conformity with municipal law. General cooperation. Inspection and observation. Public information. Use of facilities. Indemnities and reimbursements. Local currency. Claims and settlements. Tax exemptions. Recognition. Customs exemptions. Domestic obligation. Materials, equipment and services. Aid missions. Joint defense. Defense and security. Self-defense. Military assistance. Security of information. Exchange of defense information. Restrictions on transfer.
INTL ORGS: North Atlantic Treaty Organization. United Nations.
TREATY REF: 34UNTS243.
PROCEDURE: Amendment. Duration. Future Procedures Contemplated. Registration. Termination.
PARTIES:
 Denmark
 USA (United States)

100741 Bilateral Treaty **48 UNTS 135**
SIGNED: 18 Mar 48   FORCE: 18 Mar 48
REGISTERED: 15 Mar 50 USSR (Soviet Union)
ARTICLES: 6 LANGUAGE: Bulgarian. Russian.
HEADNOTE: FRIENDSHIP COOPERATION MUTUAL ASSISTANCE
TOPIC: General Military
CONCEPTS: Friendship and amity. Non-prejudice to UN charter. Peaceful relations. General cultural cooperation. General trade. Defense and security. Military assistance.
PROCEDURE: Denunciation. Duration. Ratification. Termination.
PARTIES:
 Bulgaria
 USSR (Soviet Union)

100742 Bilateral Treaty **48 UNTS 149**
SIGNED: 6 Apr 48   FORCE: 31 May 48
REGISTERED: 15 Mar 50 USSR (Soviet Union)
ARTICLES: 8 LANGUAGE: Finnish. Russian.
HEADNOTE: FRIENDSHIP COOPERATION MUTUAL ASSISTANCE
TOPIC: General Military
CONCEPTS: Friendship and amity. Non-prejudice to UN charter. General cultural cooperation. General trade. Defense and security. Military assistance.
INTL ORGS: United Nations.
TREATY REF: 48UNTS203;.
PROCEDURE: Denunciation. Duration. Ratification. Termination.
PARTIES:
 Finland
 USSR (Soviet Union)

100743 Bilateral Treaty **48 UNTS 163**
SIGNED: 18 Feb 48 FORCE: 22 Apr 48
REGISTERED: 15 Mar 50 USSR (Soviet Union)
ARTICLES: 6 LANGUAGE: Hungarian. Russian.
HEADNOTE: FRIENDSHIP COOPERATION MUTUAL ASSISTANCE
TOPIC: General Military
CONCEPTS: Friendship and amity. Non-prejudice to UN charter. Peaceful relations. General cultural cooperation. General trade. Defense and security. Military assistance.
PROCEDURE: Denunciation. Duration. Ratification. Termination.
PARTIES:
Hungary
USSR (Soviet Union)

100744 Bilateral Treaty **48 UNTS 177**
SIGNED: 27 Feb 46 FORCE: 26 Apr 46
REGISTERED: 15 Mar 50 USSR (Soviet Union)
ARTICLES: 3 LANGUAGE: Mongolian. Russian.
HEADNOTE: FRIENDSHIP MUTUAL ASSISTANCE
TOPIC: General Military
CONCEPTS: Defense and security. Military assistance. Withdrawal of forces.
PROCEDURE: Denunciation. Duration. Ratification.
PARTIES:
Mongolia
USSR (Soviet Union)

100745 Bilateral Treaty **48 UNTS 189**
SIGNED: 4 Feb 48 FORCE: 4 Feb 48
REGISTERED: 15 Mar 50 USSR (Soviet Union)
ARTICLES: 6 LANGUAGE: Russian. Romanian.
HEADNOTE: FRIENDSHIP COOPERATION MUTUAL ASSISTANCE
TOPIC: General Military
CONCEPTS: Friendship and amity. Non-prejudice to UN charter. Peaceful relations. Defense and security. Military assistance.
PROCEDURE: Denunciation. Duration. Ratification. Termination.
PARTIES:
Romania
USSR (Soviet Union)

100746 Multilateral Treaty **48 UNTS 203**
SIGNED: 10 Feb 47 FORCE: 15 Sep 47
REGISTERED: 15 Mar 50 USSR (Soviet Union)
ARTICLES: 36 LANGUAGE: English. French. Finnish. Polish.
HEADNOTE: PEACE
TOPIC: Peace/Disarmament
CONCEPTS: Definition of terms. Time limit. Annex or appendix reference. Repatriation of nationals. Nazi organizations. Democratic institutions. Human rights. Free passage and transit. General property. Revival of treaties. Investigation of violations. Arbitration. Procedure. Conciliation. Competence of tribunal. Archives and objects. Assets transfer. Most favored nation clause. National treatment. Rearmament restrictions and controls. Procurement and logistics. Armistice and peace. Reparations and restrictions. Post-war claims settlement. Disarmament and demilitarization. Withdrawal of occupation. Markers and definitions.
INTL ORGS: League of Nations. Permanent Court of International Justice. United Nations. Conciliation Commission.
PARTIES:
Australia SIGNED: 10 Feb 47 RATIFIED: 10 Jul 48 FORCE: 10 Jul 48
Byelorussia SIGNED: 10 Feb 47 RATIFIED: 15 Sep 47 FORCE: 15 Sep 47
Canada SIGNED: 10 Feb 47 RATIFIED: 19 Sep 47 FORCE: 19 Sep 47
Czechoslovakia SIGNED: 10 Feb 47 RATIFIED: 14 Oct 47 FORCE: 14 Oct 47
Finland SIGNED: 10 Feb 47 RATIFIED: 15 Sep 47 FORCE: 15 Sep 47
India SIGNED: 10 Feb 47 RATIFIED: 19 Sep 47 FORCE: 19 Sep 47
New Zealand SIGNED: 10 Feb 47 RATIFIED: 31 Dec 47 FORCE: 31 Dec 47
South Africa SIGNED: 10 Feb 47 RATIFIED: 17 May 48 FORCE: 17 May 48
UK Great Britain SIGNED: 10 Feb 47 RATIFIED: 15 Sep 47 FORCE: 15 Sep 47
Ukrainian SSR SIGNED: 10 Feb 47 RATIFIED: 15 Sep 47 FORCE: 15 Sep 47

USSR (Soviet Union) SIGNED: 10 Feb 47 RATIFIED: 15 Sep 47 FORCE: 15 Sep 47

100747 Multilateral Treaty **49 UNTS 3**
SIGNED: 10 Feb 47 FORCE: 15 Sep 47
REGISTERED: 15 Mar 50 USA (United States)
ARTICLES: 90 LANGUAGE: English. French. Italian. Russian.
HEADNOTE: PEACE
TOPIC: Peace/Disarmament
CONCEPTS: Nazi organizations. Democratic institutions. Procedure. Compensation. Currency. Claims and settlements. Rearmament restrictions and controls. Status of military forces. Reconversion to normalcy. Armistice and peace. Loss and/or damage. Claims arising from occupation of territories. Reparations and restrictions. Disarmament and demilitarization. Industrial controls. Control and occupation machinery. Withdrawal of occupation. Markers and definitions. Frontier peoples and personnel.
INTL ORGS: League of Nations. International Finance Corporation. Permanent Court of International Justice. United Nations.
PROCEDURE: Ratification.
PARTIES:
Albania RATIFIED: 20 Oct 47 FORCE: 20 Oct 47
Australia SIGNED: 10 Feb 47 RATIFIED: 9 Jul 48 FORCE: 9 Jul 48
Belgium SIGNED: 10 Feb 47 RATIFIED: 4 Sep 48 FORCE: 4 Sep 48
Brazil SIGNED: 10 Feb 47 RATIFIED: 4 Jan 49 FORCE: 4 Jan 49
Byelorussia SIGNED: 10 Feb 47
Canada SIGNED: 10 Feb 47 RATIFIED: 15 Sep 47 FORCE: 15 Sep 47
Taiwan SIGNED: 10 Feb 47 RATIFIED: 24 Nov 47 FORCE: 24 Nov 47
Czechoslovakia SIGNED: 10 Feb 47 RATIFIED: 14 Oct 47 FORCE: 14 Oct 47
Ethiopia SIGNED: 10 Feb 47 RATIFIED: 6 Nov 47 FORCE: 6 Nov 47
France SIGNED: 10 Feb 47 RATIFIED: 15 Sep 47 FORCE: 15 Sep 47
Greece SIGNED: 10 Feb 47 RATIFIED: 28 Oct 47 FORCE: 28 Oct 47
India SIGNED: 10 Feb 47 RATIFIED: 15 Sep 47 FORCE: 15 Sep 47
Italy SIGNED: 10 Feb 47 RATIFIED: 15 Sep 47 FORCE: 15 Sep 47
Mexico RATIFIED: 10 Apr 48 FORCE: 10 Apr 48
Netherlands SIGNED: 10 Feb 47 RATIFIED: 7 Feb 49 FORCE: 7 Feb 49
New Zealand SIGNED: 10 Feb 47 RATIFIED: 24 Dec 47 FORCE: 24 Dec 47
Pakistan RATIFIED: 15 Sep 47 FORCE: 15 Sep 47
Poland SIGNED: 10 Feb 47 RATIFIED: 4 Feb 48 FORCE: 4 Feb 48
South Africa SIGNED: 10 Feb 47 RATIFIED: 4 Nov 47 FORCE: 4 Nov 47
UK Great Britain SIGNED: 10 Feb 47 RATIFIED: 15 Sep 47 FORCE: 15 Sep 47
USA (United States) SIGNED: 10 Feb 47 RATIFIED: 15 Sep 47 FORCE: 15 Sep 47
Ukrainian SSR SIGNED: 10 Feb 47
USSR (Soviet Union) SIGNED: 10 Feb 47 RATIFIED: 15 Sep 47 FORCE: 15 Sep 47
Yugoslavia SIGNED: 10 Feb 47 RATIFIED: 4 Sep 47 FORCE: 15 Sep 47

100748 Bilateral Exchange **51 UNTS 3**
SIGNED: 16 Nov 49 FORCE: 17 Aug 49
REGISTERED: 16 Mar 50 Belgium
ARTICLES: 2 LANGUAGE: French.
HEADNOTE: COMPENSATION WAR DAMAGE PRIVATE PROPERTY
TOPIC: Reparations
CONCEPTS: Exceptions and exemptions. Compensation. Loss and/or damage. Post-war claims settlement.
PARTIES:
Belgium
Canada

100749 Bilateral Agreement **51 UNTS 11**
SIGNED: 15 Dec 49 FORCE: 15 Dec 49
REGISTERED: 22 Mar 50 Denmark
ARTICLES: 12 LANGUAGE: English. French.
HEADNOTE: FINANCE
TOPIC: Finance

CONCEPTS: Definition of terms. Annex or appendix reference. Previous treaty replacement. General cooperation. Licenses and permits. Existing tribunals. Import quotas. Accounting procedures. Banking. Balance of payments. Currency. Exchange rates and regulations. Interest rates. Payment schedules.
INTL ORGS: International Monetary Fund. Special Commission.
TREATY REF: 45 UNTS 3.
PROCEDURE: Duration. Renewal or Revival. Termination.
PARTIES:
Denmark
Germany, West

100750 Bilateral Exchange **51 UNTS 33**
SIGNED: 3 Nov 47 FORCE: 3 Nov 47
REGISTERED: 24 Mar 50 USA (United States)
ARTICLES: 2 LANGUAGE: English. Spanish.
HEADNOTE: CIVIL AIR MISSION
TOPIC: Air Transport
CONCEPTS: Conditions. Time limit. Personnel. Responsibility and liability. Use of facilities. Accounting procedures. Compensation. Indemnities and reimbursements. Financial programs. Tax exemptions. Customs exemptions. Special projects. Aid missions. Air transport.
PROCEDURE: Amendment.
PARTIES:
Bolivia
USA (United States)

100751 Bilateral Exchange **51 UNTS 45**
SIGNED: 22 Dec 47 FORCE: 22 Dec 47
REGISTERED: 24 Mar 50 USA (United States)
ARTICLES: 3 LANGUAGE: English. Spanish.
HEADNOTE: CULTURAL
TOPIC: Air Transport
CONCEPTS: Treaty implementation. Friendship and amity. Specialists exchange. Teacher and student exchange. Exchange. General cultural cooperation. Artists. Athletes. Scientific exchange. Publications exchange. Mass media exchange. Press and wire services.
PROCEDURE: Duration. Ratification. Renewal or Revival. Termination.
PARTIES:
Colombia
USA (United States)

100752 Bilateral Agreement **51 UNTS 57**
SIGNED: 19 Aug 47 FORCE: 19 Aug 47
REGISTERED: 24 Mar 50 USA (United States)
ARTICLES: 29 LANGUAGE: English. Spanish.
HEADNOTE: MILITARY AVIATION MISSION
TOPIC: Military Mission
CONCEPTS: Definition of terms. Use of facilities. Compensation. Indemnities and reimbursements. Exchange rates and regulations. Expense sharing formulae. Tax exemptions. Customs exemptions. Military assistance. Military training. Security of information. Airforce-army-navy personnel ratio. Ranks and privileges. Conditions for assistance missions. Third country military personnel. Status of forces.
PROCEDURE: Denunciation.
PARTIES:
El Salvador
USA (United States)
ANNEX
181 UNTS 329. USA (United States). Prolongation 31 Oct 51. Force 31 Oct 51.
181 UNTS 329. El Salvador. Prolongation 30 Oct 51. Force 31 Oct 51.
181 UNTS 332. USA (United States). Prolongation 6 Jun 52. Force 6 Jun 52.
181 UNTS 332. El Salvador. Prolongation 30 May 52. Force 6 Jun 52.
229 UNTS 289. USA (United States). Prolongation 11 Mar 54. Force 11 Mar 54.
229 UNTS 289. El Salvador. Prolongation 2 Dec 53. Force 11 Mar 54.
289 UNTS 312. USA (United States). Prolongation 26 Aug 57. Force 26 Aug 57.
289 UNTS 312. El Salvador. Prolongation 23 Aug 57. Force 26 Aug 57.

100753 Bilateral Exchange **51 UNTS 77**
SIGNED: 9 Feb 50 FORCE: 1 Mar 50

REGISTERED: 29 Mar 50 Belgium
ARTICLES: 2 LANGUAGE: French.
HEADNOTE: MUTUAL ABOLITION PASSPORT
  VISAS
TOPIC: Visas
CONCEPTS: Territorial application. Time limit. Visa
  abolition. Resident permits. Non-visa travel docu-
  ments.
PARTIES:
  Belgium
  Finland
          ANNEX
309 UNTS 358.   Belgium.   Supplementation
  29 Apr 58. Force 1 May 58.
309 UNTS 358.   Finland.   Supplementation
  30 Apr 58. Force 1 May 58.

100754   Bilateral Exchange   **51 UNTS 83**
SIGNED: 30 Dec 49   FORCE: 15 Jan 50
REGISTERED: 29 Mar 50 Belgium
ARTICLES: 2 LANGUAGE: French. Italian.
HEADNOTE: ABOLITION PASSPORT VISAS
TOPIC: Visas
CONCEPTS: Territorial application. Time limit. Visa
  abolition. Border traffic and migration. Resident
  permits. Conformity with municipal law.
PARTIES:
  Belgium
  Italy
          ANNEX
68 UNTS 282.   Belgium.   Supplementation
  20 Jun 50. Force 20 Jun 50.
68 UNTS 282. Italy. Supplementation 12 Jun 50.
  Force 20 Jun 50.
207 UNTS 332. Belgium. Amendment 23 Feb 55.
  Force 1 Mar 55.
207 UNTS 332.   Italy.   Amendment   19 Feb 55.
  Force 1 Mar 55.

100755   Bilateral Exchange   **51 UNTS 93**
SIGNED: 6 Feb 50   FORCE: 15 Feb 50
REGISTERED: 29 Mar 50 Belgium
ARTICLES: 2 LANGUAGE: French.
HEADNOTE: MUTUAL ABOLITION PASSPORTS
TOPIC: Visas
CONCEPTS: Time limit. Passports non-diplomatic.
  Resident permits. Non-visa travel documents.
PARTIES:
  Belgium
  Monaco
          ANNEX
357 UNTS 334. Belgium. Amendment 4 Mar 60.
  Force 15 Mar 60.
357 UNTS 334. Monaco. Amendment 15 Mar 60.
  Force 15 Mar 60.

100756   Bilateral Exchange   **51 UNTS 101**
SIGNED: 17 Feb 50   FORCE: 1 Mar 50
REGISTERED: 29 Mar 50 Belgium
ARTICLES: 2 LANGUAGE: French.
HEADNOTE: AMEND PROVISIONAL CONVENTION
  MAESTRICHT CANAL
TOPIC: Water Transport
CONCEPTS: Annex type material. Personnel. Com-
  pensation. Navigational conditions. Canal im-
  provement.
TREATY REF: 16DEMARTENS773.
PARTIES:
  Belgium
  Netherlands

100757   Bilateral Exchange   **51 UNTS 107**
SIGNED: 14 Dec 49   FORCE: 1 Jan 50
REGISTERED: 29 Mar 50 Belgium
ARTICLES: 2 LANGUAGE: French. Italian.
HEADNOTE: ABOLITION PASSPORT VISAS
TOPIC: Visas
CONCEPTS: Change of circumstances. Territorial
  application. Time limit. Visa abolition. Border
  traffic and migration. Resident permits. Confor-
  mity with municipal law.
PROCEDURE: Amendment.
PARTIES:
  Belgium
  San Marino

100758   Unilateral Instrument   **51 UNTS 115**
SIGNED: 10 Mar 50   FORCE: 29 Mar 50
REGISTERED: 29 Mar 50 United Nations

ARTICLES: 1 LANGUAGE: French.
HEADNOTE: ACCEPTANCE ICJ JURISDICTION
TOPIC: ICJ Option Clause
CONCEPTS: Funding procedures. Optional clause
  ICJ. Compulsory jurisdiction.
INTL ORGS: International Court of Justice. United
  Nations.
PARTIES:
  Liechtenstein

100759   Unilateral Instrument   **51 UNTS 119**
SIGNED: 10 Mar 50   FORCE: 29 Mar 50
REGISTERED: 29 Mar 50 United Nations
ARTICLES: 1 LANGUAGE: French.
HEADNOTE: ACCEPTANCE ICJ JURISDICTION
TOPIC: ICJ Option Clause
CONCEPTS: Compulsory jurisdiction.
INTL ORGS: International Court of Justice.
PARTIES:
  Liechtenstein

100760   Bilateral Exchange   **51 UNTS 123**
SIGNED: 22 Nov 49   FORCE: 1 Jan 50
REGISTERED: 29 Mar 50 New Zealand
ARTICLES: 2 LANGUAGE: English.
HEADNOTE: MUTUAL ABOLITION VISAS
TOPIC: Visas
CONCEPTS: Territorial application. Visa abolition.
  Conformity with municipal law.
PARTIES:
  New Zealand
  Norway

100761   Bilateral Exchange   **51 UNTS 129**
SIGNED: 13 May 49   FORCE: 13 May 49
REGISTERED: 4 Apr 50 USA (United States)
ARTICLES: 2 LANGUAGE: English. French.
HEADNOTE: AMENDING AIR TRANSPORT SER-
  VICES
TOPIC: Air Transport
CONCEPTS: Annex or appendix reference. Annex
  type material. Previous treaty replacement. Pro-
  cedure. Special tribunals. Competence of tribu-
  nal. Indemnities and reimbursements.
INTL ORGS: International Civil Aviation Organiza-
  tion. Arbitration Commission.
TREATY REF: 51UNTS232.
PARTIES:
  Switzerland
  USA (United States)
          ANNEX
279 UNTS 294. USA (United States). Implementa-
  tion 1 Mar 57. Force 4 Mar 57.
279 UNTS 294.   Switzerland.   Implementation
  4 Mar 57. Force 4 Mar 57.

100762   Bilateral Agreement   **51 UNTS 145**
SIGNED: 19 Jul 49   FORCE: 19 Jul 49
REGISTERED: 4 Apr 50 USA (United States)
ARTICLES: 12 LANGUAGE: English. Spanish.
HEADNOTE: AIR TRANSPORT
TOPIC: Air Transport
CONCEPTS: Exceptions and exemptions. Annex or
  appendix reference. Non-prejudice to third party.
  Conformity with municipal law. Licenses and
  permits. Recognition of legal documents. Use of
  facilities. Arbitration. Procedure. Special tribu-
  nals. Competence of tribunal. Indemnities and
  reimbursements. Fees and exemptions. Most fa-
  vored nation clause. National treatment. Cus-
  toms exemptions. Competency certificate.
  Routes and logistics. Navigational conditions.
  Permit designation. Air transport. Airport facilities. Conditions of airlines operating permission.
  Operating authorizations and regulations. Licenses and certificates of nationality.
INTL ORGS: International Civil Aviation Organiza-
  tion. Arbitration Commission.
TREATY REF: 15UNTS295.
PROCEDURE: Amendment. Registration. Termina-
  tion.
PARTIES:
  Dominican Republic
  USA (United States)

100763   Bilateral Exchange   **51 UNTS 167**
SIGNED: 10 Feb 50   FORCE: 1 Mar 50
REGISTERED: 7 Apr 50 Australia
ARTICLES: 2 LANGUAGE: English.

HEADNOTE: ABOLITION VISA FEES
TOPIC: Visas
CONCEPTS: Visas. Fees and exemptions.
PARTIES:
  Australia
  USA (United States)

100764   Bilateral Agreement   **51 UNTS 173**
SIGNED: 10 Dec 47   FORCE: 10 Dec 47
REGISTERED: 10 Apr 50 Pakistan
ARTICLES: 9 LANGUAGE: English.
HEADNOTE: DOUBLE TAXATION INCOME
TOPIC: Taxation
CONCEPTS: Conformity with municipal law. Do-
  mestic legislation. Taxation. General.
PROCEDURE: Amendment. Termination.
PARTIES:
  India
  Pakistan

100765   Bilateral Agreement   **51 UNTS 187**
SIGNED: 24 Aug 46   FORCE: 1 Sep 46
REGISTERED: 12 Apr 50 UK Great Britain
ARTICLES: 12 LANGUAGE: Afrikaans. English.
HEADNOTE: EXCHANGE TELEGRAPH MONEY OR-
  DERS
TOPIC: Telecommunications
CONCEPTS: Responsibility and liability. Payment
  schedules. Regulations. Money orders and
  postal checks. Rates and charges. Advice lists
  and orders. Radio-telephone-telegraphic com-
  munications. Conformity with IGO decisions.
TREATY   REF: 15UNTS340;   175UNTS269;
  185LTS458.
PARTIES:
  South Africa
  UK Great Britain

100766   Bilateral Exchange   **51 UNTS 201**
SIGNED: 22 Feb 50   FORCE: 22 Feb 50
REGISTERED: 17 Apr 50 Australia
ARTICLES: 2 LANGUAGE: English.
HEADNOTE: RELEASE ASSETS ENEMY OCCUPA-
  TION
TOPIC: Claims and Debts
CONCEPTS: Definition of terms. General provi-
  sions. General property. Fees and exemptions.
  Assets. Assets transfer. National treatment.
  Enemy financial interests.
PARTIES:
  Australia
  Yugoslavia

100767   Bilateral Agreement   **51 UNTS 213**
SIGNED: 27 Jan 50   FORCE: 30 Mar 50
REGISTERED: 19 Apr 50 Belgium
ARTICLES: 8 LANGUAGE: English. French.
HEADNOTE: MUTUAL DEFENSE ASSISTANCE
TOPIC: Milit Assistance
CONCEPTS: Annex or appendix reference. Non-
  prejudice to UN charter. Privileges and immunities. Conformity with municipal law. General co-
  operation. Inspection and observation. Public in-
  formation. Use of facilities. Local currency.
  Claims and settlements. Tax exemptions. Recog-
  nition. Customs exemptions. Domestic obliga-
  tion. Materials, equipment and services. Aid mis-
  sions. Joint defense. Defense and security. Self-
  defense. Military assistance. Security of
  information. Exchange of defense information.
  Restrictions on transfer. Raw materials.
INTL ORGS: North Atlantic Treaty Organization.
  United Nations.
TREATY REF: 34UNTS243.
PROCEDURE: Amendment. Future Procedures
  Contemplated. Registration. Termination.
PARTIES:
  Belgium
  USA (United States)
          ANNEX
222 UNTS 391. USA (United States). Amendment
  14 Oct 53. Force 14 Oct 53.
222 UNTS 391. Belgium. Amendment 14 Oct 53.
  Force 14 Oct 53.
253 UNTS 312. USA (United States). Amendment
  4 Apr 55. Force 25 Apr 55.
253 UNTS 312. Belgium. Amendment 25 Apr 55.
  Force 25 Apr 55.
256 UNTS 334. Belgium. Amendment 3 Sep 55.
  Force 3 Sep 55.

256 UNTS 334. USA (United States). Amendment 24 Aug 55. Force 3 Sep 55.

283 UNTS 304. USA (United States). Amendment 15 Apr 57. Force 9 May 57.

283 UNTS 304. Belgium. Amendment 9 May 57. Force 9 May 57.

357 UNTS 338. Belgium. Amendment 4 Oct 57. Force 15 Oct 57.

357 UNTS 338. USA (United States). Amendment 15 Oct 57. Force 15 Oct 57.

357 UNTS 342. USA (United States). Amendment 21 Apr 59. Force 29 Apr 59.

357 UNTS 342. Belgium. Amendment 29 Apr 59. Force 29 Apr 59.

361 UNTS 238. Belgium. Amendment 27 Oct 59. Force 1 Dec 59.

361 UNTS 238. USA (United States). Amendment 1 Dec 59. Force 1 Dec 59.

405 UNTS 294. Belgium. Amendment 23 Dec 60. Force 23 Dec 60.

405 UNTS 294. USA (United States). Amendment 1 Dec 60. Force 23 Dec 60.

416 UNTS 301. Belgium. Implementation 7 Jul 61. Force 7 Jul 61.

416 UNTS 301. USA (United States). Implementation 7 Jul 61. Force 7 Jul 61.

433 UNTS 334. Belgium. Amendment 29 Nov 61. Force 11 Dec 61.

433 UNTS 334. Belgium. Amendment 11 Dec 61. Force 11 Dec 61.

461 UNTS 215. Belgium. Amendment 20 Nov 62. Force 20 Nov 62.

461 UNTS 215. USA (United States). Amendment 29 Oct 62. Force 20 Nov 62.

524 UNTS 302. USA (United States). Amendment 6 Feb 64. Force 11 Mar 64.

524 UNTS 302. Belgium. Amendment 11 Mar 64. Force 11 Mar 64.

100768 Bilateral Protocol **52 UNTS 3**
SIGNED: 18 Dec 47   FORCE: 23 May 49
REGISTERED: 19 Apr 50 Norway
ARTICLES: 1 LANGUAGE: Norwegian. Russian.
HEADNOTE: FRONTIER DESCRIPTION PROTOCOL
TOPIC: Territory Boundary
CONCEPTS: Boundaries of territory. Markers and definitions. Frontier crossing points.
INTL ORGS: Special Commission.
PARTIES:
 Norway
 USSR (Soviet Union)

100769 Bilateral Instrument **53 UNTS 3**
SIGNED: 16 Sep 49   FORCE: 16 Sep 49
REGISTERED: 22 Apr 50 Norway
ARTICLES: 10 LANGUAGE: English.
HEADNOTE: AGREED MINUTES TRADE DISCUSSION
TOPIC: General Trade
CONCEPTS: Annex or appendix reference. General cooperation. Licenses and permits. Trade procedures. Commodity trade. Quotas.
PARTIES:
 Allied Milit Occup
 Norway

100770 Multilateral Protocol **53 UNTS 13**
SIGNED: 12 Nov 47   FORCE: 12 Nov 47
REGISTERED: 24 Apr 50 United Nations
ARTICLES: 7 LANGUAGE: Chinese. English. French. Russian. Spanish.
HEADNOTE: 1921 & 1933 CONVENTION WOMEN CHILDREN
TOPIC: Admin Cooperation
CONCEPTS: Annex or appendix reference. Previous treaty extension.
INTL ORGS: League of Nations. United Nations.
PARTIES:
 Afghanistan SIGNED: 12 Nov 47 FORCE: 12 Nov 47
 Albania RATIFIED: 25 Jul 49 FORCE: 25 Jul 49
 Australia SIGNED: 13 Nov 47 FORCE: 13 Nov 47
 Belgium SIGNED: 12 Nov 47 FORCE: 12 Nov 47
 Brazil SIGNED: 17 Mar 48 RATIFIED: 6 Apr 50 FORCE: 6 Apr 50
 Canada SIGNED: 24 Nov 47 FORCE: 24 Nov 47
 Taiwan SIGNED: 12 Nov 47 FORCE: 12 Nov 47
 Czechoslovakia SIGNED: 12 Nov 47 FORCE: 12 Nov 47
 Denmark SIGNED: 12 Nov 47 RATIFIED: 21 Nov 49 FORCE: 21 Nov 49

 United Arab Rep SIGNED: 12 Nov 47 FORCE: 12 Nov 47
 Finland RATIFIED: 6 Jan 49 FORCE: 6 Jan 49
 India SIGNED: 12 Nov 47 FORCE: 12 Nov 47
 Lebanon SIGNED: 12 Nov 47 FORCE: 12 Nov 47
 Luxembourg SIGNED: 12 Nov 47
 Mexico SIGNED: 12 Nov 47 FORCE: 12 Nov 47
 Netherlands SIGNED: 12 Nov 47 RATIFIED: 17 Mar 47 FORCE: 17 Mar 47
 Nicaragua SIGNED: 12 Nov 47 RATIFIED: 24 Apr 50 FORCE: 24 Apr 50
 Norway SIGNED: 12 Nov 47 RATIFIED: 28 Nov 47 FORCE: 28 Nov 47
 Pakistan SIGNED: 12 Nov 47 FORCE: 12 Nov 47
 South Africa SIGNED: 12 Nov 47 FORCE: 12 Nov 47
 Sweden SIGNED: 9 Jun 48 FORCE: 9 Jun 48
 Syria SIGNED: 17 Nov 47 FORCE: 17 Nov 47
 Turkey SIGNED: 12 Nov 47 FORCE: 12 Nov 47
 USSR (Soviet Union) SIGNED: 18 Dec 47 FORCE: 18 Dec 47
 Yugoslavia SIGNED: 12 Nov 47 FORCE: 12 Nov 47
ANNEX
65 UNTS 332. Austria. Signature without Reservation as to Approval 7 Jun 50.
76 UNTS 280. Romania. Signature without Reservation as to Approval 2 Nov 50.
77 UNTS 364. Poland. Acceptance 21 Dec 50.
207 UNTS 337. Luxembourg. Acceptance 14 Mar 55.
354 UNTS 393. Greece. Acceptance 5 Apr 60.
401 UNTS 246. Ireland. Acceptance 19 Jul 61.
435 UNTS 306. Sierra Leone. Signature without Reservation as to Approval 13 Aug 62.
443 UNTS 332. Ivory Coast. Signature without Reservation as to Approval 5 Nov 62.
520 UNTS 424. Niger. Acceptance 7 Dec 64.
528 UNTS 290. Jamaica. Acceptance 16 Mar 65.

100771 Multilateral Convention **53 UNTS 39**
SIGNED: 12 Nov 47   FORCE: 24 Apr 50
REGISTERED: 24 Apr 50 United Nations
ARTICLES: 13 LANGUAGE: English. French.
HEADNOTE: SUPPRESSION TRAFFIC WOMEN CHILDREN
TOPIC: Admin Cooperation
CONCEPTS: Previous treaty amendment. Extradition, deportation and repatriation. Domestic legislation. Investigation of violations. Penal sanctions.
INTL ORGS: United Nations.
TREATY REF: 9LTS415; 1LTS84; 3LTS278.
PROCEDURE: Accession. Denunciation. Ratification. Registration.
PARTIES:
 Afghanistan FORCE: 24 Apr 50
 Albania FORCE: 24 Apr 50
 Australia FORCE: 24 Apr 50
 Belgium FORCE: 24 Apr 50
 Brazil FORCE: 24 Apr 50
 Burma FORCE: 24 Apr 50
 Canada FORCE: 24 Apr 50
 Taiwan FORCE: 24 Apr 50
 Czechoslovakia FORCE: 24 Apr 50
 Denmark FORCE: 24 Apr 50
 United Arab Rep FORCE: 24 Apr 50
 Finland FORCE: 24 Apr 50
 Hungary FORCE: 24 Apr 50
 India FORCE: 24 Apr 50
 Italy FORCE: 24 Apr 50
 Lebanon FORCE: 24 Apr 50
 Mexico FORCE: 24 Apr 50
 Netherlands FORCE: 24 Apr 50
 Nicaragua FORCE: 24 Apr 50
 Norway FORCE: 24 Apr 50
 Pakistan FORCE: 24 Apr 50
 South Africa FORCE: 24 Apr 50
 Sweden FORCE: 24 Apr 50
 Syria FORCE: 24 Apr 50
 Turkey FORCE: 24 Apr 50
 USSR (Soviet Union) FORCE: 24 Apr 50
 Yugoslavia FORCE: 24 Apr 50
ANNEX
65 UNTS 333. Austria. Accession 7 Jun 50.
76 UNTS 281. Romania. Accession 2 Nov 50.
77 UNTS 364. Poland. Accession 21 Dec 50.
199 UNTS 319. Philippines. Accession 30 Sep 54.
207 UNTS 338. Luxembourg. Acceptance 14 Mar 55.
324 UNTS 299. Libya. Accession 17 Feb 59.
354 UNTS 394. Greece. Acceptance 5 Apr 60.

401 UNTS 247. Ireland. Acceptance 19 Jul 61.
435 UNTS 307. Sierra Leone. Acceptance 13 Aug 62.
453 UNTS 346. Madagascar. Accession 18 Feb 63.
480 UNTS 319. Algeria. Accession 31 Oct 63.
528 UNTS 291. Jamaica. Acceptance 16 Mar 65.
557 UNTS 245. Malawi. Accession 25 Feb 66.

100772 Multilateral Convention **53 UNTS 49**
SIGNED: 12 Nov 47   FORCE: 24 Apr 50
REGISTERED: 24 Apr 50 United Nations
ARTICLES: 10 LANGUAGE: English. French.
HEADNOTE: SUPPRESSION TRAFFIC WOMEN FULL AGE
TOPIC: Admin Cooperation
CONCEPTS: Territorial application. Exchange of information. Investigation of violations. Arbitration. Procedure. Existing tribunals. Domestic obligation.
INTL ORGS: League of Nations. International Court of Justice. United Nations. Arbitration Commission.
TREATY REF: 150LTS431.
PROCEDURE: Accession. Denunciation. Ratification. Registration.
PARTIES:
 Afghanistan FORCE: 24 Apr 50
 Australia FORCE: 24 Apr 50
 Belgium FORCE: 24 Apr 50
 Brazil FORCE: 24 Apr 50
 Czechoslovakia FORCE: 24 Apr 50
 Finland FORCE: 24 Apr 50
 Hungary FORCE: 24 Apr 50
 Mexico FORCE: 24 Apr 50
 Netherlands FORCE: 24 Apr 50
 Nicaragua FORCE: 24 Apr 50
 Norway FORCE: 24 Apr 50
 South Africa FORCE: 24 Apr 50
 Sweden FORCE: 24 Apr 50
 Turkey FORCE: 24 Apr 50
 USSR (Soviet Union) FORCE: 24 Apr 50
ANNEX
65 UNTS 334. Austria. Accession 7 Jun 50.
76 UNTS 281. Romania. Accession 2 Nov 50.
77 UNTS 365. Poland. Accession 21 Dec 50.
199 UNTS 320. Philippines. Accession 30 Sep 54. Force 29 Nov 54.
207 UNTS 339. Luxembourg. Accession 14 Mar 55. Force 13 Apr 55.
324 UNTS 299. Libya. Accession 17 Feb 59. Force 19 Apr 59.
354 UNTS 394. Greece. Acceptance 5 Apr 60.
401 UNTS 248. Ireland. Acceptance 19 Jul 61.
443 UNTS 332. Ivory Coast. Accession 5 Nov 62.
480 UNTS 319. Algeria. Accession 31 Oct 63. Force 30 Dec 63.
520 UNTS 425. Niger. Acceptance 7 Dec 64.

100773 Bilateral Agreement **53 UNTS 59**
SIGNED: 6 Nov 47   FORCE: 4 Jul 49
REGISTERED: 27 Apr 50 Netherlands
ARTICLES: 12 LANGUAGE: Dutch. French. Portuguese.
HEADNOTE: AIR TRANSPORT
TOPIC: Air Transport
CONCEPTS: Definition of terms. Treaty interpretation. Annex or appendix reference. Previous treaty replacement. Conformity with municipal law. Use of facilities. Arbitration. Procedure. Interest rates. Most favored nation clause. National treatment. Customs exemptions. Routes and logistics. Permit designation. Air transport. Airport facilities. Conditions of airlines operating permission. Operating authorizations and regulations.
INTL ORGS: International Civil Aviation Organization. Arbitration Commission.
TREATY REF: 15UNTS295.
PROCEDURE: Amendment. Future Procedures Contemplated. Ratification. Registration. Termination.
PARTIES:
 Brazil
 Netherlands
ANNEX
327 UNTS 350. Netherlands. Amendment 25 Jun 57.
327 UNTS 350. Brazil. Amendment 25 Jun 57.

100774 Bilateral Agreement **53 UNTS 95**
SIGNED: 14 Dec 49   FORCE: 14 Mar 50
REGISTERED: 1 May 50 Afghanistan
ARTICLES: 14 LANGUAGE: English. Persian.
HEADNOTE: RADIO-TELEGRAPHIC COMMUNICATIONS
TOPIC: Telecommunications
CONCEPTS: Exchange of information and documents. Accounting procedures. Non-interest rates and fees. Conveyance in transit. Telegrams. Radio-telephone-telegraphic communications. Conformity with IGO decisions.
INTL ORGS: International Telecommunication Union.
PROCEDURE: Termination.
PARTIES:
　Afghanistan
　India

100775 Bilateral Exchange **53 UNTS 107**
SIGNED: 6 Oct 47   FORCE: 6 Oct 47
REGISTERED: 1 May 50 ICAO (Civil Aviat)
ARTICLES: 2 LANGUAGE: French.
HEADNOTE: AIR TRANSPORT
TOPIC: Air Transport
CONCEPTS: Privileges and immunities. Conformity with municipal law. Exchange of information and documents. Personnel. Financial programs. Non-interest rates and fees. Passenger transport. Routes and logistics. Air transport. Airport facilities. Operating authorizations and regulations. Postal services.
PROCEDURE: Denunciation. Duration. Future Procedures Contemplated.
PARTIES:
　Sweden
　Yugoslavia

100776 Bilateral Exchange **53 UNTS 115**
SIGNED: 27 May 48   FORCE: 27 May 48
REGISTERED: 1 May 50 ICAO (Civil Aviat)
ARTICLES: 2 LANGUAGE: English.
HEADNOTE: RECIPROCAL FACILITIES OPERATION COMMERCIAL AIR SERVICE
TOPIC: Air Transport
CONCEPTS: Conditions. Conformity with municipal law. Exchange of information and documents. Non-interest rates and fees. Passenger transport. Routes and logistics. Transport of goods. Air transport. Operating authorizations and regulations. Postal services.
TREATY REF: 15UNTS295.
PROCEDURE: Amendment. Duration. Termination.
PARTIES:
　Luxembourg
　UK Great Britain

100777 Bilateral Agreement **53 UNTS 123**
SIGNED: 25 Feb 49   FORCE: 27 Mar 49
REGISTERED: 1 May 50 ICAO (Civil Aviat)
ARTICLES: 12 LANGUAGE: English.
HEADNOTE: AIR TRANSPORT
TOPIC: Air Transport
CONCEPTS: Annex or appendix reference. Non-prejudice to third party. Conformity with municipal law. Licenses and permits. Recognition of legal documents. Use of facilities. Procedure. Existing tribunals. Special tribunals. Reexport of goods, etc.. Fees and exemptions. Most favored nation clause. National treatment. Customs exemptions. Competency certificate. Routes and logistics. Navigational conditions. Permit designation. Air transport. Airport facilities. Airworthiness certificates. Conditions of airlines operating permission. Operating authorizations and regulations. Licenses and certificates of nationality.
INTL ORGS: International Civil Aviation Organization. Arbitration Commission.
TREATY REF: 15UNTS295.
PROCEDURE: Registration. Termination.
PARTIES:
　Finland
　Netherlands

100778 Bilateral Agreement **53 UNTS 137**
SIGNED: 12 Jul 49   FORCE: 12 Jul 49
REGISTERED: 1 May 50 ICAO (Civil Aviat)
ARTICLES: 12 LANGUAGE: Arabic. English.
HEADNOTE: AIR TRANSPORT SERVICES

TOPIC: Air Transport
CONCEPTS: Annex or appendix reference. Conformity with municipal law. Licenses and permits. Recognition of legal documents. Use of facilities. Procedure. Existing tribunals. Special tribunals. Fees and exemptions. Most favored nation clause. National treatment. Customs exemptions. Competency certificate. Routes and logistics. Navigational conditions. Permit designation. Air transport. Airport facilities. Airworthiness certificates. Conditions of airlines operating permission. Licenses and certificates of nationality.
INTL ORGS: International Civil Aviation Organization. Arbitration Commission.
TREATY REF: 15UNTS295.
PROCEDURE: Amendment. Future Procedures Contemplated. Registration. Termination.
PARTIES:
　Iraq
　Norway

100779 Bilateral Agreement **53 UNTS 153**
SIGNED: 13 Jul 49   FORCE: 19 Jan 50
REGISTERED: 1 May 50 ICAO (Civil Aviat)
ARTICLES: 12 LANGUAGE: English.
HEADNOTE: AIR TRANSPORT
TOPIC: Air Transport
CONCEPTS: Annex or appendix reference. Non-prejudice to third party. Conformity with municipal law. Licenses and permits. Recognition of legal documents. Use of facilities. Procedure. Special tribunals. Competence of tribunal. Fees and exemptions. Most favored nation clause. National treatment. Customs exemptions. Competency certificate. Routes and logistics. Navigational conditions. Permit designation. Air transport. Airport facilities. Airworthiness certificates. Conditions of airlines operating permission. Licenses and certificates of nationality.
INTL ORGS: International Civil Aviation Organization. Arbitration Commission.
PROCEDURE: Ratification. Registration. Termination.
PARTIES:
　Czechoslovakia
　Finland

100780 Bilateral Agreement **53 UNTS 167**
SIGNED: 24 Aug 49   FORCE: 24 Aug 49
REGISTERED: 1 May 50 ICAO (Civil Aviat)
ARTICLES: 11 LANGUAGE: Finnish. Norwegian.
HEADNOTE: AIR TRANSPORT
TOPIC: Air Transport
CONCEPTS: Annex or appendix reference. Conformity with municipal law. Licenses and permits. Recognition of legal documents. Use of facilities. Arbitration. Procedure. Existing tribunals. Negotiation. Fees and exemptions. Most favored nation clause. National treatment. Customs exemptions. Competency certificate. Routes and logistics. Navigational conditions. Permit designation. Air transport. Airport facilities. Airworthiness certificates. Conditions of airlines operating permission. Operating authorizations and regulations. Licenses and certificates of nationality.
INTL ORGS: International Civil Aviation Organization. Arbitration Commission.
TREATY REF: 15UNTS295.
PROCEDURE: Amendment. Future Procedures Contemplated. Registration. Termination.
PARTIES:
　Finland
　Norway
　　　　ANNEX
563 UNTS 356. Norway. Amendment 15 Mar 63. Force 15 Mar 63.
563 UNTS 356. Finland. Amendment 9 Mar 63. Force 15 Mar 63.

100781 Bilateral Agreement **53 UNTS 191**
SIGNED: 26 Aug 49   FORCE: 26 Aug 49
REGISTERED: 1 May 50 ICAO (Civil Aviat)
ARTICLES: 11 LANGUAGE: Danish. Finnish. Swedish.
HEADNOTE: AIR TRANSPORT
TOPIC: Air Transport
CONCEPTS: Time limit. Conformity with municipal law. Licenses and permits. Recognition of legal documents. Use of facilities. Arbitration. Proce-

dure. Existing tribunals. Negotiation. Fees and exemptions. Most favored nation clause. National treatment. Customs exemptions. Competency certificate. Routes and logistics. Navigational conditions. Permit designation. Air transport. Airport facilities. Airworthiness certificates. Conditions of airlines operating permission. Operating authorizations and regulations. Licenses and certificates of nationality.
INTL ORGS: International Civil Aviation Organization. Arbitration Commission.
TREATY REF: 15UNTS295.
PROCEDURE: Amendment. Future Procedures Contemplated. Registration. Termination.
PARTIES:
　Denmark
　Finland

100782 Bilateral Agreement **53 UNTS 221**
SIGNED: 30 Aug 49   FORCE: 30 Aug 49
REGISTERED: 1 May 50 ICAO (Civil Aviat)
ARTICLES: 12 LANGUAGE: English. French.
HEADNOTE: AIR SERVICES
TOPIC: Air Transport
CONCEPTS: Definition of terms. Annex or appendix reference. Conformity with municipal law. Licenses and permits. Recognition of legal documents. Procedure. Existing tribunals. Negotiation. Quarantine. Non-interest rates and fees. National treatment. Customs duties. Competency certificate. Routes and logistics. Permit designation. Conditions of airlines operating permission. Operating authorizations and regulations. Compulsory jurisdiction.
INTL ORGS: International Civil Aviation Organization. International Court of Justice.
TREATY REF: 15UNTS295.
PROCEDURE: Amendment. Future Procedures Contemplated. Registration. Termination.
PARTIES:
　Belgium
　Canada
　　　　ANNEX
260 UNTS 434.　Belgium.　Amendment 25 May 56. Force 20 Jul 56.
260 UNTS 434. Canada. Amendment 20 Jul 56. Force 20 Jul 56.

100783 Multilateral Agreement **53 UNTS 235**
SIGNED: 15 Sep 49   FORCE: 15 Sep 49
REGISTERED: 1 May 50 ICAO (Civil Aviat)
ARTICLES: 5 LANGUAGE: English.
HEADNOTE: OPERATION REGULAR AIR SERVICES TASMAN EMPIRE LIMITED
TOPIC: Air Transport
CONCEPTS: Previous treaty extension. Responsibility and liability. Funding procedures. Routes and logistics. Air transport. Operating authorizations and regulations.
INTL ORGS: Special Commission.
PARTIES:
　Australia SIGNED: 16 Sep 49 FORCE: 15 Sep 49
　New Zealand SIGNED: 16 Sep 49 FORCE: 15 Sep 49
　UK Great Britain SIGNED: 16 Sep 49 FORCE: 15 Sep 49
　　　　ANNEX
254 UNTS 405. New Zealand. Termination 24 Jan 56. Force 31 Mar 54.
254 UNTS 405. Australia. Termination 24 Jan 56. Force 31 Mar 54.
254 UNTS 405. UK Great Britain. Termination 24 Jan 56. Force 31 Mar 54.

100784 Multilateral Agreement **53 UNTS 241**
SIGNED: 27 Oct 49   FORCE: 27 Oct 49
REGISTERED: 1 May 50 ICAO (Civil Aviat)
ARTICLES: 5 LANGUAGE: English.
HEADNOTE: AIR SERVICES
TOPIC: Air Transport
CONCEPTS: Previous treaty replacement. General cooperation. Responsibility and liability. Currency. Funding procedures. Routes and logistics. Permit designation. Air transport. Operating authorizations and regulations.
INTL ORGS: Special Commission.
TREATY REF: 28UNTS41.
PARTIES:
　Australia SIGNED: 27 Oct 49 FORCE: 27 Oct 49
　New Zealand SIGNED: 27 Oct 49 FORCE: 27 Oct 49

UK Great Britain SIGNED: 27 Oct 49 FORCE:
27 Oct 49
                         ANNEX
254 UNTS 406.   New Zealand.   Termination
24 Jan 56. Force 31 Mar 54.
254 UNTS 406.   UK Great Britain.   Termination
24 Jan 56. Force 31 Mar 54.
254 UNTS 406. Australia. Termination 24 Jan 56.
Force 31 Mar 54.

100785   Bilateral Exchange   **53 UNTS 247**
SIGNED: 15 Nov 49   FORCE: 15 Nov 49
REGISTERED: 1 May 50 ICAO (Civil Aviat)
ARTICLES: 2 LANGUAGE: English. French.
HEADNOTE: AIR TRAFFIC RIGHTS SOUTH PACIFIC
TOPIC: Air Transport
CONCEPTS: Conditions of airlines operating per-
mission. Operating authorizations and regula-
tions.
INTL ORGS: International Civil Aviation Organiza-
tion.
PARTIES:
France
New Zealand

100786   Bilateral Agreement   **53 UNTS 255**
SIGNED: 23 Nov 49   FORCE: 23 Nov 49
REGISTERED: 1 May 50 ICAO (Civil Aviat)
ARTICLES: 13 LANGUAGE: English.
HEADNOTE: AIR SERVICES
TOPIC: Air Transport
CONCEPTS: Annex or appendix reference. Confor-
mity with municipal law. Licenses and permits.
Recognition of legal documents. Use of facilities.
Arbitration. Procedure. Existing tribunals. Reex-
port of goods, etc.. Fees and exemptions. Most
favored nation clause. National treatment. Cus-
toms exemptions. Competency certificate.
Routes and logistics. Navigational conditions.
Permit designation. Air transport. Airport facili-
ties. Airworthiness certificates. Conditions of air-
lines operating permission. Licenses and certifi-
cates of nationality.
INTL ORGS: International Civil Aviation Organiza-
tion. Arbitration Commission.
TREATY REF: 15UNTS295
PROCEDURE: Amendment. Future Procedures
Contemplated. Registration. Termination.
PARTIES:
Denmark
Thailand
                         ANNEX
463 UNTS 320.   Denmark.   Amendment
27 Feb 63. Force 27 Feb 63.
463 UNTS 320. Thailand. Amendment 21 Feb 63.
Force 27 Feb 63.

100787   Bilateral Agreement   **53 UNTS 269**
SIGNED: 26 Nov 49   FORCE: 26 Nov 49
REGISTERED: 1 May 50 ICAO (Civil Aviat)
ARTICLES: 12 LANGUAGE: English.
HEADNOTE: AIR TRANSPORT SERVICES
TOPIC: Air Transport
CONCEPTS: Annex or appendix reference. Confor-
mity with municipal law. Licenses and permits.
Recognition of legal documents. Use of facilities.
Arbitration. Procedure. Existing tribunals. Reex-
port of goods, etc.. Fees and exemptions. Most
favored nation clause. National treatment. Cus-
toms exemptions. Competency certificate.
Routes and logistics. Navigational conditions.
Permit designation. Air transport. Airport facili-
ties. Airworthiness certificates. Conditions of air-
lines operating permission. Licenses and certifi-
cates of nationality.
INTL ORGS: International Civil Aviation Organiza-
tion. Arbitration Commission.
TREATY REF: 15UNTS295.
PROCEDURE: Amendment. Future Procedures
Contemplated. Registration. Termination.
PARTIES:
Norway
Thailand
                         ANNEX
463 UNTS 328. Norway. Amendment 27 Feb 63.
Force 27 Feb 63.
463 UNTS 328. Thailand. Amendment 21 Feb 63.
Force 27 Feb 63.

100788   Bilateral Agreement   **53 UNTS 281**
SIGNED: 2 Dec 49   FORCE: 15 Jan 50
REGISTERED: 1 May 50 ICAO (Civil Aviat)
ARTICLES: 11 LANGUAGE: English.
HEADNOTE: AIR TRANSPORT
TOPIC: Air Transport
CONCEPTS: Annex or appendix reference. Confor-
mity with municipal law. Licenses and permits.
Recognition of legal documents. Use of facilities.
Arbitration. Procedure. Existing tribunals. Fees
and exemptions. Most favored nation clause. Na-
tional treatment. Customs exemptions. Compe-
tency certificate. Routes and logistics. Naviga-
tional conditions. Permit designation. Air trans-
port. Airport facilities. Airworthiness certificates.
Conditions of airlines operating permission. Op-
erating authorizations and regulations. Licenses
and certificates of nationality.
INTL ORGS: International Civil Aviation Organization. Arbitration Commission.
TREATY REF: 15UNTS295.
PROCEDURE: Registration. Termination.
PARTIES:
Austria
Denmark

100789   Bilateral Agreement   **53 UNTS 295**
SIGNED: 12 Jan 50   FORCE: 12 Jan 50
REGISTERED: 1 May 50 ICAO (Civil Aviat)
ARTICLES: 17 LANGUAGE: English.
HEADNOTE: AIR SERVICES
TOPIC: Air Transport
CONCEPTS: Annex type material. Bonds. Interest
rates. Payment schedules. Claims and settle-
ments. Debts. Debt settlement. Loan and credit.
Loan repayment. Refinance of loan. Terms of
loan.
INTL ORGS: International Civil Aviation Organiza-
tion. International Court of Justice. Arbitration
Commission.
TREATY REF: 15UNTS295.
PARTIES:
Australia
Ceylon (Sri Lanka)
                         ANNEX
72 UNTS 304. Ceylon (Sri Lanka). Amendment
24 Mar 50. Force 22 Mar 50.
72 UNTS 304. Australia. Amendment 20 Mar 50.
Force 22 Mar 50.

100790   Bilateral Agreement   **53 UNTS 329**
SIGNED: 14 Feb 50   FORCE: 14 Feb 50
REGISTERED: 1 May 50 ICAO (Civil Aviat)
ARTICLES: 12 LANGUAGE: English.
HEADNOTE: AIR SERVICES
TOPIC: Air Transport
CONCEPTS: Annex or appendix reference. Confor-
mity with municipal law. Licenses and permits.
Recognition of legal documents. Use of facilities.
Procedure. Existing tribunals. Competence of tri-
bunal. Quarantine. Fees and exemptions. Most
favored nation clause. National treatment. Cus-
toms duties. Customs exemptions. Competency
certificate. Routes and logistics. Navigational
conditions. Permit designation. Airport facilities.
Airworthiness certificates. Conditions of airlines
operating permission. Operating authorizations
and regulations. Licenses and certificates of na-
tionality.
INTL ORGS: International Civil Aviation Organization.
TREATY REF: 15UNTS295.
PROCEDURE: Amendment. Future Procedures
Contemplated. Registration. Termination.
PARTIES:
Canada
Norway

100791   Bilateral Agreement   **53 UNTS 341**
SIGNED: 9 Sep 49   FORCE: 9 Sep 49
REGISTERED: 1 May 50 ICAO (Civil Aviat)
ARTICLES: 18 LANGUAGE: English. French. Span-
ish.
HEADNOTE: AIR NAVIGATION SERVICES
TOPIC: Air Transport
CONCEPTS: Definition of terms. Emergencies. An-
nex or appendix reference. Privileges and immu-
nities. General cooperation. Exchange of infor-
mation and documents. Inspection and observa-
tion. Responsibility and liability. Arbitration.
Procedure. Domestic jurisdiction. Meteorology.

Accounting procedures. Compensation. Indemnities and reimbursements. Currency. Exchange
rates and regulations. Expense sharing formulae.
Fees and exemptions. Funding procedures. Payment schedules. Customs duties. Navigational
conditions. Operating authorizations and regulations. International organizations. Status of experts.
TREATY REF: 15UNTS295; 33UNTS261;.
PROCEDURE: Amendment. Termination.
PARTIES:
Denmark
ICAO (Civil Aviat)

100792   Multilateral Convention   **54 UNTS 3**
SIGNED: 11 Jul 47   FORCE: 7 Apr 50
REGISTERED: 8 May 50 ILO (Labor Org)
ARTICLES: 39 LANGUAGE: English. French.
HEADNOTE: LABOR INSPECTION INDUSTRY
COMMERCE
TOPIC: ILO Labor
CONCEPTS: Definition of terms. Detailed regula-
tions. Exceptions and exemptions. Territorial ap-
plication. General cooperation. Inspection and
observation. Domestic legislation. Operating
agencies. Incorporation of treaty provisions into
national law. Investigation of violations. ILO conventions. Employment regulations. Labor statistics. Safety standards.
INTL ORGS: United Nations.
TREATY REF: 15UNTS35; 15UNTS386.
PROCEDURE: Amendment. Accession. Denunciation. Duration. Ratification. Registration. Renewal or Revival.
PARTIES:
Multilateral
                         ANNEX
77 UNTS 366. France. Ratification 16 Dec 50.
Force 16 Dec 51.
79 UNTS 327. Iraq. Ratification 13 Jan 51. Force
13 Jan 52.
82 UNTS 346. Turkey. Ratification 5 Mar 51.
Force 5 Mar 52.
92 UNTS 404. Ireland. Qualified Ratification
16 Jun 51. Force 16 Jun 52.
104 UNTS 350. Netherlands. Qualified Ratification 15 Sep 51. Force 15 Sep 52.
107 UNTS 82. Netherlands. Surinam.
107 UNTS 82. Netherlands. Netherlands Antilles.
122 UNTS 341.   Guatemala.   Ratification
13 Feb 52. Force 13 Feb 53.
127 UNTS 330. Haiti. Ratification 31 Mar 52.
Force 31 Mar 53.
149 UNTS 406. Italy. Ratification 22 Oct 52.
Force 22 Oct 53.
173 UNTS 394. Dominican Republic. Ratification
22 Sep 53. Force 22 Sep 54.
175 UNTS 366. Pakistan. Ratification 10 Oct 53.
Force 10 Oct 54.
178 UNTS 386. Japan. Ratification 20 Oct 53.
Force 20 Oct 54.
199 UNTS 321. Cuba. Ratification 7 Sep 54.
Force 7 Sep 55.
204 UNTS 342.   Argentina.   Ratification
17 Feb 55. Force 17 Feb 56.
211 UNTS 393. Israel. Ratification 7 Jun 55.
Force 7 Jun 56.
212 UNTS 392. France. Martinique.
212 UNTS 392. France. Guadeloupe.
212 UNTS 392. France. Reunion.
212 UNTS 392. France. French Guinea.
212 UNTS 392. Germany, West. Ratification
14 Jun 55. Force 14 Jun 56.
212 UNTS 392. Greece. Ratification 16 Jun 55.
Force 16 Jun 56.
218 UNTS 382.   Yugoslavia.   Ratification
18 Aug 55. Force 18 Aug 56.
236 UNTS 378. Ceylon (Sri Lanka). Ratification
3 Apr 56.
253 UNTS 386. United Arab Rep. Ratification
11 Oct 56. Force 11 Oct 57.
266 UNTS 378. Belgium. Ratification 5 Apr 57.
Force 5 Apr 58.
266 UNTS 378. Brazil. Ratification 25 Apr 57.
Force 25 Apr 58.
269 UNTS 282. Tunisia. Ratification 15 May 57.
Force 15 May 58.
293 UNTS 371. UK Great Britain. Tanganyika.
293 UNTS 371. UK Great Britain. Nigeria.
293 UNTS 371. UK Great Britain. Brunei.
293 UNTS 371. UK Great Britain. Uganda.
293 UNTS 371. UK Great Britain. Jamaica.
293 UNTS 371. UK Great Britain. Mauritius.

293 UNTS 371. UK Great Britain. St. Vincent.
293 UNTS 371. UK Great Britain. Singapore.
293 UNTS 371. UK Great Britain. Kenya.
293 UNTS 371. UK Great Britain. Gibralter.
293 UNTS 371. UK Great Britain. North Borneo.
293 UNTS 371. UK Great Britain. Cyprus.
293 UNTS 371. UK Great Britain. Sierra Leone.
293 UNTS 371. UK Great Britain. British Honduras.
293 UNTS 371. UK Great Britain. Hong Kong.
293 UNTS 371. UK Great Britain. Malta.
293 UNTS 371. Morocco. Ratification 14 Mar 58. Force 14 Mar 59.
293 UNTS 371. Luxembourg. Ratification 3 Mar 58. Force 3 Mar 59.
293 UNTS 371. UK Great Britain. Sarawak.
293 UNTS 371. UK Great Britain. Antigua.
293 UNTS 371. UK Great Britain. Barbados.
293 UNTS 371. UK Great Britain. Grenada.
300 UNTS 370. UK Great Britain. British Guiana.
304 UNTS 400. Panama. Ratification 3 Jun 58. Force 3 Jun 59.
312 UNTS 404. Denmark. Ratification 6 Aug 58. Force 6 Aug 59.
313 UNTS 337. Denmark. Declaration 16 Sep 58.
320 UNTS 325. UK Great Britain. Declaration 16 Dec 58.
327 UNTS 351. Guinea. Ratification 26 Mar 59. Force 26 Mar 60.
338 UNTS 333. Ghana. Ratification 2 Jul 59. Force 2 Jul 60.
345 UNTS 356. New Zealand. Ratification 30 Nov 59. Force 30 Nov 60.
353 UNTS 332. Peru. Ratification 1 Feb 60. Force 1 Feb 61.
356 UNTS 345. UK Great Britain. Fed Rhod/-Nyasaland.
358 UNTS 254. UK Great Britain. Fed Rhod/-Nyasaland. Qualified Application to Non-self-governing Territories 11 Apr 60.
361 UNTS 242. Spain. Ratification 30 May 60. Force 30 May 61.
366 UNTS 383. Costa Rica. Ratification 2 Jun 60. Force 2 Jun 61.
373 UNTS 347. United Arab Rep. Syria.
373 UNTS 349. Iraq. Implementation 5 Jul 60.
380 UNTS 409. Nigeria. Succession 17 Oct 60. Force 17 Oct 60.
381 UNTS 379. Cyprus. Succession 23 Sep 60. Force 23 Sep 60.
388 UNTS 332. UK Great Britain. Mauritius.
390 UNTS 347. UK Great Britain. Declaration 13 Feb 61.
396 UNTS 318. UK Great Britain. Sierra Leone.
401 UNTS 249. Sierra Leone. Succession 13 Jun 61.
413 UNTS 361. Syria. Ratification 30 Oct 61.
422 UNTS 326. Tanganyika. Succession 30 Jan 62. Force 30 Jan 62.
423 UNTS 299. Portugal. Ratification 12 Feb 62. Force 12 Feb 63.
423 UNTS 299. Taiwan. Qualified Ratification 13 Feb 62. Force 13 Feb 63.
435 UNTS 308. UK Great Britain. Gibralter.
435 UNTS 309. Lebanon. Ratification 26 Jul 62. Force 26 Jul 63.
443 UNTS 333. Cameroon. Succession 3 Sep 62. Force 3 Sep 62.
444 UNTS 321. Algeria. Succession 19 Oct 62. Force 19 Oct 62.
444 UNTS 321. Senegal. Ratification 22 Oct 62.
452 UNTS 364. Jamaica. Succession 26 Dec 62.
471 UNTS 371. Uganda. Ratification 4 Jun 63.
473 UNTS 391. Fed of Malaya. Ratification 1 Jul 63. Force 1 Jul 64.
483 UNTS 409. Mauritania. Ratification 8 Nov 63. Force 8 Nov 64.
483 UNTS 409. UK Great Britain. British Honduras.
485 UNTS 380. UK Great Britain. Declaration 18 Dec 63.
488 UNTS 361. Kenya. Ratification 13 Jan 64. Force 13 Jan 64.
488 UNTS 361. Vietnam, South. Ratification 6 Jan 64. Force 6 Jan 65.
495 UNTS 293. Malaysia. State of Sabah. Succession 3 Mar 64.
495 UNTS 293. Malaysia. Sarawak. Succession 3 Mar 64.
495 UNTS 293. Malaysia. Singapore. Succession 3 Mar 64.
495 UNTS 293. Mali. Ratification 2 Mar 64. Force 2 Mar 65.

495 UNTS 293. Malaysia. Malaya. Succession 3 Mar 64.
504 UNTS 353. Tanzania. Succession 22 Jun 64.
521 UNTS 426. Kuwait. Ratification 23 Nov 64. Force 23 Nov 65.
524 UNTS 361. Malta. Ratification 4 Jan 65. Force 4 Jan 65.
530 UNTS 412. UK Great Britain. Malawi. Ratification 22 Mar 65. Force 22 Mar 66.
547 UNTS 366. UK Great Britain. Declaration 24 Sep 65.
547 UNTS 366. UK Great Britain. Brit Solomon Is.
548 UNTS 398. Singapore. Ratification 25 Oct 65. Force 25 Oct 65.
549 UNTS 364. Chad. Ratification 30 Nov 65. Force 30 Nov 66.
567 UNTS 349. Guyana. Ratification 8 Jun 66. Force 8 Jun 66.
571 UNTS 329. UK Great Britain. Hong Kong.
603 UNTS 353. Venezuela. Ratification 21 Jul 67. Force 21 Jul 68.
607 UNTS 353. Paraguay. Ratification 23 Aug 67. Force 28 Aug 68.
613 UNTS 422. Colombia. Ratification 13 Nov 67. Force 13 Nov 68.
636 UNTS 425. Congo (Brazzaville). Ratification 19 Apr 68. Force 19 Apr 68.

100793 Bilateral Agreement **54 UNTS 33**
SIGNED: 31 Mar 48   FORCE: 31 Mar 48
REGISTERED: 10 May 50 India
ARTICLES: 12 LANGUAGE: English.
HEADNOTE: MODIFICATIONS PREVIOUS FINANCE AGREEMENTS
TOPIC: Finance
CONCEPTS: Detailed regulations. Annex type material. Incorporation of treaty provisions into national law. Responsibility and liability. Accounting procedures. Banking. Balance of payments. Monetary and gold transfers. Currency deposits. Exchange rates and regulations. Transportation costs. Local currency. Assets. Claims and settlements. Assets transfer.
PARTIES:
India
Pakistan

100794 Bilateral Agreement **54 UNTS 45**
SIGNED: 4 May 48   FORCE: 4 May 48
REGISTERED: 10 May 50 India
ARTICLES: 7 LANGUAGE: English.
HEADNOTE: CANAL WATER DISPUTE BETWEEN EAST & WEST PUNJAB
TOPIC: Dispute Settlement
CONCEPTS: Procedure.
PARTIES:
India
Pakistan
                    ANNEX
85 UNTS 356. Pakistan. Termination 23 Aug 50.
128 UNTS 300. India. Declaration 15 Sep 50.
394 UNTS 253. Netherlands. Implementation 14 Dec 59. Force 15 Dec 59.
394 UNTS 253. Belgium. Implementation 14 Dec 59. Force 15 Dec 59.

100795 Bilateral Agreement **54 UNTS 51**
SIGNED: 23 Apr 49   FORCE: 10 May 49
REGISTERED: 10 May 50 India
ARTICLES: 15 LANGUAGE: English.
HEADNOTE: TRANSFER DELAY TRANSFER MUSLIM ACCOUNTS
TOPIC: Finance
CONCEPTS: Detailed regulations. General cooperation. Legal protection and assistance. Immovable property. General property. Establishment of commission. Procedure. Accounting procedures. Banking. Bonds. Monetary and gold transfers. Assets. Claims and settlements. Assets transfer.
INTL ORGS: Special Commission.
PROCEDURE: Ratification.
PARTIES:
India
Pakistan

100796 Bilateral Exchange **54 UNTS 83**
SIGNED: 26 Apr 50   FORCE: 26 Apr 50
REGISTERED: 11 May 50 Australia
ARTICLES: 2 LANGUAGE: English.

HEADNOTE: RELEASE ASSETS
TOPIC: Claims and Debts
CONCEPTS: Definition of terms. Exceptions and exemptions. Territorial application. Exchange of information and documents. Informational records. General property. Responsibility and liability. Accounting procedures. Banking. Compensation. Assets. Claims and settlements. Assessment procedures. Assets transfer. Enemy financial interests.
PARTIES:
Australia
Netherlands

100797 Bilateral Agreement **54 UNTS 97**
SIGNED: 16 Jan 47   FORCE: 16 Jan 47
REGISTERED: 25 May 50 UK Great Britain
ARTICLES: 4 LANGUAGE: English.
HEADNOTE: SUPPLY AIRCRAFT EQUIPMENT
TOPIC: Milit Installation
CONCEPTS: Annex or appendix reference. Indemnities and reimbursements. Delivery schedules. Payment for war supplies. Surplus war property. Restrictions on transfer.
PARTIES:
Belgium
UK Great Britain

100798 Bilateral Agreement **54 UNTS 117**
SIGNED: 3 Dec 46   FORCE: 29 Nov 46
REGISTERED: 25 May 50 UK Great Britain
ARTICLES: 7 LANGUAGE: English. French.
HEADNOTE: FINANCIAL AGREEMENT
TOPIC: Finance
CONCEPTS: Currency. Monetary and gold transfers. Debt settlement.
PARTIES:
France
UK Great Britain
                    ANNEX
99 UNTS 312. UK Great Britain. Termination 1 Jan 48. Force 1 Apr 48.

100799 Bilateral Exchange **54 UNTS 127**
SIGNED: 3 Dec 46   FORCE: 3 Dec 46
REGISTERED: 25 May 50 UK Great Britain
ARTICLES: 2 LANGUAGE: English. French.
HEADNOTE: WAR DAMAGE COMPENSATION
TOPIC: Reparations
CONCEPTS: National treatment. Loss and/or damage. Post-war claims settlement.
PARTIES:
France
UK Great Britain
                    ANNEX
214 UNTS 354. France. Prolongation 6 Oct 54. Force 10 Dec 54.
214 UNTS 354. UK Great Britain. Prolongation 6 Oct 54. Force 10 Dec 54.
335 UNTS 288. Norway. Amendment 16 May 58. Force 16 May 58.
335 UNTS 288. Canada. Amendment 16 May 58. Force 16 May 58.

100800 Bilateral Exchange **54 UNTS 131**
SIGNED: 30 May 47   FORCE: 16 Jan 47
REGISTERED: 25 May 50 UK Great Britain
ARTICLES: 5 LANGUAGE: English. Italian.
HEADNOTE: ITALIAN WORKERS BRITISH FOUNDRIES
TOPIC: Non-ILO Labor
CONCEPTS: Annex or appendix reference. Non-ILO labor relations. Sickness and invalidity insurance.
PARTIES:
Italy
UK Great Britain

100801 Bilateral Exchange **54 UNTS 14**
SIGNED: 17 Apr 47   FORCE: 17 Apr 4
REGISTERED: 25 May 50 UK Great Britain
ARTICLES: 2 LANGUAGE: English. Italian.
HEADNOTE: PAYMENTS
TOPIC: Finance
CONCEPTS: Annex type material. Payment schedules.
PARTIES:
Italy
UK Great Britain

ANNEX
81 UNTS 334. UK Great Britain. Abrogation and Replacement 26 Nov 48. Force 26 Nov 48.
81 UNTS 334. Italy. Abrogation and Replacement 26 Nov 48. Force 26 Nov 48.

100802 Bilateral Exchange **54 UNTS 169**
SIGNED: 17 Apr 47 FORCE: 15 Sep 47
REGISTERED: 25 May 50 UK Great Britain
ARTICLES: 2 LANGUAGE: English. Italian.
HEADNOTE: PAYMENT DEBTS DUE PERSONS
TOPIC: Claims and Debts
CONCEPTS: Assets. Debts. Debt settlement.
TREATY REF: 49UNTS.
PROCEDURE: Ratification. Renewal or Revival.
PARTIES:
  Italy
  UK Great Britain
ANNEX
93 UNTS 365. UK Great Britain. Bahamas.
93 UNTS 365. UK Great Britain. Sierra Leone.
93 UNTS 365. UK Great Britain. Barbados.
93 UNTS 365. UK Great Britain. Singapore.
93 UNTS 365. UK Great Britain. Trinidad.
93 UNTS 365. UK Great Britain. Fed of Malaya.
93 UNTS 365. UK Great Britain. Nyasaland.
93 UNTS 365. UK Great Britain. Cyprus.
93 UNTS 365. UK Great Britain. Fiji Islands.
93 UNTS 365. UK Great Britain. British Somaliland.
93 UNTS 365. UK Great Britain. Gibralter.
93 UNTS 365. UK Great Britain. Swaziland.
93 UNTS 365. UK Great Britain. Jamaica.
93 UNTS 365. UK Great Britain. Gold Coast.
93 UNTS 365. UK Great Britain. Bermuda.
93 UNTS 365. UK Great Britain. Kenya.
93 UNTS 365. UK Great Britain. British Guiana.
93 UNTS 365. UK Great Britain. Leeward Islands.
93 UNTS 365. UK Great Britain. British Honduras.
93 UNTS 365. UK Great Britain. Uganda.
93 UNTS 365. UK Great Britain. Zanzibar.
93 UNTS 365. UK Great Britain. Hong Kong.
93 UNTS 365. UK Great Britain. Aden.
93 UNTS 365. UK Great Britain. Tanganyika.
93 UNTS 365. UK Great Britain. Mauritius.
93 UNTS 365. UK Great Britain. Northern Rhodesia.
93 UNTS 365. UK Great Britain. Nigeria.
93 UNTS 365. UK Great Britain. Southern Rhodesia.
93 UNTS 365. UK Great Britain. Malta.

100803 Bilateral Agreement **54 UNTS 181**
SIGNED: 5 Jun 47 FORCE: 1 Mar 47
REGISTERED: 25 May 50 UK Great Britain
ARTICLES: 14 LANGUAGE: English. Norwegian.
HEADNOTE: PARTICIPATION OCCUPATION
TOPIC: Milit Occupation
CONCEPTS: Exceptions and exemptions. Use of facilities. Operating authorizations and regulations. Facilities and equipment. Joint defense. Military training. Jurisdiction. Procurement and logistics. Control and occupation machinery.
PROCEDURE: Amendment. Future Procedures Contemplated. Renewal or Revival. Termination.
PARTIES:
  Norway
  UK Great Britain
ANNEX
66 UNTS 353. UK Great Britain. Prolongation 31 Jul 48. Force 31 Jul 48.
66 UNTS 353. Norway. Prolongation 31 Jul 48. Force 31 Jul 48.
99 UNTS 314. Norway. Amendment 30 Nov 50. Force 30 Nov 50.
99 UNTS 314. UK Great Britain. Amendment 30 Nov 50. Force 30 Nov 50.
99 UNTS 316. UK Great Britain. Prolongation 28 Feb 51. Force 28 Feb 51.
99 UNTS 316. Norway. Prolongation 28 Feb 51. Force 28 Feb 51.

100804 Multilateral Protocol **54 UNTS 193**
SIGNED: 10 Oct 47 FORCE: 15 Sep 47
REGISTERED: 25 May 50 UK Great Britain
ARTICLES: 1 LANGUAGE: English. Italian.
HEADNOTE: RETURN LOOTED GOLD
TOPIC: Claims and Debts
CONCEPTS: Claims and settlements. Post-war claims settlement.
TREATY REF: 49UNTS.

PARTIES:
  Italy SIGNED: 10 Oct 47 FORCE: 15 Sep 47
  UK Great Britain SIGNED: 10 Oct 47 FORCE: 15 Sep 47
  USA (United States) SIGNED: 10 Oct 47 FORCE: 15 Sep 47

100805 Bilateral Agreement **54 UNTS 197**
SIGNED: 6 Sep 46 FORCE: 6 Oct 46
REGISTERED: 26 May 50 USA (United States)
ARTICLES: 14 LANGUAGE: English. Portuguese.
HEADNOTE: AIR TRANSPORT
TOPIC: Air Transport
CONCEPTS: Definition of terms. Annex or appendix reference. Previous treaty replacement. Conformity with municipal law. Licenses and permits. Recognition of legal documents. Use of facilities. Arbitration. Procedure. Existing tribunals. Competence of tribunal. Fees and exemptions. National treatment. Customs exemptions. Competency certificate. Routes and logistics. Navigational conditions. Permit designation. Air transport. Airport facilities. Airworthiness certificates. Conditions of airlines operating permission. Operating authorizations and regulations. Licenses and certificates of nationality.
INTL ORGS: International Civil Aviation Organization.
TREATY REF: US DEPT. OF STATE PUB. 2282 SERIES 64. 015UNTS295.
PROCEDURE: Amendment. Future Procedures Contemplated. Registration. Termination.
PARTIES:
  Brazil
  USA (United States)
ANNEX
133 UNTS 340. USA (United States). Amendment 30 Dec 50. Force 30 Dec 50.
133 UNTS 340. Brazil. Amendment 30 Dec 50. Force 30 Dec 50.
337 UNTS 384. USA (United States). Amendment 1 Dec 58. Force 1 Dec 58.
337 UNTS 384. Brazil. Amendment 1 Dec 58. Force 1 Dec 58.

100806 Bilateral Agreement **55 UNTS 3**
SIGNED: 28 Sep 49 FORCE: 28 Sep 49
REGISTERED: 26 May 50 USA (United States)
ARTICLES: 15 LANGUAGE: English.
HEADNOTE: AIR TRANSPORT
TOPIC: Air Transport
CONCEPTS: Definition of terms. Exceptions and exemptions. Annex or appendix reference. Non-prejudice to third party. Conformity with municipal law. Licenses and permits. Recognition of legal documents. Use of facilities. Arbitration. Procedure. Special tribunals. Competence of tribunal. Fees and exemptions. Most favored nation clause. National treatment. Customs exemptions. Competency certificate. Routes and logistics. Navigational conditions. Permit designation. Airport facilities. Airworthiness certificates. Conditions of airlines operating permission. Operating authorizations and regulations. Licenses and certificates of nationality.
INTL ORGS: International Civil Aviation Organization. Arbitration Commission.
TREATY REF: 015 UNTS295.
PROCEDURE: Amendment. Future Procedures Contemplated. Registration. Termination.
PARTIES:
  Burma
  USA (United States)

100807 Bilateral Agreement **55 UNTS 21**
SIGNED: 10 May 47 FORCE: 30 Dec 48
REGISTERED: 26 May 50 USA (United States)
ARTICLES: 7 LANGUAGE: English. Spanish.
HEADNOTE: AIR TRANSPORT
TOPIC: Air Transport
CONCEPTS: Exceptions and exemptions. Annex or appendix reference. Non-prejudice to third party. Conformity with municipal law. Licenses and permits. Recognition of legal documents. Use of facilities. Arbitration. Procedure. Existing tribunals. Competence of tribunal. Fees and exemptions. Most favored nation clause. National treatment. Customs exemptions. Competency certificate. Routes and logistics. Navigational conditions. Air transport. Airport facilities. Air-

worthiness certificates. Conditions of airlines operating permission. Operating authorizations and regulations. Licenses and certificates of nationality.
INTL ORGS: International Civil Aviation Organization. Arbitration Commission.
PROCEDURE: Amendment. Future Procedures Contemplated. Ratification. Registration. Termination.
PARTIES:
  Chile
  USA (United States)

100808 Bilateral Agreement **55 UNTS 59**
SIGNED: 29 Mar 49 FORCE: 28 Apr 49
REGISTERED: 26 May 50 USA (United States)
ARTICLES: 14 LANGUAGE: English.
HEADNOTE: AIR TRANSPORT
TOPIC: Air Transport
CONCEPTS: Definition of terms. Exceptions and exemptions. Annex or appendix reference. Conformity with municipal law. General cooperation. Licenses and permits. Recognition of legal documents. Use of facilities. Procedure. Special tribunals. Competence of tribunal. Indemnities and reimbursements. Fees and exemptions. Most favored nation clause. National treatment. Customs exemptions. Competency certificate. Routes and logistics. Navigational conditions. Permit designation. Air transport. Airport facilities. Airworthiness certificates. Conditions of airlines operating permission. Operating authorizations and regulations. Licenses and certificates of nationality.
INTL ORGS: International Civil Aviation Organization. Arbitration Commission.
TREATY REF: 015 UNTS295.
PROCEDURE: Amendment. Future Procedures Contemplated. Registration. Termination.
PARTIES:
  Finland
  USA (United States)

100809 Bilateral Exchange **55 UNTS 79**
SIGNED: 29 Jun 49 FORCE: 29 Jun 49
REGISTERED: 26 May 50 USA (United States)
ARTICLES: 2 LANGUAGE: English.
HEADNOTE: AIR TRANSPORT SERVICES
TOPIC: Air Transport
CONCEPTS: General cooperation. Licenses and permits. Personnel. Fees and exemptions. Most favored nation clause. Customs exemptions. Competency certificate. Navigational conditions. Air transport. Airport facilities. Airport equipment. Airworthiness certificates. Overflights and technical stops.
PARTIES:
  Korea, South
  USA (United States)

100810 Bilateral Agreement **55 UNTS 87**
SIGNED: 31 Mar 49 FORCE: 14 Apr 49
REGISTERED: 26 May 50 USA (United States)
ARTICLES: 20 LANGUAGE: English. Spanish.
HEADNOTE: AVIATION
TOPIC: Air Transport
CONCEPTS: Definition of terms. Detailed regulations. Exceptions and exemptions. Annex or appendix reference. Non-prejudice to third party. Friendship and amity. Conformity with municipal law. General cooperation. Exchange of information and documents. Licenses and permits. Recognition of legal documents. Use of facilities. Arbitration. Procedure. Special tribunals. Competence of tribunal. Sanitation. Sanitation. Indemnities and reimbursements. Fees and exemptions. Most favored nation clause. National treatment. Customs duties. Customs exemptions. Special projects. Aid missions. Competency certificate. Routes and logistics. Navigational conditions. Permit designation. Airport facilities. Airworthiness certificates. Conditions of airlines operating permission. Operating authorizations and regulations. Licenses and certificates of nationality. Bands and frequency allocation. Facilities and equipment.
INTL ORGS: International Civil Aviation Organization. Arbitration Commission.
TREATY REF: 015 UNTS25F 55UNTS125.
PROCEDURE: Amendment. Future Procedures

Contemplated. Ratification. Registration. Termination.
PARTIES:
 Panama
 USA (United States)
                    ANNEX
174 UNTS 286. Panama. Amendment 3 Jun 52.
 Force 3 Jun 52.
174 UNTS 286. USA (United States). Amendment
 29 May 52. Force 3 Jun 52.

100811   Bilateral Exchange   **55 UNTS 125**
SIGNED: 31 Mar 49   FORCE: 14 Apr 49
REGISTERED: 26 May 50 USA (United States)
ARTICLES: 2 LANGUAGE: English. Spanish.
HEADNOTE: INSTALLATION OPERATION COMMUNICATIONS CABLE
TOPIC: Telecommunications
CONCEPTS: Conformity with municipal law. Non-interest rates and fees. General. Facilities and equipment. Cable.
TREATY REF: USA-PANAMA 1949.
PROCEDURE: Ratification.
PARTIES:
 Panama
 USA (United States)
                    ANNEX
545 UNTS 322. USA (United States). Prolongation
 9 Mar 65. Force 1 Apr 65.
545 UNTS 322. Panama. Prolongation 1 Apr 65.
 Force 1 Apr 65.

100812   Bilateral Exchange   **55 UNTS 141**
SIGNED: 31 Mar 49   FORCE: 14 Apr 49
REGISTERED: 26 May 50 USA (United States)
ARTICLES: 2 LANGUAGE: English. Spanish.
HEADNOTE: CIVIL AVIATION MISSION
TOPIC: Air Transport
CONCEPTS: Exceptions and exemptions. Personnel. Responsibility and liability. Use of facilities. Accounting procedures. Indemnities and reimbursements. Internal finance. Payment schedules. Transportation costs. Tax exemptions. Customs exemptions. General technical assistance. Materials, equipment and services. Aid missions.
TREATY REF: 055UNTS087.
PROCEDURE: Duration. Ratification. Termination.
PARTIES:
 Panama
 USA (United States)
                    ANNEX
212 UNTS 325. USA (United States). Extension
 and Amendment 14 Apr 53. Force 8 May 53.
212 UNTS 325. Panama. Extension and Amendment 8 May 53. Force 8 May 53.

100813   Bilateral Agreement   **55 UNTS 157**
SIGNED: 10 Dec 48   FORCE: 14 Dec 48
REGISTERED: 29 May 50 USA (United States)
ARTICLES: 12 LANGUAGE: English. Korean.
HEADNOTE: AID
TOPIC: Direct Aid
CONCEPTS: Territorial application. Privileges and immunities. Conformity with municipal law. Exchange of information and documents. Informational records. Inspection and observation. Personnel. Public information. Reexport of goods, etc.. Accounting procedures. Currency deposits. Most favored nation clause. Domestic obligation. General aid. Aid missions. Grants. Withdrawal conditions. Procurement. Access to materials. Press and wire services.
INTL ORGS: United Nations.
TREATY REF: 55UNTS187.
PROCEDURE: Amendment. Duration. Future Procedures Contemplated. Ratification. Registration. Termination.
PARTIES:
 Korea, South
 USA (United States)

100814   Multilateral Agreement   **55 UNTS 188**
SIGNED: 30 Oct 47   FORCE: 1 Jan 48
REGISTERED: 30 May 50 United Nations
ARTICLES: 34 LANGUAGE: English. French.
HEADNOTE: GENERAL AGREEMENT TARIFFS & TRADE
TOPIC: General Economic
CONCEPTS: Establishment of trade relations. Export quotas. Import quotas. Tariffs. Certificates of origin. Reciprocity in trade. Export subsidies. Trade agencies. Trade procedures. Banking. Balance of payments. Currency. Monetary and gold transfers. Exchange rates and regulations. Payment schedules. Claims and settlements. Debts. Delivery guarantees. Delivery schedules. Quotas. Equitable taxes. Trademarks. Laws and formalities. Recognition. Customs declarations. General technical assistance. Transport of goods.
INTL ORGS: General Agreement on Tariffs and Trade. International Monetary Fund. United Nations.
PROCEDURE: Accession. Denunciation.
PARTIES:
 Multilateral
                    ANNEX
65 UNTS 335.
66 UNTS 358.
66 UNTS 359.
68 UNTS 286.
70 UNTS 306.
71 UNTS 328.
76 UNTS 282.
77 UNTS 367.
81 UNTS 344.
81 UNTS 346.
81 UNTS 362.
90 UNTS 324.
92 UNTS 405.
104 UNTS 351.
107 UNTS 83.
107 UNTS 311.
117 UNTS 387.
123 UNTS 303.
131 UNTS 316.
135 UNTS 336.
138 UNTS 334.
138 UNTS 346.
138 UNTS 381.
138 UNTS 398.
141 UNTS 382.
147 UNTS 159.
161 UNTS 365.
163 UNTS 375.
167 UNTS 265.
172 UNTS 340.
173 UNTS 395.
180 UNTS 299.
183 UNTS 351.
189 UNTS 360.
220 UNTS 154.
225 UNTS 258.
228 UNTS 366.
230 UNTS 430.
234 UNTS 310.
247 UNTS 386.
248 UNTS 359.
250 UNTS 290.
250 UNTS 292.
250 UNTS 297.
250 UNTS 301.
253 UNTS 316.
256 UNTS 338.
256 UNTS 339.
257 UNTS 362.
258 UNTS 384.
261 UNTS 390.
265 UNTS 328.
271 UNTS 386.
274 UNTS 322.
277 UNTS 345.
278 UNTS 168.
278 UNTS 246.
280 UNTS 350.
281 UNTS 394.
283 UNTS 308.
283 UNTS 310.
283 UNTS 312.
285 UNTS 372.
285 UNTS 378.
287 UNTS 343.
287 UNTS 344.
300 UNTS 371.
306 UNTS 332.
306 UNTS 334.
309 UNTS 362.
309 UNTS 364.
317 UNTS 317.
317 UNTS 318.
320 UNTS 326.
321 UNTS 244.
324 UNTS 300.
328 UNTS 290.
330 UNTS 352.
338 UNTS 334.
344 UNTS 304.
346 UNTS 312.
346 UNTS 322.
347 UNTS 362.
349 UNTS 314.
350 UNTS 1.
351 UNTS 380.
355 UNTS 406.
355 UNTS 407.
358 UNTS 256.
362 UNTS 324.
363 UNTS 402.
367 UNTS 314.
373 UNTS 350.
376 UNTS 406.
377 UNTS 396.
381 UNTS 380.
382 UNTS 330.
386 UNTS 376.
387 UNTS 330.
388 UNTS 334.
390 UNTS 348.
398 UNTS 316.
402 UNTS 308.
405 UNTS 298.
411 UNTS 296.
419 UNTS 344.
421 UNTS 286.
421 UNTS 290.
424 UNTS 324.
424 UNTS 334.
424 UNTS 342.
425 UNTS 314.
425 UNTS 314.
429 UNTS 268.
431 UNTS 202.
431 UNTS 204.
431 UNTS 205.
431 UNTS 206.
431 UNTS 208.
431 UNTS 242.
431 UNTS 244.
435 UNTS 310.
438 UNTS 342.
442 UNTS 302.
444 UNTS 322.
445 UNTS 290.
445 UNTS 292.
445 UNTS 294.
445 UNTS 304.
449 UNTS 280.
449 UNTS 282.
452 UNTS 282.
452 UNTS 286.
452 UNTS 288.
452 UNTS 290.
452 UNTS 298.
452 UNTS 386.
456 UNTS 488.
456 UNTS 490.
460 UNTS 296.
462 UNTS 330.
463 UNTS 336.
463 UNTS 338.
468 UNTS 410.
468 UNTS 412.
471 UNTS 296.
474 UNTS 302.
475 UNTS 348.
475 UNTS 352.
475 UNTS 354.
476 UNTS 254.
478 UNTS 408.
483 UNTS 288.
483 UNTS 289.
483 UNTS 290.
483 UNTS 292.
483 UNTS 294.
483 UNTS 296.
489 UNTS 370.
489 UNTS 372.
489 UNTS 374.
496 UNTS 326.
501 UNTS 296.
501 UNTS 298.
501 UNTS 300.
501 UNTS 302.
501 UNTS 304.
525 UNTS 264.
525 UNTS 266.
525 UNTS 268.
525 UNTS 270.

525 UNTS 276.
525 UNTS 278.
525 UNTS 284.
525 UNTS 286.
525 UNTS 288.
525 UNTS 296.
525 UNTS 298.
525 UNTS 304.
525 UNTS 306.
525 UNTS 308.
543 UNTS 338.
543 UNTS 340.
543 UNTS 342.
543 UNTS 344.
543 UNTS 346.
543 UNTS 348.
543 UNTS 350.
543 UNTS 352.
543 UNTS 354.
543 UNTS 356.
551 UNTS 268.
557 UNTS 246.
557 UNTS 248.
557 UNTS 254.
557 UNTS 256.
557 UNTS 258.
557 UNTS 264.
557 UNTS 266.
567 UNTS 328.
567 UNTS 334.
572 UNTS 296.
572 UNTS 320.
609 UNTS 206.
620 UNTS 254.
621 UNTS 1.
640 UNTS 336.
651 UNTS 310.
655 UNTS 3.
662 UNTS 1.
663 UNTS 3.
668 UNTS 348.
761 UNTS 3.
762 UNTS 3.

100815   Bilateral Agreement   **65 UNTS 22**
SIGNED: 23 Aug 47   FORCE: 23 Aug 47
REGISTERED: 1 Jun 50 United Nations
ARTICLES: 9 LANGUAGE: English.
HEADNOTE: UNICEF ACTIVITIES
TOPIC: Tech Assistance
CONCEPTS: Privileges and immunities. General
cooperation. Personnel. Payment schedules. As-
sets transfer. Commodities and services. Domes-
tic obligation. Assistance. Aid missions. Status
of experts.
INTL ORGS: United Nations.
TREATY REF: 65UNTS4.
PARTIES:
  Poland
  UNICEF (Children)
                    ANNEX
406 UNTS 291.   UNICEF   (Children).   Force
  24 Aug 61.
406 UNTS 291. Poland. Force 24 Aug 61.

100816   Bilateral Agreement   **65 UNTS 26**
SIGNED: 3 Oct 47   FORCE: 3 Oct 47
REGISTERED: 1 Jun 50 United Nations
ARTICLES: 9 LANGUAGE: English. French.
HEADNOTE: UNICEF ACTIVITIES
TOPIC: Tech Assistance
CONCEPTS: Domestic obligation. Assistance.
INTL ORGS: United Nations.
PARTIES:
  Czechoslovakia
  UNICEF (Children)

100817   Bilateral Agreement   **65 UNTS 28**
SIGNED: 20 Nov 47   FORCE: 20 Nov 47
REGISTERED: 1 Jun 50 United Nations
ARTICLES: 9 LANGUAGE: English.
HEADNOTE: UNICEF ACTIVITIES
TOPIC: Tech Assistance
CONCEPTS: Privileges and immunities. General
cooperation. Exchange of information and docu-
ments. Informational records. Personnel. Public
information. Procedure. Tax exemptions. Cus-
toms exemptions. Domestic obligation. Assis-
tance. Aid missions. Headquarters and facilities.
Status of experts.
INTL ORGS: United Nations.

TREATY REF: 65UNTS4.
PROCEDURE: Duration.
PARTIES:
  UNICEF (Children)
  Yugoslavia

100818   Bilateral Agreement   **65 UNTS 38**
SIGNED: 21 May 48   FORCE: 21 May 48
REGISTERED: 1 Jun 50 United Nations
ARTICLES: 9 LANGUAGE: Chinese. English.
HEADNOTE: UNICEF ACTIVITIES
TOPIC: Tech Assistance
CONCEPTS: Privileges and immunities. Personnel.
  Assistance. Status of experts.
INTL ORGS: United Nations.
TREATY REF: 65UNTS4.
PARTIES:
  Taiwan
  UNICEF (Children)

100819   Bilateral Agreement   **65 UNTS 48**
SIGNED: 20 Nov 48   FORCE: 20 Nov 48
REGISTERED: 1 Jun 50 United Nations
ARTICLES: 9 LANGUAGE: English.
HEADNOTE: UNICEF ACTIVITIES
TOPIC: Tech Assistance
CONCEPTS: Assistance.
INTL ORGS: United Nations.
TREATY REF: 65UNTS4.
PARTIES:
  Philippines
  UNICEF (Children)
                    ANNEX
398 UNTS 340.   UNESCO   (Educ/Cult).   Sup-
  plementation 7 Dec 60. Force 7 Dec 60.
398 UNTS 340. Philippines. Supplementation
  7 Dec 60. Force 7 Dec 60.

100820   Bilateral Agreement   **65 UNTS 50**
SIGNED: 17 Jun 49   FORCE: 17 Jun 49
REGISTERED: 1 Jun 50 United Nations
ARTICLES: 9 LANGUAGE: English.
HEADNOTE: UNICEF ACTIVITIES
TOPIC: Tech Assistance
CONCEPTS: Guarantees and safeguards. Proxy di-
plomacy. General cooperation. Monetary and
gold transfers. Payment schedules. Local cur-
rency. Assets transfer. Expense sharing formu-
lae. Domestic obligation. Assistance. Materials,
equipment and services.
INTL ORGS: United Nations.
TREATY REF: 65UNTS4.
PARTIES:
  UNICEF (Children)
  UK Great Britain

100821   Bilateral Agreement   **65 UNTS 54**
SIGNED: 17 Jun 49   FORCE: 17 Jun 49
REGISTERED: 1 Jun 50 United Nations
ARTICLES: 9 LANGUAGE: English.
HEADNOTE: UNICEF ACTIVITIES
TOPIC: Tech Assistance
CONCEPTS: Assistance.
INTL ORGS: United Nations.
TREATY REF: 65UNTS4.
PARTIES:
  UNICEF (Children)
  UK Great Britain

100822   Bilateral Agreement   **65 UNTS 54**
SIGNED: 17 Jun 49   FORCE: 17 Jun 49
REGISTERED: 1 Jun 50 United Nations
ARTICLES: 9 LANGUAGE: English.
HEADNOTE: UNICEF ACTIVITIES
TOPIC: Tech Assistance
CONCEPTS: Assistance.
INTL ORGS: United Nations.
TREATY REF: 65UNTS4.
PARTIES:
  UNICEF (Children)
  UK Great Britain

100823   Bilateral Agreement   **65 UNTS 56**
SIGNED: 17 Jun 49   FORCE: 17 Jun 49
REGISTERED: 1 Jun 50 United Nations
ARTICLES: 9 LANGUAGE: English.
HEADNOTE: UNICEF ACTIVITIES
TOPIC: Tech Assistance

CONCEPTS: Assistance.
INTL ORGS: United Nations.
TREATY REF: 65UNTS4.
PARTIES:
  UNICEF (Children)
  UK Great Britain

100824   Bilateral Agreement   **65 UNTS 56**
SIGNED: 17 Jun 49   FORCE: 17 Jun 49
REGISTERED: 1 Jun 50 United Nations
ARTICLES: 9 LANGUAGE: English.
HEADNOTE: UNICEF ACTIVITIES
TOPIC: Tech Assistance
CONCEPTS: Assistance.
INTL ORGS: United Nations.
TREATY REF: 65UNTS4.
PARTIES:
  UNICEF (Children)
  UK Great Britain

100825   Bilateral Agreement   **65 UNTS 58**
SIGNED: 13 Jun 49   FORCE: 13 Jul 49
REGISTERED: 1 Jun 50 United Nations
ARTICLES: 9 LANGUAGE: English.
HEADNOTE: UNICEF ACTIVITIES
TOPIC: Tech Assistance
CONCEPTS: Assistance.
INTL ORGS: United Nations.
TREATY REF: 65UNTS4.
PARTIES:
  UNICEF (Children)
  UK Great Britain

100826   Bilateral Agreement   **65 UNTS 60**
SIGNED: 20 Jun 49   FORCE: 20 Jul 49
REGISTERED: 1 Jun 50 United Nations
ARTICLES: 8 LANGUAGE: English.
HEADNOTE: UNICEF ACTIVITIES
TOPIC: Tech Assistance
CONCEPTS: Assistance. IGO status.
INTL ORGS: United Nations.
TREATY REF: 65UNTS4.
PARTIES:
  Pakistan
  UNICEF (Children)
                    ANNEX
214 UNTS 360. UNICEF (Children). Supplementa-
  tion 9 Sep 55. Force 9 Sep 55.
214 UNTS 360.   Pakistan.   Supplementation
  6 Sep 55. Force 9 Sep 55.

100827   Bilateral Agreement   **65 UNTS 62**
SIGNED: 12 Oct 49   FORCE: 12 Oct 49
REGISTERED: 1 Jun 50 United Nations
ARTICLES: 9 LANGUAGE: English. Spanish.
HEADNOTE: UNICEF ACTIVITIES
TOPIC: Tech Assistance
CONCEPTS: Assistance.
INTL ORGS: United Nations.
TREATY REF: 65UNTS4.
PARTIES:
  Ecuador
  UNICEF (Children)

100828   Bilateral Agreement   **65 UNTS 64**
SIGNED: 19 Dec 49   FORCE: 19 Dec 49
REGISTERED: 1 Jun 50 United Nations
ARTICLES: 9 LANGUAGE: English.
HEADNOTE: UNICEF ACTIVITIES
TOPIC: Tech Assistance
CONCEPTS: Guarantees and safeguards. General
cooperation. Financial programs. Domestic obli-
gation. Assistance. Materials, equipment and
services. Headquarters and facilities.
INTL ORGS: United Nations.
TREATY REF: 65UNTS4.
PARTIES:
  UNICEF (Children)
  UK Great Britain

100829   Bilateral Agreement   **65 UNTS 68**
SIGNED: 20 Dec 49   FORCE: 20 Dec 49
REGISTERED: 1 Jun 50 United Nations
ARTICLES: 9 LANGUAGE: English. French.
HEADNOTE: UNICEF ACTIVITIES
TOPIC: Tech Assistance
CONCEPTS: General cooperation. Domestic obli-

gation. Assistance. Materials, equipment and services. Headquarters and facilities.
INTL ORGS: United Nations.
TREATY REF: 65UNTS4.
PARTIES:
Haiti
UNICEF (Children)

100830 Bilateral Agreement **65 UNTS 70**
SIGNED: 14 Jan 50 FORCE: 14 Jun 50
REGISTERED: 1 Jun 50 United Nations
ARTICLES: 9 LANGUAGE: English. Spanish.
HEADNOTE: UNICEF ACTIVITIES
TOPIC: Tech Assistance
CONCEPTS: Financial programs. Domestic obligation. Assistance. Headquarters and facilities.
INTL ORGS: United Nations.
TREATY REF: 65UNTS4.
PARTIES:
Costa Rica
UNICEF (Children)
ANNEX
222 UNTS 395. UNICEF (Children). Supplementation 1 Dec 55. Force 1 Dec 55.
222 UNTS 395. Costa Rica. Supplementation 20 Sep 55. Force 1 Dec 55.

100831 Bilateral Agreement **65 UNTS 74**
SIGNED: 17 Jan 50 FORCE: 17 Jan 50
REGISTERED: 1 Jun 50 United Nations
ARTICLES: 9 LANGUAGE: English. Spanish.
HEADNOTE: UNICEF ACTIVITIES
TOPIC: Tech Assistance
CONCEPTS: Assistance.
INTL ORGS: United Nations.
TREATY REF: 65UNTS4.
PARTIES:
Honduras
UNICEF (Children)
ANNEX
231 UNTS 352. UNICEF (Children). Supplementation 13 Mar 56. Force 3 Apr 56.
231 UNTS 352. Honduras. Supplementation 3 Apr 56. Force 3 Apr 56.

100832 Bilateral Agreement **65 UNTS 76**
SIGNED: 17 Jan 50 FORCE: 17 Jan 50
REGISTERED: 1 Jun 50 United Nations
ARTICLES: 9 LANGUAGE: English. Spanish.
HEADNOTE: UNICEF ACTIVITIES
TOPIC: Tech Assistance
CONCEPTS: Assistance.
INTL ORGS: United Nations.
TREATY REF: 65UNTS4.
PARTIES:
Nicaragua
UNICEF (Children)
ANNEX
651 UNTS 347. Nicaragua. Signature 9 Jul 68. Force 9 Jul 68.

100833 Bilateral Agreement **65 UNTS 78**
SIGNED: 18 Jan 50 FORCE: 18 Jan 50
REGISTERED: 1 Jun 50 United Nations
ARTICLES: 9 LANGUAGE: English. Spanish.
HEADNOTE: UNICEF ACTIVITIES
TOPIC: Tech Assistance
CONCEPTS: Assistance.
INTL ORGS: United Nations.
TREATY REF: 65UNTS4.
PARTIES:
El Salvador
UNICEF (Children)
ANNEX
264 UNTS 329. UNICEF (Children). Supplementation 2 Dec 55. Force 2 Dec 55.
264 UNTS 329. El Salvador. Supplementation 2 Dec 55. Force 2 Dec 55.

100834 Bilateral Agreement **65 UNTS 80**
SIGNED: 31 Jan 50 FORCE: 31 Jan 50
REGISTERED: 1 Jun 50 United Nations
ARTICLES: 9 LANGUAGE: English. Spanish.
HEADNOTE: UNICEF ACTIVITIES
TOPIC: Tech Assistance
CONCEPTS: Assistance. Headquarters and facilities.
INTL ORGS: United Nations.
TREATY REF: 65UNTS4.

PARTIES:
Peru
UNICEF (Children)
ANNEX
220 UNTS 380. UNICEF (Children). Supplementation 12 Nov 55. Force 12 Nov 55.
220 UNTS 380. Peru. Supplementation 12 Nov 55. Force 12 Nov 55.

100835 Bilateral Agreement **65 UNTS 82**
SIGNED: 3 Feb 50 FORCE: 3 Feb 50
REGISTERED: 1 Jun 50 United Nations
ARTICLES: 9 LANGUAGE: English. Spanish.
HEADNOTE: UNICEF ACTIVITIES
TOPIC: Tech Assistance
CONCEPTS: Assistance. Headquarters and facilities.
INTL ORGS: United Nations.
TREATY REF: 65UNTS4.
PARTIES:
Bolivia
UNICEF (Children)
ANNEX
214 UNTS 362. UNICEF (Children). Supplementation 1 Sep 55. Force 1 Sep 55.
214 UNTS 362. Bolivia. Supplementation 1 Sep 55. Force 1 Sep 55.

100836 Bilateral Agreement **65 UNTS 84**
SIGNED: 9 Feb 50 FORCE: 9 Feb 50
REGISTERED: 1 Jun 50 United Nations
ARTICLES: 9 LANGUAGE: English. Spanish.
HEADNOTE: UNICEF ACTIVITIES
TOPIC: Tech Assistance
CONCEPTS: Assistance.
INTL ORGS: United Nations.
TREATY REF: 65UNTS4.
PARTIES:
Guatemala
UNICEF (Children)

100837 Bilateral Agreement **65 UNTS 86**
SIGNED: 10 Feb 50 FORCE: 1 Jan 50
REGISTERED: 1 Jun 50 United Nations
ARTICLES: 11 LANGUAGE: English.
HEADNOTE: UNICEF ACTIVITIES
TOPIC: Direct Aid
CONCEPTS: Annex or appendix reference. Human rights. Privileges and immunities. General cooperation. Exchange of information and documents. Informational records. Inspection and observation. Personnel. Public information. Use of facilities. Procedure. Public health. Vocational training. Financial programs. Funding procedures. Assets transfer. Tax exemptions. Laws and formalities. Domestic obligation. Assistance. Special projects. Materials, equipment and services. IGO status.
INTL ORGS: United Nations.
PROCEDURE: Duration. Future Procedures Contemplated. Termination.
PARTIES:
UNICEF (Children)
UK Great Britain

100838 Bilateral Agreement **65 UNTS 104**
SIGNED: 15 Mar 50 FORCE: 15 Mar 50
REGISTERED: 1 Jun 50 United Nations
ARTICLES: 9 LANGUAGE: English. Spanish.
HEADNOTE: UNICEF ACTIVITIES
TOPIC: Tech Assistance
CONCEPTS: Assistance. Headquarters and facilities.
INTL ORGS: United Nations.
TREATY REF: 65UNTS4.
PARTIES:
Colombia
UNICEF (Children)
ANNEX
274 UNTS 332. Colombia. Supplementation 20 Jun 57. Force 20 Jun 57.
274 UNTS 332. UNICEF (Children). Supplementation 20 Jun 57. Force 20 Jun 57.

100839 Bilateral Exchange **65 UNTS 107**
SIGNED: 30 Jan 46 FORCE: 30 Jan 46
REGISTERED: 6 Jun 50 Brazil
ARTICLES: 2 LANGUAGE: Portuguese. Spanish.

HEADNOTE: EXCHANGE OFFICIAL CORRESPONDENCE AIR
TOPIC: Consul/Citizenship
CONCEPTS: Previous treaty extension. Diplomatic correspondence.
PARTIES:
Brazil
Venezuela

100840 Bilateral Agreement **65 UNTS 117**
SIGNED: 14 Apr 49 FORCE: 23 Apr 49
REGISTERED: 9 Jun 50 Belgium
ARTICLES: 16 LANGUAGE: French.
HEADNOTE: FRONTIER PASSES TERRITORY BELGIUM BRITISH OCCUPATION
TOPIC: Visas
CONCEPTS: Emergencies. Border traffic and migration. Denial of admission. Frontier permits. Fees and exemptions. Markers and definitions. Frontier peoples and personnel.
TREATY REF: 27UNTS135.
PROCEDURE: Amendment. Duration. Termination.
PARTIES:
Belgium
UK Great Britain

100841 Bilateral Exchange **65 UNTS 133**
SIGNED: 13 May 49 FORCE: 15 May 49
REGISTERED: 9 Jun 50 Belgium
ARTICLES: 2 LANGUAGE: Dutch. French.
HEADNOTE: DESIGNATION INTERNATIONAL CUSTOMS HOUSE ROUTE
TOPIC: Customs
CONCEPTS: Customs duties. Routes and logistics.
TREATY REF: 32UNTS153.
PARTIES:
Belgium
Netherlands

100842 Bilateral Exchange **65 UNTS 139**
SIGNED: 14 Mar 50 FORCE: 7 Mar 50
REGISTERED: 9 Jun 50 Belgium
ARTICLES: 2 LANGUAGE: French.
HEADNOTE: MOVEMENT PERSONS
TOPIC: Visas
CONCEPTS: Border traffic and migration. Passports diplomatic. Non-visa travel documents. Visas. Frontier permits.
PARTIES:
Belgium
France
ANNEX
314 UNTS 326. Belgium. Amendment 8 Aug 58. Force 1 Jun 58.
314 UNTS 326. France. Amendment 3 Sep 58. Force 1 Jun 58.

100843 Bilateral Exchange **65 UNTS 147**
SIGNED: 6 Apr 50 FORCE: 7 Mar 50
REGISTERED: 9 Jun 50 Belgium
ARTICLES: 2 LANGUAGE: French.
HEADNOTE: FREEDOM MOVEMENT PERSONS
TOPIC: Visas
CONCEPTS: Previous treaty replacement. Passports non-diplomatic. Denial of admission. Non-visa travel documents.
TREATY REF: 41UNTS265; 41UNTS13.
PARTIES:
Belgium
Luxembourg
ANNEX
79 UNTS 328. Belgium. Supplementation 13 Sep 50. Force 13 Jan 52.
79 UNTS 328. Luxembourg. Supplementation 19 Sep 50. Force 19 Sep 50.
336 UNTS 342. Belgium. Amendment 9 Apr 59. Force 9 Apr 59.
336 UNTS 342. Luxembourg. Amendment 9 Apr 59. Force 9 Apr 59.

100844 Unilateral Instrument **65 UNTS 157**
SIGNED: 20 May 50 FORCE: 13 Jun 50
REGISTERED: 13 Jun 50 United Nations
ARTICLES: 1 LANGUAGE: English.
HEADNOTE: ACCEPTANCE ICJ JURISDICTION
TOPIC: ICJ Option Clause
CONCEPTS: Previous treaty extension. Compulsory jurisdiction.
INTL ORGS: International Court of Justice.

TREATY REF: 88LTS280; 200LTS484.
PROCEDURE: Duration.
PARTIES:
Thailand

100845   Bilateral Exchange   **66 UNTS 3**
SIGNED: 17 May 49   FORCE: 17 May 49
REGISTERED: 14 Jun 50 USA (United States)
ARTICLES: 2 LANGUAGE: English. Spanish.
HEADNOTE: AMENDING EXTENDING AGREE-
MENT MILITARY AVIATION MISSION
TOPIC: Military Mission
CONCEPTS: Annex type material. Previous treaty
extension. Military assistance missions.
PARTIES:
Ecuador
USA (United States)
ANNEX
253 UNTS 333.   Ecuador.   Prolongation
10 May 55. Force 23 May 55.
253 UNTS 333. USA (United States). Prolongation
23 May 55. Force 23 May 55.
347 UNTS 364. USA (United States). Amendment
25 Feb 59. Force 22 May 59.
347 UNTS 364. Ecuador. Amendment 22 May 59.
Force 22 May 59.

100846   Bilateral Exchange   **66 UNTS 13**
SIGNED: 15 Aug 49   FORCE: 20 Oct 49
REGISTERED: 14 Jun 50 USA (United States)
ARTICLES: 2 LANGUAGE: English. Spanish.
HEADNOTE: ESTABLISHING WEATHER STA-
TIONS
TOPIC: Scientific Project
CONCEPTS: Previous treaty replacement. Operat-
ing agencies. General property. Research and
scientific projects. Research cooperation.
Meteorology. Research and development. In-
demnities and reimbursements.
TREATY REF: 66UNTS307,331,293.
PROCEDURE: Duration. Renewal or Revival. Termi-
nation.
PARTIES:
Mexico
USA (United States)
ANNEX
181 UNTS 340. USA (United States). Prolongation
7 Apr 52. Force 22 Aug 52.
181 UNTS 340. Mexico. Prolongation 22 Aug 52.
Force 22 Aug 52.
204 UNTS 343. USA (United States). Prolongation
30 Jun 53. Force 30 Jun 53.
204 UNTS 343. Mexico. Prolongation 30 Jun 53.
Force 20 Jun 53.
290 UNTS 286. USA (United States). Supplementation 23 Aug 57. Force 29 Aug 57.
290 UNTS 286.   Mexico.   Supplementation
29 Aug 57. Force 29 Aug 57.
458 UNTS 278. Mexico. Extension and Amendment 8 Aug 62. Force 8 Aug 62.
458 UNTS 278. USA (United States). Extension
and Amendment 8 Aug 62. Force 8 Aug 62.
473 UNTS 333. Mexico. Prolongation 15 Mar 63.
Force 15 Mar 63.
473 UNTS 333. USA (United States). Prolongation
15 Mar 63. Force 15 Mar 63.

100847   Multilateral Instrument   **66 UNTS 25**
SIGNED: 24 Jul 48   FORCE: 1 Jan 50
REGISTERED: 20 Jun 50 WHO (World Health)
ARTICLES: 24 LANGUAGE: English. French.
HEADNOTE: WHO NOMENCLATURE RESPECTING
DISEASE CAUSES DEATH
TOPIC: Sanitation
CONCEPTS: Definition of terms. Territorial applica-
tion. Exchange of information and documents.
Disease control. Research results.
PROCEDURE: Amendment. Accession. Ratifica-
tion. Termination.
PARTIES:
Afghanistan FORCE: 1 Jan 50
Albania FORCE: 1 Jan 50
Australia FORCE: 1 Jan 50
Belgium FORCE: 1 Jan 50
Brazil FORCE: 1 Jan 50
Bulgaria FORCE: 1 Jan 50
Burma FORCE: 1 Jan 50
Byelorussia FORCE: 1 Jan 50
Canada FORCE: 1 Jan 50
Ceylon (Sri Lanka) FORCE: 1 Jan 50

Czechoslovakia FORCE: 1 Jan 50
Denmark FORCE: 1 Jan 50
Dominican Republic FORCE: 1 Jan 50
United Arab Rep FORCE: 1 Jan 50
El Salvador FORCE: 1 Jan 50
Ethiopia FORCE: 1 Jan 50
Finland FORCE: 1 Jan 50
France FORCE: 1 Jan 50
Greece FORCE: 1 Jan 50
Haiti FORCE: 1 Jan 50
Hungary FORCE: 1 Jan 50
Iceland FORCE: 1 Jan 50
India FORCE: 1 Jan 50
Iran FORCE: 1 Jan 50
Iraq FORCE: 1 Jan 50
Ireland FORCE: 1 Jan 50
Italy FORCE: 1 Jan 50
Liberia FORCE: 1 Jan 50
Mexico FORCE: 1 Jan 50
Monaco FORCE: 1 Jan 50
Netherlands FORCE: 1 Jan 50
New Zealand FORCE: 1 Jan 50
Norway FORCE: 1 Jan 50
Philippines FORCE: 1 Jan 50
Poland FORCE: 1 Jan 50
Portugal FORCE: 1 Jan 50
Romania FORCE: 1 Jan 50
Saudi Arabia FORCE: 1 Jan 50
Siam FORCE: 1 Jan 50
South Africa FORCE: 1 Jan 50
Sweden FORCE: 1 Jan 50
Switzerland FORCE: 1 Jan 50
Syria FORCE: 1 Jan 50
Transjordan FORCE: 1 Jan 50
Turkey FORCE: 1 Jan 50
USA (United States) FORCE: 1 Jan 50
Ukrainian SSR FORCE: 1 Jan 50
USSR (Soviet Union) FORCE: 1 Jan 50
Venezuela FORCE: 1 Jan 50
Yugoslavia FORCE: 1 Jan 50
ANNEX
81 UNTS 378.   UK   Great   Britain.   Southern
Rhodesia.
86 UNTS 316. Israel. Force 29 Aug 50. Reservation 29 Aug 50.
86 UNTS 316. Honduras. Force 29 Aug 50.
86 UNTS 316. Guatemala. Force 29 Aug 50.
86 UNTS 316. Ecuador. Force 29 Aug 50.
86 UNTS 316. Costa Rica. Force 29 Aug 50.
86 UNTS 316. Uruguay. Force 29 Aug 50.
86 UNTS 316. Peru. Force 25 Nov 50.
86 UNTS 316. Bolivia. Force 13 Jan 51.
86 UNTS 316. Indonesia. Force 5 Jun 50.
86 UNTS 316. Laos. Force 5 Jun 50.
86 UNTS 316. Vietnam. Force 5 Jun 50.
86 UNTS 316. Chile. Force 29 Aug 50.
86 UNTS 316. Argentina. Force 29 Aug 50.
86 UNTS 316. Korea, South. Force 29 Aug 50.
86 UNTS 316. Lebanon. Force 29 Aug 50.
86 UNTS 316. Luxembourg. Force 29 Aug 50.
86 UNTS 316. Paraguay. Force 29 Aug 50.
86 UNTS 316. Cambodia. Force 5 Jun 50.
92 UNTS 406. Cambodia. Force 5 Jun 51.
92 UNTS 406. Panama. Force 5 May 51.
92 UNTS 406. Indonesia. Force 5 Jun 51.
92 UNTS 406. Vietnam. Force 5 Jun 51.
125 UNTS 301. Panama. Force 6 Feb 52.
147 UNTS 394. Germany, West. Force 5 Jun 52.
147 UNTS 394. Japan. Force 5 Jun 52.
147 UNTS 394. Spain. Force 5 Jun 52.
204 UNTS 349. Libya. Force 9 Jul 53.
204 UNTS 349. Netherlands. Dutch New Guinea.
204 UNTS 349. Nepal. Force 16 Sep 54.
204 UNTS 349. Yemen. Force 9 Dec 54.
214 UNTS 365. Netherlands. Surinam.
214 UNTS 365.   Netherlands.   Netherlands Antilles.
433 UNTS 338. Mauritania. Force 5 Apr 62.
454 UNTS 550. Ivory Coast. Force 9 Jan 62.
454 UNTS 550. Senegal. Force 9 Jan 62.
454 UNTS 550. Cyprus. Force 5 Apr 62.
454 UNTS 550. Kuwait. Force 2 Jan 61.
454 UNTS 550. Togo. Force 2 Jan 61.
454 UNTS 550. Sierra Leone. Force 30 Jan 63.
454 UNTS 550. Nigeria. Force 5 Apr 62.
454 UNTS 550. Mali. Force 9 Jan 62.
454 UNTS 550. Ghana. Force 3 Feb 59.
454 UNTS 550. Fed of Malaya. Force 29 Jul 59.
454 UNTS 550. Somalia. Force 5 Apr 62.
454 UNTS 550. Cameroon. Force 2 Jan 61.
454 UNTS 550. Central Afri Rep. Force 9 Jan 62.
454 UNTS 550.   Congo   (Brazzaville).   Force
9 Jan 62.
454 UNTS 550. Niger. Force 9 Jan 62.

454 UNTS 550. Upper Volta. Force 9 Jan 62.
454 UNTS 550. Dahomey. Force 9 Jan 62.
454 UNTS 550. Chad. Force 5 Apr 62.
454 UNTS 550. Colombia. Force 18 Jun 60.
454 UNTS 550. Guinea. Force 18 Jun 60.
454 UNTS 550. Madagascar. Force 5 Apr 62.
454 UNTS 552. Sierra Leone. Force 30 Mar 62.
454 UNTS 552. Ghana. Force 3 Apr 58.
454 UNTS 552. Guinea. Force 16 Aug 59.
454 UNTS 552. Mali. Force 9 Mar 61.
454 UNTS 552. Kuwait. Force 31 Jul 60.
454 UNTS 552. Fed of Malaya. Force 26 Sep 68.
454 UNTS 552. Colombia. Force 16 Aug 59.
454 UNTS 552. Cameroon. Force 31 Jul 60.
454 UNTS 552. Senegal. Force 9 Mar 61.
454 UNTS 552.   Congo   (Brazzaville).   Force
9 Mar 61.
454 UNTS 552. Dahomey. Force 9 Mar 61.
454 UNTS 552. Ivory Coast. Force 9 Mar 61.
454 UNTS 552. Togo. Force 31 Jul 60.
454 UNTS 552. Madagascar. Force 3 Jan 61.
454 UNTS 552. Upper Volta. Force 9 Mar 61.
454 UNTS 552. Central Afri Rep. Force 9 Mar 61.
454 UNTS 552. Niger. Force 9 Mar 61.
454 UNTS 552. Chad. Force 3 Jan 61.
454 UNTS 552. Mauritania. Force 3 Jan 61.
454 UNTS 552. Cyprus. Force 3 Jun 61.
454 UNTS 552. Gabon. Force 3 Jan 61.
454 UNTS 552. Nigeria. Force 3 Jan 61.
454 UNTS 552. Somalia. Force 3 Jan 61.

100848   Bilateral Agreement   **66 UNTS 75**
SIGNED: 9 Jun 50   FORCE: 9 Jun 50
REGISTERED: 23 Jun 50 United Nations
ARTICLES: 9 LANGUAGE: English. Portuguese.
HEADNOTE: UNICEF ACTIVITIES
TOPIC: IGO Operations
CONCEPTS: Privileges and immunities. Location
of crime. Funding procedures. Materials, equip-
ment and services. Assistance to United Nations.
INTL ORGS: United Nations.
PROCEDURE: Duration.
PARTIES:
Brazil
UNICEF (Children)
ANNEX
607 UNTS 256. UNICEF (Children). Termination
23 Oct 67.
607 UNTS 256. Brazil. Termination 23 Oct 67.

100849   Bilateral Agreement   **66 UNTS 91**
SIGNED: 28 Mar 47   FORCE: 8 Apr 47
REGISTERED: 30 Jun 50 UK Great Britain
ARTICLES: 12 LANGUAGE: English. Spanish.
HEADNOTE: FINANCE
TOPIC: Finance
CONCEPTS: Definition of terms. Detailed regula-
tions. Territorial application. Previous treaty re-
placement. General cooperation. Accounting
procedures. Banking. Balance of payments. Cur-
rency. Monetary and gold transfers. Currency de-
posits. Investments. Exchange rates and regula-
tions. Internal finance. Payment schedules. Local
currency.
TREATY REF: 23LTS157.
PROCEDURE: Amendment. Duration. Termination.
PARTIES:
Spain
UK Great Britain

100850   Bilateral Exchange   **66 UNTS 113**
SIGNED: 18 May 48   FORCE: 18 May 48
REGISTERED: 30 Jun 50 UK Great Britain
ARTICLES: 2 LANGUAGE: English.
HEADNOTE: TRANSFER WAIVER CLAIMS CON-
CERNING SHIPS
TOPIC: Milit Assistance
CONCEPTS: Time limit. Claims and settlements.
Lease of military property. Military assistance.
Naval vessels. Return of equipment and recap-
ture. Post-war claims settlement.
PARTIES:
Taiwan
UK Great Britain

100851   Bilateral Agreement   **66 UNTS 121**
SIGNED: 21 May 48   FORCE: 21 May 48
REGISTERED: 30 Jun 50 UK Great Britain
ARTICLES: 29 LANGUAGE: English. Portuguese.
HEADNOTE: TRADE PAYMENTS

TOPIC: Finance
CONCEPTS: Definition of terms. Detailed regulations. General provisions. General cooperation. Licenses and permits. Import quotas. Accounting procedures. Banking. Balance of payments. Currency. Exchange rates and regulations. Payment schedules. Local currency. Claims and settlements. Commodity trade. Delivery schedules.
PROCEDURE: Termination.
PARTIES:
Brazil
UK Great Britain
ANNEX
83 UNTS 400. UK Great Britain. Prolongation 3 Feb 49. Force 1 Jan 49.
83 UNTS 400. Brazil. Prolongation 3 Feb 49. Force 1 Jan 49.
131 UNTS 325. UK Great Britain. Prolongation 2 Apr 51. Force 1 Apr 51.
131 UNTS 325. Brazil. Prolongation 13 Apr 51. Force 1 Apr 51.
172 UNTS 347. UK Great Britain. Prolongation 31 Mar 53. Force 1 Apr 53.
172 UNTS 347. Brazil. Prolongation 31 Mar 53. Force 1 Apr 53.
196 UNTS 341. UK Great Britain. Prolongation 31 Mar 54. Force 1 Apr 54.
196 UNTS 341. Brazil. Prolongation 31 Mar 54. Force 1 Apr 54.
213 UNTS 376. UK Great Britain. Prolongation 31 Mar 55. Force 1 Apr 55.
213 UNTS 376. Brazil. Prolongation 31 Mar 55. Force 1 Apr 55.
214 UNTS 366. UK Great Britain. Prolongation 30 Jun 55. Force 1 Jul 55.
214 UNTS 366. Brazil. Prolongation 30 Jun 55. Force 1 Jul 55.
221 UNTS 428. Brazil. Amendment 16 Aug 55. Force 16 Aug 55.
221 UNTS 428. UK Great Britain. Amendment 16 Aug 55. Force 16 Aug 55.
310 UNTS 324. UK Great Britain. Prolongation 19 Sep 57. Force 1 Oct 57.
310 UNTS 324. Brazil. Prolongation 19 Sep 57. Force 1 Oct 57.
349 UNTS 319. UK Great Britain. Prolongation 30 Sep 58. Force 1 Oct 58.
349 UNTS 319. Brazil. Prolongation 30 Sep 58. Force 1 Oct 58.
398 UNTS 342. UK Great Britain. Prolongation 28 Sep 59. Force 1 Oct 59.
398 UNTS 342. Brazil. Prolongation 28 Sep 59. Force 1 Oct 59.

100852   Bilateral Agreement   **66 UNTS 151**
SIGNED: 11 Jun 48   FORCE: 5 Jul 48
REGISTERED: 30 Jun 50 UK Great Britain
ARTICLES: 31 LANGUAGE: English. French.
HEADNOTE: SOCIAL SECURITY
TOPIC: Non-ILO Labor
CONCEPTS: Exceptions and exemptions. General provisions. Domestic legislation. Incorporation of treaty provisions into national law. Old age and invalidity insurance. Non-ILO labor relations. Family allowances. Administrative cooperation. Old age insurance. Sickness and invalidity insurance. Social security. Fees and exemptions. Payment schedules. National treatment.
PARTIES:
France
UK Great Britain
ANNEX
133 UNTS 346. UK Great Britain. Supplementation 25 Oct 49. Force 1 Nov 49.
133 UNTS 346. France. Supplementation 25 Oct 49. Force 1 Nov 49.
133 UNTS 352. France. Supplementation 7 Feb 52. Force 1 Jan 52.
133 UNTS 352. UK Great Britain. Supplementation 7 Feb 52. Force 1 Jan 52.
158 UNTS 484. France. Acknowledgement 4 Jun 52. Force 16 Aug 52.
158 UNTS 484. UK Great Britain. Jersey Island. Force 16 Aug 52.
183 UNTS 357. UK Great Britain. Prolongation 5 Jun 53. Force 5 Jun 53.
183 UNTS 357. France. Prolongation 5 Jun 53. Force 5 Jun 53.
214 UNTS 367. France. Acknowledgement 25 Nov 54. Force 25 Apr 55.
214 UNTS 367. UK Great Britain. Jersey Island. Force 25 Apr 55.

100853   Bilateral Exchange   **66 UNTS 183**
SIGNED: 11 Jun 48   FORCE: 23 Mar 48
REGISTERED: 30 Jun 50 UK Great Britain
ARTICLES: 2 LANGUAGE: English.
HEADNOTE: REGULATION TRADE PAYMENTS
TOPIC: General Economic
CONCEPTS: Annex or appendix reference. General trade. Payment schedules.
PARTIES:
Netherlands
UK Great Britain

100854   Bilateral Agreement   **66 UNTS 193**
SIGNED: 23 Jun 48   FORCE: 23 Jun 48
REGISTERED: 30 Jun 50 UK Great Britain
ARTICLES: 3 LANGUAGE: English. Spanish.
HEADNOTE: TRADE PAYMENTS
TOPIC: General Economic
CONCEPTS: Annex type material. Establishment of commission. General trade. Payment schedules.
PROCEDURE: Termination.
PARTIES:
Spain
UK Great Britain
ANNEX
82 UNTS 403. Spain. Prolongation 6 Apr 49. Force 8 Apr 49.
82 UNTS 403. UK Great Britain. Prolongation 6 Apr 49. Force 8 Apr 49.
138 UNTS 466. UK Great Britain. Prolongation 19 Jun 52. Force 1 Jul 52.
138 UNTS 466. Spain. Prolongation 25 Jun 52. Force 1 Jul 52.

100855   Bilateral Agreement   **66 UNTS 197**
SIGNED: 20 Jul 48   FORCE: 1 Aug 48
REGISTERED: 30 Jun 50 UK Great Britain
ARTICLES: 11 LANGUAGE: English. Spanish.
HEADNOTE: PAYMENTS
TOPIC: Finance
CONCEPTS: Detailed regulations. General cooperation. Accounting procedures. Banking. Balance of payments. Currency. Monetary and gold transfers. Exchange rates and regulations. Payment schedules. Most favored nation clause.
PROCEDURE: Duration. Renewal or Revival. Termination.
PARTIES:
Peru
UK Great Britain
ANNEX
105 UNTS 299. Peru. Prolongation 23 Jul 51. Force 23 Jul 51.
105 UNTS 299. UK Great Britain. Prolongation 23 Jul 51. Force 23 Jul 51.
199 UNTS 322. UK Great Britain. Prolongation 9 Jul 54. Force 1 Aug 54.
199 UNTS 322. Peru. Prolongation 9 Jul 54. Force 1 Aug 54.
221 UNTS 429. UK Great Britain. Prolongation 27 Jul 55. Force 1 Aug 55.
221 UNTS 429. Peru. Prolongation 27 Jul 55. Force 1 Aug 55.

100856   Bilateral Agreement   **66 UNTS 211**
SIGNED: 11 Aug 46   FORCE: 11 Aug 46
REGISTERED: 3 Jul 50 USA (United States)
ARTICLES: 11 LANGUAGE: Arabic. English.
HEADNOTE: AIR TRANSPORT
TOPIC: Air Transport
CONCEPTS: Exceptions and exemptions. Annex or appendix reference. Conformity with municipal law. Licenses and permits. Recognition of legal documents. Use of facilities. Procedure. Existing tribunals. Competence of tribunal. Fees and exemptions. Most favored nation clause. National treatment. Customs exemptions. Competency certificate. Routes and logistics. Navigational conditions. Permit designation. Air transport. Airport facilities. Airworthiness certificates. Conditions of airlines operating permission. Operating authorizations and regulations. Licenses and certificates of nationality.
INTL ORGS: International Civil Aviation Organization.
TREATY REF: US DEPT. OF STATE PUB. 2282 SERIES 64.
PROCEDURE: Registration. Termination.
PARTIES:
Lebanon
USA (United States)

100857   Bilateral Agreement   **66 UNTS 233**
SIGNED: 23 May 47   FORCE: 23 May 47
REGISTERED: 3 Jul 50 USA (United States)
ARTICLES: 11 LANGUAGE: Afrikaans. English.
HEADNOTE: AIR SERVICES
TOPIC: Air Transport
CONCEPTS: Definition of terms. Annex or appendix reference. Conformity with municipal law. General cooperation. Exchange of information and documents. Licenses and permits. Recognition of legal documents. Use of facilities. Procedure. Special tribunals. Competence of tribunal. Indemnities and reimbursements. Fees and exemptions. Most favored nation clause. National treatment. Temporary importation. Competency certificate. Routes and logistics. Navigational conditions. Permit designation. Airport facilities. Airworthiness certificates. Conditions of airlines operating permission. Operating authorizations and regulations. Licenses and certificates of nationality.
INTL ORGS: International Civil Aviation Organization.
TREATY REF: 15UNTS295.
PROCEDURE: Amendment. Registration. Termination. Application to Non-self-governing Territories.
PARTIES:
South Africa
USA (United States)
ANNEX
206 UNTS 334. USA (United States). Amendment 21 Jul 53. Force 2 Nov 53.
206 UNTS 334. South Africa. Amendment 2 Nov 53. Force 2 Nov 53.

100858   Bilateral Agreement   **66 UNTS 269**
SIGNED: 13 Oct 47   FORCE: 13 Oct 47
REGISTERED: 3 Jul 50 USA (United States)
ARTICLES: 14 LANGUAGE: English.
HEADNOTE: STANDARDIZATION DISTANCE MEASURING EQUIPMENT CIVIL AVIATION
TOPIC: Air Transport
CONCEPTS: Exceptions and exemptions. Territorial application. Standardization. General cooperation. Exchange of information and documents. Navigational equipment. Airport equipment. Bands and frequency allocation. Facilities and equipment.
INTL ORGS: International Civil Aviation Organization.
PROCEDURE: Amendment.
PARTIES:
UK Great Britain
USA (United States)

100859   Bilateral Exchange   **66 UNTS 277**
SIGNED: 23 Oct 47   FORCE: 23 Oct 47
REGISTERED: 3 Jul 50 USA (United States)
ARTICLES: 2 LANGUAGE: English.
HEADNOTE: DELIMITATION AREA WITHIN TERRITORIAL WATERS
TOPIC: Territory Boundary
CONCEPTS: Annex or appendix reference. Markers and definitions.
PARTIES:
UK Great Britain
USA (United States)

100860   Multilateral Protocol   **66 UNTS 285**
SIGNED: 8 Apr 50   FORCE: 8 Apr 50
REGISTERED: 3 Jul 50 Belgium
ARTICLES: 1 LANGUAGE: French.
HEADNOTE: COMMITTEE POLLUTED WATER
TOPIC: IGO Establishment
CONCEPTS: Exchange of information and documents. Technical education. Admission. Subsidiary organ. Establishment. Internal structure.
INTL ORGS: Special Commission.
PARTIES:
Belgium SIGNED: 8 Apr 50 FORCE: 8 Apr 50
France SIGNED: 8 Apr 50 FORCE: 8 Apr 50
Luxembourg SIGNED: 8 Apr 50 FORCE: 8 Apr 50

100861   Bilateral Exchange   **66 UNTS 293**
SIGNED: 12 Apr 46   FORCE: 12 Apr 46
REGISTERED: 6 Jul 50 USA (United States)
ARTICLES: 2 LANGUAGE: English. Spanish.
HEADNOTE: WEATHER STATION GUADALUPE ISLAND

TOPIC: Scientific Project
CONCEPTS: General cooperation. Personnel. Use of facilities. Research and scientific projects. Research cooperation. Meteorology. Research results. Communication satellites testing. Expense sharing formulae. Domestic obligation. Materials, equipment and services. Facilities and equipment.
TREATY REF: 66UNTS331.
PARTIES:
Mexico
USA (United States)

100862   Bilateral Exchange   **67 UNTS 3**
SIGNED: 27 Jan 48   FORCE: 27 Jan 48
REGISTERED: 6 Jul 50 USA (United States)
ARTICLES: 2 LANGUAGE: English. Spanish.
HEADNOTE: WEATHER STATIONS CUBA
TOPIC: Scientific Project
CONCEPTS: Previous treaty extension. Exchange of information and documents. Personnel. General property. Technical and commercial staff. Research cooperation. Meteorology. Research and development. Expense sharing formulae. Domestic obligation. Materials, equipment and services. Facilities and equipment. Repatriation of civilians.
TREATY REF: 67UNTS221.
PROCEDURE: Duration. Renewal or Revival. Termination.
PARTIES:
Cuba
USA (United States)
            ANNEX
89 UNTS 378. Cuba. Extension and Amendment 30 Jun 50. Force 30 Jun 50.
89 UNTS 378. USA (United States). Extension and Amendment 30 Jun 50. Force 30 Jun 50.
204 UNTS 350. Cuba. Extension and Amendment 30 Jun 53. Force 30 Jun 53.
204 UNTS 350. USA (United States). Extension and Amendment 30 Jun 53. Force 30 Jun 53.

100863   Bilateral Exchange   **67 UNTS 15**
SIGNED: 3 Sep 47   FORCE: 15 Sep 47
REGISTERED: 11 Jul 50 USA (United States)
ARTICLES: 2 LANGUAGE: English. Italian.
HEADNOTE: MILITARY CIVIL AFFAIRS
TOPIC: Status of Forces
CONCEPTS: Annex or appendix reference. Jurisdiction. Status of forces. Reconversion to normalcy. Withdrawal of occupation.
TREATY REF: 49UNTS.
PARTIES:
Italy
USA (United States)

100864   Bilateral Exchange   **67 UNTS 33**
SIGNED: 25 Feb 48   FORCE: 25 Feb 48
REGISTERED: 11 Jul 50 USA (United States)
ARTICLES: 2 LANGUAGE: English. French.
HEADNOTE: MILITARY OBLIGATIONS PERSONS HAVING DUAL NATIONALITY
TOPIC: Milit Servic/Citiz
CONCEPTS: Annex type material. Dual nationality. Certificates of service.
PROCEDURE: Duration.
PARTIES:
France
USA (United States)
            ANNEX
185 UNTS 396. USA (United States). Amendment 18 Nov 52. Force 31 Dec 52.
185 UNTS 396. France. Amendment 31 Dec 52.

100865   Bilateral Agreement   **67 UNTS 43**
SIGNED: 9 Nov 49   FORCE: 22 Sep 49
REGISTERED: 11 Jul 50 WHO (World Health)
ARTICLES: 12 LANGUAGE: English. French.
HEADNOTE: PRIVILEGES & IMMUNITIES WHO
TOPIC: IGO Status/Immunit
CONCEPTS: Privileges and immunities. Procedure. Medical assistance and/or facilities. Special status.
INTL ORGS: International Court of Justice. United Nations.
PROCEDURE: Denunciation.
PARTIES:
India
WHO (World Health)

100866   Bilateral Exchange   **67 UNTS 71**
SIGNED: 15 Dec 48   FORCE: 15 Dec 48
REGISTERED: 14 Jul 50 Denmark
ARTICLES: 2 LANGUAGE: Spanish.
HEADNOTE: EXEMPT TAX INCOME DERIVED SHIP AIR TRANSPORT
TOPIC: Taxation
CONCEPTS: Definition of terms. Conformity with municipal law. Taxation. Tax exemptions. Air transport. Merchant vessels.
PARTIES:
Argentina
Denmark

100867   Bilateral Exchange   **67 UNTS 81**
SIGNED: 19 Apr 50   FORCE: 19 Apr 50
REGISTERED: 14 Jul 50 New Zealand
ARTICLES: 2 LANGUAGE: English.
HEADNOTE: RELEASE ITALIAN ASSETS
TOPIC: Claims and Debts
CONCEPTS: Attachment of funds. Compensation. Indemnities and reimbursements. Monetary and gold transfers.
PARTIES:
Italy
New Zealand

100868   Bilateral Agreement   **67 UNTS 89**
SIGNED: 21 Jun 47   FORCE: 21 Jun 47
REGISTERED: 18 Jul 50 USA (United States)
ARTICLES: 4 LANGUAGE: English.
HEADNOTE: SETTLEMENT WAR ACCOUNTS CLAIMS
TOPIC: Reparations
CONCEPTS: Definition of terms. Time limit. Exchange of information and documents. Inspection and observation. Accounting procedures. Currency. Lump sum settlements. Assets transfer. Loss and/or damage. Post-war claims settlement.
PARTIES:
Austria
USA (United States)

100869   Bilateral Agreement   **67 UNTS 99**
SIGNED: 21 Jun 47   FORCE: 1 Jul 47
REGISTERED: 18 Jul 50 USA (United States)
ARTICLES: 15 LANGUAGE: English.
HEADNOTE: PAYMENT OCCUPATION COSTS
TOPIC: Milit Occupation
CONCEPTS: General property. Use of facilities. Indemnities and reimbursements. Monetary and gold transfers. Payment schedules. Claims and settlements. Occupation regime.
PROCEDURE: Amendment. Denunciation.
PARTIES:
Austria
USA (United States)

100870   Bilateral Exchange   **67 UNTS 109**
SIGNED: 2 Feb 48   FORCE: 2 Feb 48
REGISTERED: 18 Jul 50 USA (United States)
ARTICLES: 2 LANGUAGE: English. Portuguese.
HEADNOTE: STATIONING MILITARY PERSONNEL
TOPIC: Status of Forces
CONCEPTS: Airforce-army-navy personnel ratio. Status of military forces.
INTL ORGS: United Nations. Special Commission.
PARTIES:
Brazil
USA (United States)

100871   Bilateral Exchange   **67 UNTS 115**
SIGNED: 14 Feb 48   FORCE: 14 Feb 48
REGISTERED: 18 Jul 50 USA (United States)
ARTICLES: 2 LANGUAGE: English. Italian.
HEADNOTE: FINAL SETTLEMENT WARTIME CLAIMS ITALIAN NATIONALS FORMERLY PRISONERS WAR
TOPIC: Reparations
CONCEPTS: Annex or appendix reference. War claims and reparations. Post-war claims settlement.
PARTIES:
Italy
USA (United States)

100872   Bilateral Agreement   **67 UNTS 139**
SIGNED: 11 Oct 40   FORCE: 13 Mar 48
REGISTERED: 18 Jul 50 USSR (Soviet Union)
ARTICLES: 4 LANGUAGE: Finnish. Russian.
HEADNOTE: AALAND ISLANDS
TOPIC: Territory Boundary
CONCEPTS: Consular relations establishment. Inspection and observation. Rearmament restrictions and controls. Markers and definitions.
PROCEDURE: Ratification.
PARTIES:
Finland
USSR (Soviet Union)

100873   Bilateral Convention   **67 UNTS 153**
SIGNED: 28 Oct 22   FORCE: 13 Mar 48
REGISTERED: 18 Jul 50 USSR (Soviet Union)
ARTICLES: 1 LANGUAGE: Finnish. Russian. Swedish.
HEADNOTE: FLOATING TIMBER WATERCOURSES
TOPIC: Specific Resources
CONCEPTS: Annex type material.
PARTIES:
Finland
USSR (Soviet Union)

100874   Bilateral Convention   **67 UNTS 157**
SIGNED: 28 Oct 22   FORCE: 13 Mar 48
REGISTERED: 18 Jul 50 USSR (Soviet Union)
ARTICLES: 1 LANGUAGE: Finnish. Russian. Swedish.
HEADNOTE: MAINTENANCE RIVER CHANNELS REGULATION FISHING WATER COURSES
TOPIC: Specific Resources
CONCEPTS: Annex type material. Previous treaty extension.
TREATY REF: 19LTS183; 48UNTS203.
PARTIES:
Finland
USSR (Soviet Union)

100875   Bilateral Exchange   **67 UNTS 161**
SIGNED: 18 May 48   FORCE: 18 May 48
REGISTERED: 18 Jul 50 USA (United States)
ARTICLES: 2 LANGUAGE: English. Spanish.
HEADNOTE: SUPPLEMENTING AGREEMENT INTER AMERICAN HIGHWAY
TOPIC: Land Transport
CONCEPTS: Conditions. Conformity with municipal law. General cooperation. Fees and exemptions. Financial programs. National treatment. Tax exemptions. Roads and highways.
TREATY REF: 28UNTS377.
PARTIES:
Guatemala
USA (United States)
            ANNEX
237 UNTS 294. USA (United States). Amendment 28 Jul 54. Force 28 Aug 54.
237 UNTS 294. Guatemala. Amendment 28 Aug 54. Force 28 Aug 54.

100876   Bilateral Agreement   **67 UNTS 171**
SIGNED: 23 Dec 48   FORCE: 23 Dec 48
REGISTERED: 18 Jul 50 USA (United States)
ARTICLES: 6 LANGUAGE: English. French.
HEADNOTE: FREE ENTRY FREE INLAND TRANSPORTATION RELIEF SUPPLIES
TOPIC: Direct Aid
CONCEPTS: Annex type material. Accounting procedures. Indemnities and reimbursements. Transportation costs. Customs exemptions. Relief supplies.
TREATY REF: 19UNTS9.
PROCEDURE: Amendment. Duration. Termination.
PARTIES:
France
USA (United States)
            ANNEX
93 UNTS 367. USA (United States). Amendment 3 Aug 50. Force 3 Aug 50.
93 UNTS 367. France. Amendment 3 Aug 50. Force 3 Aug 50.
181 UNTS 345. USA (United States). Amendment 2 Jul 52. Force 5 Aug 52.
181 UNTS 345. France. Amendment 5 Aug 52. Force 5 Aug 52.

100877 Bilateral Exchange **67 UNTS 189**
SIGNED: 7 Feb 49 FORCE: 7 Feb 49
REGISTERED: 18 Jul 50 USA (United States)
ARTICLES: 2 LANGUAGE: English. French.
HEADNOTE: DUTY-FREE ENTRY PAYMENT TRANSPORTATION COSTS RELIEF SUPPLIES PACKAGES
TOPIC: Direct Aid
CONCEPTS: Definition of terms. Annex type material. Accounting procedures. Indemnities and reimbursements. Transportation costs. Customs exemptions. Relief supplies. Occupation regime.
TREATY REF: 24UNTS103.
PROCEDURE: Amendment. Duration. Termination.
PARTIES:
France
USA (United States)

100878 Bilateral Exchange **67 UNTS 199**
SIGNED: 16 May 49 FORCE: 16 May 49
REGISTERED: 18 Jul 50 USA (United States)
ARTICLES: 3 LANGUAGE: English.
HEADNOTE: TRANSFER MILITARY BASES
TOPIC: Milit Installation
CONCEPTS: Annex or appendix reference. Surplus property. Surplus war property. Bases and facilities.
TREATY REF: 7UNTS53.
PARTIES:
Philippines
USA (United States)

100879 Bilateral Exchange **68 UNTS 3**
SIGNED: 31 Oct 49 FORCE: 31 Oct 49
REGISTERED: 18 Jul 50 USA (United States)
ARTICLES: 2 LANGUAGE: English.
HEADNOTE: DUTY-FREE ENTRY PAYMENT TRANSPORTATION CHARGES RELIEF SUPPLIES
TOPIC: Direct Aid
CONCEPTS: Annex type material. Accounting procedures. Indemnities and reimbursements. Transportation costs. Customs exemptions. Relief supplies.
TREATY REF: 20UNTS185.
PROCEDURE: Amendment. Duration. Termination.
PARTIES:
Norway
USA (United States)

100880 Bilateral Exchange **68 UNTS 11**
SIGNED: 1 Nov 49 FORCE: 1 Nov 49
REGISTERED: 18 Jul 50 USA (United States)
ARTICLES: 2 LANGUAGE: English.
HEADNOTE: SETTLEMENT US OBLIGATIONS REQUISITIONING FINNISH VESSELS
TOPIC: Claims and Debts
CONCEPTS: Compensation. Claims and settlements.
PARTIES:
Finland
USA (United States)

100881 Multilateral Convention **68 UNTS 17**
SIGNED: 9 Jul 48 FORCE: 4 Jul 50
REGISTERED: 19 Jul 50 ILO (Labor Org)
ARTICLES: 21 LANGUAGE: English. French.
HEADNOTE: FREEDOM ASSOCIATION RIGHT TO ORGANIZE
TOPIC: ILO Labor
CONCEPTS: Territorial application. Conformity with municipal law. Juridical personality. Incorporation of treaty provisions into national law. ILO conventions. Right to organize.
INTL ORGS: United Nations.
TREATY REF: 15UNTS40.
PROCEDURE: Amendment. Denunciation. Ratification. Registration. Renewal or Revival.
PARTIES:
Multilateral
ANNEX
70 UNTS 307.
76 UNTS 283.
81 UNTS 382.
92 UNTS 410.
94 UNTS 312.
100 UNTS 291.
109 UNTS 321.
122 UNTS 341.
134 UNTS 378.
184 UNTS 335.

196 UNTS 342.
210 UNTS 331.
211 UNTS 394.
248 UNTS 402.
249 UNTS 453.
253 UNTS 387.
256 UNTS 340.
261 UNTS 391.
264 UNTS 332.
272 UNTS 254.
282 UNTS 363.
293 UNTS 373.
302 UNTS 357.
304 UNTS 401.
312 UNTS 405.
320 UNTS 328.
323 UNTS 374.
325 UNTS 340.
327 UNTS 352.
337 UNTS 392.
338 UNTS 336.
348 UNTS 347.
349 UNTS 320.
356 UNTS 346.
366 UNTS 384.
373 UNTS 352.
380 UNTS 410.
381 UNTS 395.
384 UNTS 357.
386 UNTS 374.
390 UNTS 352.
396 UNTS 320.
401 UNTS 250.
410 UNTS 290.
413 UNTS 362.
422 UNTS 327.
422 UNTS 328.
425 UNTS 318.
431 UNTS 286.
434 UNTS 283.
435 UNTS 312.
443 UNTS 334. Cameroon. Succession 3 Sep 62. Force 3 Sep 62.
444 UNTS 324.
449 UNTS 284.
452 UNTS 365.
455 UNTS 462.
457 UNTS 356.
463 UNTS 378.
468 UNTS 433.
471 UNTS 372.
480 UNTS 476.
483 UNTS 410.
488 UNTS 362.
488 UNTS 363.
495 UNTS 294. UK Great Britain. Barbados.
504 UNTS 354.
524 UNTS 362.
541 UNTS 373.
607 UNTS 361. Guyana. Ratification 25 Sep 67.
607 UNTS 361. UK Great Britain. Gilbert Islands. Declaration 15 Aug 67.
609 UNTS 337. Nicaragua. Ratification 31 Oct 67. Force 31 Oct 68.

100882 Bilateral Exchange **68 UNTS 31**
SIGNED: 19 Sep 49 FORCE: 19 Sep 49
REGISTERED: 19 Jul 50 USA (United States)
ARTICLES: 2 LANGUAGE: English.
HEADNOTE: MODIFYING AGREEMENT LEASED NAVAL AIR BASES
TOPIC: Milit Installation
CONCEPTS: Annex or appendix reference. Use of facilities. Claims and settlements. Land transport. Bases and facilities.
PARTIES:
UK Great Britain
USA (United States)

100883 Bilateral Exchange **68 UNTS 45**
SIGNED: 29 Mar 50 FORCE: 1 Apr 50
REGISTERED: 20 Jul 50 Belgium
ARTICLES: 2 LANGUAGE: Dutch.
HEADNOTE: ABOLITION PASSPORT OBLIGATION
TOPIC: Visas
CONCEPTS: Visa abolition. Non-visa travel documents. Frontier permits.
PARTIES:
Belgium
Netherlands

100884 Bilateral Agreement **68 UNTS 55**
SIGNED: 5 Jul 49 FORCE: 5 Jul 49
REGISTERED: 21 Jul 50 USA (United States)

ARTICLES: 26 LANGUAGE: English. Spanish.
HEADNOTE: AIR FORCE LIAISON OFFICERS
TOPIC: Military Mission
CONCEPTS: Definition of terms. Use of facilities. Compensation. Indemnities and reimbursements. Exchange rates and regulations. Expense sharing formulae. Tax exemptions. Customs exemptions. Military assistance. Military training. Security of information. Airforce-army-navy personnel ratio. Ranks and privileges. Conditions for assistance missions. Third country military personnel. Status of forces.
PROCEDURE: Denunciation. Duration. Renewal or Revival. Termination.
PARTIES:
Mexico
USA (United States)
ANNEX
200 UNTS 276. USA (United States). Prolongation 4 Sep 51. Force 5 Jul 51.
200 UNTS 276. Mexico. Prolongation 19 Oct 51. Force 5 Jul 51.

100885 Bilateral Agreement **68 UNTS 75**
SIGNED: 19 Feb 48 FORCE: 19 Feb 48
REGISTERED: 1 Aug 50 United Nations
ARTICLES: 11 LANGUAGE: English. French.
HEADNOTE: UNICEF ACTIVITIES
TOPIC: IGO Operations
CONCEPTS: Non-visa travel documents. Diplomatic privileges. Privileges and immunities. Existing tribunals. Funding procedures. Materials, equipment and services. Assistance to United Nations. UN administrative tribunal.
INTL ORGS: United Nations.
PROCEDURE: Duration.
PARTIES:
France
UNICEF (Children)
ANNEX
161 UNTS 366. UNICEF (Children). Amendment 13 Mar 53. Force 13 Mar 53.
161 UNTS 366. France. Amendment 13 Mar 53. Force 13 Mar 53.

100886 Bilateral Agreement **68 UNTS 94**
SIGNED: 1 Dec 48 FORCE: 1 Dec 48
REGISTERED: 1 Aug 50 United Nations
ARTICLES: 9 LANGUAGE: English. French.
HEADNOTE: UNICEF ACTIVITIES
TOPIC: IGO Operations
CONCEPTS: Diplomatic privileges. Privileges and immunities. Accounting procedures. Materials, equipment and services. Assistance to United Nations.
INTL ORGS: United Nations.
PROCEDURE: Duration.
PARTIES:
UNICEF (Children)
Thailand
ANNEX
248 UNTS 360. Siam. Supplementation 20 Aug 56. Force 20 Aug 56.
248 UNTS 360. UNICEF (Children). Supplementation 15 Aug 56. Force 20 Aug 56.

100887 Bilateral Agreement **68 UNTS 96**
SIGNED: 10 May 49 FORCE: 10 May 49
REGISTERED: 1 Aug 50 United Nations
ARTICLES: 9 LANGUAGE: English.
HEADNOTE: UNICEF ACTIVITIES
TOPIC: IGO Operations
CONCEPTS: Materials, equipment and services. Relief supplies. Distribution. Extension of functions. IGO status. Status of experts.
INTL ORGS: United Nations.
PROCEDURE: Duration.
PARTIES:
India
UNICEF (Children)
ANNEX
249 UNTS 432. UNICEF (Children). Supplementation 23 Aug 56. Force 5 Sep 56.
249 UNTS 432. India. Supplementation 5 Sep 56. Force 5 Sep 56.
390 UNTS 354. India. Sikkim.

100888 Bilateral Agreement **68 UNTS 96**
SIGNED: 22 Apr 50 FORCE: 22 Apr 50
REGISTERED: 1 Aug 50 United Nations

ARTICLES: 9 LANGUAGE: English.
HEADNOTE: UNICEF ACTIVITIES
TOPIC: IGO Operations
CONCEPTS: Diplomatic privileges. Privileges and immunities. Accounting procedures. Materials, equipment and services. Regional offices. Assistance to United Nations.
INTL ORGS: United Nations.
PROCEDURE: Duration.
PARTIES:
Burma
UNICEF (Children)
ANNEX
228 UNTS 368. UNICEF (Children). Supplementation 18 Feb 56. Force 18 Feb 56.
228 UNTS 368. Burma. Supplementation 20 Jan 56. Force 18 Feb 56.

100889 Multilateral Instrument **68 UNTS 99**
SIGNED: 8 Apr 50 FORCE: 8 Apr 50
REGISTERED: 8 Aug 50 Belgium
ARTICLES: 4 LANGUAGE: French.
HEADNOTE: INSTALLATION PERMANENT STORES EXPLOSIVE SUBSTANCES
TOPIC: Specif Goods/Equip
CONCEPTS: Establishment of commission. Negotiation. Specific goods and equipment.
INTL ORGS: Special Commission.
PARTIES:
Belgium SIGNED: 8 Apr 50 FORCE: 8 Apr 50
France SIGNED: 8 Apr 50 FORCE: 8 Apr 50
Luxembourg SIGNED: 8 Apr 50 FORCE: 8 Apr 50

100890 Bilateral Agreement **68 UNTS 105**
SIGNED: 13 Aug 49 FORCE: 9 Jun 50
REGISTERED: 9 Aug 50 Denmark
ARTICLES: 7 LANGUAGE: English.
HEADNOTE: TRADE COMMERCE
TOPIC: General Trade
CONCEPTS: Definition of terms. Detailed regulations. Exceptions and exemptions. Annex type material. Import quotas.
INTL ORGS: General Agreement on Tariffs and Trade.
TREATY REF: 55UNTS194.
PROCEDURE: Ratification. Termination.
PARTIES:
Denmark
UK Great Britain

100891 Bilateral Convention **68 UNTS 117**
SIGNED: 27 Mar 50 FORCE: 7 Jul 50
REGISTERED: 9 Aug 50 Denmark
ARTICLES: 22 LANGUAGE: Danish. English.
HEADNOTE: DOUBLE TAXATION FISCAL EVASION
TOPIC: Taxation
CONCEPTS: Definition of terms. Territorial application. Conformity with municipal law. Exchange of official publications. Teacher and student exchange. Wages and salaries. Taxation. Tax credits. Equitable taxes. General. Air transport. Merchant vessels.
TREATY REF: 32LTS90.
PROCEDURE: Duration. Ratification. Termination.
PARTIES:
Denmark
UK Great Britain
ANNEX
211 UNTS 396. UK Great Britain. Cyprus. Force 22 Dec 54.
211 UNTS 396. UK Great Britain. Antigua. Force 22 Dec 54.
211 UNTS 396. UK Great Britain. Barbados. Force 22 Dec 54.
211 UNTS 396. UK Great Britain. Fiji Islands. Force 22 Dec 54.
211 UNTS 396. UK Great Britain. Gambia. Force 22 Dec 54.
211 UNTS 396. UK Great Britain. Gilbert Islands. Force 22 Dec 54.
211 UNTS 396. UK Great Britain. Gold Coast. Force 22 Dec 54.
211 UNTS 396. UK Great Britain. Jamaica. Force 22 Dec 54.
211 UNTS 396. UK Great Britain. Fed of Malaya. Force 22 Dec 54.
211 UNTS 396. UK Great Britain. Mauritius. Force 22 Dec 54.
211 UNTS 396. UK Great Britain. Montserrat. Force 22 Dec 54.

211 UNTS 396. UK Great Britain. Nigeria. Force 22 Dec 54.
211 UNTS 396. UK Great Britain. North Borneo. Force 22 Dec 54.
211 UNTS 396. UK Great Britain. St. Christopher. Force 22 Dec 54.
211 UNTS 396. UK Great Britain. Aden. Force 22 Dec 54.
211 UNTS 396. UK Great Britain. Nevis. Force 22 Dec 54.
211 UNTS 396. UK Great Britain. British Honduras. Force 22 Dec 54.
211 UNTS 396. UK Great Britain. Anguilla. Force 22 Dec 54.
211 UNTS 396. UK Great Britain. St. Lucia. Force 22 Dec 54.
211 UNTS 396. UK Great Britain. Falkland Islands. Force 22 Dec 54.
211 UNTS 396. UK Great Britain. Brit Solomon Is. Force 22 Dec 54.
211 UNTS 396. UK Great Britain. Seychelles. Force 22 Dec 54.
211 UNTS 396. UK Great Britain. Dominican Republic. Force 22 Dec 54.
211 UNTS 396. UK Great Britain. Sierra Leone. Force 22 Dec 54.
211 UNTS 396. UK Great Britain. Singapore. Force 22 Dec 54.
211 UNTS 396. UK Great Britain. Trinidad/Tobago. Force 22 Dec 54.
211 UNTS 396. UK Great Britain. Brit Virgin Islands. Force 22 Dec 54.
211 UNTS 396. Denmark. Acknowledgement 22 Dec 54. Force 22 Dec 54.
221 UNTS 396. UK Great Britain. St. Vincent. Force 22 Dec 54.
351 UNTS 382. UK Great Britain. Fed Rhod/Nyasaland. Force 17 Jan 59.
351 UNTS 382. Denmark. Acknowledgement 17 Jan 59. Force 17 Jan 59.
351 UNTS 382. UK Great Britain. Kenya. Force 17 Jan 59.
351 UNTS 382. UK Great Britain. Uganda. Force 17 Jan 59.
351 UNTS 382. UK Great Britain. Tanganyika. Force 17 Jan 59.
351 UNTS 382. UK Great Britain. Zanzibar. Force 17 Jan 59.
398 UNTS 343. Denmark. Acknowledgement 6 Nov 58.
414 UNTS 376. Denmark. Faroe Islands. Force 19 Apr 61.
414 UNTS 376. UK Great Britain. Acknowledgement 31 Oct 60. Force 19 Apr 61.
419 UNTS 348. Denmark. Amendment 31 Oct 60. Force 31 Oct 60.
419 UNTS 348. UK Great Britain. Amendment 31 Oct 60. Force 31 Oct 60.
492 UNTS 338. Denmark. Acknowledgement 21 Jan 64. Force 21 Jan 64.
492 UNTS 338. UK Great Britain. Northern Rhodesia. Force 21 Jan 64.
492 UNTS 338. UK Great Britain. Nyasaland. Force 21 Jan 64.
492 UNTS 338. UK Great Britain. Southern Rhodesia. Force 21 Jan 64.
640 UNTS 364. Denmark. Acknowledgement 24 Oct 67.
640 UNTS 364. UK Great Britain. Faroe Islands.

100892 Bilateral Agreement **68 UNTS 157**
SIGNED: 22 Feb 46 FORCE: 22 Feb 46
REGISTERED: 11 Aug 50 Belgium
ARTICLES: 14 LANGUAGE: French.
HEADNOTE: CULTURAL AGREEMENT
TOPIC: Culture
CONCEPTS: Detailed regulations. Friendship and amity. Standardization. Conformity with municipal law. Operating agencies. Establishment of commission. Teacher and student exchange. Professorships. Scholarships and grants. Exchange. Artists. Scientific exchange. Recognition. Customs exemptions. Publications exchange.
INTL ORGS: Special Commission.
PROCEDURE: Denunciation. Duration. Renewal or Revival.
PARTIES:
Belgium
France
ANNEX
135 UNTS 352. Belgium. Amendment 25 Jun 52. Force 25 Jun 52.

135 UNTS 352. France. Amendment 25 Jun 52. Force 25 Jun 52.

100893 Bilateral Exchange **68 UNTS 165**
SIGNED: 5 Jul 50 FORCE: 5 Jul 50
REGISTERED: 11 Aug 50 Belgium
ARTICLES: 3 LANGUAGE: Arabic. French.
HEADNOTE: RELEASE ASSETS
TOPIC: Claims and Debts
CONCEPTS: Assets transfer.
PARTIES:
Belgium
Iraq

100894 Bilateral Agreement **69 UNTS 3**
SIGNED: 2 Nov 49 FORCE: 27 Dec 49
REGISTERED: 14 Aug 50 Netherlands
ARTICLES: 30 LANGUAGE: Dutch. English. Indonesian.
HEADNOTE: TRANSFER SOVEREIGNTY
TOPIC: Recognition
CONCEPTS: Status of state. Democratic institutions. Transition period. Recognition. Self-determination. Union with other states. Human rights. Arbitration. Procedure. Exchange. Finances and payments.
INTL ORGS: International Court of Justice. United Nations.
PARTIES:
Indonesia
Netherlands

100895 Bilateral Agreement **70 UNTS 3**
SIGNED: 8 Dec 47 FORCE: 8 Dec 47
REGISTERED: 18 Aug 50 USA (United States)
ARTICLES: 10 LANGUAGE: Chinese. English.
HEADNOTE: TRANSFER NAVAL VESSELS EQUIPMENT
TOPIC: Milit Installation
CONCEPTS: Exceptions and exemptions. Annex or appendix reference. Previous treaty replacement. Exchange of information and documents. Responsibility and liability. Indemnities and reimbursements. Delivery schedules. Materials, equipment and services. Security of information. Surplus war property. Restrictions on transfer.
PROCEDURE: Termination.
PARTIES:
Taiwan
USA (United States)

100896 Bilateral Convention **70 UNTS 27**
SIGNED: 12 Jan 48 FORCE: 19 Mar 50
REGISTERED: 18 Aug 50 USA (United States)
ARTICLES: 15 LANGUAGE: English. Spanish.
HEADNOTE: CONSULAR CONVENTION
TOPIC: Consul/Citizenship
CONCEPTS: Definition of terms. Territorial application. General consular functions. Diplomatic privileges. Consular relations establishment. Inviolability. Privileges and immunities. Diplomatic correspondence. Responsibility and liability. Use of facilities. Fees and exemptions. Tax exemptions. Customs exemptions. Shipwreck and salvage. Foreign nationals.
PROCEDURE: Duration. Ratification. Termination.
PARTIES:
Costa Rica
USA (United States)

100897 Bilateral Exchange **70 UNTS 71**
SIGNED: 20 Dec 49 FORCE: 20 Dec 49
REGISTERED: 18 Aug 50 USA (United States)
ARTICLES: 2 LANGUAGE: English. Spanish.
HEADNOTE: FLIGHTS MILITARY AIRCRAFT
TOPIC: Status of Forces
CONCEPTS: Previous treaty replacement. Conformity with municipal law. Fees and exemptions. Airport facilities. Airport equipment. Overflights and technical stops. Airforce-army-navy personnel ratio. Ranks and privileges. Procurement and logistics.
PROCEDURE: Renewal or Revival. Termination.
PARTIES:
Guatemala
USA (United States)

100898 Multilateral Convention **70 UNTS 85**
SIGNED: 9 Jul 48   FORCE: 10 Aug 50
REGISTERED: 22 Aug 50 ILO (Labor Org)
ARTICLES: 22 LANGUAGE: English. French.
HEADNOTE: ORGANIZATION EMPLOYMENT SER-
VICE
TOPIC: ILO Labor
CONCEPTS: Detailed regulations. Territorial appli-
cation. Conformity with municipal law. General
cooperation. Operating agencies. Personnel. ILO
conventions. Employment regulations. Labor statistics.
INTL ORGS: United Nations.
PROCEDURE: Amendment. Denunciation. Duration. Ratification. Registration. Renewal or Revival.
PARTIES:
Multilateral
ANNEX
70 UNTS 308. Canada. Ratification 24 Aug 50.
Force 24 Aug 51.
92 UNTS 411. Iraq. Ratification 22 Jun 51. Force
22 Jun 52.
100 UNTS 292. Netherlands. Surinam.
100 UNTS 292. Netherlands. Netherlands Antilles.
120 UNTS 298. Switzerland. Ratification
19 Jan 52. Force 19 Jan 53.
122 UNTS 342. Guatemala. Ratification
13 Feb 52. Force 13 Feb 53.
131 UNTS 332. Cuba. Ratification 29 Apr 52.
Force 29 Apr 53.
149 UNTS 406. Italy. Ratification 15 Oct 52.
Force 15 Oct 53.
162 UNTS 344. Belgium. Ratification 16 Mar 53.
Force 16 Mar 54.
173 UNTS 396. Dominican Republic. Ratification
22 Sep 53. Force 22 Sep 54.
178 UNTS 387. Japan. Ratification 20 Oct 53.
Force 20 Oct 54.
184 UNTS 336. Philippines. Ratification
29 Dec 53. Force 29 Dec 54.
193 UNTS 351. Germany, West. Ratification
22 Jun 54. Force 22 Jun 55.
196 UNTS 343. United Arab Rep. Ratification
3 Jul 54. Force 3 Jul 55.
212 UNTS 393. Greece. Ratification 16 Jun 55.
Force 16 Jun 56.
212 UNTS 393. France. Martinique.
212 UNTS 393. France. Guadeloupe.
212 UNTS 393. France. Reunion.
212 UNTS 393. France. French Guinea.
253 UNTS 388. Argentina. Ratification
24 Sep 56. Force 24 Sep 57.
266 UNTS 379. Brazil. Ratification 25 Apr 57.
Force 25 Apr 58.
293 UNTS 373. Luxembourg. Ratification
3 Mar 58. Force 3 Mar 59.
302 UNTS 358. UK Great Britain. Sierra Leone.
312 UNTS 406. Yugoslavia. Ratification
23 Jul 58. Force 23 Jul 59.
328 UNTS 304. UK Great Britain. Nigeria.
337 UNTS 393. India. Ratification 24 Jun 59.
Force 24 Jun 60.
340 UNTS 340. Israel. Ratification 21 Aug 59.
Force 21 Aug 60.
361 UNTS 243. Spain. Ratification 30 May 60.
Force 30 May 61.
366 UNTS 386. Costa Rica. Ratification 2 Jun 60.
Force 2 Jun 61.
373 UNTS 353. United Arab Rep. Syria.
381 UNTS 396. Cyprus. Succession 23 Sep 60.
Force 23 Sep 60.
390 UNTS 356. UK Great Britain. Declaration
13 Feb 61.
396 UNTS 322. UK Great Britain. West Indies.
Declaration 13 Mar 61.
396 UNTS 322. Bulgaria. Denunciation
13 Mar 61. Force 13 Mar 62.
396 UNTS 322. Ghana. Ratification 4 Apr 61.
Force 4 Apr 62.
401 UNTS 251. Sierra Leone. Succession
13 Jun 61.
401 UNTS 251. Nigeria. Ratification 19 Jun 61.
Force 19 Jun 62.
413 UNTS 363. Syria. Ratification 30 Oct 61.
422 UNTS 329. Tanganyika. Succession
30 Jan 62. Force 30 Jan 62.
429 UNTS 270. Peru. Ratification 4 Apr 62. Force
4 Apr 63.
434 UNTS 284. Libya. Ratification 20 Jun 62.
Force 20 Jun 63.
444 UNTS 325. Algeria. Succession 19 Oct 62.

471 UNTS 373. Ethiopia. Ratification 4 Jun 63.
Force 4 Jun 64.
488 UNTS 364. Kenya. Ratification 13 Jan 64.
Force 13 Jan 64.
495 UNTS 294. UK Great Britain. Mauritius.
495 UNTS 294. Malaysia. Singapore. Succession
3 Mar 64.
504 UNTS 355. Tanzania. Succession 22 Jun 64.
504 UNTS 355. Central Afri Rep. Ratification
9 Jun 64. Force 9 Jun 65.
510 UNTS 362. UK Great Britain. British Honduras.
521 UNTS 426. Venezuela. Ratification
16 Nov 64. Force 16 Nov 65.
524 UNTS 363. Malta. Ratification 4 Jan 65.
Force 4 Jan 65.
548 UNTS 399. Singapore. Ratification
25 Oct 65. Force 25 Oct 65.
649 UNTS 382. Tunisia. Ratification 11 Oct 68.
Force 11 Oct 69.
660 UNTS 428. Thailand. Ratification 26 Feb 69.
Force 26 Feb 70.

100899 Bilateral Agreement **70 UNTS 105**
SIGNED: 2 Jan 48   FORCE: 2 Jun 48
REGISTERED: 23 Aug 50 Netherlands
ARTICLES: 12 LANGUAGE: French.
HEADNOTE: ADMISSION STUDENT EMPLOYEES
TOPIC: Visas
CONCEPTS: Detailed regulations. Previous treaty
replacement. Non-visa travel documents. Gen-
eral cooperation. Teacher and student ex-
change.
INTL ORGS: Special Commission.
TREATY REF: 125LTS29.
PROCEDURE: Denunciation. Renewal or Revival.
PARTIES:
France
Netherlands

100900 Bilateral Exchange **70 UNTS 115**
SIGNED: 22 Jun 50   FORCE: 22 Jun 50
REGISTERED: 24 Aug 50 USA (United States)
ARTICLES: 2 LANGUAGE: English.
HEADNOTE: WEATHER STATIONS PACIFIC
TOPIC: Scientific Project
CONCEPTS: General cooperation. Research and
scientific projects. Research cooperation.
Meteorology. Research and development. Do-
mestic obligation. Liaison with other IGO's.
INTL ORGS: International Civil Aviation Organiza-
tion.
PARTIES:
Canada
USA (United States)
ANNEX
87 UNTS 390. USA (United States). Amendment
25 Sep 50. Force 16 Feb 51.
87 UNTS 390. Canada. Amendment 16 Feb 51.
Force 16 Feb 51.
207 UNTS 340. USA (United States). Amendment
22 Jan 52. Force 22 Feb 52.
207 UNTS 340. Canada. Amendment 22 Feb 52.
Force 22 Feb 52.
238 UNTS 306. USA (United States). Implementation 4 Jun 54. Force 28 Jun 54.
238 UNTS 306. Canada. Implementation
28 Jun 54. Force 28 Jun 54.

100901 Bilateral Exchange **70 UNTS 123**
SIGNED: 26 Apr 49   FORCE: 26 Apr 49
REGISTERED: 29 Aug 50 Netherlands
ARTICLES: 2 LANGUAGE: English.
HEADNOTE: DRAWING RIGHTS OBLIGATIONS
TOPIC: Finance
CONCEPTS: Detailed regulations. Accounting pro-
cedures. Exchange rates and regulations.
TREATY REF: 20UNTS91.
PARTIES:
Netherlands
USA (United States)

100902 Bilateral Treaty **70 UNTS 133**
SIGNED: 27 Sep 47   FORCE: 25 Jul 48
REGISTERED: 2 Sep 50 Philippines
ARTICLES: 8 LANGUAGE: English. Spanish.
HEADNOTE: FRIENDSHIP
TOPIC: General Amity
CONCEPTS: Friendship and amity. Diplomatic mis-

sions. Dispute settlement. Procedure. Special tri-
bunals.
INTL ORGS: Arbitration Commission. Conciliation
Commission.
PROCEDURE: Duration. Ratification.
PARTIES:
Philippines
Spain

100903 Bilateral Treaty **70 UNTS 143**
SIGNED: 20 May 48   FORCE: 22 Dec 48
REGISTERED: 2 Sep 50 Philippines
ARTICLES: 22 LANGUAGE: English. Spanish.
HEADNOTE: CIVIL RIGHTS CONSULAR PREROGA-
TIVES
TOPIC: Consul/Citizenship
CONCEPTS: Resident permits. Alien status. Gen-
eral consular functions. Diplomatic privileges.
Consular relations establishment. Inviolability.
Privileges and immunities. Nationality and citi-
zenship. General property. Responsibility and lia-
bility. National treatment. Shipwreck and sal-
vage. Foreign nationals.
PROCEDURE: Duration. Ratification. Termination.
PARTIES:
Philippines
Spain

100904 Bilateral Treaty **70 UNTS 183**
SIGNED: 17 Oct 47   FORCE: 4 Jan 48
REGISTERED: 7 Sep 50 UK Great Britain
ARTICLES: 15 LANGUAGE: English.
HEADNOTE: RECOGNITION BURMESE INDEPEN-
DENCE RELATED MATTERS
TOPIC: Recognition
CONCEPTS: Annex or appendix reference. Non-
prejudice to UN charter. Continuity of rights and
obligations. Recognition. Dual citizenship. Diplo-
matic relations establishment. Nationality and
citizenship. General property. Private contracts.
Procedure. Existing tribunals. Payment sched-
ules. Lump sum settlements. Debt settlement.
Postal services. Surplus war property.
INTL ORGS: International Court of Justice.
PROCEDURE: Future Procedures Contemplated.
Ratification.
PARTIES:
Burma
UK Great Britain
ANNEX
86 UNTS 322. UK Great Britain. Supplementation
24 Dec 49. Force 24 Dec 49.
86 UNTS 322. Burma. Supplementation
24 Dec 49. Force 24 Dec 49.
199 UNTS 323. UK Great Britain. Supplementation 1 Feb 54. Force 19 Feb 54.
199 UNTS 323. Burma. Supplementation
19 Feb 54. Force 19 Feb 54.
267 UNTS 370. Burma. Termination 3 Jan 53.
Force 3 Jan 54.

100905 Bilateral Exchange **70 UNTS 215**
SIGNED: 21 Feb 47   FORCE: 21 Feb 47
REGISTERED: 7 Sep 50 UK Great Britain
ARTICLES: 2 LANGUAGE: English.
HEADNOTE: AIR SERVICE
TOPIC: Air Transport
CONCEPTS: Routes and logistics. Permit designa-
tion. Conditions of airlines operating permission.
Operating authorizations and regulations.
TREATY REF: 35UNTS163.
PARTIES:
Greece
UK Great Britain

100906 Bilateral Agreement **71 UNTS 3**
SIGNED: 4 Jul 50   FORCE: 4 Jul 50
REGISTERED: 12 Sep 50 United Nations
ARTICLES: 9 LANGUAGE: English.
HEADNOTE: ACTIVITIES UNICEF
TOPIC: IGO Operations
CONCEPTS: Detailed regulations. Diplomatic privi-
leges. Privileges and immunities. Exchange of in-
formation and documents. Incorporation of
treaty provisions into national law. Accounting
procedures. Domestic obligation. Materials,
equipment and services. IGO obligations.
INTL ORGS: United Nations.
PROCEDURE: Duration.

PARTIES:
Afghanistan
UNICEF (Children)
ANNEX
236 UNTS 379. UNICEF (Children). Supplementation 28 Apr 56. Force 28 Apr 56.
236 UNTS 379. Afghanistan. Supplementation 21 Apr 56. Force 28 Apr 56.

100907   Bilateral Agreement   **71 UNTS 17**
SIGNED: 20 Sep 48   FORCE: 20 Sep 48
REGISTERED: 12 Sep 50 United Nations
ARTICLES: 9 LANGUAGE: English. French.
HEADNOTE: ACTIVITIES UNICEF
TOPIC: Direct Aid
CONCEPTS: Diplomatic privileges. Privileges and immunities. Exchange of information and documents. Accounting procedures. Investments. Materials, equipment and services. Regional offices.
INTL ORGS: United Nations.
PROCEDURE: Duration.
PARTIES:
Israel
UNICEF (Children)
ANNEX
209 UNTS 332. UNICEF (Children). Supplementation 18 Mar 55. Force 8 May 55.
209 UNTS 332.   Israel.   Supplementation 8 May 55. Force 8 May 55.

100908   Bilateral Agreement   **71 UNTS 31**
SIGNED: 3 Nov 49   FORCE: 3 Nov 49
REGISTERED: 13 Sep 50 USA (United States)
ARTICLES: 12 LANGUAGE: English. French.
HEADNOTE: EDUCATIONAL EXCHANGE PROGRAM
TOPIC: Education
CONCEPTS: Definition of terms. Conformity with municipal law. Inspection and observation. Personnel. General property. Responsibility and liability. Exchange. Commissions and foundations. Teacher and student exchange. Scholarships and grants. Research and development. Accounting procedures. Indemnities and reimbursements. Currency. Financial programs. Funding procedures.
PROCEDURE: Amendment.
PARTIES:
United Arab Rep
USA (United States)

100909   Bilateral Exchange   **71 UNTS 45**
SIGNED: 29 Dec 49   FORCE: 29 Dec 49
REGISTERED: 13 Sep 50 USA (United States)
ARTICLES: 2 LANGUAGE: English.
HEADNOTE: COPYRIGHT LAWS
TOPIC: Patents/Copyrights
CONCEPTS: Conformity with municipal law. Domestic legislation. Laws and formalities. Postwar adjustment.
PARTIES:
Australia
USA (United States)

100910   Bilateral Agreement   **71 UNTS 64**
SIGNED: 22 Sep 48   FORCE: 22 Sep 48
REGISTERED: 13 Sep 50 USA (United States)
ARTICLES: 17 LANGUAGE: English.
HEADNOTE: USE FUNDS SETTLEMENT LEND-LEASE AID SURPLUS WAR PROPERTY CLAIMS
TOPIC: Milit Assistance
CONCEPTS: Definition of terms. Exceptions and exemptions. General provisions. Exchange. Commissions and foundations. Teacher and student exchange. Scholarships and grants. Monetary and gold transfers. Lend lease.
TREATY REF: 4UNTS92.
PROCEDURE: Amendment. Application to Non-self-governing Territories.
PARTIES:
UK Great Britain
USA (United States)
ANNEX
79 UNTS 332. UK Great Britain. British Guiana.
79 UNTS 332. UK Great Britain. Nigeria.
79 UNTS 332. UK Great Britain. Gibralter.
79 UNTS 332. UK Great Britain. Bahamas.
79 UNTS 332. UK Great Britain. Bermuda.
79 UNTS 332. UK Great Britain. British Honduras.

79 UNTS 332. UK Great Britain. Brit Solomon Is.
79 UNTS 332. UK Great Britain. Uganda.
79 UNTS 332. UK Great Britain. Barbados.
79 UNTS 332. UK Great Britain. Aden.
79 UNTS 332. UK Great Britain. Tonga.
79 UNTS 332. UK Great Britain. Basutoland.
79 UNTS 332. UK Great Britain. Tanganyika.
79 UNTS 332. UK Great Britain. Windward Islands.
79 UNTS 332. UK Great Britain. Trinidad.
79 UNTS 332. UK Great Britain. Zanzibar.
79 UNTS 332. UK Great Britain. Malta.
79 UNTS 332. UK Great Britain. Northern Rhodesia.
79 UNTS 332. UK Great Britain. Swaziland.
79 UNTS 332. UK Great Britain. Fiji Islands.
79 UNTS 332. UK Great Britain. Bechuanaland.
79 UNTS 332. UK Great Britain. Falkland Islands.
79 UNTS 332. UK Great Britain. North Borneo.
79 UNTS 332. UK Great Britain. St. Helena.
79 UNTS 332. UK Great Britain. British Somaliland.
79 UNTS 332. UK Great Britain. Gambia.
79 UNTS 332. UK Great Britain. Jamaica.
79 UNTS 332. UK Great Britain. Nyasaland.
79 UNTS 332. UK Great Britain. Mauritius.
79 UNTS 332. UK Great Britain. Gold Coast.
79 UNTS 332. UK Great Britain. Kenya.
79 UNTS 332. UK Great Britain. Leeward Islands.
79 UNTS 332. UK Great Britain. Fed of Malaya.
79 UNTS 332. UK Great Britain. Gilbert Islands.
79 UNTS 332. UK Great Britain. Hong Kong.
79 UNTS 332. UK Great Britain. Sarawak.
158 UNTS 490. USA (United States). Supplementation 22 Oct 52. Force 22 Oct 52.
158 UNTS 490. UK Great Britain. Supplementation 22 Oct 52. Force 22 Oct 52.
199 UNTS 326. USA (United States). Supplementation 15 Jun 54. Force 15 Jun 54.
199 UNTS 326. UK Great Britain. Supplementation 15 Jun 54. Force 15 Jun 54.
215 UNTS 412. UK Great Britain. Prolongation 23 May 55. Force 23 May 55.
215 UNTS 412. USA (United States). Prolongation 23 May 55. Force 23 May 55.
326 UNTS 300. UK Great Britain. Supplementation 22 Sep 58. Force 22 Sep 58.
326 UNTS 300. USA (United States). Supplementation 22 Sep 58. Force 22 Sep 58.
343 UNTS 342. USA (United States). Acknowledgement 19 Jul 57. Force 28 Jun 57.
343 UNTS 342. UK Great Britain. Fed Rhod/Nyasaland. Force 28 Jun 57.

100911   Bilateral Exchange   **71 UNTS 91**
SIGNED: 28 Jul 50   FORCE: 10 Aug 50
REGISTERED: 14 Sep 50 Belgium
ARTICLES: 2 LANGUAGE: French.
HEADNOTE: ABOLITION PASSPORT REQUIREMENTS
TOPIC: Visas
CONCEPTS: Territorial application. Time limit. Previous treaty replacement. Visa abolition. Border traffic and migration. Passports non-diplomatic. Resident permits. Non-visa travel documents. Tourism.
TREATY REF: 29UNTS277.
PARTIES:
Belgium
Switzerland

100912   Multilateral Protocol   **71 UNTS 101**
SIGNED: 28 Apr 49   FORCE: 20 Sep 50
REGISTERED: 20 Sep 50 United Nations
ARTICLES: 47 LANGUAGE: English. French.
HEADNOTE: REVISED GENERAL ACT PACIFIC SETTLEMENT INTERNATIONAL DISPUTES
TOPIC: Dispute Settlement
CONCEPTS: Exceptions and exemptions. Conformity with municipal law. Arbitration. Existing tribunals. Conciliation. Competence of tribunal.
INTL ORGS: International Court of Justice.
PROCEDURE: Accession. Denunciation. Duration. Registration. Renewal or Revival.
PARTIES:
Multilateral
ANNEX
94 UNTS 313. Norway. Accession 16 Jul 51. Force 14 Oct 51.
124 UNTS 315. Denmark. Accession 25 Mar 52. Force 23 Jun 52.

399 UNTS 264.   Luxembourg.   Accession 28 Jun 61. Force 26 Sep 61.
424 UNTS 344.   Upper   Volta.   Accession 27 Mar 62. Force 25 Jun 62.

100913   Bilateral Agreement   **71 UNTS 129**
SIGNED: 12 Jul 50   FORCE: 1 Jul 50
REGISTERED: 25 Sep 50 Denmark
ARTICLES: 9 LANGUAGE: French.
HEADNOTE: FINANCE
TOPIC: Finance
CONCEPTS: Detailed regulations. General cooperation. Accounting procedures. Banking. Balance of payments. Monetary and gold transfers. Exchange rates and regulations. Payment schedules.
PROCEDURE: Denunciation.
PARTIES:
Denmark
Spain

100914   Bilateral Agreement   **71 UNTS 135**
SIGNED: 12 Jul 50   FORCE: 1 Jul 50
REGISTERED: 25 Sep 50 Denmark
ARTICLES: 5 LANGUAGE: French.
HEADNOTE: EXCHANGE COMMODITIES
TOPIC: General Trade
CONCEPTS: Definition of terms. Annex or appendix reference. Establishment of commission. General trade. Export quotas. Import quotas. Reciprocity in trade. Quotas.
INTL ORGS: Special Commission.
PROCEDURE: Denunciation. Duration.
PARTIES:
Denmark
Spain

100915   Bilateral Protocol   **71 UNTS 143**
SIGNED: 9 Feb 48   FORCE: 22 Apr 48
REGISTERED: 26 Sep 50 Belgium
ARTICLES: 21 LANGUAGE: French.
HEADNOTE: RECRUITING ITALIAN WORKERS BELGIUM
TOPIC: Non-ILO Labor
CONCEPTS: Definition of terms. Jurisdiction. Private contracts. Establishment of commission. Employment regulations. Non-ILO labor relations. Unemployment. Migrant worker.
INTL ORGS: Special Commission.
TREATY REF: 19UNTS65.
PROCEDURE: Ratification.
PARTIES:
Belgium
Italy
ANNEX
137 UNTS 328. Italy. Amendment   1 Aug 52. Force 1 Aug 52.
137 UNTS 328. Belgium. Amendment 1 Aug 52. Force 1 Aug 52.

100916   Unilateral Instrument   **71 UNTS 153**
SIGNED: 25 Sep 50   FORCE: 28 Sep 50
REGISTERED: 28 Sep 50 United Nations
ARTICLES: 1 LANGUAGE: English.
HEADNOTE: ACCEPTANCE UN CHARTER
TOPIC: UN Charter
CONCEPTS: Acceptance of obligations upon admittance to UN.
INTL ORGS: United Nations.
PARTIES:
Indonesia

100917   Bilateral Agreement   **71 UNTS 157**
SIGNED: 15 Jun 46   FORCE: 8 Aug 47
REGISTERED: 30 Sep 50 USA (United States)
ARTICLES: 11 LANGUAGE: Arabic. English.
HEADNOTE: AIR TRANSPORT
TOPIC: Air Transport
CONCEPTS: Exceptions and exemptions. Annex or appendix reference. Conformity with municipal law. Licenses and permits. Recognition of legal documents. Use of facilities. Procedure. Special tribunals. Competence of tribunal. Fees and exemptions. Most favored nation clause. National treatment. Customs exemptions. Competency certificate. Routes and logistics. Navigational conditions. Permit designation. Air transport. Airport facilities. Airworthiness certificates. Conditions of airlines operating permission. Operating

authorizations and regulations. Licenses and certificates of nationality.
INTL ORGS: International Civil Aviation Organization.
TREATY REF: US DEPT. OF STATE PUB. 2282 SERIES 64.
PROCEDURE: Ratification. Registration. Termination.
PARTIES:
United Arab Rep
USA (United States)
ANNEX
290 UNTS 303. USA (United States). Amendment 24 Jun 57. Force 31 Jul 57.
290 UNTS 303. United Arab Rep. Amendment 31 Jul 57. Force 31 Jul 57.

100918 Bilateral Agreement **71 UNTS 179**
SIGNED: 15 Jul 47 FORCE: 12 Feb 48
REGISTERED: 2 Oct 50 UK Great Britain
ARTICLES: 20 LANGUAGE: English. Spanish.
HEADNOTE: PAYMENTS
TOPIC: Finance
CONCEPTS: Definition of terms. Detailed regulations. General provisions. General cooperation. Accounting procedures. Banking. Balance of payments. Currency. Monetary and gold transfers. Exchange rates and regulations. Interest rates. Payment schedules. Local currency.
PROCEDURE: Ratification.
PARTIES:
UK Great Britain
Uruguay
ANNEX
266 UNTS 380. Uruguay. Prolongation 6 Feb 53. Force 12 Feb 53.
266 UNTS 380. UK Great Britain. Prolongation 4 Feb 53. Force 12 Feb 53.

100919 Bilateral Agreement **71 UNTS 199**
SIGNED: 12 Jul 48 FORCE: 12 Jul 48
REGISTERED: 2 Oct 50 UK Great Britain
ARTICLES: 20 LANGUAGE: English.
HEADNOTE: FINANCE
TOPIC: Finance
CONCEPTS: General provisions. Annex or appendix reference. Annex type material. Currency. Payment schedules. Claims and settlements. Lump sum settlements. Lease of military property. Lend lease. Surplus war property. Bases and facilities.
TREATY REF: 4UNTS84.
PARTIES:
UK Great Britain
Uruguay

100920 Bilateral Agreement **71 UNTS 215**
SIGNED: 15 Jul 48 FORCE: 15 Jul 48
REGISTERED: 2 Oct 50 UK Great Britain
ARTICLES: 8 LANGUAGE: English. French.
HEADNOTE: SETTLEMENT INTER-CUSTODIAL CONFLICTS RELATING GERMAN ENEMY ASSETS
TOPIC: Claims and Debts
CONCEPTS: Territorial application. Treaty implementation. Annex or appendix reference. Procedure. Existing tribunals. Assets.
INTL ORGS: Allied Military Occupation.
PROCEDURE: Amendment. Accession.
PARTIES:
France
UK Great Britain

100921 **UNTS**
SIGNED:
REGISTERED:
ARTICLES:
HEADNOTE: AGREEMENT REGISTERED UNDER 100501
TOPIC:
PARTIES:

100922 Bilateral Exchange **71 UNTS 241**
SIGNED: 30 Sep 48 FORCE: 30 Sep 48
REGISTERED: 2 Oct 50 UK Great Britain
ARTICLES: 2 LANGUAGE: English.
HEADNOTE: FERROUS SCRAP EXPORTS
TOPIC: Specific Resources
CONCEPTS: Previous treaties adherence. Estab-

lishment of commission. Export quotas. Purchase authorization. Surplus war property. Raw materials.
INTL ORGS: Organization for Economic Co-operation and Development. Special Commission.
TREATY REF: 7UNTS163; 34UNTS390.
PARTIES:
UK Great Britain
USA (United States)
ANNEX
89 UNTS 388. UK Great Britain. Amendment 1 Jul 49. Force 1 Jul 49.
89 UNTS 388. USA (United States). Amendment 1 Jul 49. Force 1 Jul 49.

100923 Bilateral Exchange **71 UNTS 255**
SIGNED: 12 Oct 48 FORCE: 12 Oct 48
REGISTERED: 2 Oct 50 UK Great Britain
ARTICLES: 2 LANGUAGE: English.
HEADNOTE: CONSERVATION EXCHANGE RESOURCES
TOPIC: Finance
CONCEPTS: Definition of terms. General cooperation. Balance of payments.
PARTIES:
Burma
UK Great Britain

100924 Multilateral Protocol **72 UNTS 3**
SIGNED: 16 Dec 49 FORCE: 5 May 50
REGISTERED: 4 Oct 50 Belgium
ARTICLES: 7 LANGUAGE: French.
HEADNOTE: AMEND 1890 CONVENTION CUSTOMS TARIFFS
TOPIC: Admin Cooperation
CONCEPTS: Annex type material. Previous treaty extension.
INTL ORGS: International Union for the Publication of Customs Tariffs.
PARTIES:
Argentina SIGNED: 16 Dec 49
Australia SIGNED: 16 Dec 49 FORCE: 5 May 50
Austria SIGNED: 16 Dec 49 RATIFIED: 2 Aug 50 FORCE: 1 Sep 50
Belgium SIGNED: 16 Dec 49
Brazil SIGNED: 16 Dec 49
Canada SIGNED: 16 Dec 49 FORCE: 5 May 50
Colombia SIGNED: 16 Dec 49 FORCE: 5 May 50
Denmark SIGNED: 16 Dec 49 FORCE: 5 May 50
Dominican Republic SIGNED: 16 Dec 49
United Arab Rep SIGNED: 16 Dec 49 FORCE: 5 May 50
Finland SIGNED: 16 Dec 49 FORCE: 5 May 50
France SIGNED: 16 Dec 49 RATIFIED: 1 Sep 50 FORCE: 1 Oct 50
Germany, West SIGNED: 16 Dec 49 RATIFIED: 1 Sep 50 FORCE: 1 Oct 50
Greece SIGNED: 16 Dec 49
Haiti SIGNED: 16 Dec 49 FORCE: 5 May 50
India SIGNED: 16 Dec 50 FORCE: 5 May 50
Iraq SIGNED: 16 Dec 49 FORCE: 5 May 50
Italy SIGNED: 16 Dec 49 FORCE: 5 May 50
Japan SIGNED: 16 Dec 49 RATIFIED: 5 May 50 FORCE: 5 May 50
Lebanon SIGNED: 16 Dec 49 FORCE: 5 May 50
Luxembourg SIGNED: 16 Dec 49
Mexico SIGNED: 16 Dec 49
Netherlands SIGNED: 16 Dec 50 FORCE: 5 May 50
Norway SIGNED: 16 Dec 49
Pakistan SIGNED: 16 Dec 50 FORCE: 5 May 50
Philippines RATIFIED: 1 Nov 50 FORCE: 1 Dec 50
South Africa SIGNED: 16 Dec 50 FORCE: 5 May 50
Spain SIGNED: 16 Dec 49 FORCE: 5 May 50
Sweden SIGNED: 16 Dec 50 RATIFIED: 2 Aug 50 FORCE: 1 Sep 50
Switzerland SIGNED: 16 Dec 50 FORCE: 5 May 50
UK Great Britain SIGNED: 16 Dec 49 FORCE: 5 May 50
Yugoslavia SIGNED: 16 Dec 50 RATIFIED: 28 Mar 50 FORCE: 5 May 50
ANNEX
89 UNTS 392. Chile. Accession 15 Nov 50. Force 15 Dec 50.
89 UNTS 392. Peru. Accession 15 Jan 51. Force 14 Feb 51.
89 UNTS 392. Norway. Accession 15 May 51. Force 14 Jun 51.

100925 Bilateral Exchange **72 UNTS 25**
SIGNED: 31 May 47 FORCE: 31 May 47
REGISTERED: 5 Oct 50 Ecuador
ARTICLES: 8 LANGUAGE: Portuguese. Spanish.
HEADNOTE: EXCHANGE DIPLOMATIC CORRESPONDENCE AIRMAIL
TOPIC: Consul/Citizenship
CONCEPTS: Previous treaty extension. Personnel.
PARTIES:
Brazil
Ecuador

100926 Bilateral Instrument **72 UNTS 35**
SIGNED: 24 Aug 49 FORCE: 24 Aug 49
REGISTERED: 5 Oct 50 Ecuador
ARTICLES: 1 LANGUAGE: Italian. Spanish.
HEADNOTE: FRIENDSHIP COLLABORATION
TOPIC: General Amity
CONCEPTS: Friendship and amity. Defense and security.
PROCEDURE: Future Procedures Contemplated.
PARTIES:
Ecuador
Italy

100927 Bilateral Agreement **72 UNTS 41**
SIGNED: 26 Oct 45 FORCE: 26 Oct 45
REGISTERED: 5 Oct 50 ICAO (Civil Aviat)
ARTICLES: 9 LANGUAGE: Afrikaans. English.
HEADNOTE: ESTABLISHMENT CIVIL AIR SERVICES
TOPIC: Air Transport
CONCEPTS: Annex or appendix reference. Licenses and permits. Recognition of legal documents. Use of facilities. Arbitration. Procedure. Special tribunals. Negotiation. Fees and exemptions. Most favored nation clause. National treatment. Customs exemptions. Competency certificate. Routes and logistics. Navigational conditions. Permit designation. Airport facilities. Airworthiness certificates. Conditions of airlines operating permission. Operating authorizations and regulations. Licenses and certificates of nationality.
INTL ORGS: International Civil Aviation Organization. Arbitration Commission.
TREATY REF: US DEPT. OF STATE PUB. 2282 SERIES 64.
PROCEDURE: Future Procedures Contemplated. Registration. Termination.
PARTIES:
South Africa
UK Great Britain
ANNEX
353 UNTS 334. South Africa. Supplementation 15 Sep 59. Force 15 Sep 59.
353 UNTS 334. UK Great Britain. Supplementation 15 Sep 59. Force 15 Sep 59.

100928 Bilateral Agreement **72 UNTS 57**
SIGNED: 5 Apr 46 FORCE: 4 Jun 46
REGISTERED: 5 Oct 50 ICAO (Civil Aviat)
ARTICLES: 11 LANGUAGE: English.
HEADNOTE: AIR SERVICES
TOPIC: Air Transport
CONCEPTS: Annex or appendix reference. Conformity with municipal law. Licenses and permits. Recognition of legal documents. Use of facilities. Arbitration. Procedure. Existing tribunals. Special tribunals. Fees and exemptions. Most favored nation clause. National treatment. Customs exemptions. Competency certificate. Routes and logistics. Navigational conditions. Permit designation. Airport facilities. Airworthiness certificates. Conditions of airlines operating permission. Operating authorizations and regulations. Licenses and certificates of nationality.
INTL ORGS: International Civil Aviation Organization. Arbitration Commission.
TREATY REF: US DEPT. OF STATE PUB. 2282 SERIES 64.
PROCEDURE: Amendment. Future Procedures Contemplated. Ratification. Registration. Termination.
PARTIES:
Ireland
UK Great Britain
ANNEX
192 UNTS 320. Ireland. Amendment 18 Sep 51. Force 18 Sep 51.

192 UNTS 320. UK Great Britain. Amendment 15 Sep 51. Force 18 Sep 51.
192 UNTS 324. UK Great Britain. Amendment 14 Mar 52. Force 12 Apr 52.
192 UNTS 324. Ireland. Amendment 12 Apr 52. Force 12 Apr 52.
192 UNTS 328. Ireland. Amendment 29 Dec 52. Force 29 Dec 52.
192 UNTS 328. UK Great Britain. Amendment 28 Nov 52. Force 29 Dec 52.
310 UNTS 326. Ireland. Supplementation 31 Aug 56. Force 31 Aug 56.
310 UNTS 326. UK Great Britain. Supplementation 31 Aug 56. Force 31 Aug 56.
335 UNTS 292. Ireland. Amendment 20 Jun 58. Force 30 Jun 58.
335 UNTS 292. UK Great Britain. Amendment 30 Jun 58. Force 30 Jun 58.
353 UNTS 338. Ireland. Amendment 30 Jan 59. Force 30 Jan 59.
353 UNTS 338. UK Great Britain. Amendment 30 Jan 59. Force 30 Jan 59.
392 UNTS 338. Ireland. Amendment 15 Aug 59. Force 30 Jan 59.
392 UNTS 338. UK Great Britain. Amendment 15 Aug 59.
412 UNTS 290. Ireland. Amendment 21 Jul 60. Force 21 Jul 60.
412 UNTS 290. UK Great Britain. Amendment 21 Jul 60. Force 21 Jul 60.
412 UNTS 292. UK Great Britain. Amendment 9 May 61. Force 9 May 61.
412 UNTS 292. Ireland. Amendment 9 May 61. Force 9 May 61.
552 UNTS 361. UK Great Britain. Amendment 19 Mar 65. Force 19 Mar 65.
552 UNTS 361. Ireland. Amendment 19 Mar 65. Force 19 Mar 65.
604 UNTS 350. UK Great Britain. Amendment 22 Jun 65. Force 30 Jun 67.
604 UNTS 350. Ireland. Amendment 22 Jun 65. Force 30 Jun 67.
613 UNTS 402. Ireland. Amendment 13 Apr 67. Force 13 Apr 67.
613 UNTS 402. UK Great Britain. Amendment 13 Apr 67. Force 13 Apr 67.
618 UNTS 372. UK Great Britain. Amendment 24 Jan 67. Force 24 Jul 67.
618 UNTS 372. Ireland. Amendment 24 Jan 67. Force 24 Jul 67.

100929 Bilateral Agreement **72 UNTS 77**
SIGNED: 27 Jan 40   FORCE: 14 Nov 49
REGISTERED: 5 Oct 50 ICAO (Civil Aviat)
ARTICLES: 15 LANGUAGE: French. Portuguese.
HEADNOTE: AIR TRANSPORT
TOPIC: Air Transport
CONCEPTS: Definition of terms. Annex or appendix reference. Previous treaty replacement. Conformity with municipal law. General cooperation. Licenses and permits. Recognition of legal documents. Use of facilities. Arbitration. Procedure. Existing tribunals. Negotiation. Competence of tribunal. Fees and exemptions. Most favored nation clause. National treatment. Customs exemptions. Competency certificate. Routes and logistics. Navigational conditions. Permit designation. Air transport. Airport facilities. Airworthiness certificates. Conditions of airlines operating permission. Operating authorizations and regulations. Licenses and certificates of nationality.
INTL ORGS: International Civil Aviation Organization. Arbitration Commission.
TREATY REF: US DEPT. OF STATE PUB. 2282 SERIES 64; 15UNTS295.
PROCEDURE: Amendment. Future Procedures Contemplated. Ratification. Registration. Termination.
PARTIES:
Brazil
France

100930 Bilateral Agreement **72 UNTS 107**
SIGNED: 30 Jun 47   FORCE: 21 Dec 49
REGISTERED: 5 Oct 50 ICAO (Civil Aviat)
ARTICLES: 12 LANGUAGE: Arabic. Turkish.
HEADNOTE: CIVIL AIR TRANSPORT
TOPIC: Air Transport
CONCEPTS: Exceptions and exemptions. Annex or appendix reference. Conformity with municipal law. Licenses and permits. Recognition of legal documents. Use of facilities. Arbitration. Procedure. Existing tribunals. Negotiation. Fees and exemptions. Most favored nation clause. National treatment. Customs exemptions. Competency certificate. Routes and logistics. Navigational conditions. Permit designation. Air transport. Airport facilities. Airworthiness certificates. Conditions of airlines operating permission. Operating authorizations and regulations. Licenses and certificates of nationality.
INTL ORGS: International Civil Aviation Organization. Arbitration Commission.
TREATY REF: 15UNTS295.
PROCEDURE: Amendment. Denunciation. Future Procedures Contemplated. Ratification. Registration.
PARTIES:
Iraq
Turkey

100931 Bilateral Agreement **72 UNTS 131**
SIGNED: 22 Jul 47   FORCE: 20 Jan 50
REGISTERED: 5 Oct 50 ICAO (Civil Aviat)
ARTICLES: 11 LANGUAGE: French.
HEADNOTE: AIR TRANSPORT
TOPIC: Air Transport
CONCEPTS: Exceptions and exemptions. Annex or appendix reference. Conformity with municipal law. Licenses and permits. Recognition of legal documents. Use of facilities. Arbitration. Procedure. Existing tribunals. Fees and exemptions. Most favored nation clause. National treatment. Customs exemptions. Competency certificate. Routes and logistics. Navigational conditions. Permit designation. Air transport. Airport facilities. Airworthiness certificates. Conditions of airlines operating permission. Operating authorizations and regulations. Licenses and certificates of nationality.
INTL ORGS: International Civil Aviation Organization. Arbitration Commission.
TREATY REF: 15UNTS295.
PROCEDURE: Amendment. Denunciation. Future Procedures Contemplated. Ratification. Registration.
PARTIES:
Greece
Turkey

100932 Bilateral Agreement **72 UNTS 143**
SIGNED: 22 Dec 47   FORCE: 22 Dec 47
REGISTERED: 5 Oct 50 ICAO (Civil Aviat)
ARTICLES: 14 LANGUAGE: English. Spanish.
HEADNOTE: AIR SERVICES
TOPIC: Air Transport
CONCEPTS: Conditions. Definition of terms. Detailed regulations. Conformity with municipal law. Exchange of information and documents. Arbitration. Procedure. Existing tribunals. Negotiation. Non-interest rates and fees. Passenger transport. Routes and logistics. Permit designation. Transport of goods. Overflights and technical stops. Operating authorizations and regulations.
INTL ORGS: International Civil Aviation Organization. Arbitration Commission.
TREATY REF: 15UNTS295.
PROCEDURE: Amendment. Future Procedures Contemplated. Termination.
PARTIES:
Peru
UK Great Britain
ANNEX
404 UNTS 317. UK Great Britain. Amendment 3 Feb 61. Force 16 Feb 61.
404 UNTS 317. Peru. Amendment 16 Feb 61. Force 16 Feb 61.
566 UNTS 334. UK Great Britain. Amendment 16 Dec 65. Force 16 Dec 65.
566 UNTS 334. Peru. Amendment 16 Dec 65. Force 16 Dec 65.

100933 Bilateral Agreement **72 UNTS 175**
SIGNED: 16 Feb 49   FORCE: 16 Jun 49
REGISTERED: 5 Oct 50 ICAO (Civil Aviat)
ARTICLES: 11 LANGUAGE: French. Turkish.
HEADNOTE: PROVISIONAL AIR TRANSPORT
TOPIC: Air Transport
CONCEPTS: Detailed regulations. Exceptions and exemptions. Annex or appendix reference. Conformity with municipal law. General cooperation. Licenses and permits. Recognition of legal documents. Use of facilities. Arbitration. Procedure. Existing tribunals. Negotiation. Fees and exemptions. Non-interest rates and fees. Most favored nation clause. National treatment. Customs exemptions. Competency certificate. Routes and logistics. Navigational conditions. Permit designation. Air transport. Airport facilities. Airworthiness certificates. Conditions of airlines operating permission. Operating authorizations and regulations. Licenses and certificates of nationality.
INTL ORGS: International Civil Aviation Organization. Arbitration Commission.
TREATY REF: 15UNTS295.
PROCEDURE: Amendment. Future Procedures Contemplated. Registration. Termination.
PARTIES:
Switzerland
Turkey

100934 Bilateral Agreement **72 UNTS 191**
SIGNED: 20 Oct 49   FORCE: 20 Oct 49
REGISTERED: 5 Oct 50 ICAO (Civil Aviat)
ARTICLES: 15 LANGUAGE: English.
HEADNOTE: AIR SERVICES
TOPIC: Air Transport
CONCEPTS: Conditions. Definition of terms. Detailed regulations. Exceptions and exemptions. Annex or appendix reference. Conformity with municipal law. General cooperation. Exchange of information and documents. Arbitration. Procedure. Existing tribunals. Negotiation. Non-interest rates and fees. National treatment. Customs duties. Customs exemptions. Routes and logistics. Permit designation. Conditions of airlines operating permission. Overflights and technical stops. Operating authorizations and regulations.
INTL ORGS: International Civil Aviation Organization. Arbitration Commission.
TREATY REF: 15UNTS295.
PROCEDURE: Amendment. Future Procedures Contemplated. Termination.
PARTIES:
India
Philippines

100935 Bilateral Agreement **72 UNTS 217**
SIGNED: 23 Nov 49   FORCE: 23 Nov 49
REGISTERED: 5 Oct 50 ICAO (Civil Aviat)
ARTICLES: 13 LANGUAGE: English.
HEADNOTE: AIR SERVICES
TOPIC: Air Transport
CONCEPTS: Annex or appendix reference. Conformity with municipal law. Licenses and permits. Recognition of legal documents. Use of facilities. Arbitration. Procedure. Existing tribunals. Reexport of goods, etc.. Fees and exemptions. Most favored nation clause. National treatment. Customs exemptions. Competency certificate. Routes and logistics. Navigational conditions. Permit designation. Air transport. Airport facilities. Airworthiness certificates. Conditions of airlines operating permission. Licenses and certificates of nationality.
INTL ORGS: International Civil Aviation Organization. Arbitration Commission.
TREATY REF: 15UNTS295.
PROCEDURE: Amendment. Future Procedures Contemplated. Registration. Termination.
PARTIES:
Sweden
Thailand
ANNEX
464 UNTS 312. Sweden. Amendment 27 Feb 63. Force 27 Feb 63.
464 UNTS 312. Thailand. Amendment 21 Feb 63. Force 27 Feb 63.

100936 Bilateral Agreement **72 UNTS 230**
SIGNED: 2 Dec 49   FORCE: 15 Jan 50
REGISTERED: 5 Oct 50 ICAO (Civil Aviat)
ARTICLES: 11 LANGUAGE: English. German.
HEADNOTE: AIR TRANSPORT
TOPIC: Air Transport
CONCEPTS: Annex or appendix reference. Conformity with municipal law. Licenses and permits. Recognition of legal documents. Use of facilities. Arbitration. Procedure. Existing tribunals. Reexport of goods, etc.. Fees and exemptions. Most favored nation clause. National treatment. Cus-

toms exemptions. Competency certificate. Routes and logistics. Navigational conditions. Permit designation. Air transport. Airport facilities. Airworthiness certificates. Conditions of airlines operating permission. Operating authorizations and regulations. Licenses and certificates of nationality.
INTL ORGS: International Civil Aviation Organization. Arbitration Commission.
PROCEDURE: Future Procedures Contemplated. Registration. Termination.
PARTIES:
Austria
Norway

100937   Bilateral Agreement   **72 UNTS 247**
SIGNED: 13 Dec 49   FORCE: 15 Dec 49
REGISTERED: 5 Oct 50 ICAO (Civil Aviat)
ARTICLES: 12 LANGUAGE: English.
HEADNOTE: AIR SERVICES
TOPIC: Air Transport
CONCEPTS: Annex or appendix reference. Conformity with municipal law. Use of facilities. Arbitration. Procedure. Existing tribunals. Negotiation. Quarantine. Fees and exemptions. Most favored nation clause. National treatment. Customs duties. Customs exemptions. Routes and logistics. Permit designation. Airport facilities. Conditions of airlines operating permission. Operating authorizations and regulations.
INTL ORGS: International Civil Aviation Organization. Arbitration Commission.
TREATY REF: 15UNTS295.
PROCEDURE: Amendment. Future Procedures Contemplated. Registration. Termination.
PARTIES:
Canada
Denmark
ANNEX
353 UNTS 340.   Denmark.   Amendment 16 May 58. Force 16 May 58.
353 UNTS 340. Canada. Amendment 16 May 58. Force 16 May 58.

100938   Bilateral Agreement   **72 UNTS 261**
SIGNED: 24 Feb 50   FORCE: 24 Feb 50
REGISTERED: 5 Oct 50 ICAO (Civil Aviat)
ARTICLES: 12 LANGUAGE: English.
HEADNOTE: AIR TRANSPORT SERVICES
TOPIC: Air Transport
CONCEPTS: Annex or appendix reference. Conformity with municipal law. Licenses and permits. Recognition of legal documents. Use of facilities. Arbitration. Procedure. Existing tribunals. Reexport of goods, etc.. Fees and exemptions. Most favored nation clause. National treatment. Customs exemptions. Competency certificate. Routes and logistics. Navigational conditions. Permit designation. Air transport. Airport facilities. Airworthiness certificates. Conditions of airlines operating permission. Licenses and certificates of nationality.
INTL ORGS: International Civil Aviation Organization. Arbitration Commission.
TREATY REF: 15UNTS295.
PROCEDURE: Amendment. Future Procedures Contemplated. Registration. Termination.
PARTIES:
Ceylon (Sri Lanka)
Thailand
ANNEX
601 UNTS 332. Thailand. Amendment 23 Jan 65. Force 23 Jan 65.
601 UNTS 332. Ceylon (Sri Lanka). Amendment 23 Jan 65. Force 23 Jan 65.

100939   Bilateral Agreement   **72 UNTS 273**
SIGNED: 22 Mar 50   FORCE: 22 Mar 50
REGISTERED: 5 Oct 50 ICAO (Civil Aviat)
ARTICLES: 11 LANGUAGE: Danish. Icelandic.
HEADNOTE: AIR TRANSPORT
TOPIC: Air Transport
CONCEPTS: Annex or appendix reference. Conformity with municipal law. Licenses and permits. Recognition of legal documents. Use of facilities. Arbitration. Procedure. Existing tribunals. Most favored nation clause. National treatment. Customs exemptions. Competency certificate. Routes and logistics. Navigational conditions. Permit designation. Airport facilities. Airworthiness certificates. Conditions of airlines operat-

ing permission. Operating authorizations and regulations. Licenses and certificates of nationality.
INTL ORGS: International Civil Aviation Organization. Arbitration Commission.
TREATY REF: 15UNTS295.
PROCEDURE: Amendment. Future Procedures Contemplated. Registration. Termination.
PARTIES:
Denmark
Iceland

100940   Bilateral Agreement   **73 UNTS 3**
SIGNED: 29 Jun 50   FORCE: 29 Jun 50
REGISTERED: 5 Oct 50 ICAO (Civil Aviat)
ARTICLES: 15 LANGUAGE: English.
HEADNOTE: AIR TRANSPORT
TOPIC: Air Transport
CONCEPTS: Definition of terms. Exceptions and exemptions. Annex or appendix reference. Non-prejudice to third party. Conformity with municipal law. Licenses and permits. Recognition of legal documents. Use of facilities. Procedure. Special tribunals. Competence of tribunal. Indemnities and reimbursements. Fees and exemptions. Most favored nation clause. National treatment. Customs exemptions. Competency certificate. Routes and logistics. Navigational conditions. Permit designation. Airport facilities. Airworthiness certificates. Conditions of airlines operating permission. Operating authorizations and regulations. Licenses and certificates of nationality.
INTL ORGS: International Civil Aviation Organization. Arbitration Commission.
TREATY REF: 15UNTS295.
PROCEDURE: Amendment. Future Procedures Contemplated. Registration. Termination.
PARTIES:
Burma
Ceylon (Sri Lanka)

100941   Bilateral Agreement   **73 UNTS 21**
SIGNED: 1 Aug 50   FORCE: 1 Aug 50
REGISTERED: 5 Oct 50 ICAO (Civil Aviat)
ARTICLES: 12 LANGUAGE: English. French.
HEADNOTE: AIR SERVICES
TOPIC: Air Transport
CONCEPTS: Definition of terms. Detailed regulations. Annex or appendix reference. Conformity with municipal law. Exchange of information and documents. Arbitration. Procedure. Non-interest rates and fees. Most favored nation clause. Permit designation. Conditions of airlines operating permission. Overflights and technical stops. Operating authorizations and regulations.
INTL ORGS: International Civil Aviation Organization. Arbitration Commission.
TREATY REF: 15UNTS295.
PROCEDURE: Amendment. Future Procedures Contemplated. Registration. Termination. Application to Non-self-governing Territories.
PARTIES:
Canada
France
ANNEX
77 UNTS 368. France. Amendment 28 Sep 50. Force 1 Oct 50.
77 UNTS 368. Canada. Amendment 4 Oct 50. Force 4 Oct 50.
128 UNTS 302. Canada. Supplementation 1 Aug 50. Force 1 Aug 50.
128 UNTS 302. France. Supplementation 1 Aug 50. Force 1 Aug 50.
353 UNTS 344. Canada. Amendment 22 Oct 58. Force 22 Oct 58.
353 UNTS 344. France. Amendment 22 Oct 58. Force 22 Oct 58.

100942   Multilateral Convention   **73 UNTS 39**
SIGNED: 9 Dec 48   FORCE: 9 Oct 50
REGISTERED: 9 Oct 50 United Nations
ARTICLES: 18 LANGUAGE: English. French.
HEADNOTE: ECONOMIC STATISTICS
TOPIC: Scientific Project
CONCEPTS: Definition of terms. Detailed regulations. Exceptions and exemptions. Treaty interpretation. Annex or appendix reference. Exchange of information and documents. Public information. Dispute settlement. Research and scientific projects. Research results.

INTL ORGS: League of Nations. United Nations.
PROCEDURE: Accession. Denunciation. Duration. Registration.
PARTIES:
Australia FORCE: 9 Oct 50
Austria FORCE: 9 Oct 50
Canada FORCE: 9 Oct 50
Denmark FORCE: 9 Oct 50
United Arab Rep FORCE: 9 Oct 50
Finland FORCE: 9 Oct 50
France FORCE: 9 Oct 50
Greece FORCE: 9 Oct 50
India FORCE: 9 Oct 50
Italy FORCE: 9 Oct 50
Netherlands FORCE: 9 Oct 50
Norway FORCE: 9 Oct 50
South Africa FORCE: 9 Oct 50
Southern Rhodesia FORCE: 9 Oct 50
Sweden FORCE: 9 Oct 50
UK Great Britain FORCE: 9 Oct 50
ANNEX
77 UNTS 372. Israel. Accession 20 Dec 50. Force 28 Mar 51.
122 UNTS 340. Ireland. Accession 28 Feb 52.
122 UNTS 340. Pakistan. Accession 3 Mar 52.
128 UNTS 306. Belgium. Ratification 2 May 52.
150 UNTS 368. Japan. Accession 2 Dec 52.
171 UNTS 414. Luxembourg. Ratification 23 Jul 53. Force 21 Oct 53.
292 UNTS 361. Ghana. Acceptance 7 Apr 58.
541 UNTS 307. Nigeria. Accession 22 Jul 65. Force 21 Oct 65.

100943   Bilateral Exchange   **73 UNTS 57**
SIGNED: 5 Sep 47   FORCE: 5 Sep 47
REGISTERED: 9 Oct 50 USA (United States)
ARTICLES: 2 LANGUAGE: English.
HEADNOTE: EXCHANGE OFFICIAL PUBLICATIONS
TOPIC: Admin Cooperation
CONCEPTS: Exchange of official publications. Operating agencies.
PARTIES:
Thailand
USA (United States)

100944   Bilateral Exchange   **73 UNTS 65**
SIGNED: 16 Dec 47   FORCE: 16 Dec 47
REGISTERED: 9 Oct 50 USA (United States)
ARTICLES: 2 LANGUAGE: English.
HEADNOTE: EXCHANGE OFFICIAL PUBLICATIONS
TOPIC: Admin Cooperation
CONCEPTS: Exchange of official publications. Operating agencies. Indemnities and reimbursements.
PARTIES:
Sweden
USA (United States)

100945   Bilateral Exchange   **73 UNTS 73**
SIGNED: 5 Apr 48   FORCE: 5 Apr 48
REGISTERED: 9 Oct 50 USA (United States)
ARTICLES: 2 LANGUAGE: English.
HEADNOTE: EXCHANGE OFFICIAL PUBLICATIONS
TOPIC: Admin Cooperation
CONCEPTS: Exchange of official publications. Operating agencies. Indemnities and reimbursements.
PARTIES:
Burma
USA (United States)

100946   Bilateral Exchange   **73 UNTS 81**
SIGNED: 15 Mar 48   FORCE: 15 Mar 48
REGISTERED: 9 Oct 50 USA (United States)
ARTICLES: 2 LANGUAGE: English.
HEADNOTE: EXCHANGE OFFICIAL PUBLICATIONS
TOPIC: Admin Cooperation
CONCEPTS: Exchange of official publications. Operating agencies. Indemnities and reimbursements.
PARTIES:
Norway
USA (United States)
ANNEX
530 UNTS 346. Norway. Amendment 10 Aug 64. Force 1 Sep 64.

530 UNTS 346. USA (United States). Amendment 11 Aug 64. Force 1 Sep 64.

100947 Bilateral Exchange **73 UNTS 89**
SIGNED: 7 Jun 48 FORCE: 7 Jun 48
REGISTERED: 9 Oct 50 USA (United States)
ARTICLES: 2 LANGUAGE: English.
HEADNOTE: EXCHANGE OFFICIAL PUBLICATIONS
TOPIC: Admin Cooperation
CONCEPTS: Exchange of official publications. Operating agencies. Indemnities and reimbursements.
PARTIES:
Philippines
USA (United States)

100948 Bilateral Exchange **73 UNTS 97**
SIGNED: 16 Nov 49 FORCE: 16 Nov 49
REGISTERED: 9 Oct 50 USA (United States)
ARTICLES: 2 LANGUAGE: English.
HEADNOTE: EXCHANGE OFFICIAL PUBLICATIONS
TOPIC: Admin Cooperation
CONCEPTS: Exchange of official publications. Operating agencies. Indemnities and reimbursements.
PARTIES:
South Africa
USA (United States)

100949 Bilateral Exchange **73 UNTS 106**
SIGNED: 26 Jul 49 FORCE: 26 Jul 49
REGISTERED: 9 Oct 50 USA (United States)
ARTICLES: 2 LANGUAGE: English.
HEADNOTE: EXCHANGE OFFICIAL PUBLICATION
TOPIC: Admin Cooperation
CONCEPTS: Exchange of official publications. Operating agencies. Indemnities and reimbursements.
PARTIES:
Colombia
USA (United States)

100950 Bilateral Agreement **73 UNTS 113**
SIGNED: 6 Feb 48 FORCE: 2 Sep 48
REGISTERED: 9 Oct 50 USA (United States)
ARTICLES: 15 LANGUAGE: English. Italian.
HEADNOTE: AIR TRANSPORT
TOPIC: Air Transport
CONCEPTS: Definition of terms. Exceptions and exemptions. Annex or appendix reference. Previous treaty replacement. Conformity with municipal law. Domestic legislation. Licenses and permits. Recognition of legal documents. Use of facilities. Procedure. Special tribunals. Competence of tribunal. Currency. Fees and exemptions. Most favored nation clause. National treatment. Customs exemptions. Competency certificate. Routes and logistics. Navigational conditions. Permit designation. Airport facilities. Airworthiness certificates. Conditions of airlines operating permission. Operating authorizations and regulations. Licenses and certificates of nationality.
INTL ORGS: International Civil Aviation Organization. Arbitration Commission.
TREATY REF: 15UNTS295.
PROCEDURE: Amendment. Future Procedures Contemplated. Ratification. Registration. Termination.
PARTIES:
Italy
USA (United States)
ANNEX
89 UNTS 394. USA (United States). Amendment 21 Mar 50. Force 24 Mar 50.
89 UNTS 394. Italy. Amendment 24 Mar 50. Force 24 Mar 50.
388 UNTS 338. USA (United States). Amendment 4 Aug 60. Force 4 Aug 60.
388 UNTS 338. Italy. Amendment 4 Aug 60. Force 4 Aug 60.
529 UNTS 314. USA (United States). Interpretation 30 Jun 64. Force 30 Jun 64.
529 UNTS 314. Italy. Interpretation 30 Jun 64. Force 30 Jun 64.

100951 Bilateral Agreement **73 UNTS 143**
SIGNED: 24 Feb 48 FORCE: 24 Feb 48
REGISTERED: 9 Oct 50 USA (United States)
ARTICLES: 14 LANGUAGE: English.
HEADNOTE: USE MILITARY AIR BASES CIVILIAN AIRCRAFT
TOPIC: Milit Installation
CONCEPTS: Annex or appendix reference. Frontier formalities. General cooperation. Inspection and observation. Use of facilities. Investigation of violations. Indemnities and reimbursements. Fees and exemptions. National treatment. Customs duties. Materials, equipment and services. Airport facilities. Overflights and technical stops. Security of information. Bases and facilities.
INTL ORGS: International Civil Aviation Organization.
TREATY REF: 3UNTS253.
PROCEDURE: Amendment. Future Procedures Contemplated. Termination.
PARTIES:
UK Great Britain
USA (United States)

100952 Bilateral Exchange **73 UNTS 179**
SIGNED: 29 Aug 50 FORCE: 29 Aug 50
REGISTERED: 9 Oct 50 Norway
ARTICLES: 2 LANGUAGE: English.
HEADNOTE: COMMERCE
TOPIC: General Trade
CONCEPTS: Detailed regulations. Exceptions and exemptions. Annex or appendix reference. General cooperation. Exchange of information and documents. Licenses and permits. Public information.
INTL ORGS: Organization for Economic Co-operation and Development.
PARTIES:
India
Norway

100953 Bilateral Protocol **73 UNTS 191**
SIGNED: 8 Jul 50 FORCE: 8 Jul 50
REGISTERED: 18 Oct 50 Denmark
ARTICLES: 2 LANGUAGE: Danish. Finnish.
HEADNOTE: EXCHANGE COMMODITIES
TOPIC: General Trade
CONCEPTS: Time limit. Annex or appendix reference. General trade. Export quotas. Import quotas.
PARTIES:
Denmark
Finland

100954 Bilateral Convention **73 UNTS 203**
SIGNED: 15 Oct 48 FORCE: 18 Jul 50
REGISTERED: 23 Oct 50 Netherlands
ARTICLES: 9 LANGUAGE: Dutch. English.
HEADNOTE: DOUBLE TAXATION DUTIES PROPERTY DECEASED PERSONS
TOPIC: Taxation
CONCEPTS: Definition of terms. Territorial application. Claims and settlements. Taxation. Death duties. General.
PROCEDURE: Duration. Ratification. Termination.
PARTIES:
Netherlands
UK Great Britain
ANNEX
126 UNTS 360. Netherlands. Amendment 27 Jun 51. Force 27 Jun 51.
126 UNTS 360. UK Great Britain. Amendment 27 Jun 51. Force 27 Jun 51.

100955 Bilateral Convention **74 UNTS 3**
SIGNED: 15 Oct 48 FORCE: 18 Jul 50
REGISTERED: 23 Oct 50 Netherlands
ARTICLES: 21 LANGUAGE: Dutch. English.
HEADNOTE: DOUBLE TAXATION FISCAL EVASION
TOPIC: Taxation
CONCEPTS: Definition of terms. Territorial application. Exchange of official publications. Wages and salaries. Sickness and invalidity insurance. Taxation. Tax credits. Equitable taxes. General. Tax exemptions. Air transport. Merchant vessels.
PROCEDURE: Duration. Ratification. Termination.
PARTIES:
Netherlands
UK Great Britain

ANNEX
313 UNTS 338. UK Great Britain. Acknowledgement 29 Jul 55. Force 15 Mar 57.
313 UNTS 338. Netherlands. Netherlands Antilles. Force 15 Mar 57.
474 UNTS 306. UK Great Britain. Fed Rhod/ Nyasaland. Force 27 Dec 62.
474 UNTS 306. Netherlands. Acknowledgement 27 Dec 62. Force 27 Dec 62.
560 UNTS 240. UK Great Britain. Northern Rhodesia. Prolongation 7 Dec 63.
560 UNTS 240. UK Great Britain. Southern Rhodesia. Prolongation 7 Dec 63.
560 UNTS 240. Netherlands. Acknowledgement 23 Dec 63.
560 UNTS 240. UK Great Britain. Nyasaland. Prolongation 7 Dec 63.

100956 Bilateral Agreement **74 UNTS 41**
SIGNED: 14 Dec 48 FORCE: 29 Dec 48
REGISTERED: 26 Oct 50 Denmark
ARTICLES: 41 LANGUAGE: Dutch. Spanish.
HEADNOTE: TRADE PAYMENTS
TOPIC: General Economic
CONCEPTS: Definition of terms. Detailed regulations. Conformity with municipal law. General cooperation. Procedure. Negotiation. General trade. Reciprocity in trade. Trade agencies. Trade procedures. Finances and payments. Accounting procedures. Banking. Balance of payments. Currency. Monetary and gold transfers. Exchange rates and regulations. Financial programs. Interest rates. Payment schedules. Non-interest rates and fees. Transportation costs. Local currency. Commodity trade. Navigational conditions. Transport of goods. Water transport.
PROCEDURE: Amendment. Denunciation. Future Procedures Contemplated. Ratification.
PARTIES:
Argentina
Denmark

100957 Multilateral Protocol **74 UNTS 95**
SIGNED: 31 May 50 FORCE: 5 Sep 50
REGISTERED: 26 Oct 50 Denmark
ARTICLES: 6 LANGUAGE: English.
HEADNOTE: JOINT COMMISSION COMMODITIES EXCHANGE PROTOCOL
TOPIC: General Trade
CONCEPTS: Annex or appendix reference. Annex type material. Export quotas. Import quotas. Balance of payments. Quotas.
INTL ORGS: Special Commission.
TREATY REF: 69UNTS.
PARTIES:
Denmark SIGNED: 31 May 50 FORCE: 5 Sep 50
Indonesia SIGNED: 31 May 50 FORCE: 5 Sep 50
Netherlands SIGNED: 31 May 50 FORCE: 5 Sep 50

100958 Bilateral Agreement **74 UNTS 107**
SIGNED: 23 Apr 48 FORCE: 23 Apr 48
REGISTERED: 26 Oct 50 USA (United States)
ARTICLES: 16 LANGUAGE: English. Greek.
HEADNOTE: USE FUNDS CREDIT AGREEMENT
TOPIC: Education
CONCEPTS: Friendship and amity. Operating agencies. Responsibility and liability. Exchange. Commissions and foundations. Professorships. Scholarships and grants. Accounting procedures. Currency. Financial programs. Funding procedures. Transportation costs. Tax exemptions. Surplus property. Credit provisions.
PROCEDURE: Amendment.
PARTIES:
Greece
USA (United States)
ANNEX
223 UNTS 320. Greece. Amendment 13 Apr 54. Force 13 Apr 54.
223 UNTS 320. USA (United States). Amendment 16 Mar 51. Force 13 Apr 54.
223 UNTS 322. Greece. Amendment 28 Jun 54. Force 28 Jun 54.
223 UNTS 322. USA (United States). Amendment 28 Jun 54. Force 28 Jun 54.
232 UNTS 322. Greece. Amendment 28 Jun 54. Force 28 Jun 54.
232 UNTS 322. USA (United States). Amendment 28 Jun 54. Force 28 Jun 54.

261 UNTS 392. Greece. Amendment 4 Jun 55. Force 4 Jun 55.

261 UNTS 392. USA (United States). Amendment 12 Mar 55. Force 4 Jun 55.

406 UNTS 292. USA (United States). Amendment 23 Jan 59. Force 22 Nov 60.

406 UNTS 292. Greece. Amendment 22 Nov 60. Force 22 Nov 60.

100959 Bilateral Agreement **74 UNTS 131**
SIGNED: 9 May 47   FORCE: 28 Jan 48
REGISTERED: 31 Oct 50 Denmark
ARTICLES: 9 LANGUAGE: French.
HEADNOTE: COMMERCIAL EXCHANGES
TOPIC: General Trade
CONCEPTS: Detailed regulations. Treaty implementation. Annex or appendix reference. General cooperation. Licenses and permits. Currency. Payment schedules. Most favored nation clause.
INTL ORGS: Special Commission.
PROCEDURE: Denunciation. Duration.
PARTIES:
  Bulgaria
  Denmark

100960 Bilateral Agreement **74 UNTS 139**
SIGNED: 9 May 47   FORCE: 28 Jan 48
REGISTERED: 31 Oct 50 Denmark
ARTICLES: 10 LANGUAGE: French.
HEADNOTE: REGULATION PAYMENTS
TOPIC: Finance
CONCEPTS: Detailed regulations. Annex type material. General cooperation. Accounting procedures. Banking. Balance of payments. Currency. Currency deposits. Exchange rates and regulations. Interest rates. Payment schedules.
TREATY REF: 74UNTS131.
PARTIES:
  Bulgaria
  Denmark

100961 Bilateral Agreement **74 UNTS 147**
SIGNED: 17 Dec 49   FORCE: 17 Dec 49
REGISTERED: 31 Oct 50 Denmark
ARTICLES: 7 LANGUAGE: French.
HEADNOTE: COMMERCIAL EXCHANGES
TOPIC: General Trade
CONCEPTS: Detailed regulations. Exceptions and exemptions. Annex or appendix reference. Previous treaty replacement. General cooperation. Licenses and permits. Establishment of commission. Import quotas. Payment schedules. Quotas.
INTL ORGS: Special Commission.
TREATY REF: 23LTS139.
PROCEDURE: Denunciation. Duration.
PARTIES:
  Czechoslovakia
  Denmark

100962 Bilateral Agreement **74 UNTS 159**
SIGNED: 17 Dec 49   FORCE: 17 Dec 49
REGISTERED: 31 Oct 50 Denmark
ARTICLES: 6 LANGUAGE: French.
HEADNOTE: REGULATION PAYMENTS
TOPIC: Finance
CONCEPTS: Previous treaty replacement. General cooperation. Bonds. Balance of payments. Monetary and gold transfers. Exchange rates and regulations. Interest rates. Payment schedules. Local currency.
TREATY REF: 27NOV45 PAYMENT REGULATION.
PROCEDURE: Amendment. Denunciation. Duration. Renewal or Revival.
PARTIES:
  Czechoslovakia
  Denmark
          ANNEX
133 UNTS 362. Denmark. Amendment 4 Apr 52. Force 20 May 52.
133 UNTS 362. Czechoslovakia. Amendment 4 Apr 52. Force 20 May 52.

100963 Bilateral Agreement **74 UNTS 167**
SIGNED: 17 Feb 49   FORCE: 1 Dec 49
REGISTERED: 1 Nov 50 USA (United States)
ARTICLES: 23 LANGUAGE: English. Korean.
HEADNOTE: PARCEL POST
TOPIC: Postal Service

CONCEPTS: Conformity with municipal law. Customs duties. Customs declarations. Postal services. Regulations. Conveyance in transit. Parcel post. Rates and charges.
PROCEDURE: Termination.
PARTIES:
  Korea, South
  USA (United States)

100964 Bilateral Agreement **74 UNTS 209**
SIGNED: 8 Apr 49   FORCE: 8 Apr 49
REGISTERED: 1 Nov 50 Denmark
ARTICLES: 6 LANGUAGE: French.
HEADNOTE: TRADE
TOPIC: General Trade
CONCEPTS: Previous treaty replacement. General cooperation. Licenses and permits. Payment schedules. Quotas.
TREATY REF: 25DEMARTENS474.
PROCEDURE: Duration.
PARTIES:
  Denmark
  Portugal

100965 Bilateral Agreement **74 UNTS 221**
SIGNED: 8 Apr 49   FORCE: 8 Apr 49
REGISTERED: 1 Nov 50 Denmark
ARTICLES: 9 LANGUAGE: French.
HEADNOTE: REGULATING PAYMENTS
TOPIC: Finance
CONCEPTS: Definition of terms. General cooperation. Accounting procedures. Banking. Balance of payments. Currency. Exchange rates and regulations. Interest rates. Payment schedules.
PROCEDURE: Amendment. Denunciation.
PARTIES:
  Denmark
  Portugal

100966 Bilateral Agreement **74 UNTS 229**
SIGNED: 2 Jun 50   FORCE: 2 Jun 50
REGISTERED: 1 Nov 50 Denmark
ARTICLES: 6 LANGUAGE: French.
HEADNOTE: TRADE
TOPIC: General Trade
CONCEPTS: Annex or appendix reference. General cooperation. Licenses and permits. Payment schedules. Quotas.
PROCEDURE: Denunciation. Duration.
PARTIES:
  Denmark
  Portugal

100967 Bilateral Agreement **74 UNTS 243**
SIGNED: 29 Nov 48   FORCE: 29 Nov 48
REGISTERED: 1 Nov 50 Denmark
ARTICLES: 10 LANGUAGE: German.
HEADNOTE: TRADE
TOPIC: General Trade
CONCEPTS: Detailed regulations. Annex or appendix reference. Licenses and permits. Establishment of commission. Trade procedures. Payment schedules.
INTL ORGS: Special Commission.
PROCEDURE: Denunciation. Duration.
PARTIES:
  Austria
  Denmark
          ANNEX
135 UNTS 356. Denmark. Supplementation 14 May 52. Force 23 Feb 52.
135 UNTS 356. Austria. Supplementation 14 May 52. Force 23 Feb 52.

100968 Bilateral Agreement **74 UNTS 257**
SIGNED: 29 Nov 48   FORCE: 29 Nov 48
REGISTERED: 1 Nov 50 Denmark
ARTICLES: 10 LANGUAGE: German.
HEADNOTE: REGULATING PAYMENTS
TOPIC: Finance
CONCEPTS: Detailed regulations. General cooperation. Accounting procedures. Balance of payments. Currency. Interest rates. Payment schedules. Local currency.
PROCEDURE: Denunciation. Duration. Renewal or Revival.
PARTIES:
  Austria
  Denmark

100969 Bilateral Protocol **74 UNTS 269**
SIGNED: 23 Feb 50   FORCE: 23 Feb 50
REGISTERED: 1 Nov 50 Denmark
ARTICLES: 9 LANGUAGE: German.
HEADNOTE: TRADE PAYMENTS JOINT COMMISSION
TOPIC: General Trade
CONCEPTS: Detailed regulations. General provisions. Annex or appendix reference. Annex type material. Tourism. Licenses and permits. Free trade. Trade procedures. Balance of payments. Financial programs. Quotas. Most favored nation clause.
INTL ORGS: Organization for Economic Co-operation and Development. Special Commission.
TREATY REF: 74UNTS243.
PROCEDURE: Duration.
PARTIES:
  Austria
  Denmark
          ANNEX
98 UNTS 280. Denmark. Interpretation 17 Apr 51. Force 22 May 51.
98 UNTS 280. Austria. Interpretation 17 Apr 51. Force 22 May 51.
98 UNTS 286. Denmark. Amendment 17 Apr 51. Force 22 May 51.
98 UNTS 286. Austria. Amendment 17 Apr 51. Force 22 May 51.

100970 Multilateral Convention **75 UNTS 31**
SIGNED: 12 Aug 49   FORCE: 21 Oct 50
REGISTERED: 2 Nov 50 Switzerland
ARTICLES: 64 LANGUAGE: English. French.
HEADNOTE: TREATMENT SICK & WOUNDED IN WAR
TOPIC: Humanitarian
CONCEPTS: Detailed regulations. Previous treaty extension. Previous treaty replacement. Non-prejudice to third party. Assistance. Repatriation of nationals. Human rights. Privileges and immunities. Exchange of information and documents. Informational records. Legal protection and assistance. General property. Responsibility and liability. Investigation of violations. Dispute settlement. Disease control. Public health. Humanitarian matters. Registration certificate. Air transport. Overflights and technical stops. Prisoners of war. Responsibility for war dead. Upkeep of war graves. Special status.
INTL ORGS: International Committee of the Red Cross. United Nations.
TREATY REF: 75UNTS135; 55BFSP43; 100BFSP415.
PROCEDURE: Accession. Denunciation. Ratification.
PARTIES:
  Afghanistan SIGNED: 12 Aug 49
  Albania SIGNED: 12 Aug 49
  Argentina SIGNED: 12 Aug 49
  Australia SIGNED: 12 Aug 49
  Austria SIGNED: 12 Aug 49
  Belgium SIGNED: 12 Aug 49
  Bolivia SIGNED: 12 Aug 49
  Brazil SIGNED: 12 Aug 49
  Bulgaria SIGNED: 12 Aug 49
  Byelorussia SIGNED: 12 Aug 49
  Canada SIGNED: 12 Aug 49
  Ceylon (Sri Lanka) SIGNED: 12 Aug 49
  Chile SIGNED: 12 Aug 49
  Taiwan SIGNED: 12 Aug 49
  Colombia SIGNED: 12 Aug 49
  Cuba SIGNED: 12 Aug 49
  Czechoslovakia SIGNED: 12 Aug 49
  Denmark SIGNED: 12 Aug 49
  Ecuador SIGNED: 12 Aug 49
  United Arab Rep SIGNED: 12 Aug 49
  El Salvador SIGNED: 12 Aug 49
  Ethiopia SIGNED: 12 Aug 49
  Finland SIGNED: 12 Aug 49
  France SIGNED: 12 Aug 49
  Greece SIGNED: 12 Aug 49
  Guatemala SIGNED: 12 Aug 49
  Hungary SIGNED: 12 Aug 49
  India SIGNED: 12 Aug 49
  Iran SIGNED: 12 Aug 49
  Ireland SIGNED: 12 Aug 49
  Israel SIGNED: 12 Aug 49
  Italy SIGNED: 12 Aug 49
  Lebanon SIGNED: 12 Aug 49
  Liechtenstein SIGNED: 12 Aug 49 RATIFIED: 21 Sep 50 FORCE: 21 Mar 51
  Luxembourg SIGNED: 12 Aug 49

Mexico SIGNED: 12 Aug 49
Monaco SIGNED: 12 Aug 49 RATIFIED: 5 Jul 50
  FORCE: 5 Jan 51
Netherlands SIGNED: 12 Aug 49
New Zealand SIGNED: 12 Aug 49
Nicaragua SIGNED: 12 Aug 49
Norway SIGNED: 12 Aug 49
Pakistan SIGNED: 12 Aug 49
Paraguay SIGNED: 12 Aug 49
Peru SIGNED: 12 Aug 49
Philippines SIGNED: 12 Aug 49
Poland SIGNED: 12 Aug 49
Portugal SIGNED: 12 Aug 49
Romania SIGNED: 12 Aug 49
Spain SIGNED. 12 Aug 49
Sweden SIGNED: 12 Aug 49
Switzerland SIGNED: 12 Aug 49 RATIFIED:
  31 Mar 50 FORCE: 21 Oct 50
Syria SIGNED: 12 Aug 49
Turkey SIGNED: 12 Aug 49
UK Great Britain SIGNED: 12 Aug 49
USA (United States) SIGNED: 12 Aug 49
Ukrainian SSR SIGNED: 12 Aug 49
Uruguay SIGNED: 12 Aug 49
USSR (Soviet Union) SIGNED: 12 Aug 49
Vatican/Holy See SIGNED: 12 Aug 49
Venezuela SIGNED: 12 Aug 49
Yugoslavia SIGNED: 12 Aug 49 RATIFIED:
  21 Apr 50 FORCE: 21 Oct 50
             ANNEX
78 UNTS 365.
84 UNTS 413.
87 UNTS 394.
91 UNTS 378.
94 UNTS 323.
96 UNTS 323.
100 UNTS 293.
105 UNTS 303.
120 UNTS 298.
128 UNTS 307.
131 UNTS 332.
139 UNTS 459.
149 UNTS 409.
150 UNTS 369.
165 UNTS 326.
167 UNTS 295.
171 UNTS 415.
173 UNTS 397.
180 UNTS 301.
181 UNTS 349.
184 UNTS 337.
191 UNTS 365.
198 UNTS 384.
199 UNTS 329.
202 UNTS 330.
207 UNTS 344.
213 UNTS 378.
230 UNTS 431.
247 UNTS 388.
248 UNTS 362.
251 UNTS 372.
253 UNTS 337.
257 UNTS 364.
260 UNTS 438.
264 UNTS 333.
267 UNTS 371.
269 UNTS 283.
270 UNTS 374.
274 UNTS 335.
278 UNTS 259.
286 UNTS 337.
310 UNTS 336.
314 UNTS 330.
320 UNTS 334.
328 UNTS 305.
330 UNTS 354.
392 UNTS 339.
394 UNTS 255.
404 UNTS 322.
421 UNTS 292.
423 UNTS 300.
445 UNTS 313.
470 UNTS 374.
478 UNTS 414.
480 UNTS 320.
492 UNTS 342.
502 UNTS 364.
503 UNTS 328.
511 UNTS 266.
535 UNTS 408.
538 UNTS 330.
540 UNTS 332.
544 UNTS 286.
547 UNTS 314.

562 UNTS 324.
573 UNTS 304.
600 UNTS 328. Congo (Brazzaville). Succession
  30 Jan 67.
608 UNTS 353.
609 UNTS 253.
639 UNTS 328.
645 UNTS 344.
653 UNTS 452.

100971 Multilateral Convention **75 UNTS 85**
SIGNED: 12 Aug 49   FORCE: 21 Oct 50
REGISTERED: 2 Nov 50 Switzerland
ARTICLES: 63 LANGUAGE: English. French.
HEADNOTE: TREATMENT WOUNDED SHIP-
  WRECKED SAILORS
TOPIC: Humanitarian
CONCEPTS: Definition of terms. Detailed regulations. Previous treaty extension. Non-prejudice
  to third party. Repatriation of nationals. Human
  rights. Privileges and immunities. Non-
  diplomatic delegations. General cooperation. In-
  formational records. Inspection and observation.
  Legal protection and assistance. Personnel. Re-
  sponsibility and liability. Investigation of viola-
  tions. Dispute settlement. Public health. Human-
  itarian matters. Registration certificate. Routes
  and logistics. Overflights and technical stops.
  Water transport. Prisoners of war. Naval vessels.
  Foreign nationals. Responsibility for war dead.
  Upkeep of war graves. Special status.
INTL ORGS: International Committee of the Red
  Cross. United Nations.
TREATY REF: 100BFSP415;   75UNTS31;
  55BFSP43.
PROCEDURE: Accession. Denunciation. Ratifica-
  tion.
PARTIES:
  Afghanistan SIGNED: 12 Aug 49
  Albania SIGNED: 12 Aug 49
  Argentina SIGNED: 12 Aug 49
  Australia SIGNED: 12 Aug 49
  Austria SIGNED: 12 Aug 49
  Belgium SIGNED: 12 Aug 49
  Bolivia SIGNED: 12 Aug 49
  Brazil SIGNED: 12 Aug 49
  Bulgaria SIGNED: 12 Aug 49
  Byelorussia SIGNED: 12 Aug 49
  Canada SIGNED: 12 Aug 49
  Ceylon (Sri Lanka) SIGNED: 12 Aug 49
  Chile SIGNED: 12 Aug 49
  Taiwan SIGNED: 12 Aug 49
  Colombia SIGNED: 12 Aug 49
  Cuba SIGNED: 12 Aug 49
  Czechoslovakia SIGNED: 12 Aug 49
  Denmark SIGNED: 12 Aug 49
  Ecuador SIGNED: 12 Aug 49
  El Salvador SIGNED: 12 Aug 49
  Ethiopia SIGNED: 12 Aug 49
  Finland SIGNED: 12 Aug 49
  France SIGNED: 12 Aug 49
  Greece SIGNED: 12 Aug 49
  Guatemala SIGNED: 12 Aug 49
  Hungary SIGNED: 12 Aug 49
  India SIGNED: 12 Aug 49
  Iran SIGNED: 12 Aug 49
  Ireland SIGNED: 12 Aug 49
  Israel SIGNED: 12 Aug 49
  Italy SIGNED: 12 Aug 49
  Lebanon SIGNED: 12 Aug 49
  Liechtenstein SIGNED: 12 Aug 49 RATIFIED:
    21 Sep 50 FORCE: 21 Mar 51
  Luxembourg SIGNED: 12 Aug 49
  Mexico SIGNED: 12 Aug 49
  Monaco SIGNED: 12 Aug 49 RATIFIED: 5 Jul 50
    FORCE: 5 Jan 51
  Netherlands SIGNED: 12 Aug 49
  New Zealand SIGNED: 12 Aug 49
  Nicaragua SIGNED: 12 Aug 49
  Norway SIGNED: 12 Aug 49
  Pakistan SIGNED: 12 Aug 49
  Paraguay SIGNED: 12 Aug 49
  Peru SIGNED: 12 Aug 49
  Philippines SIGNED: 12 Aug 49
  Poland SIGNED: 12 Aug 49
  Portugal SIGNED: 12 Aug 49
  Romania SIGNED: 12 Aug 49
  Spain SIGNED: 12 Aug 49
  Sweden SIGNED: 12 Aug 49
  Switzerland SIGNED: 12 Aug 49 RATIFIED:
    31 Mar 50 FORCE: 21 Oct 50
  Syria SIGNED: 12 Aug 49
  Turkey SIGNED: 12 Aug 49

United Arab Rep SIGNED: 12 Aug 49
UK Great Britain SIGNED: 12 Aug 49
USA (United States) SIGNED: 12 Aug 49
Ukrainian SSR SIGNED: 12 Aug 49
Uruguay SIGNED: 12 Aug 49
USSR (Soviet Union) SIGNED: 12 Aug 49
Vatican/Holy See SIGNED: 12 Aug 49
Venezuela SIGNED: 12 Aug 49
Yugoslavia SIGNED: 12 Aug 49   RATIFIED:
  21 Apr 50 FORCE: 21 Oct 50
             ANNEX
84 UNTS 414.
87 UNTS 394.
91 UNTS 379.
96 UNTS 324.
100 UNTS 294.
120 UNTS 299.
128 UNTS 307.
131 UNTS 333.
139 UNTS 460.
141 UNTS 383.
149 UNTS 410.
150 UNTS 370.
165 UNTS 327.
167 UNTS 296.
171 UNTS 416.
173 UNTS 398.
180 UNTS 302.
181 UNTS 350.
184 UNTS 338.
191 UNTS 366.
198 UNTS 386.
199 UNTS 330.
202 UNTS 331.
207 UNTS 345.
213 UNTS 382.
230 UNTS 431.
247 UNTS 389.
248 UNTS 363.
253 UNTS 338.
257 UNTS 366.
260 UNTS 440.
264 UNTS 334.
267 UNTS 372.
269 UNTS 284.
270 UNTS 375.
274 UNTS 337.
278 UNTS 260.
286 UNTS 338.
310 UNTS 337.
314 UNTS 331.
320 UNTS 335.
328 UNTS 306.
330 UNTS 355.
392 UNTS 340.
394 UNTS 256.
404 UNTS 323.
421 UNTS 294.
423 UNTS 301.
445 UNTS 315.
470 UNTS 376.
478 UNTS 416.
480 UNTS 322.
492 UNTS 343.
502 UNTS 366.
503 UNTS 329.
511 UNTS 266.
535 UNTS 408.
538 UNTS 331.
540 UNTS 332.
544 UNTS 286.
547 UNTS 314.
562 UNTS 324.
573 UNTS 304.
600 UNTS 328. Congo (Brazzaville). Succession
  30 Jan 67.
608 UNTS 353.
609 UNTS 253.
639 UNTS 325.
645 UNTS 344.
653 UNTS 452.

100972 Multilateral Convention **75 UNTS 135**
SIGNED: 12 Aug 49   FORCE: 21 Oct 50
REGISTERED: 2 Nov 50 Switzerland
ARTICLES: 143 LANGUAGE: English. French.
HEADNOTE: TREATMENT PRISONERS OF WAR
TOPIC: General Military
CONCEPTS: Prisoners of war. Repatriation of civil-
  ians. Ranks and privileges. Jurisdiction. Repara-
  tions and restrictions. Responsibility for war
  dead. Establishment of war cemeteries.

INTL ORGS: International Committee of the Red
Cross. United Nations.
PARTIES:
  Afghanistan SIGNED: 12 Aug 49
  Albania SIGNED: 12 Aug 49
  Argentina SIGNED: 12 Aug 49
  Australia SIGNED: 12 Aug 49
  Austria SIGNED: 12 Aug 49
  Belgium SIGNED: 12 Aug 49
  Bolivia SIGNED: 12 Aug 49
  Brazil SIGNED: 12 Aug 49
  Bulgaria SIGNED: 12 Aug 49
  Byelorussia SIGNED: 12 Aug 49
  Canada SIGNED: 12 Aug 49
  Ceylon (Sri Lanka) SIGNED: 12 Aug 49
  Chile SIGNED: 12 Aug 49
  Taiwan SIGNED: 12 Aug 49
  Colombia SIGNED: 12 Aug 49
  Cuba SIGNED: 12 Aug 49
  Czechoslovakia SIGNED: 12 Aug 49
  Denmark SIGNED: 12 Aug 49
  Ecuador SIGNED: 12 Aug 49
  United Arab Rep SIGNED: 12 Aug 49
  El Salvador SIGNED: 12 Aug 49
  Ethiopia SIGNED: 12 Aug 49
  Finland SIGNED: 12 Aug 49
  France SIGNED: 12 Aug 49
  Greece SIGNED: 12 Aug 49
  Guatemala SIGNED: 12 Aug 49
  Hungary SIGNED: 12 Aug 49
  India SIGNED: 12 Aug 49
  Iran SIGNED: 12 Aug 49
  Ireland SIGNED: 12 Aug 49
  Israel SIGNED: 12 Aug 49
  Italy SIGNED: 12 Aug 49
  Lebanon SIGNED: 12 Aug 49
  Liechtenstein SIGNED: 12 Aug 49 RATIFIED:
    21 Sep 50 FORCE: 21 Mar 51
  Luxembourg SIGNED: 12 Aug 49
  Mexico SIGNED: 12 Aug 49 RATIFIED: 5 Jul 50
    FORCE: 5 Jan 51
  Netherlands SIGNED: 12 Aug 49
  New Zealand SIGNED: 12 Aug 49
  Nicaragua SIGNED: 12 Aug 49
  Norway SIGNED: 12 Aug 49
  Pakistan SIGNED: 12 Aug 49
  Paraguay SIGNED: 12 Aug 49
  Peru SIGNED: 12 Aug 49
  Philippines SIGNED: 12 Aug 49
  Poland SIGNED: 12 Aug 49
  Portugal SIGNED: 12 Aug 49
  Romania SIGNED: 12 Aug 49
  Spain SIGNED: 12 Aug 49
  Sweden   SIGNED: 12 Aug 49   RATIFIED:
    31 Mar 50 FORCE: 21 Oct 50
  Switzerland SIGNED: 12 Aug 49
  Syria SIGNED: 12 Aug 49
  Turkey SIGNED: 12 Aug 49
  UK Great Britain SIGNED: 12 Aug 49
  USA (United States) SIGNED: 12 Aug 49
  Ukrainian SSR SIGNED: 12 Aug 49
  Uruguay SIGNED: 12 Aug 49
  USSR (Soviet Union) SIGNED: 12 Aug 49
  Vatican/Holy See SIGNED: 12 Aug 49
  Venezuela SIGNED: 12 Aug 49
  Yugoslavia SIGNED: 12 Aug 49 RATIFIED:
    21 Apr 50 FORCE: 21 Oct 50
              ANNEX
84 UNTS 415.
87 UNTS 395.
91 UNTS 380.
96 UNTS 325.
100 UNTS 294.
120 UNTS 299.
128 UNTS 308.
131 UNTS 333.
139 UNTS 461.
141 UNTS 384.
149 UNTS 410.
150 UNTS 371.
165 UNTS 328.
167 UNTS 297.
171 UNTS 417.
173 UNTS 399.
180 UNTS 303.
181 UNTS 351.
184 UNTS 339.
191 UNTS 367.
198 UNTS 388.
199 UNTS 331.
202 UNTS 332.
207 UNTS 346.
213 UNTS 383.
230 UNTS 432.

247 UNTS 390.
248 UNTS 364.
251 UNTS 374.
253 UNTS 339.
257 UNTS 368.
260 UNTS 442.
264 UNTS 335.
267 UNTS 373.
269 UNTS 285.
270 UNTS 376.
274 UNTS 339.
278 UNTS 261.
286 UNTS 339.
310 UNTS 338.
314 UNTS 332.
320 UNTS 336.
328 UNTS 307.
330 UNTS 356.
392 UNTS 341.
394 UNTS 257.
404 UNTS 324.
421 UNTS 296.
423 UNTS 302.
445 UNTS 316.
470 UNTS 378.
478 UNTS 418.
480 UNTS 324.
492 UNTS 344.
502 UNTS 367.
503 UNTS 330.
511 UNTS 266.
535 UNTS 408.
538 UNTS 332.
540 UNTS 332.
544 UNTS 286.
547 UNTS 314.
562 UNTS 324.
573 UNTS 304.
600 UNTS 328. Congo (Brazzaville). Succession
  30 Jan 67.
608 UNTS 354.
609 UNTS 253.
639 UNTS 328.
645 UNTS 344.
653 UNTS 454.

100973 Multilateral Convention **75 UNTS 287**
SIGNED: 12 Aug 49   FORCE: 21 Oct 50
REGISTERED: 2 Nov 50 Switzerland
ARTICLES: 159 LANGUAGE: English. French.
HEADNOTE: PROTECTION CIVILIANS TIME WAR
TOPIC: Humanitarian
CONCEPTS: Detailed regulations. Treaty implementation. Previous treaty extension. Repatriation of nationals. Democratic institutions. Alien
  status. Privileges and immunities. Court procedures. Information centers. Exchange of official
  publications. Exchange of information and documents. Informational records. Inspection and observation. Domestic legislation. Personnel. General property. Succession. Jurisdiction. Investigation of violations. Dispute settlement. Public
  health. Sanitation. Humanitarian matters. General transportation. Postal services. Burial arrangements. Repatriation of combatants. Prisoners of war. Repatriation of civilians. Status of
  forces. Responsibility for war dead. Upkeep of
  war graves.
INTL ORGS: International Committee of the Red
  Cross. United Nations.
TREATY REF: 75UNTS31,85,135; 2'27DM949;
  3'3DM461;;V.
PROCEDURE: Accession. Ratification.
PARTIES:
  Afghanistan SIGNED: 12 Aug 49
  Albania SIGNED: 12 Aug 49
  Argentina SIGNED: 12 Aug 49
  Australia SIGNED: 12 Aug 49
  Austria SIGNED: 12 Aug 49
  Belgium SIGNED: 12 Aug 49
  Bolivia SIGNED: 12 Aug 49
  Brazil SIGNED: 12 Aug 49
  Bulgaria SIGNED: 12 Aug 49
  Byelorussia SIGNED: 12 Aug 49
  Canada SIGNED: 12 Aug 49
  Chile SIGNED: 12 Aug 49
  Taiwan SIGNED: 12 Aug 49
  Colombia SIGNED: 12 Aug 49
  Cuba SIGNED: 12 Aug 49
  Czechoslovakia SIGNED: 12 Aug 49
  Denmark SIGNED: 12 Aug 49
  Ecuador SIGNED: 12 Aug 49
  United Arab Rep SIGNED: 12 Aug 49

  El Salvador SIGNED: 12 Aug 49
  Ethiopia SIGNED: 12 Aug 49
  Finland SIGNED: 12 Aug 49
  France SIGNED: 12 Aug 49
  Greece SIGNED: 12 Aug 49
  Guatemala SIGNED: 12 Aug 49
  Hungary SIGNED: 12 Aug 49
  India SIGNED: 12 Aug 49
  Iran SIGNED: 12 Aug 49
  Ireland SIGNED: 12 Aug 49
  Israel SIGNED: 12 Aug 49
  Italy SIGNED: 12 Aug 49
  Lebanon SIGNED: 12 Aug 49
  Liechtenstein SIGNED: 12 Aug 49 RATIFIED:
    21 Sep 50 FORCE: 21 Mar 50
  Luxembourg SIGNED: 12 Aug 49
  Mexico SIGNED: 12 Aug 49
  Monaco SIGNED: 12 Aug 49 RATIFIED: 5 Jul 50
    FORCE: 5 Jan 51
  Netherlands SIGNED: 12 Aug 49
  New Zealand SIGNED: 12 Aug 49
  Nicaragua SIGNED: 12 Aug 49
  Norway SIGNED: 12 Aug 49
  Pakistan SIGNED: 12 Aug 49
  Paraguay SIGNED: 12 Aug 49
  Peru SIGNED: 12 Aug 49
  Philippines SIGNED: 12 Aug 49
  Poland SIGNED: 12 Aug 49
  Portugal SIGNED: 12 Aug 49
  Romania SIGNED: 12 Aug 49
  Spain SIGNED: 12 Aug 49
  Sweden SIGNED: 12 Aug 49
  Switzerland SIGNED: 12 Aug 49 RATIFIED:
    31 Mar 50 FORCE: 21 Oct 50
  Syria SIGNED: 12 Aug 49
  Turkey SIGNED: 12 Aug 49
  UK Great Britain SIGNED: 12 Aug 49
  USA (United States) SIGNED: 12 Aug 49
  Ukrainian SSR SIGNED: 12 Aug 49
  Uruguay SIGNED: 12 Aug 49
  USSR (Soviet Union) SIGNED: 12 Aug 49
  Vatican/Holy See SIGNED: 12 Aug 49
  Venezuela SIGNED: 12 Aug 49
  Yugoslavia SIGNED: 12 Aug 49 RATIFIED:
    21 Apr 50 FORCE: 21 Oct 50
              ANNEX
78 UNTS 368.
84 UNTS 416.
87 UNTS 395.
91 UNTS 381.
96 UNTS 326.
100 UNTS 295.
120 UNTS 300.
128 UNTS 308.
131 UNTS 333.
139 UNTS 462.
141 UNTS 385.
149 UNTS 411.
150 UNTS 372.
165 UNTS 329.
167 UNTS 298.
171 UNTS 418.
173 UNTS 400.
180 UNTS 304.
181 UNTS 352.
184 UNTS 340.
191 UNTS 368.
198 UNTS 390.
199 UNTS 332.
202 UNTS 333.
213 UNTS 384.
230 UNTS 433.
247 UNTS 391.
248 UNTS 365.
251 UNTS 375.
253 UNTS 340.
257 UNTS 370.
260 UNTS 444.
264 UNTS 336.
267 UNTS 374.
269 UNTS 286.
270 UNTS 377.
274 UNTS 341.
278 UNTS 262.
286 UNTS 340.
310 UNTS 339.
314 UNTS 333.
320 UNTS 337.
328 UNTS 308.
330 UNTS 357.
392 UNTS 342.
394 UNTS 258.
404 UNTS 325.
421 UNTS 298.

423 UNTS 303.
445 UNTS 317.
470 UNTS 380.
478 UNTS 420.
480 UNTS 326.
492 UNTS 345.
502 UNTS 368.
503 UNTS 331.
511 UNTS 266.
535 UNTS 408.
538 UNTS 333.
540 UNTS 332.
544 UNTS 286.
547 UNTS 314.
562 UNTS 324.
573 UNTS 304.
600 UNTS 328. Congo (Brazzaville). Succession
30 Jan 67.
608 UNTS 354.
609 UNTS 253.
639 UNTS 328.
645 UNTS 344.
653 UNTS 454.

100974   Bilateral Agreement   **76 UNTS 3**
SIGNED: 15 Dec 48   FORCE: 1 Jan 49
REGISTERED: 9 Nov 50 Denmark
ARTICLES: 10 LANGUAGE: French.
HEADNOTE: PAYMENTS
TOPIC: Finance
CONCEPTS: Detailed regulations. Conformity with
municipal law. General cooperation. Accounting
procedures. Banking. Balance of payments. Cur-
rency. Monetary and gold transfers. Currency de-
posits. Exchange rates and regulations. Payment
schedules.
TREATY REF: 76UNTS17.
PROCEDURE: Duration.
PARTIES:
Denmark
Turkey

100975   Bilateral Agreement   **76 UNTS 17**
SIGNED: 15 Dec 48   FORCE: 1 Jan 49
REGISTERED: 9 Nov 50 Denmark
ARTICLES: 7 LANGUAGE: French.
HEADNOTE: COMMERCE
TOPIC: General Trade
CONCEPTS: Exceptions and exemptions. General
provisions. Annex or appendix reference. Infor-
mational records. Licenses and permits. Export
quotas. Import quotas. Payment schedules.
TREATY REF: 76UNTS3.
PROCEDURE: Denunciation. Duration. Renewal or
Revival.
PARTIES:
Denmark
Turkey

100976   Bilateral Agreement   **76 UNTS 23**
SIGNED: 4 Aug 47   FORCE: 4 Aug 47
REGISTERED: 10 Nov 50 Belgium
ARTICLES: 17 LANGUAGE: English.
HEADNOTE: MONEY PROPERTY
TOPIC: Reparations
CONCEPTS: Definition of terms. Currency. Assets
transfer. Loss and/or damage. Post-war claims
settlement.
PROCEDURE: Future Procedures Contemplated.
PARTIES:
Belgium
India

100977   Bilateral Exchange   **76 UNTS 41**
SIGNED: 30 Oct 47   FORCE: 1 Jan 48
REGISTERED: 13 Nov 50 Netherlands
ARTICLES: 2 LANGUAGE: English.
HEADNOTE: SUPPLEMENTARY AGREEMENT TA-
RIFFS TRADE
TOPIC: General Economic
CONCEPTS: Annex type material.
TREATY REF: 55UNTS194; 185LTS329; GATT.
PARTIES:
Netherlands
New Zealand

100978   Bilateral Agreement   **76 UNTS 47**
SIGNED: 30 Oct 47   FORCE: 1 Jan 48
REGISTERED: 13 Nov 50 Netherlands

ARTICLES: 1 LANGUAGE: English.
HEADNOTE: SUPPLEMENTARY AGREEMENT TA-
RIFFS TRADE
TOPIC: General Economic
CONCEPTS: Treaty interpretation. Annex type ma-
terial.
INTL ORGS: United Nations.
TREATY REF: 55UNTS194,308,188; 188LTS239.
PROCEDURE: Termination.
PARTIES:
Netherlands
USA (United States)

100979   Bilateral Agreement   **76 UNTS 55**
SIGNED: 20 Jun 50   FORCE: 20 Jun 50
REGISTERED: 15 Nov 50 Netherlands
ARTICLES: 3 LANGUAGE: English.
HEADNOTE: CARE GIVEN FORTY REFUGEES
TOPIC: Refugees
CONCEPTS: Assistance. Sickness and invalidity in-
surance. Funding procedures.
INTL ORGS: United Nations.
PARTIES:
Netherlands
IRO (Refugee Org)
                    ANNEX
87 UNTS 396. IRO (Refugee Org). Amendment
12 Feb 51. Force 12 Feb 51.
87 UNTS 396.   Netherlands.   Amendment
12 Feb 51. Force 12 Feb 51.

100980   Bilateral Agreement   **76 UNTS 61**
SIGNED: 5 May 47   FORCE: 8 Mar 49
REGISTERED: 17 Nov 50 ICAO (Civil Aviat)
ARTICLES: 14 LANGUAGE: French. Greek.
HEADNOTE: AIR TRANSPORT
TOPIC: Air Transport
CONCEPTS: Exceptions and exemptions. Annex or
appendix reference. Previous treaty replacement. Conformity with municipal law. General
cooperation. Licenses and permits. Recognition
of legal documents. Use of facilities. Arbitration.
Procedure. Existing tribunals. Negotiation. Reexport of goods, etc.. Fees and exemptions. Most
favored nation clause. National treatment. Customs exemptions. Competency certificate.
Routes and logistics. Navigational conditions.
Permit designation. Airport facilities. Airworthiness certificates. Conditions of airlines operating permission. Operating authorizations and
regulations. Licenses and certificates of nation-
ality.
INTL ORGS: International Civil Aviation Organiza-
tion.
TREATY REF: US DEPT. OF STATE PUB. 2282 SE-
RIES 64; 131LTS201.
PROCEDURE: Amendment. Denunciation. Future
Procedures Contemplated. Ratification. Registra-
tion.
PARTIES:
France
Greece

100981   Bilateral Exchange   **76 UNTS 85**
SIGNED: 15 Mar 50   FORCE: 15 Jul 50
REGISTERED: 29 Nov 50 Belgium
ARTICLES: 2 LANGUAGE: English. French.
HEADNOTE: PROTECTION TRADEMARKS
TOPIC: Patents/Copyrights
CONCEPTS: Conformity with municipal law. Liter-
ary and artistic copyrights. Laws and formalities.
PARTIES:
Belgium
UK Great Britain

100982   Bilateral Agreement   **76 UNTS 91**
SIGNED: 28 Nov 49   FORCE: 25 Nov 50
REGISTERED: 11 Dec 50 Belgium
ARTICLES: 18 LANGUAGE: Arabic. French.
HEADNOTE: CULTURAL AGREEMENT
TOPIC: Culture
CONCEPTS: Exchange. General cultural cooper-
ation. Artists. Athletes.
INTL ORGS: Special Commission.
PROCEDURE: Denunciation. Duration.
PARTIES:
Belgium
United Arab Rep
                    ANNEX
668 UNTS 368. Belgium. Termination 17 Jan 68.

668 UNTS 368.

100983   Bilateral Exchange   **76 UNTS 107**
SIGNED: 11 Feb 47   FORCE: 11 Feb 47
REGISTERED: 15 Dec 50 Belgium
ARTICLES: 2 LANGUAGE: French.
HEADNOTE: PROTECTION INDUSTRIAL COMMER-
CIAL TRADEMARKS
TOPIC: Patents/Copyrights
CONCEPTS: Conformity with municipal law. Trade-
marks.
PROCEDURE: Duration. Termination.
PARTIES:
Belgium
Chile

100984   Bilateral Agreement   **76 UNTS 113**
SIGNED: 29 Aug 50   FORCE: 1 Jun 50
REGISTERED: 15 Dec 50 Belgium
ARTICLES: 8 LANGUAGE: English.
HEADNOTE: FINANCIAL
TOPIC: General Trade
CONCEPTS: Definition of terms. Guarantees and
safeguards. Informational records. Accounting
procedures. Bonds. Balance of payments. Cur-
rency. Payment schedules.
PROCEDURE: Future Procedures Contemplated.
Termination.
PARTIES:
Belgium
Japan
                    ANNEX
124 UNTS 316. Belgium. Amendment 4 Feb 52.
Force 10 Feb 52.
124 UNTS 316.   SCAP Japan.   Amendment
4 Feb 52. Force 10 Feb 52.

100985   Multilateral Agreement   **76 UNTS 120**
SIGNED: 15 Dec 50   FORCE: 15 Dec 50
REGISTERED: 15 Dec 50 United Nations
ARTICLES: 5 LANGUAGE: English.
HEADNOTE: BASIC AGREEMENT TECHNICAL AS-
SISTANCE
TOPIC: Tech Assistance
CONCEPTS: Treaty implementation. Annex or ap-
pendix reference. Privileges and immunities.
General cooperation. Personnel. Title and deeds.
Scholarships and grants. Research and scientific
projects. Accounting procedures. Financial pro-
grams. Funding procedures. Local currency. Do-
mestic obligation. General technical assistance.
Materials, equipment and services. IGO status.
Conformity with IGO decisions.
TREATY REF: 1UNTS15,263;   33UNTS264;
76UNTS132.
PROCEDURE: Amendment. Duration. Termination.
PARTIES:
FAO (Food Agri) SIGNED: 15 Dec 50 FORCE:
15 Dec 50
ICAO (Civil Aviat) SIGNED: 15 Dec 50 FORCE:
15 Dec 50
ILO (Labor Org) SIGNED: 15 Dec 50 FORCE:
15 Dec 50
UNESCO (Educ/Cult) SIGNED: 15 Dec 50
FORCE: 15 Dec 50
United Nations SIGNED: 15 Dec 50 FORCE:
15 Dec 50
WHO (World Health) SIGNED: 15 Dec 50 FORCE:
15 Dec 50
UK Great Britain SIGNED: 15 Dec 50 FORCE:
15 Dec 50

100986   Bilateral Exchange   **76 UNTS 151**
SIGNED: 8 Nov 45   FORCE: 8 Nov 45
REGISTERED: 19 Dec 50 USA (United States)
ARTICLES: 2 LANGUAGE: English. French.
HEADNOTE: SUPPLEMENTARY COMMERCIAL
POLICY
TOPIC: General Trade
CONCEPTS: Treaty implementation. Annex type
material. Reciprocity in trade. Investments. Pay-
ment schedules. Customs declarations.
INTL ORGS: United Nations.
TREATY REF: MASTER LEND-LEASE AGREEMENT
(ARTIIII).
PARTIES:
France
USA (United States)

100987 Bilateral Exchange **76 UNTS 157**
SIGNED: 17 Mar 48 FORCE: 17 Mar 48
REGISTERED: 19 Dec 50 USA (United States)
ARTICLES: 2 LANGUAGE: Chinese. English.
HEADNOTE: CLAIMS RESULTING ACTIVITIES MIL-
ITARY FORCES
TOPIC: Reparations
CONCEPTS: Change of circumstances. Exceptions
and exemptions. Loss and/or damage. Post-war
claims settlement.
PARTIES:
Taiwan
USA (United States)

100988 Bilateral Agreement **77 UNTS 3**
SIGNED: 5 Jan 48 FORCE: 1 Jan 48
REGISTERED: 20 Dec 50 UK Great Britain
ARTICLES: 8 LANGUAGE: English.
HEADNOTE: PAYMENTS
TOPIC: Finance
CONCEPTS: Previous treaty amendment. Previous
treaty extension. Accounting procedures. Bal-
ance of payments. Monetary and gold transfers.
Payment schedules. Loan and credit. Terms of
loan.
TREATY REF: CMD7163; CMD6582; CMD7100.
PARTIES:
United Arab Rep
UK Great Britain

100989 Bilateral Exchange **77 UNTS 23**
SIGNED: 21 Jan 48 FORCE: 21 Jan 48
REGISTERED: 20 Dec 50 UK Great Britain
ARTICLES: 2 LANGUAGE: English. Italian.
HEADNOTE: MILITARY FIXED ASSETS
TOPIC: Milit Installation
CONCEPTS: Annex or appendix reference. Military
installations and equipment.
TREATY REF: 54UNTS149.
PARTIES:
Italy
UK Great Britain

100990 Bilateral Convention **77 UNTS 33**
SIGNED: 2 Mar 48 FORCE: 30 Jun 48
REGISTERED: 20 Dec 50 UK Great Britain
ARTICLES: 11 LANGUAGE: English. French.
HEADNOTE: CULTURAL CONVENTION
TOPIC: Culture
CONCEPTS: Exchange. Teacher and student ex-
change. Exchange. General cultural cooperation.
Artists. Athletes.
INTL ORGS: Special Commission.
PROCEDURE: Denunciation. Duration. Ratification.
PARTIES:
France
UK Great Britain

100991 Bilateral Agreement **77 UNTS 47**
SIGNED: 2 Mar 48 FORCE: 10 Mar 48
REGISTERED: 20 Dec 50 UK Great Britain
ARTICLES: 12 LANGUAGE: English.
HEADNOTE: PAYMENTS
TOPIC: Finance
CONCEPTS: Definition of terms. General cooper-
ation. Accounting procedures. Banking. Cur-
rency. Currency deposits. Investments. Exchange rates and regulations. Payment schedules. Local currency.
PROCEDURE: Duration. Termination.
PARTIES:
Poland
UK Great Britain
ANNEX
99 UNTS 320. UK Great Britain. Prolongation
6 Mar 51. Force 6 Mar 51.
99 UNTS 320. Poland. Prolongation 6 Mar 51.
Force 6 Mar 51.
117 UNTS 388. Poland. Prolongation 3 Sep 51.
Force 10 Sep 51.
117 UNTS 388. UK Great Britain. Prolongation
3 Sep 51. Force 10 Sep 51.
131 UNTS 334. UK Great Britain. Prolongation
3 Mar 52. Force 10 Mar 52.
131 UNTS 334. Poland. Prolongation 28 Feb 52.
Force 10 Mar 52.
151 UNTS 377. Poland. Prolongation 9 Sep 52.
Force 10 Sep 52.
151 UNTS 377. UK Great Britain. Prolongation
9 Sep 52. Force 10 Sep 52.

158 UNTS 493. Poland. Prolongation 9 Dec 52.
Force 10 Dec 52.
158 UNTS 493. UK Great Britain. Prolongation
9 Dec 52. Force 10 Dec 52.
172 UNTS 348. Poland. Prolongation 7 Mar 53.
Force 9 Mar 53.
172 UNTS 348. UK Great Britain. Prolongation
6 Mar 53. Force 9 Mar 53.
175 UNTS 367. UK Great Britain. Prolongation
8 Jun 53. Force 10 Jun 53.
175 UNTS 367. Poland. Prolongation 9 Jul 53.
Force 10 Jun 53.
183 UNTS 360. UK Great Britain. Prolongation
2 Sep 53. Force 10 Sep 53.
183 UNTS 360. Poland. Prolongation 8 Sep 53.
Force 10 Sep 53.
191 UNTS 369. UK Great Britain. Prolongation
7 Dec 53. Force 10 Dec 53.
191 UNTS 369. UK Great Britain. Prolongation
16 Mar 54. Force 10 Mar 54.
191 UNTS 369. Poland. Prolongation 9 Dec 53.
Force 10 Dec 53.
191 UNTS 369. Poland. Prolongation 18 Mar 54.
Force 10 Mar 54.
196 UNTS 344. UK Great Britain. Prolongation
11 Jun 54. Force 10 Jun 54.
196 UNTS 344. Poland. Prolongation 15 Jun 54.
Force 10 Jun 54.
201 UNTS 367. UK Great Britain. Prolongation
6 Sep 54. Force 10 Sep 54.
201 UNTS 367. Poland. Prolongation 8 Sep 54.
Force 10 Sep 54.
204 UNTS 361. UK Great Britain. Prolongation
11 Nov 54. Force 10 Dec 54.
204 UNTS 361. Poland. Prolongation 11 Nov 54.
Force 10 Dec 54.
263 UNTS 404. Poland. Prolongation 31 Dec 56.
Force 1 Jan 57.
263 UNTS 404. UK Great Britain. Prolongation
31 Dec 56. Force 1 Jan 57.

100992 Bilateral Agreement **77 UNTS 57**
SIGNED: 4 Mar 48 FORCE: 4 Mar 48
REGISTERED: 20 Dec 50 UK Great Britain
ARTICLES: 3 LANGUAGE: English.
HEADNOTE: SUPPLY CERTAIN AIRCRAFT EQUIP-
MENT
TOPIC: Milit Assistance
CONCEPTS: Annex or appendix reference. Inspec-
tion and observation. Transportation costs. De-
livery schedules. Payment for war supplies.
Lease of military property. Military assistance.
Restrictions on transfer.
TREATY REF: 9UNTS163.
PROCEDURE: Future Procedures Contemplated.
PARTIES:
Denmark
UK Great Britain

100993 Bilateral Exchange **77 UNTS 69**
SIGNED: 11 Mar 48 FORCE: 11 Mar 48
REGISTERED: 20 Dec 50 UK Great Britain
ARTICLES: 2 LANGUAGE: English.
HEADNOTE: SETTLEMENT WAR-TIME DEBTS
TOPIC: Reparations
CONCEPTS: Interest rates. Payment schedules.
Lump sum settlements. Debt settlement. Pay-
ment for war supplies. Post-war claims settle-
ment.
PARTIES:
Netherlands
UK Great Britain
ANNEX
191 UNTS 370. UK Great Britain. Supplementa-
tion 14 Jan 54. Force 14 Jan 54.
191 UNTS 370. Netherlands. Supplementation
14 Jan 54. Force 14 Jan 54.

100994 Bilateral Treaty **77 UNTS 77**
SIGNED: 15 Mar 48 FORCE: 30 Apr 48
REGISTERED: 20 Dec 50 UK Great Britain
ARTICLES: 7 LANGUAGE: Arabic. English.
HEADNOTE: ALLIANCE
TOPIC: General Military
CONCEPTS: Friendship and amity. Peaceful rela-
tions. Defense and security.
INTL ORGS: International Court of Justice. United
Nations.
PROCEDURE: Duration. Ratification. Termination.

PARTIES:
Jordan
UK Great Britain
ANNEX
310 UNTS 340. UK Great Britain. Abrogation
13 Mar 57. Force 14 Mar 57.
310 UNTS 340. Transjordan. Abrogation
13 Mar 57. Force 14 Mar 57.
312 UNTS 407. UK Great Britain. Supplementation 26 Apr 58. Force 26 Apr 58.
312 UNTS 407. Transjordan. Supplementation
26 Apr 58. Force 26 Apr 58.
359 UNTS 392. Jordan. Amendment 7 Sep 59.
Force 7 Sep 59.
359 UNTS 392. UK Great Britain. Amendment
7 Sep 59. Force 7 Sep 59.
385 UNTS 362. UK Great Britain. Amendment
2 Jun 60. Force 2 Jun 60.
385 UNTS 362. Jordan. Amendment 2 Jun 60.
Force 2 Jun 60.
420 UNTS 337. UK Great Britain. Amendment
8 Jun 61. Force 8 Jun 61.
420 UNTS 337. Jordan. Amendment 8 Jun 61.
Force 8 Jun 61.
474 UNTS 312. UK Great Britain. Amendment
19 Mar 63. Force 19 Mar 63.
474 UNTS 312. Jordan. Amendment 17 Mar 63.
Force 19 Mar 63.
533 UNTS 319. Jordan. Amendment 24 Dec 63.
Force 20 Feb 64.
533 UNTS 319. UK Great Britain. Amendment
20 Feb 64. Force 20 Feb 64.
551 UNTS 274. UK Great Britain. Amendment
9 Nov 64. Force 9 Nov 64.
551 UNTS 274. Jordan. Amendment 20 Oct 64.
Force 9 Nov 64.

100995 Bilateral Agreement **77 UNTS 113**
SIGNED: 24 Jun 48 FORCE: 24 Jun 48
REGISTERED: 20 Dec 50 UK Great Britain
ARTICLES: 12 LANGUAGE: English. Spanish.
HEADNOTE: FINANCE
TOPIC: Finance
CONCEPTS: Definition of terms. Detailed regula-
tions. General cooperation. Use of facilities. Ac-
counting procedures. Banking. Currency. Inter-
est rates. Local currency.
PROCEDURE: Duration. Termination.
PARTIES:
Chile
UK Great Britain
ANNEX
108 UNTS 316. UK Great Britain. Prolongation
23 Jun 51. Force 23 Jun 51.
108 UNTS 316. Chile. Prolongation 18 Jun 51.
Force 23 Jun 51.

100996 Bilateral Exchange **77 UNTS 129**
SIGNED: 28 Oct 48 FORCE: 10 Nov 48
REGISTERED: 20 Dec 50 UK Great Britain
ARTICLES: 2 LANGUAGE: English. Italian.
HEADNOTE: EXTENDING VISA ABOLITION
AGREEMENT OVERSEAS BRITISH TERRITORIES
TOPIC: Visas
CONCEPTS: Territorial application. Annex type
material.
PARTIES:
Italy
UK Great Britain
ANNEX
86 UNTS 326. Italy. Acknowledgement
19 Aug 50. Force 24 Aug 50.
86 UNTS 326. UK Great Britain. Singapore. Withdrawal 10 Aug 50. Force 24 Aug 50.
86 UNTS 326. UK Great Britain. Fed of Malaya.
Withdrawal 10 Aug 50. Force 24 Aug 50.
91 UNTS 382. UK Great Britain. Newfoundland.
Withdrawal 25 Apr 49. Force 25 Apr 49.
93 UNTS 369. UK Great Britain. Kenya. Force
11 Nov 49.
117 UNTS 390. UK Great Britain. Brunei. Withdrawal 1 Oct 51. Force 15 Oct 51.
117 UNTS 390. UK Great Britain. North Borneo.
Withdrawal 1 Oct 51. Force 15 Oct 51.
175 UNTS 368. UK Great Britain. Singapore.
175 UNTS 368. UK Great Britain. Fed of Malaya.
175 UNTS 368. UK Great Britain. North Borneo.
267 UNTS 375. UK Great Britain. Gibralter. Force
20 Jul 55.
349 UNTS 321. UK Great Britain. North Borneo.
Force 1 Feb 58.

349 UNTS 321. UK Great Britain. Brunei. Force 1 Feb 58.

349 UNTS 321. UK Great Britain. Gambia. Force 1 Oct 58.

100997 Bilateral Agreement **77 UNTS 137**
SIGNED: 3 Jul 48 FORCE: 2 Nov 50
REGISTERED: 22 Dec 50 Belgium
ARTICLES: 4 LANGUAGE: French.
HEADNOTE: AMENDING COMMERCE TREATY
TOPIC: General Trade
CONCEPTS: Treaty interpretation. Annex type material. Proxy diplomacy. General cooperation. Negotiation. Customs duties.
TREATY REF: 58LTS189.
PROCEDURE: Duration. Ratification.
PARTIES:
Belgium
Czechoslovakia

100998 Multilateral Convention **77 UNTS 143**
SIGNED: 11 Oct 47 FORCE: 23 Mar 50
REGISTERED: 28 Dec 50 USA (United States)
ARTICLES: 35 LANGUAGE: English. French.
HEADNOTE: WORLD METEOROLOGICAL ORGAN
TOPIC: IGO Establishment
CONCEPTS: Default remedies. Treaty interpretation. Treaty violation. Annex type material. Privileges and immunities. Exchange of information and documents. Juridical personality. Arbitration. Procedure. Meteorology. Scientific exchange. Research and development. Accounting procedures. Funding procedures. General technical assistance. Admission. Subsidiary organ. Establishment. Regional offices. Liaison with other IGO's. Internal structure. Special status. Status of experts. Inter-agency agreements.
INTL ORGS: United Nations. World Meteorological Organization.
PROCEDURE: Amendment. Accession. Ratification. Termination.
PARTIES:
Argentina SIGNED: 11 Oct 47
Australia Nauru RATIFIED: 26 Oct 50 FORCE: 26 Oct 50
Australia New Guinea RATIFIED: 26 Oct 50 FORCE: 26 Oct 50
Australia Norfolk Islands RATIFIED: 26 Oct 50 FORCE: 26 Oct 50
Australia Papua RATIFIED: 26 Oct 50 FORCE: 26 Oct 50
Austria SIGNED: 11 Oct 47 RATIFIED: 14 Mar 49 FORCE: 23 Mar 50
Belgium Belgian Colonies RATIFIED: 11 Oct 47
Belgium SIGNED: 11 Oct 47
Brazil SIGNED: 11 Oct 47 RATIFIED: 15 Mar 50 FORCE: 14 Apr 50
Burma SIGNED: 11 Oct 47 RATIFIED: 19 Aug 49 FORCE: 23 Mar 50
Byelorussia RATIFIED: 12 Apr 48 FORCE: 23 Mar 50
Canada SIGNED: 11 Oct 47 RATIFIED: 28 Jul 50 FORCE: 27 Aug 50
Chile SIGNED: 11 Oct 47
China SIGNED: 11 Oct 47
Colombia SIGNED: 11 Oct 47
Cuba SIGNED: 11 Oct 47
Czechoslovakia SIGNED: 11 Oct 47 RATIFIED: 26 Jul 49 FORCE: 23 Mar 50
Denmark SIGNED: 11 Oct 47
Dominican Republic SIGNED: 11 Oct 47 RATIFIED: 15 Sep 49 FORCE: 23 Mar 50
Ecuador SIGNED: 11 Oct 47
United Arab Rep SIGNED: 11 Oct 47 RATIFIED: 10 Jan 50 FORCE: 23 Mar 50
Finland SIGNED: 11 Oct 47 RATIFIED: 7 Jan 50 FORCE: 23 Mar 50
France Algeria RATIFIED: 5 Dec 49 FORCE: 23 Mar 50
France Andorra RATIFIED: 5 Dec 49 FORCE: 20 Mar 50
France Cameroon RATIFIED: 5 Dec 49 FORCE: 23 Mar 50
France Fr Equatorial Afri RATIFIED: 5 Dec 49 FORCE: 23 Mar 50
France French Somaliland RATIFIED: 5 Dec 49 FORCE: 23 Mar 50
France French West Africa RATIFIED: 5 Dec 49 FORCE: 23 Mar 50
France French West Indies RATIFIED: 5 Dec 49 FORCE: 23 Mar 50

France Guyana RATIFIED: 5 Dec 49 FORCE: 23 Mar 50
France Indochina RATIFIED: 5 Dec 49 FORCE: 23 Mar 50
France Madagascar RATIFIED: 5 Dec 49 FORCE: 23 Mar 50
France Miquelon RATIFIED: 5 Dec 49 FORCE: 23 Mar 50
France Oceania RATIFIED: 5 Dec 49 FORCE: 23 Mar 50
France Reunion RATIFIED: 5 Dec 49 FORCE: 23 Mar 50
France SIGNED: 11 Oct 47 RATIFIED: 5 Dec 49 FORCE: 23 Mar 50
France Saar RATIFIED: 5 Dec 49 FORCE: 20 Mar 50
France St. Pierre RATIFIED: 5 Dec 49 FORCE: 23 Mar 50
France Togo RATIFIED: 5 Dec 49 FORCE: 23 Mar 50
France Tunisia RATIFIED: 5 Dec 49 FORCE: 23 Mar 50
Greece SIGNED: 11 Oct 47 RATIFIED: 20 Jan 50 FORCE: 23 Mar 50
Guatemala SIGNED: 11 Oct 47
Hungary SIGNED: 11 Oct 47
Iceland SIGNED: 11 Oct 47 RATIFIED: 16 Jan 48 FORCE: 23 Mar 50
India SIGNED: 11 Oct 47 RATIFIED: 27 Apr 49 FORCE: 23 Mar 50
Indonesia RATIFIED: 16 Nov 50 FORCE: 16 Dec 50
Iraq RATIFIED: 21 Feb 50 FORCE: 23 Mar 50
Ireland SIGNED: 11 Oct 47 RATIFIED: 14 Mar 50 FORCE: 13 Apr 50
Israel RATIFIED: 30 Sep 49 FORCE: 23 Mar 50
Italy SIGNED: 11 Oct 47
Lebanon RATIFIED: 22 Dec 48 FORCE: 23 Mar 50
Mexico SIGNED: 11 Oct 47 RATIFIED: 27 May 49 FORCE: 23 Mar 50
Netherlands SIGNED: 11 Oct 47
New Zealand SIGNED: 11 Oct 47 RATIFIED: 2 Apr 48 FORCE: 23 Mar 50
Norway SIGNED: 11 Oct 47 RATIFIED: 9 Dec 49 FORCE: 23 Mar 50
Pakistan SIGNED: 11 Oct 47 RATIFIED: 11 Apr 50 FORCE: 11 May 50
Paraguay SIGNED: 11 Oct 47 RATIFIED: 15 Sep 50 FORCE: 15 Oct 50
Peru RATIFIED: 30 Sep 49 FORCE: 23 Mar 50
Philippines SIGNED: 11 Oct 47 RATIFIED: 5 Apr 49 FORCE: 23 Mar 50
Poland SIGNED: 11 Oct 47 RATIFIED: 16 May 50 FORCE: 15 Jun 50
Portugal SIGNED: 11 Oct 47
Siam SIGNED: 11 Oct 47 RATIFIED: 11 Jul 49 FORCE: 23 Mar 50
South Africa SIGNED: 11 Oct 47 RATIFIED: 17 Jan 50 FORCE: 23 Mar 50
South Africa Southwest Africa RATIFIED: 17 Jan 50 FORCE: 20 Mar 50
Sweden SIGNED: 11 Oct 47 RATIFIED: 10 Nov 48 FORCE: 23 Mar 50
Turkey SIGNED: 11 Oct 47 RATIFIED: 5 Aug 49 FORCE: 23 Mar 50
UK Great Britain Aden RATIFIED: 14 Dec 48 FORCE: 23 Mar 50
UK Great Britain Basutoland RATIFIED: 14 Dec 48 FORCE: 23 Mar 50
UK Great Britain Bechuanaland RATIFIED: 14 Dec 48 FORCE: 23 Mar 50
UK Great Britain Bermuda RATIFIED: 14 Dec 48 FORCE: 23 Mar 50
UK Great Britain Brit Solomon Is RATIFIED: 14 Dec 48 FORCE: 23 Mar 50
UK Great Britain Brunei RATIFIED: 14 Dec 48 FORCE: 23 Mar 50
UK Great Britain Falkland Islands RATIFIED: 14 Dec 48 FORCE: 23 Mar 50
UK Great Britain Fiji Islands RATIFIED: 14 Dec 48 FORCE: 23 Mar 50
UK Great Britain Gambia RATIFIED: 14 Dec 48 FORCE: 23 Mar 50
UK Great Britain Gibralter RATIFIED: 14 Dec 48 FORCE: 23 Mar 50
UK Great Britain Gilbert Islands RATIFIED: 14 Dec 48 FORCE: 23 Mar 50
UK Great Britain Gold Coast RATIFIED: 14 Dec 48 FORCE: 23 Mar 50
UK Great Britain Hong Kong RATIFIED: 14 Dec 48 FORCE: 23 Mar 50
UK Great Britain Kenya RATIFIED: 14 Dec 48 FORCE: 23 Mar 50

UK Great Britain Malta RATIFIED: 14 Dec 48 FORCE: 23 Mar 50
UK Great Britain Mauritius RATIFIED: 14 Dec 48 FORCE: 23 Mar 50
UK Great Britain Nigeria RATIFIED: 14 Dec 48 FORCE: 23 Mar 50
UK Great Britain North Borneo RATIFIED: 14 Dec 48 FORCE: 23 Mar 50
UK Great Britain Northern Rhodesia RATIFIED: 14 Dec 48 FORCE: 23 Mar 50
UK Great Britain Nyasaland RATIFIED: 14 Dec 48 FORCE: 23 Mar 50
UK Great Britain SIGNED: 11 Oct 47 RATIFIED: 14 Dec 48 FORCE: 23 Mar 50
UK Great Britain Sarawak RATIFIED: 14 Dec 48 FORCE: 23 Mar 50
UK Great Britain Seychelles RATIFIED: 14 Dec 48 FORCE: 23 Mar 50
UK Great Britain Sierra Leone RATIFIED: 14 Dec 48 FORCE: 23 Mar 50
UK Great Britain Singapore RATIFIED: 14 Dec 48 FORCE: 23 Mar 50
UK Great Britain Southern Rhodesia RATIFIED: 14 Dec 48 FORCE: 23 Mar 50
UK Great Britain Swaziland RATIFIED: 14 Dec 48 FORCE: 23 Mar 50
UK Great Britain Tanganyika RATIFIED: 14 Dec 48 FORCE: 23 Mar 50
UK Great Britain Uganda RATIFIED: 14 Dec 48 FORCE: 23 Mar 50
UK Great Britain Zanzibar RATIFIED: 14 Dec 48 FORCE: 23 Mar 50
USA (United States) SIGNED: 11 Oct 47 RATIFIED: 4 May 49 FORCE: 23 Mar 50
Ukrainian SSR RATIFIED: 12 Apr 48 FORCE: 23 Mar 50
Uruguay SIGNED: 11 Oct 47
Yugoslavia SIGNED: 11 Oct 47 RATIFIED: 7 Dec 48 FORCE: 23 Mar 50
ANNEX
88 UNTS 454.
148 UNTS 406.
174 UNTS 291.
209 UNTS 334.
260 UNTS 446.
283 UNTS 314.
313 UNTS 334.
356 UNTS 350.
394 UNTS 226.
394 UNTS 260.
394 UNTS 262.
407 UNTS 236.
472 UNTS 388.
601 UNTS 338. UK Great Britain. Declaration 21 Dec 66.

100999 Bilateral Exchange **77 UNTS 191**
SIGNED: 30 Apr 48 FORCE: 30 Apr 48
REGISTERED: 28 Dec 50 USA (United States)
ARTICLES: 2 LANGUAGE: English.
HEADNOTE: SANITATION SHELL FISH INDUSTRY
TOPIC: Sanitation
CONCEPTS: General cooperation. Border control. Sanitation. Maritime products and equipment. Trade procedures.
PROCEDURE: Termination.
PARTIES:
Canada
USA (United States)

101000 Bilateral Exchange **77 UNTS 197**
SIGNED: 21 Oct 48 FORCE: 21 Oct 48
REGISTERED: 28 Dec 50 USA (United States)
ARTICLES: 2 LANGUAGE: English.
HEADNOTE: COPYRIGHT RELATIONS
TOPIC: Patents/Copyrights
CONCEPTS: Conformity with municipal law. Domestic legislation. Laws and formalities.
PARTIES:
Philippines
USA (United States)

101001 Bilateral Agreement **77 UNTS 215**
SIGNED: 20 Jun 50 FORCE: 20 Jun 50
REGISTERED: 2 Jan 51 ICAO (Civil Aviat)
ARTICLES: 12 LANGUAGE: Arabic. English.
HEADNOTE: AIR SERVICES
TOPIC: Air Transport
CONCEPTS: Definition of terms. Detailed regulations. Treaty interpretation. Annex or appendix reference. Friendship and amity. Conformity

with municipal law. General cooperation. Exchange of information and documents. Use of facilities. Arbitration. Procedure. Existing tribunals. Reexport of goods, etc.. Non-interest rates and fees. Most favored nation clause. National treatment. Customs exemptions. Competency certificate. Registration certificate. Routes and logistics. Permit designation. Airport facilities. Conditions of airlines operating permission. Overflights and technical stops. Operating authorizations and regulations.
INTL ORGS: International Civil Aviation Organization.
TREATY REF: 15UNTS295.
PROCEDURE: Amendment. Future Procedures Contemplated. Registration. Termination.
PARTIES:
Iraq
Pakistan
ANNEX
216 UNTS 382. Iraq. Amendment 14 Jun 54. Force 24 Aug 54.
216 UNTS 382. Pakistan. Amendment 24 Aug 54. Force 24 Aug 54.

101002   Bilateral Agreement   **77 UNTS 239**
SIGNED: 16 Aug 50   FORCE: 16 Aug 50
REGISTERED: 2 Jan 51 ICAO (Civil Aviat)
ARTICLES: 14 LANGUAGE: English.
HEADNOTE: AIR TRANSPORT
TOPIC: Air Transport
CONCEPTS: Definition of terms. Annex or appendix reference. Conformity with municipal law. Exchange of information and documents. Licenses and permits. Recognition of legal documents. Use of facilities. Arbitration. Procedure. Existing tribunals. Negotiation. Quarantine. Fees and exemptions. Most favored nation clause. National treatment. Customs duties. Customs exemptions. Temporary importation. Competency certificate. Routes and logistics. Navigational conditions. Permit designation. Airport facilities. Airworthiness certificates. Conditions of airlines operating permission. Operating authorizations and regulations. Licenses and certificates of nationality.
INTL ORGS: International Civil Aviation Organization. International Court of Justice.
TREATY REF: 15UNTS295.
PROCEDURE: Amendment. Future Procedures Contemplated. Termination. Application to Non-self-governing Territories.
PARTIES:
Canada
New Zealand
ANNEX
192 UNTS 332. New Zealand. Amendment 29 Sep 52. Force 29 Sep 52.
192 UNTS 332. Canada. Amendment 29 Sep 52. Force 29 Sep 52.

101003   Bilateral Exchange   **77 UNTS 259**
SIGNED: 21 Sep 48   FORCE: 21 Sep 48
REGISTERED: 3 Jan 51 Greece
ARTICLES: 2 LANGUAGE: French.
HEADNOTE: CULTURAL INSTITUTIONS
TOPIC: Culture
CONCEPTS: General property. Institute establishment. General cultural cooperation. Special status.
PARTIES:
Greece
Italy

101004   Bilateral Agreement   **77 UNTS 265**
SIGNED: 27 Dec 48   FORCE: 27 Dec 48
REGISTERED: 3 Jan 51 Greece
ARTICLES: 9 LANGUAGE: French.
HEADNOTE: COMMERCE
TOPIC: General Trade
CONCEPTS: Annex or appendix reference. Licenses and permits. Establishment of commission. Trade procedures. Payment schedules. Delivery schedules. Quotas.
INTL ORGS: Special Commission.
PARTIES:
Belgium
Greece

101005   Bilateral Agreement   **77 UNTS 293**
SIGNED: 27 Dec 48   FORCE: 27 Dec 48
REGISTERED: 3 Jan 51 Greece
ARTICLES: 9 LANGUAGE: French.
HEADNOTE: REGULATING PAYMENTS
TOPIC: Finance
CONCEPTS: Definition of terms. General cooperation. Accounting procedures. Banking. Balance of payments. Currency. Monetary and gold transfers. Exchange rates and regulations. Interest rates.
PROCEDURE: Duration. Renewal or Revival.
PARTIES:
Belgium
Greece

101006   Bilateral Agreement   **77 UNTS 307**
SIGNED: 16 Mar 49   FORCE: 16 Mar 49
REGISTERED: 3 Jan 51 Greece
ARTICLES: 7 LANGUAGE: English. French.
HEADNOTE: TRADE WITH OCCUPIED AREAS
TOPIC: General Trade
CONCEPTS: General provisions. Treaty implementation. Annex or appendix reference. Previous treaty replacement. Licenses and permits. Establishment of commission. Payment schedules.
PROCEDURE: Duration. Future Procedures Contemplated. Renewal or Revival. Termination.
PARTIES:
Germany, West
Greece

101007   Bilateral Agreement   **77 UNTS 327**
SIGNED: 16 Mar 49   FORCE: 16 Mar 49
REGISTERED: 3 Jan 51 Greece
ARTICLES: 9 LANGUAGE: English. French.
HEADNOTE: PAYMENTS
TOPIC: Finance
CONCEPTS: Detailed regulations. Annex or appendix reference. General cooperation. Accounting procedures. Banking. Currency. Interest rates. Payment schedules. Loan repayment. General military.
PROCEDURE: Denunciation.
PARTIES:
Germany, West
Greece

101008   Bilateral Agreement   **78 UNTS 3**
SIGNED: 24 Mar 49   FORCE: 24 Mar 49
REGISTERED: 3 Jan 51 Greece
ARTICLES: 10 LANGUAGE: French.
HEADNOTE: TRADE
TOPIC: General Trade
CONCEPTS: Annex or appendix reference. Licenses and permits. Establishment of commission. Trade procedures. Currency. Payment schedules. Delivery schedules. Quotas.
INTL ORGS: Special Commission.
PROCEDURE: Duration. Termination.
PARTIES:
Finland
Greece
ANNEX
187 UNTS 424.   Greece.   Supplementation 8 Oct 52. Force 8 Oct 52.
187 UNTS 424.   Finland.   Supplementation 8 Oct 52. Force 8 Oct 52.
224 UNTS 344.   Finland.   Supplementation 10 Oct 53. Force 10 Oct 53.
224 UNTS 344.   Greece.   Supplementation 10 Oct 53. Force 10 Oct 53.
227 UNTS 312.   Greece.   Supplementation 1 Jun 55. Force 1 Jun 55.
227 UNTS 312.   Finland.   Supplementation 1 Jun 55. Force 1 Jun 55.

101009   Bilateral Agreement   **78 UNTS 13**
SIGNED: 24 Mar 49   FORCE: 24 Mar 49
REGISTERED: 3 Jan 51 Greece
ARTICLES: 10 LANGUAGE: French.
HEADNOTE: FACILITATING CURRENT PAYMENTS
TOPIC: Finance
CONCEPTS: General cooperation. Licenses and permits. Import quotas. Accounting procedures. Banking. Balance of payments. Monetary and gold transfers. Exchange rates and regulations. Interest rates. Payment schedules.
PROCEDURE: Amendment. Termination.

PARTIES:
Finland
Greece

101010   Bilateral Agreement   **78 UNTS 23**
SIGNED: 2 Apr 49   FORCE: 2 Apr 49
REGISTERED: 3 Jan 51 Greece
ARTICLES: 9 LANGUAGE: French.
HEADNOTE: PAYMENTS
TOPIC: Finance
CONCEPTS: Annex or appendix reference. General cooperation. Import quotas. Accounting procedures. Banking. Balance of payments. Currency. Exchange rates and regulations. Payment schedules.
PROCEDURE: Denunciation. Duration. Renewal or Revival.
PARTIES:
Greece
Turkey

101011   Bilateral Agreement   **78 UNTS 55**
SIGNED: 21 Jul 49   FORCE: 21 Jul 49
REGISTERED: 3 Jan 51 Greece
ARTICLES: 8 LANGUAGE: French.
HEADNOTE: TRADE
TOPIC: General Trade
CONCEPTS: Detailed regulations. Exceptions and exemptions. Treaty implementation. Annex or appendix reference. Informational records. Establishment of commission. Reexport of goods, etc.. Trade procedures. Expense sharing formulae. Payment schedules. Raw materials.
INTL ORGS: Special Commission.
TREATY REF: 78UNTS23.
PARTIES:
Greece
Turkey

101012   Bilateral Protocol   **78 UNTS 65**
SIGNED: 21 Jul 49   FORCE: 5 Aug 49
REGISTERED: 3 Jan 51 Greece
ARTICLES: 6 LANGUAGE: French.
HEADNOTE: LIQUIDATION NON-COMMERCIAL ASSETS
TOPIC: Claims and Debts
CONCEPTS: Import quotas. Accounting procedures. Banking. Compensation. Balance of payments. Currency. Currency deposits. Exchange rates and regulations. Interest rates. Payment schedules. Assets. Debt settlement.
TREATY REF: 78UNTS23.
PROCEDURE: Denunciation.
PARTIES:
Greece
Turkey

101013   Bilateral Agreement   **78 UNTS 71**
SIGNED: 5 Jul 49   FORCE: 5 Jul 49
REGISTERED: 3 Jan 51 Greece
ARTICLES: 13 LANGUAGE: English.
HEADNOTE: CIVIL AIR SERVICES
TOPIC: Air Transport
CONCEPTS: Definition of terms. Exceptions and exemptions. Annex or appendix reference. Conformity with municipal law. Licenses and permits. Recognition of legal documents. Use of facilities. Procedure. Existing tribunals. Negotiation. Fees and exemptions. Most favored nation clause. National treatment. Customs exemptions. Competency certificate. Routes and logistics. Navigational conditions. Permit designation. Airport facilities. Airworthiness certificates. Conditions of airlines operating permission. Operating authorizations and regulations. Licenses and certificates of nationality.
INTL ORGS: International Civil Aviation Organization.
TREATY REF: 15UNTS295.
PROCEDURE: Amendment. Future Procedures Contemplated. Ratification. Registration. Termination.
PARTIES:
Greece
Syria

101014   Bilateral Agreement   **78 UNTS 89**
SIGNED: 31 Aug 49   FORCE: 31 Aug 49
REGISTERED: 3 Jan 51 Greece

ARTICLES: 54 LANGUAGE: French.
HEADNOTE: ECONOMIC COLLABORATION SET-
  TLEMENT QUESTIONS
TOPIC: Reparations
CONCEPTS: Definition of terms. Time limit. Annex
  or appendix reference. Exchange of information
  and documents. General property. Private con-
  tracts. Establishment of commission. Procedure.
  Conciliation. Accounting procedures. Indemnities and reimbursements. Exchange rates and
  regulations. Payment schedules. Delivery schedules. Reparations and restrictions. Post-war
  claims settlement. Raw materials.
INTL ORGS: Special Commission.
PARTIES:
  Greece
  Italy
            ANNEX
219 UNTS 326. Italy. Denunciation 30 Sep 53.
  Force 30 Sep 53.
219 UNTS 326. Greece. Denunciation 30 Sep 53.
  Force 30 Sep 53.
219 UNTS 336. Greece. Supplementation
  21 Mar 54. Force 21 Mar 54.
219 UNTS 336. Italy. Supplementation
  21 Mar 54. Force 21 Mar 54.

101015   Bilateral Agreement   **78 UNTS 165**
SIGNED: 6 Jan 51   FORCE: 6 Jan 51
REGISTERED: 6 Jan 51 United Nations
ARTICLES: 5 LANGUAGE: English. French.
HEADNOTE: TECHNICAL ASSISTANCE
TOPIC: Direct Aid
CONCEPTS: Treaty implementation. Annex or ap-
  pendix reference. Privileges and immunities.
  General cooperation. Personnel. Title and deeds.
  Scholarships and grants. Vocational training. Re-
  search and development. Expense sharing for-
  mulae. Local currency. Domestic obligation.
  General technical assistance. Materials, equip-
  ment and services. IGO status. Conformity with
  IGO decisions.
TREATY REF: 76UNTS132; 1UNTS15.
PROCEDURE: Amendment. Termination.
PARTIES:
  United Nations
  Yugoslavia
            ANNEX
94 UNTS 314. United Nations. Supplementation
  10 Jul 51. Force 10 Jul 51.
94 UNTS 314. Yugoslavia. Supplementation
  10 Jul 51. Force 10 Jul 51.
94 UNTS 320. United Nations. Supplementation
  12 Jul 51. Force 12 Jul 51.
94 UNTS 320. Yugoslavia. Supplementation
  12 Jul 51. Force 12 Jul 51.
187 UNTS 428. UNTAB (Tech Assis). Amendment
  18 Dec 53. Force 31 Dec 53.
187 UNTS 428. Yugoslavia. Amendment
  31 Dec 53. Force 31 Dec 53.
253 UNTS 341. United Nations. Force 26 Jun 56.
253 UNTS 341. Yugoslavia. Force 26 Jun 56.

101016   Multilateral Convention   **78 UNTS 181**
SIGNED: 22 Jun 33   FORCE: 29 Dec 50
REGISTERED: 9 Jan 51 ILO (Labor Org)
ARTICLES: 16 LANGUAGE: English. French.
HEADNOTE: NON-INDUSTRIAL EMPLOYMENT
  CHILDREN
TOPIC: ILO Labor
CONCEPTS: Definition of terms. Detailed regula-
  tions. Exceptions and exemptions. Incorporation
  of treaty provisions into national law. Professor-
  ships. ILO conventions. Employment regulations.
INTL ORGS: United Nations.
TREATY REF: 38UNTS3; 38UNTS143;
  40UNTS205; 40UNTS217.
PROCEDURE: Amendment. Denunciation. Dura-
  tion. Ratification. Registration. Renewal or Revival.
PARTIES:
  Multilateral
            ANNEX
149 UNTS 406. Italy. Ratification 22 Oct 52.
  Force 22 Oct 53.
199 UNTS 333. Cuba. Ratification 7 Sep 54.
  Force 7 Sep 55.
249 UNTS 454. USSR (Soviet Union). Ratification
  10 Aug 56. Force 10 Aug 57.
253 UNTS 389. Ukrainian SSR. Ratification
  14 Sep 56. Force 14 Sep 57.

253 UNTS 389. Byelorussia. Ratification
  6 Nov 56. Force 6 Nov 57.
293 UNTS 376. Luxembourg. Ratification
  3 Mar 58. Force 3 Mar 59.
406 UNTS 296. New Zealand. Denunciation
  11 Jul 61. Force 11 Jul 62.
560 UNTS 314. Paraguay. Ratification 21 Mar 66.
  Force 21 Mar 67.

101017   Multilateral Convention   **78 UNTS 198**
SIGNED: 9 Oct 46   FORCE: 29 Dec 50
REGISTERED: 9 Jan 51 ILO (Labor Org)
ARTICLES: 19 LANGUAGE: English. French.
HEADNOTE: MEDICAL EXAMINATIONS EMPLOY-
  MENT CHILDREN INDUSTRIAL JOBS
TOPIC: ILO Labor
CONCEPTS: Definition of terms. Exceptions and
  exemptions. Non-prejudice to third party. Incor-
  poration of treaty provisions into national law.
  Public health. ILO conventions. Employment reg-
  ulations. Labor statistics. Safety standards.
INTL ORGS: United Nations.
PROCEDURE: Amendment. Denunciation. Dura-
  tion. Ratification. Registration. Renewal or Revival.
PARTIES:
  Multilateral
            ANNEX
79 UNTS 334. Iraq. Ratification 13 Jan 51. Force
  13 Jan 52.
94 UNTS 312. France. Ratification 28 Jun 51.
  Force 28 Jun 51.
122 UNTS 342. Guatemala. Ratification
  13 Feb 52. Force 13 Feb 53.
149 UNTS 407. Italy. Ratification 22 Oct 52.
  Force 22 Oct 53.
183 UNTS 361. Israel. Ratification 23 Dec 53.
  Force 23 Dec 54.
184 UNTS 341. Cuba. Ratification 13 Jan 54.
  Force 13 Jan 55.
204 UNTS 362. Argentina. Ratification
  17 Feb 55. Force 17 Feb 56.
212 UNTS 393. France. Martinique.
212 UNTS 393. France. Guadeloupe.
212 UNTS 393. France. Reunion.
212 UNTS 393. France. French Guinea.
248 UNTS 403. Hungary. Ratification 8 Jun 56.
  Force 8 Jun 56.
249 UNTS 455. USSR (Soviet Union). Ratification
  10 Aug 56. Force 10 Aug 57.
253 UNTS 390. Ukrainian SSR. Ratification
  14 Sep 56. Force 14 Sep 57.
253 UNTS 390. Byelorussia. Ratification
  6 Nov 56. Force 6 Nov 57.
266 UNTS 386. Haiti. Ratification 12 Apr 57.
  Force 12 Apr 58.
272 UNTS 255. Albania. Ratification 3 Jun 57.
  Force 3 Jun 58.
293 UNTS 376. Luxembourg. Ratification
  3 Mar 58. Force 3 Mar 59.
384 UNTS 358. Philippines. Ratification
  17 Nov 60. Force 17 Nov 61.
429 UNTS 271. Peru. Ratification 6 Apr 62. Force
  6 Apr 63.
444 UNTS 326. Algeria. Succession 19 Oct 62.
560 UNTS 314. Paraguay. Ratification 21 Mar 66.
  Force 21 Mar 67.

101018   Multilateral Convention   **78 UNTS 213**
SIGNED: 9 Oct 46   FORCE: 29 Dec 50
REGISTERED: 9 Jan 51 ILO (Labor Org)
ARTICLES: 18 LANGUAGE: English. French.
HEADNOTE: EMPLOYMENT CHILDREN NON-
  IMDUSTRIAL JOBS
TOPIC: ILO Labor
CONCEPTS: Definition of terms. Exceptions and
  exemptions. Non-prejudice to third party. Incor-
  poration of treaty provisions into national law.
  Public health. ILO conventions. Employment reg-
  ulations. Labor statistics. Safety standards.
INTL ORGS: United Nations.
PARTIES:
  Multilateral
            ANNEX
94 UNTS 313. France. Ratification 28 Jun 51.
  Force 28 Jun 51.
122 UNTS 342. Guatemala. Ratification
  13 Feb 52. Force 13 Feb 53.
149 UNTS 407. Italy. Ratification 22 Oct 52.
  Force 22 Oct 53.
183 UNTS 361. Israel. Ratification 23 Dec 53.
  Force 23 Dec 54.

199 UNTS 333. Cuba. Ratification 7 Sep 54.
  Force 7 Sep 55.
204 UNTS 362. Argentina. Ratification
  17 Feb 55. Force 17 Feb 56.
212 UNTS 394. France. Martinique.
212 UNTS 394. France. Reunion.
212 UNTS 394. France. Guadeloupe.
212 UNTS 394. France. French Guinea.
248 UNTS 403. Hungary. Ratification 8 Jun 56.
  Force 8 Jun 56.
249 UNTS 456. USSR (Soviet Union). Ratification
  10 Aug 56. Force 10 Aug 57.
266 UNTS 387. Haiti. Ratification 12 Apr 57.
  Force 12 Apr 58.
272 UNTS 255. Albania. Ratification 3 Jun 57.
  Force 3 Jun 58.
293 UNTS 377. Luxembourg. Ratification
  3 Mar 58. Force 3 Mar 59.
366 UNTS 384. Costa Rica. Ratification 2 Jun 60.
  Force 2 Jun 61.
373 UNTS 354. Iraq. Ratification 5 Jul 60. Force
  5 Jul 61.
429 UNTS 272. Peru. Ratification 4 Apr 62. Force
  4 Apr 63.
444 UNTS 327. Algeria. Succession 19 Oct 62.
560 UNTS 316. Paraguay. Ratification 21 Mar 66.
  Force 21 Mar 67.

101019   Multilateral Convention   **78 UNTS 227**
SIGNED: 9 Oct 46   FORCE: 29 Dec 50
REGISTERED: 9 Jan 51 ILO (Labor Org)
ARTICLES: 17 LANGUAGE: English. French.
HEADNOTE: RESTRICTION NIGHT WORK CHIL-
  DREN NON-INDUSTRIAL OCCUPATIONS
TOPIC: ILO Labor
CONCEPTS: Definition of terms. Exceptions and
  exemptions. Non-prejudice to third party. Inspec-
  tion and observation. Incorporation of treaty pro-
  visions into national law. Investigation of viola-
  tions. ILO conventions. Employment regulations.
  Holidays and rest periods. Labor statistics.
INTL ORGS: United Nations.
PROCEDURE: Amendment. Denunciation. Duration. Ratification. Registration. Renewal or Revival.
PARTIES:
  Multilateral
            ANNEX
122 UNTS 343. Guatemala. Ratification
  13 Feb 52. Force 13 Feb 53.
149 UNTS 407. Italy. Ratification 22 Oct 52.
  Force 22 Oct 53.
173 UNTS 401. Dominican Republic. Ratification
  22 Sep 53. Force 22 Sep 54.
183 UNTS 362. Israel. Ratification 23 Dec 53.
  Force 23 Dec 54.
199 UNTS 334. Cuba. Ratification 7 Sep 54.
  Force 7 Sep 55.
204 UNTS 363. Argentina. Ratification
  17 Feb 55. Force 17 Feb 56.
249 UNTS 457. USSR (Soviet Union). Ratification
  10 Aug 56. Force 10 Aug 57.
293 UNTS 377. Luxembourg. Ratification
  3 Mar 58. Force 3 Mar 59.
429 UNTS 273. Peru. Ratification 4 Apr 62. Force
  4 Apr 63.
560 UNTS 316. Paraguay. Ratification 21 Mar 66.
  Force 21 Mar 67.

101020   Bilateral Agreement   **78 UNTS 242**
SIGNED: 28 Jun 47   FORCE: 10 Nov 47
REGISTERED: 11 Jan 51 Denmark
ARTICLES: 10 LANGUAGE: French.
HEADNOTE: TRADE PAYMENTS AGREEMENTS
TOPIC: General Economic
CONCEPTS: Licenses and permits. Establishment
  of commission. Establishment of trade relations.
  Export quotas. Import quotas. Trade procedures.
  Payment schedules. Delivery schedules. Quotas.
  Most favored nation clause. Goods in transit.
INTL ORGS: Special Commission.
PROCEDURE: Denunciation. Ratification. Termina-
  tion.
PARTIES:
  Denmark
  Yugoslavia
            ANNEX
119 UNTS 352. Yugoslavia. Supplementation
  10 Nov 51. Force 10 Nov 51.
119 UNTS 352. Denmark. Supplementation
  10 Nov 51. Force 10 Nov 51.

157 UNTS 360. Denmark. Supplementation 18 Nov 52. Force 18 Nov 52.
157 UNTS 360. Yugoslavia. Supplementation 18 Nov 52. Force 18 Nov 52.

101021 Multilateral Convention **78 UNTS 277**
SIGNED: 9 Dec 48   FORCE: 12 Jan 51
REGISTERED: 12 Jan 51 United Nations
ARTICLES: 19 LANGUAGE: Chinese. English. French. Russian. Spanish.
HEADNOTE: PREVENTION PUNISHMENT CRIME GENOCIDE
TOPIC: Humanitarian
CONCEPTS: Court procedures. Extraditable offenses. Special factors. Domestic legislation. Existing tribunals. Humanitarian matters.
INTL ORGS: International Court of Justice. United Nations.
TREATY REF: UN DOC A 64 ADD.1 (31JAN47).
PROCEDURE: Accession.
PARTIES:
Australia All Territories RATIFIED: 8 Jul 49 FORCE: 12 Jan 51
Australia SIGNED: 11 Dec 48 RATIFIED: 8 Jul 49 FORCE: 12 Jan 51
Belgium SIGNED: 12 Dec 49
Bolivia SIGNED: 11 Dec 48
Brazil SIGNED: 11 Dec 48
Bulgaria RATIFIED: 21 Jul 50 FORCE: 12 Jan 51
Burma SIGNED: 30 Dec 49
Byelorussia SIGNED: 16 Dec 49
Cambodia RATIFIED: 14 Oct 50 FORCE: 12 Jan 51
Canada SIGNED: 28 Nov 49
Ceylon (Sri Lanka) RATIFIED: 12 Oct 50 FORCE: 12 Jan 51
Chile SIGNED: 9 Dec 48
Taiwan SIGNED: 20 Jul 49
Colombia SIGNED: 28 Dec 49
Costa Rica RATIFIED: 14 Oct 50 FORCE: 12 Jan 51
Cuba SIGNED: 28 Dec 49
Czechoslovakia SIGNED: 28 Dec 49 RATIFIED: 21 Dec 50 FORCE: 12 Jan 51
Denmark SIGNED: 28 Sep 49
Dominican Republic SIGNED: 11 Dec 48
Ecuador SIGNED: 11 Dec 48 RATIFIED: 21 Dec 49 FORCE: 12 Jan 51
United Arab Rep SIGNED: 12 Dec 48
El Salvador SIGNED: 27 Apr 49 RATIFIED: 28 Sep 50 FORCE: 12 Jan 51
Ethiopia SIGNED: 11 Dec 48 RATIFIED: 1 Jul 49 FORCE: 12 Jan 51
France SIGNED: 11 Dec 48 RATIFIED: 14 Oct 50 FORCE: 12 Jan 51
Greece SIGNED: 29 Dec 49
Guatemala SIGNED: 22 Jun 49 RATIFIED: 13 Jan 50 FORCE: 12 Jan 51
Haiti SIGNED: 11 Dec 48 RATIFIED: 14 Oct 50 FORCE: 12 Jan 51
Honduras SIGNED: 22 Apr 49
Iceland SIGNED: 14 May 49 RATIFIED: 29 Aug 49 FORCE: 12 Jan 51
India SIGNED: 29 Nov 49
Iran SIGNED: 8 Dec 49
Israel SIGNED: 17 Aug 49
Jordan RATIFIED: 3 Apr 50 FORCE: 12 Jan 51
Korea, South RATIFIED: 14 Oct 50 FORCE: 12 Jan 51
Laos RATIFIED: 8 Dec 50 FORCE: 12 Jan 51
Lebanon SIGNED: 30 Dec 49
Liberia SIGNED: 11 Dec 48 RATIFIED: 9 Jun 50 FORCE: 12 Jan 51
Mexico SIGNED: 14 Dec 48
Monaco RATIFIED: 30 Mar 50 FORCE: 12 Jan 51
New Zealand SIGNED: 25 Nov 49
Norway SIGNED: 11 Dec 48 RATIFIED: 22 Jul 49 FORCE: 12 Jan 51
Pakistan SIGNED: 11 Dec 48
Panama SIGNED: 11 Dec 48 RATIFIED: 11 Jan 50 FORCE: 12 Jan 51
Paraguay SIGNED: 11 Dec 48
Peru SIGNED: 11 Dec 48
Philippines SIGNED: 11 Dec 48 RATIFIED: 2 Jul 50 FORCE: 12 Jan 51
Poland RATIFIED: 14 Nov 50 FORCE: 12 Jan 51
Romania RATIFIED: 2 Nov 50 FORCE: 12 Jan 51
Saudi Arabia RATIFIED: 13 Jul 50 FORCE: 12 Jan 51
Turkey RATIFIED: 31 Jul 50 FORCE: 12 Jan 51
USA (United States) SIGNED: 11 Dec 48
Ukrainian SSR SIGNED: 16 Dec 49
Uruguay SIGNED: 11 Dec 48
USSR (Soviet Union) SIGNED: 16 Dec 49
Vietnam, South RATIFIED: 11 Aug 50 FORCE: 12 Jan 51
Yugoslavia SIGNED: 11 Dec 48 RATIFIED: 29 Aug 50 FORCE: 12 Jan 51
ANNEX
91 UNTS 383. Denmark. Ratification 15 Jun 51. Force 13 Sep 51.
96 UNTS 327. Taiwan. Ratification 19 Jul 51.
100 UNTS 295. Belgium. Ratification 5 Sep 51. Force 4 Dec 51.
118 UNTS 306. Hungary. Qualified Accession 17 Jan 52. Force 6 Apr 52.
120 UNTS 300. Nicaragua. Accession 29 Jan 52. Force 28 Apr 52.
121 UNTS 330. United Arab Rep. Ratification 8 Feb 52. Force 8 May 52.
123 UNTS 304. Honduras. Ratification 5 Mar 52. Force 3 Jun 52.
124 UNTS 318. Belgium. Belgian Colonies.
124 UNTS 318. Belgium. Ruanda-Urundi.
127 UNTS 331. Brazil. Ratification 15 Apr 52. Force 14 Jul 52.
131 UNTS 336. Sweden. Ratification 27 May 52. Force 25 Aug 52.
131 UNTS 336. Italy. Accession 4 Jun 52. Force 2 Sep 52.
134 UNTS 379. Mexico. Ratification 22 Jul 52. Force 20 Oct 52.
136 UNTS 389. Canada. Ratification 3 Sep 52. Force 2 Dec 52.
161 UNTS 369. Cuba. Ratification 4 Mar 53. Force 2 Jun 53.
166 UNTS 369. Chile. Ratification 3 Jun 53. Force 10 Sep 53.
182 UNTS 225. Lebanon. Ratification 17 Dec 53. Force 17 Mar 54.
190 UNTS 381. USSR (Soviet Union). Qualified Ratification 3 May 54.
196 UNTS 345. Byelorussia. Qualified Ratification 11 Aug 54.
201 UNTS 368. Ukrainian SSR. Qualified Ratification 15 Nov 54.
201 UNTS 369. Germany, West. Accession 20 Nov 54.
202 UNTS 334. Greece. Ratification 8 Dec 54. Force 8 Mar 55.
210 UNTS 332. Albania. Qualified Accession 12 May 55.
211 UNTS 404. Syria. Accession 25 Jun 55. Force 23 Sep 55.
230 UNTS 435. Burma. Qualified Ratification 14 Mar 56.
230 UNTS 435. Afghanistan. Ratification 22 Mar 56.
248 UNTS 365. Iran. Ratification 14 Aug 56. Force 12 Nov 56.
254 UNTS 407. Tunisia. Accession 29 Nov 56. Force 27 Feb 57.
277 UNTS 347. Pakistan. Ratification 12 Oct 57. Force 10 Jan 58.
286 UNTS 341. Morocco. Qualified Accession 24 Jan 58.
289 UNTS 316. Austria. Accession 19 Mar 58. Force 17 Jun 58.
317 UNTS 319. Ghana. Accession 24 Dec 58. Force 24 Mar 59.
320 UNTS 338. Iraq. Accession 20 Jan 59. Force 20 Apr 59.
340 UNTS 341. India. Qualified Ratification 27 Aug 59.
344 UNTS 313. Colombia. Ratification 27 Oct 59. Force 25 Jan 60.
346 UNTS 324. Finland. Qualified Accession 18 Dec 59.
351 UNTS 392. Peru. Ratification 24 Feb 60. Force 24 May 60.
367 UNTS 316. Venezuela. Qualified Accession 12 Jul 60.
429 UNTS 274. Congo (Zaire). Succession 31 May 62.
480 UNTS 328. Algeria. Qualified Accession 31 Oct 63.
544 UNTS 288. Upper Volta. Accession 14 Sep 65. Force 13 Dec 65.
565 UNTS 280. Netherlands. Qualified Accession 20 Jun 66. Force 18 Sep 66.
600 UNTS 330. Uruguay. Ratification 11 Jul 67. Force 9 Oct 67.
645 UNTS 346. United Nations. Qualified Accession 13 Sep 68.
646 UNTS 342. Jamaica. Accession 23 Sep 68. Force 22 Dec 68.

101022 Bilateral Agreement **78 UNTS 325**
SIGNED: 25 Feb 49   FORCE: 25 Feb 49
REGISTERED: 12 Jan 51 Denmark
ARTICLES: 10 LANGUAGE: French.
HEADNOTE: TRADE
TOPIC: General Trade
CONCEPTS: Detailed regulations. Annex or appendix reference. Licenses and permits. Establishment of commission. Trade procedures. Currency. Payment schedules. Non-interest rates and fees. Commodity trade. Delivery schedules. Quotas.
INTL ORGS: Special Commission.
PROCEDURE: Denunciation. Duration.
PARTIES:
Denmark
Greece

101023 Bilateral Agreement **78 UNTS 335**
SIGNED: 25 Feb 49   FORCE: 25 Feb 49
REGISTERED: 12 Jan 51 Denmark
ARTICLES: 9 LANGUAGE: French.
HEADNOTE: FACILITATING CURRENT PAYMENTS
TOPIC: Finance
CONCEPTS: General cooperation. General trade. Accounting procedures. Banking. Balance of payments. Currency. Exchange rates and regulations. Interest rates. Payment schedules. Local currency.
PROCEDURE: Amendment. Duration.
PARTIES:
Denmark
Greece
ANNEX
81 UNTS 383. Denmark. Amendment 14 Dec 49. Force 14 Dec 49.
81 UNTS 383. Greece. Amendment 14 Dec 49. Force 14 Dec 49.

101024 Bilateral Agreement **78 UNTS 341**
SIGNED: 4 Oct 50   FORCE: 15 Oct 50
REGISTERED: 15 Jan 51 Denmark
ARTICLES: 6 LANGUAGE: French.
HEADNOTE: REGULATE RELEASE TRADE RESTRICTIONS
TOPIC: General Trade
CONCEPTS: Detailed regulations. Annex or appendix reference. Establishment of commission. General trade. Payment schedules. Quotas.
INTL ORGS: Special Commission.
PROCEDURE: Duration.
PARTIES:
Denmark
Italy

101025 Bilateral Agreement **78 UNTS 353**
SIGNED: 4 Oct 50   FORCE: 15 Oct 50
REGISTERED: 15 Jan 51 Denmark
ARTICLES: 6 LANGUAGE: French.
HEADNOTE: REGULATING PAYMENTS
TOPIC: Finance
CONCEPTS: Previous treaty replacement. General cooperation. Accounting procedures. Banking. Balance of payments. Currency deposits. Exchange rates and regulations. Interest rates. Payment schedules. Local currency.
TREATY REF: 2MARCH46 PAYMENTS AGREEMENT.
PROCEDURE: Denunciation.
PARTIES:
Denmark
Italy

101026 Bilateral Exchange **79 UNTS**
SIGNED: 26 Sep 50   FORCE: 15 Oct 50
REGISTERED: 18 Jan 51 Belgium
ARTICLES: 2 LANGUAGE: French.
HEADNOTE: ENTRY FRANCE ALGERIA BELGIAN NATIONALS RESIDENT SWITZERLAND
TOPIC: Visas
CONCEPTS: Border traffic and migration. Non-visa travel documents.
TREATY REF: 71UNTS91.
PARTIES:
Belgium
France

101027 Bilateral Agreement **79 UNTS**
SIGNED: 25 Jan 51   FORCE: 25 Jan 5

REGISTERED: 25 Jan 51 United Nations
ARTICLES: 9 LANGUAGE: English. Spanish.
HEADNOTE: UNICEF ACTIVITIES
TOPIC: IGO Operations
CONCEPTS: Diplomatic privileges. Privileges and immunities. Exchange of information and documents. Materials, equipment and services. Assistance to United Nations.
INTL ORGS: United Nations.
PROCEDURE: Duration.
PARTIES:
Paraguay
UNICEF (Children)
ANNEX
264 UNTS 337. Paraguay. Supplementation 20 Oct 56. Force 20 Oct 56.
264 UNTS 337. UNICEF (Children). Supplementation 20 Oct 56. Force 20 Oct 56.

101028 Bilateral Agreement **79 UNTS 25**
SIGNED: 19 Oct 50 FORCE: 20 Oct 50
REGISTERED: 28 Jan 51 Denmark
ARTICLES: 8 LANGUAGE: English.
HEADNOTE: MODIFYING PAYMENT ARRANGEMENTS
TOPIC: Finance
CONCEPTS: Definition of terms. Annex type material. Previous treaty replacement. General cooperation. Banking. Monetary and gold transfers. Exchange rates and regulations. Internal finance. Payment schedules.
INTL ORGS: European Payments Union.
TREATY REF: 5UNTS251; 25UNTS333; 71UNTS307.
PROCEDURE: Termination.
PARTIES:
Denmark
UK Great Britain
ANNEX
183 UNTS 363. UK Great Britain. Prolongation 3 Sep 53. Force 5 Sep 53.
183 UNTS 363. Denmark. Prolongation 5 Sep 53. Force 5 Sep 53.

101029 Bilateral Exchange **79 UNTS 33**
SIGNED: 7 Oct 50 FORCE: 7 Oct 50
REGISTERED: 7 Feb 51 Netherlands
ARTICLES: 2 LANGUAGE: English.
HEADNOTE: CREDIT BALANCES UTILIZATION PER EPU
TOPIC: Loans and Credits
CONCEPTS: Accounting procedures. Currency. Payment schedules. Credit provisions. Loan repayment.
INTL ORGS: European Payments Union.
PARTIES:
Netherlands
USA (United States)

101030 Bilateral Agreement **79 UNTS 41**
SIGNED: 17 Oct 50 FORCE: 17 Oct 50
REGISTERED: 7 Feb 51 Thailand
ARTICLES: 9 LANGUAGE: English. Thai.
HEADNOTE: MILITARY ASSISTANCE
TOPIC: Milit Assistance
CONCEPTS: Treaty interpretation. Non-prejudice to UN charter. Privileges and immunities. Conformity with municipal law. General cooperation. Inspection and observation. Public information. Use of facilities. Indemnities and reimbursements. Local currency. Claims and settlements. Recognition. Customs exemptions. Domestic obligation. Materials, equipment and services. Aid missions. Joint defense. Military assistance. Security of information. Conditions for assistance missions. Exchange of defense information. Restrictions on transfer. Raw materials.
INTL ORGS: United Nations.
PROCEDURE: Future Procedures Contemplated. Registration. Termination.
PARTIES:
Thailand
USA (United States)
ANNEX
258 UNTS 386. USA (United States). Implementation 6 Jul 55. Force 6 Jul 55.
258 UNTS 386. Thailand. Implementation 6 Jul 55. Force 6 Jul 55.

101031 Bilateral Agreement **79 UNTS 57**
SIGNED: 24 Aug 48 FORCE: 24 Aug 48
REGISTERED: 7 Feb 51 USA (United States)
ARTICLES: 5 LANGUAGE: English. Korean.
HEADNOTE: INTERIM MILITARY SECURITY MATTERS
TOPIC: General Military
CONCEPTS: Guarantees and safeguards. Treaty interpretation. Defense and security. Military assistance. Jurisdiction. Status of forces. Bases and facilities.
INTL ORGS: United Nations.
PARTIES:
Korea, South
USA (United States)

101032 Bilateral Exchange **79 UNTS 71**
SIGNED: 26 Nov 48 FORCE: 26 Nov 48
REGISTERED: 7 Feb 51 USA (United States)
ARTICLES: 4 LANGUAGE: English. Italian.
HEADNOTE: DUTY-FREE ENTRY RELIEF SUPPLIES
TOPIC: Direct Aid
CONCEPTS: Annex type material. Accounting procedures. Indemnities and reimbursements. Payment schedules. Transportation costs. Customs exemptions. Relief supplies.
TREATY REF: 20UNTS43.
PARTIES:
Italy
USA (United States)
ANNEX
181 UNTS 353. Italy. Amendment 19 Jul 52. Force 19 Jul 52.
181 UNTS 353. USA (United States). Amendment 19 Jul 52. Force 19 Jul 52.

101033 Multilateral Exchange **79 UNTS 85**
SIGNED: 16 Dec 48 FORCE: 16 Dec 48
REGISTERED: 7 Feb 51 USA (United States)
ARTICLES: 2 LANGUAGE: English.
HEADNOTE: DUTY-FREE ENTRY RELIEF SUPPLIES
TOPIC: Direct Aid
CONCEPTS: Annex type material. Accounting procedures. Indemnities and reimbursements. Payment schedules. Transportation costs. Customs exemptions. Relief supplies. Occupation regime.
TREATY REF: 23UNTS3.
PROCEDURE: Amendment. Duration. Termination.
PARTIES:
USA (United States) SIGNED: 7 Dec 48 FORCE: 16 Dec 48
British Occup Germ SIGNED: 16 Dec 48 FORCE: 16 Dec 48
US Occup Germ SIGNED: 16 Dec 48 FORCE: 16 Dec 48

101034 Bilateral Agreement **79 UNTS 95**
SIGNED: 9 Feb 49 FORCE: 9 Feb 49
REGISTERED: 7 Feb 51 USA (United States)
ARTICLES: 7 LANGUAGE: English.
HEADNOTE: DUTY-FREE ENTRY RELIEF SUPPLIES
TOPIC: Direct Aid
CONCEPTS: Treaty interpretation. Annex or appendix reference. Annex type material. Accounting procedures. Payment schedules. Transportation costs. Customs exemptions. Relief supplies.
INTL ORGS: Universal Postal Union.
TREATY REF: 23UNTS43.
PROCEDURE: Amendment. Duration. Termination.
PARTIES:
Greece
USA (United States)
ANNEX
179 UNTS 216. Greece. Amendment 7 May 52. Force 7 May 52.
179 UNTS 216. USA (United States). Amendment 19 Dec 51. Force 7 May 52.
185 UNTS 400. Greece. Amendment 22 Dec 52. Force 22 Dec 52.
185 UNTS 400. USA (United States). Amendment 18 Jul 52. Force 22 Dec 52.

101035 Bilateral Exchange **79 UNTS 113**
SIGNED: 11 Feb 49 FORCE: 11 Feb 49
REGISTERED: 7 Feb 51 USA (United States)
ARTICLES: 2 LANGUAGE: English.
HEADNOTE: DUTY-FREE ENTRY RELIEF SUPPLIES
TOPIC: Direct Aid
CONCEPTS: Annex type material. Accounting procedures. Indemnities and reimbursements. Pay-

ment schedules. Transportation costs. Customs exemptions. Relief supplies.
TREATY REF: 21UNTS29.
PROCEDURE: Amendment. Duration. Termination.
PARTIES:
Austria
USA (United States)

101036 Bilateral Agreement **79 UNTS 123**
SIGNED: 11 Feb 49 FORCE: 11 Feb 49
REGISTERED: 7 Feb 51 USA (United States)
ARTICLES: 5 LANGUAGE: English.
HEADNOTE: DUTY-FREE ENTRY RELIEF SUPPLIES
TOPIC: Direct Aid
CONCEPTS: Annex type material. Accounting procedures. Indemnities and reimbursements. Payment schedules. Transportation costs. Customs exemptions. Relief supplies. Occupation regime.
INTL ORGS: Universal Postal Union.
PARTIES:
Trieste
USA (United States)
ANNEX
180 UNTS 305. Trieste. Amendment 18 Jul 52. Force 18 Jul 52.
180 UNTS 305. USA (United States). Amendment 30 Jun 52. Force 18 Jul 52.

101037 Bilateral Agreement **79 UNTS 133**
SIGNED: 18 Dec 48 FORCE: 18 Dec 48
REGISTERED: 7 Feb 51 USA (United States)
ARTICLES: 11 LANGUAGE: English. Italian.
HEADNOTE: EDUCATIONAL EXCHANGE PROGRAM
TOPIC: Education
CONCEPTS: Definition of terms. Conformity with municipal law. Personnel. General property. Dispute settlement. Education. Exchange. Commissions and foundations. Teacher and student exchange. Professorships. Scholarships and grants. Research and development. Accounting procedures. Indemnities and reimbursements. Currency. Exchange rates and regulations. Financial programs. Funding procedures. Tax exemptions.
INTL ORGS: Special Commission.
PROCEDURE: Duration. Renewal or Revival.
PARTIES:
Italy
USA (United States)
ANNEX
237 UNTS 304. Italy. Amendment 14 Jun 54. Force 30 Jun 54.
237 UNTS 304. USA (United States). Amendment 30 Jun 54. Force 30 Jun 54.
262 UNTS 450. Italy. Amendment 30 Jun 55. Force 30 Jun 55.
262 UNTS 450. USA (United States). Amendment 22 Apr 55. Force 30 Jun 55.
347 UNTS 369. USA (United States). Amendment 17 Jun 59. Force 17 Jun 59.
347 UNTS 369. Italy. Amendment 17 Jun 59. Force 17 Jun 59.

101038 Bilateral Exchange **79 UNTS 147**
SIGNED: 1 Aug 49 FORCE: 1 Aug 49
REGISTERED: 7 Feb 51 USA (United States)
ARTICLES: 2 LANGUAGE: English.
HEADNOTE: EXCHANGE OFFICIAL PUBLICATIONS
TOPIC: Admin Cooperation
CONCEPTS: Exchange of official publications. Operating agencies.
PARTIES:
Denmark
USA (United States)

101039 Bilateral Agreement **79 UNTS 155**
SIGNED: 1 Sep 49 FORCE: 1 Sep 49
REGISTERED: 7 Feb 51 USA (United States)
ARTICLES: 12 LANGUAGE: English. Persian.
HEADNOTE: USE FUNDS FROM SALE SURPLUS PROPERTY
TOPIC: Direct Aid
CONCEPTS: Definition of terms. Detailed regulations. Conformity with municipal law. Exchange of information and documents. Personnel. Commissions and foundations. Accounting procedures. Funding procedures. Local currency. Surplus property. Internal structure.

PROCEDURE: Amendment.
PARTIES:
  Iran
  USA (United States)
          ANNEX
303 UNTS 308. USA (United States). Amendment 25 Nov 57. Force 25 Nov 57.
303 UNTS 308. Iran. Amendment 25 Nov 57. Force 25 Nov 57.
416 UNTS 306. USA (United States). Amendment 20 Jun 61. Force 20 Jun 61.
416 UNTS 306. Iran. Amendment 20 Jun 61. Force 20 Jun 61.

101040   Bilateral Treaty   **79 UNTS 171**
SIGNED: 2 Feb 48   FORCE: 26 Jul 49
REGISTERED: 7 Feb 51 USA (United States)
ARTICLES: 27 LANGUAGE: English. Italian.
HEADNOTE: FRIENDSHIP COMMERCE NAVIGATION
TOPIC: General Amity
CONCEPTS: Definition of terms. Exceptions and exemptions. General provisions. Treaty interpretation. Border traffic and migration. Alien status. Conformity with municipal law. Juridical personality. Free passage and transit. Legal protection and assistance. General property. Public information. Responsibility and liability. Procedure. Export quotas. Import quotas. Reexport of goods, etc.. Compensation. Fees and exemptions. Financial programs. Non-interest rates and fees. Most favored nation clause. General. Laws and formalities. Recognition. Navigational conditions. Inland and territorial waters. Use of ports and territorial waters. Ports and pilotage. Repatriation of civilians.
INTL ORGS: International Court of Justice. United Nations.
PROCEDURE: Duration. Ratification. Termination.
PARTIES:
  Italy
  USA (United States)
          ANNEX
404 UNTS 326. USA (United States). Supplementation 26 Sep 61. Force 2 Mar 61.
404 UNTS 326. Italy. Supplementation 26 Sep 61. Force 2 Mar 61.

101041   Bilateral Convention   **80 UNTS 3**
SIGNED: 31 May 49   FORCE: 3 Mar 50
REGISTERED: 7 Feb 51 USA (United States)
ARTICLES: 5 LANGUAGE: English. Spanish.
HEADNOTE: TUNA COMMISSION
TOPIC: IGO Establishment
CONCEPTS: Exchange of information and documents. Informational records. Domestic legislation. Research results. Scientific exchange. Research and development. Funding procedures. Establishment. Internal structure. Ocean resources.
INTL ORGS: Special Commission.
PROCEDURE: Ratification. Termination.
PARTIES:
  Costa Rica
  USA (United States)

101042   Bilateral Exchange   **80 UNTS 27**
SIGNED: 4 Jan 51   FORCE: 4 Jan 50
REGISTERED: 8 Feb 51 Australia
ARTICLES: 11 LANGUAGE: English.
HEADNOTE: RELEASE MONEYS CLAIM SETTLEMENT
TOPIC: Claims and Debts
CONCEPTS: Definition of terms. Exceptions and exemptions. Conformity with municipal law. Exchange of information and documents. Informational records. Compensation. Exchange rates and regulations. Claims and settlements. Assessment procedures. Assets transfer. General.
PARTIES:
  Australia
  Finland

101043   Bilateral Agreement   **80 UNTS 37**
SIGNED: 14 Apr 49   FORCE: 14 Apr 49
REGISTERED: 10 Feb 51 USA (United States)
ARTICLES: 30 LANGUAGE: English. French.
HEADNOTE: NAVAL MISSION
TOPIC: Military Mission
CONCEPTS: Definition of terms. Use of facilities.

Compensation. Indemnities and reimbursements. Exchange rates and regulations. Expense sharing formulae. Tax exemptions. Customs exemptions. Military assistance. Military training. Security of information. Airforce-army-navy personnel ratio. Ranks and privileges. Conditions for assistance missions. Third country military personnel. Status of forces.
PROCEDURE: Denunciation. Duration. Renewal or Revival. Termination.
PARTIES:
  Haiti
  USA (United States)
          ANNEX
207 UNTS 347. USA (United States). Prolongation 28 Jan 53. Force 14 Apr 53.
207 UNTS 347. Haiti. Prolongation 2 Mar 53. Force 14 Apr 53.

101044   Bilateral Agreement   **80 UNTS 51**
SIGNED: 6 Mar 50   FORCE: 6 Mar 50
REGISTERED: 10 Feb 51 USA (United States)
ARTICLES: 30 LANGUAGE: English. Spanish.
HEADNOTE: AIR FORCE MISSION
TOPIC: Military Mission
CONCEPTS: Definition of terms. Use of facilities. Compensation. Indemnities and reimbursements. Exchange rates and regulations. Expense sharing formulae. Tax exemptions. Customs exemptions. Military assistance. Military training. Security of information. Airforce-army-navy personnel ratio. Ranks and privileges. Conditions for assistance missions. Third country military personnel. Status of forces.
PROCEDURE: Denunciation. Duration. Renewal or Revival. Termination.
PARTIES:
  Honduras
  USA (United States)
          ANNEX
222 UNTS 399. USA (United States). Prolongation 5 Oct 53. Force 6 Mar 54.
222 UNTS 399. Honduras. Prolongation 23 Nov 53. Force 6 Mar 54.
376 UNTS 408. USA (United States). Extension and Amendment 22 Apr 60. Force 20 May 60.
376 UNTS 408. Honduras. Extension and Amendment 20 May 60. Force 20 May 60.

101045   Bilateral Agreement   **80 UNTS 71**
SIGNED: 6 Mar 50   FORCE: 6 Mar 50
REGISTERED: 10 Feb 51 USA (United States)
ARTICLES: 29 LANGUAGE: English. Spanish.
HEADNOTE: ARMY MISSION
TOPIC: Military Mission
CONCEPTS: Definition of terms. Use of facilities. Compensation. Indemnities and reimbursements. Exchange rates and regulations. Expense sharing formulae. Tax exemptions. Customs exemptions. Military assistance. Military training. Security of information. Airforce-army-navy personnel ratio. Ranks and privileges. Conditions for assistance missions. Third country military personnel. Status of forces.
PROCEDURE: Denunciation. Duration. Renewal or Revival. Termination.
PARTIES:
  Honduras
  USA (United States)
          ANNEX
222 UNTS 400. Honduras. Prolongation 23 Nov 53. Force 6 Mar 54.
222 UNTS 400. USA (United States). Prolongation 5 Oct 53. Force 6 Mar 54.
376 UNTS 414. USA (United States). Extension and Amendment 22 Apr 60. Force 20 May 60.
376 UNTS 414. Honduras. Extension and Amendment 20 May 60. Force 20 May 60.

101046   Bilateral Agreement   **80 UNTS 91**
SIGNED: 6 Oct 48   FORCE: 6 Oct 48
REGISTERED: 10 Feb 51 USA (United States)
ARTICLES: 30 LANGUAGE: English. Spanish.
HEADNOTE: MILITARY ADVISORY MISSION
TOPIC: Military Mission
CONCEPTS: Definition of terms. Use of facilities. Compensation. Indemnities and reimbursements. Exchange rates and regulations. Expense sharing formulae. Tax exemptions. Customs exemptions. Military assistance. Military training. Security of information. Airforce-army-navy per-

sonnel ratio. Ranks and privileges. Conditions for assistance missions. Third country military personnel. Status of forces.
PROCEDURE: Denunciation. Duration. Renewal or Revival. Termination.
PARTIES:
  Argentina
  USA (United States)

101047   Bilateral Agreement   **80 UNTS 111**
SIGNED: 29 Jul 48   FORCE: 29 Jul 48
REGISTERED: 10 Feb 51 USA (United States)
ARTICLES: 27 LANGUAGE: English. Portuguese.
HEADNOTE: MILITARY ADVISORY MISSION
TOPIC: Military Mission
CONCEPTS: Definition of terms. Use of facilities. Compensation. Indemnities and reimbursements. Exchange rates and regulations. Expense sharing formulae. Tax exemptions. Customs exemptions. Military assistance. Military training. Security of information. Airforce-army-navy personnel ratio. Ranks and privileges. Conditions for assistance missions. Third country military personnel. Status of forces.
PROCEDURE: Denunciation. Duration. Renewal or Revival. Termination.
PARTIES:
  Brazil
  USA (United States)
          ANNEX
232 UNTS 326. USA (United States). Prolongation 23 Sep 52. Force 23 Sep 52.
232 UNTS 326. Brazil. Prolongation 21 Jul 52. Force 23 Sep 52.
264 UNTS 340. USA (United States). Amendment 13 Apr 55. Force 16 May 55.
264 UNTS 340. Brazil. Amendment 16 May 55. Force 16 May 55.
278 UNTS 269. USA (United States). Prolongation 25 May 56. Force 25 May 56.
278 UNTS 269. Brazil. Prolongation 31 Mar 56. Force 25 May 56.
337 UNTS 394. USA (United States). Prolongation 2 Apr 58. Force 2 Apr 58.
337 UNTS 394. Brazil. Prolongation 4 Mar 58. Force 2 Apr 58.
371 UNTS 271. Brazil. Amendment 9 Jun 59. Force 17 Jun 59.
371 UNTS 271. USA (United States). Amendment 17 Jun 59. Force 17 Jun 59.

101048   Bilateral Exchange   **80 UNTS 127**
SIGNED: 21 Sep 48   FORCE: 21 Sep 48
REGISTERED: 10 Feb 51 USA (United States)
ARTICLES: 4 LANGUAGE: English. Spanish.
HEADNOTE: MODIFYING EXTENDING AGREEMENT MILITARY MISSION
TOPIC: Military Mission
CONCEPTS: Annex type material. Previous treaty extension. Military assistance missions.
TREATY REF: 80UNTS283.
PARTIES:
  Ecuador
  USA (United States)
          ANNEX
253 UNTS 342. USA (United States). Extension and Amendment 26 May 55. Force 26 May 55.
253 UNTS 342. Ecuador. Extension and Amendment 10 May 55. Force 26 May 55.
347 UNTS 375. Ecuador. Amendment 22 May 59. Force 22 May 59.
347 UNTS 375. USA (United States). Amendment 25 Feb 59. Force 22 May 59.

101049   Bilateral Exchange   **80 UNTS 137**
SIGNED: 4 Feb 49   FORCE: 4 Feb 49
REGISTERED: 10 Feb 51 USA (United States)
ARTICLES: 2 LANGUAGE: English. Spanish.
HEADNOTE: AMENDING EXTENDING AGREEMENT NAVAL MISSION
TOPIC: Military Mission
CONCEPTS: Annex type material. Previous treaty extension. Military assistance missions.
PARTIES:
  Ecuador
  USA (United States)
          ANNEX
253 UNTS 346. USA (United States). Prolongation 6 Dec 54. Force 6 Dec 54.
253 UNTS 346. Ecuador. Prolongation 30 Aug 54. Force 6 Dec 54.

347 UNTS 375. Ecuador. Amendment 22 May 59. Force 22 May 59.
347 UNTS 375. USA (United States). Amendment 25 Feb 59. Force 22 May 59.

101050 Bilateral Exchange **80 UNTS 145**
SIGNED: 27 Jan 50 FORCE: 27 Jan 50
REGISTERED: 10 Feb 51 USA (United States)
ARTICLES: 2 LANGUAGE: English. Italian.
HEADNOTE: MUTUAL DEFENSE ASSISTANCE
TOPIC: Milit Assistance
CONCEPTS: Annex or appendix reference. Non-prejudice to UN charter. Privileges and immunities. Conformity with municipal law. General co-operation. Inspection and observation. Public information. Use of facilities. Indemnities and reimbursements. Local currency. Claims and settlements. Tax exemptions. Recognition. Customs exemptions. Domestic obligation. Materials, equipment and services. Aid missions. Joint defense. Defense and security. Military assistance. Security of information. Exchange of defense information. Restrictions on transfer.
INTL ORGS: North Atlantic Treaty Organization.
TREATY REF: 34UNTS243.
PROCEDURE: Amendment. Future Procedures Contemplated. Registration. Termination.
PARTIES:
Italy
USA (United States)
ANNEX
238 UNTS 310. USA (United States). Supplementation 20 Nov 51. Force 14 Dec 51.
238 UNTS 310. Italy. Supplementation 14 Dec 51. Force 14 Dec 51.
389 UNTS 307. USA (United States). Amendment 7 Sep 60. Force 7 Sep 60.
389 UNTS 307. Italy. Amendment 7 Sep 60. Force 7 Sep 60.

101051 Bilateral Agreement **80 UNTS 171**
SIGNED: 27 Jan 50 FORCE: 27 Jan 50
REGISTERED: 10 Feb 51 USA (United States)
ARTICLES: 7 LANGUAGE: English. French.
HEADNOTE: MUTUAL DEFENSE ASSISTANCE
TOPIC: Milit Assistance
CONCEPTS: Annex or appendix reference. Non-prejudice to UN charter. Privileges and immunities. Conformity with municipal law. General co-operation. Inspection and observation. Public information. Use of facilities. Indemnities and reimbursements. Local currency. Claims and settlements. Tax exemptions. Recognition. Customs exemptions. Domestic obligation. Materials, equipment and services. Aid missions. Joint defense. Defense and security. Military assistance. Security of information. Exchange of defense information. Restrictions on transfer. Raw materials.
INTL ORGS: North Atlantic Treaty Organization.
TREATY REF: 34UNTS243.
PROCEDURE: Amendment. Future Procedures Contemplated. Ratification. Registration. Termination.
PARTIES:
France
USA (United States)
ANNEX
304 UNTS 349. USA (United States). Supplementation 30 Jan 58. Force 30 Jan 58.
304 UNTS 349. France. Supplementation 30 Jan 58. Force 30 Jan 58.
337 UNTS 397. USA (United States). Supplementation 28 Oct 58. Force 28 Oct 58.
337 UNTS 397. France. Supplementation 28 Oct 58. Force 28 Oct 58.
433 UNTS 340. USA (United States). Interpretation 20 Dec 61. Force 20 Dec 61.
433 UNTS 340. France. Interpretation 20 Dec 61. Force 20 Dec 61.

101052 Bilateral Agreement **80 UNTS 187**
SIGNED: 27 Jan 50 FORCE: 28 Mar 50
REGISTERED: 10 Feb 51 USA (United States)
ARTICLES: 8 LANGUAGE: English. French.
HEADNOTE: MUTUAL DEFENSE ASSISTANCE
TOPIC: Milit Assistance
CONCEPTS: Annex or appendix reference. Non-prejudice to UN charter. Privileges and immunities. Conformity with municipal law. General co-operation. Inspection and observation. Public in-

formation. Use of facilities. Indemnities and re-imbursements. Local currency. Tax exemptions. Recognition. Customs exemptions. Domestic obligation. Materials, equipment and services. Aid missions. Joint defense. Defense and security. Military assistance. Security of information. Exchange of defense information. Restrictions on transfer. Raw materials.
INTL ORGS: North Atlantic Treaty Organization.
TREATY REF: 34UNTS243.
PROCEDURE: Amendment. Future Procedures Contemplated. Ratification. Registration. Termination.
PARTIES:
Luxembourg
USA (United States)
ANNEX
284 UNTS 366. USA (United States). Amendment 15 Apr 57. Force 25 Apr 57.
284 UNTS 366. Luxembourg. Amendment 25 Apr 57. Force 25 Apr 57.
299 UNTS 410. USA (United States). Amendment 4 Oct 57. Force 7 Oct 57.
299 UNTS 410. Luxembourg. Amendment 7 Oct 57. Force 7 Oct 57.
344 UNTS 314. USA (United States). Amendment 21 Apr 59. Force 8 May 59.
344 UNTS 314. Luxembourg. Amendment 21 Apr 59. Force 8 May 59.
358 UNTS 262. USA (United States). Amendment 27 Oct 59. Force 31 Oct 59.
358 UNTS 262. Luxembourg. Amendment 31 Oct 59. Force 31 Oct 59.
394 UNTS 264. USA (United States). Amendment 22 Sep 60. Force 5 Oct 60.
394 UNTS 264. Luxembourg. Amendment 5 Oct 60. Force 5 Oct 60.
433 UNTS 348. USA (United States). Amendment 18 Sep 61. Force 22 Sep 61.
433 UNTS 348. Luxembourg. Amendment 22 Sep 61. Force 22 Sep 61.
531 UNTS 306. USA (United States). Amendment 24 Sep 64. Force 30 Sep 64.
531 UNTS 306. Luxembourg. Amendment 30 Sep 64. Force 30 Sep 64.

101053 Bilateral Agreement **80 UNTS 205**
SIGNED: 26 Jan 50 FORCE: 26 Jan 50
REGISTERED: 13 Feb 51 USA (United States)
ARTICLES: 8 LANGUAGE: English. Korean.
HEADNOTE: MUTUAL DEFENSE ASSISTANCE
TOPIC: Milit Assistance
CONCEPTS: Treaty interpretation. Non-prejudice to UN charter. Privileges and immunities. Conformity with municipal law. General cooperation. Inspection and observation. Public information. Use of facilities. Recognition. Customs exemptions. Domestic obligation. Materials, equipment and services. Aid missions. Joint defense. Defense and security. Military assistance. Security of information. Exchange of defense information. Restrictions on transfer. Raw materials.
INTL ORGS: United Nations.
TREATY REF: 55UNTS157.
PROCEDURE: Amendment. Future Procedures Contemplated. Ratification. Registration. Termination.
PARTIES:
Korea, South
USA (United States)

101054 Bilateral Agreement **80 UNTS 219**
SIGNED: 27 Jan 50 FORCE: 27 Jan 50
REGISTERED: 13 Feb 51 USA (United States)
ARTICLES: 6 LANGUAGE: Dutch. English.
HEADNOTE: MUTUAL DEFENSE ASSISTANCE
TOPIC: Milit Assistance
CONCEPTS: General provisions. Annex or appendix reference. Non-prejudice to UN charter. Privileges and immunities. Conformity with municipal law. General cooperation. Inspection and observation. Public information. Use of facilities. Indemnities and reimbursements. Local currency. Claims and settlements. Tax exemptions. Recognition. Customs exemptions. Domestic obligation. Materials, equipment and services. Aid missions. Joint defense. Defense and security. Military assistance. Security of information. Exchange of defense information. Restrictions on transfer. Raw materials.
INTL ORGS: North Atlantic Treaty Organization.
TREATY REF: 34UNTS243.

PROCEDURE: Amendment. Denunciation. Duration. Future Procedures Contemplated. Ratification. Registration. Renewal or Revival. Termination.
PARTIES:
Netherlands
USA (United States)

101055 Bilateral Agreement **80 UNTS 241**
SIGNED: 27 Jan 50 FORCE: 24 Feb 50
REGISTERED: 13 Feb 51 USA (United States)
ARTICLES: 6 LANGUAGE: English. Norwegian.
HEADNOTE: MUTUAL DEFENSE ASSISTANCE
TOPIC: Milit Assistance
CONCEPTS: Annex or appendix reference. Non-prejudice to UN charter. Privileges and immunities. Conformity with municipal law. General co-operation. Inspection and observation. Public information. Use of facilities. Indemnities and reimbursements. Local currency. Claims and settlements. Tax exemptions. Recognition. Customs exemptions. Domestic obligation. Materials, equipment and services. Aid missions. Joint defense. Defense and security. Military assistance. Security of information. Exchange of defense information. Restrictions on transfer.
INTL ORGS: North Atlantic Treaty Organization.
TREATY REF: 34UNTS243.
PROCEDURE: Amendment. Future Procedures Contemplated. Ratification. Registration. Termination.
PARTIES:
Norway
USA (United States)
ANNEX
157 UNTS 366. USA (United States). Amendment 30 Jun 50. Force 30 Jun 50.
157 UNTS 366. Norway. Amendment 30 Jun 50. Force 30 Jun 50.
178 UNTS 388. USA (United States). Amendment 26 Jul 51. Force 26 Jul 51.
178 UNTS 388. Norway. Amendment 26 Jul 51. Force 26 Jul 51.
223 UNTS 326. USA (United States). Amendment 20 Aug 52. Force 20 Aug 52.
223 UNTS 326. Norway. Amendment 20 Aug 52. Force 20 Aug 52.
238 UNTS 316. USA (United States). Amendment 12 Nov 53. Force 12 Nov 53.
238 UNTS 316. Norway. Amendment 12 Nov 53. Force 12 Nov 53.
266 UNTS 388. USA (United States). Amendment 15 Nov 55. Force 23 Nov 55.
266 UNTS 388. Norway. Amendment 23 Nov 55. Force 23 Nov 55.
279 UNTS 300. USA (United States). Amendment 14 Aug 56. Force 23 Aug 56.
279 UNTS 300. Norway. Amendment 23 Aug 56. Force 23 Aug 56.
303 UNTS 316. USA (United States). Amendment 24 Oct 57. Force 4 Nov 57.
303 UNTS 316. Norway. Amendment 4 Nov 57. Force 4 Nov 57.
317 UNTS 320. USA (United States). Supplementation 17 Apr 58. Force 8 May 58.
317 UNTS 320. Norway. Supplementation 8 May 58. Force 8 May 58.
335 UNTS 294. USA (United States). Amendment 25 Jul 58. Force 16 Aug 58.
335 UNTS 294. Norway. Amendment 16 Aug 58. Force 16 Aug 58.
358 UNTS 266. USA (United States). Amendment 31 Aug 59. Force 9 Sep 59.
358 UNTS 266. Norway. Amendment 9 Sep 59. Force 9 Sep 59.
388 UNTS 344. USA (United States). Amendment 21 Jul 60. Force 18 Aug 60.
388 UNTS 344. Norway. Amendment 18 Aug 60. Force 18 Aug 60.
406 UNTS 298. Norway. Amendment 23 Mar 61. Force 23 Mar 61.
406 UNTS 298. USA (United States). Amendment 6 Mar 61. Force 23 Mar 61.
421 UNTS 300. Norway. Amendment 30 Aug 61. Force 30 Aug 61.
421 UNTS 300. USA (United States). Amendment 17 Aug 61. Force 30 Aug 61.
460 UNTS 298. USA (United States). Amendment 7 Aug 62. Force 15 Aug 62.
460 UNTS 298. Norway. Amendment 15 Aug 62. Force 15 Aug 62.
471 UNTS 318. USA (United States). Prolongation 14 Jan 63. Force 14 Jan 63.

471 UNTS 318. Norway. Prolongation 16 Nov 62.
Force 14 Jan 63.
531 UNTS 310. USA (United States). Amendment
25 Aug 64. Force 2 Sep 64.
531 UNTS 310. Norway. Amendment 2 Sep 64.
Force 2 Sep 64.
606 UNTS 306. USA (United States). Amendment
6 Sep 66. Force 6 Sep 66.
606 UNTS 306. Norway. Amendment 6 Sep 66.
Force 6 Sep 66.

101056   Bilateral Agreement   **80 UNTS 261**
SIGNED: 27 Jan 50   FORCE: 27 Jan 50
REGISTERED: 13 Feb 51 USA (United States)
ARTICLES: 12 LANGUAGE: English.
HEADNOTE: MUTUAL DEFENSE ASSISTANCE
TOPIC: Milit Assistance
CONCEPTS: Annex or appendix reference. Non-
prejudice to UN charter. Privileges and immunities. Conformity with municipal law. General cooperation. Inspection and observation. Public information. Use of facilities. Indemnities and
reimbursements. Local currency. Claims and set-
tlements. Recognition. Customs exemptions. Domestic obligation. Materials, equipment and services. Aid missions. Joint defense. Defense and
security. Military assistance. Security of information. Exchange of defense information. Restrictions on transfer.
INTL ORGS: North Atlantic Treaty Organization.
TREATY REF: 34UNTS243; 22UNTS263.
PROCEDURE: Amendment. Future Procedures
Contemplated. Ratification. Termination.
PARTIES:
UK Great Britain
USA (United States)
ANNEX
164 UNTS 362. UK Great Britain. Hong Kong.
164 UNTS 362. UK Great Britain. Gambia.
164 UNTS 362. UK Great Britain. Leeward Islands.
164 UNTS 362. UK Great Britain. Falkland Islands.
164 UNTS 362. UK Great Britain. Tanganyika.
164 UNTS 362. UK Great Britain. Trinidad/-
Tobago.
164 UNTS 362. UK Great Britain. British Guiana.
164 UNTS 362. UK Great Britain. British Honduras.
164 UNTS 362. UK Great Britain. Brunei.
164 UNTS 362. UK Great Britain. Cyprus.
164 UNTS 362. UK Great Britain. Zanzibar.
164 UNTS 362. UK Great Britain. Uganda.
164 UNTS 362. UK Great Britain. Gibralter.
164 UNTS 362. UK Great Britain. Mauritius.
164 UNTS 362. UK Great Britain. Nigeria.
164 UNTS 362. UK Great Britain. Nyasaland.
164 UNTS 362. UK Great Britain. North Borneo.
164 UNTS 362. UK Great Britain. Northern
Rhodesia.
164 UNTS 362. UK Great Britain. St. Helena.
164 UNTS 362. UK Great Britain. Sarawak.
164 UNTS 362. UK Great Britain. Seychelles.
164 UNTS 362. UK Great Britain. Sierra Leone.
164 UNTS 362. UK Great Britain. British Somaliland.
164 UNTS 362. UK Great Britain. Malta.
164 UNTS 362. UK Great Britain. Gold Coast.
164 UNTS 362. UK Great Britain. Bahamas.
164 UNTS 362. UK Great Britain. Aden.
291 UNTS 300. USA (United States). Supplementation 10 May 57. Force 13 May 57.
291 UNTS 300. UK Great Britain. Supplementation 13 May 57. Force 13 May 57.
340 UNTS 342. USA (United States). Amendment
17 Dec 58. Force 30 Dec 58.
340 UNTS 342. UK Great Britain. Amendment
30 Dec 58. Force 30 Dec 58.
431 UNTS 288. USA (United States). Amendment
7 Nov 61. Force 10 Nov 61.
431 UNTS 288. UK Great Britain. Amendment
10 Nov 61. Force 10 Nov 61.
449 UNTS 286. UK Great Britain. Supplementation 29 Jun 62. Force 29 Jun 62.
449 UNTS 286. USA (United States). Supplementation 29 Jun 62. Force 29 Jun 62.
486 UNTS 398. UK Great Britain. Amendment
28 Aug 63. Force 28 Aug 63.
486 UNTS 398. USA (United States). Amendment
28 Aug 63. Force 28 Aug 63.

101057   Bilateral Exchange   **81 UNTS 3**
SIGNED: 23 May 50   FORCE: 23 May 50
REGISTERED: 13 Feb 51 USA (United States)
ARTICLES: 2 LANGUAGE: English.
HEADNOTE: MUTUAL DEFENSE ASSISTANCE
TOPIC: Milit Assistance
CONCEPTS: Non-prejudice to UN charter. General
cooperation. Inspection and observation. Public
information. Use of facilities. Claims and settle-
ments. Tax exemptions. Recognition. Customs
exemptions. Domestic obligation. Materials,
equipment and services. Aid missions. Security
of information. Exchange of defense informa-
tion. Restrictions on transfer. Raw materials.
TREATY REF: 31UNTS451; 11UNTS303.
PROCEDURE: Future Procedures Contemplated.
PARTIES:
Iran
USA (United States)
ANNEX
303 UNTS 320. USA (United States). Supplementation 12 Jul 57. Force 31 Oct 57.
303 UNTS 320. Iran. Supplementation 31 Oct 57.
Force 31 Oct 57.

101058   Bilateral Exchange   **81 UNTS 13**
SIGNED: 25 Aug 50   FORCE: 25 Aug 50
REGISTERED: 18 Feb 51 Netherlands
ARTICLES: 2 LANGUAGE: French.
HEADNOTE: PLACEMENT AGRICULTURAL WORK-
ERS
TOPIC: Non-ILO Labor
CONCEPTS: Definition of terms. Border traffic and
migration. Employment regulations. Wages and
salaries. Non-ILO labor relations. Administrative
cooperation. Social security. Migrant worker.
National treatment.
TREATY REF: 19LTS11.
PARTIES:
Luxembourg
Netherlands

101059   Bilateral Agreement   **81 UNTS 21**
SIGNED: 7 Dec 49   FORCE: 7 Dec 49
REGISTERED: 21 Feb 51 Denmark
ARTICLES: 8 LANGUAGE: French.
HEADNOTE: EXCHANGE COMMODITIES
TOPIC: Commodity Trade
CONCEPTS: Time limit. Treaty implementation.
Annex or appendix reference. Previous treaty re-
placement. Licenses and permits. Establishment
of commission. General trade. Reciprocity in
trade. Payment schedules. Quotas.
TREATY REF: 81UNTS33; 14DEC48 EXCHANGE
AGREEMENT.
PROCEDURE: Denunciation. Renewal or Revival.
PARTIES:
Denmark
Poland

101060   Bilateral Agreement   **81 UNTS 33**
SIGNED: 14 Dec 48   FORCE: 14 Dec 48
REGISTERED: 21 Feb 51 Denmark
ARTICLES: 13 LANGUAGE: French.
HEADNOTE: SETTLING TRANSFER RECIPROCAL
PAYMENTS
TOPIC: Finance
CONCEPTS: Detailed regulations. General cooper-
ation. Licenses and permits. Establishment of
commission. Existing tribunals. General trade.
Accounting procedures. Banking. Exchange
rates and regulations. Financial programs. Inter-
est rates. Payment schedules. Local currency.
PROCEDURE: Amendment. Denunciation. Dura-
tion. Renewal or Revival.
PARTIES:
Denmark
Poland

101061   Bilateral Protocol   **81 UNTS 43**
SIGNED: 1 Oct 50   FORCE: 30 Nov 50
REGISTERED: 21 Feb 51 Denmark
ARTICLES: 5 LANGUAGE: French.
HEADNOTE: EXCHANGE GOODS PAYMENTS
TOPIC: General Economic
CONCEPTS: Annex or appendix reference. Annex
type material. Licenses and permits. Export
quotas. Import quotas. Financial programs. Pay-
ment schedules. Quotas. Credit provisions.
Transport of goods.

TREATY REF: 81UNTS21,33.
PARTIES:
Denmark
Poland

101062   Bilateral Treaty   **81 UNTS 53**
SIGNED: 14 Jun 49   FORCE: 1 Aug 50
REGISTERED: 26 Feb 51 Thailand
ARTICLES: 7 LANGUAGE: English.
HEADNOTE: FRIENDSHIP
TOPIC: General Amity
CONCEPTS: Friendship and amity. Alien status.
Consular relations establishment. Diplomatic re-
lations establishment. General property. Proce-
dure. Domestic jurisdiction.
INTL ORGS: International Court of Justice.
PROCEDURE: Future Procedures Contemplated.
Ratification. Termination.
PARTIES:
Philippines
Thailand

101063   Bilateral Agreement   **81 UNTS 61**
SIGNED: 1 Jul 50   FORCE: 1 Jul 50
REGISTERED: 26 Feb 51 Thailand
ARTICLES: 13 LANGUAGE: English.
HEADNOTE: EDUCATIONAL EXCHANGE PRO-
GRAM
TOPIC: Education
CONCEPTS: Definition of terms. Privileges and im-
munities. Conformity with municipal law. Per-
sonnel. General property. Dispute settlement. Ex-
change. Commissions and foundations. Teacher
and student exchange. Professorships. Scholar-
ships and grants. Research and development.
Accounting procedures. Currency. Exchange
rates and regulations. Financial programs. Funding procedures. Tax exemptions.
PROCEDURE: Amendment.
PARTIES:
Thailand
USA (United States)
ANNEX
207 UNTS 348. USA (United States). Amendment
20 Jan 53. Force 7 Apr 53.
207 UNTS 348. Thailand. Amendment 7 Apr 53.
Force 7 Apr 53.
262 UNTS 456. USA (United States). Amendment
23 Jun 55. Force 23 Jun 55.
262 UNTS 456. Thailand. Amendment 23 Jun 55.
Force 23 Jun 55.
278 UNTS 272. Thailand. Amendment 21 Jan 57.
Force 21 Jan 57.
278 UNTS 272. USA (United States). Amendment
21 Jan 57. Force 21 Jan 57.
336 UNTS 346. USA (United States). Amendment
12 Sep 58. Force 12 Sep 58.
336 UNTS 346. Thailand. Amendment
12 Sep 58. Force 12 Sep 58.
371 UNTS 276. Thailand. Amendment 1 Feb 60.
Force 1 Feb 60.
371 UNTS 276. USA (United States). Amendment
1 Feb 60. Force 1 Feb 60.
416 UNTS 314. Thailand. Amendment
23 Dec 60. Force 23 Dec 60.
416 UNTS 314. USA (United States). Amendment
1 Dec 60. Force 23 Dec 60.

101064   Bilateral Treaty   **81 UNTS 75**
SIGNED: 4 Jan 50   FORCE: 30 Sep 50
REGISTERED: 26 Feb 51 Afghanistan
ARTICLES: 9 LANGUAGE: English. Persian.
HEADNOTE: FRIENDSHIP
TOPIC: General Amity
CONCEPTS: Treaty interpretation. Friendship and
amity. Consular relations establishment. Diplo-
matic relations establishment. Privileges and im-
munities. Negotiation. General cultural cooper-
ation. Trade agencies.
PROCEDURE: Ratification.
PARTIES:
Afghanistan
India

101065   Bilateral Exchange   **81 UNTS 85**
SIGNED: 10 Nov 48   FORCE: 8 Nov 48
REGISTERED: 2 Mar 51 UK Great Britain
ARTICLES: 2 LANGUAGE: English. French.
HEADNOTE: RECIPROCAL ABOLITION VISAS
TOPIC: Visas

CONCEPTS: Territorial application. Visa abolition. Conformity with municipal law.
PARTIES:
Monaco
UK Great Britain
ANNEX
267 UNTS 376. UK Great Britain. Gibraltar. Force 20 Jul 55.
349 UNTS 322. UK Great Britain. Seychelles. Force 1 Oct 57.

101066 Bilateral Exchange **81 UNTS 93**
SIGNED: 1 Dec 48 FORCE: 1 Dec 48
REGISTERED: 2 Mar 51 UK Great Britain
ARTICLES: 2 LANGUAGE: English.
HEADNOTE: DUTY-FREE TREATMENT RELIEF GOODS
TOPIC: Direct Aid
CONCEPTS: Annex type material. Public information. Accounting procedures. Indemnities and reimbursements. Transportation costs. Customs exemptions. Relief supplies.
TREATY REF: 22UNTS263.
PARTIES:
UK Great Britain
USA (United States)
ANNEX
87 UNTS 400. UK Great Britain. Gambia.
87 UNTS 400. UK Great Britain. W Pacif Hi Command.
87 UNTS 400. UK Great Britain. British Honduras.
87 UNTS 400. UK Great Britain. Fed of Malaya.
87 UNTS 400. UK Great Britain. Channel Islands.
87 UNTS 400. UK Great Britain. Brunei.
87 UNTS 400. UK Great Britain. Fiji Islands.
87 UNTS 400. UK Great Britain. Malta.
87 UNTS 400. UK Great Britain. British Somaliland.
87 UNTS 400. UK Great Britain. Nigeria.
87 UNTS 400. UK Great Britain. Barbados.
87 UNTS 400. UK Great Britain. Leeward Islands.
87 UNTS 400. UK Great Britain. North Borneo.
87 UNTS 400. UK Great Britain. Mauritius.
87 UNTS 400. UK Great Britain. Sarawak.
87 UNTS 400. UK Great Britain. Gibraltar.
87 UNTS 400. UK Great Britain. Windward Islands.
100 UNTS 296. USA (United States). Amendment 23 Feb 51. Force 23 Feb 51.
100 UNTS 296. UK Great Britain. Amendment 7 Apr 51. Force 23 Feb 51.
100 UNTS 300. USA (United States). Termination 1 Jun 51. Force 1 Jun 51.
100 UNTS 300. UK Great Britain. Termination 1 Jun 51. Force 1 Jun 51.

101067 Bilateral Agreement **81 UNTS 103**
SIGNED: 23 Dec 48 FORCE: 23 Dec 48
REGISTERED: 2 Mar 51 UK Great Britain
ARTICLES: 12 LANGUAGE: English.
HEADNOTE: MONEY PROPERTY SUBJECTED SPECIAL MEASURES
TOPIC: Reparations
CONCEPTS: Definition of terms. Treaty implementation. Annex or appendix reference. Legal protection and assistance. Assets transfer. National treatment. Post-war claims settlement.
TREATY REF: 81UNTS121.
PARTIES:
UK Great Britain
Yugoslavia
ANNEX
449 UNTS 294. UK Great Britain. Termination 19 Jun 62. Force 19 Jun 62.
449 UNTS 294. Yugoslavia. Termination 19 Jun 62. Force 19 Jun 62.

101068 Bilateral Agreement **81 UNTS 121**
SIGNED: 23 Dec 48 FORCE: 23 Dec 48
REGISTERED: 2 Mar 51 UK Great Britain
ARTICLES: 5 LANGUAGE: English.
HEADNOTE: COMPENSATION PROPERTY RIGHTS INTERESTS
TOPIC: Reparations
CONCEPTS: Definition of terms. Time limit. Payment schedules. Lump sum settlements. Post-war claims settlement.
TREATY REF: 81UNTS103.
PARTIES:
UK Great Britain
Yugoslavia

ANNEX
87 UNTS 402. UK Great Britain. Other 26 Dec 49. Force 26 Dec 49.
87 UNTS 402. Yugoslavia. Other 26 Dec 49. Force 26 Dec 49.
87 UNTS 404. UK Great Britain. Supplementation 26 Dec 49.
87 UNTS 404. Yugoslavia. Supplementation 26 Dec 49.
119 UNTS 358. UK Great Britain. South Africa. Force 18 Jul 49.

101069 Bilateral Agreement **81 UNTS 133**
SIGNED: 23 Dec 48 FORCE: 23 Dec 48
REGISTERED: 2 Mar 51 UK Great Britain
ARTICLES: 11 LANGUAGE: English.
HEADNOTE: INCREASING TRADE
TOPIC: General Trade
CONCEPTS: Treaty implementation. Annex or appendix reference. Licenses and permits. Procedure. Negotiation. Trade procedures. Balance of payments. Quotas. Water transport. Ports and pilotage.
PROCEDURE: Duration. Future Procedures Contemplated.
PARTIES:
UK Great Britain
Yugoslavia

101070 Multilateral Exchange **81 UNTS 147**
SIGNED: 9 Jul 48 FORCE: 27 Feb 51
REGISTERED: 5 Mar 51 ILO (Labor Org)
ARTICLES: 20 LANGUAGE: English. French.
HEADNOTE: NIGHT WORK WOMEN INDUSTRIAL EMPLOYMENT
TOPIC: ILO Labor
CONCEPTS: Definition of terms. Exceptions and exemptions. Territorial application. Domestic legislation. ILO conventions. Employment regulations. Holidays and rest periods.
INTL ORGS: International Labour Organization. United Nations.
TREATY REF: 38UNTS67; 40UNTS3.
PROCEDURE: Amendment. Denunciation. Duration. Ratification. Registration. Renewal or Revival.
PARTIES:
Multilateral
ANNEX
119 UNTS 359. Ireland. Ratification 14 Jan 52. Force 14 Jan 53.
122 UNTS 343. Guatemala. Ratification 13 Feb 52. Force 13 Feb 53.
127 UNTS 332. Belgium. Qualified Ratification 1 Apr 52. Force 1 Apr 53.
131 UNTS 338. Cuba. Ratification 29 Apr 52. Force 29 Apr 53.
149 UNTS 407. Italy. Ratification 22 Oct 52. Force 22 Oct 53.
173 UNTS 402. Dominican Republic. Ratification 22 Sep 53. Force 22 Sep 54.
173 UNTS 402. France. Ratification 21 Sep 53. Force 21 Sep 54.
184 UNTS 342. Philippines. Ratification 29 Dec 53. Force 29 Dec 54.
201 UNTS 370. Netherlands. Ratification 22 Oct 54. Force 22 Oct 55.
212 UNTS 394. France. Martinique.
212 UNTS 394. France. Guadeloupe.
212 UNTS 394. France. Reunion.
212 UNTS 394. France. French Guinea.
225 UNTS 260. Netherlands. Netherlands Antilles.
225 UNTS 260. Netherlands. Dutch New Guinea.
248 UNTS 404. Yugoslavia. Ratification 20 Jun 56. Force 20 Jun 57.
266 UNTS 392. Brazil. Ratification 25 Apr 57. Force 25 Apr 58.
269 UNTS 287. Tunisia. Ratification 15 May 57. Force 15 May 58.
272 UNTS 256. Romania. Ratification 28 May 57. Force 28 May 58.
287 UNTS 345. South Africa. Southwest Africa.
293 UNTS 378. Luxembourg. Ratification 3 Mar 58. Force 3 Mar 59.
304 UNTS 403. Spain. Ratification 24 Jun 58. Force 24 Jun 59.
328 UNTS 309. Greece. Ratification 27 Apr 59. Force 27 Apr 60.
338 UNTS 337. Ghana. Ratification 2 Jul 59. Force 2 Jul 60.

366 UNTS 388. Costa Rica. Ratification 2 Jun 60. Force 2 Jun 61.
373 UNTS 355. United Arab Rep. United Arab Rep.
381 UNTS 397. Congo (Zaire). Succession 20 Sep 60. Force 20 Sep 60.
410 UNTS 291. Kuwait. Ratification 21 Sep 61. Force 21 Sep 62.
413 UNTS 364. Syria. Ratification 30 Oct 61.
434 UNTS 285. Libya. Ratification 20 Jun 62. Force 20 Jun 63.
435 UNTS 314. Lebanon. Ratification 26 Jul 62. Force 26 Jul 62.
443 UNTS 335. Rwanda. Succession 18 Sep 62. Force 18 Sep 62.
444 UNTS 328. Senegal. Ratification 22 Oct 62. Force 22 Oct 63.
444 UNTS 328. Algeria. Succession 19 Oct 62.
457 UNTS 357. Burundi. Succession 11 Mar 63.
483 UNTS 412. Mauritania. Ratification 8 Nov 63. Force 8 Nov 64.
504 UNTS 355. Portugal. Ratification 2 Jun 64. Force 2 Jun 65.
524 UNTS 364. Malta. Ratification 4 Jan 65. Force 4 Jan 66.
527 UNTS 339. Zambia. Ratification 22 Feb 65. Force 22 Feb 66.
530 UNTS 413. UK Great Britain. Malawi. Ratification 22 Mar 65. Force 22 Mar 66.
548 UNTS 400. Cyprus. Ratification 8 Oct 65. Force 8 Oct 66.
548 UNTS 400. Vietnam, South. Ratification 26 Oct 65. Force 26 Oct 66.
549 UNTS 365. Kenya. Ratification 30 Nov 65. Force 30 Nov 66.
560 UNTS 318. Paraguay. Ratification 21 Mar 66. Force 21 Mar 67.
560 UNTS 318. Ceylon (Sri Lanka). Ratification 31 Mar 66. Force 31 Mar 67.
613 UNTS 422. Iraq. Ratification 17 Nov 67. Force 17 Nov 68.

101071 Multilateral Agreement **81 UNTS 160**
SIGNED: 2 Nov 50 FORCE: 2 Nov 50
REGISTERED: 5 Mar 51 United Nations
ARTICLES: 6 LANGUAGE: English.
HEADNOTE: BASIC AGREEMENT TECHNICAL ASSISTANCE
TOPIC: Tech Assistance
CONCEPTS: Treaty implementation. Annex or appendix reference. Privileges and immunities. General cooperation. Exchange of information and documents. Personnel. Public information. Title and deeds. Use of facilities. Arbitration. Procedure. Professorships. Scholarships and grants. Vocational training. Research and scientific projects. Expense sharing formulae. Local currency. Domestic obligation. General technical assistance. Materials, equipment and services. IGO status. Conformity with IGO decisions.
TREATY REF: 76UNTS132; 1UNTS15,263; 33UNTS261.
PROCEDURE: Amendment. Termination.
PARTIES:
Indonesia SIGNED: 2 Nov 50 FORCE: 2 Nov 50
ICAO (Civil Aviat) SIGNED: 2 Nov 50 FORCE: 2 Nov 50
ILO (Labor Org) SIGNED: 2 Nov 50 FORCE: 2 Nov 50
UNESCO (Educ/Cult) SIGNED: 2 Nov 50 FORCE: 2 Nov 50
United Nations SIGNED: 2 Nov 50 FORCE: 2 Nov 50
WHO (World Health) SIGNED: 2 Nov 50 FORCE: 2 Nov 50
ANNEX
88 UNTS 456. Indonesia. Supplementation 7 May 51. Force 7 May 51.
88 UNTS 456. United Nations. Supplementation 7 May 51. Force 7 May 51.
187 UNTS 434. India. Amendment 6 Feb 54. Force 6 Feb 54.
187 UNTS 434. UNTAB (Tech Assis). Amendment 6 Feb 54. Force 6 Feb 54.

101072 Multilateral Agreement **81 UNTS 188**
SIGNED: 24 Nov 50 FORCE: 24 Nov 50
REGISTERED: 5 Mar 51 United Nations
ARTICLES: 6 LANGUAGE: English. Spanish.
HEADNOTE: BASIC AGREEMENT TECHNICAL ASSISTANCE
TOPIC: Tech Assistance

CONCEPTS: Treaty implementation. Annex or appendix reference. Privileges and immunities. General cooperation. Exchange of information and documents. Personnel. Public information. Title and deeds. Use of facilities. Arbitration. Procedure. Professorships. Scholarships and grants. Vocational training. Research and scientific projects. Exchange rates and regulations. Expense sharing formulae. Local currency. Domestic obligation. General technical assistance. Materials, equipment and services. IGO status. Conformity with IGO decisions.
TREATY REF: 76UNTS132; 33UNTS261.
PROCEDURE: Amendment. Termination.
PARTIES:
Colombia SIGNED: 24 Nov 50 FORCE: 24 Nov 50
FAO (Food Agri) SIGNED: 24 Nov 50 FORCE: 24 Nov 50
ICAO (Civil Aviat) SIGNED: 24 Nov 50 FORCE: 24 Nov 50
ILO (Labor Org) SIGNED: 24 Nov 50 FORCE: 24 Nov 50
UNESCO (Educ/Cult) SIGNED: 24 Nov 50 FORCE: 24 Nov 50
United Nations SIGNED: 24 Nov 50 FORCE: 24 Nov 50
WHO (World Health) SIGNED: 24 Nov 50 FORCE: 24 Nov 50

101073 Multilateral Agreement **81 UNTS 233**
SIGNED: 18 Jan 51 FORCE: 18 Jan 51
REGISTERED: 5 Mar 51 United Nations
ARTICLES: 6 LANGUAGE: English.
HEADNOTE: BASIC AGREEMENT TECHNICAL ASSISTANCE
TOPIC: Tech Assistance
CONCEPTS: Treaty implementation. Annex or appendix reference. Privileges and immunities. General cooperation. Personnel. Public information. Use of facilities. Professorships. Scholarships and grants. Vocational training. Exchange. Research and scientific projects. Exchange rates and regulations. Expense sharing formulae. Local currency. Domestic obligation. General technical assistance. IGO status.
TREATY REF: 76UNTS132; 33UNTS261.
PROCEDURE: Amendment. Termination.
PARTIES:
Iran SIGNED: 18 Jan 51 FORCE: 18 Jan 51
FAO (Food Agri) SIGNED: 18 Jan 51 FORCE: 18 Jan 51
ICAO (Civil Aviat) SIGNED: 18 Jan 51 FORCE: 18 Jan 51
ILO (Labor Org) SIGNED: 18 Jan 51 FORCE: 18 Jan 51
UNESCO (Educ/Cult) SIGNED: 18 Jan 51 FORCE: 18 Jan 51
United Nations SIGNED: 18 Jan 51 FORCE: 18 Jan 51
WHO (World Health) SIGNED: 18 Jan 51 FORCE: 18 Jan 51
ANNEX
96 UNTS 328. Iran. Supplementation 18 Jan 51. Force 18 Jan 51.
96 UNTS 328. ICAO (Civil Aviat). Supplementation 18 Oct 51. Force 18 Jan 51.
227 UNTS 318. Iran. Force 2 Feb 56.
227 UNTS 318. UNTAB (Tech Assis). Force 2 Feb 56.

101074 Multilateral Agreement **81 UNTS 245**
SIGNED: 15 Feb 51 FORCE: 26 Feb 51
REGISTERED: 5 Mar 51 United Nations
ARTICLES: 5 LANGUAGE: English. Spanish.
HEADNOTE: TECHNICAL ASSISTANCE
TOPIC: Tech Assistance
CONCEPTS: Treaty implementation. Annex or appendix reference. Privileges and immunities. General cooperation. Personnel. Title and deeds. Professorships. Vocational training. Research and scientific projects. Expense sharing formulae. Local currency. Domestic obligation. General technical assistance. Materials, equipment and services. IGO status. Conformity with IGO decisions.
TREATY REF: 76UNTS132; 33UNTS261.
PROCEDURE: Amendment. Termination.
PARTIES:
El Salvador SIGNED: 26 Feb 51 FORCE: 26 Feb 51

FAO (Food Agri) SIGNED: 15 Feb 51 FORCE: 26 Feb 51
ICAO (Civil Aviat) SIGNED: 15 Feb 51 FORCE: 26 Feb 51
ILO (Labor Org) SIGNED: 15 Feb 51 FORCE: 26 Feb 51
UNESCO (Educ/Cult) SIGNED: 15 Feb 51 FORCE: 26 Feb 51
United Nations SIGNED: 15 Feb 51 FORCE: 26 Feb 51
WHO (World Health) SIGNED: 15 Feb 51 FORCE: 26 Feb 51
ANNEX
93 UNTS 370. United Nations. Supplementation 10 Jul 51. Force 10 Jul 51.
93 UNTS 370. El Salvador. Supplementation 10 Jul 51. Force 10 Jul 51.
93 UNTS 376. United Nations. Supplementation 11 Jul 51. Force 11 Jul 51.
93 UNTS 376. El Salvador. Supplementation 11 Jul 51. Force 11 Jul 51.

101075 Multilateral Agreement **81 UNTS 261**
SIGNED: 5 Mar 51 FORCE: 5 Mar 51
REGISTERED: 5 Mar 51 United Nations
ARTICLES: 5 LANGUAGE: English. French.
HEADNOTE: TECHNICAL ASSISTANCE
TOPIC: Tech Assistance
CONCEPTS: Definition of terms. Treaty implementation. Annex or appendix reference. Privileges and immunities. General cooperation. Personnel. Title and deeds. Professorships. Vocational training. Research and scientific projects. Expense sharing formulae. Local currency. Domestic obligation. General technical assistance. IGO status. Conformity with IGO decisions.
TREATY REF: 76UNTS132; 33UNTS261.
PROCEDURE: Amendment. Termination.
PARTIES:
Burma SIGNED: 5 Mar 51 FORCE: 5 Mar 51
FAO (Food Agri) SIGNED: 5 Mar 51 FORCE: 5 Mar 51
ICAO (Civil Aviat) SIGNED: 5 Mar 51 FORCE: 5 Mar 51
ILO (Labor Org) SIGNED: 5 Mar 51 FORCE: 5 Mar 51
UNESCO (Educ/Cult) SIGNED: 5 Mar 51 FORCE: 5 Mar 51
United Nations SIGNED: 5 Mar 51 FORCE: 5 Mar 51
WHO (World Health) SIGNED: 5 Mar 51 FORCE: 5 Mar 51
ANNEX
92 UNTS 412. Burma. Supplementation 29 Jun 51. Force 29 Jun 51.
92 UNTS 412. United Nations. Supplementation 29 Jun 51. Force 29 Jun 51.
92 UNTS 420. Burma. Supplementation 18 Jun 51. Force 18 Jun 51.
92 UNTS 420. United Nations. Supplementation 18 Jun 51. Force 18 Jun 51.
92 UNTS 426. Burma. Supplementation 8 Jun 51. Force 8 Jun 51.
92 UNTS 426. United Nations. Supplementation 8 Jun 51. Force 8 Jun 51.
99 UNTS 324. Burma. Supplementation 29 Jun 51. Force 29 Jun 51.
99 UNTS 324. ILO (Labor Org). Supplementation 29 Jun 51. Force 29 Jun 51.
99 UNTS 330. ILO (Labor Org). Supplementation 29 Jun 51. Force 29 Jun 51.
99 UNTS 330. Burma. Supplementation 29 Jun 51. Force 29 Jun 51.
99 UNTS 334. Burma. Supplementation 29 Jun 51. Force 29 Jun 51.
99 UNTS 334. ILO (Labor Org). Supplementation 29 Jun 51. Force 29 Jun 51.
187 UNTS 442. Burma. Amendment 26 Dec 53. Force 26 Dec 53.

101076 Bilateral Agreement **81 UNTS 273**
SIGNED: 27 Jul 49 FORCE: 30 Jul 49
REGISTERED: 6 Mar 51 Pakistan
ARTICLES: 2 LANGUAGE: English.
HEADNOTE: ESTABLISHMENT CEASE-FIRE LINE
TOPIC: Peace/Disarmament
CONCEPTS: Procedure. Armistice and peace. Disarmament and demilitarization. Markers and definitions.
INTL ORGS: United Nations.
PROCEDURE: Ratification.

PARTIES:
India
Pakistan

101077 Bilateral Exchange **81 UNTS 285**
SIGNED: 31 Mar 48 FORCE: 31 Mar 48
REGISTERED: 6 Mar 51 USA (United States)
ARTICLES: 2 LANGUAGE: English.
HEADNOTE: OPERATION · MAINTENANCE WAR-BUILT LAND LINE COMMUNICATION SYSTEM
TOPIC: Specific Property
CONCEPTS: Annex or appendix reference. Non-interest rates and fees. Facilities and equipment. Communications linkage.
PARTIES:
Canada
USA (United States)

101078 Bilateral Exchange **81 UNTS 295**
SIGNED: 23 Nov 48 FORCE: 23 Nov 48
REGISTERED: 6 Mar 51 USA (United States)
ARTICLES: 2 LANGUAGE: English.
HEADNOTE: CONTROLLING POTATO IMPORTS
TOPIC: Commodity Trade
CONCEPTS: Licenses and permits. Import quotas. Commodity trade. Quotas.
PARTIES:
Canada
USA (United States)
ANNEX
233 UNTS 298. Canada. Termination 20 Jul 49. Force 20 Jun 49.
233 UNTS 298. USA (United States). Termination 20 Jun 49. Force 20 Jun 49.

101079 Bilateral Exchange **82 UNTS 3**
SIGNED: 14 Mar 49 FORCE: 14 Mar 49
REGISTERED: 6 Mar 51 USA (United States)
ARTICLES: 2 LANGUAGE: English.
HEADNOTE: SETTLEMENTS CLAIMS ACCOUNTS
TOPIC: Reparations
CONCEPTS: Accounting procedures. Payment for war supplies. Post-war claims settlement.
PARTIES:
Canada
USA (United States)

101080 Bilateral Exchange **82 UNTS 11**
SIGNED: 23 Aug 48 FORCE: 23 Aug 48
REGISTERED: 6 Mar 51 USA (United States)
ARTICLES: 3 LANGUAGE: English.
HEADNOTE: FILING PATENT APPLICATIONS
TOPIC: Patents/Copyrights
CONCEPTS: Conformity with municipal law. Domestic legislation. Laws and formalities.
PARTIES:
Philippines
USA (United States)

101081 Bilateral Exchange **82 UNTS 23**
SIGNED: 28 Oct 47 FORCE: 28 Oct 47
REGISTERED: 6 Mar 51 USA (United States)
ARTICLES: 2 LANGUAGE: English.
HEADNOTE: PASSPORT VISAS
TOPIC: Visas
CONCEPTS: Time limit. Visas. Tourism. Fees and exemptions.
PARTIES:
Liberia
USA (United States)

101082 Bilateral Exchange **82 UNTS 31**
SIGNED: 9 Dec 47 FORCE: 9 Dec 47
REGISTERED: 6 Mar 51 USA (United States)
ARTICLES: 2 LANGUAGE: English.
HEADNOTE: PASSPORT VISAS
TOPIC: Visas
CONCEPTS: Time limit. Visas. Tourism. Fees and exemptions.
PARTIES:
Iceland
USA (United States)

101083 Bilateral Exchange **82 UNTS 37**
SIGNED: 1 Aug 49 FORCE: 1 Aug 49
REGISTERED: 6 Mar 51 USA (United States)
ARTICLES: 2 LANGUAGE: English.

HEADNOTE: PASSPORT VISAS
TOPIC: Visas
CONCEPTS: Time limit. Visa abolition. Border traffic and migration. Visas. Conformity with municipal law. Fees and exemptions.
PARTIES:
Ireland
USA (United States)

101084   Bilateral Exchange   **82 UNTS 45**
SIGNED: 8 Nov 49   FORCE: 8 Nov 49
REGISTERED: 6 Mar 51 USA (United States)
ARTICLES: 2 LANGUAGE: English. Spanish.
HEADNOTE: PASSPORT VISAS
TOPIC: Visas
CONCEPTS: Time limit. Visa abolition. Border traffic and migration. Passports non-diplomatic. Fees and exemptions.
PARTIES:
USA (United States)
Uruguay

101085   Bilateral Exchange   **82 UNTS 53**
SIGNED: 15 Oct 47   FORCE: 15 Oct 47
REGISTERED: 12 Mar 51 USA (United States)
ARTICLES: 2 LANGUAGE: English.
HEADNOTE: ALLOCATION CHANNELS FREQUENCY MODULATION BROADCASTING
TOPIC: Telecommunications
CONCEPTS: Bands and frequency allocation. Interference of broadcasts.
PARTIES:
Canada
USA (United States)

101086   Bilateral Exchange   **82 UNTS 99**
SIGNED: 1 Apr 48   FORCE: 1 Apr 48
REGISTERED: 12 Mar 51 USA (United States)
ARTICLES: 2 LANGUAGE: English.
HEADNOTE: ENGINEERING STANDARDS APPLICABLE ALLOCATION BROADCASTING STATIONS
TOPIC: Telecommunications
CONCEPTS: Standardization. Amateur radio. Bands and frequency allocation.
TREATY REF: 962; 55STAT1005; TIAS1553; 60STAT1862.
PARTIES:
Canada
USA (United States)

101087   Bilateral Exchange   **82 UNTS 109**
SIGNED: 5 Aug 48   FORCE: 5 Aug 48
REGISTERED: 12 Mar 51 USA (United States)
ARTICLES: 2 LANGUAGE: English.
HEADNOTE: RURAL RECONSTRUCTION CHINA
TOPIC: IGO Establishment
CONCEPTS: Privileges and immunities. Conformity with municipal law. Exchange of information and documents. Public information. International circulation. Public health. Sanitation. Exchange. Accounting procedures. Funding procedures. Customs exemptions. Agriculture. Assistance. Establishment. Special status. Status of experts.
INTL ORGS: Special Commission.
TREATY REF: CHINA AID ACT 1948.
PROCEDURE: Termination.
PARTIES:
Taiwan
USA (United States)

101088   Bilateral Agreement   **82 UNTS 131**
SIGNED: 23 Sep 50   FORCE: 23 Sep 50
REGISTERED: 13 Mar 51 Pakistan
ARTICLES: 15 LANGUAGE: English.
HEADNOTE: EDUCATIONAL EXCHANGE PROGRAM
TOPIC: Education
CONCEPTS: Definition of terms. Annex or appendix reference. Privileges and immunities. Conformity with municipal law. Personnel. Dispute settlement. Exchange. Commissions and foundations. Teacher and student exchange. Professorships. Scholarships and grants. Vocational training. Accounting procedures. Indemnities and reimbursements. Exchange rates and regulations. Financial programs. Funding procedures. Tax exemptions. Customs exemptions.

TREATY REF: 4UNTS183.
PROCEDURE: Amendment.
PARTIES:
Pakistan
USA (United States)
ANNEX
293 UNTS 336. USA (United States). Amendment 16 Sep 57. Force 5 Oct 57.
293 UNTS 336. Pakistan. Amendment 5 Oct 57. Force 5 Oct 57.
453 UNTS 348. Pakistan. Amendment 13 Nov 61. Force 13 Nov 61.
453 UNTS 348. USA (United States). Amendment 29 Jul 60. Force 13 Nov 61.

101089   Bilateral Agreement   **82 UNTS 147**
SIGNED: 29 Aug 50   FORCE: 29 Aug 50
REGISTERED: 14 Mar 51 Belgium
ARTICLES: 4 LANGUAGE: English.
HEADNOTE: TRADE
TOPIC: General Trade
CONCEPTS: General cooperation. Trade procedures. Currency.
PROCEDURE: Amendment. Termination.
PARTIES:
Belgium
Japan

101090   Bilateral Agreement   **82 UNTS 153**
SIGNED: 18 Jan 51   FORCE: 1 Jan 51
REGISTERED: 14 Mar 51 Norway
ARTICLES: 5 LANGUAGE: Danish. Norwegian.
HEADNOTE: RECOGNITION PREMIUMS UNEMPLOYMENT INSURANCE
TOPIC: Non-ILO Labor
CONCEPTS: Detailed regulations. Annex or appendix reference. Domestic legislation. Recognition and enforcement of legal decisions. Recognition of legal documents. Non-ILO labor relations. Unemployment. Payment schedules.
PROCEDURE: Termination.
PARTIES:
Denmark
Norway

101091   Multilateral Agreement   **82 UNTS 172**
SIGNED: 20 Mar 51   FORCE: 20 Mar 51
REGISTERED: 20 Mar 51 United Nations
ARTICLES: 5 LANGUAGE: French.
HEADNOTE: PROVISION TECHNICAL ASSISTANCE
TOPIC: IGO Operations
CONCEPTS: General technical assistance. Assistance. Distribution. IGO operations.
INTL ORGS: United Nations.
PROCEDURE: Termination.
PARTIES:
France SIGNED: 20 Mar 51 FORCE: 20 Mar 51
FAO (Food Agri) SIGNED: 20 Mar 51 FORCE: 20 Mar 51
ICAO (Civil Aviat) SIGNED: 20 Mar 51 FORCE: 20 Mar 51
ILO (Labor Org) SIGNED: 20 Mar 51 FORCE: 20 Mar 51
UNESCO (Educ/Cult) SIGNED: 20 Mar 51 FORCE: 20 Mar 51
United Nations SIGNED: 20 Mar 51 FORCE: 20 Mar 51

101092   Bilateral Exchange   **82 UNTS 191**
SIGNED: 29 Sep 47   FORCE: 29 Sep 47
REGISTERED: 20 Mar 51 UK Great Britain
ARTICLES: 2 LANGUAGE: English.
HEADNOTE: DESCRIPTION KENYA-ETHIOPIA BOUNDARY
TOPIC: Territory Boundary
CONCEPTS: Previous treaty amendment. Annex or appendix reference. Establishment of commission. Markers and definitions.
TREATY REF: 3'2DEMARTENS832;O.
PARTIES:
Ethiopia
UK Great Britain
ANNEX
99 UNTS 338. Ethiopia. Implementation 3 Jul 50. Force 3 Jul 50.
99 UNTS 338. UK Great Britain. Implementation 3 Jul 50. Force 3 Jul 50.
99 UNTS 348. UK Great Britain. Amendment 2 Jan 51. Force 2 Jan 51.

99 UNTS 348. Ethiopia. Amendment 29 Dec 50. Force 2 Jan 51.
191 UNTS 374. UK Great Britain. Prolongation 15 Dec 53. Force 17 Mar 54.
191 UNTS 374. Ethiopia. Prolongation 11 Jan 54. Force 17 Mar 54.
211 UNTS 406. Ethiopia. Prolongation 11 Apr 55. Force 1 Apr 55.
211 UNTS 406. UK Great Britain. Prolongation 22 Mar 55. Force 1 Apr 55.

101093   Bilateral Exchange   **82 UNTS 203**
SIGNED: 16 Oct 47   FORCE: 11 Oct 47
REGISTERED: 20 Mar 51 UK Great Britain
ARTICLES: 2 LANGUAGE: English. Portuguese.
HEADNOTE: APPOINTMENT DOCTORS HOSPITALS
TOPIC: Sanitation
CONCEPTS: Alien status. Standardization. Conformity with municipal law. Public health.
PROCEDURE: Denunciation. Duration. Ratification. Renewal or Revival.
PARTIES:
Portugal
UK Great Britain

101094   Bilateral Agreement   **82 UNTS 209**
SIGNED: 27 Oct 47   FORCE: 8 Oct 48
REGISTERED: 20 Mar 51 UK Great Britain
ARTICLES: 7 LANGUAGE: English. Spanish.
HEADNOTE: MILITARY SERVICE
TOPIC: Milit Servic/Citiz
CONCEPTS: Exchange of information and documents. Certificates of service. Foreign nationals. Service in foreign army.
PROCEDURE: Ratification. Termination.
PARTIES:
Chile
UK Great Britain

101095   Bilateral Agreement   **82 UNTS 219**
SIGNED: 6 Mar 45   FORCE: 25 Nov 47
REGISTERED: 20 Mar 51 UK Great Britain
ARTICLES: 9 LANGUAGE: English.
HEADNOTE: MODIFYING ARRANGEMENTS
TOPIC: Finance
CONCEPTS: Definition of terms. Detailed regulations. Previous treaty amendment. Annex type material. Previous treaty replacement. Conformity with municipal law. General cooperation. Accounting procedures. Banking. Balance of payments. Currency. Monetary and gold transfers. Exchange rates and regulations. Internal finance. Payment schedules. Local currency.
TREATY REF: UK TREATY SERIES 55 (1947) CMD 7170.
PROCEDURE: Amendment. Duration. Renewal or Revival. Termination.
PARTIES:
Sweden
UK Great Britain

101096   Multilateral Protocol   **82 UNTS 237**
SIGNED: 16 Dec 47   FORCE: 15 Sep 47
REGISTERED: 20 Mar 51 UK Great Britain
ARTICLES: 1 LANGUAGE: English. French.
HEADNOTE: RESTRICTION MONETARY GOLD
TOPIC: Reparations
CONCEPTS: Monetary and gold transfers. Enemy financial interests. Reparations and restrictions.
INTL ORGS: Allied Military Occupation.
TREATY REF: 49UNTS.
PARTIES:
France SIGNED: 16 Dec 47 FORCE: 15 Sep 47
Italy SIGNED: 16 Dec 47 FORCE: 15 Sep 47
UK Great Britain SIGNED: 16 Dec 47 FORCE: 15 Sep 47
USA (United States) SIGNED: 16 Dec 47 FORCE: 15 Sep 47

101097   Bilateral Exchange   **82 UNTS 243**
SIGNED: 6 Dec 47   FORCE: 1 Jan 48
REGISTERED: 20 Mar 51 UK Great Britain
ARTICLES: 2 LANGUAGE: English. Italian.
HEADNOTE: MUTUAL ABOLITION VISAS
TOPIC: Visas
CONCEPTS: Territorial application. Visa abolition. Border traffic and migration. Conformity with municipal law.

PARTIES:
Italy
UK Great Britain
ANNEX
218 UNTS 383. UK Great Britain. Sarawak. Force
1 Oct 55.
264 UNTS 347. UK Great Britain. Cyprus. Withdrawal 6 Nov 56. Force 12 Nov 56.
398 UNTS 345. UK Great Britain. Cyprus.
560 UNTS 242. UK Great Britain. Southern
Rhodesia.

101098   Bilateral Exchange   **82 UNTS 251**
SIGNED: 27 Dec 47   FORCE: 15 Jan 48
REGISTERED: 20 Mar 51 UK Great Britain
ARTICLES: 2 LANGUAGE: English. Russian.
HEADNOTE: PAYMENTS
TOPIC: Finance
CONCEPTS: Detailed regulations. Conformity with
municipal law. Accounting procedures. Banking.
Monetary and gold transfers. Payment sched-
ules.
PARTIES:
UK Great Britain
USSR (Soviet Union)

101099   Bilateral Convention   **82 UNTS 259**
SIGNED: 7 Jul 48   FORCE: 26 Feb 50
REGISTERED: 20 Mar 51 UK Great Britain
ARTICLES: 19 LANGUAGE: Dutch. English.
HEADNOTE: CULTURAL CONVENTION
TOPIC: Culture
CONCEPTS: Definition of terms. Territorial applica-
tion. Annex or appendix reference. Friendship
and amity. Standardization. Conformity with mu-
nicipal law. Establishment of commission. Rec-
ognition of degrees. Teacher and student ex-
change. Professorships. Institute establishment.
Scholarships and grants. General cultural coop-
eration. Scientific exchange. Publications exchange. Mass media exchange.
INTL ORGS: Special Commission.
PROCEDURE: Amendment. Denunciation. Duration. Ratification. Renewal or Revival.
PARTIES:
Netherlands
UK Great Britain
ANNEX
299 UNTS 414. UK Great Britain. Amendment
10 May 57. Force 19 Feb 58.
299 UNTS 414. Netherlands. Amendment
10 May 57. Force 19 Feb 58.

101100   Bilateral Agreement   **83 UNTS 3**
SIGNED: 14 Jan 49   FORCE: 14 Jan 49
REGISTERED: 20 Mar 51 UK Great Britain
ARTICLES: 21 LANGUAGE: English. Polish.
HEADNOTE: PROMOTION TRADE FINANCIAL
QUESTIONS
TOPIC: General Economic
CONCEPTS: Conditions. Detailed regulations. Gen-
eral provisions. Time limit. Annex or appendix
reference. General cooperation. Licenses and
permits. Negotiation. Export quotas. Import
quotas. Trade procedures. Accounting proce-
dures. Banking. Currency. Financial programs.
Payment schedules. Debt settlement. Quotas.
Smuggling. Credit provisions. Transport of
goods. Enemy financial interests.
TREATY REF: U.K. TREATY SERIES 23(1948) CMD
7403; 77UNTS47.
PROCEDURE: Future Procedures Contemplated.
Duration. Termination.
PARTIES:
Poland
UK Great Britain

101101   Bilateral Agreement   **83 UNTS 51**
SIGNED: 14 Jan 49   FORCE: 14 Jan 49
REGISTERED: 20 Mar 51 UK Great Britain
ARTICLES: 13 LANGUAGE: English.
HEADNOTE: MONEY PROPERTY
TOPIC: Reparations
CONCEPTS: Definition of terms. Treaty implemen-
tation. Annex or appendix reference. Legal pro-
tection and assistance. General property. Cur-
rency. Assets transfer. Post-war claims settle-
ment.

PARTIES:
Poland
UK Great Britain

101102   Bilateral Exchange   **83 UNTS 67**
SIGNED: 17 Jan 49   FORCE: 24 Nov 48
REGISTERED: 20 Mar 51 UK Great Britain
ARTICLES: 2 LANGUAGE: English.
HEADNOTE: RELEASE MONEY PROPERTY
TOPIC: Reparations
CONCEPTS: Annex or appendix reference. Annex
type material. Assets transfer. War claims and
reparations. Post-war claims settlement.
PARTIES:
Netherlands
UK Great Britain

101103   Bilateral Agreement   **83 UNTS 85**
SIGNED: 16 Oct 48   FORCE: 27 May 49
REGISTERED: 20 Mar 51 UK Great Britain
ARTICLES: 2 LANGUAGE: English. Turkish.
HEADNOTE: DRAWING RIGHTS
TOPIC: Finance
CONCEPTS: Finances and payments. Credit provi-
sions.
INTL ORGS: Organization for Economic Co-opera-
tion and Development.
PROCEDURE: Ratification.
PARTIES:
Turkey
UK Great Britain

101104   Bilateral Agreement   **83 UNTS 95**
SIGNED: 3 Mar 49   FORCE: 3 Mar 49
REGISTERED: 20 Mar 51 UK Great Britain
ARTICLES: 6 LANGUAGE: Czechoslovakian. En-
glish.
HEADNOTE: MUTUAL UPKEEP WAR GRAVES
TOPIC: Other Military
CONCEPTS: Exchange of information and docu-
ments. Informational records. Title and deeds.
Indemnities and reimbursements. Responsibility
for war dead. Upkeep of war graves. Establish-
ment of war cemeteries.
PARTIES:
Czechoslovakia
UK Great Britain

101105   Multilateral Agreement   **83 UNTS 105**
SIGNED: 28 Apr 49   FORCE: 28 Apr 49
REGISTERED: 20 Mar 51 UK Great Britain
ARTICLES: 35 LANGUAGE: English. French.
HEADNOTE: RUHR INTERNATIONAL AUTHORITY
TOPIC: IGO Establishment
CONCEPTS: Default remedies. Definition of terms.
Treaty interpretation. Treaty violation. Privileges
and immunities. General cooperation. Exchange
of information and documents. Informational
records. Accounting procedures. Expense shar-
ing formulae. Funding procedures. Quotas. Cus-
toms duties. Subsidiary organ. Establishment.
Headquarters and facilities. Internal structure.
Special status. Status of experts. Inter-agency
agreements. Raw materials.
INTL ORGS: International Authority for the Ruhr.
United Nations.
TREATY REF: 1UNTS115,263;1.
PROCEDURE: Amendment.
PARTIES:
Belgium SIGNED: 28 Apr 49 FORCE: 28 Apr 49
France SIGNED: 28 Apr 49 FORCE: 28 Apr 49
Luxembourg   SIGNED: 28 Apr 49   FORCE:
28 Apr 49
Netherlands   SIGNED: 28 Apr 49   FORCE:
28 Apr 49
UK Great Britain SIGNED: 28 Apr 49 FORCE:
28 Apr 49
USA (United States) SIGNED: 28 Apr 49 FORCE:
28 Apr 49
ANNEX
331 UNTS 368. Netherlands. Supplementation
19 Oct 51. Force 19 Oct 51.
331 UNTS 368. UK Great Britain. Supplementation 19 Oct 51. Force 19 Oct 51.
331 UNTS 368. Belgium. Supplementation
19 Oct 51. Force 19 Oct 51.
331 UNTS 368. Luxembourg. Supplementation
19 Oct 51. Force 19 Oct 51.
331 UNTS 368. USA (United States). Supplementation 19 Oct 51. Force 19 Oct 51.

331 UNTS 370.   Belgium.   Supplementation
25 Jul 52. Force 25 Jun 52.
331 UNTS 370. UK Great Britain. Supplementation 25 Jul 52. Force 25 Jun 52.
331 UNTS 370. Luxembourg. Supplementation
25 Jul 52. Force 25 Jun 52.
331 UNTS 370. Netherlands. Supplementation
25 Jul 52. Force 25 Jun 52.
331 UNTS 370. USA (United States). Supplementation 25 Jul 52. Force 25 Jun 52.

101106   Bilateral Agreement   **83 UNTS 139**
SIGNED: 31 Mar 49   FORCE: 1 Jan 49
REGISTERED: 20 Mar 51 UK Great Britain
ARTICLES: 16 LANGUAGE: English.
HEADNOTE: PAYMENTS
TOPIC: Finance
CONCEPTS: Definition of terms. Detailed regula-
tions. General cooperation. Exchange of infor-
mation and documents. Accounting procedures.
Banking. Currency. Monetary and gold transfers.
Currency deposits. Exchange rates and regula-
tions. Funding procedures. Payment schedules.
Loan and credit. Credit provisions.
INTL ORGS: International Monetary Fund.
PROCEDURE: Duration. Renewal or Revival. Termi-
nation.
PARTIES:
United Arab Rep
UK Great Britain

101107   Bilateral Exchange   **83 UNTS 183**
SIGNED: 17 Apr 49   FORCE: 17 Apr 49
REGISTERED: 20 Mar 51 UK Great Britain
ARTICLES: 2 LANGUAGE: English. French.
HEADNOTE: EQUITY TREATMENT REGARD WAR
DAMAGE COMPENSATION
TOPIC: Reparations
CONCEPTS: Definition of terms. Annex or appen-
dix reference. National treatment. Loss and/or
damage. Post-war claims settlement.
PARTIES:
United Arab Rep
UK Great Britain

101108   Bilateral Exchange   **83 UNTS 193**
SIGNED: 14 Mar 49   FORCE: 14 Mar 49
REGISTERED: 20 Mar 51 UK Great Britain
ARTICLES: 2 LANGUAGE: English. Spanish.
HEADNOTE: DOUBLE   TAXATION   INCOME
DERIVED SEA AIR
TOPIC: Taxation
CONCEPTS: Taxation. Tax exemptions. Air trans-
port. Merchant vessels.
PROCEDURE: Termination.
PARTIES:
Argentina
UK Great Britain

101109   Bilateral Agreement   **83 UNTS 20**
SIGNED: 19 Apr 48   FORCE: 19 Apr 4
REGISTERED: 20 Mar 51 UK Great Britain
ARTICLES: 9 LANGUAGE: English. French.
HEADNOTE: AIR TRANSPORT FACILITIES
TOPIC: Status of Forces
CONCEPTS: Annex or appendix reference. Confor-
mity with municipal law. General cooperation.
Humanitarian matters. Expense sharing formu-
lae. Overflights and technical stops. Operating
authorizations and regulations. Airforce-army-
navy personnel ratio. Procurement and logistics.
INTL ORGS: International Monetary Fund.
PROCEDURE: Amendment. Future Procedures
Contemplated. Termination.
PARTIES:
France
UK Great Britain

101110   Bilateral Agreement   **83 UNTS 21**
SIGNED: 27 Jun 49   FORCE: 1 Jul 4
REGISTERED: 20 Mar 51 UK Great Britain
ARTICLES: 27 LANGUAGE: English. Spanish.
HEADNOTE: TRADE PAYMENTS
TOPIC: General Economic
CONCEPTS: Definition of terms. Detailed regula-
tions. Annex or appendix reference. General co-
operation. Licenses and permits. Use of facili-
ties. Establishment of commission. General
trade. Accounting procedures. Banking. Balance

of payments. Currency. Exchange rates and regulations. Payment schedules. Non-interest rates and fees. Commodity trade. Delivery schedules.
INTL ORGS: Special Commission.
PROCEDURE: Duration. Termination.
PARTIES:
  Argentina
  UK Great Britain
ANNEX
160 UNTS 382. Argentina. Supplementation 31 Dec 52. Force 31 Dec 52.
160 UNTS 382. UK Great Britain. Supplementation 31 Dec 52. Force 31 Dec 52.
191 UNTS 378. Argentina. Supplementation 8 Feb 54. Force 8 Feb 54.
191 UNTS 378. UK Great Britain. Supplementation 8 Feb 54. Force 8 Feb 54.

101111 Bilateral Agreement **83 UNTS 269**
SIGNED: 16 Oct 50   FORCE: 16 Oct 50
REGISTERED: 21 Mar 51 Netherlands
ARTICLES: 18 LANGUAGE: English.
HEADNOTE: MIGRATION AGREEMENT
TOPIC: Non-ILO Labor
CONCEPTS: Conditions. Border traffic and migration. Acquisition of nationality. General cooperation. Private contracts. Employment regulations. Safety standards. Family allowances. Social security. Indemnities and reimbursements. Expense sharing formulae. Transportation costs. National treatment.
TREATY REF: IN.NAT.LAW CONF.,CONV.AND RECOMENDATIONS,1919-49.
PROCEDURE: Duration. Future Procedures Contemplated. Termination.
PARTIES:
  Netherlands
  New Zealand
ANNEX
152 UNTS 304. New Zealand. Implementation 28 Jul 52. Force 28 Jul 52.
152 UNTS 304. Netherlands. Implementation 28 Jul 52. Force 28 Jul 52.

101112 Bilateral Agreement **83 UNTS 291**
SIGNED: 29 Dec 49   FORCE: 30 Oct 50
REGISTERED: 22 Mar 51 Norway
ARTICLES: 40 LANGUAGE: Norwegian. Russian.
HEADNOTE: REGIME NORWEGIAN-SOVIET FRONTIER
TOPIC: Territory Boundary
CONCEPTS: Frontier permits. Inspection and observation. Negotiation. Currency. Fish, wildlife, and natural resources. Markers and definitions. Frontier peoples and personnel. Frontier waterways.
INTL ORGS: Special Commission.
TREATY REF: 52UNTS3.
PROCEDURE: Denunciation. Duration. Ratification. Renewal or Revival.
PARTIES:
  Norway
  USSR (Soviet Union)

101113 Bilateral Exchange **84 UNTS 3**
SIGNED: 13 Mar 46   FORCE: 13 Mar 46
REGISTERED: 30 Mar 51 USA (United States)
ARTICLES: 4 LANGUAGE: English.
HEADNOTE: PASSPORT VISA FEES
TOPIC: Visas
CONCEPTS: Frontier formalities. Fees and exemptions.
PARTIES:
  Netherlands
  USA (United States)

101114 Bilateral Exchange **84 UNTS 11**
SIGNED: 20 Aug 47   FORCE: 20 Aug 47
REGISTERED: 30 Mar 51 USA (United States)
ARTICLES: 2 LANGUAGE: English.
HEADNOTE: PASSPORT VISAS
TOPIC: Visas
CONCEPTS: Territorial application. Time limit. Visa abolition.
PARTIES:
  Netherlands
  USA (United States)

101115 Bilateral Exchange **84 UNTS 19**
SIGNED: 16 Sep 47   FORCE: 16 Sep 47
REGISTERED: 30 Mar 51 USA (United States)
ARTICLES: 5 LANGUAGE: English. French.
HEADNOTE: PASSPORT VISA FEES
TOPIC: Visas
CONCEPTS: Frontier formalities. Fees and exemptions.
TREATY REF: 15UNTS265.
PARTIES:
  France
  USA (United States)

101116 Bilateral Exchange **84 UNTS 33**
SIGNED: 30 Apr 47   FORCE: 30 Apr 47
REGISTERED: 30 Mar 51 USA (United States)
ARTICLES: 3 LANGUAGE: English.
HEADNOTE: PASSPORT VISA FEES
TOPIC: Visas
CONCEPTS: Visa abolition. Border traffic and migration. Conformity with municipal law. Fees and exemptions.
PARTIES:
  Sweden
  USA (United States)

101117 Bilateral Exchange **84 UNTS 43**
SIGNED: 29 Sep 48   FORCE: 29 Sep 48
REGISTERED: 30 Mar 51 USA (United States)
ARTICLES: 2 LANGUAGE: English. Italian.
HEADNOTE: PASSPORT VISAS
TOPIC: Visas
CONCEPTS: Time limit. Visa abolition. Visas.
PARTIES:
  Italy
  USA (United States)

101118 Bilateral Exchange **84 UNTS 51**
SIGNED: 30 Nov 50   FORCE: 9 Feb 51
REGISTERED: 2 Apr 51 Denmark
ARTICLES: 2 LANGUAGE: English.
HEADNOTE: EXEMPTION LOCAL GOVERNMENT TAXATION INCOME SHIPPING AIRCRAFT
TOPIC: Taxation
CONCEPTS: Definition of terms. Taxation. Tax exemptions. Air transport. Merchant vessels.
PARTIES:
  Denmark
  South Africa

101119 Bilateral Instrument **84 UNTS 59**
SIGNED: 28 May 46   FORCE: 28 May 46
REGISTERED: 2 Apr 51 USA (United States)
ARTICLES: 8 LANGUAGE: English. French.
HEADNOTE: SETTLEMENT LEND-LEASE RECIPROCAL AID SURPLUS WAR PROPERTY CLAIMS
TOPIC: Milit Assistance
CONCEPTS: Emergencies. Annex or appendix reference. General property. Exchange. Monetary and gold transfers. Interest rates. Payment schedules. Lump sum settlements. Post-war adjustment. Payment for war supplies. Lend lease. Naval vessels. Return of equipment and recapture. Surplus war property. Restrictions on transfer. Post-war claims settlement.
INTL ORGS: International Monetary Fund.
TREATY REF: 76UNTS193.
PROCEDURE: Future Procedures Contemplated. Ratification.
PARTIES:
  France
  USA (United States)

101120 Bilateral Agreement **84 UNTS 79**
SIGNED: 28 May 46   FORCE: 28 May 46
REGISTERED: 2 Apr 51 USA (United States)
ARTICLES: 12 LANGUAGE: English.
HEADNOTE: TRANSFER SURPLUS US ARMY NAVY PROPERTY INSTALLATIONS FRANCE
TOPIC: Milit Assistance
CONCEPTS: Exceptions and exemptions. Annex or appendix reference. General property. Expense sharing formulae. Surplus war property. Restrictions on transfer.
INTL ORGS: United Nations Relief and Rehabilitation Administration.
TREATY REF: 84UNTS59; 42UNTS183.

PARTIES:
  France
  USA (United States)

101121 Bilateral Agreement **84 UNTS 93**
SIGNED: 28 May 46   FORCE: 28 May 46
REGISTERED: 2 Apr 51 USA (United States)
ARTICLES: 7 LANGUAGE: English. French.
HEADNOTE: COMBINED STATEMENT RELATING DISPOSITION CLAIMS
TOPIC: Reparations
CONCEPTS: Annex or appendix reference. Indemnities and reimbursements. Lump sum settlements. Payment for war supplies. Lend lease. Post-war claims settlement. Naval vessels
TREATY REF: 76UNTS183.
PARTIES:
  France
  USA (United States)

101122 Bilateral Agreement **84 UNTS 113**
SIGNED: 28 May 46   FORCE: 28 May 46
REGISTERED: 2 Apr 51 USA (United States)
ARTICLES: 3 LANGUAGE: English. French.
HEADNOTE: SHIPPING CLAIMS
TOPIC: Reparations
CONCEPTS: Annex or appendix reference. Conformity with municipal law. Responsibility and liability. Indemnities and reimbursements. Lump sum settlements. Payment for war supplies. Naval vessels. Post-war claims settlement.
PARTIES:
  France
  USA (United States)

101123 Bilateral Agreement **84 UNTS 121**
SIGNED: 28 May 46   FORCE: 28 May 46
REGISTERED: 2 Apr 51 USA (United States)
ARTICLES: 1 LANGUAGE: English. French.
HEADNOTE: RECOMMENDATIONS TROOP PAY
TOPIC: Status of Forces
CONCEPTS: Annex or appendix reference. Accounting procedures. Indemnities and reimbursements. Currency. Financial programs. Local currency. Materials, equipment and services. Status of military forces. Procurement and logistics. Post-war claims settlement.
TREATY REF: 84UNTS141.
PARTIES:
  France
  USA (United States)

101124 Bilateral Agreement **84 UNTS 141**
SIGNED: 28 May 46   FORCE: 28 May 46
REGISTERED: 2 Apr 51 USA (United States)
ARTICLES: 8 LANGUAGE: English. French.
HEADNOTE: EXPENDITURES ARMED FORCES
TOPIC: Status of Forces
CONCEPTS: Accounting procedures. Exchange rates and regulations. Financial programs. Local currency. Materials, equipment and services. Surplus property. Airforce-army-navy personnel ratio.
PARTIES:
  France
  USA (United States)

101125 Bilateral Agreement **84 UNTS 151**
SIGNED: 28 May 46   FORCE: 28 May 46
REGISTERED: 2 Apr 51 USA (United States)
ARTICLES: 8 LANGUAGE: English. French.
HEADNOTE: COMMERCE POLICY TRADE STATEMENTS
TOPIC: General Trade
CONCEPTS: General provisions. Licenses and permits. General property. Trade agencies. Trade procedures. Balance of payments. Non-interest rates and fees. Commodity trade. Quotas. Recognition. Customs declarations. Reparations and restrictions.
PROCEDURE: Future Procedures Contemplated.
PARTIES:
  France
  USA (United States)

101126 Bilateral Agreement **84 UNTS 161**
SIGNED: 28 May 46   FORCE: 28 May 46
REGISTERED: 2 Apr 51 USA (United States)

ARTICLES: 1 LANGUAGE: English. French.
HEADNOTE: MOTION PICTURES
TOPIC: Mass Media
CONCEPTS: Detailed regulations. Dispute settlement. Import quotas. Mass media exchange.
PROCEDURE: Amendment. Termination.
PARTIES:
France
USA (United States)

101127 Bilateral Instrument **84 UNTS 167**
SIGNED: 28 May 46 FORCE: 28 May 46
REGISTERED: 2 Apr 51 USA (United States)
ARTICLES: 1 LANGUAGE: English.
HEADNOTE: ECONOMIC FINANCIAL PROBLEMS
TOPIC: General Economic
CONCEPTS: General economics. Commodity trade. Economic assistance. Surplus property. Loan and credit. Water transport. Payment for war supplies. Surplus war property.
INTL ORGS: International Bank for Reconstruction and Development. United Nations.
PARTIES:
France
USA (United States)

101128 Bilateral Agreement **84 UNTS 173**
SIGNED: 22 Oct 48 FORCE: 18 Nov 48
REGISTERED: 2 Apr 51 USA (United States)
ARTICLES: 13 LANGUAGE: English. French.
HEADNOTE: SETTLEMENT INTER-GOVERNMENTAL DEBTS
TOPIC: Education
CONCEPTS: Detailed regulations. Time limit. Currency. Interest rates. Claims and settlements. Debt settlement. Loan repayment. Payment for war supplies. Surplus war property. Reparations and restrictions. Post-war claims settlement.
TREATY REF: 84UNTS51.
PARTIES:
France
USA (United States)
ANNEX
234 UNTS 312. USA (United States). Amendment 18 Jun 54. Force 30 Jun 54.
234 UNTS 312. France. Amendment 30 Jun 54. Force 30 Jun 54.
262 UNTS 462. USA (United States). Amendment 30 Jun 55. Force 30 Jun 55.
262 UNTS 462. France. Amendment 30 Jun 55. Force 30 Jun 55.
373 UNTS 356. France. Amendment 29 Apr 60. Force 29 Apr 60.

101129 Bilateral Agreement **84 UNTS 185**
SIGNED: 16 Sep 48 FORCE: 1 Jul 48
REGISTERED: 2 Apr 51 USA (United States)
ARTICLES: 5 LANGUAGE: English. French.
HEADNOTE: MOTION PICTURES
TOPIC: Culture
CONCEPTS: Annex or appendix reference. Import quotas. Balance of payments. Mass media exchange.
TREATY REF: 55UNTS208; 84UNTS161.
PROCEDURE: Amendment. Duration.
PARTIES:
France
USA (United States)

101130 Multilateral Agreement **84 UNTS 201**
SIGNED: 19 Oct 48 FORCE: 19 Oct 48
REGISTERED: 2 Apr 51 USA (United States)
ARTICLES: 1 LANGUAGE: English. French.
HEADNOTE: CLAIMS
TOPIC: Specif Claim/Waive
CONCEPTS: Annex or appendix reference. Specific claims or waivers.
PARTIES:
Australia SIGNED: 19 Oct 48 FORCE: 19 Oct 48
France SIGNED: 19 Oct 48 FORCE: 19 Oct 48
USA (United States) SIGNED: FORCE: 19 Oct 48

101131 Bilateral Exchange **84 UNTS 207**
SIGNED: 27 Feb 48 FORCE: 27 Feb 48
REGISTERED: 2 Apr 51 USA (United States)
ARTICLES: 2 LANGUAGE: English.
HEADNOTE: SETTLEMENT CLAIMS
TOPIC: Reparations

CONCEPTS: Indemnities and reimbursements. Lump sum settlements. Payment for war supplies. Post-war claims settlement. Inspection and observation.
TREATY REF: 84UNTS207.
PARTIES:
France
USA (United States)

101132 Bilateral Agreement **84 UNTS 225**
SIGNED: 14 Mar 49 FORCE: 14 Mar 49
REGISTERED: 2 Apr 51 USA (United States)
ARTICLES: 9 LANGUAGE: English. French.
HEADNOTE: RESPECTING MARITIME CLAIMS LITIGATION
TOPIC: Claims and Debts
CONCEPTS: Time limit.
TREATY REF: 84UNTS59.
PARTIES:
France
USA (United States)

101133 Bilateral Agreement **84 UNTS 237**
SIGNED: 14 Mar 49 FORCE: 14 Mar 49
REGISTERED: 2 Apr 51 USA (United States)
ARTICLES: 10 LANGUAGE: English. French.
HEADNOTE: SETTLEMENT RESIDUAL FINANCIAL CLAIMS
TOPIC: Claims and Debts
CONCEPTS: Detailed regulations. General provisions. Time limit. Annex or appendix reference. General property. Payment schedules. Claims and settlements. Debts. Assessment procedures. Post-war adjustment. Lend lease. Surplus war property. War claims and reparations. Loss and-/or damage. Enemy financial interests. Post-war claims settlement.
TREATY REF: 84UNTS59; 84UNTS207; 84UNTS201.
PARTIES:
France
USA (United States)

101134 Bilateral Exchange **84 UNTS 255**
SIGNED: 3 Feb 47 FORCE: 17 Feb 49
REGISTERED: 5 Apr 51 USA (United States)
ARTICLES: 4 LANGUAGE: English. French.
HEADNOTE: PASSPORT VISA FEES
TOPIC: Visas
CONCEPTS: Time limit. Visas.
PARTIES:
Belgium
USA (United States)

101135 Bilateral Exchange **84 UNTS 265**
SIGNED: 26 Oct 48 FORCE: 26 Oct 48
REGISTERED: 5 Apr 51 USA (United States)
ARTICLES: 2 LANGUAGE: English.
HEADNOTE: PASSPORT VISAS
TOPIC: Visas
CONCEPTS: Time limit. Visa abolition. Passports non-diplomatic. Non-visa travel documents. Conformity with municipal law. Fees and exemptions. Ranks and privileges.
TREATY REF: 84UNTS255.
PARTIES:
Belgium
USA (United States)

101136 Bilateral Exchange **84 UNTS 275**
SIGNED: 12 Nov 48 FORCE: 12 Nov 48
REGISTERED: 5 Apr 51 USA (United States)
ARTICLES: 2 LANGUAGE: English.
HEADNOTE: PASSPORT VISA FEES
TOPIC: Visas
CONCEPTS: Time limit. Visa abolition. Denial of admission. Resident permits. Conformity with municipal law.
PARTIES:
UK Great Britain
USA (United States)

101137 Bilateral Exchange **84 UNTS 283**
SIGNED: 31 Mar 49 FORCE: 31 Mar 49
REGISTERED: 5 Apr 51 USA (United States)
ARTICLES: 2 LANGUAGE: English. French.
HEADNOTE: PASSPORT VISA FEES
TOPIC: Visas

CONCEPTS: Territorial application. Time limit. Visa abolition. Visas.
PARTIES:
France
USA (United States)

101138 Bilateral Exchange **84 UNTS 291**
SIGNED: 12 Jul 49 FORCE: 12 Jul 49
REGISTERED: 5 Apr 51 USA (United States)
ARTICLES: 3 LANGUAGE: English. German.
HEADNOTE: PASSPORT VISA FEES
TOPIC: Visas
CONCEPTS: Frontier formalities. Visas. Currency.
PARTIES:
Austria
USA (United States)

101139 Multilateral Agreement **84 UNTS 299**
SIGNED: 5 Apr 51 FORCE: 5 Apr 51
REGISTERED: 5 Apr 51 United Nations
ARTICLES: 6 LANGUAGE: English.
HEADNOTE: TECHNICAL ASSISTANCE
TOPIC: Tech Assistance
CONCEPTS: Treaty implementation. Annex or appendix reference. Privileges and immunities. Personnel. Public information. Title and deeds. Use of facilities. Professorships. Scholarships and grants. Vocational training. Research and scientific projects. Exchange rates and regulations. Expense sharing formulae. Local currency. Domestic obligation. General technical assistance. Materials, equipment and services. IGO status. Conformity with IGO decisions.
INTL ORGS: United Nations.
TREATY REF: 76UNTS132; 1UNTS15,263; 33UNTS261.
PROCEDURE: Amendment. Termination.
PARTIES:
Philippines SIGNED: 5 Apr 51 FORCE: 5 Apr 51
ICAO (Civil Aviat) SIGNED: 5 Apr 51 FORCE: 5 Apr 51
ILO (Labor Org) SIGNED: 5 Apr 51 FORCE: 5 Apr 51
UNESCO (Educ/Cult) SIGNED: 5 Apr 51 FORCE: 5 Apr 51
United Nations SIGNED: 5 Apr 51 FORCE: 5 Apr 51
WHO (World Health) SIGNED: 5 Apr 51 FORCE: 5 Apr 51

101140 Bilateral Agreement **84 UNTS 313**
SIGNED: 16 May 49 FORCE: 1 Oct 49
REGISTERED: 6 Apr 51 Poland
ARTICLES: 14 LANGUAGE: Bulgarian. Polish.
HEADNOTE: AIR COMMUNICATIONS
TOPIC: Air Transport
CONCEPTS: Exceptions and exemptions. Representation. Annex or appendix reference. Previous treaty replacement. Friendship and amity. Conformity with municipal law. General cooperation. Informational records. Licenses and permits. Personnel. Recognition of legal documents. Use of facilities. Procedure. Negotiation. Humanitarian matters. Fees and exemptions. Tax exemptions. Customs declarations. Customs exemptions. Competency certificate. Routes and logistics. Navigational conditions. Permit designation. Airport facilities. Airworthiness certificates. Conditions of airlines operating permission. Operating authorizations and regulations. Licenses and certificates of nationality.
PROCEDURE: Amendment. Denunciation. Future Procedures Contemplated. Ratification.
PARTIES:
Bulgaria
Poland

101141 Bilateral Convention **84 UNTS 347**
SIGNED: 12 Nov 48 FORCE: 7 Sep 49
REGISTERED: 6 Apr 51 Poland
ARTICLES: 32 LANGUAGE: Czechoslovakian. Polish.
HEADNOTE: PRIVILEGED RAIL TRANSIT THROUGH POLAND
TOPIC: Land Transport
CONCEPTS: Detailed regulations. Annex or appendix reference. Non-visa travel documents. Conformity with municipal law. General cooperation. Exchange of information and documents. Free passage and transit. Recognition of legal docu

ments. Responsibility and liability. Investigation of violations. Arbitration. Mediation and good offices. Procedure. Humanitarian matters. Compensation. Indemnities and reimbursements. Fees and exemptions. Non-interest rates and fees. Claims and settlements. Customs duties. Customs exemptions. Passenger transport. Transport of goods. Operating authorizations and regulations. Railway border crossing. Railways. Regulations.
PROCEDURE: Denunciation. Ratification.
PARTIES:
Czechoslovakia
Poland

101142 Bilateral Convention **85 UNTS 3**
SIGNED: 22 Jan 49 FORCE: 1 Sep 49
REGISTERED: 6 Apr 51 Poland
ARTICLES: 9 LANGUAGE: Czechoslovakian. Polish.
HEADNOTE: PROTECTION AGRICULTURAL PLANTS PESTS DISEASES
TOPIC: Sanitation
CONCEPTS: General cooperation. Domestic legislation. Programs. Specialists exchange. Quarantine. Border control. Disease control. Insect control. Research results. Agriculture. Specific technical assistance.
PROCEDURE: Denunciation. Duration. Ratification. Renewal or Revival.
PARTIES:
Czechoslovakia
Poland

101143 Bilateral Treaty **85 UNTS 21**
SIGNED: 26 Jan 49 FORCE: 29 Nov 49
REGISTERED: 6 Apr 51 Poland
ARTICLES: 6 LANGUAGE: Polish. Romanian.
HEADNOTE: FRIENDSHIP COOPERATION MUTUAL ASSISTANCE
TOPIC: General Military
CONCEPTS: Friendship and amity. Non-prejudice to UN charter. Peaceful relations. General cultural cooperation. General trade. Defense and security. Military assistance.
INTL ORGS: United Nations.
PROCEDURE: Denunciation. Duration. Ratification. Termination.
PARTIES:
Poland
Romania

101144 Bilateral Agreement **85 UNTS 35**
SIGNED: 28 Feb 48 FORCE: 24 Feb 48
REGISTERED: 7 Apr 51 Denmark
ARTICLES: 9 LANGUAGE: German.
HEADNOTE: REGULATING PAYMENTS
TOPIC: Finance
CONCEPTS: General cooperation. Import quotas. Accounting procedures. Banking. Bonds. Balance of payments. Currency. Monetary and gold transfers. Exchange rates and regulations. Funding procedures. Interest rates. Local currency. Credit provisions.
PROCEDURE: Termination.
PARTIES:
Denmark
Hungary
ANNEX
162 UNTS 345. Denmark. Prolongation 27 Feb 53. Force 27 Feb 53.
162 UNTS 345. Hungary. Prolongation 27 Feb 53. Force 27 Feb 53.

101145 Bilateral Agreement **85 UNTS 49**
SIGNED: 10 Feb 51 FORCE: 10 Feb 51
REGISTERED: 7 Apr 51 Denmark
ARTICLES: 5 LANGUAGE: German.
HEADNOTE: EXCHANGE GOODS
TOPIC: General Trade
CONCEPTS: Detailed regulations. Annex or appendix reference. Previous treaty replacement. Extradition, deportation and repatriation. Licenses and permits. Negotiation. Payment schedules. Quotas.
PARTIES:
Denmark
Hungary

ANNEX
162 UNTS 346. Denmark. Prolongation 27 Feb 53. Force 27 Feb 53.
162 UNTS 346. Hungary. Prolongation 27 Feb 53. Force 27 Feb 53.

101146 Bilateral Convention **85 UNTS 62**
SIGNED: 4 Apr 47 FORCE: 7 Dec 48
REGISTERED: 9 Apr 51 Poland
ARTICLES: 5 LANGUAGE: Czechoslovakian. Polish.
HEADNOTE: ECONOMIC COOPERATION
TOPIC: General Economic
CONCEPTS: Treaty implementation. Annex or appendix reference. Arbitration. Procedure. General economics. Economic assistance.
INTL ORGS: Special Commission.
TREATY REF: 25LTS231,206,208,210.
PARTIES:
Czechoslovakia
Poland

101147 Bilateral Agreement **86 UNTS 3**
SIGNED: 5 Jun 46 FORCE: 6 Nov 46
REGISTERED: 10 Apr 51 UK Great Britain
ARTICLES: 11 LANGUAGE: English.
HEADNOTE: DOUBLE TAXATION FISCAL EVASION
TOPIC: Taxation
CONCEPTS: Definition of terms. Territorial application. Treaty implementation. Claims and settlements. Taxation. Death duties. General. Taxation of immovable property.
PROCEDURE: Duration. Termination.
PARTIES:
Canada
UK Great Britain

101148 Bilateral Agreement **86 UNTS 19**
SIGNED: 11 Nov 47 FORCE: 4 Feb 48
REGISTERED: 10 Apr 51 UK Great Britain
ARTICLES: 5 LANGUAGE: English.
HEADNOTE: DEFENSE AGREEMENT
TOPIC: Milit Assistance
CONCEPTS: General cooperation. Defense and security. Military assistance. Jurisdiction. Bases and facilities.
PROCEDURE: Future Procedures Contemplated.
PARTIES:
Ceylon (Sri Lanka)
UK Great Britain

101149 Bilateral Agreement **86 UNTS 25**
SIGNED: 11 Nov 47 FORCE: 4 Feb 48
REGISTERED: 10 Apr 51 UK Great Britain
ARTICLES: 7 LANGUAGE: English.
HEADNOTE: EXTERNAL AFFAIRS
TOPIC: Consul/Citizenship
CONCEPTS: Proxy diplomacy.
PARTIES:
Ceylon (Sri Lanka)
UK Great Britain

101150 Bilateral Agreement **86 UNTS 31**
SIGNED: 11 Nov 47 FORCE: 4 Feb 48
REGISTERED: 10 Apr 51 UK Great Britain
ARTICLES: 6 LANGUAGE: English.
HEADNOTE: PUBLIC OFFICERS
TOPIC: Admin Cooperation
CONCEPTS: Definition of terms. Personnel. Post-colonial administration. Social security.
PARTIES:
Ceylon (Sri Lanka)
UK Great Britain

101151 Bilateral Agreement **86 UNTS 37**
SIGNED: 31 Jul 48 FORCE: 12 Aug 48
REGISTERED: 10 Apr 51 UK Great Britain
ARTICLES: 7 LANGUAGE: English.
HEADNOTE: TRADE
TOPIC: General Trade
CONCEPTS: Detailed regulations. Annex or appendix reference. Previous treaty extension. Export quotas. Import quotas. Trade procedures. Balance of payments. Non-interest rates and fees. Commodity trade. Quotas. Customs duties.
TREATY REF: UK'CMD 5728;.
PROCEDURE: Amendment. Duration. Termination.

PARTIES:
Ireland
UK Great Britain
ANNEX
552 UNTS 362. UK Great Britain. Amendment 17 Jun 53. Force 29 Jun 53.
552 UNTS 362. Ireland. Amendment 17 Jun 53. Force 29 Jun 53.

101152 Bilateral Agreement **86 UNTS 51**
SIGNED: 14 Oct 46 FORCE: 13 Feb 47
REGISTERED: 10 Apr 51 UK Great Britain
ARTICLES: 11 LANGUAGE: Afrikaans. English.
HEADNOTE: DOUBLE TAXATION FISCAL EVASION ESTATE DUTIES
TOPIC: Taxation
CONCEPTS: Definition of terms. Territorial application. Treaty implementation. Conformity with municipal law. Exchange of official publications. Claims and settlements. Taxation. Death duties. General.
PROCEDURE: Duration. Termination.
PARTIES:
South Africa
UK Great Britain

101153 Bilateral Agreement **86 UNTS 77**
SIGNED: 14 Oct 46 FORCE: 13 Feb 47
REGISTERED: 10 Apr 51 UK Great Britain
ARTICLES: 28 LANGUAGE: Afrikaans. English.
HEADNOTE: DOUBLE TAXATION FISCAL EVASION
TOPIC: Taxation
CONCEPTS: Definition of terms. Territorial application. Previous treaty replacement. Conformity with municipal law. Exchange of official publications. Wages and salaries. Taxation. Tax credits. General. Tax exemptions.
TREATY REF: 20JUL1939.
PROCEDURE: Duration. Termination.
PARTIES:
South Africa
UK Great Britain
ANNEX
412 UNTS 296. UK Great Britain. Extension and Amendment 6 Aug 60. Force 5 Oct 60.
412 UNTS 296. South Africa. Extension and Amendment 6 Aug 60. Force 5 Oct 60.

101154 Bilateral Exchange **86 UNTS 113**
SIGNED: 3 Aug 49 FORCE: 3 Aug 49
REGISTERED: 11 Apr 51 UK Great Britain
ARTICLES: 2 LANGUAGE: English. Portuguese.
HEADNOTE: TRADE
TOPIC: General Trade
CONCEPTS: Annex or appendix reference. Annex type material. Licenses and permits. Reexport of goods, etc.. Balance of payments. Payment schedules. Non-interest rates and fees. Quotas.
TREATY REF: 66UNTS121.
PROCEDURE: Duration. Future Procedures Contemplated. Termination.
PARTIES:
Brazil
UK Great Britain

101155 Bilateral Agreement **86 UNTS 129**
SIGNED: 18 Aug 49 FORCE: 19 Aug 49
REGISTERED: 11 Apr 51 UK Great Britain
ARTICLES: 10 LANGUAGE: Czechoslovakian. English.
HEADNOTE: PAYMENTS
TOPIC: Finance
CONCEPTS: Definition of terms. Detailed regulations. General cooperation. Accounting procedures. Banking. Currency. Monetary and gold transfers. Currency deposits. Investments. Exchange rates and regulations. Payment schedules.
INTL ORGS: International Monetary Fund.
TREATY REF: 2UNTS104.
PROCEDURE: Termination.
PARTIES:
Czechoslovakia
UK Great Britain
ANNEX
131 UNTS 339. UK Great Britain. Amendment 28 Dec 50. Force 28 Dec 50.
131 UNTS 339. Czechoslovakia. Amendment 28 Dec 50. Force 28 Dec 50.

138 UNTS 470. UK Great Britain. Prolongation
1 Aug 52. Force 19 Aug 52.
138 UNTS 470. Czechoslovakia. Prolongation
1 Aug 52. Force 19 Aug 52.
222 UNTS 401. UK Great Britain. Prolongation
18 Aug 55. Force 20 Aug 55.
222 UNTS 401. Czechoslovakia. Prolongation
1 Sep 55. Force 20 Aug 55.
231 UNTS 355. UK Great Britain. Prolongation
17 Nov 55. Force 20 Nov 55.
231 UNTS 355. Czechoslovakia. Prolongation
29 Nov 55. Force 20 Nov 55.
249 UNTS 434. UK Great Britain. Prolongation
18 May 56. Force 20 May 56.
249 UNTS 434. Czechoslovakia. Prolongation
1 Jun 56. Force 20 May 56.
256 UNTS 341. UK Great Britain. Prolongation
18 Aug 56. Force 20 Aug 56.
256 UNTS 341. Czechoslovakia. Prolongation
24 Aug 56. Force 20 Aug 56.
269 UNTS 288. UK Great Britain. Prolongation
15 Feb 57. Force 19 Feb 57.
269 UNTS 288. Czechoslovakia. Prolongation
19 Feb 57. Force 19 Feb 57.

101156 Bilateral Agreement **86 UNTS 141**
SIGNED: 28 Sep 49   FORCE: 28 Sep 49
REGISTERED: 11 Apr 51 UK Great Britain
ARTICLES: 12 LANGUAGE: Czechoslovakian. English.
HEADNOTE: TRADE FINANCE
TOPIC: General Economic
CONCEPTS: Conditions. Detailed regulations. Annex or appendix reference. Licenses and permits. Establishment of commission. Export quotas. Import quotas. Trade procedures. Finances and payments. Funding procedures. Payment schedules. Debt settlement. Quotas.
INTL ORGS: Special Commission.
TREATY REF: 29LTS377; 45LTS128; 54LTS396; 86UNTS175,161.
PROCEDURE: Future Procedures Contemplated. Termination.
PARTIES:
 Czechoslovakia
 UK Great Britain

101157 Bilateral Agreement **86 UNTS 161**
SIGNED: 28 Sep 49   FORCE: 28 Sep 49
REGISTERED: 11 Apr 51 UK Great Britain
ARTICLES: 7 LANGUAGE: Czechoslovakian. English.
HEADNOTE: COMPENSATION PROPERTY RIGHTS INTERESTS
TOPIC: Reparations
CONCEPTS: Definition of terms. Annex or appendix reference. General cooperation. Exchange of information and documents. General property. Compensation. Payment schedules. Claims and settlements. Post-war claims settlement.
PARTIES:
 Czechoslovakia
 UK Great Britain
          ANNEX
263 UNTS 405. UK Great Britain. Supplementation 22 Oct 56. Force 22 Oct 56.
263 UNTS 405. Czechoslovakia. Supplementation 22 Oct 56. Force 22 Oct 56.

101158 Bilateral Agreement **86 UNTS 175**
SIGNED: 28 Sep 49   FORCE: 28 Sep 49
REGISTERED: 11 Apr 51 UK Great Britain
ARTICLES: 10 LANGUAGE: Czechoslovakian. English.
HEADNOTE: INTER-GOVERNMENTAL DEBTS
TOPIC: Claims and Debts
CONCEPTS: Debt settlement. Credit provisions. Loan repayment. Refinance of loan.
PARTIES:
 Czechoslovakia
 UK Great Britain
          ANNEX
263 UNTS 410. Czechoslovakia. Supplementation 22 Oct 56. Force 22 Oct 56.
263 UNTS 410. Czechoslovakia. Supplementation 22 Oct 56. Force 22 Oct 56.
344 UNTS 318. UK Great Britain. Supplementation 4 Feb 59. Force 4 Feb 59.
344 UNTS 318. Czechoslovakia. Supplementation 4 Feb 59. Force 4 Feb 59.

437 UNTS 343. UK Great Britain. Supplementation 20 Mar 62. Force 20 Mar 62.
437 UNTS 343. Czechoslovakia. Supplementation 20 Mar 62. Force 20 Mar 62.
470 UNTS 382. Czechoslovakia. Supplementation 20 Dec 62. Force 20 Dec 62.
470 UNTS 382. UK Great Britain. Supplementation 20 Dec 62. Force 20 Dec 62.
502 UNTS 369. UK Great Britain. Interpretation 18 Nov 63. Force 18 Nov 63.
502 UNTS 369. Czechoslovakia. Interpretation 18 Nov 63. Force 18 Nov 63.

101159 Bilateral Exchange **86 UNTS 191**
SIGNED: 28 Dec 49   FORCE: 28 Dec 49
REGISTERED: 11 Apr 51 UK Great Britain
ARTICLES: 2 LANGUAGE: English.
HEADNOTE: INSURANCE CONTRACT
TOPIC: Peace/Disarmament
CONCEPTS: Annex or appendix reference. Responsibility and liability. Reconversion to normalcy.
PARTIES:
 Finland
 UK Great Britain

101160 Bilateral Exchange **86 UNTS 203**
SIGNED: 29 Jun 49   FORCE: 4 Jul 49
REGISTERED: 11 Apr 51 UK Great Britain
ARTICLES: 2 LANGUAGE: English.
HEADNOTE: FINANCE
TOPIC: Finance
CONCEPTS: Accounting procedures. Loan and credit. Credit provisions.
INTL ORGS: Organization for Economic Co-operation and Development.
TREATY REF: UK MISCELLANEOUS 8 (1948) CMD 7546.
PARTIES:
 Greece
 UK Great Britain

101161 Bilateral Exchange **86 UNTS 211**
SIGNED: 10 Feb 50   FORCE: 10 Feb 50
REGISTERED: 11 Apr 51 UK Great Britain
ARTICLES: 2 LANGUAGE: English. Hebrew.
HEADNOTE: DOUBLE TAXATION FISCAL EVASION
TOPIC: Taxation
CONCEPTS: Previous treaty extension. Taxation.
TREATY REF: ARRANGEMENT OF 1947.
PARTIES:
 Israel
 UK Great Britain

101162 Bilateral Agreement **86 UNTS 231**
SIGNED: 30 Mar 50   FORCE: 30 Mar 50
REGISTERED: 11 Apr 51 UK Great Britain
ARTICLES: 12 LANGUAGE: English.
HEADNOTE: FINANCE SETTLEMENT MANDATE TERMINATION
TOPIC: Claims and Debts
CONCEPTS: Definition of terms. Detailed regulations. Exceptions and exemptions. General cooperation. Exchange of information and documents. Informational records. General property. Responsibility and liability. Use of facilities. Old age and invalidity insurance. Bonds. Balance of payments. Monetary and gold transfers. Currency deposits. Exchange rates and regulations. Financial programs. Interest rates. Payment schedules. Claims and settlements. Assets transfer. Enemy financial interests.
PARTIES:
 Israel
 UK Great Britain

101163 Bilateral Exchange **87 UNTS 3**
SIGNED: 24 Jan 48   FORCE: 24 Jan 46
REGISTERED: 11 Apr 51 UK Great Britain
ARTICLES: 2 LANGUAGE: English. Polish.
HEADNOTE: COMPENSATION NATIONALIZED ASSETS
TOPIC: Claims and Debts
CONCEPTS: Expropriation. Compensation.
PARTIES:
 Poland
 UK Great Britain

101164 Bilateral Exchange **87 UNTS 37**
SIGNED: 12 Sep 49   FORCE: 1 Oct 49
REGISTERED: 11 Apr 51 UK Great Britain
ARTICLES: 2 LANGUAGE: English. Italian.
HEADNOTE: ABOLITION VISAS
TOPIC: Visas
CONCEPTS: Visa abolition. Frontier permits.
PARTIES:
 San Marino
 UK Great Britain
          ANNEX
218 UNTS 383. UK Great Britain. Sarawak. Force 1 Oct 55.
267 UNTS 377. UK Great Britain. Gibralter. Force 20 Jul 55.
349 UNTS 323. UK Great Britain. Gambia. Force 1 Oct 58.
349 UNTS 323. UK Great Britain. Amendment 27 Oct 58. Force 27 Oct 58.
349 UNTS 323. San Marino. Amendment 27 Oct 58. Force 27 Oct 58.
560 UNTS 242. UK Great Britain. Southern Rhodesia.

101165 Bilateral Agreement **87 UNTS 49**
SIGNED: 15 Dec 48   FORCE: 15 Dec 48
REGISTERED: 11 Apr 51 UK Great Britain
ARTICLES: 11 LANGUAGE: English. Spanish.
HEADNOTE: PAYMENTS
TOPIC: Finance
CONCEPTS: Definition of terms. Previous treaty replacement. General cooperation. Accounting procedures. Banking. Currency. Monetary and gold transfers. Currency deposits. Investments. Exchange rates and regulations. Payment schedules. Local currency.
TREATY REF: 66UNTS91.
PROCEDURE: Duration. Termination.
PARTIES:
 Spain
 UK Great Britain

101166 Bilateral Agreement **87 UNTS 59**
SIGNED: 30 Dec 49   FORCE: 1 Jan 50
REGISTERED: 11 Apr 51 UK Great Britain
ARTICLES: 12 LANGUAGE: English.
HEADNOTE: FINANCE
TOPIC: Finance
CONCEPTS: Definition of terms. Detailed regulations. General cooperation. Accounting procedures. Banking. Balance of payments. Currency. Monetary and gold transfers. Currency deposits. Investments. Exchange rates and regulations. Internal finance. Loan and credit.
INTL ORGS: International Monetary Fund.
TREATY REF: 2UNTS39; 19UNTS280.
PROCEDURE: Duration. Termination.
PARTIES:
 Sweden
 UK Great Britain

101167 Bilateral Agreement **87 UNTS 71**
SIGNED: 26 Dec 49   FORCE: 1 Jan 50
REGISTERED: 11 Apr 51 UK Great Britain
ARTICLES: 10 LANGUAGE: English. Serbo-Croat.
HEADNOTE: TRADE LONG TERM BASIS
TOPIC: General Trade
CONCEPTS: Exceptions and exemptions. Territorial application. Treaty implementation. Annex or appendix reference. Annex type material. General cooperation. Licenses and permits. Financial programs. Funding procedures. Payment schedules. Commodity trade. Delivery schedules. Quotas. Credit provisions. Purchase authorization. Water transport. Ports and pilotage.
TREATY REF: 81UNTS103.
PROCEDURE: Duration.
PARTIES:
 UK Great Britain
 Yugoslavia
          ANNEX
158 UNTS 494. UK Great Britain. Implementation 21 Oct 52. Force 21 Oct 52.
158 UNTS 494. Yugoslavia. Implementation 21 Oct 52. Force 21 Oct 52.

101168 Multilateral Instrument **87 UNTS 103**
SIGNED: 5 May 49   FORCE: 3 Aug 49
REGISTERED: 11 Apr 51 UK Great Britain
ARTICLES: 42 LANGUAGE: English. French.

HEADNOTE: STATUTE COUNCIL OF EUROPE
TOPIC: IGO Establishment
CONCEPTS: Definition of terms. Friendship and amity. Privileges and immunities. Expense sharing formulae. Funding procedures. Admission. Subsidiary organ. Establishment. Procedure. Headquarters and facilities. Internal structure. Special status. Status of experts.
INTL ORGS: Council of Europe. United Nations.
PROCEDURE: Amendment. Denunciation. Ratification.
PARTIES:
Belgium SIGNED: 5 May 49 RATIFIED: 8 Aug 49 FORCE: 8 Aug 49
Denmark SIGNED: 5 May 49 RATIFIED: 14 Jul 49 FORCE: 3 Aug 49
France SIGNED: 5 May 49 RATIFIED: 4 Aug 49 FORCE: 4 Aug 49
Ireland SIGNED: 5 May 49 RATIFIED: 30 Jul 49 FORCE: 3 Aug 49
Italy SIGNED: 5 May 49 RATIFIED: 3 Aug 49 FORCE: 3 Aug 49
Luxembourg SIGNED: 5 May 49 RATIFIED: 3 Aug 49 FORCE: 3 Aug 49
Netherlands SIGNED: 5 May 49 RATIFIED: 5 Aug 49 FORCE: 5 Aug 49
Norway SIGNED: 5 May 49 RATIFIED: 2 Aug 49 FORCE: 3 Aug 49
Sweden SIGNED: 5 May 49 RATIFIED: 20 Jul 49 FORCE: 3 Aug 49
UK Great Britain SIGNED: 5 May 49 RATIFIED: 26 Jul 49 FORCE: 3 Aug 49
ANNEX
100 UNTS 302. Iceland. Accession 7 Mar 50.
100 UNTS 302. Saar. Accession 13 May 50.
100 UNTS 302. Germany, West. Accession 13 Jul 50.
196 UNTS 347. Council of Europe. Amendment 4 May 53. Force 4 May 53.
614 UNTS 296. Malta. Accession 29 Apr 65.
614 UNTS 296. Greece. Accession 9 Aug 49.
614 UNTS 296. Turkey. Accession 13 Apr 50.
614 UNTS 296. Council of Europe. Force 24 May 65.
614 UNTS 296. Austria. Accession 16 Apr 56.
614 UNTS 296. Switzerland. Accession 6 May 63.
614 UNTS 296. Cyprus. Accession 24 May 61.

101169 Multilateral Instrument **87 UNTS 131**
SIGNED: 12 Aug 49   FORCE: 24 Feb 50
REGISTERED: 11 Apr 51 UK Great Britain
ARTICLES: 1 LANGUAGE: English.
HEADNOTE: TELECOMMUNICATION AGREEMENT
TOPIC: IGO Establishment
CONCEPTS: Definition of terms. Exceptions and exemptions. Previous treaty amendment. Treaty interpretation. Previous treaty replacement. General cooperation. Indemnities and reimbursements. Currency. Exchange rates and regulations. Non-interest rates and fees. Most favored nation clause. Communications linkage. Cable. Radio-telephone-telegraphic communications.
TREATY REF: 9UNTS101.
PROCEDURE: Amendment. Termination.
PARTIES:
Australia SIGNED: 12 Aug 49 RATIFIED: 28 Nov 49 FORCE: 24 Feb 50
Canada SIGNED: 12 Aug 49 RATIFIED: 18 Feb 50 FORCE: 24 Feb 50
Ceylon (Sri Lanka) SIGNED: 12 Aug 49 RATIFIED: 16 Feb 50 FORCE: 24 Feb 50
India SIGNED: 12 Aug 49 RATIFIED: 24 Feb 50 FORCE: 24 Feb 50
New Zealand SIGNED: 12 Aug 49 RATIFIED: 21 Nov 49 FORCE: 24 Feb 50
Pakistan SIGNED: 12 Aug 49 RATIFIED: 22 Feb 50 FORCE: 24 Feb 50
South Africa SIGNED: 12 Aug 49 RATIFIED: 3 Feb 50 FORCE: 24 Feb 50
Southern Rhodesia SIGNED: 12 Aug 49 RATIFIED: 16 Feb 50 FORCE: 24 Feb 50
UK Great Britain SIGNED: 12 Aug 49 RATIFIED: 30 Oct 49 FORCE: 24 Feb 50
USA (United States) SIGNED: 12 Aug 49 RATIFIED: 13 Jan 50 FORCE: 24 Feb 50
ANNEX
151 UNTS 378. Ceylon (Sri Lanka). Amendment 1 Oct 52. Force 1 Oct 52.
151 UNTS 378. Southern Rhodesia. Amendment 1 Oct 52. Force 1 Oct 52.
151 UNTS 378. UK Great Britain. Amendment 1 Oct 52. Force 1 Oct 52.

151 UNTS 378. USA (United States). Amendment 1 Oct 52. Force 1 Oct 52.
151 UNTS 378. Canada. Amendment 1 Oct 52. Force 1 Oct 52.
151 UNTS 378. Australia. Amendment 1 Oct 52. Force 1 Oct 52.
151 UNTS 378. New Zealand. Amendment 1 Oct 52. Force 1 Oct 52.
151 UNTS 378. South Africa. Amendment 1 Oct 52. Force 1 Oct 52.
151 UNTS 378. India. Amendment 1 Oct 52. Force 1 Oct 52.
151 UNTS 378. Pakistan. Amendment 1 Oct 52. Force 1 Oct 52.

101170 Multilateral Agreement **87 UNTS 153**
SIGNED: 28 Jun 50   FORCE: 28 Jun 50
REGISTERED: 11 Apr 51 UK Great Britain
ARTICLES: 6 LANGUAGE: English.
HEADNOTE: LOAN
TOPIC: Loans and Credits
CONCEPTS: Definition of terms. Responsibility and liability. Financial programs. Funding procedures. Interest rates. Payment schedules. Loan and credit. Loan repayment.
PARTIES:
Australia SIGNED: 28 Jun 50 FORCE: 28 Jun 50
Burma SIGNED: 28 Jun 50 FORCE: 28 Jun 50
Ceylon (Sri Lanka) SIGNED: 28 Jun 50 FORCE: 28 Jun 50
India SIGNED: 28 Jun 50 FORCE: 28 Jun 50
Pakistan SIGNED: 28 Jun 50 FORCE: 28 Jun 50
UK Great Britain SIGNED: 28 Jun 50 FORCE: 28 Jun 50

101171 Bilateral Agreement **87 UNTS 161**
SIGNED: 26 Jan 51   FORCE: 26 Jan 51
REGISTERED: 13 Apr 51 Denmark
ARTICLES: 11 LANGUAGE: Danish. Spanish.
HEADNOTE: FINANCE
TOPIC: Finance
CONCEPTS: Guarantees and safeguards. General cooperation. Licenses and permits. General trade. Trade agencies. Trade procedures. Accounting procedures. Banking. Balance of payments. Currency deposits. Non-interest rates and fees. Commodity trade.
PROCEDURE: Denunciation. Duration. Renewal or Revival.
PARTIES:
Colombia
Denmark

101172 Bilateral Protocol **87 UNTS 179**
SIGNED: 12 May 49   FORCE: 12 May 49
REGISTERED: 16 Apr 51 Denmark
ARTICLES: 14 LANGUAGE: French.
HEADNOTE: INTEREST ASSETS
TOPIC: Claims and Debts
CONCEPTS: Detailed regulations. Diplomatic and consular relations. Consular functions in property. Conformity with municipal law. Exchange of information and documents. Informational records. Juridical personality. Expropriation. Immovable property. General property. Establishment of commission. Arbitration. Procedure. Negotiation. Compensation. Interest rates. Claims and settlements. Debts. Most favored nation clause. Patents, copyrights and trademarks. Grants.
INTL ORGS: Special Commission.
PROCEDURE: Future Procedures Contemplated.
PARTIES:
Denmark
Poland

101173 Bilateral Protocol **87 UNTS 197**
SIGNED: 6 Apr 50   FORCE: 6 Apr 50
REGISTERED: 16 Apr 51 Denmark
ARTICLES: 1 LANGUAGE: German.
HEADNOTE: TRADE
TOPIC: General Trade
CONCEPTS: Annex or appendix reference. Annex type material.
TREATY REF: TRADE AGREEMENT 15JUL40.
PARTIES:
Denmark
Switzerland

101174 Bilateral Agreement **87 UNTS 223**
SIGNED: 20 Jan 51   FORCE: 1 Mar 51
REGISTERED: 16 Apr 51 Denmark
ARTICLES: 10 LANGUAGE: German.
HEADNOTE: PAYMENTS
TOPIC: Finance
CONCEPTS: Detailed regulations. Territorial application. Previous treaty replacement. General cooperation. Accounting procedures. Banking. Exchange rates and regulations. Payment schedules. Assets.
INTL ORGS: European Payments Union.
TREATY REF: LIECHTENSTEIN 15JUL40; 6MAR41 PAYMENT AGREEMENTS.
PROCEDURE: Denunciation.
PARTIES:
Denmark
Switzerland

101175 Bilateral Exchange **87 UNTS 239**
SIGNED: 13 Feb 51   FORCE: 13 Feb 51
REGISTERED: 17 Apr 51 Netherlands
ARTICLES: 2 LANGUAGE: English.
HEADNOTE: ASSISTANCE TO REFUGEES
TOPIC: IGO Operations
CONCEPTS: Assistance. IGO operations.
INTL ORGS: United Nations.
PARTIES:
Netherlands
IRO (Refugee Org)

101176 Multilateral Agreement **87 UNTS 247**
SIGNED: 20 Jan 47   FORCE: 20 Jan 47
REGISTERED: 17 Apr 51 Netherlands
ARTICLES: 5 LANGUAGE: English.
HEADNOTE: RESTITUTION INLAND TRANSPORT CRAFT
TOPIC: Water Transport
CONCEPTS: Merchant vessels. Inland and territorial waters.
INTL ORGS: Inter-Allied Reparations Agency. Special Commission.
PARTIES:
Netherlands SIGNED: 20 Jan 47 FORCE: 20 Jan 47
British Occup Germ SIGNED: 20 Jan 47 FORCE: 20 Jan 47
US Occup Germ SIGNED: 20 Jan 47 FORCE: 20 Jan 47

101177 Bilateral Agreement **87 UNTS 257**
SIGNED: 14 Dec 50   FORCE: 14 Dec 50
REGISTERED: 17 Apr 51 Netherlands
ARTICLES: 1 LANGUAGE: Dutch. English. French. German.
HEADNOTE: SETTLEMENT QUESTIONS RESTITUTION INLAND WATERCRAFT
TOPIC: Water Transport
CONCEPTS: Conditions. Exceptions and exemptions. Annex or appendix reference. Continuity of rights and obligations. General cooperation. Exchange of information and documents. Personnel. General property. Private contracts. Establishment of commission. Procedure. Indemnities and reimbursements. Non-interest rates and fees. National treatment. Navigational conditions. Merchant vessels. Inland and territorial waters. Reparations and restrictions. Specific claims or waivers.
INTL ORGS: Allied Military Occupation.
PARTIES:
Germany, West
Netherlands

101178 Bilateral Exchange **87 UNTS 343**
SIGNED: 29 Jul 47   FORCE: 29 Jul 47
REGISTERED: 19 Apr 51 USA (United States)
ARTICLES: 2 LANGUAGE: English.
HEADNOTE: PASSPORT VISA REQUIREMENTS
TOPIC: Visas
CONCEPTS: Time limit. Visa abolition. Fees and exemptions.
PARTIES:
Norway
USA (United States)

101179 Bilateral Treaty **87 UNTS 351**
SIGNED: 6 Oct 48   FORCE: 28 Aug 50
REGISTERED: 23 Apr 51 Greece

ARTICLES: 34 LANGUAGE: French.
HEADNOTE: CONSULAR NAVIGATION CIVIL & COMMERCIAL ESTABLISHMENT
TOPIC: Consul/Citizenship
CONCEPTS: Passports diplomatic. General consular functions. Diplomatic privileges. Dual citizenship. Inviolability. Privileges and immunities. Notarial acts and services. General cooperation. Juridical personality. Legal protection and assistance. General property. Arbitration. Existing tribunals. Education. Establishment of trade relations. Fees and exemptions. Most favored nation clause. National treatment. General. Trademarks. Navigational conditions. Use of ports and territorial waters. Shipwreck and salvage. Repatriation of civilians.
INTL ORGS: Arab League. International Court of Justice. Special Commission.
PROCEDURE: Denunciation. Ratification.
PARTIES:
  Greece
  Lebanon

101180   Bilateral Exchange   **88 UNTS 3**
SIGNED: 26 Nov 48   FORCE: 26 Nov 48
REGISTERED: 1 May 51 USA (United States).
ARTICLES: 2 LANGUAGE: English. Portuguese.
HEADNOTE: SURVEY PROGRAM MINERAL RESOURCES
TOPIC: Scientific Project
CONCEPTS: Exchange of information and documents. Operating agencies. Use of facilities. Specialists exchange. Research and scientific projects. Research results. Research and development. Fees and exemptions. Financial programs. Funding procedures. Tax exemptions. Domestic obligation. Natural resources.
PROCEDURE: Denunciation. Duration. Renewal or Revival. Termination.
PARTIES:
  Brazil
  USA (United States)

101181   Bilateral Exchange   **88 UNTS 21**
SIGNED: 31 Jan 49   FORCE: 31 Jan 49
REGISTERED: 1 May 51 USA (United States).
ARTICLES: 2 LANGUAGE: English.
HEADNOTE: EXCHANGE OFFICIAL PUBLICATIONS
TOPIC: Admin Cooperation
CONCEPTS: Exchange of official publications. Operating agencies.
PARTIES:
  Ceylon (Sri Lanka)
  USA (United States)

101182   Bilateral Exchange   **88 UNTS 29**
SIGNED: 21 Feb 49   FORCE: 21 Feb 49
REGISTERED: 1 May 51 USA (United States).
ARTICLES: 2 LANGUAGE: English.
HEADNOTE: EXTENSION FACILITIES TRAINING EXERCISES
TOPIC: Status of Forces
CONCEPTS: Use of facilities. Military training. Status of military forces.
PARTIES:
  Greece
  USA (United States)

101183   Bilateral Exchange   **88 UNTS 35**
SIGNED: 29 Jan 49   FORCE: 29 Jan 49
REGISTERED: 1 May 51 USA (United States).
ARTICLES: 2 LANGUAGE: English. French.
HEADNOTE: REDUCTION NON-IMMIGRANT PASSPORT VISAS EXTENSION PERIOD VALIDITY
TOPIC: Visas
CONCEPTS: Time limit. Visas. Fees and exemptions.
PARTIES:
  Greece
  USA (United States)

101184   Bilateral Agreement   **88 UNTS 43**
SIGNED: 25 May 50   FORCE: 25 May 50
REGISTERED: 1 May 51 USA (United States)
ARTICLES: 1 LANGUAGE: English. Spanish.
HEADNOTE: TERMINATION 1935 TRADE AGREEMENT
TOPIC: General Trade

CONCEPTS: Annex type material.
INTL ORGS: General Agreement on Tariffs and Trade.
TREATY REF: 55UNTS187.
PROCEDURE: Termination.
PARTIES:
  Sweden
  USA (United States)

101185   Bilateral Agreement   **88 UNTS 47**
SIGNED: 17 Sep 46   FORCE: 17 Sep 46
REGISTERED: 14 May 51 UK Great Britain
ARTICLES: 4 LANGUAGE: English. Spanish.
HEADNOTE: ECONOMIC AGREEMENT
TOPIC: General Economic
CONCEPTS: Exceptions and exemptions. Annex or appendix reference. Immovable property. Negotiation. Banking. Compensation. Funding procedures. Internal finance. Payment schedules. Commodity trade. Quotas. Railways.
PROCEDURE: Amendment. Duration. Future Procedures Contemplated.
PARTIES:
  Argentina
  UK Great Britain

101186   Bilateral Exchange   **88 UNTS 93**
SIGNED: 23 Dec 46   FORCE: 18 Dec 46
REGISTERED: 14 May 51 UK Great Britain
ARTICLES: 3 LANGUAGE: English. German.
HEADNOTE: FINANCIAL AID CREDITS
TOPIC: General Aid
CONCEPTS: Import quotas. Financial programs. Materials, equipment and services. Grants. Credit provisions.
INTL ORGS: United Nations Relief and Rehabilitation Administration.
PARTIES:
  Austria
  UK Great Britain

101187   Bilateral Agreement   **88 UNTS 107**
SIGNED: 31 Jan 51   FORCE: 31 Jan 51
REGISTERED: 14 May 51 UK Great Britain
ARTICLES: 9 LANGUAGE: English.
HEADNOTE: STERLING PAYMENTS
TOPIC: Finance
CONCEPTS: Detailed regulations. Annex type material. General cooperation. Banking. Currency. Monetary and gold transfers. Payment schedules.
INTL ORGS: European Payments Union. International Monetary Fund.
PROCEDURE: Termination.
PARTIES:
  Austria
  UK Great Britain
                    ANNEX
191 UNTS 385. UK Great Britain. Prolongation 27 Nov 53. Force 28 Dec 53.
191 UNTS 385. Austria. Prolongation 28 Dec 53. Force 28 Dec 53.

101188   Bilateral Exchange   **88 UNTS 115**
SIGNED: 18 Sep 50   FORCE: 1 Jul 50
REGISTERED: 14 May 51 UK Great Britain
ARTICLES: 2 LANGUAGE: English. Portuguese.
HEADNOTE: COMMERCE
TOPIC: General Trade
CONCEPTS: Annex or appendix reference. General cooperation. Establishment of commission. Export quotas. Import quotas. Reexport of goods, etc.. Trade agencies. Banking. Balance of payments. Payment schedules. Non-interest rates and fees.
INTL ORGS: Special Commission.
TREATY REF: 66UNTS121.
PROCEDURE: Duration. Renewal or Revival.
PARTIES:
  Brazil
  UK Great Britain

101189   Bilateral Agreement   **88 UNTS 133**
SIGNED: 13 Dec 49   FORCE: 1 May 50
REGISTERED: 14 May 51 UK Great Britain
ARTICLES: 28 LANGUAGE: English. Spanish.
HEADNOTE: MONEY ORDER AGREEMENT
TOPIC: Finance
CONCEPTS: Definition of terms. Conformity with

municipal law. Accounting procedures. Exchange rates and regulations. Payment schedules. Postal services. Money orders and postal checks. Rates and charges. Advice lists and orders.
PARTIES:
  Colombia
  UK Great Britain

101190   Bilateral Exchange   **88 UNTS 191**
SIGNED: 2 Mar 51   FORCE: 17 Mar 51
REGISTERED: 14 May 51 UK Great Britain
ARTICLES: 2 LANGUAGE: English. Spanish.
HEADNOTE: ABOLITION VISAS
TOPIC: Visas
CONCEPTS: Territorial application. Visa abolition. Border traffic and migration. Denial of admission. Resident permits. Conformity with municipal law.
PARTIES:
  Cuba
  UK Great Britain
                    ANNEX
267 UNTS 378. UK Great Britain. Channel Islands. Force 25 May 51.
267 UNTS 378. UK Great Britain. Gibralter. Force 20 Jul 55.

101191   Bilateral Exchange   **88 UNTS 199**
SIGNED: 17 Feb 51   FORCE: 17 Feb 51
REGISTERED: 14 May 51 UK Great Britain
ARTICLES: 2 LANGUAGE: English. French.
HEADNOTE: FINANCE
TOPIC: Finance
CONCEPTS: Accounting procedures. Debt settlement.
TREATY REF: 54UNTS117.
PARTIES:
  France
  UK Great Britain

101192   Bilateral Exchange   **88 UNTS 205**
SIGNED: 21 Feb 51   FORCE: 21 Feb 51
REGISTERED: 14 May 51 UK Great Britain
ARTICLES: 2 LANGUAGE: English.
HEADNOTE: COMMERCE NAVIGATION AMENDMENT
TOPIC: General Economic
CONCEPTS: Annex type material.
TREATY REF: 62UNTS121; 61LTS15; 88LTS356.
PROCEDURE: Amendment. Duration.
PARTIES:
  Greece
  UK Great Britain

101193   Bilateral Exchange   **88 UNTS 211**
SIGNED: 10 Dec 50   FORCE: 10 Dec 50
REGISTERED: 14 May 51 UK Great Britain
ARTICLES: 2 LANGUAGE: English.
HEADNOTE: INDUSTRIAL PROPERTY
TOPIC: Patents/Copyrights
CONCEPTS: Previous treaty extension. Trademarks. Laws and formalities.
TREATY REF: 092LTS17; 205LTS218; 269UNTS269; 32UNTS406.
PARTIES:
  Israel
  UK Great Britain

101194 Multilateral Agreement **88 UNTS 221**
SIGNED: 29 Nov 50   FORCE: 29 Nov 50
REGISTERED: 14 May 51 UK Great Britain
ARTICLES: 2 LANGUAGE: English. French. Italian.
HEADNOTE: PATENTS
TOPIC: Patents/Copyrights
CONCEPTS: Previous treaty extension. Post-war adjustment.
TREATY REF: CMD7359; CMD7223; 49UNTS49.
PROCEDURE: Registration.
PARTIES:
  France SIGNED: 28 Nov 50 FORCE: 29 Nov 50
  Italy SIGNED: 28 Nov 50 FORCE: 29 Nov 50
  UK Great Britain SIGNED: 28 Nov 50 FORCE: 29 Nov 50
  USA (United States) SIGNED: 28 Nov 50 FORCE: 29 Nov 50

101195 Multilateral Agreement **88 UNTS 229**
SIGNED: 5 Aug 49　　　　FORCE: 5 Aug 49
REGISTERED: 14 May 51 UK Great Britain
ARTICLES: 11 LANGUAGE: English. French.
HEADNOTE: PAYMENTS
TOPIC: Finance
CONCEPTS: Definition of terms. Detailed regulations. General cooperation. Negotiation. Accounting procedures. Banking. Balance of payments. Currency. Monetary and gold transfers. Currency deposits. Investments. Exchange rates and regulations. Financial programs. Payment schedules.
INTL ORGS: International Monetary Fund.
TREATY REF: 34UNTS390; 67UNTS336.
PROCEDURE: Duration. Renewal or Revival.
PARTIES:
　French Occup Germ SIGNED: 5 Aug 49 FORCE: 5 Aug 49
　UK Great Britain SIGNED: 5 Aug 49 FORCE: 5 Aug 49
　British Occup Germ SIGNED: 5 Aug 49 FORCE: 5 Aug 49
　US Occup Germ SIGNED: 5 Aug 49 FORCE: 5 Aug 49

101196　Bilateral Agreement　**88 UNTS 247**
SIGNED: 9 Dec 50　　　　FORCE: 9 Dec 50
REGISTERED: 14 May 51 UK Great Britain
ARTICLES: 10 LANGUAGE: English. German.
HEADNOTE: PAYMENTS
TOPIC: Finance
CONCEPTS: Definition of terms. Previous treaty replacement. Banking. Currency. Monetary and gold transfers. Exchange rates and regulations. Financial programs.
INTL ORGS: European Payments Union. International Monetary Fund.
TREATY REF: 2UNTS39; 19UNTS280.
PROCEDURE: Renewal or Revival. Termination.
PARTIES:
　Germany, West
　UK Great Britain

101197　Bilateral Agreement　**88 UNTS 257**
SIGNED: 6 Nov 50　　　　FORCE: 6 Nov 50
REGISTERED: 14 May 51 UK Great Britain
ARTICLES: 8 LANGUAGE: English.
HEADNOTE: MONETARY
TOPIC: Finance
CONCEPTS: Definition of terms. Previous treaty replacement. General cooperation. Banking. Currency. Monetary and gold transfers. Exchange rates and regulations. Financial programs. Payment schedules.
INTL ORGS: European Payments Union. International Monetary Fund.
TREATY REF: 2UNTS39; 19UNTS280; 5UNTS27,11,412.
PROCEDURE: Renewal or Revival. Termination.
PARTIES:
　Norway
　UK Great Britain
ANNEX
183 UNTS 365. UK Great Britain. Prolongation 30 Jun 53. Force 25 Jul 53.
183 UNTS 365. Norway. Prolongation 25 Jul 53. Force 25 Jul 53.

101198　Bilateral Agreement　**88 UNTS 265**
SIGNED: 10 Nov 50　　　FORCE: 10 Nov 50
REGISTERED: 14 May 51 UK Great Britain
ARTICLES: 8 LANGUAGE: English.
HEADNOTE: MONETARY
TOPIC: Finance
CONCEPTS: Definition of terms. Previous treaty replacement. General cooperation. Banking. Currency. Exchange rates and regulations. Funding procedures.
INTL ORGS: European Payments Union. International Monetary Fund.
TREATY REF: 2UNTS39; 19UNTS280; 87UNTS59.
PROCEDURE: Renewal or Revival. Termination.
PARTIES:
　Sweden
　UK Great Britain

101199　Bilateral Exchange　**88 UNTS 273**
SIGNED: 1 Aug 50　　　　FORCE: 1 Aug 50

REGISTERED: 14 May 51 UK Great Britain
ARTICLES: 2 LANGUAGE: English.
HEADNOTE: MODIFICATION LEASED BASES AGREEMENT
TOPIC: Milit Installation
CONCEPTS: Annex or appendix reference. Military installations and equipment.
PARTIES:
　UK Great Britain
　USA (United States)

101200　Bilateral Agreement　**88 UNTS 287**
SIGNED: 9 Feb 50　　　　FORCE: 1 Aug 50
REGISTERED: 14 May 51 UK Great Britain
ARTICLES: 28 LANGUAGE: English. French.
HEADNOTE: MONEY ORDER
TOPIC: Finance
CONCEPTS: Definition of terms. Conformity with municipal law. Accounting procedures. Exchange rates and regulations. Payment schedules. Postal services. Money orders and postal checks. Rates and charges. Advice lists and orders.
PARTIES:
　UK Great Britain
　Yugoslavia

101201　Bilateral Exchange　**88 UNTS 329**
SIGNED: 28 Dec 50　　　FORCE: 28 Dec 50
REGISTERED: 14 May 51 UK Great Britain
ARTICLES: 2 LANGUAGE: English.
HEADNOTE: CREDIT PURCHASE CONSUMER GOODS
TOPIC: Loans and Credits
CONCEPTS: Conditions. Definition of terms. Annex or appendix reference. Financial programs. Interest rates. Payment schedules. Loan and credit. Credit provisions. Purchase authorization. Canal improvement.
PARTIES:
　UK Great Britain
　Yugoslavia

101202　Bilateral Agreement　**88 UNTS 339**
SIGNED: 22 Jan 51　　　　FORCE: 1 Feb 51
REGISTERED: 18 May 51 Norway
ARTICLES: 5 LANGUAGE: French.
HEADNOTE: PAYMENTS
TOPIC: Finance
CONCEPTS: Previous treaty replacement. General cooperation. Accounting procedures. Banking. Currency. Exchange rates and regulations. Payment schedules.
INTL ORGS: European Payments Union.
PROCEDURE: Denunciation.
PARTIES:
　Italy
　Norway

101203　Bilateral Exchange　**88 UNTS 357**
SIGNED: 16 Mar 51　　　　FORCE: 1 Apr 51
REGISTERED: 25 May 51 Belgium
ARTICLES: 2 LANGUAGE: French.
HEADNOTE: RECIPROCAL ABOLITION DIPLOMATIC SERVICE PASSPORTS OBTAIN TRAVEL VISAS
TOPIC: Visas
CONCEPTS: Visa abolition.
PARTIES:
　Austria
　Belgium

101204　Bilateral Exchange　**89 UNTS 3**
SIGNED: 21 Jun 49　　　　FORCE: 21 Jun 49
REGISTERED: 1 Jun 51 USA (United States)
ARTICLES: 2 LANGUAGE: English. Spanish.
HEADNOTE: ANTHROPOLOGICAL RESEARCH
TOPIC: Scientific Project
CONCEPTS: Previous treaty replacement. General cooperation. Vocational training. Anthropology and archeology. Research results. Research and development. Tax exemptions. Indemnities and reimbursements.
PROCEDURE: Duration. Termination.
PARTIES:
　Mexico
　USA (United States)

ANNEX
139 UNTS 463. USA (United States). Force 1 Jul 52.
139 UNTS 463. Mexico. Force 1 Jul 52.

101205　Bilateral Exchange　**89 UNTS 15**
SIGNED: 25 Mar 49　　　FORCE: 25 Mar 49
REGISTERED: 1 Jun 51 USA (United States)
ARTICLES: 2 LANGUAGE: English. Spanish.
HEADNOTE: ANTHROPOLOGICAL RESEARCH
TOPIC: Scientific Project
CONCEPTS: General provisions. Previous treaty replacement. Technical and commercial staff. Vocational training. Research and scientific projects. Anthropology and archeology. Research results. Expense sharing formulae. Tax exemptions. Domestic obligation. Repatriation of civilians.
PROCEDURE: Amendment. Duration. Renewal or Revival. Termination.
PARTIES:
　Peru
　USA (United States)
ANNEX
139 UNTS 464. USA (United States). Force 1 Jul 52.
139 UNTS 464. Peru. Force 1 Jul 52.

101206　Bilateral Exchange　**89 UNTS 27**
SIGNED: 5 Nov 48　　　　FORCE: 5 Nov 48
REGISTERED: 1 Jun 51 USA (United States)
ARTICLES: 2 LANGUAGE: English. Spanish.
HEADNOTE: PASSPORT VISA REQUIREMENTS
TOPIC: Visas
CONCEPTS: Time limit. Fees and exemptions.
PARTIES:
　Panama
　USA (United States)

101207　Bilateral Exchange　**89 UNTS 37**
SIGNED: 14 Jun 49　　　　FORCE: 14 Jun 49
REGISTERED: 1 Jun 51 USA (United States)
ARTICLES: 2 LANGUAGE: English. Spanish.
HEADNOTE: DIPLOMATIC OFFICIAL VISAS VALID RECIPROCAL BASIS
TOPIC: Visas
CONCEPTS: Border traffic and migration. Passports diplomatic.
PARTIES:
　Panama
　USA (United States)

101208　Bilateral Agreement　**89 UNTS 43**
SIGNED: 19 Jul 48　　　　FORCE: 19 Jul 48
REGISTERED: 1 Jun 51 USA (United States)
ARTICLES: 12 LANGUAGE: English.
HEADNOTE: PECUNIARY CLAIMS
TOPIC: Claims and Debts
CONCEPTS: Detailed regulations. Exceptions and exemptions. Time limit. Conformity with municipal law. General cooperation. Exchange of information and documents. Informational records. Juridical personality. Expropriation. General property. General trade. Currency. Assets. Claims and settlements. Assets transfer. Most favored nation clause. National treatment. Trademarks. Loss and/or damage. Enemy financial interests.
PARTIES:
　USA (United States)
　Yugoslavia

101209　Bilateral Exchange　**89 UNTS 63**
SIGNED: 20 Jul 50　　　　FORCE: 20 Jul 50
REGISTERED: 3 Jun 51 USA (United States)
ARTICLES: 2 LANGUAGE: English. Spanish.
HEADNOTE: AVOIDANCE DOUBLE TAXATION OPERATION SHIPS AIRCRAFT
TOPIC: Taxation
CONCEPTS: Domestic legislation. Taxation. Tax exemptions. Air transport. Merchant vessels.
PARTIES:
　Argentina
　USA (United States)

101210　Bilateral Exchange　**89 UNTS 71**
SIGNED: 14 May 48　　　　FORCE: 16 Apr 48
REGISTERED: 3 Jun 51 USA (United States)

ARTICLES: 3 LANGUAGE: English. Spanish.
HEADNOTE: AGRICULTURAL EXPERIMENT STATION
TOPIC: Scientific Project
CONCEPTS: Previous treaty replacement. Personnel. General property. Use of facilities. Research and scientific projects. Research results. Research and development. Expense sharing formulae. Tax exemptions. Domestic obligation. Agriculture. Special projects.
INTL ORGS: Special Commission.
PARTIES:
Ecuador
USA (United States)

101211 Bilateral Agreement **89 UNTS 99**
SIGNED: 20 May 49 FORCE: 20 May 49
REGISTERED: 3 Jun 51 USA (United States)
ARTICLES: 8 LANGUAGE: English.
HEADNOTE: LEND-LEASE SETTLEMENT
TOPIC: Milit Assistance
CONCEPTS: Definition of terms. General cooperation. General property. Exchange. Exchange rates and regulations. Payment schedules. Local currency. Lump sum settlements. Payment for war supplies. Lend lease. Return of equipment and recapture. Restrictions on transfer. Post-war claims settlement.
INTL ORGS: International Monetary Fund.
PROCEDURE: Future Procedures Contemplated.
PARTIES:
Ethiopia
USA (United States)

101212 Bilateral Exchange **89 UNTS 111**
SIGNED: 25 Oct 47 FORCE: 25 Oct 47
REGISTERED: 3 Jun 51 USA (United States)
ARTICLES: 2 LANGUAGE: English. French.
HEADNOTE: FRENCH RECRUITMENT GERMAN LABOR
TOPIC: Non-ILO Labor
CONCEPTS: Detailed regulations. Non-ILO labor relations. Administrative cooperation. Migrant worker. Indemnities and reimbursements. Reconversion to normalcy.
PROCEDURE: Future Procedures Contemplated.
PARTIES:
France
USA (United States)

101213 Bilateral Exchange **89 UNTS 119**
SIGNED: 3 Dec 47 FORCE: 3 Dec 47
REGISTERED: 3 Jun 51 USA (United States)
ARTICLES: 2 LANGUAGE: English.
HEADNOTE: TRANSFER NAVAL VESSELS EQUIPMENT
TOPIC: Milit Assistance
CONCEPTS: Title and deeds. Claims and settlements. Delivery schedules. General technical assistance. Materials, equipment and services. Military assistance. Naval vessels. Security of information. Military assistance missions. Exchange of defense information. Restrictions on transfer.
PARTIES:
Greece
USA (United States)

101214 Bilateral Agreement **89 UNTS 127**
SIGNED: 2 Feb 50 FORCE: 2 Feb 50
REGISTERED: 3 Jun 51 USA (United States)
ARTICLES: 15 LANGUAGE: English.
HEADNOTE: EDUCATIONAL EXCHANGE PROGRAM
TOPIC: Education
CONCEPTS: Definition of terms. Conformity with municipal law. Inspection and observation. Personnel. General property. Dispute settlement. Exchange. Commissions and foundations. Teacher and student exchange. Professorships. Scholarships and grants. Accounting procedures. Indemnities and reimbursements. Currency. Exchange rates and regulations. Financial programs. Funding procedures. Tax exemptions. Customs exemptions.
INTL ORGS: Special Commission.
PROCEDURE: Amendment.
PARTIES:
India
USA (United States)

ANNEX
222 UNTS 402. USA (United States). Amendment 29 May 53. Force 24 Jun 53.
222 UNTS 402. India. Amendment 24 Jun 53. Force 24 Jun 53.
358 UNTS 270. USA (United States). Amendment 30 Jan 59. Force 6 Feb 59.
358 UNTS 270. India. Amendment 6 Feb 59. Force 6 Feb 59.
388 UNTS 348. USA (United States). Amendment 9 May 60. Force 29 Jul 60.
388 UNTS 348. India. Amendment 29 Jul 60. Force 29 Jul 60.

101215 Bilateral Agreement **89 UNTS 141**
SIGNED: 14 Apr 49 FORCE: 14 Apr 49
REGISTERED: 3 Jun 51 USA (United States)
ARTICLES: 5 LANGUAGE: English. Japanese.
HEADNOTE: AGREEMENT CLAIM SETTLEMENT
TOPIC: Specif Claim/Waive
CONCEPTS: Claims and settlements. Merchant vessels. Specific claims or waivers.
PARTIES:
Japan
USA (United States)

101216 Bilateral Agreement **89 UNTS 155**
SIGNED: 11 Sep 48 FORCE: 20 Sep 48
REGISTERED: 3 Jun 51 USA (United States)
ARTICLES: 14 LANGUAGE: English. Korean.
HEADNOTE: FINANCIAL PROPERTY SETTLEMENT
TOPIC: Milit Assistance
CONCEPTS: Guarantees and safeguards. Treaty interpretation. General property. Accounting procedures. Monetary and gold transfers. Exchange rates and regulations. Interest rates. Payment schedules. Claims and settlements. Debts. Debt settlement. Most favored nation clause. Surplus property. Post-war reconstruction. Payment for war supplies. Lease of military property. Restrictions on transfer. Post-war claims settlement. Status of experts.
PROCEDURE: Future Procedures Contemplated. Ratification.
PARTIES:
Korea, South
USA (United States)
ANNEX
316 UNTS 278. USA (United States). Replacement 13 Jun 49. Force 28 Dec 49.
316 UNTS 278. Korea, South. Replacement 13 Jun 49. Force 28 Dec 49.

101217 Bilateral Exchange **89 UNTS 191**
SIGNED: 1 Jan 48 FORCE: 1 Jun 48
REGISTERED: 3 Jun 51 USA (United States)
ARTICLES: 2 LANGUAGE: English. Spanish.
HEADNOTE: AGRICULTURAL EXPERIMENT STATION
TOPIC: Scientific Project
CONCEPTS: Annex type material. Previous treaty replacement. Research and scientific projects. Research cooperation. Research and development. Agriculture.
PARTIES:
Paraguay
USA (United States)

101218 Bilateral Agreement **89 UNTS 199**
SIGNED: 16 Mar 50 FORCE: 16 Mar 50
REGISTERED: 3 Jun 51 USA (United States)
ARTICLES: 4 LANGUAGE: English.
HEADNOTE: AIR SERVICE
TOPIC: Air Transport
CONCEPTS: General property. Title and deeds. Use of facilities. Meteorology. Fees and exemptions. Special projects. Routes and logistics. Navigational conditions. Air transport. Airport facilities. Operating authorizations and regulations. Bands and frequency allocation. Facilities and equipment.
INTL ORGS: International Civil Aviation Organization.
PROCEDURE: Duration.
PARTIES:
Philippines
USA (United States)

101219 Bilateral Exchange **89 UNTS 209**
SIGNED: 24 Dec 49 FORCE: 24 Dec 49
REGISTERED: 3 Jun 51 USA (United States)
ARTICLES: 2 LANGUAGE: English.
HEADNOTE: AIR TRANSPORT SERVICES
TOPIC: Air Transport
CONCEPTS: Conformity with municipal law. Licenses and permits. Recognition of legal documents. Use of facilities. Fees and exemptions. National treatment. Customs duties. Customs exemptions. Competency certificate. Passenger transport. Routes and logistics. Navigational conditions. Permit designation. Transport of goods. Air transport. Airport facilities. Airworthiness certificates. Overflights and technical stops. Operating authorizations and regulations. Licenses and certificates of nationality. General military.
INTL ORGS: International Civil Aviation Organization.
PROCEDURE: Amendment. Registration. Termination.
PARTIES:
USA (United States)
Yugoslavia
ANNEX
340 UNTS 346. Yugoslavia. Termination 3 Jun 59. Force 3 Aug 59.

101220 Bilateral Exchange **89 UNTS 219**
SIGNED: 12 Aug 46 FORCE: 27 Aug 46
REGISTERED: 4 Jun 51 UK Great Britain
ARTICLES: 3 LANGUAGE: English.
HEADNOTE: PAYMENTS
TOPIC: Finance
CONCEPTS: Annex or appendix reference. Payment schedules.
PARTIES:
Hungary
UK Great Britain
ANNEX
351 UNTS 394. UK Great Britain. Termination 15 Jul 59. Force 12 Sep 59.
351 UNTS 394. Hungary. Termination 12 Sep 59. Force 12 Sep 59.

101221 Bilateral Exchange **89 UNTS 241**
SIGNED: 15 Jan 46 FORCE: 15 Jan 46
REGISTERED: 5 Jun 51 USA (United States)
ARTICLES: 0 LANGUAGE: English. Spanish.
HEADNOTE: AIR TRANSPORT
TOPIC: Air Transport
CONCEPTS: Conditions of airlines operating permission. Operating authorizations and regulations.
PARTIES:
Spain
USA (United States)
ANNEX
232 UNTS 329. Spain. Amendment 21 Jul 52. Force 21 Jul 54.
232 UNTS 329. USA (United States). Amendment 21 Jul 52. Force 4 Feb 60.

101222 Multilateral Agreement **90 UNTS 3**
SIGNED: 21 Dec 50 FORCE: 1 Jan 51
REGISTERED: 7 Jun 51 Denmark
ARTICLES: 7 LANGUAGE: Danish. Norwegian. Swedish.
HEADNOTE: IMPLEMENTATION DOMESTIC NATIONALITY ACTS
TOPIC: Admin Cooperation
CONCEPTS: Acquisition of nationality. Nationality and citizenship. Domestic legislation.
PROCEDURE: Denunciation.
PARTIES:
Denmark SIGNED: 21 Dec 50 FORCE: 1 Jan 51
Norway SIGNED: 21 Dec 50 FORCE: 1 Jan 51
Sweden SIGNED: 21 Dec 50 FORCE: 1 Jan 51

101223 Bilateral Agreement **90 UNTS 19**
SIGNED: 25 Jul 47 FORCE: 25 Jul 47
REGISTERED: 8 Jun 51 USA (United States)
ARTICLES: 12 LANGUAGE: English.
HEADNOTE: SETTLEMENT WAR ACCOUNTS CLAIMS
TOPIC: Reparations
CONCEPTS: Annex or appendix reference. Inspection and observation. Use of facilities. Accounting procedures. Currency. Exchange rates and

regulations. Lump sum settlements. Materials, equipment and services. Withdrawal of forces. Loss and/or damage. Post-war claims settlement.
PARTIES:
Czechoslovakia
USA (United States)

101224 Bilateral Agreement **90 UNTS 35**
SIGNED: 16 Sep 48 FORCE: 16 Sep 48
REGISTERED: 8 Jun 51 USA (United States)
ARTICLES: 5 LANGUAGE: Czechoslovakian. English.
HEADNOTE: SETTLEMENT LEND-LEASE CERTAIN CLAIMS
TOPIC: Milit Assistance
CONCEPTS: Definition of terms. Non-prejudice to UN charter. Title and deeds. Exchange rates and regulations. Lump sum settlements. Payment for war supplies. Lend lease. Return of equipment and recapture. Restrictions on transfer. Post-war claims settlement.
PARTIES:
Czechoslovakia
USA (United States)
ANNEX
380 UNTS 411. Yugoslavia. Accession 18 Nov 60.

101225 Bilateral Agreement **90 UNTS 45**
SIGNED: 11 Jun 51 FORCE: 11 Jun 51
REGISTERED: 11 Jun 51 United Nations
ARTICLES: 6 LANGUAGE: English.
HEADNOTE: TECHNICAL ASSISTANCE
TOPIC: Tech Assistance
CONCEPTS: Definition of terms. Treaty implementation. Annex or appendix reference. Privileges and immunities. General cooperation. Personnel. Title and deeds. Professorships. Vocational training. Expense sharing formulae. Local currency. Domestic obligation. General technical assistance. Materials, equipment and services. IGO status. Conformity with IGO decisions.
PROCEDURE: Amendment. Registration. Termination.
PARTIES:
United Nations
Thailand
ANNEX
360 UNTS 383. United Nations. Force 4 Jun 60.
360 UNTS 383. Thailand. Force 4 Jun 60.

101226 Bilateral Exchange **90 UNTS 59**
SIGNED: 12 Jul 47 FORCE: 15 Jul 47
REGISTERED: 12 Jun 51 Norway
ARTICLES: 2 LANGUAGE: French.
HEADNOTE: MUTUAL ABOLITION VISAS
TOPIC: Visas
CONCEPTS: Visa abolition. Conformity with municipal law.
PARTIES:
Luxembourg
Norway

101227 Bilateral Exchange **90 UNTS 65**
SIGNED: 1 Aug 47 FORCE: 15 Aug 47
REGISTERED: 12 Jun 51 Norway
ARTICLES: 2 LANGUAGE: French.
HEADNOTE: MUTUAL ABOLITION VISAS
TOPIC: Visas
CONCEPTS: Territorial application. Visa abolition. Visas. Conformity with municipal law.
PARTIES:
Norway
Switzerland

101228 Bilateral Exchange **90 UNTS 71**
SIGNED: 17 Dec 47 FORCE: 1 Jan 48
REGISTERED: 12 Jun 51 Norway
ARTICLES: 2 LANGUAGE: English.
HEADNOTE: MUTUAL ABOLITION VISAS
TOPIC: Visas
CONCEPTS: Time limit. Visa abolition. Denial of admission. Conformity with municipal law.
PARTIES:
Ireland
Norway

101229 Bilateral Exchange **90 UNTS 77**
SIGNED: 16 Jul 48 FORCE: 1 Aug 48
REGISTERED: 12 Jun 51 Norway
ARTICLES: 2 LANGUAGE: French.
HEADNOTE: MUTUAL ABOLITION VISAS
TOPIC: Visas
CONCEPTS: Territorial application. Time limit. Visa abolition. Passports diplomatic. Resident permits. Conformity with municipal law.
PARTIES:
Monaco
Norway

101230 Bilateral Agreement **90 UNTS 83**
SIGNED: 12 Jul 48 FORCE: 28 Aug 48
REGISTERED: 12 Jun 51 UK Great Britain
ARTICLES: 20 LANGUAGE: English. French.
HEADNOTE: EXCHANGE MONEY ORDERS
TOPIC: Postal Service
CONCEPTS: Accounting procedures. Exchange rates and regulations. Interest rates. Payment schedules. Postal services. Money orders and postal checks. Rates and charges. Services. Telegrams.
PROCEDURE: Denunciation. Duration.
PARTIES:
France
UK Great Britain

101231 Bilateral Exchange **90 UNTS 131**
SIGNED: 8 Jun 49 FORCE: 1 Jul 49
REGISTERED: 12 Jun 51 Norway
ARTICLES: 2 LANGUAGE: English.
HEADNOTE: MUTUAL ABOLITION TREATIES
TOPIC: Visas
CONCEPTS: Visa abolition. Conformity with municipal law.
PARTIES:
Norway
Pakistan

101232 Bilateral Agreement **90 UNTS 137**
SIGNED: 20 Jun 49 FORCE: 1 Oct 49
REGISTERED: 12 Jun 51 UK Great Britain
ARTICLES: 29 LANGUAGE: English. French.
HEADNOTE: EXCHANGE MONEY ORDERS
TOPIC: Postal Service
CONCEPTS: Definition of terms. Conformity with municipal law. Operating agencies. Exchange rates and regulations. Postal services. Money orders and postal checks. Rates and charges.
PROCEDURE: Duration. Termination.
PARTIES:
Lebanon
UK Great Britain

101233 **UNTS**
SIGNED:
REGISTERED:
ARTICLES:
HEADNOTE: AGREEMENT REGISTERED UNDER 100760
TOPIC:
PARTIES:

101234 Bilateral Exchange **90 UNTS 175**
SIGNED: 30 Dec 49 FORCE: 15 Jan 50
REGISTERED: 12 Jun 51 Norway
ARTICLES: 2 LANGUAGE: Norwegian. Swedish.
HEADNOTE: MUTUAL ABOLITION VISAS
TOPIC: Visas
CONCEPTS: Visa abolition. Border traffic and migration. Denial of admission. Resident permits.
PARTIES:
Finland
Norway

101235 Bilateral Exchange **90 UNTS 181**
SIGNED: 13 Mar 50 FORCE: 1 Apr 50
REGISTERED: 12 Jun 51 Norway
ARTICLES: 2 LANGUAGE: English.
HEADNOTE: CERTAIN FACILITIES GRANTING VISAS
TOPIC: Visas
CONCEPTS: Time limit. Visa abolition. Denial of admission. Conformity with municipal law. Fees and exemptions.

PARTIES:
Canada
Norway
ANNEX
392 UNTS 343. Norway. Amendment 14 Jul 58. Force 14 Jul 58.
392 UNTS 343. Canada. Amendment 14 Jul 58. Force 14 Jul 58.

101236 Bilateral Exchange **90 UNTS 187**
SIGNED: 24 Jul 50 FORCE: 15 Aug 50
REGISTERED: 12 Jun 51 Norway
ARTICLES: 2 LANGUAGE: French. Italian.
HEADNOTE: MUTUAL ABOLITION VISAS
TOPIC: Visas
CONCEPTS: Visa abolition. Conformity with municipal law.
PARTIES:
Italy
Norway

101237 Bilateral Agreement **90 UNTS 193**
SIGNED: 24 Jan 51 FORCE: 1 Mar 51
REGISTERED: 12 Jun 51 UK Great Britain
ARTICLES: 36 LANGUAGE: English. French.
HEADNOTE: EXCHANGE MONEY ORDERS
TOPIC: Postal Service
CONCEPTS: Annex or appendix reference.
PROCEDURE: Denunciation. Duration.
PARTIES:
France
UK Great Britain

101238 Multilateral Protocol **90 UNTS 229**
SIGNED: 27 Jul 46 FORCE: 30 Nov 46
REGISTERED: 12 Jun 51 UK Great Britain
ARTICLES: 11 LANGUAGE: English. French.
HEADNOTE: PATENTS
TOPIC: Patents/Copyrights
CONCEPTS: Territorial application. Exchange of official publications. Licenses and permits. Laws and formalities.
PROCEDURE: Registration.
PARTIES:
Australia
Belgium Belgian Colonies RATIFIED: 22 Nov 47 FORCE: 22 Nov 47
Belgium Ruanda-Urundi RATIFIED: 22 Nov 47 FORCE: 22 Nov 47
Belgium SIGNED: 20 Jul 46 FORCE: 30 Nov 46
Bolivia RATIFIED: 13 Dec 46 FORCE: 13 Dec 46
Canada SIGNED: 20 Jul 46 FORCE: 30 Nov 46
Chile RATIFIED: 31 Dec 46 FORCE: 31 Dec 46
Cuba RATIFIED: 31 Jul 47 FORCE: 31 Jul 47
Czechoslovakia SIGNED: 20 Jul 46 FORCE: 30 Nov 46
Denmark SIGNED: 20 Jul 46 FORCE: 30 Nov 46
Dominican Republic RATIFIED: 31 Dec 46 FORCE: 31 Dec 46
Ecuador RATIFIED: 28 Dec 46 FORCE: 28 Dec 46
United Arab Rep RATIFIED: 30 Jul 47 FORCE: 30 Jul 47
El Salvador RATIFIED: 2 Aug 47 FORCE: 2 Aug 47
Ethiopia RATIFIED: 10 May 47 FORCE: 10 May 47
France SIGNED: 20 Jul 46 FORCE: 30 Nov 46
Guatemala RATIFIED: 31 Dec 46 FORCE: 31 Dec 46
Haiti RATIFIED: 29 Jul 47 FORCE: 29 Jul 47
Honduras RATIFIED: 31 Jan 47 FORCE: 31 Jan 47
India RATIFIED: 4 Nov 46 FORCE: 30 Nov 46
Iran RATIFIED: 31 Dec 46 FORCE: 31 Dec 46
Iraq RATIFIED: 31 Dec 46 FORCE: 31 Dec 46
Lebanon RATIFIED: 31 Dec 46 FORCE: 31 Dec 46
Luxembourg SIGNED: 20 Jul 46 FORCE: 30 Nov 46
Netherlands SIGNED: 20 Jul 46 FORCE: 30 Nov 46
New Zealand RATIFIED: 21 Nov 46 FORCE: 30 Nov 46
Nicaragua RATIFIED: 9 Dec 46 FORCE: 9 Dec 46
Panama RATIFIED: 23 Jul 47 FORCE: 23 Jul 47
Panama RATIFIED: 31 Dec 46 FORCE: 31 Dec 46
Poland RATIFIED: 31 Dec 46 FORCE: 31 Dec 46
Saudi Arabia RATIFIED: 14 Jun 47 FORCE: 14 Jun 47

South Africa SIGNED: 30 Nov 46 FORCE: 30 Nov 46
Syria RATIFIED: 31 Dec 46 FORCE: 31 Dec 46
Turkey RATIFIED: 30 Dec 46 FORCE: 30 Dec 46
UK Great Britain Ceylon (Sri Lanka) RATIFIED: 19 May 47 FORCE: 19 May 47
UK Great Britain Falkland Islands RATIFIED: 19 May 47 FORCE: 19 May 47
UK Great Britain Jamaica RATIFIED: 22 Aug 47 FORCE: 22 Aug 47
UK Great Britain Malta RATIFIED: 19 May 47 FORCE: 19 May 47
UK Great Britain Newfoundland RATIFIED: 31 Dec 46 FORCE: 31 Dec 46
UK Great Britain Nigeria RATIFIED: 19 May 47 FORCE: 19 May 47
UK Great Britain Northern Rhodesia RATIFIED: 19 May 47 FORCE: 19 May 47
UK Great Britain Palestine RATIFIED: 19 May 47 FORCE: 19 May 47
UK Great Britain SIGNED: 27 Jul 46 FORCE: 30 Nov 46
UK Great Britain Southern Rhodesia RATIFIED: 24 Dec 46 FORCE: 24 Dec 46
UK Great Britain Tanganyika RATIFIED: 19 May 47 FORCE: 19 May 47
UK Great Britain Zanzibar RATIFIED: 22 Aug 47 FORCE: 22 Aug 47
USA (United States) SIGNED: 27 Jul 46 FORCE: 30 Nov 46
Venezuela RATIFIED: 23 Dec 46 FORCE: 23 Dec 46
Yugoslavia RATIFIED: 30 Dec 46 FORCE: 30 Dec 46

101239 Multilateral Convention **91 UNTS 3**
SIGNED: 10 Jul 48   FORCE: 12 Jun 51
REGISTERED: 13 Jun 51 ILO (Labor Org)
ARTICLES: 18 LANGUAGE: English. French.
HEADNOTE: NIGHT WORK YOUNG PERSONS EMPLOYED INDUSTRY
TOPIC: ILO Labor
CONCEPTS: Definition of terms. Exceptions and exemptions. Territorial application. Previous treaty extension. Incorporation of treaty provisions into national law. ILO conventions. Employment regulations. Holidays and rest periods. Labor statistics.
INTL ORGS: United Nations.
PROCEDURE: Amendment. Denunciation. Duration. Ratification. Registration. Renewal or Revival.
PARTIES:
Multilateral
ANNEX
122 UNTS 343. Guatemala. Ratification 13 Feb 52. Force 13 Feb 53.
131 UNTS 341. Cuba. Ratification 29 Apr 52. Force 29 Apr 53.
149 UNTS 408. Italy. Ratification 22 Oct 52. Force 22 Oct 53.
183 UNTS 367. Israel. Ratification 23 Dec 53. Force 23 Dec 54.
184 UNTS 343. Philippines. Ratification 29 Dec 53. Force 29 Dec 54.
201 UNTS 370. Netherlands. Ratification 22 Oct 54. Force 22 Oct 55.
225 UNTS 261. Netherlands. Netherlands Antilles.
248 UNTS 404. Mexico. Ratification 20 Jun 56. Force 20 Jun 57.
249 UNTS 458. USSR (Soviet Union). Ratification 10 Aug 56. Force 10 Aug 57.
261 UNTS 398. Yugoslavia. Ratification 20 Feb 57. Force 20 Feb 58.
266 UNTS 393. Haiti. Ratification 12 Apr 57. Force 12 Apr 58.
268 UNTS 357. Norway. Ratification 20 May 57. Force 20 May 58.
276 UNTS 361. Dominican Republic. Ratification 12 Aug 57. Force 12 Aug 58.
293 UNTS 378. Luxembourg. Ratification 3 Mar 58. Force 3 Mar 59.
330 UNTS 360. Ceylon (Sri Lanka). Ratification 18 May 59. Force 18 May 60.
366 UNTS 389. Costa Rica. Ratification 2 Jun 60. Force 2 Jun 61.
396 UNTS 323. Ghana. Ratification 4 Apr 61. Force 4 Apr 62.
396 UNTS 323. Tunisia. Ratification 26 Apr 61. Force 26 Apr 62.
425 UNTS 320. Greece. Ratification 30 Mar 62. Force 30 Mar 63.

435 UNTS 315. Lebanon. Ratification 26 Jul 62. Force 26 Jul 62.
483 UNTS 413. Mauritania. Ratification 8 Nov 63. Force 8 Nov 64.
548 UNTS 401. Cyprus. Ratification 8 Oct 65. Force 8 Oct 66.
560 UNTS 320. Paraguay. Ratification 21 Mar 66. Force 21 Mar 67.
640 UNTS 384. Poland. Ratification 26 Jun 68. Force 26 Jun 69.

101240 Multilateral Agreement **91 UNTS 21**
SIGNED: 25 Apr 51   FORCE: 25 Apr 51
REGISTERED: 14 Jun 51 USA (United States)
ARTICLES: 5 LANGUAGE: English. French.
HEADNOTE: SUBMISSION ARBITRATOR CLAIMS
TOPIC: Reparations
CONCEPTS: Time limit. Arbitration. Procedure. Competence of tribunal. Post-war claims settlement.
INTL ORGS: International Court of Justice. Special Commission.
PARTIES:
France SIGNED: 25 Apr 51 FORCE: 25 Apr 51
UK Great Britain SIGNED: 25 Apr 51 FORCE: 25 Apr 51
USA (United States) SIGNED: 25 Apr 51 FORCE: 25 Apr 51
ANNEX
100 UNTS 304. USA (United States).
100 UNTS 304. UK Great Britain.
100 UNTS 304. France.

101241 Bilateral Convention **91 UNTS 31**
SIGNED: 3 Dec 49   FORCE: 1 May 51
REGISTERED: 14 Jun 51 Belgium
ARTICLES: 35 LANGUAGE: French.
HEADNOTE: SOCIAL SECURITY
TOPIC: Non-ILO Labor
CONCEPTS: Detailed regulations. Exceptions and exemptions. General provisions. Previous treaty replacement. Conformity with municipal law. Domestic legislation. Dispute settlement. Old age and invalidity insurance. Non-ILO labor relations. Family allowances. Administrative cooperation. Old age insurance. Sickness and invalidity insurance. Social security. Payment schedules. National treatment.
PROCEDURE: Duration. Ratification. Renewal or Revival. Termination.
PARTIES:
Belgium
Luxembourg
ANNEX
261 UNTS 400. Belgium. Supplementation 5 Nov 55. Force 1 Jul 55.
261 UNTS 400. Luxembourg. Supplementation 5 Nov 55. Force 1 Jul 55.

101242 Bilateral Exchange **91 UNTS 75**
SIGNED: 8 May 51   FORCE: 8 May 51
REGISTERED: 14 Jun 51 Belgium
ARTICLES: 2 LANGUAGE: French.
HEADNOTE: EXEMPTION CUSTOMS DUTY DIPLOMATIC AGENTS
TOPIC: Consul/Citizenship
CONCEPTS: Diplomatic privileges.
PARTIES:
Belgium
Brazil
ANNEX
229 UNTS 294. Mexico. Accession 21 Feb 56. Force 21 May 56.

101243 Bilateral Agreement **91 UNTS 83**
SIGNED: 24 Apr 46   FORCE: 24 Apr 46
REGISTERED: 14 Jun 51 France
ARTICLES: 10 LANGUAGE: French.
HEADNOTE: SETTLEMENT RECIPROCAL PAYMENT QUESTION
TOPIC: Finance
CONCEPTS: Accounting procedures. Banking. Balance of payments. Currency. Monetary and gold transfers. Exchange rates and regulations. Payment schedules. Assets.
PROCEDURE: Denunciation.
PARTIES:
France
Greece

101244 Bilateral Agreement **91 UNTS 95**
SIGNED: 6 Aug 49   FORCE: 5 Jul 49
REGISTERED: 14 Jun 51 Greece
ARTICLES: 10 LANGUAGE: French.
HEADNOTE: COMMERCE
TOPIC: General Trade
CONCEPTS: Detailed regulations. Territorial application. Treaty implementation. Annex or appendix reference. Previous treaty replacement. Licenses and permits. Public information. Delivery schedules. Most favored nation clause.
INTL ORGS: Special Commission.
PROCEDURE: Duration.
PARTIES:
France
Greece

101245 Bilateral Protocol **91 UNTS 113**
SIGNED: 27 Dec 47   FORCE: 27 Dec 47
REGISTERED: 18 Jun 51 UK Great Britain
ARTICLES: 1 LANGUAGE: English. Russian.
HEADNOTE: TRADE FINANCE
TOPIC: General Economic
CONCEPTS: Annex or appendix reference. Establishment of trade relations.
PARTIES:
UK Great Britain
USSR (Soviet Union)

101246 Bilateral Exchange **91 UNTS 137**
SIGNED: 25 Jun 46   FORCE: 1 Jul 46
REGISTERED: 18 Jun 51 UK Great Britain
ARTICLES: 2 LANGUAGE: English. Spanish.
HEADNOTE: TEMPORARY COMMERCIAL AGREEMENT
TOPIC: General Trade
CONCEPTS: Exceptions and exemptions. Most favored nation clause.
INTL ORGS: Special Commission.
PROCEDURE: Denunciation. Duration. Future Procedures Contemplated.
PARTIES:
Chile
UK Great Britain
ANNEX
93 UNTS 385. UK Great Britain. Prolongation 1 Jul 48. Force 1 Jul 48.
93 UNTS 385. Chile. Prolongation 1 Jul 48. Force 1 Jul 48.

101247 Bilateral Agreement **91 UNTS 149**
SIGNED: 21 Mar 46   FORCE: 21 Mar 46
REGISTERED: 18 Jun 51 UK Great Britain
ARTICLES: 17 LANGUAGE: English.
HEADNOTE: RESTORATION MONEY & PROPERTY DUE TO WAR
TOPIC: Claims and Debts
CONCEPTS: Detailed regulations. General provisions. Treaty interpretation. General cooperation. Legal protection and assistance. Immovable property. General property. Bonds. Fees and exemptions. Payment schedules. Claims, debts and assets. Assets. Claims and settlements. Debt settlement. National treatment.
PARTIES:
Greece
UK Great Britain
ANNEX
199 UNTS 335. Greece. Termination 13 Aug 54. Force 13 Aug 54.
199 UNTS 335. UK Great Britain. Termination 13 Aug 54. Force 13 Aug 54.

101248 Bilateral Exchange **91 UNTS 161**
SIGNED: 27 Sep 46   FORCE: 1 Oct 46
REGISTERED: 18 Jun 51 UK Great Britain
ARTICLES: 2 LANGUAGE: English. Spanish.
HEADNOTE: TRANSMISSION DIPLOMATIC CORRESPONDENCE
TOPIC: Consul/Citizenship
CONCEPTS: Inviolability. Personnel. Fees and exemptions.
PARTIES:
Mexico
UK Great Britain

101249 Bilateral Exchange **91 UNTS 169**
SIGNED: 13 Aug 47   FORCE: 13 Aug 47
REGISTERED: 18 Jun 51 UK Great Britain

ARTICLES: 2 LANGUAGE: English. French.
HEADNOTE: EMPLOYMENT FRANCE POLISH
WORKERS BRITAIN
TOPIC: Non-ILO Labor
CONCEPTS: Detailed regulations. Privileges and
immunities. Use of facilities. Non-ILO labor rela-
tions. Administrative cooperation. Social secu-
rity. Migrant worker. Indemnities and reimburse-
ments. National treatment.
INTL ORGS: International Refugees Organization.
PARTIES:
France
UK Great Britain

101250   Bilateral Exchange   **91 UNTS 177**
SIGNED: 30 Apr 51   FORCE: 30 Apr 51
REGISTERED: 18 Jun 51 UK Great Britain
ARTICLES: 2 LANGUAGE: English.
HEADNOTE: RECIPROCAL WAIVER STAMP DU-
TIES REGISTRATION DUES
TOPIC: Consul/Citizenship
CONCEPTS: Diplomatic and consular relations.
Fees and exemptions.
PARTIES:
Netherlands
UK Great Britain

101251   Bilateral Exchange   **91 UNTS 183**
SIGNED: 26 Jan 46   FORCE: 26 Jan 46
REGISTERED: 18 Jun 51 UK Great Britain
ARTICLES: 2 LANGUAGE: English. French.
HEADNOTE: USE DISPOSAL VESSELS
TOPIC: Reparations
CONCEPTS: Annex or appendix reference. Naval
vessels. Surplus war property.
PARTIES:
France
UK Great Britain

101252   Bilateral Agreement   **91 UNTS 197**
SIGNED: 22 Jun 48   FORCE: 3 Jul 48
REGISTERED: 20 Jun 51 Pakistan
ARTICLES: 32 LANGUAGE: English.
HEADNOTE: EXCHANGE PARCELS POST
TOPIC: Postal Service
CONCEPTS: Payment schedules. Claims and set-
tlements. Debt settlement. Customs duties.
Postal services. Insured letters and boxes. Con-
veyance in transit. Parcel post. Rates and
charges.
INTL ORGS: Universal Postal Union.
PROCEDURE: Duration. Termination.
PARTIES:
Burma
Pakistan

101253   Bilateral Agreement   **91 UNTS 235**
SIGNED: 28 Jun 48   FORCE: 26 Jul 48
REGISTERED: 20 Jun 51 Pakistan
ARTICLES: 33 LANGUAGE: English.
HEADNOTE: EXCHANGE PARCELS POST
TOPIC: Postal Service
CONCEPTS: Detailed regulations. Conformity with
municipal law. Payment schedules. Claims and
settlements. Debt settlement. Customs duties.
Postal services. Insured letters and boxes. Con-
veyance in transit. Parcel post. Rates and
charges.
INTL ORGS: Universal Postal Union.
PROCEDURE: Duration.
PARTIES:
New Zealand
Pakistan

101254   Bilateral Agreement   **91 UNTS 275**
SIGNED: 17 Sep 48   FORCE: 9 Nov 48
REGISTERED: 20 Jun 51 Pakistan
ARTICLES: 32 LANGUAGE: English.
HEADNOTE: EXCHANGE MONEY ORDERS
TOPIC: Postal Service
CONCEPTS: Conformity with municipal law. Ac-
counting procedures. Currency. Payment sched-
ules. Regulations. Money orders and postal
checks. Rates and charges. Advice lists and or-
ders. Telegrams.
PROCEDURE: Duration. Termination.
PARTIES:
New Zealand
Pakistan

101255   Bilateral Agreement   **91 UNTS 303**
SIGNED: 15 Dec 48   FORCE: 1 Feb 49
REGISTERED: 20 Jun 51 Pakistan
ARTICLES: 33 LANGUAGE: English.
HEADNOTE: EXCHANGE PARCELS POST
TOPIC: Postal Service
CONCEPTS: Detailed regulations. Conformity with
municipal law. Compensation. Claims and settle-
ments. Customs duties. Postal services. Insured
letters and boxes. Parcel post. Rates and
charges.
INTL ORGS: Universal Postal Union.
PROCEDURE: Duration. Termination.
PARTIES:
Ceylon (Sri Lanka)
Pakistan

101256   Bilateral Agreement   **92 UNTS 3**
SIGNED: 20 Dec 50   FORCE: 17 Apr 51
REGISTERED: 20 Jun 51 Norway
ARTICLES: 10 LANGUAGE: Norwegian. Swedish.
HEADNOTE: FISHING
TOPIC: Specific Resources
CONCEPTS: Detailed regulations.
PROCEDURE: Duration. Ratification. Renewal or
Revival. Termination.
PARTIES:
Norway
Sweden
ANNEX
460 UNTS 302. Norway. Amendment 29 Mar 63.
Force 1 Apr 63.
460 UNTS 302. Sweden. Amendment 29 Mar 63.
Force 1 Apr 63.

101257   Multilateral Agreement   **92 UNTS 19**
SIGNED: 4 May 49   FORCE: 21 Jun 51
REGISTERED: 21 Jun 51 United Nations
ARTICLES: 9 LANGUAGE: French.
HEADNOTE: SUPPRESSION WHITE SLAVE TRAF-
FIC
TOPIC: Admin Cooperation
CONCEPTS: Extradition, deportation and repatria-
tion. Exchange of information and documents.
Investigation of violations. Indemnities and reim-
bursements.
INTL ORGS: United Nations.
PROCEDURE: Accession. Denunciation. Ratifica-
tion.
PARTIES:
Australia FORCE: 21 Jun 51
Austria FORCE: 21 Jun 51
Canada FORCE: 21 Jun 51
Ceylon (Sri Lanka) FORCE: 21 Jun 51
Chile FORCE: 21 Jun 51
Taiwan FORCE: 21 Jun 51
Czechoslovakia FORCE: 21 Jun 51
Denmark FORCE: 21 Jun 51
United Arab Rep FORCE: 21 Jun 51
Finland FORCE: 21 Jun 51
France FORCE: 21 Jun 51
India FORCE: 21 Jun 51
Iraq FORCE: 21 Jun 51
Netherlands FORCE: 21 Jun 51
Norway FORCE: 21 Jun 51
Switzerland FORCE: 21 Jun 51
Turkey FORCE: 21 Jun 51
UK Great Britain FORCE: 21 Jun 51
USA (United States) FORCE: 21 Jun 51
Yugoslavia FORCE: 21 Jun 51
ANNEX
98 UNTS 292.   South   Africa.   Accession
14 Aug 51.
121 UNTS 330. Sweden. Accession 25 Feb 52.
133 UNTS 364. Pakistan. Accession 16 Jun 52.
140 UNTS 438. Belgium. Accession 13 Oct 52.
149 UNTS 411. Italy. Accession 13 Nov 52.
207 UNTS 352.   Luxembourg.   Accession
14 Mar 55.
229 UNTS 293. Mexico. Accession 21 Feb 56.
Force 21 Aug 56.
253 UNTS 351. Morocco. Succession 7 Nov 56.
292 UNTS 361. Ghana. Acceptance 7 Apr 58.
347 UNTS 377. Iran. Acceptance 30 Dec 59.
399 UNTS 265. Nigeria. Succession 26 Jun 61.
401 UNTS 252. Ireland. Acceptance 19 Jul 61.
405 UNTS 302. Niger. Succession 25 Aug 61.
412 UNTS 302. Cameroon. Succession 3 Nov 61.
415 UNTS 427.   Ivory   Coast.   Succession
8 Dec 61.
423 UNTS 304.   Sierra   Leone.   Succession
13 Mar 62.

424 UNTS 345. Dahomey. Succession 4 Apr 62.
437 UNTS 346. Central Afri Rep. Succession
4 Sep 62.
442 UNTS 313. Congo (Brazzaville). Succession
15 Oct 62.
456 UNTS 492.   Tanganyika.   Accession
15 Mar 63. Force 18 Sep 63.
463 UNTS 340. Senegal. Succession 2 May 63.
466 UNTS 381. Cyprus. Succession 16 May 63.
479 UNTS 356.   Madagascar.   Succession
9 Oct 63.
480 UNTS 330. Algeria. Accession 31 Oct 63.
Force 30 Apr 64.
503 UNTS 332. Jamaica. Succession 30 Jul 64.
538 UNTS 334. Malawi. Accession 10 Jun 65.
Force 10 Dec 65.
541 UNTS 308. Cuba. Acceptance 4 Aug 65.
560 UNTS 244. Trinidad/Tobago.   Succession
11 Apr 66. Force 31 Aug 62.

101258   Multilateral Agreement   **92 UNTS 27**
SIGNED: 25 Jun 51   FORCE: 25 Jun 51
REGISTERED: 25 Jun 51 United Nations
ARTICLES: 5 LANGUAGE: English.
HEADNOTE: TECHNICAL ASSISTANCE
TOPIC: Tech Assistance
CONCEPTS: Definition of terms. Treaty implemen-
tation. Annex or appendix reference. Privileges
and immunities. General cooperation. Person-
nel. Responsibility and liability. Title and deeds.
Professorships. Vocational training. Research
and scientific projects. Expense sharing formu-
lae. Local currency. General technical assis-
tance. Materials, equipment and services. IGO
status. Conformity with IGO decisions. Trusteeship.
PROCEDURE: Amendment. Termination.
PARTIES:
FAO (Food Agri) SIGNED: 25 Jun 51 FORCE:
25 Jun 51
ICAO (Civil Aviat) SIGNED: 25 Jun 51 FORCE:
25 Jun 51
ILO (Labor Org) SIGNED: 25 Jun 51 FORCE:
25 Jun 51
UNESCO (Educ/Cult) SIGNED: 25 Jun 51
FORCE: 25 Jun 51
United Nations SIGNED: 25 Jun 51 FORCE:
25 Jun 51
WHO (World Health) SIGNED: 25 Jun 51 FORCE:
25 Jun 51
UK Great Britain SIGNED: 25 Jun 51 FORCE:
25 Jun 51
ANNEX
366 UNTS 390.   Multilateral.   Termination
8 Jul 60. Force 8 Jul 60.

101259   Bilateral Agreement   **92 UNTS 39**
SIGNED: 25 Aug 50   FORCE: 7 Dec 50
REGISTERED: 26 Jun 51 United Arab Rep
ARTICLES: 11 LANGUAGE: English.
HEADNOTE: WHO SERVICES
TOPIC: IGO Operations
CONCEPTS: Treaty implementation. Diplomatic
privileges. Privileges and immunities. Mediation
and good offices. Exchange rates and regula-
tions. Funding procedures. General technical as-
sistance. Materials, equipment and services.
Special status.
INTL ORGS: United Nations. Arbitration Commis-
sion.
PROCEDURE: Amendment. Denunciation. Termi-
nation.
PARTIES:
WHO (World Health)
United Arab Rep
ANNEX
141 UNTS 386. WHO (World Health). Interpretation 30 Jun 52. Force 30 Jun 52.
141 UNTS 386. United Arab Rep. Interpretation
11 Mar 52. Force 30 Jun 52.

101260   Bilateral Agreement   **92 UNTS 51**
SIGNED: 7 May 51   FORCE: 4 Jun 51
REGISTERED: 26 Jun 51 Norway
ARTICLES: 10 LANGUAGE: German. Norwegian.
HEADNOTE: CLAIMS RESPECT DAMAGE FISHING
GEAR
TOPIC: Claims and Debts
CONCEPTS: Detailed regulations. General cooper-

131

ation. Establishment of commission. Procedure. Compensation. Claims and settlements. Specific claims or waivers.
INTL ORGS: Claims Commission.
PROCEDURE: Denunciation.
PARTIES:
Germany, West
Norway

101261 Bilateral Exchange **92 UNTS 65**
SIGNED: 13 Dec 48 FORCE: 1 Jan 49
REGISTERED: 28 Jun 51 New Zealand
ARTICLES: 2 LANGUAGE: English.
HEADNOTE: MUTUAL ABOLITION VISAS
TOPIC: Visas
CONCEPTS: Territorial application. Visa abolition. Passports non-diplomatic. Denial of admission. Resident permits. Conformity with municipal law.
PARTIES:
Denmark
New Zealand

101262 Bilateral Agreement **92 UNTS 71**
SIGNED: 31 Dec 49 FORCE: 31 Dec 49
REGISTERED: 28 Jun 51 Greece
ARTICLES: 7 LANGUAGE: French.
HEADNOTE: COMMERCE
TOPIC: General Trade
CONCEPTS: Detailed regulations. Annex or appendix reference. Licenses and permits. Establishment of commission. Trade procedures. Payment schedules. Quotas. Most favored nation clause.
INTL ORGS: Special Commission.
PROCEDURE: Duration. Renewal or Revival. Termination.
PARTIES:
Greece
Portugal
ANNEX
225 UNTS 262. Portugal. Supplementation 24 May 55. Force 17 Feb 55.
225 UNTS 262. Greece. Supplementation 24 May 55. Force 17 Feb 55.

101263 Bilateral Agreement **92 UNTS 83**
SIGNED: 31 Dec 49 FORCE: 31 Dec 49
REGISTERED: 28 Jun 51 Greece
ARTICLES: 6 LANGUAGE: French.
HEADNOTE: FACILITATING PAYMENTS
TOPIC: Finance
CONCEPTS: General cooperation. Accounting procedures. Banking. Balance of payments. Currency. Exchange rates and regulations. Interest rates. Payment schedules.
PARTIES:
Greece
Portugal

101264 Multilateral Instrument **92 UNTS 91**
SIGNED: 16 Sep 50 FORCE: 16 Sep 50
REGISTERED: 1 Jul 51 United Nations
ARTICLES: 8 LANGUAGE: English. French.
HEADNOTE: CONSTRUCTION MAIN INTERNATIONAL TRAFFIC
TOPIC: General Transport
CONCEPTS: Annex or appendix reference. Routes and logistics. Roads and highways.
INTL ORGS: United Nations.
PROCEDURE: Amendment. Accession.
PARTIES:
Belgium SIGNED: 16 Sep 50
France SIGNED: 16 Sep 50 FORCE: 16 Sep 50
Luxembourg SIGNED: 16 Sep 50
Netherlands SIGNED: 16 Sep 50
UK Great Britain SIGNED: 16 Sep 50 FORCE: 16 Sep 50
ANNEX
104 UNTS 352. Austria. Accession 1 Oct 51.
108 UNTS 321. Multilateral. Modification 2 Jul 51. Force 2 Jul 51.
126 UNTS 364. Sweden. Accession 31 Mar 52.
133 UNTS 365. UK Great Britain. Amendment 6 Jun 52.
133 UNTS 365. Luxembourg. Withdrawal 27 Jun 52.
133 UNTS 365. Austria. Amendment 6 Jun 52.
133 UNTS 365. Greece. Accession 1 Jul 52.

133 UNTS 365. Luxembourg. Amendment 6 Jun 52.
133 UNTS 365. Netherlands. Amendment 6 Jun 52.
133 UNTS 365. France. Amendment 6 Jun 52.
133 UNTS 365. Greece. Amendment 6 Jun 52.
133 UNTS 365. Belgium. Amendment 6 Jun 52.
133 UNTS 365. Sweden. Amendment 6 Jun 52.
150 UNTS 373. Netherlands. Withdrawal 4 Dec 52.
182 UNTS 226. Norway. Accession 15 Dec 53.
184 UNTS 344. Multilateral. Amendment 15 Dec 53.
189 UNTS 362. Belgium. Ratification 23 Apr 54.
191 UNTS 389. Turkey. Accession 10 Jun 54.
203 UNTS 336. Multilateral. Amendment 26 Nov 54.
281 UNTS 398. Germany, West. Accession 13 Nov 57.
354 UNTS 395. Spain. Accession 25 Mar 60.
375 UNTS 343. Poland. Accession 26 Sep 60.
426 UNTS 338. Bulgaria. Accession 8 May 62.
447 UNTS 355. Hungary. Accession 5 Dec 62.
451 UNTS 326. Multilateral. Amendment 4 Dec 55.
530 UNTS 338. Romania. Accession 7 Apr 65.
544 UNTS 289. Finland. Accession 9 Sep 65.
636 UNTS 363. Ireland. Accession 20 May 68.
645 UNTS 348. Multilateral. Amendment 16 Sep 50.
651 UNTS 350. Sweden. Amendment 25 Nov 68.
651 UNTS 350. Greece. Amendment 25 Nov 68.
651 UNTS 350. Austria. Amendment 25 Nov 68.
651 UNTS 350. Belgium. Amendment 25 Nov 68.
651 UNTS 350. Spain. Amendment 25 Nov 68.
651 UNTS 350. Hungary. Amendment 25 Nov 68.
651 UNTS 350. Turkey. Amendment 25 Nov 68.
651 UNTS 350. Romania. Amendment 25 Nov 68.
651 UNTS 350. Poland. Amendment 25 Nov 68.
651 UNTS 350. Germany, West. Amendment 25 Nov 68.
651 UNTS 350. Finland. Amendment 25 Nov 68.
651 UNTS 350. Norway. Amendment 25 Nov 68.

101265 Bilateral Agreement **92 UNTS 125**
SIGNED: 7 Nov 50 FORCE: 7 Nov 50
REGISTERED: 4 Jul 51 USA (United States)
ARTICLES: 5 LANGUAGE: English.
HEADNOTE: TECHNICAL COOPERATION
TOPIC: Tech Assistance
CONCEPTS: Exceptions and exemptions. Previous treaty replacement. Diplomatic privileges. General cooperation. Exchange of information and documents. Personnel. Public information. Tax exemptions. Domestic obligation. General technical assistance. Materials, equipment and services.
PROCEDURE: Amendment. Duration. Future Procedures Contemplated.
PARTIES:
Ceylon (Sri Lanka)
USA (United States)

101266 Bilateral Instrument **92 UNTS 135**
SIGNED: 19 Oct 50 FORCE: 19 Oct 50
REGISTERED: 4 Jul 51 USA (United States)
ARTICLES: 10 LANGUAGE: English. Persian.
HEADNOTE: TECHNICAL COOPERATION RURAL IMPROVEMENT
TOPIC: Tech Assistance
CONCEPTS: Personnel. Public information. Sanitation. Education. Vocational training. Expense sharing formulae. Tax exemptions. Customs exemptions. Domestic obligation. General technical assistance. Agriculture. Special projects. Materials, equipment and services. Information agency. Subsidiary organ.
INTL ORGS: Special Commission.
PROCEDURE: Termination.
PARTIES:
Iran
USA (United States)

101267 Bilateral Agreement **92 UNTS 145**
SIGNED: 22 Dec 50 FORCE: 22 Jan 51
REGISTERED: 4 Jul 51 USA (United States)
ARTICLES: 5 LANGUAGE: English.
HEADNOTE: TECHNICAL ASSISTANCE COOPERATION
TOPIC: Tech Assistance

CONCEPTS: Exceptions and exemptions. Previous treaty replacement. Diplomatic privileges. General cooperation. Exchange of information and documents. Personnel. Public information. Financial programs. Tax exemptions. Domestic obligation. General technical assistance. Materials, equipment and services.
PROCEDURE: Amendment. Duration. Future Procedures Contemplated. Termination.
PARTIES:
Liberia
USA (United States)
ANNEX
180 UNTS 308. Liberia. Amendment 22 Jan 52. Force 22 Jan 52.
180 UNTS 308. USA (United States). Amendment 7 Jan 52. Force 22 Jan 52.

101268 Bilateral Agreement **92 UNTS 155**
SIGNED: 23 Dec 50 FORCE: 23 Dec 50
REGISTERED: 4 Jul 51 USA (United States)
ARTICLES: 5 LANGUAGE: English. Spanish.
HEADNOTE: TECHNICAL COOPERATION
TOPIC: Tech Assistance
CONCEPTS: Exceptions and exemptions. Previous treaty replacement. Diplomatic privileges. General cooperation. Exchange of information and documents. Personnel. Public information. Financial programs. Tax exemptions. Domestic obligation. General technical assistance.
PROCEDURE: Amendment. Duration. Future Procedures Contemplated. Termination.
PARTIES:
Nicaragua
USA (United States)
ANNEX
180 UNTS 311. Nicaragua. Amendment 24 Dec 51. Force 24 Dec 51.
180 UNTS 311. USA (United States). Amendment 18 Dec 51. Force 24 Dec 51.

101269 Bilateral Agreement **92 UNTS 167**
SIGNED: 20 Dec 50 FORCE: 30 Dec 50
REGISTERED: 4 Jul 51 USA (United States)
ARTICLES: 5 LANGUAGE: English. Spanish.
HEADNOTE: TECHNICAL COOPERATION
TOPIC: Tech Assistance
CONCEPTS: Exceptions and exemptions. Previous treaty replacement. Diplomatic privileges. General cooperation. Exchange of information and documents. Licenses and permits. Personnel. Public information. Tax exemptions. General technical assistance. Materials, equipment and services.
PROCEDURE: Amendment. Duration. Future Procedures Contemplated. Termination.
PARTIES:
Panama
USA (United States)
ANNEX
180 UNTS 318. Panama. Amendment 7 Jan 52. Force 7 Jan 52.
180 UNTS 318. USA (United States). Amendment 17 Dec 51. Force 7 Jan 52.

101270 Bilateral Agreement **92 UNTS 179**
SIGNED: 11 Jan 51 FORCE: 11 Jan 51
REGISTERED: 4 Jul 51 USA (United States)
ARTICLES: 5 LANGUAGE: English. Spanish.
HEADNOTE: TECHNICAL COOPERATION
TOPIC: Tech Assistance
CONCEPTS: Exceptions and exemptions. Previous treaty replacement. Diplomatic privileges. General cooperation. Exchange of information and documents. Personnel. Public information. Financial programs. Tax exemptions. General technical assistance. Materials, equipment and services.
PROCEDURE: Amendment. Duration. Future Procedures Contemplated. Termination.
PARTIES:
Costa Rica
USA (United States)
ANNEX
140 UNTS 439. USA (United States). Amendment 19 Dec 51. Force 20 Dec 51.
140 UNTS 439. Costa Rica. Amendment 20 Dec 51. Force 20 Dec 51.

101271 Bilateral Exchange **92 UNTS 191**
SIGNED: 12 Dec 49 FORCE: 12 Dec 49
REGISTERED: 5 Jul 51 USA (United States)
ARTICLES: 2 LANGUAGE: English.
HEADNOTE: WAIVER VISA REQUIREMENTS
MALTA
TOPIC: Visas
CONCEPTS: Time limit. Visa abolition.
PARTIES:
UK Great Britain
USA (United States)

101272 Bilateral Agreement **92 UNTS 197**
SIGNED: 18 Jan 50 FORCE: 18 Jan 50
REGISTERED: 5 Jul 51 USA (United States)
ARTICLES: 1 LANGUAGE: English. Finnish.
HEADNOTE: TERMINATION TARIFF TRADE
AGREEMENT
TOPIC: General Economic
CONCEPTS: Conditions. Tariffs.
INTL ORGS: General Agreement on Tariffs and
Trade.
PROCEDURE: Future Procedures Contemplated.
Termination.
PARTIES:
Finland
USA (United States)

101273 Bilateral Agreement **92 UNTS 201**
SIGNED: 6 Jun 50 FORCE: 6 Jun 50
REGISTERED: 5 Jul 51 USA (United States)
ARTICLES: 13 LANGUAGE: English. German.
HEADNOTE: EDUCATIONAL EXCHANGE PRO-
GRAM
TOPIC: Education
CONCEPTS: Definition of terms. Conformity with
municipal law. Inspection and observation. Personnel. General property. Dispute settlement. Ex-
change. Commissions and foundations. Teacher
and student exchange. Professorships. Scholarships and grants. Accounting procedures. Indemnities and reimbursements. Currency. Exchange rates and regulations. Financial programs. Funding procedures. Tax exemptions.
PARTIES:
Austria
USA (United States)
ANNEX
262 UNTS 468. Austria. Amendment 6 Jun 55.
Force 6 Jun 55.
262 UNTS 468. USA (United States). Amendment
6 Jun 55. Force 6 Jun 55.
435 UNTS 316. Austria. Amendment 13 Mar 61.
Force 13 Mar 61.
435 UNTS 316. USA (United States). Amendment
9 Jan 61. Force 13 Mar 62.

101274 Bilateral Exchange **92 UNTS 219**
SIGNED: 24 Feb 50 FORCE: 24 Feb 50
REGISTERED: 5 Jul 51 USA (United States)
ARTICLES: 2 LANGUAGE: English. Portuguese.
HEADNOTE: WAIVER CERTAIN VISA REQUIRE-
MENTS
TOPIC: Visas
CONCEPTS: Time limit. Visa abolition. Tourism.
Fees and exemptions.
PROCEDURE: Termination.
PARTIES:
Portugal
USA (United States)
ANNEX
98 UNTS 293. USA (United States). Confirmation
4 Aug 50.
98 UNTS 293. Portugal. Madeira. Force 4 Aug 50.

101275 Bilateral Agreement **92 UNTS 227**
SIGNED: 21 Feb 49 FORCE: 21 Feb 49
REGISTERED: 6 Jul 51 USA (United States)
ARTICLES: 29 LANGUAGE: English. Spanish.
HEADNOTE: ARMY MISSION
TOPIC: Military Mission
CONCEPTS: Definition of terms. Use of facilities.
Compensation. Indemnities and reimburse-
ments. Exchange rates and regulations. Expense
sharing formulae. Tax exemptions. Customs ex-
emptions. Military assistance. Military training.
Security of information. Airforce-army-navy per-
sonnel ratio. Ranks and privileges. Conditions
for assistance missions. Third country military
personnel. Status of forces.

PROCEDURE: Denunciation. Duration. Renewal or
Revival. Termination.
PARTIES:
Colombia
USA (United States)
ANNEX
237 UNTS 311. USA (United States). Prolongation
6 Oct 54. Force 4 Nov 54.
237 UNTS 311. Colombia. Prolongation
4 Nov 54. Force 4 Nov 54.
342 UNTS 349. Colombia. Amendment
31 Mar 59. Force 31 Mar 59.
342 UNTS 349. USA (United States). Amendment
18 Feb 59. Force 31 Mar 59.

101276 Bilateral Agreement **92 UNTS 249**
SIGNED: 20 Jun 49 FORCE: 20 Jun 49
REGISTERED: 6 Jul 51 USA (United States)
ARTICLES: 30 LANGUAGE: English. Spanish.
HEADNOTE: ARMY MISSION
TOPIC: Military Mission
CONCEPTS: Definition of terms. Licenses and per-
mits. Compensation. Indemnities and reimburse-
ments. Exchange rates and regulations. Expense
sharing formulae. Tax exemptions. Customs ex-
emptions. Military assistance. Military training.
Security of information. Airforce-army-navy per-
sonnel ratio. Ranks and privileges. Conditions
for assistance missions. Third country military
personnel. Status of forces.
PROCEDURE: Denunciation. Duration. Renewal or
Revival. Termination.
PARTIES:
Peru
USA (United States)
ANNEX
279 UNTS 304. USA (United States). Prolongation
10 Jul 56. Force 17 Jul 56.
279 UNTS 304. Peru. Prolongation 17 Jul 56.
Force 17 Jul 56.

101277 Bilateral Agreement **92 UNTS 269**
SIGNED: 15 Dec 49 FORCE: 29 Dec 49
REGISTERED: 6 Jul 51 USA (United States)
ARTICLES: 15 LANGUAGE: English. German.
HEADNOTE: ECONOMIC COOPERATION
TOPIC: Direct Aid
CONCEPTS: Definition of terms. Territorial application. General provisions. Guarantees and safeguards. Treaty implementation. Annex or appendix reference. Tourism. Continuity of rights and
obligations. Privileges and immunities. Confor-
mity with municipal law. General cooperation.
Exchange of information and documents. Per-
sonnel. Public information. Accounting procedures. Funding procedures. Local currency. Domestic obligation. Economic assistance. Aid missions. Procurement. Access to materials.
INTL ORGS: International Bank for Reconstruction
and Development. Organization for Economic
Co-operation and Development. United Nations.
PROCEDURE: Amendment. Duration. Registration.
Termination.
PARTIES:
Germany, West
USA (United States)
ANNEX
141 UNTS 390. USA (United States). Amendment
27 Feb 51. Force 28 Mar 51.
141 UNTS 390. Germany, West. Amendment
28 Mar 51. Force 28 Mar 51.
212 UNTS 329. USA (United States). Amendment
14 Nov 52. Force 30 Dec 52.
212 UNTS 329. Germany, West. Amendment
30 Dec 52. Force 30 Dec 52.

101278 Bilateral Exchange **92 UNTS 329**
SIGNED: 11 Aug 50 FORCE: 11 Aug 50
REGISTERED: 6 Jul 51 USA (United States)
ARTICLES: 2 LANGUAGE: English. Spanish.
HEADNOTE: FLIGHTS MILITARY AIRCRAFT
TOPIC: Status of Forces
CONCEPTS: Definition of terms. Conformity with
municipal law. Fees and exemptions. Overflights
and technical stops. Operating authorizations
and regulations. Airforce-army-navy personnel
ratio. Procurement and logistics.
PARTIES:
Dominican Republic
USA (United States)

101279 Bilateral Agreement **92 UNTS 341**
SIGNED: 23 Aug 50 FORCE: 23 Aug 50
REGISTERED: 10 Jul 51 USA (United States)
ARTICLES: 30 LANGUAGE: English. Spanish.
HEADNOTE: NAVAL MISSION
TOPIC: Military Mission
CONCEPTS: Definition of terms. Use of facilities.
Compensation. Indemnities and reimburse-
ments. Exchange rates and regulations. Expense
sharing formulae. Tax exemptions. Customs ex-
emptions. Military assistance. Military training.
Security of information. Airforce-army-navy personnel ratio. Ranks and privileges. Conditions
for assistance missions. Third country military
personnel. Status of forces.
PROCEDURE: Denunciation. Duration. Renewal or
Revival. Termination.
PARTIES:
USA (United States)
Venezuela
ANNEX
270 UNTS 378. USA (United States). Prolongation
9 Apr 54. Force 12 Aug 54.
270 UNTS 378. Venezuela. Prolongation
12 Aug 54. Force 12 Aug 54.
366 UNTS 392. USA (United States). Amendment
31 Mar 59. Force 29 Apr 59.
366 UNTS 392. Venezuela. Amendment
29 Apr 59. Force 29 Apr 59.

101280 Bilateral Agreement **92 UNTS 361**
SIGNED: 13 Sep 50 FORCE: 10 Oct 50
REGISTERED: 10 Jul 51 USA (United States)
ARTICLES: 5 LANGUAGE: Burmese. English.
HEADNOTE: ECONOMIC COOPERATION
TOPIC: Direct Aid
CONCEPTS: Annex or appendix reference. Privi-
leges and immunities. Conformity with munici-
pal law. General cooperation. Exchange of infor-
mation and documents. Personnel. Commodities
and services. Domestic obligation. Economic as-
sistance. Aid missions. Procurement. Distribu-
tion.
INTL ORGS: United Nations.
PROCEDURE: Amendment. Registration. Termina-
tion.
PARTIES:
Burma
USA (United States)

101281 Bilateral Exchange **92 UNTS 387**
SIGNED: 24 Mar 50 FORCE: 24 Mar 50
REGISTERED: 10 Jul 51 USA (United States)
ARTICLES: 2 LANGUAGE: English.
HEADNOTE: ASSUMPTION OBLIGATIONS ECO-
NOMIC COOPERATION
TOPIC: Direct Aid
CONCEPTS: Continuity of rights and obligations.
Conformity with municipal law. Exchange of in-
formation and documents. Funding procedures.
Domestic obligation. Economic assistance. Ac-
cess to materials.
INTL ORGS: Organization for Economic Co-opera-
tion and Development.
PARTIES:
Indonesia
USA (United States)

101282 Bilateral Exchange **93 UNTS 3**
SIGNED: 24 Feb 50 FORCE: 24 Feb 50
REGISTERED: 10 Jul 51 USA (United States)
ARTICLES: 2 LANGUAGE: English.
HEADNOTE: EXCHANGE OFFICIAL PUBLICA-
TIONS
TOPIC: Admin Cooperation
CONCEPTS: Exchange of official publications. Op-
erating agencies.
PARTIES:
Switzerland
USA (United States)

101283 Bilateral Exchange **93 UNTS 11**
SIGNED: 24 Mar 50 FORCE: 24 Mar 50
REGISTERED: 10 Jul 51 USA (United States)
ARTICLES: 2 LANGUAGE: English. Spanish.
HEADNOTE: SUPERSEDING EXCHANGE OFFICIAL
PUBLICATIONS
TOPIC: Admin Cooperation
CONCEPTS: Previous treaty replacement. Ex-

change of official publications. Operating agencies. Indemnities and reimbursements.
PARTIES:
Honduras
USA (United States)

101284   Bilateral Agreement   **93 UNTS 21**
SIGNED: 28 Apr 50   FORCE: 28 Apr 50
REGISTERED: 10 Jul 51 USA (United States)
ARTICLES: 13 LANGUAGE: English. Korean.
HEADNOTE: EDUCATIONAL EXCHANGE PROGRAM
TOPIC: Education
CONCEPTS: Definition of terms. Conformity with municipal law. Inspection and observation. Personnel. General property. Dispute settlement. Exchange. Commissions and foundations. Teacher and student exchange. Professorships. Scholarships and grants. Accounting procedures. Indemnities and reimbursements. Currency. Exchange rates and regulations. Financial programs. Funding procedures. Tax exemptions.
PROCEDURE: Amendment.
PARTIES:
Korea, South
USA (United States)
ANNEX
380 UNTS 412. USA (United States). Amendment 30 Jun 60. Force 30 Jun 60.
380 UNTS 412. Korea, South. Amendment 30 Jun 60. Force 30 Jun 60.

101285   Bilateral Exchange   **93 UNTS 39**
SIGNED: 21 Nov 50   FORCE: 21 Nov 50
REGISTERED: 10 Jul 51 USA (United States)
ARTICLES: 2 LANGUAGE: English.
HEADNOTE: HANDLING DISTRIBUTION FOODSTUFFS PUBLICITY EMERGENCY FOOD ASSISTANCE
TOPIC: Direct Aid
CONCEPTS: Exchange of information and documents. Inspection and observation. Public information. Relief supplies. Distribution. Press and wire services.
PARTIES:
USA (United States)
Yugoslavia

101286   Bilateral Exchange   **93 UNTS 45**
SIGNED: 21 Nov 50   FORCE: 21 Nov 50
REGISTERED: 10 Jul 51 USA (United States)
ARTICLES: 2 LANGUAGE: English.
HEADNOTE: MUTUAL DEFENSE ASSISTANCE
TOPIC: Milit Assistance
CONCEPTS: Non-prejudice to UN charter. Conformity with municipal law. Local currency. Agricultural commodities. Defense and security. Restrictions on transfer. Raw materials.
PROCEDURE: Future Procedures Contemplated.
PARTIES:
USA (United States)
Yugoslavia

101287   Bilateral Exchange   **93 UNTS 53**
SIGNED: 28 Apr 47   FORCE: 28 Apr 47
REGISTERED: 10 Jul 51 UK Great Britain
ARTICLES: 2 LANGUAGE: English. German.
HEADNOTE: DEFERMENT CLAIMS
TOPIC: Reparations
CONCEPTS: Time limit. Payment schedules. Most favored nation clause. Post-war claims settlement.
PARTIES:
Austria
UK Great Britain

101288   Multilateral Protocol   **93 UNTS 61**
SIGNED: 4 Nov 47   FORCE: 4 Nov 47
REGISTERED: 10 Jul 51 UK Great Britain
ARTICLES: 3 LANGUAGE: English. French.
HEADNOTE: RESTITUTION LOOTED MONETARY GOLD
TOPIC: Reparations
CONCEPTS: Monetary and gold transfers. Lump sum settlements. Enemy financial interests. Reparations and restrictions.
INTL ORGS: Allied Military Occupation.

PARTIES:
Austria SIGNED: 4 Nov 47 FORCE: 4 Nov 47
France SIGNED: 4 Nov 47 FORCE: 4 Nov 47
UK Great Britain SIGNED: 4 Nov 47 FORCE: 4 Nov 47
USA (United States) SIGNED: 4 Nov 47 FORCE: 4 Nov 47

101289   **UNTS**
SIGNED:
REGISTERED:
ARTICLES:
HEADNOTE: AGREEMENT REGISTERED UNDER 100039
TOPIC:
PARTIES:

101290   Bilateral Exchange   **93 UNTS 67**
SIGNED: 12 Jun 50   FORCE: 12 Jun 50
REGISTERED: 10 Jul 51 UK Great Britain
ARTICLES: 2 LANGUAGE: English.
HEADNOTE: REBATE CUSTOMS DUTIES
TOPIC: Customs
CONCEPTS: Customs duties. Customs exemptions.
INTL ORGS: General Agreement on Tariffs and Trade.
PARTIES:
South Africa
UK Great Britain

101291   Bilateral Exchange   **93 UNTS 75**
SIGNED: 22 Feb 49   FORCE: 22 Feb 49
REGISTERED: 10 Jul 51 UK Great Britain
ARTICLES: 2 LANGUAGE: English.
HEADNOTE: TRANSFER MARION & PRINCE EDWARD ISLANDS
TOPIC: Territory Boundary
CONCEPTS: Definition of territory. Changes of territory.
PARTIES:
South Africa
UK Great Britain

101292   Bilateral Exchange   **93 UNTS 81**
SIGNED: 19 Dec 50   FORCE: 19 Dec 50
REGISTERED: 10 Jul 51 UK Great Britain
ARTICLES: 2 LANGUAGE: English.
HEADNOTE: TRANSFER HEARD & MACDONALD ISLANDS
TOPIC: Territory Boundary
CONCEPTS: Definition of territory. Fish, wildlife, and natural resources.
PARTIES:
Australia
UK Great Britain

101293   Bilateral Convention   **93 UNTS 87**
SIGNED: 29 Aug 49   FORCE: 1 Jun 51
REGISTERED: 10 Jul 51 Belgium
ARTICLES: 8 LANGUAGE: French.
HEADNOTE: MILITARY SERVICE
TOPIC: Milit Servic/Citiz
CONCEPTS: Time limit. Previous treaty replacement. Dual nationality. Certificates of service. Foreign nationals. Service in foreign army.
PROCEDURE: Denunciation. Termination.
PARTIES:
Belgium
France

101294   Bilateral Exchange   **93 UNTS 97**
SIGNED: 15 Mar 51   FORCE: 6 Feb 51
REGISTERED: 10 Jul 51 Belgium
ARTICLES: 2 LANGUAGE: Dutch.
HEADNOTE: RECIPROCAL SETTLEMENT CLAIMS
TOPIC: Reparations
CONCEPTS: Time limit. Conformity with municipal law. General cooperation. Procedure. Compensation. Loss and/or damage. Post-war claims settlement.
INTL ORGS: Special Commission.
PARTIES:
Belgium
Netherlands

101295   Bilateral Exchange   **93 UNTS 109**
SIGNED: 16 Mar 51   FORCE: 12 Mar 51
REGISTERED: 10 Jul 51 Belgium
ARTICLES: 5 LANGUAGE: English. French.
HEADNOTE: RECIPROCITY COMPENSATION WAR DAMAGE PRIVATE PROPERTY
TOPIC: Reparations
CONCEPTS: Time limit. Nationality and citizenship. Compensation. National treatment. Loss and/or damage. Post-war claims settlement.
PARTIES:
Belgium
USA (United States)

101296   Multilateral Convention   **93 UNTS 129**
SIGNED: 22 Feb 49   FORCE: 30 Jun 49
REGISTERED: 11 Jul 51 UK Great Britain
ARTICLES: 11 LANGUAGE: English. French.
HEADNOTE: PERMANENT CONTROL OUTBREAK AREAS RED LOCUST
TOPIC: Sanitation
CONCEPTS: Definition of terms. Territorial application. Previous treaty extension. Insect control. Research results. Research and development. Accounting procedures. Expense sharing formulae. Subsidiary organ.
INTL ORGS: International Red Locust Control Service.
PROCEDURE: Accession. Denunciation. Duration. Ratification.
PARTIES:
Belgium SIGNED: 22 Feb 49 RATIFIED: 9 Jan 50 FORCE: 9 Jan 50
Portugal Angola RATIFIED: 15 Jun 50 FORCE: 15 Jun 50
Portugal Mozambique RATIFIED: 15 Jun 50 FORCE: 15 Jun 50
South Africa SIGNED: 22 Feb 49 RATIFIED: 5 Aug 49 FORCE: 5 Aug 49
Southern Rhodesia SIGNED: 22 Feb 49 RATIFIED: 30 Jun 49 FORCE: 30 Jun 49
UK Great Britain SIGNED: 22 Feb 49 RATIFIED: 14 Apr 49 FORCE: 30 Jun 49
ANNEX
183 UNTS 368. South Africa. Amendment 29 Oct 53. Force 29 Oct 53.
183 UNTS 368. Belgium. Amendment 29 Oct 53. Force 29 Oct 53.
183 UNTS 368. Portugal. Amendment 29 Oct 53. Force 29 Oct 53.
183 UNTS 368. UK Great Britain. Amendment 29 Oct 53. Force 29 Oct 53.
183 UNTS 368. Southern Rhodesia. Amendment 29 Oct 53. Force 29 Oct 53.
466 UNTS 382. Tanganyika. Accession 15 Oct 62.
466 UNTS 382. Burundi. Accession 23 Oct 62.
565 UNTS 282. Belgium. Denunciation 20 Nov 64. Force 20 Nov 65.
571 UNTS 316. Malawi. Accession 5 Aug 65.

101297   Bilateral Protocol   **93 UNTS 143**
SIGNED: 24 Oct 45   FORCE: 24 Oct 45
REGISTERED: 11 Jul 51 UK Great Britain
ARTICLES: 8 LANGUAGE: English.
HEADNOTE: MUTUAL AID
TOPIC: Milit Assistance
CONCEPTS: General cooperation. Wages and salaries. Indemnities and reimbursements. Funding procedures. Defense and security. Military assistance. Return of equipment and recapture.
PROCEDURE: Termination.
PARTIES:
Denmark
UK Great Britain

101298   Bilateral Exchange   **93 UNTS 151**
SIGNED: 1 Dec 47   FORCE: 1 Dec 47
REGISTERED: 11 Jul 51 UK Great Britain
ARTICLES: 2 LANGUAGE: English.
HEADNOTE: SETTLEMENT CLAIMS
TOPIC: Reparations
CONCEPTS: Annex or appendix reference. Post-war claims settlement.
PARTIES:
Denmark
UK Great Britain

101299   Bilateral Agreement   **93 UNTS 165**
SIGNED: 30 Jun 47   FORCE: 14 Jul 47

REGISTERED: 11 Jul 51 UK Great Britain
ARTICLES: 11 LANGUAGE: English.
HEADNOTE: TEMPORARY ARRANGEMENT DEAL-
ING STERLING BALANCES
TOPIC: Finance
CONCEPTS: Definition of terms. Detailed regula-
tions. Annex or appendix reference. General co-
operation. Accounting procedures. Banking. Bal-
ance of payments. Monetary and gold transfers.
Financial programs. Delivery guarantees. Loan
and credit. Purchase authorization. Terms of
loan.
PROCEDURE: Duration. Termination.
PARTIES:
United Arab Rep
UK Great Britain

101300 Bilateral Agreement **93 UNTS 185**
SIGNED: 17 Oct 49 FORCE: 1 Jan 50
REGISTERED: 11 Jul 51 UK Great Britain
ARTICLES: 35 LANGUAGE: English. French.
HEADNOTE: REGULATION EXCHANGE MONEY
ORDERS
TOPIC: Postal Service
CONCEPTS: Definition of terms. Previous treaty re-
placement. Accounting procedures. Payment
schedules. Postal services. Money orders and
postal checks. Rates and charges. Advice lists
and orders. Telegrams.
PROCEDURE: Termination.
PARTIES:
Greece
UK Great Britain

101301 Bilateral Agreement **93 UNTS 225**
SIGNED: 17 Jan 51 FORCE: 1 Apr 51
REGISTERED: 11 Jul 51 UK Great Britain
ARTICLES: 36 LANGUAGE: English. Swedish.
HEADNOTE: EXCHANGE MONEY ORDERS
TOPIC: Postal Service
CONCEPTS: Definition of terms. Previous treaty re-
placement. Conformity with municipal law. Ac-
counting procedures. Currency. Payment sched-
ules. Postal services. Money orders and postal
checks. Rates and charges. Advice lists and or-
ders. Telegrams.
PROCEDURE: Denunciation. Duration.
PARTIES:
Sweden
UK Great Britain

101302 Bilateral Treaty **94 UNTS 3**
SIGNED: 31 Jul 50 FORCE: 31 Jul 50
REGISTERED: 13 Jul 51 India
ARTICLES: 10 LANGUAGE: English.
HEADNOTE: PEACE FRIENDSHIP
TOPIC: General Amity
CONCEPTS: Friendship and amity. Alien status.
Consular relations establishment. Diplomatic re-
lations establishment. Privileges and immuni-
ties. Exchange of information and documents.
Defense and security.
PROCEDURE: Duration. Termination.
PARTIES:
India
Nepal

101303 Multilateral Convention **94 UNTS 11**
SIGNED: 29 Jun 46 FORCE: 14 Jul 51
REGISTERED: 14 Jul 51 ILO (Labor Org)
ARTICLES: 12 LANGUAGE: English. French.
HEADNOTE: CERTIFICATION ABLE SEAMEN
TOPIC: ILO Labor
CONCEPTS: Detailed regulations. Previous treaty
extension. Domestic legislation. Recognition of
legal documents. ILO conventions. Competency
certificate.
INTL ORGS: International Labour Organization.
United Nations.
PROCEDURE: Amendment. Denunciation. Dura-
tion. Ratification. Registration. Renewal or Re-
vival.
PARTIES:
Multilateral
ANNEX
117 UNTS 391. Belgium. Qualified Ratification
5 Dec 51. Force 15 Dec 52.
118 UNTS 307. Netherlands. Netherlands Antilles.

131 UNTS 342. UK Great Britain. Ratification
13 May 52. Force 13 May 53.
133 UNTS 366. Portugal. Ratification 13 Jun 52.
Force 13 Jun 53.
164 UNTS 364. USA (United States). Ratification
9 Apr 53. Force 9 Apr 54.
189 UNTS 363. Poland. Ratification 13 Apr 54.
Force 13 Apr 55.
212 UNTS 395. France. French Guinea.
212 UNTS 395. France. Martinique.
212 UNTS 395. France. Guadeloupe.
212 UNTS 395. France. Reunion.
256 UNTS 342. UK Great Britain. Jersey Island.
256 UNTS 342. UK Great Britain. Isle of Man.
256 UNTS 342. UK Great Britain. Guernsey Island.
272 UNTS 256. Ireland. Ratification 21 Jun 57.
Force 21 Jun 58.
318 UNTS 419. UK Great Britain. Declaration
3 Nov 58.
338 UNTS 338. UK Great Britain. Declaration
7 Jul 59.
396 UNTS 324. UK Great Britain. British Guiana.
Declaration 13 Mar 61.
396 UNTS 324. UK Great Britain. Brit Solomon Is.
Declaration 13 Mar 61.
396 UNTS 324. UK Great Britain. Mauritius. Declaration 13 Mar 61.
396 UNTS 324. UK Great Britain. Uganda. Declaration 13 Mar 61.
396 UNTS 324. UK Great Britain. Bahamas. Declaration 13 Mar 61.
396 UNTS 324. UK Great Britain. Aden. Declaration 13 Mar 61.
396 UNTS 324. UK Great Britain. St. Helena. Declaration 13 Mar 61.
396 UNTS 324. UK Great Britain. Sarawak. Declaration 13 Mar 61.
396 UNTS 324. UK Great Britain. British Honduras. Declaration 13 Mar 61.
396 UNTS 324. UK Great Britain. Brit Virgin Islands. Declaration 13 Mar 61.
396 UNTS 324. UK Great Britain. Fiji Islands. Declaration 13 Mar 61.
396 UNTS 324. UK Great Britain. Hong Kong.
Declaration 13 Mar 61.
396 UNTS 324. UK Great Britain. Kenya. Declaration 13 Mar 61.
396 UNTS 324. UK Great Britain. Malta. Declaration 13 Mar 61.
396 UNTS 324. UK Great Britain. Gambia. Declaration 13 Mar 61.
396 UNTS 324. UK Great Britain. Brunei. Declaration 13 Mar 61.
396 UNTS 324. UK Great Britain. West Indies.
Declaration 13 Mar 61.
396 UNTS 324. UK Great Britain. Singapore. Declaration 13 Mar 61.
396 UNTS 324. UK Great Britain. Bermuda. Declaration 13 Mar 61.
396 UNTS 324. UK Great Britain. Gibralter. Declaration 13 Mar 61.
396 UNTS 324. UK Great Britain. Tanganyika.
Declaration 13 Mar 61.
396 UNTS 324. UK Great Britain. Falkland Islands. Declaration 13 Mar 61.
396 UNTS 324. UK Great Britain. Gilbert Islands.
Declaration 13 Mar 61.
396 UNTS 324. UK Great Britain. North Borneo.
Declaration 13 Mar 61.
396 UNTS 324. UK Great Britain. Seychelles. Declaration 13 May 61.
396 UNTS 324. UK Great Britain. Zanzibar.
401 UNTS 253. USA (United States). Canal Zone.
Declaration 7 Jun 61.
401 UNTS 253. USA (United States). Micronesia
(US). Declaration 7 Jun 61.
401 UNTS 253. USA (United States). Virgin Islands.
401 UNTS 253. USA (United States). American
Samoa. Declaration 7 Jun 61.
401 UNTS 253. USA (United States). Guam.
401 UNTS 253. USA (United States). Puerto Rico.
420 UNTS 341. New Zealand. Ratification
5 Dec 61. Force 5 Dec 62.
420 UNTS 341. Yugoslavia. Ratification
22 Dec 61. Force 22 Dec 62.
444 UNTS 329. Algeria. Succession 19 Oct 62.
475 UNTS 379. UK Great Britain. Mauritius.
495 UNTS 296. UK Great Britain. Barbados.
530 UNTS 414. Ghana. Ratification 18 Mar 65.
Force 18 Mar 66.

101304 Bilateral Agreement **94 UNTS 21**
SIGNED: 19 Jul 50 FORCE: 14 Jul 50
REGISTERED: 16 Jul 51 United Nations
ARTICLES: 9 LANGUAGE: English.
HEADNOTE: UNICEF & CHINA
TOPIC: IGO Operations
CONCEPTS: Diplomatic privileges. Privileges and
immunities. Exchange of information and docu-
ments. Funding procedures. Materials, equip-
ment and services. Assistance to United Nations.
INTL ORGS: United Nations.
PROCEDURE: Duration.
PARTIES:
Taiwan
UNICEF (Children)
ANNEX
402 UNTS 310. UNICEF (Children). Implementa-
tion 8 Jul 61. Force 31 Jul 61.
402 UNTS 310. Taiwan. Implementation
31 Jul 61. Force 31 Jul 61.
500 UNTS 320. Taiwan. Force 12 May 64.

101305 Bilateral Agreement **94 UNTS 35**
SIGNED: 27 Apr 51 FORCE: 8 Jun 51
REGISTERED: 16 Jul 51 Denmark
ARTICLES: 14 LANGUAGE: Danish. English.
HEADNOTE: DEFENSE GREENLAND
TOPIC: General Military
CONCEPTS: Jurisdiction. Procurement and logis-
tics. Exchange of defense information. Bases
and facilities. Restrictions on transfer.
INTL ORGS: North Atlantic Treaty Organization.
PROCEDURE: Duration. Ratification.
PARTIES:
Denmark
USA (United States)

101306 Bilateral Exchange **94 UNTS 59**
SIGNED: 14 Mar 47 FORCE: 14 Mar 47
REGISTERED: 18 Jul 51 ICAO (Civil Aviat)
ARTICLES: 2 LANGUAGE: French.
HEADNOTE: PRIVILEGES & IMMUNITIES
TOPIC: IGO Status/Immunit
CONCEPTS: Privileges and immunities. Diplomatic
correspondence. Exchange of official publica-
tions. Juridical personality. Free passage and
transit. Operating agencies. Procedure. Existing
tribunals. Regional offices. IGO status. Special
status. Status of experts.
PROCEDURE: Amendment. Duration.
PARTIES:
France
ICAO (Civil Aviat)

101307 Bilateral Agreement **94 UNTS 73**
SIGNED: 8 Apr 47 FORCE: 8 Apr 47
REGISTERED: 18 Jul 51 ICAO (Civil Aviat)
ARTICLES: 11 LANGUAGE: French.
HEADNOTE: OPERATION REGULAR AIR SERVICES
TOPIC: Air Transport
CONCEPTS: Exceptions and exemptions. Annex or
appendix reference. Conformity with municipal
law. Licenses and permits. Recognition of legal
documents. Use of facilities. Arbitration. Proce-
dure. Special tribunals. Fees and exemptions.
Most favored nation clause. National treatment.
Customs exemptions. Competency certificate.
Routes and logistics. Navigational conditions.
Permit designation. Airworthiness certificates.
Conditions of airlines operating permission. Op-
erating authorizations and regulations. Licenses
and certificates of nationality. Airport facilities.
INTL ORGS: International Civil Aviation Organiza-
tion. Arbitration Commission.
PROCEDURE: Amendment. Future Procedures
Contemplated. Ratification. Registration. Termi-
nation.
PARTIES:
Greece
Sweden
ANNEX
216 UNTS 390. Sweden. Supplementation
6 Feb 52. Force 6 Feb 52.
216 UNTS 390. Greece. Supplementation
6 Feb 52. Force 6 Feb 52.

101308 Bilateral Agreement **94 UNTS 87**
SIGNED: 25 Apr 47 FORCE: 25 Apr 47
REGISTERED: 18 Jul 51 ICAO (Civil Aviat)
ARTICLES: 12 LANGUAGE: English. Portuguese.

HEADNOTE: AIR SERVICES
TOPIC: Air Transport
CONCEPTS: Annex or appendix reference. Conformity with municipal law. Licenses and permits. Recognition of legal documents. Use of facilities. Arbitration. Procedure. Existing tribunals. Fees and exemptions. Most favored nation clause. National treatment. Customs exemptions. Competency certificate. Routes and logistics. Navigational conditions. Permit designation. Airport facilities. Airworthiness certificates. Conditions of airlines operating permission. Operating authorizations and regulations. Licenses and certificates of nationality.
INTL ORGS: International Civil Aviation Organization. Arbitration Commission.
PROCEDURE: Amendment. Future Procedures Contemplated. Registration. Termination.
PARTIES:
Canada
Portugal
                    ANNEX
311 UNTS 332. Canada. Amendment 24 Apr 57. Force 30 Apr 57.
311 UNTS 332. Portugal. Amendment 30 Apr 57. Force 30 Apr 57.
412 UNTS 303. Canada. Amendment 5 Mar 58. Force 5 Mar 58.
412 UNTS 303. Portugal. Amendment 31 Mar 58. Force 31 Mar 58.

101309   Bilateral Convention   **94 UNTS 107**
SIGNED: 21 Jun 47   FORCE: 22 Sep 47
REGISTERED: 18 Jul 51 ICAO (Civil Aviat)
ARTICLES: 13 LANGUAGE: Norwegian. Swedish.
HEADNOTE: DOUBLE TAXATION TAXES INCOME PROPERTY
TOPIC: Taxation
CONCEPTS: Territorial application. Nationality and citizenship. Taxation. Tax exemptions. Air transport. Merchant vessels.
PROCEDURE: Denunciation. Ratification.
PARTIES:
Norway
Sweden

101310   Bilateral Agreement   **94 UNTS 139**
SIGNED: 14 Nov 47   FORCE: 10 Mar 49
REGISTERED: 18 Jul 51 ICAO (Civil Aviat)
ARTICLES: 12 LANGUAGE: French. Portuguese. Swedish.
HEADNOTE: AIR TRANSPORT
TOPIC: Air Transport
CONCEPTS: Definition of terms. Treaty interpretation. Annex or appendix reference. Previous treaty replacement. Friendship and amity. Conformity with municipal law. Use of facilities. Arbitration. Procedure. Fees and exemptions. Most favored nation clause. National treatment. Customs exemptions. Routes and logistics. Permit designation. Air transport. Airport facilities. Conditions of airlines operating permission. Operating authorizations and regulations.
INTL ORGS: International Civil Aviation Organization. Arbitration Commission.
PROCEDURE: Amendment. Future Procedures Contemplated. Ratification. Registration. Termination.
PARTIES:
Brazil
Sweden

101311   Bilateral Agreement   **94 UNTS 175**
SIGNED: 18 Mar 48   FORCE: 20 Dec 50
REGISTERED: 18 Jul 51 ICAO (Civil Aviat)
ARTICLES: 18 LANGUAGE: Danish. Spanish.
HEADNOTE: AIR TRANSPORT
TOPIC: Air Transport
CONCEPTS: Definition of terms. Guarantees and safeguards. Annex or appendix reference. Non-prejudice to third party. Friendship and amity. Conformity with municipal law. General cooperation. Licenses and permits. Personnel. Recognition of legal documents. Use of facilities. Investigation of violations. Arbitration. Procedure. Reexport of goods, etc.. Fees and exemptions. Most favored nation clause. National treatment. Customs exemptions. Competency certificate. Routes and logistics. Navigational conditions. Permit designation. Air transport. Airport facilities. Airworthiness certificates. Conditions of air-

lines operating permission. Operating authorizations and regulations. Licenses and certificates of nationality.
INTL ORGS: International Civil Aviation Organization.
PROCEDURE: Amendment. Future Procedures Contemplated. Ratification. Registration. Termination. Application to Non-self-governing Territories.
PARTIES:
Argentina
Denmark

101312   Bilateral Agreement   **94 UNTS 217**
SIGNED: 26 May 48   FORCE: 26 May 48
REGISTERED: 18 Jul 51 ICAO (Civil Aviat)
ARTICLES: 13 LANGUAGE: French. Greek.
HEADNOTE: AIR SERVICES
TOPIC: Air Transport
CONCEPTS: Exceptions and exemptions. Annex or appendix reference. Conformity with municipal law. General cooperation. Licenses and permits. Recognition of legal documents. Use of facilities. Arbitration. Procedure. Existing tribunals. Negotiation. Reexport of goods, etc.. Fees and exemptions. Most favored nation clause. National treatment. Customs exemptions. Competency certificate. Routes and logistics. Navigational conditions. Permit designation. Airport facilities. Airworthiness certificates. Conditions of airlines operating permission. Operating authorizations and regulations. Licenses and certificates of nationality.
INTL ORGS: International Civil Aviation Organization. Arbitration Commission.
PROCEDURE: Amendment. Future Procedures Contemplated. Ratification. Registration. Termination.
PARTIES:
Greece
Switzerland

101313   Bilateral Agreement   **94 UNTS 239**
SIGNED: 25 Jun 48   FORCE: 24 Oct 50
REGISTERED: 18 Jul 51 ICAO (Civil Aviat)
ARTICLES: 15 LANGUAGE: English. Italian.
HEADNOTE: AIR SERVICES
TOPIC: Air Transport
CONCEPTS: Change of circumstances. Definition of terms. Detailed regulations. Exceptions and exemptions. Conformity with municipal law. General cooperation. Exchange of information and documents. Domestic legislation. Arbitration. Procedure. Existing tribunals. Negotiation. Non-interest rates and fees. Routes and logistics. Permit designation. Conditions of airlines operating permission. Overflights and technical stops. Operating authorizations and regulations.
INTL ORGS: International Civil Aviation Organization. Arbitration Commission.
PROCEDURE: Amendment. Future Procedures Contemplated. Ratification. Termination.
PARTIES:
Italy
UK Great Britain
                    ANNEX
474 UNTS 316. UK Great Britain. Correction 27 Nov 62. Force 27 Nov 62.
474 UNTS 316. Italy. Correction 27 Nov 62. Force 27 Nov 62.
496 UNTS 336. UK Great Britain. Amendment 28 Aug 63. Force 22 Nov 63.
496 UNTS 336. Italy. Amendment 22 Nov 63. Force 22 Nov 63.
605 UNTS 329. Italy. Modification 10 Feb 67.
605 UNTS 329. UK Great Britain. Modification 10 Feb 67.

101314   Bilateral Agreement   **94 UNTS 269**
SIGNED: 10 Aug 48   FORCE: 23 Aug 49
REGISTERED: 18 Jul 51 ICAO (Civil Aviat)
ARTICLES: 12 LANGUAGE: French. Portuguese.
HEADNOTE: REGULAR AIR TRANSPORT SERVICES
TOPIC: Air Transport
CONCEPTS: Definition of terms. Annex or appendix reference. Conformity with municipal law. General cooperation. Licenses and permits. Use of facilities. Arbitration. Procedure. Fees and exemptions. Most favored nation clause. National treatment. Customs exemptions. Routes and lo-

gistics. Air transport. Airport facilities. Conditions of airlines operating permission. Operating authorizations and regulations.
INTL ORGS: International Civil Aviation Organization. Arbitration Commission.
PROCEDURE: Amendment. Future Procedures Contemplated. Ratification. Registration. Termination.
PARTIES:
Brazil
Switzerland
                    ANNEX
231 UNTS 356. Brazil. Amendment 27 Aug 54.

101315   Bilateral Agreement   **95 UNTS 3**
SIGNED: 22 Oct 48   FORCE: 22 Oct 48
REGISTERED: 18 Jul 51 ICAO (Civil Aviat)
ARTICLES: 22 LANGUAGE: Spanish.
HEADNOTE: INTERNATIONAL AVIATION & PERU
TOPIC: IGO Status/Immunit
CONCEPTS: Diplomatic privileges. Diplomatic missions. Inviolability. Privileges and immunities. Property. Diplomatic correspondence. Juridical personality. Procedure. Existing tribunals. Regional offices. IGO status. Special status. Status of experts.
INTL ORGS: International Court of Justice.
PROCEDURE: Amendment. Duration.
PARTIES:
Peru
ICAO (Civil Aviat)

101316   Bilateral Agreement   **95 UNTS 21**
SIGNED: 29 Oct 48   FORCE: 14 Oct 50
REGISTERED: 18 Jul 51 ICAO (Civil Aviat)
ARTICLES: 20 LANGUAGE: Dutch. French. Spanish.
HEADNOTE: REGULAR AIR SERVICES
TOPIC: Air Transport
CONCEPTS: Conditions. Definition of terms. Annex or appendix reference. Non-prejudice to third party. Visas. Conformity with municipal law. General cooperation. Licenses and permits. Recognition of legal documents. Responsibility and liability. Use of facilities. Investigation of violations. Arbitration. Procedure. Competence of tribunal. Reexport of goods, etc.. Fees and exemptions. Most favored nation clause. National treatment. Customs exemptions. Competency certificate. Routes and logistics. Navigational conditions. Permit designation. Airport facilities. Airworthiness certificates. Conditions of airlines operating permission. Operating authorizations and regulations. Licenses and certificates of nationality.
INTL ORGS: International Civil Aviation Organization.
PROCEDURE: Amendment. Future Procedures Contemplated. Ratification. Registration. Termination.
PARTIES:
Argentina
Netherlands

101317   Bilateral Exchange   **95 UNTS 73**
SIGNED: 21 Feb 49   FORCE: 21 Feb 49
REGISTERED: 18 Jul 51 ICAO (Civil Aviat)
ARTICLES: 2 LANGUAGE: French.
HEADNOTE: REGULATION AIR TRANSPORT SERVICES
TOPIC: Air Transport
CONCEPTS: Annex type material. Previous treaty replacement. Routes and logistics. Permit designation. Airport facilities. Airport equipment. Operating authorizations and regulations.
PARTIES:
Belgium
Sweden

101318   Bilateral Agreement   **95 UNTS 83**
SIGNED: 26 Apr 49   FORCE: 1 May 49
REGISTERED: 18 Jul 51 ICAO (Civil Aviat)
ARTICLES: 11 LANGUAGE: Finnish. Swedish.
HEADNOTE: AIR TRANSPORT
TOPIC: Air Transport
CONCEPTS: Annex or appendix reference. Conformity with municipal law. Licenses and permits. Recognition of legal documents. Use of facilities.

Arbitration. Procedure. Existing tribunals. Negotiation. Fees and exemptions. Most favored nation clause. National treatment. Customs exemptions. Competency certificate. Routes and logistics. Navigational conditions. Permit designation. Air transport. Airport facilities. Airworthiness certificates. Conditions of airlines operating permission. Operating authorizations and regulations. Licenses and certificates of nationality.
INTL ORGS: International Civil Aviation Organization.
PROCEDURE: Amendment. Future Procedures Contemplated. Registration. Termination.
PARTIES:
Finland
Sweden
ANNEX
496 UNTS 340. Sweden. Amendment 25 Aug 62.
496 UNTS 340. Finland. Amendment 25 Aug 62.
601 UNTS 339. Finland. Amendment 26 Mar 64. Force 26 Mar 64.
601 UNTS 339. Sweden. Amendment 26 Mar 64. Force 26 Mar 64.
646 UNTS 343. Sweden. Amendment 5 Apr 66. Force 5 Apr 66.
646 UNTS 343. Finland. Amendment 5 Apr 66. Force 5 Apr 66.

101319   Bilateral Agreement   **95 UNTS 109**
SIGNED: 24 Jun 49   FORCE: 24 Jun 49
REGISTERED: 18 Jul 51 ICAO (Civil Aviat)
ARTICLES: 14 LANGUAGE: English. French.
HEADNOTE: AIR SERVICES
TOPIC: Air Transport
CONCEPTS: Definition of terms. Detailed regulations. Annex or appendix reference. Conformity with municipal law. General cooperation. Exchange of information and documents. Licenses and permits. Recognition of legal documents. Use of facilities. Arbitration. Procedure. Existing tribunals. Negotiation. Fees and exemptions. Non-interest rates and fees. Most favored nation clause. National treatment. Customs exemptions. Routes and logistics. Permit designation. Airport facilities. Airworthiness certificates. Conditions of airlines operating permission. Operating authorizations and regulations. Licenses and certificates of nationality.
INTL ORGS: International Civil Aviation Organization.
PROCEDURE: Amendment. Future Procedures Contemplated. Registration. Termination.
PARTIES:
India
Switzerland

101320   Bilateral Agreement   **95 UNTS 123**
SIGNED: 8 Dec 49   FORCE: 20 Sep 50
REGISTERED: 18 Jul 51 ICAO (Civil Aviat)
ARTICLES: 19 LANGUAGE: Arabic. Dutch. English.
HEADNOTE: ESTABLISHMENT AIR SERVICES
TOPIC: Air Transport
CONCEPTS: Definition of terms. Detailed regulations. Annex or appendix reference. Conformity with municipal law. General cooperation. Exchange of information and documents. Arbitration. Procedure. Existing tribunals. Negotiation. Non-interest rates and fees. Customs exemptions. Routes and logistics. Navigational conditions. Permit designation. Air transport. Conditions of airlines operating permission. Operating authorizations and regulations.
INTL ORGS: International Civil Aviation Organization.
PROCEDURE: Amendment. Future Procedures Contemplated. Ratification. Registration. Termination.
PARTIES:
Netherlands
United Arab Rep
ANNEX
200 UNTS 278. United Arab Rep. Amendment 20 Jul 54. Force 20 Jul 54.
200 UNTS 278.   Netherlands.   Amendment 21 Jun 54. Force 20 Jul 54.
216 UNTS 394.   Netherlands.   Amendment 21 Sep 53. Force 19 Oct 53.
216 UNTS 394. United Arab Rep. Amendment 19 Oct 53. Force 19 Oct 53.
311 UNTS 338.   Netherlands.   Amendment 14 Jul 56. Force 8 Aug 56.

311 UNTS 338. United Arab Rep. Amendment 8 Aug 56. Force 8 Aug 56.

101321   Bilateral Agreement   **95 UNTS 157**
SIGNED: 11 Mar 50   FORCE: 30 Sep 50
REGISTERED: 18 Jul 51 ICAO (Civil Aviat)
ARTICLES: 19 LANGUAGE: Arabic. English. Norwegian.
HEADNOTE: ESTABLISHMENT SCHEDULED AIR SERVICES
TOPIC: Air Transport
CONCEPTS: Definition of terms. Detailed regulations. Exceptions and exemptions. Annex or appendix reference. Conformity with municipal law. General cooperation. Exchange of information and documents. Arbitration. Procedure. Existing tribunals. Negotiation. Non-interest rates and fees. Customs exemptions. Routes and logistics. Navigational conditions. Permit designation. Air transport. Conditions of airlines operating permission. Operating authorizations and regulations.
INTL ORGS: International Civil Aviation Organization.
PROCEDURE: Amendment. Future Procedures Contemplated. Ratification. Registration. Termination.
PARTIES:
Norway
United Arab Rep
ANNEX
163 UNTS 376. Norway. Amendment 9 Aug 52. Force 12 Oct 52.
163 UNTS 376. United Arab Rep. Amendment 12 Oct 52. Force 12 Oct 52.
200 UNTS 284. Norway. Amendment 9 May 54. Force 4 Jun 54.
200 UNTS 284. United Arab Rep. Amendment 4 Jun 54. Force 4 Jun 54.

101322   Bilateral Agreement   **95 UNTS 197**
SIGNED: 14 Mar 50   FORCE: 30 Sep 50
REGISTERED: 18 Jul 51 ICAO (Civil Aviat)
ARTICLES: 19 LANGUAGE: Arabic. Danish. English.
HEADNOTE: ESTABLISHMENT SCHEDULED AIR SERVICES
TOPIC: Air Transport
CONCEPTS: Definition of terms. Detailed regulations. Exceptions and exemptions. Annex or appendix reference. Conformity with municipal law. General cooperation. Exchange of information and documents. Arbitration. Procedure. Existing tribunals. Negotiation. Non-interest rates and fees. Customs exemptions. Routes and logistics. Navigational conditions. Permit designation. Air transport. Conditions of airlines operating permission. Operating authorizations and regulations.
INTL ORGS: International Civil Aviation Organization.
PROCEDURE: Amendment. Future Procedures Contemplated. Ratification. Registration. Termination.
PARTIES:
Denmark
United Arab Rep
ANNEX
150 UNTS 374.   Denmark.   Amendment 16 Jun 52. Force 15 Jul 52.
150 UNTS 374. United Arab Rep. Amendment 15 Jul 52. Force 15 Jul 52.
200 UNTS 291. Denmark. Amendment 8 May 54. Force 4 Jun 54.
200 UNTS 291. United Arab Rep. Amendment 4 Jun 54. Force 4 Jun 54.

101323   Bilateral Agreement   **95 UNTS 237**
SIGNED: 22 Mar 50   FORCE: 22 Mar 50
REGISTERED: 18 Jul 51 ICAO (Civil Aviat)
ARTICLES: 11 LANGUAGE: English.
HEADNOTE: AIR TRANSPORTATION
TOPIC: Air Transport
CONCEPTS: Exceptions and exemptions. Annex or appendix reference. Conformity with municipal law. Licenses and permits. Recognition of legal documents. Use of facilities. Arbitration. Procedure. Existing tribunals. Negotiation. Competence of tribunal. Reexport of goods, etc.. Fees and exemptions. Most favored nation clause. National treatment. Customs exemptions. Compe-

tency certificate. Routes and logistics. Navigational conditions. Permit designation. Air transport. Airport facilities. Airworthiness certificates. Conditions of airlines operating permission. Operating authorizations and regulations. Licenses and certificates of nationality.
INTL ORGS: International Civil Aviation Organization.
PROCEDURE: Amendment. Registration. Termination.
PARTIES:
Iceland
Netherlands

101324   Bilateral Exchange   **95 UNTS 249**
SIGNED: 28 Apr 50   FORCE: 28 Apr 50
REGISTERED: 18 Jul 51 ICAO (Civil Aviat)
ARTICLES: 2 LANGUAGE: English.
HEADNOTE: AIR SERVICES
TOPIC: Air Transport
CONCEPTS: Licenses and certificates of nationality.
PARTIES:
Australia
UK Great Britain

101325   Bilateral Agreement   **95 UNTS 255**
SIGNED: 15 May 50   FORCE: 1 Feb 51
REGISTERED: 18 Jul 51 ICAO (Civil Aviat)
ARTICLES: 19 LANGUAGE: Arabic. French.
HEADNOTE: REGULAR AIR TRANSPORT SERVICES
TOPIC: Air Transport
CONCEPTS: Detailed regulations. Exceptions and exemptions. Annex or appendix reference. Conformity with municipal law. General cooperation. Exchange of information and documents. Arbitration. Procedure. Existing tribunals. Negotiation. Non-interest rates and fees. Customs exemptions. Routes and logistics. Navigational conditions. Permit designation. Air transport. Conditions of airlines operating permission. Operating authorizations and regulations.
INTL ORGS: International Civil Aviation Organization.
PROCEDURE: Amendment. Denunciation. Future Procedures Contemplated. Ratification. Registration. Termination.
PARTIES:
Switzerland
United Arab Rep
ANNEX
496 UNTS 344.   Switzerland.   Amendment 13 Apr 59.
496 UNTS 344. United Arab Rep. Amendment 13 Apr 59.

101326   Bilateral Agreement   **95 UNTS 277**
SIGNED: 26 May 50   FORCE: 10 Jan 51
REGISTERED: 18 Jul 51 ICAO (Civil Aviat)
ARTICLES: 14 LANGUAGE: English. Icelandic.
HEADNOTE: CERTAIN AIR TRANSPORT SERVICES
TOPIC: Air Transport
CONCEPTS: Airport facilities. Airport equipment. Airworthiness certificates. Operating authorizations and regulations.
INTL ORGS: International Civil Aviation Organization.
PARTIES:
Iceland
UK Great Britain

101327   Bilateral Agreement   **95 UNTS 303**
SIGNED: 20 Jun 50   FORCE: 20 Jun 50
REGISTERED: 18 Jul 51 ICAO (Civil Aviat)
ARTICLES: 15 LANGUAGE: Dutch. Spanish.
HEADNOTE: REGULATION CIVIL AIRLINES
TOPIC: Air Transport
CONCEPTS: Annex or appendix reference. General cooperation. Licenses and permits. Recognition of legal documents. Use of facilities. Investigation of violations. Arbitration. Procedure. Competence of tribunal. Reexport of goods, etc.. Compensation. Fees and exemptions. Non-interest rates and fees. National treatment. Customs duties. Customs exemptions. Competency certificate. Routes and logistics. Navigational conditions. Permit designation. Air transport. Airport facilities. Airworthiness certificates. Conditions of airlines operating permission. Operating au-

thorizations and regulations. Licenses and certificates of nationality.
PROCEDURE: Amendment. Denunciation.
PARTIES:
Netherlands
Spain

ANNEX
200 UNTS 294. Netherlands. Amendment 10 Jun 53. Force 20 Jul 53.
200 UNTS 294. Spain. Amendment 20 Jul 53. Force 20 Jul 53.
200 UNTS 298. Netherlands. Amendment 27 Mar 54. Force 24 Mar 54.
200 UNTS 298. Spain. Amendment 27 Mar 54. Force 24 Mar 54.
311 UNTS 339. Netherlands. Amendment 14 Apr 56. Force 18 Jun 56.
311 UNTS 339. Spain. Amendment 18 Jun 56. Force 18 Jun 56.

101328 Bilateral Agreement **96 UNTS 3**
SIGNED: 22 Jun 50 FORCE: 11 May 51
REGISTERED: 18 Jul 51 ICAO (Civil Aviat)
ARTICLES: 9 LANGUAGE: Danish. French.
HEADNOTE: AIR SERVICES
TOPIC: Air Transport
CONCEPTS: Air transport. Airport facilities. Conditions of airlines operating permission. Operating authorizations and regulations. Licenses and certificates of nationality.
INTL ORGS: International Civil Aviation Organization.
PROCEDURE: Termination.
PARTIES:
Denmark
Switzerland

ANNEX
192 UNTS 338. Denmark. Amendment 4 Aug 53. Force 4 Aug 53.
192 UNTS 338. Switzerland. Amendment 4 Aug 53. Force 4 Aug 53.
496 UNTS 348. Switzerland. Amendment 14 Mar 57.
496 UNTS 348. Denmark. Amendment 14 Mar 57.

101329 Bilateral Agreement **96 UNTS 23**
SIGNED: 31 Jul 50 FORCE: 31 Jul 50
REGISTERED: 18 Jul 51 ICAO (Civil Aviat)
ARTICLES: 13 LANGUAGE: English. French.
HEADNOTE: AIR SERVICES
TOPIC: Air Transport
CONCEPTS: Definition of terms. Detailed regulations. Exceptions and exemptions. Annex or appendix reference. Conformity with municipal law. General cooperation. Exchange of information and documents. Arbitration. Procedure. Existing tribunals. Reexport of goods, etc.. Non-interest rates and fees. Most favored nation clause. Customs exemptions. Routes and logistics. Permit designation. Airport facilities. Conditions of airlines operating permission. Operating authorizations and regulations.
INTL ORGS: International Civil Aviation Organization.
PROCEDURE: Amendment. Future Procedures Contemplated. Registration. Termination.
PARTIES:
France
Pakistan

101330 Bilateral Agreement **96 UNTS 45**
SIGNED: 14 Sep 50 FORCE: 14 Sep 50
REGISTERED: 18 Jul 51 ICAO (Civil Aviat)
ARTICLES: 14 LANGUAGE: English.
HEADNOTE: AIR TRANSPORT
TOPIC: Air Transport
CONCEPTS: Definition of terms. Exceptions and exemptions. Annex or appendix reference. Nonprejudice to third party. Conformity with municipal law. Licenses and permits. Recognition of legal documents. Use of facilities. Procedure. Special tribunals. Competence of tribunal. Indemnities and reimbursements. Fees and exemptions. Most favored nation clause. National treatment. Customs exemptions. Competency certificate. Routes and logistics. Navigational conditions. Permit designation. Air transport. Airport facilities. Airworthiness certificates. Conditions of airlines operating permission. Operating

authorizations and regulations. Licenses and certificates of nationality.
INTL ORGS: International Civil Aviation Organization.
PROCEDURE: Amendment. Future Procedures Contemplated. Registration. Termination.
PARTIES:
Burma
Sweden

ANNEX
216 UNTS 398. Burma. Supplementation 15 Feb 52. Force 15 Feb 52.
216 UNTS 398. Sweden. Supplementation 12 Feb 52. Force 15 Feb 52.

101331 Bilateral Exchange **96 UNTS 63**
SIGNED: 6 Oct 50 FORCE: 1 Jan 51
REGISTERED: 18 Jul 51 ICAO (Civil Aviat)
ARTICLES: 2 LANGUAGE: English. French.
HEADNOTE: NON-SCHEDULED COMMERCIAL AIR SERVICES
TOPIC: Air Transport
CONCEPTS: Exceptions and exemptions. Territorial application. Domestic legislation. Registration certificate. Passenger transport. Routes and logistics. Transport of goods. Air transport. Conditions of airlines operating permission. Overflights and technical stops. Operating authorizations and regulations.
INTL ORGS: International Civil Aviation Organization.
PROCEDURE: Termination. Application to Non-self-governing Territories.
PARTIES:
France
UK Great Britain

ANNEX
425 UNTS 321. UK Great Britain. Termination 10 Feb 60. Force 11 Apr 60.

101332 Bilateral Agreement **96 UNTS 77**
SIGNED: 10 Nov 50 FORCE: 10 Nov 50
REGISTERED: 18 Jul 51 ICAO (Civil Aviat)
ARTICLES: 13 LANGUAGE: English. Thai.
HEADNOTE: AIR SERVICES
TOPIC: Air Transport
CONCEPTS: Air transport. Airport facilities. Conditions of airlines operating permission. Operating authorizations and regulations. Licenses and certificates of nationality.
INTL ORGS: International Civil Aviation Organization.
PROCEDURE: Termination.
PARTIES:
Thailand
UK Great Britain

ANNEX
192 UNTS 342. Thailand. Amendment 5 Apr 54. Force 5 Apr 54.
192 UNTS 342. UK Great Britain. Amendment 5 Apr 54. Force 5 Apr 54.
254 UNTS 408. UK Great Britain. Amendment 6 Sep 56. Force 8 Oct 56.
254 UNTS 408. Thailand. Amendment 8 Oct 56. Force 8 Oct 56.
412 UNTS 308. Thailand. Amendment 5 Nov 59. Force 5 Nov 59.
412 UNTS 308. UK Great Britain. Amendment 26 Oct 51. Force 5 Nov 59.
412 UNTS 310. Thailand. Amendment 28 Dec 60. Force 22 Dec 61.
412 UNTS 310. UK Great Britain. Amendment 22 Dec 61. Force 22 Dec 61.
420 UNTS 342. UK Great Britain. Amendment 2 Jun 61. Force 2 Jun 61.
420 UNTS 342. Thailand. Amendment 15 Feb 61. Force 2 Jun 61.
659 UNTS 330.
659 UNTS 330. Thailand. Amendment 16 Aug 68. Force 16 Aug 68.

101333 Bilateral Agreement **96 UNTS 123**
SIGNED: 2 Feb 51 FORCE: 2 Feb 51
REGISTERED: 18 Jul 51 ICAO (Civil Aviat)
ARTICLES: 6 LANGUAGE: English.
HEADNOTE: TECHNICAL ASSISTANCE
TOPIC: Tech Assistance
CONCEPTS: Definition of terms. Treaty implementation. Annex or appendix reference. Privileges and immunities. General cooperation. Exchange of information and documents. Personnel. Public

information. Responsibility and liability. Title and deeds. Use of facilities. Professorships. Scholarships and grants. Vocational training. Research and scientific projects. Accounting procedures. Exchange rates and regulations. Expense sharing formulae. Local currency. Claims and settlements. Domestic obligation. General technical assistance. Materials, equipment and services. IGO status. Conformity with IGO decisions.
PROCEDURE: Amendment. Termination.
PARTIES:
Ethiopia
ICAO (Civil Aviat)

101334 Bilateral Agreement **96 UNTS 141**
SIGNED: 19 Feb 51 FORCE: 19 Feb 51
REGISTERED: 18 Jul 51 ICAO (Civil Aviat)
ARTICLES: 7 LANGUAGE: English.
HEADNOTE: TECHNICAL ASSISTANCE
TOPIC: Tech Assistance
CONCEPTS: Definition of terms. Annex or appendix reference. Privileges and immunities. General cooperation. Personnel. Responsibility and liability. Title and deeds. Scholarships and grants. Vocational training. Research and scientific projects. Exchange rates and regulations. Expense sharing formulae. Local currency. Claims and settlements. Domestic obligation. General technical assistance. Materials, equipment and services. IGO status. Conformity with IGO decisions.
PROCEDURE: Amendment. Termination.
PARTIES:
Israel
ICAO (Civil Aviat)

101335 Bilateral Agreement **96 UNTS 155**
SIGNED: 14 Apr 51 FORCE: 1 May 51
REGISTERED: 18 Jul 51 ICAO (Civil Aviat)
ARTICLES: 9 LANGUAGE: English. French.
HEADNOTE: HEADQUARTERS CIVIL AVIATION ORGANIZATION
TOPIC: IGO Status/Immunit
CONCEPTS: Airport facilities. IGO status.
INTL ORGS: International Court of Justice. United Nations.
PARTIES:
Canada
ICAO (Civil Aviat)

101336 Bilateral Agreement **96 UNTS 181**
SIGNED: 19 Apr 51 FORCE: 19 Apr 51
REGISTERED: 18 Jul 51 ICAO (Civil Aviat)
ARTICLES: 7 LANGUAGE: English.
HEADNOTE: TECHNICAL ASSISTANCE
TOPIC: Tech Assistance
CONCEPTS: Definition of terms. Annex or appendix reference. Privileges and immunities. General cooperation. Personnel. Responsibility and liability. Title and deeds. Professorships. Scholarships and grants. Vocational training. Research and scientific projects. Expense sharing formulae. Local currency. Domestic obligation. General technical assistance. Materials, equipment and services. IGO status. Conformity with IGO decisions.
PROCEDURE: Amendment. Termination.
PARTIES:
ICAO (Civil Aviat)
Thailand

101337 Bilateral Agreement **96 UNTS 193**
SIGNED: 7 Jun 51 FORCE: 7 Jun 51
REGISTERED: 18 Jul 51 ICAO (Civil Aviat)
ARTICLES: 7 LANGUAGE: English.
HEADNOTE: TECHNICAL ASSISTANCE
TOPIC: Tech Assistance
CONCEPTS: Definition of terms. Annex or appendix reference. Privileges and immunities. General cooperation. Responsibility and liability. Title and deeds. Professorships. Vocational training. Research and scientific projects. Exchange rates and regulations. Expense sharing formulae. Local currency. Domestic obligation. General technical assistance. Materials, equipment and services. IGO status. Conformity with IGO decisions.
PROCEDURE: Amendment. Termination.

PARTIES:
Iceland
ICAO (Civil Aviat)

101338 Bilateral Treaty **96 UNTS 207**
SIGNED: 24 Mar 50 FORCE: 6 Jun 51
REGISTERED: 20 Jul 51 Turkey
ARTICLES: 25 LANGUAGE: French.
HEADNOTE: FRIENDSHIP CONCILIATION JUDI-
CIAL SETTLEMENT
TOPIC: General Amity
CONCEPTS: Treaty implementation. Treaty inter-
pretation. Friendship and amity. Domestic legis-
lation. Establishment of commission. Domestic
jurisdiction. Existing tribunals. Conciliation.
INTL ORGS: International Court of Justice. Special
Commission.
PROCEDURE: Denunciation. Duration. Ratification.
PARTIES:
Italy
Turkey
ANNEX
137 UNTS 340. Pakistan. Implementation
30 Jun 52. Force 30 Jun 52.
137 UNTS 340. USA (United States). Implementation 30 Jun 52. Force 30 Jun 52.
137 UNTS 348. Pakistan. Implementation
30 Jun 52. Force 30 Jun 52.
137 UNTS 348. USA (United States). Implementation 30 Jun 52. Force 30 Jun 52.
137 UNTS 352. Pakistan. Implementation
30 Jun 52. Force 30 Jun 52.
137 UNTS 352. USA (United States). Implementation 30 Jun 52. Force 30 Jun 52.
137 UNTS 356. Pakistan. Implementation
17 May 52. Force 17 May 52.
137 UNTS 356. USA (United States). Implementa
tion 17 May 52. Force 17 May 52.
137 UNTS 362. USA (United States). Implementation 17 May 52. Force 17 May 52.
137 UNTS 362. Pakistan. Implementation
17 May 52. Force 17 May 52.
137 UNTS 370. Pakistan. Implementation
17 May 52. Force 17 May 52.
137 UNTS 370. USA (United States). Implementation 17 May 52. Force 17 May 52.
137 UNTS 376. USA (United States). Implementation 17 May 52. Force 17 May 52.
137 UNTS 376. Pakistan. Implementation
17 May 52. Force 17 May 52.
137 UNTS 382. Pakistan. Implementation
30 Jun 52. Force 30 Jun 52.
137 UNTS 382. USA (United States). Implementation 30 Jun 52. Force 30 Jun 52.
137 UNTS 386. Pakistan. Implementation
17 May 52. Force 17 May 52.
137 UNTS 386. USA (United States). Implementation 17 May 52. Force 17 May 52.

101339 Bilateral Treaty **96 UNTS 223**
SIGNED: 4 Mar 48 FORCE: 1 Jul 51
REGISTERED: 24 Jul 51 Denmark
ARTICLES: 5 LANGUAGE: Danish. Spanish.
HEADNOTE: TREATY COMMERCE NAVIGATION
TOPIC: General Economic
CONCEPTS: Exceptions and exemptions. Annex or
appendix reference. General property. Establish-
ment of trade relations. Most favored nation
clause. Navigational conditions.
PROCEDURE: Denunciation. Ratification.
PARTIES:
Denmark
Guatemala

101340 Multilateral Convention **96 UNTS 237**
SIGNED: 1 Jul 49 FORCE: 18 Jul 51
REGISTERED: 24 Jul 51 ILO (Labor Org)
ARTICLES: 25 LANGUAGE: English. French.
HEADNOTE: FEE-CHARGING EMPLOYMENT
AGENCIES
TOPIC: ILO Labor
CONCEPTS: Definition of terms. Detailed regula-
tions. Exceptions and exemptions. Annex type
material. Previous treaty extension. Exchange of
information and documents. Incorporation of
treaty provisions into national law. Jurisdiction.
Investigation of violations. ILO conventions. Em-
ployment regulations. Labor statistics.
INTL ORGS: International Labour Organization.
United Nations.
PROCEDURE: Amendment. Denunciation. Dura-

tion. Ratification. Registration. Renewal or Revival.
PARTIES:
Multilateral
ANNEX
118 UNTS 308. Finland. Ratification 22 Dec 51.
Force 22 Dec 52.
124 UNTS 319. Turkey. Ratification 23 Jan 52.
Force 23 Jan 53.
131 UNTS 343. Netherlands. Ratification
20 May 52. Force 20 May 53.
131 UNTS 343. Pakistan. Ratification 26 May 52.
Force 26 May 53.
152 UNTS 314. Guatemala. Ratification 3 Jan 53.
Force 3 Jan 54.
157 UNTS 369. Italy. Ratification 9 Jan 53. Force
9 Jan 54.
160 UNTS 403. Cuba. Ratification 3 Feb 53.
Force 3 Feb 53.
165 UNTS 330. France. Ratification 10 Mar 53.
Force 10 Mar 54.
198 UNTS 392. Bolivia. Ratification 19 Jul 54.
Force 19 Jul 55.
199 UNTS 336. Germany, West. Ratification
8 Sep 54. Force 8 Sep 55.
201 UNTS 371. Poland. Ratification 25 Oct 54.
Force 25 Oct 55.
212 UNTS 395. France. Martinique.
212 UNTS 395. France. Guadeloupe.
212 UNTS 395. Netherlands. Dutch New Guinea.
Declaration 10 Jun 55.
212 UNTS 395. Netherlands. Netherlands Antilles. Declaration 10 Jun 55.
212 UNTS 395. France. Reunion.
212 UNTS 395. France. French Guinea.
212 UNTS 395. Netherlands. Surinam.
248 UNTS 405. Japan. Ratification 11 Jun 56.
Force 11 Jun 57.
272 UNTS 257. Brazil. Ratification 21 Jun 57.
Force 21 Jun 58.
272 UNTS 257. Syria. Ratification 7 Jun 57.
Force 7 Jun 58.
300 UNTS 372. Ceylon (Sri Lanka). Ratification
30 Apr 58. Force 30 Apr 59.
312 UNTS 411. Belgium.
312 UNTS 411. Belgium. Ratification 4 Jul 58.
Force 4 Jul 59.
320 UNTS 339. Luxembourg. Ratification
15 Dec 58. Force 15 Dec 59.
366 UNTS 397. Costa Rica. Ratification 2 Jun 60.
Force 2 Jun 61.
373 UNTS 361. United Arab Rep. United Arab
Rep.
399 UNTS 266. Ivory Coast. Ratification
22 May 61. Force 22 May 62.
401 UNTS 254. Gabon. Ratification 13 Jun 61.
Force 13 Jun 62.
401 UNTS 254. Israel. Ratification 19 Jun 61.
Force 19 Jun 62.
413 UNTS 365. Syria. Ratification 30 Oct 61.
434 UNTS 286. Libya. Qualified Ratification
20 Jun 62. Force 20 Jun 63.
444 UNTS 330. Algeria. Succession 19 Oct 62.
444 UNTS 330. Senegal. Qualified Ratification
22 Oct 62.
495 UNTS 297. Mauritania. Ratification
31 Mar 64. Force 31 Mar 65.

101341 Multilateral Convention **96 UNTS 257**
SIGNED: 1 Jul 49 FORCE: 18 Jul 51
REGISTERED: 24 Jul 51 ILO (Labor Org)
ARTICLES: 16 LANGUAGE: English. French.
HEADNOTE: RIGHT TO ORGANIZE BARGAIN COL-
LECTIVELY
TOPIC: ILO Labor
CONCEPTS: Detailed regulations. Territorial appli-
cation. Non-prejudice to third party. Missing per-
sons. Domestic legislation. Incorporation of
treaty provisions into national law. ILO conven-
tions. Anti-discrimination. Employment regula-
tions. Right to organize.
INTL ORGS: International Labour Organization.
United Nations.
PROCEDURE: Amendment. Denunciation. Duration. Ratification. Registration. Renewal or Revival.
PARTIES:
Multilateral
ANNEX
109 UNTS 322.
118 UNTS 309.
121 UNTS 331.
122 UNTS 344.
131 UNTS 344.

134 UNTS 380.
149 UNTS 412.
173 UNTS 403.
178 UNTS 391.
182 UNTS 227.
184 UNTS 345.
196 UNTS 348.
207 UNTS 353.
211 UNTS 410.
212 UNTS 396.
214 UNTS 372.
248 UNTS 406.
249 UNTS 459.
261 UNTS 402.
264 UNTS 348.
266 UNTS 394.
268 UNTS 358.
269 UNTS 289.
272 UNTS 258.
274 UNTS 343.
293 UNTS 379.
302 UNTS 358.
304 UNTS 404.
312 UNTS 412.
318 UNTS 420.
320 UNTS 340.
327 UNTS 355.
330 UNTS 361.
337 UNTS 405.
338 UNTS 339.
356 UNTS 354.
366 UNTS 398.
380 UNTS 418.
381 UNTS 398.
384 UNTS 359.
396 UNTS 326.
396 UNTS 327.
399 UNTS 267
401 UNTS 255.
406 UNTS 302.
413 UNTS 366.
422 UNTS 330. UK Great Britain. Gambia.
422 UNTS 331.
425 UNTS 322.
429 UNTS 276.
431 UNTS 292.
434 UNTS 287.
443 UNTS 336.
444 UNTS 332.
449 UNTS 298.
452 UNTS 366.
455 UNTS 464.
457 UNTS 358.
468 UNTS 434.
471 UNTS 374.
483 UNTS 414.
488 UNTS 365.
495 UNTS 298.
504 UNTS 356.
524 UNTS 365.
530 UNTS 415. UK Great Britain. Malawi. Ratification 22 Mar 65.
547 UNTS 367.
548 UNTS 402.
560 UNTS 320.
567 UNTS 350.
609 UNTS 339.
638 UNTS 334.
655 UNTS 412.

101342 Multilateral Convention **96 UNTS 271**
SIGNED: 21 Mar 50 FORCE: 25 Jul 51
REGISTERED: 25 Jul 51 United Nations
ARTICLES: 28 LANGUAGE: Chinese. English.
French. Russian. Spanish.
HEADNOTE: SUPPRESSION TRAFFIC PERSONS
EXPLOITATION PROSTITUTION OTHERS
TOPIC: Admin Cooperation
CONCEPTS: Human rights. Extradition, deporta-
tion and repatriation. Conformity with municipal
law. General cooperation. Informational records.
Domestic legislation. Public information. Investi-
gation of violations. Existing tribunals. Educa-
tion.
INTL ORGS: International Court of Justice. United
Nations.
PROCEDURE: Accession. Denunciation. Ratifica-
tion.
PARTIES:
Denmark SIGNED: 12 Feb 51
Ecuador SIGNED: 24 Mar 50
India SIGNED: 9 May 50
Israel RATIFIED: 28 Dec 50 FORCE: 25 Jul 51
Liberia SIGNED: 21 Mar 50
Luxembourg SIGNED: 9 Oct 50

Pakistan SIGNED: 21 Mar 50
Philippines SIGNED: 20 Dec 50
South Africa SIGNED: 16 Oct 50
Yugoslavia SIGNED: 6 Feb 51 RATIFIED:
28 Apr 51 FORCE: 25 Jul 51
ANNEX
119 UNTS 360. Norway. Accession 23 Jan 52.
Force 22 Apr 52.
131 UNTS 345. Poland. Accession 2 Jun 52.
Force 31 Aug 52.
134 UNTS 381. Pakistan. Ratification 11 Jul 52.
Force 9 Oct 52.
136 UNTS 389. Cuba. Accession 4 Sep 52. Force
3 Dec 52.
137 UNTS 339. Philippines. Ratification
19 Sep 52. Force 18 Dec 52.
152 UNTS 315. India. Ratification 9 Jan 53. Force
9 Apr 53.
172 UNTS 349. Haiti. Accession 26 Aug 53.
Force 24 Nov 53.
196 UNTS 349. USSR (Soviet Union). Qualified
Accession 11 Aug 54. Force 9 Nov 54.
201 UNTS 372. Ukrainian SSR. Qualified Accession 15 Nov 54. Force 13 Feb 55.
216 UNTS 402. Iraq. Accession 22 Sep 55. Force
21 Dec 55.
256 UNTS 343. Libya. Accession 3 Dec 56. Force
3 Mar 57.
281 UNTS 399. Argentina. Accession 15 Nov 57.
Force 13 Feb 58.
288 UNTS 363. Czechoslovakia. Accession
14 Mar 58. Force 12 Jun 58.
293 UNTS 342. Ceylon (Sri Lanka). Accession
15 Apr 58. Force 14 Jul 58.
299 UNTS 418. Japan. Accession 1 May 58.
Force 30 Jul 58.
308 UNTS 311. Ceylon (Sri Lanka). Accession
7 Aug 58. Force 5 Nov 58.
312 UNTS 413. Brazil. Ratification 12 Sep 58.
Force 11 Dec 58.
314 UNTS 337. Albania. Qualified Accession
6 Nov 58. Force 4 Feb 59.
330 UNTS 362. United Arab Rep. Accession
12 Jun 59. Force 10 Sep 59.
380 UNTS 419. France. Qualified Accession
19 Nov 60. Force 17 Feb 61.
381 UNTS 399. Argentina. Accession 1 Dec 60.
Force 1 Mar 61.
422 UNTS 332. Korea, South. Accession
13 Feb 62. Force 14 May 62.
426 UNTS 339. Guinea. Accession 26 Apr 62.
Force 25 Jul 62.
431 UNTS 293. Spain. Accession 18 Jun 62.
Force 16 Sep 62.
435 UNTS 320. Spain. Other 23 Aug 62.
435 UNTS 320. Upper Volta. Accession
24 Aug 62. Force 26 Nov 62.
480 UNTS 331. Algeria. Qualified Accession
31 Oct 63.
539 UNTS 352. Belgium. Accession 22 Jun 65.
Force 20 Sep 65.
653 UNTS 456. Venezuela. Accession 18 Dec 68.
Force 18 Mar 69.

101343 Bilateral Agreement **97 UNTS 3**
SIGNED: 14 Jun 51 FORCE: 14 Jun 51
REGISTERED: 26 Jul 51 United Nations
ARTICLES: 9 LANGUAGE: English. Spanish.
HEADNOTE: UNICEF ACTIVITIES
TOPIC: IGO Operations
CONCEPTS: General consular functions. Diplo-
matic privileges. Privileges and immunities. Ex-
change of information and documents. Assis-
tance to United Nations.
INTL ORGS: United Nations.
PROCEDURE: Duration.
PARTIES:
Panama
UNICEF (Children)
ANNEX
222 UNTS 406. UNICEF (Children). Supplementa-
tion 8 Dec 55. Force 8 Dec 55.
222 UNTS 406. Panama. Supplementation
24 Nov 55. Force 8 Dec 55.

101344 Bilateral Agreement **97 UNTS 21**
SIGNED: 25 Jun 51 FORCE: 26 Jul 51
REGISTERED: 26 Jul 51 United Nations
ARTICLES: 6 LANGUAGE: English. French.
HEADNOTE: TECHNICAL ASSISTANCE
TOPIC: Tech Assistance
CONCEPTS: Treaty implementation. Annex or ap-

pendix reference. Privileges and immunities.
General cooperation. Personnel. Title and deeds.
Professorships. Vocational training. Research
and scientific projects. Expense sharing formulae. Local currency. Domestic obligation. General technical assistance. Materials, equipment
and services. IGO status. Conformity with IGO
decisions.
PROCEDURE: Amendment. Registration. Termination.
PARTIES:
Israel
United Nations

ANNEX
286 UNTS 342. Israel. Force 15 Jul 57.
286 UNTS 342. United Nations. Force 15 Jul 57.

101345 Multilateral Convention **97 UNTS 31**
SIGNED: 17 Sep 48 FORCE: 15 Mar 50
REGISTERED: 31 Jul 51 UK Great Britain
ARTICLES: 14 LANGUAGE: English. French. Rus-
sian.
HEADNOTE: MARITIME MOBILE RADIO SERVICE
TOPIC: Telecommunications
CONCEPTS: Definition of terms. Previous treaty re-
placement. Bands and frequency allocation. Ra-
dio-telephone-telegraphic communications.
Conformity with IGO decisions.
INTL ORGS: International Telecommunication
Union.
PROCEDURE: Amendment. Accession. Denuncia-
tion. Ratification. Registration. Termination.
PARTIES:
Belgium SIGNED: 17 Sep 48 RATIFIED:
6 Dec 49 FORCE: 15 Mar 50
Denmark SIGNED: 17 Sep 48 RATIFIED:
2 Feb 49 FORCE: 15 Mar 50
France SIGNED: 17 Sep 48 RATIFIED:
19 Mar 50 FORCE: 19 Mar 50
France Morocco RATIFIED: 19 Mar 50 FORCE:
19 Mar 50
France Tunisia RATIFIED: 19 Mar 50 FORCE:
19 Mar 50
Greece SIGNED: 17 Sep 48
Iceland SIGNED: 17 Sep 48 RATIFIED: 4 Feb 50
FORCE: 4 Feb 50
Ireland SIGNED: 17 Sep 48 RATIFIED: 17 Jul 50
FORCE: 19 Jul 50
Italy SIGNED: 17 Sep 48
Monaco SIGNED: 17 Sep 48 FORCE: 29 Jun 50
Morocco SIGNED: 17 Sep 48
Netherlands SIGNED: 17 Sep 48 FORCE:
15 Mar 50
Norway SIGNED: 17 Sep 48 FORCE: 15 Mar 50
Portugal SIGNED: 17 Sep 48
Sweden SIGNED: 17 Sep 48 RATIFIED: 2 Jan 50
FORCE: 15 Mar 50
Tunisia SIGNED: 17 Sep 48
Turkey SIGNED: 17 Sep 48
UK Great Britain Cyprus RATIFIED: 15 Dec 49
FORCE: 15 Mar 50
UK Great Britain Gilbert Islands RATIFIED:
15 Dec 49 FORCE: 15 Mar 50
UK Great Britain Malta RATIFIED: 15 Dec 49
FORCE: 15 Mar 50
UK Great Britain SIGNED: 17 Sep 48 RATIFIED:
15 Dec 49 FORCE: 15 Mar 50

101346 Bilateral Treaty **97 UNTS 121**
SIGNED: 30 Oct 50 FORCE: 3 May 51
REGISTERED: 2 Aug 51 UK Great Britain
ARTICLES: 10 LANGUAGE: English. Nepalese.
HEADNOTE: PEACE FRIENDSHIP
TOPIC: General Amity
CONCEPTS: Definition of terms. Territorial applica-
tion. Previous treaty extension. Previous treaty
renunciation. Friendship and amity. Border traf-
fic and migration. Alien status. Diplomatic rela-
tions establishment.
PROCEDURE: Duration. Ratification. Termination.
PARTIES:
Nepal
UK Great Britain
ANNEX
100 UNTS 308. UK Great Britain. Southern
Rhodesia. Force 4 May 51.

101347 Bilateral Exchange **97 UNTS 137**
SIGNED: 6 Mar 51 FORCE: 6 Mar 51
REGISTERED: 2 Aug 51 UK Great Britain
ARTICLES: 2 LANGUAGE: English.

HEADNOTE: LEASE FLEET ANCHORAGE
TOPIC: Status of Forces
CONCEPTS: General cooperation. Innocent pas-
sage. Inland and territorial waters. Lease of mili-
tary property. Naval vessels. Airforce-army-navy
personnel ratio. Status of military forces.
PARTIES:
UK Great Britain
USA (United States)

101348 Bilateral Agreement **97 UNTS 149**
SIGNED: 23 Jan 50 FORCE: 7 Mar 51
REGISTERED: 2 Aug 51 UK Great Britain
ARTICLES: 4 LANGUAGE: English. French.
HEADNOTE: COMPENSATION WAR INJURY
TOPIC: Reparations
CONCEPTS: Definition of terms. Compensation.
National treatment. Loss and/or damage. Post-
war claims settlement.
PROCEDURE: Denunciation.
PARTIES:
France
UK Great Britain

101349 Bilateral Agreement **97 UNTS 155**
SIGNED: 28 Jan 50 FORCE: 1 Apr 51
REGISTERED: 2 Aug 51 UK Great Britain
ARTICLES: 31 LANGUAGE: English. French.
HEADNOTE: SOCIAL SECURITY
TOPIC: Non-ILO Labor
CONCEPTS: Detailed regulations. Exceptions and
exemptions. General provisions. Annex type material. General cooperation. Legal protection and
assistance. Domestic legislation. Dispute settlement. Old age and invalidity insurance. Non-ILO
labor relations. Administrative cooperation. Old
age insurance. Sickness and invalidity insurance. Social security. Payment schedules. National treatment.
PROCEDURE: Duration. Renewal or Revival. Termination.
PARTIES:
France
UK Great Britain
ANNEX
138 UNTS 474. UK Great Britain. Supplementation 9 May 52. Force 1 Jun 52.
138 UNTS 474. France. Supplementation
9 May 52. Force 1 Jun 52.

101350 Bilateral Agreement **97 UNTS 183**
SIGNED: 26 Jan 50 FORCE: 13 Jan 50
REGISTERED: 2 Aug 51 UK Great Britain
ARTICLES: 11 LANGUAGE: English.
HEADNOTE: STERLING PAYMENTS
TOPIC: Finance
CONCEPTS: General cooperation. Accounting pro-
cedures. Banking. Currency. Monetary and gold
transfers. Currency deposits. Investments. Ex-
change rates and regulations. Payment sched-
ules.
PROCEDURE: Amendment. Duration. Termination.
PARTIES:
Austria
UK Great Britain

101351 Bilateral Agreement **97 UNTS 193**
SIGNED: 21 Jul 50 FORCE: 21 Jul 50
REGISTERED: 2 Aug 51 UK Great Britain
ARTICLES: 26 LANGUAGE: English.
HEADNOTE: LONG RANGE PROVING GROUND
GUIDED MISSILES
TOPIC: Milit Installation
CONCEPTS: Definition of terms. Annex or appen-
dix reference. Visa abolition. Court procedures.
Legal protection and assistance. Use of facilities.
Compensation. Claims and settlements. Tax ex-
emptions. Customs exemptions. Ports and pilot-
age. Facilities and equipment. Postal services.
Security of information. Jurisdiction. Status of
forces. Testing ranges and sites.
PROCEDURE: Amendment. Termination.
PARTIES:
UK Great Britain
USA (United States)
ANNEX
218 UNTS 384. UK Great Britain. Amendment
11 Jul 55. Force 22 Jul 55.
218 UNTS 384. USA (United States). Amendment
22 Jul 55. Force 22 Jul 55.

266 UNTS 396. USA (United States). Amendment
4 Jan 57. Force 4 Jan 57.
266 UNTS 396. UK Great Britain. Amendment
6 Dec 56. Force 4 Jan 57.
288 UNTS 364. UK Great Britain. Amendment
1 Apr 57. Force 1 Apr 57.
288 UNTS 364. USA (United States). Amendment
1 Apr 57. Force 1 Apr 57.
619 UNTS 331. UK Great Britain. Amendment
17 Jul 67. Force 17 Jul 67.
619 UNTS 331. USA (United States). Amendment
17 Jul 67. Force 17 Jul 67.
648 UNTS 358. UK Great Britain. Amendment
3 May 68. Force 3 May 68.
648 UNTS 358. USA (United States). Amendment
3 May 68. Force 3 May 68.

101352 Multilateral Agreement **97 UNTS 227**
SIGNED: 6 Feb 47   FORCE: 29 Jul 48
REGISTERED: 10 Aug 51 Australia
ARTICLES: 21 LANGUAGE: Dutch. English. French.
HEADNOTE: ESTABLISHMENT SOUTH PACIFIC
COMMISSION
TOPIC: IGO Establishment
CONCEPTS: Establishment of commission. Fund-
ing procedures. IGO status.
INTL ORGS: United Nations. South Pacific Health
Service.
PROCEDURE: Ratification.
PARTIES:
Australia   SIGNED: 6 Feb 47   RATIFIED:
16 Apr 47 FORCE: 29 Jul 48
France SIGNED: 6 Feb 47 RATIFIED: 22 Jul 48
FORCE: 29 Jul 48
Netherlands   SIGNED: 6 Feb 47   RATIFIED:
29 Jul 48 FORCE: 29 Jul 48
New Zealand SIGNED: 6 Feb 47 RATIFIED:
26 Feb 47 FORCE: 29 Jul 48
UK Great Britain SIGNED: 6 Feb 47 RATIFIED:
25 Jun 47 FORCE: 29 Jul 48
USA (United States) SIGNED: 6 Feb 47 RATI-
FIED: 16 Feb 48 FORCE: 29 Jul 48
ANNEX
124 UNTS 320. Australia. Amendment 7 Nov 51.
Force 7 Nov 51.
124 UNTS 320. France. Amendment 7 Nov 51.
Force 7 Nov 51.
124 UNTS 320. Netherlands. Amendment
7 Nov 51. Force 7 Nov 51.
124 UNTS 320. New Zealand. Amendment
7 Nov 51. Force 7 Nov 51.
124 UNTS 320. UK Great Britain. Amendment
7 Nov 51. Force 7 Nov 51.
124 UNTS 320. USA (United States). Amendment
7 Nov 51. Force 7 Nov 51.
201 UNTS 374. Netherlands. Supplementation
5 Apr 54. Force 1 Jul 54.
201 UNTS 374. UK Great Britain. Supplementation 5 Apr 54. Force 1 Jul 54.
201 UNTS 374. USA (United States). Supplementation 5 Apr 54. Force 1 Jul 54.
201 UNTS 374. Australia. Supplementation
5 Apr 54. Force 1 Jul 54.
201 UNTS 374. France. Supplementation
5 Apr 54. Force 1 Jul 54.
201 UNTS 374. New Zealand. Supplementation
5 Apr 54. Force 1 Jul 54.
542 UNTS 350. USA (United States). Amendment
6 Oct 64. Force 15 Jul 65.
542 UNTS 350. Australia. Amendment 6 Oct 64.
Force 15 Jul 65.
542 UNTS 350. France. Amendment 15 Jul 65.
Force 15 Jul 65.
542 UNTS 350. New Zealand. Amendment
6 Oct 64. Force 15 Jul 65.
542 UNTS 350. UK Great Britain. Amendment
6 Oct 64. Force 15 Jul 65.
547 UNTS 316. Malawi. Qualified Accession
13 Oct 65.

101353 Bilateral Exchange **97 UNTS 271**
SIGNED: 28 Jul 47   FORCE: 28 Jul 47
REGISTERED: 10 Aug 51 Australia
ARTICLES: 2 LANGUAGE: English. French.
HEADNOTE: MONEY PROPERTY SUBJECTED SPE-
CIAL MEASURES ENEMY OCCUPATION
TOPIC: Reparations
CONCEPTS: Definition of terms. Exceptions and
exemptions. General cooperation. Legal protec-
tion and assistance. General property. Indemni-
ties and reimbursements. Currency. Payment
schedules. Post-war claims settlement.

PARTIES:
Australia
France

101354 Bilateral Exchange **97 UNTS 283**
SIGNED: 20 Feb 51   FORCE: 1 Apr 51
REGISTERED: 10 Aug 51 Australia
ARTICLES: 2 LANGUAGE: English.
HEADNOTE: MODIFICATION VISA REGULATIONS
TOPIC: Visas
CONCEPTS: Time limit. Visa abolition. Denial of
admission. Conformity with municipal law. Fees
and exemptions.
PROCEDURE: Termination.
PARTIES:
Australia
Netherlands

101355 Bilateral Agreement **98 UNTS 3**
SIGNED: 19 Oct 48   FORCE: 19 Oct 48
REGISTERED: 10 Aug 51 USA (United States)
ARTICLES: 8 LANGUAGE: English. French.
HEADNOTE: AIR SERVICE FACILITIES
TOPIC: Air Transport
CONCEPTS: Definition of terms. Detailed regulations. Exceptions and exemptions. Annex or appendix reference. Conformity with municipal
law. General cooperation. Exchange of information and documents. Personnel. Use of facilities.
Procedure. Existing tribunals. Negotiation.
Meteorology. Fees and exemptions. Non-interest
rates and fees. Most favored nation clause. National treatment. Customs exemptions. Routes
and logistics. Navigational equipment. Permit
designation. Airport equipment. Conditions of
airlines operating permission. Overflights and
technical stops. Operating authorizations and
regulations. Bands and frequency allocation. Facilities and equipment. Lend lease. Return of
equipment and recapture.
INTL ORGS: International Civil Aviation Organization.
PROCEDURE: Amendment. Future Procedures
Contemplated. Registration. Termination. Application to Non-self-governing Territories.
PARTIES:
France
USA (United States)

101356 Bilateral Agreement **98 UNTS 11**
SIGNED: 22 Dec 50   FORCE: 1 Aug 51
REGISTERED: 11 Aug 51 Turkey
ARTICLES: 11 LANGUAGE: French.
HEADNOTE: EXCHANGE STUDENT EMPLOYEES
TOPIC: Non-ILO Labor
CONCEPTS: Definition of terms. Detailed regula-
tions. Resident permits. Conformity with munici-
pal law. Vocational training. Employment regula-
tions. Wages and salaries. Non-ILO labor rela-
tions. Administrative cooperation. Migrant
worker. National treatment.
PROCEDURE: Denunciation. Duration. Future Pro-
cedures Contemplated. Renewal or Revival.
PARTIES:
France
Turkey

101357 Bilateral Instrument **98 UNTS 21**
SIGNED: 16 Aug 49   FORCE: 16 Aug 49
REGISTERED: 13 Aug 51 Netherlands
ARTICLES: 1 LANGUAGE: French.
HEADNOTE: REVIVAL PRE-WAR BILATERAL TREA-
TIES
TOPIC: Admin Cooperation
CONCEPTS: Revival of treaties.
PARTIES:
Italy
Netherlands

101358 Multilateral Convention **98 UNTS 101**
SIGNED: 4 May 49   FORCE: 14 Aug 51
REGISTERED: 14 Aug 51 United Nations
ARTICLES: 12 LANGUAGE: French.
HEADNOTE: SUPPRESSION WHITE SLAVE TRAF-
FIC
TOPIC: Admin Cooperation
CONCEPTS: Territorial application. Annex or ap-
pendix reference. General cooperation. Domes-
tic legislation. Investigation of violations.

INTL ORGS: United Nations.
PROCEDURE: Accession. Denunciation.
PARTIES:
Australia FORCE: 14 Aug 51
Austria FORCE: 14 Aug 51
Canada FORCE: 14 Aug 51
Ceylon (Sri Lanka) FORCE: 14 Aug 51
Chile FORCE: 14 Aug 51
Taiwan FORCE: 14 Aug 51
Czechoslovakia FORCE: 14 Aug 51
Denmark FORCE: 14 Aug 51
United Arab Rep FORCE: 14 Aug 51
Finland FORCE: 14 Aug 51
France FORCE: 14 Aug 51
India FORCE: 14 Aug 51
Iraq FORCE: 14 Aug 51
Netherlands FORCE: 14 Aug 51
Norway FORCE: 14 Aug 51
South Africa FORCE: 14 Aug 51
Switzerland FORCE: 14 Aug 51
Turkey FORCE: 14 Aug 51
UK Great Britain FORCE: 14 Aug 51
Yugoslavia FORCE: 14 Aug 51
ANNEX
121 UNTS 331. Sweden. Accession 25 Feb 52.
133 UNTS 367. Pakistan. Accession 16 Jun 52.
149 UNTS 413. Italy. Accession 13 Nov 52.
207 UNTS 354.   Luxembourg.   Accession
14 Mar 55.
229 UNTS 295. Mexico. Accession 21 Feb 56.
Force 21 Aug 56.
253 UNTS 352. Morocco. Succession 7 Nov 56.
292 UNTS 361. Ghana. Acceptance 7 Apr 58.
347 UNTS 378. Iran. Acceptance 30 Dec 59.
401 UNTS 256. Ireland. Acceptance 19 Jul 61.
405 UNTS 303. Niger. Succession 25 Aug 61.
412 UNTS 317. Cameroon. Succession 3 Nov 61.
415 UNTS 427.   Ivory   Coast.   Succession
8 Dec 61.
423 UNTS 305.   Sierra   Leone.   Succession
13 Mar 62.
424 UNTS 346. Dahomey. Succession 4 Apr 62.
437 UNTS 347. Central Afri Rep. Succession
4 Sep 62.
442 UNTS 313. Congo (Brazzaville). Succession
15 Oct 62.
456 UNTS 493.   Tanganyika.   Accession
16 Mar 63. Force 18 Sep 63.
463 UNTS 340. Senegal. Succession 2 May 63.
466 UNTS 383. Cyprus. Succession 16 May 63.
479 UNTS 356.   Madagascar.   Succession
9 Oct 63.
480 UNTS 332. Algeria. Accession 31 Oct 63.
Force 30 Apr 64.
528 UNTS 292. Jamaica. Succession 17 Mar 65.
538 UNTS 335. Malawi. Accession 10 Jun 65.
Force 10 Dec 65.
541 UNTS 309. Cuba. Acceptance 4 Aug 65.
560 UNTS 244.   Trinidad/Tobago.   Succession
11 Apr 66. Force 31 Aug 62.

101359 Bilateral Agreement **98 UNTS 115**
SIGNED: 14 Aug 51   FORCE: 14 Aug 51
REGISTERED: 14 Aug 51 United Nations
ARTICLES: 4 LANGUAGE: English.
HEADNOTE: PROVISION TECHNICAL ASSIS-
TANCE
TOPIC: Tech Assistance
CONCEPTS: Currency. Assistance. Status of ex-
perts.
PROCEDURE: Termination.
PARTIES:
India
United Nations

101360 Bilateral Agreement **98 UNTS 123**
SIGNED: 29 Apr 46   FORCE: 29 Apr 46
REGISTERED: 15 Aug 51 UK Great Britain
ARTICLES: 4 LANGUAGE: English. French.
HEADNOTE: FINANCE PAYMENTS
TOPIC: Finance
CONCEPTS: Detailed regulations. Treaty imple-
mentation. General cooperation. Accounting
procedures. Banking. Monetary and gold trans-
fers. Exchange rates and regulations. Financial
programs. Funding procedures. Interest rates.
Payment schedules. Loan repayment. Military as-
sistance. Surplus war property.
PARTIES:
France
UK Great Britain

101361　Bilateral Agreement　**98 UNTS 141**
SIGNED: 27 Dec 49　　　FORCE: 21 Mar 50
REGISTERED: 21 Aug 51 USA (United States)
ARTICLES: 14 LANGUAGE: English. Turkish.
HEADNOTE: USE FUNDS
TOPIC: Direct Aid
CONCEPTS: Definition of terms. Detailed regulations. Conformity with municipal law. Exchange of information and documents. Personnel. Establishment of commission. Exchange. Currency deposits. Exchange rates and regulations. Funding procedures. Local currency. Surplus property. Loan and credit. Internal structure.
PROCEDURE: Amendment. Ratification.
PARTIES:
　Turkey
　USA (United States)
　　　　　ANNEX
266 UNTS 404. USA (United States). Amendment 8 Jan 57. Force 8 Jan 57.
266 UNTS 404. Turkey. Amendment 8 Jan 57. Force 8 Jan 57.
371 UNTS 282. USA (United States). Amendment 1 Feb 60. Force 1 Feb 60.
371 UNTS 282. Turkey. Amendment 1 Feb 60. Force 1 Feb 60.
409 UNTS 302. Turkey. Amendment 30 May 61. Force 30 May 61.
409 UNTS 302. USA (United States). Amendment 21 Apr 61. Force 30 May 61.

101362　Bilateral Exchange　**98 UNTS 167**
SIGNED: 7 Jun 50　　　FORCE: 7 Jun 50
REGISTERED: 21 Aug 51 USA (United States)
ARTICLES: 2 LANGUAGE: English. Indonesian.
HEADNOTE: EXCHANGE OFFICIAL PUBLICATIONS
TOPIC: Admin Cooperation
CONCEPTS: Exchange of official publications. Operating agencies. Indemnities and reimbursements.
PARTIES:
　Indonesia
　USA (United States)

101363　Bilateral Exchange　**98 UNTS 175**
SIGNED: 8 May 50　　　FORCE: 8 May 50
REGISTERED: 21 Aug 51 USA (United States)
ARTICLES: 2 LANGUAGE: English. Spanish.
HEADNOTE: EXCHANGE OFFICIAL PUBLICATIONS
TOPIC: Admin Cooperation
CONCEPTS: Exchange of official publications. Operating agencies. Indemnities and reimbursements.
PARTIES:
　Spain
　USA (United States)

101364　Bilateral Exchange　**98 UNTS 183**
SIGNED: 30 Aug 49　　　FORCE: 30 Aug 49
REGISTERED: 21 Aug 51 USA (United States)
ARTICLES: 2 LANGUAGE: English. Spanish.
HEADNOTE: US MEXICO CULTURAL COOPERATION
TOPIC: IGO Establishment
CONCEPTS: Exchange. General cultural cooperation. Establishment. Headquarters and facilities.
INTL ORGS: Special Commission.
PARTIES:
　Mexico
　USA (United States)

101365　Bilateral Exchange　**98 UNTS 195**
SIGNED: 25 Mar 50　　　FORCE: 25 Mar 50
REGISTERED: 21 Aug 51 USA (United States)
ARTICLES: 2 LANGUAGE: English.
HEADNOTE: ISSUANCE ENTRY EXIT VISAS US CITIZENS VISITING YUGOSLAVIA
TOPIC: Visas
CONCEPTS: Border traffic and migration. Visas.
PARTIES:
　USA (United States)
　Yugoslavia

101366　Bilateral Exchange　**98 UNTS 201**
SIGNED: 3 May 50　　　FORCE: 3 May 50
REGISTERED: 21 Aug 51 USA (United States)

ARTICLES: 4 LANGUAGE: English. Spanish.
HEADNOTE: PASSPORT VISA FEES
TOPIC: Visas
CONCEPTS: Time limit. Non-visa travel documents. Visas. Tourism. Fees and exemptions.
PARTIES:
　Mexico
　USA (United States)

101367　Bilateral Convention　**99 UNTS 3**
SIGNED: 25 Jan 49　　　FORCE: 11 Jul 50
REGISTERED: 21 Aug 51 USA (United States)
ARTICLES: 3 LANGUAGE: English. Spanish.
HEADNOTE: TUNA RESEARCH
TOPIC: IGO Establishment
CONCEPTS: Operating agencies. Personnel. General property. Establishment of commission. Research and scientific projects. Research results. Communication satellites testing. Indemnities and reimbursements. IGO constitution.
INTL ORGS: Special Commission.
PROCEDURE: Duration. Ratification. Termination.
PARTIES:
　Mexico
　USA (United States)

101368　Bilateral Exchange　**99 UNTS 25**
SIGNED: 1 Feb 50　　　FORCE: 1 Feb 50
REGISTERED: 21 Aug 51 USA (United States)
ARTICLES: 2 LANGUAGE: English. Spanish.
HEADNOTE: TECHNICAL AGRICULTURAL MISSION
TOPIC: Tech Assistance
CONCEPTS: Investigation of violations. Banking. General technical assistance. Prisoners of war. Enemy financial interests.
INTL ORGS: Special Commission.
PARTIES:
　Nicaragua
　USA (United States)

101369　Bilateral Agreement　**99 UNTS 39**
SIGNED: 28 Dec 50　　　FORCE: 28 Dec 50
REGISTERED: 21 Aug 51 USA (United States)
ARTICLES: 5 LANGUAGE: English.
HEADNOTE: TECHNICAL COOPERATION
TOPIC: Tech Assistance
CONCEPTS: Exceptions and exemptions. Treaty implementation. Previous treaty replacement. General cooperation. Exchange of information and documents. Personnel. Public information. Reexport of goods, etc.. Financial programs. Tax exemptions. Customs duties. Customs exemptions. Domestic obligation. General technical assistance. Materials, equipment and services.
PROCEDURE: Amendment. Duration. Termination.
PARTIES:
　India
　USA (United States)

101370　Bilateral Agreement　**99 UNTS 49**
SIGNED: 26 Jan 51　　　FORCE: 26 Jan 51
REGISTERED: 21 Aug 51 USA (United States)
ARTICLES: 5 LANGUAGE: English. Spanish.
HEADNOTE: TECHNICAL COOPERATION
TOPIC: Tech Assistance
CONCEPTS: General technical assistance. Assistance.
PROCEDURE: Duration. Termination.
PARTIES:
　Honduras
　USA (United States)
　　　　　ANNEX
180 UNTS 327. Honduras. Amendment 3 Jan 52. Force 3 Jan 52.
180 UNTS 327. USA (United States). Amendment 12 Dec 51. Force 3 Jan 52.

101371　Bilateral Convention　**99 UNTS 61**
SIGNED: 23 Dec 49　　　FORCE: 9 Feb 51
REGISTERED: 23 Aug 51 UK Great Britain
ARTICLES: 17 LANGUAGE: English. French.
HEADNOTE: STATUS FORCES
TOPIC: Status of Forces
CONCEPTS: Definition of terms. Annex or appendix reference. Privileges and immunities. General cooperation. Use of facilities. Materials, equipment and services. Joint defense. Defense

and security. Military training. Jurisdiction. Status of forces.
INTL ORGS: Allied Military Occupation.
PROCEDURE: Amendment. Termination.
PARTIES:
　Belgium
　UK Great Britain

101372　Bilateral Agreement　**99 UNTS 81**
SIGNED: 3 Apr 50　　　FORCE: 30 Jun 50
REGISTERED: 23 Aug 51 UK Great Britain
ARTICLES: 15 LANGUAGE: English. Spanish.
HEADNOTE: TRADE & PAYMENTS
TOPIC: General Economic
CONCEPTS: Definition of terms. Exceptions and exemptions. Territorial application. Licenses and permits. General trade. Accounting procedures. Banking. Balance of payments. Currency. Monetary and gold transfers. Exchange rates and regulations. Payment schedules. Local currency. Most favored nation clause. Customs duties.
PROCEDURE: Duration. Future Procedures Contemplated. Ratification. Termination.
PARTIES:
　Paraguay
　UK Great Britain
　　　　　ANNEX
121 UNTS 332. UK Great Britain. Gold Coast. Force 22 Oct 51.
121 UNTS 332. UK Great Britain. Uganda. Force 22 Oct 51.
121 UNTS 332. UK Great Britain. Tanganyika. Force 22 Oct 51.
121 UNTS 332. UK Great Britain. Mauritius. Force 22 Oct 51.
121 UNTS 332. UK Great Britain. Aden Colony. Force 22 Oct 51.
121 UNTS 332. UK Great Britain. North Borneo. Force 22 Oct 51.
121 UNTS 332. UK Great Britain. Cyprus. Force 22 Oct 51.
121 UNTS 332. UK Great Britain. Malta. Force 22 Oct 51.
121 UNTS 332. UK Great Britain. Gibralter. Force 22 Oct 51.
121 UNTS 332. UK Great Britain. Windward Islands. Force 22 Oct 51.
121 UNTS 332. UK Great Britain. Zanzibar. Force 22 Oct 51.
121 UNTS 332. UK Great Britain. St. Helena. Force 22 Oct 51.
121 UNTS 332. UK Great Britain. Northern Rhodesia. Force 22 Oct 51.
121 UNTS 332. UK Great Britain. Hong Kong. Force 22 Oct 51.
121 UNTS 332. UK Great Britain. Leeward Islands. Force 22 Oct 51.
121 UNTS 332. UK Great Britain. Jamaica. Force 22 Oct 51.
121 UNTS 332. UK Great Britain. Sierra Leone. Force 22 Oct 51.
121 UNTS 332. UK Great Britain. British Honduras. Force 22 Oct 51.
121 UNTS 332. UK Great Britain. Trinidad. Force 22 Oct 51.
121 UNTS 332. UK Great Britain. Gambia. Force 22 Oct 51.
183 UNTS 370. UK Great Britain. Prolongation 26 May 53. Force 1 Jul 53.
183 UNTS 370. Paraguay. Prolongation 1 Jul 53. Force 1 Jul 53.
199 UNTS 337. UK Great Britain. Extension and Amendment 10 Jun 54. Force 1 Jul 54.
199 UNTS 337. Paraguay. Extension and Amendment 30 Jun 54. Force 1 Jul 54.
215 UNTS 416. UK Great Britain. Prolongation 28 Jun 55. Force 1 Jul 55.
215 UNTS 416. Paraguay. Prolongation 29 Jun 55. Force 1 Jul 55.

101373　Bilateral Exchange　**99 UNTS 97**
SIGNED: 25 Apr 51　　　FORCE: 25 Apr 51
REGISTERED: 23 Aug 51 UK Great Britain
ARTICLES: 2 LANGUAGE: English.
HEADNOTE: AREA CIVIL AIRPORT FACILITIES
TOPIC: Specific Property
CONCEPTS: Use of facilities. Materials, equipment and services. Operating authorizations and regulations. Facilities and property.
PARTIES:
　UK Great Britain
　USA (United States)

ANNEX
373 UNTS 362. UK Great Britain. Supplementation 25 May 60. Force 25 May 60.
373 UNTS 362. USA (United States). Supplementation 25 May 60. Force 25 May 60.
649 UNTS 318. UK Great Britain. Force 4 Jun 68.
649 UNTS 318. USA (United States). Force 4 Jun 68.

101374 Bilateral Agreement **99 UNTS 107**
SIGNED: 5 Apr 50   FORCE: 8 Jun 51
REGISTERED: 23 Aug 51 UK Great Britain
ARTICLES: 14 LANGUAGE: English. French.
HEADNOTE: AIR SERVICES
TOPIC: Air Transport
CONCEPTS: Conditions. Definition of terms. Detailed regulations. Annex or appendix reference. Previous treaty replacement. Conformity with municipal law. General cooperation. Exchange of information and documents. Arbitration. Procedure. Special tribunals. Negotiation. Non-interest rates and fees. Most favored nation clause. Customs exemptions. Routes and logistics. Permit designation. Air transport. Conditions of airlines operating permission. Operating authorizations and regulations.
INTL ORGS: International Civil Aviation Organization.
PROCEDURE: Amendment. Future Procedures Contemplated. Ratification. Registration. Termination. Application to Non-self-governing Territories.
PARTIES:
  Switzerland.
  UK Great Britain
          ANNEX
310 UNTS 359. UK Great Britain. Amendment 1 May 57. Force 1 May 57.
310 UNTS 359. Switzerland. Amendment 1 May 57. Force 1 May 57.
360 UNTS 384. UK Great Britain. Amendment 12 Nov 59. Force 12 Nov 59.
360 UNTS 384. Switzerland. Amendment 12 Nov 59. Force 12 Nov 59.

101375 Multilateral Agreement **99 UNTS 131**
SIGNED: 1 Jan 46   FORCE: 1 Jan 46
REGISTERED: 23 Aug 51 UK Great Britain
ARTICLES: 24 LANGUAGE: English.
HEADNOTE: TERMINATION STATE WAR
TOPIC: Peace/Disarmament
CONCEPTS: Definition of terms. Time limit. Non-prejudice to UN charter. Free passage and transit. Revival of treaties. Compensation. Most favored nation clause. Agricultural commodities. Air transport. Withdrawal of forces. Armistice and peace. Post-war claims settlement. Upkeep of war graves.
INTL ORGS: United Nations. Special Commission.
PROCEDURE: Future Procedures Contemplated.
PARTIES:
  India SIGNED: 1 Jan 46 FORCE: 1 Jan 46
  Siam SIGNED: 1 Jan 46 FORCE: 1 Jan 46
  UK Great Britain SIGNED: 1 Jan 46 FORCE: 1 Jan 46
          ANNEX
191 UNTS 390. UK Great Britain. Termination 14 Jan 54. Force 14 Jan 54.
191 UNTS 390. Thailand. Termination 14 Jan 54. Force 14 Jan 54.

101376 Bilateral Exchange **99 UNTS 149**
SIGNED: 6 Jan 47   FORCE: 6 Jan 47
REGISTERED: 23 Aug 51 UK Great Britain
ARTICLES: 2 LANGUAGE: English.
HEADNOTE: CLAIMS
TOPIC: Reparations
CONCEPTS: Procedure. Claims and settlements. Prisoners of war.
INTL ORGS: Claims Commission.
PARTIES:
  Thailand
  UK Great Britain

101377 Bilateral Exchange **99 UNTS 169**
SIGNED: 1 May 46   FORCE: 1 May 46
REGISTERED: 23 Aug 51 UK Great Britain
ARTICLES: 2 LANGUAGE: English.
HEADNOTE: RICE EXPORT
TOPIC: Commodity Trade

CONCEPTS: Import quotas. Non-interest rates and fees. Commodity trade. Delivery schedules. Quotas.
INTL ORGS: Special Commission.
PARTIES:
  Thailand
  UK Great Britain

101378 Bilateral Exchange **99 UNTS 175**
SIGNED: 1 May 46   FORCE: 1 May 46
REGISTERED: 23 Aug 51 UK Great Britain
ARTICLES: 2 LANGUAGE: English.
HEADNOTE: PREMIUM QUANTITIES RICE DELIVERED
TOPIC: Commodity Trade
CONCEPTS: Non-interest rates and fees. Commodity trade.
PARTIES:
  Thailand
  UK Great Britain

101379 Multilateral Agreement **99 UNTS 181**
SIGNED: 6 May 46   FORCE: 6 May 46
REGISTERED: 23 Aug 51 UK Great Britain
ARTICLES: 3 LANGUAGE: English. Siamese.
HEADNOTE: RICE OTHER COMMODITIES
TOPIC: Commodity Trade
CONCEPTS: Establishment of commission. Export quotas. Import quotas. Trade agencies. Non-interest rates and fees. Commodity trade.
INTL ORGS: Special Commission.
PROCEDURE: Duration. Renewal or Revival.
PARTIES:
  Siam SIGNED: 6 May 46 FORCE: 6 May 46
  UK Great Britain SIGNED: 6 May 46 FORCE: 6 May 46
  USA (United States) SIGNED: 6 May 46 FORCE: 6 May 46

101380 Bilateral Exchange **99 UNTS 193**
SIGNED: 6 May 46   FORCE: 6 May 46
REGISTERED: 23 Aug 51 UK Great Britain
ARTICLES: 2 LANGUAGE: English.
HEADNOTE: RICE
TOPIC: Commodity Trade
CONCEPTS: Treaty interpretation. Commodity trade.
PARTIES:
  Thailand
  UK Great Britain

101381 Bilateral Exchange **99 UNTS 199**
SIGNED: 6 May 46   FORCE: 6 May 46
REGISTERED: 23 Aug 51 UK Great Britain
ARTICLES: 2 LANGUAGE: English.
HEADNOTE: PERSONNEL COMBINED SIAM RICE COMMISSION
TOPIC: Admin Cooperation
CONCEPTS: Personnel. Expense sharing formulae.
INTL ORGS: Special Commission.
PARTIES:
  UK Great Britain
  USA (United States)

101382 Bilateral Agreement **99 UNTS 205**
SIGNED: 21 Apr 51   FORCE: 21 Apr 51
REGISTERED: 23 Aug 51 ILO (Labor Org)
ARTICLES: 5 LANGUAGE: Spanish.
HEADNOTE: TECHNICAL ASSISTANCE
TOPIC: Tech Assistance
CONCEPTS: Treaty implementation. Annex or appendix reference. Privileges and immunities. General cooperation. Exchange of information and documents. Personnel. Title and deeds. Arbitration. Procedure. Professorships. Vocational training. Exchange rates and regulations. Expense sharing formulae. Local currency. Domestic obligation. General technical assistance. Materials, equipment and services. IGO status. Conformity with IGO decisions.
INTL ORGS: United Nations.
PROCEDURE: Amendment. Termination.
PARTIES:
  Cuba
  ILO (Labor Org)

101383 Bilateral Agreement **100 UNTS 3**
SIGNED: 18 Jun 51   FORCE: 18 Jun 51

REGISTERED: 23 Aug 51 ILO (Labor Org)
ARTICLES: 5 LANGUAGE: Spanish.
HEADNOTE: TECHNICAL ASSISTANCE
TOPIC: Tech Assistance
CONCEPTS: Treaty implementation. Privileges and immunities. General cooperation. Exchange of information and documents. Personnel. Title and deeds. Arbitration. Procedure. Scholarships and grants. Vocational training. Exchange rates and regulations. Expense sharing formulae. Local currency. Domestic obligation. General technical assistance. Materials, equipment and services. Conformity with IGO decisions.
INTL ORGS: United Nations.
PARTIES:
  Dominican Republic
  ILO (Labor Org)

101384 Bilateral Agreement **100 UNTS 19**
SIGNED: 26 Apr 51   FORCE: 26 Apr 51
REGISTERED: 23 Aug 51 ILO (Labor Org)
ARTICLES: 5 LANGUAGE: English.
HEADNOTE: TECHNICAL ASSISTANCE
TOPIC: Tech Assistance
CONCEPTS: Treaty implementation. Privileges and immunities. General cooperation. Exchange of information and documents. Personnel. Title and deeds. Arbitration. Procedure. Scholarships and grants. Vocational training. Exchange rates and regulations. Expense sharing formulae. Local currency. Domestic obligation. General technical assistance. Materials, equipment and services. IGO status. Conformity with IGO decisions.
INTL ORGS: United Nations.
PROCEDURE: Amendment. Termination.
PARTIES:
  India
  ILO (Labor Org)

101385 Bilateral Agreement **100 UNTS 31**
SIGNED: 13 Apr 51   FORCE: 13 Apr 51
REGISTERED: 23 Aug 51 ILO (Labor Org)
ARTICLES: 5 LANGUAGE: Spanish.
HEADNOTE: TECHNICAL ASSISTANCE
TOPIC: Tech Assistance
CONCEPTS: Treaty implementation. Privileges and immunities. General cooperation. Exchange of information and documents. Personnel. Title and deeds. Arbitration. Procedure. Scholarships and grants. Vocational training. Exchange rates and regulations. Expense sharing formulae. Local currency. Domestic obligation. General technical assistance. Materials, equipment and services. IGO status. Conformity with IGO decisions.
INTL ORGS: United Nations.
PROCEDURE: Amendment. Termination.
PARTIES:
  Peru
  ILO (Labor Org)

101386 Bilateral Exchange **100 UNTS 47**
SIGNED: 8 May 47   FORCE: 8 May 47
REGISTERED: 24 Aug 51 UK Great Britain
ARTICLES: 2 LANGUAGE: English.
HEADNOTE: RESUMPTION BANKING BUSINESS
TOPIC: Claims and Debts
CONCEPTS: Reconversion to normalcy. Arms limitations. Claims and settlements.
PARTIES:
  Thailand
  UK Great Britain

101387 Bilateral Exchange **100 UNTS 53**
SIGNED: 2 Jul 51   FORCE: 2 Jul 51
REGISTERED: 28 Aug 51 Norway
ARTICLES: 2 LANGUAGE: English.
HEADNOTE: COMMERCE TRADE
TOPIC: General Trade
CONCEPTS: General provisions. Annex or appendix reference. Licenses and permits. Revival of treaties. Trade agencies. Fees and exemptions. Payment schedules. Most favored nation clause. Equitable taxes.
INTL ORGS: Organization for Economic Co-operation and Development.
PROCEDURE: Termination.
PARTIES:
  Ireland
  Norway

101388 Bilateral Agreement **100 UNTS 67**
SIGNED: 9 Feb 51 FORCE: 9 Feb 51
REGISTERED: 29 Aug 51 Pakistan
ARTICLES: 5 LANGUAGE: English.
HEADNOTE: TECHNICAL COOPERATION
TOPIC: Tech Assistance
CONCEPTS: Exceptions and exemptions. Treaty
implementation. Previous treaty replacement.
General cooperation. Exchange of information
and documents. Personnel. Public information.
Financial programs. Tax exemptions. Customs
duties. Customs exemptions. Domestic obligation. General technical assistance. Materials,
equipment and services.
PROCEDURE: Amendment. Duration. Termination.
PARTIES:
Pakistan
USA (United States)
ANNEX
131 UNTS 346. USA (United States). Supplementation 2 Feb 52. Force 2 Feb 52.
131 UNTS 346. Pakistan. Supplementation
2 Feb 52. Force 2 Feb 52.
157 UNTS 370. USA (United States). Amendment
8 Jan 52. Force 8 Jan 52.
157 UNTS 370. Pakistan. Amendment 8 Jan 52.
Force 8 Jan 52.
172 UNTS 350. USA (United States). Supplementation 27 Mar 53. Force 27 Mar 53.
172 UNTS 350. Pakistan. Supplementation
27 Mar 53. Force 27 Mar 53.
172 UNTS 354. USA (United States). Supplementation 1 Apr 53. Force 1 Apr 53.
172 UNTS 354. Pakistan. Supplementation
1 Apr 53. Force 1 Apr 53.
172 UNTS 358. USA (United States). Supplementation 1 Apr 53. Force 1 Apr 53.
172 UNTS 358. Pakistan. Supplementation
1 Apr 53. Force 1 Apr 53.
172 UNTS 364. Pakistan. Supplementation
1 Apr 53. Force 1 Apr 53.
172 UNTS 364. USA (United States). Supplementation 1 Apr 53. Force 1 Apr 53.
172 UNTS 368. USA (United States). Supplementation 1 Apr 53. Force 1 Apr 53.
172 UNTS 368. Pakistan. Supplementation
1 Apr 53. Force 1 Apr 53.
172 UNTS 372. Pakistan. Supplementation
15 Apr 53. Force 15 Apr 53.
172 UNTS 372. USA (United States). Supplementation 15 Apr 53. Force 15 Apr 53.
172 UNTS 376. Pakistan. Supplementation
1 Apr 53. Force 1 Apr 53.
172 UNTS 376. USA (United States). Supplementation 1 Apr 53. Force 1 Apr 53.
172 UNTS 382. USA (United States). Amendment
1 Apr 53. Force 1 Apr 53.
172 UNTS 382. Pakistan. Amendment 1 Apr 53.
Force 1 Apr 53.
184 UNTS 346. Pakistan. Amendment 1 Apr 53.
Force 1 Apr 53.
184 UNTS 346. USA (United States). Amendment
1 Apr 53. Force 1 Apr 53.
222 UNTS 410. Pakistan. Supplementation
28 Dec 53. Force 28 Dec 53.
222 UNTS 410. USA (United States). Supplementation 28 Dec 53. Force 28 Dec 53.
233 UNTS 302. USA (United States). Amendment
24 Jun 54. Force 24 Jun 54.
233 UNTS 302. Pakistan. Amendment 24 Jun 54.
Force 24 Jun 54.
239 UNTS 358. Pakistan. Supplementation
18 Jan 55. Force 18 Jan 55.
239 UNTS 358. USA (United States). Supplementation 18 Jan 55. Force 18 Jan 55.
275 UNTS 302. Pakistan. Amendment 4 Jun 53.
Force 4 Jun 53.
275 UNTS 302. USA (United States). Amendment
4 Jun 53. Force 4 Jun 53.

101389 Bilateral Agreement **100 UNTS 77**
SIGNED: 19 Apr 51 FORCE: 19 Apr 51
REGISTERED: 30 Aug 51 ILO (Labor Org)
ARTICLES: 5 LANGUAGE: Spanish.
HEADNOTE: TECHNICAL ASSISTANCE
TOPIC: Tech Assistance
CONCEPTS: Treaty implementation. Privileges and
immunities. General cooperation. Exchange of
information and documents. Personnel. Title and
deeds. Arbitration. Procedure. Scholarships and
grants. Vocational training. Exchange rates and
regulations. Expense sharing formulae. Local
currency. Domestic obligation. General techni-

cal assistance. Materials, equipment and ser-
vices. IGO status. Conformity with IGO decisions.
INTL ORGS: United Nations.
PROCEDURE: Amendment. Termination.
PARTIES:
Ecuador
ILO (Labor Org)

101390 Bilateral Agreement **100 UNTS 93**
SIGNED: 25 Apr 51 FORCE: 25 Apr 51
REGISTERED: 30 Aug 51 ILO (Labor Org)
ARTICLES: 5 LANGUAGE: French.
HEADNOTE: TECHNICAL ASSISTANCE
TOPIC: Tech Assistance
CONCEPTS: Treaty implementation. Privileges and
immunities. General cooperation. Exchange of
information and documents. Personnel. Title and
deeds. Arbitration. Procedure. Scholarships and
grants. Vocational training. Exchange rates and
regulations. Expense sharing formulae. Local
currency. General technical assistance. Materi-
als, equipment and services. IGO status. Confor-
mity with IGO decisions.
INTL ORGS: United Nations.
PROCEDURE: Amendment. Termination.
PARTIES:
Greece
ILO (Labor Org)

101391 Bilateral Agreement **100 UNTS 105**
SIGNED: 19 Feb 51 FORCE: 19 Feb 51
REGISTERED: 30 Aug 51 ILO (Labor Org)
ARTICLES: 5 LANGUAGE: English.
HEADNOTE: TECHNICAL ASSISTANCE
TOPIC: Tech Assistance
CONCEPTS: Treaty implementation. Privileges and
immunities. General cooperation. Exchange of
information and documents. Personnel. Title and
deeds. Use of facilities. Arbitration. Procedure.
Scholarships and grants. Vocational training. Ex-
change rates and regulations. Expense sharing
formulae. Local currency. Domestic obligation.
General technical assistance. Materials, equip-
ment and services. IGO status. Conformity with
IGO decisions.
INTL ORGS: United Nations.
PROCEDURE: Amendment. Termination.
PARTIES:
Israel
ILO (Labor Org)

101392 Bilateral Agreement **100 UNTS 117**
SIGNED: 2 Apr 51 FORCE: 2 Apr 51
REGISTERED: 30 Aug 51 ILO (Labor Org)
ARTICLES: 5 LANGUAGE: English.
HEADNOTE: TECHNICAL ASSISTANCE
TOPIC: Tech Assistance
CONCEPTS: Treaty implementation. Privileges and
immunities. Conformity with municipal law. Gen-
eral cooperation. Exchange of information and
documents. Personnel. Title and deeds. Use of
facilities. Arbitration. Procedure. Education.
Scholarships and grants. Exchange rates and
regulations. Expense sharing formulae. Local
currency. Domestic obligation. Materials, equip-
ment and services. Conformity with IGO deci-
sions.
INTL ORGS: United Nations.
PROCEDURE: Amendment. Termination.
PARTIES:
Liberia
ILO (Labor Org)

101393 Bilateral Agreement **100 UNTS 131**
SIGNED: 6 Apr 51 FORCE: 6 Apr 51
REGISTERED: 30 Aug 51 ILO (Labor Org)
ARTICLES: 5 LANGUAGE: Spanish.
HEADNOTE: TECHNICAL ASSISTANCE
TOPIC: Tech Assistance
CONCEPTS: Treaty implementation. Privileges and
immunities. General cooperation. Exchange of
information and documents. Personnel. Title and
deeds. Procedure. Scholarships and grants. Vo-
cational training. Expense sharing formulae. Lo-
cal currency. Domestic obligation. General tech-
nical assistance. Materials, equipment and ser-
vices. IGO status. Conformity with IGO decisions.
INTL ORGS: United Nations.
PROCEDURE: Amendment. Termination.

PARTIES:
Mexico
ILO (Labor Org)

101394 Bilateral Agreement **100 UNTS 147**
SIGNED: 16 May 51 FORCE: 16 May 51
REGISTERED: 23 Aug 51 ILO (Labor Org)
ARTICLES: 5 LANGUAGE: English.
HEADNOTE: TECHNICAL ASSISTANCE
TOPIC: Tech Assistance
CONCEPTS: Treaty implementation. Privileges and
immunities. General cooperation. Exchange of
information and documents. Personnel. Title and
deeds. Arbitration. Procedure. Scholarships and
grants. Vocational training. Exchange rates and
regulations. Expense sharing formulae. Domes-
tic obligation. General technical assistance. IGO
status. Conformity with IGO decisions.
INTL ORGS: United Nations.
PROCEDURE: Amendment. Termination.
PARTIES:
Pakistan
ILO (Labor Org)

101395 Bilateral Agreement **100 UNTS 159**
SIGNED: 11 Jul 51 FORCE: 6 Aug 51
REGISTERED: 30 Aug 51 ILO (Labor Org)
ARTICLES: 5 LANGUAGE: English.
HEADNOTE: TECHNICAL ASSISTANCE
TOPIC: Tech Assistance
CONCEPTS: Treaty implementation. Privileges and
immunities. General cooperation. Exchange of
information and documents. Personnel. Title and
deeds. Arbitration. Procedure. Scholarships and
grants. Vocational training. Exchange rates and
regulations. Expense sharing formulae. Local
currency. Domestic obligation. General techni-
cal assistance. Materials, equipment and ser-
vices. IGO status. Conformity with IGO decisions.
INTL ORGS: United Nations.
PARTIES:
ILO (Labor Org)
Thailand

101396 Bilateral Exchange **100 UNTS 170**
SIGNED: 22 Nov 46 FORCE: 22 Nov 46
REGISTERED: 7 Sep 51 USA (United States)
ARTICLES: 8 LANGUAGE: English. Spanish.
HEADNOTE: FOOD PRODUCTION SERVICE
TOPIC: Non-IBRD Project
CONCEPTS: Previous treaty extension. Accounting
procedures. Financial programs. Use restrictions. Non-bank projects.
PROCEDURE: Termination.
PARTIES:
Peru
USA (United States)
ANNEX
135 UNTS 366. USA (United States). Prolongation
15 Sep 50. Force 22 Sep 50.
135 UNTS 366. Peru. Prolongation 21 Sep 50.
Force 22 Sep 50.
162 UNTS 347. USA (United States). Supplementation 7 Jun 51. Force 19 Jun 51.
162 UNTS 347. Peru. Supplementation
15 Jun 51. Force 19 Jun 51.
198 UNTS 393. USA (United States). Supplementation 24 Jun 52. Force 22 Feb 52.
198 UNTS 393. Peru. Supplementation
22 Feb 52. Force 22 Feb 52.
252 UNTS 310. USA (United States). Prolongation
23 Feb 55. Force 10 Mar 55.
252 UNTS 310. Peru. Prolongation 9 Mar 55.
Force 10 Mar 55.

101397 Bilateral Exchange **101 UNTS**
SIGNED: 14 Jun 51 FORCE: 14 Jun 51
REGISTERED: 7 Sep 51 Belgium
ARTICLES: 2 LANGUAGE: Dutch.
HEADNOTE: RECIPROCAL REPARATION WAR
DAMAGE
TOPIC: Reparations
CONCEPTS: Detailed regulations. Time limit. Ex-
change of information and documents. Loss and
/or damage. Post-war claims settlement.
PARTIES:
Belgium
Netherlands

ANNEX
124 UNTS 325. Belgium. Amendment 10 Jul 51.
Force 21 Sep 51.
124 UNTS 325. Netherlands. Amendment
21 Sep 51. Force 21 Sep 51.

101398 Bilateral Exchange **101 UNTS 17**
SIGNED: 3 Jul 51 FORCE: 1 Aug 51
REGISTERED: 7 Sep 51 Belgium
ARTICLES: 2 LANGUAGE: French. Portuguese.
HEADNOTE: ABOLITION REQUIREMENT TRAVEL
VISAS
TOPIC: Visas
CONCEPTS: Territorial application. Time limit. Visa
abolition. Conformity with municipal law.
PROCEDURE: Denunciation.
PARTIES:
Belgium
Portugal

101399 Bilateral Exchange **101 UNTS 25**
SIGNED: 28 Jul 50 FORCE: 28 Jul 50
REGISTERED: 7 Sep 51 UK Great Britain
ARTICLES: 2 LANGUAGE: English. Italian.
HEADNOTE: EMPLOYMENT AGREEMENT
TOPIC: Non-ILO Labor
CONCEPTS: Annex or appendix reference. Em-
ployment regulations. Non-ILO labor relations.
Sickness and invalidity insurance. National treat-
ment. General.
PARTIES:
Italy
UK Great Britain

101400 Bilateral Exchange **101 UNTS 39**
SIGNED: 20 Jan 51 FORCE: 20 Jan 51
REGISTERED: 7 Sep 51 UK Great Britain
ARTICLES: 2 LANGUAGE: Arabic. English.
HEADNOTE: REGARDING RELATIONS
TOPIC: General Amity
CONCEPTS: Diplomatic relations establishment.
Administrative cooperation. General cooper-
ation. Expropriation. Establishment of commis-
sion. Procedure. Customs duties. Adherence to
UN Charter.
INTL ORGS: United Nations. Special Commission.
PARTIES:
UK Great Britain
Yemen

101401 Bilateral Agreement **101 UNTS 51**
SIGNED: 3 Jul 51 FORCE: 1 Jul 51
REGISTERED: 8 Sep 51 Denmark
ARTICLES: 5 LANGUAGE: French.
HEADNOTE: GOODS EXCHANGE
TOPIC: General Trade
CONCEPTS: Territorial application. Annex or ap-
pendix reference. Establishment of commission.
Quotas.
INTL ORGS: Special Commission.
PROCEDURE: Duration.
PARTIES:
Denmark
Spain

101402 Bilateral Agreement **101 UNTS 61**
SIGNED: 5 Jun 51 FORCE: 5 Jun 51
REGISTERED: 8 Sep 51 Denmark
ARTICLES: 6 LANGUAGE: French.
HEADNOTE: TRADE
TOPIC: General Trade
CONCEPTS: Territorial application. Annex or ap-
pendix reference. Previous treaty extension. Es-
tablishment of commission. Quotas.
INTL ORGS: Organization for Economic Co-opera-
tion and Development. Special Commission.
PROCEDURE: Future Procedures Contemplated.
PARTIES:
Denmark
Portugal

101403 Bilateral Exchange **101 UNTS 71**
SIGNED: 29 Jun 51 FORCE: 1 Jul 51
REGISTERED: 13 Sep 51 New Zealand
ARTICLES: 2 LANGUAGE: English.
HEADNOTE: MUTUAL ABOLITION VISAS
TOPIC: Visas
CONCEPTS: Territorial application. Visa abolition.

Denial of admission. Conformity with municipal
law.
PARTIES:
Luxembourg
New Zealand

101404 Bilateral Agreement **101 UNTS 77**
SIGNED: 25 May 51 FORCE: 11 Jun 51
REGISTERED: 13 Sep 51 Nicaragua
ARTICLES: 4 LANGUAGE: English.
HEADNOTE: SOUTH PACIFIC HEALTH SERVICE
TOPIC: Sanitation
CONCEPTS: Definition of terms. Territorial applica-
tion. Previous treaty extension. Personnel. Spe-
cialists exchange. Disease control. Public health.
Nursing. Commissions and foundations. Institute
establishment. Vocational training. Research
and development. Subsidiary organ.
INTL ORGS: South Pacific Health Service.
PROCEDURE: Duration.
PARTIES:
Nicaragua
UK Great Britain

101405 Multilateral Agreement **101 UNTS 91**
SIGNED: 12 May 40 FORCE: 13 Jan 50
REGISTERED: 14 Sep 51 UK Great Britain
ARTICLES: 18 LANGUAGE: English. French. Span-
ish.
HEADNOTE: WEATHER STATIONS
TOPIC: Scientific Project
CONCEPTS: Definition of terms. Annex or appen-
dix reference. Previous treaty replacement. Use
of facilities. Dispute settlement. Research and
scientific projects. Research cooperation.
Meteorology. Scientific exchange. Expense shar-
ing formulae. Domestic obligation. Amateur ra-
dio. Facilities and equipment. Repatriation of ci-
vilians.
INTL ORGS: International Civil Aviation Organiza-
tion. World Meteorological Organization.
PROCEDURE: Amendment. Accession. Duration.
Renewal or Revival.
PARTIES:
Belgium SIGNED: 12 May 47
Canada SIGNED: 12 May 47 RATIFIED: 8 Feb 50
FORCE: 8 Feb 50
Denmark SIGNED: 12 May 49
France SIGNED: 12 May 49
Ireland SIGNED: 27 Jun 49 RATIFIED: 2 May 50
FORCE: 2 May 50
Netherlands SIGNED: 12 May 49
Norway SIGNED: 12 May 49 RATIFIED:
28 Jun 50 FORCE: 28 Jun 50
Portugal SIGNED: 12 May 49 RATIFIED:
3 Aug 50 FORCE: 3 Aug 50
Sweden SIGNED: 12 May 49
UK Great Britain SIGNED: 12 May 49 RATIFIED:
13 Jan 50 FORCE: 13 Jan 50
USA (United States) RATIFIED: 23 Aug 49
FORCE: 13 Jan 50
ANNEX
108 UNTS 322. Denmark. Acceptance 27 Jun 51.
108 UNTS 322. Belgium. Acceptance 31 Jul 51.
124 UNTS 331. Sweden. Acceptance 4 Feb 52.
150 UNTS 380. Portugal. Prolongation
28 May 52. Force 28 May 52.
150 UNTS 380. Netherlands. Prolongation
28 May 52. Force 28 May 52.
150 UNTS 380. Norway. Prolongation
28 May 52. Force 28 May 52.
150 UNTS 380. Sweden. Prolongation
28 May 52. Force 28 May 52.
150 UNTS 380. Denmark. Prolongation
19 Jun 52. Force 19 Jun 52.
150 UNTS 380. France. Prolongation 19 Jun 52.
Force 19 Jun 52.
150 UNTS 380. USA (United States). Prolongation
28 May 52. Force 28 May 52.
150 UNTS 380. Belgium. Prolongation
28 May 52. Force 28 May 52.
150 UNTS 380. Ireland. Prolongation 28 May 52.
Force 28 May 52.
150 UNTS 380. UK Great Britain. Prolongation
28 May 52. Force 28 May 52.
150 UNTS 380. Canada. Prolongation 19 Jun 52.
Force 19 Jun 52.
150 UNTS 388. Iceland. Accession 4 Jun 52.

101406 Bilateral Exchange **102 UNTS 3**
SIGNED: 30 Dec 48 FORCE: 14 Jan 49

REGISTERED: 16 Sep 51 USA (United States)
ARTICLES: 2 LANGUAGE: English. Portuguese.
HEADNOTE: HEALTH SANITATION PROGRAM
TOPIC: Sanitation
CONCEPTS: Annex type material. Previous treaty
extension. Personnel. Programs. Public health.
Sanitation. Expense sharing formulae. Financial
programs. Funding procedures.
PROCEDURE: Duration.
PARTIES:
Brazil
USA (United States)

101407 Bilateral Exchange **102 UNTS 13**
SIGNED: 31 Aug 49 FORCE: 4 Oct 49
REGISTERED: 16 Sep 51 USA (United States)
ARTICLES: 4 LANGUAGE: English. Portuguese.
HEADNOTE: HEALTH SANITATION PROGRAM
TOPIC: Sanitation
CONCEPTS: Annex type material. Previous treaty
extension. Programs. Public health. Sanitation.
Accounting procedures. Expense sharing formu-
lae. Financial programs.
PROCEDURE: Duration. Renewal or Revival.
PARTIES:
Brazil
USA (United States)
ANNEX
166 UNTS 370. USA (United States). Prolongation
13 Jun 50. Force 25 Aug 50.
166 UNTS 370. Brazil. Prolongation 29 Jun 50.
Force 25 Aug 50.

101408 Bilateral Exchange **102 UNTS 29**
SIGNED: 10 May 51 FORCE: 10 May 51
REGISTERED: 17 Sep 51 UK Great Britain
ARTICLES: 2 LANGUAGE: English.
HEADNOTE: CREDIT PURCHASE RAW MATERI-
ALS
TOPIC: Loans and Credits
CONCEPTS: Conditions. Definition of terms. An-
nex or appendix reference. Accounting proce-
dures. Funding procedures. Interest rates. Pay-
ment schedules. Loan and credit. Credit provi-
sions. Purchase authorization.
PARTIES:
UK Great Britain
Yugoslavia

101409 Bilateral Agreement **102 UNTS 39**
SIGNED: 14 Oct 47 FORCE: 21 Sep 49
REGISTERED: 18 Sep 51 United Nations
ARTICLES: 9 LANGUAGE: English.
HEADNOTE: UN INTERNATIONAL CHILDRENS
EMERGENCY FUND
TOPIC: Humanitarian
CONCEPTS: Definition of terms. Annex or appen-
dix reference. Privileges and immunities. Gen-
eral cooperation. Informational records. Operat-
ing agencies. Personnel. General property. Pub-
lic information. Use of facilities. Programs.
Humanitarian matters. Family allowances. Ex-
port quotas. Indemnities and reimbursements.
Exchange rates and regulations. Expense sharing formulae. Financial programs. Funding procedures. Tax exemptions. Domestic obligation.
Materials, equipment and services. Regional offices. Status of experts. Conformity with IGO decisions.
INTL ORGS: United Nations.
PROCEDURE: Duration. Future Procedures Contemplated. Ratification.
PARTIES:
Greece
UNICEF (Children)
ANNEX
277 UNTS 348. UNICEF (Children). Supplementation 19 Nov 54. Force 13 Oct 55.
277 UNTS 348. Greece. Supplementation
15 Oct 55. Force 13 Oct 56.

101410 Bilateral Treaty **102 UNTS 53**
SIGNED: 10 Sep 49 FORCE: 13 Feb 51
REGISTERED: 18 Sep 51 Guatemala
ARTICLES: 8 LANGUAGE: Italian. Spanish.
HEADNOTE: PEACE FRIENDSHIP COOPERATION
TOPIC: General Amity
CONCEPTS: Previous treaty extension. Existing tri-
bunals. Armistice and peace. Reparations and
restrictions.

INTL ORGS: International Court of Justice.
PROCEDURE: Future Procedures Contemplated.
Ratification.
PARTIES:
Guatemala
Italy

101411 Bilateral Exchange **102 UNTS 67**
SIGNED: 1 Oct 47 FORCE: 1 Oct 47
REGISTERED: 20 Sep 51 USA (United States)
ARTICLES: 2 LANGUAGE: English. French.
HEADNOTE: HAITIAN FINANCES
TOPIC: Other Ad Hoc
CONCEPTS: Annex type material. Control of internal finance.
PARTIES:
Haiti
USA (United States)

101412 Bilateral Exchange **102 UNTS 73**
SIGNED: 18 Jun 51 FORCE: 18 Jun 51
REGISTERED: 20 Sep 51 Saudi Arabia
ARTICLES: 2 LANGUAGE: Arabic. English.
HEADNOTE: AIRFIELD
TOPIC: Specific Property
CONCEPTS: Annex or appendix reference. Democratic institutions. Inviolability. General property. Use of facilities. Public health. Humanitarian matters. Compensation. Customs exemptions. General technical assistance. Aid missions. Airport facilities. Airport equipment. Overflights and technical stops. Railways. Military training. Security of information. Jurisdiction. Status of forces.
PROCEDURE: Duration. Future Procedures Contemplated. Renewal or Revival. Termination.
PARTIES:
Saudi Arabia
USA (United States)

101413 Bilateral Agreement **102 UNTS 103**
SIGNED: 20 May 51 FORCE: 20 May 51
REGISTERED: 20 Sep 51 United Nations
ARTICLES: 11 LANGUAGE: Spanish.
HEADNOTE: ARRANGEMENTS UN/ECLA
TOPIC: IGO Operations
CONCEPTS: Non-visa travel documents. Diplomatic missions. Personnel. Accounting procedures. IGO operations.
INTL ORGS: Organization of American States.
PROCEDURE: Duration.
PARTIES:
Mexico
United Nations

101414 Bilateral Agreement **102 UNTS 117**
SIGNED: 4 Dec 49 FORCE: 4 Dec 49
REGISTERED: 20 Sep 51 WHO (World Health)
ARTICLES: 11 LANGUAGE: English.
HEADNOTE: SERVICES
TOPIC: Direct Aid
CONCEPTS: Treaty implementation. Privileges and immunities. Personnel. Use of facilities. Arbitration. Procedure. Negotiation. Exchange rates and regulations. Expense sharing formulae. Tax exemptions. Customs exemptions. General technical assistance. Materials, equipment and services. IGO status. Conformity with IGO decisions.
PROCEDURE: Amendment. Termination.
PARTIES:
Afghanistan
WHO (World Health)

101415 Bilateral Agreement **102 UNTS 127**
SIGNED: 17 Jul 51 FORCE: 17 Jul 51
REGISTERED: 20 Sep 51 WHO (World Health)
ARTICLES: 1 LANGUAGE: English.
HEADNOTE: TECHNICAL ADVISORY ASSISTANCE
TOPIC: Tech Assistance
CONCEPTS: Financial programs. General technical assistance. Special projects.
INTL ORGS: United Nations.
PARTIES:
Burma
WHO (World Health)

101416 Bilateral Agreement **102 UNTS 131**
SIGNED: 9 Jul 51 FORCE: 9 Jul 51

REGISTERED: 20 Sep 51 WHO (World Health)
ARTICLES: 1 LANGUAGE: English.
HEADNOTE: DEVELOPMENT SHORT-TERM COURSE SISTER TUTORS AT HOSPITAL
TOPIC: Sanitation
CONCEPTS: Nursing. Exchange. Financial programs. Domestic obligation.
PARTIES:
Burma
WHO (World Health)

101417 Bilateral Agreement **102 UNTS 139**
SIGNED: 5 Jan 51 FORCE: 21 Feb 51
REGISTERED: 20 Sep 51 WHO (World Health)
ARTICLES: 6 LANGUAGE: English.
HEADNOTE: VACCINATION CAMPAIGN AGAINST WHOOPING-COUGH DIPHTHERIA
TOPIC: Sanitation
CONCEPTS: Definition of terms. General cooperation. Programs. Specialists exchange. Disease control. WHO used as agency. Exchange. Vocational training. Research results. Research and development. Currency. Expense sharing formulae. Financial programs. Funding procedures. Specific technical assistance. Technical cooperation. Materials, equipment and services. IGO obligations.
INTL ORGS: Pan-American Health Organization. United Nations Children's Fund.
PROCEDURE: Duration.
PARTIES:
Colombia
WHO (World Health)
ANNEX
131 UNTS 352. WHO (World Health). Prolongation 11 Mar 52. Force 18 Apr 52.
131 UNTS 352. Colombia. Prolongation 18 Apr 52. Force 18 Apr 52.

101418 Bilateral Agreement **102 UNTS 151**
SIGNED: 14 Jun 51 FORCE: 14 Jun 51
REGISTERED: 20 Sep 51 WHO (World Health)
ARTICLES: 4 LANGUAGE: English. Spanish.
HEADNOTE: TECHNICAL ASSISTANCE FOR NURSE TRAINING
TOPIC: Sanitation
CONCEPTS: Definition of terms. Annex or appendix reference. Privileges and immunities. Exchange of information and documents. Personnel. General property. Public information. Jurisdiction. Responsibility and liability. Establishment of commission. Nursing. WHO used as agency. Exchange. Scholarships and grants. Vocational training. Domestic obligation. Materials, equipment and services.
INTL ORGS: Pan-American Health Organization.
PROCEDURE: Amendment. Duration. Renewal or Revival. Termination.
PARTIES:
Costa Rica
WHO (World Health)
ANNEX
141 UNTS 396. Costa Rica. Supplementation 28 Aug 52. Force 28 Aug 52.
141 UNTS 396. WHO (World Health). Supplementation 31 Jul 52. Force 28 Aug 52.
161 UNTS 370. WHO (World Health). Prolongation 25 Nov 52. Force 25 Nov 52.
161 UNTS 370. Costa Rica. Prolongation 25 Nov 52. Force 25 Nov 52.
172 UNTS 386. Costa Rica.
172 UNTS 386. WHO (World Health). Force 4 Jul 53.

101419 Bilateral Agreement **103 UNTS 3**
SIGNED: 13 Apr 51 FORCE: 1 Jan 51
REGISTERED: 20 Sep 51 WHO (World Health)
ARTICLES: 6 LANGUAGE: English.
HEADNOTE: INSECT CONTROL PROGRAM
TOPIC: Sanitation
CONCEPTS: Definition of terms. Previous treaty extension. Privileges and immunities. General cooperation. Programs. Disease control. Public health. Insect control. WHO used as agency. Vocational training. Expense sharing formulae. Financial programs. Assistance. Specific technical assistance.
INTL ORGS: Pan-American Health Organization. United Nations Children's Fund.
PROCEDURE: Duration. Ratification.
PARTIES:
Costa Rica
WHO (World Health)

101420 Bilateral Agreement **103 UNTS 13**
SIGNED: 21 Apr 50 FORCE: 21 Apr 50
REGISTERED: 20 Sep 51 WHO (World Health)
ARTICLES: 3 LANGUAGE: English. Spanish.
HEADNOTE: TUBERCULOSIS CONTROL DEMONSTRATION
TOPIC: Sanitation
CONCEPTS: Definition of terms. Diplomatic correspondence. General cooperation. General property. Responsibility and liability. Programs. Disease control. WHO used as agency. Research results. Accounting procedures. Expense sharing formulae. Financial programs. Special projects. Specific technical assistance. Materials, equipment and services.
PROCEDURE: Duration.
PARTIES:
El Salvador
WHO (World Health)

101421 Bilateral Agreement **103 UNTS 29**
SIGNED: 2 Jan 51 FORCE: 2 Jan 51
REGISTERED: 20 Sep 51 WHO (World Health)
ARTICLES: 6 LANGUAGE: English.
HEADNOTE: INSECT CONTROL PROGRAM
TOPIC: Sanitation
CONCEPTS: Definition of terms. Previous treaty extension. Privileges and immunities. General cooperation. Programs. Disease control. Insect control. WHO used as agency. Vocational training. Research results. Research and development. Expense sharing formulae. Financial programs. Assistance.
INTL ORGS: Pan-American Health Organization. United Nations Children's Fund.
PARTIES:
El Salvador
WHO (World Health)

101422 Bilateral Agreement **103 UNTS 39**
SIGNED: 2 Jul 51 FORCE: 2 Jul 51
REGISTERED: 20 Sep 51 WHO (World Health)
ARTICLES: 6 LANGUAGE: English.
HEADNOTE: TECHNICAL ASSISTANCE
TOPIC: Tech Assistance
CONCEPTS: Treaty implementation. Annex or appendix reference. Privileges and immunities. General cooperation. Exchange of information and documents. Personnel. Title and deeds. Use of facilities. Arbitration. Procedure. Public health. Scholarships and grants. Vocational training. Research and scientific projects. Exchange rates and regulations. Financial programs. Local currency. Domestic obligation. General technical assistance. Materials, equipment and services. IGO status. Conformity with IGO decisions.
PROCEDURE: Amendment. Termination.
PARTIES:
Ethiopia
WHO (World Health)

101423 Bilateral Agreement **103 UNTS 51**
SIGNED: 28 Nov 50 FORCE: 2 Jan 51
REGISTERED: 20 Sep 51 WHO (World Health)
ARTICLES: 6 LANGUAGE: English.
HEADNOTE: INSECT CONTROL PROGRAM
TOPIC: Sanitation
CONCEPTS: Definition of terms. Previous treaty extension. Privileges and immunities. General cooperation. Programs. Disease control. Insect control. WHO used as agency. Vocational training. Research results. Research and development. Expense sharing formulae. Financial programs. Assistance.
INTL ORGS: Pan-American Health Organization. United Nations Children's Fund.
PARTIES:
Guatemala
WHO (World Health)

101424 Bilateral Agreement **103 UNTS 61**
SIGNED: 21 Jun 50 FORCE: 21 Jun 50
REGISTERED: 20 Sep 51 WHO (World Health)
ARTICLES: 4 LANGUAGE: English. French.
HEADNOTE: YAWS ERADICATION SYPHILIS CONTROL PROJECT
TOPIC: Sanitation
CONCEPTS: Definition of terms. Privileges and immunities. Personnel. Programs. Disease control.

Public health. WHO used as agency. Professorships. Research results. Expense sharing formulae. Financial programs. Specific technical assistance. Mass media exchange.
INTL ORGS: Pan-American Health Organization. United Nations Children's Fund.
PARTIES:
Haiti
WHO (World Health)
ANNEX
134 UNTS 382. WHO (World Health). Prolongation 29 Apr 52. Force 21 Jun 52.
134 UNTS 382. Haiti. Prolongation 29 Apr 52. Force 21 Jun 52.

101425 Bilateral Agreement **103 UNTS 71**
SIGNED: 28 Mar 51 FORCE: 28 Mar 51
REGISTERED: 20 Sep 51 WHO (World Health)
ARTICLES: 14 LANGUAGE: English.
HEADNOTE: TECHNICAL ADVISORY ASSISTANCE OTHER SERVICES
TOPIC: Tech Assistance
CONCEPTS: Change of circumstances. Treaty implementation. Annex or appendix reference. Privileges and immunities. General cooperation. Personnel. Public information. Arbitration. Procedure. Negotiation. Competence of tribunal. Financial programs. Claims and settlements. Tax exemptions. Customs exemptions. Domestic obligation. Special projects. IGO status.
INTL ORGS: International Court of Justice.
PROCEDURE: Amendment. Termination.
PARTIES:
Indonesia
WHO (World Health)

101426 Bilateral Agreement **103 UNTS 83**
SIGNED: 11 Jun 51 FORCE: 11 Jun 51
REGISTERED: 20 Sep 51 WHO (World Health)
ARTICLES: 14 LANGUAGE: English.
HEADNOTE: TECHNICAL ADVISORY ASSISTANCE
TOPIC: Tech Assistance
CONCEPTS: Change of circumstances. Treaty implementation. Annex or appendix reference. Privileges and immunities. General cooperation. Personnel. Public information. Arbitration. Procedure. Negotiation. Competence of tribunal. Financial programs. Claims and settlements. Tax exemptions. Customs exemptions. Special projects. Materials, equipment and services. IGO status.
INTL ORGS: International Court of Justice.
PROCEDURE: Amendment. Termination.
PARTIES:
Liberia
WHO (World Health)

101427 Bilateral Agreement **103 UNTS 95**
SIGNED: 30 Apr 51 FORCE: 30 Apr 51
REGISTERED: 20 Sep 51 WHO (World Health)
ARTICLES: 3 LANGUAGE: English. Spanish.
HEADNOTE: TECHNICAL ASSISTANCE EDUCATION TRAINING CENTER
TOPIC: Tech Assistance
CONCEPTS: Privileges and immunities. General cooperation. Personnel. Education. Scholarships and grants. Research and scientific projects. Expense sharing formulae. Financial programs. Domestic obligation. Special projects. Materials, equipment and services. Conformity with IGO decisions.
INTL ORGS: United Nations.
PROCEDURE: Amendment. Termination.
PARTIES:
Mexico
WHO (World Health)
ANNEX
161 UNTS 371. WHO (World Health). Prolongation 4 Dec 52.
161 UNTS 371. Mexico. Prolongation 7 Jan 53.

101428 Bilateral Agreement **103 UNTS 107**
SIGNED: 2 Jan 51 FORCE: 2 Jan 51
REGISTERED: 20 Sep 51 WHO (World Health)
ARTICLES: 6 LANGUAGE: English.
HEADNOTE: INSECT CONTROL PROGRAM
TOPIC: Sanitation
CONCEPTS: Definition of terms. Previous treaty extension. Privileges and immunities. General cooperation. Programs. Disease control. Insect

control. WHO used as agency. Vocational training. Research results. Research and development. Expense sharing formulae. Financial programs. Assistance.
INTL ORGS: Pan-American Health Organization. United Nations Children's Fund.
PARTIES:
Nicaragua
WHO (World Health)

101429 Bilateral Agreement **103 UNTS 117**
SIGNED: 2 May 51 FORCE: 2 May 51
REGISTERED: 20 Sep 51 WHO (World Health)
ARTICLES: 5 LANGUAGE: English.
HEADNOTE: TECHNICAL ASSISTANCE
TOPIC: Tech Assistance
CONCEPTS: Treaty implementation. Privileges and immunities. General cooperation. Personnel. Title and deeds. Arbitration. Procedure. Scholarships and grants. Vocational training. Research and scientific projects. Expense sharing formulae. Local currency. Domestic obligation. General technical assistance. Materials, equipment and services. IGO status. Conformity with IGO decisions.
INTL ORGS: United Nations.
PROCEDURE: Amendment. Termination.
PARTIES:
WHO (World Health)
Yugoslavia

101430 Bilateral Treaty **104 UNTS 3**
SIGNED: 31 Jul 50 FORCE: 1 Nov 50
REGISTERED: 27 Sep 51 India
ARTICLES: 8 LANGUAGE: English.
HEADNOTE: FACILITATING TRADE COMMERCE
TOPIC: General Economic
CONCEPTS: Previous treaty replacement. Border traffic and migration. Export quotas. Import quotas. Reexport of goods, etc.. Customs duties. Customs exemptions. Transport of goods. Overflights and technical stops.
PROCEDURE: Duration. Renewal or Revival. Termination.
PARTIES:
India
Nepal

101431 Bilateral Exchange **104 UNTS 17**
SIGNED: 11 Aug 51 FORCE: 11 Aug 51
REGISTERED: 27 Sep 51 Belgium
ARTICLES: 2 LANGUAGE: French.
HEADNOTE: CUSTOMS IMMUNITY DIPLOMATIC OFFICERS
TOPIC: Consul/Citizenship
CONCEPTS: Diplomatic privileges.
PARTIES:
Belgium
Brazil

101432 Bilateral Treaty **104 UNTS 25**
SIGNED: 13 Mar 48 FORCE: 13 Mar 48
REGISTERED: 27 Jan 51 UK Great Britain
ARTICLES: 1 LANGUAGE: English.
HEADNOTE: MONEY ORDER AGREEMENT
TOPIC: Postal Service
CONCEPTS: Money orders and postal checks.
INTL ORGS: United Nations.
PROCEDURE: Amendment. Renewal or Revival.
PARTIES:
Bulgaria
UK Great Britain

101433 Bilateral Instrument **104 UNTS 29**
SIGNED: 12 Mar 48 FORCE: 12 Mar 48
REGISTERED: 27 Sep 51 UK Great Britain
ARTICLES: 1 LANGUAGE: English.
HEADNOTE: REVIVAL PRE-WAR BILATERAL TREATIES
TOPIC: Admin Cooperation
CONCEPTS: Revival of treaties.
INTL ORGS: United Nations.
PARTIES:
Finland
UK Great Britain

101434 Bilateral Instrument **104 UNTS 35**
SIGNED: 12 Mar 48 FORCE: 12 Mar 48

REGISTERED: 27 Sep 51 UK Great Britain
ARTICLES: 1 LANGUAGE: English.
HEADNOTE: REVIVAL PRE-WAR BILATERAL TREATIES
TOPIC: Admin Cooperation
CONCEPTS: Revival of treaties.
INTL ORGS: United Nations.
PARTIES:
Hungary
UK Great Britain

101435 Bilateral Instrument **104 UNTS 41**
SIGNED: 13 Mar 48 FORCE: 13 Mar 48
REGISTERED: 27 Sep 51 UK Great Britain
ARTICLES: 1 LANGUAGE: English.
HEADNOTE: REVIVAL PRE-WAR BILATERAL TREATIES
TOPIC: Admin Cooperation
CONCEPTS: Revival of treaties.
INTL ORGS: United Nations.
PARTIES:
Italy
UK Great Britain

101436 Bilateral Instrument **104 UNTS 117**
SIGNED: 13 Mar 48 FORCE: 13 Mar 48
REGISTERED: 27 Sep 51 UK Great Britain
ARTICLES: 1 LANGUAGE: English.
HEADNOTE: REVIVAL PRE-WAR BILATERAL TREATIES
TOPIC: Admin Cooperation
CONCEPTS: Revival of treaties.
INTL ORGS: United Nations.
PARTIES:
Romania
UK Great Britain

101437 Bilateral Exchange **104 UNTS 157**
SIGNED: 9 Jun 47 FORCE: 9 Jun 47
REGISTERED: 1 Oct 51 USA (United States)
ARTICLES: 2 LANGUAGE: English. Italian.
HEADNOTE: AIR SERVICE FACILITIES
TOPIC: Air Transport
CONCEPTS: Annex or appendix reference. Personnel. Meteorology. Fees and exemptions. Routes and logistics. Air transport. Airport facilities. Operating authorizations and regulations. Bands and frequency allocation. Facilities and equipment. Surplus war property. Bases and facilities.
INTL ORGS: International Civil Aviation Organization.
PARTIES:
Italy
USA (United States)

101438 Bilateral Agreement **104 UNTS 167**
SIGNED: 7 Feb 51 FORCE: 1 Jan 51
REGISTERED: 1 Oct 51 WHO (World Health)
ARTICLES: 6 LANGUAGE: English.
HEADNOTE: NATIONWIDE TYPHUS CONTROL
TOPIC: Sanitation
CONCEPTS: Disease control. Public health. WHO used as agency.
INTL ORGS: Pan-American Health Organization. United Nations Children's Fund.
PROCEDURE: Duration.
PARTIES:
Bolivia
WHO (World Health)

101439 Bilateral Agreement **104 UNTS 175**
SIGNED: 9 Jul 51 FORCE: 9 Jul 51
REGISTERED: 1 Oct 51 WHO (World Health)
ARTICLES: 4 LANGUAGE: English.
HEADNOTE: NURSING PROJECT
TOPIC: Sanitation
CONCEPTS: Definition of terms. Diplomatic privileges. Privileges and immunities. Personnel. Programs. Nursing. WHO used as agency. Expense sharing formulae. Financial programs. Specific technical assistance. Aid missions. Surplus commodities. General transportation.
INTL ORGS: International Court of Justice. United Nations Children's Fund. Arbitration Commission.
PROCEDURE: Duration. Termination.
PARTIES:
Burma
WHO (World Health)

101440 Bilateral Agreement **104 UNTS 187**
SIGNED: 9 Jul 51   FORCE: 9 Jul 51
REGISTERED: 1 Oct 51 WHO (World Health)
ARTICLES: 4 LANGUAGE: English.
HEADNOTE: PROVISION LECTURER TUBERCULO-
SIS
TOPIC: Sanitation
CONCEPTS: Definition of terms. Privileges and im-
munities. Personnel. Arbitration. Existing tribu-
nals. Public health. WHO used as agency. Ex-
change. Teacher and student exchange. Profes-
sorships. Vocational training. Expense sharing
formulae. Funding procedures. Specific techni-
cal assistance. Materials, equipment and ser-
vices. General transportation.
INTL ORGS: International Court of Justice. United
Nations Children's Fund. Arbitration Commis-
sion.
PROCEDURE: Duration. Termination.
PARTIES:
  Burma
  WHO (World Health)

101441 Multilateral Agreement **104 UNTS 197**
SIGNED: 4 Aug 51   FORCE: 4 Aug 51
REGISTERED: 1 Oct 51 WHO (World Health)
ARTICLES: 4 LANGUAGE: English.
HEADNOTE: TRAINING COURSE NUTRITION
TOPIC: Sanitation
CONCEPTS: Definition of terms. Privileges and im-
munities. General cooperation. Personnel. Gen-
eral property. Public health. WHO used as
agency. Exchange. Scholarships and grants. Vo-
cational training. Indemnities and reimburse-
ments. Currency. Expense sharing formulae. Fi-
nancial programs. Specific technical assistance.
PARTIES:
  India SIGNED: 4 Aug 51 FORCE: 4 Aug 51
  FAO (Food Agri) SIGNED: 4 Aug 51 FORCE:
    4 Aug 51
  WHO (World Health) SIGNED: 4 Aug 51 FORCE:
    4 Aug 51

101442 Bilateral Agreement **104 UNTS 213**
SIGNED: 7 Aug 51   FORCE: 26 Jul 51
REGISTERED: 1 Oct 51 WHO (World Health)
ARTICLES: 6 LANGUAGE: English.
HEADNOTE: TECHNICAL ASSISTANCE
TOPIC: Tech Assistance
CONCEPTS: Treaty implementation. Annex or ap-
pendix reference. Privileges and immunities.
General cooperation. Exchange of information
and documents. Personnel. Use of facilities. Ar-
bitration. Procedure. Public health. Scholarships
and grants. Vocational training. Research and
scientific projects. Exchange rates and regula-
tions. Expense sharing formulae. Local currency.
Domestic obligation. General technical assis-
tance. Materials, equipment and services. IGO
status. Conformity with IGO decisions.
INTL ORGS: United Nations.
PROCEDURE: Amendment. Termination.
PARTIES:
  Israel
  WHO (World Health)

101443 Bilateral Instrument **104 UNTS 225**
SIGNED: 5 Jun 51   FORCE: 5 Jun 51
REGISTERED: 1 Oct 51 WHO (World Health)
ARTICLES: 7 LANGUAGE: English.
HEADNOTE: MICROFILM PRODUCTION LABORA-
TORY
TOPIC: Scientific Project
CONCEPTS: Definition of terms. Responsibility
and liability. WHO used as agency. Research and
scientific projects. Research cooperation. Re-
search and development. Tax exemptions. Do-
mestic obligation. Materials, equipment and ser-
vices.
PARTIES:
  Lebanon
  WHO (World Health)

101444 Bilateral Agreement **104 UNTS 233**
SIGNED: 26 Sep 50   FORCE: 1 Oct 50
REGISTERED: 1 Oct 51 WHO (World Health)
ARTICLES: 6 LANGUAGE: English.
HEADNOTE: TYPHUS CONTROL PROJECT
TOPIC: Sanitation
CONCEPTS: Definition of terms. Previous treaty ex-

tension. Exchange of information and documents. Personnel. Programs. Disease control. Insect control. WHO used as agency. Vocational
training. Research results. Expense sharing formulae. Financial programs. Specific technical
assistance. Materials, equipment and services.
INTL ORGS: Pan-American Health Organization.
United Nations Children's Fund.
PARTIES:
  Peru
  WHO (World Health)
                    ANNEX
131 UNTS 356. WHO (World Health). Prolongation 5 May 52. Force 5 May 52.
131 UNTS 356. Peru. Prolongation 14 Apr 52.
  Force 5 May 52.

101445 Bilateral Agreement **104 UNTS 243**
SIGNED: 14 Feb 51   FORCE: 1 Jan 49
REGISTERED: 1 Oct 51 WHO (World Health)
ARTICLES: 1 LANGUAGE: English.
HEADNOTE: SALMONELLA RESEARCH
TOPIC: Sanitation
CONCEPTS: Programs. Disease control. WHO
used as agency. Institute establishment. Re-
search and development. Debt settlement. Mate-
rials, equipment and services.
PROCEDURE: Duration. Termination.
PARTIES:
  Denmark
  WHO (World Health)

101446 Multilateral Agreement **104 UNTS 249**
SIGNED: 1 Oct 51   FORCE: 1 Oct 51
REGISTERED: 1 Oct 51 United Nations
ARTICLES: 6 LANGUAGE: English. Spanish.
HEADNOTE: TECHNICAL ASSISTANCE
TOPIC: Tech Assistance
CONCEPTS: Definition of terms. Treaty implemen-
tation. Privileges and immunities. General coop-
eration. Personnel. Title and deeds. Scholarships
and grants. Vocational training. Research and
scientific projects. Expense sharing formulae.
Local currency. Domestic obligation. General
technical assistance. Materials, equipment and
services. IGO status. Conformity with IGO deci-
sions.
INTL ORGS: United Nations.
PROCEDURE: Amendment. Registration. Termina-
tion.
PARTIES:
  Bolivia SIGNED: 1 Oct 51 FORCE: 1 Oct 51
  FAO (Food Agri) SIGNED: 1 Oct 51 FORCE:
    1 Oct 51
  ICAO (Civil Aviat) SIGNED: 1 Oct 51 FORCE:
    1 Oct 51
  ILO (Labor Org) SIGNED: 1 Oct 51 FORCE:
    1 Oct 51
  United Nations SIGNED: 1 Oct 51 FORCE:
    1 Oct 51
                    ANNEX
264 UNTS 349. UNTAB (Tech Assis). Force
  1 Mar 57.

101447 Bilateral Agreement **104 UNTS 263**
SIGNED: 1 Oct 51   FORCE: 1 Oct 51
REGISTERED: 1 Oct 51 United Nations
ARTICLES: 26 LANGUAGE: English. Spanish.
HEADNOTE: TECHNICAL ASSISTANCE
TOPIC: Tech Assistance
CONCEPTS: Exceptions and exemptions. Treaty
implementation. Annex or appendix reference.
Privileges and immunities. General cooperation.
Personnel. Responsibility and liability. Arbitra-
tion. Procedure. Negotiation. Scholarships and
grants. Expense sharing formulae. Funding pro-
cedures. Local currency. Domestic obligation.
General technical assistance. Materials, equip-
ment and services. IGO status. Conformity with
IGO decisions.
INTL ORGS: International Bank for Reconstruction
and Development. International Court of Justice.
International Labour Organization. International
Monetary Fund.
PROCEDURE: Amendment. Duration. Termination.
PARTIES:
  Bolivia
  United Nations
                    ANNEX
165 UNTS 331. Bolivia. Amendment 2 May 53.
  Force 2 May 53.

165 UNTS 331. United Nations. Amendment
  2 May 53. Force 2 May 53.
264 UNTS 350. Bolivia. Force 1 Mar 57.
264 UNTS 350. United Nations. Force 1 Mar 57.

101448 Bilateral Agreement **104 UNTS 301**
SIGNED: 2 Oct 51   FORCE: 2 Oct 51
REGISTERED: 2 Oct 51 United Nations
ARTICLES: 10 LANGUAGE: English.
HEADNOTE: ACTIVITIES UNICEF
TOPIC: Direct Aid
CONCEPTS: Privileges and immunities. General
cooperation. Exchange of information and docu-
ments. Informational records. Inspection and ob-
servation. Personnel. Public information. Title
and deeds. Procedure. Negotiation. Indemnities
and reimbursements. Fees and exemptions. Tax
exemptions. Customs exemptions. Commodities
and services. Domestic obligation. Assistance.
General aid. Distribution. IGO status.
PROCEDURE: Amendment. Termination.
PARTIES:
  UNICEF (Children)
  UK Great Britain

101449 Bilateral Exchange **104 UNTS 313**
SIGNED: 30 Jun 47   FORCE: 1 Jul 47
REGISTERED: 4 Oct 51 Norway
ARTICLES: 3 LANGUAGE: French.
HEADNOTE: MUTUAL ABOLITION VISAS
TOPIC: Visas
CONCEPTS: Territorial application. Time limit. Visa
abolition. Border traffic and migration. Denial of
admission. Conformity with municipal law.
PARTIES:
  France
  Norway

101450 Bilateral Exchange **105 UNTS 3**
SIGNED: 15 Nov 46   FORCE: 15 Nov 46
REGISTERED: 9 Oct 51 USA (United States)
ARTICLES: 2 LANGUAGE: English. Spanish.
HEADNOTE: TERMINATING AGREEMENT
TOPIC: Non-ILO Labor
CONCEPTS: Previous treaty renunciation. Non-ILO
labor relations.
PARTIES:
  Mexico
  USA (United States)

101451 Bilateral Exchange **105 UNTS 15**
SIGNED: 10 Dec 46   FORCE: 10 Dec 46
REGISTERED: 10 Oct 51 UK Great Britain
ARTICLES: 2 LANGUAGE: English.
HEADNOTE: UTILIZATION PROFITS
TOPIC: Specif Claim/Waive
CONCEPTS: Annex or appendix reference. Ex-
change of information and documents. Account-
ing procedures. Payment schedules. Agriculture.
INTL ORGS: Special Commission.
PARTIES:
  United Arab Rep
  UK Great Britain

101452 Bilateral Convention **105 UNTS 27**
SIGNED: 14 Dec 46   FORCE: 30 Jul 51
REGISTERED: 10 Oct 51 UK Great Britain
ARTICLES: 26 LANGUAGE: English. French.
HEADNOTE: AVOIDANCE DOUBLE TAXATION
TOPIC: Taxation
CONCEPTS: Taxation. Equitable taxes. General.
Tax exemptions.
PROCEDURE: Termination.
PARTIES:
  France
  UK Great Britain
                    ANNEX
502 UNTS 372. UK Great Britain. Fed Rhod/-
  Nyasaland. Force 5 Nov 63.
502 UNTS 372. France. Acknowledgement
  5 Nov 63. Force 5 Nov 63.
502 UNTS 377. UK Great Britain. Prolongation
  31 Dec 63. Force 31 Dec 63.
502 UNTS 377. France. Prolongation 31 Dec 63.
  Force 31 Dec 63.

101453 Bilateral Agreement **105 UNTS 61**
SIGNED: 20 Jul 51   FORCE: 16 Apr 51

REGISTERED: 10 Oct 51 UK Great Britain
ARTICLES: 7 LANGUAGE: English. Portuguese.
HEADNOTE: MONETARY
TOPIC: Finance
CONCEPTS: Definition of terms. General cooperation. Banking. Currency. Monetary and gold transfers. Exchange rates and regulations. Internal finance. Payment schedules. Local currency.
INTL ORGS: European Payments Union. International Monetary Fund.
PROCEDURE: Termination.
PARTIES:
Portugal
UK Great Britain
ANNEX
199 UNTS 338. UK Great Britain. Prolongation 5 May 54. Force 30 Jun 54.
199 UNTS 338. Portugal. Prolongation 30 Jun 54. Force 30 Jun 54.

101454 Bilateral Agreement **105 UNTS 71**
SIGNED: 13 Jul 51 FORCE: 13 Jul 51
REGISTERED: 10 Oct 51 UK Great Britain
ARTICLES: 5 LANGUAGE: English.
HEADNOTE: TECHNICAL COOPERATION
TOPIC: Tech Assistance
CONCEPTS: Exceptions and exemptions. Treaty implementation. General cooperation. Exchange of information and documents. Public information. Expense sharing formulae. Tax exemptions. Customs exemptions. Domestic obligation. General technical assistance. Materials, equipment and services.
PROCEDURE: Amendment. Duration. Termination. Application to Non-self-governing Territories.
PARTIES:
UK Great Britain
USA (United States)
ANNEX
213 UNTS 385. UK Great Britain. British Honduras. Force 14 Aug 54.
213 UNTS 385. UK Great Britain. Antigua. Force 14 Aug 54.
213 UNTS 385. UK Great Britain. Jamaica. Force 14 Aug 54.
213 UNTS 385. UK Great Britain. Bahamas. Force 14 Aug 54.
213 UNTS 385. UK Great Britain. Anguilla. Force 14 Aug 54.
213 UNTS 385. UK Great Britain. Brit Virgin Islands. Force 14 Aug 54.
213 UNTS 385. UK Great Britain. St. Christopher. Force 14 Aug 54.
213 UNTS 385. UK Great Britain. Nevis. Force 14 Aug 54.
213 UNTS 385. UK Great Britain. Montserrat. Force 14 Aug 54.
213 UNTS 385. UK Great Britain. St. Vincent. Force 14 Aug 54.
213 UNTS 385. UK Great Britain. Trinidad/-Tobago. Force 14 Aug 54.
213 UNTS 385. UK Great Britain. Dominican Republic. Force 14 Aug 54.
213 UNTS 385. UK Great Britain. Grenada. Force 14 Aug 54.
213 UNTS 385. UK Great Britain. St. Lucia. Force 14 Aug 54.
213 UNTS 385. UK Great Britain. Barbados. Force 14 Aug 54.
213 UNTS 385. UK Great Britain. British Guiana. Force 14 Aug 54.
560 UNTS 246. UK Great Britain. Fed Rhod/-Nyasaland. Force 8 Apr 60.

101455 Bilateral Exchange **105 UNTS 81**
SIGNED: 30 Jul 51 FORCE: 30 Jul 51
REGISTERED: 10 Oct 51 UK Great Britain
ARTICLES: 2 LANGUAGE: English.
HEADNOTE: EXCHANGE OFFICIAL PUBLICATIONS
TOPIC: Admin Cooperation
CONCEPTS: Exchange of official publications. Operating agencies. Indemnities and reimbursements.
PARTIES:
UK Great Britain
USA (United States)

101456 Bilateral Agreement **106 UNTS 3**
SIGNED: 11 Apr 51 FORCE: 11 Apr 51
REGISTERED: 15 Oct 51 UK Great Britain

ARTICLES: 6 LANGUAGE: English. French.
HEADNOTE: COMPENSATION NATIONALIZED GAS ELECTRICITY
TOPIC: Claims and Debts
CONCEPTS: Annex or appendix reference. Expropriation. Arbitration. Procedure. Existing tribunals. Negotiation. Compensation. Currency. Interest rates. Claims and settlements. Most favored nation clause. Credit provisions. Specific claims or waivers.
INTL ORGS: International Court of Justice.
PARTIES:
France
UK Great Britain

101457 Bilateral Agreement **106 UNTS 61**
SIGNED: 7 Sep 49 FORCE: 7 Sep 49
REGISTERED: 16 Oct 51 UK Great Britain
ARTICLES: 11 LANGUAGE: English. French.
HEADNOTE: LOAN AGREEMENT
TOPIC: Loans and Credits
CONCEPTS: Annex or appendix reference. Annex type material. Exchange rates and regulations. Financial programs. Funding procedures. Interest rates. Payment schedules. Loan and credit. Credit provisions. Loan repayment. Conformity with IGO decisions.
INTL ORGS: Bank for International Settlements. Organization for Economic Co-operation and Development.
PROCEDURE: Ratification.
PARTIES:
Belgium
UK Great Britain

101458 Bilateral Exchange **106 UNTS 81**
SIGNED: 20 Apr 51 FORCE: 20 Apr 51
REGISTERED: 16 Oct 51 UK Great Britain
ARTICLES: 2 LANGUAGE: English. French.
HEADNOTE: REGULATION CIVIL AVIATION NEW HEBRIDES
TOPIC: Air Transport
CONCEPTS: General cooperation. Routes and logistics. Air transport. Overflights and technical stops. Operating authorizations and regulations.
PROCEDURE: Termination.
PARTIES:
France
UK Great Britain

101459 Bilateral Agreement **106 UNTS 87**
SIGNED: 15 Dec 50 FORCE: 31 Aug 51
REGISTERED: 16 Oct 51 UK Great Britain
ARTICLES: 9 LANGUAGE: English. Norwegian.
HEADNOTE: TRADE
TOPIC: General Trade
CONCEPTS: Definition of terms. Territorial application. Previous treaty replacement. Licenses and permits. Procedure. Existing tribunals. Fees and exemptions. Most favored nation clause. Recognition. Transport of goods.
INTL ORGS: International Court of Justice.
PROCEDURE: Duration. Ratification. Termination.
PARTIES:
Norway
UK Great Britain

101460 Bilateral Convention **106 UNTS 101**
SIGNED: 2 May 51 FORCE: 31 Aug 51
REGISTERED: 16 Oct 51 UK Great Britain
ARTICLES: 22 LANGUAGE: English. Norwegian.
HEADNOTE: DOUBLE TAXATION FISCAL EVASION TAXES ON INCOME
TOPIC: Taxation
CONCEPTS: Definition of terms. Territorial application. Conformity with municipal law. Exchange of official publications. Teacher and student exchange. Taxation. Death duties. Tax credits. Equitable taxes. General. Tax exemptions. Merchant vessels.
PROCEDURE: Duration. Ratification. Termination.
PARTIES:
Norway
UK Great Britain
ANNEX
219 UNTS 340. UK Great Britain. St. Vincent. Force 18 May 55.
219 UNTS 340. UK Great Britain. Trinidad/-Tobago. Force 18 May 55.

219 UNTS 340. UK Great Britain. St. Lucia. Force 18 May 55.
219 UNTS 340. UK Great Britain. Sierra Leone. Force 18 May 55.
219 UNTS 340. UK Great Britain. Seychelles. Force 18 May 55.
219 UNTS 340. UK Great Britain. Brit Virgin Islands. Force 18 May 55.
219 UNTS 340. UK Great Britain. Singapore. Force 18 May 55.
219 UNTS 340. UK Great Britain. Cyprus. Force 18 May 55.
219 UNTS 340. UK Great Britain. Gambia. Force 18 May 55.
219 UNTS 340. UK Great Britain. Jamaica. Force 18 May 55.
219 UNTS 340. UK Great Britain. Gold Coast. Force 18 May 55.
219 UNTS 340. UK Great Britain. North Borneo. Force 18 May 55.
219 UNTS 340. UK Great Britain. British Honduras. Force 18 May 55.
219 UNTS 340. UK Great Britain. Falkland Islands. Force 18 May 55.
219 UNTS 340. Norway. Acknowledgement 18 May 55. Force 18 May 55.
219 UNTS 340. UK Great Britain. Dominican Republic. Force 18 May 55.
219 UNTS 340. UK Great Britain. Aden. Force 18 May 55.
219 UNTS 340. UK Great Britain. Antigua. Force 18 May 55.
219 UNTS 340. UK Great Britain. Barbados. Force 18 May 55.
219 UNTS 340. UK Great Britain. Brit Solomon Is. Force 18 May 55.
219 UNTS 340. UK Great Britain. Fiji Islands. Force 18 May 55.
219 UNTS 340. UK Great Britain. Montserrat. Force 18 May 55.
219 UNTS 340. UK Great Britain. Nigeria. Force 18 May 55.
219 UNTS 340. UK Great Britain. Gilbert Islands. Force 18 May 55.
219 UNTS 340. UK Great Britain. Grenada. Force 18 May 55.
219 UNTS 340. UK Great Britain. Nevis. Force 18 May 55.
219 UNTS 340. UK Great Britain. Anguilla. Force 18 May 55.
219 UNTS 340. UK Great Britain. Fed of Malaya. Force 18 May 55.
219 UNTS 340. UK Great Britain. St. Christopher. Force 18 May 55.
219 UNTS 340. UK Great Britain. Mauritius. Force 18 May 55.
357 UNTS 346. Norway. Acknowledgement 23 Mar 60. Force 23 Mar 60.
357 UNTS 346. Fed Rhod/-Nyasaland. Force 23 Mar 60.
414 UNTS 382. Norway. Force 1 Jan 54.
414 UNTS 382. UK Great Britain. Force 12 Jun 59.
463 UNTS 342. Norway. Acknowledgement 25 May 62. Force 1 Jan 60.
463 UNTS 342. UK Great Britain. Fed Rhod/-Nyasaland. Force 1 Apr 60.
560 UNTS 248. UK Great Britain. Northern Rhodesia. Prolongation 13 Dec 63.
560 UNTS 248. UK Great Britain. Southern Rhodesia. Prolongation 13 Dec 63.
560 UNTS 248. Norway. Acknowledgement 21 Dec 63.
560 UNTS 248. UK Great Britain. Nyasaland. Prolongation 13 Dec 63.
605 UNTS 335. UK Great Britain. Amendment 29 Jun 66.
605 UNTS 335. Norway. Amendment 29 Jun 66.

101461 Multilateral Exchange **106 UNTS 141**
SIGNED: 6 Mar 51 FORCE: 6 Mar 51
REGISTERED: 16 Oct 51 UK Great Britain
ARTICLES: 2 LANGUAGE: English. French. German.
HEADNOTE: EXTERNAL DEBTS
TOPIC: Claims and Debts
CONCEPTS: Change of circumstances. Time limit. Responsibility and liability. Bonds. Exchange rates and regulations. Financial programs. Internal finance. Claims and settlements. Debts. Economic assistance.

PARTIES:
France SIGNED: 6 Mar 51 FORCE: 6 Mar 51
Germany, West SIGNED: 6 Mar 51 FORCE: 6 Mar 51
UK Great Britain SIGNED: 6 Mar 51 FORCE: 6 Mar 51
USA (United States) SIGNED: 6 Mar 51 FORCE: 6 Mar 51

101462 Bilateral Exchange **107 UNTS 3**
SIGNED: 3 Dec 45 FORCE: 3 Dec 45
REGISTERED: 19 Oct 51 USA (United States)
ARTICLES: 2 LANGUAGE: English. Spanish.
HEADNOTE: FORCE AGREEMENT NAVAL MISSION
TOPIC: Military Mission
CONCEPTS: Annex type material. Previous treaty extension. Military assistance missions.
PARTIES:
Colombia
USA (United States)

101463 Bilateral Agreement **107 UNTS 9**
SIGNED: 9 Jul 51 FORCE: 9 Jul 51
REGISTERED: 22 Oct 51 WHO (World Health)
ARTICLES: 4 LANGUAGE: English.
HEADNOTE: PROVISION LEPROSY CONSULTANT
TOPIC: Sanitation
CONCEPTS: Definition of terms. Privileges and immunities. General property. Responsibility and liability. Specialists exchange. Public health. WHO used as agency. Institute establishment. Indemnities and reimbursements. Expense sharing formulae. Special projects. Specific technical assistance. General transportation.
INTL ORGS: United Nations.
PROCEDURE: Amendment. Termination.
PARTIES:
Burma
WHO (World Health)

101464 Multilateral Instrument **107 UNTS 19**
SIGNED: 1 Aug 51 FORCE: 1 Jul 51
REGISTERED: 22 Oct 51 WHO (World Health)
ARTICLES: 5 LANGUAGE: English.
HEADNOTE: BCG VACCINATION PROGRAM
TOPIC: Sanitation
CONCEPTS: Definition of terms. General cooperation. Personnel. General property. Programs. Public health. WHO used as agency. Vocational training. Research results. Research and development. Accounting procedures. Indemnities and reimbursements. Expense sharing formulae. Assistance. Specific technical assistance. Materials, equipment and services.
PROCEDURE: Amendment. Duration. Renewal or Revival. Termination.
PARTIES:
United Arab Rep SIGNED: 1 Aug 51 FORCE: 1 Jul 51
UNICEF (Children) SIGNED: 16 Aug 51 FORCE: 1 Jul 51
WHO (World Health) SIGNED: 1 Aug 51 FORCE: 1 Jul 51

101465 Bilateral Agreement **108 UNTS 3**
SIGNED: 2 Dec 49 FORCE: 15 Jan 50
REGISTERED: 23 Oct 51 ICAO (Civil Aviat)
ARTICLES: 11 LANGUAGE: English.
HEADNOTE: AIR TRANSPORT
TOPIC: Air Transport
CONCEPTS: Annex or appendix reference. Conformity with municipal law. Licenses and permits. Recognition of legal documents. Use of facilities. Arbitration. Procedure. Existing tribunals. Reexport of goods, etc. Fees and exemptions. Most favored nation clause. National treatment. Customs exemptions. Competency certificate. Routes and logistics. Navigational conditions. Permit designation. Airport facilities. Airworthiness certificates. Conditions of airlines operating permission. Operating authorizations and regulations. Licenses and certificates of nationality.
INTL ORGS: International Civil Aviation Organization. Arbitration Commission.
PROCEDURE: Amendment. Future Procedures Contemplated. Registration. Termination.

PARTIES:
Austria
Sweden

101466 Bilateral Agreement **108 UNTS 15**
SIGNED: 12 Dec 49 FORCE: 1 Apr 51
REGISTERED: 23 Oct 51 ICAO (Civil Aviat)
ARTICLES: 19 LANGUAGE: Arabic. English. Swedish.
HEADNOTE: ESTABLISHMENT SCHEDULED AIR SERVICES
TOPIC: Air Transport
CONCEPTS: Definition of terms. Detailed regulations. Exceptions and exemptions. Annex or appendix reference. Conformity with municipal law. General cooperation. Exchange of information and documents. Arbitration. Procedure. Existing tribunals. Negotiation. Non-interest rates and fees. Customs exemptions. Routes and logistics. Navigational conditions. Permit designation. Air transport. Conditions of airlines operating permission. Overflights and technical stops. Operating authorizations and regulations.
INTL ORGS: International Civil Aviation Organization. Arbitration Commission.
PROCEDURE: Amendment. Future Procedures Contemplated. Ratification. Registration. Termination.
PARTIES:
Sweden
United Arab Rep
ANNEX
150 UNTS 389. Sweden. Amendment 15 Jul 52. Force 15 Jul 52.
150 UNTS 389. United Arab Rep. Amendment 16 Jun 52. Force 15 Jul 52.
200 UNTS 302. United Arab Rep. Amendment 4 Jun 54. Force 4 Jun 54.
200 UNTS 302. Sweden. Amendment 4 May 54. Force 4 Jun 54.
327 UNTS 356. Sweden. Amendment 3 Oct 57. Force 8 Oct 57.
327 UNTS 356. United Arab Rep. Amendment 8 Oct 57. Force 8 Oct 57.
392 UNTS 348. Sweden. Amendment 28 May 58. Force 28 May 58.
392 UNTS 348. United Arab Rep. Amendment 28 May 58. Force 28 May 58.

101467 Bilateral Agreement **108 UNTS 53**
SIGNED: 13 Feb 50 FORCE: 4 Apr 51
REGISTERED: 23 Oct 51 ICAO (Civil Aviat)
ARTICLES: 12 LANGUAGE: English.
HEADNOTE: CIVIL AIR SERVICES
TOPIC: Air Transport
CONCEPTS: Exceptions and exemptions. Annex or appendix reference. Conformity with municipal law. Licenses and permits. Recognition of legal documents. Use of facilities. Procedure. Existing tribunals. Negotiation. Fees and exemptions. Most favored nation clause. National treatment. Customs exemptions. Competency certificate. Routes and logistics. Navigational conditions. Permit designation. Airport facilities. Airworthiness certificates. Conditions of airlines operating permission. Operating authorizations and regulations. Licenses and certificates of nationality.
INTL ORGS: International Civil Aviation Organization.
PROCEDURE: Amendment. Future Procedures Contemplated. Ratification. Registration. Termination.
PARTIES:
Netherlands
Syria
ANNEX
163 UNTS 379. Netherlands. Amendment 31 May 52. Force 15 Jul 52.
163 UNTS 379. Syria. Amendment 15 Jul 52. Force 15 Jul 52.
311 UNTS 340. Syria. Amendment 19 Sep 56. Force 19 Sep 56.
311 UNTS 340. Netherlands. Amendment 26 Jul 56. Force 19 Sep 56.

101468 Bilateral Agreement **108 UNTS 67**
SIGNED: 21 Oct 50 FORCE: 21 Oct 50
REGISTERED: 23 Oct 51 ICAO (Civil Aviat)
ARTICLES: 11 LANGUAGE: French. Portuguese.
HEADNOTE: AIR TRANSPORT

TOPIC: Air Transport
CONCEPTS: Definition of terms. Annex or appendix reference. Non-prejudice to third party. Conformity with municipal law. General cooperation. Licenses and permits. Recognition of legal documents. Use of facilities. Arbitration. Procedure. Existing tribunals. Negotiation. Fees and exemptions. Most favored nation clause. National treatment. Customs exemptions. Competency certificate. Routes and logistics. Navigational conditions. Permit designation. Air transport. Airport facilities. Airworthiness certificates. Conditions of airlines operating permission. Operating authorizations and regulations. Licenses and certificates of nationality.
INTL ORGS: International Civil Aviation Organization. Arbitration Commission.
PROCEDURE: Amendment. Future Procedures Contemplated. Registration. Termination.
PARTIES:
Luxembourg
Portugal

101469 Bilateral Agreement **108 UNTS 87**
SIGNED: 9 Mar 51 FORCE: 9 Mar 51
REGISTERED: 23 Oct 51 ICAO (Civil Aviat)
ARTICLES: 14 LANGUAGE: Portuguese. Spanish.
HEADNOTE: CIVIL AIR TRANSPORT
TOPIC: Air Transport
CONCEPTS: Definition of terms. Exceptions and exemptions. Annex or appendix reference. Non-prejudice to third party. Conformity with municipal law. Licenses and permits. Recognition of legal documents. Use of facilities. Arbitration. Procedure. Existing tribunals. Reexport of goods, etc.. Fees and exemptions. Most favored nation clause. National treatment. Customs exemptions. Competency certificate. Routes and logistics. Navigational conditions. Permit designation. Air transport. Airport facilities. Airworthiness certificates. Conditions of airlines operating permission. Operating authorizations and regulations. Licenses and certificates of nationality.
INTL ORGS: International Civil Aviation Organization. Arbitration Commission.
PROCEDURE: Amendment. Future Procedures Contemplated. Registration. Termination.
PARTIES:
Colombia
Portugal

101470 Bilateral Agreement **108 UNTS 121**
SIGNED: 19 Apr 51 FORCE: 17 Apr 51
REGISTERED: 23 Oct 51 ICAO (Civil Aviat)
ARTICLES: 15 LANGUAGE: Arabic. English.
HEADNOTE: AIR SERVICES
TOPIC: Air Transport
CONCEPTS: Definition of terms. Detailed regulations. Exceptions and exemptions. Annex or appendix reference. Conformity with municipal law. General cooperation. Exchange of information and documents. Arbitration. Procedure. Existing tribunals. Negotiation. Non-interest rates and fees. Most favored nation clause. Routes and logistics. Permit designation. Conditions of airlines operating permission. Overflights and technical stops. Operating authorizations and regulations.
INTL ORGS: International Civil Aviation Organization. Arbitration Commission.
PROCEDURE: Amendment. Future Procedures Contemplated. Registration. Termination. Application to Non-self-governing Territories.
PARTIES:
Iraq
UK Great Britain

101471 Bilateral Agreement **108 UNTS 151**
SIGNED: 24 May 51 FORCE: 17 Jun 51
REGISTERED: 23 Oct 51 ICAO (Civil Aviat)
ARTICLES: 15 LANGUAGE: English.
HEADNOTE: AIR SERVICES
TOPIC: Air Transport
CONCEPTS: Detailed regulations. Annex or appendix reference. Previous treaty replacement. Conformity with municipal law. General cooperation. Exchange of information and documents. Arbitration. Procedure. Existing tribunals. Negotiation. Non-interest rates and fees. Most favored nation clause. National treatment. Routes and lo-

gistics. Permit designation. Air transport. Conditions of airlines operating permission. Operating authorizations and regulations.
INTL ORGS: International Civil Aviation Organization. International Court of Justice. Arbitration Commission.
PROCEDURE: Amendment. Future Procedures Contemplated. Termination.
PARTIES:
India
Netherlands

101472 Bilateral Agreement **108 UNTS 167**
SIGNED: 30 Jul 51   FORCE: 30 Jul 51
REGISTERED: 23 Oct 51 ICAO (Civil Aviat)
ARTICLES: 15 LANGUAGE: English.
HEADNOTE: AIR TRANSPORT
TOPIC: Air Transport
CONCEPTS: Definition of terms. Exceptions and exemptions. Annex or appendix reference. Nonprejudice to third party. Conformity with municipal law. Licenses and permits. Recognition of legal documents. Use of facilities. Arbitration. Procedure. Special tribunals. Competence of tribunal. Indemnities and reimbursements. Fees and exemptions. Most favored nation clause. National treatment. Customs exemptions. Competency certificate. Routes and logistics. Navigational conditions. Permit designation. Air transport. Airport facilities. Airworthiness certificates. Conditions of airlines operating permission. Operating authorizations and regulations. Licenses and certificates of nationality.
INTL ORGS: International Civil Aviation Organization. Arbitration Commission.
PROCEDURE: Amendment. Future Procedures Contemplated. Registration. Termination.
PARTIES:
Burma
Denmark

101473 Bilateral Agreement **108 UNTS 187**
SIGNED: 6 Sep 51   FORCE: 6 Sep 51
REGISTERED: 23 Oct 51 ICAO (Civil Aviat)
ARTICLES: 15 LANGUAGE: English.
HEADNOTE: AIR TRANSPORT
TOPIC: Air Transport
CONCEPTS: Definition of terms. Exceptions and exemptions. Annex or appendix reference. Nonprejudice to third party. Conformity with municipal law. Licenses and permits. Recognition of legal documents. Use of facilities. Arbitration. Procedure. Special tribunals. Reexport of goods, etc.. Indemnities and reimbursements. Fees and exemptions. Most favored nation clause. National treatment. Customs exemptions. Competency certificate. Routes and logistics. Navigational conditions. Permit designation. Air transport. Airport facilities. Airworthiness certificates. Conditions of airlines operating permission. Operating authorizations and regulations. Licenses and certificates of nationality.
INTL ORGS: International Civil Aviation Organization. Arbitration Commission.
PROCEDURE: Amendment. Future Procedures Contemplated. Registration. Termination.
PARTIES:
Burma
Netherlands

101474 Bilateral Agreement **108 UNTS 205**
SIGNED: 20 Sep 49   FORCE: 3 Aug 51
REGISTERED: 23 Oct 51 ICAO (Civil Aviat)
ARTICLES: 11 LANGUAGE: French.
HEADNOTE: AIR TRANSPORT
TOPIC: Air Transport
CONCEPTS: Exceptions and exemptions. Annex or appendix reference. Conformity with municipal law. Domestic legislation. Licenses and permits. Recognition of legal documents. Use of facilities. Arbitration. Procedure. Existing tribunals. Negotiation. Reexport of goods, etc.. Fees and exemptions. Most favored nation clause. National treatment. Customs exemptions. Competency certificate. Routes and logistics. Navigational conditions. Permit designation. Air transport. Airport facilities. Airworthiness certificates. Conditions of airlines operating permission. Operating authorizations and regulations. Licenses and certificates of nationality.
INTL ORGS: International Civil Aviation Organiza-

tion. International Court of Justice. Arbitration Commission.
PROCEDURE: Amendment. Denunciation. Ratification. Registration.
PARTIES:
Lebanon
Netherlands
ANNEX
231 UNTS 360. Lebanon. Amendment 5 Nov 54.
231 UNTS 360. Netherlands. Amendment 5 Nov 54.
311 UNTS 341. Lebanon. Amendment 16 Oct 56. Force 16 Oct 56.
311 UNTS 341. Netherlands. Amendment 16 Oct 56. Force 16 Oct 56.

101475 Bilateral Agreement **108 UNTS 219**
SIGNED: 18 Sep 51   FORCE: 18 Sep 51
REGISTERED: 23 Oct 51 ICAO (Civil Aviat)
ARTICLES: 6 LANGUAGE: English.
HEADNOTE: TECHNICAL ASSISTANCE
TOPIC: Tech Assistance
CONCEPTS: Treaty implementation. Annex or appendix reference. Privileges and immunities. General cooperation. Exchange of information and documents. Personnel. Title and deeds. Use of facilities. Scholarships and grants. Vocational training. Research and scientific projects. Exchange rates and regulations. Expense sharing formulae. Local currency. Domestic obligation. General technical assistance. Materials, equipment and services. IGO status. Conformity with IGO decisions.
INTL ORGS: United Nations.
PROCEDURE: Amendment. Termination.
PARTIES:
Iraq
ICAO (Civil Aviat)

101476 Bilateral Agreement **108 UNTS 231**
SIGNED: 28 Mar 51   FORCE: 24 Oct 51
REGISTERED: 24 Oct 51 United Nations
ARTICLES: 8 LANGUAGE: English. French.
HEADNOTE: POSTAL
TOPIC: Postal Service
CONCEPTS: Conformity with municipal law. Postal services. Rates and charges. Headquarters and facilities.
PROCEDURE: Amendment. Denunciation. Termination.
PARTIES:
United Nations
USA (United States)
ANNEX
149 UNTS 414. United Nations. Amendment 17 Nov 52. Force 17 Nov 52.
149 UNTS 414. USA (United States). Amendment 7 Nov 52. Force 17 Nov 52.
531 UNTS 314. USA (United States). Amendment 15 Apr 65. Force 19 Apr 65.
531 UNTS 314. United Nations. Amendment 19 Apr 65. Force 19 Apr 65.

101477 Unilateral Instrument **108 UNTS 239**
SIGNED: 4 Sep 50   FORCE: 25 Oct 51
REGISTERED: 25 Oct 51 United Nations
ARTICLES: 1 LANGUAGE: French.
HEADNOTE: ACCEPTANCE ICJ JURISDICTION
TOPIC: ICJ Option Clause
CONCEPTS: Exchange of information and documents. Compulsory jurisdiction.
INTL ORGS: International Court of Justice.
PROCEDURE: Duration.
PARTIES:
Israel

101478 Bilateral Agreement **108 UNTS 243**
SIGNED: 10 Aug 51   FORCE: 9 Sep 51
REGISTERED: 26 Oct 51 UK Great Britain
ARTICLES: 7 LANGUAGE: English. Spanish.
HEADNOTE: TRADE
TOPIC: General Trade
CONCEPTS: Annex or appendix reference. Administrative cooperation. Commodity trade. Delivery schedules. Quotas. Customs duties.
PROCEDURE: Duration. Termination.
PARTIES:
Cuba
UK Great Britain

101479 Bilateral Agreement **108 UNTS 263**
SIGNED: 20 Aug 51   FORCE: 20 Aug 51
REGISTERED: 26 Oct 51 UK Great Britain
ARTICLES: 8 LANGUAGE: English. French.
HEADNOTE: MONETARY
TOPIC: Finance
CONCEPTS: Definition of terms. Previous treaty replacement. General cooperation. Monetary and gold transfers. Exchange rates and regulations. Payment schedules.
INTL ORGS: European Payments Union. International Monetary Fund.
PROCEDURE: Termination.
PARTIES:
France
UK Great Britain
ANNEX
191 UNTS 393. UK Great Britain. Prolongation 9 Feb 54. Force 9 Feb 54.
191 UNTS 393. France. Prolongation 9 Feb 54. Force 9 Feb 54.

101480 Bilateral Agreement **108 UNTS 273**
SIGNED: 31 Aug 51   FORCE: 31 Aug 51
REGISTERED: 26 Oct 51 UK Great Britain
ARTICLES: 9 LANGUAGE: English.
HEADNOTE: PAYMENTS
TOPIC: Finance
CONCEPTS: Definition of terms. Accounting procedures. Banking. Currency. Monetary and gold transfers. Exchange rates and regulations. Payment schedules. Local currency.
PROCEDURE: Future Procedures Contemplated. Termination.
PARTIES:
Japan
UK Great Britain

101481 Multilateral Agreement **108 UNTS 287**
SIGNED: 10 Jul 51   FORCE: 10 Jul 51
REGISTERED: 28 Oct 51 Netherlands
ARTICLES: 10 LANGUAGE: Dutch. English.
HEADNOTE: GRAVES MEMBERS ARMED FORCES
TOPIC: Other Military
CONCEPTS: Definition of terms. General property. Title and deeds. Establishment of commission. Tax exemptions. Upkeep of war graves. Establishment of war cemeteries.
INTL ORGS: Special Commission.
PARTIES:
Australia SIGNED: 10 Jul 51 FORCE: 10 Jul 51
Canada SIGNED: 10 Jul 51 FORCE: 10 Jul 51
India SIGNED: 10 Jul 51 FORCE: 10 Jul 51
Netherlands SIGNED: 10 Jul 51 FORCE: 10 Jul 51
New Zealand SIGNED: 10 Jul 51 FORCE: 10 Jul 51
Pakistan SIGNED: 10 Jul 51 FORCE: 10 Jul 51
South Africa SIGNED: 10 Jul 51 FORCE: 10 Jul 51
UK Great Britain SIGNED: 10 Jul 51 FORCE: 10 Jul 51

101482 Bilateral Exchange **108 UNTS 303**
SIGNED: 25 Jul 51   FORCE: 25 Aug 51
REGISTERED: 31 Oct 51 Belgium
ARTICLES: 2 LANGUAGE: English.
HEADNOTE: VISAS
TOPIC: Visas
CONCEPTS: Territorial application. Time limit. Visa abolition. Resident permits. Visas. Fees and exemptions.
INTL ORGS: Special Commission.
PROCEDURE: Denunciation.
PARTIES:
Australia
Belgium

101483 Bilateral Exchange **109 UNTS 3**
SIGNED: 2 May 51   FORCE: 2 May 51
REGISTERED: 1 Nov 51 Belgium
ARTICLES: 2 LANGUAGE: Czechoslovakian. French.
HEADNOTE: TAXES MOTOR VEHICLES DRIVEN TRANSPORT GOODS
TOPIC: Taxation
CONCEPTS: Frontier permits. Tax exemptions. Driving permits. Motor vehicles and combinations.

PARTIES:
Belgium
Czechoslovakia

101484 Bilateral Exchange **109 UNTS 9**
SIGNED: 2 Mar 48 FORCE: 2 Mar 48
REGISTERED: 9 Nov 51 USA (United States)
ARTICLES: 2 LANGUAGE: English.
HEADNOTE: RENEWING NAVAL MISSION AGREEMENT
TOPIC: Military Mission
CONCEPTS: Annex type material. Previous treaty extension. Military assistance missions.
PARTIES:
Peru
USA (United States)
ANNEX
165 UNTS 358. USA (United States). Prolongation 24 May 52. Force 24 Mar 52.
165 UNTS 358. Peru. Prolongation 18 Jan 52. Force 24 Mar 52.
271 UNTS 388. USA (United States). Prolongation 27 Jan 56. Force 14 Mar 56.
271 UNTS 388. Peru. Prolongation 14 Mar 56. Force 14 Mar 56.
541 UNTS 310. USA (United States). Prolongation 15 Mar 61. Force 13 Aug 65.
541 UNTS 310. Peru. Prolongation 2 Jun 61. Force 13 Aug 65.

101485 Bilateral Exchange **109 UNTS 15**
SIGNED: 19 Aug 46 FORCE: 19 Aug 46
REGISTERED: 9 Nov 51 USA (United States)
ARTICLES: 2 LANGUAGE: English.
HEADNOTE: EXTENDING NAVAL AVIATION MISSION
TOPIC: Military Mission
CONCEPTS: Annex type material. Previous treaty extension. Military assistance missions.
PARTIES:
Peru
USA (United States)

101486 Bilateral Exchange **109 UNTS 25**
SIGNED: 30 Jan 48 FORCE: 30 Jan 48
REGISTERED: 9 Nov 51 USA (United States)
ARTICLES: 2 LANGUAGE: English. Spanish.
HEADNOTE: EXTENDING MILITARY AVIATION MISSION
TOPIC: Military Mission
CONCEPTS: Annex type material. Previous treaty extension. Military assistance missions.
PARTIES:
USA (United States)
Venezuela

101487 Bilateral Exchange **109 UNTS 31**
SIGNED: 5 Sep 51 FORCE: 5 Oct 51
REGISTERED: 10 Nov 51 Australia
ARTICLES: 2 LANGUAGE: English.
HEADNOTE: MUTUAL ABOLITION VISAS
TOPIC: Visas
CONCEPTS: Time limit. Visa abolition. Denial of admission. Visas. Conformity with municipal law. Fees and exemptions.
PROCEDURE: Termination.
PARTIES:
Australia
Luxembourg

101488 Bilateral Exchange **109 UNTS 39**
SIGNED: 26 Sep 51 FORCE: 1 Nov 51
REGISTERED: 10 Nov 51 Australia
ARTICLES: 2 LANGUAGE: English.
HEADNOTE: MUTUAL ABOLITION VISAS VISA FEES
TOPIC: Visas
CONCEPTS: Time limit. Denial of admission. Tourism. Conformity with municipal law. Fees and exemptions.
PROCEDURE: Termination.
PARTIES:
Australia
Sweden
ANNEX
301 UNTS 440. Australia. Amendment 30 Apr 58. Force 1 May 58.
301 UNTS 440. Sweden. Amendment 30 Apr 58. Force 1 May 58.

101489 Bilateral Agreement **109 UNTS 45**
SIGNED: 18 Sep 51 FORCE: 10 Oct 51
REGISTERED: 12 Nov 51 WHO (World Health)
ARTICLES: 1 LANGUAGE: English. Spanish.
HEADNOTE: EXTENSION PROVISIONS TECHNICAL ASSISTANCE AGREEMENT
TOPIC: Tech Assistance
CONCEPTS: Previous treaty extension. General technical assistance.
INTL ORGS: United Nations.
PARTIES:
Colombia
WHO (World Health)

101490 Bilateral Agreement **109 UNTS 49**
SIGNED: 16 Oct 51 FORCE: 22 Oct 51
REGISTERED: 12 Nov 51 WHO (World Health)
ARTICLES: 5 LANGUAGE: English.
HEADNOTE: TECHNICAL ASSISTANCE SERVICES OF PRINCIPAL FOR MEDICAL COLLEGE
TOPIC: Tech Assistance
CONCEPTS: Privileges and immunities. General cooperation. Personnel. Arbitration. Procedure. Negotiation. Expense sharing formulae. Claims and settlements. Domestic obligation. Special projects. IGO status. Conformity with IGO decisions.
INTL ORGS: Arbitration Commission.
PROCEDURE: Amendment. Termination.
PARTIES:
India
WHO (World Health)

101491 Bilateral Agreement **109 UNTS 59**
SIGNED: 23 Oct 51 FORCE: 23 Oct 51
REGISTERED: 12 Nov 51 WHO (World Health)
ARTICLES: 3 LANGUAGE: English.
HEADNOTE: NURSING PROJECT INDIA
TOPIC: Sanitation
CONCEPTS: Previous treaty extension. Personnel. Specialists exchange. Nursing. WHO used as agency. Exchange. Vocational training. Indemnities and reimbursements. Expense sharing formulae. Financial programs. Specific technical assistance. Materials, equipment and services. General transportation.
PARTIES:
India
WHO (World Health)

101492 Bilateral Agreement **109 UNTS 77**
SIGNED: 4 Oct 51 FORCE: 16 Oct 51
REGISTERED: 12 Nov 51 WHO (World Health)
ARTICLES: 4 LANGUAGE: English.
HEADNOTE: PROVISION CONSULTANT MENTAL HEALTH
TOPIC: Sanitation
CONCEPTS: Definition of terms. Privileges and immunities. General property. Responsibility and liability. Specialists exchange. Public health. WHO used as agency. Vocational training. Research and development. Indemnities and reimbursements. Expense sharing formulae. Assistance. Specific technical assistance.
PROCEDURE: Amendment. Termination.
PARTIES:
WHO (World Health)
Thailand

101493 Bilateral Agreement **109 UNTS 85**
SIGNED: 4 Oct 51 FORCE: 16 Oct 51
REGISTERED: 12 Nov 51 WHO (World Health)
ARTICLES: 4 LANGUAGE: English.
HEADNOTE: FILARIASIS SURVEY TEAM
TOPIC: Scientific Project
CONCEPTS: Definition of terms. Privileges and immunities. Personnel. Use of facilities. Public health. Vocational training. Wages and salaries. Research and scientific projects. Research and development. Domestic obligation. Repatriation of civilians. IGO obligations.
PROCEDURE: Amendment. Duration. Termination.
PARTIES:
WHO (World Health)
Thailand

101494 Bilateral Treaty **109 UNTS 95**
SIGNED: 29 Aug 50 FORCE: 4 Sep 51
REGISTERED: 15 Nov 51 Syria

ARTICLES: 5 LANGUAGE: Arabic. English.
HEADNOTE: FRIENDSHIP
TOPIC: General Amity
CONCEPTS: Friendship and amity. Consular relations establishment. Diplomatic relations establishment. Privileges and immunities. Procedure.
PROCEDURE: Future Procedures Contemplated. Ratification.
PARTIES:
Pakistan
Syria

101495 Bilateral Agreement **109 UNTS 103**
SIGNED: 26 Jul 51 FORCE: 26 Jul 51
REGISTERED: 15 Nov 51 Netherlands
ARTICLES: 4 LANGUAGE: French.
HEADNOTE: TAX EXEMPTION PROFITS SEA AIR TRANSPORT
TOPIC: Taxation
CONCEPTS: Previous treaty replacement. Tax exemptions. Air transport. Merchant vessels.
PROCEDURE: Denunciation.
PARTIES:
Greece
Netherlands

101496 Bilateral Agreement **110 UNTS 3**
SIGNED: 6 Apr 51 FORCE: 6 Apr 51
REGISTERED: 21 Nov 51 Belgium
ARTICLES: 8 LANGUAGE: English. French.
HEADNOTE: CONSTRUCTION DEEP WATER PORT
TOPIC: Specific Property
CONCEPTS: Time limit. Private contracts. Indemnities and reimbursements. Funding procedures. Payment schedules. Special projects. Materials, equipment and services. Ports and pilotage. Facilities and property.
PARTIES:
Belgium
UK Great Britain

101497 Bilateral Convention **110 UNTS 21**
SIGNED: 12 Sep 50 FORCE: 1 Jan 50
REGISTERED: 21 Nov 51 Belgium
ARTICLES: 4 LANGUAGE: French.
HEADNOTE: EXCISE DUTIES
TOPIC: Customs
CONCEPTS: Annex type material. Customs duties.
PROCEDURE: Ratification.
PARTIES:
Belgium
Luxembourg

101498 Bilateral Instrument **110 UNTS 27**
SIGNED: 20 Mar 51 FORCE: 27 Jul 51
REGISTERED: 21 Nov 51 Belgium
ARTICLES: 13 LANGUAGE: French.
HEADNOTE: ADMISSION STUDENT EMPLOYEES
TOPIC: Non-ILO Labor
CONCEPTS: Conditions. Definition of terms. Resident permits. Conformity with municipal law. Dispute settlement. Employment regulations. Safety standards. Non-ILO labor relations. Family allowances. Quotas.
PROCEDURE: Denunciation. Ratification. Renewal or Revival.
PARTIES:
Belgium
Finland

101499 Bilateral Exchange **110 UNTS 39**
SIGNED: 24 Oct 50 FORCE: 24 Oct 50
REGISTERED: 21 Nov 51 Belgium
ARTICLES: 2 LANGUAGE: French.
HEADNOTE: DELIVERY EXTRACTS CIVIL REGISTERS
TOPIC: Admin Cooperation
CONCEPTS: Exchange of information and documents.
PARTIES:
Belgium
Italy

101500 Bilateral Exchange **110 UNTS 45**
SIGNED: 11 Oct 51 FORCE: 15 Nov 51
REGISTERED: 21 Nov 51 Belgium
ARTICLES: 2 LANGUAGE: French.
HEADNOTE: MOVEMENT PERSONS

TOPIC: Visas
CONCEPTS: Exceptions and exemptions. Territorial application. Time limit. Visa abolition. Denial of admission. Resident permits. Conformity with municipal law. Fees and exemptions.
PROCEDURE: Denunciation.
PARTIES:
Austria
Belgium

101501 Bilateral Agreement **110 UNTS 55**
SIGNED: 15 Sep 51 FORCE: 15 Sep 51
REGISTERED: 25 Nov 51 Denmark
ARTICLES: 7 LANGUAGE: German.
HEADNOTE: TRADE
TOPIC: General Trade
CONCEPTS: Territorial application. Annex or appendix reference. Licenses and permits. Public information. Payment schedules. Quotas.
PROCEDURE: Future Procedures Contemplated.
PARTIES:
Denmark
Switzerland

101502 Bilateral Agreement **110 UNTS 69**
SIGNED: 3 Mar 51 FORCE: 3 Mar 51
REGISTERED: 25 Nov 51 ILO (Labor Org)
ARTICLES: 6 LANGUAGE: French.
HEADNOTE: TECHNICAL ASSISTANCE
TOPIC: Tech Assistance
CONCEPTS: Treaty implementation. Privileges and immunities. Conformity with municipal law. General cooperation. Exchange of information and documents. Personnel. Title and deeds. Use of facilities. Arbitration. Procedure. Scholarships and grants. Vocational training. Exchange rates and regulations. Expense sharing formulae. Local currency. Domestic obligation. General technical assistance. Materials, equipment and services. IGO status. Conformity with IGO decisions.
INTL ORGS: United Nations.
PROCEDURE: Amendment. Termination.
PARTIES:
ILO (Labor Org)
Syria

101503 Bilateral Agreement **110 UNTS 83**
SIGNED: 4 May 51 FORCE: 4 May 51
REGISTERED: 26 Nov 51 WHO (World Health)
ARTICLES: 14 LANGUAGE: English. Spanish.
HEADNOTE: TECHNICAL ADVISORY ASSISTANCE OTHER SERVICES
TOPIC: Tech Assistance
CONCEPTS: Change of circumstances. Treaty implementation. Treaty interpretation. Annex or appendix reference. Privileges and immunities. General cooperation. Personnel. Public information. Arbitration. Procedure. Negotiation. Competence of tribunal. Financial programs. Claims and settlements. Tax exemptions. Customs exemptions. Special projects. Materials, equipment and services. IGO status.
INTL ORGS: International Court of Justice.
PROCEDURE: Amendment. Termination.
PARTIES:
Colombia
WHO (World Health)

101504 Bilateral Agreement **110 UNTS 99**
SIGNED: 27 Jun 50 FORCE: 27 Jun 50
REGISTERED: 26 Nov 51 WHO (World Health)
ARTICLES: 14 LANGUAGE: English. French.
HEADNOTE: TECHNICAL ADVISORY ASSISTANCE OTHER SERVICES
TOPIC: Tech Assistance
CONCEPTS: Change of circumstances. Treaty implementation. Treaty interpretation. Annex or appendix reference. Privileges and immunities. General cooperation. Personnel. Public information. Arbitration. Procedure. Negotiation. Competence of tribunal. Financial programs. Claims and settlements. Tax exemptions. Customs exemptions. Special projects. Materials, equipment and services. IGO status.
INTL ORGS: International Court of Justice.
PROCEDURE: Amendment. Termination.
PARTIES:
Haiti
WHO (World Health)

101505 Bilateral Agreement **110 UNTS 111**
SIGNED: 20 Apr 51 FORCE: 26 Apr 51
REGISTERED: 26 Nov 51 WHO (World Health)
ARTICLES: 14 LANGUAGE: English. Spanish.
HEADNOTE: TECHNICAL ADVISORY ASSISTANCE OTHER SERVICES
TOPIC: Tech Assistance
CONCEPTS: Change of circumstances. Treaty implementation. Treaty interpretation. Annex or appendix reference. Privileges and immunities. General cooperation. Personnel. Public information. Arbitration. Procedure. Negotiation. Competence of tribunal. Financial programs. Claims and settlements. Tax exemptions. Customs exemptions. Special projects. Materials, equipment and services. IGO status.
INTL ORGS: International Court of Justice.
PROCEDURE: Amendment. Termination.
PARTIES:
Honduras
WHO (World Health)

101506 Bilateral Agreement **110 UNTS 127**
SIGNED: 6 Oct 50 FORCE: 6 Oct 50
REGISTERED: 26 Nov 51 WHO (World Health)
ARTICLES: 14 LANGUAGE: English. French.
HEADNOTE: TECHNICAL ADVISORY ASSISTANCE
TOPIC: Tech Assistance
CONCEPTS: Change of circumstances. Treaty implementation. Treaty interpretation. Annex or appendix reference. Privileges and immunities. General cooperation. Personnel. Public information. Arbitration. Procedure. Negotiation. Competence of tribunal. Financial programs. Claims and settlements. Tax exemptions. Customs exemptions. Special projects. Materials, equipment and services. IGO status.
INTL ORGS: International Court of Justice.
PROCEDURE: Amendment. Termination.
PARTIES:
Iceland
WHO (World Health)

101507 Bilateral Agreement **110 UNTS 139**
SIGNED: 1 Jul 51 FORCE: 14 Aug 51
REGISTERED: 26 Nov 51 WHO (World Health)
ARTICLES: 14 LANGUAGE: Arabic. English.
HEADNOTE: TECHNICAL ADVISORY ASSISTANCE OTHER SERVICES
TOPIC: Tech Assistance
CONCEPTS: Change of circumstances. Treaty implementation. Treaty interpretation. Annex or appendix reference. Privileges and immunities. General cooperation. Personnel. Public information. Arbitration. Procedure. Negotiation. Competence of tribunal. Financial programs. Claims and settlements. Tax exemptions. Customs exemptions. Special projects. Materials, equipment and services. IGO status.
INTL ORGS: International Court of Justice.
PROCEDURE: Amendment. Termination.
PARTIES:
Iraq
WHO (World Health)

101508 Bilateral Agreement **110 UNTS 155**
SIGNED: 10 Nov 50 FORCE: 26 Jan 51
REGISTERED: 26 Nov 51 WHO (World Health)
ARTICLES: 14 LANGUAGE: English. Spanish.
HEADNOTE: TECHNICAL ADVISORY ASSISTANCE OTHER SERVICES
TOPIC: Tech Assistance
CONCEPTS: Change of circumstances. Time limit. Treaty implementation. Treaty interpretation. Privileges and immunities. General cooperation. Personnel. Public information. Arbitration. Procedure. Negotiation. Competence of tribunal. Financial programs. Claims and settlements. Tax exemptions. Customs exemptions. Special projects. Materials, equipment and services. IGO status.
INTL ORGS: International Court of Justice.
PROCEDURE: Amendment. Termination.
PARTIES:
Nicaragua
WHO (World Health)

101509 Bilateral Agreement **110 UNTS 171**
SIGNED: 15 Feb 51 FORCE: 15 Mar 51
REGISTERED: 26 Nov 51 WHO (World Health)

ARTICLES: 14 LANGUAGE: English. Spanish.
HEADNOTE: TECHNICAL ADVISORY ASSISTANCE OTHER SERVICES
TOPIC: Tech Assistance
CONCEPTS: Change of circumstances. Treaty implementation. Treaty interpretation. Annex or appendix reference. Privileges and immunities. General cooperation. Personnel. Public information. Arbitration. Procedure. Negotiation. Competence of tribunal. Financial programs. Claims and settlements. Tax exemptions. Customs exemptions. Special projects. Materials, equipment and services. IGO status.
INTL ORGS: International Court of Justice.
PROCEDURE: Amendment. Termination.
PARTIES:
Paraguay
WHO (World Health)

101510 Bilateral Agreement **110 UNTS 187**
SIGNED: 10 Nov 50 FORCE: 21 Nov 50
REGISTERED: 26 Nov 51 WHO (World Health)
ARTICLES: 14 LANGUAGE: English. Spanish.
HEADNOTE: TECHNICAL ADVISORY ASSISTANCE OTHER SERVICES
TOPIC: Tech Assistance
CONCEPTS: Change of circumstances. Treaty implementation. Treaty interpretation. Annex or appendix reference. Privileges and immunities. General cooperation. Personnel. Public information. Arbitration. Procedure. Negotiation. Competence of tribunal. Financial programs. Claims and settlements. Tax exemptions. Customs exemptions. Special projects. Materials, equipment and services. IGO status.
INTL ORGS: International Court of Justice.
PROCEDURE: Amendment. Termination.
PARTIES:
Peru
WHO (World Health)

101511 Bilateral Agreement **110 UNTS 203**
SIGNED: 28 Dec 50 FORCE: 28 Dec 50
REGISTERED: 26 Nov 51 WHO (World Health)
ARTICLES: 14 LANGUAGE: English. French.
HEADNOTE: TECHNICAL ADVISORY ASSISTANCE
TOPIC: Tech Assistance
CONCEPTS: Change of circumstances. Treaty implementation. Treaty interpretation. Annex or appendix reference. Privileges and immunities. General cooperation. Personnel. Public information. Arbitration. Procedure. Negotiation. Competence of tribunal. Financial programs. Claims and settlements. Tax exemptions. Customs exemptions. Special projects. Materials, equipment and services. IGO status.
INTL ORGS: International Court of Justice.
PROCEDURE: Amendment. Termination.
PARTIES:
Philippines
WHO (World Health)

101512 Bilateral Agreement **110 UNTS 215**
SIGNED: 19 Oct 50 FORCE: 19 Oct 50
REGISTERED: 26 Nov 51 WHO (World Health)
ARTICLES: 14 LANGUAGE: English. French. Turkish.
HEADNOTE: TECHNICAL ADVISORY ASSISTANCE
TOPIC: Tech Assistance
CONCEPTS: Change of circumstances. Treaty implementation. Annex or appendix reference. Privileges and immunities. General cooperation. Personnel. Public information. Arbitration. Procedure. Negotiation. Competence of tribunal. Financial programs. Claims and settlements. Tax exemptions. Customs exemptions. Special projects. Materials, equipment and services. IGO status.
INTL ORGS: International Court of Justice.
PROCEDURE: Amendment. Termination.
PARTIES:
WHO (World Health)
Turkey

101513 Bilateral Agreement **110 UNTS 237**
SIGNED: 11 Sep 50 FORCE: 20 Apr 51
REGISTERED: 26 Nov 51 WHO (World Health)
ARTICLES: 14 LANGUAGE: English. Spanish.
HEADNOTE: TECHNICAL ASSISTANCE OTHER SERVICES

TOPIC: Tech Assistance
CONCEPTS: Change of circumstances. Treaty implementation. Treaty interpretation. Annex or appendix reference. Privileges and immunities. General cooperation. Personnel. Public information. Arbitration. Procedure. Negotiation. Competence of tribunal. Financial programs. Claims and settlements. Tax exemptions. Customs exemptions. Special projects. Materials, equipment and services. IGO status.
INTL ORGS: International Court of Justice.
PARTIES:
WHO (World Health)
Venezuela

101514 Bilateral Agreement **110 UNTS 253**
SIGNED: 5 Nov 51　　　FORCE: 5 Nov 51
REGISTERED: 26 Nov 51 WHO (World Health)
ARTICLES: 6 LANGUAGE: English.
HEADNOTE: HEALTH PROJECTS
TOPIC: Sanitation
CONCEPTS: Arbitration. Public health. WHO used as agency.
INTL ORGS: United Nations.
PROCEDURE: Termination.
PARTIES:
Denmark
WHO (World Health)

101515 Bilateral Agreement **110 UNTS 263**
SIGNED: 16 Oct 51　　　FORCE: 16 Oct 51
REGISTERED: 26 Nov 51 WHO (World Health)
ARTICLES: 6 LANGUAGE: English. Spanish.
HEADNOTE: TECHNICAL ADVISORY ASSISTANCE DEVELOPMENT HEALTH PROJECT
TOPIC: Tech Assistance
CONCEPTS: Treaty implementation. Privileges and immunities. General cooperation. Personnel. Title and deeds. Arbitration. Procedure. Scholarships and grants. Vocational training. Research and scientific projects. Expense sharing formulae. Special projects. Materials, equipment and services. IGO status.
INTL ORGS: United Nations.
PROCEDURE: Amendment. Registration. Termination.
PARTIES:
Ecuador
WHO (World Health)

101516 Bilateral Agreement **110 UNTS 277**
SIGNED: 29 Aug 51　　　FORCE: 2 Oct 51
REGISTERED: 26 Nov 51 WHO (World Health)
ARTICLES: 6 LANGUAGE: Arabic.
HEADNOTE: TECHNICAL ASSISTANCE
TOPIC: Tech Assistance
CONCEPTS: Treaty implementation. Annex or appendix reference. General cooperation. Exchange of information and documents. Personnel. Use of facilities. Arbitration. Procedure. Scholarships and grants. Vocational training. Research and scientific projects. Exchange rates and regulations. Expense sharing formulae. Local currency. Tax exemptions. Customs exemptions. Domestic obligation. General technical assistance. Special projects. Materials, equipment and services. Conformity with IGO decisions.
INTL ORGS: United Nations.
PROCEDURE: Amendment. Termination.
PARTIES:
WHO (World Health)
Saudi Arabia

101517 Bilateral Agreement **111 UNTS 3**
SIGNED: 1 Jul 46　　　FORCE: 1 Jul 46
REGISTERED: 27 Nov 51 Yugoslavia
ARTICLES: 10 LANGUAGE: French.
HEADNOTE: STRENGTHEN EXTEND COMMERCIAL RELATIONS
TOPIC: General Economic
CONCEPTS: Conditions. Time limit. Annex or appendix reference. Annex type material. Private contracts. Establishment of commission. Export quotas. Import quotas. Trade procedures. Banking. Currency. Exchange rates and regulations. Financial programs. Payment schedules. Transport of goods.
INTL ORGS: Special Commission.

PARTIES:
Albania
Yugoslavia

101518 Bilateral Agreement **111 UNTS 81**
SIGNED: 1 Jul 46　　　FORCE: 1 Jul 46
REGISTERED: 27 Nov 51 Yugoslavia
ARTICLES: 6 LANGUAGE: French.
HEADNOTE: CREDIT EXTENSION
TOPIC: Loans and Credits
CONCEPTS: Indemnities and reimbursements. Currency. Financial programs. Interest rates. Payment schedules. Loan and credit. Credit provisions. Purchase authorization. Loan repayment.
PARTIES:
Albania
Yugoslavia

101519 Bilateral Protocol **111 UNTS 87**
SIGNED: 3 Oct 46　　　FORCE: 3 Oct 46
REGISTERED: 27 Nov 51 Yugoslavia
ARTICLES: 5 LANGUAGE: French.
HEADNOTE: TRANSFER CREDITS
TOPIC: Loans and Credits
CONCEPTS: Detailed regulations. Exchange of information and documents. Accounting procedures. Currency deposits. Loan and credit. Credit provisions.
PARTIES:
Albania
Yugoslavia

101520 Bilateral Agreement **111 UNTS 93**
SIGNED: 28 Nov 46　　　FORCE: 28 Nov 46
REGISTERED: 27 Nov 51 Yugoslavia
ARTICLES: 15 LANGUAGE: French.
HEADNOTE: OIL PROSPECTING DEVELOPMENT COMPANY
TOPIC: Non-IBRD Project
CONCEPTS: Conformity with municipal law. Establishment of commission. Research and development. Expense sharing formulae. Assets. Tax exemptions. Natural resources.
INTL ORGS: Special Commission.
PARTIES:
Albania
Yugoslavia

101521 Bilateral Protocol **111 UNTS 105**
SIGNED: 28 Nov 46　　　FORCE: 28 Nov 46
REGISTERED: 27 Nov 51 Yugoslavia
ARTICLES: 2 LANGUAGE: French.
HEADNOTE: OIL REFINERY
TOPIC: Non-IBRD Project
CONCEPTS: Natural resources.
PARTIES:
Albania
Yugoslavia

101522 Bilateral Protocol **111 UNTS 109**
SIGNED: 28 Nov 46　　　FORCE: 28 Nov 46
REGISTERED: 27 Nov 51 Yugoslavia
ARTICLES: 2 LANGUAGE: French.
HEADNOTE: HYDROELECTRIC STATION
TOPIC: Non-IBRD Project
CONCEPTS: Indemnities and reimbursements. Hydro-electric power.
PARTIES:
Albania
Yugoslavia

101523 Bilateral Agreement **111 UNTS 113**
SIGNED: 28 Nov 46　　　FORCE: 28 Nov 46
REGISTERED: 27 Nov 51 Yugoslavia
ARTICLES: 15 LANGUAGE: French.
HEADNOTE: ELECTRICITY COMPANY
TOPIC: Non-IBRD Project
CONCEPTS: Conformity with municipal law. Assets. Assessment procedures. Tax exemptions. Hydro-electric power.
INTL ORGS: Special Commission.
PARTIES:
Albania
Yugoslavia

101524 Bilateral Protocol **111 UNTS 123**
SIGNED: 28 Nov 46　　　FORCE: 28 Nov 46
REGISTERED: 27 Nov 51 Yugoslavia
ARTICLES: 2 LANGUAGE: French.
HEADNOTE: CONSTRUCTION POWER STATION
TOPIC: Non-IBRD Project
CONCEPTS: Hydro-electric power.
PARTIES:
Albania
Yugoslavia

101525 Bilateral Agreement **111 UNTS 127**
SIGNED: 28 Nov 46　　　FORCE: 28 Nov 46
REGISTERED: 27 Nov 51 Yugoslavia
ARTICLES: 19 LANGUAGE: French.
HEADNOTE: CONSTRUCTION OPERATION RAILWAYS
TOPIC: Non-IBRD Project
CONCEPTS: Personnel. Non-interest rates and fees. Assets. Assessment procedures. Non-bank projects. Railways.
INTL ORGS: Special Commission.
PARTIES:
Albania
Yugoslavia

101526 Bilateral Protocol **111 UNTS 139**
SIGNED: 28 Nov 46　　　FORCE: 28 Nov 46
REGISTERED: 27 Nov 51 Yugoslavia
ARTICLES: 2 LANGUAGE: French.
HEADNOTE: CONSTRUCTION RAILWAY LINES
TOPIC: Land Transport
CONCEPTS: Annex type material. Materials, equipment and services. Railways.
PARTIES:
Albania
Yugoslavia

101527 Bilateral Agreement **111 UNTS 143**
SIGNED: 28 Nov 46　　　FORCE: 28 Nov 46
REGISTERED: 27 Nov 51 Yugoslavia
ARTICLES: 12 LANGUAGE: French.
HEADNOTE: MONETARY
TOPIC: Finance
CONCEPTS: Detailed regulations. Nationality and citizenship. Conformity with municipal law. General cooperation. Personnel. Banking. Financial programs. Funding procedures. Loan and credit.
INTL ORGS: Special Commission.
PARTIES:
Albania
Yugoslavia

101528 Bilateral Agreement **111 UNTS 151**
SIGNED: 28 Nov 46　　　FORCE: 28 Nov 46
REGISTERED: 27 Nov 51 Yugoslavia
ARTICLES: 15 LANGUAGE: French.
HEADNOTE: MINERAL PROSPECTING DEVELOPMENT
TOPIC: Non-IBRD Project
CONCEPTS: Funding procedures. Assets. Assessment procedures. Tax exemptions. Natural resources. Raw materials.
INTL ORGS: Special Commission.
PARTIES:
Albania
Yugoslavia

101529 Bilateral Protocol **111 UNTS 163**
SIGNED: 28 Nov 46　　　FORCE: 28 Nov 46
REGISTERED: 27 Nov 51 Yugoslavia
ARTICLES: 5 LANGUAGE: French.
HEADNOTE: PERSONNEL
TOPIC: Non-ILO Labor
CONCEPTS: Conformity with municipal law. Safety standards. Wages and salaries. Non-ILO labor relations. Administrative cooperation. Sickness and invalidity insurance. Indemnities and reimbursements. Transportation costs.
PARTIES:
Albania
Yugoslavia

101530 Bilateral Protocol **111 UNTS 171**
SIGNED: 28 Nov 46　　　FORCE: 28 Nov 46
REGISTERED: 27 Nov 51 Yugoslavia
ARTICLES: 3 LANGUAGE: French.
HEADNOTE: PAYMENT INITIAL CAPITAL

TOPIC: Finance
CONCEPTS: Funding procedures.
PARTIES:
   Albania
   Yugoslavia

101531   Bilateral Agreement   **111 UNTS 177**
SIGNED: 12 Jun 47   FORCE: 12 Jun 47
REGISTERED: 27 Nov 51 Yugoslavia
ARTICLES: 6 LANGUAGE: French.
HEADNOTE: CREDIT ECONOMIC REHABILITATION
DEVELOPMENT
TOPIC: Direct Aid
CONCEPTS: Treaty implementation. Commodities
   and services. Economic assistance. Materials,
   equipment and services. Loan and credit.
PROCEDURE: Future Procedures Contemplated.
PARTIES:
   Albania
   Yugoslavia

101532   Bilateral Protocol   **111 UNTS 183**
SIGNED: 12 Jun 47   FORCE: 12 Jun 47
REGISTERED: 27 Nov 51 Yugoslavia
ARTICLES: 7 LANGUAGE: French.
HEADNOTE: ESTABLISHMENT   ALBANIAN-
YUGOSLAV BOARD ARBITRATION
TOPIC: Dispute Settlement
CONCEPTS: Arbitration. Procedure.
INTL ORGS: Arbitration Commission.
PARTIES:
   Albania
   Yugoslavia

101533   Bilateral Protocol   **111 UNTS 189**
SIGNED: 12 Jun 47   FORCE: 12 Jun 47
REGISTERED: 27 Nov 51 Yugoslavia
ARTICLES: 6 LANGUAGE: French.
HEADNOTE: CONDITION DELIVERY GOODS PUR-
CHASED CREDIT
TOPIC: Loans and Credits
CONCEPTS: Inspection and observation. Dispute
   settlement. Currency. Claims and settlements.
   Loan and credit. Credit provisions. Purchase au-
   thorization.
PARTIES:
   Albania
   Yugoslavia

101534   Bilateral Agreement   **111 UNTS 195**
SIGNED: 12 Jun 47   FORCE: 12 Jun 47
REGISTERED: 27 Nov 51 Yugoslavia
ARTICLES: 6 LANGUAGE: French.
HEADNOTE: PAYMENT SHARE CAPITAL
TOPIC: Finance
CONCEPTS: Annex type material. Accounting pro-
   cedures. Banking. Exchange rates and regula-
   tions. Funding procedures. Interest rates. Pay-
   ment schedules. Credit provisions.
PARTIES:
   Albania
   Yugoslavia

101535   Bilateral Protocol   **111 UNTS 201**
SIGNED: 12 Jun 47   FORCE: 12 Jun 47
REGISTERED: 27 Nov 51 Yugoslavia
ARTICLES: 6 LANGUAGE: French.
HEADNOTE: ESTABLISHMENT   COORDINATION
COMMISSION
TOPIC: IGO Establishment
CONCEPTS: Special tribunals. IGO constitution.
INTL ORGS: Special Commission.
PARTIES:
   Albania
   Yugoslavia

101536   Bilateral Agreement   **111 UNTS 207**
SIGNED: 22 Jun 47   FORCE: 22 Jun 47
REGISTERED: 27 Nov 51 Yugoslavia
ARTICLES: 11 LANGUAGE: French.
HEADNOTE: COMMERCE
TOPIC: General Trade
CONCEPTS: Treaty implementation. Annex or ap-
   pendix reference. Reexport of goods, etc.. Trade
   agencies. Trade procedures. Accounting proce-
   dures. Banking. Currency. Financial programs.
   Interest rates. Payment schedules. Non-interest

rates and fees. Delivery schedules. Transport of
   goods.
PROCEDURE: Duration.
PARTIES:
   Albania
   Yugoslavia

101537   Bilateral Agreement   **111 UNTS 227**
SIGNED: 3 Oct 46   FORCE: 3 Oct 46
REGISTERED: 27 Nov 51 Yugoslavia
ARTICLES: 12 LANGUAGE: Albanian. French. Ser-
bo-Croat.
HEADNOTE: ESTABLISHMENT IMPORT-EXPORT
COMPANY
TOPIC: General Trade
CONCEPTS: Detailed regulations. Annex type ma-
   terial. Trade agencies. Banking. Currency. Ex-
   change rates and regulations. Expense sharing
   formulae. Inadequacy of funds. Assets. Tax ex-
   emptions.
INTL ORGS: Special Commission.
PROCEDURE: Duration. Renewal or Revival.
PARTIES:
   Albania
   Yugoslavia

101538   Bilateral Protocol   **111 UNTS 241**
SIGNED: 22 Aug 47   FORCE: 22 Aug 47
REGISTERED: 27 Nov 51 Yugoslavia
ARTICLES: 1 LANGUAGE: Bulgarian. Serbo-Croat.
HEADNOTE: CLEARING ARRANGEMENTS
TOPIC: Finance
CONCEPTS: Annex type material. Banking. Bal-
   ance of payments. Monetary and gold transfers.
PROCEDURE: Duration.
PARTIES:
   Bulgaria
   Yugoslavia

101539   Bilateral Agreement   **112 UNTS 3**
SIGNED: 25 Feb 47   FORCE: 25 Feb 47
REGISTERED: 27 Nov 51 Yugoslavia
ARTICLES: 11 LANGUAGE: Czechoslovakian. Ser-
bo-Croat.
HEADNOTE: DELIVERY CAPITAL GOODS
TOPIC: General Trade
CONCEPTS: Treaty implementation. Annex or ap-
   pendix reference. Annex type material. Previous
   treaty replacement. Establishment of commis-
   sion. Negotiation. Trade agencies. Banking. Ex-
   change rates and regulations. Payment sched-
   ules. Non-interest rates and fees. Debt settle-
   ment. Commodity trade. Delivery schedules.
INTL ORGS: Claims Commission.
PARTIES:
   Czechoslovakia
   Yugoslavia

101540   Bilateral Agreement   **112 UNTS 91**
SIGNED: 4 Sep 47   FORCE: 4 Sep 47
REGISTERED: 27 Nov 51 Yugoslavia
ARTICLES: 8 LANGUAGE: Czechoslovakian. Ser-
bo-Croat.
HEADNOTE: ASSET NATIONALIZATION
TOPIC: Claims and Debts
CONCEPTS: Expropriation. Establishment of com-
   mission. Financial programs. Assets. Claims and
   settlements. Assessment procedures. Assets
   transfer.
PROCEDURE: Amendment.
PARTIES:
   Czechoslovakia
   Yugoslavia

101541   Bilateral Agreement   **112 UNTS 101**
SIGNED: 10 Apr 48   FORCE: 1 Oct 48
REGISTERED: 27 Nov 51 Yugoslavia
ARTICLES: 1 LANGUAGE: Czechoslovakian. Ser-
bo-Croat.
HEADNOTE: SUPPLEMENT TRADE NAVIGATION
TOPIC: General Economic
CONCEPTS: Annex type material. Previous treaty
   replacement. Trade procedures. Commodity
   trade. Customs duties. Customs declarations.
PROCEDURE: Denunciation. Ratification.
PARTIES:
   Czechoslovakia
   Yugoslavia

101542   Bilateral Agreement   **112 UNTS 111**
SIGNED: 24 May 48   FORCE: 24 May 48
REGISTERED: 27 Nov 51 Yugoslavia
ARTICLES: 13 LANGUAGE: Czechoslovakian. Ser-
bo-Croat.
HEADNOTE: TRADE
TOPIC: General Trade
CONCEPTS: Definition of terms. Treaty implemen-
   tation. Annex or appendix reference. Licenses
   and permits. Establishment of commission. Pro-
   cedure. Trade procedures. Payment schedules.
   Non-interest rates and fees. Debt settlement. De-
   livery schedules. Quotas. Transport of goods.
INTL ORGS: Special Commission.
PROCEDURE: Duration.
PARTIES:
   Czechoslovakia
   Yugoslavia

101543   Bilateral Agreement   **112 UNTS 183**
SIGNED: 24 May 48   FORCE: 24 May 48
REGISTERED: 27 Nov 51 Yugoslavia
ARTICLES: 7 LANGUAGE: Czechoslovakian. Ser-
bo-Croat.
HEADNOTE: PAYMENTS
TOPIC: Finance
CONCEPTS: Detailed regulations. General cooper-
   ation. Accounting procedures. Banking. Balance
   of payments. Currency. Financial programs. In-
   terest rates. Payment schedules.
PARTIES:
   Czechoslovakia
   Yugoslavia

101544   Bilateral Protocol   **112 UNTS 215**
SIGNED: 24 May 48   FORCE: 24 May 48
REGISTERED: 27 Nov 51 Yugoslavia
ARTICLES: 6 LANGUAGE: Czechoslovakian. Ser-
bo-Croat.
HEADNOTE: SUPPLIES MACHINERY EQUIPMENT
TOPIC: Specif Goods/Equip
CONCEPTS: Operating agencies. Licenses and
   permits. Purchase authorizations. Materials,
   equipment and services. Specific goods and
   equipment.
INTL ORGS: Special Commission.
PARTIES:
   Czechoslovakia
   Yugoslavia

101545   Bilateral Protocol   **112 UNTS 225**
SIGNED: 24 May 48   FORCE: 24 May 48
REGISTERED: 27 Nov 51 Yugoslavia
ARTICLES: 4 LANGUAGE: Czechoslovakian. Ser-
bo-Croat.
HEADNOTE: PAYMENTS
TOPIC: Finance
CONCEPTS: Accounting procedures. Banking.
   Monetary and gold transfers. Interest rates. Pay-
   ment schedules.
PARTIES:
   Czechoslovakia
   Yugoslavia

101546   Bilateral Agreement   **112 UNTS 241**
SIGNED: 1 Mar 49   FORCE: 1 Mar 49
REGISTERED: 27 Nov 51 Yugoslavia
ARTICLES: 6 LANGUAGE: Czechoslovakian. Ser-
bo-Croat.
HEADNOTE: PAYMENTS
TOPIC: Finance
CONCEPTS: Detailed regulations. Annex type ma-
   terial. General cooperation. Accounting proce-
   dures. Banking. Balance of payments. Currency.
   Exchange rates and regulations. Payment sched-
   ules.
PARTIES:
   Czechoslovakia
   Yugoslavia

101547   Bilateral Agreement   **113 UNTS 3**
SIGNED: 1 Mar 49   FORCE: 1 Mar 49
REGISTERED: 27 Nov 51 Yugoslavia
ARTICLES: 13 LANGUAGE: Czechoslovakian. Ser-
bo-Croat.

HEADNOTE: TRADE EXPANSION
TOPIC: General Trade
CONCEPTS: Definition of terms. Treaty implementation. Annex or appendix reference. Licenses and permits. Establishment of commission. Procedure. Negotiation. Payment schedules. Non-interest rates and fees. Debt settlement. Delivery schedules. Quotas. Transport of goods.
INTL ORGS: Special Commission.
PARTIES:
Czechoslovakia
Yugoslavia

101548 Bilateral Agreement **113 UNTS 63**
SIGNED: 1 Jan 47 FORCE: 1 Jan 47
REGISTERED: 27 Nov 51 Yugoslavia
ARTICLES: 11 LANGUAGE: Hungarian. Serbo-Croat.
HEADNOTE: EXCHANGE OF GOODS
TOPIC: General Trade
CONCEPTS: Establishment of trade relations. Trade agencies. Trade procedures. Financial programs.
INTL ORGS: Special Commission.
PROCEDURE: Duration.
PARTIES:
Hungary
Yugoslavia

101549 Bilateral Agreement **113 UNTS 125**
SIGNED: 23 Dec 46 FORCE: 23 Dec 46
REGISTERED: 27 Nov 51 Yugoslavia
ARTICLES: 11 LANGUAGE: Hungarian. Serbo-Croat.
HEADNOTE: FACILITATE NON-COMMERCIAL PAYMENTS
TOPIC: Finance
CONCEPTS: Detailed regulations. Conformity with municipal law. General cooperation. Import quotas. Accounting procedures. Banking. Balance of payments. Currency. Exchange rates and regulations. Interest rates. Payment schedules. Non-interest rates and fees. Debt settlement.
PROCEDURE: Duration. Renewal or Revival. Termination.
PARTIES:
Hungary
Yugoslavia

101550 Bilateral Agreement **113 UNTS 141**
SIGNED: 18 Mar 48 FORCE: 18 Mar 48
REGISTERED: 27 Nov 51 Yugoslavia
ARTICLES: 11 LANGUAGE: Hungarian. Serbo-Croat.
HEADNOTE: TRADE
TOPIC: General Trade
CONCEPTS: Detailed regulations. Treaty implementation. Annex or appendix reference. Procedure. Trade agencies. Trade procedures. Attachment of funds. Banking. Payment schedules. Non-interest rates and fees. Quotas. Transport of goods.
INTL ORGS: Special Commission.
PROCEDURE: Termination.
PARTIES:
Hungary
Yugoslavia

101551 Bilateral Agreement **113 UNTS 201**
SIGNED: 18 Mar 48 FORCE: 18 Mar 48
REGISTERED: 27 Nov 51 Yugoslavia
ARTICLES: 10 LANGUAGE: Hungarian. Serbo-Croat.
HEADNOTE: NON-COMMERCIAL PAYMENTS
TOPIC: Finance
CONCEPTS: Detailed regulations. Exceptions and exemptions. Annex or appendix reference. Conformity with municipal law. General cooperation. Licenses and permits. Export quotas. Trade procedures. Accounting procedures. Banking. Balance of payments. Currency. Interest rates. Payment schedules. Non-interest rates and fees. Local currency.
INTL ORGS: Special Commission.
PROCEDURE: Denunciation. Duration. Renewal or Revival.
PARTIES:
Hungary
Yugoslavia

101552 Bilateral Agreement **113 UNTS 219**
SIGNED: 18 Mar 48 FORCE: 18 Mar 48
REGISTERED: 27 Nov 51 Yugoslavia
ARTICLES: 5 LANGUAGE: Hungarian. Serbo-Croat.
HEADNOTE: PAYMENTS
TOPIC: Finance
CONCEPTS: Treaty implementation. Annex or appendix reference. General trade. Accounting procedures. Balance of payments. Currency. Payment schedules. Non-interest rates and fees. Debts.
INTL ORGS: Special Commission.
PARTIES:
Hungary
Yugoslavia

101553 Bilateral Agreement **113 UNTS 233**
SIGNED: 13 Aug 44 FORCE: 13 Aug 49
REGISTERED: 27 Nov 51 Yugoslavia
ARTICLES: 12 LANGUAGE: Hungarian. Serbo-Croat.
HEADNOTE: MIXED COMMISSION INVESTIGATING ASCERTAINING FRONTIER INCIDENTS
TOPIC: Dispute Settlement
CONCEPTS: Privileges and immunities. Informational records. Establishment of commission.
INTL ORGS: Special Commission.
PROCEDURE: Denunciation.
PARTIES:
Hungary
Yugoslavia

101554 Bilateral Agreement **114 UNTS 3**
SIGNED: 24 Jul 47 FORCE: 24 Jul 47
REGISTERED: 27 Nov 51 Yugoslavia
ARTICLES: 14 LANGUAGE: Hungarian. Serbo-Croat.
HEADNOTE: DELIVERIES TRADE GOODS
TOPIC: General Trade
CONCEPTS: Detailed regulations. Treaty implementation. Annex or appendix reference. General cooperation. Establishment of commission. Arbitration. Procedure. Special tribunals. Negotiation. General trade. Trade agencies. Balance of payments. Currency. Financial programs. Payment schedules. Non-interest rates and fees. Delivery guarantees. Delivery schedules.
INTL ORGS: Arbitration Commission. Special Commission.
PROCEDURE: Duration.
PARTIES:
Hungary
Yugoslavia

101555 Bilateral Protocol **115 UNTS 3**
SIGNED: 23 Nov 45 FORCE: 23 Nov 45
REGISTERED: 27 Nov 51 Yugoslavia
ARTICLES: 11 LANGUAGE: Polish. Serbo-Croat.
HEADNOTE: PROVISIONAL ECONOMIC RELATIONS
TOPIC: General Economic
CONCEPTS: Conditions. General provisions. Annex or appendix reference. Negotiation. Establishment of trade relations. Reciprocity in trade. Banking. Indemnities and reimbursements. Currency. Non-interest rates and fees. Delivery guarantees. Delivery schedules. Quotas. Transport of goods.
PARTIES:
Poland
Yugoslavia

101556 Bilateral Protocol **115 UNTS 21**
SIGNED: 2 Jan 46 FORCE: 2 Jan 46
REGISTERED: 27 Nov 51 Yugoslavia
ARTICLES: 12 LANGUAGE: Polish. Serbo-Croat.
HEADNOTE: EMIGRATION POLES YUGOSLAVIA
TOPIC: Visas
CONCEPTS: Definition of terms. Detailed regulations. Border traffic and migration. General property. Jurisdiction. Establishment of commission. Dispute settlement. Sickness and invalidity insurance. Most favored nation clause. Foreign nationals.
INTL ORGS: Special Commission.
PROCEDURE: Denunciation. Duration. Renewal or Revival.
PARTIES:
Poland
Yugoslavia

101557 Bilateral Agreement **115 UNTS 37**
SIGNED: 24 May 47 FORCE: 1 Jun 47
REGISTERED: 27 Nov 51 Yugoslavia
ARTICLES: 12 LANGUAGE: Polish. Serbo-Croat.
HEADNOTE: TRADE
TOPIC: General Trade
CONCEPTS: Treaty implementation. Annex or appendix reference. Licenses and permits. Balance of payments. Payment schedules. Non-interest rates and fees. Debt settlement. Delivery schedules. Quotas. Transport of goods.
INTL ORGS: Special Commission.
PARTIES:
Poland
Yugoslavia

101558 Bilateral Agreement **115 UNTS 69**
SIGNED: 24 May 47 FORCE: 24 May 47
REGISTERED: 27 Nov 51 Yugoslavia
ARTICLES: 10 LANGUAGE: Polish. Serbo-Croat.
HEADNOTE: NON-COMMERCIAL PAYMENTS
TOPIC: Finance
CONCEPTS: Detailed regulations. Conformity with municipal law. General cooperation. Accounting procedures. Banking. Balance of payments. Interest rates. Payment schedules. Local currency.
PROCEDURE: Denunciation.
PARTIES:
Poland
Yugoslavia

101559 Bilateral Protocol **115 UNTS 83**
SIGNED: 18 Jan 46 FORCE: 24 May 47
REGISTERED: 27 Nov 51 Yugoslavia
ARTICLES: 4 LANGUAGE: Polish. Serbo-Croat.
HEADNOTE: DELIVERIES
TOPIC: General Trade
CONCEPTS: Annex type material. Accounting procedures. Banking. Payment schedules. Delivery guarantees.
PARTIES:
Poland
Yugoslavia

101560 Bilateral Treaty **115 UNTS 89**
SIGNED: 24 May 47 FORCE: 24 May 47
REGISTERED: 27 Nov 51 Yugoslavia
ARTICLES: 10 LANGUAGE: Polish. Serbo-Croat.
HEADNOTE: ECONOMIC COOPERATION TRADE
TOPIC: General Trade
CONCEPTS: General provisions. Annex or appendix reference. Establishment of commission. Research results. Scientific exchange. Delivery schedules. Quotas. Most favored nation clause. General technical assistance. Ports and pilotage.
INTL ORGS: Special Commission.
PROCEDURE: Denunciation. Duration.
PARTIES:
Poland
Yugoslavia

101561 Bilateral Agreement **115 UNTS 137**
SIGNED: 7 Nov 47 FORCE: 7 Nov 47
REGISTERED: 27 Nov 51 Yugoslavia
ARTICLES: 12 LANGUAGE: Polish. Serbo-Croat.
HEADNOTE: ECONOMIC COOPERATION
TOPIC: General Economic
CONCEPTS: Conditions. Annex or appendix reference. Annex type material. Licenses and permits. Private contracts. Trade agencies. Trade procedures. Banking. Exchange rates and regulations. Payment schedules. Non-interest rates and fees. Delivery guarantees. Delivery schedules. Quotas. General transportation. Transport of goods.
PROCEDURE: Duration.
PARTIES:
Poland
Yugoslavia

101562 Bilateral Agreement **115 UNTS 155**
SIGNED: 21 Jan 48 FORCE: 21 Jan 48
REGISTERED: 27 Nov 51 Yugoslavia
ARTICLES: 9 LANGUAGE: Polish. Serbo-Croat.
HEADNOTE: CONSTRUCTION POWDER FACTORY
TOPIC: Non-IBRD Project
CONCEPTS: Exchange of official publications. Personnel. Quotas. Materials, equipment and services. Plans and standards. Industry.

PARTIES:
Poland
Yugoslavia

101563   Bilateral Agreement   **115 UNTS 167**
SIGNED: 12 Apr 48   FORCE: 1 Jun 48
REGISTERED: 27 Nov 51 Yugoslavia
ARTICLES: 12 LANGUAGE: Polish. Serbo-Croat.
HEADNOTE: TRADE
TOPIC: General Trade
CONCEPTS: Detailed regulations. Treaty implementation. Annex or appendix reference. General cooperation. Licenses and permits. Free trade. Trade agencies. Trade procedures. Accounting procedures. Balance of payments. Payment settlement. Debt settlement. Delivery schedules. Quotas. Transport of goods.
INTL ORGS: Special Commission.
PROCEDURE: Duration.
PARTIES:
Poland
Yugoslavia

101564   Bilateral Agreement   **115 UNTS 241**
SIGNED: 16 Jan 49   FORCE: 1 Jan 49
REGISTERED: 27 Nov 51 Yugoslavia
ARTICLES: 12 LANGUAGE: Polish. Serbo-Croat.
HEADNOTE: TRADE
TOPIC: General Trade
CONCEPTS: Treaty implementation. Annex or appendix reference. Licenses and permits. Trade agencies. Balance of payments. Payment schedules. Debt settlement. Delivery guarantees. Quotas. Transport of goods.
INTL ORGS: Special Commission.
PROCEDURE: Duration.
PARTIES:
Poland
Yugoslavia

101565   Bilateral Agreement   **116 UNTS 3**
SIGNED: 15 Dec 45   FORCE: 15 Dec 45
REGISTERED: 27 Nov 51 Yugoslavia
ARTICLES: 16 LANGUAGE: French.
HEADNOTE: COMMERCIAL EXCHANGES SETTLEMENT PAYMENTS
TOPIC: General Economic
CONCEPTS: Currency. Payment schedules. Quotas.
PROCEDURE: Denunciation. Duration.
PARTIES:
Romania
Yugoslavia

101566   Bilateral Agreement   **116 UNTS 21**
SIGNED: 26 Jun 46   FORCE: 26 Jun 46
REGISTERED: 27 Nov 51 Yugoslavia
ARTICLES: 11 LANGUAGE: French.
HEADNOTE: REGULATE NON-COMMERCIAL PAYMENTS
TOPIC: Finance
CONCEPTS: Detailed regulations. Annex or appendix reference. Licenses and permits. General trade. Export quotas. Trade procedures. Accounting procedures. Banking. Exchange rates and regulations. Interest rates. Payment schedules. Non-interest rates and fees. Local currency. Loan and credit. Credit provisions.
PROCEDURE: Denunciation. Duration. Renewal or Revival.
PARTIES:
Romania
Yugoslavia

101567   Bilateral Convention   **116 UNTS 33**
SIGNED: 23 Dec 46   FORCE: 23 Dec 46
REGISTERED: 27 Nov 51 Yugoslavia
ARTICLES: 5 LANGUAGE: French.
HEADNOTE: LOAN GRAIN
TOPIC: Loans and Credits
CONCEPTS: Definition of terms. General cooperation. Operating agencies. Indemnities and reimbursements. Transportation costs. Agriculture. Agricultural commodities. Loan and credit.
PARTIES:
Romania
Yugoslavia

101568   Bilateral Convention   **116 UNTS 39**
SIGNED: 26 Jun 47   FORCE: 20 Jan 48
REGISTERED: 27 Nov 51 Yugoslavia
ARTICLES: 7 LANGUAGE: Romanian. Serbo-Croat.
HEADNOTE: CULTURAL COOPERATION
TOPIC: Culture
CONCEPTS: Friendship and amity. Operating agencies. Establishment of commission. Recognition of degrees. Teacher and student exchange. Professorships. Institute establishment. Scholarships and grants. Vocational training. Exchange. General cultural cooperation. Artists. Athletes. Research cooperation. Scientific exchange. Accounting procedures. Publications exchange. Mass media exchange.
INTL ORGS: Special Commission.
PROCEDURE: Denunciation. Duration. Ratification. Renewal or Revival.
PARTIES:
Romania
Yugoslavia

101569   Bilateral Agreement   **116 UNTS 57**
SIGNED: 30 Jun 47   FORCE: 31 Jul 47
REGISTERED: 27 Nov 51 Yugoslavia
ARTICLES: 16 LANGUAGE: French.
HEADNOTE: AIR TRANSPORT
TOPIC: Air Transport
CONCEPTS: Definition of terms. Exceptions and exemptions. Annex or appendix reference. Previous treaty replacement. Conformity with municipal law. General cooperation. Informational records. Licenses and permits. Personnel. Recognition of legal documents. Use of facilities. Procedure. Negotiation. Humanitarian matters. Fees and exemptions. National treatment. Customs exemptions. Competency certificate. Registration certificate. Routes and logistics. Navigational conditions. Navigational equipment. Permit designation. Air transport. Airport facilities. Airworthiness certificates. Conditions of airlines operating permission. Operating authorizations and regulations. Licenses and certificates of nationality.
PROCEDURE: Amendment. Denunciation. Future Procedures Contemplated.
PARTIES:
Romania
Yugoslavia

101570   Bilateral Agreement   **116 UNTS 71**
SIGNED: 30 Sep 47   FORCE: 30 Sep 47
REGISTERED: 27 Nov 51 Yugoslavia
ARTICLES: 8 LANGUAGE: French.
HEADNOTE: REGULATION RECIPROCAL PAYMENTS
TOPIC: Finance
CONCEPTS: Detailed regulations. General cooperation. Informational records. Accounting procedures. Banking. Balance of payments. Currency. Interest rates. Payment schedules. General technical assistance. Loan and credit.
PROCEDURE: Denunciation.
PARTIES:
Romania
Yugoslavia

101571   Bilateral Treaty   **116 UNTS 89**
SIGNED: 19 Dec 47   FORCE: 19 Dec 47
REGISTERED: 27 Nov 51 Yugoslavia
ARTICLES: 7 LANGUAGE: Romanian. Serbo-Croat.
HEADNOTE: FRIENDSHIP PEACEFUL COOPERATION MUTUAL AID
TOPIC: General Amity
CONCEPTS: Exceptions and exemptions. Non-prejudice to UN charter. General cooperation. Defense and security.
PROCEDURE: Duration. Ratification. Termination.
PARTIES:
Romania
Yugoslavia

101572   Bilateral Protocol   **116 UNTS 103**
SIGNED: 31 Dec 48   FORCE: 31 Dec 48
REGISTERED: 27 Nov 51 Yugoslavia
ARTICLES: 20 LANGUAGE: Romanian. Serbo-Croat.
HEADNOTE: CROSSING FRONTIERS OFFICIALS WATER CONTROL SERVICES
TOPIC: Visas

CONCEPTS: Emergencies. Annex or appendix reference. Border traffic and migration. Visas. Frontier permits. General cooperation. Fees and exemptions. Frontier peoples and personnel.
PROCEDURE: Renewal or Revival.
PARTIES:
Romania
Yugoslavia

101573   Bilateral Agreement   **116 UNTS 139**
SIGNED: 13 Nov 45   FORCE: 13 Nov 45
REGISTERED: 27 Nov 51 Yugoslavia
ARTICLES: 10 LANGUAGE: Russian. Serbo-Croat.
HEADNOTE: CONDITIONS WORK EXPERTS
TOPIC: Scientific Project
CONCEPTS: Detailed regulations. Conformity with municipal law. Personnel. Safety standards. Wages and salaries. Research and scientific projects. Claims and settlements. Tax exemptions.
PROCEDURE: Duration.
PARTIES:
USSR (Soviet Union)
Yugoslavia

101574   Bilateral Agreement   **116 UNTS 153**
SIGNED: 30 Nov 45   FORCE: 30 Nov 45
REGISTERED: 27 Nov 51 Yugoslavia
ARTICLES: 4 LANGUAGE: Russian. Serbo-Croat.
HEADNOTE: PETROLEUM PRODUCTS DELIVERIES TRADE
TOPIC: General Trade
CONCEPTS: Commodity trade. Quotas.
PROCEDURE: Termination.
PARTIES:
USSR (Soviet Union)
Yugoslavia

101575   Bilateral Agreement   **116 UNTS 163**
SIGNED: 26 Apr 46   FORCE: 26 Apr 46
REGISTERED: 27 Nov 51 Yugoslavia
ARTICLES: 5 LANGUAGE: Russian. Serbo-Croat.
HEADNOTE: GRAIN & PULSE DELIVERIES TRADE
TOPIC: General Trade
CONCEPTS: Treaty implementation. Payment schedules. Commodity trade. Delivery schedules.
PARTIES:
USSR (Soviet Union)
Yugoslavia

101576   Bilateral Agreement   **116 UNTS 171**
SIGNED: 4 Feb 47   FORCE: 4 Feb 47
REGISTERED: 27 Nov 51 Yugoslavia
ARTICLES: 16 LANGUAGE: Russian. Serbo-Croat.
HEADNOTE: CREATION JOINT-STOCK COMPANY
TOPIC: Admin Cooperation
CONCEPTS: Annex or appendix reference. Operating agencies. Use of facilities. Expense sharing formulae. Financial programs. Tax exemptions.
PROCEDURE: Duration.
PARTIES:
USSR (Soviet Union)
Yugoslavia

101577   Bilateral Agreement   **116 UNTS 281**
SIGNED: 23 Aug 47   FORCE: 23 Aug 47
REGISTERED: 27 Nov 51 Yugoslavia
ARTICLES: 8 LANGUAGE: Russian. Serbo-Croat.
HEADNOTE: SALE WAR BOOTY
TOPIC: Reparations
CONCEPTS: Annex or appendix reference. Use of facilities. Interest rates. Delivery schedules. Agricultural commodities. Surplus war property.
PARTIES:
USSR (Soviet Union)
Yugoslavia
ANNEX
149 UNTS 418. Yugoslavia. Implementation 10 Jan 48. Force 10 Jan 48.
149 UNTS 418. USSR (Soviet Union). Implementation 10 Jan 48. Force 10 Jan 48.

101578   Bilateral Agreement   **116 UNTS 313**
SIGNED: 15 Dec 47   FORCE: 15 Dec 47
REGISTERED: 27 Nov 51 Yugoslavia
ARTICLES: 9 LANGUAGE: Russian. Serbo-Croat.

HEADNOTE: FINANCIAL MAINTENANCE STU-
DENTS
TOPIC: Education
CONCEPTS: Detailed regulations. Visas. Confor-
mity with municipal law. Personnel. Recognition
of degrees. Exchange. Teacher and student ex-
change. Scholarships and grants. Accounting
procedures. Indemnities and reimbursements.
PROCEDURE: Duration.
PARTIES:
  USSR (Soviet Union)
  Yugoslavia

101579 Bilateral Protocol **116 UNTS 327**
SIGNED: 27 Dec 48 FORCE: 27 Dec 48
REGISTERED: 27 Nov 51 Yugoslavia
ARTICLES: 3 LANGUAGE: Russian. Serbo-Croat.
HEADNOTE: TRADE
TOPIC: General Trade
CONCEPTS: Annex or appendix reference. Ac-
counting procedures. Banking. Payment sched-
ules. Non-interest rates and fees. Debt settle-
ment. Commodity trade.
PARTIES:
  USSR (Soviet Union)
  Yugoslavia

101580 Bilateral Protocol **116 UNTS 345**
SIGNED: 31 Aug 49 FORCE: 31 Aug 49
REGISTERED: 27 Nov 51 Yugoslavia
ARTICLES: 7 LANGUAGE: Russian. Serbo-Croat.
HEADNOTE: LIQUIDATION JOINT-STOCK COM-
PANY
TOPIC: Admin Cooperation
CONCEPTS: Annex or appendix reference. Previ-
ous treaty replacement. Operating agencies. Re-
sponsibility and liability. Lump sum settlements.
Assets transfer. Tax exemptions.
PARTIES:
  USSR (Soviet Union)
  Yugoslavia

101581 Bilateral Convention **117 UNTS 3**
SIGNED: 7 Sep 49 FORCE: 7 Sep 49
REGISTERED: 30 Nov 51 Belgium
ARTICLES: 11 LANGUAGE: French.
HEADNOTE: LOAN CONVENTION
TOPIC: Loans and Credits
CONCEPTS: Annex or appendix reference. Gen-
eral cooperation. Operating agencies. Expense
sharing formulae. Financial programs. Funding
procedures. Interest rates. Payment schedules.
Loan and credit. Credit provisions. Loan repay-
ment. Terms of loan.
INTL ORGS: Bank for International Settlements.
Organization for Economic Co-operation and De-
velopment.
PARTIES:
  Belgium
  Netherlands

101582 Bilateral Agreement **117 UNTS 19**
SIGNED: 1 May 51 FORCE: 1 May 51
REGISTERED: 30 Nov 51 UK Great Britain
ARTICLES: 14 LANGUAGE: Arabic. English.
HEADNOTE: TERMINATION MANDATE
TOPIC: Finance
CONCEPTS: Detailed regulations. General cooper-
ation. General property. Responsibility and liabil-
ity. Use of facilities. Payment schedules. Assets.
Claims and settlements. Debt settlement. Gen-
eral aid. Trusteeship.
PARTIES:
  Jordan
  UK Great Britain

101583 Bilateral Agreement **117 UNTS 49**
SIGNED: 18 Jul 51 FORCE: 18 Jul 51
REGISTERED: 30 Nov 51 UK Great Britain
ARTICLES: 16 LANGUAGE: English.
HEADNOTE: DEVELOPMENT RHODESIA RAIL-
WAYS
TOPIC: Land Transport
CONCEPTS: Change of circumstances. Default
remedies. Definition of terms. Remedies. Time
limit. Annex or appendix reference. General co-
operation. Inspection and observation. Domestic
legislation. Programs. Accounting procedures.
Currency deposits. Interest rates. Payment

schedules. Economic assistance. Loan and
credit. Credit provisions. Purchase authorization.
Terms of loan. Natural resources. Railways.
PROCEDURE: Amendment. Termination.
PARTIES:
  UK Great Britain
  USA (United States)
                    ANNEX
204 UNTS 364. USA (United States). Amendment
  21 Oct 54. Force 18 Jul 54.
204 UNTS 364. UK Great Britain. Amendment
  30 Sep 54. Force 18 Jul 54.

101584 Bilateral Exchange **117 UNTS 79**
SIGNED: 18 Mar 47 FORCE: 18 Mar 47
REGISTERED: 6 Dec 51 USA (United States)
ARTICLES: 2 LANGUAGE: English.
HEADNOTE: AMENDING FOX SKINS AGREEMENT
TOPIC: Commodity Trade
CONCEPTS: Annex type material. Negotiation.
Commodity trade. Quotas. Customs duties.
PARTIES:
  Canada
  USA (United States)

101585 Multilateral Agreement **117 UNTS 85**
SIGNED: 29 Jul 51 FORCE: 20 Jul 51
REGISTERED: 11 Dec 51 UK Great Britain
ARTICLES: 13 LANGUAGE: English. French.
HEADNOTE: WAR CEMETERIES
TOPIC: Other Military
CONCEPTS: Definition of terms. Previous treaty re-
placement. Title and deeds. Establishment of
commission. Tax exemptions. Customs exemp-
tions. Upkeep of war graves. Establishment of
war cemeteries.
INTL ORGS: Special Commission.
PARTIES:
  Australia SIGNED: 20 Jul 51 FORCE: 20 Jul 51
  Belgium SIGNED: 20 Jul 51 FORCE: 20 Jul 51
  Canada SIGNED: 20 Jul 51 FORCE: 20 Jul 51
  India SIGNED: 20 Jul 51 FORCE: 20 Jul 51
  New Zealand SIGNED: 20 Jul 51 FORCE:
    20 Jul 51
  Pakistan SIGNED: 20 Jul 51 FORCE: 20 Jul 51
  South Africa SIGNED: 20 Jul 51 FORCE:
    20 Jul 51
  UK Great Britain SIGNED: 20 Jul 51 FORCE:
    20 Jul 51

101586 Bilateral Exchange **117 UNTS 99**
SIGNED: 28 Jun 51 FORCE: 28 Jun 51
REGISTERED: 11 Dec 51 UK Great Britain
ARTICLES: 2 LANGUAGE: English. German.
HEADNOTE: CONTINUED APPLICATION CONVEN-
TION
TOPIC: Admin Cooperation
CONCEPTS: Previous treaty extension.
PARTIES:
  Austria
  UK Great Britain

101587 Bilateral Exchange **117 UNTS 107**
SIGNED: 28 Sep 51 FORCE: 28 Sep 51
REGISTERED: 11 Dec 51 UK Great Britain
ARTICLES: 2 LANGUAGE: English.
HEADNOTE: SHORT-TERM ECONOMIC ASSIS-
TANCE
TOPIC: Finance
CONCEPTS: Annex or appendix reference. Confor-
mity with municipal law. General cooperation.
Accounting procedures. Banking. Payment
schedules. Purchase authorizations. Grants.
Credit provisions.
PARTIES:
  UK Great Britain
  Yugoslavia

101588 Bilateral Agreement **117 UNTS 115**
SIGNED: 13 Jun 51 FORCE: 13 Jun 51
REGISTERED: 11 Dec 51 WHO (World Health)
ARTICLES: 1 LANGUAGE: English.
HEADNOTE: MALARIA CONTROL DEMONSTRA-
TION PROJECT
TOPIC: Sanitation
CONCEPTS: Personnel. Programs. Disease con-
trol. Public health. Insect control. WHO used as
agency. Institute establishment. Vocational
training. Research and development. Indemni-

ties and reimbursements. Expense sharing for-
mulae. Special projects. Materials, equipment
and services. General transportation.
INTL ORGS: International Court of Justice.
PROCEDURE: Duration.
PARTIES:
  Burma
  WHO (World Health)

101589 Bilateral Instrument **117 UNTS 131**
SIGNED: 24 Aug 48 FORCE: 19 Nov 51
REGISTERED: 17 Dec 51 Belgium
ARTICLES: 8 LANGUAGE: French.
HEADNOTE: SUPPLEMENTARY DECLARATION
TOPIC: Extradition
CONCEPTS: Annex type material. Previous treaty
extension.
PARTIES:
  Belgium
  Luxembourg

101590 Bilateral Agreement **117 UNTS 139**
SIGNED: 22 Oct 51 FORCE: 22 Oct 51
REGISTERED: 26 Dec 51 ILO (Labor Org)
ARTICLES: 5 LANGUAGE: Spanish.
HEADNOTE: TECHNICAL ASSISTANCE
TOPIC: Tech Assistance
CONCEPTS: Treaty implementation. Privileges and
immunities. General cooperation. Exchange of
information and documents. Personnel. Title and
deeds. Arbitration. Procedure. Scholarships and
grants. Vocational training. Exchange rates and
regulations. Expense sharing formulae. Local
currency. Domestic obligation. General techni-
cal assistance. Materials, equipment and ser-
vices. Conformity with IGO decisions.
INTL ORGS: United Nations.
PROCEDURE: Amendment. Termination.
PARTIES:
  ILO (Labor Org)
  Venezuela

101591 Bilateral Agreement **117 UNTS 155**
SIGNED: 12 Jul 51 FORCE: 20 Aug 51
REGISTERED: 26 Dec 51 ILO (Labor Org)
ARTICLES: 5 LANGUAGE: Spanish.
HEADNOTE: TECHNICAL ASSISTANCE
TOPIC: Tech Assistance
CONCEPTS: Treaty implementation. Privileges and
immunities. General cooperation. Exchange of
information and documents. Personnel. Title and
deeds. Arbitration. Procedure. Scholarships and
grants. Vocational training. Exchange rates and
regulations. Expense sharing formulae. Local
currency. Domestic obligation. General techni-
cal assistance. Materials, equipment and ser-
vices. Conformity with IGO decisions.
INTL ORGS: United Nations.
PROCEDURE: Termination.
PARTIES:
  Paraguay
  ILO (Labor Org)

101592 Bilateral Agreement **118 UNTS 3**
SIGNED: 30 Nov 51 FORCE: 5 Dec 51
REGISTERED: 2 Jan 52 ILO (Labor Org)
ARTICLES: 8 LANGUAGE: English.
HEADNOTE: TUBERCULOSIS IMMUNIZATION RE-
SEARCH CENTER
TOPIC: Scientific Project
CONCEPTS: Definition of terms. Privileges and im-
munities. Operating agencies. Personnel. Estab-
lishment of commission. Public health. WHO
used as agency. Research and scientific
projects. Research cooperation. Research and
development.
INTL ORGS: United Nations. Special Commission.
PROCEDURE: Future Procedures Contemplated.
Termination.
PARTIES:
  Denmark
  WHO (World Health)

101593 Bilateral Agreement **118 UNTS 13**
SIGNED: 1 Nov 51 FORCE: 1 Nov 51
REGISTERED: 2 Jan 52 ILO (Labor Org)
ARTICLES: 4 LANGUAGE: English.
HEADNOTE: EPIDEMIOLOGICAL INVESTIGATION
CHOLERA

TOPIC: Scientific Project
CONCEPTS: Definition of terms. Privileges and immunities. Operating agencies. Personnel. General property. Use of facilities. Public health. Wages and salaries. Research and scientific projects. Research and development. Expense sharing formulae. Domestic obligation. IGO obligations.
INTL ORGS: United Nations.
PROCEDURE: Amendment. Duration. Termination.
PARTIES:
India
WHO (World Health)

101594 Bilateral Agreement **118 UNTS 27**
SIGNED: 11 Oct 51 FORCE: 22 Oct 51
REGISTERED: 2 Jan 52 WHO (World Health)
ARTICLES: 5 LANGUAGE: English.
HEADNOTE: FOOD PRODUCTION
TOPIC: Non-IBRD Project
CONCEPTS: Personnel. Arbitration. Negotiation. Public health. WHO used as agency. Claims and settlements. Agriculture. Assistance. Use restrictions. Hydro-electric power. IGO constitution. IGO status. Status of experts.
INTL ORGS: United Nations.
PARTIES:
India
WHO (World Health)

101595 Bilateral Agreement **118 UNTS 43**
SIGNED: 9 Nov 51 FORCE: 26 Nov 51
REGISTERED: 2 Jan 52 WHO (World Health)
ARTICLES: 6 LANGUAGE: English. Spanish.
HEADNOTE: HEALTH PROJECTS PANAMA
TOPIC: Sanitation
CONCEPTS: Definition of terms. Privileges and immunities. Personnel. General property. Arbitration. Specialists exchange. Public health. WHO used as agency. Scholarships and grants. Vocational training. Research and development. Indemnities and reimbursements. Currency. Financial programs. Assistance. Specific technical assistance.
INTL ORGS: United Nations.
PROCEDURE: Amendment. Termination.
PARTIES:
Panama
WHO (World Health)

101596 Multilateral Agreement **118 UNTS 57**
SIGNED: 1 Jun 51 FORCE: 22 Aug 51
REGISTERED: 2 Jan 52 WHO (World Health)
ARTICLES: 4 LANGUAGE: English. Spanish.
HEADNOTE: EXTENDING TRAINING FACILITIES INSTITUTE NUTRITION WORKERS
TOPIC: Tech Assistance
CONCEPTS: Privileges and immunities. General cooperation. Personnel. Institute establishment. Scholarships and grants. Financial programs. Domestic obligation. Special projects. Materials, equipment and services.
INTL ORGS: Institute of Nutrition of Central America and Panama. United Nations.
PARTIES:
Costa Rica SIGNED: 28 May 51 FORCE: 28 May 51
El Salvador SIGNED: 1 Jun 51 FORCE: 1 Jun 51
Guatemala SIGNED: 21 Jun 51 FORCE: 21 Jun 51
Honduras SIGNED: 25 May 51 FORCE: 25 May 51
Panama SIGNED: 23 May 51 FORCE: 23 May 51
FAO (Food Agri) SIGNED: 25 Jul 51 FORCE: 25 Jul 51
WHO (World Health) SIGNED: 2 Aug 51 FORCE: 2 Aug 51

101597 Bilateral Exchange **118 UNTS 73**
SIGNED: 20 Jan 47 FORCE: 20 Jan 47
REGISTERED: 4 Jan 52 UK Great Britain
ARTICLES: 2 LANGUAGE: English.
HEADNOTE: USE DANISH TELEGRAPH TELEPHONE SERVICE
TOPIC: Telecommunications
CONCEPTS: Employment regulations. Non-interest rates and fees. Facilities and equipment. Telegrams. Radio-telephone-telegraphic communications. Military assistance missions.

PARTIES:
Denmark
UK Great Britain

101598 Bilateral Agreement **118 UNTS 91**
SIGNED: 24 Oct 51 FORCE: 24 Oct 51
REGISTERED: 6 Jan 52 Denmark
ARTICLES: 8 LANGUAGE: French.
HEADNOTE: COMMERCIAL AGREEMENT
TOPIC: General Trade
CONCEPTS: Tariffs. Reciprocity in trade. Trade procedures. Banking. Monetary and gold transfers. Customs declarations. Customs exemptions.
INTL ORGS: Organization for Economic Co-operation and Development. Special Commission.
PARTIES:
Denmark
Italy

101599 Bilateral Exchange **118 UNTS 103**
SIGNED: 17 May 51 FORCE: 17 May 51
REGISTERED: 6 Jan 52 Netherlands
ARTICLES: 2 LANGUAGE: English.
HEADNOTE: CARRIAGE DANGEROUS GOODS AIRCRAFT
TOPIC: Air Transport
CONCEPTS: Territorial application. Registration certificate. Dangerous goods. Permit designation. Air transport.
PROCEDURE: Termination. Application to Non-self-governing Territories.
PARTIES:
Netherlands
UK Great Britain

101600 Bilateral Exchange **118 UNTS 115**
SIGNED: 28 Jun 51 FORCE: 28 Jun 51
REGISTERED: 7 Jan 52 UK Great Britain
ARTICLES: 2 LANGUAGE: English. Italian.
HEADNOTE: DISPOSAL PRIVATE PROPERTY
TOPIC: Claims and Debts
CONCEPTS: Annex or appendix reference. General property. Assets transfer.
INTL ORGS: United Nations.
PARTIES:
Italy
UK Great Britain

101601 Bilateral Exchange **118 UNTS 133**
SIGNED: 7 Nov 51 FORCE: 7 Nov 51
REGISTERED: 7 Jan 52 UK Great Britain
ARTICLES: 2 LANGUAGE: English. Italian.
HEADNOTE: DISPOSAL ADMINISTRATION PROPERTY
TOPIC: Claims and Debts
CONCEPTS: Annex or appendix reference. General property. Assets transfer.
TREATY REF: 118UNTS115.
PARTIES:
Italy
UK Great Britain

101602 Bilateral Exchange **118 UNTS 143**
SIGNED: 24 Oct 51 FORCE: 24 Oct 51
REGISTERED: 7 Jan 52 UK Great Britain
ARTICLES: 2 LANGUAGE: English. Italian.
HEADNOTE: CARRIAGE DANGEROUS GOODS AIRCRAFT
TOPIC: Air Transport
CONCEPTS: Exceptions and exemptions. Registration certificate. Dangerous goods. Permit designation. Air transport.
PROCEDURE: Termination. Application to Non-self-governing Territories.
PARTIES:
Italy
UK Great Britain

101603 Bilateral Agreement **118 UNTS 149**
SIGNED: 29 Dec 50 FORCE: 24 Sep 51
REGISTERED: 7 Jan 52 UK Great Britain
ARTICLES: 4 LANGUAGE: English. French.
HEADNOTE: SUBMISSION ICJ DIFFERENCES SOVEREIGNITY MINQUIERS ECREHOS ISLETS
TOPIC: Dispute Settlement
CONCEPTS: Existing tribunals.
INTL ORGS: International Court of Justice.

PROCEDURE: Ratification.
PARTIES:
France
UK Great Britain

101604 Multilateral Agreement **118 UNTS 154**
SIGNED: 28 Jun 51 FORCE: 8 Jan 52
REGISTERED: 8 Jan 52 United Nations
ARTICLES: 7 LANGUAGE: English. French.
HEADNOTE: TECHNICAL ASSISTANCE
TOPIC: Tech Assistance
CONCEPTS: Treaty implementation. Privileges and immunities. General cooperation. Exchange of information and documents. Title and deeds. Use of facilities. Arbitration. Procedure. Scholarships and grants. Vocational training. Research and scientific projects. Exchange rates and regulations. Expense sharing formulae. Local currency. Domestic obligation. General technical assistance. Materials, equipment and services. IGO status. Conformity with IGO decisions.
TREATY REF: 76UNTS132; 33UNTS261.
PROCEDURE: Amendment. Ratification. Termination.
PARTIES:
Haiti SIGNED: 28 Jun 51 RATIFIED: 8 Jan 52 FORCE: 8 Jan 52
FAO (Food Agri) SIGNED: 28 Jun 51 FORCE: 8 Jan 52
ILO (Labor Org) SIGNED: 28 Jun 51 FORCE: 8 Jan 52
UNESCO (Educ/Cult) SIGNED: 28 Jun 51 FORCE: 8 Jan 52
United Nations SIGNED: 28 Jun 51 FORCE: 8 Jan 52
WHO (World Health) SIGNED: 28 Jun 51 FORCE: 8 Jan 52
ANNEX
321 UNTS 283. United Nations. Force 24 Jul 56.
321 UNTS 283. Haiti. Force 24 Jul 56.

101605 Bilateral Exchange **118 UNTS 169**
SIGNED: 1 Nov 51 FORCE: 15 Nov 51
REGISTERED: 10 Jan 52 New Zealand
ARTICLES: 2 LANGUAGE: English.
HEADNOTE: MUTUAL ABOLITION VISAS
TOPIC: Visas
CONCEPTS: Territorial application. Time limit. Visa abolition. Denial of admission. Resident permits. Conformity with municipal law.
PROCEDURE: Termination.
PARTIES:
Belgium
New Zealand

101606 Bilateral Agreement **118 UNTS 175**
SIGNED: 12 Jan 52 FORCE: 12 Jan 52
REGISTERED: 12 Jan 52 United Nations
ARTICLES: 4 LANGUAGE: English.
HEADNOTE: ORGANIZATION SEMINAR PRODUCTION USE POWER ALCOHOL
TOPIC: Tech Assistance
CONCEPTS: Privileges and immunities. General cooperation. Personnel. Use of facilities. Expense sharing formulae. Local currency. Domestic obligation. Conferences.
TREATY REF: 1UNTS15,263.
PROCEDURE: Amendment. Termination.
PARTIES:
India
United Nations
ANNEX
136 UNTS 390. United Nations. Amendment 5 Sep 52. Force 5 Sep 52.
136 UNTS 390. India. Amendment 5 Sep 52. Force 5 Sep 52.

101607 Bilateral Agreement **118 UNTS 183**
SIGNED: 6 Dec 48 FORCE: 1 Apr 49
REGISTERED: 15 Jan 52 UK Great Britain
ARTICLES: 28 LANGUAGE: English.
HEADNOTE: CUSTOMS UNION
TOPIC: Customs
CONCEPTS: Definition of terms. Territorial application. Annex or appendix reference. Previous treaty replacement. Export quotas. Import quotas. Tariffs. Commodity trade. Most favored nation clause. Customs duties. Customs exemptions. Temporary importation.
INTL ORGS: Special Commission.

PROCEDURE: Duration. Termination.
PARTIES:
  South Africa
  UK Great Britain

101608 Bilateral Agreement **118 UNTS 221**
SIGNED: 26 Sep 51   FORCE: 20 Oct 48
REGISTERED: 15 Jan 52 UK Great Britain
ARTICLES: 39 LANGUAGE: English.
HEADNOTE: EXCHANGE MONEY ORDERS
TOPIC: Postal Service
CONCEPTS: Definition of terms. Annex or appendix reference. Conformity with municipal law. Accounting procedures. Postal services. Money orders and postal checks. Rates and charges. Advice lists and orders. Telegrams.
INTL ORGS: International Telecommunication Union.
TREATY REF: 151LTS5.
PROCEDURE: Duration. Termination.
PARTIES:
  Pakistan
  UK Great Britain

101609 Multilateral Instrument **119 UNTS 3**
SIGNED: 30 Apr 48   FORCE: 13 Dec 51
REGISTERED: 16 Jan 52 OAS (Am States)
ARTICLES: 112 LANGUAGE: English. French. Portuguese. Spanish.
HEADNOTE: OAS
TOPIC: IGO Establishment
CONCEPTS: Friendship and amity. Non-prejudice to UN charter. Peaceful relations. Privileges and immunities. Conformity with municipal law. Juridical personality. Procedure. Special tribunals. Education. Culture. Anti-discrimination. Accounting procedures. Funding procedures. Defense and security. Admission. Subsidiary organ. Establishment. Procedure. Headquarters and facilities. Internal structure. Special status. Status of experts. Assistance to United Nations. Acceptance of UN obligations.
INTL ORGS: Organization of American States. United Nations.
PROCEDURE: Amendment. Denunciation. Ratification.
PARTIES:
  Argentina SIGNED: 30 Apr 48
  Bolivia SIGNED: 30 Apr 48 RATIFIED: 18 Oct 50 FORCE: 13 Dec 51
  Brazil SIGNED: 30 Apr 48 RATIFIED: 13 Mar 50 FORCE: 13 Dec 51
  Chile SIGNED: 30 Apr 48
  Colombia SIGNED: 30 Apr 48 RATIFIED: 13 Dec 51 FORCE: 13 Dec 51
  Costa Rica SIGNED: 30 Apr 48 RATIFIED: 16 Nov 48 FORCE: 13 Dec 51
  Cuba SIGNED: 30 Apr 48
  Dominican Republic SIGNED: 30 Apr 48 RATIFIED: 22 Apr 49 FORCE: 13 Dec 51
  Ecuador SIGNED: 30 Apr 48 RATIFIED: 28 Dec 50 FORCE: 13 Dec 51
  El Salvador SIGNED: 30 Apr 48 RATIFIED: 11 Sep 50 FORCE: 13 Dec 51
  Guatemala SIGNED: 30 Apr 48
  Haiti SIGNED: 30 Apr 48 RATIFIED: 28 Mar 51 FORCE: 13 Dec 51
  Honduras SIGNED: 30 Apr 48 RATIFIED: 7 Feb 50 FORCE: 13 Dec 51
  Mexico SIGNED: 30 Apr 48 RATIFIED: 23 Nov 48 FORCE: 13 Dec 51
  Nicaragua SIGNED: 30 Apr 48 RATIFIED: 26 Jul 50 FORCE: 13 Dec 51
  Panama SIGNED: 30 Apr 48 RATIFIED: 22 Mar 51 FORCE: 13 Dec 51
  Paraguay SIGNED: 30 Apr 48 RATIFIED: 3 May 50 FORCE: 13 Dec 51
  Peru SIGNED: 30 Apr 48
  USA (United States) SIGNED: 30 Apr 48 RATIFIED: 19 Jun 51 FORCE: 13 Dec 51
  Uruguay SIGNED: 30 Apr 48
  Venezuela SIGNED: 30 Apr 48 RATIFIED: 29 Dec 51 FORCE: 29 Dec 51
          ANNEX
134 UNTS 388. Cuba. Ratification 16 Jul 52.
171 UNTS 419. Chile. Ratification 5 Jun 53.
209 UNTS 338. Guatemala. Qualified Ratification 6 Apr 55.
233 UNTS 304. Argentina. Ratification 10 Apr 56.
377 UNTS 400. Uruguay. Ratification 1 Sep 55.

101610 Multilateral Convention **119 UNTS 99**
SIGNED: 6 Apr 50   FORCE: 24 Jan 52
REGISTERED: 24 Jan 52 United Nations
ARTICLES: 20 LANGUAGE: Chinese. English. French. Russian. Spanish.
HEADNOTE: DECLARATION DEATH MISSING PERSONS
TOPIC: Admin Cooperation
CONCEPTS: Definition of terms. Exchange of information and documents. Free passage and transit. Recognition and enforcement of legal decisions. Public information. Existing tribunals. Special tribunals. Fees and exemptions. Subsidiary organ.
INTL ORGS: International Court of Justice. United Nations. Special Commission.
PROCEDURE: Accession. Duration.
PARTIES:
  Belgium SIGNED: 6 Apr 50
  Bolivia SIGNED: 6 Apr 50
  Brazil SIGNED: 6 Apr 50
  Burma SIGNED: 6 Apr 50
  Canada SIGNED: 6 Apr 50
  Taiwan RATIFIED: 20 Dec 50 FORCE: 24 Jan 52
  Cuba SIGNED: 6 Apr 50
  Denmark SIGNED: 6 Apr 50
  Ecuador SIGNED: 6 Apr 50
  United Arab Rep SIGNED: 6 Apr 50
  Israel SIGNED: 6 Apr 50
  Mexico SIGNED: 6 Apr 50
  Netherlands SIGNED: 6 Apr 50
  Nicaragua SIGNED: 6 Apr 50
  Pakistan SIGNED: 6 Apr 50
  Peru SIGNED: 6 Apr 50
  Philippines SIGNED: 6 Apr 50
  Sweden SIGNED: 6 Apr 50
  Syria SIGNED: 6 Apr 50
  Thailand SIGNED: 6 Apr 50
  Turkey SIGNED: 6 Apr 50
  UK Great Britain SIGNED: 6 Apr 50
  Venezuela SIGNED: 6 Apr 50
  Yugoslavia SIGNED: 6 Apr 50
          ANNEX
128 UNTS 309. Israel. Qualified Accession 7 May 52.
171 UNTS 420. Belgium. Accession 22 Jul 53. Force 21 Aug 53.
222 UNTS 416. Pakistan. Accession 6 Dec 55. Force 5 Jan 56.
227 UNTS 320. Germany, West. Berlin.
227 UNTS 320. Germany, West. Qualified Accession 30 Jan 56. Force 29 Feb 56.
258 UNTS 392. United Nations. Prolongation 16 Jan 57. Force 22 Jan 57.
258 UNTS 392. Israel. Accession 22 Jan 57. Force 22 Jan 57.
258 UNTS 392. Pakistan. Accession 21 Jan 57. Force 22 Jan 57.
274 UNTS 344. Cambodia. Accession 30 Jul 57.
276 UNTS 362. Taiwan. Accession 9 Sep 57.
291 UNTS 308. Italy. Accession 25 Mar 58. Force 24 Apr 58.
291 UNTS 308. Italy. Accession 25 Mar 58. Force 25 Mar 58.
314 UNTS 339. Germany, West. Qualified Accession 23 Oct 58.
402 UNTS 312. Guatemala. Accession 8 Aug 61.
603 UNTS 296. Cambodia. Accession 11 Aug 67.
605 UNTS 343. Israel. Accession 15 Sep 67.

101611 Bilateral Agreement **119 UNTS 163**
SIGNED: 30 Oct 47   FORCE: 30 Oct 47
REGISTERED: 24 Jan 52 USA (United States)
ARTICLES: 5 LANGUAGE: English. Spanish.
HEADNOTE: SUPPLEMENT GATT
TOPIC: General Economic
CONCEPTS: Annex or appendix reference. Annex type material. Previous treaty replacement. Non-interest rates and fees. Most favored nation clause. Customs declarations.
INTL ORGS: General Agreement on Tariffs and Trade. United Nations.
TREATY REF: 55UNTS187; TS427; 153LTS369; 202LTS71; 31MARTENS47.
PARTIES:
  Cuba
  USA (United States)

101612 Bilateral Exchange **120 UNTS 3**
SIGNED: 5 Mar 46   FORCE: 5 Mar 46
REGISTERED: 24 Jan 52 USA (United States)
ARTICLES: 2 LANGUAGE: English. Spanish.

HEADNOTE: REHABILITATION RAILWAYS
TOPIC: Claims and Debts
CONCEPTS: Previous treaty extension. General technical assistance. Railways.
TREATY REF: 4UNTS184; 4UNTS196.
PROCEDURE: Duration. Termination.
PARTIES:
  Mexico
  USA (United States)

101613 Multilateral Instrument **120 UNTS 13**
SIGNED: 29 Nov 48   FORCE: 4 Jan 49
REGISTERED: 24 Jan 52 FAO (Food Agri)
ARTICLES: 9 LANGUAGE: English.
HEADNOTE: INTERNATIONAL RICE COMMISSION
TOPIC: IGO Establishment
CONCEPTS: Exchange of official publications. Research cooperation. Scientific exchange. Funding procedures. Agriculture. Specific technical assistance. IGO constitution. Establishment. Liaison with other IGO's. Internal structure. UN administrative tribunal. Inter-agency agreements.
INTL ORGS: International Rice Commission. Food and Agricultural Organization of the United Nations. United Nations.
PROCEDURE: Amendment. Accession. Denunciation.
PARTIES:
  Burma RATIFIED: 29 Nov 48 FORCE: 4 Jan 49
  Cambodia RATIFIED: 16 Jul 51 FORCE: 16 Jul 51
  Ceylon (Sri Lanka) RATIFIED: 27 Sep 48 FORCE: 4 Jan 49
  Taiwan RATIFIED: 11 Jul 49 FORCE: 11 Jul 49
  Cuba RATIFIED: 10 Jan 49 FORCE: 10 Jan 49
  Dominican Republic RATIFIED: 29 Mar 51 FORCE: 29 Mar 51
  Ecuador RATIFIED: 6 Sep 48 FORCE: 4 Jan 49
  United Arab Rep RATIFIED: 29 Nov 48 FORCE: 4 Jan 49
  France RATIFIED: 10 Aug 48 FORCE: 4 Jan 49
  India RATIFIED: 12 Oct 48 FORCE: 4 Jan 49
  Indonesia RATIFIED: 15 Mar 50 FORCE: 15 Mar 50
  Italy RATIFIED: 6 Oct 48 FORCE: 4 Jan 49
  Mexico RATIFIED: 17 Dec 48 FORCE: 4 Jan 49
  Netherlands RATIFIED: 12 Nov 48 FORCE: 4 Jan 49
  Pakistan RATIFIED: 5 Oct 48 FORCE: 4 Jan 49
  Paraguay RATIFIED: 20 Apr 50 FORCE: 20 Apr 50
  Philippines RATIFIED: 4 Jan 48 FORCE: 4 Jan 49
  Thailand RATIFIED: 1 Nov 48 FORCE: 4 Jan 49
  UK Great Britain RATIFIED: 28 Feb 49 FORCE: 28 Feb 49
  USA (United States) RATIFIED: 28 Feb 49 FORCE: 28 Feb 49
  Vietnam RATIFIED: 13 Jun 51 FORCE: 13 Jun 51
          ANNEX
135 UNTS 373. Japan. Acceptance 28 Apr 52.
171 UNTS 421. Australia. Acceptance 1 Jul 53.
183 UNTS 371. Korea, South. Acceptance 21 Nov 53.
187 UNTS 448. Taiwan. Force 21 Jul 52.
193 UNTS 352. FAO (Food Agri). Amendment 10 Dec 53. Force 10 Dec 53.
196 UNTS 351. Laos. Acceptance 21 Jul 54.
202 UNTS 335. Iran. Acceptance 30 Sep 54.
202 UNTS 335. Portugal. Acceptance 9 Dec 54.
229 UNTS 296. Int Rice Commission. Amendment 18 Nov 55. Force 18 Nov 55.
313 UNTS 345. Fed of Malaya. Acceptance 15 Sep 58.
417 UNTS 349. Nigeria. Acceptance 13 Nov 61.
417 UNTS 349. Venezuela. Acceptance 27 Nov 61.
418 UNTS 334. Int Rice Commission. Amendment 23 Nov 61. Force 23 Nov 61.
469 UNTS 417. Mali. Acceptance 4 Jun 63.
507 UNTS 265. Brazil. Acceptance 21 Aug 64.
511 UNTS 268. Sierra Leone. Acceptance 22 Sep 64.
515 UNTS 304. Guatemala. Acceptance 23 Oct 64.
601 UNTS 342. Nepal. Acceptance 11 Jul 67.
633 UNTS 384. Ghana. Acceptance 8 Mar 68.
635 UNTS 345. Uruguay. Acceptance 4 Apr 68.
646 UNTS 348. Colombia. Acceptance 6 Sep 68.
653 UNTS 457. Nicaragua. Acceptance 10 Dec 68.

101614 Bilateral Convention **120 UNTS 25**
SIGNED: 7 Jan 50 FORCE: 1 Nov 51
REGISTERED: 27 Jan 52 Netherlands
ARTICLES: 36 LANGUAGE: French.
HEADNOTE: SOCIAL SECURITY OLD-AGE BENE-
FITS
TOPIC: Non-ILO Labor
CONCEPTS: Detailed regulations. Exceptions and
exemptions. General provisions. Conformity
with municipal law. Domestic legislation. Incor-
poration of treaty provisions into national law.
Old age and invalidity insurance. Non-ILO labor
relations. Family allowances. Administrative cooperation. Old age insurance. Sickness and invalidity insurance. Social security. Payment schedules. National treatment.
PROCEDURE: Duration. Future Procedures Contemplated. Ratification. Renewal or Revival. Termination.
PARTIES:
France
Netherlands
ANNEX
135 UNTS 374. Netherlands. Implementation
27 Mar 52. Force 27 Mar 52.
135 UNTS 374. France. Implementation
27 Mar 52. Force 27 Mar 52.
328 UNTS 310. France. Supplementation
11 Jan 58. Force 1 Dec 58.
328 UNTS 310. Netherlands. Supplementation
11 Jan 58. Force 1 Dec 58.
328 UNTS 314. Netherlands. Supplementation
11 Jan 58. Force 1 Dec 58.
328 UNTS 314. France. Supplementation
11 Jan 58. Force 1 Dec 58.
495 UNTS 249. Netherlands. Supplementation
7 Jan 64. Force 1 Nov 51.
495 UNTS 249. France. Supplementation
7 Jan 64. Force 1 Nov 51.
495 UNTS 251. France. Implementation
17 Aug 61. Force 1 Apr 61.
495 UNTS 251. Netherlands. Implementation
17 Aug 60. Force 1 Apr 61.
609 UNTS 256. Netherlands. Implementation
1 Jun 64. Force 1 Jun 54.
609 UNTS 256. France. Implementation
1 Jun 64. Force 1 Jun 54.

101615 Multilateral Agreement **120 UNTS 59**
SIGNED: 15 Nov 48 FORCE: 9 Nov 48
REGISTERED: 28 Jan 52 FAO (Food Agri)
ARTICLES: 10 LANGUAGE: English.
HEADNOTE: ESTABLISHMENT INDO-PACIFIC
FISHERIES COUNCIL
TOPIC: IGO Establishment
CONCEPTS: Subsidiary organ. Establishment.
Headquarters and facilities. Liaison with other
IGO's. Internal structure. Ocean resources.
INTL ORGS: Indo-Pacific Fisheries Council. Food
and Agricultural Organization of the United Na-
tions. United Nations.
PARTIES:
Australia RATIFIED: 10 Mar 49 FORCE:
10 Mar 49
Burma RATIFIED: 7 Jan 49 FORCE: 7 Jan 49
Cambodia RATIFIED: 19 Jan 51 FORCE:
19 Jan 51
Ceylon (Sri Lanka) RATIFIED: 21 Feb 49 FORCE:
21 Feb 49
Taiwan RATIFIED: 31 Jan 49 FORCE: 31 Jan 49
France RATIFIED: 30 Jun 48 FORCE: 9 Nov 48
India RATIFIED: 9 Nov 48 FORCE: 9 Nov 48
Indonesia RATIFIED: 29 Mar 50 FORCE:
29 Mar 50
Korea, South RATIFIED: 19 Jan 50 FORCE:
19 Jan 50
Netherlands RATIFIED: 12 Nov 48 FORCE:
12 Nov 48
Pakistan RATIFIED: 1 Aug 49 FORCE: 1 Aug 49
Philippines RATIFIED: 23 Jul 48 FORCE:
9 Nov 48
Thailand RATIFIED: 6 Oct 48 FORCE: 9 Nov 48
UK Great Britain RATIFIED: 28 Feb 49 FORCE:
28 Feb 49
USA (United States) RATIFIED: 3 Sep 48 FORCE:
9 Nov 48
Vietnam RATIFIED: 3 Feb 51 FORCE: 3 Feb 51
ANNEX
140 UNTS 446. Japan. Acceptance 3 Oct 52.
187 UNTS 449. Taiwan. Force 21 Jul 52.
190 UNTS 383. Indo-Pac Fish Coun. Amendment
7 Nov 52. Force 9 Dec 52.

227 UNTS 322. Indo-Pac Fish Coun. Amendment
14 Oct 55. Force 31 Oct 55.
313 UNTS 346. Fed of Malaya. Acceptance
15 Sep 58.
343 UNTS 343. Indo-Pac Fish Coun. Amendment
22 Dec 58. Force 12 Dec 58.
418 UNTS 348. Indo-Pac Fish Coun. Amendment
23 Nov 61. Force 23 Nov 61.
572 UNTS 355. New Zealand. Acceptance
6 Sep 66.

101616 Multilateral Convention **120 UNTS 71**
SIGNED: 1 Jul 49 FORCE: 22 Jan 52
REGISTERED: 28 Jan 52 ILO (Labor Org)
ARTICLES: 23 LANGUAGE: English. French.
HEADNOTE: MIGRATION EMPLOYMENT
TOPIC: Non-ILO Labor
CONCEPTS: Definition of terms. Border traffic and
migration. Conformity with municipal law. Exchange of information and documents. Public information. Public health. ILO conventions. Safety
standards. Right to organize. Wages and salaries. Family allowances. Administrative cooperation. Sickness and invalidity insurance. Social
security. Migrant worker.
INTL ORGS: International Labour Organization.
PROCEDURE: Amendment. Denunciation. Duration. Ratification. Registration. Renewal or Revival.
PARTIES:
Multilateral
ANNEX
122 UNTS 344. Guatemala. Ratification
13 Feb 52. Force 13 Feb 53.
131 UNTS 360. Cuba. Ratification 29 Apr 52.
Force 29 Apr 53.
131 UNTS 360. Netherlands. Ratification
20 May 52. Force 20 May 53.
149 UNTS 408. Italy. Ratification 22 Oct 52.
Force 22 Oct 53.
163 UNTS 382. Israel. Ratification 30 Mar 53.
Force 30 Mar 54.
172 UNTS 387. Belgium. Ratification 27 Jul 53.
Force 27 Jul 53.
207 UNTS 355. Norway. Ratification 17 Feb 55.
Force 17 Feb 56.
212 UNTS 396. France. French Guinea.
212 UNTS 396. France. Martinique.
212 UNTS 396. Netherlands. Surinam. Declaration 10 Jun 55.
212 UNTS 396. France. Reunion.
212 UNTS 396. Netherlands. Dutch New Guinea.
Declaration 10 Jun 55.
212 UNTS 396. Netherlands. Netherlands Antilles. Declaration 10 Jun 55.
212 UNTS 396. France. Guadeloupe.
231 UNTS 362. UK Great Britain. Guernsey Island.
231 UNTS 362. UK Great Britain. Isle of Man.
231 UNTS 362. UK Great Britain. Jersey Island.
320 UNTS 341. UK Great Britain. North Borneo.
320 UNTS 341. UK Great Britain. Kenya.
320 UNTS 341. UK Great Britain. Nigeria.
320 UNTS 341. UK Great Britain. Zanzibar.
320 UNTS 341. UK Great Britain. Tanganyika.
320 UNTS 341. UK Great Britain. Uganda.
320 UNTS 341. UK Great Britain. Mauritius.
320 UNTS 341. UK Great Britain. Cyprus.
320 UNTS 341. UK Great Britain. Gambia.
325 UNTS 341. UK Great Britain. Declaration
23 Feb 59.
337 UNTS 406. Germany, West. Ratification
22 Jun 59. Force 22 Jun 60.
380 UNTS 420. Nigeria. Succession 17 Oct 60.
Force 17 Oct 60.
381 UNTS 400. UK Great Britain. Barbados.
381 UNTS 400. UK Great Britain. Dominican
Republic.
381 UNTS 400. UK Great Britain. Grenada.
381 UNTS 400. UK Great Britain. St. Lucia.
381 UNTS 401. UK Great Britain. Brit Virgin Islands.
381 UNTS 401. UK Great Britain. St. Vincent.
381 UNTS 401. Cyprus. Succession 23 Sep 60.
Force 23 Sep 60.
381 UNTS 401. UK Great Britain. Trinidad.
381 UNTS 401. UK Great Britain. British Guiana.
381 UNTS 401. UK Great Britain. Antigua.
381 UNTS 401. UK Great Britain. Montserrat.
381 UNTS 401. UK Great Britain. St. Christopher.
388 UNTS 352. UK Great Britain. Declaration
5 Jan 61.
390 UNTS 357. UK Great Britain. Bahamas.

396 UNTS 328. UK Great Britain. Northern
Rhodesia. Declaration 29 Mar 61.
396 UNTS 328. UK Great Britain. Singapore. Declaration 13 Mar 61.
401 UNTS 257. Upper Volta. Ratification
9 Jun 61. Force 9 Jun 62.
444 UNTS 333. Algeria. Succession 19 Oct 62.
452 UNTS 367. Jamaica. Succession 26 Dec 62.
455 UNTS 466. UK Great Britain. Northern
Rhodesia.
468 UNTS 435. Trinidad/Tobago. Ratification
24 May 63. Force 24 May 63.
495 UNTS 300. Malaysia. State of Sabah. Succession 3 Mar 64.
504 UNTS 357. Tanzania. Succession 22 Jun 64.
522 UNTS 380. Zambia. Ratification 2 Dec 64.
Force 2 Dec 64.
530 UNTS 416. UK Great Britain. Malawi. Ratification 22 Mar 65. Force 22 Mar 66.
541 UNTS 374. Brazil. Ratification 18 Jun 65.
Force 18 Jun 66.
547 UNTS 368. UK Great Britain. Declaration
24 Sep 65.
547 UNTS 368. UK Great Britain. Bechuanaland.
549 UNTS 366. Kenya. Ratification 30 Nov 65.
Force 30 Nov 66.
567 UNTS 352. Guyana. Ratification 8 Jun 66.
Force 8 Jun 66.
655 UNTS 413. Yugoslavia. Declaration
4 Dec 68. Ratification 4 Dec 68.

101617 Bilateral Agreement **120 UNTS 105**
SIGNED: 27 Sep 51 FORCE: 27 Sep 51
REGISTERED: 31 Jan 52 United Nations
ARTICLES: 5 LANGUAGE: Spanish.
HEADNOTE: TECHNICAL ASSISTANCE
TOPIC: Tech Assistance
CONCEPTS: Treaty implementation. Annex or ap-
pendix reference. Privileges and immunities.
General cooperation. Personnel. Title and deeds.
Scholarships and grants. Vocational training. Re-
search and scientific projects. Expense sharing
formulae. Local currency. Assets transfer. Do-
mestic obligation. General technical assistance.
Materials, equipment and services. IGO status.
Conformity with IGO decisions.
TREATY REF: 1UNTS15,263.
PROCEDURE: Amendment. Termination.
PARTIES:
Paraguay
United Nations

101618 Bilateral Agreement **120 UNTS 119**
SIGNED: 14 Jan 52 FORCE: 14 Jan 52
REGISTERED: 4 Feb 52 Norway
ARTICLES: 10 LANGUAGE: Danish. Norwegian.
HEADNOTE: CLAIMS RESPECT FISHING GEAR
TOPIC: Claims and Debts
CONCEPTS: General cooperation. Legal protec-
tion and assistance. Establishment of commis-
sion. Procedure. Claims and settlements. Spe-
cific claims or waivers.
INTL ORGS: Special Commission.
PROCEDURE: Denunciation.
PARTIES:
Denmark
Norway

101619 Bilateral Agreement **120 UNTS 133**
SIGNED: 17 Dec 51 FORCE: 17 Dec 51
REGISTERED: 4 Feb 52 WHO (World Health)
ARTICLES: 6 LANGUAGE: English. Spanish.
HEADNOTE: HEALTH PROJECTS GUATEMALA
TOPIC: Sanitation
CONCEPTS: Definition of terms. Privileges and im-
munities. General property. Arbitration. Special-
ists exchange. Public health. WHO used as
agency. Scholarships and grants. Vocational
training. Research and development. Indemni-
ties and reimbursements. Financial programs.
Assistance. Specific technical assistance.
INTL ORGS: United Nations.
TREATY REF: 14UNTS185; 76UNTS132;
33UNTS261.
PROCEDURE: Amendment. Termination.
PARTIES:
Guatemala
WHO (World Health)

101620 Bilateral Agreement **120 UNTS 147**
SIGNED: 4 Feb 52 FORCE: 4 Feb 52
REGISTERED: 4 Feb 52 United Nations
ARTICLES: 10 LANGUAGE: English.
HEADNOTE: UNICEF ACTIVITIES ADEN
TOPIC: Direct Aid
CONCEPTS: Definition of terms. Territorial application. Privileges and immunities. General cooperation. Informational records. Operating agencies. General property. Public information. Use of facilities. Programs. Public health. Humanitarian matters. Export quotas. Indemnities and reimbursements. Exchange rates and regulations. Expense sharing formulae. Financial programs. Tax exemptions. Assistance. Materials, equipment and services. Regional offices. Status of experts. Conformity with IGO decisions.
TREATY REF: UN DOC. A 64 ADD.1.
PROCEDURE: Amendment. Future Procedures Contemplated. Termination.
PARTIES:
UNICEF (Children)
UK Great Britain

101621 Bilateral Agreement **121 UNTS 3**
SIGNED: 6 Feb 52 FORCE: 6 Feb 52
REGISTERED: 6 Feb 52 United Nations
ARTICLES: 18 LANGUAGE: English.
HEADNOTE: TECHNICAL ASSISTANCE
TOPIC: Tech Assistance
CONCEPTS: Exceptions and exemptions. Treaty implementation. Annex or appendix reference. Privileges and immunities. General cooperation. Exchange of information and documents. Personnel. Responsibility and liability. Arbitration. Procedure. Negotiation. Financial programs. Funding procedures. Claims and settlements. Domestic obligation. General technical assistance.
INTL ORGS: International Court of Justice. Arbitration Commission.
TREATY REF: 76UNTS132.
PROCEDURE: Amendment.
PARTIES:
Indonesia
United Nations
ANNEX
137 UNTS 390. United Nations. Amendment 16 Sep 52. Force 16 Sep 52.
137 UNTS 390. Indonesia. Amendment 16 Sep 52. Force 16 Sep 52.
191 UNTS 396. United Nations. Extension and Amendment 28 May 54. Force 28 May 54.
191 UNTS 396. Indonesia. Extension and Amendment 28 May 54. Force 28 May 54.
233 UNTS 305. United Nations. Force 17 Apr 56.
233 UNTS 305. Indonesia. Force 17 Apr 56.

101622 Bilateral Exchange **121 UNTS 25**
SIGNED: 4 Jan 52 FORCE: 1 Feb 52
REGISTERED: 11 Feb 52 Belgium
ARTICLES: 2 LANGUAGE: French.
HEADNOTE: VISA EXEMPTION NATIONALS HOLDING DIPLOMATIC VISAS
TOPIC: Visas
CONCEPTS: Exceptions and exemptions. Visa abolition. Border traffic and migration.
PARTIES:
Belgium
Spain

101623 Bilateral Exchange **121 UNTS 31**
SIGNED: 8 Oct 48 FORCE: 8 Oct 48
REGISTERED: 13 Feb 52 USA (United States)
ARTICLES: 2 LANGUAGE: English.
HEADNOTE: EXTENDING MILITARY MISSION
TOPIC: Military Mission
CONCEPTS: Annex type material. Previous treaty extension. Military assistance missions.
PARTIES:
Guatemala
USA (United States)

101624 Bilateral Exchange **121 UNTS 37**
SIGNED: 8 Oct 48 FORCE: 8 Oct 48
REGISTERED: 13 Feb 52 USA (United States)
ARTICLES: 2 LANGUAGE: English.
HEADNOTE: EXTENDING MILITARY AVIATION MISSION
TOPIC: Military Mission

CONCEPTS: Annex type material. Previous treaty extension. Military assistance missions.
PARTIES:
Guatemala
USA (United States)

101625 Bilateral Agreement **121 UNTS 43**
SIGNED: 15 Feb 52 FORCE: 15 Feb 52
REGISTERED: 15 Feb 52 United Nations
ARTICLES: 9 LANGUAGE: English. Spanish.
HEADNOTE: UNICEF ACTIVITIES
TOPIC: Humanitarian
CONCEPTS: Definition of terms. Privileges and immunities. General cooperation. Exchange of information and documents. Informational records. Operating agencies. General property. Public information. Use of facilities. Humanitarian matters. Indemnities and reimbursements. Exchange rates and regulations. Financial programs. Tax exemptions. Customs exemptions. Assistance. Materials, equipment and services. Regional offices. Status of experts. Conformity with IGO decisions.
INTL ORGS: United Nations.
TREATY REF: UN DOC. A 64 ADD.1; 1UNTS15; 4UNTS461.
PROCEDURE: Duration. Future Procedures Contemplated.
PARTIES:
Dominican Republic
UNICEF (Children)

101626 Bilateral Agreement **121 UNTS 63**
SIGNED: 15 Feb 52 FORCE: 15 Feb 52
REGISTERED: 15 Feb 52 UK Great Britain
ARTICLES: 10 LANGUAGE: English.
HEADNOTE: UNICEF ACTIVITIES
TOPIC: Direct Aid
CONCEPTS: Agriculture. Materials, equipment and services. Distribution.
INTL ORGS: United Nations.
PROCEDURE: Termination.
PARTIES:
UNICEF (Children)
UK Great Britain

101627 Bilateral Agreement **121 UNTS 75**
SIGNED: 7 Feb 52 FORCE: 7 Feb 52
REGISTERED: 15 Feb 52 United Nations
ARTICLES: 5 LANGUAGE: English.
HEADNOTE: TECHNICAL ADVISORY ASSISTANCE
TOPIC: Tech Assistance
CONCEPTS: Definition of terms. Treaty implementation. Annex or appendix reference. Privileges and immunities. General cooperation. Personnel. Title and deeds. Scholarships and grants. Vocational training. Research and scientific projects. Expense sharing formulae. Local currency. Domestic obligation. Special projects. Materials, equipment and services. IGO status. Conformity with IGO decisions.
INTL ORGS: United Nations.
TREATY REF: 14UNTS185; 76UNTS132; 1UNTS15,263.
PROCEDURE: Amendment. Termination.
PARTIES:
WHO (World Health)
UK Great Britain
ANNEX
521 UNTS 386. UK Great Britain. Supplementation 18 Nov 64. Force 18 Nov 64.
521 UNTS 386. WHO (World Health). Supplementation 18 Nov 64. Force 18 Nov 64.

101628 Bilateral Exchange **121 UNTS 89**
SIGNED: 21 Dec 51 FORCE: 21 Dec 51
REGISTERED: 19 Feb 52 UK Great Britain
ARTICLES: 2 LANGUAGE: English. Italian.
HEADNOTE: REVISION CERTAIN CLAUSES ITALIAN PEACE TREATY
TOPIC: Peace/Disarmament
CONCEPTS: Annex type material. Armistice and peace.
INTL ORGS: United Nations.
TREATY REF: 49UNTS3.
PARTIES:
Italy
UK Great Britain

101629 Bilateral Agreement **121 UNTS 97**
SIGNED: 30 Jan 51 FORCE: 24 Sep 51
REGISTERED: 19 Feb 52 UK Great Britain
ARTICLES: 8 LANGUAGE: English. French.
HEADNOTE: REGARDING RIGHTS FISHERY AREAS ECREHOS MINQUIERS
TOPIC: Privil/Immunities
CONCEPTS: Definition of terms. Regulation of natural resources.
TREATY REF: 27BFSP983; 86LTS429.
PROCEDURE: Ratification.
PARTIES:
France
UK Great Britain

101630 Bilateral Agreement **121 UNTS 107**
SIGNED: 12 Sep 50 FORCE: 12 Sep 50
REGISTERED: 25 Feb 52 United Nations
ARTICLES: 7 LANGUAGE: English. French.
HEADNOTE: REFUGEES NEAR EAST
TOPIC: Refugees
CONCEPTS: Assistance. Refugees. Relief supplies.
INTL ORGS: United Nations.
PARTIES:
UN Relief Palestin
United Arab Rep

101631 Multilateral Instrument **122 UNTS 3**
SIGNED: 14 Oct 51 FORCE: 9 Jan 52
REGISTERED: 25 Feb 52 El Salvador
ARTICLES: 22 LANGUAGE: Spanish.
HEADNOTE: ORGAN CENTRAL AMERICAN STATES
TOPIC: IGO Establishment
CONCEPTS: Peaceful relations. Economic assistance. Admission. Subsidiary organ. Establishment. Procedure. Headquarters and facilities. Internal structure.
INTL ORGS: Organization of American States. Organization of Central American States. United Nations.
PROCEDURE: Ratification.
PARTIES:
Costa Rica SIGNED: 14 Oct 51 RATIFIED: 14 Dec 51 FORCE: 9 Jan 52
El Salvador SIGNED: 14 Oct 51 RATIFIED: 3 Dec 51 FORCE: 9 Jan 52
Guatemala SIGNED: 14 Oct 51 RATIFIED: 14 Dec 51 FORCE: 9 Jan 52
Honduras SIGNED: 14 Oct 51 RATIFIED: 9 Jan 52 FORCE: 9 Jan 52
Nicaragua SIGNED: 14 Oct 51 RATIFIED: 14 Dec 51 FORCE: 9 Jan 52

101632 Bilateral Exchange **122 UNTS 21**
SIGNED: 10 Sep 51 FORCE: 10 Sep 51
REGISTERED: 26 Feb 52 Pakistan
ARTICLES: 2 LANGUAGE: English.
HEADNOTE: PRINCIPLES ECONOMIC DEVELOPMENT UNDER COLOMBO PLAN
TOPIC: Direct Aid
CONCEPTS: Annex or appendix reference. General cooperation. Economic assistance.
INTL ORGS: Colombo Plan.
PARTIES:
Canada
Pakistan

101633 Bilateral Agreement **122 UNTS 29**
SIGNED: 17 Oct 51 FORCE: 17 Oct 51
REGISTERED: 27 Feb 52 United Nations
ARTICLES: 5 LANGUAGE: Spanish.
HEADNOTE: TECHNICAL ASSISTANCE
TOPIC: Tech Assistance
CONCEPTS: Treaty implementation. Annex or appendix reference. Privileges and immunities. General cooperation. Personnel. Title and deeds. Scholarships and grants. Vocational training. Expense sharing formulae. Local currency. Assets transfer. Domestic obligation. General technical assistance. Materials, equipment and services. IGO status. Conformity with IGO decisions.
TREATY REF: 76UNTS132; 1UNTS15,263.
PROCEDURE: Amendment. Termination.
PARTIES:
United Nations
Uruguay

101634 Bilateral Exchange **122 UNTS 43**
SIGNED: 29 Aug 50   FORCE: 1 Sep 50
REGISTERED: 29 Feb 52 USA (United States)
ARTICLES: 2 LANGUAGE: English. Spanish.
HEADNOTE: PASSPORT VISAS
TOPIC: Visas
CONCEPTS: Time limit. Visas. Fees and exemptions.
PARTIES:
  Chile
  USA (United States)

101635 Bilateral Exchange **122 UNTS 51**
SIGNED: 13 Sep 50   FORCE: 13 Sep 50
REGISTERED: 29 Feb 52 USA (United States)
ARTICLES: 2 LANGUAGE: English.
HEADNOTE: WAIVER CERTAIN PASSPORT VISA
  REQUIREMENTS SOUTHERN RHODESIA
TOPIC: Visas
CONCEPTS: Time limit. Visa abolition.
PARTIES:
  UK Great Britain
  USA (United States)

101636 Multilateral Instrument **122 UNTS 57**
SIGNED: 31 Mar 49   FORCE: 8 Apr 49
REGISTERED: 29 Feb 52 USA (United States)
ARTICLES: 1 LANGUAGE: English. French.
HEADNOTE: RETENTION REMOVAL INDUSTRIAL
  PLANTS
TOPIC: Reparations
CONCEPTS: Annex or appendix reference. Enemy
  financial interests. Reparations and restrictions.
  Industrial controls.
PARTIES:
  France SIGNED: 31 Mar 49 RATIFIED: 8 Apr 49
    FORCE: 8 Apr 49
  UK Great Britain SIGNED: 31 Mar 49 RATIFIED:
    8 Apr 49 FORCE: 8 Apr 49
  USA (United States) SIGNED: 31 Mar 49 RATI-
    FIED: 8 Apr 49 FORCE: 8 Apr 49

101637 Bilateral Agreement **122 UNTS 63**
SIGNED: 6 Nov 50   FORCE: 6 Nov 50
REGISTERED: 29 Feb 52 USA (United States)
ARTICLES: 3 LANGUAGE: English.
HEADNOTE: CLAIMS PAYMENT
TOPIC: Finance
CONCEPTS: Detailed regulations. General cooper-
  ation. Negotiation. Currency. Exchange rates
  and regulations. Interest rates. Payment sched-
  ules. Claims and settlements. Lump sum settle-
  ments.
PARTIES:
  Philippines
  USA (United States)
              ANNEX
405 UNTS 304. Philippines. Supplementation
  27 Mar 61. Force 27 Mar 61.
405 UNTS 304. USA (United States). Supplementation 27 Mar 61. Force 27 Mar 61.

101638 Bilateral Exchange **122 UNTS 81**
SIGNED: 6 Nov 50   FORCE: 6 Nov 50
REGISTERED: 29 Feb 52 USA (United States)
ARTICLES: 2 LANGUAGE: English.
HEADNOTE: FURNISHING CERTAIN VESSELS
TOPIC: Milit Assistance
CONCEPTS: Non-prejudice to UN charter. Privi-
  leges and immunities. Conformity with munici-
  pal law. General property. Local currency. Do-
  mestic obligation. Defense and security. Pay-
  ment for war supplies. Military assistance. Naval
  vessels. Military assistance missions. Restric-
  tions on transfer.
INTL ORGS: United Nations.
PARTIES:
  Burma
  USA (United States)

101639 Bilateral Exchange **122 UNTS 89**
SIGNED: 15 Dec 50   FORCE: 15 Dec 50
REGISTERED: 29 Feb 52 USA (United States)
ARTICLES: 2 LANGUAGE: English.
HEADNOTE: TRANSFER MILITARY SUPPLIES
TOPIC: Milit Assistance
CONCEPTS: Exceptions and exemptions. Non-
  prejudice to UN charter. Peaceful relations. De-
  fense and security. Military assistance. Security

of information. Exchange of defense informa-
tion. Restrictions on transfer.
INTL ORGS: United Nations.
PROCEDURE: Future Procedures Contemplated.
PARTIES:
  Pakistan
  USA (United States)

101640 Bilateral Agreement **122 UNTS 97**
SIGNED: 22 Dec 50   FORCE: 22 Dec 50
REGISTERED: 29 Feb 52 USA (United States)
ARTICLES: 30 LANGUAGE: English. Spanish.
HEADNOTE: AIR FORCE MISSION
TOPIC: Military Mission
CONCEPTS: Definition of terms. Use of facilities.
  Reexport of goods, etc.. Compensation. Indemni-
  ties and reimbursements. Exchange rates and
  regulations. Expense sharing formulae. Tax ex-
  emptions. Customs exemptions. Military assis-
  tance. Security of information. Airforce-army-
  navy personnel ratio. Ranks and privileges. Conditions for assistance missions. Third country
  military personnel. Status of forces.
PROCEDURE: Denunciation. Duration. Renewal or
  Revival. Termination.
PARTIES:
  Cuba
  USA (United States)
              ANNEX
181 UNTS 357. USA (United States). Prolongation
  26 Sep 52. Force 26 Sep 52.
181 UNTS 357. Cuba. Prolongation 11 Aug 52.
  Force 26 Sep 52.
222 UNTS 417. USA (United States). Prolongation
  7 Jul 53. Force 22 Dec 53.
222 UNTS 417. Cuba. Prolongation 13 Oct 53.
  Force 22 Dec 53.
264 UNTS 351. USA (United States). Prolongation
  17 May 55. Force 17 May 55.
264 UNTS 351. Cuba. Prolongation 3 May 55.
  Force 17 May 55.

101641 Bilateral Exchange **122 UNTS 117**
SIGNED: 19 Feb 50   FORCE: 19 Feb 50
REGISTERED: 29 Feb 52 USA (United States)
ARTICLES: 2 LANGUAGE: English.
HEADNOTE: EXCHANGE OFFICIAL PUBLICA-
  TIONS
TOPIC: Admin Cooperation
CONCEPTS: Exchange of official publications. Op-
  erating agencies. Indemnities and reimburse-
  ments.
PARTIES:
  Israel
  USA (United States)

101642 Bilateral Agreement **122 UNTS 125**
SIGNED: 11 Jan 51   FORCE: 11 Jan 51
REGISTERED: 29 Feb 52 USA (United States)
ARTICLES: 27 LANGUAGE: English.
HEADNOTE: ARMY MISSION
TOPIC: Military Mission
CONCEPTS: Use of facilities. Compensation. In-
  demnities and reimbursements. Exchange rates
  and regulations. Expense sharing formulae. Tax
  exemptions. Customs exemptions. Military assis-
  tance. Military training. Security of information.
  Airforce-army-navy personnel ratio. Ranks and
  privileges. Conditions for assistance missions.
  Third country military personnel. Status of
  forces.
PROCEDURE: Denunciation. Duration. Renewal or
  Revival. Termination.
PARTIES:
  Liberia
  USA (United States)
              ANNEX
238 UNTS 320. USA (United States). Prolongation
  23 Oct 53. Force 23 Oct 53.
238 UNTS 320. Liberia. Prolongation 7 Aug 53.
  Force 23 Oct 53.
303 UNTS 328. USA (United States). Prolongation
  2 Dec 57. Force 2 Dec 57.
303 UNTS 328. Liberia. Prolongation 18 Nov 57.
  Force 2 Dec 57.
405 UNTS 310. USA (United States). Amendment
  27 Mar 59. Force 31 Mar 59.
405 UNTS 310. Liberia. Amendment 31 Mar 59.
  Force 31 Mar 59.
409 UNTS 306. Liberia. Prolongation 24 Apr 61.
  Force 24 Apr 61.

409 UNTS 306. USA (United States). Prolongation
  19 Apr 61. Force 24 Apr 61.
526 UNTS 320. Liberia. Extension and Amendment 24 Apr 64. Force 26 Apr 64.
526 UNTS 320. USA (United States). Extension
  and Amendment 17 Dec 63. Force 26 Apr 64.

101643 Bilateral Agreement **122 UNTS 137**
SIGNED: 6 Jan 51   FORCE: 6 Jan 51
REGISTERED: 29 Feb 52 USA (United States)
ARTICLES: 4 LANGUAGE: English. Serbo-Croat.
HEADNOTE: RELIEF ASSISTANCE
TOPIC: Direct Aid
CONCEPTS: Conformity with municipal law. In-
  spection and observation. Public information.
  Funding procedures. Local currency. Commodi-
  ties and services. Domestic obligation. Relief
  supplies. Withdrawal conditions. Procurement.
  Mass media. Press and wire services.
PARTIES:
  USA (United States)
  Yugoslavia

101644 Bilateral Exchange **122 UNTS 147**
SIGNED: 27 Nov 50   FORCE: 27 Nov 50
REGISTERED: 29 Feb 52 USA (United States)
ARTICLES: 3 LANGUAGE: English. Spanish.
HEADNOTE: ESTABLISHMENT JOINT COMMIS-
  SION ECONOMIC DEVELOPMENT
TOPIC: Direct Aid
CONCEPTS: Conformity with municipal law. Estab-
  lishment of commission. Funding procedures.
  Economic assistance. Internal structure.
INTL ORGS: Special Commission.
PARTIES:
  Paraguay
  USA (United States)
              ANNEX
238 UNTS 324.   Paraguay.   Termination
  13 Feb 53. Force 24 Feb 54.
238 UNTS 324. USA (United States). Termination
  24 Feb 54. Force 24 Feb 54.

101645 Bilateral Agreement **122 UNTS 157**
SIGNED: 29 Dec 50   FORCE: 29 Dec 50
REGISTERED: 29 Feb 52 USA (United States)
ARTICLES: 5 LANGUAGE: English. Spanish.
HEADNOTE: TECHNICAL COOPERATION
TOPIC: Tech Assistance
CONCEPTS: Exceptions and exemptions. Treaty
  implementation. Previous treaty replacement.
  Diplomatic privileges. General cooperation. Ex-
  change of information and documents. Person-
  nel. Public information. Financial programs. Tax
  exemptions. Customs exemptions. Domestic ob-
  ligation. General technical assistance. Materials,
  equipment and services.
PROCEDURE: Amendment. Duration. Termination.
PARTIES:
  Paraguay
  USA (United States)
              ANNEX
180 UNTS 334. Paraguay. Amendment 5 Jan 52.
  Force 5 Jan 52.
180 UNTS 334. USA (United States). Amendment
  18 Dec 51. Force 5 Jan 52.

101646 Bilateral Exchange **122 UNTS 169**
SIGNED: 9 Apr 49   FORCE: 9 Apr 49
REGISTERED: 29 Feb 52 USA (United States)
ARTICLES: 2 LANGUAGE: English. Spanish.
HEADNOTE: CUSTOMS CONCESSIONS AUTO-
  MOBILES
TOPIC: Customs
CONCEPTS: Customs duties. Motor vehicles and
  combinations.
TREATY REF: 58UNTS58; 55UNTS187.
PROCEDURE: Duration.
PARTIES:
  Chile
  USA (United States)
              ANNEX
174 UNTS 292. USA (United States). Prolongation
  8 Apr 52. Force 8 Apr 52.
174 UNTS 292. Chile. Prolongation 8 Apr 52.
  Force 8 Apr 52.
229 UNTS 299. USA (United States). Prolongation
  8 Jun 53. Force 23 Jun 53.
229 UNTS 299. Chile. Prolongation 23 Jun 53.
  Force 23 Jun 53.

101647 Bilateral Exchange **122 UNTS 191**
SIGNED: 17 Aug 51   FORCE: 17 Aug 51
REGISTERED: 1 Mar 52 United Nations
ARTICLES: 2 LANGUAGE: French.
HEADNOTE: SIXTH SESSION UN/GA
TOPIC: IGO Operations
CONCEPTS: Non-visa travel documents. Diplomatic privileges. Diplomatic missions. Privileges and immunities. Diplomatic correspondence. Procedure. Finances and payments. Status of experts.
PROCEDURE: Duration.
PARTIES:
France
United Nations

101648 Bilateral Exchange **122 UNTS 229**
SIGNED: 12 Apr 47   FORCE: 12 Apr 47
REGISTERED: 5 Mar 52 USA (United States)
ARTICLES: 2 LANGUAGE: English.
HEADNOTE: AIR TRANSPORT
TOPIC: Air Transport
CONCEPTS: Air transport. Conditions of airlines operating permission. Operating authorizations and regulations.
TREATY REF: 122UNTS261.
PARTIES:
Canada
USA (United States)

101649 Bilateral Agreement **122 UNTS 237**
SIGNED: 4 Jun 49   FORCE: 4 Jun 49
REGISTERED: 5 Mar 52 USA (United States)
ARTICLES: 15 LANGUAGE: English.
HEADNOTE: AIR TRANSPORT
TOPIC: Air Transport
CONCEPTS: Definition of terms. Exceptions and exemptions. Annex or appendix reference. Previous treaty replacement. Non-prejudice to third party. Conformity with municipal law. Licenses and permits. Recognition of legal documents. Use of facilities. Procedure. Special tribunals. Competence of tribunal. Quarantine. Indemnities and reimbursements. Fees and exemptions. Most favored nation clause. National treatment. Customs duties. Customs exemptions. Competency certificate. Routes and logistics. Navigational conditions. Permit designation. Air transport. Airport facilities. Airworthiness certificates. Conditions of airlines operating permission. Operating authorizations and regulations. Licenses and certificates of nationality.
INTL ORGS: International Civil Aviation Organization. Special Commission.
TREATY REF: 15UNTS295; 122UNTS229.
PROCEDURE: Amendment. Future Procedures Contemplated. Registration. Termination.
PARTIES:
Canada
USA (United States)
ANNEX
343 UNTS 344. Canada. Amendment 9 Apr 59. Force 9 Apr 59.
343 UNTS 344. USA (United States). Amendment 9 Apr 59. Force 9 Apr 59.

101650 Bilateral Agreement **123 UNTS 3**
SIGNED: 5 Mar 52   FORCE: 5 Mar 52
REGISTERED: 5 Mar 52 United Nations
ARTICLES: 6 LANGUAGE: English. French.
HEADNOTE: TECHNICAL ASSISTANCE
TOPIC: Tech Assistance
CONCEPTS: Definition of terms. Treaty implementation. Privileges and immunities. General cooperation. Personnel. Title and deeds. Scholarships and grants. Vocational training. Research and development. Expense sharing formulae. Local currency. Domestic obligation. General technical assistance. Materials, equipment and services. IGO status. Conformity with IGO decisions.
TREATY REF: 76UNTS132; 1UNTS15,263.
PROCEDURE: Amendment. Termination.
PARTIES:
Greece
United Nations

101651 Bilateral Agreement **123 UNTS 13**
SIGNED: 7 Sep 49   FORCE: 1 Mar 52
REGISTERED: 6 Mar 52 Belgium
ARTICLES: 11 LANGUAGE: French.

HEADNOTE: LOAN AGREEMENT
TOPIC: Loans and Credits
CONCEPTS: Annex or appendix reference. General cooperation. Operating agencies. Expense sharing formulae. Financial programs. Funding procedures. Interest rates. Payment schedules. Loan and credit. Credit provisions. Loan repayment. Terms of loan.
INTL ORGS: Bank for International Settlements. Organization for Economic Co-operation and Development.
PARTIES:
Belgium
France

101652 Bilateral Convention **123 UNTS 29**
SIGNED: 9 Oct 48   FORCE: 9 Oct 48
REGISTERED: 6 Mar 52 Belgium
ARTICLES: 9 LANGUAGE: French.
HEADNOTE: DOUBLE TAXATION CAPITAL
TOPIC: Taxation
CONCEPTS: Conformity with municipal law. Domestic legislation. Negotiation. Assets. Taxation. General.
PROCEDURE: Ratification.
PARTIES:
Belgium
Luxembourg

101653 Bilateral Exchange **123 UNTS 39**
SIGNED: 21 Jan 52   FORCE: 21 Jan 52
REGISTERED: 6 Mar 52 Belgium
ARTICLES: 2 LANGUAGE: French.
HEADNOTE: LIQUIDATION CLEARING OPERATIONS
TOPIC: Claims and Debts
CONCEPTS: Detailed regulations. Banking. Payment schedules. Claims and settlements.
PARTIES:
Belgium
Norway

101654 Multilateral Convention **123 UNTS 45**
SIGNED: 18 Feb 50   FORCE: 19 Nov 51
REGISTERED: 6 Mar 52 Belgium
ARTICLES: 24 LANGUAGE: Dutch. French.
HEADNOTE: EXCISE DUTIES FEES
TOPIC: Customs
CONCEPTS: Previous treaty replacement. Non-interest rates and fees. Customs duties. Customs exemptions.
TREATY REF: 32UNTS143.
PROCEDURE: Ratification. Termination.
PARTIES:
Belgium   SIGNED: 18 Feb 50   RATIFIED: 19 Nov 51 FORCE: 19 Nov 51
Luxembourg SIGNED: 18 Feb 50   RATIFIED: 19 Nov 51 FORCE: 19 Nov 51
Netherlands SIGNED: 18 Feb 50   RATIFIED: 19 Nov 51 FORCE: 19 Nov 51
ANNEX
180 UNTS 341. Netherlands. Amendment 27 May 52. Force 20 Oct 53.
180 UNTS 341. Belgium. Amendment 27 May 52. Force 20 Oct 53.
180 UNTS 341. Luxembourg. Amendment 27 May 52. Force 20 Oct 53.
387 UNTS 334. Belgium. Supplementation 11 Dec 58. Force 13 Jan 61.
387 UNTS 334. Luxembourg. Supplementation 11 Dec 58. Force 13 Jan 61.
387 UNTS 334. Netherlands. Supplementation 11 Dec 58. Force 13 Jan 61.
548 UNTS 328. Belgium. Amendment 29 Mar 62. Force 30 Jun 65.
548 UNTS 328. Luxembourg. Amendment 29 Mar 62. Force 30 Jun 65.
548 UNTS 328. Netherlands. Amendment 29 Mar 62. Force 30 Jun 65.
548 UNTS 328. Belgium. Ratification 30 Jun 65.
548 UNTS 328. Luxembourg. Ratification 26 Feb 64.
548 UNTS 328. Netherlands. Ratification 14 Aug 63.

101655 Bilateral Convention **123 UNTS 81**
SIGNED: 25 Sep 48   FORCE: 25 Sep 48
REGISTERED: 6 Mar 52 Belgium
ARTICLES: 9 LANGUAGE: Dutch. French.
HEADNOTE: DOUBLE TAXATION CAPITAL

TOPIC: Taxation
CONCEPTS: Domestic legislation. Negotiation. Assets. Taxation. General. Tax exemptions.
PROCEDURE: Ratification.
PARTIES:
Belgium
Netherlands

101656 Bilateral Exchange **123 UNTS 91**
SIGNED: 14 Nov 51   FORCE: 1 Jan 52
REGISTERED: 6 Mar 52 Belgium
ARTICLES: 3 LANGUAGE: Dutch.
HEADNOTE: PROVISIONAL INCREASES PILOTAGE CHARGES RIVER SCHELDT
TOPIC: Admin Cooperation
CONCEPTS: Administrative cooperation. Fees and exemptions. Ports and pilotage.
PARTIES:
Belgium
Netherlands
ANNEX
191 UNTS 398. Belgium. Prolongation 24 Dec 53. Force 1 Jan 54.
191 UNTS 398. Netherlands. Prolongation 24 Dec 53. Force 1 Jan 54.
209 UNTS 340. Belgium. Prolongation 22 Dec 54. Force 1 Jan 55.
209 UNTS 340. Netherlands. Prolongation 22 Dec 54. Force 1 Jan 55.
260 UNTS 448. Belgium. Prolongation 17 Dec 56. Force 1 Jan 57.
260 UNTS 448. Luxembourg. Prolongation 17 Dec 56. Force 1 Jan 57.
266 UNTS 410. Netherlands. Prolongation 19 Dec 55. Force 1 Jan 56.
266 UNTS 410. Belgium. Prolongation 19 Dec 55. Force 1 Jan 56.

101657 Bilateral Agreement **123 UNTS 101**
SIGNED: 15 Dec 50   FORCE: 23 Jan 52
REGISTERED: 6 Mar 52 Netherlands
ARTICLES: 58 LANGUAGE: Dutch. Portuguese.
HEADNOTE: EMIGRATION SETTLEMENT
TOPIC: Non-ILO Labor
CONCEPTS: Detailed regulations. General provisions. Friendship and amity. Border traffic and migration. Non-visa travel documents. Visas. Assistance. General cooperation. General property. Establishment of commission. Programs. Financial programs. Transportation costs. Passenger transport.
INTL ORGS: Special Commission.
PROCEDURE: Amendment. Denunciation. Future Procedures Contemplated. Ratification.
PARTIES:
Brazil
Netherlands

101658 Bilateral Agreement **123 UNTS 167**
SIGNED: 13 Dec 51   FORCE: 13 Dec 51
REGISTERED: 6 Mar 52 UK Great Britain
ARTICLES: 6 LANGUAGE: Arabic. English.
HEADNOTE: FINANCIAL ASSISTANCE
TOPIC: Direct Aid
CONCEPTS: Definition of terms. General cooperation. Personnel. Financial programs. Domestic obligation. General aid. Economic assistance.
PROCEDURE: Duration.
PARTIES:
Libya
UK Great Britain

101659 Bilateral Exchange **123 UNTS 177**
SIGNED: 30 Nov 51   FORCE: 30 Nov 51
REGISTERED: 6 Mar 52 UK Great Britain
ARTICLES: 2 LANGUAGE: English.
HEADNOTE: EXCHANGE THROUGH POSTAL CHANNELS
TOPIC: Postal Service
CONCEPTS: Privileges and immunities. Diplomatic correspondence. Postal services. Regulations. Insured letters and boxes. Rates and charges.
PARTIES:
Netherlands
UK Great Britain

101660 Bilateral Agreement **123 UNTS 187**
SIGNED: 20 Dec 51   FORCE: 15 Dec 51
REGISTERED: 6 Mar 52 UK Great Britain

ARTICLES: 9 LANGUAGE: English. Spanish.
HEADNOTE: PAYMENTS
TOPIC: Finance
CONCEPTS: Definition of terms. Detailed regulations. General cooperation. Accounting procedures. Currency. Monetary and gold transfers. Exchange rates and regulations. Payment schedules. Local currency.
PROCEDURE: Amendment. Duration. Termination.
PARTIES:
Spain
UK Great Britain
ANNEX
443 UNTS 337. Cameroon. Succession 3 Sep 62. Force 3 Sep 62.

101661 Bilateral Agreement **123 UNTS 197**
SIGNED: 27 Jan 50 FORCE: 5 Feb 52
REGISTERED: 12 Mar 52 Netherlands
ARTICLES: 8 LANGUAGE: Dutch. Spanish.
HEADNOTE: COMMERCIAL
TOPIC: General Trade
CONCEPTS: Establishment of trade relations. Trade agencies. Trade procedures. National treatment.
INTL ORGS: International Court of Justice.
PROCEDURE: Duration. Termination.
PARTIES:
Mexico
Netherlands

101662 Multilateral Agreement **124 UNTS 3**
SIGNED: 4 Feb 52 FORCE: 11 Feb 52
REGISTERED: 13 Mar 52 Belgium
ARTICLES: 1 LANGUAGE: English.
HEADNOTE: MONETARY ACCOUNT
TOPIC: General Economic
CONCEPTS: Assets transfer. Peace and disarmament.
TREATY REF: 76UNTS; 113UNTS; 316UNTS.
PARTIES:
Belgium SIGNED: 4 Feb 52 FORCE: 11 Feb 52
Belgium Belgian Colonies RATIFIED: 4 Feb 52 FORCE: 11 Feb 52
Belgium Ruanda-Urundi RATIFIED: 4 Feb 52 FORCE: 11 Feb 52
Japan SIGNED: 4 Feb 52 FORCE: 11 Feb 52
SCAP Japan SIGNED: 4 Feb 52 FORCE: 11 Feb 52

101663 Bilateral Agreement **124 UNTS 9**
SIGNED: 18 Jan 52 FORCE: 18 Jan 52
REGISTERED: 18 Mar 52 Belgium
ARTICLES: 15 LANGUAGE: French. German.
HEADNOTE: STUDENT EMPLOYEES
TOPIC: Education
CONCEPTS: Resident permits. Conformity with municipal law. Negotiation. Teacher and student exchange. Employment regulations.
PROCEDURE: Denunciation. Duration. Renewal or Revival.
PARTIES:
Belgium
Germany, West
ANNEX
173 UNTS 404. Belgium. Prolongation 8 Aug 53. Force 8 Aug 53.
173 UNTS 404. Germany, West. Prolongation 13 Jul 53. Force 8 Aug 53.

101664 Bilateral Exchange **124 UNTS 25**
SIGNED: 14 Sep 50 FORCE: 14 Sep 50
REGISTERED: 20 Mar 52 USA (United States)
ARTICLES: 2 LANGUAGE: English. Spanish.
HEADNOTE: TERMINATION POINT V AGREEMENT
TOPIC: Land Transport
CONCEPTS: Annex type material. Roads and highways.
TREATY REF: 124UNTS221.
PARTIES:
Panama
USA (United States)
ANNEX
222 UNTS 418. USA (United States). Prolongation 11 Aug 53. Force 14 Sep 53.
222 UNTS 418. Panama. Prolongation 14 Sep 53. Force 14 Sep 53.
234 UNTS 318. USA (United States). Prolongation 26 Aug 54. Force 14 Sep 54.

234 UNTS 318. Panama. Prolongation 30 Aug 54. Force 14 Sep 54.

101665 Bilateral Exchange **124 UNTS 34**
SIGNED: 30 Jun 48 FORCE. 30 Jul 48
REGISTERED: 20 Mar 52 USA (United States)
ARTICLES: 2 LANGUAGE: English. Spanish.
HEADNOTE: HEALTH SANITATION PROGRAM
TOPIC: Sanitation
CONCEPTS: Annex type material. Previous treaty extension. Personnel. Programs. Public health. Sanitation. Assistance. Specific technical assistance. Grants.
TREATY REF: 124UNTS243.
PARTIES:
Paraguay
USA (United States)
ANNEX
152 UNTS 316. USA (United States). Implementation 10 Sep 51. Force 29 Oct 51.
152 UNTS 316. Paraguay. Implementation 29 Oct 51. Force 29 Oct 51.
157 UNTS 373. USA (United States). Supplementation 5 Nov 51. Force 13 Dec 51.
157 UNTS 373. Paraguay. Supplementation 7 Dec 51. Force 13 Dec 51.
178 UNTS 392. USA (United States). Supplementation 8 Apr 52. Force 30 Apr 52.
178 UNTS 392. Paraguay. Supplementation 30 Apr 52. Force 30 Apr 52.
269 UNTS 290. USA (United States). Prolongation 5 Apr 55. Force 5 Apr 55.
269 UNTS 290. Paraguay. Prolongation 5 Apr 55. Force 5 Apr 55.

101666 Bilateral Exchange **124 UNTS 57**
SIGNED: 29 Mar 46 FORCE: 29 Mar 46
REGISTERED: 20 Mar 52 USA (United States)
ARTICLES: 2 LANGUAGE: English. Spanish.
HEADNOTE: RUBBER PRODUCTION
TOPIC: Specific Resources
CONCEPTS: Export subsidies. Raw materials.
PARTIES:
USA (United States)
Venezuela

101667 Bilateral Agreement **124 UNTS 63**
SIGNED: 30 Jan 51 FORCE: 30 Jan 51
REGISTERED: 20 Mar 52 USA (United States)
ARTICLES: 18 LANGUAGE: English. Spanish.
HEADNOTE: COOPERATIVE PROGRAM AGRICULTURE
TOPIC: Direct Aid
CONCEPTS: Agriculture. Assistance. Materials, equipment and services. Aid missions. Credit provisions.
PROCEDURE: Duration. Termination.
PARTIES:
Honduras
USA (United States)
ANNEX
140 UNTS 447. USA (United States). Amendment 7 Aug 51. Force 14 Aug 51.
140 UNTS 447. Honduras. Amendment 14 Aug 51. Force 14 Aug 51.
157 UNTS 380. USA (United States). Supplementation 9 Jan 52. Force 16 Jan 52.
157 UNTS 380. Honduras. Supplementation 16 Jan 52. Force 16 Jan 52.
269 UNTS 296. USA (United States). Supplementation 27 Apr 55. Force 27 Apr 55.
269 UNTS 296. Honduras. Supplementation 27 Apr 55. Force 27 Apr 55.

101668 Bilateral Agreement **124 UNTS 89**
SIGNED: 29 Dec 51 FORCE: 1 Jan 52
REGISTERED: 24 Mar 52 WHO (World Health)
ARTICLES: 4 LANGUAGE: English. Spanish.
HEADNOTE: VENEREAL DISEASE INVESTIGATION LABORATORY TRAINING CENTER
TOPIC: Sanitation
CONCEPTS: Definition of terms. Privileges and immunities. General cooperation. Personnel. General property. Specialists exchange. Disease control. WHO used as agency. Institute establishment. Scholarships and grants. Vocational training. Research results. Research and development. Indemnities and reimbursements. Expense sharing formulae. Assistance. Specific

technical assistance. Materials, equipment and services. General transportation.
INTL ORGS: United Nations.
TREATY REF: OFF. REC. WHO NO.28 P.68; 76UNTS132; 33UNTS261.
PROCEDURE: Amendment. Termination.
PARTIES:
Guatemala
WHO (World Health)
ANNEX
175 UNTS 369. Guatemala. Prolongation 24 Jun 53. Force 9 Jul 53.
175 UNTS 369. WHO (World Health). Prolongation 9 Jul 53. Force 9 Jul 53.

101669 Bilateral Agreement **124 UNTS 109**
SIGNED: 20 Dec 51 FORCE: 26 Dec 51
REGISTERED: 24 Mar 52 WHO (World Health)
ARTICLES: 4 LANGUAGE: English.
HEADNOTE: TECHNICAL ASSISTANCE PROFESSOR PHARMACOLOGY TEACHING EQUIPMENT
TOPIC: Tech Assistance
CONCEPTS: Privileges and immunities. General cooperation. Personnel. Title and deeds. Arbitration. Procedure. Negotiation. Professorships. Institute establishment. Vocational training. Claims and settlements. Domestic obligation. Special projects. Materials, equipment and services. IGO status.
INTL ORGS: International Court of Justice. United Nations. Special Commission.
TREATY REF: 76UNTS132.
PROCEDURE: Amendment. Termination.
PARTIES:
India
WHO (World Health)

101670 Bilateral Agreement **124 UNTS 121**
SIGNED: 17 Dec 51 FORCE: 17 Dec 51
REGISTERED: 24 Mar 52 WHO (World Health)
ARTICLES: 4 LANGUAGE: English. Spanish.
HEADNOTE: TECHNICAL ASSISTANCE CONDUCTING COURSE NURSING INSTRUCTORS
TOPIC: Tech Assistance
CONCEPTS: Annex or appendix reference. Privileges and immunities. General cooperation. Exchange of information and documents. Personnel. Title and deeds. Exchange. Scholarships and grants. Vocational training. Expense sharing formulae. Domestic obligation. Special projects. Materials, equipment and services. IGO status.
INTL ORGS: United Nations.
TREATY REF: 76UNTS132; 33UNTS26; 1UNTS15,263; UN.CHT.ART.102.
PROCEDURE: Amendment. Registration. Termination.
PARTIES:
Mexico
WHO (World Health)

101671 Multilateral Convention **125 UNTS 3**
SIGNED: 19 Sep 49 FORCE: 19 Sep 49
REGISTERED: 26 Mar 52 United Nations
ARTICLES: 35 LANGUAGE: English. French.
HEADNOTE: ROAD TRAFFIC
TOPIC: Land Transport
CONCEPTS: Conditions. Definition of terms. Detailed regulations. Exceptions and exemptions. Territorial application. Annex or appendix reference. Previous treaty replacement. Non-prejudice to UN charter. Standardization. Conformity with municipal law. Exchange of information and documents. Recognition of legal documents. Investigation of violations. Procedure. Negotiation. Customs duties. Registration certificate. Passenger transport. Transport of goods. Driving permits. Motor vehicles and combinations. Roads and highways. Road rules. Paragraph 2, Article 36.
INTL ORGS: International Court of Justice. United Nations.
TREATY REF: 108LTS123; 98LTS83.
PROCEDURE: Amendment. Accession. Denunciation. Ratification.
PARTIES:
Austria SIGNED: 19 Sep 49
Belgium SIGNED: 19 Sep 49
Czechoslovakia SIGNED: 28 Dec 49 RATIFIED: 3 Nov 50 FORCE: 26 Mar 52
Denmark SIGNED: 19 Sep 49
Dominican Republic SIGNED: 19 Sep 49

United Arab Rep SIGNED: 19 Sep 49
France   SIGNED: 19 Sep 49   RATIFIED:
    15 Sep 50 FORCE: 26 Mar 52
India SIGNED: 19 Sep 49
Israel SIGNED: 19 Sep 49
Italy SIGNED: 19 Sep 49
Lebanon SIGNED: 19 Sep 49
Luxembourg SIGNED: 19 Sep 49
Monaco RATIFIED: 3 Aug 51 FORCE: 26 Mar 52
Netherlands SIGNED: 19 Sep 49
Norway SIGNED: 19 Sep 49
Philippines SIGNED: 19 Sep 49
South Africa SIGNED: 19 Sep 49
Sweden   SIGNED: 19 Sep 49   RATIFIED:
    25 Feb 52 FORCE: 26 Mar 52
Switzerland SIGNED: 19 Sep 49
UK Great Britain SIGNED: 19 Sep 49
USA (United States) All Territories RATIFIED:
    30 Aug 50 FORCE: 26 Mar 52
USA (United States) SIGNED: 19 Sep 49 RATI-
    FIED: 30 Aug 50 FORCE: 26 Mar 52
Yugoslavia SIGNED: 19 Sep 49
                             ANNEX
133 UNTS 367.
133 UNTS 368.
137 UNTS 394.
139 UNTS 464.
141 UNTS 399.
147 UNTS 395.
150 UNTS 395.
151 UNTS 386.
157 UNTS 387.
173 UNTS 407.
179 UNTS 220.
182 UNTS 228.
182 UNTS 286.
189 UNTS 364.
189 UNTS 366.
198 UNTS 399.
202 UNTS 336.
202 UNTS 337.
220 UNTS 383.
225 UNTS 266.
227 UNTS 324.
230 UNTS 436.
251 UNTS 376.
251 UNTS 378.
253 UNTS 353.
253 UNTS 354.
260 UNTS 449.
265 UNTS 330.
266 UNTS 411.
266 UNTS 412.
268 UNTS 359.
271 UNTS 390.
273 UNTS 249.
274 UNTS 345.
280 UNTS 354.
286 UNTS 343.
286 UNTS 344.
302 UNTS 360.
312 UNTS 414.
312 UNTS 418.
314 UNTS 340.
314 UNTS 341.
317 UNTS 326.
325 UNTS 342.
327 UNTS 359.
328 UNTS 318.
337 UNTS 407.
348 UNTS 348.
349 UNTS 324.
354 UNTS 396.
356 UNTS 356.
360 UNTS 388.
372 UNTS 356.
376 UNTS 415.
381 UNTS 402.
381 UNTS 403.
384 UNTS 360.
387 UNTS 346.
387 UNTS 348.
390 UNTS 358.
392 UNTS 352.
394 UNTS 268.
395 UNTS 270.
402 UNTS 313.
405 UNTS 316.
415 UNTS 428.
419 UNTS 356.
422 UNTS 333.
423 UNTS 306.
424 UNTS 347.
424 UNTS 348.

431 UNTS 294.
433 UNTS 352.
434 UNTS 288.
434 UNTS 290.
434 UNTS 292.
435 UNTS 322.
437 UNTS 348.
438 UNTS 344.
438 UNTS 346.
442 UNTS 314.
443 UNTS 338.
444 UNTS 334.
453 UNTS 354.
453 UNTS 356.
466 UNTS 384.
469 UNTS 418.
472 UNTS 390.
473 UNTS 338.
482 UNTS 364.
502 UNTS 380.
503 UNTS 333.
505 UNTS 306.
514 UNTS 254.
525 UNTS 315.
531 UNTS 318.
541 UNTS 311.
547 UNTS 317.
550 UNTS 401.
551 UNTS 279.
562 UNTS 326.
608 UNTS 355.

101672   Bilateral Agreement   **125 UNTS 103**
SIGNED: 30 Oct 47   FORCE: 30 Oct 47
REGISTERED: 26 Mar 52 USA (United States)
ARTICLES: 1 LANGUAGE: English. French.
HEADNOTE: INOPERATIVE
TOPIC: General Economic
CONCEPTS: Previous treaty replacement.
TREATY   REF: 55UNTS187;   160LTS27;
    32UNTS143.
PROCEDURE: Amendment. Termination.
PARTIES:
    Belgium
    USA (United States)

101673   Bilateral Exchange   **125 UNTS 111**
SIGNED: 30 Jun 48   FORCE: 30 Jun 48
REGISTERED: 26 Mar 52 USA (United States)
ARTICLES: 2 LANGUAGE: English. Portuguese.
HEADNOTE: TRADE
TOPIC: General Trade
CONCEPTS: Annex type material. Previous treaty
    replacement.
INTL ORGS: United Nations.
TREATY REF: GATT.
PARTIES:
    Brazil
    USA (United States)

101674   Multilateral Exchange   **125 UNTS 119**
SIGNED: 18 Jul 46   FORCE: 28 Mar 47
REGISTERED: 26 Mar 52 USA (United States)
ARTICLES: 32 LANGUAGE: English. French.
HEADNOTE: LIQUIDATION PROPERTY
TOPIC: Reparations
CONCEPTS: Treaty implementation. Annex or ap-
    pendix reference. Exchange of information and
    documents. Inspection and observation. General
    property. Arbitration. Procedure. Compensation.
    Indemnities and reimbursements. Enemy finan-
    cial interests. Reparations and restrictions.
INTL ORGS: Intergovernmental Committee on Ref-
    ugees.
PARTIES:
    France SIGNED: 18 Jul 46 FORCE: 28 Mar 47
    Sweden   SIGNED: 18 Jul 46   RATIFIED:
        28 Mar 47 FORCE: 28 Mar 47
    UK Great Britain SIGNED: 18 Jul 46 FORCE:
        28 Mar 47
    USA (United States) SIGNED: 18 Jul 46 FORCE:
        28 Mar 47

101675   Bilateral Exchange   **125 UNTS 165**
SIGNED: 18 Jul 46   FORCE: 18 Jul 46
REGISTERED: 26 Mar 52 USA (United States)
ARTICLES: 2 LANGUAGE: English. French.
HEADNOTE: ALLOCATION LIQUIDATION PRO-
    CEEDS
TOPIC: Reparations

CONCEPTS: Enemy financial interests. Repara-
    tions and restrictions. Post-war claims settle-
    ment.
TREATY REF: 125UNTS119.
PARTIES:
    France
    USA (United States)

101676   Bilateral Agreement   **125 UNTS 171**
SIGNED: 30 Oct 47   FORCE: 30 Oct 47
REGISTERED: 26 Mar 52 USA (United States)
ARTICLES: 1 LANGUAGE: English. French.
HEADNOTE: SUPPLEMENTARY   AGREEMENT
GATT
TOPIC: General Economic
CONCEPTS: Treaty interpretation. Annex type ma-
    terial. Previous treaty replacement.
INTL ORGS: United Nations.
TREATY REF: 55UNTS187; 199LTS259.
PROCEDURE: Termination.
PARTIES:
    France
    USA (United States)

101677   Bilateral Agreement   **125 UNTS 179**
SIGNED: 12 Sep 46   FORCE: 9 Apr 47
REGISTERED: 26 Mar 52 USA (United States)
ARTICLES: 17 LANGUAGE: English. Spanish.
HEADNOTE: PROMOTION TRADE
TOPIC: General Trade
CONCEPTS: Detailed regulations. Exceptions and
    exemptions. Territorial application. Treaty imple-
    mentation. Annex or appendix reference. Con-
    formity with municipal law. General cooperation.
    Recognition and enforcement of legal decisions.
    Public information. Establishment of commis-
    sion. Procedure. Export quotas. Import quotas.
    Reciprocity in trade. Trade agencies. Trade pro-
    cedures. Payment schedules. Non-interest rates
    and fees. Quotas. Most favored nation clause.
    National treatment.
PROCEDURE: Duration. Termination.
PARTIES:
    Paraguay
    USA (United States)
                             ANNEX
442 UNTS 315. Paraguay. Amendment 2 Apr 62.
    Force 2 Apr 62.
442 UNTS 315. USA (United States). Amendment
    2 Apr 62. Force 2 Apr 62.
461 UNTS 219. USA (United States). Prolongation
    1 Oct 62. Force 1 Oct 62.
461 UNTS 219.   Paraguay.   Prolongation
    30 Sep 62. Force 1 Oct 62.
473 UNTS 340. USA (United States). Prolongation
    29 Mar 63. Force 29 Mar 63.
473 UNTS 340.   Paraguay.   Prolongation
    27 Feb 63. Force 29 Mar 63.
487 UNTS 334. USA (United States). Amendment
    26 Jun 63. Force 26 Jun 63.
487 UNTS 334.   Paraguay.   Amendment
    26 Jun 63. Force 26 Jun 63.

101678   Bilateral Exchange   **126 UNTS 3**
SIGNED: 17 May 46   FORCE: 17 May 46
REGISTERED: 26 Mar 52 USA (United States)
ARTICLES: 2 LANGUAGE: English. Portuguese.
HEADNOTE: SISAL
TOPIC: Commodity Trade
CONCEPTS: Time limit. Commodity trade.
PARTIES:
    Portugal
    USA (United States)

101679   Bilateral Agreement   **126 UNTS 13**
SIGNED: 6 Dec 45   FORCE: 15 Jul 46
REGISTERED: 26 Mar 52 USA (United States)
ARTICLES: 12 LANGUAGE: English.
HEADNOTE: PAYMENTS
TOPIC: Finance
CONCEPTS: Definition of terms. Detailed regula-
    tions. General cooperation. General trade. Im-
    port quotas. Accounting procedures. Balance of
    payments. Monetary and gold transfers. Ex-
    change rates and regulations. Financial pro-
    grams. Interest rates. Payment schedules. Pur-
    chase authorizations. Customs duties. Loan and
    credit. Credit provisions. Purchase authorization.
INTL ORGS: International Monetary Fund.
TREATY REF: 2UNTS39; 19UNTS280.

PROCEDURE: Amendment. Future Procedures Contemplated.
PARTIES:
UK Great Britain
USA (United States)
ANNEX
303 UNTS 332. USA (United States). Amendment 6 Mar 57. Force 25 Apr 57.
303 UNTS 332. UK Great Britain. Amendment 6 Mar 57. Force 25 Apr 57.

101680 Bilateral Agreement **126 UNTS 39**
SIGNED: 30 Oct 47 FORCE: 30 Oct 47
REGISTERED: 26 Mar 52 USA (United States)
ARTICLES: 1 LANGUAGE: English.
HEADNOTE: SUPPLEMENTARY AGREEMENT GATT
TOPIC: General Economic
CONCEPTS: Treaty interpretation. Annex type material. Previous treaty replacement.
INTL ORGS: United Nations.
TREATY REF: 55UNTS194; 304UNTS188; 200LTS293.
PARTIES:
UK Great Britain
USA (United States)
ANNEX
458 UNTS 286. USA (United States). Termination 27 Jun 62. Force 28 Jul 62.
458 UNTS 286. UK Great Britain. Termination 28 Jun 62. Force 28 Jul 62.

101681 Multilateral Exchange **126 UNTS 47**
SIGNED: 23 Dec 46 FORCE: 23 Dec 46
REGISTERED: 26 Mar 52 USA (United States)
ARTICLES: 3 LANGUAGE: English. Portuguese.
HEADNOTE: MODIFY SURPLUSES EXPORTABLE RICE
TOPIC: Commodity Trade
CONCEPTS: Annex type material. Commodity trade. Quotas.
TREATY REF: 65UNTS231.
PARTIES:
Brazil SIGNED: 23 Dec 46 FORCE: 23 Dec 46
UK Great Britain SIGNED: 23 Dec 46 FORCE: 23 Dec 46
USA (United States) SIGNED: 23 Dec 46 FORCE: 23 Dec 46

101682 Bilateral Agreement **126 UNTS 57**
SIGNED: 10 Dec 51 FORCE: 10 Dec 51
REGISTERED: 28 Mar 52 United Nations
ARTICLES: 9 LANGUAGE: Arabic. English.
HEADNOTE: ACTIVITIES UNICEF
TOPIC: Direct Aid
CONCEPTS: Privileges and immunities. General cooperation. Exchange of information and documents. Informational records. Inspection and observation. Public information. Use of facilities. Procedure. Existing tribunals. Export quotas. Financial programs. Tax exemptions. Commodities and services. Assistance. General aid. Procurement. Distribution. IGO status.
INTL ORGS: United Nations.
TREATY REF: 1UNTS15.
PROCEDURE: Duration.
PARTIES:
Iraq
UNICEF (Children)
ANNEX
248 UNTS 366. UNICEF (Children). Supplementation 7 Aug 56. Force 7 Aug 56.
248 UNTS 366. Iraq. Supplementation 7 Aug 56. Force 7 Aug 56.
482 UNTS 366. UNICEF (Children). Force 3 Dec 63.
482 UNTS 366. Iraq. Force 3 Dec 63.

101683 Bilateral Agreement **126 UNTS 77**
SIGNED: 25 Oct 51 FORCE: 1 Jan 52
REGISTERED: 31 Mar 52 WHO (World Health)
ARTICLES: 4 LANGUAGE: English.
HEADNOTE: MALARIA INSECT CONTROL PROGRAM
TOPIC: Sanitation
CONCEPTS: Definition of terms. Privileges and immunities. General cooperation. Personnel. General property. Specialists exchange. Disease control. Insect control. WHO used as agency. Vocational training. Research and development. Ex-

pense sharing formulae. Financial programs. Assistance. Specific technical assistance. Materials, equipment and services.
INTL ORGS: United Nations.
TREATY REF: OFF. REC. WHO NO.28 P.68; 76UNTS132; 33UNTS261.
PROCEDURE: Amendment. Duration. Termination.
PARTIES:
Taiwan
WHO (World Health)

101684 Bilateral Agreement **126 UNTS 101**
SIGNED: 7 Oct 51 FORCE: 16 Nov 51
REGISTERED: 31 Mar 52 WHO (World Health)
ARTICLES: 6 LANGUAGE: English.
HEADNOTE: TECHNICAL ASSISTANCE
TOPIC: Tech Assistance
CONCEPTS: Exceptions and exemptions. Treaty implementation. Annex or appendix reference. Privileges and immunities. General cooperation. Exchange of information and documents. Personnel. Use of facilities. Arbitration. Procedure. Scholarships and grants. Vocational training. Research and scientific projects. Expense sharing formulae. Local currency. Domestic obligation. Special projects. Materials, equipment and services. IGO status. Conformity with IGO decisions.
INTL ORGS: United Nations. Special Commission.
TREATY REF: 76UNTS132.
PROCEDURE: Amendment. Termination.
PARTIES:
Pakistan
WHO (World Health)

101685 Bilateral Agreement **126 UNTS 119**
SIGNED: 3 Mar 50 FORCE: 3 Mar 50
REGISTERED: 31 Mar 52 United Nations
ARTICLES: 9 LANGUAGE: English. Spanish.
HEADNOTE: ACITIVITIES UNICEF
TOPIC: Direct Aid
CONCEPTS: Privileges and immunities. General cooperation. Exchange of information and documents. Informational records. Inspection and observation. Public information. Use of facilities. Procedure. Existing tribunals. Export quotas. Financial programs. Tax exemptions. Commodities and services. General technical assistance. General aid. Procurement. Distribution. IGO status.
INTL ORGS: United Nations.
PARTIES:
Chile
UNICEF (Children)
ANNEX
354 UNTS 397. UNICEF (Children). Supplementation 11 Jun 56. Force 18 Jan 60.
354 UNTS 397. Chile. Supplementation 11 Jun 56. Force 18 Jan 60.

101686 Bilateral Exchange **126 UNTS 139**
SIGNED: 29 Feb 52 FORCE: 29 Feb 52
REGISTERED: 1 Apr 52 Denmark
ARTICLES: 2 LANGUAGE: English.
HEADNOTE: RESUMPTION DIPLOMATIC RELATIONS
TOPIC: Consul/Citizenship
CONCEPTS: Peaceful relations. Diplomatic relations establishment. Diplomatic relations resumption.
PARTIES:
Denmark
Japan

101687 Bilateral Agreement **126 UNTS 145**
SIGNED: 2 Apr 52 FORCE: 2 Apr 52
REGISTERED: 2 Apr 52 United Nations
ARTICLES: 6 LANGUAGE: English.
HEADNOTE: TECHNICAL ASSISTANCE
TOPIC: Tech Assistance
CONCEPTS: Definition of terms. Treaty implementation. Privileges and immunities. General cooperation. Personnel. Title and deeds. Scholarships and grants. Vocational training. Education. Research and development. Expense sharing formulae. Local currency. Domestic obligation. General technical assistance. Materials, equipment and services. IGO status. Conformity with IGO decisions.
TREATY REF: 76UNTS132; 1UNTS15,263.
PROCEDURE: Amendment. Termination.

PARTIES:
India
United Nations
ANNEX
249 UNTS 435. United Nations. Force 31 Aug 56.
249 UNTS 435. India. Force 31 Aug 56.

101688 Bilateral Agreement **126 UNTS 157**
SIGNED: 12 Nov 51 FORCE: 9 Jan 52
REGISTERED: 2 Apr 52 Netherlands
ARTICLES: 8 LANGUAGE: French. Dutch.
HEADNOTE: DOUBLE TAXATION FISCAL EVASION DEATH DUTIES
TOPIC: Taxation
CONCEPTS: Privileges and immunities. Immovable property. Claims and settlements. Taxation. Death duties. Equitable taxes.
PROCEDURE: Denunciation. Ratification.
PARTIES:
Netherlands
Switzerland

101689 Bilateral Agreement **126 UNTS 173**
SIGNED: 12 Nov 51 FORCE: 9 Jan 52
REGISTERED: 2 Apr 52 Netherlands
ARTICLES: 15 LANGUAGE: Dutch. French.
HEADNOTE: DOUBLE TAXATION TAXES INCOME PROPERTY
TOPIC: Taxation
CONCEPTS: Territorial application. Domestic legislation. Immovable property. Wages and salaries. Claims and settlements. Taxation. General. Tax exemptions.
PROCEDURE: Ratification. Termination.
PARTIES:
Netherlands
Switzerland

101690 Bilateral Agreement **126 UNTS 221**
SIGNED: 7 Jun 51 FORCE: 30 Jun 51
REGISTERED: 4 Apr 52 WHO (World Health)
ARTICLES: 6 LANGUAGE: Arabic. English.
HEADNOTE: TECHNICAL ASSISTANCE
TOPIC: Tech Assistance
CONCEPTS: Treaty implementation. Annex or appendix reference. Privileges and immunities. General cooperation. Personnel. Use of facilities. Arbitration. Procedure. Scholarships and grants. Research and scientific projects. Expense sharing formulae. Local currency. Domestic obligation. General technical assistance. Materials, equipment and services. Conformity with IGO decisions.
INTL ORGS: United Nations. Arbitration Commission.
TREATY REF: 76UNTS132; 1UNTS263,15.
PROCEDURE: Amendment. Termination.
PARTIES:
Lebanon
WHO (World Health)

101691 Multilateral Agreement **126 UNTS 237**
SIGNED: 24 Sep 49 FORCE: 20 Feb 52
REGISTERED: 5 Apr 52 FAO (Food Agri)
ARTICLES: 10 LANGUAGE: French.
HEADNOTE: MEDITERRANEAN FISHERIES
TOPIC: IGO Establishment
CONCEPTS: Diplomatic relations establishment. Exchange of information and documents. Research results. Scientific exchange. Funding procedures. General technical assistance. Establishment. Liaison with other IGO's. Internal structure. Ocean resources.
INTL ORGS: Food and Agricultural Organization of the United Nations.
PROCEDURE: Amendment. Accession. Denunciation.
PARTIES:
United Arab Rep RATIFIED: 19 Feb 51 FORCE: 20 Feb 52
Israel RATIFIED: 20 Feb 52 FORCE: 20 Feb 52
Italy RATIFIED: 29 May 50 FORCE: 20 Feb 52
UK Great Britain RATIFIED: 20 Nov 50 FORCE: 20 Feb 52
Yugoslavia RATIFIED: 12 Oct 51 FORCE: 20 Feb 52
ANNEX
135 UNTS 398. France. Acceptance 8 Jul 52.
135 UNTS 398. Greece. Acceptance 7 Apr 52.
179 UNTS 221. Spain. Acceptance 19 Oct 53.

189 UNTS 380. Turkey. Acceptance 6 Apr 54.
191 UNTS 403. Monaco. Acceptance 14 May 54.
191 UNTS 403. France. Tunisia.
251 UNTS 380. Morocco. Acceptance 17 Sep 56.
382 UNTS 332. Lebanon. Acceptance 14 Nov 60.
471 UNTS 322. Libya. Acceptance 13 May 63.
490 UNTS 444. Medit Fish Council. Amendment 5 Dec 63. Force 3 Dec 63.
535 UNTS 410. Malta. Acceptance 29 Apr 65.
540 UNTS 334. Cyprus. Acceptance 10 Jun 65.
560 UNTS 250. Medit Fish Council. Declaration 4 Dec 65.
614 UNTS 304. Algeria. Acceptance 11 Dec 67.
635 UNTS 346. UK Great Britain. Withdrawal 25 Mar 68. Force 25 Jun 68.

101692 Bilateral Agreement **126 UNTS 249**
SIGNED: 13 Apr 51 FORCE: 14 May 51
REGISTERED: 7 Apr 52 ILO (Labor Org)
ARTICLES: 5 LANGUAGE: English. Spanish.
HEADNOTE: TECHNICAL ASSISTANCE
TOPIC: Tech Assistance
CONCEPTS: Treaty implementation. Privileges and immunities. General cooperation. Exchange of information and documents. Personnel. Title and deeds. Arbitration. Procedure. Scholarships and grants. Vocational training. Exchange rates and regulations. Expense sharing formulae. Local currency. Domestic obligation. General technical assistance. Conformity with IGO decisions.
INTL ORGS: United Nations. Arbitration Commission.
TREATY REF: 76UNTS132; 33UNTS261.
PROCEDURE: Amendment. Termination.
PARTIES:
Guatemala
ILO (Labor Org)

101693 Bilateral Agreement **126 UNTS 269**
SIGNED: 10 Nov 51 FORCE: 17 Dec 51
REGISTERED: 7 Apr 52 ILO (Labor Org)
ARTICLES: 5 LANGUAGE: Spanish.
HEADNOTE: TECHNICAL ASSISTANCE
TOPIC: Tech Assistance
CONCEPTS: Treaty implementation. Privileges and immunities. General cooperation. Exchange of information and documents. Personnel. Title and deeds. Arbitration. Procedure. Scholarships and grants. Vocational training. Exchange rates and regulations. Expense sharing formulae. Local currency. Domestic obligation. General technical assistance. Materials, equipment and services. Conformity with IGO decisions.
INTL ORGS: United Nations. Arbitration Commission.
TREATY REF: 76UNTS132; 33UNTS261.
PROCEDURE: Amendment. Termination.
PARTIES:
Panama
ILO (Labor Org)

101694 Multilateral Convention **126 UNTS 285**
SIGNED: 17 Apr 50 FORCE: 12 Mar 52
REGISTERED: 7 Apr 52 UK Great Britain
ARTICLES: 16 LANGUAGE: English. French.
HEADNOTE: STUDENT EMPLOYEES
TOPIC: Non-ILO Labor
CONCEPTS: Detailed regulations. Treaty implementation. Annex or appendix reference. Resident permits. Conformity with municipal law. Dispute settlement. Employment regulations. Non-ILO labor relations. Administrative cooperation. National treatment.
INTL ORGS: Western European Union. Arbitration Commission.
TREATY REF: 19UNTS51.
PROCEDURE: Accession. Denunciation. Duration. Ratification. Registration.
PARTIES:
Belgium SIGNED: 17 Apr 50
France SIGNED: 17 Apr 50
Luxembourg SIGNED: 17 Apr 50 RATIFIED: 12 Jan 52 FORCE: 12 Mar 52
Netherlands SIGNED: 17 Apr 50 RATIFIED: 10 Aug 51 FORCE: 12 Mar 52
UK Great Britain SIGNED: 17 Apr 50 RATIFIED: 29 Jul 50 FORCE: 12 Mar 52
ANNEX
267 UNTS 379. UK Great Britain. Channel Islands. Force 1 Feb 53.

267 UNTS 379. UK Great Britain. Isle of Man. Force 1 Feb 53.
385 UNTS 366. Germany, West. Qualified Accession 13 Sep 60. Force 13 Sep 60.
385 UNTS 366. Italy. Qualified Accession 15 Jan 59. Force 13 Sep 60.

101695 Bilateral Exchange **126 UNTS 297**
SIGNED: 12 Feb 52 FORCE: 12 Feb 52
REGISTERED: 7 Apr 52 UK Great Britain
ARTICLES: 2 LANGUAGE: English. Italian.
HEADNOTE: DISPOSAL PRIVATE PROPERTY
TOPIC: Claims and Debts
CONCEPTS: Annex or appendix reference. General property. Assets transfer.
INTL ORGS: United Nations.
PARTIES:
Italy
UK Great Britain

101696 Bilateral Exchange **126 UNTS 307**
SIGNED: 8 Jan 52 FORCE: 8 Jan 52
REGISTERED: 7 Apr 52 UK Great Britain
ARTICLES: 2 LANGUAGE: English.
HEADNOTE: ECONOMIC AID
TOPIC: Direct Aid
CONCEPTS: Conformity with municipal law. General cooperation. Attachment of funds. Monetary and gold transfers. Currency deposits. Financial programs. Garnishment of funds. Seizure funds. Domestic obligation. Economic assistance. Return of equipment and recapture.
TREATY REF: 22UNTS263; 80UNTS261.
PROCEDURE: Future Procedures Contemplated.
PARTIES:
UK Great Britain
USA (United States)
ANNEX
164 UNTS 366. UK Great Britain. Sarawak. Force 8 Jan 52.
164 UNTS 366. UK Great Britain. Nigeria. Force 8 Jan 52.
164 UNTS 366. UK Great Britain. North Borneo. Force 8 Jan 52.
164 UNTS 366. UK Great Britain. Tanganyika. Force 8 Jan 52.
164 UNTS 366. UK Great Britain. Kenya. Force 8 Jan 52.
164 UNTS 366. UK Great Britain. Leeward Islands. Force 8 Jan 52.
164 UNTS 366. UK Great Britain. Cyprus. Force 8 Jan 52.
164 UNTS 366. UK Great Britain. Gambia. Force 8 Jan 52.
164 UNTS 366. UK Great Britain. Gibralter. Force 8 Jan 52.
164 UNTS 366. UK Great Britain. Fiji Islands. Force 8 Jan 52.
164 UNTS 366. UK Great Britain. Singapore. Force 8 Jan 52.
164 UNTS 366. UK Great Britain. Bahamas. Force 8 Jan 52.
164 UNTS 366. UK Great Britain. British Guiana. Force 8 Jan 52.
164 UNTS 366. UK Great Britain. British Somaliland. Force 8 Jan 52.
164 UNTS 366. UK Great Britain. Falkland Islands. Force 8 Jan 52.
164 UNTS 366. UK Great Britain. Northern Rhodesia. Force 8 Jan 52.
164 UNTS 366. UK Great Britain. Nyasaland. Force 8 Jan 52.
164 UNTS 366. UK Great Britain. Gold Coast. Force 8 Jan 52.
164 UNTS 366. UK Great Britain. Hong Kong. Force 8 Jan 52.
164 UNTS 366. UK Great Britain. Jamaica. Force 8 Jan 52.
164 UNTS 366. UK Great Britain. W Pacif Hi Command. Force 8 Jan 52.
164 UNTS 366. UK Great Britain. Southern Rhodesia. Force 8 Jan 52.
164 UNTS 366. UK Great Britain. Brunei. Force 8 Jan 52.
164 UNTS 366. UK Great Britain. Fed of Malaya. Force 8 Jan 52.
164 UNTS 366. UK Great Britain. Malta. Force 8 Jan 52.
164 UNTS 366. UK Great Britain. Windward Islands. Force 8 Jan 52.
164 UNTS 366. UK Great Britain. Zanzibar. Force 8 Jan 52.

164 UNTS 366. UK Great Britain. Barbados. Force 20 Mar 52.
164 UNTS 366. UK Great Britain. British Honduras. Force 8 Jan 52.
164 UNTS 366. UK Great Britain. Sierra Leone. Force 8 Jan 52.
164 UNTS 366. UK Great Britain. Trinidad. Force 8 Jan 52.
164 UNTS 366. UK Great Britain. St. Helena. Force 8 Jan 52.
164 UNTS 366. UK Great Britain. Mauritius. Force 8 Jan 52.
164 UNTS 366. UK Great Britain. Seychelles. Force 8 Jan 52.
164 UNTS 366. UK Great Britain. Uganda. Force 8 Jan 52.
164 UNTS 366. UK Great Britain. Aden. Force 8 Jan 52.
272 UNTS 259. UK Great Britain. Fed Rhod/Nyasaland. Force 5 Nov 54.

101697 Bilateral Agreement **127 UNTS 3**
SIGNED: 15 Jan 52 FORCE: 15 Jan 52
REGISTERED: 7 Apr 52 UK Great Britain
ARTICLES: 26 LANGUAGE: English.
HEADNOTE: EXTENSION BAHAMAS LONG-RANGE PROVING GROUNDS
TOPIC: Milit Installation
CONCEPTS: Definition of terms. Annex or appendix reference. Visa abolition. Court procedures. Legal protection and assistance. Use of facilities. Compensation. Claims and settlements. Tax exemptions. Customs exemptions. Ports and pilotage. Facilities and equipment. Postal services. Security of information. Jurisdiction. Procurement and logistics. Status of forces. Bases and facilities.
TREATY REF: 97UNTS193.
PARTIES:
UK Great Britain
USA (United States)

101698 Bilateral Agreement **127 UNTS 43**
SIGNED: 18 Feb 52 FORCE: 18 Feb 52
REGISTERED: 14 Apr 52 WHO (World Health)
ARTICLES: 4 LANGUAGE: English.
HEADNOTE: MEDICAL SCIENTISTS PROJECT
TOPIC: Scientific Project
CONCEPTS: Definition of terms. Privileges and immunities. Personnel. Use of facilities. Specialists exchange. Public health. WHO used as agency. Vocational training. Research and scientific projects. Scientific exchange. Research and development. Domestic obligation. Publications exchange. IGO obligations.
TREATY REF: 33UNTS261; 43UNTS342.
PROCEDURE: Amendment.
PARTIES:
Burma
WHO (World Health)

101699 Bilateral Convention **127 UNTS 57**
SIGNED: 12 Jun 50 FORCE: 21 Nov 50
REGISTERED: 15 Apr 52 USA (United States)
ARTICLES: 7 LANGUAGE: English.
HEADNOTE: DOUBLE TAXATION FISCAL EVASION ESTATE TAXES SUCCESSION DUTIES
TOPIC: Taxation
CONCEPTS: Previous treaty replacement. Claims and settlements. Debts. Taxation. Death duties. Tax credits. Tax exemptions.
PROCEDURE: Ratification. Termination.
PARTIES:
Canada
USA (United States)

101700 Bilateral Convention **127 UNTS 67**
SIGNED: 12 Jun 50 FORCE: 21 Nov 51
REGISTERED: 15 Apr 52 USA (United States)
ARTICLES: 2 LANGUAGE: English.
HEADNOTE: DOUBLE TAXATION FISCAL EVASION INCOME TAXES
TOPIC: Taxation
CONCEPTS: Previous treaty amendment. Annex type material. Teacher and student exchange. Wages and salaries. Taxation. Tax exemptions. Conformity with IGO decisions.
TREATY REF: 124UNTS271.
PROCEDURE: Ratification.

PARTIES:
Canada
USA (United States)
ANNEX
293 UNTS 344. USA (United States). Supplementation 8 Aug 56. Force 26 Sep 57.
293 UNTS 344. Canada. Supplementation 8 Aug 56. Force 26 Sep 57.

101701 Bilateral Convention **127 UNTS 89**
SIGNED: 13 Sep 49 FORCE: 20 Dec 51
REGISTERED: 15 Apr 52 USA (United States)
ARTICLES: 23 LANGUAGE: English.
HEADNOTE: DOUBLE TAXATION FISCAL EVASION TAXES INCOME
TOPIC: Taxation
CONCEPTS: Definition of terms. Conformity with municipal law. Exchange of official publications. Domestic legislation. Responsibility and liability. Teacher and student exchange. Wages and salaries. Taxation. Tax credits. Equitable taxes. General. Tax exemptions. Air transport. Merchant vessels.
PROCEDURE: Duration. Ratification. Termination.
PARTIES:
Ireland
USA (United States)

101702 Bilateral Convention **127 UNTS 119**
SIGNED: 13 Sep 49 FORCE: 20 Dec 51
REGISTERED: 15 Apr 52 USA (United States)
ARTICLES: 9 LANGUAGE: English.
HEADNOTE: DOUBLE TAXATION FISCAL EVASION ESTATES DECEASED PERSONS
TOPIC: Taxation
CONCEPTS: Definition of terms. Conformity with municipal law. Exchange of official publications. Immovable property. Claims and settlements. Taxation. Death duties. Tax credits.
PROCEDURE: Duration. Ratification. Termination.
PARTIES:
Ireland
USA (United States)

101703 Bilateral Convention **127 UNTS 133**
SIGNED: 16 Mar 48 FORCE: 18 Dec 51
REGISTERED: 15 Apr 52 USA (United States)
ARTICLES: 22 LANGUAGE: English.
HEADNOTE: DOUBLE TAXATION FISCAL EVASION TAXES INCOME
TOPIC: Taxation
CONCEPTS: Definition of terms. Territorial application. Conformity with municipal law. Exchange of official publications. Domestic legislation. Teacher and student exchange. Wages and salaries. Claims and settlements. Taxation. Tax credits. Tax exemptions. Air transport. Merchant vessels. Services. Mass media exchange.
PARTIES:
New Zealand
USA (United States)

101704 Bilateral Convention **127 UNTS 163**
SIGNED: 13 Jun 49 FORCE: 11 Dec 51
REGISTERED: 15 Apr 52 USA (United States)
ARTICLES: 14 LANGUAGE: English. Norwegian.
HEADNOTE: DOUBLE TAXATION FISCAL EVASION ESTATES INHERITANCES
TOPIC: Taxation
CONCEPTS: Definition of terms. Privileges and immunities. General cooperation. Exchange of official publications. Immovable property. Negotiation. Claims and settlements. Taxation. Death duties. Tax credits. Tax exemptions.
PROCEDURE: Duration. Ratification. Termination.
PARTIES:
Norway
USA (United States)

101705 Bilateral Convention **127 UNTS 189**
SIGNED: 13 Jun 49 FORCE: 11 Dec 51
REGISTERED: 15 Apr 52 USA (United States)
ARTICLES: 22 LANGUAGE: English. Norwegian.
HEADNOTE: DOUBLE TAXATION FISCAL EVASION TAXES INCOME
TOPIC: Taxation
CONCEPTS: Definition of terms. Conformity with municipal law. General cooperation. Exchange of official publications. Domestic legislation. Im-

movable property. Negotiation. Teacher and student exchange. Wages and salaries. Claims and settlements. Taxation. General. Tax exemptions. Air transport. Merchant vessels.
TREATY REF: 67LTS417; 104LTS512.
PARTIES:
Norway
USA (United States)
ANNEX
346 UNTS 326. USA (United States). Supplementation 10 Jul 58. Force 21 Oct 59.
346 UNTS 326. Norway. Supplementation 10 Jul 58. Force 21 Oct 59.

101706 Bilateral Convention **127 UNTS 227**
SIGNED: 24 May 51 FORCE: 27 Sep 51
REGISTERED: 15 Apr 52 USA (United States)
ARTICLES: 20 LANGUAGE: English. French. German.
HEADNOTE: DOUBLE TAXATION TAXES INCOME
TOPIC: Taxation
CONCEPTS: Definition of terms. Privileges and immunities. Conformity with municipal law. Exchange of official publications. Domestic legislation. Immovable property. Negotiation. Teacher and student exchange. Wages and salaries. Claims and settlements. Taxation. General. Tax exemptions. Air transport. Merchant vessels.
PROCEDURE: Duration. Ratification. Termination.
PARTIES:
Switzerland
USA (United States)

101707 Bilateral Exchange **127 UNTS 263**
SIGNED: 28 Nov 51 FORCE: 28 Nov 51
REGISTERED: 19 Apr 52 New Zealand
ARTICLES: 2 LANGUAGE: English.
HEADNOTE: SPECIFIC SUGAR TRADE
TOPIC: General Trade
CONCEPTS: Non-interest rates and fees. Commodity trade.
PARTIES:
New Zealand
UK Great Britain
ANNEX
280 UNTS 355. UK Great Britain. Force 1 Jan 57.
280 UNTS 355. New Zealand. Force 1 Jan 57.

101708 Multilateral Agreement **127 UNTS 269**
SIGNED: 23 Jan 52 FORCE: 23 Jan 52
REGISTERED: 24 Apr 52 United Nations
ARTICLES: 5 LANGUAGE: English. French.
HEADNOTE: TECHNICAL ASSISTANCE
TOPIC: Tech Assistance
CONCEPTS: Definition of terms. Treaty implementation. Annex or appendix reference. Privileges and immunities. General cooperation. Title and deeds. Scholarships and grants. Vocational training. Research and scientific projects. Expense sharing formulae. Domestic obligation. General technical assistance. Materials, equipment and services. IGO status. Conformity with IGO decisions.
TREATY REF: 76UNTS132; 1UNTS15,263; 33UNTS261.
PROCEDURE: Amendment. Termination.
PARTIES:
Afghanistan SIGNED: 23 Jan 52 FORCE: 23 Jan 52
ICAO (Civil Aviat) SIGNED: 23 Jan 52 FORCE: 23 Jan 52
ILO (Labor Org) SIGNED: 23 Jan 52 FORCE: 23 Jan 52
United Nations SIGNED: 23 Jan 52 FORCE: 23 Jan 52
ANNEX
187 UNTS 450. UNTAB (Tech Assis). Amendment 12 Dec 53. Force 12 Dec 53.
187 UNTS 450. Afghanistan. Amendment 12 Dec 53. Force 12 Dec 53.

101709 Bilateral Exchange **127 UNTS 281**
SIGNED: 14 Apr 50 FORCE: 14 Apr 50
REGISTERED: 24 Apr 52 ICAO (Civil Aviat)
ARTICLES: 4 LANGUAGE: English.
HEADNOTE: TEMPORARY AIR AGREEMENT
TOPIC: Air Transport
CONCEPTS: Conditions. Exceptions and exemptions. Conformity with municipal law. Exchange of information and documents. Routes and logis-

tics. Permit designation. Air transport. Overflights and technical stops. Operating authorizations and regulations. Procurement and logistics.
TREATY REF: 84UNTS389; 15UNTS295.
PROCEDURE: Duration. Termination.
PARTIES:
Australia
Philippines

101710 Bilateral Agreement **127 UNTS 293**
SIGNED: 8 Aug 50 FORCE: 25 Oct 51
REGISTERED: 24 Apr 52 ICAO (Civil Aviat)
ARTICLES: 19 LANGUAGE: Arabic. French.
HEADNOTE: REGULAR AIR TRANSPORT SERVICES
TOPIC: Air Transport
CONCEPTS: Definition of terms. Detailed regulations. Exceptions and exemptions. Annex or appendix reference. Conformity with municipal law. General cooperation. Exchange of information and documents. Arbitration. Procedure. Existing tribunals. Special tribunals. Non-interest rates and fees. Customs exemptions. Routes and logistics. Navigational conditions. Permit designation. Air transport. Conditions of airlines operating permission. Overflights and technical stops. Operating authorizations and regulations.
INTL ORGS: International Civil Aviation Organization. International Court of Justice.
TREATY REF: 15UNTS295; 84UNTS389.
PROCEDURE: Amendment. Future Procedures Contemplated. Ratification. Registration. Termination.
PARTIES:
France
United Arab Rep

101711 Bilateral Agreement **128 UNTS 3**
SIGNED: 12 Apr 50 FORCE: 2 Apr 51
REGISTERED: 24 Apr 52 ICAO (Civil Aviat)
ARTICLES: 19 LANGUAGE: Arabic. Turkish.
HEADNOTE: ESTABLISHMENT SCHEDULED AIR SERVICES
TOPIC: Air Transport
CONCEPTS: Definition of terms. Detailed regulations. Exceptions and exemptions. Annex or appendix reference. Conformity with municipal law. General cooperation. Exchange of information and documents. Arbitration. Procedure. Existing tribunals. Negotiation. Non-interest rates and fees. Customs exemptions. Routes and logistics. Navigational conditions. Permit designation. Air transport. Conditions of airlines operating permission. Operating authorizations and regulations.
INTL ORGS: International Civil Aviation Organization.
TREATY REF: 15UNTS295.
PROCEDURE: Amendment. Future Procedures Contemplated. Ratification. Registration. Termination.
PARTIES:
Turkey
United Arab Rep

101712 Bilateral Agreement **128 UNTS 39**
SIGNED: 1 Dec 51 FORCE: 1 Apr 51
REGISTERED: 24 Apr 52 ICAO (Civil Aviat)
ARTICLES: 16 LANGUAGE: English.
HEADNOTE: AIR SERVICES
TOPIC: Air Transport
CONCEPTS: Conditions. Definition of terms. Detailed regulations. Emergencies. Annex or appendix reference. Conformity with municipal law. General cooperation. Exchange of information and documents. Arbitration. Procedure. Existing tribunals. Negotiation. Non-interest rates and fees. Most favored nation clause. National treatment. Customs exemptions. Routes and logistics. Permit designation. Conditions of airlines operating permission. Overflights and technical stops. Operating authorizations and regulations.
INTL ORGS: International Civil Aviation Organization.
TREATY REF: 15UNTS295.
PROCEDURE: Amendment. Future Procedures Contemplated. Registration. Termination. Application to Non-self-governing Territories.

PARTIES:
India
UK Great Britain
ANNEX
166 UNTS 377. India. Amendment 16 Mar 53. Force 16 Mar 53.
166 UNTS 377. UK Great Britain. Amendment 16 Mar 53. Force 16 Mar 53.
192 UNTS 346. UK Great Britain. Amendment 14 Aug 53. Force 14 Aug 53.
192 UNTS 346. India. Amendment 14 Aug 53. Force 14 Aug 53.
192 UNTS 350. UK Great Britain. Amendment 14 Nov 53. Force 14 Nov 53.
192 UNTS 350. India. Amendment 14 Nov 53. Force 14 Nov 53.
311 UNTS 342. UK Great Britain. Amendment 25 Mar 57. Force 25 Mar 57.
311 UNTS 342. India. Amendment 25 Mar 57. Force 25 Mar 57.
353 UNTS 350. UK Great Britain. Amendment 8 Jun 59. Force 8 Jun 59.
353 UNTS 350. India. Amendment 8 Jun 59. Force 8 Jun 59.
613 UNTS 404. UK Great Britain. Amendment 9 May 67. Force 9 May 67.
613 UNTS 404. India. Amendment 9 May 67. Force 9 May 67.

101713 Bilateral Agreement **128 UNTS 63**
SIGNED: 25 Sep 51 FORCE: 25 Sep 51
REGISTERED: 24 Apr 52 ICAO (Civil Aviat)
ARTICLES: 12 LANGUAGE: English.
HEADNOTE: CONSULAR CONVENTION
TOPIC: Air Transport
CONCEPTS: Definition of terms. Territorial application. Previous treaty replacement. General consular functions. Diplomatic privileges. Consular relations establishment. Privileges and immunities. Consular functions in shipping. Consular functions in property. Responsibility and liability. Procedure.
INTL ORGS: International Civil Aviation Organization.
TREATY REF: 15UNTS295.
PROCEDURE: Amendment. Ratification. Termination.
PARTIES:
Australia
Netherlands

101714 Bilateral Agreement **128 UNTS 83**
SIGNED: 14 Feb 52 FORCE: 14 Feb 52
REGISTERED: 24 Apr 52 ICAO (Civil Aviat)
ARTICLES: 7 LANGUAGE: English.
HEADNOTE: TECHNICAL ASSISTANCE
TOPIC: Tech Assistance
CONCEPTS: Definition of terms. Annex or appendix reference. Privileges and immunities. General cooperation. Personnel. Responsibility and liability. Title and deeds. Scholarships and grants. Vocational training. Research and scientific projects. Exchange rates and regulations. Expense sharing formulae. Claims and settlements. Domestic obligation. General technical assistance. Materials, equipment and services. IGO status. Conformity with IGO decisions.
INTL ORGS: United Nations.
TREATY REF: 76UNTS132; 33UNTS261.
PROCEDURE: Amendment. Termination.
PARTIES:
Lebanon
ICAO (Civil Aviat)

101715 Bilateral Agreement **128 UNTS 97**
SIGNED: 6 Feb 52 FORCE: 6 Feb 52
REGISTERED: 24 Apr 52 ICAO (Civil Aviat)
ARTICLES: 7 LANGUAGE: English.
HEADNOTE: TECHNICAL ASSISTANCE
TOPIC: Tech Assistance
CONCEPTS: Definition of terms. Annex or appendix reference. Privileges and immunities. General cooperation. Personnel. Responsibility and liability. Title and deeds. Scholarships and grants. Vocational training. Research and scientific projects. Exchange rates and regulations. Expense sharing formulae. Claims and settlements. Domestic obligation. General technical assistance. Materials, equipment and services. IGO status. Conformity with IGO decisions.
INTL ORGS: United Nations.

TREATY REF: 76UNTS132.
PARTIES:
ICAO (Civil Aviat)
Yugoslavia

101716 Bilateral Exchange **128 UNTS 109**
SIGNED: 19 Oct 51 FORCE: 19 Nov 51
REGISTERED: 25 Apr 52 Australia
ARTICLES: 2 LANGUAGE: English.
HEADNOTE: VISAS & VISA FEES
TOPIC: Visas
CONCEPTS: Visa abolition. Denial of admission. Visas. Conformity with municipal law. Fees and exemptions.
PROCEDURE: Termination.
PARTIES:
Australia
Norway
ANNEX
301 UNTS 444. Australia. Amendment 30 Apr 58. Force 1 May 58.
301 UNTS 444. Norway. Amendment 30 Apr 58. Force 1 May 58.

101717 Bilateral Agreement **128 UNTS 115**
SIGNED: 22 Feb 51 FORCE: 1 Apr 51
REGISTERED: 25 Apr 52 Netherlands
ARTICLES: 23 LANGUAGE: Dutch. English.
HEADNOTE: ASSISTED MIGRATION
TOPIC: Non-ILO Labor
CONCEPTS: Definition of terms. Detailed regulations. Annex or appendix reference. Border traffic and migration. Repatriation of nationals. Exchange of information and documents. Responsibility and liability. Administrative cooperation. Accounting procedures. Transportation costs.
PROCEDURE: Duration.
PARTIES:
Australia
Netherlands

101718 Multilateral Instrument **128 UNTS 141**
SIGNED: 20 Jun 49 FORCE: 21 Sep 49
REGISTERED: 25 Apr 52 UK Great Britain
ARTICLES: 11 LANGUAGE: English. French.
HEADNOTE: ALLIED HIGH COMMISSION FOR GERMANY
TOPIC: IGO Establishment
CONCEPTS: Treaty interpretation. Annex type material. Previous treaty renunciation. Privileges and immunities. Inspection and observation. General trade. Accounting procedures. Funding procedures. Rearmament restrictions and controls. Jurisdiction. Equipment and supplies. Reparations and restrictions. Post-war claims settlement. Disarmament and demilitarization. Industrial controls. Control and occupation machinery. Subsidiary organ. Establishment. Headquarters and facilities. Conformity with IGO decisions. Inter-agency agreements.
INTL ORGS: Allied Military Occupation. League of Nations. United Nations.
PARTIES:
France SIGNED: 20 Jun 49 FORCE: 21 Sep 49
UK Great Britain SIGNED: 20 Jun 49 FORCE: 21 Sep 49
USA (United States) SIGNED: 20 Jun 49 FORCE: 21 Sep 49

101719 Multilateral Convention **128 UNTS 171**
SIGNED: 13 May 50 FORCE: 1 Apr 51
REGISTERED: 30 Apr 52 Switzerland
ARTICLES: 4 LANGUAGE: French.
HEADNOTE: INTERNATIONAL CONVENTION TRANSPORT GOODS RAIL
TOPIC: Land Transport
CONCEPTS: Annex or appendix reference. Annex type material. Transport of goods. Operating authorizations and regulations. Motor vehicles and combinations. Railways. Decisions. Subsidiary organ.
INTL ORGS: Special Commission.
TREATY REF: 195LTS389.
PROCEDURE: Accession. Ratification.
PARTIES:
Austria SIGNED: 13 May 50 RATIFIED: 18 Dec 50 FORCE: 1 Apr 51
Belgium SIGNED: 13 May 50 RATIFIED: 21 May 51 FORCE: 1 Jul 51

Denmark SIGNED: 16 Aug 50 RATIFIED: 21 Jan 51 FORCE: 1 Apr 51
Finland SIGNED: 18 Aug 50 RATIFIED: 24 Oct 50 FORCE: 1 Apr 51
France SIGNED: 13 May 50 RATIFIED: 13 Sep 50 FORCE: 1 Apr 51
Greece SIGNED: 21 Aug 50
Italy SIGNED: 2 Jun 50
Liechtenstein SIGNED: 13 May 50 RATIFIED: 14 Dec 51 FORCE: 1 Feb 52
Luxembourg SIGNED: 13 May 50 RATIFIED: 25 Mar 52 FORCE: 1 Jun 52
Netherlands SIGNED: 13 May 50 RATIFIED: 3 Sep 51 FORCE: 1 Nov 51
Norway SIGNED: 13 May 50 RATIFIED: 10 Apr 51 FORCE: 1 Jun 52
Portugal RATIFIED: 6 Nov 50 FORCE: 1 Apr 51
Spain SIGNED: 13 May 50
Sweden SIGNED: 13 May 50 RATIFIED: 7 Dec 50 FORCE: 1 Apr 51
Switzerland SIGNED: 13 May 50 RATIFIED: 3 Jan 51 FORCE: 1 Apr 51
Turkey SIGNED: 13 May 50 RATIFIED: 19 Jan 52 FORCE: 1 Mar 52
Yugoslavia SIGNED: 22 Aug 50 RATIFIED: 19 Jun 51 FORCE: 1 Aug 51

101720 Bilateral Agreement **128 UNTS 191**
SIGNED: 28 Apr 52 FORCE: 28 Apr 52
REGISTERED: 1 May 52 United Nations
ARTICLES: 6 LANGUAGE: English.
HEADNOTE: TECHNICAL ASSISTANCE
TOPIC: Tech Assistance
CONCEPTS: Definition of terms. Treaty implementation. Privileges and immunities. General cooperation. Personnel. Title and deeds. Exchange. Vocational training. Research and development. Expense sharing formulae. Domestic obligation. General technical assistance. Materials, equipment and services. IGO status. Conformity with IGO decisions.
TREATY REF: 76UNTS132; 1UNTS15,263.
PROCEDURE: Amendment. Termination.
PARTIES:
Pakistan
United Nations
ANNEX
187 UNTS 456. Pakistan. Amendment 8 Dec 53. Force 8 Dec 53.
187 UNTS 456. UNTAB (Tech Assis). Amendment 8 Dec 53. Force 8 Dec 53.
540 UNTS 335. United Nations. Force 2 Jul 65.
540 UNTS 335. Pakistan. Force 2 Jul 65.

101721 Bilateral Exchange **128 UNTS 201**
SIGNED: 20 Mar 50 FORCE: 20 Mar 50
REGISTERED: 5 May 52 UK Great Britain
ARTICLES: 2 LANGUAGE: English. Italian.
HEADNOTE: TRANSFER ITALY PROVISIONAL ADMINISTRATION SOMALIA
TOPIC: Territory Boundary
CONCEPTS: Annex or appendix reference. Disposition of territory. Definition of territory. Fish, wildlife, and natural resources.
INTL ORGS: United Nations.
PARTIES:
Italy
UK Great Britain
ANNEX
211 UNTS 412. UK Great Britain. Implementation 10 Mar 55. Force 10 Mar 55.
211 UNTS 412. Italy. Implementation 10 Mar 55. Force 10 Mar 55.

101722 Bilateral Exchange **128 UNTS 225**
SIGNED: 21 Mar 50 FORCE: 21 Mar 50
REGISTERED: 5 May 52 UK Great Britain
ARTICLES: 2 LANGUAGE: English. Italian.
HEADNOTE: TRANSFER ITALY PROVISIONAL ADMINISTRATION SOMALIA
TOPIC: Territory Boundary
CONCEPTS: Acceptance of UN obligations. Disposition of territory. Definition of territory. Fish, wildlife, and natural resources.
INTL ORGS: Special Commission.
TREATY REF: 49UNTS3; 50UNTS3; 118UNTS225; CMD7015.
PARTIES:
Italy
UK Great Britain

101723 Bilateral Agreement **128 UNTS 233**
SIGNED: 7 Mar 52 FORCE: 13 Mar 52
REGISTERED: 5 May 52 WHO (World Health)
ARTICLES: 4 LANGUAGE: English.
HEADNOTE: NURSING EDUCATION PROJECT
TOPIC: Sanitation
CONCEPTS: Definition of terms. Previous treaty extension. General cooperation. Personnel. Specialists exchange. Nursing. WHO used as agency. Institute establishment. Scholarships and grants. Vocational training. Research results. Research and development. Indemnities and reimbursements. Expense sharing formulae. Assistance. Special projects. Specific technical assistance. Materials, equipment and services.
TREATY REF: OFF.REC.WHO NO.28 P.68.
PROCEDURE: Amendment. Duration. Termination.
PARTIES:
Taiwan
WHO (World Health)

101724 Bilateral Agreement **128 UNTS 251**
SIGNED: 11 Jun 51 FORCE: 7 Jan 52
REGISTERED: 5 May 52 WHO (World Health)
ARTICLES: 14 LANGUAGE: English. Spanish.
HEADNOTE: TECHNICAL ADVISORY ASSISTANCE OTHER SERVICES
TOPIC: Tech Assistance
CONCEPTS: Change of circumstances. Treaty implementation. Treaty interpretation. Annex or appendix reference. Privileges and immunities. General cooperation. Personnel. Public information. Arbitration. Procedure. Negotiation. Competence of tribunal. Financial programs. Claims and settlements. Tax exemptions. Customs exemptions. Special projects. Materials, equipment and services. IGO status.
INTL ORGS: International Court of Justice. Arbitration Commission.
TREATY REF: 33UNTS261.
PROCEDURE: Amendment. Termination.
PARTIES:
WHO (World Health)
Uruguay

101725 Bilateral Agreement **129 UNTS 3**
SIGNED: 11 May 46 FORCE: 11 May 46
REGISTERED: 9 May 52 Yugoslavia
ARTICLES: 12 LANGUAGE: Hungarian. Serbo-Croat.
HEADNOTE: SUPPLY GOODS MATERIALS REPARATIONS
TOPIC: Reparations
CONCEPTS: Annex or appendix reference. Establishment of commission. Indemnities and reimbursements. Lump sum settlements. Delivery schedules. Loss and/or damage. Enemy financial interests. Reparations and restrictions. Post-war claims settlement.
PARTIES:
Hungary
Yugoslavia

101726 Bilateral Agreement **130 UNTS 3**
SIGNED: 25 Jan 47 FORCE: 25 Jan 47
REGISTERED: 9 May 52 Yugoslavia
ARTICLES: 4 LANGUAGE: Hungarian. Serbo-Croat.
HEADNOTE: SPECIFYING DELIVERY GOODS
TOPIC: Reparations
CONCEPTS: Treaty implementation. Annex or appendix reference. Exchange of information and documents. Lump sum settlements. Enemy financial interests. Reparations and restrictions. Post-war claims settlement.
TREATY REF: 129UNTS.
PARTIES:
Hungary
Yugoslavia

101727 Bilateral Agreement **130 UNTS 101**
SIGNED: 17 Apr 48 FORCE: 17 Apr 48
REGISTERED: 9 May 52 Yugoslavia
ARTICLES: 4 LANGUAGE: Hungarian. Serbo-Croat.
HEADNOTE: TRANSFER REPARATION DELIVERIES
TOPIC: Reparations
CONCEPTS: Accounting procedures. Exchange rates and regulations. Payment schedules. Enemy financial interests. Reparations and restrictions. Post-war claims settlement.
TREATY REF: 129UNTS3.

PARTIES:
Hungary
Yugoslavia

101728 Bilateral Agreement **130 UNTS 111**
SIGNED: 17 Apr 48 FORCE: 17 Apr 48
REGISTERED: 9 May 52 Yugoslavia
ARTICLES: 6 LANGUAGE: Hungarian. Serbo-Croat.
HEADNOTE: AMENDMENT PROVISIONS REPARATIONS DELIVERIES
TOPIC: Reparations
CONCEPTS: Treaty implementation. Enemy financial interests. Reparations and restrictions. Post-war claims settlement.
TREATY REF: 129UNTS3.
PROCEDURE: Future Procedures Contemplated.
PARTIES:
Hungary
Yugoslavia

101729 Bilateral Agreement **130 UNTS 121**
SIGNED: 17 Apr 48 FORCE: 17 Apr 48
REGISTERED: 9 May 52 Yugoslavia
ARTICLES: 10 LANGUAGE: Hungarian. Serbo-Croat.
HEADNOTE: DELIVERY REPARATION GOODS
TOPIC: Reparations
CONCEPTS: Annex or appendix reference. Delivery schedules. Enemy financial interests. Reparations and restrictions. Post-war claims settlement.
PARTIES:
Hungary
Yugoslavia

101730 Bilateral Agreement **130 UNTS 171**
SIGNED: 11 May 47 FORCE: 11 May 47
REGISTERED: 9 May 52 Yugoslavia
ARTICLES: 8 LANGUAGE: German. Hungarian. Serbo-Croat.
HEADNOTE: ECONOMIC COOPERATION ALUMINUM INDUSTRY
TOPIC: Direct Aid
CONCEPTS: Treaty implementation. Annex or appendix reference. General cooperation. Establishment of commission. Arbitration. Procedure. Exchange rates and regulations. Financial programs. Purchase authorizations. Tax exemptions. Customs exemptions. Domestic obligation. Special projects. Economic assistance. Industry.
INTL ORGS: Arbitration Commission. Special Commission.
PROCEDURE: Denunciation. Duration. Renewal or Revival.
PARTIES:
Hungary
Yugoslavia

101731 Bilateral Agreement **130 UNTS 235**
SIGNED: 4 Feb 47 FORCE: 4 Feb 47
REGISTERED: 9 May 52 Yugoslavia
ARTICLES: 18 LANGUAGE: Russian. Serbo-Croat.
HEADNOTE: ESTABLISHMENT YUGOSLAV-SOVIET CIVIL AVIATION COMPANY
TOPIC: Air Transport
CONCEPTS: Annex or appendix reference. Conformity with municipal law. Licenses and permits. Personnel. Title and deeds. Meteorology. Currency. Investments. Funding procedures. Non-interest rates and fees. Tax exemptions. Customs exemptions. Competency certificate. Navigational equipment. Air transport. Airport facilities. Airport equipment. Operating authorizations and regulations. Facilities and equipment.
PROCEDURE: Duration.
PARTIES:
USSR (Soviet Union)
Yugoslavia

101732 Bilateral Agreement **130 UNTS 315**
SIGNED: 25 Jul 47 FORCE: 25 Jul 47
REGISTERED: 9 May 52 Yugoslavia
ARTICLES: 14 LANGUAGE: Russian. Serbo-Croat.
HEADNOTE: DELIVERY INDUSTRIAL EQUIPMENT CREDIT
TOPIC: Tech Assistance
CONCEPTS: Guarantees and safeguards. Time

limit. Treaty implementation. Annex or appendix reference. General cooperation. Exchange of information and documents. Operating agencies. Vocational training. Research and scientific projects. Accounting procedures. Bonds. Indemnities and reimbursements. Interest rates. Payment schedules. Claims and settlements. Delivery guarantees. Delivery schedules. Patents, copyrights and trademarks. General technical assistance. Special projects. Credit provisions.
PROCEDURE: Future Procedures Contemplated.
PARTIES:
USSR (Soviet Union)
Yugoslavia

101733 Bilateral Agreement **131 UNTS 3**
SIGNED: 8 Apr 50 FORCE: 8 Apr 50
REGISTERED: 12 May 52 Pakistan
ARTICLES: 7 LANGUAGE: English.
HEADNOTE: AGREEMENT
TOPIC: Visas
CONCEPTS: Peaceful relations. Border traffic and migration. Human rights. Legal protection and assistance. Domestic legislation. Immovable property. General property. Establishment of commission.
TREATY REF: INTER-DOMINION AGREEMENT DEC,1948.
PARTIES:
India
Pakistan

101734 Multilateral Agreement **131 UNTS 25**
SIGNED: 22 Nov 50 FORCE: 21 May 52
REGISTERED: 21 May 52 United Nations
ARTICLES: 18 LANGUAGE: English. French.
HEADNOTE: IMPORTATION EDUCATIONAL SCIENTIFIC CULTURAL MATERIALS
TOPIC: Culture
CONCEPTS: Time limit. Annex or appendix reference. Non-prejudice to third party. Conformity with municipal law. General cooperation. Licenses and permits. Dispute settlement. General cultural cooperation. Import quotas. Reexport of goods, etc.. Customs exemptions. Publications exchange. Mass media exchange.
INTL ORGS: General Agreement on Tariffs and Trade. United Nations Educational, Scientific and Cultural Organization. United Nations.
TREATY REF: 4UNTS275.
PROCEDURE: Amendment. Accession. Denunciation. Ratification.
PARTIES:
Afghanistan SIGNED: 8 Oct 51
Belgium SIGNED: 22 Nov 50
Bolivia SIGNED: 22 Nov 50
Cambodia RATIFIED: 5 Nov 51 FORCE: 21 May 52
Taiwan SIGNED: 22 Nov 50
Colombia SIGNED: 22 Nov 50
Dominican Republic SIGNED: 22 Nov 50
Ecuador SIGNED: 22 Nov 50
United Arab Rep SIGNED: 22 Nov 50 RATIFIED: 8 Feb 52 FORCE: 21 May 52
El Salvador SIGNED: 4 Dec 50
France SIGNED: 14 May 51
Greece SIGNED: 22 Nov 50
Guatemala SIGNED: 22 Nov 50
Haiti SIGNED: 22 Nov 50
Iran SIGNED: 9 Feb 51
Israel SIGNED: 22 Nov 50 RATIFIED: 27 Mar 52 FORCE: 21 May 52
Laos RATIFIED: 28 Feb 52 FORCE: 21 May 52
Luxembourg SIGNED: 22 Nov 50
Netherlands SIGNED: 22 Nov 50
New Zealand SIGNED: 16 Mar 51
Pakistan SIGNED: 9 May 51 RATIFIED: 17 Jan 52 FORCE: 21 May 52
Philippines SIGNED: 22 Nov 50
Sweden SIGNED: 20 Nov 51 RATIFIED: 21 May 52 FORCE: 21 May 52
Switzerland SIGNED: 22 Nov 50
Thailand SIGNED: 22 Nov 50 RATIFIED: 18 Jun 51 FORCE: 21 May 52
UK Great Britain SIGNED: 22 Nov 50
ANNEX
131 UNTS 361. Vietnam. Acceptance 1 Jun 52.
136 UNTS 392. Cuba. Acceptance 27 Aug 52.
163 UNTS 384. Switzerland. Qualified Ratification 7 Apr 53.
167 UNTS 299. El Salvador. Ratification 24 Jun 53.

187 UNTS 462. UK Great Britain. Aden.
187 UNTS 462. UK Great Britain. Nigeria.
187 UNTS 462. UK Great Britain. Barbados.
187 UNTS 462. UK Great Britain. British Guiana.
187 UNTS 462. UK Great Britain. British Honduras.
187 UNTS 462. UK Great Britain. St. Helena.
187 UNTS 462. UK Great Britain. Brunei.
187 UNTS 462. UK Great Britain. Fiji Islands.
187 UNTS 462. UK Great Britain. Gambia.
187 UNTS 462. UK Great Britain. Gibralter.
187 UNTS 462. UK Great Britain. St. Christopher.
187 UNTS 462. UK Great Britain. Anguilla.
187 UNTS 462. UK Great Britain. Brit Virgin Islands.
187 UNTS 462. UK Great Britain. Fed of Malaya.
187 UNTS 462. UK Great Britain. Malta.
187 UNTS 462. UK Great Britain. Mauritius.
187 UNTS 462. UK Great Britain. Gold Coast.
187 UNTS 462. UK Great Britain. Sarawak.
187 UNTS 462. UK Great Britain. Kenya.
187 UNTS 462. UK Great Britain. Antigua.
187 UNTS 462. UK Great Britain. Montserrat.
187 UNTS 462. UK Great Britain. Seychelles.
187 UNTS 462. UK Great Britain. British Somaliland.
187 UNTS 462. UK Great Britain. Nevis.
187 UNTS 462. UK Great Britain. Tanganyika.
187 UNTS 462. UK Great Britain. Trinidad/Tobago.
187 UNTS 462. UK Great Britain. Uganda.
187 UNTS 462. UK Great Britain. W Pacif Hi Command.
187 UNTS 462. UK Great Britain. Zanzibar.
187 UNTS 462. UK Great Britain. Ratification 11 Mar 54.
187 UNTS 462. UK Great Britain. Aden Colony.
187 UNTS 462. UK Great Britain. Hong Kong.
187 UNTS 462. UK Great Britain. Jamaica.
187 UNTS 462. UK Great Britain. Sierra Leone.
187 UNTS 462. UK Great Britain. Singapore.
190 UNTS 384. Haiti. Ratification 14 May 54.
199 UNTS 343. UK Great Britain. St. Lucia.
199 UNTS 343. UK Great Britain. Dominican Republic.
199 UNTS 343. UK Great Britain. North Borneo.
199 UNTS 343. UK Great Britain. Grenada.
199 UNTS 343. UK Great Britain. St. Vincent.
199 UNTS 343. UK Great Britain. Tonga.
199 UNTS 343. UK Great Britain. Cyprus.
199 UNTS 343. UK Great Britain. Falkland Islands.
210 UNTS 334. UK Great Britain. Channel Islands.
210 UNTS 334. UK Great Britain. Isle of Man.
212 UNTS 334. Spain. Acceptance 7 Jul 55.
223 UNTS 330. Greece. Ratification 12 Dec 55.
230 UNTS 437. UK Great Britain. Fed Rhod/Nyasaland.
236 UNTS 381. Finland. Acceptance 30 Apr 56.
274 UNTS 346. Germany, West. Acceptance 9 Aug 57.
277 UNTS 350. France. Ratification 14 Oct 57.
277 UNTS 350. Germany, West. Berlin.
280 UNTS 356. Belgium. Belgian Colonies.
280 UNTS 356. Belgium. Ruanda-Urundi.
280 UNTS 356. Luxembourg. Ratification 31 Oct 57.
280 UNTS 356. Netherlands. Ratification 31 Oct 57.
280 UNTS 356. Netherlands. Surinam.
280 UNTS 356. Netherlands. Dutch New Guinea.
280 UNTS 356. Belgium. Ratification 31 Oct 57.
289 UNTS 317. Afghanistan. Ratification 19 Mar 58. Force 17 Jun 58.
292 UNTS 362. Ghana. Acceptance 7 Apr 58.
302 UNTS 362. Austria. Acceptance 12 Jun 58.
318 UNTS 421. Jordan. Acceptance 31 Dec 58.
327 UNTS 360. Norway. Acceptance 2 Apr 59.
343 UNTS 362. UK Great Britain. Bahamas.
354 UNTS 400. Denmark. Acceptance 4 Apr 60.
366 UNTS 400. Guatemala. Ratification 8 Jun 60.
399 UNTS 268. Nigeria. Succession 26 Jun 61.
423 UNTS 307. Sierra Leone. Succession 13 Mar 62.
426 UNTS 340. Congo (Zaire). Succession 3 May 62.
429 UNTS 281. Madagascar. Acceptance 23 May 62.
431 UNTS 296. New Zealand. Ratification 29 Jun 62.
431 UNTS 296. New Zealand. Tokelau Islands.
437 UNTS 349. Gabon. Acceptance 4 Sep 62.
445 UNTS 318. Italy. Acceptance 26 Nov 62.

457 UNTS 301. Tanganyika. Acceptance 26 Mar 63.
466 UNTS 385. Cyprus. Accession 16 May 63.
471 UNTS 323. Ivory Coast. Acceptance 19 Jul 63.
483 UNTS 300. Greece. Amendment 2 May 56. Force 1 Jan 66.
483 UNTS 300. Bulgaria. Amendment 2 May 56. Force 1 Jan 66.
483 UNTS 300. Greece. Amendment 2 May 56. Force 1 Jan 66.
483 UNTS 300. Nicaragua. Acceptance 17 Dec 63. Force 1 Jan 66.
483 UNTS 300. Nicaragua. Amendment 2 May 56. Force 1 Jan 66.
489 UNTS 376. New Zealand. Cook Islands.
496 UNTS 352. Cameroon. Acceptance 15 May 64. Force 18 Aug 64.
519 UNTS 348. Rwanda. Succession 1 Dec 64.
531 UNTS 320. Uganda. Acceptance 15 Apr 65.
543 UNTS 358. Malawi. Acceptance 17 Aug 65.
544 UNTS 290. Upper Volta. Acceptance 14 Sep 65.
551 UNTS 280. Iran. Ratification 7 Jan 66.
560 UNTS 257. Trinidad/Tobago. Succession 11 Apr 66.
634 UNTS 426. Niger. Accession 22 Apr 68.
640 UNTS 368. Morocco. Acceptance 25 Jul 68.
643 UNTS 390. Congo (Brazzaville). Acceptance 26 Aug 68.

101735 Bilateral Agreement **131 UNTS 53**
SIGNED: 13 Mar 50　　　FORCE: 26 Mar 52
REGISTERED: 21 May 52 UK Great Britain
ARTICLES: 19 LANGUAGE: English.
HEADNOTE: DOUBLE TAXATION FISCAL EVASION TAXES INCOME
TOPIC: Taxation
CONCEPTS: Definition of terms. Territorial application. Exchange of official publications. Teacher and student exchange. Taxation. Tax credits. Equitable taxes. General. Tax exemptions.
PROCEDURE: Duration. Ratification. Termination.
PARTIES:
　Burma
　UK Great Britain

101736 Multilateral Treaty **131 UNTS 83**
SIGNED: 1 Sep 51　　　FORCE: 29 Apr 52
REGISTERED: 22 May 52 Australia
ARTICLES: 11 LANGUAGE: English.
HEADNOTE: SECURITY TREATY
TOPIC: General Military
CONCEPTS: Definition of terms. Non-prejudice to UN charter. Peaceful relations. General cooperation. Defense and security. Military assistance. Subsidiary organ.
INTL ORGS: United Nations. Special Commission.
PROCEDURE: Denunciation. Ratification.
PARTIES:
　Australia　SIGNED:　1 Sep 51　RATIFIED: 29 Apr 52 FORCE: 29 Apr 52
　New Zealand SIGNED:　1 Sep 51　RATIFIED: 29 Apr 52 FORCE: 29 Apr 52
　USA (United States) SIGNED: 1 Sep 51 RATIFIED: 29 Apr 52 FORCE: 29 Apr 52

101737 Bilateral Exchange **131 UNTS 91**
SIGNED: 8 May 52　　　FORCE: 8 May 52
REGISTERED: 28 May 52 Denmark
ARTICLES: 2 LANGUAGE: English.
HEADNOTE: EQUAL TREATMENT PERSONS REGARDING COMPENSATION WAR DAMAGES
TOPIC: Reparations
CONCEPTS: General property. National treatment. Loss and/or damage. Post-war claims settlement.
PARTIES:
　Denmark
　Netherlands

101738 Multilateral Convention **131 UNTS 99**
SIGNED: 17 Apr 50　　　FORCE: 10 Oct 51
REGISTERED: 28 May 52 UK Great Britain
ARTICLES: 12 LANGUAGE: Dutch. English. French.
HEADNOTE: TYPHUS CONTROL PROJECT
TOPIC: Visas
CONCEPTS: Definition of terms. Previous treaty extension. Exchange of information and documents. Personnel. Programs. Disease control. In-

sect control. WHO used as agency. Vocational training. Research results. Expense sharing formulae. Financial programs. Specific technical assistance. Materials, equipment and services.
INTL ORGS: Western European Union.
PARTIES:
　Belgium　SIGNED:　17 Apr 50　RATIFIED: 12 Oct 50 FORCE: 10 Oct 51
　France SIGNED: 17 Apr 50 RATIFIED: 17 Dec 51 FORCE: 1 Jan 52
　Luxembourg SIGNED:　17 Apr 50　RATIFIED: 12 Jan 52 FORCE: 1 Feb 52
　Netherlands　SIGNED:　17 Apr 50　RATIFIED: 10 Aug 51 FORCE: 10 Oct 51
　UK Great Britain SIGNED: 17 Apr 50 RATIFIED: 29 Jul 50 FORCE: 10 Oct 51
　　　　　　　ANNEX
385 UNTS 366. Italy. Qualified Accession 15 Jan 59. Force 13 Sep 60.
385 UNTS 366. Germany, West. Qualified Accession 13 Sep 60. Force 13 Sep 60.

101739 Multilateral Agreement **131 UNTS 115**
SIGNED: 22 May 52　　　FORCE: 22 May 52
REGISTERED: 3 Jun 52 United Nations
ARTICLES: 4 LANGUAGE: English. Hebrew.
HEADNOTE: TECHNICAL ASSISTANCE
TOPIC: Tech Assistance
CONCEPTS: Time limit. Privileges and immunities. General cooperation. Personnel. Negotiation. Scholarships and grants. Expense sharing formulae. General technical assistance. Special projects. Headquarters and facilities. Conformity with IGO decisions.
TREATY REF: 76UNTS132; 1UNTS15,263; 33UNTS261.
PROCEDURE: Amendment. Termination.
PARTIES:
　Israel SIGNED: 22 May 52 FORCE: 22 May 52
　FAO (Food Agri) SIGNED: 22 May 52 FORCE: 22 May 52
　ICAO (Civil Aviat) SIGNED: 22 May 52 FORCE: 22 May 52
　ILO (Labor Org) SIGNED: 22 May 52 FORCE: 22 May 52
　UNESCO (Educ/Cult) SIGNED: 22 May 52 FORCE: 22 May 52
　United Nations SIGNED: 22 May 52 FORCE: 22 May 52
　WHO (World Health) SIGNED: 22 May 52 FORCE: 22 May 52

101740 Bilateral Treaty **131 UNTS 131**
SIGNED: 14 Dec 51　　　FORCE: 17 May 52
REGISTERED: 4 Jun 52 Guatemala
ARTICLES: 23 LANGUAGE: Spanish.
HEADNOTE: TREATY PROMOTING ECONOMIC UNITY INTEGRATION
TOPIC: General Economic
CONCEPTS: Exceptions and exemptions. Treaty implementation. Annex or appendix reference. General cooperation. Exchange of information and documents. Establishment of commission. Arbitration. Procedure. Export quotas. Import quotas. Free trade. Reciprocity in trade. Export subsidies. Trade agencies. Trade procedures. Banking. Currency. Investments. Exchange rates and regulations. Non-interest rates and fees. Private investment guarantee. Most favored nation clause. Taxation. Equitable taxes. Customs declarations. General transportation. Routes and logistics. Navigational conditions. Transport of goods. Commercial road vehicles. Roads and highways. Road rules. Conservation of specific resources.
INTL ORGS: Arbitration Commission. Special Commission.
PROCEDURE: Amendment. Future Procedures Contemplated. Ratification. Duration.
PARTIES:
　El Salvador
　Guatemala
　　　　　　　ANNEX
286 UNTS 345. Guatemala. Supplementation 5 Feb 57. Force 20 Aug 57.
286 UNTS 345. El Salvador. Supplementation 5 Feb 57. Force 20 Aug 57.

101741 Bilateral Agreement **131 UNTS 187**
SIGNED: 29 Mar 51　　　FORCE: 1 Aug 51
REGISTERED: 5 Jun 52 Australia

ARTICLES: 19 LANGUAGE: English. Italian.
HEADNOTE: ASSISTED MIGRATION
TOPIC: Non-ILO Labor
CONCEPTS: Definition of terms. Detailed regulations. Emergencies. Annex or appendix reference. Border traffic and migration. Repatriation of nationals. Exchange of information and documents. Responsibility and liability. Administrative cooperation. Accounting procedures. Financial programs. Transportation costs. National treatment.
PROCEDURE: Amendment. Duration. Termination.
PARTIES:
Australia
Italy

101742   Bilateral Exchange   **131 UNTS 221**
SIGNED: 21 Feb 52   FORCE: 21 Feb 52
REGISTERED: 6 Jun 52 WHO (World Health)
ARTICLES: 2 LANGUAGE: English.
HEADNOTE: COMMON RATES SUBSISTENCE WHO/UNICEF PROJECTS
TOPIC: IGO Operations
CONCEPTS: Assistance. Status of experts.
INTL ORGS: United Nations Technical Assistance Board. United Nations Children's Fund.
PARTIES:
Pakistan
WHO (World Health)

101743   Bilateral Agreement   **131 UNTS 227**
SIGNED: 2 Apr 52   FORCE: 9 Apr 52
REGISTERED: 10 Jun 52 WHO (World Health)
ARTICLES: 4 LANGUAGE: English.
HEADNOTE: PLAGUE SURVEY PROJECT
TOPIC: Sanitation
CONCEPTS: Definition of terms. Previous treaty extension. Privileges and immunities. Personnel. General property. Disease control. WHO used as agency. Research results. Research and development. Indemnities and reimbursements. Expense sharing formulae. Assistance. Specific technical assistance. Aid missions.
TREATY REF: 33UNTS261.
PROCEDURE: Amendment. Duration. Termination.
PARTIES:
India
WHO (World Health)

101744   Bilateral Agreement   **131 UNTS 241**
SIGNED: 17 Apr 52   FORCE: 24 Apr 52
REGISTERED: 10 Jun 52 WHO (World Health)
ARTICLES: 4 LANGUAGE: English.
HEADNOTE: TECHNICAL ASSISTANCE SERVICES PROFESSOR PHYSIOLOGY INDUSTRIAL HYGIENE
TOPIC: Tech Assistance
CONCEPTS: Time limit. Privileges and immunities. General cooperation. Personnel. Arbitration. Procedure. Negotiation. Exchange. Professorships. Vocational training. Research and scientific projects. Expense sharing formulae. Claims and settlements. Domestic obligation. General technical assistance. Special projects. IGO status. Conformity with IGO decisions.
INTL ORGS: International Court of Justice. Arbitration Commission.
TREATY REF: 76UNTS132; 33UNTS261.
PROCEDURE: Amendment. Termination.
PARTIES:
India
WHO (World Health)

101745   Bilateral Agreement   **131 UNTS 253**
SIGNED: 19 Apr 52   FORCE: 24 Apr 52
REGISTERED: 10 Jun 52 WHO (World Health)
ARTICLES: 4 LANGUAGE: English.
HEADNOTE: TECHNICAL ASSISTANCE SERVICES PHYSIOTHERAPY SCHOOL TRAINING CENTER
TOPIC: Tech Assistance
CONCEPTS: Time limit. Privileges and immunities. General cooperation. Personnel. Title and deeds. Arbitration. Procedure. Negotiation. Exchange. Vocational training. Financial programs. Claims and settlements. Domestic obligation. General technical assistance. Special projects. Materials, equipment and services. IGO status. Conformity with IGO decisions.
INTL ORGS: International Court of Justice. Arbitration Commission.

TREATY REF: 76UNTS132.
PROCEDURE: Amendment. Termination.
PARTIES:
India
WHO (World Health)

101746   Bilateral Agreement   **131 UNTS 265**
SIGNED: 14 Apr 52   FORCE: 7 May 52
REGISTERED: 10 Jun 52 WHO (World Health)
ARTICLES: 4 LANGUAGE: English.
HEADNOTE: ASSISTANCE
TOPIC: Tech Assistance
CONCEPTS: Border control. Public health. WHO used as agency. General technical assistance.
PROCEDURE: Termination.
PARTIES:
India
WHO (World Health)

101747   Bilateral Agreement   **131 UNTS 281**
SIGNED: 9 May 52   FORCE: 6 May 52
REGISTERED: 10 Jun 52 WHO (World Health)
ARTICLES: 14 LANGUAGE: English. French.
HEADNOTE: TECHNICAL ADVISORY ASSISTANCE OTHER SERVICES
TOPIC: Tech Assistance
CONCEPTS: Change of circumstances. Treaty implementation. Treaty interpretation. Annex or appendix reference. Privileges and immunities. Exchange of information and documents. Personnel. Arbitration. Procedure. Negotiation. Competence of tribunal. Financial programs. Claims and settlements. Tax exemptions. Customs exemptions. General technical assistance. Special projects. Materials, equipment and services. IGO status.
INTL ORGS: International Court of Justice. Arbitration Commission.
TREATY REF: 33UNTS261.
PROCEDURE: Amendment. Termination.
PARTIES:
Norway
WHO (World Health)

101748   Multilateral Convention   **132 UNTS 3**
SIGNED: 7 Nov 49   FORCE: 27 Apr 51
REGISTERED: 11 Jun 52 Belgium
ARTICLES: 11 LANGUAGE: English. French.
HEADNOTE: CONVENTION SOCIAL MEDICAL ASSISTANCE
TOPIC: Sanitation
CONCEPTS: Conditions. Definition of terms. Territorial application. Legal status. Repatriation of nationals. Arbitration. Procedure. Negotiation. Public health. Sickness and invalidity insurance. Social security. Indemnities and reimbursements.
INTL ORGS: Western European Union.
PROCEDURE: Future Procedures Contemplated. Ratification. Termination.
PARTIES:
Belgium SIGNED: 7 Nov 49 RATIFIED: 30 Jul 50 FORCE: 27 Apr 51
France SIGNED: 7 Nov 49 RATIFIED: 5 Apr 51 FORCE: 1 May 51
Luxembourg SIGNED: 7 Nov 49 RATIFIED: 12 Jan 52 FORCE: 1 Feb 52
Netherlands SIGNED: 7 Nov 49 RATIFIED: 27 Feb 51 FORCE: 27 Apr 51
UK Great Britain SIGNED: 7 Nov 49 RATIFIED: 29 Jul 50 FORCE: 27 Apr 51

101749   Multilateral Convention   **132 UNTS 31**
SIGNED: 7 Nov 49   FORCE: 15 May 51
REGISTERED: 11 Jun 52 Belgium
ARTICLES: 13 LANGUAGE: English. French.
HEADNOTE: COORDINATE SOCIAL SECURITY SCHEMES
TOPIC: Non-ILO Labor
CONCEPTS: Definition of terms. Detailed regulations. Dispute settlement. Wages and salaries. Non-ILO labor relations. Sickness and invalidity insurance. Social security. Payment schedules. National treatment.
INTL ORGS: Western European Union.
PROCEDURE: Denunciation. Duration. Future Procedures Contemplated. Ratification. Registration.

PARTIES:
Belgium   SIGNED: 7 Nov 49   RATIFIED: 20 Sep 51 FORCE: 1 Oct 51
France SIGNED: 7 Nov 49 RATIFIED: 15 Mar 51 FORCE: 15 May 51
Luxembourg   SIGNED: 7 Nov 49   RATIFIED: 12 Jan 52 FORCE: 1 Feb 52
Netherlands   SIGNED: 7 Nov 49   RATIFIED: 27 Feb 51 FORCE: 15 May 51
UK Great Britain SIGNED: 7 Nov 49 RATIFIED: 5 May 50 FORCE: 15 May 51

101750   Bilateral Exchange   **132 UNTS 45**
SIGNED: 1 Apr 52   FORCE: 1 Apr 52
REGISTERED: 11 Jun 52 Belgium
ARTICLES: 2 LANGUAGE: French. German.
HEADNOTE: RECIPROCAL GRANTING FREE VISAS OFFICIALLY RECOGNIZED JOURNALISTS
TOPIC: Visas
CONCEPTS: Frontier formalities. Passports diplomatic. Fees and exemptions.
PARTIES:
Belgium
Germany, West

101751   Multilateral Agreement   **132 UNTS 51**
SIGNED: 15 Feb 52   FORCE: 2 May 52
REGISTERED: 12 Jun 52 UNESCO (Educ/Cult)
ARTICLES: 9 LANGUAGE: English. French.
HEADNOTE: NUCLEAR RESEARCH LABORATORY
TOPIC: Scientific Project
CONCEPTS: Exceptions and exemptions. Annex or appendix reference. General cooperation. Juridical personality. Operating agencies. Use of facilities. Establishment of commission. Research and scientific projects. Nuclear research. Research and development. Funding procedures. General. Peaceful use. Liaison with other IGO's.
INTL ORGS: European Organization for Nuclear Research. United Nations Educational, Scientific and Cultural Organization. United Nations.
PROCEDURE: Duration. Ratification. Registration. Renewal or Revival.
PARTIES:
Belgium SIGNED: 15 Feb 52
Denmark SIGNED: 15 Feb 52
France SIGNED: 15 Feb 52 RATIFIED: 11 Apr 52 FORCE: 2 May 52
Germany, West SIGNED: 15 Feb 52 FORCE: 2 May 52
Greece SIGNED: 15 Feb 52
Italy SIGNED: 15 Feb 52
Netherlands   SIGNED: 15 Feb 52   FORCE: 2 May 52
Norway SIGNED: 15 Feb 52
Sweden   SIGNED: 15 Feb 52   RATIFIED: 2 May 52 FORCE: 2 May 52
Switzerland SIGNED: 15 Feb 52
Yugoslavia   SIGNED: 15 Feb 52   FORCE: 2 May 52
ANNEX
209 UNTS 342.   Italy.   Supplementation 30 Jun 53. Force 30 Jun 53.
209 UNTS 342.   Denmark.   Supplementation 30 Jun 53. Force 30 Jun 53.
209 UNTS 342.   France.   Supplementation 27 Jan 54. Force 27 Jan 54.
209 UNTS 342.   Sweden.   Supplementation 30 Jun 53. Force 30 Jun 53.
209 UNTS 342.   Yugoslavia.   Supplementation 30 Jun 53. Force 30 Jun 53.
209 UNTS 342.   Greece.   Supplementation 7 Jul 54. Force 7 Jul 54.
209 UNTS 342.   Norway.   Supplementation 31 Dec 53. Force 31 Dec 53.
209 UNTS 342. Germany, West. Supplementation 30 Jun 53. Force 30 Jun 53.
209 UNTS 342.   Belgium.   Supplementation 30 Jun 53. Force 30 Jun 53.
209 UNTS 342.   Netherlands.   Supplementation 30 Jun 53. Force 30 Jun 53.
209 UNTS 342.   Switzerland.   Supplementation 30 Jun 53. Force 30 Jun 53.
211 UNTS 418. Denmark. Ratification 3 Jun 52.
211 UNTS 418.   Switzerland.   Ratification 30 Jul 52.
211 UNTS 418. Belgium. Ratification 20 Aug 53.
211 UNTS 418. Norway. Ratification 10 Dec 53.
211 UNTS 418. Greece. Ratification 13 Jan 54.
211 UNTS 418. Italy. Ratification 24 Feb 55.

101752 Bilateral Agreement **132 UNTS 71**
SIGNED: 29 Sep 51 FORCE: 29 Sep 51
REGISTERED: 14 Jun 52 India
ARTICLES: 3 LANGUAGE: English.
HEADNOTE: TRADE
TOPIC: General Trade
CONCEPTS: Annex or appendix reference. General cooperation. Licenses and permits. Non-interest rates and fees. Commodity trade. Quotas. Customs duties.
PROCEDURE: Duration.
PARTIES:
  Burma
  India

101753 Bilateral Instrument **132 UNTS 80**
SIGNED: 24 Sep 46 FORCE: 24 Sep 46
REGISTERED: 14 Jun 52 USA (United States)
ARTICLES: 14 LANGUAGE: English.
HEADNOTE: SETTLEMENT LEND-LEASE SURPLUS PROPERTY AND CLAIMS
TOPIC: Claims and Debts
CONCEPTS: Procedure. Claims and settlements. Debts. Debt settlement. Loan repayment.
INTL ORGS: International Monetary Fund.
PARTIES:
  Belgium
  USA (United States)
      ANNEX
229 UNTS 304. Belgium. Amendment 2 Apr 54. Force 2 Apr 54.
229 UNTS 304. USA (United States). Amendment 20 Jan 54. Force 2 Apr 54.

101754 Bilateral Exchange **132 UNTS 135**
SIGNED: 19 Apr 47 FORCE: 19 Apr 47
REGISTERED: 14 Jun 52 USA (United States)
ARTICLES: 3 LANGUAGE: English. French.
HEADNOTE: COAL EXPORTS
TOPIC: General Trade
CONCEPTS: Commodity trade.
INTL ORGS: European Coal and Steel Community.
PARTIES:
  France
  USA (United States)

101755 Bilateral Instrument **132 UNTS 145**
SIGNED: 9 Jun 47 FORCE: 8 Jul 47
REGISTERED: 14 Jun 52 USA (United States)
ARTICLES: 4 LANGUAGE: English.
HEADNOTE: PASSPORT VISA FEES
TOPIC: Visas
CONCEPTS: Time limit. Visa abolition. Fees and exemptions.
PARTIES:
  Denmark
  USA (United States)

101756 Bilateral Exchange **132 UNTS 155**
SIGNED: 3 May 48 FORCE: 3 May 48
REGISTERED: 14 Jun 52 USA (United States)
ARTICLES: 2 LANGUAGE: English. Spanish.
HEADNOTE: FINANCE
TOPIC: Finance
CONCEPTS: Finances and payments. Post-war claims settlement.
PARTIES:
  Spain
  USA (United States)

101757 Bilateral Exchange **132 UNTS 163**
SIGNED: 21 Oct 49 FORCE: 21 Oct 49
REGISTERED: 14 Jun 52 USA (United States)
ARTICLES: 2 LANGUAGE: English.
HEADNOTE: SETTLEMENT WAR CLAIMS
TOPIC: Reparations
CONCEPTS: Lump sum settlements. Post-war claims settlement.
PARTIES:
  Switzerland
  USA (United States)

101758 Bilateral Agreement **132 UNTS 169**
SIGNED: 28 Feb 50 FORCE: 28 Feb 50
REGISTERED: 14 Jun 52 USA (United States)
ARTICLES: 1 LANGUAGE: English. Spanish.
HEADNOTE: TRADE & TARIFFS
TOPIC: General Trade

CONCEPTS: Annex type material. Narcotic drugs.
INTL ORGS: General Agreement on Tariffs and Trade.
TREATY REF: GATT.
PARTIES:
  Nicaragua
  USA (United States)

101759 Bilateral Exchange **132 UNTS 177**
SIGNED: 4 Apr 50 FORCE: 4 Apr 50
REGISTERED: 14 Jun 52 USA (United States)
ARTICLES: 2 LANGUAGE: English.
HEADNOTE: TRADE
TOPIC: General Trade
CONCEPTS: Annex or appendix reference. Annex type material. Previous treaty replacement. Balance of payments. Internal finance. Customs duties.
TREATY REF: 18 1LTS 183.
PARTIES:
  Costa Rica
  USA (United States)

101760 Bilateral Exchange **132 UNTS 189**
SIGNED: 4 May 50 FORCE: 4 May 50
REGISTERED: 14 Jun 52 USA (United States)
ARTICLES: 2 LANGUAGE: English.
HEADNOTE: COPYRIGHT RELATIONS
TOPIC: Patents/Copyrights
CONCEPTS: Conformity with municipal law. Domestic legislation. Laws and formalities.
PARTIES:
  Israel
  USA (United States)

101761 Bilateral Agreement **132 UNTS 199**
SIGNED: 19 Sep 50 FORCE: 19 Sep 50
REGISTERED: 14 Jun 52 USA (United States)
ARTICLES: 5 LANGUAGE: English. Thai.
HEADNOTE: ECONOMIC TECHNICAL COOPERATION
TOPIC: Tech Assistance
CONCEPTS: Annex or appendix reference. Privileges and immunities. Exchange of information and documents. Personnel. Domestic obligation. General technical assistance. Economic assistance. Aid missions. Procurement. Distribution.
INTL ORGS: United Nations.
PROCEDURE: Amendment. Duration. Registration. Termination.
PARTIES:
  Thailand
  USA (United States)
      ANNEX
134 UNTS 390. USA (United States). Amendment 12 Jul 51. Force 25 Jul 51.
134 UNTS 390. Thailand. Amendment 25 Jul 51. Force 25 Jul 51.

101762 Bilateral Treaty **132 UNTS 223**
SIGNED: 27 Feb 50 FORCE: 10 Oct 50
REGISTERED: 14 Jun 52 USA (United States)
ARTICLES: 10 LANGUAGE: English.
HEADNOTE: USES WATER NIAGARA RIVER
TOPIC: Specific Resources
CONCEPTS: Previous treaty replacement. Inspection and observation. Regulation of natural resources.
INTL ORGS: Special Commission.
TREATY REF: 203LTS267; 204LTS199.
PROCEDURE: Duration. Ratification. Termination.
PARTIES:
  Canada
  USA (United States)
      ANNEX
236 UNTS 382. USA (United States). Supplementation 13 Sep 54. Force 13 Sep 54.
236 UNTS 382. Canada. Supplementation 13 Sep 54. Force 13 Sep 54.

101763 Bilateral Convention **132 UNTS 233**
SIGNED: 26 Jan 50 FORCE: 11 Oct 50
REGISTERED: 14 Jun 52 USA (United States)
ARTICLES: 8 LANGUAGE: English. Spanish.
HEADNOTE: CLAIMS CONVENTION
TOPIC: Claims and Debts
CONCEPTS: Detailed regulations. General provisions. Exchange of information and documents.

Claims and settlements. Lump sum settlements. Specific claims or waivers.
INTL ORGS: Special Commission.
PROCEDURE: Ratification.
PARTIES:
  Panama
  USA (United States)

101764 Bilateral Exchange **132 UNTS 247**
SIGNED: 26 Oct 50 FORCE: 26 Oct 50
REGISTERED: 14 Jun 52 USA (United States)
ARTICLES: 2 LANGUAGE: English.
HEADNOTE: ECONOMIC COOPERATION INDUSTRIAL MOBILIZATION MUTUAL DEFENSE
TOPIC: Direct Aid
CONCEPTS: Annex or appendix reference. Economic assistance. Defense and security.
INTL ORGS: Special Commission.
TREATY REF: US DEPT OF STATE BULLETIN APR 26,1941 P.494.
PARTIES:
  Canada
  USA (United States)

101765 Bilateral Exchange **132 UNTS 255**
SIGNED: 10 Jan 51 FORCE: 11 Jan 51
REGISTERED: 14 Jun 52 USA (United States)
ARTICLES: 4 LANGUAGE: English.
HEADNOTE: RADIO COMMUNICATIONS AMATEUR STATIONS BEHALF THIRD PARTIES
TOPIC: Gen Communications
CONCEPTS: Territorial application. Domestic legislation. Amateur radio. Amateur third party message. Radio-telephone-telegraphic communications.
PROCEDURE: Termination.
PARTIES:
  Liberia
  USA (United States)

101766 Bilateral Agreement **132 UNTS 265**
SIGNED: 7 Feb 51 FORCE: 7 Feb 51
REGISTERED: 14 Jun 52 USA (United States)
ARTICLES: 5 LANGUAGE: English.
HEADNOTE: TECHNICAL COOPERATION
TOPIC: Tech Assistance
CONCEPTS: Exceptions and exemptions. Treaty implementation. Previous treaty replacement. Diplomatic privileges. General cooperation. Exchange of information and documents. Personnel. Public information. Financial programs. Tax exemptions. Domestic obligation. General technical assistance. Materials, equipment and services.
PROCEDURE: Amendment. Duration. Termination.
PARTIES:
  Afghanistan
  USA (United States)
      ANNEX
177 UNTS 341. USA (United States). Amendment 2 Jan 52. Force 24 Jan 52.
177 UNTS 341. Afghanistan. Amendment 24 Jan 52. Force 24 Jan 52.

101767 Bilateral Exchange **132 UNTS 273**
SIGNED: 9 Feb 51 FORCE: 9 Feb 51
REGISTERED: 14 Jun 52 USA (United States)
ARTICLES: 2 LANGUAGE: Chinese. English.
HEADNOTE: MUTUAL DEFENSE ASSISTANCE
TOPIC: Milit Assistance
CONCEPTS: Privileges and immunities. Conformity with municipal law. Inspection and observation. Use of facilities. Aid missions. Defense and security. Self-defense. Military assistance. Security of information. Exchange of defense information. Restrictions on transfer.
PARTIES:
  Taiwan
  USA (United States)
      ANNEX
184 UNTS 348. USA (United States). Amendment 23 Oct 52. Force 1 Nov 52.
184 UNTS 348. Taiwan. Amendment 1 Nov 52. Force 1 Nov 52.

101768 Bilateral Exchange **132 UNTS 287**
SIGNED: 12 Dec 51 FORCE: 12 Feb 51
REGISTERED: 14 Jun 52 USA (United States)
ARTICLES: 2 LANGUAGE: English. Spanish.

HEADNOTE: VOCATIONAL EDUCATION MISSION
TOPIC: Education
CONCEPTS: Definition of terms. General cooperation. Specialists exchange. Exchange. Vocational training. Scientific exchange. Expense sharing formulae. Tax exemptions. Customs exemptions. General technical assistance. Aid missions.
PARTIES:
El Salvador
USA (United States)
ANNEX
140 UNTS 452. El Salvador. Extension and Amendment 25 Jun 51. Force 25 Jun 51.
140 UNTS 452. USA (United States). Extension and Amendment 25 Jun 51. Force 25 Jun 51.
177 UNTS 346. USA (United States). Extension and Amendment 19 Feb 52. Force 28 Feb 52.
177 UNTS 346. El Salvador. Extension and Amendment 28 Feb 52. Force 28 Feb 52.

101769 Bilateral Exchange **132 UNTS 297**
SIGNED: 20 Feb 51 FORCE: 20 Feb 51
REGISTERED: 14 Jun 52 USA (United States)
ARTICLES: 2 LANGUAGE: English.
HEADNOTE: MUTUAL DEFENSE ASSISTANCE
TOPIC: Milit Assistance
CONCEPTS: Non-prejudice to UN charter. Peaceful relations. Conformity with municipal law. Domestic obligation. Defense and security. Military assistance. Security of information. Exchange of defense information. Restrictions on transfer.
PARTIES:
Australia
USA (United States)

101770 Bilateral Exchange **132 UNTS 305**
SIGNED: 20 Feb 51 FORCE: 20 Feb 51
REGISTERED: 14 Jun 52 USA (United States)
ARTICLES: 2 LANGUAGE: English. Spanish.
HEADNOTE: TECHNICAL COOPERATION
TOPIC: Tech Assistance
CONCEPTS: Exceptions and exemptions. Treaty implementation. Previous treaty replacement. Diplomatic privileges. General cooperation. Exchange of information and documents. Personnel. Public information. Financial programs. Tax exemptions. Domestic obligation. General technical assistance. Materials, equipment and services.
PROCEDURE: Amendment. Duration. Termination.
PARTIES:
Dominican Republic
USA (United States)
ANNEX
179 UNTS 222. Dominican Republic. Amendment 5 Jan 52. Force 5 Jan 52.
179 UNTS 222. USA (United States). Amendment 12 Dec 51. Force 5 Jan 52.

101771 Bilateral Agreement **132 UNTS 319**
SIGNED: 14 Mar 51 FORCE: 14 Mar 41
REGISTERED: 14 Jun 52 USA (United States)
ARTICLES: 5 LANGUAGE: English. Spanish.
HEADNOTE: TECHNICAL COOPERATION
TOPIC: Tech Assistance
CONCEPTS: Exceptions and exemptions. Treaty implementation. Previous treaty replacement. Diplomatic privileges. General cooperation. Exchange of information and documents. Personnel. Public information. Financial programs. Tax exemptions. Domestic obligation. General technical assistance. Materials, equipment and services.
PROCEDURE: Amendment. Duration. Termination.
PARTIES:
Bolivia
USA (United States)
ANNEX
180 UNTS 346. Bolivia. Amendment 8 Jan 52. Force 8 Jan 52.
180 UNTS 346. USA (United States). Amendment 7 Jan 52. Force 8 Jan 52.

101772 Bilateral Exchange **132 UNTS 333**
SIGNED: 27 Mar 51 FORCE: 27 Mar 51
REGISTERED: 14 Jun 52 USA (United States)
ARTICLES: 2 LANGUAGE: English.
HEADNOTE: CIVIL DEFENSE COOPERATION
TOPIC: Milit Assistance

CONCEPTS: Detailed regulations. General cooperation. Public information. Establishment of commission. Expense sharing formulae. Materials, equipment and services. Joint defense. Defense and security. Military training.
PARTIES:
Canada
USA (United States)

101773 Bilateral Agreement **133 UNTS 3**
SIGNED: 17 Apr 52 FORCE: 28 Apr 52
REGISTERED: 16 Jun 52 United Nations
ARTICLES: 10 LANGUAGE: English.
HEADNOTE: ACTIVITIES UNICEF
TOPIC: Direct Aid
CONCEPTS: Treaty implementation. Privileges and immunities. General cooperation. Exchange of information and documents. Informational records. Inspection and observation. Public information. Use of facilities. Procedure. Existing tribunals. Export quotas. Financial programs. Commodities and services. Assistance. General aid. Procurement. Distribution. IGO status.
INTL ORGS: United Nations.
TREATY REF: 1UNTS15.
PROCEDURE: Duration.
PARTIES:
Liberia
UNICEF (Children)

101774 Bilateral Exchange **133 UNTS 15**
SIGNED: 12 Oct 49 FORCE: 12 Oct 49
REGISTERED: 17 Jun 52 USA (United States)
ARTICLES: 2 LANGUAGE: English. Spanish.
HEADNOTE: TRADE
TOPIC: General Trade
CONCEPTS: Annex type material. Previous treaty replacement.
TREATY REF: 17OLTS293; GATT.
PARTIES:
Colombia
USA (United States)

101775 Bilateral Agreement **133 UNTS 21**
SIGNED: 29 Dec 49 FORCE: 29 Dec 49
REGISTERED: 17 Jun 52 USA (United States)
ARTICLES: 1 LANGUAGE: English. French.
HEADNOTE: TRADE
TOPIC: General Trade
CONCEPTS: Annex type material. Previous treaty replacement.
TREATY REF: GATT.
PARTIES:
Haiti
USA (United States)

101776 Bilateral Exchange **133 UNTS 25**
SIGNED: 9 Oct 50 FORCE: 9 Oct 50
REGISTERED: 17 Jun 52 USA (United States)
ARTICLES: 2 LANGUAGE: English.
HEADNOTE: EXCHANGE OFFICIAL PUBLICATIONS
TOPIC: Admin Cooperation
CONCEPTS: Exchange of official publications. Operating agencies. Indemnities and reimbursements.
PARTIES:
USA (United States)
Yugoslavia

101777 Bilateral Exchange **133 UNTS 33**
SIGNED: 13 Oct 50 FORCE: 13 Oct 50
REGISTERED: 17 Jun 52 USA (United States)
ARTICLES: 2 LANGUAGE: English. French.
HEADNOTE: TRADE
TOPIC: General Trade
CONCEPTS: Exceptions and exemptions. Previous treaty amendment. Annex type material. General cooperation. Procedure. Negotiation. Trade procedures.
PROCEDURE: Termination.
PARTIES:
Switzerland
USA (United States)
ANNEX
239 UNTS 362. Switzerland. Supplementation 8 Jun 55. Force 11 Jul 55.
239 UNTS 362. USA (United States). Supplementation 8 Jun 55. Force 11 Jul 55.

361 UNTS 244. USA (United States). Amendment 30 Dec 59. Force 1 Jan 60.
361 UNTS 244. Switzerland. Amendment 30 Dec 59. Force 1 Jan 60.
471 UNTS 324. Switzerland. Amendment 20 Dec 62. Force 1 Jan 63.
471 UNTS 324. USA (United States). Amendment 28 Dec 62. Force 1 Jan 63.

101778 Bilateral Exchange **133 UNTS 41**
SIGNED: 24 Oct 50 FORCE: 24 Oct 50
REGISTERED: 17 Jun 52 USA (United States)
ARTICLES: 2 LANGUAGE: English.
HEADNOTE: EXCHANGE OFFICIAL PUBLICATIONS
TOPIC: Admin Cooperation
CONCEPTS: Exchange of official publications. Operating agencies. Indemnities and reimbursements.
PARTIES:
Greece
USA (United States)

101779 Bilateral Exchange **133 UNTS 49**
SIGNED: 24 Nov 50 FORCE: 24 Nov 50
REGISTERED: 17 Jun 52 USA (United States)
ARTICLES: 2 LANGUAGE: English. Spanish.
HEADNOTE: ANTHROPOLOGICAL RESEARCH
TOPIC: Scientific Project
CONCEPTS: General provisions. Previous treaty extension. Operating agencies. Use of facilities. Vocational training. Wages and salaries. Research and scientific projects. Anthropology and archeology. Research results. Expense sharing formulae. Tax exemptions. Domestic obligation.
PROCEDURE: Amendment. Duration. Renewal or Revival. Termination.
PARTIES:
Colombia
USA (United States)
ANNEX
139 UNTS 465. USA (United States). Force 1 Jul 52.
139 UNTS 465. Colombia. Force 1 Jul 52.

101780 Bilateral Exchange **133 UNTS 61**
SIGNED: 2 Dec 50 FORCE: 2 Dec 50
REGISTERED: 17 Jun 52 USA (United States)
ARTICLES: 2 LANGUAGE: English. Spanish.
HEADNOTE: EXCHANGE OFFICIAL PUBLICATIONS
TOPIC: Admin Cooperation
CONCEPTS: Exchange of official publications. Operating agencies. Indemnities and reimbursements.
PARTIES:
Costa Rica
USA (United States)

101781 Bilateral Instrument **133 UNTS 69**
SIGNED: 22 Dec 50 FORCE: 22 Dec 50
REGISTERED: 17 Jun 52 USA (United States)
ARTICLES: 1 LANGUAGE: English.
HEADNOTE: ESTABLISHMENT JOINT COMMISSION ECONOMIC DEVELOPMENT
TOPIC: Direct Aid
CONCEPTS: Annex type material. Conformity with municipal law. Personnel. Use of facilities. Establishment of commission. Financial programs. Domestic obligation. Economic assistance.
INTL ORGS: Special Commission.
TREATY REF: 92UNTS145.
PARTIES:
Liberia
USA (United States)

101782 Bilateral Agreement **133 UNTS 75**
SIGNED: 5 Jan 51 FORCE: 5 Jan 51
REGISTERED: 17 Jun 52 USA (United States)
ARTICLES: 7 LANGUAGE: English. Portuguese.
HEADNOTE: MUTUAL DEFENSE ASSISTANCE
TOPIC: Milit Assistance
CONCEPTS: Annex or appendix reference. Non-prejudice to UN charter. Privileges and immunities. Conformity with municipal law. General cooperation. Inspection and observation. Public information. Use of facilities. Indemnities and reimbursements. Local currency. Claims and settlements. Recognition. Customs exemptions. Do-

mestic obligation. Materials, equipment and services. Aid missions. Joint defense. Security of information. Exchange of defense information. Restrictions on transfer. Raw materials.
INTL ORGS: North Atlantic Treaty Organization. United Nations.
TREATY REF: 34UNTS243; 126UNTS350.
PROCEDURE: Amendment. Future Procedures Contemplated. Registration. Termination.
PARTIES:
Portugal
USA (United States)

101783   Bilateral Agreement   **133 UNTS 95**
SIGNED: 15 Feb 51   FORCE: 15 Feb 51
REGISTERED: 17 Jun 52 USA (United States)
ARTICLES: 6 LANGUAGE: English. Spanish.
HEADNOTE: AIR FORCE MISSION
TOPIC: Military Mission
CONCEPTS: Definition of terms. Use of facilities. Compensation. Indemnities and reimbursements. Exchange rates and regulations. Expense sharing formulae. Tax exemptions. Customs exemptions. Military assistance. Military training. Security of information. Airforce-army-navy personnel ratio. Ranks and privileges. Conditions for assistance missions. Third country military personnel. Status of forces.
PROCEDURE: Denunciation. Duration. Renewal or Revival. Termination.
PARTIES:
Chile
USA (United States)
ANNEX
227 UNTS 325. USA (United States). Extension and Amendment 15 Mar 54. Force 15 Mar 54.
227 UNTS 325. Chile. Extension and Amendment 9 Sep 53.
266 UNTS 413. USA (United States). Prolongation 28 Dec 56. Force 17 Jan 57.
266 UNTS 413. Chile. Prolongation 17 Jan 57. Force 17 Jan 57.

101784   Bilateral Agreement   **133 UNTS 117**
SIGNED: 15 Feb 51   FORCE: 15 Feb 51
REGISTERED: 17 Jun 52 USA (United States)
ARTICLES: 5 LANGUAGE: English. Spanish.
HEADNOTE: NAVAL MISSION
TOPIC: Military Mission
CONCEPTS: Definition of terms. Use of facilities. Compensation. Indemnities and reimbursements. Exchange rates and regulations. Expense sharing formulae. Tax exemptions. Customs exemptions. Military assistance. Military training. Security of information. Airforce-army-navy personnel ratio. Ranks and privileges. Conditions for assistance missions. Third country military personnel. Status of forces.
PROCEDURE: Denunciation. Duration. Renewal or Revival. Termination.
PARTIES:
Chile
USA (United States)
ANNEX
206 UNTS 345. USA (United States). Amendment 22 Aug 52. Force 20 Oct 52.
206 UNTS 345. Chile. Amendment 20 Oct 52. Force 20 Oct 52.
215 UNTS 417. USA (United States). Extension and Amendment 26 Oct 53. Force 26 Oct 53.
215 UNTS 417. Chile. Extension and Amendment 6 Oct 53. Force 26 Oct 53.

101785   Bilateral Exchange   **133 UNTS 137**
SIGNED: 17 Nov 51   FORCE: 17 Nov 51
REGISTERED: 19 Jun 52 Australia
ARTICLES: 2 LANGUAGE: English. German.
HEADNOTE: REVIVING PRE-WAR TREATIES
TOPIC: Admin Cooperation
CONCEPTS: Territorial application. Revival of treaties.
TREATY REF: 127LTS167;   134LTS435; 156LTS242; 160LTS399.
PARTIES:
Australia
Austria

101786   Bilateral Agreement   **133 UNTS 143**
SIGNED: 16 Sep 47   FORCE: 3 Apr 52
REGISTERED: 19 Jun 52 UK Great Britain

ARTICLES: 14 LANGUAGE: English. Spanish.
HEADNOTE: AIR SERVICES
TOPIC: Air Transport
CONCEPTS: Conditions. Definition of terms. Detailed regulations. Exceptions and exemptions. Conformity with municipal law. Exchange of information and documents. Arbitration. Procedure. Existing tribunals. Negotiation. Non-interest rates and fees. Routes and logistics. Navigational conditions. Permit designation. Conditions of airlines operating permission. Overflights and technical stops. Operating authorizations and regulations.
INTL ORGS: International Civil Aviation Organization.
TREATY REF: 15UNTS295.
PROCEDURE: Amendment. Future Procedures Contemplated. Ratification. Termination.
PARTIES:
Chile
UK Great Britain

101787   Multilateral Agreement   **133 UNTS 165**
SIGNED: 19 Jun 52   FORCE: 19 Jun 52
REGISTERED: 19 Jun 52 United Nations
ARTICLES: 6 LANGUAGE: English. Spanish.
HEADNOTE: TECHNICAL ASSISTANCE
TOPIC: Tech Assistance
CONCEPTS: Definition of terms. Treaty implementation. Privileges and immunities. General cooperation. Exchange of information and documents. Personnel. Title and deeds. Exchange. Scholarships and grants. Vocational training. Research and development. Expense sharing formulae. Local currency. Domestic obligation. General technical assistance. Materials, equipment and services. IGO status. Conformity with IGO decisions.
TREATY REF: 76UNTS132; 1UNTS15,263; 33UNTS261.
PROCEDURE: Amendment. Termination.
PARTIES:
Cuba SIGNED: 19 Jun 52 FORCE: 19 Jun 52
FAO (Food Agri) SIGNED: 19 Jun 52 FORCE: 19 Jun 52
ICAO (Civil Aviat) SIGNED: 19 Jun 52 FORCE: 19 Jun 52
UNESCO (Educ/Cult) SIGNED: 19 Jun 52 FORCE: 19 Jun 52
United Nations SIGNED: 19 Jun 52 FORCE: 19 Jun 52
WHO (World Health) SIGNED: 19 Jun 52 FORCE: 19 Jun 52

101788   Bilateral Agreement   **133 UNTS 181**
SIGNED: 1 Jul 50   FORCE: 30 Apr 52
REGISTERED: 20 Jun 52 Denmark
ARTICLES: 7 LANGUAGE: French.
HEADNOTE: PATENTS
TOPIC: Patents/Copyrights
CONCEPTS: Non-prejudice to third party. Domestic legislation. Non-interest rates and fees. Laws and formalities. Post-war adjustment.
PROCEDURE: Ratification.
PARTIES:
Denmark
Italy

101789   Bilateral Exchange   **133 UNTS 187**
SIGNED: 18 Sep 51   FORCE: 18 Sep 51
REGISTERED: 30 Jun 52 Belgium
ARTICLES: 2 LANGUAGE: French.
HEADNOTE: STUDENT EMPLOYEES
TOPIC: Non-ILO Labor
CONCEPTS: Definition of terms. Detailed regulations. Resident permits. Conformity with municipal law. Exchange of information and documents. Dispute settlement. Employment regulations. Non-ILO labor relations. Administrative cooperation. Quotas. National treatment.
PROCEDURE: Denunciation. Duration. Renewal or Revival.
PARTIES:
Belgium
Sweden

101790   Bilateral Exchange   **133 UNTS 199**
SIGNED: 20 Feb 52   FORCE: 20 Feb 52
REGISTERED: 30 Jun 52 Belgium
ARTICLES: 2 LANGUAGE: English. French.

HEADNOTE: RECIPROCAL EXTRADITION FUGITIVE CRIMINALS
TOPIC: Extradition
CONCEPTS: Revival of treaties.
TREATY REF: 2'20DEMARTEN617; 3'1DEMARTENS758; 3'5DEMARTENS395;.
PARTIES:
Belgium
Pakistan
ANNEX
173 UNTS 408. Pakistan. Confirmation 28 Jul 53. Force 28 Jul 53.
173 UNTS 408. Belgium. Belgian Colonies. Force 28 Jul 53.
173 UNTS 408. Belgium. Ruanda-Urundi. Force 28 Jul 53.

101791   Bilateral Exchange   **133 UNTS 205**
SIGNED: 26 Nov 51   FORCE: 26 Nov 51
REGISTERED: 1 Jul 52 UK Great Britain
ARTICLES: 28 LANGUAGE: English. Spanish.
HEADNOTE: EXTENDING USE LONG-RANGE PROVING GROUND MISSILES
TOPIC: Milit Installation
CONCEPTS: Annex or appendix reference. Military installations and equipment.
PARTIES:
Dominican Republic
UK Great Britain

101792   Bilateral Agreement   **133 UNTS 245**
SIGNED: 4 Apr 52   FORCE: 20 May 52
REGISTERED: 1 Jul 52 Denmark
ARTICLES: 7 LANGUAGE: French.
HEADNOTE: COMMERCIAL EXCHANGE
TOPIC: General Trade
CONCEPTS: Exceptions and exemptions. Treaty implementation. Annex or appendix reference. Previous treaty extension. Licenses and permits. Establishment of commission. Payment schedules. Quotas.
TREATY REF: 74UNTS147.
PROCEDURE: Denunciation. Duration. Ratification.
PARTIES:
Czechoslovakia
Denmark

101793   Bilateral Agreement   **133 UNTS 257**
SIGNED: 8 Sep 51   FORCE: 1 Sep 50
REGISTERED: 7 Jul 52 Pakistan
ARTICLES: 31 LANGUAGE: English.
HEADNOTE: EXCHANGE MONEY ORDERS
TOPIC: Postal Service
CONCEPTS: Annex or appendix reference. Conformity with municipal law. Currency. Payment schedules. Money orders and postal checks. Rates and charges. Advice lists and orders.
PROCEDURE: Duration. Termination.
PARTIES:
Pakistan
United Arab Rep

101794   Bilateral Exchange   **134 UNTS 3**
SIGNED: 19 May 52   FORCE: 19 May 52
REGISTERED: 7 Jul 52 Netherlands
ARTICLES: 2 LANGUAGE: Dutch. German.
HEADNOTE: RESTITUTION GERMAN SECURITIES
TOPIC: Reparations
CONCEPTS: Accounting procedures. Interest rates. Payment schedules. Lump sum settlements. Tax exemptions. Enemy financial interests. Post-war claims settlement.
INTL ORGS: Allied Military Occupation.
PARTIES:
Germany, West
Netherlands

101795   Bilateral Agreement   **134 UNTS 19**
SIGNED: 29 Dec 50   FORCE: 14 May 52
REGISTERED: 7 Jul 52 Netherlands
ARTICLES: 29 LANGUAGE: Dutch. English. Norwegian.
HEADNOTE: DOUBLE TAXATION FISCAL EVASION INCOME CAPITAL
TOPIC: Taxation
CONCEPTS: Definition of terms. Conformity with municipal law. Exchange of official publications. Teacher and student exchange. Claims and settlements. Taxation. Death duties. Equitable

taxes. General. Tax exemptions. Merchant vessels.
TREATY REF: 85LTS409.
PROCEDURE: Duration. Ratification. Termination.
PARTIES:
Netherlands
Norway
ANNEX
613 UNTS 405. Netherlands. Force 6 Jun 67.
613 UNTS 405. Norway. Force 6 Jun 67.

101796 Bilateral Exchange **134 UNTS 70**
SIGNED: 15 Feb 48　　　FORCE: 15 Feb 48
REGISTERED: 7 Jul 52 UK Great Britain
ARTICLES: 10 LANGUAGE: English.
HEADNOTE: FINANCE
TOPIC: Finance
CONCEPTS: Definition of terms. Detailed regulations. Territorial application. Previous treaty extension. General cooperation. Accounting procedures. Banking.
INTL ORGS: International Monetary Fund.
TREATY REF: 11JUNT371.
PROCEDURE: Termination.
PARTIES:
India
UK Great Britain

101797 Bilateral Exchange **134 UNTS 128**
SIGNED: 21 Feb 48　　　FORCE: 21 Feb 48
REGISTERED: 7 Jul 52 UK Great Britain
ARTICLES: 10 LANGUAGE: English.
HEADNOTE: FINANCE
TOPIC: Finance
CONCEPTS: Detailed regulations. Treaty interpretation. Annex or appendix reference. Previous treaty extension. Accounting procedures. Balance of payments.
TREATY REF: 11JUNT371.
PROCEDURE: Duration. Future Procedures Contemplated.
PARTIES:
Pakistan
UK Great Britain

101798 Bilateral Agreement **134 UNTS 183**
SIGNED: 29 Sep 51　　　FORCE: 29 Sep 51
REGISTERED: 7 Jul 52 UK Great Britain
ARTICLES: 11 LANGUAGE: English.
HEADNOTE: NEW AGREEMENT STERLING BALANCES
TOPIC: Finance
CONCEPTS: Definition of terms. Detailed regulations. Previous treaty extension. Previous treaty replacement. General cooperation. Accounting procedures. Banking. Balance of payments. Monetary and gold transfers. Payment schedules.
INTL ORGS: International Monetary Fund.
TREATY REF: 2UNTS39; 19UNTS280; 11UNTS371; 134UNTS128.
PROCEDURE: Duration. Renewal or Revival. Termination.
PARTIES:
Pakistan
UK Great Britain

101799 Bilateral Exchange **134 UNTS 195**
SIGNED: 24 Jul 51　　　FORCE: 24 Jul 51
REGISTERED: 8 Jul 52 USA (United States)
ARTICLES: 2 LANGUAGE: English. Portuguese.
HEADNOTE: ESTABLISHMENT JOINT GROUP EMERGENCY SUPPLY PROBLEMS
TOPIC: Direct Aid
CONCEPTS: Establishment of commission. Procedure. Economic assistance. Distribution.
INTL ORGS: Special Commission.
TREATY REF: USA'TIAS 2240;.
PARTIES:
Brazil
USA (United States)

101800 Bilateral Exchange **134 UNTS 205**
SIGNED: 18 Apr 51　　　FORCE: 18 Apr 51
REGISTERED: 8 Jul 52 USA (United States)
ARTICLES: 2 LANGUAGE: English.
HEADNOTE: DISPOSAL EXCESS PROPERTY
TOPIC: Milit Assistance
CONCEPTS: Detailed regulations. Exceptions and

exemptions. General property. Accounting procedures. Customs duties. Surplus property.
TREATY REF: 101UNTS257.
PROCEDURE: Termination.
PARTIES:
Canada
USA (United States)

101801 Bilateral Exchange **134 UNTS 215**
SIGNED: 17 Jan 51　　　FORCE: 17 Jan 51
REGISTERED: 8 Jul 52 USA (United States)
ARTICLES: 2 LANGUAGE: English.
HEADNOTE: AMENDING AGREEMENT CONSTRUCTION INTER-AMERICAN HIGHWAY
TOPIC: Land Transport
CONCEPTS: Conformity with municipal law. General cooperation. Licenses and permits. Recognition of legal documents. Private contracts. Expense sharing formulae. Fees and exemptions. Financial programs. National treatment. Tax exemptions. Materials, equipment and services. Registration certificate. Roads and highways.
INTL ORGS: Organization of American States.
TREATY REF: 23UNTS285; USA'TIAS 1567;.
PARTIES:
Costa Rica
USA (United States)

101802 Bilateral Agreement **134 UNTS 225**
SIGNED: 28 Aug 51　　　FORCE: 28 Aug 51
REGISTERED: 8 Jul 52 USA (United States)
ARTICLES: 6 LANGUAGE: English. Spanish.
HEADNOTE: ARMY MISSION
TOPIC: Military Mission
CONCEPTS: Definition of terms. Use of facilities. Compensation. Indemnities and reimbursements. Exchange rates and regulations. Expense sharing formulae. Tax exemptions. Customs exemptions. Military assistance. Military training. Security of information. Airforce-army-navy personnel ratio. Ranks and privileges. Conditions for assistance missions. Third country military personnel. Status of forces.
PROCEDURE: Denunciation. Duration. Renewal or Revival. Termination.
PARTIES:
Cuba
USA (United States)
ANNEX
232 UNTS 335. USA (United States). Prolongation 13 Oct 53. Force 14 Oct 53.
232 UNTS 335. Cuba. Prolongation 21 Sep 53. Force 13 Oct 53.
264 UNTS 355. USA (United States). Prolongation 17 May 55. Force 17 May 55.
264 UNTS 355. Cuba. Prolongation 3 May 55. Force 17 May 55.

101803 Bilateral Exchange **134 UNTS 245**
SIGNED: 19 Mar 51　　　FORCE: 19 Mar 51
REGISTERED: 8 Jul 52 USA (United States)
ARTICLES: 2 LANGUAGE: English.
HEADNOTE: AGREEMENT AMENDING CONSTRUCTION INTER-AMERICAN HIGHWAY
TOPIC: Land Transport
CONCEPTS: Conformity with municipal law. General cooperation. Licenses and permits. Recognition of legal documents. Private contracts. Expense sharing formulae. Fees and exemptions. Financial programs. National treatment. Tax exemptions. Materials, equipment and services. Registration certificate. Roads and highways.
INTL ORGS: Organization of American States.
TREATY REF: 23UNTS293; USA'TIAS 1567;.
PARTIES:
El Salvador
USA (United States)

101804 Bilateral Exchange **134 UNTS 255**
SIGNED: 15 Aug 50　　　FORCE: 15 Aug 50
REGISTERED: 8 Jul 52 USA (United States)
ARTICLES: 2 LANGUAGE: English.
HEADNOTE: MILITARY ASSISTANCE
TOPIC: Milit Assistance
CONCEPTS: Guarantees and safeguards. Privileges and immunities. Conformity with municipal law. Public information. Local currency. Domestic obligation. Materials, equipment and services. Military assistance. Military assistance missions.

PROCEDURE: Duration. Future Procedures Contemplated. Termination.
PARTIES:
Indonesia
USA (United States)
ANNEX
198 UNTS 400. USA (United States). Amendment 5 Jan 53. Force 12 Jan 53.
198 UNTS 400. Indonesia. Amendment 12 Jan 53. Force 12 Jan 53.

101805 Bilateral Exchange **134 UNTS 265**
SIGNED: 23 May 51　　　FORCE: 23 May 51
REGISTERED: 8 Jul 52 USA (United States)
ARTICLES: 2 LANGUAGE: English.
HEADNOTE: EXCHANGE OFFICIAL PUBLICATIONS
TOPIC: Admin Cooperation
CONCEPTS: Exchange of official publications. Operating agencies. Indemnities and reimbursements.
PARTIES:
Pakistan
USA (United States)
ANNEX
237 UNTS 312. USA (United States). Amendment 29 Dec 53. Force 29 Dec 53.
237 UNTS 312. Pakistan. Amendment 22 Apr 53. Force 29 Dec 53.

101806 Bilateral Agreement **134 UNTS 273**
SIGNED: 9 Jun 52　　　FORCE: 19 Jun 52
REGISTERED: 21 Jul 52 WHO (World Health)
ARTICLES: 4 LANGUAGE: English.
HEADNOTE: LEPROSY SPECIALIST
TOPIC: Sanitation
CONCEPTS: Definition of terms. Annex type material. Privileges and immunities. General cooperation. General property. Responsibility and liability. Specialists exchange. Public health. WHO used as agency. Institute establishment. Scholarships and grants. Indemnities and reimbursements. Expense sharing formulae. Assistance. Special projects. Specific technical assistance.
TREATY REF: 33UNTS261; 107UNTS9.
PROCEDURE: Amendment. Termination.
PARTIES:
Burma
WHO (World Health)

101807 Bilateral Agreement **134 UNTS 285**
SIGNED: 26 Mar 52　　　FORCE: 28 Apr 52
REGISTERED: 21 Jul 52 WHO (World Health)
ARTICLES: 6 LANGUAGE: English.
HEADNOTE: SALMONELLA ESCHERICHIA RESEARCH
TOPIC: Scientific Project
CONCEPTS: Definition of terms. Public health. WHO used as agency. Scholarships and grants. Research and scientific projects. Research cooperation. Research and development. Indemnities and reimbursements.
TREATY REF: 107UNTS243.
PROCEDURE: Termination.
PARTIES:
Denmark
WHO (World Health)

101808 Bilateral Agreement **134 UNTS 291**
SIGNED: 15 Feb 52　　　FORCE: 22 Apr 52
REGISTERED: 21 Jul 52 WHO (World Health)
ARTICLES: 4 LANGUAGE: English. Spanish.
HEADNOTE: INSECT CONTROL PROGRAM
TOPIC: Sanitation
CONCEPTS: Definition of terms. Privileges and immunities. General cooperation. Personnel. General property. Specialists exchange. Disease control. Insect control. WHO used as agency. Vocational training. Research results. Research and development. Accounting procedures. Indemnities and reimbursements. Expense sharing formulae. Specific technical assistance. Aid missions.
INTL ORGS: United Nations.
TREATY REF: 76UNTS132; 33UNTS261.
PARTIES:
Dominican Republic
WHO (World Health)

101809 Bilateral Agreement **134 UNTS 307**
SIGNED: 19 Jun 52 FORCE: 15 Jun 52
REGISTERED: 21 Jul 52 WHO (World Health)
ARTICLES: 4 LANGUAGE: English.
HEADNOTE: PROVISION WHO PEDIATRIC NURSE
TOPIC: Sanitation
CONCEPTS: Definition of terms. Privileges and immunities. General cooperation. Personnel. Responsibility and liability. Public health. Nursing. WHO used as agency. Exchange. Scholarships and grants. Vocational training. Indemnities and reimbursements. Assistance. Materials, equipment and services.
TREATY REF: 33UNTS261.
PROCEDURE: Amendment. Duration. Renewal or Revival.
PARTIES:
India
WHO (World Health)

101810 Bilateral Agreement **134 UNTS 319**
SIGNED: 28 May 52 FORCE: 4 Jun 52
REGISTERED: 21 Jul 52 WHO (World Health)
ARTICLES: 4 LANGUAGE: English. Spanish.
HEADNOTE: RABIES CONTROL PROGRAM
TOPIC: Sanitation
CONCEPTS: Definition of terms. Previous treaty extension. Privileges and immunities. General cooperation. Personnel. Specialists exchange. Disease control. WHO used as agency. Research results. Research and development. Indemnities and reimbursements. Expense sharing formulae. Financial programs. Specific technical assistance. Materials, equipment and services.
INTL ORGS: United Nations.
TREATY REF: 33UNTS261.
PROCEDURE: Amendment. Renewal or Revival. Termination.
PARTIES:
Mexico
WHO (World Health)
ANNEX
172 UNTS 388. WHO (World Health). Force 25 Jun 53.
172 UNTS 388. Mexico. Force 25 Jun 53.

101811 Bilateral Agreement **135 UNTS 3**
SIGNED: 5 Jun 51 FORCE: 1 Sep 49
REGISTERED: 24 Jul 52 UK Great Britain
ARTICLES: 29 LANGUAGE: English.
HEADNOTE: EXCHANGE MONEY ORDERS
TOPIC: Postal Service
CONCEPTS: Definition of terms. Annex or appendix reference. Accounting procedures. Payment schedules. Postal services. Regulations. Money orders and postal checks. Rates and charges. Advice lists and orders.
PROCEDURE: Denunciation. Duration.
PARTIES:
India
UK Great Britain
ANNEX
613 UNTS 406. UK Great Britain. Abrogation 5 Jan 67. Force 1 Jan 67.
613 UNTS 406. India. Abrogation 5 Jan 67. Force 1 Jan 67.

101812 Bilateral Agreement **135 UNTS 37**
SIGNED: 25 Jul 52 FORCE: 25 Jul 52
REGISTERED: 25 Jul 52 United Nations
ARTICLES: 10 LANGUAGE: English.
HEADNOTE: ACTIVITIES UNICEF
TOPIC: Direct Aid
CONCEPTS: Treaty implementation. Privileges and immunities. General cooperation. Exchange of information and documents. Informational records. Inspection and observation. Public information. Title and deeds. Use of facilities. Procedure. Negotiation. Export quotas. Financial programs. Tax exemptions. Customs exemptions. Commodities and services. Assistance. General aid. Procurement. Distribution. IGO status.
INTL ORGS: United Nations.
TREATY REF: 1UNTS15.
PROCEDURE: Amendment. Termination.
PARTIES:
UNICEF (Children)
UK Great Britain

101813 Bilateral Exchange **135 UNTS 49**
SIGNED: 14 Jun 49 FORCE: 14 Jun 49
REGISTERED: 30 Jul 52 UK Great Britain
ARTICLES: 2 LANGUAGE: English.
HEADNOTE: RETURN SUBMARINE CABLES
TOPIC: Specific Property
CONCEPTS: Indemnities and reimbursements. Materials, equipment and services. Facilities and property.
PARTIES:
Italy
UK Great Britain

101814 Bilateral Exchange **135 UNTS 55**
SIGNED: 12 Nov 51 FORCE: 12 Nov 51
REGISTERED: 30 Jul 52 UK Great Britain
ARTICLES: 2 LANGUAGE: English.
HEADNOTE: RECOVERY SUBMARINE CABLE
TOPIC: Specif Claim/Waive
CONCEPTS: Indemnities and reimbursements. Materials, equipment and services. Facilities and property.
TREATY REF: 135UNTS49.
PARTIES:
Italy
UK Great Britain

101815 Bilateral Agreement **135 UNTS 61**
SIGNED: 17 Jul 52 FORCE: 17 Jul 52
REGISTERED: 1 Aug 52 United Nations
ARTICLES: 4 LANGUAGE: English. Spanish.
HEADNOTE: EXPERT WORKING GROUP MEETING STEEL IRON INDUSTRY
TOPIC: Tech Assistance
CONCEPTS: Detailed regulations. Time limit. Privileges and immunities. Personnel. Use of facilities. Expense sharing formulae. Domestic obligation. IGO constitution. IGO operations. Conferences.
TREATY REF: 81UNTS188.
PARTIES:
Colombia
United Nations

101816 Bilateral Exchange **135 UNTS 74**
SIGNED: 27 Feb 48 FORCE: 27 Feb 48
REGISTERED: 1 Aug 52 USA (United States)
ARTICLES: 2 LANGUAGE: English. Spanish.
HEADNOTE: COOPERATIVE PROGRAM AGRICULTURE
TOPIC: Direct Aid
CONCEPTS: Wages and salaries. Funding procedures. Agriculture. Assistance.
TREATY REF: 135UNTS76.
PARTIES:
Costa Rica
USA (United States)
ANNEX
165 UNTS 361. USA (United States). Supplementation 10 Jan 52. Force 25 Jan 52.
165 UNTS 361. Costa Rica. Supplementation 25 Jan 52. Force 25 Jan 52.
178 UNTS 401. Costa Rica. Supplementation 10 Jun 52. Force 10 Jun 52.
178 UNTS 401. USA (United States). Supplementation 3 Jun 52. Force 10 Jun 52.
264 UNTS 359. Costa Rica. Prolongation 7 Feb 55. Force 22 Apr 55.
264 UNTS 359. USA (United States). Prolongation 18 Jan 55. Force 22 Apr 55.

101817 Bilateral Exchange **135 UNTS 104**
SIGNED: 5 Jan 48 FORCE: 6 May 47
REGISTERED: 1 Aug 52 USA (United States)
ARTICLES: 2 LANGUAGE: English. Spanish.
HEADNOTE: COOPERATIVE EDUCATIONAL PROGRAM
TOPIC: Education
CONCEPTS: Annex or appendix reference. Annex type material. Privileges and immunities. Exchange. Commissions and foundations. Accounting procedures. Indemnities and reimbursements. Currency. Expense sharing formulae. Financial programs. Funding procedures. Tax exemptions. Customs exemptions.
TREATY REF: TAIS 2073; 135UNTS315.
PARTIES:
Guatemala
USA (United States)

101818 Bilateral Exchange **135 UNTS 130**
SIGNED: 19 Dec 47 FORCE: 5 Jan 48
REGISTERED: 1 Aug 52 USA (United States)
ARTICLES: 2 LANGUAGE: English. French.
HEADNOTE: COOPERATIVE PROGRAM FOOD PRODUCTION
TOPIC: Direct Aid
CONCEPTS: Annex type material. Financial programs. Agriculture. Assistance.
TREATY REF: USA'TIAS 2061;C.
PARTIES:
Haiti
USA (United States)
ANNEX
162 UNTS 354. USA (United States). Supplementation 28 Jun 51. Force 29 Jun 51.
162 UNTS 354. Haiti. Supplementation 28 Jun 51. Force 29 Jun 51.
162 UNTS 358. USA (United States). Supplementation 23 Aug 51. Force 28 Sep 51.
162 UNTS 358. Haiti. Supplementation 28 Sep 51. Force 28 Sep 51.
177 UNTS 351. Haiti. Supplementation 9 Apr 52. Force 9 Apr 52.
177 UNTS 351. USA (United States). Supplementation 29 Jan 52. Force 9 Apr 52.
253 UNTS 355. Haiti. Prolongation 3 Feb 55. Force 24 Mar 55.
253 UNTS 355. USA (United States). Prolongation 28 Jan 55. Force 24 Mar 55.

101819 Bilateral Exchange **135 UNTS 156**
SIGNED: 3 Mar 47 FORCE: 3 Mar 47
REGISTERED: 1 Aug 52 USA (United States)
ARTICLES: 2 LANGUAGE: English. Spanish.
HEADNOTE: EXTENSION AGREEMENT COOPERATIVE PROGRAM AGRICULTURE
TOPIC: Tech Assistance
CONCEPTS: Previous treaty extension. Financial programs. Payment schedules. Agriculture.
PROCEDURE: Future Procedures Contemplated.
PARTIES:
Paraguay
USA (United States)
ANNEX
160 UNTS 404. USA (United States). Supplementation 10 Sep 51. Force 24 Oct 51.
160 UNTS 404. Paraguay. Supplementation 24 Oct 51. Force 24 Oct 51.
167 UNTS 300. USA (United States). Supplementation 22 Jun 51. Force 30 Jan 52.
167 UNTS 300. Paraguay. Supplementation 22 Jun 51. Force 30 Jan 52.
177 UNTS 356. USA (United States). Supplementation 31 Jan 52. Force 31 Mar 52.
177 UNTS 356. Paraguay. Supplementation 31 Mar 52. Force 31 Mar 52.
269 UNTS 299. Paraguay. Prolongation 5 Apr 55. Force 5 Apr 55.
269 UNTS 299. USA (United States). Prolongation 5 Apr 55. Force 5 Apr 55.

101820 Bilateral Agreement **135 UNTS 185**
SIGNED: 4 Aug 52 FORCE: 4 Aug 52
REGISTERED: 4 Aug 52 United Nations
ARTICLES: 5 LANGUAGE: English. Portuguese.
HEADNOTE: SEMINAR PREVENTION CRIME TREATMENT OFFENDERS
TOPIC: Tech Assistance
CONCEPTS: Definition of terms. Detailed regulations. Time limit. Privileges and immunities. Personnel. Use of facilities. Expense sharing formulae. Local currency. Domestic obligation. General technical assistance. IGO status. IGO operations. Conferences.
TREATY REF: 1UNTS15,263.
PROCEDURE: Amendment. Termination.
PARTIES:
Brazil
United Nations

101821 Bilateral Exchange **135 UNTS 199**
SIGNED: 7 Mar 52 FORCE: 7 Mar 52
REGISTERED: 5 Aug 52 Netherlands
ARTICLES: 2 LANGUAGE: English.
HEADNOTE: TAXES EXPENDITURES DEFENSE
TOPIC: Taxation
CONCEPTS: General. Military installations and equipment.
INTL ORGS: North Atlantic Treaty Organization.

PARTIES:
Netherlands
USA (United States)
ANNEX
234 UNTS 320. Netherlands. Supplementation
29 May 53. Force 22 Jun 53.
234 UNTS 320. USA (United States). Supplementation 22 Jun 53. Force 22 Jun 53.

101822 Bilateral Agreement **135 UNTS 209**
SIGNED: 9 Jun 52 FORCE: 9 Jun 52
REGISTERED: 6 Aug 52 Denmark
ARTICLES: 9 LANGUAGE: French.
HEADNOTE: COMMERCIAL EXCHANGES
TOPIC: General Trade
CONCEPTS: Annex or appendix reference. Licenses and permits. Establishment of commission. Reciprocity in trade. Payment schedules. Delivery schedules. Quotas.
INTL ORGS: Special Commission.
TREATY REF: 135UNTS221.
PROCEDURE: Denunciation. Duration. Renewal or Revival.
PARTIES:
Denmark
Poland

101823 Bilateral Agreement **135 UNTS 221**
SIGNED: 9 Jun 52 FORCE: 9 Jun 52
REGISTERED: 6 Aug 52 Denmark
ARTICLES: 9 LANGUAGE: French.
HEADNOTE: PAYMENTS
TOPIC: Finance
CONCEPTS: Currency. Payment schedules.
INTL ORGS: Special Commission.
PROCEDURE: Denunciation. Duration.
PARTIES:
Denmark
Poland

101824 Bilateral Agreement **135 UNTS 229**
SIGNED: 8 Jul 50 FORCE: 1 Jun 52
REGISTERED: 11 Aug 52 Netherlands
ARTICLES: 28 LANGUAGE: French.
HEADNOTE: SOCIAL SECURITY
TOPIC: Non-ILO Labor
CONCEPTS: General provisions. Notarial acts and services. General cooperation. Operating agencies. Dispute settlement. Old age and invalidity insurance. Non-ILO labor relations. Family allowances. Administrative cooperation. Old age insurance. Sickness and invalidity insurance. Social security. Fees and exemptions. Payment schedules. National treatment.
PROCEDURE: Duration. Ratification. Renewal or Revival. Termination.
PARTIES:
Luxembourg
Netherlands

101825 Bilateral Agreement **135 UNTS 255**
SIGNED: 28 Jul 52 FORCE: 1 Jul 52
REGISTERED: 15 Aug 52 Denmark
ARTICLES: 6 LANGUAGE: French.
HEADNOTE: EXCHANGE COMMODITIES
TOPIC: Commodity Trade
CONCEPTS: Definition of terms. Annex or appendix reference. Licenses and permits. Establishment of commission. General trade. Export quotas. Import quotas. Quotas.
PROCEDURE: Duration.
PARTIES:
Denmark
Spain

101826 Bilateral Agreement **135 UNTS 265**
SIGNED: 23 Jan 52 FORCE: 23 Jun 52
REGISTERED: 15 Aug 52 WHO (World Health)
ARTICLES: 6 LANGUAGE: English. Spanish.
HEADNOTE: HEALTH PROJECTS
TOPIC: Sanitation
CONCEPTS: Definition of terms. Privileges and immunities. Personnel. General property. Arbitration. Procedure. Specialists exchange. Public health. WHO used as agency. Scholarships and grants. Vocational training. Research and development. Indemnities and reimbursements. Expense sharing formulae. Assistance. Specific

technical assistance. Materials, equipment and services.
INTL ORGS: United Nations. Arbitration Commission.
TREATY REF: 14UNTS185; OFF.REC.WHO NO.28 P.68; 76UNTS132.
PROCEDURE: Amendment. Termination.
PARTIES:
Costa Rica
WHO (World Health)

101827 Bilateral Agreement **135 UNTS 279**
SIGNED: 4 Jun 52 FORCE: 9 Jun 52
REGISTERED: 15 Aug 52 WHO (World Health)
ARTICLES: 4 LANGUAGE: English
HEADNOTE: NURSING PROJECT BOMBAY
TOPIC: Sanitation
CONCEPTS: Definition of terms. Privileges and immunities. General cooperation. Personnel. Responsibility and liability. Arbitration. Existing tribunals. Public health. Nursing. Scholarships and grants. Vocational training. Indemnities and reimbursements. Expense sharing formulae. Assistance. Specific technical assistance. Materials, equipment and services.
INTL ORGS: International Court of Justice. United Nations. Arbitration Commission.
PROCEDURE: Amendment. Duration. Termination.
PARTIES:
India
WHO (World Health)

101828 Bilateral Agreement **135 UNTS 291**
SIGNED: 16 Jul 52 FORCE: 16 Jul 52
REGISTERED: 15 Aug 52 WHO (World Health)
ARTICLES: 6 LANGUAGE: English.
HEADNOTE: TECHNICAL ADVISORY ASSISTANCE HEALTH PROJECTS
TOPIC: Tech Assistance
CONCEPTS: Treaty implementation. Privileges and immunities. General cooperation. Exchange of information and documents. Personnel. Title and deeds. Exchange. Scholarships and grants. Vocational training. Research and development. Expense sharing formulae. Local currency. Domestic obligation. General technical assistance. Special projects. Materials, equipment and services. IGO status. Conformity with IGO decisions.
INTL ORGS: United Nations.
TREATY REF: 76UNTS132; 67UNTS43.
PROCEDURE: Amendment. Termination.
PARTIES:
India
WHO (World Health)

101829 Bilateral Agreement **136 UNTS 3**
SIGNED: 20 Aug 52 FORCE: 20 Aug 52
REGISTERED: 20 Aug 52 United Nations
ARTICLES: 6 LANGUAGE: English. Spanish.
HEADNOTE: TECHNICAL ASSISTANCE
TOPIC: Tech Assistance
CONCEPTS: Treaty implementation. Privileges and immunities. General cooperation. Exchange of information and documents. Personnel. Title and deeds. Exchange. Scholarships and grants. Vocational training. Research and development. Expense sharing formulae. Local currency. Domestic obligation. General technical assistance. Materials, equipment and services. IGO status. Conformity with IGO decisions.
TREATY REF: 76UNTS132; 1UNTS15,263.
PROCEDURE: Amendment. Termination.
PARTIES:
Panama
United Nations
ANNEX
274 UNTS 347. United Nations. Force 27 Apr 57.
274 UNTS 347. Panama. Force 27 Apr 57.

101830 Bilateral Agreement **136 UNTS 17**
SIGNED: 10 Jul 52 FORCE: 10 Jul 52
REGISTERED: 20 Aug 52 United Nations
ARTICLES: 9 LANGUAGE: English.
HEADNOTE: ACTIVITIES UNICEF
TOPIC: Direct Aid
CONCEPTS: Treaty implementation. Privileges and immunities. General cooperation. Exchange of information and documents. Informational records. Inspection and observation. Public information. Use of facilities. Procedure. Existing

tribunals. Export quotas. Financial programs. Tax exemptions. Customs exemptions. Commodities and services. Assistance. General aid. Distribution. IGO status.
INTL ORGS: United Nations.
TREATY REF: 1UNTS15.
PROCEDURE: Duration.
PARTIES:
UNICEF (Children)
Syria
ANNEX
634 UNTS 427. Syria. Force 22 Apr 68.
634 UNTS 427. UNICEF (Children). Force 22 Apr 68.

101831 Bilateral Treaty **136 UNTS 31**
SIGNED: 23 Oct 50 FORCE: 11 Jul 52
REGISTERED: 21 Aug 52 Netherlands
ARTICLES: 7 LANGUAGE: Dutch. French.
HEADNOTE: MINING BOUNDARY BETWEEN COAL MINES
TOPIC: Territory Boundary
CONCEPTS: Conformity with municipal law. Exchange of information and documents. Fish, wildlife, and natural resources. Markers and definitions.
PROCEDURE: Ratification.
PARTIES:
Belgium
Netherlands
ANNEX
507 UNTS 270. Netherlands. Implementation 5 Apr 63. Force 31 Aug 64.
507 UNTS 270. Belgium. Implementation 5 Apr 63. Force 31 Aug 64.

101832 Multilateral Treaty **136 UNTS 45**
SIGNED: 8 Sep 51 FORCE: 28 Apr 52
REGISTERED: 21 Aug 52 USA (United States)
ARTICLES: 27 LANGUAGE: English. French. Japanese. Spanish.
HEADNOTE: PEACE TREATY
TOPIC: Peace/Disarmament
CONCEPTS: Previous treaty renunciation. Non-prejudice to UN charter. Peaceful relations. Recognition. Legal protection and assistance. General property. Revival of treaties. Investigation of violations. Abolition of extraterritorial rights. Procedure. Existing tribunals. Competence of tribunal. Compensation. Claims and settlements. Most favored nation clause. Recognition. Customs and excise cooperation. Air transport. Armistice and peace. Reparations and restrictions. Post-war claims settlement. Disposition of territory. Definition of territory. Ocean resources. Raw materials.
INTL ORGS: Bank for International Settlements. International Civil Aviation Organization. International Court of Justice. United Nations.
TREATY REF: 8UNTS189.
PROCEDURE: Ratification.
PARTIES:
Argentina SIGNED: 8 Sep 51 RATIFIED: 9 Apr 52 FORCE: 28 Apr 52
Australia SIGNED: 8 Sep 51 RATIFIED: 10 Apr 52 FORCE: 28 Apr 52
Belgium SIGNED: 8 Sep 51
Bolivia SIGNED: 8 Sep 51
Brazil SIGNED: 8 Sep 51 RATIFIED: 20 May 52 FORCE: 20 May 52
Cambodia SIGNED: 8 Sep 51 RATIFIED: 2 Jun 52 FORCE: 2 Jun 52
Canada SIGNED: 8 Sep 51 RATIFIED: 17 Apr 52 FORCE: 28 Apr 52
Ceylon (Sri Lanka) SIGNED: 8 Sep 51 RATIFIED: 28 Apr 52 FORCE: 28 Apr 52
Chile SIGNED: 8 Sep 51
Colombia SIGNED: 8 Sep 51
Costa Rica SIGNED: 8 Sep 51
Cuba SIGNED: 8 Sep 51
Dominican Republic SIGNED: 8 Sep 51 RATIFIED: 6 Jun 52 FORCE: 6 Jun 52
Ecuador SIGNED: 8 Sep 51
United Arab Rep SIGNED: 8 Sep 51
El Salvador SIGNED: 8 Sep 51 RATIFIED: 6 May 52 FORCE: 6 May 52
Ethiopia SIGNED: 8 Sep 51 RATIFIED: 12 Jun 52 FORCE: 12 Jun 52
France SIGNED: 8 Sep 51 RATIFIED: 18 Apr 52 FORCE: 28 Apr 52
Greece SIGNED: 8 Sep 51
Guatemala SIGNED: 8 Sep 51

Haiti SIGNED: 8 Sep 51
Indonesia SIGNED: 8 Sep 51
Iran SIGNED: 8 Sep 51
Iraq SIGNED: 8 Sep 51
Japan SIGNED: 17 Sep 51 RATIFIED: 28 Nov 51
FORCE: 28 Apr 52
Laos SIGNED: 8 Sep 51 RATIFIED: 20 Jun 52
FORCE: 20 Jun 52
Lebanon SIGNED: 8 Sep 51
Liberia SIGNED: 8 Sep 51
Luxembourg SIGNED: 8 Sep 51
Mexico SIGNED: 8 Sep 51 RATIFIED: 3 Mar 52
FORCE: 28 Apr 52
Netherlands SIGNED: 8 Sep 51 RATIFIED:
17 Jun 52 FORCE: 17 Jun 52
New Zealand SIGNED: 8 Sep 51 RATIFIED:
10 Apr 52 FORCE: 28 Apr 52
Nicaragua SIGNED: 8 Sep 51
Norway SIGNED: 8 Sep 51 RATIFIED: 19 Jun 52
FORCE: 19 Jun 52
Pakistan SIGNED: 8 Sep 51 RATIFIED:
17 Apr 52 FORCE: 28 Apr 52
Panama SIGNED: 8 Sep 51
Paraguay SIGNED: 8 Sep 51
Peru SIGNED: 8 Sep 51 RATIFIED: 17 Jun 52
FORCE: 17 Jun 52
Philippines SIGNED: 8 Sep 51
Saudi Arabia SIGNED: 8 Sep 51
South Africa SIGNED: 8 Sep 51
Syria SIGNED: 8 Sep 51
Turkey SIGNED: 8 Sep 51
UK Great Britain SIGNED: 8 Sep 51 RATIFIED:
3 Jan 52 FORCE: 28 Apr 52
USA (United States) SIGNED: 8 Sep 51 RATI-
FIED: 28 Apr 52 FORCE: 28 Apr 5
Uruguay SIGNED: 8 Sep 51
Venezuela SIGNED: 8 Sep 51 RATIFIED:
20 Jun 52 FORCE: 20 Jun 52
Vietnam SIGNED: 8 Sep 51 RATIFIED:
18 Jun 52 FORCE: 18 Jun 52
ANNEX
163 UNTS 385. Turkey. Ratification 24 Jul 52.
163 UNTS 385. Cuba. Ratification 12 Aug 52.
163 UNTS 385. Belgium. Ratification 22 Aug 52.
163 UNTS 385. South Africa. Ratification
10 Sep 52.
163 UNTS 385. Costa Rica. Ratification
17 Sep 52.
184 UNTS 358. Nicaragua. Ratification 4 Nov 52.
184 UNTS 358. Uruguay. Ratification 2 Dec 52.
184 UNTS 358. Liberia. Ratification 29 Dec 52.
184 UNTS 358. Syria. Ratification 29 Dec 52.
184 UNTS 358. United Arab Rep. Ratification
30 Dec 52.
184 UNTS 358. Paraguay. Ratification 15 Jan 53.
184 UNTS 358. Panama. Ratification 10 Apr 53.
184 UNTS 358. Haiti. Ratification 1 May 53.
184 UNTS 358. Greece. Ratification 19 May 53.
184 UNTS 358. Honduras. Ratification 4 Sep 53.
199 UNTS 344. Lebanon. Ratification 7 Jan 54.
199 UNTS 344. Saudi Arabia. Ratification
13 Mar 54.
199 UNTS 344. Chile. Ratification 28 Apr 54.
260 UNTS 450. Philippines. Ratification
23 Jul 56.
260 UNTS 450. Iran. Ratification 29 Aug 56.

101833 Multilateral Protocol **136 UNTS 165**
SIGNED: 8 Sep 51 FORCE: 28 Apr 52
REGISTERED: 21 Aug 52 USA (United States)
ARTICLES: 7 LANGUAGE: English. French. Japa-
nese. Spanish.
HEADNOTE: CONTRACTS INSURANCE RESTORA-
TION PEACE JAPAN
TOPIC: General Military
CONCEPTS: Private contracts. General military. Ar-
mistice and peace. Post-war claims settlement.
PARTIES:
Australia SIGNED: 8 Sep 51 FORCE: 28 Apr 52
Belgium SIGNED: 8 Sep 51
Cambodia SIGNED: 8 Sep 51 FORCE: 2 Jun 52
Canada SIGNED: 8 Sep 51 FORCE: 28 Apr 52
Ceylon (Sri Lanka) SIGNED: 8 Sep 51 FORCE:
28 Apr 52
Dominican Republic SIGNED: 8 Sep 51 FORCE:
6 Jun 52
United Arab Rep SIGNED: 8 Sep 51
Ethiopia SIGNED: 8 Sep 51 FORCE: 12 Jun 52
France SIGNED: 8 Sep 51 FORCE: 28 Apr 52
Greece SIGNED: 8 Sep 51
Haiti SIGNED: 8 Sep 51
Indonesia SIGNED: 8 Sep 51
Iran SIGNED: 8 Sep 51

Iraq SIGNED: 8 Sep 51
Japan SIGNED: 8 Sep 51 FORCE: 28 Apr 52
Laos SIGNED: 8 Sep 51 FORCE: 20 Jun 52
Lebanon SIGNED: 8 Sep 51
Liberia SIGNED: 8 Sep 51
Luxembourg SIGNED: 8 Sep 51
Netherlands SIGNED: 8 Sep 51 FORCE:
17 Jun 52
Pakistan SIGNED: 8 Sep 51 FORCE: 28 Apr 52
Saudi Arabia SIGNED: 8 Sep 51
Syria SIGNED: 8 Sep 51
Turkey SIGNED: 8 Sep 51
UK Great Britain SIGNED: 8 Sep 51 FORCE:
28 Apr 52
Uruguay SIGNED: 8 Sep 51
Vietnam SIGNED: 8 Sep 51 FORCE: 18 Jun 52
ANNEX
163 UNTS 386. Turkey. Force 24 Jul 52.
163 UNTS 386. Belgium. Force 22 Aug 52.
179 UNTS 229. Greece. Force 19 May 53.
179 UNTS 229. Uruguay. Force 2 Dec 52.
179 UNTS 229. Liberia. Force 29 Dec 52.
179 UNTS 229. Syria. Force 29 Dec 52.
179 UNTS 229. United Arab Rep. Force
30 Dec 52.
179 UNTS 229. Haiti. Force 1 May 53.
199 UNTS 345. Lebanon. Force 7 Jan 54.
199 UNTS 345. Saudi Arabia. Force 13 Mar 54.
260 UNTS 451. Iran. Force 29 Aug 56.

101834 Bilateral Exchange **136 UNTS 203**
SIGNED: 8 Sep 51 FORCE: 28 Apr 52
REGISTERED: 21 Aug 52 USA (United States)
ARTICLES: 2 LANGUAGE: English.
HEADNOTE: ASSISTANCE GIVEN SUPPORT UN
ACTIONS
TOPIC: Milit Assistance
CONCEPTS: Non-prejudice to UN charter. Title and
deeds. Indemnities and reimbursements. Ex-
pense sharing formulae. Materials, equipment
and services. Defense and security.
INTL ORGS: United Nations.
PROCEDURE: Future Procedures Contemplated.
PARTIES:
Japan
USA (United States)

101835 Bilateral Treaty **136 UNTS 211**
SIGNED: 8 Sep 51 FORCE: 28 Apr 52
REGISTERED: 21 Aug 52 USA (United States)
ARTICLES: 5 LANGUAGE: English. Japanese.
HEADNOTE: SECURITY TREATY
TOPIC: General Military
CONCEPTS: Defense and security. Military assis-
tance.
INTL ORGS: United Nations.
TREATY REF: 136UNTS45.
PROCEDURE: Future Procedures Contemplated.
Ratification.
PARTIES:
Japan
USA (United States)
ANNEX
247 UNTS 392. Japan. Supplementation
6 Apr 54. Force 6 Apr 54.
247 UNTS 392. USA (United States). Supplemen-
tation 6 Apr 54. Force 6 Apr 54.

101836 Bilateral Exchange **136 UNTS 221**
SIGNED: 20 Jun 52 FORCE: 20 Jun 52
REGISTERED: 27 Aug 52 Netherlands
ARTICLES: 2 LANGUAGE: Dutch. German.
HEADNOTE: RELEASE SECURITIES
TOPIC: Reparations
CONCEPTS: Accounting procedures. Assets trans-
fer. Reparations and restrictions.
PARTIES:
Germany, West
Netherlands

101837 Bilateral Exchange **136 UNTS 229**
SIGNED: 25 Jun 52 FORCE: 25 Jun 52
REGISTERED: 29 Aug 52 Taiwan
ARTICLES: 2 LANGUAGE: Chinese. English.
HEADNOTE: GUARANTEES
TOPIC: Direct Aid
CONCEPTS: Guarantees and safeguards. Annex
type material. Arbitration. Currency. Monetary
and gold transfers. Claims and settlements. Eco-
nomic assistance.

INTL ORGS: International Court of Justice. Arbitration Commission.
PARTIES:
Taiwan
USA (United States)
ANNEX
284 UNTS 370. USA (United States). Amendment
3 May 57. Force 3 May 57.
284 UNTS 370. Taiwan. Amendment 3 May 57.
Force 3 May 57.
505 UNTS 308. Taiwan. Amendment 30 Dec 63.
Force 30 Dec 63.
505 UNTS 308. USA (United States). Amendment
30 Dec 63. Force 30 Dec 63.

101838 Bilateral Exchange **136 UNTS 238**
SIGNED: 14 Jul 48 FORCE: 14 Jul 48
REGISTERED: 3 Sep 52 USA (United States)
ARTICLES: 2 LANGUAGE: English. Spanish.
HEADNOTE: HEALTH SANITATION
TOPIC: Sanitation
CONCEPTS: Annex type material. Previous treaty
extension. Public health.
PARTIES:
Bolivia
USA (United States)
ANNEX
152 UNTS 323. USA (United States). Supplementation 24 Jul 51. Force 16 Oct 51.
152 UNTS 323. Bolivia. Supplementation
17 Sep 51. Force 16 Oct 51.
174 UNTS 297. USA (United States). Supplementation 27 Aug 51. Force 19 Oct 51.
174 UNTS 297. Bolivia. Supplementation
19 Oct 51. Force 19 Oct 51.
223 UNTS 331. Bolivia. Supplementation
27 Jun 52. Force 27 Jun 52.
223 UNTS 331. USA (United States). Supplementation 7 Feb 52. Force 27 Jun 52.
251 UNTS 381. USA (United States). Prolongation
25 Feb 55. Force 23 Mar 55.
251 UNTS 381. Bolivia. Prolongation 3 Mar 55.
Force 23 Mar 55.

101839 Bilateral Exchange **136 UNTS 258**
SIGNED: 27 Sep 47 FORCE: 27 Sep 47
REGISTERED: 3 Sep 52 USA (United States)
ARTICLES: 2 LANGUAGE: English. French.
HEADNOTE: HEALTH SANITATION
TOPIC: Sanitation
CONCEPTS: Annex type material. Previous treaty
extension. Public health.
PARTIES:
Haiti
USA (United States)
ANNEX
152 UNTS 330. Haiti. Supplementation
28 Sep 51. Force 28 Sep 51.
152 UNTS 330. USA (United States). Supplementation 23 Aug 51. Force 28 Sep 51.
177 UNTS 365. Haiti. Supplementation 9 Apr 52.
Force 9 Apr 52.
177 UNTS 365. USA (United States). Supplementation 3 Mar 52. Force 9 Apr 52.
177 UNTS 370. Haiti. Supplementation
31 Mar 52. Force 6 May 52.
177 UNTS 370. USA (United States). Supplementation 17 Oct 51. Force 6 May 52.
269 UNTS 306. USA (United States). Prolongation
28 Jan 55. Force 7 Feb 55.
269 UNTS 306. Haiti. Prolongation 3 Feb 55.
Force 7 Feb 55.

101840 Bilateral Exchange **136 UNTS 284**
SIGNED: 19 Apr 47 FORCE: 19 Apr 47
REGISTERED: 3 Sep 52 USA (United States)
ARTICLES: 2 LANGUAGE: English. Spanish.
HEADNOTE: HEALTH SANITATION
TOPIC: Sanitation
CONCEPTS: Annex type material. Previous treaty
extension. Public health.
PARTIES:
Peru
USA (United States)
ANNEX
223 UNTS 339. USA (United States). Supplemen-
tation 30 Jan 52. Force 9 Apr 53.
223 UNTS 339. Peru. Supplementation 9 Apr 53.
Force 9 Apr 53.
269 UNTS 310. USA (United States). Prolongation
23 Feb 55. Force 5 Apr 55.

269 UNTS 310. Peru. Prolongation 22 Mar 55. Force 5 Apr 55.

101841 Bilateral Agreement **136 UNTS 323**
SIGNED: 31 May 52　　FORCE: 18 Jun 52
REGISTERED: 5 Sep 52 WHO (World Health)
ARTICLES: 6 LANGUAGE: English. Spanish.
HEADNOTE: VACCINATION AGAINST WHOOP-ING-COUGH & DIPTHERIA
TOPIC: Sanitation
CONCEPTS: Annex or appendix reference. General cooperation. Operating agencies. Personnel. Public information. Public health. WHO used as agency. Vocational training. Research results. Research and development. Funding procedures. Domestic obligation. General technical assistance. Materials, equipment and services. IGO obligations.
INTL ORGS: United Nations Children's Fund.
PROCEDURE: Duration. Renewal or Revival.
PARTIES:
Chile
WHO (World Health)

101842 Unilateral Instrument **137 UNTS 3**
SIGNED: 24 Nov 51　　FORCE: 10 Dec 51
REGISTERED: 12 Sep 52 United Nations
ARTICLES: 1 LANGUAGE: English.
HEADNOTE: ACCEPTANCE ICJ JURISDICTION
TOPIC: ICJ Option Clause
CONCEPTS: Compulsory jurisdiction.
INTL ORGS: International Court of Justice. United Nations.
TREATY REF: 136UNTS45.
PARTIES:
Japan

101843 Unilateral Instrument **137 UNTS 7**
SIGNED: 23 Apr 52　　FORCE: 2 May 52
REGISTERED: 12 Sep 52 United Nations
ARTICLES: 1 LANGUAGE: English.
HEADNOTE: ACCEPTANCE ICJ JURISDICTION
TOPIC: UN Charter
CONCEPTS: Compulsory jurisdiction.
INTL ORGS: International Court of Justice.
TREATY REF: 136UNTS45.
PARTIES:
Ceylon (Sri Lanka)

101844 Unilateral Instrument **137 UNTS 11**
SIGNED: 17 Jul 52　　FORCE: 22 Jul 52
REGISTERED: 12 Sep 52 United Nations
ARTICLES: 1 LANGUAGE: French.
HEADNOTE: ACCEPTANCE ICJ JURISDICTION
TOPIC: UN Charter
CONCEPTS: Compulsory jurisdiction.
INTL ORGS: International Court of Justice.
TREATY REF: 136UNTS45.
PARTIES:
Cambodia

101845 Bilateral Treaty **137 UNTS 15**
SIGNED: 14 Dec 51　　FORCE: 9 Aug 52
REGISTERED: 19 Sep 52 India
ARTICLES: 9 LANGUAGE: English. Hindi. Turkish.
HEADNOTE: FRIENDSHIP
TOPIC: General Amity
CONCEPTS: Treaty interpretation. Friendship and amity. Alien status. Consular relations establishment. Diplomatic relations establishment. Privileges and immunities. Legal protection and assistance. Procedure.
PROCEDURE: Ratification.
PARTIES:
India
Turkey

101846 Bilateral Agreement **137 UNTS 27**
SIGNED: 11 Jul 52　　FORCE: 28 Jul 52
REGISTERED: 22 Sep 52 WHO (World Health)
ARTICLES: 4 LANGUAGE: English. Spanish.
HEADNOTE: TECHNICAL ASSISTANCE ANTIBIOT-·ICS
TOPIC: Tech Assistance
CONCEPTS: Conditions. Treaty implementation. Privileges and immunities. General cooperation. Exchange of information and documents. Informational records. Personnel. Scholarships and grants. Vocational training. Financial programs. Local currency. Domestic obligation. General technical assistance. Special projects. IGO status. Conformity with IGO decisions.
INTL ORGS: United Nations Children's Fund. United Nations.
TREATY REF: 76UNTS132; 33UNTS261.
PROCEDURE: Amendment. Application to Non-self-governing Territories.
PARTIES:
Chile
WHO (World Health)

101847 Bilateral Exchange **137 UNTS 43**
SIGNED: 23 Oct 51　　FORCE: 23 Oct 51
REGISTERED: 23 Sep 52 USA (United States)
ARTICLES: 2 LANGUAGE: English. Spanish.
HEADNOTE: ECONOMIC DEVELOPMENT MISSION
TOPIC: Direct Aid
CONCEPTS: Non-visa travel documents. Conformity with municipal law. General cooperation. Exchange of information and documents. Personnel. Public information. Indemnities and reimbursements. Financial programs. Tax exemptions. Customs exemptions. Domestic obligation. Economic assistance. Aid missions.
TREATY REF: U.S.-SALVADOR NOTE,27MAR51.
PROCEDURE: Amendment. Duration. Termination.
PARTIES:
El Salvador
USA (United States)

101848 Bilateral Agreement **137 UNTS 57**
SIGNED: 26 Feb 51　　FORCE: 26 Feb 51
REGISTERED: 23 Sep 52 USA (United States)
ARTICLES: 5 LANGUAGE: English. Hebrew.
HEADNOTE: TECHNICAL COOPERATION
TOPIC: Tech Assistance
CONCEPTS: Exceptions and exemptions. Treaty implementation. Previous treaty replacement. Diplomatic privileges. General cooperation. Exchange of information and documents. Personnel. Public information. Financial programs. Tax exemptions. Domestic obligation. General technical assistance. Materials, equipment and services.
PROCEDURE: Amendment. Duration. Termination.
PARTIES:
Israel
USA (United States)
ANNEX
219 UNTS 348. Israel. Amendment 21 Jun 54. Force 21 Jun 54.
219 UNTS 348. USA (United States). Amendment 21 Jun 54. Force 21 Jun 54.

101849 Bilateral Exchange **137 UNTS 69**
SIGNED: 26 Jan 51　　FORCE: 26 Jan 51
REGISTERED: 23 Sep 52 USA (United States)
ARTICLES: 2 LANGUAGE: English. Spanish.
HEADNOTE: AMENDING AGREEMENT CONSTRUCTION INTER-AMERICAN HIGHWAY
TOPIC: Land Transport
CONCEPTS: Conformity with municipal law. General cooperation. Licenses and permits. Recognition of legal documents. Private contracts. Expense sharing formulae. Fees and exemptions. Financial programs. National treatment. Tax exemptions. Materials, equipment and services. Registration certificate. Roads and highways.
INTL ORGS: Organization of American States.
TREATY REF: 21UNTS269.
PARTIES:
Panama
USA (United States)

101850 Bilateral Agreement **137 UNTS 81**
SIGNED: 3 Jun 51　　FORCE: 1 Aug 51
REGISTERED: 23 Sep 52 USA (United States)
ARTICLES: 37 LANGUAGE: English.
HEADNOTE: PARCEL POST
TOPIC: Postal Service
CONCEPTS: Detailed regulations. Previous treaty replacement. Conformity with municipal law. Payment schedules. Customs duties. Regulations. Insured letters and boxes. Conveyance in transit. Parcel post.
INTL ORGS: Universal Postal Union.
TREATY REF: 94LTS17.
PROCEDURE: Termination.

PARTIES:
UK Great Britain
USA (United States)

101851 Bilateral Agreement **137 UNTS 131**
SIGNED: 14 Aug 50　　FORCE: 1 Jan 50
REGISTERED: 23 Sep 52 USA (United States)
ARTICLES: 30 LANGUAGE: English. French.
HEADNOTE: EXCHANGE PARCEL POST
TOPIC: Postal Service
CONCEPTS: Detailed regulations. Previous treaty replacement. Payment schedules. Customs duties. Postal services. Regulations. Insured letters and boxes. Conveyance in transit. Parcel post. Rates and charges.
INTL ORGS: Universal Postal Union.
TREATY REF: UPOSTU CONVENTION; 195LTS259.
PROCEDURE: Duration. Ratification. Termination.
PARTIES:
USA (United States)
Yugoslavia

101852 Bilateral Exchange **137 UNTS 175**
SIGNED: 12 Dec 51　　FORCE: 12 Dec 51
REGISTERED: 23 Sep 52 USA (United States)
ARTICLES: 2 LANGUAGE: English. Italian.
HEADNOTE: COPYRIGHT LAWS
TOPIC: Patents/Copyrights
CONCEPTS: Conformity with municipal law. Domestic legislation. Laws and formalities. Postwar adjustment.
PARTIES:
Italy
USA (United States)

101853 Bilateral Agreement **137 UNTS 189**
SIGNED: 19 Sep 49　　FORCE: 26 Aug 52
REGISTERED: 24 Sep 52 Belgium
ARTICLES: 19 LANGUAGE: Arabic. French.
HEADNOTE: REGULAR AIR TRANSPORT SERVICES
TOPIC: Air Transport
CONCEPTS: Change of circumstances. Definition of terms. Detailed regulations. Exceptions and exemptions. Annex or appendix reference. Conformity with municipal law. General cooperation. Exchange of information and documents. Arbitration. Procedure. Existing tribunals. Negotiation. Non-interest rates and fees. Customs exemptions. Routes and logistics. Navigational conditions. Permit designation. Air transport. Conditions of airlines operating permission. Overflights and technical stops. Operating authorizations and regulations.
INTL ORGS: International Civil Aviation Organization. Arbitration Commission.
TREATY REF: 15UNTS295; 84UNTS389.
PROCEDURE: Amendment. Future Procedures Contemplated. Ratification. Registration. Termination. Application to Non-self-governing Territories.
PARTIES:
Belgium
United Arab Rep
ANNEX
271 UNTS 394. United Arab Rep. Amendment 18 Dec 56. Force 14 Jun 56.
271 UNTS 394. Belgium. Amendment 21 Nov 56. Force 14 Jun 56.

101854 Bilateral Agreement **137 UNTS 215**
SIGNED: 21 Jun 49　　FORCE: 26 Aug 52
REGISTERED: 24 Sep 52 Belgium
ARTICLES: 14 LANGUAGE: French. Greek.
HEADNOTE: AIR TRANSPORT
TOPIC: Air Transport
CONCEPTS: Exceptions and exemptions. Annex or appendix reference. Conformity with municipal law. General cooperation. Licenses and permits. Recognition of legal documents. Use of facilities. Arbitration. Procedure. Existing tribunals. Negotiation. Reexport of goods, etc.. Fees and exemptions. Most favored nation clause. National treatment. Customs exemptions. Competency certificate. Routes and logistics. Navigational conditions. Permit designation. Air transport. Airport facilities. Airworthiness certificates. Conditions of airlines operating permission. Operating

authorizations and regulations. Licenses and certificates of nationality.
INTL ORGS: International Civil Aviation Organization. Arbitration Commission.
TREATY REF: 15UNTS295.
PROCEDURE: Amendment. Future Procedures Contemplated. Registration. Registration. Termination. Application to Non-self-governing Territories.
PARTIES:
Belgium
Greece
ANNEX
216 UNTS 404. Greece. Amendment 13 Aug 55. Force 13 Aug 55.
216 UNTS 404. Belgium. Amendment 13 Aug 55. Force 13 Aug 55.

101855 Bilateral Exchange **137 UNTS 239**
SIGNED: 25 Jun 52   FORCE: 15 Jul 52
REGISTERED: 24 Sep 52 Belgium
ARTICLES: 2 LANGUAGE: French. Italian.
HEADNOTE: COLLECTIVE CONVEYANCE PERSONS
TOPIC: Visas
CONCEPTS: Time limit. Passports non-diplomatic. Visas. Tourism. Reexport of goods, etc.. Currency. Fees and exemptions.
PARTIES:
Belgium
Italy

101856 Bilateral Agreement **137 UNTS 249**
SIGNED: 21 Mar 52   FORCE: 1 Jul 52
REGISTERED: 24 Sep 52 Belgium
ARTICLES: 12 LANGUAGE: French.
HEADNOTE: INTERNATIONAL TRANSPORT GOODS ROAD
TOPIC: Land Transport
CONCEPTS: Territorial application. Licenses and permits. Recognition of legal documents. Investigation of violations. Establishment of commission. Fees and exemptions. Transport of goods. Driving permits. Motor vehicles and combinations. Roads and highways. Road rules. Boundaries of territory.
INTL ORGS: Special Commission.
PROCEDURE: Denunciation. Duration. Renewal or Revival.
PARTIES:
Belgium
France

101857 Bilateral Exchange **137 UNTS 259**
SIGNED: 30 Jun 52   FORCE: 15 Jul 52
REGISTERED: 24 Sep 52 Belgium
ARTICLES: 2 LANGUAGE: French.
HEADNOTE: EXEMPT TRAFFIC TAX DAILY COMMERCIAL TRANSPORT VEHICLES
TOPIC: General Transport
CONCEPTS: Territorial application. Tax exemptions. Customs exemptions. Registration certificate. Transport of goods. Commercial road vehicles.
TREATY REF: 45UNTS149; 137UNTS249.
PROCEDURE: Denunciation.
PARTIES:
Belgium
France

101858 Bilateral Treaty **138 UNTS 3**
SIGNED: 28 Apr 52   FORCE: 5 Aug 52
REGISTERED: 25 Sep 52 Taiwan
ARTICLES: 14 LANGUAGE: Chinese. English. Japanese.
HEADNOTE: TREATY PEACE
TOPIC: Peace/Disarmament
CONCEPTS: Treaty interpretation. Annex or appendix reference. Previous treaty renunciation. Non-prejudice to UN charter. Peaceful relations. Abolition of extraterritorial rights. Procedure. Negotiation. Air transport. Armistice and peace. Post-war claims settlement. Ocean resources.
INTL ORGS: United Nations.
TREATY REF: 136UNTS45.
PROCEDURE: Future Procedures Contemplated. Ratification.
PARTIES:
Taiwan
Japan

101859 Bilateral Exchange **138 UNTS 57**
SIGNED: 20 Apr 51   FORCE: 20 Apr 51
REGISTERED: 25 Sep 52 USA (United States)
ARTICLES: 2 LANGUAGE: English.
HEADNOTE: AMENDING
TOPIC: Land Transport
CONCEPTS: Conformity with municipal law. General cooperation. Licenses and permits. Recognition of legal documents. Private contracts. Expense sharing formulae. Fees and exemptions. Financial programs. National treatment. Tax exemptions. Materials, equipment and services. Registration certificate. Roads and highways.
TREATY REF: 24UNTS145.
PARTIES:
Nicaragua
USA (United States)

101860 Multilateral Exchange **138 UNTS 67**
SIGNED: 6 Mar 51   FORCE: 6 Mar 51
REGISTERED: 25 Sep 52 USA (United States)
ARTICLES: 2 LANGUAGE: English. German.
HEADNOTE: DEFENSE MATERIALS
TOPIC: Milit Assistance
CONCEPTS: Exceptions and exemptions. Materials, equipment and services. Defense and security. Military assistance. Raw materials.
PARTIES:
France SIGNED: 6 Mar 51 FORCE: 6 Mar 51
Germany, West SIGNED: 6 Mar 51 FORCE: 6 Mar 51
UK Great Britain SIGNED: 6 Mar 51 FORCE: 6 Mar 51
USA (United States) SIGNED: 6 Mar 51 FORCE: 6 Mar 51

101861 Bilateral Exchange **138 UNTS 75**
SIGNED: 5 Nov 45   FORCE: 5 Nov 45
REGISTERED: 25 Sep 52 USA (United States)
ARTICLES: 3 LANGUAGE: English.
HEADNOTE: CENTRAL COMMISSION RHINE
TOPIC: IGO Establishment
CONCEPTS: Funding procedures. Inland and territorial waters. Admission.
INTL ORGS: European Inland Transportation Organization. Central Commission for the Navigation of the Rhine.
TREATY REF: 1ORTF177; 3TIAS3493; EAS494.
PARTIES:
UK Great Britain
USA (United States)

101862 Multilateral Agreement **138 UNTS 85**
SIGNED: 28 Jun 46   FORCE: 28 Jun 46
REGISTERED: 25 Sep 52 USA (United States)
ARTICLES: 14 LANGUAGE: English. French. Russian.
HEADNOTE: CONTROL AUSTRIA
TOPIC: Milit Occupation
CONCEPTS: Democratic institutions. General military. Post-war reconstruction.
INTL ORGS: Allied Military Occupation. United Nations.
PARTIES:
France SIGNED: 28 Jun 46 FORCE: 28 Jun 46
UK Great Britain SIGNED: 28 Jun 46 FORCE: 28 Jun 46
USA (United States) SIGNED: 28 Jun 46 FORCE: 28 Jun 46
USSR (Soviet Union) SIGNED: 28 Jun 46 FORCE: 28 Jun 46

101863 Multilateral Instrument **138 UNTS 111**
SIGNED: 14 Aug 47   FORCE: 14 Aug 47
REGISTERED: 25 Sep 52 USA (United States)
ARTICLES: 9 LANGUAGE: English. French. Italian.
HEADNOTE: GERMAN ASSETS ITALY
TOPIC: Reparations
CONCEPTS: Definition of terms. Annex or appendix reference. Exchange of information and documents. Establishment of commission. Accounting procedures. Indemnities and reimbursements. Assets transfer. Enemy financial interests. Reparations and restrictions.
INTL ORGS: Special Commission.
TREATY REF: 49UNTS.
PARTIES:
France SIGNED: 14 Aug 47 FORCE: 14 Aug 47
Italy SIGNED: 14 Aug 47 FORCE: 14 Aug 47

UK Great Britain SIGNED: 14 Aug 47 FORCE: 14 Aug 47
USA (United States) SIGNED: 14 Aug 47 FORCE: 14 Aug 47

101864 Multilateral Agreement **138 UNTS 123**
SIGNED: 4 May 49   FORCE: 4 May 49
REGISTERED: 25 Sep 52 USA (United States)
ARTICLES: 1 LANGUAGE: English. French. Russian.
HEADNOTE: REMOVAL RESTRICTIONS BETWEEN BERLIN EASTERN WESTERN ZONES GERMANY
TOPIC: Milit Occupation
CONCEPTS: Control and occupation machinery.
PROCEDURE: Future Procedures Contemplated.
PARTIES:
France SIGNED: 4 May 49 FORCE: 4 May 49
UK Great Britain SIGNED: 4 May 49 FORCE: 4 May 49
USA (United States) SIGNED: 4 May 49 FORCE: 4 May 49

101865 Bilateral Protocol **138 UNTS 127**
SIGNED: 23 Jul 51   FORCE: 23 Jul 51
REGISTERED: 25 Sep 52 USA (United States)
ARTICLES: 2 LANGUAGE: English. Spanish.
HEADNOTE: APPOINTMENT CENSUS MISSION
TOPIC: Direct Aid
CONCEPTS: Personnel. Expense sharing formulae. Aid missions.
PARTIES:
El Salvador
USA (United States)

101866 Bilateral Protocol **138 UNTS 137**
SIGNED: 26 May 47   FORCE: 26 May 47
REGISTERED: 25 Sep 52 USA (United States)
ARTICLES: 2 LANGUAGE: English. Spanish.
HEADNOTE: CHANGE ALIGNMENT COLON CORRIDOR
TOPIC: Territory Boundary
CONCEPTS: Previous treaty amendment. Previous treaties adherence. Conformity with municipal law. Use of facilities. Markers and definitions.
TREATY REF: 200LTS17.
PARTIES:
Panama
USA (United States)

101867 Bilateral Agreement **138 UNTS 153**
SIGNED: 30 Jun 52   FORCE: 30 Jun 52
REGISTERED: 26 Sep 52 UK Great Britain
ARTICLES: 13 LANGUAGE: English. German.
HEADNOTE: MONEY PROPERTY
TOPIC: Reparations
CONCEPTS: Definition of terms. General provisions. General cooperation. Operating agencies. General property. Currency. Claims and settlements. Assets transfer. Loss and/or damage. Enemy financial interests. Post-war claims settlement.
PARTIES:
Austria
UK Great Britain

101868 Bilateral Agreement **138 UNTS 171**
SIGNED: 7 Jul 50   FORCE: 8 Jul 50
REGISTERED: 26 Sep 52 UK Great Britain
ARTICLES: 10 LANGUAGE: English.
HEADNOTE: STERLING PAYMENTS
TOPIC: Finance
CONCEPTS: Payment schedules.
TREATY REF: AGREEMENT-STERLING PAYMENTS, LOUELOU, 7 JULY 1950.
PROCEDURE: Duration. Termination.
PARTIES:
Finland
UK Great Britain
ANNEX
151 UNTS 387. UK Great Britain. Prolongation 7 Oct 52. Force 8 Oct 52.
151 UNTS 387. Finland. Prolongation 7 Oct 52. Force 8 Oct 52.
172 UNTS 389. UK Great Britain. Prolongation 7 Apr 53. Force 8 Apr 53.
172 UNTS 389. Finland. Prolongation 7 Apr 53. Force 8 Apr 53.
172 UNTS 389. UK Great Britain. Prolongation 17 Jun 53. Force 17 Jun 53.

172 UNTS 389. Finland. Prolongation 17 Jun 53. Force 17 Jun 53.
191 UNTS 404. UK Great Britain. Prolongation 30 Mar 54. Force 1 Apr 54.
191 UNTS 404. Finland. Prolongation 30 Mar 54. Force 1 Apr 54.
196 UNTS 352. UK Great Britain. Prolongation 17 Jun 54. Force 1 Jul 54.
196 UNTS 352. Finland. Prolongation 22 Jun 54. Force 1 Jul 54.

101869 Multilateral Agreement **138 UNTS 183**
SIGNED: 12 Jun 52   FORCE: 12 Jun 52
REGISTERED: 26 Sep 52 USA (United States)
ARTICLES: 9 LANGUAGE: English. French. Japanese. Spanish.
HEADNOTE: SETTLEMENT DISPUTES ARISING ARTICLE 15 (A) TREATY PERU WITH JAPAN
TOPIC: Dispute Settlement
CONCEPTS: Establishment of commission. Procedure. Claims and settlements.
INTL ORGS: International Court of Justice. Special Commission.
PARTIES:
Australia SIGNED: 12 Aug 52 FORCE: 12 Aug 52
Belgium SIGNED: 1 Jul 52 FORCE: 22 Aug 52
Cambodia SIGNED: 13 Aug 52 FORCE: 13 Aug 52
Canada SIGNED: 13 Jun 52 FORCE: 13 Jun 52
Ceylon (Sri Lanka) SIGNED: 16 Jun 52 FORCE: 16 Jun 52
Chile SIGNED: 8 Aug 52
Cuba SIGNED: 15 Aug 52 FORCE: 15 Aug 52
Dominican Republic SIGNED: 12 Jun 52 FORCE: 12 Jun 52
France SIGNED: 24 Jul 52 FORCE: 24 Jul 52
Greece SIGNED: 20 Jun 52
Haiti SIGNED: 15 Sep 52
Japan SIGNED: 12 Jun 52
Liberia SIGNED: 5 Aug 52
Mexico SIGNED: 11 Aug 52 FORCE: 11 Aug 52
New Zealand SIGNED: 19 Jun 52 FORCE: 19 Jun 52
Norway SIGNED: 9 Sep 52 FORCE: 9 Sep 52
Pakistan SIGNED: 16 Jul 52 FORCE: 16 Jul 52
Turkey SIGNED: 18 Jul 52 FORCE: 24 Jul 52
UK Great Britain SIGNED: 14 Jul 52 FORCE: 14 Jul 52
USA (United States) SIGNED: 19 Jun 52 FORCE: 19 Jun 52
ANNEX
150 UNTS 396. Argentina. Signature 3 Oct 52.
150 UNTS 396. Lebanon. Signature 3 Oct 52.
150 UNTS 396. Argentina. Force 3 Oct 52.
150 UNTS 396. Japan. Force 3 Oct 52.
184 UNTS 359. South Africa. Signature 7 Jan 53. Force 7 Jan 53.
184 UNTS 359. Netherlands. Signature Subject to Ratification 5 Mar 53. Force 10 Sep 53.
184 UNTS 359. Iraq. Ratification 15 May 53.
184 UNTS 359. Liberia. Force 29 Dec 52.
184 UNTS 359. Haiti. Force 1 May 53.
184 UNTS 359. Greece. Force 19 May 53.
199 UNTS 346. Venezuela. Signature 3 Feb 54. Force 3 Feb 54.
199 UNTS 346. Lebanon. Force 7 Feb 54.
199 UNTS 346. Chile. Force 28 Apr 54.

101870 Multilateral Convention **138 UNTS 207**
SIGNED: 29 Jun 49   FORCE: 20 Sep 52
REGISTERED: 29 Sep 52 ILO (Labor Org)
ARTICLES: 19 LANGUAGE: English. French.
HEADNOTE: LABOR CLAUSES PUBLIC CONTRACTS
TOPIC: ILO Labor
CONCEPTS: Definition of terms. Detailed regulations. Exceptions and exemptions. Exchange of information and documents. Incorporation of treaty provisions into national law. Private contracts. Investigation of violations. ILO conventions. Employment regulations. Holidays and rest periods. Labor statistics. Safety standards. Administering authority.
INTL ORGS: International Labour Organization. United Nations.
TREATY REF: 15UNTS35; 18UNTS386.
PROCEDURE: Amendment. Denunciation. Duration. Ratification. Registration. Renewal or Revival.
PARTIES:
Multilateral

ANNEX
149 UNTS 408. Italy. Ratification 13 Oct 52. Force 13 Oct 53.
163 UNTS 387. Israel. Ratification 30 Mar 53. Force 30 Mar 54.
184 UNTS 360. Philippines. Ratification 29 Dec 53. Force 29 Dec 54.
212 UNTS 397. France. Martinique.
212 UNTS 397. France. Guadeloupe.
212 UNTS 397. France. Reunion.
212 UNTS 397. France. French Guinea.
212 UNTS 397. Netherlands. Netherlands Antilles.
212 UNTS 397. Netherlands. Dutch New Guinea. Declaration 10 Jun 55.
212 UNTS 397. Netherlands. Surinam.
214 UNTS 373. Denmark. Ratification 15 Aug 55. Force 15 Aug 56.
222 UNTS 420. Bulgaria. Ratification 7 Nov 55. Force 7 Nov 56.
231 UNTS 363. Belgium. Belgian Colonies.
231 UNTS 363. Belgium. Ruanda-Urundi.
272 UNTS 260. Syria. Ratification 7 Jun 57. Force 7 Jun 58.
293 UNTS 380. UK Great Britain. Dominican Republic.
293 UNTS 380. UK Great Britain. Grenada.
293 UNTS 380. UK Great Britain. Jamaica.
293 UNTS 380. UK Great Britain. Singapore.
293 UNTS 380. UK Great Britain. British Honduras.
293 UNTS 380. UK Great Britain. Sarawak.
293 UNTS 380. UK Great Britain. Kenya.
293 UNTS 380. UK Great Britain. British Somaliland.
293 UNTS 380. UK Great Britain. Tanganyika.
293 UNTS 380. UK Great Britain. Uganda.
293 UNTS 380. UK Great Britain. Antigua.
293 UNTS 380. UK Great Britain. Bahamas.
293 UNTS 380. UK Great Britain. Burma.
293 UNTS 380. UK Great Britain. Aden Colony.
293 UNTS 380. UK Great Britain. British Guiana.
293 UNTS 380. UK Great Britain. Brunei.
293 UNTS 380. UK Great Britain. Cyprus.
293 UNTS 380. UK Great Britain. Gibralter.
293 UNTS 380. UK Great Britain. Gilbert Islands.
293 UNTS 380. UK Great Britain. Nigeria.
293 UNTS 380. UK Great Britain. Mauritius.
293 UNTS 380. UK Great Britain. St. Vincent.
293 UNTS 380. UK Great Britain. St. Lucia.
293 UNTS 380. UK Great Britain. North Borneo.
293 UNTS 380. UK Great Britain. Barbados.
293 UNTS 380. UK Great Britain. Zanzibar.
293 UNTS 380. UK Great Britain. Malta.
293 UNTS 380. UK Great Britain. Trinidad.
300 UNTS 373. UK Great Britain. Brit Virgin Islands.
356 UNTS 360. UK Great Britain. Sierra Leone.
356 UNTS 360. UK Great Britain. Fed Rhod/-Nyasaland.
366 UNTS 401. Costa Rica. Ratification 2 Jun 60. Force 2 Jun 61.
366 UNTS 401. UK Great Britain. Fiji Islands.
373 UNTS 368. United Arab Rep. United Arab Rep.
380 UNTS 421. Nigeria. Succession 17 Oct 60. Force 17 Oct 60.
381 UNTS 405. Cyprus. Succession 23 Sep 60. Force 23 Sep 60.
381 UNTS 405. Congo (Zaire). Succession 20 Sep 60. Force 20 Sep 60.
384 UNTS 362. Somalia. Succession 18 Nov 60. Force 18 Nov 60.
396 UNTS 329. Turkey. Ratification 29 Mar 61. Force 29 Mar 62.
396 UNTS 329. Ghana. Ratification 4 Apr 61. Force 4 Apr 62.
396 UNTS 329. UK Great Britain. Northern Rhodesia. Declaration 29 Mar 61.
401 UNTS 258. Sierra Leone. Ratification 15 Jun 61. Force 15 Jun 62.
413 UNTS 367. Syria. Ratification 30 Oct 61.
422 UNTS 334. Tanganyika. Succession 30 Jan 62. Force 30 Jan 62.
443 UNTS 340. Rwanda. Succession 18 Sep 62. Force 18 Sep 62.
443 UNTS 340. Cameroon. Succession 3 Sep 62. Force 3 Sep 62.
444 UNTS 335. Algeria. Succession 19 Oct 62.
452 UNTS 368. Jamaica. Succession 26 Dec 62.
455 UNTS 468. Cameroon. Ratification 29 Jan 63.
457 UNTS 360. Burundi. Succession 11 Mar 63.
471 UNTS 375. Uganda. Ratification 4 Jun 63.

483 UNTS 415. UK Great Britain. British Honduras.
483 UNTS 415. Mauritania. Ratification 8 Nov 63. Force 8 Nov 64.
488 UNTS 366. Kenya. Ratification 13 Jan 64. Force 13 Jan 64.
495 UNTS 301. Malaysia. State of Sabah. Succession 3 Mar 64.
495 UNTS 301. Malaysia. Sarawak. Succession 3 Mar 64.
495 UNTS 301. Malaysia. Singapore. Succession 3 Mar 64.
504 UNTS 357. Tanzania. Succession 22 Jun 64.
504 UNTS 357. Central Afri Rep. Ratification 9 Jun 64. Force 9 Jun 65.
510 UNTS 363. UK Great Britain. Swaziland.
522 UNTS 381. UK Great Britain. Bechuanaland.
541 UNTS 375. Brazil. Ratification 18 Jun 65. Force 18 Jun 66.
548 UNTS 403. Singapore. Ratification 25 Oct 65. Force 25 Oct 65.
551 UNTS 348. UK Great Britain. St. Christopher.
551 UNTS 348. UK Great Britain. Nevis.
551 UNTS 348. UK Great Britain. Anguilla.
567 UNTS 352. Guyana. Ratification 8 Jun 66. Force 8 Jun 66.

101871 Unilateral Convention **138 UNTS 225**
SIGNED: 1 Jul 49   FORCE: 24 Sep 52
REGISTERED: 29 Sep 52 ILO (Labor Org)
ARTICLES: 27 LANGUAGE: English. French.
HEADNOTE: PROTECTION WAGES
TOPIC: ILO Labor
CONCEPTS: Definition of terms. Detailed regulations. Exceptions and exemptions. Territorial application. Exchange of information and documents. Domestic legislation. Incorporation of treaty provisions into national law. ILO conventions. Wages and salaries. Administrative cooperation.
INTL ORGS: International Labour Organization. United Nations.
TREATY REF: 15UNTS35; 18UNTS386.
PROCEDURE: Amendment. Denunciation. Duration. Ratification. Registration. Renewal or Revival.
PARTIES:
Multilateral

ANNEX
149 UNTS 408.
184 UNTS 361.
196 UNTS 353.
201 UNTS 378.
212 UNTS 398.
219 UNTS 352.
222 UNTS 420.
231 UNTS 364.
248 UNTS 407.
258 UNTS 402.
266 UNTS 414.
272 UNTS 261.
293 UNTS 382.
300 UNTS 374.
302 UNTS 363.
304 UNTS 406.
312 UNTS 420.
323 UNTS 375.
356 UNTS 361.
361 UNTS 271.
366 UNTS 403.
373 UNTS 369.
380 UNTS 422.
381 UNTS 406.
384 UNTS 363.
386 UNTS 375.
388 UNTS 353.
390 UNTS 359.
396 UNTS 330.
396 UNTS 331.
399 UNTS 269.
401 UNTS 259.
406 UNTS 303.
413 UNTS 368.
416 UNTS 328.
422 UNTS 335.
434 UNTS 294.
443 UNTS 341.
444 UNTS 336.
449 UNTS 300.
455 UNTS 469.
471 UNTS 376.
495 UNTS 302.
504 UNTS 358.

522 UNTS 382.
524 UNTS 366.
560 UNTS 320.
567 UNTS 352.

101872 Multilateral Protocol **139 UNTS 3**
SIGNED: 3 Sep 46   FORCE: 1 Oct 46
REGISTERED: 1 Oct 52 USA (United States)
ARTICLES: 4 LANGUAGE: English. French. Portuguese. Spanish.
HEADNOTE: EXTENSION INTER-AMERICAN COFFEE AGREEMENT
TOPIC: Commodity Trade
CONCEPTS: Annex type material. Commodity trade.
INTL ORGS: Inter-American Coffee Board. Organization of American States. United Nations.
PROCEDURE: Accession. Registration.
PARTIES:
Brazil SIGNED: 1 Nov 46 FORCE: 1 Oct 46
Colombia SIGNED: 1 Nov 46 FORCE: 1 Oct 46
Costa Rica SIGNED: 1 Nov 46 FORCE: 1 Oct 46
Cuba SIGNED: 1 Nov 46 FORCE: 1 Oct 46
Dominican Republic SIGNED: 1 Nov 46 FORCE: 1 Oct 46
Ecuador SIGNED: 1 Nov 46 FORCE: 1 Oct 46
El Salvador SIGNED: 1 Nov 46 FORCE: 1 Oct 46
Guatemala SIGNED: 1 Nov 46
Haiti SIGNED: 1 Nov 46 FORCE: 1 Oct 46
Honduras SIGNED: 1 Nov 46 FORCE: 1 Oct 46
Mexico SIGNED: 1 Nov 46 FORCE: 1 Oct 46
Nicaragua SIGNED: 1 Nov 46 FORCE: 1 Oct 46
Peru SIGNED: 1 Nov 46 FORCE: 1 Oct 46
USA (United States) SIGNED: 1 Nov 46
Venezuela SIGNED: 1 Nov 46 FORCE: 1 Oct 46

101873 Bilateral Exchange **139 UNTS 29**
SIGNED: 14 Aug 52   FORCE: 1 Sep 52
REGISTERED: 1 Oct 52 Belgium
ARTICLES: 2 LANGUAGE: French. German.
HEADNOTE: RE-ENTRY FORCE CONVENTION ON CIVIL PROCEDURES
TOPIC: Admin Cooperation
CONCEPTS: Revival of treaties.
TREATY REF: 3'2DEMARTENS243;E.
PARTIES:
Belgium
Germany, West
             ANNEX
180 UNTS 356.   Belgium.   Confirmation 14 Aug 52. Force 14 Sep 53.
180 UNTS 356. Germany, West. Berlin. Force 15 Sep 53.

101874 Multilateral Exchange **139 UNTS 35**
SIGNED: 16 Apr 52   FORCE: 16 Apr 52
REGISTERED: 1 Oct 52 Belgium
ARTICLES: 4 LANGUAGE: English. French.
HEADNOTE: FINANCIAL AGREEMENT
TOPIC: General Economic
CONCEPTS: Definition of terms. Treaty interpretation. Previous treaty extension. Proxy diplomacy.
INTL ORGS: Allied Military Occupation. Universal Postal Union.
TREATY REF: 136UNTS45; 82UNTS147; 76UNTS113; 124UNTS3.
PROCEDURE: Amendment. Termination.
PARTIES:
Belgium SIGNED: 16 Apr 52 FORCE: 16 Apr 52
Japan SIGNED: 16 Apr 52 FORCE: 16 Apr 52
Luxembourg SIGNED: 16 Apr 52 FORCE: 16 Apr 52

101875 Bilateral Agreement **139 UNTS 45**
SIGNED: 25 Oct 45   FORCE: 30 Nov 45
REGISTERED: 2 Oct 52 USA (United States)
ARTICLES: 18 LANGUAGE: English. Spanish.
HEADNOTE: PARCEL POST
TOPIC: Postal Service
CONCEPTS: Conformity with municipal law. Domestic legislation. Payment schedules. Postal services. Regulations. Insured letters and boxes. Parcel post. Rates and charges.
TREATY REF: 131LTS447; UPOSTU.
PROCEDURE: Duration. Termination.
PARTIES:
Guatemala
USA (United States)

101876 Bilateral Exchange **139 UNTS 79**
SIGNED: 15 May 51   FORCE: 15 May 51
REGISTERED: 8 Oct 52 USA (United States)
ARTICLES: 2 LANGUAGE: English.
HEADNOTE: ECONOMIC COOPERATION
TOPIC: Direct Aid
CONCEPTS: Monetary and gold transfers. Currency deposits. Financial programs. Local currency. Commodities and services. General technical assistance. Economic assistance. Grants.
INTL ORGS: European Payments Union.
TREATY REF: 21UNTS29; USA'TIAS 2380;.
PARTIES:
Austria
USA (United States)

101877 Bilateral Exchange **139 UNTS 85**
SIGNED: 2 May 51   FORCE: 27 Feb 51
REGISTERED: 8 Oct 52 USA (United States)
ARTICLES: 3 LANGUAGE: English.
HEADNOTE: HIGHWAY PROJECT
TOPIC: Direct Aid
CONCEPTS: Annex type material. Resident permits. Non-visa travel documents. Visas. Conformity with municipal law. Personnel. Responsibility and liability. Indemnities and reimbursements. Exchange rates and regulations. Expense sharing formulae. Financial programs. Local currency. Tax exemptions. Customs exemptions. World Bank projects.
INTL ORGS: International Bank for Reconstruction and Development.
TREATY REF: 157UNTS213; 157UNTS233.
PROCEDURE: Amendment. Termination.
PARTIES:
Ethiopia
USA (United States)

101878 Bilateral Exchange **139 UNTS 105**
SIGNED: 29 Dec 45   FORCE: 29 Dec 45
REGISTERED: 8 Oct 52 USA (United States)
ARTICLES: 3 LANGUAGE: English. French.
HEADNOTE: AIR TRANSPORT SERVICES
TOPIC: Air Transport
CONCEPTS: Conditions. Annex type material. Routes and logistics. Air transport. Operating authorizations and regulations.
TREATY REF: 199LTS207.
PROCEDURE: Termination.
PARTIES:
France
USA (United States)

101879 Bilateral Agreement **139 UNTS 114**
SIGNED: 27 Mar 46   FORCE: 27 Mar 46
REGISTERED: 8 Oct 52 USA (United States)
ARTICLES: 13 LANGUAGE: English. French.
HEADNOTE: AIR SERVICES
TOPIC: Air Transport
CONCEPTS: Definition of terms. Annex or appendix reference. Previous treaty replacement. Non-prejudice to third party. Conformity with municipal law. General cooperation. Licenses and permits. Recognition of legal documents. Use of facilities. Procedure. Existing tribunals. Fees and exemptions. Most favored nation clause. National treatment. Customs exemptions. Competency certificate. Routes and logistics. Navigational conditions. Permit designation. Air transport. Airport facilities. Airworthiness certificates. Conditions of airlines operating permission. Overflights and technical stops. Operating authorizations and regulations. Licenses and certificates of nationality.
INTL ORGS: International Civil Aviation Organization.
TREATY REF: 15UNTS295; 199LTS207; 139UNTS105.
PROCEDURE: Amendment. Future Procedures Contemplated. Registration. Termination. Application to Non-self-governing Territories.
PARTIES:
France
USA (United States)
             ANNEX
358 UNTS 274. France. Prolongation 23 Jul 59. Force 23 Jul 59.
358 UNTS 274. USA (United States). Prolongation 23 Jul 59. Force 23 Jul 59.
458 UNTS 292. USA (United States). Supplementation 5 Apr 60. Force 5 Apr 60.

458 UNTS 292.   France.   Supplementation 5 Apr 60. Force 5 Apr 60.

101880 Bilateral Exchange **140 UNTS 3**
SIGNED: 23 Oct 51   FORCE: 23 Oct 51
REGISTERED: 8 Oct 52 USA (United States)
ARTICLES: 2 LANGUAGE: English. Spanish.
HEADNOTE: ADDITIONAL FINANCIAL CONTRIBUTIONS COOPERATIVE PROGRAM EDUCATION
TOPIC: Direct Aid
CONCEPTS: Exchange. Financial programs. General aid.
TREATY REF: USA&PANAMA'12OCT1950; COOPERATIVE EDUCATION PROGRA.
PARTIES:
Panama
USA (United States)

101881 Bilateral Agreement **140 UNTS 11**
SIGNED: 30 Sep 52   FORCE: 10 Oct 52
REGISTERED: 10 Oct 52 United Nations
ARTICLES: 6 LANGUAGE: English.
HEADNOTE: TECHNICAL ASSISTANCE
TOPIC: Tech Assistance
CONCEPTS: Treaty implementation. Privileges and immunities. General cooperation. Exchange of information and documents. Personnel. Title and deeds. Vocational training. Expense sharing formulae. Local currency. Domestic obligation. General technical assistance. Materials, equipment and services. IGO status. Conformity with IGO decisions.
TREATY REF: 76UNTS132; 1UNTS15,263.
PROCEDURE: Amendment. Duration. Termination.
PARTIES:
United Nations
Trieste

101882 Bilateral Convention **140 UNTS 23**
SIGNED: 18 Oct 46   FORCE: 17 Oct 49
REGISTERED: 13 Oct 52 USA (United States)
ARTICLES: 19 LANGUAGE: English. French.
HEADNOTE: DOUBLE TAXATION FISCAL ASSISTANCE
TOPIC: Taxation
CONCEPTS: Definition of terms. Territorial application. Previous treaty amendment. Previous treaty extension. Conformity with municipal law. General cooperation. Exchange of official publications. Negotiation. Claims and settlements. Taxation. Death duties. Tax credits.
TREATY REF: 125UNTS259.
PROCEDURE: Duration. Ratification. Termination.
PARTIES:
France
USA (United States)

101883 Bilateral Agreement **140 UNTS 57**
SIGNED: 28 Jul 50   FORCE: 28 Jul 50
REGISTERED: 13 Oct 52 USA (United States)
ARTICLES: 9 LANGUAGE: English. Korean.
HEADNOTE: EXPENDITURES FORCES UN
TOPIC: Finance
CONCEPTS: Treaty interpretation. Previous treaty replacement. Accounting procedures. Indemnities and reimbursements. Currency. Local currency. Claims and settlements.
INTL ORGS: United Nations.
PROCEDURE: Registration. Termination.
PARTIES:
Korea, South
USA (United States)

101884 Bilateral Convention **140 UNTS 73**
SIGNED: 21 Jan 46   FORCE: 1 Jul 47
REGISTERED: 13 Oct 52 USA (United States)
ARTICLES: 26 LANGUAGE: English. French.
HEADNOTE: EXCHANGE POSTAL MONEY ORDERS
TOPIC: Postal Service
CONCEPTS: Definition of terms. Conformity with municipal law. Accounting procedures. Exchange rates and regulations. Payment schedules. Postal services. Regulations. Money orders and postal checks. Rates and charges. Advice lists and orders.
PROCEDURE: Duration. Termination.

PARTIES:
Lebanon
USA (United States)

101885 Bilateral Exchange **140 UNTS 101**
SIGNED: 29 Aug 46 FORCE: 29 Aug 46
REGISTERED: 13 Oct 52 USA (United States)
ARTICLES: 2 LANGUAGE: English.
HEADNOTE: SETTLEMENT CLAIMS
TOPIC: Reparations
CONCEPTS: Annex or appendix reference. War claims and reparations.
PARTIES:
Luxembourg
USA (United States)

101886 Multilateral Protocol **140 UNTS 111**
SIGNED: 10 Feb 47 FORCE: 10 Feb 47
REGISTERED: 13 Oct 52 USA (United States)
ARTICLES: 2 LANGUAGE: English. French. Russian.
HEADNOTE: ESTABLISHMENT FOUR POWER NAVAL COMMISSION
TOPIC: Reparations
CONCEPTS: Annex or appendix reference. Establishment of commission. Naval vessels. Reparations and restrictions.
INTL ORGS: Allied Military Occupation.
PARTIES:
France SIGNED: 10 Feb 47 FORCE: 10 Feb 47
UK Great Britain SIGNED: 10 Feb 47 FORCE: 10 Feb 47
USA (United States) SIGNED: 10 Feb 47 FORCE: 10 Feb 47
USSR (Soviet Union) SIGNED: 10 Feb 47 FORCE: 10 Feb 47

101887 Multilateral Instrument **140 UNTS 129**
SIGNED: 10 May 48 FORCE: 10 May 48
REGISTERED: 13 Oct 52 USA (United States)
ARTICLES: 16 LANGUAGE: English. French. Spanish.
HEADNOTE: ELIMINATION ECONOMIC DANGER PEACE
TOPIC: Reparations
CONCEPTS: Definition of terms. Annex or appendix reference. Exchange of information and documents. General property. Arbitration. Procedure. Accounting procedures. Enemy financial interests. Reparations and restrictions. Post-war claims settlement.
PARTIES:
France SIGNED: 10 May 48 FORCE: 10 May 48
Spain SIGNED: 10 May 48 FORCE: 10 May 48
UK Great Britain SIGNED: 10 May 48 FORCE: 10 May 48
USA (United States) SIGNED: 10 May 48 FORCE: 10 May 48
ANNEX
351 UNTS 398. Spain. Termination 9 Aug 58. Force 2 Jul 59.
351 UNTS 398. UK Great Britain. Termination 9 Aug 58. Force 2 Jul 59.

101888 Multilateral Exchange **140 UNTS 187**
SIGNED: 13 May 48 FORCE: 13 May 48
REGISTERED: 13 Oct 52 USA (United States)
ARTICLES: 4 LANGUAGE: English. French.
HEADNOTE: AGREEMENT LOOTED GOLD
TOPIC: Reparations
CONCEPTS: Monetary and gold transfers. Enemy financial interests. Reparations and restrictions. Post war claims settlement.
PARTIES:
France SIGNED: 13 May 48 FORCE: 13 May 48
Bank Int Settlement SIGNED: 13 May 48 FORCE: 13 May 48
UK Great Britain SIGNED: 13 May 48 FORCE: 13 May 48
USA (United States) SIGNED: 13 May 48 FORCE: 13 May 48

101889 Multilateral Agreement **140 UNTS 196**
SIGNED: 8 Apr 49 FORCE: 8 Apr 49
REGISTERED: 13 Oct 52 USA (United States)
ARTICLES: 9 LANGUAGE: English. French.
HEADNOTE: ALLIED POWERS RESPONSIBILITES RESTORED GERMANY
TOPIC: Milit Occupation

CONCEPTS: Annex or appendix reference. Annex type material. Democratic institutions. Exchange of information and documents. Juridical personality. Establishment of commission. Reconversion to normalcy. Disarmament and demilitarization. Industrial controls. Control and occupation machinery. Withdrawal of occupation.
INTL ORGS: Allied Military Occupation. Organization for Economic Co-operation and Development.
TREATY REF: 68UNTS189.
PROCEDURE: Future Procedures Contemplated.
PARTIES:
France SIGNED: 8 Apr 49 FORCE: 8 Apr 49
UK Great Britain SIGNED: 8 Apr 49 FORCE: 8 Apr 49
USA (United States) SIGNED: 8 Apr 49 FORCE: 8 Apr 49
ANNEX
141 UNTS 400. US Occup Germ. Amendment 6 Mar 51. Force 7 Mar 51.
141 UNTS 400. French Occup Germ. Amendment 6 Mar 51. Force 7 Mar 51.
141 UNTS 400. British Occup Germ. Amendment 6 Mar 51. Force 7 Mar 51.

101890 Bilateral Exchange **140 UNTS 223**
SIGNED: 16 Aug 50 FORCE: 16 Aug 50
REGISTERED: 14 Oct 52 USA (United States)
ARTICLES: 2 LANGUAGE: English. Portuguese.
HEADNOTE: TECHNICAL ASSISTANCE OIL SHALE STUDIES
TOPIC: Tech Assistance
CONCEPTS: Time limit. General cooperation. Exchange of information and documents. Personnel. Research and development. Currency deposits. Financial programs. Funding procedures. Local currency. Domestic obligation. General technical assistance. Special projects.
PROCEDURE: Duration. Termination.
PARTIES:
Brazil
USA (United States)
ANNEX
184 UNTS 362. Brazil. Extension and Amendment 27 Jun 52. Force 20 Aug 52.
184 UNTS 362. USA (United States). Extension and Amendment 20 Aug 52. Force 20 Aug 52.
227 UNTS 330. USA (United States). Extension and Amendment 11 Aug 53. Force 31 Oct 53.
227 UNTS 330. Brazil. Extension and Amendment 31 Oct 53. Force 31 Oct 53.
237 UNTS 316. USA (United States). Prolongation 30 Jun 54. Force 30 Jun 54.
237 UNTS 316. Brazil. Prolongation 23 Jun 54. Force 30 Jun 54.
256 UNTS 344. USA (United States). Prolongation 27 Jul 55. Force 19 Oct 55.
256 UNTS 344. Brazil. Prolongation 19 Oct 55. Force 19 Oct 55.

101891 Bilateral Agreement **140 UNTS 239**
SIGNED: 28 Aug 51 FORCE: 28 Aug 51
REGISTERED: 14 Oct 52 USA (United States)
ARTICLES: 30 LANGUAGE: English. Spanish.
HEADNOTE: NAVAL MISSION
TOPIC: Military Mission
CONCEPTS: Definition of terms. Use of facilities. Compensation. Indemnities and reimbursements. Exchange rates and regulations. Expense sharing formulae. Tax exemptions. Customs exemptions. Military assistance. Military training. Security of information. Airforce-army-navy personnel ratio. Ranks and privileges. Conditions for assistance missions. Third country military personnel. Status of forces.
PROCEDURE: Denunciation. Duration. Renewal or Revival. Termination.
PARTIES:
Cuba
USA (United States)
ANNEX
204 UNTS 370. Cuba. Prolongation 14 Apr 53. Force 2 Jul 53.
204 UNTS 370. USA (United States). Prolongation 2 Jul 53. Force 2 Jul 53.
253 UNTS 360. Cuba. Prolongation 3 May 55. Force 17 May 55.
253 UNTS 360. USA (United States). Prolongation 17 May 55. Force 17 May 55.

101892 Bilateral Exchange **140 UNTS 259**
SIGNED: 19 Jul 51 FORCE: 19 Jul 51
REGISTERED: 14 Oct 52 USA (United States)
ARTICLES: 2 LANGUAGE: English. Spanish.
HEADNOTE: FISHERIES MISSION
TOPIC: Tech Assistance
CONCEPTS: Time limit. Diplomatic privileges. General cooperation. Exchange of information and documents. Personnel. Public information. Research and development. Expense sharing formulae. Tax exemptions. Domestic obligation. General technical assistance. Special projects.
PROCEDURE: Amendment.
PARTIES:
El Salvador
USA (United States)
ANNEX
180 UNTS 360. El Salvador. Prolongation 20 Nov 52. Force 20 Nov 52.
180 UNTS 360. USA (United States). Prolongation 20 Sep 52. Force 20 Nov 52.
204 UNTS 373. USA (United States). Prolongation 28 Aug 53. Force 28 Aug 53.
204 UNTS 373. El Salvador. Prolongation 18 Aug 53. Force 28 Aug 53.
239 UNTS 376. USA (United States). Prolongation 25 Jul 55. Force 25 Jul 55.
239 UNTS 376. El Salvador. Prolongation 13 Sep 54. Force 25 Jul 55.

101893 Bilateral Exchange **140 UNTS 273**
SIGNED: 16 Nov 51 FORCE: 16 Nov 51
REGISTERED: 14 Oct 52 USA (United States)
ARTICLES: 2 LANGUAGE: English.
HEADNOTE: COPYRIGHT LAWS
TOPIC: Patents/Copyrights
CONCEPTS: Conformity with municipal law. Domestic legislation. Post-war adjustment.
PARTIES:
Finland
USA (United States)

101894 Bilateral Agreement **140 UNTS 287**
SIGNED: 24 Apr 51 FORCE: 24 Apr 51
REGISTERED: 14 Oct 52 USA (United States)
ARTICLES: 18 LANGUAGE: English. Spanish.
HEADNOTE: COOPERATIVE EDUCATION PROGRAM
TOPIC: Education
CONCEPTS: Definition of terms. Detailed regulations. Friendship and amity. Alien status. Privileges and immunities. General cooperation. Inspection and observation. Domestic legislation. Personnel. General property. Private contracts. Specialists exchange. Education. Exchange. Commissions and foundations. Teacher and student exchange. Vocational training. Research and development. Accounting procedures. Indemnities and reimbursements. Currency. Exchange rates and regulations. Expense sharing formulae. Financial programs. Funding procedures. Tax exemptions. Customs exemptions. General technical assistance.
TREATY REF: 99UNTS49.
PROCEDURE: Amendment. Duration. Future Procedures Contemplated. Renewal or Revival. Termination.
PARTIES:
Honduras
USA (United States)
ANNEX
174 UNTS 301. Honduras. Supplementation 8 Sep 51. Force 8 Sep 51.
174 UNTS 301. USA (United States). Supplementation 7 Aug 51. Force 8 Sep 51.
177 UNTS 375. USA (United States). Supplementation 9 Jan 52. Force 7 Apr 52.
177 UNTS 375. Honduras. Supplementation 7 Apr 52. Force 7 Apr 52.
269 UNTS 314. USA (United States). Supplementation 27 Apr 55. Force 27 Apr 55.
269 UNTS 314. Honduras. Supplementation 27 Apr 55. Force 27 Apr 55.

101895 Bilateral Agreement **140 UNTS 313**
SIGNED: 17 Sep 51 FORCE: 17 Sep 51
REGISTERED: 14 Oct 52 USA (United States)
ARTICLES: 9 LANGUAGE: English.
HEADNOTE: SURGICAL HOSPITAL KOREA
TOPIC: Milit Assistance
CONCEPTS: General cooperation. Responsibility

and liability. Procedure. Humanitarian matters. Accounting procedures. Indemnities and reimbursements. Currency. Materials, equipment and services. Return of equipment and recapture.
INTL ORGS: United Nations.
PROCEDURE: Future Procedures Contemplated.
PARTIES:
Norway
USA (United States)

101896 Bilateral Agreement **140 UNTS 321**
SIGNED: 30 Jul 51 FORCE: 30 Jul 51
REGISTERED: 14 Oct 52 USA (United States)
ARTICLES: 9 LANGUAGE: English. Spanish.
HEADNOTE: COOPERATIVE AGRICULTURAL DEVELOPMENT
TOPIC: Direct Aid
CONCEPTS: Annex type material. Operating agencies. Personnel. Exchange. Vocational training. Indemnities and reimbursements. Expense sharing formulae. Tax exemptions. Customs exemptions. Domestic obligation. Agriculture. Materials, equipment and services.
TREATY REF: 92UNTS167.
PROCEDURE: Amendment. Duration. Termination.
PARTIES:
Panama
USA (United States)

101897 Bilateral Agreement **140 UNTS 335**
SIGNED: 17 Jan 51 FORCE: 17 Jan 51
REGISTERED: 14 Oct 52 USA (United States)
ARTICLES: 5 LANGUAGE: Arabic. English.
HEADNOTE: TECHNICAL COOPERATION
TOPIC: Direct Aid
CONCEPTS: Treaty implementation. Previous treaty replacement. Diplomatic privileges. General cooperation. Exchange of information and documents. Personnel. Public information. Financial programs. Tax exemptions. Customs exemptions. Domestic obligation. General technical assistance. Materials, equipment and services.
PROCEDURE: Amendment. Termination.
PARTIES:
Saudi Arabia
USA (United States)
ANNEX
179 UNTS 230. USA (United States). Amendment 22 Dec 51. Force 8 Jan 52.
179 UNTS 230. Saudi Arabia. Amendment 8 Jan 52. Force 8 Jan 52.

101898 Bilateral Agreement **140 UNTS 345**
SIGNED: 10 Aug 51 FORCE: 10 Aug 51
REGISTERED: 14 Oct 52 USA (United States)
ARTICLES: 31 LANGUAGE: English. Spanish.
HEADNOTE: ARMY MISSION
TOPIC: Military Mission
CONCEPTS: Definition of terms. Use of facilities. Compensation. Indemnities and reimbursements. Exchange rates and regulations. Expense sharing formulae. Tax exemptions. Customs exemptions. Military assistance. Military training. Security of information. Airforce-army-navy personnel ratio. Ranks and privileges. Conditions for assistance missions. Third country military personnel. Status of forces.
PROCEDURE: Denunciation. Duration. Renewal or Revival. Termination.
PARTIES:
USA (United States)
Venezuela
ANNEX
279 UNTS 308. USA (United States). Prolongation 11 Feb 57. Force 15 Feb 57.
279 UNTS 308. Venezuela. Prolongation 15 Feb 57. Force 15 Feb 57.
366 UNTS 405. USA (United States). Amendment 13 Mar 59. Force 29 Apr 59.
366 UNTS 405. Venezuela. Amendment 29 Apr 59. Force 29 Apr 59.

101899 Bilateral Exchange **140 UNTS 365**
SIGNED: 19 Dec 50 FORCE: 19 Dec 50
REGISTERED: 14 Oct 52 USA (United States)
ARTICLES: 3 LANGUAGE: English. Portuguese.
HEADNOTE: JOINT COMMISSION ECONOMIC DEVELOPMENT
TOPIC: Direct Aid

CONCEPTS: Annex or appendix reference. Conformity with municipal law. Establishment of commission. Expense sharing formulae. Economic assistance.
INTL ORGS: Special Commission.
PARTIES:
Brazil
USA (United States)
ANNEX
223 UNTS 346. USA (United States). Termination 20 Jul 53. Force 20 Jul 53.
223 UNTS 346. Brazil. Termination 20 Jul 53. Force 20 Jul 53.

101900 Bilateral Exchange **141 UNTS 3**
SIGNED: 19 Dec 50 FORCE: 19 Dec 50
REGISTERED: 14 Oct 52 USA (United States)
ARTICLES: 2 LANGUAGE: English. Portuguese.
HEADNOTE: TECHNICAL COOPERATION
TOPIC: Tech Assistance
CONCEPTS: Exceptions and exemptions. Treaty implementation. Previous treaty replacement. General cooperation. Exchange of information and documents. Personnel. Public information. Financial programs. Tax exemptions. Customs exemptions. Domestic obligation. General technical assistance. Materials, equipment and services.
PROCEDURE: Amendment. Termination.
PARTIES:
Brazil
USA (United States)
ANNEX
200 UNTS 306. USA (United States). Amendment 8 Jan 52. Force 8 Jan 52.
200 UNTS 306. Brazil. Amendment 8 Jan 52. Force 8 Jan 52.

101901 Bilateral Exchange **141 UNTS 15**
SIGNED: 9 Mar 51 FORCE: 9 Mar 51
REGISTERED: 14 Oct 52 USA (United States)
ARTICLES: 5 LANGUAGE: English. Spanish.
HEADNOTE: TECHNICAL COOPERATION
TOPIC: Tech Assistance
CONCEPTS: Exceptions and exemptions. Treaty implementation. Previous treaty replacement. Diplomatic privileges. General cooperation. Exchange of information and documents. Personnel. Public information. Exchange rates and regulations. Inadequacy of funds. Tax exemptions. Domestic obligation. General technical assistance. Materials, equipment and services.
PROCEDURE: Amendment. Duration. Termination.
PARTIES:
Colombia
USA (United States)
ANNEX
179 UNTS 235. USA (United States). Amendment 20 Dec 51. Force 27 Dec 51.
179 UNTS 235. Colombia. Amendment 27 Dec 51. Force 27 Dec 51.

101902 Bilateral Agreement **141 UNTS 27**
SIGNED: 3 May 51 FORCE: 3 May 51
REGISTERED: 14 Oct 52 USA (United States)
ARTICLES: 5 LANGUAGE: English. Spanish.
HEADNOTE: TECHNICAL COOPERATION
TOPIC: Tech Assistance
CONCEPTS: Exceptions and exemptions. Treaty implementation. Previous treaty replacement. Diplomatic privileges. General cooperation. Exchange of information and documents. Personnel. Public information. Funding procedures. Tax exemptions. Domestic obligation. General technical assistance. Materials, equipment and services.
PROCEDURE: Amendment. Duration. Termination.
PARTIES:
Ecuador
USA (United States)
ANNEX
179 UNTS 242. USA (United States). Amendment 21 Dec 51. Force 8 Jan 52.
179 UNTS 242. Ecuador. Amendment 8 Jan 52. Force 8 Jan 52.

101903 Bilateral Exchange **141 UNTS 37**
SIGNED: 18 Apr 51 FORCE: 18 Apr 51
REGISTERED: 14 Oct 52 USA (United States)
ARTICLES: 2 LANGUAGE: English. Spanish.

HEADNOTE: TECHNICAL COOPERATION
TOPIC: Tech Assistance
CONCEPTS: General cooperation. Public information. Vocational training. Domestic obligation. General technical assistance. Grants.
PARTIES:
El Salvador
USA (United States)

101904 Bilateral Exchange **141 UNTS 47**
SIGNED: 16 Mar 51 FORCE: 16 Mar 51
REGISTERED: 14 Oct 52 USA (United States)
ARTICLES: 2 LANGUAGE: English.
HEADNOTE: MUTUAL DEFENSE
TOPIC: Milit Assistance
CONCEPTS: Exceptions and exemptions. Friendship and amity. Non-prejudice to UN charter. Conformity with municipal law. Payment schedules. Materials, equipment and services. Military assistance. Restrictions on transfer.
INTL ORGS: United Nations.
PARTIES:
India
USA (United States)
ANNEX
461 UNTS 224. India. Supplementation 14 Nov 62. Force 14 Nov 62.
461 UNTS 224. USA (United States). Supplementation 14 Nov 62. Force 14 Nov 62.

101905 Bilateral Agreement **141 UNTS 55**
SIGNED: 27 Feb 51 FORCE: 27 Feb 51
REGISTERED: 14 Oct 52 USA (United States)
ARTICLES: 5 LANGUAGE: Arabic. English.
HEADNOTE: TECHNICAL COOPERATION
TOPIC: Tech Assistance
CONCEPTS: Exceptions and exemptions. Treaty implementation. Previous treaty replacement. Diplomatic privileges. General cooperation. Exchange of information and documents. Public information. Funding procedures. Tax exemptions. Domestic obligation. General technical assistance. Materials, equipment and services.
PROCEDURE: Amendment. Duration. Termination.
PARTIES:
Jordan
USA (United States)
ANNEX
179 UNTS 249. USA (United States). Amendment 3 Jan 52. Force 5 Jan 52.
179 UNTS 249. Jordan. Amendment 5 Jan 52. Force 5 Jan 52.

101906 Bilateral Exchange **141 UNTS 67**
SIGNED: 18 Jun 51 FORCE: 18 Jun 51
REGISTERED: 14 Oct 52 USA (United States)
ARTICLES: 2 LANGUAGE: Arabic. English.
HEADNOTE: MUTUAL DEFENSE
TOPIC: Milit Assistance
CONCEPTS: Exceptions and exemptions. Friendship and amity. Non-prejudice to UN charter. Conformity with municipal law. Accounting procedures. Indemnities and reimbursements. Payment schedules. Military assistance. Military training. Military assistance missions. Restrictions on transfer.
INTL ORGS: United Nations.
PARTIES:
Saudi Arabia
USA (United States)
ANNEX
212 UNTS 335. USA (United States). Implementation 27 Jun 53. Force 27 Jun 53.
212 UNTS 335. Saudi Arabia. Implementation 27 Jun 53. Force 27 Jun 53.

101907 Bilateral Agreement **141 UNTS 79**
SIGNED: 15 Jun 51 FORCE: 15 Jun 51
REGISTERED: 14 Oct 52 USA (United States)
ARTICLES: 6 LANGUAGE: English.
HEADNOTE: TECHNICAL ASSISTANCE
TOPIC: Tech Assistance
CONCEPTS: Exceptions and exemptions. Treaty implementation. Diplomatic privileges. General cooperation. Exchange of information and documents. Personnel. Public information. Establishment of commission. Financial programs. Funding procedures. Tax exemptions. Domestic obligation. General technical assistance. Materials, equipment and services.

INTL ORGS: Special Commission.
PROCEDURE: Duration. Termination.
PARTIES:
  UK Great Britain
  USA (United States)
          ANNEX
180 UNTS 364. UK Great Britain. Supplementation 7 Jan 52. Force 7 Jan 52.
180 UNTS 364. USA (United States). Supplementation 7 Jan 52. Force 7 Jan 52.
267 UNTS 380. UK Great Britain. Termination 12 Jun 52. Force 15 Sep 52.

101908 Bilateral Agreement **141 UNTS 89**
SIGNED: 10 Apr 52   FORCE: 10 Apr 52
REGISTERED: 15 Oct 52 United Nations
ARTICLES: 7 LANGUAGE: English.
HEADNOTE: DEMONSTRATION CENTER REHABILITATION PHYSICALLY HANDICAPPED
TOPIC: Tech Assistance
CONCEPTS: Detailed regulations. Exchange of information and documents. Inspection and observation. Title and deeds. Vocational training. Domestic obligation. General technical assistance. Special projects. Materials, equipment and services.
PROCEDURE: Amendment. Termination.
PARTIES:
  United Nations
  Yugoslavia

101909 Multilateral Agreement **141 UNTS 96**
SIGNED: 15 Oct 52   FORCE: 15 Oct 52
REGISTERED: 15 Oct 52 United Nations
ARTICLES: 6 LANGUAGE: English.
HEADNOTE: TECHNICAL ASSISTANCE
TOPIC: Tech Assistance
CONCEPTS: Treaty implementation. General cooperation. Exchange of information and documents. Personnel. Title and deeds. Exchange. Scholarships and grants. Vocational training. Research and development. Expense sharing formulae. Local currency. Domestic obligation. General technical assistance. Materials, equipment and services. IGO status. Conformity with IGO decisions.
TREATY REF: 76UNTS132; 33UNTS261.
PROCEDURE: Amendment. Termination.
PARTIES:
  United Arab Rep SIGNED: 15 Oct 52 FORCE: 15 Oct 52
  FAO (Food Agri) SIGNED: 15 Oct 52 FORCE: 15 Oct 52
  ICAO (Civil Aviat) SIGNED: 15 Oct 52 FORCE: 15 Oct 52
  ILO (Labor Org) SIGNED: 15 Oct 52 FORCE: 15 Oct 52
  UNESCO (Educ/Cult) SIGNED: 15 Oct 52 FORCE: 15 Oct 52
  United Nations SIGNED: 15 Oct 52 FORCE: 15 Oct 52
  WHO (World Health) SIGNED: 15 Oct 52 FORCE: 15 Oct 52
          ANNEX
480 UNTS 333. UNTAB (Tech Assis). Force 10 Sep 63.
480 UNTS 333. United Arab Rep. Force 10 Sep 63.

101910 Bilateral Exchange **141 UNTS 111**
SIGNED: 26 Sep 52   FORCE: 1 Oct 52
REGISTERED: 17 Oct 52 Belgium
ARTICLES: 2 LANGUAGE: French.
HEADNOTE: RECIPROCAL REPARATION WAR DAMAGES PRIVATE PROPERTY
TOPIC: Reparations
CONCEPTS: Definition of terms. Treaty implementation. General cooperation. Enemy financial interests. Reparations and restrictions. Post-war claims settlement.
PARTIES:
  Belgium
  Luxembourg
          ANNEX
425 UNTS 324. Belgium. Supplementation 20 Dec 61. Force 20 Dec 61.
425 UNTS 324. Luxembourg. Supplementation 20 Dec 61. Force 20 Dec 61.

101911 Multilateral Agreement **141 UNTS 121**
SIGNED: 17 Oct 52   FORCE: 17 Oct 52
REGISTERED: 17 Oct 52 United Nations
ARTICLES: 5 LANGUAGE: English.
HEADNOTE: ECONOMIC DEVELOPMENT
TOPIC: Direct Aid
CONCEPTS: Treaty implementation. Privileges and immunities. Personnel. Financial programs. Assets transfer. General technical assistance. Economic assistance. Materials, equipment and services. Conformity with IGO decisions.
INTL ORGS: United Nations Educational, Scientific and Cultural Organization.
TREATY REF: 126UNTS145.
PROCEDURE: Termination.
PARTIES:
  India SIGNED: 17 Oct 52 FORCE: 17 Oct 52
  Norway SIGNED: 17 Oct 52 FORCE: 17 Oct 52
  United Nations SIGNED: 17 Oct 52 FORCE: 17 Oct 52

101912 Multilateral Agreement **141 UNTS 129**
SIGNED: 21 Aug 52   FORCE: 21 Aug 52
REGISTERED: 17 Oct 52 United Nations
ARTICLES: 6 LANGUAGE: English. Spanish.
HEADNOTE: TECHNICAL ASSISTANCE INTER-AMERICAN CENTER BIOSTATICS
TOPIC: Tech Assistance
CONCEPTS: Definition of terms. Detailed regulations. Time limit. Privileges and immunities. General cooperation. Exchange of official publications. Informational records. Operating agencies. Personnel. Institute establishment. Vocational training. Expense sharing formulae. Domestic obligation. General technical assistance. Assistance. Materials, equipment and services. Grants. IGO status.
INTL ORGS: Special Commission.
PROCEDURE: Amendment. Duration. Termination.
PARTIES:
  Chile SIGNED: 21 Aug 52 FORCE: 21 Aug 52
  United Nations SIGNED: 21 Aug 52 FORCE: 21 Aug 52
  WHO (World Health) SIGNED: 21 Aug 52 FORCE: 21 Aug 52

101913 Bilateral Exchange **141 UNTS 159**
SIGNED: 14 May 51   FORCE: 14 May 51
REGISTERED: 17 Oct 52 USA (United States)
ARTICLES: 2 LANGUAGE: English.
HEADNOTE: USE FACILITIES RADIO CEYLON
TOPIC: Gen Communications
CONCEPTS: Indemnities and reimbursements. Non-interest rates and fees. Assets transfer. Tax exemptions. Customs exemptions. Commercial and public radio. Bands and frequency allocation. Facilities and equipment.
PROCEDURE: Duration. Termination.
PARTIES:
  Ceylon (Sri Lanka)
  USA (United States)
          ANNEX
445 UNTS 319. Ceylon (Sri Lanka). Extension and Amendment 30 Apr 62. Force 30 Apr 62.
445 UNTS 319. USA (United States). Extension and Amendment 30 Apr 62. Force 30 Apr 62.

101914 Bilateral Agreement **141 UNTS 169**
SIGNED: 13 Feb 51   FORCE: 3 Feb 51
REGISTERED: 17 Oct 52 USA (United States)
ARTICLES: 18 LANGUAGE: English. Spanish.
HEADNOTE: HEALTH SANITATION PROGRAM
TOPIC: Sanitation
CONCEPTS: Conditions. Definition of terms. Friendship and amity. General cooperation. Personnel. Programs. Specialists exchange. Disease control. Public health. Insect control. Nursing. Sanitation. Exchange. Research and development. Assistance. Special projects. Specific technical assistance.
TREATY REF: 92UNTS179.
PARTIES:
  Costa Rica
  USA (United States)
          ANNEX
165 UNTS 368. USA (United States). Supplementation 10 Jan 52. Force 24 Jan 52.
165 UNTS 368. Costa Rica. Supplementation 24 Jan 52. Force 24 Jan 52.
264 UNTS 363. USA (United States). Supplementation 25 Apr 55. Force 25 Apr 55.

264 UNTS 363. Costa Rica. Supplementation 25 Apr 55. Force 25 Apr 55.

101915 Bilateral Exchange **141 UNTS 191**
SIGNED: 11 May 51   FORCE: 11 Jun 51
REGISTERED: 17 Oct 52 USA (United States)
ARTICLES: 2 LANGUAGE: English. Spanish.
HEADNOTE: MODIFYING PREVIOUS AGREEMENT AGRICULTURAL EXPERIMENT STATION
TOPIC: Direct Aid
CONCEPTS: Annex type material. Agriculture.
TREATY REF: 122UNTS277.
PARTIES:
  El Salvador
  USA (United States)
          ANNEX
184 UNTS 369. El Salvador. Prolongation 8 Oct 52. Force 21 Oct 52.
184 UNTS 369. USA (United States). Prolongation 21 Oct 52. Force 21 Oct 52.
212 UNTS 350. El Salvador. Prolongation 21 Apr 53. Force 21 Apr 53.
212 UNTS 350. USA (United States). Prolongation 16 Apr 53. Force 21 Apr 53.
215 UNTS 421. El Salvador. Prolongation 30 Jul 53. Force 30 Jun 53.
215 UNTS 421. USA (United States). Prolongation 30 Jun 53. Force 30 Jun 53.

101916 Bilateral Exchange **141 UNTS 211**
SIGNED: 27 Jun 51   FORCE: 27 Jun 51
REGISTERED: 17 Oct 52 USA (United States)
ARTICLES: 2 LANGUAGE: English. Spanish.
HEADNOTE: TECHNICAL COOPERATION
TOPIC: Tech Assistance
CONCEPTS: Exceptions and exemptions. Treaty implementation. Previous treaty replacement. Privileges and immunities. General cooperation. Exchange of information and documents. Public information. Funding procedures. Taxation. Tax exemptions. Customs duties. Domestic obligation. General technical assistance. Materials, equipment and services.
TREATY REF: 125UNTS301.
PROCEDURE: Amendment. Termination.
PARTIES:
  Mexico
  USA (United States)
          ANNEX
200 UNTS 312. Mexico. Implementation 22 Jan 52. Force 22 Jan 52.
200 UNTS 312. USA (United States). Implementation 21 Jan 52. Force 22 Jan 52.
233 UNTS 306. USA (United States). Amendment 13 Apr 54. Force 13 Apr 54.
233 UNTS 306. Mexico. Amendment 13 Apr 54. Force 13 Apr 54.

101917 Bilateral Instrument **141 UNTS 221**
SIGNED: 19 Jan 51   FORCE: 19 Jan 51
REGISTERED: 17 Oct 52 USA (United States)
ARTICLES: 1 LANGUAGE: English.
HEADNOTE: CLAIMS LOOTED SECURITIES
TOPIC: Reparations
CONCEPTS: Annex or appendix reference. Exchange of information and documents. Accounting procedures. Indemnities and reimbursements. Assets transfer. Post-war claims settlement.
INTL ORGS: United Nations.
PARTIES:
  Netherlands
  USA (United States)

101918 Bilateral Exchange **141 UNTS 273**
SIGNED: 7 Jun 51   FORCE: 7 Jun 51
REGISTERED: 17 Oct 52 USA (United States)
ARTICLES: 2 LANGUAGE: English. Spanish.
HEADNOTE: TECHNICAL COOPERATION TRAINING GRANTS
TOPIC: Tech Assistance
CONCEPTS: Detailed regulations. General cooperation. Public information. Vocational training. Domestic obligation. General technical assistance. Technical cooperation.

PROCEDURE: Termination.
PARTIES:
USA (United States)
Venezuela
ANNEX
205 UNTS 331. USA (United States). Amendment
18 Apr 52. Force 18 Apr 52.
205 UNTS 331. Venezuela. Amendment
8 Jan 52. Force 18 Apr 52.

101919 Multilateral Agreement **141 UNTS 281**
SIGNED: 14 Apr 49　　　　FORCE: 14 Apr 51
REGISTERED: 17 Oct 52 USA (United States)
ARTICLES: 12 LANGUAGE: English. French.
HEADNOTE: PROHIBITED LIMITED INDUSTRIES
TOPIC: Milit Occupation
CONCEPTS: Time limit. Treaty implementation.
Annex or appendix reference. Merchant vessels.
Disarmament and demilitarization. Industrial
controls.
INTL ORGS: Allied Military Occupation.
PROCEDURE: Future Procedures Contemplated.
PARTIES:
French Occup Germ SIGNED: 14 Apr 49 FORCE:
14 Apr 49
British Occup Germ SIGNED: 14 Apr 49 FORCE:
14 Apr 49
US Occup Germ SIGNED: 14 Apr 49 FORCE:
14 Apr 49

101920 Multilateral Agreement **141 UNTS 303**
SIGNED: 3 Apr 51　　　　FORCE: 3 Apr 51
REGISTERED: 17 Oct 52 USA (United States)
ARTICLES: 9 LANGUAGE: English. French.
HEADNOTE: INDUSTRIAL CONTROLS
TOPIC: Milit Occupation
CONCEPTS: Time limit. Annex or appendix refer-
ence. Merchant vessels. Disarmament and
demilitarization. Industrial controls.
INTL ORGS: Allied Military Occupation.
PARTIES:
France SIGNED: 3 Apr 51 FORCE: 3 Apr 51
UK Great Britain SIGNED: 3 Apr 51 FORCE:
3 Apr 51
USA (United States) SIGNED: 3 Apr 51 FORCE:
3 Apr 51
ANNEX
181 UNTS 362. France. Amendment 25 Jul 52.
Force 25 Jul 52.
181 UNTS 362. USA (United States). Amendment
25 Jul 52. Force 25 Jul 52.
181 UNTS 362. UK Great Britain. Amendment
25 Jul 52. Force 25 Jul 52.
185 UNTS 404. UK Great Britain. Supplementation 31 Dec 52. Force 1 Jan 53.
185 UNTS 404. France. Supplementation
31 Dec 52. Force 1 Jan 53.
185 UNTS 404. USA (United States). Supplementation 31 Dec 52. Force 1 Jan 53.

101921 Bilateral Exchange **141 UNTS 319**
SIGNED: 2 Mar 49　　　　FORCE: 2 Mar 49
REGISTERED: 23 Oct 52 Pakistan
ARTICLES: 2 LANGUAGE: English.
HEADNOTE: MUTUAL GRANT VISAS
TOPIC: Visas
CONCEPTS: Visas.
PARTIES:
Iraq
Pakistan

101922 Bilateral Exchange **141 UNTS 325**
SIGNED: 27 May 49　　　　FORCE: 25 Jun 49
REGISTERED: 23 Oct 52 Pakistan
ARTICLES: 2 LANGUAGE: English.
HEADNOTE: MUTUAL GRANT VISAS
TOPIC: Visas
CONCEPTS: Time limit. Passports diplomatic.
Visas.
PARTIES:
Pakistan
Turkey

101923 Bilateral Exchange **141 UNTS 333**
SIGNED: 18 Oct 49　　　　FORCE: 15 Nov 49
REGISTERED: 23 Oct 52 Pakistan
ARTICLES: 2 LANGUAGE: English.
HEADNOTE: MUTUAL REDUCTION VISA FEES
TOPIC: Visas

CONCEPTS: Tourism. Fees and exemptions.
PARTIES:
Pakistan
USA (United States)
ANNEX
204 UNTS 378. USA (United States). Amendment
8 Apr 53. Force 8 Apr 53.
204 UNTS 378. Pakistan. Amendment 19 Mar 53.
Force 8 Apr 53.
240 UNTS 438. USA (United States). Amendment
25 Nov 55. Force 1 Dec 55.
240 UNTS 438. Pakistan. Amendment 29 Nov 55.
Force 1 Dec 55.

101924 Bilateral Protocol **147 UNTS 3**
SIGNED: 7 Feb 52　　　　FORCE: 7 Feb 52
REGISTERED: 29 Oct 52 Belgium
ARTICLES: 2 LANGUAGE: French.
HEADNOTE: DOUBLE TAXATION DIRECT TAXES
TOPIC: Taxation
CONCEPTS: Previous treaty amendment. Annex
type material. Taxation. General.
TREATY REF: 137LTS267.
PARTIES:
Belgium
Luxembourg

101925 Bilateral Agreement **147 UNTS 11**
SIGNED: 16 Jan 51　　　　FORCE: 16 Jan 51
REGISTERED: 29 Oct 52 USA (United States)
ARTICLES: 18 LANGUAGE: English. Spanish.
HEADNOTE: FINANCE COMMERCE
TOPIC: Education
CONCEPTS: Definition of terms. Annex or appen-
dix reference. Previous treaty replacement. Dip-
lomatic relations resumption. General property.
Public information. Use of facilities. Finances
and payments. Banking. Bonds. Claims, debts
and assets. Claims and settlements. Lump sum
settlements.
PARTIES:
Chile
USA (United States)

101926 Bilateral Exchange **147 UNTS 33**
SIGNED: 27 Dec 50　　　　FORCE: 13 Feb 51
REGISTERED: 29 Oct 52 USA (United States)
ARTICLES: 2 LANGUAGE: English. Portuguese.
HEADNOTE: HEALTH SANITATION PROGRAM
TOPIC: Sanitation
CONCEPTS: Annex type material. Previous treaty
extension. Friendship and amity. Personnel. Disease control. Public health. Sanitation. Indemnities and reimbursements. Currency. Expense
sharing formulae. Funding procedures. Assistance. Special projects. Specific technical assistance. Economic assistance.
PROCEDURE: Duration.
PARTIES:
Brazil
USA (United States)
ANNEX
165 UNTS 374. USA (United States). Supplementation 28 Dec 51. Force 31 Dec 51.
165 UNTS 374. Brazil. Supplementation
29 Dec 51. Force 31 Dec 51.
177 UNTS 382. USA (United States). Supplementation 28 Feb 52. Force 8 Jul 52.
177 UNTS 382. Brazil. Supplementation
18 Apr 52. Force 8 Jul 52.
263 UNTS 413. USA (United States). Prolongation
8 Feb 55. Force 8 Feb 55.
263 UNTS 413. Brazil. Prolongation 7 Jan 55.
Force 8 Feb 55.
371 UNTS 290. Brazil. Extension and Amendment
31 Dec 59. Force 31 Dec 59.
371 UNTS 290. USA (United States). Extension
and Amendment 31 Dec 59. Force 31 Dec 59.

101927 Bilateral Agreement **147 UNTS 43**
SIGNED: 9 Jul 51　　　　FORCE: 9 Jul 51
REGISTERED: 29 Oct 52 USA (United States)
ARTICLES: 4 LANGUAGE: English.
HEADNOTE: INLAND TRANSPORTATION
CHARGES
TOPIC: Customs
CONCEPTS: Customs exemptions. Relief supplies.
Transport of goods.
PROCEDURE: Duration. Termination.

PARTIES:
India
USA (United States)
ANNEX
223 UNTS 354. USA (United States). Implementation 17 Oct 51. Force 26 Mar 52.
223 UNTS 354. India. Implementation 26 Mar 52.
Force 26 Mar 52.
223 UNTS 358. India. Prolongation 27 Aug 52.
Force 27 Aug 52.
223 UNTS 358. USA (United States). Prolongation
26 Aug 52. Force 27 Aug 52.
545 UNTS 326. USA (United States). Amendment
21 Jan 61. Force 21 Jan 65.
545 UNTS 326. India. Amendment 21 Jan 61.
Force 21 Jan 65.

101928 Bilateral Agreement **147 UNTS 49**
SIGNED: 23 Aug 51　　　　FORCE: 23 Aug 51
REGISTERED: 29 Oct 52 USA (United States)
ARTICLES: 13 LANGUAGE: Danish. English.
HEADNOTE: EDUCATIONAL EXCHANGE PRO-
GRAM
TOPIC: Education
CONCEPTS: Definition of terms. Standardization.
Conformity with municipal law. Exchange of information and documents. Personnel. General
property. Exchange. Commissions and foundations. Teacher and student exchange. Professorships. Scholarships and grants. Research and
development. Accounting procedures. Indemnities and reimbursements. Currency. Exchange
rates and regulations. Funding procedures. Purchase authorization.
PARTIES:
Denmark
USA (United States)
ANNEX
272 UNTS 262. USA (United States). Amendment
17 Feb 56. Force 17 Feb 56.
272 UNTS 262. Denmark. Amendment
17 Feb 56. Force 17 Feb 56.

101929 Bilateral Agreement **147 UNTS 65**
SIGNED: 16 Aug 51　　　　FORCE: 16 Aug 51
REGISTERED: 29 Oct 52 USA (United States)
ARTICLES: 12 LANGUAGE: Arabic. English.
HEADNOTE: EDUCATIONAL EXCHANGE PRO-
GRAM
TOPIC: Education
CONCEPTS: Definition of terms. Standardization.
Conformity with municipal law. Exchange of in-
formation and documents. Personnel. General
property. Commissions and foundations.
Teacher and student exchange. Professorships.
Scholarships and grants. Research and develop-
ment. Accounting procedures. Indemnities and
reimbursements. Currency. Exchange rates and
regulations. Funding procedures. Purchase au-
thorization.
PARTIES:
Iraq
USA (United States)

101930 Bilateral Exchange **147 UNTS 81**
SIGNED: 28 Aug 51　　　　FORCE: 28 Aug 51
REGISTERED: 29 Oct 52 USA (United States)
ARTICLES: 2 LANGUAGE: English. Japanese.
HEADNOTE: EDUCATIONAL COMMISSION
TOPIC: Education
CONCEPTS: Definition of terms. Annex or appen-
dix reference. Friendship and amity. Privileges
and immunities. Conformity with municipal law.
Inspection and observation. Personnel. General
property. Specialists exchange. Exchange. Com-
missions and foundations. Teacher and student
exchange. Vocational training. Research and de-
velopment. Accounting procedures. Indemnities
and reimbursements. Currency. Financial pro-
grams. Funding procedures. Aid missions.
INTL ORGS: International Monetary Fund. Special
Commission.
PARTIES:
Japan
USA (United States)

101931 Bilateral Agreement **148 UNTS 3**
SIGNED: 20 Jun 51　　　　FORCE: 20 Jun 51
REGISTERED: 30 Oct 52 USA (United States)
ARTICLES: 5 LANGUAGE: English. Spanish.

HEADNOTE: TECHNICAL COOPERATION
TOPIC: Tech Assistance
CONCEPTS: Exceptions and exemptions. Treaty implementation. Previous treaty replacement. General cooperation. Exchange of information and documents. Personnel. Public information. Funding procedures. Tax exemptions. Customs exemptions. Domestic obligation. General technical assistance. Materials, equipment and services.
PROCEDURE: Amendment. Duration. Termination.
PARTIES:
Cuba
USA (United States)
ANNEX
179 UNTS 254. USA (United States). Amendment 7 Jan 52. Force 8 Jan 52.
179 UNTS 254. Cuba. Amendment 8 Jan 52. Force 8 Jan 52.

101932 Bilateral Exchange **148 UNTS 15**
SIGNED: 16 Mar 51   FORCE: 16 Mar 51
REGISTERED: 30 Oct 52 USA (United States)
ARTICLES: 2 LANGUAGE: English. Spanish.
HEADNOTE: VOCATIONAL EDUCATION
TOPIC: Education
CONCEPTS: Definition of terms. Friendship and amity. Privileges and immunities. Conformity with municipal law. General cooperation. Exchange of information and documents. Inspection and observation. Personnel. General property. Specialists exchange. Exchange. Commissions and foundations. Vocational training. Research and development. Indemnities and reimbursements. Expense sharing formulae. Financial programs. Funding procedures.
TREATY REF: 132UNTS305.
PROCEDURE: Amendment. Duration. Termination.
PARTIES:
Dominican Republic
USA (United States)
ANNEX
152 UNTS 334. USA (United States). Supplementation 10 Sep 51. Force 19 Sep 51.
152 UNTS 334. Dominican Republic. Supplementation 19 Sep 51. Force 19 Sep 51.
177 UNTS 389. USA (United States). Supplementation 12 Feb 52. Force 4 Apr 52.
177 UNTS 389. Dominican Republic. Supplementation 4 Apr 52. Force 4 Apr 52.
236 UNTS 388. USA (United States). Amendment 19 Feb 54. Force 19 Mar 54.
236 UNTS 388. Dominican Republic. Amendment 19 Mar 54. Force 19 Mar 54.
269 UNTS 317. USA (United States). Prolongation 19 Apr 55. Force 5 May 55.
269 UNTS 317. Dominican Republic. Prolongation 5 May 55. Force 5 May 55.
378 UNTS 371. USA (United States). Extension and Amendment 2 Jun 60. Force 7 Jun 60.
378 UNTS 371. Dominican Republic. Extension and Amendment 7 Jun 60. Force 7 Jun 60.

101933 Bilateral Agreement **148 UNTS 39**
SIGNED: 16 Jun 51   FORCE: 16 Jun 51
REGISTERED: 30 Oct 52 USA (United States)
ARTICLES: 5 LANGUAGE: English.
HEADNOTE: TECHNICAL COOPERATION
TOPIC: Tech Assistance
CONCEPTS: Exceptions and exemptions. Treaty implementation. Previous treaty replacement. Diplomatic privileges. General cooperation. Exchange of information and documents. Public information. Funding procedures. Tax exemptions. Domestic obligation. General technical assistance. Materials, equipment and services.
PROCEDURE: Amendment. Duration. Termination.
PARTIES:
Ethiopia
USA (United States)
ANNEX
179 UNTS 261. USA (United States). Amendment 8 Jan 52. Force 8 Jan 52.
179 UNTS 261. Ethiopia. Amendment 27 Dec 51. Force 8 Jan 52.
205 UNTS 340. USA (United States). Implementation 24 Dec 52. Force 30 Mar 53.
205 UNTS 340. Ethiopia. Eritrea.
232 UNTS 340. USA (United States). Acknowledgement 18 May 54. Force 12 Jun 54.
232 UNTS 340. Ethiopia. Eritrea. Force 12 Jun 54.

273 UNTS 250. USA (United States). Prolongation 4 Apr 56. Force 12 Jun 56.
273 UNTS 250. Ethiopia. Prolongation 12 Jun 56. Force 12 Jun 56.

101934 Bilateral Exchange **148 UNTS 49**
SIGNED: 11 Jan 51   FORCE: 11 Jan 51
REGISTERED: 30 Oct 52 USA (United States)
ARTICLES: 2 LANGUAGE: English.
HEADNOTE: EXCHANGE OFFICIAL PUBLICATIONS
TOPIC: Admin Cooperation
CONCEPTS: Exchange of official publications.
PARTIES:
India
USA (United States)

101935 Bilateral Exchange **148 UNTS 57**
SIGNED: 13 Feb 51   FORCE: 13 Feb 51
REGISTERED: 30 Oct 52 USA (United States)
ARTICLES: 2 LANGUAGE: English. Italian.
HEADNOTE: US ITALY CONCILIATION COMMISSION
TOPIC: IGO Establishment
CONCEPTS: Conciliation. Funding procedures. Admission.
INTL ORGS: Conciliation Commission.
TREATY REF: 49UNTS; 50UNTS.
PROCEDURE: Denunciation.
PARTIES:
Italy
USA (United States)

101936 Multilateral Agreement **148 UNTS 67**
SIGNED: 15 Jun 51   FORCE: 15 Jun 51
REGISTERED: 30 Oct 52 USA (United States)
ARTICLES: 6 LANGUAGE: English. French.
HEADNOTE: TECHNICAL ASSISTANCE
TOPIC: Tech Assistance
CONCEPTS: Detailed regulations. Exceptions and exemptions. Diplomatic privileges. Exchange of information and documents. Public information. Establishment of commission. Financial programs. Tax exemptions. Domestic obligation. General technical assistance. Materials, equipment and services.
INTL ORGS: Special Commission.
PROCEDURE: Duration. Termination.
PARTIES:
France SIGNED: 15 Jun 51 FORCE: 15 Jun 51
UK Great Britain SIGNED: 15 Jun 51 FORCE: 15 Jun 51
USA (United States) SIGNED: 15 Jun 51 FORCE: 15 Jun 51

101937 Bilateral Agreement **148 UNTS 77**
SIGNED: 27 Jun 51   FORCE: 27 Jun 51
REGISTERED: 30 Oct 52 USA (United States)
ARTICLES: 9 LANGUAGE: English.
HEADNOTE: RED CROSS FIELD HOSPITAL KOREA
TOPIC: Milit Assistance
CONCEPTS: Extraditable offenses. General cooperation. Responsibility and liability. Humanitarian matters. Accounting procedures. Indemnities and reimbursements. Currency. Materials, equipment and services. Return of equipment and recapture.
INTL ORGS: United Nations.
PROCEDURE: Future Procedures Contemplated.
PARTIES:
Sweden
USA (United States)

101938 Bilateral Treaty **148 UNTS 85**
SIGNED: 18 Dec 47   FORCE: 30 Apr 51
REGISTERED: 30 Oct 52 USA (United States)
ARTICLES: 15 LANGUAGE: Afrikaans. English.
HEADNOTE: EXTRADITION
TOPIC: Extradition
CONCEPTS: Territorial application. Time limit. Previous treaty replacement. Extradition, deportation and repatriation. Extraditable offenses. Location of crime. Refusal of extradition. Pre-treaty crimes. Extradition postponement. Conformity with municipal law. Indemnities and reimbursements.
TREATY REF: 3DM456; 2'16DM850; 29DM570; 35DM541;,.

PROCEDURE: Accession. Ratification. Termination.
PARTIES:
South Africa
USA (United States)
ANNEX
151 UNTS 388. South Africa. Southwest Africa.

101939 Bilateral Exchange **148 UNTS 104**
SIGNED: 2 Apr 47   FORCE: 2 Apr 51
REGISTERED: 3 Nov 52 USA (United States)
ARTICLES: 2 LANGUAGE: English. Spanish.
HEADNOTE: AGRICULTURAL WORKERS AGREEMENTS
TOPIC: Non-ILO Labor
CONCEPTS: Annex or appendix reference. Annex type material. Previous treaty extension. Previous treaty replacement.
PARTIES:
Mexico
USA (United States)
ANNEX
167 UNTS 306. USA (United States). Supplementation 9 Mar 51. Force 9 Mar 51.
167 UNTS 306. Mexico. Supplementation 9 Mar 51. Force 9 Mar 51.

101940 Bilateral Agreement **148 UNTS 303**
SIGNED: 1 Oct 47   FORCE: 1 Oct 47
REGISTERED: 6 Nov 52 USA (United States)
ARTICLES: 11 LANGUAGE: English. French.
HEADNOTE: INTERNMENT REMOVAL
TOPIC: Other Military
CONCEPTS: Previous treaty replacement. Title and deeds. Use of facilities. Sanitation. Indemnities and reimbursements. Customs exemptions. Materials, equipment and services. Upkeep of war graves. Establishment of war cemeteries.
PROCEDURE: Termination.
PARTIES:
France
USA (United States)

101941 Bilateral Exchange **148 UNTS 313**
SIGNED: 9 Aug 46   FORCE: 9 Aug 46
REGISTERED: 6 Nov 52 USA (United States)
ARTICLES: 3 LANGUAGE: English.
HEADNOTE: INTERNMENT MILITARY PERSONNEL
TOPIC: Other Military
CONCEPTS: Exchange of information and documents. Informational records. General property. Title and deeds. Use of facilities. Sanitation. Indemnities and reimbursements. Tax exemptions. Responsibility for war dead. Establishment of war cemeteries.
INTL ORGS: Allied Military Occupation. United Nations.
PARTIES:
Hungary
USA (United States)

101942 Bilateral Exchange **148 UNTS 323**
SIGNED: 24 Sep 46   FORCE: 24 Sep 46
REGISTERED: 6 Nov 52 USA (United States)
ARTICLES: 2 LANGUAGE: English.
HEADNOTE: DISPOSITION CASE REMAINS
TOPIC: Other Military
CONCEPTS: Annex or appendix reference. Annex type material. Establishment of war cemeteries.
PARTIES:
Italy
USA (United States)

101943 Bilateral Exchange **148 UNTS 343**
SIGNED: 11 Apr 47   FORCE: 11 Apr 47
REGISTERED: 6 Nov 52 USA (United States)
ARTICLES: 2 LANGUAGE: English.
HEADNOTE: WAR GRAVES
TOPIC: Other Military
CONCEPTS: Title and deeds. Use of facilities. Sanitation. Tax exemptions. Customs exemptions. Responsibility for war dead. Upkeep of war graves. Establishment of war cemeteries.
PARTIES:
Netherlands
USA (United States)
ANNEX
149 UNTS 426. USA (United States). Amendment 1 Feb 51.

149 UNTS 426. Netherlands. Amendment 2 Mar 51.
279 UNTS 310. USA (United States). Prolongation 9 Mar 56. Force 18 Mar 57.
279 UNTS 310. Netherlands. Prolongation 29 Aug 55. Force 18 Mar 57.

101944 Bilateral Exchange **148 UNTS 355**
SIGNED: 28 Jun 46 FORCE: 28 Jun 46
REGISTERED: 6 Nov 52 USA (United States)
ARTICLES: 2 LANGUAGE: English. Romanian.
HEADNOTE: WAR GRAVES REGISTRATION
TOPIC: Other Military
CONCEPTS: Annex or appendix reference. Title and deeds. Responsibility for war dead. Establishment of war cemeteries.
PARTIES:
Romania
USA (United States)

101945 Bilateral Exchange **149 UNTS 3**
SIGNED: 6 Dec 46 FORCE: 6 Dec 46
REGISTERED: 6 Nov 52 USA (United States)
ARTICLES: 2 LANGUAGE: English.
HEADNOTE: NAVAL VESSELS TRAINING
TOPIC: Milit Assistance
CONCEPTS: Technical education. Joint defense. Defense and security. Naval vessels. Exchange of defense information.
INTL ORGS: Special Commission.
TREATY REF: 149UNTS334; 149UNTS350; 149UNTS356.
PARTIES:
Canada
USA (United States)

101946 Bilateral Exchange **149 UNTS 11**
SIGNED: 11 Feb 48 FORCE: 11 Feb 48
REGISTERED: 6 Nov 52 USA (United States)
ARTICLES: 2 LANGUAGE: English. French.
HEADNOTE: PLANTATION RUBBER INVESTIGATION
TOPIC: Specific Resources
CONCEPTS: Annex type material. Raw materials.
TREATY REF: USA'TIAS 1771 P.1;.
PARTIES:
Haiti
USA (United States)

101947 Bilateral Instrument **149 UNTS 19**
SIGNED: 12 Sep 46 FORCE: 12 Sep 46
REGISTERED: 6 Nov 52 USA (United States)
ARTICLES: 1 LANGUAGE: English. French.
HEADNOTE: CLAIMS
TOPIC: Reparations
CONCEPTS: Claims and settlements. War claims and reparations.
PARTIES:
Luxembourg
USA (United States)

101948 Bilateral Agreement **149 UNTS 23**
SIGNED: 27 Sep 49 FORCE: 27 Sep 49
REGISTERED: 6 Nov 52 USA (United States)
ARTICLES: 11 LANGUAGE: English. Russian.
HEADNOTE: RETURN NAVAL VESSELS
TOPIC: Milit Assistance
CONCEPTS: Detailed regulations. Annex or appendix reference. General cooperation. Use of facilities. Ports and pilotage. Naval vessels. Return of equipment and recapture.
PARTIES:
USA (United States)
USSR (Soviet Union)

101949 Bilateral Treaty **149 UNTS 35**
SIGNED: 7 Jul 51 FORCE: 31 Jan 52
REGISTERED: 7 Nov 52 India
ARTICLES: 8 LANGUAGE: Burmese. English. Hindi.
HEADNOTE: FRIENDSHIP
TOPIC: General Amity
CONCEPTS: Treaty interpretation. Friendship and amity. Diplomatic relations resumption. Privileges and immunities. General cooperation. Procedure.
PROCEDURE: Duration. Future Procedures Contemplated. Ratification. Termination.

PARTIES:
Burma
India

101950 Bilateral Agreement **149 UNTS 49**
SIGNED: 29 Aug 52 FORCE: 29 Aug 52
REGISTERED: 19 Nov 52 Denmark
ARTICLES: 6 LANGUAGE: French.
HEADNOTE: TRADE
TOPIC: General Trade
CONCEPTS: Territorial application. Previous treaty amendment. Annex or appendix reference. Previous treaty extension. Establishment of commission. Reexport of goods, etc.. Trade procedures. Quotas.
TREATY REF: 25DEMARTENS474.
PARTIES:
Denmark
Portugal

ANNEX
199 UNTS 347. Portugal. Prolongation 18 Jun 54. Force 1 Jul 54.
199 UNTS 347. Denmark. Prolongation 9 Jun 54. Force 1 Jul 54.

101951 Bilateral Exchange **149 UNTS 57**
SIGNED: 6 Sep 52 FORCE: 6 Sep 52
REGISTERED: 19 Nov 52 UK Great Britain
ARTICLES: 2 LANGUAGE: English.
HEADNOTE: FINANCIAL ARRANGEMENTS
TOPIC: Finance
CONCEPTS: Finances and payments. Claims and settlements.
PARTIES:
Ethiopia
UK Great Britain

101952 Bilateral Convention **149 UNTS 71**
SIGNED: 29 Mar 51 FORCE: 1 Nov 52
REGISTERED: 22 Nov 52 Netherlands
ARTICLES: 38 LANGUAGE: Dutch. German.
HEADNOTE: SOCIAL INSURANCE
TOPIC: Non-ILO Labor
CONCEPTS: Exceptions and exemptions. General provisions. Assistance. Conformity with municipal law. Domestic legislation. Incorporation of treaty provisions into national law. Old age and invalidity insurance. Non-ILO labor relations. Administrative cooperation. Old age insurance. Sickness and invalidity insurance. Social security. Payment schedules. National treatment.
INTL ORGS: International Refugees Organization. Arbitration Commission.
TREATY REF: 18UNTS18.
PARTIES:
Germany, West
Netherlands

101953 Bilateral Agreement **149 UNTS 197**
SIGNED: 22 Jul 51 FORCE: 29 Sep 52
REGISTERED: 24 Nov 52 WHO (World Health)
ARTICLES: 12 LANGUAGE: English. French.
HEADNOTE: PRIVILEGES IMMUNITIES & FACILITIES
TOPIC: IGO Status/Immunit
CONCEPTS: Definition of terms. Non-visa travel documents. Diplomatic privileges. Diplomatic missions. Inviolability. Privileges and immunities. Property. Diplomatic correspondence. Juridical personality. Procedure. Special tribunals. Status of experts.
INTL ORGS: International Court of Justice. United Nations.
TREATY REF: 1UNTS44.
PROCEDURE: Amendment. Registration.
PARTIES:
Philippines
WHO (World Health)

101954 Bilateral Exchange **149 UNTS 221**
SIGNED: 21 Jun 52 FORCE: 21 Jun 52
REGISTERED: 24 Nov 52 UK Great Britain
ARTICLES: 2 LANGUAGE: Arabic. English.
HEADNOTE: EXCHANGE OFFICIAL PUBLICATIONS
TOPIC: Admin Cooperation
CONCEPTS: Exchange of official publications. Operating agencies. Indemnities and reimbursements.

TREATY REF: 172LTS175.
PARTIES:
Iraq
UK Great Britain

101955 Bilateral Agreement **149 UNTS 227**
SIGNED: 31 Aug 51 FORCE: 28 Apr 52
REGISTERED: 24 Nov 52 UK Great Britain
ARTICLES: 9 LANGUAGE: English. Japanese.
HEADNOTE: PAYMENTS
TOPIC: Finance
CONCEPTS: Financial programs. Payment schedules.
INTL ORGS: International Monetary Fund.
PROCEDURE: Termination.
PARTIES:
Japan
UK Great Britain

ANNEX
160 UNTS 411. Japan. Prolongation 27 Dec 52. Force 27 Dec 52.
160 UNTS 411. UK Great Britain. Prolongation 27 Dec 52. Force 27 Dec 52.

101956 Bilateral Treaty **149 UNTS 247**
SIGNED: 20 Dec 51 FORCE: 19 May 52
REGISTERED: 24 Nov 52 UK Great Britain
ARTICLES: 17 LANGUAGE: Arabic. English.
HEADNOTE: FRIENDSHIP
TOPIC: General Amity
CONCEPTS: Non-prejudice to third party. Friendship and amity. National treatment. Customs declarations.
PROCEDURE: Duration. Ratification.
PARTIES:
Muscat and Oman
UK Great Britain

ANNEX
305 UNTS 430. Muscat and Oman. Amendment 10 Mar 58. Force 6 Feb 58.
305 UNTS 430. UK Great Britain. Amendment 25 Apr 57. Force 6 Feb 58.

101957 Unilateral Instrument **149 UNTS 285**
SIGNED: 24 Oct 52 FORCE: 31 Oct 52
REGISTERED: 25 Nov 52 United Nations
ARTICLES: 1 LANGUAGE: French.
HEADNOTE: ICJ JURISDICTION PEACE TREATY JAPAN
TOPIC: UN Charter
CONCEPTS: Anti-discrimination. IGO operations. Adherence to UN Charter.
INTL ORGS: International Court of Justice.
TREATY REF: 136UNTS45.
PARTIES:
Laos

101958 Bilateral Exchange **149 UNTS 289**
SIGNED: 16 Oct 52 FORCE: 1 Dec 52
REGISTERED: 28 Nov 52 Belgium
ARTICLES: 2 LANGUAGE: French.
HEADNOTE: VISA ABOLITION
TOPIC: Visas
CONCEPTS: Emergencies. Time limit. Visa abolition. Passports diplomatic. Passports non-diplomatic. Denial of admission. Tourism.
PARTIES:
Belgium
Turkey

ANNEX
228 UNTS 370. Belgium. Abrogation 1 Feb 56.
228 UNTS 370. Turkey. Abrogation 1 Feb 56.

101959 Bilateral Exchange **149 UNTS 297**
SIGNED: 14 Nov 47 FORCE: 14 Nov 47
REGISTERED: 28 Nov 52 USA (United States)
ARTICLES: 2 LANGUAGE: English. Spanish.
HEADNOTE: COOPERATIVE EDUCATION PROGRAM
TOPIC: Education
CONCEPTS: Definition of terms. Detailed regulations. Annex or appendix reference. Annex type material. Previous treaty replacement. Alien status. Conformity with municipal law. General cooperation. Inspection and observation. Personnel. General property. Private contracts. Specialists exchange. Exchange. Commissions and foundations. Teacher and student exchange. Professorships. Scholarships and grants. Voca-

tional training. Research and development. Accounting procedures. Currency. Exchange rates and regulations. Expense sharing formulae. Fees and exemptions. Financial programs. Funding procedures. Tax exemptions. Customs exemptions. Materials, equipment and services. Aid missions.
TREATY REF: 24UNTS273.
PARTIES:
Ecuador
USA (United States)
ANNEX
152 UNTS 340. USA (United States). Supplementation 27 Sep 51. Force 27 Sep 51.
152 UNTS 340. Ecuador. Supplementation 27 Sep 51. Force 27 Sep 51.
162 UNTS 362. USA (United States). Prolongation 16 Aug 48. Force 25 Aug 48.
162 UNTS 362. Ecuador. Prolongation 21 Aug 48. Force 25 Aug 48.
162 UNTS 365. Ecuador. Prolongation 15 Aug 49. Force 25 Aug 49.
162 UNTS 365. USA (United States). Prolongation 24 Aug 49. Force 25 Aug 49.
174 UNTS 307. USA (United States). Supplementation 18 Mar 52. Force 31 Mar 52.
174 UNTS 307. Ecuador. Supplementation 31 Mar 52. Force 31 Mar 52.
269 UNTS 322. USA (United States). Prolongation 17 Mar 55. Force 26 Apr 55.
269 UNTS 322. Ecuador. Prolongation 12 Apr 55. Force 26 Apr 55.

101960 Bilateral Agreement **150 UNTS 3**
SIGNED: 31 Jan 51 FORCE: 31 Jan 51
REGISTERED: 28 Nov 52 USA (United States)
ARTICLES: 18 LANGUAGE: English. Spanish.
HEADNOTE: COOPERATIVE EDUCATION PROGRAM
TOPIC: Education
CONCEPTS: Conditions. Definition of terms. Friendship and amity. Alien status. Privileges and immunities. Conformity with municipal law. General cooperation. Inspection and observation. Personnel. General property. Private contracts. Existing tribunals. Specialists exchange. Exchange. Commissions and foundations. Teacher and student exchange. Scholarships and grants. Research and development. Accounting procedures. Indemnities and reimbursements. Currency. Exchange rates and regulations. Expense sharing formulae. Fees and exemptions. Financial programs. Funding procedures. Assistance. Special projects. Aid missions.
TREATY REF: 92UNTS155.
PROCEDURE: Duration. Termination.
PARTIES:
Nicaragua
USA (United States)
ANNEX
152 UNTS 346. USA (United States). Supplementation 23 Oct 51. Force 5 Nov 51.
152 UNTS 346. Nicaragua. Supplementation 5 Nov 51. Force 5 Nov 51.
174 UNTS 314. USA (United States). Supplementation 27 Mar 52. Force 25 Apr 52.
174 UNTS 314. Nicaragua. Supplementation 25 Apr 52. Force 25 Apr 52.
180 UNTS 368. USA (United States). Supplementation 17 Oct 52. Force 17 Oct 52.
180 UNTS 368. Nicaragua. Supplementation 17 Oct 52. Force 17 Oct 52.
269 UNTS 327. USA (United States). Prolongation 27 Apr 55. Force 27 Apr 55.
269 UNTS 327. Nicaragua. Prolongation 27 Apr 55. Force 27 Apr 55.

101961 Bilateral Exchange **150 UNTS 25**
SIGNED: 24 Sep 48 FORCE: 24 Sep 48
REGISTERED: 28 Nov 52 USA (United States)
ARTICLES: 2 LANGUAGE: English. Spanish.
HEADNOTE: COOPERATIVE EDUCATION PROGRAM
TOPIC: Education
CONCEPTS: Annex or appendix reference. Annex type material. Friendship and amity. Conformity with municipal law. General cooperation. Exchange. Vocational training. Accounting procedures. Currency. Expense sharing formulae. Financial programs. Funding procedures.

TREATY REF: 39UNTS367; 140UNTS3; TIAS2148; EAS504.
PARTIES:
Panama
USA (United States)
ANNEX
227 UNTS 339. USA (United States). Supplementation 29 Feb 52. Force 9 Apr 52.
227 UNTS 339. Panama. Supplementation 9 Apr 52. Force 9 Apr 52.
256 UNTS 350. USA (United States). Prolongation 24 Mar 55. Force 30 Apr 55.
256 UNTS 350. Panama. Prolongation 30 Apr 55. Force 30 Apr 55.

101962 Bilateral Exchange **150 UNTS 45**
SIGNED: 30 Jun 48 FORCE: 6 Jul 48
REGISTERED: 28 Nov 52 USA (United States)
ARTICLES: 3 LANGUAGE: English. Spanish.
HEADNOTE: COOPERATIVE EDUCATION PROGRAM
TOPIC: Education
CONCEPTS: Annex or appendix reference. Annex type material. Friendship and amity. Conformity with municipal law. General cooperation. Exchange. Vocational training. Accounting procedures. Currency. Expense sharing formulae. Financial programs. Funding procedures.
TREATY REF: TIAS 2117; 150UNTS317.
PROCEDURE: Amendment.
PARTIES:
Peru
USA (United States)
ANNEX
152 UNTS 352. USA (United States). Supplementation 18 Oct 51. Force 23 Oct 51.
152 UNTS 352. Peru. Supplementation 23 Oct 51. Force 23 Oct 51.
174 UNTS 321. USA (United States). Supplementation 8 Aug 51. Force 19 Sep 51.
174 UNTS 321. Peru. Supplementation 6 Sep 51. Force 19 Sep 51.
174 UNTS 324. Peru. Supplementation 15 Feb 52. Force 15 Feb 52.
174 UNTS 324. USA (United States). Supplementation 17 Jan 52. Force 15 Feb 52.
264 UNTS 369. USA (United States). Prolongation 23 Feb 55. Force 28 Apr 55.
264 UNTS 369. Peru. Prolongation 26 Apr 55. Force 28 Apr 55.

101963 Multilateral Convention **150 UNTS 67**
SIGNED: 6 Dec 51 FORCE: 3 Apr 52
REGISTERED: 29 Nov 52 FAO (Food Agri)
ARTICLES: 15 LANGUAGE: English. French. Spanish.
HEADNOTE: INTERNATIONAL PLANT PROTECTION
TOPIC: Admin Cooperation
CONCEPTS: Definition of terms. Territorial application. Annex or appendix reference. General cooperation. Recognition of legal documents. Procedure. Disease control. Import quotas. Subsidiary organ.
INTL ORGS: Food and Agricultural Organization of the United Nations.
TREATY REF: 2'8DEMARTENS435; 15DEMARTENS570; 126LTS305;5.
PROCEDURE: Amendment. Accession. Denunciation. Ratification.
PARTIES:
Australia SIGNED: 30 Apr 52 RATIFIED: 27 Aug 52 FORCE: 27 Aug 52
Austria SIGNED: 6 Dec 51 RATIFIED: 22 Oct 52 FORCE: 22 Oct 52
Belgium SIGNED: 6 Dec 51 RATIFIED: 22 Jul 52 FORCE: 22 Jul 52
Brazil SIGNED: 6 Dec 51
Cambodia RATIFIED: 10 Jun 52 FORCE: 10 Jun 52
Canada SIGNED: 6 Dec 51
Ceylon (Sri Lanka) SIGNED: 7 Dec 51 FORCE: 3 Apr 52
Chile SIGNED: 3 Apr 52 FORCE: 3 Apr 52
Colombia SIGNED: 29 Apr 52
Costa Rica SIGNED: 28 Apr 52
Cuba SIGNED: 6 Dec 51
Denmark SIGNED: 6 Dec 51
Dominican Republic RATIFIED: 23 Jun 52 FORCE: 23 Jun 52
Ecuador SIGNED: 12 Mar 52
United Arab Rep SIGNED: 6 Dec 51

El Salvador SIGNED: 6 Dec 51
France SIGNED: 6 Dec 51
Germany, West SIGNED: 30 Apr 52
Guatemala SIGNED: 23 Apr 52
India SIGNED: 30 Apr 52 RATIFIED: 9 Jun 52 FORCE: 9 Jun 52
Indonesia SIGNED: 6 Dec 51
Ireland SIGNED: 6 Dec 51
Israel SIGNED: 6 Dec 51
Italy SIGNED: 2 Feb 52
Japan SIGNED: 6 Dec 51 RATIFIED: 11 Aug 52 FORCE: 11 Aug 52
Luxembourg SIGNED: 16 Jan 52
Netherlands SIGNED: 6 Dec 51
New Zealand Cook Islands RATIFIED: 16 Oct 52 FORCE: 16 Oct 52
New Zealand Niue RATIFIED: 16 Oct 52 FORCE: 16 Oct 52
New Zealand SIGNED: 6 Dec 51 RATIFIED: 16 Sep 52 FORCE: 16 Sep 52
New Zealand Western Samoa RATIFIED: 16 Oct 52 FORCE: 16 Oct 52
Philippines SIGNED: 6 Dec 51
Portugal SIGNED: 6 Dec 51
South Africa SIGNED: 6 Dec 51
Spain SIGNED: 10 Dec 51 FORCE: 3 Apr 52
Sweden SIGNED: 11 Dec 51 RATIFIED: 30 May 52 FORCE: 30 May 52
Switzerland SIGNED: 6 Dec 51
Thailand SIGNED: 6 Dec 51
UK Great Britain SIGNED: 6 Dec 51
USA (United States) SIGNED: 6 Dec 51
Uruguay SIGNED: 30 Apr 52
Yugoslavia SIGNED: 6 Dec 51
ANNEX
161 UNTS 372. El Salvador. Ratification 12 Feb 53.
161 UNTS 372. Denmark. Ratification 13 Feb 53.
172 UNTS 391. Canada. Ratification 10 Jul 53.
172 UNTS 391. United Arab Rep. Ratification 22 Jul 53.
173 UNTS 411. UK Great Britain. Ratification 7 Sep 53.
175 UNTS 370. UK Great Britain. Isle of Man. Force 31 Oct 53.
175 UNTS 370. UK Great Britain. Jersey Island.
193 UNTS 360. Iraq. Adherence 1 Jul 54.
196 UNTS 354. Australia. Amendment 14 Dec 53. Force 11 Jul 54.
196 UNTS 354. Chile. Amendment 26 May 54. Force 11 Jul 54.
196 UNTS 354. Spain. Amendment 30 Mar 54. Force 11 Jul 54.
196 UNTS 354. United Arab Rep. Amendment 6 Dec 53. Force 11 Jul 54.
196 UNTS 354. India. Amendment 29 May 54. Force 11 Jul 54.
196 UNTS 354. New Zealand. Amendment 11 Jun 54. Force 11 Jul 54.
196 UNTS 354. Cambodia. Acceptance 17 May 54. Force 11 Jul 54.
196 UNTS 354. Austria. Amendment 11 Dec 53. Force 11 Jul 54.
196 UNTS 354. UK Great Britain. Amendment 11 Dec 53. Force 11 Jul 54.
196 UNTS 354. Korea, South. Amendment 12 Dec 53. Force 11 Jul 54.
196 UNTS 354. Canada. Amendment 31 Dec 53. Force 11 Jul 54.
196 UNTS 354. Denmark. Acceptance 29 Jan 54. Force 11 Jul 54.
196 UNTS 354. Sweden. Amendment 14 Jan 54. Force 11 Jul 54.
199 UNTS 348. Australia. New Guinea. Force 8 Sep 54.
199 UNTS 348. Australia. Papua. Force 8 Sep 54.
199 UNTS 348. Australia. Nauru. Force 8 Sep 54.
199 UNTS 348. Australia. Norfolk Islands. Force 8 Sep 54.
201 UNTS 379. Pakistan. Adherence 10 Nov 54.
201 UNTS 379. Netherlands. Ratification 26 Oct 54.
201 UNTS 379. Argentina. Adherence 23 Sep 54.
202 UNTS 338. Greece. Adherence 9 Dec 54.
203 UNTS 337. Luxembourg. Ratification 13 Jan 55.
204 UNTS 390. Yugoslavia. Ratification 11 Feb 55.
207 UNTS 356. Laos. Adherence 28 Feb 55.
209 UNTS 347. Ireland. Ratification 31 Mar 55.
211 UNTS 419. Guatemala. Ratification 25 May 55.
214 UNTS 374. Italy. Ratification 3 Aug 55.
220 UNTS 384. Portugal. Ratification 20 Oct 55.

247 UNTS 400. Portugal. Supplementation 2 Jul 56. Force 2 Jul 56.

247 UNTS 400. Vietnam. Supplementation 2 Jul 56. Force 2 Jul 56.

247 UNTS 400. Australia. Supplementation 27 Feb 56. Force 2 Jul 56.

247 UNTS 400. Ceylon (Sri Lanka). Supplementation 27 Feb 56. Force 2 Jul 56.

247 UNTS 400. India. Supplementation 7 Feb 56. Force 2 Jul 56.

248 UNTS 368. Nicaragua. Adherence 2 Aug 56.

250 UNTS 312. Israel. Ratification 3 Sep 56.

251 UNTS 386. South Africa. Ratification 21 Sep 56.

256 UNTS 355. Thailand. Adherence 3 Dec 56.

256 UNTS 355. UK Great Britain. Ratification 3 Dec 56.

267 UNTS 381. Germany, West. Berlin.

267 UNTS 381. Germany, West. Ratification 3 May 57.

274 UNTS 347. Netherlands. Dutch New Guinea. Ratification 19 Jul 57.

276 UNTS 363. France. Adherence 20 Aug 57.

282 UNTS 364. Fed of Malaya. Adherence 20 Nov 57.

286 UNTS 378. Pakistan. Adherence 8 Jan 58.

313 UNTS 347. France. Ratification 17 Sep 58. Force 20 Aug 57.

346 UNTS 332. Burma. Adherence 4 Nov 59.

359 UNTS 400. Laos. Ratification 17 Mar 60.

360 UNTS 389. Hungary. Adherence 17 May 60.

369 UNTS 447. Finland. Adherence 22 Jun 60.

382 UNTS 333. Bolivia. Adherence 27 Oct 60.

411 UNTS 300. Brazil. Ratification 14 Sep 61.

434 UNTS 295. Philippines. Adherence 11 Jun 62.

527 UNTS 308. Netherlands. Force 1 Oct 62.

543 UNTS 359. Nepal. Adherence 12 Aug 65.

562 UNTS 328. UK Great Britain. Guernsey Island. Force 8 Apr 66.

617 UNTS 363. Indonesia. Ratification 21 Dec 67.

634 UNTS 428. Paraguay. Adherence 5 Apr 68.

657 UNTS 400. Cambodia. Adherence 27 Jan 69.

101964   Bilateral Agreement   **150 UNTS 103**
SIGNED: 15 Jun 51   FORCE: 15 Jun 51
REGISTERED: 1 Dec 52 Netherlands
ARTICLES: 13 LANGUAGE: French.
HEADNOTE: SETTLEMENT ECONOMIC PROVISIONS PEACE TREATY
TOPIC: Reparations
CONCEPTS: Time limit. Exchange of information and documents. Establishment of commission. Procedure. Conciliation. Compensation. Post-war claims settlement.
INTL ORGS: Conciliation Commission.
PROCEDURE: Future Procedures Contemplated.
PARTIES:
   Italy
   Netherlands

101965   Bilateral Agreement   **150 UNTS 113**
SIGNED: 22 Sep 52   FORCE: 22 Sep 52
REGISTERED: 1 Dec 52 Netherlands
ARTICLES: 7 LANGUAGE: French.
HEADNOTE: SETTLEMENT QUESTIONS INDUSTRIAL PROPERTY
TOPIC: Reparations
CONCEPTS: General property. Post-war adjustment. Enemy financial interests. Reparations and restrictions. Post-war claims settlement.
TREATY REF: 49UNTS.
PARTIES:
   Italy
   Netherlands

101966   Bilateral Agreement   **150 UNTS 119**
SIGNED: 4 Nov 52   FORCE: 1 Nov 52
REGISTERED: 1 Dec 52 WHO (World Health)
ARTICLES: 6 LANGUAGE: English. Spanish.
HEADNOTE: WHO HEALTH PROJECTS CHILE
TOPIC: Sanitation
CONCEPTS: Definition of terms. Friendship and amity. Privileges and immunities. General cooperation. Personnel. General support. Specialists exchange. Public health. WHO used as agency. Teacher and student exchange. Scholarships and grants. Vocational training. Indemnities and reimbursements. Currency. Expense sharing formulae. Assistance. Specific technical assistance. Materials, equipment and services.
INTL ORGS: United Nations.
TREATY REF: 76UNTS132; 33UNTS261.
PROCEDURE: Amendment. Termination.
PARTIES:
   Chile
   WHO (World Health)

101967   Bilateral Agreement   **150 UNTS 133**
SIGNED: 10 Oct 52   FORCE: 10 Oct 52
REGISTERED: 1 Dec 52 WHO (World Health)
ARTICLES: 6 LANGUAGE: English. Spanish.
HEADNOTE: HEALTH PROJECTS
TOPIC: Sanitation
CONCEPTS: Disease control. Public health. WHO used as agency. Medical assistance and/or facilities.
INTL ORGS: United Nations. Arbitration Commission.
PARTIES:
   Dominican Republic
   WHO (World Health)

101968   Unilateral Instrument   **150 UNTS 147**
SIGNED: 5 Nov 52   FORCE: 12 Nov 52
REGISTERED: 3 Dec 52 United Nations
ARTICLES: 1 LANGUAGE: French.
HEADNOTE: ACCEPTANCE ICJ JURISDICTION
TOPIC: ICJ Option Clause
CONCEPTS: Compulsory jurisdiction.
INTL ORGS: International Court of Justice.
TREATY REF: 136UNTS45.
PARTIES:
   Vietnam, South

101969   Bilateral Exchange   **150 UNTS 151**
SIGNED: 13 Jan 50   FORCE: 13 Jan 50
REGISTERED: 5 Dec 52 New Zealand
ARTICLES: 2 LANGUAGE: English. French.
HEADNOTE: REPAYMENT ADVANCES
TOPIC: Reparations
CONCEPTS: Lump sum settlements. Payment for war supplies.
PARTIES:
   France
   New Zealand

101970   Bilateral Exchange   **150 UNTS 157**
SIGNED: 20 Dec 51   FORCE: 20 Dec 51
REGISTERED: 5 Dec 52 New Zealand
ARTICLES: 2 LANGUAGE: English.
HEADNOTE: REVISION PEACE TREATY
TOPIC: Peace/Disarmament
CONCEPTS: Annex type material. Armistice and peace.
INTL ORGS: United Nations.
TREATY REF: 49UNTS.
PARTIES:
   Italy
   New Zealand

101971   Bilateral Agreement   **150 UNTS 165**
SIGNED: 27 Feb 51   FORCE: 27 Feb 51
REGISTERED: 5 Dec 52 New Zealand
ARTICLES: 13 LANGUAGE: English.
HEADNOTE: MONEY PROPERTY SUBJECTED ENEMY OCCUPATION
TOPIC: Reparations
CONCEPTS: Definition of terms. Treaty implementation. General property. Monetary and gold transfers. Assets transfer. National treatment. Post-war claims settlement.
TREATY REF: 81UNTS121.
PARTIES:
   New Zealand
   Yugoslavia

101972   Bilateral Agreement   **150 UNTS 179**
SIGNED: 23 May 49   FORCE: 23 May 49
REGISTERED: 11 Dec 52 Yugoslavia
ARTICLES: 12 LANGUAGE: French.
HEADNOTE: PROPERTY RIGHTS INTERESTS
TOPIC: Reparations
CONCEPTS: Definition of terms. Detailed regulations. General property. Establishment of commission. Procedure. Bonds. Lump sum settlements. Post-war claims settlement.

INTL ORGS: Arbitration Commission. Special Commission.
PROCEDURE: Future Procedures Contemplated.
PARTIES:
   Italy
   Yugoslavia

101973   Bilateral Agreement   **150 UNTS 191**
SIGNED: 23 Dec 50   FORCE: 23 Dec 50
REGISTERED: 11 Dec 52 Yugoslavia
ARTICLES: 5 LANGUAGE: French.
HEADNOTE: PAYMENTS
TOPIC: Finance
CONCEPTS: Detailed regulations. Previous treaty amendment. General cooperation. Accounting procedures. Banking. Exchange rates and regulations. Funding procedures. Interest rates. Payment schedules.
TREATY REF: 150UNTS199.
PROCEDURE: Future Procedures Contemplated.
PARTIES:
   Italy
   Yugoslavia

101974   Bilateral Agreement   **150 UNTS 199**
SIGNED: 23 Dec 50   FORCE: 23 Dec 50
REGISTERED: 11 Dec 52 Yugoslavia
ARTICLES: 9 LANGUAGE: French.
HEADNOTE: TRANSFER OPTANTS MOVABLE PROPERTY
TOPIC: Admin Cooperation
CONCEPTS: Licenses and permits. General property. Funding procedures.
TREATY REF: 49UNTS; 50UNTS.
PARTIES:
   Italy
   Yugoslavia

101975   Bilateral Agreement   **150 UNTS 213**
SIGNED: 23 Dec 50   FORCE: 23 Dec 50
REGISTERED: 11 Dec 52 Yugoslavia
ARTICLES: 4 LANGUAGE: French.
HEADNOTE: ALLOCATION ROLLING STOCK
TOPIC: Reparations
CONCEPTS: Annex or appendix reference. War claims and reparations.
TREATY REF: 49UNTS.
PARTIES:
   Italy
   Yugoslavia
                ANNEX
386 UNTS 380. Italy. Supplementation 23 Dec 50. Force 23 Dec 50.

386 UNTS 380. Yugoslavia. Supplementation 23 Dec 50. Force 23 Dec 50.

101976   Bilateral Agreement   **150 UNTS 227**
SIGNED: 26 Nov 51   FORCE: 26 Nov 51
REGISTERED: 11 Dec 52 Dominican Republic
ARTICLES: 1 LANGUAGE: English. Spanish.
HEADNOTE: PROVING GROUND MISSILES
TOPIC: Milit Installation
CONCEPTS: Bases and facilities.
PARTIES:
   Dominican Republic
   USA (United States)
                ANNEX
461 UNTS 228. USA (United States). Force 20 Nov 61.

461 UNTS 228. USA (United States). Termination 26 Nov 61. Prolongation 20 Nov 61.

461 UNTS 228. Dominican Republic. Termination 26 Nov 61. Prolongation 13 Nov 62.

461 UNTS 228. Dominican Republic. Force 20 Nov 61.

101977   Bilateral Exchange   **150 UNTS 231**
SIGNED: 19 Nov 49   FORCE: 1 Dec 49
REGISTERED: 12 Nov 52 Canada
ARTICLES: 2 LANGUAGE: English. French.
HEADNOTE: VISA REQUIREMENTS NON-IMMIGRANT TRAVELLERS
TOPIC: Visas
CONCEPTS: Territorial application. Denial of admission. Visas. Conformity with municipal law. Fees and exemptions.
PARTIES:
   Belgium
   Canada

281 UNTS 400. Canada. Amendment 19 Sep 57.
Force 1 Oct 57.
281 UNTS 400. Belgium. Amendment 1 Oct 57.
Force 1 Oct 57.

101978 Bilateral Agreement **150 UNTS 237**
SIGNED: 25 Oct 52   FORCE: 25 Oct 52
REGISTERED: 12 Nov 52 ICAO (Civil Aviat)
ARTICLES: 16 LANGUAGE: English.
HEADNOTE: AIR TRANSPORT
TOPIC: Air Transport
CONCEPTS: Conditions. Definition of terms. Detailed regulations. Exceptions and exemptions. Annex or appendix reference. Conformity with municipal law. General cooperation. Exchange of information and documents. Arbitration. Procedure. Special tribunals. Negotiation. Reexport of goods, etc.. Indemnities and reimbursements. Non-interest rates and fees. Most favored nation clause. National treatment. Customs exemptions. Routes and logistics. Permit designation. Air transport. Conditions of airlines operating permission. Overflights and technical stops. Operating authorizations and regulations.
INTL ORGS: International Civil Aviation Organization. Arbitration Commission.
TREATY REF: 15UNTS295.
PROCEDURE: Amendment. Future Procedures Contemplated. Registration. Termination.
PARTIES:
  Burma
  UK Great Britain
ANNEX
173 UNTS 412. Burma. Amendment 12 Aug 53. Force 12 Aug 53.
173 UNTS 412. UK Great Britain. Amendment 4 Aug 53. Force 12 Aug 53.
264 UNTS 373. UK Great Britain. Amendment 9 Jan 57. Force 9 Jan 57.
264 UNTS 373. Burma. Amendment 9 Jan 57. Force 9 Jan 57.
551 UNTS 282. UK Great Britain. Amendment 8 Apr 65. Force 20 Jul 65.
551 UNTS 282. Burma. Amendment 20 Jul 65. Force 20 Jul 65.

101979 Bilateral Agreement **150 UNTS 257**
SIGNED: 29 Aug 52   FORCE: 29 Aug 52
REGISTERED: 12 Nov 52 ICAO (Civil Aviat)
ARTICLES: 14 LANGUAGE: English.
HEADNOTE: AIR SERVICES
TOPIC: Air Transport
CONCEPTS: Definition of terms. Detailed regulations. Annex or appendix reference. Conformity with municipal law. General cooperation. Exchange of information and documents. Arbitration. Procedure. Existing tribunals. Negotiation. Reexport of goods, etc.. Non-interest rates and fees. Most favored nation clause. National treatment. Customs exemptions. Routes and logistics. Permit designation. Airport facilities. Conditions of airlines operating permission. Operating authorizations and regulations.
INTL ORGS: International Civil Aviation Organization. International Court of Justice. Arbitration Commission.
TREATY REF: 15UNTS295; 84UNTS389.
PROCEDURE: Amendment. Future Procedures Contemplated. Registration. Termination.
PARTIES:
  Ethiopia
  Pakistan

101980 Bilateral Agreement **150 UNTS 277**
SIGNED: 17 Jul 52   FORCE: 17 Jul 52
REGISTERED: 12 Nov 52 ICAO (Civil Aviat)
ARTICLES: 14 LANGUAGE: English.
HEADNOTE: AIR SERVICES
TOPIC: Air Transport
CONCEPTS: Definition of terms. Detailed regulations. Exceptions and exemptions. Time limit. Conformity with municipal law. General cooperation. Exchange of information and documents. Arbitration. Procedure. Existing tribunals. Negotiation. Non-interest rates and fees. Most favored nation clause. National treatment. Customs duties. Routes and logistics. Permit designation. Air transport. Conditions of airlines operating permission. Overflights and technical stops. Operating authorizations and regulations.

INTL ORGS: International Civil Aviation Organization. International Court of Justice. Arbitration Commission.
TREATY REF: 15UNTS295; 84UNTS389.
PROCEDURE: Amendment. Future Procedures Contemplated. Termination. Application to Non-self-governing Territories.
PARTIES:
  Netherlands
  Pakistan
ANNEX
353 UNTS 364.   Pakistan.   Amendment 29 May 57. Force 29 May 57.
353 UNTS 364.   Netherlands.   Amendment 29 May 57. Force 29 May 57.
412 UNTS 318. Pakistan. Amendment 31 Dec 60. Force 31 Dec 60.
412 UNTS 318.   Netherlands.   Amendment 31 Dec 60. Force 31 Dec 60.
601 UNTS 344.   Netherlands.   Amendment 23 Apr 65. Force 23 Apr 65.
601 UNTS 344. Pakistan. Amendment 23 Apr 65. Force 23 Apr 65.

101981 Bilateral Agreement **150 UNTS 299**
SIGNED: 21 Sep 50   FORCE: 7 Mar 52
REGISTERED: 12 Nov 52 ICAO (Civil Aviat)
ARTICLES: 12 LANGUAGE: French.
HEADNOTE: AIR TRANSPORT
TOPIC: Air Transport
CONCEPTS: Definition of terms. Exceptions and exemptions. Annex or appendix reference. Conformity with municipal law. Licenses and permits. Recognition of legal documents. Use of facilities. Arbitration. Procedure. Fees and exemptions. Most favored nation clause. National treatment. Customs exemptions. Competency certificate. Routes and logistics. Navigational conditions. Permit designation. Air transport. Airport facilities. Airworthiness certificates. Conditions of airlines operating permission. Operating authorizations and regulations. Licenses and certificates of nationality.
INTL ORGS: International Civil Aviation Organization. Arbitration Commission.
TREATY REF: 15UNTS295.
PROCEDURE: Amendment. Future Procedures Contemplated. Ratification. Registration. Termination.
PARTIES:
  Brazil
  Turkey

101982 Bilateral Agreement **151 UNTS 3**
SIGNED: 23 Jun 52   FORCE: 23 Jun 52
REGISTERED: 12 Nov 52 ICAO (Civil Aviat)
ARTICLES: 14 LANGUAGE: Danish. English.
HEADNOTE: AIR SERVICES
TOPIC: Air Transport
CONCEPTS: Definition of terms. Detailed regulations. Annex or appendix reference. Conformity with municipal law. General cooperation. Licenses and permits. Recognition of legal documents. Arbitration. Procedure. Existing tribunals. Negotiation. Most favored nation clause. National treatment. Customs exemptions. Competency certificate. Routes and logistics. Navigational conditions. Permit designation. Air transport. Airworthiness certificates. Conditions of airlines operating permission. Operating authorizations and regulations. Licenses and certificates of nationality.
INTL ORGS: International Civil Aviation Organization. Arbitration Commission.
TREATY REF: 15UNTS295.
PROCEDURE: Amendment. Future Procedures Contemplated. Registration. Termination. Application to Non-self-governing Territories.
PARTIES:
  Denmark
  UK Great Britain
ANNEX
172 UNTS 392. UK Great Britain. Amendment 13 Mar 53. Force 13 Mar 53.
172 UNTS 392.   Denmark.   Amendment 13 Mar 53. Force 13 Mar 53.

101983 Bilateral Agreement **151 UNTS 33**
SIGNED: 6 Dec 50   FORCE: 6 Dec 50
REGISTERED: 12 Nov 52 ICAO (Civil Aviat)
ARTICLES: 15 LANGUAGE: English. Hebrew.
HEADNOTE: AIR SERVICES
TOPIC: Air Transport
CONCEPTS: Airport facilities. Airport equipment. Airworthiness certificates. Conditions of airlines operating permission. Overflights and technical stops. Operating authorizations and regulations. Licenses and certificates of nationality.
INTL ORGS: International Civil Aviation Organization. Arbitration Commission.
TREATY REF: COUV. ON CIVIL AVIATION, DEC 7, 1944 CHICAGO.
PARTIES:
  Israel
  UK Great Britain
ANNEX
360 UNTS 390. UK Great Britain. Amendment 4 Nov 59. Force 29 Dec 59.
360 UNTS 390. Israel. Amendment 29 Dec 59. Force 29 Dec 59.

101984 Bilateral Exchange **151 UNTS 69**
SIGNED: 31 Mar 52   FORCE: 31 Mar 52
REGISTERED: 12 Nov 52 ICAO (Civil Aviat)
ARTICLES: 4 LANGUAGE: Arabic. English.
HEADNOTE: TEMPORARY CIVIL AVIATION
TOPIC: Air Transport
CONCEPTS: Exchange of information and documents. Expense sharing formulae. Air transport. Airport facilities. Airport equipment. Operating authorizations and regulations.
PROCEDURE: Duration. Future Procedures Contemplated. Renewal or Revival. Termination.
PARTIES:
  Libya
  UK Great Britain

101985 Bilateral Agreement **151 UNTS 81**
SIGNED: 23 Jun 52   FORCE: 23 Jun 52
REGISTERED: 12 Nov 52 ICAO (Civil Aviat)
ARTICLES: 15 LANGUAGE: Arabic. Norwegian.
HEADNOTE: AIR SERVICES
TOPIC: Air Transport
CONCEPTS: Air transport. Airport facilities. Airport equipment. Airworthiness certificates. Conditions of airlines operating permission. Overflights and technical stops.
INTL ORGS: International Civil Aviation Organization. Arbitration Commission.
TREATY REF: 15UNTS295; 6UNTS235.
PROCEDURE: Amendment. Future Procedures Contemplated. Registration. Termination. Application to Non-self-governing Territories.
PARTIES:
  Norway
  UK Great Britain
ANNEX
172 UNTS 396. Norway. Amendment 13 Mar 53. Force 13 Mar 53.
172 UNTS 396. UK Great Britain. Amendment 13 Mar 53. Force 13 Mar 53.
223 UNTS 362. UK Great Britain. Amendment 29 Aug 52. Force 29 Aug 52.
223 UNTS 362. Norway. Amendment 29 Aug 52. Force 29 Aug 52.
264 UNTS 374. UK Great Britain. Amendment 25 Oct 56. Force 25 Oct 56.
264 UNTS 374. Norway. Amendment 25 Oct 56. Force 25 Oct 56.
543 UNTS 360. Norway. Amendment 22 Jan 65. Force 22 Jan 65.
543 UNTS 360. UK Great Britain. Amendment 22 Jan 65. Force 22 Jan 65.

101986 Bilateral Agreement **151 UNTS 111**
SIGNED: 6 Mar 52   FORCE: 6 Mar 52
REGISTERED: 12 Nov 52 ICAO (Civil Aviat)
ARTICLES: 6 LANGUAGE: English.
HEADNOTE: TECHNICAL ASSISTANCE
TOPIC: Tech Assistance
CONCEPTS: Treaty implementation. Annex or appendix reference. Privileges and immunities. General cooperation. Exchange of information and documents. Personnel. Title and deeds. Use of facilities. Scholarships and grants. Vocational training. Research and scientific projects. Exchange rates and regulations. Expense sharing formulae. Local currency. Domestic obligation. General technical assistance. Materials, equipment and services. IGO status. Conformity with IGO decisions.
INTL ORGS: United Nations.

TREATY REF: 76UNTS132; 33UNTS261.
PROCEDURE: Amendment. Termination.
PARTIES:
    ICAO (Civil Aviat)
    United Arab Rep

101987 Bilateral Agreement **151 UNTS 123**
SIGNED: 29 Apr 52   FORCE: 29 Apr 52
REGISTERED: 12 Nov 52 ICAO (Civil Aviat)
ARTICLES: 7 LANGUAGE: English.
HEADNOTE: TECHNICAL ASSISTANCE
TOPIC: Tech Assistance
CONCEPTS: Definition of terms. Treaty implementation. Annex or appendix reference. Privileges
and immunities. General cooperation. Exchange
of information and documents. Personnel. Responsibility and liability. Title and deeds. Use of
facilities. Scholarships and grants. Vocational
training. Research and scientific projects. Exchange rates and regulations. Expense sharing
formulae. Claims and settlements. Domestic obligation. General technical assistance. Materials,
equipment and services. IGO status. Conformity
with IGO decisions.
INTL ORGS: United Nations.
TREATY REF: 76UNTS132; 33UNTS261.
PROCEDURE: Amendment. Termination.
PARTIES:
    India
    ICAO (Civil Aviat)

101988 Bilateral Exchange **151 UNTS 135**
SIGNED: 15 Jun 46   FORCE: 15 Jun 46
REGISTERED: 16 Dec 52 USA (United States)
ARTICLES: 2 LANGUAGE: English.
HEADNOTE: USE PAYNE FIELD INTERNATIONAL
CIVIL AIR TRAFFIC
TOPIC: Air Transport
CONCEPTS: Time limit. Personnel. Special
projects. Navigational equipment. Air transport.
Airport facilities. Airport equipment. Operating
authorizations and regulations.
INTL ORGS: International Civil Aviation Organiza-
tion.
PARTIES:
    United Arab Rep
    USA (United States)

101989 Bilateral Exchange **151 UNTS 141**
SIGNED: 23 May 50   FORCE: 23 May 50
REGISTERED: 16 Dec 52 USA (United States)
ARTICLES: 2 LANGUAGE: English. Portuguese.
HEADNOTE: AMEND EXCHANGE OFFICIAL PUBLI-
CATIONS 1940 AGREEMENT
TOPIC: Admin Cooperation
CONCEPTS: Annex type material.
TREATY REF: 203LTS227.
PARTIES:
    Brazil
    USA (United States)

101990 Bilateral Agreement **151 UNTS 147**
SIGNED: 16 Jan 51   FORCE: 27 Jul 51
REGISTERED: 16 Dec 52 USA (United States)
ARTICLES: 5 LANGUAGE: English. Spanish.
HEADNOTE: TECHNICAL COOPERATION
TOPIC: Tech Assistance
CONCEPTS: Exceptions and exemptions. Treaty
implementation. Previous treaty replacement.
Diplomatic privileges. General cooperation. Exchange of information and documents. Personnel. Public information. Funding procedures. Tax
exemptions. Domestic obligation. General technical assistance. Materials, equipment and services.
PROCEDURE: Amendment. Duration. Termination.
PARTIES:
    Chile
    USA (United States)
            ANNEX
179 UNTS 265. Chile. Amendment 8 Jan 52.
Force 8 Jan 52.
179 UNTS 265. USA (United States). Amendment
8 Jan 52. Force 8 Jan 52.
184 UNTS 376. Chile. Amendment 17 Oct 52.
Force 17 Oct 52.
184 UNTS 376. USA (United States). Amendment
17 Oct 52. Force 17 Oct 52.

101991 Bilateral Instrument **151 UNTS 159**
SIGNED: 11 Mar 47   FORCE: 13 Mar 47
REGISTERED: 16 Dec 52 USA (United States)
ARTICLES: 3 LANGUAGE: English. French.
HEADNOTE: REPATRIATION LIBERATION PRISON-
ERS
TOPIC: Humanitarian
CONCEPTS: Detailed regulations. Time limit. Repa-
triation of nationals. General cooperation. Ex-
change of information and documents. Human-
itarian matters. Prisoners of war.
TREATY REF: 117LTS343; 122LTS367.
PROCEDURE: Future Procedures Contemplated.
PARTIES:
    France
    USA (United States)

101992 Bilateral Exchange **151 UNTS 171**
SIGNED: 24 Jan 50   FORCE: 24 Jan 50
REGISTERED: 16 Dec 52 USA (United States)
ARTICLES: 2 LANGUAGE: English.
HEADNOTE: CLAIMS DAMAGES
TOPIC: Specif Claim/Waive
CONCEPTS: Accounting procedures. Claims and
settlements. Specific claims or waivers.
TREATY REF: 162LTS73.
PARTIES:
    Canada
    USA (United States)

101993 Bilateral Agreement **151 UNTS 179**
SIGNED: 10 Apr 51   FORCE: 2 Jun 51
REGISTERED: 16 Dec 52 USA (United States)
ARTICLES: 5 LANGUAGE: Arabic. English.
HEADNOTE: TECHNICAL COOPERATION
TOPIC: Tech Assistance
CONCEPTS: Exceptions and exemptions. Treaty
implementation. Diplomatic privileges. General
cooperation. Exchange of information and docu-
ments. Personnel. Public information. Funding
procedures. Tax exemptions. Domestic obliga-
tion. General technical assistance. Materials,
equipment and services.
INTL ORGS: United Nations.
PROCEDURE: Amendment. Duration. Termination.
PARTIES:
    Iraq
    USA (United States)

101994 Bilateral Exchange **151 UNTS 191**
SIGNED: 2 May 51   FORCE: 2 May 51
REGISTERED: 16 Dec 52 USA (United States)
ARTICLES: 2 LANGUAGE: English. French.
HEADNOTE: TECHNICAL COOPERATION
TOPIC: Tech Assistance
CONCEPTS: Exceptions and exemptions. Treaty
implementation. Previous treaty replacement.
Diplomatic privileges. General cooperation. Ex-
change of information and documents. Public in-
formation. Funding procedures. Tax exemptions.
Domestic obligation. General technical assis-
tance. Materials, equipment and services.
PROCEDURE: Amendment. Duration. Termination.
PARTIES:
    Haiti
    USA (United States)
            ANNEX
180 UNTS 372. USA (United States). Amendment
15 Dec 51. Force 8 Jan 51.
180 UNTS 372. Haiti. Amendment 8 Jan 51.
Force 8 Jan 51.

101995 Bilateral Exchange **151 UNTS 199**
SIGNED: 27 Jul 49   FORCE: 27 Jul 49
REGISTERED: 16 Dec 52 USA (United States)
ARTICLES: 3 LANGUAGE: English. Spanish.
HEADNOTE: HEALTH SANITATION PROGRAM
TOPIC: Sanitation
CONCEPTS: Conditions. Annex type material. Pre-
vious treaty extension. Personnel. Public health.
Sanitation. Indemnities and reimbursements.
Currency. Expense sharing formulae. Assistance.
Grants.
TREATY REF: 106UNTS311.
PROCEDURE: Duration.
PARTIES:
    USA (United States)
    Uruguay

101996 Bilateral Exchange **151 UNTS 207**
SIGNED: 3 Jul 52   FORCE: 3 Jul 52
REGISTERED: 18 Dec 52 UK Great Britain
ARTICLES: 2 LANGUAGE: English.
HEADNOTE: FACILITIES MILITARY AIRCRAFT
TOPIC: Status of Forces
CONCEPTS: Use of facilities. Indemnities and re-
imbursements. Airport facilities. Overflights and
technical stops. Status of military forces.
PARTIES:
    Ethiopia
    UK Great Britain
            ANNEX
172 UNTS 400. UK Great Britain. Amendment
11 Mar 53. Force 13 Mar 53.
172 UNTS 400. Ethiopia. Amendment 31 Mar 53.
Force 31 Mar 53.

101997 Bilateral Exchange **151 UNTS 215**
SIGNED: 9 Sep 52   FORCE: 9 Sep 52
REGISTERED: 18 Dec 52 UK Great Britain
ARTICLES: 2 LANGUAGE: English. German.
HEADNOTE: PRACTICE BOMBING RANGE
TOPIC: Milit Installation
CONCEPTS: Annex or appendix reference. Testing
ranges and sites.
PARTIES:
    Germany, West
    UK Great Britain
            ANNEX
207 UNTS 357. Germany, West. Amendment
15 Oct 54. Force 18 Oct 54.
207 UNTS 357. UK Great Britain. Amendment
18 Oct 54. Force 18 Oct 54.
331 UNTS 376. Germany, West. Supplementation 22 May 57. Force 31 May 57.
331 UNTS 376. UK Great Britain. Supplementation 31 May 57. Force 31 May 57.

101998 Bilateral Exchange **151 UNTS 227**
SIGNED: 10 Jul 52   FORCE: 15 Jul 52
REGISTERED: 18 Dec 52 UK Great Britain
ARTICLES: 2 LANGUAGE: English.
HEADNOTE: FINANCE
TOPIC: Finance
CONCEPTS: Previous treaty replacement. Fi-
nances and payments. Accounting procedures.
Monetary and gold transfers.
TREATY REF: 9UNTS259; 88UNTS418.
PARTIES:
    Iraq
    UK Great Britain

101999 Bilateral Exchange **151 UNTS 233**
SIGNED: 9 Oct 52   FORCE: 9 Nov 52
REGISTERED: 18 Dec 52 UK Great Britain
ARTICLES: 2 LANGUAGE: English. Turkish.
HEADNOTE: ABOLITION VISAS
TOPIC: Visas
CONCEPTS: Emergencies. Territorial application.
Visa abolition. Passports non-diplomatic. Denial
of admission. Conformity with municipal law.
PARTIES:
    Turkey
    UK Great Britain

102000 Bilateral Convention **151 UNTS 241**
SIGNED: 30 Jun 51   FORCE: 1 Oct 52
REGISTERED: 19 Dec 52 Denmark
ARTICLES: 35 LANGUAGE: Danish. French.
HEADNOTE: SOCIAL SECURITY
TOPIC: Non-ILO Labor
CONCEPTS: General provisions. Conformity with
municipal law. Domestic legislation. Incorporation of treaty provisions into national law. Penal
sanctions. ILO conventions. Old age and invalidity insurance. Non-ILO labor relations. Administrative cooperation. Old age insurance. Sickness
and invalidity insurance. Social security. Compensation. Payment schedules. National treatment.
PARTIES:
    Denmark
    France
            ANNEX
306 UNTS 336. France. Supplementation
27 Mar 58. Force 1 Apr 58.
306 UNTS 336. Denmark. Supplementation
27 Mar 58. Force 1 Apr 58.

102001 Bilateral Agreement **151 UNTS 281**
SIGNED: 16 Jan 52   FORCE: 1 Jun 51
REGISTERED: 23 Dec 52 Pakistan
ARTICLES: 33 LANGUAGE: English.
HEADNOTE: EXCHANGE POSTAL PARCELS
TOPIC: Postal Service
CONCEPTS: Detailed regulations. Conformity with municipal law. Payment schedules. Customs duties. Regulations. Insured letters and boxes. Conveyance in transit. Parcel post. Rates and charges.
INTL ORGS: Universal Postal Union.
PROCEDURE: Duration.
PARTIES:
    Australia
    Pakistan

102002 Multilateral Agreement **151 UNTS 317**
SIGNED: 29 Dec 52   FORCE: 29 Dec 52
REGISTERED: 29 Dec 52 United Nations
ARTICLES: 6 LANGUAGE: English. Spanish.
HEADNOTE: TECHNICAL ASSISTANCE
TOPIC: Tech Assistance
CONCEPTS: Definition of terms. Treaty implementation. Privileges and immunities. General cooperation. Exchange of information and documents. Personnel. Title and deeds. Exchange. Scholarships and grants. Vocational training. Research and development. Expense sharing formulae. Local currency. Domestic obligation. General technical assistance. Materials, equipment and services. IGO status. Conformity with IGO decisions.
TREATY REF: 76UNTS132;   15UNTS261;
33UNTS261.
PROCEDURE: Amendment. Termination.
PARTIES:
    Honduras   SIGNED: 29 Dec 52   FORCE:
        29 Dec 52
    ICAO (Civil Aviat) SIGNED: 29 Dec 52 FORCE:
        29 Dec 52
    ILO (Labor Org) SIGNED: 29 Dec 52 FORCE:
        29 Dec 52
    UNESCO   (Educ/Cult)   SIGNED: 29 Dec 52
        FORCE: 29 Dec 52
    United Nations SIGNED: 29 Dec 52 FORCE:
        29 Dec 52
    WHO (World Health) SIGNED: 29 Dec 52 FORCE:
        29 Dec 52
                    ANNEX
274 UNTS 348. Honduras. Force 9 Jul 57.
274 UNTS 348. UNTAB (Tech Assis). Force
    9 Jul 57.

102003 Bilateral Agreement **151 UNTS 333**
SIGNED: 12 Jun 52   FORCE: 9 Sep 52
REGISTERED: 30 Dec 52 WHO (World Health)
ARTICLES: 1 LANGUAGE: Portuguese.
HEADNOTE: EXPERT IMMUNO-CHEMISTRY
TOPIC: Scientific Project
CONCEPTS: Privileges and immunities. Use of facilities. Specialists exchange. WHO used as agency. Vocational training. Research and scientific projects. Research and development. Transportation costs. Economic assistance.
INTL ORGS: United Nations.
PARTIES:
    Brazil
    WHO (World Health)

102004 Bilateral Agreement **151 UNTS 339**
SIGNED: 24 Oct 52   FORCE: 4 Nov 52
REGISTERED: 30 Dec 52 WHO (World Health)
ARTICLES: 4 LANGUAGE: English. Spanish.
HEADNOTE: ENVIRONMENTAL   SANITATION
TRAINING WHO
TOPIC: Sanitation
CONCEPTS: Definition of terms. Privileges and immunities. General cooperation. Personnel. General property. Sanitation. WHO used as agency. Commissions and foundations. Teacher and student exchange. Professorships. Institute establishment. Scholarships and grants. Vocational training. Research results. Indemnities and reimbursements. Expense sharing formulae. Financial programs. Assistance. Specific technical assistance. Economic assistance. Materials, equipment and services. Mass media exchange.
INTL ORGS: United Nations.
TREATY REF: 33UNTS261;76UNTS132.
PROCEDURE: Amendment. Duration. Termination.

PARTIES:
    Chile
    WHO (World Health)

102005 Bilateral Agreement **151 UNTS 359**
SIGNED: 16 Dec 52   FORCE: 31 Dec 52
REGISTERED: 31 Dec 52 United Nations
ARTICLES: 10 LANGUAGE: English.
HEADNOTE: ACTIVITIES UNICEF
TOPIC: Direct Aid
CONCEPTS: Territorial application. Treaty implementation. Privileges and immunities. General cooperation. Exchange of information and documents. Informational records. Inspection and observation. Public information. Procedure. Negotiation. Export quotas. Tax exemptions. Customs exemptions. Commodities and services. Assistance. General aid. Distribution. IGO status.
INTL ORGS: United Nations.
TREATY REF: 1UNTS15.
PROCEDURE: Amendment. Termination.
PARTIES:
    UNICEF (Children)
    UK Great Britain

102006 Bilateral Exchange **152 UNTS 3**
SIGNED: 1 May 52   FORCE: 1 May 52
REGISTERED: 7 Jan 53 Australia
ARTICLES: 2 LANGUAGE: English.
HEADNOTE: VISAS VISA FEES
TOPIC: Visas
CONCEPTS: Territorial application. Time limit. Denial of admission. Visas. Conformity with municipal law. Fees and exemptions.
PROCEDURE: Termination.
PARTIES:
    Australia
    Denmark
                    ANNEX
301 UNTS 448.   Denmark.   Amendment
    30 Apr 58. Force 1 May 58.
301 UNTS 448. Australia. Amendment 30 Apr 58.
    Force 1 May 58.

102007 Bilateral Exchange **152 UNTS 11**
SIGNED: 6 Dec 52   FORCE: 1 Jan 53
REGISTERED: 8 Jan 53 Belgium
ARTICLES: 2 LANGUAGE: French. German.
HEADNOTE: ABOLISHING VISA REQUIREMENTS
BEARERS OFFICIAL PASSPORTS
TOPIC: Visas
CONCEPTS: Time limit. Visa abolition.
INTL ORGS: Council of Europe.
PARTIES:
    Belgium
    Germany, West
                    ANNEX
163 UNTS 388. Belgium. Amendment 27 Feb 53.
    Force 27 Feb 53.
163 UNTS 388. Germany, West. Amendment
    27 Feb 53. Force 27 Feb 53.

102008 Bilateral Exchange **152 UNTS 17**
SIGNED: 22 Nov 50   FORCE: 27 Nov 50
REGISTERED: 8 Jan 53 USA (United States)
ARTICLES: 2 LANGUAGE: English. Spanish.
HEADNOTE: COOPERATIVE EDUCATION PROGRAM
TOPIC: Education
CONCEPTS: Annex type material. Friendship and amity. Conformity with municipal law. Exchange. Vocational training. Expense sharing formulae. Currency. Financial programs. Funding procedures.
PROCEDURE: Future Procedures Contemplated.
PARTIES:
    Bolivia
    USA (United States)
                    ANNEX
165 UNTS 379.   Bolivia.   Supplementation
    13 Dec 51. Force 13 Dec 51.
165 UNTS 379. USA (United States). Supplementation 24 Jul 51. Force 13 Dec 51.
167 UNTS 327.   Bolivia.   Supplementation
    9 Nov 51. Force 9 Nov 51.
167 UNTS 327. USA (United States). Supplementation 14 Aug 51. Force 9 Nov 51.
229 UNTS 312. USA (United States). Supplementation 17 Jan 52. Force 28 Feb 52.

229 UNTS 312.   Bolivia.   Supplementation
    28 Feb 52. Force 28 Feb 52.
229 UNTS 316. USA (United States). Supplementation 30 Jun 52. Force 30 Jun 52.
229 UNTS 316.   Bolivia.   Supplementation
    30 Jun 52. Force 30 Jun 52.
251 UNTS 387. USA (United States). Prolongation
    25 Feb 55. Force 18 Mar 55.
251 UNTS 387. Bolivia. Prolongation 3 Mar 55.
    Force 18 Mar 55.

102009 Bilateral Agreement **152 UNTS 27**
SIGNED: 10 Aug 51   FORCE: 26 Sep 51
REGISTERED: 8 Jan 53 USA (United States)
ARTICLES: 2 LANGUAGE: English. Spanish.
HEADNOTE: ALLOCATION TELEVISION CHANNELS
TOPIC: Telecommunications
CONCEPTS: Bands and frequency allocation. Facilities and equipment. Telecommunications. Mass media.
PARTIES:
    Mexico
    USA (United States)
                    ANNEX
180 UNTS 378. USA (United States). Amendment
    4 Jun 52. Force 25 Jun 52.
180 UNTS 378. Mexico. Amendment 25 Jun 52.
    Force 25 Jun 52.
445 UNTS 325. USA (United States). Amendment
    8 Sep 59. Force 24 Sep 59.
445 UNTS 325. Mexico. Amendment 24 Sep 59.
    Force 24 Sep 59.

102010 Bilateral Agreement **152 UNTS 41**
SIGNED: 4 Dec 51   FORCE: 4 Dec 51
REGISTERED: 8 Jan 53 USA (United States)
ARTICLES: 28 LANGUAGE: English. Spanish.
HEADNOTE: AIR FORCE MISSION
TOPIC: Military Mission
CONCEPTS: Definition of terms. Use of facilities. Compensation. Indemnities and reimbursements. Exchange rates and regulations. Expense sharing formulae. Tax exemptions. Customs exemptions. Military assistance. Military training. Security of information. Airforce-army-navy personnel ratio. Ranks and privileges. Conditions for assistance missions. Third country military personnel. Status of forces.
PROCEDURE: Denunciation. Duration. Renewal or Revival. Termination.
PARTIES:
    USA (United States)
    Uruguay

102011 Bilateral Agreement **152 UNTS 61**
SIGNED: 8 Jan 52   FORCE: 8 Jan 52
REGISTERED: 8 Jan 53 USA (United States)
ARTICLES: 9 LANGUAGE: English. Serbo-Croat.
HEADNOTE: ECONOMIC COOPERATION
TOPIC: Direct Aid
CONCEPTS: Treaty implementation. Privileges and immunities. Conformity with municipal law. Exchange of information and documents. Inspection and observation. Personnel. Public information. Negotiation. Accounting procedures. Exchange rates and regulations. Funding procedures. Local currency. Customs exemptions. Commodities and services. Domestic obligation. Economic assistance. Relief supplies. Procurement. Access to materials.
INTL ORGS: United Nations.
TREATY REF: 122UNTS137.
PROCEDURE: Amendment. Duration. Registration. Termination.
PARTIES:
    USA (United States)
    Yugoslavia
                    ANNEX
207 UNTS 360. USA (United States). Amendment
    25 Feb 53. Force 10 Mar 53.
207 UNTS 360.   Yugoslavia.   Amendment
    10 Mar 53. Force 10 Mar 53.

102012 Bilateral Exchange **152 UNTS 87**
SIGNED: 17 Dec 51   FORCE: 17 Dec 51
REGISTERED: 8 Jan 53 USA (United States)
ARTICLES: 2 LANGUAGE: English.
HEADNOTE: EXEMPTION NAVIGATIONAL DUES
REQUIREMENTS ENTRY CLEARANCE

TOPIC: Visas
CONCEPTS: Frontier formalities. Fees and exemptions. Customs duties. Ports and pilotage.
PARTIES:
Cuba
USA (United States)

102013 Bilateral Exchange **152 UNTS 93**
SIGNED: 27 Dec 46 FORCE: 27 Dec 46
REGISTERED: 8 Jan 53 USA (United States)
ARTICLES: 2 LANGUAGE: English. Spanish.
HEADNOTE: CIVIL AVIATION MISSION
TOPIC: Air Transport
CONCEPTS: Exceptions and exemptions. Time limit. Diplomatic privileges. Conformity with municipal law. Personnel. Responsibility and liability. Use of facilities. Indemnities and reimbursements. Financial programs. Transportation costs. Customs exemptions. Assistance. Aid missions. Air transport. Airport facilities. Facilities and equipment.
PROCEDURE: Amendment. Duration. Renewal or Revival. Termination.
PARTIES:
Peru
USA (United States)
            ANNEX
238 UNTS 328. USA (United States). Prolongation 27 Dec 49. Force 8 Feb 50.
238 UNTS 328. Peru. Prolongation 8 Feb 50. Force 8 Feb 50.

102014 Bilateral Agreement **152 UNTS 111**
SIGNED: 9 May 47 FORCE: 9 Jun 47
REGISTERED: 13 Jan 53 IBRD (World Bank)
ARTICLES: 5 LANGUAGE: English. French.
HEADNOTE: GUARANTEE AGREEMENT
TOPIC: IBRD Project
CONCEPTS: Annex or appendix reference. Informational records. Inspection and observation. Fees and exemptions. Tax exemptions. Domestic obligation. Loan regulations. Loan guarantee. Guarantor non-interference.
PROCEDURE: Ratification.
PARTIES:
France
IBRD (World Bank)

102015 Bilateral Agreement **152 UNTS 165**
SIGNED: 7 Aug 47 FORCE: 11 Sep 47
REGISTERED: 13 Jan 53 IBRD (World Bank)
ARTICLES: 11 LANGUAGE: English.
HEADNOTE: LOAN AGREEMENT
TOPIC: IBRD Project
CONCEPTS: Default remedies. Definition of terms. Annex or appendix reference. Conformity with municipal law. Informational records. Inspection and observation. Arbitration. Procedure. Reexport of goods, etc.. Accounting procedures. Bonds. Currency. Fees and exemptions. Interest rates. Tax exemptions. Domestic obligation. Loan repayment. Loan regulations. Loan guarantee. Guarantor non-interference.
INTL ORGS: Arbitration Commission.
TREATY REF: 2UNTS134.
PROCEDURE: Ratification. Termination.
PARTIES:
Netherlands
IBRD (World Bank)

102016 Bilateral Agreement **152 UNTS 223**
SIGNED: 22 Aug 47 FORCE: 17 Oct 47
REGISTERED: 13 Jan 53 IBRD (World Bank)
ARTICLES: 11 LANGUAGE: English.
HEADNOTE: LOAN AGREEMENT
TOPIC: IBRD Project
CONCEPTS: Default remedies. Definition of terms. Annex or appendix reference. Conformity with municipal law. Informational records. Inspection and observation. Arbitration. Procedure. Reexport of goods, etc.. Accounting procedures. Bonds. Currency. Fees and exemptions. Interest rates. Tax exemptions. Domestic obligation. Loan repayment. Loan regulations. Loan guarantee. Guarantor non-interference.
INTL ORGS: Arbitration Commission.
TREATY REF: 2UNTS134.
PROCEDURE: Ratification. Termination.

PARTIES:
Denmark
IBRD (World Bank)

102017 Bilateral Agreement **153 UNTS 3**
SIGNED: 28 Aug 47 FORCE: 24 Oct 47
REGISTERED: 13 Jan 53 IBRD (World Bank)
ARTICLES: 11 LANGUAGE: English.
HEADNOTE: LOAN AGREEMENT
TOPIC: IBRD Project
CONCEPTS: Default remedies. Definition of terms. Annex or appendix reference. Conformity with municipal law. Informational records. Inspection and observation. Arbitration. Procedure. Reexport of goods, etc.. Accounting procedures. Bonds. Currency. Fees and exemptions. Interest rates. Tax exemptions. Domestic obligation. Loan repayment. Loan regulations. Loan guarantee. Guarantor non-interference.
INTL ORGS: Arbitration Commission.
TREATY REF: 2UNTS134.
PROCEDURE: Ratification. Termination.
PARTIES:
Luxembourg
IBRD (World Bank)

102018 Bilateral Agreement **153 UNTS 61**
SIGNED: 23 Mar 49 FORCE: 7 Apr 49
REGISTERED: 13 Jan 53 IBRD (World Bank)
ARTICLES: 6 LANGUAGE: English.
HEADNOTE: GUARANTEE AGREEMENT
TOPIC: IBRD Project
CONCEPTS: Definition of terms. Annex or appendix reference. Informational records. Inspection and observation. Fees and exemptions. Tax exemptions. Domestic obligation. Loan regulations. Loan guarantee. Guarantor non-interference.
PARTIES:
Chile
IBRD (World Bank)

102019 Bilateral Agreement **153 UNTS 141**
SIGNED: 23 Mar 49 FORCE: 7 Apr 49
REGISTERED: 13 Jan 53 IBRD (World Bank)
ARTICLES: 6 LANGUAGE: English.
HEADNOTE: GUARANTEE AGREEMENT
TOPIC: IBRD Project
CONCEPTS: Annex or appendix reference. Informational records. Inspection and observation. Fees and exemptions. Tax exemptions. Domestic obligation. Loan regulations. Loan guarantee. Guarantor non-interference.
PARTIES:
Chile
IBRD (World Bank)

102020 Bilateral Agreement **153 UNTS 211**
SIGNED: 15 Jul 48 FORCE: 3 Aug 48
REGISTERED: 13 Jan 53 IBRD (World Bank)
ARTICLES: 8 LANGUAGE: English.
HEADNOTE: GUARANTEE
TOPIC: IBRD Project
CONCEPTS: Banking. Credit provisions.
PARTIES:
Netherlands
IBRD (World Bank)

102021 Bilateral Agreement **153 UNTS 259**
SIGNED: 15 Jul 48 FORCE: 3 Aug 48
REGISTERED: 13 Jan 53 IBRD (World Bank)
ARTICLES: 8 LANGUAGE: English.
HEADNOTE: GUARANTEE AGREEMENT
TOPIC: IBRD Project
CONCEPTS: Annex or appendix reference. Informational records. Inspection and observation. Fees and exemptions. Tax exemptions. Domestic obligation. Loan regulations. Loan guarantee. Guarantor non-interference. Merchant vessels.
TREATY REF: 153UNTS211.
PARTIES:
Netherlands
IBRD (World Bank)

102022 Bilateral Agreement **153 UNTS 259**
SIGNED: 15 Jul 48 FORCE: 3 Aug 48
REGISTERED: 13 Jan 53 IBRD (World Bank)
ARTICLES: 8 LANGUAGE: English.

HEADNOTE: GUARANTEE AGREEMENT
TOPIC: IBRD Project
CONCEPTS: Annex or appendix reference. Informational records. Inspection and observation. Fees and exemptions. Tax exemptions. Domestic obligation. Loan regulations. Guarantor non-interference. Merchant vessels.
PARTIES:
Netherlands
IBRD (World Bank)

102023 Bilateral Agreement **153 UNTS 259**
SIGNED: 15 Jul 48 FORCE: 3 Aug 48
REGISTERED: 13 Jan 53 IBRD (World Bank)
ARTICLES: 8 LANGUAGE: English.
HEADNOTE: GUARANTEE AGREEMENT
TOPIC: IBRD Project
CONCEPTS: Annex or appendix reference. Informational records. Inspection and observation. Fees and exemptions. Tax exemptions. Domestic obligation. Loan regulations. Loan guarantee. Guarantor non-interference. Merchant vessels.
PARTIES:
Netherlands
IBRD (World Bank)

102024 Bilateral Agreement **153 UNTS 259**
SIGNED: 15 Jul 48 FORCE: 3 Aug 48
REGISTERED: 13 Jan 53 IBRD (World Bank)
ARTICLES: 8 LANGUAGE: English.
HEADNOTE: GUARANTEE AGREEMENT
TOPIC: IBRD Project
CONCEPTS: Annex or appendix reference. Informational records. Inspection and observation. Fees and exemptions. Tax exemptions. Domestic obligation. Loan regulations. Loan guarantee. Guarantor non-interference. Merchant vessels.
PARTIES:
Netherlands
IBRD (World Bank)

102025 Bilateral Agreement **153 UNTS 259**
SIGNED: 15 Jul 48 FORCE: 3 Aug 48
REGISTERED: 13 Jan 53 IBRD (World Bank)
ARTICLES: 8 LANGUAGE: English.
HEADNOTE: GUARANTEE AGREEMENT
TOPIC: IBRD Project
CONCEPTS: Annex or appendix reference. Informational records. Inspection and observation. Fees and exemptions. Tax exemptions. Domestic obligation. Loan regulations. Loan guarantee. Guarantor non-interference. Merchant vessels.
PARTIES:
Netherlands
IBRD (World Bank)

102026 Bilateral Agreement **153 UNTS 264**
SIGNED: 27 Jan 49 FORCE: 9 May 49
REGISTERED: 13 Jan 53 IBRD (World Bank)
ARTICLES: 10 LANGUAGE: English.
HEADNOTE: LOAN AGREEMENT TRACTION LIGHT POWER COMPANY
TOPIC: IBRD Project
CONCEPTS: Default remedies. Annex or appendix reference. Conformity with municipal law. Fees and exemptions. Tax exemptions. Domestic obligation. Loan regulations. Loan guarantee.
INTL ORGS: Arbitration Commission.
PARTIES:
Brazil
IBRD (World Bank)

102027 Bilateral Agreement **154 UNTS 3**
SIGNED: 6 Jan 49 FORCE: 15 Mar 49
REGISTERED: 13 Jan 53 IBRD (World Bank)
ARTICLES: 8 LANGUAGE: English.
HEADNOTE: GUARANTEE AGREEMENT
TOPIC: IBRD Project
CONCEPTS: Definition of terms. Annex or appendix reference. Conformity with municipal law. Informational records. Inspection and observation. Fees and exemptions. Tax exemptions. Domestic obligation. Loan regulations. Loan guarantee. Guarantor non-interference.
INTL ORGS: Arbitration Commission.
PARTIES:
Mexico
IBRD (World Bank)

102028 Bilateral Agreement **154 UNTS 81**
SIGNED: 6 Jan 49 FORCE: 15 Mar 49
REGISTERED: 13 Jan 53 IBRD (World Bank)
ARTICLES: 6 LANGUAGE: English.
HEADNOTE: GUARANTEE AGREEMENT
TOPIC: IBRD Project
CONCEPTS: Definition of terms. Annex or appendix reference. Conformity with municipal law. Informational records. Inspection and observation. Arbitration. Procedure. Fees and exemptions. Tax exemptions. Domestic obligation. Loan regulations. Loan guarantee. Guarantor non-interference.
INTL ORGS: Arbitration Commission.
PROCEDURE: Termination.
PARTIES:
    Mexico
    IBRD (World Bank)

102029 Bilateral Agreement **154 UNTS 133**
SIGNED: 1 Mar 49 FORCE: 1 Mar 49
REGISTERED: 13 Jan 53 IBRD (World Bank)
ARTICLES: 10 LANGUAGE: English.
HEADNOTE: LOAN AGREEMENT
TOPIC: IBRD Project
CONCEPTS: Default remedies. Definition of terms. Annex or appendix reference. Conformity with municipal law. Informational records. Inspection and observation. Arbitration. Procedure. Reexport of goods, etc.. Accounting procedures. Bonds. Currency. Fees and exemptions. Interest rates. Tax exemptions. Domestic obligation. Loan repayment. Loan regulations. Loan guarantee. Guarantor non-interference.
INTL ORGS: Arbitration Commission.
TREATY REF: 2UNTS134.
PROCEDURE: Ratification. Termination.
PARTIES:
    Belgium
    IBRD (World Bank)

102030 Bilateral Agreement **154 UNTS 178**
SIGNED: 26 Jul 49 FORCE: 13 Sep 49
REGISTERED: 13 Jan 53 IBRD (World Bank)
ARTICLES: 8 LANGUAGE: English.
HEADNOTE: GUARANTEE AGREEMENT
TOPIC: IBRD Project
CONCEPTS: Annex or appendix reference. Conformity with municipal law. Informational records. Inspection and observation. Arbitration. Procedure. Bonds. Fees and exemptions. Tax exemptions. Domestic obligation. Loan regulations. Loan guarantee. Guarantor non-interference.
INTL ORGS: Arbitration Commission.
TREATY REF: 2UNTS134.
PROCEDURE: Termination.
PARTIES:
    Netherlands
    IBRD (World Bank)

102031 Bilateral Agreement **154 UNTS 269**
SIGNED: 18 Aug 49 FORCE: 2 Nov 49
REGISTERED: 13 Jan 53 IBRD (World Bank)
ARTICLES: 11 LANGUAGE: English.
HEADNOTE: LOAN AGREEMENT
TOPIC: IBRD Project
CONCEPTS: Default remedies. Definition of terms. Annex or appendix reference. Conformity with municipal law. Informational records. Inspection and observation. Arbitration. Procedure. Accounting procedures. Bonds. Currency. Fees and exemptions. Interest rates. Tax exemptions. Domestic obligation. Loan repayment. Loan regulations. Loan guarantee. Guarantor non-interference.
INTL ORGS: Arbitration Commission.
PROCEDURE: Ratification. Termination.
PARTIES:
    India
    IBRD (World Bank)

102032 Bilateral Agreement **154 UNTS 329**
SIGNED: 19 Aug 49 FORCE: 22 Oct 49
REGISTERED: 13 Jan 53 IBRD (World Bank)
ARTICLES: 8 LANGUAGE: English.
HEADNOTE: GUARANTEE AGREEMENT
TOPIC: IBRD Project
CONCEPTS: Annex or appendix reference. Conformity with municipal law. Informational records. Inspection and observation. Arbitration. Procedure. Bonds. Fees and exemptions. Tax exemptions. Domestic obligation. Loan regulations. Loan guarantee. Guarantor non-interference.
INTL ORGS: Arbitration Commission.
TREATY REF: 2UNTS134.
PROCEDURE: Termination.
PARTIES:
    Colombia
    IBRD (World Bank)

102033 Bilateral Agreement **154 UNTS 393**
SIGNED: 29 Sep 49 FORCE: 1 Dec 49
REGISTERED: 13 Jan 53 IBRD (World Bank)
ARTICLES: 11 LANGUAGE: English.
HEADNOTE: LOAN AGREEMENT
TOPIC: IBRD Project
CONCEPTS: Default remedies. Definition of terms. Annex or appendix reference. Standardization. Conformity with municipal law. Informational records. Inspection and observation. Procedure. Accounting procedures. Bonds. Currency. Fees and exemptions. Interest rates. Tax exemptions. Domestic obligation. Loan repayment. Loan guarantee. Guarantor non-interference.
INTL ORGS: Arbitration Commission.
TREATY REF: 2UNTS134.
PARTIES:
    India
    IBRD (World Bank)

102034 Bilateral Agreement **155 UNTS 3**
SIGNED: 17 Sep 49 FORCE: 24 Jan 50
REGISTERED: 13 Jan 53 IBRD (World Bank)
ARTICLES: 10 LANGUAGE: English.
HEADNOTE: LOAN AGREEMENT
TOPIC: IBRD Project
CONCEPTS: Default remedies. Definition of terms. Annex or appendix reference. Conformity with municipal law. Informational records. Inspection and observation. Arbitration. Procedure. Accounting procedures. Bonds. Currency. Fees and exemptions. Interest rates. Tax exemptions. Domestic obligation. Loan repayment. Loan regulations. Loan guarantee. Guarantor non-interference.
INTL ORGS: Arbitration Commission.
TREATY REF: 2UNTS134.
PARTIES:
    IBRD (World Bank)
    Yugoslavia

102035 Bilateral Agreement **155 UNTS 43**
SIGNED: 14 Dec 49 FORCE: 15 Sep 50
REGISTERED: 13 Jan 53 IBRD (World Bank)
ARTICLES: 13 LANGUAGE: English.
HEADNOTE: GUARANTEE AGREEMENT
TOPIC: IBRD Project
CONCEPTS: Annex or appendix reference. Conformity with municipal law. Informational records. Inspection and observation. Arbitration. Procedure. Bonds. Fees and exemptions. Tax exemptions. Domestic obligation. Loan regulations. Loan guarantee. Guarantor non-interference.
INTL ORGS: Arbitration Commission.
TREATY REF: 2UNTS134.
PARTIES:
    El Salvador
    IBRD (World Bank)

102036 Bilateral Agreement **155 UNTS 117**
SIGNED: 18 Apr 50 FORCE: 21 Feb 51
REGISTERED: 13 Jan 53 IBRD (World Bank)
ARTICLES: 11 LANGUAGE: English.
HEADNOTE: LOAN AGREEMENT
TOPIC: IBRD Project
CONCEPTS: Definition of terms. Annex or appendix reference. Conformity with municipal law. Informational records. Inspection and observation. Arbitration. Procedure. Accounting procedures. Bonds. Currency. Fees and exemptions. Interest rates. Tax exemptions. Loan repayment. Loan regulations. Loan guarantee. Guarantor non-interference.
INTL ORGS: Arbitration Commission.
TREATY REF: 2UNTS134.
PARTIES:
    India
    IBRD (World Bank)

102037 Bilateral Agreement **155 UNTS 185**
SIGNED: 28 Apr 50 FORCE: 30 Jun 50
REGISTERED: 13 Jan 53 IBRD (World Bank)
ARTICLES: 10 LANGUAGE: English.
HEADNOTE: GUARANTEE AGREEMENT
TOPIC: IBRD Project
CONCEPTS: Annex or appendix reference. Conformity with municipal law. Informational records. Inspection and observation. Arbitration. Procedure. Bonds. Fees and exemptions. Tax exemptions. Domestic obligation. Loan regulations. Loan guarantee. Guarantor non-interference.
INTL ORGS: Arbitration Commission.
TREATY REF: 2UNTS134.
PARTIES:
    Mexico
    IBRD (World Bank)

102038 Bilateral Agreement **155 UNTS 267**
SIGNED: 15 Jun 50 FORCE: 12 Jul 51
REGISTERED: 13 Jan 53 IBRD (World Bank)
ARTICLES: 12 LANGUAGE: English.
HEADNOTE: LOAN AGREEMENT
TOPIC: IBRD Project
CONCEPTS: Default remedies. Definition of terms. Annex or appendix reference. Conformity with municipal law. Informational records. Inspection and observation. Arbitration. Procedure. Accounting procedures. Bonds. Currency. Fees and exemptions. Interest rates. Tax exemptions. Domestic obligation. Loan repayment. Loan regulations. Loan guarantee. Guarantor non-interference.
INTL ORGS: Arbitration Commission.
TREATY REF: 2UNTS39.
PARTIES:
    Iraq
    IBRD (World Bank)

102039 Bilateral Agreement **156 UNTS 3**
SIGNED: 7 Jul 50 FORCE: 28 Nov 50
REGISTERED: 13 Jan 53 IBRD (World Bank)
ARTICLES: 12 LANGUAGE: English.
HEADNOTE: LOAN AGREEMENT
TOPIC: IBRD Project
CONCEPTS: Default remedies. Definition of terms. Annex or appendix reference. Conformity with municipal law. Informational records. Inspection and observation. Arbitration. Procedure. Accounting procedures. Bonds. Currency. Fees and exemptions. Interest rates. Tax exemptions. Domestic obligation. Loan repayment. Loan regulations. Loan guarantee. Guarantor non-interference.
INTL ORGS: Arbitration Commission.
TREATY REF: 2UNTS40.
PARTIES:
    IBRD (World Bank)
    Turkey

102040 Bilateral Agreement **156 UNTS 75**
SIGNED: 7 Jul 50 FORCE: 23 Jan 51
REGISTERED: 13 Jan 53 IBRD (World Bank)
ARTICLES: 12 LANGUAGE: English.
HEADNOTE: LOAN AGREEMENT
TOPIC: IBRD Project
CONCEPTS: Default remedies. Definition of terms. Annex or appendix reference. Conformity with municipal law. Informational records. Inspection and observation. Arbitration. Procedure. Accounting procedures. Bonds. Currency. Fees and exemptions. Interest rates. Tax exemptions. Domestic obligation. Loan repayment. Loan regulations. Loan guarantee. Guarantor non-interference.
INTL ORGS: World Health Organization. Arbitration Commission.
TREATY REF: 2UNTS40.
PARTIES:
    IBRD (World Bank)
    Turkey
                ANNEX
338 UNTS 340. Turkey. Supplementation 26 Feb 55. Force 11 Jan 54.
338 UNTS 340. IBRD (World Bank). Supplementation 25 Feb 55. Force 11 Jan 54.

102041 Bilateral Agreement **156 UNTS 147**
SIGNED: 14 Nov 50 FORCE: 27 Dec 50
REGISTERED: 13 Jan 53 IBRD (World Bank)

ARTICLES: 6 LANGUAGE: English.
HEADNOTE: LOAN AGREEMENT
TOPIC: IBRD Project
CONCEPTS: Default remedies. Annex or appendix reference. Conformity with municipal law. Exchange of information and documents. Informational records. Inspection and observation. Accounting procedures. Bonds. Fees and exemptions. Interest rates. Tax exemptions. Domestic obligation. Terms of loan. Loan regulations. Loan guarantee. Guarantor non-interference.
PARTIES:
Australia
IBRD (World Bank)

102042 Bilateral Agreement **156 UNTS 203**
SIGNED: 25 Aug 50 FORCE: 28 May 51
REGISTERED: 13 Jan 53 IBRD (World Bank)
ARTICLES: 13 LANGUAGE: English.
HEADNOTE: GUARANTEE AGREEMENT
TOPIC: IBRD Project
CONCEPTS: Annex or appendix reference. Conformity with municipal law. Informational records. Inspection and observation. Arbitration. Procedure. Bonds. Fees and exemptions. Tax exemptions. Domestic obligation. Loan regulations. Loan guarantee. Guarantor non-interference.
INTL ORGS: Arbitration Commission.
TREATY REF: 2UNTS134.
PARTIES:
IBRD (World Bank)
Uruguay

102043 Bilateral Agreement **157 UNTS 3**
SIGNED: 16 Jan 51 FORCE: 16 Jan 51
REGISTERED: 14 Jan 53 USA (United States)
ARTICLES: 18 LANGUAGE: English. Spanish.
HEADNOTE: TECHNICAL AGREEMENT COOPERATIVE PROGRAM AGRICULTURE LIVESTOCK
TOPIC: Direct Aid
CONCEPTS: Treaty implementation. Annex type material. Privileges and immunities. Conformity with municipal law. General cooperation. Exchange of information and documents. Informational records. Inspection and observation. Domestic legislation. Operating agencies. Personnel. Private contracts. Title and deeds. Use of facilities. Vocational training. Research and development. Exchange rates and regulations. Expense sharing formulae. Local currency. Assets. Domestic obligation. Agriculture. Materials, equipment and services.
TREATY REF: 151UNTS147.
PROCEDURE: Duration. Termination.
PARTIES:
Chile
USA (United States)
ANNEX
174 UNTS 332. USA (United States). Supplementation 30 Jan 52. Force 5 Feb 52.
174 UNTS 332. Chile. Supplementation 5 Feb 52. Force 5 Feb 52.
258 UNTS 403. USA (United States). Prolongation 27 Apr 55. Force 27 Apr 55.
258 UNTS 403. Chile. Prolongation 27 Apr 55. Force 27 Apr 55.
401 UNTS 260. Chile. Prolongation 15 Jun 60.
401 UNTS 260. USA (United States). Prolongation 15 Jun 60.

102044 Bilateral Exchange **157 UNTS 25**
SIGNED: 4 Feb 52 FORCE: 4 Feb 52
REGISTERED: 14 Jan 53 USA (United States)
ARTICLES: 2 LANGUAGE: English.
HEADNOTE: COPYRIGHT
TOPIC: Patents/Copyrights
CONCEPTS: Recognition.
PARTIES:
Denmark
USA (United States)

102045 Bilateral Agreement **157 UNTS 39**
SIGNED: 5 Jan 52 FORCE: 5 Jan 52
REGISTERED: 14 Jan 53 USA (United States)
ARTICLES: 10 LANGUAGE: English.
HEADNOTE: TECHNICAL COOPERATION
TOPIC: Tech Assistance
CONCEPTS: Detailed regulations. Treaty implementation. Privileges and immunities. General cooperation. Exchange of information and documents. Informational records. Operating agencies. Personnel. Attachment of funds. Currency deposits. Funding procedures. Garnishment of funds. Seizure funds. Local currency. Customs

exemptions. Domestic obligation. General technical assistance. Grants. Loan and credit.
INTL ORGS: Special Commission.
TREATY REF: 99UNTS39.
PROCEDURE: Amendment. Duration. Termination.
PARTIES:
India
USA (United States)
ANNEX
288 UNTS 368. India. Prolongation 29 Jun 57. Force 29 Jun 57.
288 UNTS 368. USA (United States). Prolongation 29 Jun 57. Force 29 Jun 57.

102046 Bilateral Exchange **157 UNTS 53**
SIGNED: 7 Dec 51 FORCE: 7 Dec 51
REGISTERED: 14 Jan 53 USA (United States)
ARTICLES: 2 LANGUAGE: English.
HEADNOTE: ECONOMIC ASSISTANCE TECHNICAL COOPERATION RELIEF RESETTLEMENT REFUGEES
TOPIC: Tech Assistance
CONCEPTS: Conditions. Refugees and stateless persons. Assistance. Accounting procedures. Attachment of funds. Financial programs. Garnishment of funds. Seizure funds. Local currency. General technical assistance. Economic assistance.
PARTIES:
Israel
USA (United States)

102047 Bilateral Exchange **157 UNTS 63**
SIGNED: 28 Dec 51 FORCE: 28 Dec 51
REGISTERED: 14 Jan 53 USA (United States)
ARTICLES: 2 LANGUAGE: English. Italian.
HEADNOTE: EXTENSION GUARANTEES PRIVATE INVESTMENTS
TOPIC: General Economic
CONCEPTS: General cooperation. Expropriation. General property. Title and deeds. Arbitration. Negotiation. Compensation. Investments. Seizure funds. Assets. Claims and settlements. Private investment guarantee. Assets transfer.
INTL ORGS: International Court of Justice.
TREATY REF: USA 62STAT144; 63STAT51; 64STAT198.
PARTIES:
Italy
USA (United States)
ANNEX
291 UNTS 309. Italy. Amendment 18 Oct 57. Force 18 Oct 57.
291 UNTS 309. USA (United States). Amendment 18 Oct 57. Force 18 Oct 57.

102048 Bilateral Agreement **157 UNTS 69**
SIGNED: 20 Dec 51 FORCE: 20 Dec 51
REGISTERED: 14 Jan 53 USA (United States)
ARTICLES: 9 LANGUAGE: Arabic. English.
HEADNOTE: ECONOMIC ASSISTANCE PURSUANT GENERAL AGREEMENT TECHNICAL COOPERATION
TOPIC: Tech Assistance
CONCEPTS: Annex type material. General cooperation. Public information. Existing tribunals. Export quotas. Accounting procedures. Attachment of funds. Currency deposits. Exchange rates and regulations. Financial programs. Garnishment of funds. Seizure funds. Local currency. Claims and settlements. Most favored nation clause. Commodities and services. Domestic obligation. Economic assistance.
INTL ORGS: International Court of Justice.
TREATY REF: 141UNTS55.
PROCEDURE: Amendment. Duration. Termination.
PARTIES:
Jordan
USA (United States)

102049 Multilateral Exchange **157 UNTS 85**
SIGNED: 6 May 46 FORCE: 6 May 46
REGISTERED: 15 Jan 53 UK Great Britain
ARTICLES: 6 LANGUAGE: English.
HEADNOTE: RICE
TOPIC: Commodity Trade
CONCEPTS: Treaty interpretation. Commodity trade.
TREATY REF: 99UNTS181.

PARTIES:
Siam SIGNED: 6 May 46 FORCE: 6 May 46
UK Great Britain SIGNED: 6 May 46 FORCE: 6 May 46
USA (United States) SIGNED: 6 May 46 FORCE: 6 May 46

102050 Multilateral Exchange **157 UNTS 103**
SIGNED: 7 Dec 46 FORCE: 7 Dec 46
REGISTERED: 15 Jan 53 UK Great Britain
ARTICLES: 5 LANGUAGE: English.
HEADNOTE: STIMULATE FLOW TIN
TOPIC: Commodity Trade
CONCEPTS: Treaty interpretation. Negotiation. Commodity trade.
PARTIES:
Australia SIGNED: 7 Dec 46 FORCE: 7 Dec 46
Siam SIGNED: 7 Dec 46 FORCE: 7 Dec 46
UK Great Britain SIGNED: 7 Dec 46 FORCE: 7 Dec 46

102051 Bilateral Exchange **157 UNTS 121**
SIGNED: 22 Sep 52 FORCE: 22 Sep 52
REGISTERED: 15 Jan 53 Belgium
ARTICLES: 2 LANGUAGE: French.
HEADNOTE: EXEMPTION IMPORT DUTIES
TOPIC: Customs
CONCEPTS: Definition of terms. Diplomatic privileges. Customs exemptions.
PROCEDURE: Denunciation.
PARTIES:
Belgium
Italy

102052 Multilateral Convention **157 UNTS 129**
SIGNED: 15 Dec 50 FORCE: 4 Nov 52
REGISTERED: 12 Jan 53 Belgium
ARTICLES: 20 LANGUAGE: English. French.
HEADNOTE: CUSTOMS COOPERATION COUNCIL
TOPIC: Customs
CONCEPTS: Annex or appendix reference. Establishment of commission. Financial programs. Customs duties. Headquarters and facilities. Liaison with other IGO's. Internal structure.
INTL ORGS: Customs Co-operation Council. United Nations.
PROCEDURE: Amendment. Accession. Duration. Ratification. Registration.
PARTIES:
Belgium SIGNED: 15 Dec 50 RATIFIED: 11 Dec 52 FORCE: 11 Dec 52
Denmark SIGNED: 15 Dec 50 RATIFIED: 19 Oct 51 FORCE: 4 Nov 52
France SIGNED: 15 Dec 50 RATIFIED: 6 Oct 52 FORCE: 4 Nov 52
Germany, West SIGNED: 15 Dec 50 RATIFIED: 4 Nov 52 FORCE: 4 Nov 52
Greece SIGNED: 15 Dec 50 RATIFIED: 10 Dec 51 FORCE: 4 Nov 52
Iceland SIGNED: 15 Dec 50
Italy SIGNED: 15 Dec 50 RATIFIED: 20 Nov 52 FORCE: 20 Nov 52
Luxembourg SIGNED: 15 Dec 50
Netherlands SIGNED: 15 Dec 50
Norway SIGNED: 15 Dec 50 RATIFIED: 6 Aug 51 FORCE: 4 Nov 52
Portugal SIGNED: 15 Dec 50
Spain RATIFIED: 13 Jul 52 FORCE: 4 Nov 52
Spain Spanish Colonies RATIFIED: 13 Jul 52 FORCE: 4 Nov 52
Spain Spanish Morroco RATIFIED: 13 Jul 52 FORCE: 4 Nov 52
Sweden SIGNED: 15 Dec 50 RATIFIED: 17 Oct 52 FORCE: 4 Nov 52
UK Great Britain SIGNED: 15 Dec 50 RATIFIED: 12 Sep 52 FORCE: 4 Nov 52
ANNEX
347 UNTS 379. Austria. Qualified Accession 21 Jan 53. Force 21 Jan 53.
347 UNTS 379. Pakistan. Accession 16 Nov 55. Force 16 Nov 55.
347 UNTS 379. United Arab Rep. Accession 26 Oct 56. Force 26 Oct 56.
347 UNTS 379. Syria. Accession 3 Nov 59. Force 3 Nov 59.
347 UNTS 379. Indonesia. Accession 30 Apr 57. Force 30 Apr 57.
347 UNTS 379. Haiti. Accession 31 Jan 58. Force 31 Jan 58.
347 UNTS 379. Iran. Accession 16 Oct 59. Force 16 Oct 59.

347 UNTS 379.   Luxembourg.   Ratification
23 Jan 53. Force 23 Jan 53.
347 UNTS 379. Israel.   Accession   23 May 58.
Force 23 May 58.
347 UNTS 379.   Netherlands.   Ratification
23 Jan 53. Force 23 Jan 53.

102053 Multilateral Convention **157 UNTS 157**
SIGNED: 8 Feb 49   FORCE: 3 Jul 50
REGISTERED: 19 Jan 53 USA (United States)
ARTICLES: 17 LANGUAGE: English.
HEADNOTE: NORTHWEST ATLANTIC FISHERIES
TOPIC: Specific Resources
CONCEPTS: Definition of terms. Territorial applica-
tion. Time limit. Treaty implementation. Annex or
appendix reference. Establishment of commis-
sion. Research cooperation. Research results.
Research and development. Accounting proce-
dures. Expense sharing formulae. Financial pro-
grams. Funding procedures. Liaison with other
IGO's. Conformity with IGO decisions. Ocean re-
sources.
INTL ORGS: Northwest Atlantic Fisheries Commis-
sion. Food and Agricultural Organization of the
United Nations. United Nations.
PROCEDURE: Accession. Duration. Ratification.
Registration. Renewal or Revival.
PARTIES:
Canada SIGNED: 8 Feb 49 RATIFIED: 3 Jul 50
FORCE: 3 Jul 50
Canada Newfoundland RATIFIED: 3 Jul 50
FORCE: 3 Jul 50
Denmark SIGNED: 8 Feb 49   RATIFIED:
14 Dec 50 FORCE: 14 Dec 50
France SIGNED: 8 Feb 49
Iceland SIGNED: 8 Feb 49 RATIFIED: 13 Feb 50
FORCE: 3 Jul 50
Italy SIGNED: 8 Feb 49 .RATIFIED: 19 Aug 52
FORCE: 19 Aug 52
Newfoundland SIGNED: 8 Feb 49
Norway SIGNED: 8 Feb 49 RATIFIED: 2 Jul 52
FORCE: 2 Jul 52
Portugal SIGNED: 8 Feb 49 RATIFIED: 19 Jul 52
FORCE: 19 Jul 52
Spain SIGNED: 8 Feb 49 RATIFIED: 17 Jan 52
FORCE: 17 Jan 52
UK Great Britain SIGNED: 8 Feb 49 RATIFIED:
15 Dec 49 FORCE: 3 Jul 50
USA (United States) SIGNED: 8 Feb 49 RATI-
FIED: 1 Sep 49 FORCE: 3 Jul 50
ANNEX
200 UNTS 317. NW Atlantic Fish. Amendment
11 Jun 53. Force 1 Jan 54.
200 UNTS 317. NW Atlantic Fish. Supplementation 15 Jul 52. Force 13 Jun 53.
308 UNTS 312. Germany, West. Berlin.
308 UNTS 312. USSR (Soviet Union). Adherence
10 Apr 58.
308 UNTS 312. NW Atlantic Fish. Amendment
28 Jun 56. Force 26 Mar 57.
308 UNTS 312. Germany, West. Adherence
27 Jun 57.
331 UNTS 388. UK Great Britain. Supplementation 25 Jun 56. Force 10 Jan 59.
331 UNTS 388. USA (United States). Supplementation 25 Jun 56. Force 10 Jan 59.
331 UNTS 388.   Portugal.   Supplementation
25 Jun 56. Force 10 Jan 59.
331 UNTS 388.   Canada.   Supplementation
25 Jun 59. Force 10 Jan 59.
331 UNTS 388.   Denmark.   Supplementation
25 Jun 56. Force 10 Jan 59.
331 UNTS 388.   France.   Supplementation
25 Jun 56. Force 10 Jan 59.
331 UNTS 388.   Iceland.   Supplementation
25 Jun 56. Force 10 Jan 59.
331 UNTS 388.   Italy.   Supplementation
25 Jun 56. Force 10 Jan 59.
331 UNTS 388.   Norway.   Supplementation
25 Jun 56. Force 10 Jan 59.
331 UNTS 388.   Spain.   Supplementation
25 Jun 56. Force 10 Jan 59.
458 UNTS 296. NW Atlantic Fish. Amendment
21 Jun 57. Force 28 Sep 58.
478 UNTS 422. Poland. Adherence 21 Nov 61.
480 UNTS 334. Italy. Interpretation 14 Sep 61.
Force 5 Jun 63.
480 UNTS 334. France. Interpretation 5 May 61.
Force 5 Jun 63.
480 UNTS 334. USSR (Soviet Union). Interpretation 8 May 61. Force 5 Jun 63.
480 UNTS 334. UK Great Britain. Interpretation
2 May 61. Force 5 Jun 63.

480 UNTS 334. Iceland. Interpretation 8 May 61.
Force 5 Jun 63.
480 UNTS 334. Norway. Interpretation 8 May 61.
Force 5 Jun 63.
480 UNTS 334. Spain. Interpretation 5 May 61.
Force 5 Jun 63.
480 UNTS 334. Germany, West. Interpretation
8 May 61. Force 5 Jun 63.
480 UNTS 334.   Portugal.   Interpretation
8 May 61. Force 5 Jun 63.
480 UNTS 334. Poland. Interpretation 5 Jun 63.
Force 5 Jun 63.
480 UNTS 334.   Canada.   Interpretation
15 Sep 61. Force 5 Jun 63.
480 UNTS 334. USA (United States). Interpretation 9 Feb 62. Force 5 Jun 63.
480 UNTS 334.   Denmark.   Interpretation
2 May 61. Force 5 Jun 63.

102054   Bilateral Agreement   **157 UNTS 185**
SIGNED: 22 Jul 52   FORCE: 1 Sep 49
REGISTERED: 23 Jan 53 UK Great Britain
ARTICLES: 26 LANGUAGE: English.
HEADNOTE: EXCHANGE MONEY ORDERS
TOPIC: Postal Service
CONCEPTS: Definition of terms. Annex or appen-
dix reference. Accounting procedures. Exchange
rates and regulations. Postal services. Money or-
ders and postal checks. Advice lists and orders.
PROCEDURE: Denunciation. Duration.
PARTIES:
Pakistan
UK Great Britain
ANNEX
613 UNTS 407. UK Great Britain. Abrogation
7 Feb 67. Force 1 Jan 67.
613 UNTS 407. Pakistan. Abrogation 7 Feb 67.
Force 1 Jan 67.

102055   Bilateral Agreement   **157 UNTS 213**
SIGNED: 13 Sep 50   FORCE: 28 Feb 51
REGISTERED: 28 Jan 53 IBRD (World Bank)
ARTICLES: 7 LANGUAGE: English.
HEADNOTE: LOAN AGREEMENT
TOPIC: IBRD Project
CONCEPTS. Default remedies. Definition of terms.
Conformity with municipal law. Exchange of in-
formation and documents. Informational
records. Inspection and observation. Accounting
procedures. Bonds. Fees and exemptions. Inter-
est rates. Tax exemptions. Domestic obligation.
Terms of loan. Loan regulations. Loan guarantee.
Guarantor non-interference.
PARTIES:
Ethiopia
IBRD (World Bank)

102056   Bilateral Agreement   **157 UNTS 233**
·SIGNED: 13 Sep 50   FORCE: 1 Jun 51
REGISTERED: 28 Jan 53 IBRD (World Bank)
ARTICLES: 7 LANGUAGE: English.
HEADNOTE: LOAN AGREEMENT
TOPIC: IBRD Project
CONCEPTS: Default remedies. Definition of terms.
Conformity with municipal law. Exchange of in-
formation and documents. Informational
records. Inspection and observation. Accounting
procedures. Bonds. Fees and exemptions. Inter-
est rates. Tax exemptions. Domestic obligation.
Terms of loan. Loan regulations. Loan guarantee.
Guarantor non-interference.
PARTIES:
Ethiopia
IBRD (World Bank)

102057   Bilateral Agreement   **157 UNTS 259**
SIGNED: 18 Oct 50   FORCE: 20 Jul 51
REGISTERED: 28 Jan 53 IBRD (World Bank)
ARTICLES: 5 LANGUAGE: English.
HEADNOTE: GUARANTEE AGREEMENT
TOPIC: IBRD Project
CONCEPTS: Default remedies. Annex or appendix
reference. Conformity with municipal law. Infor-
mational records. Inspection and observation.
Bonds. Fees and exemptions. Tax exemptions.
Domestic obligation. Loan regulations. Loan
guarantee. Guarantor non-interference.
PARTIES:
Mexico
IBRD (World Bank)

102058   Bilateral Agreement   **157 UNTS 333**
SIGNED: 19 Oct 50   FORCE: 28 Feb 51
REGISTERED: 28 Jan 53 IBRD (World Bank)
ARTICLES: 4 LANGUAGE: English.
HEADNOTE: GUARANTEE AGREEMENT
TOPIC: IBRD Project
CONCEPTS: Annex or appendix reference. Ex-
change of information and documents. Informa-
tional records. Inspection and observation. Ac-
counting procedures. Currency. Exchange rates
and regulations. Fees and exemptions. Tax ex-
emptions. Domestic obligation. Loan regula-
tions. Loan guarantee. Guarantor non-interfer-
ence.
PARTIES:
IBRD (World Bank)
Turkey

102059   Bilateral Agreement   **158 UNTS 3**
SIGNED: 27 Oct 50   FORCE: 24 Feb 51
REGISTERED: 28 Jan 53 IBRD (World Bank)
ARTICLES: 6 LANGUAGE: English.
HEADNOTE: LOAN AGREEMENT
TOPIC: IBRD Project
CONCEPTS: Default remedies. Annex or appendix
reference. Exchange of information and docu-
ments. Informational records. Inspection and ob-
servation. Accounting procedures. Bonds. Fees
and exemptions. Interest rates. Tax exemptions.
Domestic obligation. Terms of loan. Loan regula-
tions. Loan guarantee. Guarantor non-interfer-
ence.
PARTIES:
IBRD (World Bank)
Thailand

102060   Bilateral Agreement   **158 UNTS 25**
SIGNED: 27 Oct 50   FORCE: 24 Feb 51
REGISTERED: 28 Jan 53 IBRD (World Bank)
ARTICLES: 6 LANGUAGE: English.
HEADNOTE: LOAN AGREEMENT
TOPIC: IBRD Project
CONCEPTS: Default remedies. Exchange of infor-
mation and documents. Informational records.
Inspection and observation. Accounting proce-
dures. Bonds. Fees and exemptions. Interest
rates. Tax exemptions. Domestic obligation.
Terms of loan. Loan regulations. Loan guarantee.
Guarantor non-interference.
PARTIES:
IBRD (World Bank)
Thailand

102061   Bilateral Agreement   **158 UNTS 43**
SIGNED: 27 Oct 50   FORCE: 29 Aug 51
REGISTERED: 28 Jan 53 IBRD (World Bank)
ARTICLES: 6 LANGUAGE: English.
HEADNOTE: LOAN AGREEMENT
TOPIC: IBRD Project
CONCEPTS: Default remedies. Exchange of infor-
mation and documents. Informational records.
Inspection and observation. Accounting proce-
dures. Bonds. Fees and exemptions. Interest
rates. Tax exemptions. Domestic obligation.
Terms of loan. Loan regulations. Loan guarantee.
Guarantor non-interference.
PARTIES:
IBRD (World Bank)
Thailand

102062   Bilateral Agreement   **158 UNTS 59**
SIGNED: 2 Nov 50   FORCE: 28 Feb 51
REGISTERED: 28 Jan 53 IBRD (World Bank)
ARTICLES: 7 LANGUAGE: English.
HEADNOTE: GUARANTEE
TOPIC: IBRD Project
CONCEPTS: Bonds. Currency. Inadequacy of
funds. Credit provisions.
PARTIES:
Colombia
IBRD (World Bank)

102063   Bilateral Agreement   **158 UNTS 87**
SIGNED: 28 Dec 50   FORCE: 29 Mar 51
·REGISTERED: 28 Jan 53 IBRD (World Bank)
ARTICLES: 7 LANGUAGE: English.
HEADNOTE: GUARANTEE AGREEMENT
TOPIC: IBRD Project
CONCEPTS: Definition of terms. Annex or appen-

dix reference. Exchange of information and documents. Informational records. Inspection and observation. Bonds. Currency. Fees and exemptions. Tax exemptions. Domestic obligation. Loan regulations. Loan guarantee. Guarantor non-interference.
PARTIES:
Colombia
IBRD (World Bank)

102064 Bilateral Agreement **158 UNTS 115**
SIGNED: 23 Jan 51 FORCE: 4 Apr 51
REGISTERED: 28 Jan 53 IBRD (World Bank)
ARTICLES: 6 LANGUAGE: English.
HEADNOTE: LOAN AGREEMENT
TOPIC: IBRD Project
CONCEPTS: Default remedies. Annex or appendix reference. Exchange of information and documents. Informational records. Inspection and observation. Accounting procedures. Bonds. Fees and exemptions. Tax exemptions. Domestic obligation. Terms of loan. Loan regulations. Loan guarantee. Guarantor non-interference.
PARTIES:
IBRD (World Bank)
South Africa

102065 Bilateral Agreement **158 UNTS 135**
SIGNED: 23 Jan 51 FORCE: 4 Apr 51
REGISTERED: 28 Jan 53 IBRD (World Bank)
ARTICLES: 4 LANGUAGE: English.
HEADNOTE: GUARANTEE AGREEMENT
TOPIC: IBRD Project
CONCEPTS: Annex or appendix reference. Exchange of information and documents. Informational records. Inspection and observation. Fees and exemptions. Tax exemptions. Domestic obligation. Loan regulations. Loan guarantee. Guarantor non-interference.
PARTIES:
IBRD (World Bank)
South Africa

102066 Bilateral Agreement **158 UNTS 155**
SIGNED: 10 Apr 51 FORCE: 6 Jul 51
REGISTERED: 28 Jan 53 IBRD (World Bank)
ARTICLES: 7 LANGUAGE: English.
HEADNOTE: LOAN AGREEMENT
TOPIC: IBRD Project
CONCEPTS: Default remedies. Definition of terms. Annex or appendix reference. Exchange of information and documents. Informational records. Inspection and observation. Accounting procedures. Bonds. Fees and exemptions. Interest rates. Tax exemptions. Domestic obligation. Terms of loan. Loan regulations. Loan guarantee. Guarantor non-interference.
PARTIES:
Colombia
IBRD (World Bank)

102067 Bilateral Agreement **158 UNTS 215**
SIGNED: 7 Jun 51 FORCE: 22 Aug 51
REGISTERED: 28 Jan 53 IBRD (World Bank)
ARTICLES: 5 LANGUAGE: English.
HEADNOTE: GUARANTEE AGREEMENT
TOPIC: IBRD Project
CONCEPTS: Definition of terms. Annex or appendix reference. Exchange of information and documents. Informational records. Inspection and observation. Bonds. Fees and exemptions. Tax exemptions. Domestic obligation. Loan regulations. Loan guarantee. Guarantor non-interference.
PARTIES:
Nicaragua
IBRD (World Bank)

102068 Bilateral Agreement **158 UNTS 277**
SIGNED: 7 Jun 51 FORCE: 17 Aug 51
REGISTERED: 28 Jan 53 IBRD (World Bank)
ARTICLES: 6 LANGUAGE: English.
HEADNOTE: LOAN AGREEMENT
TOPIC: IBRD Project
CONCEPTS: Default remedies. Definition of terms. Annex or appendix reference. Exchange of information and documents. Informational records. Inspection and observation. Accounting procedures. Bonds. Currency. Fees and exemptions.

Interest rates. Tax exemptions. Domestic obligation. Terms of loan. Loan regulations. Loan guarantee. Guarantor non-interference.
PARTIES:
Nicaragua
IBRD (World Bank)

102069 Bilateral Agreement **158 UNTS 301**
SIGNED: 20 Jun 51 FORCE: 21 Jul 51
REGISTERED: 28 Jan 53 IBRD (World Bank)
ARTICLES: 8 LANGUAGE: English.
HEADNOTE: LOAN AGREEMENT
TOPIC: IBRD Project
CONCEPTS: Default remedies. Definition of terms. Exchange of information and documents. Informational records. Inspection and observation. Accounting procedures. Bonds. Fees and exemptions. Interest rates. Tax exemptions. Domestic obligation. Terms of loan. Loan regulations. Loan guarantee. Guarantor non-interference.
PARTIES:
Iceland
IBRD (World Bank)

102070 Bilateral Agreement **158 UNTS 323**
SIGNED: 13 Sep 51 FORCE: 26 Jan 52
REGISTERED: 28 Jan 53 IBRD (World Bank)
ARTICLES: 5 LANGUAGE: English.
HEADNOTE: GUARANTEE AGREEMENT
TOPIC: IBRD Project
CONCEPTS: Annex or appendix reference. Exchange of information and documents. Informational records. Inspection and observation. Bonds. Fees and exemptions. Tax exemptions. Domestic obligation. Terms of loan. Loan regulations. Loan guarantee.
PARTIES:
Belgium
IBRD (World Bank)

102071 Bilateral Agreement **158 UNTS 349**
SIGNED: 13 Sep 51 FORCE: 26 Jan 52
REGISTERED: 28 Jan 53 IBRD (World Bank)
ARTICLES: 8 LANGUAGE: English.
HEADNOTE: LOAN AGREEMENT
TOPIC: IBRD Project
CONCEPTS: Default remedies. Definition of terms. Annex or appendix reference. Accounting procedures. Bonds. Fees and exemptions. Interest rates. Tax exemptions. Domestic obligation. Loan regulations. Loan guarantee. Guarantor non-interference.
PARTIES:
Belgium
IBRD (World Bank)

102072 Bilateral Agreement **158 UNTS 369**
SIGNED: 10 Oct 51 FORCE: 15 Feb 52
REGISTERED: 28 Jan 53 IBRD (World Bank)
ARTICLES: 5 LANGUAGE: English.
HEADNOTE: GUARANTEE AGREEMENT
TOPIC: IBRD Project
CONCEPTS: Annex or appendix reference. Exchange of information and documents. Informational records. Inspection and observation. Fees and exemptions. Interest rates. Tax exemptions. Domestic obligation. Loan regulations. Loan guarantee. Guarantor non-interference.
PARTIES:
Chile
IBRD (World Bank)

102073 Bilateral Agreement **158 UNTS 391**
SIGNED: 11 Dec 52 FORCE: 17 Dec 52
REGISTERED: 29 Jan 53 WHO (World Health)
ARTICLES: 4 LANGUAGE: English.
HEADNOTE: WHO TUBERCULOSIS CONTROL PROJECT
TOPIC: Sanitation
CONCEPTS: Conditions. Definition of terms. Annex or appendix reference. Previous treaty extension. Friendship and amity. Privileges and immunities. Personnel. General property. Specialists exchange. Disease control. Public health. WHO used as agency. Institute establishment. Vocational training. Research results. Indemnities and reimbursements. Expense sharing formulae. Fees and exemptions. Tax exemptions.

Assistance. Special projects. Specific technical assistance. Technical cooperation. Economic assistance. Materials, equipment and services. Status of experts.
INTL ORGS: United Nations.
TREATY REF: 67UNTS3.
PROCEDURE: Amendment. Termination.
PARTIES:
India
WHO (World Health)

102074 Multilateral Agreement **158 UNTS 407**
SIGNED: 16 Dec 52 FORCE: 16 Dec 52
REGISTERED: 1 Feb 53 United Nations
ARTICLES: 6 LANGUAGE: English. Spanish.
HEADNOTE: TECHNICAL ASSISTANCE
TOPIC: Tech Assistance
CONCEPTS: Treaty implementation. Privileges and immunities. General cooperation. Exchange of information and documents. Personnel. Title and deeds. Exchange. Scholarships and grants. Vocational training. Research and development. Expense sharing formulae. Local currency. Domestic obligation. General technical assistance. Materials, equipment and services. IGO status. Conformity with IGO decisions.
INTL ORGS: United Nations.
TREATY REF: 76UNTS132; 1UNTS15,263; 33UNTS261.
PROCEDURE: Amendment. Termination.
PARTIES:
Nicaragua SIGNED: 16 Dec 52 FORCE: 16 Dec 52
ICAO (Civil Aviat) SIGNED: 16 Dec 52 FORCE: 16 Dec 52
ILO (Labor Org) SIGNED: 16 Dec 52 FORCE: 16 Dec 52
UNESCO (Educ/Cult) SIGNED: 16 Dec 52 FORCE: 16 Dec 52
United Nations SIGNED: 16 Dec 52 FORCE: 16 Dec 52
WHO (World Health) SIGNED: 16 Dec 52 FORCE: 16 Dec 52
ANNEX
248 UNTS 369. UNTAB (Tech Assis). Force 2 Jul 56.
248 UNTS 369. Nicaragua. Force 2 Jul 56.

102075 Bilateral Exchange **158 UNTS 423**
SIGNED: 19 Oct 52 FORCE: 19 Oct 52
REGISTERED: 3 Feb 53 UK Great Britain
ARTICLES: 2 LANGUAGE: English.
HEADNOTE: RENEWAL PROVISIONAL COMMERCIAL AGREEMENT
TOPIC: General Trade
CONCEPTS: Territorial application. Annex type material. Previous treaty extension.
TREATY REF: 107LTS267.
PROCEDURE: Termination.
PARTIES:
United Arab Rep
UK Great Britain
ANNEX
196 UNTS 359. UK Great Britain. St. Vincent.
196 UNTS 359. UK Great Britain. Zanzibar.
196 UNTS 359. United Arab Rep. Acknowledgement 3 Apr 54.
196 UNTS 359. UK Great Britain. Brunei.
196 UNTS 359. UK Great Britain. Windward Islands.
196 UNTS 359. UK Great Britain. Dominican Republic.
196 UNTS 359. UK Great Britain. Grenada.
196 UNTS 359. UK Great Britain. St. Lucia.
196 UNTS 359. UK Great Britain. Fed Rhod/-Nyasaland.

102076 Bilateral Exchange **158 UNTS 431**
SIGNED: 6 Nov 52 FORCE: 6 Nov 52
REGISTERED: 3 Feb 53 UK Great Britain
ARTICLES: 2 LANGUAGE: English. Italian.
HEADNOTE: AGREEMENT SALVAGE
TOPIC: Specif Claim/Waive
CONCEPTS: Responsibility and liability. Shipwreck and salvage. Naval vessels. Specific claims or waivers.
PARTIES:
Italy
UK Great Britain

102077 Bilateral Exchange **158 UNTS 439**
SIGNED: 20 Aug 52 FORCE: 20 Aug 52
REGISTERED: 3 Feb 53 UK Great Britain
ARTICLES: 2 LANGUAGE: English.
HEADNOTE: FINANCIAL ARRANGEMENTS
TOPIC: Finance
CONCEPTS: Banking. Currency. Monetary and
gold transfers.
INTL ORGS: International Monetary Fund.
PARTIES:
UK Great Britain
Yugoslavia

102078 Bilateral Exchange **158 UNTS 445**
SIGNED: 10 Dec 52 FORCE: 19 Jan 53
REGISTERED: 4 Feb 53 Belgium
ARTICLES: 2 LANGUAGE: French.
HEADNOTE: INDUSTRIAL COMMERCIAL TRADE-
MARKS
TOPIC: Patents/Copyrights
CONCEPTS: Conformity with municipal law. Trade-
marks.
PROCEDURE: Denunciation. Duration.
PARTIES:
Belgium
Iceland

102079 Bilateral Agreement **158 UNTS 451**
SIGNED: 8 May 51 FORCE: 21 Jan 53
REGISTERED: 4 Feb 53 Belgium
ARTICLES: 15 LANGUAGE: English. French.
HEADNOTE: AIR SERVICES
TOPIC: Air Transport
CONCEPTS: Conditions. Definition of terms. De-
tailed regulations. Exceptions and exemptions.
Previous treaty replacement. Conformity with
municipal law. General cooperation. Exchange
of information and documents. Arbitration. Pro-
cedure. Existing tribunals. Negotiation. Non-
interest rates and fees. Most favored nation
clause. Routes and logistics. Permit designation.
Conditions of airlines operating permission.
Overflights and technical stops. Operating au-
thorizations and regulations.
INTL ORGS: International Civil Aviation Organization. International Court of Justice. Arbitration
Commission.
TREATY REF: 15UNTS295.
PROCEDURE: Amendment. Future Procedures
Contemplated. Ratification. Registration. Termination. Application to Non-self-governing Terri-
tories.
PARTIES:
Belgium
UK Great Britain
ANNEX
172 UNTS 404. UK Great Britain. Amendment
16 Mar 53. Force 16 Mar 53.
172 UNTS 404. Belgium. Amendment 16 Mar 53.
Force 16 Mar 53.
398 UNTS 346. UK Great Britain. Amendment
22 Dec 58. Force 22 Dec 58.
398 UNTS 346. Belgium. Amendment 22 Dec 58.
Force 22 Dec 58.

102080 Bilateral Exchange **158 UNTS 469**
SIGNED: 26 Sep 51 FORCE: 26 Sep 51
REGISTERED: 4 Feb 53 Netherlands
ARTICLES: 2 LANGUAGE: English.
HEADNOTE: AMERICAN WAR CEMETERY
TOPIC: Milit Installation
CONCEPTS: Time limit. Annex or appendix refer-
ence. Title and deeds. Tax exemptions. Respon-
sibility for war dead. Upkeep of war graves.
TREATY REF: 148UNTS343.
PARTIES:
Netherlands
USA (United States)

102081 Bilateral Agreement **159 UNTS 3**
SIGNED: 11 Oct 51 FORCE: 28 Dec 51
REGISTERED: 9 Feb 53 IBRD (World Bank)
ARTICLES: 7 LANGUAGE: English.
HEADNOTE: LOAN AGREEMENT
TOPIC: IBRD Project
CONCEPTS: Default remedies. Definition of terms.
Annex or appendix reference. Exchange of infor-
mation and documents. Informational records.
Inspection and observation. Accounting proce-

dures. Bonds. Fees and exemptions. Tax exemp-
tions. Domestic obligation. Terms of loan.
PARTIES:
IBRD (World Bank)
Yugoslavia

102082 Bilateral Agreement **159 UNTS 35**
SIGNED: 29 Oct 51 FORCE: 13 Feb 52
REGISTERED: 9 Feb 53 IBRD (World Bank)
ARTICLES: 8 LANGUAGE: English.
HEADNOTE: LOAN AGREEMENT
TOPIC: IBRD Project
CONCEPTS: Default remedies. Definition of terms.
Annex or appendix reference. Exchange of infor-
mation and documents. Informational records.
Inspection and observation. Bonds. Fees and ex-
emptions. Interest rates. Tax exemptions. Do-
mestic obligation. Terms of loan. Loan regula-
tions. Loan guarantee. Guarantor non-interfer-
ence.
PARTIES:
Nicaragua
IBRD (World Bank)

102083 Bilateral Agreement **159 UNTS 55**
SIGNED: 1 Nov 51 FORCE: 26 Feb 52
REGISTERED: 9 Feb 53 IBRD (World Bank)
ARTICLES: 7 LANGUAGE: English.
HEADNOTE: LOAN AGREEMENT
TOPIC: IBRD Project
CONCEPTS: Default remedies. Definition of terms.
Annex or appendix reference. Exchange of infor-
mation and documents. Informational records.
Inspection and observation. Accounting proce-
dures. Bonds. Fees and exemptions. Interest
rates. Domestic obligation. Terms of loan. Loan
regulations. Loan guarantee. Guarantor non-
interference.
PARTIES:
Iceland
IBRD (World Bank)

102084 Bilateral Agreement **159 UNTS 75**
SIGNED: 13 Oct 51 FORCE: 26 Feb 52
REGISTERED: 9 Feb 53 IBRD (World Bank)
ARTICLES: 5 LANGUAGE: English.
HEADNOTE: GUARANTEE AGREEMENT
TOPIC: IBRD Project
CONCEPTS: Annex or appendix reference. Ex-
change of information and documents. Informa-
tional records. Inspection and observation.
Bonds. Fees and exemptions. Tax exemptions.
Domestic obligation. Loan regulations. Loan
guarantee. Guarantor non-interference.
PARTIES:
Colombia
IBRD (World Bank)

102085 Bilateral Agreement **159 UNTS 103**
SIGNED: 7 Dec 51 FORCE: 5 Sep 52
REGISTERED: 9 Feb 53 IBRD (World Bank)
ARTICLES: 8 LANGUAGE: English.
HEADNOTE: LOAN AGREEMENT
TOPIC: IBRD Project
CONCEPTS: Default remedies. Definition of terms.
Annex or appendix reference. Exchange of infor-
mation and documents. Informational records.
Inspection and observation. Accounting proce-
dures. Bonds. Fees and exemptions. Interest
rates. Tax exemptions. Domestic obligation.
Terms of loan. Loan regulations. Loan guarantee.
Guarantor non-interference.
PARTIES:
Paraguay
IBRD (World Bank)
ANNEX
248 UNTS 370. IBRD (World Bank). Supplementa-
tion 12 Jan 55. Force 14 Mar 55.
248 UNTS 370. Paraguay. Supplementation
14 Mar 55. Force 14 Mar 55.
312 UNTS 422. Paraguay. Amendment 7 Apr 58.
Force 7 Apr 58.
312 UNTS 422. IBRD (World Bank). Amendment
7 Apr 58. Force 7 Apr 58.

102086 Bilateral Agreement **159 UNTS 129**
SIGNED: 11 Jan 52 FORCE: 10 Jun 52
REGISTERED: 11 Feb 53 IBRD (World Bank)
ARTICLES: 5 LANGUAGE: English.

HEADNOTE: GUARANTEE COMMISSION FEDERAL
POWER PROGRAM
TOPIC: IBRD Project
CONCEPTS: Definition of terms. Annex or appendix reference. Exchange of information and documents. Informational records. Inspection and
observation. Bonds. Indemnities and reimbursements. Fees and exemptions. Domestic obligation. Loan regulations. Loan guarantee. Guarantor non-interference.
PARTIES:
Mexico
IBRD (World Bank)

102087 Bilateral Agreement **159 UNTS 163**
SIGNED: 23 Jan 52 FORCE: 4 Jun 52
REGISTERED: 11 Feb 53 IBRD (World Bank)
ARTICLES: 7 LANGUAGE: English.
HEADNOTE: LOAN AGREEMENT
TOPIC: IBRD Project
CONCEPTS: Default remedies. Annex or appendix
reference. Exchange of information and docu-
ments. Informational records. Inspection and ob-
servation. Accounting procedures. Bonds. Fees
and exemptions. Interest rates. Tax exemptions.
Domestic obligation. Terms of loan. Loan regula-
tions. Loan guarantee. Guarantor non-interfer-
ence.
PARTIES:
Peru
IBRD (World Bank)

102088 Bilateral Agreement **159 UNTS 181**
SIGNED: 27 Feb 52 FORCE: 1 May 52
REGISTERED: 11 Feb 53 IBRD (World Bank)
ARTICLES: 5 LANGUAGE: English.
HEADNOTE: GUARANTEE AGREEMENT
TOPIC: IBRD Project
CONCEPTS: Definition of terms. Annex or appen-
dix reference. Exchange of information and doc-
uments. Informational records. Inspection and
observation. Bonds. Fees and exemptions. Tax
exemptions. Domestic obligation. Loan regula-
tions. Loan guarantee. Guarantor non-interfer-
ence.
PARTIES:
IBRD (World Bank)
UK Great Britain

102089 Bilateral Agreement **159 UNTS 207**
SIGNED: 20 Mar 52 FORCE: 25 Apr 52
REGISTERED: 11 Feb 53 IBRD (World Bank)
ARTICLES: 6 LANGUAGE: English.
HEADNOTE: GUARANTEE AGREEMENT
TOPIC: IBRD Project
CONCEPTS: Definition of terms. Annex or appen-
dix reference. Exchange of information and doc-
uments. Informational records. Inspection and
observation. Fees and exemptions. Tax exemp-
tions. Domestic obligation. Loan regulations.
Loan guarantee. Guarantor non-interference.
PARTIES:
Netherlands
IBRD (World Bank)

102090 Bilateral Agreement **159 UNTS 251**
SIGNED: 27 Mar 52 FORCE: 3 Jun 52
REGISTERED: 11 Feb 53 IBRD (World Bank)
ARTICLES: 7 LANGUAGE: English.
HEADNOTE: LOAN AGREEMENT
TOPIC: IBRD Project
CONCEPTS: Default remedies. Definition of terms.
Annex or appendix reference. Exchange of infor-
mation and documents. Informational records.
Inspection and observation. Accounting proce-
dures. Fees and exemptions. Interest rates. Tax
exemptions. Domestic obligation. Terms of loan.
Loan regulations. Loan guarantee. Guarantor
non-interference.
PARTIES:
Pakistan
IBRD (World Bank)

102091 Bilateral Agreement **159 UNTS 269**
SIGNED: 18 Jun 52 FORCE: 27 Sep 52
REGISTERED: 11 Feb 53 IBRD (World Bank)
ARTICLES: 7 LANGUAGE: English.
HEADNOTE: LOAN AGREEMENT
TOPIC: IBRD Project

CONCEPTS: Default remedies. Annex or appendix reference. Exchange of information and documents. Informational records. Inspection and observation. Accounting procedures. Bonds. Fees and exemptions. Interest rates. Tax exemptions. Domestic obligation. Terms of loan. Loan regulations. Loan guarantee. Guarantor non-interference.
PARTIES:
IBRD (World Bank)
Turkey

102092 Bilateral Agreement **159 UNTS 295**
SIGNED: 8 Jul 52 FORCE: 18 Nov 52
REGISTERED: 11 Feb 53 IBRD (World Bank)
ARTICLES: 7 LANGUAGE: English.
HEADNOTE: LOAN AGREEMENT
TOPIC: IBRD Project
CONCEPTS: Default remedies. Annex or appendix reference. Exchange of information and documents. Informational records. Inspection and observation. Accounting procedures. Bonds. Fees and exemptions. Interest rates. Tax exemptions. Domestic obligation. Terms of loan. Loan regulations. Loan guarantee. Guarantor non-interference.
PARTIES:
Australia
IBRD (World Bank)

102093 Bilateral Agreement **159 UNTS 321**
SIGNED: 8 Jul 52 FORCE: 31 Jul 52
REGISTERED: 11 Feb 53 IBRD (World Bank)
ARTICLES: 8 LANGUAGE: English.
HEADNOTE: LOAN AGREEMENT
TOPIC: IBRD Project
CONCEPTS: Default remedies. Definition of terms. Annex or appendix reference. Exchange of information and documents. Informational records. Inspection and observation. Accounting procedures. Bonds. Fees and exemptions. Interest rates. Tax exemptions. Domestic obligation. Terms of loan. Loan regulations. Loan guarantee. Guarantor non-interference.
PARTIES:
Peru
IBRD (World Bank)

102094 Bilateral Agreement **159 UNTS 339**
SIGNED: 26 Aug 52 FORCE: 23 Dec 52
REGISTERED: 11 Feb 53 IBRD (World Bank)
ARTICLES: 7 LANGUAGE: English.
HEADNOTE: LOAN AGREEMENT
TOPIC: IBRD Project
CONCEPTS: Default remedies. Definition of terms. Annex or appendix reference. Exchange of information and documents. Informational records. Inspection and observation. Accounting procedures. Bonds. Fees and exemptions. Interest rates. Tax exemptions. Domestic obligation. Terms of loan. Loan regulations. Loan guarantee. Guarantor non-interference.
PARTIES:
Colombia
IBRD (World Bank)

102095 Bilateral Agreement **159 UNTS 363**
SIGNED: 26 Aug 52 FORCE: 28 Oct 52
REGISTERED: 11 Feb 53 IBRD (World Bank)
ARTICLES: 8 LANGUAGE: English.
HEADNOTE: LOAN AGREEMENT
TOPIC: IBRD Project
CONCEPTS: Default remedies. Definition of terms. Annex or appendix reference. Exchange of information and documents. Informational records. Inspection and observation. Accounting procedures. Bonds. Fees and exemptions. Interest rates. Tax exemptions. Terms of loan. Loan regulations. Loan guarantee. Guarantor non-interference.
PARTIES:
Iceland
IBRD (World Bank)

102096 Bilateral Agreement **160 UNTS 3**
SIGNED: 11 Feb 53 FORCE: 11 Feb 53
REGISTERED: 11 Feb 53 United Nations
ARTICLES: 5 LANGUAGE: English.
HEADNOTE: TECHNICAL ASSISTANCE

TOPIC: Tech Assistance
CONCEPTS: Privileges and immunities. General cooperation. Exchange of information and documents. Operating agencies. Exchange. Financial programs. Domestic obligation. General technical assistance. Special projects. IGO status.
TREATY REF: 1UNTS15,263.
PROCEDURE: Amendment. Termination.
PARTIES:
United Nations
Sweden

102097 Bilateral Exchange **160 UNTS 11**
SIGNED: 29 Aug 46 FORCE: 29 Aug 46
REGISTERED: 12 Feb 53 USA (United States)
ARTICLES: 2 LANGUAGE: English. Polish.
HEADNOTE: CRIMINAL OFFENSES COMMITTED MEMBERS ARMED FORCES
TOPIC: Status of Forces
CONCEPTS: Indemnities and reimbursements. Jurisdiction. Status of forces.
PROCEDURE: Duration. Termination.
PARTIES:
Poland
USA (United States)

102098 Bilateral Exchange **160 UNTS 27**
SIGNED: 5 Jan 46 FORCE: 5 Jan 46
REGISTERED: 12 Feb 53 USA (United States)
ARTICLES: 2 LANGUAGE: English. French.
HEADNOTE: ESTABLISHMENT CUSTOMS PUBLIC HEALTH POLICE CONTROLS
TOPIC: Status of Forces
CONCEPTS: Conformity with municipal law. Use of facilities. Investigation of violations. Border control. Customs duties. Jurisdiction. Status of forces.
PARTIES:
United Arab Rep
USA (United States)

102099 Bilateral Exchange **160 UNTS 35**
SIGNED: 28 Sep 51 FORCE: 28 Sep 51
REGISTERED: 12 Feb 53 USA (United States)
ARTICLES: 2 LANGUAGE: English. Spanish.
HEADNOTE: TRADE
TOPIC: General Trade
CONCEPTS: Annex type material. Previous treaty replacement.
INTL ORGS: General Agreement on Tariffs and Trade.
TREATY REF: GATT.
PARTIES:
Peru
USA (United States)

102100 Bilateral Exchange **160 UNTS 41**
SIGNED: 9 Nov 51 FORCE: 9 Nov 51
REGISTERED: 12 Feb 53 USA (United States)
ARTICLES: 2 LANGUAGE: English.
HEADNOTE: MUTUAL DEFENSE ASSISTANCE
TOPIC: Milit Assistance
CONCEPTS: Exceptions and exemptions. Guarantees and safeguards. Accounting procedures. Payment schedules. Materials, equipment and services. Self-defense. Military assistance. Security of information. Exchange of defense information. Restrictions on transfer.
INTL ORGS: United Nations.
PARTIES:
South Africa
USA (United States)

102101 Bilateral Agreement **160 UNTS 49**
SIGNED: 29 May 51 FORCE: 13 Dec 51
REGISTERED: 12 Feb 53 USA (United States)
ARTICLES: 8 LANGUAGE: Arabic. English.
HEADNOTE: TECHNICAL COOPERATION
TOPIC: Tech Assistance
CONCEPTS: Conditions. Exceptions and exemptions. Treaty implementation. Previous treaty replacement. Exchange of information and documents. Personnel. Public information. Vocational training. Expense sharing formulae. Tax exemptions. Customs duties. Customs exemptions. Domestic obligation. General technical assistance. Materials, equipment and services.
INTL ORGS: United Nations.
PROCEDURE: Amendment. Termination.

PARTIES:
Lebanon
USA (United States)

102102 Bilateral Exchange **160 UNTS 63**
SIGNED: 21 Jan 52 FORCE: 21 Jan 52
REGISTERED: 12 Feb 53 USA (United States)
ARTICLES: 2 LANGUAGE: English. Spanish.
HEADNOTE: PASSPORT VISA REQUIREMENTS
TOPIC: Visas
CONCEPTS: Time limit. Visa abolition. Denial of admission. Visas. Conformity with municipal law. Fees and exemptions.
PARTIES:
Spain
USA (United States)

102103 Bilateral Exchange **160 UNTS 75**
SIGNED: 14 Feb 49 FORCE: 14 Feb 49
REGISTERED: 12 Feb 53 USA (United States)
ARTICLES: 2 LANGUAGE: English. Spanish.
HEADNOTE: HEALTH SANITATION PROGRAM MEXICO
TOPIC: Sanitation
CONCEPTS: Definition of terms. Annex or appendix reference. Annex type material. Previous treaty extension. Privileges and immunities. Domestic legislation. Personnel. Public health. Sanitation. Accounting procedures. Indemnities and reimbursements. Financial programs. Funding procedures. Assistance. Grants.
TREATY REF: TIAS2091; EAS347; 57STAT1121; 160UNTS76.
PROCEDURE: Duration.
PARTIES:
Mexico
USA (United States)
ANNEX
179 UNTS 270. Mexico. Supplementation 15 May 52. Force 15 May 52.
179 UNTS 270. USA (United States). Supplementation 31 Jan 52. Force 15 May 52.

102104 Bilateral Exchange **160 UNTS 103**
SIGNED: 23 Apr 46 FORCE: 23 Apr 46
REGISTERED: 12 Feb 53 USA (United States)
ARTICLES: 2 LANGUAGE: English. Spanish.
HEADNOTE: HEALTH SANITATION URUGUAY
TOPIC: Sanitation
CONCEPTS: Conditions. Annex or appendix reference. Annex type material. Previous treaty extension. Personnel. Specialists exchange. Public health. Sanitation. Funding procedures. Assistance. Specific technical assistance. Grants.
TREATY REF: 106UNTS311.
PROCEDURE: Duration. Termination.
PARTIES:
USA (United States)
Uruguay

102105 Bilateral Agreement **160 UNTS 121**
SIGNED: 31 Jan 51 FORCE: 31 Jan 51
REGISTERED: 12 Feb 53 USA (United States)
ARTICLES: 18 LANGUAGE: English. Spanish.
HEADNOTE: HEALTH SANITATION PROGRAM
TOPIC: Sanitation
CONCEPTS: Definition of terms. Treaty violation. Friendship and amity. Privileges and immunities. General cooperation. Inspection and observation. Domestic legislation. Personnel. Private contracts. Public health. Nursing. Sanitation. Scholarships and grants. Vocational training. Research and development. Accounting procedures. Indemnities and reimbursements. Currency. Exchange rates and regulations. Expense sharing formulae. Financial programs. Funding procedures. Debts. Assistance. Special projects. Specific technical assistance.
PROCEDURE: Duration. Termination.
PARTIES:
Nicaragua
USA (United States)
ANNEX
179 UNTS 278. USA (United States). Supplementation 16 Jan 52. Force 14 Jun 52.
179 UNTS 278. Nicaragua. Supplementation 14 Jun 52. Force 14 Jun 52.
269 UNTS 332. USA (United States). Prolongation 27 Apr 55. Force 27 Apr 55.

269 UNTS 332. Nicaragua. Prolongation 27 Apr 55. Force 27 Apr 55.

102106 Bilateral Agreement **160 UNTS 153**
SIGNED: 26 Feb 51 FORCE: 26 Feb 51
REGISTERED: 12 Feb 53 USA (United States)
ARTICLES: 18 LANGUAGE: English. Spanish.
HEADNOTE: HEALTH SANITATION PROGRAM
TOPIC: Sanitation
CONCEPTS: Definition of terms. Annex or appendix reference. Friendship and amity. Privileges and immunities. General cooperation. Inspection and observation. Domestic legislation. Personnel. Private contracts. Public health. Nursing. Sanitation. Accounting procedures. Indemnities and reimbursements. Reciprocity in financial treatment. Currency. Exchange rates and regulations. Expense sharing formulae. Financial programs. Funding procedures. Debts. Assistance. Special projects. Specific technical assistance. Technical cooperation.
PROCEDURE: Duration. Termination.
PARTIES:
Panama
USA (United States)
ANNEX
223 UNTS 366. USA (United States). Supplementation 11 Feb 52. Force 9 Apr 52.
223 UNTS 366. Panama. Supplementation 9 Apr 52. Force 9 Apr 52.
223 UNTS 370. Panama. Amendment 19 Jun 53. Force 19 Jun 53.
223 UNTS 370. USA (United States). Amendment 19 Jun 53. Force 19 Jun 53.
256 UNTS 356. Panama. Supplementation 14 Apr 55. Force 14 Apr 55.
256 UNTS 356. USA (United States). Supplementation 14 Apr 55. Force 14 Apr 55.

102107 Bilateral Exchange **160 UNTS 185**
SIGNED: 21 Jan 49 FORCE: 22 Jan 49
REGISTERED: 12 Feb 53 USA (United States)
ARTICLES: 4 LANGUAGE: English. Spanish.
HEADNOTE: HEALTH SANITATION PROGRAM
TOPIC: Sanitation
CONCEPTS: Conditions. Annex or appendix reference. Annex type material. Previous treaty extension. Privileges and immunities. General cooperation. Public health. Sanitation. Accounting procedures. Indemnities and reimbursements. Currency. Expense sharing formulae. Funding procedures. Assistance.
PARTIES:
Chile
USA (United States)
ANNEX
180 UNTS 385. USA (United States). Supplementation 30 Jan 52. Force 5 Feb 52.
180 UNTS 385. Chile. Supplementation 5 Feb 52. Force 5 Feb 52.

102108 Bilateral Exchange **160 UNTS 217**
SIGNED: 14 Nov 52 FORCE: 28 Nov 52
REGISTERED: 14 Feb 53 Belgium
ARTICLES: 2 LANGUAGE: French. German.
HEADNOTE: RECOGNIZE EQUIVALENT NATIONAL PASSPORTS SEAMENS BOOKS
TOPIC: Visas
CONCEPTS: Non-visa travel documents.
PARTIES:
Belgium
Germany, West

102109 Multilateral Convention **160 UNTS 223**
SIGNED: 18 Jun 49 FORCE: 29 Jan 53
REGISTERED: 17 Feb 53 ILO (Labor Org)
ARTICLES: 27 LANGUAGE: English. French.
HEADNOTE: CREW ACCOMODATION SHIPS
TOPIC: ILO Labor
CONCEPTS: Definition of terms. Detailed regulations. Territorial application. Domestic legislation. Incorporation of treaty provisions into national law. Sanitation. ILO conventions. Safety standards. Merchant vessels.
INTL ORGS: International Labour Organization. United Nations.
PROCEDURE: Amendment. Denunciation. Duration. Ratification. Registration. Renewal or Revival.

PARTIES:
Multilateral
ANNEX
172 UNTS 408. UK Great Britain. Ratification 6 Aug 53. Force 6 Feb 54.
189 UNTS 381. Poland. Ratification 13 Apr 54. Force 13 Oct 54.
191 UNTS 405. Brazil. Ratification 8 Jun 54. Force 8 Dec 54.
212 UNTS 399. France. Martinique.
212 UNTS 399. France. Guadeloupe.
212 UNTS 399. France. Reunion.
212 UNTS 399. France. French Guinea.
304 UNTS 408. Netherlands. Ratification 17 Jun 58. Force 17 Dec 58.
318 UNTS 422. UK Great Britain. Declaration 3 Nov 58.
318 UNTS 422. Netherlands. Declaration 14 Nov 58.
330 UNTS 363. Netherlands. Netherlands Antilles. Declaration 15 May 59.
356 UNTS 362. UK Great Britain. Guernsey Island.
356 UNTS 362. UK Great Britain. Jersey Island.
366 UNTS 410. Costa Rica. Ratification 2 Jun 60. Force 2 Dec 60.
381 UNTS 407. Denmark. Faroe Islands.
390 UNTS 360. UK Great Britain. Isle of Man.
396 UNTS 332. UK Great Britain. Uganda. Declaration 8 Mar 61.
396 UNTS 332. UK Great Britain. Aden. Declaration 8 Mar 61.
396 UNTS 332. UK Great Britain. British Guiana. Declaration 8 Mar 61.
396 UNTS 332. UK Great Britain. Sarawak. Declaration 8 Mar 61.
396 UNTS 332. UK Great Britain. British Honduras. Declaration 8 Mar 61.
396 UNTS 332. UK Great Britain. Brit Solomon Is. Declaration 8 Mar 61.
396 UNTS 332. UK Great Britain. Brit Virgin Islands. Declaration 8 Mar 61.
396 UNTS 332. UK Great Britain. Brunei. Declaration 8 Mar 61.
396 UNTS 332. UK Great Britain. Falkland Islands. Declaration 8 Mar 61.
396 UNTS 332. UK Great Britain. Fiji Islands.
396 UNTS 332. UK Great Britain. Gambia. Declaration 8 Mar 61.
396 UNTS 332. UK Great Britain. Gibralter. Declaration 8 Mar 61.
396 UNTS 332. UK Great Britain. Gilbert Islands. Declaration 8 Mar 61.
396 UNTS 332. UK Great Britain. Zanzibar. Declaration 8 Mar 61.
396 UNTS 332. UK Great Britain. Hong Kong. Declaration 8 Mar 61.
396 UNTS 332. UK Great Britain. Kenya. Declaration 8 Mar 61.
396 UNTS 332. UK Great Britain. Fed Rhod/Nyasaland. Declaration 8 Mar 61.
396 UNTS 332. UK Great Britain. Malta. Declaration 8 Mar 61.
396 UNTS 332. UK Great Britain. North Borneo. Declaration 8 Mar 61.
396 UNTS 332. UK Great Britain. St. Helena. Declaration 8 Mar 61.
396 UNTS 332. UK Great Britain. Seychelles. Declaration 8 Mar 61.
396 UNTS 333. UK Great Britain. Singapore. Declaration 8 Mar 61.
396 UNTS 333. UK Great Britain. Bahamas. Declaration 8 Mar 61.
396 UNTS 333. UK Great Britain. Bermuda. Declaration 8 Mar 61.
396 UNTS 333. UK Great Britain. Tanganyika. Declaration 8 Mar 61.
396 UNTS 333. UK Great Britain. Mauritius. Declaration 8 Mar 61.
437 UNTS 350. Belgium. Ratification 30 Aug 62. Force 28 Feb 63.
444 UNTS 337. Algeria. Succession 19 Oct 62.
510 UNTS 364. UK Great Britain. Hong Kong.
530 UNTS 417. Ghana. Ratification 18 Mar 65. Force 18 Mar 65.

102110 Bilateral Exchange **160 UNTS 261**
SIGNED: 29 Nov 52 FORCE: 29 Nov 52
REGISTERED: 18 Feb 53 Belgium
ARTICLES: 2 LANGUAGE: French.
HEADNOTE: ISSUE FREE CHARGE TEMPORARY RESIDENCE VISA
TOPIC: Visas

CONCEPTS: Resident permits. Visas. Fees and exemptions.
PARTIES:
Belgium
France

102111 Multilateral Protocol **160 UNTS 267**
SIGNED: 15 Dec 50 FORCE: 30 Mar 51
REGISTERED: 18 Feb 53 Belgium
ARTICLES: 1 LANGUAGE: English. French.
HEADNOTE: EUROPEAN CUSTOMS UNION STUDY GROUP
TOPIC: IGO Operations
CONCEPTS: Accounting procedures. IGO operations.
INTL ORGS: Customs Co-operation Council. Organization for Economic Co-operation and Development.
TREATY REF: 157 UNTS 3.
PROCEDURE: Accession. Ratification.
PARTIES:
Austria SIGNED: 15 Dec 50 RATIFIED: 21 Jan 53 FORCE: 21 Jan 53
Belgium SIGNED: 15 Dec 50 RATIFIED: 11 Dec 52 FORCE: 11 Dec 52
Denmark SIGNED: 15 Dec 50 RATIFIED: 30 Mar 51 FORCE: 30 Mar 51
France SIGNED: 15 Dec 50 RATIFIED: 6 Oct 52 FORCE: 6 Oct 52
Germany, West SIGNED: 15 Dec 50 RATIFIED: 30 Mar 51 FORCE: 30 Mar 51
Greece SIGNED: 15 Dec 50 RATIFIED: 10 Dec 51 FORCE: 10 Dec 51
Iceland SIGNED: 15 Dec 50 RATIFIED: 18 Jul 51 FORCE: 18 Jul 51
Ireland SIGNED: 15 Dec 50 RATIFIED: 23 Sep 52 FORCE: 23 Sep 52
Italy SIGNED: 15 Dec 50 RATIFIED: 30 Mar 51 FORCE: 30 Mar 51
Luxembourg SIGNED: 15 Dec 50 RATIFIED: 23 Jan 53 FORCE: 23 Jan 53
Netherlands SIGNED: 15 Dec 50 RATIFIED: 23 Jan 53 FORCE: 23 Jan 53
Norway SIGNED: 15 Dec 50 RATIFIED: 6 Aug 51 FORCE: 6 Aug 51
Portugal SIGNED: 15 Dec 50
Sweden SIGNED: 15 Dec 51 RATIFIED: 17 Oct 52 FORCE: 17 Oct 52
UK Great Britain SIGNED: 15 Dec 50 RATIFIED: 12 Sep 52 FORCE: 12 Sep 52
ANNEX
347 UNTS 381. Turkey. Ratification 29 Apr 53. Force 29 Apr 53.
347 UNTS 381. Portugal. Ratification 29 May 53. Force 29 May 53.

102112 Bilateral Instrument **160 UNTS 275**
SIGNED: 14 Nov 52 FORCE: 14 Nov 52
REGISTERED: 18 Feb 53 Denmark
ARTICLES: 1 LANGUAGE: English.
HEADNOTE: MOST FAVORED NATION TREATMENT
TOPIC: General Economic
CONCEPTS: Exceptions and exemptions. Export quotas. Import quotas. Trade procedures. Most favored nation clause. Customs duties. Navigational conditions.
PROCEDURE: Future Procedures Contemplated. Termination.
PARTIES:
Denmark
Israel

102113 Bilateral Agreement **160 UNTS 279**
SIGNED: 14 Nov 52 FORCE: 14 Nov 52
REGISTERED: 18 Feb 53 Denmark
ARTICLES: 8 LANGUAGE: English.
HEADNOTE: TRADE
TOPIC: General Trade
CONCEPTS: Treaty implementation. Conformity with municipal law. Licenses and permits. Establishment of commission. Establishment of trade relations. Free trade. Maritime products and equipment. Trade procedures. Payment schedules. Commodity trade. Quotas. Agricultural commodities. Irrigation.
TREATY REF: 160 UNTS 289.
PROCEDURE: Duration. Termination.
PARTIES:
Denmark
Israel

102114 Bilateral Agreement **160 UNTS 289**
SIGNED: 14 Nov 52   FORCE: 14 Nov 52
REGISTERED: 18 Feb 53 Denmark
ARTICLES: 7 LANGUAGE: English.
HEADNOTE: PAYMENTS AGREEMENT
TOPIC: Finance
CONCEPTS: Conformity with municipal law. Accounting procedures. Balance of payments. Currency. Exchange rates and regulations. Interest rates. Payment schedules.
PROCEDURE: Duration. Termination.
PARTIES:
  Denmark
  Israel

102115 Bilateral Agreement **160 UNTS 297**
SIGNED: 16 Oct 47   FORCE: 4 Sep 52
REGISTERED: 18 Feb 53 UK Great Britain
ARTICLES: 13 LANGUAGE: English. Spanish.
HEADNOTE: AIR SERVICES
TOPIC: Air Transport
CONCEPTS: Definition of terms. Annex or appendix reference. Conformity with municipal law. Licenses and permits. Recognition of legal documents. Use of facilities. Arbitration. Procedure. Existing tribunals. Negotiation. Fees and exemptions. Most favored nation clause. National treatment. Customs exemptions. Competency certificate. Routes and logistics. Navigational conditions. Permit designation. Airport facilities. Airworthiness certificates. Conditions of airlines operating permission. Operating authorizations and regulations. Licenses and certificates of nationality.
INTL ORGS: International Civil Aviation Organization. Arbitration Commission.
TREATY REF: 15UNTS295.
PROCEDURE: Amendment. Future Procedures Contemplated. Ratification. Registration. Termination.
PARTIES:
  Colombia
  UK Great Britain

102116 Bilateral Agreement **160 UNTS 327**
SIGNED: 15 Aug 51   FORCE: 23 Dec 52
REGISTERED: 18 Feb 53 UK Great Britain
ARTICLES: 14 LANGUAGE: Arabic. English. French.
HEADNOTE: AIR SERVICES
TOPIC: Air Transport
CONCEPTS: Conditions. Definition of terms. Detailed regulations. Exceptions and exemptions. Conformity with municipal law. General cooperation. Exchange of information and documents. Arbitration. Procedure. Existing tribunals. Negotiation. Non-interest rates and fees. Most favored nation clause. Customs exemptions. Routes and logistics. Permit designation. Conditions of airlines operating permission. Overflights and technical stops. Operating authorizations and regulations.
INTL ORGS: International Civil Aviation Organization. Arbitration Commission.
TREATY REF: 15UNTS295.
PROCEDURE: Amendment. Future Procedures Contemplated. Ratification. Registration. Termination. Application to Non-self-governing Territories.
PARTIES:
  Lebanon
  UK Great Britain
                    ANNEX
175 UNTS 371. UK Great Britain. Amendment 24 Jun 53. Force 24 Jun 53.
175 UNTS 371. Lebanon. Amendment 24 Jun 53.
351 UNTS 406. UK Great Britain. Amendment 8 Jun 59. Force 8 Jun 59.
351 UNTS 406. Lebanon. Amendment 8 Jun 59. Force 8 Jun 59.
457 UNTS 302. UK Great Britain. Amendment 27 Oct 62. Force 1 Nov 62.
457 UNTS 302. Lebanon. Amendment 27 Oct 62. Force 1 Nov 62.

102117 Bilateral Agreement **161 UNTS 3**
SIGNED: 19 Jan 53   FORCE: 19 Jan 53
REGISTERED: 18 Feb 53 UK Great Britain
ARTICLES: 12 LANGUAGE: English.
HEADNOTE: INTERCHANGE PATENTS TECHNICAL INFORMATION DEFENSE PURPOSES

TOPIC: General Military
CONCEPTS: Definition of terms. Exceptions and exemptions. Territorial application. Licenses and permits. Establishment of commission. Procedure. Claims and settlements. Patents, copyrights and trademarks. Laws and formalities. General technical assistance. Defense and security. Security of information. Exchange of defense information. Restrictions on transfer.
INTL ORGS: United Nations.
TREATY REF: 80UNTS261.
PROCEDURE: Amendment. Registration. Termination.
PARTIES:
  UK Great Britain
  USA (United States)
                    ANNEX
205 UNTS 346. USA (United States). Interpretation 19 Jan 53. Force 19 Jan 53.
205 UNTS 346. UK Great Britain. Interpretation 19 Jan 53. Force 19 Jan 53.

102118 Bilateral Treaty **161 UNTS 15**
SIGNED: 15 Mar 50   FORCE: 31 Dec 51
REGISTERED: 25 Feb 53 Iran
ARTICLES: 5 LANGUAGE: English. Persian.
HEADNOTE: FRIENDSHIP
TOPIC: General Amity
CONCEPTS: Friendship and amity. Consular relations establishment. Diplomatic relations establishment. General cooperation. Arbitration. Procedure.
INTL ORGS: Arbitration Commission.
PROCEDURE: Ratification.
PARTIES:
  India
  Iran

102119 Bilateral Treaty **161 UNTS 23**
SIGNED: 18 Feb 50   FORCE: 17 May 52
REGISTERED: 25 Feb 53 Iran
ARTICLES: 6 LANGUAGE: English. Persian.
HEADNOTE: FRIENDSHIP
TOPIC: General Amity
CONCEPTS: Friendship and amity. Consular relations establishment. Diplomatic relations establishment. Procedure.
INTL ORGS: International Court of Justice.
PROCEDURE: Future Procedures Contemplated. Ratification.
PARTIES:
  Iran
  Pakistan

102120 Multilateral Agreement **161 UNTS 31**
SIGNED: 26 Feb 53   FORCE: 26 Feb 53
REGISTERED: 26 Feb 53 United Nations
ARTICLES: 8 LANGUAGE: English.
HEADNOTE: TECHNICAL ASSISTANCE DEMONSTRATION CENTER BLIND
TOPIC: Tech Assistance
CONCEPTS: Time limit. Privileges and immunities. General cooperation. Exchange of information and documents. Inspection and observation. Personnel. Title and deeds. Establishment of commission. Exchange. Scholarships and grants. Vocational training. Financial programs. Domestic obligation. General technical assistance. Special projects. Materials, equipment and services. IGO status.
TREATY REF: 1UNTS15,263; 33UNTS261.
PROCEDURE: Amendment. Termination.
PARTIES:
  United Arab Rep SIGNED: 26 Feb 53 FORCE: 26 Feb 53
  ILO (Labor Org) SIGNED: 26 Feb 53 FORCE: 26 Feb 53
  United Nations SIGNED: 26 Feb 53 FORCE: 26 Feb 53

102121 Bilateral Agreement **161 UNTS 45**
SIGNED: 27 Feb 53   FORCE: 27 Feb 53
REGISTERED: 27 Feb 53 United Nations
ARTICLES: 6 LANGUAGE: English. Spanish.
HEADNOTE: TECHNICAL ASSISTANCE
TOPIC: Tech Assistance
CONCEPTS: Treaty implementation. Privileges and immunities. General cooperation. Exchange of information and documents. Personnel. Title and deeds. Exchange. Scholarships and grants. Vo-

cational training. Research and development. Expense sharing formulae. Local currency. Domestic obligation. General technical assistance. Materials, equipment and services. IGO status. Conformity with IGO decisions.
TREATY REF: 1UNTS15,263; 76UNTS132.
PROCEDURE: Amendment. Termination.
PARTIES:
  Costa Rica
  United Nations

102122 Bilateral Exchange **161 UNTS 59**
SIGNED: 13 Nov 52   FORCE: 17 Nov 52
REGISTERED: 2 Mar 53 Australia
ARTICLES: 2 LANGUAGE: English.
HEADNOTE: IMPORTATION MATTERS
TOPIC: General Trade
CONCEPTS: Exceptions and exemptions. Most favored nation clause.
INTL ORGS: General Agreement on Tariffs and Trade.
TREATY REF: GATT.
PROCEDURE: Duration. Termination.
PARTIES:
  Australia
  Iceland

102123 Bilateral Exchange **161 UNTS 65**
SIGNED: 24 May 52   FORCE: 24 May 52
REGISTERED: 2 Mar 53 Australia
ARTICLES: 2 LANGUAGE: English. Italian.
HEADNOTE: RELEASE PROPERTY SETTLEMENT CLAIMS
TOPIC: Reparations
CONCEPTS: Definition of terms. Time limit. General property. Indemnities and reimbursements. Post-war claims settlement.
INTL ORGS: United Nations. Arbitration Commission.
TREATY REF: 49UNTS.
PARTIES:
  Australia
  Italy

102124 Multilateral Convention **161 UNTS 72**
SIGNED: 2 Dec 46   FORCE: 10 Nov 48
REGISTERED: 4 Mar 53 USA (United States)
ARTICLES: 11 LANGUAGE: English.
HEADNOTE: REGULATION WHALING
TOPIC: Specific Resources
CONCEPTS: Definition of terms. Inspection and observation. Establishment of commission. Research cooperation. Research results. Internal structure. Regulation of natural resources.
INTL ORGS: United Nations. International Whaling Commission.
TREATY REF: 196LTS131; 11UNTS43; 190LTS179; 32UNTS304.
PROCEDURE: Accession. Ratification.
PARTIES:
  Argentina SIGNED: 2 Dec 46
  Australia SIGNED: 2 Dec 46 RATIFIED: 1 Dec 47 FORCE: 10 Nov 48
  Brazil SIGNED: 2 Dec 46 RATIFIED: 9 May 50 FORCE: 9 May 50
  Canada SIGNED: 2 Dec 46 RATIFIED: 25 Feb 49 FORCE: 25 Feb 49
  Chile SIGNED: 2 Dec 46
  Denmark SIGNED: 2 Dec 46 RATIFIED: 23 May 50 FORCE: 23 May 50
  France SIGNED: 2 Dec 46 RATIFIED: 3 Dec 48 FORCE: 3 Dec 48
  Iceland RATIFIED: 10 Mar 47 FORCE: 10 Nov 48
  Japan RATIFIED: 21 Apr 51 FORCE: 21 Apr 51
  Mexico RATIFIED: 30 Jun 49 FORCE: 30 Jun 49
  Netherlands SIGNED: 2 Dec 46 RATIFIED: 10 Nov 48 FORCE: 10 Nov 48
  New Zealand SIGNED: 22 Dec 46 RATIFIED: 2 Aug 49 FORCE: 2 Aug 49
  Norway SIGNED: 22 Dec 46 RATIFIED: 3 Mar 48 FORCE: 10 Nov 48
  Panama RATIFIED: 30 Sep 48 FORCE: 10 Nov 48
  Peru SIGNED: 22 Dec 46
  Sweden RATIFIED: 28 Jan 49 FORCE: 28 Jan 49
  UK Great Britain SIGNED: 22 Dec 46 RATIFIED: 17 Jun 47 FORCE: 10 Nov 48
  USA (United States) SIGNED: 22 Dec 46 RATIFIED: 18 Jul 47 FORCE: 10 Nov 48
  USSR (Soviet Union) SIGNED: 22 Dec 46 RATIFIED: 11 Sep 47 FORCE: 10 Nov 48

ANNEX

177 UNTS 396. Int Whaling Com. Amendment 19 Nov 51. Force 18 Nov 51.
181 UNTS 364. Int Whaling Com. Amendment 24 Sep 52. Force 12 Sep 52.
252 UNTS 316. Int Whaling Com. Amendment 19 Oct 53. Force 8 Oct 53.
252 UNTS 324. Int Whaling Com. Amendment 6 Aug 54. Force 8 Nov 54.
252 UNTS 330. Int Whaling Com. Amendment 5 Aug 55. Force 8 Nov 55.
278 UNTS 278. Int Whaling Com. Amendment 20 Jul 56.
300 UNTS 376. Int Whaling Com. Amendment 28 Jun 57. Force 4 Oct 57.
337 UNTS 408. Int Whaling Com. Amendment 27 Jun 58. Force 29 Jan 59.
338 UNTS 366. South Africa. Amendment 25 Apr 57. Force 4 May 59.
338 UNTS 366. Sweden. Amendment 6 Jun 57. Force 4 May 59.
338 UNTS 366. UK Great Britain. Amendment 23 May 57. Force 4 May 59.
338 UNTS 366. Australia. Amendment 8 Apr 57. Force 4 May 59.
338 UNTS 366. France. Amendment 14 Apr 58. Force 4 May 59.
338 UNTS 366. Brazil. Amendment 4 May 59. Force 4 May 59.
338 UNTS 366. Canada. Amendment 14 Jun 57. Force 4 May 59.
338 UNTS 366. Iceland. Amendment 23 Nov 56. Force 4 May 59.
338 UNTS 366. Denmark. Amendment 26 Jul 57. Force 4 May 59.
338 UNTS 366. USA (United States). Amendment 30 Aug 57. Force 4 May 59.
338 UNTS 366. Japan. Amendment 24 May 57. Force 4 May 59.
338 UNTS 366. Netherlands. Amendment 23 Dec 57. Force 4 May 59.
338 UNTS 366. New Zealand. Amendment 21 Jun 57. Force 4 May 59.
338 UNTS 366. USSR (Soviet Union). Amendment 3 Jul 57. Force 4 May 59.
338 UNTS 366. Norway. Amendment 15 Apr 57. Force 4 May 59.
338 UNTS 366. Panama. Amendment 9 Feb 59. Force 4 May 59.
356 UNTS 363. Norway. Withdrawal 29 Dec 58. Force 30 Jun 59.
356 UNTS 363. Netherlands. Withdrawal 31 Dec 58.
361 UNTS 272. Int Whaling Com. Amendment 1 Jul 59. Force 3 Jan 60.
388 UNTS 366. Mexico. Amendment 9 Mar 59. Force 4 May 59.
435 UNTS 324. Int Whaling Com. Amendment 24 Jun 60.
435 UNTS 328. Int Whaling Com. Amendment 23 Jun 61.
495 UNTS 254. Int Whaling Com. Amendment 5 Jul 62. Force 9 Oct 62.
495 UNTS 254. Int Whaling Com. Amendment 6 Jul 62. Force 9 Oct 62.

102125 Multilateral Convention **161 UNTS 113**
SIGNED: 11 Jul 47   FORCE: 13 Feb 53
REGISTERED: 6 Mar 53 ILO (Labor Org)
ARTICLES: 16 LANGUAGE: English. French.
HEADNOTE: MAXIMUM LENGTH EMPLOYMENT CONTRACTS
TOPIC: ILO Labor
CONCEPTS: Definition of terms. Detailed regulations. Exceptions and exemptions. Territorial application. Exchange of information and documents. Private contracts. ILO conventions.
INTL ORGS: International Labour Organization. United Nations.
TREATY REF: 15UNTS35; 18UNTS386.
PROCEDURE: Amendment. Denunciation. Duration. Ratification. Registration. Renewal or Revival.
PARTIES:
Multilateral
ANNEX
325 UNTS 344. UK Great Britain. Brit Solomon Is.
325 UNTS 344. UK Great Britain. Sarawak.
356 UNTS 364. UK Great Britain. Swaziland.
366 UNTS 411. UK Great Britain. St. Helena.
381 UNTS 408. UK Great Britain. Tanganyika.
388 UNTS 354. UK Great Britain. Brunei.

396 UNTS 334. UK Great Britain. Gilbert Islands. Declaration 8 Mar 61.
396 UNTS 335. UK Great Britain. Gambia. Declaration 8 Mar 61.
396 UNTS 335. UK Great Britain. British Guiana. Declaration 8 Mar 61.
396 UNTS 335. UK Great Britain. Falkland Islands. Declaration 8 Mar 61.
396 UNTS 335. UK Great Britain. Uganda. Declaration 8 Mar 61.
396 UNTS 335. UK Great Britain. North Borneo. Declaration 8 Mar 61.
396 UNTS 335. UK Great Britain. St. Helena. Declaration 8 Mar 61.
396 UNTS 335. UK Great Britain. Sarawak. Declaration 8 May 61.
396 UNTS 335. UK Great Britain. Seychelles. Declaration 8 May 61.
396 UNTS 335. UK Great Britain. Zanzibar. Declaration 8 May 61.
396 UNTS 335. UK Great Britain. West Indies. Declaration 8 May 61.
396 UNTS 335. UK Great Britain. Aden. Declaration 8 Mar 61.
396 UNTS 335. UK Great Britain. Brit Virgin Islands. Declaration 8 Mar 61.
396 UNTS 335. UK Great Britain. British Honduras. Declaration 8 Mar 61.
396 UNTS 335. UK Great Britain. Brit Solomon Is. Declaration 8 May 61.
396 UNTS 335. UK Great Britain. Brunei. Declaration 8 Mar 61.
396 UNTS 335. UK Great Britain. Fiji Islands. Declaration 8 Mar 61.
396 UNTS 335. UK Great Britain. Gibralter. Declaration 8 Mar 61.
396 UNTS 335. UK Great Britain. Gilbert Islands. Declaration 8 Mar 61.
396 UNTS 335. UK Great Britain. Kenya. Declaration 8 Mar 61.
396 UNTS 335. UK Great Britain. Hong Kong. Declaration 8 Mar 61.
396 UNTS 335. UK Great Britain. Malta. Declaration 8 Mar 61.
396 UNTS 336. UK Great Britain. Bermuda. Declaration 8 May 61.
396 UNTS 336. UK Great Britain. Mauritius. Declaration 8 May 61.
396 UNTS 336. UK Great Britain. Bahamas. Declaration 8 May 61.
396 UNTS 336. UK Great Britain. Singapore. Declaration 8 May 61.
396 UNTS 336. UK Great Britain. Tanganyika. Declaration 8 May 61.
401 UNTS 266. Sierra Leone. Succession 13 Jun 61.
406 UNTS 304. UK Great Britain. Brit Solomon Is.
422 UNTS 336. Tanganyika. Succession 30 Jan 62. Force 30 Jan 62.
431 UNTS 297. UK Great Britain. Bechuanaland.
452 UNTS 369. Jamaica. Succession 26 Dec 62.
471 UNTS 377. UK Great Britain. Nyasaland.
471 UNTS 377. Uganda. Ratification 4 Jun 63.
488 UNTS 367. Kenya. Ratification 13 Jan 64. Force 13 Jan 64.
495 UNTS 303. Malaysia. Sarawak. Succession 3 Mar 64.
495 UNTS 303. Malaysia. State of Sabah. Succession 3 Mar 64.
495 UNTS 303. Malaysia. Singapore. Succession 3 Mar 64.
504 UNTS 358. Tanzania. Succession 22 Jun 64.
522 UNTS 383. Zambia. Ratification 2 Dec 64. Force 2 Dec 64.
530 UNTS 418. UK Great Britain. Malawi. Ratification 22 Mar 65.
548 UNTS 404. Singapore. Ratification 25 Oct 65. Force 25 Oct 65.
567 UNTS 352. Guyana. Ratification 8 Jun 66. Force 8 Jun 66.

102126 Bilateral Treaty **161 UNTS 127**
SIGNED: 23 Jan 46   FORCE: 28 Mar 46
REGISTERED: 12 Mar 53 Taiwan
ARTICLES: 10 LANGUAGE: Chinese. English. Siamese.
HEADNOTE: AMITY
TOPIC: General Amity
CONCEPTS: Treaty interpretation. Friendship and amity. Alien status. Consular relations establishment. Diplomatic relations establishment. Privileges and immunities. Legal protection and assistance.

PROCEDURE: Duration. Future Procedures Contemplated. Ratification. Termination.
PARTIES:
Taiwan
Thailand

102127 Bilateral Agreement **161 UNTS 157**
SIGNED: 12 Feb 53   FORCE: 12 Feb 53
REGISTERED: 18 Mar 53 United Arab Rep
ARTICLES: 15 LANGUAGE: English.
HEADNOTE: SELF-GOVERNMENT SELF-DETERMINATION SUDAN
TOPIC: Recognition
CONCEPTS: Annex or appendix reference. Democratic institutions. Governor-general functions. Transition period. Self-determination. Self-government. Establishment of commission. Withdrawal of forces.
PARTIES:
United Arab Rep
UK Great Britain

102128 Bilateral Exchange **161 UNTS 185**
SIGNED: 28 Sep 51   FORCE: 28 Sep 51
REGISTERED: 20 Mar 53 Australia
ARTICLES: 2 LANGUAGE: English. French.
HEADNOTE: COMPENSATION FOR PROPERTY LOSSES
TOPIC: Reparations
CONCEPTS: General property. National treatment. Loss and/or damage. Reparations and restrictions. Post-war claims settlement.
PROCEDURE: Application to Non-self-governing Territories.
PARTIES:
Australia
France

102129 Bilateral Exchange **162 UNTS 3**
SIGNED: 16 May 49   FORCE: 16 May 49
REGISTERED: 20 Mar 53 USA (United States)
ARTICLES: 2 LANGUAGE: English. Spanish.
HEADNOTE: COOPERATIVE EDUCATION PROGRAM
TOPIC: Education
CONCEPTS: Exchange.
PARTIES:
Bolivia
USA (United States)

102130 Bilateral Exchange **162 UNTS 21**
SIGNED: 15 Feb 46   FORCE: 15 Feb 46
REGISTERED: 20 Mar 53 USA (United States)
ARTICLES: 2 LANGUAGE: English. Portuguese.
HEADNOTE: COOPERATIVE RURAL EDUCATION PROGRAM
TOPIC: Education
CONCEPTS: General cooperation. General property. Specialists exchange. Exchange. Indemnities and reimbursements. Expense sharing formulae. Financial programs. Funding procedures. General technical assistance. Aid missions.
PROCEDURE: Termination.
PARTIES:
Brazil
USA (United States)

102131 Bilateral Exchange **162 UNTS 30**
SIGNED: 12 Mar 48   FORCE: 12 Mar 48
REGISTERED: 20 Mar 53 USA (United States)
ARTICLES: 4 LANGUAGE: English. Spanish.
HEADNOTE: COOPERATIVE EDUCATION PROGRAM
TOPIC: Education
CONCEPTS: Definition of terms. Detailed regulations. Annex or appendix reference. Annex type material. Alien status. General cooperation. Inspection and observation. Domestic legislation. Personnel. General property. Private contracts. Specialists exchange. Exchange. Commissions and foundations. Teacher and student exchange. Vocational training. Research and development. Accounting procedures. Indemnities and reimbursements. Currency. Exchange rates and regulations. Expense sharing formulae. Financial programs. Funding procedures. Tax exemptions. Customs exemptions.
TREATY REF: TAIS 1815; TAIS 1991.

PROCEDURE: Duration. Renewal or Revival. Termination.
PARTIES:
Paraguay
USA (United States)
ANNEX
174 UNTS 339. USA (United States). Supplementation 31 Jan 52. Force 25 Mar 52.
174 UNTS 339. Paraguay. Supplementation 25 Mar 52. Force 25 Mar 52.
269 UNTS 337. USA (United States). Prolongation 5 Apr 55. Force 5 Apr 55.
269 UNTS 337. Paraguay. Prolongation 5 Apr 55. Force 5 Apr 55.

102132 Bilateral Exchange **162 UNTS 85**
SIGNED: 28 Sep 50   FORCE: 28 Sep 50
REGISTERED: 21 Mar 53 USA (United States).
ARTICLES: 2 LANGUAGE: English. Spanish.
HEADNOTE: HEALTH SANITATION PROGRAM
TOPIC: Sanitation
CONCEPTS: Annex or appendix reference. Previous treaty extension. Friendship and amity. Disease control. Public health. Sanitation. Exchange. Expense sharing formulae. Financial programs. Funding procedures. Assistance. Special projects. Specific technical assistance. Economic assistance.
TREATY REF: USA 64STAT204.
PROCEDURE: Duration.
PARTIES:
Honduras.
USA (United States)
ANNEX
265 UNTS 331. Honduras. Prolongation 27 Apr 55. Force 29 Apr 55.
265 UNTS 331. USA (United States). Prolongation 27 Apr 55. Force 29 Apr 55.

102133 Bilateral Exchange **162 UNTS 103**
SIGNED: 11 Aug 51   FORCE: 11 Aug 51
REGISTERED: 21 Mar 53 USA (United States).
ARTICLES: 2 LANGUAGE: English. Spanish.
HEADNOTE: EMPLOYMENT AGRICULTURAL WORKERS
TOPIC: Non-ILO Labor
CONCEPTS: Definition of terms. Detailed regulations. Guarantees and safeguards. Border traffic and migration. Alien status. Inspection and observation. Legal protection and assistance. Private contracts. Investigation of violations. Negotiation. Employment regulations. Old age and invalidity insurance. Labor statistics. Safety standards. Right to organize. Wages and salaries. Non-ILO labor relations. Family allowances. Administrative cooperation. Sickness and invalidity insurance. Migrant worker. Transportation costs. Claims and settlements. Quotas. Foreign nationals.
PROCEDURE: Duration.
PARTIES:
Mexico
USA (United States)
ANNEX
178 UNTS 407. USA (United States). Amendment 10 Jan 52. Force 31 Jan 52.
178 UNTS 407. Mexico. Amendment 31 Jan 52. Force 31 Jan 52.
178 UNTS 409. USA (United States). Prolongation 8 Feb 52. Force 8 Feb 52.
178 UNTS 409. Mexico. Prolongation 8 Feb 52. Force 8 Feb 52.
178 UNTS 411. USA (United States). Prolongation 31 Mar 52. Force 9 Apr 52.
178 UNTS 411. Mexico. Prolongation 9 Apr 52. Force 9 Apr 52.
179 UNTS 285. USA (United States). Extension and Amendment 19 May 52. Force 19 May 52.
179 UNTS 285. Mexico. Extension and Amendment 19 May 52. Force 19 May 52.
227 UNTS 346. Mexico. Prolongation 30 Dec 53. Force 31 Dec 53.
227 UNTS 346. USA (United States). Prolongation 31 Dec 53. Force 31 Dec 53.
227 UNTS 350. Mexico. Extension and Amendment 10 Mar 54. Force 10 Mar 54.
227 UNTS 350. USA (United States). Extension and Amendment 10 Mar 54. Force 10 Mar 54.
227 UNTS 360. Mexico. Amendment 10 Mar 54. Force 10 Mar 54.
227 UNTS 360. USA (United States). Amendment 10 Mar 54. Force 10 Mar 54.

227 UNTS 365. USA (United States). Implementation 10 Mar 54. Force 10 Mar 54.
227 UNTS 365. Mexico. Implementation 10 Mar 54. Force 10 Mar 54.
227 UNTS 369. USA (United States). Correction 10 Mar 54. Force 10 Mar 54.
227 UNTS 369. Mexico. Correction 10 Mar 54. Force 10 Mar 54.
234 UNTS 330. USA (United States). Amendment 16 Jul 54. Force 16 Jul 54.
234 UNTS 330. Mexico. Amendment 16 Jul 54. Force 16 Jul 54.
234 UNTS 337. USA (United States). Amendment 6 Aug 54. Force 6 Aug 54.
234 UNTS 337. Mexico. Amendment 6 Aug 54. Force 6 Aug 54.
265 UNTS 336. USA (United States). Prolongation 20 Dec 56. Force 20 Dec 56.
265 UNTS 336. Mexico. Prolongation 20 Dec 56. Force 20 Dec 56.
271 UNTS 398. USA (United States). Extension and Amendment 29 Jun 56. Force 29 Jun 56.
271 UNTS 398. Mexico. Extension and Amendment 29 Jun 56. Force 29 Jun 56.
291 UNTS 314. USA (United States). Interpretation 17 Jun 57. Force 17 Jun 57.
291 UNTS 314. Mexico. Interpretation 17 Jun 57. Force 17 Jun 57.
291 UNTS 318. USA (United States). Interpretation 30 Jul 57. Force 30 Jul 57.
291 UNTS 318. Mexico. Interpretation 30 Jul 57. Force 30 Jul 57.
357 UNTS 354. Mexico. Prolongation 27 Jun 59. Force 27 Jun 59.
357 UNTS 354. USA (United States). Prolongation 24 Jun 59. Force 27 Jun 59.
357 UNTS 357. USA (United States). Prolongation 30 Jul 59. Force 30 Jul 59.
357 UNTS 357. Mexico. Prolongation 28 Jul 59. Force 30 Jul 59.
357 UNTS 360. Mexico. Prolongation 31 Aug 59. Force 31 Aug 59.
357 UNTS 360. USA (United States). Prolongation 31 Aug 59. Force 31 Aug 59.
361 UNTS 278. Mexico. Extension and Amendment 23 Oct 59. Force 23 Oct 59.
361 UNTS 278. USA (United States). Extension and Amendment 23 Oct 59. Force 23 Oct 59.
416 UNTS 329. Mexico. Prolongation 27 Jun 61. Supplementation 27 Jun 61.
416 UNTS 329. USA (United States). Prolongation 27 Jun 61. Supplementation 27 Jun 61.
416 UNTS 329. Mexico. Force 27 Jun 61.
433 UNTS 355. USA (United States). Prolongation 11 Dec 61. Force 11 Dec 61.
433 UNTS 355. Mexico. Prolongation 11 Dec 61. Force 11 Dec 61.
461 UNTS 238. USA (United States). Extension and Amendment 29 Dec 61. Force 1 Feb 62.
461 UNTS 238. Mexico. Extension and Amendment 29 Dec 61. Force 1 Feb 62.
474 UNTS 322. Mexico. Amendment 25 Feb 63. Force 25 Feb 63.
474 UNTS 322. USA (United States). Amendment 10 Jan 63. Force 25 Feb 63.
494 UNTS 291. USA (United States). Prolongation 20 Dec 63. Force 20 Dec 63.
494 UNTS 291. Mexico. Prolongation 20 Dec 63. Force 20 Dec 63.

102134 Bilateral Exchange **162 UNTS 173**
SIGNED: 17 Apr 51   FORCE: 17 Apr 51
REGISTERED: 21 Mar 53 USA (United States)
ARTICLES: 2 LANGUAGE: English.
HEADNOTE: MUTUAL DEFENSE ASSISTANCE
TOPIC: Milit Assistance
CONCEPTS: Exceptions and exemptions. Non-prejudice to UN charter. Privileges and immunities. Conformity with municipal law. General cooperation. Inspection and observation. Public information. Use of facilities. Indemnities and reimbursements. Exchange rates and regulations. Local currency. Agricultural commodities. Aid missions. Defense and security. Restrictions on transfer. Raw materials.
TREATY REF: 93UNTS39; 93UNTS45; 122UNTS137.
PARTIES:
USA (United States)
Yugoslavia
ANNEX
207 UNTS 364. USA (United States). Amendment 25 Feb 53. Force 10 Mar 53.

207 UNTS 364. Yugoslavia. Amendment 10 Mar 53. Force 10 Mar 53.
238 UNTS 336. USA (United States). Amendment 2 Sep 54. Force 2 Sep 54.
238 UNTS 336. Philippines. Amendment 2 Sep 54. Force 2 Sep 54.

102135 Bilateral Agreement **162 UNTS 183**
SIGNED: 17 Oct 52   FORCE: 28 Feb 53
REGISTERED: 26 Mar 53 Belgium
ARTICLES: 14 LANGUAGE: French. German.
HEADNOTE: CULTURAL AGREEMENT
TOPIC: Culture
CONCEPTS: Friendship and amity. Tourism. Conformity with municipal law. General cooperation. Operating agencies. Establishment of commission. Recognition of degrees. Exchange. Teacher and student exchange. Institute establishment. Scholarships and grants. Exchange. General cultural cooperation. Artists. Research and development. Recognition. Publications exchange. Mass media exchange.
INTL ORGS: Special Commission.
PROCEDURE: Amendment. Denunciation. Duration. Ratification. Renewal or Revival.
PARTIES:
Austria
Belgium

102136 Bilateral Exchange **162 UNTS 197**
SIGNED: 12 Nov 48   FORCE: 12 Nov 48
REGISTERED: 26 Mar 53 UK Great Britain
ARTICLES: 2 LANGUAGE: English.
HEADNOTE: DEFENSE AGREEMENT
TOPIC: Milit Assistance
CONCEPTS: Emergencies. Indemnities and reimbursements. Claims and settlements. Lump sum settlements. Payment for war supplies. Military assistance.
PROCEDURE: Future Procedures Contemplated.
PARTIES:
New Zealand
UK Great Britain
ANNEX
247 UNTS 428. UK Great Britain. Amendment 21 Mar 55. Force 21 Mar 55.
247 UNTS 428. New Zealand. Amendment 13 Dec 54. Force 21 Mar 55.

102137 Bilateral Agreement **162 UNTS 205**
SIGNED: 10 Sep 52   FORCE: 27 Mar 53
REGISTERED: 27 Mar 53 Israel
ARTICLES: 17 LANGUAGE: English. German.
HEADNOTE: AGREEMENT
TOPIC: Reparations
CONCEPTS: Change of circumstances. Annex or appendix reference. Privileges and immunities. Non-diplomatic delegations. Private contracts. Establishment of commission. Arbitration. Procedure. Reexport of goods, etc.. Accounting procedures. Payment schedules. Lump sum settlements. Delivery schedules. Commodities and services. Reparations and restrictions.
INTL ORGS: International Court of Justice. United Nations. Arbitration Commission. Special Commission.
PROCEDURE: Ratification.
PARTIES:
Germany, West
Israel

102138 Multilateral Convention **163 UNTS 3**
SIGNED: 10 Jan 52   FORCE: 1 Apr 53
REGISTERED: 1 Apr 53 United Nations
ARTICLES: 17 LANGUAGE: English. French.
HEADNOTE: FACILITATE CROSSING FRONTIERS PASSENGER BAGGAGE CARRIED RAIL
TOPIC: Visas
CONCEPTS: Border traffic and migration. General cooperation. Inspection and observation. Existing tribunals. Negotiation. Customs duties. Customs exemptions. Railway border crossing.
INTL ORGS: European Economic Community. United Nations. Arbitration Commission.
PROCEDURE: Amendment. Accession. Denunciation. Registration. Termination.
PARTIES:
Belgium SIGNED: 10 Jan 52
France SIGNED: 10 Jan 52 RATIFIED: 1 Apr 53 FORCE: 1 Apr 53

Italy SIGNED: 10 Jan 52
Luxembourg SIGNED: 10 Jan 52
Netherlands SIGNED: 10 Jan 52 RATIFIED:
25 May 52 FORCE: 1 Apr 53
Norway SIGNED: 10 Jan 52 RATIFIED:
28 Oct 52 FORCE: 1 Apr 53
Sweden SIGNED: 10 Jan 52
Switzerland SIGNED: 10 Jan 52
ANNEX
171 UNTS 422. Belgium. Ratification 22 Jul 53.
185 UNTS 406. Luxembourg. Ratification
26 Jan 54.
211 UNTS 420. Italy. Ratification 22 Jun 55.
250 UNTS 312. Portugal. Accession 24 Sep 56.
269 UNTS 344. Switzerland. Ratification
5 Jun 57.
328 UNTS 319. Italy. Force 24 May 59.

102139 Multilateral Convention **163 UNTS 27**
SIGNED: 10 Jan 52 FORCE: 1 Apr 53
REGISTERED: 1 Apr 53 United Nations
ARTICLES: 17 LANGUAGE: English. French.
HEADNOTE: CROSSING FRONTIERS GOODS CAR-
RIED RAIL
TOPIC: Visas
CONCEPTS: General provisions. Annex or appen-
dix reference. Conformity with municipal law.
General cooperation. Existing tribunals. Negotia-
tion. Tax exemptions. Customs declarations.
Transport of goods. Railway border crossing.
Frontier peoples and personnel.
INTL ORGS: European Economic Community.
United Nations. Arbitration Commission.
PROCEDURE: Amendment. Accession. Denuncia-
tion. Ratification. Registration. Termination.
PARTIES:
Belgium SIGNED: 10 Jan 52
France SIGNED: 10 Jan 52 RATIFIED: 1 Apr 53
FORCE: 1 Apr 53
Italy SIGNED: 10 Jan 52
Luxembourg SIGNED: 10 Jan 52
Netherlands SIGNED: 10 Jan 52 RATIFIED:
25 May 52 FORCE: 1 Apr 53
Norway SIGNED: 10 Jan 52 RATIFIED:
28 Oct 52 FORCE: 1 Apr 53
Sweden SIGNED: 10 Jan 52
Switzerland SIGNED: 10 Jan 52
ANNEX
171 UNTS 423. Belgium. Ratification 22 Jul 53.
185 UNTS 407. Luxembourg. Ratification
26 Jan 54.
211 UNTS 421. Italy. Ratification 22 Jun 55.
250 UNTS 313. Portugal. Accession 24 Sep 56.
269 UNTS 344. Switzerland. Ratification
5 Jun 57.
328 UNTS 319. Italy. Force 24 May 59.
425 UNTS 328. Spain. Accession 17 Apr 62.

102140 Bilateral Agreement **163 UNTS 43**
SIGNED: 11 Feb 53 FORCE: 19 Feb 53
REGISTERED: 1 Apr 53 WHO (World Health)
ARTICLES: 4 LANGUAGE: English.
HEADNOTE: OPERATION NURSING PROJECT UN-
DER TECHNICAL ASSISTANCE BUDGET
TOPIC: Tech Assistance
CONCEPTS: Time limit. Privileges and immunities.
General cooperation. Personnel. Nursing. Ex-
change. Scholarships and grants. Vocational
training. Expense sharing formulae. Claims and
settlements. Domestic obligation. General tech-
nical assistance. Special projects. Materials,
equipment and services. IGO status.
TREATY REF: 33UNTS261.
PROCEDURE: Amendment. Duration. Renewal or
Revival.
PARTIES:
India
WHO (World Health)

102141 Bilateral Treaty **163 UNTS 55**
SIGNED: 25 Feb 52 FORCE: 5 Dec 52
REGISTERED: 3 Apr 53 India
ARTICLES: 7 LANGUAGE: Arabic. Hindi. English.
HEADNOTE: FRIENDSHIP COMMERCE
TOPIC: General Amity
CONCEPTS: Friendship and amity. Consular rela-
tions establishment. Diplomatic relations estab-
lishment. Privileges and immunities. General co-
operation. Arbitration. Negotiation. General cul-
tural cooperation. Export quotas. Import quotas.
PROCEDURE: Duration. Ratification. Termination.

PARTIES:
India
Syria

102142 Bilateral Agreement **163 UNTS 73**
SIGNED: 7 Apr 53 FORCE: 7 Apr 53
REGISTERED: 7 Apr 53 United Nations
ARTICLES: 6 LANGUAGE: Arabic. French.
HEADNOTE: TECHNICAL ASSISTANCE
TOPIC: Tech Assistance
CONCEPTS: Treaty implementation. Privileges and
immunities. General cooperation. Exchange of
information and documents. Personnel. Title and
deeds. Exchange. Scholarships and grants. Vo-
cational training. Research and development. Ex-
pense sharing formulae. Local currency. Domes-
tic obligation. General technical assistance. Ma-
terials, equipment and services. IGO status.
Conformity with IGO decisions.
TREATY REF: 1UNTS15,263; 76UNTS132.
PROCEDURE: Amendment. Termination.
PARTIES:
United Nations
Yemen

102143 Bilateral Agreement **163 UNTS 89**
SIGNED: 9 Apr 53 FORCE: 9 Apr 53
REGISTERED: 15 Apr 53 United Nations
ARTICLES: 10 LANGUAGE: English.
HEADNOTE: ACTIVITIES UNICEF
TOPIC: Direct Aid
CONCEPTS: Treaty implementation. Privileges and
immunities. Extraditable offenses. General coop-
eration. Exchange of information and docu-
ments. Informational records. Inspection and ob-
servation. Existing tribunals. Export quotas. In-
demnities and reimbursements. Financial
programs. Local currency. Tax exemptions. Cus-
toms exemptions. Commodities and services.
Assistance. General aid. Distribution. IGO status.
TREATY REF: 1UNTS15.
PROCEDURE: Duration.
PARTIES:
Netherlands
United Nations

102144 Bilateral Exchange **163 UNTS 103**
SIGNED: 8 Aug 49 FORCE: 28 Jul 49
REGISTERED: 15 Apr 53 USA (United States)
ARTICLES: 2 LANGUAGE: English.
HEADNOTE: ADJUTANT GENERAL RECORDS DE-
POSITORY
TOPIC: Milit Installation
CONCEPTS: Annex or appendix reference. Ex-
change of information and documents. Use of
facilities. Indemnities and reimbursements. Se-
curity of information. Bases and facilities.
TREATY REF: 43UNTS271.
PARTIES:
Philippines
USA (United States)

102145 Unilateral Instrument **163 UNTS 117**
SIGNED: 3 Mar 52 FORCE: 17 Apr 53
REGISTERED: 17 Apr 53 United Nations
ARTICLES: 1 LANGUAGE: English.
HEADNOTE: RECOGNIZING COMPULSORY ICJ
JURISDICTION
TOPIC: ICJ Option Clause
CONCEPTS: Compulsory jurisdiction.
INTL ORGS: International Court of Justice.
PROCEDURE: Duration.
PARTIES:
Liberia

102146 Bilateral Exchange **163 UNTS 121**
SIGNED: 20 Nov 52 FORCE: 20 Nov 52
REGISTERED: 21 Apr 53 Netherlands
ARTICLES: 2 LANGUAGE: French.
HEADNOTE: STUDENT EMPLOYMENT
TOPIC: Non-ILO Labor
CONCEPTS: Definition of terms. Detailed regula-
tions. General cooperation. Operating agencies.
Employment regulations. Wages and salaries.
Non-ILO labor relations. Administrative cooper-
ation. Social security. Quotas.
PROCEDURE: Denunciation. Duration. Renewal or
Revival.

PARTIES:
Netherlands
Switzerland

102147 Bilateral Agreement **163 UNTS 131**
SIGNED: 25 Apr 52 FORCE: 5 Feb 53
REGISTERED: 21 Apr 53 Netherlands
ARTICLES: 34 LANGUAGE: Dutch. Swedish.
HEADNOTE: DOUBLE TAXATION ADMINISTRA-
TIVE ASSISTANCE TAXES INCOME PROPERTY
TOPIC: Taxation
CONCEPTS: Definition of terms. Territorial applica-
tion. Conformity with municipal law. General co-
operation. Exchange of official publications. Ne-
gotiation. Teacher and student exchange.
Claims and settlements. Taxation. Equitable
taxes. General. Tax exemptions. Air transport.
Merchant vessels. Mass media exchange.
PARTIES:
Netherlands
Sweden

102148 Bilateral Agreement **163 UNTS 195**
SIGNED: 25 Apr 52 FORCE: 5 Feb 53
REGISTERED: 21 Apr 53 Netherlands
ARTICLES: 18 LANGUAGE: Dutch. Swedish.
HEADNOTE: DOUBLE TAXATION ADMINISTRA-
TIVE ASSISTANCE DEATH DUTIES
TOPIC: Taxation
CONCEPTS: Exchange of official publications.
Claims and settlements. Debts. Taxation. Death
duties. Tax exemptions.
PROCEDURE: Duration. Ratification. Termination.
PARTIES:
Netherlands
Sweden

102149 Bilateral Agreement **163 UNTS 229**
SIGNED: 24 Apr 50 FORCE: 12 Apr 52
REGISTERED: 22 Apr 53 ICAO (Civil Aviat)
ARTICLES: 19 LANGUAGE: Arabic. English. Greek.
HEADNOTE: ESTABLISHMENT SCHEDULED AIR
SERVICES
TOPIC: Air Transport
CONCEPTS: Definition of terms. Detailed regulations. Exceptions and exemptions. Annex or appendix reference. Conformity with municipal
law. General cooperation. Exchange of information and documents. Arbitration. Procedure. Ex-
isting tribunals. Negotiation. Non-interest rates
and fees. Customs exemptions. Routes and logistics. Navigational conditions. Permit designation. Air transport. Conditions of airlines operating permission. Operating authorizations and
regulations.
INTL ORGS: International Civil Aviation Organization. Arbitration Commission.
TREATY REF: 15UNTS295.
PROCEDURE: Amendment. Future Procedures
Contemplated. Ratification. Registration. Termination.
PARTIES:
Greece
United Arab Rep
ANNEX
533 UNTS 324. United Arab Rep. Replacement
29 Nov 62. Force 6 May 63.
533 UNTS 324. Greece. Replacement 6 May 63.
Force 6 May 63.

102150 Bilateral Agreement **163 UNTS 265**
SIGNED: 14 Jul 51 FORCE: 14 Jul 51
REGISTERED: 22 Apr 53 ICAO (Civil Aviat)
ARTICLES: 11 LANGUAGE: Icelandic. Norwegian.
HEADNOTE: AIR TRANSPORT
TOPIC: Air Transport
CONCEPTS: Annex or appendix reference. Conformity with municipal law. Licenses and permits.
Recognition of legal documents. Use of facilities.
Arbitration. Procedure. Negotiation. Fees and exemptions. Most favored nation clause. National
treatment. Customs exemptions. Competency
certificate. Routes and logistics. Navigational
conditions. Permit designation. Air transport. Airport facilities. Airworthiness certificates. Conditions of airlines operating permission. Operating
authorizations and regulations. Licenses and certificates of nationality.
INTL ORGS: International Civil Aviation Organization. Arbitration Commission.

TREATY REF: 15UNTS295.
PROCEDURE: Amendment. Future Procedures Contemplated. Registration. Termination.
PARTIES:
Iceland
Norway

102151 Multilateral Agreement **163 UNTS 293**
SIGNED: 20 Dec 51   FORCE: 28 May 52
REGISTERED: 22 Apr 53 ICAO (Civil Aviat)
ARTICLES: 8 LANGUAGE: Danish. Norwegian. Swedish.
HEADNOTE: COOPERATION CIVIL AVIATION
TOPIC: Air Transport
CONCEPTS: Change of circumstances. General cooperation. Arbitration. Procedure. Negotiation. Commodity trade. Registration certificate. Air transport. Operating authorizations and regulations. Licenses and certificates of nationality.
INTL ORGS: Arbitration Commission.
PROCEDURE: Ratification. Termination.
PARTIES:
Denmark   SIGNED: 20 Dec 51   RATIFIED: 28 May 52 FORCE: 28 May 52
Norway   SIGNED: 20 Dec 51   RATIFIED: 28 May 52 FORCE: 28 May 52
Sweden   SIGNED: 20 Dec 51   RATIFIED: 28 May 52 FORCE: 28 May 52
ANNEX
344 UNTS 321. Norway. Amendment 20 Aug 59. Force 20 Aug 59.
344 UNTS 321.   Denmark.   Amendment 20 Aug 59. Force 20 Aug 59.
344 UNTS 321. Sweden. Amendment 20 Aug 59. Force 20 Aug 59.

102152 Multilateral Agreement **163 UNTS 309**
SIGNED: 20 Dec 51   FORCE: 20 Dec 51
REGISTERED: 22 Apr 53 ICAO (Civil Aviat)
ARTICLES: 4 LANGUAGE: Danish. Norwegian. Swedish.
HEADNOTE: FINANCIAL GUARANTEES AIRLINES
TOPIC: Air Transport
CONCEPTS: General cooperation. Indemnities and reimbursements. Funding procedures. Internal finance. Interest rates. Air transport.
PARTIES:
Denmark SIGNED: 20 Dec 51 FORCE: 20 Dec 51
Norway SIGNED: 20 Dec 51 FORCE: 20 Dec 51
Sweden SIGNED: 20 Dec 51 FORCE: 20 Dec 51

102153 Bilateral Agreement **163 UNTS 321**
SIGNED: 17 Apr 52   FORCE: 17 Apr 52
REGISTERED: 22 Apr 53 ICAO (Civil Aviat)
ARTICLES: 2 LANGUAGE: French. Spanish.
HEADNOTE: AIR TRANSPORT
TOPIC: Air Transport
CONCEPTS: Definition of terms. Detailed regulations. Exceptions and exemptions. Annex or appendix reference. Conformity with municipal law. General cooperation. Exchange of information and documents. Licenses and permits. Recognition of legal documents. Use of facilities. Arbitration. Procedure. Negotiation. Competence of tribunal. Reexport of goods, etc.. Fees and exemptions. Non-interest rates and fees. Most favored nation clause. National treatment. Customs exemptions. Competency certificate. Routes and logistics. Navigational conditions. Permit designation. Air transport. Airport facilities. Airworthiness certificates. Conditions of airlines operating permission. Overflights and technical stops. Operating authorizations and regulations. Licenses and certificates of nationality.
INTL ORGS: International Civil Aviation Organization.
TREATY REF: 15UNTS295.
PROCEDURE: Amendment. Denunciation. Future Procedures Contemplated. Registration. Termination.
PARTIES:
France
Mexico
ANNEX
216 UNTS 408.   France. Amendment 7 Jan 54. Force 7 Jan 54.
216 UNTS 408. Mexico. Amendment 7 Jan 54. Force 7 Jan 54.

102154 Bilateral Agreement **163 UNTS 341**
SIGNED: 13 Oct 52   FORCE: 13 Oct 52
REGISTERED: 22 Apr 53 ICAO (Civil Aviat)
ARTICLES: 2 LANGUAGE: Dutch. English. Spanish.
HEADNOTE: AIR TRANSPORT
TOPIC: Air Transport
CONCEPTS: Definition of terms. Exceptions and exemptions. Annex or appendix reference. Conformity with municipal law. Licenses and permits. Recognition of legal documents. Use of facilities. Arbitration. Procedure. Special tribunals. Indemnities and reimbursements. Fees and exemptions. Most favored nation clause. National treatment. Customs exemptions. Competency certificate. Routes and logistics. Navigational conditions. Permit designation. Air transport. Airport facilities. Airworthiness certificates. Conditions of airlines operating permission. Operating authorizations and regulations. Licenses and certificates of nationality.
INTL ORGS: International Civil Aviation Organization. Arbitration Commission.
PROCEDURE: Amendment. Future Procedures Contemplated. Registration. Termination. Application to Non-self-governing Territories.
PARTIES:
Mexico
Netherlands
ANNEX
200 UNTS 321. Mexico. Amendment 24 Apr 53. Force 24 Apr 53.
200 UNTS 321.   Netherlands.   Amendment 17 Apr 53. Force 24 Apr 53.
335 UNTS 298.   Netherlands.   Amendment 28 Oct 57. Force 29 Oct 57.
335 UNTS 298. Mexico. Amendment 29 Oct 57. Force 29 Oct 57.

102155 Bilateral Exchange **164 UNTS 3**
SIGNED: 20 Feb 53   FORCE: 20 Feb 53
REGISTERED: 22 Apr 53 ICAO (Civil Aviat)
ARTICLES: 2 LANGUAGE: English.
HEADNOTE: OPERATION AIR SERVICES
TOPIC: Air Transport
CONCEPTS: Export quotas. Routes and logistics. Navigational conditions. Navigational equipment. Overflights and technical stops. Operating authorizations and regulations.
INTL ORGS: International Civil Aviation Organization.
PARTIES:
India
Pakistan

102156 Bilateral Agreement **164 UNTS 15**
SIGNED: 28 Nov 52   FORCE: 28 Nov 52
REGISTERED: 22 Apr 53 ICAO (Civil Aviat)
ARTICLES: 6 LANGUAGE: Spanish.
HEADNOTE: TECHNICAL ASSISTANCE
TOPIC: Tech Assistance
CONCEPTS: Exceptions and exemptions. Treaty implementation. Inviolability. Privileges and immunities. General cooperation. Exchange of information and documents. Personnel. Title and deeds. Exchange. Scholarships and grants. Vocational training. Research and development. Accounting procedures. Exchange rates and regulations. Expense sharing formulae. Claims and settlements. Most favored nation clause. Tax exemptions. Customs exemptions. Domestic obligation. General technical assistance. Materials, equipment and services. IGO status. Conformity with IGO decisions.
INTL ORGS: United Nations.
TREATY REF: 76UNTS132.
PROCEDURE: Amendment. Termination.
PARTIES:
Mexico
ICAO (Civil Aviat)

102157 Multilateral Convention **164 UNTS 37**
SIGNED: 27 Jun 46   FORCE: 22 Apr 53
REGISTERED: 27 Apr 53 ILO (Labor Org)
ARTICLES: 14 LANGUAGE: English. French.
HEADNOTE: CERTIFICATION SHIPS COOKS
TOPIC: ILO Labor
CONCEPTS: Definition of terms. Detailed regulations. Previous treaty extension. Standardization. Conformity with municipal law. Domestic legislation. Vocational training. ILO conventions.

Employment regulations. Competency certificate. Information agency.
INTL ORGS: International Labour Organization. United Nations.
TREATY REF: 38UNTS3; 44UNTS343.
PROCEDURE: Amendment. Denunciation. Duration. Ratification. Registration.
PARTIES:
Multilateral
ANNEX
189 UNTS 381. Poland. Ratification 13 Apr 54. Force 13 Oct 54.
212 UNTS 399. France. French Guinea.
212 UNTS 399. France. Guadeloupe.
212 UNTS 399. France. Reunion.
212 UNTS 399. France. Martinique.
318 UNTS 423. UK Great Britain. Declaration 3 Nov 58.
318 UNTS 423. UK Great Britain. Declaration 3 Nov 58.
338 UNTS 372. UK Great Britain. Declaration 7 Jul 59.
396 UNTS 335.   Yugoslavia.   Ratification 6 Mar 61. Force 6 Sep 61.
429 UNTS 282. Peru. Ratification 4 Apr 62. Force 4 Oct 62.
444 UNTS 338. Algeria. Succession 19 Oct 62.
480 UNTS 480. Greece. Ratification 9 Oct 63. Force 9 Apr 64.
530 UNTS 419. Ghana. Ratification 22 Mar 65.

102158 Bilateral Protocol **164 UNTS 49**
SIGNED: 27 Feb 53   FORCE: 1 Jul 52
REGISTERED: 29 Apr 53 Belgium
ARTICLES: 3 LANGUAGE: French.
HEADNOTE: OLD-AGE ALLOWANCES
TOPIC: Non-ILO Labor
CONCEPTS: Non-ILO labor relations. Old age insurance. Payment schedules.
PARTIES:
Belgium
France

102159 Bilateral Agreement **164 UNTS 53**
SIGNED: 17 Apr 46   FORCE: 17 May 46
REGISTERED: 29 Apr 53 UK Great Britain
ARTICLES: 13 LANGUAGE: English. Spanish.
HEADNOTE: AIR SERVICES
TOPIC: Air Transport
CONCEPTS: Definition of terms. Guarantees and safeguards. Annex or appendix reference. Conformity with municipal law. Licenses and permits. Recognition of legal documents. Use of facilities. Fees and exemptions. Most favored nation clause. National treatment. Customs exemptions. Competency certificate. Routes and logistics. Navigational conditions. Permit designation. Air transport. Airport facilities. Airworthiness certificates. Conditions of airlines operating permission. Operating authorizations and regulations. Licenses and certificates of nationality.
PROCEDURE: Amendment. Duration. Future Procedures Contemplated. Ratification. Renewal or Revival. Termination. Application to Non-self-governing Territories.
PARTIES:
Argentina
UK Great Britain
ANNEX
310 UNTS 364. UK Great Britain. Prolongation 17 Oct 56. Force 17 May 57.
310 UNTS 364.   Argentina.   Prolongation 17 Oct 56. Force 17 May 57.
312 UNTS 424. UK Great Britain. Prolongation 17 Nov 57. Force 17 May 58.
312 UNTS 424.   Argentina.   Prolongation 17 Nov 57. Force 17 May 58.
349 UNTS 325. UK Great Britain. Prolongation 17 Nov 58. Force 17 May 59.
349 UNTS 325.   Argentina.   Prolongation 17 Nov 58. Force 17 May 59.
360 UNTS 394. UK Great Britain. Prolongation 17 Dec 59. Force 17 May 60.
360 UNTS 394.   Argentina.   Prolongation 17 Dec 59. Force 17 May 60.
398 UNTS 348. UK Great Britain. Prolongation 19 Nov 60. Force 17 May 61.
398 UNTS 348.   Argentina.   Prolongation 19 Nov 60. Force 17 May 61.

102160 Bilateral Exchange **164 UNTS 91**
SIGNED: 13 May 52 FORCE: 10 Feb 53
REGISTERED: 29 Apr 53 UK Great Britain
ARTICLES: 2 LANGUAGE: English. French.
HEADNOTE: AIR SERVICES
TOPIC: Air Transport
CONCEPTS: Exceptions and exemptions. Territorial application. Exchange of information and documents. Most favored nation clause. Competency certificate. Routes and logistics. Air transport. Conditions of airlines operating permission. Overflights and technical stops. Operating authorizations and regulations.
TREATY REF: 99UNTS107; 15UNTS295.
PROCEDURE: Ratification. Termination.
PARTIES:
Switzerland
UK Great Britain
ANNEX
398 UNTS 349. UK Great Britain. Termination 10 Feb 60. Force 11 Apr 60.

102161 Bilateral Exchange **164 UNTS 101**
SIGNED: 4 Nov 52 FORCE: 4 Nov 52
REGISTERED: 29 Apr 53 UK Great Britain
ARTICLES: 2 LANGUAGE: English.
HEADNOTE: JAPANESE OWNERSHIP JAPANESE LEGATION
TOPIC: Specific Property
CONCEPTS: Post-war claims settlement. Facilities and property.
PARTIES:
Japan
UK Great Britain

102162 Bilateral Exchange **164 UNTS 107**
SIGNED: 4 Nov 52 FORCE: 4 Nov 52
REGISTERED: 29 Apr 53 UK Great Britain
ARTICLES: 2 LANGUAGE: English.
HEADNOTE: JAPANESE OWNERSHIP PERSONAL EFFECTS ARCHIVES
TOPIC: Specific Property
CONCEPTS: Post-war claims settlement. Facilities and property.
PARTIES:
Japan
UK Great Britain

102163 Multilateral Convention **164 UNTS 113**
SIGNED: 10 Jun 48 FORCE: 19 Nov 52
REGISTERED: 29 Apr 53 UK Great Britain
ARTICLES: 15 LANGUAGE: English. French.
HEADNOTE: SAFETY OF LIFE AT SEA CONVENTION
TOPIC: Humanitarian
CONCEPTS: Definition of terms. Detailed regulations. Emergencies. Previous treaty renunciation. Territorial application. Humanitarian matters. General transportation. Registration certificate. Passenger transport. Water transport. Merchant vessels. Tonnage. Facilities and equipment. Meteorology.
INTL ORGS: Inter-Governmental Maritime Consultative Organization. United Nations.
PROCEDURE: Amendment. Denunciation. Registration.
PARTIES:
Argentina SIGNED: 10 Jun 48
Australia SIGNED: 10 Jun 48
Belgium SIGNED: 10 Jun 48 RATIFIED: 5 Dec 51 FORCE: 19 Nov 52
Brazil SIGNED: 10 Jun 48
Canada SIGNED: 10 Jun 48 RATIFIED: 1 Feb 51 FORCE: 19 Nov 52
Chile SIGNED: 10 Jun 48
Taiwan SIGNED: 10 Jun 48
Denmark SIGNED: 10 Jun 48 RATIFIED: 15 Oct 51 FORCE: 19 Nov 52
United Arab Rep SIGNED: 10 Jun 48
Finland SIGNED: 10 Jun 48
France SIGNED: 10 Jun 48 RATIFIED: 8 Feb 50 FORCE: 19 Nov 52
Greece SIGNED: 10 Jun 48
Iceland SIGNED: 10 Jun 48 RATIFIED: 19 Oct 50 FORCE: 19 Nov 52
India SIGNED: 10 Jun 48 RATIFIED: 19 Nov 52 FORCE: 19 Nov 52
Ireland SIGNED: 10 Jun 48
Israel RATIFIED: 2 Jul 52 FORCE: 19 Nov 52
Italy SIGNED: 10 Jun 48 RATIFIED: 19 Nov 51 FORCE: 19 Nov 52
Japan RATIFIED: 23 Jul 52 FORCE: 19 Nov 52

Netherlands SIGNED: 10 Jun 48 RATIFIED: 18 Apr 50 FORCE: 19 Nov 52
Norway SIGNED: 10 Jun 48 RATIFIED: 12 Jun 50 FORCE: 19 Nov 52
Pakistan SIGNED: 10 Jun 48 RATIFIED: 1 Feb 51 FORCE: 19 Nov 52
Panama SIGNED: 10 Jun 48
Philippines SIGNED: 10 Jun 48 RATIFIED: 2 Oct 52 FORCE: 19 Nov 52
Poland SIGNED: 10 Jun 48
Portugal SIGNED: 10 Jun 48 RATIFIED: 30 Nov 50 FORCE: 19 Nov 52
South Africa SIGNED: 10 Jun 48 RATIFIED: 18 Aug 50 FORCE: 19 Nov 52
Spain RATIFIED: 26 Dec 52 FORCE: 26 Mar 53
Spain Spanish Colonies RATIFIED: 26 Dec 52 FORCE: 26 Mar 53
Spain Spanish Morroco RATIFIED: 26 Dec 52 FORCE: 26 Mar 53
Sweden SIGNED: 10 Jun 48 RATIFIED: 16 May 50 FORCE: 19 Nov 52
UK Great Britain SIGNED: 10 Jun 48 RATIFIED: 30 Sep 49 FORCE: 19 Nov 52
USA (United States) Alaska RATIFIED: 5 Jan 50 FORCE: 19 Nov 52
USA (United States) Hawaii RATIFIED: 5 Jan 50 FORCE: 19 Nov 52
USA (United States) Puerto Rico RATIFIED: 5 Jan 50 FORCE: 19 Nov 52
USA (United States) SIGNED: 10 Jun 48 RATIFIED: 5 Jan 50 FORCE: 19 Nov 52
ANNEX
167 UNTS 338. Liberia. Acceptance 13 Jan 53. Force 13 Apr 53.
167 UNTS 338. UK Great Britain. Hong Kong. Force 7 Apr 53.
172 UNTS 409. Chile. Acceptance 5 Jun 53. Force 5 Sep 53.
173 UNTS 416. Italy. Italian Somaliland. Force 6 Jul 53.
175 UNTS 374. Vietnam. Acceptance 12 Sep 53. Force 12 Dec 53.
175 UNTS 374. Finland. Acceptance 13 Aug 53. Force 13 Nov 53.
175 UNTS 374. Ireland. Acceptance 19 Aug 53. Force 19 Nov 53.
183 UNTS 372. UK Great Britain. Singapore. Acceptance 12 Sep 53. Force 5 Aug 53.
183 UNTS 372. UK Great Britain. Fed of Malaya. 3 Oct 63
187 UNTS 464. Panama. Acceptance 8 Jan 54. Force 8 Apr 54.
187 UNTS 464. Greece. Acceptance 21 Jan 54. Force 21 Apr 54.
191 UNTS 363. USSR (Soviet Union). Acceptance 10 May 54. Force 10 Aug 54.
191 UNTS 406. Nicaragua. Acceptance 19 Feb 54. Force 19 May 54.
193 UNTS 361. Haiti. Acceptance 26 May 54. Force 26 Aug 54.
193 UNTS 361. Switzerland. Acceptance 19 May 54. Force 19 Aug 54.
193 UNTS 361. Cambodia. Acceptance 2 Mar 54. Force 2 Jun 54.
198 UNTS 404. United Arab Rep. Acceptance 11 Jun 54. Force 11 Sep 54.
198 UNTS 404. Poland. Acceptance 11 Jun 54. Force 11 Sep 54.
200 UNTS 326. Cuba. Acceptance 26 Aug 54. Force 26 Nov 54.
200 UNTS 326. Germany, West. Acceptance 19 Aug 54. Force 19 Nov 54.
202 UNTS 339. Romania. Acceptance 30 Sep 54. Force 30 Dec 54.
210 UNTS 335. Dominican Republic. Acceptance 29 Mar 55. Force 29 Jun 55.
212 UNTS 351. France. Morocco. Force 22 Apr 55.
212 UNTS 351. France. All Territories. Force 31 May 55.
212 UNTS 351. France. Tunisia. Force 22 Apr 55.
218 UNTS 390. Netherlands. Netherlands Antilles. Force 11 Jan 55.
230 UNTS 438. Venezuela. Acceptance 8 Feb 56. Force 8 May 56.
230 UNTS 438. Brazil. Acceptance 17 Jan 56. Force 17 Apr 56.
250 UNTS 313. Argentina. Acceptance 31 Jul 56. Force 31 Oct 56.
252 UNTS 334. Bulgaria. Acceptance 17 Aug 56. Force 17 Nov 56.
252 UNTS 334. Hungary. Acceptance 15 Aug 56. Force 15 Nov 56.

253 UNTS 364. Turkey. Acceptance 19 Oct 56. Force 19 Jan 57.
267 UNTS 382. Multilateral. Force 17 May 57.
267 UNTS 382. Czechoslovakia. Acceptance 25 Mar 57. Force 25 Jun 57.
274 UNTS 349. Portugal. Timor. Force 23 Feb 57.
274 UNTS 349. Portugal. Macao. Force 23 Feb 57.
274 UNTS 349. Portugal. St. Tome. Force 23 Feb 57.
274 UNTS 349. Portugal. Portuguese India. Force 23 Feb 57.
274 UNTS 349. Portugal. Mozambique. Force 23 Feb 57.
274 UNTS 349. Portugal. Portuguese Guinea. Force 23 Feb 57.
274 UNTS 349. Portugal. Cape Verde Islands. Force 23 Feb 57.
274 UNTS 349. Portugal. Angola. Force 23 Feb 57.
327 UNTS 361. Ghana. Acceptance 22 Nov 57. Force 22 Feb 58.
327 UNTS 361. Ghana. Acceptance 22 Nov 57. Force 22 Feb 58.
344 UNTS 326. Australia. Acceptance 6 Oct 59. Force 6 Jan 60.
355 UNTS 410. Korea, South. Acceptance 10 Mar 60. Force 10 Jun 60.
357 UNTS 361. Kuwait. Acceptance 12 Jan 59. Force 12 Apr 59.
389 UNTS 312. Uruguay. Acceptance 15 Feb 61. Force 15 May 61.
419 UNTS 357. Mexico. Acceptance 4 Jan 67. Force 4 Apr 62.
466 UNTS 386. Tunisia. Acceptance 20 May 63. Force 20 Aug 63.
470 UNTS 386. Nigeria. Acceptance 3 Jul 63. Force .
486 UNTS 402. Algeria. Acceptance 20 Jan 64. Force 20 Apr 64.
531 UNTS 321. Vietnam, South. Denunciation 23 Mar 65. Force 26 May 66.
531 UNTS 321. Yugoslavia. Denunciation 22 Apr 65. Force 26 May 66.
531 UNTS 321. Netherlands. Denunciation 16 Oct 64. Force 26 May 66.
535 UNTS 411. Germany, West. Denunciation 25 May 65. Force 26 May 66.
535 UNTS 411. Finland. Denunciation 11 May 65. Force 26 May 66.
535 UNTS 411. UK Great Britain. Denunciation 23 Apr 65. Force 26 May 66.
535 UNTS 411. Taiwan. Acceptance 23 Feb 65. Force 23 Mar 65.
536 UNTS 476. Kuwait. Denunciation 25 May 65. Force 26 May 66.
536 UNTS 476. Norway. Denunciation 25 May 65. Force 26 May 66.
536 UNTS 476. Japan. Denunciation 25 May 65. Force 26 May 66.
536 UNTS 476. Denmark. Denunciation 25 May 65. Force 26 May 66.
543 UNTS 361. Iceland. Denunciation 27 Jul 65. Force 27 Jul 65.
543 UNTS 361. Iceland. Denunciation 23 Jul 63. Force 23 Jul 65.
547 UNTS 318. Liberia. Denunciation 27 Oct 65. Force 27 Oct 66.
547 UNTS 318. Greece. Denunciation 18 Oct 65. Force 18 Oct 66.
551 UNTS 290. Spain. Denunciation 29 Oct 65. Force 29 Oct 66.
557 UNTS 272. Pakistan. Denunciation 24 Feb 66. Force 24 Feb 67.
557 UNTS 272. New Zealand. Denunciation 14 Feb 66. Force 14 Feb 67.
561 UNTS 346. USA (United States). Puerto Rico. Denunciation 26 May 65. Force 26 May 65.
561 UNTS 346. Belgium. Denunciation 22 Mar 66. Force 22 Mar 67.
561 UNTS 346. Switzerland. Denunciation 21 Mar 66. Force 12 Apr 67.
561 UNTS 346. USA (United States). Denunciation 26 May 65. Force 26 May 66.
565 UNTS 283. Poland. Denunciation 24 Jun 66. Force 24 Jun 67.
572 UNTS 356. Argentina. Denunciation 5 Sep 66. Force 5 Sep 67.
603 UNTS 297. Ghana. Denunciation 9 Aug 67. Force 9 Aug 68.
607 UNTS 257. India. Denunciation 6 Oct 66. Force 6 Oct 67.
607 UNTS 257. Israel. Denunciation 13 Oct 67. Force 13 Oct 68.

614 UNTS 305. South Africa. Denunciation 13 Dec 67. Force 13 Dec 68.
616 UNTS 493. Portugal. All Territories. Denunciation 13 Nov 67. Force 13 Nov 68.
616 UNTS 493. Australia. Denunciation 20 Dec 67. Force 20 Dec 68.

102164 Bilateral Exchange **165 UNTS 3**
SIGNED: 18 Dec 51 FORCE: 18 Dec 51
REGISTERED: 1 May 53 USA (United States)
ARTICLES: 2 LANGUAGE: English. Spanish.
HEADNOTE: CONTROL ELECTROMAGNETIC RADIATION EVENT ATTACK
TOPIC: General Military
CONCEPTS: Guarantees and safeguards. Bands and frequency allocation. Defense and security.
PROCEDURE: Duration. Future Procedures Contemplated. Termination.
PARTIES:
Cuba
USA (United States)

102165 Bilateral Agreement **165 UNTS 11**
SIGNED: 7 Mar 52 FORCE: 7 Mar 52
REGISTERED: 1 May 53 USA (United States)
ARTICLES: 11 LANGUAGE: English. Spanish.
HEADNOTE: MILITARY ASSISTANCE
TOPIC: Milit Assistance
CONCEPTS: Exceptions and exemptions. Guarantees and safeguards. Non-prejudice to UN·charter. Peaceful relations. Privileges and immunities. Conformity with municipal law. General cooperation. Inspection and observation. Public information. Use of facilities. Indemnities and reimbursements. Garnishment of funds. Local currency. Claims and settlements. Most favored nation clause. Recognition. Customs exemptions. Domestic obligation. Materials, equipment and services. Aid missions. Joint defense. Defense and security. Self-defense. Military assistance. Return of equipment and recapture. Security of information. Exchange of defense information. Restrictions on transfer. Raw materials.
INTL ORGS: United Nations.
TREATY REF: 21UNTS77; 26UNTS417.
PROCEDURE: Amendment. Future Procedures Contemplated. Registration. Termination.
PARTIES:
Cuba
USA (United States)
ANNEX
258 UNTS 408. USA (United States). Implementation 18 Mar 55. Force 3 May 55.
258 UNTS 408. Cuba. Implementation 3 May 55. Force 3 May 55.

102166 Bilateral Agreement **165 UNTS 31**
SIGNED: 22 Feb 52 FORCE: 26 Apr 52
REGISTERED: 1 May 53 USA (United States)
ARTICLES: 11 LANGUAGE: English. Spanish.
HEADNOTE: MILITARY ASSISTANCE
TOPIC: Milit Assistance
CONCEPTS: Exceptions and exemptions. Guarantees and safeguards. Non-prejudice to UN charter. Peaceful relations. Privileges and immunities. Conformity with municipal law. General cooperation. Inspection and observation. Public information. Use of facilities. Indemnities and reimbursements. Garnishment of funds. Local currency. Claims and settlements. Most favored nation clause. Recognition. Customs exemptions. Domestic obligation. Materials, equipment and services. Aid missions. Joint defense. Defense and security. Self-defense. Military assistance. Return of equipment and recapture. Security of information. Exchange of defense information. Restrictions on transfer. Raw materials.
INTL ORGS: United Nations.
TREATY REF: 21UNTS77; 26UNTS417.
PROCEDURE: Amendment. Future Procedures Contemplated. Registration. Termination.
PARTIES:
Peru
USA (United States)
ANNEX
258 UNTS 415. USA (United States). Implementation 22 Mar 55. Force 30 Apr 55.
258 UNTS 415. Peru. Implementation 30 Apr 55. Force 30 Apr 55.

102167 Bilateral Convention **165 UNTS 51**
SIGNED: 9 Jul 51 FORCE: 17 Sep 52
REGISTERED: 1 May 53 USA (United States)
ARTICLES: 8 LANGUAGE: English. German.
HEADNOTE: DOUBLE TAXATION TAXES ESTATES INHERITANCES
TOPIC: Taxation
CONCEPTS: Definition of terms. Exchange of official publications. Negotiation. Claims and settlements. Taxation. Death duties. Tax credits. Tax exemptions.
PROCEDURE: Duration. Ratification. Termination.
PARTIES:
Switzerland
USA (United States)

102168 Bilateral Exchange **165 UNTS 67**
SIGNED: 3 Mar 51 FORCE: 3 Mar 52
REGISTERED: 1 May 53 USA (United States)
ARTICLES: 2 LANGUAGE: English.
HEADNOTE: TECHNICAL COOPERATION TRAINING CENTERS OTHER SERVICES
TOPIC: Tech Assistance
CONCEPTS: Exceptions and exemptions. Treaty implementation. Privileges and immunities. General cooperation. Operating agencies. Personnel. Institute establishment. Funding procedures. General technical assistance.
PROCEDURE: Amendment. Termination.
PARTIES:
OAS (Am States)
USA (United States)

102169 Multilateral Agreement **165 UNTS 77**
SIGNED: 11 Feb 52 FORCE: 11 Feb 52
REGISTERED: 1 May 53 USA (United States)
ARTICLES: 5 LANGUAGE: English.
HEADNOTE: ECONOMIC COOPERATION
TOPIC: Direct Aid
CONCEPTS: Annex or appendix reference. Previous treaty replacement. Continuity of rights and obligations. Transition period. Local currency. Assets transfer. Economic assistance.
TREATY REF: 20UNTS91; 69UNTS53; 92UNTS287; 70UNTS123.
PROCEDURE: Amendment.
PARTIES:
Indonesia SIGNED: 11 Feb 52 FORCE: 11 Feb 52
Netherlands SIGNED: 11 Feb 52 FORCE: 11 Feb 52
USA (United States) SIGNED: 11 Feb 52 FORCE: 11 Feb 52

102170 Bilateral Exchange **165 UNTS 89**
SIGNED: 8 Jan 51 FORCE: 8 Jan 51
REGISTERED: 11 May 53 USA (United States)
ARTICLES: 2 LANGUAGE: English. Spanish.
HEADNOTE: TRANSFER NAVAL VESSELS
TOPIC: Milit Assistance
CONCEPTS: Non-prejudice to UN charter. Conformity with municipal law. Materials, equipment and services. Defense and security. Payment for war supplies. Naval vessels. Exchange of defense information. Restrictions on transfer.
TREATY REF: 21UNTS77; 26UNTS417.
PARTIES:
Argentina
USA (United States)

102171 Bilateral Exchange **165 UNTS 97**
SIGNED: 4 Jan 51 FORCE: 4 Jan 51
REGISTERED: 11 May 53 USA (United States)
ARTICLES: 2 LANGUAGE: English. Portuguese.
HEADNOTE: TRANSFER NAVAL VESSELS
TOPIC: Milit Assistance
CONCEPTS: Non-prejudice to UN charter. Conformity with municipal law. Materials, equipment and services. Defense and security. Payment for war supplies. Naval vessels. Security of information. Exchange of defense information. Restrictions on transfer.
TREATY REF: 21UNTS77; 26UNTS417.
PARTIES:
Brazil
USA (United States)

102172 Bilateral Exchange **165 UNTS 105**
SIGNED: 4 Jan 51 FORCE: 4 Jan 51

REGISTERED: 11 May 53 USA (United States)
ARTICLES: 2 LANGUAGE: English.
HEADNOTE: TRANSFER NAVAL VESSELS
TOPIC: Milit Assistance
CONCEPTS: Non-prejudice to UN charter. Conformity with municipal law. Materials, equipment and services. Defense and security. Payment for war supplies. Naval vessels. Security of information. Exchange of defense information. Restrictions on transfer.
PARTIES:
Chile
USA (United States)

102173 Bilateral Exchange **165 UNTS 113**
SIGNED: 7 Mar 51 FORCE: 8 Mar 51
REGISTERED: 11 May 53 USA (United States)
ARTICLES: 2 LANGUAGE: English. Spanish.
HEADNOTE: HEALTH SANITATION PROGRAM
TOPIC: Sanitation
CONCEPTS: Previous treaty extension. Friendship and amity. Disease control. Public health. Narcotic drugs. Exchange. Financial programs. Funding procedures. Assistance. Special projects. Specific technical assistance. Economic assistance.
TREATY REF: USA 64STAT204.
PARTIES:
USA (United States)
Uruguay
ANNEX
174 UNTS 348. USA (United States). Supplementation 16 Jan 52. Force 26 Mar 52.
174 UNTS 348. Uruguay. Supplementation 26 Mar 52. Force 26 Mar 52.

102174 Bilateral Convention **165 UNTS 121**
SIGNED: 6 Jun 51 FORCE: 7 Sep 52
REGISTERED: 11 May 53 USA (United States)
ARTICLES: 29 LANGUAGE: English.
HEADNOTE: CONSULAR OFFICERS
TOPIC: Consul/Citizenship
CONCEPTS: Definition of terms. Previous treaty replacement. General consular functions. Diplomatic privileges. Consular relations establishment. Inviolability. Privileges and immunities. Protection of nationals. Diplomatic correspondence. Notarial acts and services. Immovable property. General property. Responsibility and liability. Fees and exemptions.
TREATY REF: 2DEMARTENS582.
PROCEDURE: Ratification. Termination.
PARTIES:
UK Great Britain
USA (United States)

102175 Bilateral Agreement **165 UNTS 167**
SIGNED: 18 Jul 52 FORCE: 18 Jul 52
REGISTERED: 11 May 53 USA (United States)
ARTICLES: 12 LANGUAGE: English. German.
HEADNOTE: EDUCATIONAL EXCHANGE PROGRAM
TOPIC: Education
CONCEPTS: Definition of terms. Standardization. Conformity with municipal law. General cooperation. Inspection and observation. Personnel. General property. Responsibility and liability. Specialists exchange. Exchange. Commissions and foundations. Teacher and student exchange. Professorships. Scholarships and grants. Scientific exchange. Research and development. Accounting procedures. Currency. Exchange rates and regulations. Expense sharing formulae. Financial programs. Funding procedures.
INTL ORGS: Allied Military Occupation. International Monetary Fund. Special Commission.
TREATY REF: USA 58STAT782; USA 60STAT754; 2UNTS39.
PROCEDURE: Amendment.
PARTIES:
Germany, West
USA (United States)
ANNEX
316 UNTS 342. USA (United States). Amendment 14 May 58. Force 14 May 58.
316 UNTS 342. Germany, West. Amendment 14 May 58. Force 14 May 58.

102176 Bilateral Agreement **165 UNTS 187**
SIGNED: 26 Mar 52 FORCE: 26 Mar 52
REGISTERED: 11 May 53 USA (United States)
ARTICLES: 12 LANGUAGE: Afrikaans. English.
HEADNOTE: EDUCATIONAL EXCHANGE PRO-
GRAMS
TOPIC: Education
CONCEPTS: International circulation. Exchange.
Commissions and foundations. Teacher and stu-
dent exchange. Scholarships and grants.
INTL ORGS: Allied Military Occupation. Interna-
tional Monetary Fund. Special Commission.
PARTIES:
South Africa
USA (United States)

102177 Bilateral Agreement **165 UNTS 203**
SIGNED: 2 Jul 52 FORCE: 2 Jul 52
REGISTERED: 11 May 53 USA (United States)
ARTICLES: 11 LANGUAGE: English. Finnish.
HEADNOTE: FINANCING EDUCATIONAL EX-
CHANGE
TOPIC: Education
CONCEPTS: Definition of terms. Standardization.
Conformity with municipal law. General cooper-
ation. Inspection and observation. Personnel.
General property. Responsibility and liability.
Specialists exchange. Exchange. Commissions
and foundations. Professorships. Scholarships
and grants. Research and development. Ac-
counting procedures. Currency. Exchange rates
and regulations. Expense sharing formulae. Fi-
nancial programs. Funding procedurés.
INTL ORGS: Allied Military Occupation. International Monetary Fund. Special Commission.
TREATY REF: USA 58STAT782; 60STAT754.
PARTIES:
Finland
USA (United States)
ANNEX
263 UNTS 418. USA (United States). Amendment
30 Nov 56. Force 30 Nov 56.
263 UNTS 418. Finland. Amendment 30 Nov 56.
Force 30 Nov 56.
346 UNTS 334. USA (United States). Amendment
30 May 59. Force 30 May 59.
346 UNTS 334. Finland. Amendment 30 May 59.
Force 30 May 59.
400 UNTS 382. Finland. Amendment 14 Nov 60.
Force 14 Nov 60.
400 UNTS 382. USA (United States). Amendment
14 Nov 60. Force 14 Nov 60.

102178 Bilateral Agreement **165 UNTS 219**
SIGNED: 20 Jun 52 FORCE: 13 Jul 52
REGISTERED: 11 May 53 WHO (World Health)
ARTICLES: 6 LANGUAGE: English.
HEADNOTE: TECHNICAL ASSISTANCE
TOPIC: Tech Assistance
CONCEPTS: Treaty implementation. Annex or ap-
pendix reference. Privileges and immunities.
General cooperation. Exchange of information
and documents. Operating agencies. Personnel.
Use of facilities. Arbitration. Procedure. Educa-
tion. Scholarships and grants. Vocational train-
ing. Expense sharing formulae. Local currency.
Domestic obligation. General technical assis-
tance. Materials, equipment and services.
INTL ORGS: United Nations.
TREATY REF: 76UNTS132; 33UNTS261.
PROCEDURE: Amendment. Termination.
PARTIES:
WHO (World Health)
Syria

102179 Bilateral Agreement **165 UNTS 231**
SIGNED: 11 Feb 53 FORCE: 8 May 53
REGISTERED: 22 May 53 IBRD (World Bank)
ARTICLES: 7 LANGUAGE: English.
HEADNOTE: LOAN AGREEMENT
TOPIC: IBRD Project
CONCEPTS: Default remedies. Definition of terms.
Annex or appendix reference. Exchange of infor-
mation and documents. Informational records.
Inspection and observation. Accounting proce-
dures. Bonds. Fees and exemptions. Interest
rates. Tax exemptions. Domestic obligation.
Terms of loan. Loan regulations. Loan guarantee.
Guarantor non-interference.

PARTIES:
IBRD (World Bank)
Yugoslavia

102180 Bilateral Exchange **165 UNTS 297**
SIGNED: 26 Mar 53 FORCE: 26 May 53
REGISTERED: 26 May 53 Belgium
ARTICLES: 2 LANGUAGE: Dutch.
HEADNOTE: LIBERALIZATION MINOR FRONTIER
TRAFFIC
TOPIC: Visas
CONCEPTS: Border traffic and migration. Non-visa
travel documents. Frontier permits.
PARTIES:
Belgium
Netherlands
ANNEX
213 UNTS 387. Belgium. Amendment 5 Mar 55.
Force 8 May 55.
213 UNTS 387. Netherlands. Amendment
24 Feb 55. Force 8 May 55.

102181 Multilateral Convention **165 UNTS 303**
SIGNED: 29 Jun 51 FORCE: 23 May 53
REGISTERED: 28 May 53 ILO (Labor Org)
ARTICLES: 14 LANGUAGE: English. French.
HEADNOTE: EQUAL PAY WOMEN
TOPIC: ILO Labor
CONCEPTS: Definition of terms. Territorial applica-
tion. Treaty implementation. Exchange of infor-
mation and documents. Incorporation of treaty
provisions into national law. Jurisdiction. ILO
conventions. Anti-discrimination. Wages and sal-
aries.
INTL ORGS: International Labour Organization.
United Nations.
TREATY REF: 15UNTS35.
PROCEDURE: Amendment. Denunciation. Duration. Ratification. Registration. Renewal or Revival.
PARTIES:
Multilateral
ANNEX
173 UNTS 417. Dominican Republic. Ratification
22 Sep 53. Force 22 Sep 54.
179 UNTS 347. Austria. Ratification 29 Oct 53.
Force 29 Oct 54.
184 UNTS 381. Philippines. Ratification
29 Dec 53. Force 29 Dec 54.
184 UNTS 381. Cuba. Ratification 13 Jan 54.
Force 13 Jan 55.
201 UNTS 380. Poland. Ratification 25 Oct 54.
Force 25 Oct 55.
212 UNTS 400. France. Martinique.
212 UNTS 400. France. Reunion.
212 UNTS 400. France. Guadeloupe.
212 UNTS 400. France. French Guinea.
222 UNTS 420. Bulgaria. Ratification 7 Nov 55.
Force 7 Nov 56.
238 UNTS 331. USSR (Soviet Union). Ratification
30 Apr 56. Force 30 Apr 57.
248 UNTS 407. Italy. Ratification 8 Jun 56. Force
8 Jun 57.
248 UNTS 407. Hungary. Ratification 8 Jun 56.
Force 8 Jun 57.
248 UNTS 407. Hungary. Ratification 8 Jun 56.
Force 8 Jun 57.
248 UNTS 407. Germany, West. Ratification
8 Jun 56. Force 8 Jun 57.
249 UNTS 460. Honduras. Ratification 9 Aug 56.
Force 9 Aug 57.
249 UNTS 460. Ukrainian SSR. Ratification
10 Aug 56. Force 10 Aug 57.
249 UNTS 460. Byelorussia. Ratification
21 Aug 56. Force 21 Aug 57.
264 UNTS 375. Ecuador. Ratification 11 Mar 57.
Force 11 Mar 58.
266 UNTS 415. Brazil. Ratification 25 Apr 57.
Force 25 Apr 58.
272 UNTS 268. Romania. Ratification 28 May 57.
Force 28 May 58.
272 UNTS 268. Albania. Ratification 3 Jun 57.
Force 3 Jun 58.
272 UNTS 268. Syria. Ratification 7 Jun 57.
Force 7 Jun 58.
276 UNTS 364. Italy. Declaration 20 Aug 57.
280 UNTS 357. Czechoslovakia. Ratification
30 Oct 57. Force 30 Oct 58.
287 UNTS 346. Iceland. Ratification 17 Feb 58.
Force 17 Feb 58.
293 UNTS 384. Haiti. Ratification 4 Mar 58. Force
4 Mar 59.
302 UNTS 364. Taiwan. Ratification 1 May 58.
Force 1 May 59.

304 UNTS 408. Panama. Ratification 3 Jun 58.
Force 3 Jun 59.
312 UNTS 425. Indonesia. Ratification
11 Aug 58. Force 11 Aug 59.
313 UNTS 348. India. Ratification 25 Sep 58.
Force 25 Sep 59.
343 UNTS 350. Norway. Ratification 24 Sep 59.
Force 24 Sep 60.
353 UNTS 368. Peru. Ratification 1 Feb 60. Force
1 Feb 61.
366 UNTS 412. Denmark. Ratification 22 Jun 60.
Force 22 Jun 61.
366 UNTS 412. Costa Rica. Ratification 2 Jun 60.
Force 2 Jun 61.
373 UNTS 370. United Arab Rep. United Arab
Rep.
399 UNTS 270. Ivory Coast. Ratification
5 May 61. Force 5 May 62.
401 UNTS 267. Gabon. Ratification 13 Jun 61.
Force 13 Jun 61.
406 UNTS 305. Guatemala. Ratification
2 Aug 61. Force 2 Aug 62.
413 UNTS 369. Syria. Ratification 30 Oct 61.
434 UNTS 296. Libya. Ratification 20 Jun 63.
Force 20 Jun 63.
434 UNTS 296. Sweden. Ratification 20 Jun 63.
Force 20 Jun 63.
437 UNTS 351. Madagascar. Ratification
10 Aug 62. Force 10 Aug 63.
444 UNTS 339. Algeria. Succession 19 Oct 62.
449 UNTS 301. Senegal. Ratification 22 Oct 62.
Force 22 Oct 63.
455 UNTS 470. Finland. Ratification 14 Jan 63.
Force 14 Jan 64.
471 UNTS 378. Colombia. Ratification 7 Jun 63.
Force 7 Jun 64.
475 UNTS 380. Iraq. Ratification 28 Aug 63.
Force 28 Aug 64.
504 UNTS 359. Central Afri Rep. Ratification
9 Jun 64. Force 9 Jun 65.
504 UNTS 359. Paraguay. Ratification 24 Jun 64.
Force 24 Jun 65.
530 UNTS 420. Malawi. Ratification 22 Mar 65.
Force 22 Mar 66.
541 UNTS 376. Israel. Ratification 9 Jun 65.
Force 9 Jun 65.
560 UNTS 322. Chad. Ratification 29 Mar 66.
Force 29 Mar 67.
603 UNTS 354. Turkey. Ratification 19 Jul 67.
Force 19 Jul 68.
607 UNTS 363. Luxembourg. Ratification
23 Aug 67. Force 23 Aug 68.
607 UNTS 363. Guinea. Ratification 11 Aug 67.
Force 11 Aug 68.
607 UNTS 363. Japan. Ratification 24 Aug 67.
Force 24 Aug 68.
609 UNTS 339. Nicaragua. Ratification
31 Oct 67. Force 31 Oct 68.
613 UNTS 423. Spain. Ratification 6 Nov 67.
Force 6 Nov 68.
634 UNTS 474. Ghana. Ratification 14 Mar 68.
Force 14 Mar 69.
638 UNTS 334. Dahomey. Ratification
16 May 68.
642 UNTS 394. Mali. Ratification 12 Jul 68. Force
12 Jul 68.
649 UNTS 382. Tunisia. Ratification 11 Oct 68.
Force 11 Oct 68.

102182 Bilateral Exchange **166 UNTS 3**
SIGNED: 28 Apr 52 FORCE: 28 Apr 52
REGISTERED: 2 Jun 53 ICAO (Civil Aviat)
ARTICLES: 2 LANGUAGE: English.
HEADNOTE: CIVIL AIR TRAFFIC RIGHTS
TOPIC: Air Transport
CONCEPTS: Guarantees and safeguards. Confor-
mity with municipal law. Licenses and permits.
Air transport. Airport facilities. Operating autho-
rizations and regulations.
TREATY REF: 136UNTS45.
PARTIES:
Denmark
Japan

102183 Bilateral Exchange **166 UNTS 9**
SIGNED: 21 Apr 52 FORCE: 21 Apr 52
REGISTERED: 2 Jun 53 ICAO (Civil Aviat)
ARTICLES: 2 LANGUAGE: French.
HEADNOTE: OPERATION REGULAR AIR TRANS-
PORT SERVICES
TOPIC: Air Transport
CONCEPTS: Previous treaty replacement. Regis-

tration certificate. Routes and logistics. Permit designation. Air transport. Operating authorizations and regulations.
TREATY REF: 95UNTS73; 15UNTS295.
PROCEDURE: Amendment. Denunciation.
PARTIES:
  Belgium
  Sweden

102184 Bilateral Agreement **166 UNTS 15**
SIGNED: 18 Feb 50 FORCE: 18 Feb 50
REGISTERED: 2 Jun 53 ICAO (Civil Aviat)
ARTICLES: 17 LANGUAGE: Spanish. Swedish.
HEADNOTE: AIR NAVIGATION
TOPIC: Air Transport
CONCEPTS: Definition of terms. Exceptions and exemptions. Annex or appendix reference. Non-visa travel documents. Conformity with municipal law. Licenses and permits. Recognition of legal documents. Use of facilities. Investigation of violations. Arbitration. Procedure. Reexport of goods, etc.. Compensation. Fees and exemptions. National treatment. Customs duties. Customs exemptions. Competency certificate. Routes and logistics. Navigational conditions. Permit designation. Airport facilities. Airworthiness certificates. Conditions of airlines operating permission. Overflights and technical stops. Operating authorizations and regulations. Licenses and certificates of nationality.
PROCEDURE: Termination. Application to Non-self-governing Territories.
PARTIES:
  Spain
  Sweden
ANNEX
645 UNTS 352. Spain. Signature 5 May 65. Force 5 May 65.
645 UNTS 352. Sweden. Signature 5 May 65. Force 5 May 65.

102185 Bilateral Agreement **166 UNTS 49**
SIGNED: 18 Oct 50 FORCE: 18 Oct 50
REGISTERED: 2 Jun 53 ICAO (Civil Aviat)
ARTICLES: 9 LANGUAGE: French. Swedish.
HEADNOTE: AIR SERVICE
TOPIC: Air Transport
CONCEPTS: Annex or appendix reference. Conformity with municipal law. General cooperation. Licenses and permits. Recognition of legal documents. Use of facilities. Procedure. Existing tribunals. Special tribunals. Negotiation. Fees and exemptions. Most favored nation clause. National treatment. Customs exemptions. Competency certificate. Routes and logistics. Navigational conditions. Permit designation. Airport facilities. Airworthiness certificates. Conditions of airlines operating permission. Operating authorizations and regulations. Licenses and certificates of nationality.
INTL ORGS: International Civil Aviation Organization.
TREATY REF: 15UNTS295.
PROCEDURE: Amendment. Future Procedures Contemplated. Ratification. Registration. Termination.
PARTIES:
  Sweden
  Switzerland
ANNEX
192 UNTS 352. Sweden. Amendment 12 Aug 53. Force 12 Aug 53.
192 UNTS 352. Switzerland. Amendment 12 Aug 53. Force 12 Aug 53.
335 UNTS 300. Switzerland. Amendment 25 Feb 57. Force 25 Feb 57.
335 UNTS 300. Sweden. Amendment 25 Feb 57. Force 25 Feb 57.
646 UNTS 349. Sweden. Amendment 26 Apr 27. Force 26 Apr 67.
646 UNTS 349. Switzerland. Amendment 26 Apr 27. Force 26 Apr 67.

102186 Multilateral Agreement **166 UNTS 73**
SIGNED: 27 Jul 50 FORCE: 1 Jun 53
REGISTERED: 11 Jun 53 ILO (Labor Org)
ARTICLES: 36 LANGUAGE: French.
HEADNOTE: SOCIAL SECURITY RHINE BOATMEN
TOPIC: Non-ILO Labor
CONCEPTS: Detailed regulations. General provisions. Annex or appendix reference. Conformity

with municipal law. Domestic legislation. Operating agencies. Dispute settlement. Public health. Old age and invalidity insurance. Non-ILO labor relations. Family allowances. Administrative cooperation. Old age insurance. Sickness and invalidity insurance. Social security. Fees and exemptions. Payment schedules.
INTL ORGS: Administrative Centre of Social Security for Rhine Boatmen. International Labour Organization. United Nations.
PROCEDURE: Denunciation. Duration. Registration. Renewal or Revival.
PARTIES:
  Belgium SIGNED: 27 Jul 50 RATIFIED: 4 Mar 53 FORCE: 1 Jun 53
  France SIGNED: 27 Jul 50 RATIFIED: 1 Jul 52 FORCE: 1 Jun 53
  Germany, West SIGNED: 27 Jul 50 RATIFIED: 18 Jun 52 FORCE: 1 Jun 53
  Netherlands SIGNED: 27 Jul 50 RATIFIED: 8 Sep 52 FORCE: 1 Jun 53
  Switzerland SIGNED: 27 Jul 50 RATIFIED: 7 Apr 52 FORCE: 1 Jun 53

102187 Bilateral Exchange **166 UNTS 104**
SIGNED: 19 Feb 46 FORCE: 19 Feb 46
REGISTERED: 12 Jun 53 USA (United States)
ARTICLES: 2 LANGUAGE: English. Spanish.
HEADNOTE: HEALTH SANITATION PROGRAM
TOPIC: Sanitation
CONCEPTS: Annex or appendix reference. Annex type material. Previous treaty extension. General cooperation. Personnel. Specialists exchange. Public health. Sanitation. Vocational training. Accounting procedures. Indemnities and reimbursements. Currency. Expense sharing formulae. Financial programs. Funding procedures. Assistance. Specific technical assistance.
TREATY REF: 105UNTS109; 166UNTS382; TIAS1623.
PARTIES:
  Colombia
  USA (United States)
ANNEX
179 UNTS 348. USA (United States). Supplementation 8 May 52. Force 21 May 52.
179 UNTS 348. Colombia. Supplementation 21 May 52. Force 21 May 52.
180 UNTS 391. USA (United States). Supplementation 26 Jun 52. Force 28 Jun 52.
180 UNTS 391. Colombia. Supplementation 28 Jun 52. Force 28 Jun 52.
270 UNTS 379. USA (United States). Prolongation 31 May 55. Force 10 Jun 55.
270 UNTS 379. Colombia. Prolongation 2 May 55. Force 10 Jun 55.
270 UNTS 384. Colombia. Implementation 10 Jun 55. Force 10 Jun 55.
270 UNTS 384. USA (United States). Implementation 10 Jun 55. Force 10 Jun 55.
273 UNTS 254. USA (United States). Prolongation 25 Apr 56. Force 25 May 56.
273 UNTS 254. Colombia. Prolongation 17 May 56. Force 25 May 56.
290 UNTS 313. Colombia. Prolongation 15 Mar 57. Force 26 Mar 57.
290 UNTS 313. USA (United States). Prolongation 31 Dec 56. Force 26 Mar 57.

102188 Bilateral Exchange **166 UNTS 149**
SIGNED: 13 Dec 50 FORCE: 24 Jan 51
REGISTERED: 12 Jun 53 USA (United States)
ARTICLES: 2 LANGUAGE: English. Spanish.
HEADNOTE: HEALTH SANITATION PROJECT
TOPIC: Sanitation
CONCEPTS: Previous treaty extension. Friendship and amity. Disease control. Public health. Sanitation. Exchange. Currency. Expense sharing formulae. Financial programs. Funding procedures. Assistance. Special projects.
TREATY REF: 21UNTS15.
PROCEDURE: Ratification.
PARTIES:
  El Salvador
  USA (United States)
ANNEX
181 UNTS 368. USA (United States). Supplementation 7 Jul 52. Force 15 Jul 52.
181 UNTS 368. El Salvador. Supplementation 15 Jul 52. Force 15 Jul 52.

265 UNTS 343. USA (United States). Prolongation 7 Mar 55. Force 27 Jun 55.
265 UNTS 343. El Salvador. Prolongation 14 Jun 55. Force 27 Jun 55.
474 UNTS 327. El Salvador. Prolongation 27 Jun 60. Force 27 Jun 60.
474 UNTS 327. USA (United States). Prolongation 17 Jun 60. Force 27 Jun 60.

102189 Bilateral Exchange **166 UNTS 159**
SIGNED: 13 May 47 FORCE: 13 May 47
REGISTERED: 12 Jun 53 USA (United States)
ARTICLES: 2 LANGUAGE: English. Spanish.
HEADNOTE: HEALTH SANITATION PROJECT
TOPIC: Sanitation
CONCEPTS: Conditions. Definition of terms. Treaty implementation. Annex or appendix reference. Annex type material. Previous treaty extension. Privileges and immunities. Inspection and observation. Personnel. General property. Public health. Sanitation. Research and development. Accounting procedures. Currency. Expense sharing formulae. Fees and exemptions. Financial programs. Funding procedures. Tax exemptions. Customs exemptions. Assistance. Special projects.
TREATY REF: TAIS 1557 PP19-23,P6 P21.
PROCEDURE: Amendment. Duration.
PARTIES:
  Honduras
  USA (United States)

102190 Bilateral Exchange **166 UNTS 198**
SIGNED: 30 Jun 47 FORCE: 30 Jun 47
REGISTERED: 12 Jun 53 USA (United States)
ARTICLES: 2 LANGUAGE: English. Spanish.
HEADNOTE: HEALTH SANITATION PROGRAM
TOPIC: Sanitation
CONCEPTS: Annex or appendix reference. Annex type material. Previous treaty extension. Privileges and immunities. General cooperation. Personnel. Public health. Sanitation. Vocational training. Accounting procedures. Currency. Expense sharing formulae. Fees and exemptions. Financial programs. Funding procedures. Assistance. Special projects. Specific technical assistance.
TREATY REF: 21UNTS225; 106UNTS328.
PARTIES:
  USA (United States)
  Venezuela
ANNEX
168 UNTS 323. Venezuela. Amendment 16 Mar 52. Force 16 Mar 52.
168 UNTS 323. USA (United States). Amendment 14 Feb 52. Force 16 Mar 52.
179 UNTS 354. Venezuela. Supplementation 5 Jun 52. Force 5 Jun 52.
179 UNTS 354. USA (United States). Supplementation 4 Mar 52. Force 5 Jun 52.
205 UNTS 350. USA (United States). Amendment 18 Apr 52. Force 18 Apr 52.
205 UNTS 350. Venezuela. Amendment 8 Jan 52. Force 18 Apr 52.
265 UNTS 348. USA (United States). Prolongation 21 Mar 55. Force 23 Apr 55.
265 UNTS 348. Venezuela. Prolongation 23 Apr 55. Force 23 Apr 55.

102191 Bilateral Agreement **166 UNTS 261**
SIGNED: 24 Apr 52 FORCE: 24 Apr 52
REGISTERED: 16 Jun 53 Greece
ARTICLES: 9 LANGUAGE: French.
HEADNOTE: PAYMENTS
TOPIC: Finance
CONCEPTS: Definition of terms. Territorial application. Previous treaty replacement. Proxy diplomacy. General cooperation. Accounting procedures. Banking. Reciprocity in financial treatment. Financial programs. Funding procedures. Payment schedules. Local currency.
INTL ORGS: European Payments Union.
TREATY REF: 77UNTS293.
PROCEDURE: Denunciation. Termination.
PARTIES:
  Belgium
  Greece

102192 Bilateral Agreement **166 UNTS 271**
SIGNED: 4 Apr 52 FORCE: 4 Apr 52

REGISTERED: 16 Jun 53 Greece
ARTICLES: 8 LANGUAGE: French.
HEADNOTE: TRANSFER PAYMENTS
TOPIC: Finance
CONCEPTS: Detailed regulations. Previous treaty replacement. Accounting procedures. Banking. Exchange rates and regulations. Financial programs. Interest rates. Payment schedules. Local currency. Debts. Debt settlement.
PROCEDURE: Denunciation.
PARTIES:
Greece
Switzerland

102193 Bilateral Exchange **166 UNTS 281**
SIGNED: 16 Nov 50 FORCE: 16 Nov 50
REGISTERED: 16 Jun 53 Greece
ARTICLES: 2 LANGUAGE: English.
HEADNOTE: DOUBLE TAXATION PROFITS DERIVED AIR TRANSPORT
TOPIC: Taxation
CONCEPTS: Definition of terms. Taxation. Tax exemptions. Air transport. Merchant vessels.
PROCEDURE: Termination.
PARTIES:
Greece
UK Great Britain

102194 Bilateral Agreement **166 UNTS 289**
SIGNED: 16 Jun 53 FORCE: 16 Jun 53
REGISTERED: 16 Jun 53 United Nations
ARTICLES: 6 LANGUAGE: English. Spanish.
HEADNOTE: TECHNICAL ASSISTANCE
TOPIC: Tech Assistance
CONCEPTS: Exceptions and exemptions. Treaty implementation. Privileges and immunities. General cooperation. Exchange of information and documents. Personnel. Title and deeds. Exchange. Scholarships and grants. Vocational training. Research and development. Expense sharing formulae. Local currency. Domestic obligation. General technical assistance. Materials, equipment and services. IGO status. Conformity with IGO decisions.
TREATY REF: 76UNTS132; 1UNTS15,263.
PROCEDURE: Amendment. Termination.
PARTIES:
Ecuador
United Nations
ANNEX
228 UNTS 370. Ecuador. Abrogation 10 Feb 56.
228 UNTS 370. United Nations. Abrogation 10 Feb 56.

102195 Bilateral Exchange **166 UNTS 305**
SIGNED: 18 Apr 51 FORCE: 18 Apr 51
REGISTERED: 17 Jun 53 Greece
ARTICLES: 2 LANGUAGE: English.
HEADNOTE: RELEASE MONIES PROPERTIES
TOPIC: Reparations
CONCEPTS: Definition of terms. Treaty implementation. General property. Most favored nation clause. Post-war claims settlement.
PARTIES:
Greece
India

102196 Bilateral Exchange **166 UNTS 315**
SIGNED: 9 Dec 50 FORCE: 9 Dec 50
REGISTERED: 17 Jun 53 Greece
ARTICLES: 2 LANGUAGE: French.
HEADNOTE: DOUBLE TAXATION PROFITS AIR SEA TRANSPORTATION
TOPIC: Taxation
CONCEPTS: Previous treaty amendment. Taxation. Tax exemptions. Air transport. Merchant vessels.
PARTIES:
France
Greece

102197 Bilateral Treaty **167 UNTS 3**
SIGNED: 3 Mar 51 FORCE: 1 May 53
REGISTERED: 17 Jun 53 India
ARTICLES: 7 LANGUAGE: English. Indonesian.
HEADNOTE: FRIENDSHIP
TOPIC: General Amity
CONCEPTS: Friendship and amity. Alien status. Consular relations establishment. Diplomatic relations establishment. Privileges and immunities. General cooperation. Arbitration. Negotiation.
PROCEDURE: Future Procedures Contemplated. Ratification.
PARTIES:
India
Indonesia

102198 Bilateral Exchange **167 UNTS 13**
SIGNED: 16 Mar 53 FORCE: 15 Apr 53
REGISTERED: 25 Jun 53 Norway
ARTICLES: 2 LANGUAGE: Spanish.
HEADNOTE: MUTUAL ABOLITION VISAS
TOPIC: Visas
CONCEPTS: Time limit. Visa abolition. Conformity with municipal law. Fees and exemptions.
PARTIES:
Chile
Norway

102199 Multilateral Treaty **167 UNTS 21**
SIGNED: 28 Feb 53 FORCE: 29 May 53
REGISTERED: 26 Jun 53 Yugoslavia
ARTICLES: 10 LANGUAGE: French.
HEADNOTE: FRIENDSHIP COLLABORATION
TOPIC: General Amity
CONCEPTS: Friendship and amity. Peaceful relations. General cooperation. Procedure.
INTL ORGS: United Nations.
TREATY REF: 34UNTS243; 126UNTS350.
PROCEDURE: Accession. Duration. Future Procedures Contemplated. Ratification. Termination.
PARTIES:
Greece SIGNED: 28 Feb 53 RATIFIED: 21 May 53 FORCE: 29 May 53
Turkey SIGNED: 28 Feb 53 RATIFIED: 29 May 53 FORCE: 29 May 53
Yugoslavia SIGNED: 28 Feb 53 RATIFIED: 6 Apr 53 FORCE: 29 May 53

102200 Bilateral Exchange **167 UNTS 30**
SIGNED: 17 Mar 47 FORCE: 17 Mar 47
REGISTERED: 26 Jun 53 USA (United States)
ARTICLES: 2 LANGUAGE: English. Spanish.
HEADNOTE: ERADICATION HOOF-MOUTH DISEASE
TOPIC: Sanitation
CONCEPTS: Annex or appendix reference. Previous treaty extension. General cooperation. Personnel. Establishment of commission. Quarantine. Disease control. Veterinary. Research and development. Accounting procedures. Banking. Expense sharing formulae. Funding procedures. Assistance. Special projects. Materials, equipment and services.
INTL ORGS: Special Commission.
PARTIES:
Mexico
USA (United States)

102201 Bilateral Treaty **167 UNTS 105**
SIGNED: 4 Apr 50 FORCE: 24 Mar 52
REGISTERED: 29 Jun 53 Afghanistan
ARTICLES: 18 LANGUAGE: English. Persian.
HEADNOTE: TRADE COMMERCE
TOPIC: General Trade
CONCEPTS: Definition of terms. Detailed regulations. Exceptions and exemptions. Annex or appendix reference. Conformity with municipal law. Informational records. Juridical personality. Expropriation. Free passage and transit. Legal protection and assistance. Immovable property. General property. Procedure. Negotiation. Export quotas. Import quotas. Transportation costs. Most favored nation clause. Equitable taxes. Customs duties. Transport of goods.
PROCEDURE: Duration. Ratification. Termination.
PARTIES:
Afghanistan
India

102202 Bilateral Agreement **167 UNTS 125**
SIGNED: 28 Oct 52 FORCE: 28 Oct 52
REGISTERED: 1 Jul 53 Denmark
ARTICLES: 5 LANGUAGE: French.
HEADNOTE: COMMERCE REGULATION
TOPIC: General Trade
CONCEPTS: General provisions. Annex or appendix reference. Licenses and permits. Establishment of commission. Payment schedules.
INTL ORGS: Organization for Economic Co-operation and Development. Special Commission.
TREATY REF: 76UNTS353.
PARTIES:
Denmark
Italy

102203 Bilateral Exchange **167 UNTS 135**
SIGNED: 11 Jun 46 FORCE: 11 Jun 46
REGISTERED: 3 Jul 53 USA (United States)
ARTICLES: 2 LANGUAGE: Spanish.
HEADNOTE: MILITARY AIR TRANSIT RIGHTS
TOPIC: Status of Forces
CONCEPTS: Overflights and technical stops. Status of military forces.
PARTIES:
Ecuador
USA (United States)

102204 Bilateral Exchange **167 UNTS 141**
SIGNED: 19 Nov 51 FORCE: 19 Nov 51
REGISTERED: 3 Jul 53 USA (United States)
ARTICLES: 2 LANGUAGE: English.
HEADNOTE: MUTUAL DEFENSE ASSISTANCE
TOPIC: Milit Assistance
CONCEPTS: Military assistance. Military assistance. Military training.
INTL ORGS: United Nations.
PARTIES:
Liberia
USA (United States)
ANNEX
361 UNTS 316. USA (United States). Supplementation 10 Apr 58. Force 19 Jul 58.
361 UNTS 316. Liberia. Supplementation 19 Jul 58. Force 19 Jul 58.

102205 Bilateral Exchange **167 UNTS 151**
SIGNED: 12 Dec 51 FORCE: 12 Dec 51
REGISTERED: 3 Jul 53 USA (United States)
ARTICLES: 2 LANGUAGE: English. Spanish.
HEADNOTE: AIR TRANSIT RIGHTS MILITARY AIRCRAFT
TOPIC: Status of Forces
CONCEPTS: Previous treaty replacement. Inviolability. Conformity with municipal law. General cooperation. Overflights and technical stops. Airforce-army-navy personnel ratio. Ranks and privileges. Status of military forces. Procurement and logistics.
PROCEDURE: Renewal or Revival. Termination.
PARTIES:
Nicaragua
USA (United States)

102206 Bilateral Exchange **167 UNTS 163**
SIGNED: 21 Dec 51 FORCE: 21 Dec 51
REGISTERED: 3 Jul 53 USA (United States)
ARTICLES: 2 LANGUAGE: English. Italian.
HEADNOTE: RELEASE OBLIGATIONS PEACE TREATY
TOPIC: Peace/Disarmament
CONCEPTS: Annex type material. Armistice and peace.
INTL ORGS: United Nations.
TREATY REF: 49UNTS.
PARTIES:
Italy
USA (United States)

102207 Bilateral Convention **167 UNTS 171**
SIGNED: 13 Dec 46 FORCE: 15 Jul 52
REGISTERED: 3 Jul 53 USA (United States)
ARTICLES: 18 LANGUAGE: Afrikaans. English.
HEADNOTE: DOUBLE TAXATION ADMINISTRATIVE ASSISTANCE TAXES INCOME
TOPIC: Taxation
CONCEPTS: Definition of terms. Conformity with municipal law. Exchange of official publications. Teacher and student exchange. Claims and settlements. Taxation. Tax credits. Equitable taxes. Tax exemptions.
PROCEDURE: Duration. Ratification. Termination.
PARTIES:
South Africa
USA (United States)

102208 Bilateral Convention **167 UNTS 211**
SIGNED: 10 Apr 47   FORCE: 15 Jul 52
REGISTERED: 3 Jul 53 USA (United States)
ARTICLES: 14 LANGUAGE: Afrikaans. English.
HEADNOTE: TAXES ESTATES DECEASED PERSONS
TOPIC: Taxation
CONCEPTS: Definition of terms. Conformity with municipal law. Exchange of official publications. Claims and settlements. Death duties. Tax credits. General.
PROCEDURE: Duration. Ratification. Termination.
PARTIES:
South Africa
USA (United States)

102209 Bilateral Exchange **168 UNTS 3**
SIGNED: 27 Feb 52   FORCE: 27 Feb 52
REGISTERED: 3 Jul 53 USA (United States)
ARTICLES: 2 LANGUAGE: English. Spanish.
HEADNOTE: RADIO COMMUNICATIONS AMATEUR STATIONS BEHALF THIRD PARTIES
TOPIC: Gen Communications
CONCEPTS: Territorial application. Domestic legislation. Amateur radio. Amateur third party message. Radio-telephone-telegraphic communications.
PROCEDURE: Termination.
PARTIES:
Cuba
USA (United States)

102210 Multilateral Exchange **168 UNTS 9**
SIGNED: 1 Mar 52   FORCE: 1 Mar 52
REGISTERED: 3 Jul 53 USA (United States)
ARTICLES: 4 LANGUAGE: English.
HEADNOTE: SCIENTIFIC INVESTIGATION FUR SEALS NORTH PACIFIC
TOPIC: Specific Resources
CONCEPTS: Inspection and observation. Research cooperation. Research results. Funding procedures. Materials, equipment and services. Ocean resources. Wildlife.
TREATY REF: 26UNTS363; 27UNTSl9.
PARTIES:
Canada SIGNED: 1 Mar 52 FORCE: 1 Mar 52
Japan SIGNED: 8 Feb 52 FORCE: 8 Feb 52
USA (United States) SIGNED: 7 Feb 52 FORCE: 8 Feb 52

102211 Bilateral Agreement **168 UNTS 25**
SIGNED: 12 Feb 52   FORCE: 12 Feb 52
REGISTERED: 3 Jul 53 USA (United States)
ARTICLES: 12 LANGUAGE: Arabic. English.
HEADNOTE: TECHNICAL COOPERATION
TOPIC: Tech Assistance
CONCEPTS: Treaty implementation. Annex type material. Privileges and immunities. General cooperation. Exchange of information and documents. Informational records. Domestic legislation. Personnel. General property. Sanitation. Sanitation. Education. Vocational training. Research and development. Accounting procedures. Attachment of funds. Currency deposits. Exchange rates and regulations. Funding procedures. Seizure funds. Local currency. Assets. General technical assistance. Agriculture. Special projects. Economic assistance. Materials, equipment and services. Aid missions. Industry. General transportation. Roads and highways. Regulation of natural resources.
INTL ORGS: International Monetary Fund. North Atlantic Treaty Organization.
TREATY REF: 141UNTS55; 157UNTS69.
PROCEDURE: Duration. Termination.
PARTIES:
Jordan
USA (United States)
ANNEX
212 UNTS 354. USA (United States). Amendment 7 Apr 53. Force 7 Apr 53.
212 UNTS 354. Jordan. Amendment 7 Apr 53. Force 7 Apr 53.
229 UNTS 325. USA (United States). Amendment 31 Dec 53. Force 31 Dec 53.
229 UNTS 325. Jordan. Amendment 31 Dec 53. Force 31 Dec 53.
266 UNTS 416. Jordan. Amendment 7 Dec 54. Force 7 Dec 54.
266 UNTS 416. USA (United States). Amendment 7 Dec 54. Force 7 Dec 54.

102212 Bilateral Exchange **168 UNTS 57**
SIGNED: 13 Mar 52   FORCE: 13 Mar 52
REGISTERED: 3 Jul 53 USA (United States)
ARTICLES: 2 LANGUAGE: English. French.
HEADNOTE: TAXATION EXPENDITURES DEFENSE
TOPIC: Taxation
CONCEPTS: General. Military installations and equipment.
INTL ORGS: North Atlantic Treaty Organization.
TREATY REF: 80UNTS187.
PARTIES:
Luxembourg
USA (United States)

102213 Multilateral Instrument **168 UNTS 65**
SIGNED: 9 May 52   FORCE: 9 May 52
REGISTERED: 3 Jul 53 USA (United States)
ARTICLES: 10 LANGUAGE: English. Italian.
HEADNOTE: ADMINISTRATION TRIESTE
TOPIC: Milit Occupation
CONCEPTS: General military. Occupation regime. Industrial controls. Control and occupation machinery.
TREATY REF: 49,50UNTS.
PARTIES:
Italy SIGNED: 9 May 52 FORCE: 9 May 52
UK Great Britain SIGNED: 9 May 52 FORCE: 9 May 52
USA (United States) SIGNED: 9 May 52 FORCE: 9 May 52

102214 Bilateral Exchange **168 UNTS 75**
SIGNED: 16 Nov 51   FORCE: 16 Nov 51
REGISTERED: 3 Jul 53 USA (United States)
ARTICLES: 2 LANGUAGE: English.
HEADNOTE: TECHNICAL ASSISTANCE SNOWY MOUNTAINS HYDROELECTRIC AUTHORITY
TOPIC: Tech Assistance
CONCEPTS: Annex or appendix reference. Personnel. Vocational training. General technical assistance. Materials, equipment and services. Hydroelectric power.
PARTIES:
Australia
USA (United States)

102215 Bilateral Exchange **168 UNTS 89**
SIGNED: 16 May 47   FORCE: 16 May 47
REGISTERED: 3 Jul 53 USA (United States)
ARTICLES: 2 LANGUAGE: English. Spanish.
HEADNOTE: APPROVAL OF MEMORANDUM AGRICULTURAL EXPERIMENT STATION
TOPIC: Tech Assistance
CONCEPTS: General cooperation. Personnel. Establishment of commission. Research and development. Agriculture.
TREATY REF: 68UNTS94.
PARTIES:
Bolivia
USA (United States)
ANNEX
199 UNTS 349. USA (United States). Amendment 17 May 48. Force 4 Jun 48.
199 UNTS 349. Bolivia. Amendment 4 Jun 48. Force 4 Jun 48.
199 UNTS 353. Bolivia. Amendment 16 Jun 52. Force 16 Jun 54.
199 UNTS 353. USA (United States). Amendment 16 Jun 52. Force 16 Jun 54.

102216 Bilateral Exchange **168 UNTS 109**
SIGNED: 12 Jan 52   FORCE: 12 Jan 52
REGISTERED: 3 Jul 53 USA (United States)
ARTICLES: 2 LANGUAGE: English. Spanish.
HEADNOTE: AGRICULTURAL EDUCATION PROGRAM
TOPIC: Education
CONCEPTS: Specialists exchange. Exchange. Teacher and student exchange. Vocational training. Indemnities and reimbursements. Funding procedures. Tax exemptions. Customs exemptions. Agriculture. Materials, equipment and services.
PARTIES:
Colombia
USA (United States)

102217 Bilateral Exchange **168 UNTS 119**
SIGNED: 27 Nov 48   FORCE: 27 Nov 48

REGISTERED: 3 Jul 53 USA (United States)
ARTICLES: 2 LANGUAGE: English. French.
HEADNOTE: AERIAL MAPPING PROJECT
TOPIC: Scientific Project
CONCEPTS: Annex or appendix reference. Research and development.
PARTIES:
France
USA (United States)

102218 Multilateral Agreement **168 UNTS 143**
SIGNED: 9 Jul 49   FORCE: 13 Apr 52
REGISTERED: 3 Jul 53 USA (United States)
ARTICLES: 13 LANGUAGE: English. French. Portuguese. Spanish.
HEADNOTE: INTER-AMERICAN RADIO AGREEMENT
TOPIC: Telecommunications
CONCEPTS: Standardization. Amateur radio. Amateur third party message. Bands and frequency allocation. Facilities and equipment. Interference of broadcasts. Radio-telephone-telegraphic communications.
INTL ORGS: International Telecommunication Union.
PROCEDURE: Accession.
PARTIES:
Argentina SIGNED: 9 Jul 49
Bolivia SIGNED: 9 Jul 49
Brazil SIGNED: 9 Jul 49
Canada SIGNED: 9 Jul 49
Chile SIGNED: 9 Jul 49
Colombia SIGNED: 9 Jul 49
Costa Rica SIGNED: 9 Jul 49 RATIFIED: 15 May 52 FORCE: 15 May 52
Cuba SIGNED: 9 Jul 49 RATIFIED: 3 Dec 52 FORCE: 3 Dec 52
Dominican Republic SIGNED: 9 Jul 49
Ecuador SIGNED: 9 Jul 49
Guatemala SIGNED: 9 Jul 49
Honduras SIGNED: 9 Jul 49 RATIFIED: 6 Feb 52 FORCE: 13 Apr 52
Mexico SIGNED: 9 Jul 49 RATIFIED: 28 Nov 51 FORCE: 13 Apr 52
Nicaragua SIGNED: 9 Jul 49 RATIFIED: 14 Mar 52 FORCE: 13 Apr 52
Panama SIGNED: 9 Jul 49
Paraguay SIGNED: 9 Jul 49 RATIFIED: 16 Oct 50 FORCE: 13 Apr 52
USA (United States) SIGNED: 9 Jul 49 RATIFIED: 23 Jun 50 FORCE: 13 Apr 52
Uruguay SIGNED: 9 Jul 49
Venezuela SIGNED: 9 Jul 49
ANNEX
184 UNTS 382. Dominican Republic. Acceptance 16 Apr 53.
184 UNTS 382. Haiti. Acceptance 26 Aug 53.

102219 Bilateral Agreement **168 UNTS 281**
SIGNED: 2 Apr 51   FORCE: 2 Apr 51
REGISTERED: 10 Jul 53 UK Great Britain
ARTICLES: 14 LANGUAGE: English.
HEADNOTE: TRADE
TOPIC: General Trade
CONCEPTS: Exceptions and exemptions. Territorial application. Annex or appendix reference. Previous treaty replacement. General cooperation. Non-interest rates and fees. Customs duties.
TREATY REF: GATT;.
PROCEDURE: Duration. Termination.
PARTIES:
Pakistan
UK Great Britain

102220 Multilateral Convention **169 UNTS 3**
SIGNED: 11 Jul 52   FORCE: 1 Jul 53
REGISTERED: 14 Jul 53 Belgium
ARTICLES: 83 LANGUAGE: French.
HEADNOTE: UNIVERSAL POSTAL CONVENTION
TOPIC: IGO Establishment
CONCEPTS: Detailed regulations. Treaty violation. Free passage and transit. Arbitration. Attachment of funds. Monetary and gold transfers. Exchange rates and regulations. Funding procedures. Customs exemptions. Postal services. Regulations. Admission. Subsidiary organ. Establishment. Headquarters and facilities. Internal structure. Conformity with IGO decisions. Interagency agreements.

INTL ORGS: United Nations. Universal Postal Union.
TREATY REF: 75UNTS135,287.
PROCEDURE: Denunciation. Ratification.
PARTIES:
Afghanistan SIGNED: 11 Jul 52
Albania SIGNED: 11 Jul 52
Algeria SIGNED: 11 Jul 52
Argentina SIGNED: 11 Jul 52
Australia SIGNED: 11 Jul 52
Austria SIGNED: 11 Jul 52
Belgium Rwanda RATIFIED: 12 Mar 53 FORCE: 1 Jul 53
Belgium SIGNED: 11 Jul 52 RATIFIED: 12 Mar 53 FORCE: 1 Jul 53
Belgian Colonies SIGNED: 11 Jul 52 RATIFIED: 12 Mar 53 FORCE: 1 Jul 53
Bolivia SIGNED: 11 Jul 52
Brazil SIGNED: 11 Jul 52
Bulgaria SIGNED: 11 Jul 52
Burma SIGNED: 11 Jul 52
Byelorussia SIGNED: 11 Jul 52
Cambodia SIGNED: 11 Jul 52
Canada SIGNED: 11 Jul 52 RATIFIED: 18 Mar 53 FORCE: 1 Jul 53
Ceylon (Sri Lanka) SIGNED: 11 Jul 52
Chile SIGNED: 11 Jul 52
Taiwan SIGNED: 11 Jul 52
Colombia SIGNED: 11 Jul 52
Costa Rica SIGNED: 11 Jul 52
Cuba SIGNED: 11 Jul 52
Czechoslovakia SIGNED: 11 Jul 52
Denmark SIGNED: 11 Jul 52 RATIFIED: 20 Feb 53 FORCE: 1 Jul 53
Dominican Republic SIGNED: 11 Jul 52
Ecuador SIGNED: 11 Jul 52
United Arab Rep SIGNED: 11 Jul 52
El Salvador SIGNED: 11 Jul 52
Ethiopia SIGNED: 11 Jul 52
Finland SIGNED: 11 Jul 52
France SIGNED: 11 Jul 52
Pakistan SIGNED: 11 Jul 52
Panama SIGNED: 11 Jul 52
Paraguay SIGNED: 11 Jul 52
Peru SIGNED: 11 Jul 52
Philippines SIGNED: 11 Jul 52
Poland SIGNED: 11 Jul 52
Portugal All Territories RATIFIED: 11 Jul 52
Portugal SIGNED: 11 Jul 52
Romania SIGNED: 11 Jul 52
San Marino SIGNED: 11 Jul 52
South Africa SIGNED: 11 Jul 52
Spain SIGNED: 11 Jul 52
Spain Spanish Colonies RATIFIED: 11 Jul 52
Spain Spanish Morroco RATIFIED: 11 Jul 52
Sweden SIGNED: 11 Jul 52 RATIFIED: 20 Nov 52 FORCE: 1 Jul 53
Switzerland SIGNED: 11 Jul 52 RATIFIED: 16 May 53 FORCE: 1 Jul 53
Syria SIGNED: 11 Jul 52
Thailand SIGNED: 11 Jul 52
Tunisia SIGNED: 11 Jul 52
Turkey SIGNED: 11 Jul 52
UK Great Britain All Territories RATIFIED: 11 Jul 52
UK Great Britain SIGNED: 11 Jul 52
USA (United States) All Territories RATIFIED: 11 Jul 52 FORCE: 1 Jul 53
USA (United States) SIGNED: 11 Jul 52 RATIFIED: 24 Mar 53 FORCE: 1 Jul 53
Ukrainian SSR SIGNED: 11 Jul 52
Uruguay SIGNED: 11 Jul 52
USSR (Soviet Union) SIGNED: 11 Jul 52
Vatican/Holy See SIGNED: 11 Jul 52
Venezuela SIGNED: 11 Jul 52
Vietnam SIGNED: 11 Jul 52
Yugoslavia SIGNED: 11 Jul 52
ANNEX
202 UNTS 340.
227 UNTS 390.

02221 Multilateral Agreement 170 UNTS 3
SIGNED: 11 Jul 52 FORCE: 1 Jul 53
REGISTERED: 14 Jul 53 Belgium
ARTICLES: 18 LANGUAGE: French.
HEADNOTE: INSURED LETTERS BOXES
TOPIC: Postal Service
CONCEPTS: Detailed regulations. Responsibility and liability. Claims and settlements. Postal services. Regulations. Insured letters and boxes. Rates and charges.
TREATY REF: 169UNTS3.

PROCEDURE: Duration. Future Procedures Contemplated.
PARTIES:
Albania SIGNED: 11 Jul 52
Algeria SIGNED: 11 Jul 52
Argentina SIGNED: 11 Jul 52
Austria SIGNED: 11 Jul 52
Belgium Ruanda-Urundi RATIFIED: 12 Mar 53 FORCE: 1 Jul 53
Belgium SIGNED: 11 Jul 52 RATIFIED: 12 Mar 53 FORCE: 1 Jul 53
Belgian Colonies SIGNED: 11 Jul 52 RATIFIED: 12 Mar 53 FORCE: 1 Jul 53
Bolivia SIGNED: 11 Jul 52
Brazil SIGNED: 11 Jul 52
Bulgaria SIGNED: 11 Jul 52
Burma SIGNED: 11 Jul 52
Byelorussia SIGNED: 11 Jul 52
Cambodia SIGNED: 11 Jul 52
Ceylon (Sri Lanka) SIGNED: 11 Jul 52
Chile SIGNED: 11 Jul 52
Taiwan SIGNED: 11 Jul 52
Colombia SIGNED: 11 Jul 52
Cuba SIGNED: 11 Jul 52
Czechoslovakia SIGNED: 11 Jul 52
Denmark SIGNED: 11 Jul 52 RATIFIED: 20 Feb 53 FORCE: 1 Jul 53
Dominican Republic SIGNED: 11 Jul 52
United Arab Rep SIGNED: 11 Jul 52
Finland SIGNED: 11 Jul 52
France All Territories RATIFIED: 11 Jul 52
France SIGNED: 11 Jul 52
Greece SIGNED: 11 Jul 52
Haiti SIGNED: 11 Jul 52
Honduras SIGNED: 11 Jul 52
Hungary SIGNED: 11 Jul 52
Iceland SIGNED: 11 Jul 52 RATIFIED: 6 May 53 FORCE: 1 Jul 53
India SIGNED: 11 Jul 52
Indonesia SIGNED: 11 Jul 52
Iran SIGNED: 11 Jul 52
Iraq SIGNED: 11 Jul 52
Italy SIGNED: 11 Jul 52
Japan SIGNED: 11 Jul 52
Korea, South SIGNED: 11 Jul 52
Laos SIGNED: 11 Jul 52 RATIFIED: 17 Apr 53 FORCE: 1 Jul 53
Lebanon SIGNED: 11 Jul 52 RATIFIED: 11 May 53 FORCE: 1 Jul 53
Luxembourg SIGNED: 11 Jul 52
Morocco SIGNED: 11 Jul 52
Netherlands SIGNED: 11 Jul 52
Netherlands Netherlands Antilles RATIFIED: 11 Jul 52
Netherlands Surinam RATIFIED: 11 Jul 52
New Zealand SIGNED: 11 Jul 52
Nicaragua SIGNED: 11 Jul 52
Norway SIGNED: 11 Jul 52 RATIFIED: 12 Mar 53 FORCE: 1 Jul 53
Pakistan SIGNED: 11 Jul 52
Paraguay SIGNED: 11 Jul 52
Poland SIGNED: 11 Jul 52
Portugal All Territories RATIFIED: 11 Jul 52
Portugal SIGNED: 11 Jul 52
Romania SIGNED: 11 Jul 52
San Marino SIGNED: 11 Jul 52
Spain SIGNED: 11 Jul 52
Spanish Colonies SIGNED: 11 Jul 52
Spanish Morroco SIGNED: 11 Jul 52
Sweden SIGNED: 11 Jul 52 RATIFIED: 20 Nov 52 FORCE: 1 Jul 53
Switzerland SIGNED: 11 Jul 52 RATIFIED: 16 May 53 FORCE: 1 Jul 53
Syria SIGNED: 11 Jul 52
Thailand SIGNED: 11 Jul 52
Tunisia SIGNED: 11 Jul 52
Turkey SIGNED: 11 Jul 52
UK Great Britain SIGNED: 11 Jul 52
UK Great Britain All Territories RATIFIED: 11 Jul 52
Ukrainian SSR SIGNED: 11 Jul 52
Uruguay SIGNED: 11 Jul 52
USSR (Soviet Union) SIGNED: 11 Jul 52
Vatican/Holy See SIGNED: 11 Jul 52
Venezuela SIGNED: 11 Jul 52
Vietnam SIGNED: 11 Jul 52
Yugoslavia SIGNED: 11 Jul 52
ANNEX
202 UNTS 344. UK Great Britain. Aden. Force 19 Mar 54.
202 UNTS 344. UK Great Britain. Uganda. Force 19 Mar 54.
202 UNTS 344. UK Great Britain. Zanzibar. Force 19 Mar 54.

202 UNTS 344. UK Great Britain. Trinidad. Force 19 Mar 54.
202 UNTS 344. UK Great Britain. Tonga. Force 19 Mar 54.
202 UNTS 344. UK Great Britain. Tanganyika. Force 19 Mar 54.
202 UNTS 344. UK Great Britain. British Somali land. Force 19 Mar 54.
202 UNTS 344. UK Great Britain. Singapore. Force 19 Mar 54.
202 UNTS 344. UK Great Britain. Sierra Leone. Force 19 Mar 54.
202 UNTS 344. UK Great Britain. Seychelles. Force 19 Mar 54.
202 UNTS 344. UK Great Britain. Sarawak. Force 19 Mar 54.
202 UNTS 344. UK Great Britain. St. Helena. Force 19 Mar 54.
202 UNTS 344. UK Great Britain. Cameroon. Force 19 Mar 54.
202 UNTS 344. UK Great Britain. Nigeria. Force 19 Mar 54.
202 UNTS 344. UK Great Britain. Mauritius. Force 19 Mar 54.
202 UNTS 344. UK Great Britain. Malta. Force 19 Mar 54.
202 UNTS 344. UK Great Britain. Fed of Malaya. Force 19 Mar 54.
202 UNTS 344. UK Great Britain. Leeward Islands. Force 19 Mar 54.
202 UNTS 344. UK Great Britain. Windward Islands. Force 19 Mar 54.
202 UNTS 344. UK Great Britain. Kenya. Force 19 Mar 54.
202 UNTS 344. UK Great Britain. Jamaica. Force 19 Mar 54.
202 UNTS 344. UK Great Britain. Hong Kong. Force 19 Mar 54.
202 UNTS 344. UK Great Britain. British Honduras. Force 19 Mar 54.
202 UNTS 344. UK Great Britain. British Guiana. Force 19 Mar 54.
202 UNTS 344. UK Great Britain. Gibralter. Force 19 Mar 54.
202 UNTS 344. UK Great Britain. Gambia. Force 19 Mar 54.
202 UNTS 344. UK Great Britain. Fiji Islands. Force 19 Mar 54.
202 UNTS 344. UK Great Britain. Falkland Islands. Force 19 Mar 54.
202 UNTS 344. UK Great Britain. Gold Coast. Force 19 Mar 54.
202 UNTS 344. UK Great Britain. Cyprus. Force 19 Mar 54.
202 UNTS 344. UK Great Britain. Brunei. Force 19 Mar 54.
202 UNTS 344. UK Great Britain. North Borneo. Force 19 Mar 54.
202 UNTS 344. UK Great Britain. Bermuda. Force 19 Mar 54.
202 UNTS 344. UK Great Britain. Barbados. Force 19 Mar 54.
202 UNTS 344. Hungary. Ratification 3 Sep 54.
202 UNTS 344. Ireland. Ratification 26 May 54.
202 UNTS 344. Greece. Ratification 5 Apr 54.
202 UNTS 344. Bulgaria. Ratification 2 Oct 54.
202 UNTS 344. France. All Territories. Force 25 Jun 54.
202 UNTS 344. Austria. Ratification 9 Mar 54.
202 UNTS 344. France.
202 UNTS 344. Netherlands. Ratification 29 Apr 54.
202 UNTS 344. Romania. Ratification 27 Sep 54.
202 UNTS 344. Netherlands. Dutch New Guinea. Force 29 Apr 54.
202 UNTS 344. UK Great Britain. Channel Islands. Force 1 Mar 54.
202 UNTS 344. UK Great Britain. Isle of Man. Force 1 Mar 54.
202 UNTS 344. UK Great Britain. Ratification 1 Mar 54.
202 UNTS 344. Netherlands. Surinam. Force 29 Apr 54.
202 UNTS 344. Netherlands. Netherlands Antilles. Force 29 Apr 54.
227 UNTS 392. New Zealand. Tokelau Islands. Force 19 Feb 55.
227 UNTS 392. Germany, West. Accession 21 Mar 55.
227 UNTS 392. United Arab Rep. Ratification 24 Mar 55.
227 UNTS 392. Chile. Ratification 13 Dec 55.
227 UNTS 392. Yugoslavia. Ratification 21 Jun 55.

227 UNTS 392. Venezuela. Ratification 12 Jan 55.
227 UNTS 392. South Africa. Ratification 24 Mar 54.
227 UNTS 392. Turkey. Ratification 20 Nov 55.
227 UNTS 392. Spain. Spanish Morroco. Force 12 May 55.
227 UNTS 392. Spain. Spanish Colonies. Force 12 May 55.
227 UNTS 392. Spain. Ratification 12 May 55.
227 UNTS 392. Poland. Ratification 3 Jun 55.
227 UNTS 392. New Zealand. Ratification 19 Feb 55.
227 UNTS 392. Burma. Ratification 2 Aug 55.
227 UNTS 392. Argentina. Ratification 16 Mar 55.
227 UNTS 392. Korea, South. Ratification 10 Mar 55.
227 UNTS 392. New Zealand. Cook Islands. Force 19 Feb 55.
227 UNTS 392. New Zealand. Western Samoa. Force 19 Feb 55.

102222 Multilateral Agreement **170 UNTS 63**
SIGNED: 11 Jul 52   FORCE: 1 Jul 53
REGISTERED: 14 Jul 53 Belgium
ARTICLES: 46 LANGUAGE: French.
HEADNOTE: POSTAL PARCELS
TOPIC: Postal Service
CONCEPTS: Definition of terms. Detailed regulations. Treaty implementation. Treaty interpretation. Conformity with municipal law. Responsibility and liability. Compensation. Indemnities and reimbursements. Payment schedules. Delivery schedules. Quotas. Customs duties. Postal services. Regulations. Insured letters and boxes. Parcel post. Rates and charges. Prisoners of war.
INTL ORGS: Universal Postal Union.
TREATY REF: 71UNTS3.
PROCEDURE: Future Procedures Contemplated.
PARTIES:
Afghanistan SIGNED: 11 Jul 52
Albania SIGNED: 11 Jul 52
Algeria SIGNED: 11 Jul 52
Argentina SIGNED: 11 Jul 52
Austria SIGNED: 11 Jul 52
Belgium SIGNED: 11 Jul 52
Belgian Colonies SIGNED: 11 Jul 52
Bolivia SIGNED: 11 Jul 52
Brazil SIGNED: 11 Jul 52
Bulgaria SIGNED: 11 Jul 52
Cambodia SIGNED: 11 Jul 52
Chile SIGNED: 11 Jul 52
Taiwan SIGNED: 11 Jul 52
Colombia SIGNED: 11 Jul 52
Costa Rica SIGNED: 11 Jul 52
Cuba SIGNED: 11 Jul 52
Czechoslovakia SIGNED: 11 Jul 52
Denmark SIGNED: 11 Jul 52 RATIFIED: 20 Feb 53 FORCE: 1 Jul 53
Dominican Republic SIGNED: 11 Jul 52
Ecuador SIGNED: 11 Jul 52
United Arab Rep SIGNED: 11 Jul 52
El Salvador SIGNED: 11 Jul 52
Ethiopia SIGNED: 11 Jul 52
Finland SIGNED: 11 Jul 52
France SIGNED: 11 Jul 52
France All Territories RATIFIED: 11 Jul 52
Greece SIGNED: 11 Jul 52
Guatemala SIGNED: 11 Jul 52
Haiti SIGNED: 11 Jul 52
Honduras SIGNED: 11 Jul 52
Hungary SIGNED: 11 Jul 52
Iceland SIGNED: 11 Jul 52
India SIGNED: 11 Jul 52
Indonesia SIGNED: 11 Jul 52
Iran SIGNED: 11 Jul 52
Iraq SIGNED: 11 Jul 52
Ireland SIGNED: 11 Jul 52 RATIFIED: 6 May 53 FORCE: 1 Jul 53
Italy SIGNED: 11 Jul 52
Japan SIGNED: 11 Jul 52
Jordan SIGNED: 11 Jul 52 RATIFIED: 11 May 53 FORCE: 1 Jul 53
Korea, South SIGNED: 11 Jul 52
Laos SIGNED: 11 Jul 52 RATIFIED: 17 Apr 53 FORCE: 1 Jul 53
Lebanon SIGNED: 11 Jul 52 RATIFIED: 11 May 53 FORCE: 1 Jul 53
Liberia SIGNED: 11 Jul 52
Luxembourg SIGNED: 11 Jul 52
Mexico SIGNED: 11 Jul 52
Morocco SIGNED: 11 Jul 52

Netherlands Netherlands Antilles RATIFIED: 11 Jul 52
Netherlands SIGNED: 11 Jul 52
Netherlands Surinam RATIFIED: 11 Jul 52
Nicaragua SIGNED: 11 Jul 52
Norway SIGNED: 11 Jul 52 RATIFIED: 12 Mar 53 FORCE: 1 Jul 53
Pakistan SIGNED: 11 Jul 52
Panama SIGNED: 11 Jul 52
Paraguay SIGNED: 11 Jul 52
Peru SIGNED: 11 Jul 52
Poland SIGNED: 11 Jul 52
Portugal SIGNED: 11 Jul 52
Portugal All Territories RATIFIED: 11 Jul 52
Romania SIGNED: 11 Jul 52
San Marino SIGNED: 11 Jul 52
Spain SIGNED: 11 Jul 52
Spanish Colonies SIGNED: 11 Jul 52
Spanish Morroco SIGNED: 11 Jul 52
Sweden SIGNED: 11 Jul 52 RATIFIED: 28 Nov 52 FORCE: 1 Jul 53
Switzerland SIGNED: 11 Jul 52 RATIFIED: 16 May 53 FORCE: 1 Jul 53
Syria SIGNED: 11 Jul 52
Thailand SIGNED: 11 Jul 52
Tunisia SIGNED: 11 Jul 52
Turkey SIGNED: 11 Jul 52
Uruguay SIGNED: 11 Jul 52
Vatican/Holy See SIGNED: 11 Jul 52
Venezuela SIGNED: 11 Jul 52
Vietnam SIGNED: 11 Jul 52
Yemen SIGNED: 11 Jul 52
Yugoslavia SIGNED: 11 Jul 52
ANNEX
202 UNTS 348. Mexico. Ratification 4 Oct 54.
202 UNTS 348. Austria. Ratification 9 Mar 54.
202 UNTS 348. Netherlands. Ratification 29 Apr 54.
202 UNTS 348. Romania. Ratification 27 Sep 54.
202 UNTS 348. Hungary. Ratification 6 Sep 54.
202 UNTS 348. Greece. Ratification 5 Apr 54.
202 UNTS 348. France. Ratification 25 Jun 54.
202 UNTS 348. France. All Territories.
202 UNTS 348. Bulgaria. Ratification 2 Oct 54.
227 UNTS 394. United Arab Rep. Ratification 24 Mar 55.
227 UNTS 394. Turkey. Ratification 12 Nov 55.
227 UNTS 394. Yugoslavia. Ratification 21 Jun 55.
227 UNTS 394. Chile. Ratification 13 Dec 55.
227 UNTS 394. Spain. Ratification 12 May 55.
227 UNTS 394. Spain. Spanish Morroco.
227 UNTS 394. Spain. Spanish Colonies.
227 UNTS 394. Korea, South. Ratification 10 Mar 55.
227 UNTS 394. Poland. Ratification 3 Jun 55.
227 UNTS 394. Argentina. Ratification 16 Mar 55.
227 UNTS 394. Albania. Ratification 12 Feb 55.
227 UNTS 394. Germany, West. Accession 21 Mar 55.

102223 Multilateral Agreement **170 UNTS 269**
SIGNED: 11 Jul 52   FORCE: 1 Jul 53
REGISTERED: 14 Jul 53 Belgium
ARTICLES: 40 LANGUAGE: French.
HEADNOTE: POSTAL MONEY ORDERS
TOPIC: Postal Service
CONCEPTS: Treaty implementation. Conformity with municipal law. Domestic legislation. Responsibility and liability. Accounting procedures. Exchange rates and regulations. Interest rates. Claims and settlements. Payment schedules. Postal services. Regulations. Money orders and postal checks. Rates and charges.
INTL ORGS: International Telecommunication Union.
TREATY REF: 169UNTS311.
PROCEDURE: Duration. Registration.
PARTIES:
Albania SIGNED: 11 Jul 52
Algeria SIGNED: 11 Jul 52
Argentina SIGNED: 11 Jul 52
Austria SIGNED: 11 Jul 52
Belgium SIGNED: 11 Jul 52 RATIFIED: 12 Mar 53 FORCE: 1 Jul 53
Bolivia SIGNED: 11 Jul 52
Bulgaria SIGNED: 11 Jul 52
Cambodia SIGNED: 11 Jul 52
Chile SIGNED: 11 Jul 52
Taiwan SIGNED: 11 Jul 52
Colombia SIGNED: 11 Jul 52
Cuba SIGNED: 11 Jul 52

Czechoslovakia SIGNED: 11 Jul 52
Denmark SIGNED: 11 Jul 52 RATIFIED: 20 Feb 53 FORCE: 1 Jul 53
Dominican Republic SIGNED: 11 Jul 52
United Arab Rep SIGNED: 11 Jul 52
El Salvador SIGNED: 11 Jul 52
Finland SIGNED: 11 Jul 52
France SIGNED: 11 Jul 52
France All Territories RATIFIED: 11 Jul 52
Greece SIGNED: 11 Jul 52
Haiti SIGNED: 11 Jul 52
Honduras SIGNED: 11 Jul 52
Hungary SIGNED: 11 Jul 52
Iceland SIGNED: 11 Jul 52 RATIFIED: 6 May 53 FORCE: 1 Jul 53
Indonesia SIGNED: 11 Jul 52
Iran SIGNED: 11 Jul 52
Italy SIGNED: 11 Jul 52
Japan SIGNED: 11 Jul 52
Jordan RATIFIED: 11 May 53 FORCE: 1 Jul 53
Korea, South SIGNED: 11 Jul 52
Laos SIGNED: 11 Jul 52 RATIFIED: 11 Apr 53 FORCE: 1 Jul 53
Lebanon SIGNED: 11 Jul 52 RATIFIED: 11 May 53 FORCE: 1 Jul 53
Liberia SIGNED: 11 Jul 52
Luxembourg SIGNED: 11 Jul 52
Morocco SIGNED: 11 Jul 52
Netherlands SIGNED: 11 Jul 52
Netherlands Netherlands Antilles RATIFIED: 11 Jul 52
Netherlands Surinam RATIFIED: 11 Jul 52
Nicaragua SIGNED: 11 Jul 52
Norway SIGNED: 11 Jul 52 RATIFIED: 12 Mar 53 FORCE: 1 Jul 53
Panama SIGNED: 11 Jul 52
Paraguay SIGNED: 11 Jul 52
Peru SIGNED: 11 Jul 52
Poland SIGNED: 11 Jul 52
Portugal All Territories RATIFIED: 11 Jul 52
Portugal SIGNED: 11 Jul 52
Romania SIGNED: 11 Jul 52
San Marino SIGNED: 11 Jul 52
Spain SIGNED: 11 Jul 52
Spanish Colonies SIGNED: 11 Jul 52
Sweden SIGNED: 11 Jul 52 RATIFIED: 29 Nov 52 FORCE: 1 Jul 53
Switzerland SIGNED: 11 Jul 52 RATIFIED: 16 May 53 FORCE: 1 Jul 53
Syria SIGNED: 11 Jul 52
Thailand SIGNED: 11 Jul 52
Tunisia SIGNED: 11 Jul 52
Turkey SIGNED: 11 Jul 52
Uruguay SIGNED: 11 Jul 52
Vatican/Holy See SIGNED: 11 Jul 52
Venezuela SIGNED: 11 Jul 52
Vietnam SIGNED: 11 Jul 52
Yemen SIGNED: 11 Jul 52
Yugoslavia SIGNED: 11 Jul 52
ANNEX
202 UNTS 350. Mexico. Ratification 6 May 54.
202 UNTS 350. Netherlands. Surinam.
202 UNTS 350. Netherlands. Dutch New Guinea.
202 UNTS 350. Netherlands. Netherlands Antilles.
202 UNTS 350. Netherlands. Ratification 29 Apr 54.
202 UNTS 350. Hungary. Ratification 3 Sep 54.
202 UNTS 350. France. All Territories.
202 UNTS 350. Greece. Ratification 5 Apr 54.
202 UNTS 350. Austria. Ratification 9 Mar 54.
202 UNTS 350. Romania. Ratification 27 Sep 54.
202 UNTS 350. Bulgaria. Ratification 2 Oct 54.
202 UNTS 350. France. Ratification 25 Jun 54.
227 UNTS 394. Chile. Ratification 13 Dec 55.
227 UNTS 394. Spain. Spanish Colonies.
227 UNTS 394. United Arab Rep. Ratification 24 Mar 55.
227 UNTS 394. Poland. Ratification 3 Jun 55.
227 UNTS 394. Spain. Spanish Morroco.
227 UNTS 394. Turkey. Ratification 12 Nov 55.
227 UNTS 394. Argentina. Ratification 16 Mar 55.
227 UNTS 394. Korea, South. Ratification 10 Mar 55.
227 UNTS 394. Spain. Ratification 12 May 55.

102224 Multilateral Agreement **171 UNTS 3**
SIGNED: 11 Jul 52   FORCE: 1 Jul 53
REGISTERED: 14 Jul 53 Belgium
ARTICLES: 28 LANGUAGE: French.
HEADNOTE: POSTAL CHECK ACCOUNTS
TOPIC: Postal Service

CONCEPTS: Detailed regulations. General provisions. Treaty implementation. Responsibility and liability. Accounting procedures. Currency. Payment schedules. Claims and settlements. Postal services. Regulations. Money orders and postal checks. Advice lists and orders. Radio-telephone-telegraphic communications. Conformity with IGO decisions.
INTL ORGS: Universal Postal Union. Arbitration Commission.
TREATY REF: 170UNTS269, INTER. TELECOMM. CONV.;169UNTS3.
PROCEDURE: Duration. Registration.
PARTIES:
Albania SIGNED: 11 Jul 52
Algeria SIGNED: 11 Jul 52
Argentina SIGNED: 11 Jul 52
Austria SIGNED: 11 Jul 52
Belgium   SIGNED: 11 Jul 52   RATIFIED: 12 Mar 53 FORCE: 1 Jul 53
Bolivia SIGNED: 11 Jul 52
Colombia SIGNED: 11 Jul 52
Cuba SIGNED: 11 Jul 52
Denmark   SIGNED: 11 Jul 52   RATIFIED: 20 Feb 53 FORCE: 1 Jul 53
Dominican Republic SIGNED: 11 Jul 52
Finland SIGNED: 11 Jul 52
France SIGNED: 11 Jul 52
Greece SIGNED: 11 Jul 52
Haiti SIGNED: 11 Jul 52
Honduras SIGNED: 11 Jul 52
Indonesia SIGNED: 11 Jul 52
Italy SIGNED: 11 Jul 52
Japan SIGNED: 11 Jul 52
Korea, South SIGNED: 11 Jul 52
Laos SIGNED: 11 Jul 52 RATIFIED: 17 Apr 53 FORCE: 1 Jul 53
Lebanon SIGNED: 11 Jul 52
Luxembourg SIGNED: 11 Jul 52
Morocco SIGNED: 11 Jul 52
Netherlands SIGNED: 11 Jul 52
Nicaragua SIGNED: 11 Jul 52
Norway   SIGNED: 11 Jul 52   RATIFIED: 12 Mar 53 FORCE: 1 Jul 53
Portugal All Territories SIGNED: 11 Jul 52 RATIFIED: 11 Jul 52
Romania SIGNED: 11 Jul 52
San Marino SIGNED: 11 Jul 52
Spain SIGNED: 11 Jul 52
Spanish Colonies SIGNED: 11 Jul 52
Spanish Morroco SIGNED: 11 Jul 52
Sweden   SIGNED: 11 Jul 52   RATIFIED: 29 Nov 52 FORCE: 1 Jul 53
Switzerland   SIGNED: 11 Jul 52   RATIFIED: 16 May 53 FORCE: 1 Jul 53
Tunisia SIGNED: 11 Jul 52
Turkey SIGNED: 11 Jul 52
Uruguay SIGNED: 11 Jul 52
Vatican/Holy See SIGNED: 11 Jul 52
Venezuela SIGNED: 11 Jul 52
Yugoslavia SIGNED: 11 Jul 52
ANNEX
202 UNTS 352. France. Tunisia.
202 UNTS 352. Netherlands. Dutch New Guinea.
202 UNTS 352. Romania. Ratification 27 Sep 54.
202 UNTS 352.   Netherlands.   Ratification 29 Apr 54.
202 UNTS 352. France. Morocco.
202 UNTS 352. France. Algeria.
202 UNTS 352. Austria. Ratification 9 Mar 54.
202 UNTS 352. France. Ratification 25 Jun 54.
227 UNTS 396. Spain. Spanish Colonies.
227 UNTS 396. Turkey. Ratification 12 Nov 55.
227 UNTS 396.   Korea,   South.   Ratification 10 Mar 55.
227 UNTS 396.   Germany,   West.   Accession 21 Mar 55.
227 UNTS 396. Spain. Ratification 12 May 55.
227 UNTS 396. Spain. Spanish Morroco.
227 UNTS 396.   Argentina.   Ratification 16 Mar 55.
227 UNTS 396. Chile. Ratification 13 Dec 55.

102225 Multilateral Agreement **171 UNTS 89**
SIGNED: 11 Jul 52   FORCE: 1 Jul 53
REGISTERED: 14 Jul 53 Belgium
ARTICLES: 16 LANGUAGE: French.
HEADNOTE: CASH-ON-DELIVERY ITEMS
TOPIC: Postal Service
CONCEPTS: Detailed regulations. Treaty implementation. Responsibility and liability. Indemnities and reimbursements. Payment schedules. Claims and settlements. Regulations. Insured let-

ters and boxes. Money orders and postal checks. Rates and charges. Conformity with IGO decisions.
TREATY   REF: 169UNTS3;   170UNTS3; 170UNTS63; 170UNTS269.
PROCEDURE: Duration. Registration.
PARTIES:
Albania SIGNED: 11 Jul 52
Algeria SIGNED: 11 Jul 52
Argentina SIGNED: 11 Jul 52
Austria SIGNED: 11 Jul 52
Belgium   SIGNED: 11 Jul 52   RATIFIED: 12 Mar 53 FORCE: 1 Jul 53
Bolivia SIGNED: 11 Jul 52
Cambodia SIGNED: 11 Jul 52
Chile SIGNED: 11 Jul 52
Taiwan SIGNED: 11 Jul 52
Colombia SIGNED: 11 Jul 52
Cuba SIGNED: 11 Jul 52
Czechoslovakia SIGNED: 11 Jul 52
Denmark   SIGNED: 11 Jul 52   RATIFIED: 20 Feb 53 FORCE: 1 Jul 53
Dominican Republic SIGNED: 11 Jul 52
United Arab Rep SIGNED: 11 Jul 52
Finland SIGNED: 11 Jul 52
France SIGNED: 11 Jul 52
France All Territories RATIFIED: 11 Jul 52
Greece SIGNED: 11 Jul 52
Hungary SIGNED: 11 Jul 52
Iceland SIGNED: 11 Jul 52 RATIFIED: 6 May 53 FORCE: 1 Jul 53
Indonesia SIGNED: 11 Jul 52
Italy SIGNED: 11 Jul 52
Japan SIGNED: 11 Jul 52
Korea, South SIGNED: 11 Jul 52
Laos SIGNED: 11 Jul 52 RATIFIED: 17 Apr 53 FORCE: 1 Jul 53
Lebanon SIGNED: 11 Jul 52
Luxembourg SIGNED: 11 Jul 52
Mexico SIGNED: 11 Jul 52
Morocco SIGNED: 11 Jul 52
Netherlands Netherlands Antilles RATIFIED: 11 Jul 52
Netherlands SIGNED: 11 Jul 52
Netherlands Surinam RATIFIED: 11 Jul 52
Nicaragua SIGNED: 11 Jul 52
Norway   SIGNED: 11 Jul 52   RATIFIED: 12 Mar 53 FORCE: 1 Jul 53
Paraguay SIGNED: 11 Jul 52
Poland SIGNED: 11 Jul 52
Portugal All Territories RATIFIED: 11 Jul 52
Portugal SIGNED: 11 Jul 52
Romania SIGNED: 11 Jul 52
San Marino SIGNED: 11 Jul 52
Spain SIGNED: 11 Jul 52
Spanish Colonies SIGNED: 11 Jul 52
Spanish Morroco SIGNED: 11 Jul 52
Sweden   SIGNED: 11 Jul 52   RATIFIED: 29 Nov 52 FORCE: 1 Jul 53
Switzerland   SIGNED: 11 Jul 52   RATIFIED: 16 May 53 FORCE: 1 Jul 53
Syria SIGNED: 11 Jul 52
Thailand SIGNED: 11 Jul 52
Tunisia SIGNED: 11 Jul 52
Turkey SIGNED: 11 Jul 52
Uruguay SIGNED: 11 Jul 52
Vatican/Holy See SIGNED: 11 Jul 52
Venezuela SIGNED: 11 Jul 52
Yugoslavia SIGNED: 11 Jul 52
ANNEX
202 UNTS 354. France. Ratification 25 Jun 54.
202 UNTS 354. France. All Territories.
202 UNTS 354. Austria. Ratification 9 Mar 54.
202 UNTS 354. Greece. Ratification 5 Apr 54.
202 UNTS 354. Hungary. Ratification 3 Sep 54.
202 UNTS 354. Mexico. Ratification 4 Oct 54.
202 UNTS 354.   Netherlands.   Ratification 29 Apr 54.
202 UNTS 354.   Netherlands.   Netherlands Antilles.
202 UNTS 354. Netherlands. Dutch New Guinea.
202 UNTS 354. Netherlands. Surinam.
202 UNTS 354. Romania. Ratification 27 Sep 54.
227 UNTS 396.   Argentina.   Ratification 16 Mar 55.
227 UNTS 396.   Germany,   West.   Accession 21 Mar 55.
227 UNTS 396. Spain. Spanish Morroco.
227 UNTS 396.   Korea,   South.   Ratification 10 Mar 55.
227 UNTS 396. Spain. Ratification 12 May 55.
227 UNTS 396. Chile. Ratification 13 Dec 55.
227 UNTS 396. Spain. Spanish Colonies.

227 UNTS 396. United Arab Rep. Ratification 24 Mar 55.
227 UNTS 396. Poland. Ratification 3 Jun 55.

102226 Multilateral Agreement **171 UNTS 143**
SIGNED: 11 Jul 52   FORCE: 1 Jul 53
REGISTERED: 14 Jul 53 Belgium
ARTICLES: 23 LANGUAGE: French.
HEADNOTE: COLLECTION BILLS DRAFTS ETC.
TOPIC: Postal Service
CONCEPTS: Detailed regulations. General provisions. Time limit. Treaty implementation. Responsibility and liability. Accounting procedures. Currency. Payment schedules. Local currency. Postal services. Regulations. Money orders and postal checks. Rates and charges. Conformity with IGO decisions.
PROCEDURE: Duration. Registration.
PARTIES:
Albania SIGNED: 11 Jul 52
Algeria SIGNED: 11 Jul 52
Argentina SIGNED: 11 Jul 52
Austria SIGNED: 11 Jul 52
Belgium   SIGNED: 11 Jul 52   RATIFIED: 12 Mar 53 FORCE: 1 Jul 53
Bolivia SIGNED: 11 Jul 52
Cambodia SIGNED: 11 Jul 52
Chile SIGNED: 11 Jul 52
Colombia SIGNED: 11 Jul 52
Cuba SIGNED: 11 Jul 52
Denmark   SIGNED: 11 Jul 52   RATIFIED: 20 Feb 53 FORCE: 1 Jul 53
Dominican Republic SIGNED: 11 Jul 52
United Arab Rep SIGNED: 11 Jul 52
Finland SIGNED: 11 Jul 52
France SIGNED: 11 Jul 52
Greece SIGNED: 11 Jul 52
Haiti SIGNED: 11 Jul 52
Honduras SIGNED: 11 Jul 52
Hungary SIGNED: 11 Jul 52
Iceland SIGNED: 11 Jul 52 RATIFIED: 6 May 53 FORCE: 1 Jul 53
Indonesia SIGNED: 11 Jul 52
Italy SIGNED: 11 Jul 52
Laos SIGNED: 11 Jul 52 RATIFIED: 17 Apr 53 FORCE: 1 Jul 53
Lebanon SIGNED: 11 Jul 52
Luxembourg SIGNED: 11 Jul 52
Morocco SIGNED: 11 Jul 52
Netherlands SIGNED: 11 Jul 52
Netherlands Netherlands Antilles RATIFIED: 11 Jul 52
Netherlands Surinam RATIFIED: 11 Jul 52
Nicaragua SIGNED: 11 Jul 52
Norway   SIGNED: 11 Jul 52   RATIFIED: 12 Mar 53 FORCE: 1 Jul 53
Paraguay SIGNED: 11 Jul 52
Portugal SIGNED: 11 Jul 52
Portugal All Territories RATIFIED: 11 Jul 52
Romania SIGNED: 11 Jul 52
San Marino SIGNED: 11 Jul 52
Spain SIGNED: 11 Jul 52
Spanish Colonies SIGNED: 11 Jul 52
Spanish Morroco SIGNED: 11 Jul 52
Sweden   SIGNED: 11 Jul 52   RATIFIED: 29 Nov 52 FORCE: 1 Jul 53
Switzerland   SIGNED: 11 Jul 52   RATIFIED: 13 May 53 FORCE: 1 Jul 53
Thailand SIGNED: 11 Jul 52
Tunisia SIGNED: 11 Jul 52
Turkey SIGNED: 11 Jul 52
Uruguay SIGNED: 11 Jul 52
Vatican/Holy See SIGNED: 11 Jul 52
Venezuela SIGNED: 11 Jul 52
Yugoslavia SIGNED: 11 Jul 52
ANNEX
202 UNTS 356. Netherlands. Dutch New Guinea.
202 UNTS 356.   Netherlands.   Ratification 29 Apr 54.
202 UNTS 356. Austria. Ratification 9 Mar 54.
202 UNTS 356. France. Ratification 25 Jun 54.
202 UNTS 356. France. Algeria.
202 UNTS 356. France. Morocco.
202 UNTS 356. France. Tunisia.
202 UNTS 356.   Netherlands.   Netherlands Antilles.
202 UNTS 356. Hungary. Ratification 3 Sep 54.
202 UNTS 356. Romania. Ratification 27 Sep 54.
202 UNTS 356. Netherlands. Surinam.
227 UNTS 398. Chile. Ratification 13 Dec 55.
227 UNTS 398.   Korea,   South.   Ratification 10 Mar 55.

227 UNTS 398. United Arab Rep. Ratification 24 Mar 55.
227 UNTS 398. Argentina. Ratification 16 Mar 55.
227 UNTS 398. Spain. Ratification 12 May 55.
227 UNTS 398. Spain. Spanish Colonies.
227 UNTS 398. Spain. Spanish Morroco.
227 UNTS 398. Germany, West. Accession 21 Mar 55.

102227 Multilateral Agreement **171 UNTS 191**
SIGNED: 11 Jul 52   FORCE: 1 Jul 53
REGISTERED: 14 Jul 53 Belgium
ARTICLES: 16 LANGUAGE: French.
HEADNOTE: SUBSCRIPTIONS NEWSPAPERS PERIODICALS
TOPIC: Postal Service
CONCEPTS: Detailed regulations. General provisions. Responsibility and liability. Postal services. Regulations. Rates and charges. Publications exchange. Press and wire services. Conformity with IGO decisions.
INTL ORGS: Universal Postal Union. Arbitration Commission.
TREATY REF: 169UNTS19.
PROCEDURE: Duration. Registration.
PARTIES:
  Belgium RATIFIED: 12 Mar 53 FORCE: 1 Jul 53
  Denmark RATIFIED: 20 Feb 53 FORCE: 1 Jul 53
  Laos RATIFIED: 17 Apr 53 FORCE: 1 Jul 53
  Norway RATIFIED: 12 Mar 53 FORCE: 1 Jul 53
                    ANNEX
202 UNTS 358. Hungary. Ratification 3 Sep 54.
202 UNTS 358. Netherlands. Ratification 29 Apr 54.
202 UNTS 358. Netherlands. Dutch New Guinea.
202 UNTS 358. Romania. Ratification 27 Sep 54.
202 UNTS 358. Austria. Ratification 9 Mar 54.
202 UNTS 358. Bulgaria. Ratification 2 Oct 54.
202 UNTS 358. France. Ratification 25 Jun 54.
202 UNTS 358. France. Algeria.
202 UNTS 358. France. Morocco.
202 UNTS 358. France. Tunisia.
227 UNTS 398. Chile. Ratification 13 Dec 55.
227 UNTS 398. Spain. Ratification 12 May 55.
227 UNTS 398. Poland. Ratification 3 Jun 55.
227 UNTS 398. Argentina. Ratification 16 Mar 55.
227 UNTS 398. Korea, South. Ratification 10 Mar 55.
227 UNTS 398. Spain. Spanish Colonies.
227 UNTS 398. Spain. Spanish Morroco.
227 UNTS 398. Germany, West. Accession 21 Mar 55.
227 UNTS 398. United Arab Rep. Ratification 24 Mar 55.

102228 Bilateral Agreement **171 UNTS 249**
SIGNED: 17 Jun 52   FORCE: 17 Jun 53
REGISTERED: 22 Jul 53 United Nations
ARTICLES: 10 LANGUAGE: English. French.
HEADNOTE: ACTIVITIES UNICEF
TOPIC: Direct Aid
CONCEPTS: Territorial application. Treaty implementation. Annex or appendix reference. Privileges and immunities. General cooperation. Exchange of information and documents. Informational records. Inspection and observation. Public information. Procedure. Existing tribunals. Export quotas. Indemnities and reimbursements. Local currency. Tax exemptions. Customs exemptions. Commodities and services. Assistance. General aid. Distribution. IGO status.
INTL ORGS: United Nations.
TREATY REF: 1UNTS15.
PROCEDURE: Duration.
PARTIES:
  Belgium
  UNICEF (Children)

102229 Bilateral Exchange **171 UNTS 263**
SIGNED: 10 Jun 52   FORCE: 10 Jun 52
REGISTERED: 23 Jul 53 New Zealand
ARTICLES: 2 LANGUAGE: English. German.
HEADNOTE: CONCERNING 1931 CONVENTION
TOPIC: Admin Cooperation
CONCEPTS: Territorial application.
TREATY REF: 127LTS167; 134LTS435; 156LTS242; 160LTS399.

PARTIES:
  Austria
  New Zealand

102230 Bilateral Exchange **171 UNTS 269**
SIGNED: 13 Jun 52   FORCE: 1 Jul 52
REGISTERED: 23 Jul 53 New Zealand
ARTICLES: 2 LANGUAGE: English. French.
HEADNOTE: MUTUAL ABOLITION VISAS
TOPIC: Visas
CONCEPTS: Visa abolition. Denial of admission. Conformity with municipal law.
PARTIES:
  Monaco
  New Zealand

102231 Bilateral Exchange **171 UNTS 275**
SIGNED: 9 Oct 52   FORCE: 9 Oct 52
REGISTERED: 23 Jul 53 New Zealand
ARTICLES: 2 LANGUAGE: English.
HEADNOTE: TRADE
TOPIC: General Trade
CONCEPTS: Annex type material.
TREATY REF: 189LTS167.
PARTIES:
  New Zealand
  Switzerland
                    ANNEX
247 UNTS 434. Switzerland. Amendment 3 Jun 55. Force 3 Jun 55.
247 UNTS 434. New Zealand. Amendment 3 Jun 55. Force 3 Jun 55.
247 UNTS 438. Switzerland. Amendment 21 Dec 55. Force 21 Dec 55.
247 UNTS 438. New Zealand. Amendment 21 Dec 55. Force 21 Dec 55.
274 UNTS 350. Switzerland. Amendment 6 Mar 57. Force 6 Mar 57.
274 UNTS 350. New Zealand. Amendment 6 Mar 57. Force 6 Mar 57.

102232 Bilateral Agreement **171 UNTS 279**
SIGNED: 13 Apr 49   FORCE: 1 May 49
REGISTERED: 23 Jul 53 Yugoslavia
ARTICLES: 13 LANGUAGE: French.
HEADNOTE: FISHING
TOPIC: Commodity Trade
CONCEPTS: Detailed regulations. Annex or appendix reference. Standardization. General cooperation. Inspection and observation. Licenses and permits. Procedure. Payment schedules. Fish, wildlife, and natural resources.
INTL ORGS: Inter-Governmental Maritime Consultative Organization.
TREATY REF: 136LTS81.
PROCEDURE: Duration. Renewal or Revival. Termination.
PARTIES:
  Italy
  Yugoslavia
                    ANNEX
175 UNTS 375. Yugoslavia. Prolongation 26 Feb 51. Force 26 Feb 51.
175 UNTS 375. Italy. Prolongation 26 Feb 51. Force 26 Feb 51.

102233 Bilateral Agreement **171 UNTS 291**
SIGNED: 23 Dec 50   FORCE: 23 Dec 50
REGISTERED: 23 Jul 53 Yugoslavia
ARTICLES: 10 LANGUAGE: French.
HEADNOTE: APPORTIONMENT ARCHIVES DOCUMENTS ADMINISTRATIVE CHARACTER
TOPIC: Admin Cooperation
CONCEPTS: Definition of terms. Annex or appendix reference. Exchange of information and documents. Establishment of commission. Tax exemptions.
INTL ORGS: Special Commission.
PARTIES:
  Italy
  Yugoslavia

102234 Multilateral Convention **171 UNTS 305**
SIGNED: 15 Dec 50   FORCE: 28 Jul 53
REGISTERED: 28 Jul 53 Belgium
ARTICLES: 18 LANGUAGE: English. French.
HEADNOTE: VALUATION GOODS CUSTOMS PURPOSES
TOPIC: Customs

CONCEPTS: Definition of terms. Territorial application. Annex or appendix reference. Previous treaty renunciation. Previous treaties adherence. Conformity with municipal law. Incorporation of treaty provisions into national law. Establishment of commission. Arbitration. Negotiation. Customs declarations.
INTL ORGS: Special Commission.
TREATY REF: 157UNTS129.
PROCEDURE: Amendment. Accession. Duration. Ratification. Registration.
PARTIES:
  Belgium SIGNED: 15 Dec 50 RATIFIED: 3 Jan 53 FORCE: 28 Jul 53
  Denmark SIGNED: 15 Dec 50
  France SIGNED: 15 Dec 50 RATIFIED: 27 Apr 53 FORCE: 28 Jul 53
  Germany, West SIGNED: 15 Dec 50 RATIFIED: 4 Nov 52 FORCE: 28 Jul 53
  Greece SIGNED: 15 Dec 50 RATIFIED: 10 Dec 51 FORCE: 28 Jul 53
  Iceland SIGNED: 15 Dec 50
  Italy SIGNED: 15 Dec 50
  Luxembourg SIGNED: 15 Dec 50 RATIFIED: 23 Jan 53 FORCE: 28 Jul 53
  Netherlands SIGNED: 15 Dec 50 RATIFIED: 23 Jan 53 FORCE: 28 Jul 53
  Norway SIGNED: 15 Dec 50
  Portugal SIGNED: 15 Dec 50
  Sweden SIGNED: 15 Dec 50
  UK Great Britain SIGNED: 15 Dec 50 RATIFIED: 27 Sep 52 FORCE: 28 Jul 53
                    ANNEX
347 UNTS 382. Haiti. Accession 31 Jan 58. Force 1 May 58.
347 UNTS 382. Portugal. Ratification 11 Jun 53. Force 12 Sep 53.
347 UNTS 382. Denmark. Ratification 6 Mar 59. Force 7 Jun 59.
347 UNTS 382. Austria. Accession 4 Nov 55. Force 5 Feb 56.
347 UNTS 382. Italy. Ratification 17 Jun 53. Force 18 Sep 53.
347 UNTS 382. Pakistan. Accession 14 Oct 57. Force 15 Jan 58.

102235 Multilateral Convention **171 UNTS 329**
SIGNED: 19 Jun 47   FORCE: 1 Jul 53
REGISTERED: 30 Jul 53 ILO (Labor Org)
ARTICLES: 19 LANGUAGE: English. French.
HEADNOTE: RIGHT ASSOCIATION NON-METROPOLITAN AREAS
TOPIC: ILO Labor
CONCEPTS: Exceptions and exemptions. Territorial application. General cooperation. Informational records. Dispute settlement. ILO conventions. Right to organize.
INTL ORGS: International Labour Organization.
TREATY REF: 15UNTS35.
PROCEDURE: Amendment. Denunciation. Duration. Ratification. Registration. Renewal or Revival.
PARTIES:
  Multilateral
                    ANNEX
198 UNTS 405. France. Ratification 26 Jul 54. Force 26 Jul 55.
202 UNTS 360. France. Fr Equatorial Afri.
202 UNTS 360. France. Madagascar.
202 UNTS 360. France. French West Africa.
202 UNTS 360. France. French Somaliland.
202 UNTS 360. France. Miquelon.
202 UNTS 360. France. Oceania.
202 UNTS 360. France. French Togoland.
202 UNTS 360. France. St. Pierre.
202 UNTS 360. France. French Cameroon.
203 UNTS 338. Belgium. Ratification 27 Jan 55. Force 27 Jan 56.
212 UNTS 400. France. Martinique.
212 UNTS 400. France. Reunion.
212 UNTS 400. France. French Guinea.
212 UNTS 400. France. Guadeloupe.
277 UNTS 351. Belgium. Belgian Colonies.
277 UNTS 351. Belgium. Ruanda-Urundi.
410 UNTS 292. UK Great Britain. Brit Solomon Is
444 UNTS 340. UK Great Britain. Brunei.
504 UNTS 360. UK Great Britain. Gilbert Islands

102236 Bilateral Exchange **172 UNTS 3**
SIGNED: 30 Oct 52   FORCE: 30 Oct 52
REGISTERED: 14 Aug 53 UK Great Britain
ARTICLES: 2 LANGUAGE: English.

HEADNOTE: ADVANCE RELEASE STERLING RE-
LEASES AGREEMENT
TOPIC: Finance
CONCEPTS: Licenses and permits. Accounting
procedures. Balance of payments. Monetary and
gold transfers. Financial programs.
TREATY REF: UKTS67(1951),CMD.8336.
PARTIES:
United Arab Rep
UK Great Britain

102237   Bilateral Convention   **172 UNTS 9**
SIGNED: 12 Dec 52   FORCE: 25 Apr 53
REGISTERED: 14 Aug 53 UK Great Britain
ARTICLES: 18 LANGUAGE: English. German.
HEADNOTE: CULTURAL CONVENTION
TOPIC: Culture
CONCEPTS: Definition of terms. Non-prejudice to
third party. Friendship and amity. Conformity
with municipal law. General cooperation. Oper-
ating agencies. Establishment of commission.
Recognition of degrees. Teacher and student ex-
change. Professorships. Institute establishment.
Scholarships and grants. Vocational training.
General cultural cooperation. Artists. Research
and development. Publications exchange. Mass
media exchange.
INTL ORGS: Special Commission.
PROCEDURE: Amendment. Denunciation. Dura-
tion. Ratification. Renewal or Revival.
PARTIES:
Austria
UK Great Britain

102238   Bilateral Convention   **172 UNTS 27**
SIGNED: 28 Nov 51   FORCE: 6 May 53
REGISTERED: 14 Aug 53 UK Great Britain
ARTICLES: 21 LANGUAGE: English. Italian.
HEADNOTE: CULTURAL CONVENTION
TOPIC: Culture
CONCEPTS: Definition of terms. Non-prejudice to
third party. Friendship and amity. Conformity
with municipal law. General cooperation. Oper-
ating agencies. Establishment of commission.
Recognition of degrees. Teacher and student ex-
change. Professorships. Institute establishment.
Scholarships and grants. Vocational training.
General cultural cooperation. Artists. Research
and development. Publications exchange. Mass
media exchange.
INTL ORGS: Special Commission.
PARTIES:
Italy
UK Great Britain
ANNEX
175 UNTS 379. UK Great Britain. Implementation
1 Jul 53. Force 1 Jul 53.
175 UNTS 379. Italy. Implementation 1 Jul 53.
Force 1 Jul 53.

102239   Bilateral Convention   **172 UNTS 45**
SIGNED: 12 Dec 51   FORCE: 8 Jan 53
REGISTERED: 14 Aug 53 UK Great Britain
ARTICLES: 26 LANGUAGE: English. Finnish.
HEADNOTE: DOUBLE TAXATION FISCAL EVA-
SION TAXES INCOME
TOPIC: Taxation
CONCEPTS: Definition of terms. Territorial applica-
tion. Conformity with municipal law. Teacher
and student exchange. Taxation. Tax credits. Eq-
uitable taxes.
PROCEDURE: Duration. Ratification. Termination.
PARTIES:
Finland
UK Great Britain
ANNEX
605 UNTS 344. UK Great Britain. Amendment
16 Jun 66.
605 UNTS 344. Finland. Amendment 16 Jun 66.

102240   Bilateral Exchange   **172 UNTS 85**
SIGNED: 21 Mar 53   FORCE: 21 Mar 53
REGISTERED: 14 Aug 53 UK Great Britain
ARTICLES: 2 LANGUAGE: Arabic. English.
HEADNOTE: CERTAIN FINANCIAL MILITARY MAT-
TERS
TOPIC: General Military
CONCEPTS: Exceptions and exemptions. Eco-
nomic assistance. Defense and security.
TREATY REF: 151UNTS69.

PROCEDURE: Duration. Future Procedures Con-
templated.
PARTIES:
Libya
UK Great Britain

102241   Bilateral Agreement   **172 UNTS 93**
SIGNED: 22 Jun 53   FORCE: 22 Jun 53
REGISTERED: 19 Aug 53 United Nations
ARTICLES: 6 LANGUAGE: English.
HEADNOTE: TECHNICAL ASSISTANCE
TOPIC: Tech Assistance
CONCEPTS: Definition of terms. Treaty implemen-
tation. Privileges and immunities. General coop-
eration. Exchange of information and docu-
ments. Personnel. Title and deeds. Exchange.
Scholarships and grants. Vocational training. Re-
search and development. Expense sharing for-
mulae. Local currency. Domestic obligation.
General technical assistance. Materials, equip-
ment and services. IGO status. Conformity with
IGO decisions.
INTL ORGS: United Nations.
TREATY REF: 76UNTS132; 1UNTS15,263.
PROCEDURE: Amendment. Termination.
PARTIES:
Ethiopia
United Nations
ANNEX
292 UNTS 363. Ethiopia. Force 15 Mar 58.
292 UNTS 363. United Nations. Force 15 Mar 58.

102242   Bilateral Treaty   **172 UNTS 103**
SIGNED: 10 Nov 52   FORCE: 28 Apr 53
REGISTERED: 20 Aug 53 India
ARTICLES: 7 LANGUAGE: Arabic. English. Hindi.
HEADNOTE: FRIENDSHIP
TOPIC: General Amity
CONCEPTS: Treaty interpretation. Friendship and
amity. Alien status. Consular relations establish-
ment. Diplomatic relations establishment. Privi-
leges and immunities. Conformity with munici-
pal law. Arbitration. Negotiation.
PROCEDURE: Future Procedures Contemplated.
Ratification.
PARTIES:
India
Iraq

102243   Bilateral Agreement   **172 UNTS 115**
SIGNED: 11 Mar 53   FORCE: 3 Jun 53
REGISTERED: 22 Aug 53 IBRD (World Bank)
ARTICLES: 5 LANGUAGE: English.
HEADNOTE: GUARANTEE AGREEMENT
TOPIC: IBRD Project
CONCEPTS: Definition of terms. Territorial applica-
tion. Annex or appendix reference. Exchange of
information and documents. Informational
records. Inspection and observation. Bonds. Do-
mestic obligation. Terms of loan. Loan regula-
tions. Loan guarantee. Guarantor non-interfer-
ence.
PARTIES:
IBRD (World Bank)
UK Great Britain

102244 Multilateral Convention **172 UNTS 159**
SIGNED: 28 Jun 51   FORCE: 23 Aug 53
REGISTERED: 28 Aug 53 ILO (Labor Org)
ARTICLES: 15 LANGUAGE: English. French.
HEADNOTE: MINIMUM WAGES AGRICULTURE
TOPIC: ILO Labor
CONCEPTS: Territorial application. Conformity
with municipal law. Incorporation of treaty provi-
sions into national law. Public information. ILO
conventions. Wages and salaries. Agriculture.
INTL ORGS: International Labour Organization.
PROCEDURE: Amendment. Denunciation. Dura-
tion. Ratification. Registration. Renewal or Re-
vival.
PARTIES:
Multilateral
ANNEX
180 UNTS 396. Austria. Ratification 29 Oct 53.
Force 29 Oct 54.
184 UNTS 383. Cuba. Ratification 13 Jan 54.
Force 13 Jan 55.
184 UNTS 383. Philippines. Ratification
29 Dec 53. Force 29 Dec 54.

187 UNTS 465. Germany, West. Ratification
25 Feb 54. Force 25 Feb 55.
191 UNTS 407. Netherlands. Ratification
11 Jun 54. Force 11 Jun 55.
222 UNTS 422. France. Martinique.
222 UNTS 422. France. French Guinea.
222 UNTS 422. France. Guadeloupe.
222 UNTS 422. France. Reunion.
225 UNTS 267. Netherlands. Dutch New Guinea.
225 UNTS 267. Netherlands. Netherlands Antilles.
231 UNTS 365. UK Great Britain. Isle of Man.
236 UNTS 395. UK Great Britain. Jersey Island.
266 UNTS 420. Brazil. Ratification 25 Apr 57.
Force 25 Apr 58.
293 UNTS 385. UK Great Britain. Nyasaland.
307 UNTS 364. UK Great Britain. Seychelles. Declaration 15 Aug 67.
320 UNTS 343. UK Great Britain. Mauritius.
320 UNTS 343. UK Great Britain. Sierra Leone.
323 UNTS 375. Tunisia. Ratification 12 Jan 59.
Force 12 Jan 60.
343 UNTS 351. UK Great Britain. Guernsey Island.
353 UNTS 369. Peru. Ratification 1 Feb 60. Force
1 Feb 61.
366 UNTS 413. Costa Rica. Ratification 2 Jun 60.
Force 2 Jun 61.
380 UNTS 423. Morocco. Ratification 14 Oct 60.
Force 14 Oct 61.
396 UNTS 337. UK Great Britain. Bahamas. Declaration 13 Mar 61.
399 UNTS 271. Ivory Coast. Ratification
5 May 61. Force 5 May 62.
401 UNTS 268. Gabon. Ratification 13 Jun 61.
Force 13 Jun 61.
401 UNTS 268. Sierra Leone. Succession
13 Jun 61.
406 UNTS 306. Guatemala. Ratification
4 Aug 61. Force 4 Aug 62.
444 UNTS 341. Senegal. Ratification 22 Oct 62.
Force 22 Oct 63.
444 UNTS 341. Algeria. Succession 19 Oct 62.
457 UNTS 361. UK Great Britain. Gambia.
468 UNTS 436. UK Great Britain. Brit Solomon Is.
468 UNTS 436. UK Great Britain. St. Christopher.
483 UNTS 416. UK Great Britain. British Honduras.
488 UNTS 368. Czechoslovakia. Ratification
21 Jan 64. Force 21 Jan 65.
504 UNTS 361. Central Afri Rep. Ratification
9 Jun 64. Force 9 Jun 65.
504 UNTS 361. Paraguay. Ratification 24 Jun 64.
Force 24 Jun 65.
530 UNTS 421. UK Great Britain. Malawi. Ratification 22 Mar 65.
545 UNTS 380. Syria. Ratification 10 Aug 65.
Force 10 Aug 66.
559 UNTS 384. UK Great Britain. Grenada.
649 UNTS 383. Belgium. Ratification 17 Oct 68.
Force 17 Oct 68.

102245   Bilateral Exchange   **172 UNTS 173**
SIGNED: 13 Apr 53   FORCE: 13 Apr 53
REGISTERED: 31 Aug 53 UK Great Britain
ARTICLES: 2 LANGUAGE: English. French.
HEADNOTE: EXCHANGE OFFICIAL PUBLICA-
TIONS
TOPIC: Admin Cooperation
CONCEPTS: Exchange of official publications. Op-
erating agencies.
PARTIES:
France
UK Great Britain

102246   Bilateral Agreement   **172 UNTS 179**
SIGNED: 22 May 53   FORCE: 3 Jun 53
REGISTERED: 31 Aug 53 UK Great Britain
ARTICLES: 8 LANGUAGE: English. German.
HEADNOTE: MONETARY
TOPIC: Finance
CONCEPTS: Definition of terms. Treaty implemen-
tation. Previous treaty replacement. General co-
operation. Banking. Currency. Monetary and
gold transfers. Financial programs. Internal fi-
nance. Payment schedules.
INTL ORGS: International Monetary Fund.
TREATY REF: CMD8064; 2UNTS40; 14UNTS335;
88UNTS242.
PROCEDURE: Termination.

PARTIES:
Germany, West
UK Great Britain

102247 Multilateral Agreement **172 UNTS 193**
SIGNED: 31 Oct 51   FORCE: 31 Oct 51
REGISTERED: 31 Aug 53 UK Great Britain
ARTICLES: 16 LANGUAGE: English. French.
HEADNOTE: WAR GRAVES
TOPIC: Other Military
CONCEPTS: Definition of terms. Territorial application. Previous treaty replacement. Title and deeds. Use of facilities. Establishment of commission. Sanitation. Tax exemptions. Customs exemptions. Establishment of war cemeteries.
INTL ORGS: Special Commission.
PARTIES:
Australia SIGNED: 31 Oct 51 FORCE: 31 Oct 51
Canada SIGNED: 31 Oct 51 FORCE: 31 Oct 51
France SIGNED: 31 Oct 51 FORCE: 31 Oct 51
India SIGNED: 31 Oct 51 FORCE: 31 Oct 51
New Zealand SIGNED: 31 Oct 51 FORCE: 31 Oct 51
Pakistan SIGNED: 31 Oct 51 FORCE: 31 Oct 51
South Africa SIGNED: 31 Oct 51 FORCE: 31 Oct 51
UK Great Britain SIGNED: 31 Oct 51 FORCE: 31 Oct 51

102248 Bilateral Convention **172 UNTS 205**
SIGNED: 28 Nov 51   FORCE: 1 May 53
REGISTERED: 31 Aug 53 UK Great Britain
ARTICLES: 40 LANGUAGE: English. Italian.
HEADNOTE: SOCIAL SECURITY
TOPIC: Non-ILO Labor
CONCEPTS: Definition of terms. General provisions. Conformity with municipal law. Domestic legislation. Incorporation of treaty provisions into national law. Dispute settlement. Old age and invalidity insurance. Non-ILO labor relations. Family allowances. Administrative cooperation. Old age insurance. Sickness and invalidity insurance. Social security. Fees and exemptions. Payment schedules.
PROCEDURE: Denunciation. Duration. Ratification. Renewal or Revival.
PARTIES:
Italy
UK Great Britain
ANNEX
344 UNTS 327. Italy. Jersey Island. Acknowledgement 19 May 58. Force 1 May 58.
344 UNTS 327. UK Great Britain. Jersey Island. Force 1 May 58.
618 UNTS 374. UK Great Britain. Prolongation 7 Jun 68. Force 1 Jul 68.
618 UNTS 374. Italy. Prolongation 7 Jun 68. Force 1 Jul 68.

102249 Bilateral Exchange **172 UNTS 257**
SIGNED: 2 Mar 53   FORCE: 2 Mar 53
REGISTERED: 31 Aug 53 UK Great Britain
ARTICLES: 2 LANGUAGE: English.
HEADNOTE: HIGH ALTITUDE INTERCEPTOR RANGE
TOPIC: Milit Installation
CONCEPTS: Annex or appendix reference. General cooperation. Testing ranges and sites.
TREATY REF: 97UNTS193.
PROCEDURE: Termination.
PARTIES:
UK Great Britain
USA (United States)

102250 Bilateral Exchange **172 UNTS 265**
SIGNED: 1 Jun 53   FORCE: 16 Jun 53
REGISTERED: 31 Aug 53 UK Great Britain
ARTICLES: 2 LANGUAGE: English.
HEADNOTE: RECIPROCAL ABOLITION VISAS
TOPIC: Visas
CONCEPTS: Emergencies. Territorial application. Visa abolition. Denial of admission. Conformity with municipal law.
PARTIES:
Greece
UK Great Britain
ANNEX
267 UNTS 383. UK Great Britain. Gibralter. Force 20 Jul 55.

102251 Bilateral Exchange **172 UNTS 271**
SIGNED: 13 Apr 53   FORCE: 13 Apr 53
REGISTERED: 31 Aug 53 UK Great Britain
ARTICLES: 2 LANGUAGE: English.
HEADNOTE: RECIPROCAL PAYMENT COMPENSATION
TOPIC: Reparations
CONCEPTS: Time limit. Annex or appendix reference. Payment schedules. Lump sum settlements. National treatment. Loss and/or damage. Reparations and restrictions.
PROCEDURE: Application to Non-self-governing Territories.
PARTIES:
Italy
UK Great Britain

102252 Bilateral Agreement **172 UNTS 281**
SIGNED: 25 Mar 53   FORCE: 25 Mar 53
REGISTERED: 31 Aug 53 UK Great Britain
ARTICLES: 4 LANGUAGE: Arabic. English.
HEADNOTE: FINANCE
TOPIC: Finance
CONCEPTS: Detailed regulations. Democratic institutions. Independence maintenance. Private contracts. Interest rates. Payment schedules. Claims and settlements. Loan and credit. Credit provisions. Loan repayment. Surplus war property.
INTL ORGS: United Nations.
PARTIES:
Libya
UK Great Britain

102253 Bilateral Agreement **172 UNTS 293**
SIGNED: 16 Jun 51   FORCE: 16 Jun 51
REGISTERED: 31 Aug 53 UK Great Britain
ARTICLES: 9 LANGUAGE: English. Italian.
HEADNOTE: PATENTS INVENTIONS
TOPIC: Patents/Copyrights
CONCEPTS: Definition of terms. Territorial application. Non-prejudice to third party. Conformity with municipal law. Laws and formalities.
PROCEDURE: Ratification. Termination.
PARTIES:
Italy
UK Great Britain

102254 Bilateral Exchange **172 UNTS 303**
SIGNED: 21 Nov 52   FORCE: 21 Nov 52
REGISTERED: 31 Aug 53 UK Great Britain
ARTICLES: 2 LANGUAGE: English.
HEADNOTE: SETTLEMENT PRE-WAR EXTERNAL BONDED DEBTS
TOPIC: Reparations
CONCEPTS: Treaty implementation. Annex or appendix reference. Currency. Debt settlement. Post-war claims settlement.
TREATY REF: 149UNTS227.
PARTIES:
Japan
UK Great Britain

102255 Multilateral Agreement **173 UNTS 2**
SIGNED: 11 Apr 52   FORCE: 11 Apr 52
REGISTERED: 1 Sep 53 United Nations
ARTICLES: 4 LANGUAGE: English.
HEADNOTE: TECHNICAL ASSISTANCE
TOPIC: Tech Assistance
CONCEPTS: Detailed regulations. Time limit. Privileges and immunities. General cooperation. Personnel. Scholarships and grants. Expense sharing formulae. Domestic obligation. General technical assistance. Conformity with IGO decisions.
INTL ORGS: Special Commission.
TREATY REF: 76UNTS132; 1UNTS15,263; 33UNTS261.
PROCEDURE: Amendment. Termination.
PARTIES:
FAO (Food Agri) SIGNED: 11 Apr 52 FORCE: 11 Apr 52
ICAO (Civil Aviat) SIGNED: 11 Apr 52 FORCE: 11 Apr 52
ILO (Labor Org) SIGNED: 11 Apr 52 FORCE: 11 Apr 52
UNESCO (Educ/Cult) SIGNED: 11 Apr 52 FORCE: 11 Apr 52
United Nations SIGNED: 11 Apr 52 FORCE: 11 Apr 52

Yugoslavia SIGNED: 11 Apr 52 FORCE: 11 Apr 52
ANNEX
356 UNTS 365. UNTAB (Tech Assis). Amendment 18 Jun 59. Force 23 Dec 59.
356 UNTS 365. Yugoslavia. Amendment 4 Apr 59. Force 23 Dec 59.

102256 Multilateral Agreement **173 UNTS 15**
SIGNED: 5 Sep 51   FORCE: 2 Sep 51
REGISTERED: 1 Sep 53 United Nations
ARTICLES: 5 LANGUAGE: English. French.
HEADNOTE: TECHNICAL ASSISTANCE
TOPIC: Tech Assistance
CONCEPTS: Treaty implementation. Annex or appendix reference. Privileges and immunities. General cooperation. Personnel. Title and deeds. Scholarships and grants. Vocational training. Expense sharing formulae. Local currency. Domestic obligation. General technical assistance. Materials, equipment and services. IGO status. Conformity with IGO decisions.
TREATY REF: 76UNTS132; 1UNTS15.
PROCEDURE: Amendment. Ratification. Termination.
PARTIES:
FAO (Food Agri) SIGNED: 5 Sep 51 FORCE: 5 Sep 51
ICAO (Civil Aviat) SIGNED: 5 Sep 51 FORCE: 5 Sep 51
ILO (Labor Org) SIGNED: 5 Sep 51 FORCE: 5 Sep 51
United Nations SIGNED: 5 Sep 51 FORCE: 5 Sep 51
WHO (World Health) SIGNED: 5 Sep 51 FORCE: 5 Sep 51
Turkey SIGNED: 5 Sep 51 FORCE: 5 Sep 51
ANNEX
259 UNTS 444. UNTAB (Tech Assis). Force 23 Jan 57.
259 UNTS 444. Turkey. Force 23 Jan 57.

102257 Bilateral Exchange **173 UNTS 31**
SIGNED: 29 Sep 52   FORCE: 29 Sep 52
REGISTERED: 2 Sep 53 Thailand
ARTICLES: 2 LANGUAGE: English.
HEADNOTE: COMMERCE NAVIGATION
TOPIC: General Economic
CONCEPTS: Previous treaty extension.
TREATY REF: 188LTS33; 197LTS400; 200LTS558; 2UNTS215.
PROCEDURE: Duration. Termination.
PARTIES:
Thailand
UK Great Britain

102258 Bilateral Instrument **173 UNTS 37**
SIGNED: 27 Mar 53   FORCE: 27 Jun 53
REGISTERED: 7 Sep 53 South Africa
ARTICLES: 1 LANGUAGE: English.
HEADNOTE: REVIVAL PRE-WAR TREATIES
TOPIC: Admin Cooperation
CONCEPTS: Revival of treaties.
TREATY REF: 136UNTS45; 16UNTS207; 19LTS288.
PARTIES:
Japan
South Africa

102259 Bilateral Treaty **173 UNTS 41**
SIGNED: 25 Jun 52   FORCE: 12 May 53
REGISTERED: 10 Sep 53 Pakistan
ARTICLES: 8 LANGUAGE: Burmese. English. Urdu.
HEADNOTE: FRIENDSHIP
TOPIC: General Amity
CONCEPTS: Friendship and amity. Consular relations establishment. Diplomatic relations establishment. Privileges and immunities. General cooperation. Procedure.
PROCEDURE: Duration. Future Procedures Contemplated. Ratification. Termination.
PARTIES:
Burma
Pakistan

102260 Bilateral Exchange **173 UNTS 53**
SIGNED: 5 Aug 53   FORCE: 1 Sep 53
REGISTERED: 19 Sep 53 Belgium
ARTICLES: 2 LANGUAGE: French.

HEADNOTE: RECIPROCAL ABOLITION VISAS
TOPIC: Visas
CONCEPTS: Time limit. Visa abolition. Denial of admission. Resident permits. Non-visa travel documents. Conformity with municipal law. Fees and exemptions.
INTL ORGS: Council of Europe.
PROCEDURE: Denunciation.
PARTIES:
  Belgium
  Greece

102261 Bilateral Exchange **173 UNTS 61**
SIGNED: 29 Apr 53   FORCE: 29 Apr 53
REGISTERED: 19 Sep 53 Belgium
ARTICLES: 2 LANGUAGE: Dutch.
HEADNOTE: ISSUE FREE CHARGE EXTRACTS FROM CIVIL STATUS
TOPIC: Admin Cooperation
CONCEPTS: Exchange of information and documents. Fees and exemptions.
PARTIES:
  Belgium
  Netherlands

102262 Bilateral Convention **173 UNTS 67**
SIGNED: 28 Oct 48   FORCE: 1 Jan 53
REGISTERED: 24 Sep 53 Belgium
ARTICLES: 23 LANGUAGE: English. French.
HEADNOTE: DOUBLE TAXATION FISCAL EVASION TAXES INCOME
TOPIC: Taxation
CONCEPTS: Definition of terms. Territorial application. Conformity with municipal law. Exchange of official publications. Domestic legislation. Teacher and student exchange. Claims and settlements. Taxation. General. Tax exemptions. Air transport. Merchant vessels.
PROCEDURE: Duration. Ratification. Termination.
PARTIES:
  Belgium
  USA (United States)
             ANNEX
356 UNTS 366.   Belgium.   Supplementation 22 Aug 57. Force 10 Jul 59.
356 UNTS 366. USA (United States). Supplementation 22 Aug 57. Force 10 Jul 59.
617 UNTS 364.   Belgium.   Prolongation 11 Dec 67. Force 11 Dec 67.
617 UNTS 364. USA (United States). Prolongation 11 Dec 67. Force 11 Dec 67.

102263 Bilateral Agreement **173 UNTS 99**
SIGNED: 24 Jan 48   FORCE: 16 Feb 49
REGISTERED: 24 Sep 53 France
ARTICLES: 24 LANGUAGE: French.
HEADNOTE: MONETARY & FINANCIAL RELATIONS
TOPIC: Finance
CONCEPTS: Detailed regulations. Annex or appendix reference. Previous treaty replacement. Conformity with municipal law. General cooperation. Exchange of information and documents. Informational records. Licenses and permits. General property. Procedure. Existing tribunals. Meteorology. Export quotas. Import quotas. Accounting procedures. Banking. Bonds. Currency. Exchange rates and regulations. Financial programs. Interest rates. Payment schedules. Local currency. Assets. Claims and settlements. Debt settlement. Assets transfer. Quotas. Tax exemptions. Credit provisions. Telecommunications. Surplus war property.
INTL ORGS: International Monetary Fund. Special Commission.
TREATY REF: 173UNTS727.
PROCEDURE: Amendment. Duration. Ratification. Renewal or Revival.
PARTIES:
  France
  Lebanon

102264 Multilateral Protocol **173 UNTS 143**
SIGNED: 7 Feb 53   FORCE: 1 Jul 53
REGISTERED: 25 Sep 53 Norway
ARTICLES: 9 LANGUAGE: Finnish. Norwegian. Russian.
HEADNOTE: MAINTENANCE FRONTIER MARK MUOTKAUAARA
TOPIC: Territory Boundary

CONCEPTS: Definition of terms. Inspection and observation. Markers and definitions.
INTL ORGS: Special Commission.
PROCEDURE: Denunciation. Duration. Renewal or Revival.
PARTIES:
  Finland SIGNED: 7 Feb 53 FORCE: 1 Jul 53
  Norway SIGNED: 7 Feb 53 FORCE: 1 Jul 53
  USSR (Soviet Union) SIGNED: 7 Feb 53 FORCE: 1 Jul 53

102265 Bilateral Agreement **173 UNTS 163**
SIGNED: 20 May 53   FORCE: 20 May 53
REGISTERED: 25 Sep 53 Norway
ARTICLES: 6 LANGUAGE: Finnish. Norwegian.
HEADNOTE: FISHING REGULATIONS
TOPIC: Specific Resources
CONCEPTS: Annex or appendix reference. Previous treaty replacement. Conformity with municipal law. Inspection and observation. Fees and exemptions. Aquisition of property. Ocean resources.
TREATY REF: 187LTS231; 34UNTS9.
PROCEDURE: Termination.
PARTIES:
  Finland
  Norway
             ANNEX
338 UNTS 373.   Norway.   Supplementation 2 Jun 59. Force 1 Jun 59.
338 UNTS 373.   Finland.   Supplementation 2 Jun 59. Force 1 Jun 59.

102266 Bilateral Exchange **173 UNTS 193**
SIGNED: 13 Dec 49   FORCE: 1 Jan 50
REGISTERED: 3 Oct 53 Belgium
ARTICLES: 2 LANGUAGE: French.
HEADNOTE: EXCHANGE OFFICIAL PUBLICATIONS
TOPIC: Admin Cooperation
CONCEPTS: Exchange of official publications. Operating agencies.
PARTIES:
  Belgium
  Denmark

102267 Bilateral Agreement **173 UNTS 199**
SIGNED: 28 May 53   FORCE: 28 May 53
REGISTERED: 5 Oct 53 ICAO (Civil Aviat)
ARTICLES: 6 LANGUAGE: English.
HEADNOTE: TECHNICAL ASSISTANCE
TOPIC: Tech Assistance
CONCEPTS: Treaty implementation. Privileges and immunities. General cooperation. Exchange of information and documents. Personnel. Title and deeds. Exchange. Scholarships and grants. Vocational training. Expense sharing formulae. Local currency. Domestic obligation. General technical assistance. Materials, equipment and services. IGO status. Conformity with IGO decisions.
INTL ORGS: United Nations.
TREATY REF: 76UNTS132; 1UNTS15,263; 33UNTS261.
PROCEDURE: Amendment. Termination.
PARTIES:
  ICAO (Civil Aviat)
  Syria

102268 Bilateral Agreement **173 UNTS 209**
SIGNED: 14 Jun 52   FORCE: 18 Dec 52
REGISTERED: 5 Oct 53 ICAO (Civil Aviat)
ARTICLES: 19 LANGUAGE: Arabic. English.
HEADNOTE: ESTABLISHMENT SCHEDULED AIR SERVICES
TOPIC: Air Transport
CONCEPTS: Definition of terms. Detailed regulations. Exceptions and exemptions. Annex or appendix reference. Conformity with municipal law. General cooperation. Exchange of information and documents. Arbitration. Procedure. Existing tribunals. Negotiation. Non-interest rates and fees. Most favored nation clause. Customs exemptions. Routes and logistics. Navigational conditions. Permit designation. Air transport. Conditions of airlines operating permission. Overflights and technical stops. Operating authorizations and regulations.
INTL ORGS: International Civil Aviation Organization.
TREATY REF: 15UNTSI95; 84UNTSI95.

PROCEDURE: Amendment. Future Procedures Contemplated. Ratification. Registration. Termination.
PARTIES:
  India
  United Arab Rep

102269 Bilateral Agreement **173 UNTS 241**
SIGNED: 14 Jun 52   FORCE: 12 Oct 52
REGISTERED: 5 Oct 53 ICAO (Civil Aviat)
ARTICLES: 27 LANGUAGE: Arabic. English.
HEADNOTE: ESTABLISHMENT SCHEDULED AIR SERVICES
TOPIC: Air Transport
CONCEPTS: Definition of terms. Detailed regulations. Exceptions and exemptions. Annex or appendix reference. Conformity with municipal law. General cooperation. Exchange of information and documents. Arbitration. Procedure. Existing tribunals. Negotiation. Non-interest rates and fees. Customs exemptions. Routes and logistics. Air transport. Conditions of airlines operating permission. Overflights and technical stops. Operating authorizations and regulations.
INTL ORGS: International Civil Aviation Organization.
TREATY REF: 15UNTS295; 84UNTS389.
PROCEDURE: Amendment. Future Procedures Contemplated. Ratification. Registration. Termination.
PARTIES:
  Australia
  United Arab Rep
             ANNEX
335 UNTS 302. Australia. Amendment 25 Jul 55. Force 1 Aug 55.
335 UNTS 302. United Arab Rep. Amendment 1 Aug 55. Force 1 Aug 55.

102270 Bilateral Agreement **173 UNTS 277**
SIGNED: 17 Nov 52   FORCE: 17 Nov 52
REGISTERED: 5 Oct 53 ICAO (Civil Aviat)
ARTICLES: 11 LANGUAGE: French. Swedish.
HEADNOTE: AIR SERVICES
TOPIC: Air Transport
CONCEPTS: Definition of terms. Annex or appendix reference. Conformity with municipal law. General cooperation. Licenses and permits. Recognition of legal documents. Use of facilities. Arbitration. Procedure. Existing tribunals. Negotiation. Fees and exemptions. Non-interest rates and fees. Most favored nation clause. National treatment. Customs exemptions. Competency certificate. Routes and logistics. Navigational conditions. Permit designation. Air transport. Airport facilities. Airworthiness certificates. Conditions of airlines operating permission. Operating authorizations and regulations. Licenses and certificates of nationality.
INTL ORGS: International Civil Aviation Organization.
TREATY REF: 15UNTS295.
PROCEDURE: Amendment. Future Procedures Contemplated. Ratification. Registration. Termination.
PARTIES:
  Luxembourg
  Sweden

102271 Bilateral Exchange **173 UNTS 299**
SIGNED: 9 Jan 53   FORCE: 9 Jan 53
REGISTERED: 5 Oct 53 ICAO (Civil Aviat)
ARTICLES: 2 LANGUAGE: English.
HEADNOTE: REGULATION AIR SERVICES
TOPIC: Air Transport
CONCEPTS: Definition of terms. Exceptions and exemptions. Responsibility and liability. Non-interest rates and fees. Routes and logistics. Air transport. Overflights and technical stops. Operating authorizations and regulations.
INTL ORGS: International Civil Aviation Organization.
TREATY REF: 15UNTS295.
PROCEDURE: Duration. Renewal or Revival. Termination. Application to Non-self-governing Territories.
PARTIES:
  South Africa
  Sweden

102272 Bilateral Agreement **173 UNTS 307**
SIGNED: 20 Feb 53 FORCE: 24 Jul 53
REGISTERED: 5 Oct 53 ICAO (Civil Aviat)
ARTICLES: 19 LANGUAGE: English.
HEADNOTE: AIR SERVICES
TOPIC: Air Transport
CONCEPTS: Definition of terms. Detailed regulations. Exceptions and exemptions. Conformity
with municipal law. General cooperation. Exchange of information and documents. Use of
facilities. Arbitration. Procedure. Special tribunals. Negotiation. Fees and exemptions. Non-
interest rates and fees. Most favored nation
clause. National treatment. Customs exemptions. Routes and logistics. Permit designation.
Air transport. Airport facilities. Conditions of airlines operating permission. Overflights and technical stops. Operating authorizations and regulations.
INTL ORGS: International Civil Aviation Organization.
TREATY REF: 15UNTS295.
PROCEDURE: Amendment. Future Procedures
Contemplated. Ratification. Registration. Termination. Application to Non-self-governing Territories.
PARTIES:
Japan
Sweden
        ANNEX
216 UNTS 414. Sweden. Amendment 19 Jul 54.
Force 19 Jul 54.
216 UNTS 414. Japan. Amendment 19 Jul 54.
Force 19 Jul 54.

102273 Bilateral Agreement **173 UNTS 329**
SIGNED: 26 Feb 53 FORCE: 14 Jul 53
REGISTERED: 5 Oct 53 ICAO (Civil Aviat)
ARTICLES: 19 LANGUAGE: English.
HEADNOTE: AIR SERVICES
TOPIC: Air Transport
CONCEPTS: Definition of terms. Detailed regulations. Exceptions and exemptions. Conformity
with municipal law. General cooperation. Exchange of information and documents. Use of
facilities. Arbitration. Procedure. Fees and exemptions. Non-interest rates and fees. Most favored nation clause. National treatment. Customs exemptions. Routes and logistics. Permit
designation. Air transport. Airport facilities. Conditions of airlines operating permission. Overflights and technical stops. Operating authorizations and regulations.
INTL ORGS: International Civil Aviation Organization.
TREATY REF: 15UNTS295.
PROCEDURE: Amendment. Future Procedures
Contemplated. Registration. Termination. Application to Non-self-governing Territories.
PARTIES:
Denmark
Japan
        ANNEX
231 UNTS 366. Denmark. Amendment 19 Jul 54.
Force 19 Jul 54.
231 UNTS 366. Japan. Amendment 19 Jul 54.
Force 19 Jul 54.

102274 Bilateral Agreement **174 UNTS 3**
SIGNED: 27 Apr 53 FORCE: 27 Apr 53
REGISTERED: 5 Oct 53 ICAO (Civil Aviat)
ARTICLES: 13 LANGUAGE: English.
HEADNOTE: AIR SERVICES
TOPIC: Air Transport
CONCEPTS: Definition of terms. Exceptions and
exemptions. Annex or appendix reference. Conformity with municipal law. Use of facilities. Arbitration. Procedure. Existing tribunals. Negotiation. Reexport of goods, etc.. Fees and exemptions. Most favored nation clause. National
treatment. Customs exemptions. Competency
certificate. Routes and logistics. Navigational
conditions. Permit designation. Air transport. Airport facilities. Airworthiness certificates. Conditions of airlines operating permission. Operating
authorizations and regulations. Licenses and certificates of nationality.
INTL ORGS: International Civil Aviation Organization.
TREATY REF: 15UNTS295.
PROCEDURE: Amendment. Future Procedures
Contemplated. Registration. Termination.

PARTIES:
Philippines
Thailand

102275 Bilateral Exchange **174 UNTS 19**
SIGNED: 30 Apr 53 FORCE: 10 Jan 53
REGISTERED: 5 Oct 53 ICAO (Civil Aviat)
ARTICLES: 2 LANGUAGE: English.
HEADNOTE: REGULATION AIR SERVICES
TOPIC: Air Transport
CONCEPTS: Definition of terms. Exceptions and
exemptions. Responsibility and liability. Non-
interest rates and fees. Routes and logistics. Air
transport. Overflights and technical stops. Oper-
ating authorizations and regulations.
INTL ORGS: International Civil Aviation Organiza-
tion.
PROCEDURE: Duration. Renewal or Revival. Termi-
nation. Application to Non-self-governing Terri-
tories.
PARTIES:
Denmark
South Africa

102276 Bilateral Agreement **174 UNTS 29**
SIGNED: 19 Jun 53 FORCE: 14 Jul 53
REGISTERED: 5 Oct 53 ICAO (Civil Aviat)
ARTICLES: 19 LANGUAGE: English.
HEADNOTE: AIR SERVICES
TOPIC: Air Transport
CONCEPTS: Definition of terms. Detailed regulations. Exceptions and exemptions. Annex or appendix reference. Previous treaty replacement.
Conformity with municipal law. General cooperation. Use of facilities. Arbitration. Procedure.
Special tribunals. Negotiation. Fees and exemptions. Non-interest rates and fees. Most favored
nation clause. National treatment. Customs exemptions. Routes and logistics. Permit designation. Air transport. Airport facilities. Conditions
of airlines operating permission. Overflights and
technical stops. Operating authorizations and
regulations.
INTL ORGS: International Civil Aviation Organization.
TREATY REF: 15UNTS295; 200LTS197.
PROCEDURE: Amendment. Future Procedures
Contemplated. Ratification. Registration. Termination. Application to Non-self-governing Territories.
PARTIES:
Japan
Thailand
        ANNEX
464 UNTS 320. Japan. Amendment 6 Jul 62.
Force 6 Jul 62.
464 UNTS 320. Thailand. Amendment 6 Jul 62.
Force 6 Jul 62.
601 UNTS 348. Japan. Amendment 22 Jan 65.
Force 22 Jan 65.
601 UNTS 348. Thailand. Amendment 22 Jan 65.
Force 22 Jan 65.

102277 Bilateral Agreement **174 UNTS 49**
SIGNED: 22 Jun 53 FORCE: 22 Jun 53
REGISTERED: 5 Oct 53 ICAO (Civil Aviat)
ARTICLES: 15 LANGUAGE: English.
HEADNOTE: AIR TRANSPORT
TOPIC: Air Transport
CONCEPTS: Definition of terms. Exceptions and
exemptions. Annex or appendix reference. Non-
prejudice to third party. Conformity with municipal law. Licenses and permits. Recognition of
legal documents. Use of facilities. Special tribunals. Competence of tribunal. Indemnities and
reimbursements. Fees and exemptions. Most favored nation clause. National treatment. Customs exemptions. Competency certificate.
Routes and logistics. Navigational conditions.
Permit designation. Air transport. Airport facilities. Airworthiness certificates. Conditions of airlines operating permission. Operating authorizations and regulations. Licenses and certificates
of nationality.
INTL ORGS: International Civil Aviation Organization.
TREATY REF: 15UNTS295.
PROCEDURE: Amendment. Future Procedures
Contemplated. Registration. Termination.

PARTIES:
Burma
Norway

102278 Bilateral Agreement **174 UNTS 71**
SIGNED: 30 Apr 53 FORCE: 30 Apr 53
REGISTERED: 6 Oct 53 WHO (World Health)
ARTICLES: 6 LANGUAGE: French.
HEADNOTE: TECHNICAL ADVISORY ASSISTANCE
TOPIC: Tech Assistance
CONCEPTS: Definition of terms. Treaty implemen-
tation. Privileges and immunities. General coop-
eration. Exchange of information and docu-
ments. Personnel. Title and deeds. Exchange.
Scholarships and grants. Vocational training.
Research and development. Expense sharing for-
mulae. Local currency. Domestic obligation.
General technical assistance. Special projects.
Materials, equipment and services. IGO status.
Conformity with IGO decisions.
INTL ORGS: United Nations.
TREATY REF: 76UNTS132; 33UNTS261.
PROCEDURE: Amendment. Termination.
PARTIES:
France
WHO (World Health)

102279 Bilateral Agreement **174 UNTS 83**
SIGNED: 2 Apr 53 FORCE: 2 Apr 53
REGISTERED: 6 Oct 53 WHO (World Health)
ARTICLES: 6 LANGUAGE: French.
HEADNOTE: TECHNICAL ADVISORY ASSISTANCE
TOPIC: Tech Assistance
CONCEPTS: Definition of terms. Treaty implemen-
tation. Privileges and immunities. General coop-
eration. Exchange of information and docu-
ments. Personnel. Title and deeds. Education. Ex-
change. Scholarships and grants. Vocational
training. Research and development. Expense
sharing formulae. Local currency. Domestic obli-
gation. General technical assistance. Special
projects. Materials, equipment and services.
Conformity with IGO decisions.
INTL ORGS: United Nations.
TREATY REF: 76UNTS132; 33UNTS261.
PROCEDURE: Amendment. Termination.
PARTIES:
France
WHO (World Health)

102280 Bilateral Agreement **174 UNTS 95**
SIGNED: 23 Apr 53 FORCE: 28 Jul 53
REGISTERED: 6 Oct 53 Denmark
ARTICLES: 7 LANGUAGE: French.
HEADNOTE: COMMERCE
TOPIC: General Trade
CONCEPTS: Detailed regulations. Exceptions and
exemptions. Annex or appendix reference. Previ-
ous treaty replacement. General cooperation. Li-
censes and permits. Establishment of commis-
sion. Export quotas. Payment schedules. Quotas.
INTL ORGS: Special Commission.
TREATY REF: 23LTS139.
PROCEDURE: Denunciation. Duration. Ratification.
PARTIES:
Czechoslovakia
Denmark

102281 Bilateral Agreement **174 UNTS 107**
SIGNED: 23 Apr 53 FORCE: 23 Apr 53
REGISTERED: 6 Oct 53 Denmark
ARTICLES: 6 LANGUAGE: French.
HEADNOTE: PAYMENTS
TOPIC: Finance
CONCEPTS: Previous treaty replacement. Confor-
mity with municipal law. General cooperation.
Accounting procedures. Banking. Balance of
payments. Currency. Exchange rates and regula-
tions. Financial programs. Inadequacy of funds.
Interest rates. Payment schedules. Local cur-
rency.
TREATY REF: 133UNTS363.
PROCEDURE: Amendment. Duration. Renewal or
Revival.
PARTIES:
Czechoslovakia
Denmark

102282 Bilateral Agreement **174 UNTS 115**
SIGNED: 8 Sep 51　　　　FORCE: 17 Sep 51
REGISTERED: 7 Oct 53 USA (United States)
ARTICLES: 5 LANGUAGE: English. French. Cambodian.
HEADNOTE: ECONOMIC COOPERATION
TOPIC: Direct Aid
CONCEPTS: Treaty interpretation. Annex or appendix reference. Privileges and immunities. Conformity with municipal law. General cooperation. Exchange of information and documents. Inspection and observation. Personnel. Commodities and services. Domestic obligation. General technical assistance. Economic assistance. Aid missions. Procurement. Distribution.
PROCEDURE: Registration. Termination.
PARTIES:
　Cambodia
　USA (United States)

102283 Bilateral Agreement **174 UNTS 141**
SIGNED: 9 Sep 51　　　　FORCE: 9 Sep 51
REGISTERED: 7 Oct 53 USA (United States)
ARTICLES: 5 LANGUAGE: English. French. Laotian.
HEADNOTE: ECONOMIC COOPERATION AGREEMENT
TOPIC: Direct Aid
CONCEPTS: Treaty interpretation. Annex or appendix reference. Privileges and immunities. Conformity with municipal law. General cooperation. Exchange of information and documents. Inspection and observation. Personnel. Commodities and services. Domestic obligation. General technical assistance. Economic assistance. Aid missions. Procurement. Distribution.
PROCEDURE: Registration. Termination.
PARTIES:
　Laos
　USA (United States)

102284 Bilateral Agreement **174 UNTS 165**
SIGNED: 7 Sep 51　　　　FORCE: 7 Sep 51
REGISTERED: 7 Oct 53 USA (United States)
ARTICLES: 5 LANGUAGE: English. French. Vietnamese.
HEADNOTE: ECONOMIC COOPERATION
TOPIC: Direct Aid
CONCEPTS: Treaty interpretation. Annex or appendix reference. Privileges and immunities. Conformity with municipal law. General cooperation. Exchange of information and documents. Inspection and observation. Personnel. Commodities and services. Domestic obligation. General technical assistance. Economic assistance. Aid missions. Procurement. Distribution.
PROCEDURE: Registration. Termination.
PARTIES:
　USA (United States)
　Vietnam, South
ANNEX
458 UNTS 300. Vietnam, South. Amendment 7 Jun 62. Force 7 Jun 62.
458 UNTS 300. USA (United States). Amendment 7 Jun 62. Force 7 Jun 62.

102285 Bilateral Exchange **174 UNTS 187**
SIGNED: 30 May 46　　　　FORCE: 30 May 46
REGISTERED: 7 Oct 53 USA (United States)
ARTICLES: 4 LANGUAGE: English. Portuguese.
HEADNOTE: AIR TRANSIT FACILITIES AZORES
TOPIC: Air Transport
CONCEPTS: Exceptions and exemptions. Time limit. Previous treaty extension. General cooperation. Personnel. Use of facilities. Financial programs. Tax exemptions. Customs duties. Air transport. Airport facilities. Overflights and technical stops. Operating authorizations and regulations. Status of military forces. Facilities and property.
TREATY REF: TAIS 2338.
PROCEDURE: Denunciation. Duration. Renewal or Revival.
PARTIES:
　Portugal
　USA (United States)

102286 Bilateral Agreement **174 UNTS 201**
SIGNED: 14 Nov 51　　　　FORCE: 14 Nov 51
REGISTERED: 7 Oct 53 USA (United States)
ARTICLES: 7 LANGUAGE: English. Serbo-Croat.

HEADNOTE: MILITARY ASSISTANCE
TOPIC: Milit Assistance
CONCEPTS: Exceptions and exemptions. Non-prejudice to UN charter. Privileges and immunities. Conformity with municipal law. Inspection and observation. Public information. Use of facilities. Indemnities and reimbursements. Local currency. Recognition. Customs exemptions. Domestic obligation. Materials, equipment and services. Self-defense. Security of information. Exchange of defense information. Restrictions on transfer. Raw materials.
PROCEDURE: Amendment. Future Procedures Contemplated. Registration. Termination.
PARTIES:
　USA (United States)
　Yugoslavia
ANNEX
258 UNTS 420. Yugoslavia. Implementation 22 May 55. Force 22 May 55.
258 UNTS 420. USA (United States). Implementation 19 May 55. Force 22 May 55.

102287 Bilateral Exchange **174 UNTS 215**
SIGNED: 17 Apr 52　　　　FORCE: 17 Apr 52
REGISTERED: 7 Oct 53 USA (United States)
ARTICLES: 2 LANGUAGE: English. Spanish.
HEADNOTE: MILITARY ASSISTANCE
TOPIC: Milit Assistance
CONCEPTS: Exceptions and exemptions. Guarantees and safeguards. Non-prejudice to UN charter. Peaceful relations. Privileges and immunities. Conformity with municipal law. General cooperation. Inspection and observation. Public information. Indemnities and reimbursements. Garnishment of funds. Local currency. Claims and settlements. Most favored nation clause. Recognition. Customs exemptions. Domestic obligation. Materials, equipment and services. Joint defense. Defense and security. Self-defense. Military assistance. Return of equipment and recapture. Security of information. Exchange of defense information. Restrictions on transfer.
INTL ORGS: United Nations.
TREATY REF: 132UNTS305.
PROCEDURE: Amendment. Future Procedures Contemplated. Registration. Termination.
PARTIES:
　Colombia
　USA (United States)
ANNEX
270 UNTS 392. Colombia. Supplementation 14 Mar 56. Force 14 Mar 56.
270 UNTS 392. USA (United States). Supplementation 22 Feb 56. Force 14 Mar 56.

102288 Bilateral Exchange **174 UNTS 233**
SIGNED: 25 Feb 52　　　　FORCE: 25 Feb 52
REGISTERED: 7 Oct 53 USA (United States)
ARTICLES: 2 LANGUAGE: English. Spanish.
HEADNOTE: MILITARY AIR TRANSIT RIGHTS
TOPIC: Status of Forces
CONCEPTS: Previous treaty replacement. Inviolability. Conformity with municipal law. General cooperation. Overflights and technical stops. Air-force-army-navy personnel ratio. Ranks and privileges. Status of military forces. Procurement and logistics.
INTL ORGS: International Civil Aviation Organization.
PARTIES:
　Costa Rica
　USA (United States)

102289 Bilateral Exchange **174 UNTS 243**
SIGNED: 7 Jan 52　　　　FORCE: 22 Jan 52
REGISTERED: 7 Oct 53 USA (United States)
ARTICLES: 2 LANGUAGE: English. Spanish.
HEADNOTE: COOPERATIVE PROGRAM AGRICULTURE
TOPIC: Direct Aid
CONCEPTS: Annex type material. Personnel. Wages and salaries. Attachment of funds. Funding procedures. Garnishment of funds. Seizure funds. Domestic obligation. Agriculture.
PROCEDURE: Duration. Termination.
PARTIES:
　Dominican Republic
　USA (United States)

102290 Bilateral Agreement **174 UNTS 251**
SIGNED: 27 Apr 51　　　　FORCE: 21 May 51
REGISTERED: 7 Oct 53 USA (United States)
ARTICLES: 5 LANGUAGE: English.
HEADNOTE: ECONOMIC TECHNICAL COOPERATION
TOPIC: Direct Aid
CONCEPTS: Treaty implementation. Annex or appendix reference. Privileges and immunities. Conformity with municipal law. General cooperation. Exchange of information and documents. Inspection and observation. Public information. Domestic obligation. General technical assistance. Economic assistance. Aid missions.
PROCEDURE: Ratification. Registration. Termination.
PARTIES:
　Philippines
　USA (United States)

102291 Bilateral Exchange **174 UNTS 267**
SIGNED: 19 Mar 52　　　　FORCE: 19 Mar 52
REGISTERED: 7 Oct 53 USA (United States)
ARTICLES: 2 LANGUAGE: English.
HEADNOTE: MODIFYING AGREEMENT LEASED BASES
TOPIC: Status of Forces
CONCEPTS: Previous treaty amendment. General cooperation. Taxation. Customs exemptions. Postal services. Jurisdiction. Status of forces. Bases and facilities.
INTL ORGS: United States-Canadian Defense Organization.
PARTIES:
　Canada
　USA (United States)

102292 Bilateral Protocol **175 UNTS 3**
SIGNED: 17 Jul 53　　　　FORCE: 17 Jul 53
REGISTERED: 7 Oct 53 Denmark
ARTICLES: 1 LANGUAGE: Danish. Russian.
HEADNOTE: SUPPLY OF GOODS
TOPIC: General Trade
CONCEPTS: Annex or appendix reference. Annex type material.
TREATY REF: 8JULY46.
PARTIES:
　Denmark
　USSR (Soviet Union)

102293 Bilateral Exchange **175 UNTS 13**
SIGNED: 21 Jan 53　　　　FORCE: 21 Jan 53
REGISTERED: 13 Oct 53 UK Great Britain
ARTICLES: 2 LANGUAGE: English. Portuguese.
HEADNOTE: PORTUGUESE PARTICIPATION SHIRE VALLEY PROJECT
TOPIC: Non-IBRD Project
CONCEPTS: Non-bank projects. Frontier waterways. Regulation of natural resources.
PARTIES:
　Portugal
　UK Great Britain

102294 Bilateral Agreement **175 UNTS 23**
SIGNED: 19 Mar 48　　　　FORCE: 28 May 53
REGISTERED: 13 Oct 53 UK Great Britain
ARTICLES: 13 LANGUAGE: English. Spanish.
HEADNOTE: AIR SERVICES
TOPIC: Air Transport
CONCEPTS: Definition of terms. Annex or appendix reference. Conformity with municipal law. Licenses and permits. Recognition of legal documents. Use of facilities. Arbitration. Procedure. Existing tribunals. Competence of tribunal. Fees and exemptions. Most favored nation clause. National treatment. Customs exemptions. Competency certificate. Routes and logistics. Navigational conditions. Permit designation. Airport facilities. Airworthiness certificates. Conditions of airlines operating permission. Operating authorizations and regulations. Licenses and certificates of nationality.
INTL ORGS: International Civil Aviation Organization.
TREATY REF: 15UNTSI95.
PROCEDURE: Amendment. Future Procedures Contemplated. Ratification. Registration. Termination.

PARTIES:
Cuba
UK Great Britain
ANNEX
310 UNTS 365. UK Great Britain. Amendment 28 Jun 57. Force 28 Jun 57.
310 UNTS 365. Cuba. Amendment 28 Jun 57. Force 28 Jun 57.

102295 Bilateral Agreement **175 UNTS 55**
SIGNED: 8 Dec 50 FORCE: 2 Apr 53
REGISTERED: 13 Oct 53 UK Great Britain
ARTICLES: 14 LANGUAGE: English. French.
HEADNOTE: CLAIM SETTLEMENT GERMAN ASSETS
TOPIC: Claims and Debts
CONCEPTS: Definition of terms. Territorial application. Conformity with municipal law. General cooperation. General property. Accounting procedures. Assets. Claims and settlements. Liens.
PARTIES:
Switzerland
UK Great Britain

102296 Multilateral Agreement **175 UNTS 69**
SIGNED: 28 Aug 52 FORCE: 19 Mar 53
REGISTERED: 13 Oct 53 UK Great Britain
ARTICLES: 6 LANGUAGE: English. French.
HEADNOTE: PROPERTY
TOPIC: Claims and Debts
CONCEPTS: Annex or appendix reference. Conformity with municipal law. General property. Accounting procedures. Banking. Currency. Lump sum settlements.
TREATY REF: UK,SWITZERLAND NO 1.(1946) CMD.
PARTIES:
France SIGNED: 28 Aug 52 FORCE: 19 Mar 52
Switzerland SIGNED: 28 Aug 52 FORCE: 19 Mar 52
UK Great Britain SIGNED: 28 Aug 52 FORCE: 19 Mar 52
USA (United States) SIGNED: 28 Aug 52 FORCE: 19 Mar 52

102297 Multilateral Agreement **175 UNTS 89**
SIGNED: 30 Apr 53 FORCE: 1 May 53
REGISTERED: 13 Oct 53 UK Great Britain
ARTICLES: 3 LANGUAGE: English.
HEADNOTE: LIBRARIES PROPERTIES
TOPIC: Admin Cooperation
CONCEPTS: Exchange of information and documents. Expropriation. General property. Public information.
PARTIES:
France SIGNED: 30 Apr 53 FORCE: 1 May 53
Germany, West SIGNED: 30 Apr 53 FORCE: 1 May 53
Italy SIGNED: 30 Apr 53 FORCE: 1 May 53
UK Great Britain SIGNED: 30 Apr 53 FORCE: 1 May 53
USA (United States) SIGNED: 30 Apr 53 FORCE: 1 May 53

102298 Bilateral Exchange **175 UNTS 97**
SIGNED: 22 May 52 FORCE: 9 Jul 52
REGISTERED: 13 Oct 53 UK Great Britain
ARTICLES: 2 LANGUAGE: Arabic. English.
HEADNOTE: TRANSFER PROPERTY
TOPIC: Claims and Debts
CONCEPTS: General property. Responsibility and liability. Claims and settlements. Debts.
TREATY REF: 118LTS231; 132LTS363.
PROCEDURE: Ratification.
PARTIES:
Iraq
UK Great Britain

102299 Bilateral Agreement **175 UNTS 129**
SIGNED: 29 Dec 52 FORCE: 31 Jul 53
REGISTERED: 13 Oct 53 UK Great Britain
ARTICLES: 19 LANGUAGE: English. Japanese.
HEADNOTE: AIR SERVICES
TOPIC: Air Transport
CONCEPTS: Air transport.
INTL ORGS: International Civil Aviation Organization.
TREATY REF: 15UNTS295.

PARTIES:
Japan
UK Great Britain

102300 Bilateral Exchange **175 UNTS 179**
SIGNED: 13 May 53 FORCE: 13 May 53
REGISTERED: 13 Oct 53 UK Great Britain
ARTICLES: 2 LANGUAGE: English.
HEADNOTE: CONVERSION STERLING AIRWAYS EARNINGS
TOPIC: Finance
CONCEPTS: Balance of payments. Currency. Monetary and gold transfers. Exchange rates and regulations. Local currency. Air transport.
TREATY REF: 151UNTS33.
PROCEDURE: Amendment. Duration. Termination.
PARTIES:
Israel
UK Great Britain

102301 Bilateral Agreement **175 UNTS 187**
SIGNED: 21 Dec 50 FORCE: 21 Dec 50
REGISTERED: 13 Oct 53 UK Great Britain
ARTICLES: 11 LANGUAGE: English. Italian.
HEADNOTE: PAYMENTS
TOPIC: Finance
CONCEPTS: Definition of terms. Treaty implementation. Previous treaty replacement. General cooperation. Accounting procedures. Banking. Currency. Monetary and gold transfers. Financial programs. Payment schedules. Local currency.
INTL ORGS: International Monetary Fund.
TREATY REF: CMD7775; CMD7877; CMD8014; CMD8024; CMD8085; 2UNTS.
PARTIES:
Italy
UK Great Britain
ANNEX
183 UNTS 373. UK Great Britain. Amendment 19 Sep 53. Force 19 Sep 53.
183 UNTS 373. Italy. Amendment 19 Sep 53. Force 19 Sep 53.

102302 Multilateral Agreement **175 UNTS 205**
SIGNED: 7 Mar 52 FORCE: 26 Jan 53
REGISTERED: 19 Oct 53 Norway
ARTICLES: 9 LANGUAGE: Norwegian.
HEADNOTE: PROTECTION STOCKS DEEP-SEA PRAWNS
TOPIC: Specific Resources
CONCEPTS: Inspection and observation. Establishment of commission. Ocean resources.
INTL ORGS: Special Commission.
PROCEDURE: Denunciation. Ratification.
PARTIES:
Denmark SIGNED: 7 Mar 52 RATIFIED: 26 Nov 52 FORCE: 26 Jan 53
Norway SIGNED: 7 Mar 52 RATIFIED: 26 Nov 52 FORCE: 26 Jan 53
Sweden SIGNED: 7 Mar 52 RATIFIED: 26 Nov 52 FORCE: 26 Jan 53
ANNEX
427 UNTS 365. Sweden. Amendment 14 Oct 59. Force 14 Oct 59.
427 UNTS 365. Norway. Amendment 14 Oct 59. Force 14 Oct 59.
427 UNTS 365. Denmark. Amendment 14 Oct 59. Force 14 Oct 59.

102303 Multilateral Instrument **175 UNTS 215**
SIGNED: 25 May 51 FORCE: 1 Oct 52
REGISTERED: 19 Oct 53 WHO (World Health)
ARTICLES: 115 LANGUAGE: English. French.
HEADNOTE: WHO REGULATIONS 2
TOPIC: Status of Forces
CONCEPTS: Definition of terms. Detailed regulations. Treaty implementation. Annex or appendix reference. General cooperation. Exchange of information and documents. Inspection and observation. Use of facilities. Procedure. Existing tribunals. Quarantine. Border control. Disease control. Public health. Insect control. Sanitation. Veterinary. WHO used as agency. Airport facilities.
INTL ORGS: United Nations.
TREATY REF: 14UNTS185; 15UNTS447.
PROCEDURE: Accession. Registration. Application to Non-self-governing Territories.

PARTIES:
Afghanistan FORCE: 1 Oct 52
Argentina FORCE: 3 Feb 53
Austria FORCE: 1 Oct 52
Belgium FORCE: 1 Oct 52
Bolivia FORCE: 1 Oct 52
Brazil FORCE: 1 Oct 52
Cambodia FORCE: 1 Oct 52
Canada FORCE: 1 Oct 52
Ceylon (Sri Lanka) SIGNED: 25 May 51 FORCE: 22 Oct 52
Taiwan FORCE: 1 Oct 52
Costa Rica FORCE: 1 Oct 52
Cuba FORCE: 1 Oct 52
Denmark FORCE: 27 Apr 53
Dominican Republic FORCE: 1 Oct 52
Ecuador FORCE: 1 Oct 52
El Salvador FORCE: 1 Oct 52
Ethiopia FORCE: 1 Oct 52
Finland FORCE: 1 Oct 52
France All Territories FORCE: 11 Dec 52
France FORCE: 1 Oct 52
Greece SIGNED: 25 May 51 FORCE: 1 Oct 52
Guatemala FORCE: 1 Oct 52
Haiti FORCE: 1 Oct 52
Honduras FORCE: 1 Oct 52
Iceland FORCE: 1 Oct 52
India SIGNED: 25 May 51 FORCE: 2 Mar 53
Indonesia FORCE: 1 Oct 52
Iran FORCE: 1 Oct 52
Iraq FORCE: 1 Oct 52
Ireland FORCE: 1 Oct 52
Israel FORCE: 1 Oct 52
Italy FORCE: 1 Oct 52
Japan FORCE: 1 Oct 52
Jordan FORCE: 1 Oct 52
Korea, South FORCE: 1 Oct 52
Laos FORCE: 1 Oct 52
Lebanon FORCE: 1 Oct 52
Liberia FORCE: 1 Oct 52
Libya FORCE: 1 Jan 53
Luxembourg FORCE: 1 Oct 52
Mexico FORCE: 1 Oct 52
Monaco FORCE: 1 Oct 52
Netherlands All Territories FORCE: 11 Dec 52
Netherlands FORCE: 1 Oct 52
New Zealand FORCE: 1 Oct 52
New Zealand All Territories FORCE: 11 Dec 52
Nicaragua FORCE: 1 Oct 52
Norway FORCE: 1 Oct 52
Pakistan SIGNED: 25 May 51 FORCE: 1 Oct 52
Panama FORCE: 1 Oct 52
Paraguay FORCE: 1 Oct 52
Peru FORCE: 1 Oct 52
Philippines SIGNED: 25 May 51 FORCE: 1 Oct 52
Portugal All Territories FORCE: 11 Dec 52
Portugal FORCE: 1 Oct 52
Saudi Arabia SIGNED: 25 May 51 FORCE: 1 Oct 52
South Africa SIGNED: 25 May 51 FORCE: 1 Oct 52
Spain FORCE: 1 Oct 52
Sweden FORCE: 13 Oct 52
Switzerland FORCE: 28 Oct 52
Syria FORCE: 1 Oct 52
Thailand FORCE: 1 Oct 52
Turkey FORCE: 1 Oct 52
UK Great Britain FORCE: 1 Oct 52
UK Great Britain All Territories FORCE: 11 Dec 52
USA (United States) FORCE: 1 Oct 52
Vatican/Holy See FORCE: 1 Oct 52
Venezuela FORCE: 1 Oct 52
Yugoslavia FORCE: 1 Oct 52
ANNEX
204 UNTS 391.
219 UNTS 354.
252 UNTS 336.
252 UNTS 338.
324 UNTS 334.
327 UNTS 362.
456 UNTS 494.
466 UNTS 387.

102304 Bilateral Treaty **177 UNTS 3**
SIGNED: 25 Nov 51 FORCE: 18 Mar 53
REGISTERED: 22 Oct 53 Pakistan
ARTICLES: 5 LANGUAGE: Arabic. English.
HEADNOTE: FRIENDSHIP
TOPIC: General Amity
CONCEPTS: Friendship and amity. Privileges and

immunities. Procedure. Most favored nation clause. Boundaries of territory.
PROCEDURE: Future Procedures Contemplated.
PARTIES:
  Pakistan
  Saudi Arabia

102305   Bilateral Exchange   **177 UNTS 13**
SIGNED: 4 Apr 52   FORCE: 4 Apr 52
REGISTERED: 22 Oct 53 USA (United States)
ARTICLES: 2 LANGUAGE: English.
HEADNOTE: REGISTRATION W/ITU FREQUEN-CIES USED US
TOPIC: Telecommunications
CONCEPTS: Bands and frequency allocation. Services. Conformity with IGO decisions.
INTL ORGS: International Telecommunication Union.
PARTIES:
  Denmark
  USA (United States)

102306   Bilateral Exchange   **177 UNTS 21**
SIGNED: 13 Mar 52   FORCE: 13 Mar 52
REGISTERED: 22 Oct 53 USA (United States)
ARTICLES: 2 LANGUAGE: English. French.
HEADNOTE: TAX RELIEF PURCHASES MADE COMMON DEFENSE
TOPIC: Milit Assistance
CONCEPTS: Detailed regulations. Annex or appendix reference. Indemnities and reimbursements. Fees and exemptions. Tax exemptions. Customs exemptions.
PROCEDURE: Future Procedures Contemplated.
PARTIES:
  France
  USA (United States)

102307   Bilateral Exchange   **177 UNTS 33**
SIGNED: 18 Mar 52   FORCE: 18 Mar 52
REGISTERED: 22 Oct 53 USA (United States)
ARTICLES: 2 LANGUAGE: English.
HEADNOTE: RELIEF TAXATION COMMON DE-FENSE EXPENDITURES
TOPIC: Milit Assistance
CONCEPTS: Detailed regulations. Annex or appendix reference. Tax exemptions. Customs exemptions.
TREATY REF: 80UNTS261; 164UNTS362.
PROCEDURE: Future Procedures Contemplated.
PARTIES:
  UK Great Britain
  USA (United States)

102308   Bilateral Agreement   **177 UNTS 43**
SIGNED: 20 Feb 52   FORCE: 20 Feb 52
REGISTERED: 22 Oct 53 USA (United States)
ARTICLES: 11 LANGUAGE: English. Spanish.
HEADNOTE: MILITARY AGREEMENT
TOPIC: Milit Assistance
CONCEPTS: Exceptions and exemptions. Guarantees and safeguards. Non-prejudice to UN charter. Peaceful relations. Privileges and immunities. Conformity with municipal law. General co-operation. Inspection and observation. Public information. Use of facilities. Indemnities and reimbursements. Garnishment of funds. Local currency. Claims and settlements. Most favored nation clause. Recognition. Customs exemptions. Domestic obligation. Materials, equipment and services. Aid missions. Joint defense. Defense and security. Self-defense. Payment for war supplies. Military assistance. Return of equipment and recapture. Security of information. Exchange of defense information. Restrictions on transfer. Raw materials.
INTL ORGS: United Nations.
TREATY REF: 21UNTS77; 26UNTS417.
PROCEDURE: Amendment. Future Procedures Contemplated. Registration. Termination.
PARTIES:
  Ecuador
  USA (United States)

102309   Bilateral Agreement   **177 UNTS 63**
SIGNED: 9 May 52   FORCE: 9 May 52
REGISTERED: 22 Oct 53 USA (United States)
ARTICLES: 19 LANGUAGE: English.
HEADNOTE: TECHNICAL COOPERATION

TOPIC: Tech Assistance
CONCEPTS: Exceptions and exemptions. Treaty implementation. Annex type material. Privileges and immunities. General cooperation. Exchange of information and documents. Domestic legislation. Operating agencies. Personnel. General property. Vocational training. Scientific exchange. Accounting procedures. Attachment of funds. Currency deposits. Exchange rates and regulations. Funding procedures. Garnishment of funds. Seizure funds. Local currency. Assets. Domestic obligation. General technical assistance. Materials, equipment and services. Aid missions.
INTL ORGS: International Monetary Fund. Special Commission
TREATY REF: 137UNTS57; 177UNTS123.
PROCEDURE: Future Procedures Contemplated. Termination.
PARTIES:
  Israel
  USA (United States)
                    ANNEX
180 UNTS 398. USA (United States). Amendment 17 Aug 52. Force 17 Aug 52.
180 UNTS 398. Israel. Amendment 17 Aug 52. Force 17 Aug 52.
205 UNTS 351. USA (United States). Amendment 11 Mar 53. Force 11 Mar 53.
205 UNTS 351. Israel. Amendment 11 Mar 53. Force 11 Mar 53.
219 UNTS 366. USA (United States). Amendment 21 Jun 54. Force 21 Jun 54.
219 UNTS 366. Israel. Amendment 21 Jun 54. Force 21 Jun 54.
219 UNTS 372. Israel. Amendment 29 Jun 54. Force 29 Jun 54.
219 UNTS 372. USA (United States). Amendment 29 Jun 54. Force 29 Jun 54.
314 UNTS 342. USA (United States). Amendment 10 Jun 58.
314 UNTS 342. Israel. Amendment 25 Jul 58.
345 UNTS 360. USA (United States). Amendment 26 Jun 59. Force 24 Sep 59.
345 UNTS 360. Israel. Amendment 24 Sep 59. Force 24 Sep 59.

102310   Bilateral Exchange   **177 UNTS 81**
SIGNED: 20 May 52   FORCE: 20 May 52
REGISTERED: 22 Oct 53 USA (United States)
ARTICLES: 2 LANGUAGE: English.
HEADNOTE: COOPERATIVE PROGRAM EDUCA-TION PURSUANT GENERAL TECHNICAL COOP-ERATION
TOPIC: Tech Assistance
CONCEPTS: Annex type material. Personnel. Exchange. Vocational training. Financial programs. Domestic obligation. General technical assistance.
TREATY REF: TAIS 2524.
PROCEDURE: Duration. Termination.
PARTIES:
  Libya
  USA (United States)
                    ANNEX
200 UNTS 327. Libya. Amendment 19 Jun 52. Force 19 Jun 52.
200 UNTS 327. USA (United States). Amendment 19 Jun 52. Force 19 Jun 52.

102311   Bilateral Exchange   **177 UNTS 89**
SIGNED: 1 May 52   FORCE: 1 May 52
REGISTERED: 22 Oct 53 USA (United States)
ARTICLES: 2 LANGUAGE: English.
HEADNOTE: EMERGENCY ECONOMIC ASSIS-TANCE
TOPIC: Direct Aid
CONCEPTS: Conditions. Conformity with municipal law. Exchange of information and documents. Personnel. Indemnities and reimbursements. Financial programs. Economic assistance. Grants.
PROCEDURE: Future Procedures Contemplated.
PARTIES:
  Israel
  USA (United States)

102312   Bilateral Exchange   **177 UNTS 103**
SIGNED: 12 May 50   FORCE: 12 May 52
REGISTERED: 22 Oct 53 USA (United States)
ARTICLES: 3 LANGUAGE: English.

HEADNOTE: EXEMPTION CONSULAR OFFICERS CUSTOMS DUTIES RELATED TAXES
TOPIC: Consul/Citizenship
CONCEPTS: Diplomatic privileges. Conformity with municipal law.
PARTIES:
  Chile
  USA (United States)

102313   Bilateral Exchange   **177 UNTS 115**
SIGNED: 17 Mar 52   FORCE: 12 Mar 50
REGISTERED: 22 Oct 53 USA (United States)
ARTICLES: 2 LANGUAGE: English. Spanish.
HEADNOTE: RADIO COMMUNICATIONS AMA-TEUR STATIONS BEHALF THIRD PARTIES
TOPIC: Telecommunications
CONCEPTS: Amateur radio. Amateur third party message. Radio-telephone-telegraphic communications.
PROCEDURE: Termination.
PARTIES:
  Ecuador
  USA (United States)

102314   Bilateral Exchange   **177 UNTS 123**
SIGNED: 27 Feb 52   FORCE: 27 Feb 52
REGISTERED: 22 Oct 53 USA (United States)
ARTICLES: 2 LANGUAGE: English.
HEADNOTE: RELIEF RESETTLEMENT REFUGEES
TOPIC: Direct Aid
CONCEPTS: Refugees and stateless persons. Assistance. Conformity with municipal law. Inspection and observation. Accounting procedures. Attachment of funds. Exchange rates and regulations. Financial programs. Garnishment of funds. Payment schedules. Seizure funds. Local currency. Aid and development. Commodities and services.
INTL ORGS: International Monetary Fund.
TREATY REF: 157UNTS50.
PARTIES:
  Israel
  USA (United States)
                    ANNEX
179 UNTS 362. USA (United States). Supplementation 13 Aug 52. Force 13 Aug 52.
179 UNTS 362. Israel. Supplementation 13 Aug 52. Force 13 Aug 52.

102315   Bilateral Treaty   **177 UNTS 133**
SIGNED: 30 Aug 51   FORCE: 27 Aug 52
REGISTERED: 22 Oct 53 USA (United States)
ARTICLES: 8 LANGUAGE: English.
HEADNOTE: MUTUAL DEFENSE
TOPIC: Milit Assistance
CONCEPTS: Definition of terms. Non-prejudice to UN charter. Peaceful relations. Defense and security. Military assistance.
INTL ORGS: United Nations.
PROCEDURE: Future Procedures Contemplated. Ratification. Termination.
PARTIES:
  Philippines
  USA (United States)

102316   Bilateral Convention   **177 UNTS 141**
SIGNED: 3 Mar 52   FORCE: 18 Dec 52
REGISTERED: 22 Oct 53 USA (United States)
ARTICLES: 8 LANGUAGE: English. Finnish.
HEADNOTE: DOUBLE TAXATION FISCAL EVA-SION ESTATES INHERITANCES
TOPIC: Taxation
CONCEPTS: Definition of terms. Privileges and immunities. Exchange of official publications. Taxation. Death duties. Tax credits. General.
PROCEDURE: Duration. Ratification. Termination.
PARTIES:
  Finland
  USA (United States)

102317   Bilateral Convention   **177 UNTS 163**
SIGNED: 3 Mar 52   FORCE: 18 Dec 52
REGISTERED: 22 Oct 53 USA (United States)
ARTICLES: 23 LANGUAGE: English. Finnish.
HEADNOTE: DOUBLE TAXATION FISCAL EVA-SION TAXES INCOME
TOPIC: Taxation
CONCEPTS: Definition of terms. Conformity with municipal law. Exchange of official publications.

Teacher and student exchange. Claims and settlements. Taxation. Equitable taxes. General. Tax exemptions. Air transport. Merchant vessels.
PROCEDURE: Duration. Ratification. Termination.
PARTIES:
Finland
USA (United States)

102318   Bilateral Exchange   **177 UNTS 195**
SIGNED: 31 Mar 52   FORCE: 31 Mar 52
REGISTERED: 22 Oct 53 USA (United States)
ARTICLES: 2 LANGUAGE: French.
HEADNOTE: RECIPROCAL WAIVER PASSPORT VISA FEES
TOPIC: Visas
CONCEPTS: Time limit. Visa abolition. Fees and exemptions.
PARTIES:
Monaco
USA (United States)

102319   Bilateral Agreement   **177 UNTS 203**
SIGNED: 20 Nov 52   FORCE: 20 Nov 52
REGISTERED: 22 Oct 53 USA (United States)
ARTICLES: 12 LANGUAGE: English. Swedish.
HEADNOTE: EDUCATION EXCHANGE PROGRAM
TOPIC: Education
CONCEPTS: Conformity with municipal law. Operating agencies. Education. Exchange. Commissions and foundations. Scholarships and grants. Research and development. Currency. Funding procedures. Payment schedules. Transportation costs. Credit provisions. Surplus war property.
PROCEDURE: Amendment.
PARTIES:
Sweden
USA (United States)
ANNEX
360 UNTS 396. USA (United States). Amendment 20 Nov 59. Force 20 Nov 59.
360 UNTS 396. Sweden. Amendment 20 Nov 59. Force 20 Nov 59.
479 UNTS 358. USA (United States). Amendment 28 Oct 63. Force 28 Oct 63.
479 UNTS 358. Sweden. Amendment 28 Oct 63. Force 28 Oct 63.

102320   Bilateral Agreement   **177 UNTS 219**
SIGNED: 4 Apr 52   FORCE: 4 Apr 52
REGISTERED: 22 Oct 53 USA (United States)
ARTICLES: 5 LANGUAGE: English. Spanish.
HEADNOTE: TECHNICAL COOPERATION
TOPIC: Tech Assistance
CONCEPTS: Exceptions and exemptions. Treaty implementation. Previous treaty replacement. Diplomatic privileges. General cooperation. Exchange of information and documents. Public information. Funding procedures. Tax exemptions. Domestic obligation. General technical assistance. Materials, equipment and services.
PROCEDURE: Amendment. Duration. Termination.
PARTIES:
El Salvador
USA (United States)

102321   Bilateral Agreement   **177 UNTS 233**
SIGNED: 15 May 52   FORCE: 15 May 52
REGISTERED: 22 Oct 53 USA (United States)
ARTICLES: 9 LANGUAGE: English.
HEADNOTE: OPERATIONS KOREA
TOPIC: Milit Assistance
CONCEPTS: Accounting procedures. Indemnities and reimbursements. Monetary and gold transfers. Funding procedures. Local currency. Claims and settlements. Materials, equipment and services. Defense and security. Payment for war supplies. Return of equipment and recapture.
PROCEDURE: Future Procedures Contemplated.
PARTIES:
Netherlands
USA (United States)

102322   Bilateral Agreement   **177 UNTS 241**
SIGNED: 24 Jun 52   FORCE: 24 Jun 52
REGISTERED: 22 Oct 53 USA (United States)
ARTICLES: 9 LANGUAGE: English.
HEADNOTE: OPERATIONS KOREA
TOPIC: Milit Assistance
CONCEPTS: Accounting procedures. Indemnities

and reimbursements. Monetary and gold transfers. Funding procedures. Local currency. Claims and settlements. Materials, equipment and services. Defense and security. Lend lease. Return of equipment and recapture.
PROCEDURE: Future Procedures Contemplated.
PARTIES:
South Africa
USA (United States)

102323   Bilateral Exchange   **177 UNTS 249**
SIGNED: 7 Jan 52   FORCE: 7 Jan 52
REGISTERED: 22 Oct 53 USA (United States)
ARTICLES: 2 LANGUAGE: English.
HEADNOTE: DISPOSAL SURPLUS MILITARY EQUIPMENT MATERIAL
TOPIC: Milit Assistance
CONCEPTS: Detailed regulations. Conformity with municipal law. Title and deeds. Reexport of goods, etc.. Accounting procedures. Delivery schedules. Surplus property. Payment for war supplies. Return of equipment and recapture. Surplus war property.
PARTIES:
Greece
USA (United States)

102324   Bilateral Exchange   **177 UNTS 257**
SIGNED: 7 Apr 52   FORCE: 9 Apr 52
REGISTERED: 22 Oct 53 USA (United States)
ARTICLES: 2 LANGUAGE: English.
HEADNOTE: TAX EXEMPTION EXPENDITURES COMMON DEFENSE
TOPIC: Milit Assistance
CONCEPTS: Detailed regulations. Tax exemptions. Customs exemptions.
PARTIES:
Denmark
USA (United States)

102325   Bilateral Exchange   **177 UNTS 263**
SIGNED: 18 Mar 52   FORCE: 18 Mar 52
REGISTERED: 22 Oct 53 USA (United States)
ARTICLES: 2 LANGUAGE: English.
HEADNOTE: RELIEF TAXATION COMMON DEFENSE EXPENDITURES
TOPIC: Taxation
CONCEPTS: Tax exemptions. Customs exemptions.
PROCEDURE: Future Procedures Contemplated.
PARTIES:
Iceland
USA (United States)

102326   Bilateral Agreement   **177 UNTS 269**
SIGNED: 9 May 52   FORCE: 9 May 52
REGISTERED: 22 Oct 53 USA (United States)
ARTICLES: 10 LANGUAGE: English.
HEADNOTE: ECONOMIC ASSISTANCE PURSUANT GENERAL TECHNICAL COOPERATION
TOPIC: Tech Assistance
CONCEPTS: Detailed regulations. Exceptions and exemptions. Time limit. Annex type material. General cooperation. Inspection and observation. Public information. Existing tribunals. Accounting procedures. Attachment of funds. Compensation. Indemnities and reimbursements. Currency deposits. Exchange rates and regulations. Garnishment of funds. Seizure funds. Local currency. Claims and settlements. Most favored nation clause. Commodities and services. Domestic obligation. General technical assistance. Economic assistance. Credit provisions. Optional clause ICJ. Raw materials.
TREATY REF: 1UNTS9.
PROCEDURE: Termination.
PARTIES:
Israel
USA (United States)

102327   Bilateral Exchange   **177 UNTS 283**
SIGNED: 23 Apr 52   FORCE: 29 Apr 52
REGISTERED: 22 Oct 53 USA (United States)
ARTICLES: 2 LANGUAGE: English.
HEADNOTE: GUARANTIES
TOPIC: Direct Aid
CONCEPTS: Guaranties and safeguards. Conformity with municipal law. Arbitration. Negotiation. Accounting procedures. Local currency.

Claims and settlements. Assets transfer. Economic assistance.
TREATY REF: 23UNTS43.
PARTIES:
Greece
USA (United States)
ANNEX
476 UNTS 332. USA (United States). Supplementation 19 Apr 63. Force 19 Apr 63.
476 UNTS 332. Greece. Supplementation 19 Apr 63. Force 19 Apr 63.

102328   Bilateral Exchange   **177 UNTS 291**
SIGNED: 1 Apr 52   FORCE: 3 Apr 52
REGISTERED: 22 Oct 53 USA (United States)
ARTICLES: 2 LANGUAGE: English.
HEADNOTE: GUARANTIES
TOPIC: Direct Aid
CONCEPTS: Guarantees and safeguards. Conformity with municipal law. Arbitration. Accounting procedures. Local currency. Claims and settlements. Assets transfer. Economic assistance.
TREATY REF: 20UNTS185.
PARTIES:
Norway
USA (United States)

102329   Bilateral Exchange   **177 UNTS 299**
SIGNED: 16 Feb 52   FORCE: 20 Feb 52
REGISTERED: 22 Oct 53 USA (United States)
ARTICLES: 2 LANGUAGE: English.
HEADNOTE: GUARANTIES
TOPIC: Direct Aid
CONCEPTS: Guarantees and safeguards. Conformity with municipal law. Arbitration. Accounting procedures. Local currency. Claims and settlements. Assets transfer. Economic assistance.
TREATY REF: 21UNTSI9.
PARTIES:
Austria
USA (United States)

102330   Bilateral Exchange   **177 UNTS 307**
SIGNED: 19 Feb 52   FORCE: 19 Feb 52
REGISTERED: 22 Oct 53 USA (United States)
ARTICLES: 2 LANGUAGE: English.
HEADNOTE: GUARANTIES
TOPIC: Direct Aid
CONCEPTS: Guarantees and safeguards. Conformity with municipal law. Arbitration. Accounting procedures. Local currency. Claims and settlements. Assets transfer. Economic assistance.
PARTIES:
Philippines
USA (United States)
ANNEX
303 UNTS 336. USA (United States). Amendment 12 Dec 55. Force 10 Feb 58.
303 UNTS 336. Philippines. Amendment 10 Feb 58. Force 10 Feb 58.
607 UNTS 258. USA (United States). Supplementation 15 Aug 66. Force 15 Aug 66.
607 UNTS 258. Philippines. Supplementation 15 Aug 66. Force 15 Aug 66.

102331   Bilateral Exchange   **177 UNTS 315**
SIGNED: 15 Nov 51   FORCE: 15 Nov 51
REGISTERED: 22 Oct 53 USA (United States)
ARTICLES: 2 LANGUAGE: English.
HEADNOTE: GUARANTIES
TOPIC: Direct Aid
CONCEPTS: Guarantees and safeguards. Conformity with municipal law. General cooperation. Accounting procedures. Local currency. Assets transfer. National treatment. Economic assistance.
TREATY REF: 24UNTS67.
PARTIES:
Turkey
USA (United States)
ANNEX
531 UNTS 322. USA (United States). Supplementation 27 Nov 64. Force 27 Nov 64.
531 UNTS 322. Turkey. Supplementation 27 Nov 64. Force 27 Nov 64.

102332   Bilateral Agreement   **178 UNTS 3**
SIGNED: 26 Feb 53   FORCE: 5 Oct 53
REGISTERED: 23 Oct 53 Denmark

ARTICLES: 7 LANGUAGE: Danish. German.
HEADNOTE: REPAYMENT EXPENDITURE REF-
UGEES
TOPIC: Claims and Debts
CONCEPTS: Detailed regulations. Attachment of
funds. Banking. Currency. Interest rates. Pay-
ment schedules. Loan repayment. Specific
claims or waivers.
INTL ORGS: European Payments Union.
PROCEDURE: Amendment. Future Procedures
Contemplated. Ratification.
PARTIES:
Denmark
Germany, West

102333 Bilateral Agreement **178 UNTS 17**
SIGNED: 20 Apr 51 FORCE: 10 Sep 52
REGISTERED: 27 Oct 53 Greece
ARTICLES: 21 LANGUAGE: French.
HEADNOTE: CULTURAL AGREEMENT
TOPIC: Culture
CONCEPTS: Annex or appendix reference. Friendship and amity. Visas. Non-diplomatic delega-
tions. Conformity with municipal law. Exchange
of official publications. Personnel. Establishment
of commission. Specialists exchange. Recogni-
tion of degrees. Teacher and student exchange.
Professorships. Institute establishment. Scholar-
ships and grants. Vocational training. Exchange.
General cultural cooperation. Anthropology and
archeology. Research results. Scientific exchange. Fees and exemptions. Publications exchange. Mass media exchange.
INTL ORGS: Special Commission.
PROCEDURE: Amendment. Denunciation. Duration. Ratification. Renewal or Revival.
PARTIES:
Greece
Turkey

102334 Bilateral Convention **178 UNTS 29**
SIGNED: 10 Jun 49 FORCE: 14 Jan 53
REGISTERED: 27 Oct 53 Greece
ARTICLES: 10 LANGUAGE: French.
HEADNOTE: CULTURAL CONVENTION
TOPIC: Culture
CONCEPTS: Friendship and amity. Tourism. Con-
formity with municipal law. General cooperation.
Recognition of degrees. Teacher and student ex-
change. Professorships. Scholarships and
grants. Exchange. General cultural cooperation.
Artists. Athletes. Scientific exchange. Publica-
tions exchange.
PROCEDURE: Denunciation. Ratification.
PARTIES:
Greece
Lebanon

102335 Bilateral Agreement **178 UNTS 37**
SIGNED: 6 Sep 48 FORCE: 6 Sep 48
REGISTERED: 27 Oct 53 Greece
ARTICLES: 13 LANGUAGE: French.
HEADNOTE: ESTABLISHMENT AIR COMMUNICA-
TIONS
TOPIC: Air Transport
CONCEPTS: Exceptions and exemptions. Annex or
appendix reference. Conformity with municipal
law. General cooperation. Licenses and permits.
Recognition of legal documents. Use of facilities.
Arbitration. Procedure. Existing tribunals. Nego-
tiation. Reexport of goods, etc.. Fees and exemp-
tions. Most favored nation treatment. National treat-
ment. Customs exemptions. Competency certifi-
cate. Routes and logistics. Navigational
conditions. Permit designation. Airport facilities.
Airworthiness certificates. Conditions of airlines
operating permission. Operating authorizations
and regulations. Licenses and certificates of nationality.
INTL ORGS: International Civil Aviation Organization.
TREATY REF: 15UNTS295.
PROCEDURE: Amendment. Future Procedures
Contemplated. Ratification. Registration. Termination.
PARTIES:
Greece
Lebanon

102336 Bilateral Agreement **178 UNTS 51**
SIGNED: 28 Aug 52 FORCE: 11 Oct 52
REGISTERED: 28 Oct 53 USA (United States)
ARTICLES: 13 LANGUAGE: English. Spanish.
HEADNOTE: COMMERCE
TOPIC: General Trade
CONCEPTS: Detailed regulations. Exceptions and
exemptions. Territorial application. Previous
treaty amendment. Treaty implementation. An-
nex or appendix reference. Annex type material.
General cooperation. Investigation of violations.
Establishment of commission. Procedure. Gen-
eral trade. Trade procedures. Payment sched-
ules. Quotas. Most favored nation clause. Na-
tional treatment. Customs duties.
TREATY REF: 203LTS273.
PROCEDURE: Termination.
PARTIES:
USA (United States)
Venezuela
ANNEX
505 UNTS 316. USA (United States). Amendment
15 Jul 63. Force 23 Jul 63.
505 UNTS 316. Venezuela. Amendment
23 Jul 63. Force 23 Jul 63.

102337 Bilateral Agreement **178 UNTS 97**
SIGNED: 26 Jan 50 FORCE: 26 Jan 50
REGISTERED: 28 Oct 53 USA (United States)
ARTICLES: 14 LANGUAGE: English. Korean.
HEADNOTE: MILITARY ADVISORY GROUP
TOPIC: Military Mission
CONCEPTS: Treaty interpretation. Use of facilities.
Compensation. Indemnities and reimburse-
ments. Exchange rates and regulations. Expense
sharing formulae. Local currency. Tax exemp-
tions. Customs exemptions. Defense and secu-
rity. Military assistance. Military training. Secu-
rity of information. Airforce-army-navy personnel
ratio. Ranks and privileges. Conditions for assistance missions. Third country military personnel.
Exchange of defense information.
INTL ORGS: United Nations.
PROCEDURE: Ratification. Registration. Termination.
PARTIES:
Korea, South
USA (United States)
ANNEX
400 UNTS 386. USA (United States). Amendment
21 Oct 60. Force 21 Oct 60.
400 UNTS 386. Korea, South. Amendment
21 Oct 60. Force 21 Oct 60.

102338 Bilateral Agreement **178 UNTS 113**
SIGNED: 27 May 52 FORCE: 1 Aug 52
REGISTERED: 28 Oct 53 USA (United States)
ARTICLES: 23 LANGUAGE: English.
HEADNOTE: EXCHANGE PARCEL POST
TOPIC: Postal Service
CONCEPTS: Detailed regulations. Territorial appli-
cation. Previous treaty replacement. Conformity
with municipal law. Domestic legislation. Re-
sponsibility and liability. Compensation. Indem-
nities and reimbursements. Claims and settle-
ments. Customs duties. Postal services. Regula-
tions. Insured letters and boxes. Parcel post.
Rates and charges.
INTL ORGS: Universal Postal Union.
TREATY REF: USA'34STAT PT.3,
P.2872;169UNTS3;.
PROCEDURE: Duration. Termination.
PARTIES:
Australia
USA (United States)

102339 Bilateral Exchange **178 UNTS 155**
SIGNED: 20 May 52 FORCE: 20 May 52
REGISTERED: 28 Oct 53 USA (United States)
ARTICLES: 2 LANGUAGE: English.
HEADNOTE: COOPERATIVE PROGRAM HEALTH
PURSUANT GENERAL TECHNICAL COOPER-
ATION
TOPIC: Tech Assistance
CONCEPTS: General cooperation. Personnel. Vo-
cational training. Financial programs. Domestic
obligation. General technical assistance. Assis-
tance. Materials, equipment and services.
INTL ORGS: Special Commission.
TREATY REF: TAIS 2524.
PROCEDURE: Duration. Termination.

PARTIES:
Libya
USA (United States)

102340 Bilateral Exchange **178 UNTS 163**
SIGNED: 30 Jul 51 FORCE: 30 Jul 51
REGISTERED: 28 Oct 53 USA (United States)
ARTICLES: 2 LANGUAGE: English. Spanish.
HEADNOTE: EXTENDING AGREEMENT MILITARY
AVIATION MISSION
TOPIC: Military Mission
CONCEPTS: Annex type material. Previous treaty
extension. Military assistance missions.
PARTIES:
Paraguay
USA (United States)
ANNEX
343 UNTS 352. USA (United States). Amendment
20 Feb 59. Force 30 Mar 59.
343 UNTS 352. Paraguay. Amendment
30 Mar 59. Force 30 Mar 59.

102341 Bilateral Instrument **178 UNTS 169**
SIGNED: 22 Apr 53 FORCE: 22 Jul 53
REGISTERED: 28 Oct 53 USA (United States)
ARTICLES: 1 LANGUAGE: English.
HEADNOTE: REVIVAL PRE-WAR TREATIES
TOPIC: Admin Cooperation
CONCEPTS: Revival of treaties.
TREATY REF: 178UNTS173; 191LTS43;
181LTS217; 101LTS63; 108LTS4.
PARTIES:
Japan
USA (United States)

102342 Bilateral Agreement **178 UNTS 243**
SIGNED: 10 Mar 52 FORCE: 10 Mar 52
REGISTERED: 29 Oct 53 Belgium
ARTICLES: 17 LANGUAGE: French. Spanish.
HEADNOTE: AIR TRANSPORT
TOPIC: Air Transport
CONCEPTS: Definition of terms. Annex or appen-
dix reference. Non-visa travel documents. Conformity with municipal law. General cooperation.
Licenses and permits. Personnel. Recognition of
legal documents. Use of facilities. Arbitration.
Procedure. Existing tribunals. Special tribunals.
Negotiation. Fees and exemptions. Most favored
nation clause. National treatment. Customs ex-
emptions. Competency certificate. Navigational
conditions. Permit designation. Air transport. Airport facilities. Airworthiness certificates. Conditions of airlines operating permission. Operating
authorizations and regulations. Licenses and cer-
tificates of nationality. Postal services.
INTL ORGS: International Civil Aviation Organiza-
tion.
TREATY REF: 15UNTS295.
PROCEDURE: Amendment. Future Procedures
Contemplated. Ratification. Registration. Termination.
PARTIES:
Belgium
Spain
ANNEX
330 UNTS 364. Belgium. Amendment 20 Mar 59.
Force 20 Mar 59.
330 UNTS 364. Spain. Amendment 20 Mar 59.
Force 20 Mar 59.

102343 Bilateral Agreement **178 UNTS 265**
SIGNED: 27 Mar 48 FORCE: 14 Oct 53
REGISTERED: 29 Oct 53 Belgium
ARTICLES: 13 LANGUAGE: French.
HEADNOTE: CULTURAL AGREEMENT
TOPIC: Culture
CONCEPTS: Tourism. Standardization. Conformity
with municipal law. Exchange of information and
documents. Domestic legislation. Operating
agencies. Establishment of commission. Special-
ists exchange. Recognition of degrees. Ex-
change. Teacher and student exchange. Scholar-
ships and grants. Exchange. General cultural co-
operation. Artists. Scientific exchange.
Publications exchange. Mass media exchange.
INTL ORGS: Special Commission.
PROCEDURE: Denunciation. Duration. Ratification.
Renewal or Revival.

PARTIES:
Belgium
Luxembourg

102344 Bilateral Agreement **178 UNTS 275**
SIGNED: 4 Sep 53   FORCE: 17 Oct 53
REGISTERED: 29 Oct 53 IBRD (World Bank)
ARTICLES: 5 LANGUAGE: English.
HEADNOTE: GUARANTEE AGREEMENT
TOPIC: IBRD Project
CONCEPTS: Definition of terms. Annex or appendix reference. Exchange of information and documents. Informational records. Inspection and observation. Bonds. Fees and exemptions. Tax exemptions. Domestic obligation. Terms of loan. Loan regulations. Loan guarantee. Guarantor non-interference.
PARTIES:
Iceland
IBRD (World Bank)

102345 Bilateral Exchange **178 UNTS 297**
SIGNED: 9 Jun 52   FORCE: 9 Jun 52
REGISTERED: 30 Oct 53 USA (United States)
ARTICLES: 5 LANGUAGE: English.
HEADNOTE: MEDIA GUARANTY PROGRAM
TOPIC: Mass Media
CONCEPTS: Annex type material. Media guaranty.
PARTIES:
Israel
USA (United States)

102346 Bilateral Exchange **178 UNTS 307**
SIGNED: 20 May 52   FORCE: 20 May 52
REGISTERED: 30 Oct 53 USA (United States)
ARTICLES: 2 LANGUAGE: English.
HEADNOTE: COOPERATIVE PROGRAM NATURAL RESOURCES DEVELOPMENT
TOPIC: Direct Aid
CONCEPTS: Annex type material. Personnel. Financial programs. Domestic obligation. General technical assistance. Assistance. Natural resources.
INTL ORGS: Special Commission.
TREATY REF: TAIS 2524.
PROCEDURE: Duration.
PARTIES:
Libya
USA (United States)
          ANNEX
179 UNTS 367. USA (United States). Amendment 19 Jul 52. Force 19 Jun 52.
179 UNTS 367. Libya. Amendment 19 Jun 52. Force 19 Jun 52.

102347 Bilateral Exchange **178 UNTS 315**
SIGNED: 19 Jun 52   FORCE: 19 Jun 52
REGISTERED: 30 Oct 53 USA (United States)
ARTICLES: 2 LANGUAGE: English.
HEADNOTE: MUTUAL DEFENSE ASSISTANCE
TOPIC: Milit Assistance
CONCEPTS: Friendship and amity. Defense and security.
INTL ORGS: United Nations.
PARTIES:
New Zealand
USA (United States)
          ANNEX
380 UNTS 424. USA (United States). Amendment 25 Mar 60. Force 25 Mar 60.
380 UNTS 424. New Zealand. Amendment 25 Mar 60. Force 25 Mar 60.

102348 Bilateral Agreement **178 UNTS 323**
SIGNED: 23 Jul 52   FORCE: 23 Jul 52
REGISTERED: 30 Oct 53 ILO (Labor Org)
ARTICLES: 5 LANGUAGE: Spanish.
HEADNOTE: TECHNICAL ASSISTANCE
TOPIC: Tech Assistance
CONCEPTS: Treaty implementation. General cooperation. Exchange of information and documents. Personnel. Title and deeds. Exchange. Scholarships and grants. Vocational training. Research and development. Expense sharing formulae. Local currency. Domestic obligation. General technical assistance. Materials, equipment and services. Conformity with IGO decisions.
INTL ORGS: United Nations.

228

TREATY REF: 76UNTS132.
PROCEDURE: Amendment. Termination.
PARTIES:
Chile
ILO (Labor Org)

102349 Bilateral Agreement **178 UNTS 337**
SIGNED: 13 Feb 53   FORCE: 13 Feb 53
REGISTERED: 30 Oct 53 ILO (Labor Org)
ARTICLES: 5 LANGUAGE: English.
HEADNOTE: TECHNICAL ASSISTANCE
TOPIC: Tech Assistance
CONCEPTS: Treaty implementation. General cooperation. Exchange of information and documents. Personnel. Title and deeds. Exchange. Scholarships and grants. Vocational training. Research and development. Expense sharing formulae. Local currency. Domestic obligation. General technical assistance. Materials, equipment and services. Conformity with IGO decisions.
INTL ORGS: United Nations.
TREATY REF: 76UNTS132.
PROCEDURE: Amendment. Termination.
PARTIES:
Taiwan
ILO (Labor Org)

102350 Bilateral Agreement **178 UNTS 347**
SIGNED: 12 Aug 49   FORCE: 29 Aug 49
REGISTERED: 30 Oct 53 WHO (World Health)
ARTICLES: 11 LANGUAGE: English.
HEADNOTE: SERVICES WHO THAILAND
TOPIC: Sanitation
CONCEPTS: Privileges and immunities. Personnel. Responsibility and liability. Arbitration. Public health. WHO used as agency. Vocational training. Old age and invalidity insurance. Accounting procedures. Indemnities and reimbursements. Currency. Exchange rates and regulations. Expense sharing formulae. Tax exemptions. Assistance. Specific technical assistance. Aid missions.
TREATY REF: 33UNTS261.
PARTIES:
WHO (World Health)
Thailand

102351 Bilateral Exchange **179 UNTS 3**
SIGNED: 5 Mar 52   FORCE: 5 Mar 52
REGISTERED: 2 Nov 53 USA (United States)
ARTICLES: 2 LANGUAGE: English. Italian.
HEADNOTE: TAXES EXPENDITURES DEFENSE
TOPIC: Taxation
CONCEPTS: General. Military installations and equipment.
TREATY REF: 19UNTS127; 31UNTS485.
PARTIES:
Italy
USA (United States)

102352 Bilateral Exchange **179 UNTS 15**
SIGNED: 12 May 52   FORCE: 12 May 52
REGISTERED: 2 Nov 53 USA (United States)
ARTICLES: 2 LANGUAGE: English.
HEADNOTE: GUARANTEES ECONOMIC COOPERATION ACT
TOPIC: Finance
CONCEPTS: Financial programs. Private investment guarantee. National treatment.
PARTIES:
Belgium
USA (United States)

102353 Bilateral Agreement **179 UNTS 23**
SIGNED: 24 May 52   FORCE: 24 May 52
REGISTERED: 7 Nov 53 USA (United States)
ARTICLES: 6 LANGUAGE: English. Korean.
HEADNOTE: ECONOMIC COORDINATION
TOPIC: Direct Aid
CONCEPTS: Guarantees and safeguards. Annex or appendix reference. Privileges and immunities. General cooperation. Exchange of information and documents. Informational records. Inspection and observation. Operating agencies. Personnel. Public information. Responsibility and liability. Establishment of commission. Export quotas. Accounting procedures. Attachment of funds. Indemnities and reimbursements. Ex-

change rates and regulations. Garnishment of funds. Seizure funds. General. Customs duties. Domestic obligation. Economic assistance. Materials, equipment and services. Procurement. Distribution. Joint defense.
INTL ORGS: United Nations. United Nations Unified Command in Korea.
PROCEDURE: Duration. Registration. Termination.
PARTIES:
Korea, South
USA (United States)

102354 Bilateral Exchange **179 UNTS 65**
SIGNED: 8 Jan 52   FORCE: 8 Jan 52
REGISTERED: 7 Nov 53 USA (United States)
ARTICLES: 2 LANGUAGE: English.
HEADNOTE: MUTUAL SECURITY
TOPIC: Milit Assistance
CONCEPTS: Guarantees and safeguards. Peaceful relations. Conformity with municipal law. Migrant worker. Accounting procedures. Garnishment of funds. Domestic obligation. Defense and security. Self-defense. Military assistance. Return of equipment and recapture.
TREATY REF: 48UNTS115; 22UNTS217.
PARTIES:
Denmark
USA (United States)

102355 Bilateral Exchange **179 UNTS 73**
SIGNED: 5 Jan 52   FORCE: 5 Jan 52
REGISTERED: 7 Nov 53 USA (United States)
ARTICLES: 2 LANGUAGE: English.
HEADNOTE: MUTUAL SECURITY
TOPIC: Milit Assistance
CONCEPTS: Peaceful relations. Migrant worker. Accounting procedures. Garnishment of funds. General military.
TREATY REF: 21UNTS29; 79UNTS288.
PARTIES:
Austria
USA (United States)

102356 Bilateral Exchange **179 UNTS 81**
SIGNED: 7 Jan 52   FORCE: 7 Jan 52
REGISTERED: 7 Nov 53 USA (United States)
ARTICLES: 3 LANGUAGE: English. French.
HEADNOTE: MUTUAL SECURITY
TOPIC: Milit Assistance
CONCEPTS: Guarantees and safeguards. Peaceful relations. Conformity with municipal law. Migrant worker. Accounting procedures. Garnishment of funds. Domestic obligation. Defense and security. Self-defense. Military assistance. Return of equipment and recapture.
PARTIES:
Belgium
USA (United States)

102357 Bilateral Exchange **179 UNTS 91**
SIGNED: 9 Feb 52   FORCE: 9 Feb 52
REGISTERED: 10 Nov 53 USA (United States)
ARTICLES: 2 LANGUAGE: English.
HEADNOTE: MUTUAL SECURITY
TOPIC: Milit Assistance
CONCEPTS: Non-prejudice to UN charter. Peaceful relations. Defense and security.
INTL ORGS: United Nations.
TREATY REF: 92UNTS261.
PARTIES:
Burma
USA (United States)

102358 Bilateral Exchange **179 UNTS 97**
SIGNED: 28 Dec 51   FORCE: 28 Dec 51
REGISTERED: 10 Nov 53 USA (United States)
ARTICLES: 2 LANGUAGE: English. French.
HEADNOTE: MUTUAL SECURITY
TOPIC: Milit Assistance
CONCEPTS: Conditions. Guarantees and safeguards. Time limit. Peaceful relations. Conformity with municipal law. Garnishment of funds. Domestic obligation. Defense and security. Self-defense. Military assistance. Return of equipment and recapture.
TREATY REF: 174UNTS115.

PARTIES:
Cambodia
USA (United States)

102359 Bilateral Exchange **179 UNTS 105**
SIGNED: 7 Jan 52 FORCE: 7 Jan 52
REGISTERED: 10 Nov 53 USA (United States)
ARTICLES: 2 LANGUAGE: English.
HEADNOTE: MUTUAL SECURITY
TOPIC: Milit Assistance
CONCEPTS: Guarantees and safeguards. Peaceful
relations. Conformity with municipal law. Gar-
nishment of funds. Domestic obligation. Defense
and security. Self-defense. Military assistance.
Return of equipment and recapture.
TREATY REF: 80UNTS205.
PARTIES:
Korea, South
USA (United States)

102360 Bilateral Exchange **179 UNTS 113**
SIGNED: 29 Dec 51 FORCE: 29 Dec 51
REGISTERED: 10 Nov 53 USA (United States)
ARTICLES: 2 LANGUAGE: English.
HEADNOTE: MUTUAL SECURITY
TOPIC: Milit Assistance
CONCEPTS: Guarantees and safeguards. Peaceful
relations. Conformity with municipal law. Gar-
nishment of funds. Domestic obligation. Defense
and security. Self-defense. Military assistance.
Return of equipment and recapture.
TREATY REF: 132UNTS199; 134UNTS390.
PARTIES:
Thailand
USA (United States)

102361 Bilateral Exchange **179 UNTS 121**
SIGNED: 7 Jan 52 FORCE: 7 Jan 52
REGISTERED: 10 Nov 53 USA (United States)
ARTICLES: 2 LANGUAGE: English.
HEADNOTE: MUTUAL SECURITY
TOPIC: Milit Assistance
CONCEPTS: Guarantees and safeguards. Peaceful
relations. Conformity with municipal law. Ac-
counting procedures. Garnishment of funds. Do-
mestic obligation. Defense and security. Self-
defense. Military assistance.
TREATY REF: 7UNTS199; 24UNTS67.
PARTIES:
Turkey
USA (United States)

102362 Bilateral Agreement **179 UNTS 129**
SIGNED: 29 Jul 52 FORCE: 29 Jul 52
REGISTERED: 10 Nov 53 USA (United States)
ARTICLES: 6 LANGUAGE: English.
HEADNOTE: UTILIZATION LEASED BASE AREAS
TOPIC: Status of Forces
CONCEPTS: Inspection and observation. Respon-
sibility and liability. Indemnities and reimburse-
ments. Purchase authorizations. Lease of mili-
tary property. Bases and facilities.
TREATY REF: 76UNTS142.
PARTIES:
UK Great Britain
USA (United States)

102363 Bilateral Exchange **179 UNTS 139**
SIGNED: 23 Jul 52 FORCE: 23 Jul 52
REGISTERED: 10 Nov 53 USA (United States)
ARTICLES: 2 LANGUAGE: English.
HEADNOTE: MUTUAL DEFENSE ASSISTANCE
TOPIC: Milit Assistance
CONCEPTS: Conditions. Exceptions and exemp-
tions. Guarantees and safeguards. Non-preju-
dice to UN charter. Peaceful relations. Confor-
mity with municipal law. Accounting proce-
dures. Payment schedules. Defense and
security. Self-defense. Military assistance. Secu-
rity of information. Exchange of defense informa-
tion. Restrictions on transfer.
PARTIES:
Israel
USA (United States)

102364 Bilateral Treaty **179 UNTS 147**
SIGNED: 18 Jan 52 FORCE: 30 Jul 53
REGISTERED: 12 Nov 53 Netherlands

ARTICLES: 6 LANGUAGE: Dutch. German.
HEADNOTE: MINING BOUNDARY BETWEEN
COALFIELDS
TOPIC: Specific Property
CONCEPTS: Juridical personality. Immovable
property. Markers and definitions. Raw materi-
als.
TREATY REF: 199UNTS239.
PROCEDURE: Duration. Ratification.
PARTIES:
Germany, West
Netherlands
ANNEX
450 UNTS 408. Netherlands. Amendment
8 Nov 60. Force 25 Nov 61.
450 UNTS 408. Germany, West. Amendment
8 Nov 60. Force 25 Nov 61.

102365 Bilateral Exchange **179 UNTS 165**
SIGNED: 7 Jan 52 FORCE: 7 Jan 52
REGISTERED: 14 Nov 53 USA (United States)
ARTICLES: 2 LANGUAGE: English. Italian.
HEADNOTE: MUTUAL SECURITY
TOPIC: Milit Assistance
CONCEPTS: Guarantees and safeguards. Peaceful
relations. Conformity with municipal law. Mi-
grant worker. Accounting procedures. Garnish-
ment of funds. Domestic obligation. Defense and
security. Self-defense. Military assistance. Re-
turn of equipment and recapture.
INTL ORGS: United Nations.
TREATY REF: 80UNTS145; 20UNTS43.
PARTIES:
Italy
USA (United States)

102366 Bilateral Exchange **179 UNTS 175**
SIGNED: 8 Jan 52 FORCE: 8 Jan 52
REGISTERED: 14 Nov 53 USA (United States)
ARTICLES: 2 LANGUAGE: English.
HEADNOTE: MUTUAL SECURITY
TOPIC: Milit Assistance
CONCEPTS: Guarantees and safeguards. Peaceful
relations. Conformity with municipal law. Mi-
grant worker. Accounting procedures. Garnish-
ment of funds. Domestic obligation. Defense and
security. Self-defense. Military assistance. Re-
turn of equipment and recapture.
INTL ORGS: United Nations.
TREATY REF: 20UNTS91; 80UNTS219.
PARTIES:
Netherlands
USA (United States)

102367 Bilateral Exchange **179 UNTS 185**
SIGNED: 8 Jan 52 FORCE: 8 Jan 52
REGISTERED: 14 Nov 53 USA (United States)
ARTICLES: 2 LANGUAGE: English.
HEADNOTE: MUTUAL SECURITY
TOPIC: Milit Assistance
CONCEPTS: Guarantees and safeguards. Peaceful
relations. Conformity with municipal law. Mi-
grant worker. Accounting procedures. Garnish-
ment of funds. Domestic obligation. Defense and
security. Self-defense. Military assistance. Re-
turn of equipment and recapture.
INTL ORGS: United Nations.
TREATY REF: 29UNTS185; 80UNTS241.
PARTIES:
Norway
USA (United States)

102368 Bilateral Exchange **179 UNTS 193**
SIGNED: 7 Jan 52 FORCE: 7 Jan 52
REGISTERED: 14 Nov 53 USA (United States)
ARTICLES: 2 LANGUAGE: English.
HEADNOTE: MUTUAL SECURITY
TOPIC: Milit Assistance
CONCEPTS: Guarantees and safeguards. Peaceful
relations. Conformity with municipal law. Gar-
nishment of funds. Domestic obligation. Defense
and security. Self-defense. Military assistance.
Return of equipment and recapture.
TREATY REF: 174UNTS251; 45UNTS47.
PARTIES:
Philippines
USA (United States)

102369 Bilateral Exchange **179 UNTS 201**
SIGNED: 8 Jan 52 FORCE: 8 Jan 52
REGISTERED: 14 Nov 53 USA (United States)
ARTICLES: 2 LANGUAGE: English.
HEADNOTE: MUTUAL SECURITY
TOPIC: Milit Assistance
CONCEPTS: Guarantees and safeguards. Peaceful
relations. Conformity with municipal law. Ac-
counting procedures. Monetary and gold trans-
fers. Garnishment of funds. Domestic obligation.
Defense and security. Self-defense. Return of
equipment and recapture.
INTL ORGS: United Nations.
TREATY REF: 22UNTS263; 80UNTS261.
PROCEDURE: Future Procedures Contemplated.
Termination. Application to Non-self-governing
Territories.
PARTIES:
UK Great Britain
USA (United States)

102370 Bilateral Exchange **180 UNTS 3**
SIGNED: 20 May 53 FORCE: 20 May 53
REGISTERED: 14 Nov 53 Belgium
ARTICLES: 2 LANGUAGE: French. German.
HEADNOTE: RE-ENTRY FORCE 1929 CONVEN-
TION
TOPIC: Admin Cooperation
CONCEPTS: Revival of treaties.
TREATY REF: 137LTS11; 142LTS393;
147LTS355.
PARTIES:
Belgium
Germany, West
ANNEX
211 UNTS 422. Belgium. Acknowledgement
30 Dec 54. Force 30 Dec 54.
211 UNTS 422. Germany, West. Berlin. Force
30 Dec 54.

102371 Bilateral Exchange **180 UNTS 9**
SIGNED: 18 Jul 53 FORCE: 18 Jul 53
REGISTERED: 19 Nov 53 Belgium
ARTICLES: 2 LANGUAGE: English. French.
HEADNOTE: DOUBLE TAXATION PROFITS AIR-
CRAFT
TOPIC: Taxation
CONCEPTS: General.
PROCEDURE: Termination.
PARTIES:
Belgium
USA (United States)

102372 Bilateral Agreement **180 UNTS 15**
SIGNED: 12 Nov 52 FORCE: 22 Oct 53
REGISTERED: 19 Nov 53 Belgium
ARTICLES: 9 LANGUAGE: English. French.
HEADNOTE: ESTABLISHMENT MILITARY BASE
TOPIC: Status of Forces
CONCEPTS: Use of facilities. Arbitration. Proce-
dure. Expense sharing formulae. Defense and se-
curity. Procurement and logistics. Status of
forces.
INTL ORGS: North Atlantic Treaty Organization.
PROCEDURE: Future Procedures Contemplated.
Ratification.
PARTIES:
Belgium
UK Great Britain

102373 Bilateral Convention **180 UNTS 23**
SIGNED: 17 Jun 52 FORCE: 1 Nov 53
REGISTERED: 19 Nov 53 Belgium
ARTICLES: 19 LANGUAGE: French.
HEADNOTE: SOCIAL INSURANCE
TOPIC: Non-ILO Labor
CONCEPTS: General provisions. Annex type mate-
rial. Domestic legislation. Operating agencies.
Incorporation of treaty provisions into national
law. Dispute settlement. Old age and invalidity
insurance. Non-ILO labor relations. Administra-
tive cooperation. Old age insurance. Sickness
and invalidity insurance. Social security. Fees
and exemptions. Payment schedules.
PROCEDURE: Denunciation. Duration. Ratification.
Renewal or Revival.
PARTIES:
Belgium
Switzerland

102374   Bilateral Agreement   **180 UNTS 45**
SIGNED: 19 Nov 53   FORCE: 19 Nov 53
REGISTERED: 19 Nov 53 United Nations
ARTICLES: 6 LANGUAGE: English. Spanish.
HEADNOTE: TECHNICAL ASSISTANCE
TOPIC: Tech Assistance
CONCEPTS: Treaty implementation. Privileges and immunities. General cooperation. Exchange of information and documents. Personnel. Title and deeds. Exchange. Scholarships and grants. Vocational training. Research and development. Expense sharing formulae. Local currency. Domestic obligation. General technical assistance. Materials, equipment and services. IGO status. Conformity with IGO decisions.
TREATY REF: 11NTS15,263; 76UNTS132.
PROCEDURE: Amendment. Termination.
PARTIES:
     Dominican Republic
     United Nations
             ANNEX
251 UNTS 392. Dominican Republic. Force 5 Oct 56.
251 UNTS 392. United Nations. Force 5 Oct 56.

102375   Bilateral Agreement   **180 UNTS 59**
SIGNED: 7 Oct 53   FORCE: 7 Oct 53
REGISTERED: 19 Nov 53 United Nations
ARTICLES: 10 LANGUAGE: English.
HEADNOTE: ASSISTANCE
TOPIC: Tech Assistance
CONCEPTS: Conditions. Definition of terms. Treaty implementation. Previous treaty replacement. Privileges and immunities. General cooperation. Exchange of information and documents. Informational records. Inspection and observation. Personnel. Public information. Title and deeds. Procedure. Negotiation. Export quotas. Import quotas. Indemnities and reimbursements. Fees and exemptions. Claims and settlements. General. Customs duties. Commodities and services. Domestic obligation. Assistance. Headquarters and facilities. IGO status.
INTL ORGS: United Nations.
TREATY REF: 1UNTS15,263.
PROCEDURE: Amendment. Termination. Application to Non-self-governing Territories.
PARTIES:
     UNICEF (Children)
     UK Great Britain
             ANNEX
337 UNTS 412. UNICEF (Children). Supplementation 7 Jul 59. Force 7 Jul 59.
337 UNTS 412. UK Great Britain. Supplementation 7 Jul 59. Force 7 Jul 59.
634 UNTS 429. UK Great Britain. Bahrain. Force 18 Jan 68.
634 UNTS 429. UK Great Britain. Qatar. Force 9 Apr 68.
660 UNTS 396. UK Great Britain. Trucial States. Force 7 Mar 69.

102376   Bilateral Agreement   **180 UNTS 73**
SIGNED: 28 Aug 53   FORCE: 6 Nov 53
REGISTERED: 20 Nov 53 IBRD (World Bank)
ARTICLES: 7 LANGUAGE: English.
HEADNOTE: LOAN AGREEMENT
TOPIC: IBRD Project
CONCEPTS: Default remedies. Annex or appendix reference. Exchange of information and documents. Informational records. Inspection and observation. Accounting procedures. Bonds. Fees and exemptions. Interest rates. Tax exemptions. Domestic obligation. Terms of loan. Loan regulations. Loan guarantee. Guarantor non-interference.
PARTIES:
     IBRD (World Bank)
     South Africa

102377   Bilateral Agreement   **180 UNTS 91**
SIGNED: 28 Aug 53   FORCE: 4 Nov 53
REGISTERED: 20 Nov 53 IBRD (World Bank)
ARTICLES: 5 LANGUAGE: English.
HEADNOTE: GUARANTEE AGREEMENT
TOPIC: IBRD Project
CONCEPTS: Annex or appendix reference. Exchange of information and documents. Informational records. Inspection and observation. Bonds. Fees and exemptions. Tax exemptions. Domestic obligation. Terms of loan. Loan regula-

tions. Loan guarantee. Guarantor non-interference.
PARTIES:
     IBRD (World Bank)
     South Africa

102378   Bilateral Exchange   **180 UNTS 115**
SIGNED: 1 Apr 47   FORCE: 1 Apr 47
REGISTERED: 21 Nov 53 Greece
ARTICLES: 2 LANGUAGE: French.
HEADNOTE: MOST FAVORED NATION TREATMENT VESSELS
TOPIC: Mostfavored Nation
CONCEPTS: Most favored nation clause. Navigational conditions.
TREATY REF: 63UNTS27.
PARTIES:
     Greece
     Switzerland

102379   Bilateral Exchange   **180 UNTS 119**
SIGNED: 8 Oct 46   FORCE: 18 Apr 47
REGISTERED: 21 Nov 53 Greece
ARTICLES: 6 LANGUAGE: English.
HEADNOTE: RELEASE ASSETS
TOPIC: Claims and Debts
CONCEPTS: Detailed regulations. Conformity with municipal law. General property. Accounting procedures. Banking. Financial programs. Assets. Debts. Assessment procedures. Assets transfer. General. Enemy financial interests.
PARTIES:
     Greece
     USA (United States)

102380   Bilateral Exchange   **180 UNTS 144**
SIGNED: 7 Sep 48   FORCE: 7 Sep 48
REGISTERED: 21 Nov 53 Greece
ARTICLES: 6 LANGUAGE: English. French.
HEADNOTE: MAINTENANCE MILITARY MISSION
TOPIC: Status of Forces
CONCEPTS: Indemnities and reimbursements. Payment schedules. Materials, equipment and services. Defense and security. Status of military forces.
PARTIES:
     Greece
     UK Great Britain

102381   Bilateral Exchange   **180 UNTS 161**
SIGNED: 19 Sep 51   FORCE: 1 Oct 51
REGISTERED: 28 Nov 53 USA (United States)
ARTICLES: 2 LANGUAGE: English. German.
HEADNOTE: EXPORT FERROUS SCRAP
TOPIC: General Trade
CONCEPTS: Detailed regulations. Annex type material. General cooperation. Licenses and permits. Commodity trade. Delivery schedules. Quotas.
PROCEDURE: Duration.
PARTIES:
     Germany, West
     USA (United States)

102382   Bilateral Exchange   **180 UNTS 171**
SIGNED: 7 Jan 52   FORCE: 7 Jan 52
REGISTERED: 28 Nov 53 USA (United States)
ARTICLES: 4 LANGUAGE: English.
HEADNOTE: MUTUAL SECURITY
TOPIC: Milit Assistance
CONCEPTS: Guarantees and safeguards. Previous treaty extension. Peaceful relations. Conformity with municipal law. Inspection and observation. Migrant worker. Accounting procedures. Garnishment of funds. Domestic obligation. Defense and security. Self-defense. Military assistance. Return of equipment and recapture.
TREATY REF: 7UNTS267.
PROCEDURE: Future Procedures Contemplated.
PARTIES:
     Greece
     USA (United States)
             ANNEX
407 UNTS 238. Greece. Amendment 18 Apr 61. Force 18 Apr 61.
407 UNTS 238. USA (United States). Amendment 17 Apr 61. Force 18 Apr 61.

102383   Bilateral Exchange   **180 UNTS 183**
SIGNED: 8 Jan 52   FORCE: 8 Jan 52
REGISTERED: 28 Nov 53 USA (United States)
ARTICLES: 2 LANGUAGE: English.
HEADNOTE: MUTUAL SECURITY
TOPIC: Milit Assistance
CONCEPTS: Guarantees and safeguards. Friendship and amity. Peaceful relations. Conformity with municipal law. Migrant worker. Accounting procedures. Garnishment of funds. Domestic obligation. Defense and security. Self-defense. Military assistance.
INTL ORGS: United Nations.
TREATY REF: 20UNTS141.
PARTIES:
     Iceland
     USA (United States)

102384   Bilateral Exchange   **180 UNTS 191**
SIGNED: 8 Jan 52   FORCE: 8 Jan 52
REGISTERED: 28 Nov 53 USA (United States)
ARTICLES: 2 LANGUAGE: English. French.
HEADNOTE: MUTUAL SECURITY
TOPIC: Milit Assistance
CONCEPTS: Guarantees and safeguards. Peaceful relations. Conformity with municipal law. Migrant worker. Accounting procedures. Garnishment of funds. Domestic obligation. Defense and security. Self-defense. Military assistance. Return of equipment and recapture.
INTL ORGS: United Nations.
TREATY REF: 24UNTS35; 80UNTS187.
PARTIES:
     Luxembourg
     USA (United States)

102385   Bilateral Exchange   **180 UNTS 199**
SIGNED: 5 Jan 52   FORCE: 5 Jan 52
REGISTERED: 28 Nov 53 USA (United States)
ARTICLES: 2 LANGUAGE: Arabic. English.
HEADNOTE: TECHNICAL COOPERATION
TOPIC: Tech Assistance
CONCEPTS: General technical assistance.
INTL ORGS: United Nations.
TREATY REF: 160UNTS49.
PARTIES:
     Lebanon
     USA (United States)

102386   Bilateral Agreement   **180 UNTS 207**
SIGNED: 17 Nov 52   FORCE: 17 Nov 52
REGISTERED: 28 Nov 53 USA (United States)
ARTICLES: 12 LANGUAGE: English.
HEADNOTE: EDUCATIONAL PROGRAM
TOPIC: Education
CONCEPTS: Definition of terms. Friendship and amity. Alien status. Privileges and immunities. Conformity with municipal law. Inspection and observation. Personnel. General property. Private contracts. Exchange. Commissions and foundations. Teacher and student exchange. Institute establishment. Vocational training. Research cooperation. Research and development. Accounting procedures. Indemnities and reimbursements. Currency. Exchange rates and regulations. Financial programs. Funding procedures. Customs exemptions. General technical assistance. Aid missions.
TREATY REF: USA 58STAT782; 60STAT754.
PARTIES:
     Ceylon (Sri Lanka)
     USA (United States)
             ANNEX
361 UNTS 320. Ceylon (Sri Lanka). Amendment 7 Oct 59. Force 7 Oct 59.
361 UNTS 320. USA (United States). Amendment 29 Jul 59. Force 7 Oct 59.
479 UNTS 364. Ceylon (Sri Lanka). Amendment 17 Jun 63. Force 17 Jun 63.
479 UNTS 364. USA (United States). Amendment 17 Jun 63. Force 17 Jun 63.

102387   Bilateral Exchange   **180 UNTS 219**
SIGNED: 27 Jul 49   FORCE: 19 Sep 49
REGISTERED: 28 Nov 53 USA (United States)
ARTICLES: 2 LANGUAGE: English. Spanish.
HEADNOTE: HEALTH SANITATION PROGRAM
TOPIC: Sanitation
CONCEPTS: Previous treaty extension. Public

health. Sanitation. Currency. Expense sharing formulae. Funding procedures. Assistance.
TREATY REF: 21UNTS215; 166UNTS149.
PROCEDURE: Ratification.
PARTIES:
El Salvador
USA (United States)

102388 Bilateral Agreement **180 UNTS 227**
SIGNED: 15 May 52 FORCE: 5 May 52
REGISTERED: 28 Nov 53 USA (United States)
ARTICLES: 13 LANGUAGE: Amharic. English.
HEADNOTE: AGRICULTURAL EDUCATION
TOPIC: Education
CONCEPTS: Definition of terms. Friendship and amity. Alien status. Privileges and immunities. Conformity with municipal law. General cooperation. Exchange of information and documents. Inspection and observation. Personnel. General property. Private contracts. Exchange. Commissions and foundations. Institute establishment. Vocational training. Accounting procedures. Currency. Exchange rates and regulations. Expense sharing formulae. Financial programs. Funding procedures. Garnishment of funds. Tax exemptions. Customs exemptions. Agriculture. Economic assistance. Mass media exchange.
TREATY REF: 148UNTS39.
PROCEDURE: Duration. Future Procedures Contemplated. Renewal or Revival. Termination.
PARTIES:
Ethiopia
USA (United States)
ANNEX
212 UNTS 358. Ethiopia. Amendment 25 Jun 53. Force 25 Jun 53.
212 UNTS 358. USA (United States). Amendment 25 Jun 53. Force 25 Jun 53.

102389 Bilateral Exchange **180 UNTS 251**
SIGNED: 9 Jul 52 FORCE: 9 Jul 52
REGISTERED: 28 Nov 53 USA (United States)
ARTICLES: 4 LANGUAGE: English. Portuguese.
HEADNOTE: DISPOSITION SURPLUS MUTUAL DEFENSE ASSISTANCE EQUIPMENT
TOPIC: Milit Assistance
CONCEPTS: Conformity with municipal law. General cooperation. Exchange of information and documents. Reexport of goods, etc.. Delivery schedules. Surplus property. Return of equipment and recapture. Surplus war property.
TREATY REF: 133UNTS75.
PARTIES:
Portugal
USA (United States)
ANNEX
393 UNTS 315. USA (United States). Amendment 15 Sep 60. Force 15 Sep 60.
393 UNTS 315. Portugal. Amendment 15 Sep 60. Force 15 Sep 60.

102390 Bilateral Agreement **180 UNTS 263**
SIGNED: 10 Nov 51 FORCE: 10 Nov 52
REGISTERED: 28 Nov 53 USA (United States)
ARTICLES: 4 LANGUAGE: Arabic. English.
HEADNOTE: AERIAL SURVEY PROJECT
TOPIC: Scientific Project
CONCEPTS: Privileges and immunities. Operating agencies. Responsibility and liability. Use of facilities. Research and scientific projects. Scientific exchange. Research and development. Expense sharing formulae. Tax exemptions. Domestic obligation. General technical assistance. Regulation of natural resources.
TREATY REF: 140UNTS335.
PROCEDURE: Duration. Termination.
PARTIES:
Saudi Arabia
USA (United States)

102391 Bilateral Agreement **180 UNTS 275**
SIGNED: 16 Nov 51 FORCE: 28 Apr 52
REGISTERED: 28 Nov 53 USA (United States)
ARTICLES: 2 LANGUAGE: English.
HEADNOTE: REDISTRIBUTABLE EXCESS MUTUAL DEFENSE ASSISTANCE PROGRAM PROPERTY
TOPIC: Milit Assistance
CONCEPTS: Detailed regulations. General cooperation. Exchange of information and documents.

Title and deeds. Reexport of goods, etc.. Delivery schedules. Surplus property. Return of equipment and recapture. Surplus war property.
PARTIES:
Denmark
USA (United States)
ANNEX
388 UNTS 356. USA (United States). Amendment 12 Sep 60. Force 12 Sep 60.
388 UNTS 356. Denmark. Amendment 12 Sep 60. Force 12 Sep 60.

102392 Bilateral Exchange **180 UNTS 283**
SIGNED: 20 Mar 51 FORCE: 11 Jun 52
REGISTERED: 28 Nov 53 USA (United States)
ARTICLES: 3 LANGUAGE: English. French.
HEADNOTE: ESTABLISHMENT PERMANENT CEMETERY
TOPIC: Other Military
CONCEPTS: Annex or appendix reference. Title and deeds. Upkeep of war graves. Establishment of war cemeteries.
PARTIES:
Luxembourg
USA (United States)

102393 Bilateral Exchange **181 UNTS 3**
SIGNED: 13 Jun 52 FORCE: 13 Jun 52
REGISTERED: 28 Nov 53 USA (United States)
ARTICLES: 2 LANGUAGE: English. French.
HEADNOTE: TAXATION DEFENSE EXPENDITURES
TOPIC: Taxation
CONCEPTS: General. Military installations and equipment.
PARTIES:
France
USA (United States)
ANNEX
265 UNTS 356. France. Amendment 27 Nov 56. Force 27 Nov 56.
265 UNTS 356. USA (United States). Amendment 27 Nov 56. Force 27 Nov 56.

102394 Bilateral Exchange **181 UNTS 15**
SIGNED: 4 Aug 49 FORCE: 4 Aug 49
REGISTERED: 28 Nov 53 USA (United States)
ARTICLES: 5 LANGUAGE: English.
HEADNOTE: SETTLEMENT WAR CLAIMS
TOPIC: Reparations
CONCEPTS: Annex or appendix reference. Lump sum settlements. Loss and/or damage. Post-war claims settlement.
PARTIES:
Portugal
USA (United States)

102395 Bilateral Exchange **181 UNTS 31**
SIGNED: 8 Jan 52 FORCE: 8 Jan 52
REGISTERED: 28 Nov 53 USA (United States)
ARTICLES: 2 LANGUAGE: English. Spanish.
HEADNOTE: TECHNICAL COOPERATION
TOPIC: Tech Assistance
CONCEPTS: Conditions. Annex or appendix reference. General cooperation. Attachment of funds. Garnishment of funds. Seizure funds. General technical assistance.
PARTIES:
Guatemala
USA (United States)

102396 Bilateral Exchange **181 UNTS 37**
SIGNED: 8 Aug 52 FORCE: 8 Aug 52
REGISTERED: 28 Nov 53 USA (United States)
ARTICLES: 2 LANGUAGE: English.
HEADNOTE: GUARANTIES
TOPIC: Direct Aid
CONCEPTS: Guarantees and safeguards. Conformity with municipal law. Arbitration. Negotiation. Local currency. Claims and settlements. Assets transfer. Economic assistance.
PARTIES:
Israel
USA (United States)
ANNEX
289 UNTS 318. USA (United States). Amendment 31 Jul 57. Force 11 Aug 57.
289 UNTS 318. Israel. Amendment 11 Aug 57. Force 11 Aug 57.

474 UNTS 332. USA (United States). Supplementation 5 Feb 63. Force 20 Feb 63.
474 UNTS 332. Israel. Supplementation 20 Feb 63. Force 20 Feb 63.

102397 Bilateral Exchange **181 UNTS 45**
SIGNED: 28 Dec 51 FORCE: 28 Dec 51
REGISTERED: 28 Nov 53 USA (United States)
ARTICLES: 2 LANGUAGE: English. German.
HEADNOTE: MUTUAL SECURITY
TOPIC: Milit Assistance
CONCEPTS: General cooperation. Migrant worker. Indemnities and reimbursements. Garnishment of funds. Economic assistance. Defense and security.
TREATY REF: 92UNTS269; 141UNTS390.
PARTIES:
Germany, West
USA (United States)

102398 Bilateral Exchange **181 UNTS 53**
SIGNED: 25 Jun 52 FORCE: 25 Jun 52
REGISTERED: 28 Nov 53 USA (United States)
ARTICLES: 3 LANGUAGE: English.
HEADNOTE: AIR SERVICE
TOPIC: Air Transport
CONCEPTS: Annex or appendix reference. Meteorology. Surplus property. Routes and logistics. Navigational equipment. Airport facilities. Airport equipment. Operating authorizations and regulations. Bands and frequency allocation. Facilities and equipment. Military installations and equipment.
INTL ORGS: International Civil Aviation Organization.
TREATY REF: USA'62STAT137; 22USC-1501ET SEQ;.
PROCEDURE: Termination.
PARTIES:
Greece
USA (United States)

102399 Multilateral Agreement **181 UNTS 61**
SIGNED: 28 Mar 51 FORCE: 28 Mar 51
REGISTERED: 30 Nov 53 ILO (Labor Org)
ARTICLES: 6 LANGUAGE: English. Spanish.
HEADNOTE: TECHNICAL ASSISTANCE
TOPIC: Tech Assistance
CONCEPTS: Treaty implementation. Annex or appendix reference. Privileges and immunities. General cooperation. Exchange of information and documents. Personnel. Title and deeds. Use of facilities. Arbitration. Procedure. Scholarships and grants. Vocational training. Research and scientific projects. Exchange rates and regulations. Expense sharing formulae. Local currency. Domestic obligation. General technical assistance. Materials, equipment and services. IGO status. Conformity with IGO decisions.
INTL ORGS: United Nations.
TREATY REF: 33UNTS261.
PROCEDURE: Amendment. Termination.
PARTIES:
Costa Rica SIGNED: 28 Mar 51 FORCE: 28 Mar 51
ILO (Labor Org) SIGNED: 28 Mar 51 FORCE: 28 Mar 51
UNESCO (Educ/Cult) SIGNED: 28 Mar 51 FORCE: 28 Mar 51

102400 Bilateral Treaty **181 UNTS 81**
SIGNED: 19 Feb 53 FORCE: 21 Sep 53
REGISTERED: 30 Nov 53 Taiwan
ARTICLES: 11 LANGUAGE: Chinese. English. Spanish.
HEADNOTE: AMITY
TOPIC: General Amity
CONCEPTS: Friendship and amity. National treatment.
INTL ORGS: Permanent Court of Arbitration. Arbitration Commission.
TREATY REF: PRELIM TREATY AMITY&COMM.;-CHINA-SPAIN 27DEC28.
PROCEDURE: Ratification.
PARTIES:
Taiwan
Spain

102401 Bilateral Agreement **181 UNTS 95**
SIGNED: 30 Mar 53   FORCE: 29 Jul 53
REGISTERED: 1 Dec 53 Belgium
ARTICLES: 7 LANGUAGE: English. French.
HEADNOTE: TRANSIT THROUGH STATIONING FORCES
TOPIC: Status of Forces
CONCEPTS: Use of facilities. Most favored nation clause. Defense and security. Procurement and logistics.
PROCEDURE: Future Procedures Contemplated. Ratification. Termination.
PARTIES:
Belgium
Canada

102402 Bilateral Exchange **181 UNTS 101**
SIGNED: 23 Sep 48   FORCE: 23 Oct 48
REGISTERED: 1 Dec 53 USA (United States)
ARTICLES: 2 LANGUAGE: English. Spanish.
HEADNOTE: HEALTH SANITATION
TOPIC: Sanitation
CONCEPTS: Previous treaty extension. General co-operation. Programs. Public health. Sanitation. Currency. Expense sharing formulae. Financial programs. Funding procedures.
PROCEDURE: Duration.
PARTIES:
El Salvador
USA (United States)

102403 Bilateral Exchange **181 UNTS 109**
SIGNED: 2 Jun 52   FORCE: 2 Jun 52
REGISTERED: 1 Dec 53 USA (United States)
ARTICLES: 2 LANGUAGE: English. Portuguese.
HEADNOTE: AERONAUTIC CHARTING TOPOGRAPHIC MAPPING
TOPIC: Scientific Project
CONCEPTS: General cooperation. Operating agencies. General property. Establishment of commission. Programs. Research and scientific projects. Research results. Scientific exchange. Research and development. Domestic obligation. Materials, equipment and services.
INTL ORGS: Special Commission.
PROCEDURE: Future Procedures Contemplated. Termination.
PARTIES:
Brazil
USA (United States)

102404 Bilateral Agreement **181 UNTS 121**
SIGNED: 30 Jun 52   FORCE: 30 Jun 52
REGISTERED: 1 Dec 53 USA (United States)
ARTICLES: 19 LANGUAGE: English. Spanish.
HEADNOTE: COOPERATIVE PROGRAM AGRICULTURE
TOPIC: Tech Assistance
CONCEPTS: Time limit. Treaty implementation. Annex type material. Privileges and immunities. General cooperation. Exchange of information and documents. Informational records. Inspection and observation. Domestic legislation. Operating agencies. General property. Title and deeds. Establishment of commission. Vocational training. Communication satellites testing. Attachment of funds. Currency deposits. Exchange rates and regulations. Funding procedures. Garnishment of funds. Seizure funds. Assets. Commodities and services. Domestic obligation. Agriculture. Materials, equipment and services. Aid missions.
TREATY REF: 92UNTS167.
PROCEDURE: Duration. Termination.
PARTIES:
Panama
USA (United States)
ANNEX
257 UNTS 372. USA (United States). Prolongation 23 Apr 55. Force 23 Apr 55.
257 UNTS 372. Panama. Prolongation 23 Apr 55. Force 23 Apr 55.

102405 Bilateral Agreement **181 UNTS 147**
SIGNED: 22 Jun 52   FORCE: 22 Jul 52
REGISTERED: 1 Dec 53 USA (United States)
ARTICLES: 4 LANGUAGE: English. Spanish.
HEADNOTE: PRIVILEGES & IMMUNITIES
TOPIC: IGO Status/Immunit

CONCEPTS: Privileges and immunities. IGO status. Status of experts.
PARTIES:
OAS (Am States)
USA (United States)

102406 Bilateral Exchange **181 UNTS 155**
SIGNED: 24 Nov 52   FORCE: 24 Nov 52
REGISTERED: 1 Dec 53 USA (United States)
ARTICLES: 2 LANGUAGE: English.
HEADNOTE: WAIVER NON-IMMIGRANT PASSPORT VISA FEES
TOPIC: Visas
CONCEPTS: Passports non-diplomatic. Visas. Fees and exemptions.
PROCEDURE: Amendment. Termination.
PARTIES:
Philippines
USA (United States)

102407 Bilateral Exchange **181 UNTS 161**
SIGNED: 2 Jan 52   FORCE: 2 Jan 52
REGISTERED: 1 Dec 53 USA (United States)
ARTICLES: 2 LANGUAGE: Chinese. English.
HEADNOTE: ASSURANCES UNDER MUTUAL SECURITY ACT
TOPIC: Milit Assistance
CONCEPTS: Guarantees and safeguards. Peaceful relations. Conformity with municipal law. Accounting procedures. Garnishment of funds. Domestic obligation. Defense and security. Military assistance. Return of equipment and recapture.
TREATY REF: 17UNTS119; 132UNTS273.
PARTIES:
Taiwan
USA (United States)

102408 Bilateral Exchange **181 UNTS 177**
SIGNED: 5 Jan 52   FORCE: 5 Jan 52
REGISTERED: 1 Dec 53 USA (United States)
ARTICLES: 2 LANGUAGE: English. French.
HEADNOTE: ASSURANCES MUTUAL SECURITY ACT
TOPIC: Milit Assistance
CONCEPTS: Friendship and amity. Peaceful relations. Economic assistance. Prisoners of war.
INTL ORGS: United Nations.
TREATY REF: 80UNTS171; 19UNTS9;T.
PARTIES:
France
USA (United States)

102409 Bilateral Agreement **181 UNTS 187**
SIGNED: 26 Jun 52   FORCE: 26 Jun 52
REGISTERED: 1 Dec 53 USA (United States)
ARTICLES: 11 LANGUAGE: Arabic. English.
HEADNOTE: TECHNICAL COOPERATION
TOPIC: Tech Assistance
CONCEPTS: General technical assistance. Assistance. Economic assistance. Materials, equipment and services. Loan and credit.
PARTIES:
Lebanon
USA (United States)
ANNEX
212 UNTS 360. Lebanon. Amendment 14 Apr 53. Force 14 Apr 53.
212 UNTS 360. USA (United States). Amendment 14 Apr 53. Force 14 Apr 53.
247 UNTS 442. USA (United States). Amendment 30 Apr 54. Force 30 Apr 54.
247 UNTS 442. Lebanon. Amendment 30 Apr 54. Force 30 Apr 54.
247 UNTS 446. USA (United States). Amendment 30 Apr 54. Force 30 Apr 54.
247 UNTS 446. Lebanon. Amendment 30 Apr 54. Force 30 Apr 54.

102410 Bilateral Exchange **181 UNTS 207**
SIGNED: 18 Jun 52   FORCE: 18 Jun 52
REGISTERED: 1 Dec 53 USA (United States)
ARTICLES: 2 LANGUAGE: English.
HEADNOTE: COOPERATIVE PROGRAM TECHNICAL SCIENCE EDUCATION
TOPIC: Tech Assistance
CONCEPTS: Annex type material. General cooperation. Personnel. Exchange. Vocational training. Currency deposits. Expense sharing formulae.

Domestic obligation. General technical assistance. Assistance.
INTL ORGS: Special Commission.
TREATY REF: 148UNTS39.
PROCEDURE: Duration. Renewal or Revival. Termination.
PARTIES:
Ethiopia
USA (United States)
ANNEX
212 UNTS 363. USA (United States). Implementation 19 Jun 53. Force 25 Jun 53.
212 UNTS 363. Ethiopia. Implementation 25 Jun 53. Force 25 Jun 53.

102411 Bilateral Exchange **181 UNTS 215**
SIGNED: 24 Jun 52   FORCE: 24 Jun 52
REGISTERED: 1 Dec 53 USA (United States)
ARTICLES: 2 LANGUAGE: English.
HEADNOTE: TECHNICAL COOPERATION PROGRAM WATER RESOURCES DEVELOPMENT
TOPIC: Tech Assistance
CONCEPTS: Annex type material. General cooperation. Informational records. Personnel. Vocational training. Research and development. Currency deposits. Expense sharing formulae. Domestic obligation. Assistance. Regulation of natural resources.
INTL ORGS: Special Commission.
TREATY REF: 148UNTS39.
PROCEDURE: Duration. Renewal or Revival. Termination.
PARTIES:
Ethiopia
USA (United States)
ANNEX
212 UNTS 366. USA (United States). Prolongation 27 Jun 53. Force 20 Jun 53.
212 UNTS 366. Ethiopia. Prolongation 30 Jun 53. Force 30 Jun 53.
232 UNTS 346. USA (United States). Prolongation 27 Apr 54. Force 11 May 54.
232 UNTS 346. Ethiopia. Prolongation 11 Apr 54. Force 11 May 54.
271 UNTS 424. USA (United States). Extension and Amendment 26 Jun 56. Force 27 Jun 56.
271 UNTS 424. Ethiopia. Extension and Amendment 26 Jun 56. Force 27 Jun 56.

102412 Bilateral Agreement **181 UNTS 225**
SIGNED: 10 Nov 52   FORCE: 10 Nov 52
REGISTERED: 4 Dec 53 USA (United States)
ARTICLES: 5 LANGUAGE: Arabic. English.
HEADNOTE: TECHNICAL COOPERATION PROGRAM NATURAL RESOURCES
TOPIC: Tech Assistance
CONCEPTS: Treaty implementation. Annex type material. Personnel. Vocational training. Research and development. Financial programs. Assistance. Materials, equipment and services. Regulation of natural resources.
TREATY REF: 140UNTS335.
PROCEDURE: Duration. Termination.
PARTIES:
Saudi Arabia
USA (United States)

102413 Bilateral Agreement **181 UNTS 235**
SIGNED: 10 Nov 52   FORCE: 10 Nov 52
REGISTERED: 4 Dec 53 USA (United States)
ARTICLES: 5 LANGUAGE: Arabic. English.
HEADNOTE: TECHNICAL COOPERATION
TOPIC: Tech Assistance
CONCEPTS: General technical assistance. Assistance.
PARTIES:
Saudi Arabia
USA (United States)

102414 Bilateral Exchange **181 UNTS 249**
SIGNED: 8 Aug 52   FORCE: 9 Aug 52
REGISTERED: 4 Dec 53 USA (United States)
ARTICLES: 2 LANGUAGE: English.
HEADNOTE: GUARANTIES
TOPIC: Direct Aid
CONCEPTS: Guarantees and safeguards. Conformity with municipal law. Local currency. Claims and settlements. Assets transfer. Economic assistance.
TREATY REF: 22UNTS217.

PARTIES:
Denmark
USA (United States)

102415 Bilateral Exchange **181 UNTS 257**
SIGNED: 8 Aug 52 FORCE: 8 Aug 52
REGISTERED: 4 Dec 53 USA (United States)
ARTICLES: 2 LANGUAGE: English. Spanish.
HEADNOTE: PANAMA HEADQUARTERS CIVIL AVIATION SPECIALISTS LATIN AMERICA
TOPIC: Air Transport
CONCEPTS: Privileges and immunities. Personnel. Financial programs. Assistance. Materials, equipment and services. Aid missions. Air transport. Headquarters and facilities.
TREATY REF: 92UNTS167.
PARTIES:
Panama
USA (United States)

102416 Bilateral Agreement **181 UNTS 263**
SIGNED: 15 Jul 52 FORCE: 1 Aug 52
REGISTERED: 4 Dec 53 USA (United States)
ARTICLES: 2 LANGUAGE: English. Spanish.
HEADNOTE: FLIGHT NOTIFICATIONS NON-SCHEDULED, PRIVATE COMMERCIAL INDUSTRIAL FLIGHTS
TOPIC: Air Transport
CONCEPTS: Detailed regulations. Border traffic and migration. Informational records. Fees and exemptions. Funding procedures. Air transport. Airport facilities. Operating authorizations and regulations. Facilities and equipment.
PARTIES:
Mexico
USA (United States)

102417 Bilateral Exchange **181 UNTS 285**
SIGNED: 21 Jul 52 FORCE: 21 Jul 52
REGISTERED: 4 Dec 53 USA (United States)
ARTICLES: 4 LANGUAGE: English. Spanish.
HEADNOTE: EXTENSION AGREEMENT ADVISOR TO MINISTER FOREIGN AFFAIRS.
TOPIC: Tech Assistance
CONCEPTS: Previous treaty extension. Personnel. Veterinary. General technical assistance.
TREATY REF: 9UNTS289; 9UNTS400.
PARTIES:
Panama
USA (United States)
ANNEX
293 UNTS 352. USA (United States). Prolongation 2 Oct 57. Force 2 Oct 57.
293 UNTS 352. Panama. Prolongation 25 Jul 57. Force 2 Oct 57.

102418 Bilateral Agreement **181 UNTS 295**
SIGNED: 10 Nov 52 FORCE: 10 Nov 52
REGISTERED: 4 Dec 53 USA (United States)
ARTICLES: 5 LANGUAGE: Arabic. English.
HEADNOTE: TECHNICAL COOPERATION PROGRAM AGRICULTURE
TOPIC: Direct Aid
CONCEPTS: Treaty implementation. Annex type material. Personnel. Vocational training. Expense sharing formulae. Agriculture. Assistance. Materials, equipment and services.
TREATY REF: 140UNTS335.
PROCEDURE: Duration.
PARTIES:
Saudi Arabia
USA (United States)

102419 Bilateral Agreement **181 UNTS 307**
SIGNED: 10 Nov 52 FORCE: 10 Nov 52
REGISTERED: 4 Dec 53 USA (United States)
ARTICLES: 4 LANGUAGE: Arabic. English.
HEADNOTE: COOPERATIVE RAILWAY SURVEY PROJECT
TOPIC: Direct Aid
CONCEPTS: Exchange of information and documents. Operating agencies. Personnel. Responsibility and liability. Research and development. Expense sharing formulae. Tax exemptions. Customs exemptions. Domestic obligation. Assistance. Materials, equipment and services. Railways.
TREATY REF: 140UNTS335; 181UNTS242.
PROCEDURE: Duration. Termination.

102420 Bilateral Exchange **181 UNTS 319**
SIGNED: 22 Jul 52 FORCE: 24 Jul 52
REGISTERED: 4 Dec 53 USA (United States)
ARTICLES: 2 LANGUAGE: English. French.
HEADNOTE: GUARANTIES
TOPIC: Direct Aid
CONCEPTS: Guarantees and safeguards. Conformity with municipal law. Local currency. Claims and settlements. Public debt ceiling. Assets transfer. Economic assistance.
TREATY REF: 19UNTS9.
PARTIES:
France
USA (United States)

102421 Bilateral Exchange **182 UNTS 2**
SIGNED: 30 Apr 48 FORCE: 1 Jun 48
REGISTERED: 7 Dec 53 UK Great Britain
ARTICLES: 17 LANGUAGE: English.
HEADNOTE: FINANCE
TOPIC: Finance
CONCEPTS: Detailed regulations. General provisions. Annex or appendix reference. Incorporation of treaty provisions into national law. Balance of payments. Financial programs. Payment schedules. Economic assistance. Materials, equipment and services.
INTL ORGS: International Bank for Reconstruction and Development. International Monetary Fund.
PROCEDURE: Future Procedures Contemplated.
PARTIES:
Ceylon (Sri Lanka)
UK Great Britain

102422 Multilateral Protocol **182 UNTS 51**
SIGNED: 7 Dec 53 FORCE: 7 Dec 53
REGISTERED: 7 Dec 53 United Nations
ARTICLES: 5 LANGUAGE: Chinese. English. French. Russian. Spanish.
HEADNOTE: AMENDING SLAVERY CONVENTION
TOPIC: Admin Cooperation
CONCEPTS: Annex type material. Previous treaty extension.
INTL ORGS: United Nations.
PARTIES:
Australia SIGNED: 9 Dec 53 FORCE: 9 Dec 53
Austria SIGNED: 7 Dec 53
Canada SIGNED: 17 Dec 53 FORCE: 17 Dec 53
Taiwan SIGNED: 7 Dec 53
Greece SIGNED: 7 Dec 53
Liberia SIGNED: 7 Dec 53 FORCE: 7 Dec 53
Netherlands SIGNED: 15 Dec 53
New Zealand SIGNED: 16 Dec 53 FORCE: 16 Dec 53
Switzerland SIGNED: 7 Dec 53 FORCE: 7 Dec 53
UK Great Britain SIGNED: 7 Dec 53 FORCE: 7 Dec 53
USA (United States) SIGNED: 16 Dec 53
ANNEX
183 UNTS 378. South Africa. Signature without Reservation as to Approval 29 Dec 53.
185 UNTS 408. Mexico. Signature without Reservation as to Approval 3 Feb 54.
185 UNTS 408. Italy. Signature without Reservation as to Approval 4 Feb 54.
187 UNTS 466. Finland. Acceptance 19 Mar 54.
187 UNTS 466. Denmark. Signature without Reservation as to Approval 3 Mar 54.
187 UNTS 466. India. Signature without Reservation as to Approval 12 Mar 54.
191 UNTS 408. Cuba. Signature without Reservation as to Approval 28 Jun 54.
196 UNTS 361. Syria. Acceptance 4 Aug 54.
196 UNTS 361. Austria. Acceptance 16 Jul 54.
198 UNTS 406. Afghanistan. Signature without Reservation as to Approval 16 Aug 54.
198 UNTS 406. Sweden. Signature without Reservation as to Approval 17 Aug 54.
199 UNTS 356. United Arab Rep. Acceptance 29 Sep 54.
201 UNTS 381. Monaco. Acceptance 12 Nov 54.
202 UNTS 361. Turkey. Signature without Reservation as to Approval 14 Jan 55.
207 UNTS 365. Yugoslavia. Acceptance 21 Mar 55.
210 UNTS 336. Iraq. Acceptance 23 May 55.

212 UNTS 370. Netherlands. Signature Subject to Ratification 15 Dec 53.
212 UNTS 370. Netherlands. Acceptance 7 Jul 53.
212 UNTS 370. Netherlands. Surinam.
212 UNTS 370. Netherlands. Netherlands Antilles.
212 UNTS 370. Netherlands. Dutch New Guinea.
214 UNTS 375. Ecuador. Acceptance 17 Aug 55.
214 UNTS 375. Israel. Acceptance 12 Sep 55.
223 UNTS 376. Greece. Acceptance 12 Dec 55.
223 UNTS 376. Taiwan. Acceptance 14 Dec 55.
230 UNTS 439. USA (United States). Acceptance 7 Mar 56.
265 UNTS 361. Norway. Acceptance 11 Apr 57.
265 UNTS 361. Burma. Acceptance 29 Apr 57.
281 UNTS 404. Romania. Signature without Reservation as to Approval 13 Nov 57.
287 UNTS 347. Hungary. Acceptance 26 Feb 58.
328 UNTS 332. Morocco. Acceptance 11 May 59.
406 UNTS 307. Ireland. Acceptance 31 Aug 61.
433 UNTS 356. Guinea. Acceptance 12 Jul 62.
448 UNTS 328. Belgium. Acceptance 13 Dec 62.
453 UNTS 357. France. Acceptance 14 Feb 63.
520 UNTS 426. Niger. Acceptance 7 Dec 64.

102423 Bilateral Exchange **182 UNTS 73**
SIGNED: 26 Jul 48 FORCE: 26 Jul 48
REGISTERED: 11 Dec 53 USA (United States)
ARTICLES: 2 LANGUAGE: English.
HEADNOTE: DESIGNATION PERMANENT FREE PORT AREA
TOPIC: Customs
CONCEPTS: Customs exemptions. Boundaries of territory.
PARTIES:
Liberia
USA (United States)

102424 Bilateral Protocol **182 UNTS 85**
SIGNED: 28 Jul 52 FORCE: 28 Jul 52
REGISTERED: 21 Dec 53 Greece
ARTICLES: 8 LANGUAGE: Greek. German.
HEADNOTE: ECONOMIC RELATIONS
TOPIC: General Trade
CONCEPTS: Detailed regulations. Previous treaty amendment. Annex or appendix reference. Annex type material. General cooperation. Licenses and permits. General property. Accounting procedures. Banking. Balance of payments. Payment schedules. Commodity trade. Quotas. Patents, copyrights and trademarks. Trademarks. Transport of goods. Ports and pilotage. Reparations and restrictions.
INTL ORGS: European Payments Union.
PARTIES:
Germany, West
Greece

102425 Bilateral Agreement **182 UNTS 187**
SIGNED: 26 Apr 49 FORCE: 22 Sep 53
REGISTERED: 21 Dec 53 Netherlands
ARTICLES: 12 LANGUAGE: Dutch. French.
HEADNOTE: CULTURAL AGREEMENT
TOPIC: Culture
CONCEPTS: Tourism. Standardization. Conformity with municipal law. Exchange of information and documents. Domestic legislation. Operating agencies. Establishment of commission. Specialists exchange. Recognition of degrees. Exchange. Teacher and student exchange. Scholarships and grants. Exchange. Artists. Scientific exchange. Publications exchange. Mass media exchange.
INTL ORGS: Special Commission.
PARTIES:
Luxembourg
Netherlands

102426 Bilateral Exchange **183 UNTS 3**
SIGNED: 9 Mar 48 FORCE: 9 Mar 48
REGISTERED: 23 Dec 53 USA (United States)
ARTICLES: 2 LANGUAGE: English.
HEADNOTE: REVIVAL PRE-WAR TREATIES
TOPIC: Admin Cooperation
CONCEPTS: Revival of treaties.
PARTIES:
Hungary
USA (United States)

102427 Bilateral Agreement **183 UNTS 177**
SIGNED: 21 Jan 52   FORCE: 21 Jan 52
REGISTERED: 31 Dec 53 USA (United States)
ARTICLES: 8 LANGUAGE: English.
HEADNOTE: TECHNICAL COOPERATION
TOPIC: Tech Assistance
CONCEPTS: Detailed regulations. Exceptions and
exemptions. Treaty implementation. Continuity
of rights and obligations. Diplomatic privileges.
Exchange of information and documents. Public
information. Currency deposits. Financial pro-
grams. Assets. Tax exemptions. Domestic obli-
gation. General technical assistance. Materials,
equipment and services. Aid missions.
INTL ORGS: Special Commission.
PROCEDURE: Duration. Termination.
PARTIES:
Libya
USA (United States)

102428 Bilateral Exchange **183 UNTS 197**
SIGNED: 30 Nov 45   FORCE: 30 Nov 45
REGISTERED: 4 Jan 54 Greece
ARTICLES: 2 LANGUAGE: English.
HEADNOTE: USE DISPOSAL VESSELS
TOPIC: Reparations
CONCEPTS: Naval vessels. Return of equipment
and recapture.
TREATY REF: 183UNTS329.
PARTIES:
Greece
UK Great Britain

102429 Bilateral Exchange **183 UNTS 203**
SIGNED: 10 Sep 53   FORCE: 10 Sep 53
REGISTERED: 5 Jan 54 UK Great Britain
ARTICLES: 2 LANGUAGE: English. French.
HEADNOTE: EXCHANGE OFFICIAL PUBLICA-
TIONS
TOPIC: Admin Cooperation
CONCEPTS: Exchange of official publications. Op-
erating agencies.
PARTIES:
Belgium
UK Great Britain

102430 Bilateral Exchange **183 UNTS 207**
SIGNED: 1 Oct 53   FORCE: 1 Oct 53
REGISTERED: 5 Jan 54 UK Great Britain
ARTICLES: 2 LANGUAGE: English. Portuguese.
HEADNOTE: SETTLEMENT COMMERCIAL AF-
FAIRS
TOPIC: Claims and Debts
CONCEPTS: Definition of terms. Detailed regula-
tions. General trade. Banking. Currency. Ex-
change rates and regulations. Debts. Debt settle-
ment.
INTL ORGS: International Monetary Fund.
PARTIES:
Brazil
UK Great Britain
ANNEX
221 UNTS 430. UK Great Britain. Amendment
16 Aug 55. Force 16 Aug 55.
221 UNTS 430. Brazil. Amendment 16 Aug 55.
Force 16 Aug 55.

102431 Bilateral Convention **183 UNTS 217**
SIGNED: 27 Jun 50   FORCE: 2 Oct 53
REGISTERED: 5 Jan 54 UK Great Britain
ARTICLES: 11 LANGUAGE: English. French.
HEADNOTE: CULTURAL CONVENTION
TOPIC: Culture
CONCEPTS: Definition of terms. Friendship and
amity. Tourism. Operating agencies. Establish-
ment of commission. Recognition of degrees. Ex-
change. Teacher and student exchange. Scholar-
ships and grants. Vocational training. Exchange.
General cultural cooperation. Artists. Scientific
exchange. Publications exchange. Mass media
exchange.
INTL ORGS: Special Commission.
PROCEDURE: Denunciation. Duration. Ratification.
Renewal or Revival.
PARTIES:
Luxembourg
UK Great Britain
ANNEX
247 UNTS 454.   Luxembourg.   Amendment
22 Mar 56. Force 22 Mar 56.

247 UNTS 454. UK Great Britain. Amendment
22 Mar 56. Force 22 Mar 56.

102432 Bilateral Exchange **183 UNTS 225**
SIGNED: 26 Jun 53   FORCE: 26 Jun 53
REGISTERED: 5 Jan 54 UK Great Britain
ARTICLES: 2 LANGUAGE: English.
HEADNOTE: LOAN DEVELOPMENT PORT FACILI-
TIES
TOPIC: Loans and Credits
CONCEPTS: Annex or appendix reference. Confor-
mity with municipal law. Exchange of informa-
tion and documents. Operating agencies. Ex-
change. Financial programs. Funding proce-
dures. Interest rates. Payment schedules.
Economic assistance. Loan and credit. Loan re-
payment. Canal improvement.
INTL ORGS: Special Commission.
PROCEDURE: Amendment. Duration. Termination.
PARTIES:
UK Great Britain
USA (United States)

102433 Bilateral Agreement **183 UNTS 245**
SIGNED: 22 Sep 53   FORCE: 5 Dec 53
REGISTERED: 6 Jan 54 Norway
ARTICLES: 2 LANGUAGE: Finnish. Norwegian.
Swedish.
HEADNOTE: EXEMPTION COMPULSORY MILI-
TARY SERVICE
TOPIC: Milit Servic/Citiz
CONCEPTS: Foreign nationals.
PROCEDURE: Denunciation. Ratification.
PARTIES:
Finland
Norway

102434 Bilateral Agreement **183 UNTS 251**
SIGNED: 2 Jun 52   FORCE: 19 Sep 53
REGISTERED: 6 Jan 54 Syria
ARTICLES: 7 LANGUAGE: Arabic. French.
HEADNOTE: TRADE
TOPIC: General Trade
CONCEPTS: Exceptions and exemptions. Stan-
dardization. Licenses and permits. Establish-
ment of commission. Export quotas. Import
quotas. Payment schedules. Commodity trade.
Most favored nation clause. Routes and logistics.
INTL ORGS: Special Commission.
PROCEDURE: Denunciation. Duration. Ratification.
Renewal or Revival.
PARTIES:
Greece
Syria

102435 Bilateral Agreement **183 UNTS 263**
SIGNED: 30 Jun 52   FORCE: 23 Dec 53
REGISTERED: 8 Jan 54 Belgium
ARTICLES: 15 LANGUAGE: French. Hebrew.
HEADNOTE: AIR SERVICES
TOPIC: Air Transport
CONCEPTS: Conditions. Definition of terms. De-
tailed regulations. Exceptions and exemptions.
Annex or appendix reference. Conformity with
municipal law. General cooperation. Exchange
of information and documents. Arbitration. Pro-
cedure. Special tribunals. Negotiation. Non-inter-
est rates and fees. Most favored nation clause.
Customs exemptions. Routes and logistics. Per-
mit designation. Conditions of airlines operating
permission. Overflights and technical stops. Operating authorizations and regulations.
INTL ORGS: International Civil Aviation Organization. International Court of Justice.
TREATY REF: 15UNTS295;.
PROCEDURE: Amendment. Future Procedures
Contemplated. Ratification. Registration. Termination. Application to Non-self-governing Terri-
tories.
PARTIES:
Belgium
Israel

102436 Bilateral Instrument **184 UNTS 3**
SIGNED: 8 Jun 53   FORCE: 16 Aug 53
REGISTERED: 13 Jan 54 Syria
ARTICLES: 4 LANGUAGE: French.
HEADNOTE: COMMERCE
TOPIC: General Trade

CONCEPTS: Annex or appendix reference. Cur-
rency. Monetary and gold transfers. Payment
schedules. Delivery schedules. Quotas. Most fa-
vored nation clause.
PROCEDURE: Denunciation. Duration. Renewal or
Revival.
PARTIES:
Japan
Syria

102437 Bilateral Agreement **184 UNTS 15**
SIGNED: 4 Jun 53   FORCE: 8 Jul 53
REGISTERED: 13 Jan 54 Syria
ARTICLES: 14 LANGUAGE: Arabic.
HEADNOTE: UTILIZATION YARMUK WATERS
TOPIC: Specific Resources
CONCEPTS: Definition of terms. Inspection and
observation. Establishment of commission. Fi-
nancial programs. Funding procedures. Materi-
als, equipment and services. Hydro-electric
power. Facilities and property. Frontier crossing
points. Regulation of natural resources.
INTL ORGS: Special Commission.
PROCEDURE: Duration. Ratification. Termination.
PARTIES:
Jordan
Syria

102438 Multilateral Protocol **184 UNTS 42**
SIGNED: 17 Oct 53   FORCE: 31 Dec 53
REGISTERED: 18 Jan 54 Belgium
ARTICLES: 16 LANGUAGE: English. French.
HEADNOTE: EUROPEAN CONFERENCE MINIS-
TERS TRANSPORT
TOPIC: General Transport
CONCEPTS: Territorial application. Annex or ap-
pendix reference. Domestic legislation. Use of
facilities. Indemnities and reimbursements. Land
transport. Establishment. Headquarters and fa-
cilities. Inter-agency agreements.
INTL ORGS: European Conference of Ministers of
Transportation. Organization for Economic Co-
operation and Development.
PROCEDURE: Amendment. Accession. Ratifica-
tion. Termination.
PARTIES:
Belgium   SIGNED: 17 Oct 53   RATIFIED:
17 Nov 53 FORCE: 31 Dec 53
Denmark SIGNED: 17 Oct 53
France SIGNED: 17 Oct 53 FORCE: 31 Dec 53
Germany, West SIGNED: 17 Oct 53 FORCE:
31 Dec 53
Italy FORCE: 31 Dec 53
Luxembourg SIGNED: 17 Oct 53
Netherlands SIGNED: 17 Oct 53
Norway SIGNED: 17 Oct 53
Portugal SIGNED: 17 Oct 53
Spain SIGNED: 17 Oct 53
Sweden SIGNED: 17 Oct 53 RATIFIED: 8 Jan 54
FORCE: 8 Jan 54
Switzerland   SIGNED: 17 Oct 53   FORCE:
31 Dec 53
Trieste SIGNED: 17 Oct 53 RATIFIED: 31 Dec 53
FORCE: 31 Dec 53
Turkey SIGNED: 17 Oct 53
ANNEX
213 UNTS 392. UK Great Britain. Ratification
1 Mar 54.
213 UNTS 392.   Netherlands.   Ratification
9 Mar 54.
213 UNTS 392. Denmark. Ratification 13 Jul 54.
213 UNTS 392. Norway. Ratification 13 Jul 54.
213 UNTS 392. Austria. Signature without Reservation as to Approval 26 Apr 54.
213 UNTS 392. Spain. Ratification 13 Jan 54.
213 UNTS 392. Turkey. Ratification 12 May 54.
213 UNTS 392. Portugal. Ratification 24 Jul 54.
213 UNTS 392.   Luxembourg.   Ratification
26 Feb 55.
213 UNTS 392. Greece. Signature Subject to
Ratification 5 Apr 54. Ratification 3 Aug 55.
219 UNTS 376. Yugoslavia. Accession 2 Sep 55.

102439 Bilateral Agreement **184 UNTS 65**
SIGNED: 23 Jan 51   FORCE: 23 Jan 51
REGISTERED: 19 Jan 54 USA (United States)
ARTICLES: 5 LANGUAGE: English.

HEADNOTE: TECHNICAL COOPERATION
TOPIC: Tech Assistance
CONCEPTS: Exceptions and exemptions. Treaty implementation. Previous treaty replacement. General cooperation. Exchange of information and documents. Public information. Reexport of goods, etc.. Garnishment of funds. Tax exemptions. Customs duties. Customs exemptions. Domestic obligation. General technical assistance. Materials, equipment and services.
PROCEDURE: Amendment. Termination.
PARTIES:
Nepal
USA (United States)

102440   Bilateral Agreement   **184 UNTS 79**
SIGNED: 18 Jan 52   FORCE: 18 Jan 52
REGISTERED: 19 Jan 54 USA (United States)
ARTICLES: 3 LANGUAGE: English.
HEADNOTE: MUTUAL   ASSISTANCE   RAW MATIERIALS
TOPIC: Commodity Trade
CONCEPTS: General cooperation. Export quotas. Import quotas. Currency. Payment schedules. Non-interest rates and fees. Commodity trade. Delivery schedules. Quotas. Raw materials.
PARTIES:
UK Great Britain
USA (United States)

102441   Bilateral Exchange   **184 UNTS 97**
SIGNED: 15 Aug 52   FORCE: 15 Aug 52
REGISTERED: 20 Jan 54 USA (United States)
ARTICLES: 2 LANGUAGE: English.
HEADNOTE: GUARANTIES
TOPIC: Direct Aid
CONCEPTS: Guarantees and safeguards. Conformity with municipal law. Arbitration. Mediation and good offices. Negotiation. Local currency. Claims and settlements. Assets transfer. Economic assistance.
PROCEDURE: Duration.
PARTIES:
USA (United States)
Yugoslavia

102442   Bilateral Exchange   **184 UNTS 105**
SIGNED: 9 Oct 52   FORCE: 9 Oct 52
REGISTERED: 20 Jan 54 USA (United States)
ARTICLES: 2 LANGUAGE: English.
HEADNOTE: RECIPROCAL CUSTOMS PRIVILEGES FORIEGN SERVICE PERSONNEL
TOPIC: Consul/Citizenship
CONCEPTS: Diplomatic privileges.
PARTIES:
Nicaragua
USA (United States)

102443   Bilateral Agreement   **184 UNTS 111**
SIGNED: 12 Nov 52   FORCE: 27 Dec 52
REGISTERED: 20 Jan 54 USA (United States)
ARTICLES: 8 LANGUAGE: English. Japanese.
HEADNOTE: LEASING VESSELS
TOPIC: Milit Assistance
CONCEPTS: Annex or appendix reference. Compensation. Payment for war supplies. Lease of military property. Naval vessels. Return of equipment and recapture. Restrictions on transfer.
PROCEDURE: Future Procedures Contemplated.
PARTIES:
Japan
USA (United States)
ANNEX
04 UNTS 355. Japan. Prolongation 13 Jan 58. Force 13 Jan 58.
04 UNTS 355. USA (United States). Prolongation 13 Jan 58. Force 13 Jan 58.

02444   Bilateral Exchange   **184 UNTS 131**
IGNED: 18 Aug 52   FORCE: 18 Aug 52
EGISTERED: 20 Jan 54 USA (United States)
RTICLES: 2 LANGUAGE: Arabic. English.
EADNOTE: COOPERATIVE PROGRAM SOCIAL WELFARE
OPIC: Direct Aid

CONCEPTS: Treaty implementation. Annex type material. Personnel. Vocational training. Expense sharing formulae. Domestic obligation. Assistance.
TREATY REF: 151UNTS179.
PROCEDURE: Duration. Termination.
PARTIES:
Iraq
USA (United States)

102445   Bilateral Exchange   **184 UNTS 139**
SIGNED: 5 Nov 52   FORCE: 5 Nov 52
REGISTERED: 20 Jan 54 USA (United States)
ARTICLES: 2 LANGUAGE: English.
HEADNOTE: LOCUST OTHER INSECT CONTROL PROGRAM
TOPIC: Sanitation
CONCEPTS: Conditions. Privileges and immunities. General cooperation. Personnel. Establishment of commission. Programs. Specialists exchange. Insect control. Vocational training. Indemnities and reimbursements. Expense sharing formulae. Specific technical assistance. Materials, equipment and services.
TREATY REF: 148UNTS39; 179UNTS261.
PROCEDURE: Duration. Termination.
PARTIES:
Ethiopia
USA (United States)

102446   Bilateral Agreement   **184 UNTS 147**
SIGNED: 29 Aug 52   FORCE: 29 Aug 52
REGISTERED: 21 Jan 54 Australia
ARTICLES: 21 LANGUAGE: English. German.
HEADNOTE: ASSISTED MIGRATION
TOPIC: Non-ILO Labor
CONCEPTS: Definition of terms. Detailed regulations. Annex or appendix reference. Border traffic and migration. Repatriation of nationals. General cooperation. Exchange of information and documents. Operating agencies. Responsibility and liability. Administrative cooperation. Accounting procedures. Indemnities and reimbursements. Monetary and gold transfers. Transportation costs. Domestic obligation.
PARTIES:
Australia
Germany, West

102447   Bilateral Exchange   **184 UNTS 185**
SIGNED: 19 Jun 51   FORCE: 1 Aug 51
REGISTERED: 21 Jan 54 Australia
ARTICLES: 2 LANGUAGE: English. Italian.
HEADNOTE: VISA
TOPIC: Visas
CONCEPTS: Emergencies. Territorial application. Time limit. Visa abolition. Denial of admission. Conformity with municipal law. Fees and exemptions.
PARTIES:
Australia
Italy

102448   Bilateral Agreement   **184 UNTS 193**
SIGNED: 22 Oct 53   FORCE: 22 Oct 53
REGISTERED: 21 Jan 54 Australia
ARTICLES: 18 LANGUAGE: English.
HEADNOTE: EXCHANGE POSTAL PARCELS
TOPIC: Postal Service
CONCEPTS: Territorial application. Conformity with municipal law. Domestic legislation. Responsibility and liability. Accounting procedures. Compensation. Payment schedules. Postal services. Regulations. Insured letters and boxes. Conveyance in transit. Parcel post. Rates and charges.
INTL ORGS: Universal Postal Union.
TREATY REF: 170UNTS63.
PROCEDURE: Duration. Termination.
PARTIES:
Australia
Netherlands
ANNEX
376 UNTS 416. Australia. Amendment 4 Aug 59. Force 30 Sep 60.
376 UNTS 416.   Netherlands.   Amendment 4 Aug 59. Force 30 Sep 60.
405 UNTS 318. Australia. Amendment 18 Oct 60. Force 10 Aug 61.

405 UNTS 318.   Netherlands.   Amendment 18 Oct 60. Force 10 Aug 61.

102449   Bilateral Agreement   **184 UNTS 209**
SIGNED: 7 Jul 52   FORCE: 7 Jul 52
REGISTERED: 21 Jan 54 Australia
ARTICLES: 4 LANGUAGE: English.
HEADNOTE: TECHNICAL ASSISTANCE EUCALYPTUS STUDY TOUR
TOPIC: Tech Assistance
CONCEPTS: Time limit. Privileges and immunities. Conformity with municipal law. General cooperation. Exchange of information and documents. Personnel. Exchange. Vocational training. Expense sharing formulae. Tax exemptions. Customs exemptions. Domestic obligation. General technical assistance. Special projects. IGO status.
INTL ORGS: United Nations.
PARTIES:
Australia
FAO (Food Agri)

102450   Bilateral Agreement   **184 UNTS 217**
SIGNED: 11 May 50   FORCE: 11 May 50
REGISTERED: 21 Jan 54 Greece
ARTICLES: 10 LANGUAGE: French.
HEADNOTE: TRADE
TOPIC: General Trade
CONCEPTS: Annex or appendix reference. Licenses and permits. Establishment of commission. Balance of payments. Currency. Payment schedules. Delivery schedules. Quotas. Most favored nation clause.
INTL ORGS: Special Commission.
PROCEDURE: Denunciation. Duration.
PARTIES:
Austria
Greece
ANNEX
225 UNTS 269.   Greece.   Supplementation 7 Nov 53. Force 1 Oct 53.
225 UNTS 269.   Australia.   Supplementation 7 Nov 53. Force 1 Oct 53.
225 UNTS 283.   Greece.   Supplementation 12 Nov 54. Force 1 Oct 54.
225 UNTS 283.   Australia.   Supplementation 12 Nov 54. Force 1 Oct 54.

102451   Bilateral Agreement   **184 UNTS 230**
SIGNED: 16 May 46   FORCE: 16 May 46
REGISTERED: 21 Jan 54 Greece
ARTICLES: 7 LANGUAGE: English.
HEADNOTE: PURCHASE SURPLUS PROPERTY
TOPIC: Direct Aid
CONCEPTS: Annex or appendix reference. General cooperation. General property. Exchange rates and regulations. Interest rates. Payment schedules. Local currency. Surplus property.
INTL ORGS: International Monetary Fund.
PARTIES:
Greece
USA (United States)

102452   Bilateral Exchange   **184 UNTS 271**
SIGNED: 27 Jun 52   FORCE: 27 Jun 52
REGISTERED: 25 Jan 54 USA (United States)
ARTICLES: 6 LANGUAGE: English.
HEADNOTE: RELIEF FROM TAXATION DEFENSE EXPENDITURES
TOPIC: Tech Assistance
CONCEPTS: Detailed regulations. Treaty interpretation. Previous treaty extension. General cooperation. Negotiation. Export quotas. Indemnities and reimbursements. Tax exemptions. Customs exemptions. Assistance. Self-defense. Military installations and equipment.
INTL ORGS: Organization for Economic Co-operation and Development.
TREATY REF: 34UNTS243.
PROCEDURE: Future Procedures Contemplated.
PARTIES:
Norway
USA (United States)

102453   Bilateral Exchange   **184 UNTS 285**
SIGNED: 7 Nov 52   FORCE: 7 Nov 52
REGISTERED: 25 Jan 54 USA (United States)
ARTICLES: 2 LANGUAGE: English.

HEADNOTE: TECHNICAL COOPERATION PRO-
GRAM VOCATIONAL INDUSTRIAL CRAFTS
TOPIC: Tech Assistance
CONCEPTS: Annex type material. General cooper-
ation. Exchange of information and documents.
Inspection and observation. Personnel. Institute
establishment. Vocational training. Currency de-
posits. Financial programs. Garnishment of
funds. Assets. Domestic obligation. Assistance.
Special projects.
TREATY REF: 148UNTS39.
PROCEDURE: Duration. Termination.
PARTIES:
Ethiopia
USA (United States)

102454 Bilateral Exchange **184 UNTS 295**
SIGNED: 9 Apr 52 FORCE: 21 Apr 52
REGISTERED: 25 Jan 54 USA (United States)
ARTICLES: 2 LANGUAGE: English. Spanish.
HEADNOTE: PROGRAM AGRICULTURAL EXPERI-
MENTATION
TOPIC: Tech Assistance
CONCEPTS: Time limit. Personnel. Scholarships
and grants. Research and development. Ac-
counting procedures. Currency deposits. Ex-
pense sharing formulae. Funding procedures.
Domestic obligation. Agriculture. Assistance.
Mutual exchange of technical knowledge. Mate-
rials, equipment and services.
PARTIES:
Peru
USA (United States)
ANNEX
212 UNTS 371. USA (United States). Prolongation
13 Jan 53. Force 26 Jan 53.
212 UNTS 371. Peru. Prolongation 26 Jan 53.
Force 26 Jan 53.
235 UNTS 366. Peru. Termination 11 May 54.
Force 11 May 54.
235 UNTS 366. USA (United States). Termination
27 Apr 54. Force 11 May 54.

102455 Bilateral Exchange **184 UNTS 303**
SIGNED: 29 Jun 51 FORCE: 29 Jun 51
REGISTERED: 25 Jan 54 USA (United States)
ARTICLES: 2 LANGUAGE: English. Portuguese.
HEADNOTE: ASSIGNMENT SPECIALISTS
TOPIC: Tech Assistance
CONCEPTS: Specialists exchange. Public health.
Vocational training. Expense sharing formulae.
Assistance.
TREATY REF: 141UNTS3.
PROCEDURE: Termination.
PARTIES:
Brazil
USA (United States)

102456 Multilateral Agreement **185 UNTS 3**
SIGNED: 23 Dec 50 FORCE: 23 Dec 50
REGISTERED: 26 Jan 54 USA (United States)
ARTICLES: 5 LANGUAGE: Cambodian. English.
French. Laotian. Vietnamese.
HEADNOTE: MUTUAL DEFENSE ASSISTANCE
TOPIC: Tech Assistance
CONCEPTS: Guarantees and safeguards. Treaty
implementation. Treaty interpretation. Annex or
appendix reference. Conformity with municipal
law. General cooperation. Inspection and obser-
vation. Personnel. Title and deeds. Use of facili-
ties. Export quotas. Import quotas. Local cur-
rency. Assets transfer. Tax exemptions. Customs
exemptions. Domestic obligation. Materials,
equipment and services. Burial arrangements.
Military assistance. Raw materials.
INTL ORGS: United Nations.
PROCEDURE: Denunciation. Registration.
PARTIES:
Cambodia SIGNED: 23 Dec 50 FORCE:
23 Dec 50
France SIGNED: 23 Dec 50 FORCE: 23 Dec 50
Laos SIGNED: 23 Dec 50 FORCE: 23 Dec 50
USA (United States) SIGNED: 23 Dec 50 FORCE:
23 Dec 50
Vietnam SIGNED: 23 Dec 50 FORCE: 23 Dec 50
ANNEX
237 UNTS 319. Vietnam. Amendment 17 Sep 51.
Force 7 Jan 52.
237 UNTS 319. USA (United States). Amendment
16 Aug 51. Force 7 Jan 52.

237 UNTS 319. Laos. Amendment 6 Nov 51.
Force 7 Jan 52.
237 UNTS 319. France. Amendment 8 Sep 51.
Force 7 Jan 52.
237 UNTS 319. Cambodia. Amendment 7 Jan 52.
Force 7 Jan 52.
280 UNTS 358. USA (United States). Amendment
16 Jul 53. Force 7 Sep 53.
280 UNTS 358. France. Amendment 20 Jun 53.
Force 7 Sep 53.
280 UNTS 358. Laos. Amendment 16 Jul 53.
Force 7 Sep 53.
280 UNTS 358. Cambodia. Amendment
30 Jul 53. Force 7 Sep 53.
280 UNTS 358. Vietnam. Amendment 7 Sep 53.
Force 7 Sep 53.

102457 Bilateral Agreement **185 UNTS 45**
SIGNED: 15 Dec 52 FORCE: 15 Dec 52
REGISTERED: 26 Jan 54 USA (United States)
ARTICLES: 10 LANGUAGE: English.
HEADNOTE: JOINT FUND AERIAL PHOTOGRAPHY
PROJECT
TOPIC: Tech Assistance
CONCEPTS: Non-diplomatic delegations. General
cooperation. Inspection and observation. Per-
sonnel. General property. Establishment of com-
mission. Programs. Accounting procedures. Cur-
rency. Financial programs. Funding procedures.
Economic assistance.
INTL ORGS: Special Commission.
TREATY REF: 92UNTS145; 80UNTS308;
133UNTS69.
PROCEDURE: Duration. Termination.
PARTIES:
Liberia
USA (United States)

102458 Bilateral Agreement **185 UNTS 55**
SIGNED: 15 Dec 52 FORCE: 15 Dec 52
REGISTERED: 26 Jan 54 USA (United States)
ARTICLES: 5 LANGUAGE: Arabic. English.
HEADNOTE: TECHNICAL COOPERATION PRO-
GRAM PUBLIC HEALTH DISEASE CONTROL
TOPIC: Direct Aid
CONCEPTS: Annex type material. Conformity with
municipal law. Personnel. Sanitation. Vocational
training. Expense sharing formulae. Assistance.
Materials, equipment and services.
TREATY REF: 140UNTS.
PROCEDURE: Duration. Termination.
PARTIES:
Saudi Arabia
USA (United States)

102459 Bilateral Agreement **185 UNTS 67**
SIGNED: 15 Dec 52 FORCE: 15 Dec 52
REGISTERED: 26 Jan 54 USA (United States)
ARTICLES: 7 LANGUAGE: Arabic. English.
HEADNOTE: PROJECT AGREEMENT RURAL COM-
MUNTIY DEVELOPMENT PROJECTS
TOPIC: Tech Assistance
CONCEPTS: Annex type material. General cooper-
ation. Exchange of information and documents.
Operating agencies. General property. Public
health. Vocational training. Expense sharing for-
mulae. Funding procedures. Agriculture. Assis-
tance. Materials, equipment and services. Roads
and highways.
TREATY REF: 140UNTS335.
PROCEDURE: Duration. Termination.
PARTIES:
Saudi Arabia
USA (United States)

102460 Bilateral Agreement **185 UNTS 79**
SIGNED: 30 Jun 52 FORCE: 30 Jun 52
REGISTERED: 26 Jan 54 USA (United States)
ARTICLES: 7 LANGUAGE: English. Portuguese.
HEADNOTE: PROGRAM INDUSTRIAL APPREN-
TICESHIP
TOPIC: Tech Assistance
CONCEPTS: Privileges and immunities. Use of fa-
cilities. Scholarships and grants. Vocational
training. Indemnities and reimbursements. Gar-
nishment of funds. General technical assistance.
Assistance.
TREATY REF: 141UNTS53.

PARTIES:
Brazil
USA (United States)
ANNEX
206 UNTS 346. USA (United States). Prolongation
29 Jun 53. Force 30 Jun 53.
206 UNTS 346. Brazil. Prolongation 29 Jun 53.
Force 30 Jun 53.
234 UNTS 363. Brazil. Prolongation 2 Jun 54.
Force 30 Jun 54.
234 UNTS 363. USA (United States). Prolongation
30 Jun 54. Force 30 Jun 54.
265 UNTS 362. USA (United States). Prolongation
29 Jul 55. Force 29 Jul 55.
265 UNTS 362. Brazil. Prolongation 30 Jun 55.
Force 29 Jul 55.

102461 Bilateral Exchange **185 UNTS 93**
SIGNED: 23 Mar 53 FORCE: 23 Mar 53
REGISTERED: 26 Jan 54 USA (United States)
ARTICLES: 2 LANGUAGE: English. Japanese.
HEADNOTE: SETTLEMENT COSTS FOR CLAIMS
TOPIC: Direct Aid
CONCEPTS: Treaty implementation. Domestic leg-
islation. Indemnities and reimbursements. Ex-
pense sharing formulae. Claims and settlements.
TREATY REF: 136UNTS211.
PARTIES:
Japan
USA (United States)

102462 Bilateral Agreement **185 UNTS 103**
SIGNED: 25 Oct 48 FORCE: 25 Nov 48
REGISTERED: 28 Jan 54 Greece
ARTICLES: 10 LANGUAGE: English.
HEADNOTE: APPOINTMENT IKA HEAD
TOPIC: General Trade
CONCEPTS: Detailed regulations. Diplomatic and
consular relations. Decisions. Procedure. Inter-
nal structure. Status of experts.
TREATY REF: 23UNTS43; 79UNTS298;
132UNTS384.
PARTIES:
Greece
USA (United States)

102463 Bilateral Agreement **185 UNTS 115**
SIGNED: 30 Jul 47 FORCE: 1 Aug 47
REGISTERED: 28 Jan 54 Greece
ARTICLES: 8 LANGUAGE: French.
HEADNOTE: TRADE
TOPIC: Finance
CONCEPTS: Annex or appendix reference. Confor-
mity with municipal law. Licenses and permits.
Establishment of commission. General trade.
Trade procedures. Balance of payments. Pay-
ment schedules. Non-interest rates and fees.
Quotas.
INTL ORGS: International Emergency Food Orga-
nization. Special Commission.
PROCEDURE: Denunciation. Duration. Renewal or
Revival. Termination.
PARTIES:
Czechoslovakia
Greece

102464 Bilateral Agreement **185 UNTS 133**
SIGNED: 30 Jul 47 FORCE: 1 Aug 47
REGISTERED: 28 Jan 54 Greece
ARTICLES: 14 LANGUAGE: French.
HEADNOTE: PAYMENTS
TOPIC: General Trade
CONCEPTS: Payment schedules.
TREATY REF: 121UNTS123.
PROCEDURE: Duration.
PARTIES:
Czechoslovakia
Greece

102465 Bilateral Protocol **185 UNTS 143**
SIGNED: 30 Jul 47 FORCE: 30 Jul 47
REGISTERED: 28 Jan 54 Greece
ARTICLES: 1 LANGUAGE: French.
HEADNOTE: LIQUIDATION COMMERCIAL TRANS-
ACTIONS
TOPIC: Claims and Debts
CONCEPTS: Export quotas. Commodity trade.
TREATY REF: 185UNTS115.

PARTIES:
Czechoslovakia
Greece

102466 Bilateral Protocol **185 UNTS 149**
SIGNED: 30 Jul 47 FORCE: 30 Jul 47
REGISTERED: 28 Jan 54 Greece
ARTICLES: 17 LANGUAGE: French.
HEADNOTE: LIQUIDATION CLAIMS DEBTS
TOPIC: Reparations
CONCEPTS: Definition of terms. Conformity with
municipal law. Exchange of information and doc-
uments. Export quotas. Accounting procedures.
Currency. Exchange rates and regulations. Debt
settlement. Most favored nation clause. Post-war
claims settlement.
PARTIES:
Czechoslovakia
Greece

102467 Bilateral Exchange **185 UNTS 161**
SIGNED: 28 Jul 47 FORCE: 28 Jul 47
REGISTERED: 28 Jan 54 Greece
ARTICLES: 2 LANGUAGE: English.
HEADNOTE: RELEASE FUNDS PROPERTY
TOPIC: Reparations
CONCEPTS: Definition of terms. General cooper-
ation. Exchange of information and documents.
Responsibility and liability. Compensation. In-
demnities and reimbursements. Exchange rates
and regulations. Most favored nation clause.
Loss and/or damage. Enemy financial interests.
Post-war claims settlement.
PARTIES:
Greece
South Africa

102468 Bilateral Instrument **185 UNTS 169**
SIGNED: 1 Nov 48 FORCE: 1 Nov 48
REGISTERED: 28 Jan 54 Greece
ARTICLES: 4 LANGUAGE: English.
HEADNOTE: FINANCING CAPITAL GOODS PRO-
CUREMENT
TOPIC: Direct Aid
CONCEPTS: Loan and credit.
TREATY REF: 23UNTS43.
PROCEDURE: Duration.
PARTIES:
Greece
USA (United States)

102469 Bilateral Agreement **185 UNTS 183**
SIGNED: 3 Dec 52 FORCE: 3 Dec 52
REGISTERED: 1 Feb 54 USA (United States)
ARTICLES: 5 LANGUAGE: English. Serbo-Croat.
HEADNOTE: DUTY-FREE ENTRY DEFRAY INLAND
TRANSPORT COSTS RELIEF SUPPLIES
TOPIC: Direct Aid
CONCEPTS: Annex type material. Indemnities and
reimbursements. Transportation costs. Customs
exemptions. Relief supplies.
TREATY REF: 152UNTS61.
PROCEDURE: Amendment. Duration.
PARTIES:
USA (United States)
Yugoslavia

102470 Bilateral Exchange **185 UNTS 193**
SIGNED: 24 Dec 52 FORCE: 24 Dec 52
REGISTERED: 1 Feb 54 USA (United States)
ARTICLES: 2 LANGUAGE: English.
HEADNOTE: OFFSHORE PROCUREMENT
TOPIC: Milit Assistance
CONCEPTS: Annex or appendix reference. Military
assistance.
PARTIES:
Greece
USA (United States)

102471 Bilateral Exchange **185 UNTS 203**
SIGNED: 29 May 52 FORCE: 30 May 52
REGISTERED: 1 Feb 54 USA (United States)
ARTICLES: 2 LANGUAGE: English. Spanish.
HEADNOTE: COOPERATIVE PROGRAM AGRICUL-
TURE
TOPIC: Tech Assistance
CONCEPTS: Time limit. Previous treaty replace-

ment. Expense sharing formulae. Funding proce-
dures. Agriculture. Assistance.
TREATY REF: 141UNTS27; 89UNTS71.
PROCEDURE: Duration. Future Procedures Con-
templated.
PARTIES:
Ecuador
USA (United States)
ANNEX
256 UNTS 360. USA (United States). Prolongation
17 Mar 55. Force 14 Apr 55.
256 UNTS 360. Ecuador. Prolongation 6 Apr 55.
Force 14 Apr 55.

102472 Bilateral Agreement **185 UNTS 213**
SIGNED: 25 Jan 54 FORCE: 25 Jan 54
REGISTERED: 1 Feb 54 United Nations
ARTICLES: 6 LANGUAGE: English.
HEADNOTE: UN REGIONAL TRAINING CENTER
RAILWAY OPERATIONS SIGNALLING
TOPIC: Tech Assistance
CONCEPTS: Definition of terms. Privileges and im-
munities. General cooperation. Inspection and
observation. Personnel. Title and deeds. Use of
facilities. Institute establishment. Indemnities
and reimbursements. Expense sharing formulae.
Domestic obligation. General technical assis-
tance. Materials, equipment and services. Rail-
ways. IGO status.
TREATY REF: 1UNTS15,263.
PROCEDURE: Amendment. Termination.
PARTIES:
Pakistan
United Nations

102473 Bilateral Agreement **185 UNTS 225**
SIGNED: 1 Apr 53 FORCE: 30 Dec 53
REGISTERED: 4 Feb 54 Belgium
ARTICLES: 26 LANGUAGE: French. Swedish.
HEADNOTE: DOUBLE TAXATION INCOME POR-
ERTY
TOPIC: Taxation
CONCEPTS: Definition of terms. Conformity with
municipal law. Exchange of official publications.
Claims and settlements. Taxation. General. Tax
exemptions.
PROCEDURE: Duration. Ratification. Termination.
PARTIES:
Belgium
Sweden
ANNEX
274 UNTS 358. Belgium. Belgian Colonies. Force
31 Jul 57.
274 UNTS 358. Sweden. Acknowledgement
12 Dec 55. Force 31 Jul 57.
274 UNTS 358. Belgium. Ruanda-Urundi. Force
31 Jul 57.

102474 Bilateral Exchange **185 UNTS 277**
SIGNED: 19 Dec 53 FORCE: 1 Jan 54
REGISTERED: 4 Feb 54 Belgium
ARTICLES: 2 LANGUAGE: French. German.
HEADNOTE: ABOLITION PASSPORT VISA RE-
QUIREMENTS
TOPIC: Visas
CONCEPTS: Emergencies. Territorial application.
Time limit. Visa abolition. Denial of admission.
Resident permits. Non-visa travel documents.
PROCEDURE: Denunciation.
PARTIES:
Belgium
Germany, West
ANNEX
201 UNTS 382. Belgium. Supplementation
28 Sep 54. Force 1 Nov 54.
201 UNTS 382. Germany, West. Supplementa-
tion 1 Oct 54. Force 1 Nov 54.

102475 Bilateral Exchange **185 UNTS 285**
SIGNED: 16 Dec 53 FORCE: 1 Jan 54
REGISTERED: 4 Feb 54 Belgium
ARTICLES: 2 LANGUAGE: French. Spanish.
HEADNOTE: ABOLITION PASSPORT VISA RE-
QUIREMENT
TOPIC: Visas
CONCEPTS: Territorial application. Time limit. Visa
abolition. Denial of admission. Resident permits.
Conformity with municipal law.

PARTIES:
Belgium
Cuba

102476 Bilateral Exchange **185 UNTS 293**
SIGNED: 5 Jul 47 FORCE: 5 Jul 47
REGISTERED: 5 Feb 54 USA (United States)
ARTICLES: 2 LANGUAGE: English.
HEADNOTE: FLIGHTS MILITARY AIRCRAFT
TOPIC: Status of Forces
CONCEPTS: Military assistance.
PARTIES:
India
USA (United States)

102477 Multilateral Protocol **185 UNTS 307**
SIGNED: 22 Nov 49 FORCE: 22 Nov 49
REGISTERED: 5 Feb 54 USA (United States)
ARTICLES: 10 LANGUAGE: English. French. Ger-
man.
HEADNOTE: INCORPORATION GERMANY EU-
ROPEAN COMMUNITY NATIONS
TOPIC: Recognition
CONCEPTS: Treaty implementation. Nazi organiza-
tions. Democratic institutions. Merchant vessels.
Reconversion to normalcy. Disarmament and
demilitarization. Admission.
INTL ORGS: Council of Europe. Organization for
Economic Co-operation and Development.
TREATY REF: 87UNTS103; 83UNTS105;
140UNTS196.
PARTIES:
France SIGNED: 22 Nov 49 FORCE: 22 Nov 49
Germany, West SIGNED: 22 Nov 49 FORCE:
22 Nov 49
UK Great Britain SIGNED: 22 Nov 49 FORCE:
22 Nov 49
USA (United States) SIGNED: 22 Nov 49 FORCE:
22 Nov 49

102478 Bilateral Agreement **186 UNTS 3**
SIGNED: 19 Nov 52 FORCE: 19 Nov 52
REGISTERED: 5 Feb 54 USA (United States)
ARTICLES: 30 LANGUAGE: English. Spanish.
HEADNOTE: AIR FORCE MISSION
TOPIC: Military Mission
CONCEPTS: Definition of terms. Use of facilities.
Compensation. Indemnities and reimburse-
ments. Payment schedules. Tax exemptions.
Customs exemptions. Defense and security. Mili-
tary training. Security of information. Airforce-
army-navy personnel ratio. Ranks and privileges.
Conditions for assistance missions. Jurisdiction.
PROCEDURE: Duration. Termination.
PARTIES:
Nicaragua
USA (United States)
ANNEX
277 UNTS 352. USA (United States). Prolongation
21 Aug 56. Force 27 Aug 56.
277 UNTS 352. Nicaragua. Prolongation
27 Aug 56. Force 27 Aug 56.
357 UNTS 369. USA (United States). Amendment
25 Mar 59. Force 22 May 59.
357 UNTS 369. Nicaragua. Amendment
22 May 59. Force 22 May 59.

102479 Bilateral Exchange **186 UNTS 23**
SIGNED: 29 Sep 52 FORCE: 29 Sep 52
REGISTERED: 5 Feb 54 USA (United States)
ARTICLES: 2 LANGUAGE: English. Spanish.
HEADNOTE: TECHNICAL COOPERATION
TOPIC: Tech Assistance
CONCEPTS: General technical assistance. Assis-
tance.
PARTIES:
USA (United States)
Venezuela

102480 Bilateral Exchange **186 UNTS 35**
SIGNED: 29 Aug 52 FORCE: 29 Aug 52
REGISTERED: 5 Feb 54 USA (United States)
ARTICLES: 2 LANGUAGE: English. French.
HEADNOTE: NAVIGATION STATION
TOPIC: Direct Aid
CONCEPTS: General technical assistance. Testing
ranges and sites.

PARTIES:
Haiti
USA (United States)

102481 Bilateral Exchange **186 UNTS 43**
SIGNED: 24 Sep 52 FORCE: 24 Sep 52
REGISTERED: 5 Feb 54 USA (United States)
ARTICLES: 2 LANGUAGE: English. French.
HEADNOTE: COPYRIGHT RELATIONS
TOPIC: Patents/Copyrights
CONCEPTS: Conformity with municipal law. Domestic legislation. Laws and formalities.
PARTIES:
Monaco
USA (United States)

102482 Bilateral Agreement **186 UNTS 53**
SIGNED: 9 Apr 52 FORCE: 11 Jul 52
REGISTERED: 5 Feb 54 USA (United States)
ARTICLES: 11 LANGUAGE: English. Spanish.
HEADNOTE: MILITARY ASSISTANCE
TOPIC: Milit Assistance
CONCEPTS: Exceptions and exemptions. Treaty implementation. Non-prejudice to UN charter. Privileges and immunities. Conformity with municipal law. Exchange of information and documents. Public information. Use of facilities. Garnishment of funds. Local currency. Most favored nation clause. Tax exemptions. Recognition. Customs exemptions. Domestic obligation. Materials, equipment and services. Joint defense. Defense and security. Military assistance. Return of equipment and recapture. Security of information. Restrictions on transfer. Raw materials.
INTL ORGS: United Nations.
TREATY REF: 21UNTS77.
PROCEDURE: Amendment. Ratification. Registration. Termination.
PARTIES:
Chile
USA (United States)
ANNEX
266 UNTS 421. USA (United States). Supplementation 30 Nov 56. Force 28 Dec 56.
266 UNTS 421. Chile. Supplementation 28 Dec 56. Force 28 Dec 56.

102483 Bilateral Convention **186 UNTS 69**
SIGNED: 23 Dec 52 FORCE: 27 Jan 54
REGISTERED: 5 Feb 54 Belgium
ARTICLES: 6 LANGUAGE: French. German.
HEADNOTE: CLAIMS
TOPIC: Claims and Debts
CONCEPTS: Currency. Claims and settlements.
PROCEDURE: Ratification.
PARTIES:
Belgium
Germany, West

102484 Unilateral Instrument **186 UNTS 77**
SIGNED: 6 Feb 54 FORCE: 6 Feb 54
REGISTERED: 6 Feb 54 United Nations
ARTICLES: 1 LANGUAGE: English.
HEADNOTE: RECOGNIZE COMPULSORY ICJ JURISDICTION
TOPIC: ICJ Option Clause
CONCEPTS: Previous treaty renunciation. Compulsory jurisdiction.
INTL ORGS: International Court of Justice.
TREATY REF: 7LTS379; 200LTS494.
PROCEDURE: Duration.
PARTIES:
Australia

102485 Bilateral Agreement **186 UNTS 85**
SIGNED: 5 Feb 54 FORCE: 9 Feb 54
REGISTERED: 9 Feb 54 United Nations
ARTICLES: 6 LANGUAGE: English.
HEADNOTE: TECHNICAL ASSISTANCE
TOPIC: Tech Assistance
CONCEPTS: Assistance.
PROCEDURE: Termination.
PARTIES:
Taiwan
United Nations

102486 Bilateral Agreement **186 UNTS 101**
SIGNED: 19 Feb 51 FORCE: 2 Feb 54

REGISTERED: 12 Feb 54 IBRD (World Bank)
ARTICLES: 7 LANGUAGE: English.
HEADNOTE: LOAN AGREEMENT TELECOMMUNICATIONS PROJECT
TOPIC: IBRD Project
CONCEPTS: Default remedies. Definition of terms. Annex or appendix reference. Exchange of information and documents. Informational records. Inspection and observation. Accounting procedures. Bonds. Fees and exemptions. Interest rates. Tax exemptions. Domestic obligation. Terms of loan. Loan regulations. Loan guarantee. Guarantor non-interference. Telecommunications.
PARTIES:
Ethiopia
IBRD (World Bank)
ANNEX
192 UNTS 356. IBRD (World Bank). Implementation 13 Feb 52. Force 13 Feb 52.
192 UNTS 356. Ethiopia. Implementation 13 Feb 52. Force 13 Feb 52.

102487 Bilateral Agreement **186 UNTS 117**
SIGNED: 4 Sep 53 FORCE: 15 Oct 53
REGISTERED: 17 Feb 54 IBRD (World Bank)
ARTICLES: 7 LANGUAGE: English.
HEADNOTE: LOAN AGREEMENT HIGHWAY PROJECT
TOPIC: IBRD Project
CONCEPTS: Default remedies. Definition of terms. Annex or appendix reference. Exchange of information and documents. Informational records. Inspection and observation. Accounting procedures. Bonds. Fees and exemptions. Interest rates. Tax exemptions. Domestic obligation. Terms of loan. Loan regulations. Loan guarantee. Guarantor non-interference. Roads and highways.
PARTIES:
Nicaragua
IBRD (World Bank)

102488 Bilateral Agreement **186 UNTS 137**
SIGNED: 4 Sep 53 FORCE: 15 Oct 53
REGISTERED: 17 Feb 54 IBRD (World Bank)
ARTICLES: 7 LANGUAGE: English.
HEADNOTE: LOAN MANAGUA DIESEL POWER PROJECT
TOPIC: IBRD Project
CONCEPTS: Default remedies. Definition of terms. Annex or appendix reference. Exchange of information and documents. Informational records. Inspection and observation. Accounting procedures. Bonds. Fees and exemptions. Interest rates. Tax exemptions. Domestic obligation. Terms of loan. Loan regulations. Loan guarantee. Guarantor non-interference.
PARTIES:
Nicaragua
IBRD (World Bank)

102489 Bilateral Exchange **186 UNTS 151**
SIGNED: 14 Oct 53 FORCE: 15 Nov 53
REGISTERED: 18 Feb 54 UK Great Britain
ARTICLES: 2 LANGUAGE: English. French.
HEADNOTE: TRANSIT SEAMEN
TOPIC: Admin Cooperation
CONCEPTS: Frontier permits.
PROCEDURE: Termination.
PARTIES:
France
UK Great Britain

102490 Bilateral Exchange **186 UNTS 157**
SIGNED: 18 Dec 53 FORCE: 1 Jan 54
REGISTERED: 18 Feb 54 UK Great Britain
ARTICLES: 2 LANGUAGE: English. Spanish.
HEADNOTE: COMMERCIAL RELATIONS
TOPIC: General Trade
CONCEPTS: Establishment of trade relations. Export quotas. Import quotas.
PARTIES:
Cuba
UK Great Britain
ANNEX
247 UNTS 457. UK Great Britain. Amendment 15 Feb 56. Force 15 Feb 56.
247 UNTS 457. Cuba. Amendment 15 Feb 56. Force 15 Feb 56.

269 UNTS 345. Cuba. Extension and Amendment 8 Jan 57. Force 8 Jan 57.
269 UNTS 345. UK Great Britain. Extension and Amendment 8 Jan 57. Force 8 Jan 57.
313 UNTS 349. UK Great Britain. Extension and Amendment 2 Jan 58. Force 1 Jan 58.
313 UNTS 349. UK Great Britain. Extension and Amendment 2 Jan 58. Force 1 Jan 58.
331 UNTS 394. UK Great Britain. Amendment 23 Dec 58. Force 23 Dec 58.
331 UNTS 394. Cuba. Amendment 23 Dec 58. Force 23 Dec 58.

102491 Bilateral Treaty **186 UNTS 185**
SIGNED: 29 Jul 53 FORCE: 7 Dec 53
REGISTERED: 18 Feb 54 UK Great Britain
ARTICLES: 7 LANGUAGE: English. Arabic.
HEADNOTE: FRIENDSHIP ALLIANCE
TOPIC: General Amity
CONCEPTS: Non-prejudice to third party. Acceptance of UN obligations.
INTL ORGS: International Court of Justice. United Nations.
PROCEDURE: Duration. Ratification. Termination.
PARTIES:
Libya
UK Great Britain
ANNEX
486 UNTS 403. UK Great Britain. Other 7 Feb 63. Force 7 Feb 63.
486 UNTS 403. Libya. Other 7 Feb 63. Force 7 Feb 63.

102492 Bilateral Agreement **186 UNTS 201**
SIGNED: 29 Jul 53 FORCE: 7 Dec 53
REGISTERED: 18 Feb 54 UK Great Britain
ARTICLES: 35 LANGUAGE: English. Arabic.
HEADNOTE: MILITARY EQUIPMENT
TOPIC: Status of Forces
CONCEPTS: Definition of terms. Annex or appendix reference. Non-prejudice to UN charter. Visa abolition. Conformity with municipal law. General cooperation. Exchange of information and documents. Legal protection and assistance. General property. Recognition of legal documents. Title and deeds. Use of facilities. Investigation of violations. Arbitration. Procedure. Sanitation. Compensation. Claims and settlements. Tax exemptions. Customs exemptions. Ports and pilotage. Facilities and equipment. Postal services. Money orders and postal checks. Joint defense. Military assistance. Military training. Security of information. Jurisdiction. Procurement and logistics. Status of forces. Bases and facilities.
INTL ORGS: International Court of Justice. Arbitration Commission.
PROCEDURE: Amendment. Duration. Ratification. Termination.
PARTIES:
Libya
UK Great Britain
ANNEX
486 UNTS 403. UK Great Britain. Other 7 Feb 63. Force 7 Feb 63.
486 UNTS 403. Libya. Other 7 Feb 63. Force 7 Feb 63.

102493 Bilateral Agreement **186 UNTS 27**
SIGNED: 29 Jul 53 FORCE: 7 Dec 53
REGISTERED: 18 Feb 54 UK Great Britain
ARTICLES: 5 LANGUAGE: English. Arabic.
HEADNOTE: FINANCIAL
TOPIC: Finance
CONCEPTS: Finances and payments. Payment schedules. Grants.
PROCEDURE: Ratification. Termination.
PARTIES:
Libya
UK Great Britain
ANNEX
486 UNTS 403. Libya. Other 7 Feb 63. Force 7 Feb 63.
486 UNTS 403. UK Great Britain. Other 7 Feb 63. Force 7 Feb 63.

102494 Bilateral Exchange **186 UNTS 28**
SIGNED: 19 Oct 53 FORCE: 19 Oct 5
REGISTERED: 18 Feb 54 UK Great Britain
ARTICLES: 2 LANGUAGE: English. Arabic.

HEADNOTE: LIBYAN PUBLIC DEVELOPMENT STA-
BILIZATION AGENCY
TOPIC: Admin Cooperation
CONCEPTS: Conformity with municipal law. Gen-
eral cooperation. Domestic legislation. Establish-
ment of commission. Financial programs. Fund-
ing procedures. Internal structure.
TREATY REF: 186UNTS277; 186UNTS185.
PARTIES:
Libya
UK Great Britain

102495 Unilateral Instrument **186 UNTS 295**
SIGNED: 11 Jan 54　　FORCE: 18 Feb 54
REGISTERED: 18 Feb 54 United Nations
ARTICLES: 1 LANGUAGE: Italian.
HEADNOTE: ACCEPTING COMPULSORY ICJ JU-
RISDICTION
TOPIC: ICJ Option Clause
CONCEPTS: Acceptance of UN obligations. Com-
pulsory jurisdiction.
INTL ORGS: International Court of Justice. United
Nations.
PARTIES:
San Marino

102496 Bilateral Protocol **186 UNTS 301**
SIGNED: 26 Feb 53　　FORCE: 6 Aug 53
REGISTERED: 24 Feb 54 Denmark
ARTICLES: 9 LANGUAGE: French.
HEADNOTE: INTEREST & ASSETS
TOPIC: Claims and Debts
CONCEPTS: Claims, debts and assets. Claims and
settlements. Debt settlement.
PARTIES:
Denmark
Poland

102497 Bilateral Exchange **187 UNTS 3**
SIGNED: 1 Jul 52　　FORCE: 1 Jul 52
REGISTERED: 2 Mar 54 Sweden
ARTICLES: 2 LANGUAGE: English.
HEADNOTE: PROCURING MILITARY EQUIPMENT
MATERIALS SERVICES
TOPIC: Milit Assistance
CONCEPTS: Exceptions and exemptions. Non-
prejudice to UN charter. Materials, equipment
and services. Self-defense. Lease of military
property. Security of information. Exchange of
defense information. Restrictions on transfer.
INTL ORGS: United Nations.
PARTIES:
Sweden
USA (United States)
ANNEX
404 UNTS 340. Sweden. Supplementation
30 Jan 61. Force 30 Jan 61.
404 UNTS 340. USA (United States). Supplemen-
tation 30 Jan 61. Force 30 Jan 61.

102498 Bilateral Agreement **187 UNTS 9**
SIGNED: 5 Mar 54　　FORCE: 5 Mar 54
REGISTERED: 5 Mar 54 United Nations
ARTICLES: 6 LANGUAGE: English. Spanish.
HEADNOTE: TECHNICAL ASSISTANCE
TOPIC: Tech Assistance
CONCEPTS: Treaty implementation. Privileges and
immunities. General cooperation. Exchange of
information and documents. Personnel. Title and
deeds. Exchange. Scholarships and grants. Vo-
cational training. Research and development. Ex-
change rates and regulations. Expense sharing
formulae. Local currency. Domestic obligation.
General technical assistance. Materials, equip-
ment and services. IGO status. Conformity with
IGO decisions.
TREATY REF: 76UNTS132; 1UNTS15;
1UNTS263.
PROCEDURE: Amendment. Termination.
PARTIES:
United Nations
Venezuela

102499 Bilateral Agreement **187 UNTS 25**
SIGNED: 20 Sep 52　　FORCE: 24 Dec 53
REGISTERED: 5 Mar 54 ILO (Labor Org)
ARTICLES: 5 LANGUAGE: Spanish.
HEADNOTE: TECHNICAL ASSISTANCE
TOPIC: Tech Assistance

CONCEPTS: Definition of terms. Treaty implementation. Privileges and immunities. Personnel. Title and deeds. Scholarships and grants. Vocational training. Expense sharing formulae. Local
currency. Domestic obligation. General technical assistance. Materials, equipment and services. IGO status. Conformity with IGO decisions.
TREATY REF: 76UNTS132; 33UNTS261.
PROCEDURE: Amendment. Ratification.
PARTIES:
ILO (Labor Org)
Uruguay

102500 Bilateral Instrument **187 UNTS 41**
SIGNED: 25 Apr 53　　FORCE: 25 Jul 53
REGISTERED: 5 Mar 54 France
ARTICLES: 8 LANGUAGE: French.
HEADNOTE: REVIVAL PRE-WAR TREATIES
TOPIC: Admin Cooperation
CONCEPTS: Revival of treaties.
TREATY REF: 136UNTS45; 163UNTS385;
184UNTS358; 187UNTS55,56,58.
PARTIES:
France
Japan

102501 Bilateral Agreement **187 UNTS 61**
SIGNED: 9 Mar 54　　FORCE: 9 Mar 54
REGISTERED: 9 Mar 54 United Nations
ARTICLES: 6 LANGUAGE: English.
HEADNOTE: TECHNICAL ASSISTANCE
TOPIC: Tech Assistance
CONCEPTS: Treaty implementation. Privileges and
immunities. General cooperation. Exchange of
information and documents. Personnel. Title and
deeds. Exchange. Scholarships and grants. Vo-
cational training. Research and development. Ex-
pense sharing formulae. Local currency. Domes-
tic obligation. General technical assistance. Ma-
terials, equipment and services. IGO status.
Conformity with IGO decisions.
TREATY REF: 76UNTS132; 1UNTS15.
PROCEDURE: Amendment. Termination.
PARTIES:
Liberia
United Nations
ANNEX
285 UNTS 380. United Nations. Force 5 Nov 57.
285 UNTS 380. Liberia. Force 5 Nov 57.

102502 Bilateral Agreement **187 UNTS 71**
SIGNED: 10 Sep 53　　FORCE: 17 Feb 54
REGISTERED: 15 Mar 54 IBRD (World Bank)
ARTICLES: 5 LANGUAGE: English.
HEADNOTE: GUARANTEE AGREEMENT
TOPIC: IBRD Project
CONCEPTS: Definition of terms. Annex or appen-
dix reference. Exchange of information and doc-
uments. Informational records. Inspection and
observation. Accounting procedures. Bonds.
Currency. Fees and exemptions. Tax exemp-
tions. Domestic obligation. Terms of loan. Loan
regulations. Loan guarantee. Guarantor non-
interference.
PARTIES:
IBRD (World Bank)
Turkey

102503 Bilateral Exchange **187 UNTS 97**
SIGNED: 20 Jun 53　　FORCE: 1 Jul 53
REGISTERED: 17 Mar 54 Netherlands
ARTICLES: 2 LANGUAGE: French.
HEADNOTE: INTERNATIONAL TRANSPORT
GOODS ROAD
TOPIC: Land Transport
CONCEPTS: General cooperation. Exchange of in-
formation and documents. Transport of goods.
Driving permits. Roads and highways. Road
rules.
PARTIES:
France
Netherlands

102504 Bilateral Exchange **187 UNTS 107**
SIGNED: 10 Sep 47　　FORCE: 10 Sep 47
REGISTERED: 18 Mar 54 Greece
ARTICLES: 2 LANGUAGE: French.
HEADNOTE: ABOLITION MIXED COURTS LEBA-
NON

TOPIC: Dispute Settlement
CONCEPTS: Conformity with municipal law. Juridi-
cal personality.
PARTIES:
Greece
Lebanon

102505 Bilateral Exchange **187 UNTS 113**
SIGNED: 3 Sep 51　　FORCE: 3 Sep 51
REGISTERED: 18 Mar 54 Greece
ARTICLES: 2 LANGUAGE: French.
HEADNOTE: MOST FAVORED NATION TREAT-
MENT VESSELS
TOPIC: Mostfavored Nation
CONCEPTS: Territorial application. Most favored
nation clause. Navigational conditions.
TREATY REF: 95LTS401.
PARTIES:
France
Greece

102506 Bilateral Agreement **187 UNTS 119**
SIGNED: 22 Oct 51　　FORCE: 22 Nov 51
REGISTERED: 18 Mar 54 Greece
ARTICLES: 13 LANGUAGE: French. Greek.
HEADNOTE: AIR TRANSPORT
TOPIC: Air Transport
CONCEPTS: Exceptions and exemptions. Annex or
appendix reference. Conformity with municipal
law. General cooperation. Licenses and permits.
Recognition of legal documents. Use of facilities.
Arbitration. Procedure. Existing tribunals. Negotiation. Reexport of goods, etc.. Fees and exemptions. Most favored nation clause. National treatment. Customs exemptions. Competency certifi-
cate. Routes and logistics. Navigational
conditions. Permit designation. Air transport. Airport facilities. Airworthiness certificates. Conditions of airlines operating permission. Operating
authorizations and regulations. Licenses and certificates of nationality.
INTL ORGS: International Civil Aviation Organization.
TREATY REF: 15UNTS295.
PROCEDURE: Amendment. Denunciation. Future
Procedures Contemplated. Ratification. Registration.
PARTIES:
Greece
Luxembourg

102507 Bilateral Agreement **187 UNTS 141**
SIGNED: 28 May 51　　FORCE: 28 May 51
REGISTERED: 18 Mar 54 Greece
ARTICLES: 12 LANGUAGE: French.
HEADNOTE: OPERATION REGULAR AIR SERVICES
TOPIC: Air Transport
CONCEPTS: Exceptions and exemptions. Annex or
appendix reference. Conformity with municipal
law. Licenses and permits. Recognition of legal
documents. Use of facilities. Arbitration. Proce-
dure. Existing tribunals. Fees and exemptions.
Most favored nation clause. National treatment.
Customs exemptions. Competency certificate.
Routes and logistics. Navigational conditions.
Permit designation. Airport facilities. Airworthi-
ness certificates. Conditions of airlines operat-
ing permission. Operating authorizations and
regulations. Licenses and certificates of nation-
ality.
INTL ORGS: International Civil Aviation Organiza-
tion.
PROCEDURE: Amendment. Denunciation. Future
Procedures Contemplated. Ratification. Registra-
tion.
PARTIES:
Greece
Norway

102508 Bilateral Exchange **187 UNTS 157**
SIGNED: 5 Jul 52　　FORCE: 1 Aug 52
REGISTERED: 18 Mar 54 Greece
ARTICLES: 2 LANGUAGE: French. Italian.
HEADNOTE: RECIPROCAL ABOLITION PASSPORT
VISAS
TOPIC: Visas
CONCEPTS: Emergencies. Exceptions and exemp-
tions. Time limit. Visa abolition. Denial of admis-
sion. Resident permits. Non-visa travel docu-

ments. Conformity with municipal law. Fees and exemptions.
INTL ORGS: Council of Europe.
PROCEDURE: Denunciation.
PARTIES:
    Greece
    Italy

102509 Bilateral Exchange **187 UNTS 163**
SIGNED: 5 Aug 52 FORCE: 1 Sep 52
REGISTERED: 18 Mar 54 Greece
ARTICLES: 2 LANGUAGE: French.
HEADNOTE: ABOLITION PASSPORT VISAS
TOPIC: Visas
CONCEPTS: Emergencies. Exceptions and exemptions. Time limit. Visa abolition. Denial of admission. Resident permits. Conformity with municipal law.
INTL ORGS: Council of Europe.
PROCEDURE: Denunciation.
PARTIES:
    Greece
    Turkey

102510 Bilateral Instrument **187 UNTS 169**
SIGNED: 31 Jul 52 FORCE: 31 Jul 52
REGISTERED: 18 Mar 54 Greece
ARTICLES: 1 LANGUAGE: French.
HEADNOTE: MODUS VIVENDI GOVERNING TRADE
TOPIC: General Trade
CONCEPTS: Annex type material. Previous treaty extension. Licenses and permits. Quotas.
INTL ORGS: Organization for Economic Co-operation and Development.
PARTIES:
    France
    Greece

102511 Bilateral Agreement **187 UNTS 175**
SIGNED: 23 Dec 52 FORCE: 1 Jan 53
REGISTERED: 18 Mar 54 Greece
ARTICLES: 7 LANGUAGE: French.
HEADNOTE: COMMERCE
TOPIC: General Trade
CONCEPTS: Territorial application. General provisions. Annex or appendix reference. Previous treaty replacement. General cooperation. Licenses and permits. Establishment of commission. Payment schedules. Quotas. Most favored nation clause.
INTL ORGS: European Payments Union. Special Commission.
PROCEDURE: Duration.
PARTIES:
    France
    Greece
                ANNEX
225 UNTS 289. Greece. Extension and Amendment 21 Apr 54. Force 21 Apr 54.
225 UNTS 289. France. Extension and Amendment 21 Apr 54. Force 21 Apr 54.

102512 Bilateral Protocol **187 UNTS 191**
SIGNED: 20 Sep 52 FORCE: 20 Sep 52
REGISTERED: 18 Mar 54 Greece
ARTICLES: 5 LANGUAGE: French.
HEADNOTE: TRADE
TOPIC: General Trade
CONCEPTS: Detailed regulations. Annex or appendix reference. Annex type material. Previous treaty extension. Licenses and permits. Trade procedures. Balance of payments. Payment schedules. Quotas.
INTL ORGS: European Payments Union. Special Commission.
PROCEDURE: Duration. Denunciation.
PARTIES:
    Austria
    Greece

102513 Bilateral Protocol **187 UNTS 207**
SIGNED: 15 Sep 52 FORCE: 15 Sep 52
REGISTERED: 18 Mar 54 Greece
ARTICLES: 4 LANGUAGE: French.
HEADNOTE: TRADE PROTOCOL
TOPIC: General Trade
CONCEPTS: Trade procedures. Quotas.
INTL ORGS: European Payments Union.

TREATY REF: 78UNTS325.
PROCEDURE: Duration.
PARTIES:
    Denmark
    Greece

102514 Bilateral Exchange **187 UNTS 213**
SIGNED: 21 Mar 50 FORCE: 21 Mar 50
REGISTERED: 23 Mar 54 Greece
ARTICLES: 2 LANGUAGE: Spanish.
HEADNOTE: TAXATION SHIPPING PROFITS
TOPIC: Taxation
CONCEPTS: Domestic legislation. General. Merchant vessels.
PARTIES:
    Argentina
    Greece

102515 Bilateral Agreement **187 UNTS 221**
SIGNED: 8 Oct 49 FORCE: 8 Oct 49
REGISTERED: 23 Mar 54 Greece
ARTICLES: 14 LANGUAGE: English.
HEADNOTE: AIR TRANSPORT
TOPIC: Air Transport
CONCEPTS: Definition of terms. Exceptions and exemptions. Annex or appendix reference. Conformity with municipal law. Licenses and permits. Recognition of legal documents. Use of facilities. Arbitration. Procedure. Existing tribunals. Negotiation. Fees and exemptions. Non-interest rates and fees. Most favored nation clause. National treatment. Customs exemptions. Competency certificate. Routes and logistics. Navigational conditions. Air transport. Airport facilities. Airworthiness certificates. Conditions of airlines operating permission. Operating authorizations and regulations. Licenses and certificates of nationality.
INTL ORGS: International Civil Aviation Organization.
TREATY REF: 15UNTS295.
PROCEDURE: Amendment. Future Procedures Contemplated. Ratification. Registration. Termination.
PARTIES:
    Greece
    Philippines

102516 Bilateral Agreement **187 UNTS 237**
SIGNED: 15 Mar 51 FORCE: 15 Mar 51
REGISTERED: 23 Mar 54 Greece
ARTICLES: 16 LANGUAGE: French.
HEADNOTE: AIR SERVICES
TOPIC: Air Transport
CONCEPTS: Annex or appendix reference. Previous treaty replacement. Conformity with municipal law. General cooperation. Exchange of information and documents. Informational records. Licenses and permits. Recognition of legal documents. Use of facilities. Arbitration. Procedure. Indemnities and reimbursements. Fees and exemptions. Non-interest rates and fees. Most favored nation clause. National treatment. Customs duties. Customs exemptions. Competency certificate. Registration certificate. Routes and logistics. Navigational conditions. Permit designation. Air transport. Airport facilities. Airworthiness certificates. Conditions of airlines operating permission. Operating authorizations and regulations. Licenses and certificates of nationality.
INTL ORGS: International Civil Aviation Organization.
PROCEDURE: Amendment. Ratification. Termination.
PARTIES:
    Greece
    Yugoslavia
                ANNEX
200 UNTS 332. Greece. Abrogation and Replacement 13 Jul 54. Force 13 Jul 54.
200 UNTS 332. Yugoslavia. Abrogation and Replacement 13 Jul 54. Force 13 Jul 54.

102517 Bilateral Protocol **187 UNTS 255**
SIGNED: 22 Mar 52 FORCE: 22 Mar 52
REGISTERED: 23 Mar 54 Greece
ARTICLES: 1 LANGUAGE: French.
HEADNOTE: TRADE PAYMENTS
TOPIC: General Economic

CONCEPTS: Annex or appendix reference. Annex type material. Previous treaty replacement. Licenses and permits. Export quotas. Import quotas. Banking. Currency. Claims and settlements. Debts. Debt settlement. Post-war adjustment. Post-war claims settlement.
INTL ORGS: Special Commission.
PROCEDURE: Denunciation. Future Procedures Contemplated.
PARTIES:
    Austria
    Greece

102518 Bilateral Exchange **187 UNTS 263**
SIGNED: 30 Mar 46 FORCE: 30 Mar 46
REGISTERED: 23 Mar 54 Greece
ARTICLES: 2 LANGUAGE: French.
HEADNOTE: RELEASE RESTORATION EGYPTIAN GREEK PROPERY
TOPIC: Reparations
CONCEPTS: Arbitration. Procedure. Post-war claims settlement.
INTL ORGS: Special Commission.
PARTIES:
    Greece
    United Arab Rep

102519 Bilateral Agreement **188 UNTS 3**
SIGNED: 4 Sep 53 FORCE: 19 Nov 53
REGISTERED: 25 Mar 54 IBRD (World Bank)
ARTICLES: 5 LANGUAGE: English.
HEADNOTE: GUARANTEE AGREEMENT TRANSMITTER PROJECT
TOPIC: IBRD Project
CONCEPTS: Definition of terms. Annex or appendix reference. Exchange of information and documents. Inspection and observation. Bonds. Fees and exemptions. Tax exemptions. Domestic obligation. Terms of loan. Loan regulations. Loan guarantee. Guarantor non-interference. Facilities and equipment.
PARTIES:
    Iceland
    IBRD (World Bank)

102520 Bilateral Agreement **188 UNTS 25**
SIGNED: 10 Sep 53 FORCE: 10 Dec 53
REGISTERED: 25 Mar 54 IBRD (World Bank)
ARTICLES: 6 LANGUAGE: English.
HEADNOTE: GUARANTEE AGREEMENT
TOPIC: IBRD Project
CONCEPTS: Definition of terms. Annex or appendix reference. Exchange of information and documents. Inspection and observation. Bonds. Fees and exemptions. Tax exemptions. Domestic obligation. Terms of loan. Loan regulations. Loan guarantee. Guarantor non-interference.
PARTIES:
    Chile
    IBRD (World Bank)

102521 Bilateral Agreement **188 UNTS 71**
SIGNED: 25 Sep 53 FORCE: 20 Feb 54
REGISTERED: 25 Mar 54 IBRD (World Bank)
ARTICLES: 5 LANGUAGE: English.
HEADNOTE: GUARANTEE AGREEMENT AGRICULTURAL MACHINERY
TOPIC: IBRD Project
CONCEPTS: Definition of terms. Annex or appendix reference. Exchange of information and documents. Inspection and observation. Bonds. Fees and exemptions. Tax exemptions. Domestic obligation. Agriculture. Terms of loan. Loan regulations. Loan guarantee. Guarantor non-interference.
PARTIES:
    Panama
    IBRD (World Bank)

102522 Bilateral Agreement **188 UNTS 95**
SIGNED: 25 Sep 53 FORCE: 20 Feb 54
REGISTERED: 25 Mar 54 IBRD (World Bank)
ARTICLES: 5 LANGUAGE: English.
HEADNOTE: GUARANTEE AGREEMENT GRAIN STORAGE
TOPIC: IBRD Project
CONCEPTS: Definition of terms. Annex or appendix reference. Exchange of information and documents. Inspection and observation. Bonds.

Fees and exemptions. Tax exemptions. Domestic obligation. Agriculture. Terms of loan. Loan regulations. Loan guarantee. Guarantor non-interference.
PARTIES:
Panama
IBRD (World Bank)

102523 Bilateral Agreement **188 UNTS 119**
SIGNED: 16 Sep 50   FORCE: 7 Feb 51
REGISTERED: 26 Mar 54 Belgium
ARTICLES: 8 LANGUAGE: French. Spanish.
HEADNOTE: TRADE
TOPIC: General Trade
CONCEPTS: Procedure. Establishment of trade relations. National treatment.
INTL ORGS: International Court of Justice.
PROCEDURE: Ratification. Termination.
PARTIES:
Belgium
Mexico

102524 Unilateral Instrument **188 UNTS 137**
SIGNED: 25 Mar 54   FORCE: 2 Apr 54
REGISTERED: 2 Apr 54 United Nations
ARTICLES: 1 LANGUAGE: Japanese.
HEADNOTE: STATUTE ICJ
TOPIC: ICJ Option Clause
CONCEPTS: Acceptance of UN obligations.
INTL ORGS: International Court of Justice. United Nations.
PARTIES:
Japan

102525 Bilateral Convention **188 UNTS 141**
SIGNED: 30 Jan 53   FORCE: 18 Mar 54
REGISTERED: 2 Apr 54 Belgium
ARTICLES: 17 LANGUAGE: French.
HEADNOTE: ESTABLISH NATIONAL CONTROL OFFICES FRONTIER
TOPIC: Visas
CONCEPTS: Frontier formalities. Markers and definitions. Frontier peoples and personnel. Frontier waterways.
PROCEDURE: Denunciation. Ratification. Termination.
PARTIES:
Belgium
France
ANNEX
193 UNTS 362. Belgium. Implementation 10 May 54. Force 10 May 54.
193 UNTS 362. France. Implementation 10 May 54. Force 10 May 54.
202 UNTS 362. Belgium. Implementation 29 Dec 54. Force 29 Dec 54.
202 UNTS 362. France. Implementation 29 Dec 54. Force 29 Dec 54.
445 UNTS 332. France. Supplementation 1 Oct 62. Force 1 Oct 62.
445 UNTS 332. Belgium. Supplementation 1 Oct 62. Force 1 Oct 62.

102526 Bilateral Convention **188 UNTS 153**
SIGNED: 27 Mar 53   FORCE: 17 Mar 54
REGISTERED: 5 Apr 54 Belgium
ARTICLES: 23 LANGUAGE: English. French.
HEADNOTE: DOUBLE TAXATION
TOPIC: Taxation
CONCEPTS: Equitable taxes.
PARTIES:
Belgium
UK Great Britain

102527 Bilateral Convention **188 UNTS 187**
SIGNED: 18 May 52   FORCE: 17 Sep 52
REGISTERED: 7 Apr 54 Norway
ARTICLES: 34 LANGUAGE: Norwegian. Finnish.
HEADNOTE: CONSTRUCTION MAINTENANCE REINDEER FENCES
TOPIC: Specific Resources
CONCEPTS: Previous treaty replacement. Exchange of official publications. Inspection and observation. Establishment of commission. Arbitration. Currency. Financial programs. Pasturage in frontier zones. Fish, wildlife, and natural resources. Wildlife.
INTL ORGS: Arbitration Commission. Special Commission.

TREATY REF: 169LTS33; 197LTS361; 32UNTS3.
PROCEDURE: Denunciation. Duration. Ratification. Renewal or Revival.
PARTIES:
Finland
Norway
ANNEX
219 UNTS 377. Finland. Amendment 24 Aug 55. Force 24 Aug 55.
219 UNTS 377. Norway. Amendment 23 Aug 55. Force 24 Aug 55.
317 UNTS 332. Norway. Amendment 20 Oct 58. Force 25 Oct 58.
317 UNTS 332. Finland. Amendment 25 Oct 58. Force 25 Oct 58.

102528 Bilateral Exchange **188 UNTS 251**
SIGNED: 8 Feb 54   FORCE: 8 Mar 54
REGISTERED: 8 Apr 54 Belgium
ARTICLES: 2 LANGUAGE: French.
HEADNOTE: PROVISIONAL EXTRADITION AGREEMENT
TOPIC: Extradition
CONCEPTS: Extradition, deportation and repatriation.
PARTIES:
Belgium
Israel
ANNEX
207 UNTS 366. Belgium. Prolongation 2 Mar 55. Force 8 Mar 55.
207 UNTS 366. Israel. Prolongation 28 Feb 55. Force 8 Mar 55.
234 UNTS 366. Belgium. Prolongation 28 Mar 56. Force 8 Mar 56.
234 UNTS 366. Israel. Prolongation 23 Mar 56. Force 8 Mar 56.

102529 Bilateral Exchange **188 UNTS 259**
SIGNED: 3 Mar 54   FORCE: 3 Mar 54
REGISTERED: 8 Apr 54 Belgium
ARTICLES: 3 LANGUAGE: French. German.
HEADNOTE: SUPPRESSION COUNTERFEIT CURRENCY
TOPIC: Admin Cooperation
CONCEPTS: Investigation of violations. Currency.
TREATY REF: 112LTS371.
PARTIES:
Belgium
Germany, West

102530 Bilateral Exchange **188 UNTS 267**
SIGNED: 17 Dec 52   FORCE: 1 Jan 53
REGISTERED: 9 Apr 54 Australia
ARTICLES: 2 LANGUAGE: English.
HEADNOTE: VISAS
TOPIC: Visas
CONCEPTS: Frontier formalities. Visa abolition.
PARTIES:
Australia
Germany, West

102531 Multilateral Agreement **188 UNTS 273**
SIGNED: 22 Feb 54   FORCE: 24 Mar 54
REGISTERED: 9 Apr 54 Denmark
ARTICLES: 5 LANGUAGE: Danish. English.
HEADNOTE: WAR GRAVES MEMORIALS
TOPIC: Other Military
CONCEPTS: Establishment of commission. Responsibility for war dead. Upkeep of war graves. Establishment of war cemeteries.
INTL ORGS: Conciliation Commission.
PARTIES:
Australia SIGNED: 22 Feb 54 FORCE: 24 Mar 54
Canada SIGNED: 22 Feb 54 FORCE: 24 Mar 54
Denmark SIGNED: 22 Feb 54 FORCE: 24 Mar 54
India SIGNED: 22 Feb 54 FORCE: 24 Mar 54
New Zealand SIGNED: 22 Feb 54 FORCE: 24 Mar 54
Pakistan SIGNED: 22 Feb 54 FORCE: 24 Mar 54
South Africa SIGNED: 22 Feb 54 FORCE: 24 Mar 54
UK Great Britain SIGNED: 22 Feb 54 FORCE: 24 Mar 54

102532 Bilateral Agreement **188 UNTS 283**
SIGNED: 24 Sep 53   FORCE: 1 Feb 54
REGISTERED: 9 Apr 54 Denmark
ARTICLES: 4 LANGUAGE: French.

HEADNOTE: SUPPLEMENT 30 JAN 26 CONVENTION
TOPIC: Dispute Settlement
CONCEPTS: Annex type material.
INTL ORGS: International Court of Justice. Permanent Court of International Justice. United Nations.
TREATY REF: 51LTS367; 6LTS390.
PARTIES:
Denmark
Finland

102533 Bilateral Agreement **188 UNTS 289**
SIGNED: 31 May 51   FORCE: 11 May 53
REGISTERED: 12 Apr 54 Netherlands
ARTICLES: 8 LANGUAGE: Dutch. Afrikaans. English.
HEADNOTE: CULTURAL AGREEMENT
TOPIC: Culture
CONCEPTS: Definition of terms. Friendship and amity. Conformity with municipal law. Establishment of commission. Exchange. Teacher and student exchange. Culture. Scientific exchange. Research and development. Publications exchange. Mass media exchange.
PROCEDURE: Duration. Ratification. Renewal or Revival. Termination.
PARTIES:
Netherlands
South Africa

102534 Bilateral Exchange **188 UNTS 303**
SIGNED: 6 Sep 51   FORCE: 17 Sep 51
REGISTERED: 15 Apr 54 Australia
ARTICLES: 2 LANGUAGE: English.
HEADNOTE: MOST FAVORED NATION TREATMENT
TOPIC: Mostfavored Nation
CONCEPTS: Detailed regulations. Most favored nation clause.
TREATY REF: 55UNTS187-FN2.
PROCEDURE: Termination.
PARTIES:
Australia
Israel

102535 Bilateral Agreement **188 UNTS 311**
SIGNED: 2 Feb 52   FORCE: 8 Apr 54
REGISTERED: 16 Apr 54 Greece
ARTICLES: 9 LANGUAGE: French.
HEADNOTE: EPIZOOTIC DISEASES
TOPIC: Sanitation
CONCEPTS: Detailed regulations. Border traffic and migration. Operating agencies. Conformity with municipal law. Exchange of information and documents. Use of facilities. Sanitation. Disease control. Veterinary. Indemnities and reimbursements. General technical assistance. Fish, wildlife, and natural resources.
PROCEDURE: Denunciation. Duration. Ratification. Renewal or Revival.
PARTIES:
Greece
Yugoslavia

102536 Bilateral Treaty **188 UNTS 323**
SIGNED: 26 Jul 51   FORCE: 27 Aug 52
REGISTERED: 16 Apr 54 Pakistan
ARTICLES: 5 LANGUAGE: English. Turkish. Urdu.
HEADNOTE: FRIENDSHIP
TOPIC: General Amity
CONCEPTS: Friendship and amity. Arbitration.
INTL ORGS: United Nations.
PROCEDURE: Ratification.
PARTIES:
Pakistan
Turkey

102537 Bilateral Treaty **188 UNTS 333**
SIGNED: 3 Mar 51   FORCE: 7 May 53
REGISTERED: 16 Apr 54 Pakistan
ARTICLES: 5 LANGUAGE: English. Indonesian. Urdu.
HEADNOTE: FRIENDSHIP
TOPIC: General Amity
CONCEPTS: Friendship and amity.
INTL ORGS: United Nations.

PARTIES:
Indonesia
Pakistan

102538 Bilateral Exchange **189 UNTS 3**
SIGNED: 4 Feb 53 FORCE: 4 Feb 53
REGISTERED: 19 Apr 54 Greece
ARTICLES: 2 LANGUAGE: English.
HEADNOTE: IMPLEMENTATION COMMON DE-
FENSE PROGRAM FOREIGN AID PROGRAMS
TOPIC: Milit Assistance
CONCEPTS: Annex or appendix reference. Privi-
leges and immunities. Conformity with munici-
pal law. Extraterritorial rights. Tax exemptions.
Materials, equipment and services. Defense and
security.
PROCEDURE: Future Procedures Contemplated.
PARTIES:
Greece
USA (United States)

102539 Multilateral Agreement **189 UNTS 11**
SIGNED: 20 Apr 54 FORCE: 20 Apr 54
REGISTERED: 20 Apr 54 United Nations
ARTICLES: 6 LANGUAGE: English.
HEADNOTE: TECHNICAL ASSISTANCE
TOPIC: Tech Assistance
CONCEPTS: Definition of terms. Privileges and im-
munities. General cooperation. Exchange of in-
formation and documents. Personnel. Responsi-
bility and liability. Title and deeds. Exchange.
Scholarships and grants. Vocational training. Re-
search and development. Expense sharing for-
mulae. Local currency. Domestic obligation.
General technical assistance. Materials, equip-
ment and services. IGO status. Conformity with
IGO decisions.
TREATY REF: 76UNTS132; 1UNTS15;
1UNTS263; 33UNTS261.
PARTIES:
Burma SIGNED: 20 Apr 54 FORCE: 20 Apr 54
FAO (Food Agri) SIGNED: 20 Apr 54 FORCE:
20 Apr 54
ICAO (Civil Aviat) SIGNED: 20 Apr 54 FORCE:
20 Apr 54
ILO (Labor Org) SIGNED: 20 Apr 54 FORCE:
20 Apr 54
UNESCO (Educ/Cult) SIGNED: 20 Apr 54 FORCE:
20 Apr 54
United Nations SIGNED: 20 Apr 54 FORCE:
20 Apr 54
WHO (World Health) SIGNED: 20 Apr 54 FORCE:
20 Apr 54

102540 Bilateral Exchange **189 UNTS 25**
SIGNED: 21 Dec 53 FORCE: 5 Jan 54
REGISTERED: 21 Apr 54 Netherlands
ARTICLES: 2 LANGUAGE: French. Italian.
HEADNOTE: SIMPLIFICATION ENTRY REQUIRE-
MENTS PROCEDURES FLIGHT PERSONNEL
TOPIC: Visas
CONCEPTS: Non-visa travel documents. Licenses
and permits. Air transport.
PROCEDURE: Termination.
PARTIES:
Italy
Netherlands

102541 Multilateral Instrument **189 UNTS 33**
SIGNED: 12 Feb 49 FORCE: 4 Jan 54
REGISTERED: 21 Apr 54 Netherlands
ARTICLES: 5 LANGUAGE: French.
HEADNOTE: TARIFF
TOPIC: Customs
CONCEPTS: Detailed regulations. Tariffs. Customs
duties.
TREATY REF: 105LTS9.
PROCEDURE: Denunciation. Duration. Ratification.
PARTIES:
Bel-Lux Econ Union SIGNED: 12 Feb 49 RATI-
FIED: 15 Dec 53 FORCE: 4 Jan 54
Netherlands SIGNED: 12 Feb 49 RATIFIED:
15 Dec 53 FORCE: 4 Jan 54
Switzerland SIGNED: 12 Feb 49 RATIFIED:
15 Dec 53 FORCE: 4 Jan 54

102542 Bilateral Agreement **189 UNTS 55**
SIGNED: 29 Apr 52 FORCE: 29 Apr 52
REGISTERED: 22 Apr 54 Israel

ARTICLES: 20 LANGUAGE: French. Hebrew.
HEADNOTE: AIR TRANSPORT
TOPIC: Air Transport
CONCEPTS: Definition of terms. Detailed regulations. Exceptions and exemptions. Annex or appendix reference. Conformity with municipal
law. General cooperation. Exchange of information and documents. Licenses and permits. Establishment of commission. Arbitration. Procedure. Special tribunals. Negotiation. Reexport of
goods, etc.. Non-interest rates and fees. Most favored nation clause. Equitable taxes. Customs
exemptions. Competency certificate. Routes and
logistics. Navigational conditions. Permit designation. Airport facilities. Airworthiness certificates. Conditions of airlines operating permission. Overflights and technical stops. Operating
authorizations and regulations.
INTL ORGS: International Civil Aviation Organization. International Court of Justice. Special Commission.
TREATY REF: 15UNTS295.
PROCEDURE: Amendment. Future Procedures
Contemplated. Registration. Termination.
PARTIES:
France
Israel
ANNEX
464 UNTS 324. Israel. Amendment 7 May 62.
Force 7 May 62.
464 UNTS 324. France. Amendment 7 May 62.
Force 7 May 62.

102543 Bilateral Agreement **189 UNTS 89**
SIGNED: 23 Oct 50 FORCE: 23 Oct 50
REGISTERED: 22 Apr 54 Israel
ARTICLES: 12 LANGUAGE: Dutch. English. Hebrew.
HEADNOTE: AIR TRANSPORT
TOPIC: Air Transport
CONCEPTS: Exceptions and exemptions. Treaty interpretation. Annex or appendix reference. Conformity with municipal law. Licenses and permits. Recognition of legal documents. Use of facilities. Arbitration. Procedure. Special tribunals.
Negotiation. Reexport of goods, etc.. Fees and
exemptions. Most favored nation clause. National treatment. Customs exemptions. Competency certificate. Routes and logistics. Navigational conditions. Permit designation. Air transport. Airport facilities. Airworthiness certificates.
Conditions of airlines operating permission. Operating authorizations and regulations. Licenses
and certificates of nationality.
INTL ORGS: International Civil Aviation Organization.
TREATY REF: INTER.CIVIL AVIA.CONF.INOV1944.
PROCEDURE: Amendment. Registration. Termination.
PARTIES:
Israel
Netherlands
ANNEX
311 UNTS 346. Israel. Amendment 25 May 56.
Force 25 May 56.
311 UNTS 346. Netherlands. Amendment
26 Apr 56. Force 25 May 56.

102544 Bilateral Protocol **189 UNTS 117**
SIGNED: 19 Aug 52 FORCE: 19 Aug 52
REGISTERED: 22 Apr 54 Greece
ARTICLES: 1 LANGUAGE: French.
HEADNOTE: TRADE
TOPIC: General Trade
CONCEPTS: Annex or appendix reference. Annex
type material. Licenses and permits. Trade pro-
cedures. Quotas.
INTL ORGS: European Payments Union. Special
Commission.
PARTIES:
Greece
Sweden

102545 Multilateral Convention **189 UNTS 137**
SIGNED: 2 Jul 51 FORCE: 22 Apr 54
REGISTERED: 22 Apr 54 United Nations
ARTICLES: 46 LANGUAGE: English. French.
HEADNOTE: STATUS REFUGEES
TOPIC: Refugees
CONCEPTS: Definition of terms. Exceptions and
exemptions. Territorial application. General pro-

visions. Border traffic and migration. Denial of
admission. Resident permits. Legal status. Refugees. Alien status. Human rights. General cooperation. Legal protection and assistance. Immovable property. General property. Procedure. Education. Anti-discrimination. Employment
regulations. Social security. Fees and exemptions. Assets transfer. Most favored nation
clause. National treatment.
INTL ORGS: International Court of Justice. Interna-
tional Refugees Organization. United Nations.
TREATY REF: 139LTS47,53,63(SEE ALSO)FN ON
P.152 UNTS VOL 189.
PROCEDURE: Amendment. Accession. Denuncia-
tion. Ratification.
PARTIES:
Austria SIGNED: 28 Jul 51
Belgium SIGNED: 28 Jul 51 RATIFIED: 22 Jul 53
FORCE: 22 Apr 54
Brazil SIGNED: 15 Jul 52
Colombia SIGNED: 28 Jul 51
Denmark SIGNED: 28 Jul 51 RATIFIED:
4 Dec 52 FORCE: 22 Apr 54
France SIGNED: 11 Sep 52
Germany, West SIGNED: 29 Nov 51 RATIFIED:
1 Dec 53 FORCE: 22 Apr 54
Greece SIGNED: 10 Apr 52
Israel SIGNED: 1 Aug 51
Italy SIGNED: 23 Jul 52
Liechtenstein SIGNED: 28 Jul 51
Luxembourg SIGNED: 28 Jul 51 RATIFIED:
23 Jul 53 FORCE: 22 Apr 54
Netherlands SIGNED: 28 Jul 51
Norway SIGNED: 28 Jul 51 RATIFIED:
23 Mar 53 FORCE: 22 Apr 54
Sweden SIGNED: 28 Jul 51
Switzerland SIGNED: 28 Jul 51
Turkey SIGNED: 24 Aug 51
UK Great Britain SIGNED: 28 Jul 51 RATIFIED:
11 Mar 54 FORCE: 22 Apr 54
Vatican/Holy See SIGNED: 22 May 52
Yugoslavia SIGNED: 28 Jul 51
ANNEX
190 UNTS 385. Monaco. Qualified Accession
18 May 54. Force 16 Aug 54.
191 UNTS 409. France. Qualified Ratification
23 Jun 54. Force 21 Sep 54.
199 UNTS 357. Israel. Qualified Ratification
1 Oct 54. Force 30 Dec 54.
200 UNTS 336. Sweden. Qualified Ratification
26 Oct 54. Force 24 Jan 55.
201 UNTS 387. Austria. Qualified Ratification
1 Nov 54. Force 30 Jan 55.
201 UNTS 389. Italy. Ratification 5 Nov 54. Force
13 Feb 55.
202 UNTS 368. Switzerland. Qualified Ratification 21 Jan 55. Force 21 Apr 55.
214 UNTS 376. Ecuador. Qualified Accession
17 Aug 55. Force 15 Nov 55.
223 UNTS 377. Germany, West. Berlin. Force
22 Apr 54.
230 UNTS 440. Vatican/Holy See. Qualified
Ratification 15 Mar 56. Force 13 Jun 56.
237 UNTS 335. Netherlands. Qualified Ratification 3 May 56. Force 1 Aug 56.
252 UNTS 354. UK Great Britain. St. Helena.
Force 23 Jan 57.
252 UNTS 354. UK Great Britain. St. Vincent.
Force 23 Jan 57.
252 UNTS 354. UK Great Britain. Dominican
Republic. Force 23 Jan 57.
252 UNTS 354. UK Great Britain. Fiji Islands.
Force 23 Jan 57.
252 UNTS 354. UK Great Britain. Solomon Islands. Force 23 Jan 57.
252 UNTS 354. UK Great Britain. Gambia. Force
23 Jan 57.
252 UNTS 354. UK Great Britain. Falkland Islands. Force 23 Jan 57.
252 UNTS 354. UK Great Britain. Gilbert Islands.
Force 23 Jan 57.
252 UNTS 354. UK Great Britain. Kenya. Force
23 Jan 57.
252 UNTS 354. UK Great Britain. Grenada. Force
23 Jan 57.
252 UNTS 354. UK Great Britain. Mauritius. Force
23 Jan 57.
252 UNTS 354. UK Great Britain. Jamaica. Force
23 Jan 57.
252 UNTS 354. UK Great Britain. Zanzibar. Force
23 Jan 57.
252 UNTS 354. UK Great Britain. Cyprus. Force
23 Jan 57.

252 UNTS 354. UK Great Britain. British Somaliland. Force 23 Jan 57.

252 UNTS 354. UK Great Britain. Seychelles.
Force 23 Jan 57.

253 UNTS 365. Morocco. Succession 7 Nov 56.

254 UNTS 412. Ireland. Qualified Accession
29 Nov 56. Force 27 Feb 57.

261 UNTS 404. Liechtenstein. Qualified Ratification 8 Mar 57. Force 6 Jun 57.

270 UNTS 398. UK Great Britain. British Honduras. Force 17 Sep 57.

278 UNTS 282. Tunisia. Declaration 24 Oct 57.

346 UNTS 338. Yugoslavia. Qualified Ratification
15 Dec 59. Force 14 Mar 60.

354 UNTS 402. Greece. Qualified Ratification
5 Apr 60. Force 4 Jul 60.

363 UNTS 404. New Zealand. Qualified Accession 30 Jun 60. Force 28 Sep 60.

366 UNTS 414. UK Great Britain. Fed Rhod/-
Nyasaland. Force 9 Oct 60.

380 UNTS 428. UK Great Britain. Basutoland.
Force 9 Feb 61.

380 UNTS 428. UK Great Britain. Bechuanaland.
Force 9 Feb 61.

380 UNTS 428. UK Great Britain. Swaziland.
Force 9 Feb 61.

380 UNTS 430. Brazil. Qualified Ratification
16 Nov 60. Force 14 Feb 61.

383 UNTS 314. Portugal. Qualified Accession
22 Dec 60. Force 22 Mar 61.

394 UNTS 269. Sweden. Withdrawal of Reservation 20 Apr 61. Force 1 Jul 61.

405 UNTS 322. Niger. Succession 25 Aug 61.

410 UNTS 293. Colombia. Qualified Ratification
10 Oct 61. Force 8 Jan 62.

411 UNTS 301. Cameroon.

413 UNTS 370. Argentina. Qualified Accession
15 Nov 61. Force 13 Feb 62.

413 UNTS 370. Vatican/Holy See. Implementation 17 Nov 61.

415 UNTS 430. Ivory Coast. Succession
8 Dec 61.

418 UNTS 364. Cameroon. Notification
29 Dec 61.

423 UNTS 308. Togo. Succession 27 Feb 62.

424 UNTS 349. Turkey. Qualified Ratification
30 Mar 62. Force 28 Jun 62.

424 UNTS 350. Dahomey. Succession 4 Apr 62.

435 UNTS 332. Denmark. Withdrawal of Reservation 1 Oct 61.

437 UNTS 352. Central Afri Rep. Succession
4 Sep 62.

442 UNTS 320. Central Afri Rep. Prolongation
15 Oct 62.

442 UNTS 320. Congo (Brazzaville). Succession
15 Oct 62.

443 UNTS 342. Togo. Prolongation 23 Oct 62.

453 UNTS 358. Switzerland. Withdrawal of Reservation 18 Feb 63.

454 UNTS 554. Algeria. Succession 21 Feb 63.

456 UNTS 495. Ghana. Accession 18 Mar 63.
Force 16 Jun 63.

463 UNTS 344. Senegal. Succession 2 May 63.

466 UNTS 388. Cyprus. Succession 16 May 63.

471 UNTS 330. Burundi. Accession 19 Jul 63.
Force 17 Oct 63.

494 UNTS 292. Gabon. Qualified Accession
27 Apr 64. Force 26 Jul 64.

495 UNTS 260. Tanzania. Qualified Accession
12 May 64. Force 10 Aug 64.

503 UNTS 334. Jamaica. Succession 30 Jul 64.

511 UNTS 269. Liberia. Qualified Accession
15 Oct 64. Force 13 Jan 65.

511 UNTS 269. Senegal. Notification 12 Oct 64.
Force 13 Jan 65.

514 UNTS 268. Italy. Withdrawal of Reservation
20 Oct 64.

520 UNTS 427. Niger. Acceptance 7 Dec 64.

521 UNTS 390. Peru. Qualified Accession
21 Dec 64. Force 21 Mar 65.

541 UNTS 312. Congo (Zaire). Qualified Accession 19 Jul 65. Force 17 Oct 65.

550 UNTS 403. Guinea. Succession 28 Dec 65.

562 UNTS 329. Kenya. Qualified Accession
16 May 66. Force 14 Aug 66.

572 UNTS 357. Gambia. Accession 7 Sep 66.

607 UNTS 262. Nigeria. Accession 23 Oct 67.
Force 21 Jan 68.

613 UNTS 408. Australia. Withdrawal of Reservation 1 Dec 67. Extension and Amendment
1 Dec 67.

614 UNTS 306. Madagascar. Accession
18 Dec 67. Force 17 Mar 68.

633 UNTS 385. Denmark. Withdrawal of Reservation 25 Mar 68.

645 UNTS 353. UK Great Britain. Montserrat.
Force 3 Dec 68.

645 UNTS 353. UK Great Britain. St. Lucia. Force
3 Dec 68.

648 UNTS 366. Finland. Accession 10 Oct 68.
Force 8 Jan 69.

649 UNTS 325. Ireland. Withdrawal of Reservation 23 Oct 68.

655 UNTS 389. Botswana. Accession 6 Jan 69.
Force 6 Apr 69.

102546 Unilateral Instrument **189 UNTS 223**
SIGNED: 26 Feb 54   FORCE: 26 Feb 54
REGISTERED: 23 Apr 54 Finland
ARTICLES: 1 LANGUAGE: French.
HEADNOTE: SUBMIT DISPUTE TO ICJ
TOPIC: Dispute Settlement
CONCEPTS: Dispute settlement. Procedure. Exist-
ing tribunals. Anti-discrimination. Adherence to
UN Charter.
INTL ORGS: International Court of Justice. United
Nations.
TREATY REF: 188UNTS; 51LTS36;.
PARTIES:
Finland

102547 Bilateral Instrument **189 UNTS 227**
SIGNED: 7 Jan 49   FORCE: 7 Jan 49
REGISTERED: 23 Apr 54 Australia
ARTICLES: 1 LANGUAGE: English.
HEADNOTE: REVIVAL PRE-WAR TREATIES
TOPIC: Admin Cooperation
CONCEPTS: Revival of treaties.
INTL ORGS: United Nations.
TREATY REF: 48UNTS203; 34LTS79; 50LTS161;
28LTS512.
PARTIES:
Australia
Finland

102548 Bilateral Instrument **189 UNTS 233**
SIGNED: 7 Jan 49   FORCE: 7 Jan 49
REGISTERED: 23 Apr 54 Australia
ARTICLES: 1 LANGUAGE: English.
HEADNOTE: REVIVAL PRE-WAR TREATIES
TOPIC: Admin Cooperation
CONCEPTS: Revival of treaties.
INTL ORGS: United Nations.
TREATY REF: 41UNTS135;   2'33DM112;
170LTS51;M.
PARTIES:
Australia
Hungary

102549 Bilateral Instrument **189 UNTS 239**
SIGNED: 7 Jan 49   FORCE: 7 Jan 49
REGISTERED: 23 Apr 54 Australia
ARTICLES: 1 LANGUAGE: English.
HEADNOTE: REVIVAL PRE-WAR TREATIES
TOPIC: Admin Cooperation
CONCEPTS: Revival of treaties.
INTL ORGS: United Nations.
TREATY REF: 49UNTS3; 104UNTS48; 131LTS78;
165LTS107.
PARTIES:
Australia
Italy

102550 Bilateral Instrument **189 UNTS 263**
SIGNED: 7 Jan 49   FORCE: 7 Jan 49
REGISTERED: 23 Apr 54 Australia
ARTICLES: 1 LANGUAGE: English.
HEADNOTE: REVIVAL PRE-WAR TREATIES
TOPIC: Admin Cooperation
CONCEPTS: Revival of treaties.
INTL ORGS: United Nations.
TREATY REF: 2'20DEMARTENS760; 42UNTS3;
83UNTS480;.
PARTIES:
Australia
Romania

102551 Bilateral Agreement **189 UNTS 269**
SIGNED: 4 Feb 53   FORCE: 4 Feb 53
REGISTERED: 28 Apr 54 Greece
ARTICLES: 8 LANGUAGE: French.

HEADNOTE: TRADE
TOPIC: General Trade
CONCEPTS: Previous treaty replacement. Confor-
mity with municipal law. Licenses and permits.
Establishment of commission. Trade proce-
dures. Currency. Payment schedules. Quotas.
INTL ORGS: European Payments Union. Organiza-
tion for Economic Co-operation and Develop-
ment. Special Commission.
TREATY REF: 189UNTS295.
PROCEDURE: Denunciation. Duration. Renewal or
Revival.
PARTIES:
Greece
Italy

102552 Bilateral Agreement **189 UNTS 295**
SIGNED: 4 Feb 53   FORCE: 4 Feb 53
REGISTERED: 28 Apr 54 Greece
ARTICLES: 12 LANGUAGE: French.
HEADNOTE: PAYMENTS
TOPIC: Finance
CONCEPTS: Detailed regulations. Treaty imple-
mentation. Conformity with municipal law. Gen-
eral cooperation. Licenses and permits. Account-
ing procedures. Banking. Financial programs. In-
adequacy of funds. Interest rates. Payment
schedules. Local currency.
INTL ORGS: European Payments Union. Interna-
tional Monetary Fund. Special Commission.
TREATY REF: 189UNTS269.
PROCEDURE: Amendment. Denunciation.
PARTIES:
Greece
Italy

102553 Bilateral Exchange **189 UNTS 309**
SIGNED: 24 Jul 53   FORCE: 24 Jul 53
REGISTERED: 28 Apr 54 Greece
ARTICLES: 2 LANGUAGE: French.
HEADNOTE: TRADE
TOPIC: General Trade
CONCEPTS: Annex type material. Trade proce-
dures.
PARTIES:
Greece
Sweden

102554 Bilateral Agreement **190 UNTS 3**
SIGNED: 30 Jun 53   FORCE: 30 Jun 53
REGISTERED: 1 May 54 United Nations
ARTICLES: 7 LANGUAGE: English.
HEADNOTE: ECONOMIC ENGINEERING SURVEYS
DEVELOPMENT PROJECTS
TOPIC: Tech Assistance
CONCEPTS: Annex or appendix reference. Assis-
tance. Exchange of information and documents.
Domestic legislation. Research and develop-
ment. Financial programs. General technical as-
sistance. Assistance.
PROCEDURE: Future Procedures Contemplated.
PARTIES:
UN Relief Palestin
United Arab Rep

102555 Bilateral Agreement **190 UNTS 13**
SIGNED: 14 Oct 53   FORCE: 14 Oct 53
REGISTERED: 1 May 54 United Nations
ARTICLES: 22 LANGUAGE: English.
HEADNOTE: PROJECT AGREEMENT (WITH AN-
NEXES)
TOPIC: Tech Assistance
CONCEPTS: Detailed regulations. Annex or appen-
dix reference. Assistance. General cooperation.
Exchange of information and documents. Oper-
ating agencies. Establishment of commission.
Communication satellites testing. Import quotas.
Reexport of goods, etc.. Accounting procedures.
Funding procedures. Domestic obligation. Assis-
tance. Materials, equipment and services. Irriga-
tion. Regulation of natural resources.
INTL ORGS: Special Commission.
PARTIES:
UN Relief Palestin
United Arab Rep

102556 Bilateral Exchange **190 UNTS 43**
SIGNED: 1 Apr 54   FORCE: 1 Jun 53
REGISTERED: 3 May 54 Belgium

ARTICLES: 2 LANGUAGE: French. German.
HEADNOTE: RENEWAL INTERNATIONAL LOAD LINE CONVENTION
TOPIC: Admin Cooperation
CONCEPTS: Detailed regulations. Revival of treaties.
TREATY REF: 135LTS301.
PARTIES:
Belgium
Germany, West
ANNEX
277 UNTS 353. Germany, West. Berlin. Force 1 Jun 53.
277 UNTS 353. Belgium. Acknowledgement 26 Apr 55. Force 1 Jun 53.

102557 Multilateral Agreement **190 UNTS 49**
SIGNED: 9 Oct 53   FORCE: 7 May 54
REGISTERED: 7 May 54 United Nations
ARTICLES: 6 LANGUAGE: French. Arabic.
HEADNOTE: TECHNICAL ASSISTANCE
TOPIC: Tech Assistance
CONCEPTS: Definition of terms. Detailed regulations. Treaty implementation. Privileges and immunities. General cooperation. Exchange of information and documents. Personnel. Title and deeds. Exchange. Scholarships and grants. Vocational training. Research and development. Expense sharing formulae. General technical assistance. Materials, equipment and services. Domestic obligation. IGO status. Conformity with IGO decisions.
INTL ORGS: United Nations.
TREATY REF: 76UNTS132; 1UNTS15; 1UNTS263.
PROCEDURE: Amendment. Termination.
PARTIES:
Lebanon SIGNED: 9 Oct 53 RATIFIED: 7 May 54 FORCE: 7 May 54
ICAO (Civil Aviat) SIGNED: 9 Oct 53 RATIFIED: 7 May 54 FORCE: 7 May 54
ILO (Labor Org) SIGNED: 9 Oct 53 RATIFIED: 7 May 54 FORCE: 7 May 54
UNESCO (Educ/Cult) SIGNED: 9 Oct 53 RATIFIED: 7 May 54 FORCE: 7 May 54
United Nations SIGNED: 9 Oct 53 RATIFIED: 7 May 54 FORCE: 7 May 54
WHO (World Health) SIGNED: 9 Oct 53 RATIFIED: 7 May 54 FORCE: 7 May 54
ANNEX
202 UNTS 370. UNTAB (Tech Assis). Amendment 12 Jan 55. Force 20 Jan 55.
202 UNTS 370. Lebanon. Amendment 20 Jan 55. Force 20 Jan 55.
455 UNTS 442. UNTAB (Tech Assis). Force 11 Sep 62.
455 UNTS 442. Lebanon. Force 11 Sep 62.

102558 Bilateral Exchange **190 UNTS 63**
SIGNED: 30 Mar 54   FORCE: 1 Apr 54
REGISTERED: 13 May 54 Belgium
ARTICLES: 2 LANGUAGE: French. German.
HEADNOTE: RENEWAL
TOPIC: Admin Cooperation
CONCEPTS: Territorial application. Revival of treaties.
TREATY REF: 27LTS157; 31LTS260; 117UNTS394.
PARTIES:
Belgium
Germany, West

102559 Bilateral Treaty **190 UNTS 69**
SIGNED: 15 Mar 53   FORCE: 2 Mar 54
REGISTERED: 13 May 54 India
ARTICLES: 11 LANGUAGE: Hindi. Arabic. English.
HEADNOTE: FRIENDSHIP COMMERCE NAVIGATION
TOPIC: General Amity
CONCEPTS: Friendship and amity. Alien status. Consular relations establishment. Privileges and immunities. Legal protection and assistance. Immovable property. General property. Most favored nation clause. Overflights and technical stops. Inland and territorial waters. Shipwreck and salvage.
PROCEDURE: Duration. Ratification. Termination.
PARTIES:
India
Muscat and Oman

102560 Bilateral Agreement **190 UNTS 85**
SIGNED: 27 Jun 52   FORCE: 17 Jan 53
REGISTERED: 13 May 54 IBRD (World Bank)
ARTICLES: 5 LANGUAGE: English.
HEADNOTE: GUARANTEE AGREEMENT
TOPIC: IBRD Project
CONCEPTS: Annex or appendix reference. Exchange of information and documents. Informational records. Inspection and observation. Accounting procedures. Bonds. Fees and exemptions. Tax exemptions. Domestic obligation. Terms of loan. Loan regulations. Loan guarantee. Guarantor non-interference.
PARTIES:
Brazil
IBRD (World Bank)

102561 Bilateral Agreement **190 UNTS 115**
SIGNED: 27 Jun 52   FORCE: 17 Jan 53
REGISTERED: 13 May 54 IBRD (World Bank)
ARTICLES: 8 LANGUAGE: English.
HEADNOTE: LOAN AGREEMENT
TOPIC: IBRD Project
CONCEPTS: Default remedies. Definition of terms. Annex or appendix reference. Exchange of information and documents. Informational records. Inspection and observation. Bonds. Fees and exemptions. Interest rates. Tax exemptions. Domestic obligation. Terms of loan. Loan regulations. Loan guarantee. Guarantor non-interference.
PARTIES:
Brazil
IBRD (World Bank)

102562 Bilateral Agreement **190 UNTS 133**
SIGNED: 30 Apr 53   FORCE: 5 Nov 53
REGISTERED: 13 May 54 IBRD (World Bank)
ARTICLES: 8 LANGUAGE: English.
HEADNOTE: LOAN AGREEMENT
TOPIC: IBRD Project
CONCEPTS: Default remedies. Definition of terms. Annex or appendix reference. Exchange of information and documents. Informational records. Inspection and observation. Accounting procedures. Bonds. Fees and exemptions. Interest rates. Tax exemptions. Domestic obligation. Terms of loan. Loan regulations. Loan guarantee. Guarantor non-interference.
PARTIES:
Brazil
IBRD (World Bank)

102563 Bilateral Agreement **190 UNTS 149**
SIGNED: 17 Jul 53   FORCE: 6 Nov 53
REGISTERED: 13 May 54 IBRD (World Bank)
ARTICLES: 5 LANGUAGE: English.
HEADNOTE: GUARANTEE AGREEMENT
TOPIC: IBRD Project
CONCEPTS: Definition of terms. Annex or appendix reference. Exchange of information and documents. Informational records. Inspection and observation. Accounting procedures. Bonds. Fees and exemptions. Tax exemptions. Domestic obligation. Terms of loan. Loan regulations. Loan guarantee. Guarantor non-interference.
PARTIES:
Brazil
IBRD (World Bank)

102564 Bilateral Agreement **190 UNTS 179**
SIGNED: 18 Dec 53   FORCE: 3 Mar 54
REGISTERED: 13 May 54 IBRD (World Bank)
ARTICLES: 5 LANGUAGE: English.
HEADNOTE: GUARANTEE AGREEMENT
TOPIC: IBRD Project
CONCEPTS: Annex or appendix reference. Exchange of information and documents. Informational records. Inspection and observation. Bonds. Fees and exemptions. Interest rates. Tax exemptions. Domestic obligation. Terms of loan. Loan regulations. Loan guarantee. Guarantor non-interference.
PARTIES:
Brazil
IBRD (World Bank)
ANNEX
599 UNTS 372. IBRD (World Bank). Interpretation 26 Apr 67.
599 UNTS 372. Brazil. Interpretation 26 Apr 67.

102565 Bilateral Agreement **190 UNTS 207**
SIGNED: 22 Jan 54   FORCE: 21 Apr 54
REGISTERED: 17 May 54 Netherlands
ARTICLES: 6 LANGUAGE: Dutch. English.
HEADNOTE: TECHNICAL COOPERATION
TOPIC: Tech Assistance
CONCEPTS: Exceptions and exemptions. Treaty implementation. Previous treaty replacement. General cooperation. Exchange of information and documents. Public information. Funding procedures. Tax exemptions. Customs exemptions. Domestic obligation. General technical assistance. Materials, equipment and services.
INTL ORGS: Caribbean Commission.
PROCEDURE: Amendment. Termination. Application to Non-self-governing Territories.
PARTIES:
Netherlands
USA (United States)

102566 Bilateral Exchange **190 UNTS 223**
SIGNED: 20 Dec 51   FORCE: 20 Dec 51
REGISTERED: 19 May 54 Australia
ARTICLES: 2 LANGUAGE: English.
HEADNOTE: REVISION PEACE TREATY
TOPIC: Peace/Disarmament
CONCEPTS: Annex type material. Armistice and peace.
INTL ORGS: United Nations.
PARTIES:
Australia
Italy

102567 Bilateral Agreement **190 UNTS 231**
SIGNED: 12 Apr 54   FORCE: 4 May 54
REGISTERED: 20 May 54 IBRD (World Bank)
ARTICLES: 8 LANGUAGE: English.
HEADNOTE: LOAN AGREEMENT
TOPIC: IBRD Project
CONCEPTS: Default remedies. Annex or appendix reference. Exchange of information and documents. Informational records. Inspection and observation. Accounting procedures. Bonds. Fees and exemptions. Interest rates. Tax exemptions. Domestic obligation. Terms of loan. Loan regulations. Loan guarantee. Guarantor non-interference.
PARTIES:
Peru
IBRD (World Bank)

102568 Bilateral Exchange **190 UNTS 247**
SIGNED: 3 Apr 54   FORCE: 1 Jan 54
REGISTERED: 21 May 54 Belgium
ARTICLES: 2 LANGUAGE: French. German.
HEADNOTE: RENEWAL
TOPIC: Admin Cooperation
CONCEPTS: Territorial application. Revival of treaties.
TREATY REF: 7LTS187,236; 81LTS317; 139LTS301.
PARTIES:
Belgium
Germany, West

102569 Bilateral Exchange **190 UNTS 253**
SIGNED: 15 Apr 54   FORCE: 1 Dec 53
REGISTERED: 21 May 54 Belgium
ARTICLES: 2 LANGUAGE: French. German.
HEADNOTE: RENEWAL
TOPIC: Admin Cooperation
CONCEPTS: Revival of treaties.
TREATY REF: 30LTS371; 135UNTS400.
PARTIES:
Belgium
Germany, West

102570 Bilateral Convention **190 UNTS 260**
SIGNED: 29 Sep 51   FORCE: 30 Jan 54
REGISTERED: 24 May 54 UK Great Britain
ARTICLES: 21 LANGUAGE: English. French. Greek.
HEADNOTE: CULTURAL CONVENTION
TOPIC: Culture
CONCEPTS: Definition of terms. Friendship and amity. Conformity with municipal law. Operating agencies. Establishment of commission. Specialists exchange. Recognition of degrees. Teacher and student exchange. Professorships. Institute establishment. Scholarships and grants. Ex-

change. General cultural cooperation. Artists. Scientific exchange. Import quotas. Publications exchange. Mass media exchange.
INTL ORGS: Special Commission.
PROCEDURE: Denunciation. Duration. Ratification. Renewal or Revival.
PARTIES:
Greece
UK Great Britain

102571 Bilateral Convention **190 UNTS 281**
SIGNED: 25 Jun 53   FORCE: 15 Jan 54
REGISTERED: 24 May 54 UK Great Britain
ARTICLES: 21 LANGUAGE: English. Greek.
HEADNOTE: DOUBLE TAXATION FISCAL EVASION TAXES INCOME
TOPIC: Taxation
CONCEPTS: Definition of terms. Territorial application. Conformity with municipal law. Exchange of official publications. Teacher and student exchange. Taxation. Equitable taxes. General. Tax exemptions. Air transport. Merchant vessels.
PROCEDURE: Duration. Ratification. Termination.
PARTIES:
Greece
UK Great Britain

102572 Bilateral Agreement **190 UNTS 319**
SIGNED: 29 Jan 54   FORCE: 1 Feb 54
REGISTERED: 24 May 54 UK Great Britain
ARTICLES: 9 LANGUAGE: English.
HEADNOTE: STERLING PAYMENTS
TOPIC: Finance
CONCEPTS: Definition of terms. Accounting procedures. Banking. Currency. Monetary and gold transfers. Exchange rates and regulations. Financial programs. Payment schedules.
TREATY REF: 2UNTS40; 19UNTS280; 141UNTS355.
PROCEDURE: Duration. Termination.
PARTIES:
Japan
UK Great Britain
ANNEX
201 UNTS 390. UK Great Britain. Prolongation 1 Oct 54. Force 1 Oct 54.
201 UNTS 390. Japan. Prolongation 1 Oct 54. Force 1 Oct 54.
213 UNTS 393. UK Great Britain. Prolongation 31 Mar 55. Force 1 Apr 55.
213 UNTS 393. Japan. Prolongation 31 Mar 55. Force 1 Apr 55.
215 UNTS 425. UK Great Britain. Prolongation 30 Jun 55. Force 30 Jun 55.
215 UNTS 425. Japan. Prolongation 30 Jun 55. Force 30 Jun 55.
218 UNTS 391. UK Great Britain. Prolongation 29 Jul 55. Force 1 Aug 55.
218 UNTS 391. Japan. Prolongation 29 Jul 55. Force 1 Aug 55.
223 UNTS 378. UK Great Britain. Prolongation 31 Aug 55. Force 31 Aug 55.
223 UNTS 378. Japan. Prolongation 31 Aug 55. Force 31 Aug 55.
264 UNTS 376. Japan. Prolongation 28 Sep 56. Force 1 Oct 56.
264 UNTS 376. Japan. Prolongation 31 Oct 56. Force 1 Nov 56.
264 UNTS 376. UK Great Britain. Prolongation 28 Sep 56. Force 1 Oct 56.
264 UNTS 376. UK Great Britain. Prolongation 31 Oct 56. Force 1 Nov 56.
264 UNTS 376. UK Great Britain. Prolongation 30 Nov 56. Force 1 Dec 56.
264 UNTS 376. Japan. Prolongation 30 Nov 56. Force 1 Dec 56.
264 UNTS 376. Japan. Prolongation 31 Dec 56. Force 1 Jan 56.
264 UNTS 376. UK Great Britain. Prolongation 31 Dec 56. Force 1 Jan 56.

102573 Bilateral Exchange **190 UNTS 329**
SIGNED: 29 Aug 52   FORCE: 29 Aug 52
REGISTERED: 24 May 54 UK Great Britain
ARTICLES: 2 LANGUAGE: English.
HEADNOTE: REGARDING FEDERATION ERITREA
TOPIC: Trusteeship
CONCEPTS: Acceptance of UN obligations. Disposition of territory.
INTL ORGS: United Nations.
PROCEDURE: Ratification.

PARTIES:
Ethiopia
UK Great Britain

102574 Bilateral Exchange **190 UNTS 335**
SIGNED: 31 Dec 53   FORCE: 31 Dec 53
REGISTERED: 24 May 54 UK Great Britain
ARTICLES: 2 LANGUAGE: English.
HEADNOTE: IMPORT OF BOOKS
TOPIC: Education
CONCEPTS: Detailed regulations. Annex or appendix reference. Scientific exchange. Import quotas. Trade procedures. Publications exchange.
PARTIES:
UK Great Britain
Yugoslavia
ANNEX
313 UNTS 356. Yugoslavia. Force 30 Jun 57.
313 UNTS 356. UK Great Britain. Force 30 Jun 57.

102575 Bilateral Exchange **190 UNTS 343**
SIGNED: 11 Feb 54   FORCE: 11 Feb 54
REGISTERED: 24 May 54 UK Great Britain
ARTICLES: 4 LANGUAGE: English.
HEADNOTE: REPAYMENT CREDITS ARMAMENTS
TOPIC: Milit Assistance
CONCEPTS: Exchange rates and regulations. Payment schedules. Local currency. Claims and settlements. Lump sum settlements. Payment for war supplies. Surplus war property.
TREATY REF: 190UNTSU21; 197LTS414; 200LTS167.
PARTIES:
Turkey
UK Great Britain
ANNEX
385 UNTS 370. UK Great Britain. Supplementation 9 Dec 60. Force 9 Dec 60.
385 UNTS 370. Turkey. Supplementation 9 Dec 60. Force 9 Dec 60.
414 UNTS 384. UK Great Britain. Prolongation 31 May 61. Force 31 May 61.
414 UNTS 384. Turkey. Prolongation 31 May 61. Force 31 May 61.
431 UNTS 297. UK Great Britain. Amendment 25 Oct 61. Force 4 Sep 61.
431 UNTS 297. Turkey. Amendment 25 Oct 61. Force 4 Sep 61.
437 UNTS 353. Turkey. Prolongation 30 Nov 61. Force 30 Nov 61.
437 UNTS 353. UK Great Britain. Prolongation 30 Nov 61. Force 30 Nov 61.
449 UNTS 302. UK Great Britain. Amendment 23 Jun 62. Force 1 Jun 62.
449 UNTS 302. Turkey. Amendment 23 Jun 62. Force 1 Jun 62.
470 UNTS 387. UK Great Britain. Amendment 27 Dec 62. Force 27 Dec 62.
470 UNTS 387. Turkey. Amendment 27 Dec 62. Force 27 Dec 62.
478 UNTS 423. UK Great Britain. Amendment 17 Jun 63. Force 17 Jun 63.
478 UNTS 423. Turkey. Amendment 17 Jun 63. Force 17 Jun 63.
507 UNTS 273. UK Great Britain. Implementation 16 Jan 64. Force 16 Jan 64.
507 UNTS 273. Turkey. Implementation 16 Jan 64. Force 16 Jan 64.
541 UNTS 313. UK Great Britain. Implementation 20 Aug 64. Force 20 Aug 64.
541 UNTS 313. Turkey. Implementation 20 Aug 64. Force 20 Aug 64.
541 UNTS 316. Turkey. Amendment 14 Jan 65. Force 14 Jan 65.
541 UNTS 316. UK Great Britain. Amendment 14 Jan 65. Force 14 Jan 65.
659 UNTS 336. UK Great Britain. Amendment 15 Jul 68. Force 15 Jul 68.
659 UNTS 336. Turkey. Amendment 15 Jul 68. Force 15 Jul 68.

102576 Multilateral Instrument **191 UNTS 3**
SIGNED: 10 Jun 48   FORCE: 10 Jun 48
REGISTERED: 24 May 54 UK Great Britain
ARTICLES: 1 LANGUAGE: English. French.
HEADNOTE: SAFETY LIFE SEA
TOPIC: Humanitarian
CONCEPTS: Annex or appendix reference. Previous treaty extension. Humanitarian matters. Ad-

mission. Subsidiary organ. Liaison with other IGO's. UN recommendations.
INTL ORGS: Inter-Governmental Maritime Consultative Organization.
TREATY REF: 136LTS81; 164UNTS113; 167UNTS338; 191UNTS20.
PARTIES:
Argentina SIGNED: 10 Jun 48
Australia SIGNED: 10 Jun 48
Belgium SIGNED: 10 Jun 48
Brazil SIGNED: 10 Jun 48
Canada SIGNED: 10 Jun 48
Chile SIGNED: 10 Jun 48
Taiwan SIGNED: 10 Jun 48
Denmark SIGNED: 10 Jun 48
United Arab Rep SIGNED: 10 Jun 48
Finland SIGNED: 10 Jun 48
France SIGNED: 10 Jun 48
Greece SIGNED: 10 Jun 48
Iceland SIGNED: 10 Jun 48
India SIGNED: 10 Jun 48
Ireland SIGNED: 10 Jun 48
Italy SIGNED: 10 Jun 48
Netherlands SIGNED: 10 Jun 48
New Zealand SIGNED: 10 Jun 48
Norway SIGNED: 10 Jun 48
Pakistan SIGNED: 10 Jun 48
Panama SIGNED: 10 Jun 48
Philippines SIGNED: 10 Jun 48
Poland SIGNED: 10 Jun 48
Portugal SIGNED: 10 Jun 48
South Africa SIGNED: 10 Jun 48
Sweden SIGNED: 10 Jun 48
UK Great Britain SIGNED: 10 Jun 48
USA (United States) SIGNED: 10 Jun 48
ANNEX
199 UNTS 358. Haiti. Acceptance 26 May 54.
199 UNTS 358. Panama. Acceptance 4 Feb 54.
199 UNTS 358. Germany, West. Acceptance 22 Jan 54.
220 UNTS 385. Uruguay. Acceptance 18 Aug 55.
227 UNTS 400. Czechoslovakia. Acceptance 9 Nov 55.
250 UNTS 314. Argentina. Acceptance 31 Jul 56.
267 UNTS 384. Cuba. Acceptance 22 Feb 57.
277 UNTS 354. Switzerland. Acceptance 11 Jan 57.
355 UNTS 411. Monaco. Acceptance 12 Apr 55.
355 UNTS 411. Ghana. Acceptance 11 Jul 58.

102577 Bilateral Agreement **191 UNTS 59**
SIGNED: 22 May 53   FORCE: 22 May 53
REGISTERED: 28 May 54 USA (United States)
ARTICLES: 25 LANGUAGE: English.
HEADNOTE: UTILIZATION DEFENSE INSTALLATIONS
TOPIC: Milit Installation
CONCEPTS: Definition of terms. Visa abolition. Court procedures. Conformity with municipal law. General cooperation. Recognition of legal documents. Responsibility and liability. Use of facilities. Investigation of violations. Disease control. Compensation. Indemnities and reimbursements. Currency. Tax exemptions. Customs exemptions. Materials, equipment and services. Airport facilities. Overflights and technical stops. Facilities and equipment. Postal services. Defense and security. Lease of military property. Security of information. Jurisdiction. Procurement and logistics. Status of forces. Bases and facilities. Restrictions on transfer.
PROCEDURE: Termination.
PARTIES:
Ethiopia
USA (United States)

102578 Bilateral Agreement **191 UNTS 85**
SIGNED: 13 Jun 52   FORCE: 10 Feb 54
REGISTERED: 28 May 54 IBRD (World Bank)
ARTICLES: 8 LANGUAGE: English.
HEADNOTE: LOAN AGREEMENT PUNJAB AGRICULTURAL MACHINERY
TOPIC: IBRD Project
CONCEPTS: Default remedies. Annex or appendix reference. Exchange of information and documents. Informational records. Inspection and observation. Accounting procedures. Bonds. Fees and exemptions. Interest rates. Tax exemptions. Domestic obligation. Terms of loan. Loan regulations. Loan guarantee. Guarantor non-interference.

PARTIES:
Pakistan
IBRD (World Bank)

102579 Bilateral Agreement **191 UNTS 103**
SIGNED: 2 Mar 54   FORCE: 25 May 54
REGISTERED: 28 May 54 IBRD (World Bank)
ARTICLES: 7 LANGUAGE: English.
HEADNOTE: LOAN AGREEMENT
TOPIC: IBRD Project
CONCEPTS: Default remedies. Annex or appendix reference. Exchange of information and documents. Informational records. Inspection and observation. Accounting procedures. Bonds. Fees and exemptions. Interest rates. Tax exemptions. Domestic obligation. Terms of loan. Loan regulations. Loan guarantee. Guarantor non-interference.
PARTIES:
Australia
IBRD (World Bank)

102580 Bilateral Agreement **191 UNTS 125**
SIGNED: 24 May 54   FORCE: 24 May 54
REGISTERED: 31 May 54 Australia
ARTICLES: 8 LANGUAGE: English. Japanese.
HEADNOTE: REGULATING PEARLING PENDING DECISION ICJ
TOPIC: Specif Claim/Waive
CONCEPTS: Definition of terms. General cooperation. Inspection and observation. Specific claims or waivers. Ocean resources.
INTL ORGS: International Court of Justice.
PARTIES:
Australia
Japan

102581 Multilateral Instrument **191 UNTS 143**
SIGNED: 25 Jun 53   FORCE: 20 May 54
REGISTERED: 1 Jun 54 ILO (Labor Org)
ARTICLES: 6 LANGUAGE: English. French.
HEADNOTE: AMENDMENT ILO CONSTITUTION INSTRUMENT
TOPIC: ILO Labor
CONCEPTS: Annex type material. Previous treaty extension.
INTL ORGS: United Nations.
PARTIES:
Multilateral
ANNEX
196 UNTS 362. Turkey. Ratification 21 May 54.
196 UNTS 362. Luxembourg. Ratification 28 May 54.
196 UNTS 362. Haiti. Ratification 22 Jun 54.
196 UNTS 362. France. Ratification 28 Jun 54.
196 UNTS 362. Venezuela. Acceptance 2 Jul 54.
200 UNTS 338. Ukrainian SSR. Ratification 7 Oct 54.
200 UNTS 338. USSR (Soviet Union). Ratification 7 Oct 54.
200 UNTS 338. Hungary. Ratification 16 Oct 54.
200 UNTS 338. Byelorussia. Ratification 7 Oct 54.
202 UNTS 381. Argentina. Ratification 15 Nov 54.
214 UNTS 377. Iraq. Ratification 15 Aug 55.
214 UNTS 377. Brazil. Acceptance 19 Aug 55.
230 UNTS 441. Philippines. Acceptance 29 Feb 56.
267 UNTS 385. Chile. Ratification 10 May 57.
380 UNTS 432. Guatemala. Ratification 15 Nov 60.

102582 Bilateral Convention **191 UNTS 151**
SIGNED: 17 Apr 53   FORCE: 14 Feb 54
REGISTERED: 3 Jun 54 Greece
ARTICLES: 38 LANGUAGE: English. Greek.
HEADNOTE: CONSULAR
TOPIC: Consul/Citizenship
CONCEPTS: Alien status. General consular functions. Consular relations establishment. Diplomatic missions. Inviolability. Privileges and immunities. Property. Diplomatic correspondence. Consular functions in shipping. Consular functions in property. Procedure. Existing tribunals.
INTL ORGS: International Court of Justice.
TREATY REF: 88UNTS205; 2'2DM475; 61LTS15;T.

PARTIES:
Greece
UK Great Britain

102583 Bilateral Agreement **191 UNTS 235**
SIGNED: 29 Apr 53   FORCE: 20 Mar 54
REGISTERED: 3 Jun 54 Greece
ARTICLES: 5 LANGUAGE: French.
HEADNOTE: CULTURAL AGREEMENT
TOPIC: Culture
CONCEPTS: Friendship and amity. Establishment of commission. Exchange. Teacher and student exchange. Scholarships and grants. Exchange. General cultural cooperation. Artists. Athletes. Publications exchange. Mass media exchange.
PROCEDURE: Duration. Ratification. Renewal or Revival. Termination.
PARTIES:
Greece
Netherlands

102584 Bilateral Exchange **191 UNTS 241**
SIGNED: 19 Nov 53   FORCE: 19 Nov 53
REGISTERED: 7 Jun 54 Australia
ARTICLES: 2 LANGUAGE: English.
HEADNOTE: EXCHANGE OFFICIAL PUBLICATIONS
TOPIC: Admin Cooperation
CONCEPTS: Exchange of information and documents.
PARTIES:
Australia
Yugoslavia

102585 Bilateral Exchange **191 UNTS 249**
SIGNED: 7 Nov 53   FORCE: 7 Nov 53
REGISTERED: 18 Jun 54 Australia
ARTICLES: 2 LANGUAGE: English.
HEADNOTE: EXCHANGE OFFICIAL PUBLICATIONS
TOPIC: Admin Cooperation
CONCEPTS: Exchange of information and documents.
PARTIES:
Australia
Ceylon (Sri Lanka)

102586 Bilateral Agreement **191 UNTS 255**
SIGNED: 24 May 54   FORCE: 24 May 54
REGISTERED: 18 Jun 54 Australia
ARTICLES: 17 LANGUAGE: English.
HEADNOTE: EXCHANGE POSTAL PARCELS
TOPIC: Postal Service
CONCEPTS: Responsibility and liability. Accounting procedures. Compensation. Postal services. Regulations. Insured letters and boxes. Conveyance in transit. Parcel post. Rates and charges.
INTL ORGS: Universal Postal Union.
TREATY REF: 170UNTS63; 186UNTS356.
PROCEDURE: Duration. Termination.
PARTIES:
Australia
Greece

102587 Bilateral Agreement **191 UNTS 271**
SIGNED: 10 Mar 54   FORCE: 10 Mar 54
REGISTERED: 18 Jun 54 United Nations
ARTICLES: 6 LANGUAGE: Spanish.
HEADNOTE: TECHNICAL ASSISTANCE
TOPIC: Tech Assistance
CONCEPTS: Treaty implementation. Privileges and immunities. General cooperation. Exchange of information and documents. Personnel. Title and deeds. Exchange. Scholarships and grants. Vocational training. Research and development. Expense sharing formulae. Local currency. Domestic obligation. General technical assistance. Materials, equipment and services. IGO status. Conformity with IGO decisions.
TREATY REF: 76UNTS132; 1UNTS15; 1UNTS263.
PROCEDURE: Amendment. Termination.
PARTIES:
Guatemala
United Nations
ANNEX
502 UNTS 382. United Nations. Force 10 Jul 64.
502 UNTS 382. Guatemala. Force 10 Jul 64.

102588 Multilateral Instrument **191 UNTS 285**
SIGNED: 11 Dec 53   FORCE: 10 Jun 54
REGISTERED: 21 Jun 54 FAO (Food Agri)
ARTICLES: 19 LANGUAGE: English. French. Spanish.
HEADNOTE: FOOT-MOUTH DISEASE CONTROL
TOPIC: Sanitation
CONCEPTS: Definition of terms. General cooperation. Exchange of information and documents. Procedure. Quarantine. Disease control. Sanitation. Veterinary. Research and development. Accounting procedures. Financial programs. Funding procedures. Subsidiary organ. Special status.
INTL ORGS: European Commission for the Control of Foot and Mouth Disease. United Nations.
PROCEDURE: Accession. Termination.
PARTIES:
Denmark RATIFIED: 4 Feb 54 FORCE: 12 Jun 54
Ireland RATIFIED: 16 Dec 53 FORCE: 12 Jun 54
Netherlands RATIFIED: 12 Jun 54 FORCE: 12 Jun 54
Norway RATIFIED: 11 Dec 53 FORCE: 12 Jun 54
UK Great Britain RATIFIED: 1 Mar 54
Yugoslavia RATIFIED: 14 Dec 53 FORCE: 12 Jun 54
ANNEX
203 UNTS 339. Iceland. Acceptance 17 Jan 55.
218 UNTS 392. Turkey. Acceptance 27 Sep 55.
219 UNTS 382. Italy. Acceptance 29 Sep 55.
219 UNTS 382. Portugal. Acceptance 6 Oct 55.
223 UNTS 379. Austria. Acceptance 1 Dec 55.
274 UNTS 374. Eur Foot Mouth Dis. Amendment 3 Apr 57. Force 12 Jun 57.
315 UNTS 241. Eur Foot Mouth Dis. Amendment 18 Apr 58. Force 31 Oct 58.
327 UNTS 363. Greece. Acceptance 23 Mar 59.
336 UNTS 350. Luxembourg. Accession 1 Jun 59.
344 UNTS 331. Belgium. Accession 24 Sep 59.
390 UNTS 361. Switzerland. Acceptance 23 Feb 61.
454 UNTS 556. Eur Foot Mouth Dis. Amendment 26 Oct 62. Force 26 Oct 62.
484 UNTS 409. Sweden. Acceptance 13 Dec 63.
633 UNTS 386. Finland. Acceptance 5 Mar 68.

102589 Bilateral Agreement **191 UNTS 319**
SIGNED: 12 Oct 53   FORCE: 12 Nov 53
REGISTERED: 22 Jun 54 Greece
ARTICLES: 4 LANGUAGE: Greek. English.
HEADNOTE: MILITARY FACILITIES
TOPIC: Milit Installation
CONCEPTS: Use of facilities. Compensation. Indemnities and reimbursements. National treatment. Tax exemptions. Customs exemptions. Materials, equipment and services. Postal services. Defense and security. Procurement and logistics. Bases and facilities.
INTL ORGS: North Atlantic Treaty Organization.
TREATY REF: 34UNTS243.
PARTIES:
Greece
USA (United States)
ANNEX
269 UNTS 350. USA (United States). Implementation 27 Jun 55. Force 27 Jun 55.
269 UNTS 350. Greece. Implementation 27 Jun 55. Force 27 Jun 55.

102590 Bilateral Exchange **191 UNTS 329**
SIGNED: 11 Mar 53   FORCE: 11 Mar 53
REGISTERED: 28 Jun 54 Belgium
ARTICLES: 2 LANGUAGE: French.
HEADNOTE: COMPENSATION WAR DAMAGE
TOPIC: Reparations
CONCEPTS: Definition of terms. Time limit. Annex or appendix reference. Conformity with municipal law. Exchange of information and documents. Inspection and observation. Establishment of commission. National treatment. Loss and/or damage. Reparations and restrictions. Post-war claims settlement.
PARTIES:
Belgium
France
ANNEX
209 UNTS 348. Belgium. Amendment 10 Dec 54. Force 10 Dec 54.
209 UNTS 348. France. Amendment 10 Dec 54. Force 10 Dec 54.

327 UNTS 364. Belgium. Amendment 19 Jan 59.
Force 19 Jan 59.
327 UNTS 364. France. Amendment 19 Jan 59.
Force 19 Jan 59.

102591 Bilateral Agreement **192 UNTS 3**
SIGNED: 20 May 54 FORCE: 20 May 54
REGISTERED: 28 Jun 54 United Nations
ARTICLES: 10 LANGUAGE: English. Spanish.
HEADNOTE: ACTIVITIES UNICEF
TOPIC: Direct Aid
CONCEPTS: Treaty implementation. Privileges and
immunities. Exchange of information and docu-
ments. Informational records. Inspection and ob-
servation. Public information. Procedure. Exist-
ing tribunals. Export quotas. Indemnities and re-
imbursements. Financial programs. Local
currency. Tax exemptions. Customs exemptions.
Commodities and services. Assistance. General
aid. Distribution. IGO status.
INTL ORGS: United Nations.
PROCEDURE: Duration.
PARTIES:
Mexico
UNICEF (Children)
ANNEX
230 UNTS 442. UNICEF (Children). Amendment
6 Mar 56. Force 16 Mar 56.
230 UNTS 442. Mexico. Amendment 16 Mar 56.
Force 16 Mar 56.

102592 Multilateral Agreement **192 UNTS 20**
SIGNED: 31 May 54 FORCE: 31 May 54
REGISTERED: 28 Jun 54 United Nations
ARTICLES: 5 LANGUAGE: French.
HEADNOTE: TECHNICAL ASSISTANCE
TOPIC: Tech Assistance
CONCEPTS: Definition of terms. Treaty implemen-
tation. Annex or appendix reference. Privileges
and immunities. General cooperation. Person-
nel. Responsibility and liability. Title and deeds.
Scholarships and grants. Vocational training. Re-
search and scientific projects. Expense sharing
formulae. Local currency. Domestic obligation.
General technical assistance. Materials, equip-
ment and services. IGO status. Conformity with
IGO decisions. Administering authority.
INTL ORGS: United Nations.
TREATY REF: 76UNTS133; 84UNTS310; 33UNT-
SI61; 1UNTS15; U1NTS263.
PARTIES:
France SIGNED: 31 May 54 FORCE: 31 May 54
FAO (Food Agri) SIGNED: 31 May 54 FORCE:
31 May 54
ICAO (Civil Aviat) SIGNED: 31 May 54 FORCE:
31 May 54
ILO (Labor Org) SIGNED: 31 May 54 FORCE:
31 May 54
UNESCO (Educ/Cult) SIGNED: 31 May 54
FORCE: 31 May 54
United Nations SIGNED: 31 May 54 FORCE:
31 May 54
WHO (World Health) SIGNED: 31 May 54
FORCE: 31 May 54

102593 Bilateral Exchange **192 UNTS 33**
SIGNED: 18 Jun 54 FORCE: 18 Jun 54
REGISTERED: 28 Jun 54 Luxembourg
ARTICLES: 2 LANGUAGE: English. French.
HEADNOTE: COMPENSATION WAR DAMAGE
TOPIC: Reparations
CONCEPTS: Definition of terms. Conformity with
municipal law. General cooperation. Exchange
of information and documents. Procedure. Loss
and/or damage. Post-war claims settlement.
PARTIES:
Luxembourg
UK Great Britain

102594 Bilateral Agreement **192 UNTS 39**
SIGNED: 25 Nov 49 FORCE: 10 Feb 50
REGISTERED: 30 Jun 54 ICAO (Civil Aviat)
ARTICLES: 15 LANGUAGE: French.
HEADNOTE: ESTABLISHMENT OPERATION REGU-
LAR AIR TRANSPORT SERVICES
TOPIC: Air Transport
CONCEPTS: Definition of terms. Detailed regula-
tions. Exceptions and exemptions. Annex or ap-
pendix reference. Conformity with municipal
law. General cooperation. Licenses and permits.

Recognition of legal documents. Use of facilities.
Arbitration. Procedure. Special tribunals. Negotiation. Fees and exemptions. Non-interest rates
and fees. Most favored nation clause. National
treatment. Customs exemptions. Competency
certificate. Routes and logistics. Navigational
conditions. Permit designation. Airport facilities.
Airworthiness certificates. Conditions of airlines
operating permission. Operating authorizations
and regulations. Licenses and certificates of nationality.
INTL ORGS: International Civil Aviation Organization.
TREATY REF: 15UNTS295.
PROCEDURE: Amendment. Future Procedures
Contemplated. Ratification. Registration. Termination.
PARTIES:
Italy
Turkey

102595 Bilateral Agreement **192 UNTS 53**
SIGNED: 26 Sep 50 FORCE: 3 Apr 51
REGISTERED: 30 Jun 54 ICAO (Civil Aviat)
ARTICLES: 19 LANGUAGE: Arabic. English.
HEADNOTE: ESTABLISHMENT SCHEDULED AIR
SERVICES
TOPIC: Air Transport
CONCEPTS: Definition of terms. Detailed regulations. Exceptions and exemptions. Annex or appendix reference. Conformity with municipal
law. General cooperation. Exchange of informa-
tion and documents. Arbitration. Procedure. Ex-
isting tribunals. Negotiation. Non-interest rates
and fees. Customs exemptions. Routes and logistics. Navigational conditions. Permit designation. Air transport. Conditions of airlines operating permission. Operating authorizations and
regulations.
INTL ORGS: International Civil Aviation Organization.
TREATY REF: 15UNTS295.
PROCEDURE: Future Procedures Contemplated.
Ratification. Registration. Termination.
PARTIES:
Ceylon (Sri Lanka)
United Arab Rep
ANNEX
327 UNTS 370. Ceylon (Sri Lanka). Amendment
21 Oct 57. Force 21 Oct 57.
327 UNTS 370. United Arab Rep. Amendment
21 Oct 57. Force 21 Oct 57.

102596 Bilateral Agreement **192 UNTS 81**
SIGNED: 7 Aug 51 FORCE: 7 Aug 51
REGISTERED: 30 Jun 54 ICAO (Civil Aviat)
ARTICLES: 14 LANGUAGE: English. Hebrew.
HEADNOTE: AIR SERVICES
TOPIC: Air Transport
CONCEPTS: Definition of terms. Exceptions and
exemptions. Annex or appendix reference. Conformity with municipal law. General cooperation.
Exchange of information and documents. Use of
facilities. Arbitration. Procedure. Special tribunals. Negotiation. Fees and exemptions. Non-
interest rates and fees. Most favored nation
clause. National treatment. Customs exemptions. Routes and logistics. Navigational conditions. Permit designation. Airport facilities. Conditions of airlines operating permission. Overflights and technical stops. Operating
authorizations and regulations.
INTL ORGS: International Civil Aviation Organization. International Court of Justice.
TREATY REF: 15UNTS295.
PROCEDURE: Amendment. Future Procedures
Contemplated. Registration. Termination. Application to Non-self-governing Territories.
PARTIES:
Israel
Philippines

102597 Bilateral Exchange **192 UNTS 105**
SIGNED: 21 Sep 53 FORCE: 10 Jan 53
REGISTERED: 30 Jun 54 ICAO (Civil Aviat)
ARTICLES: 2 LANGUAGE: English.
HEADNOTE: REGULATION AIR SERVICES
TOPIC: Air Transport
CONCEPTS: Exceptions and exemptions. Respon-
sibility and liability. Non-interest rates and fees.

Routes and logistics. Operating authorizations
and regulations.
TREATY REF: 15UNTS295.
PROCEDURE: Duration. Renewal or Revival. Termi-
nation. Application to Non-self-governing Terri-
tories.
PARTIES:
Norway
South Africa

102598 Bilateral Agreement **192 UNTS 115**
SIGNED: 26 Jun 51 FORCE: 10 Feb 53
REGISTERED: 30 Jun 54 ICAO (Civil Aviat)
ARTICLES: 14 LANGUAGE: Spanish. Portuguese.
HEADNOTE: ESTABLISHMENT AIR SERVICES
TOPIC: Air Transport
CONCEPTS: Definition of terms. Annex or appendix reference. Non-prejudice to third party. Conformity with municipal law. Licenses and permits. Recognition of legal documents. Use of facilities. Arbitration. Procedure. Existing
tribunals. Reexport of goods, etc.. Fees and exemptions. Most favored nation clause. National
treatment. Customs exemptions. Competency
certificate. Routes and logistics. Navigational
conditions. Permit designation. Airport facilities.
Airworthiness certificates. Conditions of airlines
operating permission. Operating authorizations
and regulations. Licenses and certificates of nationality.
INTL ORGS: International Civil Aviation Organization.
TREATY REF: 15UNTS295.
PROCEDURE: Future Procedures Contemplated.
Ratification. Registration. Termination.
PARTIES:
Cuba
Portugal

102599 Bilateral Agreement **192 UNTS 157**
SIGNED: 2 Jan 52 FORCE: 14 Apr 54
REGISTERED: 30 Jun 54 ICAO (Civil Aviat)
ARTICLES: 18 LANGUAGE: English. Arabic.
HEADNOTE: ESTABLISHMENT SCHEDULED AIR
SERVICES
TOPIC: Air Transport
CONCEPTS: Definition of terms. Detailed regulations. Exceptions and exemptions. Annex or appendix reference. Conformity with municipal
law. General cooperation. Exchange of informa-
tion and documents. Arbitration. Procedure. Ex-
isting tribunals. Negotiation. Non-interest rates
and fees. Customs exemptions. Routes and logis-
tics. Navigational conditions. Permit designa-
tion. Air transport. Conditions of airlines operating permission. Operating authorizations and
regulations.
INTL ORGS: International Civil Aviation Organization. Arbitration Commission.
TREATY REF: 15UNTS295.
PROCEDURE: Future Procedures Contemplated.
Ratification. Registration. Termination.
PARTIES:
Jordan
United Arab Rep

102600 Bilateral Exchange **192 UNTS 183**
SIGNED: 5 May 53 FORCE: 5 May 53
REGISTERED: 30 Jun 54 ICAO (Civil Aviat)
ARTICLES: 2 LANGUAGE: English.
HEADNOTE: REGULATE AIR SERVICES
TOPIC: Air Transport
CONCEPTS: Definition of terms. Exceptions and
exemptions. Non-interest rates and fees. Routes
and logistics. Operating authorizations and regu-
lations.
INTL ORGS: International Civil Aviation Organiza-
tion.
PROCEDURE: Termination. Application to Non-
self-governing Territories.
PARTIES:
Israel
South Africa
ANNEX
216 UNTS 418. Israel. Amendment 1 Sep 54.
Force 1 Sep 54.
216 UNTS 418. South Africa. Amendment
1 Sep 54. Force 1 Sep 54.

102601 Bilateral Agreement **192 UNTS 191**
SIGNED: 23 Feb 53　　　FORCE: 14 Jul 53
REGISTERED: 30 Jun 54 ICAO (Civil Aviat)
ARTICLES: 19 LANGUAGE: English.
HEADNOTE: AIR SERVICES
TOPIC: Air Transport
CONCEPTS: Definition of terms. Detailed regulations. Exceptions and exemptions. Annex or appendix reference. Conformity with municipal law. General cooperation. Exchange of information and documents. Use of facilities. Arbitration. Procedure. Special tribunals. Negotiation. Fees and exemptions. Non-interest rates and fees. Most favored nation clause. National treatment. Customs exemptions. Routes and logistics. Permit designation. Air transport. Airport facilities. Conditions of airlines operating permission. Overflights and technical stops. Operating authorizations and regulations.
INTL ORGS: International Civil Aviation Organization. International Court of Justice.
TREATY REF: 15UNTS295.
PROCEDURE: Amendment. Future Procedures Contemplated. Ratification. Registration. Termination. Application to Non-self-governing Territories.
PARTIES:
Japan
Norway
　　　　　　　　ANNEX
231 UNTS 370. Norway. Amendment 19 Jul 54. Force 19 Jul 54.
231 UNTS 370. Japan. Amendment 19 Jul 54. Force 19 Jul 54.

102602 Bilateral Agreement **192 UNTS 215**
SIGNED: 17 Feb 53　　　FORCE: 24 Jul 53
REGISTERED: 30 Jun 54 ICAO (Civil Aviat)
ARTICLES: 19 LANGUAGE: English.
HEADNOTE: AIR SERVICES
TOPIC: Air Transport
CONCEPTS: Definition of terms. Detailed regulations. Exceptions and exemptions. Annex or appendix reference. Conformity with municipal law. General cooperation. Exchange of information and documents. Use of facilities. Arbitration. Procedure. Special tribunals. Negotiation. Fees and exemptions. Non-interest rates and fees. Most favored nation clause. National treatment. Customs exemptions. Routes and logistics. Permit designation. Airport facilities. Conditions of airlines operating permission. Overflights and technical stops. Operating authorizations and regulations.
INTL ORGS: International Civil Aviation Organization. International Court of Justice.
TREATY REF: 15UNTS295.
PROCEDURE: Amendment. Future Procedures Contemplated. Ratification. Registration. Termination.
PARTIES:
Japan
Netherlands
　　　　　　　　ANNEX
335 UNTS 304. Netherlands. Amendment 7 May 58. Force 15 May 58.
335 UNTS 304. Japan. Amendment 12 May 58. Force 15 May 58.
602 UNTS 302. Japan. Amendment 25 May 64. Force 25 May 64.
602 UNTS 302. Netherlands. Amendment 25 May 64. Force 25 May 64.

102603 Bilateral Agreement **192 UNTS 237**
SIGNED: 17 Mar 52　　　FORCE: 24 Jul 53
REGISTERED: 30 Jun 54 ICAO (Civil Aviat)
ARTICLES: 15 LANGUAGE: English. French.
HEADNOTE: AIR SERVICES
TOPIC: Air Transport
CONCEPTS: Conditions. Definition of terms. Detailed regulations. Exceptions and exemptions. Annex or appendix reference. Conformity with municipal law. General cooperation. Exchange of information and documents. Use of facilities. Arbitration. Procedure. Special tribunals. Negotiation. Archives and objects. Reexport of goods, etc.. Fees and exemptions. Non-interest rates and fees. National treatment. Customs duties. Customs exemptions. Permit designation. Airport facilities. Conditions of airlines operating permission. Overflights and technical stops. Operating authorizations and regulations.

INTL ORGS: International Civil Aviation Organization.
TREATY REF: 15UNTS295; 84UNTS389.
PROCEDURE: Amendment. Future Procedures Contemplated. Ratification. Registration. Termination. Application to Non-self-governing Territories.
PARTIES:
Pakistan
Switzerland

102604 Bilateral Exchange **192 UNTS 255**
SIGNED: 27 Jul 53　　　FORCE: 27 Jul 53
REGISTERED: 30 Jun 54 ICAO (Civil Aviat)
ARTICLES: 13 LANGUAGE: English. Spanish.
HEADNOTE: AIR SERVICES
TOPIC: Air Transport
CONCEPTS: Conditions. Definition of terms. Detailed regulations. Exceptions and exemptions. Annex or appendix reference. Conformity with municipal law. General cooperation. Exchange of information and documents. Arbitration. Procedure. Special tribunals. Negotiation. Indemnities and reimbursements. Non-interest rates and fees. Most favored nation clause. National treatment. Routes and logistics. Permit designation. Conditions of airlines operating permission. Overflights and technical stops. Operating authorizations and regulations.
INTL ORGS: International Civil Aviation Organization.
TREATY REF: 15UNTS295.
PROCEDURE: Amendment. Future Procedures Contemplated. Registration. Termination. Application to Non-self-governing Territories.
PARTIES:
Canada
Mexico
　　　　　　　　ANNEX
232 UNTS 352. Canada. Amendment 28 Oct 55. Force 28 Oct 55.
232 UNTS 352. Mexico. Amendment 28 Oct 55. Force 28 Oct 55.

102605 Bilateral Exchange **192 UNTS 283**
SIGNED: 1 Sep 53　　　FORCE: 1 Sep 53
REGISTERED: 30 Jun 54 ICAO (Civil Aviat)
ARTICLES: 3 LANGUAGE: English.
HEADNOTE: TERMINATING AGREEMENT 29 APR 38 DOCUMENTS AIR CREWS
TOPIC: Air Transport
CONCEPTS: Change of circumstances. Air transport. Operating authorizations and regulations.
TREATY REF: 190LTS115; BEL.CO, U.K., N.IREL, AUSTRA, INDIA.
PROCEDURE: Application to Non-self-governing Territories.
PARTIES:
Belgium
New Zealand

102606 Bilateral Agreement **192 UNTS 291**
SIGNED: 13 Oct 52　　　FORCE: 1 Sep 53
REGISTERED: 30 Jun 54 ICAO (Civil Aviat)
ARTICLES: 12 LANGUAGE: French. German.
HEADNOTE: AIR TRANSPORT
TOPIC: Air Transport
CONCEPTS: Definition of terms. Annex or appendix reference. Conformity with municipal law. General cooperation. Licenses and permits. Recognition of legal documents. Use of facilities. Arbitration. Procedure. Reexport of goods, etc.. Fees and exemptions. Non-interest rates and fees. Most favored nation clause. National treatment. Customs exemptions. Competency certificate. Routes and logistics. Navigational conditions. Permit designation. Air transport. Airport facilities. Airworthiness certificates. Conditions of airlines operating permission. Operating authorizations and regulations. Licenses and certificates of nationality.
INTL ORGS: International Civil Aviation Organization.
TREATY REF: 15UNTS295.
PROCEDURE: Amendment. Future Procedures Contemplated. Registration. Termination.
PARTIES:
Austria
Luxembourg

102607 Bilateral Agreement **193 UNTS 3**
SIGNED: 5 Feb 51　　　FORCE: 11 Sep 53
REGISTERED: 30 Jun 54 ICAO (Civil Aviat)
ARTICLES: 15 LANGUAGE: French.
HEADNOTE: AIR TRANSPORT
TOPIC: Air Transport
CONCEPTS: Definition of terms. Exceptions and exemptions. Annex or appendix reference. Conformity with municipal law. General cooperation. Licenses and permits. Recognition of legal documents. Use of facilities. Arbitration. Procedure. Special tribunals. Negotiation. Indemnities and reimbursements. Non-interest rates and fees. Most favored nation clause. National treatment. Customs exemptions. Competency certificate. Routes and logistics. Navigational conditions. Permit designation. Air transport. Airport facilities. Airworthiness certificates. Conditions of airlines operating permission. Operating authorizations and regulations. Licenses and certificates of nationality.
INTL ORGS: International Civil Aviation Organization. Arbitration Commission.
TREATY REF: 15UNTS295.
PROCEDURE: Amendment. Future Procedures Contemplated. Ratification. Registration. Termination.
PARTIES:
Israel
Turkey

102608 Bilateral Agreement **193 UNTS 21**
SIGNED: 14 Sep 53　　　FORCE: 14 Sep 53
REGISTERED: 30 Jun 54 ICAO (Civil Aviat)
ARTICLES: 14 LANGUAGE: English.
HEADNOTE: AIR SERVICES
TOPIC: Air Transport
CONCEPTS: Conditions. Definition of terms. Detailed regulations. Exceptions and exemptions. Annex or appendix reference. Conformity with municipal law. General cooperation. Routes and logistics. Permit designation. Conditions of airlines operating permission. Overflights and technical stops. Operating authorizations and regulations.
INTL ORGS: International Civil Aviation Organization. International Court of Justice. Arbitration Commission.
TREATY REF: 15UNTS295.
PARTIES:
Ceylon (Sri Lanka)
Netherlands

102609 Bilateral Agreement **193 UNTS 39**
SIGNED: 23 Oct 52　　　FORCE: 23 Oct 52
REGISTERED: 30 Jun 54 ICAO (Civil Aviat)
ARTICLES: 11 LANGUAGE: French. Icelandic.
HEADNOTE: AIR TRANSPORT
TOPIC: Air Transport
CONCEPTS: Definition of terms. Annex or appendix reference. Conformity with municipal law. General cooperation. Licenses and permits. Recognition of legal documents. Use of facilities. Arbitration. Procedure. Existing tribunals. Negotiation. Fees and exemptions. Non-interest rates and fees. Most favored nation clause. National treatment. Customs exemptions. Competency certificate. Routes and logistics. Navigational conditions. Permit designation. Air transport. Airport facilities. Airworthiness certificates. Conditions of airlines operating permission. Operating authorizations and regulations. Licenses and certificates of nationality.
INTL ORGS: International Civil Aviation Organization. Arbitration Commission.
TREATY REF: 15UNTS295.
PROCEDURE: Amendment. Future Procedures Contemplated. Ratification. Registration.
PARTIES:
Iceland
Luxembourg

102610 Bilateral Agreement **193 UNTS 55**
SIGNED: 5 Sep 51　　　FORCE: 10 Mar 54
REGISTERED: 30 Jun 54 United Nations
ARTICLES: 9 LANGUAGE: English. French.
HEADNOTE: ACTIVITIES UNICEF
TOPIC: Direct Aid
CONCEPTS: Treaty implementation. Privileges and immunities. Exchange of information and docu-

ments. Informational records. Inspection and observation. Public information. Procedure. Existing tribunals. Export quotas. Indemnities and reimbursements. Financial programs. Local currency. Tax exemptions. Customs exemptions. Assistance. Relief supplies. Distribution. IGO status.
TREATY REF: 1UNTS15.
PROCEDURE: Duration.
PARTIES:
UNICEF (Children)
Turkey

102611 Multilateral Agreement **193 UNTS 67**
SIGNED: 30 Jun 54   FORCE: 30 Jun 54
REGISTERED: 30 Jun 54 United Nations
ARTICLES: 4 LANGUAGE: English.
HEADNOTE: TECHNICAL ASSISTANCE
TOPIC: Tech Assistance
CONCEPTS: Definition of terms. Detailed regulations. Time limit. Annex or appendix reference. Privileges and immunities. General cooperation. Personnel. General property. Negotiation. Expense sharing formulae. Funding procedures. Assets. General technical assistance. Special projects. Conformity with IGO decisions.
TREATY REF: 76UNTS132; 1UNTS15; 1UNTS263.
PROCEDURE: Amendment. Termination.
PARTIES:
Iraq SIGNED: 30 Jun 54 FORCE: 30 Jun 54
FAO (Food Agri) SIGNED: 30 Jun 54 FORCE: 30 Jun 54
ICAO (Civil Aviat) SIGNED: 30 Jun 54 FORCE: 30 Jun 54
ILO (Labor Org) SIGNED: 30 Jun 54 FORCE: 30 Jun 54
UNESCO (Educ/Cult) SIGNED: 30 Jun 54 FORCE: 30 Jun 54
United Nations SIGNED: 30 Jun 54 FORCE: 30 Jun 54

102612 Bilateral Instrument **193 UNTS 78**
SIGNED: 27 Apr 53   FORCE: 27 Jul 53
REGISTERED: 1 Jul 54 United Nations
ARTICLES: 2 LANGUAGE: English. Japanese.
HEADNOTE: REVIVAL PRE-WAR TREATIES
TOPIC: Admin Cooperation
CONCEPTS: Revival of treaties.
TREATY REF: 136UNTS45; 193UNTS84,96,126; 16LTS207; 19LTS288.
PARTIES:
Australia
Japan

102613 Multilateral Convention **193 UNTS 136**
SIGNED: 31 Mar 53   FORCE: 7 Jul 54
REGISTERED: 7 Jul 54 United Nations
ARTICLES: 11 LANGUAGE: Chinese. English. French. Russian. Spanish.
HEADNOTE: POLITICAL RIGHTS WOMEN
TOPIC: Privil/Immunities
CONCEPTS: Exceptions and exemptions. Human rights. Procedure. Existing tribunals. Negotiation.
INTL ORGS: International Court of Justice. United Nations.
PROCEDURE: Accession. Denunciation. Ratification.
PARTIES:
Argentina SIGNED: 31 Mar 53
Bolivia SIGNED: 9 Apr 53
Brazil SIGNED: 20 May 53
Bulgaria RATIFIED: 17 Mar 54 FORCE: 7 Jul 54
Byelorussia SIGNED: 31 Mar 53
Chile SIGNED: 31 Mar 53
Taiwan SIGNED: 9 Jun 53 RATIFIED: 21 Dec 53 FORCE: 7 Jul 54
Costa Rica SIGNED: 31 Mar 53
Cuba SIGNED: 31 Mar 53 RATIFIED: 8 Apr 54 FORCE: 7 Jul 54
Czechoslovakia SIGNED: 31 Mar 53
Denmark SIGNED: 29 Oct 53 RATIFIED: 7 Jul 54 FORCE: 6 Oct 54
Dominican Republic SIGNED: 31 Mar 53 RATIFIED: 11 Dec 53 FORCE: 7 Jul 54
Ecuador SIGNED: 31 Mar 53 RATIFIED: 23 Apr 54 FORCE: 22 Jul 54
El Salvador SIGNED: 24 Jun 53
Ethiopia SIGNED: 31 Mar 53
France SIGNED: 31 Mar 53

Greece SIGNED: 1 Apr 53 RATIFIED: 29 Dec 53 FORCE: 7 Jul 54
Guatemala SIGNED: 31 Mar 53
Iceland SIGNED: 25 Nov 53 RATIFIED: 30 Jun 54 FORCE: 28 Sep 54
India SIGNED: 29 Apr 53
Indonesia SIGNED: 31 Mar 53
Israel SIGNED: 14 Apr 53 RATIFIED: 6 Jul 54 FORCE: 5 Oct 54
Lebanon SIGNED: 24 Feb 54
Liberia SIGNED: 9 Dec 53
Mexico SIGNED: 31 Mar 53
Norway SIGNED: 18 Sep 53
Pakistan SIGNED: 18 May 54
Paraguay SIGNED: 16 Nov 53
Philippines SIGNED: 23 Sep 53
Poland SIGNED: 31 Mar 53
Romania SIGNED: 27 Apr 54
Sweden SIGNED: 6 Oct 53 RATIFIED: 31 Mar 54 FORCE: 4 Jul 54
Thailand SIGNED: 5 Mar 54
Turkey SIGNED: 12 Jan 54
Ukrainian SSR SIGNED: 31 Mar 53
Uruguay SIGNED: 26 May 53
USSR (Soviet Union) SIGNED: 31 Mar 53 RATIFIED: 3 May 54 FORCE: 1 Aug 54
Yugoslavia SIGNED: 31 Mar 53 RATIFIED: 23 Jun 54 FORCE: 21 Sep 54
                ANNEX
196 UNTS 363. Romania. Qualified Ratification 6 Aug 54. Force 4 Nov 54.
196 UNTS 364. Byelorussia. Qualified Ratification 11 Aug 54. Force 9 Nov 54.
196 UNTS 365. Poland. Qualified Ratification 11 Aug 54. Force 9 Nov 54.
201 UNTS 392. Ukrainian SSR. Qualified Ratification 15 Nov 54.
201 UNTS 393. Thailand. Ratification 30 Nov 54.
202 UNTS 382. Hungary. Qualified Ratification 20 Jan 55.
202 UNTS 382. Pakistan. Qualified Ratification 7 Dec 54.
212 UNTS 377. Japan. Signature 1 Apr 55.
212 UNTS 377. Japan. Ratification 13 Jul 55. Force 11 Oct 55.
248 UNTS 380. Norway. Qualified Ratification 24 Aug 56.
257 UNTS 375. Nicaragua. Accession 17 Jan 57. Force 17 Apr 57.
258 UNTS 424. Canada. Qualified Accession 30 Jan 57. Force 30 Apr 57.
265 UNTS 367. France. Ratification 22 Apr 57. Force 21 Jul 57.
276 UNTS 365. Philippines. Qualified Ratification 12 Sep 57. Force 11 Dec 57.
286 UNTS 379. Haiti. Ratification 12 Feb 58. Force 13 May 58.
313 UNTS 357. Finland. Qualified Accession 6 Oct 58. Force 4 Jan 59.
317 UNTS 337. Indonesia. Qualified Ratification 16 Dec 58. Force 16 Mar 59.
335 UNTS 308. Korea, South. Accession 23 Jun 59. Force 21 Sep 59.
342 UNTS 350. Guatemala. Qualified Ratification 7 Oct 59. Force 5 Jan 60.
348 UNTS 349. Turkey. Ratification 26 Jan 60. Force 25 Apr 60.
381 UNTS 409. Yugoslavia. Objection 26 Nov 60.
381 UNTS 409. Sweden. Objection 26 Nov 60.
381 UNTS 409. Pakistan. Objection 26 Nov 60.
381 UNTS 409. Norway. Objection 26 Nov 60.
381 UNTS 409. France. Withdrawal of Reservation 26 Nov 60.
389 UNTS 313. Argentina. Qualified Ratification 21 Feb 61. Force 28 May 61.
412 UNTS 324. India. Qualified Ratification 1 Nov 61. Force 30 Jan 62.
434 UNTS 297. Sierra Leone. Qualified Accession 25 Jul 62. Force 23 Oct 62.
437 UNTS 356. Central Afri Rep. Succession 4 Sep 62.
442 UNTS 321. Congo (Brazzaville). Succession 15 Oct 62.
463 UNTS 345. Senegal. Succession 2 May 63.
474 UNTS 336. Brazil. Ratification 13 Aug 63. Force 11 Nov 63.
496 UNTS 353. Belgium. Qualified Accession 20 May 64. Force 18 Aug 64.
520 UNTS 428. Niger. Succession 7 Dec 64.
543 UNTS 362. Mongolia. Accession 18 Aug 65. Force 16 Nov 65.
550 UNTS 404. Ghana. Accession 28 Dec 65. Force 28 Mar 66.

550 UNTS 404. Korea, South. Objection 28 Dec 65. Force 28 Mar 66.
561 UNTS 347. Nepal. Qualified Accession 26 Apr 66.
561 UNTS 347. Nepal. Accession 26 Apr 66.
565 UNTS 284. Trinidad/Tobago. Accession 24 Jun 66. Force 22 Sep 66.
565 UNTS 284. Malawi. Accession 29 Jun 66. Force 27 Sep 66.
601 UNTS 352. Costa Rica. Ratification 25 Jul 67. Force 23 Oct 67.
607 UNTS 263. Chile. Ratification 18 Oct 67. Force 16 Jan 68.
619 UNTS 334. Tunisia. Accession 24 Jan 68. Force 23 Jan 68.
619 UNTS 334. Tunisia. Reservation 24 Jan 68.
630 UNTS 396. UK Great Britain. Withdrawal of Reservation 12 Feb 68.
640 UNTS 369. Malta. Qualified Accession 9 Jul 68. Force 7 Oct 68.
649 UNTS 326. Cyprus. Accession 12 Nov 68. Ratification 12 Nov 68.
649 UNTS 326. Ireland. Accession 14 Nov 68. Ratification 14 Nov 68.

102614 Bilateral Exchange **193 UNTS 175**
SIGNED: 24 May 54   FORCE: 1 Jul 54
REGISTERED: 13 Jul 54 Australia
ARTICLES: 2 LANGUAGE: English.
HEADNOTE: VISAS VISA FEES
TOPIC: Visas
CONCEPTS: Emergencies. Time limit. Denial of admission. Conformity with municipal law. Fees and exemptions.
PROCEDURE: Termination.
PARTIES:
Australia
Greece

102615 Bilateral Exchange **193 UNTS 181**
SIGNED: 27 Jan 54   FORCE: 27 Jan 54
REGISTERED: 13 Jul 54 Denmark
ARTICLES: 2 LANGUAGE: English.
HEADNOTE: EXCHANGE OFFICIAL PUBLICATIONS
TOPIC: Admin Cooperation
CONCEPTS: Exchange of official publications. Operating agencies. Indemnities and reimbursements.
PARTIES:
Denmark
Yugoslavia

102616 Multilateral Instrument **193 UNTS 188**
SIGNED: 2 Oct 47   FORCE: 1 Jan 49
REGISTERED: 14 Jul 54 USA (United States)
ARTICLES: 49 LANGUAGE: English. French.
HEADNOTE: INTERNATIONAL TELECOMMUNICATION CONFERENCE
TOPIC: Telecommunications
CONCEPTS: Definition of terms. Territorial application. Treaty implementation. Previous treaty replacement. Responsibility and liability. Arbitration. Procedure. Accounting procedures. Non-interest rates and fees. Bands and frequency allocation. Interference of broadcasts. Money orders and postal checks. Services. Radio-telephone-telegraphic communications. Military installations and equipment. International organizations. Admission. Decisions. Subsidiary organ. Establishment. Headquarters and facilities. Liaison with other IGO's. Internal structure. Conferences. Trusteeship.
INTL ORGS: International Telecommunication Union. United Nations.
TREATY REF: 194UNTS3; 195UNTS119; 57LTS201; 88LTS347.
PROCEDURE: Accession. Ratification.
PARTIES:
Albania SIGNED: 2 Oct 47
Argentina SIGNED: 2 Oct 47
Australia SIGNED: 2 Oct 47
Austria SIGNED: 2 Oct 47
Belgium SIGNED: 2 Oct 47
Belgian Colonies SIGNED: 2 Oct 47
Brazil SIGNED: 2 Oct 47
Bulgaria SIGNED: 2 Oct 47
Burma SIGNED: 2 Oct 47
Byelorussia SIGNED: 2 Oct 47
Canada SIGNED: 2 Oct 47 RATIFIED: 5 Nov 48 FORCE: 1 Jan 49

Chile SIGNED: 2 Oct 47
Taiwan SIGNED: 2 Oct 47
Colombia SIGNED: 2 Oct 47
Cuba SIGNED: 2 Oct 47
Czechoslovakia SIGNED: 2 Oct 47 RATIFIED:
24 Aug 48 FORCE: 1 Jan 49
Denmark SIGNED: 2 Oct 47 RATIFIED: 8 Nov 48
FORCE: 1 Jan 49
Dutch East Indies SIGNED: 2 Oct 47
Dominican Republic SIGNED: 2 Oct 47
Ecuador SIGNED: 2 Oct 47
United Arab Rep SIGNED: 2 Oct 47
El Salvador SIGNED: 2 Oct 47
Ethiopia SIGNED: 2 Oct 47
Finland SIGNED: 2 Oct 47 RATIFIED: 30 Dec 48
FORCE: 1 Jan 49
France All Territories SIGNED: 2 Oct 47
France SIGNED: 2 Oct 47
Greece SIGNED: 2 Oct 47
Guatemala SIGNED: 2 Oct 47
Haiti SIGNED: 2 Oct 47
Honduras SIGNED: 2 Oct 47
Iceland SIGNED: 2 Oct 47 RATIFIED: 28 Oct 48
FORCE: 1 Jan 49
India SIGNED: 2 Oct 47
Iran SIGNED: 2 Oct 47
Iraq SIGNED: 2 Oct 47
Ireland SIGNED: 2 Oct 47 RATIFIED: 31 Dec 48
FORCE: 1 Jan 49
Italy SIGNED: 2 Oct 47
Lebanon SIGNED: 2 Oct 47
Luxembourg SIGNED: 2 Oct 47
Mexico SIGNED: 2 Oct 47
Monaco SIGNED: 2 Oct 47 RATIFIED: 17 Sep 48
FORCE: 1 Jan 49
Morocco SIGNED: 2 Oct 47
Netherlands Curacao RATIFIED: 31 Dec 48
FORCE: 1 Jan 49
Netherlands Dutch East Indies SIGNED: 2 Oct 47
RATIFIED: 31 Dec 48 FORCE: 1 Jan 49
Netherlands SIGNED: 2 Oct 47
Netherlands Surinam RATIFIED: 31 Dec 48
FORCE: 1 Jan 49
New Zealand SIGNED: 2 Oct 47 RATIFIED:
21 Sep 48 FORCE: 1 Jan 49
New Zealand Western Samoa RATIFIED:
2 Oct 47 FORCE: 1 Jan 49
Nicaragua SIGNED: 2 Oct 47
Norway SIGNED: 2 Oct 47 RATIFIED: 30 Dec 48
FORCE: 1 Jan 49
Pakistan SIGNED: 2 Oct 47
Panama SIGNED: 2 Oct 47
Peru SIGNED: 2 Oct 47
Philippines SIGNED: 2 Oct 47
Poland SIGNED: 2 Oct 47
Portugal All Territories SIGNED: 2 Oct 47
Portugal SIGNED: 2 Oct 47
Romania SIGNED: 2 Oct 47
Ruanda-Urundi SIGNED: 2 Oct 47
Saudi Arabia SIGNED: 2 Oct 47
Siam SIGNED: 2 Oct 47
South Africa SIGNED: 2 Oct 47
South Africa Southwest Africa RATIFIED:
2 Oct 47
Southern Rhodesia SIGNED: 2 Oct 47
Sweden SIGNED: 2 Oct 47 RATIFIED: 21 Dec 48
FORCE: 1 Jan 49
Switzerland SIGNED: 2 Oct 47 RATIFIED:
21 Dec 48 FORCE: 1 Jan 49
Syria SIGNED: 2 Oct 47
Tunisia SIGNED: 2 Oct 47
Turkey SIGNED: 2 Oct 47
UK Great Britain SIGNED: 2 Oct 47 RATIFIED:
29 Nov 48 FORCE: 1 Jan 49
UK Great Britain All Territories SIGNED: 2 Oct 47
USA (United States) All Territories RATIFIED:
17 Jul 48 FORCE: 1 Jan 49
USA (United States) SIGNED: 2 Oct 47 RATI-
FIED: 17 Jul 48 FORCE: 1 Jan 49
Ukrainian SSR SIGNED: 2 Oct 47
Uruguay SIGNED: 2 Oct 47
USSR (Soviet Union) SIGNED: 2 Oct 47
Vatican/Holy See SIGNED: 2 Oct 47
Venezuela SIGNED: 2 Oct 47
Yugoslavia SIGNED: 2 Oct 47

102617 Bilateral Convention **196 UNTS 3**
SIGNED: 28 Jan 49 FORCE: 1 Apr 49
REGISTERED: 19 Jul 54 Norway
ARTICLES: 12 LANGUAGE: Norwegian. Swedish.
HEADNOTE: ESTABLISHMENT JOINT REGULA-
TIONS SALMON SEA TROUT FISHING
TOPIC: Specific Resources

CONCEPTS: Fish, wildlife, and natural resources.
Ocean resources.
PROCEDURE: Duration. Termination.
PARTIES:
Norway
Sweden

102618 Bilateral Convention **196 UNTS 19**
SIGNED: 14 Dec 49 FORCE: 1 Jan 51
REGISTERED: 19 Jul 54 Norway
ARTICLES: 192 LANGUAGE: Norwegian. Swedish.
HEADNOTE: ACCESS NOMADIC LAPPS TO REIN-
DEER PASTURES
TOPIC: Specific Resources
CONCEPTS: Annex type material. Border traffic
and migration. Fish, wildlife, and natural re-
sources. Markers and definitions.
PROCEDURE: Ratification.
PARTIES:
Norway
Sweden

102619 Bilateral Exchange **196 UNTS 95**
SIGNED: 20 Jan 54 FORCE: 20 Jan 54
REGISTERED: 26 Jul 54 UK Great Britain
ARTICLES: 2 LANGUAGE: English.
HEADNOTE: TECHNICAL ASSISTANCE CARIB-
BEAN AREA
TOPIC: Tech Assistance
CONCEPTS: Treaty implementation. Annex type
material. Visas. Diplomatic privileges. Personnel.
Research and development. Indemnities and re-
imbursements. Financial programs. Tax exemp-
tions. Domestic obligation. General technical as-
sistance. Agriculture. Conservation. Special
projects. Materials, equipment and services.
TREATY REF: 105UNTS71.
PROCEDURE: Duration. Termination. Application
to Non-self-governing Territories.
PARTIES:
UK Great Britain
USA (United States)

102620 Bilateral Convention **196 UNTS 105**
SIGNED: 15 Dec 53 FORCE: 1 May 54
REGISTERED: 26 Jul 54 UK Great Britain
ARTICLES: 12 LANGUAGE: English. Danish.
HEADNOTE: COMPENSATION INDUSTRIAL INJU-
RIES
TOPIC: Non-ILO Labor
CONCEPTS: Definition of terms. Detailed regula-
tions. Territorial application. Alien status. Dis-
pute settlement. Old age and invalidity insur-
ance. Non-ILO labor relations. Sickness and inva-
lidity insurance. Payment schedules. National
treatment.
PROCEDURE: Duration. Ratification. Termination.
PARTIES:
Denmark
UK Great Britain

102621 Bilateral Convention **196 UNTS 119**
SIGNED: 16 Jan 53 FORCE: 1 Jun 54
REGISTERED: 26 Jul 54 UK Great Britain
ARTICLES: 24 LANGUAGE: English. French.
HEADNOTE: SOCIAL INSURANCE
TOPIC: Non-ILO Labor
CONCEPTS: Definition of terms. Detailed regula-
tions. Notarial acts and services. General cooper-
ation. Exchange of information and documents.
Domestic legislation. Incorporation of treaty pro-
visions into national law. Dispute settlement. Old
age and invalidity insurance. Non-ILO labor rela-
tions. Old age insurance. Sickness and invalidity
insurance. Social security. Fees and exemptions.
Payment schedules. National treatment.
INTL ORGS: International Court of Justice. Arbitration Commission.
PROCEDURE: Denunciation. Duration. Ratification.
Renewal or Revival.
PARTIES:
Switzerland
UK Great Britain
ANNEX
374 UNTS 376. UK Great Britain. Supplementation 12 Nov 59. Force 1 Jul 60.
374 UNTS 376. Switzerland. Supplementation
12 Nov 59. Force 1 Jul 60.
384 UNTS 364. UK Great Britain. Declaration
25 Nov 60.

102622 Bilateral Agreement **196 UNTS 149**
SIGNED: 12 Jun 52 FORCE: 18 May 54
REGISTERED: 26 Jul 54 UK Great Britain
ARTICLES: 26 LANGUAGE: English. Spanish.
HEADNOTE: TELECOMMUNICATION SERVICES
TOPIC: Telecommunications
CONCEPTS: Tariffs. Non-interest rates and fees.
Commercial and public radio. Amateur third
party message. Services. Telegrams. Conformity
with IGO decisions.
TREATY REF: 193UNTS188; 3DEMAR-
TENS7'288;.
PROCEDURE: Denunciation. Duration. Ratification.
PARTIES:
Mexico
UK Great Britain

102623 Bilateral Agreement **196 UNTS 175**
SIGNED: 10 Apr 54 FORCE: 15 Apr 54
REGISTERED: 29 Jul 54 Denmark
ARTICLES: 5 LANGUAGE: French.
HEADNOTE: TRADE
TOPIC: General Trade
CONCEPTS: Annex or appendix reference. Estab-
lishment of commission. Trade procedures. Pay-
ment schedules. Quotas.
INTL ORGS: Organization for Economic Co-opera-
tion and Development. Special Commission.
TREATY REF: 78UNTS353.
PROCEDURE: Duration.
PARTIES:
Denmark
Italy

102624 Multilateral Convention **196 UNTS 183**
SIGNED: 26 Jun 52 FORCE: 24 Jul 54
REGISTERED: 29 Jul 54 ILO (Labor Org)
ARTICLES: 21 LANGUAGE: English. French.
HEADNOTE: HOLIDAYS PAY AGRICULTURE
TOPIC: ILO Labor
CONCEPTS: Territorial application. Conformity
with municipal law. Exchange of information and
documents. Inspection and observation. Domes-
tic legislation. ILO conventions. Holidays and
rest periods. Labor statistics. Wages and salaries.
INTL ORGS: United Nations.
PROCEDURE: Amendment. Accession. Duration.
Ratification. Registration. Renewal or Revival.
PARTIES:
Multilateral
ANNEX
199 UNTS 359. Cuba. Ratification 7 Sep 54.
Force 7 Sep 55.
200 UNTS 339. Norway. Ratification 30 Sep 54.
Force 30 Sep 55.
202 UNTS 384. Germany, West. Ratification
5 Jan 55. Force 5 Jan 56.
210 UNTS 337. Yugoslavia. Ratification
30 Apr 55. Force 30 Apr 56.
212 UNTS 401. France. Guadeloupe.
212 UNTS 401. France. French Guinea.
212 UNTS 401. France. Martinique.
212 UNTS 401. France. Reunion.
236 UNTS 396. United Arab Rep. Ratification
9 Apr 56. Force 9 Apr 57.
248 UNTS 408. Hungary. Ratification 8 Jun 56.
Force 7 Jun 57.
248 UNTS 408. Italy. Ratification 8 Jun 56. Force
8 Jun 57.
248 UNTS 408. UK Great Britain. Ratification
25 Jun 56. Force 25 Jun 57.
266 UNTS 427. Brazil. Ratification 25 Apr 57.
Force 25 Apr 58.
276 UNTS 366. Italy. Declaration 20 Aug 57.
318 UNTS 424. Netherlands. Ratification
27 Nov 58. Force 27 Nov 59.
323 UNTS 376. UK Great Britain. Declaration
19 Jan 59.
325 UNTS 345. UK Great Britain. Barbados.
325 UNTS 345. UK Great Britain. Tanganyika.
353 UNTS 369. Peru. Ratification 1 Feb 60. Force
1 Feb 61.
356 UNTS 373. UK Great Britain. Guernsey Island.
356 UNTS 373. UK Great Britain. Jersey Island.
358 UNTS 283. UK Great Britain. Nigeria. Qualified Application to Non-self-governing Territories 11 Apr 60.
358 UNTS 283. UK Great Britain. St. Lucia.
358 UNTS 283. UK Great Britain. St. Vincent.
373 UNTS 371. United Arab Rep. Syria.

380 UNTS 432. UK Great Britain. Declaration 10 Oct 60.
380 UNTS 433. Morocco. Ratification 14 Oct 60. Force 14 Oct 61.
380 UNTS 433. UK Great Britain. Declaration 10 Oct 60.
388 UNTS 360. UK Great Britain. Nevis.
388 UNTS 360. UK Great Britain. Anguilla.
388 UNTS 360. UK Great Britain. St. Christopher.
390 UNTS 362. UK Great Britain. Declaration 23 Feb 61.
396 UNTS 338. UK Great Britain. West Indies. Declaration 13 Mar 61.
396 UNTS 338. UK Great Britain. Singapore. Qualified Application to Non-self-governing Territories 13 Mar 61.
396 UNTS 339. UK Great Britain. Isle of Man. Qualified Application to Non-self-governing Territories 13 Mar 61.
401 UNTS 269. Gabon. Ratification 13 Jun 61. Force 13 Jun 61.
401 UNTS 269. Sierra Leone. Ratification 15 Jun 61. Force 15 Jun 62.
406 UNTS 308. UK Great Britain. British Honduras.
406 UNTS 308. Guatemala. Ratification 4 Aug 61. Force 4 Aug 62.
413 UNTS 372. Syria. Ratification 30 Oct 61.
422 UNTS 337. Tanganyika. Succession 30 Jan 62. Force 30 Jan 62.
434 UNTS 298. UK Great Britain. Antigua.
437 UNTS 357. Madagascar. Ratification 10 Aug 62. Force 10 Aug 63.
444 UNTS 341. Senegal. Ratification 22 Oct 62. Force 22 Oct 63.
444 UNTS 342. Algeria. Succession 19 Oct 62.
483 UNTS 417. Mauritania. Ratification 8 Nov 63. Force 8 Nov 64.
504 UNTS 362. Netherlands. Netherlands Antilles.
504 UNTS 362. Central Afri Rep. Ratification 9 Jun 64. Force 9 Jul 65.
504 UNTS 362. Netherlands. Surinam.
504 UNTS 362. Tanzania. Succession 22 Jun 64.
560 UNTS 324. Paraguay. Ratification 21 Mar 66. Force 21 Mar 67.
561 UNTS 364. UK Great Britain. Swaziland.
561 UNTS 364. UK Great Britain. Swaziland.
600 UNTS 407. UK Great Britain. Mauritius.

102625 Bilateral Agreement **196 UNTS 199**
SIGNED: 30 Apr 51   FORCE: 1 Apr 51
REGISTERED: 2 Aug 54 India
ARTICLES: 17 LANGUAGE: English.
HEADNOTE: EXCHANGE VALUE PAYABLE ARTICLES
TOPIC: General Trade
CONCEPTS: Detailed regulations. Exceptions and exemptions. Treaty violation. General cooperation. Exchange of information and documents. Responsibility and liability. Trade agencies. Trade procedures. Balance of payments. Monetary and gold transfers. Non-interest rates and fees. Claims and settlements. Mail and money orders. Postal services. Regulations. Rates and charges.
PROCEDURE: Termination.
PARTIES:
  Ceylon (Sri Lanka)
  India

102626 Bilateral Instrument **196 UNTS 209**
SIGNED: 12 Aug 46   FORCE: 12 Aug 46
REGISTERED: 3 Aug 54 India
ARTICLES: 33 LANGUAGE: English.
HEADNOTE: EXCHANGE PARCELS PARCEL POST
TOPIC: Postal Service
CONCEPTS: Detailed regulations. Previous treaty replacement. Conformity with municipal law. Domestic legislation. Responsibility and liability. Compensation. Indemnities and reimbursements. Payment schedules. Customs duties. Postal services. Regulations. Insured letters and boxes. Parcel post. Rates and charges.
PROCEDURE: Duration. Termination.
PARTIES:
  Ceylon (Sri Lanka)
  India

102627 Bilateral Exchange **196 UNTS 245**
SIGNED: 22 Jun 54   FORCE: 22 Jul 54

REGISTERED: 6 Aug 54 Belgium
ARTICLES: 2 LANGUAGE: French.
HEADNOTE: WAIVING VISA REQUIREMENTS HOLDERS SPECIAL PASSPORTS
TOPIC: Visas
CONCEPTS: Visa abolition. Passports diplomatic.
PROCEDURE: Denunciation.
PARTIES:
  Belgium
  Israel

102628 Bilateral Agreement **196 UNTS 251**
SIGNED: 20 Jul 53   FORCE: 1 Jan 51
REGISTERED: 9 Aug 54 UK Great Britain
ARTICLES: 11 LANGUAGE: English. Hindi.
HEADNOTE: FINANCE
TOPIC: Finance
CONCEPTS: Definition of terms. Detailed regulations. Previous treaty replacement. General cooperation. General property. Accounting procedures. Banking. Monetary and gold transfers. Investments. Financial programs. Local currency. Assets transfer.
INTL ORGS: International Monetary Fund.
TREATY REF: 11UNTS371; 134UNTS70.
PROCEDURE: Duration. Termination.
PARTIES:
  India
  UK Great Britain
          ANNEX
201 UNTS 394.   India.   Supplementation 20 Jul 53.
201 UNTS 394. UK Great Britain. Supplementation 20 Jul 53.

102629 Bilateral Convention **196 UNTS 269**
SIGNED: 20 Feb 50   FORCE: 30 Dec 53
REGISTERED: 10 Aug 54 Greece
ARTICLES: 12 LANGUAGE: English. Greek.
HEADNOTE: DOUBLE TAXATION FISCAL EVASION ESTATES DECEASED PERSONS
TOPIC: Taxation
CONCEPTS: Definition of terms. Exchange of official publications. Claims and settlements. Taxation. Death duties. Tax credits. General. Tax exemptions.
PROCEDURE: Duration. Ratification. Termination.
PARTIES:
  Greece
  USA (United States)
          ANNEX
222 UNTS 423. Greece. Correction 3 Aug 54.
222 UNTS 423. USA (United States). Correction 19 Aug 54.

102630 Bilateral Convention **196 UNTS 291**
SIGNED: 20 Feb 50   FORCE: 30 Dec 53
REGISTERED: 10 Aug 54 Greece
ARTICLES: 21 LANGUAGE: English. Greek.
HEADNOTE: DOUBLE TAXATION FISCAL EVASION TAXES INCOME
TOPIC: Taxation
CONCEPTS: Definition of terms. Previous treaty replacement. Conformity with municipal law. Exchange of official publications. Domestic legislation. Teacher and student exchange. Claims and settlements. Taxation. Tax credits. Tax exemptions. Air transport. Merchant vessels.
TREATY REF: 97LTS81; 10JLTS544.
PROCEDURE: Duration. Ratification. Termination.
PARTIES:
  Greece
  USA (United States)
          ANNEX
435 UNTS 334. USA (United States). Correction 19 Dec 61. Force 19 Dec 61.
435 UNTS 334. Greece. Correction 29 Nov 61. Force 19 Dec 61.

102631 Multilateral Agreement **197 UNTS 3**
SIGNED: 15 Jul 49   FORCE: 12 Aug 54
REGISTERED: 12 Aug 54 United Nations
ARTICLES: 16 LANGUAGE: English. French.
HEADNOTE: INTERNATIONAL CIRCULATION VISUAL AUDITORY MATERIALS
TOPIC: Health/Educ/Welfare
CONCEPTS: General cooperation. Procedure. Exchange. Exchange. Scientific exchange. Customs exemptions.
INTL ORGS: International Court of Justice. United

Nations Educational, Scientific and Cultural Organization. United Nations. Arbitration Commission.
TREATY REF: CONV.,PAC. SETTLE.DISPU. HAGUE 18OCT1907;.
PROCEDURE: Accession. Denunciation. Duration. Renewal or Revival.
PARTIES:
  Afghanistan SIGNED: 29 Dec 49
  Brazil SIGNED: 15 Sep 49
  Cambodia   RATIFIED: 20 Feb 52   FORCE: 12 Aug 54
  Canada SIGNED: 17 Dec 49 RATIFIED: 4 Oct 50 FORCE: 12 Aug 54
  Denmark SIGNED: 29 Dec 49
  Dominican Republic SIGNED: 5 Aug 49
  Ecuador SIGNED: 29 Dec 49
  El Salvador SIGNED: 29 Dec 49 RATIFIED: 24 May 53 FORCE: 12 Aug 54
  Greece SIGNED: 31 Dec 49 RATIFIED: 9 Jul 54 FORCE: 12 Aug 54
  Haiti SIGNED: 2 Dec 49 RATIFIED: 14 May 54 FORCE: 12 Aug 54
  Iran SIGNED: 31 Dec 49
  Lebanon SIGNED: 30 Dec 49
  Netherlands SIGNED: 30 Dec 49
  Norway   SIGNED: 20 Dec 49   RATIFIED: 12 Jan 50 FORCE: 12 Aug 54
  Philippines SIGNED: 31 Dec 49 RATIFIED: 13 Nov 52 FORCE: 12 Aug 54
  USA (United States) SIGNED: 13 Sep 49
  Uruguay SIGNED: 31 Dec 49
          ANNEX
213 UNTS 400.   Denmark.   Acceptance 10 Aug 55. Force 8 Nov 55.
347 UNTS 384. Iran. Acceptance 30 Dec 59. Force 29 Mar 60.
354 UNTS 406. Ghana. Accession 22 Mar 60. Force 20 Jun 60.
429 UNTS 283.   Madagascar.   Accession 23 May 62. Force 21 Aug 62.
435 UNTS 338. Brazil. Acceptance 15 Aug 62. Force 13 Nov 62.
544 UNTS 291.   Trinidad/Tobago.   Accession 31 Aug 65. Force 29 Nov 65.
600 UNTS 331.   Malawi.   Accession 5 Jul 67. Force 3 Oct 67.
634 UNTS 429.   Niger.   Accession 22 Apr 68. Force 21 Jul 68.
640 UNTS 370. Morocco. Accession 25 Jul 68. Force 23 Oct 68.
640 UNTS 370.   Malta.   Accession 29 Jul 68. Force 27 Oct 68.
643 UNTS 391. Congo (Brazzaville). Accession 26 Aug 68. Force 24 Nov 68.

102632 Bilateral Exchange **197 UNTS 39**
SIGNED: 16 Mar 48   FORCE: 16 Mar 48
REGISTERED: 12 Aug 54 Sweden
ARTICLES: 2 LANGUAGE: French.
HEADNOTE: EXCHANGE STUDENT EMPLOYEES
TOPIC: Non-ILO Labor
CONCEPTS: Resident permits. General cooperation. Wages and salaries. Non-ILO labor relations. Administrative cooperation. Migrant worker. Quotas.
PROCEDURE: Amendment. Denunciation. Duration. Renewal or Revival.
PARTIES:
  Sweden
  Switzerland

102633 Bilateral Exchange **197 UNTS 47**
SIGNED: 20 Nov 48   FORCE: 20 Nov 48
REGISTERED: 12 Aug 54 Sweden
ARTICLES: 2 LANGUAGE: Spanish.
HEADNOTE: DOUBLE TAXATION SEA AIR TRANSPORT
TOPIC: Taxation
CONCEPTS: Definition of terms. Domestic legislation. Taxation. Tax exemptions. Air transport. Merchant vessels.
PARTIES:
  Argentina
  Sweden

102634 Bilateral Convention **197 UNTS 55**
SIGNED: 16 Oct 48   FORCE: 25 Mar 49
REGISTERED: 12 Aug 54 Sweden
ARTICLES: 14 LANGUAGE: Swedish. German.
HEADNOTE: DOUBLE TAXATION TAXES INCOME

TOPIC: Taxation
CONCEPTS: Conformity with municipal law. Claims and settlements. Taxation. General. Tax exemptions.
PROCEDURE: Denunciation. Ratification. Termination.
PARTIES:
Sweden
Switzerland

102635 Bilateral Convention **197 UNTS 101**
SIGNED: 16 Oct 48   FORCE: 25 Mar 49
REGISTERED: 12 Aug 54 Sweden
ARTICLES: 8 LANGUAGE: Swedish. German.
HEADNOTE: DOUBLE TAXATION DEATH DUTIES
TOPIC: Taxation
CONCEPTS: Taxation. Death duties.
PROCEDURE: Denunciation. Duration. Ratification.
PARTIES:
Sweden
Switzerland

102636 Bilateral Agreement **197 UNTS 123**
SIGNED: 17 Feb 49   FORCE: 9 Jul 49
REGISTERED: 12 Aug 54 Sweden
ARTICLES: 7 LANGUAGE: Swedish. Finnish.
HEADNOTE: TIMBER FLOATING FRONTIER RIVERS
TOPIC: Specific Resources
CONCEPTS: Annex or appendix reference. Conciliation. General. Tax exemptions. Customs exemptions. Frontier waterways. Regulation of natural resources.
TREATY REF: 70LTS201.
PROCEDURE: Denunciation. Duration. Ratification.
PARTIES:
Finland
Sweden
                    ANNEX
507 UNTS 278.   Finland.   Supplementation
23 Apr 64. Force 10 Jul 64.
507 UNTS 278.   Sweden.   Supplementation
23 Apr 64. Force 10 Jul 64.

102637 Bilateral Agreement **197 UNTS 177**
SIGNED: 8 Apr 49   FORCE: 9 Feb 51
REGISTERED: 12 Aug 54 Sweden
ARTICLES: 2 LANGUAGE: French.
HEADNOTE: DOUBLE TAXATION RECIPROCAL ADMINISTRATIVE ASSISTANCE DIRECT TAXES
TOPIC: Taxation
CONCEPTS: Territorial application. Taxation.
PROCEDURE: Ratification.
PARTIES:
France
Sweden
                    ANNEX
369 UNTS 448. Sweden. Amendment 29 Mar 56.
Force 13 Aug 57.
369 UNTS 448. France. Amendment 29 Mar 56.
Force 13 Aug 57.

102638 Bilateral Agreement **197 UNTS 183**
SIGNED: 8 Apr 49   FORCE: 9 Feb 51
REGISTERED: 12 Aug 54 Sweden
ARTICLES: 2 LANGUAGE: French.
HEADNOTE: DOUBLE TAXATION DEATH DUTIES
TOPIC: Taxation
CONCEPTS: Territorial application. Taxation. Death duties.
PROCEDURE: Ratification.
PARTIES:
France
Sweden

102639 Bilateral Exchange **197 UNTS 189**
SIGNED: 6 Jul 49   FORCE: 6 Jul 49
REGISTERED: 12 Aug 49 Sweden
ARTICLES: 2 LANGUAGE: French.
HEADNOTE: EXCHANGE STUDENT EMPLOYEES
TOPIC: Non-ILO Labor
CONCEPTS: Resident permits. General cooperation. Wages and salaries. Non-ILO labor relations. Administrative cooperation. Migrant worker. Quotas.
PROCEDURE: Denunciation. Duration. Renewal or Revival.

252

PARTIES:
Netherlands
Sweden

102640 Bilateral Convention **197 UNTS 197**
SIGNED: 17 Dec 49   FORCE: 13 Jul 50
REGISTERED: 12 Aug 54 Sweden
ARTICLES: 12 LANGUAGE: Swedish. Norwegian.
HEADNOTE: DOUBLE TAXATION DEATH DUTIES
TOPIC: Taxation
CONCEPTS: Privileges and immunities. Claims and settlements. Taxation. Death duties.
PROCEDURE: Denunciation. Duration. Ratification.
PARTIES:
Norway
Sweden

102641 Bilateral Agreement **197 UNTS 215**
SIGNED: 17 Dec 49   FORCE: 1 Aug 50
REGISTERED: 12 Aug 54 Sweden
ARTICLES: 22 LANGUAGE: Swedish. Norwegian.
HEADNOTE: TAXATION
TOPIC: Taxation
CONCEPTS: Territorial application. Conformity with municipal law. General cooperation. Exchange of official publications. Claims and settlements. Taxation. General.
TREATY REF: 94UNTS107.
PROCEDURE: Denunciation. Duration. Ratification.
PARTIES:
Norway
Sweden

102642 Bilateral Agreement **197 UNTS 243**
SIGNED: 21 Dec 49   FORCE: 28 Apr 50
REGISTERED: 12 Aug 54 Sweden
ARTICLES: 18 LANGUAGE: Swedish. Finnish.
HEADNOTE: DOUBLE TAXATION TAXES INCOME PROPERTY
TOPIC: Taxation
CONCEPTS: Previous treaty replacement. Conformity with municipal law. Taxation. Death duties. General. Tax exemptions. Air transport. Airworthiness certificates.
TREATY REF: 118LTS71.
PROCEDURE: Denunciation. Duration. Ratification.
PARTIES:
Finland
Sweden
                    ANNEX
427 UNTS 368. Sweden. Amendment 19 Jun 58.
Force 31 Dec 58.
427 UNTS 368. Finland. Amendment 19 Jun 58.
Force 31 Dec 58.

102643 Bilateral Agreement **197 UNTS 285**
SIGNED: 31 Mar 50   FORCE: 8 Aug 50
REGISTERED: 12 Aug 54 Sweden
ARTICLES: 12 LANGUAGE: Swedish. Finnish.
HEADNOTE: DOUBLE TAXATION DEATH DUTIES
TOPIC: Taxation
CONCEPTS: Privileges and immunities. Claims and settlements. Taxation. Death duties.
PROCEDURE: Denunciation. Duration. Ratification.
PARTIES:
Finland
Sweden

102644 Bilateral Agreement **197 UNTS 305**
SIGNED: 12 Oct 50   FORCE: 1 Nov 50
REGISTERED: 12 Aug 54 Sweden
ARTICLES: 7 LANGUAGE: French.
HEADNOTE: METEOROLOGICAL INFORMATION EXCHANGE
TOPIC: Scientific Project
CONCEPTS: Research and scientific projects. Meteorology. Scientific exchange. Bands and frequency allocation. Publications exchange.
PROCEDURE: Denunciation. Duration.
PARTIES:
Spain
Sweden

102645 Bilateral Agreement **197 UNTS 311**
SIGNED: 31 Oct 50   FORCE: 31 Oct 50
REGISTERED: 12 Aug 54 Sweden
ARTICLES: 7 LANGUAGE: Swedish. German.
HEADNOTE: TRANSFER PHYSICIANS

TOPIC: Non-ILO Labor
CONCEPTS: Exceptions and exemptions. Border traffic and migration. Alien status. General cooperation. Establishment of commission. Public health. Scholarships and grants. Employment regulations. Non-ILO labor relations. Migrant worker. Transportation costs.
PROCEDURE: Duration. Termination.
PARTIES:
Austria
Sweden

102646 Bilateral Exchange **197 UNTS 333**
SIGNED: 29 Dec 50   FORCE: 1 Jan 51
REGISTERED: 12 Aug 54 Sweden
ARTICLES: 2 LANGUAGE: Swedish.
HEADNOTE: FISCAL ASSISTANCE MATTER TAXES
TOPIC: Taxation
CONCEPTS: Previous treaty extension. Taxation. Death duties.
PARTIES:
Finland
Sweden

102647 Multilateral Convention **197 UNTS 341**
SIGNED: 9 Jan 51   FORCE: 1 Apr 51
REGISTERED: 12 Aug 54 Sweden
ARTICLES: 20 LANGUAGE: Swedish. Danish. Finnish. Icelandic. Norwegian.
HEADNOTE: ASSISTANCE DISTRESSED PERSONS
TOPIC: Humanitarian
CONCEPTS: Definition of terms. Detailed regulations. Territorial application. Annex or appendix reference. Previous treaty replacement. Repatriation of nationals. Privileges and immunities. Family law. Exchange of information and documents. Humanitarian matters. Indemnities and reimbursements. National treatment. General aid.
TREATY REF: 84UNTS7.
PROCEDURE: Denunciation. Ratification.
PARTIES:
Denmark   SIGNED: 9 Jan 51   RATIFIED:
   26 Feb 51 FORCE: 1 Apr 51
Finland SIGNED: 9 Jan 51 RATIFIED: 26 Feb 51
   FORCE: 1 Apr 51
Iceland SIGNED: 9 Jan 51 RATIFIED: 26 Feb 51
   FORCE: 1 Apr 51
Norway SIGNED: 9 Jan 51 RATIFIED: 26 Feb 51
   FORCE: 1 Apr 51
Sweden SIGNED: 9 Jan 51 RATIFIED: 26 Feb 51
   FORCE: 1 Apr 51

102648 Bilateral Agreement **197 UNTS 393**
SIGNED: 6 Apr 51   FORCE: 1 Sep 51
REGISTERED: 12 Aug 54 Sweden
ARTICLES: 22 LANGUAGE: Swedish. English.
HEADNOTE: FISCAL ASSISTANCE INCOME TAXES
TOPIC: Taxation
CONCEPTS: Definition of terms. Conformity with municipal law. Exchange of official publications. Domestic legislation. Teacher and student exchange. Claims and settlements. Taxation. Equitable taxes. General. Tax exemptions. Air transport. Merchant vessels.
TREATY REF: 97UNTS331.
PROCEDURE: Duration. Ratification. Termination.
PARTIES:
Canada
Sweden

102649 Bilateral Exchange **197 UNTS 421**
SIGNED: 25 May 51   FORCE: 25 May 51
REGISTERED: 12 Aug 54 Sweden
ARTICLES: 2 LANGUAGE: English.
HEADNOTE: DOUBLE TAXATION SHIPPING AIRCRAFT
TOPIC: Taxation
CONCEPTS: Taxation. Tax exemptions. Air transport. Merchant vessels.
PROCEDURE: Duration. Ratification.
PARTIES:
South Africa
Sweden

102650 Bilateral Exchange **197 UNTS 431**
SIGNED: 29 May 51 FORCE: 29 May 51
REGISTERED: 12 Aug 54 Sweden
ARTICLES: 2 LANGUAGE: German.
HEADNOTE: VALIDITY CERTAIN PREVIOUSLY CONCLUDED AGREEMENTS
TOPIC: General Amity
CONCEPTS: Annex type material. Previous treaty extension.
TREATY REF: 9LTS318; 61LTS193; 2'3DM243; 174LTS125;T.
PARTIES:
Austria
Sweden

102651 Bilateral Exchange **198 UNTS 3**
SIGNED: 15 Jun 51 FORCE: 15 Jun 51
REGISTERED: 12 Aug 54 Sweden
ARTICLES: 2 LANGUAGE: Swedish.
HEADNOTE: POSTPONEMENT FRONTIER INSPECTION
TOPIC: Visas
CONCEPTS: Treaty implementation. Inspection and observation.
INTL ORGS: Special Commission.
PARTIES:
Finland
Sweden

102652 Bilateral Exchange **198 UNTS 9**
SIGNED: 19 Jul 51 FORCE: 19 Jul 51
REGISTERED: 12 Aug 54 Sweden
ARTICLES: 2 LANGUAGE: German.
HEADNOTE: DOUBLE TAXATION FISCAL EVASION TAXES INCOME
TOPIC: Taxation
CONCEPTS: Taxation.
TREATY REF: 81LTSI81.
PARTIES:
Austria
Sweden

102653 Bilateral Exchange **198 UNTS 13**
SIGNED: 1 Aug 51 FORCE: 1 Aug 51
REGISTERED: 12 Aug 54 Sweden
ARTICLES: 2 LANGUAGE: German.
HEADNOTE: TAXATION FOREIGN MOTOR VEHICLES
TOPIC: Taxation
CONCEPTS: Domestic legislation. Tax exemptions. Motor vehicles and combinations.
PARTIES:
Austria
Sweden

102654 Multilateral Convention **198 UNTS 17**
SIGNED: 28 Aug 51 FORCE: 1 Jun 52
REGISTERED: 12 Aug 54 Sweden
ARTICLES: 8 LANGUAGE: Swedish. Finnish. Icelandic. Norwegian.
HEADNOTE: CHILD ALLOWANCES
TOPIC: Non-ILO Labor
CONCEPTS: Conditions. Definition of terms. Detailed regulations. Non-ILO labor relations. Family allowances. Administrative cooperation. Indemnities and reimbursements. Payment schedules. National treatment.
PROCEDURE: Denunciation. Ratification. Registration.
PARTIES:
Finland SIGNED: 28 Aug 51 RATIFIED: 11 Mar 52 FORCE: 1 Jun 52
Iceland SIGNED: 28 Aug 51 RATIFIED: 11 Mar 52 FORCE: 1 Jun 52
Norway SIGNED: 28 Aug 51 RATIFIED: 11 Mar 52 FORCE: 1 Jun 52
Sweden SIGNED: 28 Aug 51 RATIFIED: 11 Mar 52 FORCE: 1 Jun 52

102655 Multilateral Protocol **198 UNTS 37**
SIGNED: 14 Jul 52 FORCE: 12 Jul 52
REGISTERED: 12 Aug 54 Sweden
ARTICLES: 1 LANGUAGE: Swedish. Danish. Finnish. Norwegian.
HEADNOTE: ABOLITION PASSPORTS TRAVEL
TOPIC: Visas
CONCEPTS: Visa abolition. Border traffic and migration. Resident permits.

PARTIES:
Denmark SIGNED: 14 Jul 52 FORCE: 12 Jul 52
Finland SIGNED: 14 Jul 52 FORCE: 12 Jul 52
Norway SIGNED: 14 Jul 52 FORCE: 12 Jul 52
Sweden SIGNED: 14 Jul 52 FORCE: 12 Jul 52

102656 Multilateral Agreement **198 UNTS 47**
SIGNED: 14 Jul 52 FORCE: 12 Jul 52
REGISTERED: 12 Aug 54 Sweden
ARTICLES: 6 LANGUAGE: Swedish. Danish. Finnish. Norwegian.
HEADNOTE: READMITTANCE ALIENS
TOPIC: Consul/Citizenship
CONCEPTS: Border traffic and migration. Exchange of information and documents. Operating agencies.
PROCEDURE: Denunciation.
PARTIES:
Denmark SIGNED: 14 Jul 52 FORCE: 12 Jul 52
Finland SIGNED: 14 Jul 52 FORCE: 12 Jul 52
Norway SIGNED: 14 Jul 52 FORCE: 12 Jul 52
Sweden SIGNED: 14 Jul 52 FORCE: 12 Jul 52
ANNEX
369 UNTS 454. Sweden. Acknowledgement 3 Nov 55. Force 1 Dec 55.
369 UNTS 454. Iceland. Acceptance 3 Nov 55. Force 1 Dec 55.

102657 Bilateral Agreement **198 UNTS 61**
SIGNED: 9 Apr 53 FORCE: 13 Jul 53
REGISTERED: 12 Aug 54 Sweden
ARTICLES: 4 LANGUAGE: Swedish. Finnish. French.
HEADNOTE: SUPPLEMENT 29 JAN 26 CONVENTION
TOPIC: Dispute Settlement
CONCEPTS: Annex type material.
INTL ORGS: International Court of Justice. Permanent Court of International Justice.
PARTIES:
Finland
Sweden

102658 Bilateral Agreement **198 UNTS 71**
SIGNED: 27 Oct 53 FORCE: 18 Dec 53
REGISTERED: 12 Aug 54 Sweden
ARTICLES: 19 LANGUAGE: Swedish. Danish.
HEADNOTE: DOUBLE TAXATION INCOME PROPERTY
TOPIC: Taxation
CONCEPTS: Privileges and immunities. Negotiation. Teacher and student exchange. Claims and settlements. Taxation. Tax credits. General.
PROCEDURE: Duration. Ratification. Termination.
PARTIES:
Denmark
Sweden

102659 Bilateral Agreement **198 UNTS 111**
SIGNED: 27 Oct 53 FORCE: 18 Dec 53
REGISTERED: 12 Aug 54 Sweden
ARTICLES: 11 LANGUAGE: Swedish. Danish.
HEADNOTE: DOUBLE TAXATION DEATH DUTIES
TOPIC: Taxation
CONCEPTS: Territorial application. Privileges and immunities. Negotiation. Claims and settlements. Debts. Taxation. Death duties.
PROCEDURE: Denunciation. Duration. Termination.
PARTIES:
Denmark
Sweden

102660 Bilateral Agreement **198 UNTS 129**
SIGNED: 27 Oct 53 FORCE: 1 Jan 54
REGISTERED: 12 Aug 54 Sweden
ARTICLES: 23 LANGUAGE: Swedish. Danish.
HEADNOTE: ADMINISTRATIVE ASSITANCE TAXATION
TOPIC: Taxation
CONCEPTS: Territorial application. Conformity with municipal law. General cooperation. Exchange of official publications. Claims and settlements. Assessment procedures. General.
PROCEDURE: Denunciation. Duration. Ratification.
PARTIES:
Denmark
Sweden

ANNEX
429 UNTS 284. Denmark. Supplementation 14 Sep 61. Force 1 Apr 62.
429 UNTS 284. Sweden. Supplementation 14 Sep 61. Force 1 Apr 62.

102661 Bilateral Exchange **198 UNTS 157**
SIGNED: 12 May 54 FORCE: 12 May 54
REGISTERED: 12 Aug 54 Sweden
ARTICLES: 2 LANGUAGE: Swedish. Norwegian.
HEADNOTE: POSTPONEMENT CLEARING INSPECTION FRONTIER
TOPIC: Visas
CONCEPTS: Treaty implementation. Inspection and observation.
PARTIES:
Norway
Sweden

102662 Bilateral Agreement **198 UNTS 161**
SIGNED: 26 Nov 49 FORCE: 26 Nov 49
REGISTERED: 18 Aug 54 Australia
ARTICLES: 11 LANGUAGE: English.
HEADNOTE: REGARDING CHRISTMAS ISLAND
TOPIC: Territory Boundary
CONCEPTS: Juridical personality. Establishment of commission. Indemnities and reimbursements. Financial programs. Boundaries of territory. Regulation of natural resources.
INTL ORGS: Special Commission.
PARTIES:
Australia
New Zealand

102663 Bilateral Agreement **198 UNTS 173**
SIGNED: 26 Aug 54 FORCE: 26 Aug 54
REGISTERED: 26 Aug 54 United Nations
ARTICLES: 11 LANGUAGE: English.
HEADNOTE: ASSISTANCE
TOPIC: Direct Aid
CONCEPTS: Definition of terms. Territorial application. Guarantees and safeguards. Treaty implementation. Privileges and immunities. General cooperation. Exchange of information and documents. Inspection and observation. Public information. Procedure. Existing tribunals. Export quotas. Accounting procedures. Indemnities and reimbursements. Financial programs. Tax exemptions. Customs exemptions. Commodities and services. Domestic obligation. General aid. Distribution. IGO status.
INTL ORGS: United Nations.
TREATY REF: 1UNTS15.
PROCEDURE: Amendment. Termination.
PARTIES:
New Zealand
UNICEF (Children)

102664 Bilateral Exchange **198 UNTS 187**
SIGNED: 6 Nov 53 FORCE: 1 Jul 54
REGISTERED: 30 Aug 54 Netherlands
ARTICLES: 2 LANGUAGE: French.
HEADNOTE: FREE ISSUE COPIES CIVIL STATUS RECORDS
TOPIC: Admin Cooperation
CONCEPTS: Exchange of information and documents.
PROCEDURE: Termination.
PARTIES:
Luxembourg
Netherlands

102665 Bilateral Agreement **198 UNTS 193**
SIGNED: 12 Feb 51 FORCE: 1 Nov 53
REGISTERED: 13 Sep 54 Greece
ARTICLES: 5 LANGUAGE: Greek. German.
HEADNOTE: COMMERCE
TOPIC: General Trade
CONCEPTS: Treaty implementation. Visas. Trade procedures. Most favored nation clause. Routes and logistics. Navigational conditions. Inland and territorial waters. Ports and pilotage.
INTL ORGS: Organization for Economic Co-operation and Development.
PROCEDURE: Denunciation. Duration. Ratification. Renewal or Revival.
PARTIES:
Germany, West
Greece

229 UNTS 328. Greece. Supplementation 14 Nov 55. Force 14 Nov 55.
229 UNTS 328. Germany, West. Supplementation 14 Nov 55. Force 14 Nov 55.

102666 Bilateral Exchange **198 UNTS 225**
SIGNED: 21 Feb 52 FORCE: 21 Feb 53
REGISTERED: 15 Sep 54 USA (United States)
ARTICLES: 2 LANGUAGE: English. Arabic.
HEADNOTE: TECHNICAL COOPERATION
TOPIC: Tech Assistance
CONCEPTS: Time limit. Annex type material. Conformity with municipal law. General technical assistance.
TREATY REF: 151UNTS179.
PARTIES:
Iraq
USA (United States)

102667 Bilateral Exchange **198 UNTS 231**
SIGNED: 7 Jan 52 FORCE: 7 Jan 52
REGISTERED: 15 Sep 54 USA (United States)
ARTICLES: 3 LANGUAGE: English. Spanish.
HEADNOTE: TECHNICAL COOPERATION
TOPIC: Tech Assistance
CONCEPTS: Annex or appendix reference. Annex type material. Conformity with municipal law. Attachment of funds. Garnishment of funds. Seizure funds. General technical assistance.
PARTIES:
El Salvador
USA (United States)

102668 Bilateral Exchange **198 UNTS 243**
SIGNED: 31 Dec 51 FORCE: 31 Dec 51
REGISTERED: 15 Sep 54 USA (United States)
ARTICLES: 2 LANGUAGE: English. French.
HEADNOTE: TECHNICAL COOPERATION
TOPIC: Tech Assistance
CONCEPTS: Time limit. Conformity with municipal law. General cooperation. Attachment of funds. Garnishment of funds. Seizure funds. General technical assistance. Economic assistance. Defense and security. Military assistance. Return of equipment and recapture.
TREATY REF: 185UNTS3; 174UNTS141.
PARTIES:
Laos
USA (United States)

102669 Bilateral Exchange **198 UNTS 251**
SIGNED: 23 Apr 52 FORCE: 23 Apr 52
REGISTERED: 15 Sep 54 USA (United States)
ARTICLES: 3 LANGUAGE: English. Spanish.
HEADNOTE: FLIGHTS MILITARY AIRCRAFT
TOPIC: Status of Forces
CONCEPTS: Previous treaty replacement. Conformity with municipal law. Airport facilities. Overflights and technical stops. Airforce-army-navy personnel ratio. Ranks and privileges. Procurement and logistics.
INTL ORGS: International Civil Aviation Organization.
PROCEDURE: Renewal or Revival. Termination.
PARTIES:
Honduras
USA (United States)

102670 Bilateral Agreement **198 UNTS 265**
SIGNED: 5 May 51 FORCE: 15 Aug 51
REGISTERED: 15 Sep 54 USA (United States)
ARTICLES: 8 LANGUAGE: English. Arabic.
HEADNOTE: TECHNICAL COOPERATION
TOPIC: Tech Assistance
CONCEPTS: Exceptions and exemptions. Treaty implementation. Annex or appendix reference. Previous treaty replacement. Exchange of information and documents. Personnel. Public information. Vocational training. Reexport of goods, etc.. Expense sharing formulae. Payment schedules. Tax exemptions. Customs duties. Customs exemptions. Domestic obligation. General technical assistance. Materials, equipment and services.
INTL ORGS: United Nations.
PROCEDURE: Amendment. Ratification. Termination.

PARTIES:
United Arab Rep
USA (United States)
ANNEX
376 UNTS 422. United Arab Rep. Implementation 2 Apr 60. Force 2 Apr 60.
376 UNTS 422. USA (United States). Implementation 2 Apr 60. Force 2 Apr 60.

102671 Bilateral Exchange **198 UNTS 281**
SIGNED: 25 Jul 52 FORCE: 25 Jul 52
REGISTERED: 15 Sep 54 USA (United States)
ARTICLES: 2 LANGUAGE: English.
HEADNOTE: RELIEF TAXATION DEFENSE EXPENDITURES
TOPIC: Milit Assistance
CONCEPTS: Tax exemptions. Materials, equipment and services. Military assistance.
PARTIES:
Japan
USA (United States)

102672 Bilateral Exchange **198 UNTS 287**
SIGNED: 18 Nov 48 FORCE: 18 Nov 48
REGISTERED: 15 Sep 54 USA (United States)
ARTICLES: 2 LANGUAGE: English. Chinese.
HEADNOTE: RELIEF SUPPLIES PACKAGES
TOPIC: Direct Aid
CONCEPTS: Annex type material. General cooperation. Indemnities and reimbursements. Payment schedules. Transportation costs. Local currency. Customs exemptions. Relief supplies.
PROCEDURE: Duration.
PARTIES:
Taiwan
USA (United States)
ANNEX
237 UNTS 337. Taiwan. Amendment 26 Oct 54. Force 26 Oct 54.
237 UNTS 337. USA (United States). Amendment 12 Jul 54. Force 26 Oct 54.

102673 Bilateral Exchange **198 UNTS 305**
SIGNED: 26 Mar 54 FORCE: 26 Mar 54
REGISTERED: 15 Sep 54 Australia
ARTICLES: 2 LANGUAGE: English.
HEADNOTE: COMMERCE
TOPIC: General Trade
CONCEPTS: Annex type material. Commodity trade. Customs declarations. Customs exemptions.
TREATY REF: 177LTS271.
PARTIES:
Australia
Belgium
ANNEX
327 UNTS 371. Belgium. Termination 28 Jan 59. Force 28 Jul 59.
327 UNTS 371. Australia. Termination 28 Jan 59. Force 28 Jul 59.

102674 Multilateral Agreement **199 UNTS 3**
SIGNED: 22 May 54 FORCE: 2 Jul 54
REGISTERED: 15 Sep 54 Denmark
ARTICLES: 9 LANGUAGE: Danish. Finnish. Norwegian. Swedish.
HEADNOTE: COMMON LABOR MARKET
TOPIC: Non-ILO Labor
CONCEPTS: Emergencies. Resident permits. Exchange of information and documents. Operating agencies. Establishment of commission. Labor statistics. Non-ILO labor relations. Administrative cooperation.
INTL ORGS: Special Commission.
PROCEDURE: Denunciation. Ratification. Registration.
PARTIES:
Denmark SIGNED: 22 May 54 FORCE: 2 Jul 54
Finland SIGNED: 22 May 54 FORCE: 2 Jul 54
Norway SIGNED: 22 May 54 FORCE: 2 Jul 54
Sweden SIGNED: 22 May 54 FORCE: 2 Jul 54

102675 Multilateral Protocol **199 UNTS 29**
SIGNED: 22 May 54 FORCE: 1 Jul 54
REGISTERED: 15 Sep 54 Denmark
ARTICLES: 1 LANGUAGE: Danish. Finnish. Norwegian. Swedish.
HEADNOTE: PASSPORT RESIDENT PERMIT EXEMPTION

TOPIC: Visas
CONCEPTS: Emergencies. Visa abolition. Resident permits. Alien status. General cooperation.
PROCEDURE: Denunciation.
PARTIES:
Denmark SIGNED: 22 May 54 FORCE: 1 Jul 54
Finland SIGNED: 22 May 54 FORCE: 1 Jul 54
Norway SIGNED: 22 May 54 FORCE: 1 Jul 54
Sweden SIGNED: 22 May 54 FORCE: 1 Jul 54
ANNEX
369 UNTS 458. Sweden. Acknowledgement 3 Nov 55. Force 1 Dec 55.
369 UNTS 458. Iceland. Acceptance 3 Nov 55. Force 1 Dec 55.

102676 Bilateral Exchange **199 UNTS 43**
SIGNED: 23 Jun 54 FORCE: 23 Jun 54
REGISTERED: 25 Sep 54 Belgium
ARTICLES: 4 LANGUAGE: French.
HEADNOTE: TAXATION PROFITS SEA AIR TRANSPORT
TOPIC: Taxation
CONCEPTS: Definition of terms. General. Tax exemptions. Air transport. Merchant vessels.
PROCEDURE: Denunciation.
PARTIES:
Belgium
Greece

102677 Bilateral Agreement **199 UNTS 51**
SIGNED: 1 Sep 54 FORCE: 1 Sep 54
REGISTERED: 27 Sep 54 Guatemala
ARTICLES: 5 LANGUAGE: Spanish. English.
HEADNOTE: TECHNICAL COOPERATION
TOPIC: Tech Assistance
CONCEPTS: Exceptions and exemptions. Treaty implementation. Previous treaty replacement. General cooperation. Exchange of information and documents. Personnel. Public information. Attachment of funds. Exchange rates and regulations. Funding procedures. Garnishment of funds. Seizure funds. Tax exemptions. Customs exemptions. Domestic obligation. General technical assistance. Materials, equipment and services. Aid missions.
PROCEDURE: Amendment. Termination.
PARTIES:
Guatemala
USA (United States)

102678 Multilateral Agreement **199 UNTS 67**
SIGNED: 19 Jun 51 FORCE: 23 Aug 53
REGISTERED: 30 Sep 54 USA (United States)
ARTICLES: 20 LANGUAGE: English. French.
HEADNOTE: STATUS NATO FORCES
TOPIC: Status of Forces
CONCEPTS: Definition of terms. Territorial application. Annex or appendix reference. Court procedures. Conformity with municipal law. General cooperation. Legal protection and assistance. Recognition and enforcement of legal decisions. Recognition of legal documents. Responsibility and liability. Use of facilities. Investigation of violations. Arbitration. Procedure. Compensation. Indemnities and reimbursements. Local currency. Claims and settlements. National treatment. General. Tax exemptions. Customs duties. Temporary importation. Security of information. Ranks and privileges. Jurisdiction. Status of forces. Bases and facilities.
PROCEDURE: Amendment. Accession. Denunciation. Ratification.
PARTIES:
Belgium SIGNED: 19 Jun 51 RATIFIED: 27 Feb 53 FORCE: 23 Aug 53
Canada SIGNED: 19 Jun 51 RATIFIED: 28 Aug 53 FORCE: 27 Sep 53
Denmark SIGNED: 19 Jun 51
France SIGNED: 19 Jun 51 RATIFIED: 29 Sep 52 FORCE: 23 Aug 53
Greece RATIFIED: 26 Jul 54 FORCE: 25 Aug 54
Iceland SIGNED: 19 Jun 51
Italy SIGNED: 19 Jun 51
Luxembourg SIGNED: 19 Jun 51 RATIFIED: 19 Mar 54 FORCE: 18 Apr 54
Netherlands SIGNED: 19 Jun 51 RATIFIED: 18 Nov 53 FORCE: 18 Dec 53
Norway SIGNED: 19 Jun 51 RATIFIED: 24 Feb 53 FORCE: 23 Aug 53
Portugal SIGNED: 19 Jun 51
Turkey RATIFIED: 18 May 54 FORCE: 17 Jun 54

UK Great Britain SIGNED: 19 Jun 51 RATIFIED:
10 May 54 FORCE: 12 Jun 54
USA (United States) SIGNED: 19 Jun 51 RATI-
FIED: 24 Jul 53 FORCE: 23 Aug 53
ANNEX
200 UNTS 340. Norway. Implementation
24 Feb 53. Force 10 Apr 54.
200 UNTS 340. Turkey. Implementation
18 May 54. Force 17 Jun 54.
200 UNTS 340. Iceland. Implementation
11 May 53. Force 10 Apr 54.
200 UNTS 340. Netherlands. Implementation
22 Jun 54. Force 22 Jul 54.
200 UNTS 340. Luxembourg. Implementation
23 Jul 54. Force 22 Aug 54.
200 UNTS 340. Greece. Implementation
26 Jul 54. Force 25 Aug 54.
200 UNTS 340. Belgium. Implementation
11 Mar 54. Force 10 Apr 54.
200 UNTS 340. USA (United States). Implementation 24 Jul 53. Force 10 Apr 54.
260 UNTS 452. Portugal. Ratification 22 Nov 55.
Force 22 Dec 55.
260 UNTS 452. Portugal. Qualified Ratification
22 Nov 55. Force 22 Dec 55.
260 UNTS 452. France. Ratification 20 Jan 55.
Force 19 Feb 55.
260 UNTS 452. Italy. Ratification 22 Dec 55.
Force 21 Jan 56.
260 UNTS 452. Italy. Ratification 22 Dec 55.
Force 21 Jan 56.
260 UNTS 452. Denmark. Ratification 28 May 55.
Force 27 Jun 55.
260 UNTS 452. Denmark. Ratification 28 May 55.
Force 27 Jun 55.
286 UNTS 380. France. Algeria.
481 UNTS 588. UK Great Britain. Isle of Man.
Force 1 Mar 62.
481 UNTS 588. Germany, West. Accession
1 Jun 63. Force 1 Jul 63.
545 UNTS 330. UK Great Britain. Ratification
3 Aug 65. Force 2 Sep 65.
607 UNTS 264. France. Denunciation 30 Mar 66.
Force 31 Mar 67.

102679 Bilateral Agreement **199 UNTS 113**
SIGNED: 30 Jun 52 FORCE: 30 Jul 54
REGISTERED: 5 Oct 54 UK Great Britain
ARTICLES: 7 LANGUAGE: English. French.
HEADNOTE: DISCHARGE DEBT
TOPIC: Milit Assistance
CONCEPTS: Claims, debts and assets. Debts. Debt
settlement. Payment for war supplies.
INTL ORGS: European Payments Union.
PROCEDURE: Ratification.
PARTIES:
Belgium
UK Great Britain

102680 Bilateral Agreement **199 UNTS 135**
SIGNED: 10 Jul 54 FORCE: 10 Jul 54
REGISTERED: 5 Oct 54 UK Great Britain
ARTICLES: 10 LANGUAGE: English.
HEADNOTE: REPAYMENT OFFSET
TOPIC: Finance
CONCEPTS: General cooperation. Currency de-
posits. Exchange rates and regulations. Payment
schedules. Lump sum settlements.
INTL ORGS: European Payments Union. Organiza-
tion for Economic Co-operation and Develop-
ment.
PARTIES:
Germany, West
UK Great Britain
ANNEX
310 UNTS 368. UK Great Britain. Supplementa-
tion 26 Jul 57. Force 26 Jul 57.
310 UNTS 368. Germany, West. Supplementa-
tion 26 Jul 57. Force 26 Jul 57.

102681 Bilateral Exchange **199 UNTS 149**
SIGNED: 19 Aug 54 FORCE: 19 Aug 54
REGISTERED: 5 Oct 54 UK Great Britain
ARTICLES: 7 LANGUAGE: English.
HEADNOTE: SETTLEMENT CERTAIN FINANCIAL
MATTERS
TOPIC: Finance
CONCEPTS: Detailed regulations. Expropriation.
General property. General trade. Trade proce-
dures. Finances and payments. Payment sched-
ules. Claims and settlements.

TREATY REF: 41UNTS135.
PARTIES:
Hungary
UK Great Britain

102682 Bilateral Agreement **199 UNTS 157**
SIGNED: 9 Jul 54 FORCE: 9 Jul 54
REGISTERED: 5 Oct 54 UK Great Britain
ARTICLES: 10 LANGUAGE: English.
HEADNOTE: REPAYMENT OFFSET
TOPIC: Finance
CONCEPTS: General cooperation. Exchange rates
and regulations. Interest rates. Payment sched-
ules. Lump sum settlements.
INTL ORGS: European Payments Union. Organiza-
tion for Economic Co-operation and Develop-
ment.
PARTIES:
Netherlands
UK Great Britain
ANNEX
252 UNTS 356. UK Great Britain. Supplementa-
tion 29 Jun 56. Force 29 Jun 56.
252 UNTS 356. Netherlands. Supplementation
29 Jun 56. Force 29 Jun 56.

102683 Bilateral Agreement **199 UNTS 169**
SIGNED: 10 Jul 54 FORCE: 10 Jul 54
REGISTERED: 5 Oct 54 UK Great Britain
ARTICLES: 10 LANGUAGE: English.
HEADNOTE: REPAYMENT AMORTIZATION
TOPIC: Finance
CONCEPTS: General cooperation. Exchange rates
and regulations. Interest rates. Payment sched-
ules. Lump sum settlements.
INTL ORGS: European Payments Union. Organiza-
tion for Economic Co-operation and Develop-
ment.
PARTIES:
Portugal
UK Great Britain
ANNEX
213 UNTS 402. UK Great Britain. Prolongation
28 Apr 55. Force 28 Apr 55.
213 UNTS 402. Portugal. Prolongation
28 Apr 55. Force 28 Apr 55.

102684 Bilateral Agreement **199 UNTS 181**
SIGNED: 28 Jul 54 FORCE: 28 Jul 54
REGISTERED: 5 Oct 54 UK Great Britain
ARTICLES: 14 LANGUAGE: English.
HEADNOTE: REPAYMENT AMORTIZATION
TOPIC: Finance
CONCEPTS: General cooperation. Exchange rates
and regulations. Interest rates. Payment sched-
ules. Lump sum settlements.
INTL ORGS: European Payments Union. Organiza-
tion for Economic Co-operation and Develop-
ment.
PARTIES:
Sweden
UK Great Britain

102685 Bilateral Agreement **199 UNTS 197**
SIGNED: 16 Jul 54 FORCE: 16 Jul 54
REGISTERED: 5 Oct 54 UK Great Britain
ARTICLES: 9 LANGUAGE: English.
HEADNOTE: REPAYMENT CONSOLIDATION
TOPIC: Claims and Debts
CONCEPTS: Currency. Monetary and gold trans-
fers. Exchange rates and regulations. Financial
programs. Interest rates. Payment schedules.
Debts. Loan repayment.
INTL ORGS: European Payments Union. Organiza-
tion for Economic Co-operation and Develop-
ment.
TREATY REF: UK MISC. NO.4(1950) CMD.8064.
PARTIES:
Switzerland
UK Great Britain
ANNEX
252 UNTS 362. UK Great Britain. Supplementation 29 Jun 56. Force 29 Jun 56.
252 UNTS 362. Switzerland. Supplementation
29 Jun 56. Force 29 Jun 56.
313 UNTS 358. UK Great Britain. Supplementation 31 Mar 58. Force 31 Mar 58.
313 UNTS 358. Switzerland. Supplementation
31 Mar 58. Force 31 Mar 58.

102686 Bilateral Exchange **199 UNTS 211**
SIGNED: 18 Jun 52 FORCE: 27 Jun 52
REGISTERED: 6 Oct 54 USA (United States)
ARTICLES: 2 LANGUAGE: English. Spanish.
HEADNOTE: COOPERATIVE PROGRAM AGRICUL-
TURE
TOPIC: Tech Assistance
CONCEPTS: Time limit. Previous treaty replace-
ment. Currency deposits. Expense sharing for-
mulae. Funding procedures. Agriculture.
TREATY REF: 132UNTS319; 16,UNTS89;
199UNTS349.
PARTIES:
Bolivia
USA (United States)
ANNEX
251 UNTS 393. USA (United States). Prolongation
25 Feb 55. Force 18 Mar 55.
251 UNTS 393. Bolivia. Prolongation 3 Mar 55.
Force 18 Mar 55.

102687 Bilateral Agreement **199 UNTS 221**
SIGNED: 15 Mar 52 FORCE: 19 May 53
REGISTERED: 6 Oct 54 USA (United States)
ARTICLES: 12 LANGUAGE: English. Portuguese.
HEADNOTE: MILITARY ASSISTANCE
TOPIC: Milit Assistance
CONCEPTS: Exceptions and exemptions. Guarantees and safeguards. Non-prejudice to UN charter. Peaceful relations. Border traffic and migration. Privileges and immunities. Conformity with
municipal law. General cooperation. Inspection
and observation. Public information. Use of facilities. Indemnities and reimbursements. Local
currency. Claims and settlements. Most favored
nation clause. Recognition. Customs exemptions. Domestic obligation. Materials, equipment
and services. Aid missions. Joint defense. Defense and security. Military assistance. Return of
equipment and recapture. Security of information. Exchange of defense information. Restrictions on transfer.
PROCEDURE: Amendment.
PARTIES:
Brazil
USA (United States)

102688 Bilateral Agreement **199 UNTS 241**
SIGNED: 30 Jun 52 FORCE: 30 Jun 52
REGISTERED: 6 Oct 54 USA (United States)
ARTICLES: 19 LANGUAGE: English. Spanish.
HEADNOTE: COOPERATIVE PROGRAM TECHNI-
CAL ASSISTANCE MEDIUM SMALL INDUSTRY
TOPIC: Tech Assistance
CONCEPTS: Treaty implementation. Annex type
material. Privileges and immunities. General co-
operation. Exchange of information and docu-
ments. Informational records. Inspection and ob-
servation. Domestic legislation. Operating agen-
cies. Personnel. General property. Title and
deeds. Vocational training. Attachment of funds.
Currency deposits. Exchange rates and regulations. Funding procedures. Garnishment of
funds. Seizure funds. Assets. Domestic obligation. General technical assistance. Assistance.
Materials, equipment and services. Aid missions.
Industry.
TREATY REF: 151UNTS147.
PROCEDURE: Duration. Termination.
PARTIES:
Chile
USA (United States)
ANNEX
239 UNTS 384. USA (United States). Amendment
28 Oct 55. Force 28 Oct 55.
239 UNTS 384. Chile. Amendment 28 Oct 55.
Force 28 Oct 55.
265 UNTS 368. USA (United States). Extension
and Amendment 17 Mar 55. Force 17 Mar 55.
265 UNTS 368. Chile. Extension and Amendment
17 Mar 55. Force 17 Mar 55.

102689 Bilateral Agreement **199 UNTS 267**
SIGNED: 6 Mar 53 FORCE: 10 Jun 53
REGISTERED: 6 Oct 54 USA (United States)
ARTICLES: 11 LANGUAGE: English. Spanish.
HEADNOTE: MILITARY ASSISTANCE
TOPIC: Milit Assistance
CONCEPTS: Exceptions and exemptions. Guaran-
tees and safeguards. Non-prejudice to UN char-
ter. Privileges and immunities. Conformity with

municipal law. General cooperation. Inspection and observation. Public information. Use of facilities. Indemnities and reimbursements. Garnishment of funds. Local currency. Claims and settlements. Most favored nation clause. Recognition. Customs exemptions. Domestic obligation. Materials, equipment and services. Aid missions. Joint defense. Defense and security. Self-defense. Military assistance. Return of equipment and recapture. Security of information. Military assistance missions. Exchange of defense information. Restrictions on transfer.
TREATY REF: 21UNTS77; 26UNTS417.
PROCEDURE: Amendment. Future Procedures Contemplated. Ratification. Registration. Termination.
PARTIES:
Dominican Republic
USA (United States)

102690 Bilateral Agreement **199 UNTS 287**
SIGNED: 16 Jan 53   FORCE: 16 Jan 53
REGISTERED: 6 Oct 54 USA (United States)
ARTICLES: 31 LANGUAGE: English. Spanish.
HEADNOTE: AIR FORCE MISSION
TOPIC: Military Mission
CONCEPTS: Definition of terms. Use of facilities. Compensation. Indemnities and reimbursements. Exchange rates and regulations. Expense sharing formulae. Tax exemptions. Customs exemptions. Military assistance. Military training. Security of information. Airforce-army-navy personnel ratio. Ranks and privileges. Conditions for assistance missions. Third country military personnel. Status of forces.
PROCEDURE: Duration. Renewal or Revival. Termination.
PARTIES:
USA (United States)
Venezuela
ANNEX
279 UNTS 316. USA (United States). Prolongation 11 Feb 57. Force 15 Feb 57.
279 UNTS 316. Venezuela. Prolongation 15 Feb 57. Force 15 Feb 57.
361 UNTS 326. USA (United States). Amendment 31 Mar 59. Force 29 Apr 59.
361 UNTS 326. Venezuela. Amendment 29 Apr 59. Force 29 Apr 59.

102691 Multilateral Agreement **200 UNTS 3**
SIGNED: 20 Sep 51   FORCE: 18 May 54
REGISTERED: 6 Oct 54 USA (United States)
ARTICLES: 27 LANGUAGE: English. French.
HEADNOTE: STATUS NATIONS NATO
TOPIC: IGO Status/Immunit
CONCEPTS: Definition of terms. Diplomatic missions. Inviolability. Property. Diplomatic correspondence. Juridical personality. Procedure. Special status. Status of experts.
PROCEDURE: Denunciation.
PARTIES:
Belgium SIGNED: 20 Sep 51
Canada SIGNED: 20 Sep 51 RATIFIED: 1 Sep 54 FORCE: 1 Sep 54
Denmark SIGNED: 20 Sep 51 RATIFIED: 7 May 52 FORCE: 18 May 54
France SIGNED: 20 Sep 51
Iceland SIGNED: 20 Sep 51 RATIFIED: 11 May 53 FORCE: 18 May 54
Italy SIGNED: 20 Sep 51
Luxembourg SIGNED: 20 Sep 51 RATIFIED: 23 Jul 54 FORCE: 23 Jul 54
Netherlands SIGNED: 20 Sep 51 RATIFIED: 14 Jul 52 FORCE: 18 May 54
Norway SIGNED: 20 Sep 51 RATIFIED: 24 Feb 53 FORCE: 18 May 54
Portugal SIGNED: 20 Sep 51
Turkey SIGNED: 2 Oct 53 RATIFIED: 18 May 54 FORCE: 18 May 54
UK Great Britain SIGNED: 20 Sep 51
USA (United States) SIGNED: 20 Sep 51 RATIFIED: 24 Jul 53 FORCE: 18 May 54
ANNEX
261 UNTS 406. Greece. Signature 6 May 55.
261 UNTS 406. Germany, West. Signature 29 May 56.
261 UNTS 406. Belgium. Qualified Ratification 18 Feb 55.
261 UNTS 406. France. Ratification 20 Jan 55.
261 UNTS 406. Italy. Ratification 9 Mar 55.
261 UNTS 406. Portugal. Ratification 22 Nov 55.

256

261 UNTS 406. UK Great Britain. Ratification 10 Dec 54.
286 UNTS 381. Greece. Ratification 10 Dec 56.
317 UNTS 338. Germany, West. Ratification 25 Jul 58.

102692 Bilateral Exchange **200 UNTS 31**
SIGNED: 22 Oct 46   FORCE: 22 Oct 46
REGISTERED: 11 Oct 54 Sweden
ARTICLES: 2 LANGUAGE: French. Czechoslovakian.
HEADNOTE: VALIDITY PREVIOUSLY CONCLUDED AGREEMENTS
TOPIC: Admin Cooperation
CONCEPTS: Revival of treaties.
TREATY REF: 7LTS97; 36LTS289; 48LTS173; 134LTS135; 171LTS111.
PARTIES:
Czechoslovakia
Sweden

102693 Bilateral Exchange **200 UNTS 39**
SIGNED: 31 May 54   FORCE: 1 Jun 54
REGISTERED: 11 Oct 54 Sweden
ARTICLES: 2 LANGUAGE: German.
HEADNOTE: RECIPROCAL OBLIGATION ACCEPT CERTAIN DEPORTED OTHER COUNTRY
TOPIC: Extradition
CONCEPTS: Territorial application. Extradition, deportation and repatriation.
PARTIES:
Germany, West
Sweden

102694 Bilateral Exchange **200 UNTS 53**
SIGNED: 31 May 54   FORCE: 1 Jun 54
REGISTERED: 11 Oct 54 Denmark
ARTICLES: 2 LANGUAGE: German.
HEADNOTE: DEPORTATION PERSONS
TOPIC: Extradition
CONCEPTS: Territorial application. Extradition, deportation and repatriation.
PARTIES:
Denmark
Germany, West

102695 Bilateral Agreement **200 UNTS 67**
SIGNED: 10 Dec 46   FORCE: 7 Jul 54
REGISTERED: 18 Oct 54 ICAO (Civil Aviat)
ARTICLES: 13 LANGUAGE: Portuguese.
HEADNOTE: AIR TRANSPORT
TOPIC: Air Transport
CONCEPTS: Annex or appendix reference. Previous treaty replacement. Conformity with municipal law. Licenses and permits. Recognition of legal documents. Use of facilities. Arbitration. Procedure. Existing tribunals. Competence of tribunal. Fees and exemptions. Most favored nation clause. National treatment. Customs exemptions. Competency certificate. Routes and logistics. Navigational conditions. Permit designation. Air transport. Airport facilities. Airworthiness certificates. Conditions of airlines operating permission. Operating authorizations and regulations. Licenses and certificates of nationality.
INTL ORGS: International Civil Aviation Organization.
TREATY REF: 171UNTS345.
PROCEDURE: Future Procedures Contemplated. Ratification. Registration. Termination.
PARTIES:
Brazil
Portugal

102696 Bilateral Exchange **200 UNTS 97**
SIGNED: 15 Aug 52   FORCE: 15 Aug 52
REGISTERED: 18 Oct 54 ICAO (Civil Aviat)
ARTICLES: 2 LANGUAGE: English.
HEADNOTE: TEMPORARY AIR AGREEMENT
TOPIC: Air Transport
CONCEPTS: Friendship and amity. Routes and logistics. Permit designation. Air transport.
TREATY REF: 15UNTS295.
PARTIES:
Burma
Philippines

102697 Bilateral Exchange **200 UNTS 103**
SIGNED: 26 Oct 53   FORCE: 1 Nov 53
REGISTERED: 18 Oct 54 ICAO (Civil Aviat)
ARTICLES: 3 LANGUAGE: English.
HEADNOTE: PROVISIONAL AIR TRANSPORT AGREEMENT
TOPIC: Air Transport
CONCEPTS: General cooperation. Licenses and permits. Routes and logistics. Permit designation. Air transport. Operating authorizations and regulations.
TREATY REF: 15UNTS295.
PROCEDURE: Duration. Renewal or Revival.
PARTIES:
Korea, South
Netherlands

102698 Bilateral Exchange **200 UNTS 115**
SIGNED: 7 Jul 54   FORCE: 7 Jul 54
REGISTERED: 18 Oct 54 ICAO (Civil Aviat)
ARTICLES: 4 LANGUAGE: French.
HEADNOTE: ESTABLISHMENT AIR COMMUNICATIONS THAILAND LAOS
TOPIC: Air Transport
CONCEPTS: Routes and logistics. Air transport. Overflights and technical stops.
PROCEDURE: Duration. Renewal or Revival. Termination.
PARTIES:
Laos
Thailand
ANNEX
216 UNTS 422. Thailand. Amendment 1 Jun 55. Force 1 Jun 55.
216 UNTS 422. Laos. Amendment 1 Jun 55. Force 1 Jun 55.

102699 Bilateral Exchange **200 UNTS 121**
SIGNED: 20 Aug 54   FORCE: 20 Aug 54
REGISTERED: 18 Oct 54 ICAO (Civil Aviat)
ARTICLES: 9 LANGUAGE: English.
HEADNOTE: TEMPORARY AIR ARRANGEMENT
TOPIC: Air Transport
CONCEPTS: Detailed regulations. Conformity with municipal law. Exchange of information and documents. Routes and logistics. Permit designation. Air transport. Operating authorizations and regulations.
PARTIES:
Philippines
Sweden
ANNEX
216 UNTS 426. Sweden. Supplementation 20 Oct 54.

102700 Bilateral Agreement **200 UNTS 127**
SIGNED: 2 Sep 53   FORCE: 22 Jul 54
REGISTERED: 19 Oct 54 Belgium
ARTICLES: 16 LANGUAGE: English. French.
HEADNOTE: OFFSHORE PROCUREMENT
TOPIC: Milit Assistance
CONCEPTS: Privileges and immunities. Conformity with municipal law. General cooperation. Exchange of information and documents. Inspection and observation. Licenses and permits. General property. Private contracts. Customs exemptions. Materials, equipment and services. Defense and security. Security of information. Procurement and logistics. Exchange of defense information.
TREATY REF: 19UNTS127; 31UNTS485; 51UNTS213.
PROCEDURE: Future Procedures Contemplated. Ratification.
PARTIES:
Belgium
USA (United States)
ANNEX
233 UNTS 310. Belgium. Supplementation 19 Nov 53. Force 22 Jul 54.
233 UNTS 310. USA (United States). Supplementation 19 Nov 53. Force 22 Jul 54.
237 UNTS 342. Belgium. Amendment 19 Jul 54. Force 19 Jul 54.
237 UNTS 342. USA (United States). Amendment 13 May 54. Force 19 Jul 54.

102701 Multilateral Convention **200 UNTS 149**
SIGNED: 1 Jul 53   FORCE: 29 Sep 54
REGISTERED: 23 Oct 54 UNESCO (Educ/Cult)

ARTICLES: 20 LANGUAGE: English. French.
HEADNOTE: EUROPEAN ORGANIZATION FOR ATOMIC RESEARCH
TOPIC: IGO Establishment
CONCEPTS: Establishment of commission. Procedure. General technical assistance. General. Peaceful use. Establishment. IGO operations.
INTL ORGS: European Organization for Nuclear Research. International Court of Justice. United Nations Educational, Scientific and Cultural Organization.
PROCEDURE: Accession. Ratification.
PARTIES:
Belgium SIGNED: 1 Jul 53 RATIFIED: 19 Jul 54 FORCE: 29 Sep 54
Denmark SIGNED: 23 Dec 53 RATIFIED: 5 Apr 54 FORCE: 29 Sep 54
France SIGNED: 1 Jul 53 RATIFIED: 29 Sep 54 FORCE: 29 Sep 54
Germany, West SIGNED: 1 Jul 53 RATIFIED: 29 Sep 54 FORCE: 29 Sep 54
Greece SIGNED: 1 Jul 53 RATIFIED: 7 Jul 54 FORCE: 29 Sep 54
Italy SIGNED: 1 Jul 53
Netherlands SIGNED: 1 Jul 53 RATIFIED: 15 Jun 54 FORCE: 29 Sep 54
Norway SIGNED: 31 Dec 53 RATIFIED: 4 Oct 54 FORCE: 4 Oct 54
Sweden SIGNED: 1 Jul 53 RATIFIED: 15 Jul 54 FORCE: 29 Sep 54
Switzerland SIGNED: 17 Jul 53 RATIFIED: 12 Feb 54 FORCE: 29 Sep 54
UK Great Britain SIGNED: 1 Jul 53 RATIFIED: 30 Dec 53 FORCE: 29 Sep 54
Yugoslavia SIGNED: 1 Jun 53
ANNEX
204 UNTS 395. Germany, West. Berlin.
207 UNTS 370. Yugoslavia. Ratification 9 Feb 55.
207 UNTS 370. Italy. Ratification 24 Feb 55.
345 UNTS 364. Austria. Accession 10 Nov 59.
431 UNTS 302. Spain. Accession 6 Jun 62.
442 UNTS 322. Yugoslavia. Withdrawal 29 Sep 61. Force 31 Dec 61.

102702 Bilateral Exchange **200 UNTS 181**
SIGNED: 4 Jul 49 FORCE: 5 Jul 49
REGISTERED: 26 Oct 54 USA (United States)
ARTICLES: 9 LANGUAGE: English.
HEADNOTE: FLIGHTS MILITARY AIRCRAFT
TOPIC: Status of Forces
CONCEPTS: Use of facilities. Indemnities and reimbursements. Airport facilities. Overflights and technical stops. Conditions for assistance missions. Status of military forces.
TREATY REF: 185UNTS293.
PROCEDURE: Termination.
PARTIES:
India
USA (United States)

102703 Bilateral Exchange **200 UNTS 191**
SIGNED: 20 Jan 52 FORCE: 20 Jan 52
REGISTERED: 26 Oct 54 USA (United States)
ARTICLES: 2 LANGUAGE: English. Persian.
HEADNOTE: TECHNICAL COOPERATION
TOPIC: Tech Assistance
CONCEPTS: Time limit. Treaty implementation. Privileges and immunities. Conformity with municipal law. General cooperation. Public information. Import quotas. Attachment of funds. Indemnities and reimbursements. Currency deposits. Exchange rates and regulations. Financial programs. Funding procedures. Seizure funds. Local currency. General. Tax exemptions. Customs duties. Customs exemptions. Domestic obligation. General technical assistance. Agriculture. Materials, equipment and services. Aid missions.
PROCEDURE: Termination.
PARTIES:
Iran
USA (United States)

102704 Bilateral Exchange **200 UNTS 201**
SIGNED: 4 Jun 49 FORCE: 4 Jun 49
REGISTERED: 30 Oct 54 USA (United States)
ARTICLES: 2 LANGUAGE: English.
HEADNOTE: CIVIL AIRCRAFT AIR BASES NEWFOUNDLAND
TOPIC: Air Transport
CONCEPTS: Treaty implementation. Conformity with municipal law. Use of facilities. Naviga-

---

tional conditions. Air transport. Airport facilities. Conditions of airlines operating permission. Operating authorizations and regulations. Bases and facilities.
TREATY REF: 204LTS15.
PARTIES:
Canada
USA (United States)

102705 Bilateral Convention **200 UNTS 211**
SIGNED: 24 Mar 50 FORCE: 13 Jul 50
REGISTERED: 30 Oct 54 USA (United States)
ARTICLES: 4 LANGUAGE: English.
HEADNOTE: EXTENSION PORT PRIVILEGES
TOPIC: Customs
CONCEPTS: Customs duties. Ports and pilotage.
PROCEDURE: Duration. Ratification. Termination.
PARTIES:
Canada
USA (United States)

102706 Bilateral Agreement **201 UNTS 3**
SIGNED: 25 Jan 53 FORCE: 25 Jan 53
REGISTERED: 30 Oct 54 USA (United States)
ARTICLES: 5 LANGUAGE: English. Arabic.
HEADNOTE: EDUCATION PROGRAM
TOPIC: Education
CONCEPTS: Conformity with municipal law. Personnel. Specialists exchange. Exchange. Teacher and student exchange. Scholarships and grants. Vocational training. Research and development. Indemnities and reimbursements. Expense sharing formulae. General technical assistance. Agriculture. Materials, equipment and services.
TREATY REF: 140LTS335; 179UNTS230.
PROCEDURE: Duration. Future Procedures Contemplated. Termination.
PARTIES:
Saudi Arabia
USA (United States)

102707 Bilateral Agreement **201 UNTS 15**
SIGNED: 13 Sep 54 FORCE: 1 Oct 54
REGISTERED: 30 Oct 54 Belgium
ARTICLES: 13 LANGUAGE: English. French.
HEADNOTE: AIR SERVICES
TOPIC: Air Transport
CONCEPTS: Definition of terms. Exceptions and exemptions. Exchange of information and documents. Non-interest rates and fees. Routes and logistics. Permit designation. Conditions of airlines operating permission. Operating authorizations and regulations.
PROCEDURE: Termination. Application to Non-self-governing Territories.
PARTIES:
Belgium
South Africa

102708 Bilateral Agreement **201 UNTS 25**
SIGNED: 1 Jun 54 FORCE: 15 Oct 54
REGISTERED: 30 Oct 54 Belgium
ARTICLES: 7 LANGUAGE: French. Danish. Afrikaans. English.
HEADNOTE: CULTURAL AGREEMENT
TOPIC: Culture
CONCEPTS: Definition of terms. Friendship and amity. Non-diplomatic delegations. Conformity with municipal law. Establishment of commission. Exchange. Teacher and student exchange. Scholarships and grants. Exchange. General cultural cooperation. Artists. Scientific exchange. Publications exchange. Mass media exchange.
PROCEDURE: Denunciation. Duration. Ratification. Renewal or Revival. Termination.
PARTIES:
Belgium
South Africa

102709 Bilateral Exchange **201 UNTS 39**
SIGNED: 7 Sep 54 FORCE: 1 Nov 54
REGISTERED: 1 Nov 54 Denmark
ARTICLES: 12 LANGUAGE: German.
HEADNOTE: EXCHANGE STUDENT EMPLOYEES
TOPIC: Non-ILO Labor
CONCEPTS: Definition of terms. Resident permits. Conformity with municipal law. General cooperation. Dispute settlement. Education. Exchange.

Teacher and student exchange. Employment regulations. Wages and salaries. Non-ILO labor relations. Social security. Quotas.
PROCEDURE: Denunciation. Duration. Renewal or Revival.
PARTIES:
Austria
Denmark

102710 Multilateral Agreement **201 UNTS 51**
SIGNED: 19 Aug 54 FORCE: 19 Aug 54
REGISTERED: 1 Nov 54 United Nations
ARTICLES: 6 LANGUAGE: Spanish. English.
HEADNOTE: TECHNICAL ASSISTANCE
TOPIC: Tech Assistance
CONCEPTS: Definition of terms. Guarantees and safeguards. Previous treaty replacement. Privileges and immunities. General cooperation. Exchange of information and documents. Personnel. Responsibility and liability. Title and deeds. Exchange. Scholarships and grants. Vocational training. Research and development. Expense sharing formulae. Local currency. Domestic obligation. Materials, equipment and services. IGO status. Conformity with IGO decisions.
TREATY REF: 761NTS132; 1UNTS15; 1UNTS263; 33UNTS261; 187UNTS9.
PROCEDURE: Amendment. Termination.
PARTIES:
FAO (Food Agri) SIGNED: 19 Aug 54 FORCE: 19 Aug 54
ICAO (Civil Aviat) SIGNED: 19 Aug 54 FORCE: 19 Aug 54
ILO (Labor Org) SIGNED: 19 Aug 54 FORCE: 19 Aug 54
UNESCO (Educ/Cult) SIGNED: 19 Aug 54 FORCE: 19 Aug 54
United Nations SIGNED: 19 Aug 54 FORCE: 19 Aug 54
WHO (World Health) SIGNED: 19 Aug 54 FORCE: 19 Aug 54
Venezuela SIGNED: 19 Aug 54 FORCE: 19 Aug 54

102711 Multilateral Agreement **201 UNTS 75**
SIGNED: 6 Oct 54 FORCE: 6 Oct 54
REGISTERED: 1 Nov 54 United Nations
ARTICLES: 6 LANGUAGE: English.
HEADNOTE: TECHNICAL ASSISTANCE
TOPIC: Tech Assistance
CONCEPTS: Definition of terms. Detailed regulations. Annex or appendix reference. Privileges and immunities. General cooperation. Exchange of information and documents. Personnel. Responsibility and liability. Title and deeds. Use of facilities. Exchange. Scholarships and grants. Vocational training. Research and development. Expense sharing formulae. Local currency. Claims and settlements. Domestic obligation. General technical assistance. Materials, equipment and services. IGO status. Conformity with IGO decisions.
TREATY REF: 76UNTS132; 1UNTS15; 1UNTS263; 15UNTS263.
PROCEDURE: Amendment. Termination. Application to Non-self-governing Territories.
PARTIES:
Netherlands SIGNED: 6 Oct 54 FORCE: 6 Oct 54
FAO (Food Agri) SIGNED: 6 Oct 54 FORCE: 6 Oct 54
ICAO (Civil Aviat) SIGNED: 6 Oct 54 FORCE: 6 Oct 54
ILO (Labor Org) SIGNED: 6 Oct 54 FORCE: 6 Oct 54
UNESCO (Educ/Cult) SIGNED: 6 Oct 54 FORCE: 6 Oct 54
United Nations SIGNED: 6 Oct 54 FORCE: 6 Oct 54
WHO (World Health) SIGNED: 6 Oct 54 FORCE: 6 Oct 54
ANNEX
214 UNTS 378. UNTAB (Tech Assis). Force 31 Aug 55.
214 UNTS 378. Netherlands. Force 31 Aug 55.

102712 Multilateral Agreement **201 UNTS 95**
SIGNED: 27 Oct 54 FORCE: 27 Oct 54
REGISTERED: 1 Nov 54 United Nations
ARTICLES: 6 LANGUAGE: English.
HEADNOTE: REVISED BASIC AGREEMENT TECHNICAL ASSISTANCE

TOPIC: Tech Assistance
CONCEPTS: Definition of terms. Annex or appendix reference. Previous treaty replacement. Privileges and immunities. General cooperation. Exchange of information and documents. Personnel. Responsibility and liability. Title and deeds. Use of facilities. Exchange. Scholarships and grants. Vocational training. Research and development. Exchange rates and regulations. Expense sharing formulae. Local currency. Domestic obligation. General technical assistance. Materials, equipment and services. IGO status. Conformity with IGO decisions.
TREATY REF: ;$.
PROCEDURE: Amendment. Termination.
PARTIES:
   Philippines   SIGNED: 27 Oct 54   FORCE: 27 Oct 54
   FAO (Food Agri) SIGNED: 27 Oct 54 FORCE: 27 Oct 54
   ICAO (Civil Aviat) SIGNED: 27 Oct 54 FORCE: 27 Oct 54
   ILO (Labor Org) SIGNED: 27 Oct 54 FORCE: 27 Oct 54
   UNESCO (Educ/Cult) SIGNED: 27 Oct 54 FORCE: 27 Oct 54
   United Nations SIGNED: 27 Oct 54 FORCE: 27 Oct 54
   WHO (World Health) SIGNED: 27 Oct 54 FORCE: 27 Oct 54
ANNEX
651 UNTS 354. UNIDO (Industrial). Accession 8 Nov 68. Force 8 Nov 68.
651 UNTS 354. ITU (Telecommun). Accession 8 Nov 68. Force 8 Nov 68.
651 UNTS 354. IAEA (Atom Energy). Accession 8 Nov 68. Force 8 Nov 68.
651 UNTS 354. IMCO (Maritime Org). Accession 8 Nov 68. Force 8 Nov 68.
651 UNTS 354. UPU (Postal Union). Accession 8 Nov 68. Force 8 Nov 68.

102713 Multilateral Agreement **201 UNTS 115**
SIGNED: 29 Oct 54   FORCE: 29 Oct 54
REGISTERED: 1 Nov 54 United Nations
ARTICLES: 6 LANGUAGE: English.
HEADNOTE: REVISED BASIC AGREEMENT TECHNICAL ASSISTANCE
TOPIC: Tech Assistance
CONCEPTS: Definition of terms. Annex or appendix reference. Previous treaty replacement. Privileges and immunities. General cooperation. Exchange of information and documents. Personnel. Responsibility and liability. Title and deeds. Use of facilities. Exchange. Scholarships and grants. Vocational training. Research and development. Expense sharing formulae. Local currency. Domestic obligation. General technical assistance. Materials, equipment and services. IGO status. Conformity with IGO decisions.
TREATY REF: 76UNTS132; 1UNTS15; 1UNTS263; 33UNTS261; 81UNTS160.
PROCEDURE: Amendment. Termination.
PARTIES:
   Indonesia SIGNED: 29 Oct 54 FORCE: 29 Oct 54
   FAO (Food Agri) SIGNED: 29 Oct 54 FORCE: 29 Oct 54
   ICAO (Civil Aviat) SIGNED: 29 Oct 54 FORCE: 29 Oct 54
   ILO (Labor Org) SIGNED: 29 Oct 54 FORCE: 29 Oct 54
   UNESCO (Educ/Cult) SIGNED: 29 Oct 54 FORCE: 29 Oct 54
   United Nations SIGNED: 29 Oct 54 FORCE: 29 Oct 54
   WHO (World Health) SIGNED: 29 Oct 54 FORCE: 29 Oct 54
ANNEX
535 UNTS 412. UNTAB (Tech Assis). Termination 30 May 65. Force 17 May 65.
535 UNTS 412. Indonesia. Termination 10 Mar 65. Force 17 May 65.

102714 Bilateral Agreement **201 UNTS 131**
SIGNED: 8 Apr 54   FORCE: 11 May 54
REGISTERED: 3 Nov 54 IBRD (World Bank)
ARTICLES: 7 LANGUAGE: English.
HEADNOTE: LOAN AGREEMENT
TOPIC: IBRD Project
CONCEPTS: Default remedies. Annex or appendix reference. Exchange of information and documents. Informational records. Inspection and ob-

servation. Accounting procedures. Bonds. Fees and exemptions. Interest rates. Tax exemptions. Domestic obligation. Terms of loan. Loan regulations. Loan guarantee. Guarantor non-interference.
PARTIES:
   Norway
   IBRD (World Bank)

102715 Bilateral Agreement **201 UNTS 145**
SIGNED: 23 Jan 53   FORCE: 22 Mar 54
REGISTERED: 5 Nov 54 IBRD (World Bank)
ARTICLES: 8 LANGUAGE: English.
HEADNOTE: LOAN AGREEMENT
TOPIC: IBRD Project
CONCEPTS: Default remedies. Definition of terms. Annex or appendix reference. Exchange of information and documents. Informational records. Inspection and observation. Accounting procedures. Bonds. Fees and exemptions. Interest rates. Tax exemptions. Domestic obligation. Loan regulations. Loan guarantee. Guarantor non-interference.
PARTIES:
   India
   IBRD (World Bank)

102716 Multilateral Agreement **201 UNTS 171**
SIGNED: 2 Oct 54   FORCE: 2 Oct 54
REGISTERED: 8 Nov 54 IBRD (World Bank)
ARTICLES: 3 LANGUAGE: English.
HEADNOTE: GUARANTEE AGREEMENT
TOPIC: IBRD Project
CONCEPTS: Territorial application. Annex type material. Domestic obligation. Loan regulations.
PARTIES:
   Fed Rhod/Nyasaland SIGNED: 2 Oct 54 FORCE: 2 Oct 54
   IBRD (World Bank) SIGNED: 2 Oct 54 FORCE: 2 Oct 54
   Southern Rhodesia SIGNED: 2 Oct 54 FORCE: 2 Oct 54
   UK Great Britain SIGNED: 2 Oct 54 FORCE: 2 Oct 54

102717 Multilateral Agreement **201 UNTS 179**
SIGNED: 2 Oct 54   FORCE: 2 Oct 54
REGISTERED: 8 Nov 54 IBRD (World Bank)
ARTICLES: 3 LANGUAGE: English.
HEADNOTE: GUARANTEE AGREEMENT
TOPIC: IBRD Project
CONCEPTS: Territorial application. Annex type material. Domestic obligation. Loan regulations.
PARTIES:
   Fed Rhod/Nyasaland SIGNED: 2 Oct 54 FORCE: 2 Oct 54
   Northern Rhodesia SIGNED: 2 Oct 54 FORCE: 2 Oct 54
   IBRD (World Bank) SIGNED: 2 Oct 54 FORCE: 2 Oct 54
   Southern Rhodesia SIGNED: 2 Oct 54 FORCE: 2 Oct 54
   UK Great Britain SIGNED: 2 Oct 54 FORCE: 2 Oct 54

102718 Bilateral Agreement **201 UNTS 187**
SIGNED: 8 Jun 53   FORCE: 7 Jan 54
REGISTERED: 18 Nov 54 UK Great Britain
ARTICLES: 18 LANGUAGE: English.
HEADNOTE: SOCIAL SECURITY
TOPIC: Non-ILO Labor
CONCEPTS: Definition of terms. Detailed regulations. Operating agencies. Old age and invalidity insurance. Wages and salaries. Non-ILO labor relations. Family allowances. Administrative cooperation. Old age insurance. Sickness and invalidity insurance. Social security. Unemployment. Payment schedules.
PROCEDURE: Duration. Renewal or Revival. Termination.
PARTIES:
   Australia
   UK Great Britain

102719 Bilateral Agreement **201 UNTS 241**
SIGNED: 18 Dec 52   FORCE: 29 Oct 54
REGISTERED: 20 Nov 54 IBRD (World Bank)
ARTICLES: 5 LANGUAGE: English.
HEADNOTE: GUARANTEE AGREEMENT

TOPIC: IBRD Project
CONCEPTS: Annex or appendix reference. Exchange of information and documents. Informational records. Inspection and observation. Bonds. Fees and exemptions. Tax exemptions. Domestic obligation. Terms of loan. Loan regulations. Loan guarantee. Guarantor non-interference.
PARTIES:
   India
   IBRD (World Bank)

102720 Bilateral Agreement **201 UNTS 277**
SIGNED: 9 Jul 54   FORCE: 9 Jul 54
REGISTERED: 25 Nov 54 UK Great Britain
ARTICLES: 11 LANGUAGE: English. German.
HEADNOTE: REPAYMENT AMORTIZATION
TOPIC: Finance
CONCEPTS: Annex or appendix reference. General cooperation. Exchange rates and regulations. Interest rates. Payment schedules. Lump sum settlements.
INTL ORGS: European Payments Union. Organization for Economic Co-operation and Development.
PARTIES:
   Austria
   UK Great Britain
ANNEX
247 UNTS 462. UK Great Britain. Prolongation 19 Mar 56. Force 19 Mar 56.
247 UNTS 462. Austria. Prolongation 19 Mar 56. Force 19 Mar 56.
258 UNTS 426. UK Great Britain. Prolongation 9 Aug 56. Force 9 Aug 56.
258 UNTS 426. Austria. Prolongation 9 Aug 56. Force 9 Aug 56.
326 UNTS 304. Austria. Supplementation 30 Aug 58. Force 20 Aug 58.
326 UNTS 304. UK Great Britain. Supplementation 9 Aug 58. Force 20 Aug 58.

102721 Bilateral Agreement **201 UNTS 299**
SIGNED: 9 Jul 54   FORCE: 9 Jul 54
REGISTERED: 25 Nov 54 UK Great Britain
ARTICLES: 13 LANGUAGE: English. French.
HEADNOTE: REPAYMENT AMORTIZATION
TOPIC: Finance
CONCEPTS: General cooperation. Exchange rates and regulations. Interest rates. Payment schedules. Lump sum settlements.
INTL ORGS: European Payments Union. Organization for Economic Co-operation and Development.
PARTIES:
   Belgium
   UK Great Britain
ANNEX
249 UNTS 436. UK Great Britain. Supplementation 29 Jun 56. Force 29 Jun 56.
249 UNTS 436. Belgium. Supplementation 29 Jun 56. Force 29 Jun 56.
310 UNTS 374. UK Great Britain. Supplementation 28 Jun 57. Force 1 Jul 57.
310 UNTS 374. Belgium. Supplementation 28 Jun 57. Force 1 Jul 57.

102722 Bilateral Agreement **201 UNTS 317**
SIGNED: 30 Jul 54   FORCE: 30 Jul 54
REGISTERED: 25 Nov 54 UK Great Britain
ARTICLES: 20 LANGUAGE: English. Arabic.
HEADNOTE: ARBITRATION
TOPIC: Dispute Settlement
CONCEPTS: Treaty interpretation. Exchange of information and documents. Recognition of legal documents. Establishment of commission. Arbitration. Special tribunals. Competence of tribunal. Wages and salaries. Indemnities and reimbursements.
INTL ORGS: International Court of Justice. Arbitration Commission.
PARTIES:
   Saudi Arabia
   UK Great Britain

102723 Bilateral Exchange **201 UNTS 349**
SIGNED: 4 Oct 54   FORCE: 4 Oct 54
REGISTERED: 2 Dec 54 Australia
ARTICLES: 2 LANGUAGE: English. French.

HEADNOTE: EXCHANGE OFFICIAL PUBLICA-
TIONS
TOPIC: Admin Cooperation
CONCEPTS: Annex or appendix reference. Ex-
change of official publications. Operating agen-
cies. Indemnities and reimbursements.
PARTIES:
Australia
Vietnam, South

102724 Bilateral Exchange **201 UNTS 359**
SIGNED: 3 Nov 54 FORCE: 1 Oct 53
REGISTERED: 3 Dec 54 Belgium
ARTICLES: 2 LANGUAGE: French. German.
HEADNOTE: RE-ENTRY FORCE
TOPIC: Admin Cooperation
CONCEPTS: Revival of treaties.
TREATY REF: 67LTS63.
PARTIES:
Belgium
Germany, West
ANNEX
212 UNTS 378. Belgium. Acknowledgement
21 May 55. Force 1 Oct 53.
212 UNTS 378. Germany, West. Berlin. Force
1 Oct 53.

102725 Bilateral Agreement **202 UNTS 3**
SIGNED: 14 Aug 53 FORCE: 1 Nov 54
REGISTERED: 3 Dec 54 Denmark
ARTICLES: 48 LANGUAGE: Danish. German.
HEADNOTE: SOCIAL SECURITY
TOPIC: Non-ILO Labor
CONCEPTS: Territorial application. General provi-
sions. Conformity with municipal law. General
cooperation. Operating agencies. Dispute settle-
ment. Old age and invalidity insurance. Non-ILO
labor relations. Family allowances. Administra-
tive cooperation. Old age insurance. Sickness
and invalidity insurance. Social security. Mone-
tary and gold transfers. Exchange rates and regu-
lations. Payment schedules. National treatment.
PROCEDURE: Denunciation. Duration. Ratification.
Renewal or Revival.
PARTIES:
Denmark
Germany, West

102726 Bilateral Exchange **202 UNTS 109**
SIGNED: 23 Nov 54 FORCE: 1 Sep 54
REGISTERED: 11 Dec 54 Belgium
ARTICLES: 2 LANGUAGE: French. German.
HEADNOTE: RENEWAL TREATY
TOPIC: Admin Cooperation
CONCEPTS: Revival of treaties.
TREATY REF: 58LTS285.
PARTIES:
Belgium
Germany, West

102727 Bilateral Exchange **202 UNTS 115**
SIGNED: 30 Apr 54 FORCE: 4 Nov 54
REGISTERED: 30 Dec 54 Netherlands
ARTICLES: 2 LANGUAGE: French.
HEADNOTE: DELIVERY DUPLICATES LOOTED
TRANSFERABLE SECURITIES
TOPIC: Reparations
CONCEPTS: Recognition of legal documents. Ac-
counting procedures. Indemnities and reim-
bursements. Post-war claims settlement.
PARTIES:
France
Netherlands

102728 Bilateral Exchange **202 UNTS 123**
SIGNED: 20 Nov 54 FORCE: 20 Nov 54
REGISTERED: 30 Dec 54 United Nations
ARTICLES: 2 LANGUAGE: French.
HEADNOTE: REFUGEE AGREEMENT
TOPIC: Direct Aid
CONCEPTS: Annex or appendix reference. Assis-
tance. Privileges and immunities. Responsibility
and liability. Indemnities and reimbursements.
Financial programs. Commodities and services.
IGO status.
TREATY REF: 1UNTS15.
PARTIES:
Lebanon
UN Relief Palestin

102729 Bilateral Agreement **202 UNTS 135**
SIGNED: 31 Dec 54 FORCE: 31 Dec 54
REGISTERED: 31 Dec 54 United Nations
ARTICLES: 11 LANGUAGE: English.
HEADNOTE: ACTIVITIES UNICEF
TOPIC: Direct Aid
CONCEPTS: Treaty implementation. Privileges and
immunities. Exchange of information and docu-
ments. Informational records. Inspection and ob-
servation. Public information. Responsibility and
liability. Procedure. Existing tribunals. Export
quotas. Indemnities and reimbursements. Finan-
cial programs. Local currency. Claims and settle-
ments. Tax exemptions. Customs exemptions.
Commodities and services. Assistance. General
aid. Distribution.
TREATY REF: 1UNTS15.
PROCEDURE: Duration.
PARTIES:
Netherlands
UNICEF (Children)
ANNEX
223 UNTS 380. UNICEF (Children). Force
13 Dec 55.
223 UNTS 380. Netherlands. Force 13 Dec 55.

102730 Bilateral Exchange **202 UNTS 151**
SIGNED: 28 Jan 50 FORCE: 28 Jan 50
REGISTERED: 5 Nov 55 Norway
ARTICLES: 2 LANGUAGE: Swedish. Norwegian.
HEADNOTE: EXTENSION SWEDISH TERRITORY
ROAD FROM KVELI TO TUNSJO NORWAY
TOPIC: Land Transport
CONCEPTS: Annex type material. Funding proce-
dures. Roads and highways.
TREATY REF: 68UNTS209.
PARTIES:
Norway
Sweden

102731 Bilateral Convention **202 UNTS 157**
SIGNED: 14 Mar 52 FORCE: 24 Sep 52
REGISTERED: 5 Jan 55 Sweden
ARTICLES: 37 LANGUAGE: English. Swedish.
HEADNOTE: CONSULAR
TOPIC: Consul/Citizenship
CONCEPTS: Alien status. General consular func-
tions. Consular relations establishment. Diplo-
matic missions. Inviolability. Privileges and im-
munities. Property. Diplomatic correspondence.
Consular functions in shipping. Consular func-
tions in property. Notarial acts and services. Pro-
cedure. Existing tribunals.
INTL ORGS: International Court of Justice.
PROCEDURE: Ratification. Termination.
PARTIES:
Sweden
UK Great Britain
ANNEX
204 UNTS 396. UK Great Britain. Supplementation 21 Aug 52.
204 UNTS 396. Sweden. Supplementation
21 Aug 52.

102732 Multilateral Agreement **202 UNTS 241**
SIGNED: 23 Mar 53 FORCE: 1 Mar 54
REGISTERED: 5 Jan 55 Sweden
ARTICLES: 3 LANGUAGE: Swedish. Danish. Fin-
nish. Icelandic. Norwegian.
HEADNOTE: CHANGES IN TEXT
TOPIC: Admin Cooperation
CONCEPTS: Annex type material.
TREATY REF: 126LTS121.
PARTIES:
Denmark SIGNED: 26 Mar 53 RATIFIED:
2 Feb 54 FORCE: 1 Mar 54
Finland SIGNED: 26 Mar 53 RATIFIED: 2 Feb 54
FORCE: 1 Mar 54
Iceland SIGNED: 26 Mar 53 RATIFIED: 2 Feb 54
FORCE: 1 Mar 54
Norway SIGNED: 26 Mar 53 RATIFIED: 2 Feb 54
FORCE: 1 Mar 54
Sweden SIGNED: 26 Mar 53 RATIFIED: 2 Feb 54
FORCE: 1 Mar 54

102733 Bilateral Agreement **202 UNTS 259**
SIGNED: 29 Sep 54 FORCE: 1 Jan 55
REGISTERED: 5 Jan 55 Sweden
ARTICLES: 6 LANGUAGE: Swedish. Russian.
HEADNOTE: SAVING LIVES BALTIC SEA

TOPIC: Humanitarian
CONCEPTS: Detailed regulations. Previous treaty
replacement. Conformity with municipal law. Ex-
change of information and documents. Operat-
ing agencies. Use of facilities. Humanitarian mat-
ters. Air transport. Merchant vessels. Bands and
frequency allocation. Communications linkage.
TREATY REF: 3'7DEMARTENS728; 205LTS220;
164UNTS113; 167UNTS338.
PROCEDURE: Denunciation. Duration. Renewal or
Revival.
PARTIES:
Sweden
USSR (Soviet Union)

102734 Bilateral Agreement **202 UNTS 273**
SIGNED: 13 Oct 54 FORCE: 13 Oct 54
REGISTERED: 5 Jan 55 Sweden
ARTICLES: 15 LANGUAGE: English.
HEADNOTE: TECHNICAL ASSISTANCE FIELD VO-
CATIONAL TECHNOLOGICAL EDUCATION
TOPIC: Tech Assistance
CONCEPTS: Conditions. Detailed regulations. An-
nex or appendix reference. General property. Ti-
tle and deeds. Procedure. Exchange. Teacher
and student exchange. Institute establishment.
Scholarships and grants. Vocational training. Ex-
pense sharing formulae. Tax exemptions. Cus-
toms exemptions. Domestic obligation. General
technical assistance. Materials, equipment and
services.
PROCEDURE: Amendment. Duration. Renewal or
Revival. Termination.
PARTIES:
Ethiopia
Sweden

102735 Bilateral Agreement **202 UNTS 289**
SIGNED: 12 Oct 54 FORCE: 12 Oct 54
REGISTERED: 17 Jan 55 Belgium
ARTICLES: 9 LANGUAGE: French. English.
HEADNOTE: PATENT RIGHTS TECHNICAL INFOR-
MATION
TOPIC: Patents/Copyrights
CONCEPTS: Definition of terms. Previous treaty re-
nunciation. Responsibility and liability. Compen-
sation. Laws and formalities. Exchange of de-
fense information. Equipment and supplies.
INTL ORGS: Special Commission.
TREATY REF: 51UNTS213.
PROCEDURE: Termination.
PARTIES:
Belgium
USA (United States)

102736 Bilateral Agreement **202 UNTS 301**
SIGNED: 19 May 54 FORCE: 19 May 54
REGISTERED: 19 Jan 55 Pakistan
ARTICLES: 7 LANGUAGE: English.
HEADNOTE: MUTUAL DEFENSE ASSISTANCE
TOPIC: Milit Assistance
CONCEPTS: Exceptions and exemptions. Non-
prejudice to UN charter. Peaceful relations. Privileges and immunities. Conformity with municipal law. Inspection and observation. Public information. Use of facilities. Indemnities and
reimbursements. Garnishment of funds. Local
currency. Tax exemptions. Recognition. Customs exemptions. Domestic obligation. Materials, equipment and services. Aid missions. Self-
defense. Military assistance. Return of equipment and recapture. Security of information.
Military assistance missions. Exchange of defense information. Restrictions on transfer. Raw
materials.
INTL ORGS: United Nations.
PROCEDURE: Amendment. Future Procedures
Contemplated. Registration. Termination.
PARTIES:
Pakistan
USA (United States)
ANNEX
280 UNTS 368. USA (United States). Implementation 15 Mar 56. Force 15 May 56.
280 UNTS 368. Pakistan. Implementation
15 May 56. Force 15 May 56.

102737 Bilateral Exchange **202 UNTS 313**
SIGNED: 6 Dec 54 FORCE: 6 Dec 54
REGISTERED: 20 Jan 55 Norway

ARTICLES: 2 LANGUAGE: French.
HEADNOTE: EXEMPTION MILITARY SERVICE
TOPIC: Milit Servic/Citiz
CONCEPTS: Foreign nationals.
PARTIES:
France
Norway

102738 Bilateral Agreement **203 UNTS 3**
SIGNED: 10 Sep 53   FORCE: 21 Dec 54
REGISTERED: 27 Jan 55 IBRD (World Bank)
ARTICLES: 9 LANGUAGE: English.
HEADNOTE: LOAN AGREEMENT
TOPIC: IBRD Project
CONCEPTS: Default remedies. Definition of terms.
Annex or appendix reference. Exchange of infor-
mation and documents. Informational records.
Inspection and observation. Accounting proce-
dures. Bonds. Fees and exemptions. Interest
rates. Tax exemptions. Domestic obligation.
Terms of loan. Loan regulations. Loan guarantee.
Guarantor non-interference. Roads and high-
ways.
PARTIES:
Colombia
IBRD (World Bank)

102739 Bilateral Agreement **203 UNTS 37**
SIGNED: 12 Oct 54   FORCE: 13 Jan 55
REGISTERED: 27 Jan 55 IBRD (World Bank)
ARTICLES: 8 LANGUAGE: English.
HEADNOTE: LOAN COASTAL HIGHWAY
TOPIC: IBRD Project
CONCEPTS: Default remedies. Definition of terms.
Annex or appendix reference. Exchange of infor-
mation and documents. Informational records.
Inspection and observation. Accounting proce-
dures. Bonds. Fees and exemptions. Interest
rates. Domestic obligation. Terms of loan. Loan
regulations. Loan guarantee. Guarantor non-
interference. Roads and highways.
PARTIES:
El Salvador
IBRD (World Bank)

102740 Bilateral Exchange **203 UNTS 59**
SIGNED: 30 Aug 54   FORCE: 1 Oct 54
REGISTERED: 2 Feb 55 Pakistan
ARTICLES: 2 LANGUAGE: English.
HEADNOTE: ABOLITION VISAS
TOPIC: Visas
CONCEPTS: Time limit. Visa abolition. Passports
non-diplomatic. Denial of admission. Resident
permits. Conformity with municipal law. Fees
and exemptions.
PARTIES:
Denmark
Pakistan

102741 Bilateral Treaty **203 UNTS 73**
SIGNED: 11 Jul 52   FORCE: 29 Apr 54
REGISTERED: 2 Feb 55 India
ARTICLES: 7 LANGUAGE: English. Hindi.
HEADNOTE: FRIENDSHIP
TOPIC: General Amity
CONCEPTS: Friendship and amity. Alien status.
Consular relations establishment. Diplomatic re-
lations establishment. Privileges and immuni-
ties. Immovable property. General property. Ar-
bitration. Mediation and good offices. Proce-
dure. Domestic jurisdiction. Existing tribunals.
INTL ORGS: International Court of Justice.
PROCEDURE: Future Procedures Contemplated.
Ratification.
PARTIES:
India
Philippines

102742 Bilateral Agreement **203 UNTS 85**
SIGNED: 30 Dec 49   FORCE: 21 May 54
REGISTERED: 2 Feb 55 Netherlands
ARTICLES: 26 LANGUAGE: French. Dutch.
HEADNOTE: DOUBLE TAXATION TAXES INCOME
TOPIC: Taxation
CONCEPTS: Definition of terms. Territorial applica-
tion. Conformity with municipal law. Exchange
of official publications. Teacher and student ex-
change. Claims and settlements. Taxation. Tax

credits. Equitable taxes. General. Tax exemp-
tions.
PROCEDURE: Duration. Ratification. Termination.
PARTIES:
France
Netherlands

102743 Bilateral Agreement **203 UNTS 133**
SIGNED: 30 Dec 49   FORCE: 22 May 54
REGISTERED: 2 Feb 55 Netherlands
ARTICLES: 9 LANGUAGE: French. Dutch.
HEADNOTE: DOUBLE TAXATION TAXES PROP-
ERTY
TOPIC: Taxation
CONCEPTS: Conformity with municipal law. Do-
mestic legislation. Taxation. General.
PARTIES:
France
Netherlands

102744 Bilateral Treaty **203 UNTS 155**
SIGNED: 2 Feb 51   FORCE: 9 Jun 52
REGISTERED: 7 Feb 55 India
ARTICLES: 12 LANGUAGE: English. French.
HEADNOTE: CESSION TERRITORY FREE TOWN OF
CHANDERNAGORE
TOPIC: Territory Boundary
CONCEPTS: Annex or appendix reference. Nation-
ality and citizenship. Arbitration. Negotiation. As-
sets transfer. Paragraph 2, Article 36. Changes
of territory.
INTL ORGS: International Court of Justice.
PROCEDURE: Ratification. Registration.
PARTIES:
France
India

102745 Bilateral Agreement **203 UNTS 167**
SIGNED: 8 May 54   FORCE: 23 Jun 54
REGISTERED: 8 Feb 55 Pakistan
ARTICLES: 14 LANGUAGE: English.
HEADNOTE: RECOVERY ABDUCTED PERSONS
TOPIC: Extradition
CONCEPTS: Detailed regulations. Previous treaty
amendment. Treaty implementation. Establish-
ment of commission.
PARTIES:
India
Pakistan

102746 Multilateral Agreement **203 UNTS 179**
SIGNED: 23 Mar 49   FORCE: 1 Jul 49
REGISTERED: 11 Feb 55 USA (United States)
ARTICLES: 23 LANGUAGE: English. French. Span-
ish.
HEADNOTE: INTERNATIONAL WHEAT AGREE-
MENT
TOPIC: Commodity Trade
CONCEPTS: Definition of terms. Detailed regula-
tions. Exceptions and exemptions. Territorial ap-
plication. General provisions. Annex or appendix
reference. Responsibility and liability. Investiga-
tion of violations. Procedure. General trade.
Trade agencies. Balance of payments. Invest-
ments. Non-interest rates and fees. Commodity
trade. Quotas.
INTL ORGS: General Agreement on Tariffs and
Trade. United Nations. International Wheat
Council. Special Commission.
PROCEDURE: Amendment. Accession. Duration.
Ratification.
PARTIES:
Australia   SIGNED: 23 Mar 49   RATIFIED:
30 Jun 49 FORCE: 1 Jul 49
Austria   SIGNED: 23 Mar 49   RATIFIED:
29 Jun 49 FORCE: 1 Jul 49
Belgium   SIGNED: 23 Mar 49   RATIFIED:
17 Jun 49 FORCE: 1 Jul 49
Bolivia SIGNED: 13 Apr 49 RATIFIED: 26 Sep 49
FORCE: 26 Sep 49
Brazil SIGNED: 25 Mar 49 RATIFIED: 28 Oct 49
FORCE: 28 Oct 49
Canada   SIGNED: 23 Mar 49   RATIFIED:
12 May 49 FORCE: 1 Jul 49
Ceylon (Sri Lanka) SIGNED: 23 Mar 49 RATI-
FIED: 16 Jun 49 FORCE: 1 Jul 49
Taiwan SIGNED: 23 Mar 49
Colombia SIGNED: 23 Mar 49
Costa Rica   RATIFIED: 10 Apr 50   FORCE:
17 Apr 50

Cuba SIGNED: 23 Mar 49 RATIFIED: 27 Oct 49
FORCE: 27 Oct 49
Denmark   SIGNED: 23 Mar 49   RATIFIED:
21 Jun 49 FORCE: 1 Jul 49
Dominican Republic SIGNED: 23 Mar 49 RATI-
FIED: 5 Sep 49 FORCE: 5 Sep 49
Ecuador SIGNED: 14 Apr 49 RATIFIED: 3 Oct 49
FORCE: 3 Oct 49
United Arab Rep SIGNED: 23 Mar 49 RATIFIED:
24 Aug 49 FORCE: 24 Aug 49
El Salvador SIGNED: 23 Mar 49 RATIFIED:
22 Sep 49 FORCE: 22 Sep 49
France SIGNED: 23 Mar 49 RATIFIED: 1 Jul 49
FORCE: 1 Jul 49
Germany, West RATIFIED: 15 May 50 FORCE:
15 May 50
Greece   SIGNED: 23 Mar 49   RATIFIED:
30 Jun 49 FORCE: 1 Jul 49
Guatemala   SIGNED: 23 Mar 49   RATIFIED:
14 Nov 49 FORCE: 14 Nov 49
Haiti RATIFIED: 23 Nov 49 FORCE: 23 Nov 49
Honduras   RATIFIED: 23 Jan 51   FORCE:
23 Jan 51
Iceland RATIFIED: 2 Jan 51 FORCE: 2 Jan 51
India SIGNED: 23 Mar 49 RATIFIED: 30 Jun 49
FORCE: 1 Jul 49
Indonesia RATIFIED: 2 Nov 50 FORCE: 2 Nov 50
Ireland   SIGNED: 23 Mar 49   RATIFIED:
27 Jun 49 FORCE: 1 Jul 49
Israel SIGNED: 23 Mar 49 RATIFIED: 28 Jun 49
FORCE: 1 Jul 49
Italy SIGNED: 23 Mar 49 RATIFIED: 7 Jul 49
FORCE: 7 Jul 49
Japan RATIFIED: 23 Jul 51 FORCE: 23 Jul 51
Lebanon   SIGNED: 23 Mar 49   RATIFIED:
30 Jun 49 FORCE: 1 Jul 49
Liberia SIGNED: 23 Mar 49 RATIFIED: 19 Jun 50
FORCE: 1 Jul 49
Mexico   SIGNED: 15 Apr 49   RATIFIED:
16 Sep 49 FORCE: 16 Sep 49
Netherlands SIGNED: 23 Mar 49 RATIFIED:
29 Jun 49 FORCE: 1 Jul 49
New Zealand SIGNED: 25 Mar 49 RATIFIED:
27 Jun 49 FORCE: 1 Jul 49
Nicaragua   SIGNED: 23 Mar 49   RATIFIED:
31 Oct 49 FORCE: 31 Oct 49
Norway SIGNED: 13 Apr 49 RATIFIED: 1 Aug 49
FORCE: 1 Aug 49
Panama   SIGNED: 12 Apr 49   RATIFIED:
31 Oct 49 FORCE: 31 Oct 49
Peru SIGNED: 15 Apr 49 RATIFIED: 29 Jun 49
FORCE: 1 Jul 49
Philippines   SIGNED: 23 Mar 49   RATIFIED:
27 Feb 50 FORCE: 27 Feb 50
Portugal   SIGNED: 23 Mar 49   RATIFIED:
30 Jun 49 FORCE: 1 Jul 49
Saudi Arabia SIGNED: 23 Mar 49 RATIFIED:
30 Jun 49 FORCE: 1 Jul 49
South Africa SIGNED: 23 Mar 49 RATIFIED:
29 Jun 49 FORCE: 1 Jul 49
Spain RATIFIED: 11 Aug 50 FORCE: 11 Aug 50
Sweden   SIGNED: 11 Apr 49   RATIFIED:
28 Jun 49 FORCE: 1 Jul 49
Switzerland   SIGNED: 11 Apr 49   RATIFIED:
28 Jun 49 FORCE: 1 Jul 49
UK Great Britain SIGNED: 23 Mar 49 RATIFIED:
27 Jun 49 FORCE: 1 Jul 49
USA (United States) SIGNED: 23 Mar 49 RATI-
FIED: 17 Jun 49 FORCE: 1 Jul 49
Uruguay SIGNED: 23 Mar 49
Venezuela   SIGNED: 12 Apr 49   RATIFIED:
1 Aug 49 FORCE: 1 Aug 49
ANNEX
256 UNTS 364. Italy. Accession 10 Dec 54.

102747 Bilateral Agreement **204 UNTS 3**
SIGNED: 12 Mar 53   FORCE: 12 Mar 53
REGISTERED: 11 Feb 55 USA (United States)
ARTICLES: 12 LANGUAGE: English. Arabic.
HEADNOTE: COOPERATIVE PROGRAM PUBLIC
WORKS DEVELOPMENT
TOPIC: Tech Assistance
CONCEPTS: Time limit. Treaty implementation.
Annex type material. Privileges and immunities.
General cooperation. Exchange of information
and documents. Informational records. Inspec-
tion and observation. Domestic legislation. Oper-
ating agencies. General property. Vocational
training. Research and development. Attach-
ment of funds. Currency deposits. Exchange
rates and regulations. Expense sharing formulae.
Funding procedures. Garnishment of funds. Seizure funds. Assets. Tax exemptions. Customs ex-

emptions. Domestic obligation. Agriculture. Assistance. Aid missions. Irrigation. Natural resources. Hydro-electric power. Regulation of natural resources.
INTL ORGS: Special Commission.
TREATY REF: 198UNTS265.
PROCEDURE: Duration. Future Procedures Contemplated. Termination.
PARTIES:
United Arab Rep
USA (United States)

102748   Bilateral Agreement   **204 UNTS 29**
SIGNED: 21 May 53   FORCE: 21 May 53
REGISTERED: 11 Feb 55 USA (United States)
ARTICLES: 12 LANGUAGE: English. Arabic.
HEADNOTE: AGRICULTURAL FORESTRY FISHERIES PROGRAM AGREEMENT
TOPIC: Tech Assistance
CONCEPTS: Time limit. Treaty implementation. Annex type material. Privileges and immunities. General cooperation. Exchange of information and documents. Informational records. Inspection and observation. Domestic legislation. Operating agencies. Personnel. General property. Title and deeds. Vocational training. Research and development. Attachment of funds. Currency deposits. Exchange rates and regulations. Expense sharing formulae. Funding procedures. Garnishment of funds. Seizure funds. Assets. Customs exemptions. Agriculture. Assistance. Materials, equipment and services. Aid missions. Ocean resources.
INTL ORGS: Special Commission.
TREATY REF: 198UNTS265.
PROCEDURE: Duration. Termination. Application to Non-self-governing Territories.
PARTIES:
United Arab Rep
USA (United States)

102749   Bilateral Agreement   **204 UNTS 55**
SIGNED: 18 Jun 53   FORCE: 18 Jun 53
REGISTERED: 11 Feb 55 USA (United States)
ARTICLES: 12 LANGUAGE: English. Arabic.
HEADNOTE: EDUCATION PROGRAM
TOPIC: Education
CONCEPTS: Definition of terms. Friendship and amity. Alien status. Privileges and immunities. Conformity with municipal law. Inspection and observation. Personnel. General property. Private contracts. Exchange. Commissions and foundations. Teacher and student exchange. Institute establishment. Vocational training. Research cooperation. Research and development. Accounting procedures. Indemnities and reimbursements. Currency. Exchange rates and regulations. Financial programs. Funding procedures. Customs exemptions. General technical assistance. Aid missions.
INTL ORGS: Special Commission.
TREATY REF: 198UNTS265.
PROCEDURE: Duration. Termination.
PARTIES:
United Arab Rep
USA (United States)

102750   Bilateral Exchange   **204 UNTS 79**
SIGNED: 9 Apr 53   FORCE: 9 Apr 53
REGISTERED: 11 Feb 55 USA (United States)
ARTICLES: 7 LANGUAGE: English. German.
HEADNOTE: CULTURAL RELATIONS
TOPIC: Culture
CONCEPTS: Territorial application. Friendship and amity. Conformity with municipal law. Exchange of information and documents. Establishment of commission. Teacher and student exchange. Scholarships and grants. Exchange. General cultural cooperation. Artists. Scientific exchange.
PARTIES:
Germany, West
USA (United States)

102751   Bilateral Exchange   **204 UNTS 87**
SIGNED: 14 Oct 54   FORCE: 14 Oct 54
REGISTERED: 11 Feb 55 UK Great Britain
ARTICLES: 4 LANGUAGE: English. German.
HEADNOTE: VALIDATION FOREIGN CURRENCY BONDS
TOPIC: Claims and Debts

CONCEPTS: Annex or appendix reference. General cooperation. Negotiation.
PARTIES:
Austria
UK Great Britain

102752   Multilateral Agreement   **204 UNTS 99**
SIGNED: 30 Jun 54   FORCE: 30 Jun 54
REGISTERED: 11 Feb 55 UK Great Britain
ARTICLES: 7 LANGUAGE: English. French.
HEADNOTE: ARCHIVES ALLIED HIGH COMMISSION
TOPIC: Admin Cooperation
CONCEPTS: General cooperation. Information centers. Exchange of information and documents.
PROCEDURE: Termination.
PARTIES:
France SIGNED: 30 Jun 54 FORCE: 30 Jun 54
UK Great Britain SIGNED: 30 Jun 54 FORCE: 30 Jun 54
USA (United States) SIGNED: 30 Jun 54 FORCE: 30 Jun 54
ANNEX
341 UNTS 386. USA (United States). Amendment 5 Mar 59. Force 5 Mar 59.
341 UNTS 386. UK Great Britain. Amendment 5 Mar 59. Force 5 Mar 59.
341 UNTS 386. France. Amendment 5 Mar 59. Force 5 Mar 59.

102753   Bilateral Exchange   **204 UNTS 123**
SIGNED: 12 Jul 54   FORCE: 12 Jul 54
REGISTERED: 11 Feb 55 UK Great Britain
ARTICLES: 1 LANGUAGE: English.
HEADNOTE: TECHNICAL ASSISTANCE BRITISH GUIANA
TOPIC: Tech Assistance
CONCEPTS: General technical assistance. Assistance.
TREATY REF: 71UNTS105.
PARTIES:
UK Great Britain
USA (United States)
ANNEX
357 UNTS 374. UK Great Britain. Prolongation 22 Jun 59. Force 30 Jun 59.
357 UNTS 374. USA (United States). Prolongation 30 Jun 59. Force 30 Jun 59.
529 UNTS 324. UK Great Britain. Prolongation 22 Jun 64. Force 29 Jun 64.
529 UNTS 324. USA (United States). Prolongation 29 Jun 64. Force 29 Jun 64.

102754   Bilateral Exchange   **204 UNTS 131**
SIGNED: 25 Oct 54   FORCE: 29 Oct 54
REGISTERED: 11 Feb 55 UK Great Britain
ARTICLES: 7 LANGUAGE: English.
HEADNOTE: PAYMENT ARRANGEMENTS
TOPIC: Finance
CONCEPTS: Definition of terms. Conformity with municipal law. Accounting procedures. Currency. Payment schedules. Assets transfer.
TREATY REF: 2UNTS39; 19UNTS280; 141UNTS355.
PROCEDURE: Ratification. Termination.
PARTIES:
Iran
UK Great Britain

102755   Bilateral Agreement   **204 UNTS 137**
SIGNED: 11 Nov 54   FORCE: 11 Nov 54
REGISTERED: 11 Feb 55 UK Great Britain
ARTICLES: 12 LANGUAGE: English. Polish.
HEADNOTE: SETTLEMENT FINANCIAL MATTERS
TOPIC: Finance
CONCEPTS: Definition of terms. Detailed regulations. General cooperation. Exchange of information and documents. Informational records. Expropriation. General property. Accounting procedures. Fees and exemptions. Financial programs. Payment schedules. Claims and settlements.
TREATY REF: 83UNTS3; 204UNTS148; 1262LTS159; 83UNTS51.
PARTIES:
Poland
UK Great Britain

102756   Bilateral Exchange   **204 UNTS 177**
SIGNED: 16 Nov 54   FORCE: 16 Dec 54
REGISTERED: 11 Feb 55 UK Great Britain
ARTICLES: 9 LANGUAGE: English.
HEADNOTE: RECIPROCAL ABOLITION VISAS
TOPIC: Visas
CONCEPTS: Emergencies. Territorial application. Time limit. Visa abolition. Passports non-diplomatic. Denial of admission. Conformity with municipal law.
PROCEDURE: Denunciation.
PARTIES:
Finland
UK Great Britain
ANNEX
267 UNTS 386. UK Great Britain. Gibralter. Force 20 Jul 55.
326 UNTS 308. Finland. Amendment 1 Jul 58. Force 1 Jul 58.
326 UNTS 308. UK Great Britain. Amendment 1 Jul 58. Force 1 Jul 58.

102757   Bilateral Exchange   **204 UNTS 183**
SIGNED: 23 Nov 54   FORCE: 1 Jan 55
REGISTERED: 11 Feb 55 UK Great Britain
ARTICLES: 9 LANGUAGE: English. Portuguese.
HEADNOTE: RECIPROCAL ABOLITION VISAS
TOPIC: Visas
CONCEPTS: Territorial application. Visa abolition. Denial of admission. Resident permits. Conformity with municipal law.
PARTIES:
Portugal
UK Great Britain
ANNEX
267 UNTS 386. UK Great Britain. Gibralter. Force 20 Jul 55.

102758   Bilateral Agreement   **204 UNTS 195**
SIGNED: 17 Jan 55   FORCE: 17 Jan 55
REGISTERED: 11 Feb 55 UK Great Britain
ARTICLES: 9 LANGUAGE: English.
HEADNOTE: STERLING PAYMENTS UK EXPORTERS MERCHANTS
TOPIC: Finance
CONCEPTS: Definition of terms. Detailed regulations. General cooperation. Exchange of information and documents. Informational records. Licenses and permits. General trade. Export quotas. Import quotas. Accounting procedures. Banking. Balance of payments. Financial programs. Payment schedules. Assets transfer. Commodity trade. Quotas.
PARTIES:
Turkey
UK Great Britain
ANNEX
269 UNTS 360. Turkey. Amendment 28 Feb 57. Force 28 Feb 57.
269 UNTS 360. UK Great Britain. Amendment 28 Feb 57. Force 28 Feb 57.

102759   Bilateral Convention   **204 UNTS 207**
SIGNED: 23 Dec 53   FORCE: 3 Jun 54
REGISTERED: 16 Feb 55 Syria
ARTICLES: 55 LANGUAGE: Arabic.
HEADNOTE: JUDICIAL COOPERATION
TOPIC: Admin Cooperation
CONCEPTS: Extradition, deportation and repatriation. Extradition requests. Location of crime. Special factors. Refusal of extradition. Provisional detainment. General cooperation. Exchange of information and documents. Recognition and enforcement of legal decisions. Prizes and arbitral awards. Penal sanctions. Finances and payments. Fees and exemptions.
PROCEDURE: Denunciation. Ratification.
PARTIES:
Jordan
Syria

102760   Bilateral Agreement   **204 UNTS 255**
SIGNED: 28 Apr 53   FORCE: 1 Jul 54
REGISTERED: 16 Feb 55 Syria
ARTICLES: 17 LANGUAGE: French.
HEADNOTE: TELEPHONE TELEGRAPH SERVICES
TOPIC: Telecommunications
CONCEPTS: Accounting procedures. Non-interest rates and fees. Facilities and equipment. Tele-

grams. Radio-telephone-telegraphic communications. Conformity with IGO decisions.
TREATY REF: 193UNTS188; 194UNTS3; 195UNTS3.
PARTIES:
Syria
Turkey

102761 Bilateral Agreement **204 UNTS 267**
SIGNED: 5 Feb 54   FORCE: 1 Apr 54
REGISTERED: 16 Feb 55 Syria
ARTICLES: 8 LANGUAGE: English. French.
HEADNOTE: ESTABLISHMENT WIRELESS TELEGRAPH SERVICE
TOPIC: Telecommunications
CONCEPTS: Non-interest rates and fees. Commercial and public radio. Telegrams. Radio-telephone-telegraphic communications. Conformity with IGO decisions.
TREATY REF: 193UNTS188; 194UNTS3; 195UNTS3.
PROCEDURE: Duration.
PARTIES:
Syria
UK Great Britain

102762 Bilateral Treaty **204 UNTS 275**
SIGNED: 2 Jun 48   FORCE: 21 May 54
REGISTERED: 17 Feb 55 Netherlands
ARTICLES: 14 LANGUAGE: French.
HEADNOTE: LABOR TREATY
TOPIC: Non-ILO Labor
CONCEPTS: Detailed regulations. Border traffic and migration. Non-visa travel documents. Legal protection and assistance. Public information. Establishment of commission. Dispute settlement. Employment regulations. Wages and salaries. Non-ILO labor relations. Administrative cooperation. Social security. Unemployment. National treatment.
INTL ORGS: Special Commission.
PROCEDURE: Denunciation. Duration. Future Procedures Contemplated. Ratification. Renewal or Revival.
PARTIES:
France
Netherlands

102763 Bilateral Exchange **204 UNTS 287**
SIGNED: 20 Jul 49   FORCE: 20 Jul 49
REGISTERED: 17 Feb 55 Netherlands
ARTICLES: 2 LANGUAGE: French.
HEADNOTE: GRANTING AGRICULTURAL WORKERS MOST FAVORED NATION TREATMENT
TOPIC: Mostfavored Nation
CONCEPTS: Employment regulations. Most favored nation clause.
PARTIES:
France
Netherlands

102764 Bilateral Exchange **204 UNTS 293**
SIGNED: 10 Jan 55   FORCE: 10 Jan 55
REGISTERED: 21 Feb 55 Norway
ARTICLES: 2 LANGUAGE: Swedish. Norwegian.
HEADNOTE: REGISTRATION TRADEMARKS
TOPIC: Patents/Copyrights
CONCEPTS: Trademarks.
TREATY REF: 74LTS289.
PROCEDURE: Denunciation. Duration.
PARTIES:
Norway
Sweden

102765 Bilateral Exchange **205 UNTS 3**
SIGNED: 7 Apr 52   FORCE: 7 Apr 52
REGISTERED: 1 Mar 55 USA (United States)
ARTICLES: 4 LANGUAGE: English. French.
HEADNOTE: TAXATION DEFENSE EXPENDITURES
TOPIC: Taxation
CONCEPTS: Annex or appendix reference. Currency. General. Tax exemptions. Military assistance. Military installations and equipment.
PARTIES:
Belgium
USA (United States)

102766 Bilateral Exchange **205 UNTS 17**
SIGNED: 13 Jun 52   FORCE: 13 Jun 52
REGISTERED: 1 Mar 55 USA (United States)
ARTICLES: 2 LANGUAGE: English.
HEADNOTE: MUTUAL DEFENSE ASSISTANCE
TOPIC: Milit Assistance
CONCEPTS: Exceptions and exemptions. Non-prejudice to UN charter. Conformity with municipal law. Materials, equipment and services. Defense and security. Self-defense. Payment for war supplies. Military assistance. Security of information. Exchange of defense information. Restrictions on transfer.
INTL ORGS: United Nations.
PARTIES:
Ethiopia
USA (United States)

102767 Bilateral Exchange **205 UNTS 25**
SIGNED: 21 May 52   FORCE: 21 May 54
REGISTERED: 1 Mar 55 USA (United States)
ARTICLES: 2 LANGUAGE: English. Arabic.
HEADNOTE: TECHNICAL COOPERATION PROGRAM EDUCATION
TOPIC: Tech Assistance
CONCEPTS: Treaty implementation. Annex type material. Exchange. Vocational training. Financial programs. Domestic obligation. Assistance.
TREATY REF: 15UNTS179; TIAS2758; 205UNTS34; TIAS2724.
PROCEDURE: Duration. Termination.
PARTIES:
Iraq
USA (United States)

102768 Bilateral Exchange **205 UNTS 33**
SIGNED: 21 May 52   FORCE: 21 May 52
REGISTERED: 1 Mar 55 USA (United States)
ARTICLES: 2 LANGUAGE: English. Arabic.
HEADNOTE: TECHNICAL COOPERATION PROGRAM PUBLIC WORKS
TOPIC: Tech Assistance
CONCEPTS: Treaty implementation. Annex type material. Personnel. Vocational training. Financial programs. Domestic obligation. Assistance.
TREATY REF: 151UNTS179; TIAS2758; 205UNTS26; 205UNTS34; TIAS27.
PROCEDURE: Duration. Termination.
PARTIES:
Iraq
USA (United States)

102769 Bilateral Exchange **205 UNTS 41**
SIGNED: 1 Apr 53   FORCE: 1 Apr 53
REGISTERED: 1 Mar 55 USA (United States)
ARTICLES: 15 LANGUAGE: English. Portuguese.
HEADNOTE: TAXATION EXPENDITURES COMMON DEFENSE
TOPIC: Taxation
CONCEPTS: Currency. General. Tax exemptions. Military assistance. Military installations and equipment.
INTL ORGS: North Atlantic Treaty Organization.
TREATY REF: 34UNTS243; 126UNTS350.
PARTIES:
Portugal
USA (United States)

102770 Multilateral Convention **205 UNTS 65**
SIGNED: 9 May 52   FORCE: 12 Jun 53
REGISTERED: 1 Mar 55 USA (United States)
ARTICLES: 11 LANGUAGE: English. Japanese.
HEADNOTE: HIGH SEAS FISHERIES
TOPIC: Specific Resources
CONCEPTS: Definition of terms. Annex or appendix reference. Inspection and observation. Domestic legislation. Establishment of commission. Funding procedures. Headquarters and facilities. Internal structure. Fisheries and fishing.
INTL ORGS: International North Pacific Fisheries Commission.
PROCEDURE: Duration. Ratification. Termination.
PARTIES:
Canada SIGNED: 9 May 52 RATIFIED: 12 Jun 53 FORCE: 12 Jun 53
Japan SIGNED: 9 May 52 RATIFIED: 12 Jun 53 FORCE: 12 Jun 53
USA (United States) SIGNED: 9 May 52 RATIFIED: 12 Jun 53 FORCE: 12 Jun 53

102771 Bilateral Agreement **205 UNTS 103**
SIGNED: 27 Feb 53   FORCE: 16 Sep 53
REGISTERED: 1 Mar 55 USA (United States)
ARTICLES: 10 LANGUAGE: English. German.
HEADNOTE: SETTLEMENT OBLIGATION SURPLUS PROPERTY
TOPIC: Claims and Debts
CONCEPTS: Detailed regulations. Previous treaty replacement. Responsibility and liability. Exchange. Currency. Exchange rates and regulations. Financial programs. Funding procedures. Interest rates. Payment schedules. Transportation costs. Local currency. Claims and settlements. Debts. Economic assistance. Surplus property. Purchase authorization. Specific claims or waivers.
INTL ORGS: International Monetary Fund.
TREATY REF: 106UNTS141; 165UNTS167; 2UNTS39; TIAS2792.
PROCEDURE: Ratification.
PARTIES:
Germany, West
USA (United States)

102772 Bilateral Exchange **205 UNTS 127**
SIGNED: 19 Jan 52   FORCE: 3 Jan 52
REGISTERED: 1 Mar 55 USA (United States)
ARTICLES: 6 LANGUAGE: English. French.
HEADNOTE: MUTUAL SECURITY
TOPIC: Milit Assistance
CONCEPTS: Time limit. Peaceful relations. Conformity with municipal law. General cooperation. Garnishment of funds. Domestic obligation. Defense and security. Self-defense. Return of equipment and recapture.
PARTIES:
USA (United States)
Vietnam, South

102773 Bilateral Agreement **205 UNTS 139**
SIGNED: 25 Jun 53   FORCE: 25 Jun 53
REGISTERED: 1 Mar 55 USA (United States)
ARTICLES: 7 LANGUAGE: English.
HEADNOTE: EMERGENCY WHEAT AID
TOPIC: Direct Aid
CONCEPTS: Privileges and immunities. Conformity with municipal law. General cooperation. Exchange of information and documents. Personnel. Public information. Accounting procedures. Expense sharing formulae. Local currency. Commodities and services. General aid. Aid missions. Withdrawal conditions. Distribution. Transport of goods.
PROCEDURE: Termination.
PARTIES:
Pakistan
USA (United States)

102774 Bilateral Protocol **205 UNTS 149**
SIGNED: 4 Dec 52   FORCE: 24 Sep 53
REGISTERED: 1 Mar 55 USA (United States)
ARTICLES: 3 LANGUAGE: English. Finnish.
HEADNOTE: MODIFYING TREATY FRIENDSHIP COMMERCE CONSULAR RIGHTS
TOPIC: General Amity
CONCEPTS: Annex type material.
PROCEDURE: Duration. Ratification.
PARTIES:
Finland
USA (United States)

102775 Bilateral Agreement **205 UNTS 157**
SIGNED: 20 Dec 54   FORCE: 20 Dec 54
REGISTERED: 1 Mar 55 Australia
ARTICLES: 17 LANGUAGE: English.
HEADNOTE: EXCHANGE POSTAL PARCELS
TOPIC: Postal Service
CONCEPTS: Responsibility and liability. Accounting procedures. Compensation. Postal services. Regulations. Insured letters and boxes. Parcel post. Rates and charges.
INTL ORGS: Universal Postal Union.
TREATY REF: 170UNTS63; 186UNTS360; 202UNTS348.
PROCEDURE: Duration. Termination.
PARTIES:
Australia
Austria

102776 Bilateral Agreement **205 UNTS 173**
SIGNED: 5 May 51 FORCE: 5 May 51
REGISTERED: 3 Mar 55 USA (United States)
ARTICLES: 8 LANGUAGE: English. Icelandic.
HEADNOTE: DEFENSE AGREEMENT
TOPIC: Milit Assistance
CONCEPTS: Annex or appendix reference. Previous treaty replacement. Conformity with municipal law. Use of facilities. Materials, equipment and services. Defense and security. Military assistance. Military assistance missions. Military installations and equipment.
INTL ORGS: North Atlantic Treaty Organization.
TREATY REF: 34UNTS243; 126UNTS350; 12UNTS163.
PROCEDURE: Amendment. Future Procedures Contemplated. Ratification. Termination.
PARTIES:
Iceland
USA (United States)

102777 Bilateral Exchange **205 UNTS 213**
SIGNED: 26 Nov 53 FORCE: 26 Feb 53
REGISTERED: 3 Mar 55 USA (United States)
ARTICLES: 2 LANGUAGE: English. Spanish.
HEADNOTE: FLIGHT NOTIFICATIIONS PRIVATE AIRCRAFT
TOPIC: Air Transport
CONCEPTS: Detailed regulations. Exceptions and exemptions. Conformity with municipal law. Fees and exemptions. Registration certificate. Air transport. Airport facilities. Operating authorizations and regulations. Facilities and equipment.
PARTIES:
Cuba
USA (United States)

102778 Bilateral Convention **205 UNTS 237**
SIGNED: 14 May 53 FORCE: 14 Dec 53
REGISTERED: 3 Mar 55 USA (United States)
ARTICLES: 9 LANGUAGE: English.
HEADNOTE: DOUBLE TAXATION FISCAL EVASION TAXES GIFTS
TOPIC: Taxation
CONCEPTS: Definition of terms. Conformity with municipal law. Exchange of official publications. Responsibility and liability. Taxation. General. Tax exemptions.
PROCEDURE: Duration. Ratification. Termination.
PARTIES:
Australia
USA (United States)

102779 Bilateral Convention **205 UNTS 253**
SIGNED: 14 May 53 FORCE: 14 Dec 53
REGISTERED: 3 Mar 55 USA (United States)
ARTICLES: 21 LANGUAGE: English.
HEADNOTE: DOUBLE TAXATION FISCAL EVASION TAXES INCOME
TOPIC: Taxation
CONCEPTS: Definition of terms. Conformity with municipal law. Exchange of official publications. Domestic legislation. Teacher and student exchange. Claims and settlements. Taxation. General. Tax exemptions. Air transport. Merchant vessels.
PROCEDURE: Duration. Ratification. Termination.
PARTIES:
Australia
USA (United States)

102780 Bilateral Convention **205 UNTS 277**
SIGNED: 14 May 53 FORCE: 7 Jan 54
REGISTERED: 3 Mar 55 USA (United States)
ARTICLES: 9 LANGUAGE: English.
HEADNOTE: DOUBLE TAXATION FISCAL EVASION ESTATES DECEASED PERSONS
TOPIC: Taxation
CONCEPTS: Definition of terms. Privileges and immunities. Conformity with municipal law. Exchange of official publications. Negotiation. Claims and settlements. Taxation. Death duties. Tax credits. Tax exemptions.
PROCEDURE: Duration. Ratification. Termination.
PARTIES:
Australia
USA (United States)

102781 Bilateral Agreement **205 UNTS 293**
SIGNED: 21 Feb 52 FORCE: 13 Nov 54
REGISTERED: 3 Mar 55 USA (United States)
ARTICLES: 18 LANGUAGE: English.
HEADNOTE: SAFETY GREAT LAKES
TOPIC: Humanitarian
CONCEPTS: Definition of terms. Detailed regulations. Annex or appendix reference. Conformity with municipal law. Exchange of information and documents. Informational records. Inspection and observation. Domestic legislation. Personnel. Humanitarian matters. Registration certificate. Merchant vessels. Bands and frequency allocation. Facilities and equipment. Radio-telephone-telegraphic communications. Naval vessels.
TREATY REF: 136LTS81; 164UNTS113; TS948; 151LTS5.
PARTIES:
Canada
USA (United States)

102782 Bilateral Exchange **206 UNTS 3**
SIGNED: 21 May 52 FORCE: 21 May 52
REGISTERED: 3 Mar 55 USA (United States)
ARTICLES: 2 LANGUAGE: English. Arabic.
HEADNOTE: TECHNICAL COOPERATION PROGRAM INDUSTRIAL DEVELOPMENT
TOPIC: Tech Assistance
CONCEPTS: General technical assistance. Assistance.
TREATY REF: 151UNTS179.
PARTIES:
Iraq
USA (United States)

102783 Bilateral Exchange **206 UNTS 11**
SIGNED: 5 Dec 52 FORCE: 5 Dec 52
REGISTERED: 3 Mar 55 USA (United States)
ARTICLES: 2 LANGUAGE: English.
HEADNOTE: LEASED DEFENSE AREAS
TOPIC: Milit Installation
CONCEPTS: Time limit. Conformity with municipal law. Use of facilities. Compensation. Tax exemptions. Materials, equipment and services. Facilities and equipment. Defense and security. Payment for war supplies. Security of information. Jurisdiction. Procurement and logistics. Bases and facilities.
PARTIES:
Canada
USA (United States)

102784 Bilateral Agreement **206 UNTS 23**
SIGNED: 29 Jun 53 FORCE: 29 Jun 53
REGISTERED: 3 Mar 55 USA (United States)
ARTICLES: 5 LANGUAGE: English. Arabic.
HEADNOTE: HEALTH DISEASE CONTROL PROGRAM
TOPIC: Sanitation
CONCEPTS: Privileges and immunities. General property. Specialists exchange. Quarantine. Public health. WHO used as agency. Exchange. Institute establishment. Scholarships and grants. Vocational training. Indemnities and reimbursements. Expense sharing formulae. Funding procedures. Assistance. Special projects. Materials, equipment and services. Publications exchange. Television.
INTL ORGS: World Health Organization.
TREATY REF: 185UNTS55.
PROCEDURE: Duration. Renewal or Revival. Termination.
PARTIES:
Saudi Arabia
USA (United States)

102785 Bilateral Treaty **206 UNTS 41**
SIGNED: 7 Sep 51 FORCE: 8 Nov 53
REGISTERED: 3 Mar 55 USA (United States)
ARTICLES: 19 LANGUAGE: English. Amharic.
HEADNOTE: AMITY ECONOMIC RELATIONS
TOPIC: General Amity
CONCEPTS: Definition of terms. Exceptions and exemptions. Previous treaty replacement. Nonprejudice to third party. Friendship and amity. Border traffic and migration. Alien status. Consular relations establishment. Diplomatic relations establishment. Human rights. Inviolability. Privileges and immunities. Conformity with mu-

nicipal law. Juridical personality. Legal protection and assistance. General property. Procedure. Border control. Export quotas. Import quotas. Free trade. Maritime products and equipment. Trade procedures. Monetary and gold transfers. Exchange rates and regulations. Most favored nation clause. Tax exemptions. Recognition. Customs exemptions. Inland and territorial waters. Ports and pilotage.
TREATY REF: 3DEMARTENS7'194;0.
PROCEDURE: Duration. Ratification. Termination. Application to Non-self-governing Territories.
PARTIES:
Ethiopia
USA (United States)

102786 Bilateral Exchange **206 UNTS 93**
SIGNED: 30 Jun 53 FORCE: 30 Jun 53
REGISTERED: 3 Mar 55 USA (United States)
ARTICLES: 3 LANGUAGE: English.
HEADNOTE: HAINES-FAIRBANKS OIL PIPELINE INSTALLATION
TOPIC: Specific Property
CONCEPTS: Annex or appendix reference. Materials, equipment and services. Facilities and property.
PARTIES:
Canada
USA (United States)

102787 Bilateral Agreement **206 UNTS 117**
SIGNED: 19 Nov 53 FORCE: 19 Nov 53
REGISTERED: 3 Mar 55 USA (United States)
ARTICLES: 34 LANGUAGE: English. Spanish.
HEADNOTE: MILITARY MISSION
TOPIC: Military Mission
CONCEPTS: Definition of terms. Use of facilities. Compensation. Indemnities and reimbursements. Currency. Exchange rates and regulations. Expense sharing formulae. Tax exemptions. Customs exemptions. Military assistance. Military training. Security of information. Airforce-army-navy personnel ratio. Ranks and privileges. Conditions for assistance missions. Third country military personnel. Status of forces.
PROCEDURE: Denunciation. Termination.
PARTIES:
Nicaragua
USA (United States)
ANNEX
357 UNTS 378. USA (United States). Amendment 25 Mar 59. Force 22 May 59.
357 UNTS 378. Nicaragua. Amendment 22 May 59. Force 22 May 59.

102788 Bilateral Treaty **206 UNTS 143**
SIGNED: 2 Apr 53 FORCE: 30 Oct 53
REGISTERED: 3 Mar 55 USA (United States)
ARTICLES: 25 LANGUAGE: English. Japanese.
HEADNOTE: FRIENDSHIP COMMERCE NAVIGATION
TOPIC: General Amity
CONCEPTS: Definition of terms. Exceptions and exemptions. Territorial application. Alien status. Administrative cooperation. General cooperation. Exchange of official publications. Juridical personality. Free passage and transit. Legal protection and assistance. General property. Public information. Private contracts. Procedure. Existing tribunals. Border control. Social security. Export quotas. Import quotas. Free trade. Reciprocity in trade. Exchange rates and regulations. Most favored nation clause. Taxation. Recognition. Water transport. Inland and territorial waters. Ports and pilotage.
INTL ORGS: International Monetary Fund.
TREATY REF: GATT.
PROCEDURE: Ratification.
PARTIES:
Japan
USA (United States)

102789 Bilateral Exchange **206 UNTS 241**
SIGNED: 12 Apr 49 FORCE: 12 Apr 49
REGISTERED: 4 Mar 55 USA (United States)
ARTICLES: 3 LANGUAGE: English.
HEADNOTE: JOINT INDUSTRIAL MOBILIZATION COMMITTEE
TOPIC: Milit Assistance
CONCEPTS: Detailed regulations. General cooper-

ation. Establishment of commission. Joint defense. Defense and security.
INTL ORGS: Special Commission.
PARTIES:
Canada
USA (United States)

102790 Bilateral Convention **206 UNTS 249**
SIGNED: 17 Sep 47　　　FORCE: 1 Oct 47
REGISTERED: 4 Mar 55 USA (United States)
ARTICLES: 12 LANGUAGE: English.
HEADNOTE: POSTAL CONVENTION
TOPIC: Postal Service
CONCEPTS: Detailed regulations. Conformity with municipal law. Postal services. Regulations. Parcel post. Rates and charges.
TREATY REF: UNIVERSAL POSTAL CONVEN.
PROCEDURE: Denunciation. Duration. Ratification.
PARTIES:
Philippines
USA (United States)

102791 Bilateral Exchange **206 UNTS 263**
SIGNED: 17 Apr 46　　　FORCE: 1 May 46
REGISTERED: 4 Mar 55 USA (United States)
ARTICLES: 2 LANGUAGE: English. Italian.
HEADNOTE: RECIPROCAL APPLICATION ARTICLE 1 23 MAR 1868 RELATING EXTRADITION
TOPIC: Extradition
CONCEPTS: Previous treaty extension. Extradition, deportation and repatriation.
TREATY REF: UTS174; 15STAT629.
PARTIES:
Italy
USA (United States)

102792 Bilateral Treaty **206 UNTS 269**
SIGNED: 21 Jan 50　　　FORCE: 14 Sep 50
REGISTERED: 4 Mar 55 USA (United States)
ARTICLES: 25 LANGUAGE: English.
HEADNOTE: FRIENDSHIP COMMERCE NAVIGATION
TOPIC: General Amity
CONCEPTS: Definition of terms. Detailed regulations. Exceptions and exemptions. Territorial application. Time limit. Alien status. Administrative cooperation. General cooperation. Exchange of official publications. Juridical personality. Free passage and transit. Legal protection and assistance. General property. Private contracts. Procedure. Existing tribunals. Sickness and invalidity insurance. Export quotas. Import quotas. Free trade. Reciprocity in trade. Exchange rates and regulations. Most favored nation clause. Customs duties. Water transport. Inland and territorial waters. Service in foreign army.
INTL ORGS: General Agreement on Tariffs and Trade. International Court of Justice.
TREATY REF: 55UNTS187; ITS1938-1; EAS56.
PROCEDURE: Duration. Ratification. Termination.
PARTIES:
Ireland
USA (United States)

102793 Bilateral Exchange **206 UNTS 311**
SIGNED: 11 Sep 51　　　FORCE: 11 Sep 51
REGISTERED: 4 Mar 55 USA (United States)
ARTICLES: 2 LANGUAGE: English.
HEADNOTE: UNEMPLOYMENT INSURANCE AGREEMENT MODIFICATION
TOPIC: Non-ILO Labor
CONCEPTS: Annex type material. Non-ILO labor relations. Unemployment.
TREATY REF: 119UNTS295.
PARTIES:
Canada
USA (United States)

102794 Bilateral Convention **206 UNTS 319**
SIGNED: 26 Oct 51　　　FORCE: 11 Jul 52
REGISTERED: 4 Mar 55 USA (United States)
ARTICLES: 2 LANGUAGE: English.
HEADNOTE: SUPPLEMENTARY MUTUAL EXTRADITION FUGITIVE CRIMINALS
TOPIC: Extradition
CONCEPTS: Annex type material.
TREATY REF: UTS391; 32STAT1864.

PARTIES:
Canada
USA (United States)

102795 Bilateral Exchange **206 UNTS 325**
SIGNED: 16 May 51　　　FORCE: 16 May 51
REGISTERED: 4 Mar 55 USA (United States)
ARTICLES: 2 LANGUAGE: English. Italian.
HEADNOTE: USE FUNDS DERIVED SALE CONFISCATED PROPERTY
TOPIC: Reparations
CONCEPTS: Accounting procedures. Loss and/or damage. Enemy financial interests. Post-war claims settlement.
INTL ORGS: International Refugees Organization.
PARTIES:
Italy
USA (United States)

102796 Bilateral Exchange **207 UNTS 3**
SIGNED: 8 Nov 52　　　FORCE: 8 Nov 52
REGISTERED: 4 Mar 55 USA (United States)
ARTICLES: 5 LANGUAGE: English.
HEADNOTE: COMMUNICATIONS FACILITIES
TOPIC: Gen Communications
CONCEPTS: Facilities and equipment. Lease of military property.
INTL ORGS: North Atlantic Treaty Organization.
PARTIES:
Canada
USA (United States)
ANNEX
297 UNTS 466. USA (United States). Amendment 31 Mar 55. Force 8 Jun 55.
297 UNTS 466. Canada. Amendment 8 Jun 55. Force 8 Jun 55.

102797 Bilateral Convention **207 UNTS 17**
SIGNED: 8 Feb 51　　　FORCE: 15 May 52
REGISTERED: 4 Mar 55 USA (United States)
ARTICLES: 4 LANGUAGE: English.
HEADNOTE: RADIO EQUIPMENT STATIONS
TOPIC: Telecommunications
CONCEPTS: Conformity with municipal law. Operating authorizations and regulations. Amateur radio. Facilities and equipment. Radio-telephone-telegraphic communications.
PROCEDURE: Duration. Ratification. Termination.
PARTIES:
Canada
USA (United States)

102798 Bilateral Exchange **207 UNTS 25**
SIGNED: 23 Jun 52　　　FORCE: 23 Jun 52
REGISTERED: 4 Mar 55 USA (United States)
ARTICLES: 2 LANGUAGE: English.
HEADNOTE: ASSIGNMENT TELEVISION FREQUENCY CHANNELS
TOPIC: Telecommunications
CONCEPTS: Detailed regulations. Facilities and equipment. Telecommunications. Television.
PARTIES:
Canada
USA (United States)

102799 Bilateral Exchange **207 UNTS 51**
SIGNED: 8 Jan 52　　　FORCE: 8 Jan 52
REGISTERED: 4 Mar 55 USA (United States)
ARTICLES: 7 LANGUAGE: English. Portuguese.
HEADNOTE: ASSURANCES MUTUAL SECURITY ACT
TOPIC: General Military
CONCEPTS: Definition of terms. Friendship and amity. Non-prejudice to UN charter. Peaceful relations. Currency. Financial programs. Domestic obligation. Economic assistance. Military assistance. Return of equipment and recapture.
INTL ORGS: United Nations.
TREATY REF: 29UNTS213; 79UNTS310; 134UNTS370; 207UNTS320.
PARTIES:
Portugal
USA (United States)

102800 Bilateral Agreement **207 UNTS 61**
SIGNED: 26 Sep 53　　　FORCE: 26 Sep 53
REGISTERED: 4 Mar 55 USA (United States)
ARTICLES: 7 LANGUAGE: English. Spanish.

HEADNOTE: MUTUAL DEFENSE ASSISTANCE
TOPIC: Milit Assistance
CONCEPTS: Exceptions and exemptions. Guarantees and safeguards. Annex or appendix reference. Non-prejudice to UN charter. Peaceful relations. Privileges and immunities. Conformity with municipal law. General cooperation. Inspection and observation. Public information. Use of facilities. Indemnities and reimbursements. Garnishment of funds. Local currency. Tax exemptions. Recognition. Customs exemptions. Domestic obligation. Materials, equipment and services. Aid missions. Self-defense. Return of equipment and recapture. Security of information. Military assistance missions. Exchange of defense information. Restrictions on transfer. Arms limitations.
INTL ORGS: United Nations.
PROCEDURE: Amendment. Future Procedures Contemplated. Registration. Termination.
PARTIES:
Spain
USA (United States)
ANNEX
265 UNTS 374. USA (United States). Implementation 27 Nov 56. Force 27 Nov 56.
265 UNTS 374. Spain. Implementation 27 Nov 56. Force 27 Nov 56.

102801 Bilateral Agreement **207 UNTS 83**
SIGNED: 26 Sep 53　　　FORCE: 26 Sep 53
REGISTERED: 4 Mar 55 USA (United States)
ARTICLES: 5 LANGUAGE: English. Spanish.
HEADNOTE: DEFENSE AGREEMENT
TOPIC: Milit Assistance
CONCEPTS: Use of facilities. Materials, equipment and services. Defense and security. Military assistance. Military assistance missions. Exchange of defense information. Bases and facilities.
TREATY REF: 207UNTS61.
PROCEDURE: Renewal or Revival. Termination.
PARTIES:
Spain
USA (United States)
ANNEX
492 UNTS 346. Spain. Prolongation 26 Sep 63. Force 26 Sep 63.
492 UNTS 346. USA (United States). Prolongation 26 Sep 63. Force 26 Sep 63.

102802 Bilateral Agreement **207 UNTS 93**
SIGNED: 26 Sep 53　　　FORCE: 26 Sep 53
REGISTERED: 4 Mar 55 USA (United States)
ARTICLES: 10 LANGUAGE: English. Spanish.
HEADNOTE: ECONOMIC AID AGREEMENT
TOPIC: Direct Aid
CONCEPTS: Guarantees and safeguards. Treaty implementation. Annex or appendix reference. Privileges and immunities. Conformity with municipal law. General cooperation. Exchange of information and documents. Public information. Arbitration. Negotiation. Accounting procedures. Attachment of funds. Funding procedures. Garnishment of funds. Seizure funds. Local currency. Claims and settlements. Assets transfer. Domestic obligation. General technical assistance. Economic assistance. Aid missions. Procurement. Access to materials. Paragraph 2, Article 36.
INTL ORGS: International Court of Justice. International Monetary Fund.
TREATY REF: 1UNTS9.
PROCEDURE: Amendment. Future Procedures Contemplated. Registration. Termination.
PARTIES:
Spain
USA (United States)
ANNEX
458 UNTS 304. USA (United States). Amendment 22 Apr 62. Force 22 May 62.
458 UNTS 304. Spain. Amendment 22 May 62. Force 22 May 62.

102803 Bilateral Agreement **207 UNTS 127**
SIGNED: 22 May 53　　　FORCE: 22 May 53
REGISTERED: 11 Mar 55 USA (United States)
ARTICLES: 7 LANGUAGE: English.
HEADNOTE: MUTUAL DEFENSE
TOPIC: Milit Assistance
CONCEPTS: Friendship and amity. Defense and se-

curity. Military assistance. Airforce-army-navy personnel ratio.
INTL ORGS: United Nations.
TREATY REF: MUTUAL DEFENCE ACT 1949,MUTUAL SEC. ACT1951.
PROCEDURE: Termination.
PARTIES:
Ethiopia
USA (United States)
ANNEX
303 UNTS 342. USA (United States). Supplementation 2 Jan 58. Force 6 Jan 58.
303 UNTS 342. Ethiopia. Supplementation 6 Jan 58. Force 6 Jan 58.

102804 Bilateral Agreement **207 UNTS 139**
SIGNED: 30 Jun 52   FORCE: 11 Jun 53
REGISTERED: 11 Mar 55 Uruguay
ARTICLES: 11 LANGUAGE: English. Spanish.
HEADNOTE: MUTUAL DEFENSE ASSISTANCE
TOPIC: Milit Assistance
CONCEPTS: Exceptions and exemptions. Guarantees and safeguards. Annex or appendix reference. Non-prejudice to UN charter. Privileges and immunities. Conformity with municipal law. General cooperation. Inspection and observation. Public information. Use of facilities. Indemnities and reimbursements. Garnishment of funds. Local currency. Claims and settlements. Most favored nation clause. Tax exemptions. Recognition. Customs exemptions. Domestic obligation. Materials, equipment and services. Aid missions. Joint defense. Defense and security. Self-defense. Military assistance. Return of equipment and recapture. Security of information. Military assistance missions. Exchange of defense information. Restrictions on transfer.
INTL ORGS: United Nations.
TREATY REF: 21UNTS77; 26UNTS417.
PROCEDURE: Amendment. Future Procedures Contemplated. Ratification. Registration. Termination.
PARTIES:
USA (United States)
Uruguay
ANNEX
273 UNTS 259. Uruguay. Amendment 16 Sep 55. Force 16 Sep 55.
273 UNTS 259. USA (United States). Amendment 1 Jun 55. Force 16 Sep 55.

102805 Bilateral Agreement **207 UNTS 161**
SIGNED: 21 Aug 52   FORCE: 21 Aug 52
REGISTERED: 15 Mar 55 Pakistan
ARTICLES: 2 LANGUAGE: English.
HEADNOTE: BOUNDARY ALIGNMENT
TOPIC: Territory Boundary
CONCEPTS: Annex or appendix reference. Markers and definitions.
PARTIES:
India
Pakistan

102806 Bilateral Agreement **207 UNTS 173**
SIGNED: 10 Feb 55   FORCE: 15 Feb 55
REGISTERED: 16 Mar 55 Australia
ARTICLES: 17 LANGUAGE: English.
HEADNOTE: EXCHANGE POSTAL PARCELS
TOPIC: Postal Service
CONCEPTS: Responsibility and liability. Accounting procedures. Compensation. Payment schedules. Postal services. Regulations. Insured letters and boxes. Conveyance in transit. Parcel post. Rates and charges.
INTL ORGS: Universal Postal Union.
TREATY REF: 170UNTS63.
PROCEDURE: Duration. Termination.
PARTIES:
Australia
Hungary

102807 Multilateral Instrument **207 UNTS 189**
SIGNED: 19 Oct 53   FORCE: 30 Nov 54
REGISTERED: 21 Mar 55 Switzerland
ARTICLES: 35 LANGUAGE: English. French. Spanish.
HEADNOTE: EUROPEAN MIGRATION
TOPIC: IGO Establishment
CONCEPTS: Treaty interpretation. Treaty violation. Annex type material. Border traffic and migra-

tion. Assistance. Acquisition of nationality. Privileges and immunities. Conformity with municipal law. Juridical personality. Funding procedures. Admission. Subsidiary organ. Establishment. Headquarters and facilities. Liaison with other IGO's. Internal structure. Special status. Status of experts. Conformity with IGO decisions. Inter-agency agreements. Compulsory jurisdiction.
INTL ORGS: Intergovernmental Committee for European Migration. International Court of Justice.
PROCEDURE: Amendment. Denunciation. Termination.
PARTIES:
Argentina   RATIFIED: 18 Nov 54   FORCE: 30 Nov 54
Australia   RATIFIED: 22 Mar 54   FORCE: 30 Nov 54
Austria RATIFIED: 25 Jun 54 FORCE: 30 Nov 54
Canada RATIFIED: 29 Mar 54 FORCE: 30 Nov 54
Chile RATIFIED: 20 Oct 54 FORCE: 30 Nov 54
Denmark   RATIFIED: 26 Feb 54   FORCE: 30 Nov 54
Germany, West RATIFIED: 8 Nov 54 FORCE: 30 Nov 54
Greece RATIFIED: 8 Jul 54 FORCE: 30 Nov 54
Israel RATIFIED: 1 Mar 54 FORCE: 30 Nov 54
Italy RATIFIED: 15 Jan 54 FORCE: 30 Nov 54
Netherlands   RATIFIED: 12 Apr 54   FORCE: 30 Nov 54
Norway RATIFIED: 26 Nov 54 FORCE: 30 Nov 54
Paraguay   RATIFIED: 29 Apr 54   FORCE: 30 Nov 54
Sweden   RATIFIED: 11 Feb 54   FORCE: 30 Nov 54
Switzerland   RATIFIED: 7 Apr 54   FORCE: 30 Nov 54
USA (United States)   RATIFIED: 21 Sep 54   FORCE: 30 Nov 54

102808 Bilateral Exchange **207 UNTS 227**
SIGNED: 22 Dec 54   FORCE: 22 Dec 54
REGISTERED: 24 Mar 55 UK Great Britain
ARTICLES: 2 LANGUAGE: English.
HEADNOTE: FINANCIAL OBLIGATIONS
TOPIC: Claims and Debts
CONCEPTS: Interest rates. Debts.
TREATY REF: CMD8172;   102UNTS29;   87UNTS71; 88UNTS329.
PARTIES:
UK Great Britain
Yugoslavia
ANNEX
264 UNTS 378. UK Great Britain. Amendment 22 Sep 56. Force 22 Sep 56.
264 UNTS 378. Yugoslavia. Amendment 2 Jun 56. Force 22 Sep 56.

102809 Multilateral Protocol **207 UNTS 237**
SIGNED: 26 Oct 53   FORCE: 29 Oct 53
REGISTERED: 24 Mar 55 UK Great Britain
ARTICLES: 2 LANGUAGE: English. Japanese.
HEADNOTE: EXERCISE CRIMINAL JURISDICTION
TOPIC: Status of Forces
CONCEPTS: Annex or appendix reference. Court procedures. Conformity with municipal law. General cooperation. Exchange of information and documents. Responsibility and liability. Status of military forces. Jurisdiction. Status of forces.
INTL ORGS: United Nations.
PROCEDURE: Accession.
PARTIES:
Australia SIGNED: 26 Oct 53 FORCE: 29 Oct 53
Canada SIGNED: 26 Oct 53 FORCE: 29 Oct 53
Japan SIGNED: 26 Oct 53 FORCE: 29 Oct 53
New Zealand   SIGNED: 26 Oct 53   FORCE: 29 Oct 53
UK Great Britain SIGNED: 26 Oct 53 FORCE: 29 Oct 53
USA (United States) SIGNED: 26 Oct 53 FORCE: 29 Oct 53
ANNEX
214 UNTS 380. South Africa. Signature 29 Oct 53. Force 29 Oct 53.
214 UNTS 380. France. Signature 18 Nov 53. Force 19 Nov 53.
214 UNTS 380. Italy. Signature 3 Dec 53. Force 4 Dec 53.
214 UNTS 380. Philippines. Signature 11 Dec 53. Force 12 Dec 53.

214 UNTS 380. Netherlands. Signature Subject to Ratification 30 Jan 54.
214 UNTS 380. Belgium. Signature 28 Apr 54.

102810 Bilateral Exchange **207 UNTS 277**
SIGNED: 5 Jan 53   FORCE: 5 Jan 53
REGISTERED: 24 Mar 55 UK Great Britain
ARTICLES: 2 LANGUAGE: English. French.
HEADNOTE: CONSTRUCTION OWEN FALLS DAM
TOPIC: Specific Property
CONCEPTS: Compensation. Indemnities and reimbursements. Facilities and property.
PARTIES:
United Arab Rep
UK Great Britain

102811 Bilateral Agreement **207 UNTS 283**
SIGNED: 29 Nov 54   FORCE: 29 Nov 54
REGISTERED: 24 Mar 55 UK Great Britain
ARTICLES: 6 LANGUAGE: English.
HEADNOTE: WITHDRAWAL MILITARY ADMINISTRATION
TOPIC: Status of Forces
CONCEPTS: Annex or appendix reference. Previous treaty replacement. Legal protection and assistance. Investigation of violations. Withdrawal of forces. Pasturage in frontier zones. Frontier peoples and personnel. Frontier crossing points.
PROCEDURE: Termination.
PARTIES:
Ethiopia
UK Great Britain

102812 Multilateral Exchange **207 UNTS 293**
SIGNED: 28 Sep 54   FORCE: 28 Sep 54
REGISTERED: 24 Mar 55 UK Great Britain
ARTICLES: 10 LANGUAGE: English.
HEADNOTE: SETTLEMENT ADVANCES CURRENCY
TOPIC: Reparations
CONCEPTS: Currency. Monetary and gold transfers. Payment schedules. Lump sum settlements. Most favored nation clause. Status of military forces.
TREATY REF. 140UNTS57.
PARTIES:
Australia SIGNED: 28 Sep 54 FORCE: 28 Sep 54
Korea, South   SIGNED: 28 Sep 54   FORCE: 28 Sep 54
New Zealand   SIGNED: 28 Sep 54   FORCE: 28 Sep 54
UK Great Britain SIGNED: 28 Sep 54 FORCE: 28 Sep 54

102813 Bilateral Exchange **207 UNTS 303**
SIGNED: 24 Dec 52   FORCE: 13 Aug 53
REGISTERED: 25 Mar 55 South Africa
ARTICLES: 5 LANGUAGE: English.
HEADNOTE: DOUBLE TAXATION PROFITS FROM SEA AIR TRANSPORT
TOPIC: Taxation
CONCEPTS: Definition of terms. Taxation. Tax exemptions. Air transport. Merchant vessels.
PROCEDURE: Duration. Termination.
PARTIES:
Israel
South Africa

102814 Multilateral Convention **208 UNTS 3**
SIGNED: 10 Jun 47   FORCE: 30 Dec 54
REGISTERED: 29 Mar 55 Norway
ARTICLES: 17 LANGUAGE: English. French.
HEADNOTE: UNIFORM SYSTEM TONNAGE MEASUREMENT
TOPIC: Water Transport
CONCEPTS: Tonnage.
INTL ORGS: League of Nations.
TREATY REF: 208LTS20.
PROCEDURE: Denunciation. Ratification.
PARTIES:
Belgium SIGNED: 10 Jun 47
Denmark   SIGNED: 10 Jun 47   RATIFIED: 22 Sep 54 FORCE: 30 Dec 54
Finland SIGNED: 10 Jun 47
France SIGNED: 10 Jun 47
Iceland   SIGNED: 10 Jun 47   RATIFIED: 15 Oct 48 FORCE: 30 Dec 54
Netherlands   SIGNED: 10 Jun 47   RATIFIED: 12 Oct 49 FORCE: 30 Dec 54

Norway SIGNED: 10 Jun 47 RATIFIED: 9 Jan 48
FORCE: 30 Dec 54
Sweden SIGNED: 10 Jun 47 RATIFIED:
30 Sep 54 FORCE: 30 Dec 54
ANNEX
209 UNTS 354. Finland. Ratification 9 Apr 55.
Force 19 Jul 55.
410 UNTS 294. Poland. Ratification 5 Oct 61.
Force 5 Jan 62.
452 UNTS 308. Multilateral. Force 1 Dec 60.
640 UNTS 371. Morocco. Accession 1 Jul 68.
Force 1 Oct 68.

102815 Bilateral Agreement **208 UNTS 225**
SIGNED: 5 Jan 55 FORCE: 5 Jan 55
REGISTERED: 1 Apr 55 ILO (Labor Org)
ARTICLES: 6 LANGUAGE: Spanish.
HEADNOTE: PRIVILEGES & IMMUNITIES
TOPIC: IGO Status/Immunit
CONCEPTS: Diplomatic privileges. Diplomatic mis-
sions. Inviolability. Privileges and immunities.
Property. Diplomatic correspondence. Juridical
personality. Special status. Status of experts.
PARTIES:
Mexico
ILO (Labor Org)

102816 Multilateral Agreement **208 UNTS 239**
SIGNED: 4 Apr 55 FORCE: 4 Apr 55
REGISTERED: 4 Apr 55 United Nations
ARTICLES: 6 LANGUAGE: English.
HEADNOTE: TECHNICAL ASSISTANCE
TOPIC: Tech Assistance
CONCEPTS: Privileges and immunities. Confor-
mity with municipal law. General cooperation.
Personnel. Responsibility and liability. Title and
deeds. Use of facilities. Exchange. Scholarships
and grants. Vocational training. Research and
development. Exchange rates and regulations.
Expense sharing formulae. Local currency. Do-
mestic obligation. General technical assistance.
Materials, equipment and services. IGO status.
Conformity with IGO decisions.
TREATY REF: 76UNTS132.
PROCEDURE: Amendment. Duration. Termination.
Application to Non-self-governing Territories.
PARTIES:
United Arab Rep SIGNED: 4 Apr 55 FORCE:
4 Apr 55
FAO (Food Agri) SIGNED: 4 Apr 55 FORCE:
4 Apr 55
ICAO (Civil Aviat) SIGNED: 4 Apr 55 FORCE:
4 Apr 55
ILO (Labor Org) SIGNED: 4 Apr 55 FORCE:
4 Apr 55
ITU (Telecommun) SIGNED: 4 Apr 55 FORCE:
4 Apr 55
UNESCO (Educ/Cult) SIGNED: 4 Apr 55 FORCE:
4 Apr 55
United Nations SIGNED: 4 Apr 55 FORCE:
4 Apr 55
WHO (World Health) SIGNED: 4 Apr 55 FORCE:
4 Apr 55
WMO (Meteorology) SIGNED: 4 Apr 55 FORCE:
4 Apr 55
UK Great Britain SIGNED: 4 Apr 55 FORCE:
4 Apr 55
ANNEX
547 UNTS 319. United Nations. Termination
13 Sep 65. Force 13 Sep 65.
547 UNTS 319. United Arab Rep Termination
13 Sep 65. Force 13 Sep 65.

102817 Bilateral Agreement **208 UNTS 255**
SIGNED: 28 Feb 52 FORCE: 28 Apr 52
REGISTERED: 11 Apr 55 USA (United States)
ARTICLES: 29 LANGUAGE: English. Japanese.
HEADNOTE: ADMINISTRATIVE AGREEMENT
TOPIC: Milit Assistance
CONCEPTS: Definition of terms. Detailed regulations. Annex or appendix reference. Visa abolition. Passports non-diplomatic. Non-visa travel
documents. Diplomatic privileges. Standardization. General cooperation. Recognition and enforcement of legal decisions. Use of facilities.
Investigation of violations. Establishment of
commission. Procedure. Accounting procedures. Currency. Exchange rates and regulations. Local currency. Claims and settlements.
Most favored nation clause. General. Tax exemptions. Customs exemptions. Domestic obliga-

tion. Navigational conditions. Operating authori-
zations and regulations. Ports and pilotage.
Postal services. Telecommunications. Press and
wire services. Defense and security. Return of
equipment and recapture. Ranks and privileges.
Conditions for assistance missions. Jurisdiction.
Procurement and logistics. Status of forces.
Testing ranges and sites. Bases and facilities.
Facilities and property.
INTL ORGS: International Civil Aviation Organiza-
tion. International Monetary Fund. North Atlantic
Treaty Organization. World Meteorological Or-
ganization.
TREATY REF: 136UNTS211; 199UNTS67.
PROCEDURE: Future Procedures Contemplated.
Termination.
PARTIES:
Japan
USA (United States)
ANNEX
268 UNTS 360. USA (United States). Supplementation 19 Aug 55. Force 19 Aug 55.
268 UNTS 360. Japan. Supplementation
19 Aug 55. Force 19 Aug 55.
273 UNTS 265. USA (United States). Amendment
24 Apr 56. Force 24 Apr 56.
273 UNTS 265. Japan. Amendment 24 Apr 56.
Force 24 Apr 56.
290 UNTS 316. USA (United States). Supplementation 16 Aug 57. Force 16 Aug 57.
290 UNTS 316. Japan. Supplementation
16 Aug 57. Force 16 Aug 57.
336 UNTS 351. Japan. Supplementation
12 Aug 58. Force 12 Aug 58.
336 UNTS 351. USA (United States). Supplementation 12 Aug 58. Force 12 Aug 58.
344 UNTS 332. Japan. Supplementation
6 Apr 59. Force 6 Apr 59.
344 UNTS 332. USA (United States). Supplementation 6 Apr 59. Force 6 Apr 59.
368 UNTS 344. Japan. Supplementation
8 Jan 60. Force 8 Jan 60.
368 UNTS 344. USA (United States). Supplementation 8 Jan 60. Force 8 Jan 60.
384 UNTS 365. Japan. Supplementation
15 Jul 60. Force 15 Jul 60.
384 UNTS 365. USA (United States). Supplementation 15 Jul 60. Force 15 Jul 60.

102818 Bilateral Agreement **209 UNTS 3**
SIGNED: 22 Mar 55 FORCE: 22 Mar 55
REGISTERED: 13 Apr 55 Australia
ARTICLES: 17 LANGUAGE: English. Chinese.
HEADNOTE: EXCHANGE POSTAL PARCELS
TOPIC: Postal Service
CONCEPTS: Responsibility and liability. Account-
ing procedures. Compensation. Debt settlement.
Postal services. Regulations. Insured letters and
boxes. Conveyance in transit. Parcel post. Rates
and charges.
INTL ORGS: Universal Postal Union.
TREATY REF: 170UNTS63; 186UNTS360;
202UNTS348.
PROCEDURE: Duration. Termination.
PARTIES:
Australia
Taiwan

102819 Multilateral Instrument **209 UNTS 23**
SIGNED: 8 Sep 54 FORCE: 19 Feb 55
REGISTERED: 13 Apr 55 Philippines
ARTICLES: 11 LANGUAGE: English. French.
HEADNOTE: SOUTHEAST ASIA COLLECTIVE DE-
FENSE
TOPIC: Milit Assistance
CONCEPTS: Definition of terms. Exceptions and
exemptions. Treaty interpretation. Annex or ap-
pendix reference. Non-prejudice to UN charter.
Peaceful relations. General cooperation. Estab-
lishment of commission. General health, educa-
tion, culture, welfare and labor. Defense and se-
curity. Military assistance.
INTL ORGS: United Nations. Special Commission.
PROCEDURE: Accession. Denunciation. Ratifica-
tion.
PARTIES:
Australia SIGNED: 8 Sep 54 RATIFIED:
19 Feb 55 FORCE: 19 Feb 55
France SIGNED: 8 Sep 54 RATIFIED: 19 Feb 55
FORCE: 19 Feb 55
New Zealand SIGNED: 8 Sep 54 RATIFIED:
19 Feb 55 FORCE: 19 Feb 55

Pakistan SIGNED: 8 Sep 54
Philippines SIGNED: 8 Sep 54 RATIFIED:
19 Feb 55 FORCE: 19 Feb 55
Thailand SIGNED: 8 Sep 54 RATIFIED: 2 Dec 54
FORCE: 19 Feb 55
UK Great Britain SIGNED: 8 Sep 54 RATIFIED:
19 Feb 55 FORCE: 19 Feb 55
USA (United States) SIGNED: 8 Sep 54 RATI-
FIED: 19 Feb 55 FORCE: 19 Feb 55

102820 Multilateral Convention **209 UNTS 39**
SIGNED: 28 Jun 39 FORCE: 18 Mar 55
REGISTERED: 18 Apr 55 ILO (Labor Org)
ARTICLES: 28 LANGUAGE: English. French.
HEADNOTE: WORK REST HOURS ROAD TRANS-
PORT
TOPIC: ILO Labor
CONCEPTS: Definition of terms. Detailed regula-
tions. Emergencies. Exceptions and exemptions.
Exchange of information and documents. Inves-
tigation of violations. ILO conventions. Holidays
and rest periods. Labor statistics. Safety stan-
dards. Administrative cooperation. Commercial
road vehicles.
INTL ORGS: International Labour Organization.
TREATY REF: 15UNTS35.
PROCEDURE: Amendment. Denunciation. Duration. Ratification. Registration. Renewal or Revival.
PARTIES:
Multilateral
ANNEX
429 UNTS 292. Peru. Ratification 4 Apr 62. Force
4 Apr 63.
504 UNTS 363. Central Afri Rep. Ratification
9 Jun 64. Force 9 Jun 65.

102821 Bilateral Exchange **209 UNTS 61**
SIGNED: 21 Jun 54 FORCE: 21 Jun 54
REGISTERED: 27 Apr 55 UK Great Britain
ARTICLES: 2 LANGUAGE: English.
HEADNOTE: USE LAND MILITARY CEMETERY
TOPIC: Other Military
CONCEPTS: Annex or appendix reference. Title
and deeds. Tax exemptions. Responsibility for
war dead. Upkeep of war graves. Establishment
of war cemeteries.
PARTIES:
UK Great Britain
USA (United States)

102822 Bilateral Exchange **209 UNTS 69**
SIGNED: 5 Nov 54 FORCE: 20 Apr 55
REGISTERED: 27 Apr 55 UK Great Britain
ARTICLES: 2 LANGUAGE: English. French.
HEADNOTE: DOCUMENTS IDENTITY AIRCRAFT
PERSONNEL
TOPIC: Visas
CONCEPTS: Non-visa travel documents. Licenses
and permits. Competency certificate.
TREATY REF: 190LTS155; 15UNTS295.
PROCEDURE: Denunciation. Termination.
PARTIES:
Belgium
UK Great Britain

102823 Bilateral Exchange **209 UNTS 75**
SIGNED: 29 Oct 54 FORCE: 20 Apr 55
REGISTERED: 28 Apr 55 UK Great Britain
ARTICLES: 2 LANGUAGE: English.
HEADNOTE: TERMINATING AGREEMENT 30 MAY
38
TOPIC: Visas
CONCEPTS: Annex type material.
TREATY REF: 191LTS299.
PARTIES:
Sweden
UK Great Britain

102824 Bilateral Exchange **209 UNTS 81**
SIGNED: 31 Dec 54 FORCE: 31 Dec 54
REGISTERED: 28 Apr 55 UK Great Britain
ARTICLES: 2 LANGUAGE: English.
HEADNOTE: IMPORT BOOKS
TOPIC: Education
CONCEPTS: Detailed regulations. Scientific ex-
change. Import quotas. Trade procedures. Gen-
eral technical assistance. Publications ex-
change.

TREATY REF: 190UNTS355.
PARTIES:
UK Great Britain
Yugoslavia
ANNEX
313 UNTS 362. UK Great Britain. Force 30 Jun 57.
313 UNTS 362. Yugoslavia. Force 30 Jun 57.

102825 Bilateral Convention **209 UNTS 87**
SIGNED: 13 Oct 53 FORCE: 1 Apr 55
REGISTERED: 28 Apr 55 UK Great Britain
ARTICLES: 2 LANGUAGE: English. French.
HEADNOTE: SOCIAL SECURITY
TOPIC: Non-ILO Labor
CONCEPTS: Definition of terms. Detailed regulations. Territorial application. General provisions. Domestic legislation. Incorporation of treaty provisions into national law. Dispute settlement. Old age and invalidity insurance. Non-ILO labor relations. Family allowances. Administrative cooperation. Old age insurance. Sickness and invalidity insurance. Social security. Fees and exemptions. Payment schedules. National treatment.
PROCEDURE: Denunciation. Duration. Ratification. Renewal or Revival.
PARTIES:
Luxembourg
UK Great Britain

102826 Bilateral Convention **209 UNTS 129**
SIGNED: 30 Mar 49 FORCE: 16 Sep 49
REGISTERED: 28 Apr 55 UK Great Britain
ARTICLES: 3 LANGUAGE: English. Swedish.
HEADNOTE: DOUBLE TAXATION FISCAL EVASION TAXES INCOME
TOPIC: Taxation
CONCEPTS: Definition of terms. Territorial application. Conformity with municipal law. Exchange of official publications. Teacher and student exchange. Taxation. Death duties. Tax credits. Equitable taxes. General. Tax exemptions. Air transport. Merchant vessels.
PROCEDURE: Duration. Ratification. Termination.
PARTIES:
Sweden
UK Great Britain
ANNEX
210 UNTS 338. UK Great Britain. Supplementation 18 Feb 55.
210 UNTS 338. Sweden. Supplementation 18 Feb 55.
351 UNTS 416. UK Great Britain. Fed Rhod/-Nyasaland. Force 28 May 58.
351 UNTS 416. UK Great Britain. Tanganyika. Force 28 May 58.
351 UNTS 416. UK Great Britain. Zanzibar. Force 28 May 58.
351 UNTS 416. Sweden. Acknowledgement 28 May 58. Force 28 May 58.
351 UNTS 416. UK Great Britain. Kenya. Force 28 May 58.
351 UNTS 416. UK Great Britain. Uganda. Force 28 May 58.
560 UNTS 258. UK Great Britain. Northern Rhodesia. Prolongation 21 Dec 63.
560 UNTS 258. Sweden. Acknowledgement 21 Dec 63.
560 UNTS 258. UK Great Britain. Southern Rhodesia. Prolongation 21 Dec 63.
560 UNTS 258. UK Great Britain. Nyasaland. Prolongation 21 Dec 63.

102827 Bilateral Agreement **209 UNTS 187**
SIGNED: 24 Feb 55 FORCE: 24 Feb 55
REGISTERED: 28 Apr 55 UK Great Britain
ARTICLES: 8 LANGUAGE: English.
HEADNOTE: SUBMISSION TO ARBITRATION
TOPIC: Specif Claim/Waive
CONCEPTS: Detailed regulations. Arbitration. Procedure. Indemnities and reimbursements. Expense sharing formulae. Specific claims or waivers.
INTL ORGS: International Court of Justice. Arbitration Commission.
TREATY REF: 61LTS15.
PARTIES:
Greece
UK Great Britain

102828 Bilateral Convention **209 UNTS 197**
SIGNED: 30 Sep 54 FORCE: 23 Feb 55
REGISTERED: 28 Apr 55 UK Great Britain
ARTICLES: 24 LANGUAGE: English. French.
HEADNOTE: DOUBLE TAXATION TAXES INCOME
TOPIC: Taxation
CONCEPTS: Definition of terms. Territorial application. Conformity with municipal law. Exchange of official publications. Teacher and student exchange. Taxation. Tax credits. Equitable taxes. General. Tax exemptions. Air transport. Merchant vessels.
TREATY REF: 131LTS245.
PROCEDURE: Duration. Ratification. Termination.
PARTIES:
Switzerland
UK Great Britain
ANNEX
425 UNTS 329. UK Great Britain. Force 21 Sep 61.
425 UNTS 329. Switzerland. Acknowledgement 30 May 61. Force 21 Sep 61.
560 UNTS 259. Switzerland. Acknowledgement 18 Dec 63.
560 UNTS 259. UK Great Britain. Northern Rhodesia. Prolongation 13 Dec 63.
560 UNTS 259. UK Great Britain. Southern Rhodesia. Prolongation 13 Dec 63.
560 UNTS 259. UK Great Britain. Nyasaland. Prolongation 13 Dec 63.
603 UNTS 298. UK Great Britain. Amendment 14 Jun 66. Force 20 Dec 66.
603 UNTS 298. Switzerland. Amendment 14 Jun 66. Force 20 Dec 66.

102829 Bilateral Agreement **209 UNTS 231**
SIGNED: 23 Jul 52 FORCE: 20 May 53
REGISTERED: 2 May 55 WHO (World Health)
ARTICLES: 13 LANGUAGE: French.
HEADNOTE: PRIVILEGES IMMUNITIES & FACILITIES
TOPIC: IGO Status/Immunit
CONCEPTS: Definition of terms. Annex or appendix reference. Non-visa travel documents. Diplomatic privileges. Diplomatic missions. Inviolability. Privileges and immunities. Property. Diplomatic correspondence. Procedure. Freedom of meeting. Status of experts.
INTL ORGS: United Nations.
PROCEDURE: Denunciation.
PARTIES:
France
WHO (World Health)

102830 Bilateral Agreement **209 UNTS 261**
SIGNED: 10 Feb 54 FORCE: 1 Dec 54
REGISTERED: 4 May 55 IBRD (World Bank)
ARTICLES: 5 LANGUAGE: English.
HEADNOTE: GUARANTEE AGREEMENT
TOPIC: IBRD Project
CONCEPTS: Loan and credit. Credit provisions. Terms of loan.
PARTIES:
Ecuador
IBRD (World Bank)

102831 Bilateral Agreement **209 UNTS 287**
SIGNED: 12 Nov 54 FORCE: 10 Feb 55
REGISTERED: 4 May 55 IBRD (World Bank)
ARTICLES: 5 LANGUAGE: English.
HEADNOTE: GUARANTEE CONTRACT
TOPIC: IBRD Project
CONCEPTS: Definition of terms. Annex or appendix reference. Exchange of information and documents. Informational records. Inspection and observation. Bonds. Fees and exemptions. Tax exemptions. Domestic obligation. Terms of loan. Loan regulations. Loan guarantee. Guarantor non-interference.
PARTIES:
Peru
IBRD (World Bank)

102832 Bilateral Agreement **209 UNTS 309**
SIGNED: 18 Mar 55 FORCE: 18 Mar 55
REGISTERED: 9 May 55 Norway
ARTICLES: 4 LANGUAGE: Swedish. German.
HEADNOTE: READMITTANCE PERSONS LEGALLY ENTERED COUNTRY
TOPIC: Extradition

CONCEPTS: Time limit. Assistance. Extradition, deportation and repatriation. General cooperation. Recognition of legal documents. Indemnities and reimbursements.
PROCEDURE: Denunciation.
PARTIES:
Germany, West
Norway

102833 Bilateral Agreement **210 UNTS 3**
SIGNED: 19 Oct 54 FORCE: 19 Oct 54
REGISTERED: 10 May 55 United Arab Rep
ARTICLES: 13 LANGUAGE: Arabic. English.
HEADNOTE: AGREEMENT
TOPIC: General Amity
CONCEPTS: Annex or appendix reference. Previous treaty replacement. Non-prejudice to UN charter. General cooperation. Overflights and technical stops. Inland and territorial waters. Military assistance. Withdrawal of forces. Bases and facilities.
INTL ORGS: Arab League.
PROCEDURE: Duration. Termination.
PARTIES:
United Arab Rep
UK Great Britain
ANNEX
222 UNTS 424. United Arab Rep. Supplementation 3 May 55. Force 3 May 55.
222 UNTS 424. UK Great Britain. Supplementation 3 May 55. Force 3 May 55.
225 UNTS 292. United Arab Rep. Supplementation 19 Oct 54. Force 19 Oct 54.
225 UNTS 292. UK Great Britain. Supplementation 19 Oct 54. Force 19 Oct 54.
225 UNTS 362. UK Great Britain. Correction 19 Feb 55.
225 UNTS 362. United Arab Rep. Correction 19 Feb 55.
231 UNTS 374. United Arab Rep. Interpretation 19 Oct 54.
231 UNTS 374. UK Great Britain. Interpretation 19 Oct 54.
252 UNTS 366. United Arab Rep. Prolongation 24 Jun 56. Force 24 Jun 56.
252 UNTS 366. UK Great Britain. Prolongation 24 Jun 56. Force 24 Jun 56.
269 UNTS 366. United Arab Rep. Termination 1 Jan 57. Force 31 Oct 56.

102834 Bilateral Exchange **210 UNTS 63**
SIGNED: 13 Jan 55 FORCE: 13 Feb 55
REGISTERED: 10 May 55 Belgium
ARTICLES: 2 LANGUAGE: Dutch.
HEADNOTE: CROSSING FRONTIER PRESENTATION SEAMANS BOOK
TOPIC: Visas
CONCEPTS: Border traffic and migration. Non-visa travel documents. Repatriation of nationals.
PARTIES:
Belgium
Netherlands

102835 Bilateral Agreement **210 UNTS 71**
SIGNED: 21 Apr 55 FORCE: 21 Apr 55
REGISTERED: 12 May 55 WHO (World Health)
ARTICLES: 6 LANGUAGE: English.
HEADNOTE: TECHNICAL ADVISORY ASSISTANCE
TOPIC: Tech Assistance
CONCEPTS: Treaty implementation. Annex or appendix reference. Previous treaty replacement. Privileges and immunities. General cooperation. Exchange of information and documents. Personnel. Title and deeds. Exchange. Scholarships and grants. Vocational training. Research and development. Expense sharing formulae. Local currency. Domestic obligation. Special projects. Materials, equipment and services. IGO status.
TREATY REF: 210UNTS82; 126UNTS77; 128UNTS233; 33UNTS261.
PROCEDURE: Amendment. Termination.
PARTIES:
Taiwan
WHO (World Health)

102836 Bilateral Agreement **210 UNTS 89**
SIGNED: 10 Jun 54 FORCE: 1 Oct 54
REGISTERED: 16 May 55 IBRD (World Bank)
ARTICLES: 5 LANGUAGE: English.
HEADNOTE: GUARANTEE AGREEMENT

TOPIC: IBRD Project
CONCEPTS: Definition of terms. Annex or appendix reference. Exchange of information and documents. Informational records. Inspection and observation. Bonds. Fees and exemptions. Tax exemptions. Domestic obligation. Terms of loan. Loan regulations. Loan guarantee. Guarantor non-interference.
PARTIES:
France
IBRD (World Bank)

102837 Bilateral Agreement **210 UNTS 113**
SIGNED: 14 Dec 54   FORCE: 4 Jan 55
REGISTERED: 18 May 55 IBRD (World Bank)
ARTICLES: 6 LANGUAGE: English.
HEADNOTE: LOAN AGREEMENT
TOPIC: IBRD Project
CONCEPTS: Definition of terms. Exchange of information and documents. Informational records. Inspection and observation. Accounting procedures. Bonds. Fees and exemptions. Interest rates. Tax exemptions. Domestic obligation. Terms of loan. Loan regulations. Loan guarantee. Guarantor non-interference.
PARTIES:
Belgium
IBRD (World Bank)

102838 Multilateral Convention **210 UNTS 132**
SIGNED: 28 Jun 52   FORCE: 27 Apr 55
REGISTERED: 23 May 55 ILO (Labor Org)
ARTICLES: 87 LANGUAGE: English. French.
HEADNOTE: MINIMUM STANDARDS SOCIAL SECURITY
TOPIC: ILO Labor
CONCEPTS: Definition of terms. Territorial application. Annex or appendix reference. Standardization. Exchange of information and documents. Incorporation of treaty provisions into national law. Public health. ILO conventions. Holidays and rest periods. Old age and invalidity insurance. Wages and salaries. Administrative cooperation. Sickness and invalidity insurance. Social security. Unemployment. Lump sum settlements. Most favored nation clause.
INTL ORGS: International Labour Organization. United Nations.
TREATY REF: 15UNTS40.
PROCEDURE: Amendment. Accession. Denunciation. Duration. Ratification. Registration. Renewal or Revival.
PARTIES:
Multilateral
ANNEX
212 UNTS 402. Greece. Ratification 16 Jun 55. Force 16 Jun 56.
214 UNTS 382. Denmark. Ratification 15 Aug 55. Force 15 Aug 56.
225 UNTS 366. Israel. Ratification 16 Dec 55. Force 16 Dec 56.
248 UNTS 409. Italy. Ratification 8 Jun 56. Force 8 Jun 57.
276 UNTS 367. Italy. Declaration 20 Aug 57.
287 UNTS 348. Germany, West. Ratification 21 Feb 58. Force 21 Feb 58.
312 UNTS 426. UK Great Britain. Declaration 28 Jul 58.
320 UNTS 344. UK Great Britain. Declaration 16 Dec 58.
345 UNTS 365. Belgium. Ratification 26 Nov 59. Force 26 Nov 60.
356 UNTS 374. UK Great Britain. Jersey Island.
356 UNTS 374. UK Great Britain. Guernsey Island.
356 UNTS 374. Denmark. Implementation 3 Mar 60. Force 3 Mar 60.
381 UNTS 410. UK Great Britain. Isle of Man.
396 UNTS 340. Iceland. Ratification 20 Feb 61. Force 20 Feb 62.
406 UNTS 310. Peru. Qualified Ratification 23 Aug 61. Force 23 Aug 62.
413 UNTS 373. Mexico. Qualified Ratification 12 Oct 61. Force 12 Oct 62.
444 UNTS 343. Senegal. Qualified Ratification 22 Oct 62. Force 22 Oct 63.
444 UNTS 343. Sweden. Qualified Ratification 12 Oct 62. Force 12 Oct 63.
444 UNTS 343. Netherlands. Qualified Ratification 11 Oct 62. Force 11 Oct 63.
488 UNTS 369. Netherlands. Ratification 22 Jan 64.

510 UNTS 366. Luxembourg. Ratification 31 Aug 64. Force 31 Aug 65.
640 UNTS 385. Ireland. Ratification 17 Jun 68. Force 17 Jun 69.
642 UNTS 395. Mauritania. Ratification 15 Jul 68. Force 15 Jul 69.

102839 Multilateral Agreement **210 UNTS 197**
SIGNED: 1 Dec 54   FORCE: 1 Dec 54
REGISTERED: 26 May 55 UK Great Britain
ARTICLES: 14 LANGUAGE: English. French. German.
HEADNOTE: ADMINISTRATIVE ARBITRAL TRIBUNAL MIXED COMMISSION
TOPIC: Admin Cooperation
CONCEPTS: General provisions. Annex or appendix reference. Personnel. Wages and salaries. Expense sharing formulae. Fees and exemptions. Internal structure.
INTL ORGS: Arbitration Commission. Special Commission.
PARTIES:
France SIGNED: 1 Dec 54 FORCE: 1 Dec 54
Germany, West SIGNED: 1 Dec 54 FORCE: 1 Dec 54
UK Great Britain SIGNED: 1 Dec 54 FORCE: 1 Dec 54
USA (United States) SIGNED: 1 Dec 54 FORCE: 1 Dec 54
ANNEX
265 UNTS 380. USA (United States). Amendment 30 Nov 56. Force 30 Nov 56.
265 UNTS 380. UK Great Britain. Amendment 30 Nov 56. Force 30 Nov 56.
265 UNTS 380. France. Amendment 30 Nov 56. Force 30 Nov 56.
265 UNTS 380. Germany, West. Amendment 30 Nov 56. Force 30 Nov 56.
385 UNTS 378. UK Great Britain. Amendment 29 Aug 60. Force 29 Aug 60.
385 UNTS 378. USA (United States). Amendment 29 Aug 60. Force 29 Aug 60.
385 UNTS 378. Germany, West. Amendment 29 Aug 60. Force 29 Aug 60.
385 UNTS 378. France. Amendment 29 Aug 60. Force 29 Aug 60.

102840 Bilateral Agreement **210 UNTS 223**
SIGNED: 31 Mar 55   FORCE: 31 Mar 55
REGISTERED: 26 May 55 UK Great Britain
ARTICLES: 23 LANGUAGE: English. Spanish.
HEADNOTE: TRADE PAYMENTS AMITY ECONOMIC RELATIONS
TOPIC: General Economic
CONCEPTS: General provisions. Annex or appendix reference. Establishment of commission. General trade. Trade procedures. Finances and payments. Accounting procedures. Banking. Balance of payments. Currency. Financial programs. Inadequacy of funds. Payment schedules. Commodity trade. Quotas. Most favored nation clause. Loan and credit. Credit provisions. Purchase authorization. Loan repayment. Navigational conditions. Ports and pilotage.
INTL ORGS: Special Commission.
TREATY REF: CMD7412; 191UNTS378; 160UNTS382; 83UNTS217.
PROCEDURE: Duration. Future Procedures Contemplated. Termination.
PARTIES:
Argentina
UK Great Britain
ANNEX
218 UNTS 393. UK Great Britain. Prolongation 11 Jul 55. Force 11 Jul 55.
218 UNTS 393. Argentina. Prolongation 11 Jul 55. Force 11 Jul 55.

102841 Bilateral Agreement **210 UNTS 265**
SIGNED: 18 Nov 54   FORCE: 18 Nov 54
REGISTERED: 26 May 55 UK Great Britain
ARTICLES: 3 LANGUAGE: English. Portuguese.
HEADNOTE: NORTHERN RHODESIA-ANGOLA FRONTIER
TOPIC: Territory Boundary
CONCEPTS: Annex or appendix reference. Establishment of commission. Accounting procedures. Financial programs. Markers and definitions.
INTL ORGS: Special Commission.
TREATY REF: 2'18DEMARTENS185;.

PARTIES:
Portugal
UK Great Britain
ANNEX
539 UNTS 353. Portugal. Interpretation and Implementation 21 Oct 64. Force 21 Oct 65.
539 UNTS 353. South Africa. Acceptance 16 Oct 64.
539 UNTS 353. UK Great Britain. Interpretation and Implementation 21 Oct 64. Force 21 Oct 65.

102842 Bilateral Agreement **210 UNTS 303**
SIGNED: 20 Jan 55   FORCE: 20 Jan 55
REGISTERED: 26 May 55 UK Great Britain
ARTICLES: 12 LANGUAGE: English. Danish.
HEADNOTE: MILITARY SERVICE
TOPIC: Milit Servic/Citiz
CONCEPTS: Definition of terms. Emergencies. Territorial application. Annex or appendix reference. Exchange of information and documents. Procedure. Certificates of service. Foreign nationals. Service in foreign army.
PROCEDURE: Termination. Application to Non-self-governing Territories.
PARTIES:
Denmark
UK Great Britain
ANNEX
229 UNTS 344. UK Great Britain. Isle of Man. Force 30 Sep 55.
229 UNTS 344. Denmark. Acknowledgement 30 Sep 55. Force 30 Sep 55.
229 UNTS 344. UK Great Britain. Channel Islands. Force 30 Sep 55.

102843 Multilateral Agreement **210 UNTS 317**
SIGNED: 8 Jun 52   FORCE: 28 Feb 55
REGISTERED: 26 May 55 UK Great Britain
ARTICLES: 3 LANGUAGE: English.
HEADNOTE: WAR CEMETERIES
TOPIC: Other Military
CONCEPTS: Previous treaty extension. War graves.
TREATY REF: 184LTS445.
PARTIES:
Australia SIGNED: 8 Jun 52 FORCE: 28 Feb 55
Canada SIGNED: 8 Jun 52 FORCE: 28 Feb 55
United Arab Rep SIGNED: 8 Jun 52 FORCE: 28 Feb 55
India SIGNED: 8 Jun 52 FORCE: 28 Feb 55
New Zealand SIGNED: 8 Jun 52 FORCE: 28 Feb 55
Pakistan SIGNED: 8 Jun 52 FORCE: 28 Feb 55
South Africa SIGNED: 8 Jun 52 FORCE: 28 Feb 55
UK Great Britain SIGNED: 8 Jun 52 FORCE: 28 Feb 55

102844 Multilateral Agreement **211 UNTS 3**
SIGNED: 12 Mar 55   FORCE: 1 Jun 55
REGISTERED: 1 Jun 55 Norway
ARTICLES: 13 LANGUAGE: Swedish. Danish. Norwegian.
HEADNOTE: ROAD TRANSPORT
TOPIC: Land Transport
CONCEPTS: Default remedies. Definition of terms. Exceptions and exemptions. General provisions. Conformity with municipal law. Exchange of information and documents. Free passage and transit. Passenger transport. Transport of goods. Driving permits. Motor vehicles and combinations. Road rules. Boundaries of territory.
PROCEDURE: Termination.
PARTIES:
Denmark SIGNED: 2 Mar 55 FORCE: 1 Jun 55
Norway SIGNED: 2 Mar 55 FORCE: 1 Jun 55
Sweden SIGNED: 2 Mar 55 FORCE: 1 Jun 55

102845 Bilateral Exchange **211 UNTS 43**
SIGNED: 15 Apr 55   FORCE: 1 May 55
REGISTERED: 1 Jun 55 Belgium
ARTICLES: 2 LANGUAGE: French.
HEADNOTE: FREE ENTRY VISAS
TOPIC: Visas
CONCEPTS: Passports non-diplomatic. Visas.
PARTIES:
Belgium
Israel

102846 Bilateral Exchange **211 UNTS 49**
SIGNED: 16 Feb 55 FORCE: 4 Apr 55
REGISTERED: 1 Jun 55 Belgium
ARTICLES: 2 LANGUAGE: Dutch.
HEADNOTE: IMPROVE CONDITION FACILITATE MOVEMENT REFUGEES
TOPIC: Refugees
CONCEPTS: Emergencies. Visa abolition. Conformity with municipal law.
TREATY REF: 189UNTS137.
PROCEDURE: Denunciation. Ratification.
PARTIES:
  Belgium
  Netherlands
                    ANNEX
410 UNTS 295. Belgium. Denunciation 9 Aug 61. Force 10 Nov 61.

102847 Bilateral Exchange **211 UNTS 57**
SIGNED: 4 Apr 55 FORCE: 19 Apr 55
REGISTERED: 1 Jun 55 Belgium
ARTICLES: 2 LANGUAGE: French.
HEADNOTE: IMPROVE CONDITIONS FACILITATE MOVEMENT REFUGEES
TOPIC: Refugees
CONCEPTS: Emergencies. Visa abolition. Conformity with municipal law.
TREATY REF: 189UNTS137.
PROCEDURE: Denunciation.
PARTIES:
  Belgium
  Luxembourg
                    ANNEX
410 UNTS 296. Belgium. Denunciation 15 Jul 61. Force 16 Oct 61.

102848 Bilateral Agreement **211 UNTS 63**
SIGNED: 11 Feb 54 FORCE: 14 May 55
REGISTERED: 1 Jun 55 Belgium
ARTICLES: 25 LANGUAGE: French. Finnish.
HEADNOTE: DOUBLE TAXATION TAXES INCOME PROPERTY
TOPIC: Taxation
CONCEPTS: Exchange of official publications. Responsibility and liability. Negotiation. Teacher and student exchange. Claims and settlements. Taxation. Death duties. Equitable taxes. General. Tax exemptions. Air transport. Merchant vessels.
TREATY REF: 111LTS31.
PROCEDURE: Duration. Ratification. Termination.
PARTIES:
  Belgium
  Finland

102849 Unilateral Instrument **211 UNTS 109**
SIGNED: 2 Jun 55 FORCE: 2 Jun 55
REGISTERED: 2 Jun 55 United Nations
ARTICLES: 1 LANGUAGE: English.
HEADNOTE: ACCEPTANCE ICJ JURISDICTION
TOPIC: ICJ Option Clause
CONCEPTS: Compulsory jurisdiction.
INTL ORGS: International Court of Justice.
PROCEDURE: Duration. Termination.
PARTIES:
  UK Great Britain
                    ANNEX
219 UNTS 383. UK Great Britain. Termination 31 Oct 55.

102850 Bilateral Agreement **211 UNTS 115**
SIGNED: 5 Apr 55 FORCE: 23 May 55
REGISTERED: 2 Jun 55 IBRD (World Bank)
ARTICLES: 7 LANGUAGE: English.
HEADNOTE: LOAN AGREEMENT
TOPIC: IBRD Project
CONCEPTS: Default remedies. Definition of terms. Annex or appendix reference. Exchange of information and documents. Informational records. Inspection and observation. Accounting procedures. Bonds. Fees and exemptions. Interest rates. Tax exemptions. Domestic obligation. Terms of loan. Loan regulations. Loan guarantee. Guarantor non-interference.
PARTIES:
  Peru
  IBRD (World Bank)

102851 Bilateral Agreement **211 UNTS 135**
SIGNED: 29 Dec 54 FORCE: 3 Jun 55

REGISTERED: 10 Jun 55 IBRD (World Bank)
ARTICLES: 5 LANGUAGE: English.
HEADNOTE: GUARANTEE AGREEMENT
TOPIC: IBRD Project
CONCEPTS: Definition of terms. Annex or appendix reference. Exchange of information and documents. Informational records. Inspection and observation. Bonds. Fees and exemptions. Tax exemptions. Domestic obligation. Terms of loan. Loan regulations. Loan guarantee. Guarantor non-interference.
PARTIES:
  Colombia
  IBRD (World Bank)

102852 Bilateral Agreement **211 UNTS 159**
SIGNED: 19 Apr 55 FORCE: 26 Apr 55
REGISTERED: 10 Jun 55 IBRD (World Bank)
ARTICLES: 8 LANGUAGE: English.
HEADNOTE: LOAN AGREEMENT
TOPIC: IBRD Project
CONCEPTS: Default remedies. Definition of terms. Annex or appendix reference. Exchange of information and documents. Informational records. Inspection and observation. Accounting procedures. Bonds. Fees and exemptions. Interest rates. Tax exemptions. Domestic obligation. Terms of loan. Loan regulations. Loan guarantee. Guarantor non-interference.
PARTIES:
  Norway
  IBRD (World Bank)

102853 Bilateral Exchange **211 UNTS 215**
SIGNED: 22 Apr 54 FORCE: 27 Aug 54
REGISTERED: 16 Jun 55 South Africa
ARTICLES: 2 LANGUAGE: Afrikaans. Dutch.
HEADNOTE: DOUBLE TAXATION INCOME PROFITS SEA AIR TRANSPORT
TOPIC: Taxation
CONCEPTS: Taxation. General.
PARTIES:
  Netherlands
  South Africa

102854 Bilateral Agreement **211 UNTS 225**
SIGNED: 29 Jun 53 FORCE: 2 Jun 54
REGISTERED: 22 Jun 55 Pakistan
ARTICLES: 18 LANGUAGE: English.
HEADNOTE: CULTURAL AGREEMENT
TOPIC: Culture
CONCEPTS: Friendship and amity. Non-diplomatic delegations. Conformity with municipal law. General cooperation. Domestic legislation. Operating agencies. Establishment of commission. Recognition of degrees. Exchange. Teacher and student exchange. Professorships. Institute establishment. Scholarships and grants. General cultural cooperation. Athletes. Research cooperation. Anthropology and archeology. Fees and exemptions. General transportation. Publications exchange. Mass media exchange.
INTL ORGS: United Nations Educational, Scientific and Cultural Organization. United Nations. Special Commission.
PROCEDURE: Denunciation. Duration. Future Procedures Contemplated. Ratification. Renewal or Revival.
PARTIES:
  Pakistan
  Turkey

102855 Multilateral Treaty **211 UNTS 237**
SIGNED: 9 Aug 54 FORCE: 21 May 55
REGISTERED: 23 Jun 55 Greece
ARTICLES: 14 LANGUAGE: French.
HEADNOTE: ALLIANCE POLITICAL COOPERATION MUTUAL ASSISTANCE
TOPIC: General Amity
CONCEPTS: Non-prejudice to UN charter. Peaceful relations. General cooperation. Establishment of commission. Defense and security.
INTL ORGS: North Atlantic Treaty Organization. United Nations. Special Commission.
TREATY REF: 167UNTS21; 126UNTS350.
PROCEDURE: Denunciation. Duration. Ratification. Registration. Renewal or Revival.
PARTIES:
  Greece SIGNED: 9 Aug 54 RATIFIED: 30 Apr 55 FORCE: 21 Mar 55

Turkey SIGNED: 9 Aug 54 RATIFIED: 21 May 55 FORCE: 21 Mar 55
Yugoslavia SIGNED: 9 Aug 54 RATIFIED: 25 Feb 55 FORCE: 21 Mar 55

102856 Bilateral Exchange **211 UNTS 249**
SIGNED: 7 Mar 55 FORCE: 7 Mar 55
REGISTERED: 24 Jun 55 UK Great Britain
ARTICLES: 2 LANGUAGE: English. French.
HEADNOTE: SETTLEMENT CLAIMS
TOPIC: General Military
CONCEPTS: Claims and settlements. General military.
PARTIES:
  Greece
  UK Great Britain

102857 Bilateral Exchange **211 UNTS 255**
SIGNED: 26 Jun 53 FORCE: 30 Sep 54
REGISTERED: 28 Jun 55 South Africa
ARTICLES: 2 LANGUAGE: English.
HEADNOTE: DOUBLE TAXATION PROFTS SEA AIR TRANSPORT
TOPIC: Taxation
CONCEPTS: Definition of terms. Taxation. Tax exemptions. Air transport. Merchant vessels.
PROCEDURE: Duration. Termination.
PARTIES:
  Italy
  South Africa

102858 Bilateral Agreement **211 UNTS 263**
SIGNED: 4 Feb 54 FORCE: 12 Jun 54
REGISTERED: 28 Jun 55 Pakistan
ARTICLES: 7 LANGUAGE: English.
HEADNOTE: COOPERATION
TOPIC: General Amity
CONCEPTS: Peaceful relations. General cooperation. Exchange of information and documents. Rearmament restrictions and controls. Exchange of defense information.
INTL ORGS: United Nations.
PROCEDURE: Accession. Denunciation. Duration. Future Procedures Contemplated. Ratification. Renewal or Revival. Termination.
PARTIES:
  Pakistan
  Turkey

102859 Bilateral Exchange **212 UNTS 3**
SIGNED: 9 Jan 53 FORCE: 1 Feb 53
REGISTERED: 1 Jul 55 USA (United States)
ARTICLES: 2 LANGUAGE: English. German.
HEADNOTE: PASSPORT VISA FEES
TOPIC: Visas
CONCEPTS: Time limit. Visa abolition. Resident permits. Non-visa travel documents. Fees and exemptions.
PARTIES:
  Germany, West
  USA (United States)

102860 Bilateral Protocol **212 UNTS 13**
SIGNED: 4 Jul 55 FORCE: 4 Jul 55
REGISTERED: 4 Jul 55 United Nations
ARTICLES: 2 LANGUAGE: English.
HEADNOTE: ADDITIONAL PROTOCOL
TOPIC: Admin Cooperation
CONCEPTS: Annex type material.
PARTIES:
  Indonesia
  UNICEF (Children)

102861 Multilateral Convention **212 UNTS 17**
SIGNED: 7 Dec 50 FORCE: 7 Jul 55
REGISTERED: 7 Jul 55 United Nations
ARTICLES: 12 LANGUAGE: English. French.
HEADNOTE: SLAVERY
TOPIC: Admin Cooperation
CONCEPTS: Definition of terms. Territorial application. General cooperation. Domestic legislation. Existing tribunals.
INTL ORGS: International Court of Justice. United Nations. Arbitration Commission.
TREATY REF: 3'2DEMARTNES360; 54LTS435; 134LTS453;___.
PROCEDURE: Accession. Denunciation. Ratification.

PARTIES:
Afghanistan FORCE: 7 Jul 55
Australia FORCE: 7 Jul 55
Austria FORCE: 7 Jul 55
Canada FORCE: 7 Jul 55
Cuba FORCE: 7 Jul 55
Denmark FORCE: 7 Jul 55
United Arab Rep FORCE: 7 Jul 55
Finland FORCE: 7 Jul 55
India FORCE: 7 Jul 55
Iraq FORCE: 7 Jul 55
Italy FORCE: 7 Jul 55
Liberia FORCE: 7 Jul 55
Mexico FORCE: 7 Jul 55
Monaco FORCE: 7 Jul 55
Netherlands Netherlands Antilles RATIFIED:
  7 Dec 50 FORCE: 7 Jul 55
Netherlands Dutch New Guinea RATIFIED:
  7 Dec 50 FORCE: 7 Jul 55
Netherlands SIGNED: 7 Dec 50 FORCE: 7 Jul 55
Netherlands Surinam RATIFIED: 7 Dec 50
  FORCE: 7 Jul 55
New Zealand FORCE: 7 Jul 55
South Africa FORCE: 7 Jul 55
Sweden FORCE: 7 Jul 55
Switzerland FORCE: 7 Jul 55
Syria FORCE: 7 Jul 55
Turkey FORCE: 7 Jul 55
UK Great Britain FORCE: 7 Jul 55
Yugoslavia FORCE: 7 Jul 55
                    ANNEX
212 UNTS 383. Philippines. Accession 12 Jul 55.
214 UNTS 383. Ecuador. Accession 17 Aug 55.
214 UNTS 383. Israel. Accession 12 Sep 55.
218 UNTS 394. Pakistan. Accession 30 Sep 55.
223 UNTS 381. Greece. Acceptance 12 Dec 55.
223 UNTS 381. Taiwan. Acceptance 14 Dec 55.
230 UNTS 446. USA (United States). Accession
  7 Mar 56.
248 UNTS 381. Vietnam. Accession 14 Aug 56.
250 UNTS 314.   Byelorussia.   Accession
  13 Sep 56.
260 UNTS 454. Libya. Accession 14 Feb 57.
265 UNTS 386. Norway. Acceptance 11 Apr 57.
265 UNTS 386. Burma. Acceptance 29 Apr 57.
271 UNTS 430. Albania. Accession 2 Jul 57.
276 UNTS 368. Sudan. Acceptance 9 Sep 57.
281 UNTS 405. Romania. Acceptance 13 Nov 57.
287 UNTS 349. Hungary. Acceptance 26 Feb 58.
290 UNTS 326. Ceylon (Sri Lanka). Accession
  21 Mar 58.
320 UNTS 345.   Ukrainian   SSR.   Accession
  27 Jan 59.
327 UNTS 372. USSR (Soviet Union). Accession
  8 Aug 56.
328 UNTS 333.   Morocco.   Acceptance
  11 May 59.
328 UNTS 333. Jordan. Accession 5 May 59.
399 UNTS 272. Nigeria. Succession 26 Jun 61.
406 UNTS 311. Ireland. Acceptance 31 Aug 61.
423 UNTS 309.   Sierra   Leone.   Succession
  13 Mar 62.
433 UNTS 357. Guinea. Acceptance 12 Jul 62.
445 UNTS 334.   Tanganyika.   Accession
  28 Nov 62.
448 UNTS 329. Belgium. Accession 13 Dec 62.
450 UNTS 420. Nepal. Accession 7 Jan 63.
453 UNTS 359. France. Acceptance 14 Feb 63.
466 UNTS 389. Kuwait. Accession 28 May 63.
482 UNTS 367. Algeria. Accession 20 Nov 63.
503 UNTS 336. Jamaica. Succession 30 Jul 64.
506 UNTS 371. Uganda. Accession 12 Aug 64.
520 UNTS 429. Niger. Acceptance 7 Dec 64.
541 UNTS 322. Malawi. Accession 2 Aug 65.
551 UNTS 291. Brazil. Accession 6 Jan 66.
551 UNTS 291. Malta. Succession 3 Jan 66.
560 UNTS 261.   Trinidad/Tobago.   Succession
  11 Apr 66.
567 UNTS 336. Tunisia. Accession 15 Jul 66.
653 UNTS 458. Mongolia. Accession 20 Dec 68.

102862   Bilateral Agreement   **212 UNTS 27**
SIGNED: 11 Aug 52   FORCE: 15 Sep 53
REGISTERED: 12 Jul 55 USA (United States)
ARTICLES: 20 LANGUAGE: English. Japanese.
HEADNOTE: CIVIL AIR TRANSPORT
TOPIC: Air Transport
CONCEPTS: Definition of terms. Detailed regula-
tions. Exceptions and exemptions. Annex or ap-
pendix reference. Conformity with municipal
law. General cooperation. Domestic legislation.
Licenses and permits. Recognition of legal docu-
ments. Use of facilities. Arbitration. Procedure.
Special tribunals. Indemnities and reimburse-
ments. Fees and exemptions. Non-interest rates

and fees. National treatment. Tax exemptions.
Customs exemptions. Competency certificate.
Routes and logistics. Navigational conditions.
Permit designation. Air transport. Airport facili-
ties. Airworthiness certificates. Conditions of air-
lines operating permission. Overflights and technical stops. Operating authorizations and regula-
tions. Licenses and certificates of nationality.
INTL ORGS: International Civil Aviation Organiza-
tion. Arbitration Commission.
TREATY REF: 15UNTS295.
PROCEDURE: Amendment. Future Procedures
Contemplated. Ratification. Registration. Termination. Application to Non-self-governing Territories.
PARTIES:
Japan
USA (United States)
                    ANNEX
340 UNTS 347. USA (United States). Amendment
  14 Jan 59. Force 14 Jan 59.
340 UNTS 347. Japan. Amendment 14 Jan 59.
  Force 14 Jan 59.

102863   Bilateral Agreement   **212 UNTS 93**
SIGNED: 13 Jun 50   FORCE: 13 Jun 50
REGISTERED: 12 Jul 55 USA (United States)
ARTICLES: 13 LANGUAGE: English. Hebrew.
HEADNOTE: AIR TRANSPORT
TOPIC: Air Transport
CONCEPTS: Definition of terms. Exceptions and
exemptions. Annex or appendix reference. Con-
formity with municipal law. Licenses and per-
mits. Recognition of legal documents. Use of fa-
cilities. Arbitration. Procedure. Special tribunals.
Competence of tribunal. Fees and exemptions.
Most favored nation clause. National treatment.
Customs exemptions. Competency certificate.
Routes and logistics. Navigational conditions.
Permit designation. Air transport. Airport facili-
ties. Airworthiness certificates. Conditions of air-
lines operating permission. Operating authoriza-
tions and regulations. Licenses and certificates
of nationality.
INTL ORGS: International Civil Aviation Organiza-
tion. Arbitration Commission.
TREATY REF: 15UNTS295.
PROCEDURE: Amendment. Future Procedures
Contemplated. Registration. Termination.
PARTIES:
Israel
USA (United States)

102864   Bilateral Exchange   **212 UNTS 129**
SIGNED: 1 Jun 51   FORCE: 1 Jun 51
REGISTERED: 12 Jul 55 USA (United States)
ARTICLES: 2 LANGUAGE: English.
HEADNOTE: WAIVER PASSPORT VISA FEES CER-
TAIN AIRCRAFT CREWS
TOPIC: Visas
CONCEPTS: Visa abolition. Non-visa travel docu-
ments. Fees and exemptions.
PARTIES:
Israel
USA (United States)

102865   Bilateral Exchange   **212 UNTS 135**
SIGNED: 30 Jun 53   FORCE: 30 Jun 53
REGISTERED: 12 Jul 55 USA (United States)
ARTICLES: 2 LANGUAGE: English.
HEADNOTE: TECHNICAL COOPERATION PRO-
GRAM AGRICULTURE
TOPIC: Direct Aid
CONCEPTS: Treaty implementation. Annex type
material. General cooperation. Operating agen-
cies. Personnel. Disease control. Vocational
training. Currency deposits. Expense sharing for-
mulae. Agriculture. Assistance.
TREATY REF: 148UNTS39.
PROCEDURE: Duration. Termination.
PARTIES:
Ethiopia
USA (United States)

102866   Bilateral Exchange   **212 UNTS 143**
SIGNED: 13 Mar 53   FORCE: 2 Apr 53
REGISTERED: 12 Jul 55 USA (United States)
ARTICLES: 2 LANGUAGE: English. French.
HEADNOTE: ECONOMIC COOPERATION
TOPIC: Direct Aid

CONCEPTS: Guarantees and safeguards. Arbitra-
tion. Payment schedules. Claims and settle-
ments. Assets transfer. Economic assistance.
PARTIES:
Haiti
USA (United States)

102867   Bilateral Exchange   **212 UNTS 149**
SIGNED: 18 Mar 53   FORCE: 18 Mar 53
REGISTERED: 12 Jul 55 USA (United States)
ARTICLES: 2 LANGUAGE: English. Japanese.
HEADNOTE: TRAINING PROGRAM JAPANESE NA-
TIONAL SAFETY FORCE OFFICERS
TOPIC: Tech Assistance
CONCEPTS: Treaty implementation. Vocational
training. Assistance.
PARTIES:
Japan
USA (United States)

102868   Bilateral Exchange   **212 UNTS 157**
SIGNED: 25 Feb 53   FORCE: 25 Feb 53
REGISTERED: 12 Jul 55 USA (United States)
ARTICLES: 2 LANGUAGE: English.
HEADNOTE: ECONOMIC COOPERATION
TOPIC: Direct Aid
CONCEPTS: Annex or appendix reference. Annex
type material. Public information. Exchange. Re-
search and development. Funding procedures.
Domestic obligation. Agriculture. Economic as-
sistance. Loan and credit. Industry.
INTL ORGS: Organization for Economic Co-opera-
tion and Development.
TREATY REF: 22UNTS263.
PARTIES:
UK Great Britain
USA (United States)

102869   Bilateral Exchange   **212 UNTS 175**
SIGNED: 25 Jun 53   FORCE: 25 Jun 53
REGISTERED: 13 Jul 55 USA (United States)
ARTICLES: 2 LANGUAGE: English.
HEADNOTE: TECHNICAL COOPERATION PRO-
GRAM EDUCATION
TOPIC: Tech Assistance
CONCEPTS: Annex type material. Previous treaty
replacement. Personnel. Exchange. Vocational
training. Monetary and gold transfers. Currency
deposits. Financial programs. Funding proce-
dures. Local currency. Domestic obligation. As-
sistance.
TREATY REF: 148UNTS39; 181UNTS207.
PROCEDURE: Duration. Termination.
PARTIES:
Ethiopia
USA (United States)

102870   Bilateral Exchange   **212 UNTS 183**
SIGNED: 21 May 52   FORCE: 21 May 52
REGISTERED: 13 Jul 55 USA (United States)
ARTICLES: 3 LANGUAGE: English. Arabic.
HEADNOTE: TECHNICAL COOPERATION PRO-
GRAM WATER RESOURCE DEVELOPMENT
TOPIC: Tech Assistance
CONCEPTS: Annex type material. Personnel. Title
and deeds. Research and development. Finan-
cial programs. Domestic obligation. Assistance.
Materials, equipment and services. Irrigation.
Regulation of natural resources.
TREATY REF: 151UNTS179; 205UNTS25;,33;
206UNTS3.
PROCEDURE: Duration. Termination.
PARTIES:
Iraq
USA (United States)

102871   Bilateral Exchange   **212 UNTS 193**
SIGNED: 9 Jun 52   FORCE: 27 Jul 52
REGISTERED: 13 Jul 55 USA (United States)
ARTICLES: 2 LANGUAGE: English. Arabic.
HEADNOTE: TECHNICAL COOPERATION PRO-
GRAM HEALTH & SANITATION
TOPIC: Tech Assistance
CONCEPTS: Treaty implementation. Annex type
material. Personnel. Public health. Sanitation.
Vocational training. Financial programs. Domes-
tic obligation. Assistance.
TREATY REF: 151UNTS179.
PROCEDURE: Duration. Termination.

PARTIES:
Iraq
USA (United States)

102872 Bilateral Exchange **212 UNTS 201**
SIGNED: 23 Oct 52 FORCE: 16 Nov 52
REGISTERED: 13 Jul 55 USA (United States)
ARTICLES: 2 LANGUAGE: English. Arabic.
HEADNOTE: TECHNICAL PROGRAM ECONOMIC
DEVELOPMENT
TOPIC: Tech Assistance
CONCEPTS: Guarantees and safeguards. Time
limit. Exchange of information and documents.
Operating agencies. Personnel. Vocational train-
ing. Indemnities and reimbursements. Exchange
rates and regulations. Financial programs. Local
currency. Domestic obligation. Assistance. Eco-
nomic assistance.
TREATY REF: 151UNTS179.
PARTIES:
Iraq
USA (United States)

102873 Bilateral Exchange **212 UNTS 211**
SIGNED: 27 Aug 53 FORCE: 20 May 55
REGISTERED: 14 Jul 55 South Africa
ARTICLES: 2 LANGUAGE: English. Italian.
HEADNOTE: WAR GRAVES
TOPIC: Other Military
CONCEPTS: Use of facilities. National treatment.
Establishment of war cemeteries.
PARTIES:
Italy
South Africa

102874 Bilateral Agreement **212 UNTS 217**
SIGNED: 24 Mar 55 FORCE: 28 Jun 55
REGISTERED: 18 Jul 55 IBRD (World Bank)
ARTICLES: 5 LANGUAGE: English.
HEADNOTE: GUARANTEE AGREEMENT
TOPIC: IBRD Project
CONCEPTS: Annex or appendix reference. Ex-
change of information and documents. Informa-
tional records. Inspection and observation.
Bonds. Fees and exemptions. Tax exemptions.
Domestic obligation. Terms of loan. Loan regula-
tions. Loan guarantee. Guarantor non-interfer-
ence.
PARTIES:
Colombia
IBRD (World Bank)

102875 Bilateral Exchange **212 UNTS 249**
SIGNED: 19 Jun 53 FORCE: 19 Jun 53
REGISTERED: 19 Jul 55 USA (United States)
ARTICLES: 2 LANGUAGE: English.
HEADNOTE: NON-ASSERTION IMMUNITY SUITS
AIR TRANSPORT
TOPIC: Admin Cooperation
CONCEPTS: General cooperation. Waiver of im-
munity.
PARTIES:
Netherlands
USA (United States)

102876 Bilateral Exchange **212 UNTS 255**
SIGNED: 30 Jun 54 FORCE: 10 Jul 51
REGISTERED: 20 Jul 55 Belgium
ARTICLES: 2 LANGUAGE: English. French.
HEADNOTE: METEOROLOGICAL WATCH BEL-
GIAN CIVIL AIRCRAFT ATLANTIC
TOPIC: Air Transport
CONCEPTS: Conditions. Exchange of information
and documents. Meteorology. Currency. Pay-
ment schedules. Routes and logistics. Airport fa-
cilities.
INTL ORGS: International Civil Aviation Organiza-
tion.
PROCEDURE. Termination.
PARTIES:
Belgium
Ireland

102877 Bilateral Exchange **213 UNTS 3**
SIGNED: 9 Jun 53 FORCE: 9 Jun 53
REGISTERED: 26 Jul 55 USA (United States)
ARTICLES: 2 LANGUAGE: English. Spanish.
HEADNOTE: COOPERATIVE PROGRAM FIELD AG-

RICULTURE NATURAL RESOURCES DEVELOP-
MENT
TOPIC: Tech Assistance
CONCEPTS: Treaty implementation. Annex type
material. Privileges and immunities. Exchange of
information and documents. Domestic legisla-
tion. Operating agencies. General property. At-
tachment of funds. Financial programs. Garnish-
ment of funds. Seizure funds. Tax exemptions.
Customs exemptions. Agriculture. Assistance.
Materials, equipment and services. Natural re-
sources.
TREATY REF: 141UNTS15.
PROCEDURE: Termination.
PARTIES:
Colombia
USA (United States)

102878 Bilateral Agreement **213 UNTS 15**
SIGNED: 21 May 53 FORCE: 21 May 53
REGISTERED: 26 Jul 55 USA (United States)
ARTICLES: 31 LANGUAGE: English. Spanish.
HEADNOTE: ARMY MISSION
TOPIC: Military Mission
CONCEPTS: Definition of terms. Previous treaty re-
placement. Use of facilities. Compensation. In-
demnities and reimbursements. Exchange rates
and regulations. Expense sharing formulae. Tax
exemptions. Customs exemptions. Military assis-
tance. Military training. Security of information.
Airforce-army-navy personnel ratio. Ranks and
privileges. Conditions for assistance missions.
Third country military personnel. Status of
forces.
PROCEDURE: Denunciation. Duration. Renewal or
Revival. Termination.
PARTIES:
El Salvador
USA (United States)

102879 Bilateral Agreement **213 UNTS 37**
SIGNED: 23 Jun 53 FORCE: 23 Jun 53
REGISTERED: 26 Jul 55 USA (United States)
ARTICLES: 13 LANGUAGE: English.
HEADNOTE: COOPERATIVE PROGRAM AGRICUL-
TURE
TOPIC: Tech Assistance
CONCEPTS: Time limit. Treaty implementation.
Annex or appendix reference. Annex type mate-
rial. Privileges and immunities. General coopera-
tion. Exchange of information and documents.
Informational records. Inspection and observa-
tion. Domestic legislation. Operating agencies.
Personnel. General property. Title and deeds.
Use of facilities. Scholarships and grants. Re-
search and development. Attachment of funds.
Currency deposits. Funding procedures. Gar-
nishment of funds. Seizure funds. Assets. Tax
exemptions. Customs exemptions. Agriculture.
Assistance. Special projects. Materials, equip-
ment and services. Aid missions. Natural re-
sources. Ocean resources.
INTL ORGS: Special Commission.
TREATY REF: 92UNTS145; 133UNTS69.
PROCEDURE: Duration. Termination.
PARTIES:
Liberia
USA (United States)

102880 Bilateral Agreement **213 UNTS 57**
SIGNED: 23 Jun 53 FORCE: 23 Jun 53
REGISTERED: 26 Jul 55 USA (United States)
ARTICLES: 13 LANGUAGE: English.
HEADNOTE: EDUCATION PROGRAM
TOPIC: Education
CONCEPTS: Definition of terms. Annex or appendix reference. Friendship and amity. Alien status.
Privileges and immunities. Conformity with municipal law. Inspection and observation. Personnel. General property. Private contracts. Exchange. Commissions and foundations. Teacher
and student exchange. Institute establishment.
Vocational training. Research cooperation. Research and development. Accounting procedures. Indemnities and reimbursements. Currency. Exchange rates and regulations. Financial
programs. Funding procedures. Customs exemptions. General technical assistance. Aid missions.
INTL ORGS: Special Commission.
TREATY REF: 213UNTS38.

PROCEDURE: Duration. Termination.
PARTIES:
Liberia
USA (United States)

102881 Bilateral Exchange **213 UNTS 77**
SIGNED: 26 Jun 53 FORCE: 5 Jul 53
REGISTERED: 26 Jul 55 USA (United States)
ARTICLES: 2 LANGUAGE: English.
HEADNOTE: MUTUAL DEFENSE ASSISTANCE
TOPIC: Milit Assistance
CONCEPTS: Exceptions and exemptions. Guaran-
tees and safeguards. Previous treaty extension.
Non-prejudice to UN charter. Peaceful relations.
Privileges and immunities. Conformity with municipal law. General cooperation. Inspection and
observation. Public information. Use of facilities.
Indemnities and reimbursements. Garnishment
of funds. Local currency. Claims and settle-
ments. Tax exemptions. Recognition. Customs
exemptions. Domestic obligation. Materials,
equipment and services. Aid missions. Joint defense. Self-defense. Military assistance. Return
of equipment and recapture. Security of information. Military assistance missions. Exchange of
defense information. Restrictions on transfer.
Arms limitations. Raw materials.
INTL ORGS: United Nations.
TREATY REF: 45UNTS47; 70UNTS280.
PROCEDURE: Future Procedures Contemplated.
Registration. Termination.
PARTIES:
Philippines
USA (United States)
ANNEX
270 UNTS 400. Philippines. Implementation
3 Mar 56. Force 3 Mar 56.
270 UNTS 400. USA (United States). Implementa-
tion 27 Jul 53. Force 3 Mar 56.

102882 Bilateral Exchange **213 UNTS 91**
SIGNED: 3 Dec 53 FORCE: 3 Dec 52
REGISTERED: 26 Jul 55 USA (United States)
ARTICLES: 2 LANGUAGE: English.
HEADNOTE: AERIAL MAPPING PROJECT
TOPIC: Tech Assistance
CONCEPTS: Treaty implementation. Domestic ob-
ligation. General technical assistance. Special
projects. Materials, equipment and services.
TREATY REF: THAILAND FOREIGN MINISTRY
NOTE NO.18468-2493.
PARTIES:
Thailand
USA (United States)

102883 Bilateral Agreement **213 UNTS 99**
SIGNED: 14 Aug 53 FORCE: 22 Aug 53
REGISTERED: 26 Jul 55 USA (United States)
ARTICLES: 15 LANGUAGE: English. Spanish.
HEADNOTE: AIR TRANSPORT
TOPIC: Air Transport
CONCEPTS: Definition of terms. Exceptions and
exemptions. Annex or appendix reference. Non-
prejudice to third party. Conformity with municipal law. General cooperation. Licenses and permits. Recognition of legal documents. Use of facilities. Procedure. Special tribunals.
Competence of tribunal. Indemnities and reimbursements. Fees and exemptions. Most favored
nation clause. National treatment. Customs exemptions. Temporary importation. Competency
certificate. Routes and logistics. Navigational
conditions. Permit designation. Air transport. Airport facilities. Airworthiness certificates. Conditions of airlines operating permission. Operating
authorizations and regulations. Licenses and certificates of nationality.
INTL ORGS: International Civil Aviation Organization. International Court of Justice. Arbitration
Commission.
TREATY REF: 15UNTS295.
PROCEDURE: Amendment. Future Procedures
Contemplated. Registration. Termination.
PARTIES:
USA (United States)
Venezuela
ANNEX
234 UNTS 370. USA (United States). Amendment
30 Dec 54. Force 30 Dec 54.

234 UNTS 370.   Venezuela.   Amendment 30 Dec 54. Force 30 Dec 54.

102884 Multilateral Agreement **213 UNTS 137**
SIGNED: 27 Aug 53   FORCE: 20 May 55
REGISTERED: 8 Aug 55 UK Great Britain
ARTICLES: 12 LANGUAGE: English. Italian.
HEADNOTE: GRAVES MEMBERS ARMED FORCES
TOPIC: Other Military
CONCEPTS: Definition of terms. Annex or appendix reference. Conformity with municipal law. Title and deeds. Establishment of commission. Customs exemptions. Upkeep of war graves. Establishment of war cemeteries.
TREATY REF: 9LTS23.
PROCEDURE: Termination.
PARTIES:
Australia   SIGNED: 27 Aug 53   FORCE: 20 May 55
Canada SIGNED: 27 Aug 53 FORCE: 20 May 55
India SIGNED: 27 Aug 53 FORCE: 20 May 55
Italy SIGNED: 27 Aug 53 FORCE: 20 May 55
New Zealand SIGNED: 27 Aug 53 FORCE: 20 May 55
Pakistan SIGNED: 27 Aug 53 FORCE: 20 May 55
South Africa SIGNED: 27 Aug 53 FORCE: 20 May 55
UK Great Britain SIGNED: 27 Aug 53 FORCE: 20 May 55
ANNEX
478 UNTS 430. UK Great Britain. Supplementation 17 Apr 61. Force 23 Jun 63.
478 UNTS 430.   Italy.   Supplementation 20 Apr 61. Force 23 Jun 63.

102885   Bilateral Agreement   **213 UNTS 169**
SIGNED: 27 Apr 53   FORCE: 21 Apr 53
REGISTERED: 10 Aug 55 United Nations
ARTICLES: 10 LANGUAGE: English.
HEADNOTE: ACTIVITIES UNICEF
TOPIC: Direct Aid
CONCEPTS: Treaty implementation. Privileges and immunities. Exchange of information and documents. Informational records. Inspection and observation. Public information. Procedure. Existing tribunals. Export quotas. Indemnities and reimbursements. Financial programs. Local currency. Tax exemptions. Customs exemptions. Commodities and services. Assistance. General aid. Distribution. Freedom of action.
INTL ORGS: United Nations.
TREATY REF: 1UNTS15.
PROCEDURE: Duration. Ratification.
PARTIES:
Ethiopia
UNICEF (Children)
ANNEX
457 UNTS 311. Ethiopia. Force 1 Apr 63.
457 UNTS 311.   UNICEF   (Children).   Force 1 Apr 63.

102886   Bilateral Agreement   **213 UNTS 183**
SIGNED: 29 Jun 51   FORCE: 24 Oct 52
REGISTERED: 10 Aug 55 Turkey
ARTICLES: 12 LANGUAGE: English.
HEADNOTE: CULTURAL RELATIONS
TOPIC: Culture
CONCEPTS: Definition of terms. Friendship and amity. Conformity with municipal law. Domestic legislation. Operating agencies. Establishment of commission. Recognition of degrees. Exchange. Teacher and student exchange. Professorships. Institute establishment. Scholarships and grants. Vocational training. Exchange. General cultural cooperation. Artists. Athletes. Scientific exchange. Publications exchange. Mass media exchange.
PROCEDURE: Duration. Ratification. Renewal or Revival. Termination.
PARTIES:
India
Turkey

102887   Bilateral Exchange   **213 UNTS 193**
SIGNED: 29 Jul 55   FORCE: 1 Aug 55
REGISTERED: 10 Aug 55 Australia
ARTICLES: 2 LANGUAGE: English.
HEADNOTE: INVENTIONS TRADEMARKS
TOPIC: Patents/Copyrights

CONCEPTS: Definition of terms. Conformity with municipal law. Trademarks.
PROCEDURE: Duration.
PARTIES:
Australia
Taiwan

102888   Bilateral Agreement   **213 UNTS 199**
SIGNED: 1 Apr 55   FORCE: 1 Apr 55
REGISTERED: 10 Aug 55 Australia
ARTICLES: 18 LANGUAGE: English. Czechoslovakian.
HEADNOTE: EXCHANGE POSTAL PARCELS
TOPIC: Postal Service
CONCEPTS: Responsibility and liability. Accounting procedures. Compensation. Debt settlement. Postal services. Regulations. Insured letters and boxes. Conveyance in transit. Parcel post. Rates and charges.
INTL ORGS: Universal Postal Union.
TREATY REF: 170UNTS63;   186UNTS360; 202UNTS248.
PROCEDURE: Duration. Termination.
PARTIES:
Australia
Czechoslovakia

102889 Multilateral Convention **213 UNTS 221**
SIGNED: 4 Nov 50   FORCE: 3 Sep 53
REGISTERED: 11 Aug 55 Council of Europe
ARTICLES: 66 LANGUAGE: English. French.
HEADNOTE: HUMAN RIGHTS FUNDMENTAL FREEDOMS
TOPIC: Humanitarian
CONCEPTS: Definition of terms. Exceptions and exemptions. Territorial application. Human rights. Privileges and immunities. Court procedures. Family law. Juridical personality. Legal protection and assistance. Domestic legislation. Operating agencies. General property. Succession. Investigation of violations. Establishment of commission. Procedure. Humanitarian matters.
INTL ORGS: Council of Europe. European Court of Human Rights.
TREATY REF: 87UNTS103;   100UNTS302; 196UNTS347.
PROCEDURE: Accession. Denunciation. Ratification.
PARTIES:
Belgium SIGNED: 4 Nov 50 RATIFIED: 14 Jun 55 FORCE: 14 Jun 55
Denmark   SIGNED: 4 Nov 50   RATIFIED: 13 Apr 53 FORCE: 3 Sep 53
France SIGNED: 4 Nov 50
Germany, West Berlin RATIFIED: 5 Dec 52 FORCE: 3 Sep 53
Germany, West SIGNED: 4 Nov 50 RATIFIED: 5 Dec 52 FORCE: 3 Sep 53
Greece   SIGNED: 28 Nov 50   RATIFIED: 28 Mar 53 FORCE: 3 Sep 53
Iceland SIGNED: 4 Nov 50 RATIFIED: 29 Jun 53 FORCE: 3 Sep 53
Ireland SIGNED: 4 Nov 50 RATIFIED: 25 Feb 53 FORCE: 3 Sep 53
Italy SIGNED: 4 Nov 50
Luxembourg   SIGNED: 4 Nov 50   RATIFIED: 3 Sep 53 FORCE: 3 Sep 53
Netherlands   SIGNED: 4 Nov 50   RATIFIED: 30 Aug 54 FORCE: 31 Aug 54
Norway SIGNED: 4 Nov 50 RATIFIED: 15 Jan 52 FORCE: 3 Sep 53
Saar SIGNED: 4 Nov 50 RATIFIED: 14 Jan 53 FORCE: 3 Sep 53
Sweden SIGNED: 28 Nov 50 RATIFIED: 4 Feb 52 FORCE: 3 Sep 53
Turkey SIGNED: 4 Nov 50 RATIFIED: 18 May 54 FORCE: 18 May 54
UK Great Britain Aden Colony RATIFIED: 8 Mar 51 FORCE: 3 Sep 53
UK Great Britain Bahamas RATIFIED: 8 Mar 51 FORCE: 3 Sep 53
UK Great Britain Barbados RATIFIED: 8 Mar 51 FORCE: 3 Sep 53
UK Great Britain Basutoland RATIFIED: 8 Mar 51 FORCE: 3 Sep 53
UK Great Britain Bechuanaland RATIFIED: 8 Mar 51 FORCE: 3 Sep 53
UK Great Britain Bermuda RATIFIED: 8 Mar 51 FORCE: 3 Sep 53
UK Great Britain British Guiana RATIFIED: 8 Mar 51 FORCE: 3 Sep 53

UK Great Britain British Honduras RATIFIED: 8 Mar 51 FORCE: 3 Sep 53
UK Great Britain Brit Solomon Is RATIFIED: 8 Mar 51 FORCE: 3 Sep 53
UK Great Britain British Somaliland RATIFIED: 8 Mar 51 FORCE: 3 Sep 53
UK Great Britain Cyprus RATIFIED: 8 Mar 51 FORCE: 3 Sep 53
UK Great Britain Dominican Republic RATIFIED: 8 Mar 51 FORCE: 3 Sep 53
UK Great Britain Falkland Islands RATIFIED: 8 Mar 51 FORCE: 3 Sep 53
UK Great Britain Fiji Islands RATIFIED: 8 Mar 51 FORCE: 3 Sep 53
UK Great Britain Fed of Malaya RATIFIED: 8 Mar 51 FORCE: 3 Sep 53
UK Great Britain Gambia RATIFIED: 8 Mar 51 FORCE: 3 Sep 53
UK Great Britain Gibralter RATIFIED: 8 Mar 51 FORCE: 3 Sep 53
UK Great Britain Gilbert Islands RATIFIED: 8 Mar 51 FORCE: 3 Sep 53
UK Great Britain Gold Coast RATIFIED: 8 Mar 51 FORCE: 3 Sep 53
UK Great Britain Grenada RATIFIED: 8 Mar 51 FORCE: 3 Sep 53
UK Great Britain Guernsey Island RATIFIED: 8 Mar 51 FORCE: 3 Sep 53
UK Great Britain Isle of Man RATIFIED: 8 Mar 51 FORCE: 3 Sep 53
UK Great Britain Jamaica RATIFIED: 8 Mar 51 FORCE: 3 Sep 53
UK Great Britain Jersey Island RATIFIED: 8 Mar 51 FORCE: 3 Sep 53
UK Great Britain Kenya RATIFIED: 8 Mar 51 FORCE: 3 Sep 53
UK Great Britain SIGNED: 4 Nov 50 RATIFIED: 8 Mar 51 FORCE: 3 Sep 53
UK Great Britain Leeward Islands RATIFIED: 8 Mar 51 FORCE: 3 Sep 53
UK Great Britain Malta RATIFIED: 8 Mar 51 FORCE: 3 Sep 53
UK Great Britain Mauritius RATIFIED: 8 Mar 51 FORCE: 3 Sep 53
UK Great Britain Nigeria RATIFIED: 8 Mar 51 FORCE: 3 Sep 53
UK Great Britain North Borneo RATIFIED: 8 Mar 51 FORCE: 3 Sep 53
UK Great Britain Northern Rhodesia RATIFIED: 8 Mar 51 FORCE: 3 Sep 53
UK Great Britain Nyasaland RATIFIED: 8 Mar 51 FORCE: 3 Sep 53
UK Great Britain Sarawak RATIFIED: 8 Mar 51 FORCE: 3 Sep 53
UK Great Britain Seychelles RATIFIED: 8 Mar 51 FORCE: 3 Sep 53
UK Great Britain Sierra Leone RATIFIED: 8 Mar 51 FORCE: 3 Sep 53
UK Great Britain Singapore RATIFIED: 8 Mar 51 FORCE: 3 Sep 53
UK Great Britain St. Helena RATIFIED: 8 Mar 51 FORCE: 3 Sep 53
UK Great Britain St. Lucia RATIFIED: 8 Mar 51 FORCE: 3 Sep 53
UK Great Britain Swaziland RATIFIED: 8 Mar 51 FORCE: 3 Sep 53
UK Great Britain Tanganyika RATIFIED: 8 Mar 51 FORCE: 3 Sep 53
UK Great Britain Tonga RATIFIED: 8 Mar 51 FORCE: 3 Sep 53
UK Great Britain Trinidad RATIFIED: 8 Mar 51 FORCE: 3 Sep 53
UK Great Britain Uganda RATIFIED: 8 Mar 51 FORCE: 3 Sep 53
UK Great Britain Zanzibar RATIFIED: 8 Mar 51 FORCE: 3 Sep 53
ANNEX
223 UNTS 382. Netherlands. Netherlands Antilles. Force 31 Dec 55.
223 UNTS 382. Netherlands. Surinam. Force 31 Dec 55.
256 UNTS 365. Norway. Withdrawal of Reservation 7 Dec 56.
265 UNTS 388. Germany, West. Qualified Ratification 13 Feb 57.
265 UNTS 388. Denmark. Prolongation 2 Apr 57.
275 UNTS 306. Belgium. Renewal 16 Aug 57. Force 30 Jun 57.
310 UNTS 380. Italy. Ratification 26 Oct 55.
310 UNTS 380. Luxembourg. Force 18 Apr 58.
310 UNTS 380. Norway. Renewal 11 Dec 57.
310 UNTS 380.   Germany,   West.   Renewal 21 Jul 58.

310 UNTS 380. Germany, West. Renewal 21 Jul 58.

310 UNTS 380. Luxembourg. Declaration 28 Apr 58. Force 18 Apr 58.

310 UNTS 382. Italy. Ratification 26 Oct 55.

313 UNTS 363. Austria. Qualified Ratification 3 Sep 58.

313 UNTS 365. Austria. Declaration 3 Sep 58.

313 UNTS 365. Austria. Declaration 3 Sep 58.

313 UNTS 365. Iceland. Declaration 3 Sep 58.

313 UNTS 366. Austria. Qualified Ratification 3 Sep 58.

340 UNTS 357. Denmark. Renewal 23 Mar 59. Force 7 Apr 59.

340 UNTS 357. Belgium. Renewal 2 Jul 59. Force 30 Jun 59.

347 UNTS 385. Norway. Acknowledgement 7 Dec 59. Force 9 Dec 59.

347 UNTS 385. Norway. Renewal 7 Dec 59. Force 9 Dec 59.

363 UNTS 405. Iceland. Recognition 14 Apr 60. Prolongation 14 Apr 60.

367 UNTS 318. Netherlands. Recognition 5 Jul 60.

367 UNTS 318. Belgium. Prolongation 29 Jun 60.

395 UNTS 271. Luxembourg. Renewal 28 Apr 61. Recognition 24 Apr 61.

404 UNTS 344. Germany, West. Declaration 21 Jun 61. Force 1 Jul 61.

404 UNTS 344. Austria. Declaration 4 Aug 61. Force 3 Sep 61.

404 UNTS 344. Austria. Declaration 4 Aug 61. Force 3 Sep 61.

404 UNTS 344. Germany, West. Declaration 21 Jun 61. Force 1 Jul 61.

414 UNTS 387. Iceland. Declaration 19 Sep 61. Renewal 19 Sep 61.

418 UNTS 365. Norway. Declaration 11 Dec 61. Prolongation 11 Dec 61.

425 UNTS 334. Denmark. Declaration 4 Apr 62. Renewal 7 Apr 62.

102890 Bilateral Exchange **213 UNTS 273**
SIGNED: 15 Dec 54　　　　FORCE: 15 Dec 54
REGISTERED: 15 Aug 55 Denmark
ARTICLES: 2 LANGUAGE: English.
HEADNOTE: CERTIFICATES AIRWORTHINESS IMPORTED AIRCRAFT
TOPIC: Air Transport
CONCEPTS: Previous treaty replacement. Conformity with municipal law. Exchange of information and documents. Recognition of legal documents. Use of facilities. Reciprocity in trade. Airworthiness certificates.
TREATY REF: 149LTS93.
PROCEDURE: Termination.
PARTIES:
Denmark
USA (United States)

102891 Bilateral Exchange **213 UNTS 283**
SIGNED: 4 Apr 55　　　　FORCE: 4 Apr 55
REGISTERED: 15 Aug 55 Denmark
ARTICLES: 2 LANGUAGE: English.
HEADNOTE: EXEMPTION TAXES SHIPPING AIRCRAFT SERVICES
TOPIC: Taxation
CONCEPTS: Definition of terms. Tax exemptions. Air transport. Merchant vessels.
PROCEDURE: Termination.
PARTIES:
Denmark
Israel

102892 Bilateral Exchange **213 UNTS 291**
SIGNED: 21 Mar 55　　　　FORCE: 1 Apr 55
REGISTERED: 15 Aug 55 South Africa
ARTICLES: 2 LANGUAGE: English.
HEADNOTE: TEMPORARY SUSPENSION MARGIN PREFERENCE WOOL
TOPIC: Commodity Trade
CONCEPTS: Time limit. Commodity trade.
PARTIES:
Canada
South Africa

102893 Bilateral Treaty **213 UNTS 297**
SIGNED: 3 Mar 54　　　　FORCE: 10 Mar 55
REGISTERED: 15 Aug 55 Thailand
ARTICLES: 7 LANGUAGE: English. Thai. Indonesian.

HEADNOTE: FRIENDSHIP
TOPIC: General Amity
CONCEPTS: Friendship and amity. Alien status. Consular relations establishment. Diplomatic relations establishment. Arbitration. Mediation and good offices. Procedure. Domestic jurisdiction. Existing tribunals.
INTL ORGS: International Court of Justice.
PROCEDURE: Duration. Future Procedures Contemplated. Ratification. Termination.
PARTIES:
Indonesia
Thailand

102894 Bilateral Exchange **213 UNTS 313**
SIGNED: 23 Jul 54　　　　FORCE: 23 Jul 54
REGISTERED: 16 Aug 55 Denmark
ARTICLES: 2 LANGUAGE: English.
HEADNOTE: REGULATION FISHERIES
TOPIC: Specific Resources
CONCEPTS: Annex type material. Fisheries and fishing. Regulation of natural resources.
TREATY REF: 2'33DEMARTENS268;C.
PARTIES:
Denmark
UK Great Britain

ANNEX

337 UNTS 416. UK Great Britain. Amendment 27 Apr 59. Force 27 Apr 59.

337 UNTS 416. Denmark. Amendment 27 Apr 59. Force 27 Apr 59.

548 UNTS 338. Denmark. Force 28 Apr 63. Termination 28 Apr 62.

102895 Bilateral Exchange **213 UNTS 325**
SIGNED: 7 May 54　　　　FORCE: 30 Jul 54
REGISTERED: 16 Aug 55 Netherlands
ARTICLES: 2 LANGUAGE: English.
HEADNOTE: OFFSHORE PROCUREMENT PROGRAM
TOPIC: Milit Assistance
CONCEPTS: Annex or appendix reference. Privileges and immunities. Conformity with municipal law. General cooperation. Exchange of information and documents. Inspection and observation. Licenses and permits. General property. Private contracts. Responsibility and liability. Indemnities and reimbursements. Customs exemptions. Materials, equipment and services. Defense and security. Security of information. Exchange of defense information. Restrictions on transfer.
INTL ORGS: European Defense Community. North Atlantic Treaty Organization.
TREATY REF: 20UNTS91; 93UNTS361.
PROCEDURE: Amendment. Future Procedures Contemplated. Termination.
PARTIES:
Netherlands
USA (United States)

102896 Bilateral Treaty **214 UNTS 3**
SIGNED: 26 Feb 50　　　　FORCE: 26 Nov 52
REGISTERED: 25 Aug 55 Pakistan
ARTICLES: 5 LANGUAGE: Arabic. English.
HEADNOTE: FRIENDSHIP
TOPIC: General Amity
CONCEPTS: Friendship and amity. Consular relations establishment. Diplomatic relations establishment. Procedure. Most favored nation clause.
PROCEDURE: Future Procedures Contemplated. Ratification.
PARTIES:
Iraq
Pakistan

102897 Multilateral Agreement **214 UNTS 10**
SIGNED: 4 Jul 55　　　　FORCE: 4 Jul 55
REGISTERED: 30 Aug 55 United Nations
ARTICLES: 6 LANGUAGE: Spanish.
HEADNOTE: TECHNICAL ASSISTANCE
TOPIC: Tech Assistance
CONCEPTS: Definition of terms. Previous treaty replacement. Privileges and immunities. General cooperation. Exchange of information and documents. Personnel. Responsibility and liability. Title and deeds. Use of facilities. Exchange. Scholarships and grants. Vocational training. Research and development. Accounting procedures. Exchange rates and regulations. Ex-

pense sharing formulae. Local currency. Domestic obligation. General technical assistance. Materials, equipment and services. IGO status. Conformity with IGO decisions.
TREATY REF: 76UNTS132; 33UNTS261.
PROCEDURE: Amendment. Termination.
PARTIES:
Paraguay SIGNED: 4 Jul 55 FORCE: 4 Jul 55
FAO (Food Agri) SIGNED: 4 Jul 55 FORCE: 4 Jul 55
ICAO (Civil Aviat) SIGNED: 4 Jul 55 FORCE: 4 Jul 55
ILO (Labor Org) SIGNED: 4 Jul 55 FORCE: 4 Jul 55
ITU (Telecommun) SIGNED: 4 Jul 55 FORCE: 4 Jul 55
UNESCO (Educ/Cult) SIGNED: 4 Jul 55 FORCE: 4 Jul 55
United Nations SIGNED: 4 Jul 55 FORCE: 4 Jul 55
WHO (World Health) SIGNED: 4 Jul 55 FORCE: 4 Jul 55
WMO (Meteorology) SIGNED: 4 Jul 55 FORCE: 4 Jul 55

ANNEX

511 UNTS 270. Paraguay. Amendment 8 Aug 63. Force 10 Sep 63.

511 UNTS 270. UNTAB (Tech Assis). Amendment 10 Sep 63. Force 10 Sep 63.

643 UNTS 392. Paraguay. Amendment 26 Aug 68. Force 26 Aug 68.

643 UNTS 392. UNTAB (Tech Assis). Amendment 31 Jul 68. Force 26 Aug 68.

102898 Multilateral Convention **214 UNTS 33**
SIGNED: 11 Jul 47　　　　FORCE: 26 Jul 55
REGISTERED: 1 Sep 55 ILO (Labor Org)
ARTICLES: 17 LANGUAGE: English. French.
HEADNOTE: LABOR INSPECTORATES NON-METROPOLITAN AREAS
TOPIC: ILO Labor
CONCEPTS: Detailed regulations. Exceptions and exemptions. Territorial application. Inspection and observation. Jurisdiction. ILO conventions. Administrative cooperation.
INTL ORGS: International Labour Organization. United Nations.
TREATY REF: 15UNTS40.
PROCEDURE: Amendment. Denunciation. Duration. Ratification. Registration.
PARTIES:
Multilateral

ANNEX

277 UNTS 355. Belgium. Ruanda-Urundi.

277 UNTS 355. Belgium. Belgian Colonies.

495 UNTS 304. UK Great Britain. Swaziland.

522 UNTS 384. UK Great Britain. Bechuanaland.

567 UNTS 354. Australia. New Guinea.

567 UNTS 354. Australia. Papua.

607 UNTS 365. UK Great Britain. Fiji Islands. Declaration 15 Aug 67.

102899 Multilateral Agreement **214 UNTS 51**
SIGNED: 19 Feb 54　　　　FORCE: 11 Jun 54
REGISTERED: 1 Sep 55 Japan
ARTICLES: 25 LANGUAGE: English. Japanese.
HEADNOTE: STATUS FORCES JAPAN
TOPIC: Status of Forces
CONCEPTS: Definition of terms. Detailed regulations. Treaty implementation. Annex or appendix reference. Previous treaty replacement. Frontier formalities. Court procedures. Conformity with municipal law. General cooperation. Exchange of information and documents. Responsibility and liability. Use of facilities. Investigation of violations. Establishment of commission. Procedure. Negotiation. Conciliation. Reexport of goods, etc.. Indemnities and reimbursements. Currency. Exchange rates and regulations. National treatment. Tax exemptions. Customs duties. Customs exemptions. Materials, equipment and services. Operating authorizations and regulations. Ports and pilotage. Driving permits. Security of information. Ranks and privileges. Jurisdiction. Status of forces.
INTL ORGS: United Nations. Special Commission.
TREATY REF: 136UNTS203.
PROCEDURE: Amendment. Accession. Termination.
PARTIES:
Australia SIGNED: 19 Feb 54 RATIFIED: 11 Jun 54 FORCE: 11 Jun 54

Canada SIGNED: 19 Feb 54 RATIFIED: 11 Jun 54 FORCE: 11 Jun 54
France SIGNED: 12 Apr 54 RATIFIED: 11 Jun 54 FORCE: 11 Jun 54
Italy SIGNED: 19 May 54 RATIFIED: 11 Jun 54 FORCE: 11 Jun 54
Japan SIGNED: 19 Feb 54 RATIFIED: 11 Jun 54 FORCE: 10 Jun 54
New Zealand SIGNED: 19 Feb 54 RATIFIED: 11 Jun 54 FORCE: 11 Jun 54
Philippines SIGNED: 19 Feb 54 RATIFIED: 11 Jun 54 FORCE: 11 Jun 54
South Africa SIGNED: 19 Feb 54 RATIFIED: 30 Oct 54 FORCE: 6 Nov 54
Thailand RATIFIED: 12 Aug 54 FORCE: 24 Aug 54
UK Great Britain SIGNED: 19 Feb 54 RATIFIED: 11 Jun 54 FORCE: 11 Jun 54
USA (United States) SIGNED: 19 Feb 54 RATIFIED: 11 Jun 54 FORCE: 11 Jun 54

102900 Bilateral Treaty **214 UNTS 217**
SIGNED: 9 Dec 54 FORCE: 26 May 55
REGISTERED: 2 Sep 55 Taiwan
ARTICLES: 10 LANGUAGE: Chinese. English. Spanish.
HEADNOTE: AMITY
TOPIC: General Amity
CONCEPTS: Treaty interpretation. Friendship and amity. Peaceful relations. Alien status. Consular relations establishment. Diplomatic relations establishment. Privileges and immunities. Legal protection and assistance.
PROCEDURE: Future Procedures Contemplated. Ratification.
PARTIES:
Taiwan
El Salvador

102901 Multilateral Convention **214 UNTS 233**
SIGNED: 29 Jun 46 FORCE: 17 Aug 55
REGISTERED: 7 Sep 55 ILO (Labor Org)
ARTICLES: 17 LANGUAGE: English. French.
HEADNOTE: MEDICAL EXAMINATION SEAFARERS
TOPIC: ILO Labor
CONCEPTS: Detailed regulations. Exceptions and exemptions. Domestic legislation. Public health. ILO conventions. Employment regulations. Merchant vessels.
INTL ORGS: International Labour Organization. United Nations.
PROCEDURE: Amendment. Denunciation. Duration. Ratification. Registration.
PARTIES:
Multilateral
ANNEX
304 UNTS 409. Netherlands. Ratification 17 Jun 58. Force 17 Dec 58.
318 UNTS 425. Netherlands. Declaration 11 Nov 58.
330 UNTS 371. Netherlands. Netherlands Antilles. Declaration 15 May 59.
422 UNTS 338. Sweden. Ratification 9 Jan 62. Force 9 Jul 62.
429 UNTS 293. Peru. Ratification 4 Apr 62. Force 4 Oct 62.
444 UNTS 344. Algeria. Succession 19 Oct 62.
522 UNTS 385. Taiwan. Ratification 10 Dec 64. Force 10 Jun 65.

102902 Bilateral Treaty **214 UNTS 247**
SIGNED: 28 Aug 51 FORCE: 9 Jun 52
REGISTERED: 8 Sep 55 Pakistan
ARTICLES: 6 LANGUAGE: Arabic. English.
HEADNOTE: FRIENDSHIP
TOPIC: General Amity
CONCEPTS: Friendship and amity. Consular relations establishment. Diplomatic relations establishment. General property. Procedure. Most favored nation clause.
INTL ORGS: United Nations.
PROCEDURE: Ratification.
PARTIES:
Pakistan
United Arab Rep

102903 Bilateral Protocol **214 UNTS 255**
SIGNED: 10 Nov 52 FORCE: 1 Aug 53
REGISTERED: 12 Sep 55 UK Great Britain

ARTICLES: 7 LANGUAGE: French.
HEADNOTE: MODIFICATION 31 AUG 45 AGREEMENT
TOPIC: Admin Cooperation
CONCEPTS: Annex type material.
INTL ORGS: Committee of Control of the International Zone of Tangier.
PARTIES:
France
UK Great Britain

102904 Multilateral Convention **214 UNTS 265**
SIGNED: 10 Nov 52 FORCE: 8 Jul 53
REGISTERED: 12 Sep 55 UK Great Britain
ARTICLES: 56 LANGUAGE: French.
HEADNOTE: REFORM INTERNATIONAL JURISDICTION TANGIER ZONE
TOPIC: Admin Cooperation
CONCEPTS: Annex type material. Previous treaty extension. Special tribunals.
INTL ORGS: Committee of Control of the International Zone of Tangier.
TREATY REF: 28LTS541; 87LTS211.
PARTIES:
Belgium RATIFIED: 3 Jul 53 FORCE: 8 Jul 53
France SIGNED: 10 Nov 52 FORCE: 8 Jul 53
Italy SIGNED: 10 Nov 52 FORCE: 8 Jul 53
Netherlands RATIFIED: 23 Jun 53 FORCE: 8 Jul 53
Portugal RATIFIED: 18 Mar 53 FORCE: 8 Jul 53
Spain SIGNED: 10 Nov 52 FORCE: 8 Jul 53
Sweden RATIFIED: 27 Apr 53 FORCE: 8 Jul 53
UK Great Britain SIGNED: 10 Nov 52 FORCE: 8 Jul 53
USA (United States) RATIFIED: 8 Jul 53 FORCE: 8 Jul 53

102905 Bilateral Agreement **214 UNTS 301**
SIGNED: 15 Jun 55 FORCE: 21 Jul 55
REGISTERED: 12 Sep 55 UK Great Britain
ARTICLES: 6 LANGUAGE: English.
HEADNOTE: ATOMIC INFORMATION MATERIAL DEFENSE
TOPIC: Atomic Energy
CONCEPTS: Definition of terms. Conformity with municipal law. Research results. Scientific exchange. Rights of supplier. Defense and security. Security of information.
PROCEDURE: Termination.
PARTIES:
UK Great Britain
USA (United States)

102906 Bilateral Exchange **214 UNTS 309**
SIGNED: 19 Oct 54 FORCE: 19 Oct 54
REGISTERED: 12 Sep 55 UK Great Britain
ARTICLES: 2 LANGUAGE: English.
HEADNOTE: RELIEF IMPORT DUTY DEFENSE ARTICLES
TOPIC: Milit Assistance
CONCEPTS: Detailed regulations. Exceptions and exemptions. Annex or appendix reference. General cooperation. Indemnities and reimbursements. Tax exemptions. Customs exemptions. Domestic obligation. Materials, equipment and services. Defense and security.
PARTIES:
Canada
UK Great Britain

102907 Multilateral Convention **214 UNTS 321**
SIGNED: 28 Jun 52 FORCE: 7 Sep 55
REGISTERED: 12 Sep 55 ILO (Labor Org)
ARTICLES: 17 LANGUAGE: English. French.
HEADNOTE: MATERNITY PROTECTION
TOPIC: ILO Labor
CONCEPTS: Definition of terms. Detailed regulations. Exceptions and exemptions. Territorial application. Domestic legislation. ILO conventions. Holidays and rest periods. Administrative cooperation. Sickness and invalidity insurance.
INTL ORGS: International Labour Organization. United Nations.
TREATY REF: 15UNTS40.
PROCEDURE: Amendment. Accession. Denunciation. Duration. Ratification. Registration.
PARTIES:
Multilateral

ANNEX
248 UNTS 409. Hungary. Ratification 8 Jun 56. Force 8 Jun 57.
249 UNTS 461. USSR (Soviet Union). Ratification 10 Aug 56. Force 10 Aug 57.
423 UNTS 310. Ecuador. Ratification 5 Feb 62. Force 5 Feb 63.
541 UNTS 377. Brazil. Ratification 18 Jun 65. Force 18 Jun 66.
545 UNTS 381. Spain. Ratification 17 Aug 65. Force 17 Aug 66.

102908 Bilateral Agreement **215 UNTS 3**
SIGNED: 30 Jun 53 FORCE: 30 Jun 53
REGISTERED: 12 Sep 55 USA (United States)
ARTICLES: 9 LANGUAGE: English.
HEADNOTE: TECHNICAL COOPERATION
TOPIC: Tech Assistance
CONCEPTS: Exceptions and exemptions. Treaty implementation. Annex type material. Privileges and immunities. General cooperation. Exchange of information and documents. Informational records. Domestic legislation. Operating agencies. Personnel. General property. Public health. Sanitation. Scholarships and grants. Vocational training. Research and development. Expense sharing formulae. Funding procedures. Local currency. General technical assistance. Agriculture. Economic assistance. Materials, equipment and services. Industry. Natural resources. General transportation.
INTL ORGS: United Nations.
TREATY REF: 132UNTS265; 177UNTS346; 1UNTS15; 1UNTS263.
PROCEDURE: Duration. Termination.
PARTIES:
Afghanistan
USA (United States)
ANNEX
402 UNTS 314. USA (United States). Amendment 22 Dec 60. Force 28 Dec 60.
402 UNTS 314. Afghanistan. Amendment 28 Dec 60. Force 28 Dec 60.
445 UNTS 335. USA (United States). Extension and Amendment 30 Dec 61. Force 27 Feb 62.
445 UNTS 335. Afghanistan. Extension and Amendment 27 Feb 62. Force 27 Feb 62.
462 UNTS 339. USA (United States). Extension and Amendment 25 Sep 62. Force 7 Nov 62.
462 UNTS 339. Afghanistan. Extension and Amendment 7 Nov 62. Force 7 Nov 62.
494 UNTS 293. Afghanistan. Prolongation 17 Nov 63. Force 17 Nov 63.
494 UNTS 293. USA (United States). Prolongation 9 Nov 63. Force 17 Nov 63.
532 UNTS 373. USA (United States). Prolongation 7 Nov 64. Force 7 Nov 64.
532 UNTS 373. Afghanistan. Prolongation 7 Nov 64. Force 7 Nov 64.
545 UNTS 331. Afghanistan. Amendment 4 May 65. Force 4 May 65.
545 UNTS 331. USA (United States). Amendment 1 May 65. Force 4 May 65.
573 UNTS 306. USA (United States). Prolongation 12 Oct 65. Force 12 Oct 65.
573 UNTS 306. Afghanistan. Prolongation 12 Oct 65. Force 12 Oct 65.

102909 Bilateral Agreement **215 UNTS 17**
SIGNED: 19 Mar 53 FORCE: 19 Mar 53
REGISTERED: 12 Sep 55 USA (United States)
ARTICLES: 13 LANGUAGE: English. Arabic.
HEADNOTE: COOPERATIVE PROGRAM COMMUNITY DEVELOPMENT RURAL REHABILITATION
TOPIC: Tech Assistance
CONCEPTS: Exceptions and exemptions. Time limit. Treaty implementation. Annex type material. Privileges and immunities. General cooperation. Exchange of information and documents. Informational records. Inspection and observation. Domestic legislation. Operating agencies. Personnel. General property. Public health. Sanitation. Exchange. Institute establishment. Research and development. Attachment of funds. Currency deposits. Exchange rates and regulations. Expense sharing formulae. Funding procedures. Garnishment of funds. Seizure funds. Local currency. Assets. Customs exemptions. Domestic obligation. Agriculture. Assistance. Materials, equipment and services. Aid missions. Industry. Road rules. Regulation of natural resources.

INTL ORGS: International Monetary Fund.
TREATY REF: 198UNTS265.
PROCEDURE: Duration. Termination.
PARTIES:
United Arab Rep
USA (United States)

102910 Bilateral Agreement **215 UNTS 45**
SIGNED: 18 Jun 53 FORCE: 18 Jun 53
REGISTERED: 12 Sep 55 USA (United States)
ARTICLES: 12 LANGUAGE: English. Arabic.
HEADNOTE: PUBLIC HEALTH PROGRAM
TOPIC: Sanitation
CONCEPTS: Definition of terms. Friendship and
amity. Privileges and immunities. General cooperation. Exchange of information and documents. Inspection and observation. Domestic
legislation. Personnel. General property. Estab-
lishment of commission. Disease control. Public
health. Insect control. Nursing. Scholarships and
grants. Vocational training. Accounting proce-
dures. Currency. Currency deposits. Exchange
rates and regulations. Expense sharing formulae.
Financial programs. Funding procedures. Seizure funds. Customs exemptions. Assistance.
Special projects. Specific technical assistance.
Aid missions.
INTL ORGS: World Health Organization.
TREATY REF: 198UNTS265.
PROCEDURE: Duration. Termination.
PARTIES:
United Arab Rep
USA (United States)

102911 Bilateral Exchange **215 UNTS 69**
SIGNED: 2 Sep 53 FORCE: 2 Sep 53
REGISTERED: 12 Sep 55 USA (United States)
ARTICLES: 2 LANGUAGE: English.
HEADNOTE: SURVEYING CONSTRUCTION RAMA
ROAD NICARAGUA
TOPIC: Land Transport
CONCEPTS: Treaty implementation. General coop-
eration. Licenses and permits. Recognition of le-
gal documents. Fees and exemptions. Financial
programs. National treatment. Income taxes. Ma-
terials, equipment and services. Registration cer-
tificate. Roads and highways.
TREATY REF: USA'TIAS 1567;.
PARTIES:
Nicaragua
USA (United States)

102912 Bilateral Agreement **215 UNTS 77**
SIGNED: 26 Jun 53 FORCE: 26 Jun 53
REGISTERED: 12 Sep 55 USA (United States)
ARTICLES: 6 LANGUAGE: English. Spanish.
HEADNOTE: SPECIAL TECHNICAL SERVICES
TOPIC: Tech Assistance
CONCEPTS: Treaty implementation. Annex type
material. Privileges and immunities. General co-
operation. Exchange of information and docu-
ments. Informational records. Inspection and ob-
servation. Operating agencies. Personnel. Gen-
eral property. Vocational training. Expense
sharing formulae. Tax exemptions. Customs ex-
emptions. Special projects. Economic assis-
tance. Materials, equipment and services.
TREATY REF: 92UNTS167.
PROCEDURE: Duration. Termination.
PARTIES:
Panama
USA (United States)

102913 Multilateral Agreement **215 UNTS 97**
SIGNED: 30 Jul 53 FORCE: 30 Sep 53
REGISTERED: 12 Sep 55 USA (United States)
ARTICLES: 3 LANGUAGE: English.
HEADNOTE: DISPOSITION ACCOUNTS
TOPIC: Reparations
CONCEPTS: Accounting procedures. Armistice
and peace. Loss and/or damage. Enemy finan-
cial interests. Reparations and restrictions.
TREATY REF: 136UNTS45.
PARTIES:
Thailand SIGNED: 30 Jul 53 FORCE: 30 Jul 53
UK Great Britain SIGNED: 30 Jul 53 FORCE:
30 Jul 53
USA (United States) SIGNED: 30 Jul 53 FORCE:
30 Jul 53

102914 Bilateral Exchange **215 UNTS 103**
SIGNED: 30 Jun 53 FORCE: 30 Jun 53
REGISTERED: 12 Sep 55 USA (United States)
ARTICLES: 2 LANGUAGE: English.
HEADNOTE: TRANSFER LORAN STATION
TOPIC: General Military
CONCEPTS: Detailed regulations. Guarantees and
safeguards. General cooperation. Procedure. In-
demnities and reimbursements.
PARTIES:
Canada
USA (United States)

102915 Bilateral Exchange **215 UNTS 111**
SIGNED: 15 Oct 53 FORCE: 15 Oct 53
REGISTERED: 12 Sep 55 USA (United States)
ARTICLES: 2 LANGUAGE: English. Danish.
HEADNOTE: TRADEMARK REGISTRATION
TOPIC: Patents/Copyrights
CONCEPTS: Conformity with municipal law. Do-
mestic legislation. Trademarks.
PARTIES:
Denmark
USA (United States)

102916 Bilateral Exchange **215 UNTS 121**
SIGNED: 5 Jan 52 FORCE: 5 Jan 52
REGISTERED: 12 Sep 55 USA (United States)
ARTICLES: 2 LANGUAGE: English.
HEADNOTE: ECONOMIC TECHNICAL COOPER-
ATION
TOPIC: Tech Assistance
CONCEPTS: Conformity with municipal law. Gen-
eral property. Attachment of funds. Garnishment
of funds. Seizure funds. General technical assis-
tance. Economic assistance. Materials, equip-
ment and services. Return of equipment and re-
capture.
TREATY REF: 134UNTS255; 198UNTS400.
PARTIES:
Indonesia
USA (United States)

102917 Bilateral Agreement **215 UNTS 133**
SIGNED: 30 Jun 53 FORCE: 30 Jun 53
REGISTERED: 12 Sep 55 USA (United States)
ARTICLES: 13 LANGUAGE: English. Spanish.
HEADNOTE. COOPERATIVE PROGRAM AGRICUL-
TURE
TOPIC: Tech Assistance
CONCEPTS: Detailed regulations. Exceptions and
exemptions. Time limit. Treaty implementation.
Annex type material. Previous treaty replace-
ment. Privileges and immunities. General coop-
eration. Exchange of information and docu-
ments. Informational records. Inspection and ob-
servation. Domestic legislation. Operating
agencies. Personnel. Private contracts. Voca-
tional training. Currency deposits. Exchange
rates and regulations. Expense sharing formulae.
Funding procedures. Assets. Tax exemptions.
Customs exemptions. Agriculture. Assistance.
Materials, equipment and services. Aid missions.
TREATY REF: 92UNTS155; 99UNTS25.
PROCEDURE: Duration. Termination.
PARTIES:
Nicaragua
USA (United States)
ANNEX
233 UNTS 334. USA (United States). Implementa-
tion 23 Jun 54. Force 23 Jun 54.
233 UNTS 334. Nicaragua. Implementation
23 Jun 54. Force 23 Jun 54.

102918 Bilateral Exchange **215 UNTS 159**
SIGNED: 23 Oct 50 FORCE: 23 Oct 50
REGISTERED: 13 Sep 55 ICAO (Civil Aviat)
ARTICLES: 2 LANGUAGE: English. Chinese.
HEADNOTE: TEMPORARY AIR AGREEMENT
TOPIC: Air Transport
CONCEPTS: Previous treaty replacement. Routes
and logistics. Permit designation. Air transport.
Operating authorizations and regulations.
TREATY REF: 15UNTS295.
PROCEDURE: Duration. Renewal or Revival.
PARTIES:
Taiwan
Philippines

ANNEX
232 UNTS 357. Philippines. Prolongation
19 Apr 51. Force 23 Apr 51.
232 UNTS 357. Taiwan. Prolongation 19 Apr 51.
Force 23 Apr 51.
232 UNTS 357. Taiwan. Prolongation 21 Oct 52.
Force 23 Oct 53.
232 UNTS 357. Philippines. Prolongation
16 Apr 53. Force 23 Apr 53.
232 UNTS 357. Philippines. Prolongation
22 Apr 52. Force 23 Apr 53.
232 UNTS 357. Philippines. Prolongation
3 Apr 54. Force 23 Apr 54.
232 UNTS 357. Taiwan. Prolongation 20 Apr 53.
Force 23 Apr 53.
232 UNTS 357. Philippines. Prolongation
21 Oct 52. Force 23 Oct 53.
232 UNTS 357. Taiwan. Prolongation 22 Apr 52.
Force 23 Apr 53.
232 UNTS 357. Taiwan. Prolongation 5 Apr 54.
Force 23 Apr 54.

102919 Bilateral Exchange **215 UNTS 166**
SIGNED: 29 Sep 51 FORCE: 29 Sep 51
REGISTERED: 13 Sep 55 ICAO (Civil Aviat)
ARTICLES: 2 LANGUAGE: English. Chinese.
HEADNOTE: PROVISIONAL AIR AGREEMENT
TOPIC: Air Transport
CONCEPTS: Routes and logistics. Permit designa-
tion. Operating authorizations and regulations.
INTL ORGS: International Civil Aviation Organiza-
tion.
TREATY REF: 15UNTS295.
PROCEDURE: Duration. Renewal or Revival.
PARTIES:
Taiwan
Thailand

102920 Bilateral Agreement **215 UNTS 193**
SIGNED: 6 Oct 51 FORCE: 4 Dec 53
REGISTERED: 13 Sep 55 ICAO (Civil Aviat)
ARTICLES: 17 LANGUAGE: English. Spanish.
HEADNOTE: AIR TRANSPORT
TOPIC: Air Transport
CONCEPTS: Definition of terms. Annex or appen-
dix reference. Non-visa travel documents. Conformity with municipal law. Licenses and permits. Personnel. Recognition of legal documents. Use of facilities. Arbitration. Procedure.
Existing tribunals. Special tribunals. Competence of tribunal. Fees and exemptions. Most fa-
vored nation clause. National treatment. Customs exemptions. Competency certificate.
Routes and logistics. Navigational conditions.
Navigational equipment. Permit designation. Air
transport. Airport facilities. Airworthiness certificates. Conditions of airlines operating permis-
sion. Operating authorizations and regulations.
Licenses and certificates of nationality. Postal
services.
INTL ORGS: International Civil Aviation Organiza-
tion. Arbitration Commission.
TREATY REF: 15UNTS295.
PROCEDURE: Future Procedures Contemplated.
Ratification. Registration. Termination.
PARTIES:
Philippines
Spain

102921 Bilateral Agreement **215 UNTS 223**
SIGNED: 3 Jun 52 FORCE: 3 Jun 52
REGISTERED: 13 Sep 55 ICAO (Civil Aviat)
ARTICLES: 12 LANGUAGE: Swedish. Icelandic.
HEADNOTE: AIR TRANSPORT
TOPIC: Air Transport
CONCEPTS: Air transport.
INTL ORGS: International Civil Aviation Organiza-
tion. Arbitration Commission.
TREATY REF: 15UNTS295.
PARTIES:
Iceland
Sweden

102922 Multilateral Agreement **215 UNTS 249**
SIGNED: 25 Feb 54　　　　FORCE: 13 Sep 55
REGISTERED: 13 Sep 55 ICAO (Civil Aviat)
ARTICLES: 20 LANGUAGE: English. French. Spanish.
HEADNOTE: NORTH ATLANTIC OCEAN STATIONS
TOPIC: Air Transport
CONCEPTS: Detailed regulations. Annex or appendix reference. General cooperation. Exchange of information and documents. Informational records. Procedure. Negotiation. Meteorology. Indemnities and reimbursements. Fees and exemptions. Inadequacy of funds. Payment schedules. Navigational conditions. Navigational equipment. Operating authorizations and regulations. Water transport. Conferences. Interagency agreements.
INTL ORGS: International Civil Aviation Organization. World Meteorological Organization.
TREATY REF: 101UNTS91; 150UNTS380.
PROCEDURE: Accession. Duration. Renewal or Revival. Termination.
PARTIES:
　Belgium SIGNED: 25 Feb 54
　Canada SIGNED: 25 Feb 54 RATIFIED: 13 Jul 54
　　FORCE: 1 Feb 55
　Denmark　SIGNED:　25 Feb 54　RATIFIED:
　　1 Jun 55 FORCE: 1 Jun 55
　France SIGNED: 25 Feb 54
　Iceland SIGNED: 25 Feb 54
　Ireland　SIGNED:　25 Feb 54　RATIFIED:
　　17 May 55 FORCE: 17 May 55
　Israel SIGNED: 25 Feb 54 RATIFIED: 8 Feb 55
　　FORCE: 8 Feb 55
　Italy SIGNED: 25 Feb 54
　Netherlands SIGNED: 25 Feb 54
　Norway　SIGNED:　25 Feb 54　RATIFIED:
　　21 Apr 55 FORCE: 21 Apr 55
　Sweden SIGNED: 25 Feb 54 RATIFIED: 2 Apr 54
　　FORCE: 1 Feb 55
　Switzerland SIGNED: 25 Feb 54
　UK Great Britain SIGNED: 25 Feb 54 RATIFIED:
　　1 Feb 55 FORCE: 1 Feb 55
　USA (United States) SIGNED: 25 Feb 54 RATIFIED: 23 Jun 54 FORCE: 1 Feb 55
　　　　　ANNEX
311 UNTS 347.　Switzerland.　Acceptance
　7 Nov 55.
311 UNTS 347. Belgium. Acceptance 9 Apr 57.
311 UNTS 347.　Netherlands.　Acceptance
　24 Jan 56.
311 UNTS 347.　Germany,　West.　Accession
　15 Oct 57.
311 UNTS 347. France. Acceptance 3 May 56.
335 UNTS 308. Australia. Accession 5 Feb 59.
335 UNTS 308. Italy. Acceptance 7 Feb 58.
514 UNTS 269. Pakistan. Accession 27 Nov 63.
　Force 27 Nov 63.
514 UNTS 269.　Japan.　Qualified Accession
　28 Mar 63. Force 28 Mar 63.

102923 Bilateral Agreement **215 UNTS 303**
SIGNED: 28 Nov 49　　　　FORCE: 13 Sep 55
REGISTERED: 13 Sep 55 ICAO (Civil Aviat)
ARTICLES: 16 LANGUAGE: Spanish. Portuguese.
HEADNOTE: REGULAR AIR TRANSPORT SERVICES
TOPIC: Air Transport
CONCEPTS: Definition of terms. Annex or appendix reference. Previous treaty replacement. Conformity with municipal law. Licenses and permits. Use of facilities. Investigation of violations. Arbitration. Procedure. Reexport of goods, etc.. Fees and exemptions. National treatment. Customs duties. Customs exemptions. Competency certificate. Routes and logistics. Navigational conditions. Permit designation. Air transport. Airport facilities. Airworthiness certificates. Conditions of airlines operating permission. Operating authorizations and regulations. Licenses and certificates of nationality.
INTL ORGS: Arbitration Commission.
PROCEDURE: Amendment. Future Procedures Contemplated. Ratification. Termination.
PARTIES:
　Brazil
　Spain

102924 Bilateral Exchange **215 UNTS 365**
SIGNED: 22 Jul 52　　　　FORCE: 13 Sep 55
REGISTERED: 13 Sep 55 ICAO (Civil Aviat)
ARTICLES: 2 LANGUAGE: French.
HEADNOTE: DOUBLE TAXATION PROFITS SEA AIR TRANSPORT
TOPIC: Taxation
CONCEPTS: Taxation. Tax exemptions. Air transport. Merchant vessels.
PARTIES:
　Greece
　Israel

102925 Bilateral Agreement **215 UNTS 371**
SIGNED: 27 Aug 53　　　　FORCE: 13 Sep 55
REGISTERED: 13 Sep 55 ICAO (Civil Aviat)
ARTICLES: 12 LANGUAGE: English. French.
HEADNOTE: PRIVILEGES IMMUNITIES & FACILITIES
TOPIC: IGO Status/Immunit
CONCEPTS: Definition of terms. Annex or appendix reference. Non-visa travel documents. Diplomatic privileges. Diplomatic missions. Inviolability. Privileges and immunities. Property. Diplomatic correspondence. Juridical personality. Procedure. Status of experts. Special status.
INTL ORGS: International Court of Justice. United Nations. Arbitration Commission.
PROCEDURE: Registration.
PARTIES:
　ICAO (Civil Aviat)
　United Arab Rep

102926 Bilateral Exchange **215 UNTS 401**
SIGNED: 5 May 54　　　　FORCE: 5 May 54
REGISTERED: 13 Sep 55 ICAO (Civil Aviat)
ARTICLES: 2 LANGUAGE: English. French.
HEADNOTE: INTERIM AIR AGREEMENT
TOPIC: Air Transport
CONCEPTS: Routes and logistics. Permit designation. Air transport. Operating authorizations and regulations.
PROCEDURE: Duration.
PARTIES:
　France
　South Africa

102927 Bilateral Exchange **216 UNTS 3**
SIGNED: 20 Oct 54　　　　FORCE: 20 Oct 54
REGISTERED: 13 Sep 55 ICAO (Civil Aviat)
ARTICLES: 2 LANGUAGE: English.
HEADNOTE: TEMPORARY AIR ARRANGEMENT
TOPIC: Air Transport
CONCEPTS: Conditions. Exceptions and exemptions. Conformity with municipal law. Exchange of information and documents. Non-interest rates and fees. Routes and logistics. Permit designation. Air transport. Operating authorizations and regulations.
PARTIES:
　Denmark
　Philippines

102928 Bilateral Exchange **216 UNTS 11**
SIGNED: 20 Oct 54　　　　FORCE: 20 Oct 54
REGISTERED: 13 Sep 55 ICAO (Civil Aviat)
ARTICLES: 2 LANGUAGE: English.
HEADNOTE: TEMPORARY AIR AGREEMENT
TOPIC: Air Transport
CONCEPTS: Conditions. Exceptions and exemptions. Conformity with municipal law. Exchange of information and documents. Routes and logistics. Permit designation. Air transport. Operating authorizations and regulations.
PARTIES:
　Norway
　Philippines

102929 Bilateral Agreement **216 UNTS 19**
SIGNED: 26 Aug 54　　　　FORCE: 1 Apr 55
REGISTERED: 13 Sep 55 ICAO (Civil Aviat)
ARTICLES: 14 LANGUAGE: English. French.
HEADNOTE: AIR SERVICES
TOPIC: Air Transport
CONCEPTS: Air transport.
PARTIES:
　South Africa
　Switzerland

102930 Bilateral Agreement **216 UNTS 29**
SIGNED: 17 Sep 54　　　　FORCE: 1 Oct 54
REGISTERED: 13 Sep 55 ICAO (Civil Aviat)
ARTICLES: 13 LANGUAGE: English. French.
HEADNOTE: AIR SERVICES
TOPIC: Air Transport
CONCEPTS: Definition of terms. Detailed regulations. General cooperation. Exchange of information and documents. Non-interest rates and fees. Routes and logistics. Permit designation. Air transport. Conditions of airlines operating permission. Operating authorizations and regulations.
PROCEDURE: Termination. Application to Non-self-governing Territories.
PARTIES:
　France
　South Africa
　　　　　ANNEX
254 UNTS 414. France. Amendment 14 Sep 56. Force 24 Sep 56.
254 UNTS 414.　South　Africa.　Amendment 24 Sep 56. Force 24 Sep 56.
412 UNTS 325.　South　Africa.　Amendment 4 Apr 61. Force 4 Aug 61.
412 UNTS 325.　France.　Amendment　4 Apr 61. Force 4 Aug 61.
497 UNTS 341.　France.　Amendment 22 Jun 63. Force 22 Jun 63.
497 UNTS 341.　South　Africa.　Amendment 22 Jun 63. Force 22 Jun 63.
602 UNTS 306.　France.　Amendment 31 Jan 66. Force 31 Jan 66.
602 UNTS 306.　South　Africa.　Amendment 31 Jan 66. Force 31 Jan 66.

102931 Bilateral Exchange **216 UNTS 41**
SIGNED: 5 Jan 55　　　　FORCE: 1 Jan 55
REGISTERED: 13 Sep 55 ICAO (Civil Aviat)
ARTICLES: 2 LANGUAGE: French. Arabic.
HEADNOTE: DOUBLE TAXATION AIR TRANSPORT
TOPIC: Taxation
CONCEPTS: Definition of terms. Domestic legislation. Taxation. Tax exemptions. Air transport.
PARTIES:
　Switzerland
　United Arab Rep

102932 Bilateral Agreement **216 UNTS 51**
SIGNED: 31 Jan 55　　　　FORCE: 31 Jan 55
REGISTERED: 13 Sep 55 ICAO (Civil Aviat)
ARTICLES: 15 LANGUAGE: English.
HEADNOTE: AIR SERVICES
TOPIC: Air Transport
CONCEPTS: Conditions. Definition of terms. Detailed regulations. Exceptions and exemptions. Annex or appendix reference. Conformity with municipal law. General cooperation. Exchange of information and documents. Arbitration. Procedure. Existing tribunals. Negotiation. Non-interest rates and fees. Most favored nation clause. Customs exemptions. Routes and logistics. Permit designation. Conditions of airlines operating permission. Overflights and technical stops. Operating authorizations and regulations.
INTL ORGS: International Civil Aviation Organization. Arbitration Commission.
TREATY REF: 15UNTS295.
PROCEDURE: Amendment. Future Procedures Contemplated. Registration. Termination.

PARTIES:
Philippines
UK Great Britain
ANNEX
232 UNTS 358. Philippines. Supplementation
28 Mar 55. Force 21 Jun 55.
232 UNTS 358. UK Great Britain. Supplementation 21 Jun 55. Force 21 Jun 55.
232 UNTS 360. Philippines. Supplementation
9 Jun 55. Force 9 Jun 55.
232 UNTS 360. UK Great Britain. Supplementation 29 Mar 55. Force 9 Jun 55.
412 UNTS 330. Philippines. Amendment
14 Apr 58. Force 14 Apr 58.
412 UNTS 330. UK Great Britain. Amendment
7 Apr 58. Force 14 Apr 58.

102933 Bilateral Agreement **216 UNTS 73**
SIGNED: 11 Dec 51   FORCE: 26 Jun 53
REGISTERED: 13 Sep 55 ICAO (Civil Aviat)
ARTICLES: 17 LANGUAGE: Spanish.
HEADNOTE: AIR TRANSPORT
TOPIC: Air Transport
CONCEPTS: Definition of terms. Annex or appen-
dix reference. Non-visa travel documents. Conformity with municipal law. General cooperation.
Licenses and permits. Personnel. Recognition of
legal documents. Use of facilities. Arbitration.
Procedure. Existing tribunals. Special tribunals.
Negotiation. Fees and exemptions. Most favored
nation clause. National treatment. Customs ex-
emptions. Competency certificate. Routes and
logistics. Navigational conditions. Permit designation. Air transport. Airport facilities. Airworthiness certificates. Conditions of airlines operating permission. Operating authorizations and
regulations. Licenses and certificates of nationality. Postal services.
INTL ORGS: International Civil Aviation Organization. Arbitration Commission.
TREATY REF: 15UNTS295.
PROCEDURE: Registration.
PARTIES:
Colombia
Spain

102934   Bilateral Exchange   **216 UNTS 99**
SIGNED: 5 Feb 53   FORCE: 5 Feb 53
REGISTERED: 13 Sep 55 ICAO (Civil Aviat)
ARTICLES: 8 LANGUAGE: English.
HEADNOTE: TEMPORARY AIR ARRANGEMENT
TOPIC: Air Transport
CONCEPTS: Territorial application. Previous treaty
extension. Conformity with municipal law. Non-
interest rates and fees. Routes and logistics. Air-
port facilities. Operating authorizations and reg-
ulations.
PROCEDURE: Duration. Renewal or Revival.
PARTIES:
Netherlands
Philippines

102935 Unilateral Instrument **216 UNTS 115**
SIGNED: 12 Sep 55   FORCE: 13 Sep 55
REGISTERED: 13 Sep 55 United Nations
ARTICLES: 1 LANGUAGE: English.
HEADNOTE: ACCEPTANCE ICJ JURISDICTION
TOPIC: ICJ Option Clause
CONCEPTS: Conformity with municipal law. Proce-
dure. Compulsory jurisdiction.
INTL ORGS: International Court of Justice.
PROCEDURE: Termination.
PARTIES:
South Africa

102936   Bilateral Exchange   **216 UNTS 121**
SIGNED: 9 Jun 54   FORCE: 19 Aug 55

REGISTERED: 13 Sep 55 Belgium
ARTICLES: 2 LANGUAGE: Dutch.
HEADNOTE: MILITARY SERVICE
TOPIC: Milit Servic/Citiz
CONCEPTS: Previous treaty replacement. Ex-
change of information and documents. Dual na-
tionality. Certificates of service. Foreign nation-
als.
PROCEDURE: Denunciation. Registration. Termi-
nation.
PARTIES:
Belgium
Netherlands
ANNEX
522 UNTS 335.   Netherlands.   Amendment
25 Oct 62. Force 31 Jul 64.
522 UNTS 335. Belgium. Amendment 25 Oct 62.
Force 31 Jul 64.

102937 Multilateral Convention **216 UNTS 132**
SIGNED: 6 Sep 52   FORCE: 16 Sep 55
REGISTERED: 27 Sep 55 UNESCO (Educ/Cult)
ARTICLES: 21 LANGUAGE: English. French. Spanish.
HEADNOTE: COPYRIGHT
TOPIC: Patents/Copyrights
CONCEPTS: Definition of terms. Territorial applica-
tion. Time limit. Previous treaty renunciation.
Conformity with municipal law. Domestic legisla-
tion. Negotiation. Claims and settlements. Laws
and formalities. Subsidiary organ. Liaison with
other IGO's. Internal structure. Compulsory juris-
diction.
INTL ORGS: Intergovernmental Copyright Commit-
tee. International Union for the Protection of Lit-
erary and Artistic Works. International Court of
Justice. United Nations Educational, Scientific
and Cultural Organization.
TREATY REF: 1LTS217.
PROCEDURE: Accession. Denunciation. Ratifica-
tion. Registration.
PARTIES:
Andorra SIGNED: 6 Sep 52 RATIFIED: 22 Jan 53
  FORCE: 16 Sep 55
Argentina SIGNED: 6 Sep 52
Australia SIGNED: 6 Sep 52
Austria SIGNED: 6 Sep 52
Belgium SIGNED: 30 Dec 52
Brazil SIGNED: 6 Sep 52
Canada SIGNED: 6 Sep 52
Chile SIGNED: 6 Sep 52 RATIFIED: 18 Jan 55
  FORCE: 16 Sep 55
Cuba SIGNED: 6 Sep 52
Denmark SIGNED: 6 Sep 52
El Salvador SIGNED: 6 Sep 52
Finland SIGNED: 6 Sep 52
France SIGNED: 6 Sep 52
Germany, West SIGNED: 6 Sep 52 RATIFIED:
  3 Jun 55 FORCE: 16 Sep 55
Guatemala SIGNED: 6 Sep 52
Haiti SIGNED: 6 Sep 52 RATIFIED: 1 Sep 54
  FORCE: 16 Sep 55
Honduras SIGNED: 6 Sep 52
India SIGNED: 1 Sep 52
Ireland SIGNED: 1 Sep 52
Israel SIGNED: 16 Dec 52 RATIFIED: 6 Apr 55
  FORCE: 16 Sep 55
Italy SIGNED: 6 Sep 52
Japan SIGNED: 3 Jan 53
Liberia SIGNED: 2 Sep 52
Luxembourg SIGNED: 6 Sep 52 RATIFIED:
  15 Jul 55 FORCE: 15 Oct 55
Mexico SIGNED: 6 Sep 52
Monaco SIGNED: 6 Sep 52 RATIFIED: 16 Jun 55
  FORCE: 16 Sep 55
Netherlands SIGNED: 6 Sep 52
Nicaragua SIGNED: 6 Sep 52
Norway SIGNED: 6 Sep 52
Peru SIGNED: 2 Dec 52
Portugal SIGNED: 6 Sep 52
San Marino SIGNED: 6 Sep 52
Spain SIGNED: 6 Sep 52 RATIFIED: 27 Oct 54
  FORCE: 16 Sep 55
Sweden SIGNED: 6 Sep 52
Switzerland SIGNED: 6 Sep 52
UK Great Britain SIGNED: 6 Sep 52

USA (United States) SIGNED: 6 Sep 52 RATI-
  FIED: 6 Dec 54 FORCE: 16 Sep 55
Uruguay SIGNED: 6 Sep 52
Vatican/Holy See SIGNED: 6 Sep 52 RATIFIED:
  5 Jul 55 FORCE: 5 Oct 55
Yugoslavia SIGNED: 6 Sep 52
ANNEX
221 UNTS 437.
221 UNTS 438.
221 UNTS 438. France. Algeria. Force 14 Jan 56.
221 UNTS 438.   France.   Guadeloupe.   Force
  14 Jan 56.
228 UNTS 371.
251 UNTS 398.
253 UNTS 366.
260 UNTS 455.
261 UNTS 408.
264 UNTS 380.
265 UNTS 390.
268 UNTS 373.
272 UNTS 269.
280 UNTS 372.
282 UNTS 365.
338 UNTS 379.
344 UNTS 343.
361 UNTS 331. Belgium. Ratification 31 May 60.
  Force 31 Aug 60.
388 UNTS 361.
394 UNTS 270.
397 UNTS 330.
414 UNTS 388.
417 UNTS 350.
420 UNTS 344.
429 UNTS 294.
435 UNTS 339.
443 UNTS 343.
453 UNTS 360.
463 UNTS 346.
466 UNTS 390.
471 UNTS 331.
480 UNTS 340.
502 UNTS 384.
505 UNTS 320.
511 UNTS 277.
533 UNTS 330.
542 UNTS 359.
555 UNTS 252.
560 UNTS 262.
565 UNTS 285.
571 UNTS 317. Venezuela. Accession 30 Jun 66.
  Force 30 Jun 66.
571 UNTS 317. UK Great Britain. British Honduras. Force 19 Oct 66.
604 UNTS 352.
645 UNTS 354.
657 UNTS 401.

102938   Bilateral Agreement   **216 UNTS 221**
SIGNED: 27 Feb 46   FORCE: 27 Sep 55
REGISTERED: 27 Sep 55 USSR (Soviet Union)
ARTICLES: 3 LANGUAGE: Russian. Mongolian.
HEADNOTE: ECONOMIC CULTURAL COOPER-
ATION
TOPIC: General Economic
CONCEPTS: General provisions.
PROCEDURE: Denunciation. Duration. Future Pro-
cedures Contemplated.
PARTIES:
Mongolia
USSR (Soviet Union)

102939   Bilateral Agreement   **216 UNTS 231**
SIGNED: 3 Feb 47   FORCE: 18 Apr 47
REGISTERED: 27 Sep 55 USSR (Soviet Union)
ARTICLES: 4 LANGUAGE: Russian. Finnish.
HEADNOTE: TRANSFER TERRITORY TO SOVIET
UNION
TOPIC: Territory Boundary
CONCEPTS: Annex or appendix reference. Estab-
lishment of commission. Payment schedules.
Changes of territory. Markers and definitions.
INTL ORGS: Special Commission.
PROCEDURE: Ratification.
PARTIES:
Finland
USSR (Soviet Union)

102940   Bilateral Treaty   **216 UNTS 247**
SIGNED: 15 Jul 47   FORCE: 19 Jan 48

REGISTERED: 27 Sep 55 USSR (Soviet Union)
ARTICLES: 18 LANGUAGE: Russian. Hungarian.
HEADNOTE: TREATY COMMERCE NAVIGATION
TOPIC: General Economic
CONCEPTS: Conditions. Exceptions and exemptions. Annex or appendix reference. Privileges and immunities. Non-diplomatic delegations. Conformity with municipal law. Legal protection and assistance. Recognition and enforcement of legal decisions. Arbitration. Reciprocity in trade. Reexport of goods, etc.. Trade procedures. Commodity trade. Most favored nation clause. Customs duties. Customs declarations. Temporary importation. General transportation. Navigational conditions. Transport of goods. Licenses and certificates of nationality. Water transport. Tonnage. Ports and pilotage. Shipwreck and salvage. Land transport. Railways.
INTL ORGS: Arbitration Commission.
PROCEDURE: Ratification. Termination.
PARTIES:
Hungary
USSR (Soviet Union)

102941 Bilateral Convention **216 UNTS 285**
SIGNED: 28 Nov 47 FORCE: 4 Sep 48
REGISTERED: 27 Sep 55 USSR (Soviet Union)
ARTICLES: 9 LANGUAGE: Russian. Czechoslovakian.
HEADNOTE: QUARANTINE AGRICULTURAL PLANTS
TOPIC: Sanitation
CONCEPTS: General cooperation. Inspection and observation. Specialists exchange. Quarantine. Border control. Disease control. Insect control. Research and development. Conferences.
PROCEDURE: Amendment. Denunciation. Duration. Ratification. Renewal or Revival.
PARTIES:
Czechoslovakia
USSR (Soviet Union)

102942 Bilateral Treaty **217 UNTS 3**
SIGNED: 1 Dec 47 FORCE: 26 Apr 48
REGISTERED: 27 Sep 55 USSR (Soviet Union)
ARTICLES: 14 LANGUAGE: Russian. Czechoslovakian.
HEADNOTE: COMMERCE
TOPIC: General Trade
CONCEPTS: Arbitration. Establishment of trade relations. Trade agencies. Trade procedures. National treatment. Transport of goods. Merchant vessels.
PROCEDURE: Duration. Ratification.
PARTIES:
Finland
USSR (Soviet Union)

102943 Bilateral Treaty **217 UNTS 35**
SIGNED: 11 Dec 47 FORCE: 15 Jun 48
REGISTERED: 27 Sep 55 USSR (Soviet Union)
ARTICLES: 19 LANGUAGE: Russian. Czechoslovakian.
HEADNOTE: COMMERCE NAVIGATION
TOPIC: General Economic
CONCEPTS: Conditions. Exceptions and exemptions. General provisions. Annex or appendix reference. Previous treaty replacement. Privileges and immunities. Non-diplomatic delegations. Conformity with municipal law. Exchange of information and documents. Legal protection and assistance. Recognition and enforcement of legal decisions. Arbitration. Reciprocity in trade. Reexport of goods, etc.. Trade procedures. Commodity trade. Most favored nation clause. Customs duties. Customs declarations. Temporary importation. General transportation. Navigational conditions. Transport of goods. Water transport. Tonnage. Ports and pilotage. Shipwreck and salvage. Land transport. Railways.

TREATY REF: FRIENDSHIP TREATY, 12DEC43.
PROCEDURE: Future Procedures Contemplated. Ratification. Termination.
PARTIES:
Czechoslovakia
USSR (Soviet Union)

102944 Bilateral Treaty **217 UNTS 73**
SIGNED: 17 Mar 48 FORCE: 1 Sep 48
REGISTERED: 27 Sep 55 USSR (Soviet Union)
ARTICLES: 13 LANGUAGE: Russian. French.
HEADNOTE: COMMERCE TRADE
TOPIC: General Trade
CONCEPTS: Exceptions and exemptions. Territorial application. Juridical personality. Legal protection and assistance. Recognition and enforcement of legal decisions. Arbitration. Quotas. Most favored nation clause. Equitable taxes. Customs declarations. General transportation. Transport of goods. Water transport.
PROCEDURE: Duration. Ratification. Termination.
PARTIES:
Switzerland
USSR (Soviet Union)

102945 Bilateral Agreement **217 UNTS 87**
SIGNED: 17 Mar 48 FORCE: 1 Apr 48
REGISTERED: 27 Sep 55 USSR (Soviet Union)
ARTICLES: 8 LANGUAGE: Russian. French.
HEADNOTE: TRADE DELEGATION
TOPIC: General Trade
CONCEPTS: Detailed regulations. Exceptions and exemptions. Territorial application. Treaty implementation. Privileges and immunities. Non-diplomatic delegations. Exchange of information and documents. Public information. Trade procedures.
PROCEDURE: Duration. Termination.
PARTIES:
Switzerland
USSR (Soviet Union)

102946 Bilateral Treaty **217 UNTS 97**
SIGNED: 1 Apr 48 FORCE: 7 Aug 48
REGISTERED: 27 Sep 55 USSR (Soviet Union)
ARTICLES: 20 LANGUAGE: Russian. Bulgarian.
HEADNOTE: COMMERCE NAVIGATION
TOPIC: General Economic
CONCEPTS: Conditions. Exceptions and exemptions. General provisions. Annex or appendix reference. Privileges and immunities. Non-diplomatic delegations. Exchange of information and documents. Legal protection and assistance. Recognition and enforcement of legal decisions. Arbitration. Negotiation. Reciprocity in trade. Reexport of goods, etc.. Trade procedures. Most favored nation clause. Customs duties. Customs declarations. Temporary importation. General transportation. Navigational conditions. Transport of goods. Merchant vessels. Tonnage. Ports and pilotage. Shipwreck and salvage. Railways.
PROCEDURE: Duration. Future Procedures Contemplated. Ratification. Termination.
PARTIES:
Bulgaria
USSR (Soviet Union)

102947 Bilateral Agreement **217 UNTS 135**
SIGNED: 9 Dec 48 FORCE: 8 Apr 49
REGISTERED: 27 Sep 55 USSR (Soviet Union)
ARTICLES: 29 LANGUAGE: Russian. Finnish.
HEADNOTE: REGIME SOVIET-FINNISH FRONTIER
TOPIC: Territory Boundary
CONCEPTS: Definition of terms. Annex or appen-

dix reference. Exchange of information and documents. Inspection and observation. Operating agencies. Fish, wildlife, and natural resources. Markers and definitions. Frontier waterways. Wildlife. Regulation of natural resources.
INTL ORGS: Special Commission.
PROCEDURE: Duration. Ratification. Renewal or Revival. Termination.
PARTIES:
Finland
USSR (Soviet Union)

102948 Bilateral Treaty **217 UNTS 181**
SIGNED: 11 Dec 48 FORCE: 28 Mar 52
REGISTERED: 27 Sep 55 USSR (Soviet Union)
ARTICLES: 22 LANGUAGE: Russian. Italian.
HEADNOTE: COMMERCE NAVIGATION
TOPIC: General Economic
CONCEPTS: Exceptions and exemptions. General provisions. Annex or appendix reference. Privileges and immunities. Non-diplomatic delegations. Conformity with municipal law. Free passage and transit. Legal protection and assistance. Recognition of legal documents. Arbitration. Reciprocity in trade. Reexport of goods, etc.. Trade procedures. Commodity trade. Most favored nation clause. Customs duties. Customs declarations. Temporary importation. General transportation. Transport of goods. Licenses and certificates of nationality. Water transport. Tonnage. Ports and pilotage. Shipwreck and salvage. Postal services.
PROCEDURE: Duration. Ratification. Termination.
PARTIES:
Italy
USSR (Soviet Union)

102949 Multilateral Treaty **217 UNTS 223**
SIGNED: 15 May 55 FORCE: 27 Jul 55
REGISTERED: 27 Sep 55 USSR (Soviet Union)
ARTICLES: 38 LANGUAGE: Russian. English. French. German.
HEADNOTE: RE-ESTABLISHMENT INDENDENT DEMOCRATIC AUSTRIA
TOPIC: Recognition
CONCEPTS: General provisions. Treaty interpretation. Annex or appendix reference. Repatriation of nationals. Nazi organizations. Democratic institutions. Recognition. Re-establishment. Union with other states. Human rights. Domestic legislation. General property. Procedure. Assets. Debts. Assets transfer. Most favored nation clause. Rearmament restrictions and controls. Surplus war property. Withdrawal of forces. Foreign nationals. Arms limitations. War graves. Markers and definitions.
INTL ORGS: United Nations. Conciliation Commission.
PROCEDURE: Accession. Ratification.
PARTIES:
Austria SIGNED: 15 May 55 RATIFIED: 27 Jul 55 FORCE: 27 Jul 55
France SIGNED: 15 May 55 RATIFIED: 27 Jul 55 FORCE: 27 Jul 55
UK Great Britain SIGNED: 15 May 55 RATIFIED: 27 Jul 55 FORCE: 27 Jul 55
USA (United States) SIGNED: 15 May 55 RATIFIED: 27 Jul 55 FORCE: 27 Jul 55
USSR (Soviet Union) SIGNED: 15 May 55 RATIFIED: 27 Jul 55 FORCE: 27 Jul 55
ANNEX
221 UNTS 439. Czechoslovakia. Accession 28 Sep 55.
259 UNTS 445. Poland. Accession 20 Aug 56.
263 UNTS 424. Mexico. Accession 28 Dec 56.
316 UNTS 350. Brazil. Accession 15 Sep 58.
420 UNTS 345. Australia. Accession 10 Aug 61.

102950 Bilateral Agreement **218 UNTS 3**
SIGNED: 5 Aug 55　　　　FORCE: 8 Sep 55
REGISTERED: 28 Sep 55 IBRD (World Bank)
ARTICLES: 8 LANGUAGE: English.
HEADNOTE: LOAN AGREEMENT
TOPIC: IBRD Project
CONCEPTS: Default remedies. Annex or appendix reference. Exchange of information and documents. Informational records. Inspection and observation. Accounting procedures. Bonds. Fees and exemptions. Interest rates. Tax exemptions. Domestic obligation. Terms of loan. Loan regulations. Loan guarantee. Guarantor non-interference.
PARTIES:
　Peru
　IBRD (World Bank)

102951 Bilateral Convention **218 UNTS 19**
SIGNED: 15 Oct 54　　　　FORCE: 8 Sep 55
REGISTERED: 29 Sep 55 Belgium
ARTICLES: 12 LANGUAGE: French.
HEADNOTE: PRACTICE PROFESSION ARCHITECT
TOPIC: Admin Cooperation
CONCEPTS: General cooperation. Informational records. Recognition of degrees.
PROCEDURE: Duration. Ratification.
PARTIES:
　Belgium
　France

102952 Multilateral Convention **218 UNTS 27**
SIGNED: 11 Dec 53　　　　FORCE: 1 Jun 55
REGISTERED: 29 Sep 55 Council of Europe
ARTICLES: 11 LANGUAGE: English. French.
HEADNOTE: PATENT APPLICATIONS
TOPIC: Patents/Copyrights
CONCEPTS: Laws and formalities.
INTL ORGS: Council of Europe. International Union for the Protection of Industrial Property.
PROCEDURE: Accession. Denunciation. Ratification.
PARTIES:
　Belgium SIGNED: 11 Dec 53
　Denmark SIGNED: 11 Dec 53
　France SIGNED: 11 Dec 53
　Germany, West SIGNED: 11 Dec 53 RATIFIED: 17 May 55 FORCE: 1 Jun 55
　Greece　SIGNED:　11 Dec 53　RATIFIED: 15 Jun 55 FORCE: 1 Jul 55
　Iceland SIGNED: 11 Dec 53
　Ireland　SIGNED:　11 Dec 53　RATIFIED: 17 Jun 54 FORCE: 1 Jun 55
　Italy SIGNED: 11 Dec 53
　Luxembourg SIGNED: 11 Dec 53
　Netherlands SIGNED: 11 Dec 53
　Norway　SIGNED:　11 Dec 53　RATIFIED: 21 May 54 FORCE: 1 Jun 55
　Saar SIGNED: 11 Dec 53 RATIFIED: 8 Sep 54 FORCE: 1 Jun 55
　Sweden SIGNED: 11 Dec 53
　Turkey SIGNED: 11 Dec 53
　UK Great Britain SIGNED: 11 Dec 53 RATIFIED: 5 May 55 FORCE: 1 Jun 55
　　　　　　ANNEX
219 UNTS 384. Germany, West. Berlin. Force 5 Jun 55.
275 UNTS 307. Denmark. Ratification 3 Sep 56. Force 1 Oct 56.
275 UNTS 307. Luxembourg. Ratification 4 Jul 57. Force 1 Aug 57.
275 UNTS 307. Sweden. Ratification 28 Jun 57. Force 1 Jul 57.
275 UNTS 307. Turkey. Ratification 22 Oct 56. Force 1 Nov 56.
314 UNTS 346. South Africa. Accession 28 Nov 57. Force 1 Dec 57.
314 UNTS 346. Italy. Ratification 17 Oct 58. Force 1 Nov 58.
355 UNTS 412. Switzerland. Accession 28 Dec 59. Force 1 Jan 60.
420 UNTS 346. France. Ratification 18 Jan 62. Force 1 Feb 62.

528 UNTS 293. Belgium. Ratification 12 Mar 65. Force 1 Apr 65.
565 UNTS 286. Iceland. Ratification 24 Mar 66. Force 1 Apr 66.
565 UNTS 286. Israel. Accession 29 Apr 66. Force 1 May 66.
635 UNTS 347. Spain. Accession 28 Jun 67. Force 1 Jul 67.

102953 Multilateral Convention **218 UNTS 51**
SIGNED: 19 Dec 54　　　　FORCE: 1 Aug 55
REGISTERED: 29 Sep 55 Council of Europe
ARTICLES: 8 LANGUAGE: English. French.
HEADNOTE: PATENTS INVENTIONS
TOPIC: Patents/Copyrights
CONCEPTS: Trademarks. Laws and formalities.
INTL ORGS: Council of Europe. International Union for the Protection of Industrial Property.
PROCEDURE: Accession. Denunciation. Ratification.
PARTIES:
　Belgium　SIGNED:　19 Dec 54　RATIFIED: 16 May 55 FORCE: 1 Aug 55
　Denmark SIGNED: 19 Dec 54
　France SIGNED: 19 Dec 54 RATIFIED: 1 Jul 55 FORCE: 1 Aug 55
　Germany, West SIGNED: 19 Dec 54
　Greece SIGNED: 19 Dec 54
　Ireland　SIGNED:　19 Dec 54　RATIFIED: 11 Mar 55 FORCE: 1 Aug 55
　Italy SIGNED: 19 Dec 54
　Netherlands SIGNED: 19 Dec 54
　Norway　SIGNED:　19 Dec 54　RATIFIED: 11 Mar 55 FORCE: 1 Aug 55
　Saar SIGNED: 19 Dec 54
　Sweden SIGNED: 19 Dec 54
　Turkey SIGNED: 19 Dec 54
　UK Great Britain SIGNED: 19 Dec 54
　　　　　　ANNEX
223 UNTS 383. UK Great Britain. Qualified Ratification 28 Oct 55.
223 UNTS 383. Germany, West. Qualified Ratification 28 Nov 55. Force 1 Dec 55.
227 UNTS 401. Netherlands. Ratification 12 Jan 56. Force 1 Feb 56.
227 UNTS 401. Netherlands. Netherlands Antilles. Force 1 Feb 56.
227 UNTS 401. Netherlands. Surinam. Force 1 Feb 56.
227 UNTS 401. Netherlands. Dutch New Guinea. Force 1 Feb 56.
227 UNTS 401. UK Great Britain. Force 12 Jan 56.
275 UNTS 308. Turkey. Ratification 22 Oct 56. Force 1 Nov 56.
275 UNTS 308. Sweden. Ratification 28 Jun 57. Force 1 Jul 57.
275 UNTS 308. Italy. Ratification 9 Jan 57. Force 1 Feb 57.
288 UNTS 372. Denmark. Ratification 23 Sep 57. Force 1 Oct 57.
355 UNTS 413. Australia. Accession 24 Apr 58. Force 24 May 58.

102954 Multilateral Convention **218 UNTS 125**
SIGNED: 11 Dec 53　　　　FORCE: 20 Apr 54
REGISTERED: 29 Sep 55 Council of Europe
ARTICLES: 6 LANGUAGE: English. French.
HEADNOTE: ACEDEMIC STANDARDIZATION
TOPIC: Education
CONCEPTS: Definition of terms. Standardization. General cooperation. Exchange of information and documents. Recognition of degrees.
INTL ORGS: Council of Europe.
PROCEDURE: Accession. Ratification.
PARTIES:
　Belgium　SIGNED:　11 Dec 53　RATIFIED: 14 Jun 55 FORCE: 14 Jun 55
　Council of Europe
　Denmark　SIGNED:　11 Dec 53　RATIFIED: 20 Apr 54 FORCE: 20 Apr 54

France　　SIGNED:　　11 Dec 53　RATIFIED: 11 Mar 55 FORCE: 11 Mar 55
Germany, West SIGNED: 11 Dec 53 RATIFIED: 3 Mar 55 FORCE: 3 Mar 55
Greece SIGNED: 11 Dec 53
Iceland SIGNED: 11 Dec 53 RATIFIED: 15 Aug 5 FORCE: 5 Aug 54
Ireland　SIGNED:　11 Dec 53　RATIFIED: 31 Mar 54 FORCE: 20 Apr 54
Italy SIGNED: 11 Dec 53
Luxembourg SIGNED: 11 Dec 53 RATIFIED: 12 Jan 55 FORCE: 12 Jan 55
Netherlands SIGNED: 11 Dec 53
Norway　　SIGNED:　11 Dec 53　RATIFIED: 21 May 54 FORCE: 21 May 54
Saar SIGNED: 11 Dec 53 RATIFIED: 8 Sep 54 FORCE: 8 Sep 54
Sweden SIGNED: 11 Dec 53
Turkey SIGNED: 11 Dec 53
UK Great Britain SIGNED: 11 Dec 53 RATIFIED: 22 Mar 54 FORCE: 20 Apr 54
　　　　　ANNEX
253 UNTS 367.　Netherlands.　Ratification 27 Aug 56.
253 UNTS 367. Greece. Ratification 5 Dec 55.
253 UNTS 367.　Italy.　Qualified Ratification 31 Oct 56.
253 UNTS 367. Australia. Accession 9 Oct 56.
358 UNTS 284. Turkey. Ratification 10 Oct 57.
363 UNTS 406. Sweden. Ratification 27 May 60.
424 UNTS 351. Spain. Accession 21 Mar 62.
514 UNTS 270. Denmark. Signature 3 Jun 64. Force 4 Jul 64.
514 UNTS 270. France. Signature 3 Jun 64. Force 4 Jul 64.
514 UNTS 270. Norway. Signature 3 Jun 64. Force 4 Jul 64.
514 UNTS 270. UK Great Britain. Signature 25 Aug 64. Force 26 Sep 64.
522 UNTS 340. Council of Europe. Correction 21 Dec 64.
529 UNTS 328. Netherlands. Surinam. Force 22 Apr 65.
529 UNTS 328. Netherlands. Netherlands Antilles. Force 22 Apr 65.
529 UNTS 328. Netherlands. Ratification 21 Jan 65. Force 22 Apr 65.
565 UNTS 287. Luxembourg. Ratification 30 Nov 65. Force 31 Dec 65.
635 UNTS 348. Sweden. Signature 21 Jun 67. Force 22 Jul 67.

102955 Multilateral Convention **218 UNTS 139**
SIGNED: 19 Dec 54　　　　FORCE: 5 May 55
REGISTERED: 29 Sep 55 Council of Europe
ARTICLES: 11 LANGUAGE: English. French.
HEADNOTE: CULTURAL CONVENTION
TOPIC: Culture
CONCEPTS: Friendship and amity. Alien status. Conformity with municipal law. General cooperation. Dispute settlement. Exchange. Exchange. General cultural cooperation.
INTL ORGS: Council of Europe.
PROCEDURE: Accession. Denunciation. Duration.
PARTIES:
　Belgium　SIGNED:　19 Dec 54　RATIFIED: 11 May 55 FORCE: 11 May 55
　Denmark　SIGNED:　19 Dec 54　RATIFIED: 7 May 55 FORCE: 7 May 55
　France　SIGNED:　19 Dec 54　RATIFIED: 19 Mar 55 FORCE: 5 May 55
　Germany, West SIGNED: 19 Dec 54
　Greece SIGNED: 19 Dec 54
　Iceland SIGNED: 19 Dec 54
　Ireland　SIGNED:　19 Dec 54　RATIFIED: 11 Mar 55 FORCE: 5 May 55
　Italy SIGNED: 19 Dec 54
　Luxembourg SIGNED: 19 Dec 54
　Netherlands SIGNED: 19 Dec 54
　Norway SIGNED: 19 Dec 54
　Saar SIGNED: 19 Dec 54
　Sweden SIGNED: 19 Dec 54
　Turkey SIGNED: 19 Dec 54
　UK Great Britain SIGNED: 19 Dec 54 RATIFIED: 5 May 55 FORCE: 5 May 55

223 UNTS 384. Germany, West. Qualified Ratification 17 Nov 55.

228 UNTS 372. Netherlands. Ratification 8 Feb 56.

228 UNTS 372. Germany, West. Berlin. Force 17 Nov 55.

228 UNTS 372. Norway. Ratification 24 Jan 56.

358 UNTS 285. Iceland. Ratification 1 Mar 56.

358 UNTS 285. Italy. Ratification 16 May 57.

358 UNTS 285. Turkey. Ratification 10 Oct 57.

358 UNTS 285. Sweden. Ratification 16 Jun 58.

358 UNTS 285. Spain. Accession 4 Jul 57.

358 UNTS 285. Austria. Signature 13 Dec 57. Ratification 4 Mar 58.

358 UNTS 285. Luxembourg. Ratification 30 Jul 56.

420 UNTS 347. Greece. Ratification 10 Jan 62.

449 UNTS 308. Switzerland. Qualified Accession 13 Jul 62.

449 UNTS 308. Vatican/Holy See. Accession 10 Dec 63.

102956 Multilateral Agreement **218 UNTS 153**
SIGNED: 11 Dec 53   FORCE: 1 Jul 54
REGISTERED: 30 Sep 55 Council of Europe
ARTICLES: 16 LANGUAGE: English. French.
HEADNOTE: SOCIAL SECURITY
TOPIC: Non-ILO Labor
CONCEPTS: Definition of terms. Exceptions and exemptions. Annex or appendix reference. Alien status. Exchange of information and documents. Domestic legislation. Existing tribunals. Old age and invalidity insurance. Non-ILO labor relations. Old age insurance. Sickness and invalidity insurance. Social security. Payment schedules. National treatment.
INTL ORGS: Council of Europe. International Court of Justice.
PROCEDURE: Accession. Denunciation. Duration. Ratification. Registration. Renewal or Revival.
PARTIES:
Belgium SIGNED: 11 Dec 53
Denmark SIGNED: 11 Dec 53 RATIFIED: 30 Jun 54 FORCE: 1 Jul 54
France SIGNED: 11 Dec 53
Germany, West SIGNED: 11 Dec 53
Greece SIGNED: 11 Dec 53
Iceland SIGNED: 11 Dec 53
Ireland SIGNED: 11 Dec 53 RATIFIED: 31 Mar 54 FORCE: 1 Jul 54
Italy SIGNED: 11 Dec 53
Luxembourg SIGNED: 11 Dec 53
Netherlands SIGNED: 11 Dec 53 RATIFIED: 11 Mar 55 FORCE: 1 Apr 55
Norway SIGNED: 11 Dec 53 RATIFIED: 9 Sep 54 FORCE: 1 Oct 54
Saar SIGNED: 11 Dec 53 RATIFIED: 8 Sep 54 FORCE: 1 Oct 54
Sweden SIGNED: 11 Dec 53 RATIFIED: 2 Sep 55 FORCE: 1 Oct 55
Turkey SIGNED: 11 Dec 53
UK Great Britain SIGNED: 11 Dec 54 RATIFIED: 7 Sep 54 FORCE: 1 Oct 54

ANNEX

252 UNTS 370. France.

252 UNTS 370. Luxembourg.

252 UNTS 370. Netherlands.

252 UNTS 370. Sweden.

252 UNTS 370. UK Great Britain.

252 UNTS 370. Germany, West.

252 UNTS 370. Germany, West. Qualified Ratification 24 Aug 56. Force 1 Sep 56.

252 UNTS 370. Ireland.

252 UNTS 370. Norway.

252 UNTS 370. Belgium.

252 UNTS 370. Denmark.

256 UNTS 366. Germany, West. Berlin. Force 1 Sep 56.

269 UNTS 368. Belgium. Ratification 3 Apr 57. Force 1 May 57.

269 UNTS 368. Denmark.

292 UNTS 364. France. Ratification 18 Dec 57. Force 1 Jan 58.

292 UNTS 364. France. Amendment 18 Dec 57.

310 UNTS 384. Italy. Ratification 26 Aug 58. Force 1 Sep 58.

310 UNTS 384. Italy.

315 UNTS 242. Belgium. Amendment 6 Nov 58.

315 UNTS 242. Luxembourg. Ratification 18 Nov 58. Force 1 Dec 58.

320 UNTS 346. UK Great Britain. Amendment 9 Jan 59. Force 1 Feb 59.

324 UNTS 336. UK Great Britain. Amendment 6 Feb 59.

328 UNTS 334. France. Amendment 8 May 59.

341 UNTS 388. Luxembourg. Amendment 28 Aug 59.

349 UNTS 326. France. Amendment 12 Oct 59.

349 UNTS 326. UK Great Britain. Amendment 2 Feb 60.

349 UNTS 326. Luxembourg. Amendment 20 Nov 59.

349 UNTS 326. Sweden. Amendment 14 Dec 59.

349 UNTS 326. Italy. Amendment 8 Oct 59.

349 UNTS 330. France. Amendment 12 Oct 59.

349 UNTS 330. Italy. Amendment 8 Oct 59.

349 UNTS 330. Netherlands. Amendment 8 Jan 60.

349 UNTS 330. UK Great Britain. Amendment 2 Feb 60.

388 UNTS 362. Ireland. Amendment 4 Nov 60.

404 UNTS 346. Greece. Ratification 29 May 61. Force 1 Jun 61.

404 UNTS 346. UK Great Britain. Amendment 1 Aug 61.

404 UNTS 346. Germany, West. Amendment 27 Jul 61.

407 UNTS 242. Sweden. Withdrawal of Reservation 7 Jul 61. Force 1 Jan 61.

410 UNTS 297. Greece. Ratification 29 Sep 61. Force 1 Oct 61.

417 UNTS 351. Luxembourg. Withdrawal of Reservation 1 Dec 62. Force 1 Jan 62.

420 UNTS 348. Germany, West. Amendment 5 Dec 61.

528 UNTS 294. Iceland. Ratification 4 Dec 64. Force 1 Jan 65.

533 UNTS 331. Denmark. Ratification 5 May 65.

102957 Multilateral Agreement **218 UNTS 211**
SIGNED: 11 Dec 53   FORCE: 1 Jul 54
REGISTERED: 30 Sep 55 Council of Europe
ARTICLES: 16 LANGUAGE: English. French.
HEADNOTE: SOCIAL SECURITY OLD-AGE INVALIDITY SURVIVAL
TOPIC: Non-ILO Labor
CONCEPTS: Definition of terms. Exceptions and exemptions. Annex or appendix reference. Alien status. Exchange of information and documents. Domestic legislation. Dispute settlement. Existing tribunals. Old age and invalidity insurance. Non-ILO labor relations. Old age insurance. Sickness and invalidity insurance. Social security. Payment schedules. National treatment.
INTL ORGS: Council of Europe. International Labour Organization.
TREATY REF: 209UNTS194.
PROCEDURE: Accession. Denunciation. Duration. Ratification. Registration. Renewal or Revival.
PARTIES:
Belgium SIGNED: 11 Dec 53
Denmark SIGNED: 11 Dec 53 RATIFIED: 30 Jun 54 FORCE: 1 Jul 54
France SIGNED: 11 Dec 53
Germany, West SIGNED: 11 Dec 53
Greece SIGNED: 11 Dec 53
Iceland SIGNED: 11 Dec 53
Ireland SIGNED: 11 Dec 53 RATIFIED: 31 Mar 54 FORCE: 1 Jul 54
Italy SIGNED: 11 Dec 53
Luxembourg SIGNED: 11 Dec 53
Netherlands SIGNED: 11 Dec 53 RATIFIED: 11 Mar 55 FORCE: 1 Apr 55
Norway SIGNED: 11 Dec 53 RATIFIED: 9 Sep 54 FORCE: 1 Oct 54
Saar SIGNED: 11 Dec 53 RATIFIED: 8 Sep 54 FORCE: 1 Oct 54
Sweden SIGNED: 11 Dec 53 RATIFIED: 2 Sep 55 FORCE: 1 Oct 55
Turkey SIGNED: 11 Dec 53
UK Great Britain SIGNED: 11 Dec 54 RATIFIED: 7 Sep 54 FORCE: 1 Oct 54

252 UNTS 382. Denmark.

252 UNTS 382. France.

252 UNTS 382. Luxembourg.

252 UNTS 382. Germany, West. Qualified Ratification 24 Aug 56. Force 1 Sep 56.

252 UNTS 382. Belgium.

252 UNTS 382. UK Great Britain.

252 UNTS 382. Ireland.

252 UNTS 382. Germany, West.

253 UNTS 368. Netherlands.

256 UNTS 366. Germany, West. Berlin. Force 1 Sep 56.

269 UNTS 372. Belgium. Ratification 3 Apr 57. Force 1 May 57.

269 UNTS 372. Denmark.

292 UNTS 366. France. Amendment 18 Dec 57.

292 UNTS 366. France. Ratification 18 Dec 57. Force 1 Jan 58.

292 UNTS 366. Netherlands. Amendment 23 Jan 58.

310 UNTS 388. Italy. Ratification 26 Aug 58. Force 1 Sep 58.

310 UNTS 388. Italy.

315 UNTS 243. Luxembourg. Ratification 18 Nov 58. Force 1 Dec 58.

315 UNTS 243. Belgium. Amendment 6 Nov 58.

324 UNTS 336. UK Great Britain. Amendment 6 Feb 59.

328 UNTS 335. France. Amendment 8 May 59.

328 UNTS 336. Denmark. Amendment 14 May 59.

339 UNTS 402. Belgium. Amendment 29 Jul 59.

341 UNTS 388. Luxembourg. Amendment 28 Aug 59.

388 UNTS 364. Denmark. Amendment 16 Jan 61.

404 UNTS 346. Greece. Ratification 29 May 61. Force 1 Jun 61.

404 UNTS 346. Germany, West. Amendment 27 Jul 61.

404 UNTS 346. UK Great Britain. Amendment 1 Aug 61.

407 UNTS 243. Denmark. Withdrawal of Reservation 30 Aug 61. Force 1 Sep 61.

410 UNTS 298. Greece. Ratification 29 Sep 61. Force 1 Oct 61.

417 UNTS 352. Luxembourg. Withdrawal of Reservation 1 Dec 62. Force 1 Jan 62.

420 UNTS 349. Germany, West. Amendment 5 Dec 61.

528 UNTS 298. Iceland. Ratification 4 Dec 64. Force 1 Jan 65.

533 UNTS 331. Denmark. Ratification 5 May 65.

102958 Multilateral Convention **218 UNTS 255**
SIGNED: 11 Dec 53   FORCE: 1 Jul 54
REGISTERED: 30 Sep 55 Council of Europe
ARTICLES: 24 LANGUAGE: English. French.
HEADNOTE: SOCIAL MEDICAL ASSISTANCE
TOPIC: Non-ILO Labor
CONCEPTS: Definition of terms. Territorial application. General provisions. Annex or appendix reference. Resident permits. Repatriation of nationals. General cooperation. Exchange of information and documents. Domestic legislation. Existing tribunals. Public health. Non-ILO labor relations. Social security. Indemnities and reimbursements.
INTL ORGS: Council of Europe. International Court of Justice.
PROCEDURE: Accession. Denunciation. Duration. Ratification. Registration. Renewal or Revival.
PARTIES:
Belgium SIGNED: 11 Dec 53
Denmark SIGNED: 11 Dec 53 RATIFIED: 30 Jun 54 FORCE: 1 Jul 54
France SIGNED: 11 Dec 53
Germany, West SIGNED: 11 Dec 53
Greece SIGNED: 11 Dec 53
Iceland SIGNED: 11 Dec 53
Ireland SIGNED: 11 Dec 53 RATIFIED: 31 Mar 54 FORCE: 1 Jul 54
Italy SIGNED: 11 Dec 53
Luxembourg SIGNED: 11 Dec 53
Netherlands SIGNED: 11 Dec 53 RATIFIED: 11 Mar 55 FORCE: 1 Apr 55
Norway SIGNED: 11 Dec 53 RATIFIED: 9 Sep 54 FORCE: 1 Oct 54

Saar SIGNED: 11 Dec 53 RATIFIED: 8 Sep 54
FORCE: 1 Oct 54
Sweden SIGNED: 11 Dec 53 RATIFIED:
2 Sep 55 FORCE: 1 Oct 55
Turkey SIGNED: 11 Dec 53
UK Great Britain SIGNED: 11 Dec 53 RATIFIED:
7 Sep 54 FORCE: 1 Oct 54
ANNEX
252 UNTS 390. Germany, West. Qualified Ratification 24 Aug 56. Force 1 Sep 56.
252 UNTS 390. Germany, West.
252 UNTS 390. Ireland.
252 UNTS 390. Saar.
252 UNTS 390. Sweden.
252 UNTS 390. Belgium. Ratification 24 Jul 56.
Force 1 Aug 56.
252 UNTS 390. France.
256 UNTS 366. Germany, West. Berlin. Force
1 Sep 56.
284 UNTS 378. Sweden. Amendment 28 Nov 57.
284 UNTS 378. France. Ratification 30 Dec 57.
Force 1 Nov 57.
309 UNTS 371. Italy. Ratification 1 Jul 58. Force
1 Aug 58.
309 UNTS 371. Germany, West. Amendment
13 Aug 58.
315 UNTS 244. Luxembourg. Ratification
18 Nov 58. Force 1 Dec 58.
339 UNTS 404. Denmark. Amendment
10 Jun 59.
362 UNTS 336. Turkey. Amendment 2 Jun 60.
362 UNTS 336. Greece. Ratification 23 Jun 60.
Force 1 Jul 60.
416 UNTS 335. Ireland. Amendment 19 Oct 61.
528 UNTS 300. Iceland. Ratification 4 Dec 64.
Force 1 Jan 65.

102959 Bilateral Agreement **218 UNTS 295**
SIGNED: 18 Oct 54 FORCE: 29 Jun 55
REGISTERED: 6 Oct 55 Denmark
ARTICLES: 4 LANGUAGE: English.
HEADNOTE: DOUBLE TAXATION INCOME SEA AIR
TRANSPORT
TOPIC: Taxation
CONCEPTS: Definition of terms. Previous treaty re-
placement. Taxation. Tax exemptions. Air trans-
port. Merchant vessels.
TREATY REF: 149LTS31.
PROCEDURE: Termination.
PARTIES:
Denmark
Ireland

102960 Bilateral Convention **218 UNTS 301**
SIGNED: 18 Oct 54 FORCE: 13 Jun 55
REGISTERED: 6 Oct 55 UK Great Britain
ARTICLES: 22 LANGUAGE: English. German.
HEADNOTE: DOUBLE TAXATION FISCAL EVA-
SION TAXES INCOME
TOPIC: Taxation
CONCEPTS: Definition of terms. Territorial applica-
tion. Conformity with municipal law. Exchange
of official publications. Teacher and student ex-
change. Taxation. Tax credits. Equitable taxes.
Tax exemptions. Air transport. Merchant vessels.
PROCEDURE: Duration. Ratification. Termination.
PARTIES:
Germany, West
UK Great Britain

102961 Multilateral Convention **218 UNTS 345**
SIGNED: 11 Jul 47 FORCE: 19 Jun 55
REGISTERED: 10 Oct 55 ILO (Labor Org)
ARTICLES: 32 LANGUAGE: English. French.
HEADNOTE: SOCIAL POLICY NON-METROPOLI-
TAN AREAS
TOPIC: ILO Labor
CONCEPTS: Territorial application. Domestic leg-
islation. Vocational training. ILO conventions.
Anti-discrimination. Safety standards. Wages
and salaries. Social security. Migrant worker. Aid

and development. Economic assistance. Administering authority. Socio-economic development.
INTL ORGS: International Labour Organization.
PROCEDURE: Amendment. Accession. Denunciation. Duration. Ratification. Registration. Renewal or Revival.
PARTIES:
Multilateral
ANNEX
325 UNTS 346. UK Great Britain. Sarawak.
571 UNTS 331. UK Great Britain. Fiji Islands.
613 UNTS 424. UK Great Britain. Swaziland. Declaration 6 Nov 67.

102962 Multilateral Treaty **219 UNTS 3**
SIGNED: 14 May 55 FORCE: 6 Jun 55
REGISTERED: 10 Oct 55 Poland
ARTICLES: 11 LANGUAGE: Russian. Polish.
Czechoslovakian. German.
HEADNOTE: FRIENDSHIP COOPERATION MU-
TUAL ASSISTANCE (WARSAW PACT)
TOPIC: General Amity
CONCEPTS: Friendship and amity. Peaceful rela-
tions. General cooperation. Establishment of
commission. Dispute settlement. Joint defense.
Defense and security. Arms limitations. Subsid-
iary organ.
INTL ORGS: North Atlantic Treaty Organization.
United Nations. Special Commission.
PROCEDURE: Accession. Duration. Future Proce-
dures Contemplated. Ratification. Termination.
PARTIES:
Albania SIGNED: 14 May 55 RATIFIED: 6 Jun 55
FORCE: 6 Jun 55
Bulgaria SIGNED: 14 May 55 RATIFIED:
31 May 55 FORCE: 6 Jun 55
Czechoslovakia SIGNED: 14 May 55 RATIFIED:
27 May 55 FORCE: 6 Jun 55
Germany, East SIGNED: 14 May 55 RATIFIED:
24 May 55 FORCE: 6 Jun 55
Hungary SIGNED: 14 May 55 RATIFIED:
2 Jun 55 FORCE: 6 Jun 55
Poland SIGNED: 14 May 55 RATIFIED:
19 May 55 FORCE: 6 Jun 55
Romania SIGNED: 14 May 55 RATIFIED:
3 Jun 55 FORCE: 6 Jun 55
USSR (Soviet Union) SIGNED: 14 May 55 RATI-
FIED: 1 Jun 55 FORCE: 6 Jun 55

102963 Bilateral Exchange **219 UNTS 35**
SIGNED: 22 Nov 54 FORCE: 1 Apr 55
REGISTERED: 15 Oct 55 South Africa
ARTICLES: 2 LANGUAGE: English. French.
HEADNOTE: DOUBLE TAXATION PROFITS SHIPS
AIRCRAFT
TOPIC: Taxation
CONCEPTS: Definition of terms. Taxation. Tax ex-
emptions. Air transport. Merchant vessels.
PROCEDURE: Duration. Termination.
PARTIES:
France
South Africa

102964 Bilateral Exchange **219 UNTS 41**
SIGNED: 3 Oct 50 FORCE: 3 Oct 50
REGISTERED: 15 Oct 55 Pakistan
ARTICLES: 2 LANGUAGE: English.
HEADNOTE: RECIPROCAL GRANT VISAS GRATIS
TOPIC: Visas
CONCEPTS: Frontier formalities. Visas. Fees and
exemptions.
PARTIES:
Lebanon
Pakistan

102965 Bilateral Exchange **219 UNTS 47**
SIGNED: 22 Oct 51 FORCE: 15 Nov 51

REGISTERED: 15 Oct 55 Pakistan
ARTICLES: 3 LANGUAGE: English.
HEADNOTE: MULTIPLE JOURNEY VISAS DIPLO-
MATIC SERVICE
TOPIC: Visas
CONCEPTS: Time limit. Passports diplomatic.
Visas.
PARTIES:
Pakistan
Turkey

102966 Multilateral Protocol **219 UNTS 55**
SIGNED: 20 May 52 FORCE: 20 May 52
REGISTERED: 19 Oct 55 Belgium
ARTICLES: 5 LANGUAGE: English. French.
HEADNOTE: TERMINATION UNIFICATION PHAR-
MACOPOEIAL FORMULAS AGREEMENTS
TOPIC: Sanitation
CONCEPTS: Detailed regulations. Domestic legis-
lation. Pharmaceuticals. WHO used as agency.
Extension of functions.
INTL ORGS: International Secretariat for the Unifi-
cation of Pharmacopoeias. United Nations.
World Health Organization.
TREATY REF: 98LTS125; 57LTS583;
160LTS358.
PROCEDURE: Accession. Termination.
PARTIES:
Belgium SIGNED: 20 May 52 RATIFIED:
6 Jan 55 FORCE: 6 Jan 55
Denmark SIGNED: 20 May 52 FORCE:
20 May 52
United Arab Rep SIGNED: 20 May 52 FORCE:
20 May 52
Finland SIGNED: 20 May 52 FORCE: 20 May 52
France SIGNED: 20 May 52 FORCE: 20 May 52
Germany, West Berlin RATIFIED: 22 Jun 52
FORCE: 22 Jun 54
Germany, West SIGNED: 20 May 52 FORCE:
20 May 52
Greece SIGNED: 20 May 52 FORCE: 20 May 52
Iceland SIGNED: 20 May 52 FORCE: 20 May 52
Italy SIGNED: 20 May 52 FORCE: 20 May 52
Luxembourg SIGNED: 20 May 52 FORCE:
20 May 52
Netherlands SIGNED: 20 May 52 RATIFIED:
18 Jun 53 FORCE: 18 Jun 53
Norway SIGNED: 20 May 52 FORCE: 20 May 52
Spain SIGNED: 20 May 52 FORCE: 20 May 52
Sweden SIGNED: 20 May 52 FORCE: 20 May 52
UK Great Britain SIGNED: 20 May 52 RATIFIED:
11 Aug 55 FORCE: 11 Aug 55
USA (United States) SIGNED: 20 May 52 FORCE:
20 May 52
Yugoslavia SIGNED: 20 May 52 RATIFIED:
9 Feb 54 FORCE: 9 Feb 54

102967 Bilateral Convention **219 UNTS 73**
SIGNED: 24 Mar 54 FORCE: 31 Aug 55
REGISTERED: 19 Oct 55 Belgium
ARTICLES: 4 LANGUAGE: French.
HEADNOTE: ESTABLISHMENT MEDICAL OFFICES
TOPIC: Sanitation
CONCEPTS: Detailed regulations. General cooper-
ation. Inspection and observation. Personnel. Es-
tablishment of commission. Public health. Mate-
rials, equipment and services. Aid missions. Mer-
chant vessels.
PROCEDURE: Termination.
PARTIES:
Belgium
Norway

102968 Multilateral Agreement **219 UNTS 79**
SIGNED: 6 Jun 55 FORCE: 5 May 55
REGISTERED: 19 Oct 55 Germany, West
ARTICLES: 10 LANGUAGE: English. French. Ger-
man.
HEADNOTE: INTERNATIONAL TRACING SERVICE
TOPIC: IGO Establishment
CONCEPTS: Treaty interpretation. Annex or ap-
pendix reference. Exchange of information and
documents. Informational records. Admission.
Establishment. Headquarters and facilities. As-
sistance to United Nations. Inter-agency agree-
ments.
INTL ORGS: International Refugees Organization.
United Nations Relief and Rehabilitation Admin-

istration. United Nations. Western European Union.
PROCEDURE: Amendment. Duration. Future Procedures Contemplated. Termination.
PARTIES:
Belgium SIGNED: 6 Jun 55 FORCE: 5 May 55
France SIGNED: 6 Jun 55 FORCE: 5 May 55
Germany, West SIGNED: 6 Jun 55 FORCE: - 5 May 55
Israel SIGNED: 6 Jun 55 FORCE: 5 May 55
Italy SIGNED: 6 Jun 55 FORCE: 5 May 55
Luxembourg SIGNED: 6 Jun 55 FORCE: 5 May 55
Netherlands SIGNED: 6 Jun 55 FORCE: 5 May 55
UK Great Britain SIGNED: 6 Jun 55 FORCE: 5 May 55
USA (United States) SIGNED: 6 Jun 55 FORCE: 5 May 55
ANNEX
377 UNTS 402. France. Extension and Amendment 23 Aug 60. Force 5 May 60.
377 UNTS 402. Germany, West. Extension and Amendment 23 Aug 60. Force 5 May 60.
377 UNTS 402. Israel. Extension and Amendment 23 Aug 60. Force 5 May 60.
377 UNTS 402. Netherlands. Extension and Amendment 23 Aug 60. Force 5 May 60.
377 UNTS 402. Italy. Extension and Amendment 23 Aug 60. Force 5 May 60.
377 UNTS 402. Luxembourg. Extension and Amendment 23 Aug 60. Force 5 May 60.
377 UNTS 402. UK Great Britain. Extension and Amendment 23 Aug 60. Force 5 May 60.
377 UNTS 402. USA (United States). Extension and Amendment 23 Aug 60. Force 5 May 60.
377 UNTS 402. Belgium. Extension and Amendment 23 Aug 60. Force 5 May 60.

102969 Bilateral Agreement **219 UNTS 105**
SIGNED: 29 Apr 55   FORCE: 13 Jul 55
REGISTERED: 20 Oct 55 Netherlands
ARTICLES: 9 LANGUAGE: Danish. English.
HEADNOTE: PATENT RIGHTS TECHNICAL INFORMATION DEFENSE
TOPIC: Milit Installation
CONCEPTS: Definition of terms. Previous treaty renunciation. Responsibility and liability. Establishment of commission. Compensation. Laws and formalities. Exchange of defense information. Equipment and supplies.
INTL ORGS: International Bank for Reconstruction and Development. Special Commission.
PROCEDURE: Termination.
PARTIES:
Netherlands
USA (United States)
ANNEX
358 UNTS 286. USA (United States). Implementation 8 Oct 59. Force 8 Oct 59.
358 UNTS 286. Netherlands. Implementation 8 Oct 59. Force 8 Oct 59.

102970 Bilateral Agreement **219 UNTS 127**
SIGNED: 12 Jul 55   FORCE: 1 Sep 55
REGISTERED: 20 Oct 55 IBRD (World Bank)
ARTICLES: 8 LANGUAGE: English.
HEADNOTE: LOAN AGREEMENT
TOPIC: IBRD Project
CONCEPTS: Default remedies. Definition of terms. Annex or appendix reference. Exchange of information and documents. Informational records. Inspection and observation. Accounting procedures. Bonds. Fees and exemptions. Interest rates. Tax exemptions. Domestic obligation. Terms of loan. Loan regulations. Loan guarantee. Guarantor non-interference.
PARTIES:
Panama
IBRD (World Bank)

102971 Bilateral Agreement **219 UNTS 147**
SIGNED: 27 May 54   FORCE: 27 May 54
REGISTERED: 26 Oct 55 Greece
ARTICLES: 3 LANGUAGE: French.
HEADNOTE: TAXATION INCOME AIR TRANSPORT
TOPIC: Taxation
CONCEPTS: Definition of terms. General. Tax exemptions. Air transport.
PROCEDURE: Denunciation.

PARTIES:
Greece
Sweden

102972 Bilateral Agreement **219 UNTS 153**
SIGNED: 24 Dec 53   FORCE: 24 Dec 53
REGISTERED: 27 Oct 55 Belgium
ARTICLES: 15 LANGUAGE: French. Arabic.
HEADNOTE: AIR SERVICES BETWEEN BEYOND RESPECTIVE TERRITORIES
TOPIC: Air Transport
CONCEPTS: Conditions. Definition of terms. Detailed regulations. Exceptions and exemptions. Annex or appendix reference. Previous treaty replacement. Conformity with municipal law. General cooperation. Exchange of information and documents. Arbitration. Procedure. Existing tribunals. Negotiation. Non-interest rates and fees. Most favored nation clause. Customs exemptions. Routes and logistics. Permit designation. Conditions of airlines operating permission. Overflights and technical stops. Operating authorizations and regulations.
INTL ORGS: International Civil Aviation Organization. International Court of Justice. United Nations. Arbitration Commission.
TREATY REF: 15UNTS295.
PROCEDURE: Amendment. Future Procedures Contemplated. Ratification. Registration. Termination. Application to Non-self-governing Territories.
PARTIES:
Belgium
Lebanon

102973 Unilateral Instrument **219 UNTS 179**
SIGNED: 31 Oct 55   FORCE: 31 Oct 55
REGISTERED: 31 Oct 55 United Nations
ARTICLES: 1 LANGUAGE: English.
HEADNOTE: ACCEPTANCE ICJ JURISDICTION
TOPIC: ICJ Option Clause
CONCEPTS: Adherence to UN charter. Compulsory jurisdiction.
INTL ORGS: International Court of Justice.
PROCEDURE: Termination.
PARTIES:
UK Great Britain
ANNEX
265 UNTS 391. UK Great Britain. Termination 12 Apr 57.

102974 Bilateral Agreement **219 UNTS 185**
SIGNED: 12 Jul 55   FORCE: 12 Jul 55
REGISTERED: 1 Nov 55 Israel
ARTICLES: 10 LANGUAGE: English.
HEADNOTE: CIVIL USES ATOMIC ENERGY
TOPIC: Atomic Energy
CONCEPTS: Definition of terms. General cooperation. Exchange of information and documents. Research results. Scientific exchange. Establishment of trade relations. Nuclear materials. Nonnuclear materials. Rights of supplier. Security of information.
PROCEDURE: Duration.
PARTIES:
Israel
USA (United States)
ANNEX
368 UNTS 354. USA (United States). Amendment 20 Aug 59. Force 28 Jan 60.
368 UNTS 354. Israel. Amendment 20 Aug 59. Force 28 Jan 60.
377 UNTS 410. Israel. Amendment 11 Jun 60. Force 8 Jul 60.
377 UNTS 410. USA (United States). Amendment 11 Jun 60. Force 8 Jul 60.
448 UNTS 330. Israel. Amendment 22 Jun 62. Force 10 Jul 62.
448 UNTS 330. USA (United States). Amendment 22 Jun 62. Force 10 Jul 62.
533 UNTS 332. Israel. Amendment 19 Aug 64. Force 1 Oct 64.
533 UNTS 332. Israel. Amendment 19 Aug 64. Force 1 Oct 64.
573 UNTS 308. USA (United States). Amendment 2 Apr 65. Force 13 May 65.
573 UNTS 308. Israel. Amendment 2 Apr 65. Force 13 May 65.
606 UNTS 312. Israel. Amendment 23 Aug 66. Force 22 Sep 66.

606 UNTS 312. USA (United States). Amendment 23 Aug 66. Force 22 Sep 66.

102975 Bilateral Exchange **219 UNTS 197**
SIGNED: 29 May 53   FORCE: 24 Apr 53
REGISTERED: 1 Nov 55 Israel
ARTICLES: 3 LANGUAGE: French.
HEADNOTE: CIVIL PROCEDURES
TOPIC: Admin Cooperation
CONCEPTS: Material evidence. General cooperation.
PARTIES:
Belgium
Israel

102976 Bilateral Exchange **219 UNTS 205**
SIGNED: 25 Nov 53   FORCE: 25 Nov 53
REGISTERED: 1 Nov 55 Israel
ARTICLES: 2 LANGUAGE: English.
HEADNOTE: SPECIAL ECONOMIC ASSISTANCE
TOPIC: Direct Aid
CONCEPTS: Diplomatic privileges. Conformity with municipal law. General cooperation. Exchange of information and documents. Inspection and observation. Public information. Accounting procedures. Attachment of funds. Exchange rates and regulations. Garnishment of funds. Seizure funds. Tax exemptions. Economic assistance.
TREATY REF: 177UNTS123; 179UNTS362.
PROCEDURE: Termination.
PARTIES:
Israel
USA (United States)

102977 Bilateral Exchange **219 UNTS 215**
SIGNED: 3 Jun 51   FORCE: 27 Jul 51
REGISTERED: 1 Nov 55 Israel
ARTICLES: 2 LANGUAGE: French.
HEADNOTE: EXTRADITION
TOPIC: Extradition
CONCEPTS: Territorial application. Revival of treaties.
TREATY REF: 2'2DEMARTENS456.
PROCEDURE: Duration.
PARTIES:
France
Israel

102978 Bilateral Convention **219 UNTS 231**
SIGNED: 22 Jul 52   FORCE: 22 Jul 52
REGISTERED: 1 Nov 55 Israel
ARTICLES: 5 LANGUAGE: French.
HEADNOTE: PROMOTE DEVELOPMENT COMMERCIAL RELATIONS
TOPIC: General Economic
CONCEPTS: Definition of terms. Export quotas. Import quotas. Reciprocity in trade. Most favored nation clause. Customs duties. Passenger transport. Transport of goods. Inland and territorial waters. Ports and pilotage.
TREATY REF: 58LTS285; 69LTS102; 65LTS184.
PARTIES:
Greece
Israel

102979 Bilateral Treaty **219 UNTS 237**
SIGNED: 23 Aug 51   FORCE: 3 Apr 54
REGISTERED: 1 Nov 55 Israel
ARTICLES: 25 LANGUAGE: English. Hebrew.
HEADNOTE: FRIENDSHIP COMMERCE NAVIGATION
TOPIC: General Amity
CONCEPTS: Definition of terms. Exceptions and exemptions. Territorial application. Alien status. Human rights. Administrative cooperation. General cooperation. Exchange of information and documents. Juridical personality. Expropriation. Free passage and transit. Legal protection and assistance. General property. Procedure. Existing tribunals. Social security. Free trade. Reciprocity in trade. Compensation. Exchange rates and regulations. Fees and exemptions. Most favored nation clause. Tax exemptions. Inland and territorial waters.
INTL ORGS: International Court of Justice. International Monetary Fund.
TREATY REF: GATT.
PROCEDURE: Duration. Ratification. Termination.

PARTIES:
Israel
USA (United States)

102980 Bilateral Exchange **219 UNTS 293**
SIGNED: 8 Nov 51 FORCE: 8 Nov 51
REGISTERED: 1 Nov 55 Israel
ARTICLES: 2 LANGUAGE: French.
HEADNOTE: MOST FAVORED NATION
TOPIC: Mostfavored Nation
CONCEPTS: Most favored nation clause.
PARTIES:
Israel
Italy

102981 Bilateral Exchange **219 UNTS 297**
SIGNED: 22 May 53 FORCE: 5 Sep 53
REGISTERED: 1 Nov 55 Israel
ARTICLES: 2 LANGUAGE: French.
HEADNOTE: MOST FAVORED NATION APPLICA-
TION SHIPPING
TOPIC: Mostfavored Nation
CONCEPTS: Most favored nation clause. Naviga-
tional conditions.
PROCEDURE: Ratification. Termination.
PARTIES:
Israel
Italy

102982 Bilateral Instrument **220 UNTS 3**
SIGNED: 4 Jul 50 FORCE: 4 Jul 50
REGISTERED: 1 Nov 55 Israel
ARTICLES: 1 LANGUAGE: French.
HEADNOTE: MODUS VIVENDI MOST FAVORED
NATION
TOPIC: Mostfavored Nation
CONCEPTS: Exceptions and exemptions. Most fa-
vored nation clause. Customs duties. Naviga-
tional conditions.
PROCEDURE: Termination.
PARTIES:
Israel
Turkey

102983 Bilateral Instrument **220 UNTS 7**
SIGNED: 29 Jul 51 FORCE: 29 Jan 51
REGISTERED: 1 Nov 55 Israel
ARTICLES: 1 LANGUAGE: English.
HEADNOTE: MODUS VIVENDI MOST FAVORED
NATION
TOPIC: Mostfavored Nation
CONCEPTS: Exceptions and exemptions. Most fa-
vored nation clause. Customs duties. Naviga-
tional conditions.
PROCEDURE: Termination.
PARTIES:
Israel
Yugoslavia

102984 Bilateral Agreement **220 UNTS 11**
SIGNED: 31 Dec 54 FORCE: 1 Jan 55
REGISTERED: 1 Nov 55 Israel
ARTICLES: 27 LANGUAGE: English.
HEADNOTE: EXCHANGE POSTAL PARCELS
TOPIC: Postal Service
CONCEPTS: Conformity with municipal law. Re-
sponsibility and liability. Accounting proce-
dures. Customs declarations. Postal services.
Regulations. Insured letters and boxes. Convey-
ance in transit. Parcel post. Rates and charges.
PROCEDURE: Duration. Future Procedures Con-
templated. Termination.
PARTIES:
Israel
South Africa

102985 Bilateral Agreement **220 UNTS 29**
SIGNED: 18 Jun 54 FORCE: 1 Apr 54
REGISTERED: 1 Nov 55 Israel
ARTICLES: 17 LANGUAGE: English.
HEADNOTE: EXCHANGE POSTAL PARCELS
TOPIC: Postal Service
CONCEPTS: Responsibility and liability. Account-
ing procedures. Postal services. Regulations. In-
sured letters and boxes. Conveyance in transit.
Parcel post. Rates and charges.
INTL ORGS: Universal Postal Union.

TREATY REF: 170UNTS63; 186UNTS360;
202UNTS348.
PROCEDURE: Duration. Termination.
PARTIES:
Australia
Israel

102986 Bilateral Agreement **220 UNTS 41**
SIGNED: 1 Jul 53 FORCE: 1 Jul 53
REGISTERED: 1 Nov 55 Israel
ARTICLES: 13 LANGUAGE: French.
HEADNOTE: EXCHANGE POSTAL PARCELS
TOPIC: Postal Service
CONCEPTS: Responsibility and liability. Account-
ing procedures. Regulations. Insured letters and
boxes. Parcel post.
TREATY REF: 186UNTS360; 202UNTS348.
PROCEDURE: Termination.
PARTIES:
Israel
Switzerland

102987 Bilateral Exchange **220 UNTS 49**
SIGNED: 14 Dec 54 FORCE: 1 Jan 54
REGISTERED: 1 Nov 55 Israel
ARTICLES: 2 LANGUAGE: French.
HEADNOTE: EXCHANGE OFFICIAL PUBLICA-
TIONS
TOPIC: Admin Cooperation
CONCEPTS: Exchange of official publications. In-
demnities and reimbursements.
PARTIES:
Belgium
Israel

102988 Bilateral Agreement **220 UNTS 55**
SIGNED: 24 Jan 52 FORCE: 24 Jan 52
REGISTERED: 1 Nov 55 Israel
ARTICLES: 4 LANGUAGE: French. Hebrew.
HEADNOTE: DOUBLE TAXATION SEA AIR TRANS-
PORTS
TOPIC: Taxation
CONCEPTS: Taxation. General.
PROCEDURE: Denunciation.
PARTIES:
France
Israel

102989 Bilateral Exchange **220 UNTS 65**
SIGNED: 15 Sep 52 FORCE: 15 Sep 52
REGISTERED: 1 Nov 55 Israel
ARTICLES: 2 LANGUAGE: French.
HEADNOTE: EXEMPTION CUSTOMS DUTIES
TOPIC: Customs
CONCEPTS: Tourism. Customs exemptions.
PARTIES:
France
Israel

102990 Bilateral Exchange **220 UNTS 71**
SIGNED: 24 May 55 FORCE: 24 May 55
REGISTERED: 1 Nov 55 Israel
ARTICLES: 2 LANGUAGE: English.
HEADNOTE: EXEMPTION INCOME TAX
TOPIC: Taxation
CONCEPTS: Definition of terms. General. Air trans-
port. Merchant vessels.
PROCEDURE: Termination.
PARTIES:
Israel
Norway
ANNEX
630 UNTS 397. Israel.
630 UNTS 397. Norway.

102991 Bilateral Exchange **220 UNTS 79**
SIGNED: 28 Feb 51 FORCE: 1 Mar 51
REGISTERED: 1 Nov 55 Israel
ARTICLES: 2 LANGUAGE: English.
HEADNOTE: EXEMPTION EXCISE IMPORT TAXES
CUSTOMS DUTIES AIRCRAFT SUPPLIES
TOPIC: Taxation
CONCEPTS: Tax exemptions.
PARTIES:
Israel
USA (United States)

102992 Bilateral Exchange **220 UNTS 87**
SIGNED: 29 Apr 55 FORCE: 1 May 55
REGISTERED: 1 Nov 55 Israel
ARTICLES: 3 LANGUAGE: English.
HEADNOTE: ABOLITION VISA FEES
TOPIC: Visas
CONCEPTS: Visas. Fees and exemptions.
PARTIES:
Denmark
Israel

102993 Bilateral Exchange **220 UNTS 93**
SIGNED: 16 Jun 53 FORCE: 16 Jul 53
REGISTERED: 1 Nov 55 Israel
ARTICLES: 2 LANGUAGE: English.
HEADNOTE: VISAS EXEMPTION
TOPIC: Visas
CONCEPTS: Visa abolition.
PARTIES:
Israel
Netherlands

102994 Bilateral Exchange **220 UNTS 99**
SIGNED: 18 Jun 53 FORCE: 18 Jul 53
REGISTERED: 1 Nov 55 Israel
ARTICLES: 2 LANGUAGE: English.
HEADNOTE: GRATIS VISAS
TOPIC: Visas
CONCEPTS: Visas.
PARTIES:
Israel
Netherlands

102995 Bilateral Exchange **220 UNTS 105**
SIGNED: 2 Mar 55 FORCE: 1 Apr 55
REGISTERED: 1 Nov 55 Israel
ARTICLES: 3 LANGUAGE: English.
HEADNOTE: ABOLITION VISA FEES
TOPIC: Visas
CONCEPTS: Visas. Fees and exemptions.
PARTIES:
Israel
Sweden

102996 Bilateral Exchange **220 UNTS 113**
SIGNED: 2 Mar 55 FORCE: 15 Mar 55
REGISTERED: 8 Nov 55 Netherlands
ARTICLES: 3 LANGUAGE: English.
HEADNOTE: ABOLITION VISA FEES
TOPIC: Visas
CONCEPTS: Visas. Fees and exemptions.
PARTIES:
Israel
USA (United States)

102997 Multilateral Instrument **220 UNTS 121**
SIGNED: 9 Oct 51 FORCE: 15 Jul 55
REGISTERED: 8 Nov 55 Netherlands
ARTICLES: 15 LANGUAGE: French.
HEADNOTE: HAGUE CONFERENCE PRIVATE IN-
TERNATIONAL LAW
TOPIC: IGO Establishment
CONCEPTS: Conformity with municipal law. Gen-
eral cooperation. Exchange of information and
documents. Domestic legislation. Dispute settle-
ment. Funding procedures. Admission. Establish-
ment. Headquarters and facilities. Internal struc-
ture.
INTL ORGS: The Hague Conference on Private In-
ternational Law.
PROCEDURE: Amendment. Denunciation.
PARTIES:
Austria RATIFIED: 16 Sep 54 FORCE: 15 Jul 55
Belgium RATIFIED: 1 Sep 53 FORCE: 15 Jul 55
Denmark RATIFIED: 23 Feb 54 FORCE:
  15 Jul 55
Greece RATIFIED: 26 Aug 55 FORCE: 26 Aug 55
Ireland RATIFIED: 26 Aug 55 FORCE: 26 Aug 55
Netherlands RATIFIED: 25 Sep 54 FORCE:
  15 Jul 55
Norway RATIFIED: 15 Jul 55 FORCE: 15 Jul 55
Portugal RATIFIED: 8 Dec 53 FORCE: 15 Jul 55
Spain RATIFIED: 8 Dec 53 FORCE: 15 Jul 55
Sweden RATIFIED: 9 Dec 53 FORCE: 15 Jul 55
Turkey RATIFIED: 26 Aug 55 FORCE: 26 Aug 55
UK Great Britain RATIFIED: 3 Jan 55 FORCE:
  15 Jul 55

ANNEX

510 UNTS 317. France. Acceptance 20 Apr 64. Force 20 Apr 64.

510 UNTS 317. Italy. Acceptance 26 Jun 57. Force 26 Jun 57.

510 UNTS 317. Japan. Acceptance 27 Jun 57. Force 27 Jun 57.

510 UNTS 317. Yugoslavia. Acceptance 9 Oct 58. Force 9 Oct 58.

510 UNTS 317. Luxembourg. Acceptance 12 Mar 56. Force 12 Mar 56.

510 UNTS 317. United Arab Rep. Acceptance 24 Apr 61. Force 24 Apr 61.

510 UNTS 317. Switzerland. Acceptance 6 May 57. Force 6 Mar 57.

102998 Bilateral Agreement **220 UNTS 131**
SIGNED: 18 Mar 55   FORCE: 4 Jun 55
REGISTERED: 9 Nov 55 IBRD (World Bank)
ARTICLES: 7 LANGUAGE: English.
HEADNOTE: LOAN AGREEMENT
TOPIC: IBRD Project
CONCEPTS: Default remedies. Annex or appendix reference. Exchange of information and documents. Informational records. Inspection and observation. Accounting procedures. Bonds. Fees and exemptions. Interest rates. Tax exemptions. Domestic obligation. Terms of loan. Loan regulations. Loan guarantee. Guarantor non-interference.
PARTIES:
Australia
IBRD (World Bank)

102999 Bilateral Agreement **221 UNTS 3**
SIGNED: 17 Mar 49   FORCE: 7 Jul 49
REGISTERED: 14 Nov 55 USSR (Soviet Union)
ARTICLES: 5 LANGUAGE: Russian. Korean.
HEADNOTE: STRENGTHENING ECONOMIC CULTURAL RELATIONS
TOPIC: General Economic
CONCEPTS: General provisions. Vocational training. General cultural cooperation. Most favored nation clause. Agriculture.
PROCEDURE: Denunciation. Duration. Future Procedures Contemplated. Ratification.
PARTIES:
Korea, North
USSR (Soviet Union)

103000 Bilateral Convention **221 UNTS 13**
SIGNED: 27 May 50   FORCE: 21 Apr 51
REGISTERED: 14 Nov 55 USSR (Soviet Union)
ARTICLES: 12 LANGUAGE: Russian. Romanian.
HEADNOTE: AGRICULTURAL PLANTS THEIR PROTECTION PESTS DISEASES
TOPIC: Sanitation
CONCEPTS: Border traffic and migration. General cooperation. Exchange of information and documents. Inspection and observation. Quarantine. Border control. Disease control. Insect control. Research results. Agriculture. Materials, equipment and services. Conferences.
TREATY REF: 122UNTS319; 222UNTS269.
PROCEDURE: Duration. Termination.
PARTIES:
Romania
USSR (Soviet Union)

103001 Bilateral Convention **221 UNTS 35**
SIGNED: 13 Jul 50   FORCE: 26 Dec 50
REGISTERED: 14 Nov 55 USSR (Soviet Union)
ARTICLES: 12 LANGUAGE: Russian. Hungarian.
HEADNOTE: PROTECTION AGRICULTURAL PLANTS
TOPIC: Sanitation
CONCEPTS: Definition of terms. Detailed regulations. Border traffic and migration. General cooperation. Exchange of information and documents. Inspection and observation. Quarantine. Disease control. Insect control. Research results. General technical assistance. Agriculture. Materials, equipment and services. Conferences.
PROCEDURE: Duration. Ratification. Renewal or Revival. Termination.
PARTIES:
Hungary
USSR (Soviet Union)

103002 Bilateral Convention **221 UNTS 57**
SIGNED: 25 Aug 50   FORCE: 26 Feb 51
REGISTERED: 14 Nov 55 USSR (Soviet Union)
ARTICLES: 12 LANGUAGE: Russian. Bulgarian.
HEADNOTE: PROTECTION AGRICULTURAL PLANTS
TOPIC: Sanitation
CONCEPTS: Definition of terms. Detailed regulations. Border traffic and migration. General cooperation. Exchange of information and documents. Inspection and observation. Quarantine. Disease control. Insect control. Research results. General technical assistance. Agriculture. Materials, equipment and services. Conferences.
PROCEDURE: Duration. Renewal or Revival. Termination.
PARTIES:
Bulgaria
USSR (Soviet Union)

103003 Bilateral Agreement **221 UNTS 79**
SIGNED: 3 Sep 51   FORCE: 28 Nov 52
REGISTERED: 14 Nov 55 USSR (Soviet Union)
ARTICLES: 13 LANGUAGE: Russian. French.
HEADNOTE: TRADE
TOPIC: General Trade
CONCEPTS: Detailed regulations. Territorial application. Treaty implementation. Annex or appendix reference. Privileges and immunities. Nondiplomatic delegations. Informational records. Juridical personality. Legal protection and assistance. Recognition and enforcement of legal decisions. General property. Public information. Use of facilities. Procedure. Establishment of trade relations. Most favored nation clause. Customs declarations. Licenses and certificates of nationality. Ports and pilotage.
PROCEDURE: Duration. Ratification. Termination.
PARTIES:
France
USSR (Soviet Union)
ANNEX
338 UNTS 380. France. Prolongation 14 Nov 58. Force 15 May 59.
338 UNTS 380. USSR (Soviet Union). Prolongation 14 Nov 58. Force 15 May 59.

103004 Bilateral Agreement **221 UNTS 99**
SIGNED: 5 Aug 53   FORCE: 15 Aug 53
REGISTERED: 14 Nov 55 USSR (Soviet Union)
ARTICLES: 17 LANGUAGE: Russian. Spanish.
HEADNOTE: DEVELOPMENT TRADE RELATIONS
TOPIC: General Economic
CONCEPTS: Detailed regulations. Treaty implementation. Annex or appendix reference. Conformity with municipal law. Licenses and permits. Private contracts. Establishment of commission. General trade. Establishment of trade relations. Export quotas. Import quotas. Reciprocity in trade. Trade procedures. Accounting procedures. Banking. Balance of payments. Currency. Monetary and gold transfers. Exchange rates and regulations. Payment schedules. Debt settlement. Delivery schedules. Loan and credit. Purchase authorization. Navigational conditions.
INTL ORGS: Special Commission.
PROCEDURE: Duration. Future Procedures Contemplated.
PARTIES:
Argentina
USSR (Soviet Union)

103005 Bilateral Protocol **221 UNTS 129**
SIGNED: 22 Aug 53   FORCE: 22 Aug 53
REGISTERED: 14 Nov 55 USSR (Soviet Union)
ARTICLES: 4 LANGUAGE: Russian. German.
HEADNOTE: DISCONTINUANCE REPARATIONS PAYMENTS
TOPIC: Reparations
CONCEPTS: Treaty implementation. Establishment of commission. Indemnities and reimbursements. Debt settlement. Assets transfer. Reparations and restrictions.
PARTIES:
Germany, East
USSR (Soviet Union)

103006 Bilateral Agreement **221 UNTS 143**
SIGNED: 6 Feb 54   FORCE: 26 May 54
REGISTERED: 14 Nov 55 USSR (Soviet Union)

ARTICLES: 6 LANGUAGE: Russian. Finnish.
HEADNOTE: LOAN
TOPIC: Loans and Credits
CONCEPTS: Friendship and amity. Operating agencies. Exchange rates and regulations. Interest rates. Payment schedules. Loan and credit. Loan repayment. Terms of loan.
TREATY REF: 48UNTS149.
PROCEDURE: Duration. Ratification.
PARTIES:
Finland
USSR (Soviet Union)

103007 Bilateral Agreement **221 UNTS 153**
SIGNED: 19 Apr 55   FORCE: 5 Oct 55
REGISTERED: 15 Nov 55 IBRD (World Bank)
ARTICLES: 5 LANGUAGE: English.
HEADNOTE: GUARANTEE AGREEMENT
TOPIC: IBRD Project
CONCEPTS: Definition of terms. Annex or appendix reference. Exchange of information and documents. Informational records. Inspection and observation. Bonds. Fees and exemptions. Tax exemptions. Domestic obligation. Terms of loan. Loan regulations. Loan guarantee. Guarantor non-interference.
PARTIES:
Peru
IBRD (World Bank)

103008 Bilateral Exchange **221 UNTS 227**
SIGNED: 19 Oct 54   FORCE: 19 Oct 54
REGISTERED: 18 Nov 55 UK Great Britain
ARTICLES: 2 LANGUAGE: English.
HEADNOTE: RESERVES PETROLEUM PRODUCTS
TOPIC: Milit Installation
CONCEPTS: Annex or appendix reference. Bases and facilities.
TREATY REF: 210UNTS4.
PARTIES:
United Arab Rep
UK Great Britain

103009 Bilateral Agreement **221 UNTS 241**
SIGNED: 29 Aug 55   FORCE: 29 Aug 55
REGISTERED: 18 Nov 55 UK Great Britain
ARTICLES: 7 LANGUAGE: English.
HEADNOTE: MIGRANT LABOR
TOPIC: Non-ILO Labor
CONCEPTS: Detailed regulations. Annex or appendix reference. Border traffic and migration. Conformity with municipal law. Public health. Employment regulations. Safety standards. Non-ILO labor relations. Migrant worker. Monetary and gold transfers.
PARTIES:
Philippines
UK Great Britain

103010 Multilateral Convention **221 UNTS 255**
SIGNED: 7 Nov 52   FORCE: 20 Nov 55
REGISTERED: 20 Nov 55 United Nations
ARTICLES: 15 LANGUAGE: English. French.
HEADNOTE: IMPORTATION REGULATIONS TRADE
TOPIC: General Trade
CONCEPTS: Definition of terms. Detailed regulations. Exceptions and exemptions. Territorial application. Treaty interpretation. Informational records. Public information. Arbitration. Procedure. Existing tribunals. Negotiation. Import quotas. Reexport of goods, etc.. Trade procedures. Commodity trade. Customs exemptions. Temporary importation.
INTL ORGS: International Court of Justice. United Nations. Arbitration Commission.
TREATY REF: GATT.
PROCEDURE: Accession. Ratification. Denunciation.
PARTIES:
Belgium SIGNED: 30 Jun 53
Germany, West SIGNED: 12 Jun 53 RATIFIED: 2 Sep 55 FORCE: 20 Nov 55
Greece SIGNED: 12 Jun 53 RATIFIED: 10 Feb 55 FORCE: 20 Nov 55
Netherlands Netherlands Antilles RATIFIED: 3 May 55 FORCE: 20 Nov 55
Netherlands Dutch New Guinea RATIFIED: 3 May 55 FORCE: 20 Nov 55

Netherlands Surinam RATIFIED: 3 May 55
FORCE: 20 Nov 55
Spain RATIFIED: 9 Sep 54 FORCE: 20 Nov 55
Sweden SIGNED: 30 Jun 53 RATIFIED:
23 Feb 55 FORCE: 20 Nov 55
UK Great Britain Isle of Man RATIFIED: 21 Oct 55
FORCE: 20 Nov 55
UK Great Britain SIGNED: 30 Jun 53 RATIFIED:
21 Oct 55 FORCE: 20 Nov 55
USA (United States) SIGNED: 28 May 53
ANNEX
223 UNTS 385. Germany, West. Berlin. Force
20 Nov 55.
236 UNTS 397. Fed Rhod/Nyasaland. Accession
30 Apr 56. Force 30 May 56.
250 UNTS 315. Portugal. Accession 24 Sep 56.
Force 24 Oct 56.
256 UNTS 367. Turkey. Accession 8 Dec 56.
Force 7 Jan 57.
260 UNTS 456. UK Great Britain. North Borneo.
Force 7 Mar 57.
260 UNTS 456. UK Great Britain. St. Helena.
Force 7 Mar 57.
260 UNTS 456. UK Great Britain. British Somaliland. Force 7 Mar 57.
260 UNTS 456. UK Great Britain. Uganda. Force
7 Mar 57.
260 UNTS 456. UK Great Britain. Grenada. Force
7 Mar 57.
260 UNTS 456. UK Great Britain. St. Lucia. Force
7 Mar 57.
260 UNTS 456. UK Great Britain. Barbados. Force
7 Mar 57.
260 UNTS 456. UK Great Britain. Hong Kong.
Force 7 Mar 57.
260 UNTS 456. UK Great Britain. Montserrat.
Force 7 Mar 57.
260 UNTS 456. UK Great Britain. St. Christopher.
Force 7 Mar 57.
260 UNTS 456. UK Great Britain. Malta. Force
7 Mar 57.
260 UNTS 456. UK Great Britain. Fiji Islands.
Force 7 Mar 57.
260 UNTS 456. UK Great Britain. Gibralter. Force
7 Mar 57.
260 UNTS 456. UK Great Britain. Gold Coast.
Force 7 Mar 57.
260 UNTS 456. UK Great Britain. Jamaica. Force
7 Mar 57.
260 UNTS 456. UK Great Britain. Kenya. Force
7 Mar 57.
260 UNTS 456. UK Great Britain. Brit Virgin Islands. Force 7 Mar 57.
260 UNTS 456. UK Great Britain. Nigeria. Force
7 Mar 57.
260 UNTS 456. UK Great Britain. Anguilla. Force
7 Mar 57.
260 UNTS 456. UK Great Britain. Sarawak. Force
7 Mar 57.
260 UNTS 456. UK Great Britain. Aden. Force
7 Mar 57.
260 UNTS 456. UK Great Britain. Mauritius. Force
7 Mar 57.
260 UNTS 456. UK Great Britain. British Guiana.
Force 7 Mar 57.
260 UNTS 456. UK Great Britain. Tanganyika.
Force 7 Mar 57.
260 UNTS 456. UK Great Britain. Dominican
Republic. Force 7 Mar 57.
260 UNTS 456. UK Great Britain. St. Vincent.
Force 7 Mar 57.
260 UNTS 456. UK Great Britain. Fed of Malaya.
Force 7 Mar 57.
260 UNTS 456. UK Great Britain. Nevis. Force
7 Mar 57.
260 UNTS 456. UK Great Britain. Zanzibar. Force
7 Mar 57.
260 UNTS 456. UK Great Britain. Seychelles.
Force 7 Mar 57.
260 UNTS 456. UK Great Britain. Sierra Leone.
Force 7 Mar 57.
260 UNTS 456. UK Great Britain. Singapore.
Force 7 Mar 57.
260 UNTS 456. UK Great Britain. Trinidad/-
Tobago. Force 7 Mar 57.
260 UNTS 456. UK Great Britain. Cyprus. Force
7 Mar 57.
260 UNTS 456. UK Great Britain. Antigua. Force
7 Mar 57.
260 UNTS 456. UK Great Britain. Tonga. Force
7 Mar 57.
260 UNTS 456. UK Great Britain. British Honduras. Force 7 Mar 57.

260 UNTS 456. UK Great Britain. Gambia. Force
7 Mar 57.
260 UNTS 456. UK Great Britain. Falkland Islands. Force 7 Mar 57.
265 UNTS 392. New Zealand. Cook Islands. Force
19 May 57.
265 UNTS 392. New Zealand. Accession
19 Apr 57. Force 19 May 57.
265 UNTS 392. New Zealand. Western Samoa.
Force 19 Apr 57.
265 UNTS 392. New Zealand. Niue. Force
29 May 57.
265 UNTS 392. New Zealand. Tokelau Islands.
Force 19 May 57.
268 UNTS 373. Hungary. Accession 3 Jun 57.
Force 3 Jul 57.
276 UNTS 369. Luxembourg. Accession
9 Sep 57. Force 9 Oct 57.
276 UNTS 369. Belgium. All Territories. Force
27 Sep 57.
276 UNTS 369. Belgium. Ratification 28 Aug 57.
Force 27 Sep 57.
277 UNTS 356. USA (United States). Ratification
17 Sep 57. Force 17 Oct 57.
277 UNTS 356. Israel. Accession 8 Oct 57. Force
7 Nov 57.
286 UNTS 382. Haiti. Accession 12 Feb 58. Force
14 Mar 58.
287 UNTS 350. Italy. Accession 20 Feb 58. Force
22 Mar 58.
292 UNTS 370. Ghana. Acceptance 7 Apr 58.
309 UNTS 372. Fed of Malaya. Replacement
21 Aug 58. Force 31 Aug 57.
327 UNTS 374. Ireland. Accession 23 Apr 59.
Force 23 May 59.
335 UNTS 309. Spain. Withdrawal of Reservation
17 Jun 59.
349 UNTS 334. Ceylon (Sri Lanka). Qualified Accession 20 Oct 59. Force 27 Nov 59.
351 UNTS 426. Poland. Accession 18 Feb 60.
Force 19 Mar 60.
399 UNTS 273. Nigeria. Succession 26 Jun 61.
423 UNTS 311. Sierra Leone. Succession
13 Mar 62.
426 UNTS 341. Guinea. Accession 8 May 62.
Force 7 Jun 62.
429 UNTS 295. Congo (Zaire). Succession
31 May 62.
452 UNTS 333. Ceylon (Sri Lanka). Withdrawal of
Reservation 29 Jan 63.
463 UNTS 347. Tanganyika. Qualified Accession
28 Nov 62. Force 28 Dec 63.
466 UNTS 391. Cyprus. Succession 16 May 63.
480 UNTS 341. Jamaica. Succession 11 Nov 63.
519 UNTS 349. Rwanda. Succession 1 Dec 64.
542 UNTS 360. Uganda. Qualified Accession
15 Apr 65. Force 15 May 65.
544 UNTS 292. Kenya. Accession 3 Sep 65.
Force 3 Oct 65.
560 UNTS 263. Trinidad/Tobago. Succession
11 Apr 66.
639 UNTS 330. Malta. Succession 27 Jun 68.
Reservation 27 Jun 68.
649 UNTS 328. Romania. Accession 15 Nov 68.
Force 15 Dec 68.

103011 Bilateral Agreement **221 UNTS 283**
SIGNED: 9 Aug 55 FORCE: 16 Nov 55
REGISTERED: 22 Nov 55 IBRD (World Bank)
ARTICLES: 5 LANGUAGE: English.
HEADNOTE: GUARANTEE AGREEMENT
TOPIC: IBRD Project
CONCEPTS: Definition of terms. Annex or appen-
dix reference. Exchange of information and doc-
uments. Informational records. Inspection and
observation. Bonds. Fees and exemptions. Tax
exemptions. Domestic obligation. Terms of loan.
Loan regulations. Loan guarantee. Guarantor
non-interference.
PARTIES:
IBRD (World Bank)
Thailand

103012 Bilateral Agreement **221 UNTS 305**
SIGNED: 22 Nov 55 FORCE: 22 Nov 55
REGISTERED: 22 Nov 55 United Nations
ARTICLES: 11 LANGUAGE: Spanish.
HEADNOTE: ACTIVITIES UNICEF
TOPIC: Direct Aid
CONCEPTS: Treaty implementation. Previous
treaty replacement. Privileges and immunities.
Exchange of information and documents. Infor-

mational records. Inspection and observation.
Public information. Responsibility and liability.
Procedure. Existing tribunals. Export quotas. In-
demnities and reimbursements. Financial pro-
grams. Local currency. Claims and settlements.
Tax exemptions. Customs exemptions. Com-
modities and services. Assistance. General aid.
Distribution. IGO status.
INTL ORGS: United Nations.
TREATY REF: 1UNTS15; 65UNTS84.
PROCEDURE: Duration.
PARTIES:
Guatemala
UNICEF (Children)

103013 Bilateral Instrument **221 UNTS 325**
SIGNED: 24 Apr 53 FORCE: 24 Jul 53
REGISTERED: 22 Nov 55 Pakistan
ARTICLES: 1 LANGUAGE: English.
HEADNOTE: TREATIES KEPT FORCE REVIVED FOL-
LOWING HOSTILITIES
TOPIC: Admin Cooperation
CONCEPTS: Revival of treaties. Peace and disar-
mament. Reconversion to normalcy.
INTL ORGS: United Nations.
TREATY REF: 136UNTS45.
PARTIES:
Japan
Pakistan

103014 Bilateral Exchange **221 UNTS 331**
SIGNED: 6 Aug 54 FORCE: 6 Aug 54
REGISTERED: 30 Nov 55 USA (United States)
ARTICLES: 2 LANGUAGE: English.
HEADNOTE: AIR TRANSPORT SERVICES
TOPIC: Air Transport
CONCEPTS: Conditions. Time limit. Routes and lo-
gistics. Permit designation. Air transport. Operat-
ing authorizations and regulations.
TREATY REF: 6UNTS397.
PROCEDURE: Duration.
PARTIES:
Sweden
USA (United States)

103015 Bilateral Exchange **221 UNTS 339**
SIGNED: 3 May 54 FORCE: 3 May 54
REGISTERED: 30 Nov 55 USA (United States)
ARTICLES: 2 LANGUAGE: English.
HEADNOTE: LORAN NAVIGATION STATION
TOPIC: Milit Assistance
CONCEPTS: Annex or appendix reference. Confor-
mity with municipal law. General cooperation.
Inspection and observation. General property.
Procedure. Scientific exchange. Expense shar-
ing formulae. Tax exemptions. Customs exemp-
tions. Bands and frequency allocation. Defense
and security. Bases and facilities. Wildlife.
PARTIES:
Canada
USA (United States)

103016 Bilateral Exchange **221 UNTS 351**
SIGNED: 22 Jul 54 FORCE: 22 Jul 54
REGISTERED: 30 Nov 55 USA (United States)
ARTICLES: 2 LANGUAGE: English.
HEADNOTE: EXEMPTION AIRLINE COMPANIES
CERTAIN TAXES
TOPIC: Taxation
CONCEPTS: Tax exemptions. Air transport.
PARTIES:
Germany, West
USA (United States)

103017 Bilateral Exchange **221 UNTS 357**
SIGNED: 27 Oct 53 FORCE: 27 Oct 53
REGISTERED: 30 Nov 55 USA (United States)
ARTICLES: 2 LANGUAGE: English.
HEADNOTE: TRAINING GRANTS CONNECTION
TECHNICAL COOPERATION PROGRAM
TOPIC: Tech Assistance
CONCEPTS: Detailed regulations. Conformity with
municipal law. Exchange of information and doc-
uments. Public information. Scholarships and
grants. Domestic obligation.
PROCEDURE: Duration. Termination. Application
to Non-self-governing Territories.

PARTIES:
Netherlands
USA (United States)

103018 Bilateral Exchange **221 UNTS 365**
SIGNED: 23 Jul 53   FORCE: 23 Jul 53
REGISTERED: 30 Nov 55 USA (United States)
ARTICLES: 2 LANGUAGE: English.
HEADNOTE: TAX RELIEF OFFSHORE PROCURE-
MENT OTHER FOREIGN AID PROGRAMS
TOPIC: Taxation
CONCEPTS: Tax exemptions.
PARTIES:
USA (United States)
Yugoslavia

103019 Bilateral Exchange **222 UNTS 3**
SIGNED: 18 Jun 53   FORCE: 18 Jun 53
REGISTERED: 30 Nov 55 USA (United States)
ARTICLES: 2 LANGUAGE: English. French. Dutch.
HEADNOTE: EXEMPTION EXPORT LICENSES OFF-
SHORE PROCUREMENT GOODS
TOPIC: Milit Assistance
CONCEPTS: Detailed regulations. Exceptions and
exemptions. Annex or appendix reference. Con-
formity with municipal law. General cooperation.
Export quotas. Customs exemptions. Defense
and security.
INTL ORGS: North Atlantic Treaty Organization.
PROCEDURE: Future Procedures Contemplated.
PARTIES:
Belgium
USA (United States)

103020 Bilateral Exchange **222 UNTS 31**
SIGNED: 21 Oct 53   FORCE: 21 Oct 53
REGISTERED: 30 Nov 55 USA (United States)
ARTICLES: 2 LANGUAGE: English.
HEADNOTE: EMERGENCY WHEAT AID
TOPIC: Direct Aid
CONCEPTS: Change of circumstances. Privileges
and immunities. Conformity with municipal law.
General cooperation. Exchange of information
and documents. Inspection and observation. Per-
sonnel. Public information. Accounting proce-
dures. Local currency. Assets. Domestic obliga-
tion. Relief supplies. Withdrawal conditions. Dis-
tribution.
PROCEDURE: Termination.
PARTIES:
Jordan
USA (United States)

103021 Bilateral Agreement **222 UNTS 41**
SIGNED: 6 Nov 53   FORCE: 6 Nov 53
REGISTERED: 30 Nov 55 USA (United States)
ARTICLES: 7 LANGUAGE: English. Spanish.
HEADNOTE: ECONOMIC ASSISTANCE
TOPIC: Direct Aid
CONCEPTS: Assistance. Economic assistance.
PARTIES:
Bolivia
USA (United States)
ANNEX
367 UNTS 319. Bolivia. Amendment 11 Nov 59.
Force 11 Nov 59.
367 UNTS 319. USA (United States). Amendment
24 Aug 59. Force 11 Nov 59.

103022 Bilateral Agreement **222 UNTS 55**
SIGNED: 24 Oct 52   FORCE: 24 Oct 52
REGISTERED: 30 Nov 55 USA (United States)
ARTICLES: 6 LANGUAGE: English.
HEADNOTE: TECHNICAL COOPERATION
TOPIC: Tech Assistance
CONCEPTS: General technical assistance. Assis-
tance.
PROCEDURE: Duration.
PARTIES:
Burma
USA (United States)

103023 Bilateral Exchange **222 UNTS 67**
SIGNED: 13 Oct 53   FORCE: 13 Oct 53
REGISTERED: 30 Nov 55 USA (United States)
ARTICLES: 3 LANGUAGE: English. Persian.
HEADNOTE: RELIEF SUPPLIES PACKAGES
TOPIC: Customs

CONCEPTS: Transportation costs. Tax exemp-
tions. Customs exemptions. Relief supplies.
PROCEDURE: Future Procedures Contemplated.
Termination.
PARTIES:
Iran
USA (United States)

103024 Bilateral Convention **222 UNTS 77**
SIGNED: 2 Mar 53   FORCE: 28 Oct 53
REGISTERED: 30 Nov 55 USA (United States)
ARTICLES: 5 LANGUAGE: English.
HEADNOTE: PRESERVATION HALIBUT FISHERY
TOPIC: Specific Resources
CONCEPTS: Definition of terms. Investigation of
violations. Establishment of commission. Ocean
resources. Fisheries and fishing.
INTL ORGS: International Halibut Commission. In-
ternational Fisheries Commission.
TREATY REF: 32LTS93; 121LTS45.
PROCEDURE: Duration. Ratification. Termination.
PARTIES:
Canada
USA (United States)

103025 Bilateral Agreement **222 UNTS 87**
SIGNED: 20 May 54   FORCE: 20 May 54
REGISTERED: 30 Nov 55 USA (United States)
ARTICLES: 11 LANGUAGE: English. Spanish.
HEADNOTE: MILITARY ASSISTANCE
TOPIC: Milit Assistance
CONCEPTS: Exceptions and exemptions. Guarantees and safeguards. Non-prejudice to UN charter. Privileges and immunities. Conformity with
municipal law. General cooperation. Inspection
and observation. Public information. Use of facilities. Indemnities and reimbursements. Garnishment of funds. Local currency. Most favored nation clause. Tax exemptions. Recognition. Customs exemptions. Domestic obligation.
Materials, equipment and services. Aid missions.
Joint defense. Defense and security. Self-
defense. Military assistance. Return of equipment and recapture. Security of information. Military assistance missions. Exchange of defense
information. Restrictions on transfer. Raw materials.
INTL ORGS: United Nations.
TREATY REF: 21UNTS77; 26UNTS417.
PROCEDURE: Amendment. Future Procedures
Contemplated. Registration. Termination.
PARTIES:
Honduras
USA (United States)

103026 Bilateral Convention **222 UNTS 107**
SIGNED: 1 May 50   FORCE: 12 Jun 54
REGISTERED: 30 Nov 55 USA (United States)
ARTICLES: 30 LANGUAGE: English.
HEADNOTE: CONSULAR CONVENTION
TOPIC: Consul/Citizenship
CONCEPTS: Definition of terms. Previous treaty re-
placement. General consular functions. Diplo-
matic privileges. Consular relations establish-
ment. Protection of nationals. Consular func-
tions in shipping. Consular functions in property.
Notarial acts and services. Responsibility and lia-
bility.
TREATY REF: 2DEMARTENS582; 2'30DEMAR-
TENS235;.
PROCEDURE: Ratification. Termination.
PARTIES:
Ireland
USA (United States)

103027 Bilateral Agreement **222 UNTS 161**
SIGNED: 23 Jun 54   FORCE: 23 Jun 54
REGISTERED: 30 Nov 55 USA (United States)
ARTICLES: 12 LANGUAGE: English. Turkish.
HEADNOTE: TAX RELIEF
TOPIC: Taxation
CONCEPTS: Annex or appendix reference. Tax ex-
emptions.
INTL ORGS: North Atlantic Treaty Organization.
TREATY REF: 34UNTS243; 126UNTS350.
PARTIES:
Turkey
USA (United States)

103028 Bilateral Agreement **222 UNTS 193**
SIGNED: 24 Dec 53   FORCE: 25 Dec 53
REGISTERED: 30 Nov 55 USA (United States)
ARTICLES: 9 LANGUAGE: English. Japanese.
HEADNOTE: CONCERNING AMAMI ISLANDS
TOPIC: Territory Boundary
CONCEPTS: Definition of terms. Annex or appen-
dix reference. Currency. War claims and repara-
tions. Boundaries of territory. Changes of terri-
tory.
TREATY REF: 136UNTS45.
PARTIES:
Japan
USA (United States)

103029 Bilateral Exchange **222 UNTS 229**
SIGNED: 12 Jul 50   FORCE: 12 Jul 50
REGISTERED: 30 Nov 55 USA (United States)
ARTICLES: 2 LANGUAGE: English.
HEADNOTE: JURISDICTION OFFENSES
TOPIC: Status of Forces
CONCEPTS: Court procedures. Investigation of vi-
olations. Jurisdiction. Status of forces.
TREATY REF: 178UNTS97.
PARTIES:
Korea, South
USA (United States)

103030 Bilateral Exchange **222 UNTS 235**
SIGNED: 6 Aug 54   FORCE: 6 Aug 54
REGISTERED: 30 Nov 55 USA (United States)
ARTICLES: 2 LANGUAGE: English.
HEADNOTE: AIR TRANSPORT SERVICES
TOPIC: Air Transport
CONCEPTS: Conditions. Time limit. Routes and lo-
gistics. Permit designation. Air transport. Operat-
ing authorizations and regulations.
TREATY REF: 10UNTS213; 3UNTS301.
PROCEDURE: Duration.
PARTIES:
Denmark
USA (United States)

103031 Bilateral Exchange **222 UNTS 243**
SIGNED: 21 Jul 54   FORCE: 21 Jul 54
REGISTERED: 30 Nov 55 USA (United States)
ARTICLES: 2 LANGUAGE: English.
HEADNOTE: COMPENSATION DAMAGES PRAC-
TICE BOMBING RANGE
TOPIC: Status of Forces
CONCEPTS: Compensation. Claims and settle-
ments. Status of military forces.
PARTIES:
UK Great Britain
USA (United States)

103032 Bilateral Exchange **222 UNTS 251**
SIGNED: 21 Apr 54   FORCE: 21 Apr 54
REGISTERED: 30 Nov 55 USA (United States)
ARTICLES: 2 LANGUAGE: English. Arabic.
HEADNOTE: MILITARY ASSISTANCE
TOPIC: Milit Assistance
CONCEPTS: Non-prejudice to UN charter. Peaceful
relations. Privileges and immunities. Conformity
with municipal law. Inspection and observation.
Public information. Use of facilities. Indemnities
and reimbursements. Garnishment of funds. Lo-
cal currency. Tax exemptions. Recognition. Cus-
toms exemptions. Domestic obligation. Materi-
als, equipment and services. Aid missions. De-
fense and security. Self-defense. Military
assistance. Return of equipment and recapture.
Security of information. Exchange of defense information. Restrictions on transfer. Raw materials.
INTL ORGS: United Nations.
TREATY REF: 151UNTS179.
PROCEDURE: Termination.
PARTIES:
Iraq
USA (United States)
ANNEX
265 UNTS 393. Iraq. Supplementation 25 Jul 55.
Force 25 Jul 55.
265 UNTS 393. USA (United States). Supplemen-
tation 25 Jul 55. Force 25 Jul 55.

103033 Bilateral Exchange **222 UNTS 261**
SIGNED: 6 Aug 54   FORCE: 6 Aug 54

REGISTERED: 30 Nov 55 USA (United States)
ARTICLES: 2 LANGUAGE: English.
HEADNOTE: AIR TRANSPORT SERVICES
TOPIC: Air Transport
CONCEPTS: Conditions. Time limit. Routes and lo-
gistics. Permit designation. Air transport. Operat-
ing authorizations and regulations.
PROCEDURE: Duration.
PARTIES:
Norway
USA (United States)

103034   Bilateral Exchange   **222 UNTS 269**
SIGNED: 6 Aug 54   FORCE: 6 Aug 54
REGISTERED: 30 Nov 55 USA (United States)
ARTICLES: 2 LANGUAGE: English.
HEADNOTE: AMENDING AGREEMENT 6 OCT 45
AIR TRANSPORT SERVICES
TOPIC: Air Transport
CONCEPTS: Detailed regulations. Treaty interpre-
tation. Annex type material. General cooper-
ation. Procedure. Special tribunals. Competence
of tribunal. Indemnities and reimbursements.
Non-interest rates and fees. Air transport.
INTL ORGS: International Court of Justice. Arbitra-
tion Commission.
TREATY REF: 122UNTS319.
PROCEDURE: Amendment.
PARTIES:
Norway
USA (United States)
ANNEX
321 UNTS 284. USA (United States). Amendment
8 Jul 58. Force 8 Jul 58.
321 UNTS 284. Norway. Amendment 8 Jul 58.
Force 8 Jul 58.

103035   Bilateral Agreement   **222 UNTS 281**
SIGNED: 20 Jan 54   FORCE: 20 Jan 54
REGISTERED: 2 Dec 55 Greece
ARTICLES: 18 LANGUAGE: English.
HEADNOTE: SCHEDULED AIR SERVICES
TOPIC: Air Transport
CONCEPTS: Definition of terms. Detailed regulations. Exceptions and exemptions. Annex or appendix reference. Conformity with municipal
law. General cooperation. Exchange of informa-
tion and documents. Arbitration. Procedure. Ex-
isting tribunals. Negotiation. Non-interest rates
and fees. Customs exemptions. Routes and logis-
tics. Navigational conditions. Permit designa-
tion. Air transport. Conditions of airlines operating permission. Operating authorizations and
regulations.
INTL ORGS: International Civil Aviation Organization. Arbitration Commission.
TREATY REF: 15UNTS295.
PROCEDURE: Future Procedures Contemplated.
Ratification. Registration. Termination.
PARTIES:
Ethiopia
Greece

103036   Bilateral Agreement   **222 UNTS 299**
SIGNED: 13 May 54   FORCE: 13 May 54
REGISTERED: 2 Dec 55 Greece
ARTICLES: 10 LANGUAGE: French.
HEADNOTE: EMIGRATION
TOPIC: Non-ILO Labor
CONCEPTS: Conditions. Annex type material. Bor-
der traffic and migration. Repatriation of nation-
als. General cooperation. Juridical personality.
Public information. Establishment of commis-
sion. Public health. Safety standards. Non-ILO la-
bor relations. Monetary and gold transfers.
Transportation costs. Quotas.
INTL ORGS: Special Commission.
PROCEDURE: Denunciation. Duration. Renewal or
Revival.
PARTIES:
France
Greece

103037 Multilateral Agreement **222 UNTS 313**
SIGNED: 29 Sep 55   FORCE: 29 Sep 55
REGISTERED: 6 Dec 55 Denmark
ARTICLES: 4 LANGUAGE: Danish. Norwegian.
Swedish.
HEADNOTE: FINANCIAL GUARANTEES CERTAIN
AIRLINES

TOPIC: Air Transport
CONCEPTS: Previous treaty extension. Finances
and payments. Indemnities and reimburse-
ments. Exchange rates and regulations. Finan-
cial programs. Interest rates. Air transport.
TREATY REF: 163UNTS309.
PARTIES:
Denmark   SIGNED: 29 Sep 55   FORCE:
29 Sep 55
Norway SIGNED: 29 Sep 55 FORCE: 29 Sep 55
Sweden SIGNED: 29 Sep 55 FORCE: 29 Sep 55

103038   Bilateral Agreement   **222 UNTS 327**
SIGNED: 18 Nov 55   FORCE: 18 Nov 55
REGISTERED: 12 Dec 55 UK Great Britain
ARTICLES: 10 LANGUAGE: English.
HEADNOTE: AGREEMENT   COOPERATION
ATOMIC ENERGY
TOPIC: Atomic Energy
CONCEPTS: Definition of terms. Exceptions and
exemptions. Time limit. Exchange of information
and documents. Scientific exchange. Reexport
of goods, etc.. Laws and formalities. Domestic
obligation. Purchase authorization. Nuclear ma-
terials. Non-nuclear materials. Peaceful use.
Rights of supplier. Security of information.
PROCEDURE: Duration.
PARTIES:
Belgium
UK Great Britain
ANNEX
247 UNTS 474. Belgium. Amendment 24 Apr 56.
Force 24 Apr 56.
247 UNTS 474. UK Great Britain. Amendment
24 Apr 56. Force 24 Apr 56.

103039   Bilateral Agreement   **222 UNTS 349**
SIGNED: 22 Sep 55   FORCE: 22 Sep 55
REGISTERED: 12 Dec 55 UK Great Britain
ARTICLES: 9 LANGUAGE: English. Bulgarian.
HEADNOTE: SETTLEMENT FINANCIAL MATTERS
TOPIC: Finance
CONCEPTS: Definition of terms. Detailed regula-
tions. Exchange of information and documents.
Informational records. Expropriation. General
property. General trade. Payment schedules.
Transportation costs. Claims and settlements.
Loss and/or damage. Post-war claims settle-
ment.
TREATY REF: 41UNTS21.
PARTIES:
Bulgaria
UK Great Britain
ANNEX
344 UNTS 344. UK Great Britain. Supplementa-
tion 27 Feb 59. Force 27 Feb 59.
344 UNTS 344. Bulgaria. Supplementation
27 Feb 59. Force 27 Feb 59.

103040   Bilateral Agreement   **223 UNTS 3**
SIGNED: 15 Jul 55   FORCE: 15 Jul 55
REGISTERED: 14 Dec 55 Belgium
ARTICLES: 9 LANGUAGE: English. French.
HEADNOTE: PARTICIPATION BELGIAN FORCES
KOREA
TOPIC: Milit Assistance
CONCEPTS: General cooperation. Responsibility
and liability. Procedure. Accounting procedures.
Indemnities and reimbursements. Currency. Fi-
nancial programs. Materials, equipment and ser-
vices. Return of equipment and recapture.
INTL ORGS: United Nations.
PROCEDURE: Future Procedures Contemplated.
PARTIES:
Belgium
USA (United States)

103041   Bilateral Agreement   **223 UNTS 111**
SIGNED: 31 Aug 55   FORCE: 31 Aug 55
REGISTERED: 14 Dec 55 Belgium
ARTICLES: 4 LANGUAGE: English. French.
HEADNOTE: LOGISTICAL SUPPORT BELGIUM
KOREA
TOPIC: Milit Assistance
CONCEPTS: Indemnities and reimbursements. Ex-
pense sharing formulae. Payment schedules.
Payment for war supplies. Military assistance.
TREATY REF: 223UNTS3.

PARTIES:
Belgium
USA (United States)

103042   Bilateral Exchange   **223 UNTS 17**
SIGNED: 23 May 52   FORCE: 23 May 52
REGISTERED: 14 Dec 55 Greece
ARTICLES: 2 LANGUAGE: English.
HEADNOTE: RIGHTS PRIVILEGES AUSTRALIAN
MIGRATION OFFICE
TOPIC: Visas
CONCEPTS: Operating agencies.
PARTIES:
Australia
Greece

103043   Unilateral Instrument   **223 UNTS 23**
SIGNED: 2 Dec 48   FORCE: 14 Dec 55
REGISTERED: 14 Dec 55 United Nations
ARTICLES: 1 LANGUAGE: French.
HEADNOTE: ACCEPTANCE OBLIGATIONS UN
TOPIC: UN Charter
CONCEPTS: Acceptance of obligations upon ad-
mittance to UN.
INTL ORGS: United Nations.
PARTIES:
Albania

103044   Unilateral Instrument   **223 UNTS 27**
SIGNED: 6 Aug 52   FORCE: 14 Dec 55
REGISTERED: 14 Dec 55 United Nations
ARTICLES: 1 LANGUAGE: French.
HEADNOTE: ACCEPTANCE OBLIGATIONS UN
TOPIC: UN Charter
CONCEPTS: Acceptance of obligations upon ad-
mittance to UN. Adherence to UN Charter. Ac-
ceptance of UN obligations.
INTL ORGS: United Nations.
PARTIES:
Austria

103045   Unilateral Instrument   **223 UNTS 31**
SIGNED: 9 Oct 48   FORCE: 14 Dec 55
REGISTERED: 14 Dec 55 United Nations
ARTICLES: 1 LANGUAGE: French.
HEADNOTE: ACCEPTANCE OBLIGATIONS UN
TOPIC: UN Charter
CONCEPTS: Acceptance of obligations upon ad-
mittance to UN. Adherence to UN Charter.
INTL ORGS: United Nations.
PARTIES:
Bulgaria

103046   Unilateral Instrument   **223 UNTS 35**
SIGNED: 15 Jun 52   FORCE: 14 Dec 55
REGISTERED: 14 Dec 55 United Nations
ARTICLES: 1 LANGUAGE: French.
HEADNOTE: ACCEPTANCE OBLIGATIONS UN
TOPIC: UN Charter
CONCEPTS: Acceptance of UN obligations.
INTL ORGS: United Nations.
PARTIES:
Cambodia

103047   Unilateral Instrument   **223 UNTS 39**
SIGNED: 16 Jun 48   FORCE: 14 Dec 55
REGISTERED: 14 Dec 55 United Nations
ARTICLES: 1 LANGUAGE: English.
HEADNOTE: ACCEPTANCE OBLIGATIONS UN
TOPIC: UN Charter
CONCEPTS: Acceptance of obligations upon ad-
mittance to UN.
INTL ORGS: United Nations.
PARTIES:
Ceylon (Sri Lanka)

103048   Unilateral Instrument   **223 UNTS 43**
SIGNED: 11 Oct 55   FORCE: 14 Dec 55
REGISTERED: 14 Dec 55 United Nations
ARTICLES: 1 LANGUAGE: English.
HEADNOTE: ACCEPTANCE CHARTER UN
TOPIC: UN Charter
CONCEPTS: Adherence to UN Charter. Accep-
tance of UN obligations. Acceptance of obliga-
tions upon admittance to UN.
INTL ORGS: United Nations.

PARTIES:
Jordan

103049 Unilateral Instrument **223 UNTS 47**
SIGNED: 30 Jun 52   FORCE: 14 Dec 55
REGISTERED: 14 Dec 55 United Nations
ARTICLES: 1 LANGUAGE: French.
HEADNOTE: ACCEPTANCE OBLIGATIONS UN
TOPIC: UN Charter
CONCEPTS: Acceptance of obligations upon admittance to UN.
INTL ORGS: United Nations.
PARTIES:
Laos

103050 Unilateral Instrument **223 UNTS 51**
SIGNED: 24 Dec 51   FORCE: 14 Dec 55
REGISTERED: 14 Dec 55 United Nations
ARTICLES: 1 LANGUAGE: English.
HEADNOTE: ACCEPTANCE OBLIGATIONS UN
TOPIC: UN Charter
CONCEPTS: Acceptance of UN obligations.
INTL ORGS: United Nations.
PARTIES:
Libya

103051 Unilateral Instrument **223 UNTS 55**
SIGNED: 10 Mar 49   FORCE: 14 Dec 55
REGISTERED: 14 Dec 55 United Nations
ARTICLES: 1 LANGUAGE: English.
HEADNOTE: ACCEPTANCE OBLIGATIONS UN
TOPIC: UN Charter
CONCEPTS: Acceptance of obligations upon admittance to UN.
INTL ORGS: United Nations.
PARTIES:
Hungary

103052 Unilateral Instrument **223 UNTS 59**
SIGNED: 14 Dec 55   FORCE: 14 Dec 55
REGISTERED: 14 Dec 55 United Nations
ARTICLES: 1 LANGUAGE: French.
HEADNOTE: ACCEPTANCE OBLIGATIONS UN
TOPIC: UN Charter
CONCEPTS: Acceptance of obligations upon admittance to UN.
INTL ORGS: United Nations.
PARTIES:
Romania

103053 Unilateral Instrument **223 UNTS 63**
SIGNED: 23 Sep 55   FORCE: 14 Dec 55
REGISTERED: 14 Dec 55 United Nations
ARTICLES: 1 LANGUAGE: Spanish.
HEADNOTE: ACCEPTANCE OBLIGATIONS UN
TOPIC: UN Charter
CONCEPTS: Acceptance of obligations upon admittance to UN.
INTL ORGS: United Nations.
PARTIES:
Spain

103054 Unilateral Instrument **223 UNTS 65**
SIGNED: 15 Dec 55   FORCE: 14 Dec 55
REGISTERED: 15 Dec 55 United Nations
ARTICLES: 1 LANGUAGE: French.
HEADNOTE: ACCEPTANCE OBLIGATIONS UN
TOPIC: UN Charter
CONCEPTS: Acceptance of UN obligations.
INTL ORGS: United Nations.
PARTIES:
Nepal

103055 Unilateral Instrument **223 UNTS 69**
SIGNED: 15 Dec 55   FORCE: 14 Dec 55
REGISTERED: 19 Dec 55 United Nations
ARTICLES: 1 LANGUAGE: French.
HEADNOTE: ACCEPTANCE CHARTER UN
TOPIC: UN Charter
CONCEPTS: Adherence to UN Charter. Acceptance of UN obligations. Acceptance of obligations upon admittance to UN.
INTL ORGS: United Nations.
PARTIES:
Romania

103056 Bilateral Exchange **223 UNTS 73**
SIGNED: 16 Dec 54   FORCE: 16 Dec 54
REGISTERED: 19 Dec 55 Greece
ARTICLES: 2 LANGUAGE: French.
HEADNOTE: PAYMENT DUE SUM REPATRIATION
TOPIC: Claims and Debts
CONCEPTS: Exchange rates and regulations. Payment schedules. Local currency. Purchase authorization.
PARTIES:
Belgium
Greece

103057 Bilateral Exchange **223 UNTS 79**
SIGNED: 1 Nov 54   FORCE: 1 Nov 54
REGISTERED: 19 Dec 55 Greece
ARTICLES: 2 LANGUAGE: French.
HEADNOTE: TRADE
TOPIC: General Trade
CONCEPTS: Treaty implementation. Annex type material. Previous treaty replacement. Conformity with municipal law. Licenses and permits. Import quotas. Trade procedures. Monetary and gold transfers. Payment schedules. Commodity trade. Quotas.
INTL ORGS: Organization for Economic Co-operation and Development.
PARTIES:
Greece
Netherlands

103058 Bilateral Agreement **223 UNTS 87**
SIGNED: 25 Mar 51   FORCE: 8 Aug 51
REGISTERED: 30 Dec 55 WHO (World Health)
ARTICLES: 12 LANGUAGE: Norwegian. French.
HEADNOTE: PRIVILEGES IMMUNITIES & FACILITIES
TOPIC: IGO Status/Immunit
CONCEPTS: Definition of terms. Annex or appendix reference. Non-visa travel documents. Diplomatic privileges. Inviolability. Privileges and immunities. Property. Diplomatic correspondence. Conformity with municipal law. Juridical personality. Procedure. Special tribunals. Special status. Status of experts.
INTL ORGS: International Court of Justice. United Nations. Arbitration Commission. Arbitration Commission.
PROCEDURE: Ratification.
PARTIES:
WHO (World Health)
United Arab Rep

103059 Bilateral Exchange **223 UNTS 111**
SIGNED: 13 Jan 54   FORCE: 13 Jun 54
REGISTERED: 20 Dec 55 USA (United States)
ARTICLES: 2 LANGUAGE: English. Chinese.
HEADNOTE: LOAN NAVAL VESSELS
TOPIC: Milit Assistance
CONCEPTS: Detailed regulations. Time limit. Responsibility and liability. Title and deeds. Compensation. Indemnities and reimbursements. Delivery schedules. Lease of military property. Military assistance. Naval vessels. Return of equipment and recapture. Restrictions on transfer.
TREATY REF: 132UNTS273; 184UNTS348.
PARTIES:
Belgium
Taiwan
ANNEX
358 UNTS 296.   Belgium.   Amendment 22 Sep 59. Force 22 Sep 59.
358 UNTS 296. Taiwan. Amendment 22 Sep 59. Force 22 Sep 59.
542 UNTS 361.   Belgium.   Prolongation 23 Feb 65. Force 23 Feb 65.
542 UNTS 361. Taiwan. Prolongation 23 Feb 65. Force 23 Feb 65.

103060 Bilateral Exchange **223 UNTS 121**
SIGNED: 24 Feb 51   FORCE: 24 Feb 51
REGISTERED: 20 Dec 55 USA (United States)
ARTICLES: 3 LANGUAGE: English. French.
HEADNOTE: TECHNICAL COOPERATION PROJECT LITANY RIVER SURVEY
TOPIC: Tech Assistance
CONCEPTS: Exceptions and exemptions. Time limit. Diplomatic privileges. General cooperation. Exchange of information and documents.

Personnel. Public information. Research results. Research and development. Financial programs. Domestic obligation. Assistance. Materials, equipment and services.
PARTIES:
Lebanon
USA (United States)

103061 Bilateral Exchange **223 UNTS 131**
SIGNED: 18 Mar 52   FORCE: 18 Mar 52
REGISTERED: 20 Dec 55 USA (United States)
ARTICLES: 2 LANGUAGE: English. Arabic.
HEADNOTE: TECHNICAL COOPERATION PROGRAM AGRICULTURE DEVELOPMENT & IMPROVEMENT
TOPIC: Tech Assistance
CONCEPTS: Annex type material. Personnel. Research and development. Indemnities and reimbursements. Financial programs. Domestic obligation. Agriculture. Assistance. Materials, equipment and services.
TREATY REF: 151UNTS179.
PROCEDURE: Duration. Termination.
PARTIES:
Iraq
USA (United States)

103062 Bilateral Exchange **223 UNTS 139**
SIGNED: 12 Nov 53   FORCE: 12 Nov 53
REGISTERED: 20 Dec 55 USA (United States)
ARTICLES: 2 LANGUAGE: English.
HEADNOTE: ESTABLISHMENT JOINT COMMITTEE TRADE ECONOMIC AFFAIRS
TOPIC: General Economic
CONCEPTS: General cooperation. Exchange of information and documents. Establishment of commission. Programs. General trade. Trade procedures. Subsidiary organ.
INTL ORGS: Special Commission.
PROCEDURE: Duration. Termination.
PARTIES:
Canada
USA (United States)
ANNEX
470 UNTS 394. USA (United States). Amendment 2 Oct 61. Force 2 Oct 61.
470 UNTS 394. Canada. Amendment 2 Oct 61. Force 2 Oct 61.

103063 Bilateral Exchange **223 UNTS 145**
SIGNED: 21 Jan 54   FORCE: 21 Jan 54
REGISTERED: 20 Dec 55 USA (United States)
ARTICLES: 2 LANGUAGE: English.
HEADNOTE: TECHNICAL MISSIONS STUDY PRODUCTION DEFENSE EQUIPMENT SUPPLIES
TOPIC: Tech Assistance
CONCEPTS: Guarantees and safeguards. Conformity with municipal law. Exchange of information and documents. Indemnities and reimbursements. Recognition. Aid missions. Defense and security. Military training.
PARTIES:
Japan
USA (United States)

103064 Bilateral Agreement **223 UNTS 153**
SIGNED: 12 Feb 54   FORCE: 13 Feb 54
REGISTERED: 20 Dec 55 USA (United States)
ARTICLES: 8 LANGUAGE: English. German.
HEADNOTE: ASSISTANCE GERMAN RED CROSS HOSPITAL KOREA
TOPIC: Milit Assistance
CONCEPTS: General cooperation. Responsibility and liability. Humanitarian matters. Accounting procedures. Indemnities and reimbursements. Currency. Financial programs. Materials, equipment and services. Return of equipment and recapture.
INTL ORGS: United Nations.
TREATY REF: 75UNTS31.
PROCEDURE: Future Procedures Contemplated.
PARTIES:
Germany, West
USA (United States)

103065 Bilateral Agreement **223 UNTS 167**
SIGNED: 27 Feb 53   FORCE: 27 Feb 53
REGISTERED: 20 Dec 55 USA (United States)
ARTICLES: 18 LANGUAGE: English. German.

HEADNOTE: VALIDATION DOLLAR BONDS
TOPIC: Claims and Debts
CONCEPTS: Definition of terms. Detailed regulations. Conformity with municipal law. Exchange of information and documents. Use of facilities. Investigation of violations. Establishment of commission. Arbitration. Banking. Expense sharing formulae. Internal finance. Claims and settlements. Lump sum settlements. Conformity with IGO decisions.
INTL ORGS: Arbitration Commission. Special Commission.
PARTIES:
Germany, West
USA (United States)

103066 Bilateral Agreement **224 UNTS 3**
SIGNED: 1 Apr 53   FORCE: 16 Sep 53
REGISTERED: 20 Dec 55 USA (United States)
ARTICLES: 5 LANGUAGE: English. German.
HEADNOTE: VALIDATION BONDS
TOPIC: Claims and Debts
CONCEPTS: Time limit. Treaty implementation. Investigation of violations. Bonds.
TREATY REF: 223UNTS167; USA'TIAS 2792.
PROCEDURE: Ratification.
PARTIES:
Germany, West
USA (United States)

103067 Bilateral Agreement **224 UNTS 13**
SIGNED: 27 Feb 53   FORCE: 16 Sep 53
REGISTERED: 20 Dec 55 USA (United States)
ARTICLES: 8 LANGUAGE: English. German.
HEADNOTE: CLAIM SETTLEMENT FOR POST-WAR ECONOMIC ASSISTANCE
TOPIC: Claims and Debts
CONCEPTS: Definition of terms. Responsibility and liability. General trade. Import quotas. Banking. Bonds. Currency. Financial programs. Internal finance. Interest rates. Payment schedules. Claims and settlements. Lump sum settlements. Debt settlement. Economic assistance. Purchase authorization.
TREATY REF: 92UNTS269; 106UNTS141; TIAS2792.
PROCEDURE: Amendment. Ratification.
PARTIES:
Germany, West
USA (United States)

103068 Bilateral Agreement **224 UNTS 31**
SIGNED: 27 Feb 53   FORCE: 16 Sep 53
REGISTERED: 20 Dec 55 USA (United States)
ARTICLES: 12 LANGUAGE: English. German.
HEADNOTE: INDEBTEDNESS AWARDS CLAIMS
TOPIC: Claims and Debts
CONCEPTS: Detailed regulations. Conformity with municipal law. Procedure. Negotiation. Bonds. Financial programs. Claims and settlements. Debts. Debt settlement. Loan repayment.
INTL ORGS: Allied Military Occupation. Claims Commission.
TREATY REF: 106UNTS121; 106UNTS141; USA'TIAS 2792.
PROCEDURE: Ratification.
PARTIES:
Germany, West
USA (United States)

103069 Bilateral Agreement **224 UNTS 49**
SIGNED: 20 Aug 53   FORCE: 20 Aug 53
REGISTERED: 20 Dec 55 USA (United States)
ARTICLES: 6 LANGUAGE: English. German.
HEADNOTE: RETURN NAVAL VESSELS
TOPIC: Milit Assistance
CONCEPTS: Annex or appendix reference. Responsibility and liability. Indemnities and reimbursements. Delivery schedules. Naval vessels. Restrictions on transfer.
INTL ORGS: Allied Military Occupation.
PARTIES:
Germany, West
USA (United States)

103070 Bilateral Agreement **224 UNTS 75**
SIGNED: 26 May 53   FORCE: 30 Jun 53
REGISTERED: 20 Dec 55 USA (United States)
ARTICLES: 15 LANGUAGE: English. Spanish.

HEADNOTE: AIR TRANSPORT
TOPIC: Air Transport
CONCEPTS: Definition of terms. Exceptions and exemptions. Annex or appendix reference. Non-prejudice to third party. Conformity with municipal law. Licenses and permits. Recognition of legal documents. Use of facilities. Arbitration. Procedure. Special tribunals. Competence of tribunal. Indemnities and reimbursements. Fees and exemptions. Most favored nation clause. National treatment. Customs exemptions. Competency certificate. Routes and logistics. Navigational conditions. Permit designation. Air transport. Airport facilities. Airworthiness certificates. Conditions of airlines operating permission. Operating authorizations and regulations. Licenses and certificates of nationality.
INTL ORGS: Inter-Governmental Maritime Consultative Organization. Arbitration Commission.
TREATY REF: 15UNTS295.
PROCEDURE: Amendment. Future Procedures Contemplated. Ratification. Registration. Termination.
PARTIES:
Cuba
USA (United States)
ANNEX
289 UNTS 322. USA (United States). Amendment 30 Jul 57. Force 30 Jul 57.
289 UNTS 322. Cuba. Amendment 21 May 57. Force 30 Jul 57.

103071 Bilateral Exchange **224 UNTS 107**
SIGNED: 23 Nov 53   FORCE: 23 Nov 53
REGISTERED: 20 Dec 55 USA (United States)
ARTICLES: 2 LANGUAGE: English.
HEADNOTE: EQUIPMENT MATERIAL FOR INTERNAL POLICE USE
TOPIC: Milit Installation
CONCEPTS: Exceptions and exemptions. Guarantees and safeguards. Indemnities and reimbursements. Payment schedules. Materials, equipment and services. Security of information. Restrictions on transfer.
PARTIES:
Germany, West
USA (United States)

103072 Bilateral Exchange **224 UNTS 115**
SIGNED: 11 Aug 48   FORCE: 11 Aug 48
REGISTERED: 20 Dec 55 USA (United States)
ARTICLES: 2 LANGUAGE: English.
HEADNOTE: NON-IMMIGRANT PASSPORT VISAS
TOPIC: Visas
CONCEPTS: Visas. Fees and exemptions.
PARTIES:
India
USA (United States)

103073 Bilateral Agreement **224 UNTS 121**
SIGNED: 29 Apr 53   FORCE: 29 Apr 53
REGISTERED: 20 Dec 55 USA (United States)
ARTICLES: 12 LANGUAGE: English.
HEADNOTE: PUBLIC HEALTH PROGRAM
TOPIC: Sanitation
CONCEPTS: Definition of terms. Detailed regulations. Treaty interpretation. Annex or appendix reference. Friendship and amity. Alien status. Privileges and immunities. General cooperation. Exchange of information and documents. Inspection and observation. Personnel. General property. Programs. Disease control. Public health. Insect control. Nursing. Sanitation. Exchange. Teacher and student exchange. Scholarships and grants. Vocational training. Accounting procedures. Indemnities and reimbursements. Currency. Exchange rates and regulations. Expense sharing formulae. Financial programs. Funding procedures. Customs exemptions. General technical assistance. Special projects.
TREATY REF: 148UNTS39; TIAS2904; 205UNTS340; 179UNTS261.
PROCEDURE: Duration.
PARTIES:
Ethiopia
USA (United States)
ANNEX
235 UNTS 372. USA (United States). Amendment 30 Jun 53. Force 30 Jun 53.

235 UNTS 372. Ethiopia. Amendment 30 Jun 53. Force 30 Jun 53.
235 UNTS 374. USA (United States). Amendment 11 Jun 54. Force 11 Jun 54.
235 UNTS 374. Ethiopia. Amendment 11 Jun 54. Force 11 Jun 54.

103074 Bilateral Exchange **224 UNTS 141**
SIGNED: 24 Jun 53   FORCE: 24 Jun 53
REGISTERED: 20 Dec 55 USA (United States)
ARTICLES: 2 LANGUAGE: English.
HEADNOTE: ECONOMIC COOPERATION
TOPIC: Tech Assistance
CONCEPTS: Definition of terms. Territorial application. Annex type material. Conformity with municipal law. General cooperation. Exchange of information and documents. Informational records. Accounting procedures. Monetary and gold transfers. Funding procedures. Local currency. General technical assistance. Agriculture. General aid. Economic assistance. Terms of loan. Industry.
TREATY REF: 22UNTS263; 86UNTS304.
PARTIES:
UK Great Britain
USA (United States)

103075 Bilateral Exchange **224 UNTS 153**
SIGNED: 2 Sep 53   FORCE: 2 Sep 53
REGISTERED: 20 Dec 55 USA (United States)
ARTICLES: 2 LANGUAGE: English. French.
HEADNOTE: LOAN AIRCRAFT CARRIER
TOPIC: Milit Assistance
CONCEPTS: Detailed regulations. Time limit. Responsibility and liability. Title and deeds. Delivery schedules. Lease of military property. Military assistance. Naval vessels. Return of equipment and recapture. Restrictions on transfer.
TREATY REF: 80UNTS171; 181UNTS177.
PARTIES:
France
USA (United States)
ANNEX
272 UNTS 270. France. Amendment 3 Feb 56. Force 3 Feb 56.
272 UNTS 270. USA (United States). Amendment 3 Feb 56. Force 3 Feb 56.
336 UNTS 362. USA (United States). Amendment 22 Aug 58. Force 26 Aug 58.
336 UNTS 362. France. Amendment 26 Aug 58. Force 26 Aug 58.

103076 Bilateral Exchange **224 UNTS 161**
SIGNED: 10 Nov 53   FORCE: 10 Nov 53
REGISTERED: 20 Dec 55 USA (United States)
ARTICLES: 6 LANGUAGE: English. Japanese.
HEADNOTE: COPYRIGHT PROTECTION
TOPIC: Patents/Copyrights
CONCEPTS: Laws and formalities.
TREATY REF: 136UNTS45; 163UNTS385.
PARTIES:
Japan
USA (United States)

103077 Bilateral Exchange **224 UNTS 187**
SIGNED: 12 Nov 53   FORCE: 12 Nov 53
REGISTERED: 20 Dec 55 USA (United States)
ARTICLES: 5 LANGUAGE: English. Spanish.
HEADNOTE: VALIDITY NON-IMMIGRANT PASSPORT VISAS
TOPIC: Visas
CONCEPTS: Time limit. Visa abolition. Border traffic and migration. Resident permits. Visas. Tourism.
INTL ORGS: International Civil Aviation Organization.
PARTIES:
Mexico
USA (United States)

103078 Bilateral Agreement **224 UNTS 217**
SIGNED: 9 Sep 54   FORCE: 30 Oct 54
REGISTERED: 20 Dec 55 USA (United States)
ARTICLES: 30 LANGUAGE: English. Arabic.
HEADNOTE: USE AREAS MUTUAL DEFENSE
TOPIC: Milit Installation
CONCEPTS: Definition of terms. Annex or appendix reference. Non-prejudice to UN charter. Peaceful relations. Visa abolition. Court proce-

dures. General cooperation. Exchange of information and documents. Recognition of legal documents. Responsibility and liability. Use of facilities. Investigation of violations. Arbitration. Procedure. Public health. Compensation. Indemnities and reimbursements. Currency. Local currency. National treatment. General. Tax exemptions. Customs duties. Customs exemptions. Overflights and technical stops. Postal services. Defense and security. Military training. Jurisdiction. Procurement and logistics. Status of forces. Bases and facilities.
INTL ORGS: United Nations.
PROCEDURE: Ratification. Termination.
PARTIES:
Libya
USA (United States)
ANNEX
271 UNTS 431. Libya. Supplementation 24 Feb 55. Force 24 Feb 55.
271 UNTS 431. USA (United States). Supplementation 24 Feb 55. Force 24 Feb 55.
401 UNTS 270. USA (United States). Interpretation 30 Jun 60. Force 30 Jun 60.
401 UNTS 270. Libya. Interpretation 30 Jun 60. Force 30 Jun 60.

103079 Unilateral Instrument **224 UNTS 275**
SIGNED: 19 Dec 55   FORCE: 21 Dec 55
REGISTERED: 21 Dec 55 United Nations
ARTICLES: 1 LANGUAGE: English.
HEADNOTE: ACCEPTANCE ICJ JURISDICTION
TOPIC: ICJ Option Clause
CONCEPTS: Compulsory jurisdiction.
INTL ORGS: International Court of Justice. United Nations.
TREATY REF: 6LTS384.
PROCEDURE: Amendment. Termination.
PARTIES:
Portugal

103080 Bilateral Treaty **224 UNTS 279**
SIGNED: 3 Aug 51   FORCE: 13 Oct 54
REGISTERED: 21 Dec 55 Greece
ARTICLES: 28 LANGUAGE: English. Greek.
HEADNOTE: FRIENDSHIP COMMERCE NAVIGATION
TOPIC: General Amity
CONCEPTS: Definition of terms. Exceptions and exemptions. Territorial application. Previous treaty replacement. Non-prejudice to third party. Border traffic and migration. Alien status. Extradition, deportation and repatriation. Administrative cooperation. General cooperation. Exchange of information and documents. Juridical personality. Expropriation. Free passage and transit. Legal protection and assistance. Private contracts. Procedure. Existing tribunals. Social security. Export quotas. Import quotas. Free trade. Reciprocity in trade. Exchange rates and regulations. Fees and exemptions. Most favored nation clause. National treatment. Taxation. Inland and territorial waters. Shipwreck and salvage.
INTL ORGS: International Court of Justice. International Monetary Fund.
TREATY REF: 183LTS169.
PROCEDURE: Duration. Ratification. Termination.
PARTIES:
Greece
USA (United States)
ANNEX
238 UNTS 332. Greece. Implementation 3 Aug 51. Force 13 Oct 54.
238 UNTS 332. USA (United States). Implementation 26 Dec 51. Force 13 Oct 54.

103081 Bilateral Exchange **225 UNTS 3**
SIGNED: 3 Feb 53   FORCE: 3 Feb 53
REGISTERED: 21 Dec 55 Greece
ARTICLES: 2 LANGUAGE: French. Spanish.
HEADNOTE: INTERPRETATION CONCERNING SUCCESSION PROPERTY
TOPIC: Claims and Debts
CONCEPTS: Treaty interpretation. General property. Assets transfer.
TREATY REF: 111LTS81; 111LTS282.
PARTIES:
Greece
Spain

103082 Bilateral Exchange **225 UNTS 9**
SIGNED: 19 Oct 53   FORCE: 19 Oct 53
REGISTERED: 21 Dec 55 Greece
ARTICLES: 3 LANGUAGE: French.
HEADNOTE: TRADE
TOPIC: General Trade
CONCEPTS: Annex or appendix reference. Annex type material. Import quotas. Trade procedures. Commodity trade. Quotas.
TREATY REF: 187UNTS207.
PARTIES:
Denmark
Greece

103083 Bilateral Agreement **225 UNTS 17**
SIGNED: 19 May 54   FORCE: 1 Jun 54
REGISTERED: 21 Dec 55 Greece
ARTICLES: 8 LANGUAGE: French.
HEADNOTE: TRADE
TOPIC: General Trade
CONCEPTS: Detailed regulations. Treaty implementation. Annex or appendix reference. Incorporation of treaty provisions into national law. Establishment of commission. Export quotas. Import quotas. Payment schedules. Transportation costs. Quotas. Raw materials.
INTL ORGS: Special Commission.
TREATY REF: 225UNTS27.
PROCEDURE: Denunciation. Duration. Renewal or Revival. Termination.
PARTIES:
Greece
Romania

103084 Bilateral Agreement **225 UNTS 27**
SIGNED: 19 May 54   FORCE: 1 Jun 54
REGISTERED: 21 Dec 55 Greece
ARTICLES: 10 LANGUAGE: French.
HEADNOTE: PAYMENTS
TOPIC: Finance
CONCEPTS: Detailed regulations. Humanitarian matters. General trade. Accounting procedures. Banking. Balance of payments. Currency. Exchange rates and regulations. Inadequacy of funds. Interest rates. Debt settlement. Credit provisions.
TREATY REF: 225UNTS17.
PARTIES:
Greece
Romania

103085 Bilateral Exchange **225 UNTS 35**
SIGNED: 18 Apr 47   FORCE: 18 Apr 47
REGISTERED: 23 Dec 55 South Africa
ARTICLES: 4 LANGUAGE: English.
HEADNOTE: RELEASE FRENCH ASSETS
TOPIC: Reparations
CONCEPTS: Definition of terms. Indemnities and reimbursements. Exchange rates and regulations. Assets transfer. Most favored nation clause. Post-war claims settlement.
PARTIES:
France
South Africa

103086 Bilateral Exchange **225 UNTS 47**
SIGNED: 27 Aug 53   FORCE: 20 May 55
REGISTERED: 23 Dec 55 Australia
ARTICLES: 2 LANGUAGE: English. Italian.
HEADNOTE: CARE MAINTENANCE GRAVES
TOPIC: Other Military
CONCEPTS: National treatment. Upkeep of war graves.
TREATY REF: 213UNTS137.
PARTIES:
Australia
Italy

103087 Bilateral Instrument **225 UNTS 53**
SIGNED: 1 May 48   FORCE: 1 May 48
REGISTERED: 27 Dec 55 South Africa
ARTICLES: 1 LANGUAGE: English.
HEADNOTE: REVIVAL PRE-WAR TREATIES
TOPIC: Admin Cooperation
CONCEPTS: Revival of treaties.
INTL ORGS: United Nations.
TREATY REF: 2'10DM550; 49UNTS3; 104UNTS48; 11LTS23;T.

PARTIES:
Italy
South Africa

103088 Bilateral Instrument **225 UNTS 59**
SIGNED: 15 Nov 48   FORCE: 15 Nov 48
REGISTERED: 27 Dec 55 South Africa
ARTICLES: 1 LANGUAGE: English.
HEADNOTE: REVIVAL PRE-WAR TREATIES
TOPIC: Admin Cooperation
CONCEPTS: Revival of treaties.
INTL ORGS: United Nations.
TREATY REF: 48UNTS203; 34LTS79; 45LTS162.
PARTIES:
Finland
South Africa

103089 Bilateral Instrument **225 UNTS 65**
SIGNED: 16 Nov 48   FORCE: 16 Nov 48
REGISTERED: 27 Dec 55 South Africa
ARTICLES: 1 LANGUAGE: English.
HEADNOTE: REVIVAL PRE-WAR TREATIES
TOPIC: Admin Cooperation
CONCEPTS: Revival of treaties.
INTL ORGS: United Nations.
TREATY REF: 41UNTS135; 8LTS375; 88LTS400.
PARTIES:
Hungary
South Africa

103090 Bilateral Instrument **225 UNTS 71**
SIGNED: 16 Nov 48   FORCE: 16 Nov 48
REGISTERED: 27 Dec 55 South Africa
ARTICLES: 1 LANGUAGE: English.
HEADNOTE: REVIVAL PRE-WAR TREATIES
TOPIC: Admin Cooperation
CONCEPTS: Previous treaty replacement.
INTL ORGS: United Nations.
TREATY REF: 42UNTS3; 104UNTS132,154; 83LTS480.
PARTIES:
Romania
South Africa

103091 Bilateral Agreement **225 UNTS 77**
SIGNED: 1 Feb 54   FORCE: 27 Aug 54
REGISTERED: 28 Dec 55 Greece
ARTICLES: 7 LANGUAGE: French.
HEADNOTE: TRADE
TOPIC: General Trade
CONCEPTS: Annex or appendix reference. Juridical personality. Legal protection and assistance. Licenses and permits. Establishment of commission. Export quotas. Import quotas. Accounting procedures. Payment schedules. Transportation costs. Assets. Claims and settlements.
INTL ORGS: Special Commission.
TREATY REF: 156LTS159.
PROCEDURE: Amendment. Denunciation. Duration. Termination.
PARTIES:
Czechoslovakia
Greece
ANNEX
227 UNTS 402. Czechoslovakia. Supplementation 9 Mar 55. Force 1 Jan 55.
227 UNTS 402. Greece. Supplementation 9 Mar 55. Force 1 Jan 55.
248 UNTS 382. Greece. Supplementation 2 Feb 56. Force 1 Jan 56.
248 UNTS 382. Czechoslovakia. Supplementation 2 Feb 56. Force 1 Jan 56.

103092 Bilateral Agreement **225 UNTS 95**
SIGNED: 1 Feb 54   FORCE: 1 Feb 54
REGISTERED: 28 Dec 55 Greece
ARTICLES: 11 LANGUAGE: French.
HEADNOTE: PAYMENTS
TOPIC: Finance
CONCEPTS: Detailed regulations. General provisions. Conformity with municipal law. General cooperation. General trade. Accounting procedures. Banking. Balance of payments. Currency. Exchange rates and regulations. Financial programs. Inadequacy of funds. Interest rates. Payment schedules. Local currency. Debt settlement.
TREATY REF: 225UNTS77.
PROCEDURE: Duration. Renewal or Revival.

PARTIES:
Czechoslovakia
Greece

ANNEX
248 UNTS 394. Czechoslovakia. Supplementation 2 Feb 56. Force 1 Jan 56.
248 UNTS 394. Greece. Supplementation 2 Feb 56. Force 1 Jan 56.

103093 Bilateral Agreement **225 UNTS 107**
SIGNED: 8 Feb 54   FORCE: 1 Oct 53
REGISTERED: 28 Dec 55 Greece
ARTICLES: 14 LANGUAGE: French.
HEADNOTE: REPAIR JET ENGINES
TOPIC: Status of Forces
CONCEPTS: Treaty interpretation. Conformity with municipal law. Responsibility and liability. Use of facilities. Arbitration. Procedure. Indemnities and reimbursements. Payment schedules. Payment for war supplies.
TREATY REF: 34UNTS243.
PROCEDURE: Duration. Future Procedures Contemplated. Termination.
PARTIES:
France
Greece

103094 Bilateral Agreement **225 UNTS 121**
SIGNED: 8 Feb 54   FORCE: 8 Feb 54
REGISTERED: 28 Dec 55 Greece
ARTICLES: 14 LANGUAGE: French.
HEADNOTE: REPAIR JET ENGINES
TOPIC: Status of Forces
CONCEPTS: Treaty interpretation. Conformity with municipal law. Responsibility and liability. Use of facilities. Arbitration. Procedure. Indemnities and reimbursements. Payment schedules. Payment for war supplies.
TREATY REF: 34UNTS243.
PROCEDURE: Duration. Future Procedures Contemplated.
PARTIES:
France
Greece

103095 Bilateral Agreement **225 UNTS 135**
SIGNED: 5 Dec 53   FORCE: 5 Dec 53
REGISTERED: 29 Dec 55 Greece
ARTICLES: 7 LANGUAGE: French.
HEADNOTE: TRADE
TOPIC: General Trade
CONCEPTS: Treaty implementation. Annex or appendix reference. Establishment of commission. Export quotas. Import quotas. Payment schedules. Quotas.
INTL ORGS: Special Commission.
TREATY REF: 225UNTS145.
PROCEDURE: Denunciation. Duration. Renewal or Revival.
PARTIES:
Bulgaria
Greece

ANNEX
483 UNTS 309. Greece. Amendment 26 Apr 63. Force 1 Jan 62.
483 UNTS 309. Bulgaria. Amendment 26 Apr 63. Force 1 Jan 62.

103096 Bilateral Agreement **225 UNTS 145**
SIGNED: 5 Dec 53   FORCE: 5 Dec 53
REGISTERED: 29 Dec 55 Greece
ARTICLES: 10 LANGUAGE: French.
HEADNOTE: PAYMENTS
TOPIC: Finance
CONCEPTS: Detailed regulations. Conformity with municipal law. General cooperation. Licenses and permits. General trade. Accounting procedures. Banking. Exchange rates and regulations. Financial programs. Funding procedures. Interest rates. Payment schedules. Debt settlement. Credit provisions.
TREATY REF: 225UNTS141,143.
PROCEDURE: Denunciation. Duration. Renewal or Revival.
PARTIES:
Bulgaria
Greece

ANNEX
483 UNTS 309. Bulgaria. Amendment 26 Apr 63. Force 1 Jan 62.

483 UNTS 309. Greece. Amendment 26 Apr 63. Force 1 Jan 62.

103097 Bilateral Treaty **225 UNTS 155**
SIGNED: 28 Aug 50   FORCE: 18 Dec 54
REGISTERED: 29 Dec 55 Greece
ARTICLES: 9 LANGUAGE: English.
HEADNOTE: FRIENDSHIP CONSULAR SERVICE ESTABLISHMENT
TOPIC: General Amity
CONCEPTS: Friendship and amity. Alien status. Consular relations establishment. Diplomatic relations establishment. Privileges and immunities. Exchange of official publications. Arbitration. Mediation and good offices. Existing tribunals. Most favored nation clause.
INTL ORGS: International Court of Justice.
PROCEDURE: Future Procedures Contemplated. Ratification. Termination.
PARTIES:
Greece
Philippines

103098 Bilateral Agreement **225 UNTS 163**
SIGNED: 7 Nov 53   FORCE: 7 Nov 53
REGISTERED: 29 Dec 55 Greece
ARTICLES: 11 LANGUAGE: French.
HEADNOTE: TRADE
TOPIC: General Trade
CONCEPTS: Detailed regulations. Annex or appendix reference. Conformity with municipal law. General cooperation. Informational records. Licenses and permits. Establishment of commission. Export quotas. Import quotas. Reexport of goods, etc.. Trade procedures. Payment schedules. Debt settlement. Quotas. Raw materials.
INTL ORGS: Organization for Economic Co-operation and Development. Special Commission.
TREATY REF: 225UNTS185.
PROCEDURE: Denunciation. Duration. Renewal or Revival.
PARTIES:
Greece
Turkey

ANNEX
264 UNTS 382. Greece. Implementation 1 Nov 56. Force 1 Nov 56.
264 UNTS 382. Turkey. Implementation 1 Nov 56. Force 1 Nov 56.

103099 Bilateral Agreement **225 UNTS 199**
SIGNED: 22 Jul 54   FORCE: 1 Jul 54
REGISTERED: 30 Dec 55 Greece
ARTICLES: 7 LANGUAGE: French.
HEADNOTE: TRADE
TOPIC: General Trade
CONCEPTS: Territorial application. Annex or appendix reference. Establishment of commission. Export quotas. Import quotas. Trade procedures. Payment schedules. Quotas.
INTL ORGS: European Payments Union. Organization for Economic Co-operation and Development. Special Commission.
TREATY REF: 91UNTS83.
PROCEDURE: Duration.
PARTIES:
France
Greece

103100 Bilateral Agreement **225 UNTS 219**
SIGNED: 28 Jun 55   FORCE: 1 Jul 55
REGISTERED: 30 Dec 55 Greece
ARTICLES: 7 LANGUAGE: French.
HEADNOTE: TRADE
TOPIC: General Trade
CONCEPTS: Territorial application. Annex or appendix reference. Establishment of commission. Export quotas. Import quotas. Trade procedures. Payment schedules. Quotas.
INTL ORGS: European Payments Union. Organization for Economic Co-operation and Development. Special Commission.
PROCEDURE: Duration.
PARTIES:
France
Greece

103101 Multilateral Agreement **225 UNTS 233**
SIGNED: 2 Mar 55   FORCE: 30 Sep 55

REGISTERED: 30 Dec 55 Greece
ARTICLES: 14 LANGUAGE: French.
HEADNOTE: BALKAN CONSULTATIVE ASSEMBLY
TOPIC: IGO Establishment
CONCEPTS: Friendship and amity. Establishment. Procedure. Internal structure. Inter-agency agreements.
INTL ORGS: Balkan Alliance.
TREATY REF: TREATY OF ANKARA; TREATY OF BLED.
PROCEDURE: Amendment. Duration. Ratification. Termination.
PARTIES:
Greece SIGNED: 2 Mar 55 RATIFIED: 20 Aug 55 FORCE: 30 Sep 55
Turkey SIGNED: 2 Mar 55 RATIFIED: 30 Sep 55 FORCE: 30 Sep 55
Yugoslavia SIGNED: 2 Mar 55 RATIFIED: 28 Jun 55 FORCE: 30 Sep 55

103102 Bilateral Exchange **225 UNTS 243**
SIGNED: 30 Jul 55   FORCE: 30 Jul 55
REGISTERED: 30 Dec 55 Greece
ARTICLES: 4 LANGUAGE: French.
HEADNOTE: TRADE
TOPIC: General Trade
CONCEPTS: Treaty implementation. Commodity trade. Quotas.
PARTIES:
Greece
Sweden

103103 Bilateral Treaty **226 UNTS 3**
SIGNED: 14 Feb 50   FORCE: 11 Apr 50
REGISTERED: 3 Jan 56 USSR (Soviet Union)
ARTICLES: 6 LANGUAGE: Russian. Chinese.
HEADNOTE: FRIENDSHIP ALLIANCE & MUTUAL ASSISTANCE
TOPIC: General Amity
CONCEPTS: Friendship and amity. Peaceful relations.
PROCEDURE: Denunciation. Duration. Ratification.
PARTIES:
China People's Rep
USSR (Soviet Union)

103104 Bilateral Agreement **226 UNTS 21**
SIGNED: 14 Feb 50   FORCE: 14 Feb 50
REGISTERED: 3 Jan 56 USSR (Soviet Union)
ARTICLES: 5 LANGUAGE: Russian. Chinese.
HEADNOTE: GRANT CREDIT
TOPIC: Loans and Credits
CONCEPTS: Accounting procedures. Interest rates. Payment schedules. Materials, equipment and services. Credit provisions. Loan repayment.
PROCEDURE: Ratification.
PARTIES:
China People's Rep
USSR (Soviet Union)

103105 Bilateral Agreement **226 UNTS 31**
SIGNED: 14 Feb 50   FORCE: 11 Apr 50
REGISTERED: 3 Jan 56 USSR (Soviet Union)
ARTICLES: 4 LANGUAGE: Russian. Chinese.
HEADNOTE: CHINESE CHANG CHUN RAILWAY PORT ARTHUR & DAIREN
TOPIC: Privil/Immunities
CONCEPTS: Establishment of commission. Currency. Airforce-army-navy personnel ratio. Bases and facilities. Facilities and property. Changes of territory.
INTL ORGS: Special Commission.
PROCEDURE: Ratification.
PARTIES:
China People's Rep
USSR (Soviet Union)

103106 Bilateral Exchange **226 UNTS 45**
SIGNED: 15 Sep 52   FORCE: 15 Sep 52
REGISTERED: 3 Jan 56 USSR (Soviet Union)
ARTICLES: 2 LANGUAGE: Russian. Chinese.
HEADNOTE: EXTENSION PERIOD JOINT USE NAVAL BASE
TOPIC: Milit Installation
CONCEPTS: Annex type material. Previous treaty extension. Defense and security. Status of military forces.
TREATY REF: 226UNTS3.

PARTIES:
China People's Rep
USSR (Soviet Union)

103107 Bilateral Instrument **226 UNTS 51**
SIGNED: 12 Oct 54   FORCE: 12 Oct 54
REGISTERED: 3 Jan 56 USSR (Soviet Union)
ARTICLES: 1 LANGUAGE: Russian. Chinese.
HEADNOTE: WITHDRAWAL MILITARY UNITS
TOPIC: Milit Installation
CONCEPTS: Time limit. Defense and security.
Withdrawal of forces.
INTL ORGS: Special Commission.
TREATY REF: 226UNTS31.
PARTIES:
China People's Rep
USSR (Soviet Union)

103108 Bilateral Instrument **226 UNTS 57**
SIGNED: 12 Oct 54   FORCE: 12 Oct 54
REGISTERED: 3 Jan 56 USSR (Soviet Union)
ARTICLES: 1 LANGUAGE: Russian. Chinese.
HEADNOTE: JOINT DECLARATION
TOPIC: General Amity
CONCEPTS: Peaceful relations.
INTL ORGS: United Nations.
TREATY REF: 226UNTS3.
PARTIES:
China People's Rep
USSR (Soviet Union)

103109 Bilateral Instrument **226 UNTS 69**
SIGNED: 12 Oct 54   FORCE: 12 Oct 54
REGISTERED: 3 Jan 56 USSR (Soviet Union)
ARTICLES: 1 LANGUAGE: Russian. Chinese.
HEADNOTE: JOINT DECLARATION CONCERNING
RELATIONS WITH JAPAN
TOPIC: General Amity
CONCEPTS: Peaceful relations.
PARTIES:
China People's Rep
USSR (Soviet Union)

103110 Bilateral Treaty **226 UNTS 79**
SIGNED: 20 Feb 47   FORCE: 18 May 47
REGISTERED: 3 Jan 56 USSR (Soviet Union)
ARTICLES: 15 LANGUAGE: Russian. Romanian.
HEADNOTE: TRADE NAVIGATION
TOPIC: General Economic
CONCEPTS: Annex or appendix reference. Non-
prejudice to third party. Arbitration. Export
quotas. Import quotas. Most favored nation
clause. National treatment. Transport of goods.
Shipwreck and salvage.
PROCEDURE: Denunciation. Duration. Ratification.
Renewal or Revival. Termination.
PARTIES:
Romania
USSR (Soviet Union)

103111 Bilateral Agreement **226 UNTS 109**
SIGNED: 30 Apr 54   FORCE: 12 Sep 54
REGISTERED: 3 Jan 56 USSR (Soviet Union)
ARTICLES: 19 LANGUAGE: Russian. Arabic.
HEADNOTE: TRADE PAYMENTS
TOPIC: General Economic
CONCEPTS: Detailed regulations. Annex or appen-
dix reference. Licenses and permits. Establish-
ment of trade relations. Export quotas. Import
quotas. Tariffs. Accounting procedures. Ex-
change rates and regulations. Payment sched-
ules. Debts. Most favored nation clause. Tax ex-
emptions. Merchant vessels.
PROCEDURE: Duration. Ratification. Renewal or
Revival.
PARTIES:
Lebanon
USSR (Soviet Union)
ANNEX
511 UNTS 278. Cyprus. Accession 21 Jul 64.
Force 9 Sep 64.

103112 Multilateral Instrument **226 UNTS 153**
SIGNED: 2 Dec 54   FORCE: 2 Dec 54
REGISTERED: 3 Jan 56 USSR (Soviet Union)
ARTICLES: 1 LANGUAGE: Russian.
HEADNOTE: DECLARATION
TOPIC: General Amity

CONCEPTS: Friendship and amity. Peaceful rela-
tions.
INTL ORGS: European Defense Community. West-
ern European Union.
TREATY REF: 211UNTS342.
PARTIES:
Multilateral

103113 Bilateral Agreement **226 UNTS 187**
SIGNED: 19 Sep 55   FORCE: 28 Oct 55
REGISTERED: 3 Jan 56 USSR (Soviet Union)
ARTICLES: 5 LANGUAGE: Russian. Finnish.
HEADNOTE: RENUNCIATION RIGHTS NAVAL
BASE WITHDRAWAL ARMED FORCES
TOPIC: Milit Installation
CONCEPTS: Time limit. General property. Claims
and settlements. Withdrawal of forces. Bases
and facilities.
TREATY REF: 48UNTS149;48UNTS203.
PROCEDURE: Ratification.
PARTIES:
Finland
USSR (Soviet Union)

103114 Bilateral Treaty **226 UNTS 201**
SIGNED: 20 Sep 55   FORCE: 6 Oct 55
REGISTERED: 3 Jan 56 USSR (Soviet Union)
ARTICLES: 7 LANGUAGE: Russian. German.
HEADNOTE: CONCERNING RELATIONS
TOPIC: General Amity
CONCEPTS: Friendship and amity. Peaceful rela-
tions. General cooperation. Status of forces.
PROCEDURE: Duration. Ratification.
PARTIES:
Germany, East
USSR (Soviet Union)

103115 Bilateral Agreement **226 UNTS 215**
SIGNED: 30 Jun 55   FORCE: 6 Jul 55
REGISTERED: 4 Jan 56 Australia
ARTICLES: 6 LANGUAGE: English.
HEADNOTE: TRADE
TOPIC: General Trade
CONCEPTS: Definition of terms. Annex or appendix reference. Customs exemptions.
PROCEDURE: Duration. Ratification. Termination.
PARTIES:
Australia
Fed Rhod/Nyasaland
ANNEX
250 UNTS 316.   Australia.   Implementation
26 Jul 56. Force 30 Jul 56.
250 UNTS 316. Fed Rhod/Nyasaland. Implementation 30 Jul 56. Force 30 Jul 56.
265 UNTS 400.   Australia.   Amendment
27 Feb 57. Force 8 Mar 57.
265 UNTS 400. Fed Rhod/Nyasaland. Amendment 27 Feb 57. Force 8 Mar 57.
351 UNTS 428. Fed Rhod/Nyasaland. Amendment 16 Nov 59. Force 20 Nov 59.
351 UNTS 428.   Australia.   Amendment
16 Nov 59. Force 20 Nov 59.
351 UNTS 434. Fed Rhod/Nyasaland. Amendment 16 Nov 59. Force 20 Nov 59.
351 UNTS 434.   Australia.   Amendment
16 Nov 59. Force 20 Nov 59.
394 UNTS 272.   Australia.   Amendment
25 Jan 61. Force 3 Feb 61.
475 UNTS 356. Australia. Amendment 4 Jul 63.
Force 12 Jul 63.
475 UNTS 356. Fed Rhod/Nyasaland. Amendment 4 Jul 63. Force 12 Jul 63.

103116 Unilateral Instrument **226 UNTS 235**
SIGNED: 7 Jan 56   FORCE: 9 Jan 56
REGISTERED: 9 Jan 56 United Nations
ARTICLES: 1 LANGUAGE: English.
HEADNOTE: COMPULSORY JURISDICTION ICJ
TOPIC: ICJ Option Clause
CONCEPTS: Exceptions and exemptions. Time
limit. Optional clause ICJ. Compulsory jurisdic-
tion.
INTL ORGS: International Court of Justice.
PARTIES:
India
ANNEX
260 UNTS 459. India. Force 8 Feb 57. Termina-
tion 8 Feb 57.

103117 Bilateral Exchange **226 UNTS 241**
SIGNED: 27 Oct 54   FORCE: 26 Nov 54
REGISTERED: 12 Jan 56 Israel

ARTICLES: 2 LANGUAGE: French.
HEADNOTE: ABOLITION VISAS
TOPIC: Visas
CONCEPTS: Visa abolition. Passports diplomatic.
PROCEDURE: Denunciation.
PARTIES:
Israel
Luxembourg

103118 Bilateral Exchange **226 UNTS 247**
SIGNED: 30 Mar 55   FORCE: 1 May 55
REGISTERED: 12 Jan 56 Israel
ARTICLES: 2 LANGUAGE: French.
HEADNOTE: ABOLITION VISA FEES
TOPIC: Visas
CONCEPTS: Visas. Fees and exemptions.
PARTIES:
Israel
Luxembourg

103119 Bilateral Exchange **226 UNTS 253**
SIGNED: 15 Jul 55   FORCE: 15 Jul 55
REGISTERED: 12 Jan 56 Israel
ARTICLES: 2 LANGUAGE: Russian.
HEADNOTE: MOST FAVORED NATION TREAT-
MENT
TOPIC: Mostfavored Nation
CONCEPTS: Most favored nation clause. Merchant
vessels.
PARTIES:
Israel
USSR (Soviet Union)

103120 Bilateral Exchange **226 UNTS 257**
SIGNED: 26 Jul 55   FORCE: 15 Aug 55
REGISTERED: 12 Jan 56 Israel
ARTICLES: 4 LANGUAGE: English.
HEADNOTE: ABOLITION VISA FEES
TOPIC: Visas
CONCEPTS: Visas. Fees and exemptions.
PARTIES:
Israel
Norway

103121 Bilateral Exchange **226 UNTS 265**
SIGNED: 2 Aug 55   FORCE: 1 Sep 55
REGISTERED: 12 Jan 56 Israel
ARTICLES: 3 LANGUAGE: English.
HEADNOTE: ABOLITION VISA FEES
TOPIC: Visas
CONCEPTS: Visas. Fees and exemptions.
PARTIES:
Canada
Israel

103122 Bilateral Exchange **226 UNTS 273**
SIGNED: 31 May 49   FORCE: 31 May 49
REGISTERED: 13 Jan 56 UK Great Britain
ARTICLES: 4 LANGUAGE: English. French.
HEADNOTE: CONSTRUCTION OWEN FALLS DAM
TOPIC: Specific Resources
CONCEPTS: Operating agencies. Arbitration. Ne-
gotiation. Plans and standards. Hydro-electric
power. Facilities and property.
PARTIES:
United Arab Rep
UK Great Britain

103123 Bilateral Exchange **226 UNTS 287**
SIGNED: 20 Mar 50   FORCE: 20 Mar 50
REGISTERED: 13 Jan 56 UK Great Britain
ARTICLES: 3 LANGUAGE: English. French.
HEADNOTE: COOPERATION METEOROLOGICAL
HYDROLOGICAL SURVEYS
TOPIC: Tech Assistance
CONCEPTS: Research cooperation. Meteorology.
Research results. Assistance.
PARTIES:
United Arab Rep
UK Great Britain

103124 Multilateral Agreement **226 UNTS 297**
SIGNED: 18 Feb 54   FORCE: 15 Jun 55
REGISTERED: 13 Jan 56 UK Great Britain
ARTICLES: 3 LANGUAGE: English. Arabic.
HEADNOTE: WAR CEMETERIES GRAVES MEMORI-
ALS

TOPIC: Other Military
CONCEPTS: Previous treaty amendment. Previous treaty extension. Establishment of commission. Upkeep of war graves. Establishment of war cemeteries.
TREATY REF: 170LTS9.
PARTIES:
  Multilateral

103125 Bilateral Convention **226 UNTS 305**
SIGNED: 19 Nov 54   FORCE: 10 Nov 55
REGISTERED: 13 Jan 56 UK Great Britain
ARTICLES: 18 LANGUAGE: English. Portuguese.
HEADNOTE: CULTURAL
TOPIC: Culture
CONCEPTS: Definition of terms. Conformity with municipal law. Establishment of commission. Exchange. Teacher and student exchange. Institute establishment. Scholarships and grants. Exchange. General cultural cooperation. Artists.
INTL ORGS: Special Commission.
PROCEDURE: Denunciation. Duration. Ratification.
PARTIES:
  Portugal
  UK Great Britain

103126 Bilateral Exchange **226 UNTS 319**
SIGNED: 30 Apr 55   FORCE: 30 Apr 55
REGISTERED: 13 Jan 56 UK Great Britain
ARTICLES: 2 LANGUAGE: English. Arabic.
HEADNOTE: SETTLEMENT FINANCIAL CLAIMS
TOPIC: Claims and Debts
CONCEPTS: Responsibility and liability. Establishment of commission. Investments. Claims and settlements.
INTL ORGS: Special Commission.
PARTIES:
  Iraq
  UK Great Britain
              ANNEX
310 UNTS 390. UK Great Britain. Supplementation 27 Mar 57. Force 27 Mar 57.
310 UNTS 390.   Iraq.   Supplementation 27 Mar 57. Force 27 Mar 57.

103127 Bilateral Exchange **227 UNTS 3**
SIGNED: 12 Aug 55   FORCE: 12 Aug 55
REGISTERED: 13 Jan 56 UK Great Britain
ARTICLES: 2 LANGUAGE: English.
HEADNOTE: TERMINATION LEASE GAMBEILA ENCLAVE
TOPIC: Territory Boundary
CONCEPTS: Changes of territory.
TREATY REF: 3'2DEMARTENS826;.
PARTIES:
  Ethiopia
  UK Great Britain

103128 Bilateral Agreement **227 UNTS 9**
SIGNED: 10 Nov 54   FORCE: 1 Jul 54
REGISTERED: 26 Jan 56 Greece
ARTICLES: 7 LANGUAGE: French.
HEADNOTE: TRADE
TOPIC: General Trade
CONCEPTS: Previous treaty replacement. Licenses and permits. Establishment of commission. Trade procedures. Payment schedules.
INTL ORGS: European Payments Union. Organization for Economic Co-operation and Development. Special Commission.
TREATY REF: 189UNTS295.
PROCEDURE: Denunciation. Duration. Renewal or Revival.
PARTIES:
  Greece
  Italy
              ANNEX
231 UNTS 376.   Greece.   Supplementation 22 Dec 55. Force 1 Jul 55.
231 UNTS 376.   Italy.   Supplementation 22 Dec 55. Force 1 Jul 55.

103129 Bilateral Exchange **227 UNTS 27**
SIGNED: 14 Jul 55   FORCE: 13 Jul 55
REGISTERED: 26 Jan 56 Greece
ARTICLES: 2 LANGUAGE: French.
HEADNOTE: TRADE
TOPIC: General Trade
CONCEPTS: Licenses and permits. Private con-

tracts. Establishment of commission. Export quotas. Import quotas. Trade procedures. Commodity trade. Smuggling.
INTL ORGS: Organization for Economic Co-operation and Development. Special Commission.
PARTIES:
  Greece
  Netherlands

103130 Bilateral Instrument **227 UNTS 33**
SIGNED: 12 Mar 55   FORCE: 1 Apr 55
REGISTERED: 31 Jan 56 Greece
ARTICLES: 5 LANGUAGE: English.
HEADNOTE: TRADE
TOPIC: General Trade
CONCEPTS: Annex or appendix reference. Conformity with municipal law. General cooperation. Establishment of commission. Export quotas. Import quotas. Trade procedures. Payment schedules. Quotas.
INTL ORGS: Special Commission.
TREATY REF: 227UNTS34.
PROCEDURE: Duration. Renewal or Revival. Termination.
PARTIES:
  Greece
  Japan
              ANNEX
256 UNTS 368. Japan. Amendment 20 Sep 56. Force 20 Sep 56.
256 UNTS 368. Greece. Amendment 20 Sep 56. Force 20 Sep 56.

103131 Bilateral Agreement **227 UNTS 65**
SIGNED: 4 Jul 55   FORCE: 17 Sep 55
REGISTERED: 31 Jan 56 WHO (World Health)
ARTICLES: 6 LANGUAGE: English.
HEADNOTE: TECHNICAL ADVISORY ASSISTANCE
TOPIC: Tech Assistance
CONCEPTS: Definition of terms. Privileges and immunities. General cooperation. Exchange of information and documents. Personnel. Responsibility and liability. Title and deeds. Exchange. Scholarships and grants. Vocational training. Research and development. Expense sharing formulae. Domestic obligation. Special projects. Materials, equipment and services. IGO status. Conformity with IGO decisions.
TREATY REF: 33UNTS261.
PROCEDURE: Amendment. Termination.
PARTIES:
  Iran
  WHO (World Health)

103132 Bilateral Exchange **227 UNTS 77**
SIGNED: 17 Sep 52   FORCE: 17 Sep 52
REGISTERED: 31 Jan 56 USA (United States)
ARTICLES: 2 LANGUAGE: English.
HEADNOTE: LOAN WHEAT PURCHASE
TOPIC: Loans and Credits
CONCEPTS: Annex or appendix reference. Conformity with municipal law. General cooperation. Personnel. Accounting procedures. Indemnities and reimbursements. Agriculture. Agricultural commodities. Loan and credit. Purchase authorization. Terms of loan.
TREATY REF: USA 65STAT373; 22USC; 1651.
PARTIES:
  Pakistan
  USA (United States)

103133 Bilateral Exchange **227 UNTS 85**
SIGNED: 18 Sep 52   FORCE: 18 Sep 52
REGISTERED: 31 Jan 56 USA (United States)
ARTICLES: 3 LANGUAGE: English. Japanese.
HEADNOTE: PASSPORT VISA FEES
TOPIC: Visas
CONCEPTS: Time limit. Visas. Fees and exemptions.
PARTIES:
  Japan
  USA (United States)

103134 Bilateral Exchange **227 UNTS 101**
SIGNED: 9 Mar 53   FORCE: 13 Dec 52
REGISTERED: 31 Jan 56 USA (United States)
ARTICLES: 4 LANGUAGE: English.
HEADNOTE: ENLISTMENT PHILIPPINE CITIZENS US NAVY

TOPIC: Milit Servic/Citiz
CONCEPTS: Time limit. Return of equipment and recapture. Service in foreign army.
TREATY REF: 43UNTS271.
PROCEDURE: Termination.
PARTIES:
  Philippines
  USA (United States)
              ANNEX
232 UNTS 364. USA (United States). Amendment 20 Jul 54. Force 21 Jul 54.
232 UNTS 364.   Philippines.   Amendment 30 Jul 54. Force 21 Jul 54.

103135 Bilateral Convention **227 UNTS 111**
SIGNED: 25 May 54   FORCE: 15 Jan 55
REGISTERED: 31 Jan 56 Yugoslavia
ARTICLES: 8 LANGUAGE: Slovene. German.
HEADNOTE: WATER ECONOMY
TOPIC: Specific Resources
CONCEPTS: Annex or appendix reference. Establishment of commission. Arbitration. Special tribunals. Claims and settlements. Hydro-electric power. Regulation of natural resources.
INTL ORGS: United Nations.
PROCEDURE: Denunciation.
PARTIES:
  Austria
  Yugoslavia

103136 Bilateral Exchange **227 UNTS 147**
SIGNED: 29 Dec 55   FORCE: 1 Feb 56
REGISTERED: 1 Feb 56 Israel
ARTICLES: 2 LANGUAGE: English.
HEADNOTE: ABOLITION VISA FEES
TOPIC: Visas
CONCEPTS: Visas. Fees and exemptions.
PARTIES:
  Iceland
  Israel

103137 Multilateral Agreement **227 UNTS 153**
SIGNED: 2 Feb 56   FORCE: 2 Feb 56
REGISTERED: 2 Feb 56 United Nations
ARTICLES: 6 LANGUAGE: English. French.
HEADNOTE: REVISED STANDARD AGREEMENT TECHNICAL ASSISTANCE
TOPIC: Tech Assistance
CONCEPTS: Previous treaty replacement. Privileges and immunities. General cooperation. Exchange of information and documents. Personnel. Responsibility and liability. Title and deeds. Use of facilities. Exchange. Scholarships and grants. Vocational training. Research and development. Accounting procedures. Exchange rates and regulations. Expense sharing formulae. Local currency. Domestic obligation. General technical assistance. Materials, equipment and services. IGO status. Conformity with IGO decisions.
TREATY REF: 76UNTS132; 1UNTS15; 1UNTS263; 33UNTS261; 81UNTS233.
PROCEDURE: Amendment. Termination.
PARTIES:
  Iran SIGNED: 2 Feb 56 FORCE: 2 Feb 56
  FAO (Food Agri) SIGNED: 2 Feb 56 FORCE: 2 Feb 56
  ICAO (Civil Aviat) SIGNED: 2 Feb 56 FORCE: 2 Feb 56
  ILO (Labor Org) SIGNED: 2 Feb 56 FORCE: 2 Feb 56
  ITU (Telecommun) SIGNED: 2 Feb 56 FORCE: 2 Feb 56
  UNESCO (Educ/Cult) SIGNED: 2 Feb 56 FORCE: 2 Feb 56
  United Nations SIGNED: 2 Feb 56 FORCE: 2 Feb 56
  WHO (World Health) SIGNED: 2 Feb 56 FORCE: 2 Feb 56
  WMO (Meteorology) SIGNED: 2 Feb 56 FORCE: 2 Feb 56

103138 Multilateral Agreement **227 UNTS 169**
SIGNED: 1 Apr 53   FORCE: 1 Feb 54
REGISTERED: 3 Feb 56 Sweden
ARTICLES: 3 LANGUAGE: Swedish. Danish. Finnish. Icelandic. Norwegian.

HEADNOTE: COLLECTION MAINTENANCE AL-
LOWANCES
TOPIC: Non-ILO Labor
CONCEPTS: Annex type material.
PARTIES:
Denmark   SIGNED: 1 Apr 53   RATIFIED:
13 Jan 54 FORCE: 1 Feb 54
Finland SIGNED: 1 Apr 53 RATIFIED: 13 Jan 54
FORCE: 1 Feb 54
Iceland SIGNED: 1 Apr 53 RATIFIED: 13 Jan 54
FORCE: 1 Feb 54
Norway SIGNED: 1 Apr 53 RATIFIED: 13 Jan 54
FORCE: 1 Feb 54
Sweden SIGNED: 1 Apr 53 RATIFIED: 13 Jan 54
FORCE: 1 Feb 54

103139   Bilateral Agreement   **227 UNTS 195**
SIGNED: 15 May 53   FORCE: 1 Jul 53
REGISTERED: 3 Feb 56 Sweden
ARTICLES: 12 LANGUAGE: Swedish. German.
HEADNOTE: EXCHANGE STUDENT EMPLOYEES
TOPIC: Non-ILO Labor
CONCEPTS: Conditions. Definition of terms. Resi-
dent permits. Conformity with municipal law.
General cooperation. Operating agencies. Em-
ployment regulations. Wages and salaries. Non-
ILO labor relations. Administrative cooperation.
Migrant worker. Quotas.
PROCEDURE: Denunciation. Duration. Renewal or
Revival.
PARTIES:
Germany, West
Sweden

103140 Multilateral Convention **227 UNTS 217**
SIGNED: 20 Jul 53   FORCE: 1 Aug 54
REGISTERED: 3 Feb 56 Sweden
ARTICLES: 16 LANGUAGE: Swedish. Danish. Ice-
landic. Norwegian.
HEADNOTE: TRANSFER BENIFITS FROM SICK
FUNDS
TOPIC: Non-ILO Labor
CONCEPTS: Conditions. Detailed regulations. Pre-
vious treaty replacement. Operating agencies.
Dispute settlement. Public health. Non-ILO labor
relations. Sickness and invalidity insurance. So-
cial security. Monetary and gold transfers. Pay-
ment schedules.
TREATY   REF: 14UNTS307;   14UNTS3;
22UNTS203.
PROCEDURE: Denunciation. Duration.
PARTIES:
Denmark SIGNED: 20 Jul 53 RATIFIED: 9 Feb 54
FORCE: 1 Aug 54
Iceland SIGNED: 20 Jul 53 RATIFIED: 22 Jan 54
FORCE: 1 Aug 54
Norway   SIGNED: 20 Jul 53   RATIFIED:
13 May 54 FORCE: 1 Aug 54
Sweden   SIGNED: 20 Jul 53   RATIFIED:
29 Jan 54 FORCE: 1 Aug 54

103141   Multilateral Convention   **228 UNTS 3**
SIGNED: 20 Jul 53   FORCE: 1 Sep 54
REGISTERED: 3 Feb 56 Sweden
ARTICLES: 8 LANGUAGE: Swedish. Danish. Fin-
nish. Icelandic. Norwegian.
HEADNOTE: MATERNITY ASSISTANCE
TOPIC: Non-ILO Labor
CONCEPTS: Definition of terms. Annex or appen-
dix reference. Non-ILO labor relations. Sickness
and invalidity insurance. Indemnities and reim-
bursements. National treatment.
PROCEDURE: Denunciation. Future Procedures
Contemplated. Ratification.
PARTIES:
Denmark SIGNED: 20 Jul 53 RATIFIED: 9 Feb 54
FORCE: 1 Sep 54
Finland SIGNED: 20 Jul 53 RATIFIED: 1 Jun 54
FORCE: 1 Sep 54
Iceland SIGNED: 20 Jul 53 RATIFIED: 22 Jan 54
FORCE: 1 Sep 54
Norway   SIGNED: 20 Jul 53   RATIFIED:
13 May 54 FORCE: 1 Sep 54
Sweden   SIGNED: 20 Jul 53   RATIFIED:
29 Jan 54 FORCE: 1 Sep 54

103142 Multilateral Convention **228 UNTS 41**
SIGNED: 20 Jul 53   FORCE: 1 Sep 54
REGISTERED: 3 Feb 56 Sweden

ARTICLES: 8 LANGUAGE: Swedish. Danish. Fin-
nish. Icelandic. Norwegian.
HEADNOTE: BENEFIT REDUCED WORKING CA-
PACITY
TOPIC: Non-ILO Labor
CONCEPTS: Definition of terms. Domestic legisla-
tion. Public health. Old age and invalidity insur-
ance. Non-ILO labor relations. Old age insurance.
Sickness and invalidity insurance. Indemnities
and reimbursements. Payment schedules.
PROCEDURE: Denunciation. Ratification.
PARTIES:
Denmark SIGNED: 20 Jul 53 RATIFIED: 9 Feb 54
FORCE: 1 Sep 54
Finland SIGNED: 20 Jul 53 RATIFIED: 1 Jun 54
FORCE: 1 Sep 54
Iceland SIGNED: 20 Jul 53 RATIFIED: 22 Jan 54
FORCE: 1 Sep 54
Norway   SIGNED: 20 Jul 53   RATIFIED:
13 May 54 FORCE: 1 Sep 54
Sweden   SIGNED: 20 Jul 53   RATIFIED:
29 Jan 54 FORCE: 1 Sep 54

103143   Bilateral Exchange   **228 UNTS 85**
SIGNED: 22 Dec 54   FORCE: 22 Dec 54
REGISTERED: 3 Feb 56 Sweden
ARTICLES: 8 LANGUAGE: English. Swedish.
HEADNOTE: CERTIFICATES AIRWORTHINESS IM-
PORTED AIRCRAFT
TOPIC: Air Transport
CONCEPTS: Previous treaty replacement. Confor-
mity with municipal law. Exchange of informa-
tion and documents. Recognition of legal docu-
ments. Use of facilities. Registration certificate.
Airworthiness certificates.
TREATY REF: 144LTS183F.
PROCEDURE: Termination.
PARTIES:
Sweden
USA (United States)

103144   Multilateral Agreement   **228 UNTS 95**
SIGNED: 19 Mar 55   FORCE: 1 Apr 55
REGISTERED: 3 Feb 56 Sweden
ARTICLES: 8 LANGUAGE: Swedish. Danish. Nor-
wegian.
HEADNOTE: SANITARY CONTROL TRAFFIC
TOPIC: Sanitation
CONCEPTS: Detailed regulations. Border traffic
and migration. General cooperation. Exchange
of information and documents. Inspection and
observation. Quarantine. Sanitation.
TREATY   REF: 175UNTS215;   204UNTS39;
219UNTS354.
PROCEDURE: Denunciation.
PARTIES:
Denmark SIGNED: 19 Mar 55 FORCE: 1 Apr 55
Norway SIGNED: 19 Mar 55 FORCE: 1 Apr 55
Sweden SIGNED: 19 Mar 55 FORCE: 1 Apr 55
ANNEX
427 UNTS 376. Finland. Adherence 10 Sep 59.
Force 1 Dec 59.

103145   Bilateral Exchange   **228 UNTS 115**
SIGNED: 29 Apr 55   FORCE: 1 Jul 55
REGISTERED: 3 Feb 56 Sweden
ARTICLES: 2 LANGUAGE: Swedish. Portuguese.
HEADNOTE: REGISTRATION TRADE NAMES
TOPIC: Patents/Copyrights
CONCEPTS: Non-prejudice to third party. Confor-
mity with municipal law. Trademarks.
TREATY REF: 74BFSP44; 74LTS289.
PROCEDURE: Duration. Termination.
PARTIES:
Brazil
Sweden

103146 Bilateral Agreement **228 UNTS 121**
SIGNED: 4 Jun 55   FORCE: 4 Jun 55
REGISTERED: 3 Feb 56 Sweden
ARTICLES: 17 LANGUAGE: English.
HEADNOTE: TECHNICAL ASSISTANCE VOCA-
TIONAL TRAINING
TOPIC: Tech Assistance
CONCEPTS: Detailed regulations. General cooper-
ation. Exchange of information and documents.
Personnel. Title and deeds. Teacher and student
exchange. Institute establishment. Scholarships
and grants. Vocational training. Accounting pro-
cedures. Financial programs. Tax exemptions.

Customs exemptions. Domestic obligation. Spe-
cial projects. Materials, equipment and services.
Industry.
INTL ORGS: United Nations Technical Assistance
Board. United Nations.
PROCEDURE: Amendment. Duration. Future Proce-
dures Contemplated. Renewal or Revival. Termi-
nation.
PARTIES:
Pakistan
Sweden

103147   Bilateral Convention   **228 UNTS 137**
SIGNED: 16 Feb 54   FORCE: 23 Aug 55
REGISTERED: 3 Feb 56 Sweden
ARTICLES: 17 LANGUAGE: French.
HEADNOTE: RESIDENCE NAVIGATION
TOPIC: General Transport
CONCEPTS: Exceptions and exemptions. Territo-
rial application. Previous treaty replacement.
Frontier formalities. Border traffic and migration.
Denial of admission. Alien status. Nationality and
citizenship. Conformity with municipal law. Ex-
propriation. Legal protection and assistance.
General property. Recognition of legal docu-
ments. Use of facilities. Procedure. Existing tribu-
nals. Reexport of goods, etc.. Non-interest rates
and fees. Most favored nation clause. National
treatment. Tax exemptions. Customs exemptions. Registration certificate. Navigational con-
ditions. Ports and pilotage. Shipwreck and salvage. Foreign nationals. Optional clause ICJ.
INTL ORGS: International Court of Justice.
TREATY   REF: 95LTS894   2'9DEMAR-
TENS173,193.
PROCEDURE: Duration. Ratification. Renewal or
Revival. Termination. Application to Non-self-
governing Territories.
PARTIES:
France
Sweden

103148   Bilateral Exchange   **228 UNTS 153**
SIGNED: 24 Jun 55   FORCE: 24 Jun 55
REGISTERED: 3 Feb 56 Sweden
ARTICLES: 2 LANGUAGE: English. Chinese.
HEADNOTE: ESTABLISH CONSULAR RELATIONS
TOPIC: Consul/Citizenship
CONCEPTS: Consular relations establishment.
PARTIES:
China People's Rep
Sweden

103149   Bilateral Exchange   **228 UNTS 159**
SIGNED: 5 Jan 56   FORCE: 5 Jan 56
REGISTERED: 6 Feb 56 Belgium
ARTICLES: 2 LANGUAGE: French.
HEADNOTE: PAYMENT COMPENSATION
TOPIC: Reparations
CONCEPTS: Compensation. National treatment.
Loss and/or damage. Post-war claims settle-
ment.
PARTIES:
Belgium
Switzerland

103150 Multilateral Agreement **228 UNTS 167**
SIGNED: 10 Feb 56   FORCE: 10 Feb 56
REGISTERED: 10 Feb 56 United Nations
ARTICLES: 6 LANGUAGE: Spanish.
HEADNOTE: TECHNICAL ASSISTANCE
TOPIC: Tech Assistance
CONCEPTS: Time limit. Previous treaty replacement. Privileges and immunities. General cooperation. Exchange of information and documents. Personnel. Responsibility and liability. Title and deeds. Use of facilities. Exchange.
Scholarships and grants. Vocational training. Research and development. Accounting procedures. Exchange rates and regulations. Expense
sharing formulae. Local currency. Domestic obligation. General technical assistance. Materials,
equipment and services. IGO status. Conformity
with IGO decisions.
TREATY   REF: 33UNTS26,76UNTS132,1-
66UNTS189,100UNTS77.
PROCEDURE: Amendment. Termination.

PARTIES:
Ecuador SIGNED: 10 Feb 56 FORCE: 10 Feb 56
FAO (Food Agri) SIGNED: 10 Feb 56 FORCE:
10 Feb 56
ICAO (Civil Aviat) SIGNED: 10 Feb 56 FORCE:
10 Feb 56
ILO (Labor Org) SIGNED: 10 Feb 56 FORCE:
10 Feb 56
UNESCO (Educ/Cult) SIGNED: 10 Feb 56
FORCE: 10 Feb 56
United Nations SIGNED: 10 Feb 56 FORCE:
10 Feb 56
WHO (World Health) SIGNED: 10 Feb 56 FORCE:
10 Feb 56
ANNEX
231 UNTS 386. Ecuador. Amendment 6 Apr 56.
231 UNTS 386. UNTAB (Tech Assis). Amendment
19 Mar 56.
529 UNTS 329. Ecuador. Amendment 25 Mar 65.
Force 25 Mar 65.
529 UNTS 329. UNTAB (Tech Assis). Amendment
15 Mar 65. Force 25 Mar 65.

103151 Multilateral Agreement **228 UNTS 189**
SIGNED: 10 Feb 56 FORCE: 10 Feb 56
REGISTERED: 10 Feb 56 United Nations
ARTICLES: 6 LANGUAGE: English.
HEADNOTE: REVISED STANDARD AGREEMENT
TECHNICAL ASSISTANCE
TOPIC: Tech Assistance
CONCEPTS: Privileges and immunities. General
cooperation. Exchange of information and documents. Personnel. Responsibility and liability. Ti-
tle and deeds. Use of facilities. Exchange. Schol-
arships and grants. Vocational training. Re-
search and development. Accounting
procedures. Exchange rates and regulations. Expense sharing formulae. Local currency. Domestic obligation. General technical assistance. Materials, equipment and services. IGO status. Conformity with IGO decisions.
TREATY REF: 1UNTS15; 1UNTS263;
33UNTS261;V.
PROCEDURE: Amendment. Termination.
PARTIES:
Greece SIGNED: 10 Feb 56 FORCE: 10 Feb 56
FAO (Food Agri) SIGNED: 10 Feb 56 FORCE:
10 Feb 56
ICAO (Civil Aviat) SIGNED: 10 Feb 56 FORCE:
10 Feb 56
ILO (Labor Org) SIGNED: 10 Feb 56 FORCE:
10 Feb 56
ITU (Telecommun) SIGNED: 10 Feb 56 FORCE:
10 Feb 56
UNESCO (Educ/Cult) SIGNED: 10 Feb 56
FORCE: 10 Feb 56
United Nations SIGNED: 10 Feb 56 FORCE:
10 Feb 56
WHO (World Health) SIGNED: 10 Feb 56 FORCE:
10 Feb 56
WMO (Meteorology) SIGNED: 10 Feb 56 FORCE:
10 Feb 56
ANNEX
435 UNTS 340. Nicaragua. Implementation
23 Apr 54. Force 23 Apr 54.
435 UNTS 340. USA (United States). Implementation 23 Apr 54. Force 23 Apr 54.
519 UNTS 350. Greece. Amendment 2 Dec 64.
Force 2 Dec 64.
519 UNTS 350. UNTAB (Tech Assis). Amendment
8 Oct 63. Force 2 Dec 64.

103152 Bilateral Exchange **228 UNTS 203**
SIGNED: 2 Jan 56 FORCE: 2 Feb 56
REGISTERED: 13 Feb 56 Belgium
ARTICLES: 2 LANGUAGE: French.
HEADNOTE: ABOLITION PASSPORT VISA RE-
QUIREMENTS
TOPIC: Visas
CONCEPTS: Emergencies. Territorial application.
Visa abolition. Border traffic and migration. Pass-
ports non-diplomatic. Resident permits. Visas.
PROCEDURE: Denunciation.
PARTIES:
Belgium
Turkey

103153 Bilateral Agreement **228 UNTS 211**
SIGNED: 12 Jun 55 FORCE: 4 Oct 55
REGISTERED: 22 Feb 56 Pakistan
ARTICLES: 1 LANGUAGE: English.

HEADNOTE: FINANCE
TOPIC: Finance
CONCEPTS: Detailed regulations. General provi-
sions. Payment schedules. Assets transfer.
PROCEDURE: Ratification.
PARTIES:
India
Pakistan

103154 Bilateral Instrument **228 UNTS 227**
SIGNED: 27 Apr 53 FORCE: 15 Dec 52
REGISTERED: 22 Feb 56 UK Great Britain
ARTICLES: 8 LANGUAGE: English.
HEADNOTE: REVIVAL PRE-WAR TREATIES
TOPIC: Admin Cooperation
CONCEPTS: Revival of treaties.
TREATY REF: 136UNTS45; 3'6DM563;
2'20DM809; 6LTS333; 25LTS11;E.
PARTIES:
Japan
UK Great Britain

103155 Unilateral Instrument **229 UNTS 3**
SIGNED: 4 Feb 56 FORCE: 21 Feb 56
REGISTERED: 21 Feb 56 United Nations
ARTICLES: 1 LANGUAGE: English.
HEADNOTE: ACCEPTANCE OBLIGATIONS UN
TOPIC: UN Charter
CONCEPTS: Acceptance of obligations upon ad-
mittance to UN.
INTL ORGS: United Nations.
PARTIES:
Portugal

103156 Bilateral Exchange **229 UNTS 7**
SIGNED: 20 Mar 54 FORCE: 20 Mar 54
REGISTERED: 21 Feb 56 USA (United States)
ARTICLES: 2 LANGUAGE: English.
HEADNOTE: EMERGENCY WHEAT AID
TOPIC: Direct Aid
CONCEPTS: Privileges and immunities. Confor-
mity with municipal law. General cooperation.
Exchange of information and documents. In-
spection and observation. Personnel. Public in-
formation. Export quotas. Currency deposits. Lo-
cal currency. Relief supplies. Procurement. Dis-
tribution. Defense and security.
PARTIES:
Afghanistan
USA (United States)

103157 Bilateral Exchange **229 UNTS 15**
SIGNED: 11 Jan 54 FORCE: 11 Jan 54
REGISTERED: 21 Feb 56 USA (United States)
ARTICLES: 2 LANGUAGE: English.
HEADNOTE: EMERGENCY WHEAT AID
TOPIC: Direct Aid
CONCEPTS: Change of circumstances. Privileges
and immunities. Conformity with municipal law.
General cooperation. Exchange of information
and documents. Inspection and observation. Per-
sonnel. Public information. Title and deeds. Ex-
pense sharing formulae. Commodities and ser-
vices. Relief supplies. Withdrawal conditions.
Distribution.
TREATY REF: 183UNTS177.
PARTIES:
Libya
USA (United States)

103158 Bilateral Exchange **229 UNTS 25**
SIGNED: 30 Nov 53 FORCE: 30 Nov 53
REGISTERED: 21 Feb 56 USA (United States)
ARTICLES: 2 LANGUAGE: English. Spanish.
HEADNOTE: TRADE
TOPIC: General Trade
CONCEPTS: Annex type material. Previous treaty
replacement.
TREATY REF: GATT.
PARTIES:
USA (United States)
Uruguay

103159 Bilateral Agreement **229 UNTS 37**
SIGNED: 23 Apr 54 FORCE: 23 Apr 54
REGISTERED: 21 Feb 56 USA (United States)
ARTICLES: 11 LANGUAGE: English. Spanish.
HEADNOTE: MILITARY ASSISTANCE

TOPIC: Milit Assistance
CONCEPTS: Military assistance. Self-defense. Mili-
tary training.
INTL ORGS: United Nations.
PROCEDURE: Termination.
PARTIES:
Nicaragua
USA (United States)

103160 Bilateral Agreement **229 UNTS 53**
SIGNED: 27 Jun 53 FORCE: 27 Jun 53
REGISTERED: 21 Feb 56 USA (United States)
ARTICLES: 13 LANGUAGE: English. Spanish.
HEADNOTE: COOPERATIVE PROGRAM WATER
UTILIZATION AGRICULTURAL PRODUCTION
TOPIC: Tech Assistance
CONCEPTS: Time limit. Treaty implementation.
Annex type material. Privileges and immunities.
General cooperation. Exchange of information
and documents. Inspection and observation. Do-
mestic legislation. Operating agencies. Person-
nel. General property. Private contracts. Title
and deeds. Vocational training. Currency depos-
its. Financial programs. Funding procedures. As-
sets transfer. Domestic obligation. Agriculture.
Assistance. Materials, equipment and services.
Irrigation.
TREATY REF: 151UNTS147.
PROCEDURE: Duration. Termination.
PARTIES:
Chile
USA (United States)

103161 Bilateral Agreement **229 UNTS 73**
SIGNED: 15 Jun 55 FORCE: 21 Jul 55
REGISTERED: 23 Feb 56 UK Great Britain
ARTICLES: 11 LANGUAGE: English.
HEADNOTE: COOPERATION CIVIL USES ATOMIC
ENERGY
TOPIC: Atomic Energy
CONCEPTS: Definition of terms. Exceptions and
exemptions. Annex or appendix reference. Privileges and immunities. Exchange of information
and documents. Use of facilities. Specialists exchange. Reexport of goods, etc.. Laws and formalities. Nuclear materials. Peaceful use. Rights
of supplier. Security of information. Scientific exchange.
PROCEDURE: Duration.
PARTIES:
UK Great Britain
USA (United States)
ANNEX
252 UNTS 394. UK Great Britain. Amendment
13 Jun 56. Force 16 Jul 56.
252 UNTS 394. USA (United States). Amendment
13 Jun 56. Force 16 Jul 56.
482 UNTS 368. UK Great Britain. Amendment
5 Jun 63. Force 31 Jul 63.
482 UNTS 368. USA (United States). Amendment
5 Jun 63. Force 31 Jul 63.
532 UNTS 374. UK Great Britain. Amendment
29 Jun 64. Force 4 Dec 64.
532 UNTS 374. USA (United States). Amendment
29 Jun 64. Force 4 Dec 64.
548 UNTS 340. UK Great Britain. Amendment
15 Jul 65. Force 20 Jul 65.
548 UNTS 340. UK Great Britain. Amendment
15 Jul 65. Force 20 Jul 65.
573 UNTS 312. USA (United States). Amendment
2 Jun 66. Force 15 Jul 66.
573 UNTS 312. UK Great Britain. Amendment
2 Jun 66. Force 15 Jul 66.

103162 Bilateral Agreement **229 UNTS 97**
SIGNED: 8 Jul 55 FORCE: 8 Oct 55
REGISTERED: 23 Feb 56 IBRD (World Bank)
ARTICLES: 5 LANGUAGE: English.
HEADNOTE: GUARANTEE AGREEMENT
TOPIC: IBRD Project
CONCEPTS: Definition of terms. Annex or appen-
dix reference. Exchange of information and doc-
uments. Informational records. Inspection and
observation. Bonds. Fees and exemptions. Tax
exemptions. Domestic obligation. Terms of loan.
Loan regulations. Loan guarantee. Guarantor
non-interference.
PARTIES:
Nicaragua
IBRD (World Bank)

ANNEX
272 UNTS 274. IBRD (World Bank). Supplementation 15 Nov 56. Force 4 Jun 57.
272 UNTS 274.   Nicaragua.   Supplementation
15 Nov 56. Force 4 Jun 57.

103163   Bilateral Agreement   **229 UNTS 123**
SIGNED: 8 Jul 55   FORCE: 13 Oct 55
REGISTERED: 23 Feb 56 IBRD (World Bank)
ARTICLES: 5 LANGUAGE: English.
HEADNOTE: GUARANTEE AGREEMENT
TOPIC: IBRD Project
CONCEPTS: Definition of terms. Annex or appen-
dix reference. Standardization. Exchange of in-
formation and documents. Informational
records. Inspection and observation. Bonds.
Fees and exemptions. Tax exemptions. Domestic
obligation. Terms of loan. Loan guarantee. Guar-
antor non-interference.
PARTIES:
Nicaragua
IBRD (World Bank)
ANNEX
210 UNTS 335. Monaco. Acceptance 12 Jan 55.
Force 12 Apr 55.

103164   Bilateral Agreement   **229 UNTS 145**
SIGNED: 26 Aug 55   FORCE: 26 Nov 55
REGISTERED: 23 Feb 56 IBRD (World Bank)
ARTICLES: 5 LANGUAGE: English.
HEADNOTE: GUARANTEE AGREEMENT
TOPIC: IBRD Project
CONCEPTS: Definition of terms. Annex or appen-
dix reference. Exchange of information and doc-
uments. Informational records. Inspection and
observation. Bonds. Fees and exemptions. Tax
exemptions. Domestic obligation. Terms of loan.
Loan regulations. Loan guarantee. Guarantor
non-interference.
PARTIES:
Nicaragua
IBRD (World Bank)

103165   Bilateral Agreement   **229 UNTS 167**
SIGNED: 29 Jul 55   FORCE: 3 Nov 55
REGISTERED: 23 Feb 56 IBRD (World Bank)
ARTICLES: 7 LANGUAGE: English.
HEADNOTE: LOAN AGREEMENT
TOPIC: IBRD Project
CONCEPTS: Default remedies. Definition of terms.
Annex or appendix reference. Exchange of infor-
mation and documents. Informational records.
Inspection and observation. Accounting proce-
dures. Bonds. Fees and exemptions. Interest
rates. Tax exemptions. Domestic obligation.
Terms of loan. Loan regulations. Loan guarantee.
Guarantor non-interference.
PARTIES:
Guatemala
IBRD (World Bank)

103166   Bilateral Exchange   **229 UNTS 185**
SIGNED: 8 Aug 51   FORCE: 8 Aug 51
REGISTERED: 23 Feb 56 USA (United States)
ARTICLES: 4 LANGUAGE: English.
HEADNOTE: FREE ENTRY PRIVILEGES CONSULAR
OFFICERS
TOPIC: Visas
CONCEPTS: Diplomatic privileges.
PARTIES:
Iraq
USA (United States)

103167   Bilateral Agreement   **229 UNTS 193**
SIGNED: 27 Jun 53   FORCE: 27 Jun 53
REGISTERED: 28 Feb 56 USA (United States)
ARTICLES: 13 LANGUAGE: English. Spanish.
HEADNOTE: COOPERATIVE PROGRAM WATER
UTILIZATION
TOPIC: Tech Assistance
CONCEPTS: Detailed regulations. Treaty imple-
mentation. Annex type material. Privileges and
immunities. General cooperation. Exchange of
information and documents. Informational
records. Inspection and observation. Domestic
legislation. Operating agencies. Personnel. Gen-
eral property. Private contracts. Title and deeds.
Vocational training. Currency deposits. Exchange rates and regulations. Financial pro-

grams. Funding procedures. Domestic obliga-
tion. Assistance. Materials, equipment and ser-
vices. Irrigation. Natural resources.
TREATY REF: 151UNTS147.
PROCEDURE: Duration. Termination.
PARTIES:
Chile
USA (United States)

103168   Bilateral Exchange   **229 UNTS 213**
SIGNED: 15 Jan 54   FORCE: 15 Jan 54
REGISTERED: 28 Feb 56 USA (United States)
ARTICLES: 2 LANGUAGE: English. Spanish.
HEADNOTE: TECHNICAL COOPERATION
TOPIC: Tech Assistance
CONCEPTS: Annex type material. Conformity with
municipal law. General cooperation. Personnel.
Private contracts. Attachment of funds. Ex-
change rates and regulations. Financial pro-
grams. Funding procedures. Garnishment of
funds. Seizure funds. Tax exemptions. Customs
exemptions. General technical assistance. Mate-
rials, equipment and services. Aid missions.
TREATY REF: 132UNTS319.
PARTIES:
Bolivia
USA (United States)

103169   Bilateral Exchange   **229 UNTS 223**
SIGNED: 13 Apr 54   FORCE: 13 Apr 54
REGISTERED: 28 Feb 56 USA (United States)
ARTICLES: 2 LANGUAGE: English.
HEADNOTE: STATUS MILITARY ASSITANCE AD-
VISORY GROUP
TOPIC: Status of Forces
CONCEPTS: Exceptions and exemptions. Status of
military forces. Jurisdiction.
TREATY REF: 199UNTS67.
PARTIES:
Norway
USA (United States)

103170   Bilateral Agreement   **229 UNTS 229**
SIGNED: 23 Apr 54   FORCE: 23 Apr 54
REGISTERED: 28 Feb 56 USA (United States)
ARTICLES: 13 LANGUAGE: English.
HEADNOTE: LOAN AGREEMENT
TOPIC: Loans and Credits
CONCEPTS: Annex or appendix reference. Gen-
eral cooperation. Exchange rates and regula-
tions. Funding procedures. Interest rates. Pay-
ment schedules. Purchase authorizations. Debt
settlement. Liens. Economic assistance. Loan
and credit. Credit provisions. Loan repayment.
Terms of loan. Defense and security.
INTL ORGS: International Monetary Fund.
TREATY REF: USA'65STAT373; 22 USC; 1651;E.
PARTIES:
ECSC (Coal/Steel)
USA (United States)
ANNEX
238 UNTS 340. ECSC (Coal/Steel). Amendment
8 Dec 54. Force 8 Dec 54.
238 UNTS 340. USA (United States). Amendment
16 Dec 54. Force 16 Dec 54.

103171   Bilateral Agreement   **230 UNTS 3**
SIGNED: 10 Oct 55   FORCE: 10 Oct 55
REGISTERED: 1 Mar 56 Denmark
ARTICLES: 5 LANGUAGE: Danish. Icelandic.
HEADNOTE: DOUBLE TAXATION SEA AIR TRANS-
PORT
TOPIC: Taxation
CONCEPTS: Definition of terms. Taxation. Tax ex-
emptions. Air transport. Merchant vessels.
PROCEDURE: Termination.
PARTIES:
Denmark
Iceland

103172   Bilateral Agreement   **230 UNTS 13**
SIGNED: 9 Jul 55   FORCE: 5 Aug 55
REGISTERED: 5 Mar 56 Thailand
ARTICLES: 5 LANGUAGE: English.
HEADNOTE: SETTLEMENT SPECIAL YEN PROB-
LEM
TOPIC: Finance
CONCEPTS: Detailed regulations. Treaty imple-
mentation. Establishment of commission. Com-

pensation. Exchange rates and regulations.
Claims and settlements. Economic assistance.
INTL ORGS: Special Commission.
PROCEDURE: Ratification.
PARTIES:
Japan
Thailand
ANNEX
450 UNTS 422. Japan. Replacement 31 Jan 62.
Force 9 May 62.
450 UNTS 422.   Thailand.   Replacement
31 Jan 62. Force 9 May 62.

103173   Bilateral Exchange   **230 UNTS 19**
SIGNED: 13 Jul 54   FORCE: 13 Jul 54
REGISTERED: 6 Mar 56 Greece
ARTICLES: 2 LANGUAGE: French.
HEADNOTE: COMMERCE
TOPIC: General Trade
CONCEPTS: Annex type material. Non-interest
rates and fees. Commodity trade. Quotas.
TREATY REF: 92UNTS71.
PARTIES:
Greece
Portugal

103174   Bilateral Exchange   **230 UNTS 25**
SIGNED: 29 Aug 55   FORCE: 29 Aug 55
REGISTERED: 6 Mar 56 Greece
ARTICLES: 4 LANGUAGE: French.
HEADNOTE: COMMERCE
TOPIC: General Trade
CONCEPTS: Annex or appendix reference. Li-
censes and permits. Export quotas. Import
quotas. Trade procedures. Quotas.
TREATY REF: 92UNTS71.
PARTIES:
Denmark
Greece

103175   Bilateral Exchange   **230 UNTS 33**
SIGNED: 2 Sep 54   FORCE: 2 Sep 54
REGISTERED: 6 Mar 56 Greece
ARTICLES: 2 LANGUAGE: Greek. Russian.
HEADNOTE: TRADE
TOPIC: General Trade
CONCEPTS: Annex or appendix reference. Pay-
ment schedules.
PARTIES:
Greece
USSR (Soviet Union)

103176   Bilateral Agreement   **230 UNTS 41**
SIGNED: 20 Jun 55   FORCE: 19 Jan 56
REGISTERED: 7 Mar 56 IBRD (World Bank)
ARTICLES: 5 LANGUAGE: English.
HEADNOTE: GUARANTEE AGREEMENT
TOPIC: IBRD Project
CONCEPTS: Definition of terms. Annex or appen-
dix reference. Exchange of information and doc-
uments. Informational records. Inspection and
observation. Fees and exemptions. Tax exemp-
tions. Domestic obligation. Terms of loan. Loan
regulations. Loan guarantee. Guarantor non-
interference.
PARTIES:
Pakistan
IBRD (World Bank)

103177   Bilateral Agreement   **230 UNTS 79**
SIGNED: 4 Aug 55   FORCE: 8 Oct 55
REGISTERED: 7 Mar 56 IBRD (World Bank)
ARTICLES: 5 LANGUAGE: English.
HEADNOTE: GUARANTEE AGREEMENT
TOPIC: IBRD Project
CONCEPTS: Definition of terms. Annex or appen-
dix reference. Exchange of information and doc-
uments. Informational records. Inspection and
observation. Bonds. Fees and exemptions. Tax
exemptions. Domestic obligation. Terms of loan.
Loan regulations. Loan guarantee. Guarantor
non-interference.
PARTIES:
Pakistan
IBRD (World Bank)

103178   Bilateral Agreement   **230 UNTS 101**
SIGNED: 28 Nov 55   FORCE: 8 Dec 55

REGISTERED: 7 Mar 56 IBRD (World Bank)
ARTICLES: 8 LANGUAGE: English.
HEADNOTE: LOAN AGREEMENT
TOPIC: IBRD Project
CONCEPTS: Definition of terms. Annex or appendix reference. Exchange of information and documents. Informational records. Inspection and observation. Accounting procedures. Bonds. Fees and exemptions. Interest rates. Tax exemptions. Domestic obligation. Terms of loan. Loan regulations. Loan guarantee. Guarantor non-interference.
PARTIES:
IBRD (World Bank)
South Africa

103179   Bilateral Exchange   **230 UNTS 121**
SIGNED: 24 Mar 54   FORCE: 25 Jun 54
REGISTERED: 13 Mar 56 South Africa
ARTICLES: 2 LANGUAGE: English.
HEADNOTE: REVIVAL 21 JUN 24 AGREEMENT
TOPIC: Admin Cooperation
CONCEPTS: Revival of treaties.
TREATY REF: 28LTS511.
PARTIES:
Finland
South Africa

103180   Bilateral Agreement   **230 UNTS 127**
SIGNED: 25 Oct 45   FORCE: 25 Oct 45
REGISTERED: 13 Mar 56 Canada
ARTICLES: 10 LANGUAGE: English.
HEADNOTE: FINANCE
TOPIC: Finance
CONCEPTS: Detailed regulations. Territorial application. Conformity with municipal law. General trade. Import quotas. Accounting procedures. Banking. Bonds. Monetary and gold transfers. Exchange rates and regulations. Interest rates. Debts. Debt settlement. Loan and credit. Purchase authorization. Loan repayment. Terms of loan.
PARTIES:
Belgium
Canada

103181   Bilateral Exchange   **230 UNTS 159**
SIGNED: 13 Jul 46   FORCE: 13 Jul 46
REGISTERED: 13 Mar 56 Canada
ARTICLES: 2 LANGUAGE: English. French.
HEADNOTE: SETTLEMENT WAR CLAIMS
TOPIC: Reparations
CONCEPTS: Accounting procedures. Lump sum settlements. Materials, equipment and services. Loss and/or damage. Post-war claims settlement.
PARTIES:
Belgium
Canada

103182   Bilateral Exchange   **230 UNTS 165**
SIGNED: 22 Mar 46   FORCE: 22 Mar 46
REGISTERED: 13 Mar 56 Canada
ARTICLES: 2 LANGUAGE: English.
HEADNOTE: RELEASE PRIVATE PROPERTY
TOPIC: Reparations
CONCEPTS: Annex or appendix reference. Assets transfer. Post-war claims settlement.
PARTIES:
Canada
France

103183   Bilateral Agreement   **230 UNTS 183**
SIGNED: 8 Feb 46   FORCE: 8 Feb 46
REGISTERED: 13 Mar 56 Canada
ARTICLES: 8 LANGUAGE: English. Spanish.
HEADNOTE: COMMERCE
TOPIC: General Trade
CONCEPTS: Detailed regulations. Exceptions and exemptions. Conformity with municipal law. General cooperation. Investigation of violations. Export quotas. Import quotas. Reciprocity in trade. Trade procedures. Monetary and gold transfers. Commodity trade. Most favored nation clause. Equitable taxes.
PROCEDURE: Duration. Ratification. Termination.
PARTIES:
Canada
Mexico

103184   Bilateral Exchange   **230 UNTS 199**
SIGNED: 5 Feb 46   FORCE: 5 Feb 46
REGISTERED: 13 Mar 56 Canada
ARTICLES: 2 LANGUAGE: English.
HEADNOTE: TRADE
TOPIC: General Trade
CONCEPTS: Territorial application. Revival of treaties.
TREATY REF: 39LTS45.
PARTIES:
Canada
Netherlands

103185   Bilateral Exchange   **230 UNTS 205**
SIGNED: 30 Dec 46   FORCE: 30 Dec 46
REGISTERED: 13 Mar 56 Canada
ARTICLES: 2 LANGUAGE: English.
HEADNOTE: COMPENSATION WAR DAMAGES
TOPIC: Reparations
CONCEPTS: Territorial application. Compensation. National treatment. Post-war claims settlement.
PARTIES:
Canada
Netherlands

103186   Bilateral Exchange   **230 UNTS 213**
SIGNED: 17 Feb 56   FORCE: 18 Mar 56
REGISTERED: 18 Mar 56 South Africa
ARTICLES: 2 LANGUAGE: English.
HEADNOTE: VISA AGREEMENT
TOPIC: Visas
CONCEPTS: Time limit. Denial of admission. Visas. Conformity with municipal law. Fees and exemptions.
PARTIES:
Norway
South Africa
ANNEX
252 UNTS 400.   Norway.   Supplementation 2 Oct 56. Force 2 Oct 56.
252 UNTS 400.   South Africa.   Supplementation 10 Sep 56. Force 2 Oct 56.
384 UNTS 370.   Norway.   Amendment 12 Sep 60. Force 1 May 58.
384 UNTS 370.   South Africa.   Amendment 5 Oct 60. Force 1 May 58.

103187   Bilateral Agreement   **230 UNTS 219**
SIGNED: 6 Apr 55   FORCE: 6 Sep 55
REGISTERED: 19 Mar 56 Thailand
ARTICLES: 10 LANGUAGE: Thai. Japanese.
HEADNOTE: CULTURAL AGREEMENT
TOPIC: Culture
CONCEPTS: Friendship and amity. Domestic legislation. Recognition of degrees. Teacher and student exchange. Professorships. Scholarships and grants. General cultural cooperation. Scientific exchange. Publications exchange. Mass media exchange.
PROCEDURE: Duration. Ratification. Renewal or Revival. Termination.
PARTIES:
Japan
Thailand

103188   Bilateral Agreement   **230 UNTS 233**
SIGNED: 25 Aug 55   FORCE: 17 Feb 56
REGISTERED: 21 Mar 56 IBRD (World Bank)
ARTICLES: 5 LANGUAGE: English.
HEADNOTE: GUARANTEE AGREEMENT
TOPIC: IBRD Project
CONCEPTS: Default remedies. Definition of terms. Annex or appendix reference. Exchange of information and documents. Informational records. Inspection and observation. Accounting procedures. Fees and exemptions. Tax exemptions. Domestic obligation. Terms of loan. Loan regulations. Loan guarantee. Guarantor non-interference.
PARTIES:
Lebanon
IBRD (World Bank)

103189   Bilateral Agreement   **230 UNTS 262**
SIGNED: 22 Dec 55   FORCE: 10 Mar 56
REGISTERED: 23 Mar 56 IBRD (World Bank)
ARTICLES: 7 LANGUAGE: English.
HEADNOTE: LOAN AGREEMENT

TOPIC: IBRD Project
CONCEPTS: Default remedies. Definition of terms. Annex or appendix reference. Exchange of information and documents. Informational records. Inspection and observation. Accounting procedures. Bonds. Fees and exemptions. Interest rates. Tax exemptions. Domestic obligation. Loan regulations. Loan guarantee. Guarantor non-interference. Roads and highways.
PARTIES:
Honduras
IBRD (World Bank)

103190   Bilateral Exchange   **230 UNTS 279**
SIGNED: 7 Nov 55   FORCE: 2 Mar 56
REGISTERED: 27 Mar 56 South Africa
ARTICLES: 4 LANGUAGE: English.
HEADNOTE: DOUBLE TAXATION SHIPS AIRCRAFT
TOPIC: Taxation
CONCEPTS: Definition of terms. Taxation. Tax exemptions. Air transport. Merchant vessels.
PROCEDURE: Duration. Termination.
PARTIES:
South Africa
Switzerland
ANNEX
643 UNTS 393.   South Africa.   Termination 11 Jul 68.
643 UNTS 393.   Switzerland.   Termination 11 Jul 68.

103191   Bilateral Convention   **230 UNTS 287**
SIGNED: 28 Jul 55   FORCE: 8 Mar 56
REGISTERED: 27 Mar 56 South Africa
ARTICLES: 22 LANGUAGE: English. Afrikaans. Swedish.
HEADNOTE: DOUBLE TAXATION FISCAL EVASION TAXES ON INCOME
TOPIC: Taxation
CONCEPTS: Definition of terms. Conformity with municipal law. Exchange of official publications. Teacher and student exchange. Claims and settlements. Taxation. Death duties. Equitable taxes. General. Tax exemptions.
PROCEDURE: Duration. Ratification. Termination.
PARTIES:
South Africa
Sweden

103192   Bilateral Exchange   **230 UNTS 337**
SIGNED: 14 Dec 49   FORCE: 1 Jan 50
REGISTERED: 27 Mar 56 Canada
ARTICLES: 2 LANGUAGE: English.
HEADNOTE: NON-IMMIGRANT VISAS
TOPIC: Visas
CONCEPTS: Time limit. Visa abolition. Denial of admission. Visas. Conformity with municipal law. Fees and exemptions.
PARTIES:
Canada
Netherlands

103193   Bilateral Exchange   **230 UNTS 343**
SIGNED: 25 Mar 50   FORCE: 25 Mar 50
REGISTERED: 27 Mar 56 Canada
ARTICLES: 2 LANGUAGE: English.
HEADNOTE: SETTLEMENT WAR CLAIMS
TOPIC: Reparations
CONCEPTS: Accounting procedures. Exchange rates and regulations. Lump sum settlements. Assets transfer. Post-war claims settlement.
PARTIES:
Canada
Denmark

103194   Bilateral Exchange   **230 UNTS 349**
SIGNED: 18 Mar 50   FORCE: 18 Mar 50
REGISTERED: 27 Mar 56 Canada
ARTICLES: 2 LANGUAGE: English.
HEADNOTE: SETTLEMENT WAR CLAIMS
TOPIC: Reparations
CONCEPTS: Accounting procedures. Exchange rates and regulations. Lump sum settlements. Post-war claims settlement.
PARTIES:
Canada
Norway

103195 Bilateral Exchange **230 UNTS 357**
SIGNED: 29 Mar 50 FORCE: 29 Mar 50
REGISTERED: 27 Mar 56 Canada
ARTICLES: 2 LANGUAGE: English.
HEADNOTE: SETTLEMENT WAR CLAIMS
TOPIC: Reparations
CONCEPTS: General property. Accounting procedures. Exchange rates and regulations. Payment schedules. Local currency. Lump sum settlements. Most favored nation clause. National treatment. Post-war claims settlement.
PARTIES:
Canada
Yugoslavia

103196 Bilateral Exchange **230 UNTS 365**
SIGNED: 17 Apr 50 FORCE: 1 May 50
REGISTERED: 27 Mar 56 Canada
ARTICLES: 2 LANGUAGE: French.
HEADNOTE: MODIFYING VISA REQUIREMENTS
TOPIC: Visas
CONCEPTS: Time limit. Visa abolition. Denial of admission. Visas. Conformity with municipal law. Fees and exemptions.
PARTIES:
Canada
France

103197 Bilateral Exchange **230 UNTS 371**
SIGNED: 29 Sep 50 FORCE: 29 Sep 50
REGISTERED: 27 Mar 56 Canada
ARTICLES: 2 LANGUAGE: English. Russian.
HEADNOTE: PAYMENT SUPPLIES
TOPIC: Claims and Debts
CONCEPTS: Accounting procedures. Interest rates. Payment schedules. Payment for war supplies. Post-war claims settlement.
PARTIES:
Canada
USSR (Soviet Union)

103198 Bilateral Exchange **231 UNTS 3**
SIGNED: 11 Oct 50 FORCE: 11 Oct 50
REGISTERED: 27 Mar 56 Canada
ARTICLES: 2 LANGUAGE: English. Spanish.
HEADNOTE: MODUS VIVENDI TRADE RELATIONS
TOPIC: General Economic
CONCEPTS: Exceptions and exemptions. General cooperation. Reciprocity in trade. Exchange rates and regulations. Quotas. Most favored nation clause. General transportation.
PROCEDURE: Denunciation. Duration.
PARTIES:
Canada
Venezuela
ANNEX
399 UNTS 274. Venezuela. Prolongation 15 Oct 59. Force 15 Oct 59.
399 UNTS 274. Canada. Prolongation 17 Sep 54. Force 11 Oct 54.
399 UNTS 274. Canada. Prolongation 8 Oct 52. Force 8 Oct 52.
399 UNTS 274. Venezuela. Prolongation 8 Oct 52. Force 8 Oct 52.
399 UNTS 274. Venezuela. Prolongation 9 Oct 63. Force 9 Oct 53.
399 UNTS 274. Venezuela. Prolongation 10 Oct 58. Force 10 Oct 58.
399 UNTS 274. Canada. Prolongation 10 Oct 58. Force 10 Oct 58.
399 UNTS 274. Canada. Prolongation 30 Sep 53. Force 9 Oct 53.
399 UNTS 274. Venezuela. Prolongation 11 Oct 54. Force 11 Oct 54.
399 UNTS 274. Canada. Prolongation 19 Sep 55. Force 11 Oct 55.
399 UNTS 274. Venezuela. Prolongation 29 Sep 56. Force 29 Sep 56.
399 UNTS 274. Canada. Prolongation 13 Sep 56. Force 29 Sep 56.
399 UNTS 274. Canada. Prolongation 1 Oct 57. Force 11 Oct 57.
399 UNTS 274. Venezuela. Prolongation 11 Oct 57. Force 11 Oct 57.
399 UNTS 274. Canada. Prolongation 10 Oct 60. Force 10 Oct 60.
399 UNTS 274. Canada. Prolongation 10 Oct 59. Force 15 Oct 59.
399 UNTS 274. Venezuela. Prolongation 10 Oct 60. Force 10 Oct 60.

399 UNTS 274. Venezuela. Prolongation 11 Oct 55. Force 11 Oct 55.

103199 Bilateral Exchange **231 UNTS 15**
SIGNED: 10 Nov 50 FORCE: 1 Dec 50
REGISTERED: 27 Mar 56 Canada
ARTICLES: 2 LANGUAGE: English. Spanish.
HEADNOTE: MODUS VIVENDI TRADE RELATIONS
TOPIC: General Economic
CONCEPTS: Exceptions and exemptions. Treaty violation. Reciprocity in trade. Trade procedures. Payment schedules. Most favored nation clause. Temporary importation. General transportation.
PROCEDURE: Denunciation. Duration.
PARTIES:
Canada
Ecuador

103200 Bilateral Exchange **231 UNTS 25**
SIGNED: 18 Nov 50 FORCE: 26 Jan 51
REGISTERED: 27 Mar 56 Canada
ARTICLES: 2 LANGUAGE: English. Spanish.
HEADNOTE: MODUS VIVENDI TRADE RELATIONS
TOPIC: General Economic
CONCEPTS: General cooperation. Reciprocity in trade. Most favored nation clause. General transportation.
PROCEDURE: Denunciation. Termination.
PARTIES:
Canada
Costa Rica

103201 Bilateral Exchange **231 UNTS 37**
SIGNED: 30 Jun 49 FORCE: 1 Jul 49
REGISTERED: 27 Mar 56 Canada
ARTICLES: 2 LANGUAGE: English.
HEADNOTE: VISA REQUIREMENTS
TOPIC: Visas
CONCEPTS: Time limit. Visa abolition. Denial of admission. Visas. Conformity with municipal law. Fees and exemptions.
PARTIES:
Canada
Sweden
ANNEX
392 UNTS 354. Canada. Amendment 14 Jul 58. Force 14 Jul 58.
392 UNTS 354. Sweden. Amendment 14 Jul 58. Force 14 Jul 58.

103202 Bilateral Exchange **231 UNTS 43**
SIGNED: 6 Aug 49 FORCE: 6 Aug 49
REGISTERED: 27 Mar 56 Canada
ARTICLES: 2 LANGUAGE: English. Spanish.
HEADNOTE: DOUBLE TAXATION PROFITS SEA SIR TRANSPORT
TOPIC: Taxation
CONCEPTS: Definition of terms. Domestic legislation. Taxation. Tax exemptions. Air transport. Merchant vessels.
PARTIES:
Argentina
Canada

103203 Bilateral Exchange **231 UNTS 51**
SIGNED: 26 Nov 49 FORCE: 1 Dec 49
REGISTERED: 27 Mar 56 Canada
ARTICLES: 2 LANGUAGE: French.
HEADNOTE: VISA REQUIREMENTS
TOPIC: Visas
CONCEPTS: Time limit. Visa abolition. Denial of admission. Visas. Conformity with municipal law. Fees and exemptions.
PARTIES:
Canada
Luxembourg

103204 Bilateral Exchange **231 UNTS 57**
SIGNED: 28 Feb 49 FORCE: 30 Mar 49
REGISTERED: 27 Mar 56 Canada
ARTICLES: 2 LANGUAGE: English. French.
HEADNOTE: ISSUANCE TEMPORARY VISAS
TOPIC: Visas
CONCEPTS: Exceptions and exemptions. Time limit. Visas.
PARTIES:
Canada
Turkey

103205 Bilateral Exchange **231 UNTS 63**
SIGNED: 15 Mar 48 FORCE: 15 Mar 48
REGISTERED: 27 Mar 56 Canada
ARTICLES: 2 LANGUAGE: English.
HEADNOTE: MODUS VIVENDI TRADE RELATIONS
TOPIC: General Economic
CONCEPTS: Exceptions and exemptions. Reciprocity in trade. Customs duties.
PROCEDURE: Duration. Termination.
PARTIES:
Canada
Turkey

103206 Bilateral Exchange **231 UNTS 69**
SIGNED: 28 Apr 48 FORCE: 28 Apr 48
REGISTERED: 27 Mar 56 Canada
ARTICLES: 2 LANGUAGE: English.
HEADNOTE: MODUS VIVENDI TRADE RELATIONS
TOPIC: General Economic
CONCEPTS: Exceptions and exemptions. Previous treaty extension. Reciprocity in trade. Most favored nation clause. Customs duties.
TREATY REF: 20FEB48; 27FEB48 AGREEMENT- &NOTES.
PROCEDURE: Duration. Termination.
PARTIES:
Canada
Italy

103207 Bilateral Exchange **231 UNTS 75**
SIGNED: 17 Nov 48 FORCE: 17 Nov 48
REGISTERED: 27 Mar 56 Canada
ARTICLES: 2 LANGUAGE: English.
HEADNOTE: TRADE
TOPIC: General Trade
CONCEPTS: Most favored nation clause.
PROCEDURE: Duration. Termination.
PARTIES:
Canada
Finland

103208 Bilateral Exchange **231 UNTS 81**
SIGNED: 5 May 47 FORCE: 5 May 47
REGISTERED: 27 Mar 56 Canada
ARTICLES: 2 LANGUAGE: French.
HEADNOTE: WAR DAMAGE COMPENSATION
TOPIC: Reparations
CONCEPTS: National treatment. Loss and/or damage. Post-war claims settlement.
PARTIES:
Canada
France

103209 Bilateral Agreement **231 UNTS 87**
SIGNED: 5 May 48 FORCE: 2 Aug 49
REGISTERED: 27 Mar 56 Canada
ARTICLES: 11 LANGUAGE: English. French.
HEADNOTE: RESTORATION INDUSTRIAL PROPERTY RIGHTS
TOPIC: Reparations
CONCEPTS: Time limit. Treaty implementation. Conformity with municipal law. General property. Fees and exemptions. Post-war adjustment. Post-war claims settlement.
TREATY REF: 1UNTS269.
PARTIES:
Canada
France

103210 Bilateral Exchange **231 UNTS 95**
SIGNED: 28 Oct 48 FORCE: 28 Oct 48
REGISTERED: 27 Mar 56 Canada
ARTICLES: 2 LANGUAGE: English.
HEADNOTE: TRANSFER ARMY STORES
TOPIC: Reparations
CONCEPTS: Surplus war property. Post-war claims settlement.
PARTIES:
Canada
Netherlands

103211 Bilateral Exchange **231 UNTS 101**
SIGNED: 10 Dec 55 FORCE: 10 Dec 55
REGISTERED: 6 Apr 56 Belgium
ARTICLES: 2 LANGUAGE: French.
HEADNOTE: DOUBLE TAXATION AIR TRANSPORT
TOPIC: Taxation

CONCEPTS: Definition of terms. Taxation. Tax exemptions. Air transport.
PARTIES:
Belgium
France

103212 Bilateral Exchange **231 UNTS 108**
SIGNED: 21 Feb 49 FORCE: 4 Mar 49
REGISTERED: 6 Apr 56 USA (United States)
ARTICLES: 2 LANGUAGE: English. Spanish.
HEADNOTE: VISITS NAVAL VESSELS
TOPIC: Status of Forces
CONCEPTS: Annex or appendix reference. Naval vessels. Status of military forces.
PROCEDURE: Duration. Termination.
PARTIES:
Cuba
USA (United States)

103213 Bilateral Exchange **231 UNTS 145**
SIGNED: 12 Nov 52 FORCE: 12 Nov 52
REGISTERED: 6 Apr 56 USA (United States)
ARTICLES: 2 LANGUAGE: English.
HEADNOTE: FREE ENTRY PRIVILEGES FOREIGN SERVICE PERSONNEL
TOPIC: Visas
CONCEPTS: Diplomatic privileges.
PARTIES:
USA (United States)
Uruguay

103214 Bilateral Exchange **231 UNTS 151**
SIGNED: 2 Jun 53 FORCE: 2 Jun 53
REGISTERED: 6 Apr 56 USA (United States)
ARTICLES: 2 LANGUAGE: English.
HEADNOTE: FRIENDSHIP COMMERCE CONSULAR RIGHTS
TOPIC: General Amity
CONCEPTS: Friendship and amity. General consular functions. General trade.
PARTIES:
Germany, West
USA (United States)

103215 Bilateral Exchange **231 UNTS 157**
SIGNED: 7 May 54 FORCE: 7 May 54
REGISTERED: 6 Apr 56 USA (United States)
ARTICLES: 2 LANGUAGE: English.
HEADNOTE: FACILITIES ASSISTANCE MUTUAL DEFENSE
TOPIC: Milit Assistance
CONCEPTS: Change of circumstances. Use of facilities. Expense sharing formulae. Assistance. Materials, equipment and services. Defense and security. Military assistance. Equipment and supplies.
TREATY REF: 80UNTS241; 179UNTS185.
PROCEDURE: Future Procedures Contemplated.
PARTIES:
Norway
USA (United States)

103216 Bilateral Exchange **231 UNTS 165**
SIGNED: 14 May 54 FORCE: 14 May 54
REGISTERED: 6 Apr 56 USA (United States)
ARTICLES: 2 LANGUAGE: English. Chinese.
HEADNOTE: LOAN VESSELS SMALL CRAFT
TOPIC: Milit Installation
CONCEPTS: Time limit. Annex or appendix reference. Responsibility and liability. Title and deeds. Compensation. Delivery schedules. Lease of military property. Naval vessels. Return of equipment and recapture. Restrictions on transfer.
TREATY REF: 132UNTS273.
PARTIES:
Taiwan
USA (United States)
ANNEX
251 UNTS 399. USA (United States). Amendment 22 Mar 55. Force 31 Mar 55.
251 UNTS 399. Taiwan. Amendment 31 Mar 55. Force 31 Mar 55.
265 UNTS 406. USA (United States). Amendment 18 Jun 55. Force 18 Jun 55.
265 UNTS 406. Taiwan. Amendment 18 Jun 55. Force 18 Jun 55.
280 UNTS 373. Taiwan. Amendment 20 Oct 56. Force 20 Oct 56.

280 UNTS 373. USA (United States). Amendment 16 Oct 56. Force 20 Oct 56.
284 UNTS 380. Taiwan. Amendment 16 May 57. Force 16 May 57.
284 UNTS 380. USA (United States). Amendment 16 May 57. Force 16 May 57.
393 UNTS 320. Taiwan. Amendment 12 Oct 60. Force 12 Oct 60.
393 UNTS 320. USA (United States). Amendment 12 Oct 60. Force 12 Oct 60.
542 UNTS 361. Taiwan. Prolongation 23 Feb 65. Force 23 Feb 65.
542 UNTS 361. USA (United States). Prolongation 23 Feb 65. Force 23 Feb 65.

103217 Unilateral Instrument **231 UNTS 175**
SIGNED: 22 Feb 56 FORCE: 14 Dec 55
REGISTERED: 9 Apr 56 United Nations
ARTICLES: 1 LANGUAGE: Italian.
HEADNOTE: ACCEPTANCE OBLIGATIONS UN
TOPIC: UN Charter
CONCEPTS: Acceptance of obligations upon admittance to UN.
INTL ORGS: United Nations.
PARTIES:
Italy

103218 Bilateral Exchange **231 UNTS 179**
SIGNED: 22 Dec 55 FORCE: 22 Dec 55
REGISTERED: 11 Apr 56 UK Great Britain
ARTICLES: 2 LANGUAGE: English.
HEADNOTE: DEBT REPAYMENT
TOPIC: Claims and Debts
CONCEPTS: Debt settlement. Refinance of loan.
INTL ORGS: European Payments Union.
PARTIES:
Sweden
UK Great Britain

103219 Bilateral Exchange **231 UNTS 185**
SIGNED: 15 Nov 55 FORCE: 15 Nov 55
REGISTERED: 11 Apr 56 UK Great Britain
ARTICLES: 2 LANGUAGE: English.
HEADNOTE: CONSTRUCTION OPERATION WEATHER STATION
TOPIC: Scientific Project
CONCEPTS: Conditions. Conformity with municipal law. Exchange of information and documents. Research and scientific projects. Meteorology. Research results. Special projects. Bands and frequency allocation. Facilities and equipment. Jurisdiction.
PARTIES:
UK Great Britain
USA (United States)

103220 Bilateral Exchange **231 UNTS 193**
SIGNED: 14 Oct 55 FORCE: 14 Oct 55
REGISTERED: 11 Apr 56 UK Great Britain
ARTICLES: 2 LANGUAGE: English. French.
HEADNOTE: PROTECTION TRADEMARKS
TOPIC: Patents/Copyrights
CONCEPTS: Definition of terms. Conformity with municipal law. Trademarks.
PROCEDURE: Duration. Termination.
PARTIES:
UK Great Britain
Vietnam, South

103221 Multilateral Convention **231 UNTS 199**
SIGNED: 5 Apr 46 FORCE: 5 Apr 53
REGISTERED: 11 Apr 56 UK Great Britain
ARTICLES: 18 LANGUAGE: English. French.
HEADNOTE: REGULATION FISHING NETS SIZE LIMITS FISH
TOPIC: Specific Resources
CONCEPTS: Definition of terms. Territorial application. Annex or appendix reference. Previous treaty replacement. Establishment of commission. Headquarters and facilities. Internal structure. Ocean resources. Fisheries and fishing.
INTL ORGS: Special Commission.
TREATY REF: 3'38DEMARTENS822;.
PROCEDURE: Accession. Denunciation. Ratification. Registration.
PARTIES:
Belgium SIGNED: 5 Apr 46 RATIFIED: 9 May 51 FORCE: 5 Apr 53

Denmark SIGNED: 5 Apr 46 RATIFIED: 11 Apr 47 FORCE: 5 Apr 53
France SIGNED: 5 Apr 46 RATIFIED: 19 Jan 49 FORCE: 5 Apr 53
Germany, West RATIFIED: 11 Jun 54 FORCE: 11 Jun 54
Iceland SIGNED: 5 Apr 46 RATIFIED: 7 Sep 51 FORCE: 5 Apr 53
Ireland SIGNED: 5 Apr 46 RATIFIED: 2 Jan 50 FORCE: 5 Apr 53
Netherlands SIGNED: 5 Apr 46 RATIFIED: 10 Jan 48 FORCE: 5 Apr 53
Norway SIGNED: 5 Apr 46 RATIFIED: 21 Jul 47 FORCE: 5 Apr 53
Poland SIGNED: 5 Apr 46 RATIFIED: 22 Jan 47 FORCE: 5 Apr 53
Portugal SIGNED: 5 Apr 46 RATIFIED: 11 Jul 50 FORCE: 5 Apr 53
Spain SIGNED: 5 Apr 46 RATIFIED: 5 Feb 53 FORCE: 5 Apr 53
Sweden SIGNED: 5 Apr 46 RATIFIED: 7 Aug 46 FORCE: 5 Apr 53
UK Great Britain SIGNED: 5 Apr 46 RATIFIED: 1 Jul 46 FORCE: 5 Apr 53
ANNEX
354 UNTS 408. USSR (Soviet Union). Accession 12 Mar 58.
354 UNTS 408. NE Atlantic Fish. Amendment 1 Nov 58. Force 30 Jan 59.
431 UNTS 304. NE Atlantic Fish. Amendment 6 May 60.
456 UNTS 496. NE Atlantic Fish. Amendment 11 May 62. Force 11 May 62.
482 UNTS 372. NE Atlantic Fish. Amendment 10 May 63. Force 1 Jun 63.

103222 Bilateral Agreement **231 UNTS 219**
SIGNED: 12 Mar 48 FORCE: 30 Jun 48
REGISTERED: 11 Apr 56 ICAO (Civil Aviat)
ARTICLES: 18 LANGUAGE: English.
HEADNOTE: DOUBLE TAXATION FISCAL EVASION TAXES INCOME
TOPIC: Taxation
CONCEPTS: Definition of terms. Territorial application. Previous treaty replacement. Conformity with municipal law. Exchange of official publications. Teacher and student exchange. Taxation. Tax credits. General. Tax exemptions. Air transport. Merchant vessels.
TREATY REF: NOV3,1945 AGREEMENT BETWEEN CANADA&NEWZEA.
PROCEDURE: Duration. Termination.
PARTIES:
Canada
New Zealand

103223 Bilateral Agreement **231 UNTS 241**
SIGNED: 24 Jan 49 FORCE: 31 May 50
REGISTERED: 11 Apr 56 ICAO (Civil Aviat)
ARTICLES: 12 LANGUAGE: French.
HEADNOTE: AIR TRANSPORT
TOPIC: Air Transport
CONCEPTS: Annex or appendix reference. Conformity with municipal law. Domestic legislation. Licenses and permits. Recognition of legal documents. Use of facilities. Arbitration. Procedure. Negotiation. Reexport of goods, etc.. Fees and exemptions. Most favored nation clause. National treatment. Customs exemptions. Competency certificate. Routes and logistics. Navigational conditions. Permit designation. Air transport. Airport facilities. Airworthiness certificates. Conditions of airlines operating permission. Operating authorizations and regulations. Licenses and certificates of nationality.
INTL ORGS: International Civil Aviation Organization. International Court of Justice.
PROCEDURE: Amendment. Denunciation. Future Procedures Contemplated. Ratification. Registration.
PARTIES:
Italy
Lebanon
ANNEX
497 UNTS 344. Lebanon. Amendment 13 Feb 60. Force 11 Jun 60.
497 UNTS 344. Italy. Amendment 13 Feb 60. Force 11 Jun 60.

103224 Bilateral Agreement **231 UNTS 251**
SIGNED: 31 May 49 FORCE: 14 Apr 53

REGISTERED: 11 Apr 56 ICAO (Civil Aviat)
ARTICLES: 35 LANGUAGE: Italian. Spanish.
HEADNOTE: CIVIL AIR SERVICES
TOPIC: Air Transport
CONCEPTS: Conditions. Definition of terms. Detailed regulations. Exceptions and exemptions. Annex or appendix reference. Previous treaty replacement. Friendship and amity. Non-visa travel documents. Conformity with municipal law. General cooperation. Exchange of information and documents. Licenses and permits. Personnel. Recognition of legal documents. Use of facilities. Investigation of violations. Arbitration. Procedure. Reexport of goods, etc.. Compensation. Non-interest rates and fees. Income taxes. Customs duties. Customs exemptions. Competency certificate. Routes and logistics. Navigational conditions. Permit designation. Transport of goods. Airport facilities. Airworthiness certificates. Conditions of airlines operating permission. Overflights and technical stops. Operating authorizations and regulations. Licenses and certificates of nationality. Postal services.
PROCEDURE: Amendment. Ratification. Termination. Application to Non-self-governing Territories.
PARTIES:
Italy
Spain

103225 Bilateral Agreement **231 UNTS 301**
SIGNED: 8 Mar 52   FORCE: 25 Nov 53
REGISTERED: 11 Apr 56 ICAO (Civil Aviat)
ARTICLES: 11 LANGUAGE: English. French.
HEADNOTE: RELATING AIR SERVICES
TOPIC: Air Transport
CONCEPTS: Air transport.
INTL ORGS: International Civil Aviation Organization.
TREATY REF: 15UNTS295.
PARTIES:
Philippines
Switzerland
ANNEX
412 UNTS 334.   Switzerland.   Amendment 28 May 58. Force 10 Jun 57.
412 UNTS 334.   Philippines.   Amendment 28 May 58. Force 10 Jun 57.

103226 Bilateral Agreement **232 UNTS 3**
SIGNED: 19 Nov 52   FORCE: 13 May 55
REGISTERED: 11 Apr 56 ICAO (Civil Aviat)
ARTICLES: 13 LANGUAGE: French. Hebrew.
HEADNOTE: RELATING AIR SERVICES
TOPIC: Air Transport
CONCEPTS: Definition of terms. Detailed regulations. Annex or appendix reference. Conformity with municipal law. General cooperation. Exchange of information and documents. Licenses and permits. Recognition of legal documents. Use of facilities. Arbitration. Procedure. Special tribunals. Negotiation. Indemnities and reimbursements. Fees and exemptions. Non-interest rates and fees. Most favored nation clause. National treatment. Customs exemptions. Competency certificate. Routes and logistics. Navigational conditions. Permit designation. Air transport. Airport facilities. Airworthiness certificates. Conditions of airlines operating permission. Operating authorizations and regulations. Licenses and certificates of nationality.
INTL ORGS: International Court of Justice. Inter-Governmental Maritime Consultative Organization. Arbitration Commission.
TREATY REF: 15UNTS295.
PROCEDURE: Future Procedures Contemplated. Ratification. Registration. Termination.
PARTIES:
Israel
Switzerland
ANNEX
602 UNTS 310.   Israel.   Modification 22 Jul 65. Force 22 Jul 65.
602 UNTS 310.   Switzerland.   Modification 22 Jul 65. Force 22 Jul 65.

103227 Bilateral Agreement **232 UNTS 25**
SIGNED: 18 Nov 51   FORCE: 26 Apr 55
REGISTERED: 11 Apr 56 ICAO (Civil Aviat)
ARTICLES: 12 LANGUAGE: English. Arabic.
HEADNOTE: AIR TRANSPORT SERVICES

TOPIC: Air Transport
CONCEPTS: Annex or appendix reference. Conformity with municipal law. Licenses and permits. Recognition of legal documents. Use of facilities. Arbitration. Procedure. Existing tribunals. Fees and exemptions. Most favored nation clause. National treatment. Customs exemptions. Competency certificate. Routes and logistics. Navigational conditions. Permit designation. Air transport. Airport facilities. Airworthiness certificates. Conditions of airlines operating permission. Licenses and certificates of nationality.
INTL ORGS: Inter-Governmental Maritime Consultative Organization.
TREATY REF: 15UNTS295.
PROCEDURE: Amendment. Future Procedures Contemplated. Ratification. Registration. Termination.
PARTIES:
Denmark
Iraq

103228 Bilateral Agreement **232 UNTS 45**
SIGNED: 28 May 53   FORCE: 17 May 55
REGISTERED: 11 Apr 56 ICAO (Civil Aviat)
ARTICLES: 15 LANGUAGE: French.
HEADNOTE: AIR SERVICES
TOPIC: Air Transport
CONCEPTS: Annex or appendix reference. Conformity with municipal law. General cooperation. Informational records. Licenses and permits. Recognition of legal documents. Use of facilities. Arbitration. Procedure. Special tribunals. Competence of tribunal. Humanitarian matters. Indemnities and reimbursements. Fees and exemptions. Non-interest rates and fees. Most favored nation clause. National treatment. Customs duties. Customs exemptions. Competency certificate. Registration certificate. Routes and logistics. Navigational conditions. Permit designation. Airport facilities. Airworthiness certificates. Conditions of airlines operating permission. Operating authorizations and regulations. Licenses and certificates of nationality.
INTL ORGS: Inter-Governmental Maritime Consultative Organization. Arbitration Commission.
PROCEDURE: Amendment. Future Procedures Contemplated. Ratification. Termination.
PARTIES:
Switzerland
Yugoslavia
ANNEX
563 UNTS 358.   Switzerland.   Amendment 14 Dec 62. Force 14 Dec 62.
563 UNTS 358.   Yugoslavia.   Amendment 14 Dec 62. Force 14 Dec 62.

103229 Bilateral Exchange **232 UNTS 59**
SIGNED: 12 Aug 53   FORCE: 12 Aug 53
REGISTERED: 11 Apr 56 ICAO (Civil Aviat)
ARTICLES: 2 LANGUAGE: French.
HEADNOTE: EXEMPTION CUSTOMS DUTIES
TOPIC: Customs
CONCEPTS: Customs exemptions. Airport equipment.
PARTIES:
Sweden
Switzerland

103230 Bilateral Agreement **232 UNTS 65**
SIGNED: 31 Mar 54   FORCE: 22 Dec 55
REGISTERED: 11 Apr 56 ICAO (Civil Aviat)
ARTICLES: 17 LANGUAGE: Spanish.
HEADNOTE: AIR SERVICES
TOPIC: Air Transport
CONCEPTS: Definition of terms. Annex or appendix reference. Friendship and amity. Non-visa travel documents. Conformity with municipal law. Domestic legislation. Licenses and permits. Personnel. Recognition of legal documents. Use of facilities. Arbitration. Procedure. Existing tribunals. Special tribunals. Negotiation. Fees and exemptions. Most favored nation clause. National treatment. Customs exemptions. Competency certificate. Routes and logistics. Navigational conditions. Permit designation. Air transport. Airport facilities. Airworthiness certificates. Conditions of airlines operating permission. Operating authorizations and regulations. Licenses and certificates of nationality. Postal services.

INTL ORGS: Inter-Governmental Maritime Consultative Organization. Arbitration Commission.
TREATY REF: 15UNTS295.
PROCEDURE: Amendment. Future Procedures Contemplated. Ratification. Registration. Termination.
PARTIES:
Peru
Spain

103231 Bilateral Agreement **232 UNTS 91**
SIGNED: 27 Jul 54   FORCE: 28 Feb 55
REGISTERED: 11 Apr 56 ICAO (Civil Aviat)
ARTICLES: 10 LANGUAGE: English. French.
HEADNOTE: RESPECT AERIAL TRANSPORT BETWEEN RESPECTIVE TERRITORIES
TOPIC: Air Transport
CONCEPTS: Detailed regulations. Annex or appendix reference. Conformity with municipal law. General cooperation. Licenses and permits. Recognition of legal documents. Use of facilities. Arbitration. Procedure. Existing tribunals. Negotiation. Fees and exemptions. Non-interest rates and fees. Most favored nation clause. National treatment. Customs exemptions. Competency certificate. Routes and logistics. Navigational conditions. Permit designation. Air transport. Airport facilities. Airworthiness certificates. Conditions of airlines operating permission. Operating authorizations and regulations. Licenses and certificates of nationality.
INTL ORGS: Inter-Governmental Maritime Consultative Organization.
TREATY REF: 15UNTS295.
PROCEDURE: Future Procedures Contemplated. Ratification. Registration. Termination.
PARTIES:
Ireland
Luxembourg
ANNEX
327 UNTS 375. Ireland. Amendment 30 Sep 57. Force 19 Oct 57.
327 UNTS 375.   Luxembourg.   Amendment 19 Oct 57. Force 19 Oct 57.

103232 Bilateral Exchange **232 UNTS 103**
SIGNED: 26 Oct 54   FORCE: 26 May 55
REGISTERED: 11 Apr 56 ICAO (Civil Aviat)
ARTICLES: 2 LANGUAGE: Dutch. Spanish.
HEADNOTE: AIR SERVICES
TOPIC: Air Transport
CONCEPTS: Conditions. Detailed regulations. Exceptions and exemptions. Previous treaty replacement. Conformity with municipal law. Procedure. Non-interest rates and fees. Routes and logistics. Operating authorizations and regulations.
PROCEDURE: Amendment. Termination.
PARTIES:
Netherlands
Venezuela

103233 Bilateral Agreement **232 UNTS 115**
SIGNED: 14 Dec 54   FORCE: 6 Mar 56
REGISTERED: 11 Apr 56 ICAO (Civil Aviat)
ARTICLES: 12 LANGUAGE: Dutch. Spanish.
HEADNOTE: AIR TRANSPORT
TOPIC: Air Transport
CONCEPTS: Definition of terms. Annex or appendix reference. Conformity with municipal law. Licenses and permits. Recognition of legal documents. Use of facilities. Arbitration. Procedure. Existing tribunals. Reexport of goods, etc.. Fees and exemptions. Most favored nation clause. National treatment. Customs exemptions. Competency certificate. Routes and logistics. Navigational conditions. Permit designation. Air transport. Airport facilities. Airworthiness certificates. Conditions of airlines operating permission. Operating authorizations and regulations. Licenses and certificates of nationality.
INTL ORGS: International Court of Justice. Inter-Governmental Maritime Consultative Organization.
TREATY REF: 15UNTS295.
PROCEDURE: Ratification. Registration. Termination.
PARTIES:
Ecuador
Netherlands

103234 Bilateral Agreement **232 UNTS 143**
SIGNED: 4 Nov 55   FORCE: 29 Jul 52
REGISTERED: 11 Apr 56 ICAO (Civil Aviat)
ARTICLES: 12 LANGUAGE: English. Afrikaans.
HEADNOTE: RELATING AIR SERVICES BETWEEN
RESPECTIVE TERRITORIES
TOPIC: Air Transport
CONCEPTS: Definition of terms. Detailed regula-
tions. Exchange of information and documents.
Non-interest rates and fees. Routes and logistics.
Permit designation. Air transport. Conditions of
airlines operating permission. Operating authori-
zations and regulations.
PROCEDURE: Termination. Application to Non-
self-governing Territories.
PARTIES:
Australia
South Africa

103235 Bilateral Agreement **232 UNTS 153**
SIGNED: 17 Nov 55   FORCE: 17 Nov 55
REGISTERED: 11 Apr 56 ICAO (Civil Aviat)
ARTICLES: 12 LANGUAGE: English.
HEADNOTE: AIR TRANSPORT
TOPIC: Air Transport
CONCEPTS: Definition of terms. Annex or appen-
dix reference. Non-visa travel documents. Conformity with municipal law. General cooperation.
Licenses and permits. Recognition of legal documents. Use of facilities. Arbitration. Procedure.
Special tribunals. Negotiation. Reexport of
goods, etc.. Indemnities and reimbursements.
Fees and exemptions. Non-interest rates and
fees. Most favored nation clause. National treatment. Customs exemptions. Competency certificate. Routes and logistics. Navigational conditions. Permit designation. Air transport. Airport
facilities. Airworthiness certificates. Conditions
of airlines operating permission. Operating authorizations and regulations. Licenses and certificates of nationality.
INTL ORGS: Inter-Governmental Maritime Consultative Organization. Arbitration Commission.
TREATY REF: 15UNTS295.
PROCEDURE: Amendment. Future Procedures
Contemplated. Registration. Termination.
PARTIES:
Austria
Israel

103236 Bilateral Agreement **232 UNTS 169**
SIGNED: 8 Mar 54   FORCE: 1 May 54
REGISTERED: 11 Apr 56 USA (United States)
ARTICLES: 11 LANGUAGE: English. Japanese.
HEADNOTE: MUTUAL DEFENSE ASSISTANCE
TOPIC: Milit Assistance
CONCEPTS: Guarantees and safeguards. Annex or
appendix reference. Non-prejudice to UN charter. Privileges and immunities. Conformity with
municipal law. General cooperation. Inspection
and observation. Public information. Use of facilities. Export quotas. Indemnities and reimbursements. Garnishment of funds. Local currency.
Tax exemptions. Customs exemptions. Domestic
obligation. Materials, equipment and services.
Aid missions. Joint defense. Defense and security. Military assistance. Return of equipment and
recapture. Security of information. Military assistance missions. Exchange of defense information. Restrictions on transfer. Raw materials.
TREATY REF: 136UNTS45; 136UNTS211.
PROCEDURE: Amendment. Future Procedures
Contemplated. Ratification. Registration. Termination.
PARTIES:
Japan
USA (United States)
ANNEX
251 UNTS 404. USA (United States). Implementation 7 Jan 55. Force 7 Jan 55.
251 UNTS 404. Japan. Implementation 7 Jan 55.
Force 7 Jan 55.
265 UNTS 411. USA (United States). Supplementation 12 Jul 55. Force 12 Jul 55.
265 UNTS 411. Japan. Supplementation
12 Jul 55. Force 12 Jul 55.
272 UNTS 300. Japan. Amendment 3 Feb 56.
Force 3 Feb 56.
272 UNTS 300. USA (United States). Amendment
12 Jul 55. Force 3 Feb 56.
273 UNTS 288. USA (United States). Amendment
13 Apr 56. Force 13 Apr 56.

273 UNTS 288. Japan. Amendment 13 Apr 56.
Force 13 Apr 56.
283 UNTS 316. USA (United States). Amendment
19 Apr 57. Force 19 Apr 57.
283 UNTS 316. Japan. Amendment 19 Apr 57.
Force 19 Apr 57.
303 UNTS 348. USA (United States). Interpretation 25 Nov 57. Force 25 Nov 57.
303 UNTS 348. Japan. Interpretation 25 Nov 57.
Force 25 Nov 57.
316 UNTS 351. USA (United States). Supplementation 2 May 58. Force 2 May 58.
316 UNTS 351. Japan. Supplementation
2 May 58. Force 2 May 58.
357 UNTS 379. Japan. Implementation
11 Aug 59. Force 11 Aug 59.
357 UNTS 379. USA (United States). Implementation 11 Aug 59. Force 11 Aug 59.
388 UNTS 366. USA (United States). Supplementation 9 Aug 60. Force 9 Aug 60.
388 UNTS 366. Japan. Supplementation
9 Aug 60. Force 9 Aug 60.
434 UNTS 300. Japan. Supplementation
31 Oct 61. Force 31 Oct 61.
434 UNTS 300. USA (United States). Supplementation 31 Oct 61. Force 31 Oct 61.
461 UNTS 318. Japan. Supplementation
19 Oct 62. Force 19 Oct 62.
461 UNTS 318. USA (United States). Supplementation 19 Oct 62. Force 19 Oct 62.
487 UNTS 341. Japan. Supplementation
19 Jul 63. Force 19 Jul 63.
487 UNTS 341. USA (United States). Supplementation 19 Jul 63. Force 19 Jul 63.
529 UNTS 337. Japan. Implementation 9 Jul 64.
Force 9 Jul 64.
529 UNTS 337. USA (United States). Implementation 9 Jun 64. Force 9 Jul 64.
545 UNTS 332. USA (United States). Amendment
23 Apr 65. Force 23 Apr 65.
545 UNTS 332. Japan. Amendment 23 Apr 65.
Force 23 Apr 65.

103237 Bilateral Instrument **232 UNTS 215**
SIGNED: 8 Mar 54   FORCE: 1 May 54
REGISTERED: 11 Apr 56 USA (United States)
ARTICLES: 5 LANGUAGE: English. Japanese.
HEADNOTE: RETURN EQUIPMENT
TOPIC: Milit Assistance
CONCEPTS: General cooperation. Reexport of
goods, etc.. Delivery schedules. Surplus prop-
erty. Return of equipment and recapture.
TREATY REF: 232UNTS169.
PARTIES:
Japan
USA (United States)

103238 Bilateral Agreement **232 UNTS 227**
SIGNED: 8 Mar 54   FORCE: 1 May 54
REGISTERED: 11 Apr 56 USA (United States)
ARTICLES: 7 LANGUAGE: English. Japanese.
HEADNOTE: AGRI COMMOD
TOPIC: Direct Aid
CONCEPTS: Treaty implementation. Annex or ap-
pendix reference. Conformity with municipal
law. General cooperation. Currency deposits. Ex-
change rates and regulations. Financial pro-
grams. Local currency. Commodities and ser-
vices. Defense and security.
PARTIES:
Japan
USA (United States)

103239 Bilateral Exchange **232 UNTS 243**
SIGNED: 8 Mar 54   FORCE: 8 Mar 54
REGISTERED: 11 Apr 56 USA (United States)
ARTICLES: 2 LANGUAGE: English. Japanese.
HEADNOTE: SURPLUS AGRI COMMOD
TOPIC: Direct Aid
CONCEPTS: Annex type material. Commodities
and services. General aid.
TREATY REF: 332UNTS227.
PARTIES:
Japan
USA (United States)

103240 Bilateral Agreement **232 UNTS 251**
SIGNED: 8 Mar 54   FORCE: 1 May 54
REGISTERED: 11 Apr 56 USA (United States)
ARTICLES: 3 LANGUAGE: English. Japanese.
HEADNOTE: GUARANTY INVESTMENTS
TOPIC: Claims and Debts
CONCEPTS: Arbitration. Procedure. Existing tribu-
nals. Negotiation. Reciprocity in financial treat-

ment. Currency. Claims and settlements. Private
investment guarantee.
INTL ORGS: International Court of Justice.
PROCEDURE: Ratification.
PARTIES:
Japan
USA (United States)

103241 Bilateral Agreement **232 UNTS 267**
SIGNED: 8 Mar 54   FORCE: 1 May 54
REGISTERED: 11 Apr 56 USA (United States)
ARTICLES: 5 LANGUAGE: English. Japanese.
HEADNOTE: ECONOMIC ARRANGEMENTS
TOPIC: General Economic
CONCEPTS: Treaty implementation. Annex or ap-
pendix reference. Accounting procedures. Cur-
rency. Private investment guarantee. Assistance.
Economic assistance. Grants.
TREATY REF: 67STAT159; 232UNTS243;
62STAT144.
PARTIES:
Japan
USA (United States)

103242 Bilateral Exchange **232 UNTS 283**
SIGNED: 22 Jul 49   FORCE: 22 Jul 49
REGISTERED: 11 Apr 56 USA (United States)
ARTICLES: 2 LANGUAGE: English.
HEADNOTE: FREE ENTRY PRIVILEGES FOREIGN
SERVICE PERSONNEL
TOPIC: Visas
CONCEPTS: Diplomatic privileges.
PARTIES:
Liberia
USA (United States)

103243 Bilateral Exchange **232 UNTS 289**
SIGNED: 25 Mar 54   FORCE: 25 Mar 54
REGISTERED: 11 Apr 56 USA (United States)
ARTICLES: 2 LANGUAGE: English. Spanish.
HEADNOTE: SUMP-PUMP STATION COLON FREE
ZONE
TOPIC: Specific Property
CONCEPTS: Use of facilities. Indemnities and re-
imbursements. Materials, equipment and ser-
vices. Facilities and property.
PARTIES:
Panama
USA (United States)

103244 Bilateral Agreement **232 UNTS 299**
SIGNED: 21 Apr 54   FORCE: 21 Apr 54
REGISTERED: 11 Apr 56 USA (United States)
ARTICLES: 5 LANGUAGE: English.
HEADNOTE: SPECIAL TECHNICAL SERVICES
TOPIC: Tech Assistance
CONCEPTS: Treaty implementation. Annex type
material. Privileges and immunities. Exchange of
information and documents. Informational
records. Inspection and observation. Operating
agencies. Personnel. General property. Private
contracts. Indemnities and reimbursements. Ex-
pense sharing formulae. Tax exemptions. Cus-
toms exemptions. Special projects. Economic
assistance. Materials, equipment and services.
Aid missions.
TREATY REF: 148UNTS39.
PROCEDURE: Duration. Termination.
PARTIES:
Ethiopia
USA (United States)

103245 Bilateral Exchange **232 UNTS 311**
SIGNED: 1 Jun 54   FORCE: 1 Jun 54
REGISTERED: 11 Apr 56 USA (United States)
ARTICLES: 2 LANGUAGE: English.
HEADNOTE: TECHNICAL COOPERATION PRO-
GRAM EDUCATION
TOPIC: Direct Aid
CONCEPTS: Previous treaty extension. Informa-
tional records. Operating agencies. Title and
deeds. Attachment of funds. Exchange rates and
regulations. Funding procedures. Garnishment
of funds. Seizure funds. Assistance. Materials,
equipment and services.
INTL ORGS: International Monetary Fund.
TREATY REF: 184UNTS285; 212UNTS175.
PROCEDURE: Duration. Termination.

PARTIES:
Ethiopia
USA (United States)

103246   Bilateral Agreement   **233 UNTS 3**
SIGNED: 28 Jun 54   FORCE: 28 Jun 54
REGISTERED: 11 Apr 56 USA (United States)
ARTICLES: 13 LANGUAGE: English. Spanish.
HEADNOTE: COOPERATIVE HOUSING PROGRAM
TOPIC: Tech Assistance
CONCEPTS: Treaty implementation. Annex type
material. Privileges and immunities. Conformity
with municipal law. Exchange of information and
documents. Inspection and observation. Domes-
tic legislation. Operating agencies. Personnel.
Private contracts. Title and deeds. Indemnities
and reimbursements. Currency deposits. Ex-
change rates and regulations. Funding proce-
dures. Interest rates. Domestic obligation. Assistance. Materials, equipment and services.
PROCEDURE: Duration. Termination.
PARTIES:
Chile
USA (United States)

103247   Bilateral Instrument   **233 UNTS 23**
SIGNED: 7 Jul 54   FORCE: 7 Jul 54
REGISTERED: 11 Apr 56 USA (United States)
ARTICLES: 8 LANGUAGE: English. French.
HEADNOTE: DISPOSAL REDISTRIBUTABLE EX-
CESS PROPERTY
TOPIC: Milit Assistance
CONCEPTS: General cooperation. Reexport of
goods, etc.. Delivery schedules. Surplus prop-
erty. Return of equipment and recapture.
TREATY REF: 80UNTS187; 1801NTS191.
PARTIES:
Luxembourg
USA (United States)
ANNEX
393 UNTS 328.   Luxembourg.   Amendment
10 Jun 60. Force 10 Jun 60.
393 UNTS 328. USA (United States). Amendment
4 Mar 60. Force 10 Jun 60.

103248   Bilateral Exchange   **233 UNTS 31**
SIGNED: 17 Aug 54   FORCE: 18 Aug 54
REGISTERED: 11 Apr 56 USA (United States)
ARTICLES: 2 LANGUAGE: English.
HEADNOTE: INTERIM AGREEMENT SETTLEMENT
SURPLUS PROPERTY OBLIGATION
TOPIC: Direct Aid
CONCEPTS: Annex or appendix reference. Gen-
eral cooperation. Responsibility and liability.
Claims and settlements. Surplus property.
TREATY REF: 205UNTS103.
PARTIES:
Germany, West
USA (United States)

103249   Bilateral Protocol   **233 UNTS 39**
SIGNED: 23 Aug 55   FORCE: 23 Aug 55
REGISTERED: 12 Apr 56 Greece
ARTICLES: 1 LANGUAGE: Greek. Russian.
HEADNOTE: GOODS DELIVIERIES
TOPIC: General Trade
CONCEPTS: Annex or appendix reference. Ac-
counting procedures. Payment schedules.
Quotas.
PARTIES:
Greece
USSR (Soviet Union)

103250   Bilateral Agreement   **233 UNTS 49**
SIGNED: 4 Feb 54   FORCE: 17 Mar 56
REGISTERED: 12 Apr 56 WHO (World Health)
ARTICLES: 6 LANGUAGE: English. Portuguese.
HEADNOTE: TECHNICAL ADVISORY ASSISTANCE
TOPIC: Tech Assistance
CONCEPTS: Definition of terms. Treaty implemen-
tation. Privileges and immunities. General coop-
eration. Exchange of information and docu-
ments. Personnel. Title and deeds. Exchange.
Scholarships and grants. Vocational training. Re-
search and development. Expense sharing for-
mulae. Local currency. Domestic obligation.
Special projects. General aid. Materials, equipment and services. Conformity with IGO decisions.

INTL ORGS: United Nations.
TREATY   REF: 33UNTS261;   1UNTS15;
1UNTS263; 76UNTS132.
PROCEDURE: Amendment. Termination.
PARTIES:
Brazil
WHO (World Health)

103251   Bilateral Convention   **233 UNTS 65**
SIGNED: 26 Jan 51   FORCE: 26 Jan 51
REGISTERED: 12 Apr 56 Canada
ARTICLES: 5 LANGUAGE: French.
HEADNOTE: COMPENSATION NATIONALIZED
GAS ELECTRICITY
TOPIC: Claims and Debts
CONCEPTS: Annex or appendix reference. Expro-
priation. Arbitration. Procedure. Existing tribu-
nals. Negotiation. Compensation. Claims and
settlements. Specific claims or waivers.
PARTIES:
Canada
France

103252   Bilateral Exchange   **233 UNTS 95**
SIGNED: 9 Feb 51   FORCE: 10 Mar 51
REGISTERED: 12 Apr 56 Canada
ARTICLES: 2 LANGUAGE: French.
HEADNOTE: ISSUANCE MULTI-ENTRY VISAS DIP-
LOMATIC MISSIONS
TOPIC: Visas
CONCEPTS: Visas.
PARTIES:
Canada
Turkey

103253   Bilateral Exchange   **233 UNTS 101**
SIGNED: 4 Jul 51   FORCE: 4 Jul 51
REGISTERED: 12 Apr 56 Canada
ARTICLES: 2 LANGUAGE: English. French.
HEADNOTE: SETTLEMENT CLAIMS REQUISI-
TIONED VESSELS
TOPIC: Reparations
CONCEPTS: Definition of terms. General property.
Accounting procedures. Exchange rates and reg-
ulations. Local currency. Lump sum settlements.
Assets transfer. Naval vessels. Post-war claims
settlement.
INTL ORGS: International Monetary Fund.
PARTIES:
Canada
France

103254   Bilateral Exchange   **233 UNTS 109**
SIGNED: 1 Aug 51   FORCE: 1 Aug 51
REGISTERED: 12 Apr 56 Canada
ARTICLES: 2 LANGUAGE: English.
HEADNOTE: EXTENSION COORDINATION CONTI-
NENTAL RADAR DEFENSE
TOPIC: Milit Installation
CONCEPTS: Treaty implementation. Conformity
with municipal law. General cooperation. Title
and deeds. Indemnities and reimbursements. Ex-
pense sharing formulae. Materials, equipment
and services. Joint defense. Defense and secu-
rity. Status of military forces. Bases and facili-
ties.
INTL ORGS: Special Commission.
PARTIES:
Canada
USA (United States)

103255   Bilateral Exchange   **233 UNTS 117**
SIGNED: 29 Jan 52   FORCE: 29 Jan 52
REGISTERED: 12 Apr 56 Canada
ARTICLES: 2 LANGUAGE: Spanish.
HEADNOTE: SETTLEMENT DEBTS
TOPIC: Claims and Debts
CONCEPTS: Inspection and observation. General
trade. Banking. Debt settlement.
PARTIES:
Canada
Spain

103256   Bilateral Exchange   **233 UNTS 123**
SIGNED: 20 Mar 52   FORCE: 15 Apr 52
REGISTERED: 12 Apr 56 Canada
ARTICLES: 2 LANGUAGE: French.

HEADNOTE: NON-IMMIGRANT VISA MODIFICA-
TION
TOPIC: Visas
CONCEPTS: Time limit. Visa abolition. Fees and
exemptions.
PARTIES:
Canada
Monaco

103257   Bilateral Exchange   **233 UNTS 129**
SIGNED: 10 Apr 52   FORCE: 10 Apr 52
REGISTERED: 12 Apr 56 Canada
ARTICLES: 2 LANGUAGE: English.
HEADNOTE: LOOTED BONDS
TOPIC: Reparations
CONCEPTS: Exchange of information and docu-
ments. Informational records. Accounting proce-
dures. Banking. Bonds. Compensation. Financial
programs. Interest rates. Post-war claims settle-
ment.
PARTIES:
Canada
Netherlands

103258   Bilateral Exchange   **233 UNTS 137**
SIGNED: 10 Oct 52   FORCE: 9 Nov 52
REGISTERED: 12 Apr 56 Canada
ARTICLES: 2 LANGUAGE: English. Italian.
HEADNOTE: ISSUANCE MULTI-ENTRY VISAS
TOPIC: Visas
CONCEPTS: Passports diplomatic. Denial of ad-
mission. Visas. Conformity with municipal law.
Fees and exemptions.
PARTIES:
Canada
Italy

103259   Bilateral Exchange   **233 UNTS 145**
SIGNED: 3 Dec 52   FORCE: 3 Dec 52
REGISTERED: 12 Apr 56 Canada
ARTICLES: 2 LANGUAGE: English.
HEADNOTE: MOST FAVORED NATION TRADE
TOPIC: Mostfavored Nation
CONCEPTS: General trade. Most favored nation
clause.
PROCEDURE: Termination.
PARTIES:
Canada
United Arab Rep

103260   Bilateral Exchange   **233 UNTS 151**
SIGNED: 7 Mar 52   FORCE: 15 Feb 54
REGISTERED: 13 Apr 56 USA (United States)
ARTICLES: 2 LANGUAGE: English. Spanish.
HEADNOTE: CIVIL AVIATION MISSION
TOPIC: Tech Assistance
CONCEPTS: Exceptions and exemptions. Annex
type material. Personnel. Attachment of funds.
Indemnities and reimbursements. Exchange
rates and regulations. Garnishment of funds. Sei-
zure funds. Special projects. Aid missions.
TREATY REF: 99UNTS49.
PROCEDURE: Amendment. Duration. Termination.
PARTIES:
Honduras
USA (United States)

103261   Bilateral Exchange   **233 UNTS 163**
SIGNED: 6 Apr 54   FORCE: 6 Apr 54
REGISTERED: 13 Apr 56 USA (United States)
ARTICLES: 2 LANGUAGE: English. Spanish.
HEADNOTE: TECHNICAL COOPERATION DEVEL-
OPMENTAL ENGINEERING
TOPIC: Non-IBRD Project
CONCEPTS: Inspection and observation. Account-
ing procedures. Tax exemptions. Customs ex-
emptions. General technical assistance.
TREATY   REF: 141UNTS211;   200UNTS313;
233UNTS306.
PROCEDURE: Duration. Termination.
PARTIES:
Mexico
USA (United States)

103262   Bilateral Exchange   **233 UNTS 177**
SIGNED: 18 Jun 54   FORCE: 18 Jun 54
REGISTERED: 13 Apr 56 USA (United States)
ARTICLES: 2 LANGUAGE: English. Arabic.

HEADNOTE: SPECIAL ECONOMIC ASSISTANCE
TOPIC: Direct Aid
CONCEPTS: Annex or appendix reference. Conformity with municipal law. Exchange of information and documents. Public information. Domestic obligation. General technical assistance. Economic assistance. Procurement. Distribution.
TREATY REF: 160UNTS49.
PROCEDURE: Termination.
PARTIES:
Lebanon
USA (United States)

103263 Bilateral Agreement **233 UNTS 189**
SIGNED: 23 Jun 54   FORCE: 23 Jun 54
REGISTERED: 13 Apr 56 USA (United States)
ARTICLES: 2 LANGUAGE: English. Turkish.
HEADNOTE: STATUS FORCES
TOPIC: Status of Forces
CONCEPTS: Annex or appendix reference. Indemnities and reimbursements. Tax exemptions. Status of military forces. Jurisdiction. Status of forces. Industrial controls.
TREATY REF: 199UNTS67.
PARTIES:
Turkey
USA (United States)
ANNEX
265 UNTS 418. USA (United States). Amendment 22 Apr 55. Force 21 Jul 55.
265 UNTS 418. Turkey. Amendment 21 Jul 55. Force 21 Jul 55.

103264 Bilateral Instrument **233 UNTS 199**
SIGNED: 24 Feb 55   FORCE: 15 Apr 55
REGISTERED: 17 Apr 56 Iraq
ARTICLES: 8 LANGUAGE: Arabic. Turkish. English.
HEADNOTE: MUTUAL COOPERATION
TOPIC: General Military
CONCEPTS: Treaty interpretation. Annex or appendix reference. Non-prejudice to third party. Friendship and amity. Non-prejudice to UN charter. Peaceful relations. Establishment of commission. Joint defense. Defense and security. Military assistance.
INTL ORGS: Central Treaty Organization.
TREATY REF: 37UNTS266.
PROCEDURE: Accession. Denunciation. Duration. Future Procedures Contemplated. Ratification. Renewal or Revival.
PARTIES:
Iraq
Turkey

103265 Bilateral Agreement **233 UNTS 118**
SIGNED: 4 Apr 55   FORCE: 5 Apr 55
REGISTERED: 17 Apr 56 Iraq
ARTICLES: 9 LANGUAGE: English. Arabic.
HEADNOTE: SPECIAL AGREEMENT
TOPIC: General Military
CONCEPTS: Friendship and amity. Airforce-army-navy personnel ratio. Conditions for assistance missions.
PARTIES:
Iraq
UK Great Britain

103266 Bilateral Agreement **233 UNTS 267**
SIGNED: 17 Apr 56   FORCE: 17 Apr 56
REGISTERED: 17 Apr 56 United Nations
ARTICLES: 16 LANGUAGE: English.
HEADNOTE: TECHNICAL ASSISTANCE STATE PLANNING BUREAU
TOPIC: Non-IBRD Project
CONCEPTS: Annex or appendix reference. Previous treaty replacement. Inspection and observation. Personnel. Arbitration. Negotiation. Wages and salaries. Claims and settlements. General technical assistance. Status of experts. Conformity with IGO decisions.
INTL ORGS: International Court of Justice. Arbitration Commission.
TREATY REF: 76UNTS132; 121UNTS3; 233UNTS305.
PROCEDURE: Amendment. Duration. Termination.

PARTIES:
Indonesia
United Nations

103267 Bilateral Exchange **233 UNTS 281**
SIGNED: 28 May 54   FORCE: 28 May 54
REGISTERED: 17 Apr 56 USA (United States)
ARTICLES: 2 LANGUAGE: English. French.
HEADNOTE: TECHNICAL COOPERATION PROGRAM RURAL EDUCATION
TOPIC: Non-IBRD Project
CONCEPTS: Informational records. Operating agencies. Personnel. Education. Funding procedures. Assistance. Materials, equipment and services.
PROCEDURE: Duration. Termination.
PARTIES:
Haiti
USA (United States)
ANNEX
253 UNTS 369. USA (United States). Implementation 28 Jan 55. Force 9 Feb 55.
253 UNTS 369. Haiti. Implementation 3 Feb 55. Force 9 Feb 55.

103268 Bilateral Exchange **234 UNTS 3**
SIGNED: 29 May 54   FORCE: 29 May 54
REGISTERED: 17 Apr 56 USA (United States)
ARTICLES: 2 LANGUAGE: English. Persian.
HEADNOTE: DUTY-FREE ENTRY EXEMPTION INTERNAL TAXATION RELIEF SUPPLIES
TOPIC: Direct Aid
CONCEPTS: Export quotas. Transportation costs. Tax exemptions. Customs exemptions. Relief supplies.
PARTIES:
Afghanistan
USA (United States)
ANNEX
402 UNTS 319. Afghanistan. Amendment 12 Jan 61. Force 12 Jan 61.
402 UNTS 319. USA (United States). Amendment 27 Dec 60. Force 12 Jan 61.

103269 Bilateral Exchange **234 UNTS 11**
SIGNED: 7 Jun 54   FORCE: 7 Jun 54
REGISTERED: 17 Apr 56 USA (United States)
ARTICLES: 2 LANGUAGE: English. Spanish.
HEADNOTE: TECHNICAL COOPERATION
TOPIC: Tech Assistance
CONCEPTS: General technical assistance. Assistance.
TREATY REF: 141UNTS211,200UNTS312,2-33UNTS306.
PROCEDURE: Duration. Termination.
PARTIES:
Mexico
USA (United States)

103270 Bilateral Exchange **234 UNTS 25**
SIGNED: 12 Jun 54   FORCE: 12 Jun 54
REGISTERED: 17 Apr 56 USA (United States)
ARTICLES: 2 LANGUAGE: English.
HEADNOTE: TECHNICAL COOPERATION PROGRAM TRAINING VOCATIONAL INDUSTRIAL CRAFTS
TOPIC: Tech Assistance
CONCEPTS: Exceptions and exemptions. Treaty implementation. Annex type material. General cooperation. Personnel. General property. Private contracts. Establishment of commission. Vocational training. Attachment of funds. Currency deposits. Exchange rates and regulations. Garnishment of funds. Seizure funds. Assets. Assistance. Agricultural commodities. Materials, equipment and services.
TREATY REF: 184UNTS285.
PROCEDURE: Duration. Termination.
PARTIES:
Ethiopia
USA (United States)

103271 Bilateral Exchange **234 UNTS 35**
SIGNED: 16 Jun 54   FORCE: 16 Jun 54
REGISTERED: 17 Apr 56 USA (United States)
ARTICLES: 2 LANGUAGE: English. Spanish.
HEADNOTE: DUTY-FREE ENTRY EXEMPTION INTERNAL TAXATION RELIEF SUPPLIES
TOPIC: Direct Aid

CONCEPTS: Transportation costs. Tax exemptions. Customs exemptions. Relief supplies.
PARTIES:
Bolivia
USA (United States)

103272 Bilateral Exchange **234 UNTS 43**
SIGNED: 30 Jul 54   FORCE: 30 Jul 54
REGISTERED: 17 Apr 56 USA (United States)
ARTICLES: 2 LANGUAGE: English.
HEADNOTE: OFFSHORE PROCUREMENT
TOPIC: Milit Assistance
CONCEPTS: Detailed regulations. Annex or appendix reference. Conformity with municipal law. General cooperation. Private contracts. Indemnities and reimbursements. Security of information. Exchange of defense information. Restrictions on transfer.
TREATY REF: 185UNTS193; 189UNTS3.
PARTIES:
Greece
USA (United States)
ANNEX
251 UNTS 410. USA (United States). Supplementation 14 Oct 54. Force 12 Nov 54.
251 UNTS 410. Greece. Supplementation 12 Nov 54. Force 12 Nov 54.

103273 Bilateral Agreement **234 UNTS 71**
SIGNED: 14 May 53   FORCE: 14 May 53
REGISTERED: 17 Apr 56 USA (United States)
ARTICLES: 13 LANGUAGE: English. Spanish.
HEADNOTE: COOPERATIVE PROGRAM PRODUCTIVITY
TOPIC: Direct Aid
CONCEPTS: Treaty implementation. Annex type material. Privileges and immunities. Exchange of information and documents. Inspection and observation. Domestic legislation. Operating agencies. Personnel. Private contracts. Attachment of funds. Currency deposits. Funding procedures. Garnishment of funds. Interest rates. Seizure funds. Tax exemptions. Customs exemptions. Domestic obligation. Assistance. Economic assistance. Materials, equipment and services. Aid missions.
TREATY REF: 177UNTS219.
PROCEDURE: Duration. Termination.
PARTIES:
El Salvador
USA (United States)

103274 Bilateral Exchange **234 UNTS 97**
SIGNED: 12 Nov 53   FORCE: 12 Nov 53
REGISTERED: 17 Apr 56 USA (United States)
ARTICLES: 2 LANGUAGE: English.
HEADNOTE: ESTABLISHMENT JOINT BOARD ENGINEERS
TOPIC: IGO Establishment
CONCEPTS: Establishment of commission. Hydroelectric power. IGO constitution. Subsidiary organ.
INTL ORGS: Special Commission.
TREATY REF: 3'4DEMARTENS208;.
PARTIES:
Canada
USA (United States)

103275 Bilateral Exchange **234 UNTS 103**
SIGNED: 27 Apr 54   FORCE: 27 Apr 54
REGISTERED: 17 Apr 56 USA (United States)
ARTICLES: 2 LANGUAGE: English.
HEADNOTE: LOAN SUBMARINES
TOPIC: Milit Assistance
CONCEPTS: Detailed regulations. Time limit. Conformity with municipal law. Responsibility and liability. Use of facilities. Compensation. Indemnities and reimbursements. Delivery schedules. Lease of military property. Military assistance. Naval vessels. Return of equipment and recapture. Restrictions on transfer.
TREATY REF: 80UNTS145; 179UNTS165.
PARTIES:
Italy
USA (United States)
ANNEX
371 UNTS 295. Italy. Amendment 29 Jan 60. Force 29 Jan 60.
371 UNTS 295. USA (United States). Amendment 29 Jan 60. Force 29 Jan 60.

545 UNTS 339. USA (United States). Prolongation 31 Mar 65. Force 12 Apr 65.
545 UNTS 339. Italy. Amendment 17 Apr 65. Force 12 Apr 65.

103276 Bilateral Exchange **234 UNTS 111**
SIGNED: 26 Aug 54   FORCE: 26 Aug 54
REGISTERED: 17 Apr 56 USA (United States)
ARTICLES: 2 LANGUAGE: English. French.
HEADNOTE: RELIEF SUPPLIES EQUIPMENT
TOPIC: Direct Aid
CONCEPTS: Treaty implementation. Transportation costs. Tax exemptions. Customs exemptions. Relief supplies.
PROCEDURE: Amendment. Termination.
PARTIES:
 USA (United States)
 Vietnam, South

103277 Bilateral Exchange **234 UNTS 119**
SIGNED: 21 Oct 54   FORCE: 21 Oct 54
REGISTERED: 17 Apr 56 USA (United States)
ARTICLES: 2 LANGUAGE: English.
HEADNOTE: COPYRIGHT RELATIONS
TOPIC: Patents/Copyrights
CONCEPTS: Continuity of rights and obligations. Domestic legislation. Patents, copyrights and trademarks. Press and wire services.
PARTIES:
 India
 USA (United States)

103278 Bilateral Exchange **234 UNTS 131**
SIGNED: 27 Oct 54   FORCE: 17 Oct 54
REGISTERED: 17 Apr 56 USA (United States)
ARTICLES: 2 LANGUAGE: English.
HEADNOTE: EXCHANGE OFFICIAL PUBLICATIONS
TOPIC: Admin Cooperation
CONCEPTS: Exchange of official publications. Operating agencies. Indemnities and reimbursements.
PARTIES:
 Germany, West
 USA (United States)

103279 Bilateral Exchange **234 UNTS 139**
SIGNED: 30 Oct 54   FORCE: 30 Nov 54
REGISTERED: 17 Apr 56 USA (United States)
ARTICLES: 2 LANGUAGE: English.
HEADNOTE: RELIEF SUPPLIES EQUIPMENT
TOPIC: Direct Aid
CONCEPTS: Transportation costs. Tax exemptions. Customs exemptions. Relief supplies.
PROCEDURE: Termination.
PARTIES:
 United Arab Rep
 USA (United States)

103280 Bilateral Exchange **234 UNTS 147**
SIGNED: 1 Jul 54   FORCE: 1 Jul 54
REGISTERED: 19 Apr 56 USA (United States)
ARTICLES: 2 LANGUAGE: English.
HEADNOTE: LOAN SUBMARINES
TOPIC: Milit Assistance
CONCEPTS: Detailed regulations. Time limit. Conformity with municipal law. Responsibility and liability. Title and deeds. Compensation. Indemnities and reimbursements. Delivery schedules. Lease of military property. Military assistance. Naval vessels. Return of equipment and recapture. Restrictions on transfer.
TREATY REF: 7UNTS299; 179UNTS121.
PARTIES:
 Turkey
 USA (United States)
          ANNEX
357 UNTS 386. Turkey. Amendment 28 Aug 59. Force 28 Aug 59.
357 UNTS 386. USA (United States). Amendment 28 Aug 59. Force 28 Aug 59.

103281 Bilateral Agreement **234 UNTS 155**
SIGNED: 11 Aug 54   FORCE: 11 Aug 54
REGISTERED: 19 Apr 56 USA (United States)
ARTICLES: 7 LANGUAGE: English.
HEADNOTE: SALE PURCHASE TIN CONCENTRATES
TOPIC: Commodity Trade
CONCEPTS: Treaty implementation. General cooperation. Export quotas. Currency. Payment schedules. Non-interest rates and fees. Commodity trade. Delivery guarantees. Delivery schedules.
PROCEDURE: Amendment. Duration.
PARTIES:
 Thailand
 USA (United States)

103282 Bilateral Agreement **234 UNTS 161**
SIGNED: 18 Aug 54   FORCE: 18 Aug 54
REGISTERED: 19 Apr 56 USA (United States)
ARTICLES: 1 LANGUAGE: English. Greek.
HEADNOTE: COMMUNITY RADIOS
TOPIC: Telecommunications
CONCEPTS: Detailed regulations. Facilities and equipment. Radio-telephone-telegraphic communications.
PARTIES:
 Greece
 USA (United States)

103283 Bilateral Exchange **234 UNTS 199**
SIGNED: 30 Jun 52   FORCE: 30 Jun 52
REGISTERED: 23 Apr 56 USA (United States)
ARTICLES: 2 LANGUAGE: English.
HEADNOTE: ST LAWRENCE SEAWAY
TOPIC: Water Transport
CONCEPTS: Canal improvement. Inland and territorial waters.
INTL ORGS: Special Commission.
PARTIES:
 Canada
 USA (United States)

103284 Bilateral Exchange **234 UNTS 219**
SIGNED: 17 Aug 53   FORCE: 17 Aug 53
REGISTERED: 23 Apr 56 USA (United States)
ARTICLES: 2 LANGUAGE: English. French.
HEADNOTE: ESTABLISHMENT RADIO RANGE STATION
TOPIC: Mass Media
CONCEPTS: Customs exemptions. Facilities and equipment. Radio-telephone-telegraphic communications. Conditions for assistance missions. Equipment and supplies.
INTL ORGS: North Atlantic Treaty Organization.
TREATY REF: 168UNTS57.
PARTIES:
 Luxembourg
 USA (United States)

103285 Bilateral Exchange **234 UNTS 225**
SIGNED: 13 May 54   FORCE: 13 May 54
REGISTERED: 23 Apr 56 USA (United States)
ARTICLES: 2 LANGUAGE: English. Arabic.
HEADNOTE: SPECIAL ECONOMIC ASSISTANCE
TOPIC: Direct Aid
CONCEPTS: Annex or appendix reference. Exchange of information and documents. Domestic obligation. General technical assistance. Economic assistance. Procurement. Distribution.
TREATY REF: 141UNTS55.
PROCEDURE: Termination.
PARTIES:
 Jordan
 USA (United States)

103286 Bilateral Exchange **234 UNTS 235**
SIGNED: 30 Jul 54   FORCE: 30 Jul 54
REGISTERED: 23 Apr 56 USA (United States)
ARTICLES: 2 LANGUAGE: English. Spanish.
HEADNOTE: TRANSFER MILITARY EQUIPMENT
TOPIC: Milit Assistance
CONCEPTS: Conditions. Non-prejudice to UN charter. Peaceful relations. Payment schedules. Domestic obligation. Materials, equipment and services. Self-defense. Restrictions on transfer.
PARTIES:
 Guatemala
 USA (United States)

103287 Bilateral Exchange **234 UNTS 243**
SIGNED: 23 Aug 54   FORCE: 23 Aug 54
REGISTERED: 23 Apr 56 USA (United States)
ARTICLES: 2 LANGUAGE: English.

HEADNOTE: EMERGENCY FLOOD ASSISTANCE
TOPIC: Direct Aid
CONCEPTS: Change of circumstances. Treaty implementation. Privileges and immunities. Conformity with municipal law. General cooperation. Exchange of information and documents. Inspection and observation. Personnel. Public information. Accounting procedures. Funding procedures. Local currency. Relief supplies. Distribution.
TREATY REF: 222UNTS410.
PROCEDURE: Termination.
PARTIES:
 Pakistan
 USA (United States)

103288 Bilateral Exchange **234 UNTS 255**
SIGNED: 11 Sep 51   FORCE: 11 Sep 51
REGISTERED: 25 Apr 56 USA (United States)
ARTICLES: 2 LANGUAGE: English. Spanish.
HEADNOTE: CIVIL AIR MISSION
TOPIC: Air Transport
CONCEPTS: Time limit. Conformity with municipal law. Personnel. Responsibility and liability. Use of facilities. Accounting procedures. Indemnities and reimbursements. Financial programs. Transportation costs. Assistance. Materials, equipment and services. Aid missions. Air transport.
TREATY REF: 92UNTS179.
PROCEDURE: Amendment. Duration. Termination.
PARTIES:
 Costa Rica
 USA (United States)

103289 Bilateral Exchange **234 UNTS 267**
SIGNED: 5 Jan 54   FORCE: 5 Jan 54
REGISTERED: 25 Apr 56 USA (United States)
ARTICLES: 2 LANGUAGE: English.
HEADNOTE: ECONOMIC AID
TOPIC: Direct Aid
CONCEPTS: Time limit. Exchange of information and documents. Balance of payments. General technical assistance. Agriculture. Economic assistance. Loan and credit.
PROCEDURE: Duration.
PARTIES:
 USA (United States)
 Yugoslavia

103290 Bilateral Exchange **235 UNTS 3**
SIGNED: 24 Jun 54   FORCE: 24 Jun 54
REGISTERED: 25 Apr 56 USA (United States)
ARTICLES: 2 LANGUAGE: English. Japanese.
HEADNOTE: SPECIAL PROGRAM FACILITIES ASSISTANCE
TOPIC: Tech Assistance
CONCEPTS: Change of circumstances. Guarantees and safeguards. Conformity with municipal law. Use of facilities. Most favored nation clause. General technical assistance. Materials, equipment and services. Defense and security. Military assistance. Equipment and supplies.
TREATY REF: 80UNTS145; 179UNTS165.
PROCEDURE: Future Procedures Contemplated.
PARTIES:
 Italy
 USA (United States)
          ANNEX
341 UNTS 390. USA (United States). Supplementation 9 Jul 58. Force 16 Jul 58.
341 UNTS 390. Italy. Supplementation 16 Jul 58. Force 16 Jul 58.

103291 Bilateral Exchange **235 UNTS 11**
SIGNED: 22 Nov 54   FORCE: 25 Oct 54
REGISTERED: 25 Apr 56 USA (United States)
ARTICLES: 3 LANGUAGE: English.
HEADNOTE: TRADEMARK PROTECTION
TOPIC: Patents/Copyrights
CONCEPTS: Conformity with municipal law. Domestic legislation. Trademarks.
PARTIES:
 USA (United States)
 Vietnam, South

103292 Bilateral Exchange **235 UNTS 19**
SIGNED: 23 Nov 54   FORCE: 23 Nov 54
REGISTERED: 25 Apr 56 USA (United States)
ARTICLES: 2 LANGUAGE: English. French.

HEADNOTE: SPECIAL PROGRAM FACILITIES AS-SISTANCE
TOPIC: Tech Assistance
CONCEPTS: Change of circumstances. Guarantees and safeguards. Annex or appendix reference. Conformity with municipal law. Use of facilities. Most favored nation clause. General technical assistance. Materials, equipment and services. Defense and security. Equipment and supplies.
TREATY REF: 51UNTS213; 179UNTS81.
PROCEDURE: Future Procedures Contemplated.
PARTIES:
Belgium
USA (United States)

103293 Bilateral Exchange **235 UNTS 29**
SIGNED: 16 Jun 48   FORCE: 16 Jun 48
REGISTERED: 25 Apr 56 USA (United States)
ARTICLES: 2 LANGUAGE: English.
HEADNOTE: AIR TRANSPORT AGREEMENT US & INDIA 14 NOV 46 VALID FOR PAKISTAN
TOPIC: Air Transport
CONCEPTS: Guarantees and safeguards. Annex type material. Air transport.
TREATY REF: 22UNTS55.
PARTIES:
Pakistan
USA (United States)
ANNEX
410 UNTS 300. USA (United States). Supplementation 28 Mar 61. Force 18 Apr 61.
410 UNTS 300. Pakistan. Supplementation 18 Apr 61. Force 18 Apr 61.

103294 Bilateral Exchange **235 UNTS 35**
SIGNED: 30 Jun 54   FORCE: 30 Jun 54
REGISTERED: 25 Apr 56 USA (United States)
ARTICLES: 2 LANGUAGE: English. Spanish.
HEADNOTE: TECHNICAL COOPERATION PRO-GRAM AGRICULTURAL RESEARCH
TOPIC: Tech Assistance
CONCEPTS: Exceptions and exemptions. Treaty implementation. Annex type material. General cooperation. Personnel. Private contracts. Vocational training. Research and development. Financial programs. Tax exemptions. Customs exemptions. Domestic obligation. Agriculture. Assistance. Materials, equipment and services.
TREATY REF: 92UNTS179; 140UNTS439.
PARTIES:
Costa Rica
USA (United States)

103295 Bilateral Exchange **235 UNTS 45**
SIGNED: 30 Jul 54   FORCE: 30 Jul 54
REGISTERED: 25 Apr 56 USA (United States)
ARTICLES: 7 LANGUAGE: English. Spanish.
HEADNOTE: OFFSHORE PROCUREMENT
TOPIC: Milit Assistance
CONCEPTS: Trade agencies. Trade procedures. General. Patents, copyrights and trademarks. Military installations and equipment.
PARTIES:
Spain
USA (United States)
ANNEX
266 UNTS 428. USA (United States). Amendment 21 Dec 56. Force 27 Dec 56.
266 UNTS 428. Spain. Amendment 27 Dec 56. Force 27 Dec 56.
341 UNTS 400. USA (United States). Amendment 29 Oct 58. Force 11 Nov 58.
341 UNTS 400. Spain. Amendment 11 Nov 58. Force 11 Nov 58.

103296 Bilateral Exchange **235 UNTS 87**
SIGNED: 19 May 54   FORCE: 19 May 54
REGISTERED: 25 Apr 56 USA (United States)
ARTICLES: 3 LANGUAGE: English. Spanish.
HEADNOTE: SPECIAL PROGRAMS FACILITIES AS-SISTANCE
TOPIC: Tech Assistance
CONCEPTS: Change of circumstances. Guarantees and safeguards. Annex or appendix reference. Conformity with municipal law. Use of facilities. National treatment. General technical assistance. Materials, equipment and services. Defense and security. Equipment and supplies.

TREATY REF: MUTUAL DEFENSE ASSISTANCE AGREEMENT; SPAIN&U.S.A..
PARTIES:
Spain
USA (United States)
ANNEX
251 UNTS 416. USA (United States). Prolongation 25 May 55. Force 25 May 55.
251 UNTS 416. Spain. Prolongation 25 May 55. Force 25 May 55.
278 UNTS 283. USA (United States). Prolongation 17 Sep 56. Force 17 Sep 56.
278 UNTS 283. Spain. Prolongation 17 Sep 56. Force 17 Sep 56.

103297 Multilateral Instrument **235 UNTS 99**
SIGNED: 5 Oct 54   FORCE: 5 Oct 54
REGISTERED: 25 Apr 56 USA (United States)
ARTICLES: 17 LANGUAGE: English.
HEADNOTE: FREE TERRITORY TRIESTE
TOPIC: Territory Boundary
CONCEPTS: Annex or appendix reference. Previous treaties adherence. Nationality and citizenship. Occupation regime. Changes of territory. Markers and definitions.
INTL ORGS: United Nations. Special Commission.
TREATY REF: 49UNTS3; 50UNTS3.
PARTIES:
Italy SIGNED: 5 Oct 54 FORCE: 5 Oct 54
UK Great Britain SIGNED: 5 Oct 54 FORCE: 5 Oct 54
USA (United States) SIGNED: 5 Oct 54 FORCE: 5 Oct 54
Yugoslavia SIGNED: 5 Oct 54 FORCE: 5 Oct 54

103298 Bilateral Agreement **235 UNTS 121**
SIGNED: 29 Jul 55   FORCE: 29 Jul 55
REGISTERED: 25 Apr 56 USA (United States)
ARTICLES: 10 LANGUAGE: English.
HEADNOTE: CIVIL USES ATOMIC ENERGY
TOPIC: Atomic Energy
CONCEPTS: Definition of terms. Exchange of information and documents. Labor statistics. Research results. Scientific exchange. Establishment of trade relations. Domestic obligation. Nuclear materials. Non-nuclear materials. Rights of supplier. Security of information.
PROCEDURE: Duration.
PARTIES:
Argentina
USA (United States)
ANNEX
378 UNTS 376. USA (United States). Amendment 11 Jun 60. Force 27 Jul 60.
378 UNTS 376. Argentina. Amendment 11 Jun 60. Force 27 Jul 60.

103299 Bilateral Agreement **235 UNTS 133**
SIGNED: 15 Jun 55   FORCE: 21 Jul 55
REGISTERED: 25 Apr 56 USA (United States)
ARTICLES: 8 LANGUAGE: English. French.
HEADNOTE: CIVIL USES ATOMIC ENERGY
TOPIC: Atomic Energy
CONCEPTS: Definition of terms. Treaty implementation. Previous treaty replacement. Diplomatic missions. Exchange of information and documents. Use of facilities. Scientific exchange. Establishment of trade relations. Laws and formalities. Domestic obligation. Nuclear materials. Non-nuclear materials. Peaceful use. Rights of supplier. Security of information.
INTL ORGS: Special Commission.
PROCEDURE: Duration.
PARTIES:
Belgium
USA (United States)
ANNEX
278 UNTS 292. USA (United States). Amendment 12 Jul 56. Force 18 Jan 57.
278 UNTS 292. Belgium. Amendment 12 Jul 56. Force 18 Jan 57.
358 UNTS 304. USA (United States). Amendment 22 Jul 59. Force 29 Sep 59.
358 UNTS 304. Belgium. Amendment 22 Jul 59. Force 29 Sep 59.
489 UNTS 378. USA (United States). Amendment 7 Aug 63. Force 8 Nov 63.
489 UNTS 378. Belgium. Amendment 7 Aug 63. Force 8 Nov 63.

103300 Bilateral Agreement **235 UNTS 159**
SIGNED: 3 Aug 55   FORCE: 3 Aug 55
REGISTERED: 25 Apr 56 USA (United States)
ARTICLES: 10 LANGUAGE: English. Portuguese.
HEADNOTE: CIVIL USES ATOMIC ENERGY
TOPIC: Atomic Energy
CONCEPTS: Definition of terms. Diplomatic missions. General cooperation. Exchange of information and documents. Research results. Scientific exchange. Establishment of trade relations. Nuclear materials. Non-nuclear materials. Rights of supplier. Security of information.
PROCEDURE: Duration.
PARTIES:
Brazil
USA (United States)
ANNEX
347 UNTS 386. USA (United States). Amendment 9 Jul 58. Force 2 Jul 59.
347 UNTS 386. Brazil. Amendment 9 Jul 58. Force 2 Jul 59.
380 UNTS 434. USA (United States). Amendment 11 Jun 60. Force 2 Aug 60.
380 UNTS 434. Brazil. Amendment 11 Jun 60. Force 2 Aug 60.
459 UNTS 294. Brazil. Amendment 28 May 62. Force 20 Jul 62.
459 UNTS 294. USA (United States). Amendment 28 May 62. Force 20 Jul 62.
531 UNTS 326. USA (United States). Amendment 1 Sep 64. Force 2 Nov 64.
531 UNTS 326. Brazil. Amendment 1 Sep 64. Force 2 Nov 64.

103301 Bilateral Agreement **235 UNTS 176**
SIGNED: 15 Jun 55   FORCE: 21 Jul 55
REGISTERED: 25 Apr 56 USA (United States)
ARTICLES: 14 LANGUAGE: English.
HEADNOTE: CIVIL USES ATOMIC ENERGY
TOPIC: Atomic Energy
CONCEPTS: Definition of terms. Exceptions and exemptions. Diplomatic missions. General cooperation. Exchange of information and documents. Responsibility and liability. Use of facilities. Public health. Research cooperation. Research results. Scientific exchange. Establishment of trade relations. Reexport of goods, etc.. Laws and formalities. Nuclear materials. Non-nuclear materials. Rights of supplier. Security of information.
PROCEDURE: Duration.
PARTIES:
Canada
USA (United States)
ANNEX
279 UNTS 318. USA (United States). Amendment 26 Jun 56. Force 4 Mar 57.
279 UNTS 318. Canada. Amendment 26 Jun 56. Force 4 Mar 57.
453 UNTS 362. USA (United States). Amendment 25 May 62. Force 12 Jul 62.
453 UNTS 362. Canada. Amendment 25 May 62. Force 12 Jul 62.

103302 Bilateral Agreement **235 UNTS 201**
SIGNED: 15 Jun 55   FORCE: 22 Jul 55
REGISTERED: 25 Apr 56 USA (United States)
ARTICLES: 6 LANGUAGE: English.
HEADNOTE: TECHNICAL COOPERATION PRO-GRAM ECONOMIC DEVELOPMENT
TOPIC: Milit Assistance
CONCEPTS: Time limit. Treaty implementation. Annex or appendix reference. Annex type material. General cooperation. Exchange of information and documents. Informational records. Inspection and observation. Operating agencies. Personnel. Private contracts. Public health. Sanitation. Exchange rates and regulations. Expense sharing formulae. Funding procedures. Tax exemptions. Agriculture. Assistance. Economic assistance. Materials, equipment and services. Aid missions.
PROCEDURE: Duration. Termination.
PARTIES:
Canada
USA (United States)
ANNEX
377 UNTS 412. USA (United States). Amendment 11 Jun 60. Force 14 Jul 60.
377 UNTS 412. Canada. Amendment 11 Jun 60. Force 14 Jul 60.

103303 Bilateral Agreement **235 UNTS 209**
SIGNED: 8 Aug 55 FORCE: 8 Aug 55
REGISTERED: 25 Apr 56 USA (United States)
ARTICLES: 10 LANGUAGE: English.
HEADNOTE: CIVIL USES ATOMIC ENERGY
TOPIC: Atomic Energy
CONCEPTS: Definition of terms. Diplomatic missions. Exchange of information and documents. Research results. Scientific exchange. Establishment of trade relations. Nuclear materials. Non-nuclear materials. Rights of supplier. Security of information.
PARTIES:
Chile
USA (United States)

103304 Bilateral Agreement **235 UNTS 221**
SIGNED: 18 Jul 55 FORCE: 18 Jul 55
REGISTERED: 25 Apr 56 USA (United States)
ARTICLES: 10 LANGUAGE: English.
HEADNOTE: CIVIL USES ATOMIC ENERGY
TOPIC: Atomic Energy
CONCEPTS: Definition of terms. Diplomatic missions. General cooperation. Exchange of information and documents. Research results. Scientific exchange. Establishment of trade relations. Nuclear materials. Non-nuclear materials. Rights of supplier. Security of information.
PROCEDURE: Duration.
PARTIES:
Taiwan
USA (United States)
ANNEX
340 UNTS 358. Taiwan. Amendment 8 Dec 58. Force 2 Mar 59.
340 UNTS 358. USA (United States). Amendment 8 Dec 58. Force 2 Mar 59.
377 UNTS 416. Taiwan. Amendment 11 Jun 60. Force 15 Jul 60.
377 UNTS 416. USA (United States). Amendment 11 Jun 60. Force 15 Jul 60.
453 UNTS 368. USA (United States). Amendment 31 May 62. Force 13 Jul 62.
453 UNTS 368. Taiwan. Amendment 31 May 62. Force 13 Jul 62.
529 UNTS 344. Taiwan. Amendment 8 Jun 64. Force 6 Aug 64.
529 UNTS 344. USA (United States). Amendment 8 Jun 64. Force 6 Aug 64.
606 UNTS 316. Taiwan. Amendment 25 Aug 66. Force 28 Aug 66.
606 UNTS 316. USA (United States). Amendment 25 Aug 66. Force 28 Sep 66.

103305 Bilateral Agreement **235 UNTS 233**
SIGNED: 19 Jul 55 FORCE: 19 Jul 55
REGISTERED: 25 Apr 56 USA (United States)
ARTICLES: 10 LANGUAGE: English.
HEADNOTE: CIVIL USES ATOMIC ENERGY
TOPIC: Atomic Energy
CONCEPTS: Definition of terms. Diplomatic missions. General cooperation. Exchange of information and documents. Research results. Scientific exchange. Establishment of trade relations. Nuclear materials. Non-nuclear materials. Rights of supplier. Security of information.
PROCEDURE: Duration.
PARTIES:
Colombia
USA (United States)

103306 Bilateral Agreement **235 UNTS 245**
SIGNED: 25 Jul 55 FORCE: 25 Jul 55
REGISTERED: 25 Apr 56 USA (United States)
ARTICLES: 10 LANGUAGE: English.
HEADNOTE: CIVIL USES ATOMIC ENERGY
TOPIC: Atomic Energy
CONCEPTS: Definition of terms. Diplomatic missions. General cooperation. Exchange of information and documents. Research results. Scientific exchange. Establishment of trade relations. Nuclear materials. Non-nuclear materials. Rights of supplier. Security of information.
PROCEDURE: Duration.
PARTIES:
Denmark
USA (United States)
ANNEX
280 UNTS 378. USA (United States). Amendment 27 Jun 56. Force 14 Feb 57.

280 UNTS 378. Denmark. Amendment 27 Jun 56. Force 14 Feb 57.
335 UNTS 310. USA (United States). Amendment 26 Jun 58. Force 8 Sep 58.
335 UNTS 310. Denmark. Amendment 26 Jun 58. Force 8 Sep 58.

103307 Bilateral Agreement **235 UNTS 257**
SIGNED: 4 Aug 55 FORCE: 4 Aug 55
REGISTERED: 25 Apr 56 USA (United States)
ARTICLES: 10 LANGUAGE: English.
HEADNOTE: CIVIL USES ATOMIC ENERGY
TOPIC: Atomic Energy
CONCEPTS: Definition of terms. Diplomatic missions. Exchange of information and documents. Research results. Scientific exchange. Establishment of trade relations. Nuclear materials. Non-nuclear materials. Rights of supplier. Security of information.
PROCEDURE: Duration.
PARTIES:
Greece
USA (United States)
ANNEX
418 UNTS 366. USA (United States). Amendment 11 Jun 60. Force 13 Sep 61.
418 UNTS 366. Greece. Amendment 11 Jun 60. Force 13 Sep 61.
469 UNTS 420. USA (United States). Amendment 3 Apr 62. Force 25 Oct 63.
469 UNTS 420. Greece. Amendment 3 Apr 62. Force 25 Oct 63.
469 UNTS 424. Greece. Amendment 22 Jun 62. Force 25 Oct 62.
469 UNTS 424. USA (United States). Amendment 22 Jun 62. Force 25 Oct 62.

103308 Bilateral Exchange **235 UNTS 269**
SIGNED: 30 Apr 52 FORCE: 27 Sep 53
REGISTERED: 25 Apr 56 USA (United States)
ARTICLES: 2 LANGUAGE: English.
HEADNOTE: APPLICATION NATO STATUS FORCES AGREEMENT
TOPIC: Milit Installation
CONCEPTS: Annex type material. Status of military forces.
INTL ORGS: North Atlantic Treaty Organization. Special Commission.
TREATY REF: 199UNTS67.
PARTIES:
Canada
USA (United States)

103309 Bilateral Exchange **235 UNTS 277**
SIGNED: 11 Oct 52 FORCE: 11 Oct 52
REGISTERED: 25 Apr 56 USA (United States)
ARTICLES: 2 LANGUAGE: English.
HEADNOTE: ECONOMIC AID
TOPIC: Direct Aid
CONCEPTS: Time limit. Exchange of information and documents. Balance of payments. General technical assistance. Agriculture. Economic assistance. Loan and credit.
INTL ORGS: International Bank for Reconstruction and Development.
PROCEDURE: Duration.
PARTIES:
USA (United States)
Yugoslavia

103310 Bilateral Exchange **235 UNTS 285**
SIGNED: 30 Mar 53 FORCE: 30 Mar 53
REGISTERED: 25 Apr 56 USA (United States)
ARTICLES: 2 LANGUAGE: English. German.
HEADNOTE: SETTLEMENT OCCUPATION DAMAGE CLAIMS
TOPIC: Reparations
CONCEPTS: Lump sum settlements. Loss and/or damage. Post-war claims settlement.
PARTIES:
Germany, West
USA (United States)

103311 Bilateral Exchange **235 UNTS 293**
SIGNED: 31 Mar 54 FORCE: 31 Mar 54
REGISTERED: 25 Apr 56 USA (United States)
ARTICLES: 2 LANGUAGE: English. Italian.
HEADNOTE: OFFSHORE PROCUREMENT PROGRAM

TOPIC: Milit Assistance
CONCEPTS: General provisions. Annex or appendix reference. Privileges and immunities. Conformity with municipal law. General cooperation. Exchange of information and documents. Inspection and observation. Licenses and permits. General property. Private contracts. Responsibility and liability. Indemnities and reimbursements. Materials, equipment and services. Defense and security. Security of information. Exchange of defense information.
TREATY REF: 20UNTS43.
PROCEDURE: Future Procedures Contemplated.
PARTIES:
Italy
USA (United States)

103312 Bilateral Exchange **236 UNTS 3**
SIGNED: 23 Jan 50 FORCE: 23 Jan 50
REGISTERED: 26 Apr 56 USA (United States)
ARTICLES: 2 LANGUAGE: English. Spanish.
HEADNOTE: FREE ENTRY PRIVILEGES FOREIGN SERVICE PERSONNEL
TOPIC: Consul/Citizenship
CONCEPTS: Diplomatic privileges.
PARTIES:
Dominican Republic
USA (United States)

103313 Bilateral Agreement **236 UNTS 9**
SIGNED: 21 Jun 52 FORCE: 27 Apr 54
REGISTERED: 26 Apr 56 USA (United States)
ARTICLES: 5 LANGUAGE: English.
HEADNOTE: CLAIMS ENEMY PROPERTY
TOPIC: Reparations
CONCEPTS: Annex or appendix reference. General property. Indemnities and reimbursements. Assets transfer. Post-war claims settlement.
PARTIES:
Norway
USA (United States)

103314 Bilateral Exchange **236 UNTS 25**
SIGNED: 15 Dec 53 FORCE: 14 Jan 54
REGISTERED: 26 Apr 56 USA (United States)
ARTICLES: 2 LANGUAGE: English. Spanish.
HEADNOTE: PASSPORT VISA FEES
TOPIC: Visas
CONCEPTS: Detailed regulations. Visas. Tourism. Fees and exemptions.
PARTIES:
El Salvador
USA (United States)

103315 Bilateral Agreement **236 UNTS 41**
SIGNED: 30 Dec 53 FORCE: 30 Dec 53
REGISTERED: 26 Apr 56 USA (United States)
ARTICLES: 12 LANGUAGE: English. Spanish.
HEADNOTE: COOPERATIVE PROGRAM REFORESTATION DUNE STABILIZATION
TOPIC: Tech Assistance
CONCEPTS: Exceptions and exemptions. Time limit. Treaty implementation. Annex type material. Privileges and immunities. General cooperation. Exchange of information and documents. Informational records. Inspection and observation. Domestic legislation. Operating agencies. Personnel. General property. Private contracts. Title and deeds. Indemnities and reimbursements. Currency deposits. Exchange rates and regulations. Funding procedures. Assets. Domestic obligation. Agriculture. Assistance. Materials, equipment and services. Natural resources.
INTL ORGS: Special Commission.
TREATY REF: 151UNTS147.
PROCEDURE: Duration. Termination.
PARTIES:
Chile
USA (United States)

103316 Bilateral Exchange **236 UNTS 61**
SIGNED: 24 Feb 54 FORCE: 24 Feb 54
REGISTERED: 26 Apr 56 USA (United States)
ARTICLES: 2 LANGUAGE: English.
HEADNOTE: TECHNICAL COOPERATION
TOPIC: Tech Assistance

CONCEPTS: Annex type material. Conformity with municipal law. General cooperation. Operating agencies. Personnel. Reexport of goods, etc.. Attachment of funds. Exchange rates and regulations. Funding procedures. Garnishment of funds. Seizure funds. Tax exemptions. Customs exemptions. General technical assistance. Materials, equipment and services. Aid missions.
TREATY REF: 198UNTS265.
PARTIES:
United Arab Rep
USA (United States)
ANNEX
376 UNTS 426. USA (United States). Implementation 2 Apr 60. Force 2 Apr 60.
376 UNTS 426. United Arab Rep. Implementation 2 Apr 60. Force 2 Apr 60.

103317   Bilateral Exchange   **236 UNTS 69**
SIGNED: 6 Apr 54   FORCE: 6 Apr 54
REGISTERED: 26 Apr 56 USA (United States)
ARTICLES: 2 LANGUAGE: English. Spanish.
HEADNOTE: TECHNICAL   COOPERATION PROJECT ESTABLISH TRAINING SCHOOL
TOPIC: Tech Assistance
CONCEPTS: Exceptions and exemptions. Annex type material. Privileges and immunities. Exchange of information and documents. Informational records. Operating agencies. Personnel. Title and deeds. Institute establishment. Vocational training. Expense sharing formulae. Tax exemptions. Customs exemptions. Domestic obligation. General technical assistance. Assistance. Materials, equipment and services.
TREATY REF: 141UNTS211; 200UNTS312;9.
PROCEDURE: Duration.
PARTIES:
Mexico
USA (United States)
ANNEX
290 UNTS 327. Mexico. Amendment 29 Jun 57. Force 29 Jun 57.
290 UNTS 327. USA (United States). Amendment 29 Jun 57. Force 29 Jun 57.
358 UNTS 310. Mexico. Prolongation 22 Jun 59. Force 22 Jun 59.
358 UNTS 310. USA (United States). Prolongation 22 Jun 59. Force 22 Jun 59.

103318   Bilateral Agreement   **236 UNTS 87**
SIGNED: 13 Apr 54   FORCE: 21 May 54
REGISTERED: 26 Apr 56 USA (United States)
ARTICLES: 6 LANGUAGE: English. Spanish.
HEADNOTE: SPECIAL TECHNICAL SERVICES
TOPIC: Tech Assistance
CONCEPTS: General technical assistance. Assistance. Special projects.
INTL ORGS: Special Commission.
TREATY REF: USA'TIAS 2772;$.
PROCEDURE: Duration. Termination.
PARTIES:
Peru
USA (United States)

103319   Bilateral Agreement   **236 UNTS 107**
SIGNED: 11 May 54   FORCE: 11 May 54
REGISTERED: 26 Apr 56 USA (United States)
ARTICLES: 11 LANGUAGE: English. Spanish.
HEADNOTE: COOPERATIVE   PROGRAM   ECONOMIC DEVELOPMENT
TOPIC: Direct Aid
CONCEPTS: Treaty implementation. Privileges and immunities. Informational records. Inspection and observation. Domestic legislation. Operating agencies. Personnel. Private contracts. Title and deeds. Currency deposits. Exchange rates and regulations. Funding procedures. Assets. Tax exemptions. Customs exemptions. General technical assistance. Economic assistance. Materials, equipment and services. Aid missions.
INTL ORGS: Special Commission.
TREATY REF: 92UNTS167.
PROCEDURE: Duration. Termination.
PARTIES:
Panama
USA (United States)

103320   Bilateral Exchange   **236 UNTS 133**
SIGNED: 15 Jun 54   FORCE: 15 Jun 54
REGISTERED: 26 Apr 56 USA (United States)
ARTICLES: 2 LANGUAGE: English.
HEADNOTE: FACILITIES ASSISTANCE MUTUAL DEFENSE
TOPIC: Milit Assistance
CONCEPTS: Change of circumstances. Conformity with municipal law. General cooperation. Use of facilities. Most favored nation clause. Materials, equipment and services. Defense and security. Military assistance. Equipment and supplies.
TREATY REF: 80UNTS261.
PROCEDURE: Future Procedures Contemplated.
PARTIES:
UK Great Britain
USA (United States)
ANNEX
262 UNTS 474. UK Great Britain. Supplementation 27 Jun 55. Force 27 Jun 55.
262 UNTS 474. USA (United States). Supplementation 27 Jun 55. Force 27 Jun 55.
340 UNTS 364. USA (United States). Amendment 3 Feb 59. Force 13 Feb 59.
340 UNTS 364. UK Great Britain. Amendment 13 Feb 59. Force 13 Feb 59.

103321   Bilateral Exchange   **236 UNTS 141**
SIGNED: 31 May 54   FORCE: 31 May 54
REGISTERED: 26 Apr 56 USA (United States)
ARTICLES: 2 LANGUAGE: English. French.
HEADNOTE: PROGRAM FACILITIES ASSISTANCE
TOPIC: Milit Assistance
CONCEPTS: Change of circumstances. General cooperation. Use of facilities. Most favored nation clause. Materials, equipment and services. Defense and security. Military assistance. Equipment and supplies.
TREATY REF: 80UNTS171.
PROCEDURE: Future Procedures Contemplated.
PARTIES:
France
USA (United States)

103322   Bilateral Exchange   **236 UNTS 149**
SIGNED: 16 Jun 54   FORCE: 16 Jun 54
REGISTERED: 26 Apr 56 USA (United States)
ARTICLES: 2 LANGUAGE: English. Italian.
HEADNOTE: REVOLVING   INDUSTRIAL   LOAN FUND
TOPIC: Loans and Credits
CONCEPTS: Operating agencies. Incorporation of treaty provisions into national law. Public information. Financial programs. Funding procedures. Interest rates. Economic assistance. Loan and credit. Credit provisions. Loan repayment. Terms of loan.
TREATY REF: 20UNTS43; 55UNTS318.
PARTIES:
Italy
USA (United States)

103323   Bilateral Agreement   **236 UNTS 163**
SIGNED: 30 Jun 54   FORCE: 30 Jun 54
REGISTERED: 26 Apr 56 USA (United States)
ARTICLES: 11 LANGUAGE: English. Spanish.
HEADNOTE: COOPERATIVE PROGRAM INDUSTRY
TOPIC: Tech Assistance
CONCEPTS: Treaty implementation. Annex type material. Privileges and immunities. General cooperation. Exchange of information and documents. Informational records. Inspection and observation. Domestic legislation. Operating agencies. Personnel. General property. Private contracts. Title and deeds. Vocational training. Currency deposits. Exchange rates and regulations. Funding procedures. Assets. Tax exemptions. Customs exemptions. Domestic obligation. Assistance. Materials, equipment and services. Aid missions. Volunteer programs. Industry.
INTL ORGS: Special Commission.
TREATY REF: 141UNTS27; 179UNTS242.
PROCEDURE: Duration. Termination.
PARTIES:
Ecuador
USA (United States)

103324   Bilateral Exchange   **236 UNTS 187**
SIGNED: 2 Oct 54   FORCE: 2 Oct 54

REGISTERED: 26 Apr 56 USA (United States)
ARTICLES: 2 LANGUAGE: English.
HEADNOTE: DUTY-FREE ENTRY EXEMPTION INTERNAL TAXATION RELIEF SUPPLIES
TOPIC: Direct Aid
CONCEPTS: Transportation costs. Tax exemptions. Customs exemptions. Relief supplies.
TREATY REF: PAKISTAN-U.S.A. NOTE,6MAY53.
PROCEDURE: Termination.
PARTIES:
Pakistan
USA (United States)

103325   Bilateral Agreement   **236 UNTS 195**
SIGNED: 6 Aug 55   FORCE: 27 Mar 56
REGISTERED: 27 Apr 56 IBRD (World Bank)
ARTICLES: 5 LANGUAGE: English.
HEADNOTE: GUARANTEE AGREEMENT
TOPIC: IBRD Project
CONCEPTS: Definition of terms. Annex or appendix reference. Exchange of information and documents. Informational records. Inspection and observation. Bonds. Fees and exemptions. Tax exemptions. Domestic obligation. Terms of loan. Loan regulations. Loan guarantee. Guarantor non-interference.
PARTIES:
Pakistan
IBRD (World Bank)

103326   Bilateral Agreement   **236 UNTS 229**
SIGNED: 19 Dec 46   FORCE: 19 Dec 46
REGISTERED: 30 Apr 56 Canada
ARTICLES: 9 LANGUAGE: English. Spanish.
HEADNOTE: TRADE COMMERCE
TOPIC: General Trade
CONCEPTS: Exceptions and exemptions. Conformity with municipal law. General cooperation. Investigation of violations. Reciprocity in trade. Trade agencies. Trade procedures. Monetary and gold transfers. Most favored nation clause. Equitable taxes. Customs duties.
PROCEDURE: Duration. Ratification. Termination.
PARTIES:
Canada
Nicaragua

103327   Bilateral Exchange   **236 UNTS 245**
SIGNED: 18 Jan 52   FORCE: 18 Jan 52
REGISTERED: 30 Apr 56 Canada
ARTICLES: 2 LANGUAGE: English. German.
HEADNOTE: GIVING EFFECT CONVENTION 31 MAR 31
TOPIC: Admin Cooperation
CONCEPTS: Annex type material. Previous treaty extension.
PARTIES:
Austria
Canada

103328   Bilateral Exchange   **236 UNTS 251**
SIGNED: 20 Sep 51   FORCE: 20 Sep 51
REGISTERED: 30 Apr 56 Canada
ARTICLES: 2 LANGUAGE: English.
HEADNOTE: SETTLEMENT   WAR   CLAIMS   RELEASE ASSETS
TOPIC: Reparations
CONCEPTS: Arbitration. Procedure. Expense sharing formulae. Lump sum settlements. Assets transfer. Post-war claims settlement.
PARTIES:
Canada
Italy

103329   Bilateral Exchange   **236 UNTS 259**
SIGNED: 17 Mar 53   FORCE: 17 Mar 53
REGISTERED: 30 Apr 56 Canada
ARTICLES: 2 LANGUAGE: English.
HEADNOTE: SEALING MOBILE RADIO TRANSMITTING EQUIPMENT
TOPIC: Telecommunications
CONCEPTS: Previous treaty replacement. Licenses and permits. Amateur radio. Radio-telephone-telegraphic communications.
TREATY REF: 27UNTS3; 207UNTS17.
PARTIES:
Canada
USA (United States)

103330 Bilateral Agreement **236 UNTS 267**
SIGNED: 16 Mar 51 FORCE: 1 Jan 52
REGISTERED: 30 Apr 56 Canada
ARTICLES: 23 LANGUAGE: English. French.
HEADNOTE: DOUBLE TAXATION FISCAL EVA-
SION TAXES INCOME
TOPIC: Taxation
CONCEPTS: Definition of terms. Territorial applica-
tion. Conformity with municipal law. Exchange
of official publications. Negotiation. Teacher and
student exchange. Claims and settlements. Taxa-
tion. Tax credits. Equitable taxes. General. Tax
exemptions. Air transport. Merchant vessels.
PROCEDURE: Duration. Termination.
PARTIES:
Canada
France

103331 Bilateral Agreement **236 UNTS 297**
SIGNED: 16 Mar 51 FORCE: 28 May 53
REGISTERED: 30 Apr 56 Canada
ARTICLES: 9 LANGUAGE: English. French.
HEADNOTE: DOUBLE TAXATION FISCAL EVA-
SION SUCCESSION DUTIES
TOPIC: Taxation
CONCEPTS: Definition of terms. Territorial applica-
tion. Conformity with municipal law. Exchange
of official publications. Claims and settlements.
Taxation. Death duties. Tax credits.
PROCEDURE: Duration. Termination.
PARTIES:
Canada
France

103332 Bilateral Exchange **236 UNTS 317**
SIGNED: 30 Oct 53 FORCE: 1 Nov 53
REGISTERED: 30 Apr 56 Canada
ARTICLES: 2 LANGUAGE: English. German.
HEADNOTE: GIVING EFFECT CONVENTION 20
MAR 28
TOPIC: Admin Cooperation
CONCEPTS: Annex type material. Previous treaty
extension.
PARTIES:
Canada
Germany, West

103333 Bilateral Exchange **236 UNTS 323**
SIGNED: 15 Apr 53 FORCE: 1 May 53
REGISTERED: 30 Apr 56 Canada
ARTICLES: 2 LANGUAGE: English. German.
HEADNOTE: VISA REQUIREMENTS
TOPIC: Visas
CONCEPTS: Time limit. Visa abolition. Border traf-
fic and migration. Denial of admission. Visas.
Conformity with municipal law. Fees and exemp-
tions.
PARTIES:
Canada
Germany, West

103334 Bilateral Agreement **236 UNTS 329**
SIGNED: 31 Mar 54 FORCE: 7 Jun 54
REGISTERED: 30 Apr 56 Canada
ARTICLES: 7 LANGUAGE: English. Japanese.
HEADNOTE: REGULATING COMMERCE
TOPIC: General Trade
CONCEPTS: Detailed regulations. Exceptions and
exemptions. Treaty implementation. General co-
operation. Import quotas. Reciprocity in trade.
Trade procedures. Balance of payments. Ex-
change rates and regulations. Most favored na-
tion clause. General. Recognition. Transport of
goods.
PROCEDURE: Duration. Ratification. Termination.
PARTIES:
Canada
Japan

103335 Bilateral Convention **237 UNTS 3**
SIGNED: 29 Oct 54 FORCE: 1 Apr 56
REGISTERED: 30 Apr 56 Netherlands
ARTICLES: 15 LANGUAGE: Dutch. German.
HEADNOTE: UNEMPLOYMENT INSURANCE
TOPIC: Non-ILO Labor
CONCEPTS: Detailed regulations. Exceptions and
exemptions. General provisions. Annex or ap-
pendix reference. Annex type material. Domestic
legislation. Wages and salaries. Non-ILO labor

relations. Unemployment. Payment schedules.
Claims and settlements. National treatment.
PROCEDURE: Denunciation. Duration. Future Pro-
cedures Contemplated. Ratification. Renewal or
Revival.
PARTIES:
Germany, West
Netherlands

103336 Bilateral Agreement **237 UNTS 49**
SIGNED: 31 Aug 54 FORCE: 27 Oct 54
REGISTERED: 3 May 56 USA (United States)
ARTICLES: 13 LANGUAGE: English. Spanish.
HEADNOTE: COOPERATIVE PROGRAM PRODUC-
TIVITY
TOPIC: Non-IBRD Project
CONCEPTS: Previous treaty replacement. Operat-
ing agencies. Personnel. Accounting proce-
dures. Financial programs. Funding procedures.
Tax exemptions. Customs exemptions. General
technical assistance. Use restrictions. Aid mis-
sions. Non-bank projects.
INTL ORGS: Special Commission.
TREATY REF: 177UNTS219; 234UNTS71.
PROCEDURE: Duration. Termination.
PARTIES:
El Salvador
USA (United States)
ANNEX
252 UNTS 404. USA (United States). Supplemen-
tation 30 Dec 54. Force 30 Dec 54.
252 UNTS 404. El Salvador. Supplementation
30 Dec 54. Force 30 Dec 54.

103337 Bilateral Agreement **237 UNTS 77**
SIGNED: 16 Apr 54 FORCE: 16 Apr 54
REGISTERED: 3 May 56 USA (United States)
ARTICLES: 10 LANGUAGE: English. Serbo-Croat.
HEADNOTE: COUNTERPART RELEASE AGREE-
MENT
TOPIC: Direct Aid
CONCEPTS: Annex or appendix reference. Annex
type material. General cooperation. Exchange of
information and documents. Public information.
Accounting procedures. Funding procedures.
Economic assistance.
TREATY REF: 152UNTS61; 162UNTS173.
PROCEDURE: Amendment. Duration.
PARTIES:
USA (United States)
Yugoslavia

103338 Bilateral Agreement **237 UNTS 91**
SIGNED: 23 Sep 54 FORCE: 17 Nov 54
REGISTERED: 3 May 56 USA (United States)
ARTICLES: 31 LANGUAGE: English. Spanish.
HEADNOTE: ARMY MISSION
TOPIC: Military Mission
CONCEPTS: Definition of terms. Use of facilities.
Compensation. Indemnities and reimburse-
ments. Exchange rates and regulations. Expense
sharing formulae. Tax exemptions. Customs ex-
emptions. Military assistance. Military training.
Security of information. Airforce-army-navy per-
sonnel ratio. Ranks and privileges. Conditions
for assistance missions. Third country military
personnel. Status of forces.
PROCEDURE: Denunciation. Duration. Ratification.
Renewal or Revival. Termination.
PARTIES:
El Salvador
USA (United States)
ANNEX
338 UNTS 386. USA (United States). Prolongation
17 Nov 58. Force 17 Nov 58.
338 UNTS 386. El Salvador. Prolongation
23 Apr 58. Force 17 Nov 58.
342 UNTS 351. El Salvador. Amendment
31 Mar 59. Force 31 Mar 59.
342 UNTS 351. USA (United States). Amendment
16 Mar 59. Force 31 Mar 59.
476 UNTS 333. El Salvador. Prolongation
3 May 63. Force 3 May 63.
476 UNTS 333. USA (United States). Prolongation
27 Mar 63. Force 3 May 63.

103339 Bilateral Exchange **237 UNTS 111**
SIGNED: 29 Jun 54 FORCE: 29 Jun 54
REGISTERED: 3 May 56 USA (United States)
ARTICLES: 2 LANGUAGE: English. Arabic.

HEADNOTE: DUTY-FREE ENTRY TRANSFER RELIEF
SUPPLIES
TOPIC: Direct Aid
CONCEPTS: Customs exemptions. General aid. Ag-
ricultural commodities.
PROCEDURE: Duration. Termination.
PARTIES:
Jordan
USA (United States)
ANNEX
279 UNTS 324. Jordan. Amendment 28 Sep 55.
Force 28 Sep 55.
279 UNTS 324. USA (United States). Amendment
6 Jul 55. Force 28 Sep 55.

103340 Bilateral Agreement **237 UNTS 121**
SIGNED: 28 Jun 54 FORCE: 28 Jun 54
REGISTERED: 3 May 56 USA (United States)
ARTICLES: 12 LANGUAGE: English.
HEADNOTE: TECHNICAL COOPERATION PRO-
GRAM
TOPIC: Tech Assistance
CONCEPTS: Exceptions and exemptions. Treaty
implementation. Privileges and immunities. General cooperation. Exchange of information and
documents. Informational records. Inspection
and observation. Domestic legislation. Operating agencies. Personnel. Public information. Ti-
tle and deeds. Establishment of commission.
Public health. Education. Research and development. Attachment of funds. Currency deposits.
Exchange rates and regulations. Financial programs. Garnishment of funds. Seizure funds. Assets. Tax exemptions. Customs exemptions. Domestic obligation. Assistance. Materials, equipment and services.
INTL ORGS: Special Commission.
PROCEDURE: Duration. Termination. Application
to Non-self-governing Territories.
PARTIES:
Italy
USA (United States)
ANNEX
367 UNTS 324. USA (United States). Amendment
24 Dec 59. Force 24 Dec 59.
367 UNTS 324. Italy. Amendment 24 Dec 59.
Force 29 Dec 59.
433 UNTS 358. USA (United States). Amendment
30 Jun 60. Force 30 Jun 60.
433 UNTS 358. Italy. Amendment 30 Jun 60.
Force 30 Jun 60.

103341 Bilateral Exchange **237 UNTS 137**
SIGNED: 30 Jun 54 FORCE: 30 Jun 54
REGISTERED: 3 May 56 USA (United States)
ARTICLES: 2 LANGUAGE: English. Portuguese.
HEADNOTE: TECHNICAL COOPERATION RURAL
EDUCATION PROGRAM
TOPIC: Non-IBRD Project
CONCEPTS: Informational records. Personnel. Ex-
change. Financial programs. Funding proce-
dures. Tax exemptions. Customs exemptions.
General technical assistance. Use restrictions.
Materials, equipment and services. Non-bank
projects.
INTL ORGS: Special Commission.
PARTIES:
Brazil
USA (United States)

103342 Bilateral Exchange **237 UNTS 161**
SIGNED: 1 Dec 54 FORCE: 1 Dec 54
REGISTERED: 3 May 56 USA (United States)
ARTICLES: 2 LANGUAGE: English. Spanish.
HEADNOTE: PASSPORT VISA FEES
TOPIC: Visas
CONCEPTS: Time limit. Visas. Tourism. General
cultural cooperation. Fees and exemptions.
PROCEDURE: Termination.
PARTIES:
Guatemala
USA (United States)

103343 Bilateral Agreement **237 UNTS 169**
SIGNED: 13 Dec 54 FORCE: 13 Dec 54
REGISTERED: 3 May 56 USA (United States)
ARTICLES: 7 LANGUAGE: English. Spanish.
HEADNOTE: DEVELOPMENT ASSISTANCE
AGREEMENT
TOPIC: Direct Aid

CONCEPTS: Change of circumstances. Treaty implementation. Privileges and immunities. Conformity with municipal law. General cooperation. Exchange of information and documents. Personnel. Public information. Accounting procedures. Exchange rates and regulations. Expense sharing formulae. Local currency. Commodities and services. Domestic obligation. Economic assistance. Relief supplies. Procurement.
TREATY REF: 199UNTS51.
PROCEDURE: Termination.
PARTIES:
Guatemala
USA (United States)

103344   Bilateral Exchange   **237 UNTS 183**
SIGNED: 6 Nov 54   FORCE: 6 Nov 54
REGISTERED: 3 May 56 USA (United States)
ARTICLES: 2 LANGUAGE: English.
HEADNOTE: TECHNICAL COOPERATION PROGRAM ECONOMIC DEVELOPMENT
TOPIC: Tech Assistance
CONCEPTS: Annex or appendix reference. Exchange of information and documents. Public information. Expense sharing formulae. Commodities and services. Assistance. Economic assistance.
TREATY REF: 198UNTS265.
PROCEDURE: Termination.
PARTIES:
United Arab Rep
USA (United States)
ANNEX
376 UNTS 427. USA (United States). Implementation 2 Apr 60. Force 2 Apr 60.
376 UNTS 427. United Arab Rep. Implementation 2 Apr 60. Force 2 Apr 60.

103345   Bilateral Exchange   **237 UNTS 191**
SIGNED: 10 Dec 54   FORCE: 10 Dec 54
REGISTERED: 3 May 56 USA (United States)
ARTICLES: 2 LANGUAGE: English.
HEADNOTE: PURCHASE MILITARY EQUIPMENT MATERIALS SERVICES
TOPIC: Milit Assistance
CONCEPTS: Exceptions and exemptions. Peaceful relations. Conformity with municipal law. Defense and security. Payment for war supplies. Security of information. Surplus war property. Restrictions on transfer.
PARTIES:
Iceland
USA (United States)

103346   Bilateral Exchange   **237 UNTS 197**
SIGNED: 4 Jan 55   FORCE: 4 Jan 55
REGISTERED: 3 May 56 USA (United States)
ARTICLES: 2 LANGUAGE: English. Japanese.
HEADNOTE: SETTLEMENT CLAIMS RESULTING FROM NUCLEAR TESTS
TOPIC: Specif Claim/Waive
CONCEPTS: Claims and settlements. Lump sum settlements. Specific claims or waivers.
PARTIES:
Japan
USA (United States)

103347   Bilateral Exchange   **237 UNTS 209**
SIGNED: 1 Sep 54   FORCE: 1 Sep 54
REGISTERED: 3 May 56 USA (United States)
ARTICLES: 2 LANGUAGE: English.
HEADNOTE: INVESTMENT GUARANTIES
TOPIC: Claims and Debts
CONCEPTS: Conformity with municipal law. General property. Arbitration. Procedure. Existing tribunals. Negotiation. Reciprocity in financial treatment. Currency. Claims and settlements. Private investment guarantee.
PARTIES:
Thailand
USA (United States)
ANNEX
291 UNTS 326. USA (United States). Amendment 27 Aug 57. Force 27 Aug 57.
291 UNTS 326.   Thailand.   Amendment 27 Aug 57. Force 27 Aug 57.
551 UNTS 292. USA (United States). Amendment 22 Dec 65. Force 22 Dec 65.
551 UNTS 292.   Thailand.   Amendment 22 Dec 65. Force 22 Dec 65.

103348   Bilateral Agreement   **237 UNTS 217**
SIGNED: 6 Sep 51   FORCE: 6 Sep 51
REGISTERED: 3 May 56 USA (United States)
ARTICLES: 12 LANGUAGE: English. Portuguese.
HEADNOTE: DEFENSE AGREEMENT
TOPIC: Milit Assistance
CONCEPTS: Previous treaty replacement. General cooperation. Use of facilities. Vocational training. General technical assistance. Aid missions. Overflights and technical stops. Joint defense. Jurisdiction. Bases and facilities. Withdrawal of occupation.
INTL ORGS: North Atlantic Treaty Organization.
TREATY REF: 34UNTS243; 174UNTS187.
PROCEDURE: Denunciation. Future Procedures Contemplated.
PARTIES:
Portugal
USA (United States)
ANNEX
283 UNTS 323. USA (United States). Prolongation 2 Feb 57. Force 2 Feb 57.
283 UNTS 323.   Portugal.   Prolongation 31 Dec 57. Force 2 Feb 57.
303 UNTS 354. USA (United States). Supplementation 15 Nov 57. Force 15 Nov 57.
303 UNTS 354.   Portugal.   Supplementation 15 Nov 57. Force 15 Nov 57.

103349   Bilateral Exchange   **237 UNTS 231**
SIGNED: 1 May 54   FORCE: 1 May 54
REGISTERED: 3 May 56 USA (United States)
ARTICLES: 2 LANGUAGE: English.
HEADNOTE: INFORMATIONAL MEDIA GUARANTY PROGRAM
TOPIC: Mass Media
CONCEPTS: Local currency. Media guaranty.
TREATY REF: USA'62STAT144; 22USC PARA.1509 (B)(3);1.
PARTIES:
Pakistan
USA (United States)
ANNEX
299 UNTS 420. Pakistan. Amendment 1 Jan 57. Force 8 Jan 57.
299 UNTS 420. USA (United States). Amendment 8 Jan 57. Force 8 Jan 57.
510 UNTS 318. Pakistan. Amendment 15 Apr 63. Force 15 Apr 63.
510 UNTS 318. USA (United States). Amendment 10 Aug 62. Force 15 Apr 63.

103350   Bilateral Agreement   **237 UNTS 237**
SIGNED: 16 Jul 54   FORCE: 10 Aug 54
REGISTERED: 3 May 56 USA (United States)
ARTICLES: 12 LANGUAGE: English. Spanish.
HEADNOTE: AGRICULTURAL DEVELOPMENT
TOPIC: Non-IBRD Project
CONCEPTS: Privileges and immunities. Operating agencies. Financial programs. Funding procedures. Tax exemptions. Customs exemptions. Agriculture. Materials, equipment and services. Aid missions. Non-bank projects.
INTL ORGS: Special Commission.
PROCEDURE: Duration. Ratification. Termination.
PARTIES:
El Salvador
USA (United States)

103351   Bilateral Exchange   **237 UNTS 263**
SIGNED: 30 Jun 54   FORCE: 30 Jun 54
REGISTERED: 3 May 56 USA (United States)
ARTICLES: 2 LANGUAGE: English. Spanish.
HEADNOTE: TECHNICAL COOPERATION PROGRAM HOUSING
TOPIC: Non-IBRD Project
CONCEPTS: Tax exemptions. General technical assistance. Agricultural development/credit.
PROCEDURE: Duration. Termination.
PARTIES:
Colombia
USA (United States)
ANNEX
240 UNTS 444. USA (United States). Prolongation 1 Dec 55. Force 21 Dec 55.
240 UNTS 444.   Colombia.   Prolongation 21 Dec 55. Force 21 Dec 55.

103352   Bilateral Exchange   **237 UNTS 275**
SIGNED: 17 Jun 54   FORCE: 17 Jun 54

REGISTERED: 3 May 56 USA (United States)
ARTICLES: 2 LANGUAGE: English. Spanish.
HEADNOTE: TECHNICAL COOPERATION PROGRAM AGRICULTURAL
TOPIC: Non-IBRD Project
CONCEPTS: Personnel. Funding procedures. Tax exemptions. Customs exemptions. Agriculture. Non-bank projects.
TREATY REF: 141UNTS211; 200UNTS312; 233UNTS306.
PROCEDURE: Duration. Termination.
PARTIES:
Mexico
USA (United States)

103353   Bilateral Convention   **238 UNTS 3**
SIGNED: 16 Apr 54   FORCE: 1 Apr 55
REGISTERED: 8 May 56 USA (United States)
ARTICLES: 9 LANGUAGE: English. Japanese.
HEADNOTE: DOUBLE TAXATION FISCAL EVASION ESTATES INHERITANCES
TOPIC: Taxation
CONCEPTS: Definition of terms. Privileges and immunities. Exchange of official publications. Negotiation. Claims and settlements. Taxation. Death duties. Tax credits. General. Tax exemptions.
PROCEDURE: Ratification. Termination.
PARTIES:
Japan
USA (United States)

103354   Bilateral Convention   **238 UNTS 39**
SIGNED: 16 Apr 54   FORCE: 1 Apr 55
REGISTERED: 8 May 56 USA (United States)
ARTICLES: 20 LANGUAGE: English. Japanese.
HEADNOTE: DOUBLE TAXATION FISCAL EVASION TAXES INCOME
TOPIC: Taxation
CONCEPTS: Definition of terms. Privileges and immunities. Conformity with municipal law. Exchange of official publications. Domestic legislation. Negotiation. Teacher and student exchange. Claims and settlements. Taxation. Tax credits. General. Tax exemptions. Air transport. Merchant vessels.
PROCEDURE: Ratification. Termination.
PARTIES:
Japan
USA (United States)
ANNEX
291 UNTS 332. USA (United States). Supplementation 23 Mar 57. Force 9 Sep 57.
291 UNTS 332.   Japan.   Supplementation 23 Mar 57. Force 9 Sep 57.
530 UNTS 339. USA (United States). Force 2 Sep 64.
530 UNTS 339. Japan. Force 2 Sep 64.
530 UNTS 339. USA (United States). Supplementation 6 May 60. Amendment 7 May 60.
530 UNTS 339.   Japan.   Supplementation 7 May 60. Amendment 7 May 60.
546 UNTS 296. USA (United States). Force 6 May 65.
546 UNTS 296. Japan. Amendment 14 Aug 62. Supplementation 14 Aug 62.
546 UNTS 296. USA (United States). Amendment 14 Aug 62. Supplementation 14 Aug 62.
546 UNTS 296. Japan. Force 6 May 65.

103355   Bilateral Convention   **238 UNTS 97**
SIGNED: 10 Sep 54   FORCE: 11 Oct 55
REGISTERED: 8 May 56 USA (United States)
ARTICLES: 13 LANGUAGE: English.
HEADNOTE: GREAT LAKES FISHERIES
TOPIC: Specific Resources
CONCEPTS: Exchange of information and documents. Establishment of commission. Funding procedures. Fisheries and fishing.
INTL ORGS: Special Commission.
PROCEDURE: Duration. Ratification. Termination.
PARTIES:
Canada
USA (United States)

103356   Bilateral Exchange   **238 UNTS 109**
SIGNED: 6 Sep 55   FORCE: 6 Sep 55
REGISTERED: 8 May 56 USA (United States)
ARTICLES: 2 LANGUAGE: English.

HEADNOTE: ENTRY RIGHTS TRADERS INVES-
TORS
TOPIC: Visas
CONCEPTS: Territorial application. Annex or ap-
pendix reference. Border traffic and migration.
Denial of admission.
PROCEDURE: Duration. Termination.
PARTIES:
Philippines
USA (United States)

103357 Bilateral Agreement **238 UNTS 121**
SIGNED: 21 Jul 55   FORCE: 21 Jul 55
REGISTERED: 8 May 56 USA (United States)
ARTICLES: 10 LANGUAGE: English.
HEADNOTE: CIVIL USES ATOMIC ENERGY
TOPIC: Atomic Energy
CONCEPTS: Definition of terms. Diplomatic mis-
sions. General cooperation. Exchange of infor-
mation and documents. Research results. Scien-
tific exchange. Establishment of trade relations.
Nuclear materials. Non-nuclear materials. Rights
of supplier. Security of information.
PROCEDURE: Duration.
PARTIES:
USA (United States)
Venezuela

103358 Bilateral Agreement **238 UNTS 135**
SIGNED: 15 Nov 54   FORCE: 15 Nov 54
REGISTERED: 8 May 56 USA (United States)
ARTICLES: 4 LANGUAGE: English.
HEADNOTE: EXCHANGE COMMODITIES SALE
GRAIN
TOPIC: Commodity Trade
CONCEPTS: Detailed regulations. Annex or appen-
dix reference. Conformity with municipal law.
General cooperation. Reexport of goods, etc..
Trade procedures. Accounting procedures. Ex-
change rates and regulations. Financial programs. Payment schedules. Transportation
costs. Local currency. Commodity trade. Loan
and credit. Military assistance.
PROCEDURE: Future Procedures Contemplated.
PARTIES:
Turkey
USA (United States)
ANNEX
239 UNTS 390. Turkey. Supplementation
28 Apr 55. Force 28 Apr 55.
239 UNTS 390. USA (United States). Supplementation 28 Apr 55. Force 28 Apr 55.
239 UNTS 396. Turkey. Implementation
28 Apr 55. Force 28 Apr 55.
239 UNTS 396. USA (United States). Implementation 28 Apr 55. Force 28 Apr 55.
239 UNTS 400. Turkey. Amendment 6 Jul 55.
Force 18 Nov 55.
239 UNTS 400. USA (United States). Amendment
18 Nov 55. Force 18 Nov 55.
361 UNTS 332. USA (United States). Amendment
10 Dec 59. Force 10 Dec 59.
361 UNTS 332. Turkey. Amendment 10 Dec 59.
Force 10 Dec 59.

103359 Bilateral Agreement **238 UNTS 149**
SIGNED: 10 Jun 55   FORCE: 10 Jun 55
REGISTERED: 8 May 56 USA (United States)
ARTICLES: 10 LANGUAGE: English.
HEADNOTE: CIVIL USES ATOMIC ENERGY
TOPIC: Atomic Energy
CONCEPTS: Definition of terms. Diplomatic mis-
sions. General cooperation. Exchange of infor-
mation and documents. Research results. Scien-
tific exchange. Establishment of trade relations.
Nuclear materials. Non-nuclear materials. Rights
of supplier. Security of information.
PROCEDURE: Duration.
PARTIES:
Turkey
USA (United States)
ANNEX
407 UNTS 244. USA (United States). Amendment
27 Apr 61. Force 31 May 61.
407 UNTS 244. Turkey. Amendment 27 Apr 61.
Force 31 May 61.
549 UNTS 288. USA (United States). Amendment
3 Jun 65. Force 8 Jul 65.
549 UNTS 288. Turkey. Amendment 3 Jun 65.
Force 8 Jul 65.

103360 Bilateral Exchange **238 UNTS 161**
SIGNED: 7 Jun 51   FORCE: 29 May 51
REGISTERED: 8 May 56 USA (United States)
ARTICLES: 3 LANGUAGE: English. German.
HEADNOTE: RELIEF SUPPLIES PACKAGES
TOPIC: Direct Aid
CONCEPTS: Annex or appendix reference. Annex
type material. Transportation costs. Customs ex-
emptions. Relief supplies.
TREATY REF: GERMANY-U.S.A. NOTE 14OCT50.
PARTIES:
Germany, West
USA (United States)

103361 Bilateral Exchange **238 UNTS 179**
SIGNED: 26 Jan 55   FORCE: 26 Jan 55
REGISTERED: 8 May 56 USA (United States)
ARTICLES: 2 LANGUAGE: English. Italian.
HEADNOTE: AIRWORTHINESS CERTIFICATE IM-
PORTED AIRCRAFT
TOPIC: Air Transport
CONCEPTS: Previous treaty replacement. Confor-
mity with municipal law. Exchange of informa-
tion and documents. Recognition of legal docu-
ments. Use of facilities. Registration certificate.
Airworthiness certificates.
TREATY REF: 137LTS209.
PROCEDURE: Termination.
PARTIES:
Italy
USA (United States)

103362 Bilateral Exchange **238 UNTS 191**
SIGNED: 14 Jan 55   FORCE: 14 Jan 55
REGISTERED: 8 May 56 USA (United States)
ARTICLES: 2 LANGUAGE: English. Spanish.
HEADNOTE: INFORMATIONAL MEDIA GUARANTY
PROGRAM
TOPIC: Mass Media
CONCEPTS: Local currency. Media guaranty.
PARTIES:
Chile
USA (United States)

103363 Bilateral Treaty **238 UNTS 199**
SIGNED: 1 Oct 53   FORCE: 17 Nov 54
REGISTERED: 8 May 56 USA (United States)
ARTICLES: 6 LANGUAGE: English. Korean.
HEADNOTE: MUTUAL DEFENSE
TOPIC: General Military
CONCEPTS: Exceptions and exemptions. Non-
prejudice to UN charter. Peaceful relations. Gen-
eral cooperation. Joint defense. Defense and se-
curity. Military assistance. Status of military
forces.
INTL ORGS: United Nations.
PROCEDURE: Ratification. Termination.
PARTIES:
Korea, South
USA (United States)

103364 Bilateral Exchange **238 UNTS 207**
SIGNED: 19 Nov 54   FORCE: 19 Nov 54
REGISTERED: 8 May 56 USA (United States)
ARTICLES: 3 LANGUAGE: English. Japanese.
HEADNOTE: TRANSFER MILITARY EQUIPMENT
TOPIC: Milit Installation
CONCEPTS: Conformity with municipal law. Gen-
eral cooperation. Materials, equipment and ser-
vices. Military assistance. Surplus war property.
TREATY REF: 232UNTS.
PARTIES:
Japan
USA (United States)

103365 Bilateral Exchange **238 UNTS 217**
SIGNED: 9 Sep 54   FORCE: 9 Sep 54
REGISTERED: 8 May 56 USA (United States)
ARTICLES: 2 LANGUAGE: English. Arabic.
HEADNOTE: ECONOMIC ASSISTANCE
TOPIC: Direct Aid
CONCEPTS: Time limit. Conformity with municipal
law. Financial programs. Commodities and ser-
vices. Economic assistance.
PROCEDURE: Future Procedures Contemplated.
PARTIES:
Libya
USA (United States)

ANNEX
389 UNTS 314. USA (United States). Amendment
30 Jun 60. Force 30 Jun 60.
389 UNTS 314. Libya. Amendment 30 Jun 60.
Force 30 Jun 60.

103366 Bilateral Exchange **238 UNTS 227**
SIGNED: 3 Nov 54   FORCE: 3 Nov 54
REGISTERED: 8 May 56 USA (United States)
ARTICLES: 2 LANGUAGE: English. Arabic.
HEADNOTE: EMERGENCY WHEAT AID
TOPIC: Direct Aid
CONCEPTS: Change of circumstances. Privileges
and immunities. Conformity with municipal law.
Exchange of information and documents. In-
spection and observation. Personnel. Public in-
formation. Title and deeds. Expense sharing for-
mulae. Commodities and services. Relief sup-
plies. Withdrawal conditions.
PROCEDURE: Termination.
PARTIES:
Libya
USA (United States)

103367 Bilateral Exchange **238 UNTS 237**
SIGNED: 19 Nov 54   FORCE: 19 Nov 54
REGISTERED: 8 May 56 USA (United States)
ARTICLES: 2 LANGUAGE: English. Spanish.
HEADNOTE: SICKNESS ACCIDENT INSURANCE
TOPIC: Non-ILO Labor
CONCEPTS: Responsibility and liability. Public
health. Wages and salaries. Non-ILO labor rela-
tions. Sickness and invalidity insurance. Mone-
tary and gold transfers.
TREATY REF: 227UNTS350.
PARTIES:
Mexico
USA (United States)

103368 Bilateral Exchange **238 UNTS 247**
SIGNED: 25 Oct 54   FORCE: 29 Oct 54
REGISTERED: 8 May 56 USA (United States)
ARTICLES: 2 LANGUAGE: English. Spanish.
HEADNOTE: DUTY-FREE ENTRY EXEMPTION IN-
TERNAL TAXATION RELIEF SUPPLIES
TOPIC: Direct Aid
CONCEPTS: Transportation costs. Tax exemp-
tions. Customs exemptions. Materials, equip-
ment and services. Relief supplies.
PARTIES:
Peru
USA (United States)
ANNEX
273 UNTS 295. USA (United States). Amendment
23 Jun 55. Force 3 Aug 55.
273 UNTS 295. Peru. Amendment 3 Aug 55.
Force 3 Aug 55.

103369 Bilateral Convention **239 UNTS 3**
SIGNED: 22 Jul 54   FORCE: 20 Dec 54
REGISTERED: 8 May 56 USA (United States)
ARTICLES: 21 LANGUAGE: English. German.
HEADNOTE: DOUBLE TAXATION TAXES INCOME
TOPIC: Taxation
CONCEPTS: Definition of terms. Territorial applica-
tion. Privileges and immunities. Conformity with
municipal law. Exchange of official publications.
Domestic legislation. Negotiation. Teacher and
student exchange. Taxation. General. Tax ex-
emptions. Air transport. Merchant vessels.
PROCEDURE: Duration. Ratification. Termination.
PARTIES:
Germany, West
USA (United States)

103370 Bilateral Exchange **239 UNTS 45**
SIGNED: 23 Mar 53   FORCE: 23 Mar 53
REGISTERED: 8 May 56 USA (United States)
ARTICLES: 2 LANGUAGE: English. French.
HEADNOTE: MUTUAL DEFENSE ASSISTANCE
TOPIC: Milit Assistance
CONCEPTS: Exceptions and exemptions. Non-
prejudice to UN charter. Peaceful relations. Con-
formity with municipal law. Indemnities and re-
imbursements. Materials, equipment and ser-
vices. Defense and security. Self-defense.
Military assistance. Security of information. Ex-
change of defense information. Restrictions on
transfer.

INTL ORGS: United Nations.
PARTIES:
Lebanon
USA (United States)

103371 Bilateral Exchange **239 UNTS 53**
SIGNED: 29 Jan 55   FORCE: 29 Jan 55
REGISTERED: 8 May 56 USA (United States)
ARTICLES: 2 LANGUAGE: English.
HEADNOTE: LOAN NAVAL VESSELS
TOPIC: Milit Assistance
CONCEPTS: Time limit. Annex or appendix refer-
ence. Responsibility and liability. Compensation.
Indemnities and reimbursements. Claims and
settlements. Delivery schedules. Materials,
equipment and services. Lease of military prop-
erty. Military assistance. Naval vessels. Security
of information. Exchange of defense information. Restrictions on transfer.
TREATY REF: 80UNTS205; 179UNTS105.
PROCEDURE: Future Procedures Contemplated.
Renewal or Revival.
PARTIES:
Korea, South
USA (United States)
                ANNEX
269 UNTS 374. USA (United States). Supplementation 29 Aug 55. Force 29 Aug 55.
269 UNTS 374. Korea, South. Supplementation
29 Aug 55. Force 29 Aug 55.
371 UNTS 300. USA (United States). Supplementation 22 Oct 59. Force 29 Jan 60.
371 UNTS 300. Korea, South. Supplementation
29 Jan 60. Force 29 Jan 60.
371 UNTS 304. USA (United States). Supplementation 28 Mar 60. Force 1 Apr 60.
371 UNTS 304. Korea, South. Supplementation
1 Apr 60. Force 1 Apr 60.
401 UNTS 280. Korea, South. Supplementation
28 Oct 60. Force 4 Nov 60.
401 UNTS 280. USA (United States). Supplementation 4 Nov 60. Force 4 Nov 60.
473 UNTS 344. USA (United States). Supplementation 14 Dec 62. Force 11 Feb 63.
473 UNTS 344. Korea, South. Supplementation
11 Feb 63. Force 11 Feb 63.

103372 Bilateral Agreement **239 UNTS 61**
SIGNED: 18 Jan 55   FORCE: 18 Jan 55
REGISTERED: 9 May 56 USA (United States)
ARTICLES: 5 LANGUAGE: English.
HEADNOTE: SURPLUS AGRI COMMOD
TOPIC: US Agri Commod Aid
CONCEPTS: Treaty implementation. General coop-
eration. Local currency. Domestic obligation.
Surplus commodities.
PARTIES:
Pakistan
USA (United States)
                ANNEX
271 UNTS 438. Pakistan. Amendment 9 Feb 56.
Force 25 Feb 56.
271 UNTS 438. USA (United States). Amendment
25 Feb 56. Force 25 Feb 56.

103373 Bilateral Agreement **239 UNTS 69**
SIGNED: 29 Jul 54   FORCE: 1 Jan 55
REGISTERED: 9 May 56 USA (United States)
ARTICLES: 30 LANGUAGE: English.
HEADNOTE: PARCEL POST
TOPIC: Postal Service
CONCEPTS: Detailed regulations. Territorial appli-
cation. Responsibility and liability. Compensa-
tion. Payment schedules. Customs duties. Cus-
toms exemptions. Postal services. Regulations.
Insured letters and boxes. Parcel post. Rates and
charges.
INTL ORGS: Universal Postal Union.
TREATY REF: 169UNTS3; 186 UNTS356;
202UNTS340; 227UNTS390.
PROCEDURE: Duration. Termination.
PARTIES:
India
USA (United States)

103374 Bilateral Exchange **239 UNTS 117**
SIGNED: 20 Apr 55   FORCE: 20 Apr 55
REGISTERED: 9 May 56 USA (United States)
ARTICLES: 2 LANGUAGE: English. Spanish.
HEADNOTE: SURPLUS AGRI COMMOD

TOPIC: US Agri Commod Aid
CONCEPTS: Annex or appendix reference. Surplus
commodities.
PARTIES:
Spain
USA (United States)
                ANNEX
303 UNTS 357. USA (United States). Amendment
27 Nov 57. Force 7 Dec 57.
303 UNTS 357. Spain. Amendment 7 Dec 57.
Force 7 Dec 57.
435 UNTS 346.   Spain.   Supplementation
6 Nov 61. Force 6 Nov 61.
435 UNTS 346. USA (United States). Supplementation 18 Oct 61. Force 6 Nov 61.

103375 Bilateral Agreement **239 UNTS 135**
SIGNED: 15 Oct 54   FORCE: 2 Nov 55
REGISTERED: 9 May 56 USA (United States)
ARTICLES: 14 LANGUAGE: English. German.
HEADNOTE: TAX RELIEF DEFENSE EXPENDI-
TURES
TOPIC: Milit Assistance
CONCEPTS: Detailed regulations. Exceptions and
exemptions. Annex or appendix reference. Gen-
eral cooperation. Exchange of information and
documents. Indemnities and reimbursements.
Payment schedules. Tax exemptions. Customs
exemptions. Materials, equipment and services.
Defense and security.
PROCEDURE: Amendment. Future Procedures
Contemplated.
PARTIES:
Germany, West
USA (United States)

103376 Bilateral Exchange **239 UNTS 165**
SIGNED: 28 Oct 55   FORCE: 28 Oct 55
REGISTERED: 9 May 56 USA (United States)
ARTICLES: 2 LANGUAGE: English.
HEADNOTE: ADMINISTRATION SCHOOLS NAVAL
RESERVATION
TOPIC: Milit Installation
CONCEPTS: Conformity with municipal law. Use of
facilities. Education. Indemnities and reimburse-
ments. Bases and facilities.
PARTIES:
Philippines
USA (United States)

103377 Bilateral Exchange **239 UNTS 173**
SIGNED: 18 Nov 55   FORCE: 18 Nov 55
REGISTERED: 9 May 56 USA (United States)
ARTICLES: 3 LANGUAGE: English.
HEADNOTE: GUARANTY PRIVATE INVESTMENTS
TOPIC: Claims and Debts
CONCEPTS: Conformity with municipal law. Gen-
eral property. Responsibility and liability. Local
currency. Claims and settlements. Debt settle-
ment. Private investment guarantee.
PARTIES:
Colombia
USA (United States)

103378 Bilateral Exchange **239 UNTS 181**
SIGNED: 28 Oct 55   FORCE: 26 Oct 55
REGISTERED: 9 May 56 USA (United States)
ARTICLES: 4 LANGUAGE: English. Spanish.
HEADNOTE: MILITARY ASSISTANCE ADVISORY
GROUP
TOPIC: Military Mission
CONCEPTS: Airforce-army-navy personnel ratio.
Ranks and privileges.
TREATY REF: 165UNTS31.
PARTIES:
Peru
USA (United States)

103379 Bilateral Exchange **239 UNTS 195**
SIGNED: 3 Nov 55   FORCE: 3 Nov 55
REGISTERED: 9 May 56 USA (United States)
ARTICLES: 2 LANGUAGE: English. French.
HEADNOTE: INFORMATIONAL MEDIA GUARANTY
PROGRAM
TOPIC: Mass Media
CONCEPTS: Media guaranty.
PARTIES:
USA (United States)
Vietnam, South

103380 Bilateral Agreement **239 UNTS 201**
SIGNED: 14 Nov 55   FORCE: 14 Nov 55
REGISTERED: 9 May 56 USA (United States)
ARTICLES: 7 LANGUAGE: English.
HEADNOTE: SALE PURCHASE TIN CONCEN-
TRATES
TOPIC: Commodity Trade
CONCEPTS: Trade agencies. Attachment of funds.
Currency. Exchange rates and regulations. Fees
and exemptions. Payment schedules. Non-inter-
est rates and fees. Commodity trade. Quotas.
PROCEDURE: Duration.
PARTIES:
Thailand
USA (United States)
                ANNEX
271 UNTS 442. USA (United States). Supplemen-
tation 12 Mar 56. Force 12 Mar 56.
271 UNTS 442.   Thailand.   Supplementation
12 Mar 56. Force 12 Mar 56.

103381 Bilateral Agreement **239 UNTS 207**
SIGNED: 16 Nov 55   FORCE: 16 Nov 55
REGISTERED: 9 May 56 USA (United States)
ARTICLES: 7 LANGUAGE: English. Portuguese.
HEADNOTE: AGRI COMMOD
TOPIC: Commodity Trade
CONCEPTS: Detailed regulations. General provi-
sions. Time limit. Treaty implementation. Gen-
eral cooperation. Exchange of information and
documents. Reexport of goods, etc.. Interest
rates.
PARTIES:
Brazil
USA (United States)
                ANNEX
273 UNTS 302. USA (United States). Amendment
28 Jun 56. Force 29 Jun 56.
273 UNTS 302. Brazil. Amendment 29 Jun 56.
Force 29 Jun 56.

103382 Bilateral Agreement **239 UNTS 235**
SIGNED: 28 Jul 55   FORCE: 28 Jul 55
REGISTERED: 9 May 56 USA (United States)
ARTICLES: 10 LANGUAGE: English.
HEADNOTE: CIVIL USES ATOMIC ENERGY
TOPIC: Atomic Energy
CONCEPTS: Definition of terms. Diplomatic mis-
sions. General cooperation. Exchange of infor-
mation and documents. Research results. Scien-
tific exchange. Establishment of trade relations.
Nuclear materials. Non-nuclear materials. Rights
of supplier. Security of information.
PROCEDURE: Duration.
PARTIES:
Italy
USA (United States)

103383 Bilateral Agreement **239 UNTS 247**
SIGNED: 18 Jul 55   FORCE: 18 Jul 55
REGISTERED: 9 May 56 USA (United States)
ARTICLES: 10 LANGUAGE: English.
HEADNOTE: CIVIL USES ATOMIC ENERGY
TOPIC: Atomic Energy
CONCEPTS: Definition of terms. Diplomatic mis-
sions. General cooperation. Exchange of infor-
mation and documents. Research results. Scien-
tific exchange. Establishment of trade relations.
Nuclear materials. Non-nuclear materials. Rights
of supplier. Security of information.
PROCEDURE: Duration.
PARTIES:
Lebanon
USA (United States)

103384 Bilateral Agreement **239 UNTS 259**
SIGNED: 11 Aug 55   FORCE: 11 Aug 55
REGISTERED: 9 May 56 USA (United States)
ARTICLES: 10 LANGUAGE: English.
HEADNOTE: CIVIL USES ATOMIC ENERGY
TOPIC: Atomic Energy
CONCEPTS: Definition of terms. Diplomatic mis-
sions. General cooperation. Exchange of infor-
mation and documents. Research results. Scien-
tific exchange. Establishment of trade relations.
Nuclear materials. Non-nuclear materials. Rights
of supplier. Security of information.
PROCEDURE: Duration.

PARTIES:
Pakistan
USA (United States)

103385   Bilateral Agreement   **239 UNTS 271**
SIGNED: 27 Jul 55   FORCE: 27 Jul 55
REGISTERED: 9 May 56 USA (United States)
ARTICLES: 10 LANGUAGE: English.
HEADNOTE: CIVIL USES ATOMIC ENERGY
TOPIC: Atomic Energy
CONCEPTS: Definition of terms. Diplomatic missions. General cooperation. Exchange of information and documents. Research results. Scientific exchange. Establishment of trade relations. Nuclear materials. Non-nuclear materials. Rights of supplier. Security of information.
PROCEDURE: Duration.
PARTIES:
Philippines
USA (United States)
                    ANNEX
377 UNTS 420. USA (United States). Amendment 11 Jun 60. Force 15 Jul 60.
377 UNTS 420.   Philippines.   Amendment 11 Jun 60. Force 15 Jul 60.
531 UNTS 332. USA (United States). Amendment 7 Aug 63. Force 4 Nov 64.
531 UNTS 332.   Philippines.   Amendment 7 Aug 63. Force 4 Nov 64.
607 UNTS 266.   Philippines.   Amendment 27 Jun 66.
607 UNTS 266. USA (United States). Amendment 27 Jun 66. Force 21 Oct 66.

103386   Bilateral Agreement   **239 UNTS 283**
SIGNED: 21 Jul 55   FORCE: 21 Jul 55
REGISTERED: 9 May 56 USA (United States)
ARTICLES: 10 LANGUAGE: English. Portuguese.
HEADNOTE: CIVIL USES ATOMIC ENERGY
TOPIC: Atomic Energy
CONCEPTS: Definition of terms. Diplomatic missions. General cooperation. Exchange of information and documents. Research results. Scientific exchange. Establishment of trade relations. Nuclear materials. Non-nuclear materials. Rights of supplier. Security of information.
PROCEDURE: Duration.
PARTIES:
Portugal
USA (United States)
                    ANNEX
290 UNTS 336. Portugal. Amendment 7 Jun 57. Force 19 Sep 57.
290 UNTS 336. USA (United States). Amendment 7 Jun 57. Force 19 Sep 57.
377 UNTS 428. Portugal. Amendment 11 Jun 60. Force 19 Jul 60.
377 UNTS 428. USA (United States). Amendment 11 Jun 60. Force 19 Jul 60.
459 UNTS 298. USA (United States). Amendment 28 May 62. Force 20 Jul 62.
459 UNTS 298.   Portugal.   Amendment 28 May 62. Force 20 Jul 62.
531 UNTS 336. USA (United States). Amendment 11 Aug 64. Force 6 Nov 64.
531 UNTS 336. Portugal. Amendment 11 Aug 64. Force 6 Nov 64.

103387   Bilateral Agreement   **239 UNTS 299**
SIGNED: 19 Jul 55   FORCE: 19 Jul 55
REGISTERED: 9 May 56 USA (United States)
ARTICLES: 10 LANGUAGE: English.
HEADNOTE: CIVIL USES ATOMIC ENERGY
TOPIC: Atomic Energy
CONCEPTS: Definition of terms. Diplomatic missions. General cooperation. Exchange of information and documents. Research results. Scientific exchange. Establishment of trade relations. Nuclear materials. Non-nuclear materials. Rights of supplier. Security of information.
PROCEDURE: Duration.
PARTIES:
Spain
USA (United States)

103388   Bilateral Agreement   **239 UNTS 311**
SIGNED: 18 Jul 55   FORCE: 18 Jul 55
REGISTERED: 9 May 56 USA (United States)
ARTICLES: 11 LANGUAGE: English.
HEADNOTE: CIVIL USES ATOMIC ENERGY

TOPIC: Atomic Energy
CONCEPTS: Definition of terms. Previous treaty extension. Exchange of information and documents. Research results. Scientific exchange. Establishment of trade relations. Trade procedures. Currency. Payment schedules. Nuclear materials. Non-nuclear materials. Peaceful use.
PROCEDURE: Duration.
PARTIES:
Switzerland
USA (United States)

103389   Bilateral Exchange   **239 UNTS 325**
SIGNED: 22 Apr 55   FORCE: 22 Apr 55
REGISTERED: 9 May 56 USA (United States)
ARTICLES: 2 LANGUAGE: English. Spanish.
HEADNOTE: DISPOSITION SURPLUS EQUIPMENT MATERIALS
TOPIC: Milit Assistance
CONCEPTS: Conformity with municipal law. General cooperation. Exchange of information and documents. Reexport of goods, etc.. Delivery schedules. Materials, equipment and services. Surplus property. Return of equipment and recapture.
TREATY REF: 199UNTS267.
PARTIES:
Dominican Republic
USA (United States)

103390   Bilateral Agreement   **240 UNTS 3**
SIGNED: 10 Nov 55   FORCE: 10 Nov 55
REGISTERED: 9 May 56 USA (United States)
ARTICLES: 6 LANGUAGE: English.
HEADNOTE: AGRI COMMOD AGREE
TOPIC: US Agri Commod Aid
CONCEPTS: General provisions. Conformity with municipal law. General cooperation. Exchange of information and documents. Currency deposits. Exchange rates and regulations. Purchase authorizations. Local currency. Domestic obligation. Loan and credit. Commodities schedule. Surplus commodities.
PARTIES:
Israel
USA (United States)
                    ANNEX
288 UNTS 374.   Israel.   Amendment   10 Apr 57. Force 10 Apr 57.
288 UNTS 374. USA (United States). Amendment 9 Apr 57. Force 10 Apr 57.
314 UNTS 348. Israel. Amendment 28 Aug 58.
314 UNTS 348. USA (United States). Amendment 28 Aug 58.

103391   Bilateral Exchange   **240 UNTS 17**
SIGNED: 27 Apr 55   FORCE: 27 Apr 55
REGISTERED: 9 May 56 USA (United States)
ARTICLES: 4 LANGUAGE: English. French.
HEADNOTE: ESTABLISH JOINT COUNCIL ECONOMIC AID
TOPIC: IGO Establishment
CONCEPTS: Annex or appendix reference. Conformity with municipal law. Recognition and enforcement of legal decisions. General health, education, culture, welfare and labor. Education. General technical assistance. Economic assistance. Establishment. Internal structure.
INTL ORGS: Special Commission.
PROCEDURE: Amendment. Duration.
PARTIES:
Haiti
USA (United States)

103392   Bilateral Agreement   **240 UNTS 37**
SIGNED: 14 Dec 55   FORCE: 14 Dec 55
REGISTERED: 9 May 56 USA (United States)
ARTICLES: 6 LANGUAGE: English.
HEADNOTE: AGRI COMMOD
TOPIC: US Agri Commod Aid
CONCEPTS: General provisions. Conformity with municipal law. General cooperation. Exchange of information and documents. Currency deposits. Purchase authorizations. Local currency. Domestic obligation. Loan and credit. Commodities schedule. Surplus commodities.
PARTIES:
United Arab Rep
USA (United States)

ANNEX
272 UNTS 306. United Arab Rep. Amendment 17 Feb 56. Force 17 Feb 56.
272 UNTS 306. USA (United States). Amendment 17 Feb 56. Force 17 Feb 56.

103393   Bilateral Agreement   **240 UNTS 47**
SIGNED: 30 Jun 55   FORCE: 27 Dec 55
REGISTERED: 9 May 56 USA (United States)
ARTICLES: 11 LANGUAGE: English. German.
HEADNOTE: MUTUAL DEFENSE ASSISTANCE
TOPIC: Milit Assistance
CONCEPTS: Guarantees and safeguards. Annex or appendix reference. Non-prejudice to UN charter. Peaceful relations. Privileges and immunities. Conformity with municipal law. Exchange of information and documents. Inspection and observation. Public information. Use of facilities. Garnishment of funds. Local currency. Tax exemptions. Recognition. Domestic obligation. Materials, equipment and services. Aid missions. Joint defense. Self-defense. Return of equipment and recapture. Security of information. Military assistance missions. Exchange of defense information. Restrictions on transfer. Raw materials.
INTL ORGS: North Atlantic Treaty Organization. United Nations.
TREATY REF: 34UNTS243; 126UNTS350.
PROCEDURE: Amendment. Future Procedures Contemplated. Registration.
PARTIES:
Germany, West
USA (United States)

103394   Bilateral Exchange   **240 UNTS 69**
SIGNED: 30 Jun 55   FORCE: 27 Dec 55
REGISTERED: 9 May 56 USA (United States)
ARTICLES: 2 LANGUAGE: English. German.
HEADNOTE: DISPOSITION MILITARY EQUIPMENT
TOPIC: Milit Assistance
CONCEPTS: Annex or appendix reference. Exchange of information and documents. Reexport of goods, etc.. Delivery schedules. Surplus property. Return of equipment and recapture. Surplus war property.
TREATY REF: 240UNTS47.
PARTIES:
Germany, West
USA (United States)
                    ANNEX
405 UNTS 323. Germany, West. Amendment 9 Mar 61. Force 9 Mar 61.
405 UNTS 323. USA (United States). Amendment 9 Mar 61. Force 9 Mar 61.

103395   Bilateral Agreement   **240 UNTS 79**
SIGNED: 23 Dec 55   FORCE: 23 Dec 55
REGISTERED: 9 May 56 USA (United States)
ARTICLES: 11 LANGUAGE: English.
HEADNOTE: SALES POULTRY
TOPIC: US Agri Commod Aid
CONCEPTS: General cooperation. Currency deposits. Exchange rates and regulations. Purchase authorizations. Domestic obligation. Commodities schedule. Surplus commodities.
PARTIES:
Germany, West
USA (United States)
                    ANNEX
421 UNTS 304. USA (United States). Supplementation 19 May 61. Force 24 Aug 61.
421 UNTS 304. Germany, West. Supplementation 24 Aug 61. Force 24 Aug 61.

103396   Bilateral Exchange   **240 UNTS 87**
SIGNED: 11 Feb 55   FORCE: 11 Feb 55
REGISTERED: 9 May 56 USA (United States)
ARTICLES: 2 LANGUAGE: English. Italian.
HEADNOTE: DEFENSE SUPPORT AID
TOPIC: Milit Assistance
CONCEPTS: Conformity with municipal law. Public information. Non-ILO labor relations. Accounting procedures. Indemnities and reimbursements. Local currency. Military assistance.
TREATY REF: 20UNTS43; 55UNTS318.
PARTIES:
Italy
USA (United States)

103397 Bilateral Exchange **240 UNTS 95**
SIGNED: 28 Dec 55 FORCE: 28 Dec 55
REGISTERED: 9 May 56 USA (United States)
ARTICLES: 2 LANGUAGE: English. French.
HEADNOTE: ARTIBONITE VALLEY PROJECT
TOPIC: Non-IBRD Project
CONCEPTS: Funding procedures. Economic assistance. Non-bank projects.
TREATY REF: 151UNTS191; 180UNTS372.
PARTIES:
Haiti
USA (United States)

103398 Bilateral Agreement **240 UNTS 101**
SIGNED: 10 Jan 56 FORCE: 9 Apr 56
REGISTERED: 9 May 56 USA (United States)
ARTICLES: 9 LANGUAGE: English. Spanish.
HEADNOTE: FURNISHING SUPPLIES SERVICES NAVAL VESSELS
TOPIC: Milit Assistance
CONCEPTS: Time limit. Indemnities and reimbursements. Currency. Materials, equipment and services. Ports and pilotage. Naval vessels.
PROCEDURE: Termination.
PARTIES:
Cuba
USA (United States)

103399 Bilateral Exchange **240 UNTS 111**
SIGNED: 22 Dec 55 FORCE: 22 Dec 55
REGISTERED: 9 May 56 USA (United States)
ARTICLES: 2 LANGUAGE: English. Arabic.
HEADNOTE: DUTY-FREE ENTRY EXEMPTION INTERNAL TAXATION RELIEF SUPPLIES
TOPIC: Direct Aid
CONCEPTS: Transportation costs. Tax exemptions. Customs exemptions. Materials, equipment and services. Relief supplies.
PROCEDURE: Termination.
PARTIES:
Libya
USA (United States)

103400 Bilateral Exchange **240 UNTS 121**
SIGNED: 19 Jan 56 FORCE: 19 Jan 56
REGISTERED: 9 May 56 USA (United States)
ARTICLES: 2 LANGUAGE: English.
HEADNOTE: ECONOMIC ASSISTANCE
TOPIC: Direct Aid
CONCEPTS: Guarantees and safeguards. Conformity with municipal law. Financial programs. Interest rates. Payment schedules. Local currency. Economic assistance. Grants. Loan repayment. Terms of loan.
PROCEDURE: Future Procedures Contemplated.
PARTIES:
USA (United States)
Yugoslavia

103401 Bilateral Agreement **240 UNTS 129**
SIGNED: 3 Feb 56 FORCE: 3 Feb 56
REGISTERED: 9 May 56 USA (United States)
ARTICLES: 10 LANGUAGE: English.
HEADNOTE: CIVIL USES ATOMIC ENERGY
TOPIC: Atomic Energy
CONCEPTS: Definition of terms. Diplomatic missions. General cooperation. Exchange of information and documents. Research results. Scientific exchange. Establishment of trade relations. Nuclear materials. Non-nuclear materials. Rights of supplier. Security of information.
PROCEDURE: Duration.
PARTIES:
Korea, South
USA (United States)
ANNEX
316 UNTS 358. USA (United States). Amendment 14 Mar 58. Force 22 May 58.
316 UNTS 358. Korea, South. Amendment 14 Mar 58. Force 22 May 58.

103402 Bilateral Agreement **240 UNTS 143**
SIGNED: 2 Dec 53 FORCE: 2 Dec 53
REGISTERED: 9 May 56 USSR (Soviet Union)
ARTICLES: 10 LANGUAGE: English. Russian.
HEADNOTE: TRADE
TOPIC: General Trade
CONCEPTS: Detailed regulations. Exceptions and exemptions. General provisions. Treaty implementation. Annex or appendix reference. Conformity with municipal law. Export quotas. Import quotas. Accounting procedures. Banking. Currency. Exchange rates and regulations. Financial programs. Payment schedules. Navigational conditions. Water transport.
TREATY REF: 240UNTS151.
PROCEDURE: Duration. Renewal or Revival.
PARTIES:
India
USSR (Soviet Union)

103403 Bilateral Agreement **240 UNTS 173**
SIGNED: 17 Jul 54 FORCE: 1 Jan 56
REGISTERED: 9 May 56 USSR (Soviet Union)
ARTICLES: 11 LANGUAGE: Russian. Finnish.
HEADNOTE: DELIVERIES GOODS
TOPIC: General Trade
CONCEPTS: Payment schedules. Commodity trade. Delivery schedules.
PROCEDURE: Duration. Ratification.
PARTIES:
Finland
USSR (Soviet Union)

103404 Bilateral Agreement **240 UNTS 207**
SIGNED: 5 Jan 55 FORCE: 23 Jul 55
REGISTERED: 9 May 56 USSR (Soviet Union)
ARTICLES: 10 LANGUAGE: Russian. Serbo-Croat.
HEADNOTE: TRADE
TOPIC: General Trade
CONCEPTS: Establishment of commission. Establishment of trade relations. Reciprocity in trade. Quotas.
INTL ORGS: Special Commission.
PROCEDURE: Duration. Termination.
PARTIES:
USSR (Soviet Union)
Yugoslavia

103405 Bilateral Agreement **240 UNTS 225**
SIGNED: 5 Jan 55 FORCE: 23 Jul 55
REGISTERED: 9 May 56 USSR (Soviet Union)
ARTICLES: 7 LANGUAGE: Russian. Serbo-Croat.
HEADNOTE: PAYMENTS
TOPIC: Finance
CONCEPTS: General cooperation. General trade. Export quotas. Accounting procedures. Banking. Indemnities and reimbursements. Balance of payments. Currency. Financial programs. Inadequacy of funds. Interest rates. Payment schedules. Transportation costs. Quotas. Water transport.
TREATY REF: 240UNTS216;234UNTS234.
PARTIES:
USSR (Soviet Union)
Yugoslavia

103406 Bilateral Agreement **240 UNTS 243**
SIGNED: 24 Jan 55 FORCE: 22 Apr 55
REGISTERED: 9 May 56 USSR (Soviet Union)
ARTICLES: 6 LANGUAGE: Russian. Finnish.
HEADNOTE: LOANS
TOPIC: Loans and Credits
CONCEPTS: Friendship and amity. Operating agencies. Exchange rates and regulations. Interest rates. Payment schedules. Loan and credit. Loan repayment. Terms of loan.
TREATY REF: 48UNTS149; 226UNTS338.
PROCEDURE: Ratification.
PARTIES:
Finland
USSR (Soviet Union)

103407 Bilateral Agreement **240 UNTS 253**
SIGNED: 28 Jun 55 FORCE: 19 Sep 55
REGISTERED: 9 May 56 USSR (Soviet Union)
ARTICLES: 8 LANGUAGE: Russian. Persian.
HEADNOTE: TRANSIT QUESTIONS
TOPIC: General Transport
CONCEPTS: Customs exemptions. Transport of goods.
TREATY REF: 18DEMARTENS323.
PROCEDURE: Denunciation. Ratification.
PARTIES:
Afghanistan
USSR (Soviet Union)

103408 Bilateral Agreement **240 UNTS 267**
SIGNED: 3 Sep 55 FORCE: 28 Dec 55
REGISTERED: 9 May 56 USSR (Soviet Union)
ARTICLES: 12 LANGUAGE: Russian. Serbo-Croat.
HEADNOTE: CONCERNING AIR TRANSPORT
TOPIC: Air Transport
CONCEPTS: Conformity with municipal law. General cooperation. Exchange of information and documents. Personnel. Recognition of legal documents. Use of facilities. Meteorology. Fees and exemptions. Non-interest rates and fees. Customs duties. Customs exemptions. Registration certificate. Routes and logistics. Navigational conditions. Air transport. Airport facilities. Airport equipment. Airworthiness certificates. Operating authorizations and regulations.
PROCEDURE: Denunciation. Ratification.
PARTIES:
USSR (Soviet Union)
Yugoslavia

103409 Bilateral Treaty **240 UNTS 289**
SIGNED: 17 Oct 55 FORCE: 17 Feb 56
REGISTERED: 9 May 56 USSR (Soviet Union)
ARTICLES: 13 LANGUAGE: Russian. German.
HEADNOTE: PROMOTION ECONOMIC RELATIONS TREATY COMMERCE & NAVIGATION
TOPIC: General Economic
CONCEPTS: Exceptions and exemptions. Annex or appendix reference. Nationality and citizenship. Non-diplomatic delegations. Informational records. Juridical personality. Legal protection and assistance. Arbitration. Special tribunals. General trade. Reciprocity in trade. Trade procedures. Most favored nation clause. General transportation. Transport of goods. Licenses and certificates of nationality. Ports and pilotage.
PARTIES:
Austria
USSR (Soviet Union)

103410 Bilateral Treaty **240 UNTS 317**
SIGNED: 31 Oct 55 FORCE: 30 Mar 56
REGISTERED: 9 May 56 USSR (Soviet Union)
ARTICLES: 6 LANGUAGE: Russian. Arabic.
HEADNOTE: FRIENDSHIP
TOPIC: General Amity
CONCEPTS: Treaty interpretation. Friendship and amity. Diplomatic relations establishment. Establishment of trade relations. Reciprocity in trade.
PROCEDURE: Amendment. Denunciation. Duration. Ratification. Renewal or Revival.
PARTIES:
USSR (Soviet Union)
Yemen

103411 Bilateral Agreement **240 UNTS 329**
SIGNED: 21 Dec 55 FORCE: 21 Dec 55
REGISTERED: 9 May 56 USA (United States)
ARTICLES: 6 LANGUAGE: English. Spanish.
HEADNOTE: SALE PURCHASE SURPLUS EDIBLE OIL
TOPIC: Commodity Trade
CONCEPTS: General cooperation. Reexport of goods, etc.. Trade agencies. Accounting procedures. Banking. Balance of payments. Currency. Financial programs. Commodity trade.
PARTIES:
Argentina
USA (United States)
ANNEX
462 UNTS 344. USA (United States). Amendment 19 Sep 62. Force 26 Nov 62.
462 UNTS 344. Argentina. Amendment 26 Nov 62. Force 26 Nov 62.

103412 Bilateral Agreement **240 UNTS 347**
SIGNED: 18 Jul 55 FORCE: 30 Dec 55
REGISTERED: 9 May 56 USA (United States)
ARTICLES: 11 LANGUAGE: English.
HEADNOTE: CIVIL USES AVIATION
TOPIC: Atomic Energy
CONCEPTS: Definition of terms. Diplomatic missions. General cooperation. Exchange of information and documents. Scientific exchange. Establishment of trade relations. Nuclear materials. Non-nuclear materials. Rights of supplier. Security of information.
PROCEDURE: Duration.

PARTIES:
Netherlands
USA (United States)

103413 Bilateral Agreement **240 UNTS 361**
SIGNED: 14 Nov 55   FORCE: 27 Dec 55
REGISTERED: 9 May 56 USA (United States)
ARTICLES: 9 LANGUAGE: English. Japanese.
HEADNOTE: CIVIL USES ATOMIC ENERGY
TOPIC: Atomic Energy
CONCEPTS: Definition of terms. Diplomatic missions. Conformity with municipal law. Exchange of information and documents. Scientific exchange. Establishment of trade relations. Nuclear materials. Non-nuclear materials. Rights of supplier. Security of information.
PARTIES:
Japan
USA (United States)

103414 Bilateral Exchange **240 UNTS 391**
SIGNED: 28 Dec 50   FORCE: 28 Dec 50
REGISTERED: 11 May 56 USA (United States)
ARTICLES: 2 LANGUAGE: English.
HEADNOTE: RETURN UNUSABLE MATERIAL UNDER MUTUAL DEFENSE ASSISTANCE
TOPIC: Milit Assistance
CONCEPTS: Annex or appendix reference. General property. Reexport of goods, etc.. Delivery schedules. Surplus property. Return of equipment and recapture.
TREATY REF: 80UNTS241.
PARTIES:
Norway
USA (United States)
ANNEX
406 UNTS 312. Norway. Amendment 14 Jan 61. Force 14 Jan 61.
406 UNTS 312. USA (United States). Amendment 1 Sep 60. Force 14 Jan 61.

103415 Bilateral Agreement **240 UNTS 401**
SIGNED: 13 Jan 56   FORCE: 13 Jan 56
REGISTERED: 11 May 56 USA (United States)
ARTICLES: 10 LANGUAGE: English.
HEADNOTE: CIVIL USES ATOMIC ENERGY
TOPIC: Atomic Energy
CONCEPTS: Definition of terms. Diplomatic missions. General cooperation. Exchange of information and documents. Research results. Scientific exchange. Establishment of trade relations. Nuclear materials. Non-nuclear materials. Rights of supplier. Security of information.
PROCEDURE: Duration.
PARTIES:
USA (United States)
Uruguay

103416 Bilateral Agreement **240 UNTS 413**
SIGNED: 18 Jan 56   FORCE: 18 Jan 56
REGISTERED: 11 May 56 USA (United States)
ARTICLES: 10 LANGUAGE: English.
HEADNOTE: CIVIL USES ATOMIC ENERGY
TOPIC: Atomic Energy
CONCEPTS: Definition of terms. Diplomatic missions. General cooperation. Exchange of information and documents. Labor statistics. Research results. Scientific exchange. Establishment of trade relations. Acceptance of delivery. Nuclear materials. Rights of supplier. Security of information.
PROCEDURE: Duration.
PARTIES:
Sweden
USA (United States)
ANNEX
279 UNTS 332. USA (United States). Amendment 3 Aug 56. Force 12 Mar 57.
279 UNTS 332. Sweden. Amendment 3 Aug 56. Force 12 Mar 57.
316 UNTS 364. USA (United States). Amendment 25 Apr 58. Force 2 Jun 58.
316 UNTS 364. Sweden. Amendment 25 Apr 58. Force 2 Jun 58.
460 UNTS 306. Sweden. Amendment 20 Jul 62. Force 6 Sep 62.
460 UNTS 306. USA (United States). Amendment 20 Jul 62. Force 6 Sep 62.

103417 Bilateral Agreement **240 UNTS 425**
SIGNED: 25 Jan 56   FORCE: 25 Jan 56
REGISTERED: 11 May 56 USA (United States)
ARTICLES: 10 LANGUAGE: English.
HEADNOTE: CIVIL USES ATOMIC ENERGY
TOPIC: Atomic Energy
CONCEPTS: Definition of terms. Diplomatic missions. General cooperation. Exchange of information and documents. Research results. Scientific exchange. Establishment of trade relations. Nuclear materials. Non-nuclear materials. Rights of supplier. Security of information.
PROCEDURE: Duration.
PARTIES:
Peru
USA (United States)

103418 Bilateral Exchange **241 UNTS 3**
SIGNED: 29 Apr 52   FORCE: 29 Apr 52
REGISTERED: 14 May 56 USA (United States)
ARTICLES: 2 LANGUAGE: English.
HEADNOTE: FURNISHING MILITARY EQUIPMENT MATERIALS SERVICES EGYPT
TOPIC: Milit Assistance
CONCEPTS: Border traffic and migration. Payment schedules. Military assistance. Security of information. Military installations and equipment.
PARTIES:
United Arab Rep
USA (United States)

103419 Bilateral Exchange **241 UNTS 13**
SIGNED: 9 Feb 55   FORCE: 9 Feb 55
REGISTERED: 15 May 56 USA (United States)
ARTICLES: 2 LANGUAGE: English.
HEADNOTE: ECONOMIC AID
TOPIC: Direct Aid
CONCEPTS: Exchange of information and documents. Economic assistance.
TREATY REF: 234UNTS267.
PARTIES:
USA (United States)
Yugoslavia

103420 Bilateral Exchange **241 UNTS 19**
SIGNED: 3 Dec 55   FORCE: 3 Dec 55
REGISTERED: 15 May 56 USA (United States)
ARTICLES: 2 LANGUAGE: English. Arabic.
HEADNOTE: DISPOSITION EQUIPMENT MATERIAL PURSUANT MUTUAL DEFENSE ASSISTANCE PROGRAM
TOPIC: Milit Assistance
CONCEPTS: Payment for war supplies. Military assistance.
TREATY REF: 222UNTS251.
PARTIES:
Iraq
USA (United States)

103421 Bilateral Agreement **241 UNTS 25**
SIGNED: 20 Dec 55   FORCE: 20 Dec 55
REGISTERED: 15 May 56 USA (United States)
ARTICLES: 6 LANGUAGE: English. Spanish.
HEADNOTE: AGRI COMMOD AGREE
TOPIC: US Agri Commod Aid
CONCEPTS: Exchange of information and documents. Currency deposits. Local currency. Purchase authorization. Surplus commodities.
PARTIES:
Colombia
USA (United States)
ANNEX
283 UNTS 328. USA (United States). Interpretation 16 Apr 57. Force 16 Apr 57.
283 UNTS 328. Colombia. Interpretation 16 Apr 57. Force 16 Apr 57.

103422 Bilateral Exchange **241 UNTS 39**
SIGNED: 28 Nov 55   FORCE: 28 Nov 55
REGISTERED: 15 May 56 USA (United States)
ARTICLES: 3 LANGUAGE: English. Spanish.
HEADNOTE: TECHNICAL COOPERATION PROGRAM ECONOMIC DEVELOPMENT
TOPIC: Non-IBRD Project
CONCEPTS: Previous treaties adherence. General cooperation. Operating agencies. General technical assistance.
TREATY REF: 141UNTS15; 179UNTS235.
PROCEDURE: Duration. Termination.

PARTIES:
Colombia
USA (United States)

103423 Bilateral Exchange **241 UNTS 53**
SIGNED: 18 Jan 55   FORCE: 18 Jan 55
REGISTERED: 15 May 56 USA (United States)
ARTICLES: 2 LANGUAGE: English.
HEADNOTE: EMERGENCY RELIEF ASSISTANCE AGRICULTURAL COMMODITIES
TOPIC: Direct Aid
CONCEPTS: Conformity with municipal law. Exchange of information and documents. Informational records. Inspection and observation. Accounting procedures. Currency deposits. Agricultural commodities. Relief supplies. Purchase authorization.
PARTIES:
Pakistan
USA (United States)
ANNEX
268 UNTS 374. USA (United States). Supplementation 29 Sep 55. Force 29 Sep 55.
268 UNTS 374. Pakistan. Supplementation 29 Sep 55. Force 29 Sep 55.

103424 Bilateral Agreement **241 UNTS 63**
SIGNED: 7 Feb 55   FORCE: 7 Feb 55
REGISTERED: 15 May 56 USA (United States)
ARTICLES: 6 LANGUAGE: English. Spanish.
HEADNOTE: SURPLUS AGRICULTURAL COMMODITIES
TOPIC: Direct Aid
CONCEPTS: Currency deposits. Exchange rates and regulations. Financial programs. Local currency. Purchase authorization. Surplus commodities. Transport of goods.
PARTIES:
Peru
USA (United States)
ANNEX
257 UNTS 376. Peru. Amendment 25 Jun 55. Force 25 Jun 55.
257 UNTS 376. USA (United States). Amendment 25 Jun 55. Force 25 Jun 55.
257 UNTS 377. Peru. Amendment 20 Sep 55. Force 20 Sep 55.
257 UNTS 377. USA (United States). Amendment 20 Sep 55. Force 20 Sep 55.

103425 Bilateral Exchange **241 UNTS 77**
SIGNED: 30 Mar 50   FORCE: 30 Mar 50
REGISTERED: 15 May 56 USA (United States)
ARTICLES: 3 LANGUAGE: English. Spanish.
HEADNOTE: AIR FORCE MISSION
TOPIC: Military Mission
CONCEPTS: Annex type material. Previous treaty extension. Airforce-army-navy personnel ratio.
TREATY REF: 8UNTS345; 8UNTS348; 8UNTS388.
PARTIES:
Bolivia
USA (United States)

103426 Bilateral Exchange **241 UNTS 91**
SIGNED: 11 Feb 55   FORCE: 11 Feb 55
REGISTERED: 15 May 56 USA (United States)
ARTICLES: 2 LANGUAGE: English. Italian.
HEADNOTE: USE COUNTERPART FUNDS
TOPIC: Direct Aid
CONCEPTS: Exchange of information and documents. Informational records. Funding procedures. Loan repayment. Terms of loan.
PARTIES:
Italy
USA (United States)

103427 Bilateral Exchange **241 UNTS 101**
SIGNED: 16 Dec 55   FORCE: 1 Feb 56
REGISTERED: 15 May 56 USA (United States)
ARTICLES: 2 LANGUAGE: English. Spanish.
HEADNOTE: PASSPORT VISAS
TOPIC: Visas
CONCEPTS: Passports non-diplomatic. Visas.
PARTIES:
Dominican Republic
USA (United States)

103428 Bilateral Exchange **241 UNTS 115**
SIGNED: 26 Jan 56 FORCE: 26 Jan 56
REGISTERED: 15 May 56 USA (United States)
ARTICLES: 2 LANGUAGE: English.
HEADNOTE: STATUS FORCES
TOPIC: Status of Forces
CONCEPTS: Annex or appendix reference. Status of military forces. Status of forces.
PARTIES:
Canada
USA (United States)

103429 Bilateral Agreement **241 UNTS 129**
SIGNED: 11 Aug 54 FORCE: 19 Mar 56
REGISTERED: 16 May 56 Netherlands
ARTICLES: 5 LANGUAGE: Dutch. Indonesian.
HEADNOTE: CLAIMS
TOPIC: Claims and Debts
CONCEPTS: Claims and settlements.
PARTIES:
Indonesia
Netherlands

103430 Bilateral Convention **241 UNTS 139**
SIGNED: 24 May 50 FORCE: 11 Apr 55
REGISTERED: 22 May 56 USA (United States)
ARTICLES: 6 LANGUAGE: English. Spanish.
HEADNOTE: COLON CORRIDOR
TOPIC: Territory Boundary
CONCEPTS: Markers and definitions.
PROCEDURE: Ratification.
PARTIES:
Panama
USA (United States)

103431 Bilateral Convention **241 UNTS 159**
SIGNED: 14 Sep 50 FORCE: 11 Apr 55
REGISTERED: 22 May 56 USA (United States)
ARTICLES: 11 LANGUAGE: English. Spanish.
HEADNOTE: HIGHWAY
TOPIC: Land Transport
CONCEPTS: Routes and logistics.
PROCEDURE: Ratification. Termination.
PARTIES:
Panama
USA (United States)

103432 Bilateral Agreement **241 UNTS 173**
SIGNED: 17 Jun 54 FORCE: 16 Feb 55
REGISTERED: 22 May 56 USA (United States)
ARTICLES: 5 LANGUAGE: English.
HEADNOTE: SPECIAL ACCOUNT
TOPIC: Direct Aid
CONCEPTS: Grants.
PROCEDURE: Ratification.
PARTIES:
Ireland
USA (United States)
ANNEX
304 UNTS 374. Ireland. Supplementation 16 Mar 57. Force 23 Dec 57.
304 UNTS 374. USA (United States). Supplementation 16 Mar 57. Force 23 Dec 57.
553 UNTS 278. USA (United States). Supplementation 22 Mar 65. Force 22 Mar 65.
553 UNTS 278. Ireland. Supplementation 22 Mar 65. Force 22 Mar 65.
553 UNTS 290. Ireland. Supplementation 31 Mar 55. Force 31 Mar 55.
553 UNTS 290. USA (United States). Supplementation 31 Mar 55. Force 31 Mar 55.
553 UNTS 296. Ireland. Supplementation 31 Mar 55. Force 31 Mar 55.
553 UNTS 296. USA (United States). Supplementation 31 Mar 55. Force 31 Mar 55.
553 UNTS 304. USA (United States). Supplementation 7 Jun 55. Force 7 Jun 55.
553 UNTS 304. Ireland. Supplementation 7 Jun 55. Force 7 Jun 55.
553 UNTS 316. Ireland. Supplementation 16 Jan 56. Force 16 Jan 56.
553 UNTS 316. USA (United States). Supplementation 16 Jan 56. Force 16 Jan 56.
553 UNTS 324. Ireland. Supplementation 14 Jun 57. Force 14 Jun 57.
553 UNTS 324. USA (United States). Supplementation 14 Jun 57. Force 14 Jun 57.
553 UNTS 334. USA (United States). Supplementation 16 Apr 58. Force 16 Apr 58.

553 UNTS 334. Ireland. Supplementation 16 Apr 58. Force 16 Apr 58.

103433 Bilateral Exchange **241 UNTS 179**
SIGNED: 5 May 55 FORCE: 5 May 55
REGISTERED: 22 May 56 USA (United States)
ARTICLES: 2 LANGUAGE: English.
HEADNOTE: ESTABLISHMENT WARNING CONTROL SYSTEM
TOPIC: Milit Installation
CONCEPTS: Annex or appendix reference. Joint defense. Military installations and equipment. Bases and facilities.
PARTIES:
Canada
USA (United States)

103434 Bilateral Agreement **241 UNTS 197**
SIGNED: 31 May 55 FORCE: 25 Jun 55
REGISTERED: 22 May 56 USA (United States)
ARTICLES: 9 LANGUAGE: English. Japanese.
HEADNOTE: AGRI COMMOD
TOPIC: Direct Aid
CONCEPTS: Agricultural commodities.
PARTIES:
Japan
USA (United States)
ANNEX
275 UNTS 309. USA (United States). Amendment 10 Feb 56. Force 29 May 56.
275 UNTS 309. Japan. Amendment 10 Feb 56. Force 29 May 56.

103435 Bilateral Exchange **241 UNTS 243**
SIGNED: 31 May 55 FORCE: 31 May 55
REGISTERED: 22 May 56 USA (United States)
ARTICLES: 2 LANGUAGE: English. Japanese.
HEADNOTE: AGRI COMMOD
TOPIC: Direct Aid
CONCEPTS: Agricultural commodities.
PARTIES:
Japan
USA (United States)

103436 Bilateral Agreement **241 UNTS 255**
SIGNED: 20 Jul 55 FORCE: 1 Jan 56
REGISTERED: 22 May 56 USA (United States)
ARTICLES: 33 LANGUAGE: English.
HEADNOTE: PARCEL POST
TOPIC: Postal Service
CONCEPTS: Postal services. Regulations. Insured letters and boxes. Parcel post. Rates and charges. Advice lists and orders.
INTL ORGS: Universal Postal Union.
PROCEDURE: Duration. Termination.
PARTIES:
Pakistan
USA (United States)

103437 Bilateral Exchange **241 UNTS 305**
SIGNED: 18 Jul 55 FORCE: 18 Jul 55
REGISTERED: 22 May 56 USA (United States)
ARTICLES: 2 LANGUAGE: English.
HEADNOTE: EMERGENCY WHEAT AID
TOPIC: Direct Aid
CONCEPTS: Agricultural commodities.
PARTIES:
Libya
USA (United States)

103438 Bilateral Exchange **241 UNTS 313**
SIGNED: 15 Mar 56 FORCE: 15 Mar 56
REGISTERED: 22 May 56 Australia
ARTICLES: 2 LANGUAGE: English.
HEADNOTE: RIGHTS & PRIVILEGES CONSULATE
TOPIC: Consul/Citizenship
CONCEPTS: Privileges and immunities.
PARTIES:
Australia
Greece

103439 Bilateral Agreement **241 UNTS 319**
SIGNED: 31 Jul 54 FORCE: 5 Mar 56
REGISTERED: 23 May 56 Greece
ARTICLES: 5 LANGUAGE: French.
HEADNOTE: CULTURAL
TOPIC: Culture

CONCEPTS: Exchange.
PROCEDURE: Ratification. Termination.
PARTIES:
Ethiopia
Greece

103440 Bilateral Exchange **241 UNTS 325**
SIGNED: 27 Dec 55 FORCE: 27 Dec 55
REGISTERED: 24 May 56 Australia
ARTICLES: 2 LANGUAGE: English. French.
HEADNOTE: OFFICIAL PUBLICATION
TOPIC: Admin Cooperation
CONCEPTS: Exchange of official publications.
PARTIES:
Australia
France

103441 Bilateral Exchange **241 UNTS 331**
SIGNED: 15 Mar 56 FORCE: 1 Apr 56
REGISTERED: 24 May 56 Australia
ARTICLES: 2 LANGUAGE: English.
HEADNOTE: VISA FEES
TOPIC: Visas
CONCEPTS: Visas.
PARTIES:
Australia
Austria

103442 Multilateral Convention **241 UNTS 336**
SIGNED: 25 Oct 52 FORCE: 1 Mar 56
REGISTERED: 25 May 56 Switzerland
ARTICLES: 135 LANGUAGE: French.
HEADNOTE: GOODS RAIL & PASSENGER LUGGAGE RAIL
TOPIC: Land Transport
CONCEPTS: Arbitration. Taxation. Passenger transport. Transport of goods.
INTL ORGS: Central Office for International Rail Transport. Arbitration Commission.
PROCEDURE: Accession. Duration. Ratification.
PARTIES:
Multilateral
ANNEX
247 UNTS 478. Finland. Ratification 16 May 56. Force 1 Jul 56.
257 UNTS 385. Turkey. Ratification 11 Dec 56. Force 1 Feb 57.
300 UNTS 380. Lebanon. Ratification 22 Apr 58. Force 1 Jun 58.
375 UNTS 344. Multilateral. Amendment 1 Mar 59. Force 1 Jul 60.
423 UNTS 312. Multilateral. Force 1 Jan 62.
430 UNTS 68. Multilateral. Force 1 Jun 62.

103443 Bilateral Agreement **243 UNTS 3**
SIGNED: 18 Jan 52 FORCE: 1 May 56
REGISTERED: 28 May 56 Belgium
ARTICLES: 9 LANGUAGE: French. German.
HEADNOTE: FRONTIER WORKERS
TOPIC: Visas
CONCEPTS: Frontier permits. Migrant worker. Frontier peoples and personnel.
PROCEDURE: Termination.
PARTIES:
Belgium
Germany, West

103444 Bilateral Agreement **243 UNTS 15**
SIGNED: 10 Jun 55 FORCE: 29 Jul 55
REGISTERED: 28 May 56 Pakistan
ARTICLES: 18 LANGUAGE: English.
HEADNOTE: DOUBLE TAXATION
TOPIC: Taxation
CONCEPTS: Taxation. Equitable taxes. General. Tax exemptions.
PROCEDURE: Termination.
PARTIES:
Pakistan
UK Great Britain

103445 Bilateral Protocol **243 UNTS 43**
SIGNED: 28 May 56 FORCE: 28 May 56
REGISTERED: 28 May 56 United Nations
ARTICLES: 7 LANGUAGE: English. Italian.
HEADNOTE: ACTIVITIES UNICEF
TOPIC: Direct Aid
CONCEPTS: Annex type material. Assistance. General aid.

INTL ORGS: United Nations.
TREATY REF: 68UNTS240.
PARTIES:
Italy
UNICEF (Children)

103446 Bilateral Agreement **243 UNTS 53**
SIGNED: 28 Feb 56   FORCE: 1 Mar 56
REGISTERED: 29 May 56 Australia
ARTICLES: 17 LANGUAGE: English. Serbo-Croat.
HEADNOTE: POSTAL PARCELS
TOPIC: Postal Service
CONCEPTS: Postal services. Regulations. Insured
   letters and boxes. Parcel post. Rates and
   charges. Advice lists and orders.
INTL ORGS: Universal Postal Union.
PROCEDURE: Duration. Termination.
PARTIES:
   Australia
   Yugoslavia

103447 Bilateral Exchange **243 UNTS 73**
SIGNED: 5 Oct 53   FORCE: 5 Oct 53
REGISTERED: 1 Jun 56 UK Great Britain
ARTICLES: 2 LANGUAGE: English.
HEADNOTE: ARBITRATION DISPUTE CARGOES
   DIVERTED DURING WAR
TOPIC: Reparations
CONCEPTS: Annex or appendix reference. Arbitra-
   tion. Procedure. Exchange rates and regulations.
   Post-war claims settlement.
INTL ORGS: Arbitration Commission.
PARTIES:
   Greece
   UK Great Britain

103448 Bilateral Agreement **243 UNTS 91**
SIGNED: 17 Feb 56   FORCE: 16 Apr 56
REGISTERED: 5 Jun 56 WHO (World Health)
ARTICLES: 6 LANGUAGE: English.
HEADNOTE: TECHNICAL ADVISORY ASSISTANCE
TOPIC: Tech Assistance
CONCEPTS: Privileges and immunities. General
   technical assistance. Assistance.
INTL ORGS: United Nations.
PROCEDURE: Termination.
PARTIES:
   Ethiopia
   WHO (World Health)

103449 Multilateral Agreement **243 UNTS 103**
SIGNED: 10 May 56   FORCE: 10 May 56
REGISTERED: 18 Jun 56 United Nations
ARTICLES: 6 LANGUAGE: English. Persian.
HEADNOTE: TECHNICAL ASSISTANCE
TOPIC: Tech Assistance
CONCEPTS: Assistance.
PROCEDURE: Termination.
PARTIES:
   Afghanistan   SIGNED: 10 May 56   FORCE:
      10 May 56
   FAO (Food Agri) SIGNED: 10 May 56 FORCE:
      10 May 56
   ICAO (Civil Aviat) SIGNED: 10 May 56 FORCE:
      10 May 56
   ILO (Labor Org) SIGNED: 10 May 56 FORCE:
      10 May 56
   ITU (Telecommun) SIGNED: 10 May 56 FORCE:
      10 May 56
   UNESCO (Educ/Cult)   SIGNED: 10 May 56
      FORCE: 10 May 56
   United Nations SIGNED: 10 May 56 FORCE:
      10 May 56
   WHO (World Health) SIGNED: 10 May 56
      FORCE: 10 May 56
   WMO (Meteorology)   SIGNED: 10 May 56
      FORCE: 10 May 56
            ANNEX
651 UNTS 355. UPU (Postal Union). Accession
   2 Dec 68. Force 2 Dec 68.
651 UNTS 355. IAEA (Atom Energy). Accession
   2 Dec 68. Force 2 Dec 68.
651 UNTS 355. IMCO (Maritime Org). Accession
   2 Dec 68. Force 2 Dec 68.
651 UNTS 355. UNIDO (Industrial). Accession
   2 Dec 68. Force 2 Dec 68.

103450 Bilateral Agreement **243 UNTS 123**
SIGNED: 29 Aug 55   FORCE: 14 Mar 56

REGISTERED: 19 Jun 56 IBRD (World Bank)
ARTICLES: 5 LANGUAGE: English.
HEADNOTE: GUARANTEE AGREEMENT THERMAL
   PROJECT
TOPIC: IBRD Project
CONCEPTS: Definition of terms. Annex or appen-
   dix reference. Exchange of information and doc-
   uments. Inspection and observation. Bonds.
   Fees and exemptions. Tax exemptions. Domestic
   obligation. Terms of loan. Loan regulations. Loan
   guarantee. Guarantor non-interference.
PARTIES:
   IBRD (World Bank)
   Uruguay

103451 Multilateral Protocol **243 UNTS 147**
SIGNED: 24 Feb 56   FORCE: 24 Feb 56
REGISTERED: 19 Jun 56 Finland
ARTICLES: 3 LANGUAGE: Finnish. Norwegian.
   Russian.
HEADNOTE: REGULATION LAKE INARI
TOPIC: Specific Resources
CONCEPTS: Detailed regulations. Annex type ma-
   terial. Aquisition of property. Frontier water-
   ways.
PARTIES:
   Finland SIGNED: 24 Feb 56 FORCE: 23 Feb 56
   Norway SIGNED: 24 Feb 56 FORCE: 23 Feb 56
   USSR (Soviet Union) SIGNED: 24 Feb 56 FORCE:
      23 Feb 56

103452 Multilateral Agreement **243 UNTS 169**
SIGNED: 3 Mar 56   FORCE: 3 Mar 56
REGISTERED: 20 Jun 56 Norway
ARTICLES: 9 LANGUAGE: Danish. Norwegian.
   Swedish.
HEADNOTE: COMPULSORY MILITARY SERVICE
   NATIONALITY
TOPIC: Milit Servic/Citiz
CONCEPTS: Exchange of information and docu-
   ments. Informational records. Dual nationality.
   Certificates of service. Foreign nationals. Ser-
   vice in foreign army.
PROCEDURE: Termination.
PARTIES:
   Denmark SIGNED: 3 Mar 56 FORCE: 3 Mar 56
   Norway SIGNED: 3 Mar 56 FORCE: 3 Mar 56
   Sweden SIGNED: 3 Mar 56 FORCE: 3 Mar 56

103453 Multilateral Agreement **243 UNTS 187**
SIGNED: 12 Jun 56   FORCE: 12 Jun 56
REGISTERED: 21 Jun 56 United Nations
ARTICLES: 6 LANGUAGE: Spanish.
HEADNOTE: TECHNICAL ASSISTANCE
TOPIC: Tech Assistance
CONCEPTS: Assistance.
PROCEDURE: Termination.
PARTIES:
   Argentina   SIGNED: 12 Jun 56   FORCE:
      12 Jun 56
   FAO (Food Agri) SIGNED: 12 Jun 56 FORCE:
      12 Jun 56
   ICAO (Civil Aviat) SIGNED: 12 Jun 56 FORCE:
      12 Jun 56
   ILO (Labor Org) SIGNED: 12 Jun 56 FORCE:
      12 Jun 56
   ITU (Telecommun) SIGNED: 12 Jun 56 FORCE:
      12 Jun 56
   UNESCO (Educ/Cult)   SIGNED: 12 Jun 56
      FORCE: 12 Jun 56
   United Nations SIGNED: 12 Jun 56 FORCE:
      12 Jun 56
   WHO (World Health) SIGNED: 12 Jun 56 FORCE:
      12 Jun 56
   WMO (Meteorology) SIGNED: 12 Jun 56 FORCE:
      12 Jun 56
            ANNEX
486 UNTS 408. UNTAB (Tech Assis). Amendment
   18 Oct 63. Force 31 Dec 63.
486 UNTS 408.   Argentina.   Amendment
   31 Dec 63. Force 31 Dec 63.

103454 Bilateral Treaty   **243 UNTS 211**
SIGNED: 25 Jan 55   FORCE: 23 Aug 55
REGISTERED: 22 Jun 56 USA (United States)
ARTICLES: 13 LANGUAGE: English. Spanish.
HEADNOTE: MUTUAL UNDERSTANDING COOP-
   ERATION
TOPIC: General Ad Hoc

CONCEPTS: Friendship and amity. Disposition of
   particulars.
PROCEDURE: Ratification.
PARTIES:
   Panama
   USA (United States)

103455 Bilateral Agreement **243 UNTS 281**
SIGNED: 3 May 56   FORCE: 3 May 56
REGISTERED: 26 Jun 56 IBRD (World Bank)
ARTICLES: 8 LANGUAGE: English.
HEADNOTE: LOAN AGREEMENT
TOPIC: IBRD Project
CONCEPTS: Definition of terms. Annex or appen-
   dix reference. Exchange of information and doc-
   uments. Inspection and observation. Bonds.
   Fees and exemptions. Tax exemptions. Domestic
   obligation. Terms of loan. Loan regulations. Loan
   guarantee. Guarantor non-interference.
PARTIES:
   Norway
   IBRD (World Bank)

103456 Bilateral Exchange   **247 UNTS 3**
SIGNED: 27 Mar 46   FORCE: 15 Apr 46
REGISTERED: 29 Jun 56 Netherlands
ARTICLES: 4 LANGUAGE: French.
HEADNOTE: MUTUAL ABOLITION VISAS
TOPIC: Visas
CONCEPTS: Visa abolition. Resident permits.
   Visas.
PARTIES:
   France
   Netherlands

103457 Bilateral Agreement   **247 UNTS 11**
SIGNED: 2 Aug 51   FORCE: 2 Aug 51
REGISTERED: 1 Jul 56 United Nations
ARTICLES: 9 LANGUAGE: English.
HEADNOTE: ACTIVITIES UNICEF
TOPIC: Direct Aid
CONCEPTS: Treaty implementation. Privileges and
   immunities. General cooperation. Exchange of
   information and documents. Informational
   records. Inspection and observation. Public in-
   formation. Procedure. Existing tribunals. Export
   quotas. Tax exemptions. Customs exemptions.
   Commodities and services. Assistance. General
   aid. Distribution. IGO status.
INTL ORGS: United Nations.
TREATY REF: 1UNTS15.
PROCEDURE: Duration.
PARTIES:
   Iran
   UNICEF (Children)
            ANNEX
485 UNTS 360.   UNICEF   (Children).   Force
   21 Nov 68.
485 UNTS 360. Iran. Force 21 Nov 68.

103458 Bilateral Agreement   **247 UNTS 25**
SIGNED: 15 Apr 55   FORCE: 18 May 56
REGISTERED: 2 Jul 56 Pakistan
ARTICLES: 6 LANGUAGE: English.
HEADNOTE: RESUMPTION RAIL TRAFFIC
TOPIC: Land Transport
CONCEPTS: Annex or appendix reference. Pay-
   ment schedules. Customs duties. Routes and lo-
   gistics. Railways.
PROCEDURE: Ratification.
PARTIES:
   India
   Pakistan

103459 Bilateral Exchange   **247 UNTS 47**
SIGNED: 4 Jan 56   FORCE: 1 Feb 54
REGISTERED: 3 Jul 56 Belgium
ARTICLES: 2 LANGUAGE: English. French.
HEADNOTE: SANITARY AGREEMENT
TOPIC: Sanitation
CONCEPTS: Detailed regulations. Border traffic
   and migration. General cooperation. Disease
   control. Sanitation.
TREATY REF: 175UNTS215; 204UNTS391;
   219UNTS354.
PARTIES:
   Belgium
   UK Great Britain

103460 Bilateral Agreement **247 UNTS 54**
SIGNED: 26 Feb 53 FORCE: 1 Mar 53
REGISTERED: 3 Jul 56 Turkey
ARTICLES: 10 LANGUAGE: French.
HEADNOTE: TRADE
TOPIC: General Trade
CONCEPTS: Exceptions and exemptions. Annex or appendix reference. Conformity with municipal law. General cooperation. Informational records. Licenses and permits. Establishment of commission. Export quotas. Import quotas. Trade procedures. Monetary and gold transfers. Payment schedules. Quotas.
INTL ORGS: Special Commission.
TREATY REF: 247UNTS59.
PROCEDURE: Denunciation. Duration. Renewal or Revival.
PARTIES:
Turkey
Yugoslavia

103461 Bilateral Agreement **247 UNTS 117**
SIGNED: 20 Oct 55 FORCE: 6 Nov 55
REGISTERED: 5 Jul 56 Syria
ARTICLES: 13 LANGUAGE: Arabic.
HEADNOTE: JOINT DEFENSE AGREEMENT
TOPIC: General Military
CONCEPTS: General provisions. Guarantees and safeguards. Annex or appendix reference. Friendship and amity. Non-prejudice to UN charter. Peaceful relations. Establishment of commission. Joint defense. Military assistance. Exchange of defense information.
TREATY REF: 70UNTS237.
PROCEDURE: Duration. Ratification. Renewal or Revival. Termination.
PARTIES:
Syria
United Arab Rep

103462 Bilateral Exchange **247 UNTS 139**
SIGNED: 10 Apr 56 FORCE: 10 May 56
REGISTERED: 10 Jul 56 Australia
ARTICLES: 2 LANGUAGE: English.
HEADNOTE: VISA VISA FEES
TOPIC: Visas
CONCEPTS: Visa abolition. Denial of admission. Visas. Conformity with municipal law. Fees and exemptions.
PROCEDURE: Termination.
PARTIES:
Australia
Turkey

103463 Bilateral Exchange **247 UNTS 145**
SIGNED: 20 Mar 47 FORCE: 15 Apr 47
REGISTERED: 12 Jul 56 Netherlands
ARTICLES: 2 LANGUAGE: French.
HEADNOTE: RECIPROCAL ABOLITION VISAS
TOPIC: Visas
CONCEPTS: Time limit. Visa abolition. Denial of admission. Conformity with municipal law.
PARTIES:
Netherlands
Sweden

103464 Bilateral Exchange **247 UNTS 151**
SIGNED: 13 Jun 55 FORCE: 1 Jul 55
REGISTERED: 12 Jul 56 Canada
ARTICLES: 2 LANGUAGE: English.
HEADNOTE: WAIVING NON-IMMIGRANT VISA FEES
TOPIC: Visas
CONCEPTS: Visas. Fees and exemptions.
PARTIES:
Canada
Japan
ANNEX
450 UNTS 432. Canada. Amendment 8 Nov 60. Force 7 Dec 60.
450 UNTS 432. Japan. Amendment 8 Nov 60. Force 7 Dec 60.

103465 Bilateral Exchange **247 UNTS 157**
SIGNED: 3 Jun 55 FORCE: 3 Jun 55
REGISTERED: 12 Jul 56 Canada
ARTICLES: 2 LANGUAGE: English.
HEADNOTE: MODUS VIVENDI COMMERCIAL RELATIONS

TOPIC: General Economic
CONCEPTS: Exceptions and exemptions. Import quotas. Reciprocity in trade. Trade procedures. Balance of payments.
PROCEDURE: Duration. Termination.
PARTIES:
Canada
Ethiopia

103466 Bilateral Agreement **247 UNTS 163**
SIGNED: 8 Jun 55 FORCE: 8 Jun 55
REGISTERED: 12 Jul 56 Canada
ARTICLES: 1 LANGUAGE: English.
HEADNOTE: DUTY FISH STICKS
TOPIC: Customs
CONCEPTS: Domestic legislation. Customs duties.
TREATY REF: 61UNTS1.
PARTIES:
Canada
USA (United States)

103467 Bilateral Agreement **247 UNTS 168**
SIGNED: 29 Jun 55 FORCE: 29 Jun 56
REGISTERED: 17 Jul 56 WHO (World Health)
ARTICLES: 12 LANGUAGE: English.
HEADNOTE: WHO & DENMARK
TOPIC: IGO Status/Immunit
CONCEPTS: Definition of terms. Annex or appendix reference. Non-visa travel documents. Diplomatic privileges. Inviolability. Privileges and immunities. Property. Diplomatic correspondence. Juridical personality. Procedure. Special tribunals. Special status. Status of experts.
INTL ORGS: International Court of Justice. United Nations.
PROCEDURE: Amendment. Registration.
PARTIES:
Denmark
WHO (World Health)

103468 Bilateral Exchange **247 UNTS 193**
SIGNED: 1 May 47 FORCE: 15 May 47
REGISTERED: 18 Jul 56 Netherlands
ARTICLES: 2 LANGUAGE: English.
HEADNOTE: RECIPROCAL ABOLITION VISAS
TOPIC: Visas
CONCEPTS: Visa abolition. Denial of admission. Conformity with municipal law.
PARTIES:
Ireland
Netherlands

103469 Bilateral Exchange **247 UNTS 199**
SIGNED: 25 Sep 46 FORCE: 15 Oct 46
REGISTERED: 18 Jul 56 Netherlands
ARTICLES: 3 LANGUAGE: French.
HEADNOTE: RECIPROCAL ABOLITION VISAS
TOPIC: Visas
CONCEPTS: Visa abolition. Conformity with municipal law.
PARTIES:
Monaco
Netherlands

103470 Bilateral Exchange **247 UNTS 205**
SIGNED: 5 Jun 56 FORCE: 5 Jun 56
REGISTERED: 23 Jul 56 UK Great Britain
ARTICLES: 2 LANGUAGE: English.
HEADNOTE: SALE TABACCO CONSTRUCTION HOUSING COMMUNITY FACILITIES
TOPIC: Milit Installation
CONCEPTS: Guarantees and safeguards. Annex or appendix reference. Exchange rates and regulations. Financial programs. Local currency. Purchase authorization. Surplus commodities. Bases and facilities. Restrictions on transfer.
PARTIES:
UK Great Britain
USA (United States)
ANNEX
269 UNTS 378. UK Great Britain. Amendment 13 Mar 57. Force 13 Mar 57.
269 UNTS 378. USA (United States). Amendment 13 Mar 57. Force 13 Mar 57.
304 UNTS 382. UK Great Britain. Amendment 17 Feb 58. Force 17 Feb 58.
304 UNTS 382. USA (United States). Amendment 12 Feb 58. Force 17 Feb 58.

103471 Multilateral Agreement **247 UNTS 213**
SIGNED: 24 Aug 54 FORCE: 24 Aug 54
REGISTERED: 23 Jul 56 UK Great Britain
ARTICLES: 7 LANGUAGE: English.
HEADNOTE: WAR GRAVES
TOPIC: Other Military
CONCEPTS: Establishment of commission. Responsibility for war dead. Establishment of war cemeteries.
INTL ORGS: Special Commission.
PARTIES:
Australia SIGNED: 24 Aug 54 FORCE: 24 Aug 54
India SIGNED: 24 Aug 54 FORCE: 24 Aug 54
Thailand SIGNED: 24 Aug 54 FORCE: 24 Aug 54
UK Great Britain SIGNED: 24 Aug 54 FORCE: 24 Aug 54

103472 Bilateral Exchange **247 UNTS 223**
SIGNED: 2 Feb 52 FORCE: 2 Feb 52
REGISTERED: 25 Jul 56 USA (United States)
ARTICLES: 5 LANGUAGE: English. French.
HEADNOTE: SETTLEMENT CLAIMS
TOPIC: Reparations
CONCEPTS: Time limit. Annex or appendix reference. Conformity with municipal law. Exchange of information and documents. Recognition of legal documents. Prisoners of war. Post-war claims settlement.
TREATY REF: 19UNTS9.
PARTIES:
France
USA (United States)

103473 Bilateral Exchange **247 UNTS 247**
SIGNED: 22 Feb 55 FORCE: 22 Feb 55
REGISTERED: 25 Jul 56 USA (United States)
ARTICLES: 2 LANGUAGE: English.
HEADNOTE: RELATING CERTIFICATES AIRWORTHINESS IMPORTED AIRCRAFT
TOPIC: Air Transport
CONCEPTS: Previous treaty replacement. Conformity with municipal law. Exchange of information and documents. Recognition of legal documents. Use of facilities. Registration certificate. Airworthiness certificates.
TREATY REF: 129LTS121.
PROCEDURE: Termination.
PARTIES:
South Africa
USA (United States)

103474 Bilateral Agreement **247 UNTS 257**
SIGNED: 18 Feb 55 FORCE: 18 Feb 55
REGISTERED: 25 Jul 56 USA (United States)
ARTICLES: 8 LANGUAGE: English.
HEADNOTE: SALE FEED GRAIN PURCHASE BUILDING MATERIALS DEFENSE PURPOSE
TOPIC: Milit Assistance
CONCEPTS: Embargo. Indemnities and reimbursements. Local currency. General. Tax exemptions. Agricultural commodities. Bases and facilities.
PARTIES:
Germany, West
USA (United States)

103475 Bilateral Agreement **247 UNTS 263**
SIGNED: 26 Mar 54 FORCE: 26 Mar 54
REGISTERED: 25 Jul 56 USA (United States)
ARTICLES: 11 LANGUAGE: English. Russian.
HEADNOTE: RETURN NAVAL VESSELS UNDER LEND-LEASE ACT
TOPIC: Milit Assistance
CONCEPTS: Detailed regulations. Time limit. Annex or appendix reference. Expense sharing formulae. Delivery schedules. Ports and pilotage. Lend lease. Naval vessels. Return of equipment and recapture.
PARTIES:
USA (United States)
USSR (Soviet Union)

103476 Bilateral Agreement **247 UNTS 273**
SIGNED: 14 May 54 FORCE: 5 Jun 54
REGISTERED: 25 Jul 56 USA (United States)
ARTICLES: 10 LANGUAGE: English. Japanese.
HEADNOTE: LOAN NAVAL VESSELS
TOPIC: Milit Assistance
CONCEPTS: Time limit. Annex or appendix reference. Responsibility and liability. Title and

deeds. Compensation. Indemnities and reimbursements. Claims and settlements. Delivery schedules. Materials, equipment and services. Lease of military property. Naval vessels. Return of equipment and recapture. Security of information. Exchange of defense information. Restrictions on transfer.
TREATY REF: 232UNTS169.
PROCEDURE: Future Procedures Contemplated. Ratification.
PARTIES:
Japan
USA (United States)
ANNEX
340 UNTS 368. USA (United States). Supplementation 6 Jan 59. Force 6 Jan 59.
340 UNTS 368. Japan. Supplementation 6 Jan 59. Force 6 Jan 59.
360 UNTS 400. Japan. Prolongation 2 Oct 59. Force 2 Oct 59.
360 UNTS 400. USA (United States). Prolongation 2 Oct 59. Force 2 Oct 59.

103477 Bilateral Exchange **247 UNTS 299**
SIGNED: 10 May 54　　FORCE: 10 May 54
REGISTERED: 25 Jul 56 USA (United States)
ARTICLES: 2 LANGUAGE: English. Spanish.
HEADNOTE: CUSTOMS CONCESSIONS AUTOMOBILES
TOPIC: Customs
CONCEPTS: Customs duties. Motor vehicles and combinations.
INTL ORGS: General Agreement on Tariffs and Trade.
TREATY REF: 122UNTS169.
PARTIES:
Chile
USA (United States)

103478 Bilateral Agreement **247 UNTS 305**
SIGNED: 26 Aug 55　　FORCE: 5 Jun 56
REGISTERED: 26 Jul 56 IBRD (World Bank)
ARTICLES: 5 LANGUAGE: English.
HEADNOTE: GUARANTEE AGREEMENT
TOPIC: IBRD Project
CONCEPTS: Definition of terms. Annex or appendix reference. Exchange of information and documents. Informational records. Inspection and observation. Bonds. Fees and exemptions. Tax exemptions. Domestic obligation. Terms of loan. Loan regulations. Loan guarantee. Guarantor non-interference.
PARTIES:
France
IBRD (World Bank)

103479 Multilateral Convention **247 UNTS 329**
SIGNED: 5 Sep 52　　FORCE: 1 Jul 56
REGISTERED: 28 Jul 56 Belgium
ARTICLES: 21 LANGUAGE: French. Dutch.
HEADNOTE: CUSTOMS EXCISE
TOPIC: Customs
CONCEPTS: Conformity with municipal law. General cooperation. Exchange of official publications. Recognition and enforcement of legal decisions. Investigation of violations. Indemnities and reimbursements. Customs duties.
PROCEDURE: Denunciation. Ratification.
PARTIES:
Belgium SIGNED: 5 Sep 52 RATIFIED: 6 Jul 53 FORCE: 1 Jul 56
Luxembourg SIGNED: 5 Sep 52 RATIFIED: 18 Jan 55 FORCE: 1 Jul 56
Netherlands SIGNED: 5 Sep 52 RATIFIED: 30 Jun 56 FORCE: 1 Jul 56

103480 Bilateral Exchange **247 UNTS 353**
SIGNED: 30 Jan 47　　FORCE: 30 Jan 47
REGISTERED: 27 Jul 56 Netherlands
ARTICLES: 4 LANGUAGE: English.
HEADNOTE: RESUMPTION NORMAL FRIENDLY RELATIONS & DIPLOMATIC INTERCOURSE
TOPIC: General Amity
CONCEPTS: Annex type material. Responsibility and liability. Lump sum settlements. Air transport. General military. Reconversion to normalcy. Upkeep of war graves.
INTL ORGS: International Emergency Food Organization. United Nations.

TREATY REF: CONSULAR CONVENTION 1APR1867; 92LTS131; 193LTS13.
PROCEDURE: Future Procedures Contemplated.
PARTIES:
Netherlands
Thailand

103481 Bilateral Exchange **248 UNTS 3**
SIGNED: 20 Jan 56　　FORCE: 1 Mar 56
REGISTERED: 30 Jul 56 Belgium
ARTICLES: 2 LANGUAGE: French. German.
HEADNOTE: EXCHANGE STUDENT EMPLOYEES
TOPIC: Non-ILO Labor
CONCEPTS: Conditions. Border traffic and migration. Alien status. Operating agencies. Dispute settlement. Employment regulations. Safety standards. Wages and salaries. Non-ILO labor relations. Administrative cooperation. Social security. Migrant worker. Quotas.
PROCEDURE: Amendment. Denunciation. Duration. Renewal or Revival.
PARTIES:
Austria
Belgium

103482 Bilateral Agreement **248 UNTS 17**
SIGNED: 21 Oct 55　　FORCE: 21 Oct 55
REGISTERED: 30 Jul 56 Denmark
ARTICLES: 15 LANGUAGE: French.
HEADNOTE: AIR TRANSPORT
TOPIC: Air Transport
CONCEPTS: Arbitration. Airport facilities. Airport equipment. Airworthiness certificates. Conditions of airlines operating permission. Operating authorizations and regulations.
INTL ORGS: International Civil Aviation Organization. International Court of Justice. Arbitration Commission.
PARTIES:
Denmark
Lebanon

103483 Unilateral Instrument **248 UNTS 33**
SIGNED: 1 Aug 56　　FORCE: 6 Aug 56
REGISTERED: 1 Aug 56 United Nations
ARTICLES: 1 LANGUAGE: French.
HEADNOTE: ACCEPTANCE ICJ JURISDICTION
TOPIC: ICJ Option Clause
CONCEPTS: Compulsory jurisdiction.
INTL ORGS: International Court of Justice.
TREATY REF: 1UNTS7.
PROCEDURE: Duration.
PARTIES:
Netherlands

103484 Multilateral Agreement **248 UNTS 37**
SIGNED: 2 Jul 56　　FORCE: 2 Jul 56
REGISTERED: 1 Aug 56 United Nations
ARTICLES: 6 LANGUAGE: Spanish.
HEADNOTE: TECHNICAL ASSISTANCE
TOPIC: Tech Assistance
CONCEPTS: Definition of terms. Previous treaty replacement. Privileges and immunities. General cooperation. Exchange of information and documents. Personnel. Responsibility and liability. Title and deeds. Use of facilities. Exchange. Scholarships and grants. Vocational training. Research and development. Exchange rates and regulations. Expense sharing formulae. Local currency. Domestic obligation. General technical assistance. Materials, equipment and services. IGO status. Conformity with IGO decisions.
TREATY REF: 76UNTS132; 158UNTS407; 1UNTS15; 1UNTS263; 33UNTS26.
PROCEDURE: Amendment. Termination.
PARTIES:
Nicaragua SIGNED: 2 Jul 56 FORCE: 2 Jul 56
FAO (Food Agri) SIGNED: 2 Jul 56 FORCE: 2 Jul 56
ICAO (Civil Aviat) SIGNED: 2 Jul 56 FORCE: 2 Jul 56
ILO (Labor Org) SIGNED: 2 Jul 56 FORCE: 2 Jul 56
UNESCO (Educ/Cult) SIGNED: 2 Jul 56 FORCE: 2 Jul 56
United Nations SIGNED: 2 Jul 56 FORCE: 2 Jul 56
WHO (World Health) SIGNED: 2 Jul 56 FORCE: 2 Jul 56

ANNEX
418 UNTS 372. Nicaragua. Amendment 6 Dec 61. Force 6 Dec 61.
418 UNTS 372. UNTAB (Tech Assis). Amendment 16 Oct 61. Force 6 Dec 61.
651 UNTS 356. UNIDO (Industrial). Accession 11 Nov 68. Force 11 Nov 68.
651 UNTS 356. IMCO (Maritime Org). Accession 11 Nov 68. Force 11 Nov 68.
651 UNTS 356. UPU (Postal Union). Accession 11 Nov 68. Force 11 Nov 68.

103485 Bilateral Agreement **248 UNTS 57**
SIGNED: 22 May 56　　FORCE: 21 Jul 56
REGISTERED: 2 Aug 56 IBRD (World Bank)
ARTICLES: 5 LANGUAGE: English.
HEADNOTE: GUARANTEE
TOPIC: IBRD Project
CONCEPTS: Definition of terms. Annex or appendix reference. Exchange of information and documents. Informational records. Inspection and observation. Bonds. Fees and exemptions. Tax exemptions. Domestic obligation. Terms of loan. Loan regulations. Loan guarantee. Guarantor non-interference.
PARTIES:
Finland
IBRD (World Bank)

103486 Bilateral Exchange **248 UNTS 89**
SIGNED: 26 Jan 51　　FORCE: 26 Jan 51
REGISTERED: 6 Aug 56 Canada
ARTICLES: 2 LANGUAGE: English.
HEADNOTE: PERMANENT RESIDENCE
TOPIC: Visas
CONCEPTS: Exceptions and exemptions. Border traffic and migration. Resident permits. Conformity with municipal law.
PARTIES:
Canada
India
ANNEX
316 UNTS 376. India. Amendment 3 May 57. Force 3 May 57.
316 UNTS 376. Canada. Amendment 3 May 57. Force 3 May 57.

103487 Bilateral Exchange **248 UNTS 95**
SIGNED: 23 Oct 51　　FORCE: 23 Oct 51
REGISTERED: 6 Aug 56 Canada
ARTICLES: 2 LANGUAGE: English.
HEADNOTE: PERMANENT RESIDENCE CITIZENS
TOPIC: Visas
CONCEPTS: Exceptions and exemptions. Border traffic and migration. Resident permits. Conformity with municipal law.
PARTIES:
Canada
Pakistan

103488 Bilateral Exchange **248 UNTS 101**
SIGNED: 24 Apr 51　　FORCE: 24 Apr 51
REGISTERED: 6 Aug 56 Canada
ARTICLES: 2 LANGUAGE: English.
HEADNOTE: PERMANENT RESIDENCE
TOPIC: Visas
CONCEPTS: Exceptions and exemptions. Border traffic and migration. Resident permits. Conformity with municipal law.
PARTIES:
Canada
Ceylon (Sri Lanka)

103489 Bilateral Exchange **248 UNTS 107**
SIGNED: 26 Nov 51　　FORCE: 29 Feb 52
REGISTERED: 6 Aug 56 Canada
ARTICLES: 2 LANGUAGE: English.
HEADNOTE: DOUBLE TAXATION INCOME SHIPS AIRCRAFT
TOPIC: Taxation
CONCEPTS: Definition of terms. Taxation. Tax exemptions. Air transport. Merchant vessels.
PROCEDURE: Duration. Termination.
PARTIES:
Canada
South Africa

103490 Bilateral Exchange **248 UNTS 113**
SIGNED: 12 Jun 53   FORCE: 12 Jun 53
REGISTERED: 6 Aug 56 Canada
ARTICLES: 2 LANGUAGE: English.
HEADNOTE: INSPECTION SUPPLIES & EQUIP-
MENT
TOPIC: Admin Cooperation
CONCEPTS: Inspection and observation.
PARTIES:
Canada
India

103491 Bilateral Protocol **248 UNTS 121**
SIGNED: 18 Jul 56   FORCE: 1 Jan 54
REGISTERED: 15 Aug 56 Belgium
ARTICLES: 1 LANGUAGE: French.
HEADNOTE: OLD-AGE PENSIONS
TOPIC: Non-ILO Labor
CONCEPTS: Annex or appendix reference. Domes-
tic legislation. Non-ILO labor relations. Old age
insurance. Payment schedules. National treat-
ment.
PARTIES:
Belgium
France

103492 Bilateral Exchange **248 UNTS 129**
SIGNED: 11 Jul 56   FORCE: 15 Aug 56
REGISTERED: 15 Aug 56 Belgium
ARTICLES: 3 LANGUAGE: French. Japanese.
HEADNOTE: ABOLISHING TRAVEL VISA REQUIRE-
MENTS
TOPIC: Visas
CONCEPTS: Time limit. Visa abolition. Denial of
admission. Resident permits. Conformity with
municipal law.
PARTIES:
Belgium
Japan

103493 Bilateral Agreement **248 UNTS 139**
SIGNED: 6 Jun 56   FORCE: 21 Jul 56
REGISTERED: 20 Aug 56 IBRD (World Bank)
ARTICLES: 8 LANGUAGE: English.
HEADNOTE: LOAN AGREEMENT
TOPIC: IBRD Project
CONCEPTS: Definition of terms. Annex or appen-
dix reference. Exchange of information and doc-
uments. Informational records. Inspection and
observation. Accounting procedures. Bonds.
Fees and exemptions. Interest rates. Tax exemp-
tions. Domestic obligation. Terms of loan. Loan
regulations. Loan guarantee. Guarantor non-
interference. Roads and highways.
PARTIES:
Colombia
IBRD (World Bank)

103494 Bilateral Agreement **248 UNTS 161**
SIGNED: 15 Jun 55   FORCE: 2 Jun 56
REGISTERED: 20 Aug 56 IBRD (World Bank)
ARTICLES: 5 LANGUAGE: English.
HEADNOTE: GUARANTEE AGREEMENT
TOPIC: IBRD Project
CONCEPTS: Definition of terms. Annex or appen-
dix reference. Exchange of information and doc-
uments. Informational records. Inspection and
observation. Accounting procedures. Fees and
exemptions. Tax exemptions. Domestic obliga-
tion. Terms of loan. Loan regulations. Loan guar-
antee. Guarantor non-interference.
PARTIES:
Colombia
IBRD (World Bank)

103495 Bilateral Exchange **248 UNTS 191**
SIGNED: 30 Jun 55   FORCE: 30 Jun 55
REGISTERED: 24 Aug 56 UK Great Britain
ARTICLES: 6 LANGUAGE: English.
HEADNOTE: DEFENSE MATTERS
TOPIC: General Military
CONCEPTS: Annex or appendix reference. Estab-
lishment of commission. Repatriation of comba-
tants. Joint defense. Defense and security. Mili-
tary assistance. Naval vessels. Procurement and
logistics. Exchange of defense information.
PROCEDURE: Future Procedures Contemplated.

PARTIES:
South Africa
UK Great Britain

103496 Bilateral Treaty **248 UNTS 213**
SIGNED: 10 Dec 54   FORCE: 3 Mar 55
REGISTERED: 28 Aug 56 USA (United States)
ARTICLES: 10 LANGUAGE: English. Chinese.
HEADNOTE: MUTUAL DEFENSE TREATY
TOPIC: General Military
CONCEPTS: Annex or appendix reference. Non-
prejudice to UN charter. Peaceful relations. De-
fense and security. Military assistance.
INTL ORGS: United Nations.
PROCEDURE. Duration. Ratification. Termination.
PARTIES:
Taiwan
USA (United States)

103497 Bilateral Convention **248 UNTS 235**
SIGNED: 11 Aug 54   FORCE: 1 Jun 55
REGISTERED: 29 Aug 56 UK Great Britain
ARTICLES: 50 LANGUAGE: English. Dutch.
HEADNOTE: SOCIAL SECURITY
TOPIC: Non-ILO Labor
CONCEPTS: Definition of terms. Detailed regula-
tions. General provisions. Domestic legislation.
Dispute settlement. Old age and invalidity insur-
ance. Wages and salaries. Non-ILO labor rela-
tions. Family allowances. Administrative cooper-
ation. Old age insurance. Sickness and invalidity
insurance. Social security. Payment schedules.
National treatment.
INTL ORGS: International Court of Justice.
PROCEDURE: Denunciation. Duration. Ratification.
Renewal or Revival.
PARTIES:
Netherlands
UK Great Britain

103498 Multilateral Agreement **249 UNTS 3**
SIGNED: 22 Jun 55   FORCE: 29 Mar 56
REGISTERED: 29 Aug 56 UK Great Britain
ARTICLES: 6 LANGUAGE: English. French.
HEADNOTE: COOPERATION ATOMIC INFORMA-
TION
TOPIC: Atomic Energy
CONCEPTS: Previous treaty extension. Exchange
of information and documents. Scientific ex-
change. Rights of supplier. Defense and security.
Admission.
INTL ORGS: North Atlantic Treaty Organization.
PROCEDURE: Duration.
PARTIES:
Belgium   SIGNED: 22 Jun 55   RATIFIED:
21 Nov 55 FORCE: 29 Mar 56
Canada   SIGNED: 22 Jun 55   RATIFIED:
30 Aug 55 FORCE: 29 Mar 56
Denmark   SIGNED: 22 Jun 55   RATIFIED:
30 Nov 55 FORCE: 29 Mar 56
France SIGNED: 22 Jun 55 RATIFIED: 14 Nov 55
FORCE: 29 Mar 56
Germany, West SIGNED: 22 Jun 55 RATIFIED:
6 Dec 55 FORCE: 29 Mar 56
Greece SIGNED: 22 Jun 55 RATIFIED: 2 Dec 55
FORCE: 29 Mar 56
Iceland   SIGNED: 22 Jun 55   RATIFIED:
16 Jan 56 FORCE: 29 Mar 56
Italy SIGNED: 22 Jun 55 RATIFIED: 23 Sep 55
FORCE: 29 Mar 56
Luxembourg   SIGNED: 22 Jun 55   RATIFIED:
23 Jul 55 FORCE: 29 Mar 56
Netherlands   SIGNED: 22 Jun 55   RATIFIED:
4 Jan 56 FORCE: 29 Mar 56
Norway SIGNED: 22 Jun 55 RATIFIED: 6 Dec 55
FORCE: 29 Mar 56
Portugal   SIGNED: 22 Jun 55   RATIFIED:
2 Dec 55 FORCE: 29 Mar 56
Turkey SIGNED: 22 Jun 55 RATIFIED: 29 Mar 56
FORCE: 29 Mar 56
UK Great Britain SIGNED: 22 Jun 55 RATIFIED:
21 Oct 55 FORCE: 29 Mar 56
USA (United States) SIGNED: 22 Jun 55 RATI-
FIED: 28 Dec 55 FORCE: 29 Mar 56
ANNEX
542 UNTS 371. NATO (North Atlan). Force
12 Mar 65.

103499 Bilateral Agreement **249 UNTS 19**
SIGNED: 27 Jun 56   FORCE: 27 Jun 56

REGISTERED: 29 Aug 56 UK Great Britain
ARTICLES: 10 LANGUAGE: English. Hungarian.
HEADNOTE: SETTLEMENT FINANCIAL MATTERS
TOPIC: Claims and Debts
CONCEPTS: Definition of terms. Detailed regula-
tions. Time limit. General cooperation. Exchange
of information and documents. Informational
records. General property. Responsibility and lia-
bility. Import quotas. Banking. Payment sched-
ules. Lump sum settlements. Assessment proce-
dures. Purchase authorization.
TREATY REF: 6 UNTS 187.
PARTIES:
Hungary
UK Great Britain

103500 Multilateral Convention **249 UNTS 45**
SIGNED: 29 Jul 54   FORCE: 15 Jun 56
REGISTERED: 29 Aug 56 UK Great Britain
ARTICLES: 14 LANGUAGE: English. French.
HEADNOTE: PHYTO-SANITATION CONVENTION
TOPIC: Sanitation
CONCEPTS: Definition of terms. Detailed regula-
tions. Territorial application. General cooper-
ation. Exchange of information and documents.
Inspection and observation. Domestic legisla-
tion. Establishment of commission. Quarantine.
Disease control. Insect control. Sanitation. Re-
search and development. Accounting proce-
dures. Indemnities and reimbursements. Ex-
pense sharing formulae. Funding procedures.
General technical assistance. Agriculture.
INTL ORGS: Commission for Technical Co-opera-
tion in Africa South of the Sahara. Special Com-
mission.
PROCEDURE: Accession. Denunciation. Duration.
Ratification.
PARTIES:
Belgium SIGNED: 29 Jul 54 RATIFIED: 16 Jul 56
FORCE: 16 Jul 56
Fed Rhod/Nyasaland SIGNED: 29 Jul 54 RATI-
FIED: 27 Jul 55 FORCE: 16 Jun 56
France SIGNED: 29 Jul 54 RATIFIED: 15 Jun 56
FORCE: 15 Jun 56
Portugal SIGNED: 29 Jul 54
South Africa SIGNED: 29 Jul 54 RATIFIED:
3 Nov 55 FORCE: 15 Jun 56
UK Great Britain SIGNED: 29 Jul 54 RATIFIED:
14 Dec 54 FORCE: 15 Jun 56
ANNEX
425 UNTS 336. France. Amendment 11 Oct 61.
Force 11 Oct 61.
425 UNTS 336. Ghana. Amendment 11 Oct 61.
Force 11 Oct 61.
425 UNTS 336. Belgium. Amendment 11 Oct 61.
Force 11 Oct 61.
425 UNTS 336. Portugal. Amendment 11 Oct 61.
Force 11 Oct 61.
425 UNTS 336. Fed Rhod/Nyasaland. Amendment 11 Oct 61. Force 11 Oct 61.
425 UNTS 336. South Africa. Amendment
11 Oct 61. Force 11 Oct 61.
425 UNTS 336. UK Great Britain. Amendment
11 Oct 61. Force 11 Oct 61.
431 UNTS 308. Guinea. Accession 24 Feb 62.
431 UNTS 308. Niger. Accession 17 Oct 61.
431 UNTS 308. Liberia. Accession 5 Feb 62.
431 UNTS 308. Cameroon. Accession 28 Dec 61.
431 UNTS 308. Chad. Qualified Accession
11 Apr 62.
431 UNTS 308. Madagascar. Accession
2 Feb 62.
431 UNTS 308. Ivory Coast. Accession
22 Jan 62.
431 UNTS 308. Portugal. Ratification 16 Jul 67.
431 UNTS 308. Ghana. Accession 28 Mar 58.
431 UNTS 308. Mauritius. Accession 24 Feb 62.
431 UNTS 308. Congo (Brazzaville). Accession
5 Feb 62.
431 UNTS 308. Senegal. Accession 17 Oct 61.
431 UNTS 308. Nigeria. Accession 8 Nov 61.
431 UNTS 308. Gabon. Accession 25 Jan 62.
431 UNTS 308. Central Afri Rep. Accession
5 Jan 62.
456 UNTS 498. Sierra Leone. Accession
30 May 62.
456 UNTS 498. Tanganyika. Accession
31 May 62.
466 UNTS 392. Congo (Zaire). Accession
21 Sep 62.
466 UNTS 392. Mali. Accession 14 Jan 63.
560 UNTS 264. France. Denunciation 11 Jun 64.
Force 11 Jun 65.

560 UNTS 264. UK Great Britain. Denunciation 11 Jun 64. Force 11 Jun 65.
560 UNTS 264. Belgium. Denunciation 30 Jun 64. Force 30 Jun 65.
560 UNTS 264. South Africa. Denunciation 24 Feb 65. Force 24 Feb 66.

103501 Bilateral Agreement **249 UNTS 59**
SIGNED: 25 Jun 56　　　FORCE: 25 Jun 56
REGISTERED: 29 Aug 56 UK Great Britain
ARTICLES: 26 LANGUAGE: English.
HEADNOTE: EXTENSION BAHAMAS LONG-RANGE PROVING GROUND
TOPIC: Milit Installation
CONCEPTS: Definition of terms. Treaty implementation. Visa abolition. Court procedures. General cooperation. Legal protection and assistance. Use of facilities. Compensation. Claims and settlements. Tax exemptions. Customs exemptions. Ports and pilotage. Bands and frequency allocation. Postal services. Security of information. Jurisdiction. Procurement and logistics. Status of forces. Testing ranges and sites. Bases and facilities.
PROCEDURE: Termination.
PARTIES:
　UK Great Britain
　USA (United States)

103502 Bilateral Agreement **249 UNTS 91**
SIGNED: 25 Jun 56　　　FORCE: 25 Jun 56
REGISTERED: 29 Aug 56 UK Great Britain
ARTICLES: 26 LANGUAGE: English.
HEADNOTE: BAHAMAS LONG-RANGE TESTING GROUND
TOPIC: Milit Installation
CONCEPTS: Jurisdiction. Procurement and logistics. Status of forces. Testing ranges and sites.
PROCEDURE: Termination.
PARTIES:
　UK Great Britain
　USA (United States)
　　　　ANNEX
351 UNTS 438. USA (United States). Implementation 24 Aug 59. Force 25 Aug 59.
351 UNTS 438. UK Great Britain. Implementation 25 Aug 59. Force 25 Aug 59.

103503 Bilateral Agreement **249 UNTS 125**
SIGNED: 1 Jul 51　　　FORCE: 1 Jan 51
REGISTERED: 29 Aug 56 UK Great Britain
ARTICLES: 8 LANGUAGE: English.
HEADNOTE: STERLING RELEASES AGREEMENT
TOPIC: Finance
CONCEPTS: Detailed regulations. Accounting procedures. Banking. Assets transfer. Commodity trade. Loan and credit. Credit provisions.
PARTIES:
　United Arab Rep
　UK Great Britain

103504 Bilateral Agreement **249 UNTS 143**
SIGNED: 1 Jul 51　　　FORCE: 1 Jan 51
REGISTERED: 29 Aug 56 UK Great Britain
ARTICLES: 9 LANGUAGE: English.
HEADNOTE: STERLING PAYMENTS AGREEMENT
TOPIC: Finance
CONCEPTS: Definition of terms. General cooperation. Banking. Currency. Monetary and gold transfers. Exchange rates and regulations. Payment schedules.
INTL ORGS: International Monetary Fund.
TREATY REF: 249UNTS125.
PROCEDURE: Duration. Renewal or Revival. Termination.
PARTIES:
　United Arab Rep
　UK Great Britain

103505 Bilateral Protocol **249 UNTS 153**
SIGNED: 25 Jun 56　　　FORCE: 25 Jun 56
REGISTERED: 31 Aug 56 United Nations
ARTICLES: 2 LANGUAGE: English. French.
HEADNOTE: ACTIVITIES UNICEF
TOPIC: Direct Aid
CONCEPTS: Annex type material. Assistance. Economic assistance.

PARTIES:
　Cambodia
　UNICEF (Children)

103506 Multilateral Agreement **249 UNTS 158**
SIGNED: 31 Aug 56　　　FORCE: 31 Aug 56
REGISTERED: 31 Aug 56 United Nations
ARTICLES: 6 LANGUAGE: English.
HEADNOTE: TECHNICAL ASSISTANCE
TOPIC: Tech Assistance
CONCEPTS: Definition of terms. Previous treaty replacement. Privileges and immunities. General cooperation. Exchange of information and documents. Personnel. Responsibility and liability. Title and deeds. Use of facilities. Exchange. Scholarships and grants. Vocational training. Research and development. Expense sharing formulae. Interest rates. Local currency. Domestic obligation. General technical assistance. Materials, equipment and services. Conformity with IGO decisions.
TREATY REF: 76UNTS132; 1UNTS15; 1UNTS263.
PROCEDURE: Amendment. Termination.
PARTIES:
　India SIGNED: 31 Aug 56 FORCE: 31 Aug 56
　FAO (Food Agri) SIGNED: 31 Aug 56 FORCE: 31 Aug 56
　ICAO (Civil Aviat) SIGNED: 31 Aug 56 FORCE: 31 Aug 56
　ILO (Labor Org) SIGNED: 31 Aug 56 FORCE: 31 Aug 56
　ITU (Telecommun) SIGNED: 31 Aug 56 FORCE: 31 Aug 56
　UNESCO (Educ/Cult) SIGNED: 31 Aug 56 FORCE: 31 Aug 56
　United Nations SIGNED: 31 Aug 56 FORCE: 31 Aug 56
　WMO (Meteorology) SIGNED: 31 Aug 56 FORCE: 31 Aug 56
　　　　ANNEX
480 UNTS 342. UNTAB (Tech Assis). Amendment 3 Jul 63. Force 3 Oct 63.
480 UNTS 342. India. Amendment 3 Oct 63. Force 3 Oct 63.

103507 Bilateral Agreement **249 UNTS 175**
SIGNED: 22 Oct 54　　　FORCE: 22 Oct 54
REGISTERED: 31 Aug 56 USA (United States)
ARTICLES: 8 LANGUAGE: English.
HEADNOTE: HEADQUARTERS
TOPIC: IGO Establishment
CONCEPTS: Definition of terms. Annex or appendix reference. Diplomatic privileges. Diplomatic missions. Establishment.
PROCEDURE: Duration.
PARTIES:
　NATO (North Atlan)
　USA (United States)

103508 Bilateral Exchange **249 UNTS 187**
SIGNED: 26 Jul 56　　　FORCE: 5 Aug 56
REGISTERED: 4 Sep 56 Belgium
ARTICLES: 2 LANGUAGE: French. German.
HEADNOTE: MUTUAL ABOLITION PASSPORTS
TOPIC: Visas
CONCEPTS: Territorial application. Previous treaty replacement. Visa abolition. Denial of admission. Resident permits. Non-visa travel documents. Conformity with municipal law.
INTL ORGS: Council of Europe.
TREATY REF: 185UNTS185; 201UNTS385.
PROCEDURE: Denunciation.
PARTIES:
　Belgium
　Germany, West
　　　　ANNEX
272 UNTS 310. Germany, West. Amendment 24 Jan 57. Force 11 Mar 57.
272 UNTS 310. Belgium. Amendment 11 Mar 57. Force 11 Mar 57.

103509 Multilateral Protocol **249 UNTS 197**
SIGNED: 9 Dec 53　　　FORCE: 18 Aug 56
REGISTERED: 4 Sep 56 Belgium
ARTICLES: 9 LANGUAGE: French. Dutch.
HEADNOTE: PROTOCOL CONCERNING COMMERCIAL POLICY
TOPIC: General Economic

CONCEPTS: General provisions. Free trade. Trade procedures. Payment schedules. Quotas.
INTL ORGS: European Payments Union.
PROCEDURE: Amendment. Denunciation. Duration. Ratification. Termination.
PARTIES:
　Belgium SIGNED: 9 Dec 53 RATIFIED: 9 Jul 56 FORCE: 18 Aug 56
　Luxembourg SIGNED: 9 Dec 53 RATIFIED: 24 Jul 54 FORCE: 18 Aug 56
　Netherlands SIGNED: 9 Dec 53 RATIFIED: 18 Aug 56 FORCE: 18 Aug 56

103510 Bilateral Agreement **249 UNTS 207**
SIGNED: 2 Sep 49　　　FORCE: 28 Nov 49
REGISTERED: 4 Sep 56 Council of Europe
ARTICLES: 11 LANGUAGE: English. French.
HEADNOTE: SEAT COUNCIL OF EUROPE
TOPIC: IGO Status/Immunit
CONCEPTS: Definition of terms. Annex or appendix reference. Non-visa travel documents. Diplomatic missions. Privileges and immunities.
TREATY REF: 87UNTS103.
PARTIES:
　Council of Europe
　France

103511 Multilateral Instrument **249 UNTS 215**
SIGNED: 14 May 54　　　FORCE: 7 Aug 56
REGISTERED: 4 Sep 56 UNESCO (Educ/Cult)
ARTICLES: 1 LANGUAGE: English. French. Russian. Spanish.
HEADNOTE: PROTECTION CULTURAL PROPERTY
TOPIC: Culture
CONCEPTS: General health, education, culture, welfare and labor.
TREATY REF: 54LTS437; 54LTS439.
PROCEDURE: Ratification. Accession. Application to Non-self-governing Territories. Denunciation. Amendment.
PARTIES:
　Andorra SIGNED: 14 May 54
　Australia SIGNED: 14 May 54
　Austria SIGNED: 31 Dec 54
　Belgium SIGNED: 14 May 54
　Brazil SIGNED: 31 Dec 54
　Burma SIGNED: 14 May 54 RATIFIED: 10 Feb 56 FORCE: 7 Aug 56
　Byelorussia SIGNED: 14 May 54
　Cambodia SIGNED: 17 Dec 54
　Taiwan SIGNED: 14 May 54
　Cuba SIGNED: 14 May 54
　Czechoslovakia SIGNED: 14 May 54
　Denmark SIGNED: 18 Oct 54
　Ecuador SIGNED: 14 May 54
　United Arab Rep SIGNED: 30 Dec 54 RATIFIED: 17 Aug 55 FORCE: 7 Aug 56
　El Salvador SIGNED: 14 May 54
　France SIGNED: 14 May 54
　Germany, West SIGNED: 14 May 54
　Greece SIGNED: 14 May 54
　Hungary SIGNED: 14 May 54 RATIFIED: 17 May 56 FORCE: 17 Aug 56
　India SIGNED: 14 May 54
　Indonesia SIGNED: 24 Dec 54
　Iran SIGNED: 14 May 54
　Iraq SIGNED: 14 May 54
　Ireland SIGNED: 14 May 54
　Israel SIGNED: 14 May 54
　Italy SIGNED: 14 May 54
　Japan SIGNED: 6 Sep 54
　Jordan SIGNED: 22 Dec 54
　Lebanon SIGNED: 25 May 54
　Libya SIGNED: 14 May 54
　Luxembourg SIGNED: 14 May 54
　Mexico SIGNED: 29 Dec 54 RATIFIED: 7 May 56 FORCE: 7 Aug 56
　Monaco SIGNED: 14 May 54
　Netherlands SIGNED: 14 May 54
　New Zealand SIGNED: 20 Dec 54
　Nicaragua SIGNED: 14 May 54
　Norway SIGNED: 14 May 54
　Philippines SIGNED: 14 May 54
　Poland SIGNED: 14 May 54 RATIFIED: 6 Aug 56 FORCE: 6 Nov 56
　Portugal SIGNED: 14 May 54
　Romania SIGNED: 14 May 54
　San Marino SIGNED: 14 May 54 RATIFIED: 9 Feb 56 FORCE: 7 Aug 56
　Spain SIGNED: 14 May 54
　Syria SIGNED: 14 May 54
　UK Great Britain SIGNED: 30 Dec 54

USA (United States) SIGNED: 14 May 54
Ukrainian SSR SIGNED: 14 May 54
Uruguay SIGNED: 14 May 54
USSR (Soviet Union) SIGNED: 14 May 54
Yugoslavia SIGNED: 14 May 54 RATIFIED: 13 Feb 56 FORCE: 7 Aug 56
ANNEX
252 UNTS 407. Ecuador. Ratification 2 Oct 56. Force 2 Jan 57.
260 UNTS 22. Ratification 4 Jan 57. Force 4 Apr 57.
260 UNTS 460. Ukrainian SSR. Ratification 6 Feb 57. Force 6 May 57.
267 UNTS 387. Byelorussia. Ratification 7 May 55. Force 7 Aug 57.
270 UNTS 406. France. Ratification 7 Jun 57. Force 7 Sep 57.
277 UNTS 357. Israel. Ratification 3 Oct 57. Force 3 Jan 58.
277 UNTS 357. Jordan. Ratification 2 Oct 57. Force 2 Jan 58.
282 UNTS 366. Cuba. Ratification 26 Nov 57. Force 26 Feb 58.
282 UNTS 366. Libya. Ratification 19 Nov 57. Force 19 Feb 58.
284 UNTS 386. Monaco. Ratification 10 Dec 57. Force 10 Mar 58.
284 UNTS 386. Czechoslovakia. Ratification 6 Dec 57. Force 6 Mar 58.
287 UNTS 351. Vatican/Holy See. Accession 24 Feb 58. Force 24 May 58.
289 UNTS 325. Syria. Ratification 6 Mar 57. Force 6 Jun 57.
292 UNTS 371. Romania. Ratification 1 Mar 58. Force 21 Jun 58.
293 UNTS 357. Israel. Accession 1 Apr 58. Force 1 Jul 58.
302 UNTS 365. Italy. Ratification 9 May 58. Force 9 Aug 58.
302 UNTS 365. Thailand. Accession 2 May 58. Force 2 Aug 58.
304 UNTS 386. India. Ratification 16 Jun 58. Force 16 Sep 58.
313 UNTS 367. Brazil. Ratification 21 Sep 58. Force 12 Dec 58.
314 UNTS 352. Bulgaria. Accession 9 Oct 58. Force 9 Jan 59.
314 UNTS 352. Netherlands. Ratification 14 Oct 58. Force 12 Jan 59.
327 UNTS 378. Pakistan. Accession 27 Mar 57. Force 27 Jun 59.
336 UNTS 365. Iran. Ratification 22 Jun 59. Force 22 Sep 59.
345 UNTS 355. Nicaragua. Ratification 25 Nov 59. Force 25 Feb 60.
351 UNTS 444. Dominican Republic. Accession 5 Jan 60. Force 5 Apr 60.
358 UNTS 315. Liechtenstein. Accession 28 Apr 60. Force 28 Jul 60.
361 UNTS 336. Lebanon. Ratification 1 Jun 60. Force 1 Sep 60.
369 UNTS 459. Spain. Ratification 7 Jul 60. Force 7 Oct 60.
371 UNTS 308. Ghana. Accession 4 Aug 60. Force 25 Aug 60.
376 UNTS 428. Guinea. Accession 20 Sep 60. Force 20 Dec 60.
376 UNTS 428. Belgium. Ratification 16 Sep 60. Force 16 Dec 60.
384 UNTS 374. Albania. Accession 20 Dec 60. Force 20 Mar 60.
388 UNTS 372. Ecuador. Ratification 8 Feb 61. Force 8 May 61.
397 UNTS 331. Mali. Accession 18 May 61. Force 18 Aug 61.
399 UNTS 276. Nigeria. Accession 5 Jun 61. Force 5 Sep 61.
410 UNTS 306. Luxembourg. Ratification 29 Sep 61. Force 29 Dec 61.
414 UNTS 389. Madagascar. Accession 3 Nov 61. Force 3 Feb 62.
414 UNTS 389. Cameroon. Accession 12 Oct 61. Force 12 Jan 62.
416 UNTS 336. Guinea. Accession 11 Dec 61. Force 11 Mar 62.
416 UNTS 336. Gabon. Accession 4 Dec 61. Force 4 Mar 62.
426 UNTS 342. Cambodia. Ratification 4 Apr 62. Force 4 Jul 62.
429 UNTS 296. Switzerland. Accession 15 May 62. Force 15 Aug 62.
435 UNTS 351. Panama. Accession 17 Jul 62. Force 17 Oct 62.

454 UNTS 570. Fed of Malaya. Accession 12 Dec 60. Force 12 Mar 61.
492 UNTS 359. Austria. Ratification 25 Jun 64. Force 25 Jun 64.
515 UNTS 305. Mongolia. Accession 4 Nov 64. Force 4 Feb 65.
553 UNTS 405. Turkey. Accession 15 Dec 65. Force 15 Mar 66.
604 UNTS 354. Indonesia. Ratification 28 Jul 67. Force 26 Oct 67.
604 UNTS 354. Germany, West. Ratification 11 Aug 67. Force 11 Nov 66.
616 UNTS 494. Iraq. Ratification 21 Dec 67. Force 21 Mar 68.
646 UNTS 350. Morocco. Accession 30 Aug 68. Force 30 Nov 68.

103512 Bilateral Agreement **249 UNTS 387**
SIGNED: 28 May 54 FORCE: 17 Aug 56
REGISTERED: 5 Sep 56 Belgium
ARTICLES: 7 LANGUAGE: French. German.
HEADNOTE: ASSISTANCE EMPLOYMENT SEAMEN
TOPIC: Non-ILO Labor
CONCEPTS: Employment regulations. Labor statistics. Non-ILO labor relations. Administrative co-operation. Fees and exemptions.
PROCEDURE: Ratification.
PARTIES:
Belgium
Germany, West

103513 Bilateral Exchange **249 UNTS 395**
SIGNED: 3 Apr 56 FORCE: 1 May 56
REGISTERED: 6 Oct 56 South Africa
ARTICLES: 2 LANGUAGE: English.
HEADNOTE: VISA AGREEMENT
TOPIC: Visas
CONCEPTS: Visas. Fees and exemptions.
PARTIES:
South Africa
USA (United States)
ANNEX
300 UNTS 382. USA (United States). Supplementation 31 Mar 58. Force 1 Apr 58.
300 UNTS 382. South Africa. Supplementation 31 Mar 58. Force 1 Apr 58.

103514 Multilateral Agreement **250 UNTS 3**
SIGNED: 13 Dec 55 FORCE: 1 Jan 56
REGISTERED: 10 Sep 56 Council of Europe
ARTICLES: 11 LANGUAGE: English. French.
HEADNOTE: WAR CRIPPLES
TOPIC: Humanitarian
CONCEPTS: Humanitarian matters. Repatriation of civilians.
INTL ORGS: Council of Europe.
TREATY REF: 87UNTS103,100UNTS302,1-96UNTS347,218UNTS153.
PROCEDURE: Accession. Termination.
PARTIES:
Belgium SIGNED: 13 Dec 55
Denmark SIGNED: 13 Dec 55
France SIGNED: 13 Dec 55 FORCE: 1 Jan 56
Germany, West SIGNED: 13 Dec 55 FORCE: 1 Jan 56
Greece SIGNED: 13 Dec 55
Ireland SIGNED: 13 Dec 55 FORCE: 1 Jan 56
Italy SIGNED: 13 Dec 55
Luxembourg SIGNED: 13 Dec 55
Netherlands SIGNED: 13 Dec 55
Saar SIGNED: 13 Dec 55
Sweden SIGNED: 3 Mar 56 FORCE: 1 Apr 56
Turkey SIGNED: 13 Dec 55
UK Great Britain SIGNED: 13 Dec 55 RATIFIED: 13 Jul 56 FORCE: 1 Aug 56
ANNEX
266 UNTS 433. Italy. Ratification 17 Jan 57. Force 1 Feb 57.
266 UNTS 433. Norway. Signature without Reservation as to Approval 21 Sep 56. Force 1 Oct 56.
266 UNTS 433. Germany, West. Berlin. Force 1 Jan 56.
314 UNTS 354. Austria. Signature without Reservation as to Approval 13 Dec 57. Force 1 Jan 58.
314 UNTS 354. Denmark. Ratification 5 Jun 57. Force 1 Jul 57.
314 UNTS 354. Luxembourg. Ratification 26 Mar 58. Force 1 Apr 58.

314 UNTS 354. Netherlands. Ratification 22 Oct 58. Force 1 Nov 58.
340 UNTS 375. Belgium. Ratification 29 Apr 59. Force 1 May 59.
340 UNTS 375. Greece. Ratification 5 Jun 59. Force 1 Jul 59.
353 UNTS 370. Turkey. Ratification 7 Oct 59. Force 1 Nov 59.
635 UNTS 349. Malta. Ratification 22 Sep 67. Force 1 Oct 67.

103515 Multilateral Agreement **250 UNTS 12**
SIGNED: 2 Sep 49 FORCE: 10 Sep 52
REGISTERED: 11 Sep 56 Council of Europe
ARTICLES: 22 LANGUAGE: English. French.
HEADNOTE: PRIVILEGES IMMUNITIES COUNCIL OF EUROPE
TOPIC: IGO Status/Immunit
CONCEPTS: Diplomatic missions. Inviolability. Privileges and immunities. Property. Diplomatic correspondence. Juridical personality. Procedure. Special status. Status of experts.
INTL ORGS: Council of Europe.
PROCEDURE: Amendment. Ratification.
PARTIES:
Belgium SIGNED: 2 Sep 49 RATIFIED: 5 Apr 51 FORCE: 10 Sep 52
Denmark SIGNED: 2 Sep 49 RATIFIED: 2 Sep 53 FORCE: 2 Sep 53
France SIGNED: 2 Sep 49
Germany, West RATIFIED: 10 Sep 54 FORCE: 11 Jul 56
Greece SIGNED: 2 Sep 49 RATIFIED: 17 Nov 53 FORCE: 17 Nov 53
Iceland RATIFIED: 11 Mar 55 FORCE: 11 Jul 56
Ireland SIGNED: 2 Sep 49
Italy SIGNED: 2 Sep 49 RATIFIED: 7 Feb 52 FORCE: 10 Sep 52
Luxembourg SIGNED: 2 Sep 49 RATIFIED: 10 Sep 52 FORCE: 10 Sep 52
Netherlands SIGNED: 2 Sep 49 RATIFIED: 18 Mar 50 FORCE: 10 Sep 52
Netherlands SIGNED: 2 Sep 49 RATIFIED: 18 Mar 50 FORCE: 10 Sep 52
Norway SIGNED: 2 Sep 49 RATIFIED: 1 Dec 49 FORCE: 10 Sep 52
Saar RATIFIED: 16 Feb 54 FORCE: 11 Jul 56
Sweden SIGNED: 2 Sep 49 RATIFIED: 25 Sep 50 FORCE: 10 Sep 52
Turkey SIGNED: 2 Sep 49
UK Great Britain SIGNED: 2 Sep 49 RATIFIED: 20 Sep 50 FORCE: 10 Sep 52
ANNEX
261 UNTS 410. Belgium. Supplementation 15 Dec 56.
261 UNTS 410. France. Supplementation 15 Dec 56.
261 UNTS 410. Iceland. Supplementation 15 Dec 56. Force 15 Dec 56.
261 UNTS 410. Luxembourg. Supplementation 15 Dec 56.
261 UNTS 410. Norway. Supplementation 15 Dec 56. Force 15 Dec 56.
261 UNTS 410. Sweden. Supplementation 15 Dec 56. Force 15 Dec 56.
261 UNTS 410. Germany, West. Supplementation 15 Dec 56.
261 UNTS 410. Italy. Supplementation 15 Dec 56.
261 UNTS 410. UK Great Britain. Supplementation 15 Dec 56.
261 UNTS 410. Denmark. Supplementation 15 Dec 56. Force 15 Dec 56.
266 UNTS 434. Netherlands. Signature without Reservation as to Approval 29 Apr 57.
282 UNTS 367. Germany, West. Withdrawal of Reservation 8 Nov 57.
315 UNTS 245. Italy. Ratification 4 Jun 58.
315 UNTS 245. UK Great Britain. Ratification 8 Jul 58.
315 UNTS 245. Austria. Signature without Reservation as to Approval 13 Nov 58.
356 UNTS 375. Turkey. Ratification 7 Jan 60.
356 UNTS 375. Austria. Accession 9 May 57.
356 UNTS 375. Turkey. Ratification 7 Jan 60.
356 UNTS 375. Luxembourg. Ratification 8 Jan 60.
369 UNTS 460. Germany, West. Ratification 7 Jul 60.
376 UNTS 429. Germany, West. Berlin. Force 7 Jul 60.
388 UNTS 373. Greece. Ratification 2 Feb 61.
406 UNTS 316. Belgium. Ratification 7 Sep 61.

514 UNTS 302. Hungary. Accession 28 Oct 64. Force 26 Jan 65.

544 UNTS 294. Greece. Ratification 29 May 61. Force 15 Mar 63.

544 UNTS 294. Luxembourg. Ratification 13 Sep 60. Force 15 Mar 63.

544 UNTS 294. Italy. Ratification 15 Mar 63. Force 15 Mar 63.

544 UNTS 294. Belgium. Ratification 26 Oct 62. Force 15 Mar 63.

544 UNTS 294. Germany, West. Ratification 8 Aug 63. Force 8 Aug 63.

544 UNTS 294. Germany, West. Berlin. Force 8 Aug 63.

544 UNTS 328. Belgium. Ratification 4 Jun 64. Force 4 Jan 64.

544 UNTS 328. Germany, West. Berlin. Force 10 Dec 63.

544 UNTS 328. Austria. Signature 16 Dec 61. Force 16 Dec 61.

544 UNTS 328. Netherlands. Signature 16 Dec 61. Force 16 Dec 61.

544 UNTS 328. Norway. Signature 16 Dec 61. Force 16 Dec 61.

544 UNTS 328. Sweden. Ratification 18 Sep 62. Force 18 Sep 62.

544 UNTS 328. Greece. Ratification 24 May 65. Force 24 May 65.

544 UNTS 328. Denmark. Signature 16 Dec 61. Force 16 Dec 61.

544 UNTS 328. Germany, West. Ratification 10 Dec 63. Force 10 Dec 63.

544 UNTS 328. Luxembourg. Ratification 5 Nov 63. Force 5 Nov 63.

544 UNTS 328. Netherlands. Netherlands Antilles.

565 UNTS 288. Turkey. Force 1 Mar 65.

565 UNTS 288. Switzerland. Signature Subject to Ratification 15 Apr 64.

565 UNTS 288. Switzerland. Ratification 29 Nov 65.

565 UNTS 288. Switzerland. Ratification 29 Nov 65.

565 UNTS 288. Switzerland. Accession 29 Nov 65.

573 UNTS 316. Italy. Ratification 20 Sep 66.

635 UNTS 350. Cyprus. Accession 30 Nov 67.

635 UNTS 350. Ireland. Ratification 21 Sep 67.

660 UNTS 398. Malta. Accession 22 Jan 69.

103516 Bilateral Convention **250 UNTS 43**
SIGNED: 15 Jul 54 FORCE: 3 May 56
REGISTERED: 12 Sep 56 Denmark
ARTICLES: 10 LANGUAGE: French.
HEADNOTE: MILITARY SERVICE
TOPIC: Milit Servic/Citiz
CONCEPTS: Procedure. Dual nationality. Certificates of service. Service in foreign army.
PROCEDURE: Ratification.
PARTIES:
Denmark
Italy

103517 Bilateral Treaty **250 UNTS 51**
SIGNED: 4 Mar 53 FORCE: 29 Sep 55
REGISTERED: 12 Sep 56 Denmark
ARTICLES: 4 LANGUAGE: Danish. Spanish.
HEADNOTE: COMMERCE NAVIGATION
TOPIC: General Economic
CONCEPTS: Exceptions and exemptions. Treaty implementation. Friendship and amity. Privileges and immunities. General cooperation. Exchange of information and documents. Informational records. Establishment of trade relations. Most favored nation clause. General. Navigational conditions. Merchant vessels. Ports and pilotage.
PROCEDURE: Ratification. Termination.
PARTIES:
Denmark
Uruguay

103518 Bilateral Agreement **250 UNTS 61**
SIGNED: 20 Oct 55 FORCE: 5 Jun 56
REGISTERED: 13 Sep 56 Denmark
ARTICLES: 18 LANGUAGE: French.
HEADNOTE: CONCERNING REGULAR CIVIL AIR TRANSPORT SERVICES
TOPIC: Air Transport
CONCEPTS: Detailed regulations. Exceptions and exemptions. Annex or appendix reference. Con-

formity with municipal law. General cooperation. Licenses and permits. Recognition of legal documents. Arbitration. Procedure. Existing tribunals. Negotiation. Monetary and gold transfers. Fees and exemptions. Non-interest rates and fees. Most favored nation clause. National treatment. Customs exemptions. Competency certificate. Routes and logistics. Navigational conditions. Permit designation. Air transport. Airport facilities. Airworthiness certificates. Conditions of airlines operating permission. Overflights and technical stops. Operating authorizations and regulations. Licenses and certificates of nationality.
INTL ORGS: International Civil Aviation Organization.
PROCEDURE: Amendment. Future Procedures Contemplated. Ratification. Registration. Termination.
PARTIES:
Denmark
Syria

103519 Bilateral Instrument **250 UNTS 81**
SIGNED: 12 Jun 56 FORCE: 12 Jun 56
REGISTERED: 17 Sep 56 Netherlands
ARTICLES: 22 LANGUAGE: English. Dutch.
HEADNOTE: SOCIAL SECURITY
TOPIC: Non-ILO Labor
CONCEPTS: Definition of terms. Detailed regulations. General provisions. Old age and invalidity insurance. Wages and salaries. Non-ILO labor relations. Family allowances. Sickness and invalidity insurance. Social security. Unemployment. Payment schedules. National treatment.
TREATY REF: 248UNTS235.
PROCEDURE: Denunciation. Duration. Ratification. Renewal or Revival.
PARTIES:
Netherlands
UK Great Britain

103520 Multilateral Protocol **250 UNTS 108**
SIGNED: 24 Jul 53 FORCE: 24 Jul 56
REGISTERED: 18 Sep 56 Belgium
ARTICLES: 14 LANGUAGE: French. Dutch.
HEADNOTE: COORDINATION ECONOMIC & SOCIAL POLICIES
TOPIC: General Amity
CONCEPTS: Previous treaty amendment. Time limit. General cooperation. Arbitration. Establishment of trade relations. Export quotas. Import quotas. Reciprocity in trade. Subsidiary organ. Establishment.
INTL ORGS: Benelux Customs Union. Benelux Economic Union. International Court of Justice.
TREATY REF: ARGICULTURE PROTOCOLS 9MAY19478 21OCT19508 29DEC19.
PROCEDURE: Amendment. Duration. Ratification. Renewal or Revival.
PARTIES:
Belgium SIGNED: 24 Jul 53 RATIFIED: 20 Jul 56 FORCE: 24 Jul 56
Luxembourg SIGNED: 24 Jul 53 RATIFIED: 29 Jun 55 FORCE: 24 Jul 56
Netherlands SIGNED: 24 Jul 53 RATIFIED: 24 Jul 56 FORCE: 24 Jul 56

103521 Bilateral Agreement **250 UNTS 149**
SIGNED: 18 Jul 55 FORCE: 20 Jun 56
REGISTERED: 19 Sep 56 Finland
ARTICLES: 11 LANGUAGE: Finnish. Danish.
HEADNOTE: DOUBLE TAXATION DEATH DUTIES
TOPIC: Taxation
CONCEPTS: Debts. Taxation. Death duties. Tax exemptions.
PROCEDURE: Ratification. Termination.
PARTIES:
Denmark
Finland

103522 Bilateral Agreement **250 UNTS 167**
SIGNED: 18 Jul 55 FORCE: 1 Jul 56
REGISTERED: 19 Sep 56 Finland
ARTICLES: 24 LANGUAGE: Finnish. Danish.
HEADNOTE: ADMINISTRATIVE ASSISTANCE TAXATION
TOPIC: Taxation
CONCEPTS: Territorial application. General cooperation. Exchange of official publications. Ex-

change of information and documents. Claims and settlements. General.
PROCEDURE: Denunciation. Duration. Ratification.
PARTIES:
Denmark
Finland
ANNEX
537 UNTS 366. Finland. Supplementation 22 Mar 65. Force 1 Apr 65.

537 UNTS 366. Denmark. Supplementation 22 Mar 65. Force 1 Apr 65.

103523 Bilateral Exchange **250 UNTS 193**
SIGNED: 19 Jul 54 FORCE: 19 Jul 54
REGISTERED: 20 Sep 56 USA (United States)
ARTICLES: 2 LANGUAGE: English.
HEADNOTE: USE FIVE ISLANDS RECREATIONAL PURPOSES
TOPIC: Territory Boundary
CONCEPTS: Inspection and observation. Claims and settlements. Boundaries of territory. Changes of territory.
PARTIES:
UK Great Britain
USA (United States)

103524 Multilateral Agreement **250 UNTS 201**
SIGNED: 5 Nov 55 FORCE: 9 Sep 56
REGISTERED: 24 Sep 56 Belgium
ARTICLES: 12 LANGUAGE: French. Dutch.
HEADNOTE: INTER-PARLIAMENTARY ADVISORY COUNCIL
TOPIC: IGO Establishment
CONCEPTS: Treaty interpretation. Friendship and amity. Exchange of information and documents. Economic assistance. Establishment. Internal structure.
INTL ORGS: Benelux Parliament.
PROCEDURE: Denunciation. Future Procedures Contemplated. Ratification. Application to Non-self-governing Territories.
PARTIES:
Belgium SIGNED: 5 Nov 55 RATIFIED: 4 Jul 56 FORCE: 9 Sep 56
Luxembourg SIGNED: 5 Nov 55 RATIFIED: 3 Jul 56 FORCE: 9 Sep 56
Netherlands SIGNED: 5 Nov 55 RATIFIED: 8 Sep 56 FORCE: 9 Sep 56
ANNEX
506 UNTS 372. Netherlands. Ratification 6 Jul 58. Force 7 Nov 59.

506 UNTS 372. Luxembourg. Force 6 Nov 59. Force 7 Nov 59.

506 UNTS 372. Belgium. Ratification 3 Jul 59. Force 7 Nov 59.

103525 Bilateral Agreement **250 UNTS 213**
SIGNED: 30 Jul 55 FORCE: 12 Sep 56
REGISTERED: 24 Sep 56 Belgium
ARTICLES: 9 LANGUAGE: French. Portuguese.
HEADNOTE: CULTURAL AGREEMENT
TOPIC: Culture
CONCEPTS: Treaty interpretation. Non-prejudice to third party. Friendship and amity. Specialists exchange. Exchange. Teacher and student exchange. Professorships. Scholarships and grants. Exchange. General cultural cooperation. Artists. Scientific exchange. Publications exchange. Mass media exchange.
PROCEDURE: Denunciation. Duration. Ratification. Renewal or Revival.
PARTIES:
Belgium
Portugal

103526 Bilateral Agreement **250 UNTS 229**
SIGNED: 2 Mar 55 FORCE: 2 Mar 55
REGISTERED: 26 Sep 56 USA (United States)
ARTICLES: 11 LANGUAGE: English. Arabic.
HEADNOTE: COOPERATION PROGRAM COMMUNITY WELFARE
TOPIC: Non-IBRD Project
CONCEPTS: Previous treaty replacement. Operating agencies. Personnel. General health, education, culture, welfare and labor. Financial programs. Funding procedures. Tax exemptions. Customs exemptions. General technical assistance. Materials, equipment and services. Non-bank projects.
INTL ORGS: Special Commission.

TREATY REF: 151UNTS179; 198UNTS225; 184UNTS131.
PROCEDURE: Duration. Termination.
PARTIES:
Iraq
USA (United States)

103527 Bilateral Exchange **250 UNTS 253**
SIGNED: 5 Apr 55   FORCE: 5 Apr 55
REGISTERED: 26 Sep 56 USA (United States)
ARTICLES: 2 LANGUAGE: English. Spanish.
HEADNOTE: DUTY-FREE EXEMPTION INTERNAL TAXATION RELIEF SUPPLIES EQUIPMENT
TOPIC: Direct Aid
CONCEPTS: Transportation costs. Tax exemptions. Customs exemptions. Materials, equipment and services. Relief supplies.
PROCEDURE: Termination.
PARTIES:
Chile
USA (United States)

103528 Bilateral Agreement **250 UNTS 261**
SIGNED: 21 Mar 55   FORCE: 1 Apr 55
REGISTERED: 26 Sep 56 USA (United States)
ARTICLES: 14 LANGUAGE: English. Spanish.
HEADNOTE: AGRICULTURAL DEVELOPMENT
TOPIC: Non-IBRD Project
CONCEPTS: Treaty implementation. Previous treaty replacement. Privileges and immunities. Operating agencies. Financial programs. Funding procedures. Tax exemptions. Customs exemptions. Agriculture. Materials, equipment and services. Aid missions. Non-bank projects.
TREATY REF: 177UNTS219.
PROCEDURE: Duration. Termination.
PARTIES:
El Salvador
USA (United States)

103529 Bilateral Agreement **251 UNTS 3**
SIGNED: 6 May 55   FORCE: 6 May 55
REGISTERED: 26 Sep 56 USA (United States)
ARTICLES: 6 LANGUAGE: English.
HEADNOTE: AGRI COMMOD TITLE I
TOPIC: US Agri Commod Aid
CONCEPTS: General provisions. Annex or appendix reference. General cooperation. Exchange of information and documents. Reexport of goods, etc.. Exchange rates and regulations. Financial programs. Payment schedules. Transportation costs. Commodities schedule. Purchase authorization. Merchant vessels.
INTL ORGS: International Monetary Fund.
PARTIES:
Finland
USA (United States)
ANNEX
268 UNTS 382. USA (United States). Amendment 12 Jan 56. Force 12 Jan 51.
268 UNTS 382. Finland. Amendment 12 Jan 56. Force 12 Jan 51.
273 UNTS 306. USA (United States). Supplementation 26 Apr 56. Force 26 Apr 56.
273 UNTS 306. Finland. Supplementation 26 Apr 56. Force 26 Apr 56.
275 UNTS 314. Finland. Supplementation 26 Mar 56. Force 26 Mar 56.
275 UNTS 314. USA (United States). Supplementation 26 Mar 56. Force 26 Mar 56.
275 UNTS 320. Finland. Amendment 26 Mar 56. Force 26 Mar 56.
275 UNTS 320. USA (United States). Amendment 26 Mar 56. Force 26 Mar 56.
281 UNTS 406. Finland. Supplementation 24 Oct 56. Force 24 Oct 56.
281 UNTS 406. USA (United States). Supplementation 24 Oct 56. Force 24 Oct 56.
335 UNTS 322. Finland. Amendment 10 Feb 58. Force 17 Feb 58.
335 UNTS 322. USA (United States). Amendment 17 Feb 58. Force 17 Feb 58.

103530 Bilateral Agreement **251 UNTS 15**
SIGNED: 11 Aug 55   FORCE: 11 Aug 55
REGISTERED: 26 Sep 56 USA (United States)
ARTICLES: 7 LANGUAGE: English. French.
HEADNOTE: TITLE I AGRICULTURAL DEVELOPMENT & ASSISTANCE
TOPIC: US Agri Commod Aid

CONCEPTS: General provisions. General cooperation. Exchange of information and documents. Reexport of goods, etc.. Exchange rates and regulations. Transportation costs. Local currency. Commodities schedule. Purchase authorization. Mutual consultation.
PARTIES:
France
USA (United States)
ANNEX
410 UNTS 308. France. Supplementation 12 Jun 61. Force 12 Jun 61.
410 UNTS 308. USA (United States). Supplementation 12 Jun 61. Force 12 Jun 61.

103531 Bilateral Agreement **251 UNTS 29**
SIGNED: 5 Jan 55   FORCE: 5 Jan 55
REGISTERED: 26 Sep 56 USA (United States)
ARTICLES: 5 LANGUAGE: English.
HEADNOTE: SURPLUS COMMODITIES AGREEMENT
TOPIC: US Agri Commod Aid
CONCEPTS: Exchange of information and documents. Reexport of goods, etc.. Currency. Exchange rates and regulations. Payment schedules. Local currency. Assets transfer. Surplus commodities. Merchant vessels.
PARTIES:
USA (United States)
Yugoslavia
ANNEX
251 UNTS 422. Yugoslavia. Amendment 12 May 55. Force 12 May 55.
251 UNTS 422. USA (United States). Amendment 12 May 55. Force 12 May 55.
268 UNTS 386. Yugoslavia. Amendment 19 Jan 56. Force 19 Jan 56.
268 UNTS 386. USA (United States). Amendment 19 Jan 56. Force 19 Jan 56.
270 UNTS 408. Yugoslavia. Supplementation 1 Oct 55. Force 1 Oct 55.
270 UNTS 408. USA (United States). Supplementation 1 Oct 55. Force 1 Oct 55.
340 UNTS 376. Yugoslavia. Amendment 11 Sep 58. Force 15 Sep 58.
340 UNTS 376. USA (United States). Amendment 10 Sep 58. Force 15 Sep 58.
524 UNTS 306. USA (United States). Amendment 15 Apr 64. Force 15 Apr 64.
524 UNTS 306. Yugoslavia. Amendment 15 Apr 64. Force 15 Apr 64.

103532 Bilateral Agreement **251 UNTS 41**
SIGNED: 22 Dec 54   FORCE: 22 Dec 54
REGISTERED: 26 Sep 56 USA (United States)
ARTICLES: 11 LANGUAGE: English. Russian.
HEADNOTE: RETURN NAVAL VESSELS
TOPIC: Milit Assistance
CONCEPTS: Detailed regulations. Time limit. Annex or appendix reference. Expense sharing formulae. Delivery schedules. Ports and pilotage. Lend lease. Naval vessels. Return of equipment and recapture.
PARTIES:
USA (United States)
USSR (Soviet Union)

103533 Bilateral Agreement **251 UNTS 51**
SIGNED: 31 Dec 54   FORCE: 31 Dec 54
REGISTERED: 26 Sep 56 USA (United States)
ARTICLES: 13 LANGUAGE: English. Spanish.
HEADNOTE: COOPERATIVE EMPLOYMENT SERVICE
TOPIC: Non-ILO Labor
CONCEPTS: Definition of terms. Friendship and amity. Alien status. Operating agencies. Incorporation of treaty provisions into national law. General property. Programs. Specialists exchange. Education. Non-ILO labor relations. Administrative cooperation. Accounting procedures. Expense sharing formulae. Fees and exemptions. Financial programs. Domestic obligation. Economic assistance.
TREATY REF: USA'TIAS 2772;.
PROCEDURE: Termination.
PARTIES:
Peru
USA (United States)

ANNEX
277 UNTS 358. USA (United States). Supplementation 29 Oct 56. Force 29 Oct 56.
277 UNTS 358. Peru. Supplementation 29 Oct 56. Force 29 Oct 56.

103534 Multilateral Exchange **251 UNTS 79**
SIGNED: 13 Nov 47   FORCE: 13 Nov 47
REGISTERED: 26 Sep 56 USA (United States)
ARTICLES: 4 LANGUAGE: English.
HEADNOTE: PASSPORT VISA FEES
TOPIC: Visas
CONCEPTS: Time limit. Visa abolition. Visas. Fees and exemptions.
PARTIES:
Liechtenstein   SIGNED: 4 Nov 47   FORCE: 13 Nov 47
Switzerland   SIGNED: 4 Nov 47   FORCE: 13 Nov 47
USA (United States) SIGNED: 13 Nov 47 FORCE: 13 Nov 47

103535 Bilateral Exchange **251 UNTS 91**
SIGNED: 13 Aug 54   FORCE: 16 Nov 54
REGISTERED: 26 Sep 56 USA (United States)
ARTICLES: 2 LANGUAGE: English.
HEADNOTE: STATIONING ARMED FORCES
TOPIC: Milit Installation
CONCEPTS: Annex or appendix reference. Title and deeds. Use of facilities. Indemnities and reimbursements. Expense sharing formulae. National treatment. Tax exemptions. Customs exemptions. Defense and security. Status of military forces. Status of forces.
TREATY REF: 34UNTS243.
PROCEDURE: Termination.
PARTIES:
Netherlands
USA (United States)

103536 Bilateral Agreement **251 UNTS 105**
SIGNED: 17 Nov 53   FORCE: 10 Mar 55
REGISTERED: 26 Sep 56 USA (United States)
ARTICLES: 8 LANGUAGE: English. French.
HEADNOTE: DISPOSAL PROPERTY FURNISHED MUTUAL DEFENSE ASSISTANCE PROGRAM
TOPIC: Milit Assistance
CONCEPTS: General property. Reexport of goods, etc.. Delivery schedules. Surplus property. Return of equipment and recapture.
TREATY REF: 51UNTS213; 179UNTS81.
PARTIES:
Belgium
USA (United States)

103537 Bilateral Agreement **251 UNTS 111**
SIGNED: 11 Jan 55   FORCE: 11 Jan 55
REGISTERED: 26 Sep 56 USA (United States)
ARTICLES: 8 LANGUAGE: English.
HEADNOTE: DEFENSE SUPPORT MUTUAL SECURITY ACT
TOPIC: Milit Assistance
CONCEPTS: Peaceful relations. Privileges and immunities. Conformity with municipal law. Exchange of information and documents. Inspection and observation. Public information. Accounting procedures. Indemnities and reimbursements. Exchange rates and regulations. Financial programs. Funding procedures. Garnishment of funds. Local currency. Domestic obligation. General aid. Materials, equipment and services. Defense and security. Self-defense. Military assistance.
INTL ORGS: International Monetary Fund.
PROCEDURE: Amendment. Future Procedures Contemplated. Termination.
PARTIES:
Pakistan
USA (United States)
ANNEX
406 UNTS 318. Pakistan. Amendment 11 Mar 61. Force 11 Mar 61.
406 UNTS 318. USA (United States). Amendment 11 Mar 61. Force 11 Mar 61.

103538 Bilateral Agreement **251 UNTS 123**
SIGNED: 1 Nov 54 FORCE: 1 Oct 56
REGISTERED: 1 Oct 56 Belgium
ARTICLES: 43 LANGUAGE: French.
HEADNOTE: SOCIAL SECURITY
TOPIC: Non-ILO Labor
CONCEPTS: General provisions. Domestic legislation. Incorporation of treaty provisions into national law. Dispute settlement. Old age and invalidity insurance. Wages and salaries. Non-ILO labor relations. Family allowances. Administrative cooperation. Old age insurance. Sickness and invalidity insurance. Social security. Unemployment. Payment schedules.
PROCEDURE: Duration. Ratification. Renewal or Revival. Termination.
PARTIES:
 Belgium
 Yugoslavia

103539 Bilateral Exchange **251 UNTS 161**
SIGNED: 1 Sep 56 FORCE: 1 Oct 56
REGISTERED: 1 Oct 56 South Africa
ARTICLES: 2 LANGUAGE: English.
HEADNOTE: VISA AGREEMENT
TOPIC: Visas
CONCEPTS: Denial of admission. Visas. Conformity with municipal law. Fees and exemptions.
PARTIES:
 Israel
 South Africa

103540 Bilateral Agreement **251 UNTS 167**
SIGNED: 25 Jun 56 FORCE: 1 Jul 56
REGISTERED: 1 Oct 56 Greece
ARTICLES: 7 LANGUAGE: French.
HEADNOTE: TRADE
TOPIC: General Trade
CONCEPTS: Territorial application. Annex or appendix reference. Establishment of commission. Export quotas. Import quotas. Trade procedures. Payment schedules.
INTL ORGS: Organization for Economic Co-operation and Development. Special Commission.
TREATY REF: 251UNTS175.
PROCEDURE: Duration.
PARTIES:
 France
 Greece

103541 Multilateral Agreement **251 UNTS 181**
SIGNED: 31 May 56 FORCE: 26 Jul 56
REGISTERED: 3 Oct 56 United Nations
ARTICLES: 6 LANGUAGE: English. Arabic.
HEADNOTE: TECHNICAL ASSISTANCE
TOPIC: Tech Assistance
CONCEPTS: Definition of terms. Privileges and immunities. General cooperation. Exchange of information and documents. Personnel. Responsibility and liability. Title and deeds. Exchange. Scholarships and grants. Vocational training. Research and development. Exchange rates and regulations. Expense sharing formulae. Local currency. Domestic obligation. General technical assistance. Materials, equipment and services. IGO status. Conformity with IGO decisions.
TREATY REF: 76UNTS132; 1UNTS15; 1UNTS263; 33UNTS261.
PROCEDURE: Amendment. Termination.
PARTIES:
 FAO (Food Agri) SIGNED: 31 May 56 FORCE: 26 Jul 56
 ICAO (Civil Aviat) SIGNED: 31 May 56 FORCE: 26 Jul 56
 ILO (Labor Org) SIGNED: 31 May 56 FORCE: 26 Jul 56
 ITU (Telecommun) SIGNED: 31 May 56 FORCE: 26 Jul 56
 UNESCO (Educ/Cult) SIGNED: 31 May 56 FORCE: 26 Jul 56
 United Nations SIGNED: 31 May 56 FORCE: 26 Jul 56
 WHO (World Health) SIGNED: 31 May 56 FORCE: 26 Jul 56
 WMO (Meteorology) SIGNED: 31 May 56 FORCE: 26 Jul 56
 Yemen SIGNED: 26 Jul 56 FORCE: 26 Jul 56
ANNEX
466 UNTS 393. UNTAB (Tech Assis). Amendment 4 Apr 63. Force 14 Apr 63.

466 UNTS 393. Yemen. Amendment 14 Apr 63. Force 14 Apr 63.
654 UNTS 379. UNIDO (Industrial). Accession 10 Nov 68. Force 10 Nov 68.
654 UNTS 379. UPU (Postal Union). Accession 10 Nov 68. Force 1 Nov 68.
654 UNTS 379. IMCO (Maritime Org). Accession 10 Nov 68. Force 10 Nov 68.

103542 Bilateral Treaty **251 UNTS 201**
SIGNED: 5 Nov 54 FORCE: 16 Apr 55
REGISTERED: 4 Oct 56 Burma
ARTICLES: 10 LANGUAGE: English.
HEADNOTE: TREATY PEACE
TOPIC: Peace/Disarmament
CONCEPTS: Peaceful relations. Revival of treaties. Procedure. Existing tribunals. Negotiation. Lump sum settlements. Armistice and peace. Post-war claims settlement.
INTL ORGS: International Court of Justice.
PROCEDURE: Future Procedures Contemplated. Ratification.
PARTIES:
 Burma
 Japan

103543 Bilateral Agreement **251 UNTS 215**
SIGNED: 5 Nov 54 FORCE: 16 Apr 55
REGISTERED: 4 Oct 56 Burma
ARTICLES: 7 LANGUAGE: English.
HEADNOTE: REPARATIONS ECONOMIC COOPERATION
TOPIC: Reparations
CONCEPTS: Treaty implementation. Annex or appendix reference. Establishment of commission. Arbitration. Procedure. Reexport of goods, etc.. Payment schedules. Domestic obligation. Materials, equipment and services. Loss and/or damage. Reparations and restrictions. Post-war claims settlement.
PROCEDURE: Ratification.
PARTIES:
 Burma
 Japan

103544 Multilateral Agreement **251 UNTS 245**
SIGNED: 5 Oct 56 FORCE: 5 Oct 56
REGISTERED: 5 Oct 56 United Nations
ARTICLES: 6 LANGUAGE: Spanish.
HEADNOTE: TECHNICAL ASSISTANCE
TOPIC: Tech Assistance
CONCEPTS: Definition of terms. Previous treaty replacement. Privileges and immunities. General cooperation. Exchange of information and documents. Personnel. Responsibility and liability. Title and deeds. Use of facilities. Exchange. Scholarships and grants. Vocational training. Research and development. Exchange rates and regulations. Expense sharing formulae. Local currency. Domestic obligation. General technical assistance. Materials, equipment and services. IGO status. Conformity with IGO decisions.
TREATY REF: 76UNTS132; 1UNTS15; 1UNTS263.
PROCEDURE: Amendment. Termination.
PARTIES:
 Dominican Republic SIGNED: 5 Oct 56 FORCE: 5 Oct 56
 FAO (Food Agri) SIGNED: 5 Oct 56 FORCE: 5 Oct 56
 ICAO (Civil Aviat) SIGNED: 5 Oct 56 FORCE: 5 Oct 56
 ILO (Labor Org) SIGNED: 5 Oct 56 FORCE: 5 Oct 56
 ITU (Telecommun) SIGNED: 5 Oct 56 FORCE: 5 Oct 56
 UNESCO (Educ/Cult) SIGNED: 5 Oct 56 FORCE: 5 Oct 56
 United Nations SIGNED: 5 Oct 56 FORCE: 5 Oct 56
 WHO (World Health) SIGNED: 5 Oct 56 FORCE: 5 Oct 56
 WMO (Meteorology) SIGNED: 5 Oct 56 FORCE: 5 Oct 56
ANNEX
491 UNTS 388. Dominican Republic. Force 20 Feb 64.
491 UNTS 388. UNTAB (Tech Assis). Force 20 Feb 64.

103545 Multilateral Agreement **251 UNTS 267**
SIGNED: 5 Oct 56 FORCE: 5 Oct 56
REGISTERED: 5 Oct 56 United Nations
ARTICLES: 6 LANGUAGE: French.
HEADNOTE: TECHNICAL ASSISTANCE
TOPIC: Tech Assistance
CONCEPTS: Definition of terms. Previous treaty replacement. Privileges and immunities. General cooperation. Exchange of information and documents. Personnel. Responsibility and liability. Title and deeds. Use of facilities. Exchange. Scholarships and grants. Vocational training. Research and development. Exchange rates and regulations. Expense sharing formulae. Local currency. Domestic obligation. General technical assistance. Materials, equipment and services. IGO status. Conformity with IGO decisions.
TREATY REF: 76UNTS132; 1UNTS15; 1UNTS263.
PROCEDURE: Amendment. Termination.
PARTIES:
 Cambodia SIGNED: 5 Oct 56 FORCE: 5 Oct 56
 FAO (Food Agri) SIGNED: 28 Aug 56 FORCE: 5 Oct 56
 ICAO (Civil Aviat) SIGNED: 28 Aug 56 FORCE: 5 Oct 56
 ILO (Labor Org) SIGNED: 28 Aug 56 FORCE: 5 Oct 56
 ITU (Telecommun) SIGNED: 28 Aug 56 FORCE: 5 Oct 56
 UNESCO (Educ/Cult) SIGNED: 28 Aug 56 FORCE: 5 Oct 56
 United Nations SIGNED: 28 Aug 56 FORCE: 5 Oct 56
 WHO (World Health) SIGNED: 28 Aug 56 FORCE: 5 Oct 56
 WMO (Meteorology) SIGNED: 28 Aug 56 FORCE: 5 Oct 56

103546 Bilateral Agreement **251 UNTS 283**
SIGNED: 25 Apr 55 FORCE: 25 Apr 55
REGISTERED: 9 Oct 56 USA (United States)
ARTICLES: 6 LANGUAGE: English. Spanish.
HEADNOTE: SALE AND PURCHASE SURPLUS COTTON SEED OIL
TOPIC: US Agri Commod Aid
CONCEPTS: General provisions. Conformity with municipal law. General cooperation. Exchange of information and documents. Purchase authorizations. Local currency. Domestic obligation. Loan and credit. Commodities schedule. Surplus commodities.
PARTIES:
 Argentina
 USA (United States)
ANNEX
316 UNTS 380. USA (United States). Amendment 11 Apr 58. Force 24 Apr 58.
316 UNTS 380. Argentina. Amendment 22 Apr 58. Force 24 Apr 58.
462 UNTS 349. Argentina. Amendment 26 Nov 62. Force 26 Nov 62.
462 UNTS 349. USA (United States). Amendment 19 Sep 62. Force 26 Nov 62.

103547 Bilateral Agreement **251 UNTS 303**
SIGNED: 23 May 55 FORCE: 23 May 55
REGISTERED: 9 Oct 56 USA (United States)
ARTICLES: 6 LANGUAGE: English. Italian.
HEADNOTE: SURPLUS AGRI COMMOD TITLE I
TOPIC: US Agri Commod Aid
CONCEPTS: General provisions. Exchange of information and documents. Reexport of goods, etc.. Exchange rates and regulations. Transportation costs. Local currency. Commodities schedule. Purchase authorization. Surplus commodities. Mutual consultation.
PARTIES:
 Italy
 USA (United States)
ANNEX
270 UNTS 412. Italy. Amendment 2 Sep 55. Force 2 Sep 55.
270 UNTS 412. USA (United States). Amendment 30 Aug 55. Force 2 Sep 55.
273 UNTS 310. USA (United States). Supplementation 5 Jul 56. Force 5 Jul 56.
273 UNTS 310. Italy. Supplementation 5 Jul 56. Force 5 Jul 56.
303 UNTS 361. Italy. Amendment 11 Dec 57. Force 11 Dec 57.
303 UNTS 361. USA (United States). Amendment 2 Dec 57. Force 11 Dec 57.

103548 Bilateral Agreement **251 UNTS 321**
SIGNED: 31 May 55 FORCE: 31 May 55
REGISTERED: 9 Oct 56 USA (United States)
ARTICLES: 6 LANGUAGE: English.
HEADNOTE: SURPLUS AGRICULTURE TITLE I
TOPIC: US Agri Commod Aid
CONCEPTS: General provisions. General cooper-
ation. Exchange of information and documents.
Reexport of goods, etc.. Exchange rates and reg-
ulations. Payment schedules. Transportation
costs. Local currency. Commodities schedule.
Purchase authorization.
PARTIES:
Korea, South
USA (United States)

103549 Bilateral Exchange **251 UNTS 331**
SIGNED: 12 May 55 FORCE: 12 May 55
REGISTERED: 9 Oct 56 USA (United States)
ARTICLES: 2 LANGUAGE: English.
HEADNOTE: SURPLUS AGRI COMMOD
TOPIC: Direct Aid
CONCEPTS: Purchase authorization. Surplus com-
modities.
PARTIES:
USA (United States)
Yugoslavia

103550 Bilateral Exchange **251 UNTS 337**
SIGNED: 12 May 55 FORCE: 12 May 55
REGISTERED: 9 Oct 56 USA (United States)
ARTICLES: 2 LANGUAGE: English.
HEADNOTE: ECONOMIC AID
TOPIC: Direct Aid
CONCEPTS: Financial programs. Payment sched-
ules. Local currency. Economic assistance. Sur-
plus commodities.
PARTIES:
USA (United States)
Yugoslavia

103551 Bilateral Exchange **251 UNTS 343**
SIGNED: 12 May 55 FORCE: 12 May 55
REGISTERED: 9 Oct 56 USA (United States)
ARTICLES: 2 LANGUAGE: English.
HEADNOTE: ECONOMIC AID
TOPIC: Direct Aid
CONCEPTS: Annex or appendix reference. Confor-
mity with municipal law. Financial programs.
Economic assistance. Military assistance.
TREATY REF: 237UNTS.
PARTIES:
USA (United States)
Yugoslavia
ANNEX
338 UNTS 392. USA (United States). Amendment
17 Oct 58. Force 17 Oct 58.
338 UNTS 392. Yugoslavia. Amendment
17 Oct 58. Force 17 Oct 58.

103552 Bilateral Exchange **251 UNTS 349**
SIGNED: 27 May 55 FORCE: 27 May 55
REGISTERED: 9 Oct 56 USA (United States)
ARTICLES: 2 LANGUAGE: English.
HEADNOTE: DEFENSE FACILITIES ASSISTANCE
TOPIC: Milit Assistance
CONCEPTS: Change of circumstances. Use of fa-
cilities. General technical assistance. Materials,
equipment and services. Defense and security.
Military assistance. Equipment and supplies.
TREATY REF: 234UNTS43; 34UNTS243.
PARTIES:
Greece
USA (United States)

103553 Bilateral Exchange **251 UNTS 357**
SIGNED: 29 Apr 55 FORCE: 1 Jul 55
REGISTERED: 9 Oct 56 USA (United States)
ARTICLES: 2 LANGUAGE: English.
HEADNOTE: SPECIAL FACILITIES ASSISTANCE
PROGRAM
TOPIC: Milit Assistance
CONCEPTS: Assistance. Defense and security.
Payment for war supplies.

PARTIES:
Netherlands
USA (United States)

103554 Bilateral Protocol **252 UNTS 3**
SIGNED: 13 Mar 56 FORCE: 1 May 56
REGISTERED: 11 Oct 56 Netherlands
ARTICLES: 3 LANGUAGE: English. Japanese.
HEADNOTE: PRIVATE CLAIMS
TOPIC: Claims and Debts
CONCEPTS: Exchange rates and regulations.
Claims and settlements. Lump sum settlements.
Purchase authorization.
PARTIES:
Japan
Netherlands

103555 Bilateral Exchange **252 UNTS 13**
SIGNED: 15 Sep 49 FORCE: 15 Oct 49
REGISTERED: 11 Oct 56 Netherlands
ARTICLES: 2 LANGUAGE: French.
HEADNOTE: ABOLITION PASSPORT VISAS
TOPIC: Visas
CONCEPTS: Territorial application. Visa abolition.
Resident permits.
PARTIES:
Netherlands
Switzerland

103556 Bilateral Exchange **252 UNTS 19**
SIGNED: 8 Oct 47 FORCE: 8 Oct 47
REGISTERED: 11 Oct 56 Netherlands
ARTICLES: 2 LANGUAGE: English.
HEADNOTE: COMPENSATION WAR DAMAGE
TOPIC: Reparations
CONCEPTS: Loss and/or damage. Post-war claims
settlement.
PARTIES:
Netherlands
UK Great Britain

103557 Bilateral Agreement **252 UNTS 27**
SIGNED: 28 Feb 53 FORCE: 28 Feb 53
REGISTERED: 11 Oct 56 Greece
ARTICLES: 7 LANGUAGE: French.
HEADNOTE: EXPANDING TRADE ECONOMIC COL-
LABORATION
TOPIC: General Economic
CONCEPTS: Annex or appendix reference. Li-
censes and permits. Establishment of commis-
sion. Export quotas. Import quotas. Payment
schedules. Quotas. Most favored nation clause.
INTL ORGS: European Payments Union. Special
Commission.
PROCEDURE: Duration. Termination.
PARTIES:
Greece
Yugoslavia
ANNEX
391 UNTS 318. Greece. Supplementation
9 Apr 57. Force 9 Apr 57.
391 UNTS 318. Yugoslavia. Supplementation
9 Apr 57. Force 9 Apr 57.

103558 Bilateral Instrument **252 UNTS 83**
SIGNED: 27 Feb 56 FORCE: 1 Oct 56
REGISTERED: 11 Oct 56 UK Great Britain
ARTICLES: 10 LANGUAGE: English.
HEADNOTE: BACON IMPORTATION
TOPIC: Commodity Trade
CONCEPTS: Previous treaty replacement. General
trade. Tariffs. Commodity trade. Quotas.
INTL ORGS: General Agreement on Tariffs and
Trade.
TREATY REF: 68UNTS105; 55UNTS284;
139LTS127; 177LTS421.
PROCEDURE: Amendment. Duration. Termination.
PARTIES:
Denmark
UK Great Britain

103559 Bilateral Agreement **252 UNTS 93**
SIGNED: 31 Jul 56 FORCE: 31 Jul 56
REGISTERED: 11 Oct 56 UK Great Britain
ARTICLES: 8 LANGUAGE: English. German.
HEADNOTE: PEACEFUL USES ATOMIC ENERGY
TOPIC: Atomic Energy
CONCEPTS: General cooperation. Exchange of in-

formation and documents. Labor statistics.
Scientific exchange. Nuclear materials. Non-
nuclear materials. Peaceful use. Security of information.
PROCEDURE: Duration.
PARTIES:
Germany, West
UK Great Britain
ANNEX
313 UNTS 368. Germany, West. Berlin. Force
19 Dec 57.
313 UNTS 368. UK Great Britain. Acknowledgement 14 Nov 57. Force 19 Dec 57.

103560 Bilateral Agreement **252 UNTS 107**
SIGNED: 21 Nov 55 FORCE: 28 Jun 56
REGISTERED: 11 Oct 56 UK Great Britain
ARTICLES: 8 LANGUAGE: English. Spanish.
HEADNOTE: INCREASE TRADE FINANCIAL
TRANSACTIONS
TOPIC: General Economic
CONCEPTS: Definition of terms. Detailed regula-
tions. Exceptions and exemptions. Territorial ap-
plication. Licenses and permits. Reciprocity in
trade. Export subsidies. Monetary and gold
transfers.
PROCEDURE: Duration. Ratification. Termination.
PARTIES:
Paraguay
UK Great Britain
ANNEX
343 UNTS 359. UK Great Britain. Hong Kong.
Force 21 Feb 57.
343 UNTS 359. UK Great Britain. Barbados. Force
21 Feb 57.
343 UNTS 359. UK Great Britain. Gibralter. Force
21 Feb 57.
343 UNTS 359. UK Great Britain. Gambia. Force
21 Feb 57.
343 UNTS 359. UK Great Britain. Gold Coast.
Force 21 Feb 57.
343 UNTS 359. UK Great Britain. Leeward Islands. Force 21 Feb 57.
343 UNTS 359. UK Great Britain. Fed of Malaya.
Force 21 Feb 57.
343 UNTS 359. UK Great Britain. Mauritius. Force
21 Feb 57.
343 UNTS 359. UK Great Britain. St. Helena.
Force 21 Feb 57.
343 UNTS 359. UK Great Britain. Aden. Force
21 Feb 57.
343 UNTS 359. UK Great Britain. Sierra Leone.
Force 21 Feb 57.
343 UNTS 359. UK Great Britain. Singapore.
Force 21 Feb 57.
343 UNTS 359. UK Great Britain. Tanganyika.
Force 21 Feb 57.
343 UNTS 359. UK Great Britain. Trinidad/-
Tobago. Force 21 Feb 57.
343 UNTS 359. UK Great Britain. Uganda. Force
21 Feb 57.
343 UNTS 359. UK Great Britain. Windward Islands. Force 21 Feb 57.
343 UNTS 359. UK Great Britain. Seychelles.
Force 12 Apr 57.
343 UNTS 359. UK Great Britain. Antigua. Force
16 Jul 57.
343 UNTS 359. UK Great Britain. Malta. Force
21 Feb 57.
343 UNTS 359. Paraguay. Acknowledgement
21 Feb 57. Force 21 Feb 57.
414 UNTS 390. UK Great Britain. Prolongation
26 Jun 61. Prolongation 25 Aug 61.
414 UNTS 390. Paraguay. Prolongation
26 Jun 61. Prolongation 25 Aug 61.
425 UNTS 342. UK Great Britain. Extension and
Amendment 27 Nov 61. Force 27 Nov 61.
425 UNTS 342. Paraguay. Extension and Amendment 27 Nov 61. Force 27 Nov 61.
605 UNTS 350. UK Great Britain. Prolongation
23 Nov 66.
605 UNTS 350. Paraguay. Prolongation
23 Nov 66.
613 UNTS 409. UK Great Britain. Prolongation
27 Mar 67. Termination 27 Sep 67.
613 UNTS 409. Paraguay. Prolongation
27 Mar 67. Termination 27 Sep 67.

103561 Bilateral Exchange **252 UNTS 127**
SIGNED: 9 Aug 56 FORCE: 9 Aug 56
REGISTERED: 11 Oct 56 UK Great Britain
ARTICLES: 2 LANGUAGE: English.
HEADNOTE: PREPAYMENT POSTAGE DIPLO-
MATIC BAGS

TOPIC: Consul/Citizenship
CONCEPTS: Diplomatic correspondence. Rates and charges.
PARTIES:
Dominican Republic
UK Great Britain

103562 Bilateral Exchange **252 UNTS 129**
SIGNED: 26 Feb 55 FORCE: 25 Feb 55
REGISTERED: 11 Oct 56 USA (United States)
ARTICLES: 2 LANGUAGE: English. Spanish.
HEADNOTE: GUARANTY PRIVATE INVESTMENTS
TOPIC: Claims and Debts
CONCEPTS: Conformity with municipal law. General cooperation. Arbitration. Procedure. Existing tribunals. Negotiation. Reciprocity in financial treatment. Currency. Claims and settlements. Private investment guarantee.
TREATY REF: 252UNTS131.
PARTIES:
Costa Rica
USA (United States)

103563 Bilateral Exchange **252 UNTS 143**
SIGNED: 23 Mar 55 FORCE: 23 Mar 55
REGISTERED: 11 Oct 56 USA (United States)
ARTICLES: 2 LANGUAGE: English. Spanish.
HEADNOTE: GUARANTY PRIVATE INVESTMENTS
TOPIC: Claims and Debts
CONCEPTS: Conformity with municipal law. Arbitration. Procedure. Existing tribunals. Negotiation. Reciprocity in financial treatment. Currency. Claims and settlements. Private investment guarantee.
PARTIES:
Guatemala
USA (United States)

103564 Bilateral Exchange **252 UNTS 151**
SIGNED: 16 Mar 55 FORCE: 16 Mar 55
REGISTERED: 11 Oct 56 USA (United States)
ARTICLES: 2 LANGUAGE: English. Spanish.
HEADNOTE: GUARANTY PRIVATE INVESTMENT
TOPIC: Claims and Debts
CONCEPTS: General cooperation. Reciprocity in financial treatment. Currency. Claims and settlements. Private investment guarantee.
PARTIES:
Peru
USA (United States)

103565 Bilateral Exchange **252 UNTS 159**
SIGNED: 7 Mar 55 FORCE: 7 Mar 55
REGISTERED: 11 Oct 56 USA (United States)
ARTICLES: 2 LANGUAGE: English.
HEADNOTE: INFORMATIONAL MEDIA GUARANTY PROGRAM
TOPIC: Mass Media
CONCEPTS: Local currency. Media guaranty.
PARTIES:
United Arab Rep
USA (United States)

103566 Bilateral Agreement **252 UNTS 165**
SIGNED: 29 Feb 56 FORCE: 26 May 56
REGISTERED: 17 Oct 56 Canada
ARTICLES: 9 LANGUAGE: English. Russian.
HEADNOTE: DEVELOPING TRADE RELATIONS
TOPIC: General Trade
CONCEPTS: Exceptions and exemptions. Treaty implementation. General cooperation. Juridical personality. Legal protection and assistance. General property. Arbitration. Establishment of trade relations. Export quotas. Import quotas. Reciprocity in trade. Balance of payments. Most favored nation clause. Equitable taxes. Customs duties. Navigational conditions. Transport of goods. Merchant vessels. Ports and pilotage.
PROCEDURE: Duration. Ratification. Renewal or Revival.
PARTIES:
Canada
USSR (Soviet Union)
ANNEX
399 UNTS 278. USSR (Soviet Union). Prolongation 18 Apr 60. Force 16 Sep 60.
399 UNTS 278. Canada. Prolongation 18 Apr 60. Force 16 Sep 60.

103567 Bilateral Agreement **252 UNTS 185**
SIGNED: 29 Mar 54 FORCE: 23 Dec 55
REGISTERED: 18 Oct 56 Netherlands
ARTICLES: 30 LANGUAGE: Dutch. Finnish.
HEADNOTE: DOUBLE TAXATION TAXES INCOME PROPERTY
TOPIC: Taxation
CONCEPTS: Definition of terms. Territorial application. Conformity with municipal law. Exchange of official publications. Teacher and student exchange. Taxation. Death duties. Equitable taxes. General. Tax exemptions. Air transport. Merchant vessels.
PROCEDURE: Duration. Ratification. Termination.
PARTIES:
Finland
Netherlands
ANNEX
604 UNTS 356. Netherlands. Amendment 16 Dec 66. Force 25 Aug 67.
604 UNTS 356. Finland. Amendment 16 Dec 66. Force 25 Aug 67.

103568 Bilateral Agreement **252 UNTS 239**
SIGNED: 29 Mar 54 FORCE: 23 Dec 55
REGISTERED: 18 Oct 56 Netherlands
ARTICLES: 17 LANGUAGE: Dutch. Finnish.
HEADNOTE: DOUBLE TAXATION DEATH DUTIES
TOPIC: Taxation
CONCEPTS: Definition of terms. Territorial application. Privileges and immunities. Exchange of official publications. Negotiation. Claims and settlements. Debts. Taxation. Death duties. Tax exemptions.
PROCEDURE: Duration. Ratification. Termination.
PARTIES:
Finland
Netherlands

103569 Bilateral Agreement **252 UNTS 269**
SIGNED: 18 May 55 FORCE: 14 May 56
REGISTERED: 19 Oct 56 Netherlands
ARTICLES: 16 LANGUAGE: French.
HEADNOTE: CULTURAL AGREEMENT
TOPIC: Culture
CONCEPTS: Friendship and amity. Tourism. General cooperation. Exchange of information and documents. Operating agencies. Establishment of commission. Specialists exchange. Recognition of degrees. Exchange. Teacher and student exchange. Professorships. Scholarships and grants. Exchange. General cultural cooperation. Artists. Research cooperation. Scientific exchange. Publications exchange. Mass media exchange.
INTL ORGS: Special Commission.
PROCEDURE: Denunciation. Duration. Ratification.
PARTIES:
Netherlands
Norway

103570 Bilateral Agreement **252 UNTS 279**
SIGNED: 7 May 56 FORCE: 1 Sep 56
REGISTERED: 22 Oct 56 IBRD (World Bank)
ARTICLES: 8 LANGUAGE: English.
HEADNOTE: LOAN AGREEMENT
TOPIC: IBRD Project
CONCEPTS: Default remedies. Definition of terms. Annex or appendix reference. Exchange of information and documents. Informational records. Inspection and observation. Accounting procedures. Bonds. Fees and exemptions. Interest rates. Tax exemptions. Domestic obligation. Terms of loan. Loan regulations. Loan guarantee. Guarantor non-interference.
PARTIES:
Haiti
IBRD (World Bank)

103571 Unilateral Instrument **252 UNTS 301**
SIGNED: 3 Oct 56 FORCE: 17 Oct 56
REGISTERED: 25 Oct 56 United Nations
ARTICLES: 1 LANGUAGE: English.
HEADNOTE: ACCEPTANCE ICJ JURISDICTION
TOPIC: ICJ Option Clause
CONCEPTS: Conformity with municipal law. Compulsory jurisdiction.
INTL ORGS: International Court of Justice. United Nations.
PROCEDURE: Termination.

PARTIES:
Israel

103572 Bilateral Exchange **253 UNTS 3**
SIGNED: 21 Mar 55 FORCE: 21 Mar 55
REGISTERED: 30 Oct 56 USA (United States)
ARTICLES: 2 LANGUAGE: English. Spanish.
HEADNOTE: RELIEF SUPPLIES EQUIPMENT
TOPIC: Direct Aid
CONCEPTS: Transportation costs. Tax exemptions. Customs exemptions. Materials, equipment and services. Relief supplies.
PARTIES:
Honduras
USA (United States)

103573 Multilateral Agreement **253 UNTS 12**
SIGNED: 26 Jun 56 FORCE: 26 Jun 56
REGISTERED: 1 Nov 56 United Nations
ARTICLES: 6 LANGUAGE: English. Serbo-Croat.
HEADNOTE: TECHNICAL ASSISTANCE
TOPIC: Tech Assistance
CONCEPTS: Definition of terms. Annex or appendix reference. Previous treaty replacement. Privileges and immunities. General cooperation. Exchange of information and documents. Personnel. Responsibility and liability. Title and deeds. Use of facilities. Exchange. Scholarships and grants. Vocational training. Research and development. Exchange rates and regulations. Expense sharing formulae. Local currency. Domestic obligation. General technical assistance. Materials, equipment and services. IGO status. Conformity with IGO decisions.
TREATY REF: 76UNTS132; 1UNTS15; 1UNTS263.
PROCEDURE: Amendment. Termination.
PARTIES:
FAO (Food Agri) SIGNED: 26 Jun 56 FORCE: 26 Jun 56
ICAO (Civil Aviat) SIGNED: 26 Jun 56 FORCE: 26 Jun 56
ILO (Labor Org) SIGNED: 26 Jun 56 FORCE: 26 Jun 56
ITU (Telecommun) SIGNED: 26 Jun 56 FORCE: 26 Jun 56
UNESCO (Educ/Cult) SIGNED: 26 Jun 56 FORCE: 26 Jun 56
United Nations SIGNED: 26 Jun 56 FORCE: 26 Jun 56
WHO (World Health) SIGNED: 26 Jun 56 FORCE: 26 Jun 56
WMO (Meteorology) SIGNED: 26 Jun 56 FORCE: 26 Jun 56
Yugoslavia SIGNED: 26 Jun 56 FORCE: 26 Jun 56
ANNEX
261 UNTS 418. Yugoslavia. Acceptance 5 Mar 57. Force 5 Mar 57.
571 UNTS 318. UNTAB (Tech Assis). Amendment 4 Aug 66. Force 26 Aug 66.
571 UNTS 318. Yugoslavia. Amendment 26 Aug 66. Force 26 Aug 66.
655 UNTS 390. UNIDO (Industrial). Accession 9 Jan 69. Force 9 Jan 69.

103574 Bilateral Agreement **253 UNTS 41**
SIGNED: 22 Apr 55 FORCE: 1 Nov 56
REGISTERED: 1 Nov 56 Belgium
ARTICLES: 40 LANGUAGE: French.
HEADNOTE: SOCIAL SECURITY COORDINATION
TOPIC: Non-ILO Labor
CONCEPTS: Exceptions and exemptions. Domestic legislation. Incorporation of treaty provisions into national law. Old age and invalidity insurance. Labor statistics. Wages and salaries. Non-ILO labor relations. Family allowances. Administrative cooperation. Old age insurance. Sickness and invalidity insurance. Unemployment. Fees and exemptions. Payment schedules.
PROCEDURE: Duration. Ratification. Renewal or Revival. Termination.
PARTIES:
Belgium
San Marino

103575 Unilateral Instrument **253 UNTS 77**
SIGNED: 17 Jul 56 FORCE: 12 Nov 56
REGISTERED: 12 Nov 56 United Nations
ARTICLES: 1 LANGUAGE: French.

HEADNOTE: ACCEPTANCE OBLIGATIONS UN
TOPIC: UN Charter
CONCEPTS: Acceptance of obligations upon admittance to UN.
INTL ORGS: United Nations.
PARTIES:
  Morocco

103576 Unilateral Instrument **253 UNTS 81**
SIGNED: 12 Jan 56   FORCE: 12 Nov 56
REGISTERED: 12 Nov 56 United Nations
ARTICLES: 1 LANGUAGE: English.
HEADNOTE: ACCEPTANCE OBLIGATIONS UN
TOPIC: UN Charter
CONCEPTS: Acceptance of obligations upon admittance to UN.
INTL ORGS: United Nations.
PARTIES:
  Sudan

103577 Unilateral Instrument **253 UNTS 85**
SIGNED: 14 Jul 56   FORCE: 12 Nov 56
REGISTERED: 12 Nov 56 United Nations
ARTICLES: 1 LANGUAGE: French.
HEADNOTE: ACCEPTANCE OBLIGATIONS UN
TOPIC: UN Charter
CONCEPTS: Acceptance of obligations upon admittance to UN.
INTL ORGS: United Nations.
PARTIES:
  Tunisia

103578 Bilateral Agreement **253 UNTS 89**
SIGNED: 3 Jun 53   FORCE: 22 Oct 54
REGISTERED: 13 Nov 56 USA (United States)
ARTICLES: 6 LANGUAGE: English. German.
HEADNOTE: CONCERNING AGREEMENT 8 DEC 23 AMENDMENT
TOPIC: General Amity
CONCEPTS: Annex type material.
TREATY REF: 52LTS133; 52LTS480; 163LTS415; 231UNTS151.
PROCEDURE: Future Procedures Contemplated. Ratification. Termination.
PARTIES:
  Germany, West
  USA (United States)

103579 Bilateral Agreement **253 UNTS 105**
SIGNED: 13 Mar 56   FORCE: 13 Mar 56
REGISTERED: 13 Nov 56 USA (United States)
ARTICLES: 10 LANGUAGE: English.
HEADNOTE: CIVIL USES ATOMIC ENERGY
TOPIC: Atomic Energy
CONCEPTS: Definition of terms. Diplomatic missions. General cooperation. Exchange of information and documents. Research results. Scientific exchange. Establishment of trade relations. Nuclear materials. Non-nuclear materials. Rights of supplier. Security of information.
PROCEDURE: Duration.
PARTIES:
  Thailand
  USA (United States)
ANNEX
291 UNTS 336. USA (United States). Amendment 27 Mar 57. Force 19 Jun 57.
291 UNTS 336. Thailand. Amendment 27 Mar 57. Force 19 Jun 57.
380 UNTS 438. Thailand. Amendment 11 Jun 60. Force 26 Jul 60.
380 UNTS 438. USA (United States). Amendment 11 Jun 60. Force 26 Jul 60.
458 UNTS 310. Thailand. Amendment 31 May 62. Force 16 Aug 62.
458 UNTS 310. USA (United States). Amendment 31 May 62. Force 16 Aug 62.
542 UNTS 372. Thailand. Amendment 8 Jun 64. Force 5 Mar 65.
542 UNTS 372. USA (United States). Amendment 8 Jun 64. Force 5 Mar 65.

103580 Bilateral Agreement **253 UNTS 119**
SIGNED: 13 Feb 56   FORCE: 23 Apr 56
REGISTERED: 13 Nov 56 USA (United States)
ARTICLES: 10 LANGUAGE: English. German.
HEADNOTE: CIVIL USES ATOMIC ENERGY
TOPIC: Atomic Energy
CONCEPTS: Definition of terms. General cooper-

ation. Exchange of information and documents. Responsibility and liability. Research results. Scientific exchange. Establishment of trade relations. Nuclear materials. Non-nuclear materials. Rights of supplier. Security of information.
PROCEDURE: Duration.
PARTIES:
  Germany, West
  USA (United States)
ANNEX
279 UNTS 338. USA (United States). Amendment 29 Jun 56. Force 18 Feb 57.
279 UNTS 338. Germany, West. Amendment 29 Jun 56. Force 18 Feb 57.

103581 Bilateral Agreement **253 UNTS 139**
SIGNED: 8 Jun 56   FORCE: 13 Jul 56
REGISTERED: 13 Nov 56 USA (United States)
ARTICLES: 11 LANGUAGE: English.
HEADNOTE: CIVIL USES ATOMIC ENERGY
TOPIC: Atomic Energy
CONCEPTS: Definition of terms. Diplomatic missions. Exchange of information and documents. Responsibility and liability. Research results. Scientific exchange. Establishment of trade relations. Nuclear materials. Non-nuclear materials. Peaceful use. Rights of supplier. Security of information.
PROCEDURE: Duration.
PARTIES:
  Austria
  USA (United States)

103582 Bilateral Agreement **253 UNTS 155**
SIGNED: 13 Jun 56   FORCE: 29 Aug 56
REGISTERED: 13 Nov 56 USA (United States)
ARTICLES: 11 LANGUAGE: English.
HEADNOTE: CIVIL USES ATOMIC ENERGY
TOPIC: Atomic Energy
CONCEPTS: Definition of terms. Diplomatic missions. Conformity with municipal law. General cooperation. Exchange of information and documents. Responsibility and liability. Research results. Scientific exchange. Establishment of trade relations. Nuclear materials. Non-nuclear materials. Peaceful use. Rights of supplier. Security of information.
PROCEDURE: Duration
PARTIES:
  New Zealand
  USA (United States)
ANNEX
378 UNTS 380. USA (United States). Amendment 11 Jun 60. Force 22 Jul 60.
378 UNTS 380. New Zealand. Amendment 11 Jun 60. Force 22 Jul 60.

103583 Multilateral Agreement **253 UNTS 171**
SIGNED: 24 Sep 56   FORCE: 24 Sep 56
REGISTERED: 13 Nov 56 USA (United States)
ARTICLES: 5 LANGUAGE: English.
HEADNOTE: ATOMIC ENERGY INVENTIONS
TOPIC: Patents/Copyrights
CONCEPTS: Definition of terms. Licenses and permits. Claims and settlements. Laws and formalities. Post-war adjustment.
PARTIES:
  Canada SIGNED: 24 Sep 56 FORCE: 24 Sep 56
  UK Great Britain SIGNED: 24 Sep 56 FORCE: 24 Sep 56
  USA (United States) SIGNED: 24 Sep 56 FORCE: 24 Sep 56

103584 Bilateral Agreement **253 UNTS 179**
SIGNED: 4 May 56   FORCE: 25 Sep 56
REGISTERED: 15 Nov 56 IBRD (World Bank)
ARTICLES: 8 LANGUAGE: English.
HEADNOTE: LOAN AGREEMENT
TOPIC: IBRD Project
CONCEPTS: Default remedies. Definition of terms. Annex or appendix reference. Exchange of information and documents. Informational records. Inspection and observation. Bonds. Fees and exemptions. Interest rates. Tax exemptions. Domestic obligation. Terms of loan. Loan regulations. Loan guarantee. Guarantor non-interference. Railways.
PARTIES:
  Burma
  IBRD (World Bank)

103585 Bilateral Agreement **253 UNTS 209**
SIGNED: 4 May 56   FORCE: 10 Oct 56
REGISTERED: 15 Nov 56 IBRD (World Bank)

ARTICLES: 5 LANGUAGE: English.
HEADNOTE: GUARANTEE AGREEMENT
TOPIC: IBRD Project
CONCEPTS: Definition of terms. Annex or appendix reference. Exchange of information and documents. Informational records. Inspection and observation. Bonds. Fees and exemptions. Tax exemptions. Domestic obligation. Terms of loan. Loan regulations. Loan guarantee. Guarantor non-interference.
PARTIES:
  Burma
  IBRD (World Bank)

103586 Bilateral Agreement **253 UNTS 233**
SIGNED: 22 May 56   FORCE: 6 Nov 56
REGISTERED: 16 Nov 56 IBRD (World Bank)
ARTICLES: 5 LANGUAGE: English.
HEADNOTE: GUARANTEE AGREEMENT
TOPIC: IBRD Project
CONCEPTS: Definition of terms. Annex or appendix reference. Exchange of information and documents. Informational records. Inspection and observation. Bonds. Fees and exemptions. Tax exemptions. Domestic obligation. Terms of loan. Loan regulations. Loan guarantee. Guarantor non-interference.
PARTIES:
  Nicaragua
  IBRD (World Bank)

103587 Bilateral Exchange **253 UNTS 259**
SIGNED: 8 Sep 47   FORCE: 8 Sep 47
REGISTERED: 20 Nov 56 Canada
ARTICLES: 2 LANGUAGE: English.
HEADNOTE: APPLICATION FRENCH NATIONAL SOLIDARITY TAX
TOPIC: Taxation
CONCEPTS: General. Tax exemptions.
TREATY REF: 12MAY1933 CONVENTION.
PARTIES:
  Canada
  France

103588 Multilateral Agreement **253 UNTS 266**
SIGNED: 21 Nov 56   FORCE: 21 Nov 56
REGISTERED: 21 Nov 56 United Nations
ARTICLES: 6 LANGUAGE: English.
HEADNOTE: TECHNICAL ASSISTANCE
TOPIC: Tech Assistance
CONCEPTS: Definition of terms. Previous treaty replacement. Privileges and immunities. General cooperation. Exchange of information and documents. Personnel. Responsibility and liability. Title and deeds. Use of facilities. Exchange. Scholarships and grants. Vocational training. Research and development. Exchange rates and regulations. Expense sharing formulae. Local currency. Domestic obligation. General technical assistance. Materials, equipment and services. IGO status. Conformity with IGO decisions.
TREATY REF: 76UNTS132; 1UNTS15; 1UNTS263.
PROCEDURE: Amendment. Termination.
PARTIES:
  Iceland SIGNED: 21 Nov 56 FORCE: 21 Nov 56
  FAO (Food Agri) SIGNED: 21 Nov 56 FORCE: 21 Nov 56
  ICAO (Civil Aviat) SIGNED: 21 Nov 56 FORCE: 21 Nov 56
  ILO (Labor Org) SIGNED: 21 Nov 56 FORCE: 21 Nov 56
  ITU (Telecommun) SIGNED: 21 Nov 56 FORCE: 21 Nov 56
  UNESCO (Educ/Cult) SIGNED: 21 Nov 56 FORCE: 21 Nov 56
  United Nations SIGNED: 21 Nov 56 FORCE: 21 Nov 56
  WHO (World Health) SIGNED: 21 Nov 56 FORCE: 21 Nov 56
  WMO (Meteorology) SIGNED: 21 Nov 56 FORCE: 21 Nov 56

103589 Bilateral Agreement **254 UNTS 3**
SIGNED: 15 Sep 56   FORCE: 1 Nov 56
REGISTERED: 24 Nov 56 Finland
ARTICLES: 7 LANGUAGE: Danish. Finnish.
HEADNOTE: RECOGNITION DRIVING PERMITS MOTOR-VEHICLE REGISTRATION CERTIFICATES

TOPIC: General Transport
CONCEPTS: Conditions. Exceptions and exemptions. Time limit. Previous treaty replacement. Conformity with municipal law. Recognition of legal documents. Fees and exemptions. Registration certificate. Driving permits. Motor vehicles and combinations.
TREATY REF: 105LTS179.
PROCEDURE: Termination.
PARTIES:
Denmark
Finland

103590 Bilateral Agreement **254 UNTS 17**
SIGNED: 15 Sep 56   FORCE: 1 Nov 56
REGISTERED: 24 Nov 56 Finland
ARTICLES: 7 LANGUAGE: Finnish. Norwegian.
HEADNOTE: RECOGNITION DRIVING PERMITS MOTOR-VEHICLE REGISTRATION CERTIFICATES
TOPIC: Admin Cooperation
CONCEPTS: Exceptions and exemptions. Previous treaty replacement. Fees and exemptions. Driving permits.
TREATY REF: 47UNTS127; 288UNTS41; 3'14DEMARTENS493; 197UNTS341.
PROCEDURE: Termination.
PARTIES:
Finland
Norway

103591 Bilateral Agreement **254 UNTS 31**
SIGNED: 15 Sep 56   FORCE: 1 Nov 56
REGISTERED: 24 Nov 56 Finland
ARTICLES: 7 LANGUAGE: Finnish. Swedish.
HEADNOTE: RECOGNITION DRIVING PERMITS MOTOR-VEHICLE REGISTRATION CERTIFICATES
TOPIC: Admin Cooperation
CONCEPTS: Exceptions and exemptions. Previous treaty replacement. Fees and exemptions. Driving permits. Road rules.
TREATY REF: 105LTS343; 160LTS368.
PARTIES:
Finland
Sweden

103592 Multilateral Protocol **254 UNTS 45**
SIGNED: 15 Sep 56   FORCE: 1 Nov 56
REGISTERED: 24 Nov 56 Finland
ARTICLES: 1 LANGUAGE: Finnish. Swedish. Dutch. Norwegian.
HEADNOTE: ADDITIONAL PROTOCOL
TOPIC: Admin Cooperation
CONCEPTS: Annex type material.
PARTIES:
Denmark SIGNED: 15 Sep 56 FORCE: 1 Nov 56
Finland SIGNED: 15 Sep 56 FORCE: 1 Nov 56
Norway SIGNED: 15 Sep 56 FORCE: 1 Nov 56
Sweden SIGNED: 15 Sep 56 FORCE: 1 Nov 56

103593 Multilateral Convention **254 UNTS 55**
SIGNED: 15 Sep 55   FORCE: 1 Nov 56
REGISTERED: 24 Nov 56 Finland
ARTICLES: 36 LANGUAGE: Finnish. Swedish. Norwegian. Icelandic. Danish.
HEADNOTE: SOCIAL SECURITY
TOPIC: Non-ILO Labor
CONCEPTS: Exceptions and exemptions. General provisions. Previous treaty replacement. Nationality and citizenship. Domestic legislation. Old age and invalidity insurance. Non-ILO labor relations. Family allowances. Administrative cooperation. Old age insurance. Sickness and invalidity insurance. Social security. Unemployment. Indemnities and reimbursements. National treatment. Wages and salaries.
PROCEDURE: Denunciation. Ratification.
PARTIES:
Denmark SIGNED: 15 Sep 55 FORCE: 1 Nov 56
Finland SIGNED: 15 Sep 55 FORCE: 1 Nov 56
Iceland SIGNED: 15 Sep 55 FORCE: 1 Nov 56
Norway SIGNED: 15 Sep 55 FORCE: 1 Nov 56
Sweden SIGNED: 15 Sep 55 FORCE: 1 Nov 56
                    ANNEX
434 UNTS 306. Finland. Amendment 30 Mar 62. Force 1 Jul 62.

434 UNTS 306.   Denmark.   Amendment 15 Mar 52. Force 1 Jul 62.
434 UNTS 306. Iceland. Amendment 30 Apr 62. Force 1 Jul 62.
434 UNTS 306. Sweden. Amendment 15 Mar 62. Force 1 Jul 62.
434 UNTS 306. Norway. Amendment 15 Mar 52. Force 1 Jul 62.

103594 Unilateral Instrument **254 UNTS 223**
SIGNED: 6 Nov 56   FORCE: 14 Sep 55
REGISTERED: 29 Nov 56 United Nations
ARTICLES: 1 LANGUAGE: English.
HEADNOTE: ACCEPTANCE OBLIGATIONS UN
TOPIC: UN Charter
CONCEPTS: Acceptance of obligations upon admittance to UN.
INTL ORGS: United Nations.
PARTIES:
Ireland

103595 Bilateral Agreement **254 UNTS 227**
SIGNED: 22 May 56   FORCE: 31 Aug 56
REGISTERED: 29 Nov 56 South Africa
ARTICLES: 15 LANGUAGE: English. Afrikaans.
HEADNOTE: DOUBLE TAXATION FISCAL EVASION TAXES INCOME
TOPIC: Taxation
CONCEPTS: Definition of terms. Conformity with municipal law. Exchange of official publications. Teacher and student exchange. Taxation. Tax credits. General. Tax exemptions.
PROCEDURE: Duration. Termination.
PARTIES:
Fed Rhod/Nyasaland
South Africa
                    ANNEX
376 UNTS 430. Fed Rhod/Nyasaland. Amendment 30 Oct 59. Force 30 Oct 59.
376 UNTS 430.   South Africa.   Amendment 30 Oct 59. Force 30 Oct 59.

103596 Bilateral Agreement **254 UNTS 257**
SIGNED: 31 Oct 49   FORCE: 7 Apr 56
REGISTERED: 1 Dec 56 ICAO (Civil Aviat)
ARTICLES: 16 LANGUAGE: English. Dutch. Persian.
HEADNOTE: COMMERCIAL AIR SERVICES
TOPIC: Air Transport
CONCEPTS: Definition of terms. Detailed regulations. Exceptions and exemptions. Treaty interpretation. Annex or appendix reference. Non-prejudice to third party. Conformity with municipal law. Exchange of information and documents. Arbitration. Procedure. Existing tribunals. Negotiation. Non-interest rates and fees. Routes and logistics. Permit designation. Air transport. Conditions of airlines operating permission. Overflights and technical stops. Operating authorizations and regulations.
INTL ORGS: International Civil Aviation Organization. International Court of Justice.
TREATY REF: 15UNTS295.
PROCEDURE: Amendment. Future Procedures Contemplated. Ratification. Termination.
PARTIES:
Iran
Netherlands

103597 Bilateral Agreement **254 UNTS 287**
SIGNED: 19 Dec 49   FORCE: 19 Dec 49
REGISTERED: 1 Dec 56 ICAO (Civil Aviat)
ARTICLES: 13 LANGUAGE: German.
HEADNOTE: AIR TRANSPORT
TOPIC: Air Transport
CONCEPTS: Definition of terms. Detailed regulations. Annex or appendix reference. Conformity with municipal law. General cooperation. Licenses and permits. Recognition of legal documents. Use of facilities. Arbitration. Procedure. Existing tribunals. Negotiation. Fees and exemptions. Non-interest rates and fees. Most favored nation clause. National treatment. Customs exemptions. Competency certificate. Routes and logistics. Navigational conditions. Permit designation. Air transport. Airport facilities. Airworthiness certificates. Conditions of airlines operating permission. Operating authorizations and regulations. Licenses and certificates of nationality.

INTL ORGS: International Civil Aviation Organization.
TREATY REF: 15UNTS295.
PROCEDURE: Denunciation. Future Procedures Contemplated. Registration.
PARTIES:
Austria
Switzerland

103598 Bilateral Agreement **254 UNTS 305**
SIGNED: 4 Mar 50   FORCE: 4 Mar 50
REGISTERED: 1 Dec 56 ICAO (Civil Aviat)
ARTICLES: 13 LANGUAGE: French. Italian.
HEADNOTE: ESTABLISHMENT OPERATION SCHEDULED AIR TRANSPORT SERVICES
TOPIC: Air Transport
CONCEPTS: Definition of terms. Annex or appendix reference. Conformity with municipal law. Licenses and permits. Recognition of legal documents. Arbitration. Procedure. Special tribunals. Negotiation. Reexport of goods, etc.. National treatment. Equitable taxes. Customs duties. Customs exemptions. Competency certificate. Routes and logistics. Navigational conditions. Permit designation. Air transport. Airport facilities. Airworthiness certificates. Conditions of airlines operating permission. Operating authorizations and regulations. Licenses and certificates of nationality.
INTL ORGS: International Civil Aviation Organization.
TREATY REF: 15UNTS295.
PROCEDURE: Amendment. Ratification. Registration. Termination.
PARTIES:
Italy
Netherlands
                    ANNEX
254 UNTS 420.   Netherlands.   Amendment 21 Dec 51.
254 UNTS 420.   Netherlands.   Amendment 5 Oct 51.
254 UNTS 420. Italy. Amendment 3 Jan 52.
254 UNTS 420. Italy. Amendment 31 Oct 51.

103599 Bilateral Agreement **254 UNTS 329**
SIGNED: 5 Apr 50   FORCE: 5 Apr 50
REGISTERED: 1 Dec 56 ICAO (Civil Aviat)
ARTICLES: 14 LANGUAGE: Italian. Portuguese.
HEADNOTE: AIR TRANSPORT
TOPIC: Air Transport
CONCEPTS: Definition of terms. Exceptions and exemptions. Annex or appendix reference. Non-prejudice to third party. Conformity with municipal law. Domestic legislation. Licenses and permits. Recognition of legal documents. Use of facilities. Arbitration. Procedure. Existing tribunals. Reexport of goods, etc.. Fees and exemptions. National treatment. Customs duties. Customs exemptions. Competency certificate. Routes and logistics. Navigational conditions. Permit designation. Air transport. Airport facilities. Airworthiness certificates. Conditions of airlines operating permission. Operating authorizations and regulations. Licenses and certificates of nationality.
INTL ORGS: International Civil Aviation Organization.
TREATY REF: 15UNTS295.
PROCEDURE: Amendment. Ratification. Registration. Termination.
PARTIES:
Italy
Portugal

103600 Bilateral Agreement **254 UNTS 365**
SIGNED: 3 Aug 50   FORCE: 3 Aug 50
REGISTERED: 1 Dec 56 ICAO (Civil Aviat)
ARTICLES: 18 LANGUAGE: French. Spanish.
HEADNOTE: RELATING AIR SERVICES
TOPIC: Air Transport
CONCEPTS: Exceptions and exemptions. Annex or appendix reference. Previous treaty replacement. Non-visa travel documents. Conformity with municipal law. Licenses and permits. Personnel. Recognition of legal documents. Use of facilities. Investigation of violations. Arbitration. Procedure. Special tribunals. Negotiation. Conciliation. Compensation. Fees and exemptions. Non-interest rates and fees. Most favored nation clause. National treatment. Customs exemp-

tions. Competency certificate. Routes and logistics. Navigational conditions. Permit designation. Air transport. Airport facilities. Airworthiness certificates. Conditions of airlines operating permission. Overflights and technical stops. Operating authorizations and regulations. Licenses and certificates of nationality. Postal services.
INTL ORGS: Arbitration Commission. Special Commission.
TREATY REF: 60LTS23.
PROCEDURE: Denunciation. Future Procedures Contemplated. Ratification.
PARTIES:
  Spain
  Switzerland

103601   Bilateral Agreement   **254 UNTS 389**
SIGNED: 9 Apr 51   FORCE: 27 Feb 53
REGISTERED: 1 Dec 56 ICAO (Civil Aviat)
ARTICLES: 12 LANGUAGE: French.
HEADNOTE: REGULATING AIR RIGHTS
TOPIC: Air Transport
CONCEPTS: Air transport.
INTL ORGS: International Civil Aviation Organization.
TREATY REF: 15UNTS295.
PARTIES:
  Luxembourg
  Switzerland

103602   Bilateral Agreement   **255 UNTS 3**
SIGNED: 18 Jun 51   FORCE: 14 Jul 55
REGISTERED: 1 Dec 56 ICAO (Civil Aviat)
ARTICLES: 16 LANGUAGE: Danish. Persian. English.
HEADNOTE: COMMERCIAL AIR SERVICES
TOPIC: Air Transport
CONCEPTS: Definition of terms. Treaty implementation. General cooperation. Exchange of information and documents. Arbitration. Procedure. Existing tribunals. Special tribunals. Negotiation. Tariffs. Navigational conditions. Air transport. Overflights and technical stops. Operating authorizations and regulations.
INTL ORGS: International Civil Aviation Organization. International Court of Justice. Arbitration Commission.
TREATY REF: 15UNTS295.
PROCEDURE: Amendment. Ratification. Registration. Termination.
PARTIES:
  Denmark
  Iran

103603   Bilateral Exchange   **255 UNTS 35**
SIGNED: 1 Mar 52   FORCE: 1 Mar 52
REGISTERED: 1 Dec 56 ICAO (Civil Aviat)
ARTICLES: 2 LANGUAGE: English. Chinese.
HEADNOTE: PROVISIONAL AIR AGREEMENT
TOPIC: Air Transport
CONCEPTS: Navigational conditions. Air transport. Operating authorizations and regulations.
INTL ORGS: International Civil Aviation Organization.
TREATY REF: 15UNTS295.
PROCEDURE: Duration. Renewal or Revival.
PARTIES:
  Taiwan
  Korea, South

103604   Bilateral Agreement   **255 UNTS 49**
SIGNED: 22 Sep 52   FORCE: 1 Jun 56
REGISTERED: 1 Dec 56 ICAO (Civil Aviat)
ARTICLES: 12 LANGUAGE: Dutch. Spanish.
HEADNOTE: AIR TRANSPORT
TOPIC: Air Transport
CONCEPTS: Definition of terms. Time limit. Annex or appendix reference. General cooperation. Arbitration. Procedure. Special tribunals. Negotiation. Navigational conditions. Transport of goods. Air transport. Airport facilities. Airworthiness certificates. Conditions of airlines operating permission. Operating authorizations and regulations.
INTL ORGS: International Civil Aviation Organization. Arbitration Commission.
PROCEDURE: Amendment. Registration. Termination.

PARTIES:
  Netherlands
  Peru

103605   Bilateral Agreement   **255 UNTS 83**
SIGNED: 23 Mar 53   FORCE: 30 Dec 53
REGISTERED: 1 Dec 56 ICAO (Civil Aviat)
ARTICLES: 15 LANGUAGE: French.
HEADNOTE: AIR TRANSPORT
TOPIC: Air Transport
CONCEPTS: Annex or appendix reference. General cooperation. Arbitration. Procedure. Negotiation. Exchange rates and regulations. Fees and exemptions. Non-interest rates and fees. Most favored nation clause. Passenger transport. Navigational conditions. Transport of goods. Air transport. Airworthiness certificates. Conditions of airlines operating permission. Overflights and technical stops. Operating authorizations and regulations.
INTL ORGS: International Civil Aviation Organization. Arbitration Commission.
PROCEDURE: Amendment. Registration. Termination.
PARTIES:
  Lebanon
  Sweden

103606   Bilateral Agreement   **255 UNTS 99**
SIGNED: 16 Apr 53   FORCE: 4 May 54
REGISTERED: 1 Dec 56 ICAO (Civil Aviat)
ARTICLES: 17 LANGUAGE: French.
HEADNOTE: AIR TRANSPORT
TOPIC: Air Transport
CONCEPTS: Treaty interpretation. Annex or appendix reference. General cooperation. Procedure. Fees and exemptions. Non-interest rates and fees. Most favored nation clause. Customs duties. Transport of goods. Air transport. Airworthiness certificates. Conditions of airlines operating permission. Overflights and technical stops. Operating authorizations and regulations.
INTL ORGS: International Civil Aviation Organization. Arbitration Commission.
PROCEDURE: Amendment. Ratification. Termination.
PARTIES:
  Turkey
  Yugoslavia

103607   Bilateral Exchange   **255 UNTS 117**
SIGNED: 26 Oct 53   FORCE: 26 Oct 53
REGISTERED: 1 Dec 56 ICAO (Civil Aviat)
ARTICLES: 6 LANGUAGE: English.
HEADNOTE: AIR TRAFFIC RIGHTS
TOPIC: Air Transport
CONCEPTS: Air transport. Conditions of airlines operating permission.
PARTIES:
  Australia
  Thailand

103608   Bilateral Agreement   **255 UNTS 127**
SIGNED: 3 Mar 54   FORCE: 29 Mar 55
REGISTERED: 1 Dec 56 ICAO (Civil Aviat)
ARTICLES: 13 LANGUAGE: French. Arabic.
HEADNOTE: AIR TRANSPORT
TOPIC: Air Transport
CONCEPTS: Arbitration. Procedure. Negotiation. Fees and exemptions. Customs duties. Passenger transport. Transport of goods. Air transport. Airworthiness certificates. Conditions of airlines operating permission. Operating authorizations and regulations.
INTL ORGS: International Civil Aviation Organization. Arbitration Commission.
PROCEDURE: Amendment. Ratification. Termination.
PARTIES:
  Lebanon
  Switzerland
ANNEX
602 UNTS 312.
602 UNTS 312.

103609   Bilateral Agreement   **255 UNTS 145**
SIGNED: 26 May 54   FORCE: 11 May 55
REGISTERED: 1 Dec 56 ICAO (Civil Aviat)
ARTICLES: 17 LANGUAGE: French. Arabic.
HEADNOTE: CIVIL AIR SERVICES
TOPIC: Air Transport
CONCEPTS: Treaty implementation. Annex or appendix reference. General cooperation. Arbitration. Procedure. Existing tribunals. Negotiation. Free trade. Non-interest rates and fees. Customs duties. Air transport. Airport equipment. Airworthiness certificates. Overflights and technical stops. Operating authorizations and regulations.
INTL ORGS: International Civil Aviation Organization. Arbitration Commission.
PROCEDURE: Amendment. Registration. Termination.
PARTIES:
  Switzerland
  Syria
ANNEX
602 UNTS 314.   Switzerland.   Modification 31 Oct 57.
602 UNTS 314. Syria. Modification 31 Oct 57.

103610   Bilateral Agreement   **255 UNTS 167**
SIGNED: 13 Dec 54   FORCE: 6 Feb 56
REGISTERED: 1 Dec 56 ICAO (Civil Aviat)
ARTICLES: 19 LANGUAGE: English. Arabic.
HEADNOTE: ESTABLISHMENT AIR SERVICES
TOPIC: Air Transport
CONCEPTS: Definition of terms. Detailed regulations. Annex or appendix reference. Alien status. Exchange of information and documents. Arbitration. Procedure. Existing tribunals. Negotiation. Non-interest rates and fees. Passenger transport. Air transport. Airport equipment. Conditions of airlines operating permission. Operating authorizations and regulations.
INTL ORGS: International Civil Aviation Organization. Arbitration Commission.
TREATY REF: 15UNTS295; 26UNTS420.
PROCEDURE: Amendment. Ratification. Registration. Termination.
PARTIES:
  Pakistan
  United Arab Rep

103611   Bilateral Agreement   **255 UNTS 199**
SIGNED: 20 Feb 55   FORCE: 14 Jan 56
REGISTERED: 1 Dec 56 ICAO (Civil Aviat)
ARTICLES: 23 LANGUAGE: French. Arabic. Serbo-Croat.
HEADNOTE: AIR TRANSPORT
TOPIC: Air Transport
CONCEPTS: Detailed regulations. Annex or appendix reference. General cooperation. Exchange of information and documents. Arbitration. Procedure. Negotiation. Non-interest rates and fees. Customs duties. Passenger transport. Air transport. Airport facilities. Airport equipment. Conditions of airlines operating permission. Operating authorizations and regulations.
INTL ORGS: Permanent Court of Arbitration. United Nations. Arbitration Commission.
PROCEDURE: Amendment. Denunciation. Ratification. Termination.
PARTIES:
  United Arab Rep
  Yugoslavia

103612   Bilateral Agreement   **255 UNTS 235**
SIGNED: 10 Sep 55   FORCE: 10 Sep 55
REGISTERED: 1 Dec 56 ICAO (Civil Aviat)
ARTICLES: 13 LANGUAGE: English. French.
HEADNOTE: AIR TRANSPORT
TOPIC: Air Transport
CONCEPTS: Annex or appendix reference. General cooperation. Arbitration. Procedure. Existing tribunals. Negotiation. Non-interest rates and fees. Navigational conditions. Air transport. Airport facilities. Airport equipment. Airworthiness certificates. Conditions of airlines operating permission. Operating authorizations and regulations.
INTL ORGS: International Civil Aviation Organization. Arbitration Commission.
PROCEDURE: Amendment. Ratification. Registration. Termination.

PARTIES:
 Belgium
 Ireland
ANNEX
335 UNTS 326. Belgium. Amendment 16 Dec 57. Force 16 Dec 57.
335 UNTS 326. Ireland. Amendment 16 Dec 57. Force 16 Dec 57.

103613 Bilateral Agreement **255 UNTS 247**
SIGNED: 9 Nov 55   FORCE: 9 Nov 55
REGISTERED: 1 Dec 56 ICAO (Civil Aviat)
ARTICLES: 11 LANGUAGE: German. Russian.
HEADNOTE: AIR TRANSPORT
TOPIC: Air Transport
CONCEPTS: Annex or appendix reference. Tariffs. Finances and payments. Accounting procedures. Fees and exemptions. Payment schedules. Non-interest rates and fees. Delivery schedules. Passenger transport. Transport of goods. Air transport. Airport facilities. Conditions of airlines operating permission. Overflights and technical stops. Operating authorizations and regulations.
PROCEDURE: Termination.
PARTIES:
 Austria
 USSR (Soviet Union)

103614 Bilateral Agreement **255 UNTS 275**
SIGNED: 17 Jan 56   FORCE: 24 May 56
REGISTERED: 1 Dec 56 ICAO (Civil Aviat)
ARTICLES: 17 LANGUAGE: French. Japanese.
HEADNOTE: AIR TRANSPORT
TOPIC: Air Transport
CONCEPTS: Definition of terms. Annex or appendix reference. General cooperation. Procedure. Negotiation. Fees and exemptions. Non-interest rates and fees. Passenger transport. Transport of goods. Air transport. Airport facilities. Airport equipment. Conditions of airlines operating permission. Overflights and technical stops. Operating authorizations and regulations.
INTL ORGS: International Civil Aviation Organization. International Court of Justice. Arbitration Commission.
TREATY REF: 15UNTS295; 26UNTS420.
PROCEDURE: Amendment. Ratification. Registration. Termination.
PARTIES:
 France
 Japan
ANNEX
412 UNTS 336. France. Amendment 21 Dec 59. Force 21 Dec 59.
412 UNTS 336. Japan. Amendment 11 Dec 59. Force 21 Dec 59.
464 UNTS 326. France. Amendment 16 May 61. Force 16 May 61.
464 UNTS 326. Japan. Amendment 16 May 61. Force 16 May 61.

103615 Bilateral Exchange **255 UNTS 317**
SIGNED: 30 May 56   FORCE: 30 May 56
REGISTERED: 1 Dec 56 ICAO (Civil Aviat)
ARTICLES: 2 LANGUAGE: English.
HEADNOTE: AIR SERVICES
TOPIC: Air Transport
CONCEPTS: Exchange of information and documents. Air transport. Conditions of airlines operating permission. Operating authorizations and regulations.
PROCEDURE: Termination.
PARTIES:
 Fed Rhod/Nyasaland
 South Africa
ANNEX
412 UNTS 342. South Africa. Amendment 27 Aug 60. Force 19 Oct 60.
412 UNTS 342. Fed Rhod/Nyasaland. Amendment 29 Oct 60. Force 19 Oct 60.

103616 Bilateral Agreement **255 UNTS 323**
SIGNED: 21 May 56   FORCE: 3 Apr 56
REGISTERED: 1 Dec 56 ICAO (Civil Aviat)
ARTICLES: 14 LANGUAGE: English. Italian.
HEADNOTE: AIR SERVICES
TOPIC: Air Transport
CONCEPTS: Definition of terms. Detailed regulations. Non-prejudice to UN charter. Exchange of information and documents. Non-interest rates and fees. Passenger transport. Transport of goods. Air transport. Conditions of airlines operating permission. Operating authorizations and regulations.
PROCEDURE: Termination.
PARTIES:
 Italy
 South Africa
ANNEX
392 UNTS 358. Italy. Amendment 17 Jun 59. Force 17 Jun 59.
392 UNTS 358. South Africa. Amendment 17 Jun 59. Force 17 Jun 59.
412 UNTS 346. South Africa. Amendment 10 Apr 61. Force 10 Apr 61.
412 UNTS 346. Italy. Amendment 10 Apr 61. Force 10 Apr 61.
646 UNTS 351. Italy. Amendment 26 Jul 67. Force 26 Jul 67.
646 UNTS 351. South Africa. Amendment 26 Jul 67. Force 26 Jul 67.

103617 Bilateral Agreement **255 UNTS 341**
SIGNED: 12 Jun 56   FORCE: 12 Jun 56
REGISTERED: 1 Dec 56 ICAO (Civil Aviat)
ARTICLES: 14 LANGUAGE: English.
HEADNOTE: AIR SERVICES
TOPIC: Air Transport
CONCEPTS: Definition of terms. Detailed regulations. Exceptions and exemptions. Annex or appendix reference. Conformity with municipal law. General cooperation. Exchange of information and documents. Procedure. Tariffs. Fees and exemptions. Customs duties. Air transport. Airport equipment. Conditions of airlines operating permission. Operating authorizations and regulations.
INTL ORGS: International Civil Aviation Organization. International Court of Justice. Arbitration Commission.
TREATY REF: 15UNTS295; 26UNTS240.
PROCEDURE: Amendment.
PARTIES:
 India
 Thailand

103618 Bilateral Agreement **255 UNTS 365**
SIGNED: 14 Sep 56   FORCE: 1 Dec 56
REGISTERED: 1 Dec 56 Finland
ARTICLES: 15 LANGUAGE: Finnish. Russian.
HEADNOTE: TRACKAGE RIGHTS RAILROADS
TOPIC: Land Transport
CONCEPTS: Detailed regulations. Tariffs. Fees and exemptions. Transport of goods. Land transport. Railways.
PARTIES:
 Finland
 USSR (Soviet Union)

103619 Multilateral Agreement **256 UNTS 3**
SIGNED: 5 Sep 52   FORCE: 8 Nov 56
REGISTERED: 3 Dec 56 Belgium
ARTICLES: 10 LANGUAGE: French. Dutch.
HEADNOTE: ASSISTANCE COLLECTION TAXES
TOPIC: Taxation
CONCEPTS: Definition of terms. General cooperation. Exchange of information and documents. Procedure. General. Commercial road vehicles.
PROCEDURE: Denunciation. Ratification.
PARTIES:
 Belgium SIGNED: 5 Sep 52 RATIFIED: 6 Jul 53 FORCE: 8 Nov 56
 Luxembourg SIGNED: 5 Sep 52 RATIFIED: 9 Feb 56 FORCE: 8 Nov 56
 Netherlands SIGNED: 5 Sep 52 RATIFIED: 7 Nov 56 FORCE: 8 Nov 56

103620 Bilateral Agreement **256 UNTS 17**
SIGNED: 21 May 53   FORCE: 21 May 53
REGISTERED: 5 Dec 56 Greece
ARTICLES: 7 LANGUAGE: French.
HEADNOTE: TRADE
TOPIC: General Trade
CONCEPTS: Exceptions and exemptions. Annex type material. Licenses and permits. Establishment of commission. Reexport of goods, etc.. Trade procedures. Payment schedules. Most favored nation clause.
INTL ORGS: Special Commission.

TREATY REF: 256UNTS25.
PROCEDURE: Denunciation.
PARTIES:
 Greece
 United Arab Rep
ANNEX
268 UNTS 392. Greece. Supplementation 1 Sep 54. Force 1 Sep 54.
268 UNTS 392. United Arab Rep. Supplementation 1 Sep 54. Force 1 Sep 54.
483 UNTS 316. United Arab Rep. Supplementation 3 Aug 61. Force 3 Aug 61.
483 UNTS 316. Greece. Supplementation 3 Aug 61. Force 2 Aug 61.

103621 Bilateral Agreement **256 UNTS 25**
SIGNED: 21 May 53   FORCE: 21 May 53
REGISTERED: 5 Dec 56 Greece
ARTICLES: 7 LANGUAGE: French.
HEADNOTE: PAYMENTS
TOPIC: Finance
CONCEPTS: Conformity with municipal law. General cooperation. Accounting procedures. Banking. Currency. Exchange rates and regulations. Interest rates. Payment schedules.
PROCEDURE: Amendment. Denunciation.
PARTIES:
 Greece
 United Arab Rep
ANNEX
268 UNTS 392. United Arab Rep. Supplementation 1 Sep 54. Force 1 Sep 54.
268 UNTS 392. Greece. Supplementation 1 Sep 54. Force 1 Sep 54.
483 UNTS 316. United Arab Rep. Supplementation 3 Aug 61. Force 3 Aug 61.
483 UNTS 316. Greece. Supplementation 3 Aug 61. Force 3 Aug 61.

103622 Multilateral Agreement **256 UNTS 31**
SIGNED: 1 Mar 54   FORCE: 1 Jul 56
REGISTERED: 10 Dec 56 UK Great Britain
ARTICLES: 22 LANGUAGE: English. French. Spanish.
HEADNOTE: INTERNATIONAL TIN AGREEMENT
TOPIC: Commodity Trade
CONCEPTS: Definition of terms. Detailed regulations. Exceptions and exemptions. General provisions. Privileges and immunities. Procedure. Non-ILO labor relations. General trade. Export quotas. Finances and payments. Currency. Exchange rates and regulations. Financial programs. Non-interest rates and fees. Commodity trade. Decisions. Subsidiary organ. Internal structure.
INTL ORGS: International Civil Aviation Organization. International Tin Council.
PROCEDURE: Amendment. Accession. Duration. Ratification. Renewal or Revival. Termination.
PARTIES:
 Australia SIGNED: 28 Jun 54 RATIFIED: 20 Nov 54 FORCE: 1 Jul 56
 Belgium Belgian Colonies RATIFIED: 16 May 55
 Belgium Ruanda-Urundi RATIFIED: 16 May 55
 Belgium SIGNED: 10 Mar 54 RATIFIED: 16 May 55 FORCE: 1 Jul 56
 Bolivia SIGNED: 3 Jun 54 RATIFIED: 29 Dec 54 FORCE: 1 Jul 56
 Canada SIGNED: 28 Jun 54 RATIFIED: 13 Sep 54 FORCE: 1 Jul 56
 Denmark SIGNED: 28 Jun 54 RATIFIED: 19 Nov 54 FORCE: 1 Jul 56
 Ecuador SIGNED: 28 Jun 54 RATIFIED: 7 Mar 55 FORCE: 1 Jul 56
 France SIGNED: 25 Jun 54
 India SIGNED: 20 May 54 RATIFIED: 15 Jan 55 FORCE: 1 Jul 56
 Indonesia SIGNED: 22 Jun 54 RATIFIED: 16 May 56 FORCE: 1 Jul 56
 Italy SIGNED: 30 Jun 54 RATIFIED: 7 Aug 56 FORCE: 7 Aug 56
 Japan SIGNED: 29 Jun 54
 Lebanon SIGNED: 30 Jun 54
 Netherlands SIGNED: 12 Mar 54 RATIFIED: 5 Nov 54 FORCE: 1 Jul 56
 Spain SIGNED: 29 Jun 54 RATIFIED: 7 Jun 55 FORCE: 1 Jul 56
 Thailand SIGNED: 29 Jun 54
 Turkey SIGNED: 28 Jun 54 RATIFIED: 1 Oct 56 FORCE: 1 Oct 56
 UK Great Britain Fed of Malaya RATIFIED: 15 Dec 54 FORCE: 1 Jul 56

UK Great Britain Nigeria RATIFIED: 15 Dec 54
FORCE: 1 Jul 56
UK Great Britain SIGNED: 5 Mar 54 RATIFIED:
15 Dec 54 FORCE: 1 Jul 56
ANNEX
326 UNTS 312. UK Great Britain. Fed of Malaya.
Force 19 Jul 58.
326 UNTS 312. Belgium. Amendment 6 Jun 57.
Force 19 Jul 58.
326 UNTS 312. Belgium. Belgian Colonies. Force
19 Jul 58.
326 UNTS 312. Italy. Amendment 23 May 57.
Force 19 Jul 58.
326 UNTS 312. UK Great Britain. Amendment
22 Jul 57. Force 19 Jul 58.
326 UNTS 312. Australia. Amendment 21 Oct 57.
Force 19 Jul 58.
326 UNTS 312. Netherlands. Amendment
29 Apr 58. Force 19 Jul 58.
326 UNTS 312. Bolivia. Amendment 17 Jan 58.
Force 19 Jul 58.
326 UNTS 312. France. Amendment 16 May 58.
Force 19 Jul 58.
326 UNTS 312. India. Amendment 14 Feb 58.
Force 19 Jul 58.
326 UNTS 312. Spain. Amendment 27 Feb 57.
Force 19 Jul 58.
326 UNTS 312. Denmark. Amendment 6 Mar 58.
Force 19 Jul 58.
326 UNTS 312. Thailand. Amendment 1 Jan 58.
Force 19 Jul 58.
326 UNTS 312. Canada. Amendment 9 Jul 58.
Force 19 Jul 58.
326 UNTS 312. Austria. Amendment 13 Dec 57.
Force 19 Jul 58.
326 UNTS 312. Israel. Amendment 16 Dec 57.
Force 19 Jul 58.
326 UNTS 312. UK Great Britain. Nigeria. Force
19 Jul 58.
326 UNTS 312. Indonesia. Amendment
19 Apr 58. Force 19 Jul 58.
326 UNTS 312. Belgium. Ruanda-Urundi. Force
19 Jul 58.

103623 Bilateral Exchange **256 UNTS 125**
SIGNED: 18 Jun 56 FORCE: 18 Jun 56
REGISTERED: 10 Dec 56 UK Great Britain
ARTICLES: 2 LANGUAGE: English.
HEADNOTE: COTTON EXPORTS
TOPIC: Commodity Trade
CONCEPTS: Annex or appendix reference. Com-
modity trade.
PARTIES:
Burma
UK Great Britain
ANNEX
264 UNTS 388. Burma. Amendment 25 Oct 56.
Force 25 Oct 56.
264 UNTS 388. UK Great Britain. Amendment
25 Oct 56. Force 25 Oct 56.

103624 Bilateral Agreement **256 UNTS 139**
SIGNED: 9 Aug 56 FORCE: 9 Aug 56
REGISTERED: 10 Dec 56 UK Great Britain
ARTICLES: 7 LANGUAGE: English.
HEADNOTE: AID
TOPIC: Direct Aid
CONCEPTS: Territorial application. Treaty imple-
mentation. Privileges and immunities. General
cooperation. Responsibility and liability. Title
and deeds. Balance of payments. Expense shar-
ing formulae. Local currency. Domestic obliga-
tion. General aid. Materials, equipment and ser-
vices. IGO status.
TREATY REF: 00UNTS261.
PROCEDURE: Amendment. Termination.
PARTIES:
UNESCO (Educ/Cult)
UK Great Britain

103625 Bilateral Agreement **256 UNTS 149**
SIGNED: 9 Sep 53 FORCE: 8 Sep 55
REGISTERED: 11 Dec 56 Denmark
ARTICLES: 11 LANGUAGE: Spanish. Danish.
HEADNOTE: PAYMENTS
TOPIC: Finance
CONCEPTS: Previous treaty replacement. General
cooperation. General trade. Accounting proce-
dures. Banking. Balance of payments. Currency.
Payment schedules. Loan and credit. Credit pro-
visions.

TREATY REF: 30SEPT39 COMMERCIAL PAY-
MENTS AGREEMENT.
PROCEDURE: Duration. Ratification. Renewal or
Revival. Termination.
PARTIES:
Denmark
Uruguay

103626 Unilateral Instrument **256 UNTS 167**
SIGNED: 16 Jun 52 FORCE: 18 Dec 56
REGISTERED: 18 Dec 56 United Nations
ARTICLES: 1 LANGUAGE: English.
HEADNOTE: ACCEPTANCE OBLIGATIONS UN
TOPIC: UN Charter
CONCEPTS: Acceptance of obligations upon ad-
mittance to UN.
INTL ORGS: United Nations.
PARTIES:
Japan

103627 Multilateral Agreement **256 UNTS 171**
SIGNED: 4 Jan 56 FORCE: 5 Jul 56
REGISTERED: 18 Dec 56 USA (United States)
ARTICLES: 11 LANGUAGE: English.
HEADNOTE: NORTH ATLANTIC ICE PATROL SUP-
PORT
TOPIC: Scientific Project
CONCEPTS: Definition of terms. General cooper-
ation. Humanitarian matters. Labor statistics. In-
demnies and reimbursements. Expense sharing
formulae. Routes and logistics.
INTL ORGS: Inter-Governmental Maritime Consul-
tative Organization.
TREATY REF: 164UNTS113; 167UNTS338.
PROCEDURE: Amendment. Denunciation. Dura-
tion.
PARTIES:
Belgium SIGNED: 5 Mar 56 FORCE: 5 Jul 56
Canada SIGNED: 5 Jul 56 FORCE: 5 Jul 56
Denmark SIGNED: 19 Jan 56 FORCE: 5 Jul 56
France SIGNED: 6 Jan 56 FORCE: 5 Jul 56
Greece SIGNED: 23 Feb 56 FORCE: 5 Jul 56
Italy SIGNED: 16 Mar 56 FORCE: 5 Jul 56
Netherlands Netherlands Antilles RATIFIED:
5 Jul 56 FORCE: 5 Jul 56
Netherlands SIGNED: 17 Feb 56 FORCE:
5 Jul 56
Norway SIGNED: 10 Jan 56 FORCE: 5 Jul 56
Sweden SIGNED: 18 Jan 56 FORCE: 5 Jul 56
UK Great Britain SIGNED: 9 Feb 56 FORCE:
5 Jul 56
USA (United States) SIGNED: 4 Jan 56 FORCE:
5 Jul 56
ANNEX
317 UNTS 339. Yugoslavia. Acceptance
14 Feb 58.
317 UNTS 339. Germany, West. Acceptance
9 Jul 58.
317 UNTS 339. Liberia. Acceptance 23 Apr 58.
317 UNTS 339. Spain. Acceptance 3 Feb 58.
356 UNTS 376. Japan. Acceptance 18 Nov 59.
356 UNTS 376. Germany, West. Berlin. Force
9 Jul 58.
356 UNTS 376. Panama. Acceptance 31 Aug 59.

103628 Bilateral Exchange **256 UNTS 187**
SIGNED: 6 Sep 55 FORCE: 6 Sep 55
REGISTERED: 18 Dec 56 USA (United States)
ARTICLES: 2 LANGUAGE: English. Spanish.
HEADNOTE: DUTY-FREE ENTRY EXEMPTION IN-
TERNAL TAXATION RELIEF SUPPLIES
TOPIC: Direct Aid
CONCEPTS: Transportation costs. Tax exemp-
tions. Customs exemptions. Materials, equip-
ment and services. Relief supplies.
PROCEDURE: Termination.
PARTIES:
Ecuador
USA (United States)

103629 Bilateral Agreement **256 UNTS 197**
SIGNED: 7 Oct 55 FORCE: 7 Oct 55
REGISTERED: 18 Dec 56 USA (United States)
ARTICLES: 6 LANGUAGE: English. Spanish.
HEADNOTE: AGRI COMMOD ASSISTANCE
TOPIC: US Agri Commod Aid
CONCEPTS: General aid. Agricultural commodi-
ties. Distribution.

PARTIES:
Ecuador
USA (United States)
ANNEX
278 UNTS 308. USA (United States). Amendment
9 Oct 56. Force 9 Oct 56.
278 UNTS 308. Ecuador. Amendment 9 Oct 56.
Force 9 Oct 56.

103630 Bilateral Exchange **256 UNTS 211**
SIGNED: 14 Jun 55 FORCE: 14 Jun 55
REGISTERED: 18 Dec 56 USA (United States)
ARTICLES: 2 LANGUAGE: English. Spanish.
HEADNOTE: TECHNICAL COOPERATION PRO-
GRAM MEDICAL EDUCATION
TOPIC: Non-IBRD Project
CONCEPTS: Operating agencies. Exchange. Gen-
eral technical assistance. Non-bank projects.
TREATY REF: 141UNTS17; 179UNTS235.
PARTIES:
Colombia
USA (United States)

103631 Bilateral Exchange **256 UNTS 221**
SIGNED: 16 Sep 55 FORCE: 20 Sep 55
REGISTERED: 18 Dec 56 USA (United States)
ARTICLES: 2 LANGUAGE: English. Spanish.
HEADNOTE: MILITARY ASSISTANCE ADVISORY
GROUP
TOPIC: Military Mission
CONCEPTS: Airforce-army-navy personnel ratio.
Ranks and privileges.
TREATY REF: 174UNTS215.
PARTIES:
Colombia
USA (United States)

103632 Bilateral Exchange **256 UNTS 227**
SIGNED: 22 Sep 55 FORCE: 22 Sep 55
REGISTERED: 18 Dec 56 USA (United States)
ARTICLES: 2 LANGUAGE: English.
HEADNOTE: ESTABLISHMENT PETROLEUM
PRODUCTS PIPELINE
TOPIC: Specif Goods/Equip
CONCEPTS: Annex or appendix reference. Facili-
ties and property.
PARTIES:
Canada
USA (United States)

103633 Bilateral Exchange **256 UNTS 239**
SIGNED: 9 Sep 55 FORCE: 9 Sep 55
REGISTERED: 18 Dec 56 USA (United States)
ARTICLES: 2 LANGUAGE: English. Spanish.
HEADNOTE: EXTENSION AGREEMENT ARMY MIS-
SION
TOPIC: Military Mission
CONCEPTS: Annex type material. Previous treaty
extension. Military assistance missions.
PARTIES:
Bolivia
USA (United States)

103634 Bilateral Exchange **256 UNTS 245**
SIGNED: 20 Jul 55 FORCE: 20 Jul 55
REGISTERED: 18 Dec 56 USA (United States)
ARTICLES: 2 LANGUAGE: English.
HEADNOTE: REGISTRATION RADIO FREQUEN-
CIES DEFENSE FORCE
TOPIC: General Military
CONCEPTS: Commercial and public radio. General
military.
INTL ORGS: International Telecommunication
Union.
PARTIES:
Iceland
USA (United States)

103635 Bilateral Instrument **256 UNTS 251**
SIGNED: 17 Nov 54 FORCE: 17 Apr 54
REGISTERED: 18 Dec 56 USA (United States)
ARTICLES: 1 LANGUAGE: English.
HEADNOTE: MILITARY ECONOMIC AID
TOPIC: Milit Assistance
CONCEPTS: Exceptions and exemptions. Treaty
implementation. Annex or appendix reference.
Exchange rates and regulations. Domestic obli-

gation. Economic assistance. Joint defense. Defense and security. Military assistance.
INTL ORGS: United Nations.
PARTIES:
Korea, South
USA (United States)
ANNEX
442 UNTS 321. USA (United States). Amendment 30 Jan 62. Force 30 Jan 62.
442 UNTS 321. Korea, South. Amendment 30 Jan 62. Force 30 Jan 62.

103636 Bilateral Exchange **256 UNTS 263**
SIGNED: 29 May 55 FORCE: 29 May 55
REGISTERED: 18 Dec 56 USA (United States)
ARTICLES: 2 LANGUAGE: English.
HEADNOTE: ESTABLISH ARSENAL FACILITIES
TOPIC: Milit Installation
CONCEPTS: Indemnities and reimbursements. Materials, equipment and services. Bases and facilities. Equipment and supplies.
INTL ORGS: International Court of Justice.
TREATY REF: 256UNTS251.
PROCEDURE: Future Procedures Contemplated.
PARTIES:
Korea, South
USA (United States)

103637 Bilateral Exchange **256 UNTS 275**
SIGNED: 23 Sep 55 FORCE: 23 Sep 55
REGISTERED: 18 Dec 56 USA (United States)
ARTICLES: 2 LANGUAGE: English. Spanish.
HEADNOTE: GUARANTEES AUTHORIZED MUTUAL SECURITY ACT 1954
TOPIC: Claims and Debts
CONCEPTS: Guarantees and safeguards. Arbitration. Procedure. Negotiation. Private investment guarantee. Most favored nation clause. Economic assistance.
PARTIES:
Bolivia
USA (United States)
ANNEX
524 UNTS 312. Bolivia. Amendment 4 Mar 64. Force 4 Mar 64.
524 UNTS 312. USA (United States). Amendment 4 Mar 64. Force 4 Mar 64.

103638 Bilateral Exchange **256 UNTS 285**
SIGNED: 5 Oct 55 FORCE: 5 Oct 55
REGISTERED: 18 Dec 56 USA (United States)
ARTICLES: 2 LANGUAGE: English.
HEADNOTE: GUARANTEES AUTHORIZED MUTUAL SECURITY ACT 1954
TOPIC: Claims and Debts
CONCEPTS: Guarantees and safeguards. Arbitration. Procedure. Negotiation. Private investment guarantee. Most favored nation clause. Economic assistance.
INTL ORGS: International Court of Justice.
PARTIES:
Iceland
USA (United States)

103639 Bilateral Exchange **256 UNTS 293**
SIGNED: 15 Sep 55 FORCE: 15 Sep 55
REGISTERED: 18 Dec 56 USA (United States)
ARTICLES: 2 LANGUAGE: English.
HEADNOTE: INFORMATIONAL MEDIA GUARANTY PROGRAM
TOPIC: Mass Media
CONCEPTS: Local currency. Media guaranty.
PARTIES:
Indonesia
USA (United States)

103640 Bilateral Exchange **256 UNTS 299**
SIGNED: 24 Aug 55 FORCE: 24 Aug 55
REGISTERED: 18 Dec 56 USA (United States)
ARTICLES: 2 LANGUAGE: English. Spanish.
HEADNOTE: MILITARY ASSISTANCE ADVISORY GROUP
TOPIC: Military Mission
CONCEPTS: Airforce-army-navy personnel ratio. Ranks and privileges.
TREATY REF: 177UNTS43.
PARTIES:
Ecuador
USA (United States)

103641 Bilateral Exchange **256 UNTS 307**
SIGNED: 5 Sep 55 FORCE: 5 Sep 55
REGISTERED: 18 Dec 56 USA (United States)
ARTICLES: 2 LANGUAGE: English. Russian.
HEADNOTE: EXCHANGE MEDICAL FILMS
TOPIC: Sanitation
CONCEPTS: Detailed regulations. Friendship and amity. Exchange of information and documents. Public health. Mass media exchange.
PARTIES:
USA (United States)
USSR (Soviet Union)

103642 Unilateral Instrument **256 UNTS 315**
SIGNED: 17 Dec 56 FORCE: 19 Dec 56
REGISTERED: 19 Dec 56 United Nations
ARTICLES: 1 LANGUAGE: English.
HEADNOTE: ACCEPTANCE ICJ JURISDICTION
TOPIC: ICJ Option Clause
CONCEPTS: Standardization. Optional clause ICJ. Compulsory jurisdiction.
INTL ORGS: International Court of Justice.
PROCEDURE: Duration.
PARTIES:
Norway

103643 Bilateral Exchange **256 UNTS 319**
SIGNED: 4 Sep 56 FORCE: 4 Sep 56
REGISTERED: 28 Dec 56 Greece
ARTICLES: 2 LANGUAGE: French.
HEADNOTE: COMMERCIAL EXCHANGES
TOPIC: General Trade
CONCEPTS: Annex or appendix reference. Annex type material. Export quotas. Import quotas. Trade procedures. Quotas.
PARTIES:
Denmark
Greece

103644 Bilateral Agreement **257 UNTS 3**
SIGNED: 19 Oct 56 FORCE: 1 Jan 57
REGISTERED: 1 Jan 57 Norway
ARTICLES: 8 LANGUAGE: Norwegian. Russian.
HEADNOTE: SEARCH RESCUE COOPERATION BARENTS SEA
TOPIC: Humanitarian
CONCEPTS: Conformity with municipal law. General cooperation. Use of facilities. Humanitarian matters. Anti-discrimination. Bands and frequency allocation.
TREATY REF: 3'7DEMARTENS728; 164UNTS113;.
PROCEDURE: Denunciation. Duration. Renewal or Revival.
PARTIES:
Norway
USSR (Soviet Union)

103645 Bilateral Agreement **257 UNTS 21**
SIGNED: 3 Jan 57 FORCE: 3 Jan 57
REGISTERED: 3 Jan 57 United Nations
ARTICLES: 11 LANGUAGE: French.
HEADNOTE: ACTIVITIES UNICEF
TOPIC: Direct Aid
CONCEPTS: Treaty implementation. Privileges and immunities. General cooperation. Exchange of information and documents. Informational records. Inspection and observation. Public information. Responsibility and liability. Procedure. Existing tribunals. Export quotas. Claims and settlements. Tax exemptions. Customs exemptions. Commodities and services. Assistance. General aid. Distribution. IGO status.
TREATY REF: 1UNTS15.
PROCEDURE: Duration.
PARTIES:
UNESCO (Educ/Cult)
Tunisia

103646 Unilateral Instrument **257 UNTS 35**
SIGNED: 10 Dec 56 FORCE: 10 Dec 56
REGISTERED: 8 Jan 57 United Nations
ARTICLES: 1 LANGUAGE: French.
HEADNOTE: ACCEPTANCE ICJ JURISDICTION
TOPIC: ICJ Option Clause
CONCEPTS: Compulsory jurisdiction.
INTL ORGS: International Court of Justice.

PARTIES:
Denmark

103647 Bilateral Exchange **257 UNTS 39**
SIGNED: 16 Nov 55 FORCE: 1 Dec 55
REGISTERED: 8 Jan 57 Israel
ARTICLES: 4 LANGUAGE: English.
HEADNOTE: ABOLITION VISA FEES
TOPIC: Visas
CONCEPTS: Visas. Fees and exemptions.
PARTIES:
Finland
Israel

103648 Bilateral Exchange **257 UNTS 47**
SIGNED: 17 Jun 56 FORCE: 17 Jun 56
REGISTERED: 8 Jan 57 Israel
ARTICLES: 2 LANGUAGE: English.
HEADNOTE: EXEMPTION TAXES SHIPPING AIRCRAFT SERVICES
TOPIC: Taxation
CONCEPTS: Definition of terms. Tax exemptions. Air transport. Merchant vessels.
PROCEDURE: Termination.
PARTIES:
Israel
Sweden

103649 Bilateral Agreement **257 UNTS 55**
SIGNED: 26 Jun 56 FORCE: 26 Jul 56
REGISTERED: 8 Jan 57 Israel
ARTICLES: 12 LANGUAGE: English. Hebrew.
HEADNOTE: EDUCATION PROGRAM
TOPIC: Education
CONCEPTS: Definition of terms. Friendship and amity. Alien status. Privileges and immunities. Standardization. General cooperation. Exchange of information and documents. Personnel. Exchange. Commissions and foundations. Teacher and student exchange. Institute establishment. Vocational training. Research and development. Accounting procedures. Currency. Expense sharing formulae. Financial programs. Funding procedures. Tax exemptions. Customs exemptions.
PROCEDURE: Amendment.
PARTIES:
Israel
USA (United States)
ANNEX
407 UNTS 256. USA (United States). Amendment 30 Apr 61. Force 30 Apr 61.
407 UNTS 256. Israel. Amendment 23 Mar 61. Force 30 Apr 61.

103650 Bilateral Exchange **257 UNTS 75**
SIGNED: 8 Jan 57 FORCE: 8 Jan 57
REGISTERED: 8 Jan 57 United Nations
ARTICLES: 2 LANGUAGE: English.
HEADNOTE: CLEARANCE SUEZ CANAL
TOPIC: Specific Property
CONCEPTS: IGO status. Facilities and property.
PARTIES:
United Nations
United Arab Rep

103651 Bilateral Agreement **257 UNTS 83**
SIGNED: 30 Jun 54 FORCE: 3 Jan 56
REGISTERED: 9 Jan 57 Greece
ARTICLES: 11 LANGUAGE: French.
HEADNOTE: STUDENT EMPLOYEES
TOPIC: Non-ILO Labor
CONCEPTS: Detailed regulations. Resident permits. Conformity with municipal law. Employment regulations. Labor statistics. Non-ILO labor relations. Administrative cooperation. Social security. Migrant worker. Quotas. National treatment.
PROCEDURE: Denunciation. Duration. Ratification. Renewal or Revival.
PARTIES:
France
Greece

103652 Bilateral Exchange **257 UNTS 93**
SIGNED: 26 May 55 FORCE: 26 May 55
REGISTERED: 10 Jan 57 Pakistan
ARTICLES: 2 LANGUAGE: English.
HEADNOTE: INVESTMENT GUARANTEE PRIVATE

TOPIC: General Economic
CONCEPTS: Conformity with municipal law. Arbitration. Procedure. Existing tribunals. Negotiation. Reciprocity in financial treatment. Currency. Claims and settlements. Private investment guarantee.
INTL ORGS: International Court of Justice.
PARTIES:
Pakistan
USA (United States)

103653 Bilateral Convention **257 UNTS 99**
SIGNED: 2 Jul 53 FORCE: 17 Feb 56
REGISTERED: 10 Jan 57 Italy
ARTICLES: 15 LANGUAGE: Italian.
HEADNOTE: FRONTIER GRAZING CUSTOMS
TOPIC: Customs
CONCEPTS: Emergencies. Annex or appendix reference. Previous treaty replacement. Border traffic and migration. Frontier permits. Establishment of commission. Export quotas. Import quotas. Tax exemptions. Customs exemptions. Pasturage in frontier zones. Fish, wildlife, and natural resources. Markers and definitions. Frontier peoples and personnel.
INTL ORGS: Special Commission.
TREATY REF: 2'17DEMARTENS18; 25LTS21;.
PROCEDURE: Ratification. Renewal or Revival. Termination.
PARTIES:
Italy
Switzerland

103654 Bilateral Convention **257 UNTS 169**
SIGNED: 30 Mar 55 FORCE: 26 Oct 56
REGISTERED: 10 Jan 57 Italy
ARTICLES: 21 LANGUAGE: English. Italian.
HEADNOTE: DOUBLE TAXATION FISCAL EVASION TAXES INCOME
TOPIC: Taxation
CONCEPTS: Definition of terms. Previous treaty renunciation. Privileges and immunities. Conformity with municipal law. Exchange of official publications. Domestic legislation. Negotiation. Teacher and student exchange. Claims and settlements. Taxation. Tax credits. General. Tax exemptions. Air transport. Merchant vessels.
TREATY REF: 133LTS21.
PROCEDURE: Duration. Ratification. Termination.
PARTIES:
Italy
USA (United States)

103655 Bilateral Convention **257 UNTS 199**
SIGNED: 30 Mar 55 FORCE: 26 Oct 56
REGISTERED: 10 Jan 57 Italy
ARTICLES: 11 LANGUAGE: English. Italian.
HEADNOTE: DOUBLE TAXATION FISCAL EVASION ESTATES INHERITANCES
TOPIC: Taxation
CONCEPTS: Definition of terms. Privileges and immunities. Conformity with municipal law. Exchange of official publications. Negotiation. Claims and settlements. Taxation. Tax credits. Tax exemptions.
PROCEDURE: Duration. Ratification. Termination.
PARTIES:
Italy
USA (United States)

103656 Bilateral Exchange **257 UNTS 215**
SIGNED: 8 Aug 56 FORCE: 15 May 56
REGISTERED: 12 Jan 57 Belgium
ARTICLES: 2 LANGUAGE: French. Czechoslovakian.
HEADNOTE: RECIPROCITY ISSUE GRATIS ENTRY VISAS ATHLETES
TOPIC: Visas
CONCEPTS: Visas. Athletes. Fees and exemptions.
PARTIES:
Belgium
Czechoslovakia

103657 Bilateral Exchange **257 UNTS 221**
SIGNED: 19 Oct 56 FORCE: 15 Nov 56
REGISTERED: 12 Jan 57 Belgium
ARTICLES: 2 LANGUAGE: English.
HEADNOTE: ABOLITION TRAVEL VISA REQUIREMENT

TOPIC: Visas
CONCEPTS: Territorial application. Time limit. Visa abolition. Denial of admission. Conformity with municipal law.
PARTIES:
Belgium
Pakistan

103658 Bilateral Exchange **257 UNTS 227**
SIGNED: 9 Oct 56 FORCE: 1 Dec 56
REGISTERED: 12 Jan 57 Belgium
ARTICLES: 2 LANGUAGE: French. Spanish.
HEADNOTE: ABOLITION TRAVEL VISA REQUIREMENTS
TOPIC: Visas
CONCEPTS: Emergencies. Territorial application. Time limit. Visa abolition. Denial of admission. Tourism. Conformity with municipal law.
PROCEDURE: Denunciation.
PARTIES:
Belgium
Chile

103659 Bilateral Exchange **257 UNTS 235**
SIGNED: 31 Oct 56 FORCE: 1 Jan 56
REGISTERED: 12 Jan 57 Belgium
ARTICLES: 2 LANGUAGE: French.
HEADNOTE: EXEMPTION AIR TRANSPORT TAXES
TOPIC: Taxation
CONCEPTS: Definition of terms. Domestic legislation. Tax exemptions. Air transport.
PROCEDURE: Termination.
PARTIES:
Belgium
United Arab Rep

103660 Bilateral Agreement **257 UNTS 243**
SIGNED: 9 Dec 54 FORCE: 18 Jan 57
REGISTERED: 12 Jan 57 Belgium
ARTICLES: 14 LANGUAGE: French. Greek.
HEADNOTE: CULTURAL AGREEMENT
TOPIC: Culture
CONCEPTS: Friendship and amity. Conformity with municipal law. Operating agencies. Establishment of commission. Recognition of degrees. Exchange. Teacher and student exchange. Institute establishment. Scholarships and grants. Vocational training. Exchange. General cultural cooperation. Artists. Research cooperation. Scientific exchange. Publications exchange. Mass media exchange.
INTL ORGS: Special Commission.
PROCEDURE: Denunciation. Duration. Ratification. Renewal or Revival.
PARTIES:
Belgium
Greece

103661 Bilateral Agreement **257 UNTS 255**
SIGNED: 17 Apr 54 FORCE: 30 Sep 55
REGISTERED: 16 Jan 57 USA (United States)
ARTICLES: 18 LANGUAGE: English. French.
HEADNOTE: OFFSHORE PROCUREMENT
TOPIC: Milit Assistance
CONCEPTS: Annex or appendix reference. Privileges and immunities. Conformity with municipal law. General cooperation. Exchange of information and documents. Inspection and observation. Licenses and permits. General property. Private contracts. Responsibility and liability. National treatment. Tax exemptions. Materials, equipment and services. Defense and security. Security of information. Exchange of defense information.
INTL ORGS: European Defense Community. North Atlantic Treaty Organization.
TREATY REF: 24UNTS35.
PROCEDURE: Future Procedures Contemplated. Ratification.
PARTIES:
Luxembourg
USA (United States)

103662 Bilateral Exchange **257 UNTS 297**
SIGNED: 24 Aug 55 FORCE: 24 Aug 55
REGISTERED: 16 Jan 57 USA (United States)
ARTICLES: 2 LANGUAGE: English. Japanese.
HEADNOTE: PAYMENT DAMAGES
TOPIC: Specif Claim/Waive

CONCEPTS: Claims and settlements. Specific claims or waivers.
PARTIES:
Japan
USA (United States)

103663 Bilateral Exchange **257 UNTS 307**
SIGNED: 28 Sep 55 FORCE: 28 Sep 55
REGISTERED: 16 Jan 57 USA (United States)
ARTICLES: 2 LANGUAGE: English. Spanish.
HEADNOTE: TERMINATING TRADE AGREEMENT
TOPIC: General Trade
CONCEPTS: Annex type material.
TREATY REF: 170LTS345.
PARTIES:
Guatemala
USA (United States)

103664 Bilateral Exchange **257 UNTS 313**
SIGNED: 30 Jun 55 FORCE: 30 Jun 55
REGISTERED: 16 Jan 57 USA (United States)
ARTICLES: 2 LANGUAGE: English. Spanish.
HEADNOTE: COOPERATIVE AGRICULTURE PROGRAM
TOPIC: Non-IBRD Project
CONCEPTS: Privileges and immunities. Inspection and observation. Operating agencies. Personnel. Title and deeds. Financial programs. Funding procedures. Tax exemptions. Customs exemptions. Agriculture. Non-bank projects.
TREATY REF: 132UNTS305; 179UNTS222.
PROCEDURE: Duration. Termination.
PARTIES:
Dominican Republic
USA (United States)

103665 Bilateral Exchange **257 UNTS 349**
SIGNED: 20 Sep 55 FORCE: 20 Sep 55
REGISTERED: 16 Jan 57 USA (United States)
ARTICLES: 2 LANGUAGE: English. Portuguese.
HEADNOTE: DEFENSE COMMISSIONS
TOPIC: Military Mission
CONCEPTS: Non-prejudice to UN charter. Defense and security. Military assistance. Airforce-army-navy personnel ratio.
INTL ORGS: Special Commission.
TREATY REF: 21UNTS77.
PROCEDURE: Future Procedures Contemplated. Termination.
PARTIES:
Brazil
USA (United States)

103666 Bilateral Exchange **258 UNTS 3**
SIGNED: 2 May 55 FORCE: 2 May 55
REGISTERED: 22 Jan 57 USA (United States)
ARTICLES: 2 LANGUAGE: English.
HEADNOTE: DUTY-FREE ENTRY EXEMPTION INTERNAL TAXATION RELIEF SUPPLIES
TOPIC: Direct Aid
CONCEPTS: General cooperation. Establishment of commission. Transportation costs. Tax exemptions. Customs exemptions. Materials, equipment and services. Relief supplies.
PROCEDURE: Termination.
PARTIES:
Korea, South
USA (United States)
ANNEX
469 UNTS 428. Korea, South. Amendment 9 Nov 62. Force 28 Dec 62.
469 UNTS 428. USA (United States). Amendment 28 Dec 62. Force 28 Dec 62.

103667 Bilateral Exchange **258 UNTS 15**
SIGNED: 30 Jun 55 FORCE: 30 Jun 55
REGISTERED: 22 Jan 57 USA (United States)
ARTICLES: 2 LANGUAGE: English. Italian.
HEADNOTE: SURPLUS AGRICULTURE CHILD FEEDING
TOPIC: US Agri Commod Aid
CONCEPTS: Treaty implementation. Annex or appendix reference. Non-visa travel documents. Exchange of information and documents. Accounting procedures. Funding procedures. Payment schedules. Commodities schedule. Surplus commodities. Transport of goods. Merchant vessels.

PARTIES:
Italy
USA (United States)

103668 Bilateral Agreement **258 UNTS 37**
SIGNED: 14 Jun 55   FORCE: 14 Jun 55
REGISTERED: 22 Jan 57 USA (United States)
ARTICLES: 6 LANGUAGE: English. German.
HEADNOTE: AGRI COMMOD TITLE I
TOPIC: US Agri Commod Aid
CONCEPTS: General provisions. Exchange of infor-
mation and documents. Reexport of goods, etc..
Currency. Exchange rates and regulations. Pay-
ment schedules. Local currency. Commodities
schedule. Purchase authorization. Surplus com-
modities. Mutual consultation.
PARTIES:
Austria
USA (United States)
              ANNEX
418 UNTS 378. USA (United States). Supplementation 26 Jun 61. Force 26 Jul 61.
418 UNTS 378.   Austria.   Supplementation
26 Jul 61. Force 26 Jul 61.

103669 Bilateral Exchange **258 UNTS 51**
SIGNED: 10 Jun 55   FORCE: 10 Jun 55
REGISTERED: 22 Jan 57 USA (United States)
ARTICLES: 2 LANGUAGE: English. Spanish.
HEADNOTE: PRIVATE INVESTMENT GUARAN-
TEES
TOPIC: Claims and Debts
CONCEPTS: Conformity with municipal law. Arbi-
tration. Procedure. Existing tribunals. Negotia-
tion. Reciprocity in financial treatment. Cur-
rency. Claims and settlements. Private invest-
ment guarantee.
INTL ORGS: International Court of Justice.
PARTIES:
Honduras
USA (United States)

103670 Bilateral Exchange **258 UNTS 59**
SIGNED: 5 Dec 56   FORCE: 4 Jan 57
REGISTERED: 23 Jan 57 South Africa
ARTICLES: 2 LANGUAGE: English.
HEADNOTE: VISA
TOPIC: Visas
CONCEPTS: Time limit. Denial of admission. Resi-
dent permits. Visas. Fees and exemptions.
PARTIES:
Finland
South Africa

103671 Bilateral Agreement **258 UNTS 65**
SIGNED: 30 Jun 56   FORCE: 15 Nov 56
REGISTERED: 24 Jan 57 Denmark
ARTICLES: 17 LANGUAGE: Danish. German.
HEADNOTE: FRONTIER CROSSING POINTS
TOPIC: Visas
CONCEPTS: Emergencies. Territorial application.
Time limit. Passports non-diplomatic. Denial of
admission. Resident permits. Visas. General co-
operation.
PROCEDURE: Ratification. Termination.
PARTIES:
Denmark
Germany, West

103672 Bilateral Exchange **258 UNTS 83**
SIGNED: 7 Jul 56   FORCE: 1 Sep 56
REGISTERED: 24 Jan 57 Finland
ARTICLES: 2 LANGUAGE: Swedish.
HEADNOTE: LIABILITY RAIL SEA TRAFFIC
TOPIC: General Transport
CONCEPTS: Claims and settlements. General
transportation. Navigational conditions.
INTL ORGS: Central Office for International Rail
Transport.
PARTIES:
Finland
Sweden

103673 Bilateral Agreement **258 UNTS 89**
SIGNED: 7 Dec 56   FORCE: 1 Jan 57
REGISTERED: 24 Jan 57 Finland
ARTICLES: 9 LANGUAGE: Finnish. Russian.

HEADNOTE: COOPERATION SAVING LIVES BAL-
TIC SEAS
TOPIC: Humanitarian
CONCEPTS: Previous treaty replacement. Confor-
mity with municipal law. General cooperation.
Exchange of information and documents. Use of
facilities. Humanitarian matters. Air transport.
Merchant vessels. Bands and frequency alloca-
tion. Communications linkage.
TREATY REF: 205LTS220; 164UNTS113;
167UNTS338.
PROCEDURE: Denunciation. Duration. Renewal or
Revival.
PARTIES:
Finland
USSR (Soviet Union)

103674 Bilateral Agreement **258 UNTS 103**
SIGNED: 3 Sep 56   FORCE: 17 Sep 56
REGISTERED: 28 Jan 57 WHO (World Health)
ARTICLES: 7 LANGUAGE: English.
HEADNOTE: TUBERCULOSIS IMMUNIZATION RE-
SEARCH
TOPIC: Sanitation
CONCEPTS: Definition of terms. Annex or appen-
dix reference. Privileges and immunities. Person-
nel. General property. Establishment of commis-
sion. Disease control. Public health. WHO used
as agency. Research and development. Indemni-
ties and reimbursements. Currency. Expense
sharing formulae. General technical assistance.
Grants. Extension of functions.
TREATY REF: 118UNTS3; 247UNTS.
PROCEDURE: Termination.
PARTIES:
Denmark
WHO (World Health)

103675 Bilateral Agreement **258 UNTS 115**
SIGNED: 30 Sep 55   FORCE: 5 Sep 56
REGISTERED: 29 Jan 57 Denmark
ARTICLES: 18 LANGUAGE: Danish. English.
HEADNOTE: DOUBLE TAXATION FISCAL EVA-
SION TAXES INCOME
TOPIC: Taxation
CONCEPTS: Definition of terms. Territorial applica-
tion. Conformity with municipal law. Exchange
of official publications. Teacher and student ex-
change. Claims and settlements. Taxation. Tax
credits. General. Tax exemptions. Air transport.
Merchant vessels.
PROCEDURE: Duration. Ratification. Termination.
PARTIES:
Canada
Denmark

103676 Bilateral Agreement **258 UNTS 143**
SIGNED: 9 Oct 56   FORCE: 9 Oct 56
REGISTERED: 29 Jan 57 Thailand
ARTICLES: 6 LANGUAGE: German. Thai.
HEADNOTE: ECONOMIC TECHNICAL COOPER-
ATION
TOPIC: Direct Aid
CONCEPTS: Territorial application. Treaty imple-
mentation. Exchange of information and docu-
ments. Establishment of commission. Exchange.
Scholarships and grants. Vocational training.
General technical assistance. Economic assis-
tance.
PROCEDURE: Duration. Termination.
PARTIES:
Germany, West
Thailand

103677 Multilateral Agreement **258 UNTS 153**
SIGNED: 1 Oct 53   FORCE: 1 Jan 54
REGISTERED: 31 Jan 57 UK Great Britain
ARTICLES: 46 LANGUAGE: English. French. Chi-
nese. Russian. Spanish.
HEADNOTE: INTERNATIONAL SUGAR AGREE-
MENT
TOPIC: Commodity Trade
CONCEPTS: Definition of terms. Detailed regula-
tions. Territorial application. General provisions.
Procedure. Import quotas. Export subsidies. Fi-
nances and payments. Currency. Financial pro-
grams. Non-interest rates and fees. Commodity
trade. Quotas. Decisions. Establishment. Proce-
dure. Liaison with other IGO's. Internal structure.

INTL ORGS: International Monetary Fund. Interna-
tional Sugar Council.
PROCEDURE: Amendment. Duration. Ratification.
Termination.
PARTIES:
Australia   RATIFIED: 14 Dec 53   FORCE:
   15 Dec 53
Belgium RATIFIED: 22 Jul 54 FORCE: 22 Jul 54
Canada RATIFIED: 29 Jun 54 FORCE: 29 Jun 54
Taiwan   SIGNED: 31 Oct 53   RATIFIED:
   18 Mar 54 FORCE: 18 Mar 54
Cuba SIGNED: 26 Oct 53 RATIFIED: 16 Dec 53
   FORCE: 16 Dec 53
Czechoslovakia SIGNED: 31 Oct 53 RATIFIED:
   20 Apr 54 FORCE: 20 Apr 54
Denmark SIGNED: 31 Oct 53
Dominican Republic SIGNED: 26 Oct 53 RATI-
   FIED: 2 Feb 54 FORCE: 2 Feb 54
France SIGNED: 26 Oct 53 RATIFIED: 23 Sep 54
   FORCE: 23 Sep 54
France All Territories RATIFIED: 23 Sep 54
   FORCE: 23 Sep 54
Germany, West SIGNED: 30 Oct 53 RATIFIED:
   12 Jul 54 FORCE: 12 Jul 54
Greece   SIGNED: 31 Oct 53   RATIFIED:
   14 Sep 54 FORCE: 14 Sep 54
Haiti SIGNED: 29 Oct 53 RATIFIED: 28 Apr 54
   FORCE: 28 Apr 54
Japan SIGNED: 28 Oct 53 RATIFIED: 30 Apr 54
   FORCE: 30 Apr 54
Lebanon   SIGNED: 31 Oct 53   RATIFIED:
   23 Sep 54 FORCE: 23 Sep 54
Mexico SIGNED: 30 Oct 53 RATIFIED: 14 Apr 54
   FORCE: 14 Apr 54
Netherlands   SIGNED: 30 Oct 53   RATIFIED:
   27 Apr 54 FORCE: 27 Apr 54
Philippines   SIGNED: 30 Oct 53   RATIFIED:
   30 Apr 54 FORCE: 30 Apr 54
Poland SIGNED: 31 Oct 53 RATIFIED: 30 Apr 54
   FORCE: 30 Apr 54
Portugal   SIGNED: 30 Oct 53   RATIFIED:
   30 Apr 54 FORCE: 30 Apr 54
South Africa SIGNED: 30 Oct 53 RATIFIED:
   8 Mar 54 FORCE: 8 Mar 54
UK Great Britain SIGNED: 16 Oct 53 RATIFIED:
   12 Dec 53 FORCE: 15 Dec 53
USA (United States) SIGNED: 23 Oct 53 RATI-
   FIED: 3 May 54 FORCE: 3 May 54
USSR (Soviet Union) SIGNED: 29 Oct 53 RATI-
   FIED: 22 Mar 54 FORCE: 22 Mar 54
Yugoslavia SIGNED: 30 Oct 53
              ANNEX
264 UNTS 390.
274 UNTS 376.
326 UNTS 314.
326 UNTS 315.

103678 Multilateral Agreement **258 UNTS 322**
SIGNED: 21 Dec 54   FORCE: 23 Sep 55
REGISTERED: 31 Jan 57 UK Great Britain
ARTICLES: 15 LANGUAGE: English. French. Dutch.
German. Italian.
HEADNOTE: CONCERNING RELATIONS
TOPIC: General Amity
CONCEPTS: Definition of terms. General cooper-
ation. Exchange of information and documents.
Establishment of trade relations. Subsidiary or-
gan.
INTL ORGS: Special Commission.
PROCEDURE: Duration. Ratification.
PARTIES:
Belgium   SIGNED: 21 Dec 54   RATIFIED:
   28 Jul 55 FORCE: 23 Sep 55
France   SIGNED: 21 Dec 54   RATIFIED:
   18 Aug 55 FORCE: 23 Sep 55
Germany, West SIGNED: 21 Dec 54 RATIFIED:
   23 Sep 55 FORCE: 23 Sep 55
Italy SIGNED: 21 Dec 54 RATIFIED: 9 Sep 55
   FORCE: 23 Sep 55
Luxembourg SIGNED: 21 Dec 54 RATIFIED:
   23 Aug 55 FORCE: 23 Sep 55
Netherlands   SIGNED: 21 Dec 54   RATIFIED:
   29 Aug 55 FORCE: 23 Sep 55
ECSC (Coal/Steel) SIGNED: 21 Dec 54
UK Great Britain SIGNED: 21 Dec 54 RATIFIED:
   17 Jun 55 FORCE: 23 Sep 55

103679 Multilateral Instrument **258 UNTS 371**
SIGNED: 5 Jul 56   FORCE: 5 Jul 56
REGISTERED: 31 Jan 57 UK Great Britain
ARTICLES: 1 LANGUAGE: English. French. Italian.
HEADNOTE: GERMAN TRADEMARKS

TOPIC: Patents/Copyrights
CONCEPTS: Conformity with municipal law. Trademarks. Post-war adjustment.
TREATY REF: 49UNTS50; 138UNTS111.
PARTIES:
France SIGNED: 5 Jul 56 FORCE: 5 Jul 56
Italy SIGNED: 5 Jul 56 FORCE: 5 Jul 56
UK Great Britain SIGNED: 5 Jul 56 FORCE: 5 Jul 56
USA (United States) SIGNED: 5 Jul 56 FORCE: 5 Jul 56

103680 Bilateral Agreement **259 UNTS 3**
SIGNED: 15 Sep 56 FORCE: 1 Nov 56
REGISTERED: 31 Jan 57 Norway
ARTICLES: 7 LANGUAGE: Norwegian. Danish.
HEADNOTE: RECIPROCAL RECOGNITION DRIVING PERMITS
TOPIC: General Transport
CONCEPTS: Licenses and permits. Driving permits.
TREATY REF: 107LTS283.
PARTIES:
Denmark
Norway

103681 Bilateral Agreement **259 UNTS 17**
SIGNED: 21 Sep 56 FORCE: 9 Oct 56
REGISTERED: 31 Jan 57 IBRD (World Bank)
ARTICLES: 5 LANGUAGE: English.
HEADNOTE: GUARANTEE AGREEMENT
TOPIC: IBRD Project
CONCEPTS: Definition of terms. Annex or appendix reference. Exchange of information and documents. Informational records. Inspection and observation. Bonds. Fees and exemptions. Tax exemptions. Domestic obligation. Terms of loan. Loan regulations. Loan guarantee. Guarantor non-interference.
PARTIES:
Austria
IBRD (World Bank)

103682 Bilateral Agreement **259 UNTS 43**
SIGNED: 21 Sep 56 FORCE: 9 Oct 56
REGISTERED: 31 Jan 57 IBRD (World Bank)
ARTICLES: 5 LANGUAGE: English.
HEADNOTE: GUARANTEE AGREEMENT
TOPIC: IBRD Project
CONCEPTS: Definition of terms. Annex or appendix reference. Exchange of information and documents. Informational records. Inspection and observation. Bonds. Fees and exemptions. Tax exemptions. Domestic obligation. Terms of loan. Loan regulations. Loan guarantee. Guarantor non-interference.
PARTIES:
Austria
IBRD (World Bank)

103683 Bilateral Agreement **259 UNTS 71**
SIGNED: 16 Nov 55 FORCE: 3 Apr 56
REGISTERED: 1 Feb 57 USSR (Soviet Union)
ARTICLES: 17 LANGUAGE: Russian. Arabic.
HEADNOTE: DEVELOP STRENGTHEN TRADE RELATIONS
TOPIC: General Economic
CONCEPTS: Exceptions and exemptions. General provisions. Treaty implementation. Annex or appendix reference. General cooperation. Licenses and permits. General trade. Establishment of trade relations. Reciprocity in trade. Accounting procedures. Banking. Currency. Monetary and gold transfers. Exchange rates and regulations. Financial programs. Payment schedules. Most favored nation clause. General transportation. Routes and logistics. Transport of goods. Merchant vessels. Ports and pilotage.
PROCEDURE: Ratification. Renewal or Revival. Termination.
PARTIES:
Syria
USSR (Soviet Union)

103684 Bilateral Protocol **259 UNTS 101**
SIGNED: 18 Dec 55 FORCE: 25 Jul 56
REGISTERED: 1 Feb 57 USSR (Soviet Union)
ARTICLES: 2 LANGUAGE: Russian. Persian.
HEADNOTE: PROLONGATION 24 JUN 31 TREATY

TOPIC: Admin Cooperation
CONCEPTS: Annex type material. Previous treaty extension.
TREATY REF: 157LTS371; 177LTS470.
PARTIES:
Afghanistan
USSR (Soviet Union)

103685 Bilateral Agreement **259 UNTS 111**
SIGNED: 2 Feb 56 FORCE: 17 Apr 56
REGISTERED: 1 Feb 57 USSR (Soviet Union)
ARTICLES: 9 LANGUAGE: Russian. Serbo-Croat.
HEADNOTE: LOAN
TOPIC: Loans and Credits
CONCEPTS: Friendship and amity. Operating agencies. Exchange rates and regulations. Interest rates. Payment schedules. Loan and credit. Loan repayment. Terms of loan.
PROCEDURE: Duration. Ratification.
PARTIES:
USSR (Soviet Union)
Yugoslavia

103686 Multilateral Agreement **259 UNTS 125**
SIGNED: 26 Mar 56 FORCE: 26 Mar 56
REGISTERED: 1 Feb 57 USSR (Soviet Union)
ARTICLES: 10 LANGUAGE: Russian.
HEADNOTE: JOINT INSTITUTE NUCLEAR RESEARCH
TOPIC: IGO Establishment
CONCEPTS: Family law. Juridical personality. Research cooperation. Research results. Nuclear research. Scientific exchange. Funding procedures. General technical assistance. Admission. Establishment. Procedure. Headquarters and facilities. Internal structure.
INTL ORGS: Joint Institute for Nuclear Research.
PROCEDURE: Denunciation. Registration. Termination.
PARTIES:
Albania SIGNED: 26 Mar 56 FORCE: 26 Mar 56
Bulgaria SIGNED: 26 Mar 56 FORCE: 26 Mar 56
China People's Rep SIGNED: 26 Mar 56 FORCE: 26 Mar 56
Czechoslovakia SIGNED: 26 Mar 56 FORCE: 26 Mar 56
Germany, East SIGNED: 26 Mar 56 FORCE: 26 Mar 56
Hungary SIGNED: 26 Mar 56 FORCE: 26 Mar 56
Korea, North SIGNED: 26 Mar 56 FORCE: 26 Mar 56
Mongolia SIGNED: 26 Mar 56 FORCE: 26 Mar 56
Poland SIGNED: 26 Mar 56 FORCE: 26 Mar 56
Romania SIGNED: 26 Mar 56 FORCE: 26 Mar 56
USSR (Soviet Union) SIGNED: 26 Mar 56 FORCE: 26 Mar 56
ANNEX
274 UNTS 377. Vietnam, North. Accession 20 Sep 56.

103687 Bilateral Convention **259 UNTS 145**
SIGNED: 17 May 56 FORCE: 31 Jul 56
REGISTERED: 1 Feb 57 USSR (Soviet Union)
ARTICLES: 7 LANGUAGE: Russian. Serbo-Croat.
HEADNOTE: CULTURAL COOPERATION
TOPIC: Culture
CONCEPTS: Friendship and amity. Dispute settlement. Specialists exchange. Exchange. Teacher and student exchange. Scholarships and grants. General cultural cooperation. Artists. Athletes. Publications exchange. Mass media exchange.
PROCEDURE: Duration. Future Procedures Contemplated. Ratification. Renewal or Revival. Termination.
PARTIES:
USSR (Soviet Union)
Yugoslavia

103688 Bilateral Convention **259 UNTS 155**
SIGNED: 22 May 56 FORCE: 31 Jul 56
REGISTERED: 1 Feb 57 USSR (Soviet Union)
ARTICLES: 10 LANGUAGE: Russian. Serbo-Croat.
HEADNOTE: DUAL CITIZENSHIP
TOPIC: Consul/Citizenship
CONCEPTS: Acquisition of nationality. Dual citizenship. Nationality and citizenship.
PROCEDURE: Ratification.

PARTIES:
USSR (Soviet Union)
Yugoslavia

103689 Bilateral Agreement **259 UNTS 169**
SIGNED: 31 Mar 56 FORCE: 31 Mar 56
REGISTERED: 1 Feb 57 USSR (Soviet Union)
ARTICLES: 10 LANGUAGE: Russian. Danish.
HEADNOTE: AIR TRANSPORT
TOPIC: Air Transport
CONCEPTS: Representation. Annex or appendix reference. Conformity with municipal law. General cooperation. Exchange of information and documents. Licenses and permits. Recognition of legal documents. Use of facilities. Humanitarian matters. Meteorology. Customs exemptions. Registration certificate. Routes and logistics. Navigational conditions. Permit designation. Airport facilities. Airport equipment. Airworthiness certificates. Conditions of airlines operating permission. Operating authorizations and regulations. Facilities and equipment.
PROCEDURE: Denunciation.
PARTIES:
Denmark
USSR (Soviet Union)
ANNEX
302 UNTS 366. Denmark. Supplementation 31 Mar 58. Force 31 Mar 58.
302 UNTS 366. USSR (Soviet Union). Supplementation 31 Mar 58. Force 31 Mar 58.

103690 Bilateral Agreement **259 UNTS 205**
SIGNED: 31 Mar 56 FORCE: 31 Mar 56
REGISTERED: 1 Feb 57 USSR (Soviet Union)
ARTICLES: 10 LANGUAGE: Russian. Norwegian.
HEADNOTE: AIR TRANSPORT
TOPIC: Air Transport
CONCEPTS: Representation. Annex or appendix reference. Conformity with municipal law. General cooperation. Exchange of information and documents. Licenses and permits. Recognition of legal documents. Use of facilities. Humanitarian matters. Meteorology. Customs exemptions. Registration certificate. Routes and logistics. Navigational conditions. Permit designation. Air transport. Airport facilities. Airport equipment. Airworthiness certificates. Conditions of airlines operating permission. Operating authorizations and regulations. Facilities and equipment.
PROCEDURE: Denunciation.
PARTIES:
Norway
USSR (Soviet Union)

103691 Bilateral Agreement **259 UNTS 239**
SIGNED: 31 Mar 56 FORCE: 31 Mar 56
REGISTERED: 1 Feb 57 USSR (Soviet Union)
ARTICLES: 11 LANGUAGE: Russian. Swedish.
HEADNOTE: AIR TRANSPORT
TOPIC: Air Transport
CONCEPTS: Representation. Annex or appendix reference. Previous treaty replacement. Conformity with municipal law. General cooperation. Exchange of information and documents. Licenses and permits. Recognition of legal documents. Use of facilities. Humanitarian matters. Meteorology. Customs exemptions. Registration certificate. Routes and logistics. Navigational conditions. Permit designation. Air transport. Airport facilities. Airport equipment. Airworthiness certificates. Conditions of airlines operating permission. Operating authorizations and regulations. Facilities and equipment.
PROCEDURE: Denunciation.
PARTIES:
Sweden
USSR (Soviet Union)
ANNEX
646 UNTS 358. USSR (Soviet Union). Signature 27 Jan 67. Force 27 Jan 67.
646 UNTS 358. Sweden. Signature 27 Jan 67. Force 27 Jan 67.

103692 Bilateral Agreement **259 UNTS 279**
SIGNED: 26 Apr 56 FORCE: 19 May 56
REGISTERED: 1 Feb 57 USSR (Soviet Union)
ARTICLES: 13 LANGUAGE: Russian. German.

HEADNOTE: CULTURAL SCIENTIFIC COOPER-
ATION
TOPIC: Health/Educ/Welfare
CONCEPTS: General cooperation. Exchange.
Teacher and student exchange. Professorships.
Vocational training. Exchange. General cultural
cooperation. Artists. Athletes. Research results.
Scientific exchange.
INTL ORGS: Special Commission.
PROCEDURE: Duration. Ratification. Renewal or
Revival. Termination.
PARTIES:
Germany, East
USSR (Soviet Union)

103693 Bilateral Agreement **259 UNTS 297**
SIGNED: 24 Apr 56   FORCE: 24 Apr 56
REGISTERED: 1 Feb 57 USSR (Soviet Union)
ARTICLES: 7 LANGUAGE: Russian. Mongolian.
HEADNOTE: CULTURAL COOPERATION
TOPIC: Culture
CONCEPTS: Friendship and amity. Non-diplomatic
delegations. Establishment of commission. Ex-
change. Teacher and student exchange. Voca-
tional training. Exchange. General cultural coop-
eration. Artists. Athletes. Scientific exchange.
Accounting procedures. Publications exchange.
Mass media exchange.
INTL ORGS: Special Commission.
TREATY REF: 216UNTS211.
PROCEDURE: Duration. Ratification. Renewal or
Revival. Termination.
PARTIES:
Mongolia
USSR (Soviet Union)

103694 Bilateral Agreement **259 UNTS 311**
SIGNED: 30 Jun 56   FORCE: 22 Nov 56
REGISTERED: 1 Feb 57 USSR (Soviet Union)
ARTICLES: 12 LANGUAGE: Russian. Polish.
HEADNOTE: CULTURAL COOPERATION
TOPIC: Culture
CONCEPTS: Friendship and amity. Tourism. Non-
diplomatic delegations. Exchange of information
and documents. Operating agencies. Establish-
ment of commission. Exchange. Teacher and stu-
dent exchange. Exchange. General cultural co-
operation. Artists. Athletes. Research cooper-
ation. Scientific exchange. Accounting
procedures. Media guaranty. Press and wire ser-
vices.
INTL ORGS: Special Commission.
TREATY REF: 12UNTS371.
PROCEDURE: Duration. Ratification. Renewal or
Revival. Termination.
PARTIES:
Poland
USSR (Soviet Union)

103695 Bilateral Agreement **259 UNTS 329**
SIGNED: 5 Sep 56   FORCE: 5 Sep 56
REGISTERED: 1 Feb 57 USSR (Soviet Union)
ARTICLES: 7 LANGUAGE: Russian. Korean.
HEADNOTE: CULTURAL COOPERATION
TOPIC: Culture
CONCEPTS: Friendship and amity. Non-diplomatic
delegations. General cooperation. Establish-
ment of commission. Specialists exchange. Ex-
change. Teacher and student exchange. Ex-
change. General cultural cooperation. Artists.
Athletes. Scientific exchange. Accounting pro-
cedures. Publications exchange. Mass media ex-
change.
INTL ORGS: Special Commission.
TREATY REF: 221UNTS3.
PROCEDURE: Duration. Ratification. Renewal or
Revival. Termination.
PARTIES:
Korea, North
USSR (Soviet Union)

103696 Bilateral Agreement **259 UNTS 341**
SIGNED: 1 Jun 56   FORCE: 1 Jun 56
REGISTERED: 1 Feb 57 USSR (Soviet Union)
ARTICLES: 13 LANGUAGE: Russian. Czechoslo-
vakian.
HEADNOTE: CULTURAL COOPERATION
TOPIC: Culture
CONCEPTS: Previous treaty replacement. Friend-
ship and amity. Non-diplomatic delegations.

General cooperation. Exchange of information
and documents. Operating agencies. Establishment of commission. Specialists exchange. Recognition of degrees. Exchange. Teacher and student exchange. Professorships. Vocational training. Exchange. General cultural cooperation.
Artists. Athletes. Scientific exchange. Accounting procedures. Publications exchange. Mass
media exchange. Press and wire services.
INTL ORGS: Special Commission.
PROCEDURE: Duration. Registration. Renewal or
Revival. Termination.
PARTIES:
Czechoslovakia
USSR (Soviet Union)

103697 Bilateral Agreement **259 UNTS 363**
SIGNED: 28 Apr 56   FORCE: 28 Apr 56
REGISTERED: 1 Feb 57 USSR (Soviet Union)
ARTICLES: 7 LANGUAGE: Russian. Bulgarian.
HEADNOTE: CULTURAL COOPERATION
TOPIC: Culture
CONCEPTS: Friendship and amity. Tourism. Non-
diplomatic delegations. General cooperation. Es-
tablishment of commission. Specialists ex-
change. Exchange. Teacher and student ex-
change. Exchange. General cultural cooperation.
Artists. Athletes. Scientific exchange. Account-
ing procedures. Publications exchange. Mass
media exchange.
INTL ORGS: Special Commission.
PROCEDURE: Duration. Future Procedures Con-
templated. Renewal or Revival. Termination.
PARTIES:
Bulgaria
USSR (Soviet Union)

103698 Bilateral Agreement **259 UNTS 377**
SIGNED: 7 Apr 56   FORCE: 7 Apr 56
REGISTERED: 1 Feb 57 USSR (Soviet Union)
ARTICLES: 9 LANGUAGE: Russian. Romanian.
HEADNOTE: CULTURAL COOPERATION
TOPIC: Culture
CONCEPTS: Friendship and amity. Tourism. Non-
diplomatic delegations. Establishment of com-
mission. Recognition of degrees. Exchange.
Teacher and student exchange. Exchange. Gen-
eral cultural cooperation. Artists. Athletes. Scien-
tific exchange. Research and development. Ac-
counting procedures. Publications exchange.
Mass media exchange. Press and wire services.
INTL ORGS: Special Commission.
PROCEDURE: Duration. Renewal or Revival. Termi-
nation.
PARTIES:
Romania
USSR (Soviet Union)

103699 Bilateral Agreement **259 UNTS 391**
SIGNED: 3 May 56   FORCE: 3 May 56
REGISTERED: 1 Feb 57 USSR (Soviet Union)
ARTICLES: 5 LANGUAGE: Russian. Albanian.
HEADNOTE: CULTURAL COOPERATION
TOPIC: Culture
CONCEPTS: Friendship and amity. Tourism. Non-
diplomatic delegations. Operating agencies. Es-
tablishment of commission. Exchange. Teacher
and student exchange. Exchange. General cul-
tural cooperation. Artists. Athletes. Research re-
sults. Scientific exchange. Accounting proce-
dures. Publications exchange. Mass media ex-
change. Press and wire services.
INTL ORGS: Special Commission.
PROCEDURE: Duration. Renewal or Revival. Termination.
PARTIES:
Albania
USSR (Soviet Union)

103700 Bilateral Agreement **259 UNTS 405**
SIGNED: 28 Jun 56   FORCE: 28 Jun 56
REGISTERED: 1 Feb 57 USSR (Soviet Union)
ARTICLES: 14 LANGUAGE: Russian. Hungarian.
HEADNOTE: SCIENTIFIC CULTURAL COOPER-
ATION
TOPIC: Health/Educ/Welfare
CONCEPTS: Culture. General cultural cooperation.
Scientific exchange.
INTL ORGS: Special Commission.
PROCEDURE: Duration. Termination.

PARTIES:
Hungary
USSR (Soviet Union)

103701 Multilateral Agreement **259 UNTS 426**
SIGNED: 23 Jan 57   FORCE: 23 Jan 57
REGISTERED: 1 Feb 57 United Nations
ARTICLES: 6 LANGUAGE: English.
HEADNOTE: TECHNICAL ASSISTANCE
TOPIC: Tech Assistance
CONCEPTS: Definition of terms. Privileges and immunities. General cooperation. Exchange of in-
formation and documents. Personnel. Responsi-
bility and liability. Title and deeds. Use of facili-
ties. Exchange. Scholarships and grants.
Vocational training. Research and development.
Exchange rates and regulations. Expense shar-
ing formulae. Local currency. Domestic obliga-
tion. General technical assistance. Materials,
equipment and services. IGO status. Conformity
with IGO decisions.
TREATY   REF: 76UNTS132;   1UNTS15;
1UNTS263; 33UNTS261; 173UNTS15.
PROCEDURE: Amendment. Termination.
PARTIES:
FAO (Food Agri) SIGNED: 23 Jan 57 FORCE:
23 Jan 57
ICAO (Civil Aviat) SIGNED: 23 Jan 57 FORCE:
23 Jan 57
ILO (Labor Org) SIGNED: 23 Jan 57 FORCE:
23 Jan 57
ITU (Telecommun) SIGNED: 23 Jan 57 FORCE:
23 Jan 57
UNESCO (Educ/Cult) SIGNED: 23 Jan 57 FORCE:
23 Jan 57
United Nations SIGNED: 23 Jan 57 FORCE:
23 Jan 57
WHO (World Health) SIGNED: 23 Jan 57 FORCE:
23 Jan 57
WMO (Meteorology) SIGNED: 23 Jan 57 FORCE:
23 Jan 57
Turkey SIGNED: 23 Jan 57 FORCE: 23 Jan 57
ANNEX
561 UNTS 348. Turkey.
561 UNTS 348. UNTAB (Tech Assis). Force
21 Oct 65.

103702 Bilateral Convention **260 UNTS 3**
SIGNED: 26 Mar 56   FORCE: 2 Feb 57
REGISTERED: 2 Feb 57 Belgium
ARTICLES: 19 LANGUAGE: French. Hebrew.
HEADNOTE: EXTRADITION
TOPIC: Extradition
CONCEPTS: Territorial application. Extradition, de-
portation and repatriation. Extraditable offenses.
Location of crime. Refusal of extradition. Concur-
rent requests. Limits of prosecution. Provisional
detainment. Witnesses and experts. Material evi-
dence. Legal protection and assistance. Indem-
nities and reimbursements. Conveyance in tran-
sit.
PROCEDURE: Ratification. Termination.
PARTIES:
Belgium
Israel

103703 Bilateral Agreement **260 UNTS 35**
SIGNED: 26 May 54   FORCE: 6 Feb 57
REGISTERED: 6 Feb 57 United Nations
ARTICLES: 14 LANGUAGE: English.
HEADNOTE: HEADQUARTERS UN/ENCAFE
TOPIC: IGO Status/Immunit
CONCEPTS: Definition of terms. Annex or appen-
dix reference. Non-visa travel documents. Diplo-
matic privileges. Diplomatic missions. Inviolabil-
ity. Privileges and immunities. Property. Diplo-
matic correspondence. Juridical personality.
Procedure. Special status. Status of experts.
Conformity with IGO decisions.
PROCEDURE: Amendment.
PARTIES:
United Nations
Thailand

103704 Bilateral Exchange **260 UNTS 61**
SIGNED: 8 Feb 57   FORCE: 12 Nov 56
REGISTERED: 8 Feb 57 United Nations
ARTICLES: 2 LANGUAGE: English.
HEADNOTE: UN EMERGENCY FORCE
TOPIC: Status of Forces

CONCEPTS: Jurisdiction. Procurement and logistics. Status of forces.
INTL ORGS: International Telecommunication Union. Arbitration Commission. Claims Commission.
PARTIES:
United Nations
United Arab Rep

103705 Bilateral Convention **260 UNTS 91**
SIGNED: 29 Oct 49 FORCE: 18 Sep 50
REGISTERED: 11 Feb 57 Poland
ARTICLES: 11 LANGUAGE: Polish. Hungarian.
HEADNOTE: PEST DISEASE CONTROL PROTECTION AGRICULTURAL PLANTS
TOPIC: Sanitation
CONCEPTS: Detailed regulations. Border traffic and migration. General cooperation. Exchange of information and documents. Inspection and observation. Domestic legislation. Specialists exchange. Quarantine. Disease control. Insect control. Research results. Trade procedures. Materials, equipment and services.
PROCEDURE: Denunciation. Duration. Renewal or Revival.
PARTIES:
Hungary
Poland

103706 Bilateral Convention **260 UNTS 113**
SIGNED: 29 Oct 49 FORCE: 18 Sep 50
REGISTERED: 11 Feb 57 Poland
ARTICLES: 6 LANGUAGE: Polish. Hungarian.
HEADNOTE: VETERINARY MATTERS
TOPIC: Sanitation
CONCEPTS: Detailed regulations. Standardization. General cooperation. Exchange of information and documents. Inspection and observation. Domestic legislation. Disease control. Veterinary. Professorships. Institute establishment. Scholarships and grants. Vocational training. Research results. Trade procedures. Publications exchange. Mass media exchange. Conferences.
INTL ORGS: Special Commission.
PROCEDURE: Duration. Renewal or Revival. Termination.
PARTIES:
Hungary
Poland

103707 Bilateral Agreement **260 UNTS 131**
SIGNED: 2 Dec 50 FORCE: 18 Apr 51
REGISTERED: 11 Feb 57 Poland
ARTICLES: 11 LANGUAGE: Polish. Albanian.
HEADNOTE: CULTURAL COOPERATION
TOPIC: Culture
CONCEPTS: Friendship and amity. Operating agencies. Establishment of commission. Exchange. Teacher and student exchange. Professorships. Scholarships and grants. General cultural cooperation. Artists. Research cooperation. Scientific exchange. Press and wire services.
INTL ORGS: Special Commission.
PROCEDURE: Denunciation. Duration. Ratification. Renewal or Revival.
PARTIES:
Albania
Poland

103708 Bilateral Agreement **260 UNTS 149**
SIGNED: 2 Jul 49 FORCE: 15 May 51
REGISTERED: 11 Feb 57 Poland
ARTICLES: 25 LANGUAGE: Polish. Czechoslovakian.
HEADNOTE: PRIVILEGED RAIL TRANSIT TO POLAND THROUGH BROUMOV-MEZIMESTI
TOPIC: Land Transport
CONCEPTS: Detailed regulations. Exceptions and exemptions. General provisions. Conformity with municipal law. General cooperation. Exchange of information and documents. Free passage and transit. Recognition of legal documents. Responsibility and liability. Procedure. Compensation. Indemnities and reimbursements. Fees and exemptions. Non-interest rates and fees. Claims and settlements. Customs duties. Customs exemptions. Routes and logistics. Transport of goods. Railways. Facilities and equipment.
TREATY REF: 85UNTS62.

PROCEDURE: Duration. Ratification. Renewal or Revival.
PARTIES:
Czechoslovakia
Poland

103709 Bilateral Agreement **260 UNTS 179**
SIGNED: 2 Jul 49 FORCE: 15 May 51
REGISTERED: 11 Feb 57 Poland
ARTICLES: 30 LANGUAGE: Polish. Czechoslovakian.
HEADNOTE: PRIVILEGED RAIL TRANSIT THROUGH POLISH TERRITORY
TOPIC: Land Transport
CONCEPTS: Detailed regulations. Exceptions and exemptions. General provisions. Non-visa travel documents. Conformity with municipal law. General cooperation. Exchange of information and documents. Free passage and transit. Personnel. Recognition of legal documents. Responsibility and liability. Procedure. Compensation. Indemnities and reimbursements. Fees and exemptions. Non-interest rates and fees. Customs duties. Customs exemptions. Passenger transport. Routes and logistics. Transport of goods. Railways. Facilities and equipment. Regulations.
TREATY REF: 85UNTS62.
PROCEDURE: Denunciation. Ratification.
PARTIES:
Czechoslovakia
Poland

103710 Bilateral Agreement **260 UNTS 217**
SIGNED: 25 Jan 51 FORCE: 27 Dec 51
REGISTERED: 11 Feb 57 Poland
ARTICLES: 5 LANGUAGE: Polish. Albanian.
HEADNOTE: TECHNICAL & SCIENTIFIC COOPERATION
TOPIC: Scientific Project
CONCEPTS: Friendship and amity. Exchange of information and documents. Establishment of commission. Vocational training. Scientific exchange. Research and development. General technical assistance. Publications exchange.
INTL ORGS: Special Commission.
PROCEDURE: Duration. Ratification. Renewal or Revival. Termination.
PARTIES:
Albania
Poland

103711 Bilateral Convention **260 UNTS 227**
SIGNED: 26 Sep 49 FORCE: 29 Sep 52
REGISTERED: 11 Feb 57 Poland
ARTICLES: 11 LANGUAGE: Polish. Bulgarian.
HEADNOTE: PROTECTION AGRICULTURAL PLANTS
TOPIC: Sanitation
CONCEPTS: Detailed regulations. Border traffic and migration. General cooperation. Exchange of information and documents. Inspection and observation. Domestic legislation. Specialists exchange. Quarantine. Disease control. Insect control. Research results. Trade procedures. Materials, equipment and services. Mass media exchange.
PROCEDURE: Denunciation. Duration. Renewal or Revival.
PARTIES:
Bulgaria
Poland

103712 Bilateral Convention **260 UNTS 249**
SIGNED: 26 Sep 49 FORCE: 29 Oct 52
REGISTERED: 11 Feb 57 Poland
ARTICLES: 19 LANGUAGE: Polish. Bulgarian.
HEADNOTE: VETERINARY MATTERS
TOPIC: Sanitation
CONCEPTS: Detailed regulations. Border traffic and migration. Standardization. General cooperation. Exchange of information and documents. Inspection and observation. Domestic legislation. Establishment of commission. Disease control. Veterinary. Professorships. Institute establishment. Scholarships and grants. Vocational training. Research results. Trade procedures. Mass media exchange. Conferences.
INTL ORGS: Special Commission.

PARTIES:
Bulgaria
Poland

103713 Bilateral Agreement **260 UNTS 307**
SIGNED: 14 Jun 55 FORCE: 28 Dec 56
REGISTERED: 18 Feb 57 Italy
ARTICLES: 4 LANGUAGE: French.
HEADNOTE: CULTURAL AGREEMENT
TOPIC: Culture
CONCEPTS: Friendship and amity. Establishment of commission. Specialists exchange. Exchange. Scholarships and grants. Exchange. General cultural cooperation. Artists. Scientific exchange.
INTL ORGS: Special Commission.
PROCEDURE: Denunciation. Duration. Ratification. Renewal or Revival.
PARTIES:
Italy
Norway

103714 Bilateral Exchange **260 UNTS 315**
SIGNED: 20 Dec 55 FORCE: 20 Dec 55
REGISTERED: 18 Feb 57 Italy
ARTICLES: 2 LANGUAGE: Spanish.
HEADNOTE: SUPPLY ELECTROLYTIC PLANT
TOPIC: Specif Goods/Equip
CONCEPTS: Hydro-electric power. Specific goods and equipment.
PARTIES:
Colombia
Italy

103715 Bilateral Exchange **260 UNTS 319**
SIGNED: 16 Dec 55 FORCE: 16 Dec 55
REGISTERED: 18 Feb 57 Italy
ARTICLES: 2 LANGUAGE: Italian.
HEADNOTE: TAX EXEMPTIONS DIPLOMATIC AGENTS
TOPIC: Taxation
CONCEPTS: Privileges and immunities. Tax exemptions.
TREATY REF: 3'11DEMARTENS18;.
PARTIES:
Italy
Vatican/Holy See

103716 Bilateral Agreement **260 UNTS 327**
SIGNED: 22 Oct 55 FORCE: 1 Jan 56
REGISTERED: 18 Feb 57 Italy
ARTICLES: 15 LANGUAGE: French. German.
HEADNOTE: USE PORT OF TRIESTE
TOPIC: Specific Property
CONCEPTS: Use of facilities. Non-interest rates and fees. National treatment. Temporary importation. Transport of goods. Ports and pilotage. Railways. Facilities and property.
INTL ORGS: Special Commission.
PROCEDURE: Denunciation. Duration. Renewal or Revival.
PARTIES:
Austria
Italy

103717 Bilateral Exchange **260 UNTS 339**
SIGNED: 22 Dec 55 FORCE: 1 Jan 56
REGISTERED: 18 Feb 57 Italy
ARTICLES: 2 LANGUAGE: Italian. French.
HEADNOTE: AMENDMENTS PAYMENT AGREEMENT
TOPIC: Finance
CONCEPTS: Annex type material. Financial programs. Payment schedules.
TREATY REF: 21OCT50 PAYMENTS AGREEMENTS.
PARTIES:
Italy
Switzerland

103718 Bilateral Exchange **260 UNTS 345**
SIGNED: 28 Dec 55 FORCE: 1 Jan 56
REGISTERED: 18 Feb 57 Italy
ARTICLES: 2 LANGUAGE: Italian.
HEADNOTE: ABOLITION VISAS PASSPORTS
TOPIC: Visas
CONCEPTS: Emergencies. Time limit. Visa abolition. Passports diplomatic. Passports non-diplomatic. Denial of admission. Resident per-

mits. Conformity with municipal law. Fees and exemptions.
PROCEDURE: Denunciation.
PARTIES:
Austria
Italy

103719   Bilateral Exchange   **260 UNTS 351**
SIGNED: 30 Dec 55   FORCE: 15 Dec 55
REGISTERED: 18 Feb 57 Italy
ARTICLES: 2 LANGUAGE: English.
HEADNOTE: RECIPROCAL ABOLITION VISAS DIPLOMATIC PASSPORTS
TOPIC: Visas
CONCEPTS: Passports diplomatic. Visas. Fees and exemptions.
PARTIES:
Italy
Thailand

103720   Bilateral Agreement   **260 UNTS 357**
SIGNED: 12 May 56   FORCE: 12 May 56
REGISTERED: 18 Feb 57 Italy
ARTICLES: 5 LANGUAGE: French.
HEADNOTE: TRADE REGULATION
TOPIC: General Trade
CONCEPTS: Annex or appendix reference. Establishment of commission. Export quotas. Import quotas. Trade procedures. Payment schedules.
INTL ORGS: Special Commission.
TREATY REF: 260UNTS261; 260UNTS363.
PROCEDURE: Duration.
PARTIES:
Denmark
Italy

103721   Bilateral Agreement   **260 UNTS 369**
SIGNED: 18 Sep 56   FORCE: 13 Feb 57
REGISTERED: 20 Feb 57 IBRD (World Bank)
ARTICLES: 5 LANGUAGE: English.
HEADNOTE: GUARANTEE AGREEMENT
TOPIC: IBRD Project
CONCEPTS: Definition of terms. Annex or appendix reference. Exchange of information and documents. Informational records. Inspection and observation. Bonds. Fees and exemptions. Tax exemptions. Domestic obligation. Terms of loan. Loan regulations. Loan guarantee. Guarantor non-interference.
PARTIES:
Costa Rica
IBRD (World Bank)

103722   Bilateral Agreement   **261 UNTS 3**
SIGNED: 4 Aug 54   FORCE: 1 Sep 54
REGISTERED: 1 Mar 57 South Africa
ARTICLES: 21 LANGUAGE: English.
HEADNOTE: PARCEL POST
TOPIC: Postal Service
CONCEPTS: Responsibility and liability. Accounting procedures. Customs declarations. Customs exemptions. Postal services. Regulations. Conveyance in transit. Parcel post. Rates and charges.
PROCEDURE: Termination.
PARTIES:
Canada
South Africa

103723   Bilateral Exchange   **261 UNTS 17**
SIGNED: 6 Feb 56   FORCE: 31 Oct 56
REGISTERED: 1 Mar 57 Netherlands
ARTICLES: 2 LANGUAGE: French.
HEADNOTE: COMPENSATION WAR FLOOD DAMAGE
TOPIC: Reparations
CONCEPTS: Definition of terms. Time limit. Treaty implementation. Exchange of information and documents. Compensation. National treatment. Post-war claims settlement.
PARTIES:
Luxembourg
Netherlands

103724   Bilateral Agreement   **261 UNTS 27**
SIGNED: 1 Nov 56   FORCE: 27 Feb 57
REGISTERED: 5 Mar 57 IBRD (World Bank)
ARTICLES: 5 LANGUAGE: English.

HEADNOTE: GUARANTEE AGREEMENT
TOPIC: IBRD Project
CONCEPTS: Default remedies. Annex or appendix reference. Exchange of information and documents. Informational records. Inspection and observation. Bonds. Fees and exemptions. Tax exemptions. Domestic obligation. Terms of loan. Loan regulations. Loan guarantee. Guarantor non-interference.
PARTIES:
Chile
IBRD (World Bank)

103725   Multilateral Treaty   **261 UNTS 55**
SIGNED: 6 Apr 55   FORCE: 3 Apr 56
REGISTERED: 6 Mar 57 India
ARTICLES: 7 LANGUAGE: Hindi. Arabic. English.
HEADNOTE: FRIENDSHIP
TOPIC: General Amity
CONCEPTS: Friendship and amity. Alien status.
PROCEDURE: Ratification.
PARTIES:
Belgium   SIGNED: 18 Apr 51   RATIFIED: 22 Jul 52 FORCE: 23 Jul 52
France SIGNED: 18 Apr 51 RATIFIED: 18 Jul 52 FORCE: 23 Jul 52
Germany, West SIGNED: 18 Apr 51 RATIFIED: 23 Jul 52 FORCE: 23 Jul 52
Italy SIGNED: 18 Apr 51 RATIFIED: 22 Jul 52 FORCE: 23 Jul 52
Luxembourg SIGNED: 18 Apr 51 RATIFIED: 23 Jul 52 FORCE: 23 Jul 52
Netherlands SIGNED: 18 Apr 51 RATIFIED: 17 Jul 52 FORCE: 23 Jul 52

103726   Bilateral Agreement   **261 UNTS 71**
SIGNED: 27 Sep 56   FORCE: 30 Jan 57
REGISTERED: 6 Mar 57 Norway
ARTICLES: 27 LANGUAGE: Norwegian. Swedish.
HEADNOTE: DOUBLE TAXATION TAXES INCOME PROPERTY
TOPIC: Taxation
CONCEPTS: Definition of terms. Privileges and immunities. Nationality and citizenship. Negotiation. Taxation. Death duties. Equitable taxes. General. Air transport. Merchant vessels. Mass media exchange.
TREATY REF: 179LTS245.
PROCEDURE: Duration. Ratification. Termination.
PARTIES:
Norway
Sweden
ANNEX
348 UNTS 350.   Sweden.   Supplementation 21 May 59. Force 15 Dec 59.
348 UNTS 350.   Norway.   Supplementation 21 May 59. Force 15 Dec 59.

103727   Unilateral Instrument   **261 UNTS 113**
SIGNED: 1 Mar 57   FORCE: 8 Mar 57
REGISTERED: 8 Mar 57 United Nations
ARTICLES: 1 LANGUAGE: English.
HEADNOTE: ACCEPTANCE OBLIGATIONS UN
TOPIC: IGO Establishment
CONCEPTS: Admission. Adherence to UN charter.
INTL ORGS: United Nations.
PARTIES:
Ghana

103728   Bilateral Agreement   **261 UNTS 117**
SIGNED: 12 Oct 56   FORCE: 26 Feb 57
REGISTERED: 14 Mar 57 IBRD (World Bank)
ARTICLES: 5 LANGUAGE: English.
HEADNOTE: GUARANTEE AGREEMENT
TOPIC: IBRD Project
CONCEPTS: Definition of terms. Annex or appendix reference. Exchange of information and documents. Informational records. Inspection and observation. Bonds. Fees and exemptions. Tax exemptions. Domestic obligation. Terms of loan. Loan regulations. Loan guarantee. Guarantor non-interference. Water transport.
PARTIES:
IBRD (World Bank)
Thailand

103729   Multilateral Treaty   **261 UNTS 140**
SIGNED: 18 Apr 51   FORCE: 23 Jul 52
REGISTERED: 15 Mar 57 France

ARTICLES: 100 LANGUAGE: French. German.
HEADNOTE: EUROPEAN COAL
TOPIC: IGO Establishment
CONCEPTS: Definition of terms. Treaty implementation. Treaty interpretation. Annex or appendix reference. Treaty violation. Annex type material. Non-prejudice to third party. Border traffic and migration. Conformity with municipal law. General cooperation. Exchange of official publications. Exchange of information and documents. Juridical personality. Recognition of legal documents. Private contracts. Procedure. Special tribunals. Vocational training. Employment regulations. Old age and invalidity insurance. Migrant worker. General economics. Establishment of trade relations. Free trade. Trade procedures. Monetary and gold transfers. Investments. Financial programs. Funding procedures. Non-interest rates and fees. Customs duties. Customs declarations. Customs exemptions. Temporary importation. Economic assistance. General transportation. Establishment. Internal structure. Status of experts.
INTL ORGS: Council of Europe. General Agreement on Tariffs and Trade. Organization for Economic Co-operation and Development. United Nations.
PROCEDURE: Amendment. Accession. Denunciation. Duration. Future Procedures Contemplated. Ratification. Registration. Termination.
PARTIES:
Belgium   SIGNED: 18 Apr 51   RATIFIED: 22 Jul 52 FORCE: 23 Jul 52
France SIGNED: 18 Apr 51 RATIFIED: 18 Jul 52 FORCE: 23 Jul 52
Germany, West SIGNED: 18 Apr 51 RATIFIED: 23 Jul 52 FORCE: 23 Jul 52
Italy SIGNED: 18 Apr 51 RATIFIED: 22 Jul 52 FORCE: 23 Jul 52
Luxembourg SIGNED: 18 Apr 51 RATIFIED: 23 Jul 52 FORCE: 23 Jul 52
Netherlands SIGNED: 18 Apr 51 RATIFIED: 17 Jul 52 FORCE: 23 Jul 52
ANNEX
486 UNTS 416.   ECSC   (Coal/Steel).   Force 16 May 60.
535 UNTS 416. France. Amendment 27 Dec 56. Force 9 Oct 58.
535 UNTS 416. Belgium. Amendment 27 Aug 57. Force 9 Oct 58.
535 UNTS 416. Germany, West. Amendment 28 Dec 56. Force 9 Oct 58.
535 UNTS 416. Luxembourg. Amendment 11 Mar 57. Force 9 Oct 58.
535 UNTS 416. Italy. Amendment 12 Jun 58. Force 9 Oct 58.
535 UNTS 416.   Netherlands.   Amendment 9 Oct 58. Force 9 Oct 58.

103730   Bilateral Agreement   **261 UNTS 321**
SIGNED: 7 Jan 55   FORCE: 7 Apr 55
REGISTERED: 19 Mar 57 USA (United States)
ARTICLES: 9 LANGUAGE: English. Spanish.
HEADNOTE: FINANCIAL ARRANGEMENTS FURNISHING SUPPLIES SERVICES NAVAL VESSELS
TOPIC: Milit Assistance
CONCEPTS: Indemnities and reimbursements. Currency. Ports and pilotage. Naval vessels.
PROCEDURE: Termination.
PARTIES:
Peru
USA (United States)

103731   Bilateral Agreement   **261 UNTS 331**
SIGNED: 29 Apr 55   FORCE: 29 Apr 55
REGISTERED: 19 Mar 57 USA (United States)
ARTICLES: 6 LANGUAGE: English.
HEADNOTE: AGRI COMMOD AGREE
TOPIC: US Agri Commod Aid
CONCEPTS: Detailed regulations. General provisions. Guarantees and safeguards. Conformity with municipal law. General cooperation. Accounting procedures. Currency deposits. Exchange rates and regulations. Transportation costs. Local currency. Agricultural commodities assistance. Commodities schedule. Purchase authorization. Surplus commodities.
PARTIES:
Israel
USA (United States)

ANNEX
263 UNTS 426. USA (United States). Supplementation 15 Jun 55. Force 15 Jun 55.
263 UNTS 426. Israel. Supplementation 15 Jun 55. Force 15 Jun 55.
314 UNTS 356. USA (United States). Amendment 28 Aug 58. Force 28 Aug 58.
314 UNTS 356. Israel. Amendment 28 Aug 58. Force 28 Aug 58.

103732 Bilateral Exchange **261 UNTS 343**
SIGNED: 29 Mar 55   FORCE: 29 Mar 55
REGISTERED: 19 Mar 57 USA (United States).
ARTICLES: 2 LANGUAGE: English.
HEADNOTE: GUARANTY PRIVATE INVESTMENTS
TOPIC: Claims and Debts
CONCEPTS: Conformity with municipal law. Arbitration. Procedure. Existing tribunals. Negotiation. Reciprocity in financial treatment. Currency. Claims and settlements. Private investment guarantee.
INTL ORGS: International Court of Justice.
PARTIES:
Ecuador
USA (United States)
ANNEX
488 UNTS 262. USA (United States). Amendment 4 Sep 63. Force 4 Sep 63.
488 UNTS 262. Ecuador. Amendment 4 Sep 63. Force 4 Sep 63.

103733 Bilateral Exchange **261 UNTS 351**
SIGNED: 27 Apr 55   FORCE: 27 Apr 55
REGISTERED: 19 Mar 57 USA (United States).
ARTICLES: 2 LANGUAGE: English.
HEADNOTE: MILITARY ECONOMIC ASSISTANCE
TOPIC: Direct Aid
CONCEPTS: Exchange of information and documents. Import quotas. Accounting procedures. Funding procedures. Local currency. Tax exemptions. Customs exemptions. Commodities and services. Domestic obligation. Economic assistance. Materials, equipment and services. Procurement. Industry. Military assistance. Bases and facilities.
TREATY REF: 174UNTS251.
PROCEDURE: Termination.
PARTIES:
Philippines
USA (United States)
ANNEX
273 UNTS 316. USA (United States). Supplementation 20 Apr 56. Force 21 Apr 56.
273 UNTS 316. Philippines. Supplementation 20 Apr 56. Force 21 Apr 56.
291 UNTS 342. USA (United States). Supplementation 14 Jun 57. Force 14 Jun 57.
291 UNTS 342. Philippines. Supplementation 14 Jun 57. Force 14 Jun 57.
308 UNTS 324. USA (United States). Supplementation 14 Apr 58. Force 18 Apr 58.
308 UNTS 324. Philippines. Supplementation 14 Apr 58. Force 18 Apr 58.

103734 Bilateral Exchange **261 UNTS 361**
SIGNED: 1 Apr 55   FORCE: 1 Apr 55
REGISTERED: 19 Mar 57 USA (United States).
ARTICLES: 2 LANGUAGE: English. French.
HEADNOTE: EMERGENCY RELIEF ASSISTANCE
TOPIC: Direct Aid
CONCEPTS: Treaty implementation. Privileges and immunities. Conformity with municipal law. General cooperation. Exchange of information and documents. Inspection and observation. Personnel. Public information. Accounting procedures. Expense sharing formulae. Local currency. Assets. Tax exemptions. Customs exemptions. Domestic obligation. Relief supplies. Procurement. Distribution. Access to materials. Transport of goods.
TREATY REF: 151UNTS191.
PROCEDURE: Termination.
PARTIES:
Haiti
USA (United States)

103735 Bilateral Agreement **262 UNTS 3**
SIGNED: 27 Jan 55   FORCE: 27 Jan 55
REGISTERED: 19 Mar 57 USA (United States)
ARTICLES: 8 LANGUAGE: English. Spanish.
HEADNOTE: SURPLUS AGRI COMMOD AGREE
TOPIC: US Agri Commod Aid
CONCEPTS: General provisions. Conformity with municipal law. General cooperation. Accounting procedures. Currency deposits. Exchange rates and regulations. Purchase authorizations. Local currency. Loan repayment. Commodities schedule. Surplus commodities.
PARTIES:
Chile
USA (United States)

103736 Bilateral Agreement **262 UNTS 19**
SIGNED: 31 Mar 55   FORCE: 31 Mar 55
REGISTERED: 19 Mar 57 USA (United States)
ARTICLES: 12 LANGUAGE: English. Spanish.
HEADNOTE: EDUCATIONAL PROGRAMS
TOPIC: Education
CONCEPTS: Definition of terms. Detailed regulations. Friendship and amity. Alien status. Privileges and immunities. Conformity with municipal law. General cooperation. Inspection and observation. Personnel. General property. Exchange. Commissions and foundations. Teacher and student exchange. Scholarships and grants. Research and development. Accounting procedures. Currency. Financial programs. Funding procedures. Tax exemptions. Customs exemptions.
INTL ORGS: Special Commission.
TREATY REF: 187LTS125; 262UNTS3.
PROCEDURE: Amendment.
PARTIES:
Chile
USA (United States)
ANNEX
336 UNTS 366. Chile. Amendment 17 Sep 58. Force 17 Sep 58.
336 UNTS 366. USA (United States). Amendment 18 Aug 58. Force 17 Sep 58.
445 UNTS 340. USA (United States). Amendment 17 Nov 61. Force 8 Feb 62.
445 UNTS 340. Chile. Amendment 8 Feb 62. Force 8 Feb 62.

103737 Bilateral Exchange **262 UNTS 35**
SIGNED: 14 Dec 54   FORCE: 14 Dec 54
REGISTERED: 19 Mar 57 USA (United States)
ARTICLES: 3 LANGUAGE: English.
HEADNOTE: ESTABLISHMENT OPERATION SHAPE DEFENSE TECHNICAL CENTER
TOPIC: Milit Assistance
CONCEPTS: Annex or appendix reference. Privileges and immunities. Licenses and permits. Immovable property. Private contracts. Responsibility and liability. Use of facilities. Establishment of commission. Accounting procedures. Currency. Exchange rates and regulations. Local currency. Tax exemptions. Patents, copyrights and trademarks. Customs exemptions. Joint defense. Defense and security. Security of information. Exchange of defense information.
INTL ORGS: North Atlantic Treaty Organization.
TREATY REF: 34UNTS243; 80UNTS219.
PARTIES:
Netherlands
USA (United States)

103738 Bilateral Agreement **262 UNTS 87**
SIGNED: 21 Jun 55   FORCE: 21 Jun 55
REGISTERED: 19 Mar 57 USA (United States)
ARTICLES: 6 LANGUAGE: English.
HEADNOTE: SURPLUS AGRI COMMOD TITLE I
TOPIC: US Agri Commod Aid
CONCEPTS: General provisions. Treaty implementation. Conformity with municipal law. General cooperation. Currency deposits. Exchange rates and regulations. Financial programs. Purchase authorizations. Local currency. Procurement. Commodities schedule. Surplus commodities.
PARTIES:
Thailand
USA (United States)
ANNEX
266 UNTS 436. Thailand. Amendment 14 Dec 56. Force 14 Dec 56.
266 UNTS 436. USA (United States). Amendment 14 Dec 56. Force 14 Dec 56.

103739 Bilateral Exchange **262 UNTS 97**
SIGNED: 26 May 55   FORCE: 26 May 55
REGISTERED: 19 Mar 57 USA (United States)
ARTICLES: 2 LANGUAGE: English.
HEADNOTE: DISPOSITION SURPLUS EQUIPMENT MATERIALS
TOPIC: Milit Assistance
CONCEPTS: Exchange of information and documents. General property. Reexport of goods, etc.. Delivery schedules. Materials, equipment and services. Surplus property. Return of equipment and recapture.
TREATY REF: 179UNTS121; 7UNTS249.
PARTIES:
Turkey
USA (United States)
ANNEX
462 UNTS 350. Turkey. Amendment 10 Aug 62. Force 10 Aug 62.
462 UNTS 350. USA (United States). Amendment 10 Aug 62. Force 10 Aug 62.

103740 Bilateral Agreement **262 UNTS 105**
SIGNED: 18 Jun 55   FORCE: 18 Jun 55
REGISTERED: 19 Mar 57 USA (United States)
ARTICLES: 10 LANGUAGE: English. Spanish.
HEADNOTE: MILITARY ASSISTANCE
TOPIC: Milit Assistance
CONCEPTS: Guarantees and safeguards. Non-prejudice to UN charter. Peaceful relations. Privileges and immunities. Conformity with municipal law. General cooperation. Inspection and observation. Public information. Use of facilities. Indemnities and reimbursements. Garnishment of funds. Local currency. Most favored nation clause. Tax exemptions. Recognition. Customs exemptions. Domestic obligation. Materials, equipment and services. Aid missions. Joint defense. Self-defense. Return of equipment and recapture. Security of information. Exchange of defense information. Restrictions on transfer.
INTL ORGS: United Nations.
TREATY REF: 21UNTS77.
PROCEDURE: Amendment. Future Procedures Contemplated. Termination.
PARTIES:
Guatemala
USA (United States)
ANNEX
307 UNTS 306. USA (United States). Supplementation 16 Dec 57. Force 16 Dec 57.
307 UNTS 306. Guatemala. Supplementation 16 Dec 57. Force 16 Dec 57.

103741 Bilateral Agreement **262 UNTS 121**
SIGNED: 28 Apr 47   FORCE: 21 Jun 55
REGISTERED: 19 Mar 57 USA (United States)
ARTICLES: 11 LANGUAGE: English. Arabic.
HEADNOTE: AIR TRANSPORT
TOPIC: Air Transport
CONCEPTS: Exceptions and exemptions. Annex or appendix reference. Conformity with municipal law. Licenses and permits. Recognition of legal documents. Use of facilities. Procedure. Existing tribunals. Competence of tribunal. Fees and exemptions. Most favored nation clause. National treatment. Customs exemptions. Competency certificate. Routes and logistics. Navigational conditions. Permit designation. Air transport. Airport facilities. Airworthiness certificates. Conditions of airlines operating permission. Operating authorizations and regulations. Licenses and certificates of nationality.
INTL ORGS: International Civil Aviation Organization.
PROCEDURE: Ratification. Registration. Termination.
PARTIES:
Syria
USA (United States)
ANNEX
283 UNTS 332. USA (United States). Amendment 30 Apr 57. Force 30 Apr 57.
283 UNTS 332. Syria. Amendment 22 Oct 56. Force 30 Apr 57.

103742 Bilateral Agreement **262 UNTS 137**
SIGNED: 16 Jun 55   FORCE: 16 Jun 55
REGISTERED: 19 Mar 57 USA (United States)
ARTICLES: 9 LANGUAGE: English. Greek.

HEADNOTE: PATENT RIGHTS TECHNICAL INFOR-
MATION DEFENSE
TOPIC: Patents/Copyrights
CONCEPTS: Laws and formalities.
INTL ORGS: Special Commission.
PROCEDURE: Termination.
PARTIES:
  Greece
  USA (United States)

103743   Bilateral Agreement   **262 UNTS 151**
SIGNED: 28 May 55   FORCE: 1 Jul 54
REGISTERED: 20 Mar 57 Sweden
ARTICLES: 12 LANGUAGE: Swedish. Norwegian.
HEADNOTE: OCEAN WEATHER STATIONS
TOPIC: Scientific Project
CONCEPTS: Annex or appendix reference. Gen-
eral cooperation. Dispute settlement. Existing tri-
bunals. Wages and salaries. Research and scien-
tific projects. Research cooperation.
Meteorology. Accounting procedures. Expense
sharing formulae. Tax exemptions. Domestic ob-
ligation.
INTL ORGS: International Civil Aviation Organiza-
tion. International Court of Justice.
TREATY REF: 215UNTS249.
PROCEDURE: Amendment. Duration. Renewal or
Revival. Termination.
PARTIES:
  Norway
  Sweden

103744   Bilateral Agreement   **262 UNTS 187**
SIGNED: 31 Mar 54   FORCE: 15 Jul 54
REGISTERED: 20 Mar 57 Sweden
ARTICLES: 9 LANGUAGE: English.
HEADNOTE: INDUSTRIAL PROPERTY PROTEC-
TION
TOPIC: Claims and Debts
CONCEPTS: Laws and formalities. Post-war adjust-
ment. Recognition.
TREATY REF: 192LTS17; 174LTS289;
74BFSP44; 1UNTS269.
PARTIES:
  Japan
  Sweden

103745   Bilateral Exchange   **262 UNTS 199**
SIGNED: 30 Sep 54   FORCE: 1 Oct 54
REGISTERED: 20 Mar 57 Sweden
ARTICLES: 2 LANGUAGE: Swedish. Danish.
HEADNOTE: REGISTRATION TRADEMARKS
TOPIC: Patents/Copyrights
CONCEPTS: Trademarks.
TREATY REF: 192LTS17.
PROCEDURE: Denunciation. Duration.
PARTIES:
  Denmark
  Sweden

103746   Bilateral Exchange   **262 UNTS 205**
SIGNED: 25 Sep 54   FORCE: 1 Oct 54
REGISTERED: 20 Mar 57 Sweden
ARTICLES: 2 LANGUAGE: French.
HEADNOTE: REGISTRATION TRADEMARKS
TOPIC: Patents/Copyrights
CONCEPTS: Conformity with municipal law. Trade-
marks.
TREATY REF: 192LTS17.
PROCEDURE: Denunciation. Duration.
PARTIES:
  Sweden
  Switzerland

103747   Bilateral Exchange   **262 UNTS 211**
SIGNED: 28 Oct 54   FORCE: 28 Oct 54
REGISTERED: 20 Mar 57 Sweden
ARTICLES: 2 LANGUAGE: Swedish. Danish.
HEADNOTE: DELIVERY FOOT-MOUTH DISEASE
VACCINE
TOPIC: Sanitation
CONCEPTS: Conditions. Detailed regulations. In-
spection and observation. Responsibility and lia-
bility. International circulation. Disease control.
Export quotas. Import quotas. Reexport of goods,
etc.. Currency.
PROCEDURE: Denunciation. Duration.

PARTIES:
  Denmark
  Sweden

103748   Bilateral Exchange   **262 UNTS 229**
SIGNED: 5 Nov 54   FORCE: 5 Nov 54
REGISTERED: 20 Mar 57 Sweden
ARTICLES: 2 LANGUAGE: French.
HEADNOTE: DOUBLE TAXATION TEACHERS STU-
DENTS
TOPIC: Taxation
CONCEPTS: Annex type material. Teacher and stu-
dent exchange. Taxation.
TREATY REF: 184LTS35; 198LTS201.
PARTIES:
  France
  Sweden

103749   Bilateral Exchange   **262 UNTS 235**
SIGNED: 7 Dec 55   FORCE: 7 Dec 55
REGISTERED: 20 Mar 57 Sweden
ARTICLES: 2 LANGUAGE: Swedish. Danish.
HEADNOTE: TERMINATING 21 NOV 25 DECLARA-
TION
TOPIC: Admin Cooperation
CONCEPTS: Annex type material.
TREATY REF: 208UNTS3;42LTS55.
PARTIES:
  Denmark
  Sweden

103750   Bilateral Exchange   **262 UNTS 241**
SIGNED: 23 Sep 55   FORCE: 23 Sep 55
REGISTERED: 20 Mar 57 Sweden
ARTICLES: 2 LANGUAGE: Swedish. Icelandic.
HEADNOTE: TERMINATING 10 MAR 28 DECLARA-
TION
TOPIC: Admin Cooperation
CONCEPTS: Annex type material.
TREATY REF: 71LTS315; 208UNTS3;
209LTS354.
PARTIES:
  Iceland
  Sweden

103751   Bilateral Exchange   **262 UNTS 247**
SIGNED: 23 Nov 55   FORCE: 23 Nov 55
REGISTERED: 20 Mar 57 Sweden
ARTICLES: 2 LANGUAGE: French.
HEADNOTE: TERMINATING 24 DEC 27 DECLARA-
TION
TOPIC: Admin Cooperation
CONCEPTS: Annex type material.
TREATY REF: 71LTS391; 208UNTS3;
209UNTS354.
PARTIES:
  Netherlands
  Sweden

103752   Bilateral Exchange   **262 UNTS 253**
SIGNED: 7 Oct 55   FORCE: 7 Oct 55
REGISTERED: 20 Mar 57 Sweden
ARTICLES: 2 LANGUAGE: Swedish. Norwegian.
HEADNOTE: TERMINATING 22 DEC 24 DECLARA-
TION
TOPIC: Admin Cooperation
CONCEPTS: Annex type material.
TREATY REF: 208UNTS3; 32LTS14.
PARTIES:
  Norway
  Sweden

103753   Bilateral Agreement   **262 UNTS 259**
SIGNED: 18 Oct 54   FORCE: 25 May 55
REGISTERED: 20 Mar 57 Sweden
ARTICLES: 4 LANGUAGE: English.
HEADNOTE: DOUBLE TAXATION BUSINESS SEA
AIR TRANSPORT
TOPIC: Taxation
CONCEPTS: Definition of terms. Taxation. Air
transport. Merchant vessels.
PROCEDURE: Ratification. Termination.
PARTIES:
  Ireland
  Sweden

103754   Bilateral Exchange   **262 UNTS 265**
SIGNED: 5 Aug 55   FORCE: 15 Aug 55
REGISTERED: 20 Mar 57 Sweden
ARTICLES: 4 LANGUAGE: German.
HEADNOTE: RECOGNITION DRIVING PERMITS
MOTOR-VEHICLE REGISTRATION CERTIFI-
CATES
TOPIC: Land Transport
CONCEPTS: Driving permits. Road rules.
PROCEDURE: Termination.
PARTIES:
  Germany, West
  Sweden

103755   Bilateral Agreement   **262 UNTS 273**
SIGNED: 17 Sep 55   FORCE: 17 Sep 55
REGISTERED: 20 Mar 57 Sweden
ARTICLES: 5 LANGUAGE: Swedish. Icelandic.
HEADNOTE: TAXATION INCOME SEA AIR TRANS-
PORT
TOPIC: Taxation
CONCEPTS: Definition of terms. Taxation. Air
transport. Merchant vessels.
PROCEDURE: Termination.
PARTIES:
  Iceland
  Sweden

103756   Bilateral Exchange   **262 UNTS 283**
SIGNED: 17 Oct 55   FORCE: 1 Nov 55
REGISTERED: 20 Mar 57 Sweden
ARTICLES: 2 LANGUAGE: German.
HEADNOTE: DOUBLE TAXATION MOTOR VEHI-
CLES
TOPIC: Taxation
CONCEPTS: Taxation. Motor vehicles and combi-
nations.
PROCEDURE: Denunciation.
PARTIES:
  Austria
  Sweden

103757   Bilateral Exchange   **262 UNTS 289**
SIGNED: 3 Nov 55   FORCE: 1 Jan 56
REGISTERED: 20 Mar 57 Sweden
ARTICLES: 2 LANGUAGE: German.
HEADNOTE: EXCHANGE STUDENT EMPLOYEES
TOPIC: Non-ILO Labor
CONCEPTS: Definition of terms. Detailed regula-
tions. Resident permits. Conformity with munici-
pal law. Dispute settlement. Vocational training.
Employment regulations. Wages and salaries.
Non-ILO labor relations. Administrative cooper-
ation. Migrant worker. Quotas.
PROCEDURE: Denunciation. Duration. Renewal or
Revival.
PARTIES:
  Austria
  Sweden

103758   Bilateral Agreement   **262 UNTS 301**
SIGNED: 17 Jan 56   FORCE: 1 Mar 56
REGISTERED: 20 Mar 57 Sweden
ARTICLES: 11 LANGUAGE: German.
HEADNOTE: SATISFACTION CLAIMS
TOPIC: Reparations
CONCEPTS: Annex type material. Exchange of in-
formation and documents. Accounting proce-
dures. Debt settlement. Post-war claims settle-
ment.
PARTIES:
  Germany, West
  Sweden

103759   Bilateral Protocol   **262 UNTS 335**
SIGNED: 29 Jun 56   FORCE: 29 Jun 56
REGISTERED: 20 Mar 57 Sweden
ARTICLES: 12 LANGUAGE: Swedish. Norwegian.
HEADNOTE: CONSTRUCTION MAINTENANCE
REINDEER FENCE
TOPIC: Specific Resources
CONCEPTS: Annex or appendix reference. Inspec-
tion and observation. Arbitration. Special tribu-
nals. Indemnities and reimbursements. Financial
programs. Plans and standards. Fish, wildlife,
and natural resources. Wildlife.
INTL ORGS: Arbitration Commission.
PROCEDURE: Denunciation. Duration. Renewal or
Revival.

PARTIES:
Norway
Sweden
ANNEX
427 UNTS 379. Sweden. Amendment 13 Feb 58.
Force 13 Feb 58.
427 UNTS 379. Norway. Amendment 13 Feb 58.
Force 13 Feb 58.

103760 Bilateral Exchange **262 UNTS 355**
SIGNED: 14 Aug 56   FORCE: 14 Aug 56
REGISTERED: 20 Mar 57 Sweden
ARTICLES: 2 LANGUAGE: German.
HEADNOTE: TAX EXEMPTIONS CERTAIN INCOME
TOPIC: Taxation
CONCEPTS: Previous treaty replacement. Teacher
and student exchange. Tax exemptions.
TREATY REF: 198UNTS9; 81LTS281.
PARTIES:
Austria
Sweden

103761 Bilateral Agreement **262 UNTS 361**
SIGNED: 22 Mar 57   FORCE: 3 Sep 56
REGISTERED: 20 Mar 57 Sweden
ARTICLES: 12 LANGUAGE: Swedish. German.
HEADNOTE: GERMAN ASSETS
TOPIC: Claims and Debts
CONCEPTS: Detailed regulations. Territorial appli-
cation. General provisions. Treaty implementa-
tion. Treaty interpretation. General property. Ar-
bitration. Claims and settlements. Enemy finan-
cial interests.
INTL ORGS: International Court of Justice.
TREATY REF: 125UNTS199; 125UNTS301;
125UNTS423; 125UNTS401.
PROCEDURE: Future Procedures Contemplated.
Ratification.
PARTIES:
Germany, West
Sweden

103762 Bilateral Agreement **262 UNTS 401**
SIGNED: 22 Mar 56   FORCE: 3 Sep 56
REGISTERED: 20 Mar 57 Sweden
ARTICLES: 7 LANGUAGE: Swedish. German.
HEADNOTE: AGREEMENT EQUALIZATION BUR-
DENS SCHEME
TOPIC: Reparations
CONCEPTS: Annex type material. Exchange of in-
formation and documents. Most favored nation
clause. Loss and/or damage. Post-war claims
settlement.
TREATY REF: 262UNTS361.
PROCEDURE: Ratification.
PARTIES:
Germany, West
Sweden

103763 Bilateral Agreement **262 UNTS 423**
SIGNED: 22 Mar 56   FORCE: 3 Sep 56
REGISTERED: 20 Mar 57 Sweden
ARTICLES: 12 LANGUAGE: Swedish. German.
HEADNOTE: INDUSTRIAL PROPERTY RIGHTS
TOPIC: Patents/Copyrights
CONCEPTS: Non-prejudice to third party. Domes-
tic legislation. Fees and exemptions. Trade-
marks. Laws and formalities. Post-war adjust-
ment.
PROCEDURE: Ratification.
PARTIES:
Germany, West
Sweden

103764 Bilateral Agreement **263 UNTS 3**
SIGNED: 15 Sep 56   FORCE: 1 Nov 56
REGISTERED: 20 Mar 57 Sweden
ARTICLES: 7 LANGUAGE: Swedish. Danish.
HEADNOTE: RECOGNITION DRIVING PERMITS
MOTOR-VEHICLE REGISTRATION CERTIFI-
CATES
TOPIC: General Transport
CONCEPTS: Detailed regulations. Exceptions and
exemptions. Time limit. Previous treaty replace-
ment. Conformity with municipal law. Recogni-
tion of legal documents. Fees and exemptions.
Registration certificate. Driving permits. Motor
vehicles and combinations.
TREATY REF: 123LTS67.

PROCEDURE: Termination.
PARTIES:
Denmark
Sweden

103765 Bilateral Agreement **263 UNTS 17**
SIGNED: 15 Sep 56   FORCE: 1 Nov 56
REGISTERED: 20 Mar 57 Sweden
ARTICLES: 7 LANGUAGE: Swedish. Norwegian.
HEADNOTE: RECOGNITION DRIVING PERMITS
MOTOR-VEHICLE REGISTRATION CERTIFI-
CATES
TOPIC: Admin Cooperation
CONCEPTS: Exceptions and exemptions. Previous
treaty replacement. Fees and exemptions. Driv-
ing permits. Road rules.
PARTIES:
Norway
Sweden

103766 Bilateral Agreement **263 UNTS 31**
SIGNED: 24 Sep 56   FORCE: 22 Mar 57
REGISTERED: 22 Mar 57 Belgium
ARTICLES: 17 LANGUAGE: French. Dutch. German.
HEADNOTE: CULTURAL AGREEMENT
TOPIC: Culture
CONCEPTS: Definition of terms. Friendship and
amity. Conformity with municipal law. Exchange
of information and documents. Establishment of
commission. Specialists exchange. Recognition
of degrees. Teacher and student exchange. Insti-
tute establishment. Scholarships and grants. Vo-
cational training. Exchange. General cultural co-
operation. Artists. Accounting procedures. Publi-
cations exchange. Mass media exchange.
INTL ORGS: Special Commission.
PROCEDURE: Denunciation. Duration. Ratification.
Renewal or Revival.
PARTIES:
Belgium
Germany, West

103767 Bilateral Treaty **263 UNTS 49**
SIGNED: 22 Aug 56   FORCE: 28 Dec 56
REGISTERED: 25 Mar 57 Guatemala
ARTICLES: 23 LANGUAGE: Spanish.
HEADNOTE: FREE TRADE ECONOMIC INTEGRA-
TION
TOPIC: General Economic
CONCEPTS: Detailed regulations. Exceptions and
exemptions. Treaty implementation. Treaty interpretation. Annex or appendix reference. General
cooperation. Exchange of information and documents. Informational records. Free passage and
transit. General property. Public information. Establishment of commission. Arbitration. General
economics. Export quotas. Import quotas. Free
trade. Trade agencies. Trade procedures. Banking. Indemnities and reimbursements. Monetary
and gold transfers. Investments. Non-interest
rates and fees. Transportation costs. Quotas.
Most favored nation clause. National treatment.
General. Tax exemptions. Customs duties. Conservation. General transportation. Routes and logistics. Transport of goods.
INTL ORGS: Special Commission.
PROCEDURE: Denunciation. Duration. Ratification.
PARTIES:
Guatemala
Honduras

103768 Bilateral Instrument **263 UNTS 99**
SIGNED: 19 Oct 56   FORCE: 12 Dec 56
REGISTERED: 25 Mar 57 USSR (Soviet Union)
ARTICLES: 1 LANGUAGE: Russian. Japanese.
HEADNOTE: JOINT DECLARATION
TOPIC: General Amity
CONCEPTS: Peaceful relations. Repatriation of na-
tionals. Consular relations establishment. Diplo-
matic relations establishment. General cooper-
ation. Procedure. Claims and settlements. Repa-
rations and restrictions. Ocean resources.
INTL ORGS: United Nations.
PROCEDURE: Future Procedures Contemplated.
Ratification.
PARTIES:
Japan
USSR (Soviet Union)

103769 Bilateral Protocol **263 UNTS 119**
SIGNED: 19 Oct 56   FORCE: 12 Dec 56
REGISTERED: 25 Mar 57 USSR (Soviet Union)
ARTICLES: 1 LANGUAGE: Russian. Japanese.
HEADNOTE: EXPANSION TRADE RECIPROCAL
GRANT MOST FAVORED NATION TREATMENT
TOPIC: General Economic
CONCEPTS: Exceptions and exemptions. Most fa-
vored nation clause. Ports and pilotage.
PROCEDURE: Ratification.
PARTIES:
Japan
USSR (Soviet Union)

103770 Bilateral Agreement **263 UNTS 129**
SIGNED: 5 Jul 56   FORCE: 7 Dec 56
REGISTERED: 25 Mar 57 USSR (Soviet Union)
ARTICLES: 6 LANGUAGE: Russian. Chinese.
HEADNOTE: CULTURAL COOPERATION
TOPIC: Culture
CONCEPTS: Friendship and amity. Establishment
of commission. Exchange. Teacher and student
exchange. Exchange. General cultural cooper-
ation. Artists. Athletes. Research results. Scien-
tific exchange. Research and development. Ac-
counting procedures. Publications exchange.
Mass media exchange. Press and wire services.
PROCEDURE: Duration. Future Procedures Con-
templated. Ratification. Renewal or Revival. Ter-
mination.
PARTIES:
China People's Rep
USSR (Soviet Union)

103771 Bilateral Convention **263 UNTS 143**
SIGNED: 30 May 56   FORCE: 7 Aug 56
REGISTERED: 25 Mar 57 USSR (Soviet Union)
ARTICLES: 10 LANGUAGE: Russian. German.
HEADNOTE: PROTECTION AGRICULTURAL
PLANTS
TOPIC: Sanitation
CONCEPTS: Definition of terms. General cooper-
ation. Inspection and observation. Specialists
exchange. Quarantine. Border control. Disease
control. Insect control. Research and develop-
ment. Trade procedures. Accounting proce-
dures. General technical assistance. Materials,
equipment and services. Conferences.
PROCEDURE: Amendment. Duration. Future Proce-
dures Contemplated. Ratification. Renewal or
Revival. Termination.
PARTIES:
Germany, East
USSR (Soviet Union)

103772 Multilateral Instrument **263 UNTS 165**
SIGNED: 29 Oct 56   FORCE: 29 Oct 56
REGISTERED: 26 Mar 57 USA (United States)
ARTICLES: 1 LANGUAGE: French.
HEADNOTE: FINAL DECLARATION
TOPIC: Territory Boundary
CONCEPTS: Annex or appendix reference.
Changes of territory.
PARTIES:
Belgium SIGNED: 29 Oct 56 FORCE: 29 Oct 56
France SIGNED: 29 Oct 56 FORCE: 29 Oct 56
Italy SIGNED: 29 Oct 56 FORCE: 29 Oct 56
Morocco SIGNED: 29 Oct 56 FORCE: 29 Oct 56
Netherlands SIGNED: 29 Oct 56 FORCE:
29 Oct 56
Portugal SIGNED: 29 Oct 56 FORCE: 29 Oct 56
Spain SIGNED: 29 Oct 56 FORCE: 29 Oct 56
UK Great Britain SIGNED: 29 Oct 56 FORCE:
29 Oct 56
USA (United States) SIGNED: 29 Oct 56 FORCE:
29 Oct 56

103773 Bilateral Exchange **263 UNTS 181**
SIGNED: 11 Aug 56   FORCE: 16 Nov 56
REGISTERED: 26 Mar 57 USA (United States)
ARTICLES: 2 LANGUAGE: English. Spanish.
HEADNOTE: ESTABLISHMENT RAWINSONDE OB-
SERVATION STATION
TOPIC: Scientific Project
CONCEPTS: Operating agencies. Research coop-
eration. Meteorology.
PARTIES:
Dominican Republic
USA (United States)

103774 Bilateral Agreement **263 UNTS 193**
SIGNED: 7 Dec 56 FORCE: 7 Dec 56
REGISTERED: 26 Mar 57 USA (United States)
ARTICLES: 34 LANGUAGE: English. Spanish.
HEADNOTE: NAVAL MISSION
TOPIC: Military Mission
CONCEPTS: Definition of terms. Use of facilities. Compensation. Indemnities and reimbursements. Currency. Exchange rates and regulations. Expense sharing formulae. Claims and settlements. Tax exemptions. Customs exemptions. Military assistance. Military training. Security of information. Airforce-army-navy personnel ratio. Ranks and privileges. Conditions for assistance missions. Third country military personnel. Status of forces.
PROCEDURE: Termination.
PARTIES:
Dominican Republic
USA (United States)
ANNEX
482 UNTS 376. Dominican Republic. Force 18 Sep 60.
482 UNTS 376. USA (United States). Force 18 Sep 60.

103775 Bilateral Agreement **263 UNTS 221**
SIGNED: 30 Oct 56 FORCE: 30 Oct 56
REGISTERED: 26 Mar 57 USA (United States)
ARTICLES: 6 LANGUAGE: English. Italian.
HEADNOTE: AGRI COMMOD TITLE I
TOPIC: US Agri Commod Aid
CONCEPTS: General provisions. Exchange of information and documents. Reexport of goods, etc.. Exchange rates and regulations. Transportation costs. Local currency. Commodities schedule. Purchase authorization. Surplus commodities. Mutual consultation.
PARTIES:
Italy
USA (United States)
ANNEX
279 UNTS 344. Italy. Amendment 7 Jan 57. Force 7 Jan 57.
279 UNTS 344. USA (United States). Amendment 7 Jan 57. Force 7 Jan 57.
280 UNTS 384. Italy. Amendment 28 Jan 57. Force 1 Feb 57.
280 UNTS 384. USA (United States). Amendment 1 Feb 57. Force 1 Feb 57.
283 UNTS 336. Italy. Amendment 26 Mar 57. Force 26 Mar 57.
283 UNTS 336. USA (United States). Amendment 26 Mar 57. Force 26 Mar 57.
340 UNTS 380. USA (United States). Amendment 30 Jun 58. Force 30 Jun 58.
340 UNTS 380. Italy. Amendment 30 Jun 58. Force 30 Jun 58.
416 UNTS 337. Italy. Amendment 23 May 61. Force 23 May 61.
416 UNTS 337. USA (United States). Amendment 23 May 61. Force 23 May 61.

103776 Bilateral Exchange **263 UNTS 247**
SIGNED: 9 Mar 55 FORCE: 9 Mar 55
REGISTERED: 26 Mar 57 USA (United States)
ARTICLES: 2 LANGUAGE: English. Spanish.
HEADNOTE: TECHNICAL COOPERATION INDUSTRIAL PRODUCTIVITY
TOPIC: Tech Assistance
CONCEPTS: Exceptions and exemptions. Treaty implementation. Annex type material. Privileges and immunities. General cooperation. Exchange of information and documents. Informational records. Inspection and observation. Operating agencies. Personnel. Public information. Private contracts. Title and deeds. Vocational training. Accounting procedures. Bonds. Currency deposits. Exchange rates and regulations. Expense sharing formulae. Funding procedures. Assets. Tax exemptions. Customs exemptions. Domestic obligation. General technical assistance. Assistance. Industry.
TREATY REF: 141UNTS121; 200UNTS312.
PROCEDURE: Duration. Termination.
PARTIES:
Mexico
USA (United States)

103777 Bilateral Exchange **263 UNTS 273**
SIGNED: 16 May 55 FORCE: 16 May 55

REGISTERED: 27 Mar 57 USA (United States)
ARTICLES: 2 LANGUAGE: English. French.
HEADNOTE: MILITARY ASSISTANCE
TOPIC: Milit Assistance
CONCEPTS: Annex or appendix reference. Nonprejudice to UN charter. Peaceful relations. Conformity with municipal law. General cooperation. Inspection and observation. Use of facilities. Indemnities and reimbursements. Local currency. Aid missions. Surplus property. Self-defense. Military assistance. Return of equipment and recapture. Security of information. Military assistance missions. Ranks and privileges. Exchange of defense information. Restrictions on transfer.
PROCEDURE: Amendment. Future Procedures Contemplated. Termination.
PARTIES:
Cambodia
USA (United States)

103778 Bilateral Exchange **263 UNTS 285**
SIGNED: 7 Apr 55 FORCE: 7 Apr 55
REGISTERED: 27 Mar 57 USA (United States)
ARTICLES: 2 LANGUAGE: English. Japanese.
HEADNOTE: PRODUCTIVITY PROGRAM
TOPIC: Tech Assistance
CONCEPTS: Detailed regulations. General cooperation. Operating agencies. Personnel. Vocational training. Expense sharing formulae. Domestic obligation. Assistance. Materials, equipment and services.
PARTIES:
Japan
USA (United States)

103779 Bilateral Exchange **263 UNTS 299**
SIGNED: 25 Apr 55 FORCE: 25 Apr 55
REGISTERED: 27 Mar 57 USA (United States)
ARTICLES: 2 LANGUAGE: English.
HEADNOTE: DEFENSE FACILITIES ASSISTANCE
TOPIC: Milit Assistance
CONCEPTS: Change of circumstances. Annex or appendix reference. Use of facilities. Materials, equipment and services. Defense and security. Military assistance. Equipment and supplies.
TREATY REF: 7UNTS299.
PARTIES:
Turkey
USA (United States)

103780 Bilateral Agreement **263 UNTS 309**
SIGNED: 30 Apr 55 FORCE: 30 Apr 55
REGISTERED: 27 Mar 57 USA (United States)
ARTICLES: 13 LANGUAGE: English. Spanish.
HEADNOTE: COOPERATIVE PROGRAM IRRIGATION TRANSPORTATION INDUSTRY
TOPIC: General Aid
CONCEPTS: Previous treaty replacement. Privileges and immunities. General cooperation. Informational records. Inspection and observation. Domestic legislation. Personnel. Responsibility and liability. Title and deeds. Establishment of commission. Attachment of funds. Currency deposits. Exchange rates and regulations. Expense sharing formulae. Funding procedures. Garnishment of funds. Seizure funds. Assets. Tax exemptions. Customs exemptions. Domestic obligation. Industry. Irrigation. General transportation.
TREATY REF: US'TIAS 2772; 4UTS132;C.
PROCEDURE: Duration. Termination.
PARTIES:
Peru
USA (United States)

103781 Bilateral Agreement **263 UNTS 337**
SIGNED: 23 Jun 55 FORCE: 23 Jun 55
REGISTERED: 27 Mar 57 USA (United States)
ARTICLES: 6 LANGUAGE: English. Spanish.
HEADNOTE: AGRI COMMOD AGREE
TOPIC: US Agri Commod Aid
CONCEPTS: Detailed regulations. General provisions. Guarantees and safeguards. General cooperation. Accounting procedures. Currency deposits. Exchange rates and regulations. Local currency. Agricultural commodities assistance. Commodities schedule. Purchase authorization. Surplus commodities.
PARTIES:
Colombia
USA (United States)

ANNEX
283 UNTS 345. USA (United States). Interpretation 16 Apr 57. Force 16 Apr 57.
283 UNTS 345. Colombia. Interpretation 16 Apr 57. Force 16 Apr 57.
487 UNTS 345. USA (United States). Amendment 14 Aug 63. Force 14 Aug 63.
487 UNTS 345. Colombia. Amendment 14 Aug 63. Force 14 Aug 63.

103782 Bilateral Exchange **263 UNTS 351**
SIGNED: 14 Apr 55 FORCE: 19 Apr 55
REGISTERED: 27 Mar 57 USA (United States)
ARTICLES: 2 LANGUAGE: English.
HEADNOTE: SETTLEMENT OBLIGATION SURPLUS PROPERTY
TOPIC: General Military
CONCEPTS: Indemnities and reimbursements. Interest rates. Payment schedules. Local currency. Claims and settlements. Debts. Debt settlement. Surplus property. Surplus war property.
TREATY REF: 233UNTS231; 205UNTS103.
PARTIES:
Germany, West
USA (United States)

103783 Bilateral Agreement **263 UNTS 361**
SIGNED: 5 Feb 53 FORCE: 1 Feb 53
REGISTERED: 27 Mar 57 Greece
ARTICLES: 10 LANGUAGE: French.
HEADNOTE: TRADE
TOPIC: General Trade
CONCEPTS: Definition of terms. Territorial application. Treaty implementation. Annex or appendix reference. Previous treaty replacement. General cooperation. Licenses and permits. Establishment of commission. Trade procedures. Payment schedules. Quotas.
INTL ORGS: Organization for Economic Co-operation and Development. Special Commission.
TREATY REF: 4AUG51.
PROCEDURE: Duration. Renewal or Revival. Termination.
PARTIES:
Greece
Netherlands
ANNEX
268 UNTS 400. Netherlands. Prolongation 16 May 56. Force 23 Jun 56.
268 UNTS 400. Greece. Prolongation 23 Jun 56. Force 23 Jun 56.

103784 Bilateral Agreement **263 UNTS 381**
SIGNED: 2 Nov 55 FORCE: 26 Mar 56
REGISTERED: 27 Mar 57 UK Great Britain
ARTICLES: 12 LANGUAGE: English. Dutch.
HEADNOTE: MIGRATION
TOPIC: Non-ILO Labor
CONCEPTS: Definition of terms. Territorial application. Border traffic and migration. Resident permits. Repatriation of nationals. Exchange of information and documents. Recognition of legal documents. Non-ILO labor relations. Administrative cooperation.
PROCEDURE: Ratification.
PARTIES:
Fed Rhod/Nyasaland
Netherlands
ANNEX
528 UNTS 302. Netherlands. Implementation 13 Jul 56. Force 13 Jul 56.
528 UNTS 302. Fed Rhod/Nyasaland. Implementation 6 Jul 56. Force 13 Jul 56.
528 UNTS 302. Netherlands. Termination 29 Aug 63. Force 31 Dec 63.
528 UNTS 302. Fed Rhod/Nyasaland. Termination 29 Aug 63. Force 31 Dec 63.

103785 Bilateral Agreement **264 UNTS 3**
SIGNED: 1 Nov 56 FORCE: 1 Nov 56
REGISTERED: 27 Mar 57 UK Great Britain
ARTICLES: 26 LANGUAGE: English.
HEADNOTE: OCEANOGRAPHIC RESEARCH STATIONS
TOPIC: Scientific Project
CONCEPTS: Definition of terms. Border traffic and migration. Privileges and immunities. General cooperation. Juridical personality. Free passage and transit. Incorporation of treaty provisions into national law. General property. Use of facili-

ties. Public health. Research and scientific projects. Communication satellites testing. Claims and settlements. Taxation. Tax exemptions. Domestic obligation. Special projects. Navigational equipment. Postal services. Security of information. Jurisdiction.
PROCEDURE: Amendment. Duration. Renewal or Revival. Termination.
PARTIES:
UK Great Britain
USA (United States)
ANNEX
299 UNTS 424. UK Great Britain. Supplementation 30 Oct 57. Force 30 Oct 57.
299 UNTS 424. USA (United States). Supplementation 30 Oct 57. Force 30 Oct 57.

103786 Bilateral Agreement **264 UNTS 37**
SIGNED: 21 Dec 49   FORCE: 12 May 56
REGISTERED: 27 Mar 57 UK Great Britain
ARTICLES: 10 LANGUAGE: English. French.
HEADNOTE: MILITARY SERVICE
TOPIC: Milit Servic/Citiz
CONCEPTS: Definition of terms. Procedure. Dual nationality. Certificates of service. Service in foreign army.
PROCEDURE: Ratification. Termination.
PARTIES:
France
UK Great Britain

103787 Bilateral Convention **264 UNTS 45**
SIGNED: 9 Jul 56   FORCE: 1 Jan 57
REGISTERED: 27 Mar 57 UK Great Britain
ARTICLES: 12 LANGUAGE: English. Danish.
HEADNOTE: INDUSTRIAL INJURY COMPENSATION
TOPIC: Non-ILO Labor
CONCEPTS: Definition of terms. Territorial application. Domestic legislation. Old age and invalidity insurance. Wages and salaries. Non-ILO labor relations. Sickness and invalidity insurance. Payment schedules. National treatment.
PROCEDURE: Duration. Ratification. Termination.
PARTIES:
Denmark
UK Great Britain

103788 Bilateral Exchange **264 UNTS 61**
SIGNED: 8 Dec 56   FORCE: 8 Dec 56
REGISTERED: 27 Mar 57 UK Great Britain
ARTICLES: 2 LANGUAGE: English.
HEADNOTE: DEBT REPAYMENT
TOPIC: Claims and Debts
CONCEPTS: Compensation. Purchase authorization.
INTL ORGS: European Payments Union.
PARTIES:
Sweden
UK Great Britain

103789 Bilateral Agreement **264 UNTS 67**
SIGNED: 27 Oct 56   FORCE: 27 Oct 56
REGISTERED: 27 Mar 57 UK Great Britain
ARTICLES: 14 LANGUAGE: English. German.
HEADNOTE: AIR SERVICES BETWEEN BEYOND RESPECTIVE TERRITORIES
TOPIC: Air Transport
CONCEPTS: Conditions. Definition of terms. Detailed regulations. Exceptions and exemptions. Annex or appendix reference. Conformity with municipal law. Exchange of information and documents. Arbitration. Procedure. Existing tribunals. Negotiation. Monetary and gold transfers. Non-interest rates and fees. Most favored nation clause. National treatment. Customs exemptions. Routes and logistics. Permit designation. Conditions of airlines operating permission. Overflights and technical stops. Operating authorizations and regulations.
INTL ORGS: International Civil Aviation Organization. Organization for Economic Co-operation and Development.
TREATY REF: 15UNTS295.
PROCEDURE: Amendment. Future Procedures Contemplated. Registration. Termination. Application to Non-self-governing Territories.
PARTIES:
Austria
UK Great Britain

103790 Multilateral Agreement **264 UNTS 94**
SIGNED: 1 Mar 57   FORCE: 1 Mar 57
REGISTERED: 1 Apr 57 United Nations
ARTICLES: 6 LANGUAGE: Spanish.
HEADNOTE: TECHNICAL ASSISTANCE
TOPIC: Tech Assistance
CONCEPTS: Definition of terms. Previous treaty replacement. Privileges and immunities. General cooperation. Personnel. Public information. Responsibility and liability. Title and deeds. Use of facilities. Exchange. Scholarships and grants. Vocational training. Research and development. Accounting procedures. Exchange rates and regulations. Expense sharing formulae. Local currency. Domestic obligation. General technical assistance. Materials, equipment and services. IGO status. Conformity with IGO decisions.
INTL ORGS: Food and Agricultural Organization of the United Nations. International Labour Organization. United Nations Educational, Scientific and Cultural Organization. United Nations.
TREATY REF: 76UNTS132; 1UNTS15,263.
PROCEDURE: Amendment. Termination.
PARTIES:
Bolivia SIGNED: 1 Mar 57 FORCE: 1 Mar 57
FAO (Food Agri) SIGNED: 1 Mar 57 FORCE: 1 Mar 57
ICAO (Civil Aviat) SIGNED: 1 Mar 57 FORCE: 1 Mar 57
ILO (Labor Org) SIGNED: 1 Mar 57 FORCE: 1 Mar 57
ITU (Telecommun) SIGNED: 1 Mar 57 FORCE: 1 Mar 57
UNESCO (Educ/Cult) SIGNED: 1 Mar 57 FORCE: 1 Mar 57
United Nations SIGNED: 1 Mar 57 FORCE: 1 Mar 57
WHO (World Health) SIGNED: 1 Mar 57 FORCE: 1 Mar 57
WMO (Meteorology) SIGNED: 1 Mar 57 FORCE: 1 Mar 57
ANNEX
480 UNTS 350. UNTAB (Tech Assis). Amendment 24 Sep 63. Force 24 Sep 63.
480 UNTS 350. Bolivia. Amendment 24 Sep 63. Force 24 Sep 63.
659 UNTS 340. UNIDO (Industrial). Accession 30 Sep 68. Force 30 Sep 68.
659 UNTS 340. IMCO (Maritime Org). Accession 30 Sep 68. Force 30 Sep 68.

103791 Multilateral Agreement **264 UNTS 117**
SIGNED: 25 May 55   FORCE: 20 Jul 56
REGISTERED: 4 Apr 57 IBRD (World Bank)
ARTICLES: 9 LANGUAGE: English.
HEADNOTE: INTERNATIONAL FINANCE CORP
TOPIC: IGO Establishment
CONCEPTS: Treaty interpretation. Treaty violation. Privileges and immunities. Conformity with municipal law. Exchange of official publications. Juridical personality. Arbitration. Finances and payments. Accounting procedures. Banking. Currency deposits. Investments. Exchange rates and regulations. Expense sharing formulae. Financial programs. Funding procedures. Garnishment of funds. Legal costs. Transportation costs. Mutual exchange of technical knowledge. Admission. Headquarters and facilities. Liaison with other IGO's. Internal structure. IGO status. Special status. Status of experts. Conformity with IGO decisions. Inter-agency agreements. Socio-economic development.
INTL ORGS: International Bank for Reconstruction and Development. International Finance Corporation.
PROCEDURE: Amendment. Denunciation.
PARTIES:
Australia SIGNED: 23 Dec 55 RATIFIED: 23 Dec 55 FORCE: 20 Jul 56
Austria SIGNED: 2 Dec 55 RATIFIED: 28 Sep 56 FORCE: 28 Sep 56
Belgium SIGNED: 27 Dec 56 RATIFIED: 27 Dec 56 FORCE: 27 Dec 56
Bolivia SIGNED: 12 Apr 56 RATIFIED: 2 Apr 56 FORCE: 20 Jul 56
Brazil SIGNED: 27 Jan 56 RATIFIED: 31 Dec 56 FORCE: 31 Dec 56
Burma SIGNED: 3 Dec 56 RATIFIED: 1 Dec 56 FORCE: 3 Dec 56
Canada SIGNED: 25 Oct 55 RATIFIED: 25 Oct 55 FORCE: 20 Jul 56
Ceylon (Sri Lanka) SIGNED: 27 Feb 56 RATIFIED: 27 Feb 56 FORCE: 20 Jul 56
Chile SIGNED: 25 May 55
Colombia SIGNED: 25 May 55 RATIFIED: 16 Jul 56 FORCE: 20 Jul 56
Costa Rica SIGNED: 25 May 55 RATIFIED: 5 Jan 56 FORCE: 20 Jul 56
Cuba SIGNED: 25 May 55
Denmark SIGNED: 18 Jun 56 RATIFIED: 18 Jun 56 FORCE: 20 Jul 56
Dominican Republic SIGNED: 25 May 55 RATIFIED: 21 Feb 56 FORCE: 20 Jul 56
Ecuador SIGNED: 1 Jun 55 RATIFIED: 5 Dec 55 FORCE: 20 Jul 56
United Arab Rep SIGNED: 16 Dec 55 RATIFIED: 16 Dec 55 FORCE: 20 Jul 56
El Salvador SIGNED: 4 May 56 RATIFIED: 4 May 56 FORCE: 20 Jul 56
Ethiopia SIGNED: 26 Jan 56 RATIFIED: 26 Jan 56 FORCE: 20 Jul 56
Finland SIGNED: 2 Jun 56 RATIFIED: 22 Jun 56 FORCE: 20 Jul 56
France SIGNED: 20 Jul 56 RATIFIED: 20 Jul 56 FORCE: 20 Jul 56
Germany, West SIGNED: 20 Jul 56 RATIFIED: 20 Jul 56 FORCE: 20 Jul 56
Greece SIGNED: 25 May 55
Guatemala SIGNED: 25 May 55 RATIFIED: 10 Mar 56 FORCE: 20 Jul 56
Haiti SIGNED: 25 May 55 RATIFIED: 9 Mar 56 FORCE: 20 Jul 56
Honduras SIGNED: 25 May 55 RATIFIED: 16 Apr 56 FORCE: 20 Jul 56
Iceland SIGNED: 18 Aug 55 RATIFIED: 18 Aug 55 FORCE: 20 Jul 56
India SIGNED: 19 Oct 55 RATIFIED: 18 Apr 56 FORCE: 20 Jul 56
Indonesia SIGNED: 28 Dec 56 RATIFIED: 28 Dec 56 FORCE: 28 Dec 56
Iran SIGNED: 28 Dec 56 RATIFIED: 28 Dec 56 FORCE: 28 Dec 56
Iraq SIGNED: 9 Nov 56 RATIFIED: 27 Dec 56 FORCE: 27 Dec 56
Israel SIGNED: 26 Sep 56 RATIFIED: 26 Sep 56 FORCE: 26 Sep 56
Italy SIGNED: 27 Dec 56 RATIFIED: 27 Dec 56 FORCE: 27 Dec 56
Japan SIGNED: 15 Jun 56 RATIFIED: 15 Jun 56 FORCE: 20 Jul 56
Jordan SIGNED: 28 May 56 RATIFIED: 28 May 56 FORCE: 20 Jul 56
Lebanon SIGNED: 28 Dec 56 RATIFIED: 28 Dec 56 FORCE: 28 Dec 56
Luxembourg SIGNED: 26 Sep 56 RATIFIED: 4 Oct 56 FORCE: 4 Oct 56
Mexico SIGNED: 25 May 55 RATIFIED: 30 Dec 55 FORCE: 20 Jul 56
Netherlands SIGNED: 8 Dec 55 RATIFIED: 28 Dec 56 FORCE: 28 Dec 56
Nicaragua SIGNED: 25 May 55 RATIFIED: 14 Mar 56 FORCE: 20 Jul 56
Norway SIGNED: 1 Jun 56 RATIFIED: 11 Jun 56 FORCE: 20 Jul 56
Pakistan SIGNED: 21 Jul 55 RATIFIED: 18 May 56 FORCE: 20 Jul 56
Panama SIGNED: 25 May 55 RATIFIED: 27 Feb 56 FORCE: 20 Jul 56
Paraguay SIGNED: 25 May 55 RATIFIED: 27 Jul 56 FORCE: 27 Jul 56
Peru SIGNED: 25 May 55 RATIFIED: 6 Feb 56 FORCE: 20 Jul 56
IBRD (World Bank) SIGNED: 25 May 55
Sweden SIGNED: 6 Jun 56 RATIFIED: 6 Jun 56 FORCE: 20 Jul 56
Syria SIGNED: 30 Dec 55
Thailand SIGNED: 3 Dec 56 RATIFIED: 1 Dec 56 FORCE: 3 Dec 56
Turkey SIGNED: 18 Dec 56 RATIFIED: 19 Dec 56 FORCE: 19 Dec 56
UK Great Britain SIGNED: 25 Oct 55 RATIFIED: 3 Jan 56 FORCE: 20 Jul 56
USA (United States) SIGNED: 5 Dec 55 RATIFIED: 5 Dec 55 FORCE: 20 Jul 56
Uruguay SIGNED: 28 Sep 56
Venezuela SIGNED: 28 Dec 56 RATIFIED: 28 Dec 56 FORCE: 28 Dec 56
ANNEX
304 UNTS 387. Philippines. Signature 12 Aug 57. Acceptance 12 Aug 57.
304 UNTS 387. Fed of Malaya. Signature 20 Mar 58. Acceptance 20 Mar 58.
304 UNTS 387. South Africa. Signature 26 Mar 57. Acceptance 3 Apr 57.
304 UNTS 387. Ghana. Signature 3 Apr 58. Acceptance 3 Apr 58.
304 UNTS 387. Cuba. Acceptance 6 Sep 57.

304 UNTS 387. Chile. Acceptance 15 Apr 57.

304 UNTS 387. Afghanistan. Signature 23 Sep 57. Acceptance 23 Sep 57.

314 UNTS 357. Ireland. Signature 11 Sep 58. Acceptance 11 Sep 58.

314 UNTS 357. Libya. Signature 18 Sep 58. Acceptance 18 Sep 58.

344 UNTS 348. United Arab Rep. Replacement 10 Sep 59.

344 UNTS 348. Argentina. Signature 13 Oct 59. Acceptance 13 Oct 59.

354 UNTS 410. Spain. Signature 24 Mar 60. Acceptance 24 Mar 60.

377 UNTS 432. Sudan. Signature 21 Oct 60. Acceptance 21 Oct 60.

439 UNTS 316. Sierra Leone. Acceptance 10 Sep 62.

439 UNTS 316. Cyprus. Acceptance 2 Mar 62.

439 UNTS 316. Nigeria. Acceptance 30 Mar 61.

439 UNTS 316. Tunisia. Acceptance 25 Jul 62.

439 UNTS 316. Senegal. Acceptance 31 Aug 62.

439 UNTS 316. New Zealand. Acceptance 31 Aug 61.

439 UNTS 316. Liberia. Acceptance 28 Mar 62.

439 UNTS 316. Togo. Acceptance 4 Sep 62.

439 UNTS 316. Tanganyika. Acceptance 10 Sep 62.

439 UNTS 316. Syria. Acceptance 28 Jun 62.

439 UNTS 316. Morocco. Acceptance 30 Aug 62.

439 UNTS 316. Somalia. Acceptance 31 Aug 62.

439 UNTS 318. IFC (Finance Corp). Amendment 1 Sep 61. Force 21 Sep 61.

480 UNTS 358. Kuwait. Signature 13 Sep 62. Acceptance 13 Sep 62.

480 UNTS 358. Madagascar. Signature 27 Sep 63. Acceptance 27 Sep 63.

480 UNTS 358. Ivory Coast. Signature 11 Mar 63. Acceptance 11 Mar 63.

480 UNTS 358. Saudi Arabia. Signature 13 Sep 62. Acceptance 18 Sep 62.

480 UNTS 358. Uganda. Signature 27 Sep 63. Acceptance 27 Sep 63.

563 UNTS 362. Other Party Combin. Amendment 25 Aug 65. Force 1 Sep 65.

614 UNTS 308. Kenya. Signature 3 Feb 64. Acceptance 3 Feb 64.

614 UNTS 308. Jamaica. Signature 31 Mar 64. Acceptance 31 Mar 64.

614 UNTS 308. Vietnam, South. Signature 4 Aug 67. Acceptance 4 Aug 67.

614 UNTS 308. Malawi. Signature 19 Jul 64. Acceptance 19 Jul 64.

614 UNTS 308. Zambia. Signature 23 Sep 64. Acceptance 23 Sep 64.

614 UNTS 308. Nepal. Signature 7 Jan 66. Acceptance 7 Jan 66.

614 UNTS 308. Portugal. Signature 7 Jan 66. Acceptance 7 Jan 66.

614 UNTS 308. Guyana. Signature 4 Jan 67. Acceptance 4 Jan 66.

614 UNTS 308. Korea, South. Signature 16 Mar 64. Acceptance 16 Mar 64.

103792 Multilateral Convention **264 UNTS 163**
SIGNED: 27 Jun 46   FORCE: 24 Mar 57
REGISTERED: 4 Apr 57 ILO (Labor Org)
ARTICLES: 21 LANGUAGE: English. French.
HEADNOTE: FOOD BOARD SHIP FOR CREW
TOPIC: ILO Labor
CONCEPTS: Inspection and observation. Domestic legislation. Incorporation of treaty provisions into national law. Jurisdiction. Public health. ILO conventions. Labor statistics. Merchant vessels.
INTL ORGS: International Labour Organization.
PROCEDURE: Amendment. Denunciation. Duration. Ratification. Registration.
PARTIES:
Multilateral
                    ANNEX
304 UNTS 410. Netherlands. Ratification 17 Jun 58. Force 17 Dec 58.

318 UNTS 426. UK Great Britain. Declaration 3 Nov 58.

318 UNTS 426. Netherlands. Declaration 11 Nov 58.

318 UNTS 426. Netherlands. Declaration 11 Nov 58.

330 UNTS 372. Netherlands. Netherlands Antilles. Declaration 15 May 59.

338 UNTS 396. UK Great Britain. Declaration 7 Jul 59.

356 UNTS 377. UK Great Britain. Jersey Island.

356 UNTS 387. UK Great Britain. Guernsey Island.

381 UNTS 411. UK Great Britain. Isle of Man.

390 UNTS 363. UK Great Britain. Declaration 23 Feb 61.

429 UNTS 297. Peru. Ratification 4 Apr 62. Force 4 Apr 63.

444 UNTS 345. Algeria. Succession 19 Oct 62.

103793 Bilateral Agreement **264 UNTS 179**
SIGNED: 19 Dec 56   FORCE: 25 Mar 57
REGISTERED: 5 Apr 57 IBRD (World Bank)
ARTICLES: 5 LANGUAGE: English.
HEADNOTE: GUARANTEE AGREEMENT
TOPIC: IBRD Project
CONCEPTS: Definition of terms. Annex or appendix reference. Exchange of information and documents. Informational records. Inspection and observation. Fees and exemptions. Tax exemptions. Domestic obligation. Terms of loan. Loan regulations. Loan guarantee. Guarantor non-interference.
PARTIES:
Japan
IBRD (World Bank)

103794 Unilateral Instrument **264 UNTS 221**
SIGNED: 6 Apr 57   FORCE: 10 Apr 57
REGISTERED: 6 Apr 57 United Nations
ARTICLES: 1 LANGUAGE: French.
HEADNOTE: CREATION PERMANENT MILITARY CEMETERIES
TOPIC: ICJ Option Clause
CONCEPTS: Annex or appendix reference. Conformity with municipal law. Tax exemptions. Upkeep of war graves. Establishment of war cemeteries.
INTL ORGS: International Court of Justice.
PARTIES:
Sweden

103795 Bilateral Agreement **264 UNTS 225**
SIGNED: 3 Aug 55   FORCE: 3 Aug 55
REGISTERED: 8 Apr 57 USA (United States)
ARTICLES: 10 LANGUAGE: English. Spanish.
HEADNOTE: COOPERATIVE ROAD SERVICE
TOPIC: Non-IBRD Project
CONCEPTS: Previous treaty replacement. Operating agencies. Personnel. Title and deeds. Financial programs. Funding procedures. Non-bank projects. Roads and highways.
INTL ORGS: Special Commission.
TREATY REF: 132UNTS319; 180UNTS346.
PROCEDURE: Duration. Termination.
PARTIES:
Bolivia
USA (United States)

103796 Bilateral Agreement **264 UNTS 247**
SIGNED: 21 Jul 55   FORCE: 21 Jul 55
REGISTERED: 8 Apr 57 USA (United States)
ARTICLES: 5 LANGUAGE: English. Arabic.
HEADNOTE: TECHNICAL COOPERATION
TOPIC: Tech Assistance
CONCEPTS: Exceptions and exemptions. Treaty implementation. Previous treaty replacement. Conformity with municipal law. General cooperation. Exchange of information and documents. Inspection and observation. Personnel. Public information. Attachment of funds. Exchange rates and regulations. Funding procedures. Garnishment of funds. Seizure funds. Assets transfer. Tax exemptions. Customs exemptions. Domestic obligation. General technical assistance. Materials, equipment and services. Aid missions.
TREATY REF: 183UNTS177.
PROCEDURE: Amendment.
PARTIES:
Libya
USA (United States)

103797 Bilateral Exchange **264 UNTS 269**
SIGNED: 26 Aug 52   FORCE: 26 Aug 52
REGISTERED: 8 Apr 57 USA (United States)
ARTICLES: 2 LANGUAGE: English. Spanish.
HEADNOTE: PREVENT FOOT-MOUTH DISEASE
TOPIC: IGO Establishment
CONCEPTS: Recognition and enforcement of legal decisions. Sanitation. Quarantine. Disease con-

trol. Research cooperation. Research and development. Accounting procedures. General technical assistance. Establishment.
INTL ORGS: Special Commission.
PARTIES:
Mexico
USA (United States)

103798 Bilateral Exchange **264 UNTS 279**
SIGNED: 15 Jun 55   FORCE: 15 Jun 55
REGISTERED: 8 Apr 57 USA (United States)
ARTICLES: 2 LANGUAGE: English. French.
HEADNOTE: CLAIMS WAR DAMAGES PRIVATE PROPERTY
TOPIC: Reparations
CONCEPTS: Time limit. Treaty implementation. Exchange of information and documents. General property. National treatment. Loss and/or damage. Post-war claims settlement.
PARTIES:
Luxembourg
USA (United States)

103799 Bilateral Agreement **264 UNTS 285**
SIGNED: 9 Sep 55   FORCE: 9 Sep 55
REGISTERED: 8 Apr 57 USA (United States)
ARTICLES: 7 LANGUAGE: English.
HEADNOTE: SALE PURCHASE TIN CONCENTRATES
TOPIC: Commodity Trade
CONCEPTS: General cooperation. Currency. Exchange rates and regulations. Payment schedules. Non-interest rates and fees. Commodity trade. Delivery guarantees. Delivery schedules. Quotas. Transport of goods.
TREATY REF: 256UNTS31.
PROCEDURE: Duration. Termination.
PARTIES:
Thailand
USA (United States)

103800 Bilateral Exchange **264 UNTS 291**
SIGNED: 24 Jun 55   FORCE: 24 Jun 55
REGISTERED: 8 Apr 57 USA (United States)
ARTICLES: 2 LANGUAGE: English. French.
HEADNOTE: TECHNICAL COOPERATIVE PROJECT
TOPIC: Non-IBRD Project
CONCEPTS: Exchange of information and documents. Inspection and observation. Operating agencies. Accounting procedures. Financial programs. Funding procedures. Aid missions. Non-bank projects.
TREATY REF: 151UNTS191; 180UNTS372.
PROCEDURE: Duration. Termination.
PARTIES:
Haiti
USA (United States)

103801 Bilateral Agreement **264 UNTS 301**
SIGNED: 8 Aug 55   FORCE: 8 Aug 55
REGISTERED: 8 Apr 57 USA (United States)
ARTICLES: 10 LANGUAGE: English. Spanish.
HEADNOTE: TECHNICAL LABOR SERVICES
TOPIC: Non-IBRD Project
CONCEPTS: Privileges and immunities. Operating agencies. Non-ILO labor relations. Administrative cooperation. Financial programs. Funding procedures. Customs exemptions. Non-bank projects.
PROCEDURE: Duration. Termination.
PARTIES:
El Salvador
USA (United States)

103802 Bilateral Exchange **265 UNTS 3**
SIGNED: 22 Jul 55   FORCE: 22 Jul 55
REGISTERED: 8 Apr 57 USA (United States)
ARTICLES: 2 LANGUAGE: English. Spanish.
HEADNOTE: EXTENDING AMENDING AGREEMENT MILITARY AVIATION MISSION
TOPIC: Military Mission
CONCEPTS: Previous treaty amendment. Annex type material. Previous treaty extension. Military assistance missions.
TREATY REF: 29UNTS391.
PROCEDURE: Termination.
PARTIES:
Paraguay
USA (United States)

103803 Bilateral Exchange **265 UNTS 15**
SIGNED: 22 Jul 55 FORCE: 22 Jul 55
REGISTERED: 8 Apr 57 USA (United States)
ARTICLES: 2 LANGUAGE: English. Spanish.
HEADNOTE: EXTENDING AMENDING AGREE-
MENT MILITARY MISSION
TOPIC: Military Mission
CONCEPTS: Previous treaty amendment. Annex
type material. Previous treaty extension. Military
assistance missions.
TREATY REF: 21UNTS305.
PROCEDURE: Termination.
PARTIES:
Paraguay
USA (United States)

103804 Bilateral Exchange **265 UNTS 27**
SIGNED: 7 Jun 55 FORCE: 7 Jun 55
REGISTERED: 8 Apr 57 USA (United States)
ARTICLES: 4 LANGUAGE: English.
HEADNOTE: SURPLUS AGRICULTURAL COM-
MODITIES
TOPIC: General Military
CONCEPTS: Guarantees and safeguards. Ex-
change rates and regulations. Financial pro-
grams. Local currency. Purchase authorization.
Bases and facilities. Restrictions on transfer.
PROCEDURE: Future Procedures Contemplated.
PARTIES:
UK Great Britain
USA (United States)

103805 Bilateral Exchange **265 UNTS 41**
SIGNED: 3 Aug 55 FORCE: 10 Aug 55
REGISTERED: 8 Apr 57 USA (United States)
ARTICLES: 2 LANGUAGE: English. Spanish.
HEADNOTE: MILITARY ASSISTANCE ADVISORY
GROUP
TOPIC: Military Mission
CONCEPTS: Airforce-army-navy personnel ratio.
Ranks and privileges. Conditions for assistance
missions.
TREATY REF: 165UNTS11.
PARTIES:
Cuba
USA (United States)

103806 Bilateral Agreement **265 UNTS 49**
SIGNED: 8 Jul 55 FORCE: 6 Oct 55
REGISTERED: 8 Apr 57 USA (United States)
ARTICLES: 9 LANGUAGE: English. Spanish.
HEADNOTE: FURNISHING SUPPLIES SERVICES
NAVAL VESSELS
TOPIC: Milit Assistance
CONCEPTS: Time limit. Use of facilities. Indemni-
ties and reimbursements. Currency. Materials,
equipment and services. Ports and pilotage. Na-
val vessels.
PARTIES:
Ecuador
USA (United States)

103807 Bilateral Agreement **265 UNTS 59**
SIGNED: 25 Oct 56 FORCE: 28 Mar 57
REGISTERED: 9 Apr 57 IBRD (World Bank)
ARTICLES: 5 LANGUAGE: English.
HEADNOTE: GUARANTEE AGREEMENT
TOPIC: IBRD Project
CONCEPTS: Definition of terms. Annex or appen-
dix reference. Exchange of information and doc-
uments. Informational records. Inspection and
observation. Bonds. Tax exemptions. Domestic
obligation. Terms of loan. Loan regulations. Loan
guarantee. Guarantor non-interference.
PARTIES:
IBRD (World Bank)
Uruguay

103808 Bilateral Agreement **265 UNTS 85**
SIGNED: 15 Mar 55 FORCE: 18 Jun 55
REGISTERED: 9 Apr 57 IBRD (World Bank)
ARTICLES: 5 LANGUAGE: English.
HEADNOTE: GUARANTEE AGREEMENT
TOPIC: IBRD Project
CONCEPTS: Definition of terms. Annex or appen-
dix reference. Exchange of information and doc-
uments. Informational records. Inspection and
observation. Bonds. Fees and exemptions. Tax
exemptions. Domestic obligation. Terms of loan.

Loan regulations. Loan guarantee. Guarantor
non-interference. Water transport. Railways.
PARTIES:
IBRD (World Bank)
UK Great Britain

103809 Multilateral Agreement **265 UNTS 125**
SIGNED: 14 Jun 56 FORCE: 11 Mar 57
REGISTERED: 10 Apr 57 United Nations
ARTICLES: 6 LANGUAGE: English. Arabic.
HEADNOTE: TECHNICAL ASSISTANCE
TOPIC: Tech Assistance
CONCEPTS: Definition of terms. Annex or appen-
dix reference. Privileges and immunities. Gen-
eral cooperation. Exchange of information and
documents. Personnel. Responsibility and liabil-
ity. Title and deeds. Use of facilities. Exchange.
Scholarships and grants. Vocational training. Re-
search and development. Expense sharing for-
mulae. Local currency. Domestic obligation.
General technical assistance. Materials, equip-
ment and services. IGO status. Conformity with
IGO decisions.
TREATY REF: 76UNTS132; 1UNTS15;
1UNTS263; 33UNTS261.
PROCEDURE: Amendment. Ratification. Termina-
tion.
PARTIES:
FAO (Food Agri) SIGNED: 14 Jun 56 FORCE:
11 Mar 57
ICAO (Civil Aviat) SIGNED: 14 Jun 56 FORCE:
11 Mar 57
ILO (Labor Org) SIGNED: 14 Jun 56 FORCE:
11 Mar 57
ITU (Telecommun) SIGNED: 14 Jun 56 FORCE:
11 Mar 57
UNESCO (Educ/Cult) SIGNED: 14 Jun 56
FORCE: 11 Mar 57
United Nations SIGNED: 14 Jun 56 FORCE:
11 Mar 57
WHO (World Health) SIGNED: 14 Jun 56 FORCE:
11 Mar 57
WMO (Meteorology) SIGNED: 14 Jun 56 FORCE:
11 Mar 57
Syria SIGNED: 14 Jun 56 RATIFIED: 11 Mar 57
ANNEX
457 UNTS 312. Syria. Termination 12 Dec 62.
Force 16 Mar 63.
457 UNTS 312. UNTAB (Tech Assis). Termination
12 Dec 62. Force 16 Mar 63.

103810 Bilateral Exchange **265 UNTS 149**
SIGNED: 20 Dec 56 FORCE: 20 Dec 56
REGISTERED: 11 Apr 57 Australia
ARTICLES: 2 LANGUAGE: English.
HEADNOTE: EXCHANGE OFFICIAL PUBLICA-
TIONS
TOPIC: Admin Cooperation
CONCEPTS: Exchange of official publications. Op-
erating agencies. Indemnities and reimburse-
ments.
PARTIES:
Australia
Thailand

103811 Bilateral Agreement **265 UNTS 157**
SIGNED: 13 Jan 56 FORCE: 14 Sep 56
REGISTERED: 12 Apr 57 Poland
ARTICLES: 29 LANGUAGE: Polish. Czechoslo-
vakian.
HEADNOTE: COMMUNICATIONS AGREEMENT
TOPIC: Gen Communications
CONCEPTS: Border traffic and migration. Confor-
mity with municipal law. Negotiation. Migrant
worker. Tax exemptions. Customs exemptions.
Temporary importation. Navigational conditions.
Merchant vessels. Inland and territorial waters.
Ports and pilotage. Railway border crossing. Rail-
ways.
TREATY REF: 85UNTS62.
PROCEDURE: Amendment. Denunciation. Dura-
tion. Ratification. Renewal or Revival.
PARTIES:
Czechoslovakia
Poland

103812 Bilateral Exchange **265 UNTS 189**
SIGNED: 27 Feb 57 FORCE: 1 Apr 57
REGISTERED: 15 Apr 57 Belgium
ARTICLES: 2 LANGUAGE: French.

HEADNOTE: ISSUE GRATIS ENTRY VISAS
TOPIC: Visas
CONCEPTS: Territorial application. Time limit. Visa
abolition. Passports diplomatic. Passports non-
diplomatic. Denial of admission. Visas. Confor-
mity with municipal law. Fees and exemptions.
PROCEDURE: Denunciation.
PARTIES:
Belgium
Brazil

103813 Bilateral Agreement **265 UNTS 197**
SIGNED: 26 Feb 57 FORCE: 9 Nov 56
REGISTERED: 16 Apr 57 Australia
ARTICLES: 15 LANGUAGE: English.
HEADNOTE: TRADE & TARIFFS
TOPIC: General Trade
CONCEPTS: Definition of terms. Detailed regula-
tions. Territorial application. Annex or appendix
reference. Previous treaty replacement. General
cooperation. Negotiation. Trade procedures.
Commodity trade. Quotas. Customs duties. Cus-
toms declarations. Customs exemptions.
TREATY REF: (20AUG1932 SUPERSECDES)
265UNTS212.
PROCEDURE: Termination.
PARTIES:
Australia
UK Great Britain

103814 Unilateral Instrument **265 UNTS 221**
SIGNED: 18 Apr 57 FORCE: 18 Apr 57
REGISTERED: 18 Apr 57 United Nations
ARTICLES: 1 LANGUAGE: English.
HEADNOTE: ACCEPTANCE ICJ JURISDICTION
TOPIC: ICJ Option Clause
CONCEPTS: Exceptions and exemptions. Previous
treaty extension. Compulsory jurisdiction.
INTL ORGS: International Court of Justice.
TREATY REF: 219UNTS179.
PROCEDURE: Termination.
PARTIES:
UK Great Britain
ANNEX
316 UNTS 385. UK Great Britain. Termination
26 Nov 58.

103815 Bilateral Agreement **265 UNTS 227**
SIGNED: 15 Jun 56 FORCE: 21 Dec 56
REGISTERED: 18 Apr 57 USA (United States)
ARTICLES: 11 LANGUAGE: English.
HEADNOTE: CIVIL USES AVIATION
TOPIC: Atomic Energy
CONCEPTS: Definition of terms. Diplomatic mis-
sions. General cooperation. Exchange of infor-
mation and documents. Responsibility and liabil-
ity. Research results. Scientific exchange. Nu-
clear materials. Non-nuclear materials. Peaceful
use. Rights of supplier. Security of information.
PROCEDURE: Duration.
PARTIES:
Dominican Republic
USA (United States)

103816 Bilateral Exchange **265 UNTS 241**
SIGNED: 21 Nov 56 FORCE: 21 Nov 56
REGISTERED: 18 Apr 57 USA (United States)
ARTICLES: 2 LANGUAGE: English. Chinese.
HEADNOTE: CONSTRUCTION MILITARY INSTAL-
LATIONS FACILITIES
TOPIC: Milit Installation
CONCEPTS: Visa abolition. Recognition of legal
documents. Private contracts. Responsibility and
liability. Use of facilities. Tax exemptions. Cus-
toms exemptions. Materials, equipment and ser-
vices. Security of information. Airforce-army-
navy personnel ratio. Procurement and logistics.
Bases and facilities.
TREATY REF: 132UNTS273.
PARTIES:
Taiwan
USA (United States)

103817 Bilateral Exchange **265 UNTS 255**
SIGNED: 7 Dec 56 FORCE: 7 Dec 56
REGISTERED: 18 Apr 57 USA (United States)
ARTICLES: 2 LANGUAGE: English. French.
HEADNOTE: GUARANTEE PRIVATE INVEST-
MENTS MUTUAL SECURITY ACT 1954

TOPIC: General Military
CONCEPTS: Guarantees and safeguards. Arbitration. Procedure. Negotiation. Private investment guarantee. Most favored nation clause. Economic assistance.
PARTIES:
Luxembourg
USA (United States)

103818 Bilateral Protocol **265 UNTS 261**
SIGNED: 6 Dec 56 FORCE: 6 Dec 56
REGISTERED: 18 Apr 57 USA (United States)
ARTICLES: 4 LANGUAGE: English.
HEADNOTE: PRESENCE DEFENSE FORCES REVISION 1951 DEFENSE AGREEMENTS
TOPIC: General Military
CONCEPTS: Change of circumstances. Establishment of commission. Defense and security. Military assistance. Status of forces.
INTL ORGS: North Atlantic Treaty Organization. Special Commission.
TREATY REF: 205UNTS173; 34UNTS243; 126UNTS350; 243UNTS308.
PARTIES:
Iceland
USA (United States)

103819 Bilateral Exchange **265 UNTS 271**
SIGNED: 2 Jul 56 FORCE: 2 Jul 56
REGISTERED: 23 Apr 57 UK Great Britain
ARTICLES: 2 LANGUAGE: English.
HEADNOTE: EXPORT COTTON YARN TEXTILES
TOPIC: Commodity Trade
CONCEPTS: Export quotas. Import quotas.
PARTIES:
Indonesia
UK Great Britain

103820 Bilateral Exchange **265 UNTS 285**
SIGNED: 2 Jul 56 FORCE: 2 Jul 56
REGISTERED: 23 Apr 57 UK Great Britain
ARTICLES: 2 LANGUAGE: English.
HEADNOTE: EXPORT COTTON YARN TEXTILES
TOPIC: Commodity Trade
CONCEPTS: Export quotas. Import quotas.
PARTIES:
Indonesia
UK Great Britain
ANNEX
310 UNTS 394. UK Great Britain. Amendment 5 Apr 57. Force 5 Apr 57.
310 UNTS 394. Indonesia. Amendment 5 Apr 57. Force 5 Apr 57.

103821 Unilateral Instrument **265 UNTS 299**
SIGNED: 24 Apr 57 FORCE: 24 Apr 57
REGISTERED: 24 Apr 57 United Arab Rep
ARTICLES: 10 LANGUAGE: English.
HEADNOTE: DECLARATION SUEZ CANAL
TOPIC: General Ad Hoc
CONCEPTS: Guarantees and safeguards. Non-prejudice to UN charter. Peaceful relations. Arbitration. Procedure. Existing tribunals. Compensation. Currency deposits. Claims and settlements. Most favored nation clause. Innocent passage. Compulsory jurisdiction.
INTL ORGS: Bank for International Settlements. International Court of Justice. United Nations.
PROCEDURE: Registration.
PARTIES:
United Arab Rep

103822 Multilateral Convention **266 UNTS 3**
SIGNED: 7 Sep 56 FORCE: 30 Apr 57
REGISTERED: 30 Apr 57 United Nations
ARTICLES: 15 LANGUAGE: Chinese. English. French. Russian. Spanish.
HEADNOTE: ABOLITION SLAVERY RELATED ACTIVITIES
TOPIC: Humanitarian
CONCEPTS: Definition of terms. Exceptions and exemptions. Territorial application. Annex or appendix reference. Annex type material. Human rights. Privileges and immunities. Conformity with municipal law. Exchange of information and documents. Dispute settlement. Existing tribunals. Humanitarian matters. Employment regulations. Establishment of trade relations.
INTL ORGS: International Labour Organization.

TREATY REF: 60LTS253; 69LTS114; 39UNTS55; 54UNTS403.
PROCEDURE: Accession. Ratification.
PARTIES:
Australia SIGNED: 17 Sep 56
Belgium SIGNED: 17 Sep 56
Byelorussia SIGNED: 17 Sep 56
Canada SIGNED: 17 Sep 56
Cuba SIGNED: 10 Jan 57
Czechoslovakia SIGNED: 17 Sep 56
El Salvador SIGNED: 17 Sep 56
France SIGNED: 17 Sep 56
Germany, West SIGNED: 17 Sep 56
Greece SIGNED: 17 Sep 56
Guatemala SIGNED: 17 Sep 56
Haiti SIGNED: 17 Sep 56
Hungary SIGNED: 17 Sep 56
India SIGNED: 17 Sep 56
Iraq SIGNED: 17 Sep 56
Israel SIGNED: 17 Sep 56
Italy SIGNED: 17 Sep 56
Liberia SIGNED: 17 Sep 56
Luxembourg SIGNED: 17 Sep 56
Mexico SIGNED: 17 Sep 56
Netherlands SIGNED: 17 Sep 56
Norway SIGNED: 17 Sep 56
Pakistan SIGNED: 17 Sep 56
Peru SIGNED: 17 Sep 56
Poland SIGNED: 17 Sep 56
Portugal SIGNED: 17 Sep 56
Romania SIGNED: 17 Sep 56
San Marino SIGNED: 17 Sep 56
Sudan SIGNED: 17 Sep 56
UK Great Britain Channel Islands RATIFIED: 30 Apr 57 FORCE: 30 Apr 57
UK Great Britain Isle of Man RATIFIED: 30 Apr 57 FORCE: 30 Apr 57
UK Great Britain SIGNED: 17 Sep 56 RATIFIED: 30 Apr 57 FORCE: 30 Apr 57
Ukrainian SSR SIGNED: 17 Sep 56
USSR (Soviet Union) SIGNED: 17 Sep 56 RATIFIED: 12 Apr 57 FORCE: 30 Apr 57
Vietnam SIGNED: 17 Sep 56
Yugoslavia SIGNED: 17 Sep 56
ANNEX
269 UNTS 382.
276 UNTS 370.
277 UNTS 361.
278 UNTS 313.
280 UNTS 389.
281 UNTS 410.
282 UNTS 368.
285 UNTS 381.
286 UNTS 383.
287 UNTS 352.
290 UNTS 344.
293 UNTS 358.
301 UNTS 452.
302 UNTS 374.
304 UNTS 388.
309 UNTS 373.
314 UNTS 358.
316 UNTS 386.
320 UNTS 347.
327 UNTS 379.
328 UNTS 337.
336 UNTS 373.
338 UNTS 397.
344 UNTS 349.
347 UNTS 392.
354 UNTS 410.
357 UNTS 390.
362 UNTS 337.
399 UNTS 281.
401 UNTS 284.
401 UNTS 288.
407 UNTS 262.
423 UNTS 316.
426 UNTS 343.
429 UNTS 298.
443 UNTS 344.
445 UNTS 347.
448 UNTS 334.
450 UNTS 438.
451 UNTS 348.
463 UNTS 348.
471 UNTS 332.
474 UNTS 337.
478 UNTS 435.
479 UNTS 368.
480 UNTS 360.
496 UNTS 354.
503 UNTS 337.
506 UNTS 378.

515 UNTS 306.
541 UNTS 322.
548 UNTS 344.
551 UNTS 300.
560 UNTS 266.
567 UNTS 336.
604 UNTS 372.
613 UNTS 414.
653 UNTS 458.

103823 Bilateral Exchange **266 UNTS 89**
SIGNED: 31 Dec 56 FORCE: 26 Jan 57
REGISTERED: 30 Apr 57 USA (United States)
ARTICLES: 2 LANGUAGE: English.
HEADNOTE: FURNISH SUPPLIES SERVICES NAVAL VESSELS
TOPIC: Milit Assistance
CONCEPTS: Time limit. Use of facilities. Indemnities and reimbursements. Currency. Materials, equipment and services. Ports and pilotage. Naval vessels.
PROCEDURE: Termination.
PARTIES:
Australia
USA (United States)
ANNEX
474 UNTS 338. USA (United States). Amendment 28 Mar 63. Force 28 Mar 63.
474 UNTS 338. Australia. Amendment 28 Mar 63. Force 28 Mar 63.

103824 Bilateral Exchange **266 UNTS 99**
SIGNED: 16 Jan 57 FORCE: 16 Jan 57
REGISTERED: 30 Apr 57 USA (United States)
ARTICLES: 2 LANGUAGE: English. Portuguese.
HEADNOTE: LOAN VESSELS
TOPIC: Milit Assistance
CONCEPTS: Time limit. Responsibility and liability. Title and deeds. Compensation. Delivery schedules. Lease of military property. Naval vessels. Return of equipment and recapture.
PARTIES:
Brazil
USA (United States)
ANNEX
459 UNTS 302. Brazil. Prolongation 11 Jul 62. Force 11 Jul 62.
459 UNTS 302. USA (United States). Prolongation 20 Feb 62. Force 11 Jul 62.

103825 Bilateral Exchange **266 UNTS 109**
SIGNED: 17 Jan 57 FORCE: 17 Jan 57
REGISTERED: 30 Apr 57 USA (United States)
ARTICLES: 2 LANGUAGE: English.
HEADNOTE: USE HAINES CUT-OFF ROAD
TOPIC: Specif Goods/Equip
CONCEPTS: Use of facilities. Specific goods and equipment.
PARTIES:
Canada
USA (United States)
ANNEX
358 UNTS 316. USA (United States). Prolongation 17 Aug 59. Force 20 Aug 59.
358 UNTS 316. Canada. Prolongation 20 Aug 59. Force 20 Aug 59.
445 UNTS 348. USA (United States). Prolongation 22 Dec 61. Force 26 Jan 62.
445 UNTS 348. Canada. Prolongation 26 Jan 62. Force 26 Jan 62.

103826 Bilateral Exchange **266 UNTS 117**
SIGNED: 14 Dec 56 FORCE: 14 Dec 56
REGISTERED: 30 Apr 57 USA (United States)
ARTICLES: 2 LANGUAGE: English. French.
HEADNOTE: RELATING CERTIFICATES AIRWORTHINESS IMPORTED AIRCRAFT
TOPIC: Air Transport
CONCEPTS: Conformity with municipal law. Exchange of information and documents. Recognition of legal documents. Use of facilities. Registration certificate. Airworthiness certificates.
PROCEDURE: Termination.
PARTIES:
France
USA (United States)

103827 Bilateral Exchange **266 UNTS 125**
SIGNED: 1 May 57 FORCE: 29 Apr 57

REGISTERED: 1 May 57 United Nations
ARTICLES: 3 LANGUAGE: English.
HEADNOTE: UNEF LEAVE CENTER
TOPIC: IGO Establishment
CONCEPTS: Default remedies. Privileges and immunities. Regional offices.
PARTIES.
Lebanon
United Nations

103828   Bilateral Agreement   **266 UNTS 137**
SIGNED: 17 Jun 54   FORCE: 17 Jun 54
REGISTERED: 6 May 57 USA (United States)
ARTICLES: 9 LANGUAGE: English.
HEADNOTE: SPECIAL ECONOMIC ASSISTANCE
TOPIC: Direct Aid
CONCEPTS: Annex or appendix reference. Privileges and immunities. Operating agencies. General property. Private contracts. Establishment of commission. Indemnities and reimbursements. Currency deposits. Exchange rates and regulations. Financial programs. Local currency. Commodities and services. Economic assistance. Use restrictions. Materials, equipment and services. Procurement. Credit provisions. Commodities schedule.
PROCEDURE: Duration. Termination.
PARTIES:
Jordan
USA (United States)

103829   Bilateral Agreement   **266 UNTS 151**
SIGNED: 31 Dec 56   FORCE: 31 Dec 56
REGISTERED: 6 May 57 USA (United States)
ARTICLES: 6 LANGUAGE: English. Portuguese.
HEADNOTE: AGRI COMMOD TITLE I
TOPIC: US Agri Commod Aid
CONCEPTS: General provisions. Annex or appendix reference. Exchange of information and documents. Reexport of goods, etc.. Exchange rates and regulations. Transportation costs. Local currency. Commodities schedule. Purchase authorization. Surplus commodities. Mutual consultation.
PARTIES:
Brazil
USA (United States)
ANNEX
290 UNTS 345. Brazil. Amendment 25 Jul 57. Force 25 Jul 57.
290 UNTS 345. USA (United States). Amendment 25 Jul 57. Force 25 Jul 57.
321 UNTS 288. Brazil. Amendment 30 Jun 58. Force 30 Jun 58.
321 UNTS 288. USA (United States). Amendment 30 Jun 58. Force 30 Jun 58.
337 UNTS 422. USA (United States). Amendment 12 Dec 58. Force 12 Dec 58.
337 UNTS 422. Brazil. Amendment 12 Dec 58. Force 12 Dec 58.
341 UNTS 405. USA (United States). Amendment 2 Mar 59. Force 2 Mar 59.
341 UNTS 405. Brazil. Amendment 2 Mar 59. Force 2 Mar 59.
346 UNTS 339. USA (United States). Amendment 29 May 59. Force 29 May 59.
346 UNTS 339. Brazil. Amendment 29 May 59. Force 29 May 59.
358 UNTS 320. USA (United States). Amendment 2 Sep 59. Force 2 Sep 59.
358 UNTS 320. Brazil. Amendment 2 Sep 59. Force 2 Sep 59.
409 UNTS 316. USA (United States). Amendment 4 Jan 61. Force 18 Apr 61.
409 UNTS 316. Brazil. Amendment 18 Apr 61. Force 18 Apr 61.
435 UNTS 352. Brazil. Amendment 26 Feb 62. Force 26 Feb 62.
435 UNTS 352. USA (United States). Amendment 26 Feb 62. Force 26 Feb 62.

103830   Bilateral Treaty   **266 UNTS 179**
SIGNED: 17 Dec 56   FORCE: 27 Feb 57
REGISTERED: 13 May 57 USSR (Soviet Union)
ARTICLES: 21 LANGUAGE: Russian. Polish.
HEADNOTE: LEGAL STATUS FORCES
TOPIC: Status of Forces
CONCEPTS: Definition of terms. Court procedures. Conformity with municipal law. General cooperation. Recognition of legal documents. Responsibility and liability. Use of facilities. Investigation

of violations. Establishment of commission. Procedure. Compensation. Defense and security. Military training. Jurisdiction. Procurement and logistics. Status of forces. Bases and facilities.
INTL ORGS: Claims Commission.
PROCEDURE: Amendment. Future Procedures Contemplated. Ratification.
PARTIES:
Poland
USSR (Soviet Union)

103831   Bilateral Agreement   **266 UNTS 209**
SIGNED: 25 May 56   FORCE: 12 Mar 57
REGISTERED: 13 May 57 USSR (Soviet Union)
ARTICLES: 3 LANGUAGE: English. Russian.
HEADNOTE: FISHERIES
TOPIC: Specific Resources
CONCEPTS: Annex or appendix reference. Fisheries and fishing.
PROCEDURE: Denunciation. Duration. Ratification. Renewal or Revival.
PARTIES:
UK Great Britain
USSR (Soviet Union)
ANNEX
431 UNTS 310. USSR (Soviet Union). Termination 12 Mar 62.

103832   Multilateral Agreement   **266 UNTS 221**
SIGNED: 11 Sep 56   FORCE: 1 Apr 57
REGISTERED: 13 May 57 USSR (Soviet Union)
ARTICLES: 13 LANGUAGE: Russian. Bulgarian. Romanian.
HEADNOTE: RESCUE COOPERATION BLACK SEA
TOPIC: Humanitarian
CONCEPTS: Detailed regulations. Previous treaty replacement. Conformity with municipal law. General cooperation. Exchange of information and documents. Use of facilities. Dispute settlement. Humanitarian matters. Accounting procedures. Indemnities and reimbursements. Claims and settlements. Shipwreck and salvage. Bands and frequency allocation.
TREATY REF: 205LTS220; 164UNTS113.
PROCEDURE: Denunciation. Duration. Renewal or Revival.
PARTIES:
Bulgaria SIGNED: 11 Sep 56 FORCE: 1 Apr 57
Romania SIGNED: 11 Sep 56 FORCE: 1 Apr 57
USSR (Soviet Union) SIGNED: 11 Sep 56 FORCE: 1 Apr 57

103833   Bilateral Agreement   **266 UNTS 243**
SIGNED: 30 Nov 56   FORCE: 30 Mar 57
REGISTERED: 13 May 57 USSR (Soviet Union)
ARTICLES: 45 LANGUAGE: Russian. Czechoslovakian.
HEADNOTE: FRONTIERS INCIDENT SETTLEMENT
TOPIC: Territory Boundary
CONCEPTS: Annex or appendix reference. Border traffic and migration. General cooperation. Exchange of information and documents. Operating agencies. Investigation of violations. Establishment of commission. Dispute settlement. Domestic obligation. Boundaries of territory. Fish, wildlife, and natural resources. Markers and definitions. Frontier peoples and personnel. Frontier waterways. Regulation of natural resources.
PROCEDURE: Amendment. Denunciation. Duration. Ratification. Renewal or Revival.
PARTIES:
Czechoslovakia
USSR (Soviet Union)

103834   Bilateral Agreement   **267 UNTS 3**
SIGNED: 15 Feb 57   FORCE: 15 May 57
REGISTERED: 15 May 57 Belgium
ARTICLES: 7 LANGUAGE: French.
HEADNOTE: MOVEMENT REFUGEES
TOPIC: Refugees
CONCEPTS: Time limit. Visa abolition. Alien status. Conformity with municipal law.
TREATY REF: 189UNTS137.
PARTIES:
Belgium
France

103835   Bilateral Convention   **267 UNTS 9**
SIGNED: 5 May 53   FORCE: 1 Apr 56

REGISTERED: 15 May 57 Italy
ARTICLES: 40 LANGUAGE: Italian. German.
HEADNOTE: SOCIAL SECURITY
TOPIC: Non-ILO Labor
CONCEPTS: Detailed regulations. Territorial application. General provisions. Annex or appendix reference. General property. Existing tribunals. Old age and invalidity insurance. Wages and salaries. Non-ILO labor relations. Administrative cooperation. Old age insurance. Sickness and invalidity insurance. Social security. Exchange rates and regulations. Payment schedules.
PROCEDURE: Denunciation. Duration. Future Procedures Contemplated. Ratification. Renewal or Revival.
PARTIES:
Germany, West
Italy

103836   Bilateral Convention   **267 UNTS 89**
SIGNED: 28 Dec 53   FORCE: 11 Apr 57
REGISTERED: 15 May 57 Italy
ARTICLES: 13 LANGUAGE: French.
HEADNOTE: MILITARY SERVICE
TOPIC: Milit Servic/Citiz
CONCEPTS: Definition of terms. Procedure. Dual nationality. Certificates of service. Service in foreign army.
PROCEDURE: Denunciation. Ratification.
PARTIES:
France
Italy

103837   Bilateral Treaty   **267 UNTS 97**
SIGNED: 14 Jun 54   FORCE: 16 Dec 56
REGISTERED: 15 May 57 Italy
ARTICLES: 12 LANGUAGE: Italian. French.
HEADNOTE: TREATY COMMERCE NAVIGATION
TOPIC: General Economic
CONCEPTS: Exceptions and exemptions. Territorial application. Annex or appendix reference. Informational records. Export quotas. Banking. Currency. Payment schedules. Most favored nation clause. Customs duties. Merchant vessels. Ports and pilotage.
TREATY REF: 71LTS405.
PARTIES:
Haiti
Italy

103838   Bilateral Agreement   **267 UNTS 113**
SIGNED: 4 Nov 55   FORCE: 11 Sep 56
REGISTERED: 15 May 57 Italy
ARTICLES: 10 LANGUAGE: French.
HEADNOTE: TRADE DEVELOPMENT
TOPIC: General Trade
CONCEPTS: Exceptions and exemptions. Annex or appendix reference. General cooperation. Establishment of commission. Establishment of trade relations. Export quotas. Import quotas. Reciprocity in trade. Trade procedures. Currency. Payment schedules. Quotas. Most favored nation clause.
PROCEDURE: Denunciation. Duration. Ratification. Renewal or Revival.
PARTIES:
Italy
Lebanon

103839   Bilateral Agreement   **267 UNTS 125**
SIGNED: 11 Aug 55   FORCE: 7 Feb 57
REGISTERED: 15 May 57 Italy
ARTICLES: 12 LANGUAGE: Italian. Spanish.
HEADNOTE: CULTURAL AGREEMENT
TOPIC: Culture
CONCEPTS: Friendship and amity. Establishment of commission. Recognition of degrees. Teacher and student exchange. Professorships. Institute establishment. Scholarships and grants. Exchange. General cultural cooperation. Artists. Scientific exchange. Fees and exemptions. Tax exemptions. Publications exchange. Mass media exchange.
INTL ORGS: Special Commission.
PROCEDURE: Denunciation. Duration. Ratification.
PARTIES:
Italy
Spain

103840 Bilateral Agreement **267 UNTS 147**
SIGNED: 4 Nov 55   FORCE: 11 Sep 56
REGISTERED: 15 May 57 Italy
ARTICLES: 9 LANGUAGE: French.
HEADNOTE: STRENGTHEN DEVELOPING ECO-
NOMIC RELATIONS
TOPIC: Tech Assistance
CONCEPTS: Time limit. Treaty implementation.
Annex or appendix reference. Tourism. General
cooperation. Establishment of commission. Spe-
cialists exchange. Vocational training. Adminis-
trative cooperation. Research and development.
Private investment guarantee. Smuggling.
Patents, copyrights and trademarks. General
technical assistance. Assistance. Economic as-
sistance. Materials, equipment and services. In-
dustry.
INTL ORGS: Special Commission.
PROCEDURE: Denunciation. Duration. Future Pro-
cedures Contemplated. Ratification. Renewal or
Revival.
PARTIES:
Italy
Lebanon

103841 Bilateral Agreement **267 UNTS 157**
SIGNED: 10 Nov 55   FORCE: 27 Feb 56
REGISTERED: 15 May 57 Italy
ARTICLES: 9 LANGUAGE: French.
HEADNOTE: TRADE DEVELOPMENT
TOPIC: General Trade
CONCEPTS: Exceptions and exemptions. Confor-
mity with municipal law. General cooperation.
Licenses and permits. Establishment of commis-
sion. Establishment of trade relations. Import
quotas. Reciprocity in trade. Trade procedures.
Currency. Monetary and gold transfers. Ex-
change rates and regulations. Payment sched-
ules. Quotas. Most favored nation clause. Gen-
eral. Customs duties.
INTL ORGS: Special Commission.
PROCEDURE: Denunciation. Duration. Renewal or
Revival.
PARTIES:
Italy
Syria

103842 Bilateral Exchange **267 UNTS 175**
SIGNED: 11 Jan 56   FORCE: 15 Jan 56
REGISTERED: 15 May 57 Italy
ARTICLES: 2 LANGUAGE: French.
HEADNOTE: ABOLITION VISAS PASSPORTS
TOPIC: Visas
CONCEPTS: Time limit. Visa abolition. Denial of
admission. Resident permits. Conformity with
municipal law. Fees and exemptions.
PARTIES:
Italy
Japan

103843 Bilateral Exchange **267 UNTS 181**
SIGNED: 3 Mar 56   FORCE: 3 Mar 56
REGISTERED: 15 May 57 Italy
ARTICLES: 4 LANGUAGE: French.
HEADNOTE: SICKNESS INSURANCE
TOPIC: Non-ILO Labor
CONCEPTS: Conditions. Detailed regulations. Ex-
ceptions and exemptions. Wages and salaries.
Non-ILO labor relations. Sickness and invalidity
insurance. Migrant worker. Payment schedules.
PARTIES:
France
Italy

103844 Bilateral Agreement **267 UNTS 189**
SIGNED: 5 Mar 56   FORCE: 4 Jul 56
REGISTERED: 15 May 57 Italy
ARTICLES: 8 LANGUAGE: English.
HEADNOTE: SETTLEMENT ECONOMIC FINANCIAL
MATTERS
TOPIC: Reparations
CONCEPTS: Definition of terms. Time limit. Annex
or appendix reference. Non-diplomatic delega-
tions. Exchange of information and documents.
Private contracts. Export quotas. Import quotas.
Reexport of goods, etc.. Accounting procedures.
Garnishment of funds. Local currency. Customs
exemptions. Reparations and restrictions. Post-
war claims settlement. Raw materials.
TREATY REF: 49UNTS.

PROCEDURE: Ratification.
PARTIES:
Ethiopia
Italy

103845 Bilateral Exchange **267 UNTS 227**
SIGNED: 9 May 56   FORCE: 9 May 56
REGISTERED: 15 May 57 Italy
ARTICLES: 2 LANGUAGE: Italian. German.
HEADNOTE: RECOGNITION UNIVERSITY DE-
GREES
TOPIC: Education
CONCEPTS: Annex or appendix reference. Recog-
nition of degrees.
PARTIES:
Austria
Italy

103846 Bilateral Exchange **267 UNTS 255**
SIGNED: 23 May 56   FORCE: 23 May 56
REGISTERED: 15 May 57 Italy
ARTICLES: 2 LANGUAGE: Italian. Spanish.
HEADNOTE: TERMINATION TREATY RECIPROCAL
RELEASE PROPERTY
TOPIC: Claims and Debts
CONCEPTS: Annex type material. General prop-
erty. Assets transfer.
PARTIES:
Argentina
Italy

103847 Bilateral Agreement **267 UNTS 261**
SIGNED: 26 Oct 56   FORCE: 5 Apr 57
REGISTERED: 15 May 57 Italy
ARTICLES: 6 LANGUAGE: Italian. Danish.
HEADNOTE: CULTURAL AGREEMENT
TOPIC: Culture
CONCEPTS: Operating agencies. Exchange. Com-
missions and foundations. Teacher and student
exchange. Professorships. Exchange. General
cultural cooperation. Artists. Scientific ex-
change. Import quotas. Mass media exchange.
INTL ORGS: Special Commission.
PROCEDURE: Denunciation. Duration. Ratification.
Renewal or Revival.
PARTIES:
Denmark
Italy

103848 Bilateral Agreement **267 UNTS 270**
SIGNED: 28 Jun 53   FORCE: 1 Jul 55
REGISTERED: 16 May 57 South Africa
ARTICLES: 16 LANGUAGE: English. Afrikaans.
HEADNOTE: TRADE
TOPIC: General Trade
CONCEPTS: Definition of terms. Detailed regula-
tions. Exceptions and exemptions. Treaty imple-
mentation. Annex or appendix reference. Tourism. General cooperation. Export quotas. Import
quotas. Trade agencies. Trade procedures. Payment schedules. Commodity trade. Quotas. Customs duties. Customs exemptions.
TREATY REF: 270UNTS302; 270UNTS314;
10DEMARTENS414; 270UNTS300.
PROCEDURE: Duration. Termination.
PARTIES:
Fed Rhod/Nyasaland
South Africa
ANNEX
274 UNTS 378. South Africa. Amendment
6 Jun 57. Force 6 Jun 57.
274 UNTS 378. Fed Rhod/Nyasaland. Amendment 6 Jun 57. Force 6 Jun 57.
286 UNTS 384. Fed Rhod/Nyasaland. Amendment 28 Dec 57. Force 1 Jan 58.
286 UNTS 384. South Africa. Amendment
28 Dec 57. Force 1 Jan 58.

103849 Bilateral Agreement **267 UNTS 337**
SIGNED: 25 Jun 48   FORCE: 23 Jun 48
REGISTERED: 21 May 57 Greece
ARTICLES: 7 LANGUAGE: French.
HEADNOTE: TRADE
TOPIC: General Trade
CONCEPTS: Annex or appendix reference. Li-
censes and permits. Establishment of commis-
sion. Trade procedures. Payment schedules.
Non-interest rates and fees. Quotas. Most fa-
vored nation clause.

INTL ORGS: Special Commission.
PROCEDURE: Denunciation. Termination.
PARTIES:
Greece
Sweden
ANNEX
268 UNTS 404. Sweden. Implementation
5 Dec 56. Force 5 Dec 56.
268 UNTS 404. Greece. Implementation
5 Dec 56. Force 5 Dec 56.

103850 Multilateral Instrument **268 UNTS 3**
SIGNED: 20 Jun 56   FORCE: 25 May 57
REGISTERED: 25 May 57 United Nations
ARTICLES: 1 LANGUAGE: Chinese. English.
French. Russian. Spanish.
HEADNOTE: RECOVERY ABROAD MAINTENANCE
TOPIC: Admin Cooperation
CONCEPTS: Exceptions and exemptions. Territo-
rial application. General cooperation. Exchange
of information and documents. Operating agen-
cies. Recognition and enforcement of legal deci-
sions. Procedure. Existing tribunals. Funding pro-
cedures. Claims and settlements.
INTL ORGS: Intergovernmental Committee for Eu-
ropean Migration. International Labour Orga-
nization. United Nations.
PROCEDURE: Amendment. Accession. Denuncia-
tion. Ratification.
PARTIES:
Austria SIGNED: 21 Dec 56
Bolivia SIGNED: 20 Jun 56
Brazil SIGNED: 31 Dec 56
Byelorussia SIGNED: 20 Jun 56
Ceylon (Sri Lanka) SIGNED: 20 Jun 56
Taiwan SIGNED: 4 Dec 56
Colombia SIGNED: 16 Jul 56
Cuba SIGNED: 20 Jun 56
Denmark SIGNED: 28 Dec 56
Dominican Republic SIGNED: 20 Jun 56
Ecuador SIGNED: 20 Jun 56
El Salvador SIGNED: 20 Jun 56
France SIGNED: 5 Sep 56
Germany, West SIGNED: 20 Jun 56
Greece SIGNED: 20 Jun 56
Haiti SIGNED: 21 Dec 56
Israel SIGNED: 20 Jun 56 RATIFIED: 4 Apr 57
FORCE: 25 May 57
Italy SIGNED: 1 Aug 56
Mexico SIGNED: 20 Jun 56
Monaco SIGNED: 20 Jun 56
Netherlands SIGNED: 20 Jun 56
Philippines SIGNED: 20 Jun 56
United Nations
Sweden SIGNED: 4 Dec 56
Vatican/Holy See SIGNED: 20 Jun 56
Yugoslavia SIGNED: 30 Dec 56
ANNEX
270 UNTS 420. Taiwan. Ratification 21 Jun 57.
Force 25 Jul 57.
272 UNTS 318. Hungary. Accession 23 Jul 57.
Force 22 Aug 57.
279 UNTS 349. Norway. Accession 25 Oct 57.
Force 24 Nov 57.
286 UNTS 390. Haiti. Ratification 12 Feb 58.
Force 14 Mar 58.
307 UNTS 311. Italy. Ratification 28 Jul 58. Force
27 Aug 58.
308 UNTS 330. Ceylon (Sri Lanka). Ratification
7 Aug 58. Force 6 Sep 58.
313 UNTS 372. Sweden. Qualified Ratification
1 Oct 58. Force 31 Oct 58.
313 UNTS 372. Czechoslovakia. Accession
3 Oct 58. Force 2 Nov 58.
328 UNTS 338. Yugoslavia. Ratification
29 May 59. Force 28 Jun 59.
335 UNTS 327. Denmark. Ratification 22 Jun 59.
Force 22 Jul 59.
337 UNTS 427. Germany, West. Berlin. Force
19 Aug 59.
337 UNTS 427. Pakistan. Accession 14 Jul 59.
Force 13 Aug 59.
337 UNTS 427. Germany, West. Ratification
20 Jul 59. Force 19 Aug 59.
362 UNTS 338. France. Qualified Ratification
24 Jun 60. Force 24 Jul 60.
376 UNTS 434. Poland. Accession 13 Oct 60.
Force 12 Nov 60.
376 UNTS 434. Poland. Accession 13 Oct 60.
Force 12 Nov 60.
380 UNTS 450. Brazil. Ratification 14 Nov 60.
Force 14 Dec 60.

384 UNTS 375. Chile. Accession 9 Jan 61. Force 8 Feb 61.

399 UNTS 282. Monaco. Ratification 28 Jun 61. Force 28 Jul 61.

434 UNTS 316. Netherlands. Qualified Ratification 31 Jul 62. Force 30 Aug 62.

435 UNTS 361. Upper Volta. Accession 27 Aug 62. Force 26 Sep 62.

437 UNTS 358. Finland. Accession 13 Sep 62. Force 13 Oct 62.

442 UNTS 330. Central Afri Rep. Accession 15 Oct 62. Force 14 Nov 62.

511 UNTS 279. Vatican/Holy See. Ratification 6 Oct 64. Force 4 Nov 64.

523 UNTS 320. Portugal. Accession 25 Jan 65. Force 24 Feb 65.

525 UNTS 316. Niger. Accession 15 Feb 65. Force 17 Mar 65.

547 UNTS 320. Greece. Ratification 1 Nov 65. Force 1 Dec 65.

565 UNTS 290. Belgium. Accession 1 Jul 66. Force 31 Jul 66.

633 UNTS 387. Philippines. Ratification 21 Mar 68. Force 20 Apr 68.

649 UNTS 330. Tunisia. Accession 16 Oct 68. Force 15 Nov 68.

103851 Bilateral Exchange **268 UNTS 87**
SIGNED: 13 Jun 55   FORCE: 13 Jun 55
REGISTERED: 27 May 57 USA (United States)
ARTICLES: 2 LANGUAGE: English.
HEADNOTE: CONSTRUCTION OPERATION CERTAIN RADAR STATIONS
TOPIC: Specif Goods/Equip
CONCEPTS: Annex or appendix reference. Military installations and equipment. Specific goods and equipment.
PARTIES:
Canada
USA (United States)

103852 Bilateral Exchange **268 UNTS 101**
SIGNED: 15 Jun 55   FORCE: 15 Jun 55
REGISTERED: 27 May 57 USA (United States)
ARTICLES: 2 LANGUAGE: English.
HEADNOTE: CONSTRUCTION OPERATION CERTAIN RADAR STATIONS
TOPIC: Specif Goods/Equip
CONCEPTS: Annex or appendix reference. Military installations and equipment. Specific goods and equipment.
PARTIES:
Canada
USA (United States)

103853 Bilateral Exchange **268 UNTS 115**
SIGNED: 4 Oct 55   FORCE: 4 Oct 55
REGISTERED: 27 May 57 USA (United States)
ARTICLES: 2 LANGUAGE: English.
HEADNOTE: EMERGENCY FOOD RELIEF ASSISTANCE
TOPIC: Direct Aid
CONCEPTS: Treaty implementation. Conformity with municipal law. Relief supplies.
PARTIES:
India
USA (United States)

103854 Bilateral Agreement **268 UNTS 121**
SIGNED: 2 Aug 55   FORCE: 2 Aug 55
REGISTERED: 27 May 57 USA (United States)
ARTICLES: 1 LANGUAGE: English.
HEADNOTE: LEASE AIR NAVIGATION EQUIPMENT
TOPIC: Specif Goods/Equip
CONCEPTS: Detailed regulations. Previous treaties adherence. Responsibility and liability. Assets transfer. Navigational equipment. Airport equipment. Specific goods and equipment.
INTL ORGS: International Civil Aviation Organization.
TREATY REF: 151NTS295.
PARTIES:
Germany, West
USA (United States)
ANNEX
317 UNTS 340. USA (United States). Prolongation 24 Feb 58. Force 24 May 58.
317 UNTS 340. Germany, West. Prolongation 24 May 58. Force 24 May 58.

---

376 UNTS 435. USA (United States). Prolongation 3 Nov 59. Force 8 Jan 60.

376 UNTS 435. Germany, West. Prolongation 8 Jan 60. Force 8 Jan 60.

421 UNTS 309. USA (United States). Prolongation 14 Aug 61. Force 11 Sep 61.

421 UNTS 309. Germany, West. Prolongation 11 Sep 61. Force 11 Sep 61.

487 UNTS 350. Germany, West. Prolongation 24 Jul 63. Force 24 Jul 63.

487 UNTS 350. USA (United States). Prolongation 1 Jul 63. Force 24 Jul 63.

573 UNTS 317. USA (United States). Prolongation 30 Jul 65. Force 25 Aug 65.

573 UNTS 317. Germany, West. Prolongation 25 Aug 65. Force 25 Aug 65.

103855 Bilateral Exchange **268 UNTS 133**
SIGNED: 20 Aug 55   FORCE: 20 Aug 55
REGISTERED: 27 May 57 USA (United States)
ARTICLES: 4 LANGUAGE: English.
HEADNOTE: NON-IMMIGRANT PASSPORT VISAS
TOPIC: Visas
CONCEPTS: Time limit. Visas. Fees and exemptions.
PARTIES:
Australia
USA (United States)

103856 Bilateral Agreement **268 UNTS 143**
SIGNED: 4 Jan 56   FORCE: 4 Jan 56
REGISTERED: 27 May 57 USA (United States)
ARTICLES: 9 LANGUAGE: English. German.
HEADNOTE: INTERCHANGE PATENT RIGHTS TECHNICAL INFORMATION DEFENSE PURPOSES
TOPIC: General Military
CONCEPTS: Definition of terms. Detailed regulations. Exceptions and exemptions. Conformity with municipal law. Licenses and permits. Establishment of commission. Procedure. Claims and settlements. Patents, copyrights and trademarks. Laws and formalities. Recognition. General technical assistance. Defense and security. Security of information. Exchange of defense information.
INTL ORGS: Special Commission.
TREATY REF: 240UNTS54.
PROCEDURE: Termination.
PARTIES:
Germany, West
USA (United States)
ANNEX
361 UNTS 337. Germany, West. Supplementation 23 May 59. Force 26 May 59.
361 UNTS 337. USA (United States). Supplementation 9 Mar 59. Force 26 May 59.
529 UNTS 350. Germany, West. Amendment 14 Jan 64. Force 28 May 64.
529 UNTS 350. USA (United States). Amendment 28 May 64. Force 28 May 64.

103857 Bilateral Exchange **268 UNTS 165**
SIGNED: 14 Oct 55   FORCE: 14 Oct 55
REGISTERED: 27 May 57 USA (United States)
ARTICLES: 4 LANGUAGE: English. Chinese.
HEADNOTE: ESTABLISHMENT MEDICAL RESEARCH CENTER
TOPIC: Milit Installation
CONCEPTS: Annex or appendix reference. Privileges and immunities. Use of facilities. Disease control. Ranks and privileges.
PARTIES:
Taiwan
USA (United States)

103858 Bilateral Agreement **268 UNTS 189**
SIGNED: 4 Dec 56   FORCE: 8 Feb 56
REGISTERED: 27 May 57 USA (United States)
ARTICLES: 6 LANGUAGE: English.
HEADNOTE: AGRI COMMOD TITLE I
TOPIC: US Agri Commod Aid
CONCEPTS: General provisions. Annex or appendix reference. Exchange of information and documents. Reexport of goods, etc.. Exchange rates and regulations. Transportation costs. Local currency. Commodities schedule. Purchase authorization. Surplus commodities. Mutual consultation.

PARTIES:
Burma
USA (United States)
ANNEX
277 UNTS 362. USA (United States). Amendment 25 Jul 56. Force 25 Jul 56.
277 UNTS 362. Burma. Amendment 25 Jul 56. Force 25 Jul 56.
291 UNTS 348. USA (United States). Amendment 14 Jun 57. Force 14 Jun 57.
291 UNTS 348. Burma. Amendment 14 Jun 57. Force 14 Jun 57.

103859 Bilateral Agreement **268 UNTS 203**
SIGNED: 19 Dec 56   FORCE: 19 Mar 57
REGISTERED: 27 May 57 IBRD (World Bank)
ARTICLES: 5 LANGUAGE: English.
HEADNOTE: GUARANTEE AGRICULTURAL PROJECTS
TOPIC: IBRD Project
CONCEPTS: Definition of terms. Annex or appendix reference. Exchange of information and documents. Informational records. Inspection and observation. Bonds. Fees and exemptions. Tax exemptions. Domestic obligation. Agriculture. Terms of loan. Loan regulations. Loan guarantee. Guarantor non-interference.
PARTIES:
Japan
IBRD (World Bank)

103860 Bilateral Agreement **268 UNTS 243**
SIGNED: 20 Dec 55   FORCE: 1 Apr 56
REGISTERED: 27 May 57 New Zealand
ARTICLES: 27 LANGUAGE: English.
HEADNOTE: SOCIAL SECURITY
TOPIC: Non-ILO Labor
CONCEPTS: Definition of terms. Territorial application. General provisions. Alien status. Old age and invalidity insurance. Wages and salaries. Non-ILO labor relations. Family allowances. Administrative cooperation. Old age insurance. Sickness and invalidity insurance. Social security. Unemployment. Payment schedules.
PROCEDURE: Duration. Renewal or Revival. Termination.
PARTIES:
New Zealand
UK Great Britain

103861 Multilateral Agreement **268 UNTS 270**
SIGNED: 24 May 57   FORCE: 24 May 57
REGISTERED: 1 Jun 57 United Nations
ARTICLES: 6 LANGUAGE: English.
HEADNOTE: TECHNICAL ASSISTANCE
TOPIC: Tech Assistance
CONCEPTS: Definition of terms. Privileges and immunities. General cooperation. Exchange of information and documents. Personnel. Responsibility and liability. Title and deeds. Use of facilities. Exchange. Scholarships and grants. Vocational training. Research and development. Exchange rates and regulations. Expense sharing formulae. Local currency. Domestic obligation. General technical assistance. Materials, equipment and services. IGO status. Conformity with IGO decisions.
INTL ORGS: Food and Agricultural Organization of the United Nations. International Labour Organization. United Nations Educational, Scientific and Cultural Organization. United Nations.
TREATY REF: 76UNTS132; 1UNTS25; 1UNTS263; 33UNTS261.
PROCEDURE: Amendment. Termination.
PARTIES:
Ghana SIGNED: 24 May 57 FORCE: 24 May 57
FAO (Food Agri) SIGNED: 24 May 57 FORCE: 24 May 57
ICAO (Civil Aviat) SIGNED: 24 May 57 FORCE: 24 May 57
ILO (Labor Org) SIGNED: 24 May 57 FORCE: 24 May 57
ITU (Telecommun) SIGNED: 24 May 57 FORCE: 24 May 57
UNESCO (Educ/Cult) SIGNED: 24 May 57 FORCE: 24 May 57
United Nations SIGNED: 24 May 57 FORCE: 24 May 57
WHO (World Health) SIGNED: 24 May 57 FORCE: 24 May 57

WMO (Meteorology) SIGNED: 24 May 57
FORCE: 24 May 57
ANNEX
489 UNTS 386. UNTAB (Tech Assis). Amendment
13 Jan 64. Force 18 Feb 64.
489 UNTS 386. Ghana. Amendment 18 Feb 64.
Force 18 Feb 64.
649 UNTS 332. IMCO (Maritime Org). Accession
24 Oct 68. Force 24 Oct 68.
649 UNTS 332. UNIDO (Industrial). Accession
24 Oct 68. Force 24 Oct 68.

103862 Bilateral Agreement **268 UNTS 285**
SIGNED: 7 May 56 FORCE: 7 May 56
REGISTERED: 4 Jun 57 USA (United States)
ARTICLES: 6 LANGUAGE: English. Spanish.
HEADNOTE: SURPLUS AGRI COMMOD
TOPIC: US Agri Commod Aid
CONCEPTS: General provisions. Conformity with
municipal law. General cooperation. Exchange
of information and documents. Currency depos-
its. Exchange rates and regulations. Purchase au-
thorizations. Transportation costs. Local cur-
rency. Commodities schedule. Surplus commod-
ities.
PARTIES:
Peru
USA (United States)

103863 Bilateral Agreement **268 UNTS 299**
SIGNED: 2 May 56 FORCE: 18 May 56
REGISTERED: 4 Jun 57 USA (United States)
ARTICLES: 6 LANGUAGE: English. Spanish.
HEADNOTE: AGRICULTURAL TRADE DEVELOP-
MENT ASSISTANCE TITLE I
TOPIC: US Agri Commod Aid
CONCEPTS: General provisions. Annex or appen-
dix reference. Exchange of information and doc-
uments. Reexport of goods, etc.. Exchange rates
and regulations. Transportation costs. Local cur-
rency. Credit provisions. Internal loans. Purchase
authorization. Mutual consultation.
PARTIES:
Paraguay
USA (United States)

103864 Bilateral Exchange **268 UNTS 315**
SIGNED: 3 Apr 56 FORCE: 3 Apr 56
REGISTERED: 4 Jun 57 USA (United States)
ARTICLES: 2 LANGUAGE: English. Chinese.
HEADNOTE: DISPOSITION EQUIPMENT MATERI-
ALS MUTUAL DEFENSE ASSISTANCE
TOPIC: Milit Assistance
CONCEPTS: Conformity with municipal law. Ex-
change of information and documents. Reexport
of goods, etc.. Delivery schedules. Materials,
equipment and services. Surplus property. Re-
turn of equipment and recapture.
TREATY REF: 181UNTS162.
PARTIES:
Taiwan
USA (United States)
ANNEX
530 UNTS 355. USA (United States). Amendment
3 Jun 64. Force 3 Jun 64.
530 UNTS 355. Taiwan. Amendment 3 Jun 64.
Force 3 Jun 64.

103865 Bilateral Agreement **268 UNTS 323**
SIGNED: 24 May 56 FORCE: 24 May 56
REGISTERED: 4 Jun 57 USA (United States)
ARTICLES: 6 LANGUAGE: English.
HEADNOTE: AGRI COMMOD TITLE I
TOPIC: US Agri Commod Aid
CONCEPTS: General provisions. Exchange of infor-
mation and documents. Free trade. Exchange
rates and regulations. Transportation costs. Lo-
cal currency. Commodities schedule. Purchase
authorization. Surplus commodities. Mutual con-
sultation.
PARTIES:
Portugal
USA (United States)

103866 Bilateral Exchange **268 UNTS 333**
SIGNED: 25 May 56 FORCE: 1 Jun 56
REGISTERED: 4 Jun 57 USA (United States)
ARTICLES: 3 LANGUAGE: English. Spanish.
HEADNOTE: PASSPORT VISAS

TOPIC: Visas
CONCEPTS: Time limit. Previous treaty replace-
ment. Non-visa travel documents. Visas. Fees
and exemptions.
TREATY REF: 89UNTS27; 89UNTS37.
PARTIES:
Panama
USA (United States)

103867 Bilateral Exchange **269 UNTS 3**
SIGNED: 4 Nov 55 FORCE: 22 May 56
REGISTERED: 4 Jun 57 USA (United States)
ARTICLES: 2 LANGUAGE: English.
HEADNOTE: RELATING CERTIFICATES AIRWOR-
THINESS IMPORTED AIRCRAFT
TOPIC: Air Transport
CONCEPTS: Conformity with municipal law. Ex-
change of information and documents. Recogni-
tion of legal documents. Use of facilities. Regis-
tration certificate. Airworthiness certificates.
PROCEDURE: Duration. Termination.
PARTIES:
Netherlands
USA (United States)

103868 Bilateral Agreement **269 UNTS 15**
SIGNED: 28 May 56 FORCE: 28 May 56
REGISTERED: 4 Jun 57 USA (United States)
ARTICLES: 7 LANGUAGE: English.
HEADNOTE: CONSTRUCTION FACILITIES MEDI-
CAL DEFENSE ASSISTANCE PROGRAM
TOPIC: Milit Assistance
CONCEPTS: Definition of terms. Visa abolition. In-
spection and observation. Licenses and permits.
Private contracts. Responsibility and liability. In-
demnities and reimbursements. Tax exemptions.
Customs exemptions. Materials, equipment and
services. Bases and facilities. Equipment and
supplies.
TREATY REF: 202UNTS301.
PROCEDURE: Termination.
PARTIES:
Pakistan
USA (United States)

103869 Bilateral Exchange **269 UNTS 25**
SIGNED: 25 Apr 56 FORCE: 26 Apr 56
REGISTERED: 4 Jun 57 USA (United States)
ARTICLES: 2 LANGUAGE: English. Spanish.
HEADNOTE: MILITARY ADVISORY GROUP
TOPIC: Military Mission
CONCEPTS: Airforce-army-navy personnel ratio.
Ranks and privileges. Conditions for assistance
missions.
TREATY REF: 222UNTS87.
PARTIES:
Honduras
USA (United States)

103870 Bilateral Exchange **269 UNTS 33**
SIGNED: 11 May 56 FORCE: 11 May 56
REGISTERED: 4 Jun 57 USA (United States)
ARTICLES: 2 LANGUAGE: English. Spanish.
HEADNOTE: FREE ENTRY PRIVILEGES FOREIGN
SERVICE PERSONNEL
TOPIC: Visas
CONCEPTS: Diplomatic privileges. General coop-
eration.
PARTIES:
Paraguay
USA (United States)

103871 Bilateral Exchange **269 UNTS 39**
SIGNED: 30 Jul 54 FORCE: 30 Jul 54
REGISTERED: 4 Jun 57 USA (United States)
ARTICLES: 2 LANGUAGE: English. Spanish.
HEADNOTE: PREVENTION FOOT-MOUTH DIS-
EASE
TOPIC: Sanitation
CONCEPTS: Sanitation. Border control. Public
health. International organizations.
INTL ORGS: Special Commission.
PARTIES:
Mexico
USA (United States)

103872 Bilateral Convention **269 UNTS 49**
SIGNED: 5 Feb 57 FORCE: 5 Feb 57

REGISTERED: 10 Jun 57 Belgium
ARTICLES: 3 LANGUAGE: English. French.
HEADNOTE: MANUFACTURES COMMERCIAL
TRADEMARKS
TOPIC: Patents/Copyrights
CONCEPTS: Conformity with municipal law. Trade-
marks.
PROCEDURE: Duration. Termination.
PARTIES:
Belgium
Philippines

103873 Bilateral Exchange **269 UNTS 53**
SIGNED: 21 Jul 55 FORCE: 19 Oct 55
REGISTERED: 13 Jun 57 USA (United States)
ARTICLES: 2 LANGUAGE: English.
HEADNOTE: SURPLUS SERVICES NAVAL VES-
SELS
TOPIC: Milit Assistance
CONCEPTS: Annex or appendix reference. Military
assistance.
PROCEDURE: Termination.
PARTIES:
Canada
USA (United States)

103874 Bilateral Agreement **269 UNTS 65**
SIGNED: 6 Apr 55 FORCE: 6 Apr 55
REGISTERED: 13 Jun 57 USA (United States)
ARTICLES: 9 LANGUAGE: English.
HEADNOTE: INTERCHANGE PATENT RIGHTS
TECHNICAL INFORMATION DEFENSE PUR-
POSES
TOPIC: General Military
CONCEPTS: Definition of terms. Detailed regula-
tions. Exceptions and exemptions. Conformity
with municipal law. Licenses and permits. Estab-
lishment of commission. Procedure. Claims and
settlements. Patents, copyrights and trade-
marks. Laws and formalities. Recognition. Gen-
eral technical assistance. Defense and security.
Security of information. Exchange of defense information.
TREATY REF: 80UNTS241.
PROCEDURE: Termination.
PARTIES:
Norway
USA (United States)
ANNEX
341 UNTS 410. USA (United States). Supplementation 5 Dec 58. Force 17 Jan 59.
341 UNTS 410. Norway. Supplementation
17 Jan 59. Force 17 Jan 59.
388 UNTS 374. Norway. Amendment 12 Aug 60.
Force 12 Aug 60.
388 UNTS 374. USA (United States). Amendment
25 Apr 60. Force 12 Aug 60.

103875 Unilateral Instrument **269 UNTS 77**
SIGNED: 23 May 57 FORCE: 23 May 57
REGISTERED: 18 Jun 57 United Nations
ARTICLES: 1 LANGUAGE: English.
HEADNOTE: ACCEPTANCE ICJ JURISDICTION
TOPIC: ICJ Option Clause
CONCEPTS: Exceptions and exemptions. Ex-
change of information and documents. Compul-
sory jurisdiction.
INTL ORGS: International Court of Justice.
PARTIES:
Pakistan
ANNEX
374 UNTS 382. Pakistan. Termination 13 Sep 60.

103876 Bilateral Exchange **269 UNTS 83**
SIGNED: 19 May 55 FORCE: 19 May 55
REGISTERED: 18 Jun 57 USA (United States)
ARTICLES: 2 LANGUAGE: English. Italian.
HEADNOTE: SURPLUS AGRI COMMOD
TOPIC: Direct Aid
CONCEPTS: Currency deposits. Exchange rates
and regulations. Payment schedules. Local cur-
rency. Surplus commodities.
TREATY REF: 237UNTS121.
PARTIES:
Italy
USA (United States)

103877 Bilateral Exchange **269 UNTS 89**
SIGNED: 30 Sep 55 FORCE: 30 Sep 55

REGISTERED: 18 Jun 57 USA (United States)
ARTICLES: 2 LANGUAGE: English.
HEADNOTE: SPECIAL PROGRAM FACILITIES AS-
SISTANCE
TOPIC: General Military
CONCEPTS: Change of circumstances. Guaran-
tees and safeguards. Use of facilities. Most fa-
vored nation clause. Domestic obligation. Gen-
eral technical assistance. Assistance. Military as-
sistance. Exchange of defense information.
Equipment and supplies.
TREATY REF: 174UNTS201; 258UNTS420.
PROCEDURE: Future Procedures Contemplated.
PARTIES:
USA (United States)
Yugoslavia

103878   Bilateral Exchange   **269 UNTS 97**
SIGNED: 29 Jun 55   FORCE: 29 Jun 55
REGISTERED: 18 Jun 57 USA (United States)
ARTICLES: 4 LANGUAGE: English.
HEADNOTE: OFFSHORE PROCUREMENT PRO-
GRAM
TOPIC: Milit Assistance
CONCEPTS: Annex or appendix reference. Confor-
mity with municipal law. General cooperation.
Exchange of information and documents. In-
spection and observation. Licenses and permits.
General property. Private contracts. Responsibil-
ity and liability. Indemnities and reimburse-
ments. National treatment. Tax exemptions. Ma-
terials, equipment and services. Defense and se-
curity. Security of information. Exchange of
defense information.
TREATY REF: 34UNTS243.
PARTIES:
Turkey
USA (United States)

103879   Bilateral Convention   **269 UNTS 133**
SIGNED: 12 Jun 56   FORCE: 25 Feb 57
REGISTERED: 18 Jun 57 UK Great Britain
ARTICLES: 10 LANGUAGE: English. French.
HEADNOTE: DOUBLE   TAXATION   ESTATES
DECEASED PERSONS
TOPIC: Taxation
CONCEPTS: Definition of terms. Nationality and
citizenship. Conformity with municipal law.
Claims and settlements. Taxation. Death duties.
Tax credits.
PROCEDURE: Duration. Ratification. Termination.
PARTIES:
Switzerland
UK Great Britain

103880   Bilateral Convention   **269 UNTS 147**
SIGNED: 20 Jul 56   FORCE: 13 Mar 57
REGISTERED: 18 Jun 57 UK Great Britain
ARTICLES: 22 LANGUAGE: English. German.
HEADNOTE: AVOIDANCE DOUBLE TAXATION FIS-
CAL EVASION
TOPIC: Taxation
CONCEPTS: Definition of terms. Territorial applica-
tion. Conformity with municipal law. Exchange
of official publications. Teacher and student ex-
change. Taxation. Tax credits. General. Tax ex-
emptions. Air transport. Merchant vessels.
PROCEDURE: Duration. Ratification. Termination.
PARTIES:
Austria
UK Great Britain

103881   Bilateral Agreement   **269 UNTS 189**
SIGNED: 22 Jul 55   FORCE: 7 Mar 57
REGISTERED: 18 Jun 57 UK Great Britain
ARTICLES: 16 LANGUAGE: English. German.
HEADNOTE: AIR SERVICES BETWEEN BEYOND
RESPECTIVE TERRITORIES
TOPIC: Air Transport
CONCEPTS: Definition of terms. Detailed regulations. Exceptions and exemptions. Annex or appendix reference. Conformity with municipal
law. General cooperation. Exchange of information and documents. Use of facilities. Arbitration.
Procedure. Special tribunals. Negotiation. Currency. Monetary and gold transfers. Fees and exemptions. Non-interest rates and fees. Most favored nation clause. National treatment. Customs exemptions. Routes and logistics. Permit
designation. Airport facilities. Conditions of air-

lines operating permission. Overflights and technical stops. Operating authorizations and regulations.
INTL ORGS: International Civil Aviation Organization. Arbitration Commission.
PROCEDURE: Amendment. Future Procedures
Contemplated. Ratification. Registration. Termination. Application to Non-self-governing Territories.
PARTIES:
Germany, West
UK Great Britain
ANNEX
449 UNTS 310. UK Great Britain. Amendment
28 May 62. Force 28 May 62.
449 UNTS 310. Germany, West. Amendment
28 May 62. Force 28 May 62.

103882   Bilateral Exchange   **269 UNTS 223**
SIGNED: 22 Jul 55   FORCE: 22 Jul 55
REGISTERED: 18 Jun 57 UK Great Britain
ARTICLES: 2 LANGUAGE: English. German.
HEADNOTE: APPLICATION ICAO CONVENTION
TOPIC: Air Transport
CONCEPTS: Annex type material. Air transport.
INTL ORGS: International Civil Aviation Organiza-
tion.
TREATY REF: 15UNTS295; 84UNTS389.
PARTIES:
Germany, West
UK Great Britain

103883   Bilateral Exchange   **269 UNTS 229**
SIGNED: 31 Oct 56   FORCE: 31 Oct 56
REGISTERED: 18 Jun 57 UK Great Britain
ARTICLES: 2 LANGUAGE: English. Spanish.
HEADNOTE: CURRENCY EXCHANGE
TOPIC: Finance
CONCEPTS: Detailed regulations. Banking. Ex-
change rates and regulations.
INTL ORGS: International Monetary Fund.
PARTIES:
Argentina
UK Great Britain
ANNEX
398 UNTS 350. UK Great Britain. Termination
20 Jun 60. Force 30 Dec 58.
398 UNTS 350. Argentina. Termination
20 Jan 60. Force 30 Dec 58.

103884   Bilateral Exchange   **269 UNTS 235**
SIGNED: 30 Jun 56   FORCE: 30 Jun 56
REGISTERED: 18 Jun 57 UK Great Britain
ARTICLES: 2 LANGUAGE: English. Spanish.
HEADNOTE: INTERIM ARRANGEMENTS TRADE
PAYMENTS
TOPIC: General Economic
CONCEPTS: Previous treaty replacement. General
trade. Payment schedules. Most favored nation
clause. Navigational conditions. Ports and pilot-
age.
TREATY REF: 210UNTS233; 218UNTS393; UN-
P1948-8-2.
PARTIES:
Argentina
UK Great Britain

103885   Multilateral Agreement   **269 UNTS 241**
SIGNED: 21 Sep 55   FORCE: 22 Jun 56
REGISTERED: 18 Jun 57 UK Great Britain
ARTICLES: 10 LANGUAGE: English. Japanese.
HEADNOTE: WAR CEMETERY
TOPIC: Other Military
CONCEPTS: Definition of terms. Annex or appen-
dix reference. Conformity with municipal law. Es-
tablishment of commission. Tax exemptions.
Customs exemptions. Upkeep of war graves.
INTL ORGS: Special Commission.
TREATY REF: 136UNTS45.
PARTIES:
Austria SIGNED: 21 Sep 55 FORCE: 22 Jun 56
Canada SIGNED: 21 Sep 55 FORCE: 22 Jun 56
India SIGNED: 21 Sep 55 FORCE: 22 Jun 56
Japan SIGNED: 21 Sep 55 RATIFIED: 22 May 56
   FORCE: 22 Jun 56
New Zealand SIGNED: 21 Sep 55 FORCE:
   22 Jun 56
Pakistan SIGNED: 21 Sep 55 FORCE: 22 Jun 56
South Africa SIGNED: 21 Sep 55 FORCE:
   22 Jun 56

UK Great Britain SIGNED: 21 Sep 55 FORCE:
   22 Jun 56

103886   Bilateral Exchange   **270 UNTS 3**
SIGNED: 12 May 55   FORCE: 12 May 55
REGISTERED: 19 Jun 57 USA (United States)
ARTICLES: 2 LANGUAGE: English. Spanish.
HEADNOTE: AMEND AGREEMENT RE HIGHWAY
CONSTRUCTION
TOPIC: Direct Aid
CONCEPTS: Annex type material. Non-bank
projects. Roads and highways.
TREATY REF: 24UNTS209.
PARTIES:
Honduras
USA (United States)

103887   Bilateral Agreement   **270 UNTS 15**
SIGNED: 25 Jun 55   FORCE: 25 Jun 55
REGISTERED: 19 Jun 57 USA (United States)
ARTICLES: 1 LANGUAGE: English. Russian.
HEADNOTE: BOUNDARY SECTOR BERLIN
TOPIC: Territory Boundary
CONCEPTS: Markers and definitions.
PARTIES:
USA (United States)
USSR (Soviet Union)

103888   Bilateral Agreement   **270 UNTS 19**
SIGNED: 1 Jul 55   FORCE: 1 Jul 55
REGISTERED: 19 Jun 57 USA (United States)
ARTICLES: 11 LANGUAGE: English. French.
HEADNOTE: TRANSPORT BURIAL EMBALMING
MEMBERS ARMED FORCES
TOPIC: Other Military
CONCEPTS: Annex or appendix reference. Confor-
mity with municipal law. Exchange of informa-
tion and documents. Informational records. San-
itation. Responsibility for war dead. Upkeep of
war graves. Establishment of war cemeteries.
TREATY REF: 199UNTS67.
PARTIES:
France
USA (United States)

103889   Bilateral Agreement   **270 UNTS 29**
SIGNED: 8 Jul 55   FORCE: 8 Jul 55
REGISTERED: 19 Jun 57 USA (United States)
ARTICLES: 5 LANGUAGE: English. Italian.
HEADNOTE: FACILITIES OVERHAUL REPAIR JET
ENGINES
TOPIC: Milit Installation
CONCEPTS: Definition of terms. Treaty implemen-
tation. Use of facilities. Indemnities and reim-
bursements. Customs exemptions. Materials,
equipment and services. Surplus property. Bases
and facilities. Equipment and supplies. Restric-
tions on transfer.
TREATY REF: 34UNTS243.
PROCEDURE: Future Procedures Contemplated.
Termination.
PARTIES:
Italy
USA (United States)

103890   Bilateral Exchange   **270 UNTS 43**
SIGNED: 30 May 55   FORCE: 30 May 55
REGISTERED: 19 Jun 57 USA (United States)
ARTICLES: 2 LANGUAGE: English. Arabic.
HEADNOTE: ECONOMIC ASSISTANCE
TOPIC: Direct Aid
CONCEPTS: Annex type material. Conformity with
municipal law. Exchange of information and doc-
uments. Inspection and observation. Monetary
and gold transfers. Financial programs. Eco-
nomic assistance.
TREATY REF: 238UNTS217.
PARTIES:
Libya
USA (United States)

103891   Bilateral Exchange   **270 UNTS 51**
SIGNED: 3 Jun 55   FORCE: 3 Jun 55
REGISTERED: 19 Jun 57 USA (United States)
ARTICLES: 2 LANGUAGE: English. Japanese.
HEADNOTE: ASSEMBLY AIRPLANES MUTUAL DE-
FENSE ASSISTANCE PROGRAM
TOPIC: Milit Assistance

CONCEPTS: Conformity with municipal law. General cooperation. Indemnities and reimbursements. Materials, equipment and services. Self-defense. Military assistance. Exchange of defense information. Equipment and supplies.
TREATY REF: 232UNTS169.
PROCEDURE: Future Procedures Contemplated.
PARTIES:
Japan
USA (United States)

103892   Bilateral Agreement   **270 UNTS 61**
SIGNED: 26 May 55   FORCE: 26 May 55
REGISTERED: 19 Jun 57 USA (United States)
ARTICLES: 11 LANGUAGE: English. Russian.
HEADNOTE: RETURN NAVAL CRAFT
TOPIC: Milit Assistance
CONCEPTS: Detailed regulations. Time limit. Annex or appendix reference. Expense sharing formulae. Delivery schedules. Ports and pilotage. Lend lease. Naval vessels. Return of equipment and recapture.
PARTIES:
USA (United States)
USSR (Soviet Union)

103893   Bilateral Exchange   **270 UNTS 71**
SIGNED: 3 Aug 55   FORCE: 3 Aug 55
REGISTERED: 19 Jun 57 USA (United States)
ARTICLES: 4 LANGUAGE: English. Portuguese.
HEADNOTE: URANIUM RESOURCES
TOPIC: Scientific Project
CONCEPTS: Operating agencies. General property. Use of facilities. Specialists exchange. Research and scientific projects. Nuclear research. Research and development. Funding procedures. Tax exemptions. Domestic obligation. Materials, equipment and services. Nuclear materials. Rights of supplier. Repatriation of civilians. Regulation of natural resources.
PROCEDURE: Duration. Renewal or Revival. Termination.
PARTIES:
Brazil
USA (United States)
              ANNEX
288 UNTS 378. USA (United States). Prolongation 5 Aug 57. Force 5 Aug 57.
288 UNTS 378. Brazil. Prolongation 5 Aug 57. Force 5 Aug 57.
303 UNTS 364. USA (United States). Abrogation 26 Dec 57. Force 26 Dec 57.
303 UNTS 364. Brazil. Abrogation 26 Dec 57. Force 26 Dec 57.
380 UNTS 451. USA (United States). Amendment 2 Dec 58. Force 23 Dec 59.
380 UNTS 451. Brazil. Amendment 2 Dec 58. Force 23 Dec 59.
380 UNTS 454. Brazil. Prolongation 6 Jul 60. Force 6 Jul 60.
380 UNTS 454. USA (United States). Prolongation 6 Jan 60. Force 6 Jul 60.

103894   Bilateral Agreement   **270 UNTS 83**
SIGNED: 28 Jan 55   FORCE: 12 Sep 55
REGISTERED: 19 Jun 57 USA (United States)
ARTICLES: 11 LANGUAGE: English. French.
HEADNOTE: MILITARY ASSISTANCE
TOPIC: Milit Assistance
CONCEPTS: Exceptions and exemptions. Guarantees and safeguards. Non-prejudice to UN charter. Privileges and immunities. Conformity with municipal law. Inspection and observation. Public information. Use of facilities. Garnishment of funds. Local currency. Most favored nation clause. Tax exemptions. Recognition. Customs exemptions. Domestic obligation. Materials, equipment and services. Aid missions. Joint defense. Defense and security. Military assistance. Return of equipment and recapture. Security of information. Exchange of defense information. Restrictions on transfer. Raw materials.
INTL ORGS: United Nations.
TREATY REF: 21UNTS77.
PROCEDURE: Amendment. Future Procedures Contemplated. Ratification. Registration. Termination.
PARTIES:
Haiti
USA (United States)

103895   Bilateral Exchange   **270 UNTS 97**
SIGNED: 5 Apr 55   FORCE: 5 Apr 55
REGISTERED: 19 Jun 57 USA (United States)
ARTICLES: 2 LANGUAGE: English. French.
HEADNOTE: DISPOSITION SURPLUS EQUIPMENT MATERIALS
TOPIC: Milit Assistance
CONCEPTS: Exchange of information and documents. Reexport of goods, etc.. Delivery schedules. Materials, equipment and services. Surplus property. Return of equipment and recapture.
TREATY REF: 272UNTS83.
PARTIES:
Haiti
USA (United States)

103896 Multilateral Agreement **270 UNTS 103**
SIGNED: 25 Apr 56   FORCE: 16 Jul 56
REGISTERED: 20 Jun 57 USA (United States)
ARTICLES: 23 LANGUAGE: English. French. Spanish.
HEADNOTE: INTERNATIONAL WHEAT AGREEMENT
TOPIC: Commodity Trade
CONCEPTS: Definition of terms. Detailed regulations. Territorial application. General provisions. General cooperation. Exchange of information and documents. Recognition and enforcement of legal decisions. Responsibility and liability. Procedure. Finances and payments. Balance of payments. Non-interest rates and fees. Commodity trade. Delivery guarantees. Quotas. Decisions. Subsidiary organ. Liaison with other IGO's. Internal structure.
INTL ORGS: International Wheat Council.
TREATY REF: 203UNTS179; 256UNTS364.
PROCEDURE: Amendment. Accession. Duration. Ratification. Termination.
PARTIES:
Argentina SIGNED: 18 May 56 RATIFIED: 25 Sep 56 FORCE: 16 Jul 56
Australia SIGNED: 17 May 56 RATIFIED: 27 Nov 56 FORCE: 16 Jul 56
Austria SIGNED: 17 May 56 RATIFIED: 10 Jul 56 FORCE: 16 Jul 56
Belgium SIGNED: 15 May 56 RATIFIED: 30 Nov 56 FORCE: 16 Jul 56
Bel-Lux Econ Union SIGNED: 15 May 56 FORCE: 16 Jul 56
Bolivia SIGNED: 18 May 56 RATIFIED: 28 Nov 56 FORCE: 16 Jul 56
Brazil SIGNED: 17 May 56
Canada SIGNED: 16 May 56 FORCE: 16 Jul 56
Costa Rica SIGNED: 18 May 56 RATIFIED: 30 Nov 56 FORCE: 16 Jul 56
Denmark SIGNED: 16 May 56 RATIFIED: 22 Aug 56 FORCE: 16 Jul 56
Dominican Republic SIGNED: 18 May 56 RATIFIED: 8 Nov 56 FORCE: 16 Jul 56
Ecuador SIGNED: 15 May 56 RATIFIED: 28 Nov 56 FORCE: 16 Jul 56
United Arab Rep SIGNED: 18 May 56 RATIFIED: 1 Dec 56 FORCE: 16 Jul 56
El Salvador SIGNED: 16 May 56 RATIFIED: 23 Oct 56 FORCE: 16 Jul 56
France SIGNED: 15 May 56 RATIFIED: 30 Nov 56 FORCE: 16 Jul 56
Germany, West SIGNED: 18 May 56 RATIFIED: 30 Nov 56 FORCE: 16 Jul 56
Greece SIGNED: 15 May 56 RATIFIED: 28 Nov 56 FORCE: 16 Jul 56
Guatemala SIGNED: 18 May 56 RATIFIED: 6 Nov 56 FORCE: 16 Jul 56
Iceland RATIFIED: 23 Nov 56 FORCE: 16 Jul 56
India SIGNED: 18 May 56 RATIFIED: 19 Jul 56 FORCE: 16 Jul 56
Ireland SIGNED: 14 May 56 RATIFIED: 1 Oct 56 FORCE: 16 Jul 56
Israel SIGNED: 14 May 56 RATIFIED: 2 Nov 56 FORCE: 16 Jul 56
Italy SIGNED: 15 May 56 RATIFIED: 25 Sep 56 FORCE: 16 Jul 56
Japan SIGNED: 15 May 56 RATIFIED: 30 Nov 56 FORCE: 16 Jul 56
Korea, South SIGNED: 18 May 56 RATIFIED: 7 Jul 56 FORCE: 16 Jul 56
Lebanon SIGNED: 17 May 56 RATIFIED: 20 Mar 57 FORCE: 20 Mar 57
Liberia SIGNED: 18 May 56 RATIFIED: 1 Dec 56 FORCE: 16 Jul 56
Mexico SIGNED: 17 May 56 RATIFIED: 30 Nov 56 FORCE: 16 Jul 56
Netherlands SIGNED: 17 May 56 RATIFIED: 27 Mar 57 FORCE: 27 Mar 57
New Zealand SIGNED: 16 May 56 RATIFIED: 26 Oct 56 FORCE: 16 Jul 56
Nicaragua SIGNED: 17 May 56 RATIFIED: 27 Nov 56 FORCE: 16 Jul 56
Norway SIGNED: 15 May 56 RATIFIED: 26 Nov 56 FORCE: 16 Jul 56
Panama SIGNED: 16 May 56 RATIFIED: 14 Dec 56 FORCE: 14 Dec 56
Peru SIGNED: 16 May 56 RATIFIED: 11 Sep 56 FORCE: 16 Jul 56
Philippines SIGNED: 18 May 56 RATIFIED: 19 Nov 56 FORCE: 16 Jul 56
Portugal SIGNED: 16 May 56 RATIFIED: 19 Nov 56 FORCE: 16 Jul 56
South Africa SIGNED: 18 May 56 RATIFIED: 16 Jul 56 FORCE: 16 Jul 56
Sweden SIGNED: 16 May 56 RATIFIED: 29 Nov 56 FORCE: 16 Jul 56
Switzerland SIGNED: 18 May 56 RATIFIED: 6 Nov 56 FORCE: 16 Jul 56
USA (United States) SIGNED: 18 May 56 RATIFIED: 16 Jul 56 FORCE: 16 Jul 56
Vatican/Holy See SIGNED: 16 May 56 RATIFIED: 9 Jul 56 FORCE: 16 Jul 56
Yugoslavia SIGNED: 18 May 56 RATIFIED: 28 Nov 56 FORCE: 16 Jul 56
              ANNEX
320 UNTS 348. Brazil. Acceptance 31 Dec 57.

103897   Bilateral Exchange   **270 UNTS 199**
SIGNED: 10 Mar 56   FORCE: 10 Mar 56
REGISTERED: 25 Jun 57 USA (United States)
ARTICLES: 2 LANGUAGE: English. Spanish.
HEADNOTE: INFORMATIONAL MEDIA GUARANTY PROGRAM
TOPIC: Mass Media
CONCEPTS: Local currency. Media guaranty.
PARTIES:
Bolivia
USA (United States)

103898   Bilateral Exchange   **270 UNTS 205**
SIGNED: 6 Mar 56   FORCE: 6 Mar 56
REGISTERED: 25 Jun 57 USA (United States)
ARTICLES: 2 LANGUAGE: English. Icelandic.
HEADNOTE: TRADE LIST AMENDMENT
TOPIC: General Trade
CONCEPTS: Annex type material. Commodity trade.
TREATY REF: 29UNTS317.
PARTIES:
Iceland
USA (United States)

103899   Bilateral Agreement   **270 UNTS 211**
SIGNED: 16 Jul 55   FORCE: 1 Jan 56
REGISTERED: 25 Jun 57 USA (United States)
ARTICLES: 19 LANGUAGE: English. Khmer.
HEADNOTE: PARCEL POST
TOPIC: Postal Service
CONCEPTS: Territorial application. Domestic legislation. Responsibility and liability. Compensation. Indemnities and reimbursements. Payment schedules. Postal services. Regulations. Insured letters and boxes. Parcel post.
INTL ORGS: Universal Postal Union.
TREATY REF: TIAS2287; 169UNTS3; 186UNTS356.
PROCEDURE: Duration. Termination.
PARTIES:
Spain
USA (United States)

103900   Bilateral Agreement   **270 UNTS 245**
SIGNED: 28 Jul 55   FORCE: 28 Jul 55
REGISTERED: 25 Jun 57 USA (United States)
ARTICLES: 9 LANGUAGE: English. Arabic.
HEADNOTE: EDUCATION
TOPIC: Non-IBRD Project
CONCEPTS: Exchange of information and documents. Informational records. Operating agencies. Education. Financial programs. Funding procedures. Aid missions. Non-bank projects.
PROCEDURE: Duration. Termination.
PARTIES:
Libya
USA (United States)

103901 Bilateral Agreement **270 UNTS 269**
SIGNED: 28 Jul 55 FORCE: 28 Jul 55
REGISTERED: 25 Jun 57 USA (United States)
ARTICLES: 9 LANGUAGE: English. Arabic.
HEADNOTE: PROGRAM PUBLIC HEALTH
TOPIC: Non-IBRD Project
CONCEPTS: Exchange of information and documents. Informational records. Operating agencies. General health, education, culture, welfare and labor. Financial programs. Funding procedures. Aid missions. Non-bank projects.
TREATY REF: 264UNTS247.
PROCEDURE: Duration. Termination.
PARTIES:
Libya
USA (United States)

103902 Bilateral Agreement **270 UNTS 293**
SIGNED: 28 Jul 55 FORCE: 28 Jul 55
REGISTERED: 25 Jun 57 USA (United States)
ARTICLES: 9 LANGUAGE: English. Arabic.
HEADNOTE: NATURAL RESOURCES COOPERATION
TOPIC: Non-IBRD Project
CONCEPTS: Conservation of specific resources. Natural resources.
PROCEDURE: Duration. Termination.
PARTIES:
Libya
USA (United States)

103903 Bilateral Agreement **270 UNTS 317**
SIGNED: 28 Jul 55 FORCE: 28 Jul 55
REGISTERED: 25 Jun 57 USA (United States)
ARTICLES: 9 LANGUAGE: English. Arabic.
HEADNOTE: COOPERATIVE PROGRAM AGRICULTURE
TOPIC: Non-IBRD Project
CONCEPTS: Exchange of information and documents. Informational records. Operating agencies. Financial programs. Funding procedures. Agriculture. Aid missions. Non-bank projects.
TREATY REF: 264UNTS247.
PROCEDURE: Duration. Termination.
PARTIES:
Libya
USA (United States)

103904 Bilateral Exchange **270 UNTS 341**
SIGNED: 23 Sep 55 FORCE: 23 Sep 55
REGISTERED: 25 Jun 57 USA (United States)
ARTICLES: 4 LANGUAGE: English. French.
HEADNOTE: DISPOSITION SURPLUS EQUIPMENT MATERIALS
TOPIC: Milit Assistance
CONCEPTS: Exchange of information and documents. Reexport of goods, etc.. Delivery schedules. Materials, equipment and services. Surplus property. Return of equipment and recapture.
TREATY REF: 181UNTS177.
PARTIES:
France
USA (United States)

103905 Bilateral Agreement **270 UNTS 351**
SIGNED: 24 Jun 55 FORCE: 24 Jun 55
REGISTERED: 25 Jun 57 USA (United States)
ARTICLES: 6 LANGUAGE: English.
HEADNOTE: AGRI COMMOD TITLE I
TOPIC: US Agri Commod Aid
CONCEPTS: General provisions. Exchange of information and documents. Reexport of goods, etc.. Exchange rates and regulations. Transportation costs. Local currency. Commodities schedule. Purchase authorization. Surplus commodities. IGO obligations.
PARTIES:
Greece
USA (United States)
ANNEX
273 UNTS 322. USA (United States). Amendment 13 Feb 56. Force 17 Feb 56.
273 UNTS 322. Greece. Amendment 17 Feb 56. Force 17 Feb 56.
410 UNTS 314. USA (United States). Supplementation 3 Apr 61. Force 13 Apr 61.
410 UNTS 314. Greece. Supplementation 13 Apr 61. Force 13 Apr 61.

103906 Bilateral Agreement **270 UNTS 361**
SIGNED: 24 Jun 55 FORCE: 24 Jun 55
REGISTERED: 25 Jun 57 USA (United States)
ARTICLES: 6 LANGUAGE: English.
HEADNOTE: AGRI COMMOD TITLE I
TOPIC: US Agri Commod Aid
CONCEPTS: General provisions. Exchange of information and documents. Reexport of goods, etc.. Exchange rates and regulations. Transportation costs. Local currency. Commodities schedule. Purchase authorization. Surplus commodities. Mutual consultation.
PARTIES:
Greece
USA (United States)
ANNEX
410 UNTS 314. USA (United States). Supplementation 3 Apr 61. Force 13 Apr 61.
410 UNTS 314. Greece. Supplementation 13 Apr 61. Force 13 Apr 61.

103907 Multilateral Agreement **271 UNTS 2**
SIGNED: 17 Feb 57 FORCE: 17 Feb 57
REGISTERED: 25 Jun 57 United Nations
ARTICLES: 6 LANGUAGE: English. Arabic.
HEADNOTE: TECHNICAL ASSISTANCE
TOPIC: Tech Assistance
CONCEPTS: Definition of terms. Annex or appendix reference. Privileges and immunities. General cooperation. Exchange of information and documents. Personnel. Responsibility and liability. Title and deeds. Use of facilities. Exchange. Scholarships and grants. Vocational training. Research and development. Exchange rates and regulations. Expense sharing formulae. Local currency. Domestic obligation. General technical assistance. Materials, equipment and services. IGO status. Conformity with IGO decisions.
TREATY REF: 76UNTS132.
PROCEDURE: Amendment. Termination.
PARTIES:
FAO (Food Agri) SIGNED: 17 Feb 57 FORCE: 17 Feb 57
ICAO (Civil Aviat) SIGNED: 17 Feb 57 FORCE: 17 Feb 57
ILO (Labor Org) SIGNED: 17 Feb 57 FORCE: 17 Feb 57
ITU (Telecommun) SIGNED: 17 Feb 57 FORCE: 17 Feb 57
UNESCO (Educ/Cult) SIGNED: 17 Feb 57 FORCE: 17 Feb 57
United Nations SIGNED: 17 Feb 57 FORCE: 17 Feb 57
WHO (World Health) SIGNED: 17 Feb 57 FORCE: 17 Feb 57
WMO (Meteorology) SIGNED: 17 Feb 57 FORCE: 17 Feb 57
Saudi Arabia SIGNED: 17 Feb 57 FORCE: 17 Feb 57

103908 Multilateral Agreement **271 UNTS 30**
SIGNED: 28 Mar 57 FORCE: 28 Mar 57
REGISTERED: 25 Jun 57 United Nations
ARTICLES: 6 LANGUAGE: French.
HEADNOTE: TECHNICAL ASSISTANCE
TOPIC: Tech Assistance
CONCEPTS: Definition of terms. Annex or appendix reference. Privileges and immunities. General cooperation. Exchange of information and documents. Personnel. Responsibility and liability. Title and deeds. Use of facilities. Exchange. Scholarships and grants. Vocational training. Research and development. Exchange rates and regulations. Expense sharing formulae. Local currency. Domestic obligation. General technical assistance. Materials, equipment and services. IGO status. Conformity with IGO decisions.
TREATY REF: 76UNTS132; 1UNTS15; 33UNTS261.
PROCEDURE: Amendment. Termination.
PARTIES:
Morocco SIGNED: 28 Mar 67 FORCE: 28 Mar 67
FAO (Food Agri) SIGNED: 28 Mar 67 FORCE: 28 Mar 67
ICAO (Civil Aviat) SIGNED: 28 Mar 67 FORCE: 28 Mar 67
ILO (Labor Org) SIGNED: 28 Mar 67 FORCE: 28 Mar 67
ITU (Telecommun) SIGNED: 28 Mar 67 FORCE: 28 Mar 67
UNESCO (Educ/Cult) SIGNED: 28 Mar 67 FORCE: 28 Mar 67

United Nations SIGNED: 28 Mar 67 FORCE: 28 Mar 67
WHO (World Health) SIGNED: 28 Mar 67 FORCE: 28 Mar 67
WMO (Meteorology) SIGNED: 28 Mar 67 FORCE: 28 Mar 67

103909 Bilateral Agreement **271 UNTS 49**
SIGNED: 23 May 56 FORCE: 1 Jan 57
REGISTERED: 26 Jun 57 Denmark
ARTICLES: 22 LANGUAGE: Danish. Norwegian.
HEADNOTE: ADMINISTATIVE ASSISTANCE TAXATION
TOPIC: Taxation
CONCEPTS: Definition of terms. Territorial application. General cooperation. Exchange of official publications. Claims and settlements. Tax credits. General.
PROCEDURE: Duration. Ratification. Termination.
PARTIES:
Denmark
Norway

103910 Bilateral Agreement **271 UNTS 75**
SIGNED: 23 May 56 FORCE: 21 Dec 56
REGISTERED: 26 Jun 57 Denmark
ARTICLES: 12 LANGUAGE: Danish. Norwegian.
HEADNOTE: DOUBLE TAXATION DEATH DUTIES
TOPIC: Taxation
CONCEPTS: Privileges and immunities. Nationality and citizenship. Debts. Taxation. Death duties.
PROCEDURE: Duration. Ratification. Termination.
PARTIES:
Denmark
Norway

103911 Bilateral Agreement **271 UNTS 93**
SIGNED: 27 Oct 52 FORCE: 18 Feb 57
REGISTERED: 26 Jun 57 Denmark
ARTICLES: 19 LANGUAGE: Danish. Spanish.
HEADNOTE: AIR SERVICES
TOPIC: Air Transport
CONCEPTS: Detailed regulations. Annex or appendix reference. Conformity with municipal law. Licenses and permits. Recognition of legal documents. Use of facilities. Arbitration. Procedure. Existing tribunals. Fees and exemptions. Non-interest rates and fees. Most favored nation clause. National treatment. Customs exemptions. Competency certificate. Routes and logistics. Navigational conditions. Permit designation. Airport facilities. Airworthiness certificates. Conditions of airlines operating permission. Overflights and technical stops. Operating authorizations and regulations. Licenses and certificates of nationality.
INTL ORGS: International Civil Aviation Organization.
TREATY REF: 15UNTS295.
PROCEDURE: Future Procedures Contemplated. Ratification. Registration. Termination.
PARTIES:
Chile
Denmark

103912 Bilateral Protocol **271 UNTS 125**
SIGNED: 14 May 56 FORCE: 14 May 56
REGISTERED: 26 Jun 57 Denmark
ARTICLES: 1 LANGUAGE: Danish. Russian.
HEADNOTE: RECIPROCAL SUPPLY GOODS
TOPIC: General Trade
CONCEPTS: Treaty implementation. Annex or appendix reference. Annex type material. Licenses and permits.
TREATY REF: JOINT COMMUNIQUE 6MARCH 56.
PARTIES:
Denmark
USSR (Soviet Union)

103913 Bilateral Exchange **271 UNTS 135**
SIGNED: 27 Jun 57 FORCE: 10 Dec 56
REGISTERED: 1 Jul 57 United Nations
ARTICLES: 2 LANGUAGE: English.
HEADNOTE: SERVICE UNITED NATIONS EMERGENCY FORCE
TOPIC: Status of Forces
CONCEPTS: Annex or appendix reference. Investigation of violations. Establishment of commission. Arbitration. Procedure. Indemnities and re-

imbursements. Jurisdiction. Status of forces. IGO status. Peace-keeping force.
INTL ORGS: International Court of Justice. Arbitration Commission.
TREATY REF: 260UNTS61.
PROCEDURE: Future Procedures Contemplated.
PARTIES:
Finland
United Nations

103914 Bilateral Exchange **271 UNTS 187**
SIGNED: 1 Jul 57 FORCE: 18 Nov 56
REGISTERED: 1 Jul 57 United Nations
ARTICLES: 2 LANGUAGE: English.
HEADNOTE: UN EMERGENCY FORCE NATIONAL CONTINGENT
TOPIC: Status of Forces
CONCEPTS: Annex or appendix reference. Investigation of violations. Establishment of commission. Arbitration. Procedure. Indemnities and reimbursements. Jurisdiction. Status of forces. IGO status. Peace-keeping force.
INTL ORGS: International Court of Justice.
TREATY REF: 260UNTS61.
PARTIES:
United Nations
Sweden

103915 Multilateral Convention **271 UNTS 199**
SIGNED: 22 Jun 35 FORCE: 23 Jun 57
REGISTERED: 2 Jul 57 ILO (Labor Org)
ARTICLES: 8 LANGUAGE: English. French.
HEADNOTE: REDUCTION HOURS 40 PER WEEK
TOPIC: ILO Labor
CONCEPTS: Detailed regulations. ILO conventions. Holidays and rest periods.
INTL ORGS: International Labour Organization.
PROCEDURE: Amendment. Denunciation. Duration. Ratification. Registration. Renewal or Revival.
PARTIES:
Multilateral

103916 Bilateral Exchange **271 UNTS 207**
SIGNED: 30 Mar 55 FORCE: 1 Jan 53
REGISTERED: 2 Jul 57 New Zealand
ARTICLES: 8 LANGUAGE: English. German.
HEADNOTE: CIVIL & COMMERCIAL MATTERS
TOPIC: Admin Cooperation
CONCEPTS: Juridical personality.
PARTIES:
Germany, West
New Zealand

103917 Bilateral Exchange **271 UNTS 223**
SIGNED: 9 Jul 57 FORCE: 10 Nov 56
REGISTERED: 9 Jul 57 United Nations
ARTICLES: 2 LANGUAGE: English.
HEADNOTE: SERVICE UN EMERGENCY FORCE
TOPIC: Status of Forces
CONCEPTS: Annex or appendix reference. Investigation of violations. Establishment of commission. Arbitration. Procedure. Indemnities and reimbursements. Jurisdiction. Status of forces. IGO status. Peace-keeping force.
INTL ORGS: International Court of Justice. Arbitration Commission.
PARTIES:
Norway
United Nations

103918 Bilateral Agreement **271 UNTS 235**
SIGNED: 1 Apr 57 FORCE: 1 Apr 57
REGISTERED: 10 Jul 57 Australia
ARTICLES: 10 LANGUAGE: English.
HEADNOTE: MIGRATION SCHEME
TOPIC: Non-ILO Labor
CONCEPTS: Definition of terms. Detailed regulations. Border traffic and migration. Exchange of information and documents. Public health. Non-ILO labor relations. Administrative cooperation. Sickness and invalidity insurance. Unemployment. Accounting procedures. Expense sharing formulae. Transportation costs. General aid.
PROCEDURE: Duration. Termination.
PARTIES:
Australia
UK Great Britain

ANNEX
349 UNTS 336. Australia. Amendment 12 Jun 58. Force 19 Jun 58.
349 UNTS 336. UK Great Britain. Amendment 13 Jun 58. Force 19 Jun 58.
397 UNTS 332. UK Great Britain. Amendment 3 Sep 60. Force 3 Sep 60.
397 UNTS 332. Australia. Amendment 1 Sep 61. Force 3 Sep 60.

103919 Bilateral Agreement **271 UNTS 243**
SIGNED: 30 Jun 56 FORCE: 30 Jun 56
REGISTERED: 10 Jul 57 USA (United States)
ARTICLES: 36 LANGUAGE: English. Spanish.
HEADNOTE: AIR FORCE MISSION
TOPIC: Military Mission
CONCEPTS: Definition of terms. Visa abolition. Responsibility and liability. Use of facilities. Compensation. Indemnities and reimbursements. Currency. Exchange rates and regulations. Expense sharing formulae. Tax exemptions. Customs exemptions. Military assistance. Military training. Security of information. Airforce-army-navy personnel ratio. Ranks and privileges. Conditions for assistance missions. Third country military personnel. Status of forces.
PROCEDURE: Termination.
PARTIES:
Bolivia
USA (United States)
ANNEX
342 UNTS 356. USA (United States). Amendment 2 Apr 59. Force 3 Apr 59.
342 UNTS 356. Bolivia. Amendment 3 Apr 59. Force 3 Apr 59.

103920 Bilateral Agreement **271 UNTS 269**
SIGNED: 30 Jun 56 FORCE: 30 Jun 56
REGISTERED: 10 Jul 57 USA (United States)
ARTICLES: 35 LANGUAGE: English. Spanish.
HEADNOTE: ARMY MISSION-BOLIVIA
TOPIC: Military Mission
CONCEPTS: Payment for war supplies. Military assistance. Airforce-army-navy personnel ratio. Ranks and privileges. Conditions for assistance missions.
PARTIES:
Bolivia
USA (United States)
ANNEX
342 UNTS 360. Bolivia. Amendment 3 Apr 59. Force 3 Apr 59.
342 UNTS 360. USA (United States). Amendment 2 Apr 59. Force 3 Apr 59.

103921 Bilateral Exchange **271 UNTS 295**
SIGNED: 23 Jun 56 FORCE: 23 Jun 56
REGISTERED: 10 Jul 57 USA (United States)
ARTICLES: 2 LANGUAGE: English. Persian.
HEADNOTE: ECONOMIC DEVELOPMENT
TOPIC: Direct Aid
CONCEPTS: Treaty implementation. General cooperation. Economic assistance. Grants. Loan repayment.
PARTIES:
Afghanistan
USA (United States)

103922 Bilateral Exchange **271 UNTS 303**
SIGNED: 14 Mar 56 FORCE: 6 Jul 56
REGISTERED: 10 Jul 57 USA (United States)
ARTICLES: 3 LANGUAGE: English. Spanish.
HEADNOTE: WEATHER STATION
TOPIC: Scientific Project
CONCEPTS: General cooperation. Exchange of information and documents. Operating agencies. General property. Research and scientific projects. Research cooperation. Meteorology. Research and development. Expense sharing formulae. Tax exemptions.
PROCEDURE: Duration. Renewal or Revival. Termination.
PARTIES:
Colombia
USA (United States)

103923 Bilateral Exchange **271 UNTS 319**
SIGNED: 18 Apr 56 FORCE: 18 Apr 56
REGISTERED: 10 Jul 57 USA (United States)

ARTICLES: 2 LANGUAGE: English. German.
HEADNOTE: TRANSFER GERMAN FILES ARCHIVES
TOPIC: Admin Cooperation
CONCEPTS: Exchange of information and documents.
INTL ORGS: Allied Military Occupation.
PARTIES:
Germany, West
USA (United States)

103924 Bilateral Agreement **271 UNTS 329**
SIGNED: 5 Mar 56 FORCE: 5 Mar 56
REGISTERED: 10 Jul 57 USA (United States)
ARTICLES: 6 LANGUAGE: English. Spanish.
HEADNOTE: AGRI COMMOD TITLE I
TOPIC: US Agri Commod Aid
CONCEPTS: General provisions. Annex or appendix reference. Exchange of information and documents. Reexport of goods, etc.. Exchange rates and regulations. Transportation costs. Local currency. Commodities schedule. Purchase authorization. Surplus commodities. Mutual consultation.
PARTIES:
Spain
USA (United States)
ANNEX
275 UNTS 324. USA (United States). Supplementation 17 Mar 56. Force 17 Mar 56.
275 UNTS 324. Spain. Supplementation 17 Mar 56. Force 17 Mar 56.
277 UNTS 366. USA (United States). Supplementation 15 Sep 56. Force 15 Sep 56.
277 UNTS 366. Spain. Supplementation 15 Sep 56. Force 15 Sep 56.
277 UNTS 370. Spain. Supplementation 15 Sep 56. Force 15 Sep 56.
277 UNTS 370. USA (United States). Supplementation 15 Sep 56. Force 15 Sep 56.
277 UNTS 372. USA (United States). Amendment 20 Sep 56. Force 28 Sep 56.
277 UNTS 372. Spain. Amendment 28 Sep 56. Force 28 Sep 56.

103925 Bilateral Agreement **271 UNTS 345**
SIGNED: 2 Mar 56 FORCE: 2 Mar 56
REGISTERED: 10 Jul 57 USA (United States)
ARTICLES: 6 LANGUAGE: English.
HEADNOTE: AGRI COMMOD AGREEMENT TITLE I
TOPIC: US Agri Commod Aid
CONCEPTS: General provisions. Annex or appendix reference. Exchange of information and documents. Certificates of origin. Exchange rates and regulations. Transportation costs. Local currency. Commodities schedule. Purchase authorization. Surplus commodities. Mutual consultation.
PARTIES:
Indonesia
USA (United States)
ANNEX
335 UNTS 328. USA (United States). Amendment 22 May 58. Force 22 May 58.
335 UNTS 328. Indonesia. Amendment 22 May 58. Force 22 May 58.
377 UNTS 434. Indonesia. Amendment 11 Mar 59. Force 11 Mar 59.
377 UNTS 434. USA (United States). Amendment 18 Feb 59. Force 11 Mar 59.
401 UNTS 296. Indonesia. Amendment 7 Dec 60. Force 7 Dec 60.
401 UNTS 296. USA (United States). Amendment 7 Dec 60. Force 7 Dec 60.

103926 Bilateral Exchange **271 UNTS 361**
SIGNED: 7 Mar 56 FORCE: 7 Mar 56
REGISTERED: 10 Jul 57 USA (United States)
ARTICLES: 3 LANGUAGE: English.
HEADNOTE: ILLICIT TRAFFIC NARCOTIC DRUGS
TOPIC: Sanitation
CONCEPTS: Treaty interpretation. Previous treaty replacement. General cooperation. Exchange of information and documents. Informational records. Narcotic drugs.
TREATY REF: 79LTS235.
PARTIES:
Germany, West
USA (United States)

103927 Bilateral Agreement **271 UNTS 371**
SIGNED: 2 Mar 56 FORCE: 2 Mar 56
REGISTERED: 10 Jul 57 USA (United States)
ARTICLES: 6 LANGUAGE: English.

HEADNOTE: AGRI COMMOD TITLE I
TOPIC: US Agri Commod Aid
CONCEPTS: General provisions. Exchange of information and documents. Reexport of goods, etc.. Exchange rates and regulations. Transportation costs. Local currency. Commodities schedule. Purchase authorization. Surplus commodities. IGO obligations.
PARTIES:
Pakistan
USA (United States)

103928   Bilateral Agreement   **272 UNTS 3**
SIGNED: 13 Mar 56   FORCE: 13 Mar 56
REGISTERED: 10 Jul 57 USA (United States)
ARTICLES: 6 LANGUAGE: English.
HEADNOTE: AGRI COMMOD TITLE I
TOPIC: US Agri Commod Aid
CONCEPTS: General provisions. Annex or appendix reference. Exchange of information and documents. Reexport of goods, etc.. Currency. Exchange rates and regulations. Transportation costs. Local currency. Commodities schedule. Purchase authorization. Surplus commodities. Mutual consultation.
PARTIES:
Korea, South
USA (United States)
                    ANNEX
279 UNTS 350.   Korea, South.   Amendment 27 Jul 56. Force 27 Jul 56.
279 UNTS 350. USA (United States). Amendment 25 Jul 56. Force 27 Jul 56.
281 UNTS 412. USA (United States). Amendment 10 Oct 56. Force 15 Oct 56.
281 UNTS 412.   Korea, South.   Amendment 15 Oct 56. Force 15 Oct 56.
283 UNTS 346.   Korea, South.   Amendment 19 Apr 57. Force 19 Apr 57.
283 UNTS 346. USA (United States). Amendment 19 Apr 57. Force 19 Apr 57.
300 UNTS 386.   Korea, South.   Amendment 16 Aug 57. Force 16 Aug 57.
300 UNTS 386. USA (United States). Amendment 16 Aug 57. Force 16 Aug 57.

103929   Bilateral Agreement   **272 UNTS 21**
SIGNED: 12 Mar 56   FORCE: 12 Mar 56
REGISTERED: 10 Jul 57 USA (United States)
ARTICLES: 6 LANGUAGE: English.
HEADNOTE: AGRI COMMOD TITLE I
TOPIC: US Agri Commod Aid
CONCEPTS: General provisions. Exchange of information and documents. Reexport of goods, etc.. Exchange rates and regulations. Transportation costs. Local currency. Commodities schedule. Purchase authorization. Surplus commodities. Shipwreck and salvage. Mutual consultation.
PARTIES:
Turkey
USA (United States)
                    ANNEX
273 UNTS 326. USA (United States). Supplementation 11 May 56. Force 11 May 56.
273 UNTS 326.   Turkey.   Supplementation 11 May 56. Force 11 May 56.
336 UNTS 374. USA (United States). Amendment 8 Nov 58. Force 8 Nov 58.
336 UNTS 374. Turkey. Amendment 8 Nov 58. Force 8 Nov 58.

103930   Bilateral Agreement   **272 UNTS 31**
SIGNED: 26 Sep 55   FORCE: 26 Sep 55
REGISTERED: 12 Jul 57 USA (United States)
ARTICLES: 6 LANGUAGE: English. German.
HEADNOTE: DISPOSITION CERTAIN US PROPERTY
TOPIC: Specific Property
CONCEPTS: Annex or appendix reference. Previous treaties adherence. Financial programs. Claims and settlements. Assets transfer. Facilities and property.
TREATY REF: 67UNTS89.
PARTIES:
Austria
USA (United States)

103931   Bilateral Agreement   **272 UNTS 59**
SIGNED: 3 May 56   FORCE: 3 May 56
REGISTERED: 12 Jul 57 USA (United States)
ARTICLES: 12 LANGUAGE: English. Spanish.
HEADNOTE: FINANCING CERTAIN EDUCATIONAL EXCHANGE PROGRAMS
TOPIC: Direct Aid
CONCEPTS: Definition of terms. Conformity with municipal law. Exchange of information and documents. Establishment of commission. Exchange. Teacher and student exchange. Financial programs. Funding procedures. Local currency. Materials, equipment and services. Headquarters and facilities. Internal structure.
INTL ORGS: Special Commission.
TREATY REF: 241UNTS63.
PROCEDURE: Amendment.
PARTIES:
Peru
USA (United States)
                    ANNEX
290 UNTS 350. USA (United States). Amendment 11 Mar 57. Force 13 Jun 57.
290 UNTS 350.   Peru.   Amendment 13 Jun 57. Force 13 Jun 57.
367 UNTS 324. USA (United States). Amendment 18 Dec 59. Force 21 Dec 59.
367 UNTS 329.   Peru.   Amendment 21 Dec 59. Force 21 Dec 59.
452 UNTS 334. USA (United States). Amendment 26 Jan 62. Force 1 Feb 62.
452 UNTS 334.   Peru.   Amendment 1 Feb 62. Force 1 Feb 62.

103932   Bilateral Agreement   **272 UNTS 75**
SIGNED: 3 Feb 56   FORCE: 3 Feb 56
REGISTERED: 12 Jul 57 USA (United States)
ARTICLES: 17 LANGUAGE: English. Hindi.
HEADNOTE: AIR TRANSPORT
TOPIC: Air Transport
CONCEPTS: Definition of terms. Detailed regulations. Treaty interpretation. Conformity with municipal law. General cooperation. Exchange of information and documents. Use of facilities. Arbitration. Procedure. Special tribunals. Competence of tribunal. Indemnities and reimbursements. Fees and exemptions. Non-Interest rates and fees. Most favored nation clause. National treatment. Customs exemptions. Routes and logistics. Permit designation. Air transport. Airport facilities. Overflights and technical stops. Operating authorizations and regulations. Licenses and certificates of nationality.
INTL ORGS: International Civil Aviation Organization. International Court of Justice. Arbitration Commission.
TREATY REF: 15UNTS295.
PROCEDURE: Future Procedures Contemplated. Registration. Termination. Application to Non-self-governing Territories.
PARTIES:
India
USA (United States)
                    ANNEX
533 UNTS 334. USA (United States). Amendment 26 Oct 64. Force 26 Oct 64.
533 UNTS 334. USA (United States). Implementation 26 Oct 64.
533 UNTS 334. USA (United States). Implementation 26 Oct 64.
533 UNTS 334.   India.   Amendment 26 Oct 64. Force 26 Oct 64.

103933   Bilateral Agreement   **272 UNTS 117**
SIGNED: 7 Feb 56   FORCE: 7 Feb 56
REGISTERED: 12 Jul 57 USA (United States)
ARTICLES: 6 LANGUAGE: English. German.
HEADNOTE: AGRI COMMOD TITLE I
TOPIC: US Agri Commod Aid
CONCEPTS: General provisions. Annex or appendix reference. Exchange of information and documents. Reexport of goods, etc.. Exchange rates and regulations. Transportation costs. Local currency. Commodities schedule. Purchase authorization. Surplus commodities. Mutual consultation.
PARTIES:
Austria
USA (United States)
                    ANNEX
418 UNTS 386. USA (United States). Supplementation 26 Jun 61. Force 26 Jul 61.

418 UNTS 386.   Austria.   Supplementation 26 Jul 61. Force 26 Jul 61.

103934   Bilateral Agreement   **272 UNTS 135**
SIGNED: 20 Feb 56   FORCE: 20 Feb 56
REGISTERED: 12 Jul 57 USA (United States)
ARTICLES: 6 LANGUAGE: English.
HEADNOTE: AGRI COMMOD TITLE I
TOPIC: US Agri Commod Aid
CONCEPTS: General provisions. Exchange of information and documents. Reexport of goods, etc.. Exchange rates and regulations. Transportation costs. Local currency. Commodities schedule. Purchase authorization. Surplus commodities. Mutual consultation.
PARTIES:
Iran
USA (United States)
                    ANNEX
279 UNTS 354. USA (United States). Supplementation 13 Feb 57. Force 13 Feb 57.
279 UNTS 354.   Iran.   Supplementation 13 Feb 57. Force 13 Feb 57.
280 UNTS 390. USA (United States). Amendment 29 Jan 57. Force 30 Jan 57.
280 UNTS 390.   Iran.   Amendment 30 Jan 57. Force 30 Jan 57.
434 UNTS 318. USA (United States). Amendment 18 Sep 58. Force 16 Nov 58.
434 UNTS 318.   Iran.   Amendment 16 Nov 58. Force 16 Nov 58.
434 UNTS 321. Iran. Supplementation 2 Jul 61. Force 2 Jul 61.
434 UNTS 321. USA (United States). Supplementation 29 Mar 61. Force 2 Jul 61.

103935   Bilateral Exchange   **272 UNTS 145**
SIGNED: 11 Oct 55   FORCE: 11 Oct 55
REGISTERED: 12 Jul 57 USA (United States)
ARTICLES: 4 LANGUAGE: English.
HEADNOTE: NON-IMMIGRANT PASSPORT VISAS
TOPIC: Visas
CONCEPTS: Time limit. Visa abolition. Visas. Fees and exemptions.
PARTIES:
Turkey
USA (United States)

103936   Bilateral Treaty   **272 UNTS 157**
SIGNED: 14 Jun 41   FORCE: 14 Jul 57
REGISTERED: 14 Jul 57 Belgium
ARTICLES: 18 LANGUAGE: French. Portuguese.
HEADNOTE: EXTRADITION
TOPIC: Extradition
CONCEPTS: Extradition, deportation and repatriation. Court procedures. Extradition requests. Extraditable offenses. Location of crime. Special factors. Special factors.
PROCEDURE: Denunciation. Ratification.
PARTIES:
Belgium
Brazil
                    ANNEX
307 UNTS 312.   Belgium.   Supplementation 22 Apr 58. Force 8 Jul 58.
307 UNTS 312.   Brazil.   Supplementation 8 May 58. Force 8 Jul 58.

103937   Bilateral Convention   **272 UNTS 181**
SIGNED: 10 Jan 55   FORCE: 14 Jul 57
REGISTERED: 14 Jul 57 Belgium
ARTICLES: 5 LANGUAGE: French. Portuguese.
HEADNOTE: FREE LEGAL AID
TOPIC: Admin Cooperation
CONCEPTS: Legal protection and assistance. Operating agencies. Fees and exemptions. Tax exemptions.
PROCEDURE: Ratification.
PARTIES:
Belgium
Brazil

103938   Bilateral Agreement   **272 UNTS 191**
SIGNED: 28 Jun 57   FORCE: 28 Jun 57
REGISTERED: 16 Jul 57 Norway
ARTICLES: 11 LANGUAGE: Norwegian. Finnish.
HEADNOTE: CONSTRUCTION BRIDGE ACROSS ANARJOKKA RIVER
TOPIC: Non-IBRD Project

CONCEPTS: Inspection and observation. Establishment of commission. Financial programs. Nonbank projects. Frontier waterways. Specific goods and equipment.
PARTIES:
Finland
Norway

103939 Bilateral Agreement **272 UNTS 201**
SIGNED: 5 Mar 57　　　　FORCE: 28 Jun 57
REGISTERED: 17 Jul 57 IBRD (World Bank)
ARTICLES: 5 LANGUAGE: English.
HEADNOTE: GUARANTEE AGREEMENT
TOPIC: IBRD Project
CONCEPTS: Definition of terms. Annex or appendix reference. Exchange of information and documents. Informational records. Inspection and observation. Bonds. Fees and exemptions. Tax exemptions. Domestic obligation. Terms of loan. Loan regulations. Loan guarantee. Guarantor non-interference.
PARTIES:
India
IBRD (World Bank)

103940 Unilateral Instrument **272 UNTS 225**
SIGNED: 18 Jun 57　　　　FORCE: 22 Jul 57
REGISTERED: 22 Jul 57 United Nations
ARTICLES: 1 LANGUAGE: English.
HEADNOTE: ACCEPTANCE ICJ JURISDICTION
TOPIC: ICJ Option Clause
CONCEPTS: Compulsory jurisdiction.
INTL ORGS: International Court of Justice.
TREATY REF: 265UNTS.
PROCEDURE: Duration.
PARTIES:
United Arab Rep

103941 Bilateral Exchange **272 UNTS 229**
SIGNED: 11 Jun 57　　　　FORCE: 11 Jul 57
REGISTERED: 23 Jul 57 South Africa
ARTICLES: 2 LANGUAGE: English. German.
HEADNOTE: VISA AGREEMENT
TOPIC: Visas
CONCEPTS: Time limit. Denial of admission. Resident permits. Visas. Conformity with municipal law. Fees and exemptions.
PARTIES:
Austria
South Africa

103942 Bilateral Exchange **272 UNTS 235**
SIGNED: 28 Jun 54　　　　FORCE: 28 Jun 54
REGISTERED: 24 Jul 57 Netherlands
ARTICLES: 2 LANGUAGE: Dutch.
HEADNOTE: EXERCISE AUTHORITY REGISTERED LANDS
TOPIC: Territory Boundary
CONCEPTS: Nationality and citizenship. Markers and definitions.
PROCEDURE: Duration.
PARTIES:
Belgium
Netherlands
　　　　　ANNEX
286 UNTS 391.　Netherlands.　Prolongation 5 Dec 57. Force 7 Dec 57.
286 UNTS 391. Belgium. Prolongation 7 Dec 57. Force 7 Dec 57.

103943 Bilateral Treaty **273 UNTS 3**
SIGNED: 29 Oct 54　　　　FORCE: 14 Jul 56
REGISTERED: 25 Jul 57 USA (United States)
ARTICLES: 29 LANGUAGE: English. German.
HEADNOTE: FRIENDSHIP COMMERCE NAVIGATION
TOPIC: General Amity
CONCEPTS: Definition of terms. Exceptions and exemptions. Territorial application. Treaty interpretation. Previous treaty replacement. Passports non-diplomatic. Alien status. Administrative cooperation. General cooperation. Exchange of official publications. Juridical personality. Expropriation. Free passage and transit. Legal protection and assistance. Personnel. General property. Private contracts. Existing tribunals. Establishment of trade relations. Export quotas. Import quotas. Currency deposits. Investments. Assets transfer. Most favored na-

tion clause. National treatment. Taxation. Recognition. Navigational conditions. Inland and territorial waters. Tonnage. Ports and pilotage. Shipwreck and salvage.
INTL ORGS: International Court of Justice. International Monetary Fund.
TREATY REF: GATT; 52LTS133; 72LTS180; 163LTS415; 253UNTS89.
PROCEDURE: Duration. Ratification. Termination.
PARTIES:
Germany, West
USA (United States)

103944 Bilateral Agreement **273 UNTS 79**
SIGNED: 28 Jun 56　　　　FORCE: 28 Jun 56
REGISTERED: 25 Jul 57 USA (United States)
ARTICLES: 6 LANGUAGE: English. Polish.
HEADNOTE: SETTLEMENT LEND-LEASE CLAIMS
TOPIC: Claims and Debts
CONCEPTS: Definition of terms. Non-prejudice to UN charter. General property. Claims and settlements. Lump sum settlements. Post-war adjustment. Return of equipment and recapture. Post-war claims settlement.
PARTIES:
Poland
USA (United States)

103945 Bilateral Exchange **273 UNTS 89**
SIGNED: 27 Jun 56　　　　FORCE: 27 Jun 56
REGISTERED: 25 Jul 57 USA (United States)
ARTICLES: 2 LANGUAGE: English.
HEADNOTE: ECONOMIC DEVELOPMENT
TOPIC: Direct Aid
CONCEPTS: Detailed regulations. Treaty implementation. Financial programs. Economic assistance.
TREATY REF: EXCHA OF NOTES US&LIBYA 4APRIL1956.
PARTIES:
Libya
USA (United States)

103946 Bilateral Agreement **273 UNTS 97**
SIGNED: 28 Oct 55　　　　FORCE: 15 Nov 55
REGISTERED: 26 Jul 57 USA (United States)
ARTICLES: 6 LANGUAGE: English. Spanish.
HEADNOTE: GUARANTY PRIVATE INVESTMENT
TOPIC: Claims and Debts
CONCEPTS: Conformity with municipal law. General cooperation. Responsibility and liability. Arbitration. Procedure. Existing tribunals. Negotiation. Reciprocity in financial treatment. Currency. Claims and settlements. Private investment guarantee.
PROCEDURE: Ratification.
PARTIES:
Paraguay
USA (United States)

103947 Bilateral Agreement **273 UNTS 105**
SIGNED: 11 Jun 52　　　　FORCE: 5 May 55
REGISTERED: 26 Jul 57 USA (United States)
ARTICLES: 7 LANGUAGE: English. German.
HEADNOTE: OPERATION RADIO INSTALLATIONS
TOPIC: Mass Media
CONCEPTS: Arbitration. Domestic jurisdiction. Special tribunals. Negotiation. Competence of tribunal. Tax exemptions. Customs exemptions. Commercial and public radio. Facilities and equipment. Radio-telephone-telegraphic communications. Conformity with IGO decisions. Paragraph 2, Article 36.
TREATY REF: USA'TIAS 3425; 193UNTS3; 194UNTS3; 195UNTS3;.
PROCEDURE: Termination.
PARTIES:
Germany, West
USA (United States)

103948 Multilateral Instrument **273 UNTS 121**
SIGNED: 10 May 55　　　　FORCE: 10 May 55
REGISTERED: 26 Jul 57 USA (United States)
ARTICLES: 2 LANGUAGE: English. German.
HEADNOTE: TRANSFER PROPERTY RIGHTS & INTERESTS
TOPIC: Claims and Debts
CONCEPTS: Detailed regulations. Assets. Private

investment guarantee. Enemy financial interests. Specific claims or waivers.
INTL ORGS: United Nations.
PARTIES:
Austria SIGNED: 10 May 55 FORCE: 10 Mar 55
UK Great Britain SIGNED: 10 May 55 FORCE: 10 Mar 55
USA (United States) SIGNED: 10 May 55 FORCE: 10 Mar 55

103949 Bilateral Exchange **273 UNTS 149**
SIGNED: 27 Apr 56　　　　FORCE: 27 Apr 56
REGISTERED: 26 Jul 57 USA (United States)
ARTICLES: 2 LANGUAGE: English. Italian.
HEADNOTE: EMERGENCY RELIEF ASSISTANCE
TOPIC: Direct Aid
CONCEPTS: Conformity with municipal law. General cooperation. Public information. Commodities and services. Relief supplies. Distribution. Commodities schedule. Transport of goods.
PARTIES:
Italy
USA (United States)

103950 Bilateral Exchange **273 UNTS 157**
SIGNED: 10 May 55　　　　FORCE: 10 May 55
REGISTERED: 26 Jul 57 USA (United States)
ARTICLES: 2 LANGUAGE: English. French.
HEADNOTE: DISPOSITION EQUIPMENT MATERIALS
TOPIC: Milit Assistance
CONCEPTS: Exchange of information and documents. Reexport of goods, etc.. Delivery schedules. Materials, equipment and services. Surplus property. Return of equipment and recapture.
TREATY REF: 185UNTS3.
PARTIES:
USA (United States)
Vietnam, South

103951 Bilateral Instrument **273 UNTS 163**
SIGNED: 18 Oct 54　　　　FORCE: 18 Oct 54
REGISTERED: 26 Jul 57 USA (United States)
ARTICLES: 16 LANGUAGE: English.
HEADNOTE: OFFSHORE PROCUREMENT
TOPIC: Milit Assistance
CONCEPTS: Annex or appendix reference. Conformity with municipal law. General cooperation. Exchange of information and documents. Inspection and observation. Licenses and permits. Private contracts. Indemnities and reimbursements. Tax exemptions. Materials, equipment and services. Security of information. Exchange of defense information.
TREATY REF: 174UNTS201.
PROCEDURE: Future Procedures Contemplated.
PARTIES:
USA (United States)
Yugoslavia

103952 Bilateral Exchange **273 UNTS 209**
SIGNED: 2 Mar 56　　　　FORCE: 2 Mar 56
REGISTERED: 26 Jul 57 USA (United States)
ARTICLES: 2 LANGUAGE: English. German.
HEADNOTE: DEBT SETTLEMENT
TOPIC: Claims and Debts
CONCEPTS: Treaty interpretation. Negotiation. Bonds. Debt settlement.
PARTIES:
Germany, West
USA (United States)

103953 Bilateral Exchange **273 UNTS 223**
SIGNED: 13 Apr 56　　　　FORCE: 13 Apr 56
REGISTERED: 26 Jul 57 USA (United States)
ARTICLES: 2 LANGUAGE: English. Japanese.
HEADNOTE: ASSEMBLY AIRPLANES
TOPIC: Milit Assistance
CONCEPTS: General cooperation. Indemnities and reimbursements. Materials, equipment and services. Self-defense. Military assistance. Equipment and supplies.
TREATY REF: 232UNTS169.
PARTIES:
Japan
USA (United States)

103954 Bilateral Exchange **273 UNTS 235**
SIGNED: 27 Mar 56 FORCE: 27 Mar 56
REGISTERED: 26 Jul 57 USA (United States)
ARTICLES: 2 LANGUAGE: English. Spanish.
HEADNOTE: CIVIL AVIATION
TOPIC: Air Transport
CONCEPTS: Conditions. Treaty implementation. Previous treaty replacement. Conformity with municipal law. Exchange of information and documents. Personnel. Responsibility and liability. Use of facilities. Financial programs. Assistance. Materials, equipment and services. Aid missions. Air transport.
TREATY REF: 51UNTS45; 141UNTS15.
PROCEDURE: Duration. Termination.
PARTIES:
Colombia
USA (United States)

103955 Bilateral Exchange **274 UNTS 3**
SIGNED: 19 Apr 56 FORCE: 19 Apr 56
REGISTERED: 26 Jul 57 USA (United States)
ARTICLES: 2 LANGUAGE: English.
HEADNOTE: CONSTRUCTION OPERATION HOUSING UNITS
TOPIC: Milit Installation
CONCEPTS: Annex or appendix reference. General cooperation. Private contracts. Bases and facilities.
PARTIES:
Canada
USA (United States)

103956 Bilateral Exchange **274 UNTS 35**
SIGNED: 28 Apr 56 FORCE: 28 Apr 56
REGISTERED: 26 Jul 57 USA (United States)
ARTICLES: 2 LANGUAGE: English.
HEADNOTE: ECONOMIC ASSISTANCE
TOPIC: Direct Aid
CONCEPTS: Change of circumstances. Treaty implementation. Diplomatic privileges. Conformity with municipal law. General cooperation. Exchange of information and documents. Inspection and observation. Personnel. Public information. Accounting procedures. Attachment of funds. Exchange rates and regulations. Funding procedures. Garnishment of funds. Seizure funds. Local currency. Assets. Tax exemptions. Customs exemptions. Commodities and services. Domestic obligation. Economic assistance. Materials, equipment and services. Withdrawal conditions. Procurement. Distribution.
TREATY REF: 92UNTS125.
PROCEDURE: Termination.
PARTIES:
Ceylon (Sri Lanka)
USA (United States)

103957 Bilateral Exchange **274 UNTS 47**
SIGNED: 29 Jul 57 FORCE: 13 Nov 56
REGISTERED: 29 Jul 57 United Nations
ARTICLES: 2 LANGUAGE: English.
HEADNOTE: SERVICE UN EMERGENCY FORCE
TOPIC: Milit Assistance
CONCEPTS: Annex or appendix reference. Privileges and immunities. General cooperation. Arbitration. Procedure. Indemnities and reimbursements. Jurisdiction. Withdrawal of forces. Peace-keeping force.
INTL ORGS: International Court of Justice. Arbitration Commission.
TREATY REF: 260UNTS61.
PROCEDURE: Future Procedures Contemplated.
PARTIES:
Canada
United Nations

103958 Bilateral Agreement **274 UNTS 59**
SIGNED: 13 Mar 57 FORCE: 18 Jun 57
REGISTERED: 31 Jul 57 IBRD (World Bank)
ARTICLES: 5 LANGUAGE: English.
HEADNOTE: GUARANTEE AGREEMENT
TOPIC: IBRD Project
CONCEPTS: Definition of terms. Annex or appendix reference. Exchange of information and documents. Informational records. Inspection and observation. Bonds. Fees and exemptions. Tax exemptions. Domestic obligation. Terms of loan. Loan regulations. Loan guarantee. Guarantor non-interference.

PARTIES:
Peru
IBRD (World Bank)

103959 Bilateral Exchange **274 UNTS 81**
SIGNED: 16 Jul 57 FORCE: 10 Nov 56
REGISTERED: 1 Aug 57 United Nations
ARTICLES: 2 LANGUAGE: English.
HEADNOTE: SERVICE UN EMERGENCY FORCE
TOPIC: Milit Assistance
CONCEPTS: Annex or appendix reference. Privileges and immunities. General cooperation. Arbitration. Procedure. Indemnities and reimbursements. Jurisdiction. Withdrawal of forces. Peace-keeping force.
INTL ORGS: International Court of Justice. Arbitration Commission.
TREATY REF: 260UNTS61.
PROCEDURE: Future Procedures Contemplated.
PARTIES:
Denmark
United Nations

103960 Multilateral Agreement **274 UNTS 93**
SIGNED: 22 Feb 57 FORCE: 1 Jan 57
REGISTERED: 1 Aug 57 United Nations
ARTICLES: 8 LANGUAGE: Spanish.
HEADNOTE: ADVANCED SCHOOL PUBLIC ADMINISTRATION CENTRAL AMERICA (ESAPAC)
TOPIC: Tech Assistance
CONCEPTS: Teacher and student exchange. Institute establishment. Scholarships and grants. Expense sharing formulae. Domestic obligation. General technical assistance.
INTL ORGS: United Nations.
PROCEDURE: Amendment. Termination.
PARTIES:
Costa Rica SIGNED: 22 Feb 57 FORCE: 1 Jan 57
El Salvador SIGNED: 22 Feb 57 FORCE: 1 Jan 57
Guatemala SIGNED: 22 Feb 57 FORCE: 1 Jan 57
Honduras SIGNED: 22 Feb 57 FORCE: 1 Jan 57
Nicaragua SIGNED: 22 Feb 57 FORCE: 1 Jan 57
United Nations SIGNED: 22 Feb 57 FORCE: 1 Jan 57

103961 Bilateral Agreement **274 UNTS 105**
SIGNED: 20 Aug 56 FORCE: 30 May 57
REGISTERED: 7 Aug 57 USSR (Soviet Union)
ARTICLES: 7 LANGUAGE: Russian. Arabic.
HEADNOTE: CULTURAL COOPERATION
TOPIC: Culture
CONCEPTS: Friendship and amity. Non-diplomatic delegations. Exchange. Scholarships and grants. Exchange. General cultural exchange. Artists. Athletes. Scientific exchange. Mass media exchange.
PROCEDURE: Amendment. Duration. Ratification. Renewal or Revival. Termination.
PARTIES:
Syria
USSR (Soviet Union)

103962 Bilateral Agreement **274 UNTS 115**
SIGNED: 15 Feb 57 FORCE: 4 Jun 57
REGISTERED: 7 Aug 57 USSR (Soviet Union)
ARTICLES: 13 LANGUAGE: Russian. Vietnamese.
HEADNOTE: CULTURAL CO-OPERATION
TOPIC: Culture
CONCEPTS: Friendship and amity. Non-diplomatic delegations. General cooperation. Specialists exchange. Exchange. Teacher and student exchange. Scholarships and grants. Exchange. General cultural exchange. Artists. Athletes. Meteorology. Research results. Publications exchange. Mass media exchange. Press and wire services.
PROCEDURE: Amendment. Duration. Ratification. Renewal or Revival. Termination.
PARTIES:
USSR (Soviet Union)
Vietnam, North

103963 Bilateral Treaty **274 UNTS 133**
SIGNED: 5 Mar 57 FORCE: 4 May 57
REGISTERED: 7 Aug 57 USSR (Soviet Union)
ARTICLES: 3 LANGUAGE: Russian. Polish.
HEADNOTE: EXISTING SOVIET-POLISH STATE FRONTIER

TOPIC: Territory Boundary
CONCEPTS: Establishment of commission. Indemnities and reimbursements. Financial programs. Markers and definitions.
INTL ORGS: Special Commission.
PROCEDURE: Ratification.
PARTIES:
Poland
USSR (Soviet Union)

103964 Bilateral Agreement **274 UNTS 143**
SIGNED: 15 Apr 57 FORCE: 4 Jun 57
REGISTERED: 7 Aug 57 USSR (Soviet Union)
ARTICLES: 19 LANGUAGE: Russian. Romanian.
HEADNOTE: LEGAL STATUS FORCES
TOPIC: Status of Forces
CONCEPTS: Definition of terms. Court procedures. Conformity with municipal law. General cooperation. Recognition of legal documents. Responsibility and liability. Use of facilities. Investigation of violations. Establishment of commission. Procedure. Compensation. Defense and security. Jurisdiction. Procurement and logistics. Status of forces. Bases and facilities.
INTL ORGS: Special Commission.
PROCEDURE: Amendment. Future Procedures Contemplated. Ratification.
PARTIES:
Romania
USSR (Soviet Union)

103965 Multilateral Agreement **274 UNTS 172**
SIGNED: 9 Apr 57 FORCE: 27 Apr 57
REGISTERED: 13 Aug 57 United Nations
ARTICLES: 6 LANGUAGE: Spanish.
HEADNOTE: TECHNICAL ASSISTANCE
TOPIC: Tech Assistance
CONCEPTS: Definition of terms. Annex or appendix reference. Previous treaty replacement. Privileges and immunities. General cooperation. Exchange of information and documents. Personnel. Responsibility and liability. Title and deeds. Use of facilities. Exchange. Scholarships and grants. Vocational training. Research and development. Exchange rates and regulations. Expense sharing formulae. Local currency. Domestic obligation. General technical assistance. Materials, equipment and services. IGO status. Conformity with IGO decisions.
TREATY REF: 76UNTS132; 1UNTS15; 33UNTS261.
PROCEDURE: Amendment. Termination.
PARTIES:
Panama SIGNED: 27 Apr 57 FORCE: 27 Apr 57
FAO (Food Agri) SIGNED: 27 Apr 57 FORCE: 27 Apr 57
ICAO (Civil Aviat) SIGNED: 27 Apr 57 FORCE: 27 Apr 57
ILO (Labor Org) SIGNED: 27 Apr 57 FORCE: 27 Apr 57
ITU (Telecommun) SIGNED: 27 Apr 57 FORCE: 27 Apr 57
UNESCO (Educ/Cult) SIGNED: 27 Apr 57 FORCE: 27 Apr 57
United Nations SIGNED: 27 Apr 57 FORCE: 27 Apr 57
WHO (World Health) SIGNED: 27 Apr 57 FORCE: 27 Apr 57
WMO (Meteorology) SIGNED: 27 Apr 57 FORCE: 27 Apr 57
ANNEX
480 UNTS 361. Panama. Amendment 18 Oct 63. Force 18 Oct 63.
480 UNTS 361. UNTAB (Tech Assis). Amendment 31 Jul 63. Force 18 Oct 63.
642 UNTS 368. UNTAB (Tech Assis). Amendment 13 Aug 68. Force 13 Aug 68.

103966 Bilateral Exchange **274 UNTS 199**
SIGNED: 13 Aug 57 FORCE: 14 Jan 57
REGISTERED: 13 Aug 57 United Nations
ARTICLES: 2 LANGUAGE: English.
HEADNOTE: SERVICE UN EMERGENCY FORCE
TOPIC: Milit Assistance
CONCEPTS: Annex or appendix reference. Privileges and immunities. Arbitration. Procedure. Indemnities and reimbursements. Jurisdiction. Withdrawal of forces. Peace-keeping force.
TREATY REF: 260UNTS61.
PROCEDURE: Future Procedures Contemplated.

PARTIES:
Brazil
United Nations

103967 Bilateral Agreement **274 UNTS 211**
SIGNED: 15 May 57 FORCE: 27 Jun 57
REGISTERED: 14 Aug 57 IBRD (World Bank)
ARTICLES: 5 LANGUAGE: English.
HEADNOTE: GUARANTEE AGREEMENT
TOPIC: IBRD Project
CONCEPTS: Definition of terms. Annex or appendix reference. Exchange of information and documents. Informational records. Inspection and observation. Bonds. Fees and exemptions. Tax exemptions. Domestic obligation. Terms of loan. Loan regulations. Loan guarantee. Guarantor non-interference.
PARTIES:
Netherlands
IBRD (World Bank)

103968 Bilateral Exchange **274 UNTS 233**
SIGNED: 14 Aug 57 FORCE: 16 Nov 56
REGISTERED: 14 Aug 57 United Nations
ARTICLES: 2 LANGUAGE: English.
HEADNOTE: SERVICE UN EMERGENCY FORCE
TOPIC: Milit Assistance
CONCEPTS: Annex or appendix reference. Privileges and immunities. General cooperation. Arbitration. Procedure. Indemnities and reimbursements. Jurisdiction. Withdrawal of forces. Peace-keeping force.
INTL ORGS: International Court of Justice.
TREATY REF: 260UNTS61.
PARTIES:
India
United Nations

103969 Bilateral Exchange **274 UNTS 245**
SIGNED: 24 May 57 FORCE: 1 Jul 57
REGISTERED: 14 Aug 57 Belgium
ARTICLES: 2 LANGUAGE: French. Spanish.
HEADNOTE: ABOLISHING TRAVEL VISA REQUIREMENT
TOPIC: Visas
CONCEPTS: Territorial application. Time limit. Visa abolition. Denial of admission. Conformity with municipal law. Public health.
PARTIES:
Belgium
Colombia

103970 Bilateral Exchange **274 UNTS 251**
SIGNED: 3 May 57 FORCE: 1 Jun 57
REGISTERED: 14 Aug 57 Belgium
ARTICLES: 2 LANGUAGE: French. Spanish.
HEADNOTE: TRAVEL VISA REQUIREMENTS
TOPIC: Visas
CONCEPTS: Emergencies. Territorial application. Time limit. Visa abolition. Denial of admission. Resident permits. Conformity with municipal law.
PROCEDURE: Denunciation.
PARTIES:
Belgium
Peru

103971 Bilateral Convention **274 UNTS 259**
SIGNED: 16 Apr 56 FORCE: 22 Nov 56
REGISTERED: 19 Aug 57 New Zealand
ARTICLES: 23 LANGUAGE: English. Swedish.
HEADNOTE: DOUBLE TAXATION FISCAL EVASION TAXES INCOME
TOPIC: Taxation
CONCEPTS: Definition of terms. Conformity with municipal law. Exchange of official publications. Teacher and student exchange. Claims and settlements. Taxation. General. Tax exemptions.
PROCEDURE: Duration. Ratification. Termination.
PARTIES:
New Zealand
Sweden

103972 Multilateral Agreement **274 UNTS 300**
SIGNED: 9 Jul 57 FORCE: 9 Jul 57
REGISTERED: 19 Aug 57 United Nations
ARTICLES: 6 LANGUAGE: Spanish.
HEADNOTE: TECHNICAL ASSISTANCE

TOPIC: Tech Assistance
CONCEPTS: Definition of terms. Previous treaty replacement. Privileges and immunities. General cooperation. Exchange of information and documents. Personnel. Responsibility and liability. Title and deeds. Use of facilities. Exchange. Scholarships and grants. Vocational training. Research and development. Exchange rates and regulations. Expense sharing formulae. Local currency. Domestic obligation. General technical assistance. Materials, equipment and services. IGO status. Conformity with IGO decisions.
TREATY REF: 76UNTS132; 1UNTS15; 33UNTS261.
PROCEDURE: Amendment. Termination.
PARTIES:
Honduras SIGNED: 9 Jul 57 RATIFIED: 19 Aug 57 FORCE: 9 Jul 57
FAO (Food Agri) SIGNED: 9 Jul 57 FORCE: 9 Jul 57
ILO (Labor Org) SIGNED: 9 Jul 57 FORCE: 9 Jul 57
ITU (Telecommun) SIGNED: 9 Jul 57 FORCE: 9 Jul 57
UNESCO (Educ/Cult) SIGNED: 9 Jul 57 FORCE: 9 Jul 57
United Nations SIGNED: 9 Jul 57 FORCE: 9 Jul 57
WHO (World Health) SIGNED: 9 Jul 57 FORCE: 9 Jul 57
WMO (Meteorology) SIGNED: 9 Jul 57 FORCE: 9 Jul 57
ANNEX
482 UNTS 377. Honduras. Force 8 Nov 63.
482 UNTS 377. UNTAB (Tech Assis). Force 8 Nov 63.

103973 Bilateral Agreement **275 UNTS 3**
SIGNED: 7 Jul 55 FORCE: 16 Apr 56
REGISTERED: 20 Aug 57 USA (United States)
ARTICLES: 17 LANGUAGE: English. German.
HEADNOTE: AIR TRANSPORT
TOPIC: Air Transport
CONCEPTS: Definition of terms. Detailed regulations. Annex or appendix reference. Conformity with municipal law. General cooperation. Licenses and permits. Recognition of legal documents. Use of facilities. Procedure. Special tribunals. Competence of tribunal. Fees and exemptions. Financial programs. Non-interest rates and fees. National treatment. Customs exemptions. Competency certificate. Routes and logistics. Navigational conditions. Permit designation. Airport facilities. Airworthiness certificates. Conditions of airlines operating permission. Overflights and technical stops. Operating authorizations and regulations. Licenses and certificates of nationality.
INTL ORGS: International Civil Aviation Organization. International Court of Justice. Special Commission.
TREATY REF: 15UNTS295.
PROCEDURE: Amendment. Future Procedures Contemplated. Ratification. Registration. Termination. Application to Non-self-governing Territories.
PARTIES:
Germany, West
USA (United States)

103974 Bilateral Agreement **275 UNTS 37**
SIGNED: 19 Mar 56 FORCE: 19 Mar 56
REGISTERED: 20 Aug 57 USA (United States)
ARTICLES: 8 LANGUAGE: English. French.
HEADNOTE: WAR CEMETERIES MEMORIALS
TOPIC: Other Military
CONCEPTS: War graves. Responsibility for war dead. Upkeep of war graves. Establishment of war cemeteries.
PARTIES:
France
USA (United States)

103975 Bilateral Agreement **275 UNTS 49**
SIGNED: 13 Mar 56 FORCE: 2 Jun 56
REGISTERED: 20 Aug 57 USA (United States)
ARTICLES: 7 LANGUAGE: English. Spanish.
HEADNOTE: SURPLUS AGRICULTURAL COMMODITIES
TOPIC: US Agri Commod Aid
CONCEPTS: General provisions. Conformity with

municipal law. General cooperation. Exchange of information and documents. Currency deposits. Interest rates. Purchase authorizations. Local currency. Domestic obligation. Loan and credit. Loan repayment. Commodities schedule. Surplus commodities.
PARTIES:
Chile
USA (United States)
ANNEX
281 UNTS 416. USA (United States). Amendment 22 Oct 56. Force 23 Oct 56.
281 UNTS 416. Chile. Amendment 23 Oct 56. Force 23 Oct 56.
288 UNTS 381. Chile. Amendment 15 Apr 57. Force 15 Apr 57.
288 UNTS 381. USA (United States). Amendment 15 Apr 57. Force 15 Apr 57.
368 UNTS 366. USA (United States). Amendment 26 Jan 59. Force 21 Apr 59.
368 UNTS 366. Chile. Amendment 21 Apr 59. Force 21 Apr 59.

103976 Bilateral Exchange **275 UNTS 73**
SIGNED: 20 Feb 56 FORCE: 20 Feb 56
REGISTERED: 20 Aug 57 USA (United States)
ARTICLES: 2 LANGUAGE: English. Chinese.
HEADNOTE: NON-IMMIGRANT PASSPORT VISAS
TOPIC: Visas
CONCEPTS: Time limit. Fees and exemptions.
PARTIES:
Taiwan
USA (United States)

103977 Bilateral Instrument **275 UNTS 87**
SIGNED: 6 Oct 55 FORCE: 6 Oct 55
REGISTERED: 20 Aug 57 USA (United States)
ARTICLES: 5 LANGUAGE: English.
HEADNOTE: JOINT LIBERIAN-US COMMISSION ECONOMIC DEVELOPMENT
TOPIC: Direct Aid
CONCEPTS: Treaty interpretation. Annex type material. Economic assistance.
INTL ORGS: Special Commission.
TREATY REF: 275UNTS93.
PARTIES:
Liberia
USA (United States)

103978 Bilateral Agreement **275 UNTS 93**
SIGNED: 6 Oct 55 FORCE: 3 Feb 56
REGISTERED: 20 Aug 57 USA (United States)
ARTICLES: 7 LANGUAGE: English.
HEADNOTE: TECHNICAL ASSISTANCE COOPERATION
TOPIC: Tech Assistance
CONCEPTS: Treaty implementation. Previous treaty replacement. General cooperation. Exchange of information and documents. Personnel. Financial programs. Tax exemptions. Customs exemptions. Domestic obligation. General technical assistance. Economic assistance. Materials, equipment and services. Aid missions.
TREATY REF: 92UNTS145.
PROCEDURE: Amendment. Duration. Termination.
PARTIES:
Liberia
USA (United States)

103979 Bilateral Agreement **275 UNTS 105**
SIGNED: 10 Feb 56 FORCE: 29 May 56
REGISTERED: 20 Aug 57 USA (United States)
ARTICLES: 8 LANGUAGE: English. Japanese.
HEADNOTE: AGRI COMMOD
TOPIC: Direct Aid
CONCEPTS: General provisions. Annex or appendix reference. Conformity with municipal law. General cooperation. Accounting procedures. Financial programs. Interest rates. Payment schedules. Purchase authorizations. Local currency. Loan and credit. Loan repayment. Commodities schedule. Surplus commodities. Transport of goods.
INTL ORGS: International Monetary Fund.
TREATY REF: 232UNTS169.
PARTIES:
Japan
USA (United States)

ANNEX
278 UNTS 314. USA (United States). Supplementation 18 Jan 57. Force 18 Jan 57.
278 UNTS 314. Japan. Supplementation 18 Jan 57. Force 18 Jan 57.

103980 Bilateral Exchange **275 UNTS 157**
SIGNED: 10 Feb 56   FORCE: 29 May 56
REGISTERED: 20 Aug 57 USA (United States)
ARTICLES: 2 LANGUAGE: English. Japanese.
HEADNOTE: AGRI COMMOD SCHOOL LUNCH PROGRAM
TOPIC: Direct Aid
CONCEPTS: Annex or appendix reference. Conformity with municipal law. General cooperation. Exchange of information and documents. Inspection and observation. Public information. Commodities and services. Assistance. General aid. Grants. Commodities schedule. Surplus commodities.
TREATY REF: 241UNTS197.
PARTIES:
Japan
USA (United States)

103981 Bilateral Exchange **275 UNTS 181**
SIGNED: 10 Feb 56   FORCE: 10 Feb 56
REGISTERED: 20 Aug 57 USA (United States)
ARTICLES: 2 LANGUAGE: English. Japanese.
HEADNOTE: AGRI COMMOD SCHOOL CHILDRENS WELFARE PROGRAMS
TOPIC: Direct Aid
CONCEPTS: Commodities and services. Assistance. General aid. Grants.
TREATY REF: 275UNTS105.
PARTIES:
Japan
USA (United States)

103982 Bilateral Exchange **275 UNTS 189**
SIGNED: 4 Jun 56   FORCE: 4 Jun 56
REGISTERED: 20 Aug 57 USA (United States)
ARTICLES: 2 LANGUAGE: English.
HEADNOTE: PASSPORT VISAS
TOPIC: Visas
CONCEPTS: Time limit. Previous treaty replacement. Visas.
TREATY REF: 82UNTS31.
PARTIES:
Iceland
USA (United States)

103983 Bilateral Agreement **275 UNTS 195**
SIGNED: 22 Mar 56   FORCE: 6 Jun 56
REGISTERED: 20 Aug 57 USA (United States)
ARTICLES: 9 LANGUAGE: English. Japanese.
HEADNOTE: INTERCHANGE PATENT RIGHTS TECHNICAL INFORMATION
TOPIC: Patents/Copyrights
CONCEPTS: Patents, copyrights and trademarks. Laws and formalities.
INTL ORGS: Special Commission.
TREATY REF: 232UNTS169,251UNTS404,265UNTS272,273UNTS.
PROCEDURE: Duration. Termination.
PARTIES:
Japan
USA (United States)

103984 Bilateral Agreement **275 UNTS 231**
SIGNED: 19 Mar 56   FORCE: 1 Jul 56
REGISTERED: 20 Aug 57 USA (United States)
ARTICLES: 19 LANGUAGE: English. Spanish.
HEADNOTE: PARCEL POST
TOPIC: Postal Service
CONCEPTS: Territorial application. Previous treaty extension. Responsibility and liability. Indemnities and reimbursements. Payment schedules. Postal services. Regulations. Insured letters and boxes. Parcel post.
TREATY REF: 169UNTS3; 186UNTS356; 202UNTS340; 227UNTS390.
PROCEDURE: Duration. Termination.
PARTIES:
Nicaragua
USA (United States)

103985 Bilateral Exchange **275 UNTS 265**
SIGNED: 6 Jun 56   FORCE: 6 Jun 56
REGISTERED: 20 Aug 57 USA (United States)
ARTICLES: 2 LANGUAGE: English. Arabic.
HEADNOTE: PASSPORT VISAS
TOPIC: Visas
CONCEPTS: Exceptions and exemptions. Visas.
PARTIES:
Iraq
USA (United States)

103986 Bilateral Exchange **275 UNTS 271**
SIGNED: 30 May 56   FORCE: 30 May 56
REGISTERED: 20 Aug 57 USA (United States)
ARTICLES: 2 LANGUAGE: English. Spanish.
HEADNOTE: PASSPORT VISAS
TOPIC: Visas
CONCEPTS: Time limit. Previous treaty replacement. Visas. Fees and exemptions.
TREATY REF: 237UNTS161.
PROCEDURE: Termination.
PARTIES:
Guatemala
USA (United States)

103987 Bilateral Exchange **275 UNTS 279**
SIGNED: 27 Aug 53   FORCE: 20 Jun 55
REGISTERED: 22 Aug 57 India
ARTICLES: 2 LANGUAGE: English. Italian.
HEADNOTE: CARE MAINTENANCE GRAVES
TOPIC: Other Military
CONCEPTS: National treatment. Upkeep of war graves.
TREATY REF: 213UNTS137.
PARTIES:
India
Italy

103988 Multilateral Convention **276 UNTS 3**
SIGNED: 26 Oct 56   FORCE: 29 Jul 57
REGISTERED: 27 Aug 57 USA (United States)
ARTICLES: 23 LANGUAGE: Chinese. English. Russian. Spanish.
HEADNOTE: INTERNATIONAL ATOMIC ENERGY AGENCY
TOPIC: IGO Establishment
CONCEPTS: Definition of terms. Treaty implementation. Annex or appendix reference. Treaty violation. Annex type material. Peaceful relations. Privileges and immunities. Extraditable offenses. Conformity with municipal law. Exchange of information and documents. Informational records. Juridical personality. Establishment of commission. Disputes disrupting normal relations. Existing tribunals. Specialists exchange. Research cooperation. Research results. Nuclear research. Scientific exchange. Research and development. Accounting procedures. Expense sharing formulae. Financial programs. Funding procedures. General technical assistance. Atomic energy assistance. Nuclear materials. Non-nuclear materials. Peaceful use. Rights of supplier. Samples and testing. Admission. Establishment. Liaison with other IGO's. Internal structure. Freedom of action. Special status. Interagency agreements.
INTL ORGS: International Atomic Energy Agency. International Court of Justice. United Nations.
PROCEDURE: Amendment. Accession. Denunciation. Ratification. Registration.
PARTIES:
Afghanistan SIGNED: 23 Jan 57 RATIFIED: 31 May 57 FORCE: 29 Jul 57
Albania SIGNED: 26 Oct 56
Argentina SIGNED: 26 Oct 56
Australia SIGNED: 14 Dec 56 RATIFIED: 29 Jul 57 FORCE: 29 Jul 57
Austria SIGNED: 26 Oct 56 RATIFIED: 10 May 57 FORCE: 29 Jul 57
Belgium SIGNED: 26 Oct 56
Bolivia SIGNED: 26 Oct 56
Brazil SIGNED: 26 Oct 56 RATIFIED: 29 Jul 57 FORCE: 29 Jul 57
Bulgaria SIGNED: 26 Oct 56
Burma SIGNED: 1 Sep 57
Byelorussia SIGNED: 26 Oct 56 RATIFIED: 8 Apr 57 FORCE: 29 Jul 57
Cambodia SIGNED: 26 Oct 56
Canada SIGNED: 26 Oct 56 RATIFIED: 29 Jul 57 FORCE: 29 Jul 57
Ceylon (Sri Lanka) SIGNED: 26 Oct 56

Chile SIGNED: 26 Oct 56
Taiwan SIGNED: 26 Oct 56
Colombia SIGNED: 26 Oct 56
Costa Rica SIGNED: 26 Oct 56
Cuba SIGNED: 26 Oct 56
Czechoslovakia SIGNED: 26 Oct 56 RATIFIED: 5 Jul 57 FORCE: 29 Jul 57
Denmark SIGNED: 26 Oct 56 RATIFIED: 16 Jul 57 FORCE: 29 Jul 57
Dominican Republic SIGNED: 26 Oct 56 RATIFIED: 11 Jul 57 FORCE: 29 Jul 57
Ecuador SIGNED: 26 Oct 56
United Arab Rep SIGNED: 26 Oct 56
El Salvador SIGNED: 26 Oct 56
Ethiopia SIGNED: 26 Oct 56
France SIGNED: 26 Oct 56 RATIFIED: 29 Jul 57 FORCE: 29 Jul 57
Germany, West SIGNED: 26 Oct 56
Greece SIGNED: 26 Oct 56
Guatemala SIGNED: 26 Oct 56 RATIFIED: 29 Mar 57 FORCE: 29 Jul 57
Haiti SIGNED: 26 Oct 56
Honduras SIGNED: 26 Oct 56 RATIFIED: 9 Jul 57 FORCE: 29 Jul 57
Hungary SIGNED: 26 Oct 56 RATIFIED: 8 Aug 57 FORCE: 8 Aug 57
Iceland SIGNED: 26 Oct 56 RATIFIED: 6 Aug 57 FORCE: 6 Aug 57
India SIGNED: 26 Oct 56 RATIFIED: 16 Jul 57 FORCE: 29 Jul 57
Indonesia SIGNED: 26 Oct 56 RATIFIED: 7 Aug 57 FORCE: 7 Aug 57
Iran SIGNED: 26 Oct 56
Iraq SIGNED: 15 Jan 57
Israel SIGNED: 26 Oct 56 RATIFIED: 12 Jul 57 FORCE: 29 Jul 57
Italy SIGNED: 15 Nov 56
Japan SIGNED: 26 Oct 56 RATIFIED: 16 Jul 57 FORCE: 29 Jul 57
Korea, North SIGNED: 26 Oct 56 RATIFIED: 8 Aug 57 FORCE: 8 Aug 57
Laos SIGNED: 26 Oct 56
Lebanon SIGNED: 26 Oct 56
Liberia SIGNED: 26 Oct 56
Libya SIGNED: 26 Oct 56
Luxembourg SIGNED: 18 Jan 57
Mexico SIGNED: 7 Dec 56
Monaco SIGNED: 26 Oct 56
Morocco SIGNED: 9 Jan 57
Netherlands SIGNED: 26 Oct 56 RATIFIED: 30 Jul 57 FORCE: 30 Jul 57
New Zealand SIGNED: 26 Oct 56
Nicaragua SIGNED: 26 Oct 56
Norway SIGNED: 26 Oct 56 RATIFIED: 10 Jun 57 FORCE: 29 Jul 57
Pakistan SIGNED: 26 Oct 56 RATIFIED: 2 May 57 FORCE: 29 Jul 57
Panama SIGNED: 26 Oct 56
Paraguay SIGNED: 26 Oct 56
Peru SIGNED: 26 Oct 56
Philippines SIGNED: 5 Dec 56
Poland SIGNED: 26 Oct 56 RATIFIED: 31 Jul 57 FORCE: 31 Jul 57
Portugal SIGNED: 26 Oct 56 RATIFIED: 12 Jul 57 FORCE: 29 Jul 57
Romania SIGNED: 26 Oct 56 RATIFIED: 12 Apr 57 FORCE: 29 Jul 57
South Africa SIGNED: 26 Oct 56 RATIFIED: 6 Jun 57 FORCE: 29 Jul 57
Spain SIGNED: 26 Oct 56
Sudan SIGNED: 26 Oct 56
Sweden SIGNED: 26 Oct 56 RATIFIED: 19 Jun 57 FORCE: 29 Jul 57
Switzerland SIGNED: 26 Oct 56 RATIFIED: 5 Apr 57 FORCE: 29 Jul 57
Syria SIGNED: 26 Oct 56
Thailand SIGNED: 26 Oct 56
Tunisia SIGNED: 8 Jan 57
Turkey SIGNED: 26 Oct 56 RATIFIED: 19 Jul 57 FORCE: 29 Jul 57
UK Great Britain SIGNED: 26 Oct 56 RATIFIED: 29 Jul 57 FORCE: 29 Jul 57
USA (United States) SIGNED: 26 Oct 56 RATIFIED: 29 Jul 57 FORCE: 29 Jul 57
Ukrainian SSR SIGNED: 26 Oct 56 RATIFIED: 31 Jul 57 FORCE: 29 Jul 57
Uruguay SIGNED: 26 Oct 56
USSR (Soviet Union) SIGNED: 26 Oct 56 RATIFIED: 8 Apr 57 FORCE: 29 Jul 57
Vatican/Holy See SIGNED: 26 Oct 56
Venezuela SIGNED: 26 Oct 56
Vietnam SIGNED: 26 Oct 56
Yugoslavia SIGNED: 26 Oct 56

103989 Bilateral Exchange **276 UNTS 127**
SIGNED: 1 Dec 56   FORCE: 1 Dec 56
REGISTERED: 3 Sep 57 Netherlands
ARTICLES: 2 LANGUAGE: Danish. German.
HEADNOTE: EXTRADITION
TOPIC: Extradition
CONCEPTS: Previous treaty amendment. Revival of treaties.
TREATY REF: 2'13DEMARTENS423;.
PARTIES:
  Germany, West
  Netherlands

103990 Bilateral Agreement **276 UNTS 143**
SIGNED: 5 Feb 57   FORCE: 3 Aug 57
REGISTERED: 3 Sep 57 Belgium
ARTICLES: 13 LANGUAGE: French.
HEADNOTE: CULTURAL AGREEMENT
TOPIC: Culture
CONCEPTS: Friendship and amity. Tourism. General cooperation. Operating agencies. Establishment of commission. Exchange. Specialists exchange. Exchange. Teacher and student exchange. Scholarships and grants. Exchange. General cultural cooperation. Artists. Research cooperation. Scientific exchange. Publications exchange. Mass media exchange.
INTL ORGS: Special Commission.
PROCEDURE: Denunciation. Duration. Ratification. Renewal or Revival.
PARTIES:
  Belgium
  Yugoslavia

103991 Bilateral Agreement **276 UNTS 153**
SIGNED: 18 Dec 56   FORCE: 18 Jan 57
REGISTERED: 6 Sep 57 Netherlands
ARTICLES: 22 LANGUAGE: Danish. Hebrew. English.
HEADNOTE: EXTRADITION CRIMINALS
TOPIC: Extradition
CONCEPTS: Territorial application. Time limit. Extradition, deportation and repatriation. Extraditable offenses. Location of crime. Special factors. Refusal of extradition. Limits of prosecution. Provisional detainment. Extradition postponement. Witnesses and experts. Material evidence. Indemnities and reimbursements.
PROCEDURE: Termination.
PARTIES:
  Israel
  Netherlands

103992 Multilateral Convention **276 UNTS 191**
SIGNED: 4 Jun 54   FORCE: 4 Jun 54
REGISTERED: 11 Sep 57 United Nations
ARTICLES: 25 LANGUAGE: English. French. Spanish.
HEADNOTE: CUSTOMS FACILITIES TOURING
TOPIC: Customs
CONCEPTS: Definition of terms. Territorial application. Tourism. Investigation of violations. Arbitration. Negotiation. Customs duties. Customs exemptions.
INTL ORGS: International Court of Justice. United Nations.
PROCEDURE: Amendment. Accession. Denunciation. Ratification. Registration.
PARTIES:
  Argentina SIGNED: 4 Jun 54
  Austria SIGNED: 4 Jun 54 RATIFIED: 30 Mar 56 FORCE: 11 Sep 57

Belgium SIGNED: 4 Jun 54 RATIFIED: 21 Feb 55 FORCE: 11 Sep 57
Cambodia SIGNED: 4 Jun 54 RATIFIED: 29 Nov 55 FORCE: 11 Sep 57
Ceylon (Sri Lanka) SIGNED: 4 Jun 54 FORCE: 11 Sep 57
Costa Rica SIGNED: 20 Jul 54
Cuba SIGNED: 10 Oct 54
Dominican Republic SIGNED: 4 Jun 54
Ecuador SIGNED: 4 Jun 54
United Arab Rep SIGNED: 4 Jun 54 RATIFIED: 4 Apr 57 FORCE: 10 Sep 57
France SIGNED: 4 Jun 54
Germany, West SIGNED: 4 Jun 54
Guatemala SIGNED: 4 Jun 54
Haiti SIGNED: 4 Jun 54
Honduras SIGNED: 15 Jun 54
India SIGNED: 30 Dec 54
Italy SIGNED: 4 Jun 54
Japan SIGNED: 2 Dec 54 RATIFIED: 7 Sep 55 FORCE: 11 Sep 57
Luxembourg SIGNED: 6 Dec 54 RATIFIED: 21 Nov 56 FORCE: 11 Sep 57
Mexico SIGNED: 4 Jun 54 RATIFIED: 13 Jun 57 FORCE: 11 Sep 57
Monaco SIGNED: 4 Jun 54
Netherlands SIGNED: 4 Jun 54
Panama SIGNED: 4 Jun 54
Philippines SIGNED: 4 Jun 54
Portugal SIGNED: 4 Jun 54
Spain SIGNED: 4 Jun 54
Sweden SIGNED: 4 Jun 54 RATIFIED: 11 Jun 57 FORCE: 11 Sep 57
Switzerland SIGNED: 4 Jun 54 RATIFIED: 23 May 56 FORCE: 11 Sep 57
UK Great Britain SIGNED: 4 Jun 54 RATIFIED: 27 Feb 56 FORCE: 11 Sep 57
USA (United States) SIGNED: 4 Jun 54 RATIFIED: 25 Jul 56 FORCE: 11 Sep 57
Uruguay SIGNED: 4 Jun 54
Vatican/Holy See SIGNED: 4 Jun 54

103993 Bilateral Agreement **276 UNTS 305**
SIGNED: 29 Sep 56   FORCE: 29 Oct 56
REGISTERED: 13 Sep 57 India
ARTICLES: 9 LANGUAGE: Hindi. Polish. English.
HEADNOTE: TELECOMMUNICATIONS
TOPIC: Telecommunications
CONCEPTS: Accounting procedures. Payment schedules. Non-interest rates and fees. Telecommunications. Services. Conformity with IGO decisions.
TREATY REF: INTERNATIONAL TELECOMMUNICATIONS CONVENTION.
PROCEDURE: Duration. Termination.
PARTIES:
  India
  Poland

103994 Bilateral Convention **276 UNTS 319**
SIGNED: 1 Jun 56   FORCE: 1 Apr 57
REGISTERED: 14 Sep 57 Netherlands
ARTICLES: 43 LANGUAGE: French.
HEADNOTE: SOCIAL SECURITY
TOPIC: Non-ILO Labor
CONCEPTS: Definition of terms. Exceptions and exemptions. General provisions. Conformity with municipal law. General cooperation. Domestic legislation. Old age and invalidity insurance. Wages and salaries. Non-ILO labor relations. Family allowances. Old age insurance. Sickness and invalidity insurance. Social security. Unemployment. Payment schedules.
INTL ORGS: Arbitration Commission.
PROCEDURE: Duration. Ratification. Renewal or Revival. Termination.
PARTIES:
  Netherlands
  Yugoslavia

103995 Unilateral Instrument **277 UNTS 3**
SIGNED: 31 Aug 57   FORCE: 17 Sep 57
REGISTERED: 17 Sep 57 United Nations
ARTICLES: 1 LANGUAGE: English.
HEADNOTE: ACCEPTANCE OBLIGATIONS UN
TOPIC: UN Charter
CONCEPTS: Acceptance of obligations upon admittance to UN.
INTL ORGS: United Nations.
PARTIES:
  Fed of Malaya

103996 Bilateral Convention **277 UNTS 7**
SIGNED: 27 Dec 56   FORCE: 31 May 57
REGISTERED: 17 Sep 57 Finland
ARTICLES: 25 LANGUAGE: Finnish. German.
HEADNOTE: DOUBLE TAXATION TAXES INCOME PROPERTY
TOPIC: Taxation
CONCEPTS: Nationality and citizenship. Taxation. General. Tax exemptions.
PARTIES:
  Finland
  Switzerland

103997 Bilateral Convention **277 UNTS 59**
SIGNED: 27 Dec 56   FORCE: 31 May 57
REGISTERED: 17 Sep 57 Finland
ARTICLES: 7 LANGUAGE: Finnish. German.
HEADNOTE: DOUBLE TAXATION INHERITANCE TAXES
TOPIC: Taxation
CONCEPTS: Debts. Taxation. Death duties.
PROCEDURE: Denunciation. Duration.
PARTIES:
  Finland
  Switzerland

103998 Unilateral Instrument **277 UNTS 77**
SIGNED: 9 Sep 57   FORCE: 19 Sep 57
REGISTERED: 19 Sep 57 United Nations
ARTICLES: 1 LANGUAGE: French.
HEADNOTE: ACCEPTANCE ICJ JURISDICTION
TOPIC: ICJ Option Clause
CONCEPTS: Exceptions and exemptions. Compulsory jurisdiction.
INTL ORGS: International Court of Justice.
PROCEDURE: Termination.

PARTIES:
Cambodia

103999   Bilateral Exchange   **277 UNTS 81**
SIGNED: 25 Jul 57   FORCE: 25 Jul 57
REGISTERED: 24 Sep 57 Thailand
ARTICLES: 2 LANGUAGE: English.
HEADNOTE: EXEMPTION IMPORT DUTIES
TOPIC: Customs
CONCEPTS: Customs exemptions. Agricultural vehicles and construction.
PARTIES:
Thailand
UK Great Britain

104000   Bilateral Treaty   **277 UNTS 87**
SIGNED: 15 Oct 56   FORCE: 28 May 57
REGISTERED: 27 Sep 57 Thailand
ARTICLES: 9 LANGUAGE: Thai. Burmese. English.
HEADNOTE: FRIENDSHIP
TOPIC: General Amity
CONCEPTS: Treaty interpretation. Friendship and amity. Alien status. Consular relations establishment. Diplomatic relations establishment. Privileges and immunities. General cooperation. Arbitration. Procedure.
PROCEDURE: Duration. Future Procedures Contemplated. Ratification. Termination.
PARTIES:
Burma
Thailand

104001   Bilateral Agreement   **277 UNTS 105**
SIGNED: 23 Oct 56   FORCE: 23 Oct 56
REGISTERED: 28 Sep 57 USA (United States)
ARTICLES: 6 LANGUAGE: English. Spanish.
HEADNOTE: AGRI COMMOD
TOPIC: US Agri Commod Aid
CONCEPTS: General provisions. General cooperation. Exchange of information and documents. Currency deposits. Exchange rates and regulations. Purchase authorizations. Local currency. Commodities schedule. Surplus commodities.
PARTIES:
Spain
USA (United States)
ANNEX
279 UNTS 358. USA (United States). Amendment 1 Feb 57. Force 1 Feb 57.
279 UNTS 358. Spain. Amendment 1 Feb 57. Force 1 Feb 57.
288 UNTS 385. Spain. Amendment 26 Mar 57. Force 26 Mar 57.
288 UNTS 385. USA (United States). Amendment 26 Mar 57. Force 26 Mar 57.
340 UNTS 384. USA (United States). Amendment 12 Jun 58. Force 30 Jul 58.
340 UNTS 384. Spain. Amendment 30 Jul 58. Force 30 Jul 58.
360 UNTS 408. USA (United States). Amendment 25 Jun 59. Force 15 Jul 59.
360 UNTS 408. Spain. Amendment 15 Jul 59. Force 15 Jul 59.

104002   Bilateral Agreement   **277 UNTS 119**
SIGNED: 3 Nov 56   FORCE: 3 Nov 56
REGISTERED: 28 Sep 57 USA (United States)
ARTICLES: 5 LANGUAGE: English.
HEADNOTE: AGRI COMMOD TITLE I
TOPIC: US Agri Commod Aid
CONCEPTS: General provisions. General cooperation. Exchange of information and documents. Reexport of goods, etc.. Currency deposits. Exchange rates and regulations. Purchase authorizations. Local currency. Commodities schedule. Surplus commodities.
PARTIES:
USA (United States)
Yugoslavia
ANNEX
279 UNTS 360. USA (United States). Amendment 22 Mar 57. Force 22 Mar 57.
279 UNTS 360. Yugoslavia. Amendment 22 Mar 57. Force 22 Mar 57.
307 UNTS 316. USA (United States). Amendment 27 Dec 57. Force 27 Dec 57.
307 UNTS 316. Yugoslavia. Amendment 27 Dec 57. Force 27 Dec 57.
524 UNTS 317. USA (United States). Amendment 15 Apr 64. Force 15 Apr 64.

524 UNTS 317. Yugoslavia. Amendment 15 Apr 64. Force 15 Apr 64.

104003   Bilateral Exchange   **277 UNTS 133**
SIGNED: 7 Nov 56   FORCE: 7 Nov 56
REGISTERED: 28 Sep 57 USA (United States)
ARTICLES: 2 LANGUAGE: English. Portuguese.
HEADNOTE: LOAN NAVAL VESSELS
TOPIC: Milit Assistance
CONCEPTS: Time limit. Annex or appendix reference. Responsibility and liability. Title and deeds. Compensation. Indemnities and reimbursements. Delivery schedules. Materials, equipment and services. Lease of military property. Naval vessels. Return of equipment and recapture.
TREATY REF: 133UNTS75.
PARTIES:
Portugal
USA (United States)
ANNEX
460 UNTS 310. USA (United States). Amendment 8 Mar 62. Force 27 Jul 62.
460 UNTS 310. Portugal. Amendment 27 Jul 62. Force 27 Jul 62.

104004   Bilateral Agreement   **277 UNTS 143**
SIGNED: 5 Nov 56   FORCE: 5 Nov 56
REGISTERED: 28 Sep 57 USA (United States)
ARTICLES: 11 LANGUAGE: English. Spanish.
HEADNOTE: EDUCATIONAL PROGRAM
TOPIC: Education
CONCEPTS: Definition of terms. Friendship and amity. Standardization. Conformity with municipal law. Inspection and observation. Personnel. General property. Exchange. Commissions and foundations. Teacher and student exchange. Scholarships and grants. Research and development. Accounting procedures. Currency. Exchange rates and regulations. Expense sharing formulae. Financial programs. Funding procedures.
INTL ORGS: Special Commission.
TREATY REF: 251UNTS283.
PARTIES:
Argentina
USA (United States)
ANNEX
307 UNTS 320. USA (United States). Amendment 26 Dec 57. Force 27 Dec 57.
307 UNTS 320. Argentina. Amendment 27 Dec 57. Force 27 Dec 57.
410 UNTS 321. USA (United States). Amendment 8 May 61. Force 17 May 61.
410 UNTS 321. Argentina. Amendment 17 May 61. Force 17 May 61.

104005   Bilateral Agreement   **277 UNTS 159**
SIGNED: 22 Jun 57   FORCE: 22 Jun 57
REGISTERED: 28 Sep 57 Honduras
ARTICLES: 1 LANGUAGE: Spanish.
HEADNOTE: SUBMISSION CLAIM ICJ
TOPIC: Specif Claim/Waive
CONCEPTS: Annex or appendix reference. Procedure. Existing tribunals. Specific claims or waivers.
INTL ORGS: International Court of Justice. Organization of American States. United Nations.
TREATY REF: 21UNTS77.
PARTIES:
Honduras
Nicaragua

104006   Bilateral Exchange   **277 UNTS 191**
SIGNED: 1 Oct 57   FORCE: 17 Nov 56
REGISTERED: 1 Oct 57 United Nations
ARTICLES: 2 LANGUAGE: English.
HEADNOTE: SERVICE UN EMERGENCY FORCE
TOPIC: Milit Assistance
CONCEPTS: Annex or appendix reference. Privileges and immunities. General cooperation. Arbitration. Procedure. Indemnities and reimbursements. Jurisdiction. Withdrawal of forces. Peace-keeping force.
INTL ORGS: International Court of Justice. Arbitration Commission.
TREATY REF: 260UNTS61.
PARTIES:
United Nations
Yugoslavia

104007   Bilateral Agreement   **277 UNTS 203**
SIGNED: 8 Aug 56   FORCE: 8 Aug 56
REGISTERED: 2 Oct 57 USA (United States)
ARTICLES: 6 LANGUAGE: English.
HEADNOTE: AGRI COMMOD TITLE I
TOPIC: US Agri Commod Aid
CONCEPTS: General provisions. Annex or appendix reference. General cooperation. Exchange of information and documents. Reexport of goods, etc.. Currency deposits. Exchange rates and regulations. Purchase authorizations. Local currency. Transportation costs. Commodities schedule. Surplus commodities.
PARTIES:
Greece
USA (United States)
ANNEX
278 UNTS 320. USA (United States). Supplementation 21 Jan 57. Force 21 Jan 57.
278 UNTS 320. Greece. Supplementation 21 Jan 57. Force 21 Jan 57.
278 UNTS 324. Greece. Amendment 23 Feb 57. Force 23 Feb 57.
278 UNTS 324. USA (United States). Amendment 13 Feb 57. Force 23 Feb 57.
278 UNTS 328. USA (United States). Amendment 1 Mar 57. Force 4 Mar 57.
278 UNTS 328. Greece. Amendment 4 Mar 57. Force 4 Mar 57.
280 UNTS 394. USA (United States). Amendment 8 Jan 57. Force 25 Jan 57.
280 UNTS 394. Greece. Amendment 25 Jan 57. Force 25 Jan 57.
410 UNTS 326. USA (United States). Supplementation 3 Apr 61. Force 13 Apr 61.
410 UNTS 326. Greece. Supplementation 13 Apr 61. Force 13 Apr 61.

104008   Bilateral Agreement   **277 UNTS 215**
SIGNED: 11 Sep 56   FORCE: 11 Sep 56
REGISTERED: 2 Oct 57 USA (United States)
ARTICLES: 6 LANGUAGE: English.
HEADNOTE: AGRI COMMOD TITLE I
TOPIC: US Agri Commod Aid
CONCEPTS: General provisions. Annex or appendix reference. General cooperation. Exchange of information and documents. Reexport of goods, etc.. Currency deposits. Exchange rates and regulations. Purchase authorizations. Transportation costs. Local currency. Commodities schedule. Surplus commodities.
PARTIES:
Israel
USA (United States)
ANNEX
314 UNTS 360. USA (United States). Amendment 28 Aug 58.
314 UNTS 360. Israel. Amendment 28 Aug 58.

104009   Bilateral Agreement   **277 UNTS 231**
SIGNED: 6 Sep 56   FORCE: 6 Sep 56
REGISTERED: 2 Oct 57 USA (United States)
ARTICLES: 29 LANGUAGE: English. Spanish.
HEADNOTE: US ARMY MISSION
TOPIC: Military Mission
CONCEPTS: Payment for war supplies. Military assistance. Airforce-army-navy personnel ratio. Ranks and privileges. Conditions for assistance missions.
PARTIES:
Peru
USA (United States)
ANNEX
283 UNTS 351. USA (United States). Amendment 8 Apr 57. Force 24 Apr 57.
283 UNTS 351. Peru. Amendment 24 Apr 57. Force 24 Apr 57.

104010   Bilateral Agreement   **277 UNTS 259**
SIGNED: 10 Sep 56   FORCE: 9 Dec 56
REGISTERED: 2 Oct 57 USA (United States)
ARTICLES: 9 LANGUAGE: English.
HEADNOTE: FINANCIAL ARRANGEMENTS FURNISHING SUPPLIES SERVICES NAVAL VESSELS
TOPIC: Milit Assistance
CONCEPTS: Indemnities and reimbursements. Currency. Materials, equipment and services. Ports and pilotage. Payment for war supplies.
PROCEDURE: Termination.

PARTIES:
Pakistan
USA (United States)

104011 Bilateral Exchange **277 UNTS 267**
SIGNED: 5 Sep 56 FORCE: 5 Sep 56
REGISTERED: 2 Oct 57 USA (United States)
ARTICLES: 2 LANGUAGE: English. Japanese.
HEADNOTE: EXCHANGE OFFICIAL PUBLICA-
TIONS
TOPIC: Admin Cooperation
CONCEPTS: Exchange of official publications. Op-
erating agencies. Indemnities and reimburse-
ments.
PARTIES:
Japan
USA (United States)

104012 Bilateral Exchange **277 UNTS 279**
SIGNED: 23 Apr 55 FORCE: 23 Apr 55
REGISTERED: 2 Oct 57 USA (United States)
ARTICLES: 2 LANGUAGE: English. French.
HEADNOTE: FINANCIAL ASSISTANCE SUPPORT
ARMED FORCES
TOPIC: Milit Assistance
CONCEPTS: Indemnities and reimbursements. Fi-
nancial programs. Military assistance. Military
assistance missions.
PARTIES:
USA (United States)
Vietnam, South
ANNEX
278 UNTS 332. USA (United States). Amendment
24 Jun 55. Force 25 Jun 55.
278 UNTS 332. Vietnam, South. Amendment
25 Jun 55. Force 25 Jun 55.

104013 Bilateral Exchange **277 UNTS 285**
SIGNED: 7 Mar 55 FORCE: 7 Mar 55
REGISTERED: 2 Oct 57 USA (United States)
ARTICLES: 2 LANGUAGE: English. French.
HEADNOTE: ECONOMIC ASSISTANCE
TOPIC: Direct Aid
CONCEPTS: Exchange of information and docu-
ments. Accounting procedures. Currency depos-
its. Exchange rates and regulations. Financial
programs. Economic assistance.
TREATY REF: 174UNTS165; 205UNTS127.
PARTIES:
USA (United States)
Vietnam, South

104014 Bilateral Agreement **277 UNTS 293**
SIGNED: 20 Dec 53 FORCE: 1 Jan 54
REGISTERED: 5 Oct 57 South Africa
ARTICLES: 21 LANGUAGE: English. Italian.
HEADNOTE: PARCEL POST
TOPIC: Postal Service
CONCEPTS: Conformity with municipal law. Re-
sponsibility and liability. Accounting proce-
dures. Customs duties. Customs declarations.
Customs exemptions. Postal services. Regula-
tions. Parcel post. Rates and charges.
PROCEDURE: Termination.
PARTIES:
Italy
South Africa

104015 Bilateral Agreement **277 UNTS 315**
SIGNED: 8 Jul 57 FORCE: 8 Jul 57
REGISTERED: 9 Oct 57 Australia
ARTICLES: 4 LANGUAGE: English.
HEADNOTE: TECHNICAL ASSISTANCE TRAINING
CENTER FISHERY
TOPIC: Tech Assistance
CONCEPTS: Time limit. Privileges and immunities.
Conformity with municipal law. General cooper-
ation. Personnel. Responsibility and liability. Use
of facilities. Teacher and student exchange. Insti-
tute establishment. Expense sharing formulae.
Domestic obligation. IGO status.
INTL ORGS: Special Commission.
PARTIES:
Australia
FAO (Food Agri)

104016 Bilateral Agreement **277 UNTS 327**
SIGNED: 14 Jun 57 FORCE: 14 Jun 57

REGISTERED: 15 Oct 57 Finland
ARTICLES: 6 LANGUAGE: English.
HEADNOTE: TECHNICAL ASSISTANCE
TOPIC: Tech Assistance
CONCEPTS: Annex or appendix reference. Person-
nel. Responsibility and liability. Use of facilities.
Professorships. Indemnities and reimburse-
ments. Financial programs. Tax exemptions.
Customs exemptions. Domestic obligation. Gen-
eral technical assistance. Natural resources. Raw
materials.
PARTIES:
Finland
India

104017 Bilateral Exchange **278 UNTS 3**
SIGNED: 27 Jul 56 FORCE: 27 Jul 56
REGISTERED: 18 Oct 57 USA (United States)
ARTICLES: 2 LANGUAGE: English. German.
HEADNOTE: WAIVER IMMUNITY
TOPIC: Admin Cooperation
CONCEPTS: Waiver of immunity.
INTL ORGS: Arbitration Commission.
PARTIES:
Germany, West
USA (United States)

104018 Bilateral Exchange **278 UNTS 9**
SIGNED: 8 Oct 56 FORCE: 8 Oct 56
REGISTERED: 18 Oct 57 USA (United States)
ARTICLES: 2 LANGUAGE: English. German.
HEADNOTE: MILITARY EQUIPMENT
TOPIC: Milit Assistance
CONCEPTS: Payment schedules. Military assis-
tance.
TREATY REF: 224UNTS107.
PARTIES:
Germany, West
USA (United States)
ANNEX
393 UNTS 332. Germany, West. Amendment
24 Oct 60. Force 24 Oct 60.
393 UNTS 332. USA (United States). Amendment
15 Jun 60. Force 24 Oct 60.
434 UNTS 328. USA (United States). Supplemen-
tation 24 Nov 61. Force 24 Nov 61.
434 UNTS 328. Germany, West. Supplementation 24 Nov 61. Force 24 Nov 61.

104019 Bilateral Agreement **278 UNTS 25**
SIGNED: 29 Aug 56 FORCE: 29 Aug 56
REGISTERED: 18 Oct 57 USA (United States)
ARTICLES: 6 LANGUAGE: English.
HEADNOTE: AGRI COMMOD AGREEMENT
TOPIC: US Agri Commod Aid
CONCEPTS: General provisions. Annex or appen-
dix reference. Conformity with municipal law.
General cooperation. Exchange of information
and documents. Reexport of goods, etc.. Cur-
rency deposits. Exchange rates and regulations.
Purchase authorizations. Transportation costs.
Local currency. Assistance. Surplus commodi-
ties.
PARTIES:
India
USA (United States)
ANNEX
304 UNTS 390. India. Amendment 13 Feb 58.
Force 13 Feb 58.
304 UNTS 390. USA (United States). Amendment
13 Feb 58. Force 13 Feb 58.
358 UNTS 326. USA (United States). Amendment
1 Oct 59. Force 28 Oct 59.
358 UNTS 326. India. Amendment 28 Oct 59.
Force 28 Oct 59.

104020 Bilateral Exchange **278 UNTS 51**
SIGNED: 24 Sep 56 FORCE: 24 Sep 56
REGISTERED: 18 Oct 57 USA (United States)
ARTICLES: 2 LANGUAGE: English. Arabic.
HEADNOTE: GUARANTEES MUTUAL SECURITY
ACT
TOPIC: Milit Assistance
CONCEPTS: Guarantees and safeguards. Confor-
mity with municipal law. General cooperation.
Arbitration. Procedure. Claims and settlements.
Most favored nation clause.
PARTIES:
Jordan
USA (United States)

ANNEX
303 UNTS 377. USA (United States). Amendment
20 Nov 57. Force 22 Feb 58.
303 UNTS 377. Jordan. Amendment 22 Feb 58.
Force 22 Feb 58.
487 UNTS 356. USA (United States). Supplementation 25 Jun 63. Force 25 Jun 63.
487 UNTS 356. Jordan. Supplementation
25 Jun 63. Force 25 Jun 63.

104021 Bilateral Exchange **278 UNTS 59**
SIGNED: 8 Jul 55 FORCE: 8 Jul 55
REGISTERED: 18 Oct 57 USA (United States)
ARTICLES: 2 LANGUAGE: French.
HEADNOTE: ECONOMIC ASSISTANCE
TOPIC: Direct Aid
CONCEPTS: Annex type material. General cooper-
ation. Exchange of information and documents.
Currency deposits. Exchange rates and regula-
tions. Local currency. Economic assistance.
INTL ORGS: International Monetary Fund.
TREATY REF: 174UNTS141.
PARTIES:
Laos
USA (United States)

104022 Bilateral Exchange **278 UNTS 65**
SIGNED: 19 Oct 56 FORCE: 19 Oct 56
REGISTERED: 18 Oct 57 USA (United States)
ARTICLES: 2 LANGUAGE: English.
HEADNOTE: RADIO COMMUNICATIONS AMA-
TEUR STATIONS BEHALF THIRD PARTIES
TOPIC: Gen Communications
CONCEPTS: Domestic legislation. Amateur radio.
Amateur third party message. Radio-telephone-
telegraphic communications.
PROCEDURE: Termination.
PARTIES:
Costa Rica
USA (United States)

104023 Multilateral Convention **278 UNTS 73**
SIGNED: 15 Dec 56 FORCE: 18 Sep 57
REGISTERED: 19 Oct 57 Council of Europe
ARTICLES: 10 LANGUAGE: English. French.
HEADNOTE: UNIVERSITY STUDY
TOPIC: Education
CONCEPTS: Definition of terms. Standardization.
General cooperation. Exchange of information
and documents. Education. Recognition of de-
grees. Teacher and student exchange.
INTL ORGS: Council of Europe.
TREATY REF: 218UNTS125; 218UNTS139.
PROCEDURE: Accession. Ratification.
PARTIES:
Austria SIGNED: 3 Apr 54 RATIFIED: 2 Oct 57
FORCE: 18 Sep 57
Belgium SIGNED: 3 Apr 54
Denmark SIGNED: 3 Apr 54
France SIGNED: 3 Apr 54
Germany, West SIGNED: 3 Apr 54
Greece SIGNED: 3 Apr 54
Iceland SIGNED: 3 Apr 54
Ireland SIGNED: 3 Apr 54 RATIFIED: 20 Feb 57
FORCE: 18 Sep 57
Italy SIGNED: 3 Apr 54
Luxembourg SIGNED: 3 Apr 54
Netherlands SIGNED: 3 Apr 54
Norway SIGNED: 3 Apr 54 RATIFIED: 14 Mar 57
FORCE: 18 Sep 57
Saar SIGNED: 3 Apr 54 RATIFIED: 18 Sep 57
FORCE: 18 Sep 57
Sweden SIGNED: 3 Apr 54
Turkey SIGNED: 3 Apr 54
UK Great Britain SIGNED: 3 Apr 54 RATIFIED:
18 Sep 57 FORCE: 18 Sep 57
ANNEX
286 UNTS 396. UK Great Britain. Fed Rhod/-
Nyasaland. Force 2 Jan 58.
355 UNTS 414. France. Ratification 19 Feb 58.
355 UNTS 414. Italy. Ratification 29 Mar 58.
355 UNTS 414. Turkey. Ratification 18 Feb 60.
355 UNTS 414. Denmark. Ratification 23 Jun 58.
355 UNTS 414. Netherlands. Ratification
10 Dec 59.
376 UNTS 453. Greece. Signature 16 Sep 60.
562 UNTS 330. Germany, West. Berlin.
562 UNTS 330. Iceland. Ratification 5 Apr 63.
562 UNTS 330. Germany, West. Ratification
8 Dec 64.
635 UNTS 352. Sweden. Ratification 21 Jun 67.

635 UNTS 352.   Luxembourg.   Ratification
23 Jan 68.

104024 Bilateral Exchange   **278 UNTS 85**
SIGNED: 30 Jan 57   FORCE: 30 Jan 57
REGISTERED: 19 Oct 57 USA (United States)
ARTICLES: 2 LANGUAGE: English.
HEADNOTE: AGRICULTURAL COMMODITIES
TOPIC: US Agri Commod Aid
CONCEPTS: General provisions. Conformity with
municipal law. General cooperation. Exchange
of information and documents. Exchange
of goods, etc.. Currency deposits. Exchange rates
and regulations. Purchase authorizations. Transportation costs. Local currency. Commodities
schedule. Surplus commodities.
PARTIES:
Korea, South
USA (United States)
ANNEX
300 UNTS 394.   Korea,   South.   Amendment
16 Aug 57. Force 16 Aug 57.
300 UNTS 394. USA (United States). Amendment
16 Aug 57. Force 16 Aug 57.

104025 Bilateral Exchange   **278 UNTS 97**
SIGNED: 21 Jan 57   FORCE: 21 Jan 57
REGISTERED: 19 Oct 57 USA (United States)
ARTICLES: 2 LANGUAGE: English. Portuguese.
HEADNOTE: ESTABLISHMENT GUIDED MISSILE
STATION
TOPIC: Milit Installation
CONCEPTS: Defense and security. Testing ranges
and sites. Bases and facilities.
TREATY REF: 21UNTS77.
PROCEDURE: Denunciation. Duration.
PARTIES:
Brazil
USA (United States)

104026 Multilateral Agreement **278 UNTS 105**
SIGNED: 31 Jan 57   FORCE: 31 Jan 57
REGISTERED: 19 Oct 57 USA (United States)
ARTICLES: 6 LANGUAGE: English.
HEADNOTE: DISPOSITION GERMAN ASSETS
TOPIC: Claims and Debts
CONCEPTS: Detailed regulations. Claims and set-
tlements. Assets transfer. Enemy financial inter-
ests.
TREATY REF: 100UNTS47.
PARTIES:
France SIGNED: 31 Jan 57 FORCE: 31 Jan 57
Thailand SIGNED: 31 Jan 57 FORCE: 31 Jan 57
UK Great Britain SIGNED: 31 Jan 57 FORCE:
31 Jan 57
USA (United States) SIGNED: 31 Jan 57 FORCE:
31 Jan 57

104027 Bilateral Exchange   **278 UNTS 109**
SIGNED: 22 Sep 56   FORCE: 4 Jan 57
REGISTERED: 19 Oct 57 USA (United States)
ARTICLES: 3 LANGUAGE: English.
HEADNOTE: TRANSFER PROPERTY
TOPIC: Specific Property
CONCEPTS: Annex or appendix reference. Assets
transfer. Facilities and property.
PARTIES:
Liberia
USA (United States)

104028 Bilateral Exchange   **278 UNTS 117**
SIGNED: 8 May 56   FORCE: 8 May 56
REGISTERED: 25 Oct 57 USA (United States)
ARTICLES: 3 LANGUAGE: English. Spanish.
HEADNOTE: SURPLUS AGRI COMMOD DROUGHT
RELIEF ASSISTANCE
TOPIC: Direct Aid
CONCEPTS: Economic assistance. Relief supplies.
Loan and credit. Commodities schedule. Surplus
commodities. Transport of goods.
TREATY REF: 268UNTS3862.
PARTIES:
Peru
USA (United States)

104029 Bilateral Exchange   **278 UNTS 131**
SIGNED: 23 Mar 56   FORCE: 18 Jun 56
REGISTERED: 25 Oct 57 USA (United States)

ARTICLES: 2 LANGUAGE: English. French.
HEADNOTE: ESTABLISHMENT OBSERVATION
STATION
TOPIC: Specific Property
CONCEPTS: Exchange of information and documents. Operating agencies. Title and deeds. Research cooperation. Meteorology. Indemnities
and reimbursements. Customs exemptions. Facilities and property.
PROCEDURE: Duration. Termination.
PARTIES:
France
USA (United States)
ANNEX
357 UNTS 391. USA (United States). Supplementation 21 Jul 58. Force 3 Sep 58.
357 UNTS 391.   France.   Supplementation
3 Sep 58. Force 3 Sep 58.
400 UNTS 390. USA (United States). Amendment
23 Dec 59. Force 25 Jul 60.
400 UNTS 390. France. Amendment 25 Jul 60.
Force 25 Jul 60.
494 UNTS 299. France. Prolongation 13 Aug 63.
Force 25 Nov 63.
494 UNTS 299. USA (United States). Prolongation
25 Nov 63. Force 25 Nov 63.

104030 Bilateral Agreement   **278 UNTS 141**
SIGNED: 7 Sep 56   FORCE: 7 Sep 56
REGISTERED: 25 Oct 57 USA (United States)
ARTICLES: 5 LANGUAGE: English. Hebrew.
HEADNOTE: STATUS FORCES
TOPIC: Status of Forces
CONCEPTS: Previous treaty replacement. Court
procedures. Jurisdiction. Status of forces.
INTL ORGS: North Atlantic Treaty Organization.
TREATY REF: 191UNTS319.
PARTIES:
Greece
USA (United States)

104031 Bilateral Exchange   **279 UNTS 3**
SIGNED: 16 Aug 56   FORCE: 12 Sep 56
REGISTERED: 25 Oct 57 USA (United States)
ARTICLES: 2 LANGUAGE: English.
HEADNOTE: ESTABLISHMENT   OBSERVATION
STATIONS
TOPIC: Specific Property
CONCEPTS: Exchange of information and docu-
ments. Operating agencies. Title and deeds. Research cooperation. Meteorology. Indemnities
and reimbursements. Customs exemptions. Facilities and property.
PROCEDURE: Duration. Termination.
PARTIES:
Netherlands
USA (United States)
ANNEX
290 UNTS 358.   Netherlands.   Prolongation
29 Aug 57. Force 29 Aug 57.
290 UNTS 358. USA (United States). Prolongation
8 Jul 57. Force 29 Aug 57.
361 UNTS 354.   Netherlands.   Prolongation
10 Oct 58. Force 10 Oct 58.
361 UNTS 354. USA (United States). Prolongation
21 Jul 58. Force 10 Oct 58.

104032 Bilateral Agreement   **279 UNTS 13**
SIGNED: 3 Oct 56   FORCE: 3 Oct 56
REGISTERED: 25 Oct 57 USA (United States)
ARTICLES: 31 LANGUAGE: English. Spanish.
HEADNOTE: AIR FORCE MISSION
TOPIC: Military Mission
CONCEPTS: Definition of terms. Use of facilities.
Compensation. Indemnities and reimburse-
ments. Exchange rates and regulations. Expense
sharing formulae. Tax exemptions. Customs ex-
emptions. Military assistance. Military training.
Security of information. Airforce-army-navy per-
sonnel ratio. Ranks and privileges. Conditions
for assistance missions. Third country military
personnel. Status of forces.
PROCEDURE: Termination. Termination.
PARTIES:
Argentina
USA (United States)
ANNEX
361 UNTS 358.   Argentina.   Amendment
16 Oct 59. Force 16 Oct 59.
361 UNTS 358. USA (United States). Amendment
16 Oct 59. Force 16 Oct 59.

104033 Bilateral Agreement   **279 UNTS 41**
SIGNED: 21 Jun 56   FORCE: 29 Jan 57
REGISTERED: 25 Oct 57 USA (United States)
ARTICLES: 15 LANGUAGE: English. French.
HEADNOTE: CIVIL USES ATOMIC ENERGY
TOPIC: Atomic Energy
CONCEPTS: Definition of terms. Territorial applica-
tion. Diplomatic missions. Exchange of informa-
tion and documents. Research cooperation.
Scientific exchange. Establishment of trade rela-
tions. Nuclear materials. Non-nuclear materials.
Peaceful use. Rights of supplier. Security of in-
formation.
PROCEDURE: Amendment. Duration.
PARTIES:
Switzerland
USA (United States)
ANNEX
346 UNTS 346.   Switzerland.   Amendment
24 Apr 59. Force 8 Jun 59.
346 UNTS 346. USA (United States). Amendment
24 Apr 59. Force 8 Jun 59.
400 UNTS 396.   Switzerland.   Amendment
11 Jun 60. Force 1 Dec 60.
400 UNTS 396. USA (United States). Amendment
11 Jun 60. Force 1 Dec 60.

104034 Bilateral Agreement   **279 UNTS 73**
SIGNED: 4 Apr 55   FORCE: 7 Feb 57
REGISTERED: 25 Oct 57 USA (United States)
ARTICLES: 25 LANGUAGE: English. German.
HEADNOTE: OFFSHORE PROCUREMENT
TOPIC: Milit Assistance
CONCEPTS: Definition of terms. Privileges and im-
munities. Conformity with municipal law. Gen-
eral cooperation. Exchange of information and
documents. Licenses and permits. General prop-
erty. Private contracts. Indemnities and reim-
bursements. National treatment. Tax exemp-
tions. Customs exemptions. Materials, equipment and services. Defense and security.
Self-defense. Security of information. Exchange
of defense information.
PROCEDURE: Amendment. Future Procedures
Contemplated. Ratification.
PARTIES:
Germany, West
USA (United States)
ANNEX
289 UNTS 326. Germany, West. Implementation
4 Apr 55. Force 7 Feb 57.
289 UNTS 326. USA (United States). Implementation 4 Apr 55. Force 7 Feb 57.

104035 Bilateral Exchange   **279 UNTS 107**
SIGNED: 28 Dec 56   FORCE: 28 Dec 56
REGISTERED: 25 Oct 57 USA (United States)
ARTICLES: 2 LANGUAGE: English. French.
HEADNOTE: EMERGENCY RELIEF ASSISTANCE
TOPIC: Direct Aid
CONCEPTS: Relief supplies. Grants.
TREATY REF: 261UNTS361.
PARTIES:
Haiti
USA (United States)

104036 Bilateral Convention   **279 UNTS 113**
SIGNED: 25 Jun 56   FORCE: 1 Jan 57
REGISTERED: 25 Oct 57 USA (United States)
ARTICLES: 21 LANGUAGE: English. Spanish.
HEADNOTE: DOUBLE TAXATION FISCAL EVA-
SION TAXES INCOME
TOPIC: Taxation
CONCEPTS: Definition of terms. Privileges and im-
munities. Conformity with municipal law. Ex-
change of official publications. Domestic legisla-
tion. Negotiation. Teacher and student ex-
change. Taxation. Tax credits. Equitable taxes.
Air transport. Merchant vessels.
PROCEDURE: Duration. Ratification. Termination.
PARTIES:
Honduras
USA (United States)

104037 Bilateral Agreement   **279 UNTS 155**
SIGNED: 15 Feb 57   FORCE: 15 Feb 57
REGISTERED: 25 Oct 57 USA (United States)
ARTICLES: 6 LANGUAGE: English. Spanish.
HEADNOTE: AGRI COMMOD TITLE I
TOPIC: US Agri Commod Aid

CONCEPTS: Annex or appendix reference. General cooperation. Exchange of information and documents. Reexport of goods, etc.. Currency deposits. Exchange rates and regulations. Purchase authorizations. Transportation costs. Local currency. Loan and credit. Commodities schedule. Surplus commodities.
PARTIES:
Ecuador
USA (United States)
ANNEX
299 UNTS 431. Ecuador. Amendment 10 Sep 57. Force 10 Sep 57.
299 UNTS 431. USA (United States). Amendment 9 Sep 57. Force 10 Sep 57.

104038 Bilateral Exchange **279 UNTS 169**
SIGNED: 5 Feb 57 FORCE: 5 Feb 57
REGISTERED: 25 Oct 57 USA (United States)
ARTICLES: 2 LANGUAGE: English. Norwegian.
HEADNOTE: RELATING CERTIFICATES AIRWORTHINESS IMPORTED AIRCRAFT
TOPIC: Air Transport
CONCEPTS: Previous treaty replacement. Conformity with municipal law. Exchange of information and documents. Recognition of legal documents. Use of facilities. Registration certificate. Airworthiness certificates.
TREATY REF: 145LTS43.
PROCEDURE: Termination.
PARTIES:
Norway
USA (United States)

104039 Bilateral Exchange **279 UNTS 179**
SIGNED: 26 Feb 57 FORCE: 26 Oct 56
REGISTERED: 25 Oct 57 USA (United States)
ARTICLES: 3 LANGUAGE: English.
HEADNOTE: NAVIGATION IMPROVEMENTS GREAT LAKES CHANNELS ST. LAWRENCE SEAWAY
TOPIC: Water Transport
CONCEPTS: Conditions. Conformity with municipal law. Exchange of information and documents. Inspection and observation. Personnel. Private contracts. Responsibility and liability. Funding procedures. Non-interest rates and fees. Navigational conditions. Canal improvement. Inland and territorial waters.
PARTIES:
Canada
USA (United States)

104040 Bilateral Exchange **279 UNTS 191**
SIGNED: 9 Feb 57 FORCE: 9 Feb 57
REGISTERED: 25 Oct 57 USA (United States)
ARTICLES: 2 LANGUAGE: English. Spanish.
HEADNOTE: MILITARY ASSISTANCE ADVISORY GROUP
TOPIC: Milit Assistance
CONCEPTS: Military assistance missions. Ranks and privileges.
TREATY REF: 229UNTS37.
PARTIES:
Nicaragua
USA (United States)

104041 Bilateral Exchange **279 UNTS 199**
SIGNED: 21 Feb 57 FORCE: 21 Feb 57
REGISTERED: 25 Oct 57 USA (United States)
ARTICLES: 2 LANGUAGE: English. Spanish.
HEADNOTE: EXEMPTION MERCHANT VESSELS MEASUREMENT REQUIREMENT
TOPIC: Water Transport
CONCEPTS: Navigational conditions. Merchant vessels. Tonnage. Ports and pilotage.
PARTIES:
USA (United States)
Venezuela

104042 Bilateral Exchange **279 UNTS 205**
SIGNED: 7 Mar 57 FORCE: 5 Jun 57
REGISTERED: 25 Oct 57 USA (United States)
ARTICLES: 2 LANGUAGE: English. Spanish.
HEADNOTE: CONSTITUTING PROVISIONAL ARRANGEMENT RELATING AIR TRANSPORT SERVICE
TOPIC: Air Transport
CONCEPTS: Annex or appendix reference. Routes

and logistics. Permit designation. Air transport. Operating authorizations and regulations.
INTL ORGS: International Civil Aviation Organization. Arbitration Commission.
PROCEDURE: Duration.
PARTIES:
Mexico
USA (United States)
ANNEX
336 UNTS 380. USA (United States). Amendment 28 Jul 58. Force 28 Jul 58.
336 UNTS 380. Mexico. Amendment 24 Jul 58. Force 28 Jul 58.
354 UNTS 411. USA (United States). Prolongation 23 Jun 59. Force 1 Jul 59.
354 UNTS 411. Mexico. Prolongation 23 Jun 59. Force 1 Jul 59.
384 UNTS 377. USA (United States). Prolongation 30 Jun 60. Force 30 Jun 60.
384 UNTS 377. Mexico. Prolongation 30 Jun 60. Force 30 Jun 60.

104043 Bilateral Agreement **279 UNTS 235**
SIGNED: 4 Mar 57 FORCE: 4 Mar 57
REGISTERED: 25 Oct 57 USA (United States)
ARTICLES: 6 LANGUAGE: English.
HEADNOTE: AGRI COMMOD TITLE I
TOPIC: US Agri Commod Aid
CONCEPTS: Annex or appendix reference. General cooperation. Exchange of information and documents. Reexport of goods, etc.. Currency deposits. Exchange rates and regulations. Purchase authorizations. Transportation costs. Local currency. Commodities schedule. Surplus commodities.
PARTIES:
Thailand
USA (United States)
ANNEX
354 UNTS 416. USA (United States). Amendment 12 Mar 59. Force 9 Apr 59.
354 UNTS 416. Thailand. Amendment 9 Apr 59. Force 9 Apr 59.

104044 Bilateral Agreement **279 UNTS 249**
SIGNED: 9 Mar 57 FORCE: 19 Mar 57
REGISTERED: 25 Oct 57 USA (United States)
ARTICLES: 21 LANGUAGE: English. Spanish.
HEADNOTE: ESTABLISHMENT LORAN STATIONS
TOPIC: Gen Communications
CONCEPTS: General cooperation. Inspection and observation. Legal protection and assistance. Existing tribunals. Indemnities and reimbursements. General. Tax exemptions. Routes and logistics. Navigational conditions. Navigational equipment. Facilities and equipment. Radio-telephone-telegraphic communications. Military assistance missions. Ranks and privileges. Jurisdiction. Equipment and supplies.
INTL ORGS: International Court of Justice. Special Commission.
PROCEDURE: Duration. Termination.
PARTIES:
Dominican Republic
USA (United States)

104045 Bilateral Agreement **279 UNTS 275**
SIGNED: 12 Mar 57 FORCE: 12 Mar 57
REGISTERED: 25 Oct 57 USA (United States)
ARTICLES: 9 LANGUAGE: English. French.
HEADNOTE: PATENT RIGHTS TECHNICAL INFORMATION DEFENSE
TOPIC: Patents/Copyrights
CONCEPTS: Definition of terms. Conformity with municipal law. Currency. Press and wire services. Security of information. Exchange of defense information. Subsidiary organ.
INTL ORGS: Special Commission.
TREATY REF: 80UNTS171.
PROCEDURE: Termination.
PARTIES:
France
USA (United States)
ANNEX
367 UNTS 336. USA (United States). Implementation 28 May 59. Force 10 Jun 59.
367 UNTS 336. France. Implementation 10 Jul 59. Force 10 Jul 59.

104046 Bilateral Exchange **279 UNTS 287**
SIGNED: 12 Sep 57 FORCE: 12 Sep 57
REGISTERED: 25 Oct 57 Fed of Malaya
ARTICLES: 2 LANGUAGE: English.
HEADNOTE: SUCCESSION RIGHTS OBLIGATIONS ARISING INTERNATIONAL INSTRUMENTS
TOPIC: Recognition
CONCEPTS: Continuity of rights and obligations.
PARTIES:
Fed of Malaya
UK Great Britain

104047 Bilateral Agreement **280 UNTS 3**
SIGNED: 1 Aug 56 FORCE: 20 May 57
REGISTERED: 28 Oct 57 Netherlands
ARTICLES: 24 LANGUAGE: Dutch. English.
HEADNOTE: ASSISTED MIGRATION
TOPIC: Non-ILO Labor
CONCEPTS: Border traffic and migration. Resident permits. Repatriation of nationals. Exchange of information and documents. Recognition of legal documents. Wages and salaries. Non-ILO labor relations. Administrative cooperation. Social security. Financial programs. Transportation costs. National treatment. Domestic obligation. General aid.
PROCEDURE: Duration. Renewal or Revival. Termination.
PARTIES:
Australia
Netherlands
ANNEX
411 UNTS 302. Netherlands. Prolongation 26 Sep 61. Force 26 Sep 61.
411 UNTS 302. Australia. Prolongation 26 Sep 61. Force 26 Sep 61.
425 UNTS 350. Australia. Prolongation 29 Mar 62. Force 1 Apr 62.
425 UNTS 350. Netherlands. Prolongation 31 Mar 62. Force 1 Apr 62.
445 UNTS 352. Australia. Prolongation 29 Sep 62. Force 2 Oct 62.
445 UNTS 352. Netherlands. Prolongation 29 Sep 62. Force 2 Oct 62.
463 UNTS 350. Netherlands. Prolongation 29 Mar 63. Force 1 Apr 63.
463 UNTS 350. Australia. Prolongation 29 Mar 63. Force 1 Apr 63.
545 UNTS 344. Netherlands. Prolongation 1 Jun 65. Force 1 Jun 65.
545 UNTS 344. Australia. Prolongation 1 Jun 65. Force 1 Jun 65.

104048 Bilateral Exchange **280 UNTS 35**
SIGNED: 7 Sep 56 FORCE: 7 Sep 56
REGISTERED: 28 Oct 57 USA (United States)
ARTICLES: 2 LANGUAGE: English.
HEADNOTE: NON-IMMIGRANT PASSPORT VISAS
TOPIC: Visas
CONCEPTS: Visas. Fees and exemptions.
PARTIES:
Ceylon (Sri Lanka)
USA (United States)

104049 Bilateral Exchange **280 UNTS 45**
SIGNED: 19 Jan 57 FORCE: 19 Apr 57
REGISTERED: 28 Oct 57 USA (United States)
ARTICLES: 2 LANGUAGE: English.
HEADNOTE: SUPPLIES SERVICES NAVAL VESSELS
TOPIC: Milit Installation
CONCEPTS: Procurement and logistics.
PARTIES:
Greece
USA (United States)

104050 Bilateral Exchange **280 UNTS 55**
SIGNED: 18 Oct 56 FORCE: 18 Oct 56
REGISTERED: 28 Oct 57 USA (United States)
ARTICLES: 2 LANGUAGE: English.
HEADNOTE: TAXATION RELIEF SUUPLIES EQUIPMENT
TOPIC: Taxation
CONCEPTS: Conformity with municipal law. Export subsidies. Tax exemptions.
PARTIES:
Philippines
USA (United States)

104051 Bilateral Exchange **280 UNTS 63**
SIGNED: 12 Dec 56 FORCE: 12 Dec 56
REGISTERED: 28 Oct 57 USA (United States)
ARTICLES: 2 LANGUAGE: English. German.
HEADNOTE: TRAINING GERMAN ARMY PERSONNEL
TOPIC: Milit Assistance
CONCEPTS: Responsibility and liability. Indemnities and reimbursements. Claims and settlements. Materials, equipment and services. Military training.
TREATY REF: 240UNTS47.
PROCEDURE: Future Procedures Contemplated.
PARTIES:
Germany, West
USA (United States)

104052 Bilateral Exchange **280 UNTS 71**
SIGNED: 12 Dec 56 FORCE: 12 Dec 56
REGISTERED: 28 Oct 57 USA (United States)
ARTICLES: 2 LANGUAGE: English. German.
HEADNOTE: TRAINING GERMAN NAVY PERSONNEL
TOPIC: Milit Assistance
CONCEPTS: Responsibility and liability. Indemnities and reimbursements. Claims and settlements. Materials, equipment and services. Military training.
TREATY REF: 240UNTS47.
PROCEDURE: Future Procedures Contemplated.
PARTIES:
Germany, West
USA (United States)

104053 Bilateral Exchange **280 UNTS 79**
SIGNED: 15 Jan 57 FORCE: 15 Jan 57
REGISTERED: 28 Oct 57 USA (United States)
ARTICLES: 2 LANGUAGE: English.
HEADNOTE: GUARANTY PRIVATE INVESTMENTS
TOPIC: Claims and Debts
CONCEPTS: Conformity with municipal law. Arbitration. Procedure. Existing tribunals. Negotiation. Reciprocity in financial treatment. Private investment guarantee.
PARTIES:
Turkey
USA (United States)
ANNEX
531 UNTS 346. USA (United States). Supplementation 27 Nov 64. Force 27 Nov 64.
531 UNTS 346. Turkey. Supplementation 27 Nov 64. Force 27 Nov 64.

104054 Bilateral Treaty **280 UNTS 87**
SIGNED: 28 Feb 57 FORCE: 14 Oct 57
REGISTERED: 1 Nov 57 Norway
ARTICLES: 19 LANGUAGE: English.
HEADNOTE: TREATY COMMERCE NAVIGATION
TOPIC: General Economic
CONCEPTS: Conditions. Definition of terms. Exceptions and exemptions. Annex or appendix reference. General relations and amity. Frontier formalities. Repatriation of nationals. Consular relations establishment. Privileges and immunities. General cooperation. Juridical personality. Legal protection and assistance. Recognition and enforcement of legal decisions. Immovable property. General property. Existing tribunals. Maritime products and equipment. Reciprocity in trade. Most favored nation clause. Taxation. Customs duties. General transportation. Navigational conditions. Merchant vessels. Inland and territorial waters. Shipwreck and salvage. Foreign nationals.
INTL ORGS: International Court of Justice.
PROCEDURE: Ratification. Termination.
PARTIES:
Japan
Norway

104055 Bilateral Exchange **280 UNTS 107**
SIGNED: 7 Jun 57 FORCE: 7 Jun 57
REGISTERED: 1 Nov 57 Ceylon (Sri Lanka)
ARTICLES: 2 LANGUAGE: English.
HEADNOTE: SERVICE ESTABLISHMENTS
TOPIC: Milit Installation
CONCEPTS: Time limit. Annex or appendix reference. General cooperation. Use of facilities. Payment schedules. Lump sum settlements. Overf-

lights and technical stops. Withdrawal of forces. Bases and facilities.
PROCEDURE: Future Procedures Contemplated.
PARTIES:
Ceylon (Sri Lanka)
UK Great Britain

104056 Bilateral Treaty **280 UNTS 121**
SIGNED: 20 Dec 55 FORCE: 16 Oct 57
REGISTERED: 1 Nov 57 Guatemala
ARTICLES: 22 LANGUAGE: Spanish.
HEADNOTE: TREATY FREE TRADE ECONOMIC INTEGRATION
TOPIC: General Economic
CONCEPTS: Exceptions and exemptions. Treaty implementation. Annex or appendix reference. Exchange of information and documents. Informational records. Free passage and transit. Establishment of commission. Arbitration. Procedure. Conciliation. Free trade. Reciprocity in trade. Export subsidies. Monetary and gold transfers. Exchange rates and regulations. Non-interest rates and fees. Private investment guarantee. Quotas. Most favored nation clause. Tax exemptions. Customs declarations. Customs exemptions. General transportation. Routes and logistics. Transport of goods. Decisions.
INTL ORGS: Arbitration Commission. Special Commission.
PROCEDURE: Duration. Ratification.
PARTIES:
Costa Rica
Guatemala

104057 Bilateral Exchange **280 UNTS 177**
SIGNED: 16 May 47 FORCE: 16 May 57
REGISTERED: 5 Nov 57 USA (United States)
ARTICLES: 2 LANGUAGE: English.
HEADNOTE: LABOR RECRUITMENT
TOPIC: Non-ILO Labor
CONCEPTS: General cooperation. Exchange of information and documents. Employment regulations. Holidays and rest periods. Safety standards. Wages and salaries. Non-ILO labor relations. Sickness and invalidity insurance. Bonds.
PARTIES:
Philippines
USA (United States)

104058 Bilateral Agreement **280 UNTS 189**
SIGNED: 8 Nov 56 FORCE: 5 Nov 56
REGISTERED: 5 Nov 57 USA (United States)
ARTICLES: 6 LANGUAGE: English. French.
HEADNOTE: TRADE DEVELOPMENT ASSISTANCE ACT
TOPIC: Direct Aid
CONCEPTS: Currency. Agricultural commodities assistance.
PARTIES:
France
USA (United States)
ANNEX
410 UNTS 327. France. Supplementation 12 Jun 61. Force 12 Jun 61.
410 UNTS 327. USA (United States). Supplementation 12 Jun 61. Force 12 Jun 61.

104059 Bilateral Convention **280 UNTS 199**
SIGNED: 23 May 57 FORCE: 24 Sep 57
REGISTERED: 8 Nov 57 Israel
ARTICLES: 7 LANGUAGE: Hebrew. Spanish.
HEADNOTE: CULTURAL EXCHANGES
TOPIC: Culture
CONCEPTS: Treaty interpretation. Friendship and amity. Tourism. Conformity with municipal law. General cooperation. Specialists exchange. Teacher and student exchange. Exchange. General cultural cooperation. Artists. Research cooperation. Scientific exchange. Publications exchange. Mass media exchange.
PROCEDURE: Ratification. Termination.
PARTIES:
Argentina
Israel

104060 Bilateral Agreement **280 UNTS 209**
SIGNED: 5 Mar 56 FORCE: 11 Jun 57
REGISTERED: 8 Nov 57 Israel
ARTICLES: 4 LANGUAGE: English.

HEADNOTE: ECONOMIC COOPERATION
TOPIC: Direct Aid
CONCEPTS: General trade. Economic assistance.
PARTIES:
Burma
Israel

104061 Bilateral Exchange **280 UNTS 219**
SIGNED: 10 Jun 55 FORCE: 25 Jun 57
REGISTERED: 8 Nov 57 Israel
ARTICLES: 2 LANGUAGE: French.
HEADNOTE: DOUBLE TAXATION INCOME SEA AIR NAVIGATION
TOPIC: Taxation
CONCEPTS: Definition of terms. Taxation. Air transport. Merchant vessels.
PROCEDURE: Duration. Termination.
PARTIES:
Israel
Italy

104062 Bilateral Convention **280 UNTS 227**
SIGNED: 29 Apr 57 FORCE: 1 Nov 57
REGISTERED: 8 Nov 57 Israel
ARTICLES: 31 LANGUAGE: English. Hebrew.
HEADNOTE: SOCIAL SECURITY
TOPIC: Non-ILO Labor
CONCEPTS: Definition of terms. General provisions. Conformity with municipal law. General cooperation. Domestic legislation. Old age and invalidity insurance. Wages and salaries. Non-ILO labor relations. Family allowances. Old age insurance. Sickness and invalidity insurance. Social security. Payment schedules. Claims and settlements. National treatment.
PROCEDURE: Denunciation. Duration. Ratification. Renewal or Revival.
PARTIES:
Israel
UK Great Britain

104063 Bilateral Exchange **280 UNTS 261**
SIGNED: 9 Nov 56 FORCE: 9 Nov 56
REGISTERED: 8 Nov 57 Israel
ARTICLES: 2 LANGUAGE: English.
HEADNOTE: REFUGEES GAZA STRIP
TOPIC: Direct Aid
CONCEPTS: Humanitarian matters. Relief supplies.
PARTIES:
Israel
UN Relief Palestin

104064 Bilateral Convention **280 UNTS 269**
SIGNED: 30 Apr 53 FORCE: 20 Jun 57
REGISTERED: 8 Nov 57 Israel
ARTICLES: 4 LANGUAGE: Hebrew. Spanish.
HEADNOTE: CULTURAL EXCHANGES
TOPIC: Culture
CONCEPTS: Definition of terms. Friendship and amity. Conformity with municipal law. Exchange of information and documents. Specialists exchange. Teacher and student exchange. Professorships. Institute establishment. Exchange. General cultural cooperation. Artists. Athletes. Research cooperation. Scientific exchange. Recognition. Publications exchange. Mass media exchange. Press and wire services.
PROCEDURE: Denunciation. Ratification.
PARTIES:
Israel
Uruguay

104065 Bilateral Agreement **280 UNTS 285**
SIGNED: 1 Oct 57 FORCE: 15 Oct 57
REGISTERED: 11 Nov 57 IBRD (World Bank)
ARTICLES: 5 LANGUAGE: English.
HEADNOTE: LOAN AGREEMENT
TOPIC: IBRD Project
CONCEPTS: Default remedies. Definition of terms. Annex or appendix reference. Exchange of information and documents. Informational records. Inspection and observation. Bonds. Fees and exemptions. Interest rates. Tax exemptions. Domestic obligation. Terms of loan. Loan regulations. Loan guarantee. Guarantor non-interference.

PARTIES:
IBRD (World Bank)
South Africa

104066   Multilateral Agreement   **281 UNTS 3**
SIGNED: 13 Jul 56   FORCE: 13 Jul 56
REGISTERED: 11 Nov 57 USA (United States)
ARTICLES: 11 LANGUAGE: English. French. German.
HEADNOTE: ARBITRATION TRIBUNAL COMMISSION PROPERTY RIGHTS INTEREST GERMANY
TOPIC: Dispute Settlement
CONCEPTS: Inviolability. Personnel. Responsibility and liability. Wages and salaries. Financial programs. Payment schedules.
INTL ORGS: Arbitration Commission. Special Commission.
PARTIES:
France SIGNED: 13 Jul 56 FORCE: 13 Jul 56
Germany, West SIGNED: 13 Jul 56 FORCE: 13 Jul 56
UK Great Britain SIGNED: 13 Jul 56 FORCE: 13 Jul 56
USA (United States) SIGNED: 13 Jul 56 FORCE: 13 Jul 56

104067   Bilateral Exchange   **281 UNTS 41**
SIGNED: 2 Jul 56   FORCE: 2 Jul 56
REGISTERED: 11 Nov 57 USA (United States)
ARTICLES: 5 LANGUAGE: English.
HEADNOTE: DISPOSITION EQUIPMENT MATERIALS MUTUAL DEFENSE ASSISTANCE PROGRAM
TOPIC: Milit Assistance
CONCEPTS: Exchange of information and documents. Reexport of goods, etc.. Delivery schedules. Materials, equipment and services. Surplus property. Return of equipment and recapture.
TREATY REF: 179UNTS105.
PARTIES:
Korea, South
USA (United States)

104068   Bilateral Exchange   **281 UNTS 49**
SIGNED: 1 Aug 56   FORCE: 1 Sep 56
REGISTERED: 11 Nov 57 USA (United States)
ARTICLES: 4 LANGUAGE: English. Spanish.
HEADNOTE: RADIO COMMUNICATIONS AMATEUR STATIONS BEHALF THIRD PARTIES
TOPIC: Telecommunications
CONCEPTS: Amateur radio. Amateur third party message. Radio-telephone-telegraphic communications.
PROCEDURE: Termination.
PARTIES:
Panama
USA (United States)

104069   Bilateral Agreement   **281 UNTS 57**
SIGNED: 7 Aug 56   FORCE: 7 Aug 56
REGISTERED: 11 Nov 57 USA (United States)
ARTICLES: 8 LANGUAGE: English. Dutch.
HEADNOTE: SURPLUS AGRI COMMOD
TOPIC: US Agri Commod Aid
CONCEPTS: Currency deposits. Exchange rates and regulations. Purchase authorizations. Transportation costs. Local currency. Domestic obligation. Surplus commodities.
PROCEDURE: Duration.
PARTIES:
Netherlands
USA (United States)

104070   Bilateral Exchange   **281 UNTS 65**
SIGNED: 30 Jun 56   FORCE: 30 Jun 56
REGISTERED: 11 Nov 57 USA (United States)
ARTICLES: 8 LANGUAGE: English.
HEADNOTE: TECHNICAL SERVICES IN EXCHANGE KYAT FUNDS PURCHASE COMMODITIES
TOPIC: Tech Assistance
CONCEPTS: Treaty implementation. Personnel. Teacher and student exchange. Indemnities and reimbursements. Currency deposits. Exchange rates and regulations. Funding procedures. Payment schedules. Local currency. Special projects.
PARTIES:
Burma
USA (United States)

104071   Bilateral Agreement   **281 UNTS 75**
SIGNED: 7 Aug 56   FORCE: 7 Aug 56
REGISTERED: 11 Nov 57 USA (United States)
ARTICLES: 6 LANGUAGE: English.
HEADNOTE: AGRI COMMOD TITLE I
TOPIC: US Agri Commod Aid
CONCEPTS: General cooperation. Exchange of information and documents. Reexport of goods, etc.. Currency deposits. Purchase authorizations. Transportation costs. Local currency. Commodities schedule. Surplus commodities.
PARTIES:
Pakistan
USA (United States)
                    ANNEX
411 UNTS 306. USA (United States). Amendment 29 Jun 61. Force 29 Jun 61.
411 UNTS 306. Pakistan. Amendment 29 Jun 61. Force 29 Jun 61.

104072   Bilateral Exchange   **281 UNTS 93**
SIGNED: 21 May 56   FORCE: 30 Jul 56
REGISTERED: 11 Nov 57 USA (United States)
ARTICLES: 2 LANGUAGE: English.
HEADNOTE: FREE ENTRY PRIVILEGES CONSULAR OFFICERS
TOPIC: Visas
CONCEPTS: Diplomatic privileges.
PARTIES:
USA (United States)
Yugoslavia

104073   Bilateral Exchange   **281 UNTS 99**
SIGNED: 2 Aug 56   FORCE: 2 Aug 56
REGISTERED: 11 Nov 57 USA (United States)
ARTICLES: 2 LANGUAGE: English. Spanish.
HEADNOTE: AGREEMENT RELATING CONSTRUCTION RAMA ROAD
TOPIC: Land Transport
CONCEPTS: Responsibility and liability. Roads and highways.
TREATY REF: 215UNTS69.
PARTIES:
Nicaragua
USA (United States)

104074   Bilateral Agreement   **281 UNTS 105**
SIGNED: 16 Oct 50   FORCE: 16 Oct 50
REGISTERED: 11 Nov 57 USA (United States)
ARTICLES: 5 LANGUAGE: English. Indonesian.
HEADNOTE: ECONOMIC COOPERATION
TOPIC: Direct Aid
CONCEPTS: Annex or appendix reference. Privileges and immunities. Conformity with municipal law. General cooperation. Exchange of information and documents. Personnel. Domestic obligation. General technical assistance. Economic assistance. Aid missions. Procurement. Distribution.
INTL ORGS: United Nations.
PROCEDURE: Amendment. Duration. Registration.
PARTIES:
Indonesia
USA (United States)

104075   Bilateral Agreement   **281 UNTS 121**
SIGNED: 25 Mar 57   FORCE: 10 Jul 57
REGISTERED: 18 Nov 57 Poland
ARTICLES: 17 LANGUAGE: Polish. Russian.
HEADNOTE: TIME LIMITS PROCEDURES FURTHER REPATRIATION
TOPIC: Extradition
CONCEPTS: Detailed regulations. Exceptions and exemptions. Time limit. Acquisition of nationality. Extradition, deportation and repatriation. General cooperation. Fees and exemptions.
PROCEDURE: Ratification.
PARTIES:
Poland
USSR (Soviet Union)

104076   Bilateral Agreement   **281 UNTS 143**
SIGNED: 6 Jul 56   FORCE: 19 Feb 57
REGISTERED: 18 Nov 57 Poland
ARTICLES: 9 LANGUAGE: Polish. Serbo-Croat.
HEADNOTE: CULTURAL COOPERATION
TOPIC: Culture
CONCEPTS: Friendship and amity. Conformity with municipal law. General cooperation. Exchange of information and documents. Specialists exchange. Exchange. Teacher and student exchange. Scholarships and grants. Exchange. General cultural cooperation. Artists. Athletes. Research cooperation. Scientific exchange. Accounting procedures. Publications exchange. Mass media exchange. Press and wire services.
PROCEDURE: Denunciation. Duration. Ratification. Renewal or Revival.
PARTIES:
Poland
Yugoslavia

104077   Bilateral Treaty   **281 UNTS 157**
SIGNED: 24 Sep 50   FORCE: 10 Jan 57
REGISTERED: 19 Nov 57 Italy
ARTICLES: 6 LANGUAGE: Italian. Persian. French.
HEADNOTE: FRIENDSHIP
TOPIC: General Amity
CONCEPTS: Friendship and amity. Consular relations establishment. Diplomatic relations establishment. Procedure. Most favored nation clause.
PROCEDURE: Future Procedures Contemplated. Ratification.
PARTIES:
Iran
Italy

104078   Bilateral Treaty   **281 UNTS 167**
SIGNED: 24 Apr 52   FORCE: 23 Jun 56
REGISTERED: 19 Nov 57 Italy
ARTICLES: 11 LANGUAGE: Arabic. English. Italian.
HEADNOTE: FRIENDSHIP
TOPIC: General Amity
CONCEPTS: Friendship and amity. Alien status. Consular relations establishment. Diplomatic relations establishment. Privileges and immunities. Legal protection and assistance. Payment schedules.
PROCEDURE: Future Procedures Contemplated. Ratification. Termination.
PARTIES:
Italy
Jordan

104079   Bilateral Agreement   **281 UNTS 181**
SIGNED: 31 May 56   FORCE: 14 Jan 56
REGISTERED: 19 Nov 57 Italy
ARTICLES: 11 LANGUAGE: Italian. Spanish.
HEADNOTE: CULTURAL AGREEMENT
TOPIC: Culture
CONCEPTS: Definition of terms. Friendship and amity. Conformity with municipal law. Operating agencies. Establishment of commission. Specialists exchange. Recognition of degrees. Exchange. Teacher and student exchange. Professorships. Institute establishment. Scholarships and grants. Exchange. General cultural cooperation. Research cooperation. Publications exchange. Mass media exchange.
INTL ORGS: Special Commission.
PROCEDURE: Denunciation. Duration. Ratification.
PARTIES:
Bolivia
Italy

104080   Bilateral Protocol   **281 UNTS 195**
SIGNED: 19 Apr 56   FORCE: 19 Apr 56
REGISTERED: 19 Nov 57 Italy
ARTICLES: 3 LANGUAGE: Italian. German.
HEADNOTE: TRADE GOVERNMENT MIXED COMMISSION
TOPIC: General Trade
CONCEPTS: Detailed regulations. Previous treaty amendment. Annex or appendix reference. Trade agencies. Trade procedures. Commodity trade. Quotas.
INTL ORGS: Organization for Economic Co-operation and Development. Special Commission.
TREATY REF: 281UNTS218; 281UNTS222.
PROCEDURE: Duration.
PARTIES:
Germany, West
Italy

104081   Bilateral Exchange   **281 UNTS 239**
SIGNED: 20 Nov 56   FORCE: 1 Dec 56
REGISTERED: 20 Nov 57 Belgium
ARTICLES: 2 LANGUAGE: French.

HEADNOTE: EXEMPTION TRAFFIC TAXES VEHICLES
TOPIC: Taxation
CONCEPTS: Tax exemptions. Commercial road vehicles. Motor vehicles and combinations.
PARTIES:
Belgium
Sweden

104082 Bilateral Protocol **281 UNTS 245**
SIGNED: 7 Dec 49 FORCE: 1 Feb 50
REGISTERED: 21 Nov 57 India
ARTICLES: 12 LANGUAGE: English.
HEADNOTE: MONEY ORDERS
TOPIC: Postal Service
CONCEPTS: Mail and money orders. Money orders and postal checks.
PROCEDURE: Duration.
PARTIES:
India
UK Great Britain

104083 Bilateral Agreement **281 UNTS 257**
SIGNED: 14 Aug 56 FORCE: 14 Aug 56
REGISTERED: 25 Nov 57 USA (United States)
ARTICLES: 5 LANGUAGE: English. Chinese.
HEADNOTE: AGRI COMMOD TITLE I
TOPIC: US Agri Commod Aid
CONCEPTS: General cooperation. Exchange of information and documents. Reexport of goods, etc.. Currency deposits. Exchange rates and regulations. Purchase authorizations. Transportation costs. Local currency. Commodities schedule. Surplus commodities.
PARTIES:
Taiwan
USA (United States)

104084 Bilateral Exchange **281 UNTS 281**
SIGNED: 24 Oct 56 FORCE: 24 Oct 56
REGISTERED: 25 Nov 57 USA (United States)
ARTICLES: 2 LANGUAGE: English.
HEADNOTE: RELOCATION PART ROOSEVELT BRIDGE
TOPIC: Specif Goods/Equip
CONCEPTS: Specific goods and equipment.
PARTIES:
Canada
USA (United States)

104085 Bilateral Exchange **281 UNTS 289**
SIGNED: 27 Sep 56 FORCE: 27 Sep 56
REGISTERED: 25 Nov 57 USA (United States)
ARTICLES: 2 LANGUAGE: English.
HEADNOTE: EMERGENCY FLOOD RELIEF ASSISTANCE
TOPIC: Direct Aid
CONCEPTS: Treaty implementation. Conformity with municipal law. Relief supplies.
PARTIES:
India
USA (United States)

104086 Bilateral Agreement **281 UNTS 295**
SIGNED: 18 Jul 55 FORCE: 1 Jul 56
REGISTERED: 25 Nov 57 USA (United States)
ARTICLES: 33 LANGUAGE: English.
HEADNOTE: PARCEL POST
TOPIC: Postal Service
CONCEPTS: Detailed regulations. Domestic legislation. Responsibility and liability. Compensation. Payment schedules. Customs duties. Customs exemptions. Postal services. Regulations. Insured letters and boxes. Parcel post. Rates and charges.
TREATY REF: 169UNTS3; 186UNTS356; 202UNTS340; 227UNTS390.
PROCEDURE: Duration. Termination.
PARTIES:
Ceylon (Sri Lanka)
USA (United States)

104087 Bilateral Agreement **281 UNTS 341**
SIGNED: 19 Jun 56 FORCE: 20 Nov 56
REGISTERED: 25 Nov 57 USA (United States)
ARTICLES: 12 LANGUAGE: English. French.
HEADNOTE: CIVIL USES ATOMIC ENERGY
TOPIC: Atomic Energy

CONCEPTS: Definition of terms. Diplomatic missions. General cooperation. Exchange of information and documents. Responsibility and liability. Research results. Scientific exchange. Establishment of trade relations. Nuclear materials. Non-nuclear materials. Peaceful use. Rights of supplier. Security of information.
PROCEDURE: Duration. Termination.
PARTIES:
France
USA (United States)
ANNEX
291 UNTS 352. USA (United States). Amendment 3 Jul 57. Force 19 Aug 57.
291 UNTS 352. France. Amendment 3 Jul 57. Force 19 Aug 57.
358 UNTS 330. USA (United States). Amendment 22 Jul 59. Force 22 Sep 59.
358 UNTS 330. France. Amendment 22 Jul 59. Force 22 Sep 59.
406 UNTS 322. USA (United States). Amendment 30 Sep 60. Force 14 Apr 61.
406 UNTS 322. France. Amendment 30 Sep 60. Force 14 Apr 61.
458 UNTS 314. France. Amendment 22 Jun 62. Force 10 Aug 62.
458 UNTS 314. USA (United States). Amendment 22 Jun 62. Force 10 Aug 62.
531 UNTS 348. USA (United States). Amendment 22 Jun 64. Force 31 Aug 64.
531 UNTS 348. France. Amendment 22 Jun 64. Force 31 Aug 64.

104088 Bilateral Agreement **281 UNTS 361**
SIGNED: 23 Nov 56 FORCE: 23 Nov 56
REGISTERED: 25 Nov 57 USA (United States)
ARTICLES: 5 LANGUAGE: English.
HEADNOTE: SETTLEMENT INSURANCE COMPANIES
TOPIC: Specif Claim/Waive
CONCEPTS: Claims and settlements. Specific claims or waivers.
PARTIES:
Iceland
USA (United States)

104089 Bilateral Agreement **282 UNTS 3**
SIGNED: 15 Nov 56 FORCE: 1 Jan 57
REGISTERED: 25 Nov 57 USA (United States)
ARTICLES: 28 LANGUAGE: English. Spanish.
HEADNOTE: ARMY MISSION
TOPIC: Military Mission
CONCEPTS: Military assistance.
PROCEDURE: Termination.
PARTIES:
Chile
USA (United States)

104090 Bilateral Exchange **282 UNTS 29**
SIGNED: 16 Oct 56 FORCE: 16 Oct 56
REGISTERED: 25 Nov 57 USA (United States)
ARTICLES: 2 LANGUAGE: English. Spanish.
HEADNOTE: RADIO COMMUNICATIONS AMATEUR STATIONS BEHALF THIRD PARTIES
TOPIC: Gen Communications
CONCEPTS: Amateur radio. Amateur third party message. Radio-telephone-telegraphic communications.
PROCEDURE: Termination.
PARTIES:
Nicaragua
USA (United States)

104091 Bilateral Exchange **282 UNTS 37**
SIGNED: 23 Oct 56 FORCE: 23 Oct 56
REGISTERED: 25 Nov 57 USA (United States)
ARTICLES: 2 LANGUAGE: English.
HEADNOTE: INFORMATIONAL MEDIA GUARANTY PROGRAM
TOPIC: Mass Media
CONCEPTS: Local currency. Media guaranty.
PROCEDURE: Termination.
PARTIES:
Burma
USA (United States)

104092 Bilateral Agreement **282 UNTS 43**
SIGNED: 27 Nov 56 FORCE: 27 Nov 56
REGISTERED: 25 Nov 57 USA (United States)

ARTICLES: 26 LANGUAGE: English.
HEADNOTE: OCEANOGRAPHIC RESEARCH STATION
TOPIC: Scientific Project
CONCEPTS: Definition of terms. Border traffic and migration. Privileges and immunities. General cooperation. Juridical personality. Free passage and transit. Operating agencies. General property. Use of facilities. Public health. Vocational training. Research and scientific projects. Research and development. Claims and settlements. Taxation. Tax exemptions. Domestic obligation. Special projects. Navigational equipment. Postal services. Security of information. Jurisdiction.
PARTIES:
UK Great Britain
USA (United States)
ANNEX
372 UNTS 358. USA (United States). Supplementation 12 May 60. Force 12 May 60.
372 UNTS 358. UK Great Britain. Supplementation 12 May 60. Force 12 May 60.

104093 Bilateral Agreement **282 UNTS 77**
SIGNED: 12 Nov 56 FORCE: 12 Nov 56
REGISTERED: 25 Nov 57 USA (United States)
ARTICLES: 6 LANGUAGE: English.
HEADNOTE: AGRI COMMOD TITLE I
TOPIC: US Agri Commod Aid
CONCEPTS: General cooperation. Exchange of information and documents. Currency deposits. Exchange rates and regulations. Purchase authorizations. Transportation costs. Local currency. Technical cooperation. Commodities schedule. Surplus commodities.
PARTIES:
Turkey
USA (United States)
ANNEX
283 UNTS 356. Turkey. Amendment 20 Apr 57. Force 20 Apr 57.
283 UNTS 356. USA (United States). Amendment 20 Apr 57. Force 20 Apr 57.
336 UNTS 384. Turkey. Amendment 8 Nov 58. Force 8 Nov 58.
336 UNTS 384. USA (United States). Amendment 8 Nov 58. Force 8 Nov 58.

104094 Bilateral Exchange **282 UNTS 93**
SIGNED: 2 Nov 56 FORCE: 2 Nov 56
REGISTERED: 25 Nov 57 USA (United States)
ARTICLES: 2 LANGUAGE: English.
HEADNOTE: PURCHASE MILITARY EQUIPMENT MATERIALS SERVICES
TOPIC: Milit Assistance
CONCEPTS: Non-prejudice to UN charter. Peaceful relations. Reexport of goods, etc.. Purchase authorizations. Self-defense. Security of information. Exchange of defense information.
PARTIES:
Ceylon (Sri Lanka)
USA (United States)

104095 Bilateral Agreement **282 UNTS 99**
SIGNED: 31 Jul 57 FORCE: 31 Jul 57
REGISTERED: 27 Nov 57 United Nations
ARTICLES: 11 LANGUAGE: French.
HEADNOTE: ACTIVITIES UNICEF
TOPIC: Direct Aid
CONCEPTS: Treaty implementation. Privileges and immunities. Exchange of information and documents. Informational records. Inspection and observation. Public information. Responsibility and liability. Procedure. Existing tribunals. Export quotas. Indemnities and reimbursements. Financial programs. Local currency. Claims and settlements. Tax exemptions. Customs exemptions. Commodities and services. Assistance. General aid. Distribution. IGO status.
INTL ORGS: United Nations.
TREATY REF: 1UNTS15.
PROCEDURE: Duration.
PARTIES:
Morocco
UNICEF (Children)

104096 Bilateral Agreement **282 UNTS 113**
SIGNED: 20 Sep 57 FORCE: 20 Sep 57
REGISTERED: 3 Dec 57 WHO (World Health)

ARTICLES: 6 LANGUAGE: English.
HEADNOTE: TECHNICAL ADVISORY ASSISTANCE
TOPIC: Tech Assistance
CONCEPTS: Privileges and immunities. General cooperation. Exchange of information and documents. Personnel. Responsibility and liability. Title and deeds. Use of facilities. Exchange. Scholarships and grants. Vocational training. Research and development. Exchange rates and regulations. Expense sharing formulae. Domestic obligation. General technical assistance. Materials, equipment and services. IGO status. Conformity with IGO decisions.
TREATY REF: 33UNTS261.
PROCEDURE: Amendment. Termination.
PARTIES:
 Burma
 WHO (World Health)

104097   Bilateral Convention   **282 UNTS 125**
SIGNED: 12 Feb 57   FORCE: 26 Oct 57
REGISTERED: 12 Dec 57 Taiwan
ARTICLES: 11 LANGUAGE: Chinese. Turkish. English.
HEADNOTE: CULTURAL CONVENTION
TOPIC: Culture
CONCEPTS: Friendship and amity. Tourism. Conformity with municipal law. General cooperation. Teacher and student exchange. Professorships. Scholarships and grants. Exchange. General cultural cooperation. Artists. Athletes. Research cooperation. Scientific exchange. Publications exchange. Mass media exchange.
TREATY REF: 4UNTS275; 18UNTS383.
PROCEDURE: Duration. Ratification. Renewal or Revival. Termination.
PARTIES:
 Taiwan
 Turkey

104098   Bilateral Agreement   **282 UNTS 139**
SIGNED: 24 Jul 57   FORCE: 3 Dec 57
REGISTERED: 14 Dec 57 IBRD (World Bank)
ARTICLES: 6 LANGUAGE: English.
HEADNOTE: GUARANTEE AGREEMENT
TOPIC: IBRD Project
CONCEPTS: Default remedies. Definition of terms. Annex or appendix reference. Exchange of information and documents. Informational records. Inspection and observation. Bonds. Fees and exemptions. Tax exemptions. Domestic obligation. Terms of loan. Loan regulations. Loan guarantee. Guarantor non-interference.
PARTIES:
 Chile
 IBRD (World Bank)
            ANNEX
519 UNTS 358. Chile. Supplementation 1 Jul 64. Force 29 Sep 64.
519 UNTS 358. IBRD (World Bank). Supplementation 1 Jul 64. Force 29 Sep 64.

104099   Bilateral Agreement   **282 UNTS 189**
SIGNED: 24 Jul 57   FORCE: 3 Dec 57
REGISTERED: 14 Dec 57 IBRD (World Bank)
ARTICLES: 6 LANGUAGE: English.
HEADNOTE: GUARANTEE AGREEMENT
TOPIC: IBRD Project
CONCEPTS: Default remedies. Definition of terms. Annex or appendix reference. Exchange of information and documents. Informational records. Inspection and observation. Bonds. Fees and exemptions. Tax exemptions. Domestic obligation. Terms of loan. Loan regulations. Loan guarantee. Guarantor non-interference.
PARTIES:
 Chile
 IBRD (World Bank)
            ANNEX
519 UNTS 358. Chile. Supplementation 1 Jul 64. Force 29 Sep 64.
519 UNTS 358. IBRD (World Bank). Supplementation 1 Jul 64. Force 29 Sep 64.

104100   Bilateral Protocol   **282 UNTS 241**
SIGNED: 7 Mar 57   FORCE: 19 Nov 57
REGISTERED: 14 Dec 57 Belgium
ARTICLES: 4 LANGUAGE: French. Dutch.
HEADNOTE: SUBMISSION ICJ CERTAIN LOTS FRONTIER

TOPIC: Dispute Settlement
CONCEPTS: Existing tribunals.
INTL ORGS: International Court of Justice.
PARTIES:
 Belgium
 Netherlands

104101   Multilateral Convention   **282 UNTS 249**
SIGNED: 4 Jun 54   FORCE: 15 Dec 57
REGISTERED: 15 Dec 57 United Nations
ARTICLES: 44 LANGUAGE: English. French. Spanish.
HEADNOTE: CUSTOMS CONVENTION
TOPIC: Customs
CONCEPTS: Territorial application. Annex or appendix reference. Non-visa travel documents. Visas. Arbitration. Negotiation. Customs exemptions. Temporary importation. Motor vehicles and combinations.
INTL ORGS: International Court of Justice. United Nations.
TREATY REF: 125UNTS3.
PROCEDURE: Amendment. Accession. Denunciation. Ratification. Registration.
PARTIES:
 Argentina SIGNED: 4 Jun 54
 Austria SIGNED: 4 Jun 54 RATIFIED: 30 Mar 56 FORCE: 15 Dec 57
 Belgium Belgian Colonies RATIFIED: 21 Feb 55 FORCE: 15 Dec 57
 Belgium SIGNED: 4 Jun 54 RATIFIED: 21 Feb 55 FORCE: 15 Dec 57
 Belgium Ruanda-Urundi RATIFIED: 21 Feb 55 FORCE: 15 Dec 57
 Cambodia SIGNED: 4 Jun 54
 Ceylon (Sri Lanka) SIGNED: 4 Jun 54 RATIFIED: 28 Nov 55 FORCE: 15 Dec 57
 Costa Rica SIGNED: 20 Jul 54
 Cuba SIGNED: 12 Oct 54
 Dominican Republic SIGNED: 4 Jun 54
 Ecuador SIGNED: 4 Jun 54
 United Arab Rep SIGNED: 4 Jun 54 RATIFIED: 4 Apr 57 FORCE: 15 Dec 57
 France SIGNED: 4 Jun 54
 Germany, West Berlin RATIFIED: 16 Sep 57 FORCE: 15 Dec 57
 Germany, West SIGNED: 4 Jun 54 RATIFIED: 16 Sep 57 FORCE: 15 Dec 57
 Guatemala SIGNED: 4 Jun 54
 Haiti SIGNED: 4 Jun 54
 Honduras SIGNED: 15 Jun 54
 India SIGNED: 4 Jun 54
 Italy SIGNED: 4 Jun 54
 Japan SIGNED: 2 Dec 54
 Luxembourg SIGNED: 6 Dec 54 RATIFIED: 21 Dec 56 FORCE: 15 Dec 57
 Mexico SIGNED: 4 Jun 54 RATIFIED: 13 Jun 57 FORCE: 15 Dec 57
 Monaco SIGNED: 4 Jun 54
 Morocco RATIFIED: 25 Sep 57 FORCE: 24 Dec 57
 Netherlands SIGNED: 4 Jun 54
 Panama SIGNED: 4 Jun 54
 Philippines SIGNED: 4 Jun 54
 Portugal SIGNED: 4 Jun 54
 Spain SIGNED: 4 Jun 54
 Sweden SIGNED: 4 Jun 54 RATIFIED: 11 Jun 57 FORCE: 15 Dec 57
 Switzerland SIGNED: 4 Jun 54 RATIFIED: 23 May 56 FORCE: 15 Dec 57
 UK Great Britain British Somaliland RATIFIED: 7 Aug 57 FORCE: 15 Dec 57
 UK Great Britain Cyprus RATIFIED: 7 Aug 57 FORCE: 15 Dec 57
 UK Great Britain Fiji Islands RATIFIED: 7 Aug 57 FORCE: 15 Dec 57
 UK Great Britain Fed of Malaya RATIFIED: 7 Aug 57 FORCE: 15 Dec 57
 UK Great Britain Jamaica RATIFIED: 7 Aug 57 FORCE: 15 Dec 57
 UK Great Britain Malta RATIFIED: 7 Aug 57 FORCE: 15 Dec 57
 UK Great Britain North Borneo RATIFIED: 7 Aug 57 FORCE: 15 Dec 57
 UK Great Britain SIGNED: 4 Jun 54 RATIFIED: 27 Feb 56 FORCE: 15 Dec 57
 UK Great Britain Seychelles RATIFIED: 7 Aug 57 FORCE: 15 Dec 57
 UK Great Britain Sierra Leone RATIFIED: 7 Aug 57 FORCE: 15 Dec 57
 UK Great Britain Singapore RATIFIED: 7 Aug 57 FORCE: 15 Dec 57

 UK Great Britain Tonga RATIFIED: 7 Aug 57 FORCE: 15 Dec 57
 UK Great Britain Zanzibar RATIFIED: 7 Aug 57 FORCE: 15 Dec 57
 USA (United States) Alaska RATIFIED: 25 Jul 56 FORCE: 15 Dec 57
 USA (United States) Hawaii RATIFIED: 25 Jul 56 FORCE: 15 Dec 57
 USA (United States) Puerto Rico RATIFIED: 25 Jul 56 FORCE: 15 Dec 57
 USA (United States) SIGNED: 4 Jun 54 RATIFIED: 25 Jul 56 FORCE: 15 Dec 57
 USA (United States) Virgin Islands RATIFIED: 25 Jul 56 FORCE: 15 Dec 57
 Uruguay SIGNED: 4 Jun 54
 Vatican/Holy See SIGNED: 4 Jun 54
            ANNEX
283 UNTS 360.
285 UNTS 383.
286 UNTS 397.
287 UNTS 354.
299 UNTS 435.
300 UNTS 398.
302 UNTS 376.
304 UNTS 394.
309 UNTS 375.
312 UNTS 429.
314 UNTS 361.
320 UNTS 349.
327 UNTS 382.
334 UNTS 326.
345 UNTS 370.
348 UNTS 360.
349 UNTS 345.
367 UNTS 346.
374 UNTS 384.
375 UNTS 371. Nepal. Accession 21 Sep 60. Force 20 Dec 60.
380 UNTS 463.
384 UNTS 382.
396 UNTS 346.
399 UNTS 284.
407 UNTS 265.
410 UNTS 328.
422 UNTS 340. UK Great Britain. British Guiana.
423 UNTS 318.
431 UNTS 312.
435 UNTS 363.
437 UNTS 361.
442 UNTS 332.
445 UNTS 356.
466 UNTS 401.
475 UNTS 363.
480 UNTS 370.
490 UNTS 462.
496 UNTS 355.
519 UNTS 394.
531 UNTS 352.
551 UNTS 301.
560 UNTS 266.
603 UNTS 317.
634 UNTS 431.

104102   Bilateral Exchange   **283 UNTS 3**
SIGNED: 17 Apr 57   FORCE: 17 May 57
REGISTERED: 18 Dec 57 USA (United States)
ARTICLES: 2 LANGUAGE: English. Spanish.
HEADNOTE: ESTABLISHMENT OBSERVATION STATION
TOPIC: Scientific Project
CONCEPTS: Exchange of information and documents. Title and deeds. Research cooperation. Meteorology. Indemnities and reimbursements. Customs exemptions. Facilities and property.
PROCEDURE: Duration. Termination.
PARTIES:
 Peru
 USA (United States)
            ANNEX
340 UNTS 388. USA (United States). Prolongation 13 Nov 58. Force 24 Dec 58.
340 UNTS 388. Peru. Prolongation 24 Dec 58. Force 24 Dec 58.
371 UNTS 310. Peru. Prolongation 18 Feb 60. Force 18 Feb 60.
371 UNTS 310. USA (United States). Prolongation 30 Dec 59. Force 18 Feb 60.

104103   Bilateral Agreement   **283 UNTS 15**
SIGNED: 10 May 57   FORCE: 10 May 57
REGISTERED: 18 Dec 57 USA (United States)
ARTICLES: 5 LANGUAGE: English. German.
HEADNOTE: AGRI COMMOD
TOPIC: US Agri Commod Aid
CONCEPTS: General cooperation. Exchange of in-

formation and documents. Reexport of goods, etc.. Currency deposits. Exchange rates and regulations. Purchase authorizations. Transportation costs. Local currency. Commodities schedule. Surplus commodities.
PARTIES:
Austria
USA (United States)
ANNEX
354 UNTS 420. USA (United States). Amendment 29 Jun 59. Force 29 Jun 59.
354 UNTS 420. Austria. Amendment 29 Jun 59. Force 29 Jun 59.

104104 Bilateral Exchange **283 UNTS 33**
SIGNED: 10 May 57 FORCE: 10 May 57
REGISTERED: 18 Dec 57 USA (United States)
ARTICLES: 2 LANGUAGE: English. German.
HEADNOTE: EMERGENCY RELIEF
TOPIC: Direct Aid
CONCEPTS: Conformity with municipal law. General cooperation. Inspection and observation. Accounting procedures. Indemnities and reimbursements. Currency deposits. Transportation costs. Local currency. Customs exemptions. Relief supplies. Grants.
PARTIES:
Austria
USA (United States)

104105 Bilateral Agreement **283 UNTS 43**
SIGNED: 10 May 57 FORCE: 10 May 57
REGISTERED: 18 Dec 57 USA (United States)
ARTICLES: 6 LANGUAGE: English.
HEADNOTE: TECHNICAL ASSISTANCE
TOPIC: US Agri Commod Aid
CONCEPTS: Definition of terms. Previous treaty replacement. Privileges and immunities. General cooperation. Exchange of information and documents. Personnel. Responsibility and liability. Title and deeds. Use of facilities. Exchange. Scholarships and grants. Vocational training. Research and development. Compensation. Exchange rates and regulations. Expense sharing formulae. Local currency. Domestic obligation. General technical assistance. Materials, equipment and services. IGO status. Conformity with IGO decisions.
INTL ORGS: International Monetary Fund.
PROCEDURE: Amendment. Termination.
PARTIES:
Finland
USA (United States)
ANNEX
335 UNTS 332. USA (United States). Amendment 17 Feb 58. Force 17 Feb 58.
335 UNTS 332. Finland. Amendment 10 Feb 58. Force 17 Feb 58.

104106 Bilateral Agreement **283 UNTS 55**
SIGNED: 2 May 57 FORCE: 2 May 57
REGISTERED: 18 Dec 57 USA (United States)
ARTICLES: 6 LANGUAGE: English. Spanish.
HEADNOTE: AGRI COMMOD TITLE I
TOPIC: US Agri Commod Aid
CONCEPTS: General cooperation. Exchange of information and documents. Reexport of goods, etc.. Currency deposits. Exchange rates and regulations. Purchase authorizations. Transportation costs. Local currency. Commodities schedule. Surplus commodities.
PARTIES:
Peru
USA (United States)
ANNEX
291 UNTS 360. USA (United States). Amendment 1 Aug 57. Force 1 Aug 57.
291 UNTS 360. Peru. Amendment 10 Jul 57. Force 1 Aug 57.
336 UNTS 385. USA (United States). Amendment 15 Aug 58. Force 22 Aug 58.
336 UNTS 385. Peru. Amendment 22 Aug 58. Force 22 Aug 58.

104107 Bilateral Agreement **283 UNTS 73**
SIGNED: 23 Feb 57 FORCE: 23 Feb 57

REGISTERED: 18 Dec 57 USA (United States)
ARTICLES: 12 LANGUAGE: English. Icelandic.
HEADNOTE: EDUCATION EXCHANGE
TOPIC: Education
CONCEPTS: Definition of terms. Standardization. Conformity with municipal law. General cooperation. Inspection and observation. Personnel. General property. Exchange. Commissions and foundations. Teacher and student exchange. Scholarships and grants. Research and development. Accounting procedures. Currency. Exchange rates and regulations. Expense sharing formulae. Financial programs. Funding procedures.
INTL ORGS: Special Commission.
PROCEDURE: Amendment.
PARTIES:
Iceland
USA (United States)
ANNEX
340 UNTS 392. USA (United States). Amendment 2 Oct 58. Force 27 Nov 58.
340 UNTS 392. Iceland. Amendment 27 Nov 58. Force 27 Nov 58.
476 UNTS 338. Iceland. Amendment 5 Apr 63. Force 5 Apr 63.
476 UNTS 338. USA (United States). Amendment 19 Feb 63. Force 5 Apr 63.

104108 Bilateral Exchange **283 UNTS 89**
SIGNED: 9 Mar 57 FORCE: 9 Mar 57
REGISTERED: 18 Dec 57 USA (United States)
ARTICLES: 2 LANGUAGE: English. Spanish.
HEADNOTE: LOAN NAVAL VESSELS
TOPIC: Milit Assistance
CONCEPTS: Time limit. Annex or appendix reference. Responsibility and liability. Title and deeds. Compensation. Indemnities and reimbursements. Delivery schedules. Lend lease. Naval vessels. Return of equipment and recapture.
TREATY REF: 207UNTS61.
PARTIES:
Spain
USA (United States)
ANNEX
458 UNTS 318. Spain. Amendment 19 Jun 62. Force 19 Jun 62.
458 UNTS 318. USA (United States). Amendment 19 Jun 62. Force 19 Jun 62.

104109 Bilateral Exchange **283 UNTS 97**
SIGNED: 2 Apr 57 FORCE: 2 Apr 57
REGISTERED: 18 Dec 57 USA (United States)
ARTICLES: 2 LANGUAGE: English. Arabic.
HEADNOTE: RIGHTS DHAHRAN AIRFIELD
TOPIC: Milit Installation
CONCEPTS: Non-prejudice to UN charter. Conformity with municipal law. Use of facilities. Payment schedules. Military assistance. Military training. Military assistance missions. Bases and facilities.
TREATY REF: 141UNTS67;E.
PROCEDURE: Future Procedures Contemplated.
PARTIES:
Saudi Arabia
USA (United States)

104110 Bilateral Agreement **283 UNTS 107**
SIGNED: 11 Apr 57 FORCE: 11 Apr 57
REGISTERED: 18 Dec 57 USA (United States)
ARTICLES: 6 LANGUAGE: English.
HEADNOTE: AGRI COMMOD TITLE I
TOPIC: US Agri Commod Aid
CONCEPTS: General cooperation. Exchange of information and documents. Reexport of goods, etc.. Currency deposits. Exchange rates and regulations. Purchase authorizations. Transportation costs. Local currency. Commodities schedule. Surplus commodities.
PARTIES:
Iceland
USA (United States)
ANNEX
421 UNTS 314. USA (United States). Supplementation 3 May 61. Force 14 Sep 61.
421 UNTS 314. Iceland. Supplementation 14 Sep 61. Force 14 Sep 61.

104111 Bilateral Exchange **283 UNTS 117**
SIGNED: 26 Mar 57 FORCE: 26 Mar 57

REGISTERED: 18 Dec 57 USA (United States)
ARTICLES: 2 LANGUAGE: English. French.
HEADNOTE: ECONOMIC TECHNICAL RELATED ASSISTANCE
TOPIC: General Aid
CONCEPTS: Privileges and immunities. Conformity with municipal law. Personnel. Accounting procedures. Banking. Currency deposits. Exchange rates and regulations. Local currency. Tax exemptions. Customs exemptions. Commodities and services. Domestic obligation. General technical assistance. Economic assistance. Materials, equipment and services. Aid missions. Grants.
PROCEDURE: Termination.
PARTIES:
Tunisia
USA (United States)
ANNEX
336 UNTS 389. USA (United States). Amendment 8 Oct 58. Force 8 Oct 58.
336 UNTS 389. Tunisia. Amendment 8 Oct 58. Force 8 Oct 58.

104112 Bilateral Exchange **283 UNTS 127**
SIGNED: 1 Mar 57 FORCE: 25 Mar 57
REGISTERED: 18 Dec 57 USA (United States)
ARTICLES: 2 LANGUAGE: English. Spanish.
HEADNOTE: METEOROLOGICAL OBSERVATION STATIONS
TOPIC: Non-ILO Labor
CONCEPTS: General provisions. General cooperation. Exchange of information and documents. Operating agencies. General property. Research and scientific projects. Meteorology. Research and development. Expense sharing formulae.
TREATY REF: 151UNTS147; 179UNTS265.
PROCEDURE: Duration. Termination.
PARTIES:
Chile
USA (United States)
ANNEX
337 UNTS 428. USA (United States). Prolongation 13 Nov 58. Force 21 Nov 58.
337 UNTS 428. Chile. Prolongation 21 Nov 58. Force 21 Nov 58.
394 UNTS 277. Chile. Prolongation 7 Sep 60. Force 7 Sep 60.
394 UNTS 277. USA (United States). Prolongation 21 Jul 60. Force 7 Sep 60.

104113 Multilateral Instrument **283 UNTS 137**
SIGNED: 29 Mar 57 FORCE: 29 Mar 57
REGISTERED: 18 Dec 57 USA (United States)
ARTICLES: 9 LANGUAGE: English. French. Italian.
HEADNOTE: ASSETS
TOPIC: Claims and Debts
CONCEPTS: Previous treaty amendment. Treaty implementation. Treaty interpretation. Currency. Assets. Claims and settlements. Assets transfer. Trademarks. Purchase authorization. Enemy financial interests. Specific claims or waivers.
TREATY REF: 49UNTS; 50UNTS; 138UNTS111.
PARTIES:
France SIGNED: 29 Mar 57 FORCE: 29 Mar 57
Italy SIGNED: 29 Mar 57 FORCE: 29 Mar 57
UK Great Britain SIGNED: 29 Mar 57 FORCE: 29 Mar 57
USA (United States) SIGNED: 29 Mar 57 FORCE: 29 Mar 57

104114 Bilateral Agreement **283 UNTS 151**
SIGNED: 31 Oct 56 FORCE: 8 Mar 57
REGISTERED: 19 Dec 57 USA (United States)
ARTICLES: 11 LANGUAGE: English. Spanish.
HEADNOTE: EDUCATIONAL EXCHANGE
TOPIC: Education
CONCEPTS: Definition of terms. Friendship and amity. Standardization. Conformity with municipal law. General cooperation. Inspection and observation. Personnel. General property. Exchange. Commissions and foundations. Teacher and student exchange. Scholarships and grants. Research and development. Accounting procedures. Currency. Exchange rates and regulations. Expense sharing formulae. Financial programs. Funding procedures.
INTL ORGS: Special Commission.
TREATY REF: 256UNTS195; 187LTS125.
PROCEDURE: Amendment.

PARTIES:
Ecuador
USA (United States)
ANNEX
424 UNTS 352. Ecuador. Amendment 9 May 61.
Force 9 May 61.
424 UNTS 352. USA (United States). Amendment
9 Mar 61. Force 9 May 61.

104115 Bilateral Agreement **283 UNTS 167**
SIGNED: 18 May 56   FORCE: 2 Apr 57
REGISTERED: 19 Dec 57 USA (United States)
ARTICLES: 9 LANGUAGE: English. Turkish.
HEADNOTE: PATENT RIGHTS TECHNICAL INFOR-
MATION DEFENSE PURPOSES
TOPIC: Patents/Copyrights
CONCEPTS: Definition of terms. Conformity with
municipal law. Currency. Press and wire ser-
vices. Security of information. Exchange of de-
fense information. Subsidiary organ.
INTL ORGS: Special Commission.
PROCEDURE: Termination.
PARTIES:
Turkey
USA (United States)
ANNEX
371 UNTS 314. USA (United States). Supplemen-
tation 17 Mar 59. Force 16 Sep 59.
371 UNTS 314. Turkey. Supplementation
16 Sep 59. Force 16 Sep 59.

104116 Bilateral Exchange **283 UNTS 181**
SIGNED: 4 Apr 57   FORCE: 4 Apr 57
REGISTERED: 19 Dec 57 USA (United States)
ARTICLES: 2 LANGUAGE: English. Arabic.
HEADNOTE: ECONOMIC DEVELOPMENT
TOPIC: Tech Assistance
CONCEPTS: Change of circumstances. Conformity
with municipal law. General cooperation. Ex-
change of information and documents. Inspec-
tion and observation. Personnel. Public informa-
tion. Accounting procedures. Attachment of
funds. Currency deposits. Exchange rates and
regulations. Expense sharing formulae. Garnish-
ment of funds. Seizure funds. Local currency. As-
sets. Tax exemptions. Customs exemptions.
Commodities and services. Domestic obligation.
Economic assistance. Materials, equipment and
services. Grants.
TREATY REF: 273UNTS84; 264UNTS247.
PROCEDURE: Termination.
PARTIES:
Libya
USA (United States)

104117 Bilateral Exchange **283 UNTS 193**
SIGNED: 4 Apr 57   FORCE: 4 Apr 57
REGISTERED: 19 Dec 57 USA (United States)
ARTICLES: 4 LANGUAGE: English. Spanish.
HEADNOTE: DOUBLE TAXATION FISCAL EVA-
SION TAXES INCOME
TOPIC: Taxation
CONCEPTS: Conformity with municipal law. Ex-
change of official publications. Domestic legisla-
tion. Negotiation. Teacher and student ex-
change. Taxation. General. Tax exemptions. Air
transport. Merchant vessels.
TREATY REF: 96LTS151.
PROCEDURE: Duration. Ratification. Termination.
PARTIES:
Paraguay
USA (United States)
ANNEX
405 UNTS 328. USA (United States). Amendment
27 Dec 60. Force 7 Mar 61.
405 UNTS 328. Paraguay. Amendment 7 Mar 61.
Force 7 Mar 61.

104118 Bilateral Exchange **283 UNTS 205**
SIGNED: 25 Apr 57   FORCE: 25 Apr 57
REGISTERED: 19 Dec 57 USA (United States)
ARTICLES: 2 LANGUAGE: English.
HEADNOTE: ECONOMIC ASSISTANCE
TOPIC: Direct Aid
CONCEPTS: Change of circumstances. Treaty im-
plementation. Conformity with municipal law.
General cooperation. Exchange of information
and documents. Inspection and observation. Per-
sonnel. Public information. Accounting proce-
dures. Attachment of funds. Currency deposits.

Exchange rates and regulations. Funding proce-
dures. Garnishment of funds. Seizure funds. Lo-
cal currency. Assets. Tax exemptions. Customs
exemptions. Domestic obligation. Economic as-
sistance. Materials, equipment and services.
Withdrawal conditions. Procurement.
TREATY REF: 148UNTS39; 207UNTS27.
PROCEDURE: Termination.
PARTIES:
Ethiopia
USA (United States)

104119 Bilateral Exchange **283 UNTS 217**
SIGNED: 9 Apr 57   FORCE: 9 Apr 57
REGISTERED: 19 Dec 57 USA (United States)
ARTICLES: 3 LANGUAGE: English.
HEADNOTE: NAVIGATION IMPROVEMENTS
GREAT LAKES CHANNELS ST. LAWRENCE SEA-
WAY
TOPIC: Water Transport
CONCEPTS: Conditions. Conformity with munici-
pal law. Exchange of information and docu-
ments. Personnel. Private contracts. Responsibil-
ity and liability. Funding procedures. Naviga-
tional conditions. Canal improvement. Inland
and territorial waters.
TREATY REF: 279UNTS179.
PARTIES:
Canada
USA (United States)

104120 Bilateral Exchange **283 UNTS 233**
SIGNED: 11 Apr 57   FORCE: 11 Apr 57
REGISTERED: 19 Dec 57 USA (United States)
ARTICLES: 4 LANGUAGE: English. German.
HEADNOTE: DISBANDMENT CIVIL SERVICE OR-
GANIZATION
TOPIC: Admin Cooperation
CONCEPTS: General cooperation.
TREATY REF: 199UNTS67.
PARTIES:
Germany, West
USA (United States)

104121 Bilateral Agreement **283 UNTS 245**
SIGNED: 16 Apr 57   FORCE: 16 Apr 57
REGISTERED: 19 Dec 57 USA (United States)
ARTICLES: 6 LANGUAGE: English. Spanish.
HEADNOTE: AGRI COMMOD TITLE I
TOPIC: US Agri Commod Aid
CONCEPTS: Annex or appendix reference. General cooperation. Exchange of information and
documents. Reexport of goods, etc.. Currency
deposits. Exchange rates and regulations. Payment schedules. Transportation costs. Commodities schedule. Surplus commodities.
PARTIES:
Colombia
USA (United States)
ANNEX
291 UNTS 365. USA (United States). Supplementation 29 Aug 57. Force 11 Sep 57.
291 UNTS 365. Colombia. Supplementation
11 Sep 57. Force 11 Sep 57.
293 UNTS 361. Colombia. Amendment
30 Sep 57. Force 30 Sep 57.
293 UNTS 361. USA (United States). Amendment
6 Sep 57. Force 30 Sep 57.
336 UNTS 392. USA (United States). Amendment
18 Nov 58. Force 18 Nov 58.
336 UNTS 392. Colombia. Amendment
18 Nov 58. Force 18 Nov 58.
343 UNTS 360. Colombia. Amendment 5 Mar 59.
Force 5 Mar 59.
343 UNTS 360. USA (United States). Amendment
14 Jan 59. Force 5 Mar 59.
407 UNTS 266. USA (United States). Supplementation 20 Apr 61. Force 20 Apr 61.
407 UNTS 266. Colombia. Supplementation
20 Apr 61. Force 20 Apr 61.
487 UNTS 361. Colombia. Amendment
14 Aug 63. Force 14 Aug 63.
487 UNTS 361. USA (United States). Amendment
14 Aug 63. Force 14 Aug 63.

104122 Bilateral Agreement **283 UNTS 267**
SIGNED: 26 Apr 56   FORCE: 17 Aug 57
REGISTERED: 20 Dec 57 USA (United States)
ARTICLES: 6 LANGUAGE: English. German.
HEADNOTE: FILMS

TOPIC: Culture
CONCEPTS: Detailed regulations. Exceptions and
exemptions. Territorial application. General co-
operation. Import quotas. Mass media exchange.
TREATY REF: 131UNTS320; 55UNTS187.
PROCEDURE: Denunciation. Duration. Renewal or
Revival.
PARTIES:
Germany, West
USA (United States)

104123 Bilateral Agreement **283 UNTS 275**
SIGNED: 22 Jun 56   FORCE: 28 May 57
REGISTERED: 20 Dec 57 USA (United States)
ARTICLES: 16 LANGUAGE: English.
HEADNOTE: COOPERATION CIVIL USES ATOMIC
ENERGY
TOPIC: Atomic Energy
CONCEPTS: Definition of terms. Exchange of infor-
mation and documents. Inspection and observa-
tion. Investigation of violations. Research coop-
eration. Research results. Assets transfer. Nu-
clear materials. Non-nuclear materials. Peaceful
use. Security of information.
PROCEDURE: Duration.
PARTIES:
Australia
USA (United States)
ANNEX
404 UNTS 350. USA (United States). Amendment
14 Sep 60. Force 6 Mar 61.
638 UNTS 268. USA (United States). Amendment
11 Apr 67. Force 5 May 67.
638 UNTS 268. Australia. Force 5 May 67.

104124 Bilateral Exchange **284 UNTS 3**
SIGNED: 24 Apr 57   FORCE: 14 May 57
REGISTERED: 20 Dec 57 USA (United States)
ARTICLES: 2 LANGUAGE: English. Spanish.
HEADNOTE: ESTABLISHMENT OBSERVATION
STATION
TOPIC: Scientific Project
CONCEPTS: Exchange of information and docu-
ments. Operating agencies. Title and deeds. Re-
search cooperation. Meteorology. Indemnities
and reimbursements. Customs exemptions. Facilities and property.
PROCEDURE: Duration. Termination.
PARTIES:
Ecuador
USA (United States)
ANNEX
340 UNTS 396. USA (United States). Prolongation
18 Nov 58. Force 30 Dec 58.
340 UNTS 396. Ecuador. Prolongation
30 Dec 58. Force 30 Dec 58.
356 UNTS 382. Ecuador. Amendment 9 Jun 59.
Force 22 Jul 59.
356 UNTS 382. USA (United States). Amendment
22 Jul 59. Force 22 Jul 59.
373 UNTS 372. USA (United States). Prolongation
12 Feb 60. Force 4 May 60.
373 UNTS 372. Ecuador. Prolongation 4 May 60.
Force 4 May 60.

104125 Bilateral Exchange **284 UNTS 13**
SIGNED: 22 May 57   FORCE: 22 May 57
REGISTERED: 20 Dec 57 USA (United States)
ARTICLES: 2 LANGUAGE: English. Arabic.
HEADNOTE: ECONOMIC ASSISTANCE
TOPIC: Direct Aid
CONCEPTS: Conformity with municipal law. Eco-
nomic assistance.
TREATY REF: 151UNTS179.
PARTIES:
Iraq
USA (United States)

104126 Bilateral Agreement **284 UNTS 19**
SIGNED: 25 Feb 57   FORCE: 10 Jun 57
REGISTERED: 20 Dec 57 USA (United States)
ARTICLES: 12 LANGUAGE: English.
HEADNOTE: COOPERATION CONCERNING CIVIL
USES ATOMIC ENERGY
TOPIC: Atomic Energy
CONCEPTS: Definition of terms. Exchange of infor-
mation and documents. Inspection and observa-
tion. Investigation of violations. Research coop-
eration. Research results. Assets transfer. Nu-

clear materials. Peaceful use. Security of information.
PROCEDURE: Duration. Termination.
PARTIES:
Norway
USA (United States)

104127 Bilateral Exchange **284 UNTS 39**
SIGNED: 16 Jun 57 FORCE: 16 Jun 57
REGISTERED: 20 Dec 57 USA (United States)
ARTICLES: 2 LANGUAGE: English. Arabic.
HEADNOTE: SPECIAL PROGRAM FACILITIES ASSISTANCE
TOPIC: Tech Assistance
CONCEPTS: Change of circumstances. Conformity with municipal law. Use of facilities. Export quotas. Import quotas. Indemnities and reimbursements. Most favored nation clause. Tax exemptions. Customs exemptions. Special projects. Materials, equipment and services. Defense and security. Military assistance. Security of information. Equipment and supplies. Restrictions on transfer.
TREATY REF: 222UNTS251; 265UNTS393.
PROCEDURE: Future Procedures Contemplated.
PARTIES:
Iraq
USA (United States)

104128 Bilateral Agreement **284 UNTS 51**
SIGNED: 22 Jun 57 FORCE: 22 Jun 57
REGISTERED: 20 Dec 57 USA (United States)
ARTICLES: 3 LANGUAGE: English. Italian.
HEADNOTE: SALE WASTE MATERIAL SCRAP
TOPIC: Milit Assistance
CONCEPTS: General provisions. Exchange of information and documents. Export quotas. Import quotas. Local currency. Customs exemptions. Surplus property. Surplus war property.
PROCEDURE: Amendment. Termination.
PARTIES:
Italy
USA (United States)

104129 Bilateral Agreement **284 UNTS 63**
SIGNED: 3 Jun 57 FORCE: 3 Jun 57
REGISTERED: 20 Dec 57 USA (United States)
ARTICLES: 7 LANGUAGE: English.
HEADNOTE: TECHNICAL COOPERATION
TOPIC: Tech Assistance
CONCEPTS: Treaty implementation. Diplomatic privileges. General cooperation. Exchange of information and documents. Informational records. Personnel. Public information. Use of facilities. Export quotas. Import quotas. Attachment of funds. Exchange rates and regulations. Funding procedures. Garnishment of funds. Seizure funds. Tax exemptions. Customs exemptions. Domestic obligation. General technical assistance. Materials, equipment and services. Aid missions.
PROCEDURE: Amendment. Future Procedures Contemplated. Termination.
PARTIES:
Ghana
USA (United States)

104130 Bilateral Agreement **284 UNTS 75**
SIGNED: 27 Jun 57 FORCE: 27 Jun 57
REGISTERED: 20 Dec 57 USA (United States)
ARTICLES: 1 LANGUAGE: English.
HEADNOTE: SUPPLEMENTARY GATT
TOPIC: General Economic
CONCEPTS: Annex or appendix reference. Annex type material. Reciprocity in trade. Commodity trade. Customs duties.
TREATY REF: GATT.
PARTIES:
UK Great Britain
USA (United States)

104131 Bilateral Exchange **284 UNTS 85**
SIGNED: 1 May 57 FORCE: 1 May 57
REGISTERED: 20 Dec 57 USA (United States)
ARTICLES: 2 LANGUAGE: English. German.
HEADNOTE: LOAN NAVAL VESSELS
TOPIC: Milit Assistance
CONCEPTS: Time limit. Annex or appendix reference. Title and deeds. Compensation. Indemni-

ties and reimbursements. Delivery schedules. Lend lease. Naval vessels. Return of equipment and recapture.
TREATY REF: 240UNTS47.
PARTIES:
Germany, West
USA (United States)
ANNEX
336 UNTS 402. USA (United States). Amendment 1 Oct 58. Force 15 Oct 58.
336 UNTS 402. Germany, West. Amendment 15 Oct 58. Force 15 Oct 58.
460 UNTS 315. USA (United States). Supplementation 19 Sep 62. Force 25 Sep 62.
460 UNTS 315. Germany, West. Supplementation 25 Sep 62. Force 25 Sep 62.
573 UNTS 324. USA (United States). Prolongation 7 Oct 65. Force 7 Oct 65.
573 UNTS 324. Germany, West. Prolongation 7 Oct 65. Force 7 Oct 65.

104132 Bilateral Treaty **284 UNTS 93**
SIGNED: 15 Aug 55 FORCE: 16 Jun 57
REGISTERED: 20 Dec 57 USA (United States)
ARTICLES: 23 LANGUAGE: English. Persian.
HEADNOTE: AMITY, ECONOMIC RELATIONS, CONSULAR RIGHTS
TOPIC: General Amity
CONCEPTS: Exceptions and exemptions. Territorial application. Previous treaty replacement. Friendship and amity. Alien status. Consular relations establishment. Human rights. Inviolability. Privileges and immunities. General cooperation. Exchange of information and documents. Juridical personality. Expropriation. Legal protection and assistance. General property. Existing tribunals. Establishment of trade relations. Export quotas. Import quotas. Free trade. Investments. Most favored nation clause. Taxation. Tax exemptions. Patents, copyrights and trademarks. Customs exemptions. Navigational conditions.
TREATY REF: GATT; 3'30DEMARTENS58,885; 106UNTS155;,.
PROCEDURE: Duration. Ratification. Termination.
PARTIES:
Iran
USA (United States)

104133 Multilateral Agreement **284 UNTS 139**
SIGNED: 27 Jun 57 FORCE: 27 Jun 57
REGISTERED: 20 Dec 57 USA (United States)
ARTICLES: 1 LANGUAGE: English. French.
HEADNOTE: SUPPLEMENTARY GATT
TOPIC: General Economic
CONCEPTS: Annex or appendix reference. Annex type material. Reciprocity in trade.
TREATY REF: GATT.
PARTIES:
Belgium SIGNED: 27 Jun 57 FORCE: 27 Jun 57
Netherlands SIGNED: 27 Jun 57 FORCE: 27 Jun 57
USA (United States) SIGNED: 27 Jun 57 FORCE: 27 Jun 57

104134 Bilateral Exchange **284 UNTS 155**
SIGNED: 6 Jun 57 FORCE: 6 Jun 57
REGISTERED: 20 Dec 57 USA (United States)
ARTICLES: 2 LANGUAGE: English.
HEADNOTE: EQUIPMENT MATERIALS SERVICES OTHER ASSISTANCE
TOPIC: Tech Assistance
CONCEPTS: Exceptions and exemptions. Annex type material. Domestic obligation. Materials, equipment and services.
TREATY REF: 239UNTS45.
PROCEDURE: Termination.
PARTIES:
Lebanon
USA (United States)
ANNEX
317 UNTS 350. USA (United States). Amendment 9 Jun 58. Force 12 Jun 58.
317 UNTS 350. Lebanon. Amendment 12 Jun 58. Force 12 Jun 58.

104135 Bilateral Agreement **284 UNTS 161**
SIGNED: 4 Apr 57 FORCE: 26 Jun 57
REGISTERED: 20 Dec 57 USA (United States)
ARTICLES: 11 LANGUAGE: English. Spanish.
HEADNOTE: EDUCATION EXCHANGE

TOPIC: Education
CONCEPTS: Definition of terms. Friendship and amity. Standardization. Conformity with municipal law. General cooperation. Inspection and observation. Personnel. General property. Exchange. Commissions and foundations. Teacher and student exchange. Scholarships and grants. Research and development. Accounting procedures. Currency. Exchange rates and regulations. Expense sharing formulae. Financial programs. Funding procedures.
INTL ORGS: Special Commission.
TREATY REF: 268UNTS299; 187LTS125.
PARTIES:
Paraguay
USA (United States)
ANNEX
416 UNTS 343. Paraguay. Amendment 19 Jun 61. Force 19 Jun 61.
416 UNTS 343. USA (United States). Amendment 5 Jun 61. Force 19 Jun 61.
540 UNTS 336. Paraguay. Force 1 Oct 64.
540 UNTS 336. USA (United States). Force 1 Oct 64.

104136 Bilateral Agreement **284 UNTS 177**
SIGNED: 30 Jun 57 FORCE: 30 Jun 57
REGISTERED: 20 Dec 57 USA (United States)
ARTICLES: 8 LANGUAGE: English.
HEADNOTE: MILITARY ASSISTANCE
TOPIC: Milit Assistance
CONCEPTS: Exceptions and exemptions. Annex or appendix reference. Non-prejudice to UN charter. Peaceful relations. Privileges and immunities. Conformity with municipal law. Inspection and observation. Public information. Use of facilities. Garnishment of funds. Local currency. Tax exemptions. Recognition. Customs exemptions. Materials, equipment and services. Aid missions. Self-defense. Return of equipment and recapture. Security of information. Exchange of defense information. Raw materials.
INTL ORGS: United Nations.
TREATY REF: 70UNTS237.
PROCEDURE: Amendment. Future Procedures Contemplated. Registration. Termination.
PARTIES:
Libya
USA (United States)

104137 Bilateral Treaty **284 UNTS 193**
SIGNED: 16 Jan 53 FORCE: 18 Aug 57
REGISTERED: 20 Dec 57 Pakistan
ARTICLES: 6 LANGUAGE: English. Arabic.
HEADNOTE: FRIENDSHIP
TOPIC: General Amity
CONCEPTS: Friendship and amity. General consular functions.
PARTIES:
Lebanon
Pakistan

104138 Multilateral Protocol **284 UNTS 201**
SIGNED: 1 May 57 FORCE: 9 Dec 57
REGISTERED: 30 Dec 57 OAS (Am States)
ARTICLES: 11 LANGUAGE: English. French. Portuguese. Spanish.
HEADNOTE: DUTIES RIGHTS STATES EVENT CIVIL STRIFE
TOPIC: Admin Cooperation
CONCEPTS: Alien status. Conformity with municipal law. Arms limitations.
INTL ORGS: Organization of American States. United Nations.
TREATY REF: 134LTS45.
PROCEDURE: Denunciation. Ratification.
PARTIES:
Argentina SIGNED: 8 Aug 57 RATIFIED: 24 Oct 57 FORCE: 9 Dec 57
Brazil SIGNED: 1 May 57
Costa Rica SIGNED: 1 May 57
Cuba SIGNED: 19 Jul 57 RATIFIED: 9 Dec 57 FORCE: 9 Dec 57
Dominican Republic SIGNED: 17 Sep 57
Haiti SIGNED: 9 Aug 57
Honduras SIGNED: 18 Dec 57
Peru SIGNED: 18 Jun 57
USA (United States) SIGNED: 15 Jul 57
ANNEX
338 UNTS 397. Dominican Republic. Ratification 21 May 58.

338 UNTS 397. Haiti. Ratification 31 Jan 58.

338 UNTS 397. Costa Rica. Ratification 24 Jun 59.

377 UNTS 438. Honduras. Ratification 14 Oct 60.

377 UNTS 438. El Salvador. Ratification 13 Sep 60.

640 UNTS 396. Niger. Accession 18 Jul 68. Force 16 Oct 68.

104139 Unilateral Instrument **284 UNTS 215**
SIGNED: 30 Dec 57   FORCE: 2 Jan 58
REGISTERED: 2 Jan 58 United Nations
ARTICLES: 1 LANGUAGE: English.
HEADNOTE: ACCEPTANCE ICJ JURISDICTION
TOPIC: ICJ Option Clause
CONCEPTS: Exceptions and exemptions. Compulsory jurisdiction.
INTL ORGS: International Court of Justice.
PROCEDURE: Termination.
PARTIES:
  Sudan

104140 Bilateral Convention **284 UNTS 221**
SIGNED: 14 Mar 53   FORCE: 26 Jun 57
REGISTERED: 3 Jan 58 Italy
ARTICLES: 18 LANGUAGE: French.
HEADNOTE: CONSTRUCTION OPERATION TUNNEL UNDER MONT BLANC
TOPIC: Land Transport
CONCEPTS: Time limit. Conformity with municipal law. Personnel. Responsibility and liability. Establishment of commission. Arbitration. Procedure. Special tribunals. Indemnities and reimbursements. Expense sharing formulae. Roads and highways. Road rules.
INTL ORGS: International Court of Justice. Special Commission.
PROCEDURE: Ratification.
PARTIES:
  France
  Italy

104141 Bilateral Agreement **284 UNTS 239**
SIGNED: 18 Dec 54   FORCE: 10 Feb 56
REGISTERED: 3 Jan 58 Italy
ARTICLES: 16 LANGUAGE: French.
HEADNOTE: FINAL SETTLEMENT FINANCIAL OBLIGATIONS
TOPIC: Peace/Disarmament
CONCEPTS: Definition of terms. Annex or appendix reference. Exchange of information and documents. General property. Archives and objects. Exchange rates and regulations. Payment schedules. Post-war claims settlement.
INTL ORGS: Special Commission.
TREATY REF: 49UNTS.
PROCEDURE: Future Procedures Contemplated. Ratification.
PARTIES:
  Italy
  Yugoslavia

104142 Bilateral Agreement **284 UNTS 279**
SIGNED: 23 Jul 55   FORCE: 5 Mar 57
REGISTERED: 3 Jan 58 Italy
ARTICLES: 7 LANGUAGE: French.
HEADNOTE: ELECTRIFICATION ITALIAN STATE RAILWAYS ENTERING SWITZERLAND
TOPIC: Land Transport
CONCEPTS: Detailed regulations. Currency. Payment schedules. Loan repayment. Terms of loan. Routes and logistics. Motor vehicles and combinations. Railways.
PROCEDURE: Ratification.
PARTIES:
  Italy
  Switzerland

104143 Bilateral Agreement **284 UNTS 293**
SIGNED: 19 Nov 56   FORCE: 19 Nov 56
REGISTERED: 3 Jan 58 Italy
ARTICLES: 1 LANGUAGE: Italian. German.
HEADNOTE: SALE PROPRIETARY MEDICINES
TOPIC: Admin Cooperation
CONCEPTS: Exceptions and exemptions. Pharmaceuticals. National treatment.
TREATY REF: 3'2DEMARTENS839;.

PARTIES:
  Austria
  Italy

104144 Bilateral Exchange **284 UNTS 299**
SIGNED: 29 Jun 56   FORCE: 29 Jun 56
REGISTERED: 3 Jan 58 Italy
ARTICLES: 6 LANGUAGE: French.
HEADNOTE: REPAYMENTS AMORTIZATION WITHIN EPU
TOPIC: Finance
CONCEPTS: Detailed regulations. Exchange of information and documents. Finances and payments. Accounting procedures. Bonds. Currency. Financial programs. Interest rates. Payment schedules. Debt settlement. Loan repayment.
INTL ORGS: European Payments Union. Organization for Economic Co-operation and Development.
PROCEDURE: Future Procedures Contemplated.
PARTIES:
  Italy
  Switzerland

104145 Bilateral Agreement **284 UNTS 313**
SIGNED: 11 Sep 54   FORCE: 29 Apr 57
REGISTERED: 3 Jan 58 Italy
ARTICLES: 21 LANGUAGE: French.
HEADNOTE: CULTURAL AGREEMENT
TOPIC: Culture
CONCEPTS: Friendship and amity. Tourism. Conformity with municipal law. Exchange of information and documents. Operating agencies. Establishment of commission. Specialists exchange. Recognition of degrees. Teacher and student exchange. Professorships. Institute establishment. Scholarships and grants. Vocational training. Exchange. General cultural cooperation. Artists. Athletes. Research cooperation. Anthropology and archeology. Scientific exchange. Fees and exemptions. Publications exchange. Mass media exchange. Conferences.
INTL ORGS: Special Commission.
PROCEDURE: Denunciation. Duration. Future Procedures Contemplated. Renewal or Revival.
PARTIES:
  Greece
  Italy

104146 Bilateral Agreement **284 UNTS 325**
SIGNED: 24 Nov 54   FORCE: 8 Aug 57
REGISTERED: 3 Jan 58 Italy
ARTICLES: 23 LANGUAGE: Italian. Portuguese.
HEADNOTE: CONCILIATION JUDICIAL SETTLEMENT
TOPIC: Dispute Settlement
CONCEPTS: Time limit. Treaty interpretation. General cooperation. Recognition and enforcement of legal decisions. Establishment of commission. Procedure. Domestic jurisdiction. Existing tribunals. Conciliation. Wages and salaries.
INTL ORGS: Permanent Court of Arbitration. International Court of Justice. Conciliation Commission.
TREATY REF: 98BFSP626.
PROCEDURE: Duration. Ratification.
PARTIES:
  Brazil
  Italy

104147 Bilateral Agreement **284 UNTS 351**
SIGNED: 7 May 56   FORCE: 21 May 56
REGISTERED: 3 Jan 58 Italy
ARTICLES: 8 LANGUAGE: French.
HEADNOTE: PAYMENTS
TOPIC: Finance
CONCEPTS: Previous treaty replacement. General cooperation. Accounting procedures. Banking. Currency. Exchange rates and regulations. Financial programs. Payment schedules. Local currency. Assets transfer.
INTL ORGS: European Payments Union. International Monetary Fund. Organization for Economic Co-operation and Development.
TREATY REF: PAYMENTS AGREE., 19SEP50,2-2JUN50.
PROCEDURE: Denunciation. Future Procedures Contemplated. Termination.

PARTIES:
  Austria
  Italy

104148 Bilateral Agreement **285 UNTS 3**
SIGNED: 9 May 56   FORCE: 23 Jul 56
REGISTERED: 7 Jan 58 Philippines
ARTICLES: 20 LANGUAGE: English. Japanese.
HEADNOTE: REPARATIONS AGREEMENT
TOPIC: Reparations
CONCEPTS: Treaty implementation. Annex or appendix reference. Inviolability. Privileges and immunities. Non-diplomatic delegations. General cooperation. Private contracts. Use of facilities. Establishment of commission. Arbitration. Procedure. Reexport of goods, etc.. Indemnities and reimbursements. Tax exemptions. Enemy financial interests. Reparations and restrictions.
INTL ORGS: International Court of Justice. Arbitration Commission. Special Commission.
TREATY REF: 136UNTS45.
PROCEDURE: Ratification.
PARTIES:
  Japan
  Philippines

104149 Bilateral Agreement **285 UNTS 59**
SIGNED: 12 Oct 57   FORCE: 12 Oct 57
REGISTERED: 8 Jan 58 UK Great Britain
ARTICLES: 16 LANGUAGE: English.
HEADNOTE: EXTERNAL DEFENSE MUTUAL ASSISTANCE
TOPIC: Milit Assistance
CONCEPTS: Definition of terms. Annex or appendix reference. General cooperation. Use of facilities. Aid missions. Joint defense. Defense and security. Military assistance. Military training. Military assistance missions. Military installations and equipment. Bases and facilities.
PROCEDURE: Future Procedures Contemplated.
PARTIES:
  Fed of Malaya
  UK Great Britain

104150 Bilateral Agreement **285 UNTS 105**
SIGNED: 12 Mar 57   FORCE: 27 Apr 57
REGISTERED: 8 Jan 58 USSR (Soviet Union)
ARTICLES: 22 LANGUAGE: Russian. German.
HEADNOTE: TEMPORARY PRESENCE SOVIET FORCES
TOPIC: Status of Forces
CONCEPTS: Definition of terms. Court procedures. Conformity with municipal law. General cooperation. Recognition of legal documents. Responsibility and liability. Use of facilities. Investigation of violations. Establishment of commission. Procedure. Compensation. Claims and settlements. Military training. Jurisdiction. Procurement and logistics. Status of forces. Bases and facilities.
INTL ORGS: Special Commission.
PARTIES:
  Germany, East
  USSR (Soviet Union)

104151 Bilateral Treaty **285 UNTS 135**
SIGNED: 10 May 57   FORCE: 11 Oct 57
REGISTERED: 8 Jan 58 USSR (Soviet Union)
ARTICLES: 27 LANGUAGE: Russian. German.
HEADNOTE: CONSULAR TREATY
TOPIC: Consul/Citizenship
CONCEPTS: General consular functions. Consular relations establishment. Inviolability. Privileges and immunities. Responsibility and liability.
PROCEDURE: Denunciation. Ratification.
PARTIES:
  Germany, East
  USSR (Soviet Union)

104152 Bilateral Agreement **285 UNTS 169**
SIGNED: 14 Jun 57   FORCE: 6 Nov 57
REGISTERED: 8 Jan 58 USSR (Soviet Union)
ARTICLES: 17 LANGUAGE: Russian. German.
HEADNOTE: SETTLEMENT TECHNICAL COMMERCIAL QUESTIONS NAVIGATION DANUBE
TOPIC: Water Transport
CONCEPTS: Exceptions and exemptions. Frontier formalities. Passports non-diplomatic. Non-visa travel documents. Conformity with municipal law. General cooperation. Recognition of legal

documents. Use of facilities. Investigation of violations. Negotiation. Fees and exemptions. Most favored nation clause. General. Customs duties. Customs exemptions. Navigational conditions. Transport of goods. Merchant vessels. Ports and pilotage.
PROCEDURE: Denunciation. Ratification.
PARTIES:
Austria
USSR (Soviet Union)

104153 Bilateral Convention **285 UNTS 193**
SIGNED: 2 Apr 57   FORCE: 19 Dec 57
REGISTERED: 17 Jan 58 Netherlands
ARTICLES: 32 LANGUAGE: English. Dutch.
HEADNOTE: FISCAL EVASION TAXES ON INCOME
TOPIC: Taxation
CONCEPTS: Equitable taxes. General. Tax exemptions.
PROCEDURE: Ratification. Termination.
PARTIES:
Canada
Netherlands
ANNEX
470 UNTS 398. Canada. Amendment 28 Oct 59. Force 7 Jul 60.
470 UNTS 398. Netherlands. Amendment 28 Oct 59. Force 7 Jul 60.
543 UNTS 364. Canada. Amendment 3 Feb 65. Force 23 Jun 65.
543 UNTS 364. Netherlands. Amendment 3 Feb 65. Force 23 Jun 65.

104154 Bilateral Treaty **285 UNTS 231**
SIGNED: 27 Mar 56   FORCE: 2 Dec 57
REGISTERED: 17 Jan 58 Netherlands
ARTICLES: 30 LANGUAGE: English. Dutch.
HEADNOTE: FRIENDSHIP COMMERCE NAVIGATION
TOPIC: General Amity
CONCEPTS: Definition of terms. Exceptions and exemptions. Territorial application. General provisions. Previous treaty replacement. Tourism. Alien status. Human rights. Administrative cooperation. General cooperation. Exchange of information and documents. Juridical personality. Expropriation. Free passage and transit. Legal protection and assistance. General property. Private contracts. Existing tribunals. Export quotas. Import quotas. Free trade. Trade procedures. Exchange rates and regulations. Most favored nation clause. National treatment. Taxation. Tax exemptions. Recognition. Customs duties. Navigational conditions. Ports and pilotage. Shipwreck and salvage.
INTL ORGS: International Court of Justice. International Monetary Fund.
TREATY REF: 42LTS301; 122UNTS346.
PROCEDURE: Duration. Ratification. Termination. Application to Non-self-governing Territories.
PARTIES:
Netherlands
USA (United States)

104155 Multilateral Agreement **285 UNTS 301**
SIGNED: 5 Nov 57   FORCE: 5 Nov 57
REGISTERED: 17 Jan 58 United Nations
ARTICLES: 6 LANGUAGE: English.
HEADNOTE: TECHNICAL ASSISTANCE
TOPIC: Tech Assistance
CONCEPTS: Definition of terms. Previous treaty replacement. Privileges and immunities. General cooperation. Exchange of information and documents. Personnel. Responsibility and liability. Title and deeds. Use of facilities. Exchange. Scholarships and grants. Vocational training. Research and development. Exchange rates and regulations. Expense sharing formulae. Local currency. Domestic obligation. General technical assistance. Materials, equipment and services. IGO status. Conformity with IGO decisions.
TREATY REF: 76UNTS132; 1UNTS15; 33UNTS261; 187UNTS61.
PROCEDURE: Amendment. Termination.
PARTIES:
Liberia SIGNED: 5 Nov 57 FORCE: 5 Nov 57
FAO (Food Agri) SIGNED: 5 Nov 57 FORCE: 5 Nov 57
ICAO (Civil Aviat) SIGNED: 5 Nov 57 FORCE: 5 Nov 57

ILO (Labor Org) SIGNED: 5 Nov 57 FORCE: 5 Nov 57
ITU (Telecommun) SIGNED: 5 Nov 57 FORCE: 5 Nov 57
UNESCO (Educ/Cult) SIGNED: 5 Nov 57 FORCE: 5 Nov 57
United Nations SIGNED: 5 Nov 57 FORCE: 5 Nov 57
WHO (World Health) SIGNED: 5 Nov 57 FORCE: 5 Nov 57
WMO (Meteorology) SIGNED: 5 Nov 57 FORCE: 5 Nov 57
ANNEX
525 UNTS 317. Liberia. Force 12 Feb 65.

104156 Bilateral Agreement **285 UNTS 317**
SIGNED: 21 Jun 56   FORCE: 1 Aug 56
REGISTERED: 21 Jan 58 IBRD (World Bank)
ARTICLES: 5 LANGUAGE: English.
HEADNOTE: GUARANTEE AGREEMENT
TOPIC: IBRD Project
CONCEPTS: Annex or appendix reference. Exchange of information and documents. Inspection and observation. Bonds. Fees and exemptions. Tax exemptions. Domestic obligation. Terms of loan. Loan regulations. Loan guarantee. Guarantor non-interference.
PARTIES:
Fed Rhod/Nyasaland
IBRD (World Bank)

104157 Bilateral Agreement **285 UNTS 355**
SIGNED: 21 Jun 56   FORCE: 1 Aug 56
REGISTERED: 21 Jan 58 IBRD (World Bank)
ARTICLES: 5 LANGUAGE: English.
HEADNOTE: GUARANTEE AGREEMENT
TOPIC: IBRD Project
CONCEPTS: Annex or appendix reference. Exchange of information and documents. Inspection and observation. Bonds. Fees and exemptions. Tax exemptions. Domestic obligation. Terms of loan. Loan regulations. Loan guarantee. Guarantor non-interference.
PARTIES:
IBRD (World Bank)
UK Great Britain

104158 Bilateral Agreement **286 UNTS 3**
SIGNED: 15 May 54   FORCE: 15 May 54
REGISTERED: 24 Jan 58 Pakistan
ARTICLES: 11 LANGUAGE: English.
HEADNOTE: COMMERCE
TOPIC: General Trade
CONCEPTS: Exceptions and exemptions. Annex or appendix reference. Conformity with municipal law. General cooperation. Licenses and permits. Trade procedures. Monetary and gold transfers. Payment schedules. Quotas. Most favored nation clause. Navigational conditions.
TREATY REF: 286UNTS8; 286UNTS12.
PROCEDURE: Duration. Ratification. Renewal or Revival. Termination.
PARTIES:
Pakistan
Yugoslavia

104159 Bilateral Agreement **286 UNTS 15**
SIGNED: 23 May 55   FORCE: 1 Jul 55
REGISTERED: 24 Jan 58 Pakistan
ARTICLES: 11 LANGUAGE: English.
HEADNOTE: COMMERCIAL RELATIONS
TOPIC: General Trade
CONCEPTS: Exceptions and exemptions. Treaty implementation. Annex or appendix reference. Privileges and immunities. General cooperation. Licenses and permits. Trade procedures. Most favored nation clause. Agricultural commodities. Navigational conditions. Merchant vessels.
TREATY REF: 286UNTS20; 286UNTS22.
PROCEDURE: Termination.
PARTIES:
Ceylon (Sri Lanka)
Pakistan

104160 Bilateral Convention **286 UNTS 27**
SIGNED: 14 Jan 57   FORCE: 26 Aug 57
REGISTERED: 24 Jan 58 Denmark
ARTICLES: 14 LANGUAGE: Danish. German.

HEADNOTE: DOUBLE TAXATION INCOME PORPERTY
TOPIC: Taxation
CONCEPTS: Conformity with municipal law. Taxation. Tax credits. General. Tax exemptions.
PROCEDURE: Denunciation. Duration. Ratification.
PARTIES:
Denmark
Switzerland
ANNEX
453 UNTS 372. Switzerland. Acknowledgement 6 Sep 62. Force 6 Sep 62.
453 UNTS 372. Denmark. Faroe Islands. Force 6 Sep 62.

104161 Bilateral Convention **286 UNTS 85**
SIGNED: 14 Jan 57   FORCE: 26 Aug 57
REGISTERED: 31 Jan 58 Denmark
ARTICLES: 8 LANGUAGE: Danish. German.
HEADNOTE: DOUBLE TAXATION INHERITANCE TAXES
TOPIC: Taxation
CONCEPTS: Territorial application. Nationality and citizenship. Debts. Taxation. Death duties.
PROCEDURE: Denunciation. Duration. Ratification.
PARTIES:
Denmark
Switzerland
ANNEX
453 UNTS 372. Switzerland. Acknowledgement 6 Sep 62. Force 6 Sep 62.
453 UNTS 372. Denmark. Faroe Islands. Force 6 Sep 62.

104162 Bilateral Exchange **286 UNTS 107**
SIGNED: 4 Jun 57   FORCE: 4 Jun 57
REGISTERED: 31 Jan 58 Denmark
ARTICLES: 4 LANGUAGE: Danish. Spanish.
HEADNOTE: PAYMENTS
TOPIC: Finance
CONCEPTS: Previous treaty replacement. General trade. Export quotas. Banking. Currency. Financial programs. Interest rates. Local currency.
TREATY REF: 256UNTS149.
PROCEDURE: Denunciation.
PARTIES:
Denmark
Uruguay

104163 Bilateral Agreement **286 UNTS 117**
SIGNED: 18 May 57   FORCE: 18 May 57
REGISTERED: 31 Jan 58 Denmark
ARTICLES: 5 LANGUAGE: Danish. Spanish.
HEADNOTE: PAYMENTS
TOPIC: Finance
CONCEPTS: Previous treaty replacement. General trade. Accounting procedures. Banking. Exchange rates and regulations. Payment schedules. Local currency.
TREATY REF: 15JAN53; PAYMENTS AGREEMENT.
PROCEDURE: Denunciation. Duration. Ratification. Renewal or Revival.
PARTIES:
Denmark
Paraguay
ANNEX
620 UNTS 320. Denmark. Termination 30 Jun 67.
620 UNTS 320. Paraguay. Termination 30 Jun 67.

104164 Bilateral Agreement **286 UNTS 127**
SIGNED: 22 Feb 57   FORCE: 26 Aug 57
REGISTERED: 31 Jan 58 Denmark
ARTICLES: 30 LANGUAGE: Danish. Norwegian.
HEADNOTE: DOUBLE TAXATION INCOME PROPERTY
TOPIC: Taxation
CONCEPTS: Territorial application. Privileges and immunities. Nationality and citizenship. Conformity with municipal law. Negotiation. Teacher and student exchange. Taxation. Death duties. Equitable taxes. Tax exemptions. Air transport. Merchant vessels.
PROCEDURE: Duration. Ratification. Termination.
PARTIES:
Denmark
Norway

ANNEX
348 UNTS 362. Denmark. Supplementation
21 May 59. Force 16 Sep 59.
348 UNTS 362. Norway. Supplementation
21 May 59. Force 16 Sep 59.

104165 Multilateral Agreement **286 UNTS 171**
SIGNED: 30 Jun 57 FORCE: 15 Jul 57
REGISTERED: 1 Feb 58 United Nations
ARTICLES: 7 LANGUAGE: English.
HEADNOTE: TECHNICAL ASSISTANCE
TOPIC: Tech Assistance
CONCEPTS: Assistance.
TREATY REF: 76UNTS132; 1UNTS15;
33UNTS261; 97UNTS21.
PARTIES:
Israel SIGNED: 15 Jul 57 FORCE: 15 Jul 57
FAO (Food Agri) SIGNED: 30 Jun 57 FORCE:
15 Jul 57
ICAO (Civil Aviat) SIGNED: 30 Jun 57 FORCE:
15 Jul 57
ILO (Labor Org) SIGNED: 30 Jun 57 FORCE:
15 Jul 57
UNESCO (Educ/Cult) SIGNED: 30 Jun 57
FORCE: 15 Jul 57
United Nations SIGNED: 30 Jun 57 FORCE:
15 Jul 57
WHO (World Health) SIGNED: 30 Jun 57 FORCE:
15 Jul 57
ANNEX
496 UNTS 356. UNTAB (Tech Assis). Amendment
6 Mar 64. Force 14 May 64.
496 UNTS 356. Israel. Amendment 14 May 64.
Force 14 May 64.
651 UNTS 357. IMCO (Maritime Org). Accession
21 Nov 68. Force 21 Nov 68.
651 UNTS 357. UNIDO (Industrial). Accession
21 Nov 68. Force 21 Nov 68.

104166 Bilateral Exchange **286 UNTS 189**
SIGNED: 20 Jan 58 FORCE: 20 Jan 58
REGISTERED: 5 Feb 58 United Nations
ARTICLES: 2 LANGUAGE: English.
HEADNOTE: UN EMERGENCY FORCE AIRPORT
TRANSIT UNIT
TOPIC: Milit Installation
CONCEPTS: Annex or appendix reference. Overf-
lights and technical stops. Operating authoriza-
tions and regulations. Postal services. IGO
status. Peace-keeping force.
TREATY REF: 226UNTS125.
PARTIES:
Lebanon
United Nations

104167 Bilateral Exchange **286 UNTS 199**
SIGNED: 20 Jan 58 FORCE: 20 Jan 58
REGISTERED: 5 Feb 58 United Nations
ARTICLES: 3 LANGUAGE: English.
HEADNOTE: UN EMERGENCY FORCE POSTAL AR-
RANGEMENTS
TOPIC: Postal Service
CONCEPTS: Annex or appendix reference. Postal
services.
INTL ORGS: Universal Postal Union.
PARTIES:
Lebanon
United Nations

104168 Bilateral Agreement **286 UNTS 211**
SIGNED: 24 Aug 54 FORCE: 28 Dec 54
REGISTERED: 6 Feb 58 IBRD (World Bank)
ARTICLES: 5 LANGUAGE: English.
HEADNOTE: GUARANTEE AGREEMENT
TOPIC: IBRD Project
CONCEPTS: Definition of terms. Annex or appen-
dix reference. Inspection and observation.
Bonds. Fees and exemptions. Tax exemptions.
Domestic obligation. Terms of loan. Loan regula-
tions. Loan guarantee. Guarantor non-interfer-
ence.
PARTIES:
Mexico
IBRD (World Bank)

104169 Bilateral Exchange **286 UNTS 237**
SIGNED: 21 May 57 FORCE: 1 Jun 57
REGISTERED: 12 Feb 58 Netherlands
ARTICLES: 2 LANGUAGE: French.

HEADNOTE: RECOGNITION NATIONAL DRIVING
PERMITS
TOPIC: Land Transport
CONCEPTS: Driving permits.
TREATY REF: 125UNTS3.
PROCEDURE: Termination.
PARTIES:
Netherlands
Sweden

104170 Bilateral Agreement **286 UNTS 243**
SIGNED: 15 Feb 57 FORCE: 28 May 57
REGISTERED: 12 Feb 58 Netherlands
ARTICLES: 7 LANGUAGE: French.
HEADNOTE: MOVEMENT REFUGEES
TOPIC: Refugees
CONCEPTS: Emergencies. Time limit. Visa aboli-
tion. Denial of admission. Alien status. Confor-
mity with municipal law.
INTL ORGS: Special Commission.
TREATY REF: 189UNTS137; 11UNTS73.
PROCEDURE: Denunciation. Ratification.
PARTIES:
France
Netherlands

104171 Bilateral Exchange **286 UNTS 249**
SIGNED: 22 Feb 56 FORCE: 1 Jun 56
REGISTERED: 12 Feb 58 Netherlands
ARTICLES: 2 LANGUAGE: French.
HEADNOTE: MOVEMENT TRAVELLERS
TOPIC: Visas
CONCEPTS: Denial of admission. Non-visa travel
documents.
PROCEDURE: Denunciation. Termination.
PARTIES:
Luxembourg
Netherlands

104172 Bilateral Agreement **286 UNTS 255**
SIGNED: 31 Jan 56 FORCE: 31 Jan 56
REGISTERED: 12 Feb 58 Netherlands
ARTICLES: 9 LANGUAGE: French.
HEADNOTE: REPAYMENT AMORTIZATION
TOPIC: Finance
CONCEPTS: Detailed regulations. Territorial appli-
cation. General cooperation. Accounting proce-
dures. Banking. Bonds. Balance of payments.
Currency. Exchange rates and regulations. Inter-
est rates. Payment schedules. Local currency.
Debts. Debt settlement. Loan repayment.
INTL ORGS: European Payments Union. Organiza-
tion for Economic Co-operation and Develop-
ment.
PARTIES:
Denmark
Netherlands
ANNEX
487 UNTS 362. Denmark. Force 30 Apr 59.
487 UNTS 362. Netherlands. Force 30 Apr 59.

104173 Multilateral Convention **286 UNTS 265**
SIGNED: 1 Mar 54 FORCE: 12 Apr 57
REGISTERED: 12 Feb 58 Netherlands
ARTICLES: 33 LANGUAGE: French.
HEADNOTE: CIVIL PROCEDURE
TOPIC: Admin Cooperation
CONCEPTS: Territorial application. Previous treaty
replacement. General cooperation. Legal protec-
tion and assistance. Penal sanctions. Indemni-
ties and reimbursements. Debts.
TREATY REF: HAGUE CONVENTION 17JUL1905.
PROCEDURE: Accession. Denunciation. Duration.
Ratification.
PARTIES:
Austria SIGNED: 1 Mar 54 RATIFIED: 1 Mar 56
FORCE: 12 Apr 57
Belgium SIGNED: 1 Mar 54
Denmark SIGNED: 2 Sep 55
Finland SIGNED: 17 Sep 56 RATIFIED: 8 Jan 57
FORCE: 12 Apr 57
France SIGNED: 24 Jan 56
Germany, West SIGNED: 9 Apr 57
Italy SIGNED: 1 Mar 54 RATIFIED: 11 Feb 57
FORCE: 12 Apr 57
Luxembourg SIGNED: 28 Jun 54 RATIFIED:
3 Jul 56 FORCE: 12 Apr 57
Netherlands SIGNED: 1 Mar 54
Norway SIGNED: 23 Mar 54
Portugal SIGNED: 20 Feb 57

Spain SIGNED: 12 Apr 57
Sweden SIGNED: 28 Jun 54 RATIFIED:
21 Dec 57 FORCE: 19 Feb 58
Switzerland SIGNED: 2 Jul 54 RATIFIED:
6 May 57 FORCE: 5 Jul 57
ANNEX
510 UNTS 326. France. Guadeloupe.
510 UNTS 326. France. Reunion.
510 UNTS 326. France. Sahara Departments.
510 UNTS 326. Germany, West. Ratification
2 Nov 59. Force 1 Jan 60.
510 UNTS 326. Belgium. Ratification 24 Apr 58.
Force 23 Jun 58.
510 UNTS 326. Norway. Ratification 21 May 58.
Force 20 Jul 58.
510 UNTS 326. Denmark. Qualified Ratification
19 Sep 58. Force 18 Dec 58.
510 UNTS 326. France. New Caledonia.
510 UNTS 326. Spain. Ratification 20 Sep 61.
Force 19 Dec 61.
510 UNTS 326. France. Miquelon.
510 UNTS 326. France. French Polynesia.
510 UNTS 326. France. Martinique.
510 UNTS 326. France. Ratification 23 Apr 59.
Force 22 Jun 59.
510 UNTS 326. France. Algeria.
510 UNTS 326. France. French Guiana.
510 UNTS 326. Netherlands. Qualified Ratification 28 Apr 59. Force 27 Jun 59.
510 UNTS 326. France. French Somaliland.
510 UNTS 326. Yugoslavia. Accession 12 Oct 62.
Force 11 Dec 62.

104174 Bilateral Agreement **286 UNTS 291**
SIGNED: 10 Sep 57 FORCE: 19 Sep 57
REGISTERED: 13 Feb 58 IBRD (World Bank)
ARTICLES: 7 LANGUAGE: English.
HEADNOTE: LOAN AGREEMENT
TOPIC: IBRD Project
CONCEPTS: Default remedies. Annex or appendix
reference. Exchange of information and docu-
ments. Informational records. Bonds. Fees and
exemptions. Interest rates. Tax exemptions. Do-
mestic obligation. Terms of loan. Loan regula-
tions. Loan guarantee. Guarantor non-interfer-
ence. Water transport.
PARTIES:
Belgium
IBRD (World Bank)

104175 Bilateral Agreement **286 UNTS 307**
SIGNED: 28 Jan 57 FORCE: 4 Dec 57
REGISTERED: 13 Feb 58 IBRD (World Bank)
ARTICLES: 7 LANGUAGE: English.
HEADNOTE: LOAN AGREEMENT
TOPIC: IBRD Project
CONCEPTS: Default remedies. Annex or appendix
reference. Exchange of information and docu-
ments. Informational records. Inspection and ob-
servation. Accounting procedures. Bonds. Fees
and exemptions. Interest rates. Tax exemptions.
Domestic obligation. Terms of loan. Loan regula-
tions. Loan guarantee. Guarantor non-interfer-
ence. Roads and highways.
PARTIES:
Ethiopia
IBRD (World Bank)

104176 Bilateral Agreement **287 UNTS 3**
SIGNED: 26 Sep 57 FORCE: 1 Jan 58
REGISTERED: 20 Feb 58 South Africa
ARTICLES: 24 LANGUAGE: English.
HEADNOTE: PARCEL POST AGREEMENT
TOPIC: Postal Service
CONCEPTS: Responsibility and liability. Account-
ing procedures. Customs declarations. Customs
exemptions. Postal services. Regulations. Con-
veyance in transit. Parcel post. Rates and
charges.
PROCEDURE: Duration. Termination.
PARTIES:
Austria
South Africa

104177 Bilateral Exchange **287 UNTS 21**
SIGNED: 31 Oct 56 FORCE: 31 Oct 56
REGISTERED: 20 Feb 58 Netherlands
ARTICLES: 2 LANGUAGE: German.
HEADNOTE: RE-ENTRY FORCE PRE-WAR TREA-
TIES

TOPIC: Admin Cooperation
CONCEPTS: Revival of treaties.
INTL ORGS: Special Commission.
TREATY REF: 3LTS153.
PARTIES:
  Germany, West
  Netherlands

104178 Multilateral Agreement **287 UNTS 27**
SIGNED: 8 Jul 54   FORCE: 16 Jul 54
REGISTERED: 20 Feb 58 Netherlands
ARTICLES: 11 LANGUAGE: French. Dutch.
HEADNOTE: REMOVAL RESTRICTIONS CAPITAL
  TRANSFERS
TOPIC: Finance
CONCEPTS: Detailed regulations. General cooper-
  ation. General property. Banking. Bonds. Mone-
  tary and gold transfers. Investments. Payment
  schedules.
TREATY REF: 2UNTS281; 250UNTS109.
PROCEDURE: Duration.
PARTIES:
  Belgium SIGNED: 8 Jul 54 FORCE: 16 Jul 54
  Luxembourg   SIGNED: 8 Jul 54   FORCE:
    16 Jul 54
  Netherlands SIGNED: 8 Jul 54 FORCE: 16 Jul 54

104179 Bilateral Convention **287 UNTS 41**
SIGNED: 20 Feb 57   FORCE: 29 Jan 58
REGISTERED: 21 Feb 58 Netherlands
ARTICLES: 38 LANGUAGE: Dutch. Danish. English.
HEADNOTE: ADMINISTRATIVE   ASSISTANCE
  TAXES
TOPIC: Taxation
CONCEPTS: Definition of terms. Territorial applica-
  tion. Nationality and citizenship. General cooper-
  ation. Exchange of official publications. Teacher
  and student exchange. Claims and settlements.
  Taxation. Tax credits. Equitable taxes. General.
  Tax exemptions.
PROCEDURE: Duration. Ratification. Termination.
PARTIES:
  Denmark
  Netherlands
              ANNEX
450 UNTS 440. Netherlands. Netherlands An-
  tilles. Force 4 Oct 61.
450 UNTS 440. Denmark. Acknowledgement
  27 Jun 60. Force 4 Oct 61.

104180 Bilateral Agreement **287 UNTS 105**
SIGNED: 20 Sep 57   FORCE: 10 Jan 58
REGISTERED: 25 Feb 58 New Zealand
ARTICLES: 14 LANGUAGE: English.
HEADNOTE: CONTINUATION SOUTH PACIFIC
  HEALTH SERVICE
TOPIC: Sanitation
CONCEPTS: Definition of terms. Detailed regula-
  tions. Territorial application. Annex or appendix
  reference. Previous treaty extension. General co-
  operation. Exchange of information and docu-
  ments. Personnel. Establishment of commission.
  Quarantine. Disease control. Public health. Voca-
  tional training. Research and development. In-
  demnities and reimbursements. Expense sharing
  formulae. Conferences.
INTL ORGS: World Health Organization. South
  Pacific Health Service.
TREATY REF: 101UNTS82; 101UNTS77.
PROCEDURE: Amendment. Duration. Termination.
PARTIES:
  New Zealand
  UK Great Britain
              ANNEX
555 UNTS 253. New Zealand. Western Samoa.
  Force 7 Nov 64.
555 UNTS 253. UK Great Britain. W Pacif Hi Com-
  mand. Force 7 Nov 64.
555 UNTS 253. UK Great Britain. Tonga. Force
  7 Nov 64.
555 UNTS 253. UK Great Britain. Fiji Islands.
  Force 7 Nov 64.

104181 Bilateral Agreement **287 UNTS 121**
SIGNED: 22 Jan 56   FORCE: 8 Aug 57
REGISTERED: 27 Feb 58 Netherlands
ARTICLES: 18 LANGUAGE: English.
HEADNOTE: COOPERATION CONCERNING CIVIL
  USES ATOMIC ENERGY
TOPIC: Atomic Energy

CONCEPTS: Definition of terms. Previous treaty replacement. Exchange of information and documents. Inspection and observation. Research cooperation. Research results. Assets transfer. Nuclear materials. Peaceful use. Security of
  information.
TREATY REF: 240UNTS347.
PROCEDURE: Duration.
PARTIES:
  Netherlands
  USA (United States)
              ANNEX
358 UNTS 336.   Netherlands.   Amendment
  22 Jul 59. Force 30 Oct 59.
358 UNTS 336. USA (United States). Amendment
  22 Jul 59. Force 30 Oct 59.

104182 Bilateral Agreement **287 UNTS 159**
SIGNED: 28 Dec 54   FORCE: 23 Dec 54
REGISTERED: 3 Mar 58 Netherlands
ARTICLES: 9 LANGUAGE: French.
HEADNOTE: REPAYMENTS AMORTIZATION
TOPIC: Finance
CONCEPTS: Detailed regulations. Accounting pro-
  cedures. Banking. Bonds. Financial programs. In-
  terest rates. Payment schedules. Purchase au-
  thorization.
INTL ORGS: European Payments Union. Organiza-
  tion for Economic Co-operation and Develop-
  ment.
PARTIES:
  Iceland
  Netherlands
              ANNEX
487 UNTS 363. Iceland. Force 30 Apr 59.
487 UNTS 363. Netherlands. Force 30 Apr 59.

104183 Bilateral Agreement **287 UNTS 169**
SIGNED: 9 Jul 54   FORCE: 9 Jul 54
REGISTERED: 3 Mar 58 Netherlands
ARTICLES: 9 LANGUAGE: French.
HEADNOTE: REPAYMENT AMORTIZATION
TOPIC: Finance
CONCEPTS: Detailed regulations. Accounting pro-
  cedures. Banking. Currency. Financial programs.
  Interest rates. Payment schedules. Local cur-
  rency. Debt settlement. Purchase authorization.
INTL ORGS: European Payments Union. Organiza-
  tion for Economic Co-operation and Develop-
  ment.
PARTIES:
  France
  Netherlands
              ANNEX
486 UNTS 420. France. Force 29 Apr 59.
486 UNTS 420. Netherlands. Force 29 Apr 59.

104184 Bilateral Agreement **287 UNTS 179**
SIGNED: 9 Jun 54   FORCE: 9 Jul 54
REGISTERED: 3 Mar 58 Netherlands
ARTICLES: 15 LANGUAGE: French.
HEADNOTE: REPAYMENT AMORTIZATION
TOPIC: Finance
CONCEPTS: Detailed regulations. Accounting pro-
  cedures. Banking. Currency. Financial programs.
  Interest rates. Payment schedules. Local cur-
  rency. Debt settlement. Loan repayment.
INTL ORGS: European Payments Union. Organiza-
  tion for Economic Co-operation and Develop-
  ment.
PARTIES:
  Netherlands
  Norway
              ANNEX
487 UNTS 364. Netherlands. Force 30 Apr 59.
487 UNTS 364. Norway. Force 30 Apr 59.

104185 Bilateral Exchange **287 UNTS 193**
SIGNED: 29 Jun 56   FORCE: 29 Jun 56
REGISTERED: 3 Mar 58 Netherlands
ARTICLES: 2 LANGUAGE: French.
HEADNOTE: REPAYMENTS AMORTIZATION
TOPIC: Finance
CONCEPTS: Detailed regulations. Territorial appli-
  cation. Accounting procedures. Banking. Bonds.
  Financial programs. Interest rates. Payment
  schedules. Local currency. Debt settlement.
  Loan repayment.
INTL ORGS: European Payments Union. Organiza-

tion for Economic Co-operation and Development.
PARTIES:
  Italy
  Netherlands
              ANNEX
486 UNTS 421. Netherlands. Force 29 Apr 59.
486 UNTS 421. Italy. Force 29 Apr 59.

104186 Bilateral Exchange **287 UNTS 203**
SIGNED: 23 Oct 56   FORCE: 1 Dec 56
REGISTERED: 5 Mar 58 Netherlands
ARTICLES: 2 LANGUAGE: French.
HEADNOTE: LETTERS OF REQUEST
TOPIC: Admin Cooperation
CONCEPTS: Treaty interpretation. General cooper-
  ation.
TREATY REF: 50LTS180.
PARTIES:
  Netherlands
  Switzerland

104187 Multilateral Exchange **287 UNTS 209**
SIGNED: 29 Nov 54   FORCE: 8 May 57
REGISTERED: 5 Mar 58 Netherlands
ARTICLES: 5 LANGUAGE: French. Dutch.
HEADNOTE: LIBERALIZATION TRADE FISHING
  PRODUCTS
TOPIC: General Trade
CONCEPTS: Detailed regulations. Maritime prod-
  ucts and equipment. Trade agencies. Trade pro-
  cedures. Commodity trade. Delivery schedules.
  Quotas.
INTL ORGS: Benelux Economic Union. Special
  Commission.
PARTIES:
  Belgium SIGNED: 29 Nov 54 FORCE: 8 May 57
  Luxembourg   SIGNED: 9 Nov 54   FORCE:
    8 May 57
  Netherlands   SIGNED: 4 Nov 54   FORCE:
    8 May 57

104188 Multilateral Agreement **287 UNTS 223**
SIGNED: 16 Aug 56   FORCE: 8 May 57
REGISTERED: 5 Mar 58 Netherlands
ARTICLES: 6 LANGUAGE: French. Dutch.
HEADNOTE: LIBERALIZATION TRADE FISHING
  PRODUCTS
TOPIC: General Trade
CONCEPTS: Annex type material. Negotiation.
  Free trade. Maritime products and equipment.
  Reciprocity in trade. Transportation costs. Deliv-
  ery schedules. Smuggling. Customs duties.
  Transport of goods. Ports and pilotage.
TREATY REF: 287UNTS209.
PROCEDURE: Ratification.
PARTIES:
  Belgium SIGNED: 16 Aug 56 FORCE: 8 May 57
  Luxembourg   SIGNED: 16 Aug 56   FORCE:
    8 May 57
  Netherlands   SIGNED: 16 Aug 56   FORCE:
    8 May 57

104189 Bilateral Exchange **287 UNTS 233**
SIGNED: 25 Nov 57   FORCE: 25 Nov 57
REGISTERED: 5 Mar 58 UK Great Britain
ARTICLES: 2 LANGUAGE: English.
HEADNOTE: INHERITANCE   INTERNATIONAL
  RIGHTS OBLIGATIONS GHANA
TOPIC: Recognition
CONCEPTS: Continuity of rights and obligations.
PARTIES:
  Ghana
  UK Great Britain

104190 Bilateral Instrument **287 UNTS 239**
SIGNED: 15 Feb 57   FORCE: 15 Feb 57
REGISTERED: 7 Mar 58 Netherlands
ARTICLES: 9 LANGUAGE: English.
HEADNOTE: LEASE SPECIAL NUCLEAR MATERIAL
  (WITH APPENDIX)
TOPIC: Atomic Energy
CONCEPTS: Annex or appendix reference. Confor-
  mity with municipal law. Responsibility and lia-
  bility. Indemnities and reimbursements. Pay-
  ment schedules. Assets transfer. Nuclear materi-
  als.
TREATY REF: 240UNTS347; 240UNTS121.
PROCEDURE: Duration.

PARTIES:
Netherlands
USA (United States)

104191 Bilateral Instrument **287 UNTS 255**
SIGNED: 11 Jan 58 FORCE: 11 Jan 58
REGISTERED: 7 Mar 58 United Nations
ARTICLES: 2 LANGUAGE: English. French.
HEADNOTE: CLAIMS AGAINST UNICEF
TOPIC: Claims and Debts
CONCEPTS: Annex type material. Claims and settlements.
TREATY REF: 161UNTS323.
PARTIES:
Laos
UNICEF (Children)

104192 Bilateral Agreement **288 UNTS 3**
SIGNED: 20 Jan 58 FORCE: 20 Jan 58
REGISTERED: 10 Mar 58 Belgium
ARTICLES: 19 LANGUAGE: French.
HEADNOTE: AIR TRANSPORT
TOPIC: Air Transport
CONCEPTS: Definition of terms. Detailed regulations. Exceptions and exemptions. Annex or appendix reference. Conformity with municipal law. General cooperation. Licenses and permits. Recognition of legal documents. Use of facilities. Procedure. Negotiation. Fees and exemptions. Non-interest rates and fees. National treatment. Customs duties. Customs exemptions. Competency certificate. Routes and logistics. Navigational conditions. Permit designation. Air transport. Airport facilities. Airworthiness certificates. Conditions of airlines operating permission. Overflights and technical stops. Operating authorizations and regulations. Licenses and certificates of nationality.
INTL ORGS: International Civil Aviation Organization.
TREATY REF: 15UNTS295.
PROCEDURE: Amendment. Future Procedures Contemplated. Registration. Termination.
PARTIES:
Belgium
Morocco

104193 Bilateral Exchange **288 UNTS 23**
SIGNED: 11 Apr 57 FORCE: 12 Feb 58
REGISTERED: 10 Mar 58 Netherlands
ARTICLES: 2 LANGUAGE: Spanish.
HEADNOTE: RECOGNITION TONNAGE CERTIFICATES
TOPIC: Admin Cooperation
CONCEPTS: Recognition of legal documents. Tonnage.
PARTIES:
Netherlands
Venezuela

104194 Bilateral Exchange **288 UNTS 29**
SIGNED: 15 May 57 FORCE: 15 May 57
REGISTERED: 10 Mar 58 Netherlands
ARTICLES: 2 LANGUAGE: French.
HEADNOTE: EXEMPTION AIR TRANSPORT TAXES
TOPIC: Taxation
CONCEPTS: Definition of terms. Domestic legislation. Tax exemptions. Air transport.
PROCEDURE: Duration. Termination.
PARTIES:
Netherlands
United Arab Rep

104195 Bilateral Exchange **288 UNTS 37**
SIGNED: 15 Dec 54 FORCE: 12 Jul 55
REGISTERED: 10 Mar 58 Netherlands
ARTICLES: 8 LANGUAGE: French.
HEADNOTE: SETTLEMENT WAR FLOOD DAMAGE
TOPIC: Reparations
CONCEPTS: Definition of terms. Establishment of commission. Compensation. National treatment. Post-war claims settlement.
PARTIES:
France
Netherlands

104196 Bilateral Exchange **288 UNTS 47**
SIGNED: 26 Mar 57 FORCE: 12 Apr 57

REGISTERED: 11 Mar 58 Netherlands
ARTICLES: 2 LANGUAGE: French. Portuguese.
HEADNOTE: IDENTITY DOCUMENTS AIRCRAFT CREWS
TOPIC: Visas
CONCEPTS: Territorial application. Non-visa travel documents. Licenses and permits.
TREATY REF: 4UNTS317.
PARTIES:
Netherlands
Portugal

104197 Bilateral Exchange **288 UNTS 53**
SIGNED: 5 Mar 55 FORCE: 12 Jan 56
REGISTERED: 11 Mar 58 Netherlands
ARTICLES: 2 LANGUAGE: French.
HEADNOTE: INDUSTRIAL COMMERCIAL TRADEMARKS
TOPIC: Patents/Copyrights
CONCEPTS: Trademarks.
PARTIES:
Netherlands
Vietnam, South

104198 Bilateral Agreement **288 UNTS 59**
SIGNED: 12 Jul 54 FORCE: 12 Jul 54
REGISTERED: 13 Mar 58 Italy
ARTICLES: 9 LANGUAGE: French.
HEADNOTE: REPAYMENT AMORTIZATION
TOPIC: Finance
CONCEPTS: Detailed regulations. Annex or appendix reference. Standardization. General cooperation. Banking. Currency. Exchange rates and regulations. Fees and exemptions. Financial programs. Interest rates. Payment schedules. Debt settlement. Tax exemptions. Loan repayment.
INTL ORGS: European Payments Union. Organization for Economic Co-operation and Development.
PROCEDURE: Termination.
PARTIES:
Belgium
Italy

ANNEX
291 UNTS 370. Belgium. Supplementation 28 Jun 57. Force 1 Jul 57.
291 UNTS 370. Italy. Supplementation 28 Jun 57. Force 1 Jul 57.

104199 Bilateral Exchange **288 UNTS 83**
SIGNED: 28 Jun 54 FORCE: 28 Jun 54
REGISTERED: 13 Mar 58 Italy
ARTICLES: 2 LANGUAGE: French.
HEADNOTE: REPAYMENT EUROPEAN PAYMENTS UNION
TOPIC: Loans and Credits
CONCEPTS: Loan repayment.
INTL ORGS: European Payments Union. Organization for Economic Co-operation and Development.
PARTIES:
Germany, West
Italy

104200 Bilateral Agreement **288 UNTS 99**
SIGNED: 3 Dec 56 FORCE: 26 Apr 57
REGISTERED: 14 Mar 58 IBRD (World Bank)
ARTICLES: 7 LANGUAGE: English.
HEADNOTE: LOAN AGREEMENT
TOPIC: IBRD Project
CONCEPTS: Default remedies. Definition of terms. Annex or appendix reference. Exchange of information and documents. Informational records. Inspection and observation. Accounting procedures. Bonds. Fees and exemptions. Interest rates. Domestic obligation. Terms of loan. Loan regulations. Loan guarantee. Guarantor non-interference.
PARTIES:
Australia
IBRD (World Bank)

104201 Bilateral Agreement **288 UNTS 117**
SIGNED: 15 Nov 56 FORCE: 26 Apr 57
REGISTERED: 14 Mar 58 IBRD (World Bank)
ARTICLES: 7 LANGUAGE: English.
HEADNOTE: LOAN AGREEMENT
TOPIC: IBRD Project
CONCEPTS: Default remedies. Definition of terms.

Annex or appendix reference. Exchange of information and documents. Informational records. Inspection and observation. Accounting procedures. Bonds. Fees and exemptions. Interest rates. Domestic obligation. Terms of loan. Loan regulations. Loan guarantee. Guarantor non-interference.
PARTIES:
Australia
IBRD (World Bank)

104202 Bilateral Agreement **288 UNTS 135**
SIGNED: 12 Jul 57 FORCE: 7 Sep 57
REGISTERED: 14 Mar 58 IBRD (World Bank)
ARTICLES: 7 LANGUAGE: English.
HEADNOTE: LOAN AGREEMENT
TOPIC: IBRD Project
CONCEPTS: Default remedies. Definition of terms. Annex or appendix reference. Exchange of information and documents. Inspection and observation. Accounting procedures. Bonds. Fees and exemptions. Interest rates. Tax exemptions. Domestic obligation. Terms of loan. Loan regulations. Loan guarantee. Guarantor non-interference. Railways.
PARTIES:
India
IBRD (World Bank)

104203 Bilateral Exchange **288 UNTS 157**
SIGNED: 2 Apr 57 FORCE: 2 Apr 57
REGISTERED: 17 Mar 58 USA (United States)
ARTICLES: 2 LANGUAGE: English. French.
HEADNOTE: ECONOMIC TECHNICAL RELATED ASSISTANCE
TOPIC: General Aid
CONCEPTS: Change of circumstances. Privileges and immunities. Conformity with municipal law. General cooperation. Exchange of information and documents. Inspection and observation. Personnel. Public information. Accounting procedures. Funding procedures. Local currency. Assets. Tax exemptions. Customs exemptions. Commodities and services. Domestic obligation. General technical assistance. Economic assistance. Materials, equipment and services. Aid missions. Grants.
PROCEDURE: Termination.
PARTIES:
Morocco
USA (United States)

ANNEX
317 UNTS 354. USA (United States). Supplementation 19 May 58. Force 19 May 58.
317 UNTS 354. Morocco. Supplementation 19 May 58. Force 19 May 58.

104204 Bilateral Exchange **288 UNTS 165**
SIGNED: 9 Oct 56 FORCE: 26 Sep 56
REGISTERED: 17 Mar 58 USA (United States)
ARTICLES: 3 LANGUAGE: English. Spanish.
HEADNOTE: PASSPORT VISA FEES
TOPIC: Visas
CONCEPTS: Time limit. Visas.
PARTIES:
Peru
USA (United States)

104205 Bilateral Agreement **288 UNTS 181**
SIGNED: 15 Aug 56 FORCE: 22 Apr 57
REGISTERED: 17 Mar 58 USA (United States)
ARTICLES: 11 LANGUAGE: English. Spanish.
HEADNOTE: COOPERATION CONCERNING CIVIL USES ATOMIC ENERGY
TOPIC: Atomic Energy
CONCEPTS: Definition of terms. Non-prejudice to third party. Exchange of information and documents. Inspection and observation. Responsibility and liability. Research cooperation. Research results. Assets transfer. Nuclear materials. Non-nuclear materials. Security of information.
PROCEDURE: Duration.
PARTIES:
Guatemala
USA (United States)

104206 Bilateral Exchange **288 UNTS 201**
SIGNED: 22 Mar 57 FORCE: 21 Apr 57
REGISTERED: 17 Mar 58 USA (United States)

ARTICLES: 2 LANGUAGE: English. Japanese.
HEADNOTE: PASSPORT VISAS
TOPIC: Visas
CONCEPTS: Visas. Fees and exemptions.
PARTIES:
  Japan
  USA (United States)

104207   Bilateral Agreement   **288 UNTS 219**
SIGNED: 24 Apr 57   FORCE: 24 Apr 57
REGISTERED: 17 Mar 58 USA (United States)
ARTICLES: 17 LANGUAGE: English. Korean.
HEADNOTE: AIR TRANSPORT
TOPIC: Air Transport
CONCEPTS: Definition of terms. Detailed regula-
  tions. Annex or appendix reference. Conformity
  with municipal law. Licenses and permits. Use of
  facilities. Fees and exemptions. Customs exemp-
  tions. Competency certificate. Routes and logis-
  tics. Navigational conditions. Permit designa-
  tion. Airport facilities. Airworthiness certificates.
  Conditions of airlines operating permission.
  Overflights and technical stops. Operating au-
  thorizations and regulations. Licenses and cer-
  tificates of nationality.
INTL ORGS: International Civil Aviation Organiza-
  tion. International Court of Justice. Arbitration
  Commission.
TREATY REF: 151NTS295.
PROCEDURE: Amendment. Future Procedures
  Contemplated. Registration. Termination. Appli-
  cation to Non-self-governing Territories.
PARTIES:
  Korea, South
  USA (United States)

104208   Bilateral Exchange   **288 UNTS 263**
SIGNED: 29 Jun 57   FORCE: 29 Jun 57
REGISTERED: 17 Mar 58 USA (United States)
ARTICLES: 2 LANGUAGE: English. Arabic.
HEADNOTE: ECONOMIC ASSISTANCE
TOPIC: Direct Aid
CONCEPTS: Treaty implementation. Conformity
  with municipal law. Financial programs. Eco-
  nomic assistance.
PARTIES:
  Jordan
  USA (United States)

104209   Bilateral Exchange   **288 UNTS 269**
SIGNED: 27 Jun 57   FORCE: 1 Jul 57
REGISTERED: 17 Mar 58 USA (United States)
ARTICLES: 2 LANGUAGE: English. Arabic.
HEADNOTE: ECONOMIC TECHNICAL RELATED
  ASSISTANCE
TOPIC: General Aid
CONCEPTS: Exceptions and exemptions. Previous
  treaty replacement. Exchange of information
  and documents. Inspection and observation. Per-
  sonnel. Public information. Accounting proce-
  dures. Indemnities and reimbursements. Cur-
  rency deposits. Exchange rates and regulations.
  Funding procedures. Interest rates. Local cur-
  rency. Assets. Tax exemptions. Customs exemp-
  tions. Commodities and services. Domestic obligation. General technical assistance. Economic
  assistance. Materials, equipment and services.
  Aid missions.
PROCEDURE: Termination.
PARTIES:
  Jordan
  USA (United States)

104210   Bilateral Convention   **288 UNTS 285**
SIGNED: 12 Mar 61   FORCE: 1 Apr 51
REGISTERED: 17 Mar 58 USA (United States)
ARTICLES: 20 LANGUAGE: English.
HEADNOTE: EXCHANGE MONEY ORDERS
TOPIC: Postal Service
CONCEPTS: Accounting procedures. Currency. Ex-
  change rates and regulations. Payment sched-
  ules. Postal services. Regulations. Money orders
  and postal checks. Rates and charges. Advice
  lists and orders.
PROCEDURE: Duration. Termination.
PARTIES:
  Philippines
  USA (United States)

104211   Bilateral Exchange   **288 UNTS 299**
SIGNED: 9 Aug 57   FORCE: 9 Aug 57
REGISTERED: 17 Mar 58 USA (United States)
ARTICLES: 2 LANGUAGE: English.
HEADNOTE: MILITARY EQUIPMENT MATERIALS
  SERVICES
TOPIC: Milit Assistance
CONCEPTS: Exceptions and exemptions. Confor-
  mity with municipal law. Materials, equipment
  and services. Self-defense. Security of informa-
  tion. Exchange of defense information. Restric-
  tions on transfer.
PROCEDURE: Termination.
PARTIES:
  Austria
  USA (United States)

104212   Bilateral Agreement   **288 UNTS 305**
SIGNED: 3 Jul 57   FORCE: 7 Aug 57
REGISTERED: 17 Mar 58 USA (United States)
ARTICLES: 13 LANGUAGE: English. German.
HEADNOTE: COOPERATION CIVIL USES ATOMIC
  ENERGY
TOPIC: Atomic Energy
CONCEPTS: Definition of terms. Previous treaty re-
  placement. Non-prejudice to third party. Confor-
  mity with municipal law. Exchange of informa-
  tion and documents. Inspection and observation.
  Responsibility and liability. Investigation of viola-
  tions. Research cooperation. Assets transfer. Nuclear materials. Non-nuclear materials. Peaceful
  use. Security of information.
INTL ORGS: European Atomic Energy Commission.
TREATY REF: 253UNTS119.
PROCEDURE: Duration.
PARTIES:
  Germany, West
  USA (United States)
ANNEX
358 UNTS 344. USA (United States). Amendment
  22 Jul 59. Force 22 Sep 59.
358 UNTS 344. Germany, West. Amendment
  22 Jul 59. Force 22 Sep 59.
458 UNTS 322. USA (United States). Amendment
  15 Jul 62. Force 7 Aug 62.
458 UNTS 322. Germany, West. Amendment
  15 Jul 62. Force 7 Aug 62.

104213   Bilateral Agreement   **288 UNTS 339**
SIGNED: 28 Jun 57   FORCE: 1 Aug 57
REGISTERED: 17 Mar 58 USA (United States)
ARTICLES: 11 LANGUAGE: English. German.
HEADNOTE: COOPERATION CIVIL USES ATOMIC
  ENERGY
TOPIC: Atomic Energy
CONCEPTS: Definition of terms. Annex or appen-
  dix reference. Non-prejudice to third party. Con-
  formity with municipal law. Exchange of informa-
  tion and documents. Inspection and observation.
  Responsibility and liability. Research cooper-
  ation. Assets transfer. Nuclear materials. Non-
  nuclear materials. Peaceful use. Security of infor-
  mation.
PROCEDURE: Duration.
PARTIES:
  Germany, West
  USA (United States)
ANNEX
453 UNTS 380. USA (United States). Amendment
  29 Jun 62. Force 30 Jul 62.
453 UNTS 380. Germany, West. Amendment
  29 Jun 62. Force 30 Jul 62.

104214   Multilateral Convention   **289 UNTS 3**
SIGNED: 6 Mar 48   FORCE: 17 Mar 58
REGISTERED: 17 Mar 58 United Nations
ARTICLES: 63 LANGUAGE: English. French. Spanish.
HEADNOTE: INTERGOVERNMENTAL MARITIME
  CONSULTATIVE ORGANIZATION
TOPIC: Water Transport
CONCEPTS: Detailed regulations. Territorial application. Treaty interpretation. Annex or appendix
  reference. General cooperation. Exchange of information and documents. Informational
  records. Personnel. Procedure. Negotiation.
  Funding procedures. Transport of goods. Operating authorizations and regulations. Water
  transport. Merchant vessels. Shipwreck and salvage. Establishment. Procedure. Headquarters

and facilities. IGO status. Special status. Confer-
  ences. Inter-agency agreements. Acceptance of
  UN obligations. Optional clause ICJ.
INTL ORGS: International Court of Justice. Inter-
  Governmental Maritime Consultative Organiza-
  tion. United Nations.
TREATY REF: 331NTS261.
PROCEDURE: Amendment. Accession. Registra-
  tion. Termination.
PARTIES:
  Argentina   SIGNED: 6 Mar 48   RATIFIED:
    18 Jun 53 FORCE: 17 Mar 58
  Australia   SIGNED: 6 Mar 48   RATIFIED:
    13 Feb 52 FORCE: 17 Mar 58
  Belgium SIGNED: 6 Mar 48 RATIFIED: 9 Aug 51
    FORCE: 17 Mar 58
  Chile SIGNED: 6 Mar 48
  Colombia SIGNED: 6 Mar 48
  United Arab Rep SIGNED: 6 Mar 48
  France SIGNED: 6 Mar 48 RATIFIED: 9 Apr 52
    FORCE: 17 Mar 58
  Greece SIGNED: 6 Mar 48
  India SIGNED: 6 Mar 48
  Ireland SIGNED: 6 Mar 48 RATIFIED: 26 Feb 51
    FORCE: 17 Mar 58
  Israel RATIFIED: 20 Apr 52 FORCE: 17 Mar 58
  Italy SIGNED: 6 Mar 48 RATIFIED: 28 Jan 57
    FORCE: 17 Mar 58
  Japan RATIFIED: 17 Mar 58 FORCE: 17 Mar 58
  Lebanon SIGNED: 6 Mar 48
  Netherlands Netherlands Antilles RATIFIED:
    12 Jul 51 FORCE: 17 Mar 58
  Netherlands Dutch New Guinea RATIFIED:
    12 Jul 51 FORCE: 17 Mar 58
  Netherlands   SIGNED: 6 Mar 48   RATIFIED:
    31 Mar 49 FORCE: 17 Mar 58
  Netherlands Surinam RATIFIED: 12 Jul 51
    FORCE: 17 Mar 58
  Poland SIGNED: 6 Mar 48
  Portugal SIGNED: 6 Mar 48
  Switzerland   SIGNED: 6 Mar 48   RATIFIED:
    20 Jul 55 FORCE: 17 Mar 58
  Turkey SIGNED: 6 Mar 48
  United Arab Rep RATIFIED: 17 Mar 58 FORCE:
    17 Mar 58
  UK Great Britain SIGNED: 6 Mar 48 RATIFIED:
    14 Feb 49 FORCE: 17 Mar 58
  USA (United States) SIGNED: 6 Mar 48 RATI-
    FIED: 17 Aug 50 FORCE: 17 Mar 58
ANNEX
304 UNTS 394. Taiwan. Acceptance 1 Jul 58.
315 UNTS 246. Pakistan. Acceptance 21 Nov 58.
317 UNTS 359. Norway. Qualified Acceptance
  29 Dec 58.
317 UNTS 359. USSR (Soviet Union). Acceptance
  24 Dec 58.
318 UNTS 427. Greece. Acceptance 31 Dec 58.
318 UNTS 427. Panama. Acceptance 31 Dec 58.
320 UNTS 350. Turkey. Qualified Accession
  25 Mar 58.
320 UNTS 350. Liberia. Acceptance 6 Jan 59.
320 UNTS 350. Germany, West. Signature without Reservation as to Approval 7 Jan 59.
327 UNTS 383. Finland. Qualified Accession
  21 Apr 59.
327 UNTS 383. Sweden. Qualified Accession
  27 Apr 59.
328 UNTS 339. Denmark. Qualified Accession
  3 Jun 59.
337 UNTS 433. Ghana. Acceptance 6 Jul 59.
348 UNTS 370. UK Great Britain. Nigeria.
349 UNTS 346. Yugoslavia. Qualified Acceptance
  12 Feb 60.
351 UNTS 446.   India.   Qualified   Accession
  6 Jan 59.
354 UNTS 425. Bulgaria. Acceptance 5 Apr 60.
354 UNTS 425. Poland. Qualified Acceptance
  16 Mar 60.
363 UNTS 407. Kuwait. Acceptance 5 Jul 60.
379 UNTS 437.   Ivory   Coast.   Acceptance
  4 Nov 60.
379 UNTS 437. Senegal. Acceptance 7 Nov 60.
379 UNTS 437. Iceland. Qualified Acceptance
  8 Nov 60.
379 UNTS 437.   New   Zealand.   Acceptance
  9 Nov 60.
383 UNTS 316. Cambodia. Qualified Acceptance
  3 Jan 61.
386 UNTS 410. Indonesia. Qualified Accession
  18 Jan 61.
390 UNTS 365.   Madagascar.   Acceptance
  8 Mar 61.
395 UNTS 272.   Cameroon.   Acceptance
  1 May 61.

395 UNTS 272. Mauritius. Acceptance 8 May 61.
410 UNTS 329. UK Great Britain. Sarawak.
410 UNTS 329. UK Great Britain. North Borneo.
420 UNTS 350. Spain. Qualified Accession 23 Jan 62.
424 UNTS 360. Nigeria. Acceptance 15 Mar 62.
425 UNTS 354. Korea, South. Acceptance 10 Apr 62.
434 UNTS 336. Morocco. Qualified Accession 30 Jul 62.
452 UNTS 340. Syria. Acceptance 28 Jan 63.
455 UNTS 443. Brazil. Acceptance 4 Mar 63.
466 UNTS 402. Tunisia. Acceptance 23 May 63.
479 UNTS 369. Czechoslovakia. Acceptance 10 Oct 63.
480 UNTS 371. Algeria. Acceptance 31 Oct 63.
506 UNTS 380. UK Great Britain. Declaration 6 Aug 64.
515 UNTS 307. Philippines. Acceptance 9 Nov 64.
533 UNTS 342. Romania. Acceptance 28 Apr 65.
533 UNTS 342. Trinidad/Tobago. Acceptance 27 Apr 65.
547 UNTS 321. Indonesia. Withdrawal 9 Oct 65. Force 9 Oct 66.
551 UNTS 302. Singapore. Acceptance 17 Jan 66.
561 UNTS 349. Lebanon. Acceptance 3 May 66.
561 UNTS 349. Lebanon. Acceptance 3 May 66.
561 UNTS 349. Cuba. Acceptance 6 May 66.
561 UNTS 349. Cuba. Qualified Accession 6 May 66.
565 UNTS 291. Malta. Signature without Reservation as to Approval 22 Jun 66.
607 UNTS 276. IMCO (Maritime Org). Amendment 15 Sep 64. Force 6 Oct 67.
609 UNTS 277. Algeria. Acceptance 3 Nov 67.
613 UNTS 415. Nigeria. Acceptance 11 Dec 67.
636 UNTS 364. Uruguay. Signature 10 May 68.
649 UNTS 334. Netherlands. Acceptance 15 May 67. Force 3 Nov 68.
649 UNTS 334. Morocco. Acceptance 27 Jan 66. Force 3 Nov 68.
649 UNTS 334. Switzerland. Acceptance 13 Jan 67. Force 3 Nov 68.
649 UNTS 334. Lebanon. Acceptance 22 Feb 67. Force 3 Nov 68.
649 UNTS 334. Turkey. Acceptance 9 Jun 67. Force 3 Nov 68.
649 UNTS 334. Yugoslavia. Acceptance 28 Nov 68. Force 3 Nov 68.
649 UNTS 334. Germany, West. Acceptance 22 Jul 66. Force 3 Nov 68.
649 UNTS 334. Madagascar. Acceptance 27 Jan 66. Force 3 Nov 68.
649 UNTS 334. Poland. Acceptance 19 Aug 66. Force 3 Nov 68.
649 UNTS 334. France. Acceptance 14 Mar 66. Force 3 Nov 68.
649 UNTS 334. Romania. Acceptance 27 Jul 67. Force 3 Nov 68.
649 UNTS 334. Korea, South. Acceptance 10 Jan 67. Force 3 Nov 68.
649 UNTS 334. Spain. Acceptance 18 Feb 66. Force 3 Nov 68.
649 UNTS 334. Ivory Coast. Acceptance 20 Mar 67. Force 3 Nov 68.
649 UNTS 334. Singapore. Acceptance 18 Feb 66. Force 3 Nov 68.
649 UNTS 334. Norway. Acceptance 23 May 66. Force 3 Nov 68.
649 UNTS 334. Iceland. Acceptance 13 Mar 67. Force 3 Nov 68.
649 UNTS 334. Kuwait. Acceptance 6 Sep 68. Force 3 Nov 68.
649 UNTS 334. Israel. Acceptance 9 Feb 67. Force 3 Nov 68.
649 UNTS 334. Czechoslovakia. Acceptance 6 Oct 66. Force 3 Nov 68.
649 UNTS 334. Brazil. Acceptance 30 Dec 66. Force 3 Nov 68.
649 UNTS 334. Finland. Acceptance 20 Jan 67. Force 3 Nov 68.
649 UNTS 334. Ireland. Acceptance 23 Jun 66. Force 3 Nov 68.
649 UNTS 334. Algeria. Acceptance 3 Nov 67. Force 3 Nov 68.
649 UNTS 334. Australia. Acceptance 23 Jun 66. Force 3 Nov 68.
649 UNTS 334. Canada. Acceptance 29 Apr 66. Force 3 Nov 68.
649 UNTS 334. China. Acceptance 27 Apr 66. Force 3 Nov 68.

649 UNTS 334. Denmark. Acceptance 15 Nov 66. Force 3 Nov 68.
649 UNTS 334. India. Acceptance 13 Oct 66. Force 3 Nov 68.
649 UNTS 334. Argentina. Acceptance 5 Oct 66. Force 3 Nov 68.
649 UNTS 334. Belgium. Acceptance 6 Jun 66. Force 3 Nov 68.
649 UNTS 334. Bulgaria. Acceptance 3 Oct 66. Force 3 Nov 68.
649 UNTS 334. USSR (Soviet Union). Acceptance 7 Mar 66. Force 3 Nov 68.
649 UNTS 334. UK Great Britain. Acceptance 23 May 66. Force 3 Nov 68.
649 UNTS 334. Tunisia. Acceptance 23 Feb 66. Force 3 Nov 68.
649 UNTS 334. Nigeria. Acceptance 11 Dec 67. Force 3 Nov 68.
649 UNTS 334. USA (United States). Acceptance 1 Feb 68. Force 3 Nov 68.
649 UNTS 334. Malta. Acceptance 28 Sep 66. Force 3 Nov 68.
649 UNTS 334. United Arab Rep. Acceptance 15 Feb 67. Force 3 Nov 68.
649 UNTS 334. Maldive Islands. Acceptance 22 Apr 68. Force 3 Nov 68.
649 UNTS 334. Mexico. Acceptance 16 Oct 67. Force 3 Nov 68.
649 UNTS 334. Pakistan. Acceptance 5 Jul 66. Force 3 Nov 68.
649 UNTS 334. Philippines. Acceptance 2 Nov 66. Force 3 Nov 68.
649 UNTS 334. Trinidad/Tobago. Acceptance 20 Apr 67. Force 3 Nov 68.
649 UNTS 334. Panama. Acceptance 2 Aug 66. Force 3 Nov 68.
649 UNTS 334. Sweden. Acceptance 26 Jul 66. Force 3 Nov 68.
649 UNTS 334. Ghana. Acceptance 21 Nov 66. Force 3 Nov 68.
658 UNTS 437. Saudi Arabia. Acceptance 25 Feb 69.

104215 Multilateral Protocol **289 UNTS 111**
SIGNED: 10 May 48   FORCE: 20 Jul 51
REGISTERED: 18 Mar 58 United Nations
ARTICLES: 4 LANGUAGE: French.
HEADNOTE: MODIFYING CONVENTION INTERNATIONAL EXHIBITION
TOPIC: Culture
CONCEPTS: Annex or appendix reference.
INTL ORGS: International Exhibition Bureau.
TREATY REF: 111LTS343; 130LTS464; 266UNTS443.
PARTIES:
Austria RATIFIED: 9 Jan 57 FORCE: 9 Jan 57
Belgium SIGNED: 10 May 48 RATIFIED: 20 Jul 51 FORCE: 20 Jul 51
Canada RATIFIED: 8 Nov 57 FORCE: 8 Nov 57
Denmark SIGNED: 10 May 48 RATIFIED: 5 May 49 FORCE: 5 May 49
Finland SIGNED: 10 May 48 RATIFIED: 1 Oct 53 FORCE: 1 Oct 53
France SIGNED: 10 May 48 RATIFIED: 20 Jun 49 FORCE: 20 Jun 49
Germany, West RATIFIED: 16 Mar 57 FORCE: 16 Mar 57
Greece SIGNED: 10 May 48 RATIFIED: 6 May 53 FORCE: 6 May 53
Haiti SIGNED: 10 May 48 RATIFIED: 18 Aug 51 FORCE: 18 Aug 51
Israel RATIFIED: 31 May 52 FORCE: 30 Jun 52
Italy SIGNED: 10 May 48 RATIFIED: 26 Dec 52 FORCE: 26 Dec 52
Lebanon SIGNED: 10 May 48 RATIFIED: 9 Sep 53 FORCE: 9 Sep 53
Morocco SIGNED: 10 May 48 RATIFIED: 20 Jul 55 FORCE: 20 Jul 55
Netherlands RATIFIED: 8 Jan 51 FORCE: 8 Feb 51
New Zealand RATIFIED: 12 Jul 50 FORCE: 12 Aug 50
Norway SIGNED: 10 May 48 RATIFIED: 25 Nov 49 FORCE: 25 Nov 49
Portugal SIGNED: 10 May 48 RATIFIED: 10 Aug 55 FORCE: 10 Aug 55
Sweden SIGNED: 10 May 48 RATIFIED: 19 Apr 50 FORCE: 19 Apr 50
Switzerland SIGNED: 10 May 48 RATIFIED: 23 Apr 51 FORCE: 23 Apr 51
Tunisia RATIFIED: 20 Jul 55 FORCE: 20 Jul 55
UK Great Britain Aden RATIFIED: 15 Dec 50 FORCE: 15 Jan 51

UK Great Britain Barbados RATIFIED: 15 Dec 50 FORCE: 15 Jan 51
UK Great Britain British Guiana RATIFIED: 15 Dec 50 FORCE: 15 Jan 51
UK Great Britain British Honduras RATIFIED: 15 Dec 50 FORCE: 15 Jan 51
UK Great Britain Brunei RATIFIED: 15 Dec 50 FORCE: 15 Jan 51
UK Great Britain Falkland Islands RATIFIED: 15 Dec 50 FORCE: 15 Jan 51
UK Great Britain Fiji Islands RATIFIED: 15 Dec 50 FORCE: 15 Jan 51
UK Great Britain Fed of Malaya RATIFIED: 15 Dec 50 FORCE: 15 Jan 51
UK Great Britain Gambia RATIFIED: 15 Dec 50 FORCE: 15 Jan 51
UK Great Britain Gibralter RATIFIED: 15 Dec 50 FORCE: 15 Jan 51
UK Great Britain Gold Coast RATIFIED: 15 Dec 50 FORCE: 15 Jan 51
UK Great Britain Hong Kong RATIFIED: 15 Dec 50 FORCE: 15 Jan 51
UK Great Britain Leeward Islands RATIFIED: 15 Dec 50 FORCE: 15 Jan 51
UK Great Britain Malta RATIFIED: 15 Dec 50 FORCE: 15 Jan 51
UK Great Britain Mauritius RATIFIED: 15 Dec 50 FORCE: 15 Jan 51
UK Great Britain Nigeria RATIFIED: 15 Dec 50 FORCE: 15 Jan 51
UK Great Britain North Borneo RATIFIED: 15 Dec 50 FORCE: 15 Jan 51
UK Great Britain Northern Rhodesia RATIFIED: 15 Dec 50 FORCE: 15 Jan 51
UK Great Britain Nyasaland RATIFIED: 15 Dec 50 FORCE: 15 Jan 51
UK Great Britain RATIFIED: 2 Sep 49 FORCE: 2 Oct 49
UK Great Britain Sarawak RATIFIED: 15 Dec 50 FORCE: 15 Jan 51
UK Great Britain Seychelles RATIFIED: 15 Dec 50 FORCE: 15 Jan 51
UK Great Britain Sierra Leone RATIFIED: 15 Dec 50 FORCE: 15 Jan 51
UK Great Britain Singapore RATIFIED: 15 Dec 50 FORCE: 15 Jan 51
UK Great Britain Somalia RATIFIED: 15 Dec 50 FORCE: 15 Jan 51
UK Great Britain St. Helena RATIFIED: 15 Dec 50 FORCE: 15 Jan 51
UK Great Britain Tanganyika RATIFIED: 15 Dec 50 FORCE: 15 Jan 51
UK Great Britain Trinidad/Tobago RATIFIED: 15 Dec 50 FORCE: 15 Jan 51
UK Great Britain Uganda RATIFIED: 15 Dec 50 FORCE: 15 Jan 51
UK Great Britain Windward Islands RATIFIED: 15 Dec 50 FORCE: 15 Jan 51
UK Great Britain W Pacif Hi Command RATIFIED: 15 Dec 50 FORCE: 15 Jan 51
UK Great Britain Zanzibar RATIFIED: 15 Dec 50 FORCE: 15 Jan 51

104216 Bilateral Exchange **289 UNTS 121**
SIGNED: 14 Dec 54   FORCE: 7 Apr 55
REGISTERED: 18 Mar 58 Netherlands
ARTICLES: 2 LANGUAGE: French. Portuguese.
HEADNOTE: RECIPROCAL ABOLITION VISAS
TOPIC: Visas
CONCEPTS: Emergencies. Visa abolition. Denial of admission. Resident permits. Conformity with municipal law.
PROCEDURE: Denunciation.
PARTIES:
Netherlands
Portugal

104217 Bilateral Exchange **289 UNTS 129**
SIGNED: 21 Mar 55   FORCE: 21 Mar 55
REGISTERED: 18 Mar 58 Netherlands
ARTICLES: 2 LANGUAGE: English.
HEADNOTE: US RADIO EQUIPMENT NETHERLANDS WEATHER SHIP
TOPIC: Telecommunications
CONCEPTS: Materials, equipment and services. Navigational equipment. Merchant vessels. Facilities and equipment.
PARTIES:
Netherlands
USA (United States)

104218 Bilateral Convention **289 UNTS 144**
SIGNED: 28 Oct 52 FORCE: 1 Jan 55
REGISTERED: 18 Mar 58 Netherlands
ARTICLES: 38 LANGUAGE: French.
HEADNOTE: SOCIAL INSURANCE
TOPIC: Non-ILO Labor
CONCEPTS: General provisions. Conformity with
municipal law. Domestic legislation. Dispute set-
tlement. Old age and invalidity insurance.
Wages and salaries. Non-ILO labor relations.
Family allowances. Old age insurance. Sickness
and invalidity insurance. Social security. Unem-
ployment. Payment schedules. National treat-
ment.
PROCEDURE: Denunciation. Duration. Future Pro-
cedures Contemplated. Ratification. Renewal or
Revival.
PARTIES:
Italy
Netherlands

104219 Bilateral Exchange **289 UNTS 221**
SIGNED: 4 Dec 54 FORCE: 12 Apr 55
REGISTERED: 18 Mar 58 Netherlands
ARTICLES: 2 LANGUAGE: English.
HEADNOTE: RELEASE DUTCH ASSETS INDIA
TOPIC: Reparations
CONCEPTS: General cooperation. Assets. Claims
and settlements. Debt settlement. Assets trans-
fer. Enemy financial interests.
PARTIES:
India
Netherlands

104220 Bilateral Exchange **289 UNTS 227**
SIGNED: 25 May 55 FORCE: 24 Jun 55
REGISTERED: 18 Mar 58 Netherlands
ARTICLES: 2 LANGUAGE: English.
HEADNOTE: RETURN SILVER SUPPLIED UNDER
LEND-LEASE
TOPIC: Claims and Debts
CONCEPTS: Detailed regulations. Monetary and
gold transfers. Fees and exemptions. Debt settle-
ment. Lend lease.
PARTIES:
Netherlands
USA (United States)

104221 Bilateral Agreement **289 UNTS 237**
SIGNED: 20 Sep 57 FORCE: 3 Jan 58
REGISTERED: 18 Mar 58 IBRD (World Bank)
ARTICLES: 8 LANGUAGE: English.
HEADNOTE: LOAN AGREEMENT
TOPIC: IBRD Project
CONCEPTS: Default remedies. Definition of terms.
Annex or appendix reference. Exchange of infor-
mation and documents. Informational records.
Inspection and observation. Accounting proce-
dures. Bonds. Fees and exemptions. Interest
rates. Tax exemptions. Domestic obligation.
Terms of loan. Loan regulations. Loan guarantee.
Guarantor non-interference. Roads and high-
ways.
PARTIES:
Ecuador
IBRD (World Bank)

104222 Bilateral Agreement **289 UNTS 261**
SIGNED: 4 Jun 54 FORCE: 4 Jun 54
REGISTERED: 19 Mar 58 Netherlands
ARTICLES: 14 LANGUAGE: French.
HEADNOTE: EXCHANGE STUDENT EMPLOYEES
TOPIC: Non-ILO Labor
CONCEPTS: Definition of terms. Resident permits.
Conformity with municipal law. Exchange of in-
formation and documents. Dispute settlement.
Vocational training. Employment regulations.
Wages and salaries. Non-ILO labor relations. Ad-
ministrative cooperation. Migrant worker.
Bonds. National treatment.
PROCEDURE: Denunciation. Duration. Renewal or
Revival.
PARTIES:
Italy
Netherlands

104223 Bilateral Exchange **289 UNTS 271**
SIGNED: 19 Jul 57 FORCE: 19 Jul 57
REGISTERED: 19 Mar 58 USA (United States)

ARTICLES: 2 LANGUAGE: English.
HEADNOTE: DROUGHT RELIEF ASSISTANCE
TOPIC: Direct Aid
CONCEPTS: Conformity with municipal law. Public
information. Local currency. Assets. Relief sup-
plies. Grants. Distribution. Transport of goods.
PARTIES:
Peru
USA (United States)

104224 Bilateral Agreement **289 UNTS 279**
SIGNED: 25 Jun 57 FORCE: 25 Jun 57
REGISTERED: 19 Mar 58 USA (United States)
ARTICLES: 6 LANGUAGE: English.
HEADNOTE: AGRI COMMOD TITLE I
TOPIC: US Agri Commod Aid
CONCEPTS: General cooperation. Exchange of in-
formation and documents. Reexport of goods,
etc.. Currency deposits. Exchange rates and reg-
ulations. Purchase authorizations. Transporta-
tion costs. Local currency. Commodities sched-
ule. Surplus commodities.
PARTIES:
Philippines
USA (United States)

104225 Bilateral Exchange **289 UNTS 289**
SIGNED: 18 Jun 57 FORCE: 18 Jun 57
REGISTERED: 19 Mar 58 USA (United States)
ARTICLES: 4 LANGUAGE: English.
HEADNOTE: USE MANILA AIR STATION
TOPIC: Milit Installation
CONCEPTS: Military installations and equipment.
PARTIES:
Philippines
USA (United States)
ANNEX
307 UNTS 326. Philippines. Supplementation
27 Jan 58. Force 27 Jan 58.
307 UNTS 326. USA (United States). Supplemen-
tation 27 Jan 58. Force 27 Jan 58.
335 UNTS 334. Philippines. Amendment
31 Jul 58. Force 31 Jul 58.
335 UNTS 334. USA (United States). Amendment
31 Jul 58. Force 31 Jul 58.

104226 Bilateral Exchange **289 UNTS 301**
SIGNED: 28 Jun 57 FORCE: 28 Jun 57
REGISTERED: 19 Mar 58 USA (United States)
ARTICLES: 2 LANGUAGE: English. French.
HEADNOTE: CHILD FEEDING PROGRAM
TOPIC: Direct Aid
CONCEPTS: Time limit. Annex or appendix refer-
ence. Conformity with municipal law. Exchange
of information and documents. Informational
records. Inspection and observation. Public in-
formation. Jurisdiction. Expense sharing formu-
lae. Transportation costs. Assistance. General
aid. Grants. Distribution. Surplus commodities.
PARTIES:
Tunisia
USA (United States)

104227 Bilateral Agreement **290 UNTS 3**
SIGNED: 29 Sep 50 FORCE: 1 Oct 50
REGISTERED: 19 Mar 58 USA (United States)
ARTICLES: 27 LANGUAGE: English. Czechoslo-
vakian.
HEADNOTE: PARCEL POST
TOPIC: Postal Service
CONCEPTS: Detailed regulations. Previous treaty
replacement. Domestic legislation. Responsibil-
ity and liability. Compensation. Indemnities and
reimbursements. Payment schedules. Customs
duties. Customs exemptions. Postal services.
Regulations. Insured letters and boxes. Convey-
ance in transit. Parcel post. Rates and charges.
INTL ORGS: Universal Postal Union.
TREATY REF: 169UNTS3; 186UNTS356;
202UNTS340; 227UNTS390.
PROCEDURE: Duration. Termination.
PARTIES:
Czechoslovakia
USA (United States)

104228 Bilateral Agreement **290 UNTS 59**
SIGNED: 16 Mar 57 FORCE: 1 Aug 57
REGISTERED: 19 Mar 58 USA (United States)
ARTICLES: 30 LANGUAGE: English.

HEADNOTE: PARCEL POST
TOPIC: Postal Service
CONCEPTS: Detailed regulations. Previous treaty
replacement. Conformity with municipal law. Responsibility and liability. Compensation. Payment schedules. Customs duties. Customs exemptions. Postal services. Regulations. Insured
letters and boxes. Conveyance in transit. Parcel
post. Rates and charges.
INTL ORGS: Universal Postal Union.
TREATY REF: 169UNTS3; 186UNTS356;
202UNTS340; 227UNTS390.
PARTIES:
Liberia
USA (United States)

104229 Bilateral Protocol **290 UNTS 103**
SIGNED: 28 Dec 56 FORCE: 3 Jul 57
REGISTERED: 19 Mar 58 USA (United States)
ARTICLES: 8 LANGUAGE: English.
HEADNOTE: SOCKEYE SALMON FISHERIES
TOPIC: Specific Resources
CONCEPTS: Annex type material. Inspection and
observation. Fisheries and fishing.
INTL ORGS: Special Commission.
TREATY REF: 184LTS305.
PROCEDURE: Ratification.
PARTIES:
Canada
USA (United States)

104230 Bilateral Exchange **290 UNTS 111**
SIGNED: 29 Apr 57 FORCE: 29 Apr 57
REGISTERED: 19 Mar 58 USA (United States)
ARTICLES: 3 LANGUAGE: English. Arabic.
HEADNOTE: ECONOMIC ASSISTANCE
TOPIC: Direct Aid
CONCEPTS: Conformity with municipal law. Finan-
cial programs. Economic assistance.
PARTIES:
Jordan
USA (United States)

104231 Bilateral Exchange **290 UNTS 119**
SIGNED: 2 Apr 57 FORCE: 2 Apr 57
REGISTERED: 19 Mar 58 USA (United States)
ARTICLES: 2 LANGUAGE: English. Portuguese.
HEADNOTE: COPYRIGHT RELATIONS
TOPIC: Patents/Copyrights
CONCEPTS: Domestic legislation. Laws and for-
malities.
PARTIES:
Brazil
USA (United States)

104232 Bilateral Exchange **290 UNTS 133**
SIGNED: 27 Jun 57 FORCE: 27 Jun 57
REGISTERED: 19 Mar 58 USA (United States)
ARTICLES: 2 LANGUAGE: English.
HEADNOTE: SURPLUS AGRI COMMOD
TOPIC: Direct Aid
CONCEPTS: Financial programs. Local currency.
Surplus commodities.
TREATY REF: 247UNTS205.
PARTIES:
UK Great Britain
USA (United States)

104233 Bilateral Agreement **290 UNTS 139**
SIGNED: 12 Jul 57 FORCE: 14 Aug 57
REGISTERED: 21 Mar 58 USA (United States)
ARTICLES: 6 LANGUAGE: English.
HEADNOTE: ATOMIC INFORMATION MUTUAL DE-
FENSE
TOPIC: Milit Assistance
CONCEPTS: Definition of terms. Conformity with
municipal law. General cooperation. Atomic en-
ergy assistance. Military training. Security of in-
formation. Exchange of defense information. Re-
strictions on transfer.
PROCEDURE: Ratification. Termination.
PARTIES:
Australia
USA (United States)

104234 Bilateral Agreement **290 UNTS 147**
SIGNED: 8 Jul 57 FORCE: 22 Aug 57
REGISTERED: 21 Mar 58 USA (United States)

ARTICLES: 12 LANGUAGE: English.
HEADNOTE: COOPERATION CONCERNING CIVIL
   USES ATOMIC ENERGY
TOPIC: Atomic Energy
CONCEPTS: Definition of terms. Conformity with
   municipal law. Exchange of information and documents. Inspection and observation. Responsibility and liability. Research cooperation. Research results. Assets transfer. Nuclear materials. Non-nuclear materials. Peaceful use.
   Security of information.
PROCEDURE: Amendment. Termination.
PARTIES:
   South Africa
   USA (United States)
         ANNEX
458 UNTS 328. USA (United States). Amendment
   12 Jun 62. Force 23 Aug 62.
458 UNTS 328.   South   Africa.   Amendment
   12 Jun 62. Force 23 Aug 62.

104235   Bilateral Exchange   **290 UNTS 167**
SIGNED: 5 Aug 57   FORCE: 5 Aug 57
REGISTERED: 21 Mar 58 USA (United States)
ARTICLES: 2 LANGUAGE: English.
HEADNOTE: LOAN VESSELS SMALL CRAFT
TOPIC: Milit Assistance
CONCEPTS: Time limit. Annex or appendix refer-
   ence. Responsibility and liability. Title and
   deeds. Compensation. Indemnities and reim-
   bursements. Delivery schedules. Joint defense.
   Defense and security. Lease of military property.
   Naval vessels. Return of equipment and recap-
   ture. Restrictions on transfer.
INTL ORGS: North Atlantic Treaty Organization.
TREATY REF: 7UNTS267.
PARTIES:
   Greece
   USA (United States)
         ANNEX
426 UNTS 344. Greece. Prolongation 21 Sep 61.
   Force 9 Nov 61.
426 UNTS 344. USA (United States). Prolongation
   9 Nov 61. Force 9 Nov 61.

104236   Bilateral Exchange   **290 UNTS 175**
SIGNED: 19 Sep 57   FORCE: 19 Sep 57
REGISTERED: 21 Mar 58 USA (United States)
ARTICLES: 2 LANGUAGE: English.
HEADNOTE: GUARANTY PRIVATE INVESTMENT
TOPIC: Claims and Debts
CONCEPTS: Conformity with municipal law. Reci-
   procity in financial treatment. Currency. Pay-
   ment schedules. Private investment guarantee.
PARTIES:
   India
   USA (United States)
         ANNEX
361 UNTS 366. India. Supplementation 7 Dec 59.
   Force 7 Dec 59.
361 UNTS 366. USA (United States). Supplemen-
   tation 7 Dec 59. Force 7 Dec 59.
603 UNTS 318. USA (United States). Supplemen-
   tation 2 Feb 66. Force 2 Feb 66.
603 UNTS 318. India. Supplementation 2 Feb 66.
   Force 2 Feb 66.

104237   Bilateral Agreement   **290 UNTS 181**
SIGNED: 21 Nov 56   FORCE: 11 Sep 57
REGISTERED: 21 Mar 58 USA (United States)
ARTICLES: 16 LANGUAGE: English. German.
HEADNOTE: BONDS
TOPIC: Claims and Debts
CONCEPTS: Definition of terms. Detailed regula-
   tions. Treaty implementation. Annex or appendix
   reference. Conformity with municipal law. Ex-
   change of information and documents. Public in-
   formation. Investigation of violations. Establish-
   ment of commission. Bonds. Compensation. In-
   demnities and reimbursements.
INTL ORGS: Arbitration Commission.
TREATY REF: 290UNTS214.
PROCEDURE: Ratification.
PARTIES:
   Austria
   USA (United States)

104238   Bilateral Exchange   **290 UNTS 261**
SIGNED: 23 Sep 57   FORCE: 23 Sep 57
REGISTERED: 21 Mar 58 USA (United States)

ARTICLES: 2 LANGUAGE: English. Spanish.
HEADNOTE: ACCEPTANCE CERTIFICATES AIR-
   WORTHINESS IMPORTED AIRCRAFT
TOPIC: Air Transport
CONCEPTS: Conformity with municipal law. Ex-
   change of information and documents. Recogni-
   tion of legal documents. Use of facilities. Regis-
   tration certificate. Airworthiness certificates.
PROCEDURE: Termination.
PARTIES:
   Spain
   USA (United States)

104239   Bilateral Exchange   **290 UNTS 273**
SIGNED: 23 Nov 56   FORCE: 23 Nov 56
REGISTERED: 21 Mar 58 USA (United States)
ARTICLES: 2 LANGUAGE: English.
HEADNOTE: SURPLUS AGRICULTURAL COM-
   MODITIES
TOPIC: Direct Aid
CONCEPTS: Currency deposits. Local currency.
   Surplus commodities.
TREATY REF: 272UNTS21; 282UNTS4093.
PARTIES:
   Turkey
   USA (United States)

104240   Bilateral Exchange   **291 UNTS 3**
SIGNED: 4 May 54   FORCE: 23 Feb 55
REGISTERED: 21 Mar 58 Netherlands
ARTICLES: 2 LANGUAGE: French.
HEADNOTE: ESTABLISHMENT DENTISTS
TOPIC: Admin Cooperation
CONCEPTS: General cooperation.
PARTIES:
   Monaco
   Netherlands

104241   Bilateral Exchange   **291 UNTS 9**
SIGNED: 11 Oct 54   FORCE: 18 Jun 55
REGISTERED: 21 Mar 58 Netherlands
ARTICLES: 2 LANGUAGE: French.
HEADNOTE: REMOVAL REMAINS SERVICEMEN
TOPIC: Other Military
CONCEPTS: Informational records. Indemnities
   and reimbursements. Responsibility for war
   dead.
PARTIES:
   Germany, West
   Netherlands

104242   Bilateral Agreement   **291 UNTS 17**
SIGNED: 1 Jun 57   FORCE: 1 Jun 57
REGISTERED: 21 Mar 58 Belgium
ARTICLES: 13 LANGUAGE: French. Hungarian.
HEADNOTE: AIR TRANSPORT
TOPIC: Air Transport
CONCEPTS: Representation. Treaty implementation. Annex or appendix reference. Previous
   treaty replacement. Conformity with municipal
   law. General cooperation. Exchange of information and documents. Informational records. Licenses and permits. Recognition of legal documents. Investigation of violations. Procedure.
   Negotiation. Reexport of goods, etc.. Indemnities
   and reimbursements. Monetary and gold transfers. Non-interest rates and fees. Customs exemptions. Registration certificate. Routes and logistics. Navigational equipment. Permit designation. Air transport. Airworthiness certificates.
   Conditions of airlines operating permission. Operating authorizations and regulations.
PROCEDURE: Denunciation. Ratification.
PARTIES:
   Belgium
   Hungary

104243   Bilateral Agreement   **291 UNTS 41**
SIGNED: 7 Jun 57   FORCE: 7 Jun 57
REGISTERED: 25 Mar 58 USA (United States)
ARTICLES: 6 LANGUAGE: English. Polish.
HEADNOTE: SURPLUS AGRI COMMOD
TOPIC: Direct Aid
CONCEPTS: Annex or appendix reference. Gen-
   eral cooperation. Exchange of information and
   documents. Reexport of goods, etc.. Exchange
   rates and regulations. Interest rates. Purchase
   authorizations. Transportation costs. Local cur-

rency. Commodities schedule. Surplus commodities.
PARTIES:
   Poland
   USA (United States)
         ANNEX
307 UNTS 330. Poland. Amendment 8 Jan 58.
   Force 8 Jan 58.
307 UNTS 330. USA (United States). Amendment
   8 Jan 58. Force 8 Jan 58.
346 UNTS 350. Poland. Amendment 29 May 59.
   Force 29 May 59.
346 UNTS 350. USA (United States). Amendment
   26 May 59. Force 29 May 59.
380 UNTS 464. USA (United States). Amendment
   21 Jul 60. Force 21 Jul 60.
380 UNTS 464. Poland. Amendment 21 Jul 60.
   Force 21 Jul 60.

104244   Bilateral Agreement   **291 UNTS 61**
SIGNED: 3 Jun 57   FORCE: 3 Jun 57
REGISTERED: 25 Mar 58 USA (United States)
ARTICLES: 7 LANGUAGE: English. Spanish.
HEADNOTE: TECHNICAL COOPERATION
TOPIC: Tech Assistance
CONCEPTS: Exceptions and exemptions. Treaty
   implementation. Diplomatic privileges. General
   cooperation. Exchange of information and docu-
   ments. Informational records. Personnel. Public
   information. Attachment of funds. Exchange
   rates and regulations. Funding procedures. Gar-
   nishment of funds. Seizure funds. Tax exemptions. Customs exemptions. Domestic obligation. General technical assistance. Materials,
   equipment and services. Aid missions.
PROCEDURE: Termination.
PARTIES:
   Argentina
   USA (United States)

104245   Bilateral Agreement   **291 UNTS 77**
SIGNED: 7 Jun 57   FORCE: 7 Jun 57
REGISTERED: 25 Mar 58 USA (United States)
ARTICLES: 6 LANGUAGE: English. Spanish.
HEADNOTE: AGRI COMMOD TITLE I
TOPIC: US Agri Commod Aid
CONCEPTS: Annex or appendix reference. Gen-
   eral cooperation. Exchange of information and
   documents. Reexport of goods, etc.. Currency
   deposits. Exchange rates and regulations. Pur-
   chase authorizations. Transportation costs. Lo-
   cal currency. Commodities schedule. Surplus
   commodities.
PARTIES:
   Bolivia
   USA (United States)

104246   Bilateral Convention   **291 UNTS 101**
SIGNED: 22 Jun 56   FORCE: 13 Jun 57
REGISTERED: 25 Mar 58 USA (United States)
ARTICLES: 3 LANGUAGE: English. French.
HEADNOTE: DOUBLE TAXATION
TOPIC: Taxation
CONCEPTS: Territorial application. Annex type
   material. Previous treaty extension. Taxation.
   General. Tax exemptions.
TREATY REF: 125UNTS259; 140UNTS23.
PROCEDURE: Duration. Ratification. Termination.
PARTIES:
   France
   USA (United States)

104247   Bilateral Convention   **291 UNTS 113**
SIGNED: 2 Feb 56   FORCE: 15 Feb 58
REGISTERED: 25 Mar 58 Italy
ARTICLES: 21 LANGUAGE: French.
HEADNOTE: VETERINARY CONVENTION
TOPIC: Sanitation
CONCEPTS: Detailed regulations. Previous treaty
   extension. Inspection and observation. Arbitra-
   tion. Border control. Disease control. Insect con-
   trol. Veterinary. Export quotas. Reexport of
   goods, etc..
INTL ORGS: International Office of Epizootics. Ar-
   bitration Commission.
PROCEDURE: Amendment. Denunciation. Dura-
   tion. Ratification. Renewal or Revival.
PARTIES:
   Italy
   Switzerland

104248 Bilateral Agreement **291 UNTS 133**
SIGNED: 17 Dec 57 FORCE: 2 Jan 58
REGISTERED: 25 Mar 58 Italy
ARTICLES: 5 LANGUAGE: French.
HEADNOTE: PAYMENTS
TOPIC: Finance
CONCEPTS: Previous treaty replacement. Conformity with municipal law. Licenses and permits. Banking. Expense sharing formulae. Local currency.
TREATY REF: 5MAY51 PAYMENTS AGREEMENT 2UNTS39.
PROCEDURE: Denunciation.
PARTIES:
Finland
Italy

104249 Bilateral Convention **291 UNTS 143**
SIGNED: 23 Aug 51 FORCE: 6 Dec 57
REGISTERED: 25 Mar 58 Italy
ARTICLES: 13 LANGUAGE: French.
HEADNOTE: ESTABLISHMENT
TOPIC: Consul/Citizenship
CONCEPTS: Territorial application. General consular functions. Conformity with municipal law. Expropriation. Legal protection and assistance. Establishment of commission. Procedure. Most favored nation clause. National treatment. Taxation. Foreign nationals.
INTL ORGS: International Court of Justice. Special Commission.
PROCEDURE: Amendment. Ratification. Termination.
PARTIES:
France
Italy

104250 Bilateral Exchange **291 UNTS 163**
SIGNED: 29 Jul 57 FORCE: 29 Jul 57
REGISTERED: 25 Mar 58 Italy
ARTICLES: 2 LANGUAGE: French.
HEADNOTE: COPYRIGHT PROTECTION
TOPIC: Patents/Copyrights
CONCEPTS: Domestic legislation. Laws and formalities.
PARTIES:
France
Italy

104251 Bilateral Agreement **291 UNTS 169**
SIGNED: 12 Jul 57 FORCE: 15 Jul 57
REGISTERED: 25 Mar 58 Italy
ARTICLES: 5 LANGUAGE: French.
HEADNOTE: REGULATING TRADE
TOPIC: General Trade
CONCEPTS: Annex or appendix reference. Establishment of commission. Trade procedures. Payment schedules.
INTL ORGS: Organization for Economic Co-operation and Development. Special Commission.
TREATY REF: 291UNTS173; 291UNTS175.
PROCEDURE: Duration. Ratification.
PARTIES:
Denmark
Italy

104252 Bilateral Exchange **291 UNTS 181**
SIGNED: 12 Jul 57 FORCE: 12 Jul 57
REGISTERED: 25 Mar 58 Italy
ARTICLES: 2 LANGUAGE: French.
HEADNOTE: REPAYMENT AMORTIZATION
TOPIC: Finance
CONCEPTS: Detailed regulations. Previous treaty replacement. Exchange of information and documents. Accounting procedures. Banking. Currency. Exchange rates and regulations. Financial programs. Debt settlement. Loan repayment.
INTL ORGS: European Payments Union. Organization for Economic Co-operation and Development.
TREATY REF: 288UNTS83.
PARTIES:
Germany, West
Italy

104253 Bilateral Agreement **291 UNTS 191**
SIGNED: 28 Feb 57 FORCE: 21 Mar 57
REGISTERED: 25 Mar 58 Italy
ARTICLES: 8 LANGUAGE: French.

HEADNOTE: MOVEMENT PERSONS
TOPIC: Visas
CONCEPTS: Emergencies. Time limit. Border traffic and migration. Passports non-diplomatic. Denial of admission. Visas. Conformity with municipal law.
TREATY REF: FRENCH-ITALIAN AGREEMENT 2AUG1948.
PROCEDURE: Termination.
PARTIES:
France
Italy

104254 Bilateral Exchange **291 UNTS 197**
SIGNED: 1 Jun 57 FORCE: 15 Jun 57
REGISTERED: 25 Mar 58 Italy
ARTICLES: 2 LANGUAGE: French.
HEADNOTE: MOVEMENT PERSONS
TOPIC: Visas
CONCEPTS: Emergencies. Time limit. Border traffic and migration. Passports non-diplomatic. Denial of admission. Visas. Conformity with municipal law.
PROCEDURE: Termination.
PARTIES:
Italy
Monaco

104255 Bilateral Instrument **291 UNTS 203**
SIGNED: 28 Dec 56 FORCE: 28 Dec 56
REGISTERED: 25 Mar 58 Italy
ARTICLES: 3 LANGUAGE: French.
HEADNOTE: COST OPERATIONS CONNECTION IMMIGRANTS
TOPIC: Non-ILO Labor
CONCEPTS: Previous treaty replacement. Border traffic and migration. General cooperation. Non-ILO labor relations. Accounting procedures.
PROCEDURE: Denunciation. Duration. Renewal or Revival.
PARTIES:
France
Italy

104256 Bilateral Exchange **291 UNTS 207**
SIGNED: 16 Dec 56 FORCE: 16 Dec 56
REGISTERED: 25 Mar 58 Italy
ARTICLES: 2 LANGUAGE: French.
HEADNOTE: COPYRIGHT PROTECTION
TOPIC: Patents/Copyrights
CONCEPTS: Domestic legislation. Laws and formalities.
PARTIES:
Italy
Norway

104257 Bilateral Convention **291 UNTS 213**
SIGNED: 17 Sep 55 FORCE: 15 Feb 58
REGISTERED: 25 Mar 58 Italy
ARTICLES: 13 LANGUAGE: Italian.
HEADNOTE: REGULATION LAKE LUGANO
TOPIC: Specific Resources
CONCEPTS: Previous treaty replacement. General cooperation. Inspection and observation. Personnel. Programs. Arbitration. Procedure. Existing tribunals. Financial programs. Customs exemptions. Canal improvement. Paragraph 2, Article 36. Regulation of natural resources.
INTL ORGS: International Court of Justice. Special Commission.
PROCEDURE: Ratification.
PARTIES:
Italy
Switzerland

104258 Bilateral Exchange **291 UNTS 229**
SIGNED: 12 Oct 57 FORCE: 12 Oct 57
REGISTERED: 25 Mar 58 Italy
ARTICLES: 2 LANGUAGE: Italian. Spanish.
HEADNOTE: COPYRIGHT PROTECTION
TOPIC: Patents/Copyrights
CONCEPTS: Domestic legislation. Laws and formalities.
PARTIES:
Italy
Spain

104259 Bilateral Convention **291 UNTS 235**
SIGNED: 25 May 55 FORCE: 1 Aug 57
REGISTERED: 25 Mar 58 Italy
ARTICLES: 29 LANGUAGE: Italian. Swedish.
HEADNOTE: SOCIAL SECURITY
TOPIC: Non-ILO Labor
CONCEPTS: General provisions. Conformity with municipal law. Domestic legislation. Old age and invalidity insurance. Wages and salaries. Non-ILO labor relations. Family allowances. Administrative cooperation. Old age insurance. Sickness and invalidity insurance. Social security. Unemployment. Payment schedules. Claims and settlements.
PROCEDURE: Denunciation. Duration. Ratification. Renewal or Revival.
PARTIES:
Italy
Sweden

104260 Bilateral Exchange **291 UNTS 287**
SIGNED: 27 Feb 56 FORCE: 27 Feb 56
REGISTERED: 25 Mar 58 Italy
ARTICLES: 2 LANGUAGE: English. Italian.
HEADNOTE: PROGRAM PURCHASE SURPLUS AGRI COMMOD
TOPIC: Direct Aid
CONCEPTS: Conformity with municipal law. General cooperation. Export quotas. Accounting procedures. Indemnities and reimbursements. Currency deposits. Exchange rates and regulations. Purchase authorizations. Transportation costs. Local currency. Procurement. Surplus commodities. Transport of goods.
TREATY REF: US&ITALY 25JAN1947&-15APR1948.
PROCEDURE: Amendment.
PARTIES:
Italy
USA (United States)
ANNEX
378 UNTS 392. Italy. Supplementation 30 Jan 57. Force 30 Jan 57.
378 UNTS 394. Italy. Amendment 31 Jan 58. Force 31 Jan 58.
378 UNTS 394. USA (United States). Amendment 31 Jan 58. Force 31 Jan 58.

104261 Bilateral Agreement **292 UNTS 3**
SIGNED: 3 Jun 57 FORCE: 1 Oct 57
REGISTERED: 26 Mar 58 Czechoslovakia
ARTICLES: 8 LANGUAGE: Bulgarian. Czechoslovakian.
HEADNOTE: VETERINARY MATTERS
TOPIC: Sanitation
CONCEPTS: General cooperation. Exchange of information and documents. Specialists exchange. Disease control. Veterinary. Teacher and student exchange. Vocational training. Research results. Indemnities and reimbursements. Expense sharing formulae. Publications exchange. Conferences.
PROCEDURE: Denunciation. Duration. Future Procedures Contemplated.
PARTIES:
Bulgaria
Czechoslovakia

104262 Bilateral Exchange **292 UNTS 17**
SIGNED: 4 May 55 FORCE: 30 Jul 55
REGISTERED: 26 Mar 58 Netherlands
ARTICLES: 2 LANGUAGE: French.
HEADNOTE: MOVEMENT REFUGEES
TOPIC: Refugees
CONCEPTS: Emergencies. Visa abolition. Denial of admission. Alien status.
TREATY REF: 11UNTS73; 189UNTS137.
PROCEDURE: Denunciation. Ratification.
PARTIES:
Luxembourg
Netherlands

104263 Bilateral Exchange **292 UNTS 23**
SIGNED: 26 Sep 53 FORCE: 22 Dec 53
REGISTERED: 26 Mar 58 Netherlands
ARTICLES: 2 LANGUAGE: French.
HEADNOTE: ABOLITION VISAS
TOPIC: Visas
CONCEPTS: Emergencies. Time limit. Visa abolition. Denial of admission. Resident permits. Non-

visa travel documents. Conformity with municipal law.
INTL ORGS: Council of Europe.
PROCEDURE: Denunciation.
PARTIES:
  Greece
  Netherlands
ANNEX
528 UNTS 304. Netherlands. Force 1 Mar 64.
528 UNTS 304. Greece. Force 1 Mar 64.

104264 Bilateral Exchange **292 UNTS 31**
SIGNED: 22 Nov 55 FORCE: 6 Mar 56
REGISTERED: 26 Mar 58 Netherlands
ARTICLES: 2 LANGUAGE: French.
HEADNOTE: ABOLITION VISAS HOLDERS DIPLOMATIC SERVICE PASSPORTS
TOPIC: Visas
CONCEPTS: Emergencies. Visa abolition.
PARTIES:
  Greece
  Netherlands

104265 Bilateral Exchange **292 UNTS 37**
SIGNED: 18 Jun 54 FORCE: 2 Nov 54
REGISTERED: 26 Mar 58 Netherlands
ARTICLES: 2 LANGUAGE: Spanish.
HEADNOTE: ABOLITION VISAS
TOPIC: Visas
CONCEPTS: Exceptions and exemptions. Territorial application. Time limit. Visa abolition. Denial of admission. Fees and exemptions.
PARTIES:
  Chile
  Netherlands

104266 Bilateral Agreement **292 UNTS 45**
SIGNED: 17 Nov 54 FORCE: 1 Jun 55
REGISTERED: 26 Mar 58 Netherlands
ARTICLES: 11 LANGUAGE: Dutch. German.
HEADNOTE: EXCHANGE STUDENT EMPLOYEES
TOPIC: Non-ILO Labor
CONCEPTS: Resident permits. Conformity with municipal law. Vocational training. Employment regulations. Wages and salaries. Non-ILO labor relations. Migrant worker. Debts. National treatment.
PROCEDURE: Denunciation. Duration. Renewal or Revival.
PARTIES:
  Austria
  Netherlands

104267 Multilateral Exchange **292 UNTS 63**
SIGNED: 21 Dec 55 FORCE: 8 May 57
REGISTERED: 26 Mar 58 Netherlands
ARTICLES: 3 LANGUAGE: French. Dutch.
HEADNOTE: TRADE CUT FLOWERS
TOPIC: General Trade
CONCEPTS: Detailed regulations. Establishment of commission. Free trade. Trade agencies. Trade procedures. Commodity trade. Delivery schedules. Quotas. Customs duties. Transport of goods.
INTL ORGS: Benelux Economic Union.
TREATY REF: 250UNTS108.
PROCEDURE: Ratification.
PARTIES:
  Belgium SIGNED: 24 Aug 55 FORCE: 8 May 57
  Luxembourg SIGNED: 29 Sep 55 FORCE: 8 May 57
  Netherlands SIGNED: 21 Dec 55 FORCE: 8 May 57

104268 Bilateral Treaty **292 UNTS 75**
SIGNED: 27 Sep 57 FORCE: 8 Feb 58
REGISTERED: 27 Mar 58 USSR (Soviet Union)
ARTICLES: 17 LANGUAGE: Russian. German.
HEADNOTE: STRENGTHEN RELATIONS/TRADE NAVIGATION TREATY
TOPIC: General Economic
CONCEPTS: Exceptions and exemptions. General provisions. Annex or appendix reference. General relations and amity. Non-diplomatic delegations. Juridical personality. Recognition and enforcement of legal decisions. Arbitration. Procedure. Existing tribunals. Reciprocity in trade. Most favored nation clause. Customs duties. Customs exemptions. Transport of goods. Li-

censes and certificates of nationality. Merchant vessels. Tonnage. Ports and pilotage. Shipwreck and salvage.
TREATY REF: 226UNTS201.
PROCEDURE: Ratification. Termination.
PARTIES:
  Germany, East
  USSR (Soviet Union)

104269 Bilateral Convention **292 UNTS 107**
SIGNED: 16 Dec 57 FORCE: 5 Feb 58
REGISTERED: 27 Mar 58 USSR (Soviet Union)
ARTICLES: 10 LANGUAGE: Russian. Korean.
HEADNOTE: DUAL CITIZENSHIP
TOPIC: Consul/Citizenship
CONCEPTS: Alien status. Dual citizenship. Tax exemptions.
PROCEDURE: Ratification.
PARTIES:
  Korea, North
  USSR (Soviet Union)

104270 Bilateral Convention **292 UNTS 121**
SIGNED: 16 Dec 57 FORCE: 5 Feb 58
REGISTERED: 27 Mar 58 USSR (Soviet Union)
ARTICLES: 24 LANGUAGE: Russian. Korean.
HEADNOTE: CONSULAR CONVENTION
TOPIC: Consul/Citizenship
CONCEPTS: Definition of terms. General consular functions. Diplomatic privileges. Consular relations establishment. Inviolability. Privileges and immunities. Diplomatic correspondence. Responsibility and liability.
PROCEDURE: Ratification.
PARTIES:
  Korea, North
  USSR (Soviet Union)

104271 Bilateral Agreement **292 UNTS 151**
SIGNED: 19 Oct 57 FORCE: 11 Feb 58
REGISTERED: 27 Mar 58 United Arab Rep
ARTICLES: 11 LANGUAGE: Russian. Arabic. French.
HEADNOTE: CULTURAL AGREEMENT
TOPIC: Culture
CONCEPTS: Friendship and amity. Tourism. Non-diplomatic delegations. Exchange of information and documents. Recognition of degrees. Exchange. Teacher and student exchange. Scholarships and grants. Exchange. General cultural cooperation. Artists. Athletes. Research results. Scientific exchange. Accounting procedures. Materials, equipment and services. Publications exchange. Mass media exchange.
PROCEDURE: Denunciation. Duration. Ratification.
PARTIES:
  United Arab Rep
  USSR (Soviet Union)

104272 Bilateral Exchange **292 UNTS 165**
SIGNED: 11 Jun 57 FORCE: 1 Jan 58
REGISTERED: 31 Mar 58 Belgium
ARTICLES: 2 LANGUAGE: Dutch. Afrikaans.
HEADNOTE: DOUBLE TAXATION SEA AIR TRANSPORT
TOPIC: Taxation
CONCEPTS: Definition of terms. Taxation. Air transport. Merchant vessels.
PROCEDURE: Duration. Termination.
PARTIES:
  Belgium
  South Africa

104273 Bilateral Agreement **292 UNTS 175**
SIGNED: 27 Nov 57 FORCE: 20 Mar 58
REGISTERED: 31 Mar 58 IBRD (World Bank)
ARTICLES: 5 LANGUAGE: English.
HEADNOTE: GUARANTEE AGREEMENT
TOPIC: IBRD Project
CONCEPTS: Annex or appendix reference. Exchange of information and documents. Inspection and observation. Bonds. Fees and exemptions. Tax exemptions. Domestic obligation. Terms of loan. Loan regulations. Loan guarantee. Guarantor non-interference. Roads and highways.
PARTIES:
  Belgium
  IBRD (World Bank)

104274 Bilateral Agreement **292 UNTS 199**
SIGNED: 24 Oct 57 FORCE: 1 Mar 58
REGISTERED: 31 Mar 58 Belgium
ARTICLES: 4 LANGUAGE: French. Dutch.
HEADNOTE: AMEND 1843 SCHELDT PILOTAGE REGULATIONS
TOPIC: Water Transport
CONCEPTS: Territorial application. Annex type material. Previous treaty replacement. Ports and pilotage.
PROCEDURE: Ratification. Termination.
PARTIES:
  Belgium
  Netherlands
ANNEX
548 UNTS 346. Belgium. Amendment 27 Apr 65. Force 1 Oct 65.
548 UNTS 346. Netherlands. Amendment 27 Apr 65. Force 1 Oct 65.
548 UNTS 346. Belgium. Ratification 22 Sep 65.
548 UNTS 346. Netherlands. Ratification 22 Sep 65.
608 UNTS 356. Netherlands. Amendment 23 Mar 67.
608 UNTS 356. Belgium. Amendment 23 Mar 67.

104275 Bilateral Agreement **292 UNTS 233**
SIGNED: 29 Jan 58 FORCE: 1 Apr 58
REGISTERED: 1 Apr 58 Australia
ARTICLES: 35 LANGUAGE: English.
HEADNOTE: SOCIAL SECURITY
TOPIC: Non-ILO Labor
CONCEPTS: Definition of terms. Territorial application. General provisions. Domestic legislation. Old age and invalidity insurance. Wages and salaries. Non-ILO labor relations. Family allowances. Administrative cooperation. Old age insurance. Sickness and invalidity insurance. Social security. Unemployment. Payment schedules. Claims and settlements.
PROCEDURE: Duration. Renewal or Revival. Termination.
PARTIES:
  Australia
  UK Great Britain

104276 Multilateral Agreement **292 UNTS 273**
SIGNED: 15 Mar 58 FORCE: 15 Mar 58
REGISTERED: 1 Apr 58 United Nations
ARTICLES: 6 LANGUAGE: English.
HEADNOTE: TECHNICAL ASSISTANCE
TOPIC: Tech Assistance
CONCEPTS: Definition of terms. Previous treaty replacement. Privileges and immunities. General cooperation. Exchange of information and documents. Personnel. Responsibility and liability. Title and deeds. Use of facilities. Exchange. Scholarships and grants. Vocational training. Research and development. Exchange rates and regulations. Expense sharing formulae. Local currency. Domestic obligation. General technical assistance. Materials, equipment and services. IGO status. Conformity with IGO decisions.
TREATY REF: 76UNTS132; 1UNTS15; 33UNTS261; 172UNTS93; 243UNTS9.
PROCEDURE: Amendment. Termination.
PARTIES:
  Ethiopia SIGNED: 15 Mar 58 FORCE: 15 Mar 58
  FAO (Food Agri) SIGNED: 15 Mar 58 FORCE: 15 Mar 58
  ICAO (Civil Aviat) SIGNED: 15 Mar 58 FORCE: 15 Mar 58
  ILO (Labor Org) SIGNED: 15 Mar 58 FORCE: 15 Mar 58
  ITU (Telecommun) SIGNED: 15 Mar 58 FORCE: 15 Mar 58
  UNESCO (Educ/Cult) SIGNED: 15 Mar 58 FORCE: 15 Mar 58
  United Nations SIGNED: 15 Mar 58 FORCE: 15 Mar 58
  WHO (World Health) SIGNED: 15 Mar 58 FORCE: 15 Mar 58
  WMO (Meteorology) SIGNED: 15 Mar 58 FORCE: 15 Mar 58
ANNEX
655 UNTS 392. IMCO (Maritime Org). Accession 14 Jan 69. Force 14 Jan 69.
655 UNTS 392. UNIDO (Industrial). Accession 14 Jan 69. Force 14 Jan 69.
655 UNTS 392. IAEA (Atom Energy). Accession 14 Jan 69. Force 14 Jan 69.
655 UNTS 392.

104277 Bilateral Agreement **292 UNTS 391**
SIGNED: 26 Mar 56 FORCE: 9 Nov 56
REGISTERED: 3 Apr 58 IBRD (World Bank)
ARTICLES: 5 LANGUAGE: English.
HEADNOTE: GUARANTEE AGREEMENT
TOPIC: IBRD Project
CONCEPTS: Annex or appendix reference. Exchange of information and documents. Inspection and observation. Bonds. Fees and exemptions. Tax exemptions. Domestic obligation. Terms of loan. Loan regulations. Loan guarantee. Guarantor non-interference. Hydro-electric power.
PARTIES:
Ecuador
IBRD (World Bank)

104278 Bilateral Agreement **292 UNTS 317**
SIGNED: 6 May 57 FORCE: 13 Jan 58
REGISTERED: 3 Apr 58 Czechoslovakia
ARTICLES: 9 LANGUAGE: Czechoslovakian. Arabic. English.
HEADNOTE: SCIENTIFIC TECHNICAL COOPERATION
TOPIC: Tech Assistance
CONCEPTS: Guarantees and safeguards. Treaty implementation. Treaty interpretation. Personnel. Use of facilities. Scholarships and grants. Vocational training. Research and development. General technical assistance.
PROCEDURE: Denunciation. Ratification.
PARTIES:
Czechoslovakia
United Arab Rep

104279 Bilateral Treaty **292 UNTS 327**
SIGNED: 24 May 57 FORCE: 18 Feb 58
REGISTERED: 3 Apr 58 Czechoslovakia
ARTICLES: 24 LANGUAGE: Czechoslovakian. German.
HEADNOTE: CONSULAR TREATY
TOPIC: Consul/Citizenship
CONCEPTS: General consular functions. Diplomatic privileges. Consular relations establishment. Inviolability. Privileges and immunities. Diplomatic correspondence.
PROCEDURE: Denunciation. Duration. Ratification. Renewal or Revival.
PARTIES:
Czechoslovakia
Germany, East

104280 Bilateral Exchange **293 UNTS 3**
SIGNED: 4 Nov 53 FORCE: 11 Feb 54
REGISTERED: 10 Apr 58 Netherlands
ARTICLES: 2 LANGUAGE: French.
HEADNOTE: ABOLITION VISAS
TOPIC: Visas
CONCEPTS: Emergencies. Territorial application. Time limit. Visa abolition. Passports diplomatic. Denial of admission. Visas. Conformity with municipal law.
PROCEDURE: Denunciation.
PARTIES:
Netherlands
Turkey

104281 Bilateral Exchange **293 UNTS 11**
SIGNED: 1 May 53 FORCE: 1 Jun 53
REGISTERED: 10 Apr 58 Netherlands
ARTICLES: 2 LANGUAGE: English.
HEADNOTE: ABOLITION VISAS
TOPIC: Visas
CONCEPTS: Visa abolition. Denial of admission. Conformity with municipal law.
PARTIES:
Netherlands
Pakistan

104282 Bilateral Exchange **293 UNTS 17**
SIGNED: 30 May 53 FORCE: 30 May 53
REGISTERED: 10 Apr 58 Netherlands
ARTICLES: 2 LANGUAGE: English.
HEADNOTE: WAR CLAIMS
TOPIC: Reparations
CONCEPTS: Lump sum settlements. Post-war claims settlement.
TREATY REF: 247UNTS353.

PARTIES:
Netherlands
Thailand

104283 Bilateral Agreement **293 UNTS 23**
SIGNED: 18 Jan 56 FORCE: 1 Apr 58
REGISTERED: 14 Apr 58 Belgium
ARTICLES: 13 LANGUAGE: French. Swedish.
HEADNOTE: DOUBLE TAXATION DEATH DUTIES
TOPIC: Taxation
CONCEPTS: Nationality and citizenship. Exchange of official publications. Negotiation. Claims and settlements. Debts. Taxation. Death duties. Equitable taxes.
PROCEDURE: Duration. Ratification. Termination.
PARTIES:
Belgium
Sweden

104284 Bilateral Treaty **293 UNTS 43**
SIGNED: 30 Aug 56 FORCE: 9 Dec 57
REGISTERED: 15 Apr 58 Philippines
ARTICLES: 9 LANGUAGE: English. French.
HEADNOTE: FRIENDSHIP
TOPIC: General Amity
CONCEPTS: Friendship and amity. Alien status. Consular relations establishment. Diplomatic relations establishment. Privileges and immunities. Immovable property. General property. Arbitration. Mediation and good offices. Existing tribunals. Conciliation.
INTL ORGS: International Court of Justice.
PROCEDURE: Future Procedures Contemplated. Ratification. Termination.
PARTIES:
Philippines
Switzerland

104285 Bilateral Exchange **293 UNTS 53**
SIGNED: 3 Nov 53 FORCE: 28 Jun 54
REGISTERED: 16 Apr 58 Netherlands
ARTICLES: 2 LANGUAGE: French.
HEADNOTE: DUTIES CHARGES FUEL LUBRICANTS
TOPIC: Customs
CONCEPTS: Previous treaty renunciation. Customs duties. Air transport.
TREATY REF: 17LTS195; 35UNTS69.
PARTIES:
Netherlands
Switzerland

104286 Bilateral Agreement **293 UNTS 59**
SIGNED: 9 Aug 57 FORCE: 19 Nov 57
REGISTERED: 18 Apr 58 IBRD (World Bank)
ARTICLES: 5 LANGUAGE: English.
HEADNOTE: GUARANTEE AGREEMENT
TOPIC: IBRD Project
CONCEPTS: Definition of terms. Annex or appendix reference. Exchange of information and documents. Inspection and observation. Bonds. Fees and exemptions. Tax exemptions. Domestic obligation. Terms of loan. Loan regulations. Loan guarantee. Guarantor non-interference.
PARTIES:
Japan
IBRD (World Bank)

104287 Bilateral Agreement **293 UNTS 83**
SIGNED: 22 Nov 57 FORCE: 26 Feb 58
REGISTERED: 18 Apr 58 IBRD (World Bank)
ARTICLES: 5 LANGUAGE: English.
HEADNOTE: GUARANTEE AGREEMENT
TOPIC: IBRD Project
CONCEPTS: Definition of terms. Annex or appendix reference. Exchange of information and documents. Inspection and observation. Bonds. Fees and exemptions. Tax exemptions. Domestic obligation. Terms of loan. Loan regulations. Loan guarantee. Guarantor non-interference.
PARTIES:
Philippines
IBRD (World Bank)

104288 Bilateral Exchange **293 UNTS 115**
SIGNED: 10 Oct 53 FORCE: 15 Dec 53
REGISTERED: 21 Apr 58 Netherlands
ARTICLES: 2 LANGUAGE: Dutch. German.

HEADNOTE: ABOLITION VISAS
TOPIC: Visas
CONCEPTS: Emergencies. Territorial application. Time limit. Visa abolition. Denial of admission. Conformity with municipal law.
INTL ORGS: Council of Europe.
PROCEDURE: Denunciation.
PARTIES:
Germany, West
Netherlands
                    ANNEX
307 UNTS 334. Netherlands. Termination 9 Apr 58. Force 12 Apr 58.
307 UNTS 334. Germany, West. Termination 9 Apr 58. Force 12 Apr 58.

104289 Bilateral Exchange **293 UNTS 123**
SIGNED: 13 Mar 53 FORCE: 1 Apr 53
REGISTERED: 21 Apr 58 Netherlands
ARTICLES: 2 LANGUAGE: Dutch. German.
HEADNOTE: DELIVERY GRATIS VISAS
TOPIC: Visas
CONCEPTS: Visas. Fees and exemptions.
PARTIES:
Germany, West
Netherlands

104290 Bilateral Exchange **293 UNTS 129**
SIGNED: 17 Mar 53 FORCE: 1 Apr 53
REGISTERED: 21 Apr 58 Netherlands
ARTICLES: 2 LANGUAGE: Dutch. German.
HEADNOTE: ABOLITION VISAS
TOPIC: Visas
CONCEPTS: Visa abolition.
PARTIES:
Germany, West
Netherlands
                    ANNEX
306 UNTS 340. Netherlands. Termination 9 Apr 58. Force 12 Apr 58.
306 UNTS 340. Germany, West. Termination 9 Apr 58. Force 12 Apr 58.

104291 Bilateral Agreement **293 UNTS 135**
SIGNED: 20 Sep 57 FORCE: 12 Mar 58
REGISTERED: 22 Apr 58 IBRD (World Bank)
ARTICLES: 6 LANGUAGE: English.
HEADNOTE: GUARANTEE AGREEMENT
TOPIC: IBRD Project
CONCEPTS: Definition of terms. Annex or appendix reference. Exchange of information and documents. Inspection and observation. Bonds. Fees and exemptions. Tax exemptions. Domestic obligation. Terms of loan. Loan regulations. Loan guarantee. Guarantor non-interference.
PARTIES:
Ecuador
IBRD (World Bank)

104292 Bilateral Agreement **293 UNTS 167**
SIGNED: 14 Jan 58 FORCE: 20 Jan 58
REGISTERED: 22 Apr 58 IBRD (World Bank)
ARTICLES: 6 LANGUAGE: English.
HEADNOTE: GUARANTEE AGREEMENT
TOPIC: IBRD Project
CONCEPTS: Definition of terms. Annex or appendix reference. Exchange of information and documents. Inspection and observation. Bonds. Fees and exemptions. Tax exemptions. Domestic obligation. Terms of loan. Loan regulations. Loan guarantee. Guarantor non-interference. Hydro-electric power.
PARTIES:
Mexico
IBRD (World Bank)

104293 Bilateral Exchange **293 UNTS 247**
SIGNED: 14 Sep 57 FORCE: 14 Sep 57
REGISTERED: 23 Apr 58 USA (United States)
ARTICLES: 2 LANGUAGE: English. Japanese.
HEADNOTE: INTERPRETATION SECURITY TREATY ADMINISTRATIVE AGREEMENT
TOPIC: Admin Cooperation
CONCEPTS: Non-prejudice to UN charter. General cooperation. Procedure.
INTL ORGS: United Nations.
TREATY REF: 136UNTS211; 208UNTS255.

PARTIES:
Japan
USA (United States)

104294 Bilateral Agreement **293 UNTS 257**
SIGNED: 26 Jun 56   FORCE: 10 Oct 57
REGISTERED: 23 Apr 58 USA (United States)
ARTICLES: 11 LANGUAGE: English. Spanish.
HEADNOTE: COOPERATION CIVIL USES ATOMIC
ENERGY
TOPIC: Atomic Energy
CONCEPTS: Definition of terms. Non-prejudice to
third party. Exchange of information and documents. Inspection and observation. Responsibility and liability. Research cooperation. Assets
transfer. Nuclear materials. Non-nuclear materials. Security of information.
PROCEDURE: Duration.
PARTIES:
Cuba
USA (United States)

104295 Bilateral Exchange **293 UNTS 277**
SIGNED: 20 Apr 56   FORCE: 26 Sep 57
REGISTERED: 23 Apr 58 USA (United States)
ARTICLES: 2 LANGUAGE: English. Spanish.
HEADNOTE: URANIUM RECONNAISSANCE
TOPIC: Atomic Energy
CONCEPTS: Research cooperation. Scientific exchange. Nuclear materials.
PARTIES:
Chile
USA (United States)
ANNEX
367 UNTS 347. USA (United States). Prolongation
18 Nov 59. Force 18 Dec 59.
367 UNTS 347. Chile. Prolongation 18 Dec 59.
Force 18 Dec 59.

104296 Bilateral Exchange **293 UNTS 287**
SIGNED: 21 Sep 57   FORCE: 24 Sep 57
REGISTERED: 23 Apr 58 USA (United States)
ARTICLES: 2 LANGUAGE: English. Persian.
HEADNOTE: GUARANTY PRIVATE INVESTMENTS
TOPIC: Claims and Debts
CONCEPTS: Arbitration. Procedure. Existing tribunals. Negotiation. Private investment guarantee.
PARTIES:
Iran
USA (United States)

104297 Bilateral Exchange **293 UNTS 297**
SIGNED: 23 Sep 57   FORCE: 23 Sep 57
REGISTERED: 23 Apr 58 USA (United States)
ARTICLES: 2 LANGUAGE: English. French.
HEADNOTE: FACILITIES ASSISTANCE PROGRAM
TOPIC: Tech Assistance
CONCEPTS: Change of circumstances. Previous
treaty replacement. Use of facilities. Export
quotas. Indemnities and reimbursements. Funding procedures. Most favored nation clause. Tax
exemptions. Customs exemptions. Commodities
and services. Materials, equipment and services.
Defense and security. Military assistance. Security of information. Equipment and supplies. Restrictions on transfer.
TREATY REF: 236UNTS141; 80UNTS171.
PROCEDURE: Amendment. Future Procedures
Contemplated.
PARTIES:
France
USA (United States)

104298 Bilateral Exchange **293 UNTS 307**
SIGNED: 24 Sep 57   FORCE: 24 Sep 57
REGISTERED: 23 Apr 58 USA (United States)
ARTICLES: 2 LANGUAGE: English. Spanish.
HEADNOTE: COOPERATIVE PHOTOGRAPHING
MAPPING PROJECT
TOPIC: Tech Assistance
CONCEPTS: Treaty implementation. General cooperation. Exchange of information and documents. Personnel. Research and development.
Funding procedures. Assistance. Materials,
equipment and services.
TREATY REF: US EMBASSY IN VENEZUELA NOTE
NO.128.
PROCEDURE: Future Procedures Contemplated.

PARTIES:
USA (United States)
Venezuela

104299 Bilateral Exchange **293 UNTS 317**
SIGNED: 5 Dec 57   FORCE: 1 Jan 55
REGISTERED: 23 Apr 58 Belgium
ARTICLES: 7 LANGUAGE: French.
HEADNOTE: DOUBLE TAXATION SEA AIR TRANSPORT
TOPIC: Taxation
CONCEPTS: Definition of terms. Taxation. Air
transport. Merchant vessels.
PARTIES:
Belgium
Switzerland

104300 Multilateral Treaty **294 UNTS 2**
SIGNED: 25 Mar 57   FORCE: 1 Jan 58
REGISTERED: 24 Apr 58 Italy
ARTICLES: 248 LANGUAGE: French. German. Italian. Dutch.
HEADNOTE: FINAL ACT COMMON MARKET
TOPIC: IGO Establishment
CONCEPTS: Default remedies. Exceptions and exemptions. Annex or appendix reference. Previous treaty extension. Visa abolition. Border traffic and migration. Privileges and immunities.
Conformity with municipal law. General cooperation. Exchange of information and documents.
Juridical personality. Domestic legislation. Responsibility and liability. Dispute settlement. Anti-discrimination. Labor statistics. Right to organize. Migrant worker. Establishment of trade relations. Export quotas. Import quotas. Free trade.
Tariffs. Reciprocity in trade. Export subsidies.
Trade procedures. Balance of payments. Exchange rates and regulations. Fees and exemptions. Funding procedures. Debt settlement.
Quotas. National treatment. Equitable taxes.
General. Customs duties. Customs declarations.
Customs exemptions. Temporary importation.
Agriculture. Agricultural commodities. Economic assistance. Security of information. IGO
constitution. Admission. Subsidiary organ. Establishment. Internal structure. IGO obligations.
INTL ORGS: Council of Europe. European Coal and
Steel Community. European Economic Community. United Nations.
TREATY REF: 261UNTS140.
PARTIES:
Belgium   SIGNED: 25 Mar 57   RATIFIED:
13 Dec 57 FORCE: 1 Jan 58
France   SIGNED: 25 Mar 57   RATIFIED:
25 Nov 57 FORCE: 1 Jan 58
Germany, West SIGNED: 25 Mar 57 RATIFIED:
9 Dec 57 FORCE: 1 Jan 58
Italy SIGNED: 25 Mar 57 RATIFIED: 23 Nov 57
FORCE: 1 Jan 58
Luxembourg SIGNED: 25 Mar 57 RATIFIED:
13 Dec 57 FORCE: 1 Jan 58
Netherlands   SIGNED: 25 Mar 57   RATIFIED:
13 Dec 57 FORCE: 1 Jan 58

104301 Multilateral Treaty **294 UNTS 259**
SIGNED: 25 Mar 57   FORCE: 1 Jan 58
REGISTERED: 24 Apr 58 Italy
ARTICLES: 225 LANGUAGE: French. German. Italian. Dutch.
HEADNOTE: ESTABLISHMENT EURATOM
TOPIC: IGO Establishment
CONCEPTS: Treaty implementation. Annex or appendix reference. General cooperation. Exchange of information and documents. Labor
statistics. Research cooperation. Research results. Nuclear research. Scientific exchange. Financial programs. Economic assistance. Subsidiary organ. Establishment. Procedure. Internal
structure.
INTL ORGS: Council of Europe. General Agreement on Tariffs and Trade. Organization for Economic Co-operation and Development. United
Nations.
TREATY REF: 74LTS289.
PROCEDURE: Amendment. Duration.
PARTIES:
Belgium   SIGNED: 25 Mar 57   RATIFIED:
13 Dec 57 FORCE: 1 Jan 58
France   SIGNED: 25 Mar 57   RATIFIED:
25 Nov 57 FORCE: 1 Jan 58

Germany, West SIGNED: 25 Mar 57 RATIFIED:
9 Dec 57 FORCE: 1 Jan 58
Italy SIGNED: 25 Mar 57 RATIFIED: 23 Nov 57
FORCE: 1 Jan 58
Luxembourg SIGNED: 25 Mar 57 RATIFIED:
13 Dec 57 FORCE: 1 Jan 58
Netherlands   SIGNED: 25 Mar 57   RATIFIED:
13 Dec 57 FORCE: 1 Jan 58

104302 Multilateral Convention **294 UNTS 411**
SIGNED: 25 Mar 57   FORCE: 1 Jan 58
REGISTERED: 24 Apr 58 Italy
ARTICLES: 8 LANGUAGE: French. German. Italian.
Dutch.
HEADNOTE: INSTITUTIONS COMMON TO EUROPEAN COMMUNITIES
TOPIC: IGO Status/Immunit
CONCEPTS: Default remedies. Previous treaty replacement. Dispute settlement. Special tribunals. Financial programs. Internal structure.
INTL ORGS: European Economic Community. European Atomic Energy Commission.
TREATY REF: 261UNTS140.
PROCEDURE: Amendment.
PARTIES:
Belgium   SIGNED: 25 Mar 57   RATIFIED:
13 Dec 57 FORCE: 1 Jan 58
France   SIGNED: 25 Mar 57   RATIFIED:
25 Nov 57 FORCE: 1 Jan 58
Germany, West SIGNED: 25 Mar 57 RATIFIED:
9 Dec 57 FORCE: 1 Jan 58
Italy SIGNED: 25 Mar 57 RATIFIED: 23 Nov 57
FORCE: 1 Jan 58
Luxembourg SIGNED: 25 Mar 57 RATIFIED:
13 Dec 57 FORCE: 1 Jan 58
Netherlands   SIGNED: 25 Mar 57   RATIFIED:
13 Dec 57 FORCE: 1 Jan 58

104303 Bilateral Agreement **299 UNTS 3**
SIGNED: 28 Sep 56   FORCE: 22 Jan 58
REGISTERED: 25 Apr 58 South Africa
ARTICLES: 8 LANGUAGE: English. Afrikaans.
HEADNOTE: DOUBLE TAXATION FISCAL EVASION DEATH DUTIES
TOPIC: Taxation
CONCEPTS: Definition of terms. Conformity with
municipal law. Exchange of official publications.
Claims and settlements. Taxation. Death duties.
PROCEDURE: Duration. Ratification. Termination.
PARTIES:
Canada
South Africa

104304 Bilateral Agreement **299 UNTS 17**
SIGNED: 28 Sep 56   FORCE: 22 Jan 58
REGISTERED: 25 Apr 58 South Africa
ARTICLES: 13 LANGUAGE: English. Afrikaans.
HEADNOTE: DOUBLE TAXATION FISCAL EVASION TAXES INCOME
TOPIC: Taxation
CONCEPTS: Definition of terms. Previous treaty replacement. Conformity with municipal law. Exchange of official publications. Teacher and student exchange. Taxation. Tax credits. Tax exemptions. Air transport. Merchant vessels.
TREATY REF: 248UNTS107.
PROCEDURE: Duration. Ratification. Termination.
PARTIES:
Canada
South Africa

104305 Bilateral Exchange **299 UNTS 43**
SIGNED: 21 May 57   FORCE: 17 Mar 58
REGISTERED: 28 Apr 58 Netherlands
ARTICLES: 2 LANGUAGE: French.
HEADNOTE: MOVEMENT PERSONS
TOPIC: Visas
CONCEPTS: Emergencies. Territorial application.
Time limit. Border traffic and migration. Denial of
admission. Visas. Conformity with municipal
law.
PARTIES:
France
Netherlands
ANNEX
437 UNTS 362.   Netherlands.   Amendment
15 Mar 58. Force 15 Mar 58.
437 UNTS 362. France. Amendment 15 Mar 58.
Force 15 Mar 58.

104306 Bilateral Exchange **299 UNTS 51**
SIGNED: 21 Aug 55 FORCE: 21 Sep 55
REGISTERED: 28 Apr 58 Netherlands
ARTICLES: 2 LANGUAGE: English.
HEADNOTE: ABOLISHING VISA FEES
TOPIC: Visas
CONCEPTS: Visas. Fees and exemptions.
PARTIES:
Israel
Netherlands

104307 Bilateral Agreement **299 UNTS 57**
SIGNED: 29 Apr 54 FORCE: 3 Jun 54
REGISTERED: 28 Apr 58 India
ARTICLES: 6 LANGUAGE: Chinese. English. Hindi.
HEADNOTE: TRADE CULTURE PILGRIMAGES
TRAVEL PROMOTION
TOPIC: General Trade
CONCEPTS: Detailed regulations. Peaceful relations. Visa abolition. Border traffic and migration. Passports diplomatic. Non-visa travel documents. Visas. Privileges and immunities. Establishment of commission. Trade procedures. Routes and logistics.
PROCEDURE: Duration. Ratification. Renewal or Revival.
PARTIES:
China People's Rep
India

104308 Bilateral Agreement **299 UNTS 83**
SIGNED: 25 Nov 57 FORCE: 26 Nov 57
REGISTERED: 30 Apr 58 Denmark
ARTICLES: 23 LANGUAGE: Danish. Spanish.
HEADNOTE: FACILITATE PROMOTE ECONOMIC
RELATIONS TRADE PAYMENTS AGREEMENT
TOPIC: General Economic
CONCEPTS: General provisions. Annex or appendix reference. Previous treaty replacement. General relations and amity. Exchange of information and documents. Negotiation. Reciprocity in trade. Accounting procedures. Banking. Currency. Exchange rates and regulations. Financial programs. Funding procedures. Payment schedules. Non-interest rates and fees. Ports and pilotage.
TREATY REF: TRADE&PAYMENTS AGREEMENTS OF 18FEB1955.
PROCEDURE: Denunciation. Ratification. Renewal or Revival. Termination.
PARTIES:
Argentina
Denmark

104309 Bilateral Exchange **299 UNTS 113**
SIGNED: 5 Aug 57 FORCE: 5 Aug 57
REGISTERED: 30 Apr 58 USA (United States)
ARTICLES: 1 LANGUAGE: English. Spanish.
HEADNOTE: INSPECTION PANAMANIAN VESSELS CANAL ZONE
TOPIC: Visas
CONCEPTS: Inspection and observation. Navigational conditions.
PARTIES:
Panama
USA (United States)
ANNEX
335 UNTS 338. USA (United States). Prolongation 5 Aug 58. Force 16 Aug 58.
335 UNTS 338. Panama. Prolongation 16 Aug 58. Force 16 Aug 58.

104310 Bilateral Convention **299 UNTS 123**
SIGNED: 25 Oct 56 FORCE: 10 Oct 57
REGISTERED: 30 Apr 58 USA (United States)
ARTICLES: 20 LANGUAGE: English. German.
HEADNOTE: DOUBLE TAXATION INCOME
TOPIC: Taxation
CONCEPTS: Definition of terms. Privileges and immunities. Conformity with municipal law. Exchange of official publications. Domestic legislation. Negotiation. Teacher and student exchange. Claims and settlements. Taxation. General. Tax exemptions. Air transport. Merchant vessels.
PROCEDURE: Duration. Ratification. Termination.
PARTIES:
Austria
USA (United States)

104311 Bilateral Instrument **299 UNTS 157**
SIGNED: 29 Mar 57 FORCE: 22 Oct 57
REGISTERED: 30 Apr 58 USA (United States)
ARTICLES: 10 LANGUAGE: Italian.
HEADNOTE: WAR DAMAGE
TOPIC: Reparations
CONCEPTS: Claims and settlements. Post-war reconstruction.
INTL ORGS: Conciliation Commission.
PARTIES:
Italy
USA (United States)
ANNEX
411 UNTS 312. Italy. Supplementation 12 Jul 60. Force 15 Jun 61.
411 UNTS 312. USA (United States). Supplementation 12 Jul 60. Force 15 Jun 61.

104312 Bilateral Agreement **299 UNTS 167**
SIGNED: 1 Nov 57 FORCE: 1 Nov 57
REGISTERED: 30 Apr 58 USA (United States)
ARTICLES: 26 LANGUAGE: English.
HEADNOTE: OCEANOGRAPHIC RESEARCH STATIONS BAHAMAS
TOPIC: Scientific Project
CONCEPTS: Definition of terms. Border traffic and migration. Privileges and immunities. General cooperation. Juridical personality. Free passage and transit. General property. Use of facilities. Public health. Vocational training. Research and scientific projects. Research and development. Claims and settlements. Taxation. Tax exemptions. Special projects. Navigational equipment. Postal services. Security of information. Jurisdiction.
PARTIES:
UK Great Britain
USA (United States)
ANNEX
372 UNTS 364. USA (United States). Supplementation 12 May 60. Force 12 May 60.
372 UNTS 364. UK Great Britain. Supplementation 12 May 60. Force 12 May 60.

104313 Bilateral Agreement **299 UNTS 203**
SIGNED: 17 Oct 57 FORCE: 17 Oct 57
REGISTERED: 30 Apr 58 USA (United States)
ARTICLES: 11 LANGUAGE: French.
HEADNOTE: MUTUAL ASSISTANCE CARTOGRAPHY
TOPIC: Scientific Project
CONCEPTS: General cooperation. Exchange of information and documents. Use of facilities. Research and development. Special projects. Materials, equipment and services.
PROCEDURE: Amendment. Future Procedures Contemplated.
PARTIES:
Cambodia
USA (United States)

104314 Multilateral Convention **299 UNTS 211**
SIGNED: 27 Sep 57 FORCE: 15 Mar 58
REGISTERED: 1 May 58 Netherlands
ARTICLES: 13 LANGUAGE: French. German. English. Spanish. Italian.
HEADNOTE: ISSUE EXTRACTS CIVIL STATUS RECORDS
TOPIC: Admin Cooperation
CONCEPTS: Detailed regulations. Territorial application. Exchange of information and documents. Fees and exemptions.
INTL ORGS: International Commission on Civil Status.
PROCEDURE: Amendment. Accession. Denunciation. Duration. Ratification. Renewal or Revival.
PARTIES:
Belgium SIGNED: 27 Sep 56
France SIGNED: 27 Sep 56 RATIFIED: 12 Aug 57 FORCE: 15 Mar 58
Luxembourg SIGNED: 27 Sep 56
Netherlands SIGNED: 27 Sep 56 RATIFIED: 13 Feb 58 FORCE: 15 Mar 58
Switzerland SIGNED: 27 Sep 56
Turkey SIGNED: 27 Sep 56

104315 Bilateral Agreement **299 UNTS 231**
SIGNED: 25 Aug 56 FORCE: 14 Feb 58
REGISTERED: 5 May 58 Greece
ARTICLES: 8 LANGUAGE: French.

HEADNOTE: SETTLEMENT ECONOMIC QUESTIONS
TOPIC: Reparations
CONCEPTS: Annex or appendix reference. Exchange of information and documents. General property. Establishment of commission. Accounting procedures. Compensation. Payment schedules. Lump sum settlements. Debt settlement. Loss and/or damage. Post-war claims settlement.
INTL ORGS: Claims Commission.
TREATY REF: 42UNTS3.
PROCEDURE: Ratification.
PARTIES:
Greece
Romania

104316 Bilateral Convention **299 UNTS 247**
SIGNED: 11 Dec 56 FORCE: 9 Dec 57
REGISTERED: 5 May 58 Greece
ARTICLES: 5 LANGUAGE: French.
HEADNOTE: JUDICIAL SETTLEMENT
TOPIC: Dispute Settlement
CONCEPTS: Time limit. Procedure. Existing tribunals.
INTL ORGS: International Court of Justice.
PROCEDURE: Ratification.
PARTIES:
Greece
Sweden

104317 Bilateral Agreement **299 UNTS 253**
SIGNED: 4 Sep 56 FORCE: 17 Feb 58
REGISTERED: 5 May 58 Greece
ARTICLES: 6 LANGUAGE: French.
HEADNOTE: CULTURAL AGREEMENT
TOPIC: Culture
CONCEPTS: Friendship and amity. Conformity with municipal law. General cooperation. Recognition of degrees. Teacher and student exchange. Professorships. Institute establishment. Scholarships and grants. Exchange. General cultural cooperation. Artists. Athletes. Research cooperation. Anthropology and archeology. Scientific exchange. Publications exchange. Mass media exchange.
PROCEDURE: Denunciation. Duration. Ratification.
PARTIES:
Greece
United Arab Rep

104318 Bilateral Agreement **299 UNTS 261**
SIGNED: 15 May 54 FORCE: 15 May 54
REGISTERED: 5 May 58 Greece
ARTICLES: 8 LANGUAGE: French.
HEADNOTE: TRADE
TOPIC: General Trade
CONCEPTS: Annex or appendix reference. Previous treaty replacement. Licenses and permits. Establishment of commission. Export quotas. Import quotas. Payment schedules. Quotas.
INTL ORGS: Special Commission.
TREATY REF: 3FEB50; 299UNTS277.
PROCEDURE: Renewal or Revival. Termination.
PARTIES:
Greece
Spain

104319 Bilateral Agreement **299 UNTS 277**
SIGNED: 15 May 54 FORCE: 15 May 54
REGISTERED: 5 May 58 Greece
ARTICLES: 10 LANGUAGE: French.
HEADNOTE: PAYMENTS
TOPIC: Finance
CONCEPTS: Detailed regulations. Previous treaty replacement. Conformity with municipal law. General cooperation. Import quotas. Accounting procedures. Banking. Balance of payments. Currency. Exchange rates and regulations. Financial programs. Inadequacy of funds. Payment schedules.
TREATY REF: 299UNTS261; 23FEB50; 22DEC52; PAYMENTS AGREEMENTS.
PARTIES:
Greece
Spain

104320 Bilateral Agreement **299 UNTS 285**
SIGNED: 5 Jun 54 FORCE: 5 Jun 54

REGISTERED: 5 May 58 Greece
ARTICLES: 6 LANGUAGE: French.
HEADNOTE: TRADE
TOPIC: General Trade
CONCEPTS: Treaty implementation. Annex or appendix reference. Conformity with municipal law. Juridical personality. Expropriation. Legal protection and assistance. Licenses and permits. General property. Establishment of commission. Establishment of trade relations. Accounting procedures. Payment schedules. Claims and settlements.
INTL ORGS: Special Commission.
TREATY REF: 299UNTS295.
PROCEDURE: Denunciation. Duration. Renewal or Revival.
PARTIES:
Greece
Hungary
ANNEX
609 UNTS 378. Greece. Amendment 28 Jun 56. Force 1 Jun 56.
609 UNTS 378. Hungary. Amendment 28 Jun 56. Force 1 Jun 56.

104321 Bilateral Agreement **299 UNTS 295**
SIGNED: 5 Jun 54 FORCE: 5 Jun 54
REGISTERED: 5 May 58 Greece
ARTICLES: 10 LANGUAGE: French.
HEADNOTE: PAYMENTS
TOPIC: Finance
CONCEPTS: Detailed regulations. Previous treaty replacement. Conformity with municipal law. General cooperation. General trade. Accounting procedures. Banking. Balance of payments. Currency. Exchange rates and regulations. Fees and exemptions. Inadequacy of funds. Interest rates. Payment schedules. Local currency. Credit provisions.
TREATY REF: 299UNTS285;1JUNE53 BARTER AGREEMENT.
PROCEDURE: Denunciation. Duration. Renewal or Revival.
PARTIES:
Greece
Hungary
ANNEX
483 UNTS 322. Greece. Supplementation 3 Feb 61. Force 3 Feb 61.
483 UNTS 322. Hungary. Supplementation 3 Feb 61. Force 3 Feb 61.
483 UNTS 334. Hungary. Supplementation 24 Feb 62. Force 24 Feb 62.
483 UNTS 334. Greece. Supplementation 24 Feb 62. Force 24 Feb 62.

104322 Bilateral Agreement **299 UNTS 303**
SIGNED: 18 Oct 57 FORCE: 22 Jan 58
REGISTERED: 5 May 58 IBRD (World Bank)
ARTICLES: 7 LANGUAGE: English.
HEADNOTE: LOAN AGREEMENT
TOPIC: IBRD Project
CONCEPTS: Default remedies. Definition of terms. Annex or appendix reference. Exchange of information and documents. Informational records. Inspection and observation. Accounting procedures. Bonds. Fees and exemptions. Interest rates. Tax exemptions. Domestic obligation. Terms of loan. Loan regulations. Loan guarantee. Guarantor non-interference.
PARTIES:
Pakistan
IBRD (World Bank)

104323 Bilateral Agreement **299 UNTS 321**
SIGNED: 17 Dec 57 FORCE: 7 Mar 58
REGISTERED: 5 May 58 IBRD (World Bank)
ARTICLES: 5 LANGUAGE: English.
HEADNOTE: GUARANTEE INDUSTRIAL CREDIT & INVESTMENT
TOPIC: IBRD Project
CONCEPTS: Definition of terms. Annex or appendix reference. Exchange of information and documents. Inspection and observation. Fees and exemptions. Tax exemptions. Domestic obligation. Terms of loan. Loan regulations. Loan guarantee. Guarantor non-interference.
PARTIES:
Pakistan
IBRD (World Bank)

104324 Bilateral Agreement **299 UNTS 349**
SIGNED: 12 Sep 57 FORCE: 28 Feb 58
REGISTERED: 5 May 58 IBRD (World Bank)
ARTICLES: 6 LANGUAGE: English.
HEADNOTE: GUARANTEE AGREEMENT
TOPIC: IBRD Project
CONCEPTS: Definition of terms. Annex or appendix reference. Exchange of information and documents. Inspection and observation. Bonds. Fees and exemptions. Tax exemptions. Domestic obligation. Terms of loan. Loan regulations. Loan guarantee. Guarantor non-interference.
PARTIES:
IBRD (World Bank)
Thailand

104325 Bilateral Exchange **299 UNTS 377**
SIGNED: 28 Aug 54 FORCE: 28 Aug 54
REGISTERED: 7 May 58 USA (United States)
ARTICLES: 2 LANGUAGE: English. German.
HEADNOTE: VISAS
TOPIC: Milit Installation
CONCEPTS: Territorial application. Time limit. Visa abolition. Resident permits. Visas. Fees and exemptions.
TREATY REF: 151UNTS215.
PROCEDURE: Termination.
PARTIES:
Germany, West
USA (United States)

104326 Bilateral Exchange **300 UNTS 3**
SIGNED: 24 Sep 54 FORCE: 24 Sep 54
REGISTERED: 7 May 58 USA (United States)
ARTICLES: 2 LANGUAGE: English.
HEADNOTE: ACCEPTANCE AMENDMENT AGREEMENT PRACTICE BOMBING RANGE
TOPIC: Milit Installation
CONCEPTS: Annex or appendix reference. Military installations and equipment.
TREATY REF: 151UNTS215.
PARTIES:
UK Great Britain
USA (United States)

104327 Bilateral Agreement **300 UNTS 11**
SIGNED: 21 Mar 57 FORCE: 9 Oct 57
REGISTERED: 7 May 58 USA (United States)
ARTICLES: 7 LANGUAGE: English. Burmese.
HEADNOTE: ECONOMIC COOPERATION
TOPIC: Direct Aid
CONCEPTS: Treaty implementation. Treaty interpretation. General cooperation. Exchange of information and documents. Public information. Domestic obligation. Economic assistance. Procurement. Access to materials. Loan and credit.
INTL ORGS: United Nations.
PROCEDURE: Amendment. Registration. Termination.
PARTIES:
Burma
USA (United States)
ANNEX
358 UNTS 352. USA (United States). Amendment 12 Sep 59. Force 12 Sep 59.
358 UNTS 352. Burma. Amendment 12 Sep 59. Force 12 Sep 59.
394 UNTS 284. Burma. Supplementation 29 Jun 60. Force 29 Jun 60.
394 UNTS 284. USA (United States). Supplementation 29 Jun 60. Force 29 Jun 60.

104328 Bilateral Exchange **300 UNTS 23**
SIGNED: 5 Nov 57 FORCE: 5 Nov 57
REGISTERED: 7 May 58 USA (United States)
ARTICLES: 2 LANGUAGE: English. French.
HEADNOTE: GUARANTY PRIVATE INVESTMENT
TOPIC: Finance
CONCEPTS: Arbitration. Existing tribunals. Negotiation. Reciprocity in financial treatment. Currency. Payment schedules. Claims and settlements. Private investment guarantee. Assets transfer. Most favored nation clause. Loss and/or damage.
INTL ORGS: International Court of Justice.
PARTIES:
USA (United States)
Vietnam, South

ANNEX
488 UNTS 270. USA (United States). Supplementation 8 Aug 63. Force 8 Aug 63.
488 UNTS 270. Vietnam, South. Supplementation 8 Aug 63. Force 8 Aug 63.

104329 Bilateral Exchange **300 UNTS 29**
SIGNED: 23 Apr 56 FORCE: 23 Apr 56
REGISTERED: 7 May 58 USA (United States)
ARTICLES: 2 LANGUAGE: English.
HEADNOTE: UNEMPLOYMENT INSURANCE
TOPIC: Non-ILO Labor
CONCEPTS: Definition of terms. Non-ILO labor relations. Unemployment. Expense sharing formulae. National treatment.
PARTIES:
Canada
USA (United States)

104330 Bilateral Agreement **300 UNTS 35**
SIGNED: 23 Oct 57 FORCE: 23 Oct 57
REGISTERED: 7 May 58 USA (United States)
ARTICLES: 6 LANGUAGE: English. Spanish.
HEADNOTE: AGRI COMMOD
TOPIC: US Agri Commod Aid
CONCEPTS: Annex or appendix reference. General cooperation. Exchange of information and documents. Reexport of goods, etc.. Currency deposits. Exchange rates and regulations. Purchase authorizations. Transportation costs. Local currency. Commodities schedule. Surplus commodities.
PARTIES:
Mexico
USA (United States)
ANNEX
321 UNTS 292. Mexico. Amendment 30 Jun 58. Force 30 Jun 58.
321 UNTS 292. USA (United States). Amendment 30 Jun 58. Force 30 Jun 58.
336 UNTS 406. USA (United States). Amendment 7 Nov 58. Force 7 Nov 58.
336 UNTS 406. Mexico. Amendment 7 Nov 58. Force 7 Nov 58.
340 UNTS 400. USA (United States). Prolongation 17 Feb 59. Force 17 Feb 59.
340 UNTS 400. Mexico. Prolongation 17 Feb 59. Force 17 Feb 59.
461 UNTS 325. USA (United States). Supplementation 6 Jul 61. Force 9 Aug 62.
461 UNTS 325. Mexico. Supplementation 9 Aug 62. Force 9 Aug 62.

104331 Bilateral Agreement **300 UNTS 61**
SIGNED: 30 Jul 57 FORCE: 1 Nov 57
REGISTERED: 7 May 58 USA (United States)
ARTICLES: 18 LANGUAGE: English.
HEADNOTE: INSURED PARCEL POST
TOPIC: Postal Service
CONCEPTS: Previous treaty extension. Domestic legislation. Responsibility and liability. Compensation. Indemnities and reimbursements. Payment schedules. Claims and settlements. Postal services. Regulations. Insured letters and boxes. Parcel post.
INTL ORGS: Universal Postal Union.
TREATY REF: 169UNTS3; 186UNTS356; 202UNTS340; 227UNTS390.
PROCEDURE: Duration. Termination.
PARTIES:
Taiwan
USA (United States)

104332 Bilateral Agreement **300 UNTS 83**
SIGNED: 28 Mar 58 FORCE: 1 Jan 58
REGISTERED: 14 May 58 South Africa
ARTICLES: 9 LANGUAGE: English.
HEADNOTE: REGARD AIR SERVICES
TOPIC: Air Transport
CONCEPTS: Definition of terms. Exceptions and exemptions. Previous treaty replacement. Conformity with municipal law. Non-interest rates and fees. Routes and logistics. Permit designation. Conditions of airlines operating permission. Operating authorizations and regulations.
INTL ORGS: International Civil Aviation Organization.
TREATY REF: 15UNTS295; 192UNTS105.
PROCEDURE: Termination. Application to Non-self-governing Territories.

PARTIES:
Norway
South Africa
ANNEX
392 UNTS 364. Norway. Prolongation 15 Aug 59. Force 15 Aug 59.
392 UNTS 364. South Africa. Prolongation 15 Aug 59. Force 15 Aug 59.
392 UNTS 368. Norway. Prolongation 22 Mar 60. Force 22 Mar 60.
392 UNTS 368. South Africa. Prolongation 22 Mar 60. Force 22 Mar 60.
464 UNTS 332. South Africa. Prolongation 18 Dec 61. Force 20 Dec 61.
464 UNTS 332. Norway. Prolongation 20 Dec 61. Force 20 Dec 61.
497 UNTS 552. South Africa. Prolongation 8 May 63. Force 8 May 63.
497 UNTS 552. Norway. Prolongation 8 May 63. Force 8 May 63.
523 UNTS 328. South Africa. Prolongation 31 Mar 64. Force 31 Mar 64.
523 UNTS 328. Norway. Prolongation 31 Mar 64. Force 31 Mar 64.
602 UNTS 316. South Africa. Prolongation 29 Apr 65. Force 29 Apr 65.
602 UNTS 316. Norway. Prolongation 29 Apr 65. Force 29 Apr 65.
646 UNTS 366. South Africa. Extension and Amendment 13 Mar 67. Force 13 Mar 67.
646 UNTS 366. Norway. Extension and Amendment 13 Mar 67. Force 13 Mar 67.

104333 Bilateral Agreement **300 UNTS 95**
SIGNED: 28 Mar 58 FORCE: 1 Jan 58
REGISTERED: 14 May 58 South Africa
ARTICLES: 9 LANGUAGE: English.
HEADNOTE: REGARD AIR SERVICES
TOPIC: Air Transport
CONCEPTS: Definition of terms. Exceptions and exemptions. Previous treaty replacement. Conformity with municipal law. Non-interest rates and fees. Routes and logistics. Permit designation. Conditions of airlines operating permission. Operating authorizations and regulations.
INTL ORGS: International Civil Aviation Organization.
TREATY REF: 15UNTS295; 173UNTS299.
PROCEDURE: Termination. Application to Non-self-governing Territories.
PARTIES:
South Africa
Sweden
ANNEX
392 UNTS 372. Sweden. Prolongation 15 Aug 59. Force 15 Aug 59.
392 UNTS 372. South Africa. Prolongation 15 Aug 59. Force 15 Aug 59.
392 UNTS 376. Sweden. Prolongation 22 Mar 60. Force 22 Mar 60.
392 UNTS 376. South Africa. Prolongation 22 Mar 60. Force 22 Mar 60.
464 UNTS 336. South Africa. Prolongation 18 Dec 61. Force 18 Dec 61.
464 UNTS 336. Sweden. Prolongation 18 Dec 61. Force 18 Dec 61.
497 UNTS 356. South Africa. Prolongation 8 May 63. Force 8 May 63.
497 UNTS 356. Sweden. Prolongation 8 May 63. Force 8 May 63.
523 UNTS 332. Sweden. Prolongation 31 Mar 64. Force 31 Mar 64.
523 UNTS 332. South Africa. Prolongation 31 Mar 64. Force 31 Mar 64.
602 UNTS 324. South Africa. Prolongation 29 Apr 65. Force 29 Apr 65.
602 UNTS 324. Sweden. Prolongation 29 Apr 65. Force 29 Apr 65.
646 UNTS 370. Sweden. Extension and Amendment 13 Mar 67. Force 13 Mar 67.
646 UNTS 370. South Africa. Extension and Amendment 13 Mar 67. Force 13 Mar 67.

104334 Bilateral Agreement **300 UNTS 107**
SIGNED: 28 Mar 58 FORCE: 1 Jan 58
REGISTERED: 14 May 58 South Africa
ARTICLES: 9 LANGUAGE: English.
HEADNOTE: REGARD AIR SERVICES
TOPIC: Air Transport
CONCEPTS: Definition of terms. Exceptions and exemptions. Previous treaty replacement. Conformity with municipal law. Non-interest rates

and fees. Routes and logistics. Permit designation. Conditions of airlines operating permission. Operating authorizations and regulations.
INTL ORGS: International Civil Aviation Organization.
TREATY REF: 174UNTS19; 15UNTS295.
PROCEDURE: Termination. Application to Non-self-governing Territories.
PARTIES:
Denmark
South Africa
ANNEX
392 UNTS 380. Denmark. Prolongation 15 Aug 59. Force 15 Aug 59.
392 UNTS 380. South Africa. Prolongation 15 Aug 59. Force 15 Aug 59.
392 UNTS 384. South Africa. Prolongation 22 Mar 60. Force 22 Mar 60.
392 UNTS 384. Denmark. Prolongation 22 Mar 60. Force 22 Mar 60.
464 UNTS 340. South Africa. Prolongation 18 Dec 61. Force 18 Dec 61.
464 UNTS 340. Denmark. Prolongation 18 Dec 61. Force 18 Dec 61.
497 UNTS 360. South Africa. Prolongation 8 May 63. Force 8 May 63.
497 UNTS 360. Denmark. Prolongation 8 May 63. Force 8 May 63.
523 UNTS 336. Denmark. Prolongation 31 Mar 64. Force 31 Mar 64.
523 UNTS 336. South Africa. Prolongation 31 Mar 64. Force 31 Mar 64.
602 UNTS 332. South Africa. Prolongation 29 Apr 65. Force 29 Apr 65.
602 UNTS 332. Denmark. Prolongation 29 Apr 65. Force 29 Apr 65.
646 UNTS 374. South Africa. Extension and Amendment 13 Mar 67. Force 13 Mar 67.
646 UNTS 374. Denmark. Extension and Amendment 13 Mar 67. Force 13 Mar 67.

104335 Bilateral Protocol **300 UNTS 119**
SIGNED: 13 Feb 57 FORCE: 8 May 57
REGISTERED: 14 May 58 Czechoslovakia
ARTICLES: 6 LANGUAGE: English.
HEADNOTE: RESTORATION NORMAL RELATIONS
TOPIC: General Amity
CONCEPTS: Peaceful relations. Diplomatic relations establishment. Procedure. Post-war claims settlement.
INTL ORGS: United Nations.
PROCEDURE: Future Procedures Contemplated. Ratification.
PARTIES:
Czechoslovakia
Japan

104336 Bilateral Treaty **300 UNTS 125**
SIGNED: 13 Oct 56 FORCE: 10 Feb 58
REGISTERED: 14 May 58 Czechoslovakia
ARTICLES: 28 LANGUAGE: Czechoslovakian. Hungarian.
HEADNOTE: REGIME STATE FRONTIERS
TOPIC: Territory Boundary
CONCEPTS: Annex or appendix reference. Previous treaties adherence. Inspection and observation. Fish, wildlife, and natural resources. Markers and definitions. Frontier waterways. Regulation of natural resources.
INTL ORGS: Special Commission.
TREATY REF: 16APRIL1954.
PROCEDURE: Denunciation. Duration. Ratification. Renewal or Revival.
PARTIES:
Czechoslovakia
Hungary

104337 Bilateral Agreement **300 UNTS 177**
SIGNED: 13 Oct 56 FORCE: 4 Jul 57
REGISTERED: 14 May 58 Czechoslovakia
ARTICLES: 30 LANGUAGE: Czechoslovakian. Hungarian.
HEADNOTE: FRONTIER COMMISSIONERS
TOPIC: Territory Boundary
CONCEPTS: Annex or appendix reference. Previous treaty replacement. Inspection and observation. Operating agencies. Establishment of commission. Dispute settlement. Negotiation. Indemnities and reimbursements. Currency. Boundaries of territory. Frontier crossing points.
TREATY REF: 4MAY1949.

PROCEDURE: Denunciation.
PARTIES:
Czechoslovakia
Hungary

104338 Bilateral Agreement **300 UNTS 229**
SIGNED: 19 Nov 57 FORCE: 19 Nov 57
REGISTERED: 14 May 58 United Nations
ARTICLES: 11 LANGUAGE: English. Spanish.
HEADNOTE: ACTIVITIES UNICEF
TOPIC: Direct Aid
CONCEPTS: Treaty implementation. Recognition. Privileges and immunities. General cooperation. Informational records. Inspection and observation. Public information. Responsibility and liability. Procedure. Existing tribunals. Reexport of goods, etc.. Claims and settlements. Tax exemptions. Customs exemptions. Commodities and services. Assistance. General aid. Distribution. IGO status.
INTL ORGS: United Nations.
TREATY REF: 1UNTS15; 252UNTS308.
PROCEDURE: Duration.
PARTIES:
Argentina
UNICEF (Children)

104339 Bilateral Agreement **300 UNTS 249**
SIGNED: 29 Jan 57 FORCE: 28 Nov 57
REGISTERED: 16 May 58 Czechoslovakia
ARTICLES: 11 LANGUAGE: Czechoslovakian. Serbo-Croat.
HEADNOTE: CULTURAL OTHER COOPERATION
TOPIC: Culture
CONCEPTS: Friendship and amity. General cooperation. Exchange of information and documents. Exchange. Teacher and student exchange. Institute establishment. Scholarships and grants. General cultural cooperation. Artists. Research cooperation. Scientific exchange. Publications exchange. Press and wire services.
PROCEDURE: Denunciation. Duration. Future Procedures Contemplated. Ratification. Renewal or Revival.
PARTIES:
Czechoslovakia
Yugoslavia

104340 Bilateral Exchange **300 UNTS 263**
SIGNED: 26 Dec 56 FORCE: 26 Dec 56
REGISTERED: 19 May 58 France
ARTICLES: 2 LANGUAGE: French. Arabic.
HEADNOTE: DELIMIT FRANCO-LIBYAN FRONTIER
TOPIC: Territory Boundary
CONCEPTS: Annex or appendix reference. Markers and definitions.
PARTIES:
France
Libya

104341 Bilateral Agreement **301 UNTS 3**
SIGNED: 26 Jun 56 FORCE: 20 Nov 56
REGISTERED: 19 May 58 IBRD (World Bank)
ARTICLES: 5 LANGUAGE: English.
HEADNOTE: GUARANTEE AGREEMENT
TOPIC: IBRD Project
CONCEPTS: Annex or appendix reference. Exchange of information and documents. Inspection and observation. Bonds. Fees and exemptions. Tax exemptions. Domestic obligation. Terms of loan. Loan regulations. Loan guarantee. Guarantor non-interference.
PARTIES:
India
IBRD (World Bank)

104342 Bilateral Agreement **301 UNTS 47**
SIGNED: 20 Nov 57 FORCE: 19 Feb 58
REGISTERED: 20 May 58 IBRD (World Bank)
ARTICLES: 5 LANGUAGE: English.
HEADNOTE: GUARANTEE AGREEMENT
TOPIC: IBRD Project
CONCEPTS: Annex or appendix reference. Exchange of information and documents. Inspection and observation. Bonds. Fees and exemptions. Tax exemptions. Domestic obligation. Terms of loan. Loan regulations. Loan guarantee. Guarantor non-interference.

PARTIES:
India
IBRD (World Bank)

104343 Bilateral Agreement **301 UNTS 95**
SIGNED: 10 Oct 57   FORCE: 18 Jan 58
REGISTERED: 20 May 58 IBRD (World Bank)
ARTICLES: 5 LANGUAGE: English.
HEADNOTE: GUARANTEE AGREEMENT
TOPIC: IBRD Project
CONCEPTS: Definition of terms. Annex or appendix reference. Exchange of information and documents. Inspection and observation. Bonds. Fees and exemptions. Tax exemptions. Domestic obligation. Terms of loan. Loan regulations. Loan guarantee. Guarantor non-interference.
PARTIES:
Austria
IBRD (World Bank)

104344 Bilateral Agreement **301 UNTS 135**
SIGNED: 6 Oct 53   FORCE: 13 May 54
REGISTERED: 20 May 58 IBRD (World Bank)
ARTICLES: 6 LANGUAGE: English.
HEADNOTE: GUARANTEE AGREEMENT
TOPIC: IBRD Project
CONCEPTS: Definition of terms. Annex or appendix reference. Exchange of information and documents. Inspection and observation. Bonds. Fees and exemptions. Tax exemptions. Domestic obligation. Terms of loan. Loan regulations. Loan guarantee. Guarantor non-interference.
PARTIES:
Italy
IBRD (World Bank)

104345 Bilateral Agreement **301 UNTS 165**
SIGNED: 26 May 50   FORCE: 17 Jul 50
REGISTERED: 21 May 58 IBRD (World Bank)
ARTICLES: 9 LANGUAGE: English.
HEADNOTE: GUARANTEE AGREEMENT
TOPIC: IBRD Project
CONCEPTS: Definition of terms. Annex or appendix reference. Conformity with municipal law. Exchange of information and documents. Inspection and observation. Arbitration. Procedure. Bonds. Fees and exemptions. Tax exemptions. Domestic obligation. Terms of loan. Loan regulations. Loan guarantee. Guarantor non-interference.
PROCEDURE: Termination.
PARTIES:
Brazil
IBRD (World Bank)

104346 Bilateral Agreement **301 UNTS 229**
SIGNED: 18 Dec 53   FORCE: 2 Sep 54
REGISTERED: 21 May 58 IBRD (World Bank)
ARTICLES: 8 LANGUAGE: English.
HEADNOTE: LOAN AGREEMENT
TOPIC: IBRD Project
CONCEPTS: Default remedies. Definition of terms. Annex or appendix reference. Exchange of information and documents. Inspection and observation. Accounting procedures. Bonds. Fees and exemptions. Interest rates. Tax exemptions. Domestic obligation. Terms of loan. Loan regulations. Loan guarantee. Guarantor non-interference.
PARTIES:
Brazil
IBRD (World Bank)

104347 Bilateral Agreement **301 UNTS 249**
SIGNED: 24 Feb 54   FORCE: 28 Dec 54
REGISTERED: 21 May 58 IBRD (World Bank)
ARTICLES: 5 LANGUAGE: English.
HEADNOTE: GUARANTEE AGREEMENT
TOPIC: IBRD Project
CONCEPTS: Annex or appendix reference. Exchange of information and documents. Inspection and observation. Bonds. Fees and exemptions. Tax exemptions. Domestic obligation. Loan regulations. Loan guarantee. Guarantor non-interference. Hydro-electric power.
PARTIES:
Brazil
IBRD (World Bank)

104348 Bilateral Exchange **301 UNTS 291**
SIGNED: 18 Mar 58   FORCE: 15 Apr 58
REGISTERED: 21 May 58 Belgium
ARTICLES: 4 LANGUAGE: French. Spanish.
HEADNOTE: ABOLITION TRAVEL VISA REQUIREMENTS
TOPIC: Visas
CONCEPTS: Emergencies. Territorial application. Time limit. Visa abolition. Denial of admission. Conformity with municipal law. Fees and exemptions.
PROCEDURE: Denunciation.
PARTIES:
Belgium
Mexico

104349 Bilateral Treaty **301 UNTS 301**
SIGNED: 16 Dec 57   FORCE: 6 Mar 58
REGISTERED: 21 May 58 USSR (Soviet Union)
ARTICLES: 76 LANGUAGE: Russian. Korean.
HEADNOTE: LEGAL ASSISTANCE CIVIL FAMILY CRIMINAL CASES
TOPIC: Admin Cooperation
CONCEPTS: General provisions. Privileges and immunities. Extradition, deportation and repatriation. Extradition requests. Refusal of extradition. Concurrent requests. Provisional detainment. Extradition postponement. Witnesses and experts. Material evidence. Conformity with municipal law. General cooperation. Family law. Juridical personality. Legal protection and assistance. Recognition and enforcement of legal decisions. Immovable property. General property. Jurisdiction. Recognition of legal documents. Indemnities and reimbursements. Fees and exemptions. Assets transfer. Conveyance in transit.
PROCEDURE: Duration. Ratification. Termination.
PARTIES:
Korea, North
USSR (Soviet Union)

104350 Bilateral Agreement **301 UNTS 405**
SIGNED: 27 Jan 58   FORCE: 27 Jan 58
REGISTERED: 21 May 58 USSR (Soviet Union)
ARTICLES: 15 LANGUAGE: Russian. English.
HEADNOTE: EXCHANGES CULTURAL TECHNICAL EDUCATIONAL FIELDS
TOPIC: Health/Educ/Welfare
CONCEPTS: Exchange of information and documents. Personnel. Specialists exchange. Exchange. Teacher and student exchange. Exchange. Athletes. Scientific exchange. Air transport. Publications exchange. Mass media exchange. Press and wire services.
INTL ORGS: United Nations Educational, Scientific and Cultural Organization.
PROCEDURE: Duration.
PARTIES:
USA (United States)
USSR (Soviet Union)

104351 Bilateral Convention **302 UNTS 3**
SIGNED: 12 Dec 57   FORCE: 28 Mar 58
REGISTERED: 21 May 58 USSR (Soviet Union)
ARTICLES: 12 LANGUAGE: Russian. Bulgarian.
HEADNOTE: DUAL CITIZENSHIP
TOPIC: Consul/Citizenship
CONCEPTS: Resident permits. Dual citizenship. Procedure. Tax exemptions.
PROCEDURE: Ratification.
PARTIES:
Bulgaria
USSR (Soviet Union)

104352 Bilateral Convention **302 UNTS 21**
SIGNED: 12 Dec 57   FORCE: 28 Mar 58
REGISTERED: 21 May 58 USSR (Soviet Union)
ARTICLES: 24 LANGUAGE: Russian. Bulgarian.
HEADNOTE: CONSULAR CONVENTION
TOPIC: Consul/Citizenship
CONCEPTS: Definition of terms. General consular functions. Diplomatic privileges. Consular relations establishment. Inviolability. Privileges and immunities. Diplomatic correspondence. Responsibility and liability.
PROCEDURE: Ratification. Termination.
PARTIES:
Bulgaria
USSR (Soviet Union)

104353 Bilateral Agreement **302 UNTS 53**
SIGNED: 10 Apr 57   FORCE: 10 Apr 58
REGISTERED: 29 May 58 Denmark
ARTICLES: 14 LANGUAGE: English.
HEADNOTE: RELATING AIR SERVICES
TOPIC: Air Transport
CONCEPTS: Definition of terms. Detailed regulations. Annex or appendix reference. Previous treaty replacement. Conformity with municipal law. General cooperation. Exchange of information and documents. Use of facilities. Arbitration. Procedure. Existing tribunals. Negotiation. Fees and exemptions. Non-interest rates and fees. Most favored nation clause. National treatment. Customs duties. Customs exemptions. Routes and logistics. Permit designation. Air transport. Conditions of airlines operating permission. Overflights and technical stops. Operating authorizations and regulations.
INTL ORGS: International Civil Aviation Organization. International Court of Justice. Arbitration Commission.
TREATY REF: 15UNTS295; 171UNTS387; 44UNTS255.
PROCEDURE: Amendment. Future Procedures Contemplated. Termination. Application to Non-self-governing Territories.
PARTIES:
Denmark
Pakistan

104354 Bilateral Agreement **302 UNTS 75**
SIGNED: 29 Jan 57   FORCE: 28 Apr 58
REGISTERED: 29 May 58 Denmark
ARTICLES: 20 LANGUAGE: Danish. German.
HEADNOTE: RELATING AIR SERVICES
TOPIC: Air Transport
CONCEPTS: Definition of terms. Detailed regulations. Annex or appendix reference. Previous treaty replacement. Conformity with municipal law. General cooperation. Exchange of information and documents. Licenses and permits. Recognition of legal documents. Use of facilities. Arbitration. Procedure. Special tribunals. Reexport of goods, etc.. Currency. Monetary and gold transfers. Exchange rates and regulations. Expense sharing formulae. Fees and exemptions. Non-interest rates and fees. National treatment. Tax exemptions. Customs exemptions. Competency certificate. Routes and logistics. Navigational conditions. Permit designation. Airport facilities. Airworthiness certificates. Conditions of airlines operating permission. Overflights and technical stops. Operating authorizations and regulations. Licenses and certificates of nationality.
INTL ORGS: International Civil Aviation Organization. Arbitration Commission.
PROCEDURE: Amendment. Denunciation. Future Procedures Contemplated. Ratification. Registration. Termination.
PARTIES:
Denmark
Germany, West
                ANNEX
405 UNTS 333. Germany, West. Amendment 16 Feb 61. Force 1 Apr 61.
405 UNTS 333. Denmark. Amendment 16 Feb 61. Force 1 Apr 61.

104355 Multilateral Protocol **302 UNTS 121**
SIGNED: 3 Apr 58   FORCE: 11 Apr 58
REGISTERED: 29 May 58 United Nations
ARTICLES: 7 LANGUAGE: English. French. Spanish.
HEADNOTE: AGREEMENT OLIVE OIL
TOPIC: Commodity Trade
CONCEPTS: Annex type material. Commodity trade.
INTL ORGS: United Nations.
TREATY REF: INTL. AGREEMENT ON OLIVE OIL 17OCT55.
PROCEDURE: Registration.
PARTIES:
France SIGNED: 3 Apr 58 FORCE: 10 Apr 58
Portugal SIGNED: 8 Apr 58 FORCE: 11 Apr 58
Spain SIGNED: 9 Apr 58 FORCE: 11 Apr 58
Tunisia SIGNED: 3 Apr 58 FORCE: 11 Apr 58
                ANNEX
307 UNTS 335. Italy. Force 30 Jul 58.

104356 Bilateral Exchange **302 UNTS 141**
SIGNED: 29 Nov 56 FORCE: 14 Apr 58
REGISTERED: 11 Jun 58 United Nations
ARTICLES: 7 LANGUAGE: English.
HEADNOTE: EXEMPTION FROM DUTIES SUP-
PLIES OF FUEL AIRCRAFT
TOPIC: Air Transport
CONCEPTS: Annex type material. Fees and exemp-
tions. Customs exemptions. Air transport.
TREATY REF: 128UNTS63; 15UNTS295.
PROCEDURE: Ratification.
PARTIES:
Australia
Netherlands

104357 Bilateral Agreement **302 UNTS 147**
SIGNED: 6 Jul 57 FORCE: 22 Jul 57
REGISTERED: 13 Jun 58 Italy
ARTICLES: 6 LANGUAGE: French.
HEADNOTE: PAYMENTS
TOPIC: Finance
CONCEPTS: Annex or appendix reference. Previ-
ous treaty replacement. Conformity with munici-
pal law. Licenses and permits. Establishment of
commission. Banking. Currency. Payment sched-
ules. Local currency.
INTL ORGS: Special Commission.
TREATY REF: 302UNTS153; 8NOV52 PROVI-
SIONAL PAYMENT AGREEMENTS.
PROCEDURE: Denunciation.
PARTIES:
Italy
United Arab Rep

104358 Bilateral Agreement **302 UNTS 181**
SIGNED: 29 Jan 58 FORCE: 10 Feb 58
REGISTERED: 13 Jun 58 Italy
ARTICLES: 4 LANGUAGE: French.
HEADNOTE: PAYMENTS
TOPIC: Finance
CONCEPTS: Conformity with municipal law. Li-
censes and permits. Currency. Financial pro-
grams. Payment schedules. Local currency.
INTL ORGS: International Monetary Fund.
TREATY REF: 2UNTS40; 302UNTS189;
302UNTS193.
PROCEDURE: Denunciation.
PARTIES:
Iran
Italy

104359 Bilateral Agreement **302 UNTS 195**
SIGNED: 5 Sep 56 FORCE: 5 Sep 56
REGISTERED: 13 Jun 58 Italy
ARTICLES: 13 LANGUAGE: Italian. Spanish.
HEADNOTE: COPRODUCTION CINEMATO-
GRAPHIC FILMS
TOPIC: Mass Media
CONCEPTS: Conformity with municipal law. Estab-
lishment of commission. General cultural coop-
eration. Indemnities and reimbursements. Ex-
pense sharing formulae. Assets. Quotas. Mass
media exchange.
PROCEDURE: Denunciation. Duration.
PARTIES:
Italy
Spain

104360 Bilateral Protocol **302 UNTS 221**
SIGNED: 1 Aug 57 FORCE: 1 Aug 57
REGISTERED: 13 Jun 58 Italy
ARTICLES: 5 LANGUAGE: French.
HEADNOTE: ITALIAN BEEF WORKERS
TOPIC: Non-ILO Labor
CONCEPTS: Holidays and rest periods. Wages and
salaries. Non-ILO labor relations. Migrant
worker. Monetary and gold transfers. Quotas.
National treatment.
INTL ORGS: Special Commission.
PARTIES:
France
Italy

104361 Bilateral Protocol **302 UNTS 225**
SIGNED: 19 Sep 57 FORCE: 19 Sep 57
REGISTERED: 13 Jun 58 Italy
ARTICLES: 2 LANGUAGE: French.
HEADNOTE: ITALIAN SEASONAL WORKERS
TOPIC: Non-ILO Labor

CONCEPTS: Annex or appendix reference. Non-
ILO labor relations. Migrant worker. Monetary
and gold transfers.
TREATY REF: 30IUNTS221; 302UNTS229.
PARTIES:
France
Italy

104362 Bilateral Agreement **302 UNTS 231**
SIGNED: 28 Jan 58 FORCE: 1 Mar 58
REGISTERED: 13 Jun 58 Italy
ARTICLES: 5 LANGUAGE: French.
HEADNOTE: PAYMENTS
TOPIC: Finance
CONCEPTS: Previous treaty amendment. Annex or
appendix reference. Conformity with municipal
law. Licenses and permits. Banking. Currency.
Payment schedules. Local currency.
TREATY REF: 302UNTS235.
PROCEDURE: Denunciation.
PARTIES:
Italy
Romania

104363 Bilateral Agreement **302 UNTS 245**
SIGNED: 27 Nov 53 FORCE: 17 Sep 54
REGISTERED: 16 Jun 58 Netherlands
ARTICLES: 5 LANGUAGE: French.
HEADNOTE: RECIPROCAL COMPENSATION MA-
RINE LOSSES
TOPIC: Reparations
CONCEPTS: Accounting procedures. Exchange
rates and regulations. Lump sum settlements.
Naval vessels. Post-war claims settlement.
INTL ORGS: Arbitration Commission.
PROCEDURE: Ratification.
PARTIES:
France
Netherlands

104364 Bilateral Instrument **302 UNTS 251**
SIGNED: 3 Apr 58 FORCE: 17 Jun 58
REGISTERED: 17 Jun 58 United Nations
ARTICLES: 1 LANGUAGE: French.
HEADNOTE: ACCEPTANCE ICJ JURISDICTION
TOPIC: ICJ Option Clause
CONCEPTS: Compulsory jurisdiction.
INTL ORGS: International Court of Justice.
PROCEDURE: Duration.
PARTIES:
Belgium

104365 Bilateral Agreement **302 UNTS 255**
SIGNED: 7 Nov 57 FORCE: 7 Nov 57
REGISTERED: 17 Jun 58 USA (United States)
ARTICLES: 6 LANGUAGE: English.
HEADNOTE: AGRI COMMOD TITLE I
TOPIC: US Agri Commod Aid
CONCEPTS: General provisions. Annex or appendix reference. Exchange of information and documents. Reexport of goods, etc.. Exchange rates
and regulations. Transportation costs. Local currency. Commodities schedule. Purchase authorization. Surplus commodities. Mutual consultation.
PARTIES:
Israel
USA (United States)
ANNEX
303 UNTS 384. USA (United States). Amendment
29 Jan 58. Force 4 Feb 58.
303 UNTS 384. Israel. Amendment 4 Feb 58.
Force 4 Feb 58.
314 UNTS 362. USA (United States). Supplementation 30 Jun 58. Force 30 Jun 58.
314 UNTS 362. Israel. Supplementation
30 Jun 58. Force 30 Jun 58.
314 UNTS 366. USA (United States) Amendment
28 Aug 58. Force 28 Aug 58.
314 UNTS 366. Israel. Amendment 28 Aug 58.
Force 28 Aug 58.

104366 Bilateral Exchange **302 UNTS 273**
SIGNED: 4 Feb 57 FORCE: 29 Nov 57
REGISTERED: 17 Jun 58 USA (United States)
ARTICLES: 2 LANGUAGE: English. Spanish.
HEADNOTE: GUARANTEES PRIVATE INVEST-
MENT
TOPIC: Admin Cooperation

CONCEPTS: Guarantees and safeguards. General
cooperation. Investments. Assets transfer.
PARTIES:
Cuba
USA (United States)

104367 Bilateral Treaty **302 UNTS 281**
SIGNED: 28 Nov 56 FORCE: 7 Nov 57
REGISTERED: 17 Jun 58 USA (United States)
ARTICLES: 25 LANGUAGE: English. Korean.
HEADNOTE: FRIENDSHIP COMMERCE NAVIGA-
TION
TOPIC: General Amity
CONCEPTS: Definition of terms. Exceptions and
exemptions. Territorial application. Alien status.
Administrative cooperation. General cooper-
ation. Exchange of information and documents.
Juridical personality. Free passage and transit.
Legal protection and assistance. General prop-
erty. Existing tribunals. Social security. Export
quotas. Import quotas. Free trade. Exchange
rates and regulations. Most favored nation
clause. National treatment. Taxation. Recogni-
tion. Navigational conditions.
INTL ORGS: General Agreement on Tariffs and
Trade. International Court of Justice.
TREATY REF: GATT.
PROCEDURE: Duration. Ratification.
PARTIES:
Korea, South
USA (United States)

104368 Bilateral Exchange **303 UNTS 3**
SIGNED: 5 Nov 57 FORCE: 5 Nov 57
REGISTERED: 17 Jun 58 USA (United States)
ARTICLES: 2 LANGUAGE: English. Portuguese.
HEADNOTE: US EDUCATIONAL COMMISSION
TOPIC: Education
CONCEPTS: Definition of terms. Friendship and
amity. Standardization. Conformity with munici-
pal law. Inspection and observation. Personnel.
General property. Exchange. Commissions and
foundations. Teacher and student exchange.
Scholarships and grants. Research and develop-
ment. Accounting procedures. Currency. Ex-
change rates and regulations. Expense sharing
formulae. Financial programs. Funding procedures.
PROCEDURE: Amendment.
PARTIES:
Brazil
USA (United States)
ANNEX
401 UNTS 300. USA (United States). Amendment
14 Oct 60. Force 5 Nov 60.
401 UNTS 300. Brazil. Amendment 5 Nov 60.
Force 5 Nov 60.
488 UNTS 273. USA (United States). Amendment
20 May 63. Force 6 Jun 63.
488 UNTS 273. Brazil. Amendment 6 Jun 63.
Force 6 Jun 63.

104369 Bilateral Agreement **303 UNTS 19**
SIGNED: 21 Nov 57 FORCE: 21 Nov 57
REGISTERED: 17 Jun 58 USA (United States)
ARTICLES: 30 LANGUAGE: English. Spanish.
HEADNOTE: AIR FORCE MISSION
TOPIC: Military Mission
CONCEPTS: Definition of terms. Use of facilities.
Compensation. Indemnities and reimburse-
ments. Exchange rates and regulations. Expense
sharing formulae. Tax exemptions. Customs ex-
emptions. Military assistance. Military training.
Security of information. Airforce-army-navy personnel ratio. Ranks and privileges. Conditions
for assistance missions. Third country military
personnel. Status of forces.
PROCEDURE: Denunciation. Duration. Renewal or
Revival. Termination.
PARTIES:
El Salvador
USA (United States)
ANNEX
342 UNTS 361. USA (United States). Amendment
16 Mar 59. Force 31 Mar 59.
342 UNTS 361. El Salvador. Amendment
31 Mar 59. Force 31 Mar 59.
371 UNTS 324. USA (United States). Prolongation
15 Jan 60. Force 22 Jan 60.
371 UNTS 324. El Salvador. Prolongation
22 Jan 60. Force 22 Jan 60.

104370 Bilateral Exchange **303 UNTS 45**
SIGNED: 3 Dec 57 FORCE: 3 Dec 57
REGISTERED: 17 Jun 58 USA (United States)
ARTICLES: 2 LANGUAGE: English. French.
HEADNOTE: RELATING CERTIFICATES AIRWOR-
THINESS IMPORTED AIRCRAFT
TOPIC: Air Transport
CONCEPTS: Previous treaty replacement. Confor-
mity with municipal law. Exchange of informa-
tion and documents. Recognition of legal docu-
ments. Use of facilities. Registration certificate.
Airworthiness certificates.
TREATY REF: 137LTS389.
PROCEDURE: Termination.
PARTIES:
Belgium
USA (United States)

104371 Bilateral Convention **303 UNTS 53**
SIGNED: 20 May 57 FORCE: 1 Jun 58
REGISTERED: 17 Jun 58 Belgium
ARTICLES: 41 LANGUAGE: English. French.
HEADNOTE: SOCIAL SECURITY BENEFITS
TOPIC: Non-ILO Labor
CONCEPTS: Definition of terms. General provi-
sions. Annex or appendix reference. Domestic
legislation. Old age and invalidity insurance.
Wages and salaries. Non-ILO labor relations.
Family allowances. Administrative cooperation.
Old age insurance. Sickness and invalidity insur-
ance. Social security. Unemployment. Payment
schedules. Claims and settlements.
PROCEDURE: Denunciation. Duration. Ratification.
Renewal or Revival.
PARTIES:
Belgium
UK Great Britain

104372 Bilateral Agreement **303 UNTS 101**
SIGNED: 28 Mar 58 FORCE: 28 Mar 58
REGISTERED: 18 Jun 58 Belgium
ARTICLES: 13 LANGUAGE: French.
HEADNOTE: TRADE PHARMACEUTICAL PROD-
UCTS
TOPIC: General Trade
CONCEPTS: Detailed regulations. Treaty imple-
mentation. Treaty interpretation. General coop-
eration. Exchange of information and docu-
ments. Inspection and observation. Investigation
of violations. Procedure. Reexport of goods, etc..
Trade agencies. Trade procedures. Commodity
trade.
PROCEDURE: Denunciation. Duration. Renewal or
Revival.
PARTIES:
Belgium
Luxembourg

104373 Bilateral Agreement **303 UNTS 109**
SIGNED: 30 Apr 58 FORCE: 10 May 58
REGISTERED: 18 Jun 58 Belgium
ARTICLES: 3 LANGUAGE: English.
HEADNOTE: PAYMENTS
TOPIC: Finance
CONCEPTS: Definition of terms. Previous treaty re-
placement. Conformity with municipal law. Cur-
rency. Exchange rates and regulations. Financial
programs. Payment schedules. Local currency.
INTL ORGS: International Monetary Fund.
TREATY REF: 2UNTS40; 76UNTS113;
124UNTS316.
PROCEDURE: Amendment. Denunciation. Termi-
nation.
PARTIES:
Belgium
Japan

104374 Bilateral Agreement **303 UNTS 119**
SIGNED: 18 Jun 57 FORCE: 14 Jan 58
REGISTERED: 23 Jun 58 Czechoslovakia
ARTICLES: 9 LANGUAGE: Czechoslovakian.
Arabic.
HEADNOTE: CULTURAL COOPERATION
TOPIC: Culture
CONCEPTS: Friendship and amity. Non-diplomatic
delegations. Exchange. Teacher and student ex-
change. Exchange. General cultural cooperation.
Artists. Athletes. Research cooperation. Scien-
tific exchange. Publications exchange. Mass me-
dia exchange.

PROCEDURE: Denunciation. Duration. Ratification.
Renewal or Revival.
PARTIES:
Czechoslovakia
Syria

104375 Bilateral Exchange **303 UNTS 131**
SIGNED: 28 Apr 58 FORCE: 28 May 58
REGISTERED: 24 Jun 58 South Africa
ARTICLES: 2 LANGUAGE: English. French.
HEADNOTE: VISA
TOPIC: Visas
CONCEPTS: Visas.
PROCEDURE: Termination.
PARTIES:
Belgium
South Africa

104376 Unilateral Instrument **303 UNTS 137**
SIGNED: 25 Jun 58 FORCE: 25 Jun 58
REGISTERED: 25 Jun 58 United Nations
ARTICLES: 1 LANGUAGE: French.
HEADNOTE: ACCEPTANCE ICJ JURISDICTION
TOPIC: ICJ Option Clause
CONCEPTS: Compulsory jurisdiction.
INTL ORGS: International Court of Justice.
PROCEDURE: Denunciation.
PARTIES:
Finland

104377 Bilateral Exchange **303 UNTS 141**
SIGNED: 12 Apr 58 FORCE: 1 May 58
REGISTERED: 25 Jun 58 Belgium
ARTICLES: 3 LANGUAGE: French.
HEADNOTE: ABOLITION TRAVEL VISA REQUIRE-
MENT
TOPIC: Visas
CONCEPTS: Emergencies. Territorial application.
Time limit. Visa abolition. Denial of admission.
Resident permits.
PROCEDURE: Denunciation.
PARTIES:
Belgium
Morocco

104378 Bilateral Exchange **303 UNTS 149**
SIGNED: 18 Mar 58 FORCE: 18 Mar 58
REGISTERED: 25 Jun 58 Belgium
ARTICLES: 2 LANGUAGE: French. Japanese.
HEADNOTE: EXCHANGE OFFICIAL PUBLICALI-
TIONS
TOPIC: Admin Cooperation
CONCEPTS: Exchange of official publications. Op-
erating agencies. Indemnities and reimburse-
ments.
PARTIES:
Belgium
Japan

104379 Bilateral Agreement **303 UNTS 159**
SIGNED: 18 Dec 57 FORCE: 18 Dec 57
REGISTERED: 25 Jun 58 USA (United States)
ARTICLES: 6 LANGUAGE: English.
HEADNOTE: AGRI COMMOD TITLE I
TOPIC: US Agri Commod Aid
CONCEPTS: General provisions. Annex or appen-
dix reference. Exchange of information and documents. Reexport of goods, etc.. Exchange rates
and regulations. Payment schedules. Local currency. Commodities schedule. Purchase authorization. Surplus commodities. Mutual consultation.
PARTIES:
Greece
USA (United States)
ANNEX
308 UNTS 332. Greece. Amendment 3 Apr 58.
Force 3 Apr 58.
308 UNTS 332. USA (United States). Amendment
20 Mar 58. Force 3 Apr 58.
336 UNTS 412. Greece. Amendment 10 Nov 58.
Force 10 Nov 58.
336 UNTS 412. USA (United States). Amendment
10 Nov 58. Force 10 Nov 58.
410 UNTS 330. Greece. Supplementation
13 Apr 61. Force 13 Apr 61.
410 UNTS 330. USA (United States). Supplementation 3 Apr 61. Force 13 Apr 61.

104380 Bilateral Agreement **303 UNTS 173**
SIGNED: 15 Nov 57 FORCE: 15 Nov 57
REGISTERED: 25 Jun 58 USA (United States)
ARTICLES: 6 LANGUAGE: English.
HEADNOTE: AGRI COMMOD TITLE I
TOPIC: US Agri Commod Aid
CONCEPTS: General provisions. Annex or appen-
dix reference. Exchange of information and doc-
uments. Reexport of goods, etc.. Exchange rates
and regulations. Transportation costs. Local cur-
rency. Commodities schedule. Purchase authori-
zation. Surplus commodities. Mutual consulta-
tion.
PARTIES:
Pakistan
USA (United States)
ANNEX
411 UNTS 319. USA (United States). Amendment
29 Jun 61. Force 29 Jun 61.
411 UNTS 319. Pakistan. Amendment 29 Jun 61.
Force 29 Jun 61.

104381 Bilateral Agreement **303 UNTS 205**
SIGNED: 7 Mar 58 FORCE: 7 Mar 58
REGISTERED: 30 Jun 58 USA (United States)
ARTICLES: 6 LANGUAGE: English. Italian.
HEADNOTE: AGRI COMMOD
TOPIC: US Agri Commod Aid
CONCEPTS: Agricultural commodities.
PARTIES:
Italy
USA (United States)

104382 Bilateral Exchange **303 UNTS 227**
SIGNED: 8 Apr 57 FORCE: 8 Apr 57
REGISTERED: 30 Jun 58 USA (United States)
ARTICLES: 2 LANGUAGE: English.
HEADNOTE: EXPLOITATION MINERAL RE-
SOURCES
TOPIC: Specific Resources
CONCEPTS: Frontier permits. Claims and settle-
ments. Raw materials.
PARTIES:
Philippines
USA (United States)

104383 Bilateral Exchange **303 UNTS 237**
SIGNED: 6 Feb 57 FORCE: 6 Feb 57
REGISTERED: 30 Jun 58 USA (United States)
ARTICLES: 2 LANGUAGE: English.
HEADNOTE: DAMAGES ARISING MANEUVERS
TOPIC: Status of Forces
CONCEPTS: War claims and reparations. Loss and-
/or damage.
PARTIES:
Philippines
USA (United States)

104384 Bilateral Agreement **303 UNTS 247**
SIGNED: 27 Jan 58 FORCE: 27 Jan 58
REGISTERED: 30 Jun 58 USA (United States)
ARTICLES: 6 LANGUAGE: English. Spanish.
HEADNOTE: AGRI COMMOD TITLE I
TOPIC: US Agri Commod Aid
CONCEPTS: General provisions. Exchange of infor-
mation and documents. Reexport of goods, etc..
Exchange rates and regulations. Internal fi-
nance. Transportation costs. Local currency.
Commodities schedule. Purchase authorization.
Surplus commodities. Mutual consultation.
PARTIES:
Spain
USA (United States)
ANNEX
308 UNTS 336. USA (United States). Supplementation 10 Apr 58. Force 10 Apr 58.
308 UNTS 336. Spain. Supplementation
10 Apr 58. Force 10 Apr 58.
317 UNTS 360. USA (United States). Supplementation 30 Jun 58. Force 30 Jun 58.
317 UNTS 360. Spain. Supplementation
30 Jun 58. Force 30 Jun 58.
336 UNTS 416. USA (United States). Supplementation 21 Oct 58. Force 21 Oct 58.
336 UNTS 416. Spain. Supplementation
21 Oct 58. Force 21 Oct 58.

104385 Bilateral Exchange **303 UNTS 261**
SIGNED: 20 Feb 58 FORCE: 20 Feb 58

REGISTERED: 30 Jun 58 USA (United States)
ARTICLES: 2 LANGUAGE: English.
HEADNOTE: AGREEMENT MANEUVERS
TOPIC: Status of Forces
CONCEPTS: Time limit. Annex or appendix reference. Public information. Compensation. Claims and settlements. Status of military forces.
PARTIES:
 Philippines
 USA (United States)

104386   Bilateral Exchange   **303 UNTS 271**
SIGNED: 13 Jun 58   FORCE: 12 Jun 58
REGISTERED: 30 Jun 58 United Nations
ARTICLES: 2 LANGUAGE: English.
HEADNOTE: STATUS OBSERVERS LEBANON
TOPIC: IGO Status/Immunit
CONCEPTS: Annex or appendix reference. Diplomatic missions. Privileges and immunities. Diplomatic correspondence.
TREATY REF: 1UNTS15.
PARTIES:
 Lebanon
 United Nations

104387   Bilateral Exchange   **304 UNTS 3**
SIGNED: 20 Jan 58   FORCE: 20 Jan 58
REGISTERED: 1 Jul 58 USA (United States)
ARTICLES: 2 LANGUAGE: English.
HEADNOTE: CONSTRUCTION WEATHER STATION
TOPIC: Specific Property
CONCEPTS: Research cooperation. Meteorology. Facilities and property.
TREATY REF: 231UNTS185.
PARTIES:
 UK Great Britain
 USA (United States)

104388   Bilateral Agreement   **304 UNTS 9**
SIGNED: 30 Jan 58   FORCE: 30 Jan 58
REGISTERED: 1 Jul 58 USA (United States)
ARTICLES: 3 LANGUAGE: English. French.
HEADNOTE: POSTPONEMENT INSTALLMENTS
TOPIC: Specif Claim/Waive
CONCEPTS: Interest rates. Payment schedules. Specific claims or waivers.
TREATY REF: 84UNTS59.
PARTIES:
 France
 USA (United States)

104389   Bilateral Agreement   **304 UNTS 15**
SIGNED: 20 Jan 58   FORCE: 20 Jan 58
REGISTERED: 1 Jul 58 USA (United States)
ARTICLES: 6 LANGUAGE: English.
HEADNOTE: AGRI COMMOD TITLE I
TOPIC: US Agri Commod Aid
CONCEPTS: General provisions. Annex or appendix reference. Exchange of information and documents. Reexport of goods, etc.. Exchange rates and regulations. Transportation costs. Local currency. Commodities schedule. Purchase authorization. Surplus commodities. Mutual consultation.
PARTIES:
 Turkey
 USA (United States)
ANNEX
317 UNTS 366. USA (United States). Supplementation 25 Jun 58. Force 25 Jun 58.
317 UNTS 366. Turkey. Supplementation 25 Jun 58. Force 25 Jun 58.
336 UNTS 420. USA (United States). Amendment 8 Nov 58. Force 8 Nov 58.
336 UNTS 420. Turkey. Amendment 8 Nov 58. Force 8 Nov 58.
340 UNTS 406. USA (United States). Amendment 13 May 58. Force 9 Sep 58.
340 UNTS 406. Turkey. Amendment 9 Jun 58. Force 9 Jun 58.
340 UNTS 410. Turkey. Amendment 24 Nov 58. Force 24 Nov 58.
340 UNTS 410. USA (United States). Amendment 24 Nov 58. Force 24 Nov 58.
410 UNTS 332. Turkey. Amendment 29 Mar 61. Force 29 Mar 61.
410 UNTS 332. USA (United States). Amendment 29 Mar 61. Force 29 Mar 61.

104390   Bilateral Exchange   **304 UNTS 35**
SIGNED: 11 Jan 58   FORCE: 11 Jan 58
REGISTERED: 1 Jul 58 USA (United States)
ARTICLES: 2 LANGUAGE: English. Japanese.
HEADNOTE: US EDUCATIONAL COMMISSION
TOPIC: Education
CONCEPTS: Definition of terms. Friendship and amity. Standardization. Conformity with municipal law. General cooperation. Inspection and observation. Personnel. General property. Exchange. Commissions and foundations. Teacher and student exchange. Scholarships and grants. Research and development. Accounting procedures. Currency. Exchange rates and regulations. Expense sharing formulae. Financial programs. Funding procedures.
TREATY REF: 147UNTS81.
PARTIES:
 Japan
 USA (United States)
ANNEX
401 UNTS 307. Japan. Amendment 2 Dec 60. Force 2 Dec 60.
401 UNTS 307. USA (United States). Amendment 2 Dec 60. Force 2 Dec 60.
488 UNTS 280. USA (United States). Amendment 23 Aug 63. Force 23 Aug 63.
488 UNTS 280. Japan. Amendment 23 Aug 63. Force 23 Aug 63.

104391   Bilateral Agreement   **304 UNTS 61**
SIGNED: 31 May 57   FORCE: 6 Feb 58
REGISTERED: 1 Jul 58 USA (United States)
ARTICLES: 11 LANGUAGE: English. Spanish.
HEADNOTE: COOPERATION CIVIL USES ATOMIC ENERGY
TOPIC: Atomic Energy
CONCEPTS: Definition of terms. Non-prejudice to third party. Exchange of information and documents. Inspection and observation. Responsibility and liability. Research cooperation. Assets transfer. Nuclear materials. Non-nuclear materials. Peaceful use. Security of information.
PROCEDURE: Duration.
PARTIES:
 Ecuador
 USA (United States)

104392   Bilateral Exchange   **304 UNTS 81**
SIGNED: 25 Jan 58   FORCE: 25 Jan 58
REGISTERED: 1 Jul 58 USA (United States)
ARTICLES: 2 LANGUAGE: English. Japanese.
HEADNOTE: EQUIPMENT MATERIALS SERVICES DEFENSE ASSISTANCE
TOPIC: Milit Assistance
CONCEPTS: Conformity with municipal law. Expense sharing formulae. Materials, equipment and services. Self-defense. Military assistance.
TREATY REF: 232UNTS169.
PROCEDURE: Future Procedures Contemplated.
PARTIES:
 Japan
 USA (United States)

104393   Bilateral Convention   **304 UNTS 91**
SIGNED: 23 Jun 50   FORCE: 11 May 51
REGISTERED: 1 Jul 58 Poland
ARTICLES: 11 LANGUAGE: Polish. German.
HEADNOTE: PLANT PROTECTION
TOPIC: Sanitation
CONCEPTS: Border traffic and migration. General cooperation. Exchange of information and documents. Informational records. Inspection and observation. Expropriation. Domestic legislation. Quarantine. Disease control. Insect control. Trade procedures. Agriculture. Mass media exchange. Conferences.
PROCEDURE: Duration. Ratification. Renewal or Revival. Termination.
PARTIES:
 Germany, East
 Poland

104394   Bilateral Agreement   **304 UNTS 113**
SIGNED: 8 Jan 52   FORCE: 9 May 52
REGISTERED: 1 Jul 58 Poland
ARTICLES: 10 LANGUAGE: Polish. German.
HEADNOTE: CULTURAL COOPERATION
TOPIC: Culture
CONCEPTS: Friendship and amity. Conformity

with municipal law. Operating agencies. Establishment of commission. Specialists exchange. Exchange. Professorships. Scholarships and grants. Exchange. General cultural cooperation. Artists. Research cooperation. Scientific exchange. Accounting procedures. Publications exchange. Mass media exchange. Press and wire services. Conferences.
INTL ORGS: Special Commission.
PROCEDURE: Duration. Ratification. Renewal or Revival. Termination.
PARTIES:
 Germany, East
 Poland

104395   Bilateral Agreement   **304 UNTS 131**
SIGNED: 6 Feb 52   FORCE: 2 Aug 52
REGISTERED: 1 Jul 58 Poland
ARTICLES: 33 LANGUAGE: Polish. German.
HEADNOTE: NAVIGATION FRONTIER WATERS USE MAINTENANCE FRONTIER WATERS
TOPIC: Water Transport
CONCEPTS: Definition of terms. Exceptions and exemptions. General cooperation. Personnel. Responsibility and liability. Establishment of commission. Fees and exemptions. Navigational conditions. Ports and pilotage. Markers and definitions. Frontier waterways.
INTL ORGS: Special Commission.
PROCEDURE: Duration. Ratification. Renewal or Revival.
PARTIES:
 Germany, East
 Poland

104396   Bilateral Agreement   **304 UNTS 187**
SIGNED: 3 Apr 51   FORCE: 25 Jan 52
REGISTERED: 1 Jul 58 Poland
ARTICLES: 7 LANGUAGE: Polish. Chinese. Russian.
HEADNOTE: CULTURAL COOPERATION
TOPIC: Culture
CONCEPTS: Previous treaty replacement. Friendship and amity. Operating agencies. Establishment of commission. Exchange. Professorships. Scholarships and grants. Exchange. General cultural cooperation. Research results. Scientific exchange. Accounting procedures. Publications exchange. Mass media exchange. Press and wire services. Conferences.
INTL ORGS: Special Commission.
PROCEDURE: Denunciation. Duration. Future Procedures Contemplated. Renewal or Revival.
PARTIES:
 China People's Rep
 Poland

104397   Bilateral Exchange   **304 UNTS 207**
SIGNED: 20 Mar 58   FORCE: 10 Apr 58
REGISTERED: 3 Jul 58 Belgium
ARTICLES: 2 LANGUAGE: French. Spanish.
HEADNOTE: TRAVEL AGREEMENT
TOPIC: Visas
CONCEPTS: Emergencies. Territorial application. Time limit. Visa abolition. Denial of admission. Resident permits. Visas. Conformity with municipal law. Fees and exemptions.
PROCEDURE: Denunciation.
PARTIES:
 Belgium
 Ecuador

104398   Bilateral Agreement   **304 UNTS 214**
SIGNED: 16 Mar 57   FORCE: 16 Mar 57
REGISTERED: 8 Jul 58 Sweden
ARTICLES: 14 LANGUAGE: English.
HEADNOTE: TECHNICAL ASSISTANCE HEALTH
TOPIC: Tech Assistance
CONCEPTS: Detailed regulations. Exceptions and exemptions. Time limit. General cooperation. Personnel. General property. Title and deeds. Use of facilities. Public health. Institute establishment. Bonds. Expense sharing formulae. Tax exemptions. Customs exemptions. Domestic obligation. Special projects.
PROCEDURE: Amendment. Duration. Renewal or Revival. Termination.
PARTIES:
 Ethiopia
 Sweden

ANNEX
427 UNTS 386. Sweden. Amendment 30 Jun 58.
Force 30 Jun 58.
427 UNTS 386. Ethiopia. Amendment 30 Jun 58.
Force 30 Jun 58.

104399 Multilateral Agreement **304 UNTS 227**
SIGNED: 6 Jan 58　　　　FORCE: 6 Jan 58
REGISTERED: 8 Jul 58 USA (United States)
ARTICLES: 5 LANGUAGE: English.
HEADNOTE: DEVELOP TRANSPORTATION FACILI-
TIES
TOPIC: General Transport
CONCEPTS: Previous treaty replacement. Friend-
ship and amity. General cooperation. Personnel.
Public information. Responsibility and liability.
Title and deeds. Exchange rates and regulations.
Financial programs. Customs exemptions. Com-
modities and services. Domestic obligation. As-
sistance. Economic assistance. Materials, equip-
ment and services. Grants. General transporta-
tion.
TREATY REF: 184UNTS65.
PROCEDURE: Amendment. Termination.
PARTIES:
India SIGNED: 2 Jan 58 FORCE: 6 Jan 58
Nepal SIGNED: 2 Jan 58 FORCE: 6 Jan 58
USA (United States) SIGNED: 6 Jan 58 FORCE:
6 Jan 58
ANNEX
474 UNTS 342. USA (United States). Termination
10 Jan 63. Force 10 Jan 63.
474 UNTS 342. India. Termination 10 Jan 63.
Force 10 Jan 63.
474 UNTS 342. Nepal. Termination 10 Jan 63.
Force 10 Jan 63.

104400 Bilateral Agreement **304 UNTS 241**
SIGNED: 8 Oct 57　　　　FORCE: 1 Oct 57
REGISTERED: 8 Jul 58 USA (United States)
ARTICLES: 16 LANGUAGE: English.
HEADNOTE: EXCHANGE INTERNATIONAL MONEY
ORDERS
TOPIC: Postal Service
CONCEPTS: Annex or appendix reference. Previ-
ous treaty replacement. Conformity with munici-
pal law. Accounting procedures. Currency. Ex-
change rates and regulations. Payment sched-
ules. Postal services. Regulations. Money orders
and postal checks. Rates and charges. Advice
lists and orders.
PROCEDURE: Duration. Termination.
PARTIES:
Taiwan
USA (United States)

104401 Bilateral Agreement **304 UNTS 253**
SIGNED: 21 Feb 58　　　　FORCE: 21 Feb 58
REGISTERED: 8 Jul 58 USA (United States)
ARTICLES: 6 LANGUAGE: English.
HEADNOTE: AGRI COMMOD TITLE I
TOPIC: US Agri Commod Aid
CONCEPTS: General provisions. Annex or appen-
dix reference. Exchange of information and doc-
uments. Reexport of goods, etc.. Exchange rates
and regulations. Transportation costs. Local cur-
rency. Commodities schedule. Purchase authori-
zation. Surplus commodities. Mutual consulta-
tion.
PARTIES:
Finland
USA (United States)
ANNEX
338 UNTS 398. Finland. Amendment 29 Dec 58.
Force 2 Jan 59.
338 UNTS 398. USA (United States). Amendment
31 Dec 58. Force 2 Jan 59.

104402 Bilateral Agreement **304 UNTS 267**
SIGNED: 11 Jun 57　　　　FORCE: 7 Mar 58
REGISTERED: 8 Jul 58 USA (United States)
ARTICLES: 11 LANGUAGE: English. Spanish.
HEADNOTE: COOPERATION CIVIL USES ATOMIC
ENERGY
TOPIC: Atomic Energy
CONCEPTS: Definition of terms. Exchange of infor-
mation and documents. Inspection and observa-
tion. Assets transfer. Nuclear materials. Non-
nuclear materials. Peaceful use. Security of infor-
mation.

PROCEDURE: Future Procedures Contemplated.
PARTIES:
Nicaragua
USA (United States)

104403 Bilateral Exchange **304 UNTS 287**
SIGNED: 12 Feb 58　　　　FORCE: 12 Feb 58
REGISTERED: 8 Jul 58 USA (United States)
ARTICLES: 2 LANGUAGE: English. Polish.
HEADNOTE: INFORMATIONAL MEDIA GUARANTY
PROGRAMS
TOPIC: Mass Media
CONCEPTS: Local currency. Media guaranty.
PARTIES:
Poland
USA (United States)

104404 Bilateral Agreement **304 UNTS 293**
SIGNED: 3 Feb 58　　　　FORCE: 3 Feb 58
REGISTERED: 8 Jul 58 USA (United States)
ARTICLES: 6 LANGUAGE: English.
HEADNOTE: AGRI COMMOD TITLE I
TOPIC: US Agri Commod Aid
CONCEPTS: General provisions. Annex or appendix reference. Exchange of information and documents. Reexport of goods, etc.. Exchange rates
and regulations. Transportation costs. Local currency. Commodities schedule. Purchase authorization. Surplus commodities. Mutual consultation.
PARTIES:
USA (United States)
Yugoslavia
ANNEX
317 UNTS 370. USA (United States). Amendment
26 Jun 58. Force 26 Jun 58.
317 UNTS 370. Yugoslavia. Amendment
26 Jun 58. Force 26 Jun 58.

104405 Bilateral Exchange **304 UNTS 311**
SIGNED: 12 Dec 56　　　　FORCE: 12 Dec 56
REGISTERED: 8 Jul 58 USA (United States)
ARTICLES: 2 LANGUAGE: English.
HEADNOTE: STATUS PERSONNEL MILITARY AD-
VISORY
TOPIC: Status of Forces
CONCEPTS: Airforce-army-navy personnel ratio.
Ranks and privileges.
TREATY REF: 26UNTS452.
PARTIES:
Denmark
USA (United States)

104406 Bilateral Agreement **304 UNTS 317**
SIGNED: 28 Oct 54　　　　FORCE: 20 Dec 55
REGISTERED: 11 Jul 58 Canada
ARTICLES: 16 LANGUAGE: English.
HEADNOTE: DOUBLE TAXATION FISCAL EVA-
SION TAXES INCOME
TOPIC: Taxation
CONCEPTS: Definition of terms. Conformity with
municipal law. Exchange of official publications.
Teacher and student exchange. Taxation. Tax
credits. General. Tax exemptions. Air transport.
Merchant vessels.
PROCEDURE: Duration. Ratification. Termination.
PARTIES:
Canada
Ireland

104407 Bilateral Agreement **305 UNTS 3**
SIGNED: 28 Oct 54　　　　FORCE: 20 Dec 55
REGISTERED: 11 Jul 58 Canada
ARTICLES: 9 LANGUAGE: English.
HEADNOTE: DOUBLE TAXATION AVOIDANCE FIS-
CAL EVASION
TOPIC: Taxation
CONCEPTS: Definition of terms. Conformity with
municipal law. Exchange of official publications.
Non-interest rates and fees. Claims and settle-
ments. Taxation. Death duties.
PROCEDURE: Duration. Ratification. Termination.
PARTIES:
Canada
Ireland

104408 Bilateral Exchange **305 UNTS 17**
SIGNED: 20 Dec 55　　　　FORCE: 20 Dec 55

REGISTERED: 11 Jul 58 Canada
ARTICLES: 1 LANGUAGE: English.
HEADNOTE: LOAN FRIGATES
TOPIC: Milit Assistance
CONCEPTS: Annex or appendix reference. Re-
sponsibility and liability. Title and deeds. Com-
pensation. Indemnities and reimbursements. Ex-
pense sharing formulae. Delivery schedules.
Lease of military property. Military assistance.
Naval vessels. Return of equipment and recap-
ture. Security of information. Exchange of de-
fense information.
PROCEDURE: Termination.
PARTIES:
Canada
Norway
ANNEX
392 UNTS 388. Canada. Supplementation
1 Jul 58. Force 1 Jul 58.
392 UNTS 388. Norway. Supplementation
1 Jul 58. Force 1 Jul 58.

104409 Bilateral Exchange **305 UNTS 27**
SIGNED: 8 Mar 56　　　　FORCE: 8 Mar 56
REGISTERED: 11 Jul 58 Canada
ARTICLES: 2 LANGUAGE: English.
HEADNOTE: WHEAT
TOPIC: Commodity Trade
CONCEPTS: Trade agencies. Banking. Payment
schedules. Commodity trade. Delivery sched-
ules. Loan and credit. Credit provisions.
PARTIES:
Canada
Hungary

104410 Bilateral Exchange **305 UNTS 33**
SIGNED: 9 Jan 56　　　　FORCE: 9 Jan 56
REGISTERED: 11 Jul 58 Canada
ARTICLES: 2 LANGUAGE: English.
HEADNOTE: WAIVING OF NON-IMMIGRANT
VISAS FEES
TOPIC: Visas
CONCEPTS: Visas. Fees and exemptions.
PARTIES:
Canada
Finland

104411 Bilateral Exchange **305 UNTS 39**
SIGNED: 11 Jul 56　　　　FORCE: 18 Jul 56
REGISTERED: 11 Jul 58 Canada
ARTICLES: 2 LANGUAGE: English. Spanish.
HEADNOTE: COMMERCIAL MODUS VIVENDI
TOPIC: Mostfavored Nation
CONCEPTS: General cooperation. Procedure. Gen-
eral trade. Reciprocity in trade. Most favored na-
tion clause. Customs duties.
PROCEDURE: Denunciation. Ratification. Renewal
or Revival.
PARTIES:
Canada
Honduras

104412 Bilateral Exchange **305 UNTS 51**
SIGNED: 19 Jun 56　　　　FORCE: 1 Jul 56
REGISTERED: 11 Jul 58 Canada
ARTICLES: 2 LANGUAGE: English.
HEADNOTE: ISSUANCE OF MULTI-ENTRY VISAS
TOPIC: Visas
CONCEPTS: Time limit. Passports diplomatic.
Passports non-diplomatic. Denial of admission.
Visas. Conformity with municipal law. Fees and
exemptions.
PARTIES:
Austria
Canada

104413 Bilateral Agreement **305 UNTS 59**
SIGNED: 30 Aug 56　　　　FORCE: 30 Nov 56
REGISTERED: 11 Jul 58 Canada
ARTICLES: 5 LANGUAGE: English.
HEADNOTE: PATENTS INVENTION
TOPIC: Patents/Copyrights
CONCEPTS: Domestic legislation. Laws and for-
malities.
PROCEDURE: Duration.
PARTIES:
Canada
India

104414 Bilateral Agreement **305 UNTS 65**
SIGNED: 4 Oct 56 FORCE: 4 Oct 56
REGISTERED: 11 Jul 58 Canada
ARTICLES: 11 LANGUAGE: French.
HEADNOTE: ADMISSION TRAINEES
TOPIC: Non-ILO Labor
CONCEPTS: Annex or appendix reference. Resident permits. Conformity with municipal law. Exchange of information and documents. Vocational training. Employment regulations. Wages and salaries. Non-ILO labor relations. Administrative cooperation. Migrant worker. Quotas.
PROCEDURE: Denunciation. Duration. Renewal or Revival.
PARTIES:
Canada
France

104415 Bilateral Exchange **305 UNTS 79**
SIGNED: 4 Sep 56 FORCE: 4 Sep 56
REGISTERED: 11 Jul 58 Canada
ARTICLES: 2 LANGUAGE: French.
HEADNOTE: BURIAL ARRANGEMENTS
TOPIC: Other Military
CONCEPTS: Annex or appendix reference. Exchange of information and documents. Recognition of legal documents. Burial arrangements.
TREATY REF: 199UNTS67.
PARTIES:
Canada
France

104416 Bilateral Exchange **305 UNTS 89**
SIGNED: 21 Aug 56 FORCE: 21 Sep 56
REGISTERED: 11 Jul 58 Canada
ARTICLES: 2 LANGUAGE: English.
HEADNOTE: ISSUANCE MULTI-ENTRY VISAS
TOPIC: Visas
CONCEPTS: Emergencies. Time limit. Previous treaty replacement. Denial of admission. Resident permits. Visas. Conformity with municipal law. Fees and exemptions.
TREATY REF: 231UNTS57; 233UNTS95.
PROCEDURE: Termination.
PARTIES:
Canada
Turkey

104417 Bilateral Exchange **305 UNTS 97**
SIGNED: 16 May 56 FORCE: 28 Aug 56
REGISTERED: 14 Jul 58 Netherlands
ARTICLES: 2 LANGUAGE: English. Japanese.
HEADNOTE: ABOLITION VISAS
TOPIC: Visas
CONCEPTS: Time limit. Visa abolition. Denial of admission. Conformity with municipal law.
PROCEDURE: Termination.
PARTIES:
Japan
Netherlands

104418 Bilateral Exchange **305 UNTS 105**
SIGNED: 20 Sep 57 FORCE: 8 Mar 58
REGISTERED: 14 Jul 58 Netherlands
ARTICLES: 2 LANGUAGE: English. Japanese.
HEADNOTE: EXEMPTION VISA REQUIREMENTS
TOPIC: Visas
CONCEPTS: Time limit. Visa abolition.
TREATY REF: 305UNTS97.
PROCEDURE: Termination.
PARTIES:
Japan
Netherlands

104419 Bilateral Treaty **305 UNTS 113**
SIGNED: 28 Nov 57 FORCE: 12 Jun 58
REGISTERED: 14 Jul 58 USSR (Soviet Union)
ARTICLES: 78 LANGUAGE: Russian. German.
HEADNOTE: LEGAL ASSISTANCE CIVIL FAMILY CRIMINAL CASES
TOPIC: Admin Cooperation
CONCEPTS: General provisions. General consular functions. Privileges and immunities. Extradition, deportation and repatriation. Extradition requests. Extraditable offenses. Refusal of extradition. Concurrent requests. Provisional detainment. Extradition postponement. Witnesses and experts. Material evidence. Conformity with municipal law. General cooperation. Family law. Ex-

change of information and documents. Legal protection and assistance. Recognition and enforcement of legal decisions. Immovable property. General property. Jurisdiction. Recognition of legal documents. Indemnities and reimbursements. Assets transfer. Conveyance in transit.
PROCEDURE: Duration. Ratification. Termination.
PARTIES:
Germany, East
USSR (Soviet Union)

104420 Bilateral Agreement **305 UNTS 213**
SIGNED: 21 Dec 57 FORCE: 19 Apr 58
REGISTERED: 14 Jul 58 USSR (Soviet Union)
ARTICLES: 16 LANGUAGE: Russian. Chinese.
HEADNOTE: COMMERCIAL NAVIGATION RIVERS & LAKES ALONG FRONTIERS
TOPIC: Visas
CONCEPTS: Nationality and citizenship. Conformity with municipal law. General cooperation. Reciprocity in trade. Trade procedures. Fees and exemptions. Customs duties. Navigational conditions. Ports and pilotage. Frontier waterways.
PROCEDURE: Denunciation. Ratification.
PARTIES:
China People's Rep
USSR (Soviet Union)

104421 Bilateral Agreement **305 UNTS 235**
SIGNED: 15 Jan 58 FORCE: 15 Jan 58
REGISTERED: 14 Jul 58 USSR (Soviet Union)
ARTICLES: 7 LANGUAGE: Russian. Sinhalese.
HEADNOTE: CULTURAL COOPERATION
TOPIC: Culture
CONCEPTS: Friendship and amity. Non-diplomatic delegations. Establishment of commission. Exchange. Vocational training. Exchange. General cultural cooperation. Artists. Athletes. Scientific exchange. Mass media exchange. Conferences.
INTL ORGS: Special Commission.
PROCEDURE: Termination.
PARTIES:
Ceylon (Sri Lanka)
USSR (Soviet Union)

104422 Bilateral Agreement **305 UNTS 247**
SIGNED: 31 Dec 57 FORCE: 16 May 58
REGISTERED: 14 Jul 58 Denmark
ARTICLES: 16 LANGUAGE: Danish. French. Dutch.
HEADNOTE: CULTURAL AGREEMENT
TOPIC: Culture
CONCEPTS: Friendship and amity. Tourism. Alien status. Conformity with municipal law. Establishment of commission. Recognition of degrees. Exchange. Teacher and student exchange. Institute establishment. Scholarships and grants. Exchange. General cultural cooperation. Artists. Scientific exchange. Export quotas. Publications exchange. Mass media exchange. Conferences.
INTL ORGS: Special Commission.
PROCEDURE: Denunciation. Duration. Ratification. Renewal or Revival.
PARTIES:
Belgium
Denmark

104423 Multilateral Convention **305 UNTS 265**
SIGNED: 21 Jun 55 FORCE: 25 Mar 58
REGISTERED: 14 Jul 58 ILO (Labor Org)
ARTICLES: 7 LANGUAGE: English. French.
HEADNOTE: PENAL SANCTIONS BREACH CONTRACTS BY WORKERS
TOPIC: ILO Labor
CONCEPTS: Time limit. Previous treaty renunciation. Private contracts. Penal sanctions. ILO conventions. Anti-discrimination. Domestic obligation.
INTL ORGS: International Labour Organization.
TREATY REF: 40UNTS311.
PROCEDURE: Amendment. Denunciation. Duration. Ratification. Registration.
PARTIES:
Multilateral
ANNEX
318 UNTS 428. El Salvador. Ratification 18 Nov 58. Force 18 Nov 59.
320 UNTS 351. United Arab Rep. Acceptance 18 Dec 58.
328 UNTS 340. Iran. Ratification 13 Apr 59. Force 13 Apr 60.

358 UNTS 356. Portugal. Ratification 12 Apr 60. Force 12 Apr 61.
413 UNTS 374. Syria. Ratification 30 Oct 61.
425 UNTS 355. Niger. Ratification 23 Mar 62. Force 23 Mar 63.
431 UNTS 313. Liberia. Ratification 25 May 62. Force 25 May 63.
434 UNTS 338. Libya. Ratification 20 Jun 62. Force 20 Jun 63.
444 UNTS 346. Nigeria. Ratification 25 Oct 62. Force 25 Oct 63.
452 UNTS 369. Tunisia. Ratification 17 Dec 62. Force 17 Dec 63.
457 UNTS 362. Morocco. Ratification 27 Mar 63. Force 27 Mar 64.
504 UNTS 364. Thailand. Ratification 29 Jul 64. Force 29 Jul 65.
504 UNTS 364. Central Afri Rep. Ratification 9 Jun 64. Force 9 Jun 65.
530 UNTS 422. Malawi. Ratification 22 Mar 65. Force 22 Mar 66.
541 UNTS 378. Brazil. Ratification 18 Jun 65. Force 18 Jun 66.

104424 Bilateral Agreement **305 UNTS 275**
SIGNED: 25 Nov 57 FORCE: 26 Nov 57
REGISTERED: 14 Jul 58 Italy
ARTICLES: 30 LANGUAGE: Italian. Spanish.
HEADNOTE: EXPANDING TRADE FINANCIAL AGREEMENTS
TOPIC: General Economic
CONCEPTS: Change of circumstances. Annex or appendix reference. Previous treaty replacement. Exchange of information and documents. Licenses and permits. Establishment of commission. Procedure. Negotiation. General trade. Reciprocity in trade. Accounting procedures. Banking. Currency. Monetary and gold transfers. Financial programs. Payment schedules. General technical assistance. General transportation. Publications exchange. Mass media exchange.
INTL ORGS: Special Commission.
TREATY REF: TRADE&FINANCIAL AGREEMENT 25JUN52.
PROCEDURE: Denunciation. Future Procedures Contemplated. Renewal or Revival. Termination.
PARTIES:
Argentina
Italy

104425 Bilateral Agreement **305 UNTS 357**
SIGNED: 28 Dec 57 FORCE: 12 May 58
REGISTERED: 14 Jul 58 Italy
ARTICLES: 12 LANGUAGE: Italian. English.
HEADNOTE: COOPERATION PEACEFUL USES ATOMIC ENERGY
TOPIC: Atomic Energy
CONCEPTS: Definition of terms. Non-prejudice to third party. Exchange of information and documents. Inspection and observation. Research cooperation. Nuclear research. Nuclear materials. Non-nuclear materials. Peaceful use. Security of information.
INTL ORGS: European Atomic Energy Commission.
TREATY REF: 298UNTS167.
PROCEDURE: Ratification. Termination.
PARTIES:
Italy
UK Great Britain

104426 Bilateral Agreement **305 UNTS 387**
SIGNED: 27 Mar 58 FORCE: 1 Apr 58
REGISTERED: 14 Jul 58 Italy
ARTICLES: 10 LANGUAGE: French.
HEADNOTE: FRONTIER WORKERS
TOPIC: Visas
CONCEPTS: Frontier permits. Holidays and rest periods. Old age and invalidity insurance. Frontier peoples and personnel.
PROCEDURE: Denunciation. Duration. Renewal or Revival.
PARTIES:
France
Italy

104427 Bilateral Agreement **305 UNTS 393**
SIGNED: 8 Nov 57 FORCE: 1 Nov 57
REGISTERED: 14 Jul 58 Italy

ARTICLES: 12 LANGUAGE: French.
HEADNOTE: COPRODUCTION CINEMATO-
GRAPHIC FILMS
TOPIC: Mass Media
CONCEPTS: Previous treaty replacement. Protec-
tion of nationals. Domestic legislation. Person-
nel. Establishment of commission. Investments.
Expense sharing formulae. Payment schedules.
Assets. Mass media exchange.
INTL ORGS: Special Commission.
TREATY REF: ITALY-FRANCE AGREEMENT
15MARCH1955.
PROCEDURE: Duration. Ratification.
PARTIES:
France
Italy

104428   Bilateral Agreement   **305 UNTS 409**
SIGNED: 27 Mar 58   FORCE: 1 Apr 58
REGISTERED: 14 Jul 58 Italy
ARTICLES: 5 LANGUAGE: French.
HEADNOTE: MIGRANT WORKERS
TOPIC: Non-ILO Labor
CONCEPTS: Legal protection and assistance. Non-
ILO labor relations. Family allowances. Adminis-
trative cooperation. Old age insurance. Migrant
worker.
TREATY REF: 305UNTS415; 291UNTS203.
PROCEDURE: Ratification.
PARTIES:
France
Italy

104429   Bilateral Exchange   **306 UNTS 3**
SIGNED: 16 Aug 57   FORCE: 1 Sep 57
REGISTERED: 16 Jul 58 Pakistan
ARTICLES: 2 LANGUAGE: English.
HEADNOTE: VISAS
TOPIC: Visas
CONCEPTS: Emergencies. Time limit. Visa aboli-
tion. Denial of admission. Visas. Conformity with
municipal law. Fees and exemptions.
PROCEDURE: Termination.
PARTIES:
Austria
Pakistan

104430   Bilateral Agreement   **306 UNTS 11**
SIGNED: 8 Nov 55   FORCE: 8 Nov 55
REGISTERED: 18 Jul 58 Burma
ARTICLES: 22 LANGUAGE: Burmese. Chinese.
HEADNOTE: AIR TRANSPORT
TOPIC: Air Transport
CONCEPTS: Treaty interpretation. Conformity with
municipal law. General cooperation. Exchange
of information and documents. Informational
records. Legal protection and assistance. Licenses and permits. Personnel. Recognition of
legal documents. Use of facilities. Procedure.
Negotiation. Fees and exemptions. Non-interest
rates and fees. National treatment. Customs exemptions. Registration certificate. Routes and logistics. Navigational equipment. Permit designation. Transport of goods. Airport facilities. Airworthiness certificates. Conditions of airlines
operating permission. Operating authorizations
and regulations.
PROCEDURE: Amendment. Termination.
PARTIES:
Burma
China People's Rep

104431   Bilateral Exchange   **306 UNTS 61**
SIGNED: 20 Jun 56   FORCE: 29 May 56
REGISTERED: 18 Jul 58 Burma
ARTICLES: 2 LANGUAGE: English.
HEADNOTE: REVIVAL TREATIES
TOPIC: Admin Cooperation
CONCEPTS: Revival of treaties.
TREATY REF: 16LTS207;   19LTS288;
251LTS201.
PARTIES:
Burma
Japan

104432   Bilateral Agreement   **306 UNTS 67**
SIGNED: 13 Nov 57   FORCE: 15 May 58
REGISTERED: 21 Jul 58 Netherlands
ARTICLES: 8 LANGUAGE: English.

HEADNOTE: INTERNATIONAL TRANSPORT ROAD
TOPIC: Land Transport
CONCEPTS: Territorial application. Licenses and
permits. Passenger transport. Transport of
goods. Commercial road vehicles. Roads and
highways. Road rules.
PROCEDURE: Denunciation. Ratification.
PARTIES:
Denmark
Netherlands

104433   Bilateral Agreement   **306 UNTS 75**
SIGNED: 23 Oct 57   FORCE: 6 May 58
REGISTERED: 21 Jul 58 Netherlands
ARTICLES: 8 LANGUAGE: French.
HEADNOTE: ROAD TRANSPORT
TOPIC: Land Transport
CONCEPTS: Territorial application. General provi-
sions. Conformity with municipal law. Passenger
transport. Transport of goods. Commercial road
vehicles. Roads and highways. Road rules.
INTL ORGS: United Nations.
PROCEDURE: Denunciation. Ratification.
PARTIES:
Netherlands
Sweden

104434   Bilateral Exchange   **306 UNTS 85**
SIGNED: 12 Nov 54   FORCE: 12 Nov 54
REGISTERED: 21 Jul 58 Belgium
ARTICLES: 2 LANGUAGE: French.
HEADNOTE: SETTLEMENT CLAIMS
TOPIC: Reparations
CONCEPTS: Lump sum settlements. Loss and/or
damage. Post-war claims settlement.
TREATY REF: 19UNTS87.
PARTIES:
Belgium
France

104435   Bilateral Exchange   **306 UNTS 99**
SIGNED: 19 Oct 53   FORCE: 15 Dec 53
REGISTERED: 22 Jul 58 Netherlands
ARTICLES: 2 LANGUAGE: English.
HEADNOTE: CUSTOMS PRIVILEGES DIPLOMATS
CONSULAR OFFICIALS
TOPIC: Customs
CONCEPTS: Diplomatic privileges. Customs ex-
emptions.
PARTIES:
Netherlands
UK Great Britain

104436   Bilateral Exchange   **306 UNTS 107**
SIGNED: 11 Jun 56   FORCE: 11 Jun 56
REGISTERED: 22 Jul 58 Netherlands
ARTICLES: 2 LANGUAGE: English.
HEADNOTE: RIGHTS OBLIGATIONS FORCES
TOPIC: Status of Forces
CONCEPTS: Annex or appendix reference. Status
of military forces.
PARTIES:
Netherlands
UK Great Britain

104437   Bilateral Agreement   **307 UNTS 3**
SIGNED: 21 Jan 58   FORCE: 2 Apr 58
REGISTERED: 22 Jul 58 WHO (World Health)
ARTICLES: 6 LANGUAGE: English.
HEADNOTE: TECHNICAL ADVISORY ASSISTANCE
TOPIC: Tech Assistance
CONCEPTS: Annex or appendix reference. Privi-
leges and immunities. Exchange of information
and documents. Personnel. Responsibility and li-
ability. Title and deeds. Exchange. Scholarships
and grants. Vocational training. Research and
development. Expense sharing formulae. Local
currency. Domestic obligation. Special projects.
Materials, equipment and services. Joint de-
fense. IGO status. Conformity with IGO deci-
sions.
INTL ORGS: United Nations.
TREATY REF: 33UNTS261.
PROCEDURE: Amendment. Termination.
PARTIES:
Ghana
WHO (World Health)

104438   Bilateral Agreement   **307 UNTS 15**
SIGNED: 5 Feb 58   FORCE: 17 Feb 58
REGISTERED: 22 Jul 58 WHO (World Health)
ARTICLES: 6 LANGUAGE: English.
HEADNOTE: TECHNICAL ADVISORY ASSISTANCE
TOPIC: Tech Assistance
CONCEPTS: Definition of terms. Previous treaty re-
placement. Privileges and immunities. General
cooperation. Exchange of information and docu-
ments. Personnel. Responsibility and liability. Ti-
tle and deeds. Use of facilities. Exchange. Schol-
arships and grants. Vocational training. Re-
search and development. Exchange rates and
regulations. Expense sharing formulae. Local
currency. Domestic obligation. Special projects.
Materials, equipment and services. IGO status.
Conformity with IGO decisions.
INTL ORGS: United Nations.
TREATY REF: 33UNTS261; 103UNTS71.
PROCEDURE: Amendment. Termination.
PARTIES:
Indonesia
WHO (World Health)

104439   Bilateral Agreement   **307 UNTS 27**
SIGNED: 11 Apr 58   FORCE: 26 May 58
REGISTERED: 22 Jul 58 WHO (World Health)
ARTICLES: 6 LANGUAGE: English.
HEADNOTE: TECHNICAL ADVISORY ASSISTANCE
TOPIC: Tech Assistance
CONCEPTS: Definition of terms. Privileges and im-
munities. General cooperation. Exchange of in-
formation and documents. Personnel. Responsi-
bility and liability. Title and deeds. Exchange.
Scholarships and grants. Vocational training. Re-
search and development. Expense sharing for-
mulae. Local currency. Domestic obligation.
Special projects. Materials, equipment and ser-
vices. IGO status. Conformity with IGO decisions.
INTL ORGS: United Nations.
TREATY REF: 33UNTS261.
PARTIES:
Israel
WHO (World Health)

104440   Bilateral Exchange   **307 UNTS 39**
SIGNED: 1 Nov 57   FORCE: 1 Nov 57
REGISTERED: 24 Jul 58 USA (United States)
ARTICLES: 2 LANGUAGE: English.
HEADNOTE: CLAIMS DAMAGES MANEUVERS
TOPIC: Status of Forces
CONCEPTS: Time limit. Procedure. Compensation.
Claims and settlements. Status of military forces.
INTL ORGS: Southeast Asia Treaty Organization.
TREATY REF: 209UNTS23.
PARTIES:
Philippines
USA (United States)

104441   Bilateral Exchange   **307 UNTS 49**
SIGNED: 6 Nov 57   FORCE: 6 Nov 57
REGISTERED: 24 Jul 58 USA (United States)
ARTICLES: 3 LANGUAGE: English. Spanish.
HEADNOTE: FREE ENTRY PRIVILEGES CONSULAR
OFFICERS NON-DIPLOMATIC PERSONNEL
TOPIC: Consul/Citizenship
CONCEPTS: Diplomatic privileges.
PARTIES:
Ecuador
USA (United States)

104442   Bilateral Exchange   **307 UNTS 59**
SIGNED: 10 Dec 57   FORCE: 10 Dec 57
REGISTERED: 24 Jul 58 USA (United States)
ARTICLES: 2 LANGUAGE: English. German.
HEADNOTE: RELEASE AIR BASES TRAINING GER-
MAN AIR FORCE PERSONNEL
TOPIC: Milit Assistance
CONCEPTS: Private contracts. Responsibility and
liability. Use of facilities. Indemnities and reim-
bursements. Payment schedules. Claims and set-
tlements. Materials, equipment and services. Mil-
itary training. Military assistance missions. Con-
ditions for assistance missions. Bases and
facilities.
TREATY REF: 240UNTS47.
PROCEDURE: Future Procedures Contemplated.
PARTIES:
Germany, West
USA (United States)

104443 Bilateral Exchange **307 UNTS 71**
SIGNED: 26 Dec 57 FORCE: 26 Dec 57
REGISTERED: 24 Jul 58 USA (United States)
ARTICLES: 2 LANGUAGE: English.
HEADNOTE: FACILITIES ASSISTANCE PROGRAM
MUTUAL DEFENSE
TOPIC: Milit Assistance
CONCEPTS: Change of circumstances. Use of facilities. Indemnities and reimbursements. Customs exemptions. Materials, equipment and services. Defense and security. Security of information. Equipment and supplies. Restrictions on transfer.
TREATY REF: 207 1NTS127.
PROCEDURE: Future Procedures Contemplated.
PARTIES:
Ethiopia
USA (United States)

104444 Bilateral Agreement **307 UNTS 79**
SIGNED: 27 Dec 57 FORCE: 27 Dec 57
REGISTERED: 24 Jul 58 USA (United States)
ARTICLES: 6 LANGUAGE: English. French.
HEADNOTE: AGRI COMMOD TITLE I
TOPIC: US Agri Commod Aid
CONCEPTS: General provisions. Annex or appendix reference. Exchange of information and documents. Reexport of goods, etc.. Exchange rates and regulations. Transportation costs. Local currency. Commodities schedule. Purchase authorization. Surplus commodities. Mutual consultation.
PARTIES:
France
USA (United States)
ANNEX
321 UNTS 297. France. Amendment 30 Jun 58. Force 30 Jun 58.
321 UNTS 297. USA (United States). Amendment 30 Jun 58. Force 30 Jun 58.
410 UNTS 336. USA (United States). Supplementation 12 Jun 61. Force 12 Jun 61.
410 UNTS 336. France. Supplementation 12 Jun 61. Force 12 Jun 61.

104445 Bilateral Exchange **307 UNTS 97**
SIGNED: 9 Jun 57 FORCE: 9 Jun 57
REGISTERED: 24 Jul 58 USA (United States)
ARTICLES: 2 LANGUAGE: English. Persian.
HEADNOTE: GUARANTEES PRIVATE INTERESTS
TOPIC: Admin Cooperation
CONCEPTS: Guarantees and safeguards. General cooperation. Investments. Assets transfer.
PARTIES:
Afghanistan
USA (United States)

104446 Bilateral Agreement **307 UNTS 105**
SIGNED: 24 Jan 58 FORCE: 1 Apr 58
REGISTERED: 24 Jul 58 USA (United States)
ARTICLES: 9 LANGUAGE: English.
HEADNOTE: PATENT RIGHTS TECHNICAL INFORMATION DEFENSE PURPOSES
TOPIC: Patents/Copyrights
CONCEPTS: Definition of terms. Conformity with municipal law. Currency. Laws and formalities. Security of information. Exchange of defense information. Subsidiary organ.
INTL ORGS: Special Commission.
TREATY REF: 131UNTS83.
PROCEDURE: Termination.
PARTIES:
Australia
USA (United States)
ANNEX
421 UNTS 318. USA (United States). Supplementation 13 Sep 61. Force 2 Oct 61.
421 UNTS 318. Australia. Supplementation 2 Oct 61. Force 2 Oct 61.

104447 Bilateral Agreement **307 UNTS 121**
SIGNED: 5 Feb 58 FORCE: 5 Feb 58
REGISTERED: 24 Jul 58 USA (United States)
ARTICLES: 6 LANGUAGE: English.
HEADNOTE: AGRI COMMOD TITLE I
TOPIC: US Agri Commod Aid
CONCEPTS: General provisions. Annex or appendix reference. Exchange of information and documents. Reexport of goods, etc.. Exchange rates and regulations. Transportation costs. Local currency. Commodities schedule. Purchase authorization. Surplus commodities. Mutual consultation.
PARTIES:
Korea, South
USA (United States)

104448 Bilateral Exchange **307 UNTS 133**
SIGNED: 8 Jun 54 FORCE: 8 Jun 54
REGISTERED: 24 Jul 58 USA (United States)
ARTICLES: 1 LANGUAGE: English.
HEADNOTE: OFFSHORE PROCUREMENT PROGRAM
TOPIC: Milit Assistance
CONCEPTS: Military installations and equipment.
INTL ORGS: North Atlantic Treaty Organization.
PARTIES:
Denmark
USA (United States)

104449 Bilateral Agreement **307 UNTS 169**
SIGNED: 16 Aug 57 FORCE: 12 Feb 58
REGISTERED: 24 Jul 58 USA (United States)
ARTICLES: 12 LANGUAGE: English. Spanish.
HEADNOTE: COOPERATION CIVIL USES ATOMIC ENERGY
TOPIC: Atomic Energy
CONCEPTS: Definition of terms. Previous treaty replacement. Non-prejudice to third party. Conformity with municipal law. Exchange of information and documents. Inspection and observation. Responsibility and liability. Investigation of violations. Research cooperation. Assets transfer. Nuclear materials. Non-nuclear materials. Peaceful use. Security of information.
TREATY REF: 239UNTS299.
PROCEDURE: Duration.
PARTIES:
Spain
USA (United States)

104450 Bilateral Exchange **307 UNTS 199**
SIGNED: 3 Feb 58 FORCE: 3 Feb 58
REGISTERED: 24 Jul 58 USA (United States)
ARTICLES: 2 LANGUAGE: English.
HEADNOTE: AGRI COMMOD TITLE I
TOPIC: US Agri Commod Aid
CONCEPTS: General provisions. Annex or appendix reference. Exchange of information and documents. Reexport of goods, etc.. Exchange rates and regulations. Transportation costs. Local currency. Commodities schedule. Purchase authorization. Surplus commodities. Mutual consultation.
PARTIES:
UK Great Britain
USA (United States)
ANNEX
360 UNTS 412. UK Great Britain. Amendment 4 Feb 60. Force 4 Feb 60.
360 UNTS 412. USA (United States). Amendment 28 Jan 60. Force 4 Feb 60.

104451 Bilateral Exchange **307 UNTS 207**
SIGNED: 22 Feb 58 FORCE: 22 Feb 58
REGISTERED: 24 Jul 58 USA (United States)
ARTICLES: 2 LANGUAGE: English.
HEADNOTE: INTERMEDIATE-RANGE BALLISTIC MISSILES
TOPIC: Milit Assistance
CONCEPTS: Exceptions and exemptions. Conformity with municipal law. General cooperation. Use of facilities. Materials, equipment and services. Joint defense. Defense and security. Military assistance. Military training. Testing ranges and sites.
TREATY REF: 34UNTS243.
PROCEDURE: Amendment. Termination.
PARTIES:
UK Great Britain
USA (United States)

104452 Bilateral Agreement **307 UNTS 217**
SIGNED: 15 Feb 58 FORCE: 15 Feb 58
REGISTERED: 24 Jul 58 USA (United States)
ARTICLES: 6 LANGUAGE: English. Polish.
HEADNOTE: AGRI COMMOD
TOPIC: US Agri Commod Aid
CONCEPTS: Reexport of goods, etc.. Currency. Payment schedules. Local currency. Economic assistance. Commodities schedule. Merchant vessels. Mutual consultation.
PARTIES:
Poland
USA (United States)
ANNEX
317 UNTS 376. Poland. Amendment 6 Jun 58. Force 6 Jun 58.
317 UNTS 376. USA (United States). Amendment 6 Jun 58. Force 6 Jun 58.
346 UNTS 355. USA (United States). Amendment 26 May 59. Force 29 May 59.
346 UNTS 355. Poland. Amendment 29 May 59. Force 29 May 59.
380 UNTS 469. USA (United States). Amendment 21 Jul 60. Force 21 Jul 60.
380 UNTS 469. Poland. Amendment 21 Jul 60. Force 21 Jul 60.

104453 Bilateral Agreement **307 UNTS 235**
SIGNED: 21 Jun 58 FORCE: 14 Jul 58
REGISTERED: 29 Jul 58 WHO (World Health)
ARTICLES: 6 LANGUAGE: English. Arabic.
HEADNOTE: TECHNICAL ADVISORY ASSISTANCE
TOPIC: Tech Assistance
CONCEPTS: General cooperation. Exchange of information and documents. Domestic legislation. Personnel. Responsibility and liability. Title and deeds. Exchange. Scholarships and grants. Vocational training. Research and development. Expense sharing formulae. Local currency. Domestic obligation. Special projects. Materials, equipment and services. IGO status. Conformity with IGO decisions.
INTL ORGS: United Nations.
TREATY REF: 33UNTS261.
PROCEDURE: Amendment. Termination.
PARTIES:
WHO (World Health)
Sudan

104454 Bilateral Convention **307 UNTS 251**
SIGNED: 18 Sep 57 FORCE: 29 Apr 58
REGISTERED: 30 Jul 58 USSR (Soviet Union)
ARTICLES: 10 LANGUAGE: Russian. Albanian.
HEADNOTE: DUAL CITIZENSHIP
TOPIC: Consul/Citizenship
CONCEPTS: Time limit. Dual citizenship. Nationality and citizenship.
PROCEDURE: Ratification.
PARTIES:
Albania
USSR (Soviet Union)

104455 Bilateral Convention **307 UNTS 265**
SIGNED: 18 Sep 57 FORCE: 29 Apr 58
REGISTERED: 30 Jul 58 USSR (Soviet Union)
ARTICLES: 26 LANGUAGE: Russian. Albanian.
HEADNOTE: CONSULAR CONVENTION
TOPIC: Consul/Citizenship
CONCEPTS: Definition of terms. General consular functions. Diplomatic privileges. Consular relations establishment. Inviolability. Privileges and immunities. Diplomatic correspondence.
PROCEDURE: Ratification. Termination.
PARTIES:
Albania
USSR (Soviet Union)

104456 Bilateral Treaty **308 UNTS 3**
SIGNED: 31 Aug 57 FORCE: 10 May 58
REGISTERED: 30 Jul 58 USSR (Soviet Union)
ARTICLES: 76 LANGUAGE: Russian. Czechoslovakian.
HEADNOTE: LEGAL ASSISTANCE CIVIL FAMILY CRIMINAL
TOPIC: Admin Cooperation
CONCEPTS: General provisions. General consular functions. Privileges and immunities. Extradition, deportation and repatriation. Extradition requests. Refusal of extradition. Limits of prosecution. Provisional detainment. Extradition post-

ponement. Witnesses and experts. Material evidence. Conformity with municipal law. General cooperation. Family law. Exchange of information and documents. Juridical personality. Legal protection and assistance. Recognition and enforcement of legal decisions. Immovable property. General property. Jurisdiction. Recognition of legal documents. Indemnities and reimbursements. Assets transfer. Conveyance in transit.
PROCEDURE: Duration. Ratification. Termination.
PARTIES:
Czechoslovakia
USSR (Soviet Union)

104457   Bilateral Agreement   **308 UNTS 95**
SIGNED: 12 Oct 56   FORCE: 3 Jun 58
REGISTERED: 30 Jul 58 USSR (Soviet Union)
ARTICLES: 4 LANGUAGE: Russian. Swedish.
HEADNOTE: CULTURAL COOPERATION
TOPIC: Culture
CONCEPTS: Friendship and amity. Specialists exchange. Exchange. Exchange. General cultural cooperation. Artists. Scientific exchange.
PROCEDURE: Duration. Ratification. Termination.
PARTIES:
Norway
USSR (Soviet Union)

104458   Bilateral Exchange   **308 UNTS 105**
SIGNED: 31 Mar 58   FORCE: 31 Mar 58
REGISTERED: 1 Aug 58 USA (United States)
ARTICLES: 2 LANGUAGE: English.
HEADNOTE: ECONOMIC TECHNICAL ASSISTANCE
TOPIC: General Aid
CONCEPTS: Diplomatic privileges. Privileges and immunities. Conformity with municipal law. General cooperation. Exchange of information and documents. Personnel. Public information. Exchange rates and regulations. Tax exemptions. Customs exemptions. Domestic obligation. General technical assistance. Economic assistance. Materials, equipment and services. Aid missions.
PROCEDURE: Amendment. Termination.
PARTIES:
Sudan
USA (United States)
ANNEX
335 UNTS 342. USA (United States). Interpretation 12 Jul 58. Force 12 Jul 58.
335 UNTS 342. Sudan. Interpretation 1 Jul 58. Force 12 Jul 58.

104459   Bilateral Agreement   **308 UNTS 115**
SIGNED: 14 Mar 58   FORCE: 14 Mar 58
REGISTERED: 1 Aug 58 USA (United States)
ARTICLES: 6 LANGUAGE: English. Spanish.
HEADNOTE: AGRI COMMOD TITLE I
TOPIC: US Agri Commod Aid
CONCEPTS: General provisions. Annex or appendix reference. Exchange of information and documents. Reexport of goods, etc.. Currency. Exchange rates and regulations. Transportation costs. Local currency. Commodities schedule. Purchase authorization. Surplus commodities. Mutual consultation.
PARTIES:
Colombia
USA (United States)
ANNEX
267 UNTS 393. Spain. Force 2 Mar 56.
267 UNTS 393. Monaco. Force 29 Apr 56.
267 UNTS 393. Portugal. Force 7 Nov 49.
267 UNTS 393. Ceylon (Sri Lanka). Force 29 Dec 52.
267 UNTS 393. Italy. Force 15 Jul 55.
267 UNTS 393. Finland. Force 30 May 53.
267 UNTS 393. Sweden. Force 1 Jul 53.
267 UNTS 393. Greece. Force 27 Nov 53.
267 UNTS 393. Mexico. Force 14 Jul 55.
335 UNTS 346. USA (United States). Supplementation 30 Jun 58. Force 9 Jul 58.
335 UNTS 346. Colombia. Supplementation 9 Jul 58. Force 9 Jul 58.
337 UNTS 434. USA (United States). Amendment 18 Nov 58. Force 18 Nov 58.
337 UNTS 434. Colombia. Amendment 18 Nov 58. Force 18 Nov 58.
407 UNTS 272. Colombia. Supplementation 20 Apr 61. Force 20 Apr 61.

407 UNTS 272. USA (United States). Supplementation 20 Apr 61. Force 20 Apr 61.
487 UNTS 365. Colombia. Amendment 14 Aug 63. Force 14 Aug 63.
487 UNTS 365. USA (United States). Amendment 14 Aug 63. Force 14 Aug 63.

104460   Bilateral Agreement   **308 UNTS 147**
SIGNED: 16 Jan 57   FORCE: 17 Apr 58
REGISTERED: 1 Aug 58 USA (United States)
ARTICLES: 20 LANGUAGE: English. Persian.
HEADNOTE: AIR TRANSPORT
TOPIC: Air Transport
CONCEPTS: Definition of terms. Detailed regulations. Exceptions and exemptions. Non-prejudice to third party. Conformity with municipal law. Exchange of information and documents. Licenses and permits. Recognition of legal documents. Use of facilities. Procedure. Special tribunals. Negotiation. Competence of tribunal. Indemnities and reimbursements. Fees and exemptions. Non-interest rates and fees. National treatment. Customs exemptions. Competency certificate. Routes and logistics. Navigational conditions. Permit designation. Airport facilities. Airworthiness certificates. Conditions of airlines operating permission. Overflights and technical stops. Operating authorizations and regulations. Licenses and certificates of nationality.
INTL ORGS: International Civil Aviation Organization.
TREATY REF: 15UNTS295.
PROCEDURE: Amendment. Future Procedures Contemplated. Ratification. Registration. Termination. Application to Non-self-governing Territories.
PARTIES:
Iran
USA (United States)

104461   Bilateral Agreement   **308 UNTS 179**
SIGNED: 18 Apr 58   FORCE: 18 Apr 58
REGISTERED: 1 Aug 58 USA (United States)
ARTICLES: 6 LANGUAGE: English. Chinese.
HEADNOTE: AGRI COMMOD TITLE I
TOPIC: US Agri Commod Aid
CONCEPTS: General provisions. Exchange of information and documents. Reexport of goods, etc.. Exchange rates and regulations. Transportation costs. Local currency. Commodities schedule. Purchase authorization. Surplus commodities. Mutual consultation.
PARTIES:
Taiwan
USA (United States)
ANNEX
458 UNTS 338. USA (United States). Amendment 29 Jun 62. Force 29 Jun 62.
458 UNTS 338. Taiwan. Amendment 29 Jun 62. Force 29 Jun 62.

104462   Bilateral Agreement   **308 UNTS 195**
SIGNED: 3 Jul 57   FORCE: 15 Apr 58
REGISTERED: 1 Aug 58 USA (United States)
ARTICLES: 13 LANGUAGE: English. Italian.
HEADNOTE: COOPERATION CIVIL USES ATOMIC ENERGY
TOPIC: Atomic Energy
CONCEPTS: Definition of terms. Previous treaty replacement. Non-prejudice to third party. Exchange of information and documents. Inspection and observation. Responsibility and liability. Revival of treaties. Research cooperation. Nuclear materials. Non-nuclear materials. Peaceful use. Conformity with IGO decisions.
INTL ORGS: European Atomic Energy Commission.
TREATY REF: 239UNTS235; 298UNTS167.
PROCEDURE: Duration.
PARTIES:
Italy
USA (United States)
ANNEX
404 UNTS 358. Italy. Amendment 22 Jul 59. Force 30 Mar 61.

104463   Bilateral Treaty   **308 UNTS 227**
SIGNED: 19 Nov 57   FORCE: 20 Mar 58
REGISTERED: 4 Aug 58 Taiwan
ARTICLES: 7 LANGUAGE: Arabic. English.

HEADNOTE: AMITY
TOPIC: General Amity
CONCEPTS: Friendship and amity. Alien status. Consular relations establishment. Diplomatic relations establishment. Privileges and immunities. National treatment.
PROCEDURE: Denunciation. Future Procedures Contemplated. Ratification. Termination.
PARTIES:
Taiwan
Jordan

104464   Bilateral Convention   **308 UNTS 239**
SIGNED: 28 Nov 56   FORCE: 1 Jul 58
REGISTERED: 6 Aug 58 Belgium
ARTICLES: 35 LANGUAGE: French. Spanish.
HEADNOTE: SOCIAL SECURITY
TOPIC: Non-ILO Labor
CONCEPTS: General provisions. Conformity with municipal law. Domestic legislation. Dispute settlement. Old age and invalidity insurance. Wages and salaries. Non-ILO labor relations. Family allowances. Administrative cooperation. Old age insurance. Sickness and invalidity insurance. Social security. Unemployment. Payment schedules. Claims and settlements.
PROCEDURE: Duration. Future Procedures Contemplated. Ratification. Renewal or Revival. Termination.
PARTIES:
Belgium
Spain

104465   Bilateral Convention   **308 UNTS 285**
SIGNED: 28 Nov 56   FORCE: 1 Jul 58
REGISTERED: 6 Aug 58 Belgium
ARTICLES: 12 LANGUAGE: French. Spanish.
HEADNOTE: EMIGRATION
TOPIC: Non-ILO Labor
CONCEPTS: Detailed regulations. Border traffic and migration. Alien status. General cooperation. Public information. Private contracts. Non-ILO labor relations. Social security. Monetary and gold transfers. Transportation costs.
PROCEDURE: Denunciation.
PARTIES:
Belgium
Spain

104466   Bilateral Agreement   **309 UNTS 3**
SIGNED: 5 May 58   FORCE: 1 Jul 58
REGISTERED: 11 Aug 58 IBRD (World Bank)
ARTICLES: 5 LANGUAGE: English.
HEADNOTE: GUARANTEE AGREEMENT
TOPIC: IBRD Project
CONCEPTS: Definition of terms. Annex or appendix reference. Exchange of information and documents. Bonds. Fees and exemptions. Tax exemptions. Domestic obligation. Loan regulations. Loan guarantee. Guarantor non-interference. Hydro-electric power.
PARTIES:
Mexico
IBRD (World Bank)

104467   Bilateral Agreement   **309 UNTS 35**
SIGNED: 16 Jun 58   FORCE: 26 Jun 58
REGISTERED: 11 Aug 58 IBRD (World Bank)
ARTICLES: 5 LANGUAGE: English.
HEADNOTE: GUARANTEE AGREEMENT
TOPIC: IBRD Project
CONCEPTS: Definition of terms. Annex or appendix reference. Exchange of information and documents. Inspection and observation. Bonds. Fees and exemptions. Tax exemptions. Domestic obligation. Terms of loan. Loan regulations. Loan guarantee. Guarantor non-interference.
PARTIES:
IBRD (World Bank)
UK Great Britain

104468   Multilateral Convention   **309 UNTS 65**
SIGNED: 20 Feb 57   FORCE: 11 Aug 58
REGISTERED: 11 Aug 58 United Nations
ARTICLES: 12 LANGUAGE: English. French. Chinese. Russian. Spanish.
HEADNOTE: NATIONALITY MARRIED WOMEN
TOPIC: Consul/Citizenship
CONCEPTS: Exceptions and exemptions. Territo-

rial application. Nationality and citizenship. Existing tribunals.
INTL ORGS: International Court of Justice. United Nations.
PROCEDURE: Accession. Denunciation. Ratification.
PARTIES:
Byelorussia SIGNED: 7 Oct 57
Canada SIGNED: 20 Feb 57
Chile SIGNED: 18 Mar 57
Taiwan SIGNED: 20 Feb 57
Colombia SIGNED: 20 Feb 57
Cuba SIGNED: 20 Feb 57 RATIFIED: 5 Dec 57 FORCE: 11 Aug 58
Czechoslovakia SIGNED: 3 Sep 57
Denmark SIGNED: 20 Feb 57
Dominican Republic SIGNED: 20 Feb 57 RATIFIED: 10 Oct 57 FORCE: 11 Aug 58
Ecuador SIGNED: 16 Jan 58
Guatemala SIGNED: 20 Feb 57
Hungary SIGNED: 5 Dec 57
India SIGNED: 15 May 57
Ireland SIGNED: 24 Sep 57 RATIFIED: 25 Nov 57 FORCE: 11 Aug 58
Israel SIGNED: 12 Mar 57 RATIFIED: 7 Jun 57 FORCE: 11 Aug 58
New Zealand Cook Islands RATIFIED: 7 Jul 58
New Zealand SIGNED: 7 Jul 58
New Zealand Tokelau Islands RATIFIED: 7 Jul 58
Norway SIGNED: 9 Sep 57 RATIFIED: 20 May 58 FORCE: 18 Aug 58
Pakistan SIGNED: 10 Apr 58
Portugal SIGNED: 21 Feb 57
Sweden SIGNED: 6 May 57 RATIFIED: 13 May 58 FORCE: 11 Aug 58
UK Great Britain Aden RATIFIED: 26 Aug 57 FORCE: 11 Aug 58
UK Great Britain Bahamas RATIFIED: 26 Aug 57 FORCE: 11 Aug 58
UK Great Britain Barbados RATIFIED: 26 Aug 57 FORCE: 11 Aug 58
UK Great Britain Basutoland RATIFIED: 26 Aug 57 FORCE: 11 Aug 58
UK Great Britain Bechuanaland RATIFIED: 26 Aug 57 FORCE: 11 Aug 58
UK Great Britain Bermuda RATIFIED: 26 Aug 57 FORCE: 11 Aug 58
UK Great Britain British Guiana RATIFIED: 26 Aug 57 FORCE: 11 Aug 58
UK Great Britain British Honduras RATIFIED: 26 Aug 57 FORCE: 11 Aug 58
UK Great Britain Brit Solomon Is RATIFIED: 26 Aug 57 FORCE: 11 Aug 58
UK Great Britain British Somaliland RATIFIED: 26 Aug 57 FORCE: 11 Aug 58
UK Great Britain Brit Virgin Islands RATIFIED: 26 Aug 57 FORCE: 11 Aug 58
UK Great Britain Channel Islands RATIFIED: 26 Aug 57 FORCE: 11 Aug 58
UK Great Britain Cyprus RATIFIED: 26 Aug 57 FORCE: 11 Aug 58
UK Great Britain Falkland Islands RATIFIED: 26 Aug 57 FORCE: 11 Aug 58
UK Great Britain Fiji Islands RATIFIED: 26 Aug 57 FORCE: 11 Aug 58
UK Great Britain Fed Rhod/Nyasaland RATIFIED: 19 May 58 FORCE: 11 Aug 58
UK Great Britain Gambia RATIFIED: 26 Aug 57 FORCE: 11 Aug 58
UK Great Britain Gibralter RATIFIED: 26 Aug 57 FORCE: 11 Aug 58
UK Great Britain Gilbert Islands RATIFIED: 26 Aug 57 FORCE: 11 Aug 58
UK Great Britain Hong Kong RATIFIED: 26 Aug 57 FORCE: 11 Aug 58
UK Great Britain Isle of Man RATIFIED: 26 Aug 57 FORCE: 11 Aug 58
UK Great Britain Jamaica RATIFIED: 26 Aug 57 FORCE: 11 Aug 58
UK Great Britain Kenya RATIFIED: 26 Aug 57 FORCE: 11 Aug 58
UK Great Britain Leeward Islands RATIFIED: 26 Aug 57 FORCE: 11 Aug 58
UK Great Britain Malta RATIFIED: 26 Aug 57 FORCE: 11 Aug 58
UK Great Britain Mauritius RATIFIED: 26 Aug 57 FORCE: 11 Aug 58
UK Great Britain North Borneo RATIFIED: 26 Aug 57 FORCE: 11 Aug 58
UK Great Britain SIGNED: 20 Feb 57 RATIFIED: 28 Aug 57 FORCE: 11 Aug 58
UK Great Britain Sarawak RATIFIED: 26 Aug 57 FORCE: 11 Aug 58

UK Great Britain Seychelles RATIFIED: 26 Aug 57 FORCE: 11 Aug 58
UK Great Britain Sierra Leone RATIFIED: 26 Aug 57 FORCE: 11 Aug 58
UK Great Britain Singapore RATIFIED: 26 Aug 57 FORCE: 11 Aug 58
UK Great Britain St. Helena RATIFIED: 26 Aug 57 FORCE: 11 Aug 58
UK Great Britain Swaziland RATIFIED: 26 Aug 57 FORCE: 11 Aug 58
UK Great Britain Tanganyika RATIFIED: 26 Aug 57 FORCE: 11 Aug 58
UK Great Britain Trinidad/Tobago RATIFIED: 26 Aug 57 FORCE: 11 Aug 58
UK Great Britain Uganda RATIFIED: 26 Aug 57 FORCE: 11 Aug 58
UK Great Britain Windward Islands RATIFIED: 26 Aug 57 FORCE: 11 Aug 58
UK Great Britain Zanzibar RATIFIED: 18 Mar 58 FORCE: 11 Aug 58
Ukrainian SSR SIGNED: 15 Oct 57
Uruguay SIGNED: 20 Feb 57
USSR (Soviet Union) SIGNED: 6 Sep 57
Yugoslavia SIGNED: 27 Mar 57
ANNEX
312 UNTS 430. USSR (Soviet Union). Ratification 17 Sep 58. Force 16 Dec 58.
312 UNTS 430. Taiwan. Ratification 22 Sep 58. Force 21 Dec 58.
316 UNTS 388. Ukrainian SSR. Ratification 3 Dec 58. Force 3 Mar 59.
317 UNTS 380. New Zealand. Tokelau Islands. Force 17 Mar 59.
317 UNTS 380. Byelorussia. Ratification 23 Dec 58. Force 23 Mar 59.
317 UNTS 380. New Zealand. Ratification 17 Dec 58. Force 17 Mar 59.
317 UNTS 380. New Zealand. Cook Islands. Force 17 Mar 59.
317 UNTS 380. New Zealand. Western Samoa. Force 17 Mar 59.
324 UNTS 338. Fed of Malaya. Accession 24 Feb 59. Force 30 May 59.
325 UNTS 348. Yugoslavia. Ratification 13 Mar 59. Force 11 Jun 59.
335 UNTS 350. Denmark. Ratification 22 Jun 59. Force 20 Sep 59.
337 UNTS 442. Poland. Accession 3 Jul 59. Force 1 Oct 59.
344 UNTS 349. Canada. Ratification 21 Oct 59. Force 16 Jan 60.
345 UNTS 371. Hungary. Ratification 3 Dec 59. Force 2 Mar 60.
354 UNTS 426. Ecuador. Ratification 29 Mar 60. Force 27 Jun 60.
362 UNTS 339. Bulgaria. Accession 22 Jun 60. Force 20 Sep 60.
368 UNTS 370. Guatemala. Qualified Ratification 13 Jul 60. Force 11 Oct 60.
371 UNTS 329. Albania. Accession 27 Jul 60. Force 25 Oct 60.
379 UNTS 438. UK Great Britain. Tonga.
381 UNTS 412. Romania. Accession 2 Dec 60. Force 2 Mar 61.
390 UNTS 366. Australia. Accession 14 Mar 61. Force 12 Jun 61.
390 UNTS 366. Australia. All Territories. Force 12 Jun 61.
423 UNTS 319. Sierra Leone. Succession 13 Mar 62.
424 UNTS 361. Czechoslovakia. Ratification 5 Apr 62. Force 4 Jul 62.
439 UNTS 320. UK Great Britain. Brunei.
445 UNTS 357. Tanganyika. Accession 28 Nov 62. Force 26 Feb 63.
479 UNTS 370. Argentina. Qualified Accession 10 Oct 63. Force 8 Jan 64.
503 UNTS 338. Jamaica. Succession 30 Jul 64.
503 UNTS 339. Jamaica. Succession 30 Jul 64.
531 UNTS 354. Uganda. Accession 15 Apr 65. Force 14 Jul 65.
559 UNTS 353. Singapore. Succession 18 Mar 66.
560 UNTS 266. Trinidad/Tobago. Succession 11 Apr 66.
572 UNTS 358. Malawi. Accession 8 Sep 66. Force 7 Dec 66.
618 UNTS 379. Austria. Accession 19 Jan 68. Force 18 Apr 68.
619 UNTS 336. Tunisia. Reservation 24 Jan 68.
619 UNTS 336. Tunisia. Accession 24 Jan 68. Force 23 Apr 68.
636 UNTS 365. Finland. Accession 15 May 68. Force 13 Aug 68.

651 UNTS 358. Brazil. Ratification 4 Dec 68. Reservation 4 Dec 68.

104469 Bilateral Agreement **309 UNTS 103**
SIGNED: 12 Aug 68 FORCE: 12 Aug 58
REGISTERED: 12 Aug 58 United Nations
ARTICLES: 11 LANGUAGE: English.
HEADNOTE: ACTIVITIES UNICEF
TOPIC: Direct Aid
CONCEPTS: Treaty implementation. Privileges and immunities. General cooperation. Exchange of information and documents. Informational records. Inspection and observation. Public information. Responsibility and liability. Procedure. Existing tribunals. Export quotas. Claims and settlements. Tax exemptions. Customs exemptions. Commodities and services. Domestic obligation. Assistance. General aid. Distribution. IGO status.
INTL ORGS: United Nations.
TREATY REF: 1UNTS15.
PROCEDURE: Amendment. Termination.
PARTIES:
Ghana
UNICEF (Children)

104470 Bilateral Exchange **309 UNTS 117**
SIGNED: 14 Mar 52 FORCE: 31 Mar 52
REGISTERED: 12 Aug 58 Netherlands
ARTICLES: 2 LANGUAGE: French. Portuguese.
HEADNOTE: ABOLITION VISAS
TOPIC: Visas
CONCEPTS: Visa abolition.
PARTIES:
Netherlands
Portugal

104471 Bilateral Exchange **309 UNTS 123**
SIGNED: 21 Jun 52 FORCE: 21 Jul 52
REGISTERED: 12 Aug 58 Netherlands
ARTICLES: 2 LANGUAGE: Dutch. Afrikaans.
HEADNOTE: PASSPORT VISAS
TOPIC: Visas
CONCEPTS: Territorial application. Time limit. Visa abolition. Denial of admission. Visas. Conformity with municipal law. Fees and exemptions.
PARTIES:
Netherlands
South Africa

104472 Bilateral Agreement **309 UNTS 129**
SIGNED: 14 Mar 55 FORCE: 28 Dec 55
REGISTERED: 15 Aug 58 IBRD (World Bank)
ARTICLES: 5 LANGUAGE: English.
HEADNOTE: GUARANTEE AGREEMENT
TOPIC: IBRD Project
CONCEPTS: Annex or appendix reference. Exchange of information and documents. Inspection and observation. Bonds. Fees and exemptions. Tax exemptions. Domestic obligation. Terms of loan. Loan regulations. Loan guarantee. Guarantor non-interference.
PARTIES:
India
IBRD (World Bank)

104473 Bilateral Agreement **309 UNTS 159**
SIGNED: 19 Nov 54 FORCE: 12 Dec 55
REGISTERED: 15 Aug 58 IBRD (World Bank)
ARTICLES: 5 LANGUAGE: English.
HEADNOTE: GUARANTEE AGREEMENT
TOPIC: IBRD Project
CONCEPTS: Definition of terms. Annex or appendix reference. Exchange of information and documents. Informational records. Inspection and observation. Bonds. Fees and exemptions. Tax exemptions. Domestic obligation. Terms of loan. Loan regulations. Loan guarantee. Guarantor non-interference.
PARTIES:
India
IBRD (World Bank)

104474 Bilateral Agreement **309 UNTS 201**
SIGNED: 29 May 57 FORCE: 28 Nov 57
REGISTERED: 15 Aug 58 IBRD (World Bank)
ARTICLES: 5 LANGUAGE: English.
HEADNOTE: GUARANTEE AGREEMENT

TOPIC: IBRD Project
CONCEPTS: Definition of terms. Annex or appendix reference. Exchange of information and documents. Informational records. Inspection and observation. Bonds. Fees and exemptions. Tax exemptions. Domestic obligation. Terms of loan. Loan regulations. Loan guarantee. Guarantor non-interference.
PARTIES:
India
IBRD (World Bank)

104475 Bilateral Agreement **309 UNTS 241**
SIGNED: 1 Dec 57　　FORCE: 1 Dec 57
REGISTERED: 22 Aug 58 Denmark
ARTICLES: 5 LANGUAGE: Danish. Chinese. English.
HEADNOTE: PROMOTING TRADE RELATIONS
TOPIC: General Economic
CONCEPTS: Annex or appendix reference. Licenses and permits. Establishment of trade relations. Banking. Exchange rates and regulations. Financial programs. Payment schedules.
PROCEDURE: Duration. Renewal or Revival. Termination.
PARTIES:
China People's Rep
Denmark

104476 Bilateral Agreement **309 UNTS 269**
SIGNED: 22 Nov 57　　FORCE: 27 Jun 58
REGISTERED: 25 Aug 58 Norway
ARTICLES: 12 LANGUAGE: Norwegian. Russian.
HEADNOTE: CONSERVING STOCKS SEALS
TOPIC: Specific Resources
CONCEPTS: Annex or appendix reference. Licenses and permits. Establishment of commission. Research cooperation. Indemnities and reimbursements. Ocean resources. Wildlife.
INTL ORGS: Special Commission.
PROCEDURE: Denunciation. Ratification.
PARTIES:
Norway
USSR (Soviet Union)

104477 Bilateral Exchange **309 UNTS 291**
SIGNED: 9 Dec 57　　FORCE: 16 Jul 58
REGISTERED: 27 Aug 58 Netherlands
ARTICLES: 2 LANGUAGE: English.
HEADNOTE: ABOLITION VISAS
TOPIC: Visas
CONCEPTS: Emergencies. Visa abolition.
PROCEDURE: Denunciation.
PARTIES:
Netherlands
Thailand

104478 Bilateral Protocol **309 UNTS 297**
SIGNED: 9 Aug 58　　FORCE: 9 Aug 58
REGISTERED: 27 Aug 58 United Nations
ARTICLES: 2 LANGUAGE: English.
HEADNOTE: CLAIMS AGAINST UNICEF
TOPIC: Direct Aid
CONCEPTS: Annex type material. Responsibility and liability. Claims and settlements. Assistance.
PARTIES:
Jordan
UNICEF (Children)

104479 Bilateral Convention **309 UNTS 301**
SIGNED: 9 Jun 56　　FORCE: 1 Jun 57
REGISTERED: 3 Sep 58 UK Great Britain
ARTICLES: 37 LANGUAGE: English. Swedish.
HEADNOTE: SOCIAL SECURITY
TOPIC: Non-ILO Labor
CONCEPTS: General provisions. Conformity with municipal law. Domestic legislation. Dispute settlement. Old age and invalidity insurance. Wages and salaries. Non-ILO labor relations. Family allowances. Administrative cooperation. Old age insurance. Sickness and invalidity insurance. Social security. Unemployment. Payment schedules. Claims and settlements.
PROCEDURE: Denunciation. Duration. Ratification. Renewal or Revival.
PARTIES:
Sweden
UK Great Britain

104480 Bilateral Exchange **310 UNTS 3**
SIGNED: 1 Mar 57　　FORCE: 1 Mar 57
REGISTERED: 3 Sep 58 UK Great Britain
ARTICLES: 3 LANGUAGE: English. French.
HEADNOTE: COMMERCE NAVIGATION
TOPIC: General Economic
CONCEPTS: Exceptions and exemptions. Previous treaty replacement. Most favored nation clause. Customs duties.
TREATY REF: CONVENTION OF COMMERCE&-NAVIGATION 9DEC1856.
PARTIES:
Morocco
UK Great Britain

104481 Bilateral Instrument **310 UNTS 11**
SIGNED: 29 Mar 57　　FORCE: 29 Mar 57
REGISTERED: 3 Sep 58 UK Great Britain
ARTICLES: 7 LANGUAGE: English. Italian.
HEADNOTE: CLAIMS NATIONAL
TOPIC: Reparations
CONCEPTS: Time limit. Exchange of information and documents. Public information. Procedure. Existing tribunals. Compensation. Loss and/or damage. Post-war claims settlement.
INTL ORGS: Conciliation Commission.
TREATY REF: 49UNTS.
PARTIES:
Italy
UK Great Britain

104482 Bilateral Exchange **310 UNTS 21**
SIGNED: 16 Aug 57　　FORCE: 16 Aug 57
REGISTERED: 3 Sep 58 UK Great Britain
ARTICLES: 2 LANGUAGE: English.
HEADNOTE: PURCHASE CERTAIN SHIPS
TOPIC: Milit Assistance
CONCEPTS: Indemnities and reimbursements. Interest rates. Claims and settlements. Terms of loan. Payment for war supplies. Lend lease. Naval vessels. Surplus war property.
PARTIES:
Turkey
UK Great Britain
ANNEX
344 UNTS 350. UK Great Britain. Amendment 12 Jan 59. Force 12 Jan 59.
344 UNTS 350. Turkey. Amendment 12 Jan 59. Force 12 Jan 59.

104483 Bilateral Exchange **310 UNTS 29**
SIGNED: 28 Feb 57　　FORCE: 28 Feb 57
REGISTERED: 3 Sep 58 UK Great Britain
ARTICLES: 2 LANGUAGE: English.
HEADNOTE: TARIFF CONCESSIONS
TOPIC: Customs
CONCEPTS: Tariffs. Customs duties. Customs exemptions.
PROCEDURE: Duration. Termination.
PARTIES:
Turkey
UK Great Britain

104484 Bilateral Exchange **310 UNTS 35**
SIGNED: 12 Jun 57　　FORCE: 12 Jun 57
REGISTERED: 3 Sep 58 UK Great Britain
ARTICLES: 2 LANGUAGE: English.
HEADNOTE: PRACTICE MEDICAL DOCTORS
TOPIC: Non-ILO Labor
CONCEPTS: Detailed regulations. Standardization. Recognition of legal documents. Public health. Employment regulations. Non-ILO labor relations.
PROCEDURE: Duration. Termination.
PARTIES:
Italy
UK Great Britain

104485 Bilateral Exchange **310 UNTS 41**
SIGNED: 12 Jul 57　　FORCE: 7 Aug 57
REGISTERED: 3 Sep 58 UK Great Britain
ARTICLES: 2 LANGUAGE: English.
HEADNOTE: COOPERATION PROMOTION DEVELOPMENT PEACEFUL USES ATOMIC ENERGY
TOPIC: Atomic Energy
CONCEPTS: Exchange of information and documents. Inspection and observation. Research cooperation. General. Peaceful use. Security of information.

INTL ORGS: International Atomic Energy Agency.
PROCEDURE: Duration. Renewal or Revival. Termination.
PARTIES:
Norway
UK Great Britain
ANNEX
649 UNTS 340. UK Great Britain. Prolongation 20 Dec 67. Force 20 Dec 67.
649 UNTS 340. Norway. Prolongation 20 Dec 67. Force 20 Dec 67.

104486 Bilateral Agreement **310 UNTS 49**
SIGNED: 20 Sep 57　　FORCE: 20 Sep 57
REGISTERED: 3 Sep 58 UK Great Britain
ARTICLES: 10 LANGUAGE: English.
HEADNOTE: COOPERATION PEACEFUL USES ATOMIC ENERGY
TOPIC: Atomic Energy
CONCEPTS: Non-prejudice to third party. Exchange of information and documents. Inspection and observation. Responsibility and liability. Research cooperation. Nuclear materials. Peaceful use. Security of information.
INTL ORGS: International Atomic Energy Agency.
PROCEDURE: Duration.
PARTIES:
Sweden
UK Great Britain
ANNEX
507 UNTS 284. UK Great Britain. Supplementation 14 Feb 64. Force 14 Feb 64.
507 UNTS 284. Sweden. Supplementation 14 Feb 64. Force 14 Feb 64.

104487 Bilateral Exchange **310 UNTS 61**
SIGNED: 9 Jul 56　　FORCE: 9 Jul 56
REGISTERED: 3 Sep 58 UK Great Britain
ARTICLES: 2 LANGUAGE: English.
HEADNOTE: CONTRACTS PERIODS PRESCRIPTION
TOPIC: Non-ILO Labor
CONCEPTS: Detailed regulations. Private contracts. Non-ILO labor relations. Claims and settlements. Reconversion to normalcy.
TREATY REF: 217UNTS223; 221UNTS439.
PARTIES:
Austria
UK Great Britain

104488 Bilateral Exchange **310 UNTS 69**
SIGNED: 28 Feb 57　　FORCE: 28 Feb 57
REGISTERED: 3 Sep 58 UK Great Britain
ARTICLES: 2 LANGUAGE: English.
HEADNOTE: MATTERS RELATING COMMERCE
TOPIC: General Economic
CONCEPTS: Previous treaty replacement. General trade.
TREATY REF: CMD6907; 200LTS509; 108LTS407.
PARTIES:
Turkey
UK Great Britain

104489 Bilateral Agreement **310 UNTS 75**
SIGNED: 19 Dec 56　　FORCE: 2 Jul 57
REGISTERED: 3 Sep 58 IBRD (World Bank)
ARTICLES: 5 LANGUAGE: Chinese. Cambodian. English.
HEADNOTE: GUARANTEE AGREEMENT
TOPIC: IBRD Project
CONCEPTS: Definition of terms. Annex or appendix reference. Exchange of information and documents. Informational records. Inspection and observation. Bonds. Interest rates. Tax exemptions. Domestic obligation. Terms of loan. Loan regulations. Loan guarantee. Guarantor non-interference.
PARTIES:
India
IBRD (World Bank)

104490 Bilateral Agreement **310 UNTS 111**
SIGNED: 29 Jan 58　　FORCE: 28 Mar 58
REGISTERED: 3 Sep 58 IBRD (World Bank)
ARTICLES: 5 LANGUAGE: English.
HEADNOTE: GUARANTEE AGREEMENT (LOAN)
TOPIC: IBRD Project
CONCEPTS: Loan and credit.

PARTIES:
Japan
IBRD (World Bank)

104491 Multilateral Agreement **310 UNTS 145**
SIGNED: 3 Jun 55   FORCE: 3 Jun 55
REGISTERED: 9 Sep 58 Netherlands
ARTICLES: 3 LANGUAGE: English. French.
HEADNOTE: NORTH SEA FISHERIES
TOPIC: Specific Resources
CONCEPTS: Annex type material. Fisheries and fishing.
PROCEDURE: Ratification. Registration.
PARTIES:
  Belgium SIGNED: 3 Jun 55 RATIFIED: 25 Mar 58 FORCE: 20 Jun 58
  Denmark   SIGNED: 3 Jun 55   RATIFIED: 20 Jun 58 FORCE: 20 Jun 58
  France SIGNED: 3 Jun 55 RATIFIED: 25 Mar 58 FORCE: 20 Jun 58
  Germany, West SIGNED: 3 Jun 55 RATIFIED: 6 Sep 57 FORCE: 20 Jun 58
  Netherlands   SIGNED: 3 Jun 55   RATIFIED: 1 Oct 55 FORCE: 20 Jun 58
  UK Great Britain SIGNED: 3 Jun 55 RATIFIED: 13 Jan 58 FORCE: 20 Jun 58
              ANNEX
475 UNTS 364. UK Great Britain. Force 15 May 64.

104492 Multilateral Convention **310 UNTS 151**
SIGNED: 19 Jun 48   FORCE: 17 Sep 53
REGISTERED: 9 Sep 58 ICAO (Civil Aviat)
ARTICLES: 23 LANGUAGE: English. French. Spanish.
HEADNOTE: INTERNATIONAL RECOGNITION RIGHTS AIRCRAFT
TOPIC: Air Transport
CONCEPTS: Definition of terms. Detailed regulations. Exceptions and exemptions. Territorial application. Treaty implementation. Conformity with municipal law. Informational records. General property. Attachment of funds. Indemnities and reimbursements. Fees and exemptions. Claims, debts and assets. Claims and settlements. Registration certificate. Navigational conditions. Air transport.
INTL ORGS: United Nations.
PROCEDURE: Accession. Denunciation. Ratification. Registration. Application to Non-self-governing Territories.
PARTIES:
  Argentina   SIGNED: 19 Jun 48   RATIFIED: 31 Jan 58 FORCE: 1 May 58
  Australia SIGNED: 9 Jun 50
  Belgium SIGNED: 19 Jun 48
  Brazil SIGNED: 19 Jun 48 RATIFIED: 3 Jul 53 FORCE: 1 Oct 53
  Chile SIGNED: 19 Jun 48 RATIFIED: 19 Dec 55 FORCE: 18 Mar 56
  Taiwan SIGNED: 19 Jun 48
  Colombia SIGNED: 19 Jun 48
  Cuba SIGNED: 20 Jun 49
  Denmark SIGNED: 3 Jan 49
  Dominican Republic SIGNED: 19 Jun 48
  Ecuador SIGNED: 14 Jul 48 FORCE: 12 Oct 58
  El Salvador RATIFIED: 14 Aug 58 FORCE: 12 Nov 58
  France SIGNED: 19 Jun 48
  Greece SIGNED: 19 Jun 48
  Iceland SIGNED: 19 Jun 48
  Iran SIGNED: 18 Mar 50
  Ireland SIGNED: 19 Jun 48
  Italy SIGNED: 19 Jun 48
  Laos RATIFIED: 4 Jun 56 FORCE: 2 Sep 56
  Mexico SIGNED: 19 Jun 48
  Netherlands SIGNED: 19 Jun 48
  Norway SIGNED: 3 Jan 49 RATIFIED: 5 Mar 54 FORCE: 2 Jun 54
  Pakistan   SIGNED: 21 Aug 51   RATIFIED: 19 Jun 53 FORCE: 17 Sep 53
  Peru SIGNED: 19 Jun 48
  Portugal SIGNED: 19 Jun 48
  Sweden SIGNED: 3 Jan 49 RATIFIED: 16 Nov 55 FORCE: 14 Feb 56
  Switzerland SIGNED: 19 Jun 48
  UK Great Britain SIGNED: 19 Jun 48
  USA (United States) SIGNED: 19 Jun 48 RATIFIED: 6 Sep 49 FORCE: 17 Sep 53
  Venezuela SIGNED: 19 Jun 48

                ANNEX
418 UNTS 388. Netherlands. Ratification 1 Sep 59. Force 30 Nov 59.
418 UNTS 388.   Switzerland.   Ratification 3 Oct 60. Force 1 Jan 61.
418 UNTS 388. Haiti. Adherence 24 Mar 61. Force 22 Jun 61.
418 UNTS 388. Italy. Ratification 6 Dec 60. Force 6 Mar 61.
418 UNTS 388. Cuba. Ratification 20 Jun 61. Force 18 Sep 61.
418 UNTS 388. Germany, West. Adherence 7 Jul 59. Force 5 Oct 59.
514 UNTS 278. Denmark. Ratification 18 Jan 63. Force 18 Apr 63.
514 UNTS 278. France. Ratification 27 Feb 64. Force 27 May 64.
514 UNTS 278. Mali. Adherence 28 Dec 61. Force 28 Mar 62.
514 UNTS 278. Mauritania. Adherence 23 Jul 62. Force 21 Oct 62.
514 UNTS 278. Algeria. Adherence 10 Aug 64. Force 8 Nov 64.
514 UNTS 278. Niger. Adherence 27 Dec 62. Force 27 Mar 63.

104493 Multilateral Convention **310 UNTS 181**
SIGNED: 7 Oct 52   FORCE: 4 Feb 58
REGISTERED: 9 Sep 58 ICAO (Civil Aviat)
ARTICLES: 39 LANGUAGE: English. French. Spanish.
HEADNOTE: DAMAGE CAUSED FOREIGN AIRCRAFT TO THIRD PARTIES ON SURFACE
TOPIC: Admin Cooperation
CONCEPTS: Definition of terms. Exceptions and exemptions. Territorial application. General provisions. Responsibility and liability.
INTL ORGS: International Civil Aviation Organization.
TREATY REF: 192LTS289.
PROCEDURE: Accession. Denunciation. Ratification.
PARTIES:
  Argentina SIGNED: 7 Oct 52
  Australia SIGNED: 7 Oct 52
  Belgium SIGNED: 7 Oct 52
  Brazil SIGNED: 7 Oct 52
  Canada SIGNED: 20 Oct 53 RATIFIED: 6 Jan 56 FORCE: 4 Feb 58
  Denmark SIGNED: 7 Oct 52
  Dominican Republic SIGNED: 7 Oct 52
  Ecuador RATIFIED: 11 Aug 58
  United Arab Rep SIGNED: 7 Oct 52 RATIFIED: 23 Feb 54 FORCE: 4 Feb 58
  France SIGNED: 7 Oct 52
  Greece SIGNED: 5 Apr 55
  India SIGNED: 2 Aug 55
  Israel SIGNED: 7 Oct 52
  Italy SIGNED: 7 Oct 52
  Liberia SIGNED: 7 Oct 52
  Libya SIGNED: 11 Aug 54
  Luxembourg   SIGNED: 7 Oct 52   RATIFIED: 19 Feb 57 FORCE: 4 Feb 58
  Mexico SIGNED: 7 Oct 52
  Netherlands SIGNED: 7 Oct 52
  Norway SIGNED: 10 Dec 54
  Pakistan   SIGNED: 25 Feb 57   RATIFIED: 6 Nov 57 FORCE: 4 Feb 58
  Philippines SIGNED: 7 Oct 52
  Portugal SIGNED: 7 Oct 52
  Spain SIGNED: 7 Oct 52 RATIFIED: 1 Mar 57 FORCE: 4 Feb 58
  Sweden SIGNED: 11 Aug 54
  Switzerland SIGNED: 7 Oct 52
  Thailand SIGNED: 7 Oct 52
  UK Great Britain SIGNED: 23 Apr 53
              ANNEX
335 UNTS 350. Ceylon (Sri Lanka). Adherence 31 Mar 59. Force 29 Jun 59.
418 UNTS 390. Honduras. Adherence 5 Oct 60. Force 3 Jan 61.
418 UNTS 390. Haiti. Adherence 24 Mar 61. Force 22 Jun 61.
514 UNTS 280. Mauritania. Adherence 23 Jul 62. Force 21 Oct 62.
514 UNTS 280. Brazil. Ratification 19 Dec 62. Force 19 Mar 63.
514 UNTS 280. Tunisia. Adherence 16 Sep 63. Force 15 Dec 63.
514 UNTS 280. Morocco. Adherence 31 Mar 64. Force 29 Jun 64.
514 UNTS 280. Algeria. Adherence 13 Apr 64. Force 12 Jul 64.

514 UNTS 280. Mali. Adherence 28 Dec 61. Force 28 Mar 62.
514 UNTS 280. Niger. Adherence 27 Dec 62. Force 27 Mar 63.
514 UNTS 280. Italy. Ratification 10 Oct 63. Force 8 Jan 64.

104494 Multilateral Agreement **310 UNTS 229**
SIGNED: 30 Apr 56   FORCE: 21 Aug 57
REGISTERED: 9 Sep 58 ICAO (Civil Aviat)
ARTICLES: 11 LANGUAGE: English. French. Spanish.
HEADNOTE: COMMERCIAL RIGHTS NON-SCHEDULED AIR SERVICES EUROPE
TOPIC: Air Transport
CONCEPTS: Exceptions and exemptions. Territorial application. Exchange of information and documents. Informational records. Arbitration. Procedure. Existing tribunals. Negotiation. Air transport. Conditions of airlines operating permission. Overflights and technical stops. Operating authorizations and regulations.
INTL ORGS: European Civil Aviation Conference. International Civil Aviation Organization. International Court of Justice. Arbitration Commission.
TREATY REF: 15UNTS295.
PROCEDURE: Amendment. Accession. Denunciation. Ratification. Registration. Application to Non-self-governing Territories.
PARTIES:
  Austria   SIGNED: 30 Oct 56   RATIFIED: 21 May 57 FORCE: 21 Aug 57
  Belgium SIGNED: 30 Apr 56
  Denmark   SIGNED: 21 Nov 56   RATIFIED: 12 Sep 57 FORCE: 12 Dec 57
  Finland SIGNED: 14 Oct 57 RATIFIED: 6 Nov 57 FORCE: 6 Feb 58
  France SIGNED: 30 Apr 56 RATIFIED: 5 Jun 57 FORCE: 5 Sep 57
  Germany, West SIGNED: 29 May 56
  Iceland SIGNED: 8 Nov 56
  Ireland SIGNED: 29 May 56
  Italy SIGNED: 23 Jan 57
  Luxembourg SIGNED: 30 Apr 56
  Netherlands   SIGNED: 12 Jul 56   RATIFIED: 20 Jan 58 FORCE: 20 Apr 58
  Norway SIGNED: 8 Nov 56 RATIFIED: 5 Aug 57 FORCE: 5 Nov 57
  Portugal SIGNED: 7 May 57
  Spain SIGNED: 8 Nov 56 RATIFIED: 30 May 57 FORCE: 30 Aug 57
  Sweden   SIGNED: 23 Jan 57   RATIFIED: 13 Aug 57 FORCE: 13 Nov 57
  Switzerland   SIGNED: 30 Apr 56   RATIFIED: 2 Apr 57 FORCE: 21 Aug 57
  Turkey SIGNED: 8 Nov 56
              ANNEX
335 UNTS 351. Portugal. Ratification 17 Oct 58. Force 17 Jan 59.
335 UNTS 351. Turkey. Ratification 4 Nov 58. Force 4 Feb 59.
418 UNTS 392. Ireland. Ratification 2 Aug 61. Force 2 Nov 61.
418 UNTS 392. Iceland. Ratification 25 Sep 61. Force 25 Dec 61.
418 UNTS 392. Germany, West. Ratification 11 Sep 59. Force 11 Dec 59.
418 UNTS 392. UK Great Britain. Channel Islands. Force 11 Apr 60.
418 UNTS 392. UK Great Britain. Isle of Man. Force 11 Apr 60.
418 UNTS 392. Belgium. Ratification 22 Apr 60. Force 22 Jul 60.
418 UNTS 392. UK Great Britain. Adherence 11 Jan 60. Force 11 Apr 60.
514 UNTS 282.   Luxembourg.   Ratification 23 Dec 63. Force 23 Mar 64.
514 UNTS 282.   Luxembourg.   Ratification 23 Dec 63. Force 23 Mar 64.

104495 Bilateral Agreement **310 UNTS 251**
SIGNED: 9 Dec 46   FORCE: 9 Dec 46
REGISTERED: 9 Sep 58 ICAO (Civil Aviat)
ARTICLES: 9 LANGUAGE: French. Portuguese.
HEADNOTE: RELATING AIR TRANSPORT
TOPIC: Air Transport
CONCEPTS: Annex or appendix reference. Conformity with municipal law. General cooperation. Licenses and permits. Recognition of legal documents. Use of facilities. Arbitration. Procedure. Existing tribunals. Negotiation. Fees and exemptions. Most favored nation clause. National treat-

ment. Customs exemptions. Competency certificate. Routes and logistics. Navigational conditions. Permit designation. Air transport. Airport facilities. Airworthiness certificates. Conditions of airlines operating permission. Operating authorizations and regulations. Licenses and certificates of nationality.
INTL ORGS: International Civil Aviation Organization.
TREATY REF: 171UNTS345; 15UNTS295.
PROCEDURE: Future Procedures Contemplated. Registration. Termination.
PARTIES:
Portugal
Switzerland

104496 Bilateral Agreement **310 UNTS 279**
SIGNED: 20 Mar 52   FORCE: 20 Mar 52
REGISTERED: 9 Sep 58 ICAO (Civil Aviat)
ARTICLES: 14 LANGUAGE: Norwegian. Spanish.
HEADNOTE: AIR TRANSPORT
TOPIC: Air Transport
CONCEPTS: Definition of terms. Annex or appendix reference. Previous treaty replacement. Non-visa travel documents. Conformity with municipal law. General cooperation. Domestic legislation. Licenses and permits. Recognition of legal documents. Use of facilities. Arbitration. Procedure. Fees and exemptions. Most favored nation clause. National treatment. Customs exemptions. Competency certificate. Routes and logistics. Navigational conditions. Permit designation. Air transport. Airport facilities. Airworthiness certificates. Conditions of airlines operating permission. Operating authorizations and regulations.
INTL ORGS: International Civil Aviation Organization.
TREATY REF: 15UNTS295.
PROCEDURE: Future Procedures Contemplated. Ratification. Registration. Termination.
PARTIES:
Norway
Uruguay

104497 Bilateral Agreement **311 UNTS 3**
SIGNED: 20 Mar 52   FORCE: 20 Mar 52
REGISTERED: 9 Sep 58 ICAO (Civil Aviat)
ARTICLES: 14 LANGUAGE: Swedish. Spanish.
HEADNOTE: AIR TRANSPORT
TOPIC: Air Transport
CONCEPTS: Definition of terms. Annex or appendix reference. Previous treaty replacement. Conformity with municipal law. General cooperation. Domestic legislation. Licenses and permits. Recognition of legal documents. Use of facilities. Arbitration. Procedure. Fees and exemptions. National treatment. Customs duties. Customs exemptions. Competency certificate. Routes and logistics. Navigational conditions. Permit designation. Air transport. Airport facilities. Airworthiness certificates. Conditions of airlines operating permission. Operating authorizations and regulations. Licenses and certificates of nationality.
INTL ORGS: International Civil Aviation Organization.
TREATY REF: 15UNTS295.
PROCEDURE: Denunciation. Future Procedures Contemplated. Ratification. Registration.
PARTIES:
Sweden
Uruguay

104498 Bilateral Agreement **311 UNTS 43**
SIGNED: 31 Mar 52   FORCE: 30 Jun 56
REGISTERED: 9 Sep 58 ICAO (Civil Aviat)
ARTICLES: 11 LANGUAGE: Arabic. French.
HEADNOTE: CONCERNING AIR SERVICE
TOPIC: Air Transport
CONCEPTS: Detailed regulations. Annex or appendix reference. Court procedures. Conformity with municipal law. General cooperation. Exchange of information and documents. Licenses and permits. Recognition of legal documents. Use of facilities. Arbitration. Procedure. Existing tribunals. Negotiation. Fees and exemptions. Non-interest rates and fees. Customs duties. Customs exemptions. Competency certificate. Routes and logistics. Navigational conditions. Permit designation. Air transport. Airport facili-

ties. Airworthiness certificates. Conditions of airlines operating permission. Operating authorizations and regulations. Licenses and certificates of nationality.
INTL ORGS: International Civil Aviation Organization.
TREATY REF: 15UNTS295.
PROCEDURE: Future Procedures Contemplated. Ratification. Registration. Termination.
PARTIES:
Iraq
Switzerland

104499 Bilateral Agreement **311 UNTS 63**
SIGNED: 27 Oct 52   FORCE: 27 Oct 52
REGISTERED: 9 Sep 58 ICAO (Civil Aviat)
ARTICLES: 19 LANGUAGE: Spanish. Swedish.
HEADNOTE: CONCERNING AIR SERVICES BETWEEN BEYOND RESPECTIVE TERRITORIES
TOPIC: Air Transport
CONCEPTS: Detailed regulations. Annex or appendix reference. Non-visa travel documents. Conformity with municipal law. Licenses and permits. Recognition of legal documents. Use of facilities. Arbitration. Procedure. Existing tribunals. Fees and exemptions. Non-interest rates and fees. Most favored nation clause. National treatment. Customs exemptions. Competency certificate. Routes and logistics. Navigational conditions. Permit designation. Airport facilities. Airworthiness certificates. Conditions of airlines operating permission. Overflights and technical stops. Operating authorizations and regulations.
INTL ORGS: International Civil Aviation Organization.
TREATY REF: 15UNTS295.
PROCEDURE: Future Procedures Contemplated. Ratification. Registration. Termination.
PARTIES:
Chile
Sweden
ANNEX
609 UNTS 286. Sweden. Force 18 Feb 57.
609 UNTS 286. Chile. Force 18 Feb 57.

104500 Bilateral Agreement **311 UNTS 95**
SIGNED: 17 Nov 52   FORCE: 17 Nov 52
REGISTERED: 9 Sep 58 ICAO (Civil Aviat)
ARTICLES: 11 LANGUAGE: French. Norwegian.
HEADNOTE: AIR TRANSPORT
TOPIC: Air Transport
CONCEPTS: Definition of terms. Annex or appendix reference. Conformity with municipal law. General cooperation. Licenses and permits. Recognition of legal documents. Use of facilities. Arbitration. Procedure. Existing tribunals. Negotiation. Fees and exemptions. Non-interest rates and fees. Most favored nation clause. National treatment. Customs exemptions. Competency certificate. Routes and logistics. Navigational conditions. Permit designation. Airport facilities. Airworthiness certificates. Conditions of airlines operating permission. Operating authorizations and regulations. Licenses and certificates of nationality.
INTL ORGS: International Civil Aviation Organization.
TREATY REF: 15UNTS295.
PROCEDURE: Amendment. Future Procedures Contemplated. Ratification. Registration. Termination.
PARTIES:
Luxembourg
Norway

104501 Bilateral Agreement **311 UNTS 115**
SIGNED: 21 Feb 53   FORCE: 21 Feb 53
REGISTERED: 9 Sep 58 ICAO (Civil Aviat)
ARTICLES: 15 LANGUAGE: English. Arabic.
HEADNOTE: AIR SERVICES BETWEEN BEYOND RESPECTIVE TERRITORIES
TOPIC: Air Transport
CONCEPTS: Conditions. Definition of terms. Detailed regulations. Exceptions and exemptions. Annex or appendix reference. Conformity with municipal law. General cooperation. Exchange of information and documents. Arbitration. Procedure. Special tribunals. Negotiation. Monetary and gold transfers. Non-interest rates and fees. Most favored nation clause. National treatment.

Customs exemptions. Routes and logistics. Permit designation. Conditions of airlines operating permission. Overflights and technical stops. Operating authorizations and regulations.
INTL ORGS: International Civil Aviation Organization. Arbitration Commission.
TREATY REF: 15UNTS295.
PROCEDURE: Amendment. Future Procedures Contemplated. Ratification. Termination. Application to Non-self-governing Territories.
PARTIES:
Libya
UK Great Britain

104502 Bilateral Agreement **311 UNTS 147**
SIGNED: 30 Dec 54   FORCE: 30 Dec 54
REGISTERED: 9 Sep 58 ICAO (Civil Aviat)
ARTICLES: 11 LANGUAGE: Norwegian. French.
HEADNOTE: AIR TRANSPORT
TOPIC: Air Transport
CONCEPTS: Detailed regulations. Annex or appendix reference. Conformity with municipal law. General cooperation. Licenses and permits. Recognition of legal documents. Use of facilities. Arbitration. Procedure. Existing tribunals. Negotiation. Fees and exemptions. Non-interest rates and fees. National treatment. Customs exemptions. Competency certificate. Routes and logistics. Navigational conditions. Permit designation. Air transport. Airport facilities. Airworthiness certificates. Conditions of airlines operating permission. Operating authorizations and regulations. Licenses and certificates of nationality.
INTL ORGS: International Civil Aviation Organization.
TREATY REF: 15UNTS295.
PROCEDURE: Future Procedures Contemplated. Ratification. Registration. Termination.
PARTIES:
Norway
Switzerland
ANNEX
335 UNTS 352.   Switzerland.   Amendment 4 Jun 57. Force 4 Jun 57.
335 UNTS 352. Norway. Amendment 4 Jun 57. Force 4 Jun 57.

104503 Bilateral Agreement **311 UNTS 167**
SIGNED: 12 Jan 55   FORCE: 20 Jul 55
REGISTERED: 9 Sep 58 ICAO (Civil Aviat)
ARTICLES: 18 LANGUAGE: English. Japanese.
HEADNOTE: AIR SERVICES
TOPIC: Air Transport
CONCEPTS: Definition of terms. Detailed regulations. Exceptions and exemptions. Annex or appendix reference. Conformity with municipal law. General cooperation. Exchange of information and documents. Use of facilities. Arbitration. Procedure. Special tribunals. Negotiation. Fees and exemptions. Non-interest rates and fees. Most favored nation clause. National treatment. Customs duties. Routes and logistics. Navigational equipment. Permit designation. Airport facilities. Conditions of airlines operating permission. Overflights and technical stops. Operating authorizations and regulations.
INTL ORGS: International Civil Aviation Organization. Arbitration Commission.
TREATY REF: 15UNTS295.
PROCEDURE: Amendment. Future Procedures Contemplated. Ratification. Registration. Termination. Application to Non-self-governing Territories.
PARTIES:
Canada
Japan

104504 Bilateral Agreement **311 UNTS 199**
SIGNED: 23 Mar 55   FORCE: 7 Jun 56
REGISTERED: 9 Sep 58 ICAO (Civil Aviat)
ARTICLES: 18 LANGUAGE: English.
HEADNOTE: SCHEDULED AIR SERVICES
TOPIC: Air Transport
CONCEPTS: Definition of terms. Detailed regulations. Exceptions and exemptions. Annex or appendix reference. Conformity with municipal law. General cooperation. Exchange of information and documents. Arbitration. Procedure. Existing tribunals. Negotiation. Non-interest rates and fees. Routes and logistics. Navigational con-

ditions. Permit designation. Air transport. Conditions of airlines operating permission. Operating authorizations and regulations.
INTL ORGS: International Civil Aviation Organization.
TREATY REF: 15UNTS295.
PROCEDURE: Future Procedures Contemplated. Ratification. Registration. Termination.
PARTIES:
Iraq
United Arab Rep

104505 Bilateral Agreement **311 UNTS 217**
SIGNED: 2 Nov 55　　　FORCE: 13 Aug 56
REGISTERED: 9 Sep 58 ICAO (Civil Aviat)
ARTICLES: 18 LANGUAGE: English. Turkish.
HEADNOTE: RELATING AIR SERVICES
TOPIC: Air Transport
CONCEPTS: Definition of terms. Detailed regulations. Exceptions and exemptions. Annex or appendix reference. Conformity with municipal law. General cooperation. Exchange of information and documents. Arbitration. Procedure. Existing tribunals. Negotiation. Non-interest rates and fees. Customs exemptions. Routes and logistics. Navigational conditions. Permit designation. Air transport. Conditions of airlines operating permission. Operating authorizations and regulations.
INTL ORGS: International Civil Aviation Organization.
TREATY REF: 15UNTS295; 84UNTS389.
PROCEDURE: Future Procedures Contemplated. Ratification. Registration. Termination.
PARTIES:
Pakistan
Turkey

104506 Bilateral Agreement **311 UNTS 243**
SIGNED: 26 Nov 55　　　FORCE: 11 May 56
REGISTERED: 9 Sep 58 ICAO (Civil Aviat)
ARTICLES: 19 LANGUAGE: Hindi. Japanese. English.
HEADNOTE: AIR SERVICES
TOPIC: Air Transport
CONCEPTS: Definition of terms. Detailed regulations. Exceptions and exemptions. Treaty interpretation. Annex or appendix reference. Conformity with municipal law. General cooperation. Exchange of information and documents. Use of facilities. Arbitration. Procedure. Special tribunals. Negotiation. Non-interest rates and fees. National treatment. Customs exemptions. Routes and logistics. Permit designation. Airport facilities. Conditions of airlines operating permission. Overflights and technical stops. Operating authorizations and regulations.
INTL ORGS: International Civil Aviation Organization. International Court of Justice. Arbitration Commission.
TREATY REF: 15UNTS295.
PROCEDURE: Amendment. Duration. Future Procedures Contemplated. Ratification. Registration. Renewal or Revival. Termination.
PARTIES:
India
Japan

104507 Bilateral Agreement **311 UNTS 291**
SIGNED: 19 Jan 56　　　FORCE: 27 Apr 56
REGISTERED: 9 Sep 58 ICAO (Civil Aviat)
ARTICLES: 18 LANGUAGE: English. Japanese.
HEADNOTE: AIR SERVICES
TOPIC: Air Transport
CONCEPTS: Definition of terms. Detailed regulations. Annex or appendix reference. Conformity with municipal law. General cooperation. Exchange of information and documents. Use of facilities. Procedure. Special tribunals. Negotiation. Fees and exemptions. Non-interest rates and fees. Most favored nation clause. National treatment. Customs exemptions. Routes and logistics. Permit designation. Airport facilities. Conditions of airlines operating permission. Overflights and technical stops. Operating authorizations and regulations.
INTL ORGS: International Civil Aviation Organization. International Court of Justice. Arbitration Commission.
TREATY REF: 15UNTS295.
PROCEDURE: Amendment. Future Procedures

Contemplated. Ratification. Registration. Termination. Application to Non-self-governing Territories.
PARTIES:
Australia
Japan

104508 Bilateral Agreement **311 UNTS 319**
SIGNED: 12 Feb 56　　　FORCE: 31 Aug 56
REGISTERED: 9 Sep 58 ICAO (Civil Aviat)
ARTICLES: 13 LANGUAGE: English.
HEADNOTE: AIR SERVICES
TOPIC: Air Transport
CONCEPTS: Definition of terms. Exceptions and exemptions. Annex or appendix reference. Conformity with municipal law. Arbitration. Procedure. Negotiation. Reexport of goods, etc.. Non-interest rates and fees. Customs exemptions. Routes and logistics. Permit designation. Air transport. Conditions of airlines operating permission. Overflights and technical stops. Operating authorizations and regulations.
INTL ORGS: Arbitration Commission.
TREATY REF: 15UNTS295.
PROCEDURE: Amendment. Ratification. Termination.
PARTIES:
Netherlands
Sudan

104509 Bilateral Agreement **312 UNTS 3**
SIGNED: 24 May 56　　　FORCE: 3 Apr 57
REGISTERED: 9 Sep 58 ICAO (Civil Aviat)
ARTICLES: 18 LANGUAGE: French. Japanese.
HEADNOTE: RELATING AIR SERVICES
TOPIC: Air Transport
CONCEPTS: Definition of terms. Detailed regulations. Exceptions and exemptions. Annex or appendix reference. Conformity with municipal law. Exchange of information and documents. Use of facilities. Arbitration. Procedure. Special tribunals. Negotiation. Fees and exemptions. Non-interest rates and fees. Most favored nation clause. National treatment. Customs exemptions. Routes and logistics. Permit designation. Airport facilities. Conditions of airlines operating permission. Overflights and technical stops. Operating authorizations and regulations.
INTL ORGS: International Civil Aviation Organization. Arbitration Commission.
TREATY REF: 15UNTS295.
PROCEDURE: Amendment. Future Procedures Contemplated. Ratification. Registration. Termination. Application to Non-self-governing Territories.
PARTIES:
Japan
Switzerland

104510 Bilateral Agreement **312 UNTS 43**
SIGNED: 13 Oct 56　　　FORCE: 11 Jul 57
REGISTERED: 9 Sep 58 ICAO (Civil Aviat)
ARTICLES: 11 LANGUAGE: French. Thai.
HEADNOTE: RELATING AIR SERVICES
TOPIC: Air Transport
CONCEPTS: Detailed regulations. Annex or appendix reference. Conformity with municipal law. General cooperation. Licenses and permits. Recognition of legal documents. Use of facilities. Arbitration. Procedure. Existing tribunals. Negotiation. Fees and exemptions. Non-interest rates and fees. National treatment. Customs exemptions. Competency certificate. Routes and logistics. Navigational conditions. Permit designation. Air transport. Airport facilities. Airworthiness certificates. Conditions of airlines operating permission. Operating authorizations and regulations. Licenses and certificates of nationality.
INTL ORGS: International Civil Aviation Organization. Arbitration Commission.
TREATY REF: 15UNTS295.
PROCEDURE: Future Procedures Contemplated. Registration. Termination.
PARTIES:
Switzerland
Thailand
ANNEX
646 UNTS 378.　　Thailand.　　Amendment 28 Sep 66. Force 28 Sep 66.

646 UNTS 378.　　Switzerland.　　Amendment 28 Sep 66. Force 28 Sep 66.

104511 Bilateral Agreement **312 UNTS 63**
SIGNED: 22 Jan 57　　　FORCE: 22 Jan 57
REGISTERED: 9 Sep 58 ICAO (Civil Aviat)
ARTICLES: 15 LANGUAGE: English.
HEADNOTE: RELATING AIR TRANSPORT SERVICES
TOPIC: Air Transport
CONCEPTS: Exceptions and exemptions. Annex or appendix reference. Conformity with municipal law. General cooperation. Exchange of information and documents. Inspection and observation. Licenses and permits. Recognition of legal documents. Use of facilities. Arbitration. Procedure. Existing tribunals. Reexport of goods, etc.. Fees and exemptions. Non-interest rates and fees. National treatment. Customs exemptions. Competency certificate. Routes and logistics. Navigational conditions. Permit designation. Air transport. Airport facilities. Airworthiness certificates. Conditions of airlines operating permission. Operating authorizations and regulations. Licenses and certificates of nationality.
INTL ORGS: International Civil Aviation Organization. Arbitration Commission.
PROCEDURE: Amendment. Registration. Termination.
PARTIES:
Iceland
Thailand

104512 Bilateral Agreement **312 UNTS 75**
SIGNED: 12 Mar 57　　　FORCE: 12 Mar 57
REGISTERED: 9 Sep 58 ICAO (Civil Aviat)
ARTICLES: 12 LANGUAGE: Czechoslovakian. French.
HEADNOTE: AIR SERVICES
TOPIC: Air Transport
CONCEPTS: Definition of terms. Representation. Annex or appendix reference. Previous treaty replacement. Conformity with municipal law. General cooperation. Licenses and permits. Personnel. Recognition of legal documents. Procedure. Negotiation. Humanitarian matters. Reexport of goods, etc.. Fees and exemptions. Most favored nation clause. Customs duties. Customs exemptions. Competency certificate. Navigational conditions. Permit designation. Airworthiness certificates. Conditions of airlines operating permission. Operating authorizations and regulations.
PROCEDURE: Amendment. Denunciation.
PARTIES:
Belgium
Czechoslovakia

104513 Bilateral Agreement **312 UNTS 95**
SIGNED: 20 Jun 58　　　FORCE: 1 Jul 58
REGISTERED: 10 Sep 58 Belgium
ARTICLES: 13 LANGUAGE: French. German.
HEADNOTE: INTERNATIONAL TRANSPORT GOODS ROAD
TOPIC: Land Transport
CONCEPTS: Default remedies. Territorial application. Conformity with municipal law. Exchange of information and documents. Licenses and permits. Recognition of legal documents. Establishment of commission. Transport of goods. Operating authorizations and regulations. Driving permits. Motor vehicles and combinations. Roads and highways. Road rules.
PROCEDURE: Denunciation. Duration. Renewal or Revival.
PARTIES:
Austria
Belgium
ANNEX
509 UNTS 296. Belgium. Amendment 20 Jan 64. Force 20 Jan 64.
509 UNTS 296. Austria. Amendment 20 Jan 64. Force 20 Jan 64.

104514 Multilateral Protocol **312 UNTS 109**
SIGNED: 6 Jul 56　　　FORCE: 29 Aug 58
REGISTERED: 10 Sep 58 Belgium
ARTICLES: 12 LANGUAGE: French. Dutch.
HEADNOTE: NATIONAL TREATMENT AWARD PUBLIC WORKS CONTRACTS PURCHASE GOODS

TOPIC: Admin Cooperation
CONCEPTS: Definition of terms. Recognition and enforcement of legal decisions. Private contracts. Establishment of commission. Special tribunals. Purchase authorizations. National treatment.
INTL ORGS: Benelux Economic Union. Arbitration Commission. Special Commission.
PROCEDURE: Ratification.
PARTIES:
  Belgium SIGNED: 6 Jul 56 RATIFIED: 18 Apr 58 FORCE: 29 Aug 58
  Luxembourg SIGNED: 6 Jul 56 RATIFIED: 28 Aug 58 FORCE: 29 Aug 58
  Netherlands SIGNED: 6 Jul 56 RATIFIED: 11 Dec 57 FORCE: 29 Aug 58

104515 Bilateral Agreement **312 UNTS 131**
SIGNED: 12 Mar 57   FORCE: 5 Mar 58
REGISTERED: 10 Sep 58 India
ARTICLES: 5 LANGUAGE: Hindi. Burmese. English.
HEADNOTE: FINANCE
TOPIC: Finance
CONCEPTS: Accounting procedures. Banking. Interest rates. Payment schedules. Loan and credit. Loan repayment. Terms of loan.
PROCEDURE: Ratification.
PARTIES:
  Burma
  India

104516 Bilateral Agreement **312 UNTS 145**
SIGNED: 8 May 58   FORCE: 1 Jun 58
REGISTERED: 15 Sep 58 Belgium
ARTICLES: 11 LANGUAGE: French.
HEADNOTE: INTERNATIONAL TRANSPORT GOODS ROAD
TOPIC: Land Transport
CONCEPTS: Default remedies. Territorial application. Conformity with municipal law. Establishment of commission. Fees and exemptions. Transport of goods. Driving permits. Motor vehicles and combinations. Roads and highways. Road rules.
INTL ORGS: Special Commission.
PROCEDURE: Denunciation. Duration. Renewal or Revival.
PARTIES:
  Belgium
  Sweden

104517 Unilateral Instrument **312 UNTS 155**
SIGNED: 15 Sep 58   FORCE: 15 Sep 58
REGISTERED: 15 Sep 58 United Nations
ARTICLES: 1 LANGUAGE: English.
HEADNOTE: ACCEPTANCE ICJ JURISDICTION
TOPIC: ICJ Option Clause
CONCEPTS: Exceptions and exemptions. Compulsory jurisdiction.
INTL ORGS: International Court of Justice.
PROCEDURE: Duration.
PARTIES:
  Japan

104518 Bilateral Agreement **312 UNTS 159**
SIGNED: 13 Jun 58   FORCE: 22 Aug 58
REGISTERED: 17 Sep 58 IBRD (World Bank)
ARTICLES: 5 LANGUAGE: English.
HEADNOTE: GUARANTEE AGREEMENT
TOPIC: IBRD Project
CONCEPTS: Definition of terms. Annex or appendix reference. Exchange of information and documents. Inspection and observation. Bonds. Fees and exemptions. Tax exemptions. Domestic obligation. Terms of loan. Loan regulations. Loan guarantee. Guarantor non-interference.
PARTIES:
  Japan
  IBRD (World Bank)

104519 Bilateral Agreement **312 UNTS 193**
SIGNED: 27 Jun 58   FORCE: 22 Aug 58
REGISTERED: 17 Sep 58 IBRD (World Bank)
ARTICLES: 5 LANGUAGE: English.
HEADNOTE: GUARANTEE
TOPIC: IBRD Project
CONCEPTS: Loan and credit. Credit provisions.

PARTIES:
  Japan
  IBRD (World Bank)

104520 Bilateral Exchange **312 UNTS 225**
SIGNED: 9 Oct 57   FORCE: 1 Jul 58
REGISTERED: 22 Sep 58 Australia
ARTICLES: 4 LANGUAGE: English.
HEADNOTE: SETTLEMENT INTERCUSTODIAL CONFLICTS
TOPIC: Dispute Settlement
CONCEPTS: Procedure. Claims and settlements.
INTL ORGS: Allied Military Occupation.
PARTIES:
  Australia
  Netherlands

104521 Bilateral Agreement **312 UNTS 235**
SIGNED: 28 May 58   FORCE: 24 May 58
REGISTERED: 24 Sep 58 Denmark
ARTICLES: 16 LANGUAGE: French.
HEADNOTE: CIVIL AIR TRANSPORT
TOPIC: Air Transport
CONCEPTS: Definition of terms. Treaty implementation. Annex or appendix reference. Conformity with municipal law. General cooperation. Informational records. Licenses and permits. Personnel. Recognition of legal documents. Use of facilities. Procedure. Negotiation. Humanitarian matters. Accounting procedures. Monetary and gold transfers. Fees and exemptions. Non-interest rates and fees. Customs exemptions. Registration certificate. Routes and logistics. Navigational conditions. Permit designation. Air transport. Airport facilities. Airworthiness certificates. Conditions of airlines operating permission. Operating authorizations and regulations.
PROCEDURE: Amendment. Denunciation.
PARTIES:
  Bulgaria
  Denmark

104522 Bilateral Agreement **312 UNTS 257**
SIGNED: 18 Dec 57   FORCE: 27 Jun 58
REGISTERED: 24 Sep 58 Norway
ARTICLES: 17 LANGUAGE: Norwegian. Russian.
HEADNOTE: UTILIZATION WATER-POWER
TOPIC: Specific Resources
CONCEPTS: Currency. Materials, equipment and services. Plans and standards. Hydro-electric power. Military installations and equipment. Regulation of natural resources.
PROCEDURE: Ratification.
PARTIES:
  Norway
  USSR (Soviet Union)
              ANNEX
535 UNTS 426. USSR (Soviet Union). Implementation 24 Dec 65. Force 8 Aug 64.
535 UNTS 426. Norway. Implementation 24 Dec 65. Force 8 Aug 64.

104523 Bilateral Agreement **312 UNTS 289**
SIGNED: 15 Feb 57   FORCE: 24 Apr 57
REGISTERED: 26 Sep 58 Norway
ARTICLES: 3 LANGUAGE: Norwegian. Russian.
HEADNOTE: CONCERNING SEA FRONTIER
TOPIC: Territory Boundary
CONCEPTS: Annex or appendix reference. Establishment of commission. Funding procedures. Markers and definitions.
INTL ORGS: Special Commission.
PROCEDURE: Ratification.
PARTIES:
  Norway
  USSR (Soviet Union)

104524 Bilateral Exchange **312 UNTS 347**
SIGNED: 25 Jul 58   FORCE: 25 Jul 58
REGISTERED: 29 Sep 58 UK Great Britain
ARTICLES: 2 LANGUAGE: English.
HEADNOTE: ARMED FORCES CIVIL AVIATION AIR FORCE FACILITIES ECONOMIC DEVELOPMENT
TOPIC: General Military
CONCEPTS: Friendship and amity. Use of facilities. Exchange. Agriculture. Agricultural commodities. Airport facilities. Joint defense. Defense and security. Military assistance. Military assistance missions. Bases and facilities.

PARTIES:
  Muscat and Oman
  UK Great Britain

104525 Bilateral Agreement **312 UNTS 353**
SIGNED: 1 Jun 54   FORCE: 9 May 58
REGISTERED: 29 Sep 58 UK Great Britain
ARTICLES: 7 LANGUAGE: English. Italian.
HEADNOTE: CONTRACTS INSURANCE REINSURANCE
TOPIC: Admin Cooperation
CONCEPTS: Territorial application. Annex or appendix reference. Juridical personality. Domestic legislation. Private contracts.
TREATY REF: 49,50UNTS.
PROCEDURE: Ratification. Termination.
PARTIES:
  Italy
  UK Great Britain

104526 Bilateral Exchange **312 UNTS 373**
SIGNED: 26 Mar 58   FORCE: 26 Mar 58
REGISTERED: 29 Sep 58 UK Great Britain
ARTICLES: 2 LANGUAGE: English. Arabic.
HEADNOTE: LOAN
TOPIC: Loans and Credits
CONCEPTS: Financial programs. Payment schedules. Loan and credit. Loan repayment. Terms of loan.
PARTIES:
  Jordan
  UK Great Britain
              ANNEX
533 UNTS 343. UK Great Britain. Implementation 20 Feb 64. Force 20 Feb 64.
533 UNTS 343. Jordan. Implementation 24 Dec 63. Force 20 Feb 64.
566 UNTS 336. UK Great Britain. Supplementation 9 Nov 64. Force 9 Nov 64.
566 UNTS 336. Jordan. Supplementation 20 Oct 64. Force 9 Nov 64.

104527 Bilateral Exchange **312 UNTS 379**
SIGNED: 7 May 58   FORCE: 7 May 58
REGISTERED: 29 Sep 58 UK Great Britain
ARTICLES: 2 LANGUAGE: English. Arabic.
HEADNOTE: LOAN
TOPIC: Loans and Credits
CONCEPTS: Financial programs. Payment schedules. Loan and credit. Loan repayment. Terms of loan.
PARTIES:
  Jordan
  UK Great Britain
              ANNEX
566 UNTS 336. Jordan. Supplementation 20 Oct 64. Force 9 Nov 64.
566 UNTS 336. UK Great Britain. Supplementation 9 Nov 64. Force 9 Nov 64.

104528 Bilateral Convention **313 UNTS 3**
SIGNED: 25 Jul 57   FORCE: 1 Apr 58
REGISTERED: 29 Sep 58 UK Great Britain
ARTICLES: 39 LANGUAGE: English. Norwegian.
HEADNOTE: SOCIAL SECURITY
TOPIC: Non-ILO Labor
CONCEPTS: Definition of terms. Annex or appendix reference. Conformity with municipal law. Domestic legislation. Dispute settlement. Old age and invalidity insurance. Wages and salaries. Non-ILO labor relations. Family allowances. Administrative cooperation. Old age insurance. Sickness and invalidity insurance. Social security. Unemployment. Claims and settlements. Payment schedules.
INTL ORGS: Arbitration Commission.
PROCEDURE: Denunciation. Duration. Ratification. Renewal or Revival.
PARTIES:
  Norway
  UK Great Britain

104529 Bilateral Exchange **313 UNTS 63**
SIGNED: 30 Aug 57   FORCE: 30 Aug 57
REGISTERED: 29 Sep 58 UK Great Britain
ARTICLES: 2 LANGUAGE: English. Polish.
HEADNOTE: GRANT CONTINUOUS VISAS TRAVEL
TOPIC: Visas

CONCEPTS: Territorial application. Time limit. Visas. Fees and exemptions.
PROCEDURE: Termination.
PARTIES:
Japan
UK Great Britain

104530 Bilateral Agreement **313 UNTS 73**
SIGNED: 12 Mar 56 FORCE: 8 Feb 58
REGISTERED: 29 Sep 58 UK Great Britain
ARTICLES: 23 LANGUAGE: English. Turkish.
HEADNOTE: CULTURAL AGREEMENT
TOPIC: Culture
CONCEPTS: Definition of terms. Territorial application. Friendship and amity. Conformity with municipal law. Operating agencies. Establishment of commission. Recognition of degrees. Exchange. Teacher and student exchange. Professorships. Institute establishment. Scholarships and grants. General cultural cooperation. Athletes. Research cooperation. Export quotas. Publications exchange. Mass media exchange.
INTL ORGS: Special Commission.
PROCEDURE: Denunciation. Duration. Ratification. Renewal or Revival.
PARTIES:
Turkey
UK Great Britain

104531 Bilateral Agreement **313 UNTS 95**
SIGNED: 25 Nov 57 FORCE: 25 Nov 57
REGISTERED: 29 Sep 58 UK Great Britain
ARTICLES: 3 LANGUAGE: English. Spanish.
HEADNOTE: CONSOLIDATION DEBTS
TOPIC: Claims and Debts
CONCEPTS: Annex or appendix reference. Financial programs. Debts. Interest rates. Purchase authorization.
PARTIES:
Argentina
UK Great Britain
ANNEX
404 UNTS 367. UK Great Britain. Amendment 12 May 61. Force 12 May 61.
404 UNTS 367. Argentina. Amendment 12 May 61. Force 12 May 61.
406 UNTS 326. Turkey. Ratification 28 Jul 61.
482 UNTS 378. UK Great Britain. Amendment 5 Jun 63. Force 5 Jun 63.
482 UNTS 378. Argentina. Amendment 5 Jun 63. Force 5 Jun 63.

104532 Bilateral Agreement **313 UNTS 109**
SIGNED: 18 Jul 58 FORCE: 18 Jul 58
REGISTERED: 29 Sep 58 UK Great Britain
ARTICLES: 9 LANGUAGE: English. Portuguese.
HEADNOTE: COOPERATION PEACEFUL USES ATOMIC ENERGY
TOPIC: Atomic Energy
CONCEPTS: Non-prejudice to third party. Exchange of information and documents. Inspection and observation. Research cooperation. Nuclear materials. Research facilities. Security of information.
INTL ORGS: European Nuclear Energy Agency. International Atomic Energy Agency. Organization for Economic Co-operation and Development.
PROCEDURE: Duration. Termination.
PARTIES:
Portugal
UK Great Britain

104533 Bilateral Exchange **313 UNTS 125**
SIGNED: 24 Nov 54 FORCE: 1 Jan 55
REGISTERED: 29 Sep 58 UK Great Britain
ARTICLES: 5 LANGUAGE: English. Portuguese.
HEADNOTE: ABOLITION VISAS
TOPIC: Visas
CONCEPTS: Emergencies. Time limit. Visa abolition. Denial of admission. Conformity with municipal law.
PARTIES:
Portugal
UK Great Britain

104534 Bilateral Treaty **313 UNTS 135**
SIGNED: 23 Apr 58 FORCE: 25 Jul 58
REGISTERED: 2 Oct 58 USSR (Soviet Union)
ARTICLES: 17 LANGUAGE: Russian. Chinese.

HEADNOTE: DEVELOPMENT STRENGTHEN TRADE COMMERCE RELATIONS
TOPIC: General Economic
CONCEPTS: Exceptions and exemptions. General provisions. Annex or appendix reference. Privileges and immunities. Non-diplomatic delegations. Recognition and enforcement of legal decisions. Arbitration. Procedure. Existing tribunals. General trade. Reexport of goods, etc.. Investments. Most favored nation clause. Customs exemptions. General transportation. Transport of goods. Inland and territorial waters. Ports and pilotage.
PROCEDURE: Duration. Ratification. Termination.
PARTIES:
China People's Rep
USSR (Soviet Union)

104535 Bilateral Treaty **313 UNTS 167**
SIGNED: 3 Apr 58 FORCE: 19 Sep 58
REGISTERED: 2 Oct 58 USSR (Soviet Union)
ARTICLES: 75 LANGUAGE: Russian. Romanian.
HEADNOTE: LEGAL ASSISTANCE CIVIL FAMILY CRIMINAL
TOPIC: Admin Cooperation
CONCEPTS: General provisions. Privileges and immunities. Extradition, deportation and repatriation. Extraditable offenses. Limits of prosecution. Provisional detainment. Extradition postponement. Witnesses and experts. Material evidence. Family law. Exchange of information and documents. Juridical personality. Legal protection and assistance. Recognition and enforcement of legal decisions. Immovable property. General property. Jurisdiction. Recognition of legal documents. Indemnities and reimbursements. Conveyance in transit.
PROCEDURE: Duration. Ratification. Renewal or Revival. Termination.
PARTIES:
Romania
USSR (Soviet Union)

104536 Bilateral Treaty **313 UNTS 261**
SIGNED: 15 Feb 58 FORCE: 1 Jul 58
REGISTERED: 2 Oct 58 USSR (Soviet Union)
ARTICLES: 17 LANGUAGE: Russian. Albanian.
HEADNOTE: TRADE
TOPIC: General Economic
CONCEPTS: Exceptions and exemptions. General provisions. Non-diplomatic delegations. Conformity with municipal law. Informational records. Juridical personality. Arbitration. Procedure. Free trade. Reciprocity in trade. Delivery schedules. Most favored nation clause. Equitable taxes. Customs exemptions. General transportation. Navigational conditions. Navigational equipment. Transport of goods. Licenses and certificates of nationality. Inland and territorial waters. Ports and pilotage. Shipwreck and salvage.
PROCEDURE: Ratification. Termination.
PARTIES:
Albania
USSR (Soviet Union)

104537 Bilateral Convention **313 UNTS 291**
SIGNED: 4 Dec 57 FORCE: 28 Apr 58
REGISTERED: 2 Oct 58 USSR (Soviet Union)
ARTICLES: 14 LANGUAGE: Russian. Czechoslovakian.
HEADNOTE: COOPERATION MATTERS OF HEALTH
TOPIC: Sanitation
CONCEPTS: Detailed regulations. Friendship and amity. General cooperation. Exchange of information and documents. Specialists exchange. Quarantine. Public health. Education. Recognition of degrees. Exchange. Sickness and invalidity insurance. Research results. Scientific exchange. Research and development. Indemnities and reimbursements. Expense sharing formulae. Publications exchange. Conferences.
TREATY REF: 259 UNTS 341.
PROCEDURE: Duration. Ratification. Renewal or Revival. Termination.
PARTIES:
Czechoslovakia
USSR (Soviet Union)

104538 Bilateral Exchange **313 UNTS 309**
SIGNED: 22 Oct 57 FORCE: 5 Aug 58
REGISTERED: 2 Oct 58 Netherlands
ARTICLES: 3 LANGUAGE: English.
HEADNOTE: VALIDATION CERTIFICATES AIRWORTHINESS
TOPIC: Air Transport
CONCEPTS: Territorial application. Conformity with municipal law. Exchange of information and documents. Recognition of legal documents. Use of facilities. Registration certificate. Airworthiness certificates. Conditions of airlines operating permission.
PROCEDURE: Termination.
PARTIES:
Netherlands
UK Great Britain
ANNEX
603 UNTS 326. Netherlands. Termination 27 Jan 67. Force 25 Oct 62.
603 UNTS 326. UK Great Britain. Termination 27 Jan 67. Force 25 Oct 62.

104539 Multilateral Convention **314 UNTS 3**
SIGNED: 9 Jul 56 FORCE: 1 Oct 58
REGISTERED: 11 Oct 58 ILO (Labor Org)
ARTICLES: 25 LANGUAGE: English. French.
HEADNOTE: SOCIAL SECURITY TRANSPORT WORKERS
TOPIC: Non-ILO Labor
CONCEPTS: Definition of terms. Notarial acts and services. Conformity with municipal law. Exchange of information and documents. Domestic legislation. Dispute settlement. Public health. Old age and invalidity insurance. Wages and salaries. Non-ILO labor relations. Administrative cooperation. Sickness and invalidity insurance. Social security. Payment schedules. Claims and settlements.
INTL ORGS: International Labour Organization.
TREATY REF: 166 UNTS 73.
PROCEDURE: Amendment. Accession. Denunciation. Duration. Ratification. Registration.
PARTIES:
Belgium SIGNED: 5 Dec 56
France SIGNED: 9 Oct 56
Germany, West SIGNED: 25 Oct 56
Hungary SIGNED: 30 Oct 56
Italy SIGNED: 1 Nov 56
Luxembourg SIGNED: 1 Nov 56
Netherlands SIGNED: 12 Oct 56 RATIFIED: 4 Aug 58 FORCE: 1 Oct 58
Poland SIGNED: 26 Oct 56 RATIFIED: 24 Jan 58 FORCE: 1 Oct 58
Spain SIGNED: 1 May 58
Switzerland SIGNED: 29 Oct 56
Turkey SIGNED: 30 Oct 56
Yugoslavia SIGNED: 28 Nov 56
ANNEX
327 UNTS 385. France. Ratification 10 Apr 59. Force 1 Jun 59.
379 UNTS 439. Luxembourg. Ratification 27 Oct 60. Force 1 Dec 60.
636 UNTS 366. Belgium. Ratification 3 May 68. Force 1 Jul 68.

104540 Bilateral Exchange **314 UNTS 43**
SIGNED: 15 Aug 58 FORCE: 15 Sep 58
REGISTERED: 20 Oct 58 Finland
ARTICLES: 2 LANGUAGE: English.
HEADNOTE: VISA FACILITIES NON-IMMIGRANTS
TOPIC: Visas
CONCEPTS: Time limit. Visa abolition. Resident permits. Visas. Conformity with municipal law.
PARTIES:
Finland
USA (United States)

104541 Bilateral Agreement **314 UNTS 49**
SIGNED: 16 Feb 53 FORCE: 23 Sep 54
REGISTERED: 22 Oct 58 United Nations
ARTICLES: 12 LANGUAGE: Spanish.
HEADNOTE: HEADQUARTERS UN/ECLA
TOPIC: IGO Operations
CONCEPTS: Definition of terms. Annex or appendix reference. Non-visa travel documents. Diplomatic privileges. Privileges and immunities. Diplomatic correspondence. Juridical personality. Procedure. Exchange rates and regulations. Special status. Status of experts.
TREATY REF: 1 UNTS 263.

PROCEDURE: Amendment. Ratification.
PARTIES:
 Chile
 United Nations

104542   Bilateral Exchange   **314 UNTS 81**
SIGNED: 25 Nov 57   FORCE: 1 Jan 58
REGISTERED: 28 Oct 58 Israel
ARTICLES: 2 LANGUAGE: German.
HEADNOTE: ABOLITION VISAS
TOPIC: Visas
CONCEPTS: Passports diplomatic. Visas.
PARTIES:
 Austria
 Israel
                        ANNEX
660 UNTS 399.
660 UNTS 399. Israel. Termination 22 Dec 68.

104543   Bilateral Exchange   **314 UNTS 87**
SIGNED: 1 Mar 58   FORCE: 1 Apr 58
REGISTERED: 28 Oct 58 Israel
ARTICLES: 2 LANGUAGE: French.
HEADNOTE: ABOLITION VISAS
TOPIC: Visas
CONCEPTS: Time limit. Visa abolition. Passports
 diplomatic. Resident permits.
PARTIES:
 France
 Israel

104544   Bilateral Exchange   **314 UNTS 93**
SIGNED: 29 Apr 58   FORCE: 11 Jun 58
REGISTERED: 28 Oct 58 Israel
ARTICLES: 2 LANGUAGE: English.
HEADNOTE: ABOLITION VISA FEES
TOPIC: Visas
CONCEPTS: Denial of admission. Visas. Confor-
 mity with municipal law. Fees and exemptions.
PARTIES:
 Israel
 New Zealand

104545   Bilateral Exchange   **314 UNTS 99**
SIGNED: 20 Mar 58   FORCE: 20 Mar 58
REGISTERED: 28 Oct 58 Israel
ARTICLES: 2 LANGUAGE: English.
HEADNOTE: LANGUAGES USED
TOPIC: Admin Cooperation
CONCEPTS: General cooperation.
PARTIES:
 Israel
 Sweden

104546 Multilateral Convention **314 UNTS 105**
SIGNED: 9 Feb 57   FORCE: 14 Oct 57
REGISTERED: 30 Oct 58 USA (United States)
ARTICLES: 13 LANGUAGE: English. Japanese.
 Russian.
HEADNOTE: CONSERVATION FUR SEALS
TOPIC: Specific Resources
CONCEPTS: Definition of terms. Annex or appen-
 dix reference. Exchange of information and doc-
 uments. Inspection and observation. Incorpora-
 tion of treaty provisions into national law. Estab-
 lishment of commission. Research cooperation.
 Indemnities and reimbursements. Ocean re-
 sources.
INTL ORGS: Northern Pacific Fur Seal Commis-
 sion.
PROCEDURE: Duration. Ratification. Registration.
PARTIES:
 Canada SIGNED: 9 Feb 57 RATIFIED: 16 Sep 57
  FORCE: 14 Oct 57
 Japan SIGNED: 9 Feb 57 RATIFIED: 20 Sep 57
  FORCE: 14 Oct 57
 USA (United States) SIGNED: 9 Feb 57 RATI-
  FIED: 16 Sep 57 FORCE: 14 Oct 57
 USSR (Soviet Union) SIGNED: 9 Feb 57 RATI-
  FIED: 14 Oct 57 FORCE: 14 Oct 57
                        ANNEX
494 UNTS 303. USSR (Soviet Union). Amend-
 ment 8 Oct 63. Force 10 Apr 64.
494 UNTS 303. Japan. Amendment 8 Oct 63.
 Force 10 Apr 64.
494 UNTS 303. USA (United States). Amendment
 8 Oct 63. Force 10 Apr 64.
494 UNTS 303. USA (United States). Ratification
 6 Feb 64.

494 UNTS 303. Japan. Ratification 10 Apr 64.
494 UNTS 303. Canada. Ratification 12 Nov 63.
494 UNTS 303. Canada. Amendment 8 Oct 63.
 Force 10 Apr 64.
494 UNTS 303. USSR (Soviet Union). Ratification
 12 Mar 64.

104547   Bilateral Convention   **314 UNTS 161**
SIGNED: 7 Feb 57   FORCE: 15 Mar 58
REGISTERED: 3 Nov 58 Taiwan
ARTICLES: 9 LANGUAGE: Chinese. Spanish. En-
 glish.
HEADNOTE: CULTURAL
TOPIC: Culture
CONCEPTS: Exchange.
PARTIES:
 Taiwan
 Spain

104548   Bilateral Exchange   **314 UNTS 173**
SIGNED: 29 Jan 57   FORCE: 29 Jan 57
REGISTERED: 4 Nov 58 Netherlands
ARTICLES: 4 LANGUAGE: Dutch. German.
HEADNOTE: SETTLEMENT CLAIMS
TOPIC: Status of Forces
CONCEPTS: Time limit. Court procedures. Ex-
 change of information and documents. Compen-
 sation. Indemnities and reimbursements. Claims
 and settlements. Jurisdiction.
PROCEDURE: Duration. Renewal or Revival.
PARTIES:
 Germany, West
 Netherlands

104549   Bilateral Treaty   **314 UNTS 195**
SIGNED: 24 Sep 56   FORCE: 28 Aug 58
REGISTERED: 6 Nov 58 Belgium
ARTICLES: 26 LANGUAGE: French. German.
HEADNOTE: RECTIFICATION BELGIAN-GERMAN
 FRONTIER
TOPIC: Territory Boundary
CONCEPTS: Annex or appendix reference. Repa-
 triation of nationals. Nationality and citizenship.
 Exchange of official publications. Responsibility
 and liability. Currency. Funding procedures. Tax-
 ation. Death duties. Tax exemptions. Reparations
 and restrictions. Markers and definitions. Fron-
 tier crossing points.
INTL ORGS: Special Commission.
TREATY REF: 121LTS327.
PROCEDURE: Ratification.
PARTIES:
 Belgium
 Germany, West

104550   Bilateral Agreement   **314 UNTS 253**
SIGNED: 4 Mar 58   FORCE: 1 Jul 58
REGISTERED: 10 Nov 58 UK Great Britain
ARTICLES: 14 LANGUAGE: English. Malay.
HEADNOTE: REFERENCE APPEALS
TOPIC: Admin Cooperation
CONCEPTS: Definition of terms. Competence of
 tribunal.
PARTIES:
 Fed of Malaya
 UK Great Britain
                        ANNEX
551 UNTS 303. Fed of Malaya. Amendment
 10 Dec 63. Force 20 Dec 63.
551 UNTS 303. UK Great Britain. Amendment
 10 Dec 63. Force 20 Dec 63.

104551   Bilateral Exchange   **314 UNTS 269**
SIGNED: 28 Feb 49   FORCE: 1 Mar 49
REGISTERED: 11 Nov 58 Ceylon (Sri Lanka)
ARTICLES: 2 LANGUAGE: English.
HEADNOTE: TRANSFER RADIO CEYLON
TOPIC: Gen Communications
CONCEPTS: Title and deeds. Use of facilities. In-
 demnities and reimbursements. Assets transfer.
 Commercial and public radio. Facilities and
 equipment. Facilities and property.
PARTIES:
 Ceylon (Sri Lanka)
 UK Great Britain

104552   Bilateral Agreement   **314 UNTS 279**
SIGNED: 6 Sep 52   FORCE: 6 Sep 52

REGISTERED: 11 Nov 58 Ceylon (Sri Lanka)
ARTICLES: 5 LANGUAGE: English.
HEADNOTE: PROMOTE COMMERCE TRADE US-
 ING STERLING PAYMENTS AGREEMENT
TOPIC: General Economic
CONCEPTS: Annex or appendix reference. Gen-
 eral cooperation. Exchange of information and
 documents. Licenses and permits. Export
 quotas. Import quotas. Monetary and gold trans-
 fers. Payment schedules.
TREATY REF: 149UNTS227; 160UNTS411;
 186UNTS342.
PROCEDURE: Duration. Termination.
PARTIES:
 Ceylon (Sri Lanka)
 Japan

104553   Bilateral Exchange   **314 UNTS 297**
SIGNED: 23 Aug 54   FORCE: 23 Aug 54
REGISTERED: 11 Nov 58 Ceylon (Sri Lanka)
ARTICLES: 2 LANGUAGE: English.
HEADNOTE: BROADCAST VOICE OF AMERICA
 PROGRAM
TOPIC: Mass Media
CONCEPTS: Indemnities and reimbursements.
 Customs exemptions. Facilities and equipment.
 Radio-telephone-telegraphic communications.
 Information agency.
PROCEDURE: Duration.
PARTIES:
 Ceylon (Sri Lanka)
 USA (United States)

104554   Bilateral Agreement   **315 UNTS 3**
SIGNED: 17 Nov 54   FORCE: 17 Nov 54
REGISTERED: 11 Nov 58 Ceylon (Sri Lanka)
ARTICLES: 4 LANGUAGE: English.
HEADNOTE: COMMERCIAL RELATIONS
TOPIC: General Trade
CONCEPTS: Exceptions and exemptions. Annex or
 appendix reference. Licenses and permits. Es-
 tablishment of trade relations. Most favored na-
 tion clause. Navigational conditions.
PROCEDURE: Duration. Renewal or Revival. Termi-
 nation.
PARTIES:
 Ceylon (Sri Lanka)
 United Arab Rep

104555   Bilateral Agreement   **315 UNTS 13**
SIGNED: 4 Jun 56   FORCE: 4 Jun 56
REGISTERED: 11 Nov 58 Ceylon (Sri Lanka)
ARTICLES: 7 LANGUAGE: English.
HEADNOTE: TRADE
TOPIC: General Trade
CONCEPTS: Exceptions and exemptions. Annex or
 appendix reference. General cooperation. Li-
 censes and permits. Establishment of trade rela-
 tions. Trade procedures. Most favored nation
 clause. General transportation. Transport of
 goods.
INTL ORGS: Special Commission.
PROCEDURE: Amendment. Duration. Ratification.
 Termination.
PARTIES:
 Ceylon (Sri Lanka)
 Hungary

104556   Bilateral Agreement   **315 UNTS 23**
SIGNED: 19 Jun 56   FORCE: 19 Jun 56
REGISTERED: 11 Nov 58 Ceylon (Sri Lanka)
ARTICLES: 8 LANGUAGE: English.
HEADNOTE: TRADE
TOPIC: General Trade
CONCEPTS: Exceptions and exemptions. Annex or
 appendix reference. General cooperation. Li-
 censes and permits. Establishment of trade rela-
 tions. Trade procedures. Payment schedules.
 Most favored nation clause. Navigational condi-
 tions.
INTL ORGS: Special Commission.
PROCEDURE: Duration. Registration. Renewal or
 Revival. Termination.
PARTIES:
 Bulgaria
 Ceylon (Sri Lanka)

104557   Bilateral Agreement   **315 UNTS 33**
SIGNED: 19 Jun 56   FORCE: 19 Jun 56

REGISTERED: 11 Nov 58 Ceylon (Sri Lanka)
ARTICLES: 9 LANGUAGE: English.
HEADNOTE: PAYMENTS
TOPIC: Finance
CONCEPTS: Detailed regulations. General cooperation. Accounting procedures. Banking. Currency. Financial programs. Interest rates. Payment schedules.
INTL ORGS: Special Commission.
PROCEDURE: Amendment. Ratification. Renewal or Revival. Termination.
PARTIES:
Bulgaria
Ceylon (Sri Lanka)

104558 Bilateral Agreement **315 UNTS 41**
SIGNED: 16 Mar 56 FORCE: 19 Apr 57
REGISTERED: 11 Nov 58 Ceylon (Sri Lanka)
ARTICLES: 9 LANGUAGE: English.
HEADNOTE: TRADE
TOPIC: General Trade
CONCEPTS: Exceptions and exemptions. Annex or appendix reference. General cooperation. Licenses and permits. Establishment of trade relations. Trade agencies. Trade procedures. Payment schedules. Smuggling. Most favored nation clause.
INTL ORGS: Special Commission.
PROCEDURE: Amendment. Duration. Ratification. Renewal or Revival. Termination.
PARTIES:
Ceylon (Sri Lanka)
Romania

104559 Bilateral Agreement **315 UNTS 51**
SIGNED: 16 Mar 56 FORCE: 19 Apr 57
REGISTERED: 11 Nov 58 Ceylon (Sri Lanka)
ARTICLES: 9 LANGUAGE: English.
HEADNOTE: PAYMENTS
TOPIC: Finance
CONCEPTS: Detailed regulations. General cooperation. Negotiation. Accounting procedures. Banking. Balance of payments. Currency. Financial programs. Interest rates. Payment schedules. Credit provisions.
PROCEDURE: Amendment. Ratification. Termination.
PARTIES:
Ceylon (Sri Lanka)
Romania

104560 Bilateral Agreement **315 UNTS 59**
SIGNED: 10 Sep 56 FORCE: 8 Feb 58
REGISTERED: 11 Nov 58 Ceylon (Sri Lanka)
ARTICLES: 10 LANGUAGE: English. Hindi.
HEADNOTE: DOUBLE TAXATION INCOME
TOPIC: Taxation
CONCEPTS: Annex or appendix reference. Conformity with municipal law. Exchange of official publications. Domestic legislation. Taxation. Tax credits.
PROCEDURE: Duration. Termination.
PARTIES:
Ceylon (Sri Lanka)
India

104561 Bilateral Convention **315 UNTS 85**
SIGNED: 18 May 57 FORCE: 21 Feb 58
REGISTERED: 11 Nov 58 Ceylon (Sri Lanka)
ARTICLES: 19 LANGUAGE: English.
HEADNOTE: DOUBLE TAXATION FISCAL EVASION TAXES INCOME
TOPIC: Taxation
CONCEPTS: Definition of terms. Conformity with municipal law. Teacher and student exchange. Claims and settlements. Taxation. Tax credits. Tax exemptions. Air transport. Merchant vessels.
PROCEDURE: Duration. Ratification. Termination.
PARTIES:
Ceylon (Sri Lanka)
Sweden

104562 Bilateral Agreement **315 UNTS 107**
SIGNED: 13 Jan 58 FORCE: 1 Sep 57
REGISTERED: 11 Nov 58 Ceylon (Sri Lanka)
ARTICLES: 5 LANGUAGE: English.
HEADNOTE: TOBACCO
TOPIC: Commodity Trade

CONCEPTS: General cooperation. Tariffs. Commodity trade. Quotas.
PROCEDURE: Duration. Termination.
PARTIES:
Ceylon (Sri Lanka)
India

104563 Bilateral Exchange **315 UNTS 117**
SIGNED: 30 Jan 58 FORCE: 4 Sep 58
REGISTERED: 15 Nov 58 Netherlands
ARTICLES: 2 LANGUAGE: Dutch. German.
HEADNOTE: SAVING LIVES (RESCUE) NORTH SEA
TOPIC: Humanitarian
CONCEPTS: General cooperation. Exchange of information and documents. Domestic legislation. Humanitarian matters. Amateur radio.
PROCEDURE: Denunciation. Ratification.
PARTIES:
Germany, West
Netherlands

104564 Bilateral Exchange **315 UNTS 125**
SIGNED: 18 Nov 58 FORCE: 27 Sep 58
REGISTERED: 18 Nov 58 United Nations
ARTICLES: 3 LANGUAGE: English. Arabic.
HEADNOTE: STATIONING UN SUBSIDIARY ORGAN
TOPIC: IGO Operations
CONCEPTS: Non-visa travel documents. Diplomatic missions. Privileges and immunities. Diplomatic correspondence. Special status.
TREATY REF: 1UNTS15; 284UNTS361.
PARTIES:
Jordan
United Nations

104565 Multilateral Agreement **315 UNTS 139**
SIGNED: 13 Dec 57 FORCE: 1 Jan 58
REGISTERED: 18 Nov 58 Council of Europe
ARTICLES: 13 LANGUAGE: English. French.
HEADNOTE: MOVEMENT PEOPLE
TOPIC: Visas
CONCEPTS: Annex or appendix reference. Frontier formalities. Visa abolition. Border traffic and migration. Non-visa travel documents. Visas.
INTL ORGS: Council of Europe.
PROCEDURE: Accession. Ratification.
PARTIES:
Austria SIGNED: 13 Dec 57 RATIFIED: 30 May 58 FORCE: 1 Jun 58
Belgium SIGNED: 13 Dec 57 FORCE: 1 Jan 58
France SIGNED: 13 Dec 57 FORCE: 1 Jan 58
Germany, West Berlin RATIFIED: 11 Oct 58
Germany, West SIGNED: 13 Dec 57 RATIFIED: 30 May 58 FORCE: 1 Jun 58
Greece SIGNED: 13 Dec 57
Italy SIGNED: 13 Dec 57 FORCE: 1 Jan 58
Luxembourg SIGNED: 13 Dec 57

104566 Bilateral Exchange **315 UNTS 155**
SIGNED: 6 Jun 55 FORCE: 6 Jun 55
REGISTERED: 20 Nov 58 USA (United States)
ARTICLES: 2 LANGUAGE: English. German.
HEADNOTE: RESPONSIBILITY DIRECTION ADMINISTRATION INTERNATIONAL TRACING SERVICE
TOPIC: Humanitarian
CONCEPTS: Humanitarian matters. Indemnities and reimbursements.
TREATY REF: 219UNTS79.
PARTIES:
Germany, West
USA (United States)

104567 Bilateral Convention **315 UNTS 165**
SIGNED: 10 Apr 58 FORCE: 10 Oct 58
REGISTERED: 21 Nov 58 Taiwan
ARTICLES: 9 LANGUAGE: Chinese. Spanish. English.
HEADNOTE: CULTURAL CONVENTION
TOPIC: Culture
CONCEPTS: Friendship and amity. General cooperation. Specialists exchange. Exchange. Teacher and student exchange. Exchange. General cultural cooperation. Athletes. Scientific exchange. Mass media exchange.
TREATY REF: 4UNTS275.
PROCEDURE: Duration. Ratification. Renewal or Revival. Termination.

PARTIES:
Taiwan
Costa Rica

104568 Bilateral Agreement **315 UNTS 179**
SIGNED: 30 Jun 58 FORCE: 30 Jun 58
REGISTERED: 25 Nov 58 Netherlands
ARTICLES: 10 LANGUAGE: Dutch. German.
HEADNOTE: STUDENT EMPLOYEES
TOPIC: Non-ILO Labor
CONCEPTS: Definition of terms. Territorial application. Previous treaty replacement. Resident permits. Education. Exchange. Non-ILO labor relations. Administrative cooperation. Migrant worker. Quotas.
PROCEDURE: Denunciation. Duration. Ratification. Renewal or Revival.
PARTIES:
Germany, West
Netherlands

104569 Bilateral Agreement **315 UNTS 197**
SIGNED: 27 May 58 FORCE: 27 May 58
REGISTERED: 25 Nov 58 USA (United States)
ARTICLES: 6 LANGUAGE: English.
HEADNOTE: AGRI COMMOD TITLE I
TOPIC: US Agri Commod Aid
CONCEPTS: General provisions. Annex or appendix reference. Exchange of information and documents. Reexport of goods, etc.. Currency. Exchange rates and regulations. Transportation costs. Local currency. Commodities schedule. Purchase authorization. Surplus commodities. Mutual consultation.
PARTIES:
Burma
USA (United States)
ANNEX
344 UNTS 354. Burma. Amendment 11 Mar 59. Force 11 Mar 59.
344 UNTS 354. USA (United States). Amendment 11 Mar 59. Force 11 Mar 59.
394 UNTS 290. USA (United States). Amendment 10 Oct 60. Force 10 Oct 60.
394 UNTS 290. Burma. Amendment 10 Oct 60. Force 10 Oct 60.
409 UNTS 322. USA (United States). Amendment 1 Jun 61. Force 1 Jun 61.
409 UNTS 322. Burma. Amendment 1 Jun 61. Force 1 Jun 61.

104570 Bilateral Exchange **315 UNTS 211**
SIGNED: 28 Apr 58 FORCE: 28 Apr 58
REGISTERED: 25 Nov 58 USA (United States)
ARTICLES: 2 LANGUAGE: English. Spanish.
HEADNOTE: UN-ARMED HIGH ALTITUDE SAMPLING UNIT
TOPIC: Status of Forces
CONCEPTS: Meteorology. Tax exemptions. Customs exemptions. Materials, equipment and services. Jurisdiction. Status of forces.
PROCEDURE: Future Procedures Contemplated.
PARTIES:
Argentina
USA (United States)

104571 Bilateral Exchange **315 UNTS 221**
SIGNED: 1 May 58 FORCE: 1 May 58
REGISTERED: 25 Nov 58 USA (United States)
ARTICLES: 2 LANGUAGE: English. Arabic.
HEADNOTE: ECONOMIC ASSISTANCE EXPANSION PORT DAMMAN
TOPIC: Direct Aid
CONCEPTS: Conformity with municipal law. Exchange of information and documents. Personnel. Exchange rates and regulations. Funding procedures. Tax exemptions. Customs exemptions. Domestic obligation. Economic assistance. Materials, equipment and services.
TREATY REF: 283UNTS97.
PROCEDURE: Termination.
PARTIES:
Saudi Arabia
USA (United States)

104572 Bilateral Exchange **315 UNTS 231**
SIGNED: 30 May 58 FORCE: 30 May 58
REGISTERED: 25 Nov 58 USA (United States)
ARTICLES: 2 LANGUAGE: English. Polish.

HEADNOTE: DISTRIBUTIONS PUBLICATIONS
TOPIC: Mass Media
CONCEPTS: Publications exchange.
PARTIES:
Poland
USA (United States)

104573 Bilateral Agreement **316 UNTS 3**
SIGNED: 3 Jun 58　　　　FORCE: 3 Jun 58
REGISTERED: 25 Nov 58 USA (United States)
ARTICLES: 6 LANGUAGE: English.
HEADNOTE: AGRI COMMOD TITLE I
TOPIC: US Agri Commod Aid
CONCEPTS: General provisions. Annex or appen-
dix reference. Exchange of information and doc-
uments. Reexport of goods, etc.. Exchange rates
and regulations. Transportation costs. Local cur-
rency. Commodities schedule. Purchase authori-
zation. Mutual consultation.
INTL ORGS: International Monetary Fund.
PARTIES:
Philippines
USA (United States)

104574 Bilateral Agreement **316 UNTS 15**
SIGNED: 18 Jun 58　　　　FORCE: 18 Jun 58
REGISTERED: 25 Nov 58 USA (United States)
ARTICLES: 6 LANGUAGE: English.
HEADNOTE: AGRI COMMOD TITLE I
TOPIC: US Agri Commod Aid
CONCEPTS: Exchange of information and documents. Reexport of goods, etc.. Exchange rates
and regulations. Transportation costs. Local currency. Commodities schedule. Purchase authorization. Surplus commodities. Mutual consultation.
PARTIES:
Ceylon (Sri Lanka)
USA (United States)
　　　　ANNEX
321 UNTS 302. USA (United States). Amendment
30 Jun 58. Force 30 Jun 58.
321 UNTS 302. Ceylon (Sri Lanka). Amendment
30 Jun 58. Force 30 Jun 58.
418 UNTS 394. USA (United States). Amendment
24 Aug 61. Force 24 Aug 61.
418 UNTS 394. Ceylon (Sri Lanka). Amendment
24 Aug 61. Force 24 Aug 61.

104575 Bilateral Exchange **316 UNTS 29**
SIGNED: 9 May 58　　　　FORCE: 9 May 58
REGISTERED: 25 Nov 58 USA (United States)
ARTICLES: 2 LANGUAGE: English.
HEADNOTE: FREE ENTRY PRIVILEGES FOREIGN
SERVICE
TOPIC: Visas
CONCEPTS: Diplomatic privileges.
TREATY REF: 134LTS207.
PARTIES:
El Salvador
USA (United States)

104576 Bilateral Exchange **316 UNTS 37**
SIGNED: 9 Apr 58　　　　FORCE: 9 Apr 58
REGISTERED: 25 Nov 58 USA (United States)
ARTICLES: 6 LANGUAGE: English. Spanish.
HEADNOTE: AGRI COMMOD
TOPIC: US Agri Commod Aid
CONCEPTS: Exchange of information and docu-
ments. Reexport of goods, etc.. Currency. Ex-
change rates and regulations. Payment sched-
ules. Transportation costs. Local currency. Com-
modities schedule. Purchase authorization.
Surplus commodities. Mutual consultation.
PARTIES:
Peru
USA (United States)
　　　　ANNEX
336 UNTS 421. Peru. Amendment 12 Sep 58.
Force 12 Sep 58.
336 UNTS 421. USA (United States). Amendment
10 Sep 58. Force 12 Sep 58.
358 UNTS 357. Peru. Amendment 25 Sep 59.
Force 25 Sep 59.
358 UNTS 357. USA (United States). Amendment
11 Sep 59. Force 25 Sep 59.

104577 Unilateral Instrument **316 UNTS 59**
SIGNED: 26 Nov 58　　　　FORCE: 26 Nov 58
REGISTERED: 26 Nov 58 United Nations
ARTICLES: 1 LANGUAGE: English.
HEADNOTE: ACCEPTANCE ICJ JURISDICTION
TOPIC: ICJ Option Clause

CONCEPTS: Exceptions and exemptions. Compul-
sory jurisdiction.
INTL ORGS: International Court of Justice.
PROCEDURE: Amendment. Termination.
PARTIES:
UK Great Britain
　　　　ANNEX
482 UNTS 382. UK Great Britain. Termination
27 Nov 63.

104578 Bilateral Exchange **316 UNTS 65**
SIGNED: 15 Mar 52　　　　FORCE: 15 Mar 52
REGISTERED: 26 Nov 58 Pakistan
ARTICLES: 9 LANGUAGE: English. French.
HEADNOTE: TRADE
TOPIC: General Trade
CONCEPTS: Exceptions and exemptions. Territo-
rial application. Annex or appendix reference.
General cooperation. Establishment of commis-
sion. Negotiation. Payment schedules. Most fa-
vored nation clause.
INTL ORGS: Special Commission.
TREATY REF: 55UNTS187.
PROCEDURE: Denunciation. Duration. Ratification.
PARTIES:
Belgium
Pakistan

104579 Bilateral Agreement **316 UNTS 83**
SIGNED: 24 Dec 56　　　　FORCE: 24 Dec 56
REGISTERED: 26 Nov 58 Pakistan
ARTICLES: 6 LANGUAGE: English.
HEADNOTE: TRADE
TOPIC: General Trade
CONCEPTS: Annex or appendix reference. Gen-
eral cooperation. Licenses and permits. Trade
procedures. Currency. Monetary and gold trans-
fers. Payment schedules.
PROCEDURE: Amendment. Duration. Renewal or
Revival. Termination.
PARTIES:
Austria
Pakistan

104580 Bilateral Convention **316 UNTS 97**
SIGNED: 24 Feb 56　　　　FORCE: 9 May 58
REGISTERED: 28 Nov 58 Israel
ARTICLES: 35 LANGUAGE: Hebrew. Italian.
French.
HEADNOTE: EXTRADITION JUDICIAL ASSIS-
TANCE CRIMINAL MATTERS
TOPIC: Extradition
CONCEPTS: Territorial application. Time limit. Ex-
tradition, deportation and repatriation. Extradi-
tion requests. Extraditable offenses. Location of
crime. Special factors. Refusal of extradition.
Concurrent requests. Provisional detainment. Ex-
tradition postponement. Witnesses and experts.
Material evidence. Indemnities and reimburse-
ments. Conveyance in transit.
PROCEDURE: Ratification.
PARTIES:
Israel
Italy

104581 Bilateral Agreement **316 UNTS 137**
SIGNED: 3 May 58　　　　FORCE: 3 May 58
REGISTERED: 1 Dec 58 USA (United States)
ARTICLES: 6 LANGUAGE: English.
HEADNOTE: AGRI COMMOD TITLE I
TOPIC: US Agri Commod Aid
CONCEPTS: General provisions. Annex or appen-
dix reference. Exchange of information and doc-
uments. Reexport of goods, etc.. Currency. Ex-
change rates and regulations. Transportation
costs. Local currency. Commodities schedule.
Purchase authorization. Surplus commodities.
Mutual consultation.
PARTIES:
Iceland
USA (United States)
　　　　ANNEX
317 UNTS 382. Iceland. Supplementation
26 Jun 58. Force 26 Jun 58.
317 UNTS 382. USA (United States). Supplementation 25 Jun 58. Force 26 Jun 58.
433 UNTS 366. USA (United States). Amendment
3 Oct 61. Force 3 Oct 61.
433 UNTS 366. Iceland. Amendment 3 Oct 61.
Force 3 Oct 61.

460 UNTS 320. USA (United States). Amendment
20 Aug 62. Force 20 Aug 62.
460 UNTS 320. Iceland. Amendment 20 Aug 62.
Force 20 Aug 62.

104582 Bilateral Exchange **316 UNTS 151**
SIGNED: 12 May 58　　　　FORCE: 12 May 58
REGISTERED: 1 Dec 58 USA (United States)
ARTICLES: 2 LANGUAGE: English.
HEADNOTE: NORTH AMERICAN AIR DEFENSE
COMMAND
TOPIC: General Military
CONCEPTS: Definition of terms. Detailed regula-
tions. General cooperation. Establishment of
commission. Indemnities and reimbursements.
Joint defense. Defense and security. Security of
information. Status of forces. Exchange of de-
fense information.
TREATY REF: 34UNTS243; 199UNTS67.
PROCEDURE: Amendment. Duration. Future Proce-
dures Contemplated.
PARTIES:
Canada
USA (United States)

104583 Bilateral Exchange **316 UNTS 163**
SIGNED: 15 May 58　　　　FORCE: 15 May 58
REGISTERED: 1 Dec 58 USA (United States)
ARTICLES: 2 LANGUAGE: English.
HEADNOTE: ESTABLISHMENT MUTUAL DEFENSE
BOARD
TOPIC: Milit Assistance
CONCEPTS: Annex or appendix reference. Gen-
eral cooperation. Establishment of commission.
Joint defense.
INTL ORGS: Special Commission.
TREATY REF: 177UNTS133.
PARTIES:
Philippines
USA (United States)

104584 Bilateral Exchange **316 UNTS 177**
SIGNED: 8 May 58　　　　FORCE: 8 May 58
REGISTERED: 1 Dec 58 USA (United States)
ARTICLES: 2 LANGUAGE: English. Italian.
HEADNOTE: CHILD FEEDING PROGRAM
TOPIC: Direct Aid
CONCEPTS: Annex or appendix reference. Annex
type material. Conformity with municipal law.
Public information. Indemnities and reimburse-
ments. Domestic obligation. Assistance. General
aid. Commodities schedule. Surplus commodi-
ties.
TREATY REF: 258UNTS15.
PARTIES:
Italy
USA (United States)

104585 Bilateral Exchange **316 UNTS 201**
SIGNED: 1 Jul 57　　　　FORCE: 1 Aug 57
REGISTERED: 5 Dec 58 Canada
ARTICLES: 2 LANGUAGE: English.
HEADNOTE: VISAS
TOPIC: Visas
CONCEPTS: Passports diplomatic. Visas.
PARTIES:
Canada
Greece

104586 Bilateral Exchange **316 UNTS 207**
SIGNED: 17 Apr 57　　　　FORCE: 17 Apr 57
REGISTERED: 5 Dec 58 Canada
ARTICLES: 2 LANGUAGE: English.
HEADNOTE: CONTINUATION CANADA NATO AIR
TRAINING
TOPIC: Milit Assistance
CONCEPTS: Indemnities and reimbursements.
Payment schedules. Defense and security. Mili-
tary training.
INTL ORGS: North Atlantic Treaty Organization.
PARTIES:
Canada
Denmark
　　　　ANNEX
470 UNTS 406. Denmark. Prolongation
25 Mar 60. Force 25 Mar 60.
470 UNTS 406. Canada. Prolongation 25 Mar 60.
Force 25 Mar 60.

104587 Bilateral Exchange **316 UNTS 215**
SIGNED: 17 Apr 57 FORCE: 17 Apr 57
REGISTERED: 5 Dec 58 Canada
ARTICLES: 2 LANGUAGE: English.
HEADNOTE: CONTINUATION CANADA NATO AIR TRAINING
TOPIC: Milit Assistance
CONCEPTS: Indemnities and reimbursements. Payment schedules. Defense and security. Military training.
INTL ORGS: North Atlantic Treaty Organization.
PARTIES:
Canada
Norway
ANNEX
470 UNTS 410. Canada. Prolongation 1 Apr 60. Force 6 Apr 60.
470 UNTS 410. Norway. Prolongation 6 Apr 60. Force 6 Apr 60.
528 UNTS 306. Norway. Amendment 20 Jul 62. Force 30 Jul 62.
528 UNTS 306. Canada. Amendment 20 Jul 62. Force 20 Jul 62.

104588 Bilateral Exchange **316 UNTS 223**
SIGNED: 13 Apr 57 FORCE: 13 Apr 57
REGISTERED: 5 Dec 58 Canada
ARTICLES: 2 LANGUAGE: English.
HEADNOTE: CONTINUATION CANADA NATO AIR TRAINING
TOPIC: Milit Assistance
CONCEPTS: Indemnities and reimbursements. Payment schedules. Defense and security. Military training.
INTL ORGS: North Atlantic Treaty Organization.
PARTIES:
Canada
Netherlands

104589 Bilateral Convention **316 UNTS 231**
SIGNED: 4 Jun 56 FORCE: 5 Aug 57
REGISTERED: 5 Dec 58 Canada
ARTICLES: 23 LANGUAGE: English. German.
HEADNOTE: DOUBLE TAXATION FISCAL EVASION TAXES INCOME
TOPIC: Taxation
CONCEPTS: Definition of terms. Privileges and immunities. Conformity with municipal law. Exchange of official publications. Negotiation. Teacher and student exchange. Taxation. General. Tax exemptions.
PROCEDURE: Ratification. Termination.
PARTIES:
Canada
Germany, West

104590 Bilateral Agreement **317 UNTS 3**
SIGNED: 23 Jul 58 FORCE: 26 Sep 58
REGISTERED: 6 Dec 58 IBRD (World Bank)
ARTICLES: 8 LANGUAGE: English.
HEADNOTE: LOAN AGREEMENT
TOPIC: IBRD Project
CONCEPTS: Definition of terms. Annex or appendix reference. Exchange of information and documents. Inspection and observation. Bonds. Fees and exemptions. Tax exemptions. Domestic obligation. Terms of loan. Loan regulations. Loan guarantee. Guarantor non-interference.
PARTIES:
India
IBRD (World Bank)

104591 Bilateral Exchange **317 UNTS 31**
SIGNED: 16 Jun 58 FORCE: 16 Jun 58
REGISTERED: 9 Dec 58 USA (United States)
ARTICLES: 2 LANGUAGE: English.
HEADNOTE: RECOGNITION TONNAGE MEASUREMENT CERTIFICATE
TOPIC: Admin Cooperation
CONCEPTS: Recognition of legal documents. Regulations.
PARTIES:
USA (United States)
Yugoslavia

104592 Bilateral Exchange **317 UNTS 37**
SIGNED: 20 Jun 58 FORCE: 20 Jun 58
REGISTERED: 9 Dec 58 USA (United States)
ARTICLES: 1 LANGUAGE: English.

HEADNOTE: AERIAL REFUELING FACILITIES DEFENSE
TOPIC: Milit Assistance
CONCEPTS: Annex or appendix reference. Use of facilities. Defense and security.
INTL ORGS: United States-Canadian Defense Organization.
PARTIES:
Canada
USA (United States)

104593 Bilateral Exchange **317 UNTS 51**
SIGNED: 27 Jun 58 FORCE: 27 Jun 58
REGISTERED: 9 Dec 58 USA (United States)
ARTICLES: 2 LANGUAGE: English.
HEADNOTE: FINANCING DOLLAR COSTS CONSTRUCTING EQUIPPING FACILITIES CONFERENCE
TOPIC: Direct Aid
CONCEPTS: Conformity with municipal law. Indemnities and reimbursements. Financial programs. Interest rates. Payment schedules. Special projects. General aid. Credit provisions.
PARTIES:
Ecuador
USA (United States)
ANNEX
354 UNTS 428. Ecuador. Amendment 17 Jul 59. Force 17 Jul 59.
354 UNTS 428. USA (United States). Amendment 17 Jul 59. Force 17 Jul 59.

104594 Bilateral Exchange **317 UNTS 59**
SIGNED: 5 May 58 FORCE: 5 May 58
REGISTERED: 9 Dec 58 USA (United States)
ARTICLES: 3 LANGUAGE: English.
HEADNOTE: PASSPORT VISA FEES
TOPIC: Visas
CONCEPTS: Time limit. Visas. Fees and exemptions.
INTL ORGS: United Nations.
PARTIES:
New Zealand
USA (United States)

104595 Unilateral Instrument **317 UNTS 77**
SIGNED: 3 Dec 58 FORCE: 3 Dec 58
REGISTERED: 12 Dec 58 United Nations
ARTICLES: 1 LANGUAGE: French.
HEADNOTE: ACCEPTANCE OBLIGATIONS UN
TOPIC: UN Charter
CONCEPTS: Acceptance of obligations upon admittance to UN.
INTL ORGS: United Nations.
PARTIES:
Guinea

104596 Bilateral Agreement **317 UNTS 81**
SIGNED: 14 May 57 FORCE: 14 May 57
REGISTERED: 15 Dec 58 Belgium
ARTICLES: 12 LANGUAGE: French. Bulgarian.
HEADNOTE: AIR TRANSPORT
TOPIC: Air Transport
CONCEPTS: Territorial application. Annex or appendix reference. Conformity with municipal law. General cooperation. Informational records. Licenses and permits. Personnel. Recognition of legal documents. Procedure. Negotiation. Reexport of goods, etc.. Non-interest rates and fees. Most favored nation clause. National treatment. Customs exemptions. Registration certificate. Routes and logistics. Navigational conditions. Permit designation. Airworthiness certificates. Conditions of airlines operating permission. Operating authorizations and regulations.
PROCEDURE: Amendment. Denunciation.
PARTIES:
Belgium
Bulgaria

104597 Bilateral Agreement **317 UNTS 101**
SIGNED: 18 Jun 58 FORCE: 15 Dec 58
REGISTERED: 15 Dec 58 United Nations
ARTICLES: 10 LANGUAGE: English.
HEADNOTE: HEADQUARTERS
TOPIC: IGO Operations
CONCEPTS: Definition of terms. Treaty interpretation. Non-visa travel documents. Diplomatic privileges. Diplomatic missions. Privileges and im-

munities. Diplomatic correspondence. Procedure. Special status. Status of experts. Special tribunals.
INTL ORGS: International Court of Justice. International Telecommunication Union.
TREATY REF: 1UNTS263.
PARTIES:
Ethiopia
United Nations

104598 Bilateral Exchange **317 UNTS 117**
SIGNED: 14 May 58 FORCE: 1 Jun 58
REGISTERED: 16 Dec 58 New Zealand
ARTICLES: 2 LANGUAGE: English. German.
HEADNOTE: VISAS
TOPIC: Visas
CONCEPTS: Territorial application. Time limit. Visa abolition. Denial of admission. Resident permits. Conformity with municipal law.
PROCEDURE: Termination.
PARTIES:
Austria
New Zealand

104599 Bilateral Exchange **317 UNTS 123**
SIGNED: 5 Jun 58 FORCE: 5 Jul 58
REGISTERED: 16 Dec 58 New Zealand
ARTICLES: 2 LANGUAGE: English.
HEADNOTE: VISAS
TOPIC: Visas
CONCEPTS: Territorial application. Time limit. Visa abolition. Denial of admission. Visas. Conformity with municipal law. Fees and exemptions.
PROCEDURE: Termination.
PARTIES:
New Zealand
Turkey

104600 Bilateral Agreement **317 UNTS 129**
SIGNED: 22 Jan 57 FORCE: 19 Feb 57
REGISTERED: 18 Dec 58 IBRD (World Bank)
ARTICLES: 9 LANGUAGE: English.
HEADNOTE: LOAN AGREEMENT
TOPIC: IBRD Project
CONCEPTS: Default remedies. Definition of terms. Annex or appendix reference. Exchange of information and documents. Informational records. Inspection and observation. Accounting procedures. Bonds. Fees and exemptions. Interest rates. Tax exemptions. Domestic obligation. Terms of loan. Loan regulations. Loan guarantee. Guarantor non-interference.
PARTIES:
Iran
IBRD (World Bank)

104601 Bilateral Exchange **317 UNTS 153**
SIGNED: 25 Feb 58 FORCE: 25 Feb 58
REGISTERED: 18 Dec 58 Australia
ARTICLES: 2 LANGUAGE: English.
HEADNOTE: ESTABLISHMENT WEATHER STATION
TOPIC: Tech Assistance
CONCEPTS: Conformity with municipal law. Investigation of violations. Research cooperation. Meteorology. Compensation. Special projects. Status of forces.
INTL ORGS: Nauru Administrative Authority.
PARTIES:
Australia
USA (United States)

104602 Bilateral Agreement **317 UNTS 161**
SIGNED: 4 Dec 56 FORCE: 4 Dec 56
REGISTERED: 18 Dec 58 Belgium
ARTICLES: 15 LANGUAGE: French. Romanian.
HEADNOTE: AIR TRANSPORT
TOPIC: Air Transport
CONCEPTS: Definition of terms. Annex or appendix reference. Conformity with municipal law. General cooperation. Licenses and permits. Personnel. Recognition of legal documents. Use of facilities. Fees and exemptions. Non-interest rates and fees. Customs exemptions. Registration certificate. Routes and logistics. Navigational conditions. Permit designation. Air transport. Airport facilities. Conditions of airlines operating permission. Operating authorizations and regulations.

PROCEDURE: Amendment. Denunciation. Future
Procedures Contemplated.
PARTIES:
Belgium
Romania

104603 Bilateral Agreement **317 UNTS 181**
SIGNED: 23 Jun 58   FORCE: 23 Jun 58
REGISTERED: 18 Dec 58 USA (United States)
ARTICLES: 6 LANGUAGE: English.
HEADNOTE: AGRI COMMOD
TOPIC: US Agri Commod Aid
CONCEPTS: Agricultural commodities.
PARTIES:
India
USA (United States)
ANNEX
358 UNTS 363. India. Amendment 28 Oct 59.
Force 28 Oct 59.
358 UNTS 363. USA (United States). Amendment
1 Oct 59. Force 28 Oct 59.

104604 Bilateral Agreement **317 UNTS 195**
SIGNED: 16 Mar 56   FORCE: 9 Jul 58
REGISTERED: 18 Dec 58 USA (United States)
ARTICLES: 11 LANGUAGE: English.
HEADNOTE: COOPERATION CIVIL USES ATOMIC
ENERGY
TOPIC: Atomic Energy
CONCEPTS: Definition of terms. Non-prejudice to
third party. Exchange of information and docu-
ments. Inspection and observation. Responsibil-
ity and liability. Research cooperation. Assets
transfer. Nuclear materials. Non-nuclear materi-
als. Peaceful use. Security of information.
PROCEDURE: Duration.
PARTIES:
Ireland
USA (United States)
ANNEX
406 UNTS 328. USA (United States). Amendment
13 Feb 61. Force 30 Mar 61.
406 UNTS 328. Ireland. Amendment 13 Feb 61.
Force 30 Mar 61.
505 UNTS 321. USA (United States). Amendment
7 Aug 63. Force 10 Jan 64.
505 UNTS 321. Ireland. Amendment 7 Aug 63.
Force 10 Jan 64.

104605 Bilateral Exchange **317 UNTS 209**
SIGNED: 22 Apr 58   FORCE: 22 Apr 58
REGISTERED: 18 Dec 58 USA (United States)
ARTICLES: 2 LANGUAGE: English. Spanish.
HEADNOTE: RELATING EQUIPMENT MATERIALS
SERVICES DEFENSE PURPOSES
TOPIC: Milit Assistance
CONCEPTS: Treaty implementation. Conformity
with municipal law. Title and deeds. Financial
programs. Domestic obligation. Materials, equip-
ment and services. Military assistance. Self-
defense. Return of equipment and recapture.
PARTIES:
Bolivia
USA (United States)

104606 Bilateral Treaty **317 UNTS 217**
SIGNED: 12 Dec 57   FORCE: 28 Apr 58
REGISTERED: 29 Dec 58 USSR (Soviet Union)
ARTICLES: 75 LANGUAGE: Russian. Bulgarian.
HEADNOTE: LEGAL ASSISTANCE CIVIL FAMILY
CRIMINAL CASES
TOPIC: Admin Cooperation
CONCEPTS: General provisions. Privileges and immunities. Consular functions in property. Extradition, deportation and repatriation. Refusal of extradition. Limits of prosecution. Provisional detainment. Extradition postponement. Witnesses
and experts. Material evidence. Conformity with
municipal law. Family law. Exchange of information and documents. Juridical personality. Legal
protection and assistance. Recognition and enforcement of legal decisions. Immovable property. General property. Jurisdiction. Recognition
of legal documents. Indemnities and reimbursements. Conveyance in transit.
PROCEDURE: Ratification. Termination.
PARTIES:
Bulgaria
USSR (Soviet Union)

104607 Bilateral Convention **318 UNTS 3**
SIGNED: 24 Aug 57   FORCE: 15 Jan 58
REGISTERED: 29 Dec 58 USSR (Soviet Union)

ARTICLES: 25 LANGUAGE: Russian. Hungarian.
HEADNOTE: CONSULAR CONVENTION
TOPIC: Consul/Citizenship
CONCEPTS: Definition of terms. General consular
functions. Consular relations establishment. Invi-
olability. Privileges and immunities. Diplomatic
correspondence. Responsibility and liability.
PROCEDURE: Denunciation. Ratification.
PARTIES:
Hungary
USSR (Soviet Union)

104608 Bilateral Convention **318 UNTS 35**
SIGNED: 24 Aug 57   FORCE: 15 Jan 58
REGISTERED: 29 Dec 58 USSR (Soviet Union)
ARTICLES: 9 LANGUAGE: Russian. Hungarian.
HEADNOTE: DUAL CITIZENSHIP
TOPIC: Consul/Citizenship
CONCEPTS: Resident permits. Alien status. Dual
citizenship. Tax exemptions.
PROCEDURE: Ratification.
PARTIES:
Hungary
USSR (Soviet Union)

104609 Bilateral Convention **318 UNTS 55**
SIGNED: 4 Sep 57   FORCE: 3 Mar 58
REGISTERED: 29 Dec 58 USSR (Soviet Union)
ARTICLES: 27 LANGUAGE: Russian. Romanian.
HEADNOTE: CONSULAR CONVENTION
TOPIC: Consul/Citizenship
CONCEPTS: Definition of terms. General consular
functions. Diplomatic privileges. Consular rela-
tions establishment. Inviolability. Privileges and
immunities. Diplomatic correspondence.
PROCEDURE: Ratification. Termination.
PARTIES:
Romania
USSR (Soviet Union)

104610 Bilateral Convention **318 UNTS 89**
SIGNED: 4 Sep 57   FORCE: 3 Mar 58
REGISTERED: 29 Dec 58 USSR (Soviet Union)
ARTICLES: 9 LANGUAGE: Russian. Romanian.
HEADNOTE: DUAL CITIZENSHIP
TOPIC: Consul/Citizenship
CONCEPTS: Resident permits. Alien status. Dual
citizenship. Public information. Tax exemptions.
PROCEDURE: Ratification.
PARTIES:
Romania
USSR (Soviet Union)

104611 Bilateral Agreement **318 UNTS 103**
SIGNED: 11 Jul 58   FORCE: 24 Sep 58
REGISTERED: 30 Dec 58 IBRD (World Bank)
ARTICLES: 9 LANGUAGE: English.
HEADNOTE: PROJECT LOAN
TOPIC: IBRD Project
CONCEPTS: Credit provisions.
PARTIES:
Japan
IBRD (World Bank)

104612 Bilateral Agreement **318 UNTS 133**
SIGNED: 10 Sep 58   FORCE: 14 Nov 58
REGISTERED: 30 Dec 58 IBRD (World Bank)
ARTICLES: 5 LANGUAGE: English.
HEADNOTE: GUARANTEE AGREEMENT
TOPIC: IBRD Project
CONCEPTS: Definition of terms. Annex or appen-
dix reference. Exchange of information and doc-
uments. Inspection and observation. Bonds.
Fees and exemptions. Tax exemptions. Domestic
obligation. Terms of loan. Loan regulations. Loan
guarantee. Guarantor non-interference. Industry.
PARTIES:
Japan
IBRD (World Bank)

104613 Bilateral Agreement **318 UNTS 163**
SIGNED: 21 May 51   FORCE: 22 May 51
REGISTERED: 30 Dec 58 Pakistan
ARTICLES: 8 LANGUAGE: English.
HEADNOTE: TRADE
TOPIC: General Trade
CONCEPTS: Establishment of trade relations. Reci-

procity in trade. National treatment. General
technical assistance.
INTL ORGS: Organization for Economic Co-opera-
tion and Development.
TREATY REF: 55UNTS187.
PROCEDURE: Termination.
PARTIES:
Norway
Pakistan

104614 Bilateral Convention **318 UNTS 175**
SIGNED: 28 Mar 58   FORCE: 1 Dec 58
REGISTERED: 30 Dec 58 Netherlands
ARTICLES: 26 LANGUAGE: French.
HEADNOTE: SOCIAL INSURANCE
TOPIC: Non-ILO Labor
CONCEPTS: Detailed regulations. Exceptions and
exemptions. General provisions. Annex or ap-
pendix reference. Previous treaty replacement.
Domestic legislation. Old age and invalidity in-
surance. Wages and salaries. Non-ILO labor rela-
tions. Administrative cooperation. Old age insur-
ance. Sickness and invalidity insurance. Social
security. Monetary and gold transfers. National
treatment.
INTL ORGS: International Court of Justice. Arbitration Commission.
TREATY REF: 196LTS433.
PROCEDURE: Denunciation. Duration. Ratification.
Renewal or Revival.
PARTIES:
Netherlands
Switzerland
ANNEX
450 UNTS 444. Netherlands. Supplementation
14 Oct 60. Force 14 Oct 60.
450 UNTS 444. Switzerland. Supplementation
14 Oct 60. Force 14 Oct 60.

104615 Bilateral Exchange **318 UNTS 221**
SIGNED: 8 Jan 57   FORCE: 8 Jan 57
REGISTERED: 30 Dec 58 Japan
ARTICLES: 2 LANGUAGE: English. Spanish.
HEADNOTE: PROBLEMS CONCERNING CERTAIN
TYPES CLAIMS
TOPIC: Claims and Debts
CONCEPTS: Payment schedules. Claims and set-
tlements. Lump sum settlements. Post-war
claims settlement.
PARTIES:
Japan
Spain

104616 Bilateral Exchange **318 UNTS 227**
SIGNED: 18 Dec 56   FORCE: 1 Feb 57
REGISTERED: 30 Dec 58 Japan
ARTICLES: 2 LANGUAGE: French.
HEADNOTE: MUTUAL ABOLITION PASSPORT
VISAS FEES
TOPIC: Visas
CONCEPTS: Time limit. Visa abolition. Denial of
admission. Resident permits. Conformity with
municipal law.
PROCEDURE: Denunciation.
PARTIES:
Japan
Luxembourg

104617 Bilateral Protocol **318 UNTS 233**
SIGNED: 27 Mar 57   FORCE: 27 Mar 57
REGISTERED: 30 Dec 58 Japan
ARTICLES: 1 LANGUAGE: French. Japanese.
HEADNOTE: SETTLEMENT ACCOUNTS
TOPIC: Specif Claim/Waive
CONCEPTS: Accounting procedures. Lump sum
settlements. Specific claims or waivers.
PARTIES:
France
Japan

104618 Bilateral Exchange **318 UNTS 239**
SIGNED: 25 Mar 57   FORCE: 15 Apr 57
REGISTERED: 30 Dec 58 Japan
ARTICLES: 2 LANGUAGE: French.
HEADNOTE: MUTUAL ABOLITION PASSPORT
VISAS
TOPIC: Visas
CONCEPTS: Emergencies. Time limit. Visa aboli-

tion. Denial of admission. Resident permits. Conformity with municipal law.
PROCEDURE: Denunciation.
PARTIES:
Japan
Switzerland

104619 Bilateral Exchange **318 UNTS 245**
SIGNED: 20 Mar 57   FORCE: 19 Apr 57
REGISTERED: 30 Dec 58 Japan
ARTICLES: 2 LANGUAGE: Spanish.
HEADNOTE: RECIPROCAL WAIVING PASSPORT VISAS
TOPIC: Visas
CONCEPTS: Time limit. Visa abolition. Denial of admission. Resident permits. Conformity with municipal law.
PROCEDURE: Denunciation.
PARTIES:
Dominican Republic
Japan

104620 Bilateral Agreement **318 UNTS 251**
SIGNED: 8 Feb 57   FORCE: 18 May 57
REGISTERED: 30 Dec 58 Japan
ARTICLES: 6 LANGUAGE: French.
HEADNOTE: RE-ESTABLISHMENT NORMAL RELATIONS
TOPIC: General Amity
CONCEPTS: Peaceful relations. Diplomatic relations establishment. Procedure. Armistice and peace. Post-war claims settlement.
INTL ORGS: United Nations.
PROCEDURE: Future Procedures Contemplated. Ratification.
PARTIES:
Japan
Poland

104621 Bilateral Agreement **318 UNTS 257**
SIGNED: 8 May 57   FORCE: 20 May 57
REGISTERED: 31 Dec 58 Japan
ARTICLES: 8 LANGUAGE: English. Japanese.
HEADNOTE: LEASE SPECIAL NUCLEAR MATERIAL
TOPIC: Atomic Energy
CONCEPTS: Non-prejudice to third party. Responsibility and liability. Indemnities and reimbursements. Financial programs. Payment schedules. Assets transfer. Acceptance of delivery. Nuclear materials.
TREATY REF: 240UNTS361.
PROCEDURE: Duration.
PARTIES:
Japan
USA (United States)
ANNEX
383 UNTS 318. USA (United States). Implementation 24 Aug 60. Force 24 Aug 60.
383 UNTS 318. Japan. Implementation 24 Aug 60. Force 24 Aug 60.

104622 Bilateral Agreement **318 UNTS 289**
SIGNED: 29 Oct 56   FORCE: 24 May 57
REGISTERED: 31 Dec 58 Japan
ARTICLES: 8 LANGUAGE: English. Hindi. Japanese.
HEADNOTE: CULTURAL AGREEMENT
TOPIC: Culture
CONCEPTS: Definition of terms. Friendship and amity. Conformity with municipal law. Exchange of information and documents. Operating agencies. Establishment of commission. Exchange. Teacher and student exchange. Scholarships and grants. Exchange. General cultural cooperation. Artists. Athletes. Publications exchange. Mass media exchange.
INTL ORGS: Special Commission.
PROCEDURE: Duration. Ratification. Renewal or Revival. Termination.
PARTIES:
India
Japan

104623 Bilateral Convention **318 UNTS 309**
SIGNED: 12 Dec 56   FORCE: 1 Jun 57
REGISTERED: 31 Dec 58 Japan
ARTICLES: 20 LANGUAGE: English.
HEADNOTE: DOUBLE TAXATION FISCAL EVASION TAXES INCOME

TOPIC: Taxation
CONCEPTS: Definition of terms. Conformity with municipal law. Exchange of official publications. Negotiation. Teacher and student exchange. Claims and settlements. Taxation. General. Tax exemptions.
PROCEDURE: Duration. Ratification. Termination.
PARTIES:
Japan
Sweden

104624 Bilateral Agreement **318 UNTS 335**
SIGNED: 27 Jun 57   FORCE: 27 Jun 57
REGISTERED: 31 Dec 58 Japan
ARTICLES: 4 LANGUAGE: German. Japanese.
HEADNOTE: AUTHORIZATION PERFORM ACTS CIVIL REGISTRATION
TOPIC: Admin Cooperation
CONCEPTS: Territorial application. Notarial acts and services.
PROCEDURE: Termination.
PARTIES:
Germany, West
Japan

104625 Bilateral Agreement **318 UNTS 345**
SIGNED: 20 Mar 57   FORCE: 15 Jul 57
REGISTERED: 31 Dec 58 Japan
ARTICLES: 12 LANGUAGE: Arabic. English. Japanese.
HEADNOTE: CULTURAL AGREEMENT
TOPIC: Culture
CONCEPTS: Treaty interpretation. Friendship and amity. Visas. General cooperation. Recognition of degrees. Exchange. Teacher and student exchange. Professorships. Institute establishment. Scholarships and grants. Exchange. General cultural cooperation. Artists. Athletes. Scientific exchange. Publications exchange. Mass media exchange.
PROCEDURE: Duration. Ratification. Renewal or Revival. Termination.
PARTIES:
Japan
United Arab Rep

104626 Bilateral Agreement **318 UNTS 361**
SIGNED: 14 Feb 57   FORCE: 10 Oct 57
REGISTERED: 31 Dec 58 Japan
ARTICLES: 13 LANGUAGE: German. Japanese.
HEADNOTE: CULTURAL
TOPIC: Culture
CONCEPTS: Culture.
INTL ORGS: Special Commission.
PROCEDURE: Denunciation. Ratification.
PARTIES:
Germany, West
Japan

104627 Bilateral Agreement **318 UNTS 381**
SIGNED: 6 Jul 57   FORCE: 6 Jul 57
REGISTERED: 31 Dec 58 Japan
ARTICLES: 7 LANGUAGE: English. Japanese.
HEADNOTE: TRADE
TOPIC: General Trade
CONCEPTS: Detailed regulations. Exceptions and exemptions. General cooperation. Procedure. Negotiation. Export quotas. Import quotas. Reciprocity in trade. Trade agencies. Trade procedures. Balance of payments. Exchange rates and regulations. Most favored nation clause.
TREATY REF: GATT.
PROCEDURE: Duration. Ratification. Termination.
PARTIES:
Australia
Japan
ANNEX
517 UNTS 318. Japan. Amendment 5 Aug 63. Force 27 May 64.
517 UNTS 318. Australia. Amendment 5 Aug 63. Force 27 May 64.

104628 Bilateral Exchange **318 UNTS 411**
SIGNED: 5 Nov 57   FORCE: 5 Jan 58
REGISTERED: 31 Dec 58 Japan
ARTICLES: 2 LANGUAGE: French.
HEADNOTE: MUTUAL ABOLITION PASSPORT VISAS
TOPIC: Visas

CONCEPTS: Emergencies. Time limit. Visa abolition. Resident permits. Conformity with municipal law.
PROCEDURE: Denunciation.
PARTIES:
Japan
Turkey

104629 Bilateral Agreement **319 UNTS 3**
SIGNED: 15 Dec 58   FORCE: 15 Dec 58
REGISTERED: 1 Jan 59 United Nations
ARTICLES: 4 LANGUAGE: English.
HEADNOTE: OPERATIONAL EXECUTIVE PERSONNEL
TOPIC: Tech Assistance
CONCEPTS: Exceptions and exemptions. Treaty implementation. Annex or appendix reference. Privileges and immunities. General cooperation. Personnel. Responsibility and liability. Use of facilities. Arbitration. Procedure. Vocational training. Compensation. Expense sharing formulae. Domestic obligation. Special projects. Status of experts. Conformity with IGO decisions.
INTL ORGS: Permanent Court of Arbitration. Arbitration Commission.
PARTIES:
Burma
United Nations

104630 Multilateral Convention **319 UNTS 21**
SIGNED: 18 May 56   FORCE: 1 Jan 59
REGISTERED: 1 Jan 59 United Nations
ARTICLES: 45 LANGUAGE: English. French.
HEADNOTE: CUSTOMS CONVENTION
TOPIC: Customs
CONCEPTS: Definition of terms. Annex or appendix reference. Previous treaty renunciation. Responsibility and liability. Arbitration. Negotiation. Temporary importation.
INTL ORGS: United Nations. Arbitration Commission.
TREATY REF: 45UNTS149.
PROCEDURE: Amendment. Accession. Denunciation. Ratification. Registration.
PARTIES:
Austria   SIGNED: 18 May 56   RATIFIED: 13 Nov 57 FORCE: 1 Jan 59
Belgium SIGNED: 18 May 56
France SIGNED: 18 May 56
Germany, West SIGNED: 18 May 56
Hungary   SIGNED: 18 May 56   RATIFIED: 23 Jul 57 FORCE: 1 Jan 59
Italy SIGNED: 18 May 56
Luxembourg SIGNED: 18 May 56
Netherlands SIGNED: 18 May 56
Sweden   SIGNED: 18 May 56   RATIFIED: 16 Jan 58 FORCE: 1 Jan 59
Switzerland SIGNED: 18 May 56
UK Great Britain Guernsey Island RATIFIED: 3 Oct 58 FORCE: 1 Jan 59
UK Great Britain Isle of Man RATIFIED: 3 Oct 58 FORCE: 1 Jan 59
UK Great Britain Jersey Island RATIFIED: 3 Oct 58 FORCE: 1 Jan 59
UK Great Britain SIGNED: 18 May 56 RATIFIED: 3 Oct 58 FORCE: 1 Jan 59
ANNEX
320 UNTS 352. Denmark. Accession 8 Jan 59. Force 8 Apr 59.
328 UNTS 341. UK Great Britain. British Somaliland. Force 11 Aug 59.
328 UNTS 341. UK Great Britain. St. Helena. Force 11 Aug 59.
328 UNTS 341. UK Great Britain. Gibralter. Force 11 Aug 59.
328 UNTS 341. UK Great Britain. North Borneo. Force 11 Aug 59.
328 UNTS 341. UK Great Britain. Uganda. Force 11 Aug 59.
328 UNTS 341. UK Great Britain. Zanzibar. Force 11 Aug 59.
328 UNTS 341. UK Great Britain. Leeward Islands. Force 11 Aug 59.
328 UNTS 341. UK Great Britain. Cyprus. Force 11 Aug 59.
328 UNTS 341. UK Great Britain. Seychelles. Force 11 Aug 59.
328 UNTS 341. UK Great Britain. Aden. Force 11 Aug 59.
328 UNTS 341. UK Great Britain. British Guiana. Force 11 Aug 59.

328 UNTS 341. UK Great Britain. Brunei. Force 11 Aug 59.

328 UNTS 341. UK Great Britain. Gambia. Force 11 Aug 59.

328 UNTS 341. UK Great Britain. Sarawak. Force 11 Aug 59.

328 UNTS 341. UK Great Britain. Kenya. Force 11 Aug 59.

328 UNTS 341. UK Great Britain. Tanganyika. Force 11 Aug 59.

328 UNTS 341. UK Great Britain. Windward Islands. Force 11 Aug 59.

328 UNTS 341. UK Great Britain. Brit Solomon Is. Force 11 Aug 59.

328 UNTS 341. UK Great Britain. Singapore. Force 11 Aug 59.

328 UNTS 342. France. Ratification 20 May 59. Force 18 Aug 59.

341 UNTS 420. UK Great Britain. Jamaica. Force 14 Dec 59.

344 UNTS 358. UK Great Britain. Malta. Force 17 Jan 60.

344 UNTS 358. UK Great Britain. Sierra Leone. Force 17 Jan 60.

346 UNTS 356. France. St. Pierre. Force 13 Mar 60.

346 UNTS 356. France. Miquelon. Force 13 Mar 60.

346 UNTS 356. France. French Somaliland. Force 13 Mar 60.

346 UNTS 356. France. Comoro Islands. Force 13 Mar 60.

346 UNTS 356. France. New Caledonia. Force 13 Mar 60.

346 UNTS 356. France. French Polynesia. Force 13 Mar 60.

347 UNTS 393. France. New Hebrides Is. Force 27 Mar 60.

347 UNTS 393. UK Great Britain. New Hebrides Is. Force 27 Mar 60.

348 UNTS 371. Yugoslavia. Accession 29 Jan 60. Force 28 Apr 60.

358 UNTS 364. UK Great Britain. Falkland Islands. Force 10 Aug 60.

358 UNTS 364. UK Great Britain. Hong Kong. Force 10 Aug 60.

366 UNTS 416. Switzerland. Qualified Ratification 7 Jul 60. Force 5 Oct 60.

371 UNTS 329. Netherlands. Netherlands Antilles. Force 25 Oct 60.

371 UNTS 329. Netherlands. Dutch New Guinea. Force 25 Oct 60.

371 UNTS 329. Netherlands. Surinam. Force 25 Oct 60.

371 UNTS 329. Netherlands. Ratification 27 Jul 60. Force 25 Oct 60.

384 UNTS 382. UK Great Britain. British Honduras. Force 12 Apr 61.

388 UNTS 378. UK Great Britain. Mauritius. Force 11 May 61.

395 UNTS 273. UK Great Britain. Trinidad/-Tobago. Force 6 Aug 61.

411 UNTS 320. Germany, West. Ratification 23 Oct 61. Force 21 Jan 62.

415 UNTS 431. Germany, West. Berlin.

423 UNTS 320. Sierra Leone. Succession 13 Mar 62.

424 UNTS 362. Italy. Ratification 29 Mar 62. Force 27 Jun 62.

453 UNTS 388. Belgium. Ratification 18 Feb 63. Force 19 May 63.

480 UNTS 372. Jamaica. Succession 11 Nov 63.

480 UNTS 372. Algeria. Qualified Accession 31 Oct 63. Force 29 Jan 64.

511 UNTS 282. Luxembourg. Ratification 13 Oct 64. Force 11 Jan 65.

525 UNTS 318. Portugal. Accession 16 Feb 65. Force 17 May 65.

547 UNTS 322. Finland. Accession 30 Sep 65. Force 29 Dec 65.

560 UNTS 266. Trinidad/Tobago. Succession 11 Apr 66.

561 UNTS 350. Malta. Succession 3 May 66. Force 21 Sep 66.

561 UNTS 350. Malta. Succession 3 May 66. Force 21 Sep 64.

104631 Bilateral Agreement **319 UNTS 93**
SIGNED: 6 Jul 50 FORCE: 28 Nov 50
REGISTERED: 5 Jan 59 Poland
ARTICLES: 8 LANGUAGE: Polish. German.
HEADNOTE: DEMARCATION ESTABLISHED STATE FRONTIER

TOPIC: Territory Boundary
CONCEPTS: Annex or appendix reference. Establishment of commission. Markers and definitions. Frontier crossing points.
INTL ORGS: Special Commission.
PROCEDURE: Ratification.
PARTIES:
  Germany, East
  Poland

104632 Bilateral Treaty **319 UNTS 115**
SIGNED: 1 Feb 57 FORCE: 11 Oct 57
REGISTERED: 5 Jan 59 Poland
ARTICLES: 86 LANGUAGE: Polish. German.
HEADNOTE: LEGAL RELATIONS CIVIL FAMILY CRIMINAL CASES
TOPIC: Admin Cooperation
CONCEPTS: General provisions. Privileges and immunities. Consular functions in property. Extradition, deportation and repatriation. Extraditable offenses. Refusal of extradition. Concurrent requests. Limits of prosecution. Extradition postponement. Witnesses and experts. Material evidence. Conformity with municipal law. Family law. Exchange of information and documents. Inspection and observation. Juridical personality. Legal protection and assistance. Immovable property. General property. Recognition of legal documents. Indemnities and reimbursements. Conveyance in transit.
PROCEDURE: Duration. Ratification.
PARTIES:
  Germany, East
  Poland

104633 Bilateral Agreement **319 UNTS 221**
SIGNED: 2 Feb 57 FORCE: 29 Apr 58
REGISTERED: 5 Jan 59 Poland
ARTICLES: 7 LANGUAGE: English.
HEADNOTE: CULTURAL AGREEMENT
TOPIC: Culture
CONCEPTS: Friendship and amity. Specialists exchange. Recognition of degrees. Exchange. Teacher and student exchange. Scholarships and grants. General cultural cooperation. Artists. Athletes. Research cooperation. Scientific exchange. General trade. Customs duties. Mass media exchange.
PROCEDURE: Denunciation. Ratification.
PARTIES:
  Poland
  United Arab Rep

104634 Bilateral Treaty **319 UNTS 229**
SIGNED: 13 Jul 57 FORCE: 28 Feb 58
REGISTERED: 5 Jan 59 Poland
ARTICLES: 19 LANGUAGE: Polish. German.
HEADNOTE: COOPERATION SOCIAL POLICY
TOPIC: Health/Educ/Welfare
CONCEPTS: General cooperation. Exchange of official publications. General cultural cooperation. Old age insurance. Sickness and invalidity insurance. Unemployment. Migrant worker.
PROCEDURE: Duration. Ratification.
PARTIES:
  Germany, East
  Poland

104635 Bilateral Agreement **319 UNTS 263**
SIGNED: 27 Mar 57 FORCE: 12 Aug 58
REGISTERED: 5 Jan 59 Poland
ARTICLES: 8 LANGUAGE: Polish. Hindi. English.
HEADNOTE: CULTURAL COOPERATION
TOPIC: Culture
CONCEPTS: Friendship and amity. Conformity with municipal law. Operating agencies. Responsibility and liability. Establishment of commission. Recognition of degrees. Exchange. Institute establishment. Scholarships and grants. Vocational training. Exchange. General cultural cooperation. Artists. Athletes. Scientific exchange. Publications exchange. Mass media exchange. Press and wire services.
INTL ORGS: Special Commission.
PROCEDURE: Duration. Ratification. Renewal or Revival. Termination.
PARTIES:
  India
  Poland

104636 Bilateral Convention **319 UNTS 277**
SIGNED: 21 Jan 58 FORCE: 8 May 58
REGISTERED: 5 Jan 59 Poland
ARTICLES: 11 LANGUAGE: Polish. Russian.
HEADNOTE: DUAL CITIZENSHIP
TOPIC: Consul/Citizenship
CONCEPTS: Resident permits. Alien status. Dual citizenship. Public information. Tax exemptions.
PROCEDURE: Ratification.
PARTIES:
  Poland
  USSR (Soviet Union)

104637 Bilateral Convention **319 UNTS 291**
SIGNED: 21 Jan 58 FORCE: 8 Jun 58
REGISTERED: 5 Jan 59 Poland
ARTICLES: 33 LANGUAGE: Polish. Russian.
HEADNOTE: CONSULAR CONVENTION
TOPIC: Consul/Citizenship
CONCEPTS: Definition of terms. Previous treaty replacement. General consular functions. Diplomatic privileges. Consular relations establishment. Inviolability. Privileges and immunities. Diplomatic correspondence.
TREATY REF: 49LTS201.
PROCEDURE: Denunciation. Ratification.
PARTIES:
  Poland
  USSR (Soviet Union)

104638 Bilateral Treaty **320 UNTS 3**
SIGNED: 28 Dec 57 FORCE: 8 Jun 58
REGISTERED: 5 Jan 59 Poland
ARTICLES: 85 LANGUAGE: Polish. Russian.
HEADNOTE: LEGAL ASSISTANCE CIVIL FAMILY CRIMINAL CASES
TOPIC: Admin Cooperation
CONCEPTS: General provisions. Extradition, deportation and repatriation. Extradition requests. Refusal of extradition. Concurrent requests. Extradition postponement. Material evidence. Conformity with municipal law. Family law. Exchange of information and documents. Juridical personality. Legal protection and assistance. Recognition and enforcement of legal decisions. Immovable property. General property. Indemnities and reimbursements. Conveyance in transit.
PROCEDURE: Duration. Ratification.
PARTIES:
  Poland
  USSR (Soviet Union)

104639 Multilateral Protocol **320 UNTS 103**
SIGNED: 31 Mar 58 FORCE: 31 Mar 58
REGISTERED: 6 Jan 59 USA (United States)
ARTICLES: 1 LANGUAGE: French.
HEADNOTE: MANAGEMENT CAPE SPARTEL LIGHT
TOPIC: Specific Property
CONCEPTS: Annex or appendix reference. Assets transfer. Facilities and property.
PARTIES:
  Belgium SIGNED: 31 Mar 58 FORCE: 31 Mar 58
  France SIGNED: 31 Mar 58 FORCE: 31 Mar 58
  Italy SIGNED: 31 Mar 58 FORCE: 31 Mar 58
  Morocco SIGNED: 31 Mar 58 FORCE: 31 Mar 58
  Netherlands SIGNED: 31 Mar 58 FORCE: 31 Mar 58
  Portugal SIGNED: 31 Mar 58 FORCE: 31 Mar 58
  Spain SIGNED: 31 Mar 58 FORCE: 31 Mar 58
  Sweden SIGNED: 31 Mar 58 FORCE: 31 Mar 58
  UK Great Britain SIGNED: 31 Mar 58 FORCE: 31 Mar 58
  USA (United States) SIGNED: 31 Mar 58 FORCE: 31 Mar 58

104640 Bilateral Convention **320 UNTS 111**
SIGNED: 5 Oct 57 FORCE: 21 Jul 58
REGISTERED: 15 Jan 59 Czechoslovakia
ARTICLES: 10 LANGUAGE: Czechoslovakian. Russian.
HEADNOTE: DUAL CITIZENSHIP
TOPIC: Consul/Citizenship
CONCEPTS: Resident permits. Alien status. Dual citizenship. Public information. Tax exemptions.
PROCEDURE: Ratification.
PARTIES:
  Czechoslovakia
  USSR (Soviet Union)

104641 Bilateral Convention **320 UNTS 129**
SIGNED: 5 Oct 57 FORCE: 21 Jul 58
REGISTERED: 15 Jan 59 Czechoslovakia
ARTICLES: 26 LANGUAGE: Czechoslovakian. Russian.
HEADNOTE: CONSULAR CONVENTION
TOPIC: Consul/Citizenship
CONCEPTS: Definition of terms. Previous treaty replacement. General consular functions. Diplomatic privileges. Consular relations establishment. Inviolability. Privileges and immunities. Diplomatic correspondence.
TREATY REF: 169LTS143.
PROCEDURE: Duration. Ratification. Termination.
PARTIES:
Czechoslovakia
USSR (Soviet Union)

104642 Bilateral Agreement **320 UNTS 163**
SIGNED: 21 Jul 58 FORCE: 2 Dec 58
REGISTERED: 19 Jan 59 Denmark
ARTICLES: 27 LANGUAGE: Danish. Swedish.
HEADNOTE: DOUBLE TAXATION INCOME PROPERTY
TOPIC: Taxation
CONCEPTS: Territorial application. Previous treaty replacement. Privileges and immunities. Nationality and citizenship. Teacher and student exchange. Claims and settlements. Taxation. Death duties. Equitable taxes. General. Tax exemptions. Air transport. Merchant vessels.
TREATY REF: 198UNTS71.
PROCEDURE: Duration. Ratification. Termination.
PARTIES:
Denmark
Sweden

ANNEX
427 UNTS 390. Denmark. Supplementation 13 May 59. Force 17 Dec 59.
427 UNTS 390. Sweden. Supplementation 13 May 59. Force 17 Dec 59.

104643 Multilateral Exchange **320 UNTS 209**
SIGNED: 14 Jun 54 FORCE: 16 May 58
REGISTERED: 22 Jan 59 ICAO (Civil Aviat)
ARTICLES: 1 LANGUAGE: English. French. Spanish.
HEADNOTE: EXCHANGE OFFICIAL PUBLICATIONS
TOPIC: Air Transport
CONCEPTS: Detailed regulations. Territorial application. Exchange of official publications. Indemnities and reimbursements.
INTL ORGS: International Civil Aviation Organization.
TREATY REF: 15UNTS295.
PARTIES:
Afghanistan RATIFIED: 15 Mar 56 FORCE: 16 May 58
Argentina RATIFIED: 21 Sep 56 FORCE: 16 May 58
Australia RATIFIED: 23 Aug 57 FORCE: 16 May 58
Austria RATIFIED: 13 Apr 56 FORCE: 16 May 58
Belgium RATIFIED: 28 Jan 55 FORCE: 16 May 58
Bolivia RATIFIED: 23 May 56 FORCE: 16 May 58
Ceylon (Sri Lanka) RATIFIED: 6 Jan 55 FORCE: 16 May 58
Czechoslovakia RATIFIED: 21 Feb 57 FORCE: 16 May 58
Denmark RATIFIED: 4 Jun 55 FORCE: 16 May 58
Dominican Republic RATIFIED: 28 Dec 54 FORCE: 16 May 58
United Arab Rep RATIFIED: 15 Mar 55 FORCE: 16 May 58
Ethiopia RATIFIED: 25 Oct 54 FORCE: 16 May 58
Finland RATIFIED: 30 Dec 54 FORCE: 16 May 58
Greece RATIFIED: 12 Dec 56 FORCE: 16 May 58
Haiti RATIFIED: 13 Sep 57 FORCE: 16 May 58
Honduras RATIFIED: 1 Jun 55 FORCE: 16 May 58
Iceland RATIFIED: 5 Jul 55 FORCE: 16 May 58
India RATIFIED: 19 Jan 55 FORCE: 16 May 58
Iraq RATIFIED: 25 Mar 55 FORCE: 16 May 58
Ireland RATIFIED: 4 Jan 55 FORCE: 16 May 58
Italy RATIFIED: 24 Mar 58 FORCE: 16 May 58
Japan RATIFIED: 21 Jun 56 FORCE: 16 May 58
Korea, South RATIFIED: 23 May 57 FORCE: 16 May 58
Laos RATIFIED: 4 Jun 56 FORCE: 16 May 58

Libya RATIFIED: 6 Dec 56 FORCE: 16 May 58
Luxembourg RATIFIED: 17 Mar 55 FORCE: 16 May 58
Mexico RATIFIED: 13 May 55 FORCE: 16 May 58
Morocco RATIFIED: 21 Jun 57 FORCE: 16 May 58
Netherlands RATIFIED: 14 Dec 55 FORCE: 16 May 58
New Zealand RATIFIED: 8 May 58 FORCE: 16 May 58
Norway RATIFIED: 18 Apr 56 FORCE: 16 May 58
Pakistan RATIFIED: 21 Oct 55 FORCE: 16 May 58
Peru RATIFIED: 16 May 58 FORCE: 16 May 58
Philippines RATIFIED: 13 Aug 56 FORCE: 16 May 58
Portugal RATIFIED: 20 Sep 55 FORCE: 16 May 58
South Africa RATIFIED: 24 May 56 FORCE: 16 May 58
Spain RATIFIED: 6 Jun 55 FORCE: 16 May 58
Sweden RATIFIED: 8 Jul 55 FORCE: 16 May 58
Switzerland RATIFIED: 17 Apr 56 FORCE: 16 May 58
Syria RATIFIED: 8 Mar 56 FORCE: 16 May 58
Turkey RATIFIED: 23 Dec 55 FORCE: 16 May 58
UK Great Britain RATIFIED: 17 Feb 55 FORCE: 16 May 58
Vietnam, South RATIFIED: 30 Dec 57 FORCE: 16 May 58

ANNEX
335 UNTS 354. Canada. Ratification 2 Sep 58.
335 UNTS 354. Germany, West. Ratification 27 Apr 59.
418 UNTS 398. Guinea. Ratification 26 Jun 59.
418 UNTS 398. Fed of Malaya. Ratification 28 Mar 61.
418 UNTS 398. Sudan. Ratification 8 Apr 60.
418 UNTS 398. Ivory Coast. Ratification 20 Mar 61.
418 UNTS 398. Tunisia. Ratification 23 May 61.
418 UNTS 398. Yugoslavia. Ratification 20 Jan 61.
418 UNTS 398. Ghana. Ratification 15 Aug 61.
418 UNTS 398. Cameroon. Ratification 17 Jul 59.
418 UNTS 398. Indonesia. Ratification 24 Nov 59.
418 UNTS 398. Guatemala. Ratification 6 Oct 59.
418 UNTS 398. Costa Rica. Ratification 5 Jul 60.
418 UNTS 398. Thailand. Ratification 18 Jan 60.
418 UNTS 398. Mali. Ratification 10 Jan 61.
418 UNTS 398. Brazil. Ratification 17 Jun 59.
418 UNTS 398. Senegal. Ratification 28 Feb 61.
514 UNTS 283. Kenya. Ratification 31 May 64. Force 31 May 64.
514 UNTS 283. Nicaragua. Ratification 9 Jul 62. Force 9 Jul 62.
514 UNTS 283. Cuba. Ratification 12 Aug 63. Force 12 Aug 63.
514 UNTS 283. Chad. Ratification 28 Aug 64. Force 28 Aug 64.
514 UNTS 283. France. Ratification 21 Sep 64. Force 21 Sep 64.
514 UNTS 283. Central Afri Rep. Ratification 22 May 62. Force 22 May 62.
514 UNTS 283. Somalia. Ratification 30 Sep 64. Force 30 Sep 64.
514 UNTS 283. Madagascar. Ratification 7 Dec 62. Force 7 Dec 62.
514 UNTS 283. Tanganyika. Ratification 10 Apr 63. Force 10 Apr 63.
514 UNTS 283. Panama. Ratification 24 Sep 63. Force 24 Sep 63.
514 UNTS 283. Mauritania. Ratification 2 Apr 62. Force 2 Apr 62.
514 UNTS 283. Poland. Ratification 23 May 62. Force 23 May 62.
514 UNTS 283. Congo (Brazzaville). Ratification 26 May 62. Force 26 May 62.
514 UNTS 283. Congo (Zaire) Ratification 23 Aug 62. Force 23 Aug 62.
514 UNTS 283. Jamaica. Ratification 18 Oct 63. Force 18 Oct 63.

104644 Multilateral Exchange **320 UNTS 217**
SIGNED: 14 Jun 54 FORCE: 12 Dec 56
REGISTERED: 22 Jan 59 ICAO (Civil Aviat)
ARTICLES: 1 LANGUAGE: English. French. Spanish.
HEADNOTE: RELATING CERTAIN AMENDMENTS CONVENTION INTERNATIONAL CIVIL AVIATION
TOPIC: Air Transport

CONCEPTS: Annex type material. Air transport.
INTL ORGS: International Civil Aviation Organization.
TREATY REF: 15UNTS295.
PROCEDURE: Ratification.
PARTIES:
Afghanistan RATIFIED: 15 Mar 56 FORCE: 12 Dec 56
Argentina RATIFIED: 21 Sep 56 FORCE: 12 Dec 56
Australia RATIFIED: 22 Apr 55 FORCE: 12 Dec 56
Austria RATIFIED: 13 Apr 56 FORCE: 12 Dec 56
Belgium RATIFIED: 28 Jan 55 FORCE: 12 Dec 56
Bolivia RATIFIED: 23 May 56 FORCE: 12 Dec 56
Canada RATIFIED: 4 Nov 54 FORCE: 12 Dec 56
Ceylon (Sri Lanka) RATIFIED: 6 Jan 55 FORCE: 12 Dec 56
Taiwan RATIFIED: 16 Feb 56 FORCE: 12 Dec 56
Denmark RATIFIED: 4 Jun 55 FORCE: 12 Dec 56
Dominican Republic RATIFIED: 28 Dec 54 FORCE: 12 Dec 56
United Arab Rep RATIFIED: 15 Mar 55 FORCE: 12 Dec 56
Ethiopia RATIFIED: 25 Oct 54 FORCE: 12 Dec 56
Finland RATIFIED: 30 Dec 54 FORCE: 12 Dec 56
Greece RATIFIED: 12 Dec 56 FORCE: 12 Dec 56
Honduras RATIFIED: 1 Jun 55 FORCE: 12 Dec 56
India RATIFIED: 19 Jan 55 FORCE: 12 Dec 56
Indonesia RATIFIED: 18 Oct 55 FORCE: 12 Dec 56
Iraq RATIFIED: 25 Mar 55 FORCE: 12 Dec 56
Ireland RATIFIED: 4 Jan 55 FORCE: 12 Dec 56
Japan RATIFIED: 21 Jun 56 FORCE: 12 Dec 56
Laos RATIFIED: 4 Jun 56 FORCE: 12 Dec 56
Luxembourg RATIFIED: 17 Mar 55 FORCE: 12 Dec 56
Mexico RATIFIED: 13 May 55 FORCE: 12 Dec 56
Netherlands RATIFIED: 31 May 55 FORCE: 12 Dec 56
New Zealand RATIFIED: 8 Jun 56 FORCE: 12 Dec 56
Norway RATIFIED: 18 Apr 56 FORCE: 12 Dec 56
Pakistan RATIFIED: 21 Oct 55 FORCE: 12 Dec 56
Philippines RATIFIED: 27 Jul 55 FORCE: 12 Dec 56
Portugal RATIFIED: 20 Sep 55 FORCE: 12 Dec 56
South Africa RATIFIED: 24 May 56 FORCE: 12 Dec 56
Spain RATIFIED: 5 Jul 55 FORCE: 12 Dec 56
Sweden RATIFIED: 8 Jul 55 FORCE: 12 Dec 56
Switzerland RATIFIED: 17 Apr 56 FORCE: 12 Dec 56
Syria RATIFIED: 8 Mar 55 FORCE: 12 Dec 56
Thailand RATIFIED: 18 Jul 56 FORCE: 12 Dec 56
Turkey RATIFIED: 23 Dec 55 FORCE: 12 Dec 56
UK Great Britain RATIFIED: 17 Jan 55 FORCE: 12 Dec 56
USA (United States) RATIFIED: 22 May 56 FORCE: 12 Dec 56
Venezuela RATIFIED: 6 Jul 56 FORCE: 12 Dec 56

ANNEX
335 UNTS 355. Vietnam, South. Ratification 30 Dec 57.
335 UNTS 355. Italy. Ratification 24 Mar 58.
335 UNTS 355. Peru. Ratification 25 Sep 57.
335 UNTS 355. Czechoslovakia. Ratification 21 Feb 57.
335 UNTS 355. Burma. Ratification 16 Aug 57.
335 UNTS 355. Israel. Ratification 13 May 57.
335 UNTS 355. Korea, South. Ratification 23 May 57.
335 UNTS 355. Morocco. Ratification 21 Jun 57.
335 UNTS 355. Germany, West. Ratification 27 Apr 59.
418 UNTS 399. Guinea. Ratification 6 Oct 59.
418 UNTS 399. Guatemala. Ratification 5 Jul 60.
418 UNTS 399. Sudan. Ratification 8 Apr 60.
418 UNTS 399. Mali. Ratification 10 Jan 61.
418 UNTS 399. Tunisia. Ratification 16 Jan 61.
418 UNTS 399. Senegal. Ratification 28 Feb 61.
418 UNTS 399. Brazil. Ratification 26 Jun 59.
418 UNTS 399. Fed of Malaya. Ratification 28 Mar 61.
418 UNTS 399. Costa Rica. Ratification 5 Jul 60.
418 UNTS 399. Ivory Coast. Ratification 20 Mar 61.
418 UNTS 399. Yugoslavia. Ratification 20 Jun 61.

418 UNTS 399. Ghana. Ratification 15 Aug 61.

418 UNTS 399. Cameroon. Ratification 14 Nov 61.

514 UNTS 283. Panama. Ratification 24 Sep 63. Force 24 Sep 63.

514 UNTS 283. Jamaica. Ratification 18 Oct 63. Force 18 Oct 63.

514 UNTS 283. Tanganyika. Ratification 10 Apr 63. Force 10 Apr 63.

514 UNTS 283. Chad. Ratification 28 Aug 64. Force 28 Aug 64.

514 UNTS 283. Kenya. Ratification 31 May 64. Force 31 May 64.

514 UNTS 283. France. Ratification 21 Sep 64. Force 21 Sep 64.

514 UNTS 283. Somalia. Ratification 30 Sep 64. Force 30 Sep 64.

514 UNTS 284. Cuba. Ratification 29 Oct 62. Force 29 Oct 62.

514 UNTS 284. Congo (Brazzaville). Ratification 26 May 62. Force 26 May 62.

514 UNTS 284. Nicaragua. Ratification 9 Jul 62. Force 9 Jul 62.

514 UNTS 284. Congo (Zaire). Ratification 23 Aug 62. Force 23 Aug 62.

514 UNTS 284. Madagascar. Ratification 7 Dec 62. Force 7 Dec 62.

514 UNTS 284. Central Afri Rep. Ratification 22 May 62. Force 22 May 62.

514 UNTS 284. Poland. Ratification 23 May 62. Force 23 May 62.

514 UNTS 284. Mauritania. Ratification 2 Apr 62. Force 2 Apr 62.

104645 Bilateral Agreement **320 UNTS 225**
SIGNED: 7 Jun 58   FORCE: 7 Jul 58
REGISTERED: 23 Jan 59 Pakistan
ARTICLES: 15 LANGUAGE: English.
HEADNOTE: RELATING AIR SERVICES
TOPIC: Air Transport
CONCEPTS: Definition of terms. Detailed regulations. Annex or appendix reference. Conformity with municipal law. General cooperation. Exchange of information and documents. Procedure. Existing tribunals. Negotiation. Non-interest rates and fees. Most favored nation clause. National treatment. Routes and logistics. Permit designation. Air transport. Conditions of airlines operating permission. Overflights and technical stops. Operating authorizations and regulations.
INTL ORGS: International Civil Aviation Organization. International Court of Justice. Arbitration Commission.
TREATY REF: 15UNTS295.
PROCEDURE: Amendment. Future Procedures Contemplated. Termination. Application to Non-self-governing Territories.
PARTIES:
Pakistan
Portugal

104646 Multilateral Convention **320 UNTS 243**
SIGNED: 29 Apr 57   FORCE: 30 Apr 58
REGISTERED: 26 Jan 59 Council of Europe
ARTICLES: 41 LANGUAGE: English. French.
HEADNOTE: EUROPEAN CONVENTION PEACEFUL SETTLEMENT DISPUTES
TOPIC: Dispute Settlement
CONCEPTS: Exceptions and exemptions. Treaty interpretation. Non-prejudice to third party. Arbitration. Procedure. Domestic jurisdiction. Existing tribunals. Conciliation. Compulsory jurisdiction.
INTL ORGS: Council of Europe. International Court of Justice. Arbitration Commission. Conciliation Commission.
PROCEDURE: Denunciation. Ratification.
PARTIES:
Austria SIGNED: 13 Dec 57
Belgium SIGNED: 29 Apr 57
Denmark SIGNED: 29 Apr 57
France SIGNED: 29 Apr 57
Germany, West SIGNED: 29 Apr 57
Greece SIGNED: 29 Apr 57
Iceland SIGNED: 29 Apr 57
Ireland SIGNED: 29 Apr 57
Italy SIGNED: 29 Apr 57
Luxembourg SIGNED: 29 Apr 57
Netherlands Dutch New Guinea RATIFIED: 7 Jul 58 FORCE: 7 Jul 58
Netherlands SIGNED: 29 Apr 57 RATIFIED: 7 Jul 58 FORCE: 7 Jul 58

Netherlands Netherlands Antilles RATIFIED: 7 Jul 58 FORCE: 7 Jul 58
Netherlands Surinam RATIFIED: 7 Jul 58 FORCE: 7 Jul 58
Norway SIGNED: 29 Apr 57 RATIFIED: 27 Mar 58 FORCE: 30 Apr 58
Sweden SIGNED: 29 Apr 57 RATIFIED: 30 Apr 58 FORCE: 30 Apr 58
Turkey SIGNED: 8 May 58
UK Great Britain SIGNED: 29 Apr 57
ANNEX
351 UNTS 448. Denmark. Ratification 17 Jul 59.
351 UNTS 448. Austria. Ratification 15 Jan 60.
351 UNTS 448. Italy. Qualified Ratification 29 Jan 60.
351 UNTS 448. Council of Europe. Correction 3 Jul 59.
383 UNTS 324. UK Great Britain. Qualified Ratification 7 Dec 60.
394 UNTS 294. Germany, West. Ratification 18 Apr 61.
400 UNTS 404. Luxembourg. Ratification 5 Jul 61.
404 UNTS 371. Germany, West. Berlin. Force 18 Apr 61.
560 UNTS 268. Switzerland. Signature 15 Apr 64. Ratification 29 Nov 65.

104647 Bilateral Agreement **320 UNTS 269**
SIGNED: 18 Dec 55   FORCE: 26 Sep 57
REGISTERED: 28 Jan 59 Pakistan
ARTICLES: 8 LANGUAGE: English. Arabic.
HEADNOTE: TRADE ECONOMIC RELATIONS PROMOTION
TOPIC: General Trade
CONCEPTS: Exceptions and exemptions. Annex or appendix reference. Conformity with municipal law. Licenses and permits. Export quotas. Import quotas. Exchange rates and regulations. Payment schedules. Most favored nation clause.
PROCEDURE: Duration. Ratification. Renewal or Revival. Termination.
PARTIES:
Pakistan
Syria

104648 Multilateral Convention **320 UNTS 291**
SIGNED: 25 Jun 57   FORCE: 17 Jan 59
REGISTERED: 28 Jan 59 ILO (Labor Org)
ARTICLES: 10 LANGUAGE: English. French.
HEADNOTE: ABOLITION FORCED LABOR
TOPIC: ILO Labor
CONCEPTS: Human rights. Penal sanctions. ILO conventions. Anti-discrimination. Employment regulations. Wages and salaries.
INTL ORGS: United Nations.
TREATY REF: 39UNTS55; 3'27DM471; 60LTS253;.
PROCEDURE: Amendment. Denunciation. Duration. Ratification. Registration. Renewal or Revival.
PARTIES:
Multilateral
ANNEX
325 UNTS 349. Netherlands. Surinam.
325 UNTS 349. Netherlands. Netherlands Antilles.
325 UNTS 349. Netherlands. Dutch New Guinea.
325 UNTS 349. Netherlands. Ratification 18 Feb 59. Force 18 Feb 60.
327 UNTS 386. Taiwan. Ratification 31 Mar 59. Force 31 Mar 60.
327 UNTS 386. UK Great Britain. Isle of Man.
327 UNTS 386. UK Great Britain. Guernsey Island.
327 UNTS 386. UK Great Britain. Jersey Island.
328 UNTS 342. Iran. Ratification 13 Apr 59. Force 13 Apr 60.
330 UNTS 373. Costa Rica. Ratification 4 May 59. Force 4 May 60.
337 UNTS 443. Germany, West. Ratification 22 Jun 59. Force 22 Jun 60.
337 UNTS 443. Mexico. Ratification 1 Jun 59. Force 1 Jun 60.
337 UNTS 443. Iraq. Ratification 15 Jun 59. Force 15 Jun 60.
338 UNTS 402. UK Great Britain. Zanzibar.
338 UNTS 402. UK Great Britain. Southern Rhodesia.
338 UNTS 402. Canada. Ratification 14 Jul 59. Force 14 Jul 60.

345 UNTS 372. Portugal. Ratification 23 Nov 59. Force 23 Nov 60.
345 UNTS 372. UK Great Britain. Hong Kong.
348 UNTS 372. Guatemala. Ratification 9 Dec 59. Force 9 Dec 60.
349 UNTS 347. Argentina. Ratification 18 Jan 60. Force 18 Jan 61.
349 UNTS 347. UK Great Britain. Cyprus.
353 UNTS 371. Pakistan. Ratification 15 Feb 60. Force 15 Feb 61.
356 UNTS 387. UK Great Britain. Brit Solomon Is. Qualified Application to Non-self-governing Territories 8 Mar 60.
358 UNTS 365. UK Great Britain. Gambia.
361 UNTS 370. Finland. Qualified Ratification 27 May 60. Force 27 May 61.
366 UNTS 417. Australia. Ratification 7 Jun 60. Force 7 Jun 61.
373 UNTS 377. UK Great Britain. Nigeria.
380 UNTS 470. Nigeria. Succession 17 Oct 60. Force 17 Oct 60.
380 UNTS 470. UK Great Britain. Northern Rhodesia.
381 UNTS 413. Cyprus. Succession 23 Sep 60. Force 23 Sep 60.
384 UNTS 383. Somalia. Succession 18 Nov 60. Force 18 Nov 60.
384 UNTS 383. Iceland. Ratification 29 Nov 60. Force 29 Nov 61.
384 UNTS 383. Philippines. Ratification 17 Nov 60. Force 17 Nov 61.
386 UNTS 411. Peru. Ratification 6 Dec 60. Force 6 Dec 61.
388 UNTS 380. UK Great Britain. Nyasaland.
388 UNTS 380. Belgium. Ratification 23 Jan 61. Force 23 Jan 62.
388 UNTS 380. Belgium. Ruanda-Urundi. Force 23 Jan 62.
396 UNTS 348. UK Great Britain. British Honduras. Force 29 Mar 62.
396 UNTS 348. Turkey. Ratification 29 Mar 61. Force 29 Mar 62.
399 UNTS 285. Gabon. Ratification 29 May 61. Force 29 May 62.
399 UNTS 285. Ivory Coast. Ratification 5 May 61. Force 5 May 62.
399 UNTS 285. Dahomey. Ratification 22 May 61. Force 22 May 62.
401 UNTS 314. Sierra Leone. Succession 13 Jun 61.
401 UNTS 314. Chad. Ratification 8 Jun 61. Force 8 Jun 62.
401 UNTS 314. Libya. Ratification 13 Jun 61. Force 13 Jun 62.
406 UNTS 330. Senegal. Ratification 28 Jul 61. Force 28 Jul 62.
406 UNTS 330. Guinea. Ratification 11 Jul 61. Force 11 Jul 62.
410 UNTS 337. Kuwait. Ratification 21 Sep 61. Force 21 Sep 62.
413 UNTS 375. Australia. Papua.
413 UNTS 375. Australia. New Guinea.
413 UNTS 375. Australia. Nauru.
413 UNTS 375. Syria. Ratification 30 Oct 61.
413 UNTS 375. Australia. Norfolk Islands.
420 UNTS 351. Somalia. Succession 8 Dec 61.
422 UNTS 341. Tanganyika. Succession 30 Jan 62. Force 30 Jan 62.
423 UNTS 321. Ecuador. Ratification 5 Feb 62. Force 5 Feb 63.
425 UNTS 356. UK Great Britain. Kenya.
425 UNTS 356. UK Great Britain. Uganda.
425 UNTS 356. Niger. Ratification 23 Mar 62. Force 23 Mar 63.
425 UNTS 356. Greece. Ratification 30 Mar 62. Force 30 Mar 63.
431 UNTS 314. Liberia. Ratification 25 May 62. Force 25 May 63.
431 UNTS 314. Mali. Ratification 28 May 62. Force 25 May 63.
452 UNTS 370. Jamaica. Succession 26 Dec 62.
457 UNTS 363. Burundi. Succession 11 Mar 63.
468 UNTS 438. Afghanistan. Ratification 16 May 63. Force 16 May 64.
468 UNTS 438. Trinidad/Tobago. Ratification 24 May 63. Force 24 May 63.
471 UNTS 379. Uganda. Ratification 4 Jun 63.
471 UNTS 379. Colombia. Ratification 7 Jun 63. Force 7 Jun 64.
488 UNTS 370. Kenya. Ratification 13 Jan 64. Force 13 Jan 64.
495 UNTS 305. Malaysia. Sarawak. Succession 3 Mar 64.

495 UNTS 305. Malaysia. Singapore. Succession 3 Mar 64.

495 UNTS 305. Malaysia. State of Sabah. Succession 3 Mar 64.

495 UNTS 305. Malaysia. Malaya. Succession 3 Mar 46.

504 UNTS 365. Luxembourg. Ratification 24 Jul 64. Force 24 Jul 65.

504 UNTS 365. Central Afri Rep. Ratification 9 Jun 64. Force 9 Jun 65.

504 UNTS 365. Tanzania. Succession 22 Jun 64.

521 UNTS 427. Venezuela. Ratification 16 Nov 64. Force 16 Nov 65.

522 UNTS 386. UK Great Britain. Bechuanaland.

524 UNTS 367. Malta. Ratification 4 Jan 65. Force 4 Jan 65.

527 UNTS 340. Zambia. Ratification 22 Feb 65. Force 22 Feb 66.

541 UNTS 379. Brazil. Ratification 18 Jun 65. Force 18 Jun 66.

548 UNTS 405. Singapore. Ratification 25 Oct 65. Force 25 Oct 65.

567 UNTS 355. Guyana. Ratification 8 Jun 66. Force 8 Jun 66.

609 UNTS 340. Nicaragua. Ratification 31 Oct 67. Force 31 Oct 68.

613 UNTS 425. Spain. Ratification 6 Nov 67. Force 6 Nov 68.

634 UNTS 475. Italy. Ratification 15 Mar 68. Force 15 Mar 69.

638 UNTS 335. Paraguay. Ratification 16 May 68. Force 16 May 69.

640 UNTS 386. New Zealand. Qualified Ratification 14 Jun 68. Force 14 Jun 69.

104649 Bilateral Agreement **320 UNTS 303**
SIGNED: 27 Aug 58 FORCE: 29 Aug 57
REGISTERED: 29 Jan 59 Australia
ARTICLES: 11 LANGUAGE: English. German.
HEADNOTE: MIGRATION
TOPIC: Non-ILO Labor
CONCEPTS: Definition of terms. Detailed regulations. Border traffic and migration. Exchange of information and documents. Public health. Non-ILO labor relations. Administrative cooperation. Sickness and invalidity insurance. Unemployment. Accounting procedures. Expense sharing formulae. Transportation costs. General aid.
PROCEDURE: Duration. Renewal or Revival. Termination.
PARTIES:
Australia
Germany, West

104650 Multilateral Agreement **321 UNTS 2**
SIGNED: 26 Jun 56 FORCE: 24 Jul 56
REGISTERED: 1 Feb 59 United Nations
ARTICLES: 6 LANGUAGE: French.
HEADNOTE: TECHNICAL ASSISTANCE
TOPIC: Tech Assistance
CONCEPTS: Definition of terms. Previous treaty replacement. Privileges and immunities. General cooperation. Exchange of information and documents. Personnel. Responsibility and liability. Title and deeds. Exchange. Scholarships and grants. Vocational training. Research and development. Exchange rates and regulations. Expense sharing formulae. Local currency. Domestic obligation. General technical assistance. Materials, equipment and services. IGO status. Conformity with IGO decisions.
TREATY REF: 118UNTS54;76UNTS132; 1UNTS15.
PROCEDURE: Amendment. Ratification. Termination.
PARTIES:
Haiti SIGNED: 26 Jun 56 FORCE: 24 Jul 56
FAO (Food Agri) SIGNED: 26 Jun 56 FORCE: 24 Jul 56
ICAO (Civil Aviat) SIGNED: 26 Jun 56 FORCE: 24 Jul 56
ILO (Labor Org) SIGNED: 26 Jun 56 FORCE: 24 Jul 56
ITU (Telecommun) SIGNED: 26 Jun 56 FORCE: 24 Jul 56
UNESCO (Educ/Cult) SIGNED: 26 Jun 56 FORCE: 24 Jul 56
United Nations SIGNED: 26 Jun 56 FORCE: 24 Jul 56
WHO (World Health) SIGNED: 26 Jun 56 FORCE: 24 Jul 56

WMO (Meteorology) SIGNED: 26 Jun 56 FORCE: 24 Jul 56

104651 Bilateral Agreement **321 UNTS 23**
SIGNED: 23 Dec 58 FORCE: 7 Jan 59
REGISTERED: 1 Feb 59 United Nations
ARTICLES: 6 LANGUAGE: French.
HEADNOTE: OPERATIONAL EXECUTIVE PERSONNEL
TOPIC: Tech Assistance
CONCEPTS: Treaty implementation. Annex or appendix reference. Privileges and immunities. General cooperation. Personnel. Responsibility and liability. Arbitration. Procedure. Negotiation. Vocational training. Compensation. Expense sharing formulae. Tax exemptions. Customs exemptions. Domestic obligation. Special projects. Status of experts. Conformity with IGO decisions.
INTL ORGS: Permanent Court of Arbitration. Arbitration Commission.
PROCEDURE: Amendment. Termination.
PARTIES:
United Nations
Tunisia
ANNEX
533 UNTS 347. Tunisia. Force 8 Apr 65.
533 UNTS 347. United Nations. Force 8 Apr 65.

104652 Bilateral Agreement **321 UNTS 35**
SIGNED: 17 Jun 58 FORCE: 17 Jun 58
REGISTERED: 2 Feb 59 USA (United States)
ARTICLES: 6 LANGUAGE: English. French.
HEADNOTE: AGRICULTURAL COMMODITIES AGREEMENT
TOPIC: Atomic Energy
CONCEPTS: Currency. Currency deposits. Loan and credit. Purchase authorization.
PARTIES:
USA (United States)
Vietnam, South

104653 Bilateral Agreement **321 UNTS 51**
SIGNED: 30 Jun 58 FORCE: 1 Jul 58
REGISTERED: 2 Feb 59 USA (United States)
ARTICLES: 19 LANGUAGE: English.
HEADNOTE: FURNISHING MEDICAL TREATMENT VERERANS & FURNISHING GRANTS-IN-AID
TOPIC: Direct Aid
CONCEPTS: Definition of terms. Time limit. Treaty implementation. Previous treaty extension. Visas. Conformity with municipal law. General cooperation. Exchange of information and documents. General property. Responsibility and liability. Use of facilities. Public health. Indemnities and reimbursements. Financial programs. Funding procedures. Tax exemptions. Customs exemptions. Grants.
TREATY REF: 45UNTS63; 31UNTS147.
PROCEDURE: Amendment. Future Procedures Contemplated. Termination.
PARTIES:
Philippines
USA (United States)
ANNEX
479 UNTS 372. Philippines. Amendment 28 Jun 63. Force 28 Jun 63.
479 UNTS 372. USA (United States). Amendment 28 Jun 63. Force 28 Jun 63.

104654 Bilateral Exchange **321 UNTS 67**
SIGNED: 26 Jun 58 FORCE: 26 Jun 58
REGISTERED: 2 Feb 59 USA (United States)
ARTICLES: 2 LANGUAGE: English. Persian.
HEADNOTE: CULTURAL COOPERATION
TOPIC: Culture
CONCEPTS: Friendship and amity. Conformity with municipal law. Establishment of commission. Specialists exchange. Teacher and student exchange. Institute establishment. Scholarships and grants. Exchange. General cultural cooperation. Artists. Scientific exchange.
PARTIES:
Afghanistan
USA (United States)

104655 Bilateral Treaty **321 UNTS 77**
SIGNED: 18 Jan 58 FORCE: 5 Oct 58
REGISTERED: 3 Feb 59 USSR (Soviet Union)

ARTICLES: 51 LANGUAGE: Russian. Persian.
HEADNOTE: SOVIET-AFGHAN FRONTIERS
TOPIC: Visas
CONCEPTS: Annex or appendix reference. Border traffic and migration. General cooperation. Establishment of commission. Fish, wildlife, and natural resources. Markers and definitions. Frontier waterways.
PROCEDURE: Amendment. Denunciation. Duration. Ratification.
PARTIES:
Afghanistan
USSR (Soviet Union)

104656 Bilateral Treaty **322 UNTS 3**
SIGNED: 15 Jul 58 FORCE: 4 Jan 59
REGISTERED: 3 Feb 59 USSR (Soviet Union)
ARTICLES: 77 LANGUAGE: Russian. Hungarian.
HEADNOTE: LEGAL ASSISTANCE CIVIL FAMILY CRIMINAL
TOPIC: Admin Cooperation
CONCEPTS: General provisions. Privileges and immunities. Consular functions in property. Extradition, deportation and repatriation. Extraditable offenses. Refusal of extradition. Concurrent requests. Provisional detainment. Extradition postponement. Witnesses and experts. Material evidence. Conformity with municipal law. Family law. Exchange of information and documents. Juridical personality. Legal protection and assistance. Recognition and enforcement of legal decisions. Immovable property. General property. Recognition of legal documents. Indemnities and reimbursements. Conveyance in transit.
PROCEDURE: Duration. Ratification. Termination.
PARTIES:
Hungary
USSR (Soviet Union)

104657 Bilateral Treaty **322 UNTS 105**
SIGNED: 25 Aug 58 FORCE: 4 Jan 59
REGISTERED: 3 Feb 59 USSR (Soviet Union)
ARTICLES: 76 LANGUAGE: Russian. Mongolian.
HEADNOTE: LEGAL ASSISTANCE CIVIL FAMILY CRIMINAL
TOPIC: Admin Cooperation
CONCEPTS: General provisions. Privileges and immunities. Consular functions in property. Extradition, deportation and repatriation. Extradition requests. Extraditable offenses. Refusal of extradition. Concurrent requests. Provisional detainment. Extradition postponement. Witnesses and experts. Material evidence. Conformity with municipal law. Family law. Exchange of information and documents. Juridical personality. Legal protection and assistance. Recognition and enforcement of legal decisions. Immovable property. General property. Indemnities and reimbursements. Assets transfer. Conveyance in transit.
PROCEDURE: Future Procedures Contemplated. Ratification.
PARTIES:
Mongolia
USSR (Soviet Union)

104658 Bilateral Convention **322 UNTS 201**
SIGNED: 25 Aug 58 FORCE: 4 Dec 58
REGISTERED: 3 Feb 59 USSR (Soviet Union)
ARTICLES: 10 LANGUAGE: Russian. Mongolian.
HEADNOTE: DUAL CITIZENSHIP
TOPIC: Consul/Citizenship
CONCEPTS: Resident permits. Alien status. Dual citizenship.
PROCEDURE: Ratification.
PARTIES:
Mongolia
USSR (Soviet Union)

104659 Bilateral Convention **322 UNTS 215**
SIGNED: 25 Aug 58 FORCE: 4 Dec 58
REGISTERED: 3 Feb 59 USSR (Soviet Union)
ARTICLES: 24 LANGUAGE: Russian. Mongolian.
HEADNOTE: CONSULAR CONVENTION
TOPIC: Consul/Citizenship
CONCEPTS: Definition of terms. General consular functions. Diplomatic privileges. Consular relations establishment. Inviolability. Privileges and immunities. Diplomatic correspondence. Responsibility and liability.

PROCEDURE: Ratification. Termination.
PARTIES:
Mongolia
USSR (Soviet Union)

104660 Multilateral Convention **322 UNTS 245**
SIGNED: 12 Jul 57   FORCE: 1 May 58
REGISTERED: 5 Feb 59 Denmark
ARTICLES: 15 LANGUAGE: Danish. Finnish. Swedish. Norwegian.
HEADNOTE: WAIVER PASSPORT CONTROL INTRA-NORDIC
TOPIC: Visas
CONCEPTS: Definition of terms. Territorial application. Time limit. Annex or appendix reference. Visa abolition. Border traffic and migration. Passports diplomatic. Passports non-diplomatic. Denial of admission. Resident permits. Non-visa travel documents. Alien status. Establishment of commission.
INTL ORGS: Special Commission.
PROCEDURE: Accession. Denunciation. Ratification.
PARTIES:
Denmark SIGNED: 12 Jul 57 FORCE: 1 May 58
Finland SIGNED: 12 Jul 57 FORCE: 1 May 58
Norway SIGNED: 12 Jul 57 FORCE: 1 May 58
Sweden SIGNED: 12 Jul 57 FORCE: 1 May 58

104661 Bilateral Agreement **322 UNTS 301**
SIGNED: 26 Jun 57   FORCE: 13 Jun 58
REGISTERED: 6 Feb 59 IBRD (World Bank)
ARTICLES: 5 LANGUAGE: English.
HEADNOTE: GUARANTEE HIGHWAY & PORT
TOPIC: IBRD Project
CONCEPTS: Definition of terms. Annex or appendix reference. Exchange of information and documents. Inspection and observation. Bonds. Fees and exemptions. Tax exemptions. Domestic obligation. Terms of loan. Loan regulations. Loan guarantee. Guarantor non-interference. Water transport. Roads and highways.
PARTIES:
Belgium
IBRD (World Bank)

104662 Bilateral Agreement **323 UNTS 4**
SIGNED: 9 May 58   FORCE: 12 Dec 58
REGISTERED: 6 Feb 59 IBRD (World Bank)
ARTICLES: 9 LANGUAGE: English.
HEADNOTE: LOAN HIGHWAY
TOPIC: IBRD Project
CONCEPTS: Default remedies. Definition of terms. Annex or appendix reference. Exchange of information and documents. Inspection and observation. Accounting procedures. Bonds. Fees and exemptions. Domestic obligation. Terms of loan. Loan regulations. Loan guarantee. Guarantor non-interference. Roads and highways.
PARTIES:
Honduras
IBRD (World Bank)

104663 Bilateral Agreement **323 UNTS 27**
SIGNED: 17 Sep 58   FORCE: 25 Nov 58
REGISTERED: 6 Feb 59 IBRD (World Bank)
ARTICLES: 5 LANGUAGE: English.
HEADNOTE: GUARANTEE PORT EXPANSION
TOPIC: IBRD Project
CONCEPTS: Definition of terms. Annex or appendix reference. Exchange of information and documents. Inspection and observation. Bonds. Fees and exemptions. Tax exemptions. Domestic obligation. Terms of loan. Loan regulations. Loan guarantee. Guarantor non-interference. Water transport.
PARTIES:
Peru
IBRD (World Bank)

104664 Bilateral Agreement **323 UNTS 51**
SIGNED: 17 Sep 58   FORCE: 21 Nov 58
REGISTERED: 6 Feb 59 IBRD (World Bank)
ARTICLES: 7 LANGUAGE: French.
HEADNOTE: LOAN THERMAL PROJECT
TOPIC: IBRD Project
CONCEPTS: Default remedies. Definition of terms. Annex or appendix reference. Exchange of information and documents. Informational records.

Accounting procedures. Bonds. Fees and exemptions. Interest rates. Domestic obligation. Terms of loan. Loan regulations. Loan guarantee. Guarantor non-interference. Hydro-electric power.
PARTIES:
Ceylon (Sri Lanka)
IBRD (World Bank)

104665 Bilateral Agreement **323 UNTS 71**
SIGNED: 22 Sep 58   FORCE: 11 Dec 58
REGISTERED: 6 Feb 59 IBRD (World Bank)
ARTICLES: 5 LANGUAGE: English.
HEADNOTE: GUARANTEE AGREEMENT
TOPIC: IBRD Project
CONCEPTS: Annex or appendix reference. Exchange of information and documents. Inspection and observation. Bonds. Fees and exemptions. Tax exemptions. Domestic obligation. Terms of loan. Loan regulations. Loan guarantee. Guarantor non-interference.
PARTIES:
Fed of Malaya
IBRD (World Bank)

104666 Bilateral Agreement **323 UNTS 99**
SIGNED: 22 Jan 58   FORCE: 20 Sep 58
REGISTERED: 9 Feb 59 IBRD (World Bank)
ARTICLES: 5 LANGUAGE: English.
HEADNOTE: GUARANTEE HYDROELECTRIC PROJECT
TOPIC: IBRD Project
CONCEPTS: Definition of terms. Annex or appendix reference. Exchange of information and documents. Inspection and observation. Bonds. Fees and exemptions. Tax exemptions. Domestic obligation. Terms of loan. Loan regulations. Loan guarantee. Guarantor non-interference. Hydro-electric power.
PARTIES:
Brazil
IBRD (World Bank)
ANNEX
599 UNTS 372. IBRD (World Bank). Interpretation 26 Apr 67.
599 UNTS 372. Brazil. Interpretation 26 Apr 67.

104667 Bilateral Agreement **323 UNTS 131**
SIGNED: 25 Jun 58   FORCE: 2 Oct 58
REGISTERED: 9 Feb 59 IBRD (World Bank)
ARTICLES: 5 LANGUAGE: English.
HEADNOTE: GUARANTEE PORT
TOPIC: IBRD Project
CONCEPTS: Annex or appendix reference. Exchange of information and documents. Inspection and observation. Bonds. Fees and exemptions. Tax exemptions. Domestic obligation. Terms of loan. Loan regulations. Loan guarantee. Guarantor non-interference. Water transport.
PARTIES:
India
IBRD (World Bank)

104668 Bilateral Agreement **323 UNTS 157**
SIGNED: 25 Jun 58   FORCE: 2 Oct 58
REGISTERED: 9 Feb 59 IBRD (World Bank)
ARTICLES: 5 LANGUAGE: English.
HEADNOTE: GUARANTEE PORT
TOPIC: IBRD Project
CONCEPTS: Annex or appendix reference. Exchange of information and documents. Inspection and observation. Bonds. Fees and exemptions. Tax exemptions. Domestic obligation. Terms of loan. Loan regulations. Loan guarantee. Guarantor non-interference. Water transport.
PARTIES:
India
IBRD (World Bank)

104669 Bilateral Agreement **323 UNTS 183**
SIGNED: 21 Jul 58   FORCE: 6 Jan 59
REGISTERED: 11 Feb 59 IBRD (World Bank)
ARTICLES: 8 LANGUAGE: English.
HEADNOTE: LOAN RAILWAY
TOPIC: IBRD Project
CONCEPTS: Default remedies. Definition of terms. Annex or appendix reference. Exchange of information and documents. Inspection and observation. Accounting procedures. Bonds. Fees and

exemptions. Interest rates. Domestic obligation. Terms of loan. Loan regulations. Loan guarantee. Guarantor non-interference. Railways.
PARTIES:
IBRD (World Bank)
Sudan

104670 Bilateral Agreement **323 UNTS 205**
SIGNED: 18 Aug 58   FORCE: 10 Oct 58
REGISTERED: 11 Feb 59 IBRD (World Bank)
ARTICLES: 5 LANGUAGE: English.
HEADNOTE: GUARANTEE STEEL
TOPIC: IBRD Project
CONCEPTS: Definition of terms. Annex or appendix reference. Exchange of information and documents. Inspection and observation. Bonds. Fees and exemptions. Tax exemptions. Domestic obligation. Terms of loan. Loan regulations. Loan guarantee. Guarantor non-interference. Industry.
PARTIES:
Japan
IBRD (World Bank)

104671 Bilateral Agreement **323 UNTS 235**
SIGNED: 16 Sep 58   FORCE: 14 Oct 58
REGISTERED: 11 Feb 59 IBRD (World Bank)
ARTICLES: 7 LANGUAGE: English.
HEADNOTE: LOAN RAILWAY
TOPIC: IBRD Project
CONCEPTS: Default remedies. Definition of terms. Annex or appendix reference. Exchange of information and documents. Inspection and observation. Accounting procedures. Bonds. Fees and exemptions. Interest rates. Domestic obligation. Terms of loan. Loan regulations. Loan guarantee. Guarantor non-interference. Railways.
PARTIES:
India
IBRD (World Bank)

104672 Bilateral Agreement **323 UNTS 253**
SIGNED: 23 Apr 58   FORCE: 26 Sep 58
REGISTERED: 11 Feb 59 IBRD (World Bank)
ARTICLES: 5 LANGUAGE: English.
HEADNOTE: GUARANTEE AGREEMENT
TOPIC: IBRD Project
CONCEPTS: Definition of terms. Annex or appendix reference. Family law. Exchange of information and documents. Bonds. Fees and exemptions. Tax exemptions. Domestic obligation. Terms of loan. Loan regulations. Loan guarantee. Guarantor non-interference.
PARTIES:
Pakistan
IBRD (World Bank)

104673 Bilateral Agreement **323 UNTS 297**
SIGNED: 10 Sep 58   FORCE: 22 Dec 58
REGISTERED: 11 Feb 59 IBRD (World Bank)
ARTICLES: 5 LANGUAGE: English.
HEADNOTE: GUARANTEE AGREEMENT
TOPIC: IBRD Project
CONCEPTS: Definition of terms. Annex or appendix reference. Exchange of information and documents. Inspection and observation. Bonds. Fees and exemptions. Tax exemptions. Domestic obligation. Terms of loan. Loan regulations. Loan guarantee. Guarantor non-interference.
PARTIES:
Japan
IBRD (World Bank)

104674 Bilateral Exchange **323 UNTS 331**
SIGNED: 9 Dec 58   FORCE: 1 Jan 59
REGISTERED: 11 Feb 59 Finland
ARTICLES: 2 LANGUAGE: English.
HEADNOTE: VISA FACILITIES
TOPIC: Visas
CONCEPTS: Time limit. Visa abolition. Resident permits. Conformity with municipal law.
TREATY REF: 322UNTS322; 305UNTS33.
PARTIES:
Canada
Finland

104675 Bilateral Exchange **323 UNTS 339**
SIGNED: 4 May 56   FORCE: 4 May 56
REGISTERED: 12 Feb 59 France

ARTICLES: 4 LANGUAGE: French. Portuguese.
HEADNOTE: REDEMPTION AGREEMENT
TOPIC: Finance
CONCEPTS: Detailed regulations. Annex or appendix reference. Expropriation. Responsibility and liability. Arbitration. Mediation and good offices. Accounting procedures. Bonds. Currency. Exchange rates and regulations. Claims and settlements. Debt settlement.
INTL ORGS: International Court of Justice. Arbitration Commission.
PARTIES:
Brazil
France
ANNEX
351 UNTS 450. Brazil. Interpretation 22 Dec 59.
351 UNTS 450. France. Interpretation 22 Dec 59.

104676 Bilateral Agreement **324 UNTS 3**
SIGNED: 2 Dec 58 FORCE: 12 Dec 58
REGISTERED: 17 Feb 59 IBRD (World Bank)
ARTICLES: 8 LANGUAGE: English.
HEADNOTE: LOAN AGREEMENT
TOPIC: IBRD Project
CONCEPTS: Default remedies. Definition of terms. Annex or appendix reference. Family law. Exchange of information and documents. Informational records. Accounting procedures. Bonds. Interest rates. Domestic obligation. Terms of loan. Loan regulations. Loan guarantee. Guarantor non-interference.
PARTIES:
IBRD (World Bank)
South Africa

104677 Bilateral Agreement **324 UNTS 25**
SIGNED: 2 May 58 FORCE: 3 Jul 58
REGISTERED: 17 Feb 59 IBRD (World Bank)
ARTICLES: 5 LANGUAGE: English.
HEADNOTE: GUARANTEE RAILWAY
TOPIC: IBRD Project
CONCEPTS: Definition of terms. Annex or appendix reference. Exchange of information and documents. Inspection and observation. Bonds. Fees and exemptions. Tax exemptions. Domestic obligation. Terms of loan. Loan regulations. Loan guarantee. Guarantor non-interference. Railways.
PARTIES:
IBRD (World Bank)
UK Great Britain

104678 Bilateral Agreement **324 UNTS 59**
SIGNED: 2 Jun 54 FORCE: 17 Nov 54
REGISTERED: 17 Feb 59 IBRD (World Bank)
ARTICLES: 5 LANGUAGE: English.
HEADNOTE: GUARANTEE AGREEMENT
TOPIC: IBRD Project
CONCEPTS: Definition of terms. Annex or appendix reference. Exchange of information and documents. Inspection and observation. Bonds. Fees and exemptions. Tax exemptions. Domestic obligation. Terms of loan. Loan regulations. Loan guarantee. Guarantor non-interference.
PARTIES:
Pakistan
IBRD (World Bank)

104679 Multilateral Protocol **324 UNTS 97**
SIGNED: 26 Jun 58 FORCE: 16 Aug 58
REGISTERED: 24 Feb 59 Denmark
ARTICLES: 4 LANGUAGE: Danish. Norwegian. Swedish.
HEADNOTE: MUTUAL ASSISTANCE CONDUCT LEGAL PROCEEDINGS
TOPIC: Admin Cooperation
CONCEPTS: General cooperation. Exchange of information and documents. Indemnities and reimbursements.
TREATY REF: 50LTS180; 227UNTS169; 3'2DM243;1.
PROCEDURE: Ratification.
PARTIES:
Denmark FORCE: 16 Aug 58
Norway FORCE: 16 Aug 58
Sweden FORCE: 16 Aug 58

104680 Bilateral Exchange **324 UNTS 111**
SIGNED: 24 Dec 58 FORCE: 24 Dec 58

REGISTERED: 24 Feb 59 New Zealand
ARTICLES: 2 LANGUAGE: English.
HEADNOTE: PROVISION FACILITIES ANTARCTIC EXPEDITIONS
TOPIC: Scientific Project
CONCEPTS: Use of facilities. Nuclear research. Research and development.
PARTIES:
New Zealand
USA (United States)
ANNEX
447 UNTS 356. USA (United States). Prolongation 18 Oct 60. Force 1 Jan 60.
447 UNTS 356. New Zealand. Prolongation 18 Oct 60. Force 1 Jan 60.

104681 Bilateral Agreement **324 UNTS 121**
SIGNED: 18 Dec 58 FORCE: 24 Jan 59
REGISTERED: 24 Jan 59 WHO (World Health)
ARTICLES: 6 LANGUAGE: English.
HEADNOTE: TECHNICAL ADVISORY ASSISTANCE
TOPIC: Tech Assistance
CONCEPTS: Exceptions and exemptions. Previous treaty replacement. Privileges and immunities. General cooperation. General property. Public information. Responsibility and liability. Specialists exchange. Professorships. Institute establishment. Scholarships and grants. Vocational training. Currency. Exchange rates and regulations. Expense sharing formulae. Financial programs. General technical assistance. Materials, equipment and services.
INTL ORGS: United Nations.
TREATY REF: 33UNTS261; 102UNTS117.
PROCEDURE: Amendment. Termination.
PARTIES:
Afghanistan
WHO (World Health)

104682 Bilateral Agreement **324 UNTS 133**
SIGNED: 27 Feb 59 FORCE: 27 Feb 59
REGISTERED: 27 Feb 59 United Nations
ARTICLES: 6 LANGUAGE: English.
HEADNOTE: OPERATIONAL EXECUTIVE PERSONNEL
TOPIC: Tech Assistance
CONCEPTS: Treaty implementation. Annex or appendix reference. Privileges and immunities. General cooperation. Personnel. Responsibility and liability. Arbitration. Procedure. Negotiation. Vocational training. Compensation. Expense sharing formulae. Tax exemptions. Customs exemptions. Domestic obligation. Special projects. Status of experts. Conformity with IGO decisions.
INTL ORGS: Permanent Court of Arbitration. Arbitration Commission.
PROCEDURE: Amendment. Termination.
PARTIES:
Ghana
United Nations

104683 Bilateral Agreement **324 UNTS 145**
SIGNED: 3 Jul 56 FORCE: 6 Jan 58
REGISTERED: 1 Mar 59 United Nations
ARTICLES: 10 LANGUAGE: French.
HEADNOTE: ACTIVITIES UNICEF
TOPIC: Direct Aid
CONCEPTS: Treaty implementation. Privileges and immunities. General cooperation. Exchange of information and documents. Informational records. Inspection and observation. Public information. Responsibility and liability. Procedure. Existing tribunals. Reexport of goods, etc.. Claims and settlements. Tax exemptions. Customs exemptions. Commodities and services. Assistance. General aid. Distribution. IGO status.
INTL ORGS: United Nations.
PARTIES:
Lebanon
UNICEF (Children)

104684 Bilateral Agreement **324 UNTS 161**
SIGNED: 18 May 52 FORCE: 9 Jan 54
REGISTERED: 1 Mar 59 United Nations
ARTICLES: 9 LANGUAGE: English.
HEADNOTE: ACTIVITIES UNICEF
TOPIC: Direct Aid
CONCEPTS: Informational records. Public information. Responsibility and liability. Procedure. Ex-

port quotas. Financial programs. Tax exemptions. Loan and credit. IGO status. Special status. Status of experts.
INTL ORGS: United Nations.
TREATY REF: 18UNTS387.
PROCEDURE: Amendment. Ratification.
PARTIES:
UNICEF (Children)
United Arab Rep

104685 Bilateral Agreement **324 UNTS 177**
SIGNED: 23 Nov 56 FORCE: 14 Dec 56
REGISTERED: 2 Mar 59 Japan
ARTICLES: 6 LANGUAGE: English. Japanese.
HEADNOTE: LEASE SPECIAL NUCLEAR MATERIAL
TOPIC: Atomic Energy
CONCEPTS: Non-prejudice to third party. Responsibility and liability. Indemnities and reimbursements. Currency. Payment schedules. Assets transfer. Acceptance of delivery. Nuclear materials. Transport of goods.
PROCEDURE: Duration.
PARTIES:
Japan
USA (United States)
ANNEX
371 UNTS 330. Japan. Supplementation 8 May 57. Force 20 May 57.
371 UNTS 330. USA (United States). Supplementation 8 May 57. Force 20 May 57.
383 UNTS 328. USA (United States). Supplementation 24 Aug 60. Force 24 Aug 60.
383 UNTS 328. Japan. Supplementation 24 Aug 60. Force 24 Aug 60.

104686 Bilateral Exchange **324 UNTS 205**
SIGNED: 20 Mar 58 FORCE: 1 Apr 58
REGISTERED: 2 Mar 59 Japan
ARTICLES: 4 LANGUAGE: German.
HEADNOTE: RECIPROCAL WAIVING PASSPORT VISAS VISA FEES
TOPIC: Visas
CONCEPTS: Time limit. Visa abolition. Passports diplomatic. Denial of admission. Conformity with municipal law. Fees and exemptions.
PROCEDURE: Termination.
PARTIES:
Austria
Japan

104687 Bilateral Agreement **324 UNTS 215**
SIGNED: 4 Feb 58 FORCE: 8 Apr 58
REGISTERED: 2 Mar 59 Japan
ARTICLES: 8 LANGUAGE: English.
HEADNOTE: COMMERCE
TOPIC: General Trade
CONCEPTS: Detailed regulations. Exceptions and exemptions. Privileges and immunities. Diplomatic correspondence. Conformity with municipal law. General cooperation. Scientific exchange. Export quotas. Import quotas. Reciprocity in trade. Reexport of goods, etc.. Trade procedures. Most favored nation clause. Taxation. General. Customs duties. Economic assistance. Passenger transport. Navigational conditions. Transport of goods. Merchant vessels. Inland and territorial waters. Shipwreck and salvage.
PROCEDURE: Duration. Ratification. Termination.
PARTIES:
India
Japan

104688 Bilateral Treaty **324 UNTS 227**
SIGNED: 20 Jan 58 FORCE: 15 Apr 58
REGISTERED: 2 Mar 59 Japan
ARTICLES: 7 LANGUAGE: Japanese. Indonesian. English.
HEADNOTE: TREATY PEACE
TOPIC: Peace/Disarmament
CONCEPTS: Treaty interpretation. Peaceful relations. Procedure. Existing tribunals. Negotiation. Payment schedules. Lump sum settlements. Most favored nation clause. Armistice and peace. Reparations and restrictions.
INTL ORGS: International Court of Justice.
PROCEDURE: Future Procedures Contemplated. Ratification.

PARTIES:
Indonesia
Japan

104689 Bilateral Agreement **324 UNTS 247**
SIGNED: 20 Jan 58   FORCE: 15 Apr 58
REGISTERED: 2 Mar 59 Japan
ARTICLES: 11 LANGUAGE: English.
HEADNOTE: REPARATIONS AGREEMENT
TOPIC: Reparations
CONCEPTS: Treaty implementation. Annex or appendix reference. Inviolability. Privileges and immunities. Non-diplomatic delegations. General cooperation. Use of facilities. Establishment of commission. Arbitration. Procedure. Reexport of goods, etc.. Payment schedules. Lump sum settlements. Tax exemptions. Loss and/or damage. Reparations and restrictions.
INTL ORGS: International Court of Justice. Arbitration Commission. Special Commission.
PROCEDURE: Ratification.
PARTIES:
Indonesia
Japan

104690   Bilateral Protocol   **325 UNTS 3**
SIGNED: 20 Jan 58   FORCE: 15 Apr 58
REGISTERED: 2 Mar 59 Japan
ARTICLES: 3 LANGUAGE: English.
HEADNOTE: CLAIM SETTLEMENT
TOPIC: Claims and Debts
CONCEPTS: Accounting procedures. Balance of payments. Claims and settlements.
TREATY REF: 324UNTS227.
PROCEDURE: Ratification.
PARTIES:
Indonesia
Japan

104691   Bilateral Exchange   **325 UNTS 13**
SIGNED: 20 Jan 58   FORCE: 15 Apr 58
REGISTERED: 2 Mar 59 Japan
ARTICLES: 2 LANGUAGE: English.
HEADNOTE: COMMERCIAL LOANS
TOPIC: Loans and Credits
CONCEPTS: Conformity with municipal law. General cooperation. Arbitration. Economic assistance. Materials, equipment and services. Loan and credit. Terms of loan.
TREATY REF: 324UNTS227.
PROCEDURE: Duration. Ratification. Renewal or Revival.
PARTIES:
Indonesia
Japan

104692   Bilateral Agreement   **325 UNTS 21**
SIGNED: 27 May 57   FORCE: 21 Apr 58
REGISTERED: 2 Mar 59 Japan
ARTICLES: 11 LANGUAGE: English.
HEADNOTE: CULTURAL AGREEMENT
TOPIC: Culture
CONCEPTS: Friendship and amity. General cooperation. Recognition of degrees. Teacher and student exchange. Professorships. Scholarships and grants. Exchange. General cultural cooperation. Artists. Research cooperation. Scientific exchange. Publications exchange. Mass media exchange.
PROCEDURE: Duration. Ratification. Renewal or Revival. Termination.
PARTIES:
Japan
Pakistan

104693   Bilateral Instrument   **325 UNTS 29**
SIGNED: 20 Sep 57   FORCE: 2 May 58
REGISTERED: 2 Mar 59 Japan
ARTICLES: 5 LANGUAGE: English.
HEADNOTE: SETTLEMENT CLAIMS
TOPIC: Reparations
CONCEPTS: Conformity with municipal law. Compensation. Lump sum settlements. Reparations and restrictions. Post-war claims settlement.
PARTIES:
Japan
Sweden

104694   Bilateral Treaty   **325 UNTS 35**
SIGNED: 6 Dec 57   FORCE: 9 May 58
REGISTERED: 2 Mar 59 Japan
ARTICLES: 15 LANGUAGE: Japanese. Russian.
HEADNOTE: DEVELOPMENT COMMERCE
TOPIC: General Economic
CONCEPTS: Detailed regulations. Exceptions and exemptions. Annex or appendix reference. Friendship and amity. Non-diplomatic delegations. Exchange of information and documents. Juridical personality. Legal protection and assistance. General property. Arbitration. Establishment of trade relations. Export quotas. Import quotas. Reciprocity in trade. Balance of payments. Most favored nation clause. General. Customs duties. Temporary importation. General transportation. Navigational conditions. Transport of goods. Licenses and certificates of nationality. Inland and territorial waters. Ports and pilotage. Shipwreck and salvage.
TREATY REF: 263UNTS99.
PROCEDURE: Duration. Ratification. Termination.
PARTIES:
Japan
USSR (Soviet Union)

104695   Bilateral Treaty   **325 UNTS 91**
SIGNED: 19 Dec 57   FORCE: 10 May 58
REGISTERED: 2 Mar 59 Japan
ARTICLES: 6 LANGUAGE: Japanese. French. Amharic.
HEADNOTE: FRIENDSHIP
TOPIC: General Amity
CONCEPTS: Friendship and amity. General cooperation. Procedure.
PROCEDURE: Future Procedures Contemplated. Ratification. Termination.
PARTIES:
Ethiopia
Japan

104696   Bilateral Exchange   **325 UNTS 103**
SIGNED: 24 Jul 58   FORCE: 1 Aug 58
REGISTERED: 2 Mar 59 Japan
ARTICLES: 4 LANGUAGE: English.
HEADNOTE: SIMPLIFICATION ENTRY SOJOURN
TOPIC: Visas
CONCEPTS: Exceptions and exemptions. Time limit. Denial of admission. Visas. General cooperation. Most favored nation clause.
PARTIES:
Japan
Philippines

104697   Bilateral Agreement   **325 UNTS 113**
SIGNED: 16 Apr 57   FORCE: 20 Nov 58
REGISTERED: 2 Mar 59 Japan
ARTICLES: 6 LANGUAGE: French.
HEADNOTE: CULTURAL AGREEMENT
TOPIC: Culture
CONCEPTS: Friendship and amity. Exchange. Teacher and student exchange. Professorships. Scholarships and grants. Exchange. General cultural cooperation. Artists. Athletes. Research cooperation. Scientific exchange. Publications exchange. Mass media exchange.
PROCEDURE: Duration. Ratification. Renewal or Revival. Termination.
PARTIES:
Iran
Japan

104698   Bilateral Agreement   **325 UNTS 119**
SIGNED: 9 Sep 58   FORCE: 26 Nov 58
REGISTERED: 2 Mar 59 Japan
ARTICLES: 7 LANGUAGE: English. Japanese.
HEADNOTE: TRADE COMMERCE
TOPIC: General Trade
CONCEPTS: Exceptions and exemptions. Treaty implementation. General cooperation. Licenses and permits. Procedure. Negotiation. Export quotas. Import quotas. Reciprocity in trade. Trade procedures. Quotas. Most favored nation clause.
TREATY REF: GATT; 55UNTS187.
PROCEDURE: Ratification. Termination.
PARTIES:
Japan
New Zealand

ANNEX
485 UNTS 361. Japan. Amendment 9 Mar 62. Force 2 Oct 62.
485 UNTS 361. New Zealand. Amendment 9 Mar 62. Force 2 Oct 62.

104699 Bilateral Agreement **325 UNTS 143**
SIGNED: 19 Jun 58   FORCE: 5 Dec 58
REGISTERED: 2 Mar 59 Japan
ARTICLES: 12 LANGUAGE: English. Japanese.
HEADNOTE: COOPERATION CIVIL USES ATOMIC ENERGY
TOPIC: Atomic Energy
CONCEPTS: Definition of terms. Previous treaty replacement. Non-prejudice to third party. Conformity with municipal law. Exchange of information and documents. Inspection and observation. Responsibility and liability. Investigation of violations. Research cooperation. Assets transfer. Nuclear materials. Non-nuclear materials. Peaceful use. Security of information.
TREATY REF: 240UNTS361.
PROCEDURE: Duration.
PARTIES:
Japan
USA (United States)

ANNEX
340 UNTS 414. USA (United States). Amendment 9 Oct 58. Force 17 Feb 59.
340 UNTS 414. Japan. Amendment 9 Oct 58. Force 17 Feb 59.
517 UNTS 332. USA (United States). Amendment 7 Aug 63. Force 21 Apr 64.
517 UNTS 332. Japan. Amendment 7 Aug 63. Force 21 Apr 64.

104700 Bilateral Agreement **325 UNTS 185**
SIGNED: 16 Jun 58   FORCE: 5 Dec 58
REGISTERED: 2 Mar 59 Japan
ARTICLES: 11 LANGUAGE: English. Japanese.
HEADNOTE: PEACEFUL USES ATOMIC ENERGY
TOPIC: Atomic Energy
CONCEPTS: Nuclear materials. Peaceful use.
PROCEDURE: Termination.
PARTIES:
Japan
UK Great Britain

104701 Bilateral Agreement **325 UNTS 221**
SIGNED: 9 Dec 58   FORCE: 9 Dec 58
REGISTERED: 2 Mar 59 Japan
ARTICLES: 5 LANGUAGE: Japanese. French. Persian.
HEADNOTE: ECONOMIC TECHNICAL COOPERATION
TOPIC: General Aid
CONCEPTS: Treaty interpretation. Exchange of information and documents. Exchange. Teacher and student exchange. Vocational training. Scientific exchange. General technical assistance. Economic assistance. Aid missions.
PROCEDURE: Duration. Termination.
PARTIES:
Iran
Japan

104702 Bilateral Agreement **325 UNTS 233**
SIGNED: 18 Dec 58   FORCE: 18 Dec 58
REGISTERED: 4 Mar 59 USA (United States)
ARTICLES: 1 LANGUAGE: English. Korean.
HEADNOTE: UTILITIES CLAIMS SETTLEMENT
TOPIC: Reparations
CONCEPTS: Definition of terms. Time limit. Treaty interpretation. Annex type material. Previous treaty replacement. Exchange of information and documents. Inspection and observation. Indemnities and reimbursements. Currency. Local currency. Tax exemptions. Customs exemptions. Loss and/or damage. Post-war claims settlement.
INTL ORGS: United Nations.
PROCEDURE: Registration.
PARTIES:
Korea, South
USA (United States)

104703 Bilateral Agreement **325 UNTS 253**
SIGNED: 26 Aug 58   FORCE: 26 Aug 58
REGISTERED: 9 Mar 59 Australia

ARTICLES: 10 LANGUAGE: English.
HEADNOTE: NEW TRADING RELATIONSHIP COMMERCE
TOPIC: General Trade
CONCEPTS: Detailed regulations. Exceptions and exemptions. Treaty implementation. Annex or appendix reference. General cooperation. Licenses and permits. Procedure. Negotiation. Export quotas. Import quotas. Trade procedures. Balance of payments. Exchange rates and regulations. Commodity trade. Quotas. Most favored nation clause. Customs duties.
TREATY REF: GATT.
PROCEDURE: Termination. Duration. Ratification. Termination.
PARTIES:
Australia
Fed of Malaya

104704 Multilateral Convention **325 UNTS 279**
SIGNED: 26 Jun 57 FORCE: 4 Mar 59
REGISTERED: 10 Mar 59 ILO (Labor Org)
ARTICLES: 21 LANGUAGE: English. French.
HEADNOTE: WEEKLY REST COMMERCE OFFICES
TOPIC: ILO Labor
CONCEPTS: Detailed regulations. Emergencies. Exceptions and exemptions. Treaty implementation. Exchange of information and documents. Domestic legislation. Investigation of violations. ILO conventions. Holidays and rest periods. Safety standards. Wages and salaries. Domestic obligation.
INTL ORGS: International Labour Organization. United Nations.
TREATY REF: 15UNTS40.
PROCEDURE: Amendment. Denunciation. Duration. Ratification. Registration. Renewal or Revival.
PARTIES:
Multilateral
ANNEX
330 UNTS 374. Costa Rica. Ratification 4 May 59. Force 4 May 60.
337 UNTS 444. Mexico. Ratification 1 Jun 59. Force 1 Jun 60.
348 UNTS 373. Guatemala. Ratification 9 Dec 59. Force 9 Dec 60.
353 UNTS 371. Pakistan. Ratification 15 Feb 60. Force 15 Feb 61.
366 UNTS 418. Honduras. Ratification 20 Jun 60. Force 20 Jun 61.
373 UNTS 378. Iraq. Ratification 5 Jul 60. Force 5 Jul 61.
373 UNTS 378. Bulgaria. Ratification 22 Jul 60. Force 22 Jul 61.
380 UNTS 472. Portugal. Ratification 24 Oct 60. Force 24 Oct 61.
401 UNTS 315. Israel. Ratification 19 Jun 61. Force 19 Jun 62.
410 UNTS 338. Kuwait. Ratification 21 Sep 61. Force 21 Sep 62.
413 UNTS 376. Syria. Ratification 30 Oct 61.
468 UNTS 439. Afghanistan. Ratification 16 May 63. Force 16 May 64.
475 UNTS 381. Italy. Ratification 12 Aug 63. Force 12 Aug 64.
541 UNTS 380. Brazil. Ratification 18 Jun 65. Force 18 Jun 66.
560 UNTS 324. Paraguay. Ratification 21 Mar 66. Force 21 Mar 67.
607 UNTS 366. USSR (Soviet Union). Ratification 22 Sep 67. Force 22 Sep 68.
630 UNTS 410. Iran. Ratification 22 Jan 68. Force 22 Jan 69.
640 UNTS 387. Ukrainian SSR. Ratification 19 Jun 68. Force 19 Jun 69.

104705 Bilateral Agreement **325 UNTS 295**
SIGNED: 21 Jan 59 FORCE: 1 Feb 59
REGISTERED: 11 Mar 59 Finland
ARTICLES: 8 LANGUAGE: Finnish. Norwegian.
HEADNOTE: UNEMPLOYMENT INSURANCE
TOPIC: Non-ILO Labor
CONCEPTS: Definition of terms. Detailed regulations. Exchange of information and documents. Domestic legislation. Recognition of legal documents. Wages and salaries. Non-ILO labor relations. Unemployment.
PROCEDURE: Termination.
PARTIES:
Finland
Norway

104706 Bilateral Agreement **325 UNTS 307**
SIGNED: 18 Nov 54 FORCE: 26 Oct 55
REGISTERED: 13 Mar 59 UK Great Britain
ARTICLES: 6 LANGUAGE: English. Portuguese.
HEADNOTE: NYASALAND-MOZAMBIQUE FRONTIER
TOPIC: Territory Boundary
CONCEPTS: Annex or appendix reference. Markers and definitions. Frontier waterways.
TREATY REF: 175UNTS13; 4LTS93.
PROCEDURE: Ratification.
PARTIES:
Portugal
UK Great Britain
ANNEX
450 UNTS 448. UK Great Britain. Correction 11 Jan 63.
450 UNTS 448. Portugal. Correction 11 Jan 63.
534 UNTS 441. Portugal. Acceptance 29 Nov 63. Force 29 Nov 63.
534 UNTS 441. UK Great Britain. Acceptance 29 Nov 63. Force 29 Nov 63.

104707 Bilateral Agreement **326 UNTS 3**
SIGNED: 3 Jul 58 FORCE: 4 Aug 58
REGISTERED: 13 Mar 59 UK Great Britain
ARTICLES: 12 LANGUAGE: English.
HEADNOTE: COOPERATION USES ATOMIC ENERGY MUTUAL DEFENSE PURPOSES
TOPIC: Atomic Energy
CONCEPTS: Definition of terms. Non-prejudice to third party. Exchange of information and documents. Responsibility and liability. Research cooperation. Research results. Laws and formalities. Nuclear materials. Atomic weapons. Security of information. Equipment and supplies.
TREATY REF: 214UNTS301; 229UNTS73; 252UNTS394.
PROCEDURE: Duration. Termination.
PARTIES:
UK Great Britain
USA (United States)
ANNEX
351 UNTS 458. UK Great Britain. Amendment 7 May 59. Force 20 Jul 59.
351 UNTS 458. USA (United States). Amendment 7 May 59. Force 20 Jul 59.

104708 Bilateral Convention **326 UNTS 23**
SIGNED: 10 Jul 56 FORCE: 1 May 58
REGISTERED: 13 Mar 59 UK Great Britain
ARTICLES: 50 LANGUAGE: English. French.
HEADNOTE: SOCIAL SECURITY
TOPIC: Non-ILO Labor
CONCEPTS: Definition of terms. Annex or appendix reference. Previous treaty replacement. Conformity with municipal law. Domestic legislation. Existing tribunals. Old age and invalidity insurance. Wages and salaries. Non-ILO labor relations. Family allowances. Administrative cooperation. Old age insurance. Sickness and invalidity insurance. Social security. Payment schedules. Claims and settlements.
INTL ORGS: International Court of Justice.
TREATY REF: 66UNTS151; 97UNTS155; 326UNTS64.
PROCEDURE: Denunciation. Duration. Future Procedures Contemplated. Ratification. Renewal or Revival.
PARTIES:
France
UK Great Britain
ANNEX
360 UNTS 416. UK Great Britain. Supplementation 23 Dec 59. Force 1 Jan 60.
360 UNTS 416. France. Supplementation 23 Dec 59. Force 1 Jan 60.
548 UNTS 365. UK Great Britain. Jersey Island. Force 15 Jul 59.
560 UNTS 270. France. Acknowledgement 19 Nov 65. Force 1 Dec 65.
560 UNTS 270. UK Great Britain. Guernsey Island. Force 1 Dec 65.
560 UNTS 270. UK Great Britain. Channel Islands. Force 1 Dec 65.

104709 Bilateral Convention **326 UNTS 69**
SIGNED: 24 May 58 FORCE: 1 Sep 58
REGISTERED: 13 Mar 59 UK Great Britain
ARTICLES: 41 LANGUAGE: English. Serbo-Croat.
HEADNOTE: SOCIAL SECURITY

TOPIC: Non-ILO Labor
CONCEPTS: Definition of terms. Conformity with municipal law. Domestic legislation. Dispute settlement. Public health. Old age and invalidity insurance. Wages and salaries. Non-ILO labor relations. Family allowances. Old age insurance. Sickness and invalidity insurance. Social security. Unemployment. Claims and settlements.
PROCEDURE: Denunciation. Duration. Ratification. Renewal or Revival.
PARTIES:
UK Great Britain
Yugoslavia

104710 Bilateral Convention **326 UNTS 119**
SIGNED: 29 Jan 57 FORCE: 1 Jul 58
REGISTERED: 13 Mar 59 UK Great Britain
ARTICLES: 40 LANGUAGE: English. Italian.
HEADNOTE: SOCIAL INSURANCE
TOPIC: Non-ILO Labor
CONCEPTS: Definition of terms. Exceptions and exemptions. Territorial application. General provisions. Conformity with municipal law. Domestic legislation. Old age and invalidity insurance. Sickness and invalidity insurance. Unemployment. Payment schedules.
INTL ORGS: International Court of Justice.
PARTIES:
Italy
UK Great Britain

104711 Multilateral Agreement **326 UNTS 169**
SIGNED: 5 Mar 56 FORCE: 12 Jun 57
REGISTERED: 13 Mar 59 UK Great Britain
ARTICLES: 5 LANGUAGE: English. French. German.
HEADNOTE: WAR CEMETERIES
TOPIC: Other Military
CONCEPTS: War graves. Upkeep of war graves. Establishment of war cemeteries.
INTL ORGS: Special Commission.
PARTIES:
Australia SIGNED: 5 Mar 56 FORCE: 12 Jun 57
Canada SIGNED: 5 Mar 56 FORCE: 12 Jun 57
France SIGNED: 5 Mar 56 FORCE: 12 Jun 57
Germany, West SIGNED: 5 Mar 56 FORCE: 12 Jun 57
India SIGNED: 5 Mar 56 FORCE: 12 Jun 57
New Zealand SIGNED: 5 Mar 56 FORCE: 12 Jun 57
Pakistan SIGNED: 5 Mar 56 FORCE: 12 Jun 57
South Africa SIGNED: 5 Mar 56 FORCE: 12 Jun 57
UK Great Britain SIGNED: 5 Mar 56 FORCE: 12 Jun 57

104712 Multilateral Agreement **326 UNTS 181**
SIGNED: 5 Mar 56 FORCE: 12 Jun 57
REGISTERED: 13 Mar 59 UK Great Britain
ARTICLES: 15 LANGUAGE: English. German.
HEADNOTE: WAR GRAVES
TOPIC: Other Military
CONCEPTS: Definition of terms. Recognition of legal documents. Establishment of commission. Tax exemptions. Customs exemptions. Burial arrangements. Upkeep of war graves. Establishment of war cemeteries.
INTL ORGS: Special Commission.
PARTIES:
Australia SIGNED: 5 Mar 56 FORCE: 12 Jun 57
Canada SIGNED: 5 Mar 56 FORCE: 12 Jun 57
Germany, West SIGNED: 5 Mar 56 FORCE: 12 Jun 57
India SIGNED: 5 Mar 56 FORCE: 12 Jun 57
New Zealand SIGNED: 5 Mar 56 FORCE: 12 Jun 57
Pakistan SIGNED: 5 Mar 56 FORCE: 12 Jun 57
South Africa SIGNED: 5 Mar 56 FORCE: 12 Jun 57
UK Great Britain SIGNED: 5 Mar 56 FORCE: 12 Jun 57

104713 Bilateral Convention **326 UNTS 209**
SIGNED: 22 Feb 51 FORCE: 30 Aug 51
REGISTERED: 13 Mar 59 UK Great Britain
ARTICLES: 37 LANGUAGE: English. Norwegian.
HEADNOTE: COUNSULAR
TOPIC: Consul/Citizenship
CONCEPTS: Alien status. General consular functions. Diplomatic missions. Privileges and immu-

nities. Protection of nationals. Consular functions in shipping.
TREATY REF: 63BFSP1051,1077.
PROCEDURE: Ratification. Termination.
PARTIES:
  Norway
  UK Great Britain

104714 Multilateral Convention **327 UNTS 3**
SIGNED: 12 May 54   FORCE: 26 Jul 58
REGISTERED: 13 Mar 59 UK Great Britain
ARTICLES: 21 LANGUAGE: English. French.
HEADNOTE: PREVENTION POLLUTION SEA OIL
TOPIC: Admin Cooperation
CONCEPTS: Default remedies. Definition of terms. Emergencies. Exceptions and exemptions. Territorial application. Treaty implementation. Annex or appendix reference. Informational records. Arbitration. Existing tribunals. Merchant vessels. Ports and pilotage. Naval vessels.
INTL ORGS: United Nations.
PROCEDURE: Amendment. Accession. Denunciation. Registration. Termination.
PARTIES:
  Belgium   SIGNED: 12 May 54   RATIFIED: 16 Apr 57 FORCE: 26 Jul 58
  Canada   SIGNED: 12 May 54   RATIFIED: 19 Dec 56 FORCE: 26 Jul 58
  Ceylon (Sri Lanka) SIGNED: 12 May 54
  Denmark   SIGNED: 12 May 54   RATIFIED: 26 Nov 56 FORCE: 26 Jul 58
  Finland SIGNED: 12 May 54
  France SIGNED: 12 May 54 RATIFIED: 26 Jul 57 FORCE: 26 Jul 58
  Germany, West Berlin RATIFIED: 11 Jun 56 FORCE: 26 Jul 58
  Germany, West SIGNED: 12 May 54 RATIFIED: 11 Jun 56 FORCE: 26 Jul 58
  Greece SIGNED: 12 May 54
  Ireland   SIGNED: 12 May 54   RATIFIED: 13 Feb 57 FORCE: 26 Jul 58
  Italy SIGNED: 12 May 54
  Japan SIGNED: 12 May 54
  Liberia SIGNED: 12 May 54
  Mexico   SIGNED: 12 May 54   RATIFIED: 10 May 56 FORCE: 26 Jul 58
  Netherlands Dutch New Guinea RATIFIED: 24 Jul 58 FORCE: 26 Jul 58
  Netherlands   SIGNED: 12 May 54   RATIFIED: 24 Jul 58 FORCE: 26 Jul 58
  New Zealand SIGNED: 12 May 54
  Sweden   SIGNED: 12 May 54   RATIFIED: 24 May 56 FORCE: 26 Jul 58
  UK Great Britain SIGNED: 12 May 54 RATIFIED: 6 May 55 FORCE: 26 Jul 58
  USSR (Soviet Union) SIGNED: 12 May 54
  Yugoslavia SIGNED: 12 May 54
              ANNEX
328 UNTS 343. Finland. Acceptance 30 Dec 58. Force 31 Mar 59.
390 UNTS 367. Poland. Acceptance 28 Feb 61. Force 28 May 61.
407 UNTS 278. USA (United States). Qualified Accession 8 Sep 61. Force 8 Dec 61.
415 UNTS 432. Kuwait. Acceptance 27 Nov 61. Force 27 Feb 62.
423 UNTS 322. Iceland. Acceptance 23 Feb 62. Force 23 May 62.
425 UNTS 358. Liberia. Qualified Accession 28 Mar 62. Force 28 Jun 62.
430 UNTS 500. Ghana. Acceptance 17 May 62. Force 17 Aug 62.
434 UNTS 339. Netherlands. Netherlands Antilles.
437 UNTS 366. Australia. Acceptance 29 Aug 62. Force 29 Nov 62.
463 UNTS 354. United Arab Rep. Acceptance 22 Apr 63. Force 22 Jul 63.
463 UNTS 354. Jordan. Acceptance 8 May 63. Force 8 Aug 63.
466 UNTS 403. Dominican Republic. Acceptance 29 May 63. Force 29 Aug 63.
479 UNTS 378. Panama. Acceptance 25 Sep 63. Force 25 Dec 63.
482 UNTS 383. Philippines. Acceptance 19 Nov 63. Force 19 Feb 63.
483 UNTS 346. Venezuela. Acceptance 12 Dec 63. Force 12 Mar 64.
486 UNTS 422. Algeria. Acceptance 20 Jan 64. Force 20 Apr 64.
486 UNTS 422. Spain. Acceptance 22 Jan 64. Force 22 Apr 64.

500 UNTS 321. Italy. Qualified Acceptance 25 May 64. Force 25 Aug 64.
525 UNTS 319. Madagascar. Acceptance 1 Feb 65. Force 1 May 65.
550 UNTS 406. Israel. Qualified Acceptance 11 Nov 65. Force 11 Feb 66.
551 UNTS 309. Switzerland. Acceptance 12 Jan 66. Force 12 Apr 66.
600 UNTS 332. Multilateral. Amendment 11 Apr 62. Force 11 Apr 62.
604 UNTS 374. Japan. Acceptance 21 Aug 67. Force 21 Nov 67.
619 UNTS 337. Nigeria. Acceptance 22 Jan 68. Force 22 Apr 68.

104715 Bilateral Agreement **327 UNTS 35**
SIGNED: 25 Nov 58   FORCE: 25 Nov 58
REGISTERED: 13 Mar 59 UK Great Britain
ARTICLES: 5 LANGUAGE: English.
HEADNOTE: LOAN
TOPIC: Loans and Credits
CONCEPTS: Definition of terms. Accounting procedures. Currency. Interest rates. Payment schedules. Loan and credit. Loan repayment. Volunteer programs.
PARTIES:
  Turkey
  UK Great Britain
              ANNEX
507 UNTS 300. Turkey. Amendment 31 Mar 64. Force 31 Mar 64.
507 UNTS 300. UK Great Britain. Amendment 31 Mar 64. Force 31 Mar 64.

104716 Bilateral Exchange **327 UNTS 43**
SIGNED: 19 May 58   FORCE: 19 May 58
REGISTERED: 13 Mar 59 UK Great Britain
ARTICLES: 2 LANGUAGE: English.
HEADNOTE: LOAN ARMS
TOPIC: Milit Assistance
CONCEPTS: Annex or appendix reference. Establishment of commission. Compensation. Indemnities and reimbursements. Materials, equipment and services. Military assistance. Return of equipment and recapture. Restrictions on transfer.
PROCEDURE: Future Procedures Contemplated.
PARTIES:
  Lebanon
  UK Great Britain

104717 Bilateral Agreement **327 UNTS 51**
SIGNED: 13 Jun 57   FORCE: 12 Oct 57
REGISTERED: 20 Mar 59 Pakistan
ARTICLES: 15 LANGUAGE: English. Persian.
HEADNOTE: RELATING AIR SERVICES
TOPIC: Air Transport
CONCEPTS: Definition of terms. Exceptions and exemptions. Annex or appendix reference. Conformity with municipal law. General cooperation. Exchange of information and documents. Licenses and permits. Recognition of legal documents. Arbitration. Procedure. Existing tribunals. Negotiation. Non-interest rates and fees. Most favored nation clause. Competency certificate. Routes and logistics. Navigational conditions. Permit designation. Air transport. Airworthiness certificates. Conditions of airlines operating permission. Overflights and technical stops. Operating authorizations and regulations. Licenses and certificates of nationality.
INTL ORGS: International Civil Aviation Organization. International Court of Justice.
TREATY REF: 15UNTS295; 84UNTS389.
PROCEDURE: Amendment. Future Procedures Contemplated. Ratification. Termination. Application to Non-self-governing Territories.
PARTIES:
  Afghanistan
  Pakistan

104718 Bilateral Exchange **327 UNTS 83**
SIGNED: 28 Sep 56   FORCE: 1 Jul 58
REGISTERED: 20 Mar 59 South Africa
ARTICLES: 4 LANGUAGE: English. German.
HEADNOTE: DOUBLE TAXATION INCOME AIRCRAFT
TOPIC: Taxation
CONCEPTS: Definition of terms. Taxation. Tax exemptions. Air transport. Merchant vessels.

PROCEDURE: Duration. Termination.
PARTIES:
  Germany, West
  South Africa

104719 Bilateral Agreement **327 UNTS 95**
SIGNED: 28 Mar 59   FORCE: 28 Mar 59
REGISTERED: 28 Mar 59 United Nations
ARTICLES: 6 LANGUAGE: English.
HEADNOTE: OPERATIONAL EXECUTIVE PERSONNEL
TOPIC: Tech Assistance
CONCEPTS: Treaty implementation. Annex or appendix reference. Privileges and immunities. General cooperation. Personnel. Responsibility and liability. Arbitration. Procedure. Negotiation. Vocational training. Compensation. Expense sharing formulae. Tax exemptions. Customs exemptions. Domestic obligation. Special projects. Status of experts. Conformity with IGO decisions.
INTL ORGS: Permanent Court of Arbitration.
PROCEDURE: Amendment. Termination.
PARTIES:
  United Nations
  Sudan
              ANNEX
388 UNTS 382. United Nations. Interpretation 21 Apr 59. Force 21 Apr 59.
388 UNTS 382. Sudan. Interpretation 12 Apr 59. Force 21 Apr 59.
547 UNTS 323. United Nations. Termination 13 Sep 65. Force 13 Sep 65.
547 UNTS 323. Sudan. Termination 13 Sep 65. Force 13 Sep 65.

104720 Bilateral Agreement **327 UNTS 107**
SIGNED: 27 Oct 58   FORCE: 20 Mar 59
REGISTERED: 6 Apr 59 Belgium
ARTICLES: 14 LANGUAGE: English. Dutch. Spanish.
HEADNOTE: CULTURAL AGREEMENT
TOPIC: Culture
CONCEPTS: Friendship and amity. Tourism. Establishment of commission. Procedure. Recognition of degrees. Exchange. Professorships. Institute establishment. Scholarships and grants. General cultural cooperation. Recognition. Publications exchange. Mass media exchange.
INTL ORGS: Special Commission.
PROCEDURE: Amendment. Duration. Ratification. Renewal or Revival. Termination.
PARTIES:
  Belgium
  Spain

104721 Multilateral Convention **327 UNTS 123**
SIGNED: 18 May 56   FORCE: 8 Apr 59
REGISTERED: 8 Apr 59 United Nations
ARTICLES: 45 LANGUAGE: English. French.
HEADNOTE: CUSTOMS CONVENTION COMMERCIAL ROAD VEHICLES
TOPIC: Customs
CONCEPTS: Definition of terms. Territorial application. Previous treaty renunciation. Arbitration. Negotiation. Temporary importation. Commercial road vehicles.
INTL ORGS: United Nations.
TREATY REF: 45UNTS149.
PROCEDURE: Amendment. Accession. Denunciation. Ratification. Registration.
PARTIES:
  Austria SIGNED: 18 May 56   RATIFIED: 10 Nov 57 FORCE: 8 Apr 59
  Belgium SIGNED: 18 May 56
  Cambodia RATIFIED: 8 Apr 59 FORCE: 7 Jul 59
  France SIGNED: 18 May 56
  Germany, West SIGNED: 18 May 56
  Hungary   SIGNED: 18 May 56   RATIFIED: 23 Jul 57 FORCE: 8 Apr 59
  Italy SIGNED: 18 May 56
  Luxembourg SIGNED: 18 May 56
  Netherlands SIGNED: 18 May 56
  Poland SIGNED: 18 May 56
  Sweden   SIGNED: 18 May 56   RATIFIED: 16 Jan 58 FORCE: 8 Apr 59
  Switzerland SIGNED: 18 May 56
  UK Great Britain SIGNED: 18 May 56
              ANNEX
328 UNTS 344. France. Ratification 20 May 59. Force 18 Aug 59.

328 UNTS 344. Poland. Qualified Ratification 6 May 59. Force 4 Aug 59.

338 UNTS 403. UK Great Britain. Ratification 30 Jul 59. Force 28 Oct 59.

338 UNTS 403. UK Great Britain. Jersey Island. Force 28 Oct 59.

338 UNTS 403. UK Great Britain. Guernsey Island. Force 28 Oct 59.

338 UNTS 403. UK Great Britain. Isle of Man. Force 28 Oct 59.

342 UNTS 362. Bulgaria. Qualified Accession 7 Oct 59. Force 5 Jan 60.

344 UNTS 358. UK Great Britain. British Somaliland. Force 4 Feb 60.

344 UNTS 358. UK Great Britain. Gibraltar. Force 4 Feb 60.

344 UNTS 358. UK Great Britain. North Borneo. Force 4 Feb 60.

344 UNTS 358. UK Great Britain. Seychelles. Force 4 Feb 60.

344 UNTS 358. UK Great Britain. Singapore. Force 4 Feb 60.

344 UNTS 358. UK Great Britain. Brunei. Force 4 Feb 60.

357 UNTS 394. UK Great Britain. Cyprus. Force 28 Jul 60.

357 UNTS 394. UK Great Britain. Gambia. Force 28 Jul 60.

366 UNTS 419. Switzerland. Qualified Ratification 7 Jul 60. Force 5 Oct 60.

371 UNTS 334. Netherlands. Ratification 27 Jul 60. Force 25 Oct 60.

374 UNTS 385. UK Great Britain. Sierra Leone. Force 11 Dec 60.

375 UNTS 372. UK Great Britain. Hong Kong. Force 20 Dec 60.

397 UNTS 336. Yugoslavia. Accession 12 Jun 61. Force 10 Sep 61.

406 UNTS 331. Greece. Accession 12 Sep 61. Force 11 Dec 61.

411 UNTS 320. Germany, West. Ratification 23 Oct 61. Force 21 Jan 62.

415 UNTS 433. Germany, West. Berlin.

423 UNTS 323. Sierra Leone. Succession 13 Mar 62.

424 UNTS 363. Italy. Ratification 29 Mar 62. Force 27 Jun 62.

434 UNTS 340. UK Great Britain. Kenya. Force 17 Oct 62.

434 UNTS 340. UK Great Britain. Uganda. Force 17 Oct 62.

453 UNTS 389. Belgium. Ratification 18 Feb 63. Force 19 May 63.

480 UNTS 374. Algeria. Qualified Accession 31 Oct 63. Force 29 Jan 64.

486 UNTS 423. Luxembourg. Ratification 28 Jan 64. Force 27 Apr 64.

545 UNTS 348. Cuba. Accession 16 Sep 65. Force 15 Dec 65.

551 UNTS 310. Romania. Qualified Accession 7 Jan 66. Force 7 Apr 66.

566 UNTS 342. Norway. Accession 11 Jul 66. Force 9 Oct 66.

601 UNTS 354. Ireland. Accession 26 Jul 67. Force 24 Oct 67.

104722 Bilateral Agreement **327 UNTS 185**
SIGNED: 28 Sep 56   FORCE: 28 Apr 58
REGISTERED: 20 Apr 59 ICAO (Civil Aviat)
ARTICLES: 17 LANGUAGE: Dutch. German.
HEADNOTE: CONCERNING AIR SERVICES
TOPIC: Air Transport
CONCEPTS: Definition of terms. Detailed regulations. Territorial application. Conformity with municipal law. General cooperation. Exchange of information and documents. Licenses and permits. Personnel. Arbitration. Procedure. Special tribunals. Reexport of goods, etc.. Indemnities and reimbursements. Fees and exemptions. Non-interest rates and fees. National treatment. Customs exemptions. Routes and logistics. Permit designation. Airport facilities. Conditions of airlines operating permission. Overflights and technical stops. Operating authorizations and regulations.
INTL ORGS: International Civil Aviation Organization.
PROCEDURE: Amendment. Denunciation. Future Procedures Contemplated. Ratification. Registration. Termination. Application to Non-self-governing Territories.

PARTIES:
Germany, West
Netherlands

104723 Bilateral Agreement **327 UNTS 227**
SIGNED: 13 Mar 57   FORCE: 13 May 57
REGISTERED: 20 Apr 59 ICAO (Civil Aviat)
ARTICLES: 22 LANGUAGE: French.
HEADNOTE: RELATING SCHEDULED AIR SERVICES
TOPIC: Air Transport
CONCEPTS: Definition of terms. Detailed regulations. Annex or appendix reference. Previous treaty replacement. Conformity with municipal law. General cooperation. Exchange of information and documents. Informational records. Licenses and permits. Recognition of legal documents. Use of facilities. Arbitration. Procedure. Special tribunals. Negotiation. Competence of tribunal. Indemnities and reimbursements. Non-interest rates and fees. Most favored nation clause. Customs exemptions. Competency certificate. Registration certificate. Routes and logistics. Navigational conditions. Airport facilities. Airworthiness certificates. Conditions of airlines operating permission. Operating authorizations and regulations. Licenses and certificates of nationality. Permit designation.
INTL ORGS: International Civil Aviation Organization. International Court of Justice.
PROCEDURE: Amendment. Future Procedures Contemplated. Ratification. Termination. Application to Non-self-governing Territories.

PARTIES:
Netherlands
Yugoslavia

104724 Bilateral Treaty **327 UNTS 245**
SIGNED: 15 Dec 54   FORCE: 10 May 57
REGISTERED: 21 Apr 59 India
ARTICLES: 16 LANGUAGE: Hindi. Persian. English.
HEADNOTE: COMMERCE NAVIGATION
TOPIC: General Economic
CONCEPTS: Exceptions and exemptions. Annex or appendix reference. Conformity with municipal law. Domestic legislation. General property. Procedure. Negotiation. Reciprocity in trade. Most favored nation clause. Customs duties. General transportation. Merchant vessels. Inland and territorial waters. Ports and pilotage. Military service and citizenship.
PROCEDURE: Duration. Ratification. Termination.

PARTIES:
India
Iran

104725 Bilateral Agreement **327 UNTS 277**
SIGNED: 5 Mar 59   FORCE: 5 Mar 59
REGISTERED: 23 Apr 59 USA (United States)
ARTICLES: 6 LANGUAGE: English.
HEADNOTE: AGREEMENT COOPERATION
TOPIC: General Military
CONCEPTS: General provisions. Aid and development. Domestic obligation. Defense and security. Military assistance.
TREATY REF: 233UNTS199.
PROCEDURE: Duration. Termination.

PARTIES:
Iran
USA (United States)

104726 Bilateral Agreement **327 UNTS 285**
SIGNED: 5 Mar 59   FORCE: 5 Mar 59
REGISTERED: 23 Apr 59 USA (United States)
ARTICLES: 6 LANGUAGE: English.
HEADNOTE: AGREEMENT COOPERATION
TOPIC: General Military
CONCEPTS: General provisions. Aid and development. Domestic obligation. Defense and security. Military assistance.
TREATY REF: 233UNTS199.
PROCEDURE: Duration. Termination.

PARTIES:
Pakistan
USA (United States)

104727 Bilateral Agreement **327 UNTS 293**
SIGNED: 5 Mar 59   FORCE: 5 Mar 59
REGISTERED: 23 Apr 59 USA (United States)

ARTICLES: 6 LANGUAGE: English.
HEADNOTE: COOPERATION
TOPIC: General Military
CONCEPTS: Friendship and amity. Defense and security.
PROCEDURE: Termination.
PARTIES:
Turkey
USA (United States)

104728 Bilateral Exchange **327 UNTS 301**
SIGNED: 8 Nov 58   FORCE: 8 Nov 58
REGISTERED: 27 Apr 59 UK Great Britain
ARTICLES: 2 LANGUAGE: English.
HEADNOTE: MALA REPRESENT INTERNAL SECURITY COUNCIL
TOPIC: Recognition
CONCEPTS: Status of state.
PARTIES:
Fed of Malaya
UK Great Britain

104729 Bilateral Treaty **328 UNTS 3**
SIGNED: 30 Jun 58   FORCE: 29 Mar 59
REGISTERED: 1 May 59 USSR (Soviet Union)
ARTICLES: 75 LANGUAGE: Russian. Albanian.
HEADNOTE: LEGAL ASSISTANCE CIVIL FAMILY CRIMINAL
TOPIC: Admin Cooperation
CONCEPTS: General provisions. Privileges and immunities. Extradition, deportation and repatriation. Court procedures. Location of crime. Concurrent requests. Limits of prosecution. Provisional detainment. Extradition postponement. Witnesses and experts. Material evidence. Conformity with municipal law. Family law. Exchange of information and documents. Juridical personality. Legal protection and assistance. Recognition and enforcement of legal decisions. General property. Succession. Recognition of legal documents. Indemnities and reimbursements. Assets transfer. Income taxes. Conveyance in transit.
PROCEDURE: Ratification.
PARTIES:
Albania
USSR (Soviet Union)

104730 Bilateral Agreement **328 UNTS 95**
SIGNED: 11 Oct 58   FORCE: 3 Jan 59
REGISTERED: 1 May 59 USSR (Soviet Union)
ARTICLES: 11 LANGUAGE: Russian. Arabic.
HEADNOTE: TRADE
TOPIC: General Trade
CONCEPTS: Detailed regulations. Exceptions and exemptions. General provisions. Annex or appendix reference. Conformity with municipal law. General cooperation. Licenses and permits. Establishment of trade relations. Import quotas. Trade procedures. Accounting procedures. Currency. Monetary and gold transfers. Payment schedules. Most favored nation clause. Customs duties. General transportation. Navigational conditions. Transport of goods. Ports and pilotage.
PROCEDURE: Duration. Ratification. Renewal or Revival. Termination.
PARTIES:
Iraq
USSR (Soviet Union)

104731 Bilateral Protocol **328 UNTS 117**
SIGNED: 11 Oct 58   FORCE: 11 Oct 58
REGISTERED: 1 May 59 USSR (Soviet Union)
ARTICLES: 9 LANGUAGE: Russian. Arabic.
HEADNOTE: TRADE DELEGATION
TOPIC: General Trade
CONCEPTS: Detailed regulations. Treaty implementation. Diplomatic privileges. Privileges and immunities. Non-diplomatic delegations. General property. Responsibility and liability. Trade procedures. Claims and settlements. General.
PROCEDURE: Termination.
PARTIES:
Iraq
USSR (Soviet Union)

104732 Bilateral Exchange **328 UNTS 133**
SIGNED: 12 Feb 59   FORCE: 12 Feb 59
REGISTERED: 6 May 59 Australia

ARTICLES: 2 LANGUAGE: English.
HEADNOTE: IMPORTATION MEAT
TOPIC: Commodity Trade
CONCEPTS: Detailed regulations. Import quotas. Commodity trade.
PARTIES:
Australia
Italy

104733 Bilateral Agreement **328 UNTS 143**
SIGNED: 4 Feb 59   FORCE: 11 Feb 59
REGISTERED: 22 May 59 IBRD (World Bank)
ARTICLES: 8 LANGUAGE: English.
HEADNOTE: LOAN POWER
TOPIC: IBRD Project
CONCEPTS: Definition of terms. Annex or appendix reference. Exchange of information and documents. Bonds. Interest rates. Debts. Debt settlement. Liens. World Bank projects. Loan regulations. Guarantor non-interference. Plans and standards.
PARTIES:
Denmark
IBRD (World Bank)

104734 Bilateral Convention **328 UNTS 167**
SIGNED: 12 Nov 57   FORCE: 23 May 59
REGISTERED: 25 May 59 Belgium
ARTICLES: 10 LANGUAGE: French.
HEADNOTE: EMPLOYMENT FAIR WORKERS
TOPIC: Non-ILO Labor
CONCEPTS: Resident permits. Conformity with municipal law. Licenses and permits. Non-ILO labor relations. Migrant worker.
PROCEDURE: Denunciation. Duration. Ratification. Renewal or Revival.
PARTIES:
Belgium
France

104735 Bilateral Convention **328 UNTS 173**
SIGNED: 17 Jan 58   FORCE: 30 May 59
REGISTERED: 30 May 59 Belgium
ARTICLES: 39 LANGUAGE: French. German.
HEADNOTE: EXTRADITION JUDICIAL ASSISTANCE
TOPIC: Extradition
CONCEPTS: Territorial application. Previous treaty replacement. Privileges and immunities. Nationality and citizenship. Extradition, deportation and repatriation. Extraditable offenses. Location of crime. Special factors. Refusal of extradition. Concurrent requests. Limits of prosecution. Provisional detainment. Extradition postponement. Witnesses and experts. Material evidence. Exchange of information and documents. Informational records. Legal protection and assistance. Procedure. Indemnities and reimbursements. Conveyance in transit.
PROCEDURE: Ratification. Termination.
PARTIES:
Belgium
Germany, West

104736 Bilateral Agreement **328 UNTS 227**
SIGNED: 23 Jul 58   FORCE: 13 Feb 59
REGISTERED: 2 Jun 59 Netherlands
ARTICLES: 10 LANGUAGE: Dutch. English.
HEADNOTE: EXCHANGE MONEY ORDERS
TOPIC: Postal Service
CONCEPTS: Territorial application. Accounting procedures. Compensation. Postal services. Regulations. Money orders and postal checks.
PROCEDURE: Duration. Termination.
PARTIES:
Australia
Netherlands

104737 Bilateral Exchange **328 UNTS 241**
SIGNED: 5 Mar 56   FORCE: 12 Jun 57
REGISTERED: 4 Jun 59 Australia
ARTICLES: 2 LANGUAGE: English. German.
HEADNOTE: CARE MAINTENANCE GRAVES
TOPIC: Other Military
CONCEPTS: Burial arrangements. Upkeep of war graves.
TREATY REF: 326UNTS181.

PARTIES:
Australia
Germany, West

104738 Multilateral Convention **328 UNTS 247**
SIGNED: 26 Jun 57   FORCE: 2 Jun 59
REGISTERED: 5 Jun 59 ILO (Labor Org)
ARTICLES: 37 LANGUAGE: English. French.
HEADNOTE: PROTECTION INTEGRATION TRIBAL GROUPS INTO NATION
TOPIC: ILO Labor
CONCEPTS: Definition of terms. Alien status. Human rights. Court procedures. General cooperation. Legal protection and assistance. General property. Establishment of commission. Vocational training. ILO conventions. Anti-discrimination. Employment regulations. Social security. Socio-economic development.
INTL ORGS: Food and Agricultural Organization of the United Nations. International Labour Organization. United Nations Educational, Scientific and Cultural Organization. United Nations.
PARTIES:
Multilateral
ANNEX
349 UNTS 348.   Argentina.   Ratification 18 Jan 60. Force 18 Jan 61.
353 UNTS 372. Pakistan. Ratification 15 Feb 60. Force 15 Feb 61.
384 UNTS 384. Portugal. Ratification 22 Nov 60. Force 22 Nov 61.
386 UNTS 412. Peru. Ratification 6 Dec 60. Force 6 Dec 61.
413 UNTS 377. Syria. Ratification 30 Oct 61.
444 UNTS 347. Taiwan. Ratification 11 Oct 62. Force 11 Oct 63.
452 UNTS 371. Tunisia. Ratification 17 Dec 62. Force 17 Dec 63.
524 UNTS 368. Bolivia. Ratification 12 Jan 65. Force 12 Jan 66.
530 UNTS 423. Malawi. Ratification 22 Mar 65. Force 22 Mar 66.
541 UNTS 381. Brazil. Ratification 18 Jun 65. Force 18 Jun 66.
660 UNTS 429. Paraguay. Ratification 20 Feb 69.

104739 Multilateral Convention **330 UNTS 3**
SIGNED: 10 Jun 58   FORCE: 7 Jun 59
REGISTERED: 7 Jun 59 United Nations
ARTICLES: 16 LANGUAGE: English. French. Chinese. Russian. Spanish.
HEADNOTE: RECOGNITION ENFORCEMENT FOREIGN ARBITRAL AWARDS
TOPIC: Admin Cooperation
CONCEPTS: Definition of terms. Exceptions and exemptions. Territorial application. Previous treaty replacement. Recognition and enforcement of legal decisions. Prizes and arbitral awards. Arbitration. Competence of tribunal.
INTL ORGS: United Nations.
TREATY REF: 27LTS157; 92LTS301.
PROCEDURE: Accession. Denunciation. Ratification.
PARTIES:
Argentina SIGNED: 26 Aug 58
Belgium SIGNED: 10 Jun 58
Bulgaria SIGNED: 17 Dec 58
Byelorussia SIGNED: 29 Dec 58
Ceylon (Sri Lanka) SIGNED: 30 Dec 58
Costa Rica SIGNED: 10 Jun 58
Czechoslovakia SIGNED: 3 Oct 58
Ecuador SIGNED: 17 Dec 58
El Salvador SIGNED: 10 Jun 58
Finland SIGNED: 29 Dec 58
France SIGNED: 25 Nov 58
Germany, West SIGNED: 10 Jun 58
India SIGNED: 10 Jun 58
Israel SIGNED: 10 Jun 58 RATIFIED: 5 Jan 59 FORCE: 7 Jun 59
Jordan SIGNED: 10 Jun 58
Luxembourg SIGNED: 11 Nov 58
Monaco SIGNED: 31 Dec 58
Netherlands SIGNED: 10 Jun 58
Pakistan SIGNED: 30 Dec 58
Philippines SIGNED: 10 Jun 58
Poland SIGNED: 10 Jun 58
ANNEX
336 UNTS 426.   France. Qualified Ratification 26 Jun 59. Force 24 Sep 59.
337 UNTS 445. Czechoslovakia. Qualified Ratification 10 Jul 59. Force 8 Oct 59.

346 UNTS 357. Thailand. Accession 21 Dec 59. Force 20 Mar 60.
348 UNTS 374. Cambodia. Accession 5 Jan 60. Force 4 Apr 60.
368 UNTS 371. India. Qualified Ratification 13 Jul 60. Force 11 Oct 60.
374 UNTS 386. USSR (Soviet Union). Qualified Ratification 24 Aug 60. Force 22 Nov 60.
376 UNTS 454. Ukrainian SSR. Qualified Ratification 10 Oct 60. Force 8 Jan 61.
380 UNTS 473. Byelorussia. Qualified Ratification 15 Nov 60. Force 13 Feb 61.
390 UNTS 368. Norway. Qualified Accession 14 Mar 61. Force 12 Jun 61.
395 UNTS 274. Austria. Qualified Accession 2 May 61. Force 31 Jul 61.
398 UNTS 351. Japan. Qualified Accession 20 Jun 61. Force 18 Sep 61.
399 UNTS 286. Germany, West. Qualified Ratification 30 Jun 61. Force 28 Sep 61.
406 UNTS 332. Romania. Qualified Accession 13 Sep 61. Force 12 Dec 61.
410 UNTS 339. Poland. Ratification 3 Oct 61. Force 1 Jan 62.
410 UNTS 339. Bulgaria. Qualified Ratification 10 Oct 61. Force 8 Jan 62.
418 UNTS 400. Ecuador. Ratification 3 Jan 62. Force 3 Apr 62.
419 UNTS 358. Finland. Ratification 19 Jan 62. Force 19 Apr 62.
423 UNTS 324. Hungary. Qualified Accession 5 Mar 62. Force 3 Jun 62.
425 UNTS 359. Ceylon (Sri Lanka). Ratification 9 Apr 62. Force 8 Jul 62.
433 UNTS 371. Greece. Accession 16 Jul 62. Force 14 Oct 62.
433 UNTS 371. Madagascar. Qualified Accession 16 Jul 62. Force 14 Oct 62.
442 UNTS 333. Central Afri Rep. Qualified Accession 15 Oct 62. Force 13 Jan 63.
494 UNTS 321. Netherlands. Qualified Ratification 24 Apr 64. Force 23 Jul 64.
494 UNTS 321. Netherlands. Netherlands Antilles. Force 23 Jul 64.
494 UNTS 321. Netherlands. Surinam. Force 23 Jul 64.
511 UNTS 283. Tanzania. Qualified Accession 13 Oct 64. Force 11 Jan 65.
511 UNTS 283. Niger. Accession 14 Oct 64. Force 12 Jan 65.
536 UNTS 477. Switzerland. Qualified Ratification 1 Jun 65. Force 30 Aug 65.
555 UNTS 254. Trinidad/Tobago. Qualified Accession 14 Feb 66. Force 15 May 66.
600 UNTS 356. Philippines. Qualified Ratification 6 Jul 67. Force 4 Oct 67.
601 UNTS 355. Tunisia. Qualified Accession 17 Jul 67. Force 15 Oct 67.
634 UNTS 432. Ghana. Accession 9 Apr 68.

104740 Bilateral Exchange **330 UNTS 83**
SIGNED: 4 Feb 58   FORCE: 16 Mar 59
REGISTERED: 10 Jun 59 Netherlands
ARTICLES: 2 LANGUAGE: Dutch.
HEADNOTE: REMOVAL UNDESIRABLE PERSONS
TOPIC: Extradition
CONCEPTS: Emergencies. Passports non-diplomatic. Denial of admission. Resident permits. Indemnities and reimbursements.
PROCEDURE: Denunciation.
PARTIES:
Belgium
Netherlands

104741 Bilateral Exchange **330 UNTS 101**
SIGNED: 29 Mar 58   FORCE: 29 Mar 58
REGISTERED: 10 Jun 59 Netherlands
ARTICLES: 2 LANGUAGE: French.
HEADNOTE: ABOLITION PASSPORTS VISAS
TOPIC: Visas
CONCEPTS: Emergencies. Visa abolition. Denial of admission. Resident permits. Non-visa travel documents.
TREATY REF: 252UNTS13.
PROCEDURE: Renewal or Revival. Termination.
PARTIES:
Netherlands
Switzerland

104742 Bilateral Agreement **330 UNTS 109**
SIGNED: 29 May 58   FORCE: 29 May 59

REGISTERED: 10 Jun 59 United Nations
ARTICLES: 6 LANGUAGE: English.
HEADNOTE: COOPERATION HEALTH MATTERS
TOPIC: Tech Assistance
INTL ORGS: Permanent Court of Arbitration.
PARTIES:
    Fed of Malaya
    United Nations
                    ANNEX
636 UNTS 367. United Nations. Termination
    10 May 68. Force 10 May 68.
636 UNTS 367. Malaya. Termination 10 May 68.
    Force 10 May 68.

104743 Multilateral Agreement **330 UNTS 121**
SIGNED: 18 Jan 54   FORCE: 30 May 58
REGISTERED: 15 Jun 59 UK Great Britain
ARTICLES: 16 LANGUAGE: English. French. Por-
tuguese.
HEADNOTE: ESTABLISH SUB-SAHARA TECHNI-
CAL COOPERATION COMMISSION
TOPIC: IGO Establishment
CONCEPTS: IGO constitution. Subsidiary organ.
INTL ORGS: Commission for Technical Co-opera-
tion in Africa South of the Sahara. International
Court of Justice. Special Commission.
PARTIES:
    Belgium   SIGNED: 18 Jan 54   RATIFIED:
      12 Jun 56 FORCE: 30 May 58
    Fed Rhod/Nyasaland SIGNED: 18 Jan 54 RATI-
      FIED: 3 Jan 55 FORCE: 30 May 58
    France   SIGNED: 18 Jan 54   RATIFIED:
      30 May 58 FORCE: 30 May 58
    Ghana RATIFIED: 18 Nov 57 FORCE: 30 May 58
    Liberia RATIFIED: 20 Nov 58 FORCE: 30 May 58
    Portugal   SIGNED: 18 Jan 54   RATIFIED.
      18 Jan 55 FORCE: 30 May 58
    South Africa SIGNED: 18 Jan 54 RATIFIED:
      10 Mar 54 FORCE: 30 May 58
    UK Great Britain SIGNED: 18 Jan 54 RATIFIED:
      12 Apr 54 FORCE: 30 May 58
                    ANNEX
431 UNTS 315.   Ivory   Coast.   Accession
    24 Feb 62.
431 UNTS 315. Nigeria. Accession 29 Jan 62.
431 UNTS 315.   Central   Afri   Rep.   Accession
    29 Jan 62.
431 UNTS 315.   Congo   (Zaire).   Accession
    24 Feb 62.
431 UNTS 315. Dahomey. Accession 5 Mar 62.
431 UNTS 315. Senegal. Accession 31 Jan 62.
431 UNTS 315.   Madagascar.   Accession
    2 Feb 62.
431 UNTS 315.   Congo   (Brazzaville).   Accession
    5 Feb 62.
431 UNTS 315. Mali. Accession 24 Feb 62.
431 UNTS 315.   Upper   Volta.   Accession
    24 Feb 62.
431 UNTS 315. Somalia. Accession 24 Feb 62.
431 UNTS 315. Mauritius. Accession 24 Feb 62.
431 UNTS 315. Gabon. Accession 26 Jan 62.
456 UNTS 499. Guinea. Accession 24 Feb 62.
456 UNTS 499.   Sierra   Leone.   Accession
    26 Jun 62.
456 UNTS 499.   Tanganyika.   Accession
    31 May 62.
456 UNTS 499. Chad. Accession 23 May 62.
551 UNTS 312. Cameroon. Accession 24 Feb 62.
560 UNTS 274. Belgium. Withdrawal 15 Apr 64.
    Force 15 Apr 65.
560 UNTS 274. France. Withdrawal 15 Apr 64.
    Force 15 Apr 65.
560 UNTS 274. UK Great Britain. Withdrawal
    15 Apr 64. Force 15 Apr 65.

104744 Bilateral Convention **330 UNTS 145**
SIGNED: 31 Dec 51   FORCE: 14 Jan 58
REGISTERED: 15 Jun 59 UK Great Britain
ARTICLES: 51 LANGUAGE: English. French.
HEADNOTE: CONSULAR CONVENTION
TOPIC: Consul/Citizenship
CONCEPTS: Definition of terms. Territorial applica-
tion. Previous treaty replacement. General con-
sular functions. Diplomatic privileges. Consular
relations establishment. Privileges and immuni-
ties. Consular functions in shipping. Consular
functions in property. Responsibility and liability.
Procedure.
INTL ORGS: International Court of Justice.
PROCEDURE: Ratification. Termination.

PARTIES:
    France
    UK Great Britain

104745   Bilateral Exchange   **330 UNTS 207**
SIGNED: 26 Jan 59   FORCE: 26 Jan 59
REGISTERED: 15 Jun 59 UK Great Britain
ARTICLES: 2 LANGUAGE: English. French.
HEADNOTE: REVISION PENAL SYSTEM NEW HEB-
RIDES
TOPIC: Admin Cooperation
CONCEPTS: Annex type material. Previous treaty
extension.
TREATY REF: 10LTS333.
PARTIES:
    France
    UK Great Britain

104746   Bilateral Exchange   **330 UNTS 213**
SIGNED: 26 Jan 59   FORCE: 26 Jan 59
REGISTERED: 15 Jun 59 UK Great Britain
ARTICLES: 2 LANGUAGE: English. French.
HEADNOTE: MINING   REGULATIONS   APPLIED
NEW HEBRIDES
TOPIC: Admin Cooperation
CONCEPTS: Detailed regulations. Previous treaty
replacement.
TREATY REF: 10LTS333; 16LTS213.
PARTIES:
    France
    UK Great Britain

104747   Bilateral Agreement   **330 UNTS 217**
SIGNED: 27 Feb 53   FORCE: 16 Sep 53
REGISTERED: 15 Jun 59 UK Great Britain
ARTICLES: 10 LANGUAGE: English. German.
HEADNOTE: CLAIM SETTLEMENT REGARDING
POST-WAR ECONOMIC ASSISTANCE
TOPIC: Claims and Debts
CONCEPTS: Annex or appendix reference. Re-
sponsibility and liability. Export quotas. Import
quotas. Financial programs. Payment schedules.
Claims and settlements. Lump sum settlements.
Debts. Debt settlement. Economic assistance.
Purchase authorization. Specific claims or waiv-
ers.
TREATY REF: 106UNTS141; UKTS 7 (1959)
CMD.626.
PROCEDURE: Amendment. Ratification.
PARTIES:
    Germany, West
    UK Great Britain
                    ANNEX
414 UNTS 391. UK Great Britain. Supplementa-
    tion 25 Apr 61. Force 25 Apr 61.
414 UNTS 391. Germany, West. Supplementa-
    tion 25 Apr 61. Force 25 Apr 61.

104748   Bilateral Convention   **330 UNTS 233**
SIGNED: 30 Jul 56   FORCE: 28 Dec 57
REGISTERED: 15 Jun 59 UK Great Britain
ARTICLES: 44 LANGUAGE: English. German.
HEADNOTE: CONSULAR CONVENTION
TOPIC: Consul/Citizenship
CONCEPTS: Definition of terms. Territorial applica-
tion. General provisions. General consular func-
tions. Diplomatic privileges. Consular relations
establishment. Privileges and immunities. Con-
sular functions in shipping. Consular functions in
property. Responsibility and liability. Arbitration.
Procedure. Existing tribunals.
INTL ORGS: International Court of Justice.
PROCEDURE: Amendment. Ratification. Termina-
tion.
PARTIES:
    Germany, West
    UK Great Britain

104749   Bilateral Agreement   **331 UNTS 3**
SIGNED: 7 Jul 58   FORCE: 19 Dec 58
REGISTERED: 15 Jun 59 UK Great Britain
ARTICLES: 15 LANGUAGE: English.
HEADNOTE: AIR SERVICES BETWEEN BEYOND
RESPECTIVE TERRITORIES
TOPIC: Air Transport
CONCEPTS: Conditions. Definition of terms. De-
tailed regulations. Exceptions and exemptions.
Annex or appendix reference. Conformity with
municipal law. General cooperation. Exchange

of information and documents. Arbitration. Procedure. Special tribunals. Negotiation. Monetary
and gold transfers. Non-interest rates and fees.
Most favored nation clause. National treatment.
Customs exemptions. Routes and logistics. Permit designation. Conditions of airlines operating
permission. Overflights and technical stops. Operating authorizations and regulations.
INTL ORGS: International Civil Aviation Organization.
TREATY REF: 15UNTS295.
PROCEDURE: Amendment. Future Procedures
Contemplated. Ratification. Registration. Termination. Application to Non-self-governing Territories.
PARTIES:
    Ethiopia
    UK Great Britain

104750   Bilateral Convention   **331 UNTS 21**
SIGNED: 20 Mar 54   FORCE: 1 Apr 55
REGISTERED: 15 Jun 59 UK Great Britain
ARTICLES: 38 LANGUAGE: English. Spanish.
HEADNOTE: CONSULAR CONVENTION
TOPIC: Consul/Citizenship
CONCEPTS: Definition of terms. Territorial applica-
tion. General provisions. General consular func-
tions. Diplomatic privileges. Consular relations
establishment. Privileges and immunities. Con-
sular functions in shipping. Consular functions in
property. Responsibility and liability. Procedure.
Existing tribunals.
INTL ORGS: International Court of Justice.
PROCEDURE: Ratification. Termination.
PARTIES:
    Mexico
    UK Great Britain

104751   Bilateral Exchange   **331 UNTS 119**
SIGNED: 1 Oct 58   FORCE: 1 Nov 58
REGISTERED: 15 Jun 59 UK Great Britain
ARTICLES: 2 LANGUAGE: English. French.
HEADNOTE: MUTUAL ABOLITION VISAS
TOPIC: Visas
CONCEPTS: Emergencies. Territorial application.
Visa abolition. Denial of admission. Conformity
with municipal law.
PROCEDURE: Denunciation.
PARTIES:
    Morocco
    UK Great Britain

104752   Bilateral Agreement   **331 UNTS 125**
SIGNED: 4 Feb 59   FORCE: 4 Feb 59
REGISTERED: 15 Jun 59 UK Great Britain
ARTICLES: 19 LANGUAGE: English. French. Ger-
man. Italian. Dutch.
HEADNOTE: COOPERATION   PEACEFUL   USES
ATOMIC ENERGY
TOPIC: Atomic Energy
CONCEPTS: Definition of terms. Non-prejudice to
third party. Conformity with municipal law. Ex-
change of information and documents. Licenses
and permits. Responsibility and liability. Re-
search cooperation. Nuclear research. Purchase
authorization. Nuclear materials. Non-nuclear
materials. Peaceful use.
INTL ORGS: European Nuclear Energy Agency. In-
ternational Atomic Energy Agency.
TREATY REF: 298UNTS167.
PROCEDURE: Duration. Termination.
PARTIES:
    Euratom
    UK Great Britain

104753   Bilateral Exchange   **331 UNTS 173**
SIGNED: 11 Apr 57   FORCE: 11 Apr 57
REGISTERED: 15 Jun 59 UK Great Britain
ARTICLES: 2 LANGUAGE: English. German.
HEADNOTE: DISBANDMENT CIVILIAN SERVICE
ORGANIZATIONS
TOPIC: Status of Forces
CONCEPTS: Exceptions and exemptions. Non-ILO
labor relations. Status of military forces.
TREATY REF: 199UNTS67.
PROCEDURE: Future Procedures Contemplated.
PARTIES:
    Germany, West
    UK Great Britain

104754 Bilateral Exchange **331 UNTS 181**
SIGNED: 8 Oct 56 FORCE: 5 May 55
REGISTERED: 15 Jun 59 UK Great Britain
ARTICLES: 3 LANGUAGE: English.
HEADNOTE: RIGHTS AND OBLIGATIONS FOR-
EIGN FORCES FINANCE CONVENTION
TOPIC: Consul/Citizenship
CONCEPTS: Annex or appendix reference. Annex
type material.
TREATY REF: GBTS11 (1959) CMD654;
337UNTS4760; 4761.
PARTIES:
Denmark
UK Great Britain

104755 Bilateral Exchange **331 UNTS 192**
SIGNED: 9 Jan 56 FORCE: 5 May 55
REGISTERED: 15 Jun 59 UK Great Britain
ARTICLES: 3 LANGUAGE: English.
HEADNOTE: APPLICATION CONVENTION RIGHTS
OBLIGATIONS FOREIGN FORCES
TOPIC: Status of Forces
CONCEPTS: Annex or appendix reference. Status
of military forces.
TREATY REF: 332UNTS3.
PARTIES:
Canada
UK Great Britain
ANNEX
267 UNTS 394. UK Great Britain. Northern Ireland. Force 29 Jan 56.
267 UNTS 394. UK Great Britain. Channel Islands.
Force 29 Jan 56.
267 UNTS 394. France. French Somaliland. Force
11 Mar 56.
267 UNTS 394. France. Miquelon. Force
11 Mar 56.
267 UNTS 394. UK Great Britain. Isle of Man.
Force 29 Jan 56.
267 UNTS 394. France. Fr Equatorial Afri. Force
11 Mar 56.
267 UNTS 394. France. Cameroon. Force
11 Mar 56.
267 UNTS 394. France. Madagascar. Force
11 Mar 56.
267 UNTS 394. France. New Caledonia. Force
11 Mar 56.
267 UNTS 394. France. St. Pierre. Force
11 Mar 56.
267 UNTS 394. France. Togo. Force 11 Mar 56.

104756 Bilateral Exchange **331 UNTS 209**
SIGNED: 10 Nov 55 FORCE: 5 Nov 55
REGISTERED: 15 Jun 59 UK Great Britain
ARTICLES: 2 LANGUAGE: English. French.
HEADNOTE: STATUS FORCES
TOPIC: Status of Forces
CONCEPTS: Status of forces.
PROCEDURE: Termination.
PARTIES:
Belgium
UK Great Britain

104757 Multilateral Convention **331 UNTS 217**
SIGNED: 26 Jun 48 FORCE: 1 Aug 51
REGISTERED: 15 Jun 59 UK Great Britain
ARTICLES: 31 LANGUAGE: English. French.
HEADNOTE: PROTECTION LITERARY & ARTISTIC
WORKS
TOPIC: Culture
CONCEPTS: Definition of terms. Exceptions and
exemptions. Territorial application. Treaty inter-
pretation. Previous treaty replacement. Non-
prejudice to third party. Privileges and immuni-
ties. Conformity with municipal law. Domestic
legislation. Establishment of commission. Proce-
dure. Accounting procedures. Expense sharing
formulae. Laws and formalities. Recognition.
INTL ORGS: International Union for the Protection
of Literary and Artistic Works. International
Court of Justice.
TREATY REF: 2'12DM173; 123LTS233;P.
PROCEDURE: Amendment. Accession. Denunciation. Duration. Ratification.

PARTIES:
Australia SIGNED: 26 Jun 48
Austria SIGNED: 26 Jun 48 RATIFIED: 14 Oct 53
FORCE: 14 Oct 53
Belgium Belgian Colonies RATIFIED: 14 Feb 52
FORCE: 14 Feb 52
Belgium Ruanda-Urundi RATIFIED: 14 Feb 52
FORCE: 14 Feb 52
Belgium SIGNED: 26 Jun 48 RATIFIED:
20 Jun 51 FORCE: 1 Aug 51
Brazil SIGNED: 26 Jun 48 RATIFIED: 9 Jun 52
FORCE: 9 Jun 52
Canada SIGNED: 26 Jun 48
Czechoslovakia SIGNED: 26 Jun 48
Denmark SIGNED: 26 Jun 48
Finland SIGNED: 26 Jun 48
France Comoro Islands RATIFIED: 22 May 52
FORCE: 22 May 52
France French Cameroon RATIFIED: 22 May 52
FORCE: 22 May 52
France Fr Equatorial Afri RATIFIED: 22 May 52
FORCE: 22 May 52
France French Somaliland RATIFIED: 22 May 52
FORCE: 22 May 52
France French Togoland RATIFIED: 22 May 52
FORCE: 22 May 52
France French West Africa RATIFIED: 22 May 52
FORCE: 22 May 52
France New Hebrides Is RATIFIED: 22 May 52
FORCE: 22 May 52
France Madagascar RATIFIED: 22 May 52
FORCE: 22 May 52
France Morocco RATIFIED: 22 May 52 FORCE:
22 May 52
France New Caledonia RATIFIED: 22 May 52
FORCE: 22 May 52
France Oceania RATIFIED: 22 May 52 FORCE:
22 May 52
France SIGNED: 26 Jun 48 RATIFIED: 14 Mar 51
FORCE: 1 Aug 51
France St. Pierre RATIFIED: 22 May 52 FORCE:
22 May 52
France Tunisia RATIFIED: 22 May 52 FORCE:
22 May 52
Greece SIGNED: 26 Jun 48 RATIFIED:
14 Mar 51 FORCE: 1 Aug 51
Hungary SIGNED: 26 Jun 48
Iceland SIGNED: 26 Jun 48
India SIGNED: 26 Jun 48
Ireland SIGNED: 26 Jun 48
Israel RATIFIED: 24 Mar 50 FORCE: 24 Mar 50
Italy SIGNED: 26 Jun 48 FORCE: 12 Jul 53
Lebanon SIGNED: 26 Jun 48
Liechtenstein SIGNED: 26 Jun 48 RATIFIED:
10 Oct 50 FORCE: 1 Aug 51
Luxembourg SIGNED: 26 Jun 48 RATIFIED:
8 Apr 50 FORCE: 1 Aug 51
Monaco SIGNED: 26 Jun 48 RATIFIED:
27 Jun 51 FORCE: 1 Aug 51
Morocco SIGNED: 26 Jun 48
Netherlands SIGNED: 26 Jun 48
New Zealand SIGNED: 26 Jun 48
Norway SIGNED: 26 Jun 48
Pakistan SIGNED: 26 Jun 48
Philippines RATIFIED: 1 Aug 51 FORCE:
1 Aug 51
Portugal SIGNED: 26 Jun 48 RATIFIED: 1 Jul 61
FORCE: 1 Aug 51
Portugal All Territories SIGNED: 3 Aug 56
FORCE: 3 Aug 56
South Africa SIGNED: 26 Jun 48 RATIFIED:
29 Mar 50 FORCE: 1 Aug 51
Spain SIGNED: 26 Jun 48 RATIFIED: 30 Jun 51
FORCE: 1 Aug 51
Sweden SIGNED: 26 Jun 48
Switzerland SIGNED: 26 Jun 48 RATIFIED:
2 Jan 56 FORCE: 2 Jan 56
Syria SIGNED: 26 Jun 48
Tunisia SIGNED: 26 Jun 48
Turkey RATIFIED: 1 Jan 52 FORCE: 1 Jan 52
UK Great Britain SIGNED: 26 Jun 48 RATIFIED:
15 Dec 57 FORCE: 15 Dec 57
Vatican/Holy See SIGNED: 26 Jun 48 RATIFIED:
20 Jun 51 FORCE: 1 Aug 51
Yugoslavia SIGNED: 28 Jun 51 RATIFIED:
28 Jun 51 FORCE: 1 Aug 51
ANNEX
489 UNTS 392. UK Great Britain. Bermuda. Force
28 Jan 63.
489 UNTS 392. UK Great Britain. North Borneo.
Force 28 Jan 63.
489 UNTS 392. UK Great Britain. Zanzibar. Force
28 Jan 63.

551 UNTS 314. UK Great Britain. Bahamas. Force
19 Aug 63.
551 UNTS 314. UK Great Britain. St. Helena.
Force 18 Oct 63.
551 UNTS 314. UK Great Britain. Falkland Islands. Force 18 Oct 63.
551 UNTS 314. UK Great Britain. Seychelles.
Force 18 Oct 63.
551 UNTS 314. UK Great Britain. Brit Virgin Islands. Force 19 Aug 63.
551 UNTS 314. UK Great Britain. Kenya. Force
4 Nov 63.
642 UNTS 369. UK Great Britain. Mauritius. Force
27 Dec 64.

104758 Multilateral Protocol **331 UNTS 253**
SIGNED: 23 Oct 54 FORCE: 5 May 55
REGISTERED: 15 Jun 59 UK Great Britain
ARTICLES: 3 LANGUAGE: English. French. Ger-
man.
HEADNOTE: TERMINATION OCCUPATION
REGIME
TOPIC: Milit Occupation
CONCEPTS: Treaty implementation. Disarmament
and demilitarization. Withdrawal of occupation.
INTL ORGS: Allied Military Occupation.
PROCEDURE: Future Procedures Contemplated.
Ratification.
PARTIES:
France SIGNED: 23 Oct 54 RATIFIED: 5 May 55
FORCE: 5 May 55
Germany, West SIGNED: 23 Oct 54 RATIFIED:
20 Apr 55 FORCE: 5 May 55
UK Great Britain SIGNED: 23 Oct 54 RATIFIED:
5 May 55 FORCE: 5 May 55
USA (United States) SIGNED: 23 Oct 54 RATI-
FIED: 20 Apr 55 FORCE: 5 May 55

104759 Multilateral Convention **331 UNTS 327**
SIGNED: 23 Oct 54 FORCE: 5 May 55
REGISTERED: 15 Jun 59 UK Great Britain
ARTICLES: 11 LANGUAGE: English. French. Ger-
man.
HEADNOTE: TERMINATION OCCUPATION
TOPIC: Milit Occupation
CONCEPTS: Arbitration. Special tribunals. Disar-
mament and demilitarization. Control and occu-
pation machinery. Withdrawal of occupation.
INTL ORGS: Allied Military Occupation. United Na-
tions. Arbitration Commission.
PARTIES:
France SIGNED: 23 Oct 54 RATIFIED: 5 May 55
FORCE: 5 May 55
Germany, West SIGNED: 23 Oct 54 RATIFIED:
20 Apr 55 FORCE: 5 May 55
UK Great Britain SIGNED: 23 Oct 54 RATIFIED:
5 May 55 FORCE: 5 May 55
USA (United States) SIGNED: 23 Oct 54 RATI-
FIED: 20 Apr 55 FORCE: 5 May 55

104760 Multilateral Convention **332 UNTS 3**
SIGNED: 23 Oct 54 FORCE: 5 May 55
REGISTERED: 15 Jun 59 UK Great Britain
ARTICLES: 48 LANGUAGE: English. French. Ger-
man.
HEADNOTE: RIGHTS OBLIGATIONS FOREIGN
FORCES
TOPIC: Status of Forces
CONCEPTS: Definition of terms. Time limit. Annex
or appendix reference. Visa abolition. Inviolability. Privileges and immunities. Extradition, deportation and repatriation. Court procedures. Conformity with municipal law. General cooperation.
Recognition and enforcement of legal decisions.
General property. Private contracts. Use of facilities. Investigation of violations. Establishment of
commission. Disease control. Non-ILO labor relations. Meteorology. Currency. National treatment. Tax exemptions. Customs duties. Customs
exemptions. Materials, equipment and services.
Surplus property. Overflights and technical
stops. Driving permits. Roads and highways.
Bands and frequency allocation. Facilities and
equipment. Postal services. Defense and security. Military training. Security of information.
Surplus war property. Jurisdiction. Procurement
and logistics. Status of forces. Bases and facilities. Wildlife.
INTL ORGS: Arbitration Commission. Special Commission.
TREATY REF: 331UNTS4.

PROCEDURE: Amendment.
PARTIES:
France SIGNED: 23 Oct 54 RATIFIED: 5 May 55
FORCE: 5 May 55
Germany, West SIGNED: 23 Oct 54 RATIFIED:
20 Apr 55 FORCE: 5 May 55
UK Great Britain SIGNED: 23 Oct 54 RATIFIED:
5 May 55 FORCE: 5 May 55
USA (United States) SIGNED: 23 Oct 54 RATI-
FIED: 20 Apr 55 FORCE: 5 May 55
ANNEX
481 UNTS 589. USA (United States). Abrogation
17 Aug 61. Force 1 Jul 63.
481 UNTS 589. Germany, West. Abrogation
21 May 63. Force 1 Jul 63.
481 UNTS 589. UK Great Britain. Abrogation
5 Jul 62. Force 1 Jul 63.
481 UNTS 589. France. Abrogation 24 Jan 62.
Force 1 Jul 63.

104761 Multilateral Convention **332 UNTS 157**
SIGNED: 23 Oct 54   FORCE: 5 May 55
REGISTERED: 15 Jun 59 UK Great Britain
ARTICLES: 19 LANGUAGE: English. French. German.
HEADNOTE: FINANCE CONVENTION
TOPIC: Milit Occupation
CONCEPTS: Definition of terms. Treaty implemen-
tation. Annex or appendix reference. General co-
operation. Exchange of information and docu-
ments. Legal protection and assistance. General
property. Responsibility and liability. Use of facil-
ities. Accounting procedures. Indemnities and
reimbursements. Expense sharing formulae.
Fees and exemptions. Claims and settlements.
Materials, equipment and services. Payment for
war supplies. Procurement and logistics. Status
of forces.
INTL ORGS: North Atlantic Treaty Organization.
Special Commission.
TREATY REF: 331UNTS253.
PROCEDURE: Amendment. Future Procedures
Contemplated.
PARTIES:
France SIGNED: 23 Oct 54 RATIFIED: 5 May 55
FORCE: 5 May 55
Germany, West SIGNED: 23 Oct 54 RATIFIED:
20 Apr 55 FORCE: 5 May 55
UK Great Britain SIGNED: 23 Oct 54 RATIFIED:
5 May 55 FORCE: 5 May 55
USA (United States) SIGNED: 23 Oct 54 RATI-
FIED: 20 Apr 55 FORCE: 5 May 55
ANNEX
481 UNTS 591. UK Great Britain. Abrogation
5 Jul 62. Force 1 Jul 63.
481 UNTS 591. Germany, West. Abrogation
21 May 63. Force 1 Jul 63.
481 UNTS 591. France. Abrogation 24 Jan 62.
Force 1 Jul 63.
481 UNTS 591. USA (United States). Abrogation
17 Aug 61. Force 1 Jul 63.

104762 Multilateral Convention **332 UNTS 219**
SIGNED: 23 Oct 54   FORCE: 5 May 55
REGISTERED: 15 Jun 59 UK Great Britain
ARTICLES: 58 LANGUAGE: English. French. Ger-
man.
HEADNOTE: WAR OCCUPATION
TOPIC: Reparations
CONCEPTS: Special tribunals. Operating authori-
zations and regulations. General military. Loss
and/or damage. Enemy financial interests. Repa-
rations and restrictions. Disarmament and
demilitarization. Industrial controls.
INTL ORGS: Allied Military Occupation. European
Coal and Steel Community. Arbitration Commis-
sion. Special Commission.
PARTIES:
France SIGNED: 23 Oct 54 RATIFIED: 5 May 55
FORCE: 5 May 55
Germany, West SIGNED: 23 Oct 54 RATIFIED:
20 Apr 55 FORCE: 5 May 55
UK Great Britain SIGNED: 23 Oct 54 RATIFIED:
5 May 55 FORCE: 5 May 55
USA (United States) SIGNED: 23 Oct 54 RATI-
FIED: 20 Apr 55 FORCE: 5 May 55

104763 Multilateral Agreement **332 UNTS 387**
SIGNED: 23 Oct 54   FORCE: 5 May 55
REGISTERED: 15 Jun 59 UK Great Britain

ARTICLES: 6 LANGUAGE: English. French. Ger-
man.
HEADNOTE: TAX TREATMENT
TOPIC: Status of Forces
CONCEPTS: Definition of terms. Arbitration. Proce-
dure. Negotiation. General. Tax exemptions. Cus-
toms exemptions. Status of military forces.
INTL ORGS: Arbitration Commission.
TREATY REF: 331UNTS253.
PROCEDURE: Future Procedures Contemplated.
PARTIES:
France SIGNED: 23 Oct 54 RATIFIED: 5 May 55
FORCE: 5 May 55
Germany, West SIGNED: 23 Oct 54 RATIFIED:
20 Apr 55 FORCE: 5 May 55
UK Great Britain SIGNED: 23 Oct 54 RATIFIED:
5 May 55 FORCE: 5 May 55
USA (United States) SIGNED: 23 Oct 54 RATI-
FIED: 20 Apr 55 FORCE: 5 May 55
ANNEX
481 UNTS 591. USA (United States). Abrogation
17 Aug 61. Force 1 Jul 63.
481 UNTS 591. Germany, West. Abrogation
21 May 63. Force 1 Jul 63.
481 UNTS 591. UK Great Britain. Abrogation
5 Jul 62. Force 1 Jul 63.
481 UNTS 591. France. Abrogation 24 Jan 62.
Force 1 Jul 63.

104764 Multilateral Agreement   **333 UNTS 3**
SIGNED: 27 Feb 53   FORCE: 16 Sep 53
REGISTERED: 15 Jun 59 UK Great Britain
ARTICLES: 38 LANGUAGE: English. French. German.
HEADNOTE: DEBTS
TOPIC: Claims and Debts
CONCEPTS: Definition of terms. Detailed regulations. Territorial application. Treaty implementation. Annex or appendix reference. Previous
treaty extension. General cooperation. Establish-
ment of commission. Arbitration. Currency. Mon-
etary and gold transfers. Exchange rates and reg-
ulations. Financial programs. Payment sched-
ules. Local currency. Claims and settlements.
Debts. Debt settlement. Assets transfer. Eco-
nomic assistance. Credit provisions. Post-war
claims settlement. Specific claims or waivers.
INTL ORGS: Allied Military Occupation. Arbitration
Commission. Special Commission.
TREATY REF: 333UNTS210; 333UNTS232.
PROCEDURE: Accession. Ratification. Registra-
tion.
PARTIES:
Australia Nauru RATIFIED: 24 Nov 54 FORCE:
24 Nov 54
Australia New Guinea RATIFIED: 24 Nov 54
FORCE: 24 Nov 54
Australia Norfolk Islands RATIFIED: 24 Nov 54
FORCE: 24 Nov 54
Australia Papua RATIFIED: 24 Nov 54 FORCE:
24 Nov 54
Australia RATIFIED: 29 Sep 54 FORCE:
29 Sep 54
Austria RATIFIED: 20 Aug 58 FORCE: 20 Aug 58
Belgium Belgian Colonies RATIFIED: 18 Jan 54
FORCE: 18 Jan 54
Belgium Ruanda-Urundi RATIFIED: 14 Nov 53
FORCE: 14 Nov 53
Belgium SIGNED: 27 Feb 53 RATIFIED:
18 Jan 54 FORCE: 18 Jan 54
Cambodia RATIFIED: 16 Jul 53 FORCE:
16 Sep 53
Canada SIGNED: 27 Feb 53 RATIFIED:
14 Nov 53 FORCE: 14 Nov 53
Ceylon (Sri Lanka) SIGNED: 27 Feb 53 RATIFIED:
10 Feb 55 FORCE: 10 Feb 55
Denmark SIGNED: 27 Feb 53 RATIFIED:
13 Oct 53 FORCE: 13 Oct 53
United Arab Rep RATIFIED: 11 May 53 FORCE:
16 Sep 53
Finland RATIFIED: 26 May 55 FORCE:
26 May 55
France All Territories RATIFIED: 16 Sep 53
FORCE: 16 Sep 53
France SIGNED: 27 Feb 53 RATIFIED: 19 Jun 53
FORCE: 16 Sep 53
Germany, West RATIFIED: 4 Sep 53 FORCE:
16 Sep 53
Germany, West Berlin RATIFIED: 5 Oct 53
FORCE: 5 Oct 53
Greece SIGNED: 27 Feb 53 RATIFIED: 21 Apr 56
FORCE: 21 Apr 56

Ireland SIGNED: 27 Feb 53 RATIFIED:
12 Nov 53 FORCE: 12 Nov 53
Israel RATIFIED: 23 Oct 56 FORCE: 23 Oct 56
Liechtenstein SIGNED: 27 Feb 53 RATIFIED:
31 Dec 53 FORCE: 31 Dec 53
Luxembourg SIGNED: 27 Feb 53 RATIFIED:
29 Jun 54 FORCE: 29 Jun 54
Netherlands RATIFIED: 1 Aug 58 FORCE:
1 Aug 58
New Zealand Cook Islands RATIFIED: 4 Oct 55
FORCE: 4 Oct 55
New Zealand RATIFIED: 4 Oct 55 FORCE:
4 Oct 55
New Zealand Tokelau Islands RATIFIED:
4 Oct 55 FORCE: 4 Oct 55
New Zealand Western Samoa RATIFIED:
4 Oct 55 FORCE: 4 Oct 55
Norway SIGNED: 27 Feb 53 RATIFIED: 8 Oct 53
FORCE: 8 Oct 53
Pakistan SIGNED: 27 Feb 53 RATIFIED:
27 Oct 53 FORCE: 27 Oct 53
Peru RATIFIED: 2 Dec 55 FORCE: 2 Dec 55
South Africa SIGNED: 27 Feb 53 FORCE:
1 Jan 54
South Africa Southwest Africa RATIFIED:
1 Jan 54 FORCE: 1 Jan 54
Spain SIGNED: 27 Feb 53 RATIFIED: 25 Aug 54
FORCE: 25 Aug 54
Sweden SIGNED: 27 Feb 53 FORCE: 16 Sep 53
Switzerland SIGNED: 27 Feb 53 RATIFIED:
31 Dec 53 FORCE: 30 Dec 53
UK Great Britain Aden RATIFIED: 12 Nov 56
FORCE: 12 Nov 56
UK Great Britain Channel Islands RATIFIED:
1 Apr 54 FORCE: 1 Apr 54
UK Great Britain Falkland Islands RATIFIED:
12 Nov 56 FORCE: 12 Nov 56
UK Great Britain Gibralter RATIFIED: 12 Nov 56
FORCE: 12 Nov 56
UK Great Britain Malta RATIFIED: 12 Nov 56
FORCE: 12 Nov 56
UK Great Britain Northern Rhodesia RATIFIED:
1 Oct 54 FORCE: 1 Oct 54
UK Great Britain Nyasaland RATIFIED: 1 Oct 54
FORCE: 1 Oct 54
UK Great Britain SIGNED: 27 Feb 53 RATIFIED:
4 Sep 53 FORCE: 16 Sep 53
UK Great Britain Southern Rhodesia RATIFIED:
16 Sep 53 FORCE: 16 Sep 53
UK Great Britain Trieste RATIFIED: 4 Jun 53
FORCE: 16 Sep 53
UK Great Britain Zanzibar RATIFIED: 12 Nov 56
FORCE: 12 Nov 56
USA (United States) All Territories RATIFIED:
16 Sep 53 FORCE: 16 Sep 53
USA (United States) SIGNED: 27 Feb 53 RATI-
FIED: 16 Sep 53 FORCE: 16 Sep 53
USA (United States) Trieste RATIFIED: 4 Jun 53
FORCE: 16 Sep 53
Yugoslavia SIGNED: 27 Feb 53 RATIFIED:
15 Mar 56 FORCE: 15 Mar 56
Yugoslavia Trieste RATIFIED: 31 Mar 54 FORCE:
31 Mar 54
ANNEX
437 UNTS 367. Thailand. Accession 20 Dec 58.
437 UNTS 367. Argentina. Accession 30 Dec 58.
437 UNTS 367. Netherlands. Surinam. Force
3 Mar 59.
437 UNTS 367. Netherlands. Dutch New Guinea.
Force 10 Jun 59.
437 UNTS 367. Netherlands. Netherlands Antilles. Force 24 Jun 59.
437 UNTS 367. United Arab Rep. Syria. Force
8 Jul 60.
551 UNTS 316. Chile. Accession 15 Oct 63.

104765 Multilateral Convention **334 UNTS 3**
SIGNED: 23 Oct 54   FORCE: 6 May 55
REGISTERED: 15 Jun 59 UK Great Britain
ARTICLES: 4 LANGUAGE: English. French. Ger-
man.
HEADNOTE: PRESENCE FOREIGN FORCES
TOPIC: Status of Forces
CONCEPTS: Time limit. Defense and security. Mili-
tary training. Jurisdiction. Procurement and lo-
gistics. Status of forces.
INTL ORGS: North Atlantic Treaty Organization.
TREATY REF: 34UNTS243.
PROCEDURE: Amendment. Accession. Duration.
Ratification.
PARTIES:
Belgium RATIFIED: 22 Apr 55 FORCE: 6 May 55
Canada RATIFIED: 3 May 55 FORCE: 6 May 55

Denmark RATIFIED: 4 May 55 FORCE: 6 May 55
France SIGNED: 23 Oct 54 RATIFIED: 5 May 55
FORCE: 6 May 55
Germany, West SIGNED: 23 Oct 54 RATIFIED:
20 Apr 55 FORCE: 6 May 55
Luxembourg RATIFIED: 4 May 55 FORCE:
6 May 55
Netherlands RATIFIED: 30 Apr 55 FORCE:
6 May 55
UK Great Britain SIGNED: 23 Oct 54 RATIFIED:
5 May 55 FORCE: 6 May 55
USA (United States) SIGNED: 23 Oct 54 RATI-
FIED: 20 Apr 55 FORCE: 6 May 55

104766 Multilateral Agreement **334 UNTS 13**
SIGNED: 25 Sep 56   FORCE: 6 Jun 58
REGISTERED: 17 Jun 59 ICAO (Civil Aviat)
ARTICLES: 26 LANGUAGE: English. French. Spanish.
HEADNOTE: JOINT FINANCING CERTAIN AIR NAV-
IGATION SERVICES ICELAND
TOPIC: Air Transport
CONCEPTS: Definition of terms. Annex or appendix reference. Privileges and immunities. General cooperation. Exchange of information and
documents. Responsibility and liability. Procedure. Existing tribunals. Negotiation.
Meteorology. Accounting procedures. Compensation. Indemnities and reimbursements. Currency. Exchange rates and regulations. Expense
sharing formulae. Fees and exemptions. Pay-
ment schedules. Navigational conditions. Navi-
gational equipment. Operating authorizations
and regulations.
INTL ORGS: International Civil Aviation Organization. International Monetary Fund. United Na-
tions.
TREATY REF: 15UNTS295; 33UNTS261.
PROCEDURE: Amendment. Accession. Termina-
tion.
PARTIES:
Australia RATIFIED: 5 Mar 59 FORCE: 5 Mar 59
Belgium SIGNED: 28 Nov 66
Canada SIGNED: 28 Nov 66 RATIFIED: 8 Feb 57
FORCE: 6 Jun 58
Denmark SIGNED: 28 Nov 66 RATIFIED:
18 Dec 57 FORCE: 6 Jun 58
France SIGNED: 28 Nov 66
Germany, West SIGNED: 28 Nov 66 RATIFIED:
10 Oct 57 FORCE: 6 Jun 58
Iceland SIGNED: 28 Nov 66 RATIFIED:
18 Feb 57 FORCE: 6 Jun 58
Israel SIGNED: 28 Nov 66 RATIFIED: 13 May 57
FORCE: 6 Jun 58
Italy SIGNED: 28 Nov 66 RATIFIED: 7 Feb 58
FORCE: 6 Jun 58
Netherlands SIGNED: 28 Nov 66 RATIFIED:
6 Jun 58 FORCE: 6 Jun 58
Norway SIGNED: 28 Nov 66 RATIFIED:
10 May 57 FORCE: 6 Jun 58
Sweden SIGNED: 28 Nov 66 RATIFIED:
10 May 57 FORCE: 6 Jun 58
Switzerland SIGNED: 28 Nov 66 RATIFIED:
16 May 58 FORCE: 6 Jun 58
UK Great Britain SIGNED: 28 Nov 66 RATIFIED:
18 Oct 57 FORCE: 6 Jun 58
USA (United States) SIGNED: 28 Nov 66 RATI-
FIED: 8 Feb 57 FORCE: 6 Jun 58
ANNEX
514 UNTS 285. Japan. Accession 28 Mar 63.
Force 28 Mar 63.
514 UNTS 285. France. Qualified Accession
20 Nov 62. Force 20 Nov 62.
514 UNTS 285. Pakistan. Accession 27 Nov 63.
Force 27 Nov 63.
514 UNTS 285. Ireland. Accession 3 Jun 60.
Force 3 Jun 60.

104767 Multilateral Agreement **334 UNTS 89**
SIGNED: 25 Sep 56   FORCE: 6 Jun 58
REGISTERED: 17 Jun 59 ICAO (Civil Aviat)
ARTICLES: 26 LANGUAGE: English. French. Span-
ish.
HEADNOTE: JOINT FINANCING CERTAIN AIR NAV-
IGATION SERVICES GREENLAND FAROE IS-
LANDS
TOPIC: Air Transport
CONCEPTS: Definition of terms. Annex or appen-
dix reference. Privileges and immunities. Gen-
eral cooperation. Exchange of information and
documents. Responsibility and liability. Proce-
dure. Existing tribunals. Negotiation.

Meteorology. Accounting procedures. Indemnities and reimbursements. Currency. Exchange
rates and regulations. Expense sharing formulae.
Fees and exemptions. Payment schedules. Laws
and formalities. Navigational conditions. Naviga-
tional equipment. Operating authorizations and
regulations.
INTL ORGS: International Civil Aviation Organiza-
tion. International Monetary Fund. United Na-
tions.
TREATY REF: 15UNTS295; 33UNTS261.
PROCEDURE: Amendment. Accession. Termina-
tion.
PARTIES:
Australia RATIFIED: 5 Mar 59 FORCE: 5 Mar 59
Belgium SIGNED: 28 Nov 66
Canada SIGNED: 28 Nov 66 RATIFIED: 8 Feb 57
FORCE: 6 Jun 58
Denmark SIGNED: 28 Nov 66 RATIFIED:
18 Dec 57 FORCE: 6 Jun 58
France SIGNED: 28 Nov 66
Germany, West SIGNED: 28 Nov 66 RATIFIED:
15 Oct 57 FORCE: 6 Jun 58
Iceland SIGNED: 28 Nov 66 RATIFIED:
18 Feb 57 FORCE: 6 Jun 58
Israel SIGNED: 28 Nov 66 RATIFIED: 13 May 57
FORCE: 6 Jun 58
Italy SIGNED: 28 Nov 66 RATIFIED: 7 Feb 58
FORCE: 6 Jun 58
Netherlands SIGNED: 28 Nov 66 RATIFIED:
6 Jun 58 FORCE: 6 Jun 58
Norway SIGNED: 28 Nov 66 RATIFIED:
10 May 57 FORCE: 6 Jun 58
Sweden SIGNED: 28 Nov 66 RATIFIED:
10 May 57 FORCE: 6 Jun 58
Switzerland SIGNED: 28 Nov 66 RATIFIED:
16 May 58 FORCE: 6 Jun 58
UK Great Britain SIGNED: 28 Nov 66 RATIFIED:
18 Oct 57 FORCE: 6 Jun 58
USA (United States) SIGNED: 28 Nov 66 RATI-
FIED: 8 Feb 57 FORCE: 6 Jun 58
ANNEX
514 UNTS 286. Ireland. Accession 3 Jun 60.
Force 3 Jun 60.
514 UNTS 286. Pakistan. Qualified Accession
27 Nov 63. Force 27 Nov 63.
514 UNTS 286. France. Acceptance 20 Nov 62.
Force 20 Nov 62.
514 UNTS 286. Japan. Qualified Accession
28 Mar 63. Force 28 Mar 63.

104768 Bilateral Agreement **334 UNTS 187**
SIGNED: 6 May 48   FORCE: 6 May 48
REGISTERED: 17 Jun 59 ICAO (Civil Aviat)
ARTICLES: 11 LANGUAGE: English. French.
HEADNOTE: AIR SERVICES BETWEEN TWO
COUNTRIES
TOPIC: Air Transport
CONCEPTS: Detailed regulations. Annex or appendix reference. Conformity with municipal law.
General cooperation. Licenses and permits. Recognition of legal documents. Use of facilities. Arbitration. Procedure. Existing tribunals. Negotiation. Fees and exemptions. Non-interest rates
and fees. Most favored nation clause. National
treatment. Customs exemptions. Competency
certificate. Routes and logistics. Navigational
conditions. Permit designation. Air transport. Airport facilities. Airworthiness certificates. Conditions of airlines operating permission. Operating
authorizations and regulations. Licenses and certificates of nationality.
INTL ORGS: International Civil Aviation Organization.
TREATY REF: 15UNTS295.
PROCEDURE: Future Procedures Contemplated.
Registration. Termination.
PARTIES:
Ireland
Switzerland
ANNEX
335 UNTS 356. Ireland. Amendment 30 Sep 57.
Force 7 Nov 57.
335 UNTS 356. Switzerland. Amendment
7 Nov 57. Force 7 Nov 57.

104769 Bilateral Agreement **334 UNTS 199**
SIGNED: 5 Mar 58   FORCE: 5 Mar 58
REGISTERED: 17 Jun 59 ICAO (Civil Aviat)
ARTICLES: 14 LANGUAGE: English.
HEADNOTE: RELATING AIR SERVICES
TOPIC: Air Transport

CONCEPTS: Definition of terms. Detailed regulations. Annex or appendix reference. Previous
treaty replacement. Conformity with municipal
law. General cooperation. Exchange of information and documents. Use of facilities. Arbitration.
Procedure. Existing tribunals. Negotiation. Reexport of goods, etc.. Non-interest rates and fees.
Most favored nation clause. National treatment.
Customs exemptions. Routes and logistics. Per-
mit designation. Air transport. Airport facilities.
Conditions of airlines operating permission.
Overflights and technical stops. Operating au-
thorizations and regulations.
INTL ORGS: International Civil Aviation Organiza-
tion. International Court of Justice.
TREATY REF: 15UNTS295; 84UNTS389;
35UNTS49.
PROCEDURE: Amendment. Future Procedures
Contemplated. Termination. Application to Non-
self-governing Territories.
PARTIES:
Norway
Pakistan

104770 Bilateral Agreement **334 UNTS 221**
SIGNED: 8 Feb 56   FORCE: 1 Apr 56
REGISTERED: 17 Jun 59 ICAO (Civil Aviat)
ARTICLES: 16 LANGUAGE: German. Polish.
HEADNOTE: AIR TRANSPORT
TOPIC: Air Transport
CONCEPTS: Definition of terms. Annex or appendix reference. Conformity with municipal law.
General cooperation. Informational records. Licenses and permits. Personnel. Recognition of
legal documents. Use of facilities. Fees and exemptions. Payment schedules. Non-interest
rates and fees. Customs exemptions. Competency certificate. Registration certificate. Routes
and logistics. Navigational conditions. Permit
designation. Air transport. Airport facilities. Airworthiness certificates. Conditions of airlines operating permission. Operating authorizations
and regulations. Licenses and certificates of nationality.
PROCEDURE: Amendment. Denunciation. Future
Procedures Contemplated. Termination.
PARTIES:
Austria
Poland

104771 Bilateral Agreement **334 UNTS 257**
SIGNED: 8 Jun 56   FORCE: 8 Jun 56
REGISTERED: 17 Jun 59 ICAO (Civil Aviat)
ARTICLES: 16 LANGUAGE: French.
HEADNOTE: CIVIL AIR TRANSPORT
TOPIC: Air Transport
CONCEPTS: Definition of terms. Annex or appendix reference. Conformity with municipal law.
General cooperation. Informational records. Licenses and permits. Personnel. Recognition of
legal documents. Use of facilities. Fees and exemptions. Non-interest rates and fees. Customs
exemptions. Registration certificate. Routes and
logistics. Navigational conditions. Permit designation. Air transport. Airport facilities. Airworthiness certificates. Conditions of airlines operating permission. Operating authorizations and
regulations.
PROCEDURE: Amendment. Denunciation. Termination.
PARTIES:
Poland
Sweden

104772 Bilateral Agreement **334 UNTS 277**
SIGNED: 8 Jun 59   FORCE: 8 Jun 59
REGISTERED: 17 Jun 59 United Nations
ARTICLES: 11 LANGUAGE: French.
HEADNOTE: ACTIVITIES UNICEF
TOPIC: Direct Aid
CONCEPTS: Privileges and immunities. Claims and
settlements. Tax exemptions. Commodities and
services.
INTL ORGS: United Nations.
PROCEDURE: Duration.
PARTIES:
Guinea
UNICEF (Children)

104773 Bilateral Agreement **334 UNTS 291**
SIGNED: 28 May 57 FORCE: 22 Mar 58
REGISTERED: 17 Jun 59 ICAO (Civil Aviat)
ARTICLES: 18 LANGUAGE: English.
HEADNOTE: CONCERNING CIVIL AVIATION
TOPIC: Air Transport
CONCEPTS: Exceptions and exemptions. Guarantees and safeguards. Representation. Annex or appendix reference. Previous treaty replacement. Conformity with municipal law. General cooperation. Informational records. Licenses and permits. Personnel. Recognition of legal documents. Use of facilities. Investigation of violations. Procedure. Negotiation. Humanitarian matters. Indemnities and reimbursements. Fees and exemptions. Customs exemptions. Registration certificate. Routes and logistics. Navigational conditions. Permit designation. Air transport. Airport facilities. Airworthiness certificates. Conditions of airlines operating permission. Operating authorizations and regulations. Licenses and certificates of nationality.
PROCEDURE: Amendment. Ratification. Termination.
PARTIES:
Hungary
Netherlands

104774 Bilateral Agreement **334 UNTS 307**
SIGNED: 2 Aug 57 FORCE: 2 Aug 57
REGISTERED: 17 Jun 59 ICAO (Civil Aviat)
ARTICLES: 15 LANGUAGE: French.
HEADNOTE: CIVIL AIR TRANSPORT
TOPIC: Air Transport
CONCEPTS: Definition of terms. Representation. Annex or appendix reference. Conformity with municipal law. General cooperation. Licenses and permits. Personnel. Recognition of legal documents. Use of facilities. Humanitarian matters. Fees and exemptions. Non-interest rates and fees. Customs exemptions. Registration certificate. Navigational conditions. Permit designation. Air transport. Airport facilities. Airworthiness certificates. Conditions of airlines operating permission. Operating authorizations and regulations.
PROCEDURE: Amendment. Denunciation. Termination.
PARTIES:
Hungary
Sweden

104775 Bilateral Agreement **335 UNTS 3**
SIGNED: 18 Oct 57 FORCE: 18 Oct 57
REGISTERED: 17 Jun 59 ICAO (Civil Aviat)
ARTICLES: 15 LANGUAGE: English.
HEADNOTE: AIR SERVICES BETWEEN BEYOND RESPECTIVE TERRITORIES
TOPIC: Air Transport
CONCEPTS: Conditions. Definition of terms. Detailed regulations. Exceptions and exemptions. Conformity with municipal law. General cooperation. Exchange of information and documents. Arbitration. Procedure. Existing tribunals. Negotiation. Monetary and gold transfers. Non-interest rates and fees. Most favored nation clause. National treatment. Customs exemptions. Routes and logistics. Permit designation. Conditions of airlines operating permission. Overflights and technical stops. Operating authorizations and regulations.
INTL ORGS: International Civil Aviation Organization.
TREATY REF: 15UNTS295.
PROCEDURE: Amendment. Future Procedures Contemplated. Registration. Termination. Application to Non-self-governing Territories.
PARTIES:
Fed of Malaya
UK Great Britain

104776 Bilateral Agreement **335 UNTS 23**
SIGNED: 7 Feb 58 FORCE: 7 Feb 58
REGISTERED: 17 Jun 59 ICAO (Civil Aviat)
ARTICLES: 14 LANGUAGE: English.
HEADNOTE: AIR SERVICES BETWEEN THROUGH RESPECTIVE TERRITORIES
TOPIC: Air Transport
CONCEPTS: Conditions. Definition of terms. Detailed regulations. Exceptions and exemptions. Territorial application. General cooperation. Exchange of information and documents. Arbitration. Procedure. Special tribunals. Negotiation. Non-interest rates and fees. National treatment. Customs exemptions. Routes and logistics. Permit designation. Conditions of airlines operating permission. Overflights and technical stops. Operating authorizations and regulations.
INTL ORGS: International Civil Aviation Organization. International Court of Justice.
TREATY REF: 15UNTS295.
PROCEDURE: Amendment. Future Procedures Contemplated. Registration. Termination. Application to Non-self-governing Territories.
PARTIES:
Australia
UK Great Britain
ANNEX
497 UNTS 364. UK Great Britain. Amendment 24 Jan 63. Force 24 Jan 63.
497 UNTS 364. Australia. Amendment 24 Jan 63. Force 24 Jan 63.

104777 Bilateral Agreement **335 UNTS 45**
SIGNED: 7 Feb 58 FORCE: 11 Aug 58
REGISTERED: 17 Jun 59 ICAO (Civil Aviat)
ARTICLES: 14 LANGUAGE: French.
HEADNOTE: AIR TRANSPORT
TOPIC: Air Transport
CONCEPTS: Territorial application. Guarantees and safeguards. Annex or appendix reference. Conformity with municipal law. General cooperation. Exchange of information and documents. Informational records. Licenses and permits. Personnel. Recognition of legal documents. Use of facilities. Procedure. Negotiation. Humanitarian matters. Reexport of goods, etc.. Indemnities and reimbursements. Fees and exemptions. Payment schedules. Non-interest rates and fees. Customs exemptions. Registration certificate. Routes and logistics. Navigational conditions. Permit designation. Air transport. Airport facilities. Airworthiness certificates. Conditions of airlines operating permission. Operating authorizations and regulations. Licenses and certificates of nationality.
PROCEDURE: Amendment. Denunciation. Ratification. Termination.
PARTIES:
Bulgaria
Netherlands

104778 Bilateral Agreement **335 UNTS 63**
SIGNED: 11 Jun 58 FORCE: 1 Sep 57
REGISTERED: 17 Jun 59 ICAO (Civil Aviat)
ARTICLES: 15 LANGUAGE: English. French.
HEADNOTE: REGARD AIR SERVICES
TOPIC: Air Transport
CONCEPTS: Definition of terms. Detailed regulations. Exceptions and exemptions. Previous treaty replacement. General cooperation. Exchange of information and documents. Non-interest rates and fees. Routes and logistics. Permit designation. Conditions of airlines operating permission. Operating authorizations and regulations.
TREATY REF: 201UNTS15.
PROCEDURE: Amendment. Termination. Application to Non-self-governing Territories.
PARTIES:
Belgium
South Africa

104779 Bilateral Agreement **335 UNTS 77**
SIGNED: 17 Jun 58 FORCE: 17 Jun 58
REGISTERED: 17 Jun 59 ICAO (Civil Aviat)
ARTICLES: 14 LANGUAGE: English. Russian. Dutch.
HEADNOTE: AIR SERVICES
TOPIC: Air Transport
CONCEPTS: Territorial application. Representation. Annex or appendix reference. Conformity with municipal law. General cooperation. Licenses and permits. Personnel. Recognition of legal documents. Humanitarian matters. Reexport of goods, etc.. Customs exemptions. Registration certificate. Routes and logistics. Navigational conditions. Permit designation. Airworthiness certificates. Conditions of airlines operating permission. Overflights and technical stops. Operating authorizations and regulations.
INTL ORGS: International Civil Aviation Organization.
PROCEDURE: Ratification. Termination.
PARTIES:
Netherlands
USSR (Soviet Union)

104780 Bilateral Exchange **335 UNTS 121**
SIGNED: 26 Sep 58 FORCE: 25 Nov 57
REGISTERED: 17 Jun 59 ICAO (Civil Aviat)
ARTICLES: 15 LANGUAGE: English.
HEADNOTE: RELATING AIR SERVICES
TOPIC: Air Transport
CONCEPTS: Definition of terms. Detailed regulations. Previous treaty replacement. General cooperation. Exchange of information and documents. Non-interest rates and fees. Routes and logistics. Permit designation. Conditions of airlines operating permission. Operating authorizations and regulations.
TREATY REF: 232UNTS143; 15UNTS295.
PROCEDURE: Amendment. Termination. Application to Non-self-governing Territories.
PARTIES:
Australia
South Africa

104781 Bilateral Exchange **335 UNTS 133**
SIGNED: 28 Aug 58 FORCE: 28 Aug 58
REGISTERED: 18 Jun 59 USA (United States)
ARTICLES: 2 LANGUAGE: English.
HEADNOTE: SETTLEMENT CLAIMS USE ON LOST VESSELS
TOPIC: Reparations
CONCEPTS: Compensation. Lump sum settlements. Naval vessels. Post-war claims settlement.
PARTIES:
Denmark
USA (United States)

104782 Bilateral Agreement **335 UNTS 139**
SIGNED: 16 Jul 58 FORCE: 16 Jul 58
REGISTERED: 18 Jun 59 USA (United States)
ARTICLES: 2 LANGUAGE: English. Spanish.
HEADNOTE: ALLOCATION ULTRA HIGH FREQUENCY CHANNELS TELEVISION STATIONS
TOPIC: Telecommunications
CONCEPTS: Bands and frequency allocation. Telecommunications.
PARTIES:
Mexico
USA (United States)

104783 Bilateral Agreement **335 UNTS 161**
SIGNED: 29 May 58 FORCE: 27 Aug 58
REGISTERED: 18 Jun 59 USA (United States)
ARTICLES: 3 LANGUAGE: English. French. German. Italian. Dutch.
HEADNOTE: COOPERATION PEACEFUL APPLICATIONS ATOMIC ENERGY
TOPIC: Atomic Energy
CONCEPTS: Definition of terms. Conformity with municipal law. Peaceful use.
TREATY REF: 298UNTS167.
PARTIES:
Euratom
USA (United States)

104784 Bilateral Exchange **335 UNTS 173**
SIGNED: 6 Sep 56 FORCE: 6 Sep 56
REGISTERED: 18 Jun 59 USA (United States)
ARTICLES: 2 LANGUAGE: English. French.
HEADNOTE: MILITARY RADIO BROADCASTING STATIONS
TOPIC: Milit Installation
CONCEPTS: Facilities and equipment. Exchange of defense information. Bases and facilities.
PARTIES:
France
USA (United States)

104785 Bilateral Exchange **335 UNTS 187**
SIGNED: 13 Aug 58 FORCE: 13 Aug 58
REGISTERED: 18 Jun 59 USA (United States)
ARTICLES: 2 LANGUAGE: English.
HEADNOTE: SALE MILITARY EQUIPMENT MATERIALS SERVICES
TOPIC: Milit Assistance
CONCEPTS: Non-prejudice to UN charter. Conformity with municipal law. Materials, equipment and services. Self-defense. Payment for war supplies. Military assistance. Restrictions on transfer.
INTL ORGS: United Nations.

PARTIES:
Indonesia
USA (United States)

104786 Bilateral Exchange **335 UNTS 193**
SIGNED: 24 Jun 58   FORCE: 24 Jun 58
REGISTERED: 18 Jun 59 USA (United States)
ARTICLES: 2 LANGUAGE: English.
HEADNOTE: SALE MILITARY EQUIPMENT MATE-
RIALS SERVICES
TOPIC: Milit Assistance
CONCEPTS: Non-prejudice to UN charter. Confor-
mity with municipal law. Materials, equipment
and services. Self-defense. Payment for war sup-
plies. Military assistance. Restrictions on trans-
fer.
PARTIES:
Burma
USA (United States)

104787 Bilateral Exchange **335 UNTS 199**
SIGNED: 17 Jul 58   FORCE: 17 Jul 58
REGISTERED: 18 Jun 59 USA (United States)
ARTICLES: 2 LANGUAGE: English.
HEADNOTE: RELOCATION AIR POST OFFICE
TOPIC: Specific Property
CONCEPTS: Military installations and equipment.
Facilities and property.
TREATY REF: 289UNTS296; 307UNTS326.
PARTIES:
Philippines
USA (United States)

104788 Multilateral Instrument **335 UNTS 205**
SIGNED: 28 Jul 58   FORCE: 28 Jul 58
REGISTERED: 18 Jun 59 USA (United States)
ARTICLES: 4 LANGUAGE: English.
HEADNOTE: DECLARATION RESPECTING BAGH-
DAD PACT
TOPIC: General Military
CONCEPTS: General cooperation. Economic assis-
tance. Defense and security. Military assistance.
INTL ORGS: Central Treaty Organization.
TREATY REF: 233UNTS199.
PROCEDURE: Future Procedures Contemplated.
PARTIES:
Iran SIGNED: 28 Jul 58 FORCE: 28 Jul 58
Pakistan SIGNED: 28 Jul 58 FORCE: 28 Jul 58
Turkey SIGNED: 28 Jul 58 FORCE: 28 Jul 58
UK Great Britain SIGNED: 28 Jul 58 FORCE:
28 Jul 58
USA (United States) SIGNED: 28 Jul 58 FORCE:
28 Jul 58

104789 Multilateral Agreement **335 UNTS 211**
SIGNED: 20 Mar 58   FORCE: 20 May 59
REGISTERED: 20 Jun 59 United Nations
ARTICLES: 15 LANGUAGE: English. French.
HEADNOTE: UNIFORM CONDITIONS RECOGNI-
TION MOTOR-VEHICLE EQUIPMENT PARTS
TOPIC: Admin Cooperation
CONCEPTS: Exceptions and exemptions. Stan-
dardization. Arbitration. Procedure. Negotiation.
INTL ORGS: United Nations.
PROCEDURE: Amendment. Accession. Denuncia-
tion. Ratification.
PARTIES:
France SIGNED: 26 Jun 58 FORCE: 20 Jun 59
Germany, West SIGNED: 19 Jun 58
Hungary SIGNED: 30 Jun 58
Italy SIGNED: 28 Mar 58
Netherlands SIGNED: 30 Jun 58
ANNEX
337 UNTS 446. Belgium. Qualified Accession
7 Jul 59. Force 5 Sep 59.
357 UNTS 395. Hungary. Qualified Ratification
3 May 60. Force 2 Jul 60.
358 UNTS 366. Czechoslovakia. Qualified Accession 12 May 60. Force 11 Jul 60.
363 UNTS 408. Netherlands. Ratification
30 Jun 60. Force 29 Aug 60.
372 UNTS 370. Multilateral. Force 8 Aug 60.
374 UNTS 387. Hungary. Acceptance 12 Sep 60.
Force 8 Aug 60.
390 UNTS 369. Czechoslovakia. Acceptance
9 Mar 61. Force 8 May 61.
402 UNTS 324. Spain. Qualified Accession
11 Aug 61.
419 UNTS 359. Netherlands. Qualified Acceptance 8 Jan 62. Force 9 Mar 62.

423 UNTS 325. Yugoslavia. Accession
14 Feb 62. Force 15 Apr 62.
450 UNTS 450. UK Great Britain. Accession
15 Jan 63. Force 16 Mar 63.
454 UNTS 571. Italy. Qualified Ratification
25 Feb 63. Force 26 Apr 63.
462 UNTS 354. Multilateral. Amendment
28 Feb 63. Force 28 Apr 63.
469 UNTS 435. UK Great Britain. Force
30 Jun 63.
472 UNTS 392. Italy. Force 26 Jul 63.
480 UNTS 376. Multilateral. Force 1 Nov 63.
483 UNTS 347. Czechoslovakia. Acceptance
18 Dec 63. Force 16 Feb 64.
493 UNTS 308. Belgium. Force 15 Apr 64.
493 UNTS 308. Italy. Force 15 Apr 64.
493 UNTS 324. Italy. Implementation 22 Apr 64.
Force 21 Jun 64.
495 UNTS 262. France. Acceptance 7 May 64.
Force 6 Jul 64.
516 UNTS 378. Multilateral. Correction
24 Nov 64.
527 UNTS 309. Hungary. Implementation
10 Mar 65. Force 9 May 65.
548 UNTS 370. Germany, West. Berlin. Ratification 29 Nov 65. Force 28 Jan 66.
548 UNTS 370. Germany, West. Ratification
29 Nov 65. Force 28 Jan 66.
550 UNTS 407. Spain. Implementation
28 Dec 65. Force 26 Feb 66.
551 UNTS 317. Netherlands. Implementation
10 Jan 66. Force 11 Mar 66.
552 UNTS 370. Multilateral. Force 30 Jan 66.
557 UNTS 274. United Nations. Correction
25 Feb 66.
566 UNTS 343. Sweden. Implementation
1 Jul 66. Force 30 Aug 66.
601 UNTS 356. UK Great Britain. Application for
Membership 27 Jul 67. Force 25 Sep 67.
606 UNTS 324. Germany, West. Supplementation 30 Sep 67. Force 30 Sep 67.
606 UNTS 324. Sweden. Supplementation
30 Sep 67. Force 30 Sep 67.
606 UNTS 324. Netherlands. Supplementation
30 Sep 67. Force 30 Sep 67.
606 UNTS 324. UK Great Britain. Supplementation 30 Sep 67. Force 30 Sep 67.
607 UNTS 282. United Nations. Implementation
15 Oct 67. Force 15 Oct 67.
609 UNTS 290.
630 UNTS 398. Italy. Acceptance 12 Feb 68.
Force 12 Apr 68.
631 UNTS 350. Czechoslovakia. Acceptance
15 Feb 68. Force 15 Apr 68.
659 UNTS 342. Czechoslovakia. Accession
1 Mar 69. Force 1 Mar 69.
659 UNTS 342. Yugoslavia. Accession 1 Mar 69.
Force 1 Mar 69.
659 UNTS 342. Italy. Accession 1 Mar 69. Force
1 Mar 69.

104790 Bilateral Agreement **335 UNTS 229**
SIGNED: 29 Nov 58   FORCE: 6 Feb 59
REGISTERED: 23 Jun 59 Netherlands
ARTICLES: 5 LANGUAGE: French.
HEADNOTE: FINANCIAL ASSISTANCE
TOPIC: Direct Aid
CONCEPTS: Currency. Monetary and gold trans-
fers. Financial programs. Interest rates. Payment
schedules. Local currency. Loan repayment.
INTL ORGS: European Payments Union. Organiza-
tion for Economic Co-operation and Develop-
ment.
PARTIES:
Netherlands
Turkey

104791 Bilateral Exchange **335 UNTS 237**
SIGNED: 9 Apr 58   FORCE: 12 Apr 58
REGISTERED: 23 Jun 59 Netherlands
ARTICLES: 2 LANGUAGE: Dutch. German.
HEADNOTE: ABOLITION PASSPORT VISA RE-
QUIREMENTS
TOPIC: Visas
CONCEPTS: Emergencies. Visa abolition. Border
traffic and migration. Denial of admission. Resi-
dent permits. Non-visa travel documents. Confor-
mity with municipal law.
TREATY REF: 293UNTS129; 293UNTS115.
PARTIES:
Germany, West
Netherlands

104792 Bilateral Exchange **335 UNTS 249**
SIGNED: 2 Sep 58   FORCE: 2 Sep 58
REGISTERED: 23 Jun 59 USA (United States)
ARTICLES: 2 LANGUAGE: English.
HEADNOTE: ESTABLISHMENT CANADA-US MIN-
ISTERIAL COMMITTEE JOINT DEFENSE
TOPIC: General Military
CONCEPTS: Detailed regulations. Non-prejudice
to UN charter. General cooperation. Establish-
ment of commission. Joint defense. Defense and
security. Military assistance.
INTL ORGS: Canadian American Defense Orga-
nization.
TREATY REF: 34UNTS243.
PROCEDURE: Duration. Termination.
PARTIES:
Canada
USA (United States)

104793 Bilateral Exchange **335 UNTS 257**
SIGNED: 9 Sep 58   FORCE: 9 Sep 58
REGISTERED: 23 Jun 59 USA (United States)
ARTICLES: 2 LANGUAGE: English. French.
HEADNOTE: RELIEF SUPPLIES PACKAGES
TOPIC: Direct Aid
CONCEPTS: Transportation costs. Tax exemp-
tions. Customs exemptions. Relief supplies.
PROCEDURE: Termination.
PARTIES:
Haiti
USA (United States)

104794 Bilateral Exchange **335 UNTS 263**
SIGNED: 14 Dec 55   FORCE: 14 Dec 55
REGISTERED: 23 Jun 59 USA (United States)
ARTICLES: 2 LANGUAGE: English.
HEADNOTE: NON-IMMIGRANT VISAS
TOPIC: Visas
CONCEPTS: Time limit. Visas. Fees and exemp-
tions.
PARTIES:
Finland
USA (United States)

104795 Bilateral Exchange **336 UNTS 3**
SIGNED: 25 Aug 58   FORCE: 25 Aug 58
REGISTERED: 23 Jun 59 USA (United States)
ARTICLES: 2 LANGUAGE: English.
HEADNOTE: TEXTILES PURCHASE
TOPIC: Commodity Trade
CONCEPTS: General cooperation. Accounting pro-
cedures. Banking. Currency. Currency deposits.
Exchange rates and regulations. Payment sched-
ules. Commodity trade. Loan and credit.
TREATY REF: 278UNTS25; 304UNTS390.
PARTIES:
Burma
USA (United States)

104796 Bilateral Agreement **336 UNTS 11**
SIGNED: 30 Jun 58   FORCE: 30 Jun 58
REGISTERED: 23 Jun 59 USA (United States)
ARTICLES: 6 LANGUAGE: English. Spanish.
HEADNOTE: AGRI COMMOD TITLE I
TOPIC: US Agri Commod Aid
CONCEPTS: General provisions. Annex or appendix reference. Exchange of information and documents. Reexport of goods, etc.. Exchange rates
and regulations. Transportation costs. Local currency. Commodities schedule. Purchase authorization. Surplus commodities. Mutual consultation.
PARTIES:
Ecuador
USA (United States)
ANNEX
340 UNTS 421. USA (United States). Amendment
9 Dec 58. Force 12 Dec 58.
340 UNTS 421. Ecuador. Amendment 12 Dec 58.
Force 12 Dec 58.
342 UNTS 363. USA (United States). Amendment
27 Feb 59. Force 9 Mar 59.
342 UNTS 363. Ecuador. Amendment 9 Mar 59.
Force 9 Mar 59.

104797 Bilateral Agreement **336 UNTS 33**
SIGNED: 5 Sep 58   FORCE: 5 Sep 58
REGISTERED: 24 Jun 59 USA (United States)
ARTICLES: 12 LANGUAGE: English. Spanish.

HEADNOTE: ESTABLISHMENT LORAN TRANS-
MITTING STATION
TOPIC: Milit Installation
CONCEPTS: Annex or appendix reference. Gen-
eral. Customs duties. Customs exemptions. Ra-
dio-telephone-telegraphic communications. Mili-
tary training. Security of information. Third coun-
try military personnel. Jurisdiction. Status of
forces. Bases and facilities. Loss and/or damage.
PROCEDURE: Duration. Termination.
PARTIES:
Nicaragua
USA (United States)

104798   Bilateral Agreement   **336 UNTS 59**
SIGNED: 26 Sep 58   FORCE: 26 Sep 58
REGISTERED: 24 Jun 59 USA (United States)
ARTICLES: 6 LANGUAGE: English.
HEADNOTE: AGRI COMMOD TITLE I
TOPIC: US Agri Commod Aid
CONCEPTS: General provisions. Annex or appendix reference. Exchange of information and documents. Reexport of goods, etc.. Exchange rates
and regulations. Transportation costs. Local currency. Commodities schedule. Purchase authorization. Surplus commodities. Mutual consultation.
PARTIES:
India
USA (United States)
ANNEX
358 UNTS 367. USA (United States). Amendment
1 Oct 59. Force 28 Oct 59.
358 UNTS 367. India. Amendment 28 Oct 59.
Force 28 Oct 59.
360 UNTS 420. USA (United States). Amendment
13 Nov 59. Force 13 Nov 59.
360 UNTS 420. India. Amendment 13 Nov 59.
Force 13 Nov 59.
394 UNTS 296. India. Amendment 21 May 59.
Force 21 May 59.
394 UNTS 296. USA (United States). Amendment
13 May 59. Force 21 May 59.

104799   Bilateral Exchange   **336 UNTS 79**
SIGNED: 9 Jul 58   FORCE: 9 Jul 58
REGISTERED: 24 Jun 59 USA (United States)
ARTICLES: 2 LANGUAGE: English.
HEADNOTE: PURCHASE MILITARY EQUIPMENT
MATERIALS SERVICES
TOPIC: Milit Assistance
CONCEPTS: Exceptions and exemptions. Confor-
mity with municipal law. Self-defense. Security
of information. Exchange of defense informa-
tion. Restrictions on transfer.
PARTIES:
Fed of Malaya
USA (United States)

104800   Bilateral Exchange   **336 UNTS 85**
SIGNED: 6 Sep 58   FORCE: 6 Sep 58
REGISTERED: 24 Jun 59 USA (United States)
ARTICLES: 2 LANGUAGE: English.
HEADNOTE: REPAYMENTS DEVELOPMENT
TOPIC: Loans and Credits
CONCEPTS: Local currency. Loan repayment.
PARTIES:
Turkey
USA (United States)

104801   Bilateral Exchange   **336 UNTS 91**
SIGNED: 3 Sep 58   FORCE: 3 Sep 58
REGISTERED: 24 Jun 59 USA (United States)
ARTICLES: 2 LANGUAGE: English.
HEADNOTE: DEVELOPMENT ASSISTANCE
TOPIC: Direct Aid
CONCEPTS: Monetary and gold transfers. Finan-
cial programs. Economic assistance. Use restric-
tions.
PARTIES:
Lebanon
USA (United States)

104802   Bilateral Agreement   **336 UNTS 97**
SIGNED: 20 Jun 58   FORCE: 1 Oct 58
REGISTERED: 24 Jun 59 USA (United States)
ARTICLES: 31 LANGUAGE: English.
HEADNOTE: EXCHANGE POSTAL PARCELS
TOPIC: Postal Service

CONCEPTS: Mail and money orders. Postal ser-
vices.
INTL ORGS: Universal Postal Union.
TREATY   REF: 169UNTS3;   1861NTS356;
202UNTS340; 227UNTS390.
PROCEDURE: Duration. Termination.
PARTIES:
Australia
USA (United States)

104803   Bilateral Exchange   **336 UNTS 145**
SIGNED: 14 Oct 58   FORCE: 14 Oct 58
REGISTERED: 25 Jun 59 USA (United States)
ARTICLES: 2 LANGUAGE: English.
HEADNOTE: LOAN VESSELS
TOPIC: Milit Assistance
CONCEPTS: Time limit. Annex or appendix refer-
ence. Responsibility and liability. Title and
deeds. Compensation. Indemnities and reim-
bursements. Delivery schedules. Defense and
security. Naval vessels. Return of equipment and
recapture. Restrictions on transfer.
TREATY REF: 7UNTS299.
PARTIES:
Turkey
USA (United States)

104804   Bilateral Agreement   **336 UNTS 153**
SIGNED: 16 Oct 58   FORCE: 16 Oct 58
REGISTERED: 25 Jun 59 USA (United States)
ARTICLES: 11 LANGUAGE: English. Spanish.
HEADNOTE: EDUCATION EXCHANGE
TOPIC: Education
CONCEPTS: Definition of terms. Standardization.
Conformity with municipal law. General cooper-
ation. Inspection and observation. Personnel.
General property. Dispute settlement. Exchange.
Commissions and foundations. Scholarships
and grants. Athletes. Research and develop-
ment. Accounting procedures. Currency. Ex-
change rates and regulations. Expense sharing
formulae. Financial programs. Funding proce-
dures.
INTL ORGS: Special Commission.
TREATY REF: 239UNTS117.
PARTIES:
Spain
USA (United States)
ANNEX
400 UNTS 405. Spain. Amendment 18 Oct 60.
Force 18 Oct 60.
400 UNTS 405. USA (United States). Amendment
3 Jun 61. Force 18 Oct 60.

104805   Bilateral Exchange   **336 UNTS 169**
SIGNED: 30 Sep 58   FORCE: 30 Sep 58
REGISTERED: 25 Jun 59 USA (United States)
ARTICLES: 2 LANGUAGE: English.
HEADNOTE: GUARANTY PRIVATE INVESTMENTS
TOPIC: Admin Cooperation
CONCEPTS: Territorial application. Guarantees
and safeguards. Previous treaty replacement.
Pre-treaty crimes. General cooperation. Ex-
change of information and documents. Recogni-
tion and enforcement of legal decisions. Arbitra-
tion. Procedure. Special tribunals. Investments.
Assets transfer.
INTL ORGS: International Court of Justice.
PROCEDURE: Ratification.
PARTIES:
Ghana
USA (United States)

104806   Multilateral Agreement **336 UNTS 177**
SIGNED: 3 Apr 58   FORCE: 26 May 59
REGISTERED: 26 Jun 59 United Nations
ARTICLES: 41 LANGUAGE: English. French. Spanish.
HEADNOTE: INTERNATIONAL AGREEMENT OLIVE
OIL
TOPIC: Commodity Trade
CONCEPTS: Definition of terms. Territorial application. General provisions. Annex or appendix reference. Informational records. Procedure. Employment regulations. General trade. Balance of
payments. Commodity trade. Recognition. Subsidiary organ. Liaison with other IGO's. Internal
structure.
INTL ORGS: International Olive Oil Council. Food
and Agricultural Organization of the United Na-

tions. International Court of Justice. United Na-
tions.
PROCEDURE: Amendment. Accession. Duration.
Ratification. Registration. Renewal or Revival.
Termination.
PARTIES:
Belgium RATIFIED: 21 Apr 59 FORCE: 26 Jun 59
France RATIFIED: 3 Jun 59 FORCE: 26 Jun 59
Greece RATIFIED: 23 Apr 59 FORCE: 26 Jun 59
Israel RATIFIED: 10 Sep 58 FORCE: 26 Jun 59
Italy RATIFIED: 22 May 59 FORCE: 26 Jun 59
Morocco   RATIFIED: 11 Aug 58   FORCE:
26 Jun 59
Portugal RATIFIED: 9 Jun 59 FORCE: 26 Jun 59
Spain RATIFIED: 26 Jun 59 FORCE: 26 Jun 59
Tunisia RATIFIED: 12 May 59 FORCE: 26 Jun 59
UK Great Britain RATIFIED: 19 Jun 59 FORCE:
26 Jun 59
ANNEX
340 UNTS 424. Libya. Accession 2 Sep 59.
341 UNTS 421. Spain. Ratification 29 Sep 59.
354 UNTS 432. Tunisia. Ratification 18 Mar 60.
376 UNTS 455. Greece. Acceptance 5 Oct 60.
435 UNTS 364. Belgium. Accession 27 Aug 62.
450 UNTS 451. France. Amendment 16 Jan 63.

104807   Bilateral Exchange   **336 UNTS 235**
SIGNED: 27 Oct 58   FORCE: 27 Oct 58
REGISTERED: 26 Jun 59 USA (United States)
ARTICLES: 3 LANGUAGE: English. French.
HEADNOTE: TEMPORARY TRAINING UNIT
TOPIC: Military Mission
CONCEPTS: Military assistance missions. Airforce-
army-navy personnel ratio. Jurisdiction.
PARTIES:
Haiti
USA (United States)

104808   Bilateral Agreement   **336 UNTS 241**
SIGNED: 26 Jun 53   FORCE: 9 May 56
REGISTERED: 26 Jun 59 USA (United States)
ARTICLES: 14 LANGUAGE: English. Portuguese.
HEADNOTE: COOPERATIVE PROGRAM AGRICUL-
TURE
TOPIC: Direct Aid
CONCEPTS: Treaty implementation. Annex type
material. Privileges and immunities. Exchange of
information and documents. Informational
records. Domestic legislation. Operating agen-
cies. Personnel. General property. Private con-
tracts. Currency deposits. Expense sharing for-
mulae. Funding procedures. Interest rates. As-
sets. Tax exemptions. Customs exemptions.
Domestic obligation. Agriculture. Assistance.
Materials, equipment and services. Aid missions.
Natural resources.
INTL ORGS: Special Commission.
TREATY REF: 184UNTS303; 28OCT1940; US&-
BRAZIL;141UNTS3.
PROCEDURE: Duration. Termination.
PARTIES:
Brazil
USA (United States)
ANNEX
394 UNTS 300. Brazil. Extension and Amendment
24 Aug 60. Force 24 Aug 60.
394 UNTS 300. USA (United States). Extension
and Amendment 24 Aug 60. Force 24 Aug 60.
451 UNTS 339. Brazil. Prolongation 11 Jan 62.
Force 11 Jan 62.
451 UNTS 339. USA (United States). Prolongation
29 Dec 61. Force 11 Jan 62.
510 UNTS 330. Brazil. Force 31 Dec 63. Prolongation 30 Dec 63.
510 UNTS 330. USA (United States). Force
31 Dec 63. Prolongation 27 Dec 63.
546 UNTS 339. USA (United States). Extension
and Amendment 5 Apr 65. Force 5 Apr 65.
546 UNTS 339. Brazil. Extension and Amendment
13 Dec 64. Force 5 Apr 65.

104809   Bilateral Exchange   **336 UNTS 269**
SIGNED: 20 Aug 58   FORCE: 20 Aug 58
REGISTERED: 26 Jun 59 USA (United States)
ARTICLES: 3 LANGUAGE: English. Russian.
HEADNOTE: PASSPORT VISAS
TOPIC: Visas
CONCEPTS: Visas. Fees and exemptions.
PARTIES:
USA (United States)
USSR (Soviet Union)

104810 Bilateral Agreement **336 UNTS 275**
SIGNED: 6 Nov 58   FORCE: 6 Nov 58
REGISTERED: 26 Jun 59 USA (United States)
ARTICLES: 7 LANGUAGE: English.
HEADNOTE: AGRI COMMOD TITLE I
TOPIC: US Agri Commod Aid
CONCEPTS: Exceptions and exemptions. Annex or appendix reference. Exchange of information and documents. Reexport of goods, etc.. Exchange rates and regulations. Transportation costs. Local currency. Commodities schedule. Purchase authorization. Surplus commodities. Mutual consultation.
INTL ORGS: International Bank for Reconstruction and Development. International Finance Corporation.
PARTIES:
Israel
USA (United States)
ANNEX
341 UNTS 422. USA (United States). Supplementation 10 Mar 59. Force 10 Mar 59.
341 UNTS 422. Israel. Supplementation 10 Mar 59. Force 10 Mar 59.
413 UNTS 378. USA (United States). Amendment 15 Jun 61. Force 10 Jul 61.
413 UNTS 378. Israel. Amendment 10 Jul 61. Force 10 Jul 61.
434 UNTS 342. Israel. Amendment 8 Dec 61. Force 8 Dec 61.
434 UNTS 342. USA (United States). Amendment 5 Dec 61. Force 8 Dec 61.
445 UNTS 358. Israel. Amendment 11 Apr 62. Force 11 Apr 62.
445 UNTS 358. USA (United States). Amendment 6 Apr 62. Force 11 Apr 62.

104811 Bilateral Agreement **336 UNTS 291**
SIGNED: 27 Jun 59   FORCE: 27 Jun 59
REGISTERED: 27 Jun 59 United Nations
ARTICLES: 6 LANGUAGE: English. Arabic.
HEADNOTE: OPERATIONAL EXECUTIVE PERSONNEL
TOPIC: Tech Assistance
CONCEPTS: Treaty implementation. Annex or appendix reference. Privileges and immunities. General cooperation. Personnel. Responsibility and liability. Arbitration. Procedure. Negotiation. Vocational training. Compensation. Expense sharing formulae. Tax exemptions. Customs exemptions. Domestic obligation. Special projects. Status of experts. Conformity with IGO decisions.
INTL ORGS: Permanent Court of Arbitration.
PROCEDURE: Amendment. Termination.
PARTIES:
Libya
United Nations
ANNEX
492 UNTS 360. Libya. Supplementation 16 Mar 64. Force 16 Mar 64.
492 UNTS 360. United Nations. Supplementation 16 Mar 64. Force 16 Mar 64.

104812 Bilateral Agreement **337 UNTS 3**
SIGNED: 26 Nov 58   FORCE: 26 Nov 58
REGISTERED: 2 Jul 59 USA (United States)
ARTICLES: 6 LANGUAGE: English.
HEADNOTE: AGRI COMMOD
TOPIC: US Agri Commod Aid
CONCEPTS: General provisions. Annex or appendix reference. Exchange of information and documents. Reexport of goods, etc.. Exchange rates and regulations. Transportation costs. Local currency. Commodities schedule. Purchase authorization. Surplus commodities. Mutual consultation.
PARTIES:
Pakistan
USA (United States)
ANNEX
354 UNTS 434. USA (United States). Amendment 21 May 59. Force 21 May 59.
354 UNTS 434. Pakistan. Amendment 21 May 59. Force 21 May 59.
358 UNTS 368. USA (United States). Amendment 7 Oct 59. Force 8 Oct 59.
358 UNTS 368. Pakistan. Amendment 8 Oct 59. Force 8 Oct 59.
360 UNTS 424. USA (United States). Amendment 2 Nov 59. Force 5 Nov 59.

360 UNTS 424. Pakistan. Amendment 5 Nov 59. Force 5 Nov 59.
371 UNTS 336. USA (United States). Supplementation 28 Jan 60. Force 28 Jan 60.
371 UNTS 336. Pakistan. Supplementation 28 Jan 60. Force 28 Jan 60.
371 UNTS 344. Pakistan. Supplementation 11 Apr 60. Force 11 Apr 60.
371 UNTS 344. USA (United States). Supplementation 11 Apr 60. Force 11 Apr 60.
377 UNTS 440. Pakistan. Supplementation 27 May 60. Force 27 May 60.
377 UNTS 440. USA (United States). Supplementation 27 May 60. Force 27 May 60.
411 UNTS 321. USA (United States). Amendment 29 Jun 61. Force 29 Jun 61.
411 UNTS 321. Pakistan. Amendment 29 Jun 61. Force 29 Jun 61.

104813 Bilateral Agreement **337 UNTS 31**
SIGNED: 11 Dec 58   FORCE: 11 Dec 58
REGISTERED: 2 Jul 59 USA (United States)
ARTICLES: 8 LANGUAGE: English. German.
HEADNOTE: RELATING CERTIFICATES AIRWORTHINESS IMPORTED AIRCRAFT
TOPIC: Air Transport
CONCEPTS: Conformity with municipal law. Exchange of information and documents. Recognition of legal documents. Use of facilities. Registration certificate. Airworthiness certificates.
PROCEDURE: Termination.
PARTIES:
Germany, West
USA (United States)
ANNEX
435 UNTS 365. USA (United States). Acknowledgement 23 Jan 62. Force 23 Jan 62.
435 UNTS 365. Germany, West. Berlin. Force 23 Jan 62.

104814 Bilateral Agreement **337 UNTS 41**
SIGNED: 6 Jul 59   FORCE: 6 Jul 59
REGISTERED: 6 Jul 59 United Nations
ARTICLES: 6 LANGUAGE: French.
HEADNOTE: OPERATIONAL EXECUTIVE PERSONNEL
TOPIC: Tech Assistance
CONCEPTS: Treaty implementation. Annex or appendix reference. Privileges and immunities. General cooperation. Personnel. Responsibility and liability. Arbitration. Procedure. Negotiation. Vocational training. Compensation. Expense sharing formulae. Tax exemptions. Customs exemptions. Domestic obligation. Special projects. Conformity with IGO decisions. Inter-agency agreements.
INTL ORGS: Permanent Court of Arbitration.
PROCEDURE: Amendment. Termination.
PARTIES:
Laos
United Nations
ANNEX
603 UNTS 327. United Nations. Force 14 Jun 67.
603 UNTS 327. Laos. Force 14 Jun 67.

104815 Bilateral Convention **337 UNTS 53**
SIGNED: 1 Mar 56   FORCE: 28 May 59
REGISTERED: 7 Jul 59 Belgium
ARTICLES: 16 LANGUAGE: French.
HEADNOTE: LEGAL ASSISTANCE
TOPIC: Admin Cooperation
CONCEPTS: Recognition and enforcement of legal decisions.
INTL ORGS: International Court of Justice.
TREATY REF: DECLA 2OCT1912.
PROCEDURE: Ratification. Termination.
PARTIES:
Belgium
France

104816 Unilateral Instrument **337 UNTS 65**
SIGNED: 10 Jul 59   FORCE: 10 Jul 59
REGISTERED: 10 Jul 59 United Nations
ARTICLES: 1 LANGUAGE: French.
HEADNOTE: ACCEPTANCE ICJ JURISDICTION
TOPIC: ICJ Option Clause
CONCEPTS: Exceptions and exemptions. Compulsory jurisdiction.
INTL ORGS: International Court of Justice.
PROCEDURE: Termination.

PARTIES:
France
ANNEX
562 UNTS 331. France. Withdrawal 20 May 66.

104817 Bilateral Exchange **337 UNTS 69**
SIGNED: 1 Dec 58   FORCE: 1 Dec 58
REGISTERED: 10 Jul 59 Denmark
ARTICLES: 2 LANGUAGE: French.
HEADNOTE: EXEMPTION AIRLINES CERTAIN TAXES
TOPIC: Taxation
CONCEPTS: Definition of terms. Conformity with municipal law. Domestic legislation. Tax exemptions. Air transport.
PROCEDURE: Duration. Termination.
PARTIES:
Denmark
United Arab Rep

104818 Bilateral Agreement **337 UNTS 77**
SIGNED: 26 Jul 50   FORCE: 8 Dec 50
REGISTERED: 13 Jul 59 Ceylon (Sri Lanka)
ARTICLES: 21 LANGUAGE: English.
HEADNOTE: DOUBLE TAXATION FISCAL EVASION TAXES INCOME
TOPIC: Taxation
CONCEPTS: Definition of terms. Territorial application. Conformity with municipal law. Exchange of official publications. Domestic legislation. Teacher and student exchange. Taxation. Tax credits. Equitable taxes. General. Tax exemptions. Air transport. Merchant vessels.
PROCEDURE: Duration. Termination.
PARTIES:
Ceylon (Sri Lanka)
UK Great Britain

104819 Bilateral Agreement **337 UNTS 103**
SIGNED: 30 Jul 53   FORCE: 30 Jul 53
REGISTERED: 13 Jul 59 Ceylon (Sri Lanka)
ARTICLES: 8 LANGUAGE: English.
HEADNOTE: TRADE DEVELOPMENT
TOPIC: General Trade
CONCEPTS: Exceptions and exemptions. Annex or appendix reference. General cooperation. Licenses and permits. Establishment of trade relations. Reciprocity in trade. Trade procedures. Accounting procedures. Currency. Monetary and gold transfers. Payment schedules. Most favored nation clause. Navigational conditions. Inland and territorial waters.
PROCEDURE: Duration. Ratification. Termination.
PARTIES:
Ceylon (Sri Lanka)
Yugoslavia

104820 Bilateral Agreement **337 UNTS 115**
SIGNED: 23 Apr 57   FORCE: 1 Jun 57
REGISTERED: 13 Jul 59 Ceylon (Sri Lanka)
ARTICLES: 8 LANGUAGE: English. Italian.
HEADNOTE: TRADE DEVELOPMENT
TOPIC: General Trade
CONCEPTS: Exceptions and exemptions. Annex or appendix reference. General cooperation. Licenses and permits. Establishment of trade relations. Reciprocity in trade. Trade procedures. Currency. Monetary and gold transfers. Payment schedules. Quotas. Most favored nation clause. Customs exemptions. Navigational conditions. Ports and pilotage.
INTL ORGS: European Payments Union. Organization for Economic Co-operation and Development.
PROCEDURE: Duration. Ratification. Renewal or Revival.
PARTIES:
Ceylon (Sri Lanka)
Italy

104821 Bilateral Agreement **337 UNTS 137**
SIGNED: 19 Sep 57   FORCE: 1 Jan 58
REGISTERED: 13 Jul 59 Ceylon (Sri Lanka)
ARTICLES: 10 LANGUAGE: English. Chinese.
HEADNOTE: STRENGTHEN FRIENDSHIP ECONOMIC TRADE TIES
TOPIC: General Economic
CONCEPTS: Definition of terms. Exceptions and exemptions. Treaty implementation. Annex or

appendix reference. General relations and amity. Licenses and permits. Establishment of trade relations. Export quotas. Import quotas. Accounting procedures. Banking. Balance of payments. Currency. Monetary and gold transfers. Exchange rates and regulations. Payment schedules. Non-interest rates and fees. Quotas. Most favored nation clause. Customs duties. General transportation.
PROCEDURE: Duration. Future Procedures Contemplated.
PARTIES:
Ceylon (Sri Lanka)
China People's Rep

104822 Bilateral Agreement **337 UNTS 169**
SIGNED: 19 Sep 57 FORCE: 1 Jan 58
REGISTERED: 13 Jul 59 Ceylon (Sri Lanka)
ARTICLES: 6 LANGUAGE: English. Chinese.
HEADNOTE: ECONOMIC AID
TOPIC: Direct Aid
CONCEPTS: Time limit. Treaty implementation. Operating agencies. Accounting procedures. Indemnities and reimbursements. Commodities and services. Economic assistance.
PROCEDURE: Duration.
PARTIES:
Ceylon (Sri Lanka)
China People's Rep

104823 Bilateral Agreement **337 UNTS 177**
SIGNED: 3 Oct 58 FORCE: 7 Feb 59
REGISTERED: 13 Jul 59 IBRD (World Bank)
ARTICLES: 5 LANGUAGE: English.
HEADNOTE: GUARANTEE HYDROELECTRIC PROJECT
TOPIC: IBRD Project
CONCEPTS: Definition of terms. Annex or appendix reference. Exchange of information and documents. Inspection and observation. Bonds. Fees and exemptions. Tax exemptions. Domestic obligation. Terms of loan. Loan regulations. Loan guarantee. Guarantor non-interference. Hydroelectric power.
PARTIES:
Brazil
IBRD (World Bank)

104824 Bilateral Agreement **337 UNTS 205**
SIGNED: 17 Feb 59 FORCE: 24 Feb 59
REGISTERED: 13 Jul 59 IBRD (World Bank)
ARTICLES: 5 LANGUAGE: English.
HEADNOTE: GUARANTEE AGREEMENT
TOPIC: IBRD Project
CONCEPTS: Definition of terms. Annex or appendix reference. Exchange of information and documents. Fees and exemptions. Tax exemptions. Domestic obligation. Loan regulations. Loan guarantee. Guarantor non-interference.
PARTIES:
Japan
IBRD (World Bank)

104825 Bilateral Agreement **337 UNTS 245**
SIGNED: 11 Feb 59 FORCE: 1 May 59
REGISTERED: 13 Jul 59 IBRD (World Bank)
ARTICLES: 5 LANGUAGE: English.
HEADNOTE: GUARANTEE AGREEMENT
TOPIC: IBRD Project
CONCEPTS: Annex or appendix reference. Exchange of information and documents. Inspection and observation. Bonds. Fees and exemptions. Tax exemptions. Domestic obligation. Terms of loan. Loan regulations. Loan guarantee. Guarantor non-interference.
PARTIES:
Costa Rica
IBRD (World Bank)

104826 Bilateral Agreement **337 UNTS 269**
SIGNED: 16 Mar 59 FORCE: 16 May 59
REGISTERED: 13 Jul 59 IBRD (World Bank)
ARTICLES: 5 LANGUAGE: English.
HEADNOTE: GUARANTEE AGREEMENT
TOPIC: IBRD Project
CONCEPTS: Annex or appendix reference. Exchange of information and documents. Inspection and observation. Bonds. Fees and exemptions. Tax exemptions. Domestic obligation.

Terms of loan. Loan regulations. Loan guarantee. Guarantor non-interference.
PARTIES:
Finland
IBRD (World Bank)

104827 Bilateral Agreement **337 UNTS 299**
SIGNED: 9 Oct 58 FORCE: 20 Mar 59
REGISTERED: 13 Jul 59 IBRD (World Bank)
ARTICLES: 5 LANGUAGE: English.
HEADNOTE: GUARANTEE PORT
TOPIC: IBRD Project
CONCEPTS: Annex or appendix reference. Exchange of information and documents. Inspection and observation. Bonds. Fees and exemptions. Tax exemptions. Domestic obligation. Terms of loan. Loan regulations. Loan guarantee. Guarantor non-interference. Water transport.
PARTIES:
Ecuador
IBRD (World Bank)

104828 Bilateral Agreement **337 UNTS 327**
SIGNED: 30 Jan 59 FORCE: 5 May 59
REGISTERED: 13 Jul 59 IBRD (World Bank)
ARTICLES: 5 LANGUAGE: English.
HEADNOTE: GUARANTEE LA ESMERALDA PROJECT
TOPIC: IBRD Project
CONCEPTS: Definition of terms. Annex or appendix reference. Exchange of information and documents. Inspection and observation. Bonds. Fees and exemptions. Tax exemptions. Domestic obligation. Terms of loan. Loan regulations. Loan guarantee. Guarantor non-interference.
PARTIES:
Colombia
IBRD (World Bank)

104829 Bilateral Exchange **337 UNTS 353**
SIGNED: 17 Apr 59 FORCE: 17 Apr 59
REGISTERED: 20 Jul 59 UK Great Britain
ARTICLES: 2 LANGUAGE: English.
HEADNOTE: OVER-FLYING, LANDING STAGING FACILITIES
TOPIC: Status of Forces
CONCEPTS: Territorial application. Overflights and technical stops. Status of military forces. Jurisdiction.
PARTIES:
Ghana
UK Great Britain

104830 Bilateral Agreement **338 UNTS 3**
SIGNED: 21 Feb 59 FORCE: 4 Apr 59
REGISTERED: 23 Jul 59 USSR (Soviet Union)
ARTICLES: 11 LANGUAGE: Russian. Finnish.
HEADNOTE: FISHING SEALING
TOPIC: Specific Resources
CONCEPTS: Annex or appendix reference. Non-visa travel documents. Frontier permits. Conformity with municipal law. Claims and settlements. Inland and territorial waters. Fish, wildlife, and natural resources. Frontier crossing points. Ocean resources. Regulation of natural resources.
TREATY REF: 48UNTS149; 226UNTS338.
PROCEDURE: Duration. Ratification. Renewal or Revival. Termination.
PARTIES:
Finland
USSR (Soviet Union)
ANNEX
566 UNTS 344. USSR (Soviet Union). Prolongation 20 May 65. Force 25 May 66.
566 UNTS 344. Finland. Prolongation 20 May 65. Force 25 May 66.

104831 Bilateral Agreement **338 UNTS 29**
SIGNED: 18 Sep 58 FORCE: 30 May 59
REGISTERED: 23 Jul 59 USSR (Soviet Union)
ARTICLES: 11 LANGUAGE: Russian. Arabic. English.
HEADNOTE: SHIPPING
TOPIC: Water Transport
CONCEPTS: General cooperation. Recognition of legal documents. Responsibility and liability. Indemnities and reimbursements. Payment schedules. Claims and settlements. Most favored na-

tion clause. Routes and logistics. Navigational conditions. Permit designation. Transport of goods. Water transport. Ports and pilotage.
INTL ORGS: Special Commission.
PROCEDURE: Duration. Ratification. Renewal or Revival. Termination.
PARTIES:
United Arab Rep
USSR (Soviet Union)

104832 Bilateral Treaty **338 UNTS 49**
SIGNED: 25 Apr 58 FORCE: 24 May 59
REGISTERED: 23 Jul 59 USSR (Soviet Union)
ARTICLES: 37 LANGUAGE: Russian. German.
HEADNOTE: CONSULAR TREATY
TOPIC: Consul/Citizenship
CONCEPTS: Definition of terms. General consular functions. Diplomatic privileges. Consular relations establishment. Inviolability. Privileges and immunities. Diplomatic correspondence. Procedure.
PROCEDURE: Duration. Ratification. Termination.
PARTIES:
Germany, West
USSR (Soviet Union)

104833 Bilateral Exchange **338 UNTS 97**
SIGNED: 5 Mar 59 FORCE: 1 Apr 59
REGISTERED: 30 Jul 59 Pakistan
ARTICLES: 2 LANGUAGE: English.
HEADNOTE: ABOLITION VISAS
TOPIC: Visas
CONCEPTS: Emergencies. Visa abolition. Denial of admission. Resident permits. Conformity with municipal law.
PROCEDURE: Denunciation.
PARTIES:
Greece
Pakistan

104834 Multilateral Convention **338 UNTS 103**
SIGNED: 18 May 56 FORCE: 4 Aug 59
REGISTERED: 4 Aug 59 United Nations
ARTICLES: 23 LANGUAGE: English. French.
HEADNOTE: CUSTOMS CONVENTION CONTAINERS
TOPIC: Customs
CONCEPTS: Definition of terms. Territorial application. Annex or appendix reference. Arbitration. Negotiation. Temporary importation.
INTL ORGS: European Economic Community. United Nations.
PROCEDURE: Amendment. Accession. Denunciation. Ratification. Registration. Termination.
PARTIES:
Austria SIGNED: 18 May 56 RATIFIED: 13 Nov 57 FORCE: 4 Aug 59
Belgium SIGNED: 18 May 56
France SIGNED: 18 May 56 RATIFIED: 20 May 59 FORCE: 18 Aug 59
Germany, West SIGNED: 18 May 56
Hungary SIGNED: 18 May 56 RATIFIED: 23 Jul 57 FORCE: 4 Aug 59
Italy SIGNED: 18 May 56
Luxembourg SIGNED: 18 May 56
Netherlands SIGNED: 18 May 56
Poland SIGNED: 18 May 56 RATIFIED: 6 May 59 FORCE: 4 Aug 59
Sweden SIGNED: 18 May 56 RATIFIED: 11 Aug 59 FORCE: 9 Nov 59
Switzerland SIGNED: 18 May 56
UK Great Britain Guernsey Island RATIFIED: 23 May 58 FORCE: 4 Aug 59
UK Great Britain Isle of Man RATIFIED: 23 May 58 FORCE: 4 Aug 59
UK Great Britain Jersey Island RATIFIED: 23 May 58 FORCE: 4 Aug 59
UK Great Britain SIGNED: 18 May 56 RATIFIED: 23 May 58 FORCE: 4 Aug 59
ANNEX
32 UNTS 408. Netherlands. Surinam. Force 5 Aug 48.
32 UNTS 408. Netherlands. Indonesia. Force 5 Aug 48.
32 UNTS 408. Netherlands. West Indies. Force 5 Aug 48.
344 UNTS 359. UK Great Britain. Burma. Force 17 Jan 60.
344 UNTS 359. UK Great Britain. North Borneo. Force 17 Jan 60.

344 UNTS 359. UK Great Britain. Trinidad/-Tobago. Force 17 Jan 60.

344 UNTS 359. UK Great Britain. Dominican Republic. Force 17 Jan 60.

344 UNTS 359. UK Great Britain. Falkland Islands. Force 17 Jan 60.

344 UNTS 359. UK Great Britain. Gibralter. Force 17 Jan 60.

344 UNTS 359. UK Great Britain. Antigua. Force 17 Jan 60.

344 UNTS 359. UK Great Britain. Barbados. Force 17 Jan 60.

344 UNTS 359. UK Great Britain. Brit Solomon Is. Force 17 Jan 60.

344 UNTS 359. UK Great Britain. Brunei. Force 17 Jan 60.

344 UNTS 359. UK Great Britain. Jamaica. Force 17 Jan 60.

344 UNTS 359. UK Great Britain. Mauritius. Force 17 Jan 60.

344 UNTS 359. UK Great Britain. Montserrat. Force 17 Jan 60.

344 UNTS 359. UK Great Britain. St. Christopher. Force 17 Jan 60.

344 UNTS 359. UK Great Britain. Zanzibar. Force 17 Jan 60.

344 UNTS 359. UK Great Britain. Nevis. Force 17 Jan 60.

344 UNTS 359. UK Great Britain. Anguilla. Force 17 Jan 60.

344 UNTS 359. UK Great Britain. St. Lucia. Force 17 Jan 60.

344 UNTS 359. UK Great Britain. St. Vincent. Force 17 Jan 60.

344 UNTS 359. UK Great Britain. Sarawak. Force 17 Jan 60.

344 UNTS 359. UK Great Britain. Cyprus. Force 17 Jan 60.

344 UNTS 359. UK Great Britain. Gilbert Islands. Force 17 Jan 60.

344 UNTS 359. UK Great Britain. Gambia. Force 17 Jan 60.

344 UNTS 359. UK Great Britain. Grenada. Force 17 Jan 60.

344 UNTS 359. UK Great Britain. Sierra Leone. Force 17 Jan 60.

344 UNTS 359. UK Great Britain. Singapore. Force 17 Jan 60.

348 UNTS 375. Bulgaria. Qualified Accession 18 Jan 60. Force 17 Apr 60.

359 UNTS 401. Belgium. Ratification 27 May 60. Force 25 Aug 60.

366 UNTS 420. Switzerland. Qualified Ratification 7 Jul 60. Force 5 Oct 60.

371 UNTS 350. Netherlands. Ratification 27 Jul 60. Force 25 Oct 60.

371 UNTS 350. Netherlands. Netherlands Antilles. Force 25 Oct 60.

371 UNTS 350. Netherlands. Dutch New Guinea. Force 25 Oct 60.

377 UNTS 446. Luxembourg. Ratification 25 Oct 60. Force 23 Jan 61.

390 UNTS 370. Yugoslavia. Accession 9 Mar 61. Force 7 Jun 61.

398 UNTS 352. Finland. Accession 15 Jun 61. Force 13 Sep 61.

406 UNTS 333. Greece. Accession 12 Sep 61. Force 11 Dec 61.

411 UNTS 322. Germany, West. Ratification 23 Oct 61. Force 21 Jan 61.

414 UNTS 395. Norway. Accession 22 Nov 61. Force 20 Feb 62.

415 UNTS 434. Germany, West. Berlin.

415 UNTS 434. Germany, West. Berlin.

423 UNTS 326. Sierra Leone. Succession 13 Mar 62.

424 UNTS 363. Italy. Ratification 29 Mar 62. Force 27 Jun 62.

429 UNTS 299. Czechoslovakia. Qualified Accession 31 May 62. Force 29 Aug 62.

478 UNTS 436. Cameroon. Accession 24 Sep 63. Force 23 Dec 63.

480 UNTS 408. Algeria. Qualified Accession 31 Oct 63. Force 29 Jan 64.

480 UNTS 408. Jamaica. Succession 11 Nov 63.

494 UNTS 322. Portugal. Accession 1 May 64. Force 30 Jul 64.

541 UNTS 328. Cuba. Qualified Accession 4 Aug 65. Force 2 Nov 65.

544 UNTS 340. Denmark. Qualified Accession 3 Sep 65. Force 2 Dec 65.

560 UNTS 276. Trinidad/Tobago. Succession 11 Apr 66.

600 UNTS 357. Ireland. Accession 7 Jul 67. Force 5 Oct 67.

608 UNTS 372. Romania. Force 30 Jan 68.

609 UNTS 326. Israel. Accession 14 Nov 67. Force 12 Feb 68.

616 UNTS 495. Australia. Christmas Island. Force 2 Apr 68.

616 UNTS 495. Australia. Force 2 Apr 68.

616 UNTS 495. Australia. Papua. Force 2 Apr 68.

616 UNTS 495. Australia. Norfolk Islands. Force 2 Apr 68.

616 UNTS 495. Australia. Cocos Islands. Force 2 Apr 68.

616 UNTS 495. Australia. New Guinea. Force 2 Apr 68.

651 UNTS 359. USA (United States). Accession 3 Dec 68. Force 3 Mar 69.

104835 Bilateral Agreement **338 UNTS 135**
SIGNED: 8 Nov 58   FORCE: 18 Feb 59
REGISTERED: 6 Aug 59 USA (United States)
ARTICLES: 16 LANGUAGE: English. French. German. Italian. Dutch.
HEADNOTE: COOPERATION PEACEFUL USES ATOMIC ENERGY
TOPIC: Atomic Energy
CONCEPTS: Definition of terms. Annex or appendix reference. Non-prejudice to third party. Conformity with municipal law. Exchange of information and documents. Licenses and permits. Research cooperation. Financial programs. Laws and formalities. Purchase authorization. Nuclear materials. Non-nuclear materials. Peaceful use. Security of information.
INTL ORGS: International Atomic Energy Agency.
TREATY REF: 298UNTS167.
PROCEDURE: Duration.
PARTIES:
  Euratom
  USA (United States)
                    ANNEX
402 UNTS 325. USA (United States). Supplementation 11 Jun 60. Force 25 Jul 60.

402 UNTS 325. Euratom. Supplementation 11 Jun 60. Force 25 Jul 60.

453 UNTS 390. USA (United States). Amendment 22 May 62. Force 9 Jul 62.

453 UNTS 390. Euratom. Amendment 22 May 62. Force 9 Jul 62.

453 UNTS 400. USA (United States). Amendment 22 May 62. Force 9 Jul 62.

453 UNTS 400. Euratom. Amendment 22 May 62. Force 9 Jul 62.

488 UNTS 286. USA (United States). Amendment 27 Aug 63. Force 15 Oct 63.

488 UNTS 286. Euratom. Amendment 27 Aug 63. Force 15 Oct 63.

104836 Bilateral Agreement **338 UNTS 203**
SIGNED: 12 Aug 59   FORCE: 12 Aug 59
REGISTERED: 12 Aug 59 United Nations
ARTICLES: 10 LANGUAGE: English.
HEADNOTE: ASSISTANCE
TOPIC: Direct Aid
CONCEPTS: Detailed regulations. Treaty implementation. Visas. Privileges and immunities. Exchange of information and documents. Informational records. Inspection and observation. Operating agencies. Personnel. Public information. Responsibility and liability. Title and deeds. Use of facilities. Arbitration. Procedure. Negotiation. Import quotas. Exchange rates and regulations. Expense sharing formulae. Financial programs. Claims and settlements. Tax exemptions. Customs exemptions. Domestic obligation. General technical assistance. Economic assistance. Materials, equipment and services. IGO status.
INTL ORGS: International Atomic Energy Agency. International Court of Justice. United Nations. Arbitration Commission.
TREATY REF: 1UNTS15; 33UNTS261; 374UNTS137.
PROCEDURE: Amendment. Termination.
PARTIES:
  Ghana
  UN Special Fund

104837 Bilateral Agreement **338 UNTS 221**
SIGNED: 24 Dec 58   FORCE: 24 Dec 58
REGISTERED: 12 Aug 59 USA (United States)
ARTICLES: 5 LANGUAGE: English.

HEADNOTE: AGRI COMMOD TITLE I
TOPIC: US Agri Commod Aid
CONCEPTS: General provisions. Exchange of information and documents. Exchange rates and regulations. Transportation costs. Local currency. Commodities schedule. Purchase authorization. Surplus commodities. Reexport of goods, etc.. Mutual consultation.
PARTIES:
  United Arab Rep
  USA (United States)
                    ANNEX
344 UNTS 360. USA (United States). Supplementation 5 May 59. Force 5 May 59.

344 UNTS 360. United Arab Rep. Supplementation 5 May 59. Force 5 May 59.

358 UNTS 372. USA (United States). Amendment 14 Oct 59. Force 14 Oct 59.

358 UNTS 372. United Arab Rep. Amendment 14 Oct 59. Force 14 Oct 59.

371 UNTS 352. USA (United States). Amendment 26 Mar 60. Force 26 Mar 60.

371 UNTS 352. United Arab Rep. Amendment 26 Mar 60. Force 26 Mar 60.

104838 Bilateral Exchange **338 UNTS 233**
SIGNED: 5 Apr 58   FORCE: 5 Apr 58
REGISTERED: 12 Aug 59 USA (United States)
ARTICLES: 2 LANGUAGE: English.
HEADNOTE: TECHNICAL ASSISTANCE PROJECT
TOPIC: Tech Assistance
CONCEPTS: Previous treaty amendment. Annex or appendix reference. Import quotas. Accounting procedures. Local currency. Assets. Commodities and services. General technical assistance.
TREATY REF: 152UNTS61.
PARTIES:
  USA (United States)
  Yugoslavia

104839 Bilateral Agreement **338 UNTS 243**
SIGNED: 22 Dec 58   FORCE: 22 Dec 58
REGISTERED: 12 Aug 59 USA (United States)
ARTICLES: 6 LANGUAGE: English.
HEADNOTE: AGRI COMMOD TITLE I
TOPIC: US Agri Commod Aid
CONCEPTS: General provisions. Annex or appendix reference. Exchange of information and documents. Reexport of goods, etc.. Exchange rates and regulations. Transportation costs. Local currency. Commodities schedule. Purchase authorization. Surplus commodities. Mutual consultation.
PARTIES:
  USA (United States)
  Yugoslavia
                    ANNEX
354 UNTS 438. USA (United States). Supplementation 9 Jul 59. Force 9 Jul 59.

354 UNTS 438. Yugoslavia. Supplementation 9 Jul 59. Force 9 Jul 59.

524 UNTS 317. Yugoslavia. Amendment 15 Apr 64. Force 15 Apr 64.

524 UNTS 317. USA (United States). Amendment 15 Apr 64. Force 15 Apr 64.

104840 Bilateral Agreement **338 UNTS 265**
SIGNED: 24 Dec 58   FORCE: 24 Dec 58
REGISTERED: 12 Aug 59 USA (United States)
ARTICLES: 28 LANGUAGE: English. French.
HEADNOTE: NAVAL MISSION
TOPIC: Military Mission
CONCEPTS: Definition of terms. Use of facilities. Indemnities and reimbursements. Currency. Expense sharing formulae. Tax exemptions. Customs exemptions. Military assistance. Military training. Security of information. Airforce-army-navy personnel ratio. Ranks and privileges. Conditions for assistance missions. Third country military personnel. Status of forces.
PROCEDURE: Termination.
PARTIES:
  Haiti
  USA (United States)

104841 Bilateral Exchange **338 UNTS 281**
SIGNED: 30 Dec 58   FORCE: 30 Dec 58
REGISTERED: 12 Aug 59 USA (United States)
ARTICLES: 2 LANGUAGE: English.

HEADNOTE: ESTABLISHMENT RAWINSONDE STATION
TOPIC: Specific Property
CONCEPTS: Exchange of information and documents. Operating agencies. Title and deeds. Research cooperation. Meteorology. Indemnities and reimbursements. Facilities and property.
PARTIES:
UK Great Britain
USA (United States)
ANNEX
371 UNTS 356. USA (United States). Extension and Amendment 15 Feb 60. Force 15 Feb 60.
371 UNTS 356. UK Great Britain. Extension and Amendment 15 Feb 60. Force 15 Feb 60.

104842   Bilateral Agreement   **338 UNTS 291**
SIGNED: 4 Jun 59   FORCE: 4 Jun 59
REGISTERED: 12 Aug 59 Czechoslovakia
ARTICLES: 9 LANGUAGE: English. Chinese. Czechoslovakian. Russian. Korean.
HEADNOTE: HEALTH MATTERS
TOPIC: Sanitation
CONCEPTS: Public health.
PARTIES:
Czechoslovakia
Korea, North

104843   Bilateral Agreement   **338 UNTS 301**
SIGNED: 25 Oct 58   FORCE: 26 Jan 59
REGISTERED: 13 Aug 59 Czechoslovakia
ARTICLES: 10 LANGUAGE: Czechoslovakian. Romanian.
HEADNOTE: CULTURAL COOPERATION
TOPIC: Culture
CONCEPTS: Treaty implementation. Previous treaty replacement. Friendship and amity. Nondiplomatic delegations. Exchange of information and documents. Specialists exchange. Teacher and student exchange. Exchange. Artists. Athletes. Scientific exchange. Attachment of funds. Recognition. Publications exchange. Mass media exchange. Press and wire services.
TREATY REF: 46UNTS37.
PROCEDURE: Denunciation. Duration. Ratification. Renewal or Revival.
PARTIES:
Czechoslovakia
Romania

104844   Multilateral Convention   **339 UNTS 3**
SIGNED: 18 May 56   FORCE: 18 Aug 59
REGISTERED: 18 Aug 59 United Nations
ARTICLES: 16 LANGUAGE: English. French.
HEADNOTE: TAXATION ROAD VEHICLES PRIVATE USE INTERNATIONAL TRAFFIC
TOPIC: Land Transport
CONCEPTS: Definition of terms. Exceptions and exemptions. Territorial application. Previous treaty replacement. Conformity with municipal law. Arbitration. Procedure. Special tribunals. Negotiation. Competence of tribunal. Fees and exemptions. General. Tax exemptions. Motor vehicles and combinations. Subsidiary organ.
INTL ORGS: European Economic Community. United Nations.
TREATY REF: 138LTS149.
PROCEDURE: Amendment. Accession. Denunciation. Ratification. Termination.
PARTIES:
Austria   SIGNED: 18 May 56   RATIFIED: 12 Nov 58 FORCE: 18 Aug 59
Belgium SIGNED: 18 May 56
Finland SIGNED: 18 May 56 FORCE: 18 Aug 59
France   SIGNED: 18 May 56   RATIFIED: 20 May 59 FORCE: 18 Aug 59
Ghana RATIFIED: 18 Aug 59 FORCE: 16 Nov 59
Luxembourg SIGNED: 18 May 56
Netherlands Netherlands Antilles RATIFIED: 20 Apr 59 FORCE: 18 Aug 59
Netherlands Dutch New Guinea RATIFIED: 20 Apr 59 FORCE: 18 Aug 59
Netherlands   SIGNED: 18 May 56   RATIFIED: 20 Apr 59 FORCE: 18 Aug 59
Netherlands Surinam RATIFIED: 20 Apr 59 FORCE: 18 Aug 59
Poland SIGNED: 18 May 56
Sweden   SIGNED: 18 May 56   RATIFIED: 16 Jan 58 FORCE: 18 Aug 59
UK Great Britain SIGNED: 18 May 56

Yugoslavia SIGNED: 18 May 56
ANNEX
341 UNTS 426. Cambodia. Accession 22 Sep 59. Force 21 Dec 59.
355 UNTS 415. Yugoslavia. Ratification 8 Apr 60. Force 7 Jul 60.
395 UNTS 275. Austria. Accession 3 May 61. Force 1 Aug 61.
395 UNTS 275. Austria. Papua. Force 1 Aug 61.
395 UNTS 275. Austria. New Guinea. Force 1 Aug 61.
400 UNTS 411. Germany, West. Berlin.
429 UNTS 300. Ireland. Accession 31 May 62. Force 29 Aug 62.
431 UNTS 316. Czechoslovakia. Qualified Accession 2 Jul 62. Force 30 Sep 62.
450 UNTS 452. UK Great Britain. Ratification 15 Jan 63. Force 15 Apr 63.
450 UNTS 452. UK Great Britain. Jersey Island. Force 15 Apr 63.
450 UNTS 452. UK Great Britain. Aldernay Island. Force 15 Apr 63.
450 UNTS 452. UK Great Britain. Isle of Man. Force 15 Apr 63.
450 UNTS 452. UK Great Britain. Guernsey Island. Force 15 Apr 63.
467 UNTS 492. UK Great Britain. Falkland Islands. Force 4 Sep 63.
467 UNTS 492. UK Great Britain. Gibralter. Force 4 Sep 63.
471 UNTS 337. UK Great Britain. Seychelles. Force 16 Oct 63.
471 UNTS 337. UK Great Britain. Brit Virgin Islands.
472 UNTS 394. UK Great Britain. St. Lucia. Force 24 Oct 63.
472 UNTS 394. UK Great Britain. Montserrat. Force 24 Oct 63.
480 UNTS 410. UK Great Britain. St. Vincent. Force 6 Feb 64.
480 UNTS 410. UK Great Britain. Brunei. Force 6 Feb 64.
480 UNTS 410. UK Great Britain. Zanzibar. Force 6 Feb 64.
480 UNTS 410. UK Great Britain. British Guiana. Force 6 Feb 64.
495 UNTS 263. UK Great Britain. Mauritius. Force 4 Aug 64.
535 UNTS 430.   Luxembourg.   Ratification 28 May 65. Force 26 Aug 65.
540 UNTS 337. Norway. Accession 9 Jul 65. Force 7 Oct 65.
600 UNTS 358. Romania. Qualified Accession 10 Jul 67. Force 8 Oct 67.
630 UNTS 398. Denmark. Accession 9 Feb 68. Force 9 May 68.

104845   Multilateral Convention   **339 UNTS 23**
SIGNED: 29 Jan 58   FORCE: 20 Dec 58
REGISTERED: 18 Aug 59 Romania
ARTICLES: 18 LANGUAGE: Romanian. Bulgarian. Serbo-Croat. Russian.
HEADNOTE: FISHING DANUBE
TOPIC: Specific Resources
CONCEPTS: Annex or appendix reference. Exchange of information and documents. Establishment of commission. Ocean resources. Fisheries and fishing. Regulation of natural resources.
INTL ORGS: United Nations.
PROCEDURE: Duration. Ratification. Registration. Renewal or Revival. Termination.
PARTIES:
Bulgaria   SIGNED: 29 Jan 58   RATIFIED: 18 Nov 58 FORCE: 20 Dec 58
Romania   SIGNED: 29 Jan 58   RATIFIED: 20 Dec 58 FORCE: 20 Dec 58
USSR (Soviet Union) SIGNED: 29 Jan 58 RATIFIED: 16 May 58 FORCE: 20 Dec 58
Yugoslavia   SIGNED: 29 Jan 58   RATIFIED: 21 Oct 58 FORCE: 20 Dec 58
ANNEX
435 UNTS 369. Hungary. Accession 18 Dec 61.

104846   Bilateral Convention   **339 UNTS 77**
SIGNED: 25 Mar 58   FORCE: 2 Aug 58
REGISTERED: 18 Aug 59 Romania
ARTICLES: 7 LANGUAGE: Romanian. Czechoslovakian.
HEADNOTE: HEALTH PROTECTION COOPERATION
TOPIC: Sanitation

CONCEPTS: General cooperation. Exchange of information and documents. Specialists exchange. Public health. Exchange. Teacher and student exchange. Vocational training. Research results. Scientific exchange. Research and development. Indemnities and reimbursements. Recognition. Conferences.
PROCEDURE: Duration. Renewal or Revival. Termination.
PARTIES:
Czechoslovakia
Romania

104847   Bilateral Exchange   **339 UNTS 91**
SIGNED: 28 Jul 59   FORCE: 28 Jul 59
REGISTERED: 24 Aug 59 Thailand
ARTICLES: 2 LANGUAGE: English.
HEADNOTE: EXEMPTION IMPORT DUTIES
TOPIC: Customs
CONCEPTS: Customs exemptions. Agricultural commodities. Agricultural vehicles and construction.
INTL ORGS: Colombo Plan.
PARTIES:
Australia
Thailand

104848   Bilateral Exchange   **339 UNTS 97**
SIGNED: 10 Jul 57   FORCE: 12 May 59
REGISTERED: 24 Aug 59 Netherlands
ARTICLES: 4 LANGUAGE: German.
HEADNOTE: SUPPORT COSTS MILITARY UNITS
TOPIC: Status of Forces
CONCEPTS: Change of circumstances. Indemnities and reimbursements. Expense sharing formulae. Claims and settlements. Status of military forces.
INTL ORGS: North Atlantic Treaty Organization.
TREATY REF: 34UNTS243.
PROCEDURE: Future Procedures Contemplated. Ratification.
PARTIES:
Germany, West
Netherlands

104849   Bilateral Agreement   **339 UNTS 110**
SIGNED: 11 Dec 57   FORCE: 1 Mar 58
REGISTERED: 24 Aug 59 IAEA (Atom Energy)
ARTICLES: 20 LANGUAGE: German. Chinese. English. French. Russian.
HEADNOTE: HEADQUARTERS INTERNATIONAL ATOMIC ENERGY AGENCY
TOPIC: Atomic Energy
CONCEPTS: Definition of terms. Diplomatic privileges. Juridical personality. General property. Responsibility and liability. Special tribunals. Social security. Research cooperation. Finances and payments. National treatment. Tax exemptions. Customs exemptions. Facilities and equipment. Services. Headquarters and facilities. Special status.
INTL ORGS: International Court of Justice. United Nations. Arbitration Commission.
TREATY   REF: 276UNTS3;   293UNTS359; 312UNTS427; 316UNTS387.
PROCEDURE: Amendment. Termination.
PARTIES:
Austria
IAEA (Atom Energy)
ANNEX
425 UNTS 360. Austria. Prolongation 16 Dec 61. Force 22 Dec 61.
425 UNTS 360. IAEA (Atom Energy). Prolongation 22 Dec 61. Force 22 Dec 61.
556 UNTS 186. Austria. Interpretation 1 Mar 65. Force 1 Mar 65.
556 UNTS 186. IAEA (Atom Energy). Interpretation 20 Dec 64. Force 1 Mar 65.

104850   Bilateral Exchange   **339 UNTS 307**
SIGNED: 18 Mar 59   FORCE: 18 Mar 59
REGISTERED: 24 Aug 59 IAEA (Atom Energy)
ARTICLES: 2 LANGUAGE: English.
HEADNOTE: TECHNICAL ASSISANCE
TOPIC: Tech Assistance
CONCEPTS: Exceptions and exemptions. Guarantees and safeguards. Time limit. Previous treaty replacement. Privileges and immunities. Personnel. Arbitration. Procedure. Public health. Gen-

eral technical assistance. IGO status. Conformity with IGO decisions.
INTL ORGS: United Nations.
TREATY REF: 276UNTS3; 293UNTS359; 312UNTS359; 316UNTS387.
PARTIES:
IAEA (Atom Energy)
Thailand

104851 Bilateral Agreement **339 UNTS 315**
SIGNED: 24 Mar 59   FORCE: 24 Mar 59
REGISTERED: 24 Aug 59 IAEA (Atom Energy)
ARTICLES: 5 LANGUAGE: English.
HEADNOTE: SUPPLY URANIUM AGENCY
TOPIC: Atomic Energy
CONCEPTS: Annex or appendix reference. Special tribunals. Negotiation. Acceptance of delivery. Nuclear materials. Samples and testing.
INTL ORGS: International Court of Justice. Arbitration Commission.
PARTIES:
Canada
IAEA (Atom Energy)

104852 Bilateral Agreement **339 UNTS 327**
SIGNED: 24 Mar 59   FORCE: 24 Mar 59
REGISTERED: 24 Aug 59 IAEA (Atom Energy)
ARTICLES: 6 LANGUAGE: English.
HEADNOTE: SUPPLYING URANIUM RESEARCH REACTOR PROJECT JRR-3
TOPIC: Atomic Energy
CONCEPTS: Annex or appendix reference. Exchange of information and documents. Special tribunals. Negotiation. Acceptance of delivery. Nuclear materials. Peaceful use. Samples and testing. Security of information.
INTL ORGS: International Court of Justice. Arbitration Commission.
TREATY REF: 276UNTS3; 293UNTS359; 312UNTS427; 316UNTS387.
PARTIES:
Japan
IAEA (Atom Energy)

104853 Bilateral Agreement **339 UNTS 341**
SIGNED: 11 May 59   FORCE: 11 May 59
REGISTERED: 24 Aug 59 IAEA (Atom Energy)
ARTICLES: 9 LANGUAGE: English. Russian.
HEADNOTE: SPECIAL FISSIONABLE MATERIALS
TOPIC: Atomic Energy
CONCEPTS: Responsibility and liability. Indemnities and reimbursements. Nuclear materials. Peaceful use.
PROCEDURE: Amendment. Denunciation.
PARTIES:
IAEA (Atom Energy)
USSR (Soviet Union)

104854 Bilateral Exchange **339 UNTS 351**
SIGNED: 11 May 59   FORCE: 11 May 59
REGISTERED: 24 Aug 59 IAEA (Atom Energy)
ARTICLES: 2 LANGUAGE: English.
HEADNOTE: SPECIAL FISSIONABLE MATERIALS
TOPIC: Atomic Energy
CONCEPTS: Non-prejudice to third party. Responsibility and liability. Indemnities and reimbursements. Acceptance of delivery. Nuclear materials.
TREATY REF: 276UNTS3; 293UNTS359; 312UNTS427; 316UNTS387.
PARTIES:
IAEA (Atom Energy)
UK Great Britain

104855 Bilateral Agreement **339 UNTS 359**
SIGNED: 11 May 59   FORCE: 7 Aug 59
REGISTERED: 24 Aug 59 IAEA (Atom Energy)
ARTICLES: 6 LANGUAGE: English.
HEADNOTE: COOPERATION
TOPIC: Atomic Energy
CONCEPTS: Definition of terms. Conformity with municipal law. Responsibility and liability. Indemnities and reimbursements. Nuclear materials. Peaceful use. Security of information.
PROCEDURE: Duration.
PARTIES:
IAEA (Atom Energy)
USA (United States)

104856 Bilateral Agreement **340 UNTS 3**
SIGNED: 2 Dec 58   FORCE: 9 Dec 58
REGISTERED: 25 Aug 59 IBRD (World Bank)
ARTICLES: 5 LANGUAGE: English.
HEADNOTE: GUARANTEE AGREEMENT
TOPIC: IBRD Project
CONCEPTS: Default remedies. Definition of terms. Annex or appendix reference. Exchange of information and documents. Inspection and observation. Bonds. Fees and exemptions. Tax exemptions. Domestic obligation. Terms of loan. Loan regulations. Loan guarantee. Guarantor non-interference.
PARTIES:
Austria
IBRD (World Bank)

104857 Bilateral Agreement **340 UNTS 33**
SIGNED: 10 Jun 59   FORCE: 19 Jun 59
REGISTERED: 25 Aug 59 IBRD (World Bank)
ARTICLES: 8 LANGUAGE: English.
HEADNOTE: LOAN AGREEMENT
TOPIC: IBRD Project
CONCEPTS: Default remedies. Definition of terms. Annex or appendix reference. Exchange of information and documents. Informational records. Inspection and observation. Accounting procedures. Bonds. Fees and exemptions. Interest rates. Domestic obligation. Terms of loan. Loan regulations. Loan guarantee. Guarantor non-interference.
PARTIES:
IBRD (World Bank)
South Africa

104858 Bilateral Exchange **340 UNTS 53**
SIGNED: 9 May 59   FORCE: 1 Jul 59
REGISTERED: 31 Aug 59 Belgium
ARTICLES: 2 LANGUAGE: French. Spanish.
HEADNOTE: ABOLISHING TRAVEL VISAS
TOPIC: Visas
CONCEPTS: Emergencies. Territorial application. Time limit. Visa abolition. Denial of admission. Resident permits. Conformity with municipal law.
PARTIES:
Argentina
Belgium

104859 Bilateral Agreement **340 UNTS 61**
SIGNED: 30 Sep 58   FORCE: 1 Oct 58
REGISTERED: 2 Sep 59 Australia
ARTICLES: 15 LANGUAGE: English.
HEADNOTE: CHRISTMAS ISLAND
TOPIC: Territory Boundary
CONCEPTS: Previous treaty replacement. Title and deeds. Establishment of commission. Currency deposits. Funding procedures. Payment schedules. Tax exemptions. Customs exemptions. Frontier waterways. Regulation of natural resources.
TREATY REF: 198UNTS161.
PARTIES:
Australia
New Zealand

104860 Bilateral Exchange **340 UNTS 81**
SIGNED: 27 May 59   FORCE: 1 Jun 59
REGISTERED: 9 Sep 59 Belgium
ARTICLES: 2 LANGUAGE: French. Spanish.
HEADNOTE: ABOLISHING TRAVEL VISAS
TOPIC: Visas
CONCEPTS: Emergencies. Territorial application. Time limit. Visa abolition. Denial of admission. Resident permits. Nationality and citizenship. Conformity with municipal law.
PROCEDURE: Denunciation.
PARTIES:
Belgium
Spain

104861 Bilateral Protocol **340 UNTS 89**
SIGNED: 18 Mar 58   FORCE: 29 Jun 58
REGISTERED: 9 Sep 59 Poland
ARTICLES: 3 LANGUAGE: Polish. Russian.
HEADNOTE: DELIMITATION TERRITORIAL WATERS
TOPIC: Territory Boundary
CONCEPTS: Operating agencies. Indemnities and

reimbursements. Financial programs. Inland and territorial waters. Markers and definitions. Frontier waterways.
INTL ORGS: Special Commission.
PROCEDURE: Ratification.
PARTIES:
Poland
USSR (Soviet Union)

104862 Bilateral Convention **340 UNTS 99**
SIGNED: 25 Nov 57   FORCE: 31 Oct 58
REGISTERED: 9 Sep 59 Poland
ARTICLES: 37 LANGUAGE: Polish. German.
HEADNOTE: CONSULAR CONVENTION
TOPIC: Consul/Citizenship
CONCEPTS: Definition of terms. General consular functions. Consular relations establishment. Inviolability. Privileges and immunities. Diplomatic correspondence.
PROCEDURE: Denunciation. Duration. Ratification.
PARTIES:
Germany, East
Poland

104863 Bilateral Agreement **340 UNTS 137**
SIGNED: 16 Jan 58   FORCE: 1 Jan 59
REGISTERED: 9 Sep 59 Poland
ARTICLES: 23 LANGUAGE: Polish. Serbo-Croat.
HEADNOTE: SOCIAL INSURANCE
TOPIC: Non-ILO Labor
CONCEPTS: Exceptions and exemptions. Annex or appendix reference. Domestic legislation. Recognition of legal documents. Dispute settlement. Old age and invalidity insurance. Wages and salaries. Non-ILO labor relations. Family allowances. Administrative cooperation. Old age insurance. Sickness and invalidity insurance. Social security. Monetary and gold transfers. Payment schedules. Claims and settlements.
PROCEDURE: Denunciation. Duration. Ratification.
PARTIES:
Poland
Yugoslavia

104864 Bilateral Agreement **340 UNTS 181**
SIGNED: 16 Jan 58   FORCE: 1 Jan 59
REGISTERED: 9 Sep 59 Poland
ARTICLES: 13 LANGUAGE: Polish. Serbo-Croat.
HEADNOTE: SOCIAL POLICY
TOPIC: Non-ILO Labor
CONCEPTS: Friendship and amity. Notarial acts and services. Exchange of information and documents. Operating agencies. Establishment of commission. Public health. Exchange. Scholarships and grants. Vocational training. Holidays and rest periods. Non-ILO labor relations. Social security. Accounting procedures. National treatment.
INTL ORGS: Special Commission.
PROCEDURE: Denunciation. Duration. Future Procedures Contemplated. Ratification.
PARTIES:
Poland
Yugoslavia

104865 Bilateral Agreement **340 UNTS 199**
SIGNED: 29 Mar 58   FORCE: 9 Jan 59
REGISTERED: 9 Sep 59 Poland
ARTICLES: 10 LANGUAGE: Polish. Czechoslovakian.
HEADNOTE: SETTLEMENT OUTSTANDING PROPERTY MATTERS
TOPIC: Reparations
CONCEPTS: Definition of terms. Conformity with municipal law. General cooperation. Exchange of information and documents. Informational records. General property. Monetary and gold transfers. Loss and/or damage. Post-war claims settlement.
TREATY REF: 25UNTS207.
PROCEDURE: Ratification.
PARTIES:
Czechoslovakia
Poland

104866 Bilateral Treaty **340 UNTS 221**
SIGNED: 26 Apr 58   FORCE: 16 Jan 59
REGISTERED: 9 Sep 59 Poland
ARTICLES: 12 LANGUAGE: English.

HEADNOTE: RE-ESTABLISHMENT NORMAL TRADE RELATIONS
TOPIC: General Economic
CONCEPTS: Exceptions and exemptions. Informational records. Recognition and enforcement of legal decisions. Arbitration. Procedure. Establishment of trade relations. Trade procedures. Balance of payments. Most favored nation clause. Customs duties. Customs exemptions. Navigational conditions. Transport of goods. Operating authorizations and regulations. Merchant vessels. Inland and territorial waters. Ports and pilotage. Shipwreck and salvage.
TREATY REF: 32LTS61; 318UNTS251.
PROCEDURE: Duration. Ratification. Termination.
PARTIES:
 Japan
 Poland

104867 Bilateral Agreement **340 UNTS 235**
SIGNED: 13 Feb 59   FORCE: 13 Feb 59
REGISTERED: 10 Sep 59 USA (United States)
ARTICLES: 6 LANGUAGE: English.
HEADNOTE: AGRI COMMOD TITLE I
TOPIC: US Agri Commod Aid
CONCEPTS: General provisions. Annex or appendix reference. Exchange of information and documents. Reexport of goods, etc.. Exchange rates and regulations. Transportation costs. Local currency. Assets transfer. Commodities schedule. Purchase authorization. Surplus commodities.
PARTIES:
 Turkey
 USA (United States)
ANNEX
354 UNTS 442. USA (United States). Amendment 25 Jun 59. Force 25 Jun 59.
354 UNTS 442. Turkey. Amendment 25 Jun 59. Force 25 Jun 59.
371 UNTS 360. Turkey. Amendment 10 Mar 60. Force 10 Mar 60.
371 UNTS 360. USA (United States). Amendment 10 Mar 60. Force 10 Mar 60.

104868 Bilateral Exchange **340 UNTS 251**
SIGNED: 24 Dec 58   FORCE: 24 Dec 58
REGISTERED: 10 Sep 59 USA (United States)
ARTICLES: 2 LANGUAGE: English. Chinese.
HEADNOTE: USE CURRENCY LOAN REPAYMENT
TOPIC: Loans and Credits
CONCEPTS: Local currency. Economic assistance. Loan repayment.
PARTIES:
 Taiwan
 USA (United States)

104869 Bilateral Agreement **340 UNTS 259**
SIGNED: 30 Dec 58   FORCE: 30 Dec 58
REGISTERED: 10 Sep 59 USA (United States)
ARTICLES: 6 LANGUAGE: English.
HEADNOTE: AGRI COMMOD TITLE I
TOPIC: US Agri Commod Aid
CONCEPTS: General provisions. Annex or appendix reference. Exchange of information and documents. Reexport of goods, etc.. Exchange rates and regulations. Transportation costs. Local currency. Assets transfer. Commodities schedule. Purchase authorization. Surplus commodities.
PARTIES:
 Finland
 USA (United States)

104870 Bilateral Agreement **340 UNTS 273**
SIGNED: 14 Apr 59   FORCE: 14 Apr 59
REGISTERED: 11 Sep 59 Denmark
ARTICLES: 13 LANGUAGE: French.
HEADNOTE: AIR TRANSPORT
TOPIC: Air Transport
CONCEPTS: Detailed regulations. Annex or appendix reference. Conformity with municipal law. Licenses and permits. Recognition of legal documents. Use of facilities. Arbitration. Procedure. Negotiation. Reexport of goods, etc.. Fees and exemptions. Non-interest rates and fees. Most favored nation clause. National treatment. Customs exemptions. Competency certificate. Routes and logistics. Navigational conditions. Permit designation. Air transport. Airport facilities. Airworthiness certificates. Conditions of airlines operating permission. Overflights and tech-

nical stops. Operating authorizations and regulations. Licenses and certificates of nationality.
INTL ORGS: International Civil Aviation Organization.
TREATY REF: 15UNTS295.
PROCEDURE: Future Procedures Contemplated. Termination.
PARTIES:
 Denmark
 Tunisia
ANNEX
521 UNTS 392. Denmark. Supplementation 14 Apr 57.
521 UNTS 392. Tunisia. Supplementation 14 Apr 59.

104871 Unilateral Instrument **340 UNTS 289**
SIGNED: 14 Sep 59   FORCE: 14 Sep 59
REGISTERED: 14 Sep 59 United Nations
ARTICLES: 1 LANGUAGE: English.
HEADNOTE: ACCEPTANCE ICJ JURISDICTION
TOPIC: ICJ Option Clause
CONCEPTS: Exceptions and exemptions. Compulsory jurisdiction.
INTL ORGS: International Court of Justice. United Nations.
PROCEDURE: Termination.
PARTIES:
 India

104872 Bilateral Exchange **340 UNTS 295**
SIGNED: 9 Mar 59   FORCE: 9 Mar 59
REGISTERED: 14 Sep 59 USA (United States)
ARTICLES: 2 LANGUAGE: English.
HEADNOTE: ST. LAWRENCE SEAWAY
TOPIC: Territory Boundary
CONCEPTS: Tariffs. Frontier waterways.
PARTIES:
 Canada
 USA (United States)
ANNEX
530 UNTS 364. USA (United States). Amendment 30 Jun 64. Force 1 Jul 64.
530 UNTS 364. Canada. Amendment 30 Jun 64. Force 1 Jul 64.

104873 Bilateral Exchange **341 UNTS 3**
SIGNED: 27 Feb 59   FORCE: 27 Feb 59
REGISTERED: 14 Sep 59 USA (United States)
ARTICLES: 2 LANGUAGE: English.
HEADNOTE: ST. LAWRENCE SEAWAY
TOPIC: Specific Resources
CONCEPTS: Conformity with municipal law. Domestic legislation. Plans and standards. Canal improvement. Frontier waterways.
TREATY REF: 300UNTS009.
PARTIES:
 Canada
 USA (United States)

104874 Bilateral Exchange **341 UNTS 15**
SIGNED: 20 Mar 59   FORCE: 20 Mar 59
REGISTERED: 14 Sep 59 USA (United States)
ARTICLES: 2 LANGUAGE: English. German.
HEADNOTE: CLAIM SETTLEMENT POST-WAR ECONOMIC ASSISTANCE
TOPIC: Claims and Debts
CONCEPTS: Payment schedules. Claims and settlements. Economic assistance. Post-war claims settlement.
TREATY REF: 224UNTS13.
PARTIES:
 Germany, West
 USA (United States)
ANNEX
410 UNTS 340. USA (United States). Supplementation 25 Apr 61. Force 25 Apr 61.
410 UNTS 340. Germany, West. Supplementation 25 Apr 61. Force 25 Apr 61.

104875 Bilateral Agreement **341 UNTS 25**
SIGNED: 15 Oct 58   FORCE: 23 Jan 59
REGISTERED: 15 Sep 59 Japan
ARTICLES: 8 LANGUAGE: French.
HEADNOTE: ECONOMIC TECHNICAL COOPERATION
TOPIC: General Aid
CONCEPTS: Treaty implementation. General cooperation. Mediation and good offices. Currency

deposits. Commodities and services. Economic assistance. Grants.
INTL ORGS: Special Commission.
PROCEDURE: Future Procedures Contemplated. Ratification.
PARTIES:
 Japan
 Laos
ANNEX
450 UNTS 454. Japan. Prolongation 11 Mar 61. Force 11 Mar 61.
450 UNTS 454. Laos. Prolongation 11 Mar 61. Force 11 Mar 61.

104876 Bilateral Exchange **341 UNTS 41**
SIGNED: 22 Dec 58   FORCE: 1 Feb 59
REGISTERED: 15 Sep 59 Japan
ARTICLES: 2 LANGUAGE: English. Japanese.
HEADNOTE: RECIPROCAL WAIVING PASSPORT VISAS
TOPIC: Visas
CONCEPTS: Time limit. Visa abolition. Conformity with municipal law.
PROCEDURE: Denunciation.
PARTIES:
 Finland
 Japan

104877 Bilateral Exchange **341 UNTS 49**
SIGNED: 2 Mar 59   FORCE: 2 Mar 59
REGISTERED: 15 Sep 59 Japan
ARTICLES: 2 LANGUAGE: English.
HEADNOTE: REGARDING AIR SERVICES
TOPIC: Air Transport
CONCEPTS: Treaty implementation. Conformity with municipal law. Non-interest rates and fees. Routes and logistics. Permit designation. Conditions of airlines operating permission. Operating authorizations and regulations.
PROCEDURE: Termination.
PARTIES:
 Japan
 Philippines

104878 Bilateral Convention **341 UNTS 55**
SIGNED: 10 Mar 59   FORCE: 24 Apr 59
REGISTERED: 15 Sep 59 Japan
ARTICLES: 22 LANGUAGE: English.
HEADNOTE: DOUBLE TAXATION FISCAL EVASION TAXES INCOME
TOPIC: Taxation
CONCEPTS: Definition of terms. Territorial application. Conformity with municipal law. Exchange of official publications. Negotiation. Teacher and student exchange. Claims and settlements. Taxation. Death duties. Tax credits. Equitable taxes. General. Tax exemptions. Air transport. Merchant vessels.
PROCEDURE: Duration. Ratification. Termination.
PARTIES:
 Denmark
 Japan

104879 Bilateral Agreement **341 UNTS 83**
SIGNED: 3 Nov 58   FORCE: 1 May 59
REGISTERED: 15 Sep 59 Japan
ARTICLES: 25 LANGUAGE: English. Japanese.
HEADNOTE: PARCEL POST
TOPIC: Postal Service
CONCEPTS: Previous treaty replacement. Domestic legislation. Responsibility and liability. Compensation. Indemnities and reimbursements. Customs duties. Customs exemptions. Postal services. Regulations. Insured letters and boxes. Conveyance in transit. Parcel post. Rates and charges.
TREATY REF: 191LTS43.
PROCEDURE: Duration. Termination.
PARTIES;
 Japan
 USA (United States)
ANNEX
344 UNTS 366. USA (United States). Implementation 3 Nov 58. Force 1 May 59.
344 UNTS 366. Japan. Implementation 2 Oct 58. Force 1 May 59.

104880 Bilateral Convention **341 UNTS 127**
SIGNED: 17 Feb 59   FORCE: 14 May 59

REGISTERED: 15 Sep 59 Japan
ARTICLES: 22 LANGUAGE: English.
HEADNOTE: DOUBLE TAXATION FISCAL EVA-
SION TAXES INCOME
TOPIC: Taxation
CONCEPTS: Definition of terms. Territorial applica-
tion. Privileges and immunities. Conformity with
municipal law. Exchange of official publications.
Negotiation. Teacher and student exchange.
Claims and settlements. Taxation. Equitable
taxes. Tax exemptions.
PROCEDURE: Duration. Ratification. Termination.
PARTIES:
Japan
Pakistan
ANNEX
450 UNTS 460. Pakistan. Supplementation
28 Jun 60. Force 1 Aug 61.
450 UNTS 460. Japan. Supplementation
28 Jun 60. Force 10 Aug 61.

104881 Bilateral Agreement **341 UNTS 157**
SIGNED: 25 May 59 FORCE: 25 May 59
REGISTERED: 15 Sep 59 Japan
ARTICLES: 5 LANGUAGE: English.
HEADNOTE: SETTLEMENT CLAIMS
TOPIC: Reparations
CONCEPTS: Time limit. Payment schedules. Lump
sum settlements. Loss and/or damage. Repara-
tions and restrictions. Post-war claims settle-
ment.
PARTIES:
Denmark
Japan

104882 Bilateral Agreement **341 UNTS 163**
SIGNED: 2 Mar 59 FORCE: 6 Jul 59
REGISTERED: 15 Sep 59 Japan
ARTICLES: 8 LANGUAGE: French.
HEADNOTE: ECONOMIC TECHNICAL COOPER-
ATION AGREEMENT
TOPIC: General Economic
CONCEPTS: Treaty implementation. Annex or ap-
pendix reference. Establishment of commission.
Currency. Payment schedules. Assistance. Mate-
rials, equipment and services.
INTL ORGS: Special Commission.
PROCEDURE: Duration. Ratification.
PARTIES:
Cambodia
Japan
ANNEX
450 UNTS 466. Cambodia. Prolongation
27 Jun 62. Force 4 Jul 62.
450 UNTS 466. Japan. Prolongation 4 Jul 62.
Force 4 Jul 62.

104883 Bilateral Treaty **341 UNTS 179**
SIGNED: 28 Feb 59 FORCE: 20 Jul 59
REGISTERED: 15 Sep 59 Japan
ARTICLES: 19 LANGUAGE: English.
HEADNOTE: COMMERCE & NAVIGATION
TOPIC: General Economic
CONCEPTS: Exceptions and exemptions. Annex or
appendix reference. Consular relations estab-
lishment. Juridical personality. Legal protection
and assistance. Immovable property. General
property. Establishment of trade relations. Reci-
procity in trade. Most favored nation clause. Eq-
uitable taxes. Customs declarations. Customs ex-
emptions. General transportation. Licenses and
certificates of nationality. Foreign nationals.
INTL ORGS: International Court of Justice. United
Nations. Arbitration Commission.
TREATY REF: 42LTS99.
PARTIES:
Japan
Yugoslavia

104884 Bilateral Agreement **341 UNTS 201**
SIGNED: 20 Feb 59 FORCE: 20 Feb 59
REGISTERED: 16 Sep 59 USA (United States)
ARTICLES: 6 LANGUAGE: English. Spanish.
HEADNOTE: AGRICULTURAL COMMODITIES
TOPIC: US Agri Commod Aid
CONCEPTS: Agricultural commodities. Economic
assistance. Use restrictions. Withdrawal condi-
tions. Distribution.

PARTIES:
USA (United States)
Uruguay
ANNEX
346 UNTS 358. USA (United States). Supplementation 21 May 59. Force 21 May 59.
346 UNTS 358. Uruguay. Supplementation
21 May 59. Force 21 May 59.
360 UNTS 428. USA (United States). Supplementation 16 Nov 59. Force 16 Nov 59.
360 UNTS 428. Uruguay. Supplementation
16 Nov 59. Force 16 Nov 59.
361 UNTS 372. Uruguay. Supplementation
1 Dec 59. Force 1 Dec 59.
361 UNTS 372. USA (United States). Supplementation 1 Dec 59. Force 1 Dec 59.
368 UNTS 372. Uruguay. Supplementation
13 Jan 60. Force 13 Jan 60.
368 UNTS 372. USA (United States). Supplementation 13 Jan 60. Force 13 Jan 60.
401 UNTS 316. Uruguay. Supplementation
16 Sep 60. Force 16 Sep 60.
401 UNTS 316. USA (United States). Supplementation 13 Sep 60. Force 16 Sep 60.
401 UNTS 319. USA (United States). Supplementation 14 Oct 60. Force 14 Oct 60.
401 UNTS 319. Uruguay. Supplementation
14 Oct 60. Force 14 Oct 60.
433 UNTS 372. USA (United States). Amendment
18 Sep 61. Force 18 Sep 61.
433 UNTS 372. Uruguay. Amendment 18 Sep 61.
Force 18 Sep 61.

104885 Bilateral Exchange **341 UNTS 225**
SIGNED: 7 Feb 59 FORCE: 7 Feb 59
REGISTERED: 16 Sep 59 USA (United States)
ARTICLES: 2 LANGUAGE: English. Chinese.
HEADNOTE: VESSEL LOAN
TOPIC: Milit Assistance
CONCEPTS: Time limit. Annex or appendix reference. Responsibility and liability. Title and
deeds. Compensation. Delivery schedules. Materials, equipment and services. Lease of military
property. Naval vessels. Return of equipment
and recapture. Restrictions on transfer.
TREATY REF: 132UNTS273.
PARTIES:
Taiwan
USA (United States)
ANNEX
402 UNTS 348. USA (United States). Supplementation 18 Jan 61. Force 18 Jan 61.
402 UNTS 348. Taiwan. Supplementation
18 Jan 61. Force 18 Jan 61.
416 UNTS 350. USA (United States). Supplementation 8 Jun 61. Force 8 Jun 61.
416 UNTS 350. Taiwan. Supplementation
8 Jun 61. Force 8 Jun 61.
542 UNTS 372. Taiwan. Prolongation 23 Feb 65.
Force 23 Feb 65.
542 UNTS 372. USA (United States). Prolongation
23 Feb 65. Force 23 Feb 65.

104886 Bilateral Agreement **341 UNTS 235**
SIGNED: 3 Mar 59 FORCE: 3 Mar 59
REGISTERED: 16 Sep 59 USA (United States)
ARTICLES: 7 LANGUAGE: English.
HEADNOTE: AGRI COMMOD TITLE III
TOPIC: US Agri Commod Aid
CONCEPTS: Exchange rates and regulations. Fi-
nancial programs. Payment schedules. Com-
modities schedule.
PARTIES:
India
USA (United States)

104887 Bilateral Agreement **341 UNTS 241**
SIGNED: 13 Jan 59 FORCE: 13 Jan 59
REGISTERED: 16 Sep 59 USA (United States)
ARTICLES: 6 LANGUAGE: English. Spanish.
HEADNOTE: AGRI COMMOD TITLE I
TOPIC: US Agri Commod Aid
CONCEPTS: General provisions. Exchange of infor-
mation and documents. Reexport of goods, etc..
Exchange rates and regulations. Transportation
costs. Local currency. Commodities schedule.
Purchase authorization. Surplus commodities.
Mutual consultation.
PARTIES:
Spain
USA (United States)

104888 Bilateral Exchange **341 UNTS 255**
SIGNED: 21 Jan 59 FORCE: 21 Jan 59
REGISTERED: 16 Sep 59 USA (United States)
ARTICLES: 2 LANGUAGE: English.
HEADNOTE: CLAIMS RESPECT MANEUVERS
TOPIC: Specif Claim/Waive
CONCEPTS: Claims and settlements. Military train-
ing. Loss and/or damage. Specific claims or
waivers.
TREATY REF: 303UNTS261.
PARTIES:
Philippines
USA (United States)

104889 Bilateral Agreement **341 UNTS 261**
SIGNED: 3 Mar 59 FORCE: 3 Mar 59
REGISTERED: 16 Sep 59 USA (United States)
ARTICLES: 6 LANGUAGE: English.
HEADNOTE: AGRI COMMOD TITLE I
TOPIC: US Agri Commod Aid
CONCEPTS: General provisions. Annex or appendix reference. Exchange of information and documents. Reexport of goods, etc.. Exchange rates
and regulations. Transportation costs. Local currency. Commodities schedule. Purchase authorization. Surplus commodities. Mutual consultation.
PARTIES:
Iceland
USA (United States)
ANNEX
358 UNTS 376. USA (United States). Supplementation 3 Nov 59. Force 3 Nov 59.
358 UNTS 376. Iceland. Supplementation
3 Nov 59. Force 3 Nov 59.
372 UNTS 403. USA (United States). Amendment
10 May 60. Force 10 May 60.
372 UNTS 403. Iceland. Amendment 10 May 60.
Force 10 May 60.

104890 Bilateral Exchange **341 UNTS 277**
SIGNED: 18 May 59 FORCE: 1 Jun 59
REGISTERED: 23 Sep 59 Belgium
ARTICLES: 2 LANGUAGE: French.
HEADNOTE: ATTESTATION COPIES CIVIL
STATUS CERTIFICATES FREE OF CHARGE
TOPIC: Admin Cooperation
CONCEPTS: Exchange of information and docu-
ments. Recognition of legal documents. Fees
and exemptions.
PROCEDURE: Duration. Termination.
PARTIES:
Belgium
Sweden

104891 Bilateral Exchange **341 UNTS 283**
SIGNED: 21 May 59 FORCE: 26 Jun 59
REGISTERED: 29 Sep 59 Australia
ARTICLES: 2 LANGUAGE: English.
HEADNOTE: SUCCESSION LEGACY DUTIES
TOPIC: Taxation
CONCEPTS: Death duties.
PARTIES:
Australia
Switzerland

104892 Bilateral Treaty **341 UNTS 289**
SIGNED: 9 Jul 58 FORCE: 14 Jul 59
REGISTERED: 30 Sep 59 Denmark
ARTICLES: 8 LANGUAGE: Danish. Spanish.
HEADNOTE: MOST FAVORED NATION TREATY
TOPIC: General Economic
CONCEPTS: Exceptions and exemptions. Annex or
appendix reference. Informational records. Reci-
procity in trade. Most favored nation clause.
Transport of goods. Merchant vessels. Ports and
pilotage. Raw materials.
PROCEDURE: Duration. Future Procedures Con-
templated. Ratification. Termination.
PARTIES:
Denmark
El Salvador

104893 Bilateral Treaty **341 UNTS 305**
SIGNED: 26 Sep 56 FORCE: 27 Apr 59
REGISTERED: 30 Sep 59 Denmark
ARTICLES: 6 LANGUAGE: Danish. Spanish.
HEADNOTE: COMMERCE NAVIGATION
TOPIC: General Economic

CONCEPTS: Exceptions and exemptions. General cooperation. Informational records. General trade. Reciprocity in trade. Most favored nation clause. Equitable taxes. Merchant vessels. Inland and territorial waters. Ports and pilotage.
PROCEDURE: Ratification. Termination.
PARTIES:
Costa Rica
Denmark

104894 Bilateral Agreement **341 UNTS 319**
SIGNED: 1 Aug 59   FORCE: 1 Aug 59
REGISTERED: 30 Sep 59 United Nations
ARTICLES: 1 LANGUAGE: Spanish.
HEADNOTE: OPERATIONAL EXECUTIVE PERSONNEL
TOPIC: Tech Assistance
CONCEPTS: Treaty implementation. Annex or appendix reference. Privileges and immunities. General cooperation. Personnel. Responsibility and liability. Arbitration. Procedure. Negotiation. Vocational training. Compensation. Expense sharing formulae. Tax exemptions. Customs exemptions. Domestic obligation. Special projects. Status of experts. Conformity with IGO decisions.
INTL ORGS: Permanent Court of Arbitration. Arbitration Commission.
PROCEDURE: Amendment. Termination.
PARTIES:
Paraguay
United Nations

104895 Bilateral Agreement **342 UNTS 3**
SIGNED: 3 May 58   FORCE: 25 Apr 59
REGISTERED: 2 Oct 59 Austria
ARTICLES: 4 LANGUAGE: German. Dutch.
HEADNOTE: EXCHANGE RECORDS CONVICTION
TOPIC: Admin Cooperation
CONCEPTS: Conformity with municipal law. General cooperation. Exchange of information and documents.
PROCEDURE: Termination.
PARTIES:
Austria
Netherlands

104896 Bilateral Exchange **342 UNTS 13**
SIGNED: 17 Mar 59   FORCE: 17 Mar 59
REGISTERED: 3 Oct 59 USA (United States)
ARTICLES: 2 LANGUAGE: English.
HEADNOTE: GUARANTY PRIVATE INVESTMENTS
TOPIC: Admin Cooperation
CONCEPTS: Guarantees and safeguards. Arbitration. Currency. Investments. Claims and settlements.
INTL ORGS: International Court of Justice. Arbitration Commission.
PARTIES:
Sudan
USA (United States)
ANNEX
524 UNTS 318. USA (United States). Amendment 2 Mar 64. Force 2 Mar 64.
524 UNTS 318. Sudan. Amendment 2 Mar 64. Force 2 Mar 64.

104897 Bilateral Exchange **342 UNTS 21**
SIGNED: 9 Apr 59   FORCE: 9 Apr 59
REGISTERED: 3 Oct 59 USA (United States)
ARTICLES: 2 LANGUAGE: English.
HEADNOTE: DUTY-FREE ENTRY EXEMPTION TAXATION RELIEF SUPPLIES
TOPIC: Customs
CONCEPTS: Indemnities and reimbursements. Tax exemptions. Customs exemptions. Relief supplies.
PROCEDURE: Duration. Termination.
PARTIES:
Ghana
USA (United States)

104898 Bilateral Agreement **342 UNTS 29**
SIGNED: 5 Mar 57   FORCE: 27 Apr 59
REGISTERED: 3 Oct 59 USA (United States)
ARTICLES: 11 LANGUAGE: English.
HEADNOTE: COOPERATION CIVIL USES ATOMIC ENERGY
TOPIC: Atomic Energy

CONCEPTS: Definition of terms. Non-prejudice to third party. Conformity with municipal law. Exchange of information and documents. Inspection and observation. Responsibility and liability. Assets transfer. Nuclear materials. Non-nuclear materials. Security of information.
PROCEDURE: Duration.
PARTIES:
Iran
USA (United States)

104899 Bilateral Exchange **342 UNTS 43**
SIGNED: 13 Apr 59   FORCE: 13 Apr 59
REGISTERED: 3 Oct 59 USA (United States)
ARTICLES: 2 LANGUAGE: English.
HEADNOTE: COMMUNICATIONS FACILITIES
TOPIC: Specific Property
CONCEPTS: Annex or appendix reference. Facilities and equipment. Self-defense.
TREATY REF: 241UNTS179.
PROCEDURE: Duration.
PARTIES:
Canada
USA (United States)

104900 Bilateral Agreement **342 UNTS 51**
SIGNED: 13 Mar 59   FORCE: 13 Mar 59
REGISTERED: 3 Oct 59 USA (United States)
ARTICLES: 6 LANGUAGE: English.
HEADNOTE: AGRI COMMOD TITLE I
TOPIC: US Agri Commod Aid
CONCEPTS: General provisions. Annex or appendix reference. Exchange of information and documents. Reexport of goods, etc.. Exchange rates and regulations. Transportation costs. Local currency. Commodities schedule. Purchase authorization. Surplus commodities. Mutual consultation.
PARTIES:
Ceylon (Sri Lanka)
USA (United States)
ANNEX
346 UNTS 370. Ceylon (Sri Lanka). Amendment 28 May 59. Force 28 May 59.
346 UNTS 370. USA (United States). Amendment 28 May 59. Force 28 May 59.
418 UNTS 402. USA (United States). Amendment 1 Dec 59. Force 8 Dec 59.
418 UNTS 402. Ceylon (Sri Lanka). Amendment 8 Dec 59. Force 8 Dec 59.
418 UNTS 408. USA (United States). Amendment 24 Aug 61. Force 24 Aug 61.
418 UNTS 408. Ceylon (Sri Lanka). Amendment 24 Aug 61. Force 24 Aug 61.

104901 Bilateral Agreement **342 UNTS 71**
SIGNED: 21 Mar 59   FORCE: 21 Mar 59
REGISTERED: 3 Oct 59 USA (United States)
ARTICLES: 6 LANGUAGE: English. French.
HEADNOTE: AGRI COMMOD TITLE I
TOPIC: US Agri Commod Aid
CONCEPTS: General provisions. Annex or appendix reference. Exchange of information and documents. Reexport of goods, etc.. Exchange rates and regulations. Transportation costs. Local currency. Commodities schedule. Purchase authorization. Surplus commodities. Mutual consultation.
PARTIES:
France
USA (United States)
ANNEX
405 UNTS 339. USA (United States). Amendment 23 Feb 61. Force 23 Feb 61.
405 UNTS 339. France. Amendment 23 Feb 61. Force 23 Feb 61.

104902 Bilateral Agreement **342 UNTS 89**
SIGNED: 6 Oct 59   FORCE: 6 Oct 59
REGISTERED: 6 Oct 59 United Nations
ARTICLES: 10 LANGUAGE: English.
HEADNOTE: ASSISTANCE
TOPIC: Direct Aid
CONCEPTS: Detailed regulations. Treaty implementation. Visas. Privileges and immunities. Exchange of information and documents. Informational records. Inspection and observation. Operating agencies. Personnel. Public information. Responsibility and liability. Title and deeds. Use of facilities. Arbitration. Procedure. Negotiation.

Import quotas. Exchange rates and regulations. Expense sharing formulae. Financial programs. Claims and settlements. Tax exemptions. Customs exemptions. Domestic obligation. General technical assistance. Economic assistance. Materials, equipment and services. IGO status.
INTL ORGS: International Atomic Energy Agency. International Court of Justice. United Nations. Arbitration Commission.
TREATY REF: 1UNTS15; 33UNTS261; 374UNTS137.
PROCEDURE: Amendment. Termination.
PARTIES:
Iran
UN Special Fund

104903 Bilateral Convention **342 UNTS 107**
SIGNED: 14 Feb 53   FORCE: 14 Feb 53
REGISTERED: 7 Oct 59 Romania
ARTICLES: 8 LANGUAGE: Polish. Albanian.
HEADNOTE: CULTURAL COOPERATION
TOPIC: Culture
CONCEPTS: Friendship and amity. Exchange of information and documents. Operating agencies. Establishment of commission. Specialists exchange. Scholarships and grants. General cultural cooperation. Artists. Athletes. Scientific exchange. Publications exchange. Mass media exchange. Press and wire services.
INTL ORGS: Special Commission.
PROCEDURE: Amendment. Duration. Renewal or Revival.
PARTIES:
Albania
Romania

104904 Bilateral Agreement **342 UNTS 119**
SIGNED: 11 May 55   FORCE: 20 Jul 55
REGISTERED: 7 Oct 59 Romania
ARTICLES: 16 LANGUAGE: Polish. German.
HEADNOTE: SETTLEMENT QUESTIONS NAVIGATION DANUBE
TOPIC: Water Transport
CONCEPTS: Exceptions and exemptions. Frontier formalities. Non-visa travel documents. Visas. Conformity with municipal law. Informational records. Licenses and permits. Personnel. Recognition of legal documents. Fees and exemptions. Claims and settlements. Most favored nation clause. General. Customs duties. Customs exemptions. Navigational conditions. Transport of goods. Operating authorizations and regulations. Inland and territorial waters.
PROCEDURE: Denunciation. Duration. Renewal or Revival.
PARTIES:
Austria
Romania

104905 Bilateral Agreement **342 UNTS 141**
SIGNED: 29 Sep 50   FORCE: 29 Sep 50
REGISTERED: 7 Oct 59 Romania
ARTICLES: 5 LANGUAGE: Polish. Bulgarian.
HEADNOTE: TECHNICAL SCIENTIFIC COOPERATION
TOPIC: Scientific Project
CONCEPTS: Friendship and amity. Exchange of information and documents. Establishment of commission. Scientific exchange. General technical assistance.
INTL ORGS: Special Commission.
PROCEDURE: Duration. Renewal or Revival. Termination.
PARTIES:
Bulgaria
Romania

104906 Bilateral Convention **342 UNTS 151**
SIGNED: 14 Dec 53   FORCE: 11 Apr 54
REGISTERED: 7 Oct 59 Romania
ARTICLES: 12 LANGUAGE: Polish. Hungarian.
HEADNOTE: PROTECTION AGRICULTURAL PLANTS
TOPIC: Sanitation
CONCEPTS: Definition of terms. Border traffic and migration. General cooperation. Exchange of information and documents. Inspection and observation. Domestic legislation. Specialists exchange. Quarantine. Disease control. Insect control. Scientific exchange. Reexport of goods,

etc.. Trade procedures. Agriculture. Materials, equipment and services. Conferences.
PROCEDURE: Duration. Ratification. Renewal or Revival. Termination.
PARTIES:
Hungary
Romania

104907 Bilateral Agreement **342 UNTS 173**
SIGNED: 12 Oct 56 FORCE: 6 May 58
REGISTERED: 7 Oct 59 Romania
ARTICLES: 9 LANGUAGE: Polish. Vietnamese. French.
HEADNOTE: CULTURAL COOPERATION
TOPIC: Culture
CONCEPTS: Friendship and amity. Exchange of information and documents. Specialists exchange. Exchange. Scholarships and grants. Exchange. General cultural cooperation. Artists. Research results. Scientific exchange. Research and development. Publications exchange. Mass media exchange. Press and wire services.
PROCEDURE: Amendment. Duration. Future Procedures Contemplated. Ratification. Renewal or Revival.
PARTIES:
Romania
Vietnam, North

104908 Bilateral Agreement **342 UNTS 189**
SIGNED: 12 May 56 FORCE: 20 Jul 56
REGISTERED: 7 Oct 59 Romania
ARTICLES: 8 LANGUAGE: Polish. Korean. Russian.
HEADNOTE: CULTURAL COOPERATION
TOPIC: Culture
CONCEPTS: Friendship and amity. Specialists exchange. Exchange. Teacher and student exchange. Vocational training. Exchange. General cultural cooperation. Artists. Research results. Scientific exchange. Publications exchange. Mass media exchange. Press and wire services.
PROCEDURE: Amendment. Duration. Future Procedures Contemplated. Renewal or Revival.
PARTIES:
Korea, North
Romania

104909 Bilateral Agreement **342 UNTS 207**
SIGNED: 28 Jul 55 FORCE: 24 Oct 55
REGISTERED: 7 Oct 59 Romania
ARTICLES: 14 LANGUAGE: German. Romanian.
HEADNOTE: CIVIL AIR TRANSPORT
TOPIC: Air Transport
CONCEPTS: Annex or appendix reference. General cooperation. Exchange of information and documents. Personnel. Recognition of legal documents. Procedure. Negotiation. Import quotas. Customs exemptions. Air transport. Airport facilities. Airworthiness certificates. Conditions of airlines operating permission. Overflights and technical stops. Operating authorizations and regulations. Licenses and certificates of nationality. Conformity with IGO decisions.
PROCEDURE: Amendment. Denunciation.
PARTIES:
Germany, East
Romania

104910 Bilateral Convention **342 UNTS 229**
SIGNED: 5 Aug 55 FORCE: 24 Oct 55
REGISTERED: 7 Oct 59 Romania
ARTICLES: 15 LANGUAGE: Polish. German.
HEADNOTE: PROTECTION AGRICULTURAL PLANTS
TOPIC: Sanitation
CONCEPTS: Definition of terms. Border traffic and migration. General cooperation. Exchange of information and documents. Inspection and observation. Domestic legislation. Specialists exchange. Quarantine. Disease control. Insect control. Reexport of goods, etc.. Trade procedures. Indemnities and reimbursements. Agriculture. Materials, equipment and services. Mass media exchange. Conferences.
PROCEDURE: Duration. Future Procedures Contemplated. Ratification. Renewal or Revival. Termination.
PARTIES:
Germany, East
Romania

104911 Bilateral Agreement **342 UNTS 251**
SIGNED: 30 Apr 57 FORCE: 26 Sep 57
REGISTERED: 7 Oct 59 Romania
ARTICLES: 8 LANGUAGE: English. Hindi. Polish.
HEADNOTE: CULTURAL RELATIONS
TOPIC: Culture
CONCEPTS: Friendship and amity. Exchange. Teacher and student exchange. Vocational training. Exchange. General cultural cooperation. Artists. Athletes. Anthropology and archeology. Research results. Scientific exchange. Publications exchange. Press and wire services.
PROCEDURE: Duration. Ratification. Renewal or Revival. Termination.
PARTIES:
India
Romania

104912 Bilateral Agreement **342 UNTS 265**
SIGNED: 13 Jan 56 FORCE: 1 Aug 56
REGISTERED: 7 Oct 59 Romania
ARTICLES: 26 LANGUAGE: Polish. Serbo-Croat.
HEADNOTE: POSTAL SERVICE
TOPIC: Postal Service
CONCEPTS: Conformity with municipal law. Accounting procedures. Postal services. Regulations. Insured letters and boxes. Parcel post. Rates and charges.
TREATY REF: 169UNTS3; 186UNTS356; 202UNTS340; 227UNTS390.
PROCEDURE: Denunciation. Duration. Future Procedures Contemplated.
PARTIES:
Romania
Yugoslavia

104913 Bilateral Agreement **342 UNTS 291**
SIGNED: 8 May 56 FORCE: 8 May 56
REGISTERED: 7 Oct 59 Romania
ARTICLES: 10 LANGUAGE: Polish. Mongolian. Russian.
HEADNOTE: CULTURAL COOPERATION
TOPIC: Culture
CONCEPTS: Friendship and amity. Operating agencies. Establishment of commission. Exchange. Teacher and student exchange. Exchange. General cultural cooperation. Artists. Scientific exchange. Publications exchange. Mass media exchange. Press and wire services.
INTL ORGS: Special Commission.
PROCEDURE: Amendment. Duration. Renewal or Revival.
PARTIES:
Mongolia
Romania

104914 Bilateral Agreement **342 UNTS 309**
SIGNED: 27 Aug 57 FORCE: 27 Aug 57
REGISTERED: 7 Oct 59 Romania
ARTICLES: 17 LANGUAGE: French.
HEADNOTE: CIVIL AIR TRANSPORT
TOPIC: Air Transport
CONCEPTS: Guarantees and safeguards. Representation. Annex or appendix reference. Conformity with municipal law. General cooperation. Exchange of information and documents. Informational records. Licenses and permits. Personnel. Recognition of legal documents. Use of facilities. Procedure. Negotiation. Humanitarian matters. Reexport of goods, etc.. Fees and exemptions. Non-interest rates and fees. National treatment. Customs exemptions. Registration certificate. Routes and logistics. Navigational conditions. Permit designation. Air transport. Airport facilities. Airworthiness certificates. Conditions of airlines operating permission. Operating authorizations and regulations. Licenses and certificates of nationality.
PROCEDURE: Amendment. Denunciation. Ratification.
PARTIES:
Netherlands
Romania

104915 Bilateral Agreement **342 UNTS 325**
SIGNED: 15 Apr 57 FORCE: 15 Aug 57
REGISTERED: 7 Oct 59 Romania
ARTICLES: 15 LANGUAGE: French.
HEADNOTE: CIVIL AIR TRANSPORT
TOPIC: Air Transport

CONCEPTS: Definition of terms. Annex or appendix reference. Conformity with municipal law. General cooperation. Licenses and permits. Personnel. Recognition of legal documents. Use of facilities. Fees and exemptions. Non-interest rates and fees. Customs exemptions. Registration certificate. Routes and logistics. Navigational conditions. Permit designation. Air transport. Airport facilities. Airworthiness certificates. Conditions of airlines operating permission. Operating authorizations and regulations.
PROCEDURE: Amendment. Denunciation. Ratification.
PARTIES:
Romania
Sweden

104916 Bilateral Exchange **343 UNTS 3**
SIGNED: 21 Apr 59 FORCE: 21 Apr 59
REGISTERED: 9 Oct 59 USA (United States)
ARTICLES: 2 LANGUAGE: English.
HEADNOTE: GUARANTY PRIVATE INVESTMENTS
TOPIC: Admin Cooperation
CONCEPTS: Guarantees and safeguards. Arbitration. Currency. Investments. Claims and settlements.
INTL ORGS: International Court of Justice. Arbitration Commission.
PARTIES:
Fed of Malaya
USA (United States)

104917 Bilateral Exchange **343 UNTS 11**
SIGNED: 16 Apr 59 FORCE: 16 Apr 59
REGISTERED: 9 Oct 59 USA (United States)
ARTICLES: 2 LANGUAGE: English.
HEADNOTE: USE BAHAMAS PROVING GROUND TRACKING EARTH SATELLITES
TOPIC: IGO Status/Immunit
CONCEPTS: Special status.
TREATY REF: 127UNTS3.
PARTIES:
UK Great Britain
USA (United States)

104918 Bilateral Exchange **343 UNTS 17**
SIGNED: 19 Feb 59 FORCE: 19 Feb 59
REGISTERED: 9 Oct 59 USA (United States)
ARTICLES: 2 LANGUAGE: English. Spanish.
HEADNOTE: TRACKING ARTIFICIAL EARTH SATELLITES OTHER SPACE VEHICLES
TOPIC: Specific Property
CONCEPTS: Radio-telephone-telegraphic communications. Facilities and property.
TREATY REF: 127UNTS3.
PROCEDURE: Duration.
PARTIES:
Chile
USA (United States)

104919 Bilateral Exchange **343 UNTS 27**
SIGNED: 1 May 59 FORCE: 1 May 59
REGISTERED: 9 Oct 59 USA (United States)
ARTICLES: 2 LANGUAGE: English.
HEADNOTE: MILITARY INSTALLATION
TOPIC: Specific Property
CONCEPTS: Bases and facilities. Facilities and property.
TREATY REF: 151UNTS147; 179UNTS265; 184UNTS376.
PARTIES:
Canada
USA (United States)

104920 Bilateral Exchange **343 UNTS 41**
SIGNED: 30 Apr 59 FORCE: 30 Apr 59
REGISTERED: 9 Oct 59 USA (United States)
ARTICLES: 2 LANGUAGE: English.
HEADNOTE: CERTIFICATES AIRWORTHINESS IMPORTED AIRCRAFT
TOPIC: Air Transport
CONCEPTS: Airworthiness certificates. Recognition of legal documents. Registration certificate. Conformity with municipal law. Exchange of information and documents.
PARTIES:
Austria
USA (United States)

104921 Bilateral Agreement **343 UNTS 49**
SIGNED: 12 Jan 59 FORCE: 1 May 59
REGISTERED: 9 Oct 59 USA (United States)
ARTICLES: 31 LANGUAGE: English. Portuguese.
HEADNOTE: PARCEL POST
TOPIC: Postal Service
CONCEPTS: Detailed regulations. Responsibility
and liability. Compensation. Indemnities and re-
imbursements. Payment schedules. Claims and
settlements. Customs duties. Customs exemp-
tions. Postal services. Insured letters and boxes.
Conveyance in transit. Parcel post. Rates and
charges.
INTL ORGS: Universal Postal Union.
TREATY REF: USA'TIAS 4202;.
PROCEDURE: Duration. Termination.
PARTIES:
Portugal
USA (United States)

104922 Bilateral Exchange **343 UNTS 119**
SIGNED: 14 Apr 59 FORCE: 14 Apr 59
REGISTERED: 9 Oct 59 USA (United States)
ARTICLES: 2 LANGUAGE: English. Spanish.
HEADNOTE: GUARANTY PRIVATE INVESTMENTS
TOPIC: Admin Cooperation
CONCEPTS: Guarantees and safeguards. Arbitra-
tion. Currency. Investments. Claims and settle-
ments.
INTL ORGS: International Court of Justice. Arbitra-
tion Commission.
PARTIES:
Nicaragua
USA (United States)

104923 Multilateral Convention **343 UNTS 129**
SIGNED: 1 Mar 56 FORCE: 3 Oct 57
REGISTERED: 12 Oct 59 UK Great Britain
ARTICLES: 26 LANGUAGE: English. French.
HEADNOTE: CUSTOMS CONVENTION
TOPIC: Customs
CONCEPTS: Definition of terms. Territorial applica-
tion. Negotiation. Conciliation. Claims and settle-
ments. Customs duties. Temporary importation.
INTL ORGS: Customs Co-operation Council.
TREATY REF. 221UNTS255.
PROCEDURE: Amendment. Accession. Duration.
Ratification. Registration.
PARTIES:
Austria SIGNED: 5 Jun 56 RATIFIED: 1 Mar 57
FORCE: 3 Oct 57
Belgium SIGNED: 1 Mar 56
Denmark SIGNED: 4 Jul 56 RATIFIED:
28 Mar 58 FORCE: 28 Jun 58
France SIGNED: 9 Aug 56 RATIFIED: 3 Jul 57
FORCE: 3 Oct 57
Germany, West SIGNED: 5 Jun 56
Haiti RATIFIED: 31 Jan 58 FORCE: 30 Apr 58
Ireland SIGNED: 29 Sep 56
Italy SIGNED: 20 Sep 56 RATIFIED: 11 Oct 57
FORCE: 11 Jan 58
Luxembourg SIGNED: 4 May 56
Netherlands SIGNED: 29 Sep 56 RATIFIED:
29 Sep 58 FORCE: 29 Dec 58
Norway SIGNED: 29 Sep 56
Portugal SIGNED: 17 Jul 56
Sweden SIGNED: 29 Sep 56 RATIFIED:
27 May 57 FORCE: 3 Oct 57
Switzerland SIGNED: 7 Jun 56
Turkey SIGNED: 11 Jul 56
UK Great Britain Guernsey Island RATIFIED:
17 Jul 58 FORCE: 17 Oct 58
UK Great Britain Isle of Man RATIFIED: 17 Jul 58
FORCE: 17 Oct 58
UK Great Britain Jersey Island RATIFIED:
17 Jul 58 FORCE: 17 Oct 58
UK Great Britain SIGNED: 29 May 56 RATIFIED:
17 Jul 58 FORCE: 17 Oct 58
ANNEX
414 UNTS 396. Customs Coop Coun. Amend-
ment 15 Jun 60. Force 7 Jul 61.

104924 Bilateral Exchange **343 UNTS 153**
SIGNED: 3 Feb 59 FORCE: 3 Feb 59
REGISTERED: 12 Oct 59 UK Great Britain
ARTICLES: 2 LANGUAGE: English.
HEADNOTE: CREDIT LINE
TOPIC: Loans and Credits
CONCEPTS: Interest rates. Loan and credit. Credit
provisions. Loan repayment. Terms of loan.

PARTIES:
UK Great Britain
Yugoslavia

104925 Bilateral Agreement **343 UNTS 159**
SIGNED: 28 Feb 59 FORCE: 28 Feb 59
REGISTERED: 12 Oct 59 UK Great Britain
ARTICLES: 9 LANGUAGE: English.
HEADNOTE: FINANCIAL COMMERCIAL RELA-
TIONS
TOPIC: Finance
CONCEPTS: Establishment of trade relations.
TREATY REF: 343UNTS170; 225UNTS348;
182LTS317; 249UNTS125.
PARTIES:
United Arab Rep
UK Great Britain
ANNEX
449 UNTS 320. United Arab Rep. Supplementa-
tion 7 Aug 62. Force 7 Aug 62.
449 UNTS 320. UK Great Britain. Supplementa-
tion 7 Aug 62. Force 7 Aug 62.
633 UNTS 388. UK Great Britain. Supplementary
Agreement 24 Apr 67. Force 15 Dec 67.
633 UNTS 388. United Arab Rep. Supplementary
Agreement 24 Apr 67. Force 15 Dec 67.

104926 Bilateral Exchange **343 UNTS 201**
SIGNED: 20 Jan 59 FORCE: 20 Jan 59
REGISTERED: 12 Oct 59 UK Great Britain
ARTICLES: 2 LANGUAGE: English.
HEADNOTE: EXPORTATION COTTON TEXTILES
YARN
TOPIC: Commodity Trade
CONCEPTS: Annex or appendix reference. Com-
modity trade.
PARTIES:
Burma
UK Great Britain

104927 Bilateral Agreement **343 UNTS 223**
SIGNED: 6 Feb 59 FORCE: 6 Feb 59
REGISTERED: 12 Oct 59 UK Great Britain
ARTICLES: 3 LANGUAGE: English.
HEADNOTE: COTTON COTTON YARNS
TOPIC: Commodity Trade
CONCEPTS: Definition of terms. Detailed regula-
tions. Annex or appendix reference. Conformity
with municipal law. Informational records. Li-
censes and permits. Negotiation. Export quotas.
Import quotas. Trade agencies. Trade proce-
dures. Accounting procedures. Currency. Pay-
ment schedules. Commodity trade. Delivery
schedules.
PARTIES:
Burma
UK Great Britain

104928 Bilateral Convention **343 UNTS 241**
SIGNED: 18 Apr 58 FORCE: 17 Apr 59
REGISTERED: 12 Oct 59 UK Great Britain
ARTICLES: 21 LANGUAGE: English. German.
HEADNOTE: CULTURAL CONVENTION
TOPIC: Culture
CONCEPTS: Definition of terms. Territorial applica-
tion. Non-prejudice to third party. Friendship and
amity. Conformity with municipal law. Operating
agencies. Establishment of commission. Special-
ists exchange. Recognition of degrees. Teacher
and student exchange. Professorships. Institute
establishment. Scholarships and grants. General
cultural cooperation. Artists. Research and de-
velopment. Establishment of trade relations.
Publications exchange. Mass media exchange.
INTL ORGS: Special Commission.
PROCEDURE: Denunciation. Duration. Ratification.
Renewal or Revival.
PARTIES:
Germany, West
UK Great Britain

104929 Bilateral Exchange **343 UNTS 257**
SIGNED: 28 Apr 59 FORCE: 28 Apr 59
REGISTERED: 12 Oct 59 UK Great Britain
ARTICLES: 2 LANGUAGE: English.
HEADNOTE: REPAYMENTS DEBTS LIQUIDA-
TIONS EUROPEAN PAYMENTS UNION
TOPIC: Finance
CONCEPTS: Debt settlement.

INTL ORGS: European Payments Union. Organiza-
tion for Economic Co-operation and Develop-
ment.
TREATY REF: CMD8237; CMD8064.
PARTIES:
Denmark
UK Great Britain

104930 Bilateral Exchange **343 UNTS 263**
SIGNED: 14 Mar 59 FORCE: 14 Mar 59
REGISTERED: 12 Oct 59 UK Great Britain
ARTICLES: 2 LANGUAGE: English.
HEADNOTE: REPAYMENT DEBTS LIQUIDATIONS
EUROPEAN PAYMENTS UNION
TOPIC: Claims and Debts
CONCEPTS: Banking. Financial programs. Interest
rates. Payment schedules. Debts. Purchase au-
thorization.
INTL ORGS: European Payments Union. Organiza-
tion for Economic Co-operation and Develop-
ment.
TREATY REF: CMD8064; 201UNTS277;
326UNTS305.
PARTIES:
Austria
UK Great Britain

104931 Bilateral Agreement **343 UNTS 271**
SIGNED: 23 Apr 59 FORCE: 14 Apr 59
REGISTERED: 12 Oct 59 UK Great Britain
ARTICLES: 4 LANGUAGE: English. French.
HEADNOTE: AMORTIZATION
TOPIC: Finance
CONCEPTS: Exchange rates and regulations. Fi-
nancial programs. Interest rates. Payment sched-
ules. Local currency. Debts. Debt settlement.
Loan repayment.
INTL ORGS: European Payments Union. Organiza-
tion for Economic Co-operation and Develop-
ment.
TREATY REF: CMD8064; 201UNTS299;
310UNTS374.
PARTIES:
Belgium
UK Great Britain

104932 Bilateral Agreement **343 UNTS 277**
SIGNED: 5 Mar 59 FORCE: 5 Mar 59
REGISTERED: 12 Oct 59 UK Great Britain
ARTICLES: 5 LANGUAGE: English. French.
HEADNOTE: REPAYMENT AMORTIZATION
TOPIC: Finance
CONCEPTS: Exchange rates and regulations. Fi-
nancial programs. Interest rates. Payment sched-
ules. Local currency. Debts. Debt settlement.
Loan repayment.
INTL ORGS: European Payments Union. Organiza-
tion for Economic Co-operation and Develop-
ment.
TREATY REF: U.K. MISC.NO.14 (1950) CMD.8064.
PARTIES:
France
UK Great Britain

104933 Bilateral Agreement **343 UNTS 283**
SIGNED: 23 Apr 59 FORCE: 23 Apr 59
REGISTERED: 12 Oct 59 UK Great Britain
ARTICLES: 4 LANGUAGE: English.
HEADNOTE: AMORTIZATION
TOPIC: Finance
CONCEPTS: Exchange rates and regulations. Fi-
nancial programs. Interest rates. Payment sched-
ules. Local currency. Debts. Debt settlement.
Loan repayment.
INTL ORGS: European Payments Union. Organiza-
tion for Economic Co-operation and Develop-
ment.
TREATY REF: U.K. MISC.NO.14 (1950) CMD.8064.
PARTIES:
Norway
UK Great Britain

104934 Bilateral Exchange **343 UNTS 289**
SIGNED: 14 Apr 59 FORCE: 14 Apr 59
REGISTERED: 12 Oct 59 UK Great Britain
ARTICLES: 2 LANGUAGE: English.
HEADNOTE: REPAYMENT DEBT
TOPIC: Claims and Debts
CONCEPTS: Banking. Exchange rates and regula-

tions. Financial programs. Interest rates. Local currency. Debts. Debt settlement. Purchase authorization.
INTL ORGS: European Payments Union. Organization for Economic Co-operation and Development.
TREATY REF: U.K. MISC.NO.14 (1950) CMD.8064.
PARTIES:
Italy
UK Great Britain

104935 Bilateral Exchange **343 UNTS 295**
SIGNED: 10 Apr 59 FORCE: 10 Apr 59
REGISTERED: 12 Oct 59 UK Great Britain
ARTICLES: 2 LANGUAGE: English.
HEADNOTE: DEBT REPAYMENT
TOPIC: Claims and Debts
CONCEPTS: Currency. Exchange rates and regulations. Financial programs. Debt settlement.
INTL ORGS: European Payments Union. Organization for Economic Co-operation and Development.
TREATY REF: CMD8064; 199UNTS135.
PARTIES:
Germany, West
UK Great Britain

104936 Bilateral Agreement **343 UNTS 301**
SIGNED: 14 May 59 FORCE: 14 May 59
REGISTERED: 12 Oct 59 UK Great Britain
ARTICLES: 4 LANGUAGE: English.
HEADNOTE: AMORTIZATION
TOPIC: Finance
CONCEPTS: Exchange rates and regulations. Financial programs. Interest rates. Payment schedules. Local currency. Debts. Debt settlement. Loan repayment.
INTL ORGS: European Payments Union. Organization for Economic Co-operation and Development.
TREATY REF: U.K. MISC.NO.14 (1950) CMD.8064.
PARTIES:
Iceland
UK Great Britain

104937 Bilateral Exchange **343 UNTS 307**
SIGNED: 30 Apr 59 FORCE: 30 Apr 59
REGISTERED: 12 Oct 59 UK Great Britain
ARTICLES: 2 LANGUAGE: English.
HEADNOTE: DEBT REPAYMENT
TOPIC: Claims and Debts
CONCEPTS: Currency. Exchange rates and regulations. Financial programs. Interest rates. Debt settlement. Purchase authorization. Post-war claims settlement.
INTL ORGS: European Payments Union. Organization for Economic Co-operation and Development.
TREATY REF: CMD8064; 199UNTS157; 77UNTS69.
PARTIES:
Netherlands
UK Great Britain

104938 Bilateral Exchange **343 UNTS 315**
SIGNED: 6 May 59 FORCE: 6 May 59
REGISTERED: 12 Oct 59 UK Great Britain
ARTICLES: 2 LANGUAGE: English.
HEADNOTE: DEBT REPAYMENT
TOPIC: Claims and Debts
CONCEPTS: Detailed regulations. Currency. Exchange rates and regulations. Financial programs. Interest rates. Payment schedules. Debt settlement. Purchase authorization.
INTL ORGS: European Payments Union. Organization for Economic Co-operation and Development.
TREATY REF: CMD864; 199UNTS197.
PARTIES:
Switzerland
UK Great Britain

104939 Bilateral Agreement **344 UNTS 3**
SIGNED: 21 May 59 FORCE: 21 May 59
REGISTERED: 12 Oct 59 UK Great Britain
ARTICLES: 4 LANGUAGE: English.
HEADNOTE: REPAYMENTS DEBTS
TOPIC: Claims and Debts
CONCEPTS: Currency. Exchange rates and regula-

tions. Financial programs. Interest rates. Payment schedules. Lump sum settlements. Debt settlement.
INTL ORGS: European Payments Union. Organization for Economic Co-operation and Development.
PARTIES:
Greece
UK Great Britain

104940 Bilateral Exchange **344 UNTS 9**
SIGNED: 15 May 55 FORCE: 15 May 59
REGISTERED: 12 Oct 59 UK Great Britain
ARTICLES: 3 LANGUAGE: English. German.
HEADNOTE: CLAIMS RE-ESTABLISHMENT INDEPENDENT DEMOCRATIC AUSTRIA
TOPIC: Claims and Debts
CONCEPTS: Time limit. Conformity with municipal law. General property. Claims and settlements. Lump sum settlements. Loss and/or damage.
TREATY REF: 290UNTS181; 273UNTS121.
PARTIES:
Austria
UK Great Britain

104941 Bilateral Agreement **344 UNTS 29**
SIGNED: 15 Oct 59 FORCE: 15 Oct 59
REGISTERED: 15 Oct 59 United Nations
ARTICLES: 10 LANGUAGE: English.
HEADNOTE: ASSISTANCE
TOPIC: Direct Aid
CONCEPTS: Detailed regulations. Treaty implementation. Visas. Privileges and immunities. Exchange of information and documents. Informational records. Inspection and observation. Operating agencies. Personnel. Public information. Responsibility and liability. Title and deeds. Use of facilities. Arbitration. Procedure. Negotiation. Import quotas. Exchange rates and regulations. Expense sharing formulae. Financial programs. Claims and settlements. Tax exemptions. Customs exemptions. Domestic obligation. General technical assistance. Economic assistance. Materials, equipment and services. IGO status.
INTL ORGS: International Atomic Energy Agency. International Court of Justice. United Nations. Arbitration Commission.
TREATY REF: 1UNTS15; 33UNTS261; 374UNTS137.
PROCEDURE: Amendment. Termination.
PARTIES:
Poland
UN Special Fund

104942 Bilateral Agreement **344 UNTS 47**
SIGNED: 15 Oct 59 FORCE: 15 Oct 59
REGISTERED: 15 Oct 59 United Nations
ARTICLES: 6 LANGUAGE: French.
HEADNOTE: OPERATIONAL EXECUTIVE PERSONNEL
TOPIC: Tech Assistance
CONCEPTS: Treaty implementation. Annex or appendix reference. Privileges and immunities. General cooperation. Personnel. Responsibility and liability. Arbitration. Procedure. Negotiation. Vocational training. Compensation. Expense sharing formulae. Tax exemptions. Customs exemptions. Domestic obligation. Special projects. Status of experts. Conformity with IGO decisions.
INTL ORGS: Permanent Court of Arbitration. Arbitration Commission.
PROCEDURE: Amendment. Termination.
PARTIES:
Guinea
United Nations

104943 Bilateral Agreement **344 UNTS 59**
SIGNED: 17 Nov 46 FORCE: 17 Nov 46
REGISTERED: 16 Oct 59 France
ARTICLES: 5 LANGUAGE: French. Thai.
HEADNOTE: SETTLEMENT AGREEMENT
TOPIC: Reparations
CONCEPTS: General provisions. Annex or appendix reference. Recognition. Establishment of commission. Conciliation. Loss and/or damage. Post-war claims settlement.
INTL ORGS: United Nations. Conciliation Commission.
TREATY REF: 201UNTS113.

PROCEDURE: Future Procedures Contemplated.
PARTIES:
France
Thailand

104944 Bilateral Agreement **344 UNTS 95**
SIGNED: 28 May 59 FORCE: 28 May 59
REGISTERED: 19 Oct 59 Netherlands
ARTICLES: 10 LANGUAGE: English.
HEADNOTE: EXCHANGE STUDENT EMPLOYEES
TOPIC: Non-ILO Labor
CONCEPTS: Definition of terms. Resident permits. Conformity with municipal law. Operating agencies. Wages and salaries. Non-ILO labor relations. Administrative cooperation. Migrant worker. Quotas.
PROCEDURE: Denunciation. Duration. Renewal or Revival.
PARTIES:
Ireland
Netherlands

104945 Bilateral Agreement **344 UNTS 103**
SIGNED: 14 Apr 56 FORCE: 8 Jun 59
REGISTERED: 19 Oct 59 Belgium
ARTICLES: 20 LANGUAGE: French. German.
HEADNOTE: CONCERNING AIR SERVICES
TOPIC: Air Transport
CONCEPTS: Definition of terms. Detailed regulations. Previous treaty replacement. Conformity with municipal law. General cooperation. Exchange of information and documents. Licenses and permits. Personnel. Recognition of legal documents. Use of facilities. Arbitration. Procedure. Special tribunals. Indemnities and reimbursements. Fees and exemptions. Non-interest rates and fees. National treatment. Customs exemptions. Competency certificate. Routes and logistics. Navigational conditions. Permit designation. Airport facilities. Airworthiness certificates. Conditions of airlines operating permission. Overflights and technical stops. Operating authorizations and regulations. Licenses and certificates of nationality.
INTL ORGS: International Civil Aviation Organization. International Court of Justice. Arbitration Commission.
PROCEDURE: Amendment. Denunciation. Future Procedures Contemplated. Ratification. Registration. Termination. Application to Non-self-governing Territories.
PARTIES:
Belgium
Germany, West

104946 Bilateral Agreement **344 UNTS 143**
SIGNED: 20 Oct 59 FORCE: 20 Oct 59
REGISTERED: 20 Oct 59 United Nations
ARTICLES: 10 LANGUAGE: English.
HEADNOTE: ASSISTANCE
TOPIC: Direct Aid
CONCEPTS: Detailed regulations. Treaty implementation. Visas. Privileges and immunities. Exchange of information and documents. Informational records. Inspection and observation. Operating agencies. Personnel. Public information. Responsibility and liability. Title and deeds. Use of facilities. Arbitration. Procedure. Negotiation. Import quotas. Exchange rates and regulations. Expense sharing formulae. Financial programs. Claims and settlements. Tax exemptions. Customs exemptions. Domestic obligation. General technical assistance. Economic assistance. Materials, equipment and services. IGO status.
INTL ORGS: International Atomic Energy Agency. International Court of Justice. United Nations. Arbitration Commission.
TREATY REF: 374UNTS137; 1UNTS15; 33UNTS261.
PROCEDURE: Amendment. Termination.
PARTIES:
India
UN Special Fund

104947 Bilateral Agreement **344 UNTS 159**
SIGNED: 27 Oct 59 FORCE: 27 Oct 59
REGISTERED: 27 Oct 59 United Nations
ARTICLES: 10 LANGUAGE: English.
HEADNOTE: ASSISTANCE
TOPIC: Direct Aid

CONCEPTS: Detailed regulations. Treaty implementation. Visas. Privileges and immunities. Exchange of information and documents. Informational records. Inspection and observation. Operating agencies. Personnel. Public information. Responsibility and liability. Title and deeds. Use of facilities. Arbitration. Procedure. Negotiation. Import quotas. Exchange rates and regulations. Expense sharing formulae. Financial programs. Claims and settlements. Tax exemptions. Customs exemptions. Domestic obligation. General technical assistance. Economic assistance. Materials, equipment and services. IGO status.
INTL ORGS: International Atomic Energy Agency. International Court of Justice. United Nations. Arbitration Commission.
TREATY REF: 1UNTS15; 33UNTS261; 374UNTS137.
PROCEDURE: Amendment. Termination.
PARTIES:
UN Special Fund
Yugoslavia
ANNEX
389 UNTS 321. Yugoslavia. Force 3 Mar 51.

104948   Bilateral Exchange   **344 UNTS 179**
SIGNED: 18 Mar 59   FORCE: 18 Mar 59
REGISTERED: 27 Oct 59 USA (United States)
ARTICLES: 2 LANGUAGE: English. French.
HEADNOTE: GUARANTY PRIVATE INVESTMENTS
TOPIC: Admin Cooperation
CONCEPTS: Guarantees and safeguards. Arbitration. Currency. Investments. Claims and settlements.
INTL ORGS: International Court of Justice. Arbitration Commission.
PARTIES:
Tunisia
USA (United States)
ANNEX
474 UNTS 344.   Tunisia.   Supplementation 6 Mar 63. Force 6 Mar 63.
474 UNTS 344. USA (United States). Supplementation 22 Jan 63. Force 6 Mar 63.

104949   Bilateral Exchange   **344 UNTS 185**
SIGNED: 8 May 59   FORCE: 8 May 59
REGISTERED: 27 Oct 59 USA (United States)
ARTICLES: 2 LANGUAGE: English.
HEADNOTE: MUTUALLY-FINANCED SHIPBUILDING PROGRAM
TOPIC: Milit Assistance
CONCEPTS: Expense sharing formulae. Military assistance. Naval vessels. Equipment and supplies.
INTL ORGS: North Atlantic Treaty Organization.
TREATY REF: 48UNTS115.
PROCEDURE: Future Procedures Contemplated.
PARTIES:
Denmark
USA (United States)
ANNEX
410 UNTS 348. USA (United States). Supplementation 17 May 61. Force 17 May 61.
410 UNTS 348.   Denmark.   Supplementation 17 May 61. Force 17 May 61.

104950   Bilateral Exchange   **344 UNTS 193**
SIGNED: 8 May 59   FORCE: 1 Jul 59
REGISTERED: 27 Oct 59 USA (United States)
ARTICLES: 2 LANGUAGE: English. Spanish.
HEADNOTE: EXTENSION ESTABLISHMENT RAWISONDE OBSERVATION STATION
TOPIC: Direct Aid
CONCEPTS: Annex or appendix reference. Previous treaty extension. Exchange of information and documents. Operating agencies. Personnel. Title and deeds. Meteorology. Expense sharing formulae. Tax exemptions. Customs exemptions. General technical assistance.
TREATY REF: 271UNTS303.
PROCEDURE: Amendment. Duration. Future Procedures Contemplated. Termination.
PARTIES:
Colombia
USA (United States)

104951   Bilateral Convention   **344 UNTS 203**
SIGNED: 1 Jul 57   FORCE: 21 May 59
REGISTERED: 27 Oct 59 USA (United States)
ARTICLES: 20 LANGUAGE: English.

HEADNOTE: DOUBLE TAXATION INCOME
TOPIC: Taxation
CONCEPTS: Conditions. Definition of terms. Territorial application. General cooperation. Exchange of information and documents. Incorporation of treaty provisions into national law. Non-interest rates and fees. Taxation. Equitable taxes. General. Tax exemptions.
PROCEDURE: Duration. Ratification. Renewal or Revival. Termination.
PARTIES:
Pakistan
USA (United States)

104952   Bilateral Agreement   **344 UNTS 229**
SIGNED: 8 Jul 59   FORCE: 27 Aug 59
REGISTERED: 28 Oct 59 IBRD (World Bank)
ARTICLES: 8 LANGUAGE: English.
HEADNOTE: LOAN AGREEMENT
TOPIC: IBRD Project
CONCEPTS: Default remedies. Definition of terms. Annex or appendix reference. Exchange of information and documents. Informational records. Inspection and observation. Accounting procedures. Bonds. Fees and exemptions. Interest rates. Tax exemptions. Domestic obligation. Terms of loan. Loan regulations. Loan guarantee. Guarantor non-interference.
PARTIES:
Norway
IBRD (World Bank)

104953   Bilateral Agreement   **344 UNTS 251**
SIGNED: 20 May 59   FORCE: 14 Jul 59
REGISTERED: 29 Oct 59 IBRD (World Bank)
ARTICLES: 5 LANGUAGE: English.
HEADNOTE: GUARANTEE AGREEMENT
TOPIC: IBRD Project
CONCEPTS: Definition of terms. Annex or appendix reference. Inspection and observation. Bonds. Fees and exemptions. Tax exemptions. Domestic obligation. Terms of loan. Loan regulations. Loan guarantee. Guarantor non-interference.
PARTIES:
Colombia
IBRD (World Bank)

104954   Bilateral Agreement   **344 UNTS 281**
SIGNED: 17 Jul 58   FORCE: 9 Jul 59
REGISTERED: 6 Nov 59 Denmark
ARTICLES: 16 LANGUAGE: French.
HEADNOTE: CIVIL AIR TRANSPORT
TOPIC: Air Transport
CONCEPTS: Definition of terms. Representation. Annex or appendix reference. Conformity with municipal law. General cooperation. Licenses and permits. Personnel. Recognition of legal documents. Use of facilities. Procedure. Negotiation. Humanitarian matters. Monetary and gold transfers. Fees and exemptions. Payment schedules. Non-interest rates and fees. Customs exemptions. Registration certificate. Routes and logistics. Navigational conditions. Permit designation. Air transport. Airport facilities. Airworthiness certificates. Conditions of airlines operating permission. Operating authorizations and regulations.
PROCEDURE: Amendment. Denunciation. Ratification. Termination.
PARTIES:
Denmark
Hungary

104955   Bilateral Agreement   **345 UNTS 3**
SIGNED: 10 Nov 59   FORCE: 10 Nov 59
REGISTERED: 10 Nov 59 United Nations
ARTICLES: 10 LANGUAGE: English. Spanish.
HEADNOTE: ASSISTANCE
TOPIC: Direct Aid
CONCEPTS: Detailed regulations. Treaty implementation. Visas. Privileges and immunities. Exchange of information and documents. Informational records. Inspection and observation. Operating agencies. Personnel. Public information. Responsibility and liability. Title and deeds. Use of facilities. Arbitration. Procedure. Negotiation. Import quotas. Exchange rates and regulations. Expense sharing formulae. Financial programs. Claims and settlements. Tax exemptions. Cus-

toms exemptions. Domestic obligation. General technical assistance. Economic assistance. Materials, equipment and services. IGO status.
INTL ORGS: International Atomic Energy Agency. International Court of Justice. United Nations. Arbitration Commission.
TREATY REF. 374UNTS137; 1UNTS15; 33UNTS261.
PROCEDURE: Amendment. Termination.
PARTIES:
Ecuador
UN Special Fund
ANNEX
353 UNTS 373. UN Special Fund. Correction 8 Mar 60.
353 UNTS 373. Ecuador. Correction 8 Mar 60.

104956   Bilateral Exchange   **345 UNTS 29**
SIGNED: 11 Sep 59   FORCE: 1 Oct 59
REGISTERED: 12 Nov 59 Belgium
ARTICLES: 2 LANGUAGE: French. Spanish.
HEADNOTE: GRANT FREE PASSPORT VISAS VISITS MORE THAN THREE MONTHS
TOPIC: Visas
CONCEPTS: Time limit. Non-visa travel documents. Visas. Fees and exemptions.
PARTIES:
Belgium
Spain

104957   Bilateral Agreement   **345 UNTS 35**
SIGNED: 14 Oct 59   FORCE: 1 Jul 59
REGISTERED: 16 Nov 59 Australia
ARTICLES: 9 LANGUAGE: English. German.
HEADNOTE: COMMERCE
TOPIC: General Trade
CONCEPTS: Detailed regulations. Exceptions and exemptions. Territorial application. General provisions. Representation. Treaty implementation. Annex or appendix reference. General cooperation. Licenses and permits. Trade procedures. Balance of payments. Commodity trade. Quotas. Inland and territorial waters. Ports and pilotage.
PROCEDURE: Duration. Renewal or Revival.
PARTIES:
Australia
Germany, West
ANNEX
424 UNTS 364.   Australia.   Supplementation 18 Feb 61. Force 18 Feb 61.
424 UNTS 364. Germany, West. Supplementation 18 Feb 61. Force 18 Feb 61.
424 UNTS 368. Germany, West. Supplementation 11 Aug 66. Force 11 Aug 66.
424 UNTS 368.   Australia.   Supplementation 11 Aug 66. Force 11 Aug 66.
424 UNTS 372.   Australia.   Supplementation 22 Dec 61. Force 22 Dec 61.
424 UNTS 372. Germany, West. Supplementation 22 Dec 61. Force 22 Dec 61.

104958   Bilateral Exchange   **345 UNTS 57**
SIGNED: 1 May 59   FORCE: 1 May 59
REGISTERED: 16 Nov 59 UK Great Britain
ARTICLES: 4 LANGUAGE: English.
HEADNOTE: LOAN
TOPIC: Loans and Credits
CONCEPTS: Currency. Interest rates. Loan and credit. Loan repayment. Terms of loan.
PARTIES:
Fed of Malaya
UK Great Britain

104959   Bilateral Convention   **345 UNTS 67**
SIGNED: 14 Nov 58   FORCE: 13 Jul 59
REGISTERED: 19 Nov 59 Israel
ARTICLES: 7 LANGUAGE: Hebrew. Spanish.
HEADNOTE: CULTURAL EXCHANGES
TOPIC: Culture
CONCEPTS: Friendship and amity. Tourism. Conformity with municipal law. General cooperation. Teacher and student exchange. Exchange. Artists. Athletes. Research cooperation. Scientific exchange. Mass media exchange.
PROCEDURE: Denunciation. Ratification.
PARTIES:
El Salvador
Israel

104960 Bilateral Convention **345 UNTS 79**
SIGNED: 12 Nov 58　　FORCE: 12 Dec 58
REGISTERED: 19 Nov 59 Israel
ARTICLES: 13 LANGUAGE: Hebrew. French.
HEADNOTE: JUDICIAL ASSISTANCE CRIMINAL MATTERS
TOPIC: Admin Cooperation
CONCEPTS: Territorial application. Treaty interpretation. Witnesses and experts. Exchange of information and documents. Indemnities and reimbursements. Fees and exemptions.
PROCEDURE: Termination.
PARTIES:
France
Israel

104961 Bilateral Agreement **345 UNTS 91**
SIGNED: 10 Sep 52　　FORCE: 10 Sep 52
REGISTERED: 19 Nov 59 Israel
ARTICLES: 7 LANGUAGE: English.
HEADNOTE: AGREEMENT
TOPIC: Consul/Citizenship
CONCEPTS: General cooperation.
TREATY REF: 162UNTS205.
PROCEDURE: Future Procedures Contemplated.
PARTIES:
Germany, West
Israel

104962 Bilateral Agreement **345 UNTS 99**
SIGNED: 26 Nov 57　　FORCE: 24 Nov 58
REGISTERED: 19 Nov 59 Israel
ARTICLES: 4 LANGUAGE: French.
HEADNOTE: CULTURAL AGREEMENT
TOPIC: Culture
CONCEPTS: Friendship and amity. Exchange. Scholarships and grants. Exchange. General cultural cooperation. Scientific exchange.
PROCEDURE: Duration. Future Procedures Contemplated. Ratification. Termination.
PARTIES:
Israel
Norway

104963 Bilateral Agreement **345 UNTS 105**
SIGNED: 20 Nov 59　　FORCE: 20 Nov 59
REGISTERED: 20 Nov 59 United Nations
ARTICLES: 10 LANGUAGE: English.
HEADNOTE: ASSISTANCE
TOPIC: Direct Aid
CONCEPTS: Detailed regulations. Treaty implementation. Annex or appendix reference. Visas. Privileges and immunities. Exchange of information and documents. Informational records. Inspection and observation. Operating agencies. Personnel. Public information. Responsibility and liability. Title and deeds. Use of facilities. Arbitration. Procedure. Negotiation. Import quotas. Exchange rates and regulations. Expense sharing formulae. Financial programs. Claims and settlements. Tax exemptions. Customs exemptions. Domestic obligation. General technical assistance. Economic assistance. Materials, equipment and services. IGO status.
INTL ORGS: International Atomic Energy Agency. International Court of Justice. United Nations. Arbitration Commission.
TREATY REF: 374UNTS137; 1UNTS15; 33UNTS261.
PROCEDURE: Amendment. Termination.
PARTIES:
UN Special Fund
Turkey

104964 Bilateral Agreement **345 UNTS 125**
SIGNED: 25 Nov 59　　FORCE: 25 Nov 59
REGISTERED: 25 Nov 59 United Nations
ARTICLES: 10 LANGUAGE: English.
HEADNOTE: ASSISTANCE
TOPIC: Direct Aid
CONCEPTS: Detailed regulations. Treaty implementation. Annex or appendix reference. Privileges and immunities. Exchange of information and documents. Informational records. Inspection and observation. Operating agencies. Personnel. Public information. Responsibility and liability. Title and deeds. Use of facilities. Arbitration. Procedure. Negotiation. Import quotas. Exchange rates and regulations. Expense sharing formulae. Financial programs.

Claims and settlements. Tax exemptions. Customs exemptions. Domestic obligation. General technical assistance. Economic assistance. Materials, equipment and services. IGO status.
INTL ORGS: International Atomic Energy Agency. International Court of Justice. United Nations. Arbitration Commission.
TREATY REF: 1UNTS15; 33UNTS261; 374UNTS137.
PROCEDURE: Amendment. Termination.
PARTIES:
UN Special Fund
United Arab Rep

104965 Bilateral Agreement **345 UNTS 145**
SIGNED: 5 Jun 58　　FORCE: 5 Jun 58
REGISTERED: 27 Nov 59 Belgium
ARTICLES: 11 LANGUAGE: French. Russian.
HEADNOTE: AIR TRANSPORT
TOPIC: Air Transport
CONCEPTS: Representation. Annex or appendix reference. Conformity with municipal law. General cooperation. Use of facilities. Humanitarian matters. Customs exemptions. Registration certificate. Routes and logistics. Navigational conditions. Navigational equipment. Permit designation. Air transport. Airworthiness certificates. Conditions of airlines operating permission. Operating authorizations and regulations. Recognition of legal documents.
PROCEDURE: Denunciation. Termination.
PARTIES:
Belgium
USSR (Soviet Union)

104966 Bilateral Convention **345 UNTS 171**
SIGNED: 13 Nov 59　　FORCE: 13 Nov 59
REGISTERED: 27 Nov 59 United Nations
ARTICLES: 10 LANGUAGE: English. French.
HEADNOTE: ASSISTANCE
TOPIC: Direct Aid
CONCEPTS: Detailed regulations. Treaty implementation. Visas. Privileges and immunities. Exchange of information and documents. Informational records. Inspection and observation. Operating agencies. Personnel. Public information. Responsibility and liability. Title and deeds. Use of facilities. Arbitration. Procedure. Negotiation. Import quotas. Exchange rates and regulations. Expense sharing formulae. Financial programs. Claims and settlements. Tax exemptions. Customs exemptions. Domestic obligation. General technical assistance. Economic assistance. Materials, equipment and services. IGO status.
INTL ORGS: International Atomic Energy Agency. International Court of Justice. United Nations. Arbitration Commission.
TREATY REF: 1UNTS15; 33UNTS261; 374UNTS137.
PROCEDURE: Amendment. Termination.
PARTIES:
Greece
UN Special Fund

104967 Bilateral Agreement **345 UNTS 189**
SIGNED: 20 Nov 53　　FORCE: 20 Nov 53
REGISTERED: 1 Dec 59 Ceylon (Sri Lanka)
ARTICLES: 10 LANGUAGE: English. Irish.
HEADNOTE: ECONOMIC COMMERCIAL RELATIONS
TOPIC: General Economic
CONCEPTS: General cooperation. Use of facilities. Establishment of trade relations. Export quotas. Commodity trade. Quotas. Customs duties. Customs declarations. Transport of goods. Water transport.
PROCEDURE: Duration. Termination.
PARTIES:
Ceylon (Sri Lanka)
Ireland

104968 Bilateral Agreement **345 UNTS 197**
SIGNED: 1 Dec 59　　FORCE: 1 Dec 59
REGISTERED: 1 Dec 59 United Nations
ARTICLES: 1 LANGUAGE: English.
HEADNOTE: ASSISTANCE
TOPIC: Direct Aid
CONCEPTS: Detailed regulations. Treaty implementation. Visas. Privileges and immunities. Exchange of information and documents. Informa-

tional records. Inspection and observation. Operating agencies. Personnel. Public information. Responsibility and liability. Title and deeds. Use of facilities. Arbitration. Procedure. Negotiation. Import quotas. Exchange rates and regulations. Expense sharing formulae. Financial programs. Claims and settlements. Tax exemptions. Customs exemptions. Domestic obligation. General technical assistance. Economic assistance. Materials, equipment and services. IGO status.
INTL ORGS: International Atomic Energy Agency. International Court of Justice. United Nations. Arbitration Commission.
TREATY REF: 1UNTS15; 33UNTS261; 374UNTS137.
PROCEDURE: Amendment. Termination.
PARTIES:
Israel
UN Special Fund

104969 Bilateral Agreement **345 UNTS 215**
SIGNED: 2 Dec 59　　FORCE: 2 Dec 59
REGISTERED: 2 Dec 59 United Nations
ARTICLES: 10 LANGUAGE: English. French.
HEADNOTE: ASSISTANCE FROM UNSF
TOPIC: Direct Aid
CONCEPTS: Detailed regulations. General provisions. Privileges and immunities. General cooperation. Exchange of information and documents. Informational records. Free passage and transit. Licenses and permits. Personnel. General property. Use of facilities. Arbitration. Procedure. Negotiation. Import quotas. Exchange rates and regulations. Expense sharing formulae. Fees and exemptions. Funding procedures. Claims and settlements. Tax exemptions. Domestic obligation. Assistance. General aid. Economic assistance. Materials, equipment and services. Status of experts. IGO operations.
INTL ORGS: International Atomic Energy Agency. International Court of Justice. United Nations. Arbitration Commission.
PROCEDURE: Amendment. Termination.
PARTIES:
Guinea
UN Special Fund

104970 Bilateral Agreement **345 UNTS 231**
SIGNED: 25 Jun 58　　FORCE: 29 Aug 59
REGISTERED: 3 Dec 59 Denmark
ARTICLES: 16 LANGUAGE: French.
HEADNOTE: CIVIL AIR TRANSPORT
TOPIC: Air Transport
CONCEPTS: Definition of terms. Annex or appendix reference. Conformity with municipal law. General cooperation. Licenses and permits. Personnel. Recognition of legal documents. Use of facilities. Procedure. Negotiation. Monetary and gold transfers. Exchange rates and regulations. Fees and exemptions. Payment schedules. Non-interest rates and fees. Customs exemptions. Registration certificate. Routes and logistics. Navigational conditions. Permit designation. Airport facilities. Airworthiness certificates. Conditions of airlines operating permission. Operating authorizations and regulations.
PROCEDURE: Amendment. Denunciation. Ratification.
PARTIES:
Denmark
Romania

104971 Multilateral Agreement **345 UNTS 251**
SIGNED: 3 Dec 59　　FORCE: 3 Dec 59
REGISTERED: 3 Dec 59 United Nations
ARTICLES: 7 LANGUAGE: Spanish.
HEADNOTE: ADVANCED SCHOOL PUBLIC ADMINISTRATION CENTRAL AMERICA (ESAPAC)
TOPIC: Tech Assistance
CONCEPTS: Time limit. Personnel. Teacher and student exchange. Scholarships and grants. Expense sharing formulae. General technical assistance.
PROCEDURE: Amendment. Termination.
PARTIES:
Costa Rica SIGNED: 3 Dec 59 FORCE: 3 Dec 59
El Salvador SIGNED: 3 Dec 59 FORCE: 3 Dec 59
Guatemala SIGNED: 3 Dec 59 FORCE: 3 Dec 59
Honduras SIGNED: 3 Dec 59 FORCE: 3 Dec 59
Nicaragua SIGNED: 3 Dec 59 FORCE: 3 Dec 59

United Nations SIGNED: 3 Dec 59 FORCE:
3 Dec 59

104972 Bilateral Agreement **345 UNTS 263**
SIGNED: 4 Dec 59   FORCE: 4 Dec 59
REGISTERED: 4 Dec 59 United Nations
ARTICLES: 10 LANGUAGE: English. Spanish.
HEADNOTE: ASSISTANCE
TOPIC: Direct Aid
CONCEPTS: Detailed regulations. Treaty imple-
mentation. Visas. Privileges and immunities. Ex-
change of information and documents. Informa-
tional records. Inspection and observation. Oper-
ating agencies. Personnel. Public information.
Responsibility and liability. Title and deeds. Use
of facilities. Arbitration. Procedure. Negotiation.
Import quotas. Exchange rates and regulations.
Expense sharing formulae. Financial programs.
Claims and settlements. Tax exemptions. Cus-
toms exemptions. Domestic obligation. General
technical assistance. Economic assistance. Ma-
terials, equipment and services. IGO status.
INTL ORGS: International Atomic Energy Agency.
International Court of Justice. United Nations.
Arbitration Commission.
TREATY   REF: 1UNTS15;   33UNTS261;
374UNTS137.
PROCEDURE: Amendment. Termination.
PARTIES:
Argentina
UN Special Fund

104973 Multilateral Agreement **345 UNTS 285**
SIGNED: 21 May 54   FORCE: 1 Dec 59
REGISTERED: 4 Dec 59 ILO (Labor Org)
ARTICLES: 33 LANGUAGE: French.
HEADNOTE: CONDITION EMPLOYMENT
TOPIC: Non-ILO Labor
CONCEPTS: Definition of terms. Detailed regula-
tions. Treaty interpretation. Exchange of infor-
mation and documents. Investigation of viola-
tions. Establishment of commission. Dispute set-
tlement. Holidays and rest periods. Safety
standards. Wages and salaries. Non-ILO labor re-
lations.
INTL ORGS: Central Commission for the Naviga-
tion of the Rhine. International Labour Organiza-
tion. United Nations. Special Commission.
PROCEDURE: Accession. Denunciation. Duration.
Ratification. Registration. Renewal or Revival.
PARTIES:
Belgium   SIGNED: 21 May 54   RATIFIED:
18 Sep 59 FORCE: 1 Dec 59
France SIGNED: 21 May 54 RATIFIED: 22 Jul 57
FORCE: 1 Dec 59
Germany, West SIGNED: 21 May 54 RATIFIED:
22 Aug 57 FORCE: 1 Dec 59
Netherlands   SIGNED: 21 May 54   RATIFIED:
4 Apr 55 FORCE: 1 Dec 59
Switzerland   SIGNED: 21 May 54   RATIFIED:
8 Aug 55 FORCE: 1 Dec 59

104974 Bilateral Agreement **346 UNTS 3**
SIGNED: 15 Dec 59   FORCE: 15 Dec 59
REGISTERED: 15 Dec 59 United Nations
ARTICLES: 10 LANGUAGE: English.
HEADNOTE: ASSISTANCE
TOPIC: Direct Aid
CONCEPTS: Detailed regulations. Treaty implementation. Visas. Privileges and immunities. Exchange of information and documents. Informa-
tional records. Inspection and observation. Oper-
ating agencies. Personnel. Public information.
Title and deeds. Use of facilities. Establishment
of commission. Arbitration. Procedure. Negotia-
tion. Import quotas. Exchange rates and regula-
tions. Expense sharing formulae. Financial pro-
grams. Claims and settlements. Tax exemptions.
Customs exemptions. Domestic obligation. Gen-
eral technical assistance. Economic assistance.
Materials, equipment and services. IGO status.
INTL ORGS: International Atomic Energy Agency.
International Court of Justice. United Nations.
Arbitration Commission.
TREATY   REF: 1UNTS15;   33UNTS261;
374UNTS137.
PROCEDURE: Amendment. Termination.
PARTIES:
Jordan
UN Special Fund

ANNEX
354 UNTS 446. UN Special Fund. Amendment
20 Mar 60. Force 20 Mar 60.
354 UNTS 446. Jordan. Amendment 20 Mar 60.
Force 20 Mar 60.

104975 Bilateral Exchange **346 UNTS 21**
SIGNED: 30 Oct 59   FORCE: 30 Oct 59
REGISTERED: 16 Dec 59 Norway
ARTICLES: 2 LANGUAGE: English.
HEADNOTE: LOAN NORWAY STATION
TOPIC: Specific Property
CONCEPTS: Annex or appendix reference. Facili-
ties and property.
PARTIES:
Norway
South Africa

104976 Bilateral Agreement **346 UNTS 33**
SIGNED: 15 Jul 59   FORCE: 17 Sep 59
REGISTERED: 21 Dec 59 IBRD (World Bank)
ARTICLES: 7 LANGUAGE: English.
HEADNOTE: LOAN RAILWAY
TOPIC: IBRD Project
CONCEPTS: Default remedies. Annex or appendix
reference. Exchange of information and docu-
ments. Inspection and observation. Accounting
procedures. Bonds. Fees and exemptions. Inter-
est rates. Tax exemptions. Terms of loan. Loan
regulations. Loan guarantee. Guarantor non-
interference. Railways.
PARTIES:
India
IBRD (World Bank)

104977 Bilateral Agreement **346 UNTS 51**
SIGNED: 7 Jan 59   FORCE: 20 Nov 59
REGISTERED: 21 Dec 59 IBRD (World Bank)
ARTICLES: 7 LANGUAGE: English.
HEADNOTE: LOAN FEEDER ROAD PROGRAM
TOPIC: IBRD Project
CONCEPTS: Default remedies. Annex or appendix
reference. Exchange of information and docu-
ments. Inspection and observation. Accounting
procedures. Bonds. Fees and exemptions. Inter-
est rates. Domestic obligation. Terms of loan.
Loan regulations. Loan guarantee. Guarantor
non-interference. Roads and highways.
PARTIES:
El Salvador
IBRD (World Bank)

104978 Bilateral Agreement **346 UNTS 71**
SIGNED: 25 Apr 58   FORCE: 24 Apr 59
REGISTERED: 21 Dec 59 USSR (Soviet Union)
ARTICLES: 9 LANGUAGE: Russian. German.
HEADNOTE: DEVELOPMENT ECONOMIC RELA-
TIONS
TOPIC: General Economic
CONCEPTS: Exceptions and exemptions. Annex or
appendix reference. Non-diplomatic delega-
tions. Informational records. Recognition and en-
forcement of legal decisions. Arbitration. Estab-
lishment of trade relations. Export quotas. Import
quotas. Most favored nation clause. Registration
certificate. Navigational equipment. Licenses
and certificates of nationality. Merchant vessels.
Ports and pilotage. Shipwreck and salvage.
PROCEDURE: Duration. Future Procedures Contemplated. Ratification.
PARTIES:
Germany, West
USSR (Soviet Union)

104979 Bilateral Agreement **346 UNTS 107**
SIGNED: 16 Mar 59   FORCE: 16 Apr 59
REGISTERED: 21 Dec 59 USSR (Soviet Union)
ARTICLES: 12 LANGUAGE: Russian. Arabic.
HEADNOTE: ECONOMIC & TECHNICAL COOPER-
ATION
TOPIC: General Aid
CONCEPTS: Treaty implementation. Exchange of
information and documents. Personnel. Private
contracts. Research and development. Account-
ing procedures. Indemnities and reimburse-
ments. Currency. Currency deposits. Exchange
rates and regulations. Domestic obligation. Gen-
eral technical assistance. Economic assistance.

Use restrictions. Procurement. Loan and credit.
Loan repayment.
PROCEDURE: Ratification.
PARTIES:
Iraq
USSR (Soviet Union)
ANNEX
399 UNTS 287. USSR (Soviet Union). Supplemen-
tation 18 Aug 60. Force 9 Jan 61.
399 UNTS 287.   Iraq.   Supplementation
18 Aug 60. Force 9 Jan 61.

104980 Multilateral Agreement **346 UNTS 167**
SIGNED: 29 Apr 59   FORCE: 29 Apr 59
REGISTERED: 21 Dec 59 USSR (Soviet Union)
ARTICLES: 9 LANGUAGE: Russian. Norwegian.
Finnish.
HEADNOTE: REGULATION LAKE INARI
TOPIC: Specific Property
CONCEPTS: Annex or appendix reference. Previ-
ous treaty replacement. Establishment of com-
mission. Dispute settlement. Facilities and prop-
erty. Regulation of natural resources.
INTL ORGS: Special Commission.
TREATY REF: 243UNTS147.
PARTIES:
Finland SIGNED: 29 Apr 59 FORCE: 29 Apr 59
Norway SIGNED: 29 Apr 59 FORCE: 29 Apr 59
USSR (Soviet Union) SIGNED: 29 Apr 59 FORCE:
29 Apr 59

104981 Bilateral Protocol **346 UNTS 209**
SIGNED: 29 Apr 59   FORCE: 29 Apr 59
REGISTERED: 21 Dec 59 USSR (Soviet Union)
ARTICLES: 2 LANGUAGE: Russian. Finnish.
HEADNOTE: COMPENSATION FOR LOSS
TOPIC: Specif Claim/Waive
CONCEPTS: Lump sum settlements. Specific
claims or waivers.
TREATY REF: 346UNTS167.
PARTIES:
Finland
USSR (Soviet Union)

104982 Bilateral Agreement **346 UNTS 217**
SIGNED: 30 Jun 58   FORCE: 20 Aug 59
REGISTERED: 23 Dec 59 Norway
ARTICLES: 3 LANGUAGE: English.
HEADNOTE: COMPENSATION LOST BONDS WAR
DAMAGES
TOPIC: Reparations
CONCEPTS: Detailed regulations. Annex or appen-
dix reference. Exchange of information and doc-
uments. Compensation. Interest rates. Loss and-
/or damage. Post-war claims settlement.
PARTIES:
Netherlands
Norway

104983 Bilateral Exchange **346 UNTS 235**
SIGNED: 20 May 59   FORCE: 20 May 59
REGISTERED: 24 Dec 59 USA (United States)
ARTICLES: 2 LANGUAGE: English. Spanish.
HEADNOTE: SALE MILITARY EQUIPMENT MATE-
RIALS SERVICES
TOPIC: Milit Assistance
CONCEPTS: Definition of terms. Conformity with
municipal law. Materials, equipment and ser-
vices. Self-defense. Payment for war supplies.
Security of information. Exchange of defense in-
formation. Restrictions on transfer.
PARTIES:
Panama
USA (United States)

104984 Bilateral Exchange **346 UNTS 241**
SIGNED: 7 Jun 57   FORCE: 12 May 59
REGISTERED: 24 Dec 59 USA (United States)
ARTICLES: 5 LANGUAGE: English. German.
HEADNOTE: COST MAINTENANCE US FORCES
TOPIC: Milit Assistance
CONCEPTS: Responsibility and liability. Indemni-
ties and reimbursements. Expense sharing for-
mulae. Local currency. Claims and settlements.
Payment for war supplies. Military assistance.
INTL ORGS: North Atlantic Treaty Organization.
TREATY REF: 34UNTS243.
PROCEDURE: Future Procedures Contemplated.
Ratification.

PARTIES:
Germany, West
USA (United States)

104985 Bilateral Exchange **346 UNTS 263**
SIGNED: 22 May 59　　FORCE: 22 May 59
REGISTERED: 24 Dec 59 USA (United States)
ARTICLES: 2 LANGUAGE: English.
HEADNOTE: EXPERTS TECHNICAL IMPROVE-
MENT TAX SYSTEM
TOPIC: Tech Assistance
CONCEPTS: Time limit. Conformity with municipal
law. General cooperation. Informational records.
Personnel. Use of facilities. Specialists ex-
change. Expense sharing formulae. Fees and ex-
emptions. Financial programs. Tax exemptions.
Customs exemptions. Domestic obligation. As-
sistance.
PARTIES:
Fed of Malaya
USA (United States)

104986 Bilateral Exchange **346 UNTS 271**
SIGNED: 19 May 59　　FORCE: 19 May 59
REGISTERED: 24 Dec 59 USA (United States)
ARTICLES: 2 LANGUAGE: English.
HEADNOTE: LOAN VESSEL
TOPIC: Milit Assistance
CONCEPTS: Time limit. Annex or appendix refer-
ence. Responsibility and liability. Title and
deeds. Compensation. Delivery schedules. Lease
of military property. Naval vessels. Return of
equipment and recapture. Restrictions on trans-
fer.
TREATY REF: 79UNTS41.
PARTIES:
Thailand
USA (United States)
ANNEX
546 UNTS 339. USA (United States). Prolongation
24 Sep 65. Force 22 Apr 65.
546 UNTS 339.　　Thailand.　　Prolongation
24 Sep 65. Force 22 Apr 65.

104987 Bilateral Exchange **346 UNTS 279**
SIGNED: 15 Jun 59　　FORCE: 15 Jun 59
REGISTERED: 24 Dec 59 USA (United States)
ARTICLES: 2 LANGUAGE: English.
HEADNOTE: LOAN FLOATING DRY DOCKS
TOPIC: Milit Assistance
CONCEPTS: Time limit. Conformity with municipal
law. Responsibility and liability. Title and deeds.
Use of facilities. Compensation. Indemnities and
reimbursements. Delivery schedules. Lease of
military property. Return of equipment and re-
capture.
TREATY REF: 165UNTS31.
PARTIES:
Peru
USA (United States)

104988 Bilateral Exchange **347 UNTS 3**
SIGNED: 22 May 59　　FORCE: 22 May 59
REGISTERED: 28 Dec 59 USA (United States)
ARTICLES: 3 LANGUAGE: English. German.
HEADNOTE: SETTLEMENT CLAIMS
TOPIC: Reparations
CONCEPTS: Definition of terms. General property.
Establishment of commission. Accounting pro-
cedures. Monetary and gold transfers. Exchange
rates and regulations. Loss and/or damage.
Enemy financial interests. Reparations and re-
strictions. Post-war claims settlement.
PARTIES:
Austria
USA (United States)

104989 Bilateral Agreement **347 UNTS 41**
SIGNED: 10 Jun 59　　FORCE: 10 Jun 59
REGISTERED: 28 Dec 59 USA (United States)
ARTICLES: 6 LANGUAGE: English. Polish.
HEADNOTE: AGRI COMMOD TITLE I
TOPIC: US Agri Commod Aid
CONCEPTS: General provisions. Establishment of
trade relations. Exchange rates and regulations.
Transportation costs. Local currency. Commodi-
ties schedule. Purchase authorization. Surplus
commodities. Mutual consultation.

PARTIES:
Poland
USA (United States)
ANNEX
357 UNTS 396. Poland. Amendment 10 Nov 59.
Force 10 Nov 59.
357 UNTS 396. USA (United States). Amendment
10 Nov 59. Force 10 Nov 59.
371 UNTS 364. Poland. Amendment 11 Feb 60.
Force 11 Feb 60.
371 UNTS 364. USA (United States). Amendment
11 Feb 60. Force 11 Feb 60.
380 UNTS 474. Poland. Amendment 21 Jul 60.
Force 21 Jul 60.
380 UNTS 474. USA (United States). Amendment
21 Jul 60. Force 21 Jul 60.

104990 Bilateral Agreement **347 UNTS 59**
SIGNED: 12 Jun 59　　FORCE: 12 Jun 59
REGISTERED: 28 Dec 59 USA (United States)
ARTICLES: 6 LANGUAGE: English.
HEADNOTE: AGRI COMMOD TITLE I
TOPIC: US Agri Commod Aid
CONCEPTS: General provisions. Annex or appen-
dix reference. Exchange of information and doc-
uments. Reexport of goods, etc.. Exchange rates
and regulations. Transportation costs. Local cur-
rency. Commodities schedule. Surplus commod-
ities. Mutual consultation.
PARTIES:
Argentina
USA (United States)

104991 Bilateral Exchange **347 UNTS 77**
SIGNED: 29 May 59　　FORCE: 29 May 59
REGISTERED: 28 Dec 59 USA (United States)
ARTICLES: 2 LANGUAGE: English.
HEADNOTE: CHOLERA RESEARCH PROGRAM
TOPIC: Sanitation
CONCEPTS: Detailed regulations. General cooper-
ation. Disease control. Public health. Research
cooperation. Scientific exchange. Grants.
TREATY REF: 209UNTS23.
PARTIES:
SEATO (SE Asia)
USA (United States)

104992 Bilateral Agreement **347 UNTS 85**
SIGNED: 29 May 59　　FORCE: 29 May 59
REGISTERED: 28 Dec 59 USA (United States)
ARTICLES: 6 LANGUAGE: English.
HEADNOTE: AGRI COMMOD TITLE I
TOPIC: US Agri Commod Aid
CONCEPTS: General provisions. Annex or appendix reference. Exchange of information and documents. Reexport of goods, etc.. Exchange rates
and regulations. Transportation costs. Local currency. Commodities schedule. Purchase authorization. Surplus commodities. Mutual consultation.
PARTIES:
Indonesia
USA (United States)
ANNEX
358 UNTS 380. USA (United States). Amendment
1 Oct 59. Force 1 Oct 59.
358 UNTS 380. Indonesia. Amendment 1 Oct 59.
Force 1 Oct 59.
371 UNTS 372. USA (United States). Amendment
18 Nov 59. Force 18 Nov 59.
371 UNTS 372.　　Indonesia.　　Amendment
18 Nov 59. Force 18 Nov 59.
377 UNTS 448. USA (United States). Amendment
23 May 60. Force 8 Jun 60.
377 UNTS 448. Indonesia. Amendment 8 Jun 60.
Force 8 Jun 60.
401 UNTS 328.　　Indonesia.　　Supplementation
5 Nov 60. Force 5 Nov 60.
401 UNTS 328. USA (United States). Supplementation 5 Nov 60. Force 5 Nov 60.

104993 Bilateral Agreement **347 UNTS 113**
SIGNED: 22 Apr 59　　FORCE: 1 Sep 59
REGISTERED: 28 Dec 59 USA (United States)
ARTICLES: 12 LANGUAGE: English.
HEADNOTE: COOPERATION CIVIL USES ATOMIC
ENERGY
TOPIC: Atomic Energy
CONCEPTS: Definition of terms. Non-prejudice to
third party. Conformity with municipal law. Ex-

change of information and documents. Inspec-
tion and observation. Responsibility and liability.
Assets transfer. Nuclear materials. Non-nuclear
materials. Security of information.
INTL ORGS: International Atomic Energy Agency.
PROCEDURE: Duration.
PARTIES:
USA (United States)
Vietnam, South
ANNEX
529 UNTS 356. USA (United States). Amendment
9 Jun 64. Force 10 Aug 64.
529 UNTS 356. Vietnam, South. Amendment
9 Jun 64. Force 10 Aug 64.

104994 Multilateral Convention **347 UNTS 127**
SIGNED: 15 Dec 50　　FORCE: 11 Sep 59
REGISTERED: 30 Dec 59 Belgium
ARTICLES: 16 LANGUAGE: English. French.
HEADNOTE: CUSTOMS TARIFFS
TOPIC: Customs
CONCEPTS: Definition of terms. Territorial applica-
tion. Annex or appendix reference. Previous
treaty renunciation. Procedure. Negotiation.
Conciliation. Tariffs. Customs duties. Subsidiary
organ.
INTL ORGS: Customs Co-operation Council. Spe-
cial Commission.
PROCEDURE: Amendment. Accession. Duration.
Ratification. Registration.
PARTIES:
Austria　　SIGNED:　　15 Dec 50　　RATIFIED:
22 Aug 58 FORCE: 11 Sep 59
Belgium SIGNED: 15 Dec 50 FORCE: 11 Sep 59
Denmark　　SIGNED:　　15 Dec 50　　RATIFIED:
6 Mar 59 FORCE: 11 Sep 59
France SIGNED: 15 Dec 50 RATIFIED: 21 Jun 54
FORCE: 11 Sep 59
Germany, West SIGNED: 15 Dec 50 FORCE:
11 Sep 59
Greece　　SIGNED:　　15 Dec 50　　RATIFIED:
10 Dec 51 FORCE: 11 Sep 59
Haiti RATIFIED: 31 Jan 58
Iceland SIGNED: 15 Dec 50 FORCE: 11 Sep 59
Iran RATIFIED: 16 Oct 59
Ireland SIGNED: 15 Dec 50 FORCE: 11 Sep 59
Italy SIGNED: 15 Dec 50 RATIFIED: 23 Dec 58
FORCE: 11 Sep 59
Luxembourg　　SIGNED:　　15 Dec 50　　FORCE:
11 Sep 59
Netherlands　　SIGNED:　　15 Dec 50　　FORCE:
11 Sep 59
Norway　　SIGNED:　　15 Dec 50　　RATIFIED:
11 Jun 59 FORCE: 11 Sep 59
Portugal SIGNED: 15 Dec 50 FORCE: 11 Sep 59
Sweden　　SIGNED:　　15 Dec 50　　RATIFIED:
15 Oct 58 FORCE: 11 Sep 59
Switzerland　　SIGNED:　　15 Dec 50　　FORCE:
11 Sep 59
Turkey SIGNED: 15 Dec 50 RATIFIED: 6 Jun 51
FORCE: 11 Sep 59
UK Great Britain SIGNED: 15 Dec 50 RATIFIED:
30 Sep 58 FORCE: 11 Sep 59
ANNEX
560 UNTS 277. Greece. Ratification 18 May 65.
Force 18 Aug 65.

104995 Bilateral Exchange **348 UNTS 3**
SIGNED: 30 Jun 58　　FORCE: 20 Aug 59
REGISTERED: 5 Jan 60 Norway
ARTICLES: 2 LANGUAGE: English.
HEADNOTE: RELEASE SECURITIES CONSIDERED
ENEMY PROPERTY
TOPIC: Reparations
CONCEPTS: Annex or appendix reference. Enemy
financial interests. Reparations and restrictions.
INTL ORGS: Inter-Allied Reparations Agency.
PARTIES:
Netherlands
Norway

104996 Multilateral Convention **348 UNTS 13**
SIGNED: 15 Jan 59　　FORCE: 7 Jan 60
REGISTERED: 7 Jan 60 United Nations
ARTICLES: 51 LANGUAGE: English. French.
HEADNOTE: CUSTOMS CONVENTION
TOPIC: Customs
CONCEPTS: Definition of terms. Detailed regula-
tions. Territorial application. Annex or appendix
reference. Responsibility and liability. Investiga-
tion of violations. Arbitration. Negotiation. Reci-

procity in trade. Claims and settlements. Customs exemptions. Transport of goods.
INTL ORGS: European Economic Community. United Nations. Arbitration Commission.
TREATY REF: 45UNTS149.
PROCEDURE: Amendment. Accession. Denunciation. Ratification. Registration.
PARTIES:
Austria SIGNED: 15 Feb 59
Belgium SIGNED: 4 Mar 59
Bulgaria SIGNED: 15 Apr 59 FORCE: 7 Jan 60
Denmark SIGNED: 15 Apr 59 FORCE: 7 Jan 60
France SIGNED: 14 Apr 59 RATIFIED: 3 Jul 59 FORCE: 7 Jan 60
Germany, West SIGNED: 13 Apr 59
Italy SIGNED: 15 Apr 59
Luxembourg SIGNED: 14 Apr 59
Netherlands SIGNED: 9 Apr 59
Sweden SIGNED: 14 Apr 59 FORCE: 7 Jan 60
Switzerland SIGNED: 12 Mar 59
UK Great Britain SIGNED: 13 Apr 59 RATIFIED: 9 Oct 59 FORCE: 7 Jan 60
ANNEX
349 UNTS 349. Austria. Ratification 3 Feb 60. Force 3 May 60.
351 UNTS 466. Norway. Accession 2 Mar 60. Force 31 May 60.
366 UNTS 420. Switzerland. Qualified Ratification 7 Jul 60. Force 5 Oct 60.
371 UNTS 376. Netherlands. Ratification 27 Jul 60. Force 25 Oct 60.
373 UNTS 379. Yugoslavia. Accession 23 Aug 60. Force 21 Nov 60.
395 UNTS 276. Greece. Qualified Accession 2 May 61. Force 31 Jul 61.
396 UNTS 349. Spain. Accession 12 May 61. Force 10 Aug 61.
406 UNTS 334. Czechoslovakia. Qualified Accession 31 Aug 61.
410 UNTS 352. Poland. Qualified Accession 3 Oct 61. Force 1 Jan 62.
411 UNTS 322. Germany, West. Ratification 23 Oct 61. Force 21 Jan 61.
415 UNTS 435. Germany, West. Berlin.
415 UNTS 435. Hungary. Qualified Accession 6 Dec 61.
424 UNTS 383. Belgium. Ratification 14 Mar 62. Force 12 Jun 62.
431 UNTS 317. Luxembourg. Ratification 2 Jul 62. Force 10 Oct 62.
450 UNTS 470. Italy. Ratification 11 Jan 63. Force 11 Apr 63.
481 UNTS 598. Multilateral. Amendment 19 Nov 63. Force 19 Nov 63.
492 UNTS 364. Romania. Qualified Accession 9 Apr 64. Force 8 Jul 64.
557 UNTS 278. Turkey. Qualified Accession 23 Feb 66. Force 24 May 66.
566 UNTS 356. Multilateral. Amendment 1 Jul 66. Force 1 Jul 66.
600 UNTS 360. Ireland. Accession 7 Jul 67. Force 5 Oct 67.
651 UNTS 360. USA (United States). Accession 3 Dec 68. Force 3 Mar 69.

104997 Bilateral Agreement **348 UNTS 103**
SIGNED: 29 May 59 FORCE: 22 Sep 59
REGISTERED: 7 Jan 60 IBRD (World Bank)
ARTICLES: 8 LANGUAGE: English.
HEADNOTE: LOAN ROAD
TOPIC: IBRD Project
CONCEPTS: Default remedies. Definition of terms. Exchange of information and documents. Inspection and observation. Accounting procedures. Bonds. Fees and exemptions. Interest rates. Tax exemptions. Domestic obligation. Terms of loan. Loan regulations. Loan guarantee. Guarantor non-interference. Roads and highways.
PARTIES:
Iran
IBRD (World Bank)

104998 Bilateral Agreement **348 UNTS 131**
SIGNED: 8 Apr 59 FORCE: 16 Jul 59
REGISTERED: 7 Jan 60 IBRD (World Bank)
ARTICLES: 8 LANGUAGE: English.
HEADNOTE: LOAN POWER
TOPIC: IBRD Project
CONCEPTS: Default remedies. Definition of terms. Exchange of information and documents. Inspection and observation. Accounting proce-

dures. Bonds. Fees and exemptions. Interest rates. Tax exemptions. Domestic obligation. Terms of loan. Loan regulations. Loan guarantee. Guarantor non-interference. Hydro-electric power.
PARTIES:
India
IBRD (World Bank)

104999 Bilateral Agreement **348 UNTS 159**
SIGNED: 8 Feb 58 FORCE: 8 Feb 58
REGISTERED: 7 Jan 60 Ceylon (Sri Lanka)
ARTICLES: 10 LANGUAGE: English. Russian.
HEADNOTE: ECONOMIC TRADE RELATIONS
TOPIC: General Trade
CONCEPTS: Detailed regulations. Exceptions and exemptions. Treaty implementation. Annex or appendix reference. Conformity with municipal law. General cooperation. Licenses and permits. Establishment of commission. Establishment of trade relations. Export quotas. Import quotas. Trade procedures. Payment schedules. Most favored nation clause. Navigational conditions. Merchant vessels. Inland and territorial waters. Ports and pilotage.
INTL ORGS: Special Commission.
PROCEDURE: Duration. Termination.
PARTIES:
Ceylon (Sri Lanka)
USSR (Soviet Union)

105000 Bilateral Agreement **348 UNTS 177**
SIGNED: 7 Jan 60 FORCE: 17 Jan 60
REGISTERED: 7 Jan 60 United Nations
ARTICLES: 10 LANGUAGE: English.
HEADNOTE: ASSISTANCE
TOPIC: Direct Aid
CONCEPTS: Detailed regulations. Treaty implementation. Annex or appendix reference. Visas. Privileges and immunities. Exchange of information and documents. Informational records. Inspection and observation. Operating agencies. Personnel. Public information. Responsibility and liability. Title and deeds. Use of facilities. Arbitration. Procedure. Negotiation. Import quotas. Exchange rates and regulations. Expense sharing formulae. Financial programs. Claims and settlements. Tax exemptions. Customs exemptions. Domestic obligation. General technical assistance. Economic assistance. Materials, equipment and services. IGO status.
INTL ORGS: International Atomic Energy Agency. International Court of Justice. United Nations. Arbitration Commission.
TREATY REF: 1UNTS15; 33UNTS261; 374UNTS137.
PROCEDURE: Amendment. Termination.
PARTIES:
UN Special Fund
UK Great Britain
ANNEX
362 UNTS 340. UK Great Britain. Fed Rhod/-Nyasaland. Force 28 Jun 60.
362 UNTS 340. UN Special Fund. Acknowledgement 28 Jun 60. Force 28 Jun 60.
618 UNTS 380. UK Great Britain. Bahrain. Force 18 Jan 68.
618 UNTS 380. UK Great Britain. Qatar. Force 18 Jan 68.

105001 Bilateral Exchange **348 UNTS 201**
SIGNED: 18 Dec 59 FORCE: 18 Dec 59
REGISTERED: 8 Jan 60 Australia
ARTICLES: 2 LANGUAGE: English. German.
HEADNOTE: RELEASE PROPERTY SUBJECT SPECIAL MEASURES
TOPIC: Reparations
CONCEPTS: Definition of terms. Annex or appendix reference. General property. Accounting procedures. Debt settlement. Enemy financial interests. Reparations and restrictions. Post-war claims settlement.
PARTIES:
Australia
Austria

105002 Bilateral Agreement **348 UNTS 225**
SIGNED: 29 May 59 FORCE: 8 Sep 59
REGISTERED: 12 Jan 60 Denmark
ARTICLES: 18 LANGUAGE: English.

HEADNOTE: RELATING AIR SERVICES
TOPIC: Air Transport
CONCEPTS: Definition of terms. Detailed regulations. Annex or appendix reference. Conformity with municipal law. General cooperation. Exchange of information and documents. Licenses and permits. Recognition of legal documents. Use of facilities. Arbitration. Procedure. Existing tribunals. Reexport of goods, etc.. Monetary and gold transfers. Exchange rates and regulations. Fees and exemptions. Non-interest rates and fees. Most favored nation clause. National treatment. Customs exemptions. Competency certificate. Routes and logistics. Navigational conditions. Permit designation. Airport facilities. Airworthiness certificates. Conditions of airlines operating permission. Operating authorizations and regulations. Licenses and certificates of nationality.
INTL ORGS: International Civil Aviation Organization. Arbitration Commission.
TREATY REF: 15UNTS295.
PROCEDURE: Amendment. Future Procedures Contemplated. Registration. Termination. Application to Non-self-governing Territories.
PARTIES:
Ceylon (Sri Lanka)
Denmark

105003 Multilateral Agreement **348 UNTS 246**
SIGNED: 3 Dec 59 FORCE: 3 Dec 59
REGISTERED: 14 Jan 60 United Nations
ARTICLES: 6 LANGUAGE: French.
HEADNOTE: TECHNICAL ASSISTANCE
TOPIC: Tech Assistance
CONCEPTS: Definition of terms. Privileges and immunities. General cooperation. Exchange of information and documents. Personnel. Responsibility and liability. Title and deeds. Exchange. Scholarships and grants. Vocational training. Research and development. Exchange rates and regulations. Expense sharing formulae. Local currency. Domestic obligation. General technical assistance. Materials, equipment and services. IGO status. Conformity with IGO decisions.
TREATY REF: 76UNTS132; 1UNTS15; 33UNTS261.
PARTIES:
Guinea SIGNED: 3 Dec 59 FORCE: 3 Dec 59
FAO (Food Agri) SIGNED: 3 Dec 59 FORCE: 3 Dec 59
IAEA (Atom Energy) SIGNED: 3 Dec 59 FORCE: 3 Dec 59
ICAO (Civil Aviat) SIGNED: 3 Dec 59 FORCE: 3 Dec 59
ILO (Labor Org) SIGNED: 3 Dec 59 FORCE: 3 Dec 59
ITU (Telecommun) SIGNED: 3 Dec 59 FORCE: 3 Dec 59
UNESCO (Educ/Cult) SIGNED: 3 Dec 59 FORCE: 3 Dec 59
United Nations SIGNED: 3 Dec 59 FORCE: 3 Dec 59
WHO (World Health) SIGNED: 3 Dec 59 FORCE: 3 Dec 59
WMO (Meteorology) SIGNED: 3 Dec 59 FORCE: 3 Dec 59
ANNEX
547 UNTS 324. UNTAB (Tech Assis). Amendment 14 Sep 65. Force 24 Sep 65.
547 UNTS 324. Guinea. Amendment 24 Sep 65. Force 24 Sep 65.

105004 Bilateral Agreement **348 UNTS 261**
SIGNED: 22 Oct 53 FORCE: 27 Oct 59
REGISTERED: 27 Jan 60 Denmark
ARTICLES: 12 LANGUAGE: Danish. Spanish.
HEADNOTE: MILITARY SERVICE
TOPIC: Milit Servic/Citiz
CONCEPTS: Emergencies. Procedure. Dual nationality. Certificates of service. Service in foreign army.
PROCEDURE: Ratification. Termination.
PARTIES:
Chile
Denmark

105005 Multilateral Convention **348 UNTS 275**
SIGNED: 24 Jun 58 FORCE: 22 Jan 60
REGISTERED: 29 Jan 60 ILO (Labor Org)
ARTICLES: 99 LANGUAGE: English. French.

HEADNOTE: EMPLOYMENT PLANTATION WORK-
ERS
TOPIC: ILO Labor
CONCEPTS: Definition of terms. Exceptions and
exemptions. Exchange of information and docu-
ments. Inspection and observation. Jurisdiction.
Private contracts. Penal sanctions. Public health.
ILO conventions. Anti-discrimination. Employ-
ment regulations. Holidays and rest periods. Old
age and invalidity insurance. Safety standards.
Right to organize. Wages and salaries. Sickness
and invalidity insurance. Migrant worker. Agriculture. Basic freedoms.
INTL ORGS: United Nations.
TREATY REF: 15UNTS(SI.
PROCEDURE: Amendment. Accession. Denunciation. Duration. Ratification. Registration. Renewal or Revival.
PARTIES:
Multilateral
ANNEX
366 UNTS 421. Mexico. Ratification 20 Jun 60.
Force 20 Dec 60.
399 UNTS 293. Ivory Coast. Ratification
5 May 61. Force 6 Nov 61.
406 UNTS 335. Guatemala. Ratification
4 Aug 61. Force 4 Feb 62.
530 UNTS 424. Brazil. Ratification 1 Mar 65.
Force 1 Sep 65.
649 UNTS 384. Philippines. Ratification
10 Oct 68. Force 10 Apr 69.

105006 Bilateral Agreement **349 UNTS 3**
SIGNED: 19 Apr 57 FORCE: 23 Nov 57
REGISTERED: 29 Jan 60 Yugoslavia
ARTICLES: 10 LANGUAGE: Serbo-Croat. Bul-
garian.
HEADNOTE: DETAILED REGULATION NAVIGA-
TION DANUBE
TOPIC: Water Transport
CONCEPTS: Frontier formalities. Resident permits.
Non-visa travel documents. Visas. Conformity
with municipal law. Exchange of information and
documents. Recognition of legal documents. Tax
exemptions. Customs exemptions. Navigational
conditions. Merchant vessels. Inland and territo-
rial waters. Ports and pilotage.
TREATY REF: 33UNTS181.
PROCEDURE: Denunciation. Duration. Ratification.
Renewal or Revival.
PARTIES:
Bulgaria
Yugoslavia

105007 Bilateral Agreement **349 UNTS 21**
SIGNED: 10 Feb 56 FORCE: 27 Aug 56
REGISTERED: 29 Jan 60 Yugoslavia
ARTICLES: 4 LANGUAGE: Serbo-Croat. Bulgarian.
HEADNOTE: SCIENTIFIC TECHNICAL COOPER-
ATION
TOPIC: Scientific Project
CONCEPTS: Conformity with municipal law. Ex-
change of information and documents. Operat-
ing agencies. Establishment of commission.
Specialists exchange. Scientific exchange. Gen-
eral technical assistance. Publications ex-
change.
INTL ORGS: Special Commission.
PROCEDURE: Duration. Renewal or Revival. Termi-
nation.
PARTIES:
Bulgaria
Yugoslavia

105008 Bilateral Convention **349 UNTS 35**
SIGNED: 4 Jun 57 FORCE: 12 Mar 58
REGISTERED: 29 Jan 60 Yugoslavia
ARTICLES: 16 LANGUAGE: Serbo-Croat. Bulgarian.
HEADNOTE: PLANT PROTECTION
TOPIC: Sanitation
CONCEPTS: General cooperation. Exchange of information and documents. Inspection and observation. Domestic legislation. Establishment of
commission. Specialists exchange. Quarantine.
Disease control. Insect control. Reexport of
goods, etc.. Trade procedures. Indemnities and
reimbursements. Agriculture. Materials, equipment and services. Conferences. Markers and
definitions.
INTL ORGS: Special Commission.

PARTIES:
Bulgaria
Yugoslavia

105009 Bilateral Agreement **349 UNTS 61**
SIGNED: 21 Mar 58 FORCE: 30 Jun 58
REGISTERED: 29 Jan 60 Yugoslavia
ARTICLES: 17 LANGUAGE: Serbo-Croat. Bul-
garian.
HEADNOTE: CUSTOMS COMMERCIAL VEHICLES
TEMPORARILY IMPORTED EXPORTED
TOPIC: Land Transport
CONCEPTS: Default remedies. Exceptions and ex-
emptions. Remedies. Visas. Conformity with mu-
nicipal law. Recognition of legal documents. Re-
sponsibility and liability. Tax exemptions. Cus-
toms duties. Customs exemptions. Temporary
importation. Commercial road vehicles. Road
rules.
PROCEDURE: Duration. Ratification. Renewal or
Revival.
PARTIES:
Bulgaria
Yugoslavia

105010 Bilateral Agreement **349 UNTS 83**
SIGNED: 19 Jan 60 FORCE: 19 Jan 60
REGISTERED: 1 Feb 60 United Nations
ARTICLES: 10 LANGUAGE: English. Spanish.
HEADNOTE: ASSISTANCE
TOPIC: Direct Aid
CONCEPTS: Detailed regulations. Treaty imple-
mentation. Visas. Privileges and immunities. Ex-
change of information and documents. Informa-
tional records. Inspection and observation. Oper-
ating agencies. Personnel. Public information.
Responsibility and liability. Title and deeds. Use
of facilities. Arbitration. Procedure. Negotiation.
Import quotas. Attachment of funds. Exchange
rates and regulations. Expense sharing formulae.
Financial programs. Domestic obligation. Gen-
eral technical assistance. Economic assistance.
Materials, equipment and services. IGO status.
INTL ORGS: International Atomic Energy Agency.
International Court of Justice. United Nations.
Arbitration Commission.
TREATY REF: 1UNTS15; 33UNTS261;
374UNTS137.
PROCEDURE: Amendment. Termination.
PARTIES:
Peru
UN Special Fund

105011 Bilateral Agreement **349 UNTS 109**
SIGNED: 21 Dec 59 FORCE: 8 Jan 60
REGISTERED: 2 Feb 60 WHO (World Health)
ARTICLES: 6 LANGUAGE: English.
HEADNOTE: TECHNICAL ADVISORY ASSISTANCE
TOPIC: Tech Assistance
CONCEPTS: Previous treaty replacement. Privi-
leges and immunities. General cooperation. Ex-
change of information and documents. Person-
nel. Responsibility and liability. Title and deeds.
Use of facilities. Exchange. Scholarships and
grants. Vocational training. Research and devel-
opment. Exchange rates and regulations. Ex-
pense sharing formulae. Domestic obligation.
Special projects. Materials, equipment and ser-
vices. IGO status. Conformity with IGO decisions.
INTL ORGS: United Nations.
TREATY REF: 33UNTS261; 102UNTS309.
PROCEDURE: Amendment. Termination.
PARTIES:
Ceylon (Sri Lanka)
WHO (World Health)

105012 Bilateral Convention **349 UNTS 121**
SIGNED: 4 Jun 59 FORCE: 1 Dec 59
REGISTERED: 3 Feb 60 Czechoslovakia
ARTICLES: 19 LANGUAGE: Czechoslovakian. Ger-
man.
HEADNOTE: SOCIAL SECURITY
TOPIC: Non-ILO Labor
CONCEPTS: Definition of terms. Exceptions and
exemptions. Annex or appendix reference. Con-
formity with municipal law. Domestic legislation.
Dispute settlement. Old age and invalidity insur-
ance. Wages and salaries. Non-ILO labor rela-
tions. Old age insurance. Sickness and invalidity
insurance. Social security. Monetary and gold

transfers. Payment schedules. Claims and settle-
ments. National treatment.
INTL ORGS: Arbitration Commission.
PROCEDURE: Duration. Ratification. Renewal or
Revival. Termination.
PARTIES:
Czechoslovakia
Switzerland

105013 Multilateral Agreement **349 UNTS 167**
SIGNED: 6 Apr 59 FORCE: 16 Jul 59
REGISTERED: 8 Feb 60 USA (United States)
ARTICLES: 37 LANGUAGE: English. French. Span-
ish.
HEADNOTE: INTERNATIONAL WHEAT AGREE-
MENT
TOPIC: Commodity Trade
CONCEPTS: Definition of terms. Detailed regula-
tions. Territorial application. General provisions.
General cooperation. Responsibility and liability.
Procedure. Balance of payments. Non-interest
rates and fees. Commodity trade. Delivery sched-
ules. Decisions. Subsidiary organ. Liaison with
other IGO's. Internal structure.
INTL ORGS: Food and Agricultural Organization of
the United Nations. International Monetary Fund.
United Nations. International Wheat Council.
TREATY REF: 203UNTS179; 203UNTS179;
207UNTS103.
PROCEDURE: Amendment. Accession. Duration.
Ratification. Termination.
PARTIES:
Argentina SIGNED: 24 Apr 59 RATIFIED:
1 Dec 59 FORCE: 1 Aug 59
Australia SIGNED: 24 Apr 59 RATIFIED:
1 Dec 59 FORCE: 1 Aug 59
Austria SIGNED: 24 Apr 59 RATIFIED: 9 Jul 59
FORCE: 1 Aug 59
Belgium Ruanda-Urundi RATIFIED: 22 Apr 59
Belgium SIGNED: 22 Apr 59
Belgium Belgian Colonies RATIFIED: 22 Apr 59
Brazil SIGNED: 24 Apr 59
Canada SIGNED: 22 Apr 59 RATIFIED: 16 Jul 59
FORCE: 1 Aug 59
Cuba SIGNED: 23 Apr 59 RATIFIED: 3 Aug 59
FORCE: 1 Aug 59
Denmark SIGNED: 15 Apr 59
Dominican Republic SIGNED: 23 Apr 59 RATI-
FIED: 23 Jul 59 FORCE: 1 Aug 59
El Salvador RATIFIED: 15 Dec 59 FORCE:
15 Dec 59
France SIGNED: 23 Apr 59 RATIFIED: 9 Jul 59
FORCE: 1 Aug 59
Germany, West SIGNED: 21 Apr 59
Greece SIGNED: 23 Apr 59
Haiti SIGNED: 23 Apr 59
Iceland RATIFIED: 1 Dec 59 FORCE: 1 Dec 59
India SIGNED: 17 Apr 59 RATIFIED: 30 Jun 59
FORCE: 1 Aug 59
Indonesia SIGNED: 22 Apr 59 RATIFIED:
22 Sep 59 FORCE: 1 Aug 59
Ireland SIGNED: 21 Apr 59 RATIFIED: 1 Dec 59
FORCE: 1 Aug 59
Israel SIGNED: 22 Apr 59 RATIFIED: 21 Aug 59
FORCE: 1 Aug 59
Italy SIGNED: 26 Apr 59
Japan SIGNED: 26 Apr 59 RATIFIED: 1 Dec 59
FORCE: 1 Aug 59
Korea, South SIGNED: 24 Apr 59
Luxembourg SIGNED: 22 Apr 59
Mexico SIGNED: 23 Apr 59
Netherlands SIGNED: 24 Apr 59
New Zealand SIGNED: 22 Apr 59 RATIFIED:
26 Jun 59 FORCE: 1 Aug 59
Norway SIGNED: 21 Apr 59 RATIFIED: 13 Jul 59
FORCE: 1 Aug 59
Peru SIGNED: 24 Apr 59 RATIFIED: 3 Aug 59
FORCE: 1 Aug 59
Philippines SIGNED: 21 Apr 59 RATIFIED:
24 Aug 59 FORCE: 1 Aug 59
Portugal SIGNED: 14 Apr 59
South Africa SIGNED: 21 Apr 59 RATIFIED:
1 Jul 59 FORCE: 1 Aug 59
Spain SIGNED: 24 Apr 59 RATIFIED: 30 Nov 59
FORCE: 1 Aug 59
Sweden SIGNED: 22 Apr 59 RATIFIED:
30 Nov 59 FORCE: 1 Aug 59
Switzerland SIGNED: 20 Apr 59 RATIFIED:
8 Jul 59 FORCE: 1 Aug 59
United Arab Rep SIGNED: 22 Apr 59 RATIFIED:
9 Jul 59 FORCE: 1 Aug 59
UK Great Britain SIGNED: 24 Apr 59 RATIFIED:
14 Jul 59 FORCE: 1 Aug 59

USA (United States) SIGNED: 22 Apr 59 RATI-
FIED: 16 Jul 59 FORCE: 1 Aug 59
Vatican/Holy See SIGNED: 20 Apr 59 RATIFIED:
9 Jul 59 FORCE: 1 Aug 59
ANNEX
383 UNTS 332. UK Great Britain. Isle of Man.
383 UNTS 332. Venezuela. Accession 11 Feb 60.
Force 11 Feb 60.
383 UNTS 332. Honduras. Accession 5 Jan 60.
Force 5 Jan 60.
383 UNTS 332. Germany, West. Acceptance
15 Aug 60. Force 15 Aug 60.
383 UNTS 332. Netherlands. Surinam. Force
27 Jun 60.
383 UNTS 332. UK Great Britain. Guernsey Island.
383 UNTS 332. Portugal. Acceptance 28 Jan 60.
Force 28 Jan 60.
383 UNTS 332. Korea, South. Acceptance
23 Feb 60. Force 23 Feb 60.
383 UNTS 332. Netherlands. Netherlands Antilles. Force 27 Jun 60.
383 UNTS 332. Guatemala. Accession
18 May 60. Force 18 May 60.
383 UNTS 332. Netherlands. Acceptance
27 Jun 60. Force 27 Jun 60.
383 UNTS 332. Haiti. Acceptance 24 Feb 60.
Force 24 Feb 60.
383 UNTS 332. Netherlands. Dutch New Guinea.
Force 27 Jun 60.
383 UNTS 332. Panama. Accession 28 Jan 60.
Force 28 Jan 60.
383 UNTS 332. Belgium. Acceptance 1 Aug 60.
Force 1 Aug 60.
407 UNTS 282. Costa Rica. Accession 2 Jun 61.
407 UNTS 282. Nigeria. Accession 16 Jun 61.
425 UNTS 364. Germany, West. Berlin.
425 UNTS 364. Sierra Leone. Accession
30 Nov 61.

105014 Bilateral Agreement **349 UNTS 277**
SIGNED: 11 Feb 60   FORCE: 11 Feb 60
REGISTERED: 11 Feb 60 United Nations
ARTICLES: 10 LANGUAGE: Spanish.
HEADNOTE: ACTIVITIES UNICEF
TOPIC: Direct Aid
CONCEPTS: Treaty implementation. Privileges and
immunities. General cooperation. Exchange of
information and documents. Informational
records. Inspection and observation. Public in-
formation. Responsibility and liability. Proce-
dure. Existing tribunals. Export quotas. Claims
and settlements. Tax exemptions. Customs ex-
emptions. Commodities and services. Domestic
obligation. Assistance. General aid. Distribution.
IGO status.
INTL ORGS: United Nations.
TREATY REF: 1UNTS15.
PARTIES:
Cuba
UNICEF (Children)

105015 Bilateral Exchange **349 UNTS 293**
SIGNED: 20 Nov 59   FORCE: 20 Nov 59
REGISTERED: 16 Feb 60 USA (United States)
ARTICLES: 2 LANGUAGE: English.
HEADNOTE: ACCEPTANCE CERTIFICATES AIR-
WORTHINESS IMPORTED AIRCRAFT
TOPIC: Air Transport
CONCEPTS: Conformity with municipal law. Ex-
change of information and documents. Recogni-
tion of legal documents. Registration certificate.
Airworthiness certificates.
PROCEDURE: Termination. Application to Non-
self-governing Territories.
PARTIES:
Australia
USA (United States)

105016 Bilateral Agreement **351 UNTS 3**
SIGNED: 30 Jan 59   FORCE: 1 Dec 59
REGISTERED: 18 Feb 60 Czechoslovakia
ARTICLES: 36 LANGUAGE: Hungarian. Slovak.
HEADNOTE: SOCIAL POLICY
TOPIC: Non-ILO Labor
CONCEPTS: Definition of terms. Exceptions and
exemptions. Conformity with municipal law. Do-
mestic legislation. Dispute settlement. Old age
and invalidity insurance. Wages and salaries.
Non-ILO labor relations. Family allowances. Old
age insurance. Sickness and invalidity insur-

ance. Social security. Monetary and gold trans-
fers. Claims and settlements. National treatment.
PROCEDURE: Denunciation. Duration. Ratification.
Renewal or Revival.
PARTIES:
Czechoslovakia
Hungary

105017 Bilateral Convention **351 UNTS 57**
SIGNED: 27 Mar 59   FORCE: 20 Dec 59
REGISTERED: 18 Feb 60 Czechoslovakia
ARTICLES: 24 LANGUAGE: Czechoslovakian. Hun-
garian.
HEADNOTE: CONSULAR CONVENTION
TOPIC: Consul/Citizenship
CONCEPTS: General consular functions. Diplo-
matic privileges. Consular relations establish-
ment. Inviolability. Privileges and immunities.
Diplomatic correspondence. Responsibility and
liability.
PROCEDURE: Duration. Ratification. Termination.
PARTIES:
Czechoslovakia
Hungary

105018 Bilateral Exchange **351 UNTS 89**
SIGNED: 2 Dec 59   FORCE: 1 Jan 60
REGISTERED: 18 Feb 60 Belgium
ARTICLES: 2 LANGUAGE: English. French.
HEADNOTE: WAIVING VISA REQUIREMENTS
TOPIC: Visas
CONCEPTS: Visa abolition. Passports non-
diplomatic.
PROCEDURE: Termination.
PARTIES:
Belgium
Thailand

105019 Bilateral Agreement **351 UNTS 93**
SIGNED: 21 Feb 60   FORCE: 21 Feb 60
REGISTERED: 21 Feb 60 United Nations
ARTICLES: 10 LANGUAGE: English.
HEADNOTE: ASSISTANCE
TOPIC: Direct Aid
CONCEPTS: Detailed regulations. Treaty imple-
mentation. Annex or appendix reference. Visas.
Privileges and immunities. Exchange of informa-
tion and documents. Informational records. In-
spection and observation. Operating agencies.
Personnel. Public information. Responsibility
and liability. Title and deeds. Use of facilities.
Arbitration. Procedure. Negotiation. Import
quotas. Exchange rates and regulations. Ex-
pense sharing formulae. Financial programs.
Claims and settlements. Tax exemptions. Cus-
toms exemptions. Domestic obligation. General
technical assistance. Economic assistance. Ma-
terials, equipment and services. IGO status.
INTL ORGS: International Atomic Energy Agency.
International Court of Justice. United Nations.
TREATY REF: 1UNTS15; 33UNTS261;
374UNTS137.
PROCEDURE: Amendment. Termination.
PARTIES:
Afghanistan
UN Special Fund

105020 Bilateral Agreement **351 UNTS 115**
SIGNED: 22 Jan 60   FORCE: 22 Jan 60
REGISTERED: 22 Feb 60 United Nations
ARTICLES: 10 LANGUAGE: English. Spanish.
HEADNOTE: ASSISTANCE
TOPIC: Direct Aid
CONCEPTS: Detailed regulations. Treaty imple-
mentation. Visas. Privileges and immunities. Ex-
change of information and documents. Informa-
tional records. Inspection and observation. Oper-
ating agencies. Personnel. Public information.
Responsibility and liability. Title and deeds. Use
of facilities. Arbitration. Procedure. Negotiation.
Import quotas. Exchange rates and regulations.
Expense sharing formulae. Financial programs.
Claims and settlements. Tax exemptions. Customs exemptions. Domestic obligation. General
technical assistance. Economic assistance. Materials, equipment and services. IGO status.
INTL ORGS: International Atomic Energy Agency.
International Court of Justice. United Nations.
TREATY REF: 1UNTS15; 33UNTS261;
374UNTS137.

PROCEDURE: Amendment. Termination.
PARTIES:
Chile
UN Special Fund

105021 Bilateral Agreement **351 UNTS 141**
SIGNED: 25 Feb 60   FORCE: 25 Feb 60
REGISTERED: 25 Feb 60 United Nations
ARTICLES: 10 LANGUAGE: English.
HEADNOTE: ASSISTANCE
TOPIC: Direct Aid
CONCEPTS: Detailed regulations. Treaty imple-
mentation. Visas. Privileges and immunities. Ex-
change of information and documents. Informa-
tional records. Inspection and observation. Oper-
ating agencies. Personnel. Public information.
Responsibility and liability. Title and deeds. Use
of facilities. Arbitration. Procedure. Negotiation.
Import quotas. Exchange rates and regulations.
Expense sharing formulae. Financial programs.
Claims and settlements. Tax exemptions. Do-
mestic obligation. General technical assistance.
Economic assistance. Materials, equipment and
services.
INTL ORGS: International Atomic Energy Agency.
International Court of Justice. United Nations.
TREATY REF: 1UNTS15; 33UNTS261;
374UNTS137.
PROCEDURE: Amendment. Termination.
PARTIES:
Pakistan
UN Special Fund

105022 Multilateral Agreement **351 UNTS 159**
SIGNED: 15 Dec 58   FORCE: 1 Jan 59
REGISTERED: 29 Feb 60 Council of Europe
ARTICLES: 11 LANGUAGE: English. French.
HEADNOTE: THERAPEUTIC SUBSTANCES OF HU-
MAN ORIGIN
TOPIC: Sanitation
CONCEPTS: Conditions. Definition of terms. An-
nex or appendix reference. Standardization.
General cooperation. Public health. Trade proce-
dures. Indemnities and reimbursements. Cus-
toms exemptions.
INTL ORGS: Council of Europe.
PROCEDURE: Amendment. Accession. Duration.
Ratification. Termination.
PARTIES:
Austria SIGNED: 15 Dec 58
Belgium SIGNED: 15 Dec 58 FORCE: 1 Jan 59
France SIGNED: 15 Dec 58
Germany, West SIGNED: 15 Dec 58
Ireland SIGNED: 15 Dec 58 FORCE: 1 Jan 59
Italy SIGNED: 15 Dec 58
Luxembourg SIGNED: 15 Dec 58
Netherlands SIGNED: 26 Feb 59
Norway SIGNED: 15 Dec 58 FORCE: 1 Jan 59
Sweden SIGNED: 15 Dec 58 FORCE: 1 Jan 59
Turkey SIGNED: 15 Dec 58
ANNEX
363 UNTS 409. France. Ratification 2 Jun 60.
Force 1 Jul 60.
388 UNTS 386. Greece. Ratification 2 Feb 61.
Force 1 Mar 61.
406 UNTS 336. Italy. Ratification 23 Aug 61.
Force 1 Sep 61.
407 UNTS 284. Luxembourg. Ratification
11 Sep 61. Force 1 Oct 61.
407 UNTS 284. Netherlands. Ratification
11 Sep 61. Force 1 Oct 61.
473 UNTS 349. Germany, West. Ratification
18 Feb 63. Force 1 Mar 63.
473 UNTS 349. Germany, West. Berlin. Force
1 Mar 63.
514 UNTS 287. Denmark. Signature without Reservation as to Approval 30 Sep 64. Force
1 Oct 64.
565 UNTS 292. UK Great Britain. Signature
21 Nov 63. Qualified Ratification 8 Dec 64.
565 UNTS 292. UK Great Britain. Force 1 Jan 65.
565 UNTS 292. Switzerland. Signature
15 Apr 64. Ratification 29 Nov 65.
565 UNTS 292. Switzerland. Force 1 Dec 65.
565 UNTS 292. Turkey. Ratification 3 Jun 66.
Force 1 Jul 66.

105023 Bilateral Exchange **351 UNTS 197**
SIGNED: 24 Dec 59   FORCE: 24 Dec 59
REGISTERED: 29 Feb 60 Thailand
ARTICLES: 2 LANGUAGE: English.

HEADNOTE: EXEMPTION IMPORT DUTIES
TOPIC: Customs
CONCEPTS: Customs exemptions. Agricultural commodities. Agricultural vehicles and construction.
PARTIES:
New Zealand
Thailand

105024 Bilateral Agreement **351 UNTS 203**
SIGNED: 9 Feb 60   FORCE: 9 Feb 60
REGISTERED: 1 Mar 60 United Nations
ARTICLES: 10 LANGUAGE: English. Spanish.
HEADNOTE: ASSISTANCE
TOPIC: Direct Aid
CONCEPTS: Detailed regulations. Treaty implementation. Visas. Privileges and immunities. Exchange of information and documents. Informational records. Inspection and observation. Operating agencies. Personnel. Public information. Responsibility and liability. Title and deeds. Use of facilities. Arbitration. Procedure. Negotiation. Import quotas. Exchange rates and regulations. Expense sharing formulae. Financial programs. Claims and settlements. Tax exemptions. Domestic obligation. General technical assistance. Economic assistance. Materials, equipment and services. IGO status.
INTL ORGS: International Atomic Energy Agency. International Court of Justice. United Nations.
TREATY REF: 1UNTS15; 33UNTS261; 374UNTS137.
PROCEDURE: Amendment. Termination.
PARTIES:
Bolivia
UN Special Fund

105025 Bilateral Agreement **351 UNTS 229**
SIGNED: 10 Jan 58   FORCE: 25 Nov 59
REGISTERED: 4 Mar 60 Turkey
ARTICLES: 5 LANGUAGE: French.
HEADNOTE: CULTURAL AGREEMENT
TOPIC: Culture
CONCEPTS: Treaty implementation. Establishment of commission. Specialists exchange. Exchange. Teacher and student exchange. Scholarships and grants. Exchange. General cultural cooperation. Artists. Scientific exchange.
INTL ORGS: Special Commission.
PROCEDURE: Duration. Ratification. Renewal or Revival. Termination.
PARTIES:
Norway
Turkey

105026 Bilateral Agreement **351 UNTS 235**
SIGNED: 19 Dec 57   FORCE: 24 Mar 59
REGISTERED: 4 Mar 60 UK Great Britain
ARTICLES: 14 LANGUAGE: English. Russian.
HEADNOTE: CONCERNING AIR SERVICDS
TOPIC: Air Transport
CONCEPTS: Representation. Treaty implementation. Visas. Conformity with municipal law. General cooperation. Exchange of information and documents. Licenses and permits. Personnel. Recognition of legal documents. Humanitarian matters. Accounting procedures. Non-interest rates and fees. Tax exemptions. Customs exemptions. Registration certificate. Routes and logistics. Permit designation. Airworthiness certificates. Conditions of airlines operating permission. Operating authorizations and regulations.
PROCEDURE: Ratification. Termination.
PARTIES:
UK Great Britain
USSR (Soviet Union)
ANNEX
374 UNTS 388. UK Great Britain. Amendment 3 Mar 60. Force 29 Mar 60.
374 UNTS 388. USSR (Soviet Union). Amendment 29 Mar 60. Force 29 Mar 60.
398 UNTS 353. UK Great Britain. Amendment 14 Oct 60. Force 14 Oct 60.
398 UNTS 353. USSR (Soviet Union). Amendment 22 Sep 60. Force 14 Oct 60.

105027 Bilateral Exchange **351 UNTS 263**
SIGNED: 28 Nov 58   FORCE: 28 Nov 58
REGISTERED: 4 Mar 60 UK Great Britain
ARTICLES: 6 LANGUAGE: English. French.

HEADNOTE: TURNOVER TAX ROYALTIES
TOPIC: Taxation
CONCEPTS: Definition of terms. Responsibility and liability. General.
PROCEDURE: Termination.
PARTIES:
France
UK Great Britain

105028 Bilateral Exchange **351 UNTS 283**
SIGNED: 11 Jun 59   FORCE: 11 Jun 59
REGISTERED: 4 Mar 60 UK Great Britain
ARTICLES: 2 LANGUAGE: English. Arabic.
HEADNOTE: LOAN
TOPIC: Loans and Credits
CONCEPTS: Financial programs. Interest rates. Loan and credit. Loan repayment. Terms of loan.
PARTIES:
Jordan
UK Great Britain
ANNEX
566 UNTS 361. UK Great Britain. Implementation 9 Nov 64. Force 9 Nov 64.
566 UNTS 361. Jordan. Implementation 20 Oct 64. Force 4 Nov 64.

105029 Bilateral Exchange **351 UNTS 289**
SIGNED: 20 Jul 56   FORCE: 20 Jul 56
REGISTERED: 4 Mar 60 UK Great Britain
ARTICLES: 2 LANGUAGE: English. Spanish.
HEADNOTE: EXEMPTION MEASUREMENT SHIPS PORT
TOPIC: Admin Cooperation
CONCEPTS: Exceptions and exemptions. Ports and pilotage.
PARTIES:
UK Great Britain
Venezuela

105030 Bilateral Exchange **351 UNTS 295**
SIGNED: 3 Apr 59   FORCE: 3 Apr 59
REGISTERED: 4 Mar 60 UK Great Britain
ARTICLES: 2 LANGUAGE: English.
HEADNOTE: INTRODUCTION AIR SERVICES BETWEEN UK POLAND
TOPIC: Air Transport
CONCEPTS: Personnel. Monetary and gold transfers. Non-interest rates and fees. Customs exemptions. Routes and logistics. Permit designation. Operating authorizations and regulations.
TREATY REF: 15UNTS295.
PROCEDURE: Duration. Termination.
PARTIES:
Poland
UK Great Britain

105031 Multilateral Agreement **351 UNTS 303**
SIGNED: 27 Oct 58   FORCE: 24 Oct 59
REGISTERED: 4 Mar 60 UK Great Britain
ARTICLES: 3 LANGUAGE: English. French. Portuguese.
HEADNOTE: AGREEMENT GERMAN ASSETS CLAIMS REGARDING MONETARY GOLD
TOPIC: Reparations
CONCEPTS: Definition of terms. Previous treaty replacement. Accounting procedures. Monetary and gold transfers. Exchange rates and regulations. Payment schedules. Local currency. Lump sum settlements. Enemy financial interests. Postwar claims settlement.
PARTIES:
France SIGNED: 27 Oct 58 FORCE: 24 Oct 59
Portugal SIGNED: 27 Oct 58 FORCE: 24 Oct 59
UK Great Britain SIGNED: 27 Oct 58 FORCE: 24 Oct 59
USA (United States) SIGNED: 27 Oct 58 FORCE: 24 Oct 59

105032 Bilateral Agreement **351 UNTS 313**
SIGNED: 1 Dec 59   FORCE: 1 Dec 59
REGISTERED: 4 Mar 60 UK Great Britain
ARTICLES: 14 LANGUAGE: English. Russian.
HEADNOTE: RELATIONS SCIENTIFIC TECHNOLOGICAL EDUCATIONAL CULTURAL FIELDS
TOPIC: Health/Educ/Welfare
CONCEPTS: General cooperation. Exchange of information and documents. Personnel. Specialists exchange. Exchange. Teacher and student

exchange. General cultural cooperation. Artists. Athletes. Scientific exchange.
PROCEDURE: Duration.
PARTIES:
UK Great Britain
USSR (Soviet Union)

105033 Bilateral Agreement **351 UNTS 341**
SIGNED: 22 Oct 59   FORCE: 22 Oct 59
REGISTERED: 4 Mar 60 UK Great Britain
ARTICLES: 7 LANGUAGE: French.
HEADNOTE: AMITY TRADE
TOPIC: General Trade
CONCEPTS: Exceptions and exemptions. Territorial application. Annex or appendix reference. Border traffic and migration. Exchange of information and documents. Licenses and permits. Establishment of commission. Establishment of trade relations. Import quotas. Trade procedures. Accounting procedures. Quotas.
INTL ORGS: Organization for Economic Co-operation and Development. Special Commission.
PROCEDURE: Duration. Renewal or Revival. Termination.
PARTIES:
Guinea
UK Great Britain

105034 Bilateral Agreement **351 UNTS 355**
SIGNED: 20 Jan 60   FORCE: 15 Feb 60
REGISTERED: 7 Mar 60 WHO (World Health)
ARTICLES: 6 LANGUAGE: English.
HEADNOTE: TECHNICAL ADVISORY ASSISTANCE
TOPIC: Tech Assistance
CONCEPTS: Definition of terms. Privileges and immunities. General cooperation. Personnel. Responsibility and liability. Title and deeds. Exchange. Scholarships and grants. Vocational training. Research and development. Expense sharing formulae. Domestic obligation. Special projects. Materials, equipment and services. IGO status. Conformity with IGO decisions.
INTL ORGS: United Nations.
TREATY REF: 33UNTS261.
PROCEDURE: Amendment. Termination.
PARTIES:
Pakistan
WHO (World Health)

105035 Multilateral Protocol **352 UNTS 3**
SIGNED: 25 Jul 58   FORCE: 1 Mar 60
REGISTERED: 7 Mar 60 Belgium
ARTICLES: 4 LANGUAGE: French. Dutch.
HEADNOTE: NEW SCHEDULE IMPORT DUTIES
TOPIC: Customs
CONCEPTS: Detailed regulations. Previous treaty replacement. Import quotas. Customs duties.
INTL ORGS: Benelux Economic Union.
TREATY REF: 347UNTS127.
PARTIES:
Belgium SIGNED: 25 Jul 58 RATIFIED: 29 Jan 60 FORCE: 1 Mar 60
Luxembourg SIGNED: 25 Jul 58 RATIFIED: 20 Jan 60 FORCE: 1 Mar 60
Netherlands SIGNED: 25 Jul 58 RATIFIED: 15 Jan 60 FORCE: 1 Mar 60

105036 Bilateral Agreement **353 UNTS 3**
SIGNED: 12 Sep 58   FORCE: 12 Sep 58
REGISTERED: 11 Mar 60 ICAO (Civil Aviat)
ARTICLES: 16 LANGUAGE: German. Bulgarian.
HEADNOTE: AIR TRANSPORT
TOPIC: Air Transport
CONCEPTS: Definition of terms. Representation. Annex or appendix reference. Conformity with municipal law. General cooperation. Informational records. Licenses and permits. Personnel. Recognition of legal documents. Use of facilities. Arbitration. Procedure. Humanitarian matters. Indemnities and reimbursements. Expense sharing formulae. Fees and exemptions. Non-interest rates and fees. Customs exemptions. Competency certificate. Registration certificate. Routes and logistics. Navigational conditions. Permit designation. Air transport. Airport facilities. Airworthiness certificates. Conditions of airlines operating permission. Operating authorizations and regulations. Licenses and certificates of nationality.
PROCEDURE: Amendment. Termination.

PARTIES:
Austria
Bulgaria

105037 Bilateral Agreement **353 UNTS 39**
SIGNED: 29 Jan 57 FORCE: 28 Apr 58
REGISTERED: 11 Mar 60 ICAO (Civil Aviat)
ARTICLES: 20 LANGUAGE: German. Norwegian.
HEADNOTE: AIR SERVICES
TOPIC: Air Transport
CONCEPTS: Definition of terms. Detailed regulations. Previous treaty replacement. Conformity with municipal law. General cooperation. Exchange of information and documents. Licenses and permits. Recognition of legal documents. Use of facilities. Arbitration. Procedure. Special tribunals. Competence of tribunal. Indemnities and reimbursements. Monetary and gold transfers. Exchange rates and regulations. Expense sharing formulae. Fees and exemptions. Non-interest rates and fees. National treatment. Customs exemptions. Competency certificate. Routes and logistics. Navigational conditions. Permit designation. Airport facilities. Airworthiness certificates. Conditions of airlines operating permission. Overflights and technical stops. Operating authorizations and regulations. Licenses and certificates of nationality.
INTL ORGS: International Civil Aviation Organization. Arbitration Commission.
PROCEDURE: Amendment. Denunciation. Future Procedures Contemplated. Ratification. Registration. Termination. Application to Non-self-governing Territories.
PARTIES:
Germany, West
Norway

105038 Bilateral Agreement **353 UNTS 73**
SIGNED: 21 Nov 47 FORCE: 21 Nov 47
REGISTERED: 11 Mar 60 ICAO (Civil Aviat)
ARTICLES: 12 LANGUAGE: English. Italian.
HEADNOTE: AIR SERVICES BETWEEN TWO COUNTRIES
TOPIC: Air Transport
CONCEPTS: Annex or appendix reference. Conformity with municipal law. Licenses and permits. Recognition of legal documents. Use of facilities. Arbitration. Procedure. Special tribunals. Fees and exemptions. Most favored nation clause. National treatment. Customs exemptions. Competency certificate. Routes and logistics. Navigational conditions. Permit designation. Airport facilities. Airworthiness certificates. Conditions of airlines operating permission. Operating authorizations and regulations. Licenses and certificates of nationality.
INTL ORGS: International Civil Aviation Organization. Arbitration Commission.
TREATY REF: 15UNTS295.
PROCEDURE: Future Procedures Contemplated. Registration. Termination.
PARTIES:
Ireland
Italy

105039 Bilateral Agreement **353 UNTS 91**
SIGNED: 5 Oct 57 FORCE: 5 Oct 57
REGISTERED: 11 Mar 60 ICAO (Civil Aviat)
ARTICLES: 14 LANGUAGE: English. Italian.
HEADNOTE: RELATING AIR SERVICES
TOPIC: Air Transport
CONCEPTS: Definition of terms. Detailed regulations. Annex or appendix reference. Conformity with municipal law. General cooperation. Exchange of information and documents. Licenses and permits. Recognition of legal documents. Arbitration. Procedure. Existing tribunals. Negotiation. Reexport of goods, etc.. Non-interest rates and fees. Most favored nation clause. National treatment. Customs exemptions. Temporary importation. Competency certificate. Routes and logistics. Navigational conditions. Permit designation. Air transport. Airworthiness certificates. Conditions of airlines operating permission. Overflights and technical stops. Operating authorizations and regulations. Licenses and certificates of nationality.
INTL ORGS: International Civil Aviation Organization. International Court of Justice.
TREATY REF: 15UNTS295.

PROCEDURE: Amendment. Future Procedures Contemplated. Ratification. Termination. Application to Non-self-governing Territories.
PARTIES:
Italy
Pakistan

105040 Bilateral Agreement **353 UNTS 121**
SIGNED: 12 Jun 56 FORCE: 5 Jul 57
REGISTERED: 11 Mar 60 ICAO (Civil Aviat)
ARTICLES: 19 LANGUAGE: English. German.
HEADNOTE: AIR TRANSPORT
TOPIC: Air Transport
CONCEPTS: Definition of terms. Detailed regulations. Conformity with municipal law. General cooperation. Exchange of information and documents. Licenses and permits. Personnel. Use of facilities. Arbitration. Procedure. Special tribunals. Competence of tribunal. Expense sharing formulae. Fees and exemptions. Non-interest rates and fees. National treatment. Customs exemptions. Competency certificate. Routes and logistics. Navigational conditions. Permit designation. Air transport. Airport facilities. Airworthiness certificates. Conditions of airlines operating permission. Overflights and technical stops. Operating authorizations and regulations. Licenses and certificates of nationality. Recognition of legal documents.
INTL ORGS: International Civil Aviation Organization. Arbitration Commission.
PROCEDURE: Amendment. Future Procedures Contemplated. Ratification. Termination. Application to Non-self-governing Territories.
PARTIES:
Germany, West
Ireland
ANNEX
552 UNTS 412. Germany. West. Supplementation 24 Mar 58. Force 24 Mar 58.
552 UNTS 412. Ireland. Supplementation 24 Mar 58. Force 24 Mar 58.
602 UNTS 340. Ireland. Amendment 8 Feb 66. Force 8 Feb 66.
602 UNTS 340. Germany, West. Amendment 8 Feb 66. Force 8 Feb 66.

105041 Bilateral Agreement **353 UNTS 155**
SIGNED: 10 Jul 58 FORCE: 10 Jul 58
REGISTERED: 11 Mar 60 ICAO (Civil Aviat)
ARTICLES: 12 LANGUAGE: French.
HEADNOTE: CIVIL AIR TRANSPORT
TOPIC: Air Transport
CONCEPTS: Definition of terms. Representation. Annex or appendix reference. Conformity with municipal law. General cooperation. Licenses and permits. Personnel. Recognition of legal documents. Use of facilities. Procedure. Negotiation. Humanitarian matters. Fees and exemptions. Non-interest rates and fees. Customs exemptions. Registration certificate. Routes and logistics. Navigational conditions. Permit designation. Airport facilities. Airworthiness certificates. Conditions of airlines operating permission. Operating authorizations and regulations.
PROCEDURE: Amendment. Denunciation. Termination.
PARTIES:
Austria
Romania

105042 Bilateral Agreement **353 UNTS 173**
SIGNED: 7 Jan 59 FORCE: 7 Jan 59
REGISTERED: 11 Mar 60 ICAO (Civil Aviat)
ARTICLES: 13 LANGUAGE: French.
HEADNOTE: CONCERNING AIR SERVICE
TOPIC: Air Transport
CONCEPTS: Detailed regulations. Conformity with municipal law. General cooperation. Exchange of information and documents. Use of facilities. Arbitration. Procedure. Existing tribunals. Negotiation. Expense sharing formulae. Non-interest rates and fees. National treatment. Customs exemptions. Routes and logistics. Navigational conditions. Permit designation. Air transport. Airport facilities. Conditions of airlines operating permission. Overflights and technical stops. Operating authorizations and regulations.
INTL ORGS: International Civil Aviation Organization.

PROCEDURE: Future Procedures Contemplated. Ratification. Registration. Termination.
PARTIES:
Finland
Switzerland
ANNEX
392 UNTS 392. Finland. Amendment 10 Feb 60. Force 10 Feb 60.
392 UNTS 392. Switzerland. Amendment 13 Feb 60. Force 10 Feb 60.
646 UNTS 382. Finland. Amendment 4 Mar 67. Force 4 Mar 67.
646 UNTS 382. Switzerland. Amendment 4 Mar 67. Force 4 Mar 67.

105043 Bilateral Agreement **353 UNTS 185**
SIGNED: 19 Oct 55 FORCE: 19 Oct 55
REGISTERED: 11 Mar 60 ICAO (Civil Aviat)
ARTICLES: 10 LANGUAGE: Finnish. Russian.
HEADNOTE: AIR TRANSPORT
TOPIC: Air Transport
CONCEPTS: Representation. Conformity with municipal law. General cooperation. Exchange of information and documents. Licenses and permits. Recognition of legal documents. Use of facilities. Humanitarian matters. Registration certificate. Routes and logistics. Navigational conditions. Permit designation. Air transport. Airworthiness certificates. Conditions of airlines operating permission. Operating authorizations and regulations.
PROCEDURE: Denunciation.
PARTIES:
Finland
USSR (Soviet Union)
ANNEX
602 UNTS 345. Finland. Modification 7 Feb 64.
602 UNTS 345. USSR (Soviet Union). Modification 7 Feb 64.
646 UNTS 383. USSR (Soviet Union). Amendment 23 May 67. Force 23 May 67.

105044 Bilateral Agreement **353 UNTS 203**
SIGNED: 4 Oct 55 FORCE: 30 Sep 57
REGISTERED: 11 Mar 60 ICAO (Civil Aviat)
ARTICLES: 24 LANGUAGE: French. German.
HEADNOTE: AIR TRANSPORT
TOPIC: Air Transport
CONCEPTS: Definition of terms. Detailed regulations. Exceptions and exemptions. Conformity with municipal law. General cooperation. Exchange of information and documents. Licenses and permits. Recognition of legal documents. Use of facilities. Investigation of violations. Arbitration. Procedure. Special tribunals. Reexport of goods, etc.. Expense sharing formulae. Fees and exemptions. Non-interest rates and fees. National treatment. Customs exemptions. Competency certificate. Routes and logistics. Navigational conditions. Permit designation. Air transport. Airport facilities. Airworthiness certificates. Conditions of airlines operating permission. Overflights and technical stops. Operating authorizations and regulations. Licenses and certificates of nationality.
INTL ORGS: International Civil Aviation Organization. International Court of Justice. Arbitration Commission.
TREATY REF: 15UNTS295.
PROCEDURE: Amendment. Denunciation. Future Procedures Contemplated. Ratification.
PARTIES:
France
Germany, West

105045 Bilateral Exchange **353 UNTS 237**
SIGNED: 13 Jul 59 FORCE: 13 Jul 59
REGISTERED: 14 Mar 60 USA (United States)
ARTICLES: 2 LANGUAGE: English.
HEADNOTE: ESTABLISHMENT BALLISTIC MISSILE EARLY WARNING SYSTEM
TOPIC: Milit Assistance
CONCEPTS: Annex or appendix reference. General cooperation. Facilities and equipment. Communications linkage. Joint defense. Defense and security.
PARTIES:
Canada
USA (United States)

105046 Bilateral Agreement **353 UNTS 257**
SIGNED: 9 Jun 59 FORCE: 9 Jun 59
REGISTERED: 14 Mar 60 USA (United States)
ARTICLES: 6 LANGUAGE: English. Chinese.
HEADNOTE: AGRI COMMOD TITLE I
TOPIC: US Agri Commod Aid
CONCEPTS: General provisions. Annex or appendix reference. Exchange of information and documents. Reexport of goods, etc.. Exchange rates and regulations. Transportation costs. Local currency. Commodities schedule. Purchase authorization. Surplus commodities. Mutual consultation.
PARTIES:
Taiwan
USA (United States)
　　　ANNEX
371 UNTS 377. USA (United States). Supplementation 11 Feb 60. Force 11 Feb 60.
371 UNTS 377. Taiwan. Supplementation 11 Feb 60. Force 11 Feb 60.
388 UNTS 387. Taiwan. Supplementation 24 Aug 60. Force 24 Aug 60.
388 UNTS 387. USA (United States). Supplementation 17 Aug 60. Force 24 Aug 60.
458 UNTS 338. USA (United States). Amendment 29 Jun 62. Force 29 Jun 62.
458 UNTS 338. Taiwan. Amendment 29 Jun 62. Force 29 Jun 62.

105047 Bilateral Agreement **353 UNTS 297**
SIGNED: 30 Jun 59 FORCE: 30 Jun 59
REGISTERED: 14 Mar 60 USA (United States)
ARTICLES: 6 LANGUAGE: English.
HEADNOTE: AGRI COMMOD TITLE I
TOPIC: US Agri Commod Aid
CONCEPTS: General provisions. Exchange of information and documents. Reexport of goods, etc.. Exchange rates and regulations. Transportation costs. Local currency. Commodities schedule. Purchase authorization. Surplus commodities. Mutual consultation.
PARTIES:
Korea, South
USA (United States)
　　　ANNEX
367 UNTS 352. USA (United States). Amendment 12 Oct 59. Force 11 Dec 59.
367 UNTS 352. Korea, South. Amendment 11 Dec 59. Force 11 Dec 59.
389 UNTS 322. USA (United States). Amendment 14 Sep 60. Force 14 Sep 60.
389 UNTS 322. Korea, South. Amendment 14 Sep 60. Force 14 Sep 60.
405 UNTS 344. Korea, South. Amendment 17 Mar 61. Force 17 Mar 61.
405 UNTS 344. USA (United States). Amendment 17 Mar 61. Force 17 Mar 61.

105048 Bilateral Exchange **354 UNTS 3**
SIGNED: 23 Jun 59 FORCE: 23 Jun 59
REGISTERED: 14 Mar 60 USA (United States)
ARTICLES: 2 LANGUAGE: English.
HEADNOTE: SPECIAL ECONOMIC ASSISTANCE
TOPIC: Direct Aid
CONCEPTS: Conformity with municipal law. Import quotas. Indemnities and reimbursements. Financial programs. Interest rates. Loan and credit. Loan repayment.
PARTIES:
Iceland
USA (United States)

105049 Bilateral Exchange **354 UNTS 11**
SIGNED: 23 Jun 59 FORCE: 23 Jun 59
REGISTERED: 14 Mar 60 USA (United States)
ARTICLES: 2 LANGUAGE: English. Spanish.
HEADNOTE: LOAN VESSELS
TOPIC: Milit Assistance
CONCEPTS: Time limit. Annex or appendix reference. Responsibility and liability. Title and deeds. Compensation. Delivery schedules. Lease of military property. Naval vessels. Return of equipment and recapture. Restrictions on transfer.
TREATY REF: 20MUNTS61.
PARTIES:
Spain
USA (United States)

　　　ANNEX
394 UNTS 305. USA (United States). Supplementation 30 Sep 60. Force 30 Sep 60.
394 UNTS 305. Spain. Supplementation 30 Sep 60. Force 30 Sep 60.
541 UNTS 329. USA (United States). Prolongation 11 Jan 65. Force 11 Jan 65.
541 UNTS 329. Spain. Prolongation 11 Jan 65. Force 11 Jan 65.

105050 Bilateral Exchange **354 UNTS 21**
SIGNED: 22 May 54 FORCE: 21 Jun 57
REGISTERED: 14 Mar 60 USA (United States)
ARTICLES: 3 LANGUAGE: English. Spanish.
HEADNOTE: PASSPORT VISAS
TOPIC: Visas
CONCEPTS: Time limit.
INTL ORGS: United Nations.
PARTIES:
Colombia
USA (United States)

105051 Bilateral Exchange **354 UNTS 39**
SIGNED: 22 Jul 59 FORCE: 22 Jul 59
REGISTERED: 14 Mar 60 USA (United States)
ARTICLES: 2 LANGUAGE: English.
HEADNOTE: GUARANTY PRIVATE INVESTMENTS
TOPIC: Admin Cooperation
CONCEPTS: Guarantees and safeguards. Arbitration. Currency. Investments. Claims and settlements.
INTL ORGS: International Court of Justice.
PARTIES:
Finland
USA (United States)

105052 Bilateral Exchange **354 UNTS 47**
SIGNED: 8 Jul 59 FORCE: 8 Jul 59
REGISTERED: 14 Mar 60 USA (United States)
ARTICLES: 2 LANGUAGE: English. Chinese.
HEADNOTE: LOAN SMALL CRAFT
TOPIC: Milit Assistance
CONCEPTS: Annex or appendix reference. Responsibility and liability. Title and deeds. Compensation. Delivery schedules. Lease of military property. Naval vessels. Return of equipment and recapture.
TREATY REF: 132UNTS273.
PARTIES:
Taiwan
USA (United States)

105053 Bilateral Exchange **354 UNTS 57**
SIGNED: 26 May 59 FORCE: 26 May 59
REGISTERED: 14 Mar 60 USA (United States)
ARTICLES: 2 LANGUAGE: English.
HEADNOTE: EDUCATIONAL FACILITIES PRIVATE SCHOOLS
TOPIC: Direct Aid
CONCEPTS: Currency deposits. Financial programs. Use restrictions. Materials, equipment and services.
TREATY REF: 24UNTS67.
PARTIES:
Turkey
USA (United States)

105054 Bilateral Agreement **354 UNTS 63**
SIGNED: 22 May 59 FORCE: 27 Jul 59
REGISTERED: 14 Mar 60 USA (United States)
ARTICLES: 13 LANGUAGE: English.
HEADNOTE: COOPERATION USES ATOMIC ENERGY MUTUAL DEFENSE
TOPIC: Milit Assistance
CONCEPTS: Definition of terms. Conformity with municipal law. General cooperation. Exchange of information and documents. Licenses and permits. Research cooperation. Nuclear research. Claims and settlements. National treatment. Laws and formalities. Recognition. Atomic energy assistance. Non-nuclear materials. Rights of supplier. Joint defense. Defense and security. Atomic weapons. Military training. Security of information. Exchange of defense information. Restrictions on transfer.
PROCEDURE: Future Procedures Contemplated. Ratification. Termination.

PARTIES:
Canada
USA (United States)

105055 Bilateral Agreement **354 UNTS 83**
SIGNED: 7 May 59 FORCE: 20 Jul 59
REGISTERED: 14 Mar 60 USA (United States)
ARTICLES: 8 LANGUAGE: English. French.
HEADNOTE: COOPERATION USES ATOMIC ENERGY MUTUAL DEFENSE
TOPIC: Milit Assistance
CONCEPTS: Definition of terms. Conformity with municipal law. Compensation. Payment schedules. Atomic energy assistance. Nuclear materials. Return of equipment and recapture. Restrictions on transfer.
PROCEDURE: Ratification. Termination.
PARTIES:
France
USA (United States)

105056 Bilateral Exchange **354 UNTS 95**
SIGNED: 26 Feb 60 FORCE: 26 Feb 60
REGISTERED: 15 Mar 60 Australia
ARTICLES: 2 LANGUAGE: English.
HEADNOTE: SPACE VEHICLE TRACKING AND COMMUNICATIONS
TOPIC: Specific Property
CONCEPTS: Research results. Customs exemptions. Facilities and property.
PARTIES:
Australia
USA (United States)
　　　ANNEX
473 UNTS 350. USA (United States). Amendment 9 Jan 63. Force 11 Feb 63.
473 UNTS 350. Australia. Amendment 11 Feb 63. Force 11 Feb 63.
488 UNTS 300. Australia. Amendment 22 Oct 63. Force 22 Oct 63.
488 UNTS 300. USA (United States). Amendment 22 Oct 63. Force 22 Oct 63.
542 UNTS 378. Australia. Acknowledgement 10 Feb 65. Force 10 Feb 65.
542 UNTS 378. USA (United States). Amendment 10 Feb 65. Force 10 Feb 65.

105057 Bilateral Exchange **354 UNTS 105**
SIGNED: 7 Jul 59 FORCE: 7 Jul 59
REGISTERED: 15 Mar 60 Australia
ARTICLES: 2 LANGUAGE: English. French.
HEADNOTE: VISAS VISA FEES
TOPIC: Visas
CONCEPTS: Time limit. Visa abolition. Denial of admission. Resident permits. Conformity with municipal law.
PROCEDURE: Denunciation. Termination.
PARTIES:
Australia
Monaco

105058 Bilateral Agreement **354 UNTS 109**
SIGNED: 17 Dec 59 FORCE: 1 Jul 59
REGISTERED: 15 Mar 59 Australia
ARTICLES: 8 LANGUAGE: English.
HEADNOTE: EXPANDING TRADE
TOPIC: General Trade
CONCEPTS: Annex or appendix reference. Conformity with municipal law. General cooperation. Licenses and permits. Establishment of commission. Trade procedures. Commodity trade. Most favored nation clause. Water transport.
INTL ORGS: General Agreement on Tariffs and Trade. Special Commission.
TREATY REF: 55UNTS187.
PROCEDURE: Duration. Renewal or Revival.
PARTIES:
Australia
Indonesia
　　　ANNEX
376 UNTS 450. Australia. Prolongation 30 Jun 60. Force 30 Jun 60.
376 UNTS 450. Indonesia. Prolongation 30 Jun 60. Force 30 Jun 60.
411 UNTS 324. Australia. Prolongation 22 Aug 61. Force 1 Jul 61.
411 UNTS 324. Indonesia. Prolongation 22 Aug 61. Force 1 Jul 61.
443 UNTS 346. Australia. Prolongation 6 Sep 62. Force 6 Sep 62.

443 UNTS 346. Indonesia. Prolongation 6 Sep 62. Force 6 Sep 62.
480 UNTS 412. Australia. Prolongation 4 Sep 63. Force 4 Sep 63.
480 UNTS 412. Indonesia. Prolongation 4 Sep 63. Force 4 Sep 63.
511 UNTS 284. Australia. Prolongation 1 Sep 64. Force 16 Sep 64.
511 UNTS 284. Indonesia. Prolongation 16 Sep 64. Force 16 Sep 64.
544 UNTS 342. Indonesia. Prolongation 11 Aug 65. Force 11 Aug 65.
544 UNTS 342. Australia. Prolongation 28 Jul 65. Force 11 Aug 65.
607 UNTS 334. Australia. Prolongation 2 Sep 66. Force 2 Sep 66.
607 UNTS 334. Indonesia. Prolongation 2 Sep 66. Force 2 Sep 66.
660 UNTS 400. Indonesia. Prolongation 1 Jul 68.
660 UNTS 400. Australia. Prolongation 1 Jul 68.

105059 Bilateral Agreement **354 UNTS 119**
SIGNED: 17 Mar 60 FORCE: 17 Mar 60
REGISTERED: 17 Mar 60 United Nations
ARTICLES: 10 LANGUAGE: English. French.
HEADNOTE: ASSISTANCE
TOPIC: Direct Aid
CONCEPTS: Detailed regulations. Treaty implementation. Visas. Privileges and immunities. Exchange of information and documents. Informational records. Inspection and observation. Operating agencies. Personnel. Public information. Responsibility and liability. Title and deeds. Use of facilities. Arbitration. Procedure. Negotiation. Import quotas. Exchange rates and regulations. Expense sharing formulae. Financial programs. Claims and settlements. Tax exemptions. Domestic obligation. General technical assistance. Economic assistance. Materials, equipment and services. IGO status.
INTL ORGS: International Atomic Energy Agency. International Court of Justice. United Nations.
TREATY REF: 1UNTS15; 33UNTS261; 374UNTS137.
PROCEDURE: Amendment. Termination.
PARTIES:
France
UN Special Fund

105060 Bilateral Agreement **354 UNTS 137**
SIGNED: 29 Nov 58 FORCE: 26 Jun 59
REGISTERED: 17 Mar 60 UK Great Britain
ARTICLES: 7 LANGUAGE: English. Portuguese.
HEADNOTE: PROMOTION COMMERCE BETWEEN CONTIGUOUS STATES
TOPIC: General Trade
CONCEPTS: Exceptions and exemptions. Territorial application. Domestic legislation. Reciprocity in trade. Trade procedures. Smuggling. Most favored nation clause. Customs duties. Customs declarations.
PROCEDURE: Denunciation. Duration. Ratification. Termination.
PARTIES:
Fed Rhod/Nyasaland
Portugal

105061 Bilateral Agreement **354 UNTS 151**
SIGNED: 19 Feb 60 FORCE: 19 Feb 60
REGISTERED: 18 Mar 60 Denmark
ARTICLES: 9 LANGUAGE: English.
HEADNOTE: PATENT RIGHTS TECHNICAL INFORMATION DEFENSE PURPOSES
TOPIC: Patents/Copyrights
CONCEPTS: Definition of terms. Conformity with municipal law. Currency. Press and wire services. Security of information. Exchange of defense information. Subsidiary organ.
INTL ORGS: Special Commission.
TREATY REF: 48UNTS115.
PROCEDURE: Termination.
PARTIES:
Denmark
USA (United States)
ANNEX
378 UNTS 400. USA (United States). Implementation 13 Jun 60. Force 20 Jun 60.
378 UNTS 400. Denmark. Implementation 20 Jun 60. Force 20 Jun 60.

105062 Bilateral Agreement **354 UNTS 161**
SIGNED: 12 Aug 59 FORCE: 25 Nov 58
REGISTERED: 29 Mar 60 New Zealand
ARTICLES: 19 LANGUAGE: English.

HEADNOTE: TRADE
TOPIC: General Trade
CONCEPTS: Definition of terms. Detailed regulations. Territorial application. Annex or appendix reference. Previous treaty replacement. General cooperation. Tariffs. Reciprocity in trade. Trade procedures. Commodity trade. Smuggling. Customs duties. Customs declarations. Customs exemptions. Agricultural commodities.
INTL ORGS: General Agreement on Tariffs and Trade.
TREATY REF: 55UNTS187.
PROCEDURE: Amendment. Termination.
PARTIES:
New Zealand
UK Great Britain

105063 Bilateral Agreement **354 UNTS 197**
SIGNED: 22 Dec 59 FORCE: 12 Feb 60
REGISTERED: 31 Mar 60 IBRD (World Bank)
ARTICLES: 5 LANGUAGE: English.
HEADNOTE: GUARANTEE
TOPIC: IBRD Project
CONCEPTS: Definition of terms. Annex or appendix reference. Exchange of information and documents. Inspection and observation. Bonds. Fees and exemptions. Tax exemptions. Domestic obligation. Terms of loan. Loan regulations. Loan guarantee. Guarantor non-interference.
PARTIES:
IBRD (World Bank)
United Arab Rep

105064 Bilateral Agreement **354 UNTS 221**
SIGNED: 13 Jun 58 FORCE: 14 Feb 59
REGISTERED: 31 Mar 60 Poland
ARTICLES: 4 LANGUAGE: Polish. Czechoslovakian.
HEADNOTE: DEMARCATION STATE FRONTIER
TOPIC: Territory Boundary
CONCEPTS: Markers and definitions.
INTL ORGS: Special Commission.
PROCEDURE: Ratification.
PARTIES:
Czechoslovakia
Poland

105065 Bilateral Agreement **354 UNTS 233**
SIGNED: 15 Dec 58 FORCE: 11 Jan 60
REGISTERED: 31 Mar 60 IBRD (World Bank)
ARTICLES: 5 LANGUAGE: English.
HEADNOTE: GUARANTEE AGREEMENT
TOPIC: IBRD Project
CONCEPTS: Definition of terms. Annex or appendix reference. Exchange of information and documents. Inspection and observation. Bonds. Fees and exemptions. Tax exemptions. Domestic obligation. Terms of loan. Loan regulations. Loan guarantee. Guarantor non-interference.
PARTIES:
Colombia
IBRD (World Bank)

105066 Bilateral Agreement **354 UNTS 261**
SIGNED: 1 Apr 60 FORCE: 1 Apr 60
REGISTERED: 1 Apr 60 United Nations
ARTICLES: 10 LANGUAGE: English.
HEADNOTE: ASSISTANCE
TOPIC: Direct Aid
CONCEPTS: Detailed regulations. Treaty implementation. Visas. Privileges and immunities. Exchange of information and documents. Informational records. Inspection and observation. Operating agencies. Personnel. Public information. Responsibility and liability. Title and deeds. Use of facilities. Arbitration. Procedure. Negotiation. Import quotas. Exchange rates and regulations. Expense sharing formulae. Financial programs. Claims and settlements. Tax exemptions. Domestic obligation. General technical assistance. Economic assistance. Materials, equipment and services. IGO status.
INTL ORGS: International Atomic Energy Agency. International Court of Justice. United Nations.
TREATY REF: 1UNTS15; 33UNTS261; 374UNTS137.
PROCEDURE: Amendment. Termination.
PARTIES:
Italy
UN Special Fund

105067 Bilateral Agreement **354 UNTS 279**
SIGNED: 12 Nov 59 FORCE: 16 Jan 60
REGISTERED: 1 Apr 60 IBRD (World Bank)
ARTICLES: 5 LANGUAGE: English.
HEADNOTE: GUARANTEE AGREEMENT
TOPIC: IBRD Project
CONCEPTS: Definition of terms. Annex or appendix reference. Exchange of information and documents. Bonds. Fees and exemptions. Tax exemptions. Domestic obligation. Terms of loan. Loan regulations. Loan guarantee. Guarantor non-interference. Industry.
PARTIES:
Japan
IBRD (World Bank)

105068 Bilateral Agreement **354 UNTS 313**
SIGNED: 12 Nov 52 FORCE: 16 Jan 60
REGISTERED: 1 Apr 60 IBRD (World Bank)
ARTICLES: 5 LANGUAGE: English.
HEADNOTE: GUARANTEE AGREEMENT
TOPIC: IBRD Project
CONCEPTS: Definition of terms. Annex or appendix reference. Exchange of information and documents. Inspection and observation. Bonds. Fees and exemptions. Tax exemptions. Domestic obligation. Terms of loan. Loan regulations. Loan guarantee. Guarantor non-interference. Industry.
PARTIES:
Japan
IBRD (World Bank)

105069 Bilateral Agreement **354 UNTS 347**
SIGNED: 4 Apr 59 FORCE: 4 Apr 60
REGISTERED: 1 Apr 60 United Nations
ARTICLES: 10 LANGUAGE: English. French.
HEADNOTE: ASSISTANCE
TOPIC: Direct Aid
CONCEPTS: Detailed regulations. Treaty implementation. Annex or appendix reference. Visas. Privileges and immunities. Exchange of information and documents. Informational records. Inspection and observation. Operating agencies. Personnel. Public information. Responsibility and liability. Title and deeds. Use of facilities. Arbitration. Procedure. Negotiation. Import quotas. Exchange rates and regulations. Expense sharing formulae. Financial programs. Claims and settlements. Tax exemptions. Domestic obligation. General technical assistance. Economic assistance. Materials, equipment and services. IGO status.
INTL ORGS: International Atomic Energy Agency. International Court of Justice. United Nations.
TREATY REF: 1UNTS15; 33UNTS261; 374UNTS137.
PROCEDURE: Amendment. Termination.
PARTIES:
Morocco
UN Special Fund

105070 Bilateral Agreement **354 UNTS 367**
SIGNED: 16 Nov 59 FORCE: 16 Nov 59
REGISTERED: 5 Apr 60 UK Great Britain
ARTICLES: 8 LANGUAGE: French.
HEADNOTE: EXTENDING TRADE
TOPIC: General Trade
CONCEPTS: Territorial application. Annex or appendix reference. General cooperation. Licenses and permits. Establishment of commission. Export quotas. Import quotas. Trade procedures. Payment schedules. Quotas.
INTL ORGS: Organization for Economic Co-operation and Development. Special Commission.
PROCEDURE: Duration. Termination.
PARTIES:
Tunisia
UK Great Britain

105071 Bilateral Exchange **354 UNTS 377**
SIGNED: 5 Sep 59 FORCE: 1 Oct 59
REGISTERED: 5 Apr 60 Pakistan
ARTICLES: 2 LANGUAGE: English.
HEADNOTE: ACCEPTANCE CREW MEMBER CERTIFICATES
TOPIC: Admin Cooperation
CONCEPTS: Annex or appendix reference. Licenses and certificates of nationality.
TREATY REF: 15UNTS295.

PARTIES:
Denmark
Pakistan

105072 Bilateral Convention **355 UNTS 3**
SIGNED: 28 Mar 59 FORCE: 29 Dec 59
REGISTERED: 7 Apr 60 Finland
ARTICLES: 21 LANGUAGE: Finnish. English.
HEADNOTE: DOUBLE TAXATION FISCAL EVA-
SION TAXES INCOME
TOPIC: Taxation
CONCEPTS: Definition of terms. Privileges and im-
munities. Conformity with municipal law. Ex-
change of official publications. Negotiation.
Teacher and student exchange. Claims and set-
tlements. Taxation. Tax credits. Equitable taxes.
General. Tax exemptions. Air transport. Insured
letters and boxes.
PROCEDURE: Duration. Ratification. Termination.
PARTIES:
Canada
Finland
　　　　　ANNEX
544 UNTS 346. Finland. Amendment 30 Dec 64.
Force 15 Jun 65.
544 UNTS 346. Canada. Amendment 30 Dec 64.
Force 15 Jun 65.

105073 Bilateral Convention **355 UNTS 31**
SIGNED: 28 Jul 59 FORCE: 1 Mar 60
REGISTERED: 7 Apr 60 Finland
ARTICLES: 34 LANGUAGE: Finnish. English.
HEADNOTE: SOCIAL SECURITY
TOPIC: Non-ILO Labor
CONCEPTS: Definition of terms. Domestic legisla-
tion. Dispute settlement. Old age and invalidity
insurance. Wages and salaries. Non-ILO labor re-
lations. Family allowances. Administrative coop-
eration. Old age insurance. Sickness and invalid-
ity insurance. Social security. Unemployment.
Payment schedules. Claims and settlements.
PROCEDURE: Denunciation. Duration. Ratification.
Renewal or Revival.
PARTIES:
Finland
UK Great Britain

105074 Bilateral Agreement **355 UNTS 77**
SIGNED: 19 Sep 59 FORCE: 23 Dec 59
REGISTERED: 8 Apr 60 Czechoslovakia
ARTICLES: 12 LANGUAGE: Czechoslovakian. Bul-
garian.
HEADNOTE: HEALTH COOPERATION
TOPIC: Sanitation
CONCEPTS: General cooperation. Exchange of in-
formation and documents. Public health. Ex-
change. Commissions and foundations. Teacher
and student exchange. Vocational training. Re-
search results. Scientific exchange. Research
and development. Indemnities and reimburse-
ments. Expense sharing formulae. Mass media
exchange. Conferences.
PROCEDURE: Duration. Ratification. Renewal or
Revival. Termination.
PARTIES:
Bulgaria
Czechoslovakia

105075 Bilateral Agreement **355 UNTS 95**
SIGNED: 15 Jul 59 FORCE: 11 Dec 59
REGISTERED: 8 Apr 60 IBRD (World Bank)
ARTICLES: 5 LANGUAGE: English.
HEADNOTE: GUARANTEE AGREEMENT
TOPIC: IBRD Project
CONCEPTS: Annex or appendix reference. Ex-
change of information and documents. Inspec-
tion and observation. Bonds. Fees and exemp-
tions. Tax exemptions. Domestic obligation.
Terms of loan. Loan regulations. Loan guarantee.
Guarantor non-interference.
PARTIES:
India
IBRD (World Bank)

105076 Bilateral Agreement **355 UNTS 129**
SIGNED: 13 Aug 59 FORCE: 5 Jan 60
REGISTERED: 8 Apr 60 IBRD (World Bank)
ARTICLES: 5 LANGUAGE: English.
HEADNOTE: GUARANTEE AGREEMENT

TOPIC: IBRD Project
CONCEPTS: Definition of terms. Exchange of information and documents. Inspection and observation. Bonds. Fees and exemptions. Tax exemptions. Domestic obligation. Terms of loan. Loan
regulations. Loan guarantee. Guarantor non-
interference. Hydro-electric power.
PARTIES:
Pakistan
IBRD (World Bank)

105077 Bilateral Agreement **355 UNTS 169**
SIGNED: 25 Sep 59 FORCE: 29 Dec 59
REGISTERED: 8 Apr 60 IBRD (World Bank)
ARTICLES: 5 LANGUAGE: English.
HEADNOTE: GUARANTEE AGREEMENT
TOPIC: IBRD Project
CONCEPTS: Definition of terms. Annex or appen-
dix reference. Exchange of information and doc-
uments. Inspection and observation. Bonds.
Fees and exemptions. Tax exemptions. Domestic
obligation. Terms of loan. Loan regulations. Loan
guarantee. Guarantor non-interference.
PARTIES:
Pakistan
IBRD (World Bank)

105078 Bilateral Agreement **355 UNTS 203**
SIGNED: 30 Nov 59 FORCE: 18 Mar 60
REGISTERED: 8 Apr 60 IBRD (World Bank)
ARTICLES: 7 LANGUAGE: English.
HEADNOTE: LOAN
TOPIC: IBRD Project
CONCEPTS: Definition of terms. Annex or appen-
dix reference. Exchange of information and doc-
uments. Inspection and observation. Accounting
procedures. Bonds. Domestic obligation. Terms
of loan. Loan regulations. Loan guarantee. Guar-
antor non-interference. Railways.
PARTIES:
Pakistan
IBRD (World Bank)

105079 Bilateral Agreement **355 UNTS 223**
SIGNED: 25 Sep 59 FORCE: 6 Feb 60
REGISTERED: 8 Apr 60 IBRD (World Bank)
ARTICLES: 5 LANGUAGE: English.
HEADNOTE: LOAN GUARANTEE
TOPIC: IBRD Project
CONCEPTS: Loan repayment.
PARTIES:
Austria
IBRD (World Bank)

105080 Bilateral Agreement **355 UNTS 257**
SIGNED: 4 Feb 60 FORCE: 4 Feb 60
REGISTERED: 11 Apr 60 United Nations
ARTICLES: 10 LANGUAGE: English. Spanish.
HEADNOTE: ASSISTANCE
TOPIC: Direct Aid
CONCEPTS: Detailed regulations. Treaty imple-
mentation. Visas. Privileges and immunities. Ex-
change of information and documents. Informa-
tional records. Inspection and observation. Oper-
ating agencies. Personnel. Public information.
Responsibility and liability. Title and deeds. Use
of facilities. Arbitration. Procedure. Negotiation.
Import quotas. Exchange rates and regulations.
Expense sharing formulae. Financial programs.
Claims and settlements. Tax exemptions. Do-
mestic obligation. General technical assistance.
Economic assistance. Materials, equipment and
services. IGO status.
INTL ORGS: International Atomic Energy Agency.
International Court of Justice. United Nations.
TREATY REF: 1UNTS15; 33UNTS261;
374UNTS137.
PROCEDURE: Amendment. Termination.
PARTIES:
Colombia
UN Special Fund

105081 Bilateral Agreement **355 UNTS 283**
SIGNED: 14 Jan 59 FORCE: 14 Jan 59
REGISTERED: 11 Apr 60 ILO (Labor Org)
ARTICLES: 5 LANGUAGE: English.
HEADNOTE: ESTABLISH AFRICAN FIELD OFFICE
TOPIC: IGO Operations
CONCEPTS: Privileges and immunities. General

technical assistance. Regional offices. Recogni-
tion of specialized agency.
INTL ORGS: United Nations.
TREATY REF: 15UNTS40.
PROCEDURE: Duration.
PARTIES:
ILO (Labor Org)
UK Great Britain

105082 Bilateral Agreement **355 UNTS 289**
SIGNED: 12 Apr 60 FORCE: 12 Apr 60
REGISTERED: 12 Apr 60 United Nations
ARTICLES: 10 LANGUAGE: English. French.
HEADNOTE: ASSISTANCE
TOPIC: Direct Aid
CONCEPTS: Detailed regulations. Treaty imple-
mentation. Visas. Privileges and immunities. Ex-
change of information and documents. Informa-
tional records. Inspection and observation. Oper-
ating agencies. Personnel. Public information.
Responsibility and liability. Title and deeds. Use
of facilities. Arbitration. Procedure. Negotiation.
Import quotas. Exchange rates and regulations.
Expense sharing formulae. Financial programs.
Claims and settlements. Tax exemptions. Do-
mestic obligation. General technical assistance.
Economic assistance. Materials, equipment and
services. IGO status.
INTL ORGS: International Atomic Energy Agency.
International Court of Justice. United Nations.
TREATY REF: 1UNTS15; 33UNTS261;
374UNTS137.
PROCEDURE: Amendment. Termination.
PARTIES:
UN Special Fund
Tunisia

105083 Bilateral Agreement **355 UNTS 307**
SIGNED: 5 May 59 FORCE: 27 Jul 59
REGISTERED: 14 Apr 60 USA (United States)
ARTICLES: 11 LANGUAGE: English. German.
HEADNOTE: ATOMIC ENERGY MUTUAL DEFENSE
TOPIC: Atomic Energy
CONCEPTS: Definition of terms. Exchange of infor-
mation and documents. Assistance. Atomic en-
ergy assistance.
PROCEDURE: Duration.
PARTIES:
Germany, West
USA (United States)

105084 Bilateral Agreement **355 UNTS 327**
SIGNED: 6 May 59 FORCE: 27 Jul 59
REGISTERED: 14 Apr 60 USA (United States)
ARTICLES: 11 LANGUAGE: English.
HEADNOTE: ATOMIC ENERGY MUTUAL DEFENSE
TOPIC: Milit Installation
CONCEPTS: Definition of terms. General cooper-
ation. Exchange of information and documents.
Recognition. Non-nuclear materials. Defense
and security. Military training. Security of infor-
mation. Exchange of defense information. Re-
strictions on transfer.
TREATY REF: 80UNTS219.
PROCEDURE: Duration. Termination.
PARTIES:
Netherlands
USA (United States)

105085 Bilateral Exchange **355 UNTS 341**
SIGNED: 5 May 59 FORCE: 27 Jul 59
REGISTERED: 14 Apr 60 USA (United States)
ARTICLES: 2 LANGUAGE: English.
HEADNOTE: ATOMIC ENERGY COOPERATION
TOPIC: Milit Assistance
CONCEPTS: Military assistance. Atomic weapons.
PARTIES:
Turkey
USA (United States)

105086 Bilateral Agreement **355 UNTS 355**
SIGNED: 31 Oct 58 FORCE: 1 Jul 59
REGISTERED: 14 Apr 60 USA (United States)
ARTICLES: 18 LANGUAGE: English.
HEADNOTE: EXCHANGE INTERNATIONAL MONEY
ORDERS
TOPIC: Postal Service
CONCEPTS: Annex or appendix reference. Previ-
ous treaty replacement. Conformity with munici-

pal law. Accounting procedures. Currency. Exchange rates and regulations. Regulations. Money orders and postal checks. Rates and charges.
PROCEDURE: Duration. Termination.
PARTIES:
United Arab Rep
USA (United States)

105087   Bilateral Exchange   **355 UNTS 367**
SIGNED: 18 Jul 59   FORCE: 18 Jul 59
REGISTERED: 14 Apr 60 USA (United States)
ARTICLES: 4 LANGUAGE: English.
HEADNOTE: ESTABLISHMENT COMMUNICATIONS UNIT
TOPIC: Gen Communications
CONCEPTS: Definition of terms. Annex or appendix reference. Conformity with municipal law. Tax exemptions. Customs exemptions. Temporary importation. Facilities and equipment. Communications linkage. Radio-telephone-telegraphic communications.
TREATY REF: 269UNTS15.
PROCEDURE: Duration. Termination.
PARTIES:
Pakistan
USA (United States)

105088   Bilateral Exchange   **355 UNTS 393**
SIGNED: 30 Jul 59   FORCE: 30 Jul 59
REGISTERED: 14 Apr 60 USA (United States)
ARTICLES: 2 LANGUAGE: English. Italian.
HEADNOTE: CHILD FEEDING PROGRAM
TOPIC: Direct Aid
CONCEPTS: Previous treaty extension. Conformity with municipal law. Jurisdiction. Commodities and services. Domestic obligation. Assistance. General aid. Use restrictions.
TREATY REF: 316UNTS177.
PARTIES:
Italy
USA (United States)

105089   Bilateral Exchange   **356 UNTS 3**
SIGNED: 5 Aug 59   FORCE: 5 Aug 59
REGISTERED: 14 Apr 60 USA (United States)
ARTICLES: 2 LANGUAGE: English. Spanish.
HEADNOTE: OPENING INSPECTION STATION
TOPIC: Customs
CONCEPTS: Inspection and observation. Customs duties. Frontier crossing points.
PARTIES:
Mexico
USA (United States)

105090   Bilateral Agreement   **356 UNTS 11**
SIGNED: 19 Apr 60   FORCE: 19 Apr 60
REGISTERED: 19 Apr 60 United Nations
ARTICLES: 10 LANGUAGE: English. Arabic.
HEADNOTE: ASSISTANCE
TOPIC: Direct Aid
CONCEPTS: Detailed regulations. Treaty implementation. Visas. Privileges and immunities. Exchange of information and documents. Informational records. Inspection and observation. Operating agencies. Personnel. Public information. Responsibility and liability. Title and deeds. Use of facilities. Arbitration. Procedure. Negotiation. Import quotas. Exchange rates and regulations. Expense sharing formulae. Financial programs. Claims and settlements. Tax exemptions. Domestic obligation. General technical assistance. Economic assistance. Materials, equipment and services. IGO status.
INTL ORGS: International Atomic Energy Agency. International Court of Justice. United Nations.
TREATY REF: 1UNTS15; 33UNTS261; 374UNTS137.
PROCEDURE: Amendment. Termination.
PARTIES:
Libya
UN Special Fund

105091   Bilateral Treaty   **356 UNTS 39**
SIGNED: 28 Feb 59   FORCE: 19 Jan 60
REGISTERED: 19 Apr 60 USSR (Soviet Union)
ARTICLES: 33 LANGUAGE: Russian. German.
HEADNOTE: CONSULAR
TOPIC: Consul/Citizenship

CONCEPTS: Definition of terms. General consular functions. Diplomatic privileges. Consular relations establishment. Inviolability. Privileges and immunities. Diplomatic correspondence. Responsibility and liability.
PROCEDURE: Ratification. Termination.
PARTIES:
Austria
USSR (Soviet Union)

105092   Bilateral Agreement   **356 UNTS 83**
SIGNED: 23 Jun 59   FORCE: 19 Dec 59
REGISTERED: 19 Apr 60 USSR (Soviet Union)
ARTICLES: 26 LANGUAGE: Russian. Chinese.
HEADNOTE: CONSULAR
TOPIC: Consul/Citizenship
CONCEPTS: General consular functions. Diplomatic privileges. Consular relations establishment. Inviolability. Privileges and immunities. Diplomatic correspondence. Responsibility and liability.
PROCEDURE: Ratification.
PARTIES:
China People's Rep
USSR (Soviet Union)

105093   Bilateral Convention   **356 UNTS 111**
SIGNED: 5 Jun 59   FORCE: 15 Dec 59
REGISTERED: 19 Apr 60 USSR (Soviet Union)
ARTICLES: 27 LANGUAGE: Russian. Vietnamese.
HEADNOTE: CONSULAR
TOPIC: Consul/Citizenship
CONCEPTS: Definition of terms. General consular functions. Diplomatic privileges. Consular relations establishment. Diplomatic relations resumption. Inviolability. Privileges and immunities. Responsibility and liability.
PROCEDURE: Ratification.
PARTIES:
USSR (Soviet Union)
Vietnam, North

105094   Bilateral Treaty   **356 UNTS 149**
SIGNED: 12 Mar 58   FORCE: 2 Oct 58
REGISTERED: 19 Apr 60 USSR (Soviet Union)
ARTICLES: 17 LANGUAGE: Russian. Vietnamese.
HEADNOTE: TRADE NAVIGATION
TOPIC: General Economic
CONCEPTS: General trade. Establishment of trade relations. Maritime products and equipment. National treatment.
INTL ORGS: Arbitration Commission.
PROCEDURE: Ratification.
PARTIES:
USSR (Soviet Union)
Vietnam, North

105095   Bilateral Agreement   **356 UNTS 179**
SIGNED: 5 May 59   FORCE: 15 Nov 59
REGISTERED: 19 Apr 60 USSR (Soviet Union)
ARTICLES: 11 LANGUAGE: Russian. Arabic.
HEADNOTE: CULTURAL COOPERATION
TOPIC: Culture
CONCEPTS: Treaty implementation. Friendship and amity. Non-diplomatic delegations. Conformity with municipal law. Exchange of information and documents. Specialists exchange. Teacher and student exchange. Professorships. Scholarships and grants. Exchange. General cultural cooperation. Artists. Athletes. Anthropology and archeology. Scientific exchange. Publications exchange. Mass media exchange. Press and wire services.
PROCEDURE: Amendment. Ratification. Termination.
PARTIES:
Iraq
USSR (Soviet Union)

105096   Bilateral Agreement   **356 UNTS 193**
SIGNED: 10 Jun 58   FORCE: 10 Jun 58
REGISTERED: 20 Apr 60 Denmark
ARTICLES: 15 LANGUAGE: French. Danish.
HEADNOTE: AIR TRANSPORT
TOPIC: Air Transport
CONCEPTS: Definition of terms. Annex or appendix reference. Conformity with municipal law. General cooperation. Licenses and permits. Recognition of legal documents. Use of facilities. Ar-

bitration. Procedure. Existing tribunals. Negotiation. Fees and exemptions. Non-interest rates and fees. Most favored nation clause. National treatment. Customs exemptions. Competency certificate. Navigational conditions. Permit designation. Air transport. Airport facilities. Airworthiness certificates. Conditions of airlines operating permission. Licenses and certificates of nationality.
INTL ORGS: International Civil Aviation Organization.
TREATY REF: 15UNTS295.
PROCEDURE: Amendment. Future Procedures Contemplated. Ratification. Registration. Termination.
PARTIES:
Denmark
Luxembourg

105097   Bilateral Agreement   **356 UNTS 213**
SIGNED: 21 Apr 60   FORCE: 21 Apr 60
REGISTERED: 21 Apr 60 United Nations
ARTICLES: 10 LANGUAGE: English.
HEADNOTE: ASSISTANCE
TOPIC: Direct Aid
CONCEPTS: Detailed regulations. Treaty implementation. Visas. Privileges and immunities. Exchange of information and documents. Informational records. Inspection and observation. Operating agencies. Personnel. Public information. Responsibility and liability. Title and deeds. Use of facilities. Arbitration. Procedure. Negotiation. Import quotas. Exchange rates and regulations. Expense sharing formulae. Financial programs. Claims and settlements. Tax exemptions. Domestic obligation. General technical assistance. Economic assistance. Materials, equipment and services. IGO status.
INTL ORGS: International Atomic Energy Agency. International Court of Justice. United Nations.
TREATY REF: 1UNTS15; 33UNTS261; 374UNTS137.
PROCEDURE: Amendment. Termination.
PARTIES:
UN Special Fund
Sudan

105098   Bilateral Convention   **356 UNTS 231**
SIGNED: 21 Feb 59   FORCE: 15 Sep 59
REGISTERED: 22 Apr 60 Norway
ARTICLES: 21 LANGUAGE: English.
HEADNOTE: DOUBLE TAXATION FISCAL EVASION TAXES INCOME
TOPIC: Taxation
CONCEPTS: Definition of terms. Privileges and immunities. Conformity with municipal law. Exchange of official publications. Negotiation. Teacher and student exchange. Claims and settlements. Taxation. Death duties. Tax credits. Equitable taxes. General. Tax exemptions. Air transport. Merchant vessels.
PROCEDURE: Duration. Ratification. Termination.
PARTIES:
Japan
Norway

105099   Bilateral Agreement   **356 UNTS 257**
SIGNED: 20 Jul 59   FORCE: 23 Mar 60
REGISTERED: 22 Apr 60 Norway
ARTICLES: 21 LANGUAGE: English.
HEADNOTE: DOUBLE TAXATION INCOME
TOPIC: Taxation
CONCEPTS: Definition of terms. Conformity with municipal law. Exchange of official publications. Teacher and student exchange. Claims and settlements. Taxation. Tax exemptions. Air transport. Merchant vessels.
PROCEDURE: Duration. Ratification. Termination.
PARTIES:
India
Norway

105100   Bilateral Agreement   **356 UNTS 279**
SIGNED: 17 Oct 56   FORCE: 1 Jan 57
REGISTERED: 25 Apr 60 Belgium
ARTICLES: 15 LANGUAGE: French. Polish.
HEADNOTE: AIR TRANSPORT
TOPIC: Air Transport
CONCEPTS: Definition of terms. Territorial application. Annex or appendix reference. Conformity

with municipal law. General cooperation. Licenses and permits. Personnel. Recognition of legal documents. Use of facilities. Fees and exemptions. Non-interest rates and fees. Customs exemptions. Registration certificate. Routes and logistics. Navigational conditions. Permit designation. Air transport. Airport facilities. Airworthiness certificates. Conditions of airlines operating permission. Operating authorizations and regulations.
PROCEDURE: Amendment. Denunciation. Termination.
PARTIES:
Belgium
Poland

105101   Bilateral Exchange   **356 UNTS 303**
SIGNED: 17 Feb 60   FORCE: 16 Mar 60
REGISTERED: 26 Apr 60 Belgium
ARTICLES: 2 LANGUAGE: French. German.
HEADNOTE: RECIPROCAL WAIVER NON-IMMIGRANT PASSPORT VISA FEES
TOPIC: Visas
CONCEPTS: Visas. Fees and exemptions.
PROCEDURE: Termination.
PARTIES:
Belgium
Philippines

105102   Bilateral Convention   **356 UNTS 309**
SIGNED: 22 Apr 59   FORCE: 1 Apr 60
REGISTERED: 26 Apr 60 Belgium
ARTICLES: 2 LANGUAGE: English. French.
HEADNOTE: ADDITIONAL CONVENTION
TOPIC: Extradition
CONCEPTS: Annex type material.
PARTIES:
Austria
Belgium

105103   Bilateral Agreement   **357 UNTS 3**
SIGNED: 2 Jul 54   FORCE: 23 Nov 55
REGISTERED: 29 Apr 60 UNESCO (Educ/Cult)
ARTICLES: 32 LANGUAGE: English.
HEADNOTE: PRIVILEGES & IMMUNITIES
TOPIC: IGO Status/Immunit
CONCEPTS: Annex or appendix reference. Non-visa travel documents. Diplomatic missions. Inviolability. Privileges and immunities. Property. Diplomatic correspondence. Juridical personality. Headquarters and facilities. Special status. Status of experts.
INTL ORGS: International Court of Justice. United Nations.
TREATY REF: 33UNTS261.
PARTIES:
France
UNESCO (Educ/Cult)

105104   Bilateral Agreement   **357 UNTS 29**
SIGNED: 29 Sep 59   FORCE: 29 Sep 59
REGISTERED: 29 Apr 60 ICAO (Civil Aviat)
ARTICLES: 15 LANGUAGE: English. German.
HEADNOTE: RELATING AIR SERVICES
TOPIC: Air Transport
CONCEPTS: Definition of terms. Annex or appendix reference. Conformity with municipal law. General cooperation. Exchange of information and documents. Arbitration. Procedure. Special tribunals. Negotiation. Non-interest rates and fees. Routes and logistics. Permit designation. Overflights and technical stops. Operating authorizations and regulations.
INTL ORGS: International Civil Aviation Organization.
TREATY REF: 15UNTS295.
PROCEDURE: Amendment. Future Procedures Contemplated. Registration. Termination. Application to Non-self-governing Territories.
PARTIES:
Australia
Fed of Malaya

105105   Bilateral Agreement   **357 UNTS 45**
SIGNED: 22 May 57   FORCE: 10 Jan 59
REGISTERED: 29 Apr 60 ICAO (Civil Aviat)
ARTICLES: 16 LANGUAGE: English.
HEADNOTE: RELATING AIR TRANSPORT
TOPIC: Air Transport

CONCEPTS: Definition of terms. Detailed regulations. Conformity with municipal law. General cooperation. Exchange of information and documents. Use of facilities. Arbitration. Procedure. Special tribunals. Expense sharing formulae. Fees and exemptions. Non-interest rates and fees. National treatment. Tax exemptions. Customs exemptions. Routes and logistics. Permit designation. Airport facilities. Conditions of airlines operating permission. Overflights and technical stops. Operating authorizations and regulations.
INTL ORGS: International Civil Aviation Organization. International Court of Justice. Arbitration Commission.
PROCEDURE: Amendment. Future Procedures Contemplated. Registration. Termination. Application to Non-self-governing Territories.
PARTIES:
Australia
Germany, West

105106   Bilateral Exchange   **357 UNTS 77**
SIGNED: 25 Aug 59   FORCE: 25 Aug 59
REGISTERED: 29 Apr 60 USA (United States)
ARTICLES: 2 LANGUAGE: English.
HEADNOTE: TERMINATION MILITARY ASSISTANCE
TOPIC: Milit Assistance
CONCEPTS: Annex or appendix reference. Non-prejudice to UN charter. Exchange of information and documents. Title and deeds. Materials, equipment and services. Restrictions on transfer. Self-defense. Military assistance. Security of information. Surplus war property.
PARTIES:
USA (United States)
Yugoslavia

105107   Bilateral Exchange   **357 UNTS 87**
SIGNED: 25 Aug 59   FORCE: 25 Aug 59
REGISTERED: 29 Apr 60 USA (United States)
ARTICLES: 2 LANGUAGE: English.
HEADNOTE: SALE MILITARY EQUIPMENT MATERIALS SERVICES
TOPIC: Milit Assistance
CONCEPTS: Exceptions and exemptions. Conformity with municipal law. Materials, equipment and services. Self-defense. Military assistance. Security of information. Restrictions on transfer.
PARTIES:
USA (United States)
Yugoslavia

105108   Bilateral Agreement   **357 UNTS 93**
SIGNED: 8 Jul 59   FORCE: 8 Jul 59
REGISTERED: 29 Apr 60 USA (United States)
ARTICLES: 3 LANGUAGE: English. Spanish.
HEADNOTE: AGREEMENT COOPERATION
TOPIC: Milit Assistance
CONCEPTS: Conformity with municipal law. Defense and security. Military assistance.
INTL ORGS: United Nations.
PROCEDURE: Termination.
PARTIES:
Liberia
USA (United States)

105109   Bilateral Exchange   **357 UNTS 99**
SIGNED: 22 Aug 59   FORCE: 22 Aug 59
REGISTERED: 29 Apr 60 USA (United States)
ARTICLES: 2 LANGUAGE: English. Japanese.
HEADNOTE: ACQUISITION NUCLEAR RESEARCH TRAINING EQUIPMENT
TOPIC: Atomic Energy
CONCEPTS: Responsibility and liability. Funding procedures. Non-nuclear materials. Peaceful use.
PARTIES:
Peru
USA (United States)

105110   Bilateral Exchange   **357 UNTS 107**
SIGNED: 31 Jul 59   FORCE: 31 Jul 59
REGISTERED: 29 Apr 60 USA (United States)
ARTICLES: 2 LANGUAGE: English.
HEADNOTE: GRANT VESSELS
TOPIC: Milit Assistance
CONCEPTS: Annex or appendix reference. Lease

of military property. Naval vessels. Return of equipment and recapture.
TREATY REF: 304UNTS355.
PARTIES:
Japan
USA (United States)

105111   Bilateral Agreement   **357 UNTS 121**
SIGNED: 29 Jul 59   FORCE: 29 Jul 59
REGISTERED: 29 Apr 60 USA (United States)
ARTICLES: 6 LANGUAGE: English. Arabic.
HEADNOTE: AGRI COMMOD TITLE I
TOPIC: US Agri Commod Aid
CONCEPTS: General provisions. Annex or appendix reference. Exchange of information and documents. Reexport of goods, etc.. Exchange rates and regulations. Transportation costs. Local currency. Commodities schedule. Purchase authorization. Surplus commodities. Mutual consultation.
PARTIES:
United Arab Rep
USA (United States)
                 ANNEX
371 UNTS 390. United Arab Rep. Supplementation 26 Mar 60. Force 26 Mar 60.
371 UNTS 390. USA (United States). Supplementation 26 Mar 60. Force 26 Mar 60.

105112   Bilateral Exchange   **357 UNTS 137**
SIGNED: 30 Jun 59   FORCE: 30 Jun 59
REGISTERED: 29 Apr 60 USA (United States)
ARTICLES: 2 LANGUAGE: English.
HEADNOTE: ASSISTANCE TRANSPORTATION WHEAT
TOPIC: Direct Aid
CONCEPTS: General cooperation. Financial programs. Transportation costs. Domestic obligation.
PARTIES:
USA (United States)
Yemen
                 ANNEX
358 UNTS 386. USA (United States). Supplementation 3 Oct 59. Force 4 Oct 59.
358 UNTS 386. Yemen. Supplementation 4 Oct 59. Force 4 Oct 59.

105113   Bilateral Exchange   **357 UNTS 145**
SIGNED: 2 Mar 59   FORCE: 2 Mar 59
REGISTERED: 29 Apr 60 USA (United States)
ARTICLES: 2 LANGUAGE: English. Arabic.
HEADNOTE: CONSTITUTING ARRANGEMENT RELATING AIR TRANSPORT SERVICES
TOPIC: Air Transport
CONCEPTS: Conditions. Detailed regulations. General cooperation. Licenses and permits. Recognition of legal documents. Use of facilities. Fees and exemptions. Customs exemptions. Competency certificate. Air transport. Airport facilities. Airworthiness certificates. Overflights and technical stops. Operating authorizations and regulations.
PROCEDURE: Duration. Renewal or Revival.
PARTIES:
Indonesia
USA (United States)
                 ANNEX
378 UNTS 410. USA (United States). Prolongation 22 Mar 60. Force 21 Jun 60.
378 UNTS 410. Indonesia. Prolongation 21 Jun 60. Force 21 Jun 60.
416 UNTS 358. USA (United States). Prolongation 30 Mar 61. Force 31 May 61.
416 UNTS 358. Indonesia. Prolongation 31 May 61. Force 31 May 61.
435 UNTS 370. USA (United States). Prolongation 27 Feb 62. Force 17 Apr 62.
435 UNTS 370. Indonesia. Prolongation 17 Apr 62. Force 17 Apr 62.

105114   Bilateral Exchange   **357 UNTS 153**
SIGNED: 7 Jul 59   FORCE: 21 Jul 59
REGISTERED: 29 Apr 60 USA (United States)
ARTICLES: 2 LANGUAGE: English. Greek.
HEADNOTE: TERMINATION MILITARY ECONOMIC ASSISTANCE AGREEMENTS
TOPIC: Milit Assistance
CONCEPTS: Change of circumstances. Annex or appendix reference. Non-prejudice to UN char-

ter. Peaceful relations. Materials, equipment and services. Self-defense. Return of equipment and recapture. Restrictions on transfer.
INTL ORGS: United Nations.
TREATY REF: 222UNTS251; 265UNTS393; 284UNTS13.
PARTIES:
Iraq
USA (United States)

105115 Bilateral Exchange **357 UNTS 163**
SIGNED: 6 May 59 FORCE: 11 Aug 59
REGISTERED: 29 Apr 60 USA (United States)
ARTICLES: 2 LANGUAGE: English.
HEADNOTE: USES ATOMIC ENERGY MUTUAL DEFENSE
TOPIC: Milit Assistance
CONCEPTS: Definition of terms. Conformity with municipal law. General cooperation. Materials, equipment and services. Atomic energy assistance. Non-nuclear materials. Defense and security. Military assistance. Security of information. Exchange of defense information.
TREATY REF: 34UNTS243.
PROCEDURE: Ratification. Termination.
PARTIES:
Greece
USA (United States)

105116 Bilateral Agreement **357 UNTS 181**
SIGNED: 13 Aug 59 FORCE: 13 Aug 59
REGISTERED: 29 Apr 60 USA (United States)
ARTICLES: 8 LANGUAGE: English. Spanish.
HEADNOTE: RADIO FACILITIES
TOPIC: Telecommunications
CONCEPTS: Personnel. Tax exemptions. Customs exemptions. Facilities and equipment. Radio-telephone-telegraphic communications.
PROCEDURE: Duration.
PARTIES:
Liberia
USA (United States)
ANNEX
421 UNTS 332. USA (United States). Supplementation 8 Aug 60. Force 15 Aug 60.
421 UNTS 332. Liberia. Supplementation 15 Aug 60. Force 15 Aug 60.

105117 Bilateral Exchange **357 UNTS 187**
SIGNED: 31 Jul 59 FORCE: 30 Aug 59
REGISTERED: 2 May 60 USA (United States)
ARTICLES: 2 LANGUAGE: French.
HEADNOTE: EXCHANGE THIRD PARTY MESSAGES BETWEEN RADIO AMATEURS
TOPIC: Gen Communications
CONCEPTS: Amateur radio. Amateur third party message. Radio-telephone-telegraphic communications.
PROCEDURE: Termination.
PARTIES:
Mexico
USA (United States)

105118 Bilateral Agreement **357 UNTS 195**
SIGNED: 29 Dec 58 FORCE: 1 Apr 60
REGISTERED: 4 May 60 Belgium
ARTICLES: 17 LANGUAGE: Norwegian. German.
HEADNOTE: CULTURAL AGREEMENT
TOPIC: Culture
CONCEPTS: Annex or appendix reference. Friendship and amity. Tourism. Conformity with municipal law. Responsibility and liability. Establishment of commission. Specialists exchange. Recognition of degrees. Teacher and student exchange. Professorships. Institute establishment. Scholarships and grants. Exchange. General cultural cooperation. Artists. Research cooperation. Scientific exchange. Publications exchange. Mass media exchange.
INTL ORGS: Special Commission.
PROCEDURE: Amendment. Ratification.
PARTIES:
Belgium
Turkey

105119 Bilateral Agreement **357 UNTS 205**
SIGNED: 18 Nov 58 FORCE: 4 May 60
REGISTERED: 4 May 60 Norway
ARTICLES: 27 LANGUAGE: English.

HEADNOTE: DOUBLE TAXATION INCOME FORTUNE
TOPIC: Taxation
CONCEPTS: Definition of terms. Diplomatic privileges. Privileges and immunities. Conformity with municipal law. Exchange of official publications. Negotiation. Teacher and student exchange. Claims and settlements. Taxation. Death duties. Equitable taxes. Tax exemptions. Air transport. Merchant vessels. IGO status.
PROCEDURE: Duration. Ratification. Termination.
PARTIES:
Germany, West
Norway
ANNEX
389 UNTS 328. Norway. Correction 28 Feb 61. Force 28 Feb 61.
389 UNTS 328. Germany, West. Correction 28 Feb 61. Force 28 Feb 61.

105120 Bilateral Exchange **357 UNTS 281**
SIGNED: 15 Jan 59 FORCE: 15 Jan 59
REGISTERED: 4 May 60 USA (United States)
ARTICLES: 2 LANGUAGE: English. Chinese.
HEADNOTE: LOAN VESSELS
TOPIC: Milit Assistance
CONCEPTS: Time limit. Annex or appendix reference. Conformity with municipal law. Exchange of official publications. Responsibility and liability. Compensation. Delivery schedules. Lease of military property. Naval vessels. Return of equipment and recapture.
TREATY REF: 7UNTS267.
PARTIES:
Greece
USA (United States)
ANNEX
452 UNTS 342. USA (United States). Supplementation 4 Apr 62. Force 14 Apr 62.
452 UNTS 342. Greece. Supplementation 14 Apr 62. Force 14 Apr 62.
546 UNTS 359. USA (United States). Prolongation 16 Mar 65. Force 23 Mar 65.
546 UNTS 359. Greece. Prolongation 23 Mar 65. Force 23 Mar 65.

105121 Bilateral Exchange **357 UNTS 293**
SIGNED: 22 Jul 59 FORCE: 22 Jul 59
REGISTERED: 4 May 60 USA (United States)
ARTICLES: 2 LANGUAGE: English.
HEADNOTE: SALE EXCESS MILITARY PROPERTY
TOPIC: Milit Assistance
CONCEPTS: Detailed regulations. Annex or appendix reference. Currency. General. Tax exemptions. Customs duties. Customs exemptions. Surplus property. Surplus war property.
PROCEDURE: Future Procedures Contemplated. Termination.
PARTIES:
Taiwan
USA (United States)

105122 Bilateral Agreement **358 UNTS 3**
SIGNED: 13 Jan 59 FORCE: 1 Oct 59
REGISTERED: 4 May 60 USA (United States)
ARTICLES: 31 LANGUAGE: English.
HEADNOTE: PARCEL POST
TOPIC: Postal Service
CONCEPTS: Definition of terms. Detailed regulations. Domestic legislation. Responsibility and liability. Compensation. Indemnities and reimbursements. Payment schedules. Customs duties. Customs exemptions. Postal services. Insured letters and boxes. Conveyance in transit. Parcel post. Rates and charges.
INTL ORGS: Universal Postal Union.
TREATY REF: USA'TIAS 4202;.
PROCEDURE: Duration. Termination.
PARTIES:
United Arab Rep
USA (United States)

105123 Bilateral Exchange **358 UNTS 51**
SIGNED: 22 Oct 55 FORCE: 22 Oct 55
REGISTERED: 6 May 60 USA (United States)
ARTICLES: 3 LANGUAGE: English. Spanish.
HEADNOTE: PASSPORT VISAS
TOPIC: Visas
CONCEPTS: Visas. Fees and exemptions.

PARTIES:
Nicaragua
USA (United States)

105124 Bilateral Convention **358 UNTS 63**
SIGNED: 15 Aug 58 FORCE: 4 Sep 59
REGISTERED: 6 May 60 USA (United States)
ARTICLES: 8 LANGUAGE: English. Spanish.
HEADNOTE: CONSERVATION SHRIMP
TOPIC: Specific Resources
CONCEPTS: Exchange of information and documents. Investigation of violations. Establishment of commission. Ocean resources. Fisheries and fishing.
INTL ORGS: Special Commission.
PROCEDURE: Duration. Ratification. Termination.
PARTIES:
Cuba
USA (United States)

105125 Bilateral Exchange **358 UNTS 77**
SIGNED: 17 Dec 58 FORCE: 17 Dec 58
REGISTERED: 6 May 60 USA (United States)
ARTICLES: 2 LANGUAGE: English.
HEADNOTE: ASSURANCES REGARDING MUTUAL DEFENSE ASSISTANCE
TOPIC: Milit Assistance
CONCEPTS: Conformity with municipal law. Materials, equipment and services. Exchange of defense information.
TREATY REF: 141UNTS47.
PARTIES:
India
USA (United States)

105126 Bilateral Exchange **358 UNTS 83**
SIGNED: 17 Apr 59 FORCE: 17 Apr 59
REGISTERED: 6 May 60 USA (United States)
ARTICLES: 2 LANGUAGE: English. Spanish.
HEADNOTE: FREE-ENTRY PRIVILEGES
TOPIC: Visas
CONCEPTS: Frontier formalities. Customs exemptions.
PARTIES:
USA (United States)
Venezuela

105127 Bilateral Exchange **358 UNTS 91**
SIGNED: 24 Jun 59 FORCE: 24 Jun 59
REGISTERED: 6 May 60 USA (United States)
ARTICLES: 2 LANGUAGE: English.
HEADNOTE: SPECIAL ECONOMIC ASSISTANCE
TOPIC: Direct Aid
CONCEPTS: General cooperation. Financial programs. Economic assistance. Grants.
TREATY REF: 300UNTS11.
PARTIES:
Burma
USA (United States)

105128 Bilateral Agreement **358 UNTS 97**
SIGNED: 28 Sep 59 FORCE: 28 Sep 59
REGISTERED: 9 May 60 USA (United States)
ARTICLES: 12 LANGUAGE: English. Arabic.
HEADNOTE: EDUCATION PROGRAM
TOPIC: Education
CONCEPTS: Definition of terms. Standardization. Conformity with municipal law. General cooperation. Inspection and observation. Personnel. General property. Exchange. Commissions and foundations. Teacher and student exchange. Scholarships and grants. Research and development. Accounting procedures. Currency. Exchange rates and regulations. Expense sharing formulae. Financial programs. Funding procedures.
INTL ORGS: Special Commission.
TREATY REF: 71UNTS31.
PROCEDURE: Amendment. Termination.
PARTIES:
United Arab Rep
USA (United States)
ANNEX
487 UNTS 366. USA (United States). Amendment 28 Jun 62. Force 30 Jun 62.
487 UNTS 366. United Arab Rep. Amendment 30 Jun 62. Force 30 Jun 62.

105129 Bilateral Agreement **358 UNTS 115**
SIGNED: 1 Oct 59 FORCE: 1 Oct 59
REGISTERED: 9 May 60 USA (United States)
ARTICLES: 6 LANGUAGE: English. Korean.
HEADNOTE: DISPOSAL EXCESS PROPERTY
TOPIC: Direct Aid
CONCEPTS: Annex or appendix reference. Conformity with municipal law. General cooperation. Import quotas. Indemnities and reimbursements. Local currency. General. Customs duties. Domestic obligation. Surplus property.
PROCEDURE: Amendment. Renewal or Revival. Termination.
PARTIES:
Korea, South
USA (United States)
ANNEX
473 UNTS 354. USA (United States). Amendment 1 Feb 63. Force 1 Feb 63.
473 UNTS 354. Korea, South. Amendment 1 Feb 63. Force 1 Feb 63.

105130 Bilateral Agreement **358 UNTS 129**
SIGNED: 1 Oct 59 FORCE: 1 Oct 59
REGISTERED: 9 May 60 USA (United States)
ARTICLES: 9 LANGUAGE: English. German.
HEADNOTE: BIRKENFELD HIGH ALTITUDE AIR TRAFFIC CONTROL SERVICES
TOPIC: Air Transport
CONCEPTS: Exceptions and exemptions. Nonprejudice to third party. General cooperation. Personnel. Claims and settlements. Materials, equipment and services. Navigational conditions. Navigational equipment. Air transport. Operating authorizations and regulations.
PROCEDURE: Termination.
PARTIES:
Germany, West
USA (United States)

105131 Bilateral Exchange **358 UNTS 139**
SIGNED: 23 Feb 60 FORCE: 31 Mar 60
REGISTERED: 10 May 60 Philippines
ARTICLES: 2 LANGUAGE: English.
HEADNOTE: RECIPROCAL WAIVER NON-IMMIGRANT PASSPORT VISA FEES
TOPIC: Visas
CONCEPTS: Visas. Fees and exemptions.
PROCEDURE: Termination.
PARTIES:
Australia
Philippines

105132 Bilateral Exchange **358 UNTS 145**
SIGNED: 6 Oct 59 FORCE: 6 Oct 59
REGISTERED: 12 May 60 USA (United States)
ARTICLES: 2 LANGUAGE: English. Spanish.
HEADNOTE: SURPLUS AGRI COMMOD
TOPIC: US Agri Commod Aid
CONCEPTS: Annex or appendix reference. General cooperation. Exchange of information and documents. Reexport of goods, etc.. Currency deposits. Exchange rates and regulations. Purchase authorizations. Transportation costs. Local currency. Commodities schedule. Surplus commodities.
PARTIES:
Colombia
USA (United States)
ANNEX
407 UNTS 285. Colombia. Amendment 26 Apr 61. Force 26 Apr 61.
407 UNTS 285. USA (United States). Amendment 26 Apr 61. Force 26 Apr 61.
433 UNTS 377. Colombia. Amendment 20 Nov 62. Force 20 Nov 61.
433 UNTS 377. USA (United States). Amendment 9 Nov 61. Force 20 Nov 61.
442 UNTS 334. USA (United States). Amendment 6 Sep 61. Force 8 Sep 61.
442 UNTS 334. Colombia. Amendment 8 Sep 61. Force 8 Sep 61.
445 UNTS 362. USA (United States). Amendment 31 Jan 62. Force 14 Feb 62.
445 UNTS 362. Colombia. Amendment 14 Feb 62. Force 14 Feb 62.
458 UNTS 344. Colombia. Amendment 20 Jun 62. Force 20 Jun 62.
458 UNTS 344. USA (United States). Amendment 20 Jun 62. Force 20 Jun 62.

105133 Bilateral Exchange **358 UNTS 163**
SIGNED: 25 Sep 59 FORCE: 26 Sep 59
REGISTERED: 12 May 60 USA (United States)
ARTICLES: 2 LANGUAGE: English.
HEADNOTE: INFORMATIONAL MEDIA GUARANTY PROGRAM
TOPIC: Mass Media
CONCEPTS: Guarantees and safeguards. Export quotas. Trade procedures. Publications exchange. Mass media exchange. Media guaranty.
PROCEDURE: Termination.
PARTIES:
Korea, South
USA (United States)

105134 Bilateral Exchange **358 UNTS 169**
SIGNED: 28 Oct 59 FORCE: 28 Oct 59
REGISTERED: 12 May 60 USA (United States)
ARTICLES: 2 LANGUAGE: English. French.
HEADNOTE: CULTURAL RELATIONS
TOPIC: Culture
CONCEPTS: Friendship and amity. Tourism. Conformity with municipal law. Establishment of commission. Specialists exchange. Teacher and student exchange. Scholarships and grants. Exchange. General cultural cooperation. Artists. Scientific exchange.
PARTIES:
Guinea
USA (United States)

105135 Bilateral Exchange **358 UNTS 175**
SIGNED: 16 Sep 59 FORCE: 16 Sep 59
REGISTERED: 12 May 60 USA (United States)
ARTICLES: 2 LANGUAGE: English. Arabic.
HEADNOTE: NUCLEAR RESEARCH TRAINING EQUIPMENT
TOPIC: Scientific Project
CONCEPTS: Responsibility and liability. Institute establishment. Research and scientific projects. Research results. Research and development. Materials, equipment and services. Atomic energy assistance. Nuclear materials. Non-nuclear materials. Peaceful use.
PARTIES:
Lebanon
USA (United States)

105136 Bilateral Agreement **358 UNTS 185**
SIGNED: 7 Aug 59 FORCE: 23 Apr 60
REGISTERED: 13 May 60 Norway
ARTICLES: 4 LANGUAGE: Norwegian. German.
HEADNOTE: PAYMENTS BEHALF NATIONALS VICTIMIZED NATIONAL SOCIALIST PERSECUTION
TOPIC: Reparations
CONCEPTS: Payment schedules. Lump sum settlements. Loss and/or damage. Reparations and restrictions. Post-war claims settlement.
PROCEDURE: Ratification.
PARTIES:
Germany, West
Norway

105137 Bilateral Agreement **358 UNTS 203**
SIGNED: 1 Jun 55 FORCE: 3 Aug 55
REGISTERED: 17 May 60 IBRD (World Bank)
ARTICLES: 6 LANGUAGE: English.
HEADNOTE: GUARANTEE ELECTRIC POWER IRRIGATION INDUSTRIAL
TOPIC: IBRD Project
CONCEPTS: Definition of terms. Annex or appendix reference. Exchange of information and documents. Inspection and observation. Bonds. Fees and exemptions. Tax exemptions. Domestic obligation. Terms of loan. Loan regulations. Loan guarantee. Guarantor non-interference. Industry. Irrigation. Hydro-electric power.
PARTIES:
Italy
IBRD (World Bank)

105138 Bilateral Agreement **359 UNTS 3**
SIGNED: 11 Oct 56 FORCE: 10 Dec 56
REGISTERED: 17 May 60 IBRD (World Bank)
ARTICLES: 6 LANGUAGE: English.
HEADNOTE: GUARANTEE AGREEMENT
TOPIC: IBRD Project
CONCEPTS: Definition of terms. Annex or appendix reference. Exchange of information and documents. Inspection and observation. Bonds. Fees and exemptions. Tax exemptions. Domestic obligation. Terms of loan. Loan regulations. Loan guarantee. Guarantor non-interference.
PARTIES:
Italy
IBRD (World Bank)

105139 Bilateral Agreement **359 UNTS 47**
SIGNED: 28 Feb 58 FORCE: 8 May 58
REGISTERED: 17 May 60 IBRD (World Bank)
ARTICLES: 6 LANGUAGE: English.
HEADNOTE: GUARANTEE LOAN
TOPIC: IBRD Project
CONCEPTS: Loan and credit. Credit provisions.
PARTIES:
Italy
IBRD (World Bank)

105140 Bilateral Agreement **359 UNTS 89**
SIGNED: 28 Apr 58 FORCE: 15 Mar 60
REGISTERED: 17 May 60 IBRD (World Bank)
ARTICLES: 5 LANGUAGE: English.
HEADNOTE: GUARANTEE AGREEMENT
TOPIC: IBRD Project
CONCEPTS: Definition of terms. Annex or appendix reference. Exchange of information and documents. Inspection and observation. Bonds. Fees and exemptions. Tax exemptions. Domestic obligation. Terms of loan. Loan regulations. Loan guarantee. Guarantor non-interference.
PARTIES:
Chile
IBRD (World Bank)

105141 Bilateral Agreement **359 UNTS 119**
SIGNED: 20 May 59 FORCE: 21 Apr 60
REGISTERED: 17 May 60 IBRD (World Bank)
ARTICLES: 5 LANGUAGE: English.
HEADNOTE: GUARANTEE POWER
TOPIC: IBRD Project
CONCEPTS: Annex or appendix reference. Exchange of information and documents. Inspection and observation. Bonds. Fees and exemptions. Tax exemptions. Domestic obligation. Terms of loan. Loan regulations. Loan guarantee. Guarantor non-interference. Hydro-electric power.
PARTIES:
Honduras
IBRD (World Bank)

105142 Bilateral Agreement **359 UNTS 145**
SIGNED: 28 Apr 58 FORCE: 9 Jul 58
REGISTERED: 19 May 60 IBRD (World Bank)
ARTICLES: 5 LANGUAGE: English.
HEADNOTE: GUARANTEE INDUSTRIAL CREDIT
TOPIC: IBRD Project
CONCEPTS: Definition of terms. Annex or appendix reference. Exchange of information and documents. Inspection and observation. Bonds. Fees and exemptions. Tax exemptions. Domestic obligation. Terms of loan. Loan regulations. Loan guarantee. Guarantor non-interference.
PARTIES:
Austria
IBRD (World Bank)

105143 Bilateral Agreement **359 UNTS 191**
SIGNED: 21 Apr 59 FORCE: 24 Oct 59
REGISTERED: 19 May 60 IBRD (World Bank)
ARTICLES: 6 LANGUAGE: English.
HEADNOTE: GUARANTEE AGREEMENT
TOPIC: IBRD Project
CONCEPTS: Definition of terms. Annex or appendix reference. Exchange of information and documents. Inspection and observation. Bonds. Fees and exemptions. Tax exemptions. Domestic obligation. Terms of loan. Loan regulations. Loan guarantee. Guarantor non-interference.
PARTIES:
Italy
IBRD (World Bank)

105144 Bilateral Exchange **359 UNTS 227**
SIGNED: 7 Dec 59 FORCE: 7 Dec 59
REGISTERED: 20 May 60 USA (United States)

ARTICLES: 2 LANGUAGE: English.
HEADNOTE: RELINQUISHMENT COMMUNITY OLONGAPO
TOPIC: Milit Installation
CONCEPTS: Annex or appendix reference. General property. Responsibility and liability. Bases and facilities.
PARTIES:
Philippines
USA (United States)

105145 Bilateral Agreement **359 UNTS 259**
SIGNED: 7 Jul 59 FORCE: 10 Feb 60
REGISTERED: 23 May 60 Czechoslovakia
ARTICLES: 7 LANGUAGE: Czechoslovakian. Hindi. English.
HEADNOTE: CULTURAL COOPERATION
TOPIC: Culture
CONCEPTS: Friendship and amity. Conformity with municipal law. Establishment of commission. Recognition of degrees. Exchange. Teacher and student exchange. Institute establishment. Scholarships and grants. Exchange. General cultural cooperation. Artists. Athletes. Scientific exchange. Publications exchange. Mass media exchange.
INTL ORGS: Special Commission.
PROCEDURE: Duration. Ratification. Termination.
PARTIES:
Czechoslovakia
India

105146 Multilateral Convention **359 UNTS 273**
SIGNED: 13 Dec 57 FORCE: 18 Apr 60
REGISTERED: 24 May 60 Council of Europe
ARTICLES: 32 LANGUAGE: English. French.
HEADNOTE: EUROPEAN CONVENTION EXTRADITION
TOPIC: Extradition
CONCEPTS: Definition of terms. Exceptions and exemptions. Territorial application. Time limit. Extradition, deportation and repatriation. Extradition requests. Extraditable offenses. Location of crime. Special factors. Refusal of extradition. Concurrent requests. Provisional detainment. Extradition postponement. Material evidence. Conformity with municipal law. Indemnities and reimbursements. Conveyance in transit.
INTL ORGS: Council of Europe.
PROCEDURE: Accession. Denunciation. Ratification.
PARTIES:
Austria SIGNED: 13 Dec 57
Belgium SIGNED: 13 Dec 57
Denmark SIGNED: 13 Dec 57
France SIGNED: 13 Dec 57
Germany, West SIGNED: 13 Dec 57
Greece SIGNED: 13 Dec 57
Iceland SIGNED: 13 Dec 57
Ireland SIGNED: 13 Dec 57
Italy SIGNED: 13 Dec 57
Luxembourg SIGNED: 13 Dec 57
Netherlands SIGNED: 13 Dec 57
Norway SIGNED: 13 Dec 57 RATIFIED: 19 Jan 60 FORCE: 19 Apr 60
Sweden SIGNED: 13 Dec 57 RATIFIED: 22 Jan 59 FORCE: 19 Apr 60
Turkey SIGNED: 13 Dec 57 RATIFIED: 7 Jan 60 FORCE: 19 Apr 60
UK Great Britain SIGNED: 13 Dec 57
ANNEX
404 UNTS 372. Greece. Qualified Ratification 29 May 61. Force 27 Aug 61.
444 UNTS 348. Denmark. Qualified Ratification 13 Sep 62. Force 12 Dec 62.
475 UNTS 366. Italy. Ratification 6 Aug 63. Force 4 Nov 63.
565 UNTS 294.
565 UNTS 294. Ireland. Signature 2 May 66. Qualified Ratification 2 May 66.
645 UNTS 356. Israel. Declaration 26 Dec 67. Reservation 26 Dec 67.

105147 Bilateral Exchange **359 UNTS 305**
SIGNED: 18 Feb 59 FORCE: 15 Mar 59
REGISTERED: 24 May 60 Philippines
ARTICLES: 2 LANGUAGE: English.
HEADNOTE: RECIPROCAL WAIVER NON-IMMIGRANT PASSPORT VISA FEES
TOPIC: Visas
CONCEPTS: Visas. Fees and exemptions.

PROCEDURE: Amendment. Termination.
PARTIES:
Norway
Philippines

105148 Bilateral Exchange **359 UNTS 311**
SIGNED: 17 Feb 60 FORCE: 16 Mar 60
REGISTERED: 24 May 60 Philippines
ARTICLES: 2 LANGUAGE: English.
HEADNOTE: RECIPROCAL WAIVER NON-IMMIGRANT VISA FEES
TOPIC: Visas
CONCEPTS: Visas. Fees and exemptions.
PROCEDURE: Amendment. Termination.
PARTIES:
Luxembourg
Philippines

105149 Bilateral Exchange **359 UNTS 317**
SIGNED: 17 Feb 60 FORCE: 16 Mar 60
REGISTERED: 24 May 60 Philippines
ARTICLES: 2 LANGUAGE: English.
HEADNOTE: RECIPROCAL WAIVER NON-IMMIGRANT PASSPORT VISA FEES
TOPIC: Visas
CONCEPTS: Visas. Fees and exemptions.
PROCEDURE: Amendment. Termination.
PARTIES:
Netherlands
Philippines

105150 Multilateral Agreement **359 UNTS 323**
SIGNED: 12 Apr 60 FORCE: 12 Apr 60
REGISTERED: 25 May 60 United Nations
ARTICLES: 6 LANGUAGE: French.
HEADNOTE: TECHNICAL ASSISTANCE
TOPIC: Tech Assistance
CONCEPTS: Definition of terms. Privileges and immunities. General cooperation. Exchange of information and documents. Personnel. Responsibility and liability. Title and deeds. Use of facilities. Exchange. Scholarships and grants. Vocational training. Research and development. Exchange rates and regulations. Expense sharing formulae. Local currency. Domestic obligation. General technical assistance. Materials, equipment and services. Conformity with IGO decisions.
TREATY REF: 76UNTS132; 1UNTS15; 33UNTS261.
PROCEDURE: Amendment. Termination.
PARTIES:
FAO (Food Agri) SIGNED: 12 Apr 60 FORCE: 12 Apr 60
IAEA (Atom Energy) SIGNED: 12 Apr 60 FORCE: 12 Apr 60
ICAO (Civil Aviat) SIGNED: 12 Apr 60 FORCE: 12 Apr 60
ILO (Labor Org) SIGNED: 12 Apr 60 FORCE: 12 Apr 60
ITU (Telecommun) SIGNED: 12 Apr 60 FORCE: 12 Apr 60
UNESCO (Educ/Cult) SIGNED: 12 Apr 60 FORCE: 12 Apr 60
United Nations SIGNED: 12 Apr 60 FORCE: 12 Apr 60
WHO (World Health) SIGNED: 12 Apr 60 FORCE: 12 Apr 60
WMO (Meteorology) SIGNED: 12 Apr 60 FORCE: 12 Apr 60
Tunisia SIGNED: 12 Apr 60 FORCE: 12 Apr 60

105151 Bilateral Agreement **359 UNTS 339**
SIGNED: 3 Feb 59 FORCE: 3 Feb 59
REGISTERED: 2 Jun 60 UK Great Britain
ARTICLES: 19 LANGUAGE: English. Serbo-Croat.
HEADNOTE: CONCERNING AIR SERVICES
TOPIC: Air Transport
CONCEPTS: Definition of terms. Detailed regulations. Exceptions and exemptions. Representation. Annex or appendix reference. Previous treaty replacement. Visas. Conformity with municipal law. General cooperation. Exchange of information and documents. Informational records. Licenses and permits. Recognition of legal documents. Use of facilities. Arbitration. Procedure. Special tribunals. Negotiation. Humanitarian matters. Expense sharing formulae. Fees and exemptions. Non-interest rates and fees. Customs exemptions. Temporary importation.

Competency certificate. Registration certificate. Routes and logistics. Navigational conditions. Permit designation. Airport facilities. Airworthiness certificates. Conditions of airlines operating permission. Operating authorizations and regulations. Licenses and certificates of nationality.
INTL ORGS: International Court of Justice. Arbitration Commission.
PROCEDURE: Amendment. Future Procedures Contemplated. Ratification. Termination. Application to Non-self-governing Territories.
PARTIES:
UK Great Britain
Yugoslavia
ANNEX
566 UNTS 362. UK Great Britain. Amendment 13 Sep 65. Force 7 May 65.
566 UNTS 362. Yugoslavia. Amendment 7 May 65. Force 7 May 65.
659 UNTS 366. UK Great Britain. Amendment 4 Mar 68. Force 4 Mar 69.
659 UNTS 366. Yugoslavia. Amendment 4 Mar 69. Force 4 Mar 69.

105152 Bilateral Exchange **360 UNTS 3**
SIGNED: 13 Nov 59 FORCE: 1 Jan 60
REGISTERED: 2 Jun 60 UK Great Britain
ARTICLES: 2 LANGUAGE: English. Spanish.
HEADNOTE: RECIPROCAL ABOLITION VISAS
TOPIC: Visas
CONCEPTS: Emergencies. Territorial application. Visa abolition. Denial of admission. Resident permits. Conformity with municipal law.
PROCEDURE: Denunciation.
PARTIES:
Mexico
UK Great Britain
ANNEX
470 UNTS 414. UK Great Britain. British Honduras. Force 1 Mar 63.
470 UNTS 414. Mexico. Acknowledgement 21 Jan 63. Force 1 Mar 63.

105153 Bilateral Convention **360 UNTS 11**
SIGNED: 27 Aug 59 FORCE: 1 Mar 60
REGISTERED: 2 Jun 60 UK Great Britain
ARTICLES: 42 LANGUAGE: English. Danish.
HEADNOTE: SOCIAL SECURITY
TOPIC: Non-ILO Labor
CONCEPTS: Old age and invalidity insurance.
TREATY REF: 196UNTS105; 264UNTS45.
PROCEDURE: Denunciation. Ratification.
PARTIES:
Denmark
UK Great Britain

105154 Bilateral Exchange **360 UNTS 69**
SIGNED: 14 May 59 FORCE: 14 May 59
REGISTERED: 2 Jun 60 UK Great Britain
ARTICLES: 2 LANGUAGE: English.
HEADNOTE: FINAL SETTLEMENT CLAIMS
TOPIC: Specif Claim/Waive
CONCEPTS: Annex or appendix reference. Lump sum settlements. Specific claims or waivers.
PARTIES:
Greece
UK Great Britain

105155 Bilateral Exchange **360 UNTS 79**
SIGNED: 12 Apr 60 FORCE: 12 Apr 60
REGISTERED: 2 Jun 60 UK Great Britain
ARTICLES: 2 LANGUAGE: English.
HEADNOTE: IMPORT BOOKS FILMS
TOPIC: Culture
CONCEPTS: Definition of terms. Annex or appendix reference. Education. Culture. Import quotas. Trade procedures. Exchange rates and regulations. Local currency. Recognition. Publications exchange. Mass media exchange.
PROCEDURE: Termination.
PARTIES:
UK Great Britain
Yugoslavia
ANNEX
404 UNTS 376. UK Great Britain. Amendment 24 Jan 61. Force 15 Feb 61.
404 UNTS 376. Yugoslavia. Amendment 15 Feb 61. Force 15 Feb 61.

565 UNTS 296. Yugoslavia. Acknowledgement 9 Nov 65. Force 9 Nov 65.
565 UNTS 296. UK Great Britain. Amendment 9 Nov 65. Force 9 Nov 65.

105156 Bilateral Exchange **360 UNTS 89**
SIGNED: 18 Apr 59　　　　FORCE: 18 Apr 59
REGISTERED: 2 Jun 60 UK Great Britain
ARTICLES: 2 LANGUAGE: English.
HEADNOTE: DEBT REPAYMENT
TOPIC: Claims and Debts
CONCEPTS: Banking. Currency. Exchange rates and regulations. Financial programs. Interest rates. Payment schedules. Debt settlement.
INTL ORGS: Organization for Economic Co-operation and Development.
PARTIES:
Sweden
UK Great Britain

105157 Bilateral Agreement **360 UNTS 97**
SIGNED: 4 Jun 60　　　　FORCE: 4 Jun 60
REGISTERED: 4 Jun 60 United Nations
ARTICLES: 10 LANGUAGE: English.
HEADNOTE: SOCIAL SECURITY
TOPIC: Tech Assistance
CONCEPTS: Definition of terms. Previous treaty replacement. Conformity with municipal law. Domestic legislation. Dispute settlement. Old age and invalidity insurance. Wages and salaries. Non-ILO labor relations. Family allowances. Administrative cooperation. Old age insurance. Sickness and invalidity insurance. Social security. Unemployment. Payment schedules. Claims and settlements.
INTL ORGS: International Atomic Energy Agency. International Court of Justice. United Nations.
TREATY REF: 1UNTS15; 33UNTS261.
PROCEDURE: Denunciation. Duration. Ratification. Renewal or Revival.
PARTIES:
UN Special Fund
Thailand

105158 Multilateral Convention **360 UNTS 117**
SIGNED: 28 Sep 54　　　　FORCE: 6 Jun 60
REGISTERED: 6 Jun 60 United Nations
ARTICLES: 42 LANGUAGE: English. French. Spanish.
HEADNOTE: STATUS STATELESS PERSONS
TOPIC: Refugees
CONCEPTS: Definition of terms. Exceptions and exemptions. Territorial application. Denial of admission. Resident permits. Legal status. Stateless persons. Human rights. General cooperation. Legal protection and assistance. Domestic legislation. Immovable property. General property. Procedure. Anti-discrimination. Employment regulations. Social security. Indemnities and reimbursements. Assets transfer. Most favored nation clause. Recognition.
INTL ORGS: International Court of Justice. United Nations.
PROCEDURE: Amendment. Accession. Denunciation. Ratification.
PARTIES:
Belgium　SIGNED:　28 Sep 54　RATIFIED: 27 May 60 FORCE: 25 Aug 60
Brazil SIGNED: 28 Sep 54
Colombia SIGNED: 30 Dec 54
Costa Rica SIGNED: 28 Sep 54
Denmark　SIGNED:　28 Sep 54　RATIFIED: 17 Jan 56 FORCE: 6 Jun 60
Ecuador SIGNED: 28 Sep 54
El Salvador SIGNED: 28 Sep 54
France Algeria RATIFIED: 8 Mar 60 FORCE: 6 Jun 60
France Comoro Islands RATIFIED: 8 Mar 60 FORCE: 6 Jun 60
France French Guiana RATIFIED: 8 Mar 60 FORCE: 6 Jun 60
France French Polynesia RATIFIED: 8 Mar 60 FORCE: 6 Jun 60
France French Somaliland RATIFIED: 8 Mar 60 FORCE: 6 Jun 60
France Guadeloupe RATIFIED: 8 Mar 60 FORCE: 6 Jun 60
France Martinique RATIFIED: 8 Mar 60 FORCE: 6 Jun 60
France Miquelon RATIFIED: 8 Mar 60 FORCE: 6 Jun 60

France New Caledonia RATIFIED: 8 Mar 60 FORCE: 6 Jun 60
France SIGNED: 12 Jan 55 RATIFIED: 8 Mar 60 FORCE: 6 Jun 60
France St. Pierre RATIFIED: 8 Mar 60 FORCE: 6 Jun 60
Germany, West SIGNED: 28 Sep 54
Guatemala SIGNED: 28 Sep 54
Honduras SIGNED: 28 Sep 54
Israel SIGNED: 1 Oct 54 RATIFIED: 23 Dec 58 FORCE: 6 Jun 60
Italy SIGNED: 20 Oct 54
Liechtenstein SIGNED: 28 Sep 54
Luxembourg SIGNED: 28 Oct 55
Netherlands SIGNED: 28 Sep 54
Norway　SIGNED:　28 Sep 54　RATIFIED: 19 Nov 56 FORCE: 6 Jun 60
Philippines SIGNED: 22 Jun 55
Sweden SIGNED: 28 Sep 54
Switzerland SIGNED: 28 Sep 54
UK Great Britain Basutoland RATIFIED: 7 Dec 59 FORCE: 6 Jun 60
UK Great Britain Bechuanaland RATIFIED: 7 Dec 59 FORCE: 6 Jun 60
UK Great Britain Channel Islands RATIFIED: 7 Dec 59 FORCE: 6 Jun 60
UK Great Britain Fed Rhod/Nyasaland RATIFIED: 7 Dec 59 FORCE: 6 Jun 60
UK Great Britain Isle of Man RATIFIED: 7 Dec 59 FORCE: 6 Jun 60
UK Great Britain SIGNED: 28 Sep 54 RATIFIED: 16 Apr 59 FORCE: 6 Jun 60
UK Great Britain Swaziland RATIFIED: 7 Dec 59 FORCE: 6 Jun 60
Vatican/Holy See SIGNED: 23 Apr 54
ANNEX
362 UNTS 344.　Luxembourg.　Ratification 27 Jun 60. Force 25 Sep 60.
423 UNTS 327.　Madagascar.　Accession 20 Feb 62. Force 21 May 62.
424 UNTS 384. UK Great Britain. British Guiana.
424 UNTS 384. UK Great Britain. Sarawak. Force 17 Jun 62.
424 UNTS 384. UK Great Britain. Brit Virgin Islands. Force 17 Jun 62.
424 UNTS 384. UK Great Britain. Aden Colony. Force 17 Jun 62.
424 UNTS 384. UK Great Britain. Zanzibar.
424 UNTS 384. UK Great Britain. Fiji Islands.
424 UNTS 384. UK Great Britain. Bermuda. Force 17 Jun 62.
424 UNTS 384. Guinea. Accession 21 Mar 62. Force 19 Jun 62.
424 UNTS 384. UK Great Britain. Malta. Force 17 Jun 62.
424 UNTS 384. UK Great Britain. North Borneo.
424 UNTS 384. UK Great Britain. West Indies.
424 UNTS 384. UK Great Britain. St. Helena. Force 17 Jun 62.
424 UNTS 384. UK Great Britain. Uganda. Force 17 Jun 62.
424 UNTS 384. UK Great Britain. British Honduras.
424 UNTS 384. UK Great Britain. Brit Solomon Is.
424 UNTS 384. UK Great Britain. Falkland Islands.
424 UNTS 384. UK Great Britain. Gilbert Islands.
424 UNTS 384. UK Great Britain. Hong Kong.
424 UNTS 384. UK Great Britain. Kenya.
424 UNTS 384. UK Great Britain. Mauritius.
424 UNTS 384. UK Great Britain. Singapore.
424 UNTS 384. UK Great Britain. Seychelles. Force 17 Jun 62.
425 UNTS 366. Netherlands. Surinam. Force 11 Jul 62.
425 UNTS 366. Netherlands. Dutch New Guinea. Force 11 Jul 62.
425 UNTS 366. Netherlands. Qualified Ratification 12 Apr 62. Force 11 Jul 62.
435 UNTS 374.　Korea,　South.　Accession 22 Aug 62. Force 20 Nov 62.
435 UNTS 374. Denmark. Withdrawal of Reservation 23 Aug 62.
446 UNTS 396. Italy. Ratification 3 Dec 62. Force 3 Mar 63.
448 UNTS 336.　Ireland.　Qualified Accession 17 Dec 62. Force 17 Mar 63.
502 UNTS 386.　Algeria.　Accession　15 Jul 64. Force 13 Oct 64.
510 UNTS 334.　Liberia.　Accession　11 Sep 64. Force 10 Dec 64.
529 UNTS 362.　Madagascar.　Denunciation 2 Apr 65. Force 2 Apr 66.

529 UNTS 362.　Sweden.　Qualified Ratification 2 Apr 65. Force 1 Jul 65.
531 UNTS 355. Uganda. Accession 15 Apr 65. Force 14 Jul 65.
560 UNTS 278.　Trinidad/Tobago.　Succession 11 Apr 66.
619 UNTS 338. Italy. Withdrawal 25 Jan 68.
633 UNTS 410. Denmark. Withdrawal of Reservation 25 Mar 68.
648 UNTS 368.　Finland.　Accession　10 Oct 68. Force 8 Jan 69.
658 UNTS 438.　　Botswana.　　Succession 25 Feb 69.

105159 Multilateral Agreement **360 UNTS 208**
SIGNED: 4 Jun 60　　　　FORCE: 4 Jun 60
REGISTERED: 6 Jun 60 United Nations
ARTICLES: 6 LANGUAGE: English.
HEADNOTE: TECHNICAL ASSISTANCE
TOPIC: Tech Assistance
CONCEPTS: Definition of terms. Previous treaty replacement. Privileges and immunities. General cooperation. Exchange of information and documents. Personnel. Responsibility and liability. Title and deeds. Use of facilities. Exchange. Scholarships and grants. Vocational training. Research and development. Exchange rates and regulations. Expense sharing formulae. Local currency. Domestic obligation. General technical assistance. Materials, equipment and services. IGO status. Conformity with IGO decisions.
TREATY　REF:　76UNTS132;　1UNTS15; 33UNTS261; 90UNTS45.
PROCEDURE: Amendment. Termination.
PARTIES:
FAO (Food Agri) SIGNED: 4 Jun 60 FORCE: 4 Jun 60
IAEA (Atom Energy) SIGNED: 4 Jun 60 FORCE: 4 Jun 60
ICAO (Civil Aviat) SIGNED: 4 Jun 60 FORCE: 4 Jun 60
ILO (Labor Org) SIGNED: 4 Jun 60 FORCE: 4 Jun 60
ITU (Telecommun) SIGNED: 4 Jun 60 FORCE: 4 Jun 60
UNESCO (Educ/Cult) SIGNED: 4 Jun 60 FORCE: 4 Jun 60
United Nations SIGNED: 4 Jun 60 FORCE: 4 Jun 60
WHO (World Health) SIGNED: 4 Jun 60 FORCE: 4 Jun 60
WMO (Meteorology) SIGNED: 4 Jun 60 FORCE: 4 Jun 60
Thailand SIGNED: 4 Jun 60 FORCE: 4 Jun 60
ANNEX
519 UNTS 396.　　Thailand.　　Amendment 30 Nov 64. Force 30 Nov 64.
519 UNTS 396. UNTAB (Tech Assis). Amendment 9 Apr 64. Force 30 Nov 64.

105160 Bilateral Agreement **360 UNTS 225**
SIGNED: 7 May 60　　　　FORCE: 7 May 60
REGISTERED: 7 Jun 60 United Nations
ARTICLES: 10 LANGUAGE: English. Arabic.
HEADNOTE: ASSISTANCE
TOPIC: Tech Assistance
CONCEPTS: Conditions. Detailed regulations. Treaty implementation. Annex or appendix reference. Visas. Privileges and immunities. General cooperation. Exchange of information and documents. Inspection and observation. Operating agencies. Personnel. General property. Public information. Responsibility and liability. Title and deeds. Use of facilities. Arbitration. Procedure. Negotiation. Export quotas. Reexport of goods, etc.. Indemnities and reimbursements. Exchange rates and regulations. Expense sharing formulae. Financial programs. Tax exemptions. Customs exemptions. Domestic obligation. General technical assistance. Materials, equipment and services. IGO status. Conformity with IGO decisions.
INTL ORGS: International Atomic Energy Agency. International Court of Justice. United Nations.
TREATY REF: 1UNTS15; 33UNTS261.
PROCEDURE: Amendment. Termination.
PARTIES:
Lebanon
UN Special Fund

105161 Bilateral Exchange **360 UNTS 259**
SIGNED: 22 Oct 59　　　　FORCE: 22 Oct 59

REGISTERED: 7 Jun 60 USA (United States)
ARTICLES: 2 LANGUAGE: English.
HEADNOTE: PROGRAMS SPECIAL ECONOMIC
TECHNICAL ASSISTANCE
TOPIC: Tech Assistance
CONCEPTS: Previous treaty amendment. Import quotas. Currency deposits. Local currency. Assets. Commodities and services. General technical assistance. Economic assistance. Materials, equipment and services.
TREATY REF: 338UNTS233; 152UNTS61.
PARTIES:
USA (United States)
Yugoslavia

105162　Bilateral Exchange　360 UNTS 265
SIGNED: 28 Oct 59　FORCE: 28 Oct 59
REGISTERED: 7 Jun 60 USA (United States)
ARTICLES: 2 LANGUAGE: English.
HEADNOTE: INTRODUCTION MODERN WEAPONS
NATO DEFENSE FORCES
TOPIC: Milit Assistance
CONCEPTS: Defense and security. Atomic weapons.
INTL ORGS: North Atlantic Treaty Organization.
PROCEDURE: Future Procedures Contemplated.
PARTIES:
Turkey
USA (United States)

105163　Bilateral Agreement　360 UNTS 271
SIGNED: 16 Oct 59　FORCE: 16 Oct 59
REGISTERED: 7 Jun 60 USA (United States)
ARTICLES: 6 LANGUAGE: English. French.
HEADNOTE: AGRI COMMOD TITLE I
TOPIC: US Agri Commod Aid
CONCEPTS: General provisions. Annex or appendix reference. Exchange of information and documents. Reexport of goods, etc.. Exchange rates and regulations. Transportation costs. Local currency. Mutual consultation. Commodities schedule. Purchase authorization. Surplus commodities.
PARTIES:
USA (United States)
Vietnam, South
ANNEX
371 UNTS 396. USA (United States). Amendment 13 Feb 60. Force 13 Feb 60.
371 UNTS 396. Vietnam, South. Amendment 13 Feb 60. Force 13 Feb 60.

105164　Bilateral Agreement　360 UNTS 287
SIGNED: 13 Nov 59　FORCE: 13 Nov 59
REGISTERED: 7 Jun 60 USA (United States)
ARTICLES: 6 LANGUAGE: English.
HEADNOTE: AGRI COMMOD TITLE I
TOPIC: US Agri Commod Aid
CONCEPTS: General provisions. Annex or appendix reference. Exchange of information and documents. Reexport of goods, etc.. Exchange rates and regulations. Transportation costs. Local currency. Commodities schedule. Purchase authorization. Surplus commodities. Mutual consultation.
PARTIES:
India
USA (United States)
ANNEX
368 UNTS 371. India. Amendment 8 Jan 60. Force 8 Jan 60.
368 UNTS 371. USA (United States). Amendment 8 Jan 60. Force 8 Jan 60.
371 UNTS 402. India. Amendment 21 Mar 60. Force 21 Mar 60.
371 UNTS 402. USA (United States). Amendment 21 Mar 60.
400 UNTS 412. India. Amendment 9 Nov 60. Force 9 Nov 60.
400 UNTS 412. USA (United States). Amendment 3 Nov 60. Force 9 Nov 60.

105165　Bilateral Agreement　360 UNTS 311
SIGNED: 14 Nov 59　FORCE: 14 Nov 59
REGISTERED: 7 Jun 60 USA (United States)
ARTICLES: 6 LANGUAGE: English.
HEADNOTE: AGRI COMMOD TITLE I
TOPIC: US Agri Commod Aid
CONCEPTS: General provisions. Annex or appendix reference. Exchange of information and doc-

uments. Reexport of goods, etc.. Exchange rates and regulations. Transportation costs. Local currency. Commodities schedule. Purchase authorization. Surplus commodities.
PARTIES:
United Arab Rep
USA (United States)

105166　Bilateral Exchange　360 UNTS 327
SIGNED: 28 Jul 59　FORCE: 1 Aug 59
REGISTERED: 9 Jun 60 Pakistan
ARTICLES: 3 LANGUAGE: English.
HEADNOTE: VALIDITY CERTAIN TYPES VISAS
TOPIC: Visas
CONCEPTS: Time limit.
PARTIES:
Pakistan
USA (United States)
ANNEX
435 UNTS 376. Pakistan. Supplementation 29 Sep 61.
435 UNTS 376. USA (United States). Supplementation 16 Sep 61.

105167　Bilateral Convention　360 UNTS 335
SIGNED: 27 May 59　FORCE: 25 Apr 60
REGISTERED: 10 Jun 60 Czechoslovakia
ARTICLES: 23 LANGUAGE: Czechoslovakian. Bulgarian.
HEADNOTE: CONSULAR
TOPIC: Consul/Citizenship
CONCEPTS: General consular functions. Diplomatic privileges. Consular relations establishment. Inviolability. Privileges and immunities. Responsibility and liability.
PROCEDURE: Duration. Ratification. Renewal or Revival.
PARTIES:
Bulgaria
Czechoslovakia

105168　Bilateral Exchange　361 UNTS 3
SIGNED: 13 Nov 59　FORCE: 13 Nov 59
REGISTERED: 13 Jun 60 USA (United States)
ARTICLES: 2 LANGUAGE: English.
HEADNOTE: SALE EXCESS MILITARY PROPERTY
TOPIC: Milit Assistance
CONCEPTS: Detailed regulations. Reexport of goods, etc.. Currency. Tax exemptions. Customs exemptions. Surplus property. Surplus war property.
INTL ORGS: North Atlantic Treaty Organization.
TREATY REF: 262UNTS97.
PROCEDURE: Future Procedures Contemplated. Termination.
PARTIES:
Turkey
USA (United States)

105169　Bilateral Exchange　361 UNTS 11
SIGNED: 18 Aug 59　FORCE: 18 Aug 59
REGISTERED: 13 Jun 60 USA (United States)
ARTICLES: 2 LANGUAGE: English. Italian.
HEADNOTE: VESSEL LOAN
TOPIC: Milit Assistance
CONCEPTS: Time limit. Annex or appendix reference. Responsibility and liability. Title and deeds. Compensation. Indemnities and reimbursements. Delivery schedules. Lease of military property. Naval vessels. Return of equipment and recapture. Restrictions on transfer.
TREATY REF: 80UNTS145.
PARTIES:
Italy
USA (United States)
ANNEX
545 UNTS 349. USA (United States). Prolongation 31 Mar 65. Force 17 Apr 65.
545 UNTS 349. Italy. Prolongation 17 Apr 65. Force 17 Apr 65.

105170　Bilateral Exchange　361 UNTS 21
SIGNED: 30 Oct 59　FORCE: 30 Oct 59
REGISTERED: 13 Jun 60 USA (United States)
ARTICLES: 2 LANGUAGE: English.
HEADNOTE: AERIAL MAPPING COASTAL AREAS
TOPIC: Tech Assistance
CONCEPTS: Treaty implementation. Research results. Research and development.

TREATY REF: 324UNTS111.
PARTIES:
New Zealand
USA (United States)

105171　Bilateral Exchange　361 UNTS 27
SIGNED: 12 Nov 59　FORCE: 12 Nov 59
REGISTERED: 13 Jun 60 USA (United States)
ARTICLES: 2 LANGUAGE: English. Japanese.
HEADNOTE: EMERGENCY FLOOD RELIEF ASSISTANCE
TOPIC: Direct Aid
CONCEPTS: Inspection and observation. Public information. Jurisdiction. Use of facilities. Expense sharing formulae. Transportation costs. Domestic obligation. Relief supplies.
PARTIES:
Japan
USA (United States)

105172　Bilateral Agreement　361 UNTS 35
SIGNED: 21 Nov 59　FORCE: 1 Jan 60
REGISTERED: 13 Jun 60 USA (United States)
ARTICLES: 16 LANGUAGE: English. Russian.
HEADNOTE: EXCHANGES SCIENTIFIC EDUCATIONAL CULTURAL FIELDS
TOPIC: Culture
CONCEPTS: Definition of terms. Detailed regulations. Annex or appendix reference. Tourism. Non-diplomatic delegations. Conformity with municipal law. Operating agencies. Specialists exchange. Public health. WHO used as agency. Exchange. Teacher and student exchange. Vocational training. General cultural cooperation. Artists. Athletes. Research cooperation. Scientific exchange. Accounting procedures. Agriculture. Peaceful use. General transportation. Air transport. Publications exchange. Mass media exchange.
INTL ORGS: World Health Organization.
TREATY REF: 301UNTS405.
PROCEDURE: Duration. Future Procedures Contemplated.
PARTIES:
USA (United States)
USSR (Soviet Union)

105173　Bilateral Agreement　361 UNTS 93
SIGNED: 9 Dec 59　FORCE: 1 Jan 60
REGISTERED: 14 Jun 60 Norway
ARTICLES: 10 LANGUAGE: Norwegian. Russian.
HEADNOTE: CLAIMS DAMAGE FISHING GEAR
TOPIC: Specif Claim/Waive
CONCEPTS: Exchange of information and documents. Arbitration. Special tribunals. Claims and settlements. Specific claims or waivers.
INTL ORGS: Claims Commission.
PROCEDURE: Denunciation.
PARTIES:
Norway
USSR (Soviet Union)

105174　Bilateral Exchange　361 UNTS 107
SIGNED: 30 Nov 59　FORCE: 30 Nov 59
REGISTERED: 14 Jun 60 USA (United States)
ARTICLES: 2 LANGUAGE: English.
HEADNOTE: SPECIAL PROJECT ASSISTANCE
TOPIC: Tech Assistance
CONCEPTS: Change of circumstances. Annex type material. Use of facilities. Indemnities and reimbursements. Transportation costs. Tax exemptions. Customs exemptions. General technical assistance. Materials, equipment and services. Defense and security. Military assistance. Military installations and equipment.
PARTIES:
Turkey
USA (United States)

105175　Bilateral Exchange　361 UNTS 115
SIGNED: 2 Dec 59　FORCE: 2 Dec 59
REGISTERED: 14 Jun 60 USA (United States)
ARTICLES: 2 LANGUAGE: English.
HEADNOTE: NUCLEAR RESEARCH TRAINING
EQUIPMENT
TOPIC: Atomic Energy
CONCEPTS: Responsibility and liability. Research and scientific projects. Research results. Research and development. Indemnities and reim-

457

bursements. Payment schedules. Materials, equipment and services. Atomic energy assistance. Nuclear materials. Non-nuclear materials. Peaceful use.
PARTIES:
Taiwan
USA (United States)

105176 Bilateral Exchange **361 UNTS 123**
SIGNED: 21 May 59 FORCE: 21 May 59
REGISTERED: 14 Jun 60 USA (United States)
ARTICLES: 2 LANGUAGE: English. Arabic.
HEADNOTE: ECONOMIC ASSISTANCE
TOPIC: Tech Assistance
CONCEPTS: Previous treaty amendment. Financial programs. Economic assistance.
TREATY REF: 238UNTS217; 270UNTS43.
PROCEDURE: Future Procedures Contemplated.
PARTIES:
Libya
USA (United States)

105177 Bilateral Exchange **361 UNTS 135**
SIGNED: 1 Apr 60 FORCE: 10 Apr 60
REGISTERED: 15 Jun 60 Belgium
ARTICLES: 2 LANGUAGE: English. French.
HEADNOTE: ABOLITION PASSPORTS BELGIAN NATIONALS
TOPIC: Visas
CONCEPTS: Territorial application. Time limit. Previous treaty replacement. Visa abolition. Denial of admission. Resident permits. Conformity with municipal law.
PROCEDURE: Termination.
PARTIES:
Belgium
UK Great Britain
ANNEX
560 UNTS 280. UK Great Britain. Southern Rhodesia.

105178 Bilateral Convention **361 UNTS 155**
SIGNED: 20 Jan 59 FORCE: 12 Jun 60
REGISTERED: 17 Jun 60 Belgium
ARTICLES: 19 LANGUAGE: French.
HEADNOTE: DOUBLE TAXATION DEATH DUTIES
TOPIC: Taxation
CONCEPTS: Definition of terms. Territorial application. Privileges and immunities. Exchange of official publications. Fees and exemptions. Claims and settlements. Debts. Taxation. Death duties. Equitable taxes. Air transport. Merchant vessels.
TREATY REF: CONVENTION AT LILLE 12AUG1843.
PROCEDURE: Duration. Ratification. Termination.
PARTIES:
Belgium
France

105179 Bilateral Agreement **361 UNTS 171**
SIGNED: 30 Apr 60 FORCE: 30 Apr 60
REGISTERED: 17 Jun 60 United Nations
ARTICLES: 10 LANGUAGE: French.
HEADNOTE: ASSISTANCE
TOPIC: Tech Assistance
CONCEPTS: Conditions. Detailed regulations. Treaty implementation. Annex or appendix reference. Visas. Privileges and immunities. General cooperation. Exchange of information and documents. Inspection and observation. Operating agencies. Licenses and permits. Personnel. General property. Public information. Responsibility and liability. Title and deeds. Use of facilities. Arbitration. Procedure. Negotiation. Import quotas. Reexport of goods, etc.. Accounting procedures. Exchange rates and regulations. Fees and exemptions. Financial programs. Tax exemptions. Customs exemptions. Domestic obligation. General technical assistance. Materials, equipment and services. IGO status. Conformity with IGO decisions.
INTL ORGS: International Atomic Energy Agency. International Court of Justice. United Nations.
TREATY REF: 1UNTS15; 33UNTS261.
PROCEDURE: Amendment. Termination.
PARTIES:
Laos
UN Special Fund

105180 Bilateral Agreement **362 UNTS 3**
SIGNED: 23 Oct 59 FORCE: 23 Oct 59
REGISTERED: 17 Jun 60 Pakistan
ARTICLES: 10 LANGUAGE: English.
HEADNOTE: BORDER DISPUTES
TOPIC: Territory Boundary
CONCEPTS: Annex or appendix reference. Existing tribunals. Markers and definitions.
INTL ORGS: Special Commission.
TREATY REF: NEHRU-NOON AGREEMENT.
PARTIES:
India
Pakistan

105181 Multilateral Convention **362 UNTS 31**
SIGNED: 25 Jun 58 FORCE: 15 Jun 60
REGISTERED: 17 Jun 60 ILO (Labor Org)
ARTICLES: 14 LANGUAGE: English. French.
HEADNOTE: DISCRIMINATION EMPLOYMENT
TOPIC: ILO Labor
CONCEPTS: Definition of terms. General provisions. Human rights. Exchange of information and documents. Personnel. Establishment of commission. Vocational training. ILO conventions. Anti-discrimination. Right to organize.
INTL ORGS: International Labour Organization. United Nations.
TREATY REF: 15UNTS40.
PROCEDURE: Amendment. Denunciation. Duration. Ratification. Registration. Renewal or Revival.
PARTIES:
Multilateral
ANNEX
366 UNTS 422. India. Ratification 3 Jun 60. Force 3 Jun 61.
366 UNTS 422. Denmark. Ratification 22 Jun 60. Force 22 Jun 61.
366 UNTS 422. Honduras. Ratification 20 Jun 60. Force 20 Jun 61.
373 UNTS 380. Bulgaria. Ratification 22 Jul 60. Force 22 Jul 61.
380 UNTS 475. Guatemala. Ratification 11 Oct 60. Force 11 Oct 61.
381 UNTS 414. Guinea. Ratification 1 Sep 60. Force 1 Sep 61.
384 UNTS 385. Philippines. Ratification 17 Nov 60. Force 17 Nov 61.
388 UNTS 395. Pakistan. Ratification 24 Jan 61. Force 24 Jan 62.
390 UNTS 371. Yugoslavia. Ratification 2 Feb 61. Force 2 Feb 62.
396 UNTS 350. Ghana. Ratification 4 Apr 61. Force 4 Apr 62.
399 UNTS 294. USSR (Soviet Union). Ratification 4 May 61. Force 4 May 62.
399 UNTS 294. Dahomey. Ratification 22 May 61. Force 22 May 62.
399 UNTS 294. Poland. Ratification 30 May 61. Force 30 May 62.
399 UNTS 294. Ivory Coast. Ratification 5 May 61. Force 5 May 62.
399 UNTS 294. Gabon. Ratification 29 May 61. Force 29 May 62.
401 UNTS 332. Hungary. Ratification 20 Jun 61. Force 20 Jun 62.
401 UNTS 332. Germany, West. Ratification 15 Jun 61. Force 15 Jun 62.
401 UNTS 332. Libya. Ratification 13 Jun 61. Force 13 Jun 62.
406 UNTS 337. Byelorussia. Ratification 4 Aug 61. Force 4 Aug 62.
406 UNTS 337. Madagascar. Ratification 11 Aug 61. Force 11 Aug 62.
406 UNTS 337. Ukrainian SSR. Ratification 4 Aug 61. Force 4 Aug 62.
406 UNTS 337. Switzerland. Ratification 13 Jun 61. Force 13 Jun 62.
410 UNTS 353. Mexico. Ratification 11 Sep 61. Force 11 Sep 62.
413 UNTS 382. Syria. Ratification 30 Oct 61.
420 UNTS 352. Somalia. Ratification 8 Dec 61. Force 8 Dec 62.
423 UNTS 328. Taiwan. Ratification 13 Feb 62. Force 13 Feb 63.
425 UNTS 368. Niger. Ratification 23 Mar 62. Force 23 Mar 63.
425 UNTS 368. Costa Rica. Ratification 1 Mar 62. Force 1 Mar 63.
429 UNTS 301. Upper Volta. Ratification 16 Apr 62. Force 16 Apr 63.
434 UNTS 346. Sweden. Ratification 20 Jun 62. Force 20 Jun 63.

435 UNTS 380. Ecuador. Ratification 10 Jul 62. Force 10 Jul 63.
457 UNTS 364. Morocco. Ratification 27 Mar 63. Force 27 Mar 64.
473 UNTS 392. Jordan. Ratification 4 Jul 63. Force 4 Jul 64.
473 UNTS 392. Iceland. Ratification 29 Jul 63. Force 29 Jul 64.
475 UNTS 382. Italy. Ratification 12 Aug 63. Force 12 Aug 64.
483 UNTS 418. Mauritania. Ratification 8 Nov 63. Force 8 Nov 64.
488 UNTS 371. Czechoslovakia. Ratification 21 Jan 64. Force 21 Jan 65.
488 UNTS 371. Vietnam, South. Ratification 6 Jan 64. Force 6 Jan 65.
495 UNTS 306. Mali. Ratification 2 Mar 65.
504 UNTS 366. Central Afri Rep. Ratification 9 Jun 64. Force 9 Jun 65.
504 UNTS 366. Iran. Ratification 30 Jun 64. Force 30 Jun 65.
504 UNTS 366. Dominican Republic. Ratification 13 Jul 65. Force 13 Jul 65.
521 UNTS 427. Canada. Ratification 26 Nov 64. Force 26 Nov 65.
530 UNTS 425. Malawi. Ratification 22 Mar 65. Force 22 Mar 66.
545 UNTS 382. Cuba. Ratification 26 Aug 65. Force 26 Aug 66.
549 UNTS 367. Brazil. Ratification 26 Nov 65. Force 26 Nov 66.
560 UNTS 328. Chad. Ratification 29 Mar 66. Force 29 Mar 67.
567 UNTS 355. Ethiopia. Ratification 11 Jun 66. Force 11 Jun 67.
603 UNTS 355. Turkey. Ratification 19 Jul 67. Force 19 Jul 68.
603 UNTS 355. Paraguay. Ratification 10 Jul 67. Force 10 Jul 68.
609 UNTS 340. Nicaragua. Ratification 31 Oct 67. Force 31 Oct 68.
613 UNTS 425. Senegal. Ratification 13 Nov 67. Force 13 Nov 68.
613 UNTS 425. Spain. Ratification 6 Nov 67. Force 6 Nov 68.
640 UNTS 388. Argentina. Ratification 18 Jun 68. Force 18 Jun 69.
642 UNTS 396. Malta. Ratification 1 Jul 68. Force 1 Jul 69.

105182 Bilateral Agreement **362 UNTS 43**
SIGNED: 17 Mar 60 FORCE: 25 May 60
REGISTERED: 22 Jun 60 IBRD (World Bank)
ARTICLES: 5 LANGUAGE: English.
HEADNOTE: GUARANTEE EXPRESSWAY
TOPIC: IBRD Project
CONCEPTS: Definition of terms. Annex or appendix reference. Exchange of information and documents. Inspection and observation. Bonds. Fees and exemptions. Tax exemptions. Domestic obligation. Terms of loan. Loan regulations. Loan guarantee. Guarantor non-interference. Roads and highways.
PARTIES:
Japan
IBRD (World Bank)

105183 Bilateral Agreement **362 UNTS 75**
SIGNED: 20 Feb 59 FORCE: 18 Sep 59
REGISTERED: 23 Jun 60 IBRD (World Bank)
ARTICLES: 5 LANGUAGE: English.
HEADNOTE: GUARANTEE HYDROELECTRIC PROJECT
TOPIC: IBRD Project
CONCEPTS: Definition of terms. Annex or appendix reference. Exchange of information and documents. Inspection and observation. Bonds. Fees and exemptions. Tax exemptions. Domestic obligation. Terms of loan. Loan regulations. Loan guarantee. Guarantor non-interference. Hydroelectric power.
PARTIES:
El Salvador
IBRD (World Bank)

105184 Bilateral Convention **362 UNTS 101**
SIGNED: 22 Jul 54 FORCE: 29 Apr 55
REGISTERED: 23 Jun 60 Romania
ARTICLES: 13 LANGUAGE: Romanian. Bulgarian.
HEADNOTE: AGRICULTURAL PLANT PROTECTION
TOPIC: Sanitation

CONCEPTS: Definition of terms. Border traffic and migration. General cooperation. Exchange of information and documents. Inspection and observation. Domestic legislation. Specialists exchange. Quarantine. Disease control. Insect control. Scientific exchange. Reexport of goods, etc.. Trade procedures. Indemnities and reimbursements. Agriculture. Materials, equipment and services. Mass media exchange. Conferences.
PARTIES:
Bulgaria
Romania

105185 Bilateral Convention **362 UNTS 123**
SIGNED: 31 Jul 52   FORCE: 25 Feb 53
REGISTERED: 23 Jun 60 Romania
ARTICLES: 10 LANGUAGE: Romanian. Czechoslovakian.
HEADNOTE: AGRICULTURAL PLANT PROTECTION
TOPIC: Sanitation
CONCEPTS: Definition of terms. General cooperation. Exchange of information and documents. Domestic legislation. Quarantine. Disease control. Insect control. Scientific exchange. Establishment of trade relations. Reexport of goods, etc.. Trade procedures. Agriculture. Materials, equipment and services. Conferences.
PROCEDURE: Duration. Ratification. Renewal or Revival. Termination.
PARTIES:
Czechoslovakia
Romania

105186 Bilateral Instrument **362 UNTS 141**
SIGNED: 5 Dec 55   FORCE: 5 Jan 56
REGISTERED: 23 Jun 60 Romania
ARTICLES: 19 LANGUAGE: Romanian. Korean.
HEADNOTE: TELEGRAPH TELEPHONE SERVICES
TOPIC: Telecommunications
CONCEPTS: Detailed regulations. Accounting procedures. Currency. Non-interest rates and fees. Radio-telephone-telegraphic communications.
TREATY REF: INTERNATIONAL TELECOMMUNICATION CONVENTION.
PROCEDURE: Denunciation. Duration. Renewal or Revival.
PARTIES:
Korea, North
Romania

105187 Bilateral Instrument **362 UNTS 163**
SIGNED: 5 Dec 55   FORCE: 5 Jan 56
REGISTERED: 23 Jun 60 Romania
ARTICLES: 27 LANGUAGE: Romanian. Korean.
HEADNOTE: EXCHANGE POSTAL CORRESPONDENCE POSTAL PARCELS
TOPIC: Postal Service
CONCEPTS: Customs exemptions. Postal services. Regulations. Money orders and postal checks. Parcel post. Rates and charges.
TREATY REF: 169UNTS3; 170UNTS3.
PROCEDURE: Denunciation. Duration. Renewal or Revival.
PARTIES:
Korea, North
Romania

105188 Bilateral Convention **362 UNTS 189**
SIGNED: 8 Dec 56   FORCE: 5 Dec 56
REGISTERED: 23 Jun 60 Romania
ARTICLES: 7 LANGUAGE: Romanian. German.
HEADNOTE: VETERINARY MEDICINE COOPERATION
TOPIC: Sanitation
CONCEPTS: Standardization. General cooperation. Exchange of information and documents. Veterinary. Teacher and student exchange. Vocational training. Scientific exchange. Trade procedures. Indemnities and reimbursements. Materials, equipment and services. Publications exchange. Conferences.
PROCEDURE: Denunciation. Duration. Future Procedures Contemplated. Ratification. Renewal or Revival.
PARTIES:
Germany, East
Romania

105189 Bilateral Agreement **362 UNTS 203**
SIGNED: 1 Feb 56   FORCE: 3 Aug 56
REGISTERED: 23 Jun 60 Romania
ARTICLES: 16 LANGUAGE: Romanian. Serbo-Croat.
HEADNOTE: CONCERNING AIR SERVICES
TOPIC: Air Transport
CONCEPTS: Definition of terms. Exceptions and exemptions. Annex or appendix reference. Previous treaty replacement. Conformity with municipal law. General cooperation. Exchange of information and documents. Informational records. Licenses and permits. Recognition of legal documents. Use of facilities. Procedure. Negotiation. Humanitarian matters. Fees and exemptions. Non-interest rates and fees. Most favored nation clause. Customs exemptions. Registration certificate. Routes and logistics. Navigational conditions. Permit designation. Airport facilities. Airworthiness certificates. Operating authorizations and regulations.
PROCEDURE: Amendment. Ratification. Termination.
PARTIES:
Romania
Yugoslavia

105190 Bilateral Agreement **362 UNTS 233**
SIGNED: 3 Feb 56   FORCE: 10 May 56
REGISTERED: 23 Jun 60 Romania
ARTICLES: 16 LANGUAGE: Romanian. Hungarian.
HEADNOTE: CONCERNING AIR TRANSPORT
TOPIC: Air Transport
CONCEPTS: Representation. Previous treaty replacement. Conformity with municipal law. General cooperation. Exchange of information and documents. Informational records. Licenses and permits. Recognition of legal documents. Use of facilities. Procedure. Border control. Humanitarian matters. Indemnities and reimbursements. Tax exemptions. Customs exemptions. Competency certificate. Registration certificate. Routes and logistics. Permit designation. Air transport. Airport facilities. Airworthiness certificates. Operating authorizations and regulations.
TREATY REF: AIR TRANSPORT,26MAR47.
PROCEDURE: Duration. Ratification. Renewal or Revival. Termination.
PARTIES:
Hungary
Romania

105191 Bilateral Agreement **362 UNTS 259**
SIGNED: 26 May 58   FORCE: 1 Jun 58
REGISTERED: 28 Jun 60 Italy
ARTICLES: 4 LANGUAGE: French.
HEADNOTE: PAYMENTS
TOPIC: Finance
CONCEPTS: Annex or appendix reference. Previous treaty replacement. Licenses and permits. Currency. Payment schedules. Local currency.
TREATY REF: 17DEC54 PAYMENTS AGREEMENT.
PROCEDURE: Denunciation.
PARTIES:
Albania
Italy

105192 Bilateral Exchange **362 UNTS 273**
SIGNED: 8 Jan 58   FORCE: 8 Jan 58
REGISTERED: 28 Jun 60 Italy
ARTICLES: 2 LANGUAGE: Italian. Portuguese.
HEADNOTE: AGREEMENT WAR DAMAGE
TOPIC: Reparations
CONCEPTS: Accounting procedures. Lump sum settlements. Loss and/or damage. Post-war claims settlement.
PARTIES:
Brazil
Italy

105193 Bilateral Agreement **362 UNTS 279**
SIGNED: 25 Feb 58   FORCE: 1 Apr 58
REGISTERED: 28 Jun 60 Italy
ARTICLES: 4 LANGUAGE: French.
HEADNOTE: PAYMENTS
TOPIC: Finance
CONCEPTS: Annex or appendix reference. Licenses and permits. Accounting procedures. Currency. Payment schedules. Local currency.
PROCEDURE: Denunciation.

PARTIES:
Bulgaria
Italy

105194 Bilateral Agreement **362 UNTS 291**
SIGNED: 25 Feb 58   FORCE: 1 Mar 58
REGISTERED: 28 Jun 60 Italy
ARTICLES: 7 LANGUAGE: French.
HEADNOTE: TRADE
TOPIC: General Trade
CONCEPTS: Annex or appendix reference. Previous treaty replacement. Establishment of commission. Payment schedules. Quotas.
INTL ORGS: Special Commission.
TREATY REF: 362UNTS277.
PROCEDURE: Duration. Renewal or Revival. Termination.
PARTIES:
Bulgaria
Italy

105195 Bilateral Convention **362 UNTS 309**
SIGNED: 4 Jun 56   FORCE: 28 Oct 59
REGISTERED: 28 Jun 60 Italy
ARTICLES: 11 LANGUAGE: Italian. Spanish.
HEADNOTE: MILITARY SERVICE
TOPIC: Milit Servic/Citiz
CONCEPTS: Emergencies. Procedure. Dual nationality. Certificates of service. Service in foreign army.
PARTIES:
Chile
Italy

105196 Bilateral Convention **363 UNTS 3**
SIGNED: 30 Oct 58   FORCE: 1 Mar 60
REGISTERED: 28 Jun 60 Italy
ARTICLES: 22 LANGUAGE: French.
HEADNOTE: ESTABLISHMENT JOINT NATIONAL CONTROL OFFICE ITALO-FRENCH FRONTIER
TOPIC: Visas
CONCEPTS: Border traffic and migration. Conformity with municipal law. General cooperation. Inspection and observation. Establishment of commission. Tax exemptions. Routes and logistics. Headquarters and facilities. Markers and definitions.
INTL ORGS: Special Commission.
PROCEDURE: Termination.
PARTIES:
France
Italy

105197 Bilateral Agreement **363 UNTS 23**
SIGNED: 24 Jun 58   FORCE: 1 Jul 58
REGISTERED: 28 Jun 60 Italy
ARTICLES: 10 LANGUAGE: French.
HEADNOTE: COMMERCE TRADE
TOPIC: General Trade
CONCEPTS: Definition of terms. Annex or appendix reference. General cooperation. Exchange of information and documents. Establishment of commission. Trade procedures. Payment schedules. Quotas.
PROCEDURE: Denunciation. Duration. Renewal or Revival.
PARTIES:
Italy
Morocco

105198 Bilateral Convention **363 UNTS 45**
SIGNED: 6 Dec 57   FORCE: 1 Mar 60
REGISTERED: 28 Jun 60 Italy
ARTICLES: 19 LANGUAGE: French.
HEADNOTE: ACCIDENT DISEASE INSURANCE
TOPIC: Non-ILO Labor
CONCEPTS: Notarial acts and services. Conformity with municipal law. General cooperation. Exchange of information and documents. Domestic legislation. Dispute settlement. Old age and invalidity insurance. Wages and salaries. Non-ILO labor relations. Sickness and invalidity insurance. Monetary and gold transfers. Payment schedules. Claims and settlements. National treatment.
INTL ORGS: Special Commission.
PROCEDURE: Duration. Ratification. Renewal or Revival. Termination.

PARTIES:
Italy
Monaco

105199   Bilateral Agreement   **363 UNTS 59**
SIGNED: 6 Dec 57   FORCE: 1 Mar 60
REGISTERED: 28 Jun 60 Italy
ARTICLES: 8 LANGUAGE: French.
HEADNOTE: SOCIAL SECURITY
TOPIC: Non-ILO Labor
CONCEPTS: Definition of terms. Exchange of information and documents. Old age and invalidity insurance. Wages and salaries. Non-ILO labor relations. Family allowances. Sickness and invalidity insurance. Social security.
PROCEDURE: Duration. Future Procedures Contemplated. Ratification. Renewal or Revival. Termination.
PARTIES:
Italy
Monaco

105200   Bilateral Agreement   **363 UNTS 69**
SIGNED: 19 Sep 57   FORCE: 29 Mar 60
REGISTERED: 28 Jun 60 Italy
ARTICLES: 11 LANGUAGE: French.
HEADNOTE: MOTOR TRAFFIC ROAD TRANSPORT
TOPIC: Land Transport
CONCEPTS: General provisions. Previous treaty replacement. Non-prejudice to third party. Conformity with municipal law. Licenses and permits. Recognition of legal documents. Responsibility and liability. Fees and exemptions. Non-interest rates and fees. National treatment. General. Passenger transport. Transport of goods. Driving permits. Road rules.
PROCEDURE: Ratification. Termination.
PARTIES:
Italy
Switzerland

105201   Bilateral Convention   **363 UNTS 81**
SIGNED: 23 May 58   FORCE: 13 Jun 59
REGISTERED: 28 Jun 60 Italy
ARTICLES: 11 LANGUAGE: French.
HEADNOTE: CONSTRUCTION OPERATION ROAD TUNNEL GRAND-SAINT-BERNARD
TOPIC: Land Transport
CONCEPTS: Detailed regulations. Time limit. Treaty implementation. Conformity with municipal law. General cooperation. Establishment of commission. Procedure. Fees and exemptions. Customs duties. Routes and logistics. Roads and highways. Boundaries of territory. Markers and definitions.
INTL ORGS: Special Commission.
TREATY REF: 33LTS91.
PROCEDURE: Ratification.
PARTIES:
Italy
Switzerland

105202   Bilateral Agreement   **363 UNTS 91**
SIGNED: 29 Apr 59   FORCE: 29 Apr 59
REGISTERED: 28 Jun 60 Italy
ARTICLES: 7 LANGUAGE: French.
HEADNOTE: ECONOMIC TECHNICAL COOPERATION
TOPIC: Tech Assistance
CONCEPTS: Exceptions and exemptions. Guarantees and safeguards. Treaty implementation. Conformity with municipal law. Exchange of information and documents. Establishment of commission. Accounting procedures. Financial programs. Payment schedules. Assets. Most favored nation clause. Commodities and services. General technical assistance. Economic assistance.
INTL ORGS: Special Commission.
TREATY REF: 30IUNTS147.
PARTIES:
Italy
United Arab Rep

105203   Bilateral Agreement   **363 UNTS 99**
SIGNED: 20 May 57   FORCE: 28 Jan 58
REGISTERED: 29 Jun 60 Yugoslavia
ARTICLES: 12 LANGUAGE: Serbo-Croat. Albanian.
HEADNOTE: AGRICULTURAL PLANT PROTECTION

TOPIC: Sanitation
CONCEPTS: Definition of terms. Border traffic and migration. General cooperation. Exchange of information and documents. Inspection and observation. Domestic legislation. Quarantine. Disease control. Insect control. Research results. Scientific exchange. Reexport of goods, etc.. Trade procedures. General technical assistance. Agriculture. Canal improvement. Conferences.
PROCEDURE: Amendment. Denunciation. Duration. Ratification. Renewal or Revival. Termination.
PARTIES:
Albania
Yugoslavia

105204   Bilateral Protocol   **363 UNTS 123**
SIGNED: 23 Nov 56   FORCE: 23 Nov 56
REGISTERED: 29 Jun 60 Yugoslavia
ARTICLES: 7 LANGUAGE: Serbo-Croat. Albanian.
HEADNOTE: FLIGHT ACROSS COMMON FRONTIER
TOPIC: Air Transport
CONCEPTS: Procedure. Routes and logistics.
PROCEDURE: Amendment. Denunciation. Future Procedures Contemplated.
PARTIES:
Albania
Yugoslavia

105205   Bilateral Agreement   **363 UNTS 133**
SIGNED: 18 Jun 59   FORCE: 31 Mar 60
REGISTERED: 29 Jun 60 Yugoslavia
ARTICLES: 9 LANGUAGE: French.
HEADNOTE: HYDROECONOMIC QUESTIONS
TOPIC: Specific Resources
CONCEPTS: Annex or appendix reference. Frontier permits. Establishment of commission. Arbitration. Special tribunals. Temporary importation. Hydro-electric power. Facilities and property. Frontier waterways.
INTL ORGS: Arbitration Commission. Special Commission.
PROCEDURE: Denunciation. Duration. Ratification. Renewal or Revival.
PARTIES:
Greece
Yugoslavia

105206   Bilateral Agreement   **363 UNTS 149**
SIGNED: 11 Nov 53   FORCE: 11 Nov 53
REGISTERED: 29 Jun 60 Yugoslavia
ARTICLES: 16 LANGUAGE: French.
HEADNOTE: CONCERNING AIR SERVICES
TOPIC: Air Transport
CONCEPTS: Definition of terms. Detailed regulations. Annex or appendix reference. Conformity with municipal law. General cooperation. Informational records. Licenses and permits. Recognition of legal documents. Use of facilities. Arbitration. Procedure. Expense sharing formulae. Fees and exemptions. Non-interest rates and fees. Most favored nation clause. National treatment. Customs exemptions. Competency certificate. Registration certificate. Navigational conditions. Permit designation. Airport facilities. Airworthiness certificates. Conditions of airlines operating permission. Operating authorizations and regulations. Licenses and certificates of nationality.
INTL ORGS: International Civil Aviation Organization.
PROCEDURE: Amendment. Ratification. Termination.
PARTIES:
Austria
Yugoslavia

105207   Bilateral Convention   **363 UNTS 165**
SIGNED: 16 Jan 59   FORCE: 28 Apr 60
REGISTERED: 30 Jun 60 Czechoslovakia
ARTICLES: 24 LANGUAGE: Czechoslovakian. Albanian.
HEADNOTE: CONSULAR
TOPIC: Consul/Citizenship
CONCEPTS: General consular functions. Diplomatic privileges. Consular relations establishment. Inviolability. Privileges and immunities. Responsibility and liability.

PROCEDURE: Duration. Ratification. Renewal or Revival. Termination.
PARTIES:
Albania
Czechoslovakia

105208   Bilateral Treaty   **363 UNTS 195**
SIGNED: 16 Jan 59   FORCE: 28 May 60
REGISTERED: 30 Jun 60 Czechoslovakia
ARTICLES: 75 LANGUAGE: Czechoslovakian. Albanian.
HEADNOTE: LEGAL ASSISTANCE CIVIL FAMILY CRIMINAL MATTERS
TOPIC: Admin Cooperation
CONCEPTS: General provisions. Privileges and immunities. Consular functions in property. Extradition, deportation and repatriation. Extradition requests. Extraditable offenses. Concurrent requests. Limits of prosecution. Provisional detainment. Extradition postponement. Witnesses and experts. Material evidence. Conformity with municipal law. General cooperation. Family law. Exchange of information and documents. Juridical personality. Legal protection and assistance. Recognition and enforcement of legal decisions. Succession. Recognition of legal documents. Indemnities and reimbursements. Assets transfer. Conveyance in transit.
PROCEDURE: Duration. Ratification. Termination.
PARTIES:
Albania
Czechoslovakia

105209   Bilateral Agreement   **363 UNTS 287**
SIGNED: 18 Sep 59   FORCE: 5 May 60
REGISTERED: 30 Jun 60 Czechoslovakia
ARTICLES: 7 LANGUAGE: Czechoslovakian. German.
HEADNOTE: CUSTOMS SEALING REGULATIONS SHIPPING
TOPIC: Customs
CONCEPTS: Customs declarations. Water transport.
PROCEDURE: Accession. Ratification. Termination.
PARTIES:
Czechoslovakia
Germany, East

105210   Bilateral Convention   **363 UNTS 333**
SIGNED: 4 Jul 59   FORCE: 12 Apr 60
REGISTERED: 30 Jun 60 Czechoslovakia
ARTICLES: 16 LANGUAGE: Czechoslovakian. Polish.
HEADNOTE: MINOR FRONTIER TRAFFIC
TOPIC: Visas
CONCEPTS: Territorial application. Previous treaty replacement. Border traffic and migration. Frontier permits. General cooperation. Exchange of information and documents. Customs exemptions. Fish, wildlife, and natural resources. Markers and definitions. Frontier peoples and personnel.
TREATY REF: 47LTS397.
PROCEDURE: Denunciation. Ratification.
PARTIES:
Czechoslovakia
Poland

105211   Multilateral Convention   **364 UNTS 3**
SIGNED: 3 Oct 57   FORCE: 1 Apr 59
REGISTERED: 7 Jul 60 Canada
ARTICLES: 84 LANGUAGE: French.
HEADNOTE: UNIVERSAL POSTAL CONVENTION
TOPIC: Postal Service
CONCEPTS: Regulations. Territorial application. Establishment. Internal structure. Subsidiary organ. Assistance to United Nations. Treaty implementation. General provisions. Rates and charges. International organizations. Dispute settlement. Arbitration. Accounting procedures. Postal services. Treaty violation. Customs duties. Customs declarations. Customs exemptions. Temporary importation. Insured letters and boxes. Conveyance in transit. Detailed regulations. Liaison with other IGO's.
INTL ORGS: United Nations. Universal Postal Union.
PROCEDURE: Duration.

PARTIES:
Afghanistan SIGNED: 3 Oct 57 FORCE: 1 Apr 59
Albania SIGNED: 3 Oct 57 RATIFIED: 14 Sep 59 FORCE: 1 Apr 59
Algeria SIGNED: 3 Oct 57 FORCE: 1 Apr 59
Argentina SIGNED: 3 Oct 57 RATIFIED: 15 Apr 59 FORCE: 1 Apr 59
Australia All Territories RATIFIED: 29 Apr 59 FORCE: 29 Apr 59
Australia SIGNED: 3 Oct 57 RATIFIED: 29 Apr 59 FORCE: 1 Apr 59
Austria SIGNED: 3 Oct 57 RATIFIED: 4 May 59 FORCE: 1 Apr 59
Belgium SIGNED: 3 Oct 57 RATIFIED: 5 Mar 59 FORCE: 1 Apr 59
Belgian Colonies SIGNED: 3 Oct 57 RATIFIED: 5 Mar 59 FORCE: 1 Apr 59
Bolivia SIGNED: 3 Oct 57 FORCE: 1 Apr 59
Brazil SIGNED: 3 Oct 57 FORCE: 1 Apr 59
Bulgaria SIGNED: 3 Oct 57 FORCE: 1 Apr 59
Burma SIGNED: 3 Oct 57 FORCE: 1 Apr 59
Byelorussia SIGNED: 3 Oct 57 RATIFIED: 23 Apr 59 FORCE: 1 Apr 59
Cambodia SIGNED: 3 Oct 57 RATIFIED: 12 Jan 60 FORCE: 1 Apr 59
Canada SIGNED: 3 Oct 57 RATIFIED: 11 Aug 58 FORCE: 1 Apr 59
Ceylon (Sri Lanka) SIGNED: 3 Oct 57 RATIFIED: 16 Nov 59 FORCE: 1 Apr 59
Chile SIGNED: 3 Oct 57 FORCE: 1 Apr 59
China SIGNED: 3 Oct 57 RATIFIED: 6 Oct 59 FORCE: 1 Apr 59
Colombia SIGNED: 3 Oct 57 FORCE: 1 Apr 59
Costa Rica SIGNED: 3 Oct 57 FORCE: 1 Apr 59
Cuba SIGNED: 3 Oct 57 FORCE: 1 Apr 59
Czechoslovakia SIGNED: 3 Oct 57 RATIFIED: 13 Aug 59 FORCE: 1 Apr 59
Czechoslovakia SIGNED: 3 Oct 57 RATIFIED: 13 Aug 59 FORCE: 1 Apr 59
Denmark SIGNED: 3 Oct 57 RATIFIED: 13 Aug 58 FORCE: 1 Apr 59
Dominican Republic SIGNED: 3 Oct 57 FORCE: 1 Apr 59
Ecuador SIGNED: 3 Oct 57 FORCE: 1 Apr 59
United Arab Rep SIGNED: 3 Oct 57 RATIFIED: 15 Jan 59 FORCE: 1 Apr 59
Ethiopia SIGNED: 3 Oct 57 FORCE: 1 Apr 59
Finland SIGNED: 3 Oct 57 RATIFIED: 6 Mar 59 FORCE: 1 Apr 59
Fed of Malaya RATIFIED: 13 Mar 59 FORCE: 1 Apr 59
France All Territories RATIFIED: 8 May 59 FORCE: 1 Apr 59
France SIGNED: 3 Oct 57 RATIFIED: 8 May 59 FORCE: 1 Apr 59
Germany, West SIGNED: 3 Oct 57 FORCE: 1 Apr 59
Greece SIGNED: 3 Oct 57 RATIFIED: 2 Oct 59 FORCE: 1 Apr 59
Guatemala SIGNED: 3 Oct 57 FORCE: 1 Apr 59
Haiti SIGNED: 3 Oct 57 FORCE: 1 Apr 59
Honduras SIGNED: 3 Oct 57 FORCE: 1 Apr 59
Hungary SIGNED: 3 Oct 57 RATIFIED: 5 Apr 60 FORCE: 1 Apr 59
Iceland SIGNED: 3 Oct 57 RATIFIED: 27 Nov 58 FORCE: 1 Apr 59
India SIGNED: 3 Oct 57 RATIFIED: 21 Dec 59 FORCE: 1 Apr 59
Indonesia SIGNED: 3 Oct 57 FORCE: 1 Apr 59
Iraq SIGNED: 3 Oct 57 RATIFIED: 18 Jan 60 FORCE: 1 Apr 59
Ireland SIGNED: 3 Oct 57 FORCE: 1 Apr 59
Israel SIGNED: 3 Oct 57 RATIFIED: 23 Oct 59 FORCE: 1 Apr 59
Italy SIGNED: 3 Oct 57 RATIFIED: 9 Jun 60 FORCE: 1 Apr 59
Italy Somalia RATIFIED: 9 Jun 60 FORCE: 1 Apr 59
Japan SIGNED: 3 Oct 57 RATIFIED: 7 Nov 58 FORCE: 1 Apr 59
Jordan SIGNED: 3 Oct 57 RATIFIED: 2 Mar 59
Korea, South SIGNED: 3 Oct 57 RATIFIED: 14 Mar 60 FORCE: 1 Apr 59
Laos SIGNED: 3 Oct 57 FORCE: 1 Apr 59
Lebanon SIGNED: 3 Oct 57 RATIFIED: 23 Apr 58 FORCE: 1 Apr 59
Liberia SIGNED: 3 Oct 57 FORCE: 1 Apr 59
Libya SIGNED: 3 Oct 57 FORCE: 1 Apr 59
Luxembourg SIGNED: 3 Oct 57 RATIFIED: 13 Jan 60 FORCE: 1 Apr 59
Mexico SIGNED: 3 Oct 57 RATIFIED: 19 Apr 59 FORCE: 1 Apr 59

Monaco SIGNED: 3 Oct 57 RATIFIED: 2 Sep 59 FORCE: 1 Apr 59
Morocco SIGNED: 3 Oct 57 RATIFIED: 9 Jul 59 FORCE: 1 Apr 59
Nepal SIGNED: 3 Oct 57 FORCE: 1 Apr 59
Netherlands Netherlands Antilles RATIFIED: 27 Aug 59 FORCE: 1 Apr 59
Netherlands SIGNED: 3 Oct 57 RATIFIED: 27 Aug 59 FORCE: 1 Apr 59
Netherlands Surinam RATIFIED: 27 Aug 59 FORCE: 1 Apr 59
New Zealand Cook Islands RATIFIED: 6 Apr 59
New Zealand SIGNED: 3 Oct 57 RATIFIED: 6 Apr 59 FORCE: 1 Apr 59
New Zealand Tokelau Islands RATIFIED: 6 Apr 59
New Zealand Western Samoa RATIFIED: 6 Apr 59
Nicaragua SIGNED: 3 Oct 57 FORCE: 1 Apr 59
Norway SIGNED: 3 Oct 57 RATIFIED: 19 Aug 58 FORCE: 1 Apr 59
Pakistan SIGNED: 3 Oct 57 RATIFIED: 8 Oct 59 FORCE: 1 Apr 59
Panama SIGNED: 3 Oct 57 FORCE: 1 Apr 59
Paraguay SIGNED: 3 Oct 57 FORCE: 1 Apr 59
Peru SIGNED: 3 Oct 57 RATIFIED: 21 May 59 FORCE: 1 Apr 59
Philippines SIGNED: 3 Oct 57 RATIFIED: 18 Jun 59 FORCE: 1 Apr 59
Poland SIGNED: 3 Oct 57 FORCE: 1 Apr 59
Portugal All Territories RATIFIED: 1 Apr 59
Portugal SIGNED: 3 Oct 57 FORCE: 1 Apr 59
Romania SIGNED: 3 Oct 57 FORCE: 1 Apr 59
San Marino SIGNED: 3 Oct 57 RATIFIED: 31 Mar 59 FORCE: 1 Apr 59
Saudi Arabia SIGNED: 3 Oct 57 FORCE: 1 Apr 59
South Africa SIGNED: 3 Oct 57 RATIFIED: 7 Apr 60 FORCE: 1 Apr 59
Spain SIGNED: 3 Oct 57 RATIFIED: 29 Jul 59 FORCE: 1 Apr 59
Spain Spanish Colonies RATIFIED: 29 Jul 59 FORCE: 1 Apr 59
Sudan SIGNED: 3 Oct 57 RATIFIED: 1 Mar 60 FORCE: 1 Apr 59
Sweden SIGNED: 3 Oct 57 RATIFIED: 2 May 58 FORCE: 1 Apr 59
Switzerland SIGNED: 3 Oct 57 RATIFIED: 14 Nov 58 FORCE: 1 Apr 59
Syria SIGNED: 3 Oct 57 RATIFIED: 15 Jan 59 FORCE: 1 Apr 59
Thailand SIGNED: 3 Oct 57 FORCE: 1 Apr 59
Tunisia SIGNED: 3 Oct 57 RATIFIED: 24 Mar 59 FORCE: 1 Apr 59
Turkey SIGNED: 3 Oct 57 FORCE: 1 Apr 59
UK Great Britain SIGNED: 3 Oct 57 RATIFIED: 17 Jul 59 FORCE: 1 Apr 59
UK Great Britain All Territories RATIFIED: 17 Jul 59 FORCE: 1 Apr 59
USA (United States) SIGNED: 3 Oct 57 RATIFIED: 1 Apr 59 FORCE: 1 Apr 59
Ukrainian SSR SIGNED: 3 Oct 57 RATIFIED: 5 May 59 FORCE: 1 Apr 59
Uruguay SIGNED: 3 Oct 57 FORCE: 1 Apr 59
USSR (Soviet Union) SIGNED: 3 Oct 57 RATIFIED: 28 Apr 59 FORCE: 1 Apr 59
Vatican/Holy See SIGNED: 3 Oct 57 RATIFIED: 13 Apr 60 FORCE: 1 Apr 59
Venezuela SIGNED: 3 Oct 57 FORCE: 1 Apr 59
Vietnam, South SIGNED: 3 Oct 57 RATIFIED: 3 Dec 59 FORCE: 1 Apr 59
Yemen SIGNED: 3 Oct 57 RATIFIED: 3 Apr 59 FORCE: 1 Apr 59
Yugoslavia SIGNED: 3 Oct 57 RATIFIED: 15 Apr 59 FORCE: 1 Apr 59
ANNEX
391 UNTS 322. UK Great Britain. British Somaliland.
391 UNTS 322. UK Great Britain. Swaziland.
391 UNTS 322. Germany, West. Berlin.
391 UNTS 322. Poland. Ratification 23 Feb 61.
391 UNTS 322. UK Great Britain. Bahamas.
391 UNTS 322. Italy. Ratification 9 Jun 60.
391 UNTS 322. UK Great Britain. British Guiana.
391 UNTS 322. UK Great Britain. St. Helena.
391 UNTS 322. UK Great Britain. Singapore.
391 UNTS 322. UK Great Britain. Sierra Leone.
391 UNTS 322. UK Great Britain. Seychelles.
391 UNTS 322. UK Great Britain. Tonga.
391 UNTS 322. UK Great Britain. Fiji Islands.
391 UNTS 322. UK Great Britain. Brunei.
391 UNTS 322. UK Great Britain. Sarawak.
391 UNTS 322. UK Great Britain. W Pacif Hi Command.

391 UNTS 322. Thailand. Ratification 21 Jul 60.
391 UNTS 322. UK Great Britain. West Indies.
391 UNTS 322. UK Great Britain. Aden Colony.
391 UNTS 322. UK Great Britain. Aden.
391 UNTS 322. UK Great Britain. Uganda.
391 UNTS 322. UK Great Britain. Zanzibar.
391 UNTS 322. UK Great Britain. Tanganyika.
391 UNTS 322. Somalia. Ratification 16 Nov 60.
391 UNTS 322. UK Great Britain. Cyprus.
391 UNTS 322. UK Great Britain. Gambia.
391 UNTS 322. UK Great Britain. Gibralter.
391 UNTS 322. UK Great Britain. Hong Kong.
391 UNTS 322. UK Great Britain. Nigeria.
391 UNTS 322. UK Great Britain. North Borneo.
391 UNTS 322. UK Great Britain.
391 UNTS 322. UK Great Britain. Basutoland.
391 UNTS 322. UK Great Britain. Fed Rhod/-Nyasaland.
391 UNTS 322. UK Great Britain. Bechuanaland.
391 UNTS 322. UK Great Britain. British Honduras.
391 UNTS 322. UK Great Britain. Brit Virgin Islands.
391 UNTS 322. UK Great Britain. Falkland Islands.
391 UNTS 322. Germany, West. Ratification 30 Aug 60.
391 UNTS 322. UK Great Britain. Bermuda.
404 UNTS 380. Ireland. Ratification 19 Jun 61.
404 UNTS 380. Burma. Ratification 16 Jun 61.

105212 Multilateral Agreement **364 UNTS 331**
SIGNED: 3 Oct 57 FORCE: 1 Apr 59
REGISTERED: 7 Jul 60 Canada
ARTICLES: 18 LANGUAGE: French.
HEADNOTE: INSURED LETTERS BOXES
TOPIC: Postal Service
CONCEPTS: Detailed regulations. Responsibility and liability. Insured letters and boxes. Rates and charges.
PROCEDURE: Duration.
PARTIES:
Albania SIGNED: 3 Oct 57 FORCE: 1 Apr 59
Algeria SIGNED: 3 Oct 57 FORCE: 1 Apr 59
Argentina SIGNED: 3 Oct 57 RATIFIED: 15 Apr 59 FORCE: 1 Apr 59
Austria SIGNED: 3 Oct 57 RATIFIED: 4 May 59 FORCE: 1 Apr 59
Belgium Belgian Colonies RATIFIED: 5 Mar 59 FORCE: 1 Apr 59
Belgium Ruanda-Urundi RATIFIED: 5 Mar 59 FORCE: 1 Apr 59
Belgium SIGNED: 3 Oct 57 RATIFIED: 5 Mar 59 FORCE: 1 Apr 59
Bolivia SIGNED: 3 Oct 57 FORCE: 1 Apr 59
Brazil SIGNED: 3 Oct 57 FORCE: 1 Apr 59
Bulgaria SIGNED: 3 Oct 57 FORCE: 1 Apr 59
Burma SIGNED: 3 Oct 57 FORCE: 1 Apr 59
Byelorussia SIGNED: 3 Oct 57 RATIFIED: 23 Apr 59 FORCE: 1 Apr 59
Cambodia SIGNED: 3 Oct 57 RATIFIED: 12 Jan 60 FORCE: 1 Apr 59
Ceylon (Sri Lanka) SIGNED: 3 Oct 57 RATIFIED: 16 Nov 59 FORCE: 1 Apr 59
Chile SIGNED: 3 Oct 57 FORCE: 1 Apr 59
China SIGNED: 3 Oct 57 RATIFIED: 6 Oct 59 FORCE: 1 Apr 59
Colombia SIGNED: 3 Oct 57 FORCE: 1 Apr 59
Cuba SIGNED: 3 Oct 57 FORCE: 1 Apr 59
Czechoslovakia SIGNED: 3 Oct 57 FORCE: 1 Apr 59
Czechoslovakia RATIFIED: 13 Aug 59 FORCE: 1 Apr 59
Denmark SIGNED: 3 Oct 57 RATIFIED: 13 Aug 58 FORCE: 1 Apr 59
Dominican Republic SIGNED: 3 Oct 57 FORCE: 1 Apr 59
United Arab Rep SIGNED: 3 Oct 57 RATIFIED: 15 Jan 59 FORCE: 1 Apr 59
El Salvador SIGNED: 3 Oct 57 FORCE: 1 Apr 59
Finland SIGNED: 3 Oct 57 RATIFIED: 6 Mar 59 FORCE: 1 Apr 59
Fed of Malaya RATIFIED: 13 Mar 59 FORCE: 1 Apr 59
France All Territories RATIFIED: 8 May 59
France SIGNED: 3 Oct 57 RATIFIED: 8 May 59 FORCE: 1 Apr 59
Germany, West SIGNED: 3 Oct 57 FORCE: 1 Apr 59
Greece SIGNED: 3 Oct 57 RATIFIED: 2 Nov 59 FORCE: 1 Apr 59
Haiti SIGNED: 3 Oct 57 FORCE: 1 Apr 59
Honduras SIGNED: 3 Oct 57 FORCE: 1 Apr 59

Hungary SIGNED: 3 Oct 57 RATIFIED: 5 Apr 60
FORCE: 1 Apr 59
Iceland SIGNED: 3 Oct 57 RATIFIED: 27 Nov 58
FORCE: 1 Apr 59
India SIGNED: 3 Oct 57 RATIFIED: 21 Dec 59
FORCE: 1 Apr 59
Iran SIGNED: 3 Oct 57 FORCE: 1 Apr 59
Iraq SIGNED: 3 Oct 57 RATIFIED: 18 Jan 60
FORCE: 1 Apr 59
Ireland SIGNED: 3 Oct 57 FORCE: 1 Apr 59
Italy SIGNED: 3 Oct 57 RATIFIED: 9 Jun 60
FORCE: 1 Apr 59
Italy Somalia RATIFIED: 9 Jun 60
Japan SIGNED: 3 Oct 57 RATIFIED: 7 Nov 58
FORCE: 1 Apr 59
Jordan SIGNED: 3 Oct 57 RATIFIED: 2 Mar 59
FORCE: 1 Apr 59
Laos SIGNED: 3 Oct 57 FORCE: 1 Apr 59
Lebanon SIGNED: 3 Oct 57 RATIFIED: 23 Jul 58
FORCE: 1 Apr 59
Libya SIGNED: 3 Oct 57 FORCE: 1 Apr 59
Luxembourg SIGNED: 3 Oct 57 RATIFIED:
13 Jan 60 FORCE: 1 Apr 59
Monaco SIGNED: 3 Oct 57 RATIFIED: 2 Sep 59
FORCE: 1 Apr 59
Morocco SIGNED: 3 Oct 57 RATIFIED: 9 Jul 59
FORCE: 1 Apr 59
Netherlands Netherlands Antilles RATIFIED:
27 Aug 59
Netherlands SIGNED: 3 Oct 57 RATIFIED:
27 Aug 59 FORCE: 1 Apr 59
Netherlands Surinam RATIFIED: 27 Aug 59
New Zealand SIGNED: 3 Oct 57 RATIFIED:
6 Apr 59 FORCE: 6 Apr 59
New Zealand Cook Islands RATIFIED: 6 Apr 59
New Zealand Tokelau Islands RATIFIED:
6 Apr 59
New Zealand Western Samoa RATIFIED:
6 Apr 59
Nicaragua SIGNED: 3 Oct 57 FORCE: 1 Apr 59
Norway SIGNED: 3 Oct 57 RATIFIED: 19 Aug 58
FORCE: 1 Apr 59
Pakistan SIGNED: 3 Oct 57 RATIFIED: 8 Oct 59
FORCE: 1 Apr 59
Paraguay SIGNED: 3 Oct 57 FORCE: 1 Apr 59
Poland SIGNED: 3 Oct 57 FORCE: 1 Apr 59
Portugal All Territories RATIFIED: 3 Oct 57
FORCE: 1 Apr 59
Portugal SIGNED: 3 Oct 57 FORCE: 1 Apr 59
Romania SIGNED: 3 Oct 57 FORCE: 1 Apr 59
San Marino SIGNED: 3 Oct 57 RATIFIED:
31 Mar 59 FORCE: 1 Apr 59
Saudi Arabia SIGNED: 3 Oct 57 FORCE:
1 Apr 59
Spain SIGNED: 3 Oct 57 RATIFIED: 29 Jul 59
FORCE: 1 Apr 59
Spain Spanish Colonies RATIFIED: 29 Jul 59
FORCE: 1 Apr 59
Sweden SIGNED: 3 Oct 57 RATIFIED: 2 May 58
FORCE: 1 Apr 59
Switzerland SIGNED: 3 Oct 57 RATIFIED:
14 Nov 58 FORCE: 1 Apr 59
Syria SIGNED: 3 Oct 57 RATIFIED: 15 Jan 59
FORCE: 1 Apr 59
Thailand SIGNED: 3 Oct 57 FORCE: 1 Apr 59
Tunisia SIGNED: 3 Oct 57 RATIFIED:
24 Mar 59 FORCE: 1 Apr 59
Turkey SIGNED: 3 Oct 57 FORCE: 1 Apr 59
UK Great Britain All Territories RATIFIED:
17 Jul 59 FORCE: 1 Apr 59
UK Great Britain SIGNED: 3 Oct 57 RATIFIED:
17 Jul 59 FORCE: 1 Apr 59
Ukrainian SSR SIGNED: 3 Oct 57 RATIFIED:
5 May 59 FORCE: 1 Apr 59
Uruguay SIGNED: 3 Oct 57 FORCE: 1 Apr 59
USSR (Soviet Union) SIGNED: 3 Oct 57 RATI-
FIED: 23 Apr 59 FORCE: 1 Apr 59
Vatican/Holy See SIGNED: 3 Oct 57 RATIFIED:
13 Apr 60 FORCE: 1 Apr 59
Venezuela SIGNED: 3 Oct 57 FORCE: 1 Apr 59
Vietnam, South SIGNED: 3 Oct 57 RATIFIED:
3 Dec 59 FORCE: 1 Apr 59
Yemen SIGNED: 3 Oct 57 RATIFIED: 3 Apr 59
FORCE: 1 Apr 59
Yugoslavia SIGNED: 3 Oct 57 RATIFIED:
15 Apr 59 FORCE: 1 Apr 59
ANNEX
391 UNTS 326. UK Great Britain. Tonga.
391 UNTS 326. UK Great Britain. West Indies.
391 UNTS 326. UK Great Britain. North Borneo.
391 UNTS 326. UK Great Britain. British Guiana.
391 UNTS 326. Italy. Ratification 29 Jun 60.
391 UNTS 326. UK Great Britain. British Honduras.

391 UNTS 326. UK Great Britain. Brit Virgin Islands.
391 UNTS 326. UK Great Britain. Zanzibar.
391 UNTS 326. UK Great Britain. Brunei.
391 UNTS 326. Thailand. Ratification 21 Jul 60.
391 UNTS 326. UK Great Britain. Malta.
391 UNTS 326. UK Great Britain. Hong Kong.
391 UNTS 326. UK Great Britain. Kenya.
391 UNTS 326. UK Great Britain. Mauritius.
391 UNTS 326. Somalia. Ratification 16 Nov 60.
391 UNTS 326. UK Great Britain. Nigeria.
391 UNTS 326. UK Great Britain. St. Helena.
391 UNTS 326. UK Great Britain. Tanganyika.
391 UNTS 326. UK Great Britain. Uganda.
391 UNTS 326. UK Great Britain. Aden.
391 UNTS 326. UK Great Britain. Cyprus.
391 UNTS 326. Germany, West. Berlin.
391 UNTS 326. UK Great Britain. Aden Colony.
391 UNTS 326. UK Great Britain. Falkland Islands.
391 UNTS 326. UK Great Britain. Sarawak.
391 UNTS 326. UK Great Britain. Seychelles.
391 UNTS 326. UK Great Britain. Fiji Islands.
391 UNTS 326. UK Great Britain. British Somaliland.
391 UNTS 326. UK Great Britain. Sierra Leone.
391 UNTS 326. UK Great Britain. Singapore.
391 UNTS 326. UK Great Britain. Gambia.
391 UNTS 326. UK Great Britain. Gibralter.
391 UNTS 326. Poland. Ratification 23 Feb 61.
391 UNTS 326. Germany, West. Ratification
30 Aug 60.
391 UNTS 362. UK Great Britain. Bermuda.

105213 Multilateral Agreement **365 UNTS 3**
SIGNED: 3 Oct 57　　　　　FORCE: 1 Apr 59
REGISTERED: 7 Jul 60 Canada
ARTICLES: 17 LANGUAGE: French.
HEADNOTE: POSTAL PARCELS
TOPIC: Postal Service
CONCEPTS: Definition of terms. General provi-
sions. Responsibility and liability. Compensa-
tion. Payment schedules. Postal services. Regu-
lations. Insured letters and boxes. Parcel post.
Rates and charges. Decisions. Conformity with
IGO decisions.
INTL ORGS: Universal Postal Union.
PROCEDURE: Duration.
PARTIES:
Afghanistan SIGNED: 3 Oct 57 FORCE: 1 Apr 59
Albania SIGNED: 3 Oct 57 RATIFIED: 14 Sep 59
FORCE: 1 Apr 59
Algeria SIGNED: 3 Oct 57 FORCE: 1 Apr 59
Argentina SIGNED: 3 Oct 57 RATIFIED:
15 Apr 59 FORCE: 1 Apr 59
Austria SIGNED: 3 Oct 57 RATIFIED: 4 May 59
FORCE: 1 Apr 59
Belgium SIGNED: 3 Oct 57 FORCE: 1 Apr 59
Belgian Colonies SIGNED: 3 Oct 57 FORCE:
1 Apr 59
Bolivia SIGNED: 3 Oct 57 FORCE: 1 Apr 59
Brazil SIGNED: 3 Oct 57 FORCE: 1 Apr 59
Bulgaria SIGNED: 3 Oct 57 RATIFIED:
13 May 59 FORCE: 1 Apr 59
Byelorussia SIGNED: 3 Oct 57 RATIFIED:
23 Apr 59 FORCE: 1 Apr 59
Cambodia SIGNED: 3 Oct 57 RATIFIED:
12 Jan 60 FORCE: 1 Apr 59
Ceylon (Sri Lanka) SIGNED: 3 Oct 57 RATIFIED:
16 Nov 59 FORCE: 1 Apr 59
Chile SIGNED: 3 Oct 57 FORCE: 1 Apr 59
China SIGNED: 3 Oct 57 RATIFIED: 6 Oct 69
FORCE: 1 Apr 59
Colombia SIGNED: 3 Oct 57 FORCE: 1 Apr 59
Costa Rica SIGNED: 3 Oct 57 FORCE: 1 Apr 59
Cuba SIGNED: 3 Oct 57 FORCE: 1 Apr 59
Czechoslovakia SIGNED: 3 Oct 57 FORCE:
1 Apr 59
Czechoslovakia SIGNED: 3 Oct 57 RATIFIED:
13 Aug 59 FORCE: 1 Apr 59
Denmark SIGNED: 3 Oct 57 RATIFIED:
13 Aug 58 FORCE: 1 Apr 59
Netherlands Antilles SIGNED: 3 Oct 57 FORCE:
1 Apr 59
Dominican Republic SIGNED: 3 Oct 57 FORCE:
1 Apr 59
Ecuador SIGNED: 3 Oct 57 FORCE: 1 Apr 59
United Arab Rep SIGNED: 3 Oct 57 RATIFIED:
15 Jan 59 FORCE: 1 Apr 59
El Salvador SIGNED: 3 Oct 57 FORCE: 1 Apr 59
Ethiopia SIGNED: 3 Oct 57 FORCE: 1 Apr 59
Finland SIGNED: 3 Oct 57 RATIFIED: 6 Mar 59
FORCE: 1 Apr 59

France All Territories RATIFIED: 8 May 59
FORCE: 1 Apr 59
France SIGNED: 3 Oct 57 RATIFIED: 8 May 59
FORCE: 1 Apr 59
Germany, West SIGNED: 3 Oct 57 FORCE:
1 Apr 59
Greece SIGNED: 3 Oct 57 RATIFIED: 2 Oct 59
FORCE: 1 Apr 59
Guatemala SIGNED: 3 Oct 57 FORCE: 1 Apr 59
Haiti SIGNED: 3 Oct 57 FORCE: 1 Apr 59
Honduras SIGNED: 3 Oct 57 FORCE: 1 Apr 59
Hungary SIGNED: 3 Oct 57 RATIFIED: 5 Apr 60
FORCE: 1 Apr 59
Iceland SIGNED: 3 Oct 57 RATIFIED: 25 Nov 58
FORCE: 1 Apr 59
India SIGNED: 3 Oct 57 RATIFIED: 21 Dec 59
FORCE: 1 Apr 59
Indonesia SIGNED: 3 Oct 57 FORCE: 1 Apr 59
Iran SIGNED: 3 Oct 57 FORCE: 1 Apr 59
Iraq SIGNED: 3 Oct 57 RATIFIED: 18 Jan 60
FORCE: 1 Apr 59
Ireland SIGNED: 3 Oct 57 FORCE: 1 Apr 59
Italy SIGNED: 3 Oct 57 RATIFIED: 9 Jun 60
FORCE: 1 Apr 59
Italy Somalia RATIFIED: 9 Jun 60 FORCE:
1 Apr 59
Japan SIGNED: 3 Oct 57 RATIFIED: 7 Nov 58
FORCE: 1 Apr 59
Jordan SIGNED: 3 Oct 57 RATIFIED: 2 Mar 59
FORCE: 1 Apr 59
Korea, South SIGNED: 3 Oct 57 RATIFIED:
14 Mar 59 FORCE: 1 Apr 59
Laos SIGNED: 3 Oct 57 FORCE: 1 Apr 59
Lebanon SIGNED: 3 Oct 57 RATIFIED: 23 Jul 58
FORCE: 1 Apr 59
Liberia SIGNED: 3 Oct 57 FORCE: 1 Apr 59
Libya SIGNED: 3 Oct 57 FORCE: 1 Apr 59
Luxembourg SIGNED: 3 Oct 57 RATIFIED:
13 Jan 60 FORCE: 1 Apr 59
Malaya RATIFIED: 13 Mar 59 FORCE: 1 Apr 59
Mexico SIGNED: 3 Oct 57 RATIFIED: 19 Mar 59
FORCE: 1 Apr 59
Monaco SIGNED: 3 Oct 57 RATIFIED: 20 Sep 59
FORCE: 1 Apr 59
Morocco SIGNED: 3 Oct 57 RATIFIED: 9 Jul 59
FORCE: 1 Apr 59
Netherlands Netherlands Antilles RATIFIED:
25 Aug 59 FORCE: 1 Apr 59
Netherlands SIGNED: 3 Oct 57 RATIFIED:
25 Aug 59 FORCE: 1 Apr 59
Netherlands Surinam RATIFIED: 25 Aug 59
FORCE: 1 Apr 59
Nicaragua SIGNED: 3 Oct 57 FORCE: 1 Apr 59
Norway SIGNED: 3 Oct 57 RATIFIED: 19 Aug 58
FORCE: 1 Apr 59
Pakistan SIGNED: 3 Oct 57 RATIFIED: 8 Oct 59
FORCE: 1 Apr 59
Panama SIGNED: 3 Oct 57 FORCE: 1 Apr 59
Paraguay SIGNED: 3 Oct 57 FORCE: 1 Apr 59
Peru SIGNED: 3 Oct 57 RATIFIED: 21 May 59
FORCE: 1 Apr 59
Poland SIGNED: 3 Oct 57 FORCE: 1 Apr 59
Portugal SIGNED: 3 Oct 57 FORCE: 1 Apr 59
Portugal All Territories RATIFIED: 3 Oct 57
FORCE: 1 Apr 59
San Marino SIGNED: 3 Oct 57 RATIFIED:
31 Mar 59 FORCE: 1 Apr 59
Saudi Arabia SIGNED: 3 Oct 57 FORCE:
1 Apr 59
Spain SIGNED: 3 Oct 57 RATIFIED: 29 Jul 59
FORCE: 1 Apr 59
Spain Spanish Colonies RATIFIED: 29 Jul 59
FORCE: 1 Apr 59
Spanish Colonies SIGNED: 3 Oct 57 FORCE:
1 Apr 59
Sudan SIGNED: 3 Oct 57 RATIFIED: 1 Mar 60
FORCE: 1 Apr 59
Sweden SIGNED: 3 Oct 57 RATIFIED: 2 May 58
FORCE: 1 Apr 59
Switzerland SIGNED: 3 Oct 57 RATIFIED:
14 Nov 58 FORCE: 1 Apr 59
Syria SIGNED: 3 Oct 57 RATIFIED: 15 Jan 59
FORCE: 1 Apr 59
Thailand SIGNED: 3 Oct 57 FORCE: 1 Apr 59
Tunisia SIGNED: 3 Oct 57 RATIFIED: 24 Mar 59
FORCE: 1 Apr 59
Turkey SIGNED: 3 Oct 57 FORCE: 1 Apr 59
UK Great Britain All Territories RATIFIED:
17 Jul 59 FORCE: 1 Apr 59
UK Great Britain SIGNED: 3 Oct 57 RATIFIED:
17 Jul 59 FORCE: 1 Apr 59
Ukrainian SSR SIGNED: 3 Oct 57 RATIFIED:
5 May 59 FORCE: 1 Apr 59
Uruguay SIGNED: 3 Oct 57 FORCE: 1 Apr 59

USSR (Soviet Union) SIGNED: 3 Oct 57 RATI-
FIED: 25 Apr 59 FORCE: 1 Apr 59
Vatican/Holy See SIGNED: 3 Oct 57 RATIFIED:
13 Apr 60 FORCE: 1 Apr 59
Venezuela SIGNED: 3 Oct 57 FORCE: 1 Apr 59
Vietnam SIGNED: 3 Oct 57 RATIFIED: 3 Dec 59
FORCE: 1 Apr 59
Yemen RATIFIED: 3 Apr 59 FORCE: 1 Apr 59
Yugoslavia SIGNED: 3 Oct 57 RATIFIED:
15 Apr 59 FORCE: 1 Apr 59
ANNEX
404 UNTS 381. Ireland. Ratification 19 Jun 61.
412 UNTS 352. Congo (Zaire). Ratification
20 Sep 61.

105214 Multilateral Agreement **365 UNTS 207**
SIGNED: 3 Oct 57   FORCE: 1 Apr 59
REGISTERED: 7 Jul 60 Canada
ARTICLES: 45 LANGUAGE: French.
HEADNOTE: POSTAL MONEY ORDERS & TRA-
VELLERS CHEQUES
TOPIC: Postal Service
CONCEPTS: Detailed regulations. Responsibility
and liability. Bonds. Currency. Payment sched-
ules. Claims and settlements. Postal services.
Money orders and postal checks. Rates and
charges. Conformity with IGO decisions.
PROCEDURE: Duration.
PARTIES:
Albania SIGNED: 3 Oct 57 FORCE: 1 Apr 59
Algeria SIGNED: 3 Oct 57 FORCE: 1 Apr 59
Argentina   SIGNED: 3 Oct 57   RATIFIED:
15 Apr 59 FORCE: 1 Apr 59
Austria SIGNED: 3 Oct 57 RATIFIED: 4 May 59
FORCE: 1 Apr 59
Belgium SIGNED: 3 Oct 57 RATIFIED: 5 Mar 59
FORCE: 1 Apr 59
Bolivia SIGNED: 3 Oct 57 FORCE: 1 Apr 59
Bulgaria   SIGNED: 3 Oct 57   RATIFIED:
13 May 59 FORCE: 1 Apr 59
Cambodia   SIGNED: 3 Oct 57   RATIFIED:
12 Jan 60 FORCE: 1 Apr 59
Chile SIGNED: 3 Oct 57 FORCE: 1 Apr 59
China SIGNED: 3 Oct 57 RATIFIED: 6 Oct 59
FORCE: 1 Apr 59
Colombia SIGNED: 3 Oct 57 FORCE: 1 Apr 59
Cuba SIGNED: 3 Oct 57 FORCE: 1 Apr 59
Czechoslovakia SIGNED: 3 Oct 57 RATIFIED:
13 Aug 59 FORCE: 1 Apr 59
Denmark   SIGNED: 3 Oct 57   RATIFIED:
13 Aug 58 FORCE: 1 Apr 59
United Arab Rep SIGNED: 3 Oct 57 RATIFIED:
15 Jan 59 FORCE: 1 Apr 59
El Salvador SIGNED: 3 Oct 57 FORCE: 1 Apr 59
Finland SIGNED: 3 Oct 57 RATIFIED: 6 Mar 59
FORCE: 1 Apr 59
France SIGNED: 3 Oct 57 RATIFIED: 8 May 59
FORCE: 1 Apr 59
France All Territories RATIFIED: 8 May 59
FORCE: 1 Apr 59
Germany, West SIGNED: 3 Oct 57 FORCE:
1 Apr 59
Greece SIGNED: 3 Oct 57 RATIFIED: 2 Oct 59
FORCE: 1 Apr 59
Haiti SIGNED: 3 Oct 57 FORCE: 1 Apr 59
Honduras SIGNED: 3 Oct 57 FORCE: 1 Apr 59
Hungary SIGNED: 3 Oct 57 RATIFIED: 5 Apr 60
FORCE: 1 Apr 59
Iceland SIGNED: 3 Oct 57 RATIFIED: 27 Nov 58
FORCE: 1 Apr 59
Indonesia SIGNED: 3 Oct 57 FORCE: 1 Apr 59
Iran SIGNED: 3 Oct 57 FORCE: 1 Apr 59
Italy SIGNED: 3 Oct 57 RATIFIED: 9 Jun 60
FORCE: 1 Apr 59
Italy Somalia RATIFIED: 9 Jun 60 FORCE:
1 Apr 59
Japan SIGNED: 3 Oct 57 RATIFIED: 7 Nov 58
FORCE: 1 Apr 59
Korea, South SIGNED: 3 Oct 57 FORCE:
1 Apr 59
Laos SIGNED: 3 Oct 57 FORCE: 1 Apr 59
Lebanon SIGNED: 3 Oct 57 RATIFIED: 23 Jul 58
FORCE: 1 Apr 59
Liberia SIGNED: 3 Oct 57 FORCE: 1 Apr 59
Libya SIGNED: 3 Oct 57 FORCE: 1 Apr 59
Luxembourg SIGNED: 3 Oct 57 RATIFIED:
13 Jan 60 FORCE: 1 Apr 59
Mexico SIGNED: 3 Oct 57 RATIFIED: 19 Mar 59
Monaco SIGNED: 3 Oct 57 RATIFIED: 2 Sep 59
FORCE: 1 Apr 59
Morocco SIGNED: 3 Oct 57 RATIFIED: 9 Jul 59
FORCE: 1 Apr 59

Netherlands Netherlands Antilles RATIFIED:
25 Aug 59 FORCE: 1 Apr 59
Netherlands SIGNED: 3 Oct 57 RATIFIED:
25 Aug 59 FORCE: 1 Apr 59
Netherlands Surinam RATIFIED: 25 Aug 59
FORCE: 1 Apr 59
Nicaragua SIGNED: 3 Oct 57 FORCE: 1 Apr 59
Norway SIGNED: 3 Oct 57 RATIFIED: 19 Aug 58
FORCE: 1 Apr 59
Panama SIGNED: 3 Oct 57 FORCE: 1 Apr 59
Paraguay SIGNED: 3 Oct 57 FORCE: 1 Apr 59
Peru SIGNED: 3 Oct 57 RATIFIED: 21 May 59
FORCE: 1 Apr 59
Poland SIGNED: 3 Oct 57 FORCE: 1 Apr 59
Portugal SIGNED: 3 Oct 57 FORCE: 1 Apr 59
Portugal All Territories RATIFIED: 3 Oct 57
FORCE: 1 Apr 59
Romania SIGNED: 3 Oct 57 FORCE: 1 Apr 59
San Marino SIGNED: 3 Oct 57 RATIFIED:
31 Mar 59 FORCE: 1 Apr 59
Saudi Arabia SIGNED: 3 Oct 57 FORCE:
1 Apr 59
Spain SIGNED: 3 Oct 57 RATIFIED: 29 Jul 59
FORCE: 1 Apr 59
Spain Spanish Colonies RATIFIED: 29 Jul 59
FORCE: 1 Apr 59
Sudan SIGNED: 3 Oct 57 RATIFIED: 1 Mar 60
FORCE: 1 Apr 59
Sweden SIGNED: 3 Oct 57 RATIFIED: 2 May 58
FORCE: 1 Apr 59
Switzerland SIGNED: 3 Oct 57 RATIFIED:
14 Nov 58 FORCE: 1 Apr 59
Syria SIGNED: 3 Oct 57 RATIFIED: 15 Jan 59
FORCE: 1 Apr 59
Thailand SIGNED: 3 Oct 57 FORCE: 1 Apr 59
Tunisia SIGNED: 3 Oct 57 RATIFIED: 24 Mar 59
FORCE: 1 Apr 59
Turkey SIGNED: 3 Oct 57 FORCE: 1 Apr 59
Uruguay SIGNED: 3 Oct 57 FORCE: 1 Apr 59
Vatican/Holy See SIGNED: 3 Oct 57 RATIFIED:
13 Apr 60 FORCE: 1 Apr 59
Venezuela SIGNED: 3 Oct 57 FORCE: 1 Apr 59
Vietnam SIGNED: 3 Oct 57 FORCE: 3 Dec 59
FORCE: 1 Apr 59
Yemen RATIFIED: 3 Apr 59 FORCE: 1 Apr 59
Yugoslavia SIGNED: 3 Oct 57 FORCE: 1 Apr 59
ANNEX
391 UNTS 328. Somalia. Ratification 16 Nov 60.
391 UNTS 328. Germany, West. Berlin.
391 UNTS 328. Italy. Ratification 9 Jun 60.
391 UNTS 328. Thailand. Ratification 21 Jul 60.
391 UNTS 328. Germany, West. Ratification
30 Aug 60.
391 UNTS 328. Poland. Ratification 23 Feb 61.

105215 Multilateral Agreement   **366 UNTS 3**
SIGNED: 3 Oct 57   FORCE: 1 Apr 59
REGISTERED: 7 Jul 60 Canada
ARTICLES: 31 LANGUAGE: French.
HEADNOTE: POSTAL CHEQUE ACCOUNTS
TOPIC: Postal Service
CONCEPTS: Detailed regulations. Responsibility
and liability. Accounting procedures. Currency.
Exchange rates and regulations. Payment sched-
ules. Claims and settlements. Money orders and
postal checks. Rates and charges. Telegrams.
Conformity with IGO decisions.
INTL ORGS: Universal Postal Union.
PROCEDURE: Duration.
PARTIES:
Albania SIGNED: 3 Oct 57 FORCE: 1 Apr 59
Algeria SIGNED: 3 Oct 57 RATIFIED: 8 May 59
FORCE: 1 Apr 59
Argentina   SIGNED: 3 Oct 57   RATIFIED:
15 Apr 59 FORCE: 1 Apr 59
Austria SIGNED: 3 Oct 57 FORCE: 1 Apr 59
Belgium SIGNED: 3 Oct 57 RATIFIED: 5 Mar 59
FORCE: 1 Apr 59
Bolivia SIGNED: 3 Oct 57 FORCE: 1 Apr 59
Chile SIGNED: 3 Oct 57 FORCE: 1 Apr 59
Colombia SIGNED: 3 Oct 57 FORCE: 1 Apr 59
Cuba SIGNED: 3 Oct 57 FORCE: 1 Apr 59
Denmark   SIGNED: 3 Oct 57   RATIFIED:
13 Aug 58 FORCE: 1 Apr 59
United Arab Rep SIGNED: 3 Oct 57 RATIFIED:
15 Jan 59 FORCE: 1 Apr 59
Finland SIGNED: 3 Oct 57 RATIFIED: 6 Mar 59
FORCE: 1 Apr 59
France All Territories RATIFIED: 8 May 59
FORCE: 1 Apr 59
France SIGNED: 3 Oct 57 RATIFIED: 8 May 59
FORCE: 1 Apr 59

Germany, West SIGNED: 3 Oct 57 FORCE:
1 Apr 59
Greece SIGNED: 3 Oct 57 FORCE: 1 Apr 59
Haiti SIGNED: 3 Oct 57 FORCE: 1 Apr 59
Honduras SIGNED: 3 Oct 57 FORCE: 1 Apr 59
Indonesia SIGNED: 3 Oct 57 FORCE: 1 Apr 59
Italy SIGNED: 3 Oct 57 RATIFIED: 9 Jun 60
FORCE: 1 Apr 59
Italy Somalia RATIFIED: 9 Jun 60 FORCE:
1 Apr 59
Japan SIGNED: 3 Oct 57 RATIFIED: 7 Nov 58
FORCE: 1 Apr 59
Laos SIGNED: 3 Oct 57 FORCE: 1 Apr 59
Lebanon SIGNED: 3 Oct 57 FORCE: 1 Apr 59
Luxembourg SIGNED: 3 Oct 57 RATIFIED:
13 Jan 60 FORCE: 1 Apr 59
Monaco SIGNED: 3 Oct 57 RATIFIED: 2 Sep 59
FORCE: 1 Apr 59
Morocco SIGNED: 3 Oct 57 RATIFIED: 9 Jul 59
FORCE: 1 Apr 59
Netherlands SIGNED: 3 Oct 57 RATIFIED:
27 Aug 59 FORCE: 1 Apr 59
Nicaragua SIGNED: 3 Oct 57 FORCE: 1 Apr 59
Norway SIGNED: 3 Oct 57 RATIFIED: 19 Aug 58
FORCE: 1 Apr 59
Paraguay SIGNED: 3 Oct 57 FORCE: 1 Apr 59
Portugal All Territories RATIFIED: 3 Oct 57
FORCE: 1 Apr 59
Portugal SIGNED: 3 Oct 57 FORCE: 1 Apr 59
Romania SIGNED: 3 Oct 57 FORCE: 1 Apr 59
San Marino SIGNED: 3 Oct 57 RATIFIED:
13 Mar 59 FORCE: 1 Apr 59
Spain SIGNED: 3 Oct 57 RATIFIED: 29 Jul 59
FORCE: 1 Apr 59
Spain Spanish Colonies RATIFIED: 29 Jul 59
FORCE: 1 Apr 59
Sweden SIGNED: 3 Oct 57 RATIFIED: 2 May 58
FORCE: 1 Apr 59
Switzerland SIGNED: 3 Oct 57 RATIFIED:
14 Nov 58 FORCE: 1 Apr 59
Tunisia SIGNED: 3 Oct 57 RATIFIED: 24 Mar 59
FORCE: 1 Apr 59
Turkey SIGNED: 3 Oct 57 FORCE: 1 Apr 59
Uruguay SIGNED: 3 Oct 57 FORCE: 1 Apr 59
Vatican/Holy See SIGNED: 3 Oct 57 RATIFIED:
13 Apr 60 FORCE: 1 Apr 59
Venezuela SIGNED: 3 Oct 57 FORCE: 1 Apr 59
Vietnam SIGNED: 3 Oct 57 FORCE: 1 Apr 59
Yemen RATIFIED: 3 Apr 59 FORCE: 1 Apr 59
Yugoslavia SIGNED: 3 Oct 57 FORCE: 1 Apr 59
ANNEX
391 UNTS 329. Italy. Ratification 9 Jun 60.
391 UNTS 329. Germany, West. Ratification
30 Aug 60.
391 UNTS 329. Germany, West. Berlin.
391 UNTS 329. Somalia. Ratification 16 Nov 60.

105216 Multilateral Agreement **366 UNTS 87**
SIGNED: 3 Oct 57   FORCE: 1 Apr 59
REGISTERED: 7 Jul 60 Canada
ARTICLES: 18 LANGUAGE: French.
HEADNOTE: COMMERCIAL SCHEDULED AIR
TRANSPORT
TOPIC: Postal Service
CONCEPTS: Definition of terms. Detailed regulations. Exceptions and exemptions. Annex or appendix reference. General cooperation. Exchange of information and documents. Use of
facilities. Arbitration. Procedure. Special tribunals. Negotiation. Reexport of goods, etc.. Monetary and gold transfers. Expense sharing formulae. Fees and exemptions. Non-interest rates and
fees. National treatment. Tax exemptions. Customs exemptions. Routes and logistics. Permit
designation. Air transport. Airport facilities. Conditions of airlines operating permission. Overflights and technical stops. Operating authoriza-
tions and regulations.
INTL ORGS: Universal Postal Union.
PROCEDURE: Amendment. Future Procedures
Contemplated. Registration. Termination.
PARTIES:
Albania SIGNED: 3 Oct 57 FORCE: 1 Apr 59
Algeria SIGNED: 3 Oct 57 RATIFIED: 8 May 59
FORCE: 1 Apr 59
Argentina   SIGNED: 3 Oct 57   RATIFIED:
15 Apr 59 FORCE: 1 Apr 59
Austria SIGNED: 3 Oct 57 RATIFIED: 4 May 59
FORCE: 1 Apr 59
Belgium SIGNED: 3 Oct 57 RATIFIED: 5 Mar 59
FORCE: 1 Apr 59
Bolivia SIGNED: 3 Oct 57 FORCE: 1 Apr 59

Cambodia SIGNED: 3 Oct 57 RATIFIED: 12 Jan 60 FORCE: 1 Apr 59
China SIGNED: 3 Oct 57 RATIFIED: 6 Oct 59 FORCE: 1 Apr 59
Taiwan SIGNED: 3 Oct 57 FORCE: 1 Apr 59
Colombia SIGNED: 3 Oct 57 FORCE: 1 Apr 59
Cuba SIGNED: 3 Oct 57 FORCE: 1 Apr 59
Czechoslovakia SIGNED: 3 Oct 57 RATIFIED: 13 Aug 59 FORCE: 1 Apr 59
Denmark SIGNED: 3 Oct 57 RATIFIED: 13 Aug 58 FORCE: 1 Apr 59
Dominican Republic SIGNED: 3 Oct 57 FORCE: 1 Apr 59
United Arab Rep SIGNED: 3 Oct 57 RATIFIED: 15 Jan 59 FORCE: 1 Apr 59
Finland SIGNED: 3 Oct 57 RATIFIED: 6 Mar 59 FORCE: 1 Apr 59
France All Territories RATIFIED: 8 May 59 FORCE: 1 Apr 59
France SIGNED: 3 Oct 57 RATIFIED: 8 May 59 FORCE: 1 Apr 59
Germany, West SIGNED: 3 Oct 57 FORCE: 1 Apr 59
Greece SIGNED: 3 Oct 57 RATIFIED: 2 Oct 59 FORCE: 1 Apr 59
Hungary SIGNED: 3 Oct 57 RATIFIED: 5 Apr 60 FORCE: 1 Apr 59
Iceland SIGNED: 3 Oct 57 RATIFIED: 27 Nov 58 FORCE: 1 Apr 59
Indonesia SIGNED: 3 Oct 57 FORCE: 1 Apr 59
Iraq SIGNED: 3 Oct 57 RATIFIED: 18 Jan 61 FORCE: 1 Apr 59
Italy SIGNED: 3 Oct 57 RATIFIED: 9 Jun 60 FORCE: 1 Apr 59
Italy Somalia RATIFIED: 9 Jun 60 FORCE: 1 Apr 59
Japan SIGNED: 3 Oct 57 RATIFIED: 7 Nov 58 FORCE: 1 Apr 59
Laos SIGNED: 3 Oct 57 FORCE: 1 Apr 59
Lebanon SIGNED: 3 Oct 57 FORCE: 1 Apr 59
Libya SIGNED: 3 Oct 57 FORCE: 1 Apr 59
Luxembourg SIGNED: 3 Oct 57 RATIFIED: 13 Jan 60 FORCE: 1 Apr 59
Mexico SIGNED: 3 Oct 57 RATIFIED: 19 Mar 59 FORCE: 1 Apr 59
Monaco SIGNED: 3 Oct 57 RATIFIED: 2 Sep 59 FORCE: 1 Apr 59
Morocco SIGNED: 3 Oct 57 RATIFIED: 9 Aug 59 FORCE: 1 Apr 59
Netherlands Netherlands Antilles RATIFIED: 27 Aug 59 FORCE: 1 Apr 59
Netherlands SIGNED: 3 Oct 57 RATIFIED: 27 Aug 59 FORCE: 1 Apr 59
Netherlands Surinam RATIFIED: 27 Aug 59 FORCE: 1 Apr 59
Nicaragua SIGNED: 3 Oct 57 FORCE: 1 Apr 59
Norway SIGNED: 3 Oct 57 RATIFIED: 19 Aug 58 FORCE: 1 Apr 59
Paraguay SIGNED: 3 Oct 57 FORCE: 1 Apr 59
Poland SIGNED: 3 Oct 57 FORCE: 1 Apr 59
Portugal All Territories RATIFIED: 3 Oct 57 FORCE: 1 Apr 59
Portugal SIGNED: 3 Oct 57 FORCE: 1 Apr 59
Romania SIGNED: 3 Oct 57 FORCE: 1 Apr 59
San Marino SIGNED: 3 Oct 57 RATIFIED: 27 Aug 59 FORCE: 1 Apr 59
Spain SIGNED: 3 Oct 57 RATIFIED: 29 Jul 59 FORCE: 1 Apr 59
Spain Spanish Colonies RATIFIED: 29 Jul 59 FORCE: 1 Apr 59
Sweden SIGNED: 3 Oct 57 RATIFIED: 2 May 58 FORCE: 1 Apr 59
Switzerland SIGNED: 3 Oct 57 RATIFIED: 14 Nov 58 FORCE: 1 Apr 59
Syria SIGNED: 3 Oct 57 RATIFIED: 15 Jan 59 FORCE: 1 Apr 59
Thailand SIGNED: 3 Oct 57 FORCE: 1 Apr 59
Tunisia SIGNED: 3 Oct 57 FORCE: 1 Apr 59
Turkey SIGNED: 3 Oct 57 FORCE: 1 Apr 59
Uruguay SIGNED: 3 Oct 57 FORCE: 1 Apr 59
Vatican/Holy See SIGNED: 3 Oct 57 RATIFIED: 13 Apr 60 FORCE: 1 Apr 59
Venezuela SIGNED: 3 Oct 57 FORCE: 1 Apr 59
Vietnam SIGNED: 3 Oct 57 FORCE: 1 Apr 59
Yemen RATIFIED: 3 Apr 59
Yugoslavia SIGNED: 3 Oct 57 FORCE: 1 Apr 59
ANNEX
391 UNTS 330. Somalia. Ratification 16 Nov 60.
391 UNTS 330. Italy. Ratification 9 Jun 60.
391 UNTS 330. Thailand. Ratification 21 Jul 60.
391 UNTS 330. Germany, West. Ratification 30 Aug 60.
391 UNTS 330. Germany, West. Berlin.
391 UNTS 330. Poland. Ratification 23 Feb 61.

105217 Multilateral Agreement **366 UNTS 141**
SIGNED: 3 Oct 57 FORCE: 1 Apr 59
REGISTERED: 7 Jul 60 Canada
ARTICLES: 22 LANGUAGE: French.
HEADNOTE: COLLECTION BILL DRAFTS ETC.
TOPIC: Postal Service
CONCEPTS: Detailed regulations. Responsibility and liability. Currency. Payment schedules. Postal services. Money orders and postal checks. Rates and charges. Conformity with IGO decisions.
INTL ORGS: Universal Postal Union.
TREATY REF: 36JUNTS3.
PROCEDURE: Duration.
PARTIES:
Albania SIGNED: 3 Oct 57 FORCE: 1 Apr 59
Algeria SIGNED: 3 Oct 57 FORCE: 1 Apr 59
Argentina SIGNED: 3 Oct 57 RATIFIED: 15 Apr 59 FORCE: 1 Apr 59
Austria SIGNED: 3 Oct 57 RATIFIED: 4 May 59 FORCE: 1 Apr 59
Belgium SIGNED: 3 Oct 57 RATIFIED: 5 Mar 59 FORCE: 1 Apr 59
Bolivia SIGNED: 3 Oct 57 FORCE: 1 Apr 59
Cambodia SIGNED: 3 Oct 57 RATIFIED: 12 Jan 60 FORCE: 1 Apr 59
Chile SIGNED: 3 Oct 57 FORCE: 1 Apr 59
Colombia SIGNED: 3 Oct 57 FORCE: 1 Apr 59
Cuba SIGNED: 3 Oct 57 FORCE: 1 Apr 59
Denmark SIGNED: 3 Oct 57 RATIFIED: 13 Aug 58 FORCE: 1 Apr 59
Dominican Republic SIGNED: 3 Oct 57 FORCE: 1 Apr 59
United Arab Rep SIGNED: 3 Oct 57 RATIFIED: 15 Jan 59 FORCE: 1 Apr 59
Finland SIGNED: 3 Oct 57 RATIFIED: 6 Mar 59 FORCE: 1 Apr 59
France All Territories RATIFIED: 8 May 59 FORCE: 1 Apr 59
France SIGNED: 3 Oct 57 RATIFIED: 8 May 59 FORCE: 1 Apr 59
Germany, West SIGNED: 3 Oct 57 FORCE: 1 Apr 59
Greece SIGNED: 3 Oct 57 RATIFIED: 2 Oct 59 FORCE: 1 Apr 59
Haiti SIGNED: 3 Oct 57 FORCE: 1 Apr 59
Honduras SIGNED: 3 Oct 57 FORCE: 1 Apr 59
Hungary SIGNED: 3 Oct 57 RATIFIED: 5 Apr 60 FORCE: 1 Apr 59
Iceland SIGNED: 3 Oct 57 RATIFIED: 27 Nov 58 FORCE: 1 Apr 59
Indonesia SIGNED: 3 Oct 57 FORCE: 1 Apr 59
Italy SIGNED: 3 Oct 57 FORCE: 1 Apr 59
Italy Somalia RATIFIED: 3 Oct 57 FORCE: 1 Apr 59
Laos SIGNED: 3 Oct 57 RATIFIED: 13 Jan 60 FORCE: 1 Apr 59
Lebanon SIGNED: 3 Oct 57 FORCE: 1 Apr 59
Luxembourg SIGNED: 3 Oct 57 FORCE: 1 Apr 59
Monaco SIGNED: 3 Oct 57 RATIFIED: 2 Sep 59 FORCE: 1 Apr 59
Morocco SIGNED: 3 Oct 57 RATIFIED: 9 Jul 59 FORCE: 1 Apr 59
Netherlands SIGNED: 3 Oct 57 RATIFIED: 27 Aug 59 FORCE: 1 Apr 59
Netherlands Netherlands Antilles RATIFIED: 27 Aug 59 FORCE: 1 Apr 59
Netherlands Surinam RATIFIED: 27 Jul 59 FORCE: 1 Apr 59
Nicaragua SIGNED: 3 Oct 57 FORCE: 1 Apr 59
Norway SIGNED: 3 Oct 57 RATIFIED: 19 Aug 58 FORCE: 1 Apr 59
Paraguay SIGNED: 3 Oct 57 FORCE: 1 Apr 59
Portugal All Territories RATIFIED: 3 Oct 57 FORCE: 1 Apr 59
Portugal SIGNED: 3 Oct 57 FORCE: 1 Apr 59
Romania SIGNED: 3 Oct 57 FORCE: 1 Apr 59
San Marino SIGNED: 3 Oct 57 RATIFIED: 31 Mar 59 FORCE: 1 Apr 59
Spain SIGNED: 3 Oct 57 RATIFIED: 28 Jul 59 FORCE: 1 Apr 59
Spain Spanish Colonies RATIFIED: 29 Jul 59 FORCE: 1 Apr 59
Sweden SIGNED: 3 Oct 57 RATIFIED: 2 May 58 FORCE: 1 Apr 59
Switzerland SIGNED: 3 Oct 57 RATIFIED: 14 Nov 58 FORCE: 1 Apr 59
Thailand SIGNED: 3 Oct 57 FORCE: 1 Apr 59
Tunisia SIGNED: 3 Oct 57 RATIFIED: 24 Mar 59 FORCE: 1 Apr 59
Turkey SIGNED: 3 Oct 57 FORCE: 1 Apr 59
Uruguay SIGNED: 3 Oct 57 FORCE: 1 Apr 59
Vatican/Holy See SIGNED: 3 Oct 57 RATIFIED: 13 Apr 60 FORCE: 1 Apr 59

Venezuela SIGNED: 3 Oct 57 FORCE: 1 Apr 59
Vietnam SIGNED: 3 Oct 57 FORCE: 1 Apr 59
Yemen RATIFIED: 3 Apr 59
Yugoslavia SIGNED: 3 Oct 57 FORCE: 1 Apr 59
ANNEX
391 UNTS 331. Germany, West. Ratification 30 Aug 60.
391 UNTS 331. Somalia. Ratification 16 Nov 60.
391 UNTS 331. Italy. Ratification 9 Jun 60.
391 UNTS 331. Thailand. Ratification 21 Jul 60.
391 UNTS 331. Germany, West. Berlin.

105218 Multilateral Agreement **366 UNTS 193**
SIGNED: 3 Oct 57 FORCE: 1 Apr 59
REGISTERED: 7 Jul 60 Canada
ARTICLES: 22 LANGUAGE: French.
HEADNOTE: INTERNATIONAL SAVINGS BANK SERVICE
TOPIC: Postal Service
CONCEPTS: Detailed regulations. Responsibility and liability. Accounting procedures. Banking. Monetary and gold transfers. Currency deposits. Interest rates. Postal services. Money orders and postal checks. Conformity with IGO decisions.
INTL ORGS: Universal Postal Union.
TREATY REF: 364UNTS3.
PARTIES:
Belgium SIGNED: 5 Oct 57 FORCE: 1 Apr 59
Chile SIGNED: 5 Oct 57 FORCE: 1 Apr 59
United Arab Rep SIGNED: 5 Oct 57 RATIFIED: 15 Jan 58 FORCE: 1 Apr 59
France SIGNED: 5 Oct 57 RATIFIED: 8 May 59 FORCE: 1 Apr 59
Germany, West SIGNED: 5 Oct 57 FORCE: 1 Apr 59
Italy SIGNED: 5 Oct 57 RATIFIED: 9 Jun 60 FORCE: 1 Apr 59
Japan SIGNED: 5 Oct 57 RATIFIED: 7 Nov 58 FORCE: 1 Apr 59
Netherlands Netherlands Antilles RATIFIED: 25 Aug 59 FORCE: 1 Apr 59
Netherlands SIGNED: 3 Oct 57 RATIFIED: 25 Aug 59 FORCE: 1 Apr 59
Netherlands Surinam RATIFIED: 25 Aug 59 FORCE: 1 Apr 59
Norway SIGNED: 5 Oct 57 RATIFIED: 19 Aug 58 FORCE: 1 Apr 59
Paraguay SIGNED: 5 Oct 57 FORCE: 1 Apr 59
Spain SIGNED: 3 Oct 57 RATIFIED: 29 Jul 59 FORCE: 1 Apr 59
Spain Spanish Colonies RATIFIED: 29 Jul 59 FORCE: 1 Apr 59
Sweden SIGNED: 3 Oct 57 RATIFIED: 2 May 58 FORCE: 1 Apr 59
Turkey SIGNED: 3 Oct 57 FORCE: 1 Apr 59
Vietnam SIGNED: 3 Oct 57 FORCE: 1 Apr 59
ANNEX
391 UNTS 332. Germany, West. Ratification 30 Aug 60.
391 UNTS 332. Italy. Ratification 9 Jun 60.
391 UNTS 332. Germany, West. Berlin.

105219 Multilateral Agreement **366 UNTS 255**
SIGNED: 3 Oct 57 FORCE: 1 Apr 59
REGISTERED: 7 Jul 60 Canada
ARTICLES: 16 LANGUAGE: French.
HEADNOTE: SUBSCRIPTIONS NEWSPAPERS PERIODICALS
TOPIC: Postal Service
CONCEPTS: Responsibility and liability. Postal services. Rates and charges. Press and wire services. Conformity with IGO decisions.
INTL ORGS: Universal Postal Union.
TREATY REF: 36JUNTS3.
PROCEDURE: Duration.
PARTIES:
Albania SIGNED: 3 Oct 57 FORCE: 1 Apr 59
Algeria SIGNED: 3 Oct 57 RATIFIED: 8 May 59 FORCE: 1 Apr 59
Argentina SIGNED: 3 Oct 57 FORCE: 1 Apr 59
Austria SIGNED: 3 Oct 57 RATIFIED: 4 May 59 FORCE: 1 Apr 59
Belgium SIGNED: 3 Oct 57 RATIFIED: 5 Mar 59 FORCE: 1 Apr 59
Bolivia SIGNED: 3 Oct 57 FORCE: 1 Apr 59
Bulgaria SIGNED: 3 Oct 57 RATIFIED: 13 May 59 FORCE: 1 Apr 59
Cambodia SIGNED: 3 Oct 57 RATIFIED: 12 Jan 60 FORCE: 1 Apr 59
Chile SIGNED: 3 Oct 57 FORCE: 1 Apr 59
China SIGNED: 3 Oct 57 RATIFIED: 1 Oct 59 FORCE: 1 Apr 59

Colombia SIGNED: 3 Oct 57 FORCE: 1 Apr 59
Cuba SIGNED: 3 Oct 57 FORCE: 1 Apr 59
Denmark SIGNED: 3 Oct 57 RATIFIED:
13 Aug 58 FORCE: 1 Apr 59
Dominican Republic SIGNED: 3 Oct 57 FORCE:
1 Apr 59
United Arab Rep SIGNED: 3 Oct 57 RATIFIED:
15 Jan 59 FORCE: 1 Apr 59
Finland SIGNED: 3 Oct 57 RATIFIED: 6 Mar 59
FORCE: 1 Apr 59
France SIGNED: 3 Oct 57 RATIFIED: 8 May 59
FORCE: 1 Apr 59
Germany, West SIGNED: 3 Oct 57 RATIFIED:
15 Apr 59 FORCE: 1 Apr 59
Greece SIGNED: 3 Oct 57 RATIFIED: 2 Oct 59
FORCE: 1 Apr 59
Haiti SIGNED: 3 Oct 57 FORCE: 1 Apr 59
Honduras SIGNED: 3 Oct 57 FORCE: 1 Apr 59
Hungary SIGNED: 3 Oct 57 RATIFIED: 5 Apr 60
FORCE: 1 Apr 59
Italy SIGNED: 3 Oct 57 RATIFIED: 9 Jun 60
FORCE: 1 Apr 59
Italy Somalia RATIFIED: 3 Oct 57 FORCE:
1 Apr 59
Laos SIGNED: 3 Oct 57 FORCE: 1 Apr 59
Liberia SIGNED: 3 Oct 57 FORCE: 1 Apr 59
Luxembourg SIGNED: 3 Oct 57 RATIFIED:
13 Jan 60 FORCE: 1 Apr 59
Monaco SIGNED: 3 Oct 57 RATIFIED: 2 Sep 59
FORCE: 1 Apr 59
Morocco SIGNED: 3 Oct 57 RATIFIED: 9 Jul 59
FORCE: 1 Apr 59
Netherlands SIGNED: 3 Oct 57 RATIFIED:
27 Aug 59 FORCE: 1 Apr 59
Nicaragua SIGNED: 3 Oct 57 FORCE: 1 Apr 59
Norway SIGNED: 3 Oct 57 RATIFIED: 19 Aug 58
FORCE: 1 Apr 59
Paraguay SIGNED: 3 Oct 57 FORCE: 1 Apr 59
Poland SIGNED: 3 Oct 57 FORCE: 1 Apr 59
Portugal All Territories RATIFIED: 3 Oct 57
FORCE: 1 Apr 59
Portugal SIGNED: 3 Oct 57 FORCE: 1 Apr 59
Romania SIGNED: 3 Oct 57 FORCE: 1 Apr 59
San Marino SIGNED: 3 Oct 57 RATIFIED:
27 Jul 59 FORCE: 1 Apr 59
Spain SIGNED: 3 Oct 57 RATIFIED: 29 Jul 59
FORCE: 1 Apr 59
Spain Spanish Colonies RATIFIED: 29 Jul 59
FORCE: 1 Apr 59
Sweden SIGNED: 3 Oct 57 RATIFIED: 2 May 58
FORCE: 1 Apr 59
Switzerland SIGNED: 3 Oct 57 RATIFIED:
14 Nov 58 FORCE: 1 Apr 59
Thailand SIGNED: 3 Oct 57 FORCE: 1 Apr 59
Tunisia SIGNED: 3 Oct 57 RATIFIED: 24 Mar 59
FORCE: 1 Apr 59
Turkey SIGNED: 3 Oct 57 FORCE: 1 Apr 59
Uruguay SIGNED: 3 Oct 57 FORCE: 1 Apr 59
Vatican/Holy See SIGNED: 3 Oct 57 FORCE:
1 Apr 59
Venezuela SIGNED: 3 Oct 57 FORCE: 1 Apr 59
Vietnam SIGNED: 3 Oct 57 FORCE: 1 Apr 59
Yemen RATIFIED: 3 Apr 59 FORCE: 1 Apr 59
Yugoslavia SIGNED: 3 Oct 57 FORCE: 1 Apr 59
ANNEX
391 UNTS 333. Germany, West. Ratification
30 Aug 60.
391 UNTS 333. Italy. Ratification 9 Jun 60.
391 UNTS 333. Thailand. Ratification 21 Jul 60.
391 UNTS 333. Somalia. Ratification 16 Nov 60.
391 UNTS 333. Poland. Ratification 23 Feb 61.
391 UNTS 333. Germany, West. Berlin.

105220 Multilateral Agreement **366 UNTS 310**
SIGNED: 8 Jul 60 FORCE: 8 Jul 60
REGISTERED: 8 Jul 60 United Nations
ARTICLES: 6 LANGUAGE: English.
HEADNOTE: TECHNICAL ASSISTANCE
TOPIC: Tech Assistance
CONCEPTS: Definition of terms. Annex or appen-
dix reference. Previous treaty replacement. Privi-
leges and immunities. General cooperation. Ex-
change of information and documents. Personnel.
Responsibility and liability. Title and deeds.
Use of facilities. Exchange. Scholarships and
grants. Vocational training. Research and devel-
opment. Exchange rates and regulations. Ex-
pense sharing formulae. Local currency. Domestic obligation. General technical assistance. Materials, equipment and services. IGO status.
Conformity with IGO decisions.
TREATY REF: 76UNTS132; 92UNTS27.

PROCEDURE: Amendment. Termination. Application to Non-self-governing Territories.
PARTIES:
FAO (Food Agri) SIGNED: 8 Jul 60 FORCE:
8 Jul 60
IAEA (Atom Energy) SIGNED: 8 Jul 60 FORCE:
8 Jul 60
ICAO (Civil Aviat) SIGNED: 8 Jul 60 FORCE:
8 Jul 60
ILO (Labor Org) SIGNED: 8 Jul 60 FORCE:
8 Jul 60
ITU (Telecommun) SIGNED: 8 Jul 60 FORCE:
8 Jul 60
UNESCO (Educ/Cult) SIGNED: 8 Jul 60 FORCE:
8 Jul 60
United Nations SIGNED: 8 Jul 60 FORCE:
8 Jul 60
WHO (World Health) SIGNED: 8 Jul 60 FORCE:
8 Jul 60
WMO (Meteorology) SIGNED: 8 Jul 60 FORCE:
8 Jul 60
UK Great Britain SIGNED: 8 Jul 60 FORCE:
8 Jul 60
ANNEX
463 UNTS 356. UNTAB (Tech Assis). Amendment
10 May 63. Force 10 May 63.
463 UNTS 356. UK Great Britain. Amendment
10 May 63. Force 10 May 63.
490 UNTS 464. UK Great Britain. Supplementation 26 Feb 64. Force 26 Feb 64.
490 UNTS 464. UNTAB (Tech Assis). Supplementation 17 Feb 64. Force 26 Feb 64.

105221 Bilateral Agreement **366 UNTS 331**
SIGNED: 27 Nov 59 FORCE: 27 Nov 59
REGISTERED: 11 Jul 60 USA (United States)
ARTICLES: 8 LANGUAGE: English. French.
HEADNOTE: MILITARY CEMETERIES
TOPIC: Other Military
CONCEPTS: Definition of terms. Annex or appen-
dix reference. Previous treaty replacement. Re-
sponsibility and liability. Reexport of goods, etc..
Indemnities and reimbursements. Tax exemp-
tions. Customs exemptions. Materials, equip-
ment and services. Establishment of war ceme-
teries.
TREATY REF: 173UNTS67.
PARTIES:
Belgium
USA (United States)
ANNEX
489 UNTS 393. USA (United States). Correction
8 Jan 62. Force 24 Oct 63.
489 UNTS 393. Belgium. Correction 24 Oct 63.
Force 24 Oct 63.

105222 Bilateral Agreement **366 UNTS 343**
SIGNED: 28 Feb 58 FORCE: 28 Feb 58
REGISTERED: 11 Jul 60 USA (United States)
ARTICLES: 6 LANGUAGE: English. French.
HEADNOTE: AGRI COMMOD TITLE I
TOPIC: US Agri Commod Aid
CONCEPTS: General provisions. Annex or appendix reference. Exchange of information and documents. Reexport of goods, etc.. Exchange rates
and regulations. Transportation costs. Local currency. Commodities schedule. Purchase authorization. Surplus commodities. Mutual consultation.
PARTIES:
France
USA (United States)
ANNEX
410 UNTS 354. USA (United States). Supplementation 12 Jun 61. Force 12 Jun 61.
410 UNTS 354. France. Supplementation
12 Jun 61. Force 12 Jun 61.

105223 Bilateral Exchange **366 UNTS 361**
SIGNED: 6 Aug 58 FORCE: 6 Aug 58
REGISTERED: 11 Jul 60 USA (United States)
ARTICLES: 2 LANGUAGE: English.
HEADNOTE: STATUS FORCES
TOPIC: Status of Forces
CONCEPTS: Inviolability. Claims and settlements.
Tax exemptions. Customs exemptions. Security
of information. Jurisdiction. Procurement and lo-
gistics. Status of forces.
PARTIES:
Lebanon
USA (United States)

105224 Bilateral Treaty **367 UNTS 3**
SIGNED: 21 Jan 56 FORCE: 24 May 58
REGISTERED: 11 Jul 60 USA (United States)
ARTICLES: 25 LANGUAGE: English. Spanish.
HEADNOTE: FRIENDSHIP COMMERCE NAVIGA-
TION
TOPIC: General Amity
CONCEPTS: Definition of terms. Exceptions and
exemptions. Territorial application. Friendship
and amity. Alien status. General cooperation. Exchange of information and documents. Juridical
personality. Free passage and transit. Legal pro-
tection and assistance. Immovable property.
General property. Private contracts. Existing tri-
bunals. Export quotas. Import quotas. Free trade.
Reciprocity in trade. Exchange rates and regula-
tions. Fees and exemptions. Most favored nation
clause. National treatment. Taxation. Income
taxes. Recognition. Navigational conditions. Inland and territorial waters.
INTL ORGS: International Court of Justice.
TREATY REF: GATT.
PROCEDURE: Duration. Ratification. Termination.
PARTIES:
Nicaragua
USA (United States)

105225 Bilateral Agreement **367 UNTS 57**
SIGNED: 22 Dec 59 FORCE: 22 Dec 59
REGISTERED: 11 Jul 60 USA (United States)
ARTICLES: 6 LANGUAGE: English.
HEADNOTE: AGRI COMMOD TITLE I
TOPIC: US Agri Commod Aid
CONCEPTS: General provisions. Annex or appendix reference. Exchange of information and documents. Reexport of goods, etc.. Exchange rates
and regulations. Transportation costs. Local currency. Commodities schedule. Purchase authorization. Surplus commodities. Mutual consultation.
PARTIES:
Turkey
USA (United States)
ANNEX
378 UNTS 418. USA (United States). Amendment
31 May 60. Force 31 May 60.
378 UNTS 418. Turkey. Amendment 31 May 60.
Force 31 May 60.
401 UNTS 334. USA (United States). Amendment
22 Oct 60. Force 22 Oct 60.
401 UNTS 334. Turkey. Amendment 22 Oct 60.
Force 22 Oct 60.

105226 Bilateral Exchange **367 UNTS 75**
SIGNED: 6 Jan 60 FORCE: 5 Feb 60
REGISTERED: 11 Jul 60 USA (United States)
ARTICLES: 2 LANGUAGE: English. French.
HEADNOTE: RADIO COMMUNICATIONS AMA-
TEUR STATIONS BEHALF THIRD PARTIES
TOPIC: Gen Communications
CONCEPTS: Amateur radio. Amateur third party
message. Radio-telephone-telegraphic commu-
nications.
PROCEDURE: Termination.
PARTIES:
Haiti
USA (United States)

105227 Bilateral Exchange **367 UNTS 81**
SIGNED: 12 Nov 59 FORCE: 12 Dec 59
REGISTERED: 11 Jul 60 USA (United States)
ARTICLES: 2 LANGUAGE: English. Spanish.
HEADNOTE: RADIO COMMUNICATIONS AMA-
TEUR STATIONS BEHALF THIRD PARTIES
TOPIC: Gen Communications
CONCEPTS: Amateur radio. Amateur third party
message. Radio-telephone-telegraphic commu-
nications.
PROCEDURE: Termination.
PARTIES:
USA (United States)
Venezuela

105228 Bilateral Agreement **367 UNTS 89**
SIGNED: 4 Apr 58 FORCE: 29 Dec 59
REGISTERED: 12 Jul 60 Yugoslavia
ARTICLES: 8 LANGUAGE: Serbo-Croat. Bulgarian.
HEADNOTE: WATER-ECONOMY QUESTIONS
TOPIC: Water Transport
CONCEPTS: Frontier formalities. Passports non-

diplomatic. General cooperation. Exchange of information and documents. Establishment of commission. Procedure. Currency deposits. Fees and exemptions. Funding procedures. Tax exemptions. Customs exemptions. Water transport. Canal improvement. Inland and territorial waters. Regulation of natural resources.
INTL ORGS: Claims Commission.
PROCEDURE: Denunciation. Duration. Ratification. Renewal or Revival.
PARTIES:
Bulgaria
Yugoslavia

105229 Bilateral Agreement **367 UNTS 119**
SIGNED: 22 May 56   FORCE: 31 Jan 57
REGISTERED: 12 Jul 60 Yugoslavia
ARTICLES: 20 LANGUAGE: Serbo-Croat. Bulgarian.
HEADNOTE: ORGANIZATION FRONTIER TRANSIT SERVICE
TOPIC: Visas
CONCEPTS: Territorial application. General provisions. Previous treaty replacement. Border traffic and migration. Frontier permits. General cooperation. Exchange of information and documents. Responsibility and liability. Border control. Veterinary. Tariffs. Payment schedules. Customs duties. Routes and logistics. Agricultural vehicles and construction. Railway border crossing. Railways. Postal services. Markers and definitions. Frontier peoples and personnel.
PROCEDURE: Denunciation.
PARTIES:
Bulgaria
Yugoslavia

105230 Bilateral Treaty **367 UNTS 213**
SIGNED: 23 Mar 56   FORCE: 26 Jan 57
REGISTERED: 12 Jul 60 Yugoslavia
ARTICLES: 89 LANGUAGE: Serbo-Croat. Bulgarian.
HEADNOTE: MUTUAL LEGAL ASSISTANCE
TOPIC: Admin Cooperation
CONCEPTS: Previous treaty replacement. Consular functions in property. Extradition, deportation and repatriation. Extradition requests. Extraditable offenses. Special factors. Refusal of extradition. Family law. Exchange of information and documents. Juridical personality. Legal protection and assistance. Recognition and enforcement of legal decisions. Succession. Recognition of legal documents. Procedure. Indemnities and reimbursements. Fees and exemptions. Conveyance in transit.
TREATY REF: 26LTS85; 26LTS199.
PROCEDURE: Ratification. Termination.
PARTIES:
Bulgaria
Yugoslavia

105231 Bilateral Agreement **368 UNTS 3**
SIGNED: 18 Jun 59   FORCE: 11 Nov 59
REGISTERED: 12 Jul 60 Yugoslavia
ARTICLES: 6 LANGUAGE: French.
HEADNOTE: COMPENSATION NATIONALIZED PROPERTY
TOPIC: Claims and Debts
CONCEPTS: Exchange of information and documents. Informational records. Expropriation. General property. Balance of payments. Currency. Payment schedules. Lump sum settlements.
PROCEDURE: Ratification.
PARTIES:
Greece
Yugoslavia

105232 Bilateral Agreement **368 UNTS 9**
SIGNED: 18 Jun 59   FORCE: 11 Nov 59
REGISTERED: 12 Jul 60 Yugoslavia
ARTICLES: 4 LANGUAGE: French.
HEADNOTE: SETTLEMENT CLAIMS AND DEBTS
TOPIC: Claims and Debts
CONCEPTS: Detailed regulations. Exchange of information and documents. Informational records. Responsibility and liability. Claims and settlements. Debt settlement.
PROCEDURE: Ratification.

PARTIES:
Greece
Yugoslavia

105233 Bilateral Agreement **368 UNTS 17**
SIGNED: 18 Jun 59   FORCE: 1 Mar 60
REGISTERED: 12 Jul 60 Yugoslavia
ARTICLES: 14 LANGUAGE: French.
HEADNOTE: DEVELOPMENT TOURING
TOPIC: IGO Establishment
CONCEPTS: Tourism. General transportation. Routes and logistics. Establishment.
INTL ORGS: Special Commission.
PROCEDURE: Denunciation. Duration. Ratification.
PARTIES:
Greece
Yugoslavia

105234 Bilateral Agreement **368 UNTS 27**
SIGNED: 18 Jun 59   FORCE: 5 Oct 59
REGISTERED: 12 Jul 60 Yugoslavia
ARTICLES: 45 LANGUAGE: French.
HEADNOTE: REGULATIONS ROAD TRANSPORT PASSENGERS GOODS COMMERCIAL VEHICLES
TOPIC: Land Transport
CONCEPTS: Conditions. Default remedies. Definition of terms. General provisions. Annex or appendix reference. Passports non-diplomatic. Visas. Conformity with municipal law. General cooperation. Exchange of information and documents. Informational records. Establishment of commission. Compensation. Currency. Payment schedules. Non-interest rates and fees. Tax exemptions. Customs exemptions. Registration certificate. Passenger transport. Routes and logistics. Transport of goods. Commercial road vehicles. Driving permits. Roads and highways. Road rules.
INTL ORGS: Special Commission.
TREATY REF: 45UNTS149; 212UNTS296; 327UNTS123; 348UNTS13.
PROCEDURE: Denunciation. Duration. Ratification. Renewal or Revival.
PARTIES:
Greece
Yugoslavia

105235 Bilateral Agreement **368 UNTS 69**
SIGNED: 18 Jun 59   FORCE: 31 Mar 60
REGISTERED: 12 Jul 60 Yugoslavia
ARTICLES: 13 LANGUAGE: French.
HEADNOTE: RECOGNITION ENFORCEMENT JUDICIAL DECISIONS
TOPIC: Admin Cooperation
CONCEPTS: Recognition and enforcement of legal decisions. Arbitration. Procedure. Special tribunals.
INTL ORGS: International Court of Justice. Arbitration Commission.
PROCEDURE: Denunciation. Ratification.
PARTIES:
Greece
Yugoslavia

105236 Bilateral Convention **368 UNTS 81**
SIGNED: 18 Jun 59   FORCE: 31 Mar 60
REGISTERED: 12 Jul 60 Yugoslavia
ARTICLES: 68 LANGUAGE: French.
HEADNOTE: MUTUAL LEGAL RELATIONS
TOPIC: Admin Cooperation
CONCEPTS: General provisions. Extradition, deportation and repatriation. Extradition requests. Location of crime. Refusal of extradition. Family law. Exchange of information and documents. Juridical personality. Legal protection and assistance. Recognition of legal documents. Procedure. Indemnities and reimbursements. Fees and exemptions. Conveyance in transit.
PROCEDURE: Denunciation. Ratification.
PARTIES:
Greece
Yugoslavia

105237 Bilateral Agreement **368 UNTS 125**
SIGNED: 18 Jun 59   FORCE: 1 Mar 60
REGISTERED: 12 Jul 60 Yugoslavia
ARTICLES: 17 LANGUAGE: French.
HEADNOTE: STATUTE MIXED YUGOSLAV-GREEK COMMITTEE ECONOMIC COOPERATION

TOPIC: Admin Cooperation
CONCEPTS: Treaty implementation. General cooperation. Establishment of commission. Payment schedules. General technical assistance. Economic assistance. Conferences.
INTL ORGS: Special Commission.
PROCEDURE: Duration. Ratification. Renewal or Revival.
PARTIES:
Greece
Yugoslavia

105238 Bilateral Agreement **368 UNTS 137**
SIGNED: 18 Jun 59   FORCE: 1 Jan 60
REGISTERED: 12 Jul 60 Yugoslavia
ARTICLES: 8 LANGUAGE: French.
HEADNOTE: SCIENTIFIC CULTURAL COOPERATION
TOPIC: Culture
CONCEPTS: Friendship and amity. Conformity with municipal law. Responsibility and liability. Establishment of commission. Scholarships and grants. Exchange. General cultural cooperation. Artists. Research results. Scientific exchange. Research and development. Mass media exchange.
INTL ORGS: Special Commission.
PROCEDURE: Denunciation. Duration. Ratification. Renewal or Revival.
PARTIES:
Greece
Yugoslavia

105239 Bilateral Agreement **368 UNTS 143**
SIGNED: 13 Jul 60   FORCE: 13 Jul 60
REGISTERED: 13 Jul 60 United Nations
ARTICLES: 6 LANGUAGE: English.
HEADNOTE: OPERATIONAL EXECUTIVE PERSONNEL
TOPIC: Tech Assistance
CONCEPTS: Treaty implementation. Annex or appendix reference. Privileges and immunities. Personnel. Responsibility and liability. Arbitration. Procedure. Negotiation. Vocational training. Compensation. Expense sharing formulae. Tax exemptions. Customs exemptions. Domestic obligation. Special projects. Status of experts. Conformity with IGO decisions.
INTL ORGS: Permanent Court of Arbitration.
PROCEDURE: Amendment. Termination.
PARTIES:
Ethiopia
United Nations
ANNEX
550 UNTS 408. United Nations. Force 12 Nov 65.
550 UNTS 408. Ethiopia. Force 12 Nov 65.

105240 Bilateral Agreement **368 UNTS 159**
SIGNED: 13 Jul 60   FORCE: 13 Jul 60
REGISTERED: 13 Jul 60 United Nations
ARTICLES: 10 LANGUAGE: English.
HEADNOTE: ASSISTANCE
TOPIC: Tech Assistance
CONCEPTS: Detailed regulations. Treaty implementation. Annex or appendix reference. Visas. Privileges and immunities. General cooperation. Exchange of information and documents. Inspection and observation. Operating agencies. Licenses and permits. General property. Public information. Responsibility and liability. Title and deeds. Use of facilities. Arbitration. Procedure. Negotiation. Import quotas. Reexport of goods, etc.. Accounting procedures. Exchange rates and regulations. Fees and exemptions. Financial programs. Tax exemptions. Customs exemptions. Domestic obligation. General technical assistance. Materials, equipment and services. IGO status. Conformity with IGO decisions.
INTL ORGS: United Nations.
TREATY REF: 1UNTS15;33UNTS261.
PROCEDURE: Amendment. Ratification. Termination.
PARTIES:
Ethiopia
UN Special Fund

105241 Bilateral Agreement **368 UNTS 181**
SIGNED: 7 Jan 60   FORCE: 7 Jan 60
REGISTERED: 13 Jul 60 USA (United States)
ARTICLES: 6 LANGUAGE: English.

HEADNOTE: AGRICULTURAL COMMODITIES
TOPIC: US Agri Commod Aid
CONCEPTS: Currency. Agricultural commodities. Economic assistance.
PARTIES:
Israel
USA (United States)
ANNEX
377 UNTS 452. Israel. Supplementation 30 Jun 60. Force 30 Jun 60.
377 UNTS 452. USA (United States). Supplementation 30 Jun 60. Force 30 Jun 60.
413 UNTS 384. USA (United States). Amendment 22 Sep 61. Force 9 Oct 61.
413 UNTS 384. Israel. Amendment 9 Oct 61. Force 9 Oct 61.
434 UNTS 342. USA (United States). Amendment 5 Dec 61. Force 8 Dec 61.
434 UNTS 342. Israel. Amendment 8 Dec 61. Force 8 Dec 61.

105242 Bilateral Agreement **368 UNTS 199**
SIGNED: 22 Jul 59   FORCE: 25 Jan 60
REGISTERED: 13 Jul 60 USA (United States)
ARTICLES: 12 LANGUAGE: English.
HEADNOTE: COOPERATION CIVIL USES ATOMIC ENERGY
TOPIC: Atomic Energy
CONCEPTS: Definition of terms. Previous treaty replacement. Conformity with municipal law. Exchange of information and documents. Inspection and observation. Investigation of violations. Assets transfer. Nuclear materials. Non-nuclear materials. Peaceful use. Security of information.
INTL ORGS: International Atomic Energy Agency.
TREATY REF: 253UNTS139.
PROCEDURE: Duration.
PARTIES:
Austria
USA (United States)

105243 Bilateral Agreement **368 UNTS 221**
SIGNED: 7 Jan 60   FORCE: 7 Jan 60
REGISTERED: 13 Jul 60 USA (United States)
ARTICLES: 6 LANGUAGE: English.
HEADNOTE: AGRI COMMOD TITLE I
TOPIC: US Agri Commod Aid
CONCEPTS: General provisions. Annex or appendix reference. Exchange of information and documents. Reexport of goods, etc.. Exchange rates and regulations. Transportation costs. Local currency. Assets transfer. Commodities schedule. Purchase authorization. Surplus commodities.
PARTIES:
Greece
USA (United States)
ANNEX
407 UNTS 290. USA (United States). Supplementation 20 Apr 61. Force 29 Apr 61.
407 UNTS 290. Greece. Supplementation 29 Apr 61. Force 29 Apr 61.

105244 Multilateral Convention **368 UNTS 237**
SIGNED: 14 Dec 59   FORCE: 13 Apr 60
REGISTERED: 14 Jul 60 USSR (Soviet Union)
ARTICLES: 6 LANGUAGE: Russian.
HEADNOTE: COUNCIL MUTUAL ECONOMIC ASSISTANCE
TOPIC: IGO Status/Immunit
CONCEPTS: Diplomatic missions. Inviolability. Privileges and immunities. Property. Diplomatic correspondence. Juridical personality. IGO obligations. Special status.
INTL ORGS: Council for Mutual Economic Assistance.
PROCEDURE: Ratification.
PARTIES:
Albania   SIGNED: 14 Dec 59   RATIFIED: 13 Apr 60 FORCE: 13 Apr 60
Bulgaria   SIGNED: 14 Dec 59   RATIFIED: 13 Apr 60 FORCE: 13 Apr 60
Czechoslovakia SIGNED: 14 Dec 59 RATIFIED: 13 Apr 60 FORCE: 13 Apr 60
Germany, East SIGNED: 14 Dec 59 RATIFIED: 13 Apr 60 FORCE: 13 Apr 60
Hungary   SIGNED: 14 Dec 59   RATIFIED: 13 Apr 60 FORCE: 13 Apr 60
Poland SIGNED: 14 Dec 59 RATIFIED: 13 Apr 60 FORCE: 13 Apr 60
Romania   SIGNED: 14 Dec 59   RATIFIED: 13 Apr 60 FORCE: 13 Apr 60

USSR (Soviet Union) SIGNED: 14 Dec 59 RATIFIED: 13 Apr 60 FORCE: 13 Apr 60

105245 Multilateral Protocol **368 UNTS 253**
SIGNED: 14 Dec 59   FORCE: 13 Apr 60
REGISTERED: 14 Jul 60 USSR (Soviet Union)
ARTICLES: 17 LANGUAGE: Russian.
HEADNOTE: ECONOMIC ASSISTANCE
TOPIC: IGO Establishment
CONCEPTS: Non-prejudice to UN charter. Exchange of information and documents. Juridical personality. Research cooperation. Accounting procedures. Funding procedures. General technical assistance. Economic assistance. Admission. Subsidiary organ. Establishment. Procedure. Headquarters and facilities. Liaison with other IGO's. Internal structure. Special status. Status of experts. Conformity with IGO decisions.
INTL ORGS: Council for Mutual Economic Assistance.
PROCEDURE: Amendment. Denunciation. Ratification.
PARTIES:
Albania   SIGNED: 14 Dec 59   RATIFIED: 13 Apr 60 FORCE: 13 Apr 60
Bulgaria   SIGNED: 14 Dec 59   RATIFIED: 13 Apr 60 FORCE: 13 Apr 60
Czechoslovakia SIGNED: 14 Dec 59 RATIFIED: 13 Apr 60 FORCE: 13 Apr 60
Germany, East SIGNED: 14 Dec 59 RATIFIED: 13 Apr 60 FORCE: 13 Apr 60
Hungary   SIGNED: 14 Dec 59   RATIFIED: 13 Apr 60 FORCE: 13 Apr 60
Poland SIGNED: 14 Dec 59 RATIFIED: 13 Apr 60 FORCE: 13 Apr 60
Romania   SIGNED: 14 Dec 59   RATIFIED: 13 Apr 60 FORCE: 13 Apr 60
USSR (Soviet Union) SIGNED: 14 Dec 59 RATIFIED: 13 Apr 60 FORCE: 13 Apr 60

105246 Bilateral Agreement **368 UNTS 287**
SIGNED: 11 Dec 59   FORCE: 1 May 60
REGISTERED: 14 Jul 60 USSR (Soviet Union)
ARTICLES: 20 LANGUAGE: Russian. Bulgarian.
HEADNOTE: SOCIAL SECURITY
TOPIC: Non-ILO Labor
CONCEPTS: Information centers. Social security.
PROCEDURE: Ratification.
PARTIES:
Bulgaria
USSR (Soviet Union)

105247 Bilateral Agreement **369 UNTS 3**
SIGNED: 13 Feb 60   FORCE: 12 May 60
REGISTERED: 14 Jul 60 USSR (Soviet Union)
ARTICLES: 6 LANGUAGE: Russian. Spanish.
HEADNOTE: GRANTING CREDIT
TOPIC: Claims and Debts
CONCEPTS: Accounting procedures. Banking. Currency. Exchange rates and regulations. Interest rates. Commodity trade. General technical assistance. Materials, equipment and services. Procurement. Loan and credit. Credit provisions. Purchase authorization.
TREATY REF: 369UNTS17.
PROCEDURE: Future Procedures Contemplated. Ratification.
PARTIES:
Cuba
USSR (Soviet Union)

105248 Bilateral Agreement **369 UNTS 17**
SIGNED: 13 Feb 60   FORCE: 12 May 60
REGISTERED: 14 Jul 60 USSR (Soviet Union)
ARTICLES: 12 LANGUAGE: Russian. Spanish.
HEADNOTE: TRADE DEVELOPMENT
TOPIC: General Economic
CONCEPTS: Exceptions and exemptions. Treaty implementation. Annex or appendix reference. Licenses and permits. Establishment of commission. Establishment of trade relations. Reexport of goods, etc.. Accounting procedures. Banking. Balance of payments. Currency. Financial programs. Interest rates. Payment schedules. Commodity trade. Most favored nation clause. General. Customs duties. Merchant vessels. Ports and pilotage.
INTL ORGS: Special Commission.

PROCEDURE: Duration. Future Procedures Contemplated. Ratification.
PARTIES:
Cuba
USSR (Soviet Union)

105249 Bilateral Exchange **369 UNTS 37**
SIGNED: 4 May 53   FORCE: 4 May 53
REGISTERED: 18 Jul 60 Brazil
ARTICLES: 2 LANGUAGE: Spanish. Portuguese.
HEADNOTE: INTENSIFYING TRADE
TOPIC: General Trade
CONCEPTS: Establishment of commission. General trade.
INTL ORGS. Special Commission.
PARTIES:
Brazil
Ecuador

105250 Bilateral Agreement **369 UNTS 43**
SIGNED: 5 Mar 58   FORCE: 5 Mar 58
REGISTERED: 18 Jul 60 Brazil
ARTICLES: 8 LANGUAGE: Spanish. Portuguese.
HEADNOTE: ECONOMIC TECHNICAL COOPERATION
TOPIC: General Economic
CONCEPTS: Establishment of commission. General trade. General technical assistance. Economic assistance.
INTL ORGS: Special Commission.
PARTIES:
Brazil
Ecuador

105251 Bilateral Agreement **369 UNTS 57**
SIGNED: 1 Apr 55   FORCE: 1 Apr 55
REGISTERED: 18 Jul 60 Ceylon (Sri Lanka)
ARTICLES: 12 LANGUAGE: English. German.
HEADNOTE: COMMERCE TRADE
TOPIC: General Trade
CONCEPTS: Territorial application. Treaty implementation. Annex or appendix reference. Previous treaty replacement. General cooperation. Licenses and permits. Teacher and student exchange. Vocational training. Import quotas. Trade procedures. Accounting procedures. Payment schedules. Quotas. Customs duties. General technical assistance. General aid. Economic assistance. Materials, equipment and services.
INTL ORGS: Organization for Economic Co-operation and Development.
TREATY REF: 22NOV52 TRADE AGREEMENT.
PROCEDURE: Termination.
PARTIES:
Ceylon (Sri Lanka)
Germany, West
ANNEX
392 UNTS 393. Ceylon (Sri Lanka). Amendment 20 Mar 57. Force 20 Mar 57.
392 UNTS 393. Germany, West. Amendment 20 Mar 57. Force 20 Mar 57.

105252 Bilateral Agreement **369 UNTS 81**
SIGNED: 10 Sep 58   FORCE: 10 Sep 58
REGISTERED: 19 Jul 60 Pakistan
ARTICLES: 3 LANGUAGE: English.
HEADNOTE: BORDER DISPUTES
TOPIC: Territory Boundary
CONCEPTS: Procedure. Markers and definitions.
TREATY REF: 50LTS180.
PARTIES:
India
Pakistan

105253 Bilateral Agreement **369 UNTS 89**
SIGNED: 12 Feb 60   FORCE: 30 Jun 60
REGISTERED: 20 Jul 60 Australia
ARTICLES: 9 LANGUAGE: English.
HEADNOTE: TRADE
TOPIC: General Trade
CONCEPTS: Detailed regulations. General provisions. Annex or appendix reference. Previous treaty replacement. Conformity with municipal law. General cooperation. Tariffs. Reciprocity in trade. Trade procedures. Transportation costs. Customs duties. Transport of goods.
PROCEDURE: Duration. Ratification. Termination.

PARTIES:
Australia
Canada

105254 Bilateral Agreement **369 UNTS 119**
SIGNED: 12 May 60   FORCE: 23 Jun 60
REGISTERED: 20 Jul 60 Australia
ARTICLES: 17 LANGUAGE: English.
HEADNOTE: DOUBLE TAXATION FISCAL EVASION TAXES INCOME
TOPIC: Taxation
CONCEPTS: Definition of terms. Conformity with municipal law. Exchange of official publications. Teacher and student exchange. Taxation. Tax credits. General. Tax exemptions.
PROCEDURE: Duration. Termination.
PARTIES:
Australia
New Zealand

105255 Bilateral Agreement **369 UNTS 141**
SIGNED: 28 May 58   FORCE: 28 May 58
REGISTERED: 21 Jul 60 Brazil
ARTICLES: 8 LANGUAGE: Spanish. Portuguese.
HEADNOTE: ECONOMIC TECHNICAL COOPERATION
TOPIC: Tech Assistance
CONCEPTS: Establishment of commission. General technical assistance. Economic assistance.
INTL ORGS: Special Commission.
PARTIES:
Brazil
Colombia

105256 Bilateral Convention **369 UNTS 155**
SIGNED: 7 Mar 56   FORCE: 25 May 59
REGISTERED: 22 Jul 60 Sweden
ARTICLES: 16 LANGUAGE: French.
HEADNOTE: JUDICIAL ASSISTANCE CRIMINAL MATTERS
TOPIC: Admin Cooperation
CONCEPTS: Definition of terms. Territorial application. Witnesses and experts. Exchange of information and documents.
PROCEDURE: Ratification. Termination.
PARTIES:
France
Sweden

105257 Bilateral Convention **369 UNTS 171**
SIGNED: 7 Mar 56   FORCE: 25 May 59
REGISTERED: 22 Jul 60 Sweden
ARTICLES: 12 LANGUAGE: French.
HEADNOTE: LEGAL ASSISTANCE CIVIL COMMERCIAL MATTERS
TOPIC: Admin Cooperation
CONCEPTS: General cooperation. Legal protection and assistance.
PROCEDURE: Ratification. Termination.
PARTIES:
France
Sweden

105258 Bilateral Agreement **369 UNTS 183**
SIGNED: 25 Aug 58   FORCE: 26 Feb 59
REGISTERED: 22 Jul 60 Sweden
ARTICLES: 23 LANGUAGE: English.
HEADNOTE: DOUBLE TAXATION FISCAL EVASION TAXES INCOME
TOPIC: Taxation
CONCEPTS: Definition of terms. Territorial application. Conformity with municipal law. Exchange of official publications. Teacher and student exchange. Taxation. Death duties. Tax credits. General. Tax exemptions. Air transport.
PROCEDURE: Duration. Ratification. Termination.
PARTIES:
Pakistan
Sweden

105259 Bilateral Agreement **369 UNTS 211**
SIGNED: 30 Jul 58   FORCE: 23 Jan 59
REGISTERED: 22 Jul 60 Sweden
ARTICLES: 21 LANGUAGE: English.
HEADNOTE: DOUBLE TAXATION INCOME
TOPIC: Taxation
CONCEPTS: Definition of terms. Conformity with municipal law. Exchange of official publications.

Teacher and student exchange. Taxation. Tax exemptions. Air transport. Merchant vessels.
PROCEDURE: Duration. Ratification. Termination.
PARTIES:
India
Sweden

105260 Bilateral Convention **369 UNTS 233**
SIGNED: 17 Dec 54   FORCE: 1 Sep 55
REGISTERED: 22 Jul 60 Sweden
ARTICLES: 19 LANGUAGE: Swedish. German.
HEADNOTE: SOCIAL INSURANCE
TOPIC: Non-ILO Labor
CONCEPTS: Exceptions and exemptions. Nationality and citizenship. Notarial acts and services. Domestic legislation. Dispute settlement. Old age and invalidity insurance. Wages and salaries. Non-ILO labor relations. Administrative cooperation. Sickness and invalidity insurance. Social security. Payment schedules.
INTL ORGS: Arbitration Commission.
PROCEDURE: Denunciation. Duration. Ratification. Renewal or Revival.
PARTIES:
Sweden
Switzerland

105261 Bilateral Agreement **369 UNTS 275**
SIGNED: 6 Mar 56   FORCE: 6 Mar 56
REGISTERED: 22 Jul 60 Sweden
ARTICLES: 6 LANGUAGE: English.
HEADNOTE: SAFEGUARD DEVELOP COMMERCIAL RELATIONS
TOPIC: General Trade
CONCEPTS: Annex or appendix reference. General cooperation. Licenses and permits. General transportation. Water transport.
PROCEDURE: Duration. Termination.
PARTIES:
Burma
Sweden

105262 Bilateral Agreement **369 UNTS 285**
SIGNED: 9 Mar 56   FORCE: 1 Jul 56
REGISTERED: 22 Jul 60 Sweden
ARTICLES: 8 LANGUAGE: Swedish. Norwegian.
HEADNOTE: TRANSIT TRAFFIC VIA PARTS TRONDHEIM FIORD
TOPIC: Land Transport
CONCEPTS: Change of circumstances. Negotiation. Expense sharing formulae. Fees and exemptions. Routes and logistics. Transport of goods. Ports and pilotage. Railway border crossing. Railways. Roads and highways. Boundaries of territory.
PROCEDURE: Amendment. Denunciation. Duration. Ratification. Renewal or Revival.
PARTIES:
Norway
Sweden

105263 Bilateral Convention **369 UNTS 305**
SIGNED: 20 Dec 56   FORCE: 3 Jun 58
REGISTERED: 22 Jul 60 Sweden
ARTICLES: 12 LANGUAGE: Swedish. Italian.
HEADNOTE: DOUBLE TAXATION INHERITANCE TAXES
TOPIC: Taxation
CONCEPTS: Nationality and citizenship. Claims and settlements. Debts. Taxation. Death duties. Tax exemptions.
PROCEDURE: Duration. Ratification. Termination.
PARTIES:
Italy
Sweden

105264 Bilateral Agreement **369 UNTS 323**
SIGNED: 29 Jul 58   FORCE: 9 Jan 59
REGISTERED: 22 Jul 60 Sweden
ARTICLES: 25 LANGUAGE: English.
HEADNOTE: DOUBLE TAXATION FISCAL EVASION TAXES INCOME CAPITAL
TOPIC: Taxation
CONCEPTS: Definition of terms. Exchange of official publications. Teacher and student exchange. Taxation. Death duties. Tax credits. Equitable taxes. General. Tax exemptions.
PROCEDURE: Duration. Ratification. Termination.

PARTIES:
Sweden
United Arab Rep

105265 Bilateral Agreement **369 UNTS 357**
SIGNED: 20 Dec 56   FORCE: 3 Jun 58
REGISTERED: 22 Jul 60 Sweden
ARTICLES: 23 LANGUAGE: Swedish. Italian.
HEADNOTE: DOUBLE TAXATION TAXES INCOME FORTUNE
TOPIC: Taxation
CONCEPTS: Definition of terms. Nationality and citizenship. Exchange of official publications. Negotiation. Teacher and student exchange. Claims and settlements. Taxation. Death duties. Tax exemptions.
PROCEDURE: Duration. Ratification. Termination.
PARTIES:
Italy
Sweden

105266 Multilateral Convention **370 UNTS 3**
SIGNED: 4 Jan 60   FORCE: 3 May 60
REGISTERED: 22 Jul 60 Sweden
ARTICLES: 43 LANGUAGE: English. French.
HEADNOTE: ESTABLISHMENT EFTA
TOPIC: IGO Establishment
CONCEPTS: Establishment of trade relations. Export quotas. Import quotas. Free trade. Maritime products and equipment. Export subsidies. Monetary and gold transfers. Assets transfer. Equitable taxes. Establishment.
INTL ORGS: European Economic Community. General Agreement on Tariffs and Trade. International Monetary Fund. Organization for Economic Co-operation and Development.
PROCEDURE: Ratification. Termination.
PARTIES:
Austria SIGNED: 4 Jan 60 RATIFIED: 3 May 60 FORCE: 3 May 60
Denmark SIGNED: 4 Jan 60 RATIFIED: 3 May 60 FORCE: 3 May 60
Norway SIGNED: 4 Jan 60 RATIFIED: 3 May 60 FORCE: 3 May 60
Portugal SIGNED: 4 Jan 60 RATIFIED: 3 May 60 FORCE: 3 May 60
Sweden SIGNED: 4 Jan 60 RATIFIED: 3 May 60 FORCE: 3 May 60
Switzerland SIGNED: 4 Jan 60 RATIFIED: 3 May 60 FORCE: 3 May 60
UK Great Britain SIGNED: 4 Jan 60 RATIFIED: 3 May 60 FORCE: 3 May 60
ANNEX
397 UNTS 337. Denmark. Greenland. Qualified Application to Non-self-governing Territories 2 Jun 61. Force 1 Jul 61.

105267 Bilateral Agreement **371 UNTS 3**
SIGNED: 29 Mar 60   FORCE: 2 May 60
REGISTERED: 28 Jul 60 UK Great Britain
ARTICLES: 29 LANGUAGE: English.
HEADNOTE: SOCIAL SECURITY
TOPIC: Non-ILO Labor
CONCEPTS: Definition of terms. Previous treaty replacement. Domestic legislation. Dispute settlement. Old age and invalidity insurance. Wages and salaries. Non-ILO labor relations. Family allowances. Administrative cooperation. Old age insurance. Sickness and invalidity insurance. Social security. Unemployment. Payment schedules. Claims and settlements.
PARTIES:
Ireland
UK Great Britain

105268 Bilateral Exchange **371 UNTS 37**
SIGNED: 11 Jan 60   FORCE: 11 Jan 60
REGISTERED: 29 Jul 60 USA (United States)
ARTICLES: 2 LANGUAGE: English. Spanish.
HEADNOTE: GRANT PROCUREMENT NUCLEAR RESEARCH TRAINING EQUIPMENT MATERIAL
TOPIC: Tech Assistance
CONCEPTS: Guarantees and safeguards. Public information. Responsibility and liability. Scientific exchange. Indemnities and reimbursements. Funding procedures. Domestic obligation. Atomic energy assistance. Nuclear materials. Non-nuclear materials. Peaceful use.
TREATY REF: NOTE,31JUL59.

PARTIES:
Colombia
USA (United States)

105269 Bilateral Exchange **371 UNTS 45**
SIGNED: 15 Feb 60 FORCE: 15 Feb 60
REGISTERED: 29 Jul 60 USA (United States)
ARTICLES: 2 LANGUAGE: English.
HEADNOTE: BALLISTIC MISSILE EARLY WARN-
ING STATION
TOPIC: Milit Assistance
CONCEPTS: Annex or appendix reference. Bases
and facilities.
TREATY REF: 34UNTS248.
PARTIES:
UK Great Britain
USA (United States)

105270 Bilateral Agreement **371 UNTS 55**
SIGNED: 24 Feb 60 FORCE: 24 Feb 60
REGISTERED: 29 Jul 60 USA (United States)
ARTICLES: 9 LANGUAGE: English. Spanish.
HEADNOTE: COOPERATION TRACKING SATEL-
LITES & SPACE VEHICLES
TOPIC: Tech Assistance
CONCEPTS: General cooperation. Operating agen-
cies. Personnel. Title and deeds. Vocational
training. Research cooperation. Scientific ex-
change. Export quotas. Import quotas. Fees and
exemptions. Financial programs. Tax exemp-
tions. Assistance. Materials, equipment and ser-
vices.
PROCEDURE: Duration. Renewal or Revival.
PARTIES:
Ecuador
USA (United States)
ANNEX
546 UNTS 362. USA (United States). Prolongation
10 May 65. Force 10 May 65.
546 UNTS 362. Ecuador. Prolongation
10 May 65. Force 10 May 65.

105271 Bilateral Agreement **371 UNTS 69**
SIGNED: 8 Oct 58 FORCE: 9 Feb 60
REGISTERED: 29 Jul 60 USA (United States)
ARTICLES: 12 LANGUAGE: English. Spanish.
HEADNOTE: COOPERATION CIVIL USES ATOMIC
ENERGY
TOPIC: Atomic Energy
CONCEPTS: Definition of terms. Previous treaty re-
placement. Non-prejudice to third party. Confor-
mity with municipal law. Exchange of informa-
tion and documents. Inspection and observation.
Responsibility and liability. Investigation of vio-
lations. Research cooperation. Assets transfer. Nu-
clear materials. Non-nuclear materials. Peaceful
use. Security of information.
INTL ORGS: International Atomic Energy Agency.
TREATY REF: 238UNTS121.
PROCEDURE: Duration.
PARTIES:
USA (United States)
Venezuela

105272 Bilateral Exchange **371 UNTS 101**
SIGNED: 16 Mar 60 FORCE: 16 Mar 60
REGISTERED: 4 Aug 60 USA (United States)
ARTICLES: 2 LANGUAGE: English.
HEADNOTE: OWNERSHIP SUBMARINE TELE-
GRAPH CABLE
TOPIC: Specific Property
CONCEPTS: Treaty implementation. Indemnities
and reimbursements. Claims and settlements.
Materials, equipment and services. Facilities and
property.
PARTIES:
Germany, West
USA (United States)

105273 Bilateral Exchange **371 UNTS 109**
SIGNED: 19 Feb 60 FORCE: 17 Mar 60
REGISTERED: 4 Aug 60 USA (United States)
ARTICLES: 3 LANGUAGE: English. Spanish.
HEADNOTE: RADIO COMMUNICATIONS AMA-
TEUR STATIONS BEHALF THIRD PARTIES
TOPIC: Gen Communications
CONCEPTS: Amateur radio. Amateur third party
message. Radio-telephone-telegraphic commu-
nications.

PROCEDURE: Termination.
PARTIES:
Honduras
USA (United States)

105274 Bilateral Agreement **371 UNTS 117**
SIGNED: 23 Mar 60 FORCE: 23 Mar 60
REGISTERED: 4 Aug 60 USA (United States)
ARTICLES: 6 LANGUAGE: English.
HEADNOTE: AGRI COMMOD
TOPIC: US Agri Commod Aid
CONCEPTS: Trade procedures. Currency. Quotas.
Agricultural commodities.
PARTIES:
Finland
USA (United States)
ANNEX
372 UNTS 407. Finland. Amendment 6 May 60.
Force 6 May 60.
372 UNTS 407. USA (United States). Amendment
6 May 60. Force 6 May 60.

105275 Bilateral Agreement **371 UNTS 131**
SIGNED: 19 Mar 60 FORCE: 19 Mar 60
REGISTERED: 4 Aug 60 USA (United States)
ARTICLES: 11 LANGUAGE: English. Portuguese.
HEADNOTE: EDUCATIONAL PROGRAM
TOPIC: Education
CONCEPTS: Definition of terms. Friendship and
amity. Standardization. Conformity with munici-
pal law. Inspection and observation. Personnel.
General property. Exchange. Commissions and
foundations. Teacher and student exchange.
Scholarships and grants. Research and develop-
ment. Accounting procedures. Currency. Ex-
change rates and regulations. Expense sharing
formulae. Financial programs. Funding proce-
dures.
INTL ORGS: Special Commission.
PROCEDURE: Amendment.
PARTIES:
Portugal
USA (United States)
ANNEX
511 UNTS 288. USA (United States). Amendment
3 Jun 63. Force 4 Dec 63.
511 UNTS 288. Portugal. Amendment 4 Dec 63.
Force 4 Dec 63.

105276 Bilateral Exchange **371 UNTS 147**
SIGNED: 23 Mar 60 FORCE: 23 Mar 60
REGISTERED: 4 Aug 60 USA (United States)
ARTICLES: 2 LANGUAGE: English.
HEADNOTE: NUCLEAR RESEARCH TRAINING
EQUIPMENT
TOPIC: Atomic Energy
CONCEPTS: Responsibility and liability. Research
and scientific projects. Research results. Re-
search and development. Indemnities and reim-
bursements. Payment schedules. Materials,
equipment and services. Atomic energy assis-
tance. Nuclear materials. Non-nuclear materials.
Peaceful use.
PARTIES:
New Zealand
USA (United States)

105277 Bilateral Exchange **371 UNTS 155**
SIGNED: 29 Mar 60 FORCE: 29 Mar 60
REGISTERED: 4 Aug 60 USA (United States)
ARTICLES: 2 LANGUAGE: English.
HEADNOTE: ACCESSION GATT
TOPIC: General Trade
CONCEPTS: Treaty interpretation. Annex type ma-
terial. Previous treaty replacement. Trade proce-
dures.
INTL ORGS: General Agreement on Tariffs and
Trade.
TREATY REF: 350UNTS3; 55UNTS187;
171LTS231; 200LTS532; 133UNTS.
PARTIES:
Switzerland
USA (United States)

105278 Bilateral Agreement **371 UNTS 163**
SIGNED: 30 Mar 60 FORCE: 30 Mar 60
REGISTERED: 4 Aug 60 USA (United States)
ARTICLES: 7 LANGUAGE: English. Romanian.
HEADNOTE: FINANCE

TOPIC: Claims and Debts
CONCEPTS: Detailed regulations. Nationality and
citizenship. Expropriation. General property.
Claims and settlements. Lump sum settlements.
Loan repayment.
PARTIES:
Romania
USA (United States)

105279 Bilateral Exchange **371 UNTS 185**
SIGNED: 13 Feb 60 FORCE: 13 Feb 60
REGISTERED: 4 Aug 60 USA (United States)
ARTICLES: 2 LANGUAGE: English. Spanish.
HEADNOTE: SETTLEMENT CLAIMS ARISING
FROM CONSTRUCTION MILITARY BASES
TOPIC: Milit Installation
CONCEPTS: Annex or appendix reference. Indem-
nities and reimbursements. Claims and settle-
ments. Lump sum settlements. Bases and facili-
ties.
PARTIES:
Spain
USA (United States)

105280 Bilateral Exchange **371 UNTS 237**
SIGNED: 24 Mar 60 FORCE: 7 Apr 60
REGISTERED: 4 Aug 60 USA (United States)
ARTICLES: 2 LANGUAGE: English.
HEADNOTE: NUCLEAR RESEARCH TRAINING
EQUIPMENT
TOPIC: Atomic Energy
CONCEPTS: Responsibility and liability. Research
and scientific projects. Research results. Re-
search and development. Indemnities and reim-
bursements. Payment schedules. Materials,
equipment and services. Atomic energy assis-
tance. Nuclear materials. Non-nuclear materials.
Peaceful use.
PARTIES:
Ireland
USA (United States)

105281 Bilateral Exchange **371 UNTS 245**
SIGNED: 1 Apr 60 FORCE: 1 Apr 60
REGISTERED: 4 Aug 60 USA (United States)
ARTICLES: 2 LANGUAGE: English. Spanish.
HEADNOTE: VESSELS LOAN
TOPIC: Milit Assistance
CONCEPTS: Time limit. Annex or appendix refer-
ence. Conformity with municipal law. Exchange
of information and documents. Inspection and
observation. Responsibility and liability. Title
and deeds. Use of facilities. Compensation. Indemnities and reimbursements. Delivery schedules. Self-defense. Lease of military property. Naval vessels. Return of equipment and recapture.
Restrictions on transfer.
TREATY REF: 21UNTS77.
PARTIES:
Argentina
USA (United States)
ANNEX
402 UNTS 356. USA (United States). Supplementation 27 Dec 60. Force 29 Dec 60.
402 UNTS 356. Argentina. Supplementation
29 Dec 60. Force 29 Dec 60.
542 UNTS 382. USA (United States). Prolongation
1 Feb 65. Force 17 Feb 65.
542 UNTS 382. Argentina. Prolongation
17 Feb 65. Force 17 Feb 65.

105282 Bilateral Exchange **371 UNTS 255**
SIGNED: 19 Feb 60 FORCE: 19 Feb 60
REGISTERED: 4 Aug 60 USA (United States)
ARTICLES: 2 LANGUAGE: English. Spanish.
HEADNOTE: NUCLEAR RESEARCH TRAINING
EQUIPMENT
TOPIC: Atomic Energy
CONCEPTS: Responsibility and liability. Research
and scientific projects. Research results. Re-
search and development. Indemnities and reim-
bursements. Payment schedules. Materials,
equipment and services. Atomic energy assis-
tance. Nuclear materials. Non-nuclear materials.
Peaceful use.
PARTIES:
Chile
USA (United States)

105283 Bilateral Agreement **372 UNTS 3**
SIGNED: 29 Jan 60 FORCE: 8 Apr 60
REGISTERED: 4 Aug 60 USA (United States)
ARTICLES: 6 LANGUAGE: English. Spanish.
HEADNOTE: GUARANTY PRIVATE INVESTMENTS
TOPIC: Claims and Debts
CONCEPTS: Exchange of information and documents. Informational records. Expropriation. Arbitration. Existing tribunals. Special tribunals. Negotiation. Payment schedules. Claims and settlements. Private investment guarantee. National treatment.
INTL ORGS: International Court of Justice.
PROCEDURE: Termination.
PARTIES:
El Salvador
USA (United States)

105284 Bilateral Exchange **372 UNTS 13**
SIGNED: 18 Mar 60 FORCE: 18 Mar 60
REGISTERED: 4 Aug 60 USA (United States)
ARTICLES: 2 LANGUAGE: English. Spanish.
HEADNOTE: SPACE VEHICLE TRACKING COMMUNICATIONS
TOPIC: Scientific Project
CONCEPTS: Specialists exchange. Research cooperation. Communication satellites testing. Assets transfer. Facilities and equipment. Satellites. Facilities and property.
PARTIES:
Spain
USA (United States)
ANNEX
487 UNTS 370. Spain. Extension and Amendment 28 Jun 63. Force 1 Jul 63.
487 UNTS 370. USA (United States). Extension and Amendment 27 Jun 63. Force 1 Jul 63.

105285 Bilateral Exchange **372 UNTS 27**
SIGNED: 7 Apr 60 FORCE: 7 Apr 60
REGISTERED: 4 Aug 60 USA (United States)
ARTICLES: 2 LANGUAGE: English. Spanish.
HEADNOTE: VESSEL LOAN
TOPIC: Milit Assistance
CONCEPTS: Time limit. Annex or appendix reference. Responsibility and liability. Title and deeds. Compensation. Delivery schedules. Lease of military property. Naval vessels. Return of equipment and recapture. Restrictions on transfer.
TREATY REF: 174UNTS215.
PARTIES:
Colombia
USA (United States)
ANNEX
388 UNTS 396. USA (United States). Amendment 25 Jul 60. Force 25 Jul 60.
388 UNTS 396. Colombia. Amendment 25 Jul 60. Force 25 Jul 60.

105286 Bilateral Exchange **372 UNTS 37**
SIGNED: 2 Mar 60 FORCE: 2 Mar 60
REGISTERED: 4 Aug 60 USA (United States)
ARTICLES: 2 LANGUAGE: English.
HEADNOTE: WEAPONS PRODUCTION PROGRAMS
TOPIC: Milit Assistance
CONCEPTS: Change of circumstances. Previous treaty replacement. General cooperation. Licenses and permits. Private contracts. Use of facilities. Indemnities and reimbursements. Most favored nation clause. Customs exemptions. General technical assistance. Materials, equipment and services. Joint defense. Defense and security. Exchange of defense information. Equipment and supplies.
INTL ORGS: North Atlantic Treaty Organization.
TREATY REF: 34UNTS243.
PROCEDURE: Future Procedures Contemplated.
PARTIES:
Turkey
USA (United States)

105287 Bilateral Exchange **372 UNTS 47**
SIGNED: 12 Apr 60 FORCE: 12 Apr 60
REGISTERED: 4 Aug 60 USA (United States)
ARTICLES: 2 LANGUAGE: English. Spanish.
HEADNOTE: FACILITY SPACE VEHICLE TRACKING COMMUNICATION
TOPIC: Scientific Project

CONCEPTS: Specialists exchange. Research cooperation. Communication satellites testing. Facilities and equipment. Satellites. Facilities and property.
INTL ORGS: Special Commission.
PROCEDURE: Termination.
PARTIES:
Mexico
USA (United States)
ANNEX
479 UNTS 379. USA (United States). Extension and Amendment 16 May 63. Force 16 May 63.
479 UNTS 379. Mexico. Extension and Amendment 16 May 63. Force 16 May 63.
541 UNTS 334. USA (United States). Prolongation 27 Jan 65. Force 27 Jan 65.
541 UNTS 334. Mexico. Prolongation 27 Jan 65. Force 27 Jan 65.

105288 Bilateral Exchange **372 UNTS 63**
SIGNED: 12 Apr 60 FORCE: 12 Apr 60
REGISTERED: 4 Aug 60 USA (United States)
ARTICLES: 2 LANGUAGE: English.
HEADNOTE: BALANCE OF PAYMENTS
TOPIC: General Trade
CONCEPTS: Detailed regulations. Annex type material. Balance of payments. Customs duties.
TREATY REF: 106UNTS155.
PARTIES:
Iran
USA (United States)
ANNEX
393 UNTS 338. Iran. Termination 27 Jul 60. Force 27 Jul 60.
393 UNTS 338. USA (United States). Termination 27 Jul 60. Force 27 Jul 60.

105289 Bilateral Agreement **372 UNTS 71**
SIGNED: 6 Apr 60 FORCE: 6 Apr 60
REGISTERED: 4 Aug 60 USA (United States)
ARTICLES: 6 LANGUAGE: English.
HEADNOTE: AGRI COMMOD TITLE I
TOPIC: US Agri Commod Aid
CONCEPTS: General provisions. Annex or appendix reference. Exchange of information and documents. Reexport of goods, etc.. Exchange rates and regulations. Transportation costs. Local currency. Commodities schedule. Purchase authorization. Surplus commodities. Mutual consultation.
PARTIES:
Iceland
USA (United States)
ANNEX
405 UNTS 350. USA (United States). Amendment 27 Feb 61. Force 27 Feb 61.
405 UNTS 350. Iceland. Amendment 27 Feb 61. Force 27 Feb 61.

105290 Bilateral Agreement **372 UNTS 83**
SIGNED: 12 Feb 60 FORCE: 12 Feb 60
REGISTERED: 4 Aug 60 USA (United States)
ARTICLES: 6 LANGUAGE: English. Spanish.
HEADNOTE: AGRI COMMOD TITLE I
TOPIC: US Agri Commod Aid
CONCEPTS: General provisions. Annex or appendix reference. Exchange of information and documents. Reexport of goods, etc.. Exchange rates and regulations. Transportation costs. Local currency. Commodities schedule. Purchase authorization. Surplus commodities. Mutual consultation.
PARTIES:
Peru
USA (United States)
ANNEX
402 UNTS 360. USA (United States). Amendment 25 Oct 60. Force 24 Nov 60.
402 UNTS 360. Peru. Amendment 24 Nov 60. Force 24 Nov 60.
405 UNTS 354. USA (United States). Supplementation 4 Oct 60. Force 27 Dec 60.
405 UNTS 354. Peru. Supplementation 27 Dec 60. Force 27 Dec 60.
418 UNTS 412. USA (United States). Amendment 25 Apr 61. Force 31 Jul 61.
418 UNTS 412. Peru. Amendment 31 Jul 61. Force 31 Jul 61.
458 UNTS 349. USA (United States). Amendment 4 Jun 62. Force 18 Jun 62.

458 UNTS 349. Peru. Amendment 18 Jun 62. Force 18 Jun 62.

105291 Bilateral Exchange **372 UNTS 109**
SIGNED: 19 Feb 60 FORCE: 19 Feb 60
REGISTERED: 4 Aug 60 USA (United States)
ARTICLES: 2 LANGUAGE: English.
HEADNOTE: GUARANTY PRIVATE INVESTMENTS
TOPIC: Claims and Debts
CONCEPTS: General cooperation. General property. Arbitration. Existing tribunals. Special tribunals. Negotiation. Reciprocity in financial treatment. Currency. Payment schedules. Claims and settlements. Private investment guarantee. Most favored nation clause. War claims and reparations.
INTL ORGS: International Court of Justice.
PARTIES:
Korea, South
USA (United States)
ANNEX
546 UNTS 372. USA (United States). Amendment 16 Apr 65. Force 16 Apr 65.
546 UNTS 372. Korea, South. Amendment 16 Apr 65. Force 16 Apr 65.

105292 Bilateral Exchange **372 UNTS 117**
SIGNED: 18 Feb 60 FORCE: 18 Feb 60
REGISTERED: 4 Aug 60 USA (United States)
ARTICLES: 2 LANGUAGE: English. Japanese.
HEADNOTE: SURPLUS AGRICULTURAL COMMODITIES
TOPIC: Direct Aid
CONCEPTS: Exchange. Agricultural commodities assistance. Surplus commodities.
TREATY REF: 241UNTS197; 275UNTS105.
PARTIES:
Japan
USA (United States)

105293 Bilateral Exchange **372 UNTS 131**
SIGNED: 19 Oct 59 FORCE: 19 Oct 59
REGISTERED: 4 Aug 60 USA (United States)
ARTICLES: 2 LANGUAGE: English. Portuguese.
HEADNOTE: VESSEL LOAN
TOPIC: Milit Assistance
CONCEPTS: Time limit. Annex or appendix reference. Responsibility and liability. Title and deeds. Compensation. Delivery schedules. Lease of military property. Naval vessels. Return of equipment and recapture. Restrictions on transfer.
TREATY REF: 199UNTS221.
PARTIES:
Brazil
USA (United States)
ANNEX
405 UNTS 360. USA (United States). Supplementation 21 Nov 60. Force 27 Dec 60.
405 UNTS 360. Brazil. Supplementation 27 Dec 60. Force 27 Dec 60.
405 UNTS 363. Brazil. Supplementation 28 Dec 60. Force 29 Dec 60.
405 UNTS 363. USA (United States). Supplementation 29 Dec 60. Force 29 Dec 60.
541 UNTS 339. USA (United States). Prolongation 19 Jan 65. Force 21 Jan 65.
541 UNTS 339. Brazil. Prolongation 21 Jan 65. Force 21 Jan 65.

105294 Bilateral Exchange **372 UNTS 141**
SIGNED: 11 Feb 60 FORCE: 11 Feb 60
REGISTERED: 4 Aug 60 USA (United States)
ARTICLES: 2 LANGUAGE: English. Spanish.
HEADNOTE: VESSELS LOAN
TOPIC: Milit Assistance
CONCEPTS: Time limit. Annex or appendix reference. Responsibility and liability. Title and deeds. Compensation. Delivery schedules. Lease of military property. Naval vessels. Return of equipment and recapture.
TREATY REF: 177UNTS42.
PARTIES:
Ecuador
USA (United States)

105295 Bilateral Exchange **372 UNTS 149**
SIGNED: 19 Jul 56 FORCE: 20 Jul 56
REGISTERED: 4 Aug 60 USA (United States)

ARTICLES: 2 LANGUAGE: English. Spanish.
HEADNOTE: DISPOSITION EQUIPMENT MATERI-
ALS
TOPIC: Milit Assistance
CONCEPTS: Exchange of information and docu-
ments. Title and deeds. Delivery schedules. Sur-
plus property. Surplus war property.
TREATY REF: 177UNTS43.
PARTIES:
Ecuador
USA (United States)

105296 Multilateral Agreement **372 UNTS 159**
SIGNED: 13 Dec 57 FORCE: 10 Aug 60
REGISTERED: 10 Aug 60 United Nations
ARTICLES: 18 LANGUAGE: English. French.
HEADNOTE: ROAD MARKINGS
TOPIC: Land Transport
CONCEPTS: Definition of terms. Detailed regula-
tions. Exceptions and exemptions. Territorial ap-
plication. Arbitration. Procedure. Special tribu-
nals. Negotiation. Roads and highways. Road
rules.
INTL ORGS: United Nations.
PROCEDURE: Amendment. Accession. Denuncia-
tion. Ratification. Termination.
PARTIES:
Belgium SIGNED: 14 Jan 58 RATIFIED:
28 Aug 58 FORCE: 10 Aug 60
France SIGNED: 4 Feb 58 FORCE: 4 Feb 58
Germany, West SIGNED: 13 Dec 57
Ghana RATIFIED: 10 Aug 60 FORCE: 8 Nov 60
Italy SIGNED: 13 Feb 58
Luxembourg SIGNED: 13 Dec 57
Netherlands SIGNED: 13 Dec 57
Portugal SIGNED: 13 Dec 57 RATIFIED:
26 Mar 59 FORCE: 10 Aug 60
Switzerland SIGNED: 17 Feb 58
Turkey SIGNED: 28 Feb 58
UK Great Britain SIGNED: 25 Feb 58
ANNEX
383 UNTS 334. Spain. Accession 3 Jan 61. Force
3 Apr 61.
396 UNTS 351. Turkey. Ratification 25 May 61.
Force 23 Aug 61.
399 UNTS 295. Luxembourg. Ratification
28 Jun 61. Force 26 Sep 61.
434 UNTS 348. Hungary. Qualified Accession
30 Jul 62.
450 UNTS 471. Germany, West. Qualified Ratification 3 Jan 63. Force 3 Apr 63.
456 UNTS 500. Bulgaria. Qualified Acceptance
14 Mar 63.
483 UNTS 348. Romania. Qualified Accession
20 Dec 63. Force 19 Mar 64.

105297 Bilateral Convention **372 UNTS 177**
SIGNED: 25 Oct 57 FORCE: 8 Aug 60
REGISTERED: 10 Aug 60 Belgium
ARTICLES: 11 LANGUAGE: French. German.
HEADNOTE: RECOGNITION ENFORCEMENT JUDI-
CIAL DECISIONS
TOPIC: Admin Cooperation
CONCEPTS: Territorial application. Treaty inter-
pretation. Recognition and enforcement of legal
decisions.
PROCEDURE: Denunciation. Ratification.
PARTIES:
Austria
Belgium

105298 Bilateral Agreement **372 UNTS 193**
SIGNED: 19 May 60 FORCE: 19 May 60
REGISTERED: 11 Aug 60 WHO (World Health)
ARTICLES: 6 LANGUAGE: French.
HEADNOTE: TECHNICAL ADVISORY ASSISTANCE
TOPIC: Tech Assistance
CONCEPTS: Definition of terms. Previous treaty re-
placement. Privileges and immunities. General
cooperation. Exchange of information and docu-
ments. Personnel. Responsibility and liability. Ti-
tle and deeds. Exchange. Scholarships and
grants. Vocational training. Research and devel-
opment. Expense sharing formulae. Domestic
obligation. Special projects. Materials, equipment and services. IGO status. Conformity with
IGO decisions.
TREATY REF: 33UNTS261; 102UNTS279.
PROCEDURE: Amendment. Termination.

PARTIES:
Cambodia
WHO (World Health)

105299 Bilateral Agreement **372 UNTS 205**
SIGNED: 25 Nov 58 FORCE: 27 Apr 59
REGISTERED: 11 Aug 60 Czechoslovakia
ARTICLES: 16 LANGUAGE: Czechoslovakian. Pol-
ish.
HEADNOTE: CUSTOMS MATTERS
TOPIC: Customs
CONCEPTS: Frontier permits. General cooper-
ation. Exchange of official publications. Customs
duties. Transport of goods.
PROCEDURE: Duration. Termination.
PARTIES:
Czechoslovakia
Poland

105300 Bilateral Agreement **372 UNTS 223**
SIGNED: 16 Dec 59 FORCE: 17 May 60
REGISTERED: 11 Aug 60 Czechoslovakia
ARTICLES: 11 LANGUAGE: Czechoslovakian. Pol-
ish.
HEADNOTE: MINE RESCUE SERVICES
TOPIC: Admin Cooperation
CONCEPTS: General cooperation.
PROCEDURE: Duration. Renewal or Revival. Termi-
nation.
PARTIES:
Czechoslovakia
Poland

105301 Bilateral Treaty **372 UNTS 243**
SIGNED: 7 Feb 59 FORCE: 23 Apr 60
REGISTERED: 11 Aug 60 Czechoslovakia
ARTICLES: 9 LANGUAGE: English.
HEADNOTE: TREATY COMMERCE & NAVIGATION
TOPIC: General Economic
CONCEPTS: Exceptions and exemptions. Previous
treaty replacement. Informational records. Gen-
eral property. Most favored nation clause. Cus-
toms exemptions. Water transport. Ports and pi-
lotage.
INTL ORGS: United Nations Educational, Scientific
and Cultural Organization.
TREATY REF: 192LTS17; 205LTS218;
107UNTS179.
PROCEDURE: Duration. Ratification.
PARTIES:
Czechoslovakia
United Arab Rep

105302 Bilateral Agreement **372 UNTS 251**
SIGNED: 11 Apr 60 FORCE: 11 Apr 60
REGISTERED: 12 Aug 60 USA (United States)
ARTICLES: 6 LANGUAGE: English.
HEADNOTE: AGRI COMMOD TITLE I
TOPIC: US Agri Commod Aid
CONCEPTS: General provisions. Annex or appen-
dix reference. Recognition. Reexport of goods,
etc.. Exchange rates and regulations. Transportation costs. Local currency. Commodities schedule. Purchase authorization. Surplus commodities. Mutual consultation.
PARTIES:
Pakistan
USA (United States)
ANNEX
389 UNTS 332. USA (United States). Amendment
23 Sep 60. Force 23 Sep 60.
389 UNTS 332. Pakistan. Amendment 23 Sep 60.
Force 23 Sep 60.
406 UNTS 338. Pakistan. Amendment 11 Mar 61.
Force 11 Mar 61.
406 UNTS 338. USA (United States). Amendment
11 Mar 61. Force 11 Mar 61.
407 UNTS 294. USA (United States). Amendment
22 Apr 61. Force 22 Apr 61.
407 UNTS 294. Pakistan. Amendment 22 Apr 61.
Force 22 Apr 61.
409 UNTS 326. USA (United States). Amendment
3 Jun 61. Force 3 Jun 61.
409 UNTS 326. Pakistan. Amendment 3 Jun 61.
Force 3 Jun 61.
409 UNTS 330. Pakistan. Supplementation
14 Jun 61. Force 14 Jun 61.
409 UNTS 330. USA (United States). Supplementation 14 Jun 61. Force 14 Jun 61.

411 UNTS 328. USA (United States). Amendment
29 Jun 61. Force 29 Jun 61.
411 UNTS 328. Pakistan. Amendment 29 Jun 61.
Force 29 Jun 61.
416 UNTS 362. USA (United States). Amendment
12 Aug 61. Force 12 Aug 61.
416 UNTS 362. Pakistan. Amendment
12 Aug 61. Force 12 Aug 61.

105303 Bilateral Exchange **372 UNTS 267**
SIGNED: 15 Apr 60 FORCE: 15 Apr 60
REGISTERED: 12 Aug 60 USA (United States)
ARTICLES: 2 LANGUAGE: English. Japanese.
HEADNOTE: EQUIPMENT MATERIALS SERVICES
DEFENSE PURPOSES
TOPIC: Milit Assistance
CONCEPTS: Indemnities and reimbursements. Ma-
terials, equipment and services. Defense and se-
curity. Self-defense. Equipment and supplies.
TREATY REF: 232UNTS169.
PROCEDURE: Future Procedures Contemplated.
PARTIES:
Japan
USA (United States)

105304 Bilateral Exchange **372 UNTS 277**
SIGNED: 22 Apr 60 FORCE: 22 Apr 60
REGISTERED: 12 Aug 60 USA (United States)
ARTICLES: 2 LANGUAGE: English. French.
HEADNOTE: WEAPONS PRODUCTION PROGRAM
TOPIC: Milit Assistance
CONCEPTS: Bases and facilities.
INTL ORGS: North Atlantic Treaty Organization.
PARTIES:
Belgium
USA (United States)

105305 Bilateral Exchange **372 UNTS 289**
SIGNED: 23 Mar 60 FORCE: 23 Mar 60
REGISTERED: 12 Aug 60 USA (United States)
ARTICLES: 2 LANGUAGE: English. Japanese.
HEADNOTE: COOPERATION TECHNICAL ASSIS-
TANCE THIRD COUNTRIES
TOPIC: Tech Assistance
CONCEPTS: Conformity with municipal law. Gen-
eral cooperation. Exchange of information and
documents. Exchange. Vocational training. Ex-
pense sharing formulae. General technical assis-
tance.
PARTIES:
Japan
USA (United States)

105306 Bilateral Exchange **372 UNTS 299**
SIGNED: 26 Apr 60 FORCE: 26 Apr 60
REGISTERED: 12 Aug 60 USA (United States)
ARTICLES: 2 LANGUAGE: English.
HEADNOTE: PATENT RIGHTS TECHNICAL INFOR-
MATION DEFENSE PURPOSES
TOPIC: Patents/Copyrights
CONCEPTS: Treaty implementation. Previous trea-
ties adherence. Press and wire services.
TREATY REF: 263UNTS137.
PARTIES:
Greece
USA (United States)

105307 Bilateral Exchange **372 UNTS 313**
SIGNED: 17 May 60 FORCE: 17 May 60
REGISTERED: 12 Aug 60 USA (United States)
ARTICLES: 2 LANGUAGE: English.
HEADNOTE: GUARANTY PRIVATE INVESTMENTS
TOPIC: Claims and Debts
CONCEPTS: General cooperation. Arbitration. Ex-
isting tribunals. Special tribunals. Negotiation.
Reciprocity in financial treatment. Currency.
Claims and settlements. Private investment guar-
antee. Assets transfer. Most favored nation
clause. War claims and reparations.
INTL ORGS: International Court of Justice.
PARTIES:
Nepal
USA (United States)
ANNEX
487 UNTS 376. Nepal. Supplementation
4 Jun 63. Force 4 Jun 63.
487 UNTS 376. USA (United States). Supplemen-
tation 4 Jun 63. Force 4 Jun 63.

105308 Bilateral Exchange **372 UNTS 321**
SIGNED: 8 Jun 60 FORCE: 8 Jun 60
REGISTERED: 12 Aug 60 Thailand
ARTICLES: 2 LANGUAGE: English.
HEADNOTE: BORDER TRAFFIC
TOPIC: Visas
CONCEPTS: Time limit. Frontier permits. General
cooperation.
PARTIES:
Burma
Thailand

105309 Bilateral Agreement **372 UNTS 331**
SIGNED: 12 Aug 60 FORCE: 12 Aug 60
REGISTERED: 12 Aug 60 United Nations
ARTICLES: 10 LANGUAGE: English.
HEADNOTE: MUTUAL ABOLITION VISAS
TOPIC: Tech Assistance
CONCEPTS: Time limit. Visa abolition.
INTL ORGS: International Atomic Energy Agency.
International Court of Justice. United Nations.
TREATY REF: 1UNTS15; 33UNTS261.
PARTIES:
Netherlands
UN Special Fund
ANNEX
376 UNTS 460. UN Special Fund. Amendment
12 Oct 60. Force 12 Oct 60.
376 UNTS 460. Netherlands. Amendment
12 Oct 60. Force 12 Oct 60.
426 UNTS 348. Netherlands. Force 27 Apr 62.
511 UNTS 294. Netherlands. Amendment
12 Oct 64. Force 12 Oct 64.
511 UNTS 294. UN Special Fund. Amendment
12 Oct 64. Force 12 Oct 64.

105310 Bilateral Exchange **373 UNTS 3**
SIGNED: 20 Jan 60 FORCE: 20 Jan 60
REGISTERED: 15 Aug 60 Belgium
ARTICLES: 2 LANGUAGE: Dutch.
HEADNOTE: MAINTAINING FORCE
TOPIC: Admin Cooperation
CONCEPTS: Annex type material. Previous treaty
extension.
TREATY REF: 187LTS9.
PARTIES:
Belgium
Netherlands

105311 Bilateral Exchange **373 UNTS 9**
SIGNED: 12 Apr 60 FORCE: 12 Apr 60
REGISTERED: 17 Aug 60 USA (United States)
ARTICLES: 2 LANGUAGE: English.
HEADNOTE: WEAPONS PRODUCTION
TOPIC: Milit Assistance
CONCEPTS: Change of circumstances. Annex or
appendix reference. General cooperation. Li-
censes and permits. Private contracts. Use of fa-
cilities. Indemnities and reimbursements. Most
favored nation clause. Customs exemptions.
General technical assistance. Materials, equip-
ment and services. Defense and security. Ex-
change of defense information. Equipment and
supplies.
INTL ORGS: North Atlantic Treaty Organization.
TREATY REF: 34UNTS243.
PROCEDURE: Future Procedures Contemplated.
PARTIES:
Denmark
USA (United States)

105312 Bilateral Exchange **373 UNTS 23**
SIGNED: 23 Apr 60 FORCE: 23 Apr 60
REGISTERED: 17 Aug 60 USA (United States)
ARTICLES: 2 LANGUAGE: English. Spanish.
HEADNOTE: NUCLEAR RESEARCH TRAINING
EQUIPMENT
TOPIC: Atomic Energy
CONCEPTS: Responsibility and liability. Research
and scientific projects. Research results. Re-
search and development. Indemnities and reim-
bursements. Materials, equipment and services.
Atomic energy assistance. Nuclear materials.
Non-nuclear materials. Advice lists and orders.
PARTIES:
Guatemala
USA (United States)

105313 Bilateral Exchange **373 UNTS 31**
SIGNED: 18 May 60 FORCE: 18 May 60
REGISTERED: 17 Aug 60 USA (United States)
ARTICLES: 2 LANGUAGE: English. French.
HEADNOTE: PATENT RIGHTS TECHNICAL INFOR-
MATION DEFENSE PURPOSES
TOPIC: Patents/Copyrights
CONCEPTS: Treaty implementation. Previous trea-
ties adherence. Press and wire services.
TREATY REF: 202UNTS289.
PARTIES:
Belgium
USA (United States)

105314 Bilateral Treaty **373 UNTS 47**
SIGNED: 18 Sep 59 FORCE: 8 Feb 60
REGISTERED: 19 Aug 60 South Africa
ARTICLES: 16 LANGUAGE: Afrikaans. English. He-
brew.
HEADNOTE: EXTRADITION
TOPIC: Extradition
CONCEPTS: Time limit. Extradition, deportation
and repatriation. Extradition requests. Extradita-
ble offenses. Location of crime. Refusal of extra-
dition. Concurrent requests. Material evidence.
Indemnities and reimbursements.
PROCEDURE: Ratification. Termination.
PARTIES:
Israel
South Africa

105315 Bilateral Exchange **373 UNTS 75**
SIGNED: 11 Oct 58 FORCE: 25 Sep 59
REGISTERED: 19 Aug 60 South Africa
ARTICLES: 2 LANGUAGE: English.
HEADNOTE: WORKMENS COMPENSATION
TOPIC: Non-ILO Labor
CONCEPTS: Definition of terms. Detailed regula-
tions. Exchange of information and documents.
Old age and invalidity insurance. Wages and sal-
aries. Non-ILO labor relations. Administrative co-
operation. Sickness and invalidity insurance.
Payment schedules.
PROCEDURE: Duration. Termination.
PARTIES:
Fed Rhod/Nyasaland
South Africa

105316 Bilateral Agreement **373 UNTS 85**
SIGNED: 22 Jul 59 FORCE: 26 Oct 59
REGISTERED: 19 Aug 60 Japan
ARTICLES: 11 LANGUAGE: Japanese. Spanish.
HEADNOTE: IMMIGRATION
TOPIC: Visas
CONCEPTS: Treaty interpretation. Border traffic
and migration. Conformity with municipal law.
Establishment of commission. Tax exemptions.
Customs exemptions.
INTL ORGS: Special Commission.
PROCEDURE: Ratification.
PARTIES:
Japan
Paraguay

105317 Bilateral Agreement **373 UNTS 101**
SIGNED: 13 May 59 FORCE: 12 Jan 60
REGISTERED: 19 Aug 60 Japan
ARTICLES: 11 LANGUAGE: French. Japanese.
Vietnamese.
HEADNOTE: REPARATIONS
TOPIC: Reparations
CONCEPTS: War claims and reparations. Loss and-
/or damage.
INTL ORGS: International Court of Justice. Special
Commission.
PROCEDURE: Ratification.
PARTIES:
Japan
Vietnam, South

105318 Bilateral Agreement **373 UNTS 149**
SIGNED: 13 May 59 FORCE: 12 Jan 60
REGISTERED: 19 Aug 60 Japan
ARTICLES: 6 LANGUAGE: French. Japanese. Viet-
namese.
HEADNOTE: LOAN
TOPIC: Loans and Credits
CONCEPTS: Treaty interpretation. Dispute settle-
ment. Indemnities and reimbursements. Finan-

cial programs. Interest rates. Economic assis-
tance. Loan and credit. Purchase authorization.
Loan repayment. Terms of loan.
PROCEDURE: Ratification.
PARTIES:
Japan
Vietnam, South

105319 Bilateral Exchange **373 UNTS 173**
SIGNED: 13 May 59 FORCE: 12 Jan 60
REGISTERED: 19 Aug 60 Japan
ARTICLES: 2 LANGUAGE: French.
HEADNOTE: COMMERCIAL LOANS
TOPIC: Loans and Credits
CONCEPTS: Conformity with municipal law. Cur-
rency. Financial programs. Loan and credit. Inter-
agency agreements.
TREATY REF: 373UNTS101.
PROCEDURE: Amendment. Duration.
PARTIES:
Japan
Vietnam, South

105320 Bilateral Treaty **373 UNTS 179**
SIGNED: 19 Jan 60 FORCE: 23 Jun 60
REGISTERED: 19 Aug 60 Japan
ARTICLES: 10 LANGUAGE: English. Japanese.
HEADNOTE: MUTUAL DEFENSE COOPERATION
TOPIC: General Military
CONCEPTS: Defense and security.
INTL ORGS: United Nations.
PROCEDURE: Termination.
PARTIES:
Japan
USA (United States)

105321 Bilateral Agreement **373 UNTS 207**
SIGNED: 19 Jan 60 FORCE: 23 Jun 60
REGISTERED: 19 Aug 60 Japan
ARTICLES: 28 LANGUAGE: English. Japanese.
HEADNOTE: FACILITIES AREAS STATUS FORCES
TOPIC: Status of Forces
CONCEPTS: Definition of terms. Time limit. Annex
or appendix reference. Frontier formalities.
Court procedures. Conformity with municipal
law. General cooperation. Private contracts. Use
of facilities. Investigation of violations. Establishment of commission. Procedure. Negotiation.
Non-ILO labor relations. Meteorology. Indemni-
ties and reimbursements. Currency. Claims and
settlements. National treatment. Tax exemptions. Customs duties. Customs exemptions. Materials, equipment and services. Facilities and
equipment. Postal services. Return of equipment
and recapture. Security of information. Jurisdiction. Status of forces. Bases and facilities.
INTL ORGS: Special Commission.
PROCEDURE: Amendment. Future Procedures
Contemplated.
PARTIES:
Japan
USA (United States)
ANNEX
394 UNTS 310. USA (United States). Supplementation 22 Aug 60. Force 22 Aug 60.
394 UNTS 310. Japan. Supplementation
22 Aug 60. Force 22 Aug 60.

105322 Bilateral Agreement **373 UNTS 313**
SIGNED: 4 Aug 60 FORCE: 4 Aug 60
REGISTERED: 23 Aug 60 WHO (World Health)
ARTICLES: 6 LANGUAGE: French.
HEADNOTE: TECHNICAL ADVISORY ASSISTANCE
TOPIC: Tech Assistance
CONCEPTS: Definition of terms. Previous treaty re-
placement. Privileges and immunities. General
cooperation. Exchange of information and docu-
ments. Personnel. Responsibility and liability. Ti-
tle and deeds. Exchange. Scholarships and
grants. Vocational training. Research and devel-
opment. Expense sharing formulae. Domestic
obligation. Special projects. Materials, equip-
ment and services. IGO status. Conformity with
IGO decisions.
TREATY REF: 33UNTS261.
PROCEDURE: Amendment. Termination.
PARTIES:
Laos
WHO (World Health)

105323 Multilateral Convention **374 UNTS 3**
SIGNED: 11 Apr 60 FORCE: 1 Jul 60
REGISTERED: 24 Aug 60 Belgium
ARTICLES: 18 LANGUAGE: French. Dutch.
HEADNOTE: TRANSFER CONTROL PERSONS EXTERNAL FRONTIERS BENELUX TERRITORY
TOPIC: Visas
CONCEPTS: Definition of terms. Emergencies. Border traffic and migration. Denial of admission. Resident permits. Visas. Alien status. Conformity with municipal law. General cooperation. Procedure.
INTL ORGS: Benelux Economic Union. Benelux Parliament. Special Commission.
PROCEDURE: Ratification.
PARTIES:
Belgium SIGNED: 11 Apr 60 RATIFIED: 30 Jun 60 FORCE: 1 Jul 60
Luxembourg SIGNED: 11 Apr 60 RATIFIED: 30 Jun 60 FORCE: 1 Jul 60
Netherlands SIGNED: 11 Apr 60 RATIFIED: 30 Jun 60 FORCE: 1 Jul 60

105324 Bilateral Agreement **374 UNTS 21**
SIGNED: 27 Jul 59 FORCE: 27 Jul 59
REGISTERED: 25 Aug 60 UK Great Britain
ARTICLES: 3 LANGUAGE: English.
HEADNOTE: PUBLIC OFFICERS
TOPIC: Non-ILO Labor
CONCEPTS: Definition of terms. Detailed regulations. Exceptions and exemptions. Employment regulations. Wages and salaries. Non-ILO labor relations. Family allowances. Old age insurance. Sickness and invalidity insurance. Payment schedules. Tax exemptions.
PARTIES:
Fed of Malaya
UK Great Britain

105325 Bilateral Exchange **374 UNTS 31**
SIGNED: 26 Nov 59 FORCE: 26 Nov 59
REGISTERED: 2 Sep 60 Brazil
ARTICLES: 2 LANGUAGE: Portuguese. Spanish.
HEADNOTE: TRADE REGULATIONS
TOPIC: General Trade
CONCEPTS: Previous treaty extension. Trade procedures.
TREATY REF: 31JAN40 TRADE&NAVIGATION TREATY.
PARTIES:
Argentina
Brazil

105326 Bilateral Exchange **374 UNTS 39**
SIGNED: 26 Nov 59 FORCE: 26 Nov 59
REGISTERED: 2 Sep 60 Brazil
ARTICLES: 2 LANGUAGE: Portuguese. Spanish.
HEADNOTE: RAISING BALANCING TRADE
TOPIC: General Trade
CONCEPTS: General provisions. Use of facilities. Balance of payments.
PARTIES:
Argentina
Brazil

105327 Bilateral Exchange **374 UNTS 45**
SIGNED: 26 Nov 59 FORCE: 26 Nov 59
REGISTERED: 2 Sep 60 Brazil
ARTICLES: 2 LANGUAGE: Portuguese. Spanish.
HEADNOTE: TRADE FRUIT
TOPIC: General Trade
CONCEPTS: Tariffs. Commodity trade. Customs declarations.
PARTIES:
Argentina
Brazil

105328 Bilateral Exchange **374 UNTS 51**
SIGNED: 26 Nov 59 FORCE: 26 Nov 59
REGISTERED: 2 Sep 60 Brazil
ARTICLES: 2 LANGUAGE: Portuguese. Spanish.
HEADNOTE: SUPPRESSION VISAS
TOPIC: Visas
CONCEPTS: Time limit. Visa abolition.
PARTIES:
Argentina
Brazil

105329 Bilateral Exchange **374 UNTS 57**
SIGNED: 19 Sep 58 FORCE: 19 Sep 58
REGISTERED: 2 Sep 60 Brazil
ARTICLES: 2 LANGUAGE: Portuguese. Spanish.
HEADNOTE: ESTABLISHMENT MIXED GROUP INDUSTRIAL COOPERATION
TOPIC: Tech Assistance
CONCEPTS: General cooperation. Establishment of commission. Non-bank projects.
INTL ORGS: Special Commission.
PARTIES:
Argentina
Brazil

105330 Bilateral Agreement **374 UNTS 63**
SIGNED: 2 Dec 59 FORCE: 1 Jul 60
REGISTERED: 7 Sep 60 Czechoslovakia
ARTICLES: 20 LANGUAGE: Czechoslovakian. Russian.
HEADNOTE: SOCIAL SECURITY
TOPIC: Non-ILO Labor
CONCEPTS: Definition of terms. General provisions. Time limit. Annex or appendix reference. Friendship and amity. Exchange of information and documents. Incorporation of treaty provisions into national law. Public health. Anti-discrimination. Old age and invalidity insurance. Wages and salaries. Non-ILO labor relations. Administrative cooperation. Old age insurance. Sickness and invalidity insurance. Social security.
PROCEDURE: Denunciation. Duration. Ratification. Renewal or Revival.
PARTIES:
Czechoslovakia
USSR (Soviet Union)

105331 Bilateral Treaty **374 UNTS 101**
SIGNED: 25 Nov 59 FORCE: 15 Jun 60
REGISTERED: 7 Sep 60 Czechoslovakia
ARTICLES: 19 LANGUAGE: Czechoslovakian. Russian.
HEADNOTE: TRADE NAVIGATION
TOPIC: General Economic
CONCEPTS: Exceptions and exemptions. Informational records. Juridical personality. Free passage and transit. Reciprocity in trade. Reexport of goods, etc.. Trade agencies. Non-interest rates and fees. Most favored nation clause. Customs exemptions. General transportation. Passenger transport. Transport of goods. Licenses and certificates of nationality. Merchant vessels. Ports and pilotage.
PROCEDURE: Ratification. Termination.
PARTIES:
Czechoslovakia
Germany, East

105332 Unilateral Instrument **374 UNTS 127**
SIGNED: 12 Sep 60 FORCE: 13 Sep 60
REGISTERED: 13 Sep 60 United Nations
ARTICLES: 1 LANGUAGE: English.
HEADNOTE: ACCEPTANCE ICJ JURISDICTION
TOPIC: ICJ Option Clause
CONCEPTS: Exceptions and exemptions. Compulsory jurisdiction.
INTL ORGS: International Court of Justice.
PROCEDURE: Termination.
PARTIES:
Pakistan

105333 Bilateral Instrument **374 UNTS 133**
SIGNED: 28 Jun 60 FORCE: 30 Jun 60
REGISTERED: 13 Sep 60 IAEA (Atom Energy)
ARTICLES: 12 LANGUAGE: English.
HEADNOTE: MASTER CONTRACT FINANCING IAEA RESEARCH
TOPIC: Direct Aid
CONCEPTS: Treaty implementation. Annex or appendix reference. Exchange of information and documents. Inspection and observation. Responsibility and liability. Arbitration. Procedure. Research and development. Indemnities and reimbursements. Financial programs. Payment schedules. Patents, copyrights and trademarks.
INTL ORGS: United Nations. Arbitration Commission.
TREATY REF: 267UNTS3.
PROCEDURE: Amendment. Duration. Termination.

PARTIES:
IAEA (Atom Energy)
USA (United States)
ANNEX
556 UNTS 190. USA (United States). Amendment 23 Apr 65. Force 12 May 65.
556 UNTS 190. IAEA (Atom Energy). Amendment 12 May 65. Force 12 May 65.
603 UNTS 328. IAEA (Atom Energy). Amendment 12 Feb 67. Force 1 Feb 67.
603 UNTS 328. USA (United States). Amendment 12 Feb 67. Force 1 Feb 67.

105334 Multilateral Agreement **374 UNTS 147**
SIGNED: 1 Jul 59 FORCE: 4 Aug 60
REGISTERED: 13 Sep 60 IAEA (Atom Energy)
ARTICLES: 12 LANGUAGE: English. French. Russian. Spanish.
HEADNOTE: INTERNATIONAL ATOMIC ENERGY
TOPIC: IGO Status/Immunit
CONCEPTS: Definition of terms. Non-visa travel documents. Diplomatic privileges. Diplomatic missions. Inviolability. Privileges and immunities. Property. Diplomatic correspondence. Juridical personality. Procedure. Special status. Status of experts.
INTL ORGS: International Atomic Energy Agency. International Court of Justice. United Nations.
TREATY REF: 276UNTS3.
PROCEDURE: Amendment. Duration.
PARTIES:
Multilateral
ANNEX
396 UNTS 352. Iraq. Acceptance 23 Nov 60.
396 UNTS 352. India. Acceptance 10 Mar 61.
399 UNTS 296. New Zealand. Acceptance 22 Jun 61.
412 UNTS 353. Norway. Acceptance 9 Oct 61.
412 UNTS 353. Sweden. Acceptance 8 Sep 61.
456 UNTS 502. Denmark. Qualified Acceptance 14 Mar 62.
456 UNTS 502. Korea, South. Qualified Acceptance 17 Jan 62.
456 UNTS 503. Thailand. Qualified Acceptance 15 May 62.
456 UNTS 503. United Arab Rep. Acceptance 12 Feb 63.
456 UNTS 503. Philippines. Acceptance 17 Dec 62.
463 UNTS 362. UK Great Britain. Qualified Accession 19 Sep 61.
556 UNTS 194. Netherlands. Surinam. Acceptance 29 Aug 63.
556 UNTS 194. Ghana. Acceptance 16 Dec 63.
556 UNTS 194. Japan. Acceptance 18 Apr 63.
556 UNTS 194. Netherlands. Netherlands Antilles. Acceptance 29 Aug 63.
556 UNTS 194. Belgium. Qualified Acceptance 26 Oct 65.
556 UNTS 194. Yugoslavia. Acceptance 14 Oct 63.
556 UNTS 194. Argentina. Acceptance 15 Oct 63.
556 UNTS 194. Netherlands. Qualified Acceptance 29 Aug 63.
566 UNTS 369. Brazil. Acceptance 13 Jun 66.
566 UNTS 369. Canada. Qualified Acceptance 15 Jun 66.
604 UNTS 375. Hungary. Qualified Accession 14 Jul 67.
631 UNTS 351. Czechoslovakia. Qualified Accession 7 Feb 68.
631 UNTS 351. Tunisia. Acceptance 28 Dec 67.
642 UNTS 370. Bulgaria. Qualified Acceptance 17 Jun 68.

105335 Bilateral Exchange **374 UNTS 199**
SIGNED: 18 Mar 60 FORCE: 17 Apr 60
REGISTERED: 13 Sep 60 UK Great Britain
ARTICLES: 2 LANGUAGE: English. Spanish.
HEADNOTE: RECIPROCAL ABOLITION VISAS
TOPIC: Visas
CONCEPTS: Emergencies. Territorial application. Visa abolition. Denial of admission. Conformity with municipal law.
PROCEDURE: Denunciation.
PARTIES:
Bolivia
UK Great Britain

105336 Bilateral Agreement **374 UNTS 207**
SIGNED: 15 Jan 60   FORCE: 15 Jan 60
REGISTERED: 13 Sep 60 UK Great Britain
ARTICLES: 16 LANGUAGE: English. Czechoslovakian.
HEADNOTE: AIR SERVICES BETWEEN BEYOND RESPECTIVE TERRITORIES
TOPIC: Air Transport
CONCEPTS: Definition of terms. Detailed regulations. Exceptions and exemptions. Annex or appendix reference. Governor-general functions. Conformity with municipal law. Exchange of information and documents. Personnel. Arbitration. Procedure. Special tribunals. Negotiation. Reexport of goods, etc.. Monetary and gold transfers. Non-interest rates and fees. Most favored nation clause. National treatment. Tax exemptions. Customs exemptions. Routes and logistics. Navigational conditions. Permit designation. Conditions of airlines operating permission. Overflights and technical stops. Operating authorizations and regulations.
INTL ORGS: International Civil Aviation Organization. Arbitration Commission.
TREATY REF: 15UNTS295.
PROCEDURE: Amendment. Future Procedures Contemplated. Registration. Termination. Application to Non-self-governing Territories.
PARTIES:
  Czechoslovakia
  UK Great Britain

105337 Bilateral Agreement **374 UNTS 233**
SIGNED: 8 Apr 60   FORCE: 3 May 60
REGISTERED: 13 Sep 60 UK Great Britain
ARTICLES: 8 LANGUAGE: English.
HEADNOTE: AGRICULTURE
TOPIC: Customs
CONCEPTS: Definition of terms. Annex or appendix reference. Customs exemptions. Agricultural commodities.
PROCEDURE: Duration.
PARTIES:
  Denmark
  UK Great Britain
          ANNEX
470 UNTS 420. Denmark.   Supplementation 11 May 63. Force 11 May 63.
470 UNTS 420. UK Great Britain. Supplementation 11 May 63. Force 11 May 63.

105338 Bilateral Exchange **374 UNTS 245**
SIGNED: 20 May 60   FORCE: 20 May 60
REGISTERED: 13 Sep 60 UK Great Britain
ARTICLES: 2 LANGUAGE: English.
HEADNOTE: COOPERATION PROMOTION DEVELOPMENT PEACEFUL USES ATOMIC ENERGY
TOPIC: Atomic Energy
CONCEPTS: Exchange of information and documents. Informational records. Inspection and observation. Nuclear materials. Peaceful use. Security of information.
INTL ORGS: European Nuclear Energy Agency. Organization for Economic Co-operation and Development.
PROCEDURE: Duration. Termination.
PARTIES:
  Denmark
  UK Great Britain

105339 Bilateral Agreement **374 UNTS 253**
SIGNED: 14 Dec 59   FORCE: 28 Jun 60
REGISTERED: 13 Sep 60 UK Great Britain
ARTICLES: 16 LANGUAGE: English. Arabic.
HEADNOTE: CULTURAL
TOPIC: Culture
CONCEPTS: Exchange. General cultural cooperation.
INTL ORGS: Special Commission.
PROCEDURE: Ratification. Termination.
PARTIES:
  Iraq
  UK Great Britain

105340 Bilateral Exchange **374 UNTS 267**
SIGNED: 1 Apr 60   FORCE: 10 Apr 60
REGISTERED: 13 Sep 60 UK Great Britain
ARTICLES: 2 LANGUAGE: English.
HEADNOTE: FACILITATE TRAVEL
TOPIC: Visas

CONCEPTS: Territorial application. Time limit. Annex or appendix reference. Previous treaty replacement. Visa abolition. Denial of admission. Conformity with municipal law.
TREATY REF: 2UNTS267.
PROCEDURE: Denunciation.
PARTIES:
  Luxembourg
  UK Great Britain
          ANNEX
560 UNTS 280. UK Great Britain. Southern Rhodesia.

105341 Bilateral Exchange **374 UNTS 277**
SIGNED: 1 Apr 60   FORCE: 10 Apr 60
REGISTERED: 13 Sep 60 UK Great Britain
ARTICLES: 2 LANGUAGE: English.
HEADNOTE: FACILITATE TRAVEL
TOPIC: Visas
CONCEPTS: Emergencies. Territorial application. Time limit. Annex or appendix reference. Previous treaty replacement. Visa abolition. Denial of admission. Conformity with municipal law.
PROCEDURE: Denunciation.
PARTIES:
  Netherlands
  UK Great Britain
          ANNEX
551 UNTS 318. Netherlands. Surinam.
560 UNTS 280. UK Great Britain. Southern Rhodesia.

105342 Bilateral Exchange **374 UNTS 287**
SIGNED: 13 May 60   FORCE: 15 Jun 60
REGISTERED: 13 Sep 60 UK Great Britain
ARTICLES: 2 LANGUAGE: English. Spanish.
HEADNOTE: RECIPROCAL ABOLITION VISAS
TOPIC: Visas
CONCEPTS: Emergencies. Territorial application. Non-prejudice to third party. Denial of admission. Conformity with municipal law.
PROCEDURE: Denunciation.
PARTIES:
  Spain
  UK Great Britain

105343 Bilateral Exchange **374 UNTS 295**
SIGNED: 1 Mar 60   FORCE: 1 Apr 60
REGISTERED: 13 Sep 60 UK Great Britain
ARTICLES: 4 LANGUAGE: English.
HEADNOTE: ABOLITION VISAS
TOPIC: Visas
CONCEPTS: Emergencies. Territorial application. Annex or appendix reference. Visa abolition. Denial of admission. Resident permits. Conformity with municipal law.
TREATY REF: 229UNTS308.
PROCEDURE: Denunciation.
PARTIES:
  Turkey
  UK Great Britain
          ANNEX
431 UNTS 318. UK Great Britain. Amendment 28 Jun 61. Force 1 Aug 61.
431 UNTS 318. Turkey. Amendment 28 Jun 61. Force 1 Aug 61.
482 UNTS 384. UK Great Britain. New Hebrides Is. Withdrawal 19 May 63. Force 11 Jun 63.
482 UNTS 384. Turkey.   Acknowledgement 11 Jun 63. Force 11 Jun 63.

105344 Bilateral Agreement **374 UNTS 305**
SIGNED: 24 May 59   FORCE: 24 May 59
REGISTERED: 13 Sep 60 UK Great Britain
ARTICLES: 9 LANGUAGE: English. Russian.
HEADNOTE: TRADE
TOPIC: General Trade
CONCEPTS: General provisions. General cooperation. Informational records. Licenses and permits. Use of facilities. Reciprocity in trade. Trade procedures. Commodity trade. Quotas. Water transport. Merchant vessels.
TREATY REF: 149LTS445.
PROCEDURE: Duration.
PARTIES:
  UK Great Britain
  USSR (Soviet Union)
          ANNEX
539 UNTS 360. USSR (Soviet Union). Prolongation 23 Apr 64. Force 23 Apr 64.

539 UNTS 360. UK Great Britain. Prolongation 23 Apr 64. Force 23 Apr 64.

105345 Bilateral Exchange **374 UNTS 319**
SIGNED: 22 Jul 59   FORCE: 15 Jul 59
REGISTERED: 13 Sep 60 UK Great Britain
ARTICLES: 4 LANGUAGE: English.
HEADNOTE: RECOGNITION AIR CREW LICENSES
TOPIC: Admin Cooperation
CONCEPTS: Licenses and permits.
TREATY REF: 359UNTS339.
PARTIES:
  UK Great Britain
  Yugoslavia

105346 Bilateral Agreement **374 UNTS 331**
SIGNED: 26 Jun 60   FORCE: 26 Jun 60
REGISTERED: 13 Sep 60 UK Great Britain
ARTICLES: 8 LANGUAGE: English.
HEADNOTE: SOCIAL SECURITY
TOPIC: Direct Aid
CONCEPTS: Time limit. Annex or appendix reference. Exchange of information and documents. Incorporation of treaty provisions into national law. Public health. Old age and invalidity insurance. Wages and salaries. Non-ILO labor relations. Administrative cooperation. Old age insurance. Sickness and invalidity insurance. Social security. Payment schedules. National treatment.
PROCEDURE: Denunciation. Duration. Renewal or Revival.
PARTIES:
  Somalia
  UK Great Britain

105347 Bilateral Agreement **374 UNTS 339**
SIGNED: 26 Jun 60   FORCE: 26 Jun 60
REGISTERED: 13 Sep 60 UK Great Britain
ARTICLES: 8 LANGUAGE: English.
HEADNOTE: PUBLIC OFFICERS
TOPIC: Non-ILO Labor
CONCEPTS: Definition of terms. Detailed regulations. Exceptions and exemptions. Employment regulations. Wages and salaries. Non-ILO labor relations. Family allowances. Old age insurance. Sickness and invalidity insurance. Exchange rates and regulations. Payment schedules.
PARTIES:
  Somalia
  UK Great Britain

105348 Bilateral Agreement **374 UNTS 347**
SIGNED: 26 Jun 60   FORCE: 26 Jun 60
REGISTERED: 13 Sep 60 UK Great Britain
ARTICLES: 10 LANGUAGE: English.
HEADNOTE: INTERIM ARRANGEMENTS SOMALILAND SCOUTS
TOPIC: Non-ILO Labor
CONCEPTS: Definition of terms. Exceptions and exemptions. Employment regulations. Wages and salaries. Non-ILO labor relations. Indemnities and reimbursements. Domestic obligation.
PARTIES:
  Somalia
  UK Great Britain

105349 Bilateral Exchange **374 UNTS 357**
SIGNED: 26 Jun 60   FORCE: 26 Jun 60
REGISTERED: 13 Sep 60 UK Great Britain
ARTICLES: 2 LANGUAGE: English.
HEADNOTE: TRANSFER TREATY OBLIGATIONS
TOPIC: Recognition
CONCEPTS: Exceptions and exemptions.
PARTIES:
  Somalia
  UK Great Britain

105350 Bilateral Exchange **374 UNTS 363**
SIGNED: 26 Jun 60   FORCE: 26 Jun 60
REGISTERED: 13 Sep 60 UK Great Britain
ARTICLES: 2 LANGUAGE: English.
HEADNOTE: AVAILABILITY CURRENCY DURING TRANSITIONAL PERIOD
TOPIC: Finance
CONCEPTS: Independence maintenance. Transition period. Privileges and immunities. Currency.

PARTIES:
Somalia
UK Great Britain

105351 Bilateral Agreement **375 UNTS 3**
SIGNED: 16 Sep 60 FORCE: 16 Sep 60
REGISTERED: 16 Sep 60 United Nations
ARTICLES: 10 LANGUAGE: English. Portuguese.
HEADNOTE: ASSISTANCE
TOPIC: Tech Assistance
CONCEPTS: Detailed regulations. Treaty implementation. Treaty interpretation. Annex or appendix reference. Visas. Privileges and immunities. Conformity with municipal law. Exchange of
information and documents. Inspection and observation. Operating agencies. Licenses and permits. General property. Public information. Title
and deeds. Use of facilities. Arbitration. Procedure. Negotiation. Import quotas. Reexport of
goods, etc.. Accounting procedures. Exchange
rates and regulations. Expense sharing formulae.
Fees and exemptions. Local currency. Tax exemptions. Customs exemptions. Commodities
and services. General technical assistance. Materials, equipment and services. IGO status. Conformity with IGO decisions.
INTL ORGS: International Atomic Energy Agency.
International Court of Justice. United Nations.
Arbitration Commission.
TREATY REF: 1UNTS15; 33UNTS261;
374UNTS147.
PROCEDURE: Amendment. Termination.
PARTIES:
Brazil
UN Special Fund

105352 Bilateral Agreement **375 UNTS 29**
SIGNED: 20 Sep 60 FORCE: 20 Sep 60
REGISTERED: 20 Sep 60 United Nations
ARTICLES: 10 LANGUAGE: English.
HEADNOTE: ASSISTANCE
TOPIC: Tech Assistance
CONCEPTS: Detailed regulations. Treaty imple-
mentation. Annex or appendix reference. Visas.
Privileges and immunities. Exchange of informa-
tion and documents. Inspection and observation.
Operating agencies. Licenses and permits. Gen-
eral property. Public information. Responsibility
and liability. Title and deeds. Use of facilities.
Arbitration. Procedure. Negotiation. Import
quotas. Reexport of goods, etc.. Accounting pro-
cedures. Exchange rates and regulations. Ex-
pense sharing formulae. Fees and exemptions.
Tax exemptions. Customs exemptions. Commo-
dities and services. General technical assistance. Materials, equipment and services. IGO
status. Conformity with IGO decisions.
INTL ORGS: International Atomic Energy Agency.
International Court of Justice. United Nations.
Arbitration Commission.
TREATY REF: 1UNTS15; 33UNTS261;
374UNTS147.
PARTIES:
Taiwan
UN Special Fund

105353 Bilateral Agreement **375 UNTS 49**
SIGNED: 20 Jan 60 FORCE: 10 Aug 60
REGISTERED: 20 Sep 60 IBRD (World Bank)
ARTICLES: 5 LANGUAGE: English.
HEADNOTE: GUARANTEE POWER
TOPIC: IBRD Project
CONCEPTS: Definition of terms. Annex or appen-
dix reference. Exchange of information and doc-
uments. Inspection and observation. Bonds.
Fees and exemptions. Tax exemptions. Domestic
obligation. Terms of loan. Loan regulations. Loan
guarantee. Guarantor non-interference. Hydro-
electric power.
PARTIES:
Colombia
IBRD (World Bank)

105354 Unilateral Instrument **375 UNTS 79**
SIGNED: 13 Jan 60 FORCE: 19 Jan 60
REGISTERED: 20 Sep 60 United Nations
ARTICLES: 1 LANGUAGE: French.
HEADNOTE: ACCEPTANCE OBLIGATIONS UN
TOPIC: UN Charter
CONCEPTS: Adherence to UN charter.

INTL ORGS: United Nations.
PARTIES:
Cameroon

105355 Unilateral Instrument **375 UNTS 83**
SIGNED: 21 May 60 FORCE: 1 Jul 60
REGISTERED: 20 Sep 60 United Nations
ARTICLES: 1 LANGUAGE: French.
HEADNOTE: ACCEPTANCE OBLIGATIONS UN
TOPIC: UN Charter
CONCEPTS: Acceptance of obligations upon ad-
mittance to UN.
INTL ORGS: United Nations.
PARTIES:
Togo

105356 Unilateral Instrument **375 UNTS 87**
SIGNED: 26 Jun 60 FORCE: 20 Sep 60
REGISTERED: 20 Sep 60 United Nations
ARTICLES: 1 LANGUAGE: French.
HEADNOTE: ACCEPTANCE OBLIGATIONS UN
TOPIC: UN Charter
CONCEPTS: Acceptance of UN obligations. Adher-
ence to UN charter.
INTL ORGS: United Nations.
PARTIES:
Malagasy

105357 Unilateral Instrument **375 UNTS 91**
SIGNED: 2 Aug 60 FORCE: 20 Sep 60
REGISTERED: 20 Sep 60 United Nations
ARTICLES: 1 LANGUAGE: French.
HEADNOTE: ACCEPTANCE UN CHARTER
TOPIC: UN Charter
CONCEPTS: Adherence to UN Charter. Accep-
tance of UN obligations. Acceptance of obliga-
tions upon admittance to UN.
INTL ORGS: United Nations.
PARTIES:
Dahomey

105358 Unilateral Instrument **375 UNTS 95**
SIGNED: 7 Aug 60 FORCE: 20 Sep 60
REGISTERED: 20 Sep 60 United Nations
ARTICLES: 1 LANGUAGE: French.
HEADNOTE: ACCEPTANCE OBLIGATIONS UN
TOPIC: UN Charter
CONCEPTS: Acceptance of UN obligations. Adher-
ence to UN charter.
INTL ORGS: United Nations.
PARTIES:
Niger

105359 Unilateral Instrument **375 UNTS 99**
SIGNED: 7 Aug 60 FORCE: 20 Sep 60
REGISTERED: 20 Sep 60 United Nations
ARTICLES: 1 LANGUAGE: French.
HEADNOTE: ACCEPTANCE OBLIGATIONS UN
TOPIC: UN Charter
CONCEPTS: Acceptance of UN obligations. Adher-
ence to UN charter.
INTL ORGS: United Nations.
PARTIES:
Upper Volta

105360 Unilateral Instrument **375 UNTS 103**
SIGNED: 7 Aug 60 FORCE: 20 Sep 60
REGISTERED: 20 Sep 60 United Nations
ARTICLES: 1 LANGUAGE: French.
HEADNOTE: ACCEPTANCE OBLIGATIONS UN
TOPIC: UN Charter
CONCEPTS: Acceptance of UN obligations. Adher-
ence to UN charter.
INTL ORGS: United Nations.
PARTIES:
Ivory Coast

105361 Unilateral Instrument **375 UNTS 107**
SIGNED: 12 Aug 60 FORCE: 20 Sep 60
REGISTERED: 20 Sep 60 United Nations
ARTICLES: 1 LANGUAGE: French.
HEADNOTE: ACCEPTANCE OBLIGATIONS UN
TOPIC: UN Charter
CONCEPTS: Acceptance of UN obligations. Adher-
ence to UN charter.
INTL ORGS: United Nations.

PARTIES:
Chad

105362 Unilateral Instrument **375 UNTS 111**
SIGNED: 12 Aug 60 FORCE: 20 Sep 60
REGISTERED: 20 Sep 60 United Nations
ARTICLES: 1 LANGUAGE: French.
HEADNOTE: ACCEPTANCE OBLIGATIONS UN
TOPIC: UN Charter
CONCEPTS: Acceptance of UN obligations. Adher-
ence to UN charter.
INTL ORGS: United Nations.
PARTIES:
Congo (Brazzaville)

105363 Unilateral Instrument **375 UNTS 115**
SIGNED: 13 Aug 60 FORCE: 20 Sep 60
REGISTERED: 20 Sep 60 United Nations
ARTICLES: 1 LANGUAGE: French.
HEADNOTE: ACCEPTANCE OBLIGATIONS UN
TOPIC: UN Charter
CONCEPTS: Acceptance of UN obligations. Adher-
ence to UN charter.
INTL ORGS: United Nations.
PARTIES:
Central Afri Rep

105364 Bilateral Agreement **375 UNTS 119**
SIGNED: 11 Jan 60 FORCE: 11 Jan 60
REGISTERED: 21 Sep 60 Pakistan
ARTICLES: 4 LANGUAGE: English.
HEADNOTE: WEST PAKISTAN-INDIA BORDER DIS-
PUTES
TOPIC: Territory Boundary
CONCEPTS: Annex or appendix reference. Mark-
ers and definitions.
INTL ORGS: Special Commission.
PARTIES:
India
Pakistan

105365 Bilateral Agreement **375 UNTS 141**
SIGNED: 7 Jun 60 FORCE: 7 Jun 60
REGISTERED: 22 Sep 60 UK Great Britain
ARTICLES: 9 LANGUAGE: English.
HEADNOTE: TROPICAL FISH CULTURE RESEARCH
INSTITUTE
TOPIC: Scientific Project
CONCEPTS: Territorial application. Annex or ap-
pendix reference. Incorporation of treaty provi-
sions into national law. Research cooperation.
Fisheries and fishing.
PROCEDURE: Amendment.
PARTIES:
Fed of Malaya
UK Great Britain

105366 Bilateral Agreement **375 UNTS 159**
SIGNED: 16 Sep 59 FORCE: 1 Mar 60
REGISTERED: 23 Sep 60 IBRD (World Bank)
ARTICLES: 6 LANGUAGE: English.
HEADNOTE: GUARANTEE NUCLEAR POWER
TOPIC: IBRD Project
CONCEPTS: Definition of terms. Annex or appen-
dix reference. Exchange of information and doc-
uments. Inspection and observation. Bonds.
Fees and exemptions. Tax exemptions. Domestic
obligation. Terms of loan. General. Peaceful use.
Loan regulations. Loan guarantee. Guarantor
non-interference.
PARTIES:
Italy
IBRD (World Bank)

105367 Bilateral Agreement **375 UNTS 201**
SIGNED: 27 May 60 FORCE: 30 Jun 60
REGISTERED: 23 Sep 60 IBRD (World Bank)
ARTICLES: 5 LANGUAGE: English.
HEADNOTE: GUARANTEE AGRICULTURE
TOPIC: IBRD Project
CONCEPTS: Definition of terms. Annex or appen-
dix reference. Exchange of information and doc-
uments. Inspection and observation. Bonds.
Fees and exemptions. Tax exemptions. Domestic
obligation. Agriculture. Terms of loan. Loan regu-
lations. Loan guarantee. Guarantor non-interfer-
ence.

PARTIES:
IBRD (World Bank)
UK Great Britain

105368 Bilateral Protocol **375 UNTS 235**
SIGNED: 16 Jun 56   FORCE: 3 Aug 56
REGISTERED: 26 Sep 60 Yugoslavia
ARTICLES: 7 LANGUAGE: Serbo-Croat. Bulgarian.
HEADNOTE: NEW DESCRIPTION FRONTIER LINE
TOPIC: Territory Boundary
CONCEPTS: Frontier permits. Establishment of commission. Markers and definitions.
INTL ORGS: Special Commission.
PARTIES:
Bulgaria
Yugoslavia

105369 Bilateral Protocol **375 UNTS 249**
SIGNED: 17 Jun 57   FORCE: 30 May 58
REGISTERED: 26 Sep 60 Yugoslavia
ARTICLES: 1 LANGUAGE: Serbo-Croat. Bulgarian.
HEADNOTE: NEW DESCRIPTION FRONTIER
TOPIC: Territory Boundary
CONCEPTS: Annex or appendix reference. Markers and definitions.
INTL ORGS: Special Commission.
PARTIES:
Bulgaria
Yugoslavia

105370 Bilateral Convention **375 UNTS 287**
SIGNED: 17 Jun 55   FORCE: 16 May 56
REGISTERED: 26 Sep 60 Yugoslavia
ARTICLES: 22 LANGUAGE: Serbo-Croat. Bulgarian.
HEADNOTE: VETERINARY HEALTH CONVENTION
TOPIC: Sanitation
CONCEPTS: Definition of terms. Detailed regulations. Previous treaty extension. Border traffic and migration. Inspection and observation. Dispute settlement. Arbitration. Veterinary. Vocational training. Scientific exchange. Reexport of goods, etc.. Trade procedures. Materials, equipment and services.
PROCEDURE: Denunciation. Duration. Ratification. Renewal or Revival.
PARTIES:
Bulgaria
Yugoslavia

105371 Bilateral Agreement **375 UNTS 333**
SIGNED: 2 Nov 54   FORCE: 12 Aug 55
REGISTERED: 26 Sep 60 Yugoslavia
ARTICLES: 6 LANGUAGE: French.
HEADNOTE: INDUSTRIAL COMMERCIAL TRADEMARKS
TOPIC: Patents/Copyrights
CONCEPTS: Patents, copyrights and trademarks. Trademarks.
TREATY REF: 205LTS219; 205LTS163; 32UNTS407.
PARTIES:
Bulgaria
Yugoslavia

105372 Bilateral Convention **376 UNTS 3**
SIGNED: 18 Dec 57   FORCE: 1 Sep 58
REGISTERED: 26 Sep 60 Yugoslavia
ARTICLES: 35 LANGUAGE: Serbo-Croat. Bulgarian.
HEADNOTE: SOCIAL SECURITY
TOPIC: Non-ILO Labor
CONCEPTS: Definition of terms. Exceptions and exemptions. Annex or appendix reference. Domestic legislation. Incorporation of treaty provisions into national law. Old age and invalidity insurance. Wages and salaries. Non-ILO labor relations. Family allowances. Administrative cooperation. Old age insurance. Sickness and invalidity insurance. Social security. Unemployment. Payment schedules. Claims and settlements. National treatment.
PROCEDURE: Denunciation. Duration. Ratification.
PARTIES:
Bulgaria
Yugoslavia

105373 Bilateral Agreement **376 UNTS 53**
SIGNED: 21 Mar 58   FORCE: 14 Aug 58
REGISTERED: 26 Sep 60 Yugoslavia
ARTICLES: 18 LANGUAGE: Serbo-Croat. Bulgarian.
HEADNOTE: TRUCKING REGULATIONS & CUSTOMS
TOPIC: Customs
CONCEPTS: Commercial road vehicles. Customs declarations.
PARTIES:
Bulgaria
Yugoslavia

105374 Unilateral Instrument **376 UNTS 79**
SIGNED: 20 Sep 60   FORCE: 20 Sep 60
REGISTERED: 28 Sep 60 United Nations
ARTICLES: 1 LANGUAGE: French.
HEADNOTE: ACCEPTANCE OBLIGATIONS UN
TOPIC: UN Charter
CONCEPTS: Adherence to UN charter.
INTL ORGS: United Nations.
PARTIES:
Senegal

105375 Multilateral Agreement **376 UNTS 85**
SIGNED: 20 Apr 59   FORCE: 3 Sep 60
REGISTERED: 28 Sep 60 Council of Europe
ARTICLES: 12 LANGUAGE: English. French.
HEADNOTE: ABOLITION VISAS REFUGEES
TOPIC: Visas
CONCEPTS: Definition of terms. Emergencies. Non-prejudice to third party. Border traffic and migration. Denial of admission. Refugees. Markers and definitions.
INTL ORGS: Council of Europe.
PROCEDURE: Accession. Ratification. Termination.
PARTIES:
Belgium SIGNED: 20 Apr 59 FORCE: 3 Sep 60
Council of Europe
France SIGNED: 20 Apr 59 FORCE: 3 Sep 60
Germany, West SIGNED: 20 Apr 59
Luxembourg SIGNED: 20 Apr 59
Netherlands SIGNED: 20 Apr 59 RATIFIED: 3 Aug 60 FORCE: 3 Sep 60
ANNEX
383 UNTS 336. Sweden. Signature without Reservation as to Approval 30 Nov 60. Force 1 Jan 61.
383 UNTS 336. Norway. Signature without Reservation as to Approval 25 Nov 60. Force 1 Jan 61.
383 UNTS 336. Denmark. Signature without Reservation as to Approval 30 Nov 60. Force 1 Jan 61.
387 UNTS 350. France. Algeria.
387 UNTS 350. France. Sahara Departments.
387 UNTS 350. Denmark. Declaration 13 Dec 60.
387 UNTS 350. Norway. Declaration 13 Dec 60.
414 UNTS 400. Germany, West. Qualified Ratification 6 Nov 61. Force 7 Dec 61.
414 UNTS 400. Luxembourg. Ratification 24 Apr 61. Force 25 May 61.
565 UNTS 300. Italy. Signature Subject to Ratification 4 Dec 63. Ratification 1 Jun 65.
565 UNTS 300. Italy. Force 2 Jul 65.
572 UNTS 359. Iceland. Signature 8 Sep 66. Force 9 Oct 66.
572 UNTS 359. Iceland. Ratification 8 Sep 66. Force 9 Oct 66.

105376 Multilateral Agreement **376 UNTS 99**
SIGNED: 20 Aug 59   FORCE: 1 Oct 60
REGISTERED: 1 Oct 60 Denmark
ARTICLES: 5 LANGUAGE: Danish. Swedish. Norwegian.
HEADNOTE: FINANCIAL GUARANTEES
TOPIC: Air Transport
CONCEPTS: Private investment guarantee. Air transport.
TREATY REF: 222UNTS313.
PARTIES:
Denmark SIGNED: 20 Aug 59 FORCE: 1 Oct 60
Norway SIGNED: 20 Aug 59 FORCE: 1 Oct 60
Sweden SIGNED: 20 Aug 59 FORCE: 1 Oct 60
ANNEX
473 UNTS 359. Denmark. Implementation 18 Jun 63. Force 18 Jun 63.
473 UNTS 359. Norway. Implementation 18 Jun 63. Force 18 Jun 63.

473 UNTS 359. Sweden. Implementation 18 Jun 63. Force 18 Jun 63.
646 UNTS 385. Denmark. Prolongation 31 Aug 66. Force 31 Aug 66.
646 UNTS 385. Sweden. Prolongation 31 Aug 66. Force 31 Aug 66.
646 UNTS 385. Norway. Prolongation 31 Aug 66. Force 31 Aug 66.

105377 Multilateral Agreement **376 UNTS 111**
SIGNED: 28 Apr 60   FORCE: 9 Sep 60
REGISTERED: 1 Oct 60 Council of Europe
ARTICLES: 9 LANGUAGE: English. French.
HEADNOTE: IMPORTATION MEDICAL EQUIPMENT
TOPIC: Health/Educ/Welfare
CONCEPTS: Conditions. Detailed regulations. Non-prejudice to third party. Licenses and permits. International circulation. Trade procedures. Customs exemptions. Materials, equipment and services. Loan repayment.
INTL ORGS: Council of Europe.
PROCEDURE: Accession. Duration. Ratification. Termination.
PARTIES:
Belgium SIGNED: 8 Jun 60 FORCE: 9 Sep 60
Denmark SIGNED: 28 Apr 60
France SIGNED: 28 Apr 60 FORCE: 29 Jul 60
Germany, West SIGNED: 28 Apr 60
Greece SIGNED: 28 Apr 60
Ireland SIGNED: 28 Apr 60 FORCE: 29 Jul 60
Italy SIGNED: 28 Apr 60
Luxembourg SIGNED: 28 Apr 60
Norway SIGNED: 28 Apr 60 FORCE: 29 Jul 60
Sweden SIGNED: 28 Apr 60
UK Great Britain SIGNED: 28 Apr 60 FORCE: 29 Jul 60
ANNEX
414 UNTS 401. Austria. Signature 8 Mar 61. Force 11 Oct 61.
414 UNTS 401. Austria. Force 12 Jan 62.
424 UNTS 392. Denmark. Ratification 14 Mar 62. Force 15 Jun 62.
444 UNTS 352. Netherlands. Netherlands Antilles. Force 27 Sep 62.
444 UNTS 352. Luxembourg. Ratification 10 May 62. Force 11 Aug 62.
444 UNTS 352. Sweden. Ratification 27 Jul 62. Force 28 Oct 62.
444 UNTS 352. Netherlands. Ratification 26 Jun 62. Force 27 Sep 62.
444 UNTS 352. Netherlands. Surinam. Force 27 Sep 62.
444 UNTS 352. Netherlands. Signature 9 Sep 61.
559 UNTS 354. Italy. Ratification 14 May 63. Force 15 Aug 63.
559 UNTS 354. Greece. Ratification 24 May 65. Force 25 Aug 65.
559 UNTS 354. Switzerland. Ratification 29 Nov 65. Force 28 Feb 66.
559 UNTS 354. Germany, West. Ratification 11 Feb 66. Force 12 May 66.
559 UNTS 354. Turkey. Ratification 10 Mar 66. Force 11 Jun 66.
635 UNTS 353. Malta. Ratification 22 Sep 67. Force 23 Dec 67.

105378 Multilateral Agreement **376 UNTS 122**
SIGNED: 15 Jan 57   FORCE: 26 Sep 60
REGISTERED: 3 Oct 60 United Nations
ARTICLES: 6 LANGUAGE: English. Spanish.
HEADNOTE: TECHNICAL ASSISTANCE
TOPIC: Tech Assistance
CONCEPTS: Definition of terms. General provisions. Previous treaty replacement. Privileges and immunities. General cooperation. Exchange of information and documents. Personnel. Responsibility and liability. Title and deeds. Use of facilities. Exchange. Vocational training. Research and development. Import quotas. Expense sharing formulae. Local currency. Domestic obligation. General technical assistance. Materials, equipment and services. Conformity with IGO decisions.
TREATY REF: 76UNTS132; 1UNTS15; 33UNTS261.
PROCEDURE: Amendment. Ratification. Termination.
PARTIES:
Chile SIGNED: 15 Jan 57 RATIFIED: 26 Sep 60 FORCE: 26 Sep 60

FAO (Food Agri) SIGNED: 15 Jan 57 FORCE: 26 Sep 60
ICAO (Civil Aviat) SIGNED: 15 Jan 57 FORCE: 26 Sep 60
ILO (Labor Org) SIGNED: 15 Jan 57 FORCE: 26 Sep 60
ITU (Telecommun) SIGNED: 15 Jan 57 FORCE: 26 Sep 60
UNESCO (Educ/Cult) SIGNED: 15 Jan 57 FORCE: 26 Sep 60
United Nations SIGNED: 15 Jan 57 FORCE: 26 Sep 60
WHO (World Health) SIGNED: 15 Jan 57 FORCE: 26 Sep 60
WMO (Meteorology) SIGNED: 15 Jan 57 FORCE: 26 Sep 60

105379 Bilateral Agreement **376 UNTS 145**
SIGNED: 19 Aug 59 FORCE: 5 Aug 60
REGISTERED: 3 Oct 60 Norway
ARTICLES: 4 LANGUAGE: Swedish. Spanish.
HEADNOTE: CULTURAL AGREEMENT
TOPIC: Culture
CONCEPTS: Friendship and amity. Establishment of commission. Exchange. Scholarships and grants. Exchange. General cultural cooperation. Artists. Scientific exchange.
INTL ORGS: Special Commission.
PROCEDURE: Denunciation. Duration. Ratification.
PARTIES:
Norway
Spain

105380 Bilateral Agreement **376 UNTS 155**
SIGNED: 25 Feb 60 FORCE: 14 Sep 60
REGISTERED: 3 Oct 60 Norway
ARTICLES: 27 LANGUAGE: Swedish. German.
HEADNOTE: DOUBLE TAXATION INCOME FORTUNE
TOPIC: Taxation
CONCEPTS: Definition of terms. Territorial application. Privileges and immunities. Nationality and citizenship. Conformity with municipal law. Exchange of official publications. Negotiation. Teacher and student exchange. Claims and settlements. Taxation. Equitable taxes. Tax exemptions. Air transport. Merchant vessels.
PROCEDURE: Duration. Ratification. Termination.
PARTIES:
Austria
Norway

105381 Bilateral Agreement **376 UNTS 217**
SIGNED: 16 May 60 FORCE: 1 Jul 60
REGISTERED: 6 Oct 60 South Africa
ARTICLES: 13 LANGUAGE: Afrikaans. English.
HEADNOTE: TRADE
TOPIC: General Trade
CONCEPTS: Establishment of trade relations.
PROCEDURE: Duration. Termination.
PARTIES:
Fed Rhod/Nyasaland
South Africa
ANNEX
394 UNTS 314. South Africa. Amendment 2 Feb 61. Force 14 Feb 61.
394 UNTS 314. Fed Rhod/Nyasaland. Amendment 2 Feb 61. Force 14 Feb 61.
480 UNTS 416. South Africa. Amendment 27 Feb 63. Force 11 Mar 63.
480 UNTS 416. Fed Rhod/Nyasaland. Amendment 27 Feb 63. Force 11 Mar 63.

105382 Bilateral Agreement **376 UNTS 243**
SIGNED: 3 Jun 60 FORCE: 3 Jun 60
REGISTERED: 7 Oct 60 USA (United States)
ARTICLES: 6 LANGUAGE: English.
HEADNOTE: AGRI COMMOD
TOPIC: US Agri Commod Aid
CONCEPTS: Accounting procedures. Agricultural commodities.
PARTIES:
USA (United States)
Yugoslavia
ANNEX
421 UNTS 344. USA (United States). Amendment 1 Jul 61. Force 1 Jul 61.
421 UNTS 344. Yugoslavia. Amendment 1 Jul 61. Force 1 Jul 61.

105383 Bilateral Exchange **376 UNTS 267**
SIGNED: 15 Jun 60 FORCE: 15 Jun 60
REGISTERED: 7 Oct 60 USA (United States)
ARTICLES: 2 LANGUAGE: English.
HEADNOTE: COPYRIGHT
TOPIC: Patents/Copyrights
CONCEPTS: Conformity with municipal law. Domestic legislation. Laws and formalities. Post-war adjustment.
PARTIES:
Austria
USA (United States)

105384 Bilateral Agreement **376 UNTS 279**
SIGNED: 4 May 60 FORCE: 4 May 60
REGISTERED: 7 Oct 60 USA (United States)
ARTICLES: 6 LANGUAGE: English.
HEADNOTE: AGRI COMMOD TITLE I
TOPIC: US Agri Commod Aid
CONCEPTS: General provisions. Annex or appendix reference. Exchange of information and documents. Reexport of goods, etc.. Exchange rates and regulations. Transportation costs. Local currency. Commodities schedule. Purchase authorization. Surplus commodities. Mutual consultation.
PARTIES:
India
USA (United States)
ANNEX
384 UNTS 386. USA (United States). Supplementation 29 Jul 60. Force 29 Jul 60.
384 UNTS 386. India. Supplementation 29 Jul 60. Force 29 Jul 60.
389 UNTS 336. USA (United States). Supplementation 23 Sep 60. Force 23 Sep 60.
389 UNTS 336. India. Supplementation 23 Sep 60. Force 23 Sep 60.
406 UNTS 346. USA (United States). Amendment 9 Mar 61. Force 9 Mar 61.
406 UNTS 346. India. Amendment 9 Mar 61. Force 9 Mar 61.

105385 Bilateral Exchange **376 UNTS 301**
SIGNED: 31 May 60 FORCE: 31 May 60
REGISTERED: 7 Oct 60 USA (United States)
ARTICLES: 2 LANGUAGE: English. Japanese.
HEADNOTE: FINANCING TYPHOON REHIBILITATING ACTIVITIES
TOPIC: Direct Aid
CONCEPTS: Financial programs. Local currency. Relief supplies. Procurement.
TREATY REF: 241UNTS197; 275UNTS105.
PARTIES:
Japan
USA (United States)

105386 Bilateral Agreement **376 UNTS 311**
SIGNED: 23 Mar 56 FORCE: 22 Mar 60
REGISTERED: 7 Oct 60 USA (United States)
ARTICLES: 7 LANGUAGE: English. Spanish.
HEADNOTE: PROGRAM TECHNICAL COOPERATION
TOPIC: Tech Assistance
CONCEPTS: Exceptions and exemptions. Treaty implementation. Previous treaty replacement. Diplomatic privileges. General cooperation. Exchange of information and documents. Informational records. Personnel. Public information. Export quotas. Import quotas. Attachment of funds. Exchange rates and regulations. Fees and exemptions. Funding procedures. Garnishment of funds. Seizure funds. Tax exemptions. Domestic obligation. Assistance. Materials, equipment and services. Aid missions.
TREATY REF: TECHNICAL COOPERATION, 1-4MAR51.
PROCEDURE: Amendment. Ratification. Termination.
PARTIES:
USA (United States)
Uruguay

105387 Bilateral Agreement **376 UNTS 331**
SIGNED: 20 Sep 58 FORCE: 1 Oct 60
REGISTERED: 10 Oct 60 Belgium
ARTICLES: 9 LANGUAGE: French.
HEADNOTE: COMPENSATION DISABLEMENT DEATH DUE WAR INJURY SUFFERED CIVILIANS
TOPIC: Reparations

CONCEPTS: Definition of terms. Time limit. Recognition. Nationality and citizenship. General cooperation. Informational records. Loss and/or damage. Post-war claims settlement.
PROCEDURE: Denunciation. Ratification. Termination.
PARTIES:
Belgium
France

105388 Bilateral Agreement **376 UNTS 341**
SIGNED: 11 Oct 60 FORCE: 11 Oct 60
REGISTERED: 11 Oct 60 United Nations
ARTICLES: 10 LANGUAGE: English.
HEADNOTE: ASSISTANCE
TOPIC: Direct Aid
CONCEPTS: Detailed regulations. Treaty implementation. Visas. Privileges and immunities. Exchange of information and documents. Informational records. Inspection and observation. Operating agencies. Personnel. Public information. Responsibility and liability. Title and deeds. Use of facilities. Arbitration. Procedure. Negotiation. Import quotas. Attachment of funds. Exchange rates and regulations. Expense sharing formulae. Financial programs. Domestic obligation. General technical assistance. Economic assistance. Materials, equipment and services. IGO status.
INTL ORGS: International Atomic Energy Agency. United Nations.
TREATY REF: 1UNTS15; 33UNTS261; 374UNTS137.
PROCEDURE: Amendment. Termination.
PARTIES:
Liberia
UN Special Fund

105389 Bilateral Agreement **376 UNTS 357**
SIGNED: 19 Jun 60 FORCE: 13 Oct 60
REGISTERED: 13 Oct 60 United Nations
ARTICLES: 10 LANGUAGE: English.
HEADNOTE: ASSISTANCE
TOPIC: Direct Aid
CONCEPTS: Detailed regulations. Treaty implementation. Visas. Privileges and immunities. Exchange of information and documents. Informational records. Inspection and observation. Operating agencies. Personnel. Public information. Responsibility and liability. Title and deeds. Use of facilities. Arbitration. Procedure. Negotiation. Import quotas. Attachment of funds. Exchange rates and regulations. Expense sharing formulae. Financial programs. Domestic obligation. General technical assistance. Economic assistance. Materials, equipment and services. IGO status.
INTL ORGS: United Nations. Arbitration Commission.
TREATY REF: 1UNTS15; 33UNTS261; 374UNTS137.
PROCEDURE: Amendment. Termination.
PARTIES:
Iraq
UN Special Fund

105390 Bilateral Agreement **376 UNTS 375**
SIGNED: 4 Jan 60 FORCE: 3 May 60
REGISTERED: 14 Oct 60 Denmark
ARTICLES: 6 LANGUAGE: Swedish.
HEADNOTE: REMOVAL TRADE BARRIERS
TOPIC: General Trade
CONCEPTS: Detailed regulations. Treaty implementation. Annex type material. General cooperation. Exchange of information and documents. Reexport of goods, etc.. Trade agencies. Trade procedures. Accounting procedures. Banking. Currency. Financial programs. Interest rates. Payment schedules. Purchase authorizations. Transportation costs. Local currency. Commodity trade. Quotas. Agricultural commodities. Loan repayment. Terms of loan.
INTL ORGS: European Free Trade Association.
PROCEDURE: Ratification.
PARTIES:
Denmark
Sweden
ANNEX
633 UNTS 411. Sweden. Force 25 Jan 64.
633 UNTS 411. Denmark. Force 25 Jan 64.

105391 Multilateral Agreement **376 UNTS 382**
SIGNED: 9 Oct 59   FORCE: 9 Oct 59
REGISTERED: 14 Oct 60 United Nations
ARTICLES: 15 LANGUAGE: Spanish.
HEADNOTE: PROVISION TECHNICAL ASSISTANCE UNDER FUNDS HELD TRUST
TOPIC: Tech Assistance
CONCEPTS: Time limit. Treaty implementation. Personnel. Use of facilities. Negotiation. Scholarships and grants. Accounting procedures. Indemnities and reimbursements. Currency deposits. Expense sharing formulae. Fees and exemptions. Funding procedures. Payment schedules. General technical assistance. Materials, equipment and services.
TREATY REF: 201UNTS51.
PROCEDURE: Amendment. Termination.
PARTIES:
  FAO (Food Agri) SIGNED: 9 Oct 59 FORCE: 9 Oct 59
  IAEA (Atom Energy) SIGNED: 9 Oct 59 FORCE: 9 Oct 59
  ICAO (Civil Aviat) SIGNED: 9 Oct 59 FORCE: 9 Oct 59
  ILO (Labor Org) SIGNED: 9 Oct 59 FORCE: 9 Oct 59
  ITU (Telecommun) SIGNED: 9 Oct 59 FORCE: 9 Oct 59
  UNESCO (Educ/Cult) SIGNED: 9 Oct 59 FORCE: 9 Oct 59
  United Nations SIGNED: 9 Oct 59 FORCE: 9 Oct 59
  WHO (World Health) SIGNED: 9 Oct 59 FORCE: 9 Oct 59
  WMO (Meteorology) SIGNED: 9 Oct 59 FORCE: 9 Oct 59
  Venezuela SIGNED: 9 Oct 59 FORCE: 9 Oct 59

105392 Bilateral Exchange **377 UNTS 3**
SIGNED: 23 May 60   FORCE: 23 May 60
REGISTERED: 22 Oct 60 USA (United States)
ARTICLES: 2 LANGUAGE: English. Spanish.
HEADNOTE: NUCLEAR RESEARCH TRAINING EQUIPMENT
TOPIC: Atomic Energy
CONCEPTS: Responsibility and liability. Research and scientific projects. Research results. Research and development. Indemnities and reimbursements. Materials, equipment and services. Atomic energy assistance. Nuclear materials. Non-nuclear materials. Peaceful use.
PARTIES:
  Argentina
  USA (United States)

105393 Bilateral Agreement **377 UNTS 11**
SIGNED: 2 Jun 60   FORCE: 2 Jun 60
REGISTERED: 22 Oct 60 USA (United States)
ARTICLES: 6 LANGUAGE: English. Spanish.
HEADNOTE: AGRI COMMOD
TOPIC: US Agri Commod Aid
CONCEPTS: Currency. Agricultural commodities.
PARTIES:
  Chile
  USA (United States)
              ANNEX
388 UNTS 397. USA (United States). Amendment 12 Aug 60. Force 12 Aug 60.
388 UNTS 397. Chile. Amendment 12 Aug 60. Force 12 Aug 60.

105394 Bilateral Exchange **377 UNTS 37**
SIGNED: 13 Jun 60   FORCE: 13 Jun 60
REGISTERED: 22 Oct 60 USA (United States)
ARTICLES: 2 LANGUAGE: English.
HEADNOTE: GRANT CERTAIN NUCLEAR RESEARCH EQUIPMENT
TOPIC: Atomic Energy
CONCEPTS: Non-prejudice to third party. Exchange of information and documents. Responsibility and liability. Research cooperation. Nuclear materials. Peaceful use.
PARTIES:
  India
  USA (United States)

105395 Bilateral Exchange **377 UNTS 45**
SIGNED: 27 May 60   FORCE: 27 May 60
REGISTERED: 22 Oct 60 USA (United States)
ARTICLES: 2 LANGUAGE: English. German.

HEADNOTE: WEAPONS PRODUCTION
TOPIC: Milit Assistance
CONCEPTS: Procurement and logistics.
INTL ORGS: North Atlantic Treaty Organization.
TREATY REF: MUTUAL DEFENSE ASSISTANCE AGREE. JUNE 30, 1955..
PARTIES:
  Germany, West
  USA (United States)

105396 Bilateral Agreement **377 UNTS 63**
SIGNED: 24 Jun 60   FORCE: 24 Jun 60
REGISTERED: 22 Oct 60 USA (United States)
ARTICLES: 26 LANGUAGE: English.
HEADNOTE: ESTABLISHMENT LONG-RANGE AID TO NAVIGATION STATION
TOPIC: Gen Communications
CONCEPTS: Definition of terms. Protection of nationals. Juridical personality. Legal protection and assistance. Title and deeds. General health, education, culture, welfare and labor. Claims and settlements. Assets transfer. General. Tax exemptions. Customs exemptions. Navigational conditions. Facilities and equipment. Postal services. Radio-telephone-telegraphic communications. Security of information. Jurisdiction. Status of forces.
TREATY REF: 204LTS15; 88UNTS273.
PROCEDURE: Amendment. Duration. Termination.
PARTIES:
  UK Great Britain
  USA (United States)

105397 Bilateral Exchange **377 UNTS 95**
SIGNED: 15 Feb 60   FORCE: 15 Feb 60
REGISTERED: 22 Oct 60 USA (United States)
ARTICLES: 2 LANGUAGE: English.
HEADNOTE: WEAPONS PRODUCTION PROGRAM
TOPIC: Milit Assistance
CONCEPTS: Change of circumstances. Annex or appendix reference. Previous treaty replacement. General cooperation. Use of facilities. Reexport of goods, etc.. Indemnities and reimbursements. Most favored nation clause. Customs exemptions. General technical assistance. Materials, equipment and services. Equipment and supplies.
INTL ORGS: North Atlantic Treaty Organization.
TREATY REF: 34UNTS243.
PROCEDURE: Future Procedures Contemplated.
PARTIES:
  Greece
  USA (United States)

105398 Bilateral Agreement **377 UNTS 111**
SIGNED: 17 Jun 59   FORCE: 2 Sep 60
REGISTERED: 24 Oct 60 IBRD (World Bank)
ARTICLES: 5 LANGUAGE: English.
HEADNOTE: GUARANTEE POWER
TOPIC: IBRD Project
CONCEPTS: Definition of terms. Annex or appendix reference. Exchange of information and documents. Inspection and observation. Bonds. Fees and exemptions. Tax exemptions. Domestic obligation. Terms of loan. Loan regulations. Loan guarantee. Guarantor non-interference. Hydro-electric power.
PARTIES:
  Brazil
  IBRD (World Bank)

105399 Bilateral Agreement **377 UNTS 153**
SIGNED: 29 Jul 60   FORCE: 13 Oct 60
REGISTERED: 24 Oct 60 IBRD (World Bank)
ARTICLES: 7 LANGUAGE: English.
HEADNOTE: LOAN FIFTH RAILWAY PROJECT
TOPIC: IBRD Project
CONCEPTS: Annex or appendix reference. Exchange of information and documents. Accounting procedures. Bonds. Financial programs. Interest rates. Debt settlement. Liens. Domestic obligation. Loan repayment. Terms of loan. World Bank projects. Loan regulations. Plans and standards.
PARTIES:
  India
  IBRD (World Bank)

105400 Bilateral Agreement **377 UNTS 171**
SIGNED: 24 Oct 60   FORCE: 13 Oct 60
REGISTERED: 24 Oct 60 United Nations
ARTICLES: 10 LANGUAGE: English. Spanish.
HEADNOTE: ASSISTANCE
TOPIC: Direct Aid
CONCEPTS: Detailed regulations. Treaty implementation. Visas. Privileges and immunities. Exchange of information and documents. Informational records. Inspection and observation. Operating agencies. Personnel. Public information. Responsibility and liability. Title and deeds. Use of facilities. Arbitration. Procedure. Negotiation. Import quotas. Attachment of funds. Exchange rates and regulations. Expense sharing formulae. Financial programs. Domestic obligation. General technical assistance. Economic assistance. Materials, equipment and services. IGO status.
INTL ORGS: International Atomic Energy Agency. International Court of Justice. United Nations. Arbitration Commission.
TREATY REF: 1UNTS15; 33UNTS261; 374UNTS137.
PROCEDURE: Amendment. Termination.
PARTIES:
  El Salvador
  UN Special Fund

105401 Bilateral Exchange **377 UNTS 197**
SIGNED: 4 Jun 60   FORCE: 4 Jun 60
REGISTERED: 24 Oct 60 Ghana
ARTICLES: 2 LANGUAGE: English.
HEADNOTE: APPEALS JUDICIAL COMMITTEE PRIVY COUNCIL
TOPIC: Admin Cooperation
CONCEPTS: General cooperation.
PARTIES:
  Ghana
  UK Great Britain

105402 Multilateral Convention **377 UNTS 203**
SIGNED: 7 Jul 59   FORCE: 21 Mar 60
REGISTERED: 28 Oct 60 United Nations
ARTICLES: 15 LANGUAGE: Bulgarian. Romanian. Russian.
HEADNOTE: FISHING BLACK SEA
TOPIC: Specific Resources
CONCEPTS: Exchange of information and documents. Establishment of commission. Research results. Ports and pilotage. Fisheries and fishing.
INTL ORGS: United Nations. Special Commission.
PROCEDURE: Accession. Duration. Ratification. Registration. Renewal or Revival. Termination.
PARTIES:
  Bulgaria SIGNED: 7 Jul 59 FORCE: 21 Mar 60
  Romania SIGNED: 7 Jul 59 FORCE: 21 Mar 60
  USSR (Soviet Union) SIGNED: 7 Jul 59 FORCE: 21 Mar 60

105403 Bilateral Exchange **377 UNTS 231**
SIGNED: 19 May 59   FORCE: 15 May 59
REGISTERED: 28 Oct 60 Israel
ARTICLES: 2 LANGUAGE: French.
HEADNOTE: MOVEMENT MERCHANT SEAMEN
TOPIC: Admin Cooperation
CONCEPTS: Non-visa travel documents.
PROCEDURE: Denunciation.
PARTIES:
  France
  Israel

105404 Bilateral Agreement **377 UNTS 237**
SIGNED: 30 Nov 59   FORCE: 12 Apr 60
REGISTERED: 28 Oct 60 Israel
ARTICLES: 15 LANGUAGE: Hebrew. French.
HEADNOTE: CULTURAL AGREEMENT WITH ANNEXES
TOPIC: Culture
CONCEPTS: Annex or appendix reference. Tourism. Conformity with municipal law. General cooperation. Operating agencies. Establishment of commission. Recognition of degrees. Exchange. Teacher and student exchange. Professorships. Institute establishment. Scholarships and grants. Exchange. General cultural cooperation. Artists. Research cooperation. Anthropology and archeology. Scientific exchange. Publications exchange. Mass media exchange.
INTL ORGS: Special Commission.

PROCEDURE: Denunciation. Duration. Ratification. Renewal or Revival.
PARTIES:
France
Israel

105405   Bilateral Exchange   **377 UNTS 261**
SIGNED: 15 Jun 60   FORCE: 15 Aug 60
REGISTERED: 28 Oct 60 Israel
ARTICLES: 2 LANGUAGE: English.
HEADNOTE: TRADEMARKS
TOPIC: Patents/Copyrights
CONCEPTS: Conformity with municipal law. Trademarks.
PARTIES:
Iceland
Israel

105406   Bilateral Convention   **377 UNTS 267**
SIGNED: 15 Jun 59   FORCE: 30 Mar 60
REGISTERED: 28 Oct 60 Israel
ARTICLES: 6 LANGUAGE: Hebrew. Spanish.
HEADNOTE: CULTURAL EXCHANGES
TOPIC: Culture
CONCEPTS: Friendship and amity. Conformity with municipal law. Teacher and student exchange. Exchange. General cultural cooperation. Artists. Scientific exchange. Research and development. Publications exchange. Mass media exchange.
PROCEDURE: Denunciation. Ratification.
PARTIES:
Israel
Mexico

105407   Bilateral Agreement   **377 UNTS 277**
SIGNED: 22 Dec 59   FORCE: 3 Jun 60
REGISTERED: 28 Oct 60 Israel
ARTICLES: 22 LANGUAGE: English.
HEADNOTE: DOUBLE TAXATION INCOME CAPITAL
TOPIC: Taxation
CONCEPTS: Definition of terms. Previous treaty replacement. Conformity with municipal law. Exchange of official publications. Teacher and student exchange. Claims and settlements. Taxation. Death duties. Tax credits. Equitable taxes. General. Tax exemptions. Air transport. Merchant vessels.
TREATY REF: 257UNTS47.
PROCEDURE: Duration. Ratification. Termination.
PARTIES:
Israel
Sweden

105408   Bilateral Convention   **377 UNTS 305**
SIGNED: 31 Dec 58   FORCE: 15 Dec 59
REGISTERED: 28 Oct 60 Israel
ARTICLES: 18 LANGUAGE: Hebrew. French.
HEADNOTE: EXTRADITION
TOPIC: Extradition
CONCEPTS: Extradition, deportation and repatriation. Extradition requests. Location of crime. Refusal of extradition. Concurrent requests. Provisional detainment. Extradition postponement. Indemnities and reimbursements. Conveyance in transit.
PROCEDURE: Denunciation. Ratification.
PARTIES:
Israel
Switzerland

105409   Bilateral Exchange   **377 UNTS 325**
SIGNED: 7 Jul 60   FORCE: 5 Sep 60
REGISTERED: 28 Oct 60 Israel
ARTICLES: 2 LANGUAGE: English.
HEADNOTE: EXEMPTION VISAS
TOPIC: Visas
CONCEPTS: Visa abolition. Resident permits.
PROCEDURE: Termination.
PARTIES:
Israel
Thailand

105410   Bilateral Agreement   **377 UNTS 331**
SIGNED: 4 Apr 60   FORCE: 26 Oct 60
REGISTERED: 28 Oct 60 Israel
ARTICLES: 18 LANGUAGE: Hebrew. English.

HEADNOTE: RECIPROCAL EXTRADITION CRIMINALS
TOPIC: Extradition
CONCEPTS: Territorial application. Time limit. Extradition, deportation and repatriation. Extradition requests. Extraditable offenses. Location of crime. Refusal of extradition. Pre-treaty crimes.
PROCEDURE: Ratification.
PARTIES:
Israel
UK Great Britain

105411   Bilateral Exchange   **377 UNTS 355**
SIGNED: 29 Jun 60   FORCE: 29 Jun 60
REGISTERED: 28 Oct 60 USA (United States)
ARTICLES: 2 LANGUAGE: English. Spanish.
HEADNOTE: EMERGENCY RELIEF ASSISTANCE
TOPIC: Direct Aid
CONCEPTS: Relief supplies.
PARTIES:
Chile
USA (United States)

105412   Unilateral Instrument   **377 UNTS 361**
SIGNED: 22 Oct 60   FORCE: 28 Sep 60
REGISTERED: 28 Oct 60 United Nations
ARTICLES: 1 LANGUAGE: French.
HEADNOTE: ACCEPTANCE OBLIGATIONS UN
TOPIC: UN Charter
CONCEPTS: Acceptance of UN obligations.
INTL ORGS: United Nations.
PARTIES:
Mali

105413   Bilateral Exchange   **377 UNTS 365**
SIGNED: 14 Jun 60   FORCE: 14 Jun 60
REGISTERED: 31 Oct 60 USA (United States)
ARTICLES: 2 LANGUAGE: English.
HEADNOTE: ATMOSPHERIC RESEARCH FACILITIES
TOPIC: Scientific Project
CONCEPTS: Conditions. Annex or appendix reference. Use of facilities. Research and scientific projects. Meteorology. Special projects.
PARTIES:
Canada
USA (United States)
ANNEX
546 UNTS 376. USA (United States). Amendment 11 Jun 65. Force 14 Jun 65.
546 UNTS 376. Canada. Amendment 11 Jun 65. Force 14 Jun 65.

105414   Bilateral Agreement   **378 UNTS 3**
SIGNED: 22 Jun 60   FORCE: 22 Jun 60
REGISTERED: 31 Oct 60 USA (United States)
ARTICLES: 6 LANGUAGE: English. Spanish.
HEADNOTE: AGRI COMMOD TITLE I
TOPIC: US Agri Commod Aid
CONCEPTS: General provisions. Annex or appendix reference. Exchange of information and documents. Reexport of goods, etc.. Exchange rates and regulations. Transportation costs. Local currency. Commodities schedule. Purchase authorization. Surplus commodities. Mutual consultation.
PARTIES:
Spain
USA (United States)

105415   Bilateral Exchange   **378 UNTS 25**
SIGNED: 6 Jul 60   FORCE: 6 Jul 60
REGISTERED: 31 Oct 60 USA (United States)
ARTICLES: 2 LANGUAGE: English.
HEADNOTE: SHIP BUILDING PROGRAM
TOPIC: Milit Assistance
CONCEPTS: Private contracts. Indemnities and reimbursements. Defense and security. Naval vessels.
TREATY REF: 80UNTS241.
PROCEDURE: Future Procedures Contemplated.
PARTIES:
Norway
USA (United States)

105416   Bilateral Agreement   **378 UNTS 31**
SIGNED: 18 Jan 55   FORCE: 22 Jul 55
REGISTERED: 1 Nov 60 Yugoslavia

ARTICLES: 13 LANGUAGE: Serbo-Croat. German.
HEADNOTE: CINEMATOGRAPHIC FILMS
TOPIC: Mass Media
CONCEPTS: Establishment of commission. Special tribunals. Indemnities and reimbursements. Assets. Mass media exchange.
INTL ORGS: Special Commission.
PROCEDURE: Denunciation. Duration. Renewal or Revival.
PARTIES:
Austria
Yugoslavia

105417   Bilateral Convention   **378 UNTS 49**
SIGNED: 11 Dec 55   FORCE: 11 Aug 56
REGISTERED: 1 Nov 60 Yugoslavia
ARTICLES: 14 LANGUAGE: Serbo-Croat. Bulgarian.
HEADNOTE: SANITARY DISEASE CONTROL METHODS
TOPIC: Sanitation
CONCEPTS: Definition of terms. Detailed regulations. General cooperation. Exchange of information and documents. Negotiation. Specialists exchange. Border control. Disease control. Exchange. Research and development. Indemnities and reimbursements. Materials, equipment and services. Publications exchange. Conferences.
TREATY REF: DANUBE CONVENTION ON SANITARY CONTROL 1954.
PROCEDURE: Denunciation. Duration. Ratification. Renewal or Revival.
PARTIES:
Bulgaria
Yugoslavia

105418   Bilateral Agreement   **378 UNTS 83**
SIGNED: 29 Jun 53   FORCE: 29 Jun 53
REGISTERED: 1 Nov 60 Yugoslavia
ARTICLES: 6 LANGUAGE: English.
HEADNOTE: ECONOMIC COORDINATION TRADE
TOPIC: General Trade
CONCEPTS: Annex or appendix reference. General cooperation. Licenses and permits. Export quotas. Import quotas. Trade procedures.
PROCEDURE: Termination.
PARTIES:
Burma
Yugoslavia

105419   Bilateral Protocol   **378 UNTS 93**
SIGNED: 14 Jun 55   FORCE: 14 Jun 55
REGISTERED: 1 Nov 60 Yugoslavia
ARTICLES: 6 LANGUAGE: English.
HEADNOTE: ECONOMIC COOPERATION
TOPIC: Direct Aid
CONCEPTS: Economic assistance.
PROCEDURE: Future Procedures Contemplated.
PARTIES:
Burma
Yugoslavia

105420   Bilateral Agreement   **378 UNTS 99**
SIGNED: 7 Mar 56   FORCE: 7 Mar 56
REGISTERED: 1 Nov 60 Yugoslavia
ARTICLES: 4 LANGUAGE: English.
HEADNOTE: DEVELOPMENT INDUSTRY UTILIZATION POWER NATURAL RESOURCES OTHER FIELDS
TOPIC: Direct Aid
CONCEPTS: Treaty implementation. Economic assistance. Industry. Natural resources. Hydroelectric power. Adherence to UN Charter.
INTL ORGS: United Nations.
TREATY REF: 378UNTS93.
PROCEDURE: Duration. Termination.
PARTIES:
Burma
Yugoslavia

105421   Bilateral Agreement   **378 UNTS 105**
SIGNED: 21 Aug 53   FORCE: 21 Aug 53
REGISTERED: 1 Nov 60 Yugoslavia
ARTICLES: 6 LANGUAGE: French.
HEADNOTE: TRADE ECONOMIC COOPERATION
TOPIC: General Economic
CONCEPTS: Exceptions and exemptions. Annex or appendix reference. General cooperation. Li-

censes and permits. General economics. General trade. Establishment of trade relations. Most favored nation clause. Customs duties. Customs exemptions.
PROCEDURE: Duration. Future Procedures Contemplated. Renewal or Revival. Termination.
PARTIES:
Ethiopia
Yugoslavia

105422 Bilateral Agreement **378 UNTS 117**
SIGNED: 14 Dec 56 FORCE: 14 Dec 56
REGISTERED: 1 Nov 60 Yugoslavia
ARTICLES: 8 LANGUAGE: English.
HEADNOTE: EXPANDING ECONOMIC RELATIONS
TOPIC: General Trade
CONCEPTS: Exceptions and exemptions. Annex or appendix reference. Conformity with municipal law. General cooperation. Establishment of commission. Export quotas. Import quotas. Trade procedures. Monetary and gold transfers. Payment schedules. Most favored nation clause.
INTL ORGS: Special Commission.
PROCEDURE: Duration. Renewal or Revival. Termination.
PARTIES:
Indonesia
Yugoslavia

105423 Bilateral Agreement **378 UNTS 127**
SIGNED: 19 Dec 55 FORCE: 19 Dec 55
REGISTERED: 1 Nov 60 Yugoslavia
ARTICLES: 6 LANGUAGE: Serbo-Croat. Russian.
HEADNOTE: SCIENTIFIC TECHNICAL COOPERATION
TOPIC: Scientific Project
CONCEPTS: Conformity with municipal law. General cooperation. Exchange of information and documents. Establishment of commission. Scholarships and grants. Research results. Scientific exchange. Funding procedures. Payment schedules. Patents, copyrights and trademarks. General technical assistance. Economic assistance.
INTL ORGS: Special Commission.
PROCEDURE: Duration. Renewal or Revival. Termination.
PARTIES:
USSR (Soviet Union)
Yugoslavia

105424 Bilateral Agreement **378 UNTS 141**
SIGNED: 7 Oct 60 FORCE: 7 Oct 60
REGISTERED: 1 Nov 60 United Nations
ARTICLES: 10 LANGUAGE: English.
HEADNOTE: ASSISTANCE
TOPIC: Direct Aid
CONCEPTS: Detailed regulations. Treaty implementation. Visas. Privileges and immunities. Exchange of information and documents. Informational records. Inspection and observation. Operating agencies. Personnel. Public information. Responsibility and liability. Title and deeds. Use of facilities. Arbitration. Procedure. Negotiation. Import quotas. Attachment of funds. Exchange rates and regulations. Expense sharing formulae. Financial programs. Domestic obligation. General technical assistance. Economic assistance. Materials, equipment and services. IGO status.
INTL ORGS: United Nations. Arbitration Commission.
TREATY REF: 1UNTS15; 33UNTS261; 374UNTS137.
PROCEDURE: Amendment. Termination.
PARTIES:
Indonesia
UN Special Fund
ANNEX
535 UNTS 432. UN Special Fund. Termination 8 Apr 65. Force 18 May 65.
535 UNTS 432. Indonesia. Termination 10 Mar 65. Force 18 May 65.

105425 Multilateral Convention **378 UNTS 159**
SIGNED: 20 Oct 55 FORCE: 22 Jul 59
REGISTERED: 1 Nov 60 Switzerland
ARTICLES: 17 LANGUAGE: French. German. Italian.
HEADNOTE: ESTABLISH EUROFINA
TOPIC: IGO Establishment

CONCEPTS: Annex or appendix reference. Conformity with municipal law. Procedure. Existing tribunals. Funding procedures. Railways. Admission. Establishment. Headquarters and facilities. Conformity with IGO decisions.
INTL ORGS: European Company for the Financing of Railway Rolling Stock. United Nations.
PROCEDURE: Amendment. Accession. Duration. Ratification. Termination.
PARTIES:
Austria SIGNED: 20 Oct 55
Belgium SIGNED: 20 Oct 55 RATIFIED: 22 Feb 60 FORCE: 22 Feb 60
Denmark SIGNED: 20 Oct 55 RATIFIED: 29 Jun 56 FORCE: 22 Jul 59
France SIGNED: 20 Oct 55 RATIFIED: 6 Apr 59 FORCE: 22 Jul 59
Germany, West SIGNED: 20 Oct 55 RATIFIED: 16 Nov 56 FORCE: 22 Jul 59
Greece RATIFIED: 16 Aug 57 FORCE: 22 Jul 59
Italy SIGNED: 20 Oct 55 RATIFIED: 22 Jun 59 FORCE: 22 Jul 59
Luxembourg SIGNED: 20 Oct 55 RATIFIED: 29 Jan 57 FORCE: 22 Jul 59
Netherlands SIGNED: 20 Oct 55 RATIFIED: 28 May 56 FORCE: 22 Jul 59
Norway SIGNED: 20 Oct 55 RATIFIED: 7 May 56 FORCE: 22 Jul 59
Portugal SIGNED: 20 Oct 55 RATIFIED: 25 Jul 56 FORCE: 22 Jul 59
Spain SIGNED: 20 Oct 55 RATIFIED: 18 Mar 57 FORCE: 22 Jul 59
Sweden SIGNED: 20 Oct 55 RATIFIED: 21 Feb 56 FORCE: 22 Jul 59
Switzerland SIGNED: 20 Oct 55 RATIFIED: 30 Mar 56 FORCE: 22 Jul 59
Turkey RATIFIED: 18 Mar 57 FORCE: 22 Jul 59
Yugoslavia SIGNED: 20 Oct 55 RATIFIED: 18 Sep 56 FORCE: 22 Jul 59
ANNEX
390 UNTS 372. Austria. Ratification 6 Feb 61.

105426 Bilateral Agreement **378 UNTS 249**
SIGNED: 12 Jul 56 FORCE: 1 Jul 58
REGISTERED: 2 Nov 60 Italy
ARTICLES: 12 LANGUAGE: Italian. German.
HEADNOTE: STUDENT EMPLOYEES
TOPIC: Non-ILO Labor
CONCEPTS: Definition of terms. Dispute settlement. Employment regulations. Wages and salaries. Non-ILO labor relations. Administrative cooperation. Migrant worker. Quotas.
PROCEDURE: Denunciation. Duration. Ratification. Renewal or Revival.
PARTIES:
Austria
Italy

105427 Bilateral Exchange **378 UNTS 267**
SIGNED: 6 Oct 59 FORCE: 6 Oct 59
REGISTERED: 2 Nov 60 Italy
ARTICLES: 2 LANGUAGE: English.
HEADNOTE: TRADE
TOPIC: General Trade
CONCEPTS: General provisions. Annex or appendix reference. Conformity with municipal law. General cooperation. Licenses and permits. Public information. Establishment of commission. Migrant worker. Export quotas. Import quotas. Trade procedures. Payment schedules. Commodity trade. Quotas. Most favored nation clause. General transportation. Passenger transport. Transport of goods. Air transport. Ports and pilotage.
INTL ORGS: Special Commission.
PROCEDURE: Duration. Termination.
PARTIES:
India
Italy

105428 Bilateral Agreement **378 UNTS 289**
SIGNED: 25 Nov 57 FORCE: 3 Feb 59
REGISTERED: 2 Nov 60 Italy
ARTICLES: 11 LANGUAGE: Italian. Spanish.
HEADNOTE: EXCHANGE STUDENT EMPLOYEES
TOPIC: Non-ILO Labor
CONCEPTS: Definition of terms. Resident permits. Conformity with municipal law. Exchange of information and documents. Vocational training. Employment regulations. Wages and salaries. Non-ILO labor relations. Administrative cooper-

ation. Unemployment. Migrant worker. Quotas. National treatment.
PROCEDURE: Denunciation. Duration. Ratification. Renewal or Revival.
PARTIES:
Italy
Spain

105429 Bilateral Agreement **378 UNTS 311**
SIGNED: 4 Jun 56 FORCE: 31 May 58
REGISTERED: 2 Nov 60 Italy
ARTICLES: 14 LANGUAGE: French.
HEADNOTE: RELATING AIR SERVICES
TOPIC: Air Transport
CONCEPTS: Definition of terms. Detailed regulations. Annex or appendix reference. Previous treaty replacement. Conformity with municipal law. General cooperation. Exchange of information and documents. Licenses and permits. Recognition of legal documents. Use of facilities. Arbitration. Procedure. Existing tribunals. Negotiation. Reexport of goods, etc.. Fees and exemptions. Non-interest rates and fees. National treatment. Customs exemptions. Competency certificate. Navigational conditions. Permit designation. Air transport. Airport facilities. Airworthiness certificates. Conditions of airlines operating permission. Operating authorizations and regulations. Licenses and certificates of nationality.
INTL ORGS: International Civil Aviation Organization. Arbitration Commission. Special Commission.
TREATY REF: 15UNTS295.
PROCEDURE: Future Procedures Contemplated. Ratification. Registration. Termination.
PARTIES:
Italy
Switzerland

105430 Bilateral Agreement **378 UNTS 327**
SIGNED: 8 Apr 58 FORCE: 8 Apr 58
REGISTERED: 2 Nov 60 Italy
ARTICLES: 8 LANGUAGE: French.
HEADNOTE: TRADE
TOPIC: General Trade
CONCEPTS: Annex or appendix reference. Informational records. Licenses and permits. Establishment of commission. Export quotas. Import quotas. Trade procedures. Payment schedules. Quotas.
INTL ORGS: European Payments Union. Organization for Economic Co-operation and Development. Special Commission.
PROCEDURE: Duration.
PARTIES:
Italy
Tunisia

105431 Bilateral Agreement **378 UNTS 349**
SIGNED: 31 Oct 59 FORCE: 31 Oct 59
REGISTERED: 2 Nov 60 Italy
ARTICLES: 7 LANGUAGE: French.
HEADNOTE: TRADE
TOPIC: General Trade
CONCEPTS: Annex or appendix reference. General cooperation. Informational records. Licenses and permits. Establishment of commission. Export quotas. Import quotas. Free trade. Trade procedures. Payment schedules. Quotas.
INTL ORGS: Organization for Economic Co-operation and Development. Special Commission.
PROCEDURE: Amendment. Denunciation. Duration. Renewal or Revival.
PARTIES:
Italy
Tunisia

105432 Bilateral Convention **379 UNTS 3**
SIGNED: 26 Mar 55 FORCE: 24 Jun 60
REGISTERED: 2 Nov 60 Italy
ARTICLES: 20 LANGUAGE: French.
HEADNOTE: VETERINARY CONVENTION
TOPIC: Sanitation
CONCEPTS: Definition of terms. Detailed regulations. Exceptions and exemptions. Previous treaty extension. General cooperation. Inspection and observation. Licenses and permits. Arbitration. Procedure. Border control. Disease control. Veterinary. Trade procedures. Conferences.

PROCEDURE: Denunciation. Duration. Ratification. Renewal or Revival.
PARTIES:
Italy
Yugoslavia

105433 Bilateral Agreement **379 UNTS 23**
SIGNED: 20 Nov 58 FORCE: 5 Nov 59
REGISTERED: 2 Nov 60 Italy
ARTICLES: 18 LANGUAGE: Italian. Serbo-Croat.
HEADNOTE: FISHING ITALIAN FISHERMEN YUGO-SLAV WATERS
TOPIC: Territory Boundary
CONCEPTS: Licenses and permits. Regulation of natural resources.
PROCEDURE: Ratification.
PARTIES:
Italy
Yugoslavia

105434 Bilateral Exchange **379 UNTS 77**
SIGNED: 12 Feb 60 FORCE: 12 Feb 60
REGISTERED: 2 Nov 60 Italy
ARTICLES: 2 LANGUAGE: Italian. Serbo-Croat.
HEADNOTE: TRANSFER REMAINS
TOPIC: Other Military
CONCEPTS: Exchange of information and documents. Informational records. Indemnities and reimbursements. Burial arrangements. Responsibility for war dead.
TREATY REF: 75UNTS31.
PARTIES:
Italy
Yugoslavia

105435 Bilateral Agreement **379 UNTS 89**
SIGNED: 18 Mar 60 FORCE: 29 Jun 60
REGISTERED: 4 Nov 60 Guatemala
ARTICLES: 7 LANGUAGE: Spanish. German.
HEADNOTE: TRADE
TOPIC: General Trade
CONCEPTS: Exceptions and exemptions. Conformity with municipal law. Licenses and permits. Export quotas. Import quotas. Trade procedures. Currency. Payment schedules. Commodity trade. Most favored nation clause. Customs exemptions.
PROCEDURE: Denunciation. Ratification.
PARTIES:
Austria
Guatemala

105436 Unilateral Instrument **379 UNTS 99**
SIGNED: 2 Nov 60 FORCE: 7 Nov 60
REGISTERED: 7 Nov 60 United Nations
ARTICLES: 1 LANGUAGE: French.
HEADNOTE: ACCEPTANCE OBLIGATIONS UN
TOPIC: UN Charter
CONCEPTS: Acceptance of UN obligations. Adherence to UN charter.
INTL ORGS: United Nations.
PARTIES:
Gabon

105437 Bilateral Agreement **379 UNTS 103**
SIGNED: 30 Mar 60 FORCE: 10 Jun 60
REGISTERED: 7 Nov 60 IBRD (World Bank)
ARTICLES: 5 LANGUAGE: English.
HEADNOTE: GUARANTEE AGRICULTURE
TOPIC: IBRD Project
CONCEPTS: Definition of terms. Annex or appendix reference. Exchange of information and documents. Inspection and observation. Bonds. Fees and exemptions. Tax exemptions. Domestic obligation. Agriculture. Terms of loan. Loan regulations. Loan guarantee. Guarantor non-interference.
PARTIES:
Belgium
IBRD (World Bank)

105438 Bilateral Agreement **379 UNTS 129**
SIGNED: 30 Mar 60 FORCE: 10 Jun 60
REGISTERED: 7 Nov 60 IBRD (World Bank)
ARTICLES: 6 LANGUAGE: English.
HEADNOTE: GUARANTEE AGREEMENT
TOPIC: IBRD Project
CONCEPTS: Definition of terms. Annex or appen-

dix reference. Exchange of information and documents. Inspection and observation. Bonds. Fees and exemptions. Tax exemptions. Domestic obligation. Terms of loan. Loan regulations. Loan guarantee. Guarantor non-interference.
PARTIES:
Belgium
IBRD (World Bank)

105439 Bilateral Agreement **379 UNTS 161**
SIGNED: 30 Mar 60 FORCE: 10 Jun 60
REGISTERED: 7 Nov 60 IBRD (World Bank)
ARTICLES: 5 LANGUAGE: English.
HEADNOTE: GUARANTEE AGREEMENT
TOPIC: IBRD Project
CONCEPTS: Definition of terms. Annex or appendix reference. Exchange of information and documents. Inspection and observation. Bonds. Fees and exemptions. Tax exemptions. Domestic obligation. Terms of loan. Loan regulations. Loan guarantee. Guarantor non-interference.
PARTIES:
Belgium
IBRD (World Bank)

105440 Bilateral Exchange **379 UNTS 201**
SIGNED: 10 Dec 59 FORCE: 1 Jan 60
REGISTERED: 7 Nov 60 UK Great Britain
ARTICLES: 2 LANGUAGE: English.
HEADNOTE: SOCIAL SECURITY
TOPIC: Non-ILO Labor
CONCEPTS: Definition of terms. Detailed regulations. Domestic legislation. Public health. Wages and salaries. Non-ILO labor relations. Family allowances. Social security. Unemployment. Payment schedules. National treatment. Disposition of territory.
PROCEDURE: Duration. Termination.
PARTIES:
Canada
UK Great Britain
ANNEX
431 UNTS 322. Canada. Amendment 30 Nov 61. Force 1 Feb 62.
431 UNTS 322. UK Great Britain. Amendment 7 Nov 61. Force 1 Feb 62.

105441 Bilateral Agreement **379 UNTS 218**
SIGNED: 10 May 60 FORCE: 25 Oct 60
REGISTERED: 8 Nov 60 IBRD (World Bank)
ARTICLES: 5 LANGUAGE: English.
HEADNOTE: GUARANTEE POWER
TOPIC: IBRD Project
CONCEPTS: Definition of terms. Annex or appendix reference. Exchange of information and documents. Inspection and observation. Bonds. Fees and exemptions. Tax exemptions. Domestic obligation. Terms of loan. Loan regulations. Loan guarantee. Guarantor non-interference. Hydroelectric power.
PARTIES:
Colombia
IBRD (World Bank)

105442 Bilateral Agreement **379 UNTS 253**
SIGNED: 17 Jun 60 FORCE: 20 Aug 60
REGISTERED: 8 Nov 60 IBRD (World Bank)
ARTICLES: 7 LANGUAGE: English.
HEADNOTE: LOAN IRRIGATION
TOPIC: IBRD Project
CONCEPTS: Default remedies. Definition of terms. Annex or appendix reference. Exchange of information and documents. Informational records. Inspection and observation. Accounting procedures. Bonds. Fees and exemptions. Interest rates. Domestic obligation. Terms of loan. Loan regulations. Loan guarantee. Guarantor non-interference. Irrigation.
PARTIES:
IBRD (World Bank)
Sudan
ANNEX
507 UNTS 304. Sudan. Amendment 28 Feb 63. Force 7 May 63.
507 UNTS 304. IBRD (World Bank). Amendment 28 Feb 63. Force 7 May 63.
507 UNTS 308. IBRD (World Bank). Amendment 26 Apr 64. Force 8 Jul 64.
507 UNTS 308. Sudan. Amendment 26 Apr 64. Force 8 Jul 64.

105443 Bilateral Agreement **379 UNTS 277**
SIGNED: 23 Jun 60 FORCE: 5 Oct 60
REGISTERED: 9 Nov 60 Finland
ARTICLES: 48 LANGUAGE: Finnish. Russian.
HEADNOTE: REGIME FINNISH-SOVIET STATE FRONTIER
TOPIC: Territory Boundary
CONCEPTS: Annex or appendix reference. Previous treaty replacement. Exchange of official publications. Inspection and observation. Operating agencies. Procedure. Negotiation. Claims and settlements. Fish, wildlife, and natural resources. Markers and definitions. Frontier waterways. Wildlife. Regulation of natural resources.
TREATY REF: 3UNTS5.
PROCEDURE: Denunciation. Duration. Ratification. Renewal or Revival.
PARTIES:
Finland
USSR (Soviet Union)

105444 Bilateral Agreement **379 UNTS 381**
SIGNED: 27 May 60 FORCE: 25 Aug 60
REGISTERED: 9 Nov 60 Finland
ARTICLES: 7 LANGUAGE: Finnish. Russian.
HEADNOTE: CULTURAL COOPERATION
TOPIC: Culture
CONCEPTS: Friendship and amity. Tourism. Non-diplomatic delegations. Exchange. Teacher and student exchange. Exchange. General cultural cooperation. Artists. Athletes. Publications exchange. Mass media exchange.
TREATY REF: 48UNTS149.
PROCEDURE: Duration. Termination.
PARTIES:
Finland
USSR (Soviet Union)

105445 Bilateral Exchange **379 UNTS 391**
SIGNED: 19 Jul 60 FORCE: 19 Jul 60
REGISTERED: 9 Nov 60 Belgium
ARTICLES: 2 LANGUAGE: English.
HEADNOTE: WAIVER VISA REQUIREMENTS
TOPIC: Visas
CONCEPTS: Emergencies. Time limit. Visa abolition. Denial of admission. Resident permits. Conformity with municipal law.
PARTIES:
Belgium
Fed of Malaya

105446 Bilateral Agreement **379 UNTS 397**
SIGNED: 1 Apr 60 FORCE: 12 Jul 60
REGISTERED: 9 Nov 60 IBRD (World Bank)
ARTICLES: 5 LANGUAGE: English.
HEADNOTE: GUARANTEE AGRICULTURE
TOPIC: IBRD Project
CONCEPTS: Definition of terms. Annex or appendix reference. Exchange of information and documents. Inspection and observation. Bonds. Fees and exemptions. Tax exemptions. Domestic obligation. Terms of loan. Commodities schedule. Loan regulations. Loan guarantee. Guarantor non-interference.
PARTIES:
IBRD (World Bank)
UK Great Britain

105447 Bilateral Agreement **380 UNTS 3**
SIGNED: 25 Oct 56 FORCE: 24 Oct 60
REGISTERED: 10 Nov 60 Belgium
ARTICLES: 12 LANGUAGE: French.
HEADNOTE: AIR TRANSPORT
TOPIC: Air Transport
CONCEPTS: Exceptions and exemptions. Annex or appendix reference. Conformity with municipal law. Licenses and permits. Recognition of legal documents. Use of facilities. Arbitration. Procedure. Existing tribunals. Negotiation. Fees and exemptions. Most favored nation clause. National treatment. Customs exemptions. Competency certificate. Routes and logistics. Navigational conditions. Permit designation. Air transport. Airport facilities. Airworthiness certificates. Conditions of airlines operating permission. Operating authorizations and regulations. Licenses and certificates of nationality.
INTL ORGS: International Civil Aviation Organization.
TREATY REF: 15UNTS295.

PROCEDURE: Denunciation. Future Procedures Contemplated. Ratification.
PARTIES:
Belgium
Turkey

105448 Bilateral Agreement **380 UNTS 15**
SIGNED: 1 Jun 60 FORCE: 10 Sep 60
REGISTERED: 11 Nov 60 IBRD (World Bank)
ARTICLES: 7 LANGUAGE: English.
HEADNOTE: GUARANTEE AGRICULTURE CREDIT
TOPIC: IBRD Project
CONCEPTS: Definition of terms. Annex or appendix reference. Exchange of information and documents. Inspection and observation. Bonds. Fees and exemptions. Tax exemptions. Domestic obligation. Agriculture. Terms of loan. Loan regulations. Loan guarantee. Guarantor non-interference.
PARTIES:
Peru
IBRD (World Bank)

105449 Bilateral Agreement **380 UNTS 39**
SIGNED: 7 Jul 60 FORCE: 7 Jul 60
REGISTERED: 11 Nov 60 Denmark
ARTICLES: 8 LANGUAGE: English.
HEADNOTE: AERONAUTICAL FACILITIES SERVICES GREENLAND
TOPIC: Air Transport
CONCEPTS: Exceptions and exemptions. Annex or appendix reference. Exchange of information and documents. Personnel. Materials, equipment and services. Navigational conditions. Navigational equipment. Air transport. Facilities and equipment.
INTL ORGS: International Civil Aviation Organization.
TREATY REF: 94UNTS35; 15UNTS295.
PROCEDURE: Duration. Application to Non-self-governing Territories.
PARTIES:
Denmark
USA (United States)

105450 Bilateral Agreement **380 UNTS 59**
SIGNED: 18 Jun 59 FORCE: 13 Nov 59
REGISTERED: 14 Nov 60 South Africa
ARTICLES: 14 LANGUAGE: English. Afrikaans.
HEADNOTE: DOUBLE TAXATION FISCAL EVASION INCOME
TOPIC: Taxation
CONCEPTS: Definition of terms. Territorial application. Conformity with municipal law. Exchange of official publications. Teacher and student exchange. Claims and settlements. Taxation. Tax exemptions.
PROCEDURE: Duration. Termination.
PARTIES:
South Africa
UK Great Britain

105451 Bilateral Agreement **380 UNTS 81**
SIGNED: 18 Jun 59 FORCE: 13 Nov 59
REGISTERED: 14 Nov 60 South Africa
ARTICLES: 14 LANGUAGE: English. Afrikaans.
HEADNOTE: DOUBLE TAXATION FISCAL EVASION INCOME
TOPIC: Taxation
CONCEPTS: Definition of terms. Territorial application. Conformity with municipal law. Exchange of official publications. Teacher and student exchange. Claims and settlements. Taxation. Tax credits. Tax exemptions.
PROCEDURE: Duration. Termination.
PARTIES:
South Africa
UK Great Britain

105452 Bilateral Agreement **380 UNTS 103**
SIGNED: 18 Jun 59 FORCE: 13 Nov 59
REGISTERED: 14 Nov 60 South Africa
ARTICLES: 15 LANGUAGE: English. Afrikaans.
HEADNOTE: DOUBLE TAXATION FISCAL EVASION INCOME
TOPIC: Taxation
CONCEPTS: Definition of terms. Territorial application. Previous treaty replacement. Conformity with municipal law. Exchange of official publica-

tions. Teacher and student exchange. Claims and settlements. Taxation. Tax credits.
TREATY REF: 129LTS377.
PROCEDURE: Duration. Termination.
PARTIES:
South Africa
UK Great Britain

105453 Bilateral Exchange **380 UNTS 129**
SIGNED: 15 Jul 60 FORCE: 15 Jul 60
REGISTERED: 15 Nov 60 USA (United States)
ARTICLES: 2 LANGUAGE: English. French.
HEADNOTE: EXCHANGE OFFICIAL PUBLICATIONS
TOPIC: Admin Cooperation
CONCEPTS: Exchange of official publications. Operating agencies. Indemnities and reimbursements.
PARTIES:
Cambodia
USA (United States)

105454 Bilateral Exchange **380 UNTS 135**
SIGNED: 8 Jul 60 FORCE: 8 Jul 60
REGISTERED: 15 Nov 60 USA (United States)
ARTICLES: 2 LANGUAGE: English. French.
HEADNOTE: VESSEL LOAN
TOPIC: Milit Assistance
CONCEPTS: Time limit. Annex or appendix reference. Responsibility and liability. Title and deeds. Compensation. Delivery schedules. Lease of military property. Naval vessels. Return of equipment and recapture. Restrictions on transfer.
TREATY REF: 270UNTS83.
PARTIES:
Haiti
USA (United States)

105455 Bilateral Exchange **380 UNTS 143**
SIGNED: 7 Jul 60 FORCE: 7 Jul 60
REGISTERED: 15 Nov 60 USA (United States)
ARTICLES: 2 LANGUAGE: English. Italian.
HEADNOTE: WEAPONS PRODUCTION PROGRAM
TOPIC: Milit Assistance
CONCEPTS: Change of circumstances. Previous treaty replacement. General cooperation. Licenses and permits. Private contracts. Use of facilities. Indemnities and reimbursements. Most favored nation clause. Customs exemptions. General technical assistance. Materials, equipment and services. Defense and security. Exchange of defense information. Equipment and supplies.
TREATY REF: 34UNTS243.
PROCEDURE: Future Procedures Contemplated.
PARTIES:
Italy
USA (United States)

105456 Bilateral Agreement **380 UNTS 157**
SIGNED: 21 Jul 60 FORCE: 21 Jul 60
REGISTERED: 15 Nov 60 USA (United States)
ARTICLES: 6 LANGUAGE: English. Polish.
HEADNOTE: SURPLUS AGRICULTURE
TOPIC: US Agri Commod Aid
CONCEPTS: General provisions. Annex or appendix reference. Exchange of information and documents. Reexport of goods, etc.. Exchange rates and regulations. Transportation costs. Local currency. Commodities schedule. Purchase authorization. Surplus commodities. Mutual consultation.
PARTIES:
Poland
USA (United States)

105457 Bilateral Treaty **380 UNTS 181**
SIGNED: 20 Dec 58 FORCE: 11 Jun 60
REGISTERED: 15 Nov 60 USA (United States)
ARTICLES: 16 LANGUAGE: English. Arabic.
HEADNOTE: AMITY ECONOMIC RELATIONS CONSULAR RIGHTS
TOPIC: General Amity
CONCEPTS: Exceptions and exemptions. Territorial application. Previous treaty replacement. Friendship and amity. Alien status. Consular relations establishment. Human rights. Privileges and immunities. General cooperation. Juridical

personality. Legal protection and assistance. Free trade. Exchange rates and regulations. Most favored nation clause. National treatment. Taxation. Navigational conditions.
INTL ORGS: General Agreement on Tariffs and Trade.
TREATY REF: U.S.A. 8STAT458.
PROCEDURE: Duration. Ratification. Termination.
PARTIES:
Muscat and Oman
USA (United States)

105458 Bilateral Treaty **380 UNTS 219**
SIGNED: 7 Jan 55 FORCE: 7 Jan 55
REGISTERED: 15 Nov 60 Belgium
ARTICLES: 12 LANGUAGE: French. German.
HEADNOTE: AIR TRANSPORT
TOPIC: Air Transport
CONCEPTS: Definition of terms. Annex or appendix reference. Non-visa travel documents. Conformity with municipal law. General cooperation. Licenses and permits. Recognition of legal documents. Use of facilities. Arbitration. Procedure. Negotiation. Reexport of goods, etc.. Expense sharing formulae. Fees and exemptions. Non-interest rates and fees. Most favored nation clause. National treatment. Customs exemptions. Competency certificate. Routes and logistics. Navigational conditions. Permit designation. Airport facilities. Airworthiness certificates. Conditions of airlines operating permission. Operating authorizations and regulations. Licenses and certificates of nationality.
INTL ORGS: International Civil Aviation Organization. Arbitration Commission.
TREATY REF: 15UNTS295.
PROCEDURE: Amendment. Future Procedures Contemplated. Registration. Termination.
PARTIES:
Austria
Belgium
ANNEX
492 UNTS 365. Belgium. Amendment 23 Dec 63. Force 23 Dec 63.
492 UNTS 365. Austria. Amendment 23 Dec 63. Force 23 Dec 63.

105459 Bilateral Agreement **380 UNTS 245**
SIGNED: 23 Nov 59 FORCE: 14 May 60
REGISTERED: 15 Nov 60 IBRD (World Bank)
ARTICLES: 5 LANGUAGE: English.
HEADNOTE: GUARANTEE INDUSTRIAL DEVELOPMENT
TOPIC: IBRD Project
CONCEPTS: Definition of terms. Exchange of information and documents. Inspection and observation. Bonds. Fees and exemptions. Tax exemptions. Domestic obligation. Terms of loan. Loan regulations. Loan guarantee. Guarantor non-interference. Industry.
PARTIES:
Iran
IBRD (World Bank)

105460 Bilateral Agreement **380 UNTS 277**
SIGNED: 17 Nov 60 FORCE: 17 Nov 60
REGISTERED: 17 Nov 60 United Nations
ARTICLES: 6 LANGUAGE: English.
HEADNOTE: OPERATIONAL EXECUTIVE PERSONNEL
TOPIC: Tech Assistance
CONCEPTS: Treaty implementation. Annex or appendix reference. Privileges and immunities. General cooperation. Personnel. Responsibility and liability. Arbitration. Procedure. Negotiation. Vocational training. Compensation. Expense sharing formulae. Tax exemptions. Customs exemptions. Domestic obligation. Special projects. Status of experts. Conformity with IGO decisions.
INTL ORGS: Permanent Court of Arbitration.
PROCEDURE: Amendment. Termination.
PARTIES:
Pakistan
United Nations

105461 Bilateral Agreement **380 UNTS 289**
SIGNED: 17 Nov 60 FORCE: 17 Nov 60
REGISTERED: 17 Nov 60 United Nations
ARTICLES: 10 LANGUAGE: English.

HEADNOTE: ASSISTANCE
TOPIC: Direct Aid
CONCEPTS: Detailed regulations. Treaty implementation. Visas. Privileges and immunities. Exchange of information and documents. Inspection and observation. Operating agencies. Personnel. Public information. Responsibility and liability. Title and deeds. Use of facilities. Arbitration. Procedure. Negotiation. Import quotas. Attachment of funds. Exchange rates and regulations. Expense sharing formulae. Financial programs. Domestic obligation. General technical assistance. Economic assistance. Materials, equipment and services. IGO status.
INTL ORGS; International Court of Justice. United Nations.
TREATY REF: 1UNTS15; 33UNTS261; 374UNTS137.
PROCEDURE: Amendment. Termination.
PARTIES:
Nepal
UN Special Fund

105462 Bilateral Exchange **380 UNTS 307**
SIGNED: 10 Jun 55   FORCE: 15 Jul 55
REGISTERED: 21 Nov 60 New Zealand
ARTICLES: 2 LANGUAGE: English.
HEADNOTE: VISAS
TOPIC: Visas
CONCEPTS: Territorial application. Time limit. Visa abolition. Denial of admission. Resident permits. Visas. Conformity with municipal law. Fees and exemptions.
PROCEDURE: Termination.
PARTIES:
Germany, West
New Zealand

105463 Bilateral Exchange **380 UNTS 313**
SIGNED: 30 Dec 58   FORCE: 17 Feb 59
REGISTERED: 21 Nov 60 New Zealand
ARTICLES: 2 LANGUAGE: English.
HEADNOTE: DEATH DUTIES
TOPIC: Taxation
CONCEPTS: Previous treaty renunciation. Death duties.
TREATY REF: 2'2DEMARTENS82;.
PARTIES:
New Zealand
Switzerland

105464 Bilateral Agreement **380 UNTS 319**
SIGNED: 10 Dec 59   FORCE: 15 Apr 60
REGISTERED: 22 Nov 60 IBRD (World Bank)
ARTICLES: 5 LANGUAGE: English.
HEADNOTE: GUARANTEE AGREEMENT
TOPIC: IBRD Project
CONCEPTS: Definition of terms. Annex or appendix reference. Exchange of information and documents. Inspection and observation. Bonds. Fees and exemptions. Tax exemptions. Domestic obligation. Terms of loan. Loan regulations. Loan guarantee. Guarantor non-interference. Natural resources.
PARTIES:
France
IBRD (World Bank)

105465 Bilateral Treaty **381 UNTS 3**
SIGNED: 12 Nov 59   FORCE: 14 Jun 60
REGISTERED: 26 Nov 60 France
ARTICLES: 23 LANGUAGE: French. Amharic.
HEADNOTE: OPERATION COMPAGNIE DU CHEMIN
TOPIC: Specific Property
CONCEPTS: Annex or appendix reference. Nationality and citizenship. Arbitration. Conciliation. Bonds. Currency. Exchange rates and regulations. Interest rates. Assets transfer. General. Tax exemptions. Customs declarations. Customs exemptions. Loan and credit. Ports and pilotage. Facilities and property.
INTL ORGS: International Monetary Fund. Arbitration Commission. Conciliation Commission.
PROCEDURE: Duration. Ratification.
PARTIES:
Ethiopia
France

105466 Bilateral Convention **381 UNTS 99**
SIGNED: 20 Oct 56   FORCE: 1 Nov 56
REGISTERED: 29 Nov 60 UK Great Britain
ARTICLES: 16 LANGUAGE: English.
HEADNOTE: EXCHANGE MONEY ORDERS
TOPIC: Postal Service
CONCEPTS: Conformity with municipal law. Accounting procedures. Currency. Exchange rates and regulations. Postal services. Money orders and postal checks. Rates and charges.
PROCEDURE: Duration. Termination.
PARTIES:
Canada
UK Great Britain

105467 Bilateral Convention **381 UNTS 111**
SIGNED: 21 Jun 56   FORCE: 1 Nov 56
REGISTERED: 29 Nov 60 UK Great Britain
ARTICLES: 16 LANGUAGE: English.
HEADNOTE: EXCHANGE MONEY ORDERS
TOPIC: Postal Service
CONCEPTS: Conformity with municipal law. Accounting procedures. Currency. Exchange rates and regulations. Postal services. Money orders and postal checks. Rates and charges.
PROCEDURE: Duration. Termination.
PARTIES:
Canada
UK Great Britain

105468 Bilateral Exchange **381 UNTS 123**
SIGNED: 7 Apr 59   FORCE: 7 Apr 59
REGISTERED: 1 Dec 60 United Nations
ARTICLES: 2 LANGUAGE: Spanish.
HEADNOTE: 27 SESSION ECOSOC
TOPIC: IGO Operations
CONCEPTS: Diplomatic missions. Privileges and immunities. Funding procedures. Subsidiary organ.
PARTIES:
Mexico
United Nations

105469 Bilateral Agreement **381 UNTS 133**
SIGNED: 3 Aug 60   FORCE: 15 Sep 60
REGISTERED: 1 Dec 60 WHO (World Health)
ARTICLES: 6 LANGUAGE: English.
HEADNOTE: TECHNICAL ADVISORY ASSISTANCE
TOPIC: Tech Assistance
CONCEPTS: Treaty implementation. Previous treaty replacement. Privileges and immunities. General cooperation. Exchange of information and documents. Personnel. Responsibility and liability. Title and deeds. Exchange. Scholarships and grants. Vocational training. Research and development. Expense sharing formulae. Local currency. Domestic obligation. Special projects. Materials, equipment and services. IGO status. Conformity with IGO decisions.
TREATY REF: 33UNTS261; 110UNTS297.
PROCEDURE: Amendment. Termination.
PARTIES:
Jordan
WHO (World Health)

105470 Multilateral Treaty **381 UNTS 145**
SIGNED: 7 Jun 56   FORCE: 1 Nov 60
REGISTERED: 5 Dec 60 Belgium
ARTICLES: 19 LANGUAGE: French. Dutch.
HEADNOTE: LABOR TREATY
TOPIC: Non-ILO Labor
CONCEPTS: Definition of terms. Previous treaty replacement. Resident permits. Conformity with municipal law. Exchange of information and documents. Investigation of violations. Establishment of commission. Dispute settlement. Employment regulations. Safety standards. Wages and salaries. Non-ILO labor relations. Administrative cooperation. Unemployment. National treatment. Economic assistance.
INTL ORGS: Special Commission.
TREATY REF: 165LTS383; 174LTS11; 77LTS375.
PROCEDURE: Denunciation. Duration. Ratification.
PARTIES:
Belgium SIGNED: 7 Jun 56 RATIFIED: 1 Nov 60 FORCE: 1 Nov 60
Luxembourg SIGNED: 7 Jun 56 RATIFIED: 12 Sep 60 FORCE: 1 Nov 60

Netherlands SIGNED: 7 Jun 56 RATIFIED: 14 Jul 60 FORCE: 1 Nov 60

105471 Multilateral Treaty **381 UNTS 165**
SIGNED: 3 Feb 58   FORCE: 1 Nov 60
REGISTERED: 5 Dec 60 Belgium
ARTICLES: 100 LANGUAGE: French. Dutch.
HEADNOTE: BENELUX
TOPIC: IGO Establishment
CONCEPTS: Annex or appendix reference. Visa abolition. Border traffic and migration. Passports diplomatic. Privileges and immunities. Exchange of official publications. Exchange of information and documents. Juridical personality. Arbitration. Procedure. Export quotas. Import quotas. Free trade. Customs exemptions. Agriculture. Economic assistance. Navigational conditions. Use of ports and territorial waters. Road rules. Subsidiary organ. Establishment. Procedure. Headquarters and facilities. Internal structure. Freedom of meeting. Conformity with IGO decisions.
INTL ORGS: Benelux Economic Union. European Economic Community. International Court of Justice.
PROCEDURE: Duration. Ratification.
PARTIES:
Belgium SIGNED: 3 Feb 58 FORCE: 1 Nov 60
Luxembourg SIGNED: 3 Feb 58 FORCE: 1 Nov 60
Netherlands SIGNED: 3 Feb 58 FORCE: 1 Nov 60
ANNEX
480 UNTS 424. Belgium. Implementation 19 Sep 60. Force 1 Oct 63.
480 UNTS 424. Luxembourg. Implementation 19 Sep 60. Force 1 Oct 63.
480 UNTS 424. Netherlands. Implementation 19 Sep 60. Force 1 Oct 63.
565 UNTS 302. Belgium. Force 3 Mar 66.
565 UNTS 302. Luxembourg. Signature 14 Jan 64. Ratification 25 Nov 65.
565 UNTS 302. Luxembourg. Force 3 Mar 66.
565 UNTS 302. Belgium. Signature 14 Jan 64. Ratification 2 Mar 66.
565 UNTS 312. Netherlands. Signature 14 Jan 64. Ratification 30 Jul 65.
565 UNTS 312. Netherlands. Force 3 Mar 66.

105472 Bilateral Exchange **381 UNTS 305**
SIGNED: 3 Feb 58   FORCE: 1 Nov 60
REGISTERED: 5 Dec 60 Belgium
ARTICLES: 2 LANGUAGE: Dutch.
HEADNOTE: RHINE BOUNTIES
TOPIC: Territory Boundary
CONCEPTS: Ports and pilotage. Boundaries of territory.
INTL ORGS: Benelux Economic Union.
PARTIES:
Belgium
Netherlands

105473 Bilateral Agreement **381 UNTS 309**
SIGNED: 14 Apr 58   FORCE: 10 Nov 60
REGISTERED: 5 Dec 60 Belgium
ARTICLES: 17 LANGUAGE: French. Persian.
HEADNOTE: AIR TRANSPORT
TOPIC: Air Transport
CONCEPTS: Definition of terms. Detailed regulations. Exceptions and exemptions. Annex or appendix reference. Non-prejudice to third party. Conformity with municipal law. Exchange of information and documents. Use of facilities. Arbitration. Procedure. Existing tribunals. Negotiation. Fees and exemptions. Non-interest rates and fees. Most favored nation clause. National treatment. Customs exemptions. Routes and logistics. Permit designation. Airport facilities. Conditions of airlines operating permission. Overflights and technical stops. Operating authorizations and regulations.
INTL ORGS: International Civil Aviation Organization. International Court of Justice. Arbitration Commission.
TREATY REF: 15UNTS295.
PROCEDURE: Amendment. Future Procedures Contemplated. Ratification. Registration. Termination.
PARTIES:
Belgium
Iran

105474 Bilateral Agreement **381 UNTS 335**
SIGNED: 4 Aug 60 FORCE: 17 Sep 60
REGISTERED: 6 Dec 60 WHO (World Health)
ARTICLES: 6 LANGUAGE: French.
HEADNOTE: TECHNICAL ADVISORY ASSISTANCE
TOPIC: Tech Assistance
CONCEPTS: Definition of terms. Previous treaty replacement. Privileges and immunities. General cooperation. Exchange of information and documents. Personnel. Responsibility and liability. Use of facilities. Exchange. Scholarships and grants. Vocational training. Research and development. Expense sharing formulae. Local currency. Domestic obligation. Special projects. Materials, equipment and services. IGO status. Conformity with IGO decisions.
TREATY REF: 33UNTS261; 174UNTS83.
PROCEDURE: Amendment. Termination.
PARTIES:
 WHO (World Health)
 Tunisia

105475 Multilateral Treaty **382 UNTS 3**
SIGNED: 16 Aug 60 FORCE: 16 Aug 60
REGISTERED: 12 Dec 60 UK Great Britain
ARTICLES: 5 LANGUAGE: English. French.
HEADNOTE: GUARANTEE
TOPIC: Recognition
CONCEPTS: General relations and amity. Peaceful relations. Arbitration.
INTL ORGS: United Nations.
PARTIES:
 Cyprus SIGNED: 16 Aug 60 FORCE: 16 Aug 60
 Greece SIGNED: 16 Aug 60 FORCE: 16 Aug 60
 Turkey SIGNED: 16 Aug 60 FORCE: 16 Aug 60
 UK Great Britain SIGNED: 16 Aug 60 FORCE:
  16 Aug 60

105476 Multilateral Treaty **382 UNTS 8**
SIGNED: 16 Aug 60 FORCE: 16 Aug 60
REGISTERED: 12 Dec 60 UK Great Britain
ARTICLES: 12 LANGUAGE: English.
HEADNOTE: ESTABLISHMENT REPUBLIC CYPRUS
TOPIC: Recognition
CONCEPTS: Treaty interpretation. Annex or appendix reference. Continuity of rights and obligations. Human rights. Nationality and citizenship. General cooperation. Procedure. Special tribunals. Negotiation. General trade. Defense and security. Status of forces.
INTL ORGS: International Court of Justice.
PARTIES:
 Cyprus SIGNED: 16 Aug 60 FORCE: 16 Aug 60
 Greece SIGNED: 16 Aug 60 FORCE: 16 Aug 60
 Turkey SIGNED: 16 Aug 60 FORCE: 16 Aug 60
 UK Great Britain SIGNED: 16 Aug 60 FORCE:
  16 Aug 60

105477 Bilateral Exchange **382 UNTS 177**
SIGNED: 16 Aug 60 FORCE: 16 Aug 60
REGISTERED: 12 Dec 60 UK Great Britain
ARTICLES: 2 LANGUAGE: English.
HEADNOTE: ACCESS POWER STATIONS
TOPIC: Specific Property
CONCEPTS: Security of information. Facilities and property. Frontier peoples and personnel.
PARTIES:
 Cyprus
 UK Great Britain

105478 Bilateral Exchange **382 UNTS 183**
SIGNED: 16 Aug 60 FORCE: 16 Aug 60
REGISTERED: 12 Dec 60 UK Great Britain
ARTICLES: 2 LANGUAGE: English.
HEADNOTE: BOUNDARY COMMISSION 16 AUG 60 TREATY
TOPIC: Dispute Settlement
CONCEPTS: Annex type material.
INTL ORGS: Special Commission.
PARTIES:
 Cyprus
 UK Great Britain

105479 Bilateral Exchange **382 UNTS 189**
SIGNED: 16 Aug 60 FORCE: 16 Aug 60
REGISTERED: 12 Dec 60 UK Great Britain
ARTICLES: 2 LANGUAGE: English.

HEADNOTE: SPECIAL ARRANGEMENTS FOR SITES
TOPIC: Specific Property
CONCEPTS: Treaty implementation. Annex or appendix reference. Facilities and property.
PARTIES:
 Cyprus
 UK Great Britain

105480 Bilateral Exchange **382 UNTS 201**
SIGNED: 16 Aug 60 FORCE: 16 Aug 60
REGISTERED: 12 Dec 60 UK Great Britain
ARTICLES: 2 LANGUAGE: English.
HEADNOTE: VERY SHORT-TERM SITES
TOPIC: Specific Property
CONCEPTS: Detailed regulations. Facilities and property.
PARTIES:
 Cyprus
 UK Great Britain

105481 Bilateral Exchange **382 UNTS 207**
SIGNED: 16 Aug 60 FORCE: 16 Aug 60
REGISTERED: 12 Dec 60 UK Great Britain
ARTICLES: 2 LANGUAGE: English.
HEADNOTE: CROWN PROPERTIES SOVEREIGN BASE AREAS
TOPIC: Specific Property
CONCEPTS: Detailed regulations. Indemnities and reimbursements. Assets transfer. Facilities and property.
PARTIES:
 Cyprus
 UK Great Britain

105482 Bilateral Exchange **382 UNTS 215**
SIGNED: 16 Aug 60 FORCE: 16 Aug 60
REGISTERED: 12 Dec 60 UK Great Britain
ARTICLES: 2 LANGUAGE: English.
HEADNOTE: CUSTOMS DUTIES
TOPIC: Customs
CONCEPTS: Annex or appendix reference. Customs duties.
PARTIES:
 Cyprus
 UK Great Britain

105483 Bilateral Exchange **382 UNTS 225**
SIGNED: 16 Aug 60 FORCE: 16 Aug 60
REGISTERED: 12 Dec 60 UK Great Britain
ARTICLES: 2 LANGUAGE: English.
HEADNOTE: COLONIAL STOCK
TOPIC: Privil/Immunities
CONCEPTS: Annex type material.
TREATY REF: 382UNTS8.
PARTIES:
 Cyprus
 UK Great Britain

105484 Bilateral Exchange **382 UNTS 231**
SIGNED: 16 Aug 60 FORCE: 16 Aug 60
REGISTERED: 12 Dec 60 UK Great Britain
ARTICLES: 2 LANGUAGE: English.
HEADNOTE: FINANCIAL ASSISTANCE
TOPIC: Direct Aid
CONCEPTS: Annex or appendix reference. General cooperation. Financial programs. Claims and settlements. General aid. Grants.
TREATY REF: 382UNTS8.
PARTIES:
 Cyprus
 UK Great Britain

105485 Bilateral Exchange **382 UNTS 239**
SIGNED: 16 Aug 60 FORCE: 16 Aug 60
REGISTERED: 12 Dec 60 UK Great Britain
ARTICLES: 2 LANGUAGE: English.
HEADNOTE: FINANCIAL LIABILITIES TIME INDEPENDENCE
TOPIC: Claims and Debts
CONCEPTS: Definition of terms. Governor-general functions. Transition period. Payment schedules. Economic assistance. Materials, equipment and services.
PARTIES:
 Cyprus
 UK Great Britain

105486 Bilateral Exchange **382 UNTS 247**
SIGNED: 16 Aug 60 FORCE: 16 Aug 60
REGISTERED: 12 Dec 60 UK Great Britain
ARTICLES: 2 LANGUAGE: English.
HEADNOTE: CONCERNING BRITISH RESIDENTS CYPRUS
TOPIC: Consul/Citizenship
CONCEPTS: Annex type material.
TREATY REF: 382UNTS8.
PARTIES:
 Cyprus
 UK Great Britain

105487 Bilateral Agreement **382 UNTS 255**
SIGNED: 24 Nov 60 FORCE: 24 Nov 60
REGISTERED: 12 Dec 60 United Nations
ARTICLES: 10 LANGUAGE: English. French.
HEADNOTE: ASSISTANCE
TOPIC: Direct Aid
CONCEPTS: Detailed regulations. Treaty implementation. Visas. Privileges and immunities. Exchange of information and documents. Informational records. Inspection and observation. Operating agencies. Personnel. Public information. Responsibility and liability. Title and deeds. Use of facilities. Arbitration. Procedure. Negotiation. Import quotas. Attachment of funds. Exchange rates and regulations. Expense sharing formulae. Financial programs. Domestic obligation. General technical assistance. Economic assistance. Materials, equipment and services. IGO status.
INTL ORGS: International Atomic Energy Agency. International Court of Justice. United Nations.
TREATY REF: 1UNTS15; 33UNTS261; 374UNTS147.
PROCEDURE: Amendment. Termination.
PARTIES:
 Cambodia
 UN Special Fund

105488 Bilateral Agreement **382 UNTS 273**
SIGNED: 12 Dec 60 FORCE: 12 Dec 60
REGISTERED: 12 Dec 60 United Nations
ARTICLES: 8 LANGUAGE: English.
HEADNOTE: ACTIVITIES UNICEF
TOPIC: Direct Aid
CONCEPTS: Treaty implementation. Privileges and immunities. Exchange of information and documents. Informational records. Inspection and observation. Public information. Responsibility and liability. Indemnities and reimbursements. Claims and settlements. Tax exemptions. Customs exemptions. Assistance. General aid. Materials, equipment and services. Return of equipment and recapture. IGO status.
INTL ORGS: United Nations.
TREATY REF: 1UNTS15.
PROCEDURE: Amendment. Termination.
PARTIES:
 Nepal
 UNICEF (Children)

105489 Bilateral Agreement **382 UNTS 283**
SIGNED: 14 Dec 60 FORCE: 14 Dec 60
REGISTERED: 14 Dec 60 United Nations
ARTICLES: 6 LANGUAGE: Spanish.
HEADNOTE: OPERATIONAL EXECUTIVE PERSONNEL
TOPIC: Tech Assistance
CONCEPTS: Treaty implementation. Annex or appendix reference. Privileges and immunities. General cooperation. Personnel. Responsibility and liability. Arbitration. Procedure. Negotiation. Vocational training. Compensation. Expense sharing formulae. Tax exemptions. Customs exemptions. Domestic obligation. Special projects. Status of experts. Conformity with IGO decisions.
INTL ORGS: Permanent Court of Arbitration.
PROCEDURE: Amendment. Termination.
PARTIES:
 Bolivia
 United Nations
ANNEX
534 UNTS 480. United Nations. Force 12 May 65.
534 UNTS 480. Bolivia. Force 12 May 65.

105490 Bilateral Exchange **382 UNTS 301**
SIGNED: 15 Dec 60 FORCE: 15 Dec 60
REGISTERED: 15 Dec 60 United Nations

ARTICLES: 4 LANGUAGE: English. French.
HEADNOTE: PRESS RADIO
TOPIC: Mass Media
CONCEPTS: Radio-telephone-telegraphic communications. Press and wire services.
PARTIES:
Cambodia
Thailand

105491 Bilateral Exchange **382 UNTS 307**
SIGNED: 15 Dec 60   FORCE: 15 Dec 60
REGISTERED: 15 Dec 60 United Nations
ARTICLES: 4 LANGUAGE: English. French.
HEADNOTE: JOINT REPRESSION CRIMINAL OFFENSES FRONTIER REGION
TOPIC: Admin Cooperation
CONCEPTS: General cooperation. Penal sanctions.
INTL ORGS: United Nations.
PARTIES:
Cambodia
Thailand

105492 Bilateral Exchange **382 UNTS 315**
SIGNED: 15 Dec 60   FORCE: 15 Dec 60
REGISTERED: 15 Dec 60 United Nations
ARTICLES: 4 LANGUAGE: English. French.
HEADNOTE: REBELS POLITICAL REFUGEES
TOPIC: Extradition
CONCEPTS: Refugees.
INTL ORGS: United Nations.
PARTIES:
Cambodia
Thailand

105493 Bilateral Exchange **382 UNTS 321**
SIGNED: 15 Dec 60   FORCE: 15 Dec 60
REGISTERED: 15 Dec 60 United Nations
ARTICLES: 4 LANGUAGE: English. French.
HEADNOTE: COMMON LAW CRIMINALS
TOPIC: Extradition
CONCEPTS: Extradition, deportation and repatriation. Extraditable offenses. Conformity with municipal law.
INTL ORGS: United Nations.
PARTIES:
Cambodia
Thailand

105494 Multilateral Treaty **383 UNTS 3**
SIGNED: 6 Feb 60   FORCE: 27 Apr 60
REGISTERED: 19 Dec 60 El Salvador
ARTICLES: 31 LANGUAGE: Spanish.
HEADNOTE: DEVELOPMENT INTEGRATION ECONOMICS REGION
TOPIC: General Economic
CONCEPTS: Exceptions and exemptions. Treaty implementation. Annex or appendix reference. Border traffic and migration. Conformity with municipal law. Informational records. Juridical personality. Legal protection and assistance. General property. Establishment of commission. Procedure. Special tribunals. Negotiation. Free trade. Reciprocity in trade. Trade procedures. Currency. Funding procedures. Non-interest rates and fees. Quotas. Equitable taxes. Customs declarations. Customs exemptions. Competency certificate. Ports and pilotage.
INTL ORGS: Central American Economic Association. Arbitration Commission.
PROCEDURE: Future Procedures Contemplated. Accession. Denunciation. Duration. Ratification. Renewal or Revival.
PARTIES:
El Salvador SIGNED: 6 Feb 60 FORCE: 27 Apr 60
Guatemala SIGNED: 6 Feb 60 FORCE: 27 Apr 60
Honduras SIGNED: 6 Feb 60 FORCE: 27 Apr 60

105495 Bilateral Agreement **383 UNTS 67**
SIGNED: 17 Nov 60   FORCE: 17 Nov 60
REGISTERED: 19 Dec 60 United Nations
ARTICLES: 10 LANGUAGE: English. Spanish.
HEADNOTE: ASSISTANCE
TOPIC: Direct Aid
CONCEPTS: Detailed regulations. Visas. Privileges and immunities. Property. Exchange of information and documents. Informational records. Inspection and observation. Operating agencies. Personnel. Public information. Responsibility and liability. Title and deeds. Use of facilities.

Arbitration. Procedure. Negotiation. Import quotas. Attachment of funds. Exchange rates and regulations. Expense sharing formulae. Financial programs. Domestic obligation. Materials, equipment and services. IGO status.
INTL ORGS: International Atomic Energy Agency. International Court of Justice. United Nations.
TREATY REF: 1UNTS15; 33UNTS261; 374UNTS147.
PROCEDURE: Amendment. Termination.
PARTIES:
Guatemala
UN Special Fund
                    ANNEX
399 UNTS 297. UN Special Fund. Interpretation 30 Jun 61. Force 30 Jun 61.
399 UNTS 397. Guatemala. Interpretation 30 Jun 61. Force 30 Jun 61.
422 UNTS 342. Guatemala. Ratification 7 Feb 62. Force 7 Feb 62.

105496 Bilateral Agreement **383 UNTS 91**
SIGNED: 15 Nov 60   FORCE: 25 Nov 60
REGISTERED: 19 Dec 60 WHO (World Health)
ARTICLES: 6 LANGUAGE: French.
HEADNOTE: TECHNICAL ADVISORY ASSISTANCE
TOPIC: Tech Assistance
CONCEPTS: Definition of terms. Privileges and immunities. General cooperation. Exchange of information and documents. Personnel. Responsibility and liability. Title and deeds. Exchange. Scholarships and grants. Vocational training. Research and development. Expense sharing formulae. Local currency. Domestic obligation. Special projects. Materials, equipment and services. IGO status. Conformity with IGO decisions.
INTL ORGS: United Nations.
TREATY REF: 33UNTS261.
PROCEDURE: Amendment. Termination.
PARTIES:
WHO (World Health)
Upper Volta
                    ANNEX
633 UNTS 412. WHO (World Health). Amendment 3 Nov 67. Force 3 Nov 67.
633 UNTS 412. Upper Volta. Amendment 3 Nov 67. Force 3 Nov 67.

105497 Bilateral Agreement **383 UNTS 103**
SIGNED: 20 Dec 60   FORCE: 20 Dec 60
REGISTERED: 20 Dec 60 United Nations
ARTICLES: 10 LANGUAGE: English. Spanish.
HEADNOTE: ASSISTANCE
TOPIC: Direct Aid
CONCEPTS: Detailed regulations. Treaty implementation. Visas. Privileges and immunities. Exchange of information and documents. Informational records. Inspection and observation. Operating agencies. Personnel. Public information. Responsibility and liability. Title and deeds. Use of facilities. Arbitration. Procedure. Negotiation. Import quotas. Attachment of funds. Exchange rates and regulations. Expense sharing formulae. Financial programs. Domestic obligation. General technical assistance. Economic assistance. Materials, equipment and services. IGO status.
INTL ORGS: International Court of Justice. United Nations.
TREATY REF: 1UNTS15; 33UNTS261; 374UNTS147.
PROCEDURE: Amendment. Termination.
PARTIES:
Honduras
UN Special Fund

105498 Bilateral Exchange **383 UNTS 125**
SIGNED: 21 Nov 60   FORCE: 21 Nov 60
REGISTERED: 26 Dec 60 Finland
ARTICLES: 2 LANGUAGE: Swedish.
HEADNOTE: FERRY SERVICE
TOPIC: Territory Boundary
CONCEPTS: Indemnities and reimbursements. Financial programs. Facilities and equipment. Frontier waterways.
PARTIES:
Finland
Sweden

105499 Bilateral Agreement **383 UNTS 131**
SIGNED: 18 Nov 59   FORCE: 24 Jun 60

REGISTERED: 27 Dec 60 Norway
ARTICLES: 5 LANGUAGE: English.
HEADNOTE: PAYMENTS
TOPIC: Finance
CONCEPTS: Previous treaty replacement. General cooperation. Accounting procedures. Banking. Balance of payments. Currency. Exchange rates and regulations. Interest rates. Payment schedules. Local currency. Assets transfer.
TREATY REF: 15UNTS163.
PROCEDURE: Future Procedures Contemplated. Termination.
PARTIES:
Norway
Yugoslavia

105500 Bilateral Agreement **383 UNTS 147**
SIGNED: 30 Nov 60   FORCE: 30 Nov 60
REGISTERED: 29 Dec 60 United Nations
ARTICLES: 6 LANGUAGE: French.
HEADNOTE: PROVISION OPERATIVE EXECUTIVE PERSONNEL
TOPIC: Tech Assistance
CONCEPTS: Treaty implementation. Annex or appendix reference. Privileges and immunities. General cooperation. Personnel. Responsibility and liability. Arbitration. Procedure. Negotiation. Vocational training. Compensation. Expense sharing formulae. Tax exemptions. Customs exemptions. Domestic obligation. Special projects. Status of experts. Conformity with IGO decisions.
INTL ORGS: Permanent Court of Arbitration.
PROCEDURE: Amendment. Termination.
PARTIES:
Cambodia
United Nations
                    ANNEX
483 UNTS 350. United Nations. Supplementation 21 May 63. Force 15 Jun 63.
483 UNTS 350. Cambodia. Supplementation 15 Jun 63. Force 15 Jun 63.

105501 Bilateral Agreement **383 UNTS 159**
SIGNED: 15 Nov 60   FORCE: 1 Jan 61
REGISTERED: 1 Jan 61 Norway
ARTICLES: 10 LANGUAGE: Norwegian. Finnish.
HEADNOTE: FISHING REGULATIONS TANA RIVER
TOPIC: Specific Resources
CONCEPTS: Annex or appendix reference. Previous treaty replacement. Passports non-diplomatic. Non-visa travel documents. Inspection and observation. Operating agencies. Investigation of violations. Fees and exemptions. Fisheries and fishing.
TREATY REF: 173UNTS163; 338UNTS373.
PROCEDURE: Amendment. Duration. Termination.
PARTIES:
Finland
Norway

105502 Multilateral Agreement **383 UNTS 203**
SIGNED: 8 Sep 59   FORCE: 1 Jan 61
REGISTERED: 1 Jan 61 Norway
ARTICLES: 8 LANGUAGE: Norwegian. Danish. Finnish. Swedish. Icelandic.
HEADNOTE: UNEMPLOYMENT INSURANCE DETAILS
TOPIC: Non-ILO Labor
CONCEPTS: Definition of terms. Detailed regulations. Previous treaty replacement. Exchange of information and documents. Domestic legislation. Wages and salaries. Non-ILO labor relations. Unemployment. Payment schedules.
TREATY REF: 254UNTS55.
PARTIES:
Denmark SIGNED: 8 Sep 59 FORCE: 1 Jan 61
Finland SIGNED: 8 Sep 59 FORCE: 1 Jan 61
Iceland SIGNED: 8 Sep 59 FORCE: 1 Jan 61
Norway SIGNED: 8 Sep 59 FORCE: 1 Jan 61
Sweden SIGNED: 8 Sep 59 FORCE: 1 Jan 61

105503 Multilateral Convention **383 UNTS 229**
SIGNED: 15 Jan 58   FORCE: 1 Jan 61
REGISTERED: 1 Jan 61 United Nations
ARTICLES: 13 LANGUAGE: French.
HEADNOTE: CUSTOMS CONVENTION CONCERNING SPARE PARTS
TOPIC: Customs

CONCEPTS: Definition of terms. Arbitration. Negotiation. Customs duties. Railways.
INTL ORGS: United Nations.
PROCEDURE: Amendment. Accession. Denunciation. Ratification. Registration.
PARTIES:
Australia SIGNED: 20 Feb 58 RATIFIED: 3 Mar 59 FORCE: 1 Jan 61
Belgium SIGNED: 5 Feb 58 RATIFIED: 10 Sep 59 FORCE: 1 Jan 61
Denmark SIGNED: 5 Feb 58 RATIFIED: 5 Feb 58 FORCE: 1 Jan 61
France SIGNED: 5 Feb 58 RATIFIED: 19 Aug 59 FORCE: 1 Jan 61
Germany, West Berlin RATIFIED: 21 Oct 60 FORCE: 1 Jan 61
Germany, West SIGNED: 10 Feb 58 RATIFIED: 21 Oct 60 FORCE: 1 Jan 61
Italy SIGNED: 5 Feb 58 RATIFIED: 8 Mar 60 FORCE: 1 Jan 61
Liechtenstein RATIFIED: 7 Jul 60 FORCE: 1 Jan 61
Luxembourg SIGNED: 12 Feb 58 RATIFIED: 19 Feb 60 FORCE: 1 Jan 61 .
Netherlands SIGNED: 7 Feb 58 RATIFIED: 7 May 59 FORCE: 1 Jan 61
Switzerland SIGNED: 20 Feb 58 RATIFIED: 7 Jul 60 FORCE: 1 Jan 61

105504 Bilateral Agreement **383 UNTS 243**
SIGNED: 2 Jul 59 FORCE: 27 Jul 60
REGISTERED: 3 Jan 61 Japan
ARTICLES: 8 LANGUAGE: English. Japanese.
HEADNOTE: COOPERATION PEACEFUL USES ATOMIC ENERGY
TOPIC: Atomic Energy
CONCEPTS: Definition of terms. General cooperation. Exchange of information and documents. Informational records. Inspection and observation. Research cooperation. Nuclear materials. Peaceful use. Security of information.
INTL ORGS: International Atomic Energy Agency.
PROCEDURE: Duration. Termination.
PARTIES:
Canada
Japan

105505 Bilateral Treaty **383 UNTS 277**
SIGNED: 15 Dec 59 FORCE: 26 Sep 60
REGISTERED: 3 Jan 61 Japan
ARTICLES: 14 LANGUAGE: English.
HEADNOTE: PROMOTE DEVELOPMENT COMMERCIAL RELATIONS
TOPIC: General Trade
CONCEPTS: Exceptions and exemptions. Conformity with municipal law. General cooperation. Juridical personality. Legal protection and assistance. Recognition and enforcement of legal decisions. Arbitration. Procedure. General trade. Establishment of trade relations. Export quotas. Import quotas. Reciprocity in trade. Trade agencies. Trade procedures. Balance of payments. Most favored nation clause. General. Customs duties. Temporary importation. Routes and logistics. Navigational conditions. Transport of goods. Merchant vessels. Inland and territorial waters.
INTL ORGS: General Agreement on Tariffs and Trade.
TREATY REF: 55UNTS187;300UNTS199; 221UNTS255.
PROCEDURE: Duration. Ratification. Termination.
PARTIES:
Czechoslovakia
Japan

105506 Bilateral Agreement **383 UNTS 293**
SIGNED: 10 May 60 FORCE: 16 Aug 60
REGISTERED: 3 Jan 61 Japan
ARTICLES: 11 LANGUAGE: English.
HEADNOTE: COMMERCE
TOPIC: General Trade
CONCEPTS: Establishment of trade relations. Maritime products and equipment. National treatment. Tonnage. Shipwreck and salvage.
INTL ORGS: General Agreement on Tariffs and Trade. International Monetary Fund.
TREATY REF: GENEVA ARGEEMENT ON TARIFFS AND TRADE..
PROCEDURE: Ratification.

PARTIES:
Fed of Malaya
Japan

105507 Bilateral Agreement **384 UNTS 3**
SIGNED: 5 Jan 60 FORCE: 13 Jun 60
REGISTERED: 3 Jan 61 Japan
ARTICLES: 16 LANGUAGE: English.
HEADNOTE: DOUBLE TAXATION INCOME
TOPIC: Taxation
CONCEPTS: Definition of terms. Conformity with municipal law. Exchange of official publications. Negotiation. Teacher and student exchange. Taxation. Tax credits. Equitable taxes. General. Tax exemptions. Air transport. Merchant vessels.
PROCEDURE: Ratification. Termination.
PARTIES:
India
Japan

105508 Bilateral Agreement **384 UNTS 31**
SIGNED: 25 Jan 60 FORCE: 25 Jan 60
REGISTERED: 3 Jan 61 Japan
ARTICLES: 8 LANGUAGE: English.
HEADNOTE: ESTABLISHMENT PROTOTYPE PRODUCTION TRAINING CENTER SMALL SCALE INDUSTRIES
TOPIC: Tech Assistance
CONCEPTS: Annex or appendix reference. Privileges and immunities. Conformity with municipal law. General cooperation. Personnel. Responsibility and liability. Institute establishment. Vocational training. Expense sharing formulae. Claims and settlements. Most favored nation clause. General. Customs duties. General technical assistance. Materials, equipment and services. Industry.
PROCEDURE: Duration. Termination.
PARTIES:
India
Japan

105509 Bilateral Agreement **384 UNTS 43**
SIGNED: 12 Sep 60 FORCE: 12 Sep 60
REGISTERED: 3 Jan 61 Japan
ARTICLES: 8 LANGUAGE: English.
HEADNOTE: ESTABLISHMENT TRAINING CENTER SMALL SCALE INDUSTRIES
TOPIC: Education
CONCEPTS: Annex or appendix reference. Privileges and immunities. Conformity with municipal law. General cooperation. Personnel. Responsibility and liability. Title and deeds. Institute establishment. Vocational training. Expense sharing formulae. Most favored nation clause. General. Customs duties. Materials, equipment and services. Industry.
TREATY REF: 325UNTS221.
PROCEDURE: Duration. Termination.
PARTIES:
Iran
Japan

105510 Bilateral Exchange **384 UNTS 55**
SIGNED: 21 Jul 60 FORCE: 1 Aug 60
REGISTERED: 3 Jan 61 Japan
ARTICLES: 2 LANGUAGE: French.
HEADNOTE: MUTUAL ABOLITION PASSPORT VISAS VISA FEES
TOPIC: Visas
CONCEPTS: Time limit. Previous treaty replacement. Denial of admission. Resident permits. Conformity with municipal law. Fees and exemptions.
TREATY REF: 318UNTS227.
PROCEDURE: Denunciation.
PARTIES:
Japan
Luxembourg

105511 Bilateral Agreement **384 UNTS 63**
SIGNED: 30 Jul 60 FORCE: 30 Jul 60
REGISTERED: 3 Jan 61 Japan
ARTICLES: 8 LANGUAGE: English.
HEADNOTE: AGRICULTURAL TRAINING CENTER
TOPIC: Education
CONCEPTS: Definition of terms. Annex or appendix reference. Friendship and amity. Alien status. Conformity with municipal law. General cooper-

ation. Personnel. General property. Responsibility and liability. Institute establishment. Vocational training. Research and development. Indemnities and reimbursements. Agriculture. Materials, equipment and services.
PROCEDURE: Duration. Termination.
PARTIES:
Japan
Pakistan

105512 Bilateral Agreement **384 UNTS 73**
SIGNED: 24 Aug 60 FORCE: 24 Aug 60
REGISTERED: 3 Jan 61 Japan
ARTICLES: 9 LANGUAGE: English.
HEADNOTE: TELECOMMUNICATIONS TRAINING CENTER
TOPIC: Education
CONCEPTS: Definition of terms. Annex or appendix reference. Friendship and amity. Alien status. Conformity with municipal law. General cooperation. Personnel. General property. Responsibility and liability. Institute establishment. Scholarships and grants. Vocational training. Indemnities and reimbursements. Customs exemptions. General technical assistance. Materials, equipment and services. Telecommunications.
PROCEDURE: Duration. Renewal or Revival. Termination.
PARTIES:
Japan
Thailand

105513 Bilateral Instrument **384 UNTS 89**
SIGNED: 7 Oct 60 FORCE: 7 Oct 60
REGISTERED: 3 Jan 61 Japan
ARTICLES: 5 LANGUAGE: English. Japanese.
HEADNOTE: SETTLEMENT CLAIMS
TOPIC: Reparations
CONCEPTS: Time limit. Lump sum settlements. Loss and/or damage. Reparations and restrictions. Post-war claims settlement.
TREATY REF: 136UNTS45.
PARTIES:
Japan
UK Great Britain

105514 Bilateral Agreement **384 UNTS 105**
SIGNED: 2 Aug 60 FORCE: 2 Aug 60
REGISTERED: 6 Jan 61 USA (United States)
ARTICLES: 31 LANGUAGE: English. Spanish.
HEADNOTE: ARMY MISSION
TOPIC: Military Mission
CONCEPTS: Definition of terms. Responsibility and liability. Compensation. Indemnities and reimbursements. Exchange rates and regulations. Expense sharing formulae. Tax exemptions. Customs exemptions. Military assistance. Military training. Security of information. Airforce-army-navy personnel ratio. Ranks and privileges. Conditions for assistance missions. Third country military personnel. Status of forces.
INTL ORGS: North Atlantic Treaty Organization.
TREATY REF: 34UNTS243.
PROCEDURE: Termination.
PARTIES:
Argentina
USA (United States)
ANNEX
458 UNTS 354. USA (United States). Amendment 8 Jan 62. Force 7 Jun 62.
458 UNTS 354. Argentina. Amendment 7 Jun 62. Force 7 Jun 62.

105515 Bilateral Exchange **384 UNTS 131**
SIGNED: 27 Feb 60 FORCE: 27 Feb 60
REGISTERED: 6 Jan 61 USA (United States)
ARTICLES: 3 LANGUAGE: English. Portuguese.
HEADNOTE: GRANT FOR PROCUREMENT NUCLEAR RESEARCH TRAINING EQUIPMENT MATERIALS
TOPIC: Direct Aid
CONCEPTS: Exchange of information and documents. Public information. Responsibility and liability. Indemnities and reimbursements. Financial programs. Grants. Procurement. Atomic energy assistance. Non-nuclear materials. Peaceful use. Transport of goods.
PARTIES:
Brazil
USA (United States)

105516 Bilateral Agreement **384 UNTS 141**
SIGNED: 26 Jul 60 FORCE: 26 Jul 60
REGISTERED: 6 Jan 61 USA (United States)
ARTICLES: 6 LANGUAGE: English. Persian.
HEADNOTE: AGRI COMMOD TITLE I
TOPIC: US Agri Commod Aid
CONCEPTS: General provisions. Annex or appendix reference. Exchange of information and documents. Reexport of goods, etc.. Exchange rates and regulations. Transportation costs. Local currency. Commodities schedule. Purchase authorization. Surplus commodities. Mutual consultation.
PARTIES:
Iran
USA (United States)
ANNEX
394 UNTS 318. USA (United States). Amendment 26 Sep 60. Force 26 Sep 60.
394 UNTS 318. Iran. Amendment 26 Sep 60. Force 26 Sep 60.
394 UNTS 324. Iran. Amendment 20 Oct 60. Force 20 Oct 60.
394 UNTS 324. USA (United States). Amendment 20 Oct 60. Force 20 Oct 60.
405 UNTS 370. USA (United States). Amendment 10 Apr 61. Force 17 Apr 61.
405 UNTS 370. Iran. Amendment 17 Apr 61. Force 17 Apr 61.
410 UNTS 355. USA (United States). Amendment 18 May 61. Force 1 Jan 61.
410 UNTS 355. Iran. Amendment 1 Jun 61. Force 1 Jun 61.

105517 Bilateral Exchange **384 UNTS 159**
SIGNED: 15 Jul 60 FORCE: 15 Jul 60
REGISTERED: 6 Jan 61 USA (United States)
ARTICLES: 4 LANGUAGE: English. Spanish.
HEADNOTE: AMENDING AGREEMENTS ARMY NAVY MILITARY AVIATION MISSIONS
TOPIC: Military Mission
CONCEPTS: Previous treaty amendment. Compensation. Payment schedules. Military assistance missions.
TREATY REF: 277 1NTS231.
PARTIES:
Peru
USA (United States)

105518 Bilateral Agreement **384 UNTS 169**
SIGNED: 16 Jul 60 FORCE: 16 Jul 60
REGISTERED: 6 Jan 61 USA (United States)
ARTICLES: 8 LANGUAGE: English. Polish.
HEADNOTE: CLAIMS NATIONALS
TOPIC: Specif Claim/Waive
CONCEPTS: Treaty implementation. Annex or appendix reference. Exchange of information and documents. Payment schedules. Claims and settlements. Lump sum settlements. Specific claims or waivers.
PARTIES:
Poland
USA (United States)
ANNEX
401 UNTS 338. USA (United States). Supplementation 29 Nov 60. Force 29 Nov 60.
401 UNTS 338. Poland. Supplementation 29 Nov 60. Force 29 Nov 60.

105519 Bilateral Agreement **384 UNTS 189**
SIGNED: 1 Aug 60 FORCE: 1 Aug 60
REGISTERED: 6 Jan 61 USA (United States)
ARTICLES: 6 LANGUAGE: English.
HEADNOTE: AGRI COMMOD TITLE I
TOPIC: US Agri Commod Aid
CONCEPTS: General provisions. Annex or appendix reference. Exchange of information and documents. Reexport of goods, etc.. Exchange rates and regulations. Transportation costs. Local currency. Commodities schedule. Purchase authorization. Surplus commodities. Mutual consultation.
PARTIES:
United Arab Rep
USA (United States)
ANNEX
402 UNTS 364. United Arab Rep. Amendment 16 Jan 61. Force 16 Jan 61.
402 UNTS 364. USA (United States). Amendment 16 Jan 61. Force 16 Jan 61.

404 UNTS 382. USA (United States). Amendment 13 Feb 61. Force 13 Feb 61.
404 UNTS 382. United Arab Rep. Amendment 13 Feb 61. Force 13 Feb 61.
410 UNTS 360. United Arab Rep. Amendment 27 May 61. Force 27 May 61.
410 UNTS 360. USA (United States). Amendment 27 May 61. Force 27 May 61.
411 UNTS 330. United Arab Rep. Amendment 24 Jun 61. Force 24 Jun 61.
411 UNTS 330. USA (United States). Amendment 24 Jun 61. Force 24 Jun 61.

105520 Bilateral Exchange **384 UNTS 207**
SIGNED: 1 Oct 60 FORCE: 1 Oct 60
REGISTERED: 10 Jan 61 UK Great Britain
ARTICLES: 2 LANGUAGE: English.
HEADNOTE: INHERITANCE INTERNATIONAL RIGHTS OBLIGATIONS
TOPIC: Recognition
CONCEPTS: Continuity of rights and obligations.
PARTIES:
Nigeria
UK Great Britain

105521 Bilateral Agreement **384 UNTS 213**
SIGNED: 20 Feb 60 FORCE: 7 Sep 60
REGISTERED: 12 Jan 61 IBRD (World Bank)
ARTICLES: 8 LANGUAGE: English.
HEADNOTE: LOAN AGREEMENT
TOPIC: IBRD Project
CONCEPTS: Default remedies. Definition of terms. Annex or appendix reference. Exchange of information and documents. Informational records. Inspection and observation. Accounting procedures. Bonds. Fees and exemptions. Interest rates. Domestic obligation. Terms of loan. Loan regulations. Loan guarantee. Guarantor non-interference.
PARTIES:
Iran
IBRD (World Bank)

105522 Bilateral Agreement **384 UNTS 243**
SIGNED: 22 Jun 60 FORCE: 29 Nov 60
REGISTERED: 12 Jan 61 IBRD (World Bank)
ARTICLES: 8 LANGUAGE: English.
HEADNOTE: GUARANTEE HYDROELECTRIC PROJECT
TOPIC: IBRD Project
CONCEPTS: Definition of terms. Annex or appendix reference. Exchange of information and documents. Inspection and observation. Bonds. Fees and exemptions. Tax exemptions. Domestic obligation. Terms of loan. Loan regulations. Loan guarantee. Guarantor non-interference.
PARTIES:
Nicaragua
IBRD (World Bank)

105523 Bilateral Agreement **384 UNTS 275**
SIGNED: 30 Dec 59 FORCE: 2 Dec 60
REGISTERED: 12 Jan 61 IBRD (World Bank)
ARTICLES: 7 LANGUAGE: English.
HEADNOTE: LOAN LIVESTOCK IMPROVEMENT
TOPIC: IBRD Project
CONCEPTS: Default remedies. Definition of terms. Annex or appendix reference. Exchange of information and documents. Inspection and observation. Accounting procedures. Bonds. Fees and exemptions. Interest rates. Tax exemptions. Domestic obligation. Agriculture. Terms of loan. Loan regulations. Loan guarantee. Guarantor non-interference.
PARTIES:
IBRD (World Bank)
Uruguay

105524 Bilateral Agreement **385 UNTS 3**
SIGNED: 3 Aug 60 FORCE: 26 Nov 60
REGISTERED: 16 Jan 61 WHO (World Health)
ARTICLES: 6 LANGUAGE: English.
HEADNOTE: TECHNICAL ADVISORY ASSISTANCE
TOPIC: Tech Assistance
CONCEPTS: Definition of terms. Previous treaty replacement. Privileges and immunities. General cooperation. Exchange of information and documents. Personnel. Responsibility and liability. Title and deeds. Exchange. Scholarships and

grants. Vocational training. Research and development. Expense sharing formulae. Local currency. Domestic obligation. Special projects. Materials, equipment and services. IGO status. Conformity with IGO decisions.
INTL ORGS: United Nations.
TREATY REF: 33UNTS261; 92UNTS39; 165UNTS219.
PARTIES:
WHO (World Health)
United Arab Rep

105525 Bilateral Exchange **385 UNTS 15**
SIGNED: 21 Oct 60 FORCE: 21 Oct 60
REGISTERED: UK Great Britain
ARTICLES: 2 LANGUAGE: English.
HEADNOTE: LOAN
TOPIC: Loans and Credits
CONCEPTS: Loan and credit. Loan repayment.
PARTIES:
Chile
UK Great Britain

105526 Bilateral Agreement **385 UNTS 21**
SIGNED: 16 Oct 59 FORCE: 16 Oct 59
REGISTERED: 16 Jan 61 UK Great Britain
ARTICLES: 10 LANGUAGE: English. German.
HEADNOTE: WAR GRAVES
TOPIC: Other Military
CONCEPTS: Responsibility for war dead. Upkeep of war graves. Establishment of war cemeteries.
PARTIES:
Germany, West
UK Great Britain

105527 Bilateral Agreement **385 UNTS 39**
SIGNED: 23 Feb 60 FORCE: 1 Sep 60
REGISTERED: 16 Jan 61 UK Great Britain
ARTICLES: 7 LANGUAGE: English. German.
HEADNOTE: EXTRADITION FUGITIVE CRIMINALS
TOPIC: Extradition
CONCEPTS: Territorial application. Annex type material. Extradition requests. Revival of treaties.
INTL ORGS: United Nations.
TREATY REF: 62BFSP5.
PARTIES:
Germany, West
UK Great Britain

105528 Bilateral Exchange **385 UNTS 55**
SIGNED: 20 Jun 60 FORCE: 7 Jul 60
REGISTERED: 16 Jan 61 UK Great Britain
ARTICLES: 2 LANGUAGE: English. Persian.
HEADNOTE: FACILITATE TRAVEL
TOPIC: Visas
CONCEPTS: Territorial application. Time limit. Non-visa travel documents.
INTL ORGS: Council of Europe. Organization for Economic Co-operation and Development.
PROCEDURE: Termination.
PARTIES:
Germany, West
UK Great Britain

105529 Bilateral Exchange **385 UNTS 63**
SIGNED: 9 Apr 60 FORCE: 9 Apr 60
REGISTERED: 16 Jan 61 UK Great Britain
ARTICLES: 2 LANGUAGE: English.
HEADNOTE: DOUBLE TAXATION AIR TRANSPORT
TOPIC: Taxation
CONCEPTS: Taxation. Air transport.
PROCEDURE: Termination.
PARTIES:
Iran
UK Great Britain

105530 Bilateral Exchange **385 UNTS 71**
SIGNED: 31 Aug 60 FORCE: 1 Sep 60
REGISTERED: 16 Jan 61 UK Great Britain
ARTICLES: 2 LANGUAGE: English. Arabic.
HEADNOTE: IMPORTATION BOOKS OTHER CULTURAL MATERIAL
TOPIC: Culture
CONCEPTS: Definition of terms. Annex or appendix reference. Exchange. Import quotas. Trade procedures. Accounting procedures. Currency. Currency deposits. Publications exchange. Mass media exchange.

PROCEDURE: Duration. Renewal or Revival. Termination.
PARTIES:
Israel
UK Great Britain
ANNEX
413 UNTS 388. UK Great Britain. Termination 21 Aug 61. Force 18 Oct 61.
413 UNTS 388. Israel. Termination 18 Aug 61. Force 18 Oct 61.

105531 Bilateral Exchange **385 UNTS 81**
SIGNED: 4 May 60 FORCE: 4 May 60
REGISTERED: 16 Jan 61 UK Great Britain
ARTICLES: 2 LANGUAGE: English. Polish.
HEADNOTE: LOAN
TOPIC: Loans and Credits
CONCEPTS: Financial programs. Interest rates. Loan and credit. Loan repayment.
PARTIES:
Jordan
UK Great Britain

105532 Bilateral Agreement **385 UNTS 87**
SIGNED: 2 Jul 60 FORCE: 25 Oct 60
REGISTERED: 16 Jan 61 UK Great Britain
ARTICLES: 17 LANGUAGE: English. Romanian.
HEADNOTE: CONCERNING CIVIL AIR TRANSPORT
TOPIC: Air Transport
CONCEPTS: Definition of terms. Detailed regulations. Exceptions and exemptions. Annex or appendix reference. Previous treaty replacement. Conformity with municipal law. General cooperation. Procedure. Negotiation. Monetary and gold transfers. Non-interest rates and fees. Tax exemptions. Customs exemptions. Routes and logistics. Navigational conditions. Permit designation. Air transport. Conditions of airlines operating permission. Overflights and technical stops. Operating authorizations and regulations.
TREATY REF: 15UNTS295.
PROCEDURE: Amendment. Termination.
PARTIES:
Poland
UK Great Britain

105533 Bilateral Agreement **385 UNTS 113**
SIGNED: 10 Nov 60 FORCE: 10 Nov 60
REGISTERED: 16 Jan 61 UK Great Britain
ARTICLES: 11 LANGUAGE: Chinese. English. French. Russian. Spanish.
HEADNOTE: FINANCE
TOPIC: Finance
CONCEPTS: Definition of terms. Detailed regulations. Annex or appendix reference. Nationality and citizenship. General cooperation. Exchange of information and documents. Informational records. Expropriation. General property. Title and deeds. Negotiation. Claims and settlements. Lump sum settlements. Loan repayment.
TREATY REF: 42UNTS3.
PROCEDURE: Future Procedures Contemplated.
PARTIES:
Romania
UK Great Britain

105534 Multilateral Agreement **385 UNTS 137**
SIGNED: 1 Dec 58 FORCE: 1 Jan 59
REGISTERED: 18 Jan 61 UK Great Britain
ARTICLES: 48 LANGUAGE: German. French. Italian. Dutch.
HEADNOTE: INTERNATIONAL SUGAR AGREEMENTS
TOPIC: Commodity Trade
CONCEPTS: Definition of terms. Detailed regulations. Territorial application. General provisions. Treaty interpretation. Procedure. Employment regulations. General trade. Export quotas. Finances and payments. Balance of payments. Currency. Non-interest rates and fees. Commodity trade. Quotas. Domestic obligation. Decisions. Subsidiary organ. Liaison with other IGO's. Internal structure.
INTL ORGS: International Monetary Fund. United Nations. International Sugar Council.
PROCEDURE: Amendment. Accession. Duration. Ratification.
PARTIES:
Australia SIGNED: 19 Dec 58 RATIFIED: 23 Dec 58 FORCE: 1 Jan 59

Bel-Lux Econ Union SIGNED: 23 Dec 58 RATIFIED: 30 Mar 60 FORCE: 1 Jan 59
Brazil SIGNED: 15 Dec 58 RATIFIED: 5 Nov 59 FORCE: 1 Jan 59
Canada SIGNED: 23 Dec 58 FORCE: 1 Jan 59
Taiwan SIGNED: 23 Dec 58 RATIFIED: 29 May 59 FORCE: 1 Jan 59
Costa Rica SIGNED: 22 Dec 58 RATIFIED: 23 Jun 59 FORCE: 1 Jan 59
Cuba SIGNED: 18 Dec 58 RATIFIED: 15 Jun 59 FORCE: 1 Jan 59
Czechoslovakia SIGNED: 23 Dec 58 RATIFIED: 23 Jul 58 FORCE: 1 Jan 59
Denmark SIGNED: 23 Dec 58 RATIFIED: 29 May 59 FORCE: 1 Jan 59
Dominican Republic SIGNED: 23 Dec 58 RATIFIED: 3 Jun 59 FORCE: 1 Jan 59
France SIGNED: 23 Dec 58 RATIFIED: 1 Jun 59 FORCE: 1 Jan 59
Germany, West SIGNED: 23 Dec 58 RATIFIED: 28 Mar 60 FORCE: 1 Jan 59
Ghana SIGNED: 24 Dec 58 RATIFIED: 4 Mar 59 FORCE: 1 Jan 59
Greece SIGNED: 23 Dec 58
Guatemala SIGNED: 22 Dec 58 RATIFIED: 11 Dec 59 FORCE: 1 Jan 59
Haiti SIGNED: 23 Dec 58 RATIFIED: 6 Apr 60 FORCE: 1 Jan 59
Indonesia SIGNED: 24 Dec 58 RATIFIED: 6 Nov 59 FORCE: 1 Jan 59
Ireland SIGNED: 22 Dec 58 RATIFIED: 5 Jun 59 FORCE: 1 Jan 59
Israel SIGNED: 23 Dec 58
Italy SIGNED: 23 Dec 58
Japan SIGNED: 23 Dec 58 RATIFIED: 1 May 59 FORCE: 1 Jan 59
Mexico SIGNED: 19 Dec 58 RATIFIED: 28 Mar 60 FORCE: 1 Jan 59
Morocco SIGNED: 23 Dec 58 RATIFIED: 26 Oct 59 FORCE: 1 Jan 59
Netherlands SIGNED: 23 Dec 58
Nicaragua SIGNED: 19 Dec 58 RATIFIED: 14 Sep 59 FORCE: 1 Jan 59
Panama SIGNED: 24 Dec 58 RATIFIED: 18 Mar 59 FORCE: 1 Jan 59
Peru SIGNED: 4 Dec 58 RATIFIED: 22 Dec 58 FORCE: 1 Jan 59
Philippines SIGNED: 23 Dec 58 RATIFIED: 16 Jul 59 FORCE: 1 Jan 59
Poland SIGNED: 23 Dec 58 RATIFIED: 28 Oct 59 FORCE: 1 Jan 59
Portugal SIGNED: 23 Dec 58 RATIFIED: 21 Mar 60 FORCE: 1 Jan 59
South Africa SIGNED: 19 Dec 58 RATIFIED: 30 Dec 58 FORCE: 1 Jan 59
UK Great Britain Aden RATIFIED: 29 Dec 58 FORCE: 1 Jan 59
UK Great Britain Bahamas RATIFIED: 29 Dec 58 FORCE: 1 Jan 59
UK Great Britain Barbados RATIFIED: 29 Dec 58 FORCE: 1 Jan 59
UK Great Britain Bermuda RATIFIED: 29 Dec 58 FORCE: 1 Jan 59
UK Great Britain British Guiana RATIFIED: 29 Dec 58 FORCE: 1 Jan 59
UK Great Britain British Honduras RATIFIED: 29 Dec 58 FORCE: 1 Jan 59
UK Great Britain Brit Virgin Islands RATIFIED: 29 Dec 58 FORCE: 1 Jan 59
UK Great Britain Cayman Island RATIFIED: 29 Dec 58 FORCE: 1 Jan 59
UK Great Britain Cyprus RATIFIED: 29 Dec 58 FORCE: 1 Jan 59
UK Great Britain Falkland Islands RATIFIED: 29 Dec 58 FORCE: 1 Jan 59
UK Great Britain Fiji Islands RATIFIED: 29 Dec 58 FORCE: 1 Jan 59
UK Great Britain Gambia RATIFIED: 29 Dec 58 FORCE: 1 Jan 59
UK Great Britain Gibralter RATIFIED: 29 Dec 58 FORCE: 1 Jan 59
UK Great Britain Hong Kong RATIFIED: 29 Dec 58 FORCE: 1 Jan 59
UK Great Britain Jamaica RATIFIED: 29 Dec 58 FORCE: 1 Jan 59
UK Great Britain Kenya RATIFIED: 29 Dec 58 FORCE: 21 Mar 60
UK Great Britain Leeward Islands RATIFIED: 29 Dec 58 FORCE: 1 Jan 59
UK Great Britain Mauritius RATIFIED: 29 Dec 58 FORCE: 1 Jan 59
UK Great Britain Nigeria RATIFIED: 29 Dec 58 FORCE: 1 Jan 59

UK Great Britain SIGNED: 22 Dec 58 RATIFIED: 29 Dec 58 FORCE: 1 Jan 59
UK Great Britain Sarawak RATIFIED: 29 Dec 58 FORCE: 16 Oct 5
UK Great Britain Seychelles RATIFIED: 29 Dec 58 FORCE: 1 Jan 59
UK Great Britain Sierra Leone RATIFIED: 29 Dec 58 FORCE: 1 Jan 59
UK Great Britain St. Helena RATIFIED: 29 Dec 58 FORCE: 16 Oct 59
UK Great Britain Tanganyika RATIFIED: 29 Dec 58 FORCE: 1 Jan 59
UK Great Britain Tonga RATIFIED: 29 Dec 58 FORCE: 21 Mar 60
UK Great Britain Trinidad/Tobago RATIFIED: 29 Dec 58 FORCE: 1 Jan 59
UK Great Britain Turk-Caicose Is RATIFIED: 29 Dec 58 FORCE: 1 Jan 59
UK Great Britain Uganda RATIFIED: 29 Dec 58 FORCE: 21 Mar 60
UK Great Britain Windward Islands RATIFIED: 29 Dec 58 FORCE: 1 Jan 59
UK Great Britain W Pacif Hi Command RATIFIED: 29 Dec 58 FORCE: 1 Jan 59
UK Great Britain Zanzibar RATIFIED: 29 Dec 58 FORCE: 1 Jan 59
USA (United States) All Territories RATIFIED: 9 Oct 59 FORCE: 1 Jan 59
USSR (Soviet Union) SIGNED: 24 Dec 58 RATIFIED: 1 Jun 59 FORCE: 1 Jan 59
ANNEX
425 UNTS 370. Netherlands. Ratification 2 Feb 61.
425 UNTS 370. Colombia. Accession 15 Feb 61.
425 UNTS 370. Lebanon. Accession 3 Jul 61.
425 UNTS 370. Paraguay. Accession 11 Oct 61.
425 UNTS 370. UK Great Britain. Sierra Leone. Withdrawal 27 Apr 61.
425 UNTS 370. UK Great Britain. Tanganyika. Withdrawal 9 Dec 61.
425 UNTS 370. New Zealand. Accession 28 Nov 60.
425 UNTS 370. Ecuador. Accession 19 Jan 61.
425 UNTS 370. Nigeria. Accession 12 Dec 61.
425 UNTS 370. Germany, West. Berlin. Force 1 Jan 61.
425 UNTS 370. UK Great Britain. Cyprus. Withdrawal 16 Aug 60.
466 UNTS 404. India. Qualified Accession 13 Jul 61.
466 UNTS 404. Italy. Ratification 16 Feb 62.
466 UNTS 404. Trinidad/Tobago. Acceptance 21 Feb 63.
535 UNTS 436. UK Great Britain. Zanzibar. Withdrawal 10 Dec 63.
535 UNTS 436. UK Great Britain. Uganda. Withdrawal 9 Oct 62.
535 UNTS 436. UK Great Britain. Sarawak. Withdrawal 16 Sep 63.
535 UNTS 436. UK Great Britain. Kenya. Withdrawal 12 Dec 63.
535 UNTS 436. UK Great Britain. Somalia. Withdrawal 26 Jun 60.
535 UNTS 436. UK Great Britain. Nigeria. Withdrawal 1 Oct 62.
535 UNTS 436. UK Great Britain. Jamaica. Withdrawal 6 Aug 62.
535 UNTS 436. UK Great Britain. Trinidad/Tobago. Withdrawal 31 Aug 62.
551 UNTS 319. UK Great Britain. Swaziland. Force 12 Jul 63.
551 UNTS 319. Jamaica. Accession 20 Aug 63.
551 UNTS 319. Argentina. Accession 30 Sep 63.
617 UNTS 368. Bolivia. Accession 14 Dec 66.
617 UNTS 368. Germany, West. Berlin. Acceptance 30 Dec 66.
617 UNTS 368. Guyana. Accession 30 Dec 66.
617 UNTS 368. Nigeria. Ratification 21 Dec 66.
617 UNTS 368. Brazil. Ratification 30 Dec 66.
617 UNTS 368. Lebanon. Accession 22 Dec 66.

105535 Multilateral Agreement **386 UNTS 3**
SIGNED: 26 Jul 57 FORCE: 1 Mar 58
REGISTERED: 18 Jan 61 Austria
ARTICLES: 11 LANGUAGE: English.
HEADNOTE: RAILWAY RATES
TOPIC: Land Transport
CONCEPTS: Railways.
INTL ORGS: Special Commission.
PROCEDURE: Denunciation.
PARTIES:
Austria SIGNED: 26 Jul 57 FORCE: 1 Mar 58
Belgium SIGNED: 26 Jul 57 FORCE: 1 Mar 58

France SIGNED: 26 Jul 57 FORCE: 1 Mar 58
Germany, West SIGNED: 26 Jul 57 FORCE: 1 Mar 58
Italy SIGNED: 26 Jul 57 FORCE: 1 Mar 58
Luxembourg SIGNED: 26 Jul 57 FORCE: 1 Mar 58
Netherlands SIGNED: 26 Jul 57 FORCE: 1 Mar 58
ECSC (Coal/Steel) SIGNED: 26 Jul 57 FORCE: 1 Mar 58
ANNEX
414 UNTS 402. Austria. Supplementation 29 Nov 60. Force 6 Nov 61.
414 UNTS 402. ECSC (Coal/Steel). Supplementation 29 Nov 60. Force 6 Nov 61.

105536 Bilateral Agreement **386 UNTS 45**
SIGNED: 11 Dec 59 FORCE: 11 May 60
REGISTERED: 18 Jan 61 Czechoslovakia
ARTICLES: 5 LANGUAGE: English.
HEADNOTE: SCIENTIFIC TECHNICAL COOPERATION
TOPIC: Scientific Project
CONCEPTS: General cooperation. Specialists exchange. Scholarships and grants. Vocational training. Scientific exchange. General technical assistance. Economic assistance. Materials, equipment and services.
PROCEDURE: Duration. Ratification. Renewal or Revival. Termination.
PARTIES:
Czechoslovakia
Ethiopia

105537 Bilateral Treaty **386 UNTS 51**
SIGNED: 11 Dec 59 FORCE: 11 May 60
REGISTERED: 18 Jan 61 Czechoslovakia
ARTICLES: 4 LANGUAGE: English. Czechoslovakian. Amharic.
HEADNOTE: AMITY COOPERATION
TOPIC: General Amity
CONCEPTS: Friendship and amity. General cooperation. Procedure. Economic assistance.
PROCEDURE: Future Procedures Contemplated. Ratification. Renewal or Revival. Termination.
PARTIES:
Czechoslovakia
Ethiopia

105538 Bilateral Agreement **386 UNTS 63**
SIGNED: 30 Nov 59 FORCE: 14 Sep 60
REGISTERED: 18 Jan 61 Czechoslovakia
ARTICLES: 11 LANGUAGE: Czechoslovakian. French.
HEADNOTE: CULTURAL COOPERATION
TOPIC: Culture
CONCEPTS: Treaty implementation. Friendship and amity. Recognition of degrees. Exchange. Teacher and student exchange. Scholarships and grants. Exchange. General cultural cooperation. Artists. Athletes. Research results. Scientific exchange. Publications exchange. Mass media exchange. Press and wire services.
PROCEDURE: Denunciation. Ratification.
PARTIES:
Czechoslovakia
Guinea

105539 Bilateral Agreement **386 UNTS 73**
SIGNED: 23 Nov 56 FORCE: 16 Jul 57
REGISTERED: 18 Jan 61 Yugoslavia
ARTICLES: 16 LANGUAGE: Serbo-Croat. Albanian.
HEADNOTE: AIR SERVICES
TOPIC: Air Transport
CONCEPTS: Definition of terms. Exceptions and exemptions. Annex or appendix reference. Previous treaty replacement. Conformity with municipal law. General cooperation. Exchange of information and documents. Informational records. Licenses and permits. Recognition of legal documents. Use of facilities. Procedure. Negotiation. Fees and exemptions. Non-interest rates and fees. Most favored nation clause. Customs exemptions. Registration certificate. Routes and logistics. Airport facilities. Airworthiness certificates. Operating authorizations and regulations.
PROCEDURE: Amendment. Ratification. Termination.

PARTIES:
Albania
Yugoslavia

105540 Bilateral Exchange **386 UNTS 103**
SIGNED: 28 Apr 58 FORCE: 29 Apr 58
REGISTERED: 18 Jan 61 Yugoslavia
ARTICLES: 2 LANGUAGE: Serbo-Croat. Albanian.
HEADNOTE: FREE MEDICAL CARE DIPLOMATIC OTHER OFFICIALS
TOPIC: Consul/Citizenship
CONCEPTS: Detailed regulations. Public health.
PARTIES:
Albania
Yugoslavia

105541 Bilateral Agreement **386 UNTS 119**
SIGNED: 21 Mar 58 FORCE: 9 Oct 58
REGISTERED: 18 Jan 61 Yugoslavia
ARTICLES: 46 LANGUAGE: Serbo-Croat. Bulgarian.
HEADNOTE: REGULATIONS ROAD TRANSPORT PASSENGERS COMMERCIAL VEHICLE
TOPIC: Land Transport
CONCEPTS: Conditions. Default remedies. Definition of terms. General provisions. Annex or appendix reference. Passports non-diplomatic. Visas. Conformity with municipal law. General cooperation. Exchange of information and documents. Informational records. Establishment of commission. Compensation. Currency. Payment schedules. Non-interest rates and fees. Tax exemptions. Customs exemptions. Registration certificate. Passenger transport. Routes and logistics. Transport of goods. Commercial road vehicles. Driving permits. Roads and highways. Road rules.
INTL ORGS: Special Commission.
TREATY REF: 376UNTS53.
PROCEDURE: Denunciation. Duration. Ratification. Renewal or Revival.
PARTIES:
Bulgaria
Yugoslavia

105542 Bilateral Protocol **386 UNTS 207**
SIGNED: 7 Mar 56 FORCE: 7 Mar 56
REGISTERED: 18 Jan 61 Yugoslavia
ARTICLES: 9 LANGUAGE: English.
HEADNOTE: RICE CONSUMER GOODS MACHINERY EQUIPMENT ETC.
TOPIC: Commodity Trade
CONCEPTS: Treaty implementation. Annex or appendix reference. General trade. Trade agencies. Accounting procedures. Banking. Currency. Payment schedules. Non-interest rates and fees. Transportation costs. Commodity trade. Economic assistance.
PROCEDURE: Duration. Termination.
PARTIES:
Burma
Yugoslavia

105543 Bilateral Agreement **386 UNTS 235**
SIGNED: 7 Mar 56 FORCE: 7 Mar 56
REGISTERED: 18 Jan 61 Yugoslavia
ARTICLES: 7 LANGUAGE: English.
HEADNOTE: TECHNICAL COOPERATION
TOPIC: Tech Assistance
CONCEPTS: General cooperation. Recognition and enforcement of legal decisions. Personnel. Establishment of commission. Specialists exchange. Teacher and student exchange. Institute establishment. Research and development. Currency. Economic assistance.
INTL ORGS: Special Commission.
PROCEDURE: Duration. Termination.
PARTIES:
Burma
Yugoslavia

105544 Bilateral Agreement **386 UNTS 243**
SIGNED: 6 Jun 59 FORCE: 9 Feb 60
REGISTERED: 18 Jan 61 Yugoslavia
ARTICLES: 11 LANGUAGE: English.
HEADNOTE: DELIVERY GOOD CREDIT
TOPIC: Loans and Credits
CONCEPTS: Friendship and amity. Operating agencies. Establishment of commission. Indem-

nities and reimbursements. Currency. Interest rates. Payment schedules. Loan and credit. Credit provisions. Purchase authorization. Loan repayment. Terms of loan.
PROCEDURE: Ratification.
PARTIES:
Ethiopia
Yugoslavia

105545 Bilateral Agreement **386 UNTS 251**
SIGNED: 13 Jul 59 FORCE: 19 Dec 59
REGISTERED: 18 Jan 61 Yugoslavia
ARTICLES: 5 LANGUAGE: French.
HEADNOTE: COMPENSATION INTERESTS
TOPIC: Specif Claim/Waive
CONCEPTS: Annex or appendix reference. Compensation. Claims and settlements. Lump sum settlements.
PROCEDURE: Ratification.
PARTIES:
Denmark
Yugoslavia

105546 Bilateral Agreement **386 UNTS 263**
SIGNED: 22 Jul 58 FORCE: 25 Aug 59
REGISTERED: 18 Jan 61 Yugoslavia
ARTICLES: 11 LANGUAGE: French.
HEADNOTE: COMPENSATION REGARDING NATIONALIZATION
TOPIC: Claims and Debts
CONCEPTS: Treaty implementation. Conformity with municipal law. General cooperation. Exchange of information and documents. Informational records. Expropriation. Responsibility and liability. Procedure. Accounting procedures. Banking. Compensation. Payment schedules. Claims and settlements.
PROCEDURE: Ratification.
PARTIES:
Netherlands
Yugoslavia

105547 Bilateral Agreement **386 UNTS 271**
SIGNED: 11 Dec 58 FORCE: 11 Dec 58
REGISTERED: 18 Jan 61 Yugoslavia
ARTICLES: 12 LANGUAGE: English.
HEADNOTE: TRADE
TOPIC: General Trade
CONCEPTS: Establishment of trade relations. National treatment.
INTL ORGS: Special Commission.
PROCEDURE: Duration. Ratification. Termination.
PARTIES:
Israel
Yugoslavia

105548 Bilateral Agreement **386 UNTS 283**
SIGNED: 11 Dec 58 FORCE: 11 Dec 58
REGISTERED: 18 Jan 61 Yugoslavia
ARTICLES: 10 LANGUAGE: English.
HEADNOTE: PAYMENTS
TOPIC: Finance
CONCEPTS: Change of circumstances. Detailed regulations. Conformity with municipal law. General cooperation. Accounting procedures. Banking. Balance of payments. Currency. Inadequacy of funds. Interest rates. Payment schedules. Credit provisions.
PROCEDURE: Ratification. Renewal or Revival. Termination.
PARTIES:
Israel
Yugoslavia

105549 Bilateral Agreement **386 UNTS 293**
SIGNED: 12 Dec 57 FORCE: 20 Jun 58
REGISTERED: 18 Jan 61 Yugoslavia
ARTICLES: 18 LANGUAGE: French.
HEADNOTE: FILMS
TOPIC: Mass Media
CONCEPTS: Conformity with municipal law. Personnel. Establishment of commission. Dispute settlement. Arbitration. Indemnities and reimbursements. Expense sharing formulae. Payment schedules. Assets. Mass media exchange.
INTL ORGS: Special Commission.
PROCEDURE: Duration. Renewal or Revival.

PARTIES:
Italy
Yugoslavia

105550 Bilateral Agreement **386 UNTS 307**
SIGNED: 31 Mar 55　　　　FORCE: 28 Mar 58
REGISTERED: 18 Jan 61 Yugoslavia
ARTICLES: 13 LANGUAGE: French.
HEADNOTE: ROAD TRANSPORT PASSENGERS
TOPIC: Visas
CONCEPTS: Licenses and permits. Establishment
of commission. Customs declarations. Driving
permits. Motor vehicles and combinations. Road
rules.
INTL ORGS: Special Commission.
PROCEDURE: Denunciation. Renewal or Revival.
PARTIES:
Italy
Yugoslavia

105551 Bilateral Agreement **386 UNTS 317**
SIGNED: 31 Mar 55　　　　FORCE: 1 Apr 55
REGISTERED: 18 Jan 61 Yugoslavia
ARTICLES: 8 LANGUAGE: French.
HEADNOTE: TRADE
TOPIC: General Trade
CONCEPTS: Definition of terms. Annex or appen-
dix reference. Establishment of commission. Ex-
port quotas. Import quotas. Trade procedures.
Payment schedules.
INTL ORGS: Special Commission.
PROCEDURE: Denunciation. Duration. Renewal or
Revival.
PARTIES:
Italy
Yugoslavia

105552 Multilateral Agreement **386 UNTS 345**
SIGNED: 18 Jun 58　　　　FORCE: 1 Jul 58
REGISTERED: 18 Jan 61 Yugoslavia
ARTICLES: 6 LANGUAGE: French.
HEADNOTE: TRADE
TOPIC: General Trade
CONCEPTS: Definition of terms. Territorial applica-
tion. Previous treaty replacement. Establishment
of commission. Trade procedures. Payment
schedules.
INTL ORGS: Organization for Economic Co-opera-
tion and Development. Special Commission.
TREATY REF: 249UNTS197; 386UNTS355.
PROCEDURE: Denunciation. Renewal or Revival.
PARTIES:
Bel-Lux Econ Union SIGNED: 18 Jun 58 FORCE:
1 Jul 58
Netherlands　SIGNED:　18 Jun 58　FORCE:
1 Jul 58
Yugoslavia SIGNED: 18 Jun 58 FORCE: 1 Jul 58

105553 Multilateral Agreement **386 UNTS 355**
SIGNED: 18 Jun 58　　　　FORCE: 1 Jul 58
REGISTERED: 18 Jan 61 Yugoslavia
ARTICLES: 8 LANGUAGE: French.
HEADNOTE: PAYMENTS
TOPIC: Finance
CONCEPTS: Definition of terms. Territorial applica-
tion. Previous treaty replacement. General coop-
eration. Licenses and permits. General trade. Ac-
counting procedures. Banking. Balance of pay-
ments. Currency. Exchange rates and
regulations. Financial programs. Interest rates.
Payment schedules. Local currency.
TREATY REF: 249UNTS197.
PROCEDURE: Denunciation.
PARTIES:
Bel-Lux Econ Union SIGNED: 18 Jun 58 FORCE:
1 Jul 58
Netherlands　SIGNED:　18 Jun 58　FORCE:
1 Jul 58
Yugoslavia SIGNED: 18 Jun 58 FORCE: 1 Jul 58

105554 Bilateral Convention **387 UNTS 3**
SIGNED: 12 Jun 59　　　　FORCE: 30 Aug 60
REGISTERED: 20 Jan 61 Taiwan
ARTICLES: 9 LANGUAGE: Chinese. English. Span-
ish.
HEADNOTE: CULTURAL CONVENTION
TOPIC: Culture
CONCEPTS: Treaty interpretation. Friendship and
amity. Specialists exchange. Exchange. Teacher

and student exchange. Exchange. General cul-
tural cooperation. Artists. Athletes. Scientific ex-
change. Mass media exchange.
TREATY REF: 4UNTS275.
PROCEDURE: Duration. Ratification. Renewal or
Revival. Termination.
PARTIES:
Taiwan
Ecuador

105555 Bilateral Agreement **387 UNTS 15**
SIGNED: 20 Jan 61　　　　FORCE: 20 Jan 61
REGISTERED: 20 Jan 61 United Nations
ARTICLES: 10 LANGUAGE: English. Spanish.
HEADNOTE: ASSISTANCE
TOPIC: Direct Aid
CONCEPTS: Detailed regulations. Treaty imple-
mentation. Visas. Privileges and immunities. Ex-
change of information and documents. Informa-
tional records. Inspection and observation. Oper-
ating agencies. Personnel. Public information.
Responsibility and liability. Title and deeds. Use
of facilities. Arbitration. Procedure. Negotiation.
Import quotas. Attachment of funds. Exchange
rates and regulations. Expense sharing formulae.
Financial programs. Domestic obligation. Gen-
eral technical assistance. Economic assistance.
Materials, equipment and services. IGO status.
INTL ORGS: International Court of Justice. United
Nations. Special Commission.
TREATY　REF:　1UNTS15;　33UNTS261;
374UNTS147.
PROCEDURE: Amendment. Termination.
PARTIES:
Nicaragua
UN Special Fund

105556 Bilateral Agreement **387 UNTS 37**
SIGNED: 25 Nov 60　　　　FORCE: 25 Nov 60
REGISTERED: 25 Jan 61 WHO (World Health)
ARTICLES: 6 LANGUAGE: English.
HEADNOTE: TECHNICAL ADVISORY ASSISTANCE
TOPIC: Tech Assistance
CONCEPTS: Definition of terms. Privileges and im-
munities. General cooperation. Exchange of in-
formation and documents. Personnel. Responsi-
bility and liability. Title and deeds. Exchange.
Scholarships and grants. Vocational training. Re-
search and development. Expense sharing for-
mulae. Local currency. Domestic obligation.
Special projects. Materials, equipment and ser-
vices. IGO status. Conformity with IGO decisions.
INTL ORGS: United Nations.
TREATY REF: 33UNTS261.
PROCEDURE: Amendment. Termination.
PARTIES:
Fed of Malaya
WHO (World Health)
ANNEX
514 UNTS 288. Malaysia. Amendment 4 Sep 64.

105557 Bilateral Agreement **387 UNTS 49**
SIGNED: 8 Sep 60　　　　FORCE: 14 Oct 60
REGISTERED: 25 Jan 61 WHO (World Health)
ARTICLES: 6 LANGUAGE: French.
HEADNOTE: TECHNICAL ADVISORY ASSISTANCE
TOPIC: Tech Assistance
CONCEPTS: Definition of terms. Privileges and im-
munities. General cooperation. Exchange of in-
formation and documents. Personnel. Responsi-
bility and liability. Title and deeds. Exchange.
Scholarships and grants. Vocational training. Re-
search and development. Expense sharing for-
mulae. Local currency. Domestic obligation.
Special projects. Materials, equipment and ser-
vices. IGO status. Conformity with IGO decisions.
INTL ORGS: United Nations.
TREATY REF: 33UNTS261.
PROCEDURE: Amendment. Termination.
PARTIES:
Lebanon
WHO (World Health)

105558 Bilateral Convention **387 UNTS 61**
SIGNED: 21 Sep 59　　　　FORCE: 24 Dec 59
REGISTERED: 26 Jan 61 Romania
ARTICLES: 12 LANGUAGE: Romanian. Bulgarian.
HEADNOTE: DUAL CITIZENSHIP
TOPIC: Consul/Citizenship

CONCEPTS: Treaty interpretation. Dual citizen-
ship. Nationality and citizenship.
PROCEDURE: Ratification. Termination.
PARTIES:
Bulgaria
Romania

105559 Bilateral Convention **387 UNTS 81**
SIGNED: 23 Apr 59　　　　FORCE: 12 Aug 59
REGISTERED: 26 Jan 61 Romania
ARTICLES: 22 LANGUAGE: Romanian. Bulgarian.
HEADNOTE: CONSULAR CONVENTION
TOPIC: Consul/Citizenship
CONCEPTS: Definition of terms. General consular
functions. Consular relations establishment. Invi-
olability. Privileges and immunities. Diplomatic
correspondence. Responsibility and liability.
PROCEDURE: Denunciation. Duration. Ratification.
Renewal or Revival.
PARTIES:
Bulgaria
Romania

105560 Bilateral Agreement **387 UNTS 115**
SIGNED: 15 Jul 58　　　　FORCE: 26 Jan 59
REGISTERED: 26 Jan 61 Romania
ARTICLES: 14 LANGUAGE: Romanian. German.
HEADNOTE: CULTURAL SCIENTIFIC COOPER-
ATION
TOPIC: Health/Educ/Welfare
CONCEPTS: General cooperation. Exchange of in-
formation and documents. Exchange. Teacher
and student exchange. Professorships. Voca-
tional training. Exchange. Artists. Athletes. Re-
search results. Scientific exchange. Publications
exchange. Mass media exchange. Press and
wire services.
PROCEDURE: Denunciation. Duration.
PARTIES:
Germany, East
Romania

105561 Bilateral Convention **387 UNTS 133**
SIGNED: 15 Jul 58　　　　FORCE: 25 Mar 59
REGISTERED: 26 Jan 61 Romania
ARTICLES: 26 LANGUAGE: Romanian. German.
HEADNOTE: CONSULAR
TOPIC: Consul/Citizenship
CONCEPTS: General consular functions. Privileges
and immunities. Consular functions in property.
Overflights and technical stops. Shipwreck and
salvage.
PROCEDURE: Ratification.
PARTIES:
Germany, East
Romania

105562 Bilateral Convention **387 UNTS 167**
SIGNED: 2 May 57　　　　FORCE: 20 Mar 58
REGISTERED: 26 Jan 61 Romania
ARTICLES: 18 LANGUAGE: Romanian. Czechoslo-
vakian.
HEADNOTE: SPECIAL PROBLEMS
TOPIC: Health/Educ/Welfare
CONCEPTS: Old age and invalidity insurance. Ad-
ministrative cooperation. Sickness and invalidity
insurance. Social security.
PARTIES:
Czechoslovakia
Romania

105563 Multilateral Agreement **387 UNTS 202**
SIGNED: 28 Jan 61　　　　FORCE: 28 Jan 61
REGISTERED: 28 Jan 61 United Nations
ARTICLES: 6 LANGUAGE: English.
HEADNOTE: TECHNICAL ASSISTANCE
TOPIC: Tech Assistance
CONCEPTS: Definition of terms. Previous treaty replacement. Privileges and immunities. General
cooperation. Exchange of information and documents. Personnel. Responsibility and liability. Title and deeds. Exchange. Scholarships and
grants. Vocational training. Research and development. Expense sharing formulae. Local cur-

rency. Domestic obligation. General technical assistance. Materials, equipment and services. IGO status. Conformity with IGO decisions.
TREATY REF: 76UNTS132; 1UNTS15; 33UNTS261.
PROCEDURE: Amendment. Termination.
PARTIES:
FAO (Food Agri) SIGNED: 28 Jan 61 FORCE: 28 Jan 61
IAEA (Atom Energy) SIGNED: 28 Jan 61 FORCE: 28 Jan 61
ICAO (Civil Aviat) SIGNED: 28 Jan 61 FORCE: 28 Jan 61
ILO (Labor Org) SIGNED: 28 Jan 61 FORCE: 28 Jan 61
ITU (Telecommun) SIGNED: 28 Jan 61 FORCE: 28 Jan 61
UNESCO (Educ/Cult) SIGNED: 28 Jan 61 FORCE: 28 Jan 61
United Nations SIGNED: 28 Jan 61 FORCE: 28 Jan 61
WHO (World Health) SIGNED: 28 Jan 61 FORCE: 28 Jan 61
WMO (Meteorology) SIGNED: 28 Jan 61 FORCE: 28 Jan 61
Somalia SIGNED: 28 Jan 61 FORCE: 28 Jan 61
ANNEX
500 UNTS 322. Somalia. Amendment 9 Jun 64. Force 9 Jun 64.
500 UNTS 322. UNTAB (Tech Assis). Amendment 25 May 64. Force 9 Jun 64.
649 UNTS 344. UNIDO (Industrial). Accession 3 Nov 68. Force 3 Nov 68.
649 UNTS 344. IMCO (Maritime Org). Accession 3 Nov 68. Force 3 Nov 68.

105564 Bilateral Agreement **387 UNTS 219**
SIGNED: 3 Jan 61 FORCE: 3 Jan 61
REGISTERED: 28 Jan 61 United Nations
ARTICLES: 10 LANGUAGE: English.
HEADNOTE: ASSISTANCE
TOPIC: Direct Aid
CONCEPTS: Detailed regulations. Treaty implementation. Visas. Privileges and immunities. Exchange of information and documents. Informational records. Inspection and observation. Operating agencies. Personnel. Public information. Responsibility and liability. Title and deeds. Use of facilities. Arbitration. Procedure. Negotiation. Import quotas. Attachment of funds. Exchange rates and regulations. Expense sharing formulae. Financial programs. Domestic obligation. General technical assistance. Economic assistance. Materials, equipment and services. IGO status.
INTL ORGS: International Atomic Energy Agency. International Court of Justice. United Nations. Special Commission.
TREATY REF: 1UNTS15; 33UNTS261; 374UNTS147.
PROCEDURE: Amendment. Termination.
PARTIES:
Burma
UN Special Fund

105565 Bilateral Exchange **387 UNTS 237**
SIGNED: 21 Nov 60 FORCE: 22 Nov 60
REGISTERED: 1 Feb 61 Belgium
ARTICLES: 2 LANGUAGE: French. Spanish.
HEADNOTE: ABOLITION TRAVEL VISA REQUIREMENT
TOPIC: Visas
CONCEPTS: Emergencies. Time limit. Visa abolition. Denial of admission. Resident permits. Conformity with municipal law.
PROCEDURE: Denunciation.
PARTIES:
Belgium
Paraguay

105566 Bilateral Convention **387 UNTS 245**
SIGNED: 30 Jun 58 FORCE: 27 Jan 61
REGISTERED: 1 Feb 61 Belgium
ARTICLES: 19 LANGUAGE: French. German.
HEADNOTE: RECOGNITION ENFORCEMENT JUDICIAL DECISIONS ARBITRAL AWARDS
TOPIC: Admin Cooperation
CONCEPTS: Territorial application. Recognition and enforcement of legal decisions. Prizes and arbitral awards.
PROCEDURE: Denunciation. Ratification.

PARTIES:
Belgium
Germany, West

105567 Bilateral Agreement **387 UNTS 277**
SIGNED: 7 Dec 60 FORCE: 9 Jan 61
REGISTERED: 1 Feb 61 WHO (World Health)
ARTICLES: 6 LANGUAGE: French.
HEADNOTE: TECHNICAL ADVISORY ASSISTANCE
TOPIC: Tech Assistance
CONCEPTS: Definition of terms. Privileges and immunities. General cooperation. Exchange of information and documents. Personnel. Responsibility and liability. Title and deeds. Exchange. Scholarships and grants. Vocational training. Research and development. Expense sharing formulae. Local currency. Domestic obligation. Special projects. Materials, equipment and services. IGO status. Conformity with IGO decisions.
INTL ORGS: United Nations.
TREATY REF: 33UNTS261.
PROCEDURE: Amendment. Termination.
PARTIES:
Dahomey
WHO (World Health)

105568 Bilateral Agreement **387 UNTS 289**
SIGNED: 2 Feb 61 FORCE: 2 Feb 61
REGISTERED: 2 Feb 61 United Nations
ARTICLES: 10 LANGUAGE: English. French.
HEADNOTE: ASSISTANCE
TOPIC: Direct Aid
CONCEPTS: Detailed regulations. Treaty implementation. Visas. Privileges and immunities. Exchange of information and documents. Informational records. Inspection and observation. Operating agencies. Personnel. Public information. Responsibility and liability. Title and deeds. Use of facilities. Arbitration. Procedure. Negotiation. Import quotas. Attachment of funds. Exchange rates and regulations. Expense sharing formulae. Financial programs. Domestic obligation. General technical assistance. Economic assistance. Materials, equipment and services. IGO status.
INTL ORGS: International Atomic Energy Agency. International Court of Justice. United Nations. Special Commission.
TREATY REF: 1UNTS15; 33UNTS261; 374UNTS147.
PROCEDURE: Amendment. Termination.
PARTIES:
Gabon
UN Special Fund

105569 Bilateral Agreement **387 UNTS 305**
SIGNED: 4 Jul 58 FORCE: 4 Jul 58
REGISTERED: 6 Feb 61 Belgium
ARTICLES: 15 LANGUAGE: English. French.
HEADNOTE: RELATING AIR SERVICES
TOPIC: Air Transport
CONCEPTS: Definition of terms. Detailed regulations. Annex or appendix reference. Conformity with municipal law. General cooperation. Exchange of information and documents. Arbitration. Procedure. Existing tribunals. Negotiation. Non-interest rates and fees. Most favored nation clause. National treatment. Routes and logistics. Permit designation. Air transport. Conditions of airlines operating permission. Overflights and technical stops. Operating authorizations and regulations.
INTL ORGS: International Civil Aviation Organization. International Court of Justice.
TREATY REF: 15UNTS295; 84UNTS389.
PROCEDURE: Amendment. Future Procedures Contemplated. Ratification. Termination. Application to Non-self-governing Territories.
PARTIES:
Belgium
Pakistan

105570 Bilateral Agreement **388 UNTS 3**
SIGNED: 18 Jun 59 FORCE: 13 Nov 59
REGISTERED: 6 Feb 61 Yugoslavia
ARTICLES: 27 LANGUAGE: French.
HEADNOTE: FRONTIER TRAFFIC
TOPIC: Visas
CONCEPTS: Visas. Frontier crossing points.
INTL ORGS: Special Commission.
PROCEDURE: Termination.

PARTIES:
Greece
Yugoslavia
ANNEX
483 UNTS 354. Yugoslavia. Supplementation 16 Feb 60. Force 16 Feb 60.
483 UNTS 354. Greece. Supplementation 16 Feb 60. Force 16 Feb 60.
483 UNTS 370. Greece. Supplementation 7 Jul 60. Force 7 Jul 60.
483 UNTS 370. Yugoslavia. Supplementation 7 Jul 60. Force 7 Jul 60.

105571 Bilateral Agreement **388 UNTS 53**
SIGNED: 6 May 60 FORCE: 6 May 60
REGISTERED: 8 Feb 61 United Nations
ARTICLES: 6 LANGUAGE: French.
HEADNOTE: OPERATIONAL EXECUTIVE PERSONNEL
TOPIC: Tech Assistance
CONCEPTS: Treaty implementation. Annex or appendix reference. Privileges and immunities. General cooperation. Personnel. Responsibility and liability. Arbitration. Procedure. Negotiation. Vocational training. Compensation. Expense sharing formulae. Tax exemptions. Customs exemptions. Domestic obligation. Special projects. Status of experts. Conformity with IGO decisions.
INTL ORGS: Permanent Court of Arbitration.
PROCEDURE: Amendment. Termination.
PARTIES:
United Nations
Togo

105572 Bilateral Exchange **388 UNTS 65**
SIGNED: 13 Sep 60 FORCE: 13 Sep 60
REGISTERED: 9 Feb 61 South Africa
ARTICLES: 2 LANGUAGE: English.
HEADNOTE: ERECTION SPACE TRACKING STATIONS
TOPIC: Specific Property
CONCEPTS: Frontier formalities. Operating agencies. Title and deeds. Customs exemptions. Materials, equipment and services. Facilities and equipment. Facilities and property.
PROCEDURE: Duration. Termination.
PARTIES:
South Africa
USA (United States)

105573 Bilateral Agreement **388 UNTS 75**
SIGNED: 28 Jan 61 FORCE: 28 Jan 61
REGISTERED: 9 Feb 61 United Nations
ARTICLES: 10 LANGUAGE: English.
HEADNOTE: ASSISTANCE
TOPIC: Direct Aid
CONCEPTS: Detailed regulations. Treaty implementation. Visas. Privileges and immunities. Exchange of information and documents. Informational records. Inspection and observation. Operating agencies. Personnel. Public information. Responsibility and liability. Title and deeds. Use of facilities. Arbitration. Procedure. Negotiation. Import quotas. Attachment of funds. Exchange rates and regulations. Expense sharing formulae. Financial programs. Domestic obligation. General technical assistance. Economic assistance. Materials, equipment and services. IGO status.
INTL ORGS: International Court of Justice.
TREATY REF: 1UNTS15; 33UNTS261; 374UNTS147.
PROCEDURE: Amendment. Termination.
PARTIES:
UN Special Fund
Somalia

105574 Bilateral Convention **388 UNTS 93**
SIGNED: 1 Apr 58 FORCE: 1 Jan 61
REGISTERED: 13 Feb 61 Belgium
ARTICLES: 40 LANGUAGE: English. French. Greek.
HEADNOTE: SOCIAL SECURITY
TOPIC: Non-ILO Labor
CONCEPTS: Exceptions and exemptions. Domestic legislation. Dispute settlement. Old age and invalidity insurance. Wages and salaries. Non-ILO labor relations. Administrative cooperation. Old age insurance. Sickness and invalidity insurance. Social security. Unemployment. Payment

schedules. Claims and settlements. National treatment.
PROCEDURE: Duration. Ratification. Renewal or Revival. Termination.
PARTIES:
Belgium
Greece

105575 Bilateral Exchange **388 UNTS 143**
SIGNED: 17 Oct 60   FORCE: 17 Oct 60
REGISTERED: 13 Feb 61 United Nations
ARTICLES: 3 LANGUAGE: English.
HEADNOTE: SETTLEMENT CLAIMS
TOPIC: Specif Claim/Waive
CONCEPTS: Claims and settlements. Specific claims or waivers.
PROCEDURE: Termination.
PARTIES:
United Nations
United Arab Rep

105576 Bilateral Agreement **388 UNTS 151**
SIGNED: 23 Feb 61   FORCE: 23 Feb 61
REGISTERED: 23 Feb 61 United Nations
ARTICLES: 10 LANGUAGE: English. Spanish.
HEADNOTE: ASSISTANCE
TOPIC: Direct Aid
CONCEPTS: Detailed regulations. Treaty implementation. Annex or appendix reference. Visas. Privileges and immunities. Exchange of information and documents. Informational records. Inspection and observation. Operating agencies. Personnel. Public information. Responsibility and liability. Title and deeds. Use of facilities. Arbitration. Procedure. Negotiation. Import quotas. Attachment of funds. Exchange rates and regulations. Expense sharing formulae. Financial programs. Domestic obligation. General technical assistance. Economic assistance. Materials, equipment and services. IGO status.
INTL ORGS: International Court of Justice.
TREATY REF: 1UNTS15; 33UNTS261; 374UNTS147.
PROCEDURE: Amendment. Termination.
PARTIES:
Mexico
UN Special Fund

105577 Unilateral Instrument **388 UNTS 179**
SIGNED: 11 Feb 61   FORCE: 23 Feb 61
REGISTERED: 23 Feb 61 United Nations
ARTICLES: 1 LANGUAGE: English.
HEADNOTE: ACCEPTANCE OBLIGATIONS UN
TOPIC: UN Charter
CONCEPTS: Acceptance of UN obligations. Adherence to UN charter.
INTL ORGS: United Nations.
PARTIES:
Somalia

105578 Bilateral Exchange **388 UNTS 183**
SIGNED: 19 Aug 59   FORCE: 19 Aug 59
REGISTERED: 23 Feb 61 USA (United States)
ARTICLES: 3 LANGUAGE: English.
HEADNOTE: NON-IMMIGRANT PASSPORT VISA PROCEDURES
TOPIC: Visas
CONCEPTS: Time limit.
PARTIES:
Australia
USA (United States)

105579 Bilateral Agreement **388 UNTS 191**
SIGNED: 30 Aug 60   FORCE: 30 Aug 60
REGISTERED: 23 Feb 61 USA (United States)
ARTICLES: 6 LANGUAGE: English. Chinese.
HEADNOTE: AGRI COMMOD TITLE I
TOPIC: US Agri Commod Aid
CONCEPTS: General provisions. Annex or appendix reference. Exchange of information and documents. Reexport of goods, etc.. Exchange rates and regulations. Transportation costs. Local currency. Commodities schedule. Purchase authorization. Surplus commodities. Mutual consultation.
PARTIES:
Taiwan
USA (United States)

ANNEX
401 UNTS 347. Taiwan. Amendment 31 Oct 60. Force 31 Oct 60.
401 UNTS 347. USA (United States). Amendment 31 Oct 60. Force 31 Oct 60.
401 UNTS 353. Taiwan. Amendment 1 Dec 60. Force 1 Dec 60.
401 UNTS 353. USA (United States). Amendment 1 Dec 60. Force 1 Dec 60.
404 UNTS 386. Taiwan. Amendment 9 Feb 61. Force 9 Feb 61.
404 UNTS 386. USA (United States). Amendment 9 Feb 61. Force 9 Feb 61.
409 UNTS 336. USA (United States). Amendment 27 Apr 61. Force 27 Apr 61.
409 UNTS 336. Taiwan. Amendment 27 Apr 61. Force 27 Apr 61.
458 UNTS 359. USA (United States). Amendment 29 Jun 62. Force 29 Jun 62.
458 UNTS 359. Taiwan. Amendment 29 Jun 62. Force 29 Jun 62.

105580 Bilateral Exchange **388 UNTS 225**
SIGNED: 24 Aug 60   FORCE: 24 Aug 60
REGISTERED: 23 Feb 61 USA (United States)
ARTICLES: 2 LANGUAGE: English.
HEADNOTE: SPACE VEHICLE RADIO TRACKING
TOPIC: Scientific Project
CONCEPTS: Annex or appendix reference. General cooperation. Research and scientific projects. Communication satellites testing. Research and development.
PARTIES:
Canada
USA (United States)

105581 Bilateral Agreement **388 UNTS 237**
SIGNED: 23 Aug 60   FORCE: 23 Aug 60
REGISTERED: 23 Feb 61 USA (United States)
ARTICLES: 9 LANGUAGE: English.
HEADNOTE: MUTUAL WEAPONS DEVELOPMENT PROGRAM
TOPIC: General Military
CONCEPTS: Definition of terms. Peaceful relations. Inspection and observation. Compensation. Expense sharing formulae. Patents, copyrights and trademarks. Compliance with domestic patent and copyright laws. Laws and formalities. Recognition. Domestic obligation. Defense and security. Military assistance. Security of information. Exchange of defense information. Restrictions on transfer.
PROCEDURE: Future Procedures Contemplated.
PARTIES:
Australia
USA (United States)

105582 Bilateral Exchange **388 UNTS 249**
SIGNED: 1 Sep 60   FORCE: 1 Sep 60
REGISTERED: 23 Feb 61 USA (United States)
ARTICLES: 2 LANGUAGE: English. French.
HEADNOTE: TRANSFER MILITARY EQUIPMENT MATERIALS SERVICE
TOPIC: Milit Assistance
CONCEPTS: Exchange of information and documents. Inspection and observation. Domestic obligation. Materials, equipment and services. Self-defense. Military assistance. Security of information. Restrictions on transfer.
TREATY REF: 270UNTS97.
PARTIES:
Haiti
USA (United States)

105583 Bilateral Exchange **388 UNTS 255**
SIGNED: 13 Feb 60   FORCE: 13 Feb 60
REGISTERED: 23 Feb 61 USA (United States)
ARTICLES: 2 LANGUAGE: English.
HEADNOTE: WEAPONS PRODUCTION PROGRAM
TOPIC: Milit Assistance
CONCEPTS: Change of circumstances. Annex or appendix reference. Previous treaty replacement. General cooperation. Licenses and permits. Use of facilities. National treatment. Customs exemptions. Materials, equipment and services. Security of information. Exchange of defense information. Equipment and supplies. Restrictions on transfer.
INTL ORGS: North Atlantic Treaty Organization.
TREATY REF: 34UNTS243.

PROCEDURE: Future Procedures Contemplated.
PARTIES:
Norway
USA (United States)

105584 Bilateral Agreement **388 UNTS 271**
SIGNED: 9 Aug 60   FORCE: 9 Aug 60
REGISTERED: 23 Feb 61 USA (United States)
ARTICLES: 2 LANGUAGE: English.
HEADNOTE: AGRI COMMOD TITLE I
TOPIC: US Agri Commod Aid
CONCEPTS: General provisions. Annex or appendix reference. Exchange of information and documents. Reexport of goods, etc.. Exchange rates and regulations. Transportation costs. Local currency. Commodities schedule. Purchase authorization. Surplus commodities. Mutual consultation.
PARTIES:
United Arab Rep
USA (United States)

ANNEX
389 UNTS 342. USA (United States). Amendment 17 Sep 60. Force 17 Sep 60.
389 UNTS 342. United Arab Rep. Amendment 17 Sep 60. Force 17 Sep 60.

105585 Bilateral Agreement **388 UNTS 287**
SIGNED: 8 Jun 60   FORCE: 21 Sep 60
REGISTERED: 23 Feb 61 USA (United States)
ARTICLES: 11 LANGUAGE: English.
HEADNOTE: COOPERATION CIVIL USES ATOMIC ENERGY
TOPIC: Atomic Energy
CONCEPTS: Definition of terms. Non-prejudice to third party. Exchange of information and documents. Responsibility and liability. Assets transfer. Nuclear materials. Non-nuclear materials. Peaceful use. Security of information.
INTL ORGS: International Atomic Energy Agency.
PROCEDURE: Duration.
PARTIES:
Indonesia
USA (United States)

105586 Bilateral Exchange **388 UNTS 303**
SIGNED: 26 Nov 63   FORCE: 26 Nov 53
REGISTERED: 23 Feb 61 USA (United States)
ARTICLES: 2 LANGUAGE: English.
HEADNOTE: DISPOSITION EQUIPMENT MATERIALS
TOPIC: Milit Assistance
CONCEPTS: Annex or appendix reference. Conformity with municipal law. Exchange of information and documents. Title and deeds. Reexport of goods, etc.. Delivery schedules. Surplus property. Return of equipment and recapture. Surplus war property.
TREATY REF: 179UNTS175.
PARTIES:
Netherlands
USA (United States)

105587 Bilateral Exchange **388 UNTS 315**
SIGNED: 22 Jul 60   FORCE: 22 Jul 60
REGISTERED: 23 Feb 61 USA (United States)
ARTICLES: 2 LANGUAGE: English. Spanish.
HEADNOTE: COMMISSION EDUCATIONAL EXCHANGE
TOPIC: Education
CONCEPTS: Conditions. Standardization. Conformity with municipal law. General cooperation. Inspection and observation. Personnel. General property. Exchange. Commissions and foundations. Teacher and student exchange. Scholarships and grants. Research and development. Accounting procedures. Exchange rates and regulations. Financial programs. Funding procedures.
INTL ORGS: Special Commission.
TREATY REF: 341UNTS201.
PARTIES:
USA (United States)
Uruguay

105588 Bilateral Agreement **389 UNTS 3**
SIGNED: 24 Feb 61   FORCE: 24 Feb 61
REGISTERED: 24 Feb 61 United Nations
ARTICLES: 10 LANGUAGE: English.

HEADNOTE: ASSISTANCE
TOPIC: Direct Aid
CONCEPTS: Detailed regulations. Treaty implementation. Visas. Privileges and immunities. Exchange of information and documents. Informational records. Inspection and observation. Operating agencies. Personnel. Public information. Responsibility and liability. Title and deeds. Use of facilities. Arbitration. Procedure. Negotiation. Import quotas. Exchange rates and regulations. Expense sharing formulae. Financial programs. Domestic obligation. General technical assistance. Economic assistance. Materials, equipment and services. IGO status.
INTL ORGS: International Court of Justice.
TREATY REF: 1UNTS15; 33UNTS261; 374UNTS147.
PROCEDURE: Amendment. Termination.
PARTIES:
Cyprus
UN Special Fund

105589 Bilateral Agreement **389 UNTS 21**
SIGNED: 15 Apr 57　　　FORCE: 30 Aug 57
REGISTERED: 27 Feb 61 Romania
ARTICLES: 8 LANGUAGE: English. Arabic.
HEADNOTE: CULTURAL AGREEMENT
TOPIC: Culture
CONCEPTS: Treaty interpretation. Friendship and amity. Non-diplomatic delegations. Recognition of degrees. Teacher and student exchange. Scholarships and grants. General cultural cooperation. Artists. Athletes. Scientific exchange. Research and development. Customs exemptions. Mass media exchange. Press and wire services.
PROCEDURE: Denunciation. Duration. Ratification.
PARTIES:
Romania
United Arab Rep

105590 Bilateral Agreement **389 UNTS 33**
SIGNED: 27 Oct 56　　　FORCE: 8 May 57
REGISTERED: 27 Feb 61 Romania
ARTICLES: 8 LANGUAGE: Romanian. Serbo-Croat.
HEADNOTE: CULTURAL COOPERATION
TOPIC: Culture
CONCEPTS: Treaty implementation. Friendship and amity. Conformity with municipal law. Exchange of information and documents. Exchange. Scholarships and grants. Exchange. General cultural cooperation. Artists. Scientific exchange. Research and development. Publications exchange. Mass media exchange. Press and wire services.
PROCEDURE: Denunciation. Duration. Ratification. Renewal or Revival.
PARTIES:
Romania
Yugoslavia

105591 Bilateral Agreement **389 UNTS 43**
SIGNED: 30 Jun 58　　　FORCE: 30 Jun 58
REGISTERED: 27 Feb 61 Romania
ARTICLES: 5 LANGUAGE: Romanian. Vietnamese. Russian.
HEADNOTE: TECHNICAL SCIENTIFIC COOPERATION
TOPIC: Scientific Project
CONCEPTS: Friendship and amity. Non-diplomatic delegations. Establishment of commission. Scientific exchange. General technical assistance. Economic assistance.
INTL ORGS: Special Commission.
PROCEDURE: Denunciation. Duration. Renewal or Revival.
PARTIES:
Romania
Vietnam, North

105592 Bilateral Agreement **389 UNTS 55**
SIGNED: 27 Oct 56　　　FORCE: 6 Mar 57
REGISTERED: 27 Feb 61 Romania
ARTICLES: 7 LANGUAGE: Romanian. Serbo-Croat.
HEADNOTE: TECHNICAL SCIENTIFIC COOPERATION
TOPIC: Scientific Project
CONCEPTS: Friendship and amity. Conformity with municipal law. Operating agencies. Establishment of commission. Vocational training. Re-

search and scientific projects. Research results. Scientific exchange. Research and development. Payment schedules. General technical assistance. Economic assistance.
INTL ORGS: Special Commission.
PROCEDURE: Denunciation. Duration. Future Procedures Contemplated. Renewal or Revival.
PARTIES:
Romania
Yugoslavia

105593 Multilateral Agreement **389 UNTS 69**
SIGNED: 8 Apr 59　　　FORCE: 30 Dec 59
REGISTERED: 28 Feb 61 USA (United States)
ARTICLES: 15 LANGUAGE: English. French. Portuguese. Spanish.
HEADNOTE: ESTABLISHMENT INTER-AMERICAN DEVELOPMENT BANK
TOPIC: IGO Establishment
CONCEPTS: Privileges and immunities. Arbitration. Loan and credit. Credit provisions. Decisions. Establishment. Headquarters and facilities. Liaison with other IGO's. Internal structure.
INTL ORGS: Inter-American Bank. Organization of American States.
PARTIES:

Argentina	SIGNED: 14 Oct 59	RATIFIED: 14 Oct 59	FORCE: 30 Dec 59
Bolivia	SIGNED: 30 Dec 59	RATIFIED: 30 Dec 59	FORCE: 30 Dec 59
Brazil	SIGNED: 30 Dec 59	RATIFIED: 30 Dec 59	FORCE: 30 Dec 59
Chile	SIGNED: 17 Dec 59	RATIFIED: 17 Dec 59	FORCE: 30 Dec 59
Colombia	SIGNED: 21 Dec 59	RATIFIED: 21 Dec 59	FORCE: 30 Dec 59
Costa Rica	SIGNED: 30 Dec 59	RATIFIED: 30 Dec 59	FORCE: 30 Dec 59
Dominican Republic	SIGNED: 16 Dec 59	RATIFIED: 16 Dec 59	FORCE: 30 Dec 59
Ecuador	SIGNED: 22 Dec 59	RATIFIED: 22 Dec 59	FORCE: 30 Dec 59
El Salvador	SIGNED: 29 Dec 59	RATIFIED: 30 Dec 59	FORCE: 30 Dec 59
Guatemala	SIGNED: 16 Dec 59	RATIFIED: 16 Dec 59	FORCE: 30 Dec 59
Haiti	SIGNED: 27 Oct 59	RATIFIED: 27 Oct 59	FORCE: 30 Dec 59
Honduras	SIGNED: 29 Dec 59	RATIFIED: 29 Dec 59	FORCE: 30 Dec 59
Mexico	SIGNED: 30 Dec 59	RATIFIED: 30 Dec 59	FORCE: 30 Dec 59
Nicaragua	SIGNED: 29 Dec 59	RATIFIED: 29 Dec 59	FORCE: 30 Dec 59
Panama	SIGNED: 29 Dec 59	RATIFIED: 28 Dec 59	FORCE: 30 Dec 59
Paraguay	SIGNED: 16 Dec 59	RATIFIED: 16 Dec 59	FORCE: 30 Dec 59
Peru	SIGNED: 30 Dec 59	RATIFIED: 30 Dec 59	FORCE: 30 Dec 59
USA (United States)	SIGNED: 14 Oct 59	RATIFIED: 14 Oct 59	FORCE: 30 Dec 59
Uruguay	SIGNED: 12 Feb 60	RATIFIED: 12 Feb 60	FORCE: 12 Feb 60
Venezuela	SIGNED: 18 Nov 59	RATIFIED: 13 Feb 60	FORCE: 13 Feb 60

105594 Bilateral Agreement **389 UNTS 221**
SIGNED: 30 Sep 60　　　FORCE: 30 Sep 60
REGISTERED: 1 Mar 61 USA (United States)
ARTICLES: 5 LANGUAGE: English.
HEADNOTE: AGRI COMMOD TITLE I
TOPIC: US Agri Commod Aid
CONCEPTS: General provisions. Annex or appendix reference. Exchange of information and documents. Reexport of goods, etc.. Exchange rates and regulations. Transportation costs. Local currency. Commodities schedule. Purchase authorization. Surplus commodities. Mutual consultation.
PARTIES:
Ceylon (Sri Lanka)
USA (United States)

105595 Bilateral Exchange **389 UNTS 237**
SIGNED: 19 Jul 60　　　FORCE: 19 Jul 60
REGISTERED: 1 Mar 61 USA (United States)
ARTICLES: 2 LANGUAGE: English. Italian.
HEADNOTE: CHILD FEEDING PROGRAM
TOPIC: Direct Aid
CONCEPTS: Jurisdiction. Financial programs.

Commodities and services. Domestic obligation. Assistance. General aid.
TREATY REF: 258UNTS15; 316UNTS177; 355UNTS393.
PROCEDURE: Renewal or Revival.
PARTIES:
Italy
USA (United States)

105596 Bilateral Agreement **389 UNTS 245**
SIGNED: 6 Sep 60　　　FORCE: 12 Sep 60
REGISTERED: 1 Mar 61 USA (United States)
ARTICLES: 2 LANGUAGE: English.
HEADNOTE: GUARANTEE PRIVATE INVESTMENTS
TOPIC: Admin Cooperation
CONCEPTS: Arbitration. Currency. Claims and settlements. Guarantees and safeguards.
PARTIES:
Liberia
USA (United States)
　　　　　　　ANNEX
533 UNTS 348. Liberia. Supplementation 29 Sep 64. Force 29 Sep 64.
533 UNTS 348. USA (United States). Supplementation 26 Sep 64. Force 29 Sep 64.

105597 Bilateral Agreement **389 UNTS 253**
SIGNED: 10 Jan 61　　　FORCE: 10 Jan 61
REGISTERED: 1 Mar 61 United Nations
ARTICLES: 10 LANGUAGE: English. Spanish.
HEADNOTE: ASSISTANCE
TOPIC: Direct Aid
CONCEPTS: Detailed regulations. Treaty implementation. Visas. Privileges and immunities. Exchange of information and documents. Informational records. Inspection and observation. Operating agencies. Personnel. Public information. Responsibility and liability. Title and deeds. Use of facilities. Arbitration. Procedure. Negotiation. Import quotas. Attachment of funds. Exchange rates and regulations. Expense sharing formulae. Financial programs. Domestic obligation. General technical assistance. Economic assistance. Materials. equipment and services. IGO status.
INTL ORGS: International Court of Justice.
TREATY REF: 1UNTS15; 33UNTS261; 374UNTS147.
PROCEDURE: Amendment. Termination.
PARTIES:
Costa Rica
UN Special Fund

105598 Multilateral Convention **389 UNTS 277**
SIGNED: 13 May 58　　　FORCE: 19 Feb 61
REGISTERED: 5 Mar 61 ILO (Labor Org)
ARTICLES: 14 LANGUAGE: English. French.
HEADNOTE: SEAFARERS NATIONAL IDENTITY DOCUMENTS
TOPIC: ILO Labor
CONCEPTS: Detailed regulations. Non-visa travel documents. Domestic legislation. Recognition and enforcement of legal decisions. Recognition of legal documents. ILO conventions. Labor statistics. Domestic obligation. Merchant vessels.
INTL ORGS: International Labour Organization.
PROCEDURE: Amendment. Denunciation. Duration. Ratification. Registration. Renewal or Revival.
PARTIES:
Multilateral
　　　　　　　ANNEX
401 UNTS 363. Ireland. Ratification 17 Jun 61. Force 17 Jun 62.
410 UNTS 366. Mexico. Ratification 11 Sep 61. Force 11 Sep 62.
449 UNTS 380. Tanganyika. Ratification 26 Nov 62. Force 26 Nov 63.
475 UNTS 383. Italy. Ratification 12 Aug 63. Force 12 Aug 64.
480 UNTS 481. Greece. Ratification 9 Oct 63. Force 9 Oct 63.
483 UNTS 419. Brazil. Ratification 5 Nov 63. Force 5 Nov 64.
492 UNTS 380. UK Great Britain. Ratification 18 Feb 64. Force 18 Feb 65.
504 UNTS 367. Tanzania. Succession 22 Jun 64.
510 UNTS 367. UK Great Britain. Bermuda.
510 UNTS 367. UK Great Britain. Antigua.
510 UNTS 367. UK Great Britain. Barbados.

510 UNTS 367. UK Great Britain. Dominican Republic.

510 UNTS 367. UK Great Britain. Aden. Declaration 3 Aug 64.

510 UNTS 367. UK Great Britain. Brit Solomon Is.

510 UNTS 367. UK Great Britain. Brit Virgin Islands.

510 UNTS 367. UK Great Britain. Falkland Islands.

510 UNTS 367. UK Great Britain. Fiji Islands.

510 UNTS 367. UK Great Britain. Gibralter.

510 UNTS 367. UK Great Britain. Gilbert Islands.

510 UNTS 367. UK Great Britain. St. Helena.

510 UNTS 367. UK Great Britain. Seychelles.

510 UNTS 367. UK Great Britain. British Guiana.

510 UNTS 367. UK Great Britain. British Honduras.

510 UNTS 367. UK Great Britain. Gambia.

510 UNTS 367. UK Great Britain. Grenada.

510 UNTS 367. UK Great Britain. Malta.

510 UNTS 367. UK Great Britain. Hong Kong.

510 UNTS 367. UK Great Britain. Montserrat.

510 UNTS 367. UK Great Britain. St. Christopher.

510 UNTS 367. UK Great Britain. Nevis.

510 UNTS 367. UK Great Britain. Anguilla.

510 UNTS 367. UK Great Britain. St. Lucia.

510 UNTS 367. UK Great Britain. St. Vincent.

510 UNTS 367. UK Great Britain. Mauritania.

511 UNTS 322. UK Great Britain. Swaziland.

511 UNTS 322. UK Great Britain. Basutoland.

511 UNTS 322. UK Great Britain. Bechuanaland.

511 UNTS 322. UK Great Britain. Southern Rhodesia.

524 UNTS 369. Malta. Ratification 4 Jan 65. Force 4 Jan 65.

533 UNTS 399. UK Great Britain. Brunei.

567 UNTS 356. Guyana. Ratification 8 Jun 66. Force 8 Jun 66.

600 UNTS 408. France. Ratification 8 Jun 67. Force 8 Jun 67.

607 UNTS 366. Portugal. Ratification 3 Aug 67. Force 3 Aug 68.

105599 Bilateral Agreement **390 UNTS 3**
SIGNED: 23 Mar 60 FORCE: 1 Aug 60
REGISTERED: 6 Mar 61 Austria
ARTICLES: 7 LANGUAGE: German. Spanish.
HEADNOTE: TRADE
TOPIC: General Trade
CONCEPTS: Exceptions and exemptions. Conformity with municipal law. Licenses and permits. Establishment of commission. Currency. Exchange rates and regulations. Commodity trade. Most favored nation clause. Customs exemptions.
PROCEDURE: Denunciation. Ratification.
PARTIES:
Austria
El Salvador

105600 Bilateral Agreement **390 UNTS 17**
SIGNED: 17 Jun 60 FORCE: 17 Jun 60
REGISTERED: 7 Mar 61 Austria
ARTICLES: 10 LANGUAGE: German. Spanish.
HEADNOTE: TRADE
TOPIC: General Trade
CONCEPTS: Definition of terms. Territorial application. Annex or appendix reference. Previous treaty replacement. Informational records. Establishment of commission. Trade procedures. Monetary and gold transfers. Payment schedules. Quotas.
INTL ORGS: Organization for Economic Co-operation and Development. Special Commission.
PROCEDURE: Denunciation. Duration. Renewal or Revival.
PARTIES:
Austria
Spain

105601 Bilateral Agreement **390 UNTS 35**
SIGNED: 10 Mar 61 FORCE: 10 Mar 61
REGISTERED: 10 Mar 61 United Nations
ARTICLES: 10 LANGUAGE: English. Spanish.
HEADNOTE: ASSISTANCE
TOPIC: Direct Aid
CONCEPTS: Detailed regulations. Treaty implementation. Visas. Privileges and immunities. Exchange of information and documents. Informational records. Inspection and observation. Operating agencies. Personnel. Public information.

Responsibility and liability. Title and deeds. Use of facilities. Arbitration. Procedure. Negotiation. Import quotas. Attachment of funds. Exchange rates and regulations. Expense sharing formulae. Financial programs. Domestic obligation. General technical assistance. Economic assistance. Materials, equipment and services. IGO status.
INTL ORGS: International Court of Justice.
TREATY REF: 1UNTS15; 33UNTS261; 374UNTS147.
PROCEDURE: Amendment. Termination.
PARTIES:
Cuba
UN Special Fund

105602 Bilateral Exchange **390 UNTS 61**
SIGNED: 21 Feb 61 FORCE: 1 Mar 61
REGISTERED: 13 Mar 61 Australia
ARTICLES: 2 LANGUAGE: English.
HEADNOTE: VISAS VISA FEES
TOPIC: Visas
CONCEPTS: Time limit. Visa abolition. Denial of admission. Resident permits. Visas. Conformity with municipal law. Fees and exemptions.
PROCEDURE: Termination.
PARTIES:
Australia
Finland

105603 Bilateral Agreement **390 UNTS 69**
SIGNED: 23 Jan 61 FORCE: 2 Feb 61
REGISTERED: 13 Mar 61 United Nations
ARTICLES: 10 LANGUAGE: English. French.
HEADNOTE: ASSISTANCE
TOPIC: Direct Aid
CONCEPTS: Detailed regulations. Treaty implementation. Visas. Privileges and immunities. Exchange of information and documents. Informational records. Inspection and observation. Operating agencies. Personnel. Public information. Responsibility and liability. Title and deeds. Use of facilities. Arbitration. Procedure. Negotiation. Import quotas. Attachment of funds. Exchange rates and regulations. Expense sharing formulae. Financial programs. Domestic obligation. General technical assistance. Economic assistance. Materials, equipment and services. IGO status.
INTL ORGS: International Court of Justice.
TREATY REF: 1UNTS15; 33UNTS261; 374UNTS147.
PROCEDURE: Amendment. Termination.
PARTIES:
Chad
UN Special Fund

105604 Bilateral Agreement **390 UNTS 85**
SIGNED: 10 Feb 61 FORCE: 10 Feb 61
REGISTERED: 13 Mar 61 United Nations
ARTICLES: 10 LANGUAGE: English.
HEADNOTE: ASSISTANCE
TOPIC: Direct Aid
CONCEPTS: Detailed regulations. Treaty implementation. Visas. Privileges and immunities. Exchange of information and documents. Informational records. Inspection and observation. Operating agencies. Personnel. Public information. Responsibility and liability. Title and deeds. Use of facilities. Arbitration. Procedure. Negotiation. Import quotas. Attachment of funds. Exchange rates and regulations. Expense sharing formulae. Financial programs. Domestic obligation. General technical assistance. Economic assistance. Materials, equipment and services. IGO status.
INTL ORGS: International Court of Justice.
TREATY REF: 1UNTS15; 33UNTS261; 374UNTS147.
PROCEDURE: Amendment. Termination.
PARTIES:
Nigeria
UN Special Fund

105605 Bilateral Agreement **390 UNTS 101**
SIGNED: 29 Jul 60 FORCE: 17 Nov 60
REGISTERED: 14 Mar 61 IBRD (World Bank)
ARTICLES: 5 LANGUAGE: English.
HEADNOTE: GUARANTEE HYDROELECTRIC PROJECT
TOPIC: IBRD Project
CONCEPTS: Definition of terms. Annex or appendix reference. Exchange of information and doc-

uments. Inspection and observation. Bonds. Fees and exemptions. Tax exemptions. Domestic obligation. Terms of loan. Loan regulations. Loan guarantee. Guarantor non-interference. Hydroelectric power.
PARTIES:
El Salvador
IBRD (World Bank)

105606 Bilateral Agreement **390 UNTS 131**
SIGNED: 2 Dec 60 FORCE: 10 Jan 61
REGISTERED: 14 Mar 61 IBRD (World Bank)
ARTICLES: 7 LANGUAGE: English.
HEADNOTE: LOAN AGREEMENT
TOPIC: IBRD Project
CONCEPTS: Default remedies. Definition of terms. Annex or appendix reference. Exchange of information and documents. Informational records. Inspection and observation. Accounting procedures. Bonds. Fees and exemptions. Interest rates. Tax exemptions. Domestic obligation. Terms of loan. Loan regulations. Loan guarantee. Guarantor non-interference.
PARTIES:
Norway
IBRD (World Bank)

105607 Bilateral Agreement **390 UNTS 153**
SIGNED: 19 Aug 60 FORCE: 16 Dec 60
REGISTERED: 14 Mar 61 IBRD (World Bank)
ARTICLES: 7 LANGUAGE: English.
HEADNOTE: LOAN ROAD
TOPIC: IBRD Project
CONCEPTS: Default remedies. Definition of terms. Annex or appendix reference. Exchange of information and documents. Informational records. Inspection and observation. Accounting procedures. Bonds. Fees and exemptions. Interest rates. Tax exemptions. Domestic obligation. Loan regulations. Loan guarantee. Guarantor non-interference. Roads and highways.
PARTIES:
Panama
IBRD (World Bank)

105608 Bilateral Agreement **390 UNTS 173**
SIGNED: 20 Sep 60 FORCE: 19 Jan 61
REGISTERED: 14 Mar 61 IBRD (World Bank)
ARTICLES: 5 LANGUAGE: English.
HEADNOTE: GUARANTEE RAILROAD EQUIPMENT
TOPIC: IBRD Project
CONCEPTS: Definition of terms. Annex or appendix reference. Exchange of information and documents. Inspection and observation. Bonds. Fees and exemptions. Tax exemptions. Domestic obligation. Terms of loan. Loan regulations. Loan guarantee. Guarantor non-interference. Railways.
PARTIES:
Colombia
IBRD (World Bank)

105609 Bilateral Agreement **390 UNTS 201**
SIGNED: 4 May 60 FORCE: 12 Sep 60
REGISTERED: 14 Mar 61 IBRD (World Bank)
ARTICLES: 5 LANGUAGE: English.
HEADNOTE: LOAN VOCATIONAL EDUCATION
TOPIC: IBRD Project
CONCEPTS: Default remedies. Definition of terms. Annex or appendix reference. Exchange of information and documents. Informational records. Inspection and observation. Education. Accounting procedures. Bonds. Fees and exemptions. Interest rates. Tax exemptions. Domestic obligation. Terms of loan. Loan regulations. Loan guarantee. Guarantor non-interference.
PARTIES:
Costa Rica
IBRD (World Bank)

105610 Multilateral Agreement **390 UNTS 227**
SIGNED: 18 Nov 59 FORCE: 16 Nov 60
REGISTERED: 14 Mar 61 FAO (Food Agri)
ARTICLES: 25 LANGUAGE: English. French. Spanish.
HEADNOTE: ESTABLISH LA FOREST RESEARCH INSTITUTE
TOPIC: IGO Establishment
CONCEPTS: Annex or appendix reference. Diplo-

matic missions. Juridical personality. Personnel. Procedure. Accounting procedures. Funding procedures. Subsidiary organ. Internal structure. Inter-agency agreements.
INTL ORGS: Latin America Forestry Institute. Food and Agricultural Organization of the United Nations. United Nations.
PROCEDURE: Amendment. Denunciation. Termination.
PARTIES:
Ecuador RATIFIED: 23 Jan 61 FORCE: 23 Jan 61
France RATIFIED: 26 Oct 60 FORCE: 16 Sep 60
Guatemala RATIFIED: 5 Oct 60 FORCE: 16 Sep 60
Netherlands RATIFIED: 16 Nov 60 FORCE: 16 Sep 60
Nicaragua RATIFIED: 8 Nov 60 FORCE: 16 Sep 60
Panama RATIFIED: 16 Nov 60 FORCE: 16 Sep 60
Peru RATIFIED: 6 Dec 60 FORCE: 6 Dec 60
Venezuela RATIFIED: 11 Oct 60 FORCE: 16 Sep 60
ANNEX
394 UNTS 331. UK Great Britain. British Honduras.
394 UNTS 331. Haiti. Acceptance 13 Mar 61.
394 UNTS 331. UK Great Britain. Acceptance 17 Mar 61.
394 UNTS 331. UK Great Britain. British Guiana.
394 UNTS 331. UK Great Britain. West Indies.
402 UNTS 370. Cuba. Acceptance 17 Jul 61.
437 UNTS 368. Honduras. Acceptance 14 Aug 62.
438 UNTS 348. Nicaragua. Denunciation 30 Apr 62. Force 30 Oct 62.
447 UNTS 360. Guatemala. Denunciation 20 Nov 62. Force 20 May 63.
453 UNTS 436. Costa Rica. Acceptance 30 Jan 63.
484 UNTS 410. Brazil. Acceptance 17 Dec 63.
533 UNTS 352. Panama. Ratification 11 Feb 65.
533 UNTS 352. Dominican Republic. Acceptance 5 Apr 65.
547 UNTS 330. Brazil. Denunciation 20 Jul 65. Force 20 Jan 66.
547 UNTS 330. Chile. Acceptance 7 Oct 65.

105611 Bilateral Convention **390 UNTS 275**
SIGNED: 27 Feb 59 FORCE: 20 Jan 61
REGISTERED: 17 Mar 61 Belgium
ARTICLES: 39 LANGUAGE: French.
HEADNOTE: EXTRADITION JUDICIAL ASSISTANCE CRIMINAL MATTERS
TOPIC: Extradition
CONCEPTS: Territorial application. Time limit. Privileges and immunities. Extradition, deportation and repatriation. Extradition requests. Extraditable offenses. Location of crime. Special factors. Refusal of extradition. Concurrent requests. Provisional detainment. Extradition postponement. Witnesses and experts. Material evidence. Exchange of information and documents. Legal protection and assistance. Recognition of legal documents. Penal sanctions. Procedure. Conveyance in transit.
PROCEDURE: Ratification. Termination.
PARTIES:
Belgium
Morocco

105612 Bilateral Convention **390 UNTS 307**
SIGNED: 13 Apr 60 FORCE: 1 Jul 60
REGISTERED: 17 Mar 61 South Africa
ARTICLES: 20 LANGUAGE: English.
HEADNOTE: PARCEL POST
TOPIC: Postal Service
CONCEPTS: Responsibility and liability. Accounting procedures. Customs declarations. Postal services. Regulations. Parcel post. Rates and charges.
PROCEDURE: Duration. Termination.
PARTIES:
Ireland
South Africa

105613 Bilateral Convention **391 UNTS 3**
SIGNED: 16 Jun 56 FORCE: 28 Jan 57
REGISTERED: 17 Mar 61 Yugoslavia
ARTICLES: 9 LANGUAGE: Serbo-Croat. Bulgarian.
HEADNOTE: UPKEEP MAINTENANCE RENEWAL

BORDER LINE BORDER MARKINGS AND BORDER SIGNS
TOPIC: Territory Boundary
CONCEPTS: Previous treaty replacement. Establishment of commission. Indemnities and reimbursements. Markers and definitions.
INTL ORGS: Special Commission.
TREATY REF: 41UNTS21; 194LTS89; 3'12DEMARTENS326;.
PROCEDURE: Denunciation. Duration. Renewal or Revival.
PARTIES:
Bulgaria
Yugoslavia

105614 Bilateral Agreement **391 UNTS 23**
SIGNED: 2 Feb 61 FORCE: 2 Feb 61
REGISTERED: 17 Mar 61 United Nations
ARTICLES: 6 LANGUAGE: English.
HEADNOTE: HUMAN RIGHTS SEMINAR
TOPIC: Humanitarian
CONCEPTS: Exchange.
TREATY REF: 1UNTS15; 1UNTS263; 4UNTS461.
PARTIES:
New Zealand
United Nations

105615 Bilateral Convention **391 UNTS 33**
SIGNED: 22 May 57 FORCE: 28 Dec 57
REGISTERED: 17 Mar 61 Yugoslavia
ARTICLES: 11 LANGUAGE: Romanian. Czechoslovakian.
HEADNOTE: SOCIAL POLICY COOPERATION
TOPIC: Non-ILO Labor
CONCEPTS: General cooperation. Exchange of information and documents. Recognition of legal documents. Establishment of commission. General health, education, culture, welfare and labor. Specialists exchange. Public health. Exchange. Anti-discrimination. Social security. Scientific exchange. Publications exchange.
INTL ORGS: Special Commission.
PROCEDURE: Duration. Ratification. Termination.
PARTIES:
Czechoslovakia
Yugoslavia

105616 Bilateral Protocol **391 UNTS 47**
SIGNED: 4 Apr 56 FORCE: 4 Apr 56
REGISTERED: 17 Mar 61 Yugoslavia
ARTICLES: 7 LANGUAGE: Serbo-Croat. Bulgarian.
HEADNOTE: AIRCRAFT CROSSING FRONTIER
TOPIC: Air Transport
CONCEPTS: Exchange of information and documents. Procedure. Routes and logistics. Air transport. Operating authorizations and regulations.
PROCEDURE: Amendment. Denunciation. Termination.
PARTIES:
Bulgaria
Yugoslavia

105617 Bilateral Convention **391 UNTS 57**
SIGNED: 22 May 57 FORCE: 1 Dec 57
REGISTERED: 17 Mar 61 Yugoslavia
ARTICLES: 36 LANGUAGE: Czechoslovakian. Serbo-Croat.
HEADNOTE: SOCIAL INSURANCE
TOPIC: Non-ILO Labor
CONCEPTS: Definition of terms. Detailed regulations. Conformity with municipal law. Domestic legislation. Dispute settlement. Old age and invalidity insurance. Wages and salaries. Non-ILO labor relations. Family allowances. Administrative cooperation. Old age insurance. Sickness and invalidity insurance. Social security. Payment schedules. Claims and settlements.
PROCEDURE: Ratification. Termination.
PARTIES:
Czechoslovakia
Yugoslavia

105618 Bilateral Agreement **391 UNTS 101**
SIGNED: 5 May 59 FORCE: 29 Sep 59
REGISTERED: 17 Mar 61 Yugoslavia
ARTICLES: 9 LANGUAGE: English.
HEADNOTE: SCIENTIFIC TECHNICAL CO-OPERATION

TOPIC: Scientific Project
CONCEPTS: Conformity with municipal law. General cooperation. Specialists exchange. Research results. Scientific exchange. Payment schedules. Patents, copyrights and trademarks. General technical assistance. Economic assistance.
PROCEDURE: Duration. Future Procedures Contemplated. Renewal or Revival. Termination.
PARTIES:
Ceylon (Sri Lanka)
Yugoslavia

105619 Bilateral Agreement **391 UNTS 109**
SIGNED: 22 Apr 57 FORCE: 2 Jun 57
REGISTERED: 17 Mar 61 Yugoslavia
ARTICLES: 10 LANGUAGE: French.
HEADNOTE: DIRECT MAIL-VAN SERVICE TRAINS
TOPIC: Postal Service
CONCEPTS: Railways. Postal services. Conveyance in transit.
PROCEDURE: Denunciation. Duration.
PARTIES:
Greece
Yugoslavia

105620 Bilateral Exchange **391 UNTS 117**
SIGNED: 11 Sep 56 FORCE: 11 Sep 56
REGISTERED: 17 Mar 61 Yugoslavia
ARTICLES: 2 LANGUAGE: French.
HEADNOTE: COOPERATION TOURISM
TOPIC: Admin Cooperation
CONCEPTS: Tourism. General cooperation.
PARTIES:
Greece
Yugoslavia

105621 Bilateral Protocol **391 UNTS 127**
SIGNED: 29 Aug 57 FORCE: 25 Feb 58
REGISTERED: 17 Mar 61 Yugoslavia
ARTICLES: 11 LANGUAGE: Serbo-Croat. Albanian.
HEADNOTE: EXCHANGE POSTAL MATTER
TOPIC: Postal Service
CONCEPTS: Frontier permits. Conformity with municipal law. Administrative cooperation. Railway border crossing. Postal services. Regulations.
TREATY REF: 170UNTS3; 169UNTS3.
PROCEDURE: Duration. Termination.
PARTIES:
Albania
Yugoslavia

105622 Bilateral Agreement **391 UNTS 167**
SIGNED: 29 Aug 57 FORCE: 1 Apr 58
REGISTERED: 17 Mar 61 Yugoslavia
ARTICLES: 22 LANGUAGE: Serbo-Croat. Albanian.
HEADNOTE: POSTAL TELECOMMUNICATION SERVICE
TOPIC: Postal Service
CONCEPTS: General provisions. Treaty implementation. Tariffs. Accounting procedures. Customs exemptions. Postal services. Insured letters and boxes. Rates and charges. Services.
TREATY REF: 170UNTS3.
PROCEDURE: Denunciation.
PARTIES:
Albania
Yugoslavia

105623 Bilateral Agreement **391 UNTS 191**
SIGNED: 4 Aug 59 FORCE: 7 Oct 59
REGISTERED: 21 Mar 61 Canada
ARTICLES: 7 LANGUAGE: English.
HEADNOTE: COOPERATION PEACEFUL USES ATOMIC ENERGY
TOPIC: Atomic Energy
CONCEPTS: Definition of terms. General cooperation. Exchange of information and documents. Informational records. Inspection and observation. Nuclear materials. Non-nuclear materials. Peaceful use. Security of information.
INTL ORGS: International Atomic Energy Agency.
TREATY REF: 276INTS3.
PROCEDURE: Duration. Ratification. Termination.
PARTIES:
Australia
Canada

105624 Bilateral Exchange **391 UNTS 207**
SIGNED: 7 Jan 59 FORCE: 7 Jan 59
REGISTERED: 21 Mar 61 Canada
ARTICLES: 2 LANGUAGE: English.
HEADNOTE: OPERATION TELEVISION STATION
TOPIC: Specific Property
CONCEPTS: Previous treaties adherence. Bands and frequency allocation. Facilities and equipment. Telecommunications.
TREATY REF: 207UNTS25.
PARTIES:
Canada
USA (United States)

105625 Bilateral Exchange **391 UNTS 213**
SIGNED: 23 Jun 58 FORCE: 8 Sep 58
REGISTERED: 21 Mar 61 Canada
ARTICLES: 2 LANGUAGE: French.
HEADNOTE: ABROGATION 1872 AGREEMENT SUCCESSION DUTIES
TOPIC: Admin Cooperation
CONCEPTS: Annex type material.
TREATY REF: 2'2DEMARTENS82;.
PARTIES:
Canada
Switzerland

105626 Bilateral Exchange **391 UNTS 219**
SIGNED: 31 Oct 58 FORCE: 31 Oct 58
REGISTERED: 21 Mar 61 Canada
ARTICLES: 2 LANGUAGE: English.
HEADNOTE: CLAIMS SETTLEMENT
TOPIC: Non-ILO Labor
CONCEPTS: Treaty implementation. Treaty interpretation. Nationality and citizenship. Exchange of information and documents. Informational records. Responsibility and liability. Procedure. Banking. Bonds. Currency. Fees and exemptions. Payment schedules. Claims and settlements. Lump sum settlements.
TREATY REF: 43UNTS97; 253UNTS310; CTS 1947 NO.42.
PROCEDURE: Ratification.
PARTIES:
Canada
USA (United States)

105627 Bilateral Agreement **391 UNTS 225**
SIGNED: 5 Nov 58 FORCE: 5 Nov 58
REGISTERED: 21 Mar 61 Canada
ARTICLES: 1 LANGUAGE: English.
HEADNOTE: FINANCE
TOPIC: Loans and Credits
CONCEPTS: Currency. Financial programs. Interest rates. Payment schedules. General aid. Agricultural commodities. Loan and credit. Loan repayment. Terms of loan.
INTL ORGS: Colombo Plan.
PARTIES:
Canada
Ceylon (Sri Lanka)

105628 Bilateral Agreement **391 UNTS 231**
SIGNED: 20 Feb 58 FORCE: 20 Feb 58
REGISTERED: 21 Mar 61 Canada
ARTICLES: 1 LANGUAGE: English.
HEADNOTE: FINANCE
TOPIC: Loans and Credits
CONCEPTS: Currency. Financial programs. Interest rates. Payment schedules. General aid. Agricultural commodities. Loan and credit. Loan repayment. Terms of loan.
INTL ORGS: Colombo Plan.
PARTIES:
Canada
India

105629 Bilateral Exchange **391 UNTS 237**
SIGNED: 10 Sep 51 FORCE: 10 Sep 51
REGISTERED: 21 Mar 61 Canada
ARTICLES: 2 LANGUAGE: English.
HEADNOTE: STATEMENT PRINCIPLES COOPERATIVE ECONOMIC DEVELOPMENT
TOPIC: General Aid
CONCEPTS: Annex or appendix reference. Financial programs. Economic assistance.
INTL ORGS: Colombo Plan.

PARTIES:
Canada
India

105630 Bilateral Exchange **391 UNTS 245**
SIGNED: 11 Jul 52 FORCE: 11 Jul 52
REGISTERED: 21 Mar 61 Canada
ARTICLES: 2 LANGUAGE: English.
HEADNOTE: STATEMENT PRINCIPLES COOPERATIVE ECONOMIC DEVELOPMENT
TOPIC: General Aid
CONCEPTS: Annex or appendix reference. Financial programs. Economic assistance.
INTL ORGS: Colombo Plan.
PARTIES:
Canada
Ceylon (Sri Lanka)

105631 Bilateral Agreement **391 UNTS 253**
SIGNED: 28 May 54 FORCE: 1 Jul 54
REGISTERED: 21 Mar 61 Canada
ARTICLES: 9 LANGUAGE: English. Portuguese.
HEADNOTE: TRADE
TOPIC: General Trade
CONCEPTS: Definition of terms. Detailed regulations. Exceptions and exemptions. Territorial application. Annex or appendix reference. Previous treaty replacement. Conformity with municipal law. General cooperation. Balance of payments. Currency. Exchange rates and regulations. Commodity trade. Most favored nation clause. General. Recognition. Customs duties. Transport of goods.
TREATY REF: 10&12SEPT1928.
PROCEDURE: Duration. Ratification. Renewal or Revival. Termination.
PARTIES:
Canada
Portugal

105632 Bilateral Agreement **391 UNTS 273**
SIGNED: 26 May 54 FORCE: 1 Jul 54
REGISTERED: 21 Mar 61 Canada
ARTICLES: 10 LANGUAGE: English. Spanish.
HEADNOTE: TRADE
TOPIC: General Trade
CONCEPTS: Definition of terms. Previous treaty amendment. Annex or appendix reference. Annex type material. Conformity with municipal law. General cooperation. Trade procedures. Balance of payments. Commodity trade. Most favored nation clause. General. Recognition. Customs duties. Transport of goods.
TREATY REF: 28LTS339.
PROCEDURE: Duration. Ratification. Termination.
PARTIES:
Canada
Spain

105633 Bilateral Exchange **392 UNTS 3**
SIGNED: 10 Dec 56 FORCE: 10 Dec 56
REGISTERED: 21 Mar 61 Canada
ARTICLES: 2 LANGUAGE: English. German.
HEADNOTE: PURCHASE F-86 AIRCRAFT TRAINING OF GERMAN AIRCREW
TOPIC: Milit Assistance
CONCEPTS: Annex or appendix reference. General cooperation. Indemnities and reimbursements. Payment for war supplies. Military training. Status of military forces.
INTL ORGS: North Atlantic Treaty Organization.
TREATY REF: 34UNTS243.
PROCEDURE: Future Procedures Contemplated.
PARTIES:
Canada
Germany, West

105634 Bilateral Exchange **392 UNTS 15**
SIGNED: 24 Jan 58 FORCE: 15 Feb 58
REGISTERED: 21 Mar 61 Canada
ARTICLES: 2 LANGUAGE: English.
HEADNOTE: NON-IMMIGRANT VISA
TOPIC: Visas
CONCEPTS: Time limit. Visas. Tourism. Conformity with municipal law. Fees and exemptions.
PARTIES:
Canada
Portugal

105635 Bilateral Agreement **392 UNTS 21**
SIGNED: 22 Oct 58 FORCE: 22 Oct 58
REGISTERED: 21 Mar 61 Canada
ARTICLES: 1 LANGUAGE: English.
HEADNOTE: FINANCES
TOPIC: Finance
CONCEPTS: Detailed regulations. Currency. Financial programs. Interest rates. Payment schedules. General aid. Loan and credit. Loan repayment. Terms of loan.
PARTIES:
Canada
India

105636 Bilateral Exchange **392 UNTS 27**
SIGNED: 6 Feb 58 FORCE: 7 Feb 58
REGISTERED: 21 Mar 61 Canada
ARTICLES: 2 LANGUAGE: English.
HEADNOTE: TRADE
TOPIC: General Trade
CONCEPTS: Establishment of trade relations.
PARTIES:
Canada
Fed Rhod/Nyasaland

105637 Bilateral Convention **392 UNTS 35**
SIGNED: 15 Jan 58 FORCE: 16 Apr 58
REGISTERED: 21 Mar 61 Canada
ARTICLES: 5 LANGUAGE: English.
HEADNOTE: PATENTS INVENTION
TOPIC: Patents/Copyrights
CONCEPTS: Conformity with municipal law. Domestic legislation. Laws and formalities.
PROCEDURE: Duration.
PARTIES:
Canada
Pakistan

105638 Bilateral Agreement **392 UNTS 41**
SIGNED: 1 Oct 57 FORCE: 21 May 58
REGISTERED: 21 Mar 61 Canada
ARTICLES: 16 LANGUAGE: English.
HEADNOTE: DOUBLE TAXATION FISCAL EVASION TAXES INCOME
TOPIC: Taxation
CONCEPTS: Definition of terms. Conformity with municipal law. Exchange of official publications. Domestic legislation. Teacher and student exchange. Taxation. Tax credits. General. Tax exemptions. Air transport. Merchant vessels.
PROCEDURE: Duration. Termination.
PARTIES:
Australia
Canada

105639 Bilateral Exchange **392 UNTS 61**
SIGNED: 18 Oct 58 FORCE: 18 Oct 58
REGISTERED: 21 Mar 61 Canada
ARTICLES: 2 LANGUAGE: English.
HEADNOTE: STATEMENT PRINCIPLES COOPERATIVE ECONOMIC DEVELOPMENT
TOPIC: General Aid
CONCEPTS: Annex or appendix reference. Financial programs. Economic development. Economic assistance.
INTL ORGS: Special Commission.
PARTIES:
Canada
UK Great Britain

105640 Multilateral Agreement **392 UNTS 69**
SIGNED: 29 Jul 60 FORCE: 29 Jul 60
REGISTERED: 21 Mar 61 USSR (Soviet Union)
ARTICLES: 5 LANGUAGE: Bulgarian. Romanian. Russian.
HEADNOTE: LOAD LINE SHIPS SAILING FLAGS PORTS BLACK SEA
TOPIC: Water Transport
CONCEPTS: Annex or appendix reference. Navigational conditions. Merchant vessels. Ports and pilotage.
TREATY REF: 135LTS301.
PROCEDURE: Accession. Registration. Termination.
PARTIES:
Bulgaria SIGNED: 29 Jul 60 FORCE: 29 Jul 60
Romania SIGNED: 29 Jul 60 FORCE: 29 Jul 60
USSR (Soviet Union) SIGNED: 29 Jul 60 FORCE: 29 Jul 60

105641 Bilateral Agreement **392 UNTS 131**
SIGNED: 29 Jun 60　　　FORCE: 1 Jul 60
REGISTERED: 21 Mar 61 USSR (Soviet Union)
ARTICLES: 17 LANGUAGE: Russian. English.
HEADNOTE: EXCHANGE POSTAL PARCELS
TOPIC: Postal Service
CONCEPTS: Responsibility and liability. Accounting procedures. Postal services. Insured letters and boxes. Parcel post. Rates and charges.
INTL ORGS: Universal Postal Union.
TREATY REF: 365UNTS3; 391UNTS3.
PROCEDURE: Duration. Termination.
PARTIES:
　Australia
　USSR (Soviet Union)

105642 Bilateral Agreement **392 UNTS 153**
SIGNED: 12 Feb 60　　　FORCE: 10 Sep 60
REGISTERED: 21 Mar 61 USSR (Soviet Union)
ARTICLES: 8 LANGUAGE: Russian. Hindi. English.
HEADNOTE: CULTURAL SCIENTIFIC TECHNOLOGICAL COOPERATION
TOPIC: Culture
CONCEPTS: General cooperation. Establishment of commission. Exchange. Teacher and student exchange. Exchange. General cultural cooperation. Artists. Athletes. Scientific exchange. Domestic obligation. Publications exchange.
INTL ORGS: Special Commission.
PROCEDURE: Duration. Ratification. Termination.
PARTIES:
　India
　USSR (Soviet Union)

105643 Bilateral Agreement **392 UNTS 173**
SIGNED: 28 Feb 60　　　FORCE: 1 Jul 60
REGISTERED: 21 Mar 61 USSR (Soviet Union)
ARTICLES: 10 LANGUAGE: Russian. Indonesian.
HEADNOTE: ECONOMIC TECHNICAL COOPERATION
TOPIC: General Aid
CONCEPTS: Treaty implementation. Exchange of information and documents. Vocational training. Research and development. Accounting procedures. Banking. Indemnities and reimbursements. Exchange rates and regulations. Interest rates. General technical assistance. Agriculture. Special projects. Economic assistance. Materials, equipment and services. Loan repayment. Terms of loan. Atomic energy assistance. Peaceful use. Industry.
PROCEDURE: Future Procedures Contemplated. Ratification.
PARTIES:
　Indonesia
　USSR (Soviet Union)

105644 Bilateral Agreement **392 UNTS 191**
SIGNED: 28 Feb 60　　　FORCE: 23 Jun 60
REGISTERED: 21 Mar 61 USSR (Soviet Union)
ARTICLES: 8 LANGUAGE: Russian. Indonesian.
HEADNOTE: CULTURAL COOPERATION
TOPIC: Culture
CONCEPTS: Treaty implementation. Friendship and amity. Conformity with municipal law. General cooperation. Recognition of degrees. Exchange. Teacher and student exchange. General cultural cooperation. Artists. Athletes. Scientific exchange. Research and development. Publications exchange. Mass media exchange.
PROCEDURE: Amendment. Ratification. Termination.
PARTIES:
　Indonesia
　USSR (Soviet Union)

105645 Bilateral Treaty **392 UNTS 205**
SIGNED: 24 May 60　　　FORCE: 1 Nov 60
REGISTERED: 21 Mar 61 USSR (Soviet Union)
ARTICLES: 18 LANGUAGE: German. Russian.
HEADNOTE: SOCIAL SECURITY
TOPIC: Non-ILO Labor
CONCEPTS: Definition of terms. General provisions. Exchange of information and documents. Conformity with municipal law. Public health. Wages and salaries. Non-ILO labor relations. Family allowances. Administrative cooperation. Sickness and invalidity insurance. Social security. Indemnities and reimbursements. Payment schedules.

PROCEDURE: Denunciation. Duration. Ratification. Renewal or Revival.
PARTIES:
　Germany, East
　USSR (Soviet Union)

105646 Bilateral Agreement **392 UNTS 243**
SIGNED: 9 Mar 60　　　FORCE: 9 Mar 60
REGISTERED: 27 Mar 61 ICAO (Civil Aviat)
ARTICLES: 11 LANGUAGE: French.
HEADNOTE: AIR TRANSPORT
TOPIC: Air Transport
CONCEPTS: Territorial application. Annex or appendix reference. Conformity with municipal law. Arbitration. Procedure. Existing tribunals. Negotiation. Reexport of goods, etc.. Non-interest rates and fees. Customs exemptions. Routes and logistics. Navigational conditions. Permit designation. Air transport. Conditions of airlines operating permission. Operating authorizations and regulations.
INTL ORGS: International Civil Aviation Organization. International Court of Justice.
PROCEDURE: Amendment. Denunciation. Ratification. Registration. Termination.
PARTIES:
　Guinea
　Netherlands

105647 Bilateral Agreement **392 UNTS 255**
SIGNED: 26 Feb 60　　　FORCE: 26 Feb 60
REGISTERED: 27 Mar 61 ICAO (Civil Aviat)
ARTICLES: 15 LANGUAGE: English. Thai.
HEADNOTE: RELATING AIR SERVICES
TOPIC: Air Transport
CONCEPTS: Definition of terms. Detailed regulations. Annex or appendix reference. Conformity with municipal law. General cooperation. Exchange of information and documents. Arbitration. Procedure. Special tribunals. Negotiation. Non-interest rates and fees. Customs exemptions. Routes and logistics. Permit designation. Air transport. Conditions of airlines operating permission. Overflights and technical stops. Operating authorizations and regulations.
INTL ORGS: International Civil Aviation Organization.
TREATY REF: 15UNTS295.
PROCEDURE: Amendment. Future Procedures Contemplated. Registration. Termination. Application to Non-self-governing Territories.
PARTIES:
　Australia
　Thailand

105648 Bilateral Agreement **392 UNTS 279**
SIGNED: 26 Feb 60　　　FORCE: 26 Feb 60
REGISTERED: 27 Mar 61 ICAO (Civil Aviat)
ARTICLES: 15 LANGUAGE: French. Thai.
HEADNOTE: AIR TRANSPORT
TOPIC: Air Transport
CONCEPTS: Definition of terms. Detailed regulations. Conformity with municipal law. General cooperation. Licenses and permits. Recognition of legal documents. Use of facilities. Arbitration. Procedure. Negotiation. Reexport of goods, etc.. Non-interest rates and fees. Most favored nation clause. Equitable taxes. Customs exemptions. Competency certificate. Routes and logistics. Navigational conditions. Permit designation. Air transport. Airport facilities. Airworthiness certificates. Conditions of airlines operating permission. Operating authorizations and regulations. Licenses and certificates of nationality. Postal services.
PROCEDURE: Amendment. Denunciation. Future Procedures Contemplated. Registration.
PARTIES:
　France
　Thailand

105649 Bilateral Agreement **392 UNTS 303**
SIGNED: 14 Oct 59　　　FORCE: 14 Oct 59
REGISTERED: 27 Mar 61 ICAO (Civil Aviat)
ARTICLES: 13 LANGUAGE: Spanish.
HEADNOTE: AIR SERVICES BETWEEN RESPECTIVE TERRITORIES
TOPIC: Air Transport
CONCEPTS: Definition of terms. Annex or appendix reference. Conformity with municipal law.

Use of facilities. Arbitration. Procedure. Existing tribunals. Negotiation. Fees and exemptions. National treatment. Customs exemptions. Routes and logistics. Navigational conditions. Air transport. Airport facilities. Conditions of airlines operating permission. Operating authorizations and regulations.
INTL ORGS: International Civil Aviation Organization.
TREATY REF: 15UNTS295.
PROCEDURE: Amendment. Denunciation. Future Procedures Contemplated. Ratification. Registration. Termination.
PARTIES:
　Nicaragua
　Peru

105650 Bilateral Agreement **393 UNTS 3**
SIGNED: 2 Jun 58　　　FORCE: 2 Jun 58
REGISTERED: 27 Mar 61 ICAO (Civil Aviat)
ARTICLES: 19 LANGUAGE: Hindi. Russian. English.
HEADNOTE: RELATING AIR SERVICES
TOPIC: Air Transport
CONCEPTS: Definition of terms. Detailed regulations. Exceptions and exemptions. Representation. Annex or appendix reference. Visas. Conformity with municipal law. General cooperation. Exchange of information and documents. Informational records. Licenses and permits. Personnel. Recognition of legal documents. Use of facilities. Procedure. Negotiation. Humanitarian matters. Reexport of goods, etc.. Monetary and gold transfers. Fees and exemptions. Non-interest rates and fees. Tax exemptions. Customs duties. Customs exemptions. Registration certificate. Routes and logistics. Navigational conditions. Permit designation. Airport facilities. Airworthiness certificates. Conditions of airlines operating permission. Operating authorizations and regulations.
PROCEDURE: Amendment. Termination.
PARTIES:
　India
　USSR (Soviet Union)
　　　　　　ANNEX
497 UNTS 368. India. Amendment 3 Nov 62. Force 1 Jan 62.
497 UNTS 368. USSR (Soviet Union). Amendment 3 Nov 62. Force 1 Jan 62.

105651 Bilateral Agreement **393 UNTS 55**
SIGNED: 28 Nov 58　　　FORCE: 28 Nov 58
REGISTERED: 27 Mar 61 ICAO (Civil Aviat)
ARTICLES: 11 LANGUAGE: English.
HEADNOTE: AIR SERVICES
TOPIC: Air Transport
CONCEPTS: Definition of terms. Annex or appendix reference. Conformity with municipal law. General cooperation. Arbitration. Procedure. Existing tribunals. Negotiation. Reexport of goods, etc.. Non-interest rates and fees. Customs exemptions. Routes and logistics. Permit designation. Air transport. Conditions of airlines operating permission. Overflights and technical stops. Operating authorizations and regulations.
INTL ORGS: International Civil Aviation Organization. International Court of Justice. Arbitration Commission.
TREATY REF: 15UNTS295.
PROCEDURE: Amendment. Ratification. Termination.
PARTIES:
　Liberia
　Netherlands

105652 Bilateral Agreement **393 UNTS 67**
SIGNED: 3 Jul 55　　　FORCE: 11 Mar 56
REGISTERED: 27 Mar 61 ICAO (Civil Aviat)
ARTICLES: 19 LANGUAGE: French. Arabic.
HEADNOTE: AIR TRANSPORT
TOPIC: Air Transport
CONCEPTS: Definition of terms. Detailed regulations. Exceptions and exemptions. Annex or appendix reference. Non-prejudice to third party. General cooperation. Exchange of information and documents. Domestic legislation. Arbitration. Procedure. Existing tribunals. Negotiation. Non-interest rates and fees. Customs exemptions. Routes and logistics. Permit designation. Air transport. Conditions of airlines operating

permission. Overflights and technical stops. Operating authorizations and regulations.
INTL ORGS: International Civil Aviation Organization. International Court of Justice. Arbitration Commission.
TREATY REF: 15UNTS295.
PROCEDURE: Amendment. Future Procedures Contemplated. Ratification. Registration. Termination.
PARTIES:
Syria
United Arab Rep

105653 Bilateral Agreement **393 UNTS 97**
SIGNED: 23 Jan 56   FORCE: 1 Jul 57
REGISTERED: 27 Mar 61 ICAO (Civil Aviat)
ARTICLES: 12 LANGUAGE: French.
HEADNOTE: AIR TRANSPORT
TOPIC: Air Transport
CONCEPTS: Definition of terms. Annex or appendix reference. Previous treaty replacement. Conformity with municipal law. General cooperation. Licenses and permits. Recognition of legal documents. Arbitration. Procedure. Negotiation. Reexport of goods, etc.. Indemnities and reimbursements. Fees and exemptions. Non-interest rates and fees. Most favored nation clause. National treatment. Customs duties. Customs exemptions. Competency certificate. Routes and logistics. Navigational conditions. Permit designation. Air transport. Airport facilities. Airworthiness certificates. Conditions of airlines operating permission. Operating authorizations and regulations. Licenses and certificates of nationality.
INTL ORGS: International Civil Aviation Organization. Arbitration Commission.
TREATY REF: 15UNTS295;   100LTS41; 104LTS550.
PROCEDURE: Amendment. Future Procedures Contemplated. Registration. Termination.
PARTIES:
Austria
Italy

105654 Bilateral Agreement **393 UNTS 113**
SIGNED: 29 Jan 57   FORCE: 28 Apr 58
REGISTERED: 27 Mar 61 ICAO (Civil Aviat)
ARTICLES: 20 LANGUAGE: Swedish. German.
HEADNOTE: RELATING AIR SERVICES
TOPIC: Air Transport
CONCEPTS: Definition of terms. Detailed regulations. Previous treaty replacement. Conformity with municipal law. General cooperation. Exchange of information and documents. Licenses and permits. Recognition of legal documents. Use of facilities. Arbitration. Procedure. Special tribunals. Currency. Monetary and gold transfers. Fees and exemptions. Non-interest rates and fees. National treatment. Tax exemptions. Customs exemptions. Competency certificate. Routes and logistics. Navigational conditions. Permit designation. Airport facilities. Airworthiness certificates. Conditions of airlines operating permission. Overflights and technical stops. Operating authorizations and regulations. Licenses and certificates of nationality.
INTL ORGS: International Civil Aviation Organization. Arbitration Commission.
PROCEDURE: Amendment. Future Procedures Contemplated. Ratification. Registration. Termination.
PARTIES:
Germany, West
Sweden

105655 Bilateral Agreement **393 UNTS 161**
SIGNED: 17 Feb 58   FORCE: 17 Feb 58
REGISTERED: 27 Mar 61 ICAO (Civil Aviat)
ARTICLES: 13 LANGUAGE: English.
HEADNOTE: AIR SERVICES BETWEEN BEYOND RESPECTIVE TERRITORIES
TOPIC: Air Transport
CONCEPTS: Definition of terms. Detailed regulations. Exceptions and exemptions. General cooperation. Exchange of information and documents. Arbitration. Procedure. Special tribunals. Negotiation. Non-interest rates and fees. Most favored nation clause. National treatment. Customs exemptions. Routes and logistics. Permit designation. Conditions of airlines operating

permission. Overflights and technical stops. Operating authorizations and regulations.
INTL ORGS: International Civil Aviation Organization. Arbitration Commission.
TREATY REF: 15UNTS295.
PROCEDURE: Amendment. Future Procedures Contemplated. Ratification. Registration. Termination.
PARTIES:
Sudan
Sweden

105656 Bilateral Agreement **393 UNTS 181**
SIGNED: 6 Mar 58   FORCE: 6 Mar 58
REGISTERED: 27 Mar 61 ICAO (Civil Aviat)
ARTICLES: 14 LANGUAGE: English.
HEADNOTE: RELATING AIR SERVICES
TOPIC: Air Transport
CONCEPTS: Definition of terms. Detailed regulations. Annex or appendix reference. Previous treaty replacement. Conformity with municipal law. General cooperation. Exchange of information and documents. Use of facilities. Arbitration. Procedure. Existing tribunals. Negotiation. Reexport of goods, etc.. Non-interest rates and fees. Most favored nation clause. National treatment. Customs exemptions. Routes and logistics. Permit designation. Air transport. Airport facilities. Conditions of airlines operating permission. Overflights and technical stops. Operating authorizations and regulations.
INTL ORGS: International Civil Aviation Organization. International Court of Justice. Arbitration Commission.
TREATY   REF: 15UNTS295;   84UNTS389; 36UNTS3.
PROCEDURE: Amendment. Future Procedures Contemplated. Termination. Application to Non-self-governing Territories.
PARTIES:
Pakistan
Sweden

105657 Bilateral Agreement **393 UNTS 203**
SIGNED: 3 Apr 58   FORCE: 3 Apr 58
REGISTERED: 27 Mar 61 ICAO (Civil Aviat)
ARTICLES: 21 LANGUAGE: French.
HEADNOTE: AIR TRANSPORT
TOPIC: Air Transport
CONCEPTS: Definition of terms. Detailed regulations. Annex or appendix reference. Conformity with municipal law. General cooperation. Licenses and permits. Recognition of legal documents. Use of facilities. Arbitration. Procedure. Special tribunals. Reexport of goods, etc.. Expense sharing formulae. Fees and exemptions. Non-interest rates and fees. National treatment. Customs exemptions. Competency certificate. Routes and logistics. Navigational conditions. Permit designation. Air transport. Airport facilities. Airworthiness certificates. Conditions of airlines operating permission. Overflights and technical stops. Operating authorizations and regulations. Licenses and certificates of nationality.
INTL ORGS: International Civil Aviation Organization. Arbitration Commission.
TREATY REF: 15UNTS295.
PROCEDURE: Amendment. Denunciation. Future Procedures Contemplated. Ratification. Registration.
PARTIES:
Morocco
Portugal

105658 Bilateral Agreement **393 UNTS 225**
SIGNED: 18 Apr 58   FORCE: 18 Apr 58
REGISTERED: 27 Mar 61 ICAO (Civil Aviat)
ARTICLES: 20 LANGUAGE: French.
HEADNOTE: AIR TRANSPORT
TOPIC: Air Transport
CONCEPTS: Definition of terms. Exceptions and exemptions. Annex or appendix reference. Previous treaty replacement. Conformity with municipal law. General cooperation. Exchange of information and documents. Informational records. Licenses and permits. Recognition of legal documents. Arbitration. Procedure. Special tribunals. Negotiation. Expense sharing formulae. Fees and exemptions. Non-interest rates and fees. Most favored nation clause. Customs exemptions. Registration certificate. Routes and logis-

tics. Navigational conditions. Permit designation. Air transport. Airport facilities. Airworthiness certificates. Conditions of airlines operating permission. Operating authorizations and regulations. Licenses and certificates of nationality.
INTL ORGS: International Civil Aviation Organization. International Court of Justice. Arbitration Commission.
PROCEDURE: Amendment. Denunciation. Ratification. Termination.
PARTIES:
Sweden
Yugoslavia
                ANNEX
646 UNTS 383. Yugoslavia. Force 6 Oct 62.
646 UNTS 383. Sweden. Force 6 Oct 62.

105659 Bilateral Exchange **393 UNTS 247**
SIGNED: 31 Aug 60   FORCE: 31 Aug 60
REGISTERED: 27 Mar 61 USA (United States)
ARTICLES: 3 LANGUAGE: English.
HEADNOTE: VESSEL LOAN
TOPIC: Milit Assistance
CONCEPTS: Time limit. Exchange of information and documents. Inspection and observation. Responsibility and liability. Title and deeds. Compensation. Indemnities and reimbursements. Delivery schedules. Self-defense. Lease of military property. Naval vessels. Return of equipment and recapture. Military training.
INTL ORGS: North Atlantic Treaty Organization.
TREATY REF: 34UNTS243.
PROCEDURE: Future Procedures Contemplated.
PARTIES:
Canada
USA (United States)

105660 Bilateral Exchange **393 UNTS 257**
SIGNED: 26 Sep 60   FORCE: 26 Sep 60
REGISTERED: 28 Mar 61 USA (United States)
ARTICLES: 2 LANGUAGE: English. Portuguese.
HEADNOTE: WEAPONS PRODUCTION PROGRAM
TOPIC: Milit Assistance
CONCEPTS: Change of circumstances. General cooperation. Licenses and permits. Use of facilities. Indemnities and reimbursements. National treatment. Customs exemptions. Materials, equipment and services. Exchange of defense information. Equipment and supplies. Restrictions on transfer.
INTL ORGS: North Atlantic Treaty Organization.
TREATY REF: 34UNTS243.
PROCEDURE: Future Procedures Contemplated.
PARTIES:
Portugal
USA (United States)

105661 Bilateral Exchange **393 UNTS 271**
SIGNED: 16 Jul 60   FORCE: 16 Jul 60
REGISTERED: 28 Mar 61 USA (United States)
ARTICLES: 2 LANGUAGE: English. Spanish.
HEADNOTE: VESSEL LOAN
TOPIC: Milit Assistance
CONCEPTS: Lease of military property. Naval vessels.
TREATY REF: 186UNTS53.
PARTIES:
Chile
USA (United States)
                ANNEX
401 UNTS 364.   Chile.   Supplementation 7 Dec 60. Force 7 Dec 60.
401 UNTS 364. USA (United States). Supplementation 2 Dec 60. Force 7 Dec 60.

105662 Bilateral Exchange **393 UNTS 281**
SIGNED: 6 Oct 60   FORCE: 5 Nov 60
REGISTERED: 28 Mar 61 USA (United States)
ARTICLES: 2 LANGUAGE: English. Spanish.
HEADNOTE: RADIO COMMUNICATIONS AMATEUR STATIONS BEHALF THIRD PARTIES
TOPIC: Gen Communications
CONCEPTS: Amateur radio. Amateur third party message. Radio-telephone-telegraphic communications.
PROCEDURE: Termination.
PARTIES:
Paraguay
USA (United States)

105663 Bilateral Exchange **393 UNTS 289**
SIGNED: 21 Jul 60 FORCE: 21 Jul 60
REGISTERED: 28 Mar 61 USA (United States)
ARTICLES: 2 LANGUAGE: English. Spanish.
HEADNOTE: INTERCHANGE PATENT RIGHTS TECHNICAL INFORMATION DEFENSE PURPOSES
TOPIC: Milit Assistance
CONCEPTS: Definition of terms. Detailed regulations. Exceptions and exemptions. Conformity with municipal law. Exchange of information and documents. Establishment of commission. Compensation. Indemnities and reimbursements. Payment schedules. Recognition. Defense and security. Security of information. Exchange of defense information.
TREATY REF: 207UNTS61.
PROCEDURE: Amendment. Termination.
PARTIES:
Spain
USA (United States)

105664 Multilateral Agreement **394 UNTS 3**
SIGNED: 21 Sep 60 FORCE: 12 Jan 61
REGISTERED: 30 Mar 61 USA (United States)
ARTICLES: 7 LANGUAGE: English. French.
HEADNOTE: SECRECY INVENTIONS PATENTS
TOPIC: Patents/Copyrights
CONCEPTS: Currency. Press and wire services. Security of information.
INTL ORGS: North Atlantic Treaty Organization.
TREATY REF: 34UNTS243.
PROCEDURE: Denunciation. Ratification. Registration.
PARTIES:
Belgium SIGNED: 21 Sep 60
Canada SIGNED: 21 Sep 60
Denmark SIGNED: 21 Sep 60
France SIGNED: 21 Sep 60
Germany, West SIGNED: 21 Sep 60
Greece SIGNED: 21 Sep 60
Italy SIGNED: 21 Sep 60
Luxembourg SIGNED: 21 Sep 60
Netherlands All Territories SIGNED: 21 Sep 60
Norway SIGNED: 21 Sep 60 RATIFIED: 13 Dec 60 FORCE: 12 Jan 61
Portugal SIGNED: 21 Sep 60
Turkey SIGNED: 21 Sep 60
UK Great Britain SIGNED: 21 Sep 60
USA (United States) SIGNED: 21 Sep 60 RATIFIED: 8 Dec 60 FORCE: 12 Jan 61
ANNEX
421 UNTS 348. UK Great Britain. Ratification 13 Oct 61. Force 12 Nov 61.
421 UNTS 348. Belgium. Ratification 20 Oct 61. Force 19 Nov 61.
451 UNTS 340. Denmark. Ratification 15 Nov 61. Force 15 Dec 61.
460 UNTS 324. Turkey. Ratification 20 Feb 62. Force 22 Mar 62.
535 UNTS 438. France. Approval 18 Jan 65. Force 17 Feb 65.
545 UNTS 350. Portugal. Ratification 11 May 65. Force 10 Jun 65.

105665 Bilateral Agreement **394 UNTS 13**
SIGNED: 24 Jul 53 FORCE: 8 Nov 53
REGISTERED: 7 Apr 61 Yugoslavia
ARTICLES: 9 LANGUAGE: English.
HEADNOTE: TRADE
TOPIC: General Trade
CONCEPTS: Exceptions and exemptions. General provisions. Annex or appendix reference. Conformity with municipal law. General cooperation. Licenses and permits. Use of facilities. Trade agencies. Currency. Payment schedules. Most favored nation clause. Water transport.
PROCEDURE: Duration. Ratification.
PARTIES:
India
Yugoslavia

105666 Bilateral Agreement **394 UNTS 27**
SIGNED: 27 Feb 61 FORCE: 27 Feb 61
REGISTERED: 7 Apr 61 United Nations
ARTICLES: 6 LANGUAGE: English.
HEADNOTE: DIPLOMATIC CONFERENCE
TOPIC: IGO Status/Immunit
CONCEPTS: Arbitration. IGO status.

PARTIES:
Austria
United Nations

105667 Multilateral Protocol **394 UNTS 37**
SIGNED: 28 Jul 60 FORCE: 22 Mar 61
REGISTERED: 10 Apr 61 Sweden
ARTICLES: 21 LANGUAGE: English. French.
HEADNOTE: PRIVILEGES IMMUNITIES EFTA
TOPIC: IGO Status/Immunit
CONCEPTS: Treaty violation. Passports diplomatic. Diplomatic privileges. Inviolability. Privileges and immunities. Property. Diplomatic correspondence. Conformity with municipal law. Juridical personality. Responsibility and liability. Customs exemptions. Admission. Special status. Status of experts.
INTL ORGS: European Free Trade Association.
TREATY REF: 370UNTS3.
PARTIES:
Austria SIGNED: 28 Jul 60 RATIFIED: 22 Mar 61 FORCE: 22 Mar 61
Denmark SIGNED: 28 Jul 60 RATIFIED: 29 Nov 60 FORCE: 22 Mar 61
Norway SIGNED: 28 Jul 60 RATIFIED: 24 Sep 60 FORCE: 22 Mar 61
Portugal SIGNED: 28 Jul 60 FORCE: 22 Mar 61
Sweden SIGNED: 28 Jul 60 FORCE: 22 Mar 61
Switzerland SIGNED: 28 Jul 60 FORCE: 22 Mar 61
UK Great Britain SIGNED: 28 Jul 60 FORCE: 22 Mar 61
ANNEX
397 UNTS 338. Sweden. Acceptance 2 Jun 61.
429 UNTS 302. UK Great Britain. Ratification 26 Jun 62.
462 UNTS 356. Finland. Accession 1 Apr 63.

105668 Bilateral Treaty **394 UNTS 53**
SIGNED: 28 Aug 58 FORCE: 9 Dec 60
REGISTERED: 10 Apr 61 Thailand
ARTICLES: 9 LANGUAGE: Thai. Urdu. English.
HEADNOTE: FRIENDSHIP
TOPIC: General Amity
CONCEPTS: Friendship and amity. Alien status. Consular relations establishment. Diplomatic relations establishment. Privileges and immunities. General cooperation. Procedure.
INTL ORGS: United Nations.
PROCEDURE: Duration. Future Procedures Contemplated. Ratification. Termination.
PARTIES:
Pakistan
Thailand

105669 Bilateral Agreement **394 UNTS 69**
SIGNED: 3 Oct 57 FORCE: 9 Mar 61
REGISTERED: 13 Apr 61 Belgium
ARTICLES: 8 LANGUAGE: English. French.
HEADNOTE: COMPENSATION DISABLEMENT DEATH
TOPIC: Reparations
CONCEPTS: Definition of terms. Time limit. Nationality and citizenship. Exchange of information and documents. Loss and/or damage. Post-war claims settlement.
PROCEDURE: Denunciation. Ratification.
PARTIES:
Belgium
UK Great Britain

105670 Bilateral Convention **394 UNTS 79**
SIGNED: 15 Nov 60 FORCE: 16 Feb 61
REGISTERED: 13 Apr 61 Belgium
ARTICLES: 18 LANGUAGE: French.
HEADNOTE: WINDING-UP BANQUE CENTRALE DU CONGO BELGE
TOPIC: Finance
CONCEPTS: Responsibility and liability. Arbitration. Banking. Bonds. Reciprocity in financial treatment. Currency. Currency deposits. Debts. Assets transfer. Tax exemptions.
INTL ORGS: International Court of Justice. Special Commission.
PROCEDURE: Ratification.
PARTIES:
Belgium
Congo (Zaire)

105671 Bilateral Exchange **394 UNTS 103**
SIGNED: 30 Sep 60 FORCE: 30 Sep 60
REGISTERED: 14 Apr 61 USA (United States)
ARTICLES: 2 LANGUAGE: English. French.
HEADNOTE: ECONOMIC TECHNICAL RELATED ASSISTANCE
TOPIC: General Aid
CONCEPTS: Conformity with municipal law. Personnel. Accounting procedures. Banking. Exchange rates and regulations. Expense sharing formulae. Financial programs. Tax exemptions. Customs exemptions. Commodities and services. Domestic obligation. General technical assistance. Economic assistance. Materials, equipment and services. Aid missions. Grants.
INTL ORGS: United Nations.
PROCEDURE: Termination.
PARTIES:
Guinea
USA (United States)

105672 Bilateral Agreement **394 UNTS 113**
SIGNED: 19 Oct 60 FORCE: 19 Oct 60
REGISTERED: 14 Apr 61 USA (United States)
ARTICLES: 18 LANGUAGE: English.
HEADNOTE: SPACE VEHICLE TRACKING STATION COMMUNICATIONS
TOPIC: Scientific Project
CONCEPTS: Conditions. Personnel. General property. Responsibility and liability. Use of facilities. Research and scientific projects. Research cooperation. Research results. Communication satellites testing. Research and development. Indemnities and reimbursements. Tax exemptions. General communications. Bands and frequency allocation. Facilities and equipment.
PROCEDURE: Duration. Future Procedures Contemplated. Termination.
PARTIES:
Nigeria
USA (United States)
ANNEX
531 UNTS 356. USA (United States). Amendment 28 Apr 64. Force 21 May 64.
531 UNTS 356. Nigeria. Amendment 21 May 64. Force 21 May 64.

105673 Bilateral Agreement **394 UNTS 127**
SIGNED: 31 Oct 60 FORCE: 31 Oct 60
REGISTERED: 14 Apr 61 USA (United States)
ARTICLES: 9 LANGUAGE: English. Portuguese.
HEADNOTE: PATENT RIGHTS TECHNICAL INFORMATION DEFENSE
TOPIC: Patents/Copyrights
CONCEPTS: Definition of terms. Currency. Press and wire services. Security of information. Exchange of defense information. Subsidiary organ.
INTL ORGS: Special Commission.
TREATY REF: 133UNTS75.
PROCEDURE: Termination.
PARTIES:
Portugal
USA (United States)

105674 Bilateral Exchange **394 UNTS 141**
SIGNED: 26 Feb 60 FORCE: 26 Feb 60
REGISTERED: 14 Apr 61 USA (United States)
ARTICLES: 2 LANGUAGE: English. Russian.
HEADNOTE: VESSEL LOAN
TOPIC: Milit Assistance
CONCEPTS: Time limit. Annex or appendix reference. Responsibility and liability. Title and deeds. Compensation. Delivery schedules. Lease of military property. Naval vessels. Return of equipment and recapture.
TREATY REF: 165UNTS31.
PARTIES:
Peru
USA (United States)
ANNEX
406 UNTS 350. USA (United States). Supplementation 27 Dec 60. Force 28 Dec 60.
406 UNTS 350. Peru. Supplementation 28 Dec 60. Force 28 Dec 60.
549 UNTS 292. Peru. Acknowledgement 28 Jun 65. Force 28 Jun 65.
549 UNTS 292. USA (United States). Prolongation 8 Jun 65. Force 28 Jun 65.
616 UNTS 496. USA (United States). Prolongation 24 Aug 66. Force 24 Aug 66.

616 UNTS 496. Peru. Prolongation 24 Aug 66. Force 24 Aug 66.

105675 Bilateral Agreement **394 UNTS 149**
SIGNED: 13 Feb 61　　　　FORCE: 13 Feb 61
REGISTERED: 17 Apr 61 WHO (World Health)
ARTICLES: 6 LANGUAGE: French.
HEADNOTE: TECHNICAL ADVISORY ASSISTANCE
TOPIC: Tech Assistance
CONCEPTS: Definition of terms. Privileges and immunities. General cooperation. Exchange of information and documents. Personnel. Responsibility and liability. Title and deeds. Exchange. Scholarships and grants. Vocational training. Research and development. Expense sharing formulae. Local currency. Domestic obligation. Special projects. Materials, equipment and services. IGO status. Conformity with IGO decisions.
INTL ORGS: United Nations.
TREATY REF: 1UNTS15.
PROCEDURE: Amendment. Termination.
PARTIES:
　Central Afri Rep
　WHO (World Health)

105676 Bilateral Agreement **394 UNTS 161**
SIGNED: 3 Feb 61　　　　FORCE: 23 Mar 61
REGISTERED: 17 Apr 61 WHO (World Health)
ARTICLES: 6 LANGUAGE: French.
HEADNOTE: TECHNICAL ADVISORY ASSISTANCE
TOPIC: Tech Assistance
CONCEPTS: Definition of terms. General cooperation. Exchange of information and documents. Personnel. Responsibility and liability. Title and deeds. Exchange. Scholarships and grants. Vocational training. Research and development. Expense sharing formulae. Local currency. Domestic obligation. Special projects. Materials, equipment and services. IGO status. Conformity with IGO decisions.
INTL ORGS: United Nations.
PARTIES:
　Chad
　WHO (World Health)

105677 Bilateral Agreement **394 UNTS 173**
SIGNED: 11 Feb 61　　　　FORCE: 21 Feb 61
REGISTERED: 17 Apr 61 WHO (World Health)
ARTICLES: 6 LANGUAGE: French.
HEADNOTE: TECHNICAL ASSISTANCE
TOPIC: Tech Assistance
CONCEPTS: Assistance.
INTL ORGS: United Nations.
PROCEDURE: Termination.
PARTIES:
　Guinea
　WHO (World Health)

105678 Bilateral Agreement **394 UNTS 185**
SIGNED: 19 Apr 61　　　　FORCE: 19 Apr 61
REGISTERED: 19 Apr 61 United Nations
ARTICLES: 8 LANGUAGE: English.
HEADNOTE: ACTIVITIES UNICEF
TOPIC: Direct Aid
CONCEPTS: Treaty implementation. Privileges and immunities. Exchange of information and documents. Informational records. Public information. Responsibility and liability. Title and deeds. Attachment of funds. Tax exemptions. Customs exemptions. Domestic obligation. Assistance. General aid. Materials, equipment and services. Distribution. IGO status.
INTL ORGS: United Nations.
PROCEDURE: Amendment. Termination.
PARTIES:
　Cyprus
　UNICEF (Children)

105679 Bilateral Agreement **394 UNTS 195**
SIGNED: 28 Dec 60　　　　FORCE: 28 Dec 60
REGISTERED: 21 Apr 61 WHO (World Health)
ARTICLES: 6 LANGUAGE: French.
HEADNOTE: TECHNICAL ADVISORY ASSISTANCE
TOPIC: Tech Assistance
CONCEPTS: Definition of terms. General cooperation. Exchange of information and documents. Personnel. Responsibility and liability. Title and deeds. Exchange. Scholarships and grants. Vocational training. Research and development. Ex-

pense sharing formulae. Local currency. Domestic obligation. Special projects. Materials, equipment and services. IGO status. Conformity with IGO decisions.
INTL ORGS: United Nations.
PARTIES:
　Niger
　WHO (World Health)

105680 Bilateral Agreement **394 UNTS 207**
SIGNED: 3 Feb 61　　　　FORCE: 18 Feb 61
REGISTERED: 21 Apr 61 WHO (World Health)
ARTICLES: 6 LANGUAGE: French.
HEADNOTE: TECHNICAL ADVISORY ASSISTANCE
TOPIC: Tech Assistance
CONCEPTS: Definition of terms. Privileges and immunities. General cooperation. Exchange of information and documents. Personnel. Responsibility and liability. Title and deeds. Exchange. Scholarships and grants. Vocational training. Research and development. Expense sharing formulae. Local currency. Domestic obligation. Special projects. Materials, equipment and services. IGO status. Conformity with IGO decisions.
INTL ORGS: United Nations.
TREATY REF: 33UNTS261.
PROCEDURE: Amendment. Termination.
PARTIES:
　WHO (World Health)
　Togo
ANNEX
562 UNTS 332. WHO (World Health). Amendment 30 Dec 65. Force 9 Apr 66.
562 UNTS 332. Togo. Amendment 9 Apr 66. Force 9 Apr 66.

105681 Bilateral Treaty **395 UNTS 3**
SIGNED: 15 Jul 58　　　　FORCE: 25 Mar 59
REGISTERED: 28 Apr 61 Romania
ARTICLES: 79 LANGUAGE: Romanian. German.
HEADNOTE: LEGAL ASSISTANCE CIVIL FAMILY CRIMINAL CASES
TOPIC: Admin Cooperation
CONCEPTS: General provisions. Privileges and immunities. Consular functions in property. Extradition, deportation and repatriation. Refusal of extradition. Concurrent requests. Provisional detainment. Extradition postponement. Witnesses and experts. Material evidence. Conformity with municipal law. Family law. Exchange of information and documents. Juridical personality. Legal protection and assistance. Recognition and enforcement of legal decisions. General property. Succession. Recognition of legal documents. Prizes and arbitral awards. Indemnities and reimbursements. Assets transfer. Conveyance in transit.
PROCEDURE: Denunciation. Duration. Ratification. Renewal or Revival.
PARTIES:
　Germany, East
　Romania

105682 Bilateral Convention **395 UNTS 99**
SIGNED: 4 Aug 56　　　　FORCE: 14 Jan 57
REGISTERED: 28 Apr 61 Romania
ARTICLES: 26 LANGUAGE: Romanian. Serbo-Croat.
HEADNOTE: VETERINARY HEALTH
TOPIC: Sanitation
CONCEPTS: Definition of terms. Detailed regulations. Exceptions and exemptions. Previous treaty extension. Border traffic and migration. General cooperation. Inspection and observation. Licenses and permits. Procedure. Disease control. Veterinary. Trade procedures. Conferences.
PROCEDURE: Denunciation. Duration. Ratification. Renewal or Revival.
PARTIES:
　Romania
　Yugoslavia

105683 Bilateral Convention **395 UNTS 147**
SIGNED: 25 Sep 56　　　　FORCE: 7 Mar 57
REGISTERED: 28 Apr 61 Romania
ARTICLES: 12 LANGUAGE: Romanian. Serbo-Croat.
HEADNOTE: PROTECTION AGRICULTURAL WOODLAND PLANTS

TOPIC: Sanitation
CONCEPTS: Definition of terms. Exceptions and exemptions. Border traffic and migration. General cooperation. Exchange of information and documents. Inspection and observation. Domestic legislation. Licenses and permits. Establishment of commission. Specialists exchange. Disease control. Insect control. Scientific exchange. Reexport of goods, etc.. Trade procedures. Agriculture. Materials, equipment and services. Conferences.
INTL ORGS: Special Commission.
PROCEDURE: Denunciation. Duration. Ratification. Renewal or Revival.
PARTIES:
　Romania
　Yugoslavia

105684 Bilateral Agreement **395 UNTS 169**
SIGNED: 6 Sep 60　　　　FORCE: 4 Apr 61
REGISTERED: 1 May 61 WHO (World Health)
ARTICLES: 6 LANGUAGE: English. Arabic.
HEADNOTE: TECHNICAL ADVISORY ASSISTANCE
TOPIC: Tech Assistance
CONCEPTS: Definition of terms. Privileges and immunities. Conformity with municipal law. General cooperation. Personnel. Responsibility and liability. Title and deeds. Exchange. Scholarships and grants. Vocational training. Research and development. Expense sharing formulae. Local currency. Domestic obligation. Special projects. Materials, equipment and services. IGO status. Conformity with IGO decisions.
INTL ORGS: United Nations.
TREATY REF: 33UNTS261.
PROCEDURE: Amendment. Termination.
PARTIES:
　WHO (World Health)
　Saudi Arabia

105685 Bilateral Agreement **395 UNTS 187**
SIGNED: 3 Dec 60　　　　FORCE: 3 Dec 60
REGISTERED: 1 May 61 WHO (World Health)
ARTICLES: 6 LANGUAGE: English. Arabic.
HEADNOTE: TECHNICAL ADVISORY ASSISTANCE
TOPIC: Tech Assistance
CONCEPTS: Definition of terms. General cooperation. Exchange of information and documents. Personnel. Responsibility and liability. Title and deeds. Exchange. Scholarships and grants. Vocational training. Research and development. Expense sharing formulae. Local currency. Domestic obligation. Special projects. Materials, equipment and services. IGO status. Conformity with IGO decisions.
INTL ORGS: United Nations.
TREATY REF: 33UNTS261.
PROCEDURE: Amendment. Termination.
PARTIES:
　WHO (World Health)
　Yemen

105686 Bilateral Agreement **395 UNTS 205**
SIGNED: 30 Jan 61　　　　FORCE: 7 Feb 61
REGISTERED: 1 May 61 WHO (World Health)
ARTICLES: 6 LANGUAGE: French.
HEADNOTE: TECHNICAL ADVISORY ASSISTANCE
TOPIC: Tech Assistance
CONCEPTS: Definition of terms. Privileges and immunities. General cooperation. Exchange of information and documents. Personnel. Responsibility and liability. Title and deeds. Exchange. Scholarships and grants. Vocational training. Research and development. Expense sharing formulae. Local currency. Domestic obligation. Special projects. Materials, equipment and services. IGO status. Conformity with IGO decisions.
INTL ORGS: United Nations.
TREATY REF: 33UNTS261.
PROCEDURE: Amendment. Termination.
PARTIES:
　Ivory Coast
　WHO (World Health)

105687 Bilateral Agreement **395 UNTS 217**
SIGNED: 3 May 61　　　　FORCE: 3 May 61
REGISTERED: 3 May 61 United Nations
ARTICLES: 10 LANGUAGE: English.
HEADNOTE: ASSISTANCE
TOPIC: Direct Aid

CONCEPTS: Detailed regulations. Treaty implementation. Annex or appendix reference. Visas. Privileges and immunities. Exchange of information and documents. Informational records. Inspection and observation. Operating agencies. Personnel. Public information. Responsibility and liability. Title and deeds. Use of facilities. Arbitration. Procedure. Negotiation. Import quotas. Attachment of funds. Exchange rates and regulations. Expense sharing formulae. Financial programs. Domestic obligation. General technical assistance. Economic assistance. Materials, equipment and services. IGO status.
INTL ORGS: International Atomic Energy Agency. International Court of Justice. United Nations. Arbitration Commission.
TREATY REF: 33UNTS261; 1UNTS15; 374UNTS147.
PROCEDURE: Amendment. Termination.
PARTIES:
  Ceylon (Sri Lanka)
  UN Special Fund

105688 Unilateral Instrument **395 UNTS 237**
SIGNED: 21 Mar 61   FORCE: 8 May 61
REGISTERED: 8 May 61 United Nations
ARTICLES: 1 LANGUAGE: English.
HEADNOTE: ACCEPTANCE OBLIGATIONS UN
TOPIC: UN Charter
CONCEPTS: Acceptance of obligations upon admittance to UN.
INTL ORGS: United Nations.
PARTIES:
  Nigeria

105689 Multilateral Instrument **395 UNTS 241**
SIGNED: 30 Dec 60   FORCE: 30 Dec 60
REGISTERED: 8 May 61 IAEA (Atom Energy)
ARTICLES: 6 LANGUAGE: English.
HEADNOTE: TRASNFER ENRICHED URANIUM FOR RESEARCH REACTOR
TOPIC: Atomic Energy
CONCEPTS: Responsibility and liability. Title and deeds. Procedure. Special tribunals. Research cooperation. Payment schedules. Nuclear materials. Transport of goods.
INTL ORGS: International Court of Justice. Arbitration Commission.
TREATY REF: 339UNTS359; 276UNTS3; 293UNTS359.
PARTIES:
  Finland SIGNED: 30 Dec 60 FORCE: 30 Dec 60
  IAEA (Atom Energy) SIGNED: 23 Dec 60
  USA (United States) SIGNED: 23 Dec 60

105690 Bilateral Agreement **395 UNTS 257**
SIGNED: 30 Dec 60   FORCE: 30 Dec 60
REGISTERED: 8 May 61 IAEA (Atom Energy)
ARTICLES: 9 LANGUAGE: English.
HEADNOTE: ESTABLISHING RESEARCH REACTOR PROJECT
TOPIC: Atomic Energy
CONCEPTS: Annex or appendix reference. Exchange of information and documents. Procedure. Public health. Research cooperation. Nuclear materials. Peaceful use. Transport of goods. Security of information.
TREATY REF: 339UNTS359.
PARTIES:
  Finland
  IAEA (Atom Energy)

105691 Bilateral Agreement **396 UNTS 3**
SIGNED: 9 Mar 61   FORCE: 9 Mar 61
REGISTERED: 9 May 61 United Nations
ARTICLES: 10 LANGUAGE: English. Spanish.
HEADNOTE: ASSISTANCE
TOPIC: Direct Aid
CONCEPTS: Detailed regulations. Treaty implementation. Visas. Privileges and immunities. Exchange of information and documents. Informational records. Inspection and observation. Operating agencies. Personnel. Public information. Responsibility and liability. Title and deeds. Use of facilities. Arbitration. Procedure. Negotiation. Import quotas. Attachment of funds. Exchange rates and regulations. Expense sharing formulae. Financial programs. Domestic obligation. General technical assistance. Economic assistance. Materials, equipment and services. IGO status.

INTL ORGS: International Court of Justice. United Nations. Arbitration Commission.
TREATY REF: 1UNTS15; 33UNTS261; 374UNTS147.
PROCEDURE: Amendment. Termination.
PARTIES:
  Panama
  UN Special Fund

105692 Bilateral Agreement **396 UNTS 27**
SIGNED: 19 Jan 61   FORCE: 19 Jan 61
REGISTERED: 15 May 61 United Nations
ARTICLES: 10 LANGUAGE: English. Arabic.
HEADNOTE: ASSISTANCE
TOPIC: Direct Aid
CONCEPTS: Detailed regulations. Treaty implementation. Annex or appendix reference. Visas. Privileges and immunities. Exchange of information and documents. Informational records. Inspection and observation. Operating agencies. Personnel. Public information. Responsibility and liability. Title and deeds. Use of facilities. Arbitration. Procedure. Negotiation. Import quotas. Attachment of funds. Exchange rates and regulations. Expense sharing formulae. Financial programs. Domestic obligation. General technical assistance. Economic assistance. Materials, equipment and services. IGO status.
INTL ORGS: International Court of Justice. United Nations. Arbitration Commission.
TREATY REF: 1UNTS15; 331NTS261; 374UNTS147.
PROCEDURE: Amendment. Termination.
PARTIES:
  UN Special Fund
  Saudi Arabia
                ANNEX
439 UNTS 321. UN Special Fund. Correction 24 Jul 62. Force 8 Aug 62.
439 UNTS 321. Saudi Arabia. Correction 8 Aug 62. Force 8 Aug 62.

105693 Bilateral Protocol **396 UNTS 63**
SIGNED: 29 Dec 59   FORCE: 26 May 60
REGISTERED: 26 May 61 Yugoslavia
ARTICLES: 3 LANGUAGE: Serbo Croat. Albanian.
HEADNOTE: EXCHANGE GOODS
TOPIC: General Trade
CONCEPTS: Annex or appendix reference. Annex type material. General cooperation. Quotas.
PARTIES:
  Albania
  Yugoslavia

105694 Bilateral Agreement **396 UNTS 75**
SIGNED: 27 Nov 54   FORCE: 9 Feb 56
REGISTERED: 26 May 61 Yugoslavia
ARTICLES: 11 LANGUAGE: Serbo-Croat. German.
HEADNOTE: WATER ECONOMY QUESTIONS
TOPIC: Specific Resources
CONCEPTS: Annex or appendix reference. Previous treaties adherence. Frontier permits. Exchange of information and documents. Establishment of commission. Arbitration. Special tribunals. Financial programs. Temporary importation. Materials, equipment and services. Markers and definitions. Regulation of natural resources.
INTL ORGS: United Nations. Special Commission.
TREATY REF: 100BFSP298;54LTS435; 134LTS453.
PROCEDURE: Denunciation. Duration. Ratification. Renewal or Revival.
PARTIES:
  Austria
  Yugoslavia

105695 Bilateral Agreement **396 UNTS 117**
SIGNED: 15 Jun 56   FORCE: 18 Jul 58
REGISTERED: 26 May 61 Yugoslavia
ARTICLES: 30 LANGUAGE: Serbo-Croat. German.
HEADNOTE: VETERINARY AGREEMENT
TOPIC: Sanitation
CONCEPTS: Definition of terms. Detailed regulations. Exceptions and exemptions. Annex or appendix reference. Previous treaty extension. Border traffic and migration. General cooperation. Exchange of information and documents. Inspection and observation. Negotiation. Special-

ists exchange. Border control. Veterinary. Scientific exchange. Trade procedures.
TREATY REF: AGREEMENT CONCERNING MINOR FRONTIER TRAFFIC 19MAR5.
PROCEDURE: Denunciation. Duration. Ratification.
PARTIES:
  Austria
  Yugoslavia

105696 Bilateral Exchange **396 UNTS 179**
SIGNED: 15 Nov 55   FORCE: 16 Nov 55
REGISTERED: 26 May 61 Yugoslavia
ARTICLES: 2 LANGUAGE: Serbo-Croat. Bulgarian.
HEADNOTE: FREE MEDICAL SERVICES DIPLOMATIC OTHER OFFICERS
TOPIC: Consul/Citizenship
CONCEPTS: Detailed regulations. Public health.
PARTIES:
  Bulgaria
  Yugoslavia

105697 Bilateral Agreement **396 UNTS 191**
SIGNED: 15 Nov 55   FORCE: 1 Apr 56
REGISTERED: 26 May 61 Yugoslavia
ARTICLES: 28 LANGUAGE: Serbo-Croat. Bulgarian.
HEADNOTE: POSTAL TELECOMMUNICATION SERVICE
TOPIC: General Transport
CONCEPTS: Exceptions and exemptions. Conformity with municipal law. General cooperation. Exchange of information and documents. Accounting procedures. Monetary and gold transfers. Fees and exemptions. Internal finance. Non-interest rates and fees. Postal services. Regulations. Insured letters and boxes. Parcel post. Rates and charges. Services. Radio-telephone-telegraphic communications.
TREATY REF: 169UNTS3; 170UNTS63.
PROCEDURE: Amendment. Denunciation. Ratification.
PARTIES:
  Bulgaria
  Yugoslavia

105698 Bilateral Agreement **396 UNTS 223**
SIGNED: 1 Oct 55   FORCE: 20 Jun 56
REGISTERED: 26 May 61 Yugoslavia
ARTICLES: 16 LANGUAGE: Serbo-Croat. Bulgarian.
HEADNOTE: AIR SERVICES
TOPIC: Air Transport
CONCEPTS: Definition of terms. Exceptions and exemptions. Annex or appendix reference. Previous treaty replacement. Conformity with municipal law. Exchange of information and documents. Informational records. Licenses and permits. Recognition of legal documents. Use of facilities. Procedure. Negotiation. Fees and exemptions. Non-interest rates and fees. Most favored nation clause. National treatment. Customs exemptions. Registration certificate. Routes and logistics. Permit designation. Airport facilities. Airworthiness certificates. Operating authorizations and regulations.
INTL ORGS: International Civil Aviation Organization.
PROCEDURE: Amendment. Ratification. Termination.
PARTIES:
  Bulgaria
  Yugoslavia

105699 Bilateral Agreement **397 UNTS 3**
SIGNED: 24 Dec 56   FORCE: 15 Nov 60
REGISTERED: 26 May 61 Yugoslavia
ARTICLES: 9 LANGUAGE: Serbo-Croat. Bulgarian.
HEADNOTE: CULTURAL COOPERATION
TOPIC: Culture
CONCEPTS: Treaty implementation. Friendship and amity. Conformity with municipal law. Exchange of information and documents. Exchange. Scholarships and grants. Exchange. General cultural cooperation. Research cooperation. Research results. Scientific exchange. Publications exchange. Mass media exchange.
PROCEDURE: Duration. Ratification. Renewal or Revival. Termination.

PARTIES:
Bulgaria
Yugoslavia

105700 Bilateral Agreement **397 UNTS 13**
SIGNED: 20 Feb 54　　FORCE: 3 Apr 54
REGISTERED: 26 May 61 Yugoslavia
ARTICLES: 10 LANGUAGE: Serbo-Croat. Bulgarian.
HEADNOTE: RESTORATION MARKING FRONTIER PYRAMIDS FRONTIER LINE
TOPIC: Territory Boundary
CONCEPTS: Annex or appendix reference. Frontier permits. Establishment of commission. Negotiation. Markers and definitions.
INTL ORGS: Special Commission.
PROCEDURE: Duration.
PARTIES:
Bulgaria
Yugoslavia

105701 Bilateral Agreement **397 UNTS 43**
SIGNED: 22 Apr 54　　FORCE: 5 Jul 54
REGISTERED: 26 May 61 Yugoslavia
ARTICLES: 10 LANGUAGE: Serbo-Croat. Bulgarian.
HEADNOTE: INVESTIGATION SETTLEMENT FRONTIER INCIDENTS
TOPIC: Dispute Settlement
CONCEPTS: Annex or appendix reference. Privileges and immunities. General cooperation. Inspection and observation. Establishment of commission. Procedure.
INTL ORGS: Special Commission.
PROCEDURE: Denunciation. Ratification.
PARTIES:
Bulgaria
Yugoslavia

105702 Bilateral Agreement **397 UNTS 83**
SIGNED: 16 Mar 55　　FORCE: 18 Nov 55
REGISTERED: 26 May 61 Yugoslavia
ARTICLES: 10 LANGUAGE: Serbo-Croat. Bulgarian.
HEADNOTE: DEVELOPING TRADE
TOPIC: General Economic
CONCEPTS: Treaty implementation. Annex or appendix reference. Conformity with municipal law. Licenses and permits. Establishment of commission. Establishment of trade relations. Payment schedules. Quotas.
PROCEDURE: Denunciation. Duration. Future Procedures Contemplated.
PARTIES:
Bulgaria
Yugoslavia

105703 Bilateral Agreement **397 UNTS 135**
SIGNED: 11 Feb 56　　FORCE: 20 Dec 56
REGISTERED: 26 May 61 Yugoslavia
ARTICLES: 7 LANGUAGE: Serbo-Croat. Czechoslovakian.
HEADNOTE: SETTLEMENT PROPERTY QUESTIONS
TOPIC: Admin Cooperation
CONCEPTS: Exchange of information and documents. General property. Claims and settlements.
PROCEDURE: Ratification.
PARTIES:
Czechoslovakia
Yugoslavia

105704 Bilateral Agreement **397 UNTS 165**
SIGNED: 3 Jul 56　　FORCE: 19 Dec 56
REGISTERED: 26 May 61 Yugoslavia
ARTICLES: 7 LANGUAGE: Serbo-Croat. Czechoslovakian.
HEADNOTE: SCIENTIFIC TECHNICAL COOPERATION
TOPIC: General Economic
CONCEPTS: Annex or appendix reference. Exchange of official publications. Exchange of information and documents. Licenses and permits. Establishment of commission. Specialists exchange. Scientific exchange. Patents, copyrights and trademarks. Materials, equipment and services.
INTL ORGS: Special Commission.

PROCEDURE: Duration. Future Procedures Contemplated. Termination.
PARTIES:
Czechoslovakia
Yugoslavia

105705 Bilateral Agreement **397 UNTS 187**
SIGNED: 24 Nov 59　　FORCE: 24 Nov 59
REGISTERED: 29 May 61 United Nations
ARTICLES: 6 LANGUAGE: English.
HEADNOTE: OPERATIONAL EXECUTIVE PERSONNEL
TOPIC: Tech Assistance
CONCEPTS: Treaty implementation. Annex or appendix reference. Privileges and immunities. General cooperation. Personnel. Responsibility and liability. Arbitration. Procedure. Negotiation. Research and development. Compensation. Expense sharing formulae. Tax exemptions. Customs exemptions. Domestic obligation. Special projects. Status of experts. Conformity with IGO decisions.
INTL ORGS: Permanent Court of Arbitration.
PROCEDURE: Amendment. Termination.
PARTIES:
Afghanistan
United Nations

ANNEX
527 UNTS 310. United Nations. Force 23 Feb 65.
527 UNTS 310. Afghanistan. Force 23 Feb 65.

105706 Bilateral Agreement **397 UNTS 199**
SIGNED: 15 Mar 61　　FORCE: 5 Jun 61
REGISTERED: 5 Jun 61 United Nations
ARTICLES: 6 LANGUAGE: English.
HEADNOTE: ASIA FAR EAST INSTITUTE FOR CRIME PREVENTION & TREATMENT
TOPIC: IGO Operations
CONCEPTS: Privileges and immunities. Domestic obligation. Procedure. IGO obligations.
INTL ORGS: Asian Crime Prevention Organization.
PROCEDURE: Duration. Termination.
PARTIES:
Japan
United Nations

105707 Bilateral Agreement **397 UNTS 215**
SIGNED: 27 Apr 61　　FORCE: 20 May 61
REGISTERED: 6 Jun 61 WHO (World Health)
ARTICLES: 6 LANGUAGE: French.
HEADNOTE: TECHNICAL ADVISORY ASSISTANCE
TOPIC: Tech Assistance
CONCEPTS: Definition of terms. Privileges and immunities. General cooperation. Exchange of information and documents. Personnel. Responsibility and liability. Title and deeds. Exchange. Scholarships and grants. Vocational training. Research and development. Expense sharing formulae. Local currency. Domestic obligation. Special projects. Materials, equipment and services. IGO status. Conformity with IGO decisions.
INTL ORGS: United Nations.
TREATY REF: 33UNTS261.
PROCEDURE: Amendment. Termination.
PARTIES:
Gabon
WHO (World Health)

105708 Bilateral Convention **397 UNTS 227**
SIGNED: 4 Nov 60　　FORCE: 19 Mar 61
REGISTERED: 6 Jun 61 Czechoslovakia
ARTICLES: 10 LANGUAGE: Czechoslovakian. Hungarian.
HEADNOTE: QUESTIONS CITIZENSHIP
TOPIC: Consul/Citizenship
CONCEPTS: Alien status. Dual citizenship. Nationality and citizenship. Tax exemptions.
PROCEDURE: Ratification.
PARTIES:
Czechoslovakia
Hungary

105709 Bilateral Convention **397 UNTS 245**
SIGNED: 21 May 60　　FORCE: 24 Mar 61
REGISTERED: 6 Jun 61 Czechoslovakia
ARTICLES: 23 LANGUAGE: Czechoslovakian. Romanian.
HEADNOTE: CONSULAR
TOPIC: Consul/Citizenship

CONCEPTS: General consular functions. Diplomatic privileges. Consular relations establishment. Inviolability. Privileges and immunities.
PROCEDURE: Duration. Ratification. Termination.
PARTIES:
Czechoslovakia
Romania

105710 Bilateral Exchange **397 UNTS 275**
SIGNED: 11 Mar 61　　FORCE: 11 Mar 61
REGISTERED: 8 Jun 61 Iceland
ARTICLES: 2 LANGUAGE: English.
HEADNOTE: SETTLEMENT FISHERIES DISPUTE
TOPIC: Dispute Settlement
CONCEPTS: Procedure. Markers and definitions.
INTL ORGS: United Nations.
PARTIES:
Iceland
UK Great Britain

105711 Unilateral Instrument **397 UNTS 283**
SIGNED: 29 May 61　　FORCE: 20 Sep 60
REGISTERED: 9 Jun 61 United Nations
ARTICLES: 1 LANGUAGE: English.
HEADNOTE: ACCEPTANCE OBLIGATIONS UN
TOPIC: UN Charter
CONCEPTS: Acceptance of obligations upon admittance to UN.
INTL ORGS: United Nations.
PARTIES:
Cyprus

105712 Multilateral Treaty **397 UNTS 287**
SIGNED: 16 Aug 60　　FORCE: 16 Aug 60
REGISTERED: 12 Jun 61 Greece
ARTICLES: 6 LANGUAGE: French.
HEADNOTE: ALLIANCE
TOPIC: General Amity
CONCEPTS: Peaceful relations. General cooperation. Establishment of commission.
INTL ORGS: United Nations.
PROCEDURE: Registration.
PARTIES:
Cyprus SIGNED: 16 Aug 60 FORCE: 16 Aug 60
Greece SIGNED: 16 Aug 60 FORCE: 16 Aug 60
Turkey SIGNED: 16 Aug 60 FORCE: 16 Aug 60

105713 Bilateral Agreement **397 UNTS 297**
SIGNED: 13 Jun 61　　FORCE: 13 Jun 61
REGISTERED: 13 Jun 61 United Nations
ARTICLES: 10 LANGUAGE: English. French.
HEADNOTE: ASSISTANCE
TOPIC: Direct Aid
CONCEPTS: Detailed regulations. Treaty implementation. Visas. Privileges and immunities. Exchange of information and documents. Informational records. Inspection and observation. Operating agencies. Personnel. Public information. Responsibility and liability. Title and deeds. Use of facilities. Arbitration. Procedure. Negotiation. Import quotas. Attachment of funds. Exchange rates and regulations. Expense sharing formulae. Financial programs. Domestic obligation. General technical assistance. Economic assistance. Materials, equipment and services. IGO status.
INTL ORGS: International Court of Justice. United Nations. Arbitration Commission.
TREATY REF: 1UNTS15; 33UNTS261; 374UNTS147.
PROCEDURE: Amendment. Termination.
PARTIES:
Cameroon
UN Special Fund

105714 Bilateral Agreement **398 UNTS 3**
SIGNED: 1 May 58　　FORCE: 26 Aug 60
REGISTERED: 14 Jun 61 South Africa
ARTICLES: 4 LANGUAGE: English.
HEADNOTE: DOUBLE TAXATION SEA AIR TRANSPORT
TOPIC: Taxation
CONCEPTS: Definition of terms. Taxation. Tax exemptions. Air transport. Merchant vessels.
PROCEDURE: Duration. Termination.

PARTIES:
Ireland
South Africa

105715   Multilateral Convention   **398 UNTS 9**
SIGNED: 3 Dec 58   FORCE: 30 May 61
REGISTERED: 15 Jun 61 UNESCO (Educ/Cult)
ARTICLES: 22 LANGUAGE: English. French. Russian. Spanish.
HEADNOTE: EXCHANGE OFFICIAL PUBLICATIONS
TOPIC: Admin Cooperation
CONCEPTS: Definition of terms. Territorial application. General cooperation. Exchange of official publications. Exchange of information and documents. Non-interest rates and fees. Customs exemptions. IGO obligations.
INTL ORGS: United Nations.
PROCEDURE: Amendment. Accession. Denunciation. Ratification. Registration.
PARTIES:
Ceylon (Sri Lanka) RATIFIED: 7 Dec 59 FORCE: 30 May 61
Taiwan RATIFIED: 26 Apr 61 FORCE: 26 Apr 62
Ecuador RATIFIED: 8 Feb 61 FORCE: 8 Feb 62
France RATIFIED: 30 May 60 FORCE: 30 May 61
Guatemala RATIFIED: 23 Nov 60 FORCE: 23 Nov 61
Israel RATIFIED: 4 Jan 60 FORCE: 30 May 61
UK Great Britain Anguilla RATIFIED: 1 Jun 61 FORCE: 1 Jun 62
UK Great Britain Antigua RATIFIED: 1 Jun 61 FORCE: 1 Jun 62
UK Great Britain Bahamas RATIFIED: 1 Jun 61 FORCE: 1 Jun 62
UK Great Britain Barbados RATIFIED: 1 Jun 61 FORCE: 1 Jun 62
UK Great Britain Bermuda RATIFIED: 1 Jun 61 FORCE: 1 Jun 62
UK Great Britain British Guiana RATIFIED: 1 Jun 61 FORCE: 1 Jun 62
UK Great Britain Brit Solomon Is RATIFIED: 1 Jun 61 FORCE: 1 Jun 62
UK Great Britain Brit Virgin Islands RATIFIED: 1 Jun 61 FORCE: 1 Jun 62
UK Great Britain Dominican Republic RATIFIED: 1 Jun 61 FORCE: 1 Jun 62
UK Great Britain Fed Rhod/Nyasaland RATIFIED: 1 Jun 61 FORCE: 1 Jun 62
UK Great Britain Gilbert Islands RATIFIED: 1 Jun 61 FORCE: 1 Jun 62
UK Great Britain Grenada RATIFIED: 1 Jun 61 FORCE: 1 Jun 62
UK Great Britain Guernsey Island RATIFIED: 1 Jun 61 FORCE: 1 Jun 62
UK Great Britain Isle of Man RATIFIED: 1 Jun 61 FORCE: 1 Jun 62
UK Great Britain Jamaica RATIFIED: 1 Jun 61 FORCE: 1 Jun 62
UK Great Britain Jersey Island RATIFIED: 1 Jun 61 FORCE: 1 Jun 62
UK Great Britain Malta RATIFIED: 1 Jun 61 FORCE: 1 Jun 62
UK Great Britain Montserrat RATIFIED: 1 Jun 61 FORCE: 1 Jun 62
UK Great Britain Nevis RATIFIED: 1 Jun 61 FORCE: 1 Jun 62
UK Great Britain RATIFIED: 1 Jun 61 FORCE: 1 Jun 62
UK Great Britain Seychelles RATIFIED: 1 Jun 61 FORCE: 1 Jun 62
UK Great Britain Singapore RATIFIED: 1 Jun 61 FORCE: 1 Jun 62
UK Great Britain St. Christopher RATIFIED: 1 Jun 61 FORCE: 1 Jun 62
UK Great Britain St. Lucia RATIFIED: 1 Jun 61 FORCE: 1 Jun 62
UK Great Britain St. Vincent RATIFIED: 1 Jun 61 FORCE: 1 Jun 62
UK Great Britain Trinidad/Tobago RATIFIED: 1 Jun 61 FORCE: 1 Jun 62
ANNEX
402 UNTS 371. Italy. Acceptance 2 Aug 61. Force 2 Aug 62.
435 UNTS 381. Panama. Ratification 17 Jul 62. Force 17 Jul 63.
449 UNTS 381. Hungary. Acceptance 10 Dec 62. Force 10 Dec 63.
449 UNTS 381. Byelorussia. Ratification 10 Dec 62. Force 10 Dec 63.
450 UNTS 472. Ukrainian SSR. Ratification 19 Dec 62. Force 19 Dec 63.

453 UNTS 437. Spain. Ratification 1 Feb 63. Force 1 Feb 64.
453 UNTS 437. New Zealand. Ratification 5 Feb 63. Force 5 Feb 64.
456 UNTS 504. Bulgaria. Ratification 4 Mar 63. Force 4 Mar 64.
474 UNTS 347. Cuba. Ratification 1 Aug 63. Force 1 Aug 64.
483 UNTS 382. Ghana. Ratification 6 Dec 63. Force 6 Dec 64.
483 UNTS 382. Czechoslovakia. Acceptance 29 Nov 63. Force 29 Nov 64.
521 UNTS 396. Denmark. Ratification 10 Nov 64. Force 10 Nov 65.
539 UNTS 363. Romania, Qualified Ratification 9 Jun 65. Force 9 Jun 66.
565 UNTS 317. Malta. Succession 18 May 66.
614 UNTS 410. Luxembourg. Ratification 13 Dec 67. Force 13 Dec 68.
615 UNTS 410. Luxembourg. Ratification 13 Dec 67.
646 UNTS 398. Morocco. Acceptance 30 Aug 68. Force 30 Aug 69.
648 UNTS 370. Norway. Acceptance 19 Sep 68. Force 19 Sep 68.

105716   Bilateral Agreement   **398 UNTS 39**
SIGNED: 15 Jun 61   FORCE: 15 Jun 61
REGISTERED: 15 Jun 61 United Nations
ARTICLES: 6 LANGUAGE: English.
HEADNOTE: OPERATIONAL & EXECUTIVE PERSONNEL
TOPIC: Tech Assistance
CONCEPTS: Treaty implementation. Annex or appendix reference. Privileges and immunities. General cooperation. Personnel. Responsibility and liability. Arbitration. Procedure. Negotiation. Vocational training. Compensation. Expense sharing formulae. Tax exemptions. Customs exemptions. Domestic obligation. Special projects. Status of experts. Conformity with IGO decisions.
INTL ORGS: Permanent Court of Arbitration. Arbitration Commission.
PROCEDURE: Amendment. Termination.
PARTIES:
Cyprus
United Nations
ANNEX
527 UNTS 311. Cyprus. Force 5 Mar 65.
527 UNTS 311. United Nations. Force 5 Mar 65.

105717   Bilateral Convention   **398 UNTS 51**
SIGNED: 6 May 59   FORCE: 25 Nov 60
REGISTERED: 16 Jun 61 UK Great Britain
ARTICLES: 22 LANGUAGE: English. Persian.
HEADNOTE: CULTURAL CONVENTION
TOPIC: Culture
CONCEPTS: Definition of terms. Treaty implementation. Friendship and amity. Resident permits. Conformity with municipal law. General cooperation. Operating agencies. Establishment of commission. Specialists exchange. Recognition of degrees. Teacher and student exchange. Professorships. Institute establishment. Scholarships and grants. General cultural cooperation. Athletes. Research cooperation. Anthropology and archeology. Import quotas. Publications exchange. Mass media exchange.
INTL ORGS: Special Commission.
PROCEDURE: Denunciation. Duration. Ratification. Renewal or Revival.
PARTIES:
Iran
UK Great Britain

105718   Bilateral Agreement   **398 UNTS 71**
SIGNED: 23 Nov 60   FORCE: 23 Nov 60
REGISTERED: 16 Jun 61 UK Great Britain
ARTICLES: 14 LANGUAGE: English. Indonesian.
HEADNOTE: AIR SERVICES BETWEEN BEYOND RESPECTIVE TERRITORIES
TOPIC: Air Transport
CONCEPTS: Definition of terms. Detailed regulations. Exceptions and exemptions. Annex or appendix reference. General cooperation. Arbitration. Procedure. Special tribunals. Negotiation. Monetary and gold transfers. Exchange rates and regulations. Non-interest rates and fees. Most favored nation clause. National treatment. Customs exemptions. Routes and logistics. Per-

mit designation. Conditions of airlines operating permission. Overflights and technical stops. Operating authorizations and regulations.
INTL ORGS: International Civil Aviation Organization. Arbitration Commission.
TREATY REF: 15UNTS295.
PROCEDURE: Amendment. Future Procedures Contemplated. Registration. Termination. Application to Non-self-governing Territories.
PARTIES:
Indonesia
UK Great Britain

105719   Bilateral Agreement   **398 UNTS 101**
SIGNED: 20 Jul 50   FORCE: 15 Jan 60
REGISTERED: 16 Jun 61 UK Great Britain
ARTICLES: 18 LANGUAGE: English. Spanish.
HEADNOTE: AIR SERVICES
TOPIC: Air Transport
CONCEPTS: Definition of terms. Detailed regulations. Exceptions and exemptions. Annex or appendix reference. Previous treaty replacement. Non-visa travel documents. Conformity with municipal law. General cooperation. Exchange of information and documents. Licenses and permits. Recognition of legal documents. Use of facilities. Arbitration. Procedure. Special tribunals. Negotiation. Fees and exemptions. Non-interest rates and fees. Most favored nation clause. National treatment. Customs exemptions. General transportation. Competency certificate. Navigational conditions. Permit designation. Airport facilities. Airworthiness certificates. Conditions of airlines operating permission. Overflights and technical stops. Operating authorizations and regulations.
INTL ORGS: International Civil Aviation Organization. Arbitration Commission.
PROCEDURE: Amendment. Future Procedures Contemplated. Ratification. Termination. Application to Non-self-governing Territories.
PARTIES:
Spain
UK Great Britain

105720   Bilateral Exchange   **398 UNTS 157**
SIGNED: 12 Jan 61   FORCE: 26 Jan 61
REGISTERED: 16 Jun 61 UK Great Britain
ARTICLES: 2 LANGUAGE: English. Russian.
HEADNOTE: MAGAZINE DISTRIBUTION
TOPIC: Culture
CONCEPTS: Detailed regulations. Import quotas. Publications exchange.
PROCEDURE: Denunciation. Duration.
PARTIES:
UK Great Britain
USSR (Soviet Union)

105721   Bilateral Exchange   **398 UNTS 165**
SIGNED: 14 Oct 60   FORCE: 14 Oct 60
REGISTERED: 16 Jun 61 UK Great Britain
ARTICLES: 2 LANGUAGE: English.
HEADNOTE: SPACE VEHICLE TRACKING STATION
TOPIC: Scientific Project
CONCEPTS: General cooperation. General property. Responsibility and liability. Research results. Communication satellites testing. Research and development. Indemnities and reimbursements. Special projects. Economic assistance. Facilities and equipment.
PARTIES:
UK Great Britain
USA (United States)

105722   Bilateral Exchange   **398 UNTS 179**
SIGNED: 9 May 63   FORCE: 9 May 53
REGISTERED: 16 Jun 61 UK Great Britain
ARTICLES: 2 LANGUAGE: English. Greek.
HEADNOTE: TRANSFER LAKE COPAIS ESTATE
TOPIC: Specific Property
CONCEPTS: General property. Indemnities and reimbursements. Assets transfer. Facilities and property.
PARTIES:
Greece
UK Great Britain

105723   Bilateral Agreement   **398 UNTS 189**
SIGNED: 17 Nov 60   FORCE: 3 Mar 61

REGISTERED: 16 Jun 61 UK Great Britain
ARTICLES: 9 LANGUAGE: English. Norwegian.
HEADNOTE: FISHERY AGREEMENT
TOPIC: Specific Resources
CONCEPTS: Definition of terms. Annex or appendix reference. National treatment. Markers and definitions. Fisheries and fishing.
INTL ORGS: United Nations.
PROCEDURE: Ratification.
PARTIES:
Norway
UK Great Britain

105724 Bilateral Exchange **398 UNTS 229**
SIGNED: 21 Feb 61 FORCE: 15 Mar 61
REGISTERED: 16 Jun 61 UK Great Britain
ARTICLES: 2 LANGUAGE: English. French.
HEADNOTE: ACCEPTANCE BRITISH VISITOR PASSPORT
TOPIC: Visas
CONCEPTS: Emergencies. Time limit. Annex or appendix reference. Passports non-diplomatic. Denial of admission. Nationality and citizenship. Conformity with municipal law.
PROCEDURE: Denunciation. Duration.
PARTIES:
Belgium
UK Great Britain
ANNEX
410 UNTS 367. UK Great Britain. Supplementation 23 May 61. Force 1 Jun 61.
410 UNTS 367. Belgium. Supplementation 23 May 61. Force 1 Jun 61.

105725 Bilateral Exchange **398 UNTS 235**
SIGNED: 21 Feb 61 FORCE: 15 Mar 61
REGISTERED: 16 Jun 61 UK Great Britain
ARTICLES: 2 LANGUAGE: English.
HEADNOTE: ACCEPTANCE BRITISH VISITOR PASSPORT
TOPIC: Visas
CONCEPTS: Emergencies. Territorial application. Time limit. Annex or appendix reference. Passports non-diplomatic. Denial of admission. Resident permits. Nationality and citizenship. Conformity with municipal law.
TREATY REF: 374UNTS277.
PROCEDURE: Denunciation. Duration.
PARTIES:
Netherlands
UK Great Britain

105726 Bilateral Exchange **398 UNTS 243**
SIGNED: 21 Feb 61 FORCE: 15 Mar 61
REGISTERED: 16 Jun 61 UK Great Britain
ARTICLES: 2 LANGUAGE: English. French.
HEADNOTE: ACCEPTANCE BRITISH VISITOR PASSPORT
TOPIC: Visas
CONCEPTS: Emergencies. Territorial application. Time limit. Passports non-diplomatic. Denial of admission. Nationality and citizenship. Conformity with municipal law.
TREATY REF: 374UNTS267.
PROCEDURE: Denunciation. Duration.
PARTIES:
Luxembourg
UK Great Britain
ANNEX
414 UNTS 415. Luxembourg. Supplementation 19 Jun 61. Force 19 Jun 61.
414 UNTS 415. UK Great Britain. Supplementation 15 May 61. Force 19 Jun 61.

105727 Bilateral Exchange **398 UNTS 249**
SIGNED: 20 Feb 61 FORCE: 20 Feb 61
REGISTERED: 16 Jun 61 UK Great Britain
ARTICLES: 2 LANGUAGE: English. German.
HEADNOTE: ACCEPTANCE BRITISH VISITOR PASSPORT
TOPIC: Visas
CONCEPTS: Emergencies. Territorial application. Time limit. Passports non-diplomatic. Denial of admission. Nationality and citizenship. Conformity with municipal law.
TREATY REF: 385UNTS55.
PROCEDURE: Duration. Termination.
PARTIES:
Germany, West
UK Great Britain
ANNEX
414 UNTS 419. Germany, West. Supplementation 24 Jun 61. Force 24 Jun 61.
414 UNTS 419. UK Great Britain. Supplementation 9 Jun 61. Force 24 Jun 61.

105728 Bilateral Exchange **398 UNTS 259**
SIGNED: 9 Feb 61 FORCE: 15 Mar 61
REGISTERED: 16 Jun 61 UK Great Britain
ARTICLES: 2 LANGUAGE: English.
HEADNOTE: ACCEPTANCE BRITISH VISITOR PASSPORT
TOPIC: Visas
CONCEPTS: Emergencies. Time limit. Annex or appendix reference. Passports non-diplomatic. Denial of admission. Resident permits. Nationality and citizenship. Conformity with municipal law.
PROCEDURE: Duration. Termination.
PARTIES:
Iceland
UK Great Britain
ANNEX
414 UNTS 424. Iceland. Supplementation 29 May 61. Force 29 May 61.
414 UNTS 424. UK Great Britain. Supplementation 29 May 61. Force 29 May 61.

105729 Bilateral Exchange **398 UNTS 267**
SIGNED: 14 Feb 61 FORCE: 15 Mar 61
REGISTERED: 16 Jun 61 UK Great Britain
ARTICLES: 2 LANGUAGE: English. French.
HEADNOTE: FACILITATE TRAVEL
TOPIC: Visas
CONCEPTS: Territorial application. Time limit. Annex or appendix reference. Passports non-diplomatic. Denial of admission. Resident permits. Conformity with municipal law.
INTL ORGS: Organization for Economic Co-operation and Development.
PROCEDURE: Duration. Termination.
PARTIES:
France
UK Great Britain
ANNEX
420 UNTS 353. France. Supplementation 26 Jun 61. Force 26 Jun 61.
420 UNTS 353. UK Great Britain. Supplementation 15 Jun 61. Force 26 Jun 61.

105730 Bilateral Exchange **398 UNTS 275**
SIGNED: 7 Jun 57 FORCE: 12 May 59
REGISTERED: 16 Jun 61 UK Great Britain
ARTICLES: 6 LANGUAGE: English. German.
HEADNOTE: DEFENSE COSTS
TOPIC: Milit Assistance
CONCEPTS: General military.
INTL ORGS: North Atlantic Treaty Organization.
PARTIES:
Germany, West
UK Great Britain

105731 Bilateral Exchange **398 UNTS 293**
SIGNED: 3 Oct 58 FORCE: 6 Jun 59
REGISTERED: 16 Jun 61 UK Great Britain
ARTICLES: 2 LANGUAGE: English. German.
HEADNOTE: LOCAL DEFENSE COSTS
TOPIC: Milit Assistance
CONCEPTS: General cooperation. Financial programs. Interest rates. Payment schedules. Defense and security. Payment for war supplies.
INTL ORGS: North Atlantic Treaty Organization.
TREATY REF: 34UNTS243.
PROCEDURE: Future Procedures Contemplated. Ratification.
PARTIES:
Germany, West
UK Great Britain

105732 Bilateral Treaty **399 UNTS 3**
SIGNED: 22 Jun 60 FORCE: 3 Mar 61
REGISTERED: 26 Jun 61 USSR (Soviet Union)
ARTICLES: 17 LANGUAGE: Russian. Korean.
HEADNOTE: TRADE NAVIGATION
TOPIC: General Economic
CONCEPTS: Exceptions and exemptions. Annex or appendix reference. Friendship and amity. Conformity with municipal law. Informational records. Juridical personality. Recognition and enforcement of legal decisions. Arbitration. Procedure. Existing tribunals. Export quotas. Import quotas. Reexport of goods, etc.. Trade agencies. Most favored nation clause. Customs duties. Customs exemptions. General transportation. Passenger transport. Licenses and certificates of nationality. Merchant vessels. Ports and pilotage. Shipwreck and salvage.
INTL ORGS: Arbitration Commission.
PROCEDURE: Ratification. Termination.
PARTIES:
Korea, North
USSR (Soviet Union)

105733 Bilateral Agreement **399 UNTS 37**
SIGNED: 27 Aug 60 FORCE: 2 Mar 61
REGISTERED: 26 Jun 61 USSR (Soviet Union)
ARTICLES: 6 LANGUAGE: Russian. Arabic.
HEADNOTE: COMPLETING CONSTRUCTION ASWAN HIGH DAM FINAL STAGE
TOPIC: Tech Assistance
CONCEPTS: Previous treaty extension. General cooperation. Scholarships and grants. Research and development. Interest rates. Payment schedules. Agriculture. Assistance. Economic assistance. Materials, equipment and services. Loan and credit. Loan repayment. Irrigation. Hydroelectric power. Regulation of natural resources.
TREATY REF: USSR UAR 27DEC1958;.
PROCEDURE: Ratification.
PARTIES:
United Arab Rep
USSR (Soviet Union)

105734 Bilateral Agreement **399 UNTS 61**
SIGNED: 4 Aug 60 FORCE: 23 Dec 60
REGISTERED: 26 Jun 61 USSR (Soviet Union)
ARTICLES: 10 LANGUAGE: Russian. English.
HEADNOTE: ECONOMIC TECHNICAL COOPERATION
TOPIC: General Aid
CONCEPTS: Treaty implementation. General cooperation. Exchange of information and documents. Personnel. Vocational training. Research and development. Accounting procedures. Banking. Indemnities and reimbursements. Exchange rates and regulations. Interest rates. Payment schedules. General technical assistance. Agriculture. Special projects. Economic assistance. Materials, equipment and services. Credit provisions.
PROCEDURE: Future Procedures Contemplated. Ratification.
PARTIES:
Ghana
USSR (Soviet Union)
ANNEX
421 UNTS 350. Ghana. Supplementation 23 Dec 60. Force 20 May 61.
421 UNTS 350. USSR (Soviet Union). Supplementation 23 Dec 60. Force 20 May 61.

105735 Bilateral Agreement **399 UNTS 75**
SIGNED: 9 Feb 60 FORCE: 10 Apr 61
REGISTERED: 26 Jun 61 USSR (Soviet Union)
ARTICLES: 16 LANGUAGE: Russian. Italian.
HEADNOTE: CULTURAL AGREEMENT
TOPIC: Culture
CONCEPTS: Treaty implementation. Friendship and amity. Tourism. Conformity with municipal law. General cooperation. Exchange of information and documents. Operating agencies. Establishment of commission. Specialists exchange. Recognition of degrees. Teacher and student exchange. Professorships. Exchange. General cultural cooperation. Artists. Athletes. Scientific exchange. Publications exchange. Mass media exchange.
INTL ORGS: Special Commission.
PROCEDURE: Denunciation. Duration. Future Procedures Contemplated. Ratification.
PARTIES:
Italy
USSR (Soviet Union)

105736 Bilateral Agreement **399 UNTS 93**
SIGNED: 11 Dec 59 FORCE: 11 May 60
REGISTERED: 30 Jun 61 Czechoslovakia
ARTICLES: 10 LANGUAGE: Czechoslovakian. Amharic. English.
HEADNOTE: CULTURAL COOPERATION
TOPIC: Culture
CONCEPTS: Treaty implementation. Friendship and amity. General cooperation. Exchange of information and documents. Specialists exchange. Recognition of degrees. Exchange. Teacher and student exchange. Scholarships and grants. Exchange. General cultural cooper-

ation. Artists. Athletes. Scientific exchange. Publications exchange. Mass media exchange.
PROCEDURE: Duration. Ratification. Renewal or Revival. Termination.
PARTIES:
Czechoslovakia
Ethiopia

105737 Bilateral Agreement **399 UNTS 105**
SIGNED: 12 Dec 60   FORCE: 8 Jun 61
REGISTERED: 30 Jun 61 WHO (World Health)
ARTICLES: 6 LANGUAGE: French.
HEADNOTE: TECHNICAL ADVISORY ASSISTANCE
TOPIC: Tech Assistance
CONCEPTS: Definition of terms. Privileges and immunities. General cooperation. Exchange of information and documents. Personnel. Responsibility and liability. Title and deeds. Exchange. Scholarships and grants. Vocational training. Research and development. Expense sharing formulae. Local currency. Domestic obligation. Special projects. Materials, equipment and services. IGO status. Conformity with IGO decisions.
INTL ORGS: United Nations.
TREATY REF: 33UNTS261.
PROCEDURE: Amendment. Termination.
PARTIES:
Congo (Brazzaville)
WHO (World Health)

105738 Bilateral Agreement **399 UNTS 117**
SIGNED: 22 Jun 61   FORCE: 22 Jun 61
REGISTERED: 1 Jul 61 United Nations
ARTICLES: 10 LANGUAGE: English. Spanish.
HEADNOTE: ASSISTANCE
TOPIC: Direct Aid
CONCEPTS: Detailed regulations. Treaty implementation. Visas. Privileges and immunities. Exchange of information and documents. Informational records. Inspection and observation. Operating agencies. Personnel. Public information. Responsibility and liability. Title and deeds. Use of facilities. Arbitration. Procedure. Negotiation. Import quotas. Attachment of funds. Exchange rates and regulations. Expense sharing formulae. Financial programs. Domestic obligation. General technical assistance. Economic assistance. Materials, equipment and services. IGO status.
INTL ORGS: International Atomic Energy Agency. International Court of Justice. United Nations. Arbitration Commission.
TREATY REF: 1UNTS15; 33UNTS261; 374UNTS147.
PROCEDURE: Amendment. Termination.
PARTIES:
Paraguay
UN Special Fund

105739 Bilateral Agreement **399 UNTS 141**
SIGNED: 28 Jun 61   FORCE: 28 Jun 61
REGISTERED: 1 Jul 61 United Nations
ARTICLES: 10 LANGUAGE: English.
HEADNOTE: ASSISTANCE
TOPIC: Direct Aid
CONCEPTS: Detailed regulations. Treaty implementation. Annex or appendix reference. Visas. Privileges and immunities. Exchange of information and documents. Informational records. Inspection and observation. Operating agencies. Personnel. Public information. Responsibility and liability. Title and deeds. Use of facilities. Arbitration. Procedure. Negotiation. Import quotas. Attachment of funds. Exchange rates and regulations. Expense sharing formulae. Financial programs. Domestic obligation. General technical assistance. Economic assistance. Materials, equipment and services. IGO status.
INTL ORGS: International Atomic Energy Agency. International Court of Justice. United Nations. Arbitration Commission.
TREATY REF: 1UNTS15; 33UNTS261; 374UNTS147.
PROCEDURE: Amendment. Termination.
PARTIES:
Philippines
UN Special Fund

105740 Bilateral Agreement **399 UNTS 159**
SIGNED: 28 Jun 61   FORCE: 28 Jun 61
REGISTERED: 1 Jul 61 United Nations

ARTICLES: 6 LANGUAGE: French.
HEADNOTE: PROVISION EXPERTS OPERATIONAL EXECUTIVE PERSONNEL
TOPIC: Tech Assistance
CONCEPTS: Treaty implementation. Annex or appendix reference. Privileges and immunities. Personnel. Responsibility and liability. Arbitration. Procedure. Negotiation. Vocational training. Compensation. Expense sharing formulae. Tax exemptions. Customs exemptions. Domestic obligation. Special projects. Status of experts. Conformity with IGO decisions.
INTL ORGS: Permanent Court of Arbitration. Arbitration Commission.
PROCEDURE: Amendment. Termination.
PARTIES:
Haiti
United Nations

105741 Bilateral Agreement **399 UNTS 171**
SIGNED: 28 Jun 61   FORCE: 28 Jun 61
REGISTERED: 1 Jul 61 United Nations
ARTICLES: 10 LANGUAGE: English. French.
HEADNOTE: ASSISTANCE
TOPIC: Direct Aid
CONCEPTS: Detailed regulations. Treaty implementation. Visas. Privileges and immunities. Exchange of information and documents. Informational records. Inspection and observation. Operating agencies. Personnel. Public information. Responsibility and liability. Title and deeds. Use of facilities. Arbitration. Procedure. Negotiation. Import quotas. Attachment of funds. Exchange rates and regulations. Expense sharing formulae. Financial programs. Domestic obligation. General technical assistance. Economic assistance. Materials, equipment and services. IGO status.
INTL ORGS: International Atomic Energy Agency. International Court of Justice. United Nations. Arbitration Commission.
TREATY REF: 1UNTS15; 33UNTS261; 374UNTS147.
PROCEDURE: Amendment. Termination.
PARTIES:
Haiti
UN Special Fund

105742 Multilateral Convention **399 UNTS 189**
SIGNED: 19 May 56   FORCE: 2 Jul 61
REGISTERED: 2 Jul 61 United Nations
ARTICLES: 51 LANGUAGE: English. French.
HEADNOTE: CONTRACT INTERNATIONAL CARRIAGE GOODS ROAD
TOPIC: Land Transport
CONCEPTS: Conditions. Detailed regulations. Exceptions and exemptions. Territorial application. Time limit. Conformity with municipal law. Recognition of legal documents. Private contracts. Responsibility and liability. Arbitration. Procedure. Negotiation. Compensation. Indemnities and reimbursements. Currency. Exchange rates and regulations. Fees and exemptions. Interest rates. Claims and settlements. Dangerous goods. Goods in transit. Transport of goods. Commercial road vehicles. Roads and highways. Road rules. Paragraph 2, Article 36.
INTL ORGS: International Court of Justice. United Nations.
TREATY REF: 125UNTS3.
PROCEDURE: Amendment. Accession. Denunciation. Ratification. Termination.
PARTIES:
Austria SIGNED: 19 May 56 RATIFIED: 18 Jul 60 FORCE: 2 Jul 61
Belgium SIGNED: 19 May 56
Bulgaria SIGNED: 19 May 56
France   SIGNED: 19 May 56   RATIFIED: 20 May 59 FORCE: 2 Jul 61
Germany, West SIGNED: 19 May 56
Luxembourg SIGNED: 19 May 56
Netherlands SIGNED: 19 May 56 RATIFIED: 27 Sep 60 FORCE: 2 Jul 61
Poland SIGNED: 19 May 56
Sweden SIGNED: 19 May 56
Switzerland SIGNED: 19 May 56
Yugoslavia   SIGNED: 19 May 56   RATIFIED: 22 Oct 58 FORCE: 2 Jul 61
ANNEX
412 UNTS 354. Germany, West. Qualified Ratification 7 Nov 61. Force 5 Feb 62.
430 UNTS 501. Poland. Qualified Ratification 13 Jun 62. Force 11 Sep 62.

437 UNTS 369. Belgium. Ratification 18 Sep 62. Force 17 Dec 62.
493 UNTS 326.   Luxembourg.   Ratification 20 Apr 64. Force 19 Jul 64.
540 UNTS 337. Denmark. Accession 28 Jun 65. Force 26 Sep 65.
601 UNTS 356. UK Great Britain. Accession 21 Jul 67. Force 19 Oct 67.
649 UNTS 346. UK Great Britain. Gibralter. Force 29 Jan 69.

105743 Bilateral Exchange **399 UNTS 239**
SIGNED: 19 Jun 61   FORCE: 19 Jun 61
REGISTERED: 6 Jul 61 UK Great Britain
ARTICLES: 2 LANGUAGE: English. Arabic.
HEADNOTE: RELATIONS
TOPIC: General Amity
CONCEPTS: Previous treaty replacement. Friendship and amity. General cooperation.
TREATY REF: AGREEMENT-23JAN1899.
PROCEDURE: Termination.
PARTIES:
Kuwait
UK Great Britain
ANNEX
649 UNTS 347. Kuwait. Termination 13 May 68. Force 13 May 68.
649 UNTS 347. UK Great Britain. Termination 13 May 68. Force 13 May 68.

105744 Bilateral Agreement **400 UNTS 3**
SIGNED: 26 Jun 61   FORCE: 26 Jun 61
REGISTERED: 7 Jul 61 United Nations
ARTICLES: 10 LANGUAGE: English. French.
HEADNOTE: ASSISTANCE
TOPIC: Direct Aid
CONCEPTS: Detailed regulations. Treaty implementation. Visas. Privileges and immunities. Exchange of information and documents. Informational records. Inspection and observation. Operating agencies. Personnel. Public information. Responsibility and liability. Title and deeds. Use of facilities. Arbitration. Procedure. Negotiation. Import quotas. Attachment of funds. Expense sharing formulae. Financial programs. Exchange rates and regulations. Domestic obligation. General technical assistance. Economic assistance. Materials, equipment and services. IGO status.
INTL ORGS: International Court of Justice.
TREATY   REF: 1UNTS15;   33UNTS261; 374UNTS147.
PROCEDURE: Amendment. Termination.
PARTIES:
UN Special Fund
Upper Volta

105745 Bilateral Exchange **400 UNTS 21**
SIGNED: 19 Sep 60   FORCE: 19 Sep 60
REGISTERED: 7 Jul 61 USA (United States)
ARTICLES: 2 LANGUAGE: English. French.
HEADNOTE: WEAPONS PRODUCTION PROGRAM
TOPIC: Milit Assistance
CONCEPTS: Change of circumstances. Previous treaty replacement. General cooperation. Licenses and permits. Private contracts. Use of facilities. Indemnities and reimbursements. Customs exemptions. Materials, equipment and services. Defense and security. Security of information. Exchange of defense information. Equipment and supplies. Restrictions on transfer.
INTL ORGS: North Atlantic Treaty Organization.
TREATY REF: 341NTS243.
PROCEDURE: Future Procedures Contemplated.
PARTIES:
France
USA (United States)

105746 Bilateral Agreement **400 UNTS 35**
SIGNED: 5 Nov 60   FORCE: 5 Nov 60
REGISTERED: 7 Jul 61 USA (United States)
ARTICLES: 6 LANGUAGE: English.
HEADNOTE: AGRI COMMOD TITLE I
TOPIC: US Agri Commod Aid
CONCEPTS: General provisions. Annex or appendix reference. Exchange of information and documents. Reexport of goods, etc.. Exchange rates and regulations. Transportation costs. Local currency. Commodities schedule. Purchase authori-

zation. Surplus commodities. Mutual consultation.
PARTIES:
  Indonesia
  USA (United States)
ANNEX
405 UNTS 374. USA (United States). Supplementation 2 Mar 61. Force 2 Mar 61.
405 UNTS 374. Indonesia. Supplementation
  2 Mar 61. Force 2 Mar 61.
421 UNTS 366. USA (United States). Amendment
  8 Sep 61. Force 8 Sep 61.
421 UNTS 366. Indonesia. Amendment 8 Sep 61.
  Force 8 Sep 61.

105747   Bilateral Exchange   **400 UNTS 49**
SIGNED: 18 Nov 60   FORCE: 18 Nov 60
REGISTERED: 7 Jul 61 USA (United States)
ARTICLES: 2 LANGUAGE: English.
HEADNOTE: GRANT NUCLEAR RESEARCH TRAIN-
ING MATERIALS
TOPIC: Atomic Energy
CONCEPTS: Guarantees and safeguards. Ex-
change of information and documents. Public in-
formation. Responsibility and liability. Indemni-
ties and reimbursements. Funding procedures.
Payment schedules. Grants. Atomic energy as-
sistance. Non-nuclear materials. Peaceful use.
Transport of goods.
PARTIES:
  Korea, South
  USA (United States)

105748   Bilateral Agreement   **400 UNTS 57**
SIGNED: 7 Nov 60   FORCE: 7 Nov 60
REGISTERED: 7 Jul 61 USA (United States)
ARTICLES: 6 LANGUAGE: English.
HEADNOTE: AGRI COMMOD TITLE I
TOPIC: US Agri Commod Aid
CONCEPTS: General provisions. Annex or appen-
dix reference. Exchange of information and doc-
uments. Reexport of goods, etc.. Exchange rates
and regulations. Transportation costs. Local cur-
rency. Commodities schedule. Purchase authori-
zation. Surplus commodities. Mutual consulta-
tion.
PARTIES:
  Greece
  USA (United States)
ANNEX
411 UNTS 336. USA (United States). Amendment
  22 Jun 61. Force 22 Jun 61.
411 UNTS 336. Greece. Amendment 22 Jun 61.
  Force 22 Jun 61.

105749   Bilateral Agreement   **400 UNTS 73**
SIGNED: 16 Jan 61   FORCE: 14 Jun 61
REGISTERED: 12 Jul 61 IBRD (World Bank)
ARTICLES: 5 LANGUAGE: English.
HEADNOTE: GUARANTEE RAILWAY
TOPIC: IBRD Project
CONCEPTS: Definition of terms. Annex or appen-
dix reference. Exchange of information and doc-
uments. Inspection and observation. Bonds.
Fees and exemptions. Tax exemptions. Domestic
obligation. Terms of loan. Loan regulations. Loan
guarantee. Guarantor non-interference. Rail-
ways.
PARTIES:
  Burma
  IBRD (World Bank)

105750   Bilateral Agreement   **400 UNTS 99**
SIGNED: 29 Jun 60   FORCE: 7 Apr 61
REGISTERED: 12 Jul 61 IBRD (World Bank)
ARTICLES: 5 LANGUAGE: English.
HEADNOTE: GUARANTEE AGREEMENT
TOPIC: IBRD Project
CONCEPTS: Definition of terms. Annex or appen-
dix reference. Exchange of information and doc-
uments. Inspection and observation. Bonds.
Fees and exemptions. Tax exemptions. Domestic
obligation. Terms of loan. Loan regulations. Loan
guarantee. Guarantor non-interference.
PARTIES:
  Peru
  IBRD (World Bank)

105751   Bilateral Agreement   **400 UNTS 137**
SIGNED: 29 Jun 60   FORCE: 13 Jan 61
REGISTERED: 12 Jul 61 IBRD (World Bank)
ARTICLES: 5 LANGUAGE: English.
HEADNOTE: GUARANTEE   HYDROELECTRIC
PROJECT
TOPIC: IBRD Project
CONCEPTS: Definition of terms. Annex or appen-
dix reference. Exchange of information and doc-
uments. Inspection and observation. Bonds.
Fees and exemptions. Tax exemptions. Domestic
obligation. Terms of loan. Loan regulations. Loan
guarantee. Guarantor non-interference.
PARTIES:
  Honduras
  IBRD (World Bank)

105752   Bilateral Agreement   **400 UNTS 167**
SIGNED: 20 Dec 60   FORCE: 20 Jan 61
REGISTERED: 13 Jul 61 IBRD (World Bank)
ARTICLES: 5 LANGUAGE: English.
HEADNOTE: GUARANTEE AGREEMENT
TOPIC: IBRD Project
CONCEPTS: Definition of terms. Annex or appen-
dix reference. Exchange of information and doc-
uments. Inspection and observation. Bonds.
Fees and exemptions. Tax exemptions. Domestic
obligation. Terms of loan. Loan regulations. Loan
guarantee. Guarantor non-interference.
PARTIES:
  Japan
  IBRD (World Bank)

105753   Bilateral Agreement   **400 UNTS 201**
SIGNED: 16 Mar 61   FORCE: 3 May 61
REGISTERED: 14 Jul 61 IBRD (World Bank)
ARTICLES: 5 LANGUAGE: English.
HEADNOTE: GUARANTEE POWER
TOPIC: IBRD Project
CONCEPTS: Definition of terms. Annex or appen-
dix reference. Exchange of information and doc-
uments. Inspection and observation. Bonds.
Fees and exemptions. Tax exemptions. Domestic
obligation. Terms of loan. Loan regulations. Loan
guarantee. Guarantor non-interference. Hydro-
electric power.
PARTIES:
  Japan
  IBRD (World Bank)

105754   Bilateral Agreement   **400 UNTS 279**
SIGNED: 20 Dec 60   FORCE: 20 Jan 61
REGISTERED: 14 Jul 61 IBRD (World Bank)
ARTICLES: 5 LANGUAGE: English.
HEADNOTE: GUARANTEE AGREEMENT
TOPIC: IBRD Project
CONCEPTS: Default remedies. Annex or appendix
reference. Exchange of information and docu-
ments. Informational records. Inspection and ob-
servation. Accounting procedures. Bonds. Fees
and exemptions. Interest rates. Tax exemptions.
Domestic obligation. Terms of loan. Loan regula-
tions. Loan guarantee. Guarantor non-interfer-
ence.
PARTIES:
  Japan
  IBRD (World Bank)

105755   Bilateral Exchange   **400 UNTS 315**
SIGNED: 31 Mar 60   FORCE: 31 Mar 60
REGISTERED: 17 Jul 61 USA (United States)
ARTICLES: 2 LANGUAGE: English.
HEADNOTE: DISPOSAL PIPELINE FACILITIES
TOPIC: Specif Goods/Equip
CONCEPTS: Annex or appendix reference. Facili-
ties and property.
TREATY REF: 206UNTS93; 99UNTS273.
PARTIES:
  Canada
  USA (United States)

105756   Bilateral Agreement   **400 UNTS 323**
SIGNED: 4 Nov 60   FORCE: 4 Nov 60
REGISTERED: 17 Jul 61 USA (United States)
ARTICLES: 6 LANGUAGE: English. French.
HEADNOTE: AGRI COMMOD TITLE I
TOPIC: US Agri Commod Aid
CONCEPTS: General provisions. Annex or appen-
dix reference. Exchange of information and doc-
uments. Reexport of goods, etc.. Exchange rates
and regulations. Transportation costs. Local cur-
rency. Commodities schedule. Purchase authori-
zation. Surplus commodities. Mutual consulta-
tion.
PARTIES:
  France
  USA (United States)

105757   Bilateral Agreement   **400 UNTS 339**
SIGNED: 17 Aug 60   FORCE: 1 Jan 61
REGISTERED: 17 Jul 61 USA (United States)
ARTICLES: 19 LANGUAGE: English. Korean.
HEADNOTE: INSURED PARCEL POST
TOPIC: Postal Service
CONCEPTS: Conformity with municipal law. Do-
mestic legislation. Responsibility and liability.
Sickness and invalidity insurance. Compensa-
tion. Payment schedules. Claims and settle-
ments. Postal services. Regulations. Insured let-
ters and boxes.
TREATY REF: 364UNTS3; 391UNTS3.
PROCEDURE: Duration. Termination.
PARTIES:
  Korea, South
  USA (United States)

105758   Bilateral Agreement   **401 UNTS 3**
SIGNED: 28 Oct 60   FORCE: 28 Oct 60
REGISTERED: 17 Jul 61 USA (United States)
ARTICLES: 6 LANGUAGE: English.
HEADNOTE: AGRI COMMOD TITLE I
TOPIC: US Agri Commod Aid
CONCEPTS: General provisions. Annex or appendix reference. Exchange of information and documents. Reexport of goods, etc.. Exchange rates
and regulations. Transportation costs. Local currency. Commodities schedule. Purchase authorization. Surplus commodities. Mutual consultation.
PARTIES:
  USA (United States)
  Vietnam, South
ANNEX
433 UNTS 382. USA (United States). Amendment
  24 Jan 62. Force 24 Jan 62.
433 UNTS 382. Vietnam, South. Amendment
  24 Jan 62. Force 24 Jan 62.

105759   Bilateral Exchange   **401 UNTS 19**
SIGNED: 9 Dec 60   FORCE: 9 Dec 60
REGISTERED: 17 Jul 61 USA (United States)
ARTICLES: 2 LANGUAGE: English.
HEADNOTE: CULTURAL RELATIONS
TOPIC: Culture
CONCEPTS: Detailed regulations. Annex or appen-
dix reference. Tourism. Non-diplomatic delega-
tions. Conformity with municipal law. General
cooperation. Exchange. Teacher and student ex-
change. Exchange. General cultural cooperation.
Artists. Athletes. Research cooperation. Scien-
tific exchange. Publications exchange. Mass me-
dia exchange.
PROCEDURE: Future Procedures Contemplated.
PARTIES:
  Romania
  USA (United States)

105760   Bilateral Exchange   **401 UNTS 33**
SIGNED: 22 Dec 60   FORCE: 22 Dec 60
REGISTERED: 17 Jul 61 USA (United States)
ARTICLES: 2 LANGUAGE: English. French.
HEADNOTE: ECONOMIC ASSISTANCE
TOPIC: Direct Aid
CONCEPTS: Change of circumstances. Diplomatic
privileges. Conformity with municipal law. General cooperation. Exchange of information and
documents. Inspection and observation. Personnel. Accounting procedures. Attachment of
funds. Currency deposits. Exchange rates and
regulations. Funding procedures. Garnishment
of funds. Seizure funds. Local currency. Tax exemptions. Customs exemptions. Commodities
and services. Domestic obligation. General technical assistance. Economic assistance. Materials, equipment and services. Aid missions.
Grants. Procurement.
PROCEDURE: Termination.

PARTIES:
Togo
USA (United States)

105761 Bilateral Exchange **401 UNTS 43**
SIGNED: 30 Dec 60 FORCE: 30 Dec 60
REGISTERED: 17 Jul 61 USA (United States)
ARTICLES: 2 LANGUAGE: English.
HEADNOTE: ECONOMIC ASSISTANCE
TOPIC: Direct Aid
CONCEPTS: Import quotas. Currency deposits. Financial programs. Purchase authorizations. Local currency. Economic assistance. Grants.
TREATY REF: 20UNTS141; 233UNTS316.
PROCEDURE: Future Procedures Contemplated.
PARTIES:
Iceland
USA (United States)

105762 Bilateral Exchange **401 UNTS 51**
SIGNED: 21 Sep 59 FORCE: 1 Jan 59
REGISTERED: 18 Jul 61 New Zealand
ARTICLES: 2 LANGUAGE: English.
HEADNOTE: FINANCIAL ARRANGEMENTS DEFENSE FIJI
TOPIC: Milit Assistance
CONCEPTS: Accounting procedures. Indemnities and reimbursements. Self-defense. Payment for war supplies. Lease of military property. Surplus war property.
TREATY REF: 162UNTS197.
PROCEDURE: Renewal or Revival.
PARTIES:
New Zealand
UK Great Britain
ANNEX
521 UNTS 397. New Zealand. Prolongation 4 Apr 64. Force 31 Dec 63.

105763 Bilateral Agreement **401 UNTS 59**
SIGNED: 4 Jul 56 FORCE: 1 Feb 61
REGISTERED: 20 Jul 61 Philippines
ARTICLES: 14 LANGUAGE: English. Indonesian.
HEADNOTE: IMMIGRATION
TOPIC: Admin Cooperation
CONCEPTS: Border traffic and migration. Resident permits. Frontier permits. Repatriation of nationals. Conformity with municipal law. General cooperation. Frontier crossing points.
PROCEDURE: Amendment. Duration. Ratification. Renewal or Revival.
PARTIES:
Indonesia
Philippines

105764 Bilateral Convention **401 UNTS 75**
SIGNED: 25 Nov 59 FORCE: 21 Dec 60
REGISTERED: 20 Jul 61 USA (United States)
ARTICLES: 18 LANGUAGE: English. French.
HEADNOTE: ESTABLISHMENT
TOPIC: Admin Cooperation
CONCEPTS: Definition of terms. Exceptions and exemptions. Territorial application. Treaty interpretation. Previous treaty replacement. Alien status. Protection of nationals. Conformity with municipal law. Exchange of information and documents. Expropriation. Arbitration. Procedure. Compensation. Exchange rates and regulations. National treatment.
TREATY REF: U.S.A. TS 94; STAT.771.
PROCEDURE: Duration. Ratification. Termination.
PARTIES:
France
USA (United States)

105765 Bilateral Exchange **401 UNTS 105**
SIGNED: 28 Mar 60 FORCE: 28 Mar 60
REGISTERED: 20 Jul 61 USA (United States)
ARTICLES: 2 LANGUAGE: English. Spanish.
HEADNOTE: TRACKING STATION
TOPIC: Scientific Project
CONCEPTS: Annex type material. General cooperation. Research and scientific projects. Research cooperation. Research and development. Economic assistance.
PARTIES:
Chile
USA (United States)

ANNEX
410 UNTS 384. USA (United States). Supplementation 21 Apr 61. Force 10 May 61.
410 UNTS 384. Chile. Supplementation 10 May 61. Force 10 May 61.
442 UNTS 338. USA (United States). Amendment 25 Oct 61. Force 18 Nov 61.
442 UNTS 338. Chile. Amendment 18 Nov 61. Force 18 Nov 61.

105766 Bilateral Agreement **401 UNTS 115**
SIGNED: 27 Sep 60 FORCE: 27 Sep 60
REGISTERED: 20 Jul 61 USA (United States)
ARTICLES: 5 LANGUAGE: English. Spanish.
HEADNOTE: AGRI COMMOD TITLE I
TOPIC: US Agri Commod Aid
CONCEPTS: General provisions. Annex or appendix reference. Exchange of information and documents. Reexport of goods, etc.. Exchange rates and regulations. Transportation costs. Local currency. Commodities schedule. Purchase authorization. Surplus commodities. Mutual consultation.
PARTIES:
Ecuador
USA (United States)

105767 Bilateral Agreement **401 UNTS 137**
SIGNED: 24 Oct 60 FORCE: 24 Oct 60
REGISTERED: 20 Jul 61 USA (United States)
ARTICLES: 1 LANGUAGE: English. Spanish.
HEADNOTE: CONSTRUCTION AMISTAD DAM
TOPIC: Specific Property
CONCEPTS: Non-bank projects. Irrigation. Hydroelectric power. Facilities and property.
TREATY REF: 3UNTS313.
PARTIES:
Mexico
USA (United States)

105768 Bilateral Agreement **401 UNTS 141**
SIGNED: 21 Jul 61 FORCE: 21 Jul 61
REGISTERED: 21 Jul 61 United Nations
ARTICLES: 10 LANGUAGE: English. French.
HEADNOTE: ASSISTANCE
TOPIC: Direct Aid
CONCEPTS: Detailed regulations. Treaty implementation. Visas. Privileges and immunities. Exchange of information and documents. Informational records. Inspection and observation. Operating agencies. Personnel. Public information. Responsibility and liability. Title and deeds. Use of facilities. Arbitration. Procedure. Negotiation. Import quotas. Attachment of funds. Exchange rates and regulations. Expense sharing formulae. Financial programs. Domestic obligation. General technical assistance. Economic assistance. Materials, equipment and services. IGO status.
INTL ORGS: International Court of Justice.
TREATY REF: 1UNTS15; 33UNTS261; 374UNTS147.
PROCEDURE: Amendment. Termination.
PARTIES:
Mali
UN Special Fund

105769 Bilateral Agreement **401 UNTS 159**
SIGNED: 25 Jul 61 FORCE: 25 Jul 61
REGISTERED: 25 Jul 61 United Nations
ARTICLES: 10 LANGUAGE: English.
HEADNOTE: ASSISTANCE SPECIAL FUND
TOPIC: Direct Aid
CONCEPTS: Arbitration. Aid and development. Grants. Conditions of airlines operating permission.
INTL ORGS: International Court of Justice.
PROCEDURE: Termination.
PARTIES:
Fed of Malaya
UN Special Fund
ANNEX
484 UNTS 412. UN Special Fund. Supplementation 19 Dec 63.
484 UNTS 412. Fed of Malaya. Supplementation 28 Dec 63. Force 28 Dec 63.

105770 Bilateral Exchange **401 UNTS 177**
SIGNED: 28 Oct 60 FORCE: 28 Oct 60
REGISTERED: 28 Jul 61 USA (United States)
ARTICLES: 2 LANGUAGE: English. Spanish.
HEADNOTE: EMERGENCY RELIEF ASSISTANCE
TOPIC: Direct Aid
CONCEPTS: Accounting procedures. Exchange

rates and regulations. Financial programs. Local currency. Relief supplies. Grants.
PROCEDURE: Termination.
PARTIES:
Chile
USA (United States)

105771 Bilateral Exchange **401 UNTS 185**
SIGNED: 27 Dec 60 FORCE: 27 Dec 60
REGISTERED: 28 Jul 61 USA (United States)
ARTICLES: 2 LANGUAGE: English.
HEADNOTE: PASSPORT VISAS
TOPIC: Visas
CONCEPTS: Visas. Fees and exemptions.
PROCEDURE: Amendment. Termination.
PARTIES:
Kuwait
USA (United States)

105772 Bilateral Exchange **401 UNTS 195**
SIGNED: 19 Dec 60 FORCE: 19 Dec 60
REGISTERED: 28 Jul 61 USA (United States)
ARTICLES: 2 LANGUAGE: English.
HEADNOTE: GRANT NUCLEAR RESEARCH TRAINING EQUIPMENT
TOPIC: Direct Aid
CONCEPTS: Exchange of information and documents. Public information. Responsibility and liability. Indemnities and reimbursements. Funding procedures. Payment schedules. Transportation costs. Grants. Procurement. Atomic energy assistance. Non-nuclear materials. Peaceful use. Transport of goods.
PARTIES:
Israel
USA (United States)

105773 Bilateral Agreement **402 UNTS 3**
SIGNED: 28 Dec 60 FORCE: 28 Dec 60
REGISTERED: 28 Jul 61 USA (United States)
ARTICLES: 5 LANGUAGE: English.
HEADNOTE: AGRI COMMOD TITLE I
TOPIC: US Agri Commod Aid
CONCEPTS: General provisions. Annex or appendix reference. Exchange of information and documents. Reexport of goods, etc.. Exchange rates and regulations. Transportation costs. Local currency. Commodities schedule. Purchase authorization. Surplus commodities. Mutual consultation.
PARTIES:
Korea, South
USA (United States)
ANNEX
405 UNTS 380. USA (United States). Amendment 17 Mar 61. Force 17 Mar 61.
405 UNTS 380. Korea, South. Amendment 17 Mar 61. Force 17 Mar 61.
406 UNTS 356. USA (United States). Amendment 17 Mar 61. Force 17 Mar 61.
406 UNTS 356. Korea, South. Amendment 17 Mar 61. Force 17 Mar 61.
409 UNTS 352. USA (United States). Amendment 11 May 61. Force 11 May 61.
409 UNTS 352. Korea, South. Amendment 11 May 61. Force 11 May 61.

105774 Bilateral Exchange **402 UNTS 17**
SIGNED: 5 Jul 60 FORCE: 5 Jul 60
REGISTERED: 28 Jul 61 Ghana
ARTICLES: 2 LANGUAGE: English.
HEADNOTE: JURISDICTION COURTS
TOPIC: Admin Cooperation
CONCEPTS: General cooperation. Competence of tribunal.
PARTIES:
Ghana
UK Great Britain

105775 Bilateral Agreement **402 UNTS 23**
SIGNED: 17 Nov 60 FORCE: 23 Jun 61
REGISTERED: 1 Aug 61 United Nations
ARTICLES: 8 LANGUAGE: French.
HEADNOTE: ACTIVITIES UNICEF
TOPIC: Direct Aid
CONCEPTS: Treaty implementation. Privileges and immunities. General cooperation. Exchange of information and documents. Informational records. Public information. Responsibility and

liability. Title and deeds. Claims and settlements. Tax exemptions. Customs exemptions. Domestic obligation. Assistance. General aid. Materials, equipment and services. Distribution. IGO status.
TREATY REF: 1UNTS15.
PARTIES:
Mali
UNICEF (Children)
ANNEX
474 UNTS 348. UNICEF (Children). Correction 17 Apr 63.
474 UNTS 348. Mali. Correction 15 May 63.

105776 Bilateral Agreement **402 UNTS 33**
SIGNED: 15 Nov 60 FORCE: 23 Jun 61
REGISTERED: 1 Aug 61 United Nations
ARTICLES: 8 LANGUAGE: French.
HEADNOTE: ACTIVITIES UNICEF
TOPIC: Direct Aid
CONCEPTS: Treaty implementation. Privileges and immunities. General cooperation. Exchange of information and documents. Informational records. Public information. Responsibility and liability. Title and deeds. Claims and settlements. Tax exemptions. Customs exemptions. Domestic obligation. Assistance. General aid. Materials, equipment and services. Distribution. IGO status.
TREATY REF: 1UNTS15.
PROCEDURE: Amendment. Termination.
PARTIES:
UNICEF (Children)
Upper Volta

105777 Bilateral Agreement **402 UNTS 43**
SIGNED: 2 Aug 61 FORCE: 2 Aug 61
REGISTERED: 2 Aug 61 United Nations
ARTICLES: 10 LANGUAGE: English. Arabic.
HEADNOTE: ASSISTANCE
TOPIC: Direct Aid
CONCEPTS: Detailed regulations. Treaty implementation. Visas. Privileges and immunities. Exchange of information and documents. Informational records. Inspection and observation. Operating agencies. Personnel. Public information. Responsibility and liability. Title and deeds. Use of facilities. Arbitration. Procedure. Negotiation. Import quotas. Attachment of funds. Exchange rates and regulations. Expense sharing formulae. Financial programs. Domestic obligation. General technical assistance. Economic assistance. Materials, equipment and services. IGO status.
INTL ORGS: International Court of Justice.
TREATY REF: 1UNTS15; 33UNTS261; 374UNTS147.
PROCEDURE: Amendment. Termination.
PARTIES:
UN Special Fund
Yemen

105778 Multilateral Treaty **402 UNTS 71**
SIGNED: 1 Dec 59 FORCE: 23 Jun 61
REGISTERED: 4 Aug 61 USA (United States)
ARTICLES: 14 LANGUAGE: English. French. Russian. Spanish.
HEADNOTE: ANTARTIC TREATY
TOPIC: Territory Boundary
CONCEPTS: Inspection and observation. Procedure. Research cooperation. Scientific exchange. Research and development. Compulsory jurisdiction. Boundaries of territory.
PROCEDURE: Accession. Ratification. Registration.
PARTIES:
Argentina SIGNED: 1 Dec 59 RATIFIED: 23 Jun 61 FORCE: 23 Jun 61
Australia SIGNED: 1 Dec 59 RATIFIED: 23 Jun 61 FORCE: 23 Jun 61
Belgium SIGNED: 1 Dec 59 RATIFIED: 26 Jul 60 FORCE: 23 Jun 61
Chile SIGNED: 1 Dec 59 RATIFIED: 23 Jun 61 FORCE: 23 Jun 61
France SIGNED: 1 Dec 59 RATIFIED: 16 Sep 60 FORCE: 23 Jun 61
Japan SIGNED: 1 Dec 59 RATIFIED: 4 Aug 60 FORCE: 23 Jun 61
New Zealand SIGNED: 1 Dec 59 RATIFIED: 1 Nov 60 FORCE: 23 Jun 61
Norway SIGNED: 1 Dec 59 RATIFIED: 20 Aug 60 FORCE: 23 Jun 61
Poland SIGNED: 1 Dec 59 RATIFIED: 8 Jun 61 FORCE: 23 Jun 61

South Africa SIGNED: 1 Dec 59 RATIFIED: 21 Jun 60 FORCE: 23 Jun 61
UK Great Britain SIGNED: 1 Dec 59 RATIFIED: 31 May 60 FORCE: 23 Jun 61
USA (United States) SIGNED: 1 Dec 59 RATIFIED: 18 Aug 60 FORCE: 23 Jun 61
USSR (Soviet Union) SIGNED: 1 Dec 59 RATIFIED: 2 Nov 60 FORCE: 23 Jun 61
ANNEX
544 UNTS 349. Denmark. Accession 20 May 65.
605 UNTS 361. Netherlands. Surinam.
605 UNTS 361. Netherlands. Netherlands Antilles.
605 UNTS 361. Netherlands. Accession 30 Mar 67.

105779 Bilateral Exchange **402 UNTS 103**
SIGNED: 5 Mar 56 FORCE: 12 Jun 57
REGISTERED: 4 Aug 61 New Zealand
ARTICLES: 2 LANGUAGE: English. German.
HEADNOTE: CARE MAINTENANCE WAR GRAVES
TOPIC: Other Military
CONCEPTS: Burial arrangements. Upkeep of war graves.
TREATY REF: 326UNTS181.
PARTIES:
Germany, West
New Zealand

105780 Bilateral Exchange **402 UNTS 109**
SIGNED: 4 Jul 57 FORCE: 4 Jul 57
REGISTERED: 4 Aug 61 New Zealand
ARTICLES: 3 LANGUAGE: English.
HEADNOTE: DEFENSE ARRANGEMENTS KINGDOM OF TONGA
TOPIC: Milit Assistance
CONCEPTS: General cooperation. Exchange of information and documents. Use of facilities. Indemnities and reimbursements. Joint defense. Lease of military property. Military assistance. Military training. Bases and facilities.
PROCEDURE: Future Procedures Contemplated.
PARTIES:
New Zealand
UK Great Britain

105781 Bilateral Exchange **402 UNTS 119**
SIGNED: 9 Sep 60 FORCE: 9 Sep 60
REGISTERED: 4 Aug 61 New Zealand
ARTICLES: 2 LANGUAGE: English.
HEADNOTE: DEVELOPMENT TRADE
TOPIC: General Trade
CONCEPTS: Territorial application. General provisions. General cooperation. Establishment of trade relations. Most favored nation clause.
TREATY REF: GATT.
PROCEDURE: Duration.
PARTIES:
New Zealand
Yugoslavia
ANNEX
485 UNTS 364. New Zealand. Prolongation 21 Sep 62. Force 9 Sep 62.
485 UNTS 364. Yugoslavia. Prolongation 21 Sep 62. Force 9 Sep 62.

105782 Bilateral Agreement **402 UNTS 125**
SIGNED: 20 Apr 59 FORCE: 1 Apr 59
REGISTERED: 4 Aug 61 New Zealand
ARTICLES: 8 LANGUAGE: English. German.
HEADNOTE: TRADE
TOPIC: General Trade
CONCEPTS: Detailed regulations. Territorial application. Treaty interpretation. Annex or appendix reference. Previous treaty replacement. General cooperation. Licenses and permits. Import quotas. Trade procedures. Quotas.
INTL ORGS: European Economic Community.
TREATY REF: GATT; 11MAY55.
PROCEDURE: Duration. Termination.
PARTIES:
Germany, West
New Zealand

105783 Bilateral Exchange **402 UNTS 153**
SIGNED: 20 Jan 61 FORCE: 20 Jan 61
REGISTERED: 7 Aug 61 USA (United States)
ARTICLES: 2 LANGUAGE: English.

HEADNOTE: ESTABLISHMENT OPERATION TRACKING STATION
TOPIC: Scientific Project
CONCEPTS: General cooperation. Operating agencies. Licenses and permits. General property. Research and scientific projects. Communication satellites testing. Research and development. Indemnities and reimbursements. Fees and exemptions. Tax exemptions. Special projects. Materials, equipment and services. Bands and frequency allocation. Facilities and equipment.
TREATY REF: USA'TIAS 3266;T.
PROCEDURE: Duration. Renewal or Revival. Termination.
PARTIES:
UK Great Britain
USA (United States)
ANNEX
565 UNTS 318. USA (United States). Prolongation 17 Jan 66. Force 17 Jun 66.
565 UNTS 318. UK Great Britain. Prolongation 8 Feb 66. Force 17 Jun 66.

105784 Bilateral Exchange **402 UNTS 163**
SIGNED: 19 Jan 61 FORCE: 19 Jan 61
REGISTERED: 7 Aug 61 USA (United States)
ARTICLES: 2 LANGUAGE: English.
HEADNOTE: ECONOMIC TECHNICAL ASSISTANCE
TOPIC: General Aid
CONCEPTS: Conditions. Exceptions and exemptions. Research cooperation. Establishment of trade relations. Banking. Financial programs. Commodities and services. General technical assistance. Economic assistance.
TREATY REF: 360UNTS259; 152UNTS61; 207UNTS360.
PARTIES:
USA (United States)
Yugoslavia

105785 Bilateral Exchange **402 UNTS 169**
SIGNED: 18 Jan 61 FORCE: 18 Jan 61
REGISTERED: 7 Aug 61 USA (United States)
ARTICLES: 2 LANGUAGE: English. Spanish.
HEADNOTE: TERMINATE PARTS 1935 TRADE AGREEMENT
TOPIC: General Trade
CONCEPTS: Treaty interpretation. Establishment of trade relations.
TREATY REF: 167LTS313.
PARTIES:
Honduras
USA (United States)

105786 Bilateral Agreement **402 UNTS 177**
SIGNED: 15 Aug 60 FORCE: 15 Aug 60
REGISTERED: 7 Aug 61 USA (United States)
ARTICLES: 18 LANGUAGE: English. Spanish.
HEADNOTE: AIR TRANSPORT
TOPIC: Air Transport
CONCEPTS: Definition of terms. Detailed regulations. Annex or appendix reference. Friendship and amity. Conformity with municipal law. General cooperation. Exchange of information and documents. Licenses and permits. Recognition of legal documents. Use of facilities. Arbitration. Procedure. Special tribunals. Competence of tribunal. Indemnities and reimbursements. Fees and exemptions. Non-interest rates and fees. National treatment. Tax exemptions. Customs exemptions. Competency certificate. Routes and logistics. Navigational conditions. Permit designation. Air transport. Airport facilities. Airworthiness certificates. Conditions of airlines operating permission. Overflights and technical stops. Operating authorizations and regulations. Licenses and certificates of nationality.
INTL ORGS: International Civil Aviation Organization. International Court of Justice.
TREATY REF: 15UNTS295.
PROCEDURE: Amendment. Future Procedures Contemplated. Ratification. Registration. Termination. Application to Non-self-governing Territories.

PARTIES:
Mexico
USA (United States)
ANNEX
505 UNTS 322. USA (United States). Prolongation 14 Aug 63. Force 6 Jan 64.
505 UNTS 322. Mexico. Prolongation 14 Aug 63. Force 6 Jan 64.
531 UNTS 362. USA (United States). Implementation 14 Aug 64. Force 14 Aug 64.
531 UNTS 362. Mexico. Implementation 14 Aug 64. Force 14 Aug 64.

105787 Bilateral Treaty **402 UNTS 209**
SIGNED: 7 May 60 FORCE: 8 Jun 61
REGISTERED: 7 Aug 61 Czechoslovakia
ARTICLES: 22 LANGUAGE: Czechoslovakian. Chinese.
HEADNOTE: CONSULAR
TOPIC: Consul/Citizenship
CONCEPTS: General consular functions. Consular relations establishment. Inviolability. Privileges and immunities. Diplomatic correspondence.
PROCEDURE: Duration. Ratification. Termination.
PARTIES:
China People's Rep
Czechoslovakia

105788 Bilateral Agreement **402 UNTS 235**
SIGNED: 12 Aug 61 FORCE: 12 Aug 61
REGISTERED: 12 Aug 61 United Nations
ARTICLES: 8 LANGUAGE: French.
HEADNOTE: ACTIVITIES UNICEF
TOPIC: Direct Aid
CONCEPTS: Treaty implementation. Privileges and immunities. General cooperation. Exchange of information and documents. Informational records. Public information. Responsibility and liability. Title and deeds. Claims and settlements. Tax exemptions. Customs exemptions. Domestic obligation. Assistance. General aid. Materials, equipment and services. Distribution. IGO status.
TREATY REF: 1UNTS15.
PROCEDURE: Amendment. Termination.
PARTIES:
Cameroon
UNICEF (Children)

105789 Bilateral Exchange **402 UNTS 245**
SIGNED: 2 Dec 60 FORCE: 2 Dec 60
REGISTERED: 14 Aug 61 Denmark
ARTICLES: 2 LANGUAGE: English.
HEADNOTE: COMMITTEE GREENLAND PROJECTS
TOPIC: Milit Installation
CONCEPTS: Annex or appendix reference. Establishment of commission. Joint defense. Defense and security. Military installations and equipment.
INTL ORGS: Special Commission.
PARTIES:
Denmark
USA (United States)

105790 Bilateral Agreement **402 UNTS 255**
SIGNED: 10 Apr 61 FORCE: 15 Jun 61
REGISTERED: 15 Aug 61 IAEA (Atom Energy)
ARTICLES: 12 LANGUAGE: English.
HEADNOTE: RESEARCH REACTOR PHYSICS
TOPIC: Scientific Project
CONCEPTS: Annex or appendix reference. Post-colonial administration. Use of facilities. Establishment of commission. Dispute settlement. Public health. Research and scientific projects. Nuclear research. Funding procedures. Patents, copyrights and trademarks. Domestic obligation. Nuclear materials. Peaceful use. IGO obligations.
INTL ORGS: International Court of Justice.
TREATY REF: 339UNTS359; 276UNTS3; 293UNTS359; 402UNTS281.
PROCEDURE: Duration. Renewal or Revival. Termination.
PARTIES:
Norway
IAEA (Atom Energy)
ANNEX
501 UNTS 360. IAEA (Atom Energy). Prolongation 8 Apr 64. Force 8 Apr 64.
501 UNTS 360. Norway. Prolongation 8 Apr 64. Force 8 Apr 64.
603 UNTS 330. IAEA (Atom Energy). Prolongation 10 Apr 67. Force 10 Apr 67.

603 UNTS 330. Norway. Prolongation 10 Apr 67. Force 10 Apr 67.

105791 Multilateral Instrument **402 UNTS 281**
SIGNED: 10 Apr 61 FORCE: 15 Jun 61
REGISTERED: 15 Aug 61 IAEA (Atom Energy)
ARTICLES: 12 LANGUAGE: English.
HEADNOTE: LEASE OF ENRICHED URANIUM
TOPIC: Atomic Energy
CONCEPTS: Annex or appendix reference. Exchange of information and documents. Responsibility and liability. Title and deeds. Arbitration. Special tribunals. Research cooperation. Payment schedules. Assets transfer. Nuclear materials. Transport of goods.
INTL ORGS: International Court of Justice.
TREATY REF: 339UNTS359; 276UNTS3.
PARTIES:
Norway SIGNED: 10 Apr 61 FORCE: 15 Jun 61
IAEA (Atom Energy) SIGNED: 10 Apr 61 FORCE: 15 Jun 61
USA (United States) SIGNED: 16 Mar 61 FORCE: 15 Jun 61
ANNEX
456 UNTS 506. Norway. Amendment 3 Sep 62. Force 3 Sep 62.
456 UNTS 506. USA (United States). Amendment 27 Jul 62. Force 3 Sep 62.
501 UNTS 368. IAEA (Atom Energy). Extension and Amendment 8 Apr 64. Force 8 Apr 64.
501 UNTS 368. Norway. Extension and Amendment 8 Apr 64. Force 8 Apr 64.
603 UNTS 330. IAEA (Atom Energy). Prolongation 10 Apr 67. Force 10 Apr 67.
603 UNTS 330. USA (United States). Prolongation 10 Apr 67. Force 10 Apr 67.

105792 Multilateral Agreement **403 UNTS 3**
SIGNED: 1 Sep 60 FORCE: 1 Jul 61
REGISTERED: 16 Aug 61 UK Great Britain
ARTICLES: 22 LANGUAGE: English. French. Spanish.
HEADNOTE: SECOND INTERNATIONAL TIN
TOPIC: Commodity Trade
CONCEPTS: Definition of terms. Exceptions and exemptions. General provisions. Privileges and immunities. Procedure. Employment regulations. Export quotas. Finances and payments. Balance of payments. Currency. Exchange rates and regulations. Non-interest rates and fees. Commodity trade. Subsidiary organ. Internal structure.
INTL ORGS: International Tin Council.
PROCEDURE: Amendment. Accession. Duration. Ratification. Renewal or Revival. Termination.
PARTIES:
Australia SIGNED: 21 Dec 60 RATIFIED: 6 Mar 61 FORCE: 1 Jul 61
Austria SIGNED: 30 Dec 60 RATIFIED: 30 Jun 61 FORCE: 1 Jul 61
Belgium SIGNED: 21 Oct 60 RATIFIED: 23 May 61 FORCE: 1 Jul 61
Belgium Ruanda-Urundi RATIFIED: 21 Oct 60 FORCE: 1 Jul 61
Bolivia SIGNED: 29 Dec 60 RATIFIED: 28 Apr 61 FORCE: 1 Jul 61
Canada SIGNED: 2 Dec 60 RATIFIED: 22 Mar 61 FORCE: 1 Jul 61
Congo (Zaire) SIGNED: 25 Nov 60 RATIFIED: 8 Mar 61 FORCE: 1 Jul 61
Denmark SIGNED: 23 Dec 60 RATIFIED: 20 Mar 61 FORCE: 1 Jul 61
Fed of Malaya SIGNED: 16 Dec 60 RATIFIED: 19 Dec 60 FORCE: 1 Jul 61
France SIGNED: 2 Dec 60 RATIFIED: 31 May 61 FORCE: 1 Jul 61
India SIGNED: 29 Dec 60 RATIFIED: 9 Jun 61 FORCE: 1 Jul 61
Indonesia SIGNED: 30 Dec 60 RATIFIED: 28 Jun 61 FORCE: 1 Jul 61
Italy SIGNED: 5 Dec 60 RATIFIED: 9 May 61 FORCE: 1 Jul 61
Japan SIGNED: 29 Dec 60 RATIFIED: 29 Jun 61 FORCE: 1 Jul 61
Mexico SIGNED: 22 Dec 60 RATIFIED: 19 May 61 FORCE: 1 Jul 61
Netherlands SIGNED: 22 Dec 60 RATIFIED: 30 Jun 61 FORCE: 1 Jul 61
Nigeria SIGNED: 2 Dec 60 RATIFIED: 20 Jun 61 FORCE: 1 Jul 61
Spain SIGNED: 30 Dec 60 RATIFIED: 30 Jun 61 FORCE: 1 Jul 61

Thailand SIGNED: 27 Sep 60 RATIFIED: 27 Jun 61 FORCE: 1 Jul 61
Turkey SIGNED: 29 Sep 60 RATIFIED: 21 Jun 61 FORCE: 1 Jul 61
UK Great Britain SIGNED: 3 Nov 60 RATIFIED: 26 Jun 61 FORCE: 1 Jul 61
ANNEX
425 UNTS 372. Korea, South. Accession 21 Dec 61.
425 UNTS 372. Japan. Ratification 24 Nov 61. Force 21 Feb 62.
425 UNTS 372. Congo (Zaire). Ratification 30 Dec 61. Force 21 Feb 62.
425 UNTS 372. Spain. Ratification 27 Jan 62. Force 21 Feb 62.
425 UNTS 372. Australia. Ratification 6 Dec 61. Force 21 Feb 62.
425 UNTS 372. Bolivia. Ratification 21 Feb 62. Force 21 Feb 62.
456 UNTS 510. Mexico. Ratification 5 Jun 62.
456 UNTS 510. Belgium. Qualified Ratification 27 Jun 62.
466 UNTS 406. Italy. Ratification 10 Apr 63.
566 UNTS 370. Turkey. Ratification 23 Jul 64.

105793 Bilateral Agreement **403 UNTS 139**
SIGNED: 5 Apr 55 FORCE: 22 Nov 60
REGISTERED: 16 Aug 61 UK Great Britain
ARTICLES: 11 LANGUAGE: English. Portuguese.
HEADNOTE: MILITARY SERVICE
TOPIC: Milit Servic/Citiz
CONCEPTS: Emergencies. Territorial application. Procedure. Certificates of service. Service in foreign army.
PROCEDURE: Ratification. Termination. Application to Non-self-governing Territories.
PARTIES:
Brazil
UK Great Britain

105794 Bilateral Agreement **403 UNTS 153**
SIGNED: 18 Nov 57 FORCE: 25 Jan 61
REGISTERED: 16 Aug 61 UK Great Britain
ARTICLES: 7 LANGUAGE: English. Danish.
HEADNOTE: COMMERCIAL
TOPIC: General Trade
CONCEPTS: Trade procedures.
PROCEDURE: Ratification.
PARTIES:
Denmark
UK Great Britain

105795 Multilateral Agreement **403 UNTS 169**
SIGNED: 25 Nov 57 FORCE: 22 Oct 58
REGISTERED: 16 Aug 61 UK Great Britain
ARTICLES: 8 LANGUAGE: English. German. French. Italian. Dutch.
HEADNOTE: IRON STEEL TARIFFS
TOPIC: General Trade
CONCEPTS: Detailed regulations. Territorial application. Annex or appendix reference. Tariffs. Customs declarations.
PROCEDURE: Duration. Ratification. Termination.
PARTIES:
Belgium SIGNED: 25 Nov 57 RATIFIED: 18 Apr 58 FORCE: 22 Oct 58
France SIGNED: 25 Nov 57 RATIFIED: 24 Jun 58 FORCE: 22 Oct 58
Germany, West SIGNED: 25 Nov 57 RATIFIED: 23 May 58 FORCE: 22 Oct 58
Italy SIGNED: 25 Nov 57 RATIFIED: 28 Feb 58 FORCE: 22 Oct 58
Luxembourg SIGNED: 25 Nov 57 RATIFIED: 18 Apr 58 FORCE: 22 Oct 58
Netherlands SIGNED: 25 Nov 57 RATIFIED: 22 Oct 58 FORCE: 22 Oct 58
ECSC (Coal/Steel) SIGNED: 25 Nov 57
UK Great Britain SIGNED: 25 Nov 57 RATIFIED: 18 Mar 58 FORCE: 22 Oct 58

105796 Bilateral Exchange **403 UNTS 253**
SIGNED: 9 Mar 60 FORCE: 1 Nov 59
REGISTERED: 16 Aug 61 UK Great Britain
ARTICLES: 4 LANGUAGE: English. German.
HEADNOTE: REAPPLICATION EXTENSION UK DEPENDENT TERRITORIES
TOPIC: Admin Cooperation
CONCEPTS: Territorial application. Annex type material.

TREATY REF: 90LTS287.
PARTIES:
  Germany, West
  UK Great Britain

105797 Bilateral Exchange **403 UNTS 267**
SIGNED: 6 Apr 61   FORCE: 1 May 61
REGISTERED: 16 Aug 61 UK Great Britain
ARTICLES: 2 LANGUAGE: English.
HEADNOTE: ACCEPTANCE BRITISH VISITORS
  PASSPORT
TOPIC: Visas
CONCEPTS: Emergencies. Time limit. Annex or appendix reference. Passports non-diplomatic. Denial of admission. Conformity with municipal law.
INTL ORGS: European Economic Community.
PARTIES:
  Greece
  UK Great Britain
                    ANNEX
414 UNTS 428. UK Great Britain. Supplementation 3 Jun 61. Force 3 Jun 61.
414 UNTS 428.   Greece.   Supplementation 3 Jun 61. Force 3 Jun 61.

105798 Bilateral Convention **403 UNTS 275**
SIGNED: 1 Jun 54   FORCE: 29 Dec 57
REGISTERED: 16 Aug 61 UK Great Britain
ARTICLES: 40 LANGUAGE: English. Italian.
HEADNOTE: CONSULAR CONVENTION
TOPIC: Consul/Citizenship
CONCEPTS: Definition of terms. Territorial application. General provisions. Previous treaty replacement. General consular functions. Diplomatic privileges. Consular relations establishment. Inviolability. Privileges and immunities. Diplomatic correspondence. Consular functions in shipping. Consular functions in property. Expropriation. Responsibility and liability. Existing tribunals. Compensation.
PROCEDURE: Ratification. Termination.
PARTIES:
  Italy
  UK Great Britain

105799 Bilateral Exchange **404 UNTS 3**
SIGNED: 6 Mar 61   FORCE: 15 Mar 61
REGISTERED: 16 Aug 61 UK Great Britain
ARTICLES: 2 LANGUAGE: English. Italian.
HEADNOTE: ACCEPTANCE BRITISH VISITORS
  PASSPORT
TOPIC: Visas
CONCEPTS: Emergencies. Time limit. Annex or appendix reference. Passports non-diplomatic. Denial of admission. Resident permits. Conformity with municipal law.
PARTIES:
  Italy
  UK Great Britain

105800 Bilateral Exchange **404 UNTS 11**
SIGNED: 11 Apr 61   FORCE: 11 Apr 61
REGISTERED: 16 Aug 61 UK Great Britain
ARTICLES: 2 LANGUAGE: English. French.
HEADNOTE: ARRANGEMENTS   FACILITATE
  TRAVEL
TOPIC: Visas
CONCEPTS: Emergencies. Territorial application. Time limit. Visa abolition. Passports non-diplomatic. Denial of admission. Resident permits. Conformity with municipal law.
PROCEDURE: Termination.
PARTIES:
  Monaco
  UK Great Britain
                    ANNEX
414 UNTS 432. UK Great Britain. Supplementation 14 Jul 61. Force 29 Jul 61.
414 UNTS 432.   Monaco.   Supplementation 29 Jul 61. Force 29 Jul 61.

105801 Bilateral Exchange **404 UNTS 17**
SIGNED: 22 Aug 49   FORCE: 22 Aug 49
REGISTERED: 16 Aug 61 UK Great Britain
ARTICLES: 2 LANGUAGE: English.
HEADNOTE: WINDING-UP SOCIAL INSURANCE
  COMMITTEE POLISH MERCHANT NAVY
TOPIC: Admin Cooperation

CONCEPTS: General cooperation. Claims and settlements.
PARTIES:
  Poland
  UK Great Britain

105802 Bilateral Exchange **404 UNTS 27**
SIGNED: 21 Nov 52   FORCE: 21 Nov 52
REGISTERED: 16 Aug 61 UK Great Britain
ARTICLES: 2 LANGUAGE: English. Portuguese.
HEADNOTE: EXTENSION TRANSIT FACILITIES
TOPIC: Milit Assistance
CONCEPTS: Use of facilities. Defense and security. Military assistance.
TREATY REF: 237UNTS217.
PARTIES:
  Portugal
  UK Great Britain

105803 Bilateral Exchange **404 UNTS 33**
SIGNED: 27 Feb 61   FORCE: 15 Mar 61
REGISTERED: 16 Aug 61 UK Great Britain
ARTICLES: 2 LANGUAGE: English. Portuguese.
HEADNOTE: ACCEPTANCE BRITISH VISITORS
  PASSPORT
TOPIC: Visas
CONCEPTS: Emergencies. Territorial application. Time limit. Visa abolition. Passports non-diplomatic. Denial of admission. Resident permits. Conformity with municipal law.
INTL ORGS: Council of Europe.
PROCEDURE: Termination.
PARTIES:
  Portugal
  UK Great Britain
                    ANNEX
420 UNTS 357. UK Great Britain. Supplementation 22 May 61. Force 30 May 61.
420 UNTS 357.   Portugal.   Supplementation 30 May 61. Force 30 May 61.

105804 Bilateral Agreement **404 UNTS 41**
SIGNED: 19 Jan 60   FORCE: 29 Mar 61
REGISTERED: 16 Aug 61 UK Great Britain
ARTICLES: 8 LANGUAGE: English. Spanish.
HEADNOTE: COOPERATION PEACEFUL USES
  ATOMIC ENERGY
TOPIC: Atomic Energy
CONCEPTS: Definition of terms. Non-prejudice to third party. Exchange of information and documents. Informational records. Inspection and observation. Research results. Nuclear materials. Peaceful use. Security of information.
PARTIES:
  Spain
  UK Great Britain

105805 Bilateral Exchange **404 UNTS 75**
SIGNED: 15 Feb 61   FORCE: 15 Mar 61
REGISTERED: 16 Aug 61 UK Great Britain
ARTICLES: 2 LANGUAGE: English. Spanish.
HEADNOTE: ACCEPTANCE BRITISH VISITORS
  PASSPORT
TOPIC: Visas
CONCEPTS: Emergencies. Time limit. Passports non-diplomatic. Denial of admission. Resident permits. Conformity with municipal law.
INTL ORGS: Council of Europe.
PROCEDURE: Termination.
PARTIES:
  Spain
  UK Great Britain
                    ANNEX
420 UNTS 361. UK Great Britain. Supplementation 3 Jun 61. Force 30 May 61.
420 UNTS 361.   Spain.   Supplementation 3 Jun 61. Force 30 May 61.

105806 Bilateral Convention **404 UNTS 85**
SIGNED: 28 Jul 60   FORCE: 14 Feb 61
REGISTERED: 16 Aug 61 UK Great Britain
ARTICLES: 11 LANGUAGE: English. Swedish.
HEADNOTE: DOUBLE   TAXATION   ESTATES
  DECEASED PERSONS
TOPIC: Taxation
CONCEPTS: Definition of terms. Territorial application. Nationality and citizenship. Conformity with municipal law. Claims and settlements. Taxation. Death duties. Tax credits.

PROCEDURE: Duration. Ratification. Termination.
PARTIES:
  Sweden
  UK Great Britain

105807 Bilateral Exchange **404 UNTS 105**
SIGNED: 5 May 61   FORCE: 1 Jun 61
REGISTERED: 16 Aug 61 UK Great Britain
ARTICLES: 2 LANGUAGE: English.
HEADNOTE: ACCEPTANCE BRITISH VISITORS
  PASSPORT
TOPIC: Visas
CONCEPTS: Emergencies. Time limit. Visa abolition. Passports non-diplomatic. Denial of admission. Resident permits. Conformity with municipal law.
INTL ORGS: Council of Europe.
PROCEDURE: Duration. Termination.
PARTIES:
  Sweden
  UK Great Britain
                    ANNEX
425 UNTS 374. UK Great Britain. Implementation 25 Aug 61. Force 25 Aug 61.
425 UNTS 374.   Sweden.   Implementation 25 Aug 61. Force 25 Aug 61.

105808 Bilateral Convention **404 UNTS 113**
SIGNED: 28 Jul 60   FORCE: 14 Feb 61
REGISTERED: 16 Aug 61 UK Great Britain
ARTICLES: 30 LANGUAGE: English. Swedish.
HEADNOTE: DOUBLE TAXATION FISCAL EVASION TAXES INCOME
TOPIC: Taxation
CONCEPTS: Definition of terms. Territorial application. Previous treaty renunciation. Conformity with municipal law. Exchange of official publications. Teacher and student exchange. Taxation. Death duties. Tax credits. Equitable taxes. General. Tax exemptions. Air transport. Merchant vessels.
TREATY   REF: 32LTS291;   120LTS211; 209UNTS129.
PROCEDURE: Duration. Ratification. Termination.
PARTIES:
  Sweden
  UK Great Britain
                    ANNEX
453 UNTS 438.   Sweden.   Acknowledgement 27 Nov 61. Force 27 Nov 61.
453 UNTS 438. UK Great Britain. Swaziland. Acknowledgement 27 Nov 61. Force 27 Nov 61.
453 UNTS 438. UK Great Britain. Bechuanaland. Acknowledgement 27 Nov 61. Force 27 Nov 61.

105809 Bilateral Exchange **404 UNTS 167**
SIGNED: 27 Feb 61   FORCE: 15 Mar 61
REGISTERED: 16 Aug 61 UK Great Britain
ARTICLES: 2 LANGUAGE: English. French.
HEADNOTE: FACILITATE TRAVEL
TOPIC: Visas
CONCEPTS: Emergencies. Territorial application. Time limit. Annex or appendix reference. Visa abolition. Passports non-diplomatic. Denial of admission. Resident permits. Nationality and citizenship. Conformity with municipal law.
INTL ORGS: Council of Europe.
PROCEDURE: Duration. Termination.
PARTIES:
  Switzerland
  UK Great Britain
                    ANNEX
414 UNTS 435.   Switzerland.   Supplementation 15 Jun 61. Force 15 Jun 61.
414 UNTS 435. UK Great Britain. Supplementation 15 Jun 61. Force 15 Jun 61.

105810 Bilateral Agreement **404 UNTS 175**
SIGNED: 9 Jan 61   FORCE: 9 Jan 61
REGISTERED: 16 Aug 61 UK Great Britain
ARTICLES: 16 LANGUAGE: English. Russian.
HEADNOTE: RELATIONS SCIENTIFIC TECHNOLOGICAL EDUCATIONAL CULTURAL FIELDS
TOPIC: Health/Educ/Welfare
CONCEPTS: General cooperation. Exchange of information and documents. Personnel. Establishment of commission. Specialists exchange. Exchange. Teacher and student exchange. General cultural cooperation. Artists. Athletes. Research

results. Scientific exchange. Research and development. Mass media exchange.
TREATY REF: 351UNTS313; 4634.
PROCEDURE: Duration. Termination.
PARTIES:
UK Great Britain
USSR (Soviet Union)

105811 Bilateral Exchange **404 UNTS 207**
SIGNED: 15 Mar 61　　　FORCE: 15 Mar 61
REGISTERED: 16 Aug 61 UK Great Britain
ARTICLES: 2 LANGUAGE: English.
HEADNOTE: SPACE VEHICLE TRACKING STATION
TOPIC: Scientific Project
CONCEPTS: Personnel. General property. Research and scientific projects. Research cooperation. Research results. Research and development. Tax exemptions. Economic assistance. Facilities and equipment.
TREATY REF: 204LTS15.
PARTIES:
UK Great Britain
USA (United States)
ANNEX
486 UNTS 424. UK Great Britain. Prolongation 23 Sep 63. Force 23 Sep 63.
486 UNTS 424. USA (United States). Prolongation 23 Sep 63. Force 23 Sep 63.
642 UNTS 372. UK Great Britain. Amendment 17 Jan 68. Force 17 Jan 68.
642 UNTS 372. USA (United States). Amendment 17 Jan 68. Force 17 Jan 68.

105812 Bilateral Exchange **404 UNTS 215**
SIGNED: 6 Apr 61　　　FORCE: 6 Apr 61
REGISTERED: 16 Aug 61 UK Great Britain
ARTICLES: 2 LANGUAGE: English.
HEADNOTE: SPACE VEHICLE TRACKING STATION
TOPIC: Scientific Project　　.
CONCEPTS: General cooperation. Personnel. General property. Research and scientific projects. Research cooperation. Research and development. Indemnities and reimbursements. Economic assistance. Bands and frequency allocation. Facilities and equipment. Definition of territory.
TREATY REF: 196LTS343.
PROCEDURE: Duration. Future Procedures Contemplated. Termination.
PARTIES:
UK Great Britain
USA (United States)
ANNEX
486 UNTS 428. UK Great Britain. Prolongation 23 Sep 63. Force 23 Sep 63.
486 UNTS 428. USA (United States). Prolongation 23 Sep 63. Force 23 Sep 63.
642 UNTS 376. UK Great Britain. Termination 23 Aug 67. Force 1 Jan 68.
642 UNTS 376. USA (United States). Termination 23 Aug 67. Force 1 Jan 68.

105813 Bilateral Exchange **404 UNTS 227**
SIGNED: 18 Jul 61　　　FORCE: 18 Jul 61
REGISTERED: 16 Aug 61 UK Great Britain
ARTICLES: 2 LANGUAGE: English.
HEADNOTE: MISSILE DEFENSE ALARM SYSTEM
TOPIC: Milit Assistance
CONCEPTS: Annex or appendix reference. Bases and facilities.
TREATY REF: 34UNTS243.
PARTIES:
UK Great Britain
USA (United States)

105814 Bilateral Agreement **404 UNTS 237**
SIGNED: 18 May 56　　　FORCE: 8 Feb 61
REGISTERED: 17 Aug 61 USA (United States)
ARTICLES: 11 LANGUAGE: English.
HEADNOTE: COOPERATION CIVIL USES ATOMIC ENERGY
TOPIC: Atomic Energy
CONCEPTS: Definition of terms. Non-prejudice to third party. Conformity with municipal law. Exchange of information and documents. Inspection and observation. Responsibility and liability. Research results. Assets transfer. Nuclear materials. Non-nuclear materials. Security of information.
PROCEDURE: Duration.

PARTIES:
Costa Rica
USA (United States)

105815 Bilateral Exchange **404 UNTS 251**
SIGNED: 29 Nov 60　　　FORCE: 31 Jan 61
REGISTERED: 17 Aug 61 USA (United States)
ARTICLES: 2 LANGUAGE: English.
HEADNOTE: MUTUALLY FINANCED SHIP BUILDING PROGRAM
TOPIC: Milit Assistance
CONCEPTS: Indemnities and reimbursements. Defense and security. Naval vessels. Equipment and supplies.
TREATY REF: 80UNTS241.
PROCEDURE: Future Procedures Contemplated.
PARTIES:
Norway
USA (United States)

105816 Bilateral Treaty **404 UNTS 259**
SIGNED: 12 Nov 59　　　FORCE: 12 Feb 61
REGISTERED: 17 Aug 61 USA (United States)
ARTICLES: 24 LANGUAGE: English.
HEADNOTE: FRIENDSHIP COMMERCE
TOPIC: General Amity
CONCEPTS: Friendship and amity. Scientific exchange. National treatment.
INTL ORGS: General Agreement on Tariffs and Trade.
PROCEDURE: Ratification. Termination.
PARTIES:
Pakistan
USA (United States)

105817 Bilateral Agreement **404 UNTS 297**
SIGNED: 18 Aug 61　　　FORCE: 18 Aug 61
REGISTERED: 18 Aug 61 United Nations
ARTICLES: 6 LANGUAGE: English.
HEADNOTE: HUMAN RIGHTS SEMINAR MEXICO CITY
TOPIC: Humanitarian
CONCEPTS: Definition of terms. Human rights. Privileges and immunities. General cooperation. Legal protection and assistance. Personnel. Use of facilities. Exchange. Indemnities and reimbursements. Expense sharing formulae. Domestic obligation. Internal structure. Status of experts.
TREATY REF: 1UNTS15.
PROCEDURE: Amendment.
PARTIES:
Mexico
United Nations

105818 Bilateral Agreement **404 UNTS 307**
SIGNED: 19 Apr 61　　　FORCE: 8 Aug 61
REGISTERED: 22 Aug 61 Norway
ARTICLES: 7 LANGUAGE: English.
HEADNOTE: CULTURAL AGREEMENT
TOPIC: Culture
CONCEPTS: Treaty implementation. Friendship and amity. Non-diplomatic delegations. Conformity with municipal law. General cooperation. Establishment of commission. Specialists exchange. Recognition of degrees. Exchange. Teacher and student exchange. Exchange. General cultural cooperation. Artists. Anthropology and archeology. Scientific exchange. Publications exchange. Mass media exchange. Press and wire services.
PROCEDURE: Duration. Ratification. Renewal or Revival. Termination.
PARTIES:
India
Norway

105819 Bilateral Agreement **405 UNTS 3**
SIGNED: 23 Aug 61　　　FORCE: 23 Aug 61
REGISTERED: 23 Aug 61 United Nations
ARTICLES: 1 LANGUAGE: English.
HEADNOTE: UN CONFERENCE ENERGY SOURCES
TOPIC: IGO Operations
CONCEPTS: General cooperation. Research cooperation. Scientific exchange. Conferences.
INTL ORGS: Food and Agricultural Organization of the United Nations.

PARTIES:
Italy
United Nations

105820 Bilateral Agreement **405 UNTS 13**
SIGNED: 16 Sep 59　　　FORCE: 9 Mar 60
REGISTERED: 23 Aug 61 Denmark
ARTICLES: 22 LANGUAGE: English.
HEADNOTE: AVOIDANCE DOUBLE TAXATION
TOPIC: Taxation
CONCEPTS: Extradition, deportation and repatriation. Extradition requests. Location of crime. Refusal of extradition. Limits of prosecution. Provisional detainment. Extradition postponement. Indemnities and reimbursements.
PROCEDURE: Denunciation. Ratification.
PARTIES:
Denmark
India

105821 Bilateral Exchange **405 UNTS 37**
SIGNED: 8 Feb 61　　　FORCE: 28 Feb 61
REGISTERED: 23 Aug 61 USA (United States)
ARTICLES: 2 LANGUAGE: English.
HEADNOTE: ECONOMIC TECHNICAL ASSISTANCE
TOPIC: General Aid
CONCEPTS: Currency. General technical assistance. Assistance. Agricultural commodities. Credit provisions.
TREATY REF: 238UNTS199,80UNTS205,1-79UNTS105.
PROCEDURE: Termination.
PARTIES:
Korea, South
USA (United States)
ANNEX
413 UNTS 392. Korea, South. Implementation 8 Feb 61. Force 8 Feb 61.
413 UNTS 392. USA (United States). Implementation 8 Feb 61. Force 8 Feb 61.

105822 Bilateral Exchange **405 UNTS 55**
SIGNED: 4 Apr 61　　　FORCE: 4 Apr 61
REGISTERED: 23 Aug 61 USA (United States)
ARTICLES: 2 LANGUAGE: English.
HEADNOTE: ECONOMIC ASSISTANCE
TOPIC: Direct Aid
CONCEPTS: Privileges and immunities. Personnel. Economic assistance. Aid missions.
TREATY REF: 141UNTS15.
PARTIES:
Colombia
USA (United States)

105823 Bilateral Exchange **405 UNTS 63**
SIGNED: 31 Oct 60　　　FORCE: 1 Nov 60
REGISTERED: 23 Aug 61 USA (United States)
ARTICLES: 2 LANGUAGE: English. Spanish.
HEADNOTE: RECOGNITION MOTOR-VEHICLE LICENSES
TOPIC: Admin Cooperation
CONCEPTS: Standardization. General cooperation. Exchange of information and documents. Licenses and permits.
PROCEDURE: Termination.
PARTIES:
Panama
USA (United States)

105824 Bilateral Exchange **405 UNTS 77**
SIGNED: 4 Apr 61　　　FORCE: 4 Apr 61
REGISTERED: 23 Aug 61 USA (United States)
ARTICLES: 2 LANGUAGE: English.
HEADNOTE: EXCHANGE OFFICIAL PUBLICATIONS
TOPIC: Admin Cooperation
CONCEPTS: Exchange of official publications. Operating agencies. Indemnities and reimbursements.
PARTIES:
USA (United States)
Vietnam, South

105825 Bilateral Agreement **405 UNTS 85**
SIGNED: 8 Nov 60　　　FORCE: 8 Nov 60
REGISTERED: 23 Aug 61 USA (United States)
ARTICLES: 6 LANGUAGE: English. Spanish.

HEADNOTE: AGRI COMMOD TITLE I
TOPIC: US Agri Commod Aid
CONCEPTS: General provisions. Annex or appendix reference. Exchange of information and documents. Reexport of goods, etc.. Exchange rates and regulations. Transportation costs. Local currency. Commodities schedule. Purchase authorization. Surplus commodities. Mutual consultation.
PARTIES:
Chile
USA (United States)

105826 Bilateral Exchange **405 UNTS 107**
SIGNED: 29 Mar 61   FORCE: 29 Mar 61
REGISTERED: 23 Aug 61 USA (United States)
ARTICLES: 2 LANGUAGE: English.
HEADNOTE: COMMUNICATIONS SATELLITES
TOPIC: Scientific Project
CONCEPTS: Communication satellites testing. Research and development. Facilities and equipment. Satellites.
PARTIES:
UK Great Britain
USA (United States)

105827 Bilateral Exchange **405 UNTS 113**
SIGNED: 9 Feb 61   FORCE: 9 Feb 61
REGISTERED: 23 Aug 61 USA (United States)
ARTICLES: 2 LANGUAGE: English. Spanish.
HEADNOTE: EQUIPMENT MATERIALS SERVICES
TOPIC: Milit Assistance
CONCEPTS: Materials, equipment and services. Military assistance.
TREATY REF: 317UNTS209.
PARTIES:
Bolivia
USA (United States)

105828 Bilateral Exchange **405 UNTS 119**
SIGNED: 31 Mar 61   FORCE: 31 Mar 61
REGISTERED: 23 Aug 61 USA (United States)
ARTICLES: 2 LANGUAGE: English.
HEADNOTE: FREE ENTRY PRIVILEGES FOREIGN SERVICE PERSONNEL
TOPIC: Visas
CONCEPTS: Diplomatic privileges.
PARTIES:
Indonesia
USA (United States)

105829 Bilateral Exchange **405 UNTS 127**
SIGNED: 29 Jul 60   FORCE: 15 Feb 61
REGISTERED: 23 Aug 61 USA (United States)
ARTICLES: 2 LANGUAGE: English. Spanish.
HEADNOTE: INVESTMENT GUARANTEES
TOPIC: Admin Cooperation
CONCEPTS: Guarantees and safeguards. Arbitration Currency. Investments. Claims and settlements.
PARTIES:
Chile
USA (United States)

105830 Bilateral Exchange **405 UNTS 135**
SIGNED: 23 Dec 60   FORCE: 23 Dec 60
REGISTERED: 23 Aug 61 USA (United States)
ARTICLES: 2 LANGUAGE: English.
HEADNOTE: SEATO MEDICAL RESEARCH LAB
TOPIC: IGO Establishment
CONCEPTS: Annex type material. Specialists exchange. Sanitation. Research cooperation. Research results. Scientific exchange. Research and development. Funding procedures. IGO constitution.
INTL ORGS: Southeast Asia Treaty Organization.
PARTIES:
Thailand
USA (United States)

105831 Bilateral Instrument **405 UNTS 145**
SIGNED: 8 Dec 60   FORCE: 8 Dec 60
REGISTERED: 23 Aug 61 USA (United States)
ARTICLES: 2 LANGUAGE: English.
HEADNOTE: DELIVERY FREE DISTRIBUTION WHEAT BARLEY
TOPIC: Direct Aid
CONCEPTS: Treaty interpretation. Annex or ap-

pendix reference. Informational records. Inspection and observation. Operating agencies. Jurisdiction. Expense sharing formulae. Domestic obligation. Relief supplies. Grants. Distribution. Transport of goods.
PROCEDURE: Amendment. Termination.
PARTIES:
Cyprus
USA (United States)

105832 Bilateral Exchange **405 UNTS 165**
SIGNED: 4 Jan 61   FORCE: 4 Jan 61
REGISTERED: 23 Aug 61 USA (United States)
ARTICLES: 2 LANGUAGE: English. French.
HEADNOTE: ECONOMIC TECHNICAL ASSISTANCE
TOPIC: General Aid
CONCEPTS: Change of circumstances. Conformity with municipal law. Personnel. Accounting procedures. Currency deposits. Exchange rates and regulations. Local currency. Assets. Customs exemptions. Commodities and services. Domestic obligation. General technical assistance. Economic assistance. Materials, equipment and services. Grants.
PROCEDURE: Amendment. Termination.
PARTIES:
Mali
USA (United States)

105833 Bilateral Agreement **405 UNTS 173**
SIGNED: 11 Jan 61   FORCE: 11 Jan 61
REGISTERED: 23 Aug 61 USA (United States)
ARTICLES: 6 LANGUAGE: English.
HEADNOTE: AGRI COMMOD TITLE I
TOPIC: US Agri Commod Aid
CONCEPTS: General provisions. Annex or appendix reference. Exchange of information and documents. Reexport of goods, etc.. Exchange rates and regulations. Transportation costs. Local currency. Commodities schedule. Purchase authorization. Surplus commodities. Mutual consultation.
PARTIES:
Turkey
USA (United States)
ANNEX
409 UNTS 358. USA (United States). Amendment 29 May 61. Force 29 May 61.
409 UNTS 358. Turkey. Amendment 29 May 61. Force 29 May 61.
416 UNTS 368. USA (United States). Amendment 17 Jul 61. Force 17 Jul 61.
416 UNTS 368. Turkey. Amendment 17 Jul 61. Force 17 Jul 61.

105834 Bilateral Agreement **405 UNTS 189**
SIGNED: 14 Aug 58   FORCE: 23 Dec 58
REGISTERED: 25 Aug 61 Romania
ARTICLES: 19 LANGUAGE: Romanian. Arabic. French.
HEADNOTE: CIVIL AIR TRANSPORT
TOPIC: Air Transport
CONCEPTS: Definition of terms. Detailed regulations. Representation. Annex or appendix reference. Conformity with municipal law. General cooperation. Exchange of information and documents. Licenses and permits. Personnel. Recognition of legal documents. Use of facilities. Procedure. Negotiation. Humanitarian matters. Fees and exemptions. Non-interest rates and fees. Customs exemptions. Competency certificate. Registration certificate. Routes and logistics. Navigational conditions. Permit designation. Air transport. Airport facilities. Airworthiness certificates. Conditions of airlines operating permission. Overflights and technical stops. Operating authorizations and regulations.
PROCEDURE: Amendment. Denunciation. Ratification. Termination.
PARTIES:
Romania
United Arab Rep

105835 Bilateral Agreement **405 UNTS 223**
SIGNED: 16 Jun 58   FORCE: 19 Jun 59
REGISTERED: 25 Aug 61 Romania
ARTICLES: 16 LANGUAGE: French.
HEADNOTE: CIVIL AIR TRANSPORT
TOPIC: Air Transport

CONCEPTS: Air transport. Airport facilities. Airport equipment. Airworthiness certificates. Conditions of airlines operating permission. Overflights and technical stops. Operating authorizations and regulations. Licenses and certificates of nationality.
PROCEDURE: Denunciation.
PARTIES:
Norway
Romania

105836 Bilateral Agreement **405 UNTS 243**
SIGNED: 24 Dec 58   FORCE: 2 Jun 59
REGISTERED: 25 Aug 61 Romania
ARTICLES: 12 LANGUAGE: Romanian. Arabic. English.
HEADNOTE: DEVELOP EXTEND CONSOLIDATE TRADE
TOPIC: General Trade
CONCEPTS: Exceptions and exemptions. Annex or appendix reference. General cooperation. Licenses and permits. Establishment of commission. Establishment of trade relations. Reexport of goods, etc.. Trade procedures. Banking. Currency. Payment schedules. Quotas. Most favored nation clause. General technical assistance. Navigational conditions. Merchant vessels. Ports and pilotage.
INTL ORGS: Special Commission.
PROCEDURE: Duration. Ratification. Renewal or Revival. Termination.
PARTIES:
Iraq
Romania

105837 Bilateral Agreement **406 UNTS 3**
SIGNED: 9 Sep 60   FORCE: 18 Nov 60
REGISTERED: 25 Aug 61 IBRD (World Bank)
ARTICLES: 7 LANGUAGE: English.
HEADNOTE: LOAN PORT
TOPIC: IBRD Project
CONCEPTS: Default remedies. Definition of terms. Annex or appendix reference. Exchange of information and documents. Informational records. Inspection and observation. Accounting procedures. Bonds. Fees and exemptions. Interest rates. Domestic obligation. Terms of loan. Loan regulations. Loan guarantee. Guarantor non-interference. Water transport.
PARTIES:
Israel
IBRD (World Bank)

105838 Bilateral Agreement **406 UNTS 27**
SIGNED: 28 Oct 60   FORCE: 2 Feb 61
REGISTERED: 25 Aug 61 IBRD (World Bank)
ARTICLES: 5 LANGUAGE: English.
HEADNOTE: GUARANTEE AGREEMENT
TOPIC: IBRD Project
CONCEPTS: Definition of terms. Annex or appendix reference. Exchange of information and documents. Inspection and observation. Bonds. Fees and exemptions. Tax exemptions. Domestic obligation. Terms of loan. Loan regulations. Loan guarantee. Guarantor non-interference.
PARTIES:
India
IBRD (World Bank)

105839 Bilateral Treaty **406 UNTS 63**
SIGNED: 10 Jun 57   FORCE: 11 Mar 61
REGISTERED: 28 Aug 61 Denmark
ARTICLES: 6 LANGUAGE: Danish. Spanish.
HEADNOTE: COMMERCE & NAVIGATION
TOPIC: General Economic
CONCEPTS: Exceptions and exemptions. Annex or appendix reference. Consular relations establishment. Informational records. General property. Establishment of trade relations. Most favored nation clause. Equitable taxes. Customs duties. Navigational conditions. Merchant vessels. Inland and territorial waters. Ports and pilotage.
PROCEDURE: Denunciation. Ratification.
PARTIES:
Denmark
Peru

105840 Bilateral Agreement **406 UNTS 81**
SIGNED: 14 Jun 61 FORCE: 14 Jun 61
REGISTERED: 1 Sep 61 United Nations
ARTICLES: 7 LANGUAGE: English.
HEADNOTE: ESTABLISHMENT INTERNATIONAL
STATISTICAL TRAINING CENTER
TOPIC: Direct Aid
CONCEPTS: Privileges and immunities. Exchange
of information and documents. Personnel. Responsibility and liability. Establishment of commission. Exchange. Institute establishment.
Scholarships and grants. Accounting procedures. Expense sharing formulae. Domestic obligation. General technical assistance. Materials,
equipment and services. Internal structure. Conformity with IGO decisions.
TREATY REF: 1UNTS15.
PROCEDURE: Amendment. Duration. Renewal or
Revival. Termination.
PARTIES:
Ethiopia
United Nations

105841 Bilateral Agreement **406 UNTS 95**
SIGNED: 24 Aug 61 FORCE: 24 Aug 61
REGISTERED: 1 Sep 61 United Nations
ARTICLES: 9 LANGUAGE: English.
HEADNOTE: ACTIVITIES UNICEF
TOPIC: Direct Aid
CONCEPTS: Treaty implementation. Previous
treaty replacement. Privileges and immunities.
General cooperation. Exchange of information
and documents. Informational records. Inspection and observation. Public information. Responsibility and liability. Export quotas. Claims
and settlements. Tax exemptions. Customs exemptions. Commodities and services. Domestic
obligation. Assistance. General aid. Distribution.
IGO status.
TREATY REF: 1UNTS15.
PROCEDURE: Amendment. Termination.
PARTIES:
Poland
UNICEF (Children)

105842 Bilateral Agreement **406 UNTS 105**
SIGNED: 26 Aug 61 FORCE: 26 Aug 61
REGISTERED: 1 Sep 61 United Nations
ARTICLES: 6 LANGUAGE: French.
HEADNOTE: OPERATIONAL EXECUTIVE PERSONNEL
TOPIC: Tech Assistance
CONCEPTS: Treaty implementation. Annex or appendix reference. Privileges and immunities.
General cooperation. Personnel. Responsibility
and liability. Arbitration. Procedure. Negotiation.
Vocational training. Compensation. Expense
sharing formulae. Customs exemptions. Domestic obligation. Special projects. Tax exemptions.
Status of experts. Conformity with IGO decisions.
INTL ORGS: Permanent Court of Arbitration.
PROCEDURE: Amendment. Termination.
PARTIES:
Lebanon
United Nations

105843 Bilateral Agreement **406 UNTS 117**
SIGNED: 29 Aug 61 FORCE: 29 Aug 61
REGISTERED: 1 Sep 61 United Nations
ARTICLES: 6 LANGUAGE: English.
HEADNOTE: ESTABLISHMENT STATISTICAL
TRAINING CENTER
TOPIC: Tech Assistance
CONCEPTS: Time limit. Treaty implementation.
General cooperation. Exchange of information
and documents. Personnel. Responsibility and liability. Recognition of degrees. Institute establishment. Scholarships and grants. Vocational
training. Indemnities and reimbursements. Funding procedures. Domestic obligation. Materials,
equipment and services. Internal structure. Conformity with IGO decisions.
PROCEDURE: Amendment. Future Procedures
Contemplated. Renewal or Revival. Termination.
PARTIES:
Ghana
United Nations

105844 Bilateral Agreement **406 UNTS 129**
SIGNED: 29 Aug 61 FORCE: 29 Aug 61
REGISTERED: 1 Sep 61 United Nations
ARTICLES: 10 LANGUAGE: English. French.
HEADNOTE: ASSISTANCE
TOPIC: Direct Aid
CONCEPTS: Detailed regulations. Treaty implementation. Visas. Privileges and immunities. Exchange of information and documents. Informational records. Inspection and observation. Operating agencies. Personnel. Public information. Responsibility and liability. Title and deeds. Use
of facilities. Arbitration. Procedure. Negotiation.
Import quotas. Attachment of funds. Exchange
rates and regulations. Expense sharing formulae.
Financial programs. Domestic obligation. General technical assistance. Economic assistance.
Materials, equipment and services. IGO status.
INTL ORGS: International Court of Justice.
TREATY REF: 1UNTS15; 33UNTS261;
374UNTS147.
PROCEDURE: Amendment. Termination.
PARTIES:
Ivory Coast
UN Special Fund

105845 Bilateral Agreement **406 UNTS 147**
SIGNED: 29 May 61 FORCE: 29 May 61
REGISTERED: 1 Sep 61 United Nations
ARTICLES: 6 LANGUAGE: French.
HEADNOTE: CIVIL RIGHTS SEMINAR
TOPIC: IGO Operations
CONCEPTS: Diplomatic missions. Human rights.
Subsidiary organ. Internal structure.
PARTIES:
Romania
United Nations

105846 Bilateral Exchange **406 UNTS 157**
SIGNED: 7 Jul 61 FORCE: 1 Jan 60
REGISTERED: 1 Sep 61 Belgium
ARTICLES: 2 LANGUAGE: French.
HEADNOTE: DOUBLE TAXATION
TOPIC: Taxation
CONCEPTS: Domestic legislation. Taxation.
TREATY REF: 141LTS333.
PARTIES:
Belgium
France

105847 Bilateral Exchange **406 UNTS 165**
SIGNED: 24 Mar 60 FORCE: 24 Mar 60
REGISTERED: 5 Sep 61 USA (United States)
ARTICLES: 2 LANGUAGE: English.
HEADNOTE: WEAPONS PRODUCTION PROGRAM
TOPIC: Milit Assistance
CONCEPTS: Change of circumstances. Territorial
application. Previous treaty replacement. General cooperation. Licenses and permits. Private
contracts. Use of facilities. National treatment.
Customs exemptions. Materials, equipment and
services. Security of information. Exchange of
defense information. Equipment and supplies.
Restrictions on transfer.
INTL ORGS: North Atlantic Treaty Organization.
TREATY REF: 34UNTS243.
PROCEDURE: Future Procedures Contemplated.
Ratification.
PARTIES:
Netherlands
USA (United States)

105848 Bilateral Exchange **406 UNTS 177**
SIGNED: 13 Feb 61 FORCE: 13 Feb 61
REGISTERED: 5 Sep 61 USA (United States)
ARTICLES: 4 LANGUAGE: English. Spanish.
HEADNOTE: FREE ENTRY PRIVILEGES FOREIGN
SERVICE PERSONNEL
TOPIC: Visas
CONCEPTS: Diplomatic privileges.
PARTIES:
Peru
USA (United States)

105849 Bilateral Agreement **406 UNTS 187**
SIGNED: 25 Mar 61 FORCE: 25 Mar 61
REGISTERED: 6 Sep 61 USA (United States)
ARTICLES: 6 LANGUAGE: English.
HEADNOTE: AGRI COMMOD TITLE I

TOPIC: US Agri Commod Aid
CONCEPTS: General provisions. Annex or appendix reference. Exchange of information and documents. Reexport of goods, etc.. Exchange rates
and regulations. Sale of local currency. Local
currency. Commodities schedule. Purchase authorization. Surplus commodities. Mutual consultation.
PARTIES:
USA (United States)
Vietnam, South
                    ANNEX
433 UNTS 382. USA (United States). Amendment
24 Jan 62. Force 24 Jan 62.
433 UNTS 382. Vietnam, South. Amendment
24 Jan 62. Force 24 Jan 62

105850 Bilateral Agreement **406 UNTS 203**
SIGNED: 7 Apr 61 FORCE: 7 Apr 61
REGISTERED: 6 Sep 61 USA (United States)
ARTICLES: 6 LANGUAGE: English.
HEADNOTE: AGRI COMMOD TITLE I
TOPIC: US Agri Commod Aid
CONCEPTS: General provisions. Annex or appendix reference. Exchange of information and documents. Reexport of goods, etc.. Exchange rates
and regulations. Transportation costs. Local currency. Commodities schedule. Purchase authorization. Surplus commodities. Mutual consultation.
PARTIES:
Iceland
USA (United States)
                    ANNEX
416 UNTS 374. USA (United States). Amendment
6 Jul 61. Force 18 Jul 61.
416 UNTS 374. Iceland. Amendment 18 Jul 61.
Force 18 Jul 61.

105851 Bilateral Agreement **406 UNTS 215**
SIGNED: 22 Apr 46 FORCE: 22 Apr 46
REGISTERED: 6 Sep 61 USA (United States)
ARTICLES: 1 LANGUAGE: English. Polish.
HEADNOTE: PURCHASE SURPLUS PROPERTY
TOPIC: Loans and Credits
CONCEPTS: General property. Exchange rates and
regulations. Interest rates. Local currency. Loan
and credit. Credit provisions. Purchase authorization. Loan repayment. Terms of loan.
PARTIES:
Poland
USA (United States)

105852 Bilateral Exchange **406 UNTS 235**
SIGNED: 15 Feb 61 FORCE: 15 Feb 61
REGISTERED: 6 Sep 61 USA (United States)
ARTICLES: 2 LANGUAGE: English. Persian.
HEADNOTE: INFORMATIONAL MEDIA GUARANTY
PROGRAM
TOPIC: Mass Media
CONCEPTS: Local currency. Media guaranty.
PARTIES:
Afghanistan
USA (United States)

105853 Bilateral Exchange **406 UNTS 241**
SIGNED: 17 Mar 61 FORCE: 17 Mar 61
REGISTERED: 6 Sep 61 USA (United States)
ARTICLES: 2 LANGUAGE: English. Portuguese.
HEADNOTE: GRANT PROCUREMENT NUCLEAR
RESEARCH TRAINING EQUIPMENT MATERIAL
TOPIC: Atomic Energy
CONCEPTS: Non-prejudice to third party. Exchange of information and documents. Responsibility and liability. Research cooperation. Nuclear research. Indemnities and reimbursements. Payment schedules. Nuclear materials.
Peaceful use. Transport of goods.
PARTIES:
Brazil
USA (United States)

105854 Bilateral Exchange **406 UNTS 249**
SIGNED: 31 Mar 61 FORCE: 31 Mar 61
REGISTERED: 6 Sep 61 USA (United States)
ARTICLES: 2 LANGUAGE: English. French.
HEADNOTE: GUARANTEES PRIVATE INVESTMENTS
TOPIC: Admin Cooperation

CONCEPTS: Guarantees and safeguards. Arbitration. Currency. Investments. Claims and settlements.
PARTIES:
Morocco
USA (United States)
ANNEX
489 UNTS 399. USA (United States). Supplementation 2 Oct 63. Force 2 Oct 63.
489 UNTS 399. Morocco. Supplementation 2 Oct 63. Force 2 Oct 63.

105855 Bilateral Agreement **406 UNTS 255**
SIGNED: 11 Sep 61   FORCE: 11 Sep 61
REGISTERED: 11 Sep 61 United Nations
ARTICLES: 6 LANGUAGE: English.
HEADNOTE: OPERATIONAL EXECUTIVE PERSONNEL
TOPIC: Tech Assistance
CONCEPTS: Treaty implementation. Annex or appendix reference. Privileges and immunities. General cooperation. Personnel. Responsibility and liability. Arbitration. Procedure. Negotiation. Vocational training. Compensation. Expense sharing formulae. Tax exemptions. Customs exemptions. Domestic obligation. Special projects. Volunteer programs. Conformity with IGO decisions.
INTL ORGS: Permanent Court of Arbitration.
PROCEDURE: Amendment. Termination.
PARTIES:
Jordan
United Nations

105856 Bilateral Exchange **407 UNTS 3**
SIGNED: 3 Apr 61   FORCE: 3 Apr 61
REGISTERED: 14 Sep 61 USA (United States)
ARTICLES: 2 LANGUAGE: English. Spanish.
HEADNOTE: MILITARY EQUIPMENT MATERIALS SERVICES
TOPIC: Milit Assistance
CONCEPTS: Previous treaty amendment. Materials, equipment and services. Defense and security. Self-defense.
TREATY REF: 174UNTS215.
PARTIES:
Colombia
USA (United States)

105857 Multilateral Agreement **407 UNTS 8**
SIGNED: 13 Dec 55   FORCE: 18 Sep 61
REGISTERED: 18 Sep 61 United Nations
ARTICLES: 6 LANGUAGE: Spanish.
HEADNOTE: TECHNICAL ASSISTANCE
TOPIC: Tech Assistance
CONCEPTS: General technical assistance. Assistance. Military assistance.
PROCEDURE: Ratification.
PARTIES:
FAO (Food Agri) SIGNED: 13 Dec 55 FORCE: 18 Sep 61
ICAO (Civil Aviat) SIGNED: 13 Dec 55 FORCE: 18 Sep 61
ILO (Labor Org) SIGNED: 13 Dec 55 FORCE: 18 Sep 61
ITU (Telecommun) SIGNED: 13 Dec 55 FORCE: 18 Sep 61
UNESCO (Educ/Cult) SIGNED: 13 Dec 55 FORCE: 18 Sep 61
United Nations SIGNED: 13 Dec 55 FORCE: 18 Sep 61
WHO (World Health) SIGNED: 13 Dec 55 FORCE: 18 Sep 61
WMO (Meteorology) SIGNED: 13 Dec 55 FORCE: 18 Sep 61
Uruguay SIGNED: 13 Dec 55 RATIFIED: 18 Sep 61 FORCE: 18 Sep 61
ANNEX
614 UNTS 310. ICAO (Civil Aviat). Amendment 24 Jul 67. Force 31 Jul 67.
614 UNTS 310. ITU (Telecommun). Amendment 24 Jul 67. Force 31 Jul 67.
614 UNTS 310. WMO (Meteorology). Amendment 24 Jul 67. Force 31 Jul 67.
614 UNTS 310. Uruguay. Amendment 24 Jul 67. Force 31 Jul 67.
614 UNTS 310. United Nations. Amendment 24 Jul 67. Force 31 Jul 67.
614 UNTS 310. ILO (Labor Org). Amendment 24 Jul 67. Force 31 Jul 67.

614 UNTS 310. UNESCO (Educ/Cult). Amendment 24 Jul 67. Force 31 Jul 67.
614 UNTS 310. WHO (World Health). Amendment 24 Jul 67. Force 31 Jul 67.
614 UNTS 310. FAO (Food Agri). Amendment 24 Jul 67. Force 31 Jul 67.
651 UNTS 361. IMCO (Maritime Org). Accession 21 Oct 68. Force 21 Oct 68.
651 UNTS 361. UNIDO (Industrial). Accession 21 Oct 68. Force 21 Oct 68.

105858 Bilateral Agreement **407 UNTS 37**
SIGNED: 27 Jul 61   FORCE: 27 Jul 61
REGISTERED: 19 Sep 61 Austria
ARTICLES: 6 LANGUAGE: German. Albanian.
HEADNOTE: TRADE & PAYMENTS
TOPIC: General Economic
CONCEPTS: Annex or appendix reference. Conformity with municipal law. Licenses and permits. Establishment of commission. Currency. Monetary and gold transfers. Payment schedules.
INTL ORGS: Special Commission.
PROCEDURE: Denunciation. Duration. Renewal or Revival.
PARTIES:
Albania
Austria

105859 Multilateral Agreement **407 UNTS 52**
SIGNED: 20 Sep 61   FORCE: 20 Sep 61
REGISTERED: 25 Sep 61 United Nations
ARTICLES: 6 LANGUAGE: French.
HEADNOTE: TECHNICAL ASSISTANCE
TOPIC: Tech Assistance
CONCEPTS: Definition of terms. Privileges and immunities. General cooperation. Exchange of information and documents. Personnel. Responsibility and liability. Title and deeds. Use of facilities. Exchange. Scholarships and grants. Vocational training. Research and development. Exchange rates and regulations. Expense sharing formulae. Local currency. Domestic obligation. General technical assistance. Materials, equipment and services. IGO status. Conformity with IGO decisions.
TREATY REF: 76UNTS132; 374UNTS147; 1UNTS15; 33UNTS261.
PROCEDURE: Amendment. Termination.
PARTIES:
FAO (Food Agri) SIGNED: 20 Sep 61 FORCE: 20 Sep 61
IAEA (Atom Energy) SIGNED: 20 Sep 61 FORCE: 20 Sep 61
ICAO (Civil Aviat) SIGNED: 20 Sep 61 FORCE: 20 Sep 61
ILO (Labor Org) SIGNED: 20 Sep 61 FORCE: 20 Sep 61
ITU (Telecommun) SIGNED: 20 Sep 61 FORCE: 20 Sep 61
UNESCO (Educ/Cult) SIGNED: 20 Sep 61 FORCE: 20 Sep 61
United Nations SIGNED: 20 Sep 61 FORCE: 20 Sep 61
WHO (World Health) SIGNED: 20 Sep 61 FORCE: 20 Sep 61
WMO (Meteorology) SIGNED: 20 Sep 61 FORCE: 20 Sep 61
Togo SIGNED: 20 Sep 61 FORCE: 20 Sep 61

105860 Bilateral Agreement **407 UNTS 66**
SIGNED: 27 Apr 61   FORCE: 1 Aug 61
REGISTERED: 26 Sep 61 WHO (World Health)
ARTICLES: 6 LANGUAGE: German. Hungarian.
HEADNOTE: TECHNICAL ADVISORY ASSISTANCE
TOPIC: Tech Assistance
CONCEPTS: Definition of terms. Privileges and immunities. General cooperation. Exchange of information and documents. Personnel. Responsibility and liability. Title and deeds. Exchange. Scholarships and grants. Vocational training. Research and development. Expense sharing formulae. Local currency. Domestic obligation. Special projects. Materials, equipment and services. IGO status. Conformity with IGO decisions.
INTL ORGS: United Nations.
PROCEDURE: Amendment. Termination.
PARTIES:
Mali
WHO (World Health)

105861 Bilateral Agreement **407 UNTS 78**
SIGNED: 14 Jun 58   FORCE: 13 Sep 58
REGISTERED: 26 Sep 61 Hungary
ARTICLES: 7 LANGUAGE: Hungarian. Czechoslovakian.
HEADNOTE: HEALTH COOPERATION
TOPIC: Sanitation
CONCEPTS: General cooperation. Exchange of information and documents. Informational records. Public health. Exchange. Scholarships and grants. Vocational training. Scientific exchange. Research and development. Indemnities and reimbursements. Publications exchange. Conferences.
PROCEDURE: Denunciation. Duration. Ratification. Renewal or Revival.
PARTIES:
Germany, East
Hungary

105862 Bilateral Agreement **407 UNTS 92**
SIGNED: 8 May 58   FORCE: 22 Sep 58
REGISTERED: 26 Sep 61 Hungary
ARTICLES: 19 LANGUAGE: Hungarian. German.
HEADNOTE: CUSTOMS MATTERS
TOPIC: Customs
CONCEPTS: General cooperation. Investigation of violations. Customs duties. Frontier crossing points.
PROCEDURE: Denunciation.
PARTIES:
Czechoslovakia
Hungary

105863 Bilateral Agreement **407 UNTS 132**
SIGNED: 10 Sep 55   FORCE: 24 Jan 56
REGISTERED: 26 Sep 61 Hungary
ARTICLES: 12 LANGUAGE: Hungarian. Russian.
HEADNOTE: RELATING CIVIL AIR TRANSPORT
TOPIC: Air Transport
CONCEPTS: Representation. Annex or appendix reference. Conformity with municipal law. General cooperation. Exchange of information and documents. Licenses and permits. Recognition of legal documents. Humanitarian matters. Tax exemptions. Customs exemptions. Registration certificate. Routes and logistics. Permit designation. Air transport. Airworthiness certificates. Operating authorizations and regulations.
PROCEDURE: Amendment. Denunciation. Ratification. Termination.
PARTIES:
Germany, East
Hungary

105864 Bilateral Agreement **407 UNTS 156**
SIGNED: 27 May 55   FORCE: 16 Aug 57
REGISTERED: 26 Sep 61 Hungary
ARTICLES: 19 LANGUAGE: Hungarian. German.
HEADNOTE: LEGAL STATUS SOVIET FORCES
TOPIC: Status of Forces
CONCEPTS: Definition of terms. Court procedures. Conformity with municipal law. General cooperation. Recognition of legal documents. Responsibility and liability. Use of facilities. Investigation of violations. Establishment of commission. Procedure. Compensation. Claims and settlements. Military training. Jurisdiction. Procurement and logistics. Status of forces. Bases and facilities.
INTL ORGS: Claims Commission.
PROCEDURE: Future Procedures Contemplated.
PARTIES:
Hungary
USSR (Soviet Union)

105865 Bilateral Convention **407 UNTS 186**
SIGNED: 3 Jul 57   FORCE: 22 Feb 58
REGISTERED: 26 Sep 61 Hungary
ARTICLES: 24 LANGUAGE: Hungarian. German.
HEADNOTE: CONSULAR
TOPIC: Consul/Citizenship
CONCEPTS: General consular functions. Diplomatic privileges. Consular relations establishment. Privileges and immunities. Responsibility and liability.
PROCEDURE: Duration. Ratification.
PARTIES:
Germany, East
Hungary

105866 Bilateral Convention **407 UNTS 216**
SIGNED: 13 Nov 57   FORCE: 20 Jun 58
REGISTERED: 26 Sep 61 Hungary
ARTICLES: 7 LANGUAGE: Hungarian. German.
HEADNOTE: VETERINARY COOPERATION
TOPIC: Sanitation
CONCEPTS: Standardization. General cooperation. Exchange of information and documents. Negotiation. Specialists exchange. Veterinary. Teacher and student exchange. Vocational training. Research results. Scientific exchange. Trade procedures. Indemnities and reimbursements. Materials, equipment and services. Publications exchange.
PROCEDURE: Denunciation. Duration. Future Procedures Contemplated. Ratification. Renewal or Revival.
PARTIES:
 Germany, East
 Hungary

105867   Bilateral Treaty   **408 UNTS 4**
SIGNED: 30 Oct 57   FORCE: 23 Jun 58
REGISTERED: 26 Sep 61 Hungary
ARTICLES: 88 LANGUAGE: Hungarian. German.
HEADNOTE: LEGAL ASSISTANCE CIVIL FAMILY CRIMINAL CASES
TOPIC: Admin Cooperation
CONCEPTS: General provisions. Privileges and immunities. Consular functions in property. Extradition, deportation and repatriation. Refusal of extradition. Concurrent requests. Limits of prosecution. Provisional detainment. Extradition postponement. Witnesses and experts. Material evidence. Conformity with municipal law. Family law. Exchange of information and documents. Juridical personality. Legal protection and assistance. Recognition and enforcement of legal decisions. General property. Succession. Recognition of legal documents. Prizes and arbitral awards. Indemnities and reimbursements. Assets transfer. Conveyance in transit.
PROCEDURE: Denunciation. Duration. Ratification. Renewal or Revival.
PARTIES:
 Germany, East
 Hungary

105868 Bilateral Agreement **408 UNTS 118**
SIGNED: 24 Apr 58   FORCE: 15 Jul 58
REGISTERED: 26 Sep 61 Hungary
ARTICLES: 34 LANGUAGE: Hungarian. Russian.
HEADNOTE: MUTUAL LEGAL ASSISTANCE RELATING TEMPORARY PRESENCE SOVIET FORCES
TOPIC: Status of Forces
CONCEPTS: Legal protection and assistance. Recognition and enforcement of legal decisions. Investigation of violations. Indemnities and reimbursements. Jurisdiction.
INTL ORGS: Special Commission.
PROCEDURE: Amendment. Ratification.
PARTIES:
 Hungary
 USSR (Soviet Union)

105869 Bilateral Agreement **408 UNTS 156**
SIGNED: 25 Oct 57   FORCE: 21 Jul 58
REGISTERED: 26 Sep 61 Hungary
ARTICLES: 13 LANGUAGE: Hungarian. German.
HEADNOTE: AGRICULTURAL PLANT PROTECTION
TOPIC: Sanitation
CONCEPTS: Definition of terms. General cooperation. Exchange of information and documents. Inspection and observation. Domestic legislation. Quarantine. Border control. Disease control. Insect control. Research results. Scientific exchange. Reexport of goods, etc.. Trade procedures. Indemnities and reimbursements. General technical assistance. Agriculture. Canal improvement. Mass media exchange. Conferences.
PROCEDURE: Amendment. Denunciation. Duration. Ratification. Renewal or Revival.
PARTIES:
 Germany, East
 Hungary

105870 Bilateral Convention **408 UNTS 178**
SIGNED: 12 Mar 58   FORCE: 29 Oct 58
REGISTERED: 26 Sep 61 Hungary
ARTICLES: 9 LANGUAGE: Hungarian. Czechoslovakian.
HEADNOTE: VETERINARY COOPERATION
TOPIC: Sanitation
CONCEPTS: Standardization. General cooperation. Exchange of information and documents. Domestic legislation. Negotiation. Specialists exchange. Disease control. Veterinary. Exchange. Vocational training. Research results. Scientific exchange. Trade procedures. Indemnities and reimbursements. Economic assistance. Mass media exchange.
PROCEDURE: Denunciation. Duration. Future Procedures Contemplated. Ratification. Renewal or Revival.
PARTIES:
 Czechoslovakia
 Hungary

105871 Bilateral Agreement **408 UNTS 194**
SIGNED: 21 Jul 58   FORCE: 23 Nov 58
REGISTERED: 26 Sep 61 Hungary
ARTICLES: 11 LANGUAGE: Hungarian. Russian.
HEADNOTE: CUSTOMS MATTERS
TOPIC: Customs
CONCEPTS: General cooperation. Investigation of violations. Customs duties. Frontier crossing points.
PROCEDURE: Duration. Renewal or Revival. Termination.
PARTIES:
 Hungary
 USSR (Soviet Union)

105872 Bilateral Agreement **408 UNTS 212**
SIGNED: 8 May 58   FORCE: 20 Jan 59
REGISTERED: 26 Sep 61 Hungary
ARTICLES: 9 LANGUAGE: Hungarian. Polish.
HEADNOTE: HEALTH COOPERATION
TOPIC: Sanitation
CONCEPTS: General cooperation. Exchange of information and documents. Informational records. Domestic legislation. Public health. Pharmaceuticals. Exchange. Teacher and student exchange. Vocational training. Research results. Scientific exchange. Research and development. Indemnities and reimbursements. Publications exchange. Conferences.
PROCEDURE: Denunciation. Duration. Ratification. Renewal or Revival.
PARTIES:
 Hungary
 Poland

105873 Bilateral Agreement **408 UNTS 230**
SIGNED: 30 Jan 60   FORCE: 1 May 60
REGISTERED: 26 Sep 61 Hungary
ARTICLES: 20 LANGUAGE: Hungarian. German.
HEADNOTE: COOPERATION SOCIAL POLICY
TOPIC: Health/Educ/Welfare
CONCEPTS: General cooperation. Exchange of information and documents. Informational records. Domestic legislation. Personnel. Family allowances. Old age insurance. Sickness and invalidity insurance. Social security. Unemployment.
PROCEDURE: Denunciation. Duration. Ratification. Renewal or Revival.
PARTIES:
 Germany, East
 Hungary

105874   Bilateral Agreement   **409 UNTS 4**
SIGNED: 19 Dec 59   FORCE: 6 May 60
REGISTERED: 26 Sep 61 Hungary
ARTICLES: 15 LANGUAGE: Hungarian. German.
HEADNOTE: CULTURAL SCIENTIFIC EXCHANGE
TOPIC: Health/Educ/Welfare
CONCEPTS: Standardization. Exchange of information and documents. Personnel. Specialists exchange. Recognition of degrees. Exchange. Teacher and student exchange. Professorships. Vocational training. Exchange. Artists. Athletes. Scientific exchange. Recognition. Publications exchange. Mass media exchange. Information agency. Press and wire services.
PROCEDURE: Denunciation. Duration.
PARTIES:
 Germany, East
 Hungary

105875 Bilateral Agreement **409 UNTS 22**
SIGNED: 12 Jan 60   FORCE: 7 Sep 60
REGISTERED: 26 Sep 61 Hungary
ARTICLES: 6 LANGUAGE: Hungarian. German.
HEADNOTE: PATENTS TRADEMARKS
TOPIC: Patents/Copyrights
CONCEPTS: Patents, copyrights and trademarks. Trademarks. Recognition.
TREATY REF: 190LTS17; 1UNTS269.
PARTIES:
 Germany, East
 Hungary

105876 Unilateral Instrument **409 UNTS 44**
SIGNED: 27 Apr 61   FORCE: 27 Sep 61
REGISTERED: 27 Sep 61 United Nations
ARTICLES: 1 LANGUAGE: English.
HEADNOTE: ACCEPTANCE OBLIGATIONS UN
TOPIC: UN Charter
CONCEPTS: Acceptance of UN obligations. Acceptance of obligations upon admittance to UN.
INTL ORGS: United Nations.
PARTIES:
 Sierra Leone

105877   Bilateral Exchange   **409 UNTS 47**
SIGNED: 19 Jul 61   FORCE: 19 Jul 61
REGISTERED: 27 Sep 61 Iceland
ARTICLES: 2 LANGUAGE: German.
HEADNOTE: FISHERY ZONE AROUND ICELAND
TOPIC: Specific Resources
CONCEPTS: Compulsory jurisdiction. Markers and definitions. Frontier waterways. Ocean resources. Fisheries and fishing.
PROCEDURE: Registration.
PARTIES:
 Germany, West
 Iceland

105878 Bilateral Agreement **409 UNTS 56**
SIGNED: 5 Mar 61   FORCE: 3 Jul 61
REGISTERED: 29 Sep 61 United Nations
ARTICLES: 6 LANGUAGE: English.
HEADNOTE: EXPERTS OPERATIONAL EXECUTIVE PERSONNEL
TOPIC: Tech Assistance
CONCEPTS: Treaty implementation. Privileges and immunities. General cooperation. Personnel. Responsibility and liability. Arbitration. Procedure. Negotiation. Vocational training. Compensation. Expense sharing formulae. Tax exemptions. Customs exemptions. Domestic obligation. Special projects. Status of experts. Conformity with IGO decisions.
INTL ORGS: Permanent Court of Arbitration.
PROCEDURE: Amendment. Termination.
PARTIES:
 Iraq
 United Nations

105879 Bilateral Agreement **409 UNTS 68**
SIGNED: 10 Feb 61   FORCE: 10 Feb 61
REGISTERED: 29 Sep 61 USA (United States)
ARTICLES: 24 LANGUAGE: English.
HEADNOTE: US DEFENSE AREAS WEST INDIES
TOPIC: Milit Installation
CONCEPTS: Currency. Defense and security. Jurisdiction. Procurement and logistics. Status of forces.
INTL ORGS: United Nations. Special Commission.
PROCEDURE: Duration.
PARTIES:
 UK Great Britain
 USA (United States)
               ANNEX
531 UNTS 368. USA (United States). Replacement 20 Aug 64. Force 20 Aug 64.
531 UNTS 368. UK Great Britain. Replacement 20 Aug 64. Force 20 Aug 64.

105880   Bilateral Exchange   **409 UNTS 129**
SIGNED: 10 Feb 61   FORCE: 10 Feb 61
REGISTERED: 29 Sep 61 USA (United States)
ARTICLES: 2 LANGUAGE: English.
HEADNOTE: DEFENSE AREAS
TOPIC: Milit Installation
CONCEPTS: Annex type material. Use of facilities. Military installations and equipment
TREATY REF: 409UNTS67.

PARTIES:
UK Great Britain
USA (United States)

105881 Bilateral Exchange **409 UNTS 136**
SIGNED: 31 Mar 61 FORCE: 31 Mar 61
REGISTERED: 29 Sep 61 USA (United States)
ARTICLES: 2 LANGUAGE: English. French.
HEADNOTE: COMMUNICATION SATELLITE TESTING
TOPIC: Scientific Project
CONCEPTS: Communication satellites testing. Research and development. Facilities and equipment. Satellites.
PARTIES:
France
USA (United States)

105882 Bilateral Agreement **409 UNTS 140**
SIGNED: 3 Apr 61 FORCE: 3 Apr 61
REGISTERED: 29 Sep 61 USA (United States)
ARTICLES: 6 LANGUAGE: English. Spanish.
HEADNOTE: AGRI COMMOD TITLE I
TOPIC: US Agri Commod Aid
CONCEPTS: General provisions. Annex or appendix reference. Exchange of information and documents. Reexport of goods, etc.. Exchange rates and regulations. Transportation costs. Local currency. Commodities schedule. Purchase authorization. Surplus commodities. Mutual consultation.
PARTIES:
Ecuador
USA (United States)

105883 Bilateral Exchange **409 UNTS 163**
SIGNED: 19 Apr 61 FORCE: 19 Apr 61
REGISTERED: 29 Sep 61 USA (United States)
ARTICLES: 2 LANGUAGE: English.
HEADNOTE: GRANT PROCUREMENT NUCLEAR RESEARCH TRAINING EQUIPMENT MATERIAL
TOPIC: Direct Aid
CONCEPTS: Public information. Responsibility and liability. Indemnities and reimbursements. Financial programs. Payment schedules. Transportation costs. General aid. Grants. Procurement. Atomic energy assistance. Non-nuclear materials. Peaceful use. Transport of goods.
PARTIES:
USA (United States)
Yugoslavia

105884 Bilateral Agreement **409 UNTS 172**
SIGNED: 28 Apr 61 FORCE: 28 Apr 61
REGISTERED: 29 Sep 61 USA (United States)
ARTICLES: 6 LANGUAGE: English.
HEADNOTE: AGRI COMMOD
TOPIC: US Agri Commod Aid
CONCEPTS: General provisions. Annex or appendix reference. Exchange of information and documents. Reexport of goods, etc.. Exchange rates and regulations. Transportation costs. Local currency. Commodities schedule. Purchase authorization. Surplus commodities. Mutual consultation.
PARTIES:
USA (United States)
Yugoslavia
ANNEX
416 UNTS 378. USA (United States). Amendment 1 Jul 61. Force 1 Jul 61.
416 UNTS 378. Yugoslavia. Amendment 1 Jul 61. Force 1 Jul 61.
524 UNTS 322. USA (United States). Amendment 15 Apr 64. Force 15 Apr 64.
524 UNTS 322. Yugoslavia. Amendment 15 Apr 64. Force 15 Apr 64.

105885 Bilateral Agreement **409 UNTS 194**
SIGNED: 5 May 61 FORCE: 5 May 61
REGISTERED: 29 Sep 61 USA (United States)
ARTICLES: 6 LANGUAGE: English.
HEADNOTE: ECONOMIC TECHNICAL RELATED ASSISTANCE
TOPIC: General Aid
CONCEPTS: Change of circumstances. Exceptions and exemptions. Guarantees and safeguards. Diplomatic privileges. Privileges and immunities. Conformity with municipal law. General cooperation. Personnel. Accounting procedures. Attachment of funds. Banking. Exchange rates and regulations. Garnishment of funds. Seizure funds. Tax exemptions. Customs exemptions. Commodities and services. Domestic obligation. General technical assistance. Economic assistance. Materials, equipment and services. Aid missions. Grants.
PROCEDURE: Amendment. Duration. Termination.
PARTIES:
Sierra Leone
USA (United States)

105886 Bilateral Exchange **409 UNTS 203**
SIGNED: 9 May 61 FORCE: 9 May 61
REGISTERED: 29 Sep 61 USA (United States)
ARTICLES: 2 LANGUAGE: English.
HEADNOTE: RADIOACTIVITY ATMOSPHERE
TOPIC: Scientific Project
CONCEPTS: Operating agencies. General property. Responsibility and liability. Use of facilities. Meteorology. Nuclear research. Research and development. Tax exemptions. Economic assistance. Atomic energy assistance. Facilities and equipment.
PROCEDURE: Duration. Renewal or Revival. Termination.
PARTIES:
Australia
USA (United States)
ANNEX
462 UNTS 358. USA (United States). Prolongation 11 Sep 62. Force 30 Oct 62.
462 UNTS 358. Australia. Prolongation 30 Oct 62. Force 30 Oct 62.
638 UNTS 286. Australia. Amendment 1 Sep 66. Prolongation 1 Sep 66.
638 UNTS 286. USA (United States). Force 1 Sep 66.
638 UNTS 286. USA (United States). Amendment 1 Sep 66. Prolongation 1 Sep 66.

105887 Bilateral Exchange **409 UNTS 213**
SIGNED: 10 May 61 FORCE: 10 May 61
REGISTERED: 29 Sep 61 USA (United States)
ARTICLES: 2 LANGUAGE: English.
HEADNOTE: AGRI COMMOD TITLE I
TOPIC: US Agri Commod Aid
CONCEPTS: General provisions. Annex or appendix reference. Exchange of information and documents. Reexport of goods, etc.. Exchange rates and regulations. Transportation costs. Local currency. Commodities schedule. Purchase authorization. Surplus commodities. Mutual consultation.
PARTIES:
Israel
USA (United States)

105888 Bilateral Agreement **409 UNTS 232**
SIGNED: 13 May 61 FORCE: 10 May 61
REGISTERED: 29 Sep 61 USA (United States)
ARTICLES: 7 LANGUAGE: English. French.
HEADNOTE: ECONOMIC FINANCIAL TECHNICAL RELATED ASSISTANCE
TOPIC: General Aid
CONCEPTS: Guarantees and safeguards. Privileges and immunities. Conformity with municipal law. Personnel. Accounting procedures. Attachment of funds. Banking. Exchange rates and regulations. Financial programs. Garnishment of funds. Seizure funds. Tax exemptions. Customs exemptions. Temporary importation. Commodities and services. Domestic obligation. General technical assistance. Economic assistance. Materials, equipment and services. Aid missions. Grants.
PROCEDURE: Termination.
PARTIES:
Senegal
USA (United States)

105889 Bilateral Exchange **409 UNTS 241**
SIGNED: 17 May 61 FORCE: 17 May 61
REGISTERED: 29 Sep 61 USA (United States)
ARTICLES: 2 LANGUAGE: English. French.
HEADNOTE: ECONOMIC TECHNICAL RELATED ASSISTANCE
TOPIC: General Aid
CONCEPTS: Change of circumstances. Exceptions and exemptions. Guarantees and safeguards. Diplomatic privileges. Privileges and immunities. Conformity with municipal law. Personnel. Accounting procedures. Attachment of funds. Banking. Exchange rates and regulations. Funding procedures. Garnishment of funds. Seizure funds. Tax exemptions. Customs exemptions. Commodities and services. Domestic obligation. General technical assistance. Economic assistance. Materials, equipment and services. Aid missions. Grants.
PROCEDURE: Termination.
PARTIES:
Ivory Coast
USA (United States)

105890 Bilateral Exchange **409 UNTS 251**
SIGNED: 19 May 61 FORCE: 19 May 61
REGISTERED: 29 Sep 61 USA (United States)
ARTICLES: 2 LANGUAGE: English.
HEADNOTE: GUARANTY PRIVATE INVESTMENTS
TOPIC: Admin Cooperation
CONCEPTS: Guarantees and safeguards. Arbitration. Currency. Investments. Claims and settlements.
INTL ORGS: International Court of Justice.
PARTIES:
Sierra Leone
USA (United States)
ANNEX
494 UNTS 324. USA (United States). Amendment 28 Dec 62. Force 13 Nov 63.
494 UNTS 324. Sierra Leone. Amendment 13 Nov 63. Force 13 Nov 63.

105891 Bilateral Agreement **409 UNTS 260**
SIGNED: 22 May 61 FORCE: 22 May 61
REGISTERED: 29 Sep 61 USA (United States)
ARTICLES: 6 LANGUAGE: English. Spanish.
HEADNOTE: AGRI COMMOD TITLE I
TOPIC: US Agri Commod Aid
CONCEPTS: General provisions. Annex or appendix reference. Exchange of information and documents. Reexport of goods, etc.. Exchange rates and regulations. Transportation costs. Local currency. Commodities schedule. Purchase authorization. Surplus commodities. Mutual consultation.
PARTIES:
Spain
USA (United States)

105892 Bilateral Exchange **409 UNTS 279**
SIGNED: 5 Jun 61 FORCE: 5 Jun 61
REGISTERED: 29 Sep 61 USA (United States)
ARTICLES: 2 LANGUAGE: English.
HEADNOTE: TRANSIT NAVIGATIONAL SATELLITE PROGRAM
TOPIC: Scientific Project
CONCEPTS: Personnel. Use of facilities. Research results. Communication satellites testing. Research and development. Indemnities and reimbursements. Tax exemptions. Special projects. Navigational equipment. Facilities and equipment. Satellites.
PROCEDURE: Duration. Termination.
PARTIES:
Australia
USA (United States)

105893 Bilateral Agreement **410 UNTS 3**
SIGNED: 3 Dec 60 FORCE: 24 May 61
REGISTERED: 29 Sep 61 USA (United States)
ARTICLES: 11 LANGUAGE: English. Italian.
HEADNOTE: COOPERATION USES ATOMIC ENERGY MUTUAL DEFENSE PURPOSES
TOPIC: Atomic Energy
CONCEPTS: Definition of terms. Exchange of official publications. Exchange of information and documents. Research results. Laws and formalities. Non-nuclear materials. Atomic weapons. Military assistance. Security of information.
PROCEDURE: Duration.
PARTIES:
Italy
USA (United States)

105894 Bilateral Exchange **410 UNTS 21**
SIGNED: 12 Jun 61 FORCE: 12 Jun 61

REGISTERED: 29 Sep 61 USA (United States)
ARTICLES: 2 LANGUAGE: English.
HEADNOTE: AIR DEFENSE RELATED COOPER-
ATION
TOPIC: Milit Assistance
CONCEPTS: Annex or appendix reference. Joint
defense. Defense and security. Military assis-
tance.
INTL ORGS: North Atlantic Treaty Organization.
TREATY REF: 34UNTS243.
PARTIES:
Canada
USA (United States)

105895 Bilateral Agreement **410 UNTS 34**
SIGNED: 19 Jun 61   FORCE: 19 Jun 61
REGISTERED: 29 Sep 61 USA (United States)
ARTICLES: 8 LANGUAGE: English.
HEADNOTE: SOCIAL PROGRESS TRUST FUND
TOPIC: Direct Aid
CONCEPTS: Annex or appendix reference. Gen-
eral cooperation. Exchange of information and
documents. Informational records. Inspection
and observation. Operating agencies. Personnel.
Accounting procedures. Currency. Monetary
and gold transfers. Funding procedures. Interest
rates. Assets. General technical assistance. Economic assistance. Loan and credit. Loan repayment.
INTL ORGS: Organization of American States.
PROCEDURE: Termination.
PARTIES:
Inter-Am Devel Bnk
USA (United States)
ANNEX
511 UNTS 296. USA (United States). Implementation 17 Feb 64. Force 17 Feb 64.
511 UNTS 296. Inter-Am Devel Bnk. Implementation 17 Feb 64. Force 17 Feb 64.
606 UNTS 356. USA (United States). Supplementation 7 Sep 66. Force 7 Sep 66.
606 UNTS 356. Inter-Am Devel Bnk. Supplementation 7 Sep 66. Force 7 Sep 66.

105896 Bilateral Exchange **410 UNTS 53**
SIGNED: 22 Jun 61   FORCE: 22 Jun 61
REGISTERED: 29 Sep 61 USA (United States)
ARTICLES: 2 LANGUAGE: English.
HEADNOTE: ESTABLISHMENT JOINT TRADE ECO-
NOMICS COMMITTEE
TOPIC: General Economic
CONCEPTS: Treaty implementation. Establish-
ment of commission. General trade.
INTL ORGS: Special Commission.
TREATY REF: 373UNTS179.
PROCEDURE: Termination.
PARTIES:
Japan
USA (United States)

105897 Bilateral Convention **410 UNTS 62**
SIGNED: 13 Jan 61   FORCE: 1 Jul 61
REGISTERED: 29 Sep 61 USA (United States)
ARTICLES: 19 LANGUAGE: English.
HEADNOTE: POSTAL CONVENTION
TOPIC: Postal Service
CONCEPTS: Treaty implementation. Previous
treaty replacement. Customs declarations.
Postal services. Insured letters and boxes. Con-
veyance in transit. Parcel post. Rates and
charges.
INTL ORGS: Universal Postal Union.
TREATY REF: USA'22STAT.2226;.
PROCEDURE: Duration. Termination.
PARTIES:
Canada
USA (United States)

105898 Bilateral Exchange **410 UNTS 79**
SIGNED: 20 Aug 54   FORCE: 20 Aug 54
REGISTERED: 29 Sep 61 USA (United States)
ARTICLES: 2 LANGUAGE: English. Portuguese.
HEADNOTE: ACQUISITION MONAZITE SAND
RARE EARTH COMPOUNDS THORIUM COM-
POUNDS
TOPIC: Commodity Trade
CONCEPTS: Treaty implementation. Previous
treaty replacement. Negotiation. Trade agen-
cies. Accounting procedures. Banking. Fees and

exemptions. Interest rates. Non-interest rates
and fees. Commodity trade.
TREATY REF: 21FEB52.
PROCEDURE: Future Procedures Contemplated.
PARTIES:
Brazil
USA (United States)
ANNEX
416 UNTS 382. USA (United States). Amendment
7 Aug 61. Force 7 Aug 61.
416 UNTS 382. Brazil. Amendment 20 Jul 61.
Force 7 Aug 61.
433 UNTS 385. Brazil. Amendment 21 Dec 61.
Force 21 Dec 61.
433 UNTS 385. USA (United States). Amendment
19 Dec 61. Force 21 Dec 61.

105899 Bilateral Agreement **410 UNTS 125**
SIGNED: 25 Aug 61   FORCE: 6 Sep 61
REGISTERED: 2 Oct 61 Thailand
ARTICLES: 4 LANGUAGE: English.
HEADNOTE: REGIONAL OFFICE
TOPIC: IGO Operations
CONCEPTS: Annex or appendix reference. Privi-
leges and immunities. Regional offices.
TREATY REF: 331NTS261.
PROCEDURE: Amendment. Termination.
PARTIES:
UNESCO (Educ/Cult)
Thailand

105900 Bilateral Agreement **410 UNTS 133**
SIGNED: 4 Oct 61   FORCE: 4 Oct 61
REGISTERED: 4 Oct 61 United Nations
ARTICLES: 6 LANGUAGE: English.
HEADNOTE: COURSE AERIAL SURVEY TECH-
NIQUES
TOPIC: Education
CONCEPTS: Definition of terms. Detailed regula-
tions. Personnel. Exchange. Teacher and student
exchange. Scholarships and grants. Vocational
training. Research cooperation. Indemnities and
reimbursements. General technical assistance.
Assistance to United Nations.
PROCEDURE: Amendment. Duration.
PARTIES:
Japan
United Nations

105901 Bilateral Exchange **410 UNTS 141**
SIGNED: 17 Sep 59   FORCE: 17 Sep 59
REGISTERED: 5 Oct 61 Denmark
ARTICLES: 2 LANGUAGE: French.
HEADNOTE: TAX ROYALTIES
TOPIC: Taxation
CONCEPTS: General. Tax exemptions.
PARTIES:
Denmark
France

105902 Multilateral Convention **410 UNTS 156**
SIGNED: 19 Nov 59   FORCE: 26 Sep 61
REGISTERED: 9 Oct 61 FAO (Food Agri)
ARTICLES: 19 LANGUAGE: English. French. Span-
ish.
HEADNOTE: INTERNATIONAL POPLAR COMMIS-
SION
TOPIC: IGO Operations
CONCEPTS: Procedure. Funding procedures. Gen-
eral technical assistance. Admission. Subsidiary
organ. Headquarters and facilities. UN adminis-
trative tribunal.
INTL ORGS: International Poplar Commission.
Food and Agricultural Organization of the United
Nations. International Court of Justice. United
Nations.
PROCEDURE: Amendment. Accession. Denuncia-
tion. Termination.
PARTIES:
Argentina RATIFIED: 6 Feb 61
Austria RATIFIED: 17 Feb 61
France RATIFIED: 17 Mar 61
Germany, West RATIFIED: 15 May 61
Iran RATIFIED: 6 Mar 61
Ireland RATIFIED: 4 Jul 61
Lebanon RATIFIED: 23 Jan 61
Spain RATIFIED: 21 Apr 60
Switzerland RATIFIED: 23 Feb 61
Tunisia RATIFIED: 4 Apr 61
United Arab Rep RATIFIED: 26 Sep 61

Yugoslavia RATIFIED: 11 Jan 61
ANNEX
421 UNTS 372. Netherlands. Acceptance
22 Dec 61.
422 UNTS 343. Syria. Acceptance 19 Dec 62.
426 UNTS 349. UK Great Britain. Channel Islands.
426 UNTS 349. UK Great Britain. Acceptance
3 Apr 62.
426 UNTS 349. UK Great Britain. Isle of Man.
429 UNTS 303. Belgium. Acceptance 24 Apr 62.
434 UNTS 349. Pakistan. Acceptance 6 Jul 62.
439 UNTS 327. Morocco. Acceptance 7 Sep 62.
447 UNTS 361. Canada. Acceptance 28 Nov 62.
466 UNTS 407. Italy. Acceptance 9 May 63.
480 UNTS 436. Portugal. Acceptance 14 Aug 63.
489 UNTS 403. India. Acceptance 17 Feb 64.
489 UNTS 403. Romania. Acceptance 28 Jan 64.
541 UNTS 344. Turkey. Acceptance 27 Jul 65.
620 UNTS 321. Japan. Acceptance 23 Jan 68.
634 UNTS 433. Multilateral. Amendment
23 Nov 67. Force 23 Nov 67.

105903 Bilateral Exchange **410 UNTS 183**
SIGNED: 8 Jun 61   FORCE: 8 Jun 61
REGISTERED: 10 Oct 61 USA (United States)
ARTICLES: 2 LANGUAGE: English. Japanese.
HEADNOTE: SETTLEMENT CLAIMS
TOPIC: Reparations
CONCEPTS: Lump sum settlements. Loss and/or
damage. Post-war claims settlement.
TREATY REF: 136UNTS45.
PARTIES:
Japan
USA (United States)

105904 Bilateral Agreement **410 UNTS 193**
SIGNED: 3 Apr 57   FORCE: 3 Apr 57
REGISTERED: 10 Oct 61 USA (United States)
ARTICLES: 17 LANGUAGE: English.
HEADNOTE: AIR TRANSPORT
TOPIC: Air Transport
CONCEPTS: Definition of terms. Detailed regulations. Annex or appendix reference. Conformity
with municipal law. General cooperation. Licenses and permits. Recognition of legal documents. Use of facilities. Arbitration. Procedure.
Special tribunals. Competence of tribunal. Reexport of goods, etc.. Indemnities and reimbursements. Non-interest rates and fees. Most favored
nation clause. Customs exemptions. Competency certificate. Routes and logistics. Navigational conditions. Permit designation. Air transport. Airport facilities. Airworthiness certificates.
Conditions of airlines operating permission.
Overflights and technical stops. Operating authorizations and regulations. Licenses and certificates of nationality.
INTL ORGS: International Civil Aviation Organization. International Court of Justice.
TREATY REF: 15UNTS295.
PROCEDURE: Amendment. Future Procedures
Contemplated. Ratification. Registration. Termi-
nation. Application to Non-self-governing Terri-
tories.
PARTIES:
Netherlands
USA (United States)

105905 Bilateral Exchange **410 UNTS 213**
SIGNED: 26 May 61   FORCE: 26 May 61
REGISTERED: 10 Oct 61 USA (United States)
ARTICLES: 2 LANGUAGE: English. French.
HEADNOTE: ECONOMIC TECHNICAL RELATED
ASSISTANCE
TOPIC: General Aid
CONCEPTS: Change of circumstances. Guaran-
tees and safeguards. Diplomatic privileges. Privi-
leges and immunities. Conformity with munici-
pal law. Personnel. Accounting procedures. At-
tachment of funds. Banking. Exchange rates and
regulations. Funding procedures. Garnishment
of funds. Seizure funds. Tax exemptions. Cus-
toms exemptions. Commodities and services.
Domestic obligation. General technical assistance. Economic assistance. Materials, equipment and services. Aid missions. Grants.
PROCEDURE: Termination.
PARTIES:
Niger
USA (United States)

105906 Bilateral Exchange **410 UNTS 223**
SIGNED: 1 Jun 61 FORCE: 1 Jun 61
REGISTERED: 10 Oct 61 USA (United States)
ARTICLES: 2 LANGUAGE: English. French.
HEADNOTE: ECONOMIC TECHNICAL ASSIS-
TANCE
TOPIC: General Aid
CONCEPTS: General trade. Currency. General
technical assistance. Assistance.
PROCEDURE: Termination.
PARTIES:
USA (United States)
Upper Volta

105907 Bilateral Exchange **410 UNTS 233**
SIGNED: 17 Jun 61 FORCE: 17 Jun 61
REGISTERED: 10 Oct 61 USA (United States)
ARTICLES: 2 LANGUAGE: English.
HEADNOTE: MILITARY EQUIPMENT MATERIALS
SERVICES
TOPIC: Milit Assistance
CONCEPTS: Exceptions and exemptions. Non-
prejudice to UN charter. Materials, equipment
and services. Defense and security. Self-
defense. Military assistance. Return of equip-
ment and recapture. Security of information. Ex-
change of defense information. Restrictions on
transfer.
INTL ORGS: United Nations.
PARTIES:
Liberia
USA (United States)
ANNEX
433 UNTS 390. USA (United States). Supplementation 18 Jan 62. Force 23 Jan 62.
433 UNTS 390. Liberia. Supplementation
23 Jan 62. Force 23 Jan 62.

105908 Multilateral Agreement **410 UNTS 242**
SIGNED: 16 Oct 61 FORCE: 16 Oct 61
REGISTERED: 16 Oct 61 United Nations
ARTICLES: 6 LANGUAGE: English.
HEADNOTE: TECHNICAL ASSISTANCE
TOPIC: Tech Assistance
CONCEPTS: Definition of terms. Privileges and im-
munities. General cooperation. Exchange of in-
formation and documents. Personnel. Responsi-
bility and liability. Title and deeds. Use of facili-
ties. Exchange. Scholarships and grants.
Vocational training. Research and development.
Exchange rates and regulations. Expense shar-
ing formulae. Local currency. Domestic obliga-
tion. General technical assistance. Materials,
equipment and services. IGO status. Conformity
with IGO decisions.
TREATY REF: 76UNTS132; 1UNTS15;
33UNTS261; 374UNTS147.
PARTIES:
FAO (Food Agri) SIGNED: 16 Oct 61 FORCE:
16 Oct 61
IAEA (Atom Energy) SIGNED: 16 Oct 61 FORCE:
16 Oct 61
ICAO (Civil Aviat) SIGNED: 16 Oct 61 FORCE:
16 Oct 61
ILO (Labor Org) SIGNED: 16 Oct 61 FORCE:
16 Oct 61
ITU (Telecommun) SIGNED: 16 Oct 61 FORCE:
16 Oct 61
UNESCO (Educ/Cult) SIGNED: 16 Oct 61 FORCE:
16 Oct 61
United Nations SIGNED: 16 Oct 61 FORCE:
16 Oct 61
WHO (World Health) SIGNED: 16 Oct 61 FORCE:
16 Oct 61
WMO (Meteorology) SIGNED: 16 Oct 61 FORCE:
16 Oct 61
Sierra Leone SIGNED: 16 Oct 61 FORCE:
16 Oct 61

105909 Bilateral Exchange **410 UNTS 255**
SIGNED: 7 Apr 61 FORCE: 8 Apr 61
REGISTERED: 18 Oct 61 Belgium
ARTICLES: 2 LANGUAGE: French. Spanish.
HEADNOTE: ABOLITION TRAVEL VISA REQUIRE-
MENT
TOPIC: Visas
CONCEPTS: Emergencies. Visa abolition. Denial of
admission. Resident permits. Nationality and citi-
zenship. Conformity with municipal law.
TREATY REF: 257UNTS227.
PROCEDURE: Denunciation.

PARTIES:
Belgium
Chile

105910 Bilateral Agreement **410 UNTS 263**
SIGNED: 27 Nov 60 FORCE: 4 May 61
REGISTERED: 18 Oct 61 Czechoslovakia
ARTICLES: 8 LANGUAGE: Czechoslovakian.
Khmer. French.
HEADNOTE: CULTURAL COOPERATION
TOPIC: Culture
CONCEPTS: Friendship and amity. Exchange of in-
formation and documents. Specialists ex-
change. Exchange. Teacher and student ex-
change. Exchange. General cultural cooperation.
Artists. Athletes. Scientific exchange. Recogni-
tion. Publications exchange. Mass media ex-
change.
PROCEDURE: Denunciation. Duration. Future Pro-
cedures Contemplated. Ratification. Renewal or
Revival.
PARTIES:
Cambodia
Czechoslovakia

105911 Bilateral Agreement **411 UNTS 3**
SIGNED: 20 Jun 59 FORCE: 3 Jul 61
REGISTERED: 23 Oct 61 Belgium
ARTICLES: 18 LANGUAGE: French. Japanese.
HEADNOTE: RELATING AIR SERVICES
TOPIC: Air Transport
CONCEPTS: Definition of terms. Detailed regula-
tions. Exceptions and exemptions. Annex or ap-
pendix reference. Conformity with municipal
law. General cooperation. Exchange of informa-
tion and documents. Use of facilities. Arbitration.
Procedure. Special tribunals. Negotiation. Fees
and exemptions. Non-interest rates and fees.
Most favored nation clause. National treatment.
Customs exemptions. Routes and logistics. Per-
mit designation. Airport facilities. Conditions of
airlines operating permission. Overflights and
technical stops. Operating authorizations and
regulations.
INTL ORGS: International Civil Aviation Organiza-
tion. International Court of Justice.
TREATY REF: 15UNTS195.
PROCEDURE: Amendment. Future Procedures
Contemplated. Ratification. Registration.
PARTIES:
Belgium
Japan
ANNEX
472 UNTS 396. Japan. Amendment 30 Apr 63.
Force 30 Apr 63.
472 UNTS 396. Belgium. Amendment 30 Apr 63.
Force 30 Apr 63.

105912 Bilateral Agreement **411 UNTS 42**
SIGNED: 22 Dec 59 FORCE: 5 May 61
REGISTERED: 25 Oct 61 USA (United States)
ARTICLES: 5 LANGUAGE: English. Spanish.
HEADNOTE: GUARANTY PRIVATE INVESTMENTS
TOPIC: Admin Cooperation
CONCEPTS: Guarantees and safeguards. Arbitra-
tion. Currency. Investments. Claims and settle-
ments.
PARTIES:
Argentina
USA (United States)

105913 Bilateral Exchange **411 UNTS 49**
SIGNED: 17 Jun 61 FORCE: 17 Jun 61
REGISTERED: 25 Oct 61 USA (United States)
ARTICLES: 2 LANGUAGE: English. Spanish.
HEADNOTE: ECONOMIC ASSISTANCE
TOPIC: Direct Aid
CONCEPTS: Privileges and immunities. Economic
assistance. Aid missions.
TREATY REF: 141UNTS27.
PROCEDURE: Future Procedures Contemplated.
PARTIES:
Ecuador
USA (United States)

105914 Bilateral Agreement **411 UNTS 56**
SIGNED: 29 Jun 61 FORCE: 29 Jun 61
REGISTERED: 25 Oct 61 USA (United States)
ARTICLES: 5 LANGUAGE: English.

HEADNOTE: TECHNICAL COOPERATION
TOPIC: General Aid
CONCEPTS: General technical assistance. Assis-
tance. Special projects.
PARTIES:
Cyprus
USA (United States)

105915 Bilateral Agreement **411 UNTS 64**
SIGNED: 18 Feb 54 FORCE: 5 Jun 57
REGISTERED: 25 Oct 61 ICAO (Civil Aviat)
ARTICLES: 14 LANGUAGE: English. Spanish.
HEADNOTE: AIR SERVICES BETWEEN BEYOND
RESPECTIVE TERRITORIES
TOPIC: Air Transport
CONCEPTS: Conditions. Definition of terms. Exceptions and exemptions. Annex or appendix
reference. General cooperation. Exchange of information and documents. Arbitration. Procedure. Existing tribunals. Negotiation. Most fa-
vored nation clause. National treatment. Routes
and logistics. Permit designation. Conditions of
airlines operating permission. Overflights and
technical stops. Operating authorizations and
regulations.
INTL ORGS: International Civil Aviation Organization. Arbitration Commission.
TREATY REF: 15UNTS295.
PROCEDURE: Amendment. Future Procedures
Contemplated. Ratification. Registration. Termination. Application to Non-self-governing Territories.
PARTIES:
Canada
Peru

105916 Bilateral Agreement **411 UNTS 97**
SIGNED: 23 Nov 56 FORCE: 23 Nov 56
REGISTERED: 25 Oct 61 ICAO (Civil Aviat)
ARTICLES: 16 LANGUAGE: French. Spanish.
HEADNOTE: RELATING AIR SERVICES
TOPIC: Air Transport
CONCEPTS: Definition of terms. Detailed regulations. Exceptions and exemptions. Annex or appendix reference. Conformity with municipal
law. General cooperation. Exchange of information and documents. Licenses and permits. Recognition of legal documents. Use of facilities. Arbitration. Procedure. Existing tribunals. Negotiation. Fees and exemptions. Non-interest rates
and fees. Most favored nation clause. National
treatment. Customs duties. Competency certificate. Routes and logistics. Navigational conditions. Permit designation. Airport facilities. Airworthiness certificates. Conditions of airlines operating permission. Overflights and technical
stops. Operating authorizations and regulations.
Licenses and certificates of nationality.
INTL ORGS: International Civil Aviation Organization. Arbitration Commission.
TREATY REF: 15UNTS295.
PROCEDURE: Amendment. Future Procedures
Contemplated. Ratification. Registration. Termi-
nation.
PARTIES:
Peru
Switzerland

105917 Bilateral Agreement **411 UNTS 126**
SIGNED: 30 Jun 57 FORCE: 20 Feb 58
REGISTERED: 25 Oct 61 ICAO (Civil Aviat)
ARTICLES: 17 LANGUAGE: French.
HEADNOTE: CONCERNING SCHEDULED AIR SER-
VICES
TOPIC: Air Transport
CONCEPTS: Exceptions and exemptions. Annex or
appendix reference. Non-prejudice to third party.
Conformity with municipal law. General cooper-
ation. Exchange of information and documents.
Licenses and permits. Recognition of legal docu-
ments. Use of facilities. Arbitration. Procedure.
Negotiation. Monetary and gold transfers. Fees
and exemptions. Non-interest rates and fees.
Most favored nation clause. National treatment.
Customs exemptions. Competency certificate.
Routes and logistics. Navigational conditions.
Permit designation. Air transport. Airport facilities. Airworthiness certificates. Conditions of airlines operating permission. Overflights and technical stops. Operating authorizations and regulations. Licenses and certificates of nationality.

INTL ORGS: International Civil Aviation Organization. Arbitration Commission.
PROCEDURE: Amendment. Ratification. Registration. Termination.
PARTIES:
Czechoslovakia
United Arab Rep

105918   Bilateral Agreement   **411 UNTS 146**
SIGNED: 24 Sep 58   FORCE: 24 Sep 58
REGISTERED: 25 Oct 61 ICAO (Civil Aviat)
ARTICLES: 15 LANGUAGE: English.
HEADNOTE: AIR SERVICES BETWEEN BEYOND RESPECTIVE TERRITORIES
TOPIC: Air Transport
CONCEPTS: Conditions. Definition of terms. Detailed regulations. Exceptions and exemptions. Annex or appendix reference. General cooperation. Exchange of information and documents. Arbitration. Procedure. Negotiation. Monetary and gold transfers. Exchange rates and regulations. Non-interest rates and fees. Most favored nation clause. National treatment. Customs exemptions. Routes and logistics. Permit designation. Conditions of airlines operating permission. Overflights and technical stops. Operating authorizations and regulations.
INTL ORGS: International Civil Aviation Organization. Arbitration Commission.
TREATY REF: 15UNTS295.
PROCEDURE: Amendment. Future Procedures Contemplated. Registration. Termination. Application to Non-self-governing Territories.
PARTIES:
Ghana
UK Great Britain

105919   Bilateral Agreement   **411 UNTS 165**
SIGNED: 29 May 59   FORCE: 29 May 59
REGISTERED: 25 Oct 61 ICAO (Civil Aviat)
ARTICLES: 18 LANGUAGE: English.
HEADNOTE: RELATING AIR SERVICES
TOPIC: Air Transport
CONCEPTS: Definition of terms. Detailed regulations. Annex or appendix reference. Conformity with municipal law. General cooperation. Exchange of information and documents. Licenses and permits. Recognition of legal documents. Use of facilities. Procedure. Existing tribunals. Reexport of goods, etc.. Currency. Monetary and gold transfers. Fees and exemptions. Non-interest rates and fees. Most favored nation clause. National treatment. Customs exemptions. Competency certificate. Routes and logistics. Navigational conditions. Permit designation. Airport facilities. Airworthiness certificates. Conditions of airlines operating permission. Operating authorizations and regulations. Licenses and certificates of nationality.
INTL ORGS: International Civil Aviation Organization. Arbitration Commission.
TREATY REF: 15UNTS295.
PROCEDURE: Amendment. Future Procedures Contemplated. Registration. Termination. Application to Non-self-governing Territories.
PARTIES:
Ceylon (Sri Lanka)
Norway

105920   Bilateral Agreement   **411 UNTS 187**
SIGNED: 9 Jul 59   FORCE: 9 Jul 59
REGISTERED: 25 Oct 61 ICAO (Civil Aviat)
ARTICLES: 20 LANGUAGE: French. Arabic. Bulgarian.
HEADNOTE: CONCERNING CIVIL AIR SERVICES
TOPIC: Air Transport
CONCEPTS: Definition of terms. Detailed regulations. Exceptions and exemptions. Representation. Annex or appendix reference. Passports non-diplomatic. Visas. Conformity with municipal law. General cooperation. Exchange of information and documents. Domestic legislation. Licenses and permits. Personnel. Recognition of legal documents. Use of facilities. Procedure. Negotiation. Humanitarian matters. Fees and exemptions. Non-interest rates and fees. National treatment. Customs exemptions. Competency certificate. Registration certificate. Routes and logistics. Permit designation. Air transport. Airport facilities. Airworthiness certificates. Conditions of airlines operating permission. Overf-

lights and technical stops. Operating authorizations and regulations.
INTL ORGS: International Civil Aviation Organization.
PROCEDURE: Amendment. Denunciation.
PARTIES:
Bulgaria
United Arab Rep

105921   Bilateral Agreement   **411 UNTS 224**
SIGNED: 12 Aug 59   FORCE: 5 Jan 61
REGISTERED: 25 Oct 61 ICAO (Civil Aviat)
ARTICLES: 16 LANGUAGE: German. Icelandic.
HEADNOTE: RELATING AIR SERVICES
TOPIC: Air Transport
CONCEPTS: Definition of terms. Detailed regulations. Annex or appendix reference. Conformity with municipal law. General cooperation. Exchange of information and documents. Personnel. Use of facilities. Arbitration. Procedure. Special tribunals. Expense sharing formulae. Fees and exemptions. Non-interest rates and fees. National treatment. Customs exemptions. Routes and logistics. Permit designation. Air transport. Airport facilities. Conditions of airlines operating permission. Overflights and technical stops. Operating authorizations and regulations.
INTL ORGS: International Civil Aviation Organization. Arbitration Commission.
TREATY REF: 15UNTS295.
PROCEDURE: Amendment. Denunciation. Future Procedures Contemplated. Ratification. Registration. Termination.
PARTIES:
Germany, West
Iceland

105922   Bilateral Agreement   **411 UNTS 260**
SIGNED: 4 Sep 59   FORCE: 19 Jul 61
REGISTERED: 25 Oct 61 ICAO (Civil Aviat)
ARTICLES: 16 LANGUAGE: English. German.
HEADNOTE: AIR TRANSPORT
TOPIC: Air Transport
CONCEPTS: Definition of terms. Detailed regulations. Annex or appendix reference. Conformity with municipal law. General cooperation. Exchange of information and documents. Use of facilities. Arbitration. Procedure. Special tribunals. Expense sharing formulae. Fees and exemptions. Non-interest rates and fees. National treatment. Tax exemptions. Customs exemptions. Routes and logistics. Permit designation. Airport facilities. Conditions of airlines operating permission. Overflights and technical stops. Operating authorizations and regulations.
INTL ORGS: International Civil Aviation Organization. Arbitration Commission.
TREATY REF: 15UNTS295.
PROCEDURE: Amendment. Future Procedures Contemplated. Ratification. Registration. Termination.
PARTIES:
Canada
Germany, West

105923   Bilateral Agreement   **412 UNTS 4**
SIGNED: 24 May 60   FORCE: 24 May 60
REGISTERED: 25 Oct 61 ICAO (Civil Aviat)
ARTICLES: 14 LANGUAGE: English. Arabic.
HEADNOTE: AIR SERVICES BETWEEN BEYOND RESPECTIVE TERRITORIES
TOPIC: Air Transport
CONCEPTS: Conditions. Definition of terms. Detailed regulations. Exceptions and exemptions. Annex or appendix reference. Exchange of information and documents. Arbitration. Procedure. Existing tribunals. Negotiation. Currency. Monetary and gold transfers. Non-interest rates and fees. Customs exemptions. Routes and logistics. Permit designation. Conditions of airlines operating permission. Overflights and technical stops. Operating authorizations and regulations.
INTL ORGS: International Civil Aviation Organization. Arbitration Commission.
TREATY REF: 15UNTS295.
PROCEDURE: Amendment. Future Procedures Contemplated. Registration. Termination. Application to Non-self-governing Territories.
PARTIES:
Kuwait
UK Great Britain

ANNEX
482 UNTS 388. Kuwait. Amendment 2 Jun 63. Force 2 Jun 63.
482 UNTS 388. UK Great Britain. Amendment 2 Jun 63. Force 2 Jun 63.

105924   Bilateral Agreement   **412 UNTS 30**
SIGNED: 24 Jun 60   FORCE: 24 Jun 60
REGISTERED: 25 Oct 61 ICAO (Civil Aviat)
ARTICLES: 15 LANGUAGE: English. Portuguese.
HEADNOTE: AIR TRANSPORT
TOPIC: Air Transport
CONCEPTS: Detailed regulations. Annex or appendix reference. General cooperation. Arbitration. Procedure. Special tribunals. Negotiation. Reexport of goods, etc.. Monetary and gold transfers. Exchange rates and regulations. Non-interest rates and fees. Tax exemptions. Customs exemptions. Routes and logistics. Permit designation. Air transport. Conditions of airlines operating permission. Overflights and technical stops. Operating authorizations and regulations.
INTL ORGS: International Civil Aviation Organization. Arbitration Commission.
TREATY REF: 15UNTS295.
PROCEDURE: Amendment. Future Procedures Contemplated. Termination.
PARTIES:
Ireland
Portugal

105925   Bilateral Agreement   **412 UNTS 51**
SIGNED: 30 Jul 60   FORCE: 30 Jul 60
REGISTERED: 25 Oct 61 ICAO (Civil Aviat)
ARTICLES: 14 LANGUAGE: English.
HEADNOTE: AIR SERVICES BETWEEN BEYOND RESPECTIVE TERRITORIES
TOPIC: Air Transport
CONCEPTS: Definition of terms. Detailed regulations. Treaty violation. Conformity with municipal law. General cooperation. Arbitration. Procedure. Existing tribunals. Negotiation. Currency. Monetary and gold transfers. Exchange rates and regulations. Non-interest rates and fees. Most favored nation clause. National treatment. Customs duties. Routes and logistics. Permit designation. Conditions of airlines operating permission. Overflights and technical stops. Operating authorizations and regulations.
INTL ORGS: International Civil Aviation Organization. Arbitration Commission.
TREATY REF: 15UNTS295.
PROCEDURE: Amendment. Future Procedures Contemplated. Registration. Termination. Application to Non-self-governing Territories.
PARTIES:
Ghana
Netherlands

ANNEX
497 UNTS 374. Netherlands. Force 23 Jul 63.
497 UNTS 374. Ghana. Force 23 Jul 63.

105926   Bilateral Agreement   **412 UNTS 71**
SIGNED: 29 Aug 60   FORCE: 29 Aug 60
REGISTERED: 25 Oct 61 ICAO (Civil Aviat)
ARTICLES: 17 LANGUAGE: English. Arabic.
HEADNOTE: AIR SERVICES
TOPIC: Air Transport
CONCEPTS: Definition of terms. Detailed regulations. Exceptions and exemptions. Annex or appendix reference. Conformity with municipal law. General cooperation. Exchange of information and documents. Arbitration. Procedure. Existing tribunals. Negotiation. Monetary and gold transfers. Non-interest rates and fees. Customs exemptions. Routes and logistics. Navigational conditions. Permit designation. Conditions of airlines operating permission. Overflights and technical stops. Operating authorizations and regulations.
INTL ORGS: International Civil Aviation Organization. Arbitration Commission.
TREATY REF: 15UNTS295.
PROCEDURE: Amendment. Future Procedures Contemplated. Ratification. Registration. Termination. Application to Non-self-governing Territories.
PARTIES:
Ghana
United Arab Rep

105927 Bilateral Agreement **412 UNTS 111**
SIGNED: 17 Jan 61 FORCE: 21 Apr 61
REGISTERED: 25 Oct 61 ICAO (Civil Aviat)
ARTICLES: 18 LANGUAGE: French.
HEADNOTE: AIR TRANSPORT
TOPIC: Air Transport
CONCEPTS: Air transport. Airport facilities. Airport equipment. Airworthiness certificates. Conditions of airlines operating permission. Overflights and technical stops. Operating authorizations and regulations.
PARTIES:
Denmark
Poland
ANNEX
607 UNTS 338. Poland. Amendment 6 Jun 67.
607 UNTS 338. Denmark. Amendment 6 Jun 67.

105928 Bilateral Agreement **412 UNTS 130**
SIGNED: 17 Jan 61 FORCE: 17 Jan 61
REGISTERED: 25 Oct 61 ICAO (Civil Aviat)
ARTICLES: 18 LANGUAGE: French.
HEADNOTE: CIVIL AIR TRANSPORT
TOPIC: Air Transport
CONCEPTS: Definition of terms. Representation. Annex or appendix reference. Conformity with municipal law. General cooperation. Licenses and permits. Personnel. Recognition of legal documents. Use of facilities. Procedure. Negotiation. Humanitarian matters. Fees and exemptions. Non-interest rates and fees. Customs exemptions. Registration certificate. Routes and logistics. Navigational conditions. Permit designation. Air transport. Airworthiness certificates. Conditions of airlines operating permission. Operating authorizations and regulations. Airport facilities.
PROCEDURE: Amendment. Denunciation. Ratification. Termination.
PARTIES:
Norway
Poland

105929 Bilateral Agreement **412 UNTS 148**
SIGNED: 16 Jun 61 FORCE: 16 Jun 61
REGISTERED: 25 Oct 61 ICAO (Civil Aviat)
ARTICLES: 20 LANGUAGE: French.
HEADNOTE: AIR TRANSPORT
TOPIC: Air Transport
CONCEPTS: Detailed regulations. Annex or appendix reference. Conformity with municipal law. General cooperation. Licenses and permits. Recognition of legal documents. Arbitration. Procedure. Special tribunals. Negotiation. Reexport of goods, etc.. Expense sharing formulae. Fees and exemptions. Non-interest rates and fees. Customs exemptions. Competency certificate. Routes and logistics. Navigational conditions. Permit designation. Air transport. Airworthiness certificates. Conditions of airlines operating permission. Operating authorizations and regulations. Licenses and certificates of nationality.
INTL ORGS: International Civil Aviation Organization.
TREATY REF: 15UNTS295.
PROCEDURE: Amendment. Denunciation. Registration.
PARTIES:
Cameroon
France

105930 Bilateral Convention **412 UNTS 166**
SIGNED: 16 Nov 56 FORCE: 1 Nov 56
REGISTERED: 27 Oct 61 UK Great Britain
ARTICLES: 16 LANGUAGE: English.
HEADNOTE: EXCHANGE MONEY ORDERS
TOPIC: Postal Service
CONCEPTS: Accounting procedures. Postal services. Regulations. Money orders and postal checks. Rates and charges.
PROCEDURE: Duration. Termination.
PARTIES:
Canada
UK Great Britain

105931 Bilateral Treaty **412 UNTS 179**
SIGNED: 27 Nov 60 FORCE: 2 May 61
REGISTERED: 31 Oct 61 Czechoslovakia
ARTICLES: 4 LANGUAGE: Czechoslovakian. Khmer. French.

HEADNOTE: FRIENDSHIP COOPERATION
TOPIC: General Amity
CONCEPTS: Treaty implementation. Friendship and amity. General cooperation. Procedure.
PROCEDURE: Denunciation. Duration. Ratification.
PARTIES:
Cambodia
Czechoslovakia

105932 Bilateral Agreement **412 UNTS 192**
SIGNED: 9 Aug 61 FORCE: 15 Sep 61
REGISTERED: 31 Oct 61 WHO (World Health)
ARTICLES: 6 LANGUAGE: French.
HEADNOTE: TECHNICAL ADVISORY ASSISTANCE
TOPIC: Tech Assistance
CONCEPTS: Definition of terms. Previous treaty replacement. Privileges and immunities. General cooperation. Exchange of information and documents. Personnel. Responsibility and liability. Title and deeds. Exchange. Scholarships and grants. Vocational training. Research and development. Expense sharing formulae. Local currency. Domestic obligation. Special projects. Materials, equipment and services. IGO status. Conformity with IGO decisions.
INTL ORGS: United Nations.
TREATY REF: 33UNTS261; 174UNTS71.
PROCEDURE: Amendment. Termination.
PARTIES:
Morocco
WHO (World Health)

105933 Bilateral Exchange **412 UNTS 203**
SIGNED: 30 May 61 FORCE: 30 Jun 61
REGISTERED: 6 Nov 61 South Africa
ARTICLES: 2 LANGUAGE: English.
HEADNOTE: VISA AGREEMENT
TOPIC: Visas
CONCEPTS: Emergencies. Time limit. Visa abolition. Denial of admission. Resident permits. Visas. Conformity with municipal law. Fees and exemptions.
PARTIES:
Luxembourg
South Africa

105934 Multilateral Instrument **412 UNTS 210**
SIGNED: 4 Oct 61 FORCE: 4 Oct 61
REGISTERED: 6 Nov 61 IAEA (Atom Energy)
ARTICLES: 6 LANGUAGE: English.
HEADNOTE: TRANSFER ENRICHED URANIUM
TOPIC: Scientific Project
CONCEPTS: Conditions. Annex or appendix reference. Responsibility and liability. Existing tribunals. Research and development. Payment schedules. Acceptance of delivery. Nuclear materials. Peaceful use. Rights of supplier. Samples and testing.
INTL ORGS: International Court of Justice.
TREATY REF: 339UNTS359; 276UNTS359; 312UNTS427.
PARTIES:
IAEA (Atom Energy) SIGNED: 4 Oct 61 FORCE: 4 Oct 61
USA (United States) SIGNED: 4 Oct 61 FORCE: 4 Oct 61
Yugoslavia SIGNED: 4 Oct 61 FORCE: 4 Oct 61
ANNEX
556 UNTS 198. Yugoslavia. Amendment 28 Sep 65. Force 28 Sep 65.
556 UNTS 198. USA (United States). Amendment 28 Sep 65. Force 28 Sep 65.

105935 Bilateral Agreement **412 UNTS 226**
SIGNED: 4 Oct 61 FORCE: 4 Oct 61
REGISTERED: 6 Nov 61 IAEA (Atom Energy)
ARTICLES: 8 LANGUAGE: English.
HEADNOTE: RESEARCH REACTOR PROJECTS
TOPIC: Scientific Project
CONCEPTS: Definition of terms. Annex or appendix reference. Responsibility and liability. Existing tribunals. Public health. Research cooperation. Research results. Nuclear research. Research and development. Patents, copyrights and trademarks. General. Nuclear materials. Rights of supplier.
INTL ORGS: International Court of Justice.
TREATY REF: 339UNTS359; 276UNTS3; 293UNTS359; 412UNTS209.

PARTIES:
IAEA (Atom Energy)
Yugoslavia

105936 Bilateral Agreement **412 UNTS 240**
SIGNED: 7 Nov 61 FORCE: 7 Nov 61
REGISTERED: 7 Nov 61 United Nations
ARTICLES: 10 LANGUAGE: English. French.
HEADNOTE: ASSISTANCE
TOPIC: Direct Aid
CONCEPTS: Detailed regulations. Treaty implementation. Visas. Privileges and immunities. Exchange of information and documents. Informational records. Inspection and observation. Operating agencies. Personnel. Public information. Responsibility and liability. Title and deeds. Use of facilities. Arbitration. Procedure. Negotiation. Import quotas. Attachment of funds. Exchange rates and regulations. Expense sharing formulae. Financial programs. Domestic obligation. General technical assistance. Economic assistance. Materials, equipment and services. IGO status.
INTL ORGS: International Atomic Energy Agency. International Court of Justice. United Nations.
TREATY REF: 1UNTS15; 33UNTS261; 374UNTS147.
PROCEDURE: Amendment. Termination.
PARTIES:
Mauritania
UN Special Fund

105937 Multilateral Agreement **412 UNTS 258**
SIGNED: 7 Nov 61 FORCE: 7 Nov 61
REGISTERED: 7 Nov 61 United Nations
ARTICLES: 6 LANGUAGE: French.
HEADNOTE: TECHNICAL ASSISTANCE
TOPIC: Tech Assistance
CONCEPTS: Definition of terms. Privileges and immunities. General cooperation. Exchange of information and documents. Personnel. Responsibility and liability. Title and deeds. Use of facilities. Exchange. Scholarships and grants. Vocational training. Research and development. Exchange rates and regulations. Expense sharing formulae. Local currency. Domestic obligation. General technical assistance. Materials, equipment and services. IGO status. Conformity with IGO decisions.
TREATY REF: 76UNTS132; 1UNTS15; 33UNTS261; 374UNTS147.
PROCEDURE: Amendment. Termination.
PARTIES:
Mauritania SIGNED: 7 Nov 61 FORCE: 7 Nov 61
FAO (Food Agri) SIGNED: 7 Nov 61 FORCE: 7 Nov 61
IAEA (Atom Energy) SIGNED: 7 Nov 61 FORCE: 7 Nov 61
ICAO (Civil Aviat) SIGNED: 7 Nov 61 FORCE: 7 Nov 61
ILO (Labor Org) SIGNED: 7 Nov 61 FORCE: 7 Nov 61
ITU (Telecommun) SIGNED: 7 Nov 61 FORCE: 7 Nov 61
UNESCO (Educ/Cult) SIGNED: 7 Nov 61 FORCE: 7 Nov 61
United Nations SIGNED: 7 Nov 61 FORCE: 7 Nov 61
WHO (World Health) SIGNED: 7 Nov 61 FORCE: 7 Nov 61
WMO (Meteorology) SIGNED: 7 Nov 61 FORCE: 7 Nov 61

105938 Bilateral Agreement **413 UNTS 4**
SIGNED: 14 Nov 60 FORCE: 22 Jun 61
REGISTERED: 8 Nov 61 Czechoslovakia
ARTICLES: 22 LANGUAGE: Czechoslovakian. Polish.
HEADNOTE: VETERINARY MATTERS
TOPIC: Sanitation
CONCEPTS: Definition of terms. Detailed regulations. Exceptions and exemptions. Border traffic and migration. General cooperation. Exchange of information and documents. Inspection and observation. Domestic legislation. Procedure. Negotiation. Specialists exchange. Border control. Disease control. Veterinary. Scientific exchange. Trade procedures.
PROCEDURE: Denunciation. Duration. Ratification. Renewal or Revival.

PARTIES:
Czechoslovakia
Poland

105939 Bilateral Agreement **413 UNTS 48**
SIGNED: 21 Aug 61   FORCE: 21 Aug 61
REGISTERED: 8 Nov 61 United Nations
ARTICLES: 8 LANGUAGE: French.
HEADNOTE: ACTIVITIES UNICEF
TOPIC: Direct Aid
CONCEPTS: Treaty implementation. Privileges and
immunities. General cooperation. Exchange of
official publications. Exchange of information
and documents. Informational records. Public in-
formation. Responsibility and liability. Export
quotas. Claims and settlements. Tax exemptions.
Customs exemptions. Commodities and ser-
vices. Domestic obligation. Assistance. General
aid. Distribution. IGO status.
INTL ORGS: United Nations.
TREATY REF: 1UNTS15.
PROCEDURE: Amendment. Termination.
PARTIES:
Central Afri Rep
UNICEF (Children)

105940 Bilateral Agreement **413 UNTS 58**
SIGNED: 9 Nov 61   FORCE: 7 Nov 61
REGISTERED: 9 Nov 61 United Nations
ARTICLES: 10 LANGUAGE: English. French.
HEADNOTE: ASSISTANCE
TOPIC: Direct Aid
CONCEPTS: Detailed regulations. Treaty imple-
mentation. Visas. Privileges and immunities. Ex-
change of information and documents. Informa-
tional records. Inspection and observation. Oper-
ating agencies. Personnel. Public information.
Responsibility and liability. Title and deeds. Use
of facilities. Arbitration. Procedure. Negotiation.
Import quotas. Attachment of funds. Exchange
rates and regulations. Expense sharing formulae.
Financial programs. Domestic obligation. Gen-
eral technical assistance. Economic assistance.
Materials, equipment and services. IGO status.
INTL ORGS: International Atomic Energy Agency.
International Court of Justice. United Nations.
TREATY REF: 1UNTS15; 33UNTS261;
374UNTS147.
PROCEDURE: Amendment. Termination.
PARTIES:
Congo (Brazzaville)
UN Special Fund

105941 Bilateral Exchange **413 UNTS 73**
SIGNED: 5 Sep 60   FORCE: 1 Jan 61
REGISTERED: 10 Nov 61 Israel
ARTICLES: 2 LANGUAGE: Spanish.
HEADNOTE: ABOLITION VISA FEES
TOPIC: Visas
CONCEPTS: Visas. Fees and exemptions. Tax ex-
emptions.
PARTIES:
El Salvador
Israel

105942 Bilateral Exchange **413 UNTS 79**
SIGNED: 7 Jul 60   FORCE: 7 Jul 60
REGISTERED: 10 Nov 61 Israel
ARTICLES: 2 LANGUAGE: French.
HEADNOTE: COLLECTIVE PASSPORTS
TOPIC: Visas
CONCEPTS: Time limit. Passports non-diplomatic.
Visas.
PARTIES:
France
Israel

105943 Bilateral Agreement **413 UNTS 86**
SIGNED: 27 Aug 61   FORCE: 27 Aug 61
REGISTERED: 10 Nov 61 Israel
ARTICLES: 2 LANGUAGE: French. Hebrew.
HEADNOTE: TECHNICAL COOPERATION
TOPIC: Direct Aid

CONCEPTS: Detailed regulations. Scholarships
and grants. General technical assistance.
PARTIES:
Israel
Malagasy

105944 Bilateral Agreement **413 UNTS 95**
SIGNED: 24 Nov 60   FORCE: 24 Nov 60
REGISTERED: 10 Nov 61 Israel
ARTICLES: 3 LANGUAGE: French. Hebrew.
HEADNOTE: TECHNICAL COOPERATION
TOPIC: Tech Assistance
CONCEPTS: Detailed regulations. Personnel.
Professorships. Expense sharing formulae. Gen-
eral technical assistance.
PARTIES:
Israel
Mali

105945 Bilateral Agreement **413 UNTS 104**
SIGNED: 24 Nov 60   FORCE: 24 Nov 60
REGISTERED: 10 Nov 61 Israel
ARTICLES: 6 LANGUAGE: French. Hebrew.
HEADNOTE: CULTURAL AGREEMENT
TOPIC: Culture
CONCEPTS: Friendship and amity. Tourism. Con-
formity with municipal law. General cooperation.
Exchange of information and documents.
Teacher and student exchange. Exchange. Gen-
eral cultural cooperation. Artists. Scientific ex-
change. Publications exchange. Mass media ex-
change.
PARTIES:
Israel
Mali

105946 Bilateral Agreement **413 UNTS 113**
SIGNED: 11 Jun 61   FORCE: 11 Jun 61
REGISTERED: 10 Nov 61 Israel
ARTICLES: 3 LANGUAGE: French. Hebrew.
HEADNOTE: TECHNICAL COOPERATION
TOPIC: Tech Assistance
CONCEPTS: Detailed regulations. Scholarships
and grants. Expense sharing formulae. General
technical assistance.
PARTIES:
Israel
Upper Volta

105947 Bilateral Agreement **413 UNTS 122**
SIGNED: 4 Jul 61   FORCE: 4 Jul 61
REGISTERED: 14 Nov 61 United Nations
ARTICLES: 8 LANGUAGE: English. Arabic.
HEADNOTE: ACTIVITIES UNICEF
TOPIC: Direct Aid
CONCEPTS: Treaty implementation. Privileges and
immunities. General cooperation. Exchange of
information and documents. Informational
records. Public information. Responsibility and
liability. Title and deeds. Claims and settlements.
Tax exemptions. Customs exemptions. Domestic
obligation. Assistance. General aid. Materials,
equipment and services. Distribution. IGO status.
INTL ORGS: United Nations.
TREATY REF: 1UNTS15.
PROCEDURE: Amendment. Termination.
PARTIES:
UNICEF (Children)
Saudi Arabia

105948 Bilateral Agreement **413 UNTS 137**
SIGNED: 15 Sep 61   FORCE: 15 Sep 61
REGISTERED: 14 Nov 61 Thailand
ARTICLES: 7 LANGUAGE: English.
HEADNOTE: TRADE
TOPIC: General Trade
CONCEPTS: Exceptions and exemptions. Annex or
appendix reference. Conformity with municipal
law. General cooperation. Export quotas. Import
quotas. Reciprocity in trade. Trade procedures.
INTL ORGS: United Nations.
PROCEDURE: Amendment. Duration. Termination.
PARTIES:
Korea, South
Thailand

105949 Multilateral Convention **413 UNTS 148**
SIGNED: 19 Jun 59   FORCE: 7 Nov 61
REGISTERED: 14 Nov 61 ILO (Labor Org)
ARTICLES: 12 LANGUAGE: English. French.
HEADNOTE: MINIMUM AGE EMPLOYMENT FISH-
ERMEN

TOPIC: ILO Labor
CONCEPTS: Definition of terms. Exceptions and
exemptions. ILO conventions. Employment regulations. Safety standards.
INTL ORGS: International Labour Organization.
United Nations.
PROCEDURE: Amendment. Denunciation. Duration. Ratification. Registration. Renewal or Revival.
PARTIES:
Multilateral
ANNEX
423 UNTS 329. Taiwan. Ratification 13 Feb 62.
Force 13 Feb 63.
423 UNTS 329. Denmark. Qualified Ratification
27 Feb 62. Force 27 Feb 63.
429 UNTS 304. Peru. Ratification 4 Apr 62. Force
4 Apr 63.
455 UNTS 471. Norway. Ratification 22 Jan 63.
455 UNTS 471. Tunisia. Ratification 14 Jan 63.
Force 14 Jan 64.
457 UNTS 365. Germany, West. Ratification
11 Feb 63. Force 11 Feb 64.
468 UNTS 440. Belgium. Ratification 8 May 63.
Force 8 May 64.
483 UNTS 420. Mauritania. Ratification 8 Nov 63.
Force 8 Nov 64.
510 UNTS 368. Albania. Ratification 11 Aug 64.
Force 11 Aug 64.
522 UNTS 387. Costa Rica. Ratification
29 Dec 64. Force 29 Dec 65.
527 UNTS 342. Netherlands. Ratification
15 Feb 65. Force 15 Feb 66.
527 UNTS 342. Netherlands. Surinam. Ratification 15 Feb 65. Force 15 Feb 66.
567 UNTS 357. Poland. Ratification 20 Jun 66.
Force 20 Jun 67.
600 UNTS 408. France. Ratification 8 Jun 67.
Force 8 Jun 67.

105950 Multilateral Convention **413 UNTS 158**
SIGNED: 19 Jun 59   FORCE: 7 Nov 61
REGISTERED: 14 Nov 61 ILO (Labor Org)
ARTICLES: 13 LANGUAGE: English. French.
HEADNOTE: MEDICAL EXAMINATION FISHER-
MEN
TOPIC: ILO Labor
CONCEPTS: Definition of terms. Exceptions and
exemptions. Public health. ILO conventions.
Safety standards.
INTL ORGS: International Labour Organization.
United Nations.
PROCEDURE: Amendment. Denunciation. Dura-
tion. Ratification. Registration. Renewal or Re-
vival.
PARTIES:
Multilateral
ANNEX
423 UNTS 330. Taiwan. Ratification 13 Feb 62.
Force 13 Feb 63.
429 UNTS 305. Peru. Ratification 4 Apr 62. Force
4 Apr 63.
455 UNTS 472. Tunisia. Ratification 14 Jan 63.
Force 14 Jan 64.
468 UNTS 441. Belgium. Ratification 8 May 63.
Force 8 May 64.
522 UNTS 388. Costa Rica. Ratification
29 Dec 64. Force 29 Dec 65.
530 UNTS 426. Brazil. Ratification 1 Mar 65.
Force 1 Mar 66.
600 UNTS 409. France. Ratification 8 Jun 67.
Force 8 Jun 68.

105951 Multilateral Convention **413 UNTS 168**
SIGNED: 19 Jun 59   FORCE: 7 Nov 61
REGISTERED: 14 Nov 61 ILO (Labor Org)
ARTICLES: 20 LANGUAGE: English. French.
HEADNOTE: FISHERMANS ARTICLES AGREE-
MENT
TOPIC: ILO Labor
CONCEPTS: Definition of terms. Detailed regula-
tions. Exceptions and exemptions. Domestic leg-
islation. Private contracts. ILO conventions. Em-
ployment regulations. Labor statistics.
INTL ORGS: International Labour Organization.
United Nations.
PROCEDURE: Amendment. Denunciation. Dura-
tion. Ratification. Registration. Renewal or Re-
vival.
PARTIES:
Multilateral
ANNEX
420 UNTS 366. Yugoslavia. Ratification
22 Dec 61. Force 22 Dec 62.

423 UNTS 331. Taiwan. Ratification 13 Feb 62.
Force 13 Feb 63.
429 UNTS 306. Peru. Ratification 4 Apr 62. Force
4 Apr 63.
455 UNTS 473. Tunisia. Ratification 14 Jan 63.
Force 14 Jan 64.
468 UNTS 442. Belgium. Ratification 8 May 63.
Force 8 May 64.
483 UNTS 421. Mauritania. Ratification 8 Nov 63.
Force 8 Nov 64.
504 UNTS 368. Germany, West. Ratification
1 Jul 64. Force 1 Jul 65.
522 UNTS 389. Costa Rica. Ratification
29 Dec 64. Force 29 Dec 65.
600 UNTS 409. France. Ratification 8 Jun 67.
Force 8 Jun 68.

105952 Bilateral Agreement **413 UNTS 182**
SIGNED: 12 Apr 61 FORCE: 27 May 61
REGISTERED: 14 Nov 61 USA (United States)
ARTICLES: 6 LANGUAGE: English. Spanish.
HEADNOTE: ECONOMIC COOPERATION
TOPIC: Direct Aid
CONCEPTS: Change of circumstances. Previous
treaty replacement. Diplomatic privileges. Privi-
leges and immunities. Conformity with munici-
pal law. Exchange of information and docu-
ments. Inspection and observation. Personnel.
Public information. Accounting procedures. Ex-
change rates and regulations. Assets. Tax ex-
emptions. Customs exemptions. Commodities
and services. Domestic obligation. General tech-
nical assistance. Economic assistance. Materials, equipment and services. Aid missions.
Grants. Withdrawal conditions.
TREATY REF: 99UNTS49.
PROCEDURE: Amendment. Termination.
PARTIES:
Honduras
USA (United States)

105953 Bilateral Exchange **413 UNTS 195**
SIGNED: 26 May 61 FORCE: 26 May 61
REGISTERED: 15 Nov 61 USA (United States)
ARTICLES: 2 LANGUAGE: English. French.
HEADNOTE: ECONOMIC TECHNICAL RELATED
ASSISTANCE
TOPIC: General Aid
CONCEPTS: Change of circumstances. Exceptions
and exemptions. Guarantees and safeguards.
Diplomatic privileges. Privileges and immunities.
Conformity with municipal law. Exchange of in-
formation and documents. Personnel. General
property. Accounting procedures. Attachment of
funds. Banking. Exchange rates and regulations.
Funding procedures. Garnishment of funds. Sei-
zure funds. Tax exemptions. Customs exemp-
tions. Commodities and services. Domestic obligation. General technical assistance. Economic
assistance. Materials, equipment and services.
Aid missions. Grants.
PROCEDURE: Termination.
PARTIES:
Cameroon
USA (United States)
ANNEX
445 UNTS 367. USA (United States). Acknowledgement 8 Dec 61. Force 8 Dec 61.
445 UNTS 367. Cameroon. Amendment
14 Mar 62. Force 8 Dec 61.

105954 Bilateral Exchange **413 UNTS 205**
SIGNED: 20 May 61 FORCE: 20 May 61
REGISTERED: 15 Nov 61 USA (United States)
ARTICLES: 2 LANGUAGE: English. French.
HEADNOTE: MILITARY ASSISTANCE
TOPIC: Milit Assistance
CONCEPTS: Non-prejudice to UN charter. Materi-
als, equipment and services. Self-defense. Mili-
tary assistance. Return of equipment and recap-
ture. Restrictions on transfer.
PARTIES:
Mali
USA (United States)

105955 Bilateral Exchange **413 UNTS 211**
SIGNED: 16 Jun 61 FORCE: 16 Jun 61
REGISTERED: 15 Nov 61 USA (United States)
ARTICLES: 2 LANGUAGE: English.

HEADNOTE: CLOSING ACCOUNTS ADJUSTING
PAYMENTS
TOPIC: Claims and Debts
CONCEPTS: Conformity with municipal law. Ac-
counting procedures. Currency. Financial pro-
grams. Transportation costs. Customs duties.
Merchant vessels.
TREATY REF: 251UNTS3; 251UNTS268;
283UNTS43; 304UNTS253.
PARTIES:
Finland
USA (United States)

105956 Bilateral Exchange **413 UNTS 219**
SIGNED: 22 Jun 61 FORCE: 22 Jun 61
REGISTERED: 15 Nov 61 USA (United States)
ARTICLES: 2 LANGUAGE: English. French.
HEADNOTE: ECONOMIC TECHNICAL RELATED
ASSISTANCE
TOPIC: General Aid
CONCEPTS: Change of circumstances. Exceptions
and exemptions. Privileges and immunities. Con-
formity with municipal law. Personnel. Account-
ing procedures. Attachment of funds. Banking.
Exchange rates and regulations. Funding proce-
dures. Garnishment of funds. Seizure funds. Tax
exemptions. Customs exemptions. Temporary
importation. Commodities and services. Domes-
tic obligation. General technical assistance. Economic assistance. Materials, equipment and services. Aid missions. Grants.
PROCEDURE: Termination.
PARTIES:
Madagascar
USA (United States)

105957 Bilateral Exchange **413 UNTS 229**
SIGNED: 26 Jun 61 FORCE: 26 Jun 61
REGISTERED: 15 Nov 61 USA (United States)
ARTICLES: 2 LANGUAGE: English. Spanish.
HEADNOTE: TRANSFER POLICE EQUIPMENT
TOPIC: Direct Aid
CONCEPTS: Guarantees and safeguards. Treaty
implementation. Conformity with municipal law.
Exchange of information and documents. Title
and deeds. Materials, equipment and services.
PARTIES:
Mexico
USA (United States)

105958 Bilateral Convention **413 UNTS 236**
SIGNED: 20 Apr 60 FORCE: 1 Aug 61
REGISTERED: 20 Nov 61 UK Great Britain
ARTICLES: 51 LANGUAGE: English. German.
HEADNOTE: SOCIAL SECURITY
TOPIC: Non-ILO Labor
CONCEPTS: Definition of terms. Domestic legisla-
tion. Dispute settlement. Old age and invalidity
insurance. Wages and salaries. Non-ILO labor relations. Family allowances. Administrative cooperation. Old age insurance. Sickness and invalidity insurance. Social security. Unemployment.
Payment schedules. Claims and settlements.
INTL ORGS: League of Nations. European Economic Community. International Court of Justice.
PARTIES:
Germany, West
UK Great Britain
ANNEX
606 UNTS 360. Germany, West. Implementation
10 Dec 64. Force 1 Mar 67.
606 UNTS 360. UK Great Britain. Implementation
10 Dec 64. Force 1 Mar 67.
643 UNTS 394. Germany, West. Amendment
14 Feb 68. Force 1 Mar 67.
643 UNTS 394. UK Great Britain. Amendment
14 Feb 68. Force 1 Mar 67.

105959 Bilateral Exchange **414 UNTS 3**
SIGNED: 2 May 61 FORCE: 2 May 61
REGISTERED: 20 Nov 61 UK Great Britain
ARTICLES: 2 LANGUAGE: English. German.
HEADNOTE: ASSISTANCE CRIMINAL MATTERS
TOPIC: Admin Cooperation
CONCEPTS: Exceptions and exemptions. General
cooperation.
PARTIES:
Germany, West
UK Great Britain

105960 Bilateral Exchange **414 UNTS 9**
SIGNED: 10 May 61 FORCE: 1 Jun 61
REGISTERED: 20 Nov 61 UK Great Britain
ARTICLES: 2 LANGUAGE: English.
HEADNOTE: ACCEPTANCE BRITISH VISITORS
PASSPORT
TOPIC: Visas
CONCEPTS: Emergencies. Time limit. Annex or ap-
pendix reference. Passports non-diplomatic. De-
nial of admission. Conformity with municipal
law.
INTL ORGS: Council of Europe. Organization for
Economic Co-operation and Development.
TREATY REF: 322UNTS245.
PARTIES:
Norway
UK Great Britain
ANNEX
420 UNTS 368. UK Great Britain. Supplementa-
tion 14 Jul 61. Force 17 Jul 61.
420 UNTS 368. Norway. Supplementation
17 Jul 61. Force 17 Jul 61.

105961 Bilateral Exchange **414 UNTS 17**
SIGNED: 10 May 61 FORCE: 1 Jun 61
REGISTERED: 20 Nov 61 UK Great Britain
ARTICLES: 2 LANGUAGE: English.
HEADNOTE: ACCEPTANCE BRITISH VISITORS
PASSPORT
TOPIC: Visas
CONCEPTS: Time limit. Annex or appendix refer-
ence. Passports non-diplomatic. Denial of admis-
sion. Visas. Conformity with municipal law.
INTL ORGS: Council of Europe. Organization for
Economic Co-operation and Development.
TREATY REF: 322UNTS245.
PARTIES:
Denmark
UK Great Britain
ANNEX
420 UNTS 372. Denmark. Supplementation
27 Jul 61. Force 27 Jul 61.
420 UNTS 372. UK Great Britain. Supplementa-
tion 27 Jul 61. Force 27 Jul 61.

105962 Bilateral Agreement **414 UNTS 26**
SIGNED: 21 Jul 61 FORCE: 21 Jul 61
REGISTERED: 20 Nov 61 UK Great Britain
ARTICLES: 6 LANGUAGE: English. Portuguese.
HEADNOTE: LOAN
TOPIC: Loans and Credits
CONCEPTS: Definition of terms. Interest rates.
Payment schedules. Loan and credit. Loan repay-
ment. Terms of loan.
PARTIES:
Brazil
UK Great Britain

105963 Bilateral Exchange **414 UNTS 37**
SIGNED: 9 May 61 FORCE: 1 Jun 61
REGISTERED: 20 Nov 61 UK Great Britain
ARTICLES: 2 LANGUAGE: English. Spanish.
HEADNOTE: RECIPROCAL ABOLITION VISAS
TOPIC: Visas
CONCEPTS: Territorial application. Time limit. Visa
abolition. Denial of admission. Resident permits.
Conformity with municipal law.
PROCEDURE: Denunciation.
PARTIES:
Chile
UK Great Britain

105964 Bilateral Exchange **414 UNTS 46**
SIGNED: 8 Mar 61 FORCE: 15 Mar 61
REGISTERED: 20 Nov 61 UK Great Britain
ARTICLES: 2 LANGUAGE: English. Italian.
HEADNOTE: ACCEPTANCE BRITISH VISITORS
PASSPORT
TOPIC: Visas
CONCEPTS: Emergencies. Time limit. Annex or ap-
pendix reference. Visa abolition. Passports non-
diplomatic. Denial of admission. Resident per-
mits. Conformity with municipal law.
TREATY REF: 87UNTS37.

PARTIES:
San Marino
UK Great Britain
ANNEX
425 UNTS 378. San Marino. Implementation
31 Aug 61. Force 15 Jun 61.
425 UNTS 378. UK Great Britain. Implementation
14 Jul 61. Force 15 Jun 61.

105965 Bilateral Exchange **414 UNTS 53**
SIGNED: 9 Jun 61 FORCE: 1 Jul 61
REGISTERED: 20 Nov 61 UK Great Britain
ARTICLES: 2 LANGUAGE: English.
HEADNOTE: ACCEPTANCE BRITISH VISITORS
PASSPORT
TOPIC: Visas
CONCEPTS: Time limit. Annex or appendix refer-
ence. Visa abolition. Passports non-diplomatic.
Denial of admission. Conformity with municipal
law.
TREATY REF: 322UNTS245.
PARTIES:
Finland
UK Great Britain
ANNEX
420 UNTS 376. Finland. Supplementation
10 Aug 61. Force 10 Aug 61.
420 UNTS 376. UK Great Britain. Supplementa-
tion 10 Aug 61. Force 10 Aug 61.

105966 Bilateral Agreement **414 UNTS 61**
SIGNED: 3 Dec 60 FORCE: 8 Jul 61
REGISTERED: 20 Nov 61 UK Great Britain
ARTICLES: 15 LANGUAGE: English. Japanese.
HEADNOTE: CULTURAL AGREEMENT
TOPIC: Culture
CONCEPTS: Definition of terms. Friendship and
amity. Border traffic and migration. Conformity
with municipal law. Operating agencies. Estab-
lishment of commission. Specialists exchange.
Recognition of degrees. Teacher and student ex-
change. Professorships. Institute establishment.
Scholarships and grants. General cultural coop-
eration. Publications exchange. Mass media ex-
change.
INTL ORGS: Special Commission.
PROCEDURE: Denunciation. Duration. Ratification.
Renewal or Revival.
PARTIES:
Japan
UK Great Britain

105967 Bilateral Exchange **414 UNTS 85**
SIGNED: 26 May 61 FORCE: 26 Jun 61
REGISTERED: 20 Nov 61 UK Great Britain
ARTICLES: 2 LANGUAGE: English. Spanish.
HEADNOTE: RECIPROCAL ABOLITION VISAS
TOPIC: Visas
CONCEPTS: Emergencies. Territorial application.
Time limit. Visa abolition. Denial of admission.
Conformity with municipal law.
PROCEDURE: Denunciation.
PARTIES:
Colombia
UK Great Britain

105968 Bilateral Exchange **414 UNTS 93**
SIGNED: 28 Jun 61 FORCE: 1 Sep 61
REGISTERED: 20 Nov 61 UK Great Britain
ARTICLES: 2 LANGUAGE: English.
HEADNOTE: ACCEPTANCE BRITISH VISITORS
PASSPORT
TOPIC: Visas
CONCEPTS: Emergencies. Time limit. Visa aboli-
tion. Passports non-diplomatic. Denial of admis-
sion. Conformity with municipal law.
INTL ORGS: Council of Europe. Organization for
Economic Co-operation and Development.
PROCEDURE: Termination.
PARTIES:
Turkey
UK Great Britain
ANNEX
425 UNTS 384. UK Great Britain. Implementation
24 Nov 61. Force 24 Nov 61.
425 UNTS 384. Turkey. Implementation
24 Nov 61. Force 24 Nov 61.

105969 Bilateral Exchange **414 UNTS 101**
SIGNED: 5 May 61 FORCE: 5 Jun 61
REGISTERED: 20 Nov 61 UK Great Britain
ARTICLES: 2 LANGUAGE: English.
HEADNOTE: ABOLITION VISAS
TOPIC: Visas
CONCEPTS: Emergencies. Annex or appendix ref-
erence. Visa abolition. Denial of admission. Con-
formity with municipal law.
TREATY REF: 204UNTS177.
PROCEDURE: Denunciation.
PARTIES:
Finland
UK Great Britain

105970 Multilateral Agreement **414 UNTS 110**
SIGNED: 1 Dec 60 FORCE: 27 Feb 61
REGISTERED: 20 Nov 61 UK Great Britain
ARTICLES: 13 LANGUAGE: English. French.
HEADNOTE: SPACE RESEARCH COOPERATION
TOPIC: Scientific Project
CONCEPTS: Annex or appendix reference. Gen-
eral cooperation. Operating agencies. Establish-
ment of commission. Research and scientific
projects. Communication satellites testing.
Scientific exchange. Expense sharing formulae.
INTL ORGS: Special Commission.
PROCEDURE: Accession. Duration. Future Proce-
dures Contemplated. Ratification. Renewal or
Revival. Termination.
PARTIES:
Belgium SIGNED: 1 Dec 60 FORCE: 27 Feb 61
Denmark SIGNED: 1 Dec 60 FORCE: 27 Feb 61
France SIGNED: 1 Dec 60 RATIFIED: 27 Jan 61
FORCE: 27 Feb 61
Germany, West SIGNED: 27 Feb 61 FORCE:
27 Feb 61
Italy SIGNED: 1 Dec 60
Netherlands SIGNED: 1 Dec 60 FORCE:
27 Feb 61
Norway SIGNED: 1 Dec 60 FORCE: 27 Feb 61
Spain SIGNED: 1 Dec 60 FORCE: 27 Feb 61
Sweden SIGNED: 1 Dec 60 FORCE: 27 Feb 61
Switzerland SIGNED: 1 Dec 60 RATIFIED:
24 Feb 61 FORCE: 27 Feb 61
UK Great Britain SIGNED: 1 Dec 60 FORCE:
27 Feb 61
ANNEX
507 UNTS 312. Netherlands. Prolongation
21 Feb 62. Force 21 Feb 63.
507 UNTS 312. Spain. Prolongation 21 Feb 62.
Force 21 Feb 63.
507 UNTS 312. Sweden. Prolongation 21 Feb 62.
Force 21 Feb 63.
507 UNTS 312. UK Great Britain. Prolongation
21 Feb 62. Force 21 Feb 63.
507 UNTS 312. France. Prolongation 21 Feb 62.
Force 21 Feb 63.
507 UNTS 312. Belgium. Prolongation 21 Feb 62.
Force 21 Feb 63.
507 UNTS 312. Switzerland. Prolongation
21 Feb 62. Force 21 Feb 63.
507 UNTS 312. Denmark. Prolongation
21 Feb 62. Force 21 Feb 63.
507 UNTS 312. Austria. Prolongation 21 Feb 62.
Force 26 Sep 62.
507 UNTS 312. Norway. Prolongation 21 Feb 62.
Force 21 Feb 63.
507 UNTS 312. UK Great Britain. Prolongation
21 Feb 62. Force 21 Feb 63.
507 UNTS 312. Germany, West. Prolongation
21 Feb 62. Force 21 Feb 63.
507 UNTS 322. Germany, West. Prolongation
23 Nov 62. Force 19 Apr 63.
507 UNTS 322. Netherlands. Prolongation
23 Nov 62. Force 19 Apr 63.
507 UNTS 322. Denmark. Prolongation
23 Nov 62. Force 14 May 63.
507 UNTS 322. Spain. Prolongation 23 Nov 62.
Force 19 Apr 63.
507 UNTS 322. Sweden. Prolongation
23 Nov 62. Force 19 Apr 63.
507 UNTS 322. Switzerland. Prolongation
23 Nov 62. Force 19 Apr 63.
507 UNTS 322. UK Great Britain. Prolongation
23 Nov 62. Force 19 Apr 63.
507 UNTS 322. Belgium. Prolongation
23 Nov 62. Force 19 Apr 63.
507 UNTS 322. Austria. Prolongation 23 Nov 62.
Force 19 Apr 63.
507 UNTS 322. France. Prolongation 23 Nov 62.
Force 19 Apr 63.

507 UNTS 330. UK Great Britain. Prolongation
21 Jun 63. Force 21 Jun 63.
507 UNTS 330. France. Prolongation 21 Jun 63.
Force 21 Jun 63.
507 UNTS 330. Spain. Prolongation 21 Jun 63.
Force 21 Jun 63.
507 UNTS 330. Sweden. Prolongation 21 Jun 63.
Force 13 Aug 63.
507 UNTS 330. Denmark. Prolongation
21 Jun 63. Force 14 Oct 63.
507 UNTS 330. Belgium. Prolongation
21 Jun 63. Force 21 Jun 63.
507 UNTS 330. Switzerland. Prolongation
21 Jun 63. Force 21 Jun 63.
507 UNTS 330. Germany, West. Prolongation
21 Jun 63. Force 21 Jun 63.
507 UNTS 330. Netherlands. Prolongation
21 Jun 63. Force 21 Jun 63.
507 UNTS 338. France. Prolongation 13 Dec 63.
Force 13 Dec 63.
507 UNTS 338. Germany, West. Prolongation
13 Dec 63. Force 13 Dec 63.
507 UNTS 338. Belgium. Prolongation
13 Dec 63. Force 20 Dec 63.
507 UNTS 338. UK Great Britain. Prolongation
13 Dec 63. Force 13 Dec 63.
507 UNTS 338. Netherlands. Prolongation
13 Dec 63. Force 13 Dec 63.
507 UNTS 338. Spain. Prolongation 13 Dec 63.
Force 13 Dec 63.
507 UNTS 338. Sweden. Prolongation
13 Dec 63. Force 30 Dec 63.
507 UNTS 338. Switzerland. Prolongation
13 Dec 63. Force 13 Dec 63.
507 UNTS 338. Denmark. Prolongation
13 Dec 63. Force 7 Jan 64.
507 UNTS 338. Italy. Prolongation 13 Dec 63.
Force 13 Dec 63.

105971 Bilateral Convention **414 UNTS 123**
SIGNED: 12 Jun 60 FORCE: 14 Jun 61
REGISTERED: 20 Nov 61 UK Great Britain
ARTICLES: 21 LANGUAGE: English. Spanish.
HEADNOTE: CONVENTION CULTURAL
TOPIC: Culture
CONCEPTS: Definition of terms. Friendship and
amity. Resident permits. Tourism. Conformity
with municipal law. Operating agencies. Estab-
lishment of commission. Recognition of degrees.
Teacher and student exchange. Professorships.
Scholarships and grants. General cultural coop
eration. Import quotas. Publications exchange.
Mass media exchange.
INTL ORGS: Special Commission.
PROCEDURE: Denunciation. Duration. Ratification.
Renewal or Revival.
PARTIES:
Spain
UK Great Britain

105972 Bilateral Convention **414 UNTS 144**
SIGNED: 14 Jul 60 FORCE: 15 Jul 61
REGISTERED: 20 Nov 61 UK Great Britain
ARTICLES: 13 LANGUAGE: English. German.
HEADNOTE: RECOGNITION ENFORCEMENT
JUDGEMENTS CIVIL COMMERCIAL MATTERS
TOPIC: Admin Cooperation
CONCEPTS: Definition of terms. Territorial applica-
tion. General cooperation. Exchange of informa-
tion and documents. Recognition and enforce-
ment of legal decisions. Competence of tribunal.
PROCEDURE: Ratification. Termination.
PARTIES:
Germany, West
UK Great Britain

105973 Bilateral Agreement **414 UNTS 180**
SIGNED: 12 May 61 FORCE: 29 Jun 61
REGISTERED: 20 Nov 61 IDA (Devel Assoc)
ARTICLES: 9 LANGUAGE: English.
HEADNOTE: DEVELOPMENT CREDIT AGREEMENT
TOPIC: Loans and Credits
CONCEPTS: Definition of terms. Detailed regulations. Annex or appendix reference. Exchange of
information and documents. Inspection and observation. Dispute settlement. Currency. Financial programs. Interest rates. Payment schedules. Debt settlement. Credit provisions. Loan
regulations. Plans and standards. IDA development project.
INTL ORGS: International Bank for Reconstruction

and Development. International Court of Justice. United Nations. Arbitration Commission.
PROCEDURE: Termination.
PARTIES:
  Honduras
  IDA (Devel Assoc)

105974 Bilateral Exchange **414 UNTS 211**
SIGNED: 19 Jul 61   FORCE: 1 Aug 61
REGISTERED: 23 Nov 61 Austria
ARTICLES: 2 LANGUAGE: German.
HEADNOTE: ACCEPTANCE PERSONS FRONTIER
TOPIC: Visas
CONCEPTS: Border traffic and migration. National-
  ity and citizenship. Extradition, deportation and
  repatriation. General cooperation. Indemnities
  and reimbursements.
PROCEDURE: Denunciation.
PARTIES:
  Austria
  Germany, West

105975 Bilateral Agreement **414 UNTS 229**
SIGNED: 27 Nov 61   FORCE: 15 Jul 61
REGISTERED: 27 Nov 61 United Nations
ARTICLES: 48 LANGUAGE: French.
HEADNOTE: PRIVILEGES & IMMUNITIES
TOPIC: IGO Status/Immunit
CONCEPTS: Non-visa travel documents. Diplo-
  matic privileges. Diplomatic missions. Inviolabil-
  ity. Privileges and immunities. Property. Confor-
  mity with municipal law. Arbitration. Special tri-
  bunals. Military assistance. Jurisdiction.
  Procurement and logistics. Status of forces. Spe-
  cial status.
INTL ORGS: International Court of Justice. Interna-
  tional Telecommunication Union. Claims Com-
  mission.
PROCEDURE: Amendment. Duration.
PARTIES:
  Congo (Zaire)
  United Nations

105976 Bilateral Agreement **414 UNTS 253**
SIGNED: 26 Jul 61   FORCE: 10 Oct 61
REGISTERED: 28 Nov 61 IBRD (World Bank)
ARTICLES: 7 LANGUAGE: English.
HEADNOTE: LOAN AGREEMENT
TOPIC: IBRD Project
CONCEPTS: Default remedies. Definition of terms.
  Annex or appendix reference. Exchange of infor-
  mation and documents. Informational records.
  Inspection and observation. Accounting proce-
  dures. Bonds. Fees and exemptions. Interest
  rates. Tax exemptions. Domestic obligation.
  Terms of loan. Loan regulations. Loan guarantee.
  Guarantor non-interference.
PARTIES:
  Philippines
  IBRD (World Bank)

105977 Bilateral Agreement **414 UNTS 314**
SIGNED: 3 Feb 61   FORCE: 14 Jul 61
REGISTERED: 28 Nov 61 IBRD (World Bank)
ARTICLES: 5 LANGUAGE: English.
HEADNOTE: GUARANTEE HYDROELECTRIC
  PROJECT
TOPIC: IBRD Project
CONCEPTS: Definition of terms. Annex or appen-
  dix reference. Exchange of information and doc-
  uments. Inspection and observation. Bonds.
  Fees and exemptions. Tax exemptions. Domestic
  obligation. Terms of loan. Loan regulations. Loan
  guarantee. Guarantor non-interference. Hydro-
  electric power.
PARTIES:
  Costa Rica
  IBRD (World Bank)

105978 Bilateral Agreement **414 UNTS 349**
SIGNED: 6 Jun 61   FORCE: 29 Sep 61
REGISTERED: 28 Nov 61 IBRD (World Bank)
ARTICLES: 8 LANGUAGE: English.
HEADNOTE: LOAN POWER
TOPIC: IBRD Project
CONCEPTS: Default remedies. Definition of terms.
  Annex or appendix reference. Exchange of infor-
  mation and documents. Informational records.
  Inspection and observation. Accounting proce-

dures. Bonds. Fees and exemptions. Interest
rates. Domestic obligation. Terms of loan. Loan
regulations. Loan guarantee. Guarantor non-
interference. Hydro-electric power.
PARTIES:
  Ceylon (Sri Lanka)
  IBRD (World Bank)

105979 Multilateral Agreement **415 UNTS 4**
SIGNED: 14 Jun 61   FORCE: 19 Oct 61
REGISTERED: 28 Nov 61 IBRD (World Bank)
ARTICLES: 5 LANGUAGE: English.
HEADNOTE: ADMINISTRATION IRRIGATION
TOPIC: IBRD Project
CONCEPTS: Definition of terms. Annex or appen-
  dix reference. Exchange of information and doc-
  uments. Informational records. Inspection and
  observation. Indemnities and reimbursements.
  Domestic obligation. Terms of loan. Loan regula-
  tions. Loan guarantee. Guarantor non-interfer-
  ence. Irrigation.
PARTIES:
  IBRD (World Bank) SIGNED: 14 Jun 61 FORCE:
    19 Oct 61
  IDA (Devel Assoc) SIGNED: 14 Jun 61 FORCE:
    19 Oct 61
  Sudan SIGNED: 14 Jun 61 FORCE: 19 Oct 61
                    ANNEX
  458 UNTS 360. Vietnam, South. Amendment
    28 May 62. Force 28 May 62.
  458 UNTS 360. USA (United States). Amendment
    28 May 63. Force 28 May 62.
  549 UNTS 296. IDA (Devel Assoc). Implementa-
    tion 11 Sep 64. Force 2 Feb 65.
  549 UNTS 296. Other Party Combin. Implementa-
    tion 11 Sep 64. Force 2 Feb 65.
  549 UNTS 296. IBRD (World Bank). Implementa-
    tion 11 Sep 64. Force 2 Feb 65.
  549 UNTS 296.   Sudan.   Implementation
    11 Sep 64. Force 2 Feb 65.

105980 Bilateral Agreement **415 UNTS 26**
SIGNED: 14 Jun 61   FORCE: 19 Oct 61
REGISTERED: 28 Nov 61 IBRD (World Bank)
ARTICLES: 8 LANGUAGE: English.
HEADNOTE: LOAN IRRIGATION
TOPIC: IBRD Project
CONCEPTS: Default remedies. Definition of terms.
  Annex or appendix reference. Exchange of infor-
  mation and documents. Informational records.
  Inspection and observation. Accounting proce-
  dures. Bonds. Fees and exemptions. Interest
  rates. Domestic obligation. Terms of loan. Loan
  regulations. Loan guarantee. Guarantor non-
  interference. Irrigation.
PARTIES:
  IBRD (World Bank)
  Sudan

105981 Bilateral Agreement **415 UNTS 50**
SIGNED: 14 Jun 61   FORCE: 19 Oct 61
REGISTERED: 28 Nov 61 IDA (Devel Assoc)
ARTICLES: 7 LANGUAGE: English.
HEADNOTE: IDA CREDIT AGREEMENT
TOPIC: Loans and Credits
CONCEPTS: Definition of terms. Detailed regula-
  tions. Annex or appendix reference. Exchange of
  information and documents. Inspection and ob-
  servation. Dispute settlement. Currency. Finan-
  cial programs. Interest rates. Payment sched-
  ules. Debt settlement. Credit provisions. Loan
  regulations. Plans and standards. IDA develop-
  ment project.
INTL ORGS: International Bank for Reconstruction
  and Development.
PROCEDURE: Termination.
PARTIES:
  IDA (Devel Assoc)
  Sudan

105982 Bilateral Agreement **415 UNTS 92**
SIGNED: 23 Feb 61   FORCE: 8 Aug 61
REGISTERED: 29 Nov 61 IBRD (World Bank)
ARTICLES: 5 LANGUAGE: English.
HEADNOTE: GUARANTEE POWER
TOPIC: IBRD Project
CONCEPTS: Definition of terms. Annex or appen-
  dix reference. Exchange of information and doc-
  uments. Inspection and observation. Bonds.
  Fees and exemptions. Tax exemptions. Domestic

obligation. Terms of loan. Loan regulations. Loan
guarantee. Guarantor non-interference. Hydro-
electric power.
PARTIES:
  IBRD (World Bank)
  Yugoslavia

105983 Bilateral Agreement **415 UNTS 121**
SIGNED: 28 Apr 61   FORCE: 6 Jul 61
REGISTERED: 1 Dec 61 IBRD (World Bank)
ARTICLES: 5 LANGUAGE: English.
HEADNOTE: GUARANTEE RAILWAY
TOPIC: IBRD Project
CONCEPTS: Definition of terms. Annex or appen-
  dix reference. Exchange of information and doc-
  uments. Inspection and observation. Bonds.
  Fees and exemptions. Tax exemptions. Domestic
  obligation. Terms of loan. Loan regulations. Loan
  guarantee. Guarantor non-interference. Rail-
  ways.
PARTIES:
  IBRD (World Bank)
  Thailand

105984 Bilateral Agreement **415 UNTS 144**
SIGNED: 2 May 61   FORCE: 3 Jun 61
REGISTERED: 1 Dec 61 IBRD (World Bank)
ARTICLES: 5 LANGUAGE: English.
HEADNOTE: GUARANTEE AGREEMENT
TOPIC: IBRD Project
CONCEPTS: Definition of terms. Annex or appen-
  dix reference. Exchange of information and doc-
  uments. Inspection and observation. Bonds.
  Fees and exemptions. Tax exemptions. Domestic
  obligation. Terms of loan. Loan regulations. Loan
  guarantee. Guarantor non-interference. Rail-
  ways.
PARTIES:
  Japan
  IBRD (World Bank)

105985 Bilateral Agreement **415 UNTS 172**
SIGNED: 12 May 61   FORCE: 20 Sep 61
REGISTERED: 1 Dec 61 IBRD (World Bank)
ARTICLES: 5 LANGUAGE: English.
HEADNOTE: GUARANTEE AGREEMENT
TOPIC: IBRD Project
CONCEPTS: Definition of terms. Annex or appen-
  dix reference. Exchange of information and doc-
  uments. Inspection and observation. Bonds.
  Fees and exemptions. Tax exemptions. Domestic
  obligation. Terms of loan. Loan regulations. Loan
  guarantee. Guarantor non-interference.
PARTIES:
  Colombia
  IBRD (World Bank)

105986 Bilateral Agreement **415 UNTS 204**
SIGNED: 9 Aug 61   FORCE: 1 Sep 61
REGISTERED: 1 Dec 61 IBRD (World Bank)
ARTICLES: 5 LANGUAGE: English.
HEADNOTE: GUARANTEE AGREEMENT
TOPIC: IBRD Project
CONCEPTS: Definition of terms. Annex or appen-
  dix reference. Exchange of information and doc-
  uments. Inspection and observation. Bonds.
  Fees and exemptions. Tax exemptions. Domestic
  obligation. Terms of loan. Loan regulations. Loan
  guarantee. Guarantor non-interference.
PARTIES:
  Finland
  IBRD (World Bank)

105987 Bilateral Agreement **415 UNTS 236**
SIGNED: 4 Dec 61   FORCE: 4 Dec 61
REGISTERED: 4 Dec 61 United Nations
ARTICLES: 6 LANGUAGE: English.
HEADNOTE: OPERATIONAL EXECUTIVE ADMINIS-
  TRATIVE PERSONNEL
TOPIC: Tech Assistance
CONCEPTS: Treaty implementation. Annex or ap-
  pendix reference. Privileges and immunities.
  General cooperation. Personnel. Responsibility
  and liability. Arbitration. Procedure. Negotiation.
  Vocational training. Compensation. Expense
  sharing formulae. Tax exemptions. Customs ex-
  emptions. Domestic obligation. Special projects.
  Status of experts. Conformity with IGO deci-
  sions.

INTL ORGS: Permanent Court of Arbitration.
PROCEDURE: Amendment. Termination.
PARTIES:
Ceylon (Sri Lanka)
United Nations
ANNEX
602 UNTS 347. United Nations. Force 10 Jun 67.
602 UNTS 347. Ceylon (Sri Lanka). Force
10 Jun 67.

105988 Bilateral Agreement **415 UNTS 248**
SIGNED: 16 Jun 60   FORCE: 29 Aug 61
REGISTERED: 6 Dec 61 Czechoslovakia
ARTICLES: 8 LANGUAGE: Czechoslovakian. German.
HEADNOTE: ECONOMIC TECHNICAL SCIENTIFIC
COOPERATION
TOPIC: General Economic
CONCEPTS: General provisions. Annex or appendix reference. Previous treaty replacement. Establishment of commission. Decisions.
INTL ORGS: Special Commission.
PARTIES:
Czechoslovakia
Germany, East

105989 Bilateral Agreement **415 UNTS 269**
SIGNED: 13 Oct 61   FORCE: 24 Nov 61
REGISTERED: 6 Dec 61 IBRD (World Bank)
ARTICLES: 5 LANGUAGE: English.
HEADNOTE: GUARANTEE ANGAT PROJECT
TOPIC: IBRD Project
CONCEPTS: Definition of terms. Annex or appendix reference. Exchange of information and documents. Bonds. Fees and exemptions. Tax exemptions. Domestic obligation. Terms of loan. Loan regulations. Loan guarantee. Guarantor non-interference.
PARTIES:
Philippines
IBRD (World Bank)

105990 Bilateral Agreement **415 UNTS 300**
SIGNED: 29 Mar 61   FORCE: 30 Aug 61
REGISTERED: 7 Dec 61 IBRD (World Bank)
ARTICLES: 5 LANGUAGE: English.
HEADNOTE: GUARANTEE ELECTRICITY
TOPIC: IBRD Project
CONCEPTS: Definition of terms. Annex or appendix reference. Exchange of information and documents. Inspection and observation. Bonds. Fees and exemptions. Tax exemptions. Domestic obligation. Terms of loan. Loan regulations. Loan guarantee. Guarantor non-interference. Hydroelectric power.
PARTIES:
IBRD (World Bank)
UK Great Britain

105991 Bilateral Agreement **415 UNTS 358**
SIGNED: 23 Jun 61   FORCE: 22 Aug 61
REGISTERED: 8 Dec 61 IBRD (World Bank)
ARTICLES: 5 LANGUAGE: English.
HEADNOTE: GUARANTEE AGREEMENT
TOPIC: IBRD Project
CONCEPTS: Definition of terms. Annex or appendix reference. Exchange of information and documents. Inspection and observation. Bonds. Fees and exemptions. Tax exemptions. Domestic obligation. Terms of loan. Loan regulations. Loan guarantee. Guarantor non-interference.
PARTIES:
IBRD (World Bank)
UK Great Britain

105992 Bilateral Agreement **416 UNTS 3**
SIGNED: 28 Aug 61   FORCE: 25 Nov 61
REGISTERED: 11 Dec 61 IDA (Devel Assoc)
ARTICLES: 7 LANGUAGE: English.
HEADNOTE: CREDIT ROAD
TOPIC: Loans and Credits
CONCEPTS: Definition of terms. Annex or appendix reference. Exchange of information and documents. Currency. Financial programs. Interest rates. Payment schedules. Debt settlement. Loan and credit. Credit provisions. Purchase authorization. Loan repayment. Terms of loan. IDA development project. Roads and highways.

INTL ORGS: International Bank for Reconstruction
and Development.
PROCEDURE: Termination.
PARTIES:
Colombia
IDA (Devel Assoc)

105993 Bilateral Agreement **416 UNTS 23**
SIGNED: 28 Aug 61   FORCE: 25 Nov 61
REGISTERED: 11 Dec 61 IBRD (World Bank)
ARTICLES: 8 LANGUAGE: English.
HEADNOTE: LOAN ROAD
TOPIC: IBRD Project
CONCEPTS: Default remedies. Definition of terms. Annex or appendix reference. Exchange of information and documents. Informational records. Inspection and observation. Accounting procedures. Bonds. Fees and exemptions. Interest rates. Tax exemptions. Domestic obligation. Terms of loan. Loan regulations. Loan guarantee. Guarantor non-interference. Roads and highways.
INTL ORGS: International Development Association.
PARTIES:
Colombia
IBRD (World Bank)

105994 Multilateral Agreement **416 UNTS 45**
SIGNED: 28 Aug 61   FORCE: 25 Nov 61
REGISTERED: 11 Dec 61 IBRD (World Bank)
ARTICLES: 1 LANGUAGE: English.
HEADNOTE: DISBURSEMENT AGREEMENT
TOPIC: IBRD Project
CONCEPTS: Payment schedules. World Bank projects.
PARTIES:
Colombia   SIGNED: 28 Aug 61   FORCE:
25 Nov 61
IBRD (World Bank) SIGNED: 28 Aug 61 FORCE:
25 Nov 61
IDA (Devel Assoc) SIGNED: 28 Aug 61 FORCE:
25 Nov 61

105995 Multilateral Convention **416 UNTS 51**
SIGNED: 3 Dec 58   FORCE: 23 Nov 61
REGISTERED: 11 Dec 61 UNESCO (Educ/Cult)
ARTICLES: 21 LANGUAGE: English. French. Russian. Spanish.
HEADNOTE: EXCHANGE PUBLICATIONS
TOPIC: Admin Cooperation
CONCEPTS: Territorial application. General cooperation. Exchange of official publications. Indemnities and reimbursements. Non-interest rates and fees. Customs exemptions. IGO obligations.
INTL ORGS: United Nations Educational, Scientific and Cultural Organization.
PROCEDURE: Amendment. Accession. Denunciation. Ratification. Registration.
PARTIES:
Taiwan RATIFIED: 26 Apr 61 FORCE: 26 Apr 62
Ecuador RATIFIED: 8 Feb 61 FORCE: 8 Feb 62
France RATIFIED: 30 May 60 FORCE: 23 Nov 61
Guatemala   RATIFIED: 23 Nov 60   FORCE:
23 Nov 61
Israel RATIFIED: 4 Jan 60 FORCE: 23 Nov 61
Italy RATIFIED: 2 Aug 61 FORCE: 2 Aug 62
UK Great Britain Anguilla RATIFIED: 1 Jun 61
FORCE: 1 Jun 62
UK Great Britain Antigua RATIFIED: 1 Jun 61
FORCE: 1 Jun 62
UK Great Britain Bahamas RATIFIED: 1 Jun 61
FORCE: 1 Jun 62
UK Great Britain Barbados RATIFIED: 1 Jun 61
FORCE: 1 Jun 62
UK Great Britain Bermuda RATIFIED: 1 Jun 61
FORCE: 1 Jun 62
UK Great Britain British Guiana RATIFIED:
1 Jun 61 FORCE: 1 Jun 62
UK Great Britain Brit Solomon Is RATIFIED:
1 Jun 61 FORCE: 1 Jun 62
UK Great Britain Brit Virgin Islands RATIFIED:
1 Jun 61 FORCE: 1 Jun 62
UK Great Britain Brunei RATIFIED: 1 Jun 61
FORCE: 1 Jun 62
UK Great Britain Dominican Republic RATIFIED:
1 Jun 61 FORCE: 1 Jun 62
UK Great Britain Fed Rhod/Nyasaland RATIFIED:
1 Jun 61 FORCE: 1 Jun 62
UK Great Britain Gilbert Islands RATIFIED:
1 Jun 61 FORCE: 1 Jun 62

UK Great Britain Grenada RATIFIED: 1 Jun 61
FORCE: 1 Jun 62
UK Great Britain Guernsey Island RATIFIED:
1 Jun 61 FORCE: 1 Jun 62
UK Great Britain Isle of Man RATIFIED: 1 Jun 61
FORCE: 1 Jun 62
UK Great Britain Jamaica RATIFIED: 1 Jun 61
FORCE: 1 Jun 62
UK Great Britain Jersey Island RATIFIED:
1 Jun 61 FORCE: 1 Jun 62
UK Great Britain Montserrat RATIFIED: 1 Jun 61
FORCE: 1 Jun 62
UK Great Britain Nevis RATIFIED: 1 Jun 61
FORCE: 1 Jun 62
UK Great Britain RATIFIED: 1 Jun 61 FORCE:
1 Jun 62
UK Great Britain Singapore RATIFIED: 1 Jun 61
FORCE: 1 Jun 62
UK Great Britain St. Christopher RATIFIED:
1 Jun 61 FORCE: 1 Jun 62
UK Great Britain St. Lucia RATIFIED: 1 Jun 61
FORCE: 1 Jun 62
UK Great Britain St. Vincent RATIFIED: 1 Jun 61
FORCE: 1 Jun 62
UK Great Britain Trinidad RATIFIED: 1 Jun 61
FORCE: 1 Jun 62
ANNEX
435 UNTS 382. Panama. Ratification 17 Jul 62.
Force 17 Jul 63.
443 UNTS 352. United Arab Rep. Acceptance
22 Oct 62. Force 22 Oct 63.
443 UNTS 352. USSR (Soviet Union). Ratification
8 Oct 62. Force 8 Oct 63.
449 UNTS 382. Hungary. Acceptance 10 Dec 62.
Force 10 Dec 63.
449 UNTS 382.   Byelorussia.   Ratification
10 Dec 62. Force 10 Dec 63.
450 UNTS 473.   Ukrainian   SSR.   Ratification
19 Dec 62. Force 19 Dec 63.
453 UNTS 446.   New Zealand.   Ratification
5 Feb 63. Force 5 Feb 64.
453 UNTS 446. Spain. Ratification 1 Feb 63.
Force 1 Feb 64.
456 UNTS 512. Bulgaria. Ratification 4 Mar 63.
Force 4 Mar 64.
474 UNTS 349. Cuba. Ratification 1 Aug 63.
Force 1 Aug 64.
483 UNTS 383. Ghana. Ratification 6 Dec 63.
Force 6 Dec 64.
483 UNTS 383. Czechoslovakia. Acceptance
29 Nov 63. Force 29 Nov 64.
507 UNTS 344. Brazil. Ratification 11 Aug 64.
Force 11 Aug 65.
521 UNTS 398. Denmark. Ratification 10 Nov 64.
Force 10 Nov 65.
539 UNTS 365. Romania. Qualified Ratification
9 Jun 65. Force 9 Jun 66.
615 UNTS 410.   Luxembourg.   Ratification
13 Dec 67.
615 UNTS 410.   Luxembourg.   Ratification
13 Dec 67. Force 13 Dec 68.
646 UNTS 398. Morocco. Acceptance 30 Aug 68.
Force 30 Aug 69.
648 UNTS 370. Norway. Acceptance 19 Sep 68.
Force 19 Sep 68.

105996 Bilateral Agreement **416 UNTS 81**
SIGNED: 24 Mar 60   FORCE: 24 Mar 60
REGISTERED: 12 Dec 61 Belgium
ARTICLES: 14 LANGUAGE: French.
HEADNOTE: CONCERNING AIR SERVICES
TOPIC: Air Transport
CONCEPTS: Detailed regulations. Territorial application. Annex or appendix reference. Conformity with municipal law. General cooperation. Arbitration. Procedure. Existing tribunals. Negotiation. Indemnities and reimbursements. Monetary and gold transfers. National treatment. Customs exemptions. Routes and logistics. Navigational conditions. Permit designation. Air transport. Conditions of airlines operating permission. Overflights and technical stops. Operating authorizations and regulations. Non-interest rates and fees.
INTL ORGS: International Civil Aviation Organization. International Court of Justice.
PROCEDURE: Amendment. Future Procedures Contemplated. Ratification. Registration. Termination.
PARTIES:
Belgium
Switzerland

105997 Bilateral Exchange **416 UNTS 93**
SIGNED: 3 Jan 61 FORCE: 3 Jan 61
REGISTERED: 13 Dec 61 USA (United States)
ARTICLES: 3 LANGUAGE: English. German.
HEADNOTE: LEGAL ASSISTANCE
TOPIC: Admin Cooperation
CONCEPTS: Exchange of information and documents. Legal protection and assistance. Operating agencies.
TREATY REF: 119LTS247.
PARTIES:
    Germany, West
    USA (United States)

105998 Bilateral Agreement **416 UNTS 101**
SIGNED: 21 Jul 61 FORCE: 21 Jul 61
REGISTERED: 13 Dec 61 USA (United States)
ARTICLES: 6 LANGUAGE: English. Chinese.
HEADNOTE: AGRI COMMOD
TOPIC: US Agri Commod Aid
CONCEPTS: General provisions. Annex or appendix reference. Exchange of information and documents. Reexport of goods, etc.. Exchange rates and regulations. Transportation costs. Local currency. Commodities schedule. Purchase authorization. Mutual consultation.
PARTIES:
    Taiwan
    USA (United States)
        ANNEX
434 UNTS 350. Taiwan. Amendment 15 Nov 61. Force 15 Nov 61.
434 UNTS 350. USA (United States). Amendment 15 Nov 61. Force 15 Nov 61.
458 UNTS 359. Taiwan. Amendment 29 Jun 62. Force 29 Jun 62.
458 UNTS 359. USA (United States). Amendment 29 Jun 62. Force 29 Jun 62.

105999 Bilateral Agreement **416 UNTS 133**
SIGNED: 14 Jul 61 FORCE: 14 Jul 61
REGISTERED: 13 Dec 61 USA (United States)
ARTICLES: 6 LANGUAGE: English.
HEADNOTE: AGRI COMMOD TITLE I
TOPIC: US Agri Commod Aid
CONCEPTS: General provisions. Annex or appendix reference. Exchange of information and documents. Reexport of goods, etc.. Embargo. Transportation costs. Local currency. Commodities schedule. Purchase authorization. Surplus commodities. Mutual consultation.
PARTIES:
    USA (United States)
    Vietnam, South

106000 Unilateral Instrument **416 UNTS 147**
SIGNED: 9 Dec 61 FORCE: 14 Dec 61
REGISTERED: 14 Dec 61 United Nations
ARTICLES: 1 LANGUAGE: English.
HEADNOTE: ACCEPTANCE OBLIGATIONS UN
TOPIC: UN Charter
CONCEPTS: Acceptance of UN obligations. Acceptance of obligations upon admittance to UN.
INTL ORGS: United Nations.
PARTIES:
    Tanganyika

106001 Bilateral Agreement **416 UNTS 151**
SIGNED: 29 Jul 61 FORCE: 29 Jul 61
REGISTERED: 14 Dec 61 USA (United States)
ARTICLES: 6 LANGUAGE: English.
HEADNOTE: AGRI COMMOD TITLE I
TOPIC: US Agri Commod Aid
CONCEPTS: General provisions. Annex or appendix reference. Exchange of information and documents. Reexport of goods, etc.. Exchange rates and regulations. Transportation costs. Local currency. Commodities schedule. Purchase authorization. Surplus commodities. Mutual consultation.
PARTIES:
    Turkey
    USA (United States)
        ANNEX
426 UNTS 350. Turkey. Amendment 6 Sep 61. Force 6 Sep 61.
426 UNTS 350. USA (United States). Amendment 6 Sep 61. Force 6 Sep 61.
433 UNTS 394. Turkey. Amendment 8 Dec 61. Force 8 Dec 61.

433 UNTS 394. USA (United States). Amendment 8 Dec 61. Force 8 Dec 61.
433 UNTS 398. USA (United States). Amendment 3 Jan 62. Force 3 Jan 62.
433 UNTS 398. Turkey. Amendment 3 Jan 62. Force 3 Jan 62.
433 UNTS 402. Turkey. Amendment 5 Jan 62. Force 5 Jan 62.
433 UNTS 402. USA (United States). Amendment 5 Jan 62. Force 5 Jan 62.
445 UNTS 370. USA (United States). Amendment 14 Mar 62. Force 14 Mar 62.
445 UNTS 370. Turkey. Amendment 14 Mar 62. Force 14 Mar 62.
459 UNTS 306. Turkey. Amendment 21 Jun 62. Force 21 Jan 62.
459 UNTS 306. USA (United States). Amendment 21 Jun 62. Force 21 Jan 62.
459 UNTS 310. Turkey. Amendment 11 Oct 62. Force 11 Oct 62.
459 UNTS 310. USA (United States). Amendment 11 Oct 62. Force 11 Oct 62.
462 UNTS 362. Turkey. Amendment 21 Nov 62. Force 21 Nov 62.
462 UNTS 362. USA (United States). Amendment 21 Nov 62. Force 21 Nov 62.

106002 Bilateral Exchange **416 UNTS 167**
SIGNED: 19 Jul 61 FORCE: 19 Jul 61
REGISTERED: 14 Dec 61 USA (United States)
ARTICLES: 2 LANGUAGE: English.
HEADNOTE: PEACE CORPS PROGRAM
TOPIC: Direct Aid
CONCEPTS: Treaty implementation. Privileges and immunities. Conformity with municipal law. General cooperation. Personnel. Tax exemptions. Customs exemptions. Materials, equipment and services. Volunteer programs. Withdrawal conditions.
PROCEDURE: Termination.
PARTIES:
    Ghana
    USA (United States)

106003 Bilateral Agreement **416 UNTS 175**
SIGNED: 30 Aug 61 FORCE: 27 Nov 61
REGISTERED: 14 Dec 61 IDA (Devel Assoc)
ARTICLES: 7 LANGUAGE: English.
HEADNOTE: IDA CREDIT AGREEMENT - HARBOR DREDGING
TOPIC: Loans and Credits
CONCEPTS: Definition of terms. Annex or appendix reference. Exchange of information and documents. Currency. Financial programs. Interest rates. Payment schedules. Debt settlement. Loan and credit. Credit provisions. Purchase authorization. Loan repayment. Terms of loan. IDA development project. Canal improvement.
PROCEDURE: Termination.
PARTIES:
    Taiwan
    IDA (Devel Assoc)

106004 Bilateral Treaty **416 UNTS 199**
SIGNED: 7 Oct 58 FORCE: 7 May 59
REGISTERED: 15 Dec 61 Romania
ARTICLES: 81 LANGUAGE: Romanian. Hungarian.
HEADNOTE: LEGAL ASSISTANCE CIVIL FAMILY CRIMINAL
TOPIC: Admin Cooperation
CONCEPTS: General provisions. Previous treaty replacement. Privileges and immunities. Consular functions in property. Extradition, deportation and repatriation. Extradition requests. Refusal of extradition. Concurrent requests. Provisional detainment. Extradition postponement. Witnesses and experts. Material evidence. Conformity with municipal law. Family law. Exchange of information and documents. Juridical personality. Legal protection and assistance. Recognition and enforcement of legal decisions. General property. Succession. Recognition of legal documents. Indemnities and reimbursements. Assets transfer. Conveyance in transit.
PROCEDURE: Duration. Ratification. Renewal or Revival.
PARTIES:
    Hungary
    Romania

106005 Bilateral Convention **417 UNTS 3**
SIGNED: 18 Mar 59 FORCE: 15 Oct 59
REGISTERED: 15 Dec 61 Romania
ARTICLES: 28 LANGUAGE: Romanian. Hungarian.
HEADNOTE: CONSULAR
TOPIC: Consul/Citizenship
CONCEPTS: Definition of terms. General consular functions. Diplomatic privileges. Consular relations establishment. Inviolability. Privileges and immunities.
PROCEDURE: Denunciation. Duration. Ratification.
PARTIES:
    Hungary
    Romania

106006 Bilateral Treaty **417 UNTS 37**
SIGNED: 25 Oct 58 FORCE: 20 Apr 59
REGISTERED: 15 Dec 61 Romania
ARTICLES: 79 LANGUAGE: Romanian. Czechoslovakian.
HEADNOTE: LEGAL ASSISTANCE CIVIL FAMILY CRIMINAL
TOPIC: Admin Cooperation
CONCEPTS: General provisions. Previous treaty replacement. Privileges and immunities. Consular functions in property. Extradition, deportation and repatriation. Extradition requests. Refusal of extradition. Concurrent requests. Provisional detainment. Extradition postponement. Witnesses and experts. Material evidence. Conformity with municipal law. Family law. Exchange of information and documents. Juridical personality. Legal protection and assistance. Recognition and enforcement of legal decisions. Succession. Recognition of legal documents. Indemnities and reimbursements. Assets transfer. Conveyance in transit.
TREATY REF: 54LTS17; 54LTS51.
PARTIES:
    Czechoslovakia
    Romania

106007 Bilateral Treaty **417 UNTS 133**
SIGNED: 3 Dec 58 FORCE: 4 Jul 59
REGISTERED: 15 Dec 61 Romania
ARTICLES: 79 LANGUAGE: Romanian. Bulgarian.
HEADNOTE: LEGAL ASSISTANCE CIVIL FAMILY CRIMINAL
TOPIC: Admin Cooperation
CONCEPTS: General provisions. Previous treaty replacement. Privileges and immunities. Consular functions in property. Extradition, deportation and repatriation. Extradition requests. Refusal of extradition. Concurrent requests. Provisional detainment. Extradition postponement. Witnesses and experts. Material evidence. Conformity with municipal law. Family law. Exchange of information and documents. Juridical personality. Legal protection and assistance. Recognition and enforcement of legal decisions. Succession. Recognition of legal documents. Indemnities and reimbursements. Assets transfer. Conveyance in transit.
TREATY REF: 33LTS209; 33LTS221.
PARTIES:
    Bulgaria
    Romania

106008 Bilateral Agreement **417 UNTS 227**
SIGNED: 30 Aug 61 FORCE: 27 Nov 61
REGISTERED: 18 Dec 61 IDA (Devel Assoc)
ARTICLES: 7 LANGUAGE: English.
HEADNOTE: IDA CREDIT GROUND WATER
TOPIC: Loans and Credits
CONCEPTS: Definition of terms. Annex or appendix reference. Exchange of information and documents. Currency. Interest rates. Payment schedules. Debt settlement. Loan and credit. Credit provisions. Purchase authorization. Loan repayment. Terms of loan. Plans and standards. IDA development project. Natural resources.
PROCEDURE: Termination.
PARTIES:
    Taiwan
    IDA (Devel Assoc)
        ANNEX
491 UNTS 390. Taiwan. Supplementation 19 Dec 63. Force 19 Dec 63.
491 UNTS 390. IDA (Devel Assoc). Supplementation 19 Dec 63. Force 19 Dec 63.

106009 Bilateral Agreement **417 UNTS 253**
SIGNED: 6 Sep 61 FORCE: 27 Nov 61
REGISTERED: 18 Dec 61 IDA (Devel Assoc)
ARTICLES: 7 LANGUAGE: English.
HEADNOTE: IDA CREDIT TAIPEI WATER SUPPLY
TOPIC: Loans and Credits
CONCEPTS: Definition of terms. Annex or appendix reference. Exchange of information and documents. Currency. Interest rates. Payment schedules. Debt settlement. Loan and credit. Credit provisions. Purchase authorization. Loan repayment. Terms of loan. Plans and standards. IDA development project. Natural resources.
PROCEDURE: Termination.
PARTIES:
Taiwan
IDA (Devel Assoc)

106010 Bilateral Agreement **417 UNTS 275**
SIGNED: 19 Dec 60 FORCE: 4 Apr 61
REGISTERED: 20 Dec 61 IBRD (World Bank)
ARTICLES: 8 LANGUAGE: English.
HEADNOTE: LOAN ROAD
TOPIC: IBRD Project
CONCEPTS: Default remedies. Definition of terms. Annex or appendix reference. Exchange of information and documents. Informational records. Inspection and observation. Accounting procedures. Bonds. Fees and exemptions. Interest rates. Tax exemptions. Domestic obligation. Terms of loan. Loan regulations. Loan guarantee. Guarantor non-interference. Roads and highways.
PARTIES:
Peru
IBRD (World Bank)

106011 Bilateral Agreement **417 UNTS 297**
SIGNED: 9 Aug 61 FORCE: 18 Oct 61
REGISTERED: 20 Dec 61 IBRD (World Bank)
ARTICLES: 8 LANGUAGE: English.
HEADNOTE: LOAN COAL PRODUCTION
TOPIC: IBRD Project
CONCEPTS: Default remedies. Definition of terms. Annex or appendix reference. Exchange of information and documents. Informational records. Inspection and observation. Accounting procedures. Bonds. Fees and exemptions. Interest rates. Tax exemptions. Domestic obligation. Terms of loan. Loan regulations. Loan guarantee. Guarantor non-interference. Industry.
PARTIES:
India
IBRD (World Bank)

106012 Bilateral Agreement **417 UNTS 319**
SIGNED: 17 Aug 61 FORCE: 27 Sep 61
REGISTERED: 20 Dec 61 IBRD (World Bank)
ARTICLES: 5 LANGUAGE: English.
HEADNOTE: GUARANTEE PORT
TOPIC: IBRD Project
CONCEPTS: Default remedies. Definition of terms. Annex or appendix reference. Exchange of information and documents. Informational records. Inspection and observation. Accounting procedures. Bonds. Fees and exemptions. Interest rates. Tax exemptions. Domestic obligation. Terms of loan. Loan regulations. Loan guarantee. Guarantor non-interference. Water transport.
PARTIES:
India
IBRD (World Bank)

106013 Bilateral Agreement **418 UNTS 3**
SIGNED: 13 Oct 61 FORCE: 12 Dec 61
REGISTERED: 20 Dec 61 IBRD (World Bank)
ARTICLES: 7 LANGUAGE: English.
HEADNOTE: LOAN RAILWAY
TOPIC: IBRD Project
CONCEPTS: Default remedies. Definition of terms. Annex or appendix reference. Exchange of information and documents. Informational records. Inspection and observation. Accounting procedures. Bonds. Fees and exemptions. Tax exemptions. Domestic obligation. Terms of loan. Loan regulations. Loan guarantee. Guarantor non-interference. Railways.
PARTIES:
India
IBRD (World Bank)

106014 Bilateral Agreement **418 UNTS 19**
SIGNED: 4 Aug 61 FORCE: 14 Aug 61
REGISTERED: 20 Dec 61 USA (United States)
ARTICLES: 6 LANGUAGE: English.
HEADNOTE: AGRI COMMOD TITLE I
TOPIC: US Agri Commod Aid
CONCEPTS: General provisions. Annex or appendix reference. Exchange of information and documents. Reexport of goods, etc.. Exchange rates and regulations. Transportation costs. Local currency. Commodities schedule. Purchase authorization. Surplus commodities. Mutual consultation.
PARTIES:
Finland
USA (United States)

106015 Bilateral Agreement **418 UNTS 35**
SIGNED: 21 Aug 61 FORCE: 21 Aug 61
REGISTERED: 20 Dec 61 USA (United States)
ARTICLES: 5 LANGUAGE: English. Spanish.
HEADNOTE: AGRI COMMOD TITLE I
TOPIC: US Agri Commod Aid
CONCEPTS: General provisions. Annex or appendix reference. Exchange of information and documents. Reexport of goods, etc.. Exchange rates and regulations. Transportation costs. Local currency. Commodities schedule. Purchase authorization. Surplus commodities. Mutual consultation.
PARTIES:
El Salvador
USA (United States)

106016 Bilateral Exchange **418 UNTS 53**
SIGNED: 8 Sep 61 FORCE: 8 Sep 61
REGISTERED: 20 Dec 61 USA (United States)
ARTICLES: 2 LANGUAGE: English.
HEADNOTE: SPACE RESEARCH PROGRAM
TOPIC: Scientific Project
CONCEPTS: Conformity with municipal law. General cooperation. Operating agencies. Use of facilities. Research and scientific projects. Research results. Scientific exchange. Research and development. Tax exemptions. Economic assistance.
PROCEDURE: Duration. Renewal or Revival. Termination.
PARTIES:
UK Great Britain
USA (United States)

106017 Bilateral Agreement **418 UNTS 61**
SIGNED: 21 Jun 61 FORCE: 25 Aug 61
REGISTERED: 22 Dec 61 IDA (Devel Assoc)
ARTICLES: 6 LANGUAGE: English.
HEADNOTE: IDA CREDIT ROAD
TOPIC: Loans and Credits
CONCEPTS: Definition of terms. Annex or appendix reference. Exchange of information and documents. Currency. Interest rates. Payment schedules. Debt settlement. Loan and credit. Credit provisions. Purchase authorization. Loan repayment. Terms of loan. Plans and standards. IDA development project. Roads and highways.
PROCEDURE: Termination.
PARTIES:
India
IDA (Devel Assoc)

106018 Bilateral Agreement **418 UNTS 81**
SIGNED: 6 Sep 61 FORCE: 12 Dec 61
REGISTERED: 22 Dec 61 IDA (Devel Assoc)
ARTICLES: 7 LANGUAGE: English.
HEADNOTE: IDA CREDIT IRRIGATION
TOPIC: Loans and Credits
CONCEPTS: Definition of terms. Annex or appendix reference. Exchange of information and documents. Currency. Interest rates. Payment schedules. Debt settlement. Loan and credit. Credit provisions. Purchase authorization. Loan repayment. Terms of loan. Plans and standards. IDA development project. Irrigation.
PROCEDURE: Termination.
PARTIES:
India
IDA (Devel Assoc)

106019 Multilateral Agreement **418 UNTS 109**
SIGNED: 21 Jun 60 FORCE: 6 Sep 61
REGISTERED: 29 Dec 61 USA (United States)
ARTICLES: 6 LANGUAGE: English. French. Dutch. Spanish.
HEADNOTE: GUARANTEE ANGAT PROJECT
TOPIC: IGO Establishment
CONCEPTS: Annex or appendix reference. Mutual exchange of technical knowledge.
INTL ORGS: Caribbean Commission.
PROCEDURE: Denunciation. Duration. Termination.
PARTIES:
France French Guiana RATIFIED: 30 Dec 60 FORCE: 6 Sep 61
France Guadeloupe RATIFIED: 30 Dec 60 FORCE: 6 Sep 61
France Martinique RATIFIED: 30 Dec 60 FORCE: 6 Sep 61
France SIGNED: 21 Jun 60 RATIFIED: 27 Dec 60 FORCE: 6 Sep 61
Netherlands Netherlands Antilles RATIFIED: 25 Aug 61 FORCE: 6 Sep 61
Netherlands SIGNED: 21 Jun 60 RATIFIED: 25 Aug 61 FORCE: 6 Sep 61
Netherlands Surinam RATIFIED: 25 Aug 61
UK Great Britain SIGNED: 21 Jun 60 RATIFIED: 12 Jan 61 FORCE: 6 Sep 61
UK Great Britain British Guiana RATIFIED: 12 Jan 61 FORCE: 6 Sep 61
UK Great Britain Virgin Islands RATIFIED: 12 Jan 61 FORCE: 6 Sep 61
USA (United States) Puerto Rico RATIFIED: 12 Jul 61 FORCE: 6 Sep 61
USA (United States) SIGNED: 21 Jun 60 RATIFIED: 12 Jul 61 FORCE: 6 Sep 61
ANNEX
572 UNTS 360. France. Termination 22 Dec 64. Force 31 Dec 65.
572 UNTS 360. USA (United States). Termination 29 Dec 64. Force 31 Dec 65.
572 UNTS 360. UK Great Britain. Termination 31 Dec 64. Force 31 Dec 65.

106020 Unilateral Instrument **418 UNTS 157**
SIGNED: 31 Oct 61 FORCE: 20 Sep 60
REGISTERED: 2 Jan 62 United Nations
ARTICLES: 1 LANGUAGE: French.
HEADNOTE: ACCEPTANCE OBLIGATIONS UN
TOPIC: UN Charter
CONCEPTS: Acceptance of UN obligations. Adherence to UN charter.
INTL ORGS: United Nations.
PARTIES:
Congo (Zaire)

106021 Multilateral Protocol **418 UNTS 161**
SIGNED: 27 May 47 FORCE: 20 Mar 61
REGISTERED: 2 Jan 62 ICAO (Civil Aviat)
ARTICLES: 1 LANGUAGE: English. French. Spanish.
HEADNOTE: RELATING AMENDMENT CONVENTION INTERNATIONAL CIVIL AVIATION
TOPIC: Air Transport
CONCEPTS: Annex type material. Air transport. Constitutional amendment.
INTL ORGS: International Civil Aviation Organization. United Nations.
TREATY REF: 15UNTS295.
PROCEDURE: Ratification.
PARTIES:
Afghanistan RATIFIED: 2 Mar 48 FORCE: 20 Mar 61
Brazil RATIFIED: 14 Oct 49 FORCE: 20 Mar 61
Burma RATIFIED: 25 Oct 51 FORCE: 20 Mar 61
Canada RATIFIED: 22 Aug 47 FORCE: 20 Mar 61
Ceylon (Sri Lanka) RATIFIED: 9 Dec 48 FORCE: 20 Mar 61
Costa Rica RATIFIED: 5 Jul 60 FORCE: 20 Mar 61
Czechoslovakia RATIFIED: 21 Apr 48 FORCE: 20 Mar 61
Dominican Republic RATIFIED: 10 Nov 47 FORCE: 20 Mar 61
United Arab Rep RATIFIED: 24 Nov 49 FORCE: 20 Mar 61
Guinea RATIFIED: 23 Jun 59 FORCE: 20 Mar 61
India RATIFIED: 15 Dec 47 FORCE: 20 Mar 61
Indonesia RATIFIED: 17 Jul 61 FORCE: 17 Jul 61
Iran RATIFIED: 27 Apr 50 FORCE: 20 Mar 61
Iraq RATIFIED: 9 Dec 50 FORCE: 20 Mar 61

Italy RATIFIED: 8 Oct 52 FORCE: 20 Mar 61

Ivory Coast RATIFIED: 20 Mar 61 FORCE: 20 Mar 61

Mali RATIFIED: 10 Jan 61 FORCE: 20 Mar 61

Mexico RATIFIED: 12 Sep 49 FORCE: 20 Mar 61

Morocco RATIFIED: 21 Jun 57 FORCE: 20 Mar 61

Netherlands RATIFIED: 24 Feb 55 FORCE: 20 Mar 61

New Zealand RATIFIED: 22 Sep 47 FORCE: 20 Mar 61

Pakistan RATIFIED: 19 Jul 48 FORCE: 20 Mar 61

Philippines RATIFIED: 17 Nov 52 FORCE: 20 Mar 61

Senegal RATIFIED: 28 Feb 61 FORCE: 20 Mar 61

Sudan RATIFIED: 8 Apr 60 FORCE: 20 Mar 61

Syria RATIFIED: 23 Jan 53 FORCE: 20 Mar 61

Thailand RATIFIED: 3 Dec 57 FORCE: 20 Mar 61

Tunisia RATIFIED: 23 May 61 FORCE: 23 May 61

UK Great Britain RATIFIED: 19 Jan 48 FORCE: 20 Mar 61

Vietnam RATIFIED: 30 Dec 57 FORCE: 20 Mar 61

Yugoslavia RATIFIED: 13 Apr 60 FORCE: 20 Mar 61

ANNEX

514 UNTS 289. Mauritania. Ratification 2 Apr 62.

514 UNTS 289. Central Afri Rep. Ratification 22 May 62.

514 UNTS 289. Congo (Brazzaville). Ratification 26 May 62.

514 UNTS 289. Nicaragua. Ratification 9 Jul 62.

514 UNTS 289. Norway. Ratification 18 Jul 62.

514 UNTS 289. Fed of Malaya. Ratification 1 Oct 62.

514 UNTS 289. Madagascar. Ratification 7 Dec 62.

514 UNTS 289. Jamaica. Ratification 18 Oct 63.

514 UNTS 289. Argentina. Ratification 19 Nov 63.

514 UNTS 289. El Salvador. Ratification 22 Jan 63.

514 UNTS 289. Tanganyika. Ratification 10 Apr 63.

514 UNTS 289. Panama. Ratification 24 Sep 63.

514 UNTS 289. Cuba. Ratification 30 Sep 63.

514 UNTS 289. Kenya. Ratification 31 May 64.

514 UNTS 289. Chad. Ratification 28 Aug 64.

514 UNTS 289. Somalia. Ratification 30 Sep 64. Force 30 Sep 64.

106022 Multilateral Convention **418 UNTS 171**
SIGNED: 26 Feb 60 FORCE: 1 Dec 61
REGISTERED: 2 Jan 62 ICAO (Civil Aviat)
ARTICLES: 34 LANGUAGE: Spanish.
HEADNOTE: CENTRAL AMERICAN AIR NAVIGATION CORPORATION
TOPIC: Air Transport
CONCEPTS: Change of circumstances. Annex or appendix reference. Standardization. General cooperation. Exchange of information and documents. Juridical personality. Domestic legislation. Personnel. Responsibility and liability. Use of facilities. Arbitration. Procedure. Special tribunals. Negotiation. Facilities and equipment. Currency. Exchange rates and regulations. Funding procedures. Non-interest rates and fees. Tax exemptions. Customs exemptions. Materials, equipment and services. Loan and credit. Navigational conditions. Navigational equipment. Operating authorizations and regulations. Services.
INTL ORGS: International Civil Aviation Organization. Organization of Central American States. United Nations. Special Commission.
TREATY REF: 15UNTS295.
PROCEDURE: Amendment. Accession. Denunciation. Duration. Ratification. Registration. Renewal or Revival.
PARTIES:
Costa Rica SIGNED: 26 Feb 60
El Salvador SIGNED: 26 Feb 60 RATIFIED: 8 Nov 61 FORCE: 1 Dec 61
Guatemala SIGNED: 26 Feb 60 RATIFIED: 3 Aug 61 FORCE: 1 Dec 61
Honduras SIGNED: 26 Feb 60 RATIFIED: 5 Oct 60 FORCE: 1 Dec 61
Nicaragua SIGNED: 26 Feb 60 RATIFIED: 26 Oct 60 FORCE: 1 Dec 61

106023 Multilateral Agreement **418 UNTS 211**
SIGNED: 22 Apr 60 FORCE: 24 Aug 61
REGISTERED: 2 Jan 62 ICAO (Civil Aviat)
ARTICLES: 16 LANGUAGE: English. French. Spanish.
HEADNOTE: RELATING CERTIFICATES AIRWORTHINESS IMPORTED AIRCRAFT
TOPIC: Air Transport
CONCEPTS: Exceptions and exemptions. Annex or appendix reference. Conformity with municipal law. Exchange of information and documents. Recognition of legal documents. Import quotas. Airworthiness certificates. Operating authorizations and regulations.
INTL ORGS: International Civil Aviation Organization.
TREATY REF: 15UNTS295.
PROCEDURE: Amendment. Accession. Denunciation. Ratification. Registration. Application to Non-self-governing Territories.
PARTIES:
Austria SIGNED: 25 Apr 60 RATIFIED: 25 Jul 61 FORCE: 24 Aug 61
Belgium SIGNED: 28 Apr 60 RATIFIED: 6 Oct 61 FORCE: 5 Nov 61
Denmark SIGNED: 4 Nov 60
Finland SIGNED: 22 Apr 60
France SIGNED: 22 Apr 60
Germany, West SIGNED: 28 Mar 61
Greece SIGNED: 28 Jun 61
Ireland SIGNED: 22 Apr 60
Italy SIGNED: 22 Apr 60
Luxembourg SIGNED: 22 Apr 60
Netherlands SIGNED: 2 Sep 60
Portugal SIGNED: 22 Apr 60
Spain SIGNED: 22 Apr 60 RATIFIED: 1 Aug 61 FORCE: 31 Aug 61
Sweden SIGNED: 22 Apr 60 RATIFIED: 7 Jun 60 FORCE: 24 Aug 61
Switzerland SIGNED: 22 Apr 60 RATIFIED: 20 Sep 61 FORCE: 20 Oct 61
UK Great Britain SIGNED: 22 Apr 60 RATIFIED: 5 Dec 61 FORCE: 4 Jan 62
ANNEX
514 UNTS 290. Denmark. Ratification 13 Sep 62. Force 13 Oct 62.
514 UNTS 290. Netherlands. Netherlands Antilles. Ratification 25 Sep 62. Force 25 Oct 62.
514 UNTS 290. Norway. Ratification 11 Apr 62. Force 11 May 62.
514 UNTS 290. Germany, West. Ratification 17 Jul 62. Force 16 Aug 62.
514 UNTS 290. Germany, West. Berlin. Qualified Ratification 17 Jul 62. Force 16 Aug 62.
514 UNTS 290. France. Ratification 29 Nov 62. Force 29 Dec 62.
514 UNTS 290. Netherlands. Ratification 25 Sep 62. Force 25 Oct 62.

106024 Bilateral Agreement **418 UNTS 235**
SIGNED: 16 Aug 60 FORCE: 30 Jun 61
REGISTERED: 3 Jan 62 USA (United States)
ARTICLES: 7 LANGUAGE: English. German.
HEADNOTE: VALIDATION GERMAN BONDS
TOPIC: Claims and Debts
CONCEPTS: Detailed regulations. Territorial application. Conformity with municipal law. Investigation of violations. Bonds. Claims and settlements.
TREATY REF: 223UNTS167.
PROCEDURE: Ratification.
PARTIES:
Germany, West
USA (United States)

106025 Bilateral Agreement **418 UNTS 253**
SIGNED: 29 Jan 57 FORCE: 9 Jun 61
REGISTERED: 3 Jan 62 USA (United States)
ARTICLES: 5 LANGUAGE: English. Spanish.
HEADNOTE: RADIO BROADCASTING
TOPIC: Telecommunications
CONCEPTS: Annex or appendix reference. Amateur radio. Commercial and public radio. Bands and frequency allocation. Interference of broadcasts. Radio-telephone-telegraphic communications.
INTL ORGS: International Telecommunication Union.
PROCEDURE: Denunciation. Duration. Ratification.
PARTIES:
Mexico
USA (United States)

106026 Bilateral Exchange **419 UNTS 3**
SIGNED: 22 May 61 FORCE: 22 May 61
REGISTERED: 3 Feb 62 USA (United States)
ARTICLES: 2 LANGUAGE: English.
HEADNOTE: ULTRA-VIOLET SURVEY SOUTHERN SKIES
TOPIC: Scientific Project
CONCEPTS: Operating agencies. Use of facilities. Research and scientific projects. Scientific exchange. Research and development. Funding procedures. Economic assistance.
TREATY REF: 354UNTS95.
PARTIES:
Australia
USA (United States)

106027 Bilateral Exchange **419 UNTS 9**
SIGNED: 5 May 61 FORCE: 5 May 61
REGISTERED: 3 Feb 62 USA (United States)
ARTICLES: 2 LANGUAGE: English.
HEADNOTE: PILOTAGE SERVICES GREAT LAKES ST. LAWRENCE RIVER
TOPIC: Admin Cooperation
CONCEPTS: General cooperation. Inland and territorial waters. Ports and pilotage.
PARTIES:
Canada
USA (United States)
ANNEX
474 UNTS 350. USA (United States). Amendment 23 Oct 62. Force 21 Feb 63.
474 UNTS 350. Canada. Amendment 21 Feb 62. Force 21 Feb 63.
493 UNTS 328. USA (United States). Amendment 10 Sep 63. Force 10 Sep 63.
493 UNTS 328. Canada. Amendment 23 Aug 63. Force 10 Sep 63.
493 UNTS 334. USA (United States). Amendment 4 Dec 63. Force 4 Dec 63.
493 UNTS 334. Canada. Amendment 19 Nov 63. Force 4 Dec 63.

106028 Bilateral Agreement **419 UNTS 29**
SIGNED: 5 Jan 62 FORCE: 5 Jan 62
REGISTERED: 5 Jan 62 United Nations
ARTICLES: 10 LANGUAGE: English. French.
HEADNOTE: ASSISTANCE
TOPIC: Direct Aid
CONCEPTS: Detailed regulations. Treaty implementation. Visas. Privileges and immunities. Extraditable offenses. Exchange of information and documents. Informational records. Inspection and observation. Operating agencies. Personnel. Public officials. Responsibility and liability. Title and deeds. Use of facilities. Arbitration. Negotiation. Import quotas. Attachment of funds. Exchange rates and regulations. Expense sharing formulae. Financial programs. Domestic obligation. General technical assistance. Economic assistance. Materials, equipment and services. IGO status.
INTL ORGS: International Court of Justice. United Nations. United Nations Special Fund.
TREATY REF: 1UNTS15; 33UNTS261; 374UNTS147.
PROCEDURE: Amendment. Termination.
PARTIES:
Malagasy
UN Special Fund

106029 Bilateral Convention **419 UNTS 45**
SIGNED: 16 Jun 59 FORCE: 16 Dec 61
REGISTERED: 8 Jan 62 Belgium
ARTICLES: 12 LANGUAGE: French. German.
HEADNOTE: JUDICIAL DECISIONS ARBITRAL AWARDS
TOPIC: Admin Cooperation
CONCEPTS: Definition of terms. Territorial application. Recognition and enforcement of legal decisions. Prizes and arbitral awards. Procedure.
TREATY REF: 92LTS301.
PROCEDURE: Denunciation. Ratification.
PARTIES:
Austria
Belgium

106030 Bilateral Agreement **419 UNTS 69**
SIGNED: 13 Sep 61 FORCE: 18 Oct 61
REGISTERED: 10 Jan 62 WHO (World Health)
ARTICLES: 6 LANGUAGE: English.

HEADNOTE: TECHNICAL ADVISORY ASSISTANCE
TOPIC: Tech Assistance
CONCEPTS: Definition of terms. Previous treaty replacement. Privileges and immunities. General cooperation. Exchange of information and documents. Personnel. Responsibility and liability. Title and deeds. Exchange. Scholarships and grants. Vocational training. Research and development. Expense sharing formulae. Local currency. Domestic obligation. Special projects. Materials, equipment and services. IGO status. Conformity with IGO decisions.
INTL ORGS: United Nations.
TREATY REF: 331NTS261.
PROCEDURE: Amendment. Termination.
PARTIES:
　Iraq
　WHO (World Health)

106031 Multilateral Agreement **419 UNTS 79**
SIGNED: 20 Dec 61　　　　FORCE: 20 Dec 61
REGISTERED: 12 Jan 62 Finland
ARTICLES: 19 LANGUAGE: Finnish. Danish. Norwegian. Swedish.
HEADNOTE: COOPERATION IN ICE-BREAKING
TOPIC: Water Transport
CONCEPTS: Canal improvement.
PARTIES:
　Denmark SIGNED: 20 Dec 61 FORCE: 20 Dec 61
　Finland SIGNED: 20 Dec 61 FORCE: 20 Dec 61
　Norway SIGNED: 20 Dec 61
　Sweden SIGNED: 20 Dec 61

106032 Multilateral Treaty **419 UNTS 125**
SIGNED: 19 Sep 60　　　　FORCE: 12 Jan 61
REGISTERED: 16 Jan 62 India
ARTICLES: 12 LANGUAGE: English.
HEADNOTE: INDUS WATERS TREATY
TOPIC: IBRD Project
CONCEPTS: Definition of terms. General provisions. Annex or appendix reference. Transition period. Privileges and immunities. Exchange of information and documents. Informational records. Inspection and observation. Establishment of commission. Procedure. Scientific exchange. Indemnities and reimbursements. Payment schedules. Domestic obligation. Conservation. Special projects. Irrigation. Navigational conditions. Inland and territorial waters. Status of experts.
INTL ORGS: Permanent Court of Arbitration. United Nations.
TREATY REF: 1UNTS15.
PROCEDURE: Amendment. Ratification. Termination.
PARTIES:
　India SIGNED: 19 Sep 60 RATIFIED: 12 Jan 61 FORCE: 12 Jan 61
　Pakistan SIGNED: 19 Sep 60 RATIFIED: 12 Jan 61 FORCE: 12 Jan 61
　IBRD (World Bank) SIGNED: 19 Sep 60

106033 Multilateral Agreement **419 UNTS 294**
SIGNED: 17 Jan 62　　　　FORCE: 17 Jan 62
REGISTERED: 17 Jan 62 United Nations
ARTICLES: 6 LANGUAGE: French.
HEADNOTE: TECHNICAL ASSISTANCE
TOPIC: Tech Assistance
CONCEPTS: Definition of terms. Privileges and immunities. General cooperation. Exchange of information and documents. Personnel. Responsibility and liability. Title and deeds. Use of facilities. Exchange. Scholarships and grants. Vocational training. Research and development. Exchange rates and regulations. Expense sharing formulae. Local currency. Domestic obligation. General technical assistance. Materials, equipment and services. IGO status. Conformity with IGO decisions.
TREATY REF: 72UNTS132; 1UNTS15; 33UNTS261; 374UNTS147.
PROCEDURE: Amendment. Termination.
PARTIES:
　Dahomey SIGNED: 17 Jan 62 FORCE: 17 Jan 62
　FAO (Food Agri) SIGNED: 17 Jan 62 FORCE: 17 Jan 62
　IAEA (Atom Energy) SIGNED: 17 Jan 62 FORCE: 17 Jan 62
　ICAO (Civil Aviat) SIGNED: 17 Jan 62 FORCE: 17 Jan 62

　ILO (Labor Org) SIGNED: 17 Jan 62 FORCE: 17 Jan 62
　ITU (Telecommun) SIGNED: 17 Jan 62 FORCE: 17 Jan 62
　UNESCO (Educ/Cult) SIGNED: 17 Jan 62 FORCE: 17 Jan 62
　United Nations SIGNED: 17 Jan 62 FORCE: 17 Jan 62
　WHO (World Health) SIGNED: 17 Jan 62 FORCE: 17 Jan 62
　WMO (Meteorology) SIGNED: 17 Jan 62 FORCE: 17 Jan 62

106034 Bilateral Agreement **419 UNTS 309**
SIGNED: 25 Oct 60　　　　FORCE: 3 May 61
REGISTERED: 19 Jan 62 UK Great Britain
ARTICLES: 20 LANGUAGE: English. Hungarian.
HEADNOTE: CONCERNING CIVIL AVIATION
TOPIC: Air Transport
CONCEPTS: Definition of terms. Exceptions and exemptions. Representation. Annex or appendix reference. Previous treaty replacement. Conformity with municipal law. General cooperation. Exchange of information and documents. Informational records. Licenses and permits. Recognition of legal documents. Use of facilities. Procedure. Negotiation. Humanitarian matters. Reexport of goods, etc.. Monetary and gold transfers. Exchange rates and regulations. Fees and exemptions. Non-interest rates and fees. National treatment. Tax exemptions. Customs exemptions. Registration certificate. Routes and logistics. Navigational conditions. Permit designation. Airport facilities. Airworthiness certificates. Conditions of airlines operating permission. Operating authorizations and regulations. Licenses and certificates of nationality.
PROCEDURE: Amendment. Ratification. Termination. Application to Non-self-governing Territories.
PARTIES:
　Hungary
　UK Great Britain

106035 Bilateral Exchange **420 UNTS 3**
SIGNED: 22 Jul 61　　　　FORCE: 22 Jul 61
REGISTERED: 19 Jan 62 UK Great Britain
ARTICLES: 2 LANGUAGE: English. Italian.
HEADNOTE: SETTLEMENT SAN MARINO DAMAGE CLAIM
TOPIC: Reparations
CONCEPTS: Loss and/or damage. Post-war claims settlement.
PARTIES:
　San Marino
　UK Great Britain

106036 Bilateral Exchange **420 UNTS 11**
SIGNED: 5 May 61　　　　FORCE: 5 May 61
REGISTERED: 19 Jan 62 UK Great Britain
ARTICLES: 2 LANGUAGE: English.
HEADNOTE: INHERITANCE INTERNATIONAL RIGHTS OBLIGATIONS
TOPIC: Recognition
CONCEPTS: Continuity of rights and obligations.
PARTIES:
　Sierra Leone
　UK Great Britain

106037 Bilateral Agreement **420 UNTS 17**
SIGNED: 5 May 61　　　　FORCE: 27 Apr 61
REGISTERED: 19 Jan 62 UK Great Britain
ARTICLES: 8 LANGUAGE: English.
HEADNOTE: PUBLIC OFFICERS
TOPIC: Consul/Citizenship
CONCEPTS: Conditions. Definition of terms. General cooperation. Holidays and rest periods.
PARTIES:
　Sierra Leone
　UK Great Britain

106038 Bilateral Agreement **420 UNTS 29**
SIGNED: 28 Jan 60　　　　FORCE: 30 Nov 61
REGISTERED: 19 Jan 62 UK Great Britain
ARTICLES: 8 LANGUAGE: English. German.
HEADNOTE: CONTRACTS INSURANCE
TOPIC: Reparations
CONCEPTS: Definition of terms. Territorial applica

tion. Annex or appendix reference. Private contracts. Post-war claims settlement.
PROCEDURE: Ratification. Application to Non-self-governing Territories.
PARTIES:
　Germany, West
　UK Great Britain

106039 Bilateral Exchange **420 UNTS 53**
SIGNED: 17 Jul 61　　　　FORCE: 17 Jul 61
REGISTERED: 19 Jan 62 UK Great Britain
ARTICLES: 2 LANGUAGE: English. Arabic.
HEADNOTE: LOAN
TOPIC: Loans and Credits
CONCEPTS: Interest rates. Payment schedules. Agriculture. Loan and credit. Credit provisions. Loan repayment. Terms of loan. Plans and standards. Natural resources. Roads and highways.
PARTIES:
　Jordan
　UK Great Britain
ANNEX
431 UNTS 326. UK Great Britain. Amendment 22 Oct 61. Force 22 Oct 61.
431 UNTS 326. Jordan. Amendment 22 Oct 61. Force 22 Oct 61.

106040 Bilateral Exchange **420 UNTS 61**
SIGNED: 21 Jul 61　　　　FORCE: 21 Jul 61
REGISTERED: 19 Jan 62 UK Great Britain
ARTICLES: 2 LANGUAGE: English.
HEADNOTE: CREDIT LINE PURSUANT EXCHANGE REFORM PROGRAM
TOPIC: Loans and Credits
CONCEPTS: Exchange rates and regulations. Interest rates. Payment schedules. Loan and credit. Credit provisions. Loan repayment.
PARTIES:
　UK Great Britain
　Yugoslavia

106041 Bilateral Exchange **420 UNTS 67**
SIGNED: 15 Nov 61　　　　FORCE: 15 Nov 61
REGISTERED: 19 Jan 62 UK Great Britain
ARTICLES: 2 LANGUAGE: English
HEADNOTE: COMMISSION ENQUIRY INCIDENTS BRITISH TRAVELER RED CRUSADER
TOPIC: Dispute Settlement
CONCEPTS: Inspection and observation. Investigation of violations. Establishment of commission.
PARTIES:
　Denmark
　UK Great Britain

106042 Bilateral Convention **420 UNTS 75**
SIGNED: 11 Apr 61　　　　FORCE: 5 Sep 61
REGISTERED: 19 Jan 62 UK Great Britain
ARTICLES: 20 LANGUAGE: English.
HEADNOTE: DOUBLE TAXATION FISCAL EVASION/TAXES INCOME
TOPIC: Taxation
CONCEPTS: Definition of terms. Privileges and immunities. Conformity with municipal law. Exchange of official publications. Negotiation. Teacher and student exchange. Claims and settlements. Taxation. Tax credits. Equitable taxes. Tax exemptions. Air transport. Merchant vessels.
PROCEDURE: Ratification. Termination.
PARTIES:
　Japan
　UK Great Britain

106043 Multilateral Agreement **420 UNTS 109**
SIGNED: 27 Mar 61　　　　FORCE: 26 Jun 61
REGISTERED: 19 Jan 62 UK Great Britain
ARTICLES: 10 LANGUAGE: English. French.
HEADNOTE: FINLAND EUROPEAN FREE TRADE
TOPIC: IGO Establishment
CONCEPTS: Definition of terms. Annex or appendix reference. Annex type material. Funding procedures. IGO constitution. Subsidiary organ. Conformity with IGO decisions.
INTL ORGS: European Free Trade Association. Special Commission.
TREATY REF: 370UNTS3.
PROCEDURE: Amendment. Denunciation. Duration. Termination.

Austria SIGNED: 27 Mar 61 RATIFIED: 26 Jun 61 FORCE: 26 Jun 61

Denmark SIGNED: 27 Mar 61 RATIFIED: 29 May 61 FORCE: 26 Jun 61

Finland SIGNED: 27 Mar 61 RATIFIED: 23 May 61 FORCE: 26 Jun 61

Norway SIGNED: 27 Mar 61 RATIFIED: 23 May 61 FORCE: 26 Jun 61

Portugal SIGNED: 27 Mar 61 RATIFIED: 26 Jun 61 FORCE: 26 Jun 61

Sweden SIGNED: 27 Mar 61 RATIFIED: 2 Jun 61 FORCE: 26 Jun 61

Switzerland SIGNED: 27 Mar 61 RATIFIED: 22 Jun 61 FORCE: 26 Jun 61

UK Great Britain SIGNED: 27 Mar 61 RATIFIED: 9 Jun 61 FORCE: 26 Jun 61

106044 Bilateral Agreement **420 UNTS 133**
SIGNED: 20 Jan 62 FORCE: 20 Jan 62
REGISTERED: 20 Jan 62 United Nations
ARTICLES: 6 LANGUAGE: English.
HEADNOTE: OPERATIONAL EXECUTIVE ADMINIS-TRATIVE PERSONNEL
TOPIC: Tech Assistance
CONCEPTS: Treaty implementation. Annex or appendix reference. Privileges and immunities. Personnel. Responsibility and liability. Arbitration. Procedure. Negotiation. Vocational training. Compensation. Expense sharing formulae. Tax exemptions. Customs exemptions. Domestic obligation. Special projects. Status of experts. Conformity with IGO decisions.
PROCEDURE: Amendment. Termination.
PARTIES:
United Nations
Somalia
ANNEX
561 UNTS 351. United Nations. Force 21 Sep 65.
561 UNTS 351. Somalia. Force 21 Sep 65.

106045 Bilateral Treaty **420 UNTS 145**
SIGNED: 6 Jul 61 FORCE: 10 Sep 61
REGISTERED: 23 Jan 62 USSR (Soviet Union)
ARTICLES: 6 LANGUAGE: Russian. Korean.
HEADNOTE: FRIENDSHIP COOPERATION MU-TUAL ASSISTANCE
TOPIC: General Amity
CONCEPTS: Peaceful relations. General cooperation. Defense and security.
PROCEDURE: Denunciation. Duration. Ratification. Renewal or Revival.
PARTIES:
Korea, North
USSR (Soviet Union)

106046 Bilateral Treaty **420 UNTS 161**
SIGNED: 5 Feb 61 FORCE: 20 Sep 61
REGISTERED: 23 Jan 62 USSR (Soviet Union)
ARTICLES: 55 LANGUAGE: Russian. Polish.
HEADNOTE: COOPERATION MUTUAL ASSIS-TANCE FRONTIER MATTERS
TOPIC: Territory Boundary
CONCEPTS: Definition of terms. Annex or appendix reference. General cooperation. Exchange of information and documents. Inspection and observation. Establishment of commission. Navigational conditions. Inland and territorial waters. Railway border crossing. Railways. Road rules. Fish, wildlife, and natural resources. Markers and definitions. Frontier waterways.
TREATY REF: 340UNTS89; 37UNTS25; 37UNTS107.
PROCEDURE: Amendment. Denunciation. Duration. Ratification. Renewal or Revival.
PARTIES:
Poland
USSR (Soviet Union)

106047 Bilateral Agreement **420 UNTS 307**
SIGNED: 27 Apr 61 FORCE: 11 Oct 61
REGISTERED: 23 Jan 62 USSR (Soviet Union)
ARTICLES: 18 LANGUAGE: Russian. Turkish. French.
HEADNOTE: DIRECT RAILWAY COMMUNICA-TIONS
TOPIC: Land Transport
CONCEPTS: Treaty implementation. Treaty interpretation. Previous treaty replacement. Administrative cooperation. Conformity with municipal law. General cooperation. Exchange of information and documents. Personnel. Responsibility and liability. Establishment of commission. Procedure. Accounting procedures. Currency. Non-interest rates and fees. Tax exemptions. Customs exemptions. Temporary importation. Passenger transport. Transport of goods. Operating authorizations and regulations. Railway border crossing. Railways.
TREATY REF: 3'22DEMARTENS91;.
PROCEDURE: Denunciation. Ratification.
PARTIES:
Turkey
USSR (Soviet Union)

106048 Bilateral Agreement **421 UNTS 3**
SIGNED: 12 Dec 60 FORCE: 25 Aug 61
REGISTERED: 23 Jan 62 USSR (Soviet Union)
ARTICLES: 8 LANGUAGE: Russian. Spanish.
HEADNOTE: CULTURAL AGREEMENT
TOPIC: Culture
CONCEPTS: Friendship and amity. Non-diplomatic delegations. Exchange of information and documents. Specialists exchange. Exchange. Scholarships and grants. Exchange. General cultural cooperation. Athletes. Scientific exchange. Mass media exchange. Press and wire services.
PROCEDURE: Amendment. Denunciation. Ratification.
PARTIES:
Cuba
USSR (Soviet Union)

106049 Bilateral Agreement **421 UNTS 13**
SIGNED: 13 Jan 61 FORCE: 8 Dec 61
REGISTERED: 23 Jan 62 USSR (Soviet Union)
ARTICLES: 14 LANGUAGE: Russian. Amharic. English.
HEADNOTE: CULTURAL COOPERATION
TOPIC: Culture
CONCEPTS: Treaty implementation. Treaty interpretation. Friendship and amity. Tourism. Non-diplomatic delegations. Conformity with municipal law. Exchange of information and documents. Specialists exchange. Exchange. Teacher and student exchange. Scholarships and grants. Vocational training. Exchange. General cultural cooperation. Artists. Athletes. Scientific exchange. Finances and payments. Publications exchange. Mass media exchange.
PROCEDURE: Future Procedures Contemplated. Ratification. Renewal or Revival. Termination.
PARTIES:
Ethiopia
USSR (Soviet Union)

106050 Bilateral Agreement **421 UNTS 27**
SIGNED: 4 Aug 60 FORCE: 3 Jun 61
REGISTERED: 23 Jan 62 USSR (Soviet Union)
ARTICLES: 17 LANGUAGE: Russian. English.
HEADNOTE: TRADE
TOPIC: General Trade
CONCEPTS: Exceptions and exemptions. Annex or appendix reference. Conformity with municipal law. General cooperation. Licenses and permits. Export quotas. Import quotas. Trade agencies. Trade procedures. Accounting procedures. Banking. Currency. Exchange rates and regulations. Payment schedules. Most favored nation clause. Temporary importation. Merchant vessels.
PROCEDURE: Denunciation. Duration. Ratification. Renewal or Revival.
PARTIES:
Ghana
USSR (Soviet Union)

106051 Bilateral Agreement **421 UNTS 49**
SIGNED: 23 Jun 61 FORCE: 29 Dec 61
REGISTERED: 24 Jan 62 Finland
ARTICLES: 22 LANGUAGE: English.
HEADNOTE: DOUBLE TAXATION INCOME
TOPIC: Taxation
CONCEPTS: Definition of terms. Conformity with municipal law. Exchange of official publications. Teacher and student exchange. Claims and settlements. Taxation. General. Tax exemptions. Air transport. Merchant vessels.
PROCEDURE: Duration. Ratification. Termination.
PARTIES:
Finland
India

106052 Bilateral Exchange **421 UNTS 71**
SIGNED: 13 Oct 60 FORCE: 15 Oct 60
REGISTERED: 26 Jan 62 Belgium
ARTICLES: 2 LANGUAGE: French.
HEADNOTE: ABOLITION VISAS
TOPIC: Visas
CONCEPTS: Emergencies. Time limit. Visa abolition. Denial of admission. Resident permits. Conformity with municipal law.
PROCEDURE: Denunciation.
PARTIES:
Belgium
Tunisia

106053 Bilateral Exchange **421 UNTS 79**
SIGNED: 23 Sep 61 FORCE: 23 Sep 61
REGISTERED: 30 Jan 62 USA (United States)
ARTICLES: 2 LANGUAGE: English.
HEADNOTE: TACTICAL AIR NAVIGATION FACIL-ITY
TOPIC: Milit Installation
CONCEPTS: Indemnities and reimbursements. Joint defense. Airforce-army-navy personnel ratio. Bases and facilities.
TREATY REF: 343UNTS27.
PARTIES:
Canada
USA (United States)

106054 Bilateral Exchange **421 UNTS 85**
SIGNED: 27 Sep 61 FORCE: 27 Sep 61
REGISTERED: 30 Jan 62 USA (United States)
ARTICLES: 2 LANGUAGE: English.
HEADNOTE: IMPROVEMENTS CONTINENTAL AIR DEFENSE SYSTEM
TOPIC: Milit Assistance
CONCEPTS: Annex or appendix reference. Expense sharing formulae. Joint defense. Defense and security. Exchange of defense information. Bases and facilities.
TREATY REF: 132UNTS247.
PROCEDURE: Future Procedures Contemplated.
PARTIES:
Canada
USA (United States)
ANNEX
524 UNTS 324. Canada. Amendment 6 May 64. Force 6 May 64.
524 UNTS 324. USA (United States). Amendment 6 May 64. Force 6 May 64.
573 UNTS 330. USA (United States). Amendment 24 Nov 65. Force 24 Nov 65.
573 UNTS 330. Canada. Amendment 24 Nov 65. Force 24 Nov 65.

106055 Bilateral Exchange **421 UNTS 99**
SIGNED: 26 Sep 61 FORCE: 26 Sep 61
REGISTERED: 30 Jan 62 USA (United States)
ARTICLES: 2 LANGUAGE: English.
HEADNOTE: WEATHER STATION
TOPIC: Scientific Project
CONCEPTS: Annex type material. Research and scientific projects. Research cooperation. Meteorology. Special projects.
TREATY REF: 231UNTS185; 307UNTS3.
PARTIES:
UK Great Britain
USA (United States)

106056 Bilateral Treaty **421 UNTS 105**
SIGNED: 1 Oct 51 FORCE: 30 Jul 61
REGISTERED: 30 Jan 62 USA (United States)
ARTICLES: 26 LANGUAGE: English. Danish.
HEADNOTE: FRIENDSHIP COMMERCE NAVIGA-TION
TOPIC: General Amity
CONCEPTS: Definition of terms. Exceptions and exemptions. Territorial application. Previous treaty replacement. Alien status. Human rights. General cooperation. Exchange of information and documents. Juridical personality. Free passage and transit. Legal protection and assistance. Immovable property. General property. Procedure. Existing tribunals. Social security. Export quotas. Import quotas. Free trade. Reciproc-

ity in trade. Exchange rates and regulations. Most favored nation clause. National treatment. Taxation. Navigational conditions.
INTL ORGS: International Court of Justice.
TREATY REF: GATT; 2'6DEMARTENS919.
PROCEDURE: Duration. Ratification. Termination.
PARTIES:
Denmark
USA (United States)

106057 Bilateral Agreement **421 UNTS 161**
SIGNED: 21 Jul 61 FORCE: 21 Jul 61
REGISTERED: 30 Jan 62 Austria
ARTICLES: 14 LANGUAGE: German. Romanian.
HEADNOTE: LONG-TERM REGULATION TRADE
TOPIC: General Trade
CONCEPTS: Detailed regulations. Annex or appendix reference. Previous treaty replacement. Conformity with municipal law. General cooperation. Licenses and permits. Establishment of commission. Export quotas. Import quotas. Trade procedures. Payment schedules. Delivery schedules. Quotas.
TREATY REF: TRADE AGREE.12JUL50.
PROCEDURE: Denunciation. Duration.
PARTIES:
Austria
Romania

106058 Bilateral Exchange **421 UNTS 199**
SIGNED: 1 Sep 61 FORCE: 1 Sep 61
REGISTERED: 31 Jan 62 USA (United States)
ARTICLES: 2 LANGUAGE: English.
HEADNOTE: DISPOSAL EXCESS PROPERTY
TOPIC: Claims and Debts
CONCEPTS: Detailed regulations. General cooperation. General property. Claims and settlements. Return of equipment and recapture. Surplus war property.
TREATY REF: 134UNTS205.
PROCEDURE: Termination.
PARTIES:
Canada
USA (United States)

106059 Bilateral Exchange **421 UNTS 209**
SIGNED: 12 Aug 61 FORCE: 12 Aug 61
REGISTERED: 31 Jan 62 USA (United States)
ARTICLES: 2 LANGUAGE: English. Spanish.
HEADNOTE: WEATHER STATION
TOPIC: Scientific Project
CONCEPTS: Personnel. General property. Research and scientific projects. Meteorology. Special projects.
TREATY REF: 394UNTS277.
PARTIES:
Chile
USA (United States)

106060 Bilateral Exchange **421 UNTS 215**
SIGNED: 4 Sep 61 FORCE: 4 Sep 61
REGISTERED: 31 Jan 62 USA (United States)
ARTICLES: 2 LANGUAGE: English.
HEADNOTE: PEACE CORPS PROGRAM
TOPIC: Direct Aid
CONCEPTS: Treaty implementation. Legal protection and assistance. Personnel. Funding procedures. Tax exemptions. Customs exemptions. Domestic obligation. Materials, equipment and services. Volunteer programs.
PROCEDURE: Termination.
PARTIES:
Fed of Malaya
USA (United States)

106061 Bilateral Agreement **421 UNTS 223**
SIGNED: 9 Jun 61 FORCE: 9 Jun 61
REGISTERED: 31 Jan 62 USA (United States)
ARTICLES: 12 LANGUAGE: English. Nepalese.
HEADNOTE: EDUCATION PROGRAM
TOPIC: Education
CONCEPTS: Friendship and amity. Standardization. Conformity with municipal law. Exchange of information and documents. Inspection and observation. Personnel. General property. Exchange. Commissions and foundations. Scholarships and grants. Accounting procedures. Currency. Expense sharing formulae. Financial pro-

grams. Funding procedures. Customs exemptions. Special status.
TREATY REF: 360UNTS287.
PROCEDURE: Amendment.
PARTIES:
Nepal
USA (United States)

106062 Bilateral Agreement **421 UNTS 241**
SIGNED: 5 Sep 61 FORCE: 15 Sep 61
REGISTERED: 31 Jan 62 USA (United States)
ARTICLES: 1 LANGUAGE: English.
HEADNOTE: CONSIDERING RECIPROCAL CONCESSIONS ADVANTAGES PROMOTION TRADE
TOPIC: General Economic
CONCEPTS: Annex or appendix reference.
TREATY REF: GATT.
PARTIES:
Sweden
USA (United States)

106063 Bilateral Agreement **421 UNTS 251**
SIGNED: 2 Sep 61 FORCE: 2 Sep 61
REGISTERED: 31 Jan 62 USA (United States)
ARTICLES: 6 LANGUAGE: English.
HEADNOTE: AGRI COMMOD
TOPIC: US Agri Commod Aid
CONCEPTS: Currency. Agricultural commodities.
PARTIES:
United Arab Rep
USA (United States)
ANNEX
424 UNTS 394. USA (United States). Amendment 11 Nov 61. Force 11 Nov 61.
424 UNTS 394. United Arab Rep. Amendment 11 Nov 61. Force 11 Nov 61.
433 UNTS 406. USA (United States). Amendment 7 Oct 61. Force 7 Oct 61.
433 UNTS 406. United Arab Rep. Amendment 7 Oct 61. Force 7 Oct 61.
445 UNTS 374. USA (United States). Amendment 28 Mar 62. Force 28 Mar 62.
445 UNTS 374. United Arab Rep. Amendment 28 Mar 62. Force 28 Mar 62.

106064 Bilateral Agreement **421 UNTS 273**
SIGNED: 13 Oct 61 FORCE: 2 Nov 61
REGISTERED: 31 Jan 62 WHO (World Health)
ARTICLES: 6 LANGUAGE: French.
HEADNOTE: TECHNICAL ADVISORY ASSISTANCE
TOPIC: Tech Assistance
CONCEPTS: Definition of terms. Privileges and immunities. General cooperation. Exchange of information and documents. Personnel. Responsibility and liability. Title and deeds. Exchange. Scholarships and grants. Vocational training. Research and development. Expense sharing formulae. Local currency. Domestic obligation. Special projects. Materials, equipment and services. IGO status. Conformity with IGO decisions.
TREATY REF: 33UNTS261.
PROCEDURE: Amendment. Termination.
PARTIES:
Malagasy
WHO (World Health)

106065 Bilateral Agreement **422 UNTS 3**
SIGNED: 29 Sep 61 FORCE: 29 Sep 61
REGISTERED: 1 Feb 62 Philippines
ARTICLES: 9 LANGUAGE: English.
HEADNOTE: TRADE
TOPIC: General Trade
CONCEPTS: Annex or appendix reference. Conformity with municipal law. General cooperation. Export quotas. Import quotas. Trade procedures. Currency. Payment schedules. Most favored nation clause. Water transport. Inland and territorial waters.
PROCEDURE: Amendment. Denunciation. Duration. Renewal or Revival.
PARTIES:
Pakistan
Philippines

106066 Bilateral Agreement **422 UNTS 15**
SIGNED: 24 Feb 61 FORCE: 8 Aug 61
REGISTERED: 1 Feb 62 Czechoslovakia

ARTICLES: 11 LANGUAGE: Czechoslovakian. Hungarian.
HEADNOTE: CULTURAL COOPERATION
TOPIC: Culture
CONCEPTS: Treaty implementation. Previous treaty replacement. Friendship and amity. Conformity with municipal law. Exchange of information and documents. Specialists exchange. Recognition of degrees. Exchange. Teacher and student exchange. Professorships. General cultural cooperation. Artists. Athletes. Research cooperation. Scientific exchange. Recognition. Publications exchange. Mass media exchange. Press and wire services.
PROCEDURE: Denunciation. Duration. Ratification. Renewal or Revival.
PARTIES:
Czechoslovakia
Hungary

106067 Multilateral Agreement **422 UNTS 33**
SIGNED: 14 Dec 59 FORCE: 29 Jun 60
REGISTERED: 1 Feb 62 Council of Europe
ARTICLES: 13 LANGUAGE: Russian.
HEADNOTE: PLANT PROTECTION QUARANTINE
TOPIC: Sanitation
CONCEPTS: Treaty interpretation. Annex or appendix reference. Border traffic and migration. Standardization. Exchange of information and documents. Domestic legislation. Specialists exchange. Quarantine. Disease control. Insect control. Teacher and student exchange. Research results. Scientific exchange. Research and development. Indemnities and reimbursements. General technical assistance. Agriculture. Economic assistance. Conferences.
INTL ORGS: Special Commission.
PROCEDURE: Amendment. Accession. Denunciation. Duration. Future Procedures Contemplated. Ratification.
PARTIES:
Albania SIGNED: 14 Dec 59 RATIFIED: 19 Nov 60 FORCE: 19 Nov 60
Bulgaria SIGNED: 14 Dec 59 RATIFIED: 9 Jun 60 FORCE: 19 Oct 60
Czechoslovakia SIGNED: 14 Dec 59 RATIFIED: 8 Jul 60 FORCE: 19 Oct 60
Germany, East SIGNED: 14 Dec 59 RATIFIED: 17 Nov 60 FORCE: 17 Nov 60
Hungary SIGNED: 14 Dec 59 RATIFIED: 12 Sep 60 FORCE: 19 Oct 60
Korea, North SIGNED: 29 Jun 60 RATIFIED: 15 Nov 60 FORCE: 15 Nov 60
Mongolia RATIFIED: 23 Aug 61 FORCE: 23 Aug 61
Poland SIGNED: 14 Dec 59 RATIFIED: 27 Oct 60 FORCE: 27 Oct 60
Romania SIGNED: 14 Dec 59 RATIFIED: 19 Oct 60 FORCE: 19 Oct 60
USSR (Soviet Union) SIGNED: 14 Dec 59 RATIFIED: 28 Jun 60 FORCE: 19 Oct 60

106068 Multilateral Agreement **422 UNTS 57**
SIGNED: 14 Dec 59 FORCE: 12 Sep 60
REGISTERED: 1 Feb 62 Council of Europe
ARTICLES: 9 LANGUAGE: Russian.
HEADNOTE: VETERINARY SCIENCE
TOPIC: Sanitation
CONCEPTS: Treaty interpretation. Annex or appendix reference. Exchange of information and documents. Domestic legislation. Establishment of commission. Specialists exchange. Border control. Disease control. Veterinary. Teacher and student exchange. Research results. Scientific exchange. Research and development. Trade procedures. Indemnities and reimbursements. Materials, equipment and services. Publications exchange.
INTL ORGS: Special Commission.
PROCEDURE: Accession. Denunciation. Duration. Ratification.
PARTIES:
Albania SIGNED: 14 Dec 59 RATIFIED: 19 Nov 60 FORCE: 19 Nov 60
Bulgaria SIGNED: 14 Dec 59 RATIFIED: 9 Jun 60 FORCE: 12 Sep 60
Czechoslovakia SIGNED: 14 Dec 59 RATIFIED: 18 Jul 60 FORCE: 12 Sep 60
Germany, East SIGNED: 14 Dec 59 RATIFIED: 16 Aug 60 FORCE: 12 Sep 60
Hungary SIGNED: 14 Dec 59 RATIFIED: 12 Sep 60 FORCE: 12 Sep 60

Korea, North SIGNED: 14 Dec 59 RATIFIED:
15 Nov 60 FORCE: 15 Nov 60
Mongolia SIGNED: 14 Dec 59 RATIFIED:
19 Dec 60 FORCE: 19 Dec 60
Poland SIGNED: 14 Dec 59 RATIFIED: 27 Oct 60
FORCE: 27 Oct 60
Romania SIGNED: 14 Dec 59 RATIFIED:
19 Oct 60 FORCE: 19 Oct 60
USSR (Soviet Union) SIGNED: 14 Dec 59 RATI-
FIED: 28 Jun 60 FORCE: 12 Sep 60
ANNEX
543 UNTS 373. Cuba. Accession 30 Jul 65.

106069 Multilateral Agreement **422 UNTS 75**
SIGNED: 14 Dec 59 FORCE: 2 Aug 60
REGISTERED: 1 Feb 62 Council of Europe
ARTICLES: 8 LANGUAGE: Russian.
HEADNOTE: INTERNATIONAL DIRECT GOODS
TRAFFIC RAIL WATER
TOPIC: Land Transport
CONCEPTS: Responsibility and liability. Account-
ing procedures. Fees and exemptions. Payment
schedules. Goods in transit. Transport of goods.
Water transport. Ports and pilotage. Railways.
Road rules.
INTL ORGS: Special Commission.
PROCEDURE: Amendment. Accession. Denuncia-
tion. Ratification.
PARTIES:
Bulgaria SIGNED: 14 Dec 59 RATIFIED:
25 May 60 FORCE: 2 Aug 60
Czechoslovakia SIGNED: 14 Dec 59 RATIFIED:
2 Jul 60 FORCE: 2 Aug 60
Germany, East SIGNED: 14 Dec 59 RATIFIED:
17 May 60 FORCE: 2 Aug 60
Hungary SIGNED: 14 Dec 59 RATIFIED:
6 Jun 60 FORCE: 2 Aug 60
Poland SIGNED: 14 Dec 59 RATIFIED:
21 Mar 60 FORCE: 2 Aug 60
Romania SIGNED: 14 Dec 59 RATIFIED:
3 Jun 60 FORCE: 2 Aug 60
USSR (Soviet Union) SIGNED: 14 Dec 59 RATI-
FIED: 19 Feb 60 FORCE: 2 Aug 60

106070 Bilateral Agreement **422 UNTS 87**
SIGNED: 10 Dec 61 FORCE: 10 Dec 61
REGISTERED: 1 Feb 62 Thailand
ARTICLES: 7 LANGUAGE: English. Spanish. Thai.
HEADNOTE: TRADE
TOPIC: General Trade
CONCEPTS: Exceptions and exemptions. Treaty
implementation. Conformity with municipal law.
General cooperation. Reciprocity in trade. Trade
procedures.
PROCEDURE: Amendment. Duration. Renewal or
Revival. Termination.
PARTIES:
Argentina
Thailand

106071 Multilateral Convention **422 UNTS 101**
SIGNED: 14 Apr 61 FORCE: 11 May 61
REGISTERED: 1 Feb 62 Japan
ARTICLES: 48 LANGUAGE: English.
HEADNOTE: ASIAN PRODUCTIVITY ORGANIZA-
TION
TOPIC: IGO Establishment
CONCEPTS: Annex or appendix reference. Privi-
leges and immunities. Exchange of information
and documents. Procedure. Funding proce-
dures. Admission. Establishment. Liaison with
other IGO's. Internal structure. Status of experts.
Inter-agency agreements.
INTL ORGS: Asian Productivity Organization.
United Nations.
PROCEDURE: Amendment. Accession. Denuncia-
tion. Termination.
PARTIES:
Taiwan SIGNED: 14 Apr 61 RATIFIED:
18 May 61 FORCE: 18 May 61
Japan SIGNED: 14 Apr 61 RATIFIED: 28 Apr 61
FORCE: 11 May 61
Korea, South SIGNED: 14 Apr 61 RATIFIED:
15 May 61 FORCE: 15 May 61
Nepal SIGNED: 14 Apr 61 RATIFIED: 25 Apr 61
FORCE: 11 May 61
Pakistan SIGNED: 14 Apr 61 RATIFIED:
1 May 61 FORCE: 11 May 61
Philippines SIGNED: 14 Apr 61 RATIFIED:
11 May 61 FORCE: 11 May 61

Thailand SIGNED: 14 Apr 61 RATIFIED:
16 May 61 FORCE: 11 May 61

106072 Bilateral Agreement **422 UNTS 125**
SIGNED: 30 Aug 61 FORCE: 1 Nov 61
REGISTERED: 5 Feb 62 Thailand
ARTICLES: 3 LANGUAGE: English.
HEADNOTE: ILO LIAISON ECAFE
TOPIC: IGO Operations
CONCEPTS: Annex or appendix reference. Privi-
leges and immunities. Special status.
INTL ORGS: United Nations.
TREATY REF: 33UNTS261; 260UNTS35.
PARTIES:
ILO (Labor Org)
Thailand

106073 Bilateral Agreement **422 UNTS 131**
SIGNED: 2 Oct 61 FORCE: 2 Oct 61
REGISTERED: 6 Feb 62 United Nations
ARTICLES: 10 LANGUAGE: English.
HEADNOTE: ASSISTANCE
TOPIC: Direct Aid
CONCEPTS: Detailed regulations. Treaty imple-
mentation. Visas. Privileges and immunities. Ex-
change of information and documents. Informa-
tional records. Operating agencies. Personnel.
Public information. Responsibility and liability.
Title and deeds. Use of facilities. Arbitration. Pro-
cedure. Negotiation. Import quotas. Attachment
of funds. Exchange rates and regulations. Ex-
pense sharing formulae. Financial programs. Do-
mestic obligation. General technical assistance.
Economic assistance. Materials, equipment and
services. IGO status.
INTL ORGS: International Atomic Energy Agency.
International Court of Justice. United Nations.
Arbitration Commission.
TREATY REF: 1UNTS15; 33UNTS261;
374UNTS147.
PROCEDURE: Amendment. Termination.
PARTIES:
UN Special Fund
Sierra Leone

106074 Bilateral Agreement **422 UNTS 149**
SIGNED: 11 Dec 61 FORCE: 11 Dec 61
REGISTERED: 6 Feb 62 United Nations
ARTICLES: 10 LANGUAGE: English. Spanish.
HEADNOTE: ASSISTANCE
TOPIC: Direct Aid
CONCEPTS: Detailed regulations. Treaty imple-
mentation. Annex or appendix reference. Visas.
Privileges and immunities. Exchange of informa-
tion and documents. Informational records. In-
spection and observation. Operating agencies.
Personnel. Public information. Responsibility
and liability. Title and deeds. Use of facilities.
Arbitration. Procedure. Negotiation. Import
quotas. Attachment of funds. Exchange rates
and regulations. Expense sharing formulae. Fi-
nancial programs. Domestic obligation. General
technical assistance. Economic assistance. Materials, equipment and services. IGO status.
INTL ORGS: United Nations.
TREATY REF: 1UNTS15; 33UNTS261;
374UNTS147.
PROCEDURE: Amendment. Termination.
PARTIES:
UN Special Fund
Venezuela

106075 Bilateral Agreement **422 UNTS 177**
SIGNED: 18 Oct 60 FORCE: 5 Sep 61
REGISTERED: 8 Feb 62 IBRD (World Bank)
ARTICLES: 5 LANGUAGE: English.
HEADNOTE: GUARANTEE ROAD
TOPIC: IBRD Project
CONCEPTS: Definition of terms. Annex or appen-
dix reference. Exchange of information and doc-
uments. Inspection and observation. Bonds.
Fees and exemptions. Tax exemptions. Domestic
obligation. Terms of loan. Loan regulations. Loan
guarantee. Guarantor non-interference. Roads
and highways.
PARTIES:
Mexico
IBRD (World Bank)

106076 Bilateral Agreement **422 UNTS 203**
SIGNED: 16 Jan 61 FORCE: 8 Nov 61
REGISTERED: 8 Feb 62 IBRD (World Bank)
ARTICLES: 5 LANGUAGE: English.
HEADNOTE: GUARANTEE IRRIGATION
TOPIC: IBRD Project
CONCEPTS: Definition of terms. Annex or appen-
dix reference. Family law. Exchange of informa-
tion and documents. Bonds. Fees and exemp-
tions. Tax exemptions. Domestic obligation.
Terms of loan. Loan regulations. Loan guarantee.
Guarantor non-interference. Irrigation.
PARTIES:
Mexico
IBRD (World Bank)

106077 Bilateral Agreement **422 UNTS 231**
SIGNED: 26 Aug 61 FORCE: 4 Sep 61
REGISTERED: 13 Feb 62 United Nations
ARTICLES: 8 LANGUAGE: French.
HEADNOTE: ACTIVITIES UNICEF
TOPIC: Direct Aid
CONCEPTS: Treaty implementation. Privileges and
immunities. General cooperation. Exchange of
information and documents. Informational
records. Public information. Responsibility and
liability. Title and deeds. Attachment of funds.
Tax exemptions. Customs exemptions. Domestic
obligation. Assistance. General aid. Materials,
equipment and services. Distribution. IGO status.
INTL ORGS: United Nations.
TREATY REF: 1UNTS15.
PROCEDURE: Amendment. Termination.
PARTIES:
Chad
UNICEF (Children)

106078 Bilateral Agreement **422 UNTS 241**
SIGNED: 2 Nov 61 FORCE: 15 Nov 61
REGISTERED: 13 Feb 62 United Nations
ARTICLES: 8 LANGUAGE: French.
HEADNOTE: ACTIVITIES UNICEF
TOPIC: Direct Aid
CONCEPTS: Treaty implementation. Privileges and
immunities. General cooperation. Exchange of
information and documents. Informational
records. Public information. Responsibility and
liability. Title and deeds. Attachment of funds.
Tax exemptions. Customs exemptions. Domestic
obligation. Assistance. General aid. Materials,
equipment and services. Distribution. IGO status.
INTL ORGS: United Nations.
TREATY REF: 1UNTS15.
PROCEDURE: Amendment. Termination.
PARTIES:
Gabon
UNICEF (Children)

106079 Bilateral Agreement **422 UNTS 251**
SIGNED: 16 Nov 61 FORCE: 16 Nov 61
REGISTERED: 13 Feb 62 United Nations
ARTICLES: 8 LANGUAGE: French.
HEADNOTE: ACTIVITIES UNICEF
TOPIC: Direct Aid
CONCEPTS: Treaty implementation. Privileges and
immunities. General cooperation. Exchange of
information and documents. Informational
records. Public information. Responsibility and
liability. Title and deeds. Use of facilities. Attach-
ment of funds. Tax exemptions. Customs exemp-
tions. Domestic obligation. Assistance. General
aid. Materials, equipment and services. Distribu-
tion. IGO status.
INTL ORGS: United Nations.
TREATY REF: 1UNTS15.
PROCEDURE: Amendment. Termination.
PARTIES:
Malagasy
UNICEF (Children)

106080 Bilateral Agreement **422 UNTS 261**
SIGNED: 10 Jan 62 FORCE: 10 Jan 62
REGISTERED: 13 Feb 62 United Nations
ARTICLES: 8 LANGUAGE: French.
HEADNOTE: ACTIVITIES UNICEF
TOPIC: Direct Aid
CONCEPTS: Treaty implementation. Privileges and
immunities. General cooperation. Exchange of
information and documents. Informational
records. Public information. Responsibility and

liability. Title and deeds. Attachment of funds. Tax exemptions. Customs exemptions. Domestic obligation. Assistance. General aid. Materials, equipment and services. Distribution. IGO status.
INTL ORGS: United Nations.
TREATY REF: 1UNTS15.
PROCEDURE: Amendment. Termination.
PARTIES:
Ivory Coast
UNICEF (Children)

106081 Bilateral Agreement **422 UNTS 271**
SIGNED: 31 Jan 62 FORCE: 31 Jan 62
REGISTERED: 13 Feb 62 United Nations
ARTICLES: 8 LANGUAGE: English. Arabic.
HEADNOTE: ACTIVITIES UNICEF
TOPIC: Direct Aid
CONCEPTS: Treaty implementation. Treaty interpretation. Privileges and immunities. General cooperation. Exchange of information and documents. Informational records. Public information. Responsibility and liability. Title and deeds. Attachment of funds. Tax exemptions. Customs exemptions. Domestic obligation. Assistance. General aid. Materials, equipment and services. Distribution. IGO status.
INTL ORGS: United Nations.
TREATY REF: 1UNTS15.
PROCEDURE: Amendment. Termination.
PARTIES:
UNICEF (Children)
Yemen

106082 Bilateral Agreement **423 UNTS 3**
SIGNED: 19 Feb 62 FORCE: 19 Feb 62
REGISTERED: 19 Feb 62 United Nations
ARTICLES: 5 LANGUAGE: English.
HEADNOTE: ORGANIZATION SEMINAR FREEDOM INFORMATION
TOPIC: Direct Aid
CONCEPTS: Visas. Privileges and immunities. Professorships. Domestic obligation. Rights of supplier. Security of information. Internal structure. Status of experts. IGO obligations.
PROCEDURE: Amendment. Duration.
PARTIES:
India
United Nations

106083 Multilateral Convention **423 UNTS 11**
SIGNED: 26 Jun 61 FORCE: 5 Feb 62
REGISTERED: 19 Feb 62 ILO (Labor Org)
ARTICLES: 7 LANGUAGE: English. French.
HEADNOTE: REVISION CONVENTIONS REGARDS REPORTS
TOPIC: ILO Labor
CONCEPTS: Annex type material.
INTL ORGS: International Labour Organization. United Nations.
PARTIES:
Multilateral
ANNEX
425 UNTS 388. UK Great Britain. Ratification 9 Mar 62.
425 UNTS 388. Niger. Ratification 23 Mar 62.
425 UNTS 388. United Arab Rep. Ratification 26 Mar 62.
429 UNTS 307. Sweden. Ratification 3 Apr 62.
429 UNTS 307. Upper Volta. Ratification 16 Apr 62.
429 UNTS 307. Canada. Ratification 25 Apr 62.
434 UNTS 360. India. Ratification 21 Jun 62.
434 UNTS 360. Nigeria. Ratification 27 Jun 62.
435 UNTS 383. Denmark. Ratification 10 Jul 62.
435 UNTS 383. Spain. Ratification 17 Jul 62.
443 UNTS 354. Thailand. Ratification 24 Sep 62.
444 UNTS 353. Iraq. Ratification 26 Oct 62.
449 UNTS 383. Switzerland. Ratification 5 Nov 62.
449 UNTS 383. Taiwan. Ratification 16 Nov 62.
449 UNTS 383. Morocco. Ratification 14 Nov 62.
455 UNTS 474. Ivory Coast. Ratification 2 Jan 63.
455 UNTS 474. Norway. Ratification 22 Jan 63.
457 UNTS 366. Ireland. Ratification 27 Feb 63.
457 UNTS 366. New Zealand. Ratification 1 Mar 63.
463 UNTS 382. Kuwait. Ratification 23 Apr 63.
468 UNTS 443. Israel. Ratification 24 May 63.
471 UNTS 380. Central Afri Rep. Ratification 10 Jun 63.
473 UNTS 393. Jordan. Ratification 4 Jul 63.
475 UNTS 384. Ghana. Ratification 27 Aug 63.
480 UNTS 482. Germany, West. Ratification 7 Oct 63.
480 UNTS 482. Australia. Ratification 29 Oct 63.

483 UNTS 422. Mauritania. Ratification 8 Nov 63.
483 UNTS 422. Austria. Ratification 14 Nov 63.
488 UNTS 372. Czechoslovakia. Ratification 21 Jan 64. Force 21 Jan 65.
495 UNTS 307. Luxembourg. Ratification 4 Mar 64.
495 UNTS 307. Poland. Ratification 22 Apr 64.
504 UNTS 369. Finland. Ratification 1 Jun 64.
504 UNTS 369. Cyprus. Ratification 20 Jul 64.
504 UNTS 369. Madagascar. Ratification 1 Jun 64.
521 UNTS 428. Venezuela. Ratification 16 Nov 64.
521 UNTS 428. Honduras. Ratification 17 Nov 64.
521 UNTS 428. Netherlands. Ratification 13 Nov 64.
522 UNTS 390. Cameroon. Ratification 29 Dec 64.
524 UNTS 370. Guatemala. Ratification 25 Jan 65.
524 UNTS 370. Bolivia. Ratification 12 Jan 65.
530 UNTS 427. Yugoslavia. Ratification 9 Mar 65.
533 UNTS 400. Romania. Ratification 9 Apr 65.
545 UNTS 383. Syria. Ratification 10 Aug 65.
567 UNTS 358. Ethiopia. Ratification 11 Jun 66.
600 UNTS 410. France. Ratification 8 Jun 67.
607 UNTS 367. Congo (Zaire). Ratification 5 Sep 67.
613 UNTS 426. Pakistan. Ratification 17 Nov 67.
613 UNTS 426. Senegal. Ratification 13 Nov 67.
648 UNTS 389. Turkey. Ratification 2 Sep 68.
660 UNTS 430. Paraguay. Ratification 20 Feb 69.

106084 Bilateral Treaty **423 UNTS 19**
SIGNED: 20 Jun 60 FORCE: 21 Dec 61
REGISTERED: 19 Feb 62 Belgium
ARTICLES: 55 LANGUAGE: French. Dutch.
HEADNOTE: IMPROVEMENT TERNEUZEN & CHENT CANAL
TOPIC: Specific Property
CONCEPTS: Definition of terms. Annex or appendix reference. Visa abolition. Inspection and observation. Title and deeds. Tariffs. Indemnities and reimbursements. Currency. Funding procedures. Interest rates. Payment schedules. Non-interest rates and fees. Materials, equipment and services. Transport of goods. Inland and territorial waters. Ports and pilotage. Railways. Roads and highways. Facilities and property. Regulation of natural resources.
TREATY REF: 261UNTS140.
PROCEDURE: Ratification.
PARTIES:
Belgium
Netherlands

106085 Bilateral Agreement **423 UNTS 77**
SIGNED: 25 May 55 FORCE: 5 Feb 62
REGISTERED: 22 Feb 62 Norway
ARTICLES: 3 LANGUAGE: French.
HEADNOTE: TAX EXEMPTION AIR TRANSPORT ENTERPRISES
TOPIC: Taxation
CONCEPTS: Definition of terms. Tax exemptions. Air transport.
PROCEDURE: Ratification. Termination.
PARTIES:
Greece
Norway

106086 Bilateral Agreement **423 UNTS 83**
SIGNED: 26 Feb 62 FORCE: 26 Feb 62
REGISTERED: 26 Feb 62 United Nations
ARTICLES: 10 LANGUAGE: English. French.
HEADNOTE: ASSISTANCE
TOPIC: Direct Aid
CONCEPTS: Detailed regulations. Treaty implementation. Visas. Privileges and immunities. Exchange of information and documents. Informational records. Inspection and observation. Operating agencies. Personnel. Public information. Responsibility and liability. Title and deeds. Use of facilities. Arbitration. Procedure. Negotiation. Import quotas. Attachment of funds. Exchange rates and regulations. Expense sharing formulae. Financial programs. Domestic obligation. General technical assistance. Economic assistance. Materials, equipment and services. IGO status.

TREATY REF: 1UNTS15; 33UNTS261; 374UNTS147.
PROCEDURE: Amendment. Termination.
PARTIES:
Niger
UN Special Fund

106087 Bilateral Agreement **423 UNTS 99**
SIGNED: 11 Jan 62 FORCE: 11 Jan 62
REGISTERED: 26 Feb 62 WHO (World Health)
ARTICLES: 6 LANGUAGE: English.
HEADNOTE: TECHNICAL ADVISORY ASSISTANCE
TOPIC: Tech Assistance
CONCEPTS: Definition of terms. Previous treaty replacement. Privileges and immunities. General cooperation. Exchange of information and documents. Personnel. Responsibility and liability. Title and deeds. Exchange. Scholarships and grants. Vocational training. Research and development. Expense sharing formulae. Local currency. Domestic obligation. Special projects. Materials, equipment and services. IGO status. Conformity with IGO decisions.
TREATY REF: 33UNTS261; 243UNTS91.
PROCEDURE: Amendment. Termination.
PARTIES:
Ethiopia
WHO (World Health)

106088 Bilateral Agreement **423 UNTS 111**
SIGNED: 17 Aug 61 FORCE: 10 Jan 62
REGISTERED: 26 Feb 62 WHO (World Health)
ARTICLES: 6 LANGUAGE: English.
HEADNOTE: TECHNICAL ADVISORY ASSISTANCE
TOPIC: Tech Assistance
CONCEPTS: General cooperation. Exchange of information and documents. Personnel. Responsibility and liability. Title and deeds. Exchange. Scholarships and grants. Vocational training. Research and development. Expense sharing formulae. Local currency. Domestic obligation. Special projects. Materials, equipment and services. IGO status. Conformity with IGO decisions.
TREATY REF: 33UNTS261.
PROCEDURE: Amendment. Termination.
PARTIES:
WHO (World Health)
Somalia

106089 Multilateral Agreement **423 UNTS 122**
SIGNED: 1 Mar 62 FORCE: 1 Mar 62
REGISTERED: 1 Mar 62 United Nations
ARTICLES: 6 LANGUAGE: English.
HEADNOTE: TECHNICAL ASSISTANCE
TOPIC: Tech Assistance
CONCEPTS: Definition of terms. Previous treaty replacement. Privileges and immunities. General cooperation. Exchange of information and documents. Personnel. Responsibility and liability. Title and deeds. Use of facilities. Exchange. Scholarships and grants. Vocational training. Research and development. Exchange rates and regulations. Expense sharing formulae. Local currency. Domestic obligation. General technical assistance. Materials, equipment and services. IGO status. Conformity with IGO decisions.
TREATY REF: 76UNTS132; 1UNTS15; 33UNTS261; 374UNTS147; 92UNTS2.
PROCEDURE: Amendment. Termination.
PARTIES:
Fed of Malaya SIGNED: 1 Mar 62 FORCE: 1 Mar 62
FAO (Food Agri) SIGNED: 1 Mar 62 FORCE: 1 Mar 62
IAEA (Atom Energy) SIGNED: 1 Mar 62 FORCE: 1 Mar 62
ICAO (Civil Aviat) SIGNED: 1 Mar 62 FORCE: 1 Mar 62
ILO (Labor Org) SIGNED: 1 Mar 62 FORCE: 1 Mar 62
ITU (Telecommun) SIGNED: 1 Mar 62 FORCE: 1 Mar 62
UNESCO (Educ/Cult) SIGNED: 1 Mar 62 FORCE: 1 Mar 62
United Nations SIGNED: 1 Mar 62 FORCE: 1 Mar 62
WHO (World Health) SIGNED: 1 Mar 62 FORCE: 1 Mar 62
WMO (Meteorology) SIGNED: 1 Mar 62 FORCE: 1 Mar 62

485 UNTS 368. UNTAB (Tech Assis). Amendment 24 Oct 63. Force 28 Dec 63.
485 UNTS 368. Fed of Malaya. Amendment 28 Dec 63. Force 28 Dec 63.

106090 Bilateral Agreement **423 UNTS 139**
SIGNED: 25 Apr 61 FORCE: 10 Nov 61
REGISTERED: 5 Mar 62 Taiwan
ARTICLES: 8 LANGUAGE: Chinese. Spanish.
HEADNOTE: CULTURAL AGREEMENT
TOPIC: Culture
CONCEPTS: Friendship and amity. Exchange. Teacher and student exchange. Exchange. General cultural cooperation. Athletes. Mass media exchange. Press and wire services.
INTL ORGS: United Nations Educational, Scientific and Cultural Organization. United Nations.
TREATY REF: 4UNTS275.
PROCEDURE: Duration. Ratification. Renewal or Revival. Termination.
PARTIES:
Taiwan
Nicaragua

106091 Multilateral Agreement **423 UNTS 151**
SIGNED: 21 Feb 62 FORCE: 21 Feb 62
REGISTERED: 8 Mar 62 United Nations
ARTICLES: 6 LANGUAGE: French.
HEADNOTE: TECHNICAL ASSISTANCE
TOPIC: Tech Assistance
CONCEPTS: Definition of terms. Privileges and immunities. General cooperation. Exchange of information and documents. Personnel. Responsibility and liability. Title and deeds. Use of facilities. Exchange. Scholarships and grants. Vocational training. Research and development. Exchange rates and regulations. Expense sharing formulae. Local currency. Domestic obligation. General technical assistance. Materials, equipment and services. IGO status. Conformity with IGO decisions.
TREATY REF: 76UNTS132; 1UNTS15; 33UNTS261; 374UNTS147.
PROCEDURE: Amendment. Termination.
PARTIES:
Gabon SIGNED: 21 Feb 61 FORCE: 21 Feb 61
FAO (Food Agri) SIGNED: 21 Feb 61 FORCE: 21 Feb 61
IAEA (Atom Energy) SIGNED: 21 Feb 61 FORCE: 21 Feb 61
ICAO (Civil Aviat) SIGNED: 21 Feb 61 FORCE: 21 Feb 61
ILO (Labor Org) SIGNED: 21 Feb 61 FORCE: 21 Feb 61
ITU (Telecommun) SIGNED: 21 Feb 61 FORCE: 21 Feb 61
UNESCO (Educ/Cult) SIGNED: 21 Feb 61 FORCE: 21 Feb 61
United Nations SIGNED: 21 Feb 61 FORCE: 21 Feb 61
WHO (World Health) SIGNED: 21 Feb 61 FORCE: 21 Feb 61
WMO (Meteorology) SIGNED: 21 Feb 61 FORCE: 21 Feb 61

106092 Bilateral Agreement **423 UNTS 165**
SIGNED: 22 Jun 60 FORCE: 1 Mar 62
REGISTERED: 12 Mar 62 ILO (Labor Org)
ARTICLES: 10 LANGUAGE: Spanish.
HEADNOTE: STATUS & PRIVILEGES ILO PERU
TOPIC: IGO Status/Immunit
CONCEPTS: IGO status. Special status. Status of experts.
PARTIES:
Peru
ILO (Labor Org)

106093 Bilateral Treaty **423 UNTS 197**
SIGNED: 18 Dec 60 FORCE: 20 Aug 61
REGISTERED: 12 Mar 62 Pakistan
ARTICLES: 14 LANGUAGE: English.
HEADNOTE: FRIENDSHIP COMMERCE
TOPIC: General Amity
CONCEPTS: Exceptions and exemptions. Territorial application. Treaty interpretation. Alien status. General cooperation. Juridical personality. Expropriation. Legal protection and assistance. Arbitration. Existing tribunals. Export quotas. Import quotas. Most favored nation clause. National treatment. Taxation. Customs exemptions. Foreign nationals.
INTL ORGS: General Agreement on Tariffs and Trade. International Court of Justice. International Monetary Fund.
TREATY REF: GATT.
PROCEDURE: Duration. Ratification. Termination.
PARTIES:
Japan
Pakistan

106094 Bilateral Agreement **423 UNTS 217**
SIGNED: 24 Feb 61 FORCE: 24 Feb 61
REGISTERED: 12 Mar 62 Philippines
ARTICLES: 6 LANGUAGE: English.
HEADNOTE: DEVELOPING DIRECT TRADE RELATIONS
TOPIC: General Trade
CONCEPTS: Treaty implementation. Annex or appendix reference. Licenses and permits. Establishment of trade relations. Export quotas. Import quotas. Most favored nation clause. General. Customs duties.
INTL ORGS: United Nations.
PROCEDURE: Duration. Renewal or Revival. Termination.
PARTIES:
Korea, South
Philippines

106095 Bilateral Agreement **423 UNTS 229**
SIGNED: 5 May 60 FORCE: 24 Oct 60
REGISTERED: 13 Mar 62 Poland
ARTICLES: 24 LANGUAGE: Polish. Serbo-Croat.
HEADNOTE: VETERINARY COOPERATION
TOPIC: Sanitation
CONCEPTS: Definition of terms. Detailed regulations. Exceptions and exemptions. Border traffic and migration. General cooperation. Exchange of official publications. Exchange of information and documents. Inspection and observation. Domestic legislation. Procedure. Negotiation. Specialists exchange. Border control. Disease control. Veterinary. Scientific exchange. Research and development. Trade procedures. Indemnities and reimbursements.
PROCEDURE: Denunciation. Duration. Ratification.
PARTIES:
Poland
Yugoslavia

106096 Bilateral Convention **424 UNTS 3**
SIGNED: 17 May 60 FORCE: 22 Mar 61
REGISTERED: 13 Mar 62 Poland
ARTICLES: 28 LANGUAGE: Polish. Czechoslovakian.
HEADNOTE: CONSULAR CONVENTION
TOPIC: Consul/Citizenship
CONCEPTS: General consular functions. Diplomatic privileges. Consular relations establishment. Inviolability. Privileges and immunities. Diplomatic correspondence.
PROCEDURE: Duration. Ratification.
PARTIES:
Czechoslovakia
Poland

106097 Bilateral Agreement **424 UNTS 37**
SIGNED: 8 Jun 60 FORCE: 12 Dec 60
REGISTERED: 13 Mar 62 Poland
ARTICLES: 4 LANGUAGE: French.
HEADNOTE: CULTURAL AGREEMENT
TOPIC: Culture
CONCEPTS: Friendship and amity. Establishment of commission. Exchange. Scholarships and grants. Exchange. General cultural cooperation. Artists. Scientific exchange.
PROCEDURE: Denunciation. Duration. Ratification.
PARTIES:
Denmark
Poland

106098 Multilateral Agreement **424 UNTS 43**
SIGNED: 15 Dec 61 FORCE: 15 Dec 61
REGISTERED: 13 Mar 62 Poland
ARTICLES: 11 LANGUAGE: Russian.
HEADNOTE: COOPERATION TECHNICAL SUPERVISION CLASSIFICATION SHIPS
TOPIC: Admin Cooperation
CONCEPTS: Standardization. General cooperation. Exchange of information and documents.
PROCEDURE: Accession. Denunciation.
PARTIES:
Bulgaria FORCE: 15 Dec 61
Czechoslovakia FORCE: 15 Dec 61
Germany, East FORCE: 15 Dec 61
Hungary FORCE: 15 Dec 61
Poland FORCE: 15 Dec 61
Romania FORCE: 15 Dec 61
USSR (Soviet Union) FORCE: 15 Dec 61

106099 Bilateral Agreement **424 UNTS 55**
SIGNED: 28 Mar 62 FORCE: 28 Mar 62
REGISTERED: 28 Mar 62 United Nations
ARTICLES: 10 LANGUAGE: English. French.
HEADNOTE: ASSISTANCE
TOPIC: Tech Assistance
CONCEPTS: Detailed regulations. Treaty implementation. Visas. Privileges and immunities. Conformity with municipal law. Exchange of information and documents. Inspection and observation. Operating agencies. Licenses and permits. General property. Public information. Responsibility and liability. Title and deeds. Use of facilities. Arbitration. Procedure. Negotiation. Import quotas. Reexport of goods, etc.. Accounting procedures. Exchange rates and regulations. Expense sharing formulae. Fees and exemptions. Local currency. Tax exemptions. Customs exemptions. Commodities and services. General technical assistance. Materials, equipment and services. IGO status. Conformity with IGO decisions.
INTL ORGS: International Atomic Energy Agency. International Court of Justice. United Nations. Arbitration Commission.
TREATY REF: 1UNTS15; 33UNTS261; 374UNTS147.
PROCEDURE: Amendment. Termination.
PARTIES:
Dahomey
UN Special Fund

106100 Bilateral Agreement **424 UNTS 71**
SIGNED: 8 Nov 60 FORCE: 23 May 61
REGISTERED: 30 Mar 62 Czechoslovakia
ARTICLES: 14 LANGUAGE: Czechoslovakian. German.
HEADNOTE: ADMISSION EXCHANGE STUDENTS
TOPIC: Admin Cooperation
CONCEPTS: Detailed regulations. Operating agencies. Exchange. Indemnities and reimbursements.
PROCEDURE: Duration. Ratification. Renewal or Revival.
PARTIES:
Czechoslovakia
Germany, East

106101 Bilateral Exchange **424 UNTS 93**
SIGNED: 23 Oct 61 FORCE: 22 Nov 61
REGISTERED: 2 Apr 62 USA (United States)
ARTICLES: 2 LANGUAGE: English. Spanish.
HEADNOTE: RADIO COMMUNICATIONS AMATEUR STATIONS BEHALF THIRD PARTIES
TOPIC: Telecommunications
CONCEPTS: Amateur radio. Amateur third party message. Radio-telephone-telegraphic communications.
PROCEDURE: Termination.
PARTIES:
Bolivia
USA (United States)

106102 Bilateral Exchange **424 UNTS 101**
SIGNED: 17 Oct 61 FORCE: 17 Oct 61
REGISTERED: 2 Apr 62 USA (United States)
ARTICLES: 3 LANGUAGE: English.
HEADNOTE: CHANNEL IMPROVEMENTS LAKE ERIE
TOPIC: Water Transport
CONCEPTS: Canal improvement.
PARTIES:
Canada
USA (United States)

106103 Bilateral Exchange **424 UNTS 113**
SIGNED: 29 Sep 61 FORCE: 29 Sep 61

REGISTERED: 2 Apr 62 USA (United States)
ARTICLES: 2 LANGUAGE: English. German.
HEADNOTE: EXPERIMENTAL COMMUNICATIONS
SATELLITE
TOPIC: Scientific Project
CONCEPTS: Operating agencies. Research and scientific projects. Communication satellites testing. Research and development. Facilities and equipment.
PROCEDURE: Future Procedures Contemplated.
PARTIES:
Germany, West
USA (United States)

106104 Bilateral Agreement **424 UNTS 119**
SIGNED: 29 Nov 61   FORCE: 29 Nov 61
REGISTERED: 2 Apr 62 USA (United States)
ARTICLES: 9 LANGUAGE: English.
HEADNOTE: FUNDS
TOPIC: Direct Aid
CONCEPTS: Treaty implementation. Exchange of information and documents. Informational records. Inspection and observation. Personnel. Accounting procedures. Funding procedures. Use restrictions.
TREATY REF: CHARTER OF PUNTA DEL ESTE.
PROCEDURE: Duration. Termination.
PARTIES:
OAS (Am States)
USA (United States)
ANNEX
511 UNTS 298. USA (United States). Amendment 17 Feb 64. Force 17 Feb 64.
511 UNTS 298. OAS (Am States). Amendment 17 Feb 64. Force 17 Feb 64.

106105 Bilateral Exchange **424 UNTS 129**
SIGNED: 31 Oct 61   FORCE: 31 Oct 61
REGISTERED: 2 Apr 62 USA (United States)
ARTICLES: 2 LANGUAGE: English.
HEADNOTE: PEACE CORPS PROGRAM
TOPIC: Direct Aid
CONCEPTS: Treaty implementation. Legal protection and assistance. Personnel. Fees and exemptions. Tax exemptions. Customs exemptions. Materials, equipment and services. Aid missions. Volunteer programs.
PARTIES:
Philippines
USA (United States)

106106 Bilateral Treaty **424 UNTS 137**
SIGNED: 3 Apr 61   FORCE: 30 Nov 61
REGISTERED: 2 Apr 62 USA (United States)
ARTICLES: 15 LANGUAGE: English. Vietnamese.
HEADNOTE: AMITY, ECONOMIC RELATIONS
TOPIC: General Amity
CONCEPTS: Exceptions and exemptions. Alien status. Human rights. General cooperation. Juridical personality. Legal protection and assistance. Private contracts. Existing tribunals. Export quotas. Import quotas. Free trade. Reciprocity in trade. Trade procedures. Exchange rates and regulations. National treatment. Taxation. Customs duties. Navigational conditions.
INTL ORGS: International Court of Justice. International Monetary Fund.
TREATY REF: GATT.
PROCEDURE: Duration. Ratification. Termination.
PARTIES:
USA (United States)
Vietnam, South

106107 Bilateral Convention **424 UNTS 173**
SIGNED: 12 Jun 61   FORCE: 5 Apr 62
REGISTERED: 5 Apr 62 Norway
ARTICLES: 11 LANGUAGE: Norwegian. English.
HEADNOTE: RECOGNITION ENFORCEMENT JUDGEMENTS CIVIL MATTERS
TOPIC: Admin Cooperation
CONCEPTS: Definition of terms. Territorial application. General provisions. Legal protection and assistance.
PROCEDURE: Duration. Ratification. Termination.
PARTIES:
Norway
UK Great Britain

106108 Bilateral Exchange **424 UNTS 201**
SIGNED: 26 Sep 61   FORCE: 26 Sep 61
REGISTERED: 5 Apr 62 UK Great Britain
ARTICLES: 2 LANGUAGE: English. German.
HEADNOTE: LOGISTIC TRAINING FACILITIES
TOPIC: Milit Assistance
CONCEPTS: Use of facilities. Indemnities and re-imbursements. Customs exemptions. Materials, equipment and services. Military training. Bases and facilities.
INTL ORGS: North Atlantic Treaty Organization.
TREATY REF: 34UNTS243.
PROCEDURE: Termination.
PARTIES:
Germany, West
UK Great Britain

106109 Bilateral Exchange **424 UNTS 211**
SIGNED: 12 Jul 61   FORCE: 14 Aug 61
REGISTERED: 5 Apr 62 UK Great Britain
ARTICLES: 2 LANGUAGE: English. German.
HEADNOTE: APPLICATION NATO STATUS FORCES AGREEMENT
TOPIC: Status of Forces
CONCEPTS: Time limit. Status of forces.
INTL ORGS: North Atlantic Treaty Organization.
TREATY REF: 199UNTS67.
PROCEDURE: Termination.
PARTIES:
Germany, West
UK Great Britain

106110 Bilateral Agreement **424 UNTS 217**
SIGNED: 5 Dec 61   FORCE: 5 Dec 61
REGISTERED: 5 Apr 62 UK Great Britain
ARTICLES: 5 LANGUAGE: English. Finnish.
HEADNOTE: RECOGNITION TONNAGE CERTIFICATES MERCHANT SHIPS
TOPIC: Admin Cooperation
CONCEPTS: Territorial application. Previous treaty replacement. Recognition of legal documents. Merchant vessels.
TREATY REF: 28LTS512.
PROCEDURE: Termination.
PARTIES:
Finland
UK Great Britain

106111 Bilateral Exchange **424 UNTS 225**
SIGNED: 23 Oct 61   FORCE: 23 Jan 62
REGISTERED: 5 Apr 62 UK Great Britain
ARTICLES: 2 LANGUAGE: English. Italian.
HEADNOTE: RECOGNITION VEHICLE REAR LIGHTS RED REFLECTORS
TOPIC: Admin Cooperation
CONCEPTS: General cooperation. Road rules.
PARTIES:
Italy
UK Great Britain

106112 Bilateral Agreement **424 UNTS 233**
SIGNED: 16 Jan 61   FORCE: 10 Nov 61
REGISTERED: 5 Apr 62 UK Great Britain
ARTICLES: 14 LANGUAGE: English. Arabic.
HEADNOTE: AIR SERVICES BETWEEN BEYOND RESPECTIVE TERRITORIES
TOPIC: Air Transport
CONCEPTS: Conditions. Definition of terms. Detailed regulations. Exceptions and exemptions. Annex or appendix reference. General cooperation. Exchange of information and documents. Arbitration. Procedure. Negotiation. Non-interest rates and fees. Most favored nation clause. National treatment. Customs exemptions. Routes and logistics. Permit designation. Conditions of airlines operating permission. Overflights and technical stops. Operating authorizations and regulations.
INTL ORGS: International Civil Aviation Organization. International Court of Justice. Arbitration Commission.
TREATY REF: 15UNTS295.
PROCEDURE: Amendment. Future Procedures Contemplated. Ratification. Registration. Termination. Application to Non-self-governing Territories.
PARTIES:
Sudan
UK Great Britain

106113 Bilateral Convention **424 UNTS 267**
SIGNED: 9 Sep 59   FORCE: 1 Jun 61
REGISTERED: 5 Apr 62 UK Great Britain
ARTICLES: 40 LANGUAGE: English. Turkish.
HEADNOTE: SOCIAL INSURANCE
TOPIC: Non-ILO Labor
CONCEPTS: Definition of terms. Annex or appendix reference. Domestic legislation. Dispute settlement. Old age and invalidity insurance. Wages and salaries. Non-ILO labor relations. Family allowances. Administrative cooperation. Old age insurance. Sickness and invalidity insurance. Social security. Unemployment. Payment schedules. Claims and settlements.
INTL ORGS: International Court of Justice. Arbitration Commission.
PARTIES:
Turkey
UK Great Britain

106114 Multilateral Instrument **425 UNTS 3**
SIGNED: 5 Mar 62   FORCE: 5 Mar 62
REGISTERED: 9 Apr 62 IAEA (Atom Energy)
ARTICLES: 6 LANGUAGE: English.
HEADNOTE: TRANFER URANIUM PLUTONIUM RESEARCH REACTOR
TOPIC: Scientific Project
CONCEPTS: Definition of terms. General cooperation. Operating agencies. Responsibility and liability. Existing tribunals. Meteorology. Nuclear research. Transportation costs. Acceptance of delivery. General. Peaceful use. Samples and testing.
INTL ORGS: International Court of Justice. Arbitration Commission.
TREATY REF: 339UNTS359; 276UNTS3 293UNTS359.
PARTIES:
Pakistan SIGNED: 5 Mar 62 FORCE: 5 Mar 62
IAEA (Atom Energy) SIGNED: 5 Mar 62 FORCE: 5 Mar 62
USA (United States) SIGNED: 5 Mar 62 FORCE: 5 Mar 62

106115 Bilateral Agreement **425 UNTS 17**
SIGNED: 5 Mar 62   FORCE: 5 Mar 62
REGISTERED: 9 Apr 62 IAEA (Atom Energy)
ARTICLES: 11 LANGUAGE: English.
HEADNOTE: RESEARCH REACTOR PROJECT
TOPIC: Scientific Project
CONCEPTS: Definition of terms. Annex or appendix reference. General cooperation. Inspection and observation. Programs. Dispute settlement. Research results. Nuclear research. Research and development. Patents, copyrights and trademarks. Acceptance of delivery. General. Nuclear materials. Samples and testing.
INTL ORGS: International Court of Justice. Arbitration Commission.
TREATY REF: 339UNTS359; 276UNTS3 293UNTS359.
PARTIES:
Pakistan
IAEA (Atom Energy)

106116 Bilateral Exchange **425 UNTS 33**
SIGNED: 1 Feb 62   FORCE: 1 Apr 62
REGISTERED: 10 Apr 62 Finland
ARTICLES: 2 LANGUAGE: German.
HEADNOTE: EXCHANGE STUDENT EMPLOYEES
TOPIC: Non-ILO Labor
CONCEPTS: Definition of terms. Detailed regulations. Resident permits. Conformity with municipal law. Dispute settlement. Employment regulations. ILO conventions. Non-ILO labor relations. Administrative cooperation. Migrant worker. Quotas.
PROCEDURE: Denunciation. Duration. Renewal or Revival.
PARTIES:
Austria
Finland

106117 Bilateral Agreement **425 UNTS 45**
SIGNED: 11 Apr 62   FORCE: 11 Apr 62
REGISTERED: 11 Apr 62 United Nations
ARTICLES: 5 LANGUAGE: English.
HEADNOTE: HUMAN RIGHTS SEMINAR
TOPIC: IGO Operations
CONCEPTS: IGO constitution. Procedure.

PARTIES:
Japan
United Nations

106118   Bilateral Exchange   **425 UNTS 53**
SIGNED: 30 Sep 61   FORCE: 1 Oct 61
REGISTERED: 11 Apr 62 Belgium
ARTICLES: 2 LANGUAGE: French. Spanish.
HEADNOTE: ABOLITION PASSPORT VISA RE-
QUIREMENT
TOPIC: Visas
CONCEPTS: Emergencies. Territorial application.
Time limit. Visa abolition. Denial of admission.
Resident permits. Conformity with municipal
law.
PROCEDURE: Termination.
PARTIES:
Belgium
Bolivia

106119   Multilateral Convention   **425 UNTS 61**
SIGNED: 6 Dec 51   FORCE: 28 Nov 61
REGISTERED: 13 Apr 62 UNESCO (Educ/Cult)
ARTICLES: 14 LANGUAGE: English. French.
HEADNOTE: ESTABLISH INTERNATIONAL COM-
PUTATION CENTER
TOPIC: IGO Establishment
CONCEPTS: Annex or appendix reference. Ex-
change of official publications. Exchange of in-
formation and documents. Juridical personality.
Education. Institute establishment. Research and
scientific projects. Research cooperation. Scien-
tific exchange. Funding procedures. Establish-
ment. Headquarters and facilities. Internal struc-
ture. Freedom of meeting. IGO obligations. Inter-
agency agreements.
INTL ORGS: International Computation Centre.
United Nations.
PROCEDURE: Amendment. Accession. Denuncia-
tion.
PARTIES:
Argentina RATIFIED: 28 Nov 61
Belgium SIGNED: 6 Dec 51 RATIFIED: 21 Jul 53
FORCE: 28 Nov 61
Ceylon (Sri Lanka) RATIFIED: 16 Mar 54
Cuba SIGNED: 6 Dec 51 FORCE: 27 Mar 62
Ecuador SIGNED: 6 Dec 51 FORCE: 28 Nov 61
United Arab Rep SIGNED: 6 Dec 51 FORCE:
28 Nov 61
France RATIFIED: 18 Nov 58
Greece SIGNED: 6 Dec 51 FORCE: 28 Nov 61
Iraq SIGNED: 6 Dec 51 FORCE: 28 Nov 61
Israel SIGNED: 6 Dec 51 RATIFIED: 7 Aug 61
FORCE: 28 Nov 61
Italy SIGNED: 6 Dec 51 RATIFIED: 12 Apr 54
FORCE: 28 Nov 61
Japan SIGNED: 6 Dec 51 RATIFIED: 10 Jun 61
FORCE: 28 Nov 61
Liberia SIGNED: 6 Dec 51 FORCE: 28 Nov 61
Libya RATIFIED: 16 Feb 61
Mexico SIGNED: 6 Dec 51 RATIFIED: 16 Mar 56
FORCE: 28 Nov 61
Netherlands SIGNED: 6 Dec 51 FORCE:
28 Nov 61
Turkey SIGNED: 6 Dec 51 FORCE: 28 Nov 61
United Arab Rep RATIFIED: 19 May 60
ANNEX
435 UNTS 384. Ceylon (Sri Lanka). Withdrawal
16 Jul 62. Force 16 Aug 63.
435 UNTS 384. Ghana. Acceptance 7 Aug 62.
478 UNTS 437. Greece. Acceptance 17 Sep 63.
486 UNTS 432. Ecuador. Acceptance 24 Jan 64.
535 UNTS 439. United Arab Rep. Withdrawal
4 Jan 65. Force 4 Jan 66.

106120   Multilateral Agreement   **425 UNTS 83**
SIGNED: 27 Dec 61   FORCE: 20 Feb 62
REGISTERED: 13 Apr 62 United Nations
ARTICLES: 6 LANGUAGE: French.
HEADNOTE: TECHNICAL ASSISTANCE
TOPIC: Tech Assistance
CONCEPTS: Definition of terms. Privileges and im-
munities. General cooperation. Exchange of in-
formation and documents. Personnel. Responsi-
bility and liability. Title and deeds. Use of facili-
ties. Exchange. Scholarships and grants.
Vocational training. Research and development.
Exchange rates and regulations. Expense shar-
ing formulae. Local currency. Domestic obliga-
tion. General technical assistance. Materials,

equipment and services. IGO status. Conformity
with IGO decisions.
TREATY   REF: 76UNTS132;   1UNTS15;
33UNTS261; 374UNTS147.
PROCEDURE: Amendment. Termination.
PARTIES:
FAO (Food Agri) SIGNED: 27 Dec 61 FORCE:
20 Feb 62
IAEA (Atom Energy) SIGNED: 27 Dec 61 FORCE:
20 Feb 62
ICAO (Civil Aviat) SIGNED: 27 Dec 61 FORCE:
20 Feb 62
ILO (Labor Org) SIGNED: 27 Dec 61 FORCE:
20 Feb 62
ITU (Telecommun) SIGNED: 27 Dec 61 FORCE:
20 Feb 62
UNESCO (Educ/Cult) SIGNED: 27 Dec 61
FORCE: 20 Feb 62
United Nations SIGNED: 27 Dec 61 FORCE:
20 Feb 62
WHO (World Health) SIGNED: 27 Dec 61 FORCE:
20 Feb 62
WMO (Meteorology) SIGNED: 27 Dec 61 FORCE:
20 Feb 62
Senegal SIGNED: 27 Dec 61 FORCE: 20 Feb 62
ANNEX
654 UNTS 380. UPU (Postal Union). Accession
7 Dec 68. Force 7 Dec 68.
654 UNTS 380. IMCO (Maritime Org). Accession
7 Dec 68. Force 7 Dec 68.
654 UNTS 380. UNIDO (Industrial). Accession
7 Dec 68. Force 7 Dec 68.

106121   Bilateral Agreement   **425 UNTS 97**
SIGNED: 16 Dec 61   FORCE: 20 Feb 62
REGISTERED: 13 Apr 62 United Nations
ARTICLES: 10 LANGUAGE: English. French.
HEADNOTE: ASSISTANCE
TOPIC: Direct Aid
CONCEPTS: Detailed regulations. Treaty imple-
mentation. Annex or appendix reference. Visas.
Privileges and immunities. Exchange of informa-
tion and documents. Informational records. In-
spection and observation. Operating agencies.
Personnel. Public information. Responsibility
and liability. Title and deeds. Use of facilities.
Arbitration. Procedure. Negotiation. Import
quotas. Attachment of funds. Exchange rates
and regulations. Expense sharing formulae. Fi-
nancial programs. Domestic obligation. General
technical assistance. Economic assistance. Ma-
terials, equipment and services. IGO status.
INTL ORGS: International Court of Justice. United
Nations. Arbitration Commission.
TREATY   REF: 1UNTS15;   33UNTS261;
374UNTS147.
PROCEDURE: Amendment. Termination.
PARTIES:
UN Special Fund
Senegal

106122   Bilateral Agreement   **425 UNTS 115**
SIGNED: 23 Oct 61   FORCE: 26 Feb 62
REGISTERED: 16 Apr 62 Denmark
ARTICLES: 28 LANGUAGE: Danish. German.
HEADNOTE: DOUBLE TAXATION INCOME FOR-
TUNE
TOPIC: Taxation
CONCEPTS: Definition of terms. Territorial applica-
tion. Privileges and immunities. Nationality and
citizenship. Conformity with municipal law. Ex-
change of official publications. Teacher and stu-
dent exchange. Taxation. Death duties. Tax ex-
emptions. Air transport. Merchant vessels.
PROCEDURE: Duration. Ratification. Termination.
PARTIES:
Austria
Denmark

106123   Bilateral Convention   **425 UNTS 181**
SIGNED: 23 Oct 61   FORCE: 3 Apr 62
REGISTERED: 17 Apr 62 Belgium
ARTICLES: 9 LANGUAGE: French. Danish.
HEADNOTE: DOUBLE TAXATION AIR TRANSPORT
TOPIC: Taxation
CONCEPTS: Taxation. Tax exemptions. Air trans-
port.
PARTIES:
Belgium
Denmark

106124   Bilateral Exchange   **425 UNTS 191**
SIGNED: 1 Aug 61   FORCE: 1 Aug 61
REGISTERED: 18 Apr 62 Denmark
ARTICLES: 2 LANGUAGE: Danish. Icelandic.
HEADNOTE: HAND-LINE FISHING
TOPIC: Specific Resources
CONCEPTS: Conformity with municipal law. Fish-
eries and fishing.
PROCEDURE: Termination.
PARTIES:
Denmark
Iceland

106125   Bilateral Agreement   **425 UNTS 197**
SIGNED: 1 Dec 61   FORCE: 1 Jan 62
REGISTERED: 23 Apr 62 IBRD (World Bank)
ARTICLES: 7 LANGUAGE: English.
HEADNOTE: SOCIAL POLICY
TOPIC: IBRD Project
CONCEPTS: General provisions. Friendship and
amity. Exchange of information and documents.
Old age and invalidity insurance. Wages and sal-
aries. Non-ILO labor relations. Family allow-
ances. Old age insurance. Sickness and invalid-
ity insurance. Payment schedules. Claims and
settlements. National treatment. Publications ex-
change.
PROCEDURE: Denunciation. Duration. Ratification.
PARTIES:
IBRD (World Bank)
South Africa

106126   Bilateral Agreement   **425 UNTS 215**
SIGNED: 1 Dec 61   FORCE: 15 Jan 62
REGISTERED: 23 Apr 62 IBRD (World Bank)
ARTICLES: 5 LANGUAGE: English.
HEADNOTE: GUARANTEE AGREEMENT
TOPIC: IBRD Project
CONCEPTS: Definition of terms. Annex or appen-
dix reference. Exchange of information and doc-
uments. Inspection and observation. Bonds.
Fees and exemptions. Tax exemptions. Domestic
obligation. Terms of loan. Loan regulations. Loan
guarantee. Guarantor non-interference.
PARTIES:
IBRD (World Bank)
South Africa

106127   Bilateral Agreement   **425 UNTS 241**
SIGNED: 27 Jun 61   FORCE: 29 Dec 61
REGISTERED: 23 Apr 62 IBRD (World Bank)
ARTICLES: 5 LANGUAGE: English.
HEADNOTE: GUARANTEE AGREEMENT
TOPIC: IBRD Project
CONCEPTS: Definition of terms. Annex or appen-
dix reference. Exchange of information and doc-
uments. Inspection and observation. Bonds.
Fees and exemptions. Tax exemptions. Domestic
obligation. Terms of loan. Loan regulations. Loan
guarantee. Guarantor non-interference.
PARTIES:
Pakistan
IBRD (World Bank)

106128   Bilateral Agreement   **426 UNTS 3**
SIGNED: 29 Nov 61   FORCE: 30 Jan 62
REGISTERED: 23 Apr 62 IBRD (World Bank)
ARTICLES: 5 LANGUAGE: English.
HEADNOTE: GUARANTEE EXPRESSWAY
TOPIC: IBRD Project
CONCEPTS: Definition of terms. Annex or appen-
dix reference. Exchange of information and doc-
uments. Inspection and observation. Compensa-
tion. Fees and exemptions. Tax exemptions. Do-
mestic obligation. Terms of loan. Loan
regulations. Loan guarantee. Guarantor non-
interference. Roads and highways.
PARTIES:
Japan
IBRD (World Bank)

106129   Bilateral Agreement   **426 UNTS 33**
SIGNED: 28 Jun 61   FORCE: 21 Dec 61
REGISTERED: 23 Apr 62 IBRD (World Bank)
ARTICLES: 7 LANGUAGE: English.
HEADNOTE: LOAN HIGHWAY MAINTENANCE
TOPIC: IBRD Project
CONCEPTS: Default remedies. Definition of terms.
Annex or appendix reference. Exchange of infor-

mation and documents. Informational records. Inspection and observation. Accounting procedures. Bonds. Fees and exemptions. Interest rates. Aid and development. Terms of loan. Loan regulations. Loan guarantee. Guarantor non-interference. Roads and highways.
PARTIES:
Chile
IBRD (World Bank)

106130 Bilateral Agreement **426 UNTS 49**
SIGNED: 29 Nov 61 FORCE: 29 Mar 62
REGISTERED: 23 Apr 62 IBRD (World Bank)
ARTICLES: 5 LANGUAGE: English.
HEADNOTE: GUARANTEE AGREEMENT
TOPIC: IBRD Project
CONCEPTS: Definition of terms. Annex or appendix reference. Exchange of information and documents. Inspection and observation. Bonds. Fees and exemptions. Tax exemptions. Domestic obligation. Terms of loan. Loan regulations. Loan guarantee. Guarantor non-interference.
PARTIES:
IBRD (World Bank)
UK Great Britain
ANNEX
503 UNTS 340. UK Great Britain. Amendment 2 Apr 64. Force 18 Jul 64.
503 UNTS 340. IBRD (World Bank). Amendment 2 Apr 64. Force 18 Jul 64.
503 UNTS 340. Kenya. Amendment 2 Apr 64. Force 18 Jul 64.

106131 Bilateral Agreement **426 UNTS 89**
SIGNED: 28 Jun 61 FORCE: 19 Oct 61
REGISTERED: 23 Apr 62 IDA (Devel Assoc)
ARTICLES: 6 LANGUAGE: English.
HEADNOTE: IDA CREDIT ROADS
TOPIC: Loans and Credits
CONCEPTS: Definition of terms. Annex or appendix reference. Exchange of information and documents. Interest rates. Payment schedules. Debt settlement. Loan and credit. Credit provisions. Purchase authorization. Loan repayment. Terms of loan. Plans and standards. IDA development project. Roads and highways.
PROCEDURE: Termination.
PARTIES:
Chile
IDA (Devel Assoc)

106132 Bilateral Agreement **426 UNTS 105**
SIGNED: 1 Dec 61 FORCE: 2 Feb 62
REGISTERED: 23 Apr 62 IDA (Devel Assoc)
ARTICLES: 7 LANGUAGE: English.
HEADNOTE: IDA CREDIT DEVELOPMENT CORPORATION
TOPIC: Loans and Credits
CONCEPTS: Definition of terms. Annex or appendix reference. Exchange of information and documents. Currency. Interest rates. Payment schedules. Debt settlement. Loan and credit. Credit provisions. Purchase authorization. Loan repayment. Terms of loan. Plans and standards. IDA development project. Industry.
PROCEDURE: Termination.
PARTIES:
Taiwan
IDA (Devel Assoc)

106133 Bilateral Agreement **426 UNTS 129**
SIGNED: 14 May 59 FORCE: 18 Jul 60
REGISTERED: 24 Apr 62 Pakistan
ARTICLES: 7 LANGUAGE: English.
HEADNOTE: PEACEFUL USES ATOMIC ENERGY
TOPIC: Atomic Energy
CONCEPTS: Definition of terms. Exchange of information and documents. Inspection and observation. Nuclear materials. Peaceful use. Security of information.
INTL ORGS: International Atomic Energy Agency.
TREATY REF: 276UNTS3; 356UNTS378.
PROCEDURE: Duration. Ratification. Termination.
PARTIES:
Canada
Pakistan

106134 Bilateral Agreement **426 UNTS 145**
SIGNED: 22 Dec 60 FORCE: 3 May 61

REGISTERED: 2 May 62 Czechoslovakia
ARTICLES: 12 LANGUAGE: Czechoslovakian. Spanish.
HEADNOTE: CULTURAL COOPERATION
TOPIC: Culture
CONCEPTS: Treaty implementation. Friendship and amity. Exchange of information and documents. Specialists exchange. Recognition of degrees. Exchange. Teacher and student exchange. Scholarships and grants. Exchange. General cultural cooperation. Artists. Athletes. Scientific exchange. Publications exchange. Mass media exchange. Press and wire services.
PROCEDURE: Duration. Ratification. Termination.
PARTIES:
Cuba
Czechoslovakia

106135 Bilateral Exchange **426 UNTS 159**
SIGNED: 27 Sep 61 FORCE: 27 Oct 61
REGISTERED: 3 May 62 Australia
ARTICLES: 2 LANGUAGE: English. Spanish.
HEADNOTE: VISAS VISA FEES
TOPIC: Visas
CONCEPTS: Time limit. Denial of admission. Visas. Conformity with municipal law. Fees and exemptions.
PROCEDURE: Termination.
PARTIES:
Australia
Spain

106136 Bilateral Convention **426 UNTS 165**
SIGNED: 31 Oct 61 FORCE: 6 Mar 62
REGISTERED: 4 May 62 Belgium
ARTICLES: 22 LANGUAGE: French.
HEADNOTE: VETERINARY CONVENTION
TOPIC: Sanitation
CONCEPTS: Definition of terms. Detailed regulations. Exceptions and exemptions. Previous treaty extension. Border traffic and migration. General cooperation. Exchange of information and documents. Inspection and observation. Establishment of commission. Border control. Disease control. Veterinary. Trade procedures. Conferences.
INTL ORGS: International Office of Epizootics. Special Commission.
PROCEDURE: Amendment. Future Procedures Contemplated.
PARTIES:
Belgium
Yugoslavia

106137 Bilateral Exchange **426 UNTS 187**
SIGNED: 3 Oct 61 FORCE: 3 Oct 61
REGISTERED: 7 May 62 USA (United States)
ARTICLES: 2 LANGUAGE: English. German.
HEADNOTE: SURPLUS AGRI COMMOD
TOPIC: Direct Aid
CONCEPTS: Assistance. General cooperation. Accounting procedures. Currency deposits. Expense sharing formulae. Funding procedures. Assistance. Surplus commodities.
INTL ORGS: Office of the United Nations High Commissioner for Refugees.
PARTIES:
Austria
USA (United States)
ANNEX
459 UNTS 314. USA (United States). Amendment 18 May 62. Force 14 Jun 62.
459 UNTS 314. Austria. Amendment 14 Jun 62. Force 14 Jun 62.

106138 Bilateral Exchange **426 UNTS 201**
SIGNED: 17 Oct 61 FORCE: 17 Oct 61
REGISTERED: 7 May 62 USA (United States)
ARTICLES: 2 LANGUAGE: English.
HEADNOTE: DREDGING WOLFE ISLAND CUT
TOPIC: Specific Property
CONCEPTS: Frontier permits. Personnel. Responsibility and liability. Indemnities and reimbursements. Facilities and property. Frontier waterways.
PARTIES:
Canada
USA (United States)

106139 Bilateral Agreement **426 UNTS 209**
SIGNED: 18 Oct 61 FORCE: 18 Oct 61
REGISTERED: 7 May 62 USA (United States)
ARTICLES: 6 LANGUAGE: English.
HEADNOTE: AGRICULTURAL COMMODITIES
TOPIC: US Agri Commod Aid
CONCEPTS: Currency. Agricultural commodities.
PARTIES:
Greece
USA (United States)
ANNEX
435 UNTS 386. Greece. Amendment 13 Feb 62. Force 13 Feb 62.
435 UNTS 386. USA (United States). Amendment 13 Feb 62. Force 13 Feb 62.

106140 Bilateral Agreement **426 UNTS 225**
SIGNED: 6 Nov 61 FORCE: 6 Nov 61
REGISTERED: 7 May 62 USA (United States)
ARTICLES: 6 LANGUAGE: English.
HEADNOTE: AGRI COMMOD TITLE I
TOPIC: US Agri Commod Aid
CONCEPTS: General provisions. Annex or appendix reference. Exchange of information and documents. Reexport of goods, etc.. Exchange rates and regulations. Transportation costs. Local currency. Commodities schedule. Purchase authorization. Surplus commodities. Mutual consultation.
PARTIES:
Iceland
USA (United States)

106141 Bilateral Agreement **426 UNTS 237**
SIGNED: 14 Oct 61 FORCE: 14 Oct 61
REGISTERED: 7 May 62 USA (United States)
ARTICLES: 6 LANGUAGE: English.
HEADNOTE: AGRI COMMOD
TOPIC: US Agri Commod Aid
CONCEPTS: Currency. Agricultural commodities.
INTL ORGS: International Bank for Reconstruction and Development.
PARTIES:
Pakistan
USA (United States)
ANNEX
460 UNTS 326. Pakistan. Amendment 3 Dec 62. Force 3 Dec 62.
460 UNTS 326. USA (United States). Amendment 3 Dec 62. Force 3 Dec 62.
488 UNTS 304. Pakistan. Amendment 31 May 63. Force 31 May 63.
488 UNTS 304. USA (United States). Amendment 31 May 63. Force 31 May 63.
511 UNTS 304. Pakistan. Amendment 10 Feb 64. Force 10 Feb 64.
511 UNTS 304. USA (United States). Amendment 10 Feb 64. Force 10 Feb 64.
531 UNTS 374. Pakistan. Amendment 28 Nov 64. Force 28 Nov 64.
531 UNTS 374. USA (United States). Amendment 28 Nov 64. Force 28 Nov 64.

106142 Bilateral Agreement **426 UNTS 255**
SIGNED: 22 Nov 61 FORCE: 15 Mar 62
REGISTERED: 8 May 62 IBRD (World Bank)
ARTICLES: 6 LANGUAGE: English.
HEADNOTE: GUARANTEE LOAN
TOPIC: IBRD Project
CONCEPTS: Loan guarantee.
PARTIES:
Ethiopia
IBRD (World Bank)

106143 Bilateral Agreement **426 UNTS 287**
SIGNED: 16 Aug 61 FORCE: 19 Dec 61
REGISTERED: 8 May 62 IBRD (World Bank)
ARTICLES: 5 LANGUAGE: English.
HEADNOTE: GUARANTEE ELECTRICITY
TOPIC: IBRD Project
CONCEPTS: Definition of terms. Annex or appendix reference. Exchange of information and documents. Inspection and observation. Bonds. Fees and exemptions. Tax exemptions. Domestic obligation. Terms of loan. Loan regulations. Loan guarantee. Guarantor non-interference. Hydro-electric power.
PARTIES:
IBRD (World Bank)
UK Great Britain

106144 Bilateral Agreement **427 UNTS 3**
SIGNED: 22 Nov 61   FORCE: 3 Feb 62
REGISTERED: 8 May 62 IDA (Devel Assoc)
ARTICLES: 7 LANGUAGE: English.
HEADNOTE: FLOOD CONTROL PROJECT
TOPIC: Loans and Credits
CONCEPTS: Definition of terms. Annex or appen-
dix reference. Exchange of information and doc-
uments. Currency. Interest rates. Payment
schedules. Debt settlement. Loan and credit.
Credit provisions. Purchase authorization. Loan
repayment. Terms of loan. Plans and standards.
IDA development project. Irrigation.
PROCEDURE: Termination.
PARTIES:
India
IDA (Devel Assoc)

106145 Bilateral Agreement **427 UNTS 29**
SIGNED: 22 Nov 61   FORCE: 31 Jan 62
REGISTERED: 8 May 62 IDA (Devel Assoc)
ARTICLES: 7 LANGUAGE: English.
HEADNOTE: IDA CREDIT IRRIGATION
TOPIC: Loans and Credits
CONCEPTS: Definition of terms. Annex or appen-
dix reference. Exchange of information and doc-
uments. Currency. Interest rates. Payment
schedules. Debt settlement. Loan and credit.
Credit provisions. Purchase authorization. Loan
repayment. Terms of loan. Plans and standards.
IDA development project. Irrigation.
PROCEDURE: Termination.
PARTIES:
India
IDA (Devel Assoc)

106146 Bilateral Agreement **427 UNTS 55**
SIGNED: 22 Nov 61   FORCE: 31 Jan 62
REGISTERED: 8 May 62 IDA (Devel Assoc)
ARTICLES: 7 LANGUAGE: English.
HEADNOTE: IDA CREDIT IRRIGATION
TOPIC: Loans and Credits
CONCEPTS: Definition of terms. Annex or appen-
dix reference. Exchange of information and doc-
uments. Currency. Interest rates. Payment
schedules. Debt settlement. Loan and credit.
Credit provisions. Purchase authorization. Loan
repayment. Terms of loan. Plans and standards.
IDA development project. Irrigation.
PROCEDURE: Termination.
PARTIES:
India
IDA (Devel Assoc)

106147 Multilateral Agreement **427 UNTS 81**
SIGNED: 21 Dec 56   FORCE: 21 Dec 56
REGISTERED: 8 May 62 Sweden
ARTICLES: 14 LANGUAGE: Swedish.
HEADNOTE: MEDICAL CENTER TREATMENT
TRAINING KOREA
TOPIC: Humanitarian
CONCEPTS: Definition of terms. Exchange of infor-
mation and documents. Operating agencies. Per-
sonnel. Establishment of commission. Public
health. Humanitarian matters. Accounting proce-
dures. Indemnities and reimbursements.
INTL ORGS: Scandinavian Korea Mediation.
United Nations Commission for Korean Recon-
struction.
TREATY REF: 427UNTS245.
PARTIES:
Denmark SIGNED: 21 Dec 56 FORCE: 21 Dec 56
Norway SIGNED: 21 Dec 56 FORCE: 21 Dec 56
Sweden SIGNED: 21 Dec 56 FORCE: 21 Dec 56

106148 Multilateral Agreement **427 UNTS 93**
SIGNED: 19 Dec 56   FORCE: 1 Jan 57
REGISTERED: 8 May 62 Sweden
ARTICLES: 16 LANGUAGE: Swedish. Danish. Ice-
landic. Norwegian.
HEADNOTE: TRANSFERS BETWEEN SICK FUNDS
TOPIC: Non-ILO Labor
CONCEPTS: Detailed regulations. Previous treaty
replacement. Domestic legislation. Incorpora-
tion of treaty provisions into national law. Dis-
pute settlement. Public health. ILO conventions.
Non-ILO labor relations. Sickness and invalidity
insurance. Monetary and gold transfers. Pay-
ment schedules.
TREATY REF: 227UNTS217.

PROCEDURE: Denunciation.
PARTIES:
Denmark SIGNED: 19 Dec 56 FORCE: 1 Jan 57
Iceland SIGNED: 19 Dec 56 FORCE: 1 Jan 57
Norway SIGNED: 19 Dec 56 FORCE: 1 Jan 57
Sweden SIGNED: 19 Dec 56 FORCE: 1 Jan 57
ANNEX
603 UNTS 336. Sweden. Force 1 Apr 67.
603 UNTS 336. Denmark. Force 1 Apr 67.
603 UNTS 336. Iceland. Force 1 Apr 67.
603 UNTS 336. Norway. Force 1 Apr 67.

106149 Bilateral Exchange **427 UNTS 127**
SIGNED: 10 May 57   FORCE: 1 Jun 57
REGISTERED: 8 May 62 Sweden
ARTICLES: 2 LANGUAGE: French.
HEADNOTE: RECOGNITION DRIVING PERMITS
TOPIC: Admin Cooperation
CONCEPTS: Licenses and permits. Driving per-
mits.
PARTIES:
France
Sweden

106150 Bilateral Convention **427 UNTS 133**
SIGNED: 5 Mar 55   FORCE: 13 Aug 57
REGISTERED: 8 May 62 Sweden
ARTICLES: 46 LANGUAGE: French.
HEADNOTE: CONSULAR
TOPIC: Consul/Citizenship
CONCEPTS: Definition of terms. Territorial applica-
tion. Previous treaty replacement. General con-
sular functions. Diplomatic privileges. Consular
relations establishment. Inviolability. Privileges
and immunities. Diplomatic correspondence.
Consular functions in shipping. Consular func-
tions in property. Responsibility and liability. Pro-
cedure. Existing tribunals.
INTL ORGS: International Court of Justice.
TREATY REF: 95LTS89; 2'9DEMARTENS193;
2'12DEMARTENS695;.
PROCEDURE: Ratification. Termination.
PARTIES:
France
Sweden

106151 Bilateral Exchange **427 UNTS 167**
SIGNED: 14 Apr 58   FORCE: 1 May 58
REGISTERED: 8 May 62 Sweden
ARTICLES: 2 LANGUAGE: French.
HEADNOTE: RECOGNITION DRIVING PERMITS
TOPIC: Admin Cooperation
CONCEPTS: Licenses and permits. Driving per-
mits.
PARTIES:
Italy
Sweden

106152 Bilateral Exchange **427 UNTS 173**
SIGNED: 6 Apr 57   FORCE: 1 Jun 57
REGISTERED: 8 May 62 Sweden
ARTICLES: 2 LANGUAGE: French.
HEADNOTE: RECOGNITION DRIVING PERMITS
TOPIC: Admin Cooperation
CONCEPTS: Licenses and permits. Driving per-
mits.
PARTIES:
Luxembourg
Sweden

106153 Bilateral Exchange **427 UNTS 179**
SIGNED: 12 Mar 58   FORCE: 1 May 58
REGISTERED: 8 May 62 Sweden
ARTICLES: 2 LANGUAGE: French.
HEADNOTE: RECOGNITION DRIVING PERMITS
TOPIC: Admin Cooperation
CONCEPTS: Licenses and permits. Driving per-
mits.
PARTIES:
Luxembourg
Sweden

106154 Bilateral Agreement **427 UNTS 185**
SIGNED: 30 Mar 61   FORCE: 3 Nov 61
REGISTERED: 8 May 62 Sweden
ARTICLES: 22 LANGUAGE: French.
HEADNOTE: DOUBLE TAXATION DIRECT TAXES
TOPIC: Taxation

CONCEPTS: Definition of terms. Nationality and
citizenship. General cooperation. Exchange of
official publications. Claims and settlements.
Taxation. Air transport. Merchant vessels.
PROCEDURE: Denunciation. Duration. Ratification.
PARTIES:
Morocco
Sweden

106155 Bilateral Agreement **427 UNTS 211**
SIGNED: 19 Feb 58   FORCE: 19 Feb 58
REGISTERED: 8 May 62 Sweden
ARTICLES: 2 LANGUAGE: Swedish. German.
HEADNOTE: MOTOR SERVICES
TOPIC: Land Transport
CONCEPTS: Conformity with municipal law. Ex-
change of information and documents. Licenses
and permits. Operating authorizations and regu-
lations. Land transport.
PROCEDURE: Denunciation. Duration. Ratification.
Renewal or Revival.
PARTIES:
Austria
Sweden

106156 Bilateral Exchange **427 UNTS 221**
SIGNED: 9 Jun 58   FORCE: 1 Jul 58
REGISTERED: 8 May 62 Sweden
ARTICLES: 2 LANGUAGE: Swedish. Norwegian.
HEADNOTE: COASTING TRADE
TOPIC: Water Transport
CONCEPTS: Inland and territorial waters.
INTL ORGS: Nordic Council.
PARTIES:
Norway
Sweden

106157 Bilateral Agreement **427 UNTS 225**
SIGNED: 28 Oct 59   FORCE: 1 Jan 60
REGISTERED: 8 May 62 Sweden
ARTICLES: 11 LANGUAGE: Swedish. Norwegian.
HEADNOTE: FRONTIER CUSTOMS COOPERATION
TOPIC: Visas
CONCEPTS: Change of circumstances. Provisional
detainment. General cooperation. Responsibility
and liability. Export quotas. Import quotas. Com-
pensation. Customs duties. Markers and defini-
tions.
PROCEDURE: Ratification.
PARTIES:
Norway
Sweden

106158 Multilateral Agreement **427 UNTS 245**
SIGNED: 13 Mar 56   FORCE: 13 Mar 56
REGISTERED: 8 May 62 Sweden
ARTICLES: 13 LANGUAGE: English. Korean.
HEADNOTE: MEDICAL CENTER KOREA
TOPIC: Humanitarian
CONCEPTS: Definition of terms. Treaty interpreta-
tion. Annex or appendix reference. Friendship
and amity. Resident permits. Personnel. General
property. Use of facilities. Establishment of com-
mission. Public health. Nursing. Vocational train-
ing. Expense sharing formulae. Domestic obliga-
tion. Materials, equipment and services.
INTL ORGS: United Nations.
TREATY REF: UN-ORGA 5TH SESS. SUPP.20 (A-
1775)P.31.
PROCEDURE: Duration. Termination.
PARTIES:
Denmark SIGNED: 13 Mar 56 FORCE: 13 Mar 56
Korea, South SIGNED: 13 Mar 56 FORCE:
13 Mar 56
Norway SIGNED: 13 Mar 56 FORCE: 13 Mar 56
UNKRA (Korean Rec) SIGNED: 13 Mar 56
FORCE: 13 Mar 56
Sweden SIGNED: 13 Mar 56 FORCE: 13 Mar 56
ANNEX
503 UNTS 354. Denmark. Supplementation
19 Jun 64. Force 19 Jun 64.
503 UNTS 354. Korea, South. Supplementation
19 Jun 64. Force 19 Jun 64.
503 UNTS 354. Norway. Supplementation
19 Jun 64. Force 19 Jun 64.
503 UNTS 354. Sweden. Supplementation
19 Jun 64. Force 19 Jun 64.
503 UNTS 354. UNKRA (Korean Rec). Supplementation 19 Jun 64. Force 19 Jun 64.

106159 Bilateral Exchange **427 UNTS 277**
SIGNED: 21 Aug 57 FORCE: 6 Nov 57
REGISTERED: 8 May 62 Sweden
ARTICLES: 2 LANGUAGE: French.
HEADNOTE: RECOGNITION TONNAGE CERTIFI-
CATES
TOPIC: Admin Cooperation
CONCEPTS: General cooperation.
PARTIES:
 Poland
 Sweden

106160 Bilateral Exchange **427 UNTS 285**
SIGNED: 21 Jul 58 FORCE: 21 Jul 58
REGISTERED: 8 May 62 Sweden
ARTICLES: 3 LANGUAGE: French.
HEADNOTE: RECIPROCAL EXEMPTION AIR
TRANSPORT COMPANIES CERTAIN TAXES
TOPIC: Mostfavored Nation
CONCEPTS: Definition of terms. Reciprocity in fi-
nancial treatment. Tax exemptions. Air trans-
port.
PROCEDURE: Termination.
PARTIES:
 Sweden
 United Arab Rep

106161 Bilateral Exchange **427 UNTS 295**
SIGNED: 30 Apr 58 FORCE: 1 Jun 58
REGISTERED: 8 May 62 Sweden
ARTICLES: 2 LANGUAGE: French.
HEADNOTE: AGREEMENT CONCERNING RECIP-
ROCAL RECOGNITION DRIVING PERMITS
TOPIC: Land Transport
CONCEPTS: Recognition of legal documents. Driv-
ing permits. Motor vehicles and combinations.
PROCEDURE: Termination.
PARTIES:
 Sweden
 Switzerland

106162 Bilateral Agreement **427 UNTS 301**
SIGNED: 6 Sep 60 FORCE: 1 Jan 62
REGISTERED: 8 May 62 Sweden
ARTICLES: 23 LANGUAGE: French.
HEADNOTE: DOUBLE TAXATION ADMINISTRA-
TIVE ASSISTANCE DIRECT TAXES
TOPIC: Taxation
CONCEPTS: Definition of terms. Nationality and
citizenship. General cooperation. Exchange of
official publications. Negotiation. Claims and
settlements. Taxation. Air transport. Merchant
vessels.
PROCEDURE: Denunciation. Duration. Ratification.
PARTIES:
 Sweden
 Tunisia

106163 Bilateral Agreement **427 UNTS 327**
SIGNED: 16 Jan 59 FORCE: 16 Jan 59
REGISTERED: 8 May 62 Sweden
ARTICLES: 4 LANGUAGE: Swedish. Spanish.
HEADNOTE: MILITARY SERVICE
TOPIC: Milit Servic/Citiz
CONCEPTS: Dual nationality. Certificates of ser-
vice. Service in foreign army.
PROCEDURE: Termination.
PARTIES:
 Argentina
 Sweden

106164 Bilateral Exchange **427 UNTS 337**
SIGNED: 12 Jun 59 FORCE: 1 Aug 58
REGISTERED: 8 May 62 Sweden
ARTICLES: 2 LANGUAGE: Spanish.
HEADNOTE: FILM AGREEMENT
TOPIC: Culture
CONCEPTS: Exceptions and exemptions. Export
quotas. Trade procedures. General. Mass media
exchange.
PROCEDURE: Denunciation. Duration. Renewal or
Revival.
PARTIES:
 Argentina
 Sweden

106165 Bilateral Exchange **427 UNTS 343**
SIGNED: 10 Apr 57 FORCE: 1 Jun 57

REGISTERED: 8 May 62 Sweden
ARTICLES: 2 LANGUAGE: German.
HEADNOTE: RECOGNITION DRIVERS LICENSES
TOPIC: Admin Cooperation
CONCEPTS: Licenses and permits. Driving per-
mits.
PARTIES:
 Austria
 Sweden

106166 Bilateral Agreement **427 UNTS 349**
SIGNED: 18 Feb 58 FORCE: 18 Feb 58
REGISTERED: 8 May 62 Sweden
ARTICLES: 6 LANGUAGE: Swedish. German.
HEADNOTE: COMMERCIAL ROAD TRAFFIC
TOPIC: Land Transport
CONCEPTS: Definition of terms. Exceptions and
exemptions. General cooperation. Negotiation.
Passenger transport. Transport of goods. Roads
and highways.
INTL ORGS: United Nations Economic Commis-
sion for Europe.
PROCEDURE: Denunciation. Duration. Renewal or
Revival.
PARTIES:
 Austria
 Sweden

106167 Bilateral Agreement **428 UNTS 3**
SIGNED: 14 May 59 FORCE: 29 Dec 59
REGISTERED: 8 May 62 Sweden
ARTICLES: 27 LANGUAGE: Swedish. German.
HEADNOTE: DOUBLE TAXATION INCOME FOR-
TUNE
TOPIC: Taxation
CONCEPTS: Definition of terms. Privileges and im-
munities. Nationality and citizenship. Conformity
with municipal law. Exchange of official publica-
tions. Negotiation. Teacher and student ex-
change. Claims and settlements. Taxation. Gen-
eral. Tax exemptions. Air transport. Merchant
vessels.
PROCEDURE: Duration. Ratification. Termination.
PARTIES:
 Austria
 Sweden

106168 Bilateral Agreement **428 UNTS 65**
SIGNED: 22 May 58 FORCE: 22 May 58
REGISTERED: 8 May 62 Sweden
ARTICLES: 11 LANGUAGE: English.
HEADNOTE: TECHNICAL COOPERATION FIELD
FAMILY PLANNING
TOPIC: Tech Assistance
CONCEPTS: Time limit. General cooperation. Per-
sonnel. Assets transfer. Tax exemptions. Cus-
toms exemptions. Domestic obligation. Assis-
tance. Materials, equipment and services.
PROCEDURE: Amendment. Duration. Renewal or
Revival. Termination.
PARTIES:
 Ceylon (Sri Lanka)
 Sweden

106169 Multilateral Agreement **428 UNTS 73**
SIGNED: 5 Nov 58 FORCE: 3 Feb 59
REGISTERED: 8 May 62 Sweden
ARTICLES: 13 LANGUAGE: Swedish. Danish. Fin-
nish. Norwegian.
HEADNOTE: CARRIAGE PERSONS GOODS ROAD
TOPIC: Land Transport
CONCEPTS: Default remedies. Definition of terms.
Exceptions and exemptions. General provisions.
Previous treaty replacement. Conformity with
municipal law. Exchange of information and doc-
uments. Passenger transport. Routes and logis-
tics. Transport of goods. Commercial road vehi-
cles. Driving permits. Motor vehicles and combi-
nations. Roads and highways. Road rules.
Boundaries of territory.
TREATY REF: 211UNTS3.
PROCEDURE: Termination.
PARTIES:
 Denmark SIGNED: 5 Nov 58 FORCE: 3 Feb 59
 Finland SIGNED: 5 Nov 58 FORCE: 3 Feb 59
 Norway SIGNED: 5 Nov 58 FORCE: 3 Feb 59
 Sweden SIGNED: 5 Nov 58 FORCE: 3 Feb 59

106170 Bilateral Exchange **428 UNTS 119**
SIGNED: 22 Sep 58 FORCE: 22 Sep 58
REGISTERED: 8 May 62 Sweden
ARTICLES: 2 LANGUAGE: Swedish.
HEADNOTE: FERRY SERVICES RIVER TORNE
TOPIC: Water Transport
CONCEPTS: Expense sharing formulae. Naviga-
tional equipment. Water transport. Inland and
territorial waters. Roads and highways.
PARTIES:
 Finland
 Sweden

106171 Bilateral Exchange **428 UNTS 125**
SIGNED: 16 Oct 58 FORCE: 9 Jan 59
REGISTERED: 8 May 62 Sweden
ARTICLES: 2 LANGUAGE: Swedish.
HEADNOTE: WRITING INTEREST CULTURAL RE-
LATIONS
TOPIC: Culture
CONCEPTS: Detailed regulations. Personnel. Es-
tablishment of commission. General cultural co-
operation. Accounting procedures. Attachment
of funds. Expense sharing formulae. Financial
programs. Funding procedures. Claims and set-
tlements.
PROCEDURE: Amendment. Future Procedures
Contemplated. Ratification.
PARTIES:
 Finland
 Sweden

106172 Bilateral Agreement **428 UNTS 131**
SIGNED: 13 Apr 60 FORCE: 13 Apr 60
REGISTERED: 8 May 62 Sweden
ARTICLES: 14 LANGUAGE: Swedish. Finnish.
HEADNOTE: CULTURAL FUND
TOPIC: Culture
CONCEPTS: General cultural cooperation.
INTL ORGS: Special Commission.
PARTIES:
 Finland
 Sweden

106173 Bilateral Exchange **428 UNTS 145**
SIGNED: 18 Feb 61 FORCE: 18 Feb 61
REGISTERED: 8 May 62 Sweden
ARTICLES: 2 LANGUAGE: Swedish.
HEADNOTE: SWEDISH-FINNISH BORDER
TOPIC: Visas
CONCEPTS: General cooperation.
PARTIES:
 Finland
 Sweden

106174 Bilateral Exchange **428 UNTS 149**
SIGNED: 13 Feb 57 FORCE: 1 Mar 57
REGISTERED: 8 May 62 Sweden
ARTICLES: 2 LANGUAGE: German.
HEADNOTE: RECOGNITION DRIVING PERMITS
TOPIC: Admin Cooperation
CONCEPTS: Licenses and permits. Driving per-
mits.
PARTIES:
 Germany, West
 Sweden

106175 Bilateral Agreement **428 UNTS 155**
SIGNED: 17 Apr 59 FORCE: 17 Sep 60
REGISTERED: 8 May 62 Sweden
ARTICLES: 29 LANGUAGE: Swedish. German.
HEADNOTE: DOUBLE TAXATION INCOME FOR-
TUNE
TOPIC: Taxation
CONCEPTS: Definition of terms. Privileges and im-
munities. Exchange of official publications. Ne-
gotiation. Teacher and student exchange.
Claims and settlements. Taxation. Death duties.
Equitable taxes. General. Tax exemptions. Air
transport. Merchant vessels.
PROCEDURE: Duration. Ratification. Termination.
PARTIES:
 Germany, West
 Sweden

106176 Bilateral Exchange **428 UNTS 221**
SIGNED: 5 Dec 57 FORCE: 1 Jan 58
REGISTERED: 8 May 62 Sweden

ARTICLES: 2 LANGUAGE: English.
HEADNOTE: EXCHANGE STUDENT EMPLOYEES
TOPIC: Non-ILO Labor
CONCEPTS: Resident permits. Exchange of information and documents. Vocational training. Employment regulations. Wages and salaries. Non-ILO labor relations. Administrative cooperation. Migrant worker. Quotas.
PROCEDURE: Denunciation. Duration. Renewal or Revival.
PARTIES:
Ireland
Sweden

106177   Bilateral Agreement   **428 UNTS 231**
SIGNED: 6 Nov 59   FORCE: 19 Nov 60
REGISTERED: 8 May 62 Sweden
ARTICLES: 29 LANGUAGE: English.
HEADNOTE: AVOIDANCE DOUBLE TAXATION INCOME CAPITAL
TOPIC: Taxation
CONCEPTS: Taxation. Equitable taxes. General. Tax exemptions.
PROCEDURE: Ratification.
PARTIES:
Ireland
Sweden

106178   Bilateral Exchange   **428 UNTS 263**
SIGNED: 16 Sep 57   FORCE: 16 Sep 57
REGISTERED: 8 May 62 Sweden
ARTICLES: 2 LANGUAGE: Swedish. Norwegian.
HEADNOTE: CLEARANCE BORDER ROAD
TOPIC: Territory Boundary
CONCEPTS: Markers and definitions.
PARTIES:
Norway
Sweden

106179   Bilateral Exchange   **428 UNTS 267**
SIGNED: 8 Apr 57   FORCE: 8 Apr 57
REGISTERED: 8 May 62 Sweden
ARTICLES: 2 LANGUAGE: Chinese. English.
HEADNOTE: TRADEMARKS
TOPIC: Patents/Copyrights
CONCEPTS: Conformity with municipal law. Trademarks.
PARTIES:
China People's Rep
Sweden

106180   Bilateral Agreement   **428 UNTS 275**
SIGNED: 20 Oct 61   FORCE: 18 Jan 62
REGISTERED: 8 May 62 Sweden
ARTICLES: 22 LANGUAGE: English.
HEADNOTE: DOUBLE TAXATION INCOME CAPITAL
TOPIC: Taxation
CONCEPTS: Definition of terms. Conformity with municipal law. Exchange of official publications. Teacher and student exchange. Claims and settlements. Taxation. Equitable taxes. Tax exemptions. Air transport.
PROCEDURE: Duration. Ratification. Termination.
PARTIES:
Sweden
Thailand

106181   Bilateral Exchange   **428 UNTS 301**
SIGNED: 18 Jan 56   FORCE: 18 Jan 56
REGISTERED: 8 May 62 Sweden
ARTICLES: 2 LANGUAGE: English.
HEADNOTE: REPLACING 3 AUG 1882 AGREEMENT
TOPIC: Admin Cooperation
CONCEPTS: Annex type material. Previous treaty replacement.
PARTIES:
Sweden
UK Great Britain

106182   Bilateral Agreement   **428 UNTS 307**
SIGNED: 8 Oct 56   FORCE: 8 Oct 56
REGISTERED: 8 May 62 Sweden
ARTICLES: 11 LANGUAGE: English.
HEADNOTE: ADMITTANCE INTO SWEDEN REFUGEES FROM CHINA
TOPIC: Refugees

CONCEPTS: Assistance. Procedure. Public health. Vocational training. Funding procedures.
INTL ORGS: United Nations Refugee Fund. United Nations. Arbitration Commission.
PROCEDURE: Termination.
PARTIES:
UN Hi Com Refugees
Sweden

106183   Bilateral Exchange   **428 UNTS 315**
SIGNED: 28 Jan 57   FORCE: 23 Jan 57
REGISTERED: 8 May 62 Sweden
ARTICLES: 2 LANGUAGE: Swedish. Russian.
HEADNOTE: TRANSFER INCOME DERIVED AIR TRANSPORT
TOPIC: Finance
CONCEPTS: General cooperation. Accounting procedures. Banking. Financial programs. Air transport.
TREATY REF: 259UNTS239.
PARTIES:
Sweden
USSR (Soviet Union)

106184   Bilateral Agreement   **428 UNTS 321**
SIGNED: 28 Mar 58   FORCE: 11 Jun 58
REGISTERED: 8 May 62 Sweden
ARTICLES: 15 LANGUAGE: Swedish. Russian.
HEADNOTE: CONSTRUCTION EMBASSY BUILDINGS
TOPIC: Privil/Immunities
CONCEPTS: General cooperation. Inspection and observation. Personnel. Procedure. Import quotas. Accounting procedures. Indemnities and reimbursements.
PROCEDURE: Ratification.
PARTIES:
Sweden
USSR (Soviet Union)

106185   Bilateral Exchange   **428 UNTS 351**
SIGNED: 13 Mar 57   FORCE: 13 Mar 57
REGISTERED: 8 May 62 Sweden
ARTICLES: 2 LANGUAGE: Spanish.
HEADNOTE: RECOGNITION TONNAGE CERTIFICATES
TOPIC: Admin Cooperation
CONCEPTS: General cooperation. Tonnage.
PARTIES:
Sweden
Venezuela

106186   Bilateral Exchange   **428 UNTS 357**
SIGNED: 31 May 58   FORCE: 1 Jul 58
REGISTERED: 8 May 62 Sweden
ARTICLES: 2 LANGUAGE: English.
HEADNOTE: RECOGNITION TONNAGE CERTIFICATES
TOPIC: Admin Cooperation
CONCEPTS: General cooperation.
PARTIES:
Sweden
Yugoslavia

106187   Bilateral Convention   **428 UNTS 363**
SIGNED: 12 Jun 59   FORCE: 1 Feb 62
REGISTERED: 9 May 62 Norway
ARTICLES: 29 LANGUAGE: Norwegian. Italian.
HEADNOTE: SOCIAL SECURITY
TOPIC: Non-ILO Labor
CONCEPTS: Definition of terms. Exceptions and exemptions. Conformity with municipal law. Domestic legislation. Wages and salaries. Non-ILO labor relations. Family allowances. Administrative cooperation. Old age insurance. Sickness and invalidity insurance. Social security. Unemployment. Payment schedules. Claims and settlements.
INTL ORGS: Arbitration Commission.
PROCEDURE: Denunciation. Duration. Ratification. Renewal or Revival.
PARTIES:
Italy
Norway

106188   Bilateral Agreement   **429 UNTS 3**
SIGNED: 11 Jul 61   FORCE: 9 Nov 61
REGISTERED: 9 May 62 IBRD (World Bank)

ARTICLES: 5 LANGUAGE: English.
HEADNOTE: GUARANTEE AGREEMENT
TOPIC: IBRD Project
CONCEPTS: Definition of terms. Annex or appendix reference. Exchange of information and documents. Inspection and observation. Bonds. Fees and exemptions. Tax exemptions. Domestic obligation. Terms of loan. Loan regulations. Loan guarantee. Guarantor non-interference.
PARTIES:
Israel
IBRD (World Bank)

106189   Multilateral Agreement   **429 UNTS 46**
SIGNED: 17 May 62   FORCE: 17 May 62
REGISTERED: 17 May 62 United Nations
ARTICLES: 6 LANGUAGE: French.
HEADNOTE: TECHNICAL ASSISTANCE
TOPIC: Tech Assistance
CONCEPTS: Definition of terms. Privileges and immunities. General cooperation. Exchange of information and documents. Personnel. Responsibility and liability. Title and deeds. Use of facilities. Exchange. Scholarships and grants. Vocational training. Research and development. Exchange rates and regulations. Expense sharing formulae. Local currency. Domestic obligation. General technical assistance. Materials, equipment and services. IGO status. Conformity with IGO decisions.
INTL ORGS: United Nations Technical Assistance Board.
TREATY   REF: 76UNTS132;   1UNTS15;
33UNTS261; 374UNTS147.
PROCEDURE: Amendment. Termination.
PARTIES:
Madagascar   SIGNED: 17 May 62   FORCE:
17 May 62
FAO (Food Agri) SIGNED: 17 May 62 FORCE:
17 May 62
IAEA (Atom Energy) SIGNED: 17 May 62 FORCE:
17 May 62
ICAO (Civil Aviat) SIGNED: 17 May 62 FORCE:
17 May 62
ILO (Labor Org) SIGNED: 17 May 62 FORCE:
17 May 62
ITU (Telecommun) SIGNED: 17 May 62 FORCE:
17 May 62
UNESCO   (Educ/Cult)   SIGNED: 17 May 62
FORCE: 17 May 62
United Nations SIGNED: 17 May 62 FORCE:
17 May 62
WHO (World Health) SIGNED: 17 May 62
FORCE: 17 May 62
WMO   (Meteorology)   SIGNED: 17 May 62
FORCE: 17 May 62

106190   Bilateral Agreement   **429 UNTS 61**
SIGNED: 18 May 62   FORCE: 18 May 62
REGISTERED: 18 May 62 United Nations
ARTICLES: 6 LANGUAGE: English.
HEADNOTE: OPERATIONAL EXECUTIVE ADMINISTRATIVE PERSONNEL
TOPIC: Tech Assistance
CONCEPTS: Annex or appendix reference. Exchange of information and documents. Private contracts. Use of facilities. Arbitration. Procedure. Negotiation. Indemnities and reimbursements. Financial programs. Assistance. IGO constitution. Status of experts.
INTL ORGS: Permanent Court of Arbitration. Arbitration Commission.
PROCEDURE: Amendment. Termination.
PARTIES:
Greece
United Nations

106191   Bilateral Agreement   **429 UNTS 73**
SIGNED: 3 May 62   FORCE: 3 May 62
REGISTERED: 22 May 62 ILO (Labor Org)
ARTICLES: 6 LANGUAGE: English.
HEADNOTE: ESTABLISH EAST AFRICAN FIELD OFFICE
TOPIC: IGO Operations
CONCEPTS: Privileges and immunities. IGO constitution. Regional offices.
INTL ORGS: United Nations. United Nations Special Fund.
TREATY REF: 15UNTS40.

PARTIES:
ILO (Labor Org)
Tanganyika

106192 Multilateral Agreement **429 UNTS 78**
SIGNED: 10 Apr 62   FORCE: 10 Apr 62
REGISTERED: 24 May 62 United Nations
ARTICLES: 6 LANGUAGE: French.
HEADNOTE: TECHNICAL ASSISTANCE
TOPIC: Tech Assistance
CONCEPTS: Definition of terms. Privileges and immunities. General cooperation. Exchange of information and documents. Personnel. Responsibility and liability. Title and deeds. Use of facilities. Exchange. Scholarships and grants. Vocational training. Research and development. Exchange rates and regulations. Expense sharing formulae. Local currency. Domestic obligation. General technical assistance. Materials, equipment and services. IGO status. Conformity with IGO decisions.
INTL ORGS: United Nations Technical Assistance Board.
TREATY   REF: 76UNTS132;   11NTS15;
33UNTS261; 374UNTS147.
PROCEDURE: Amendment. Termination.
PARTIES:
Ivory Coast SIGNED: 10 Apr 62 FORCE:
10 Apr 62
FAO (Food Agri) SIGNED: 10 Apr 62 FORCE:
10 Apr 62
IAEA (Atom Energy) SIGNED: 10 Apr 62 FORCE:
10 Apr 62
ICAO (Civil Aviat) SIGNED: 10 Apr 62 FORCE:
10 Apr 62
ILO (Labor Org) SIGNED: 10 Apr 62 FORCE:
10 Apr 62
ITU (Telecommun) SIGNED: 10 Apr 62 FORCE:
10 Apr 62
UNESCO (Educ/Cult) SIGNED: 10 Apr 62 FORCE:
10 Apr 62
United Nations SIGNED: 10 Apr 62 FORCE:
10 Apr 62
WHO (World Health) SIGNED: 10 Apr 62 FORCE:
10 Apr 62
WMO (Meteorology) SIGNED: 10 Apr 62 FORCE:
10 Apr 62
ANNEX
604 UNTS 376. IMCO (Maritime Org). Accession
11 Sep 67. Force 11 Sep 67.
604 UNTS 376. UPU (Postal Union). Accession
11 Sep 67. Force 11 Sep 67.
649 UNTS 352. UNIDO (Industrial). Accession
18 Oct 68. Force 18 Oct 68.

106193 Multilateral Convention **429 UNTS 93**
SIGNED: 14 Dec 60   FORCE: 22 May 62
REGISTERED: 29 May 62 UNESCO (Educ/Cult)
ARTICLES: 19 LANGUAGE: English. French. Russian. Spanish.
HEADNOTE: DISCRIMINATION EDUCATION
TOPIC: Education
CONCEPTS: Definition of terms. Detailed regulations. Exceptions and exemptions. Territorial application. Friendship and amity. Human rights. Standardization. Conformity with municipal law. General cooperation. Exchange of information and documents. Dispute settlement. Education.
INTL ORGS: International Court of Justice. United Nations.
PROCEDURE: Amendment.
PARTIES:
Central Afri Rep RATIFIED: 22 Feb 62 FORCE:
22 May 62
France RATIFIED: 11 Sep 61 FORCE: 22 May 62
Israel RATIFIED: 22 Sep 61 FORCE: 22 May 62
Liberia RATIFIED: 17 May 62 FORCE: 17 Aug 62
United Arab Rep RATIFIED: 28 Mar 62 FORCE:
28 Jun 62
UK Great Britain RATIFIED: 14 May 62 FORCE:
14 Jun 62
ANNEX
435 UNTS 390. USSR (Soviet Union). Ratification
1 Aug 62. Force 1 Nov 62.
443 UNTS 356. Cuba. Ratification 2 Nov 62.
Force 2 Feb 63.
449 UNTS 384.   Byelorussia.   Ratification
12 Dec 62. Force 12 Mar 63.
449 UNTS 384. Bulgaria. Acceptance 4 Dec 62.
Force 4 Mar 63.
452 UNTS 346. Kuwait. Acceptance 15 Jan 63.
Force 15 Apr 63.
452 UNTS 346. Norway. Ratification 8 Jan 63.
Force 8 Apr 63.

452 UNTS 346.   Ukrainian   SSR.   Ratification
19 Dec 62. Force 19 Mar 63.
453 UNTS 447.   New   Zealand.   Ratification
12 Feb 63. Force 12 May 63.
456 UNTS 513.   Czechoslovakia.   Ratification
14 Mar 63. Force 14 Jun 63.
471 UNTS 337. Dahomey. Acceptance 9 Jul 63.
Force 9 Oct 63.
478 UNTS 438.   Costa   Rica.   Ratification
10 Sep 63. Force 10 Dec 63.
480 UNTS 437. Denmark. Ratification 4 Oct 63.
Force 4 Jan 64.
480 UNTS 437. Argentina. Ratification 30 Oct 63.
Force 30 Jan 64.
482 UNTS 392. Albania. Ratification 21 Nov 63.
Force 21 Feb 64.
486 UNTS 433. Hungary. Ratification 16 Jan 64.
Force 16 Apr 64.
500 UNTS 328. UK Great Britain. Gibralter. Force
29 Aug 64.
500 UNTS 328. UK Great Britain. Malta. Force
29 Aug 64.
500 UNTS 328. UK Great Britain. Mauritania.
Force 29 Aug 64.
500 UNTS 328. UK Great Britain. Seychelles.
Force 29 Aug 64.
500 UNTS 328. UK Great Britain. Brit Solomon Is.
Force 29 Aug 64.
500 UNTS 328. UK Great Britain. Swaziland.
Force 29 Aug 64.
500 UNTS 328. UK Great Britain. Antigua. Force
29 Aug 64.
500 UNTS 328. UK Great Britain. Montserrat.
Force 29 Aug 64.
500 UNTS 328. UK Great Britain. Basutoland.
Force 29 Aug 64.
500 UNTS 328. UK Great Britain. British Guiana.
Force 29 Aug 64.
500 UNTS 328. UK Great Britain. Brunei. Force
29 Aug 64.
500 UNTS 328. UK Great Britain. Dominican
Republic. Force 29 Aug 64.
500 UNTS 328. UK Great Britain. Nevis. Force
29 Aug 64.
500 UNTS 328. UK Great Britain. Turk-Caicose Is.
Force 29 Aug 64.
500 UNTS 328. UK Great Britain. Barbados. Force
29 Aug 64.
500 UNTS 328. UK Great Britain. Cayman Island.
Force 29 Aug 64.
500 UNTS 328. UK Great Britain. Falkland Islands. Force 29 Aug 64.
500 UNTS 328. UK Great Britain. Gambia. Force
29 Aug 64.
500 UNTS 328. UK Great Britain. Gilbert Islands.
Force 29 Aug 64.
500 UNTS 328. UK Great Britain. Grenada. Force
29 Aug 64.
500 UNTS 328. UK Great Britain. St. Vincent.
Force 29 Aug 64.
500 UNTS 328. UK Great Britain. St. Helena.
Force 29 Aug 64.
500 UNTS 328. UK Great Britain. Anguilla. Force
29 Aug 64.
500 UNTS 328. UK Great Britain. St. Lucia. Force
29 Aug 64.
500 UNTS 328. UK Great Britain. Tonga. Force
29 Aug 64.
500 UNTS 328. UK Great Britain. St. Christopher.
Force 29 Aug 64.
505 UNTS 323. Romania. Ratification 9 Jun 64.
Force 9 Oct 64.
514 UNTS 292.   Yugoslavia.   Acceptance
14 Oct 64. Force 14 Jan 65.
514 UNTS 292. Poland. Ratification 15 Sep 64.
Force 15 Dec 64.
515 UNTS 308. Mongolia. Ratification 4 Nov 64.
Force 4 Feb 65.
515 UNTS 308. Lebanon. Ratification 27 Oct 64.
Force 27 Jan 65.
521 UNTS 399.   Philippines.   Acceptance
19 Nov 64. Force 19 Feb 65.
521 UNTS 399. Guinea. Acceptance 11 Dec 64.
Force 11 Mar 65.
521 UNTS 399. UK Great Britain. Brit Virgin Islands. Force 9 Mar 65.
522 UNTS 344.   Madagascar.   Ratification
21 Dec 64. Force 21 Mar 65.
526 UNTS 324. Taiwan. Ratification 12 Feb 65.
Force 12 May 65.
557 UNTS 279. Malta. Succession 5 Jan 66.
560 UNTS 282.   Netherlands.   Ratification
25 Mar 66. Force 25 Jun 66.

573 UNTS 334. New Zealand. Cook Islands. Force
12 May 63.
573 UNTS 334. New Zealand. Tokelau Islands.
Force 12 May 63.
604 UNTS 377. Panama. Acceptance 10 Aug 67.
Force 10 Nov 67.
607 UNTS 340. Senegal. Ratification 25 Sep 67.
Force 25 Dec 6 .
634 UNTS 435. Sweden. Ratification 21 Mar 68.
Force 21 Jun 68.
635 UNTS 354. Brazil. Ratification 19 Apr 68.
Force 19 Jul 68.
639 UNTS 331. Vietnam, South. Acceptance
12 Jun 68. Force 12 Sep 68.
643 UNTS 396. Niger. Acceptance 16 Jul 68.
Force 16 Oct 68.
643 UNTS 396. Germany, West. Ratification
17 Jul 68. Force 17 Oct 68.
643 UNTS 396. Germany, West. Berlin. Force
17 Oct 68.
643 UNTS 396. Iran. Acceptance 17 Jul 68. Force
17 Oct 68.
646 UNTS 400. Morocco. Acceptance 30 Aug 68.
Force 30 Nov 68.
648 UNTS 372. Congo (Zaire). Ratification/Acceptance 9 Sep 68. Force 9 Dec 68.
648 UNTS 372. Uganda. Ratification/Acceptance
9 Sep 68. Force 9 Dec 68.
651 UNTS 362. UK Great Britain. St. Lucia. Declaration 24 May 64. Force 24 Oct 68.
651 UNTS 362. Italy. Accession 6 Oct 66. Force
24 Oct 68.
651 UNTS 362.   Philippines.   Accession
19 Nov 64. Force 24 Oct 68.
651 UNTS 362. UK Great Britain. Mauritius. Declaration 24 May 64. Force 24 Oct 68.
651 UNTS 362. UK Great Britain. Seychelles. Declaration 24 May 64. Force 24 May 64.
651 UNTS 362. UK Great Britain. Swaziland. Declaration 24 May 64. Force 24 May 64. .
651 UNTS 362.   Madagascar.   Accession
21 Dec 64. Force 24 Oct 68.
651 UNTS 362. Vietnam. Accession 12 Jun 68.
Force 24 Oct 68.
651 UNTS 362. UK Great Britain. British Honduras. Declaration 24 May 64. Force 24 Oct 68.
651 UNTS 362. UK Great Britain. Basutoland.
Declaration 24 May 64. Force 24 Oct 68.
651 UNTS 362. Senegal. Ratification 24 Jul 68.
Force 24 Oct 68.
651 UNTS 362. Uganda. Accession 9 Sep 68.
Force 24 Oct 68.
651 UNTS 362. UK Great Britain. Gambia. Declaration 24 May 64. Force 24 Oct 68.
651 UNTS 362. UK Great Britain. Gilbert Islands.
Declaration 24 May 64. Force 24 Oct 68.
651 UNTS 362. UK Great Britain. Grenada. Declaration 24 May 64. Force 24 Oct 68.
651 UNTS 362. UK Great Britain. Malta. Declaration 24 May 64. Force 24 Oct 68.
651 UNTS 362. Germany, West. Ratification
17 Jul 68. Force 24 Oct 68.
651 UNTS 362. Argentina. Ratification 17 Jul 68.
Force 24 Oct 68.
651 UNTS 362. UK Great Britain. Brunei. Declaration 24 May 64. Force 24 Oct 68.
651 UNTS 362. Germany, West. Berlin. Force
24 Oct 68.
651 UNTS 362. UK Great Britain. Barbados. Declaration 24 May 64. Force 24 Oct 68.
651 UNTS 362. UK Great Britain. St. Christopher.
Declaration 24 May 64. Force 24 Oct 68.
651 UNTS 362. UK Great Britain. Brit Solomon Is.
Declaration 24 May 64. Force 24 Oct 68.
651 UNTS 362. Panama. Ratification 10 Aug 67.
Force 24 Oct 68.
651 UNTS 362.   Netherlands.   Ratification
25 Mar 66. Force 24 Oct 68.
651 UNTS 362. UK Great Britain. Tonga. Declaration 24 May 64. Force 24 May 64.
651 UNTS 362. UK Great Britain. Turk-Caicose Is.
Declaration 24 May 64. Force 24 May 64.
651 UNTS 362. UK Great Britain. Acceptance
8 Jan 64. Force 24 Oct 68.
651 UNTS 362. UK Great Britain. British Guiana.
Declaration 24 May 64. Force 24 Oct 68.
651 UNTS 362. France. Ratification 24 Apr 64.
Force 24 Oct 68.
651 UNTS 362. UK Great Britain. St. Vincent. Declaration 24 May 64. Force 24 May 64.
651 UNTS 362. Morocco. Accession 30 Aug 68.
Force 24 Oct 68.
651 UNTS 362. UK Great Britain. Gibralter. Declaration 24 May 64. Force 24 Oct 68.

651 UNTS 362. Israel. Ratification 13 Sep 67. Force 24 Oct 68.

651 UNTS 362. Denmark. Ratification 4 Oct 63. Force 24 Oct 68.

651 UNTS 362. Malta. Succession 5 Jan 66. Force 24 Oct 68.

651 UNTS 362. Niger. Accession 12 Jun 68. Force 24 Oct 68.

651 UNTS 362. UK Great Britain. Montserrat. Declaration 24 May 64. Force 24 Oct 68.

651 UNTS 362. UK Great Britain. St. Helena. Declaration 24 May 64. Force 24 Oct 68.

651 UNTS 362. UK Great Britain. Antigua. Declaration 24 May 64. Force 24 Oct 68.

651 UNTS 362. UK Great Britain. Falkland Islands. Declaration 24 May 64. Force 24 Oct 68.

651 UNTS 362. UK Great Britain. Cayman Island. Declaration 24 May 64. Force 24 Oct 68.

651 UNTS 362. UK Great Britain. Dominican Republic. Declaration 24 May 64. Force 24 Oct 68.

653 UNTS 459. Venezuela. Ratification 16 Dec 68. Force 16 Mar 69.

655 UNTS 394. Algeria. Acceptance 24 Dec 68. Force 24 Mar 69.

106194 Bilateral Agreement **429 UNTS 123**
SIGNED: 27 Mar 62 FORCE: 27 Mar 62
REGISTERED: 31 May 62 WHO (World Health)
ARTICLES: 6 LANGUAGE: English.
HEADNOTE: TECHNICAL ADVISORY ASSISTANCE
TOPIC: Tech Assistance
CONCEPTS: Definition of terms. Privileges and immunities. General cooperation. Exchange of information and documents. Personnel. Responsibility and liability. Title and deeds. Exchange. Scholarships and grants. Vocational training. Research and development. Expense sharing formulae. Local currency. Domestic obligation. Special projects. Materials, equipment and services. IGO status. Conformity with IGO decisions.
TREATY REF: 33UNTS261.
PROCEDURE: Amendment. Termination.
PARTIES:
Nigeria
WHO (World Health)

106195 Bilateral Agreement **429 UNTS 135**
SIGNED: 1 Jun 62 FORCE: 1 Jun 62
REGISTERED: 1 Jun 62 United Nations
ARTICLES: 5 LANGUAGE: English.
HEADNOTE: HUMAN RIGHTS SEMINAR STOCKHOLM
TOPIC: Admin Cooperation
CONCEPTS: Privileges and immunities. Use of facilities. Domestic obligation. Conferences. IGO obligations.
PROCEDURE: Amendment.
PARTIES:
United Nations
Sweden

106196 Bilateral Agreement **429 UNTS 143**
SIGNED: 4 May 62 FORCE: 4 May 62
REGISTERED: 4 Jun 62 United Nations
ARTICLES: 10 LANGUAGE: English. Spanish.
HEADNOTE: ASSISTANCE
TOPIC: Direct Aid
CONCEPTS: Detailed regulations. Treaty implementation. Visas. Privileges and immunities. Exchange of information and documents. Informational records. Inspection and observation. Operating agencies. Personnel. Public information. Responsibility and liability. Title and deeds. Use of facilities. Arbitration. Procedure. Negotiation. Import quotas. Attachment of funds. Exchange rates and regulations. Expense sharing formulae. Financial programs. Domestic obligation. General technical assistance. Economic assistance. Materials, equipment and services. IGO status.
INTL ORGS: International Atomic Energy Agency. International Court of Justice. United Nations. Arbitration Commission.
TREATY REF: 1UNTS15; 33UNTS261; 374UNTS147.
PROCEDURE: Amendment. Termination.
PARTIES:
UN Special Fund
Uruguay

106197 Bilateral Agreement **429 UNTS 169**
SIGNED: 6 Jun 62 FORCE: 6 Jun 62
REGISTERED: 6 Jun 62 United Nations
ARTICLES: 10 LANGUAGE: English. Spanish.
HEADNOTE: ASSISTANCE
TOPIC: Direct Aid
CONCEPTS: Detailed regulations. Treaty implementation. Visas. Privileges and immunities. Exchange of information and documents. Informational records. Inspection and observation. Operating agencies. Personnel. Public information. Responsibility and liability. Title and deeds. Use of facilities. Arbitration. Procedure. Negotiation. Import quotas. Attachment of funds. Exchange rates and regulations. Expense sharing formulae. Financial programs. Domestic obligation. General technical assistance. Economic assistance. Materials, equipment and services. IGO status.
INTL ORGS: International Atomic Energy Agency. International Court of Justice. United Nations. Arbitration Commission.
TREATY REF: 1UNTS15; 33UNTS261; 374UNTS147.
PROCEDURE: Amendment. Termination.
PARTIES:
Dominican Republic
UN Special Fund

106198 Bilateral Exchange **429 UNTS 193**
SIGNED: 12 Feb 62 FORCE: 14 Mar 62
REGISTERED: 8 Jun 62 Belgium
ARTICLES: 2 LANGUAGE: French.
HEADNOTE: ABOLITION VISA REQUIREMENTS
TOPIC: Visas
CONCEPTS: Emergencies. Visa abolition. Denial of admission.
PROCEDURE: Denunciation.
PARTIES:
Belgium
Ivory Coast

106199 Bilateral Agreement **429 UNTS 199**
SIGNED: 28 Oct 61 FORCE: 1 Jan 62
REGISTERED: 8 Jun 62 Belgium
ARTICLES: 16 LANGUAGE: French.
HEADNOTE: FILMS
TOPIC: Culture
CONCEPTS: Detailed regulations. Alien status. Conformity with municipal law. General cooperation. Personnel. Use of facilities. Establishment of commission. Scholarships and grants. Employment regulations. Free trade. Monetary and gold transfers. Expense sharing formulae. Mass media exchange.
PROCEDURE: Denunciation. Duration. Ratification. Renewal or Revival.
PARTIES:
Belgium
Italy

106200 Multilateral Convention **429 UNTS 211**
SIGNED: 9 Dec 60 FORCE: 12 Jun 62
REGISTERED: 12 Jun 62 United Nations
ARTICLES: 16 LANGUAGE: English. French.
HEADNOTE: CUSTOMS TREATMENT PALLETS
TOPIC: Customs
CONCEPTS: Definition of terms. Territorial application. Arbitration. Negotiation. Customs duties. Customs exemptions. Transport of goods.
INTL ORGS: United Nations. Arbitration Commission.
PROCEDURE: Amendment. Accession. Denunciation. Ratification. Registration.
PARTIES:
Belgium SIGNED: 21 Jan 61 RATIFIED: 14 Mar 62 FORCE: 12 Jun 62
Bulgaria SIGNED: 28 Feb 61 FORCE: 12 Jun 62
Czechoslovakia RATIFIED: 31 Mar 62 FORCE: 29 Aug 62
Denmark SIGNED: 14 Mar 61 RATIFIED: 14 Mar 61 FORCE: 12 Jun 62
France SIGNED: 8 Mar 61 RATIFIED: 12 Mar 62 FORCE: 12 Jun 62
Germany, West SIGNED: 20 Dec 61
Italy SIGNED: 15 Mar 61
Luxembourg SIGNED: 6 Feb 61
Netherlands SIGNED: 13 Mar 61
Sweden SIGNED: 1 Mar 61 FORCE: 12 Jun 62
Switzerland SIGNED: 6 Mar 61
UK Great Britain SIGNED: 7 Feb 61

ANNEX
434 UNTS 361. Luxembourg. Ratification 31 Jul 62. Force 29 Oct 62.

439 UNTS 328. UK Great Britain. Grenada. Force 30 Dec 62.

439 UNTS 328. UK Great Britain. Hong Kong. Force 30 Dec 62.

439 UNTS 328. UK Great Britain. Isle of Man. Force 30 Dec 62.

439 UNTS 328. UK Great Britain. British Honduras. Force 30 Dec 62.

439 UNTS 328. UK Great Britain. Brit Solomon Is. Force 30 Dec 62.

439 UNTS 328. UK Great Britain. Channel Islands. Force 30 Dec 62.

439 UNTS 328. UK Great Britain. Falkland Islands. Force 30 Dec 62.

439 UNTS 328. UK Great Britain. Kenya. Force 30 Dec 62.

439 UNTS 328. UK Great Britain. Fiji Islands. Force 30 Dec 62.

439 UNTS 328. UK Great Britain. Antigua. Force 30 Dec 62.

439 UNTS 328. UK Great Britain. Bahamas. Force 30 Dec 62.

439 UNTS 328. UK Great Britain. Gambia. Force 30 Dec 62.

439 UNTS 328. UK Great Britain. Montserrat. Force 30 Dec 62.

439 UNTS 328. UK Great Britain. Aden Colony. Force 30 Dec 62.

439 UNTS 328. UK Great Britain. North Borneo. Force 30 Dec 62.

439 UNTS 328. UK Great Britain. Sarawak. Force 30 Dec 62.

439 UNTS 328. UK Great Britain. Uganda. Force 30 Dec 62.

439 UNTS 328. UK Great Britain. Gilbert Islands. Force 30 Dec 62.

442 UNTS 342. Netherlands. Ratification 22 Oct 62. Force 20 Jan 63.

442 UNTS 342. Netherlands. Netherlands Antilles. Force 20 Jan 63.

461 UNTS 331. Switzerland. Ratification 24 Apr 63. Force 23 Jul 63.

472 UNTS 398. Hungary. Qualified Accession 26 Jul 63. Force 24 Oct 63.

478 UNTS 439. Cuba. Qualified Accession 26 Sep 63. Force 25 Dec 63.

479 UNTS 385. Austria. Accession 7 Oct 63. Force 5 Jan 64.

496 UNTS 362. Romania. Qualified Accession 15 May 64. Force 13 Aug 64.

500 UNTS 330. Yugoslavia. Accession 19 Jun 64. Force 17 Sep 64.

510 UNTS 334. Germany, West. Berlin. Force 28 Dec 64.

510 UNTS 334. Germany, West. Ratification 24 Sep 64. Force 28 Dec 64.

514 UNTS 294. Norway. Accession 27 Oct 64. Force 25 Jan 65.

571 UNTS 326. Finland. Accession 19 Aug 66. Force 17 Nov 66.

617 UNTS 369. Portugal. Accession 15 Dec 68. Force 14 Apr 68.

106201 Bilateral Agreement **430 UNTS 3**
SIGNED: 23 Jan 62 FORCE: 31 May 62
REGISTERED: 13 Jun 62 IBRD (World Bank)
ARTICLES: 7 LANGUAGE: English.
HEADNOTE: LOAN AGREEMENT
TOPIC: IBRD Project
CONCEPTS: Default remedies. Definition of terms. Annex or appendix reference. Exchange of information and documents. Inspection and observation. Accounting procedures. Bonds. Fees and exemptions. Interest rates. Tax exemptions. Domestic obligation. Terms of loan. Loan regulations. Loan guarantee. Guarantor non-interference.
PARTIES:
Australia
IBRD (World Bank)

106202 Bilateral Agreement **430 UNTS 27**
SIGNED: 13 Oct 61 FORCE: 2 May 62
REGISTERED: 13 Jun 62 IBRD (World Bank)
ARTICLES: 8 LANGUAGE: English.
HEADNOTE: LOAN HIGHWAY
TOPIC: IBRD Project
CONCEPTS: Default remedies. Definition of terms. Annex or appendix reference. Exchange of infor-

mation and documents. Informational records. Inspection and observation. Accounting procedures. Bonds. Fees and exemptions. Interest rates. Domestic obligation. Terms of loan. Loan regulations. Loan guarantee. Guarantor non-interference. Roads and highways.
PARTIES:
Costa Rica
IBRD (World Bank)

106203 Bilateral Agreement **430 UNTS 47**
SIGNED: 3 Nov 61　　　　FORCE: 16 May 62
REGISTERED: 13 Jun 62 IBRD (World Bank)
ARTICLES: 8 LANGUAGE: English.
HEADNOTE: LOAN HIGHWAY MAINTENANCE
TOPIC: IBRD Project
CONCEPTS: Default remedies. Definition of terms. Annex or appendix reference. Exchange of information and documents. Informational records. Inspection and observation. Accounting procedures. Bonds. Fees and exemptions. Interest rates. Domestic obligation. Terms of loan. Loan regulations. Loan guarantee. Guarantor non-interference. Roads and highways.
PARTIES:
Peru
IBRD (World Bank)

106204 Bilateral Agreement **431 UNTS 3**
SIGNED: 13 Oct 61　　　　FORCE: 2 May 61
REGISTERED: 13 Jun 62 IDA (Devel Assoc)
ARTICLES: 7 LANGUAGE: English.
HEADNOTE: HIGHWAY PROJECT
TOPIC: Non-IBRD Project
CONCEPTS: Detailed regulations. Informational records. Accounting procedures. Interest rates. Tax exemptions. Loan and credit. Credit provisions. Loan repayment. Terms of loan. Loan regulations. Non-bank projects. IDA development project. Roads and highways.
INTL ORGS: International Bank for Reconstruction and Development.
TREATY REF: 430UNTS.
PARTIES:
Costa Rica
IDA (Devel Assoc)

106205 Bilateral Exchange **431 UNTS 21**
SIGNED: 10 Nov 60　　　　FORCE: 10 Nov 60
REGISTERED: 13 Jun 62 Denmark
ARTICLES: 2 LANGUAGE: German.
HEADNOTE: EXCHANGE INFORMATION RELATING NATURALIZATION
TOPIC: Consul/Citizenship
CONCEPTS: Definition of terms. Territorial application. Previous treaty replacement. Nationality and citizenship. Exchange of information and documents.
PROCEDURE: Denunciation.
PARTIES:
Denmark
Germany, West

106206 Bilateral Agreement **431 UNTS 29**
SIGNED: 20 Oct 61　　　　FORCE: 22 Dec 61
REGISTERED: 19 Jun 62 UK Great Britain
ARTICLES: 6 LANGUAGE: English. French.
HEADNOTE: LOAN
TOPIC: Loans and Credits
CONCEPTS: Friendship and amity. Balance of payments. Currency. Interest rates. Payment schedules. Loan and credit. Loan repayment. Terms of loan.
INTL ORGS: International Monetary Fund.
PROCEDURE: Ratification.
PARTIES:
Switzerland
UK Great Britain

106207 Bilateral Exchange **431 UNTS 35**
SIGNED: 13 Feb 62　　　　FORCE: 13 Feb 62
REGISTERED: 19 Jun 62 UK Great Britain
ARTICLES: 2 LANGUAGE: English.
HEADNOTE: BOOKS FILMS IMPORTATION
TOPIC: Culture
CONCEPTS: Annex type material. Import quotas. Publications exchange. Mass media exchange.
TREATY REF: 360UNTS79; 404UNTS376.

PARTIES:
UK Great Britain
Yugoslavia

106208 Multilateral Convention **431 UNTS 41**
SIGNED: 22 Jun 60　　　　FORCE: 17 Jun 62
REGISTERED: 25 Jun 62 ILO (Labor Org)
ARTICLES: 23 LANGUAGE: English. French.
HEADNOTE: PROTECTION IONIZING RADIATION
TOPIC: Sanitation
CONCEPTS: Detailed regulations. Standardization. General cooperation. Inspection and observation. Domestic legislation. Public health. ILO conventions. Employment regulations. General. Mass media exchange.
INTL ORGS: United Nations.
PROCEDURE: Amendment. Accession. Denunciation. Duration. Future Procedures Contemplated. Ratification. Renewal or Revival.
PARTIES:
Multilateral
ANNEX
435 UNTS 391. Spain. Ratification 17 Jul 62. Force 17 Jul 63.
444 UNTS 354. Iraq. Ratification 26 Oct 62. Force 26 Oct 63.
468 UNTS 444. UK Great Britain. Declaration 29 May 63.
468 UNTS 444. Switzerland. Ratification 29 May 63. Force 29 May 64.
471 UNTS 381. UK Great Britain. Northern Rhodesia.
475 UNTS 385. UK Great Britain. Guernsey Island.
475 UNTS 385. UK Great Britain. Jersey Island.
488 UNTS 373. Czechoslovakia. Ratification 21 Jan 64. Force 21 Jan 65.
488 UNTS 373. Syria. Ratification 15 Jan 64. Force 15 Jan 65.
495 UNTS 308. United Arab Rep. Ratification 18 Mar 64. Force 18 Mar 65.
504 UNTS 370. UK Great Britain. Basutoland. Declaration 7 Jul 64.
504 UNTS 370. UK Great Britain. Montserrat. Declaration 7 Jul 64.
504 UNTS 370. UK Great Britain. British Honduras.
504 UNTS 370. UK Great Britain. Aden. Declaration 7 Jul 64.
504 UNTS 370. UK Great Britain. St. Lucia. Declaration 12 Jun 64.
504 UNTS 370. UK Great Britain. Fiji Islands. Declaration 7 Jul 64.
511 UNTS 323. UK Great Britain. Bermuda.
515 UNTS 345. UK Great Britain. Barbados.
522 UNTS 391. UK Great Britain. Brunei. Declaration 11 Dec 64.
522 UNTS 391. Poland. Ratification 23 Dec 64. Force 23 Dec 65.
522 UNTS 391. UK Great Britain. Jersey Island.
524 UNTS 371. UK Great Britain. Antigua. Declaration 22 Jan 65.
545 UNTS 384. Belgium. Ratification 2 Jul 65. Force 2 Jul 66.
545 UNTS 384. UK Great Britain. Declaration 20 Jul 65.
547 UNTS 369. UK Great Britain. Declaration 24 Sep 65.
551 UNTS 350. UK Great Britain. Hong Kong.
559 UNTS 385. UK Great Britain. British Guiana.
567 UNTS 359. Guyana. Ratification 8 Jun 66. Force 8 Jun 66.
600 UNTS 411. UK Great Britain. Guernsey Island.
603 UNTS 356. Paraguay. Ratification 10 Jul 67. Force 10 Jul 68.
607 UNTS 368. USSR (Soviet Union). Ratification 22 Sep 67. Force 22 Sep 68.
640 UNTS 389. Hungary. Ratification 8 Jun 68. Force 8 Jun 69.
640 UNTS 389. Ukrainian SSR. Force 19 Jun 69.

106209 Bilateral Agreement **431 UNTS 55**
SIGNED: 11 Apr 62　　　　FORCE: 11 Apr 62
REGISTERED: 25 Jun 62 United Nations
ARTICLES: 8 LANGUAGE: English.
HEADNOTE: ACTIVITIES UNICEF
TOPIC: Direct Aid
CONCEPTS: Treaty implementation. Privileges and immunities. General cooperation. Exchange of information and documents. Informational records. Public information. Responsibility and

liability. Title and deeds. Attachment of funds. Tax exemptions. Customs exemptions. Domestic obligation. Assistance. General aid. Materials, equipment and services. Distribution. IGO status.
INTL ORGS: United Nations.
TREATY REF: 1UNTS15.
PROCEDURE: Amendment. Termination.
PARTIES:
UNICEF (Children)
Sierra Leone

106210 Bilateral Agreement **431 UNTS 65**
SIGNED: 9 Apr 62　　　　FORCE: 9 Apr 62
REGISTERED: 26 Jun 62 United Nations
ARTICLES: 8 LANGUAGE: French.
HEADNOTE: ACTIVITIES UNICEF
TOPIC: Direct Aid
CONCEPTS: Treaty implementation. Privileges and immunities. General cooperation. Exchange of information and documents. Informational records. Public information. Responsibility and liability. Title and deeds. Attachment of funds. Tax exemptions. Customs exemptions. Domestic obligation. Assistance. General aid. Materials, equipment and services. Distribution. IGO status.
INTL ORGS: United Nations.
TREATY REF: 1UNTS15.
PROCEDURE: Amendment. Termination.
PARTIES:
Congo (Brazzaville)
UNICEF (Children)

106211 Bilateral Agreement **431 UNTS 75**
SIGNED: 1 Apr 62　　　　FORCE: 1 Apr 62
REGISTERED: 27 Jun 62 United Nations
ARTICLES: 8 LANGUAGE: English.
HEADNOTE: ACTIVITIES
TOPIC: Direct Aid
CONCEPTS: Treaty implementation. Privileges and immunities. General cooperation. Exchange of information and documents. Informational records. Public information. Responsibility and liability. Title and deeds. Attachment of funds. Tax exemptions. Customs exemptions. Domestic obligation. Assistance. General aid. Materials, equipment and services. Distribution. IGO status.
INTL ORGS: United Nations.
TREATY REF: 1UNTS15.
PROCEDURE: Amendment. Termination.
PARTIES:
UNICEF (Children)
Somalia

106212 Bilateral Agreement **431 UNTS 85**
SIGNED: 23 Nov 60　　　　FORCE: 14 Mar 62
REGISTERED: 2 Jul 62 Czechoslovakia
ARTICLES: 8 LANGUAGE: English.
HEADNOTE: SCIENTIFIC & TECHNICAL COOPERATION
TOPIC: Tech Assistance
CONCEPTS: Detailed regulations. Guarantees and safeguards. Treaty implementation. General cooperation. Personnel. Use of facilities. Research and scientific projects. Scientific exchange. General technical assistance.
PROCEDURE: Termination.
PARTIES:
Czechoslovakia
Ghana

106213 Bilateral Agreement **431 UNTS 91**
SIGNED: 23 Nov 60　　　　FORCE: 14 Mar 62
REGISTERED: 2 Jul 62 Czechoslovakia
ARTICLES: 10 LANGUAGE: English.
HEADNOTE: CULTURAL COOPERATION
TOPIC: Culture
CONCEPTS: Treaty implementation. Friendship and amity. Specialists exchange. Recognition of degrees. Exchange. Teacher and student exchange. Scholarships and grants. Exchange. General cultural cooperation. Artists. Athletes. Scientific exchange. Publications exchange. Mass media exchange.
PROCEDURE: Duration. Ratification. Termination.
PARTIES:
Czechoslovakia
Ghana

106214 Bilateral Agreement **431 UNTS 99**
SIGNED: 31 Jan 58   FORCE: 31 May 58
REGISTERED: 10 Jul 62 Poland
ARTICLES: 27 LANGUAGE: Polish. Czechoslovakian.
HEADNOTE: RAIL TRAFFIC BETWEEN TWO COUNTRIES
TOPIC: Land Transport
CONCEPTS: Detailed regulations. General provisions. Treaty implementation. Annex or appendix reference. Previous treaty replacement. Passports non-diplomatic. Conformity with municipal law. Exchange of information and documents. Inspection and observation. Legal protection and assistance. Licenses and permits. Personnel. Responsibility and liability. Use of facilities. Indemnities and reimbursements. Currency. Fees and exemptions. Non-interest rates and fees. National treatment. Tax exemptions. Customs duties. Customs exemptions. Navigational equipment. Railway border crossing. Railways. Facilities and equipment. Regulations. Services. Markers and definitions.
INTL ORGS: Universal Postal Union.
TREATY REF: 98LTS233.
PROCEDURE: Duration. Ratification. Renewal or Revival.
PARTIES:
  Czechoslovakia
  Poland

106215 Bilateral Agreement **431 UNTS 157**
SIGNED: 14 Feb 59   FORCE: 1 Nov 59
REGISTERED: 10 Jul 62 Poland
ARTICLES: 30 LANGUAGE: Polish. Hungarian.
HEADNOTE: COOPERATION SOCIAL POLICY
TOPIC: Non-ILO Labor
CONCEPTS: Specialists exchange. General cultural cooperation. Family allowances. Administrative cooperation. Old age insurance. Sickness and invalidity insurance. Social security. Unemployment.
PROCEDURE: Denunciation. Ratification.
PARTIES:
  Hungary
  Poland

106216 Bilateral Treaty **432 UNTS 3**
SIGNED: 6 Mar 59   FORCE: 26 Feb 60
REGISTERED: 10 Jul 62 Poland
ARTICLES: 89 LANGUAGE: Polish. Hungarian.
HEADNOTE: LEGAL RELATIONS CIVIL FAMILY CRIMINAL CASES
TOPIC: Admin Cooperation
CONCEPTS: Exceptions and exemptions. General provisions. Previous treaty replacement. Human rights. Privileges and immunities. Consular functions in property. Extradition requests. Extraditable offenses. Refusal of extradition. Concurrent requests. Provisional detainment. Extradition postponement. Material evidence. Conformity with municipal law. Family law. Exchange of information and documents. Juridical personality. Legal protection and assistance. Succession. Recognition of legal documents. Prizes and arbitral awards. Indemnities and reimbursements. Assets transfer. Insured letters and boxes.
TREATY REF: 181LTS115.
PROCEDURE: Denunciation. Duration. Ratification. Renewal or Revival.
PARTIES:
  Hungary
  Poland

106217 Bilateral Convention **432 UNTS 115**
SIGNED: 20 May 59   FORCE: 6 Dec 59
REGISTERED: 10 Jul 62 Poland
ARTICLES: 28 LANGUAGE: Polish. Hungarian.
HEADNOTE: CONSULAR CONVENTION
TOPIC: Consul/Citizenship
CONCEPTS: Definition of terms. General provisions. Previous treaty replacement. General consular functions. Diplomatic privileges. Consular relations establishment. Inviolability. Privileges and immunities. Diplomatic correspondence. Responsibility and liability.
TREATY REF: 13KLTS303.
PROCEDURE: Duration. Ratification.
PARTIES:
  Hungary
  Poland

106218 Bilateral Agreement **432 UNTS 147**
SIGNED: 2 Apr 59   FORCE: 9 Dec 59
REGISTERED: 10 Jul 62 Poland
ARTICLES: 6 LANGUAGE: Polish. Arabic. English.
HEADNOTE: CULTURAL COOPERATION
TOPIC: Culture
CONCEPTS: Culture.
INTL ORGS: Special Commission.
PROCEDURE: Ratification.
PARTIES:
  Iraq
  Poland

106219 Bilateral Agreement **432 UNTS 161**
SIGNED: 11 May 56   FORCE: 31 Jan 57
REGISTERED: 10 Jul 62 Poland
ARTICLES: 7 LANGUAGE: Polish. Korean. Russian.
HEADNOTE: CULTURAL COOPERATION
TOPIC: Culture
CONCEPTS: Treaty implementation. Treaty interpretation. Friendship and amity. General cooperation. Exchange. Teacher and student exchange. Scholarships and grants. Exchange. General cultural cooperation. Research results. Scientific exchange. Publications exchange. Mass media exchange.
PROCEDURE: Denunciation. Duration. Future Procedures Contemplated. Ratification. Renewal or Revival.
PARTIES:
  Korea, North
  Poland

106220 Bilateral Agreement **432 UNTS 177**
SIGNED: 23 Dec 58   FORCE: 20 Oct 59
REGISTERED: 10 Jul 62 Poland
ARTICLES: 6 LANGUAGE: Polish. Mongolian. Russian.
HEADNOTE: CULTURAL COOPERATION
TOPIC: Culture
CONCEPTS: Treaty implementation. Treaty interpretation. Friendship and amity. Specialists exchange. Public health. Exchange. Teacher and student exchange. Vocational training. Exchange. General cultural cooperation. Artists. Athletes. Scientific exchange. Finances and payments. Publications exchange. Mass media exchange. Press and wire services.
PROCEDURE: Denunciation. Duration. Future Procedures Contemplated. Ratification. Renewal or Revival.
PARTIES:
  Mongolia
  Poland

106221 Bilateral Agreement **432 UNTS 193**
SIGNED: 17 Dec 58   FORCE: 5 May 59
REGISTERED: 10 Jul 62 Poland
ARTICLES: 4 LANGUAGE: French.
HEADNOTE: CULTURAL
TOPIC: Culture
CONCEPTS: Establishment of commission. Specialists exchange. Exchange. Scholarships and grants. Exchange. General cultural cooperation. Artists. Scientific exchange.
PROCEDURE: Duration. Future Procedures Contemplated. Ratification. Termination.
PARTIES:
  Norway
  Poland

106222 Bilateral Agreement **432 UNTS 199**
SIGNED: 15 Feb 51   FORCE: 5 Jun 51
REGISTERED: 10 Jul 62 Poland
ARTICLES: 5 LANGUAGE: Polish. Russian.
HEADNOTE: EXCHANGE SECTORS STATE TERRITORIES
TOPIC: Territory Boundary
CONCEPTS: Annex or appendix reference. Establishment of commission. Indemnities and reimbursements. Financial programs. Changes of territory. Markers and definitions.
INTL ORGS: Special Commission.
TREATY REF: 10UNTS193.
PROCEDURE: Ratification.
PARTIES:
  Poland
  USSR (Soviet Union)

106223 Bilateral Agreement **432 UNTS 221**
SIGNED: 26 Oct 57   FORCE: 8 May 58
REGISTERED: 10 Jul 62 Poland
ARTICLES: 18 LANGUAGE: Polish. Russian.
HEADNOTE: TEMPORARY STATIONING SOVIET FORCES
TOPIC: Status of Forces
CONCEPTS: Definition of terms. Court procedures. Conformity with municipal law. General cooperation. Recognition of legal documents. Responsibility and liability. Use of facilities. Investigation of violations. Establishment of commission. Procedure. Compensation. Claims and settlements. Military training. Jurisdiction. Procurement and logistics. Status of forces. Bases and facilities.
INTL ORGS: Special Commission.
PARTIES:
  Poland
  USSR (Soviet Union)

106224 Bilateral Agreement **432 UNTS 255**
SIGNED: 6 Apr 57   FORCE: 2 Jun 58
REGISTERED: 10 Jul 62 Poland
ARTICLES: 4 LANGUAGE: Polish. Vietnamese. French.
HEADNOTE: CULTURAL COOPERATION
TOPIC: Culture
CONCEPTS: Treaty implementation. Friendship and amity. Exchange of information and documents. Responsibility and liability. Establishment of commission. Specialists exchange. Exchange. Teacher and student exchange. Exchange. General cultural cooperation. Artists. Athletes. Anthropology and archeology. Publications exchange. Mass media exchange. Press and wire services.
INTL ORGS: Special Commission.
PROCEDURE: Amendment. Denunciation. Duration. Ratification. Renewal or Revival.
PARTIES:
  Poland
  Vietnam, North

106225 Bilateral Convention **432 UNTS 267**
SIGNED: 17 Nov 58   FORCE: 12 Jul 59
REGISTERED: 10 Jul 62 Poland
ARTICLES: 49 LANGUAGE: Polish. Serbo-Croat.
HEADNOTE: CONSULAR CONVENTION
TOPIC: Consul/Citizenship
CONCEPTS: Definition of terms. General provisions. General consular functions. Diplomatic privileges. Consular relations establishment. Inviolability. Privileges and immunities. Diplomatic correspondence. Responsibility and liability. Most favored nation clause.
PROCEDURE: Denunciation. Ratification.
PARTIES:
  Poland
  Yugoslavia

106226 Bilateral Agreement **432 UNTS 325**
SIGNED: 11 Mar 62   FORCE: 11 Mar 62
REGISTERED: 10 Jul 62 WHO (World Health)
ARTICLES: 6 LANGUAGE: English.
HEADNOTE: TECHNICAL ADVISORY ASSISTANCE
TOPIC: Tech Assistance
CONCEPTS: Definition of terms. Previous treaty replacement. Privileges and immunities. General cooperation. Exchange of information and documents. Personnel. Responsibility and liability. Title and deeds. Exchange. Scholarships and grants. Vocational training. Research and development. Expense sharing formulae. Local currency. Domestic obligation. Special projects. Materials, equipment and services. IGO status. Conformity with IGO decisions.
INTL ORGS: United Nations.
TREATY REF: 33UNTSI61; 307UNTS235.
PROCEDURE: Amendment. Termination.
PARTIES:
  WHO (World Health)
  Sudan

106227 Bilateral Agreement **433 UNTS 3**
SIGNED: 7 Apr 61   FORCE: 7 Apr 61
REGISTERED: 11 Jul 62 USA (United States)
ARTICLES: 6 LANGUAGE: English. Spanish.
HEADNOTE: AGRI COMMOD TITLE I
TOPIC: US Agri Commod Aid
CONCEPTS: General provisions. Annex or appen-

dix reference. Exchange of information and documents. Reexport of goods, etc.. Exchange rates and regulations. Transportation costs. Local currency. Commodities schedule. Purchase authorization. Surplus commodities. Mutual consultation.
PARTIES:
Bolivia
USA (United States)

106228 Bilateral Exchange **433 UNTS 21**
SIGNED: 3 Aug 61 FORCE: 3 Aug 61
REGISTERED: 11 Jul 62 USA (United States)
ARTICLES: 2 LANGUAGE: English. Spanish.
HEADNOTE: EMERGENCY RELIEF ASSISTANCE
TOPIC: Direct Aid
CONCEPTS: Public information. Financial programs. Relief supplies. Loan and credit.
PARTIES:
Chile
USA (United States)

106229 Bilateral Agreement **433 UNTS 29**
SIGNED: 27 Jul 61 FORCE: 9 Oct 61
REGISTERED: 11 Jul 62 USA (United States)
ARTICLES: 11 LANGUAGE: English. French.
HEADNOTE: COOPERATION OPERATION ATOMIC WEAPONS
TOPIC: Milit Assistance
CONCEPTS: Definition of terms. Conformity with municipal law. Exchange of information and documents. Recognition. Non-nuclear materials. Joint defense. Defense and security. Atomic weapons. Military training. Security of information. Exchange of defense information. Restrictions on transfer.
TREATY REF: 80UNTS171.
PROCEDURE: Ratification. Termination.
PARTIES:
France
USA (United States)

106230 Bilateral Exchange **433 UNTS 43**
SIGNED: 19 Jul 61 FORCE: 19 Jul 61
REGISTERED: 11 Jul 62 USA (United States)
ARTICLES: 2 LANGUAGE: English. Spanish.
HEADNOTE: CERTIFICATES AIRWORTHINESS IMPORTED AIRCRAFT
TOPIC: Air Transport
CONCEPTS: Exchange of information and documents. Airworthiness certificates.
PROCEDURE: Termination.
PARTIES:
Mexico
USA (United States)
ANNEX
442 UNTS 343. USA (United States). Amendment 30 Jan 62. Force 30 Jan 62.
442 UNTS 343. Mexico. Amendment 19 Jan 62. Force 30 Jan 62.

106231 Bilateral Agreement **433 UNTS 53**
SIGNED: 7 Jul 61 FORCE: 7 Jul 61
REGISTERED: 11 Jul 62 USA (United States)
ARTICLES: 6 LANGUAGE: English. Spanish.
HEADNOTE: AGRI COMMOD TITLE I
TOPIC: US Agri Commod Aid
CONCEPTS: General provisions. Annex or appendix reference. Exchange of information and documents. Reexport of goods, etc.. Exchange rates and regulations. Transportation costs. Local currency. Commodities schedule. Purchase authorization. Surplus commodities. Mutual consultation.
PARTIES:
Paraguay
USA (United States)

106232 Bilateral Exchange **433 UNTS 83**
SIGNED: 4 Oct 61 FORCE: 4 Oct 61
REGISTERED: 11 Jul 62 USA (United States)
ARTICLES: 2 LANGUAGE: English.
HEADNOTE: LOAN VESSEL
TOPIC: Specif Goods/Equip
CONCEPTS: Licenses and permits. Claims and settlements. Merchant vessels. Lend lease. Specific goods and equipment.
TREATY REF: 45UNTS47.

PARTIES:
Philippines
USA (United States)

106233 Bilateral Agreement **433 UNTS 91**
SIGNED: 4 May 61 FORCE: 4 May 61
REGISTERED: 13 Jul 62 USA (United States)
ARTICLES: 6 LANGUAGE: English. Portuguese.
HEADNOTE: AGRI COMMOD TITLE I
TOPIC: US Agri Commod Aid
CONCEPTS: General provisions. Annex or appendix reference. Exchange of information and documents. Reexport of goods, etc.. Exchange rates and regulations. Transportation costs. Local currency. Commodities schedule. Purchase authorization. Surplus commodities. Mutual consultation.
PARTIES:
Brazil
USA (United States)

106234 Bilateral Exchange **433 UNTS 113**
SIGNED: 27 Oct 61 FORCE: 27 Oct 61
REGISTERED: 13 Jul 62 USA (United States)
ARTICLES: 2 LANGUAGE: English. Portuguese.
HEADNOTE: INTERCONTINENTAL TESTING EXPERIMENTAL COMMUNICATIONS SATELLITE
TOPIC: Telecommunications
CONCEPTS: Communication satellites testing. Facilities and equipment. Arms limitations.
PARTIES:
Brazil
USA (United States)

106235 Bilateral Exchange **433 UNTS 123**
SIGNED: 1 Aug 61 FORCE: 11 Dec 61
REGISTERED: 13 Jul 62 USA (United States)
ARTICLES: 2 LANGUAGE: English.
HEADNOTE: DOUBLE TAXATION SHIPS AIRCRAFT
TOPIC: Taxation
CONCEPTS: Definition of terms. Taxation. Tax exemptions. Air transport. Merchant vessels.
PROCEDURE: Termination.
PARTIES:
Colombia
USA (United States)

106236 Bilateral Agreement **433 UNTS 133**
SIGNED: 11 Jan 62 FORCE: 11 Jan 62
REGISTERED: 13 Jul 62 USA (United States)
ARTICLES: 7 LANGUAGE: English. Spanish.
HEADNOTE: ECONOMIC TECHNICAL RELATED ASSISTANCE
TOPIC: General Aid
CONCEPTS: Change of circumstances. Exceptions and exemptions. Diplomatic privileges. Privileges and immunities. Conformity with municipal law. General cooperation. Personnel. Accounting procedures. Exchange rates and regulations. Funding procedures. Sale of local currency. Tax exemptions. Customs exemptions. Commodities and services. Domestic obligation. General technical assistance. Economic assistance. Materials, equipment and services. Aid missions. Grants.
PROCEDURE: Termination.
PARTIES:
Dominican Republic
USA (United States)

106237 Bilateral Agreement **433 UNTS 147**
SIGNED: 3 Jan 62 FORCE: 3 Jan 62
REGISTERED: 13 Jul 62 USA (United States)
ARTICLES: 9 LANGUAGE: English.
HEADNOTE: SCIENTIFIC COOPERATION BIOMEDICINE
TOPIC: Scientific Project
CONCEPTS: Friendship and amity. Operating agencies. Personnel. Use of facilities. Specialists exchange. Public health. Vocational training. Research and scientific projects. Scientific exchange. Research and development. Funding procedures. Tax exemptions.
PROCEDURE: Termination.
PARTIES:
Ghana
USA (United States)

106238 Bilateral Exchange **433 UNTS 155**
SIGNED: 24 May 54 FORCE: 24 May 54
REGISTERED: 13 Jul 62 USA (United States)
ARTICLES: 2 LANGUAGE: English. Spanish.
HEADNOTE: DISPOSITION DEFENSE EQUIPMENT MATERIALS
TOPIC: Milit Installation
CONCEPTS: Exchange of information and documents. Reexport of goods, etc.. Delivery schedules. Surplus property. Surplus war property.
TREATY REF: 222UNTS87.
PARTIES:
Honduras
USA (United States)

106239 Bilateral Exchange **433 UNTS 163**
SIGNED: 8 Jan 62 FORCE: 8 Jan 62
REGISTERED: 13 Jul 62 USA (United States)
ARTICLES: 2 LANGUAGE: English. Spanish.
HEADNOTE: APPLICATION SAFETY LIFE SEA CONVENTION
TOPIC: Humanitarian
CONCEPTS: Previous treaty extension. Humanitarian matters.
INTL ORGS: Inter-Governmental Maritime Consultative Organization.
TREATY REF: 419UNTS357; 164UNTS113; 167UNTS338.
PARTIES:
Mexico
USA (United States)

106240 Bilateral Agreement **433 UNTS 169**
SIGNED: 16 Jan 62 FORCE: 16 Jan 62
REGISTERED: 13 Jul 62 USA (United States)
ARTICLES: 13 LANGUAGE: English. Spanish.
HEADNOTE: MAPPING
TOPIC: Scientific Project
CONCEPTS: General cooperation. Exchange of information and documents. Juridical personality. Operating agencies. General property. Responsibility and liability. Use of facilities. Research and scientific projects. Research and development. Tax exemptions. Economic assistance.
PROCEDURE: Amendment. Duration. Termination.
PARTIES:
Paraguay
USA (United States)

106241 Bilateral Exchange **433 UNTS 179**
SIGNED: 4 Feb 61 FORCE: 4 Feb 61
REGISTERED: 13 Jul 62 USA (United States)
ARTICLES: 2 LANGUAGE: English. Italian.
HEADNOTE: ASSUMPTION RIGHTS OBLIGATIONS TECHNICAL COOPERATION PROGRAM
TOPIC: Tech Assistance
CONCEPTS: Continuity of rights and obligations. General technical assistance.
TREATY REF: 237UNTS121.
PARTIES:
Somalia
USA (United States)
ANNEX
476 UNTS 342. USA (United States). Prolongation 22 Mar 62. Force 26 Mar 62.
476 UNTS 342. Somalia. Prolongation 26 Mar 62. Force 26 Mar 62.
476 UNTS 344. USA (United States). Prolongation 15 Jun 62. Force 17 Jun 62.
476 UNTS 344. Somalia. Prolongation 17 Jun 62. Force 17 Jun 62.
505 UNTS 324. Somalia. Prolongation 29 Dec 63. Force 29 Dec 63.
505 UNTS 324. USA (United States). Prolongation 24 Dec 63. Force 29 Dec 63.
535 UNTS 440. Somalia. Prolongation 30 Dec 64. Force 30 Dec 64.
535 UNTS 440. USA (United States). Prolongation 29 Dec 64. Force 30 Dec 64.
546 UNTS 382. USA (United States). Prolongation 19 Apr 65. Force 19 Apr 65.
546 UNTS 382. Somalia. Prolongation 7 Apr 65. Force 19 Apr 65.

106242 Bilateral Agreement **433 UNTS 185**
SIGNED: 27 Dec 61 FORCE: 27 Dec 61
REGISTERED: 13 Jul 62 USA (United States)
ARTICLES: 6 LANGUAGE: English.
HEADNOTE: AGRI COMMOD TITLE I
TOPIC: US Agri Commod Aid

CONCEPTS: General provisions. Annex or appendix reference. Exchange of information and documents. Reexport of goods, etc.. Exchange rates and regulations. Transportation costs. Local currency. Commodities schedule. Purchase authorization. Surplus commodities. Mutual consultation.
PARTIES:
USA (United States)
Vietnam, South
ANNEX
452 UNTS 347. USA (United States). Amendment 3 May 62. Force 3 May 62.
452 UNTS 347. Vietnam, South. Amendment 3 May 62. Force 3 May 62.
459 UNTS 319. Vietnam, South. Amendment 7 Jun 62. Force 7 Jun 62.
459 UNTS 319. USA (United States). Amendment 7 Jun 62. Force 7 Jun 62.
474 UNTS 358. USA (United States). Amendment 8 Mar 63. Force 8 Mar 63.
474 UNTS 358. Vietnam, South. Amendment 8 Mar 63. Force 8 Mar 63.

106243 Bilateral Exchange **433 UNTS 199**
SIGNED: 11 Nov 61　　　FORCE: 11 Nov 61
REGISTERED: 16 Jul 62 USA (United States)
ARTICLES: 2 LANGUAGE: English. Portuguese.
HEADNOTE: PEACE CORPS PROGRAM
TOPIC: Direct Aid
CONCEPTS: Visas. Privileges and immunities. Conformity with municipal law. Legal protection and assistance. Personnel. Exchange rates and regulations. Fees and exemptions. Funding procedures. Tax exemptions. Customs exemptions. Materials, equipment and services. Volunteer programs.
PROCEDURE: Termination.
PARTIES:
Brazil
USA (United States)

106244 Bilateral Agreement **433 UNTS 207**
SIGNED: 18 Nov 61　　　FORCE: 18 Nov 61
REGISTERED: 16 Jul 62 USA (United States)
ARTICLES: 6 LANGUAGE: English. French.
HEADNOTE: AGRI COMMOD TITLE I
TOPIC: US Agri Commod Aid
CONCEPTS: General provisions. Annex or appendix reference. Exchange of information and documents. Reexport of goods, etc.. Exchange rates and regulations. Transportation costs. Local currency. Commodities schedule. Purchase authorization. Surplus commodities. Mutual consultation.
PARTIES:
Congo (Zaire)
USA (United States)
ANNEX
456 UNTS 514. USA (United States). Amendment 4 May 62. Force 11 May 62.
456 UNTS 514. Congo (Zaire). Amendment 11 May 62. Force 11 May 62.
460 UNTS 330. Congo (Zaire). Amendment 8 Jun 62. Force 8 Jun 62.
460 UNTS 330. USA (United States). Amendment 23 Apr 62. Force 8 Jun 62.
460 UNTS 333. USA (United States). Amendment 31 Aug 62. Force 3 Aug 62.
460 UNTS 333. Congo (Zaire). Amendment 31 Aug 62. Force 3 Aug 62.
460 UNTS 337. USA (United States). Amendment 2 Nov 62. Force 2 Nov 62.
460 UNTS 337. Congo (Zaire). Amendment 2 Nov 62. Force 2 Nov 62.
462 UNTS 366. USA (United States). Amendment 27 Jul 62. Force 27 Jul 62.
462 UNTS 366. Congo (Zaire). Amendment 27 Jul 62. Force 27 Jul 62.
531 UNTS 378. USA (United States). Amendment 28 Aug 64. Force 4 Sep 64.
531 UNTS 378. Congo (Zaire). Amendment 4 Sep 64. Force 4 Sep 64.

106245 Bilateral Exchange **433 UNTS 221**
SIGNED: 20 Nov 61　　　FORCE: 13 Nov 61
REGISTERED: 16 Jul 62 USA (United States)
ARTICLES: 3 LANGUAGE: English. Spanish.
HEADNOTE: PEACE CORPS PROGRAM
TOPIC: Direct Aid
CONCEPTS: Treaty implementation. Diplomatic

privileges. Legal protection and assistance. Personnel. Exchange rates and regulations. Fees and exemptions. Funding procedures. Tax exemptions. Customs exemptions. Domestic obligation. Materials, equipment and services. Volunteer programs.
PROCEDURE: Termination.
PARTIES:
El Salvador
USA (United States)

106246 Bilateral Agreement **433 UNTS 231**
SIGNED: 6 Dec 61　　　FORCE: 6 Dec 61
REGISTERED: 16 Jul 62 USA (United States)
ARTICLES: 11 LANGUAGE: English.
HEADNOTE: EDUCATIONAL PROGRAM
TOPIC: Education
CONCEPTS: Definition of terms. Friendship and amity. Standardization. Conformity with municipal law. General cooperation. Exchange of information and documents. Inspection and observation. Personnel. General property. Exchange. Commissions and foundations. Scholarships and grants. Accounting procedures. Currency. Expense sharing formulae. Financial programs. Funding procedures. Customs exemptions. Special status.
INTL ORGS: Special Commission.
PROCEDURE: Amendment.
PARTIES:
Ethiopia
USA (United States)

106247 Bilateral Exchange **433 UNTS 243**
SIGNED: 21 Sep 61　　　FORCE: 21 Sep 61
REGISTERED: 16 Jul 62 USA (United States)
ARTICLES: 2 LANGUAGE: English. French.
HEADNOTE: NON-IMMIGRANT VISAS TREATY TRADERS INVESTORS
TOPIC: Visas
CONCEPTS: Time limit. Resident permits. Visas. Fees and exemptions.
PARTIES:
France
USA (United States)

106248 Bilateral Agreement **433 UNTS 249**
SIGNED: 26 Oct 61　　　FORCE: 26 Oct 61
REGISTERED: 16 Jul 62 USA (United States)
ARTICLES: 6 LANGUAGE: English.
HEADNOTE: AGRI COMMOD TITLE I
TOPIC: US Agri Commod Aid
CONCEPTS: General provisions. Annex or appendix reference. Exchange of information and documents. Reexport of goods, etc.. Exchange rates and regulations. Transportation costs. Local currency. Commodities schedule. Purchase authorization. Surplus commodities. Mutual consultation.
PARTIES:
Indonesia
USA (United States)

106249 Bilateral Agreement **433 UNTS 269**
SIGNED: 21 Dec 61　　　FORCE: 21 Dec 61
REGISTERED: 16 Jul 62 USA (United States)
ARTICLES: 6 LANGUAGE: English. Persian.
HEADNOTE: ECONOMIC COOPERATION
TOPIC: Direct Aid
CONCEPTS: Previous treaty replacement. Diplomatic privileges. Conformity with municipal law. General cooperation. Exchange of information and documents. Personnel. Accounting procedures. Attachment of funds. Exchange rates and regulations. Garnishment of funds. Seizure funds. Tax exemptions. Customs exemptions. Commodities and services. Domestic obligation. General technical assistance. Economic assistance. Aid missions. Grants.
TREATY REF: 200UNTS91.
PROCEDURE: Amendment. Ratification. Termination.
PARTIES:
Iran
USA (United States)

106250 Bilateral Exchange **433 UNTS 287**
SIGNED: 16 Oct 61　　　FORCE: 1 Jan 62
REGISTERED: 16 Jul 62 USA (United States)

ARTICLES: 2 LANGUAGE: English. Japanese.
HEADNOTE: COTTON TEXTILES
TOPIC: General Trade
CONCEPTS: Treaty interpretation. Annex type material. Commodity trade.
PARTIES:
Japan
USA (United States)
ANNEX
445 UNTS 378. Japan. Supplementation 23 Mar 62. Force 23 Mar 62.
445 UNTS 378. USA (United States). Supplementation 23 Mar 62. Force 23 Mar 62.

106251 Bilateral Agreement **433 UNTS 315**
SIGNED: 24 Nov 61　　　FORCE: 24 Nov 61
REGISTERED: 16 Jul 62 USA (United States)
ARTICLES: 6 LANGUAGE: English.
HEADNOTE: AGRI COMMOD TITLE I
TOPIC: US Agri Commod Aid
CONCEPTS: General provisions. Annex or appendix reference. Exchange of information and documents. Reexport of goods, etc.. Exchange rates and regulations. Transportation costs. Local currency. Commodities schedule. Purchase authorization. Surplus commodities. Mutual consultation.
PARTIES:
Philippines
USA (United States)
ANNEX
473 UNTS 364. USA (United States). Supplementation 14 Aug 62. Force 5 Sep 62.
473 UNTS 364. Philippines. Supplementation 5 Sep 62. Force 5 Sep 62.

106252 Bilateral Agreement **434 UNTS 3**
SIGNED: 15 Dec 61　　　FORCE: 15 Dec 61
REGISTERED: 16 Jul 62 USA (United States)
ARTICLES: 6 LANGUAGE: English. Polish.
HEADNOTE: AGRI COMMOD TITLE I
TOPIC: US Agri Commod Aid
CONCEPTS: General provisions. Annex or appendix reference. Exchange of information and documents. Reexport of goods, etc.. Exchange rates and regulations. Transportation costs. Local currency. Commodities schedule. Purchase authorization. Surplus commodities. Mutual consultation.
PARTIES:
Poland
USA (United States)
ANNEX
445 UNTS 383. USA (United States). Amendment 19 Mar 62. Force 19 Apr 62.
445 UNTS 383. Poland. Amendment 19 Apr 62. Force 19 Apr 62.

106253 Bilateral Agreement **434 UNTS 31**
SIGNED: 28 Nov 61　　　FORCE: 28 Nov 61
REGISTERED: 16 Jul 62 USA (United States)
ARTICLES: 5 LANGUAGE: English. Portuguese.
HEADNOTE: AGRI COMMOD TITLE I
TOPIC: US Agri Commod Aid
CONCEPTS: General provisions. Annex or appendix reference. Exchange of information and documents. Reexport of goods, etc.. Exchange rates and regulations. Transportation costs. Local currency. Commodities schedule. Purchase authorization. Surplus commodities. Mutual consultation.
PARTIES:
Portugal
USA (United States)
ANNEX
487 UNTS 380. Portugal. Amendment 26 Jun 63. Force 26 Jun 63.
487 UNTS 380. USA (United States). Amendment 5 Jun 63. Force 26 Jun 63.
527 UNTS 312. USA (United States). Amendment 23 Mar 64. Force 3 Apr 64.
527 UNTS 312. Portugal. Amendment 3 Apr 64. Force 3 Apr 64.

106254 Bilateral Exchange **434 UNTS 43**
SIGNED: 29 Dec 61　　　FORCE: 29 Dec 61
REGISTERED: 16 Jul 62 USA (United States)
ARTICLES: 2 LANGUAGE: English.
HEADNOTE: PEACE CORPS PROGRAM
TOPIC: Direct Aid

CONCEPTS: Treaty implementation. Diplomatic privileges. Legal protection and assistance. Personnel. Exchange rates and regulations. Fees and exemptions. Funding procedures. Tax exemptions. Customs exemptions. Domestic obligation. Materials, equipment and services. Volunteer programs.
PROCEDURE: Termination.
PARTIES:
Sierra Leone
USA (United States)

106255 Bilateral Agreement **434 UNTS 51**
SIGNED: 14 Nov 61   FORCE: 14 Nov 61
REGISTERED: 16 Jul 62 USA (United States)
ARTICLES: 6 LANGUAGE: English. Arabic.
HEADNOTE: AGRI COMMOD TITLE I
TOPIC: US Agri Commod Aid
CONCEPTS: General provisions. Annex or appendix reference. Exchange of information and documents. Reexport of goods, etc.. Exchange rates and regulations. Transportation costs. Local currency. Commodities schedule. Purchase authorization. Surplus commodities. Mutual consultation.
PARTIES:
Sudan
USA (United States)

106256 Bilateral Exchange **434 UNTS 77**
SIGNED: 28 Nov 61   FORCE: 28 Nov 61
REGISTERED: 16 Jul 62 USA (United States)
ARTICLES: 2 LANGUAGE: English.
HEADNOTE: PEACE CORPS PROGRAM
TOPIC: Direct Aid
CONCEPTS: Treaty implementation. Diplomatic privileges. Exchange of information and documents. Legal protection and assistance. Personnel. Tax exemptions. Customs exemptions. Domestic obligation. Materials, equipment and services. Volunteer programs.
PROCEDURE: Termination.
PARTIES:
Thailand
USA (United States)

106257 Bilateral Agreement **434 UNTS 85**
SIGNED: 30 Jun 61   FORCE: 30 Jun 61
REGISTERED: 16 Jul 62 USA (United States)
ARTICLES: 6 LANGUAGE: English. French.
HEADNOTE: AGRI COMMOD TITLE I
TOPIC: US Agri Commod Aid
CONCEPTS: General provisions. Annex or appendix reference. Exchange of information and documents. Reexport of goods, etc.. Exchange rates and regulations. Transportation costs. Local currency. Commodities schedule. Purchase authorization. Surplus commodities. Mutual consultation.
PARTIES:
Tunisia
USA (United States)

106258 Bilateral Exchange **434 UNTS 103**
SIGNED: 28 Aug 61   FORCE: 28 Aug 61
REGISTERED: 16 Jul 62 USA (United States)
ARTICLES: 2 LANGUAGE: English.
HEADNOTE: ACCOUNT CLOSING PAYMENTS CERTAIN AGRI COMMOD AGREEMENTS
TOPIC: Finance
CONCEPTS: Detailed regulations. Bonds. Transportation costs. General aid. Agricultural commodities. Loan and credit. Terms of loan. Surplus commodities.
TREATY REF: 265UNTS27; 247UNTS205; 290UNTS133; 307UNTS199.
PARTIES:
UK Great Britain
USA (United States)

106259 Bilateral Agreement **434 UNTS 111**
SIGNED: 28 Dec 61   FORCE: 28 Dec 61
REGISTERED: 16 Jul 62 USA (United States)
ARTICLES: 6 LANGUAGE: English.
HEADNOTE: AGRI COMMOD
TOPIC: US Agri Commod Aid
CONCEPTS: Currency. Agricultural commodities.

PARTIES:
USA (United States)
Yugoslavia
ANNEX
442 UNTS 348. USA (United States). Amendment 21 Apr 62. Force 21 Apr 62.
442 UNTS 348. Yugoslavia. Amendment 21 Apr 62. Force 21 Apr 62.
524 UNTS 328. USA (United States). Amendment 15 Apr 64. Force 15 Apr 64.
524 UNTS 328. Yugoslavia. Amendment 15 Apr 64. Force 15 Apr 64.
546 UNTS 388. USA (United States). Amendment 21 May 65. Force 21 May 65.
546 UNTS 388. Yugoslavia. Amendment 21 May 65. Force 21 May 65.

106260 Bilateral Exchange **434 UNTS 133**
SIGNED: 23 May 62   FORCE: 23 Jun 62
REGISTERED: 17 Jul 62 Belgium
ARTICLES: 2 LANGUAGE: English. French.
HEADNOTE: ISSUE VISAS
TOPIC: Visas
CONCEPTS: Time limit. Previous treaty replacement. Visas. Fees and exemptions.
TREATY REF: 11UNTS11; 84UNTS255; 84UNTS265.
PROCEDURE: Amendment. Termination.
PARTIES:
Belgium
USA (United States)

106261 Unilateral Instrument **434 UNTS 141**
SIGNED: 4 Dec 61   FORCE: 27 Oct 61
REGISTERED: 17 Jul 62 United Nations
ARTICLES: 1 LANGUAGE: Mongolian.
HEADNOTE: ACCEPTANCE OBLIGATIONS UN
TOPIC: UN Charter
CONCEPTS: Acceptance of obligations upon admittance to UN. Adherence to UN charter.
INTL ORGS: United Nations.
PARTIES:
Mongolia

106262 Multilateral Agreement **434 UNTS 145**
SIGNED: 23 Mar 62   FORCE: 1 Jul 62
REGISTERED: 23 Jul 62 Finland
ARTICLES: 40 LANGUAGE: Finnish. Danish. Icelandic. Norwegian. Swedish.
HEADNOTE: COOPERATION
TOPIC: General Amity
CONCEPTS: Peaceful relations. Court procedures. Standardization. General cooperation. Domestic legislation. Education. General cultural cooperation. Non-ILO labor relations. Free trade. Monetary and gold transfers. Payment schedules. Economic assistance. General communications. IGO operations.
INTL ORGS: Nordic Council.
PROCEDURE: Denunciation. Ratification.
PARTIES:

Denmark	SIGNED: 23 Mar 62	RATIFIED: 29 Jun 62	FORCE: 1 Jul 62
Finland	SIGNED: 23 Mar 62	RATIFIED: 29 Jun 62	FORCE: 1 Jul 62
Iceland	SIGNED: 23 Mar 62	RATIFIED: 29 Jun 62	FORCE: 1 Jul 62
Norway	SIGNED: 23 Mar 62	RATIFIED: 29 Jun 62	FORCE: 1 Jul 62
Sweden	SIGNED: 23 Mar 62	RATIFIED: 29 Jun 62	FORCE: 1 Jul 62

106263 Bilateral Agreement **434 UNTS 199**
SIGNED: 18 Feb 61   FORCE: 1 Jun 62
REGISTERED: 23 Jul 62 Finland
ARTICLES: 13 LANGUAGE: Finnish. Italian.
HEADNOTE: EXCHANGE STUDENT EMPLOYEES
TOPIC: Non-ILO Labor
CONCEPTS: Resident permits. Conformity with municipal law. Exchange of information and documents. Dispute settlement. Vocational training. Employment regulations. Safety standards. Wages and salaries. Non-ILO labor relations. Administrative cooperation. Unemployment. Migrant worker. Quotas. National treatment.
PROCEDURE: Duration. Ratification. Renewal or Revival. Termination.
PARTIES:
Finland
Italy

106264 Bilateral Agreement **434 UNTS 219**
SIGNED: 28 May 62   FORCE: 1 Jun 62
REGISTERED: 24 Jul 62 Australia
ARTICLES: 10 LANGUAGE: English.
HEADNOTE: ASSISTED PASSAGE
TOPIC: Admin Cooperation
CONCEPTS: Border traffic and migration. General cooperation. Expense sharing formulae. Funding procedures.
PARTIES:
Australia
UK Great Britain

106265 Bilateral Agreement **434 UNTS 227**
SIGNED: 5 Apr 62   FORCE: 5 Apr 62
REGISTERED: 27 Jul 62 Sierra Leone
ARTICLES: 17 LANGUAGE: English.
HEADNOTE: AIR SERVICES BETWEEN BEYOND RESPECTIVE TERRITORIES
TOPIC: Air Transport
CONCEPTS: Conditions. Definition of terms. Detailed regulations. Exceptions and exemptions. Annex or appendix reference. General cooperation. Exchange of information and documents. Arbitration. Procedure. Special tribunals. Negotiation. Reexport of goods, etc.. Monetary and gold transfers. Exchange rates and regulations. Fees and exemptions. Non-interest rates and fees. Customs exemptions. Routes and logistics. Permit designation. Conditions of airlines operating permission. Overflights and technical stops. Operating authorizations and regulations.
INTL ORGS: International Civil Aviation Organization.
TREATY REF: 15UNTS295.
PROCEDURE: Amendment. Future Procedures Contemplated. Termination. Application to Non-self-governing Territories.
PARTIES:
Sierra Leone
UK Great Britain

106266 Bilateral Agreement **435 UNTS 3**
SIGNED: 18 Jan 62   FORCE: 18 Jan 62
REGISTERED: 2 Aug 62 USA (United States)
ARTICLES: 11 LANGUAGE: English.
HEADNOTE: EDUCATIONAL PROGRAM
TOPIC: Education
CONCEPTS: Definition of terms. Friendship and amity. Standardization. Conformity with municipal law. General cooperation. Exchange of information and documents. Inspection and observation. Personnel. General property. Exchange. Commissions and foundations. Scholarships and grants. Accounting procedures. Currency. Exchange rates and regulations. Expense sharing formulae. Financial programs. Funding procedures. Customs exemptions. Special status.
INTL ORGS: Special Commission.
TREATY REF: 400UNTS411.
PARTIES:
Cyprus
USA (United States)

106267 Bilateral Instrument **435 UNTS 15**
SIGNED: 15 Jan 62   FORCE: 15 Jan 62
REGISTERED: 2 Aug 62 USA (United States)
ARTICLES: 11 LANGUAGE: English.
HEADNOTE: PROCEEDS WHEAT SALES
TOPIC: Commodity Trade
CONCEPTS: Treaty interpretation. General cooperation. Inspection and observation. Accounting procedures. Financial programs. Transportation costs. Commodity trade. General aid. Agricultural commodities. Transport of goods.
PROCEDURE: Amendment. Termination.
PARTIES:
Cyprus
USA (United States)

106268 Bilateral Agreement **435 UNTS 23**
SIGNED: 24 Jan 62   FORCE: 24 Jan 62
REGISTERED: 2 Aug 62 USA (United States)
ARTICLES: 11 LANGUAGE: English.
HEADNOTE: EDUCATIONAL PROGRAM
TOPIC: Education
CONCEPTS: Definition of terms. Friendship and amity. Standardization. Conformity with municipal law. General cooperation. Exchange of information and documents. Inspection and observa-

tion. Personnel. General property. Exchange. Commissions and foundations. Scholarships and grants. Accounting procedures. Currency. Expense sharing formulae. Financial programs. Funding procedures. Special status.
INTL ORGS: Special Commission.
TREATY REF: 368UNTS181.
PROCEDURE: Amendment.
PARTIES:
Ghana
USA (United States)

106269   Bilateral Agreement   **435 UNTS 35**
SIGNED: 2 Feb 62   FORCE: 2 Feb 62
REGISTERED: 2 Aug 62 USA (United States)
ARTICLES: 6 LANGUAGE: English. French.
HEADNOTE: AGRI COMMOD TITLE I
TOPIC: US Agri Commod Aid
CONCEPTS: General provisions. Annex or appendix reference. Exchange of information and documents. Reexport of goods, etc.. Exchange rates and regulations. Transportation costs. Local currency. Commodities schedule. Purchase authorization. Surplus commodities. Mutual consultation.
PARTIES:
Guinea
USA (United States)
ANNEX
451 UNTS 341. USA (United States). Amendment 3 May 62. Force 3 May 62.
451 UNTS 341. Guinea. Amendment 3 May 62. Force 3 May 62.
458 UNTS 364. USA (United States). Amendment 29 Jun 62. Force 29 Jun 62.
458 UNTS 364. Guinea. Amendment 29 Jun 62. Force 29 Jun 62.

106270   Bilateral Agreement   **435 UNTS 53**
SIGNED: 29 Jan 62   FORCE: 29 Jan 62
REGISTERED: 2 Aug 62 USA (United States)
ARTICLES: 6 LANGUAGE: English.
HEADNOTE: AGRI COMMOD TITLE I
TOPIC: US Agri Commod Aid
CONCEPTS: General provisions. Annex or appendix reference. Exchange of information and documents. Reexport of goods, etc.. Exchange rates and regulations. Transportation costs. Local currency. Commodities schedule. Purchase authorization. Surplus commodities. Mutual consultation.
PARTIES:
Iran
USA (United States)
ANNEX
531 UNTS 382. USA (United States). Amendment 10 Feb 64. Force 1 Sep 64.
531 UNTS 382. Iran. Amendment 1 Sep 64. Force 1 Sep 64.

106271   Bilateral Agreement   **435 UNTS 75**
SIGNED: 9 Nov 61   FORCE: 9 Nov 61
REGISTERED: 2 Aug 62 USA (United States)
ARTICLES: 7 LANGUAGE: English. Arabic.
HEADNOTE: AGRI COMMOD TITLE I
TOPIC: US Agri Commod Aid
CONCEPTS: General provisions. Annex or appendix reference. Exchange of information and documents. Reexport of goods, etc.. Exchange rates and regulations. Local currency. Transportation costs. Commodities schedule. Purchase authorization. Surplus commodities. Mutual consultation.
PARTIES:
Syria
USA (United States)
ANNEX
445 UNTS 389. Syria. Amendment 24 Feb 62. Force 24 Feb 62.
445 UNTS 389. USA (United States). Amendment 24 Feb 62. Force 24 Feb 62.

106272   Bilateral Exchange   **435 UNTS 99**
SIGNED: 19 Jan 62   FORCE: 19 Jan 62
REGISTERED: 2 Aug 62 USA (United States)
ARTICLES: 2 LANGUAGE: English.
HEADNOTE: PROTECT MONUMENTS FROM ASWAN HIGH DAM
TOPIC: Culture
CONCEPTS: Exceptions and exemptions. Inspec-

tion and observation. Accounting procedures. Currency. Funding procedures. Grants. Disposition of particulars.
PARTIES:
UNESCO (Educ/Cult)
USA (United States)

106273   Bilateral Agreement   **435 UNTS 107**
SIGNED: 19 Jan 62   FORCE: 10 Feb 62
REGISTERED: 2 Aug 62 USA (United States)
ARTICLES: 6 LANGUAGE: English.
HEADNOTE: AGRI COMMOD TITLE I
TOPIC: US Agri Commod Aid
CONCEPTS: General provisions. Annex or appendix reference. Exchange of information and documents. Reexport of goods, etc.. Exchange rates and regulations. Transportation costs. Local currency. Commodities schedule. Purchase authorization. Surplus commodities. Mutual consultation.
PARTIES:
United Arab Rep
USA (United States)
ANNEX
445 UNTS 394. USA (United States). Amendment 28 Apr 62. Force 23 Apr 63.
445 UNTS 394. United Arab Rep. Amendment 28 Mar 62. Force 23 Mar 63.
459 UNTS 324. USA (United States). Amendment 21 May 62. Force 21 May 62.
459 UNTS 324. United Arab Rep. Amendment 21 May 62. Force 21 May 62.
460 UNTS 340. United Arab Rep. Amendment 1 Sep 62. Force 1 Sep 62.
460 UNTS 340. USA (United States). Amendment 1 Sep 62. Force 1 Sep 62.

106275   Bilateral Exchange   **435 UNTS 127**
SIGNED: 22 Feb 62   FORCE: 22 Feb 62
REGISTERED: 2 Aug 62 USA (United States)
ARTICLES: 3 LANGUAGE: English.
HEADNOTE: PEACE CORPS PROGRAM
TOPIC: Direct Aid
CONCEPTS: Treaty implementation. Diplomatic privileges. Conformity with municipal law. General cooperation. Personnel. Tax exemptions. Customs exemptions. Materials, equipment and services. Volunteer programs.
PROCEDURE: Termination.
PARTIES:
UK Great Britain
USA (United States)

106276   Bilateral Agreement   **435 UNTS 137**
SIGNED: 19 Feb 62   FORCE: 19 Feb 62
REGISTERED: 2 Aug 62 USA (United States)
ARTICLES: 6 LANGUAGE: English.
HEADNOTE: AGRI COMMOD TITLE I
TOPIC: US Agri Commod Aid
CONCEPTS: General provisions. Annex or appendix reference. Exchange of information and documents. Reexport of goods, etc.. Exchange rates and regulations. Transportation costs. Local currency. Commodities schedule. Purchase authorization. Surplus commodities. Mutual consultation.
PARTIES:
Indonesia
USA (United States)
ANNEX
451 UNTS 346. USA (United States). Amendment 15 May 63. Force 15 May 63.
451 UNTS 346. Indonesia. Amendment 15 May 63. Force 15 May 63.
460 UNTS 344. USA (United States). Amendment 11 Jul 62. Force 11 Jul 62.
460 UNTS 344. Indonesia. Amendment 11 Jul 62. Force 11 Jul 62.
469 UNTS 436. USA (United States). Amendment 10 Dec 62. Force 10 Dec 62.
469 UNTS 436. Indonesia. Amendment 10 Dec 62. Force 10 Dec 62.
479 UNTS 386. USA (United States). Amendment 21 Jun 63. Force 21 Jun 63.
479 UNTS 386. Indonesia. Amendment 21 Jun 63. Force 21 Jun 63.
479 UNTS 394. USA (United States). Amendment 28 Jun 63. Force 28 Jun 63.
479 UNTS 394. Indonesia. Amendment 28 Jun 63. Force 28 Jun 63.

530 UNTS 370. USA (United States). Amendment 13 Aug 64. Force 13 Aug 64.
530 UNTS 370. Indonesia. Amendment 13 Aug 64. Force 13 Aug 64.

106277   Bilateral Instrument   **435 UNTS 155**
SIGNED: 1 Feb 62   FORCE: 13 Mar 62
REGISTERED: 3 Aug 62 IBRD (World Bank)
ARTICLES: 4 LANGUAGE: English.
HEADNOTE: LETTER OF PLEDGE
TOPIC: IBRD Project
CONCEPTS: Annex or appendix reference. Exchange of information and documents. Recognition of legal documents. Bonds.
TREATY REF: 406UNTS3.
PARTIES:
Israel
IBRD (World Bank)

106278   Bilateral Agreement   **435 UNTS 167**
SIGNED: 7 Aug 62   FORCE: 7 Aug 62
REGISTERED: 7 Aug 62 United Nations
ARTICLES: 6 LANGUAGE: English.
HEADNOTE: EXPERTS OPERATIONAL EXECUTIVE PERSONNEL
TOPIC: Tech Assistance
CONCEPTS: Treaty implementation. Annex or appendix reference. Privileges and immunities. Personnel. Responsibility and liability. Arbitration. Procedure. Negotiation. Vocational training. Compensation. Expense sharing formulae. Tax exemptions. Customs exemptions. Domestic obligation. Special projects. Status of experts. Conformity with IGO decisions.
INTL ORGS: Permanent Court of Arbitration. Arbitration Commission.
PROCEDURE: Amendment. Termination.
PARTIES:
Nigeria
United Nations
ANNEX
636 UNTS 368. United Nations. Termination 13 May 68. Force 20 Apr 68.
636 UNTS 368. Nigeria. Termination 13 May 68. Force 20 Apr 68.

106279   Bilateral Agreement   **435 UNTS 179**
SIGNED: 6 Aug 62   FORCE: 6 Aug 62
REGISTERED: 23 Aug 62 WHO (World Health)
ARTICLES: 6 LANGUAGE: French.
HEADNOTE: TECHNICAL ADVISORY ASSISTANCE
TOPIC: Tech Assistance
CONCEPTS: Definition of terms. Privileges and immunities. General cooperation. Exchange of information and documents. Personnel. Responsibility and liability. Title and deeds. Exchange. Scholarships and grants. Vocational training. Research and development. Expense sharing formulae. Local currency. Domestic obligation. Special projects. Materials, equipment and services. IGO status. Conformity with IGO decisions.
TREATY REF: 33UNTS261.
PROCEDURE: Amendment. Termination.
PARTIES:
WHO (World Health)
Senegal

106280 Multilateral Convention **435 UNTS 191**
SIGNED: 31 Mar 53   FORCE: 24 Aug 62
REGISTERED: 24 Aug 62 United Nations
ARTICLES: 14 LANGUAGE: English. French. Chinese. Russian. Spanish.
HEADNOTE: INTERNATIONAL RIGHT CORRECTION
TOPIC: Mass Media
CONCEPTS: Territorial application. Public information. Information agency. Press and wire services.
INTL ORGS: International Court of Justice. United Nations.
PROCEDURE: Amendment. Accession. Denunciation. Ratification. Registration.
PARTIES:
Argentina SIGNED: 11 Jun 53
Chile SIGNED: 22 Apr 53
Ecuador SIGNED: 31 Mar 53
United Arab Rep SIGNED: 27 Jan 55 RATIFIED: 4 Aug 55 FORCE: 24 Aug 62
El Salvador SIGNED: 11 Mar 58 RATIFIED: 28 Oct 50 FORCE: 24 Aug 62

Ethiopia SIGNED: 31 Mar 53
France SIGNED: 2 Apr 54
Guatemala SIGNED: 1 Apr 53 RATIFIED: 9 May 57 FORCE: 24 Aug 62
Paraguay SIGNED: 16 Nov 53
Peru SIGNED: 12 Nov 59
Sierra Leone RATIFIED: 25 Jul 62 FORCE: 24 Aug 62
ANNEX
444 UNTS 355. France. Ratification 16 Nov 62. Force 16 Dec 62.

106281 Bilateral Agreement 435 UNTS 237
SIGNED: 17 Jul 62 FORCE: 17 Jul 62
REGISTERED: 24 Aug 62 United Nations
ARTICLES: 10 LANGUAGE: English.
HEADNOTE: ASSISTANCE
TOPIC: Direct Aid
CONCEPTS: Detailed regulations. Treaty implementation. Visas. Privileges and immunities. Exchange of information and documents. Informational records. Inspection and observation. Operating agencies. Personnel. Public information. Responsibility and liability. Title and deeds. Use of facilities. Arbitration. Procedure. Negotiation. Import quotas. Attachment of funds. Exchange rates and regulations. Expense sharing formulae. Financial programs. Domestic obligation. General technical assistance. Economic assistance. Materials, equipment and services. IGO status.
INTL ORGS: International Atomic Energy Agency. International Court of Justice. United Nations. Arbitration Commission.
TREATY REF: 1UNTS15; 33UNTS261; 374UNTS147.
PROCEDURE: Amendment. Termination.
PARTIES:
UN Special Fund
Tanganyika
ANNEX
551 UNTS 320. Tanzania. Prolongation 31 Dec 65.
551 UNTS 320. UN Special Fund. Prolongation 2 Dec 65.

106282 Bilateral Exchange 435 UNTS 255
SIGNED: 25 Jan 61 FORCE: 1 Mar 61
REGISTERED: 27 Aug 62 New Zealand
ARTICLES: 2 LANGUAGE: English.
HEADNOTE: VISAS
TOPIC: Visas
CONCEPTS: Time limit. Resident permits. Visas. Garnishment of funds.
PARTIES:
Italy
New Zealand

106283 Bilateral Exchange 435 UNTS 261
SIGNED: 7 Aug 62 FORCE: 7 Aug 62
REGISTERED: 28 Aug 62 Australia
ARTICLES: 2 LANGUAGE: English.
HEADNOTE: CIVIL USES ATOMIC ENERGY
TOPIC: Atomic Energy
CONCEPTS: General. Nuclear materials. Peaceful use. Security of information.
INTL ORGS: International Atomic Energy Agency.
TREATY REF: 276UNTS3.
PARTIES:
Australia
Japan

106284 Bilateral Convention 435 UNTS 267
SIGNED: 17 Oct 61 FORCE: 25 May 62
REGISTERED: 28 Aug 62 Taiwan
ARTICLES: 10 LANGUAGE: Chinese. Arabic. English.
HEADNOTE: CULTURAL CONVENTION
TOPIC: Culture
CONCEPTS: Friendship and amity. Tourism. Exchange of information and documents. Exchange. Professorships. Scholarships and grants. Exchange. General cultural cooperation. Artists. Athletes. Scientific exchange. Publications exchange. Mass media exchange. Press and wire services.
TREATY REF: 4UNTS275; 18UNTS383.
PROCEDURE: Duration. Ratification. Renewal or Revival. Termination.

PARTIES:
Taiwan
Jordan

106285 Bilateral Convention 435 UNTS 281
SIGNED: 26 Feb 60 FORCE: 28 Jun 62
REGISTERED: 28 Aug 62 Taiwan
ARTICLES: 8 LANGUAGE: Chinese. Spanish.
HEADNOTE: CULTURAL CONVENTION
TOPIC: Culture
CONCEPTS: Friendship and amity. General cooperation. Specialists exchange. Teacher and student exchange. Exchange. General cultural cooperation. Artists. Athletes. Scientific exchange. Mass media exchange. Press and wire services.
TREATY REF: 4UNTS275; 18UNTS283.
PROCEDURE: Duration. Ratification. Renewal or Revival. Termination.
PARTIES:
Taiwan
Panama

106286 Bilateral Agreement 436 UNTS 3
SIGNED: 7 Mar 62 FORCE: 1 Jul 62
REGISTERED: 28 Aug 62 USA (United States)
ARTICLES: 4 LANGUAGE: English. French.
HEADNOTE: TARIFFS
TOPIC: General Trade
CONCEPTS: Detailed regulations. Tariffs. Trade procedures.
INTL ORGS: General Agreement on Tariffs and Trade.
TREATY REF: 55UNTS187.
PROCEDURE: Termination.
PARTIES:
Canada
USA (United States)

106287 Bilateral Agreement 436 UNTS 25
SIGNED: 27 Apr 62 FORCE: 27 Apr 62
REGISTERED: 28 Aug 62 USA (United States)
ARTICLES: 4 LANGUAGE: English. Chinese.
HEADNOTE: AGRI COMMOD TITLE I
TOPIC: US Agri Commod Aid
CONCEPTS: General provisions. Annex or appendix reference. Exchange of information and documents. Reexport of goods, etc.. Exchange rates and regulations. Transportation costs. Local currency. Commodities schedule. Purchase authorization. Surplus commodities. Mutual consultation.
PARTIES:
Taiwan
USA (United States)
ANNEX
459 UNTS 328. USA (United States). Amendment 25 May 62. Force 25 May 62.
459 UNTS 328. Taiwan. Amendment 25 May 62. Force 25 May 62.
459 UNTS 333. Taiwan. Amendment 9 Jun 62. Force 9 Jun 62.
459 UNTS 333. USA (United States). Amendment 9 Jun 62. Force 9 Jun 62.

106288 Bilateral Agreement 436 UNTS 49
SIGNED: 7 Mar 62 FORCE: 7 Mar 62
REGISTERED: 28 Aug 62 USA (United States)
ARTICLES: 5 LANGUAGE: English. French.
HEADNOTE: TARIFFS
TOPIC: General Trade
CONCEPTS: Detailed regulations. Annex type material. Tariffs. Trade procedures. Delivery schedules.
INTL ORGS: European Coal and Steel Community. General Agreement on Tariffs and Trade.
TREATY REF: 62UNTS60; 55UNTS187.
PARTIES:
EEC (Econ Commnty)
USA (United States)

106289 Bilateral Exchange 436 UNTS 93
SIGNED: 24 Apr 62 FORCE: 24 Apr 62
REGISTERED: 28 Aug 62 USA (United States)
ARTICLES: 2 LANGUAGE: English.
HEADNOTE: USE ZANDERIJ AIRPORT
TOPIC: Specific Property
CONCEPTS: Definition of terms. Visa abolition. Juridical personality. Use of facilities. Negotiation. General trade. Indemnities and reimbursements.

Tax exemptions. Customs exemptions. Airport facilities. Operating authorizations and regulations.
INTL ORGS: International Civil Aviation Organization.
PROCEDURE: Duration.
PARTIES:
Netherlands
USA (United States)

106290 Bilateral Agreement 436 UNTS 101
SIGNED: 5 Mar 62 FORCE: 5 Mar 62
REGISTERED: 28 Aug 62 USA (United States)
ARTICLES: 5 LANGUAGE: English.
HEADNOTE: INTERIM GATT
TOPIC: General Trade
CONCEPTS: Detailed regulations. Tariffs. Trade procedures. Delivery schedules.
INTL ORGS: General Agreement on Tariffs and Trade.
TREATY REF: 55UNTS187.
PARTIES:
Portugal
USA (United States)

106291 Bilateral Exchange 436 UNTS 107
SIGNED: 17 Apr 62 FORCE: 17 Apr 62
REGISTERED: 28 Aug 62 USA (United States)
ARTICLES: 2 LANGUAGE: English.
HEADNOTE: PEACE CORPS PROGRAM
TOPIC: Direct Aid
CONCEPTS: Treaty implementation. Diplomatic privileges. General cooperation. Personnel. Exchange rates and regulations. Tax exemptions. Customs exemptions. Domestic obligation. Materials, equipment and services. Volunteer programs.
PARTIES:
Somalia
USA (United States)

106292 Multilateral Convention 436 UNTS 115
SIGNED: 14 Dec 56 FORCE: 29 Aug 62
REGISTERED: 29 Aug 62 United Nations
ARTICLES: 14 LANGUAGE: English. French.
HEADNOTE: TAXATION ROAD VEHICLES
TOPIC: Taxation
CONCEPTS: Territorial application. Arbitration. Negotiation. General. Tax exemptions. Temporary importation. Motor vehicles and combinations.
INTL ORGS: United Nations. Arbitration Commission.
PROCEDURE: Amendment. Accession. Denunciation. Ratification. Registration. Renewal or Revival.
PARTIES:
Austria SIGNED: 14 Dec 56 RATIFIED: 7 Apr 60 FORCE: 29 Aug 62
Ghana RATIFIED: 29 Aug 62 FORCE: 29 Aug 62
Luxembourg SIGNED: 20 Feb 57
Morocco RATIFIED: 29 Aug 62 FORCE: 29 Aug 62
Netherlands SIGNED: 15 May 57
Norway SIGNED: 17 May 57 FORCE: 29 Aug 62
Poland SIGNED: 14 Dec 56
Sweden SIGNED: 14 Dec 56 RATIFIED: 16 Jan 58 FORCE: 28 Aug 62
ANNEX
535 UNTS 444. Luxembourg. Ratification 28 May 65. Force 26 Aug 65.
555 UNTS 255. Cuba. Qualified Accession 14 Feb 66. Force 15 May 66.
630 UNTS 399. Denmark. Accession 9 Feb 68. Force 9 May 68.

106293 Multilateral Convention 436 UNTS 131
SIGNED: 14 Dec 56 FORCE: 29 Aug 62
REGISTERED: 29 Aug 62 United Nations
ARTICLES: 14 LANGUAGE: English. French.
HEADNOTE: TAXATION ROAD VEHICLES
TOPIC: Taxation
CONCEPTS: Definition of terms. Territorial application. Arbitration. Negotiation. General. Tax exemptions. Transport of goods.
INTL ORGS: United Nations. Arbitration Commission.
PROCEDURE: Amendment. Accession. Denunciation. Ratification. Registration. Renewal or Revival. Termination.

PARTIES:
Austria SIGNED: 14 Dec 56 RATIFIED: 7 Apr 60
FORCE: 29 Aug 62
Ghana RATIFIED: 29 Aug 62 FORCE: 29 Aug 62
Luxembourg SIGNED: 20 Feb 57
Netherlands SIGNED: 15 May 57
Norway SIGNED: 17 May 57 FORCE: 29 Aug 62
Poland SIGNED: 14 Dec 56
Sweden SIGNED: 10 Dec 56 RATIFIED:
16 Jan 58 FORCE: 29 Aug 62
UK Great Britain SIGNED: 17 May 57
ANNEX
450 UNTS 474. UK Great Britain. Ratification
15 Jan 63. Force 15 Jan 63.
450 UNTS 474. UK Great Britain. Jersey Island.
Force 15 Apr 63.
450 UNTS 474. UK Great Britain. Isle of Man.
Force 15 Apr 63.
467 UNTS 493. UK Great Britain. Gibralter. Force
4 Sep 63.
535 UNTS 445. Luxembourg. Ratification
28 May 65. Force 26 Aug 65.
545 UNTS 351. Cuba. Qualified Accession
16 Sep 65. Force 15 Dec 65.
630 UNTS 399. Denmark. Accession 9 Feb 68.
Force 9 May 68.
631 UNTS 353. Romania. Qualified Accession
19 Feb 68.

106294 Bilateral Agreement **436 UNTS 147**
SIGNED: 12 Jul 61 FORCE: 1 Apr 62
REGISTERED: 29 Aug 62 Poland
ARTICLES: 25 LANGUAGE: Polish. Bulgarian.
HEADNOTE: COOPERATION MATTERS SOCIAL
POLICY
TOPIC: Admin Cooperation
CONCEPTS: Exceptions and exemptions. General
provisions. General cooperation. Procedure. An-
ti-discrimination. Old age and invalidity insur-
ance. Sickness and invalidity insurance. Social
security. Claims and settlements. Assets trans-
fer.
PROCEDURE: Denunciation. Ratification.
PARTIES:
Bulgaria
Poland

106295 Bilateral Treaty **436 UNTS 189**
SIGNED: 4 Jul 61 FORCE: 19 Apr 62
REGISTERED: 29 Aug 62 Poland
ARTICLES: 96 LANGUAGE: Polish. Czechoslovakian.
HEADNOTE: LEGAL RELATIONS CIVIL FAMILY
CRIMINAL MATTERS
TOPIC: Admin Cooperation
CONCEPTS: General provisions. Time limit. Nota-
rial acts and services. Privileges and immunities.
Extradition, deportation and repatriation. Extradition requests. Special factors. Concurrent re-
quests. Limits of prosecution. Provisional detain-
ment. Extradition postponement. Witnesses and
experts. Material evidence. Family law. Ex-
change of information and documents. Juridical
personality. Legal protection and assistance.
Recognition and enforcement of legal decisions.
Immovable property. General property. Succession. Competence of tribunal. Indemnities and
reimbursements. Assets transfer. Insured letters
and boxes.
PROCEDURE: Denunciation. Duration. Ratification.
Renewal or Revival.
PARTIES:
Czechoslovakia
Poland

106296 Bilateral Convention **437 UNTS 3**
SIGNED: 5 Jul 61 FORCE: 3 Feb 62
REGISTERED: 29 Aug 62 Poland
ARTICLES: 13 LANGUAGE: Polish. Hungarian.
HEADNOTE: REGULATION OF NATIONALITY
TOPIC: Consul/Citizenship
CONCEPTS: Treaty interpretation. Dual citizen-
ship. Nationality and citizenship. Fees and ex-
emptions.
PROCEDURE: Denunciation. Duration. Ratification.
Renewal or Revival.
PARTIES:
Hungary
Poland

106297 Bilateral Agreement **437 UNTS 25**
SIGNED: 23 Apr 61 FORCE: 15 Feb 62
REGISTERED: 4 Sep 62 Czechoslovakia
ARTICLES: 10 LANGUAGE: Czechoslovakian. Per-
sian. English.
HEADNOTE: CULTURAL COOPERATION
TOPIC: Culture
CONCEPTS: Treaty implementation. Friendship
and amity. Specialists exchange. Recognition of
degrees. Exchange. Teacher and student ex-
change. Scholarships and grants. Exchange.
General cultural cooperation. Artists. Athletes.
Scientific exchange. Publications exchange.
Mass media exchange.
PROCEDURE: Denunciation. Ratification.
PARTIES:
Afghanistan
Czechoslovakia

106298 Bilateral Instrument **437 UNTS 39**
SIGNED: 6 Jun 62 FORCE: 6 Jun 62
REGISTERED: 6 Sep 62 UK Great Britain
ARTICLES: 5 LANGUAGE: English. German.
HEADNOTE: CURRENCY DIFFICULTIES MAINTE-
NANCE FORCES
TOPIC: Status of Forces
CONCEPTS: Financial programs. Status of military
forces.
INTL ORGS: North Atlantic Treaty Organization.
Western European Union.
PROCEDURE: Future Procedures Contemplated.
PARTIES:
Germany, West
UK Great Britain

106299 Bilateral Agreement **437 UNTS 47**
SIGNED: 9 Dec 61 FORCE: 11 Dec 61
REGISTERED: 6 Sep 62 UK Great Britain
ARTICLES: 8 LANGUAGE: English.
HEADNOTE: EAST AFRICAN COMMON SERVICES
ORGANIZATION
TOPIC: IGO Establishment
CONCEPTS: Annex or appendix reference. Juridi-
cal personality. Funding procedures. Establish-
ment.
INTL ORGS: East African Common Services Orga-
nization.
PROCEDURE: Amendment. Duration. Termination.
PARTIES:
Tanganyika
UK Great Britain
ANNEX
457 UNTS 314. Tanganyika. Amendment
10 Oct 62. Force 10 Oct 62.
457 UNTS 314. UK Great Britain. Amendment
10 Oct 62. Force 10 Oct 62.
457 UNTS 318. UK Great Britain. Amendment
24 Nov 62. Force 24 Nov 62.
457 UNTS 318. Tanganyika. Amendment
22 Nov 62. Force 24 Nov 62.

106300 Bilateral Agreement **437 UNTS 111**
SIGNED: 8 Jun 61 FORCE: 9 Mar 62
REGISTERED: 6 Sep 62 UK Great Britain
ARTICLES: 8 LANGUAGE: English. Serbo-Croat.
HEADNOTE: ESTABLISHMENT UK INFORMATION
AGENCY
TOPIC: Mass Media
CONCEPTS: General cultural cooperation. Tax ex-
emptions. Customs exemptions. Information
agency.
PROCEDURE: Duration. Termination.
PARTIES:
UK Great Britain
Yugoslavia

106301 Bilateral Agreement **437 UNTS 127**
SIGNED: 16 Jun 62 FORCE: 16 Jun 62
REGISTERED: 17 Sep 62 WHO (World Health)
ARTICLES: 6 LANGUAGE: English. Arabic.
HEADNOTE: TECHNICAL ADVISORY ASSISTANCE
TOPIC: Tech Assistance
CONCEPTS: Definition of terms. Previous treaty replacement. Privileges and immunities. General
cooperation. Exchange of information and documents. Personnel. Responsibility and liability. Title and deeds. Exchange. Scholarships and
grants. Vocational training. Research and development. Expense sharing formulae. Local currency. Domestic obligation. Special projects.

Materials, equipment and services. IGO status.
Conformity with IGO decisions.
TREATY REF: 33UNTS261; 219UNTS305.
PROCEDURE: Amendment. Termination.
PARTIES:
Libya
WHO (World Health)

106302 Unilateral Instrument **437 UNTS 145**
SIGNED: 1 Jul 62 FORCE: 18 Sep 62
REGISTERED: 18 Sep 62 United Nations
ARTICLES: 1 LANGUAGE: French.
HEADNOTE: ACCEPTANCE OBLIGATIONS UN
TOPIC: UN Charter
CONCEPTS: Acceptance of UN obligations. Adher-
ence to UN charter.
INTL ORGS: United Nations.
PARTIES:
Rwanda

106303 Unilateral Instrument **437 UNTS 149**
SIGNED: 4 Jul 62 FORCE: 18 Sep 62
REGISTERED: 18 Sep 62 United Nations
ARTICLES: 1 LANGUAGE: French.
HEADNOTE: ACCEPTANCE OBLIGATIONS UN
TOPIC: UN Charter
CONCEPTS: Acceptance of UN obligations. Adher-
ence to UN charter.
INTL ORGS: United Nations.
TREATY REF: 431UNTS200.
PARTIES:
Burundi

106304 Unilateral Instrument **437 UNTS 153**
SIGNED: 6 Aug 62 FORCE: 18 Sep 62
REGISTERED: 18 Sep 62 United Nations
ARTICLES: 1 LANGUAGE: English.
HEADNOTE: ACCEPTANCE UN CHARTER
TOPIC: UN Charter
CONCEPTS: Acceptance of UN obligations. Adher-
ence to UN charter.
INTL ORGS: United Nations.
PARTIES:
Jamaica

106305 Unilateral Instrument **437 UNTS 157**
SIGNED: 6 Sep 62 FORCE: 18 Sep 62
REGISTERED: 18 Sep 62 United Nations
ARTICLES: 1 LANGUAGE: English.
HEADNOTE: ACCEPTANCE OBLIGATIONS UN
TOPIC: UN Charter
CONCEPTS: Acceptance of UN obligations. Adher-
ence to UN charter.
INTL ORGS: United Nations.
PARTIES:
Trinidad/Tobago

106306 Bilateral Convention **437 UNTS 161**
SIGNED: 27 Nov 61 FORCE: 20 Jun 62
REGISTERED: 18 Sep 62 Taiwan
ARTICLES: 8 LANGUAGE: Chinese. Spanish. En-
glish.
HEADNOTE: CULTURAL CONVENTION
TOPIC: Culture
CONCEPTS: Treaty interpretation. Friendship and
amity. Exchange. Exchange. General cultural co-
operation. Artists. Athletes. Scientific exchange.
Publications exchange. Mass media exchange.
Press and wire services.
TREATY REF: 4UNTS275; 18UNTS383.
PROCEDURE: Duration. Ratification. Renewal or
Revival. Termination.
PARTIES:
Taiwan
El Salvador

106307 Bilateral Agreement **437 UNTS 175**
SIGNED: 16 Apr 62 FORCE: 1 Aug 62
REGISTERED: 19 Sep 62 Norway
ARTICLES: 8 LANGUAGE: Swedish. Russian.
HEADNOTE: FISHING
TOPIC: Specific Resources
CONCEPTS: Definition of terms. Annex or appen-
dix reference. Conformity with municipal law.
Claims and settlements. Markers and definitions.
Fisheries and fishing.
PROCEDURE: Ratification.

PARTIES:
Norway
USSR (Soviet Union)

106308 Bilateral Agreement **437 UNTS 213**
SIGNED: 4 Nov 61 FORCE: 1 Feb 62
REGISTERED: 19 Sep 62 USSR (Soviet Union)
ARTICLES: 17 LANGUAGE: Russian. English.
HEADNOTE: TRADE
TOPIC: General Trade
CONCEPTS: Treaty implementation. Annex or appendix reference. Previous treaty replacement. Conformity with municipal law. General cooperation. Legal protection and assistance. Licenses and permits. Use of facilities. Export quotas. Import quotas. Trade agencies. Trade procedures. Payment schedules. Purchase authorizations. Non-interest rates and fees. Commodity trade. Most favored nation clause. Temporary importation. Navigational conditions. Transport of goods. Merchant vessels. Ports and pilotage.
TREATY REF: 421UNTS27.
PROCEDURE: Denunciation. Ratification. Renewal or Revival.
PARTIES:
Ghana
USSR (Soviet Union)

106309 Bilateral Convention **437 UNTS 233**
SIGNED: 14 Jun 62 FORCE: 14 Jun 62
REGISTERED: 19 Sep 62 USSR (Soviet Union)
ARTICLES: 12 LANGUAGE: Russian. French.
HEADNOTE: CULTURAL COOPERATION
TOPIC: Culture
CONCEPTS: Friendship and amity. Tourism. Conformity with municipal law. Specialists exchange. Public health. Recognition of degrees. Exchange. Teacher and student exchange. Scholarships and grants. Vocational training. General cultural cooperation. Artists. Athletes. Scientific exchange. Publications exchange. Mass media exchange.
PROCEDURE: Amendment. Duration. Termination.
PARTIES:
Senegal
USSR (Soviet Union)

106310 Bilateral Agreement **437 UNTS 243**
SIGNED: 30 Aug 61 FORCE: 16 Feb 62
REGISTERED: 19 Sep 62 USSR (Soviet Union)
ARTICLES: 11 LANGUAGE: Russian. Arabic.
HEADNOTE: ECONOMIC TECHNICAL COOPERATION
TOPIC: General Aid
CONCEPTS: Treaty implementation. Conformity with municipal law. Exchange of information and documents. Personnel. Teacher and student exchange. Institute establishment. Vocational training. Research and development. Accounting procedures. Banking. Indemnities and reimbursements. Exchange rates and regulations. Interest rates. Domestic obligation. General technical assistance. Special projects. Loan repayment. Terms of loan. Regulation of natural resources.
PROCEDURE: Ratification.
PARTIES:
Tunisia
USSR (Soviet Union)

106311 Bilateral Agreement **437 UNTS 273**
SIGNED: 15 Aug 62 FORCE: 21 Sep 62
REGISTERED: 21 Sep 62 United Nations
ARTICLES: 29 LANGUAGE: English.
HEADNOTE: CONCERNING WEST NEW GUINEA
TOPIC: Territory Boundary
CONCEPTS: Annex or appendix reference. Previous treaty replacement. Self-determination. Exchange of official publications. Exchange of information and documents. Domestic legislation. Post-colonial administration. Accounting procedures. Indemnities and reimbursements. IGO status. Trusteeship. Administering authority.
INTL ORGS: United Nations. United Nations Temporary Executive Authority.
PROCEDURE: Ratification. Registration.
PARTIES:
Indonesia
Netherlands

106312 Multilateral Instrument **437 UNTS 292**
SIGNED: 15 Aug 62 FORCE: 15 Aug 62
REGISTERED: 21 Sep 62 United Nations
ARTICLES: 4 LANGUAGE: English.
HEADNOTE: CONCERNING WEST NEW GUINEA
TOPIC: Territory Boundary
CONCEPTS: Annex or appendix reference. Disposition of territory.
INTL ORGS: United Nations Temporary Executive Authority.
PARTIES:
Indonesia SIGNED: 15 Aug 62 FORCE: 15 Aug 62
Netherlands SIGNED: 15 Aug 62 FORCE: 15 Aug 62
United Nations SIGNED: 15 Aug 62 FORCE: 15 Aug 62

106313 Bilateral Treaty **438 UNTS 3**
SIGNED: 2 Nov 61 FORCE: 8 Jul 62
REGISTERED: 26 Sep 62 Czechoslovakia
ARTICLES: 86 LANGUAGE: Czechoslovakian. Hungarian.
HEADNOTE: LEGAL RELATIONS CIVIL FAMILY CRIMINAL
TOPIC: Admin Cooperation
CONCEPTS: Exceptions and exemptions. General provisions. Privileges and immunities. Notarial acts and services. Extradition, deportation and repatriation. Extradition requests. Refusal of extradition. Concurrent requests. Limits of prosecution. Provisional detainment. Extradition postponement. Witnesses and experts. Material evidence. Family law. Exchange of information and documents. Juridical personality. Legal protection and assistance. Recognition and enforcement of legal decisions. Immovable property. General property. Succession. Public information. Prizes and arbitral awards. Indemnities and reimbursements. Assets transfer. Insured letters and boxes.
PROCEDURE: Duration. Ratification. Termination.
PARTIES:
Czechoslovakia
Hungary

106314 Bilateral Convention **438 UNTS 109**
SIGNED: 18 Aug 61 FORCE: 11 May 62
REGISTERED: 27 Sep 62 Taiwan
ARTICLES: 9 LANGUAGE: Chinese. Spanish. English.
HEADNOTE: CULTURAL CONVENTION
TOPIC: Culture
CONCEPTS: Treaty interpretation. Friendship and amity. Specialists exchange. Exchange. Teacher and student exchange. Exchange. General cultural cooperation. Artists. Athletes. Scientific exchange. Mass media exchange. Press and wire services.
TREATY REF: 4UNTS275.
PROCEDURE: Duration. Ratification. Renewal or Revival. Termination.
PARTIES:
Taiwan
Paraguay

106315 Bilateral Treaty **438 UNTS 123**
SIGNED: 9 Apr 56 FORCE: 31 Jul 56
REGISTERED: 27 Sep 62 Hungary
ARTICLES: 22 LANGUAGE: Hungarian. German.
HEADNOTE: REGULATION WATER ECONOMY QUESTIONS
TOPIC: Specific Resources
CONCEPTS: Annex or appendix reference. Exchange of official publications. Establishment of commission. Accounting procedures. Financial programs. Funding procedures. Temporary importation. Frontier waterways. Frontier crossing points. Regulation of natural resources.
INTL ORGS: Special Commission.
PROCEDURE: Denunciation. Duration. Ratification.
PARTIES:
Austria
Hungary

106316 Bilateral Convention **438 UNTS 173**
SIGNED: 13 Mar 58 FORCE: 12 Aug 59
REGISTERED: 27 Sep 62 Hungary
ARTICLES: 6 LANGUAGE: Hungarian. Bulgarian.
HEADNOTE: VETERINARY COOPERATION

TOPIC: Sanitation
CONCEPTS: Standardization. General cooperation. Exchange of information and documents. Informational records. Domestic legislation. Disease control. Public health. Veterinary. Exchange. Trade procedures. Bonds. Indemnities and reimbursements. Materials, equipment and services. Publications exchange. Media guaranty. Conferences.
PROCEDURE: Denunciation. Duration. Future Procedures Contemplated. Ratification. Renewal or Revival.
PARTIES:
Bulgaria
Hungary

106317 Bilateral Agreement **438 UNTS 191**
SIGNED: 13 Mar 58 FORCE: 12 Aug 59
REGISTERED: 27 Sep 62 Hungary
ARTICLES: 21 LANGUAGE: Hungarian. Bulgarian.
HEADNOTE: IMPORT EXPORT LIVESTOCK CONTAGIOUS DISEASES
TOPIC: Sanitation
CONCEPTS: Conditions. Definition of terms. Detailed regulations. Exceptions and exemptions. General cooperation. Exchange of information and documents. Inspection and observation. Domestic legislation. Procedure. Border control. Disease control. Veterinary. Trade procedures.
PROCEDURE: Duration. Ratification.
PARTIES:
Bulgaria
Hungary

106318 Bilateral Convention **438 UNTS 235**
SIGNED: 27 Jun 58 FORCE: 3 Jun 59
REGISTERED: 27 Sep 62 Hungary
ARTICLES: 24 LANGUAGE: Hungarian. Bulgarian.
HEADNOTE: CONSULAR CONVENTION
TOPIC: Culture
CONCEPTS: Definition of terms. Previous treaty replacement. Resident permits. Diplomatic and consular relations. General consular functions. Consular relations establishment. Diplomatic missions. Inviolability. Privileges and immunities. Property. Protection of nationals. Consular functions in shipping. Consular functions in property. Notarial acts and services. Legal protection and assistance.
TREATY REF: 104BFSP695; 69LTS327.
PROCEDURE: Denunciation. Duration. Ratification. Renewal or Revival.
PARTIES:
Bulgaria
Hungary

106319 Bilateral Agreement **438 UNTS 269**
SIGNED: 3 Apr 59 FORCE: 29 Dec 59
REGISTERED: 27 Sep 62 Hungary
ARTICLES: 9 LANGUAGE: Hungarian. Bulgarian.
HEADNOTE: HEALTH COOPERATION
TOPIC: Sanitation
CONCEPTS: Exchange of official publications. Exchange of information and documents. Informational records. Domestic legislation. Specialists exchange. Public health. Pharmaceuticals. Teacher and student exchange. Vocational training. Research results. Scientific exchange. Research and development. Indemnities and reimbursements. General technical assistance. Materials, equipment and services. Publications exchange.
PROCEDURE: Denunciation. Duration. Ratification. Renewal or Revival.
PARTIES:
Bulgaria
Hungary

106320 Bilateral Agreement **438 UNTS 287**
SIGNED: 30 Jun 61 FORCE: 1 Jan 62
REGISTERED: 27 Sep 62 Hungary
ARTICLES: 37 LANGUAGE: Hungarian. Bulgarian.
HEADNOTE: COOPERATION IN SOCIAL POLICY
TOPIC: Admin Cooperation
CONCEPTS: General provisions. Time limit. General cooperation. Domestic legislation. Procedure. Old age and invalidity insurance. Sickness and invalidity insurance. Social security. Claims and settlements. Assets transfer.
PROCEDURE: Denunciation. Duration. Ratification.

106321 Bilateral Agreement **439 UNTS 3**
SIGNED: 10 Jun 59 FORCE: 10 Jun 59
REGISTERED: 27 Sep 62 Hungary
ARTICLES: 11 LANGUAGE: Hungarian. Finnish.
HEADNOTE: CULTURAL
TOPIC: Culture
CONCEPTS: Treaty implementation. Friendship and amity. Establishment of commission. Exchange. Teacher and student exchange. Professorships. Scholarships and grants. General cultural cooperation. Artists. Anthropology and archeology. Scientific exchange. Mass media exchange.
INTL ORGS: Special Commission.
PROCEDURE: Duration. Future Procedures Contemplated. Termination.
PARTIES:
 Finland
 Hungary

106322 Bilateral Agreement **439 UNTS 17**
SIGNED: 27 Apr 61 FORCE: 1 May 62
REGISTERED: 27 Sep 62 Hungary
ARTICLES: 10 LANGUAGE: English.
HEADNOTE: CULTURAL COOPERATION
TOPIC: Culture
CONCEPTS: Definition of terms. Treaty interpretation. Friendship and amity. Exchange of information and documents. Specialists exchange. Public health. Recognition of degrees. Exchange. Teacher and student exchange. Scholarships and grants. General cultural cooperation. Artists. Athletes. Scientific exchange. Publications exchange. Mass media exchange.
PROCEDURE: Ratification. Termination.
PARTIES:
 Ghana
 Hungary

106323 Bilateral Agreement **439 UNTS 25**
SIGNED: 11 Apr 59 FORCE: 10 Nov 59
REGISTERED: 27 Sep 62 Hungary
ARTICLES: 15 LANGUAGE: Hungarian. Arabic. English.
HEADNOTE: CULTURAL
TOPIC: Culture
CONCEPTS: Friendship and amity. Non-diplomatic delegations. Public information. Establishment of commission. Recognition of degrees. Exchange. Teacher and student exchange. Scholarships and grants. Exchange. General cultural cooperation. Artists. Athletes. Anthropology and archeology. Scientific exchange. Publications exchange. Mass media exchange.
INTL ORGS: Special Commission.
PROCEDURE: Denunciation. Duration. Ratification.
PARTIES:
 Hungary
 Iraq

106324 Bilateral Agreement **439 UNTS 41**
SIGNED: 17 Apr 59 FORCE: 27 Nov 59
REGISTERED: 27 Sep 62 Hungary
ARTICLES: 7 LANGUAGE: Hungarian. Russian.
HEADNOTE: HEALTH MEDICAL SCIENCE COOPERATION
TOPIC: Sanitation
CONCEPTS: Treaty implementation. Friendship and amity. General cooperation. Exchange of information and documents. Domestic legislation. Specialists exchange. Quarantine. Public health. Teacher and student exchange. Vocational training. Sickness and invalidity insurance. Research results. Research and development. Indemnities and reimbursements. Funding procedures. General technical assistance. Publications exchange. Mass media exchange.
PROCEDURE: Denunciation. Duration. Ratification. Renewal or Revival.
PARTIES:
 Hungary
 USSR (Soviet Union)

106325 Bilateral Convention **439 UNTS 61**
SIGNED: 7 Oct 57 FORCE: 1 Jul 58

REGISTERED: 27 Sep 62 Hungary
ARTICLES: 33 LANGUAGE: Hungarian. Serbo-Croat.
HEADNOTE: SOCIAL SECURITY
TOPIC: Non-ILO Labor
CONCEPTS: Definition of terms. Exceptions and exemptions. Domestic legislation. Dispute settlement. Old age and invalidity insurance. Wages and salaries. Non-ILO labor relations. Family allowances. Administrative cooperation. Old age insurance. Sickness and invalidity insurance. Social security. Unemployment. Payment schedules. Claims and settlements. National treatment.
PROCEDURE: Denunciation. Duration. Ratification. Renewal or Revival.
PARTIES:
 Hungary
 Yugoslavia

106326 Bilateral Agreement **439 UNTS 113**
SIGNED: 22 Jun 60 FORCE: 23 Feb 62
REGISTERED: 27 Sep 62 Denmark
ARTICLES: 12 LANGUAGE: Danish. Spanish.
HEADNOTE: BILATERAL AIR TRANSPORT
TOPIC: Air Transport
CONCEPTS: Definition of terms. Exceptions and exemptions. Time limit. Annex or appendix reference. Conformity with municipal law. General cooperation. Licenses and permits. Recognition of legal documents. Use of facilities. Arbitration. Procedure. Existing tribunals. Negotiation. Reexport of goods, etc.. Fees and exemptions. Most favored nation clause. National treatment. Customs exemptions. Competency certificate. Routes and logistics. Navigational conditions. Permit designation. Air transport. Airport facilities. Airworthiness certificates. Conditions of airlines operating permission. Operating authorizations and regulations. Licenses and certificates of nationality.
INTL ORGS: International Civil Aviation Organization. Arbitration Commission.
TREATY REF: 15UNTSI95.
PROCEDURE: Amendment. Ratification. Registration. Termination.
PARTIES:
 Denmark
 Peru

106327 Bilateral Agreement **439 UNTS 151**
SIGNED: 19 Jun 62 FORCE: 19 Jun 62
REGISTERED: 28 Sep 62 WHO (World Health)
ARTICLES: 6 LANGUAGE: English.
HEADNOTE: TECHNICAL ADVISORY ASSISTANCE
TOPIC: Tech Assistance
CONCEPTS: Definition of terms. Privileges and immunities. General cooperation. Exchange of information and documents. Personnel. Responsibility and liability. Title and deeds. Exchange. Scholarships and grants. Vocational training. Research and development. Expense sharing formulae. Local currency. Domestic obligation. Special projects. Materials, equipment and services. IGO status. Conformity with IGO decisions.
TREATY REF: 33UNTS261.
PROCEDURE: Amendment. Termination.
PARTIES:
 WHO (World Health)
 Sierra Leone

106328 Bilateral Agreement **439 UNTS 163**
SIGNED: 16 Aug 62 FORCE: 1 Oct 62
REGISTERED: 1 Oct 62 Australia
ARTICLES: 18 LANGUAGE: English.
HEADNOTE: SOCIAL SECURITY
TOPIC: Non-ILO Labor
CONCEPTS: Annex type material. Previous treaty extension. Non-ILO labor relations. Social security.
TREATY REF: 292UNTS233.
PARTIES:
 Australia
 UK Great Britain

106329 Bilateral Agreement **439 UNTS 181**
SIGNED: 1 Oct 62 FORCE: 1 Oct 62
REGISTERED: 1 Oct 62 United Nations
ARTICLES: 6 LANGUAGE: French.

HEADNOTE: OPERATIONAL EXECUTIVE ADMINISTRATIVE PERSONNEL
TOPIC: Tech Assistance
CONCEPTS: Treaty implementation. Annex or appendix reference. Privileges and immunities. Personnel. Responsibility and liability. Arbitration. Procedure. Negotiation. Vocational training. Compensation. Expense sharing formulae. Tax exemptions. Customs exemptions. Domestic obligation. Special projects. Status of experts. Conformity with IGO decisions.
INTL ORGS: Permanent Court of Arbitration. Arbitration Commission.
PROCEDURE: Amendment. Termination.
PARTIES:
 Niger
 United Nations

106330 Multilateral Convention **439 UNTS 193**
SIGNED: 10 May 52 FORCE: 24 Feb 56
REGISTERED: 2 Oct 62 Belgium
ARTICLES: 18 LANGUAGE: French. English.
HEADNOTE: ARREST OF SEAGOING SHIPS
TOPIC: Admin Cooperation
CONCEPTS: Definition of terms. Detailed regulations. Navigational conditions.
INTL ORGS: Diplomatic Conference of International Maritime Law. Central Commission for the Navigation of the Rhine. International Court of Justice.
PARTIES:
 Belgium SIGNED: 10 May 52 RATIFIED: 10 Apr 61 FORCE: 10 Oct 61
 Brazil SIGNED: 10 May 52
 Cambodia RATIFIED: 12 Nov 56 FORCE: 12 May 57
 Costa Rica RATIFIED: 13 Jul 55 FORCE: 24 Feb 56
 United Arab Rep SIGNED: 6 Jan 55 RATIFIED: 24 Aug 55 FORCE: 24 Aug 56
 France All Territories RATIFIED: 23 Apr 58 FORCE: 23 Oct 58
 France French Cameroon RATIFIED: 23 Apr 58 FORCE: 23 Oct 58
 France French Togoland RATIFIED: 23 Apr 58 FORCE: 23 Oct 58
 France SIGNED: 10 May 52 RATIFIED: 25 May 57 FORCE: 25 Nov 57
 Germany, West SIGNED: 10 May 52
 Greece SIGNED: 10 May 52
 Haiti RATIFIED: 4 Nov 54 FORCE: 24 Feb 56
 Italy SIGNED: 10 May 52
 Lebanon SIGNED: 25 May 54
 Monaco SIGNED: 10 May 52
 Nicaragua SIGNED: 10 May 52
 Portugal SIGNED: 16 Oct 56 RATIFIED: 4 May 57 FORCE: 4 Nov 57
 Spain SIGNED: 10 May 52 RATIFIED: 8 Dec 53 FORCE: 24 Feb 56
 UK Great Britain SIGNED: 10 May 52 RATIFIED: 18 Mar 59 FORCE: 18 Sep 59
 Vatican/Holy See SIGNED: 4 Feb 54 RATIFIED: 10 Aug 56 FORCE: 10 Feb 57
 Yugoslavia SIGNED: 10 May 52
 ANNEX
552 UNTS 414. UK Great Britain. Hong Kong. Force 29 Sep 63.
552 UNTS 414. UK Great Britain. Bermuda. Force 30 Nov 63.
552 UNTS 414. UK Great Britain. North Borneo. Force 29 Sep 63.
552 UNTS 414. UK Great Britain. Sarawak. Force 28 Feb 63.
552 UNTS 414. UK Great Britain. Fiji Islands. Force 29 Sep 63.
552 UNTS 414. UK Great Britain. Gibralter. Force 29 Sep 63.
552 UNTS 414. UK Great Britain. British Guiana. Force 29 Sep 63.
552 UNTS 414. UK Great Britain. Seychelles. Force 29 Sep 63.
552 UNTS 414. UK Great Britain. Mauritius. Force 29 Sep 63.
552 UNTS 414. UK Great Britain. Brit Virgin Islands. Force 29 Nov 63.

106331 Multilateral Convention **439 UNTS 217**
SIGNED: 10 May 52 FORCE: 14 Sep 55
REGISTERED: 2 Oct 62 Belgium
ARTICLES: 16 LANGUAGE: French. English.
HEADNOTE: CIVIL JURISDICTION MATTERS COLLISION

Also at top left of page:
PARTIES:
 Bulgaria
 Hungary

TOPIC: Admin Cooperation
CONCEPTS: Territorial application. Previous treaty replacement. Arbitration. Claims and settlements. Navigational conditions.
INTL ORGS: Diplomatic Conference of International Maritime Law. Central Commission for the Navigation of the Rhine. International Court of Justice.
TREATY REF: 20DEMARTENS355.
PROCEDURE: Accession. Denunciation. Ratification.
PARTIES:
Argentina RATIFIED: 19 Apr 61 FORCE: 19 Oct 61
Belgium SIGNED: 10 May 52 RATIFIED: 10 Apr 61 FORCE: 10 Oct 61
Brazil SIGNED: 10 May 52
Cambodia RATIFIED: 12 Nov 56 FORCE: 12 May 57
Costa Rica RATIFIED: 13 Jul 55 FORCE: 13 Jan 56
Denmark SIGNED: 10 May 52
United Arab Rep SIGNED: 6 Jan 55 RATIFIED: 24 Aug 55 FORCE: 24 Feb 56
France All Territories RATIFIED: 23 Apr 58 FORCE: 23 Oct 58
France French Cameroon RATIFIED: 23 Apr 58 FORCE: 23 Oct 58
France French Togoland RATIFIED: 23 Apr 58 FORCE: 23 Oct 58
France SIGNED: 10 May 52 RATIFIED: 25 May 57 FORCE: 25 Nov 57
Germany, West SIGNED: 10 May 52
Greece SIGNED: 10 May 52
Italy SIGNED: 10 May 52
Lebanon SIGNED: 25 May 54
Monaco SIGNED: 10 May 52
Nicaragua SIGNED: 10 May 52
Portugal SIGNED: 16 Oct 56 RATIFIED: 4 May 57 FORCE: 4 Nov 57
Spain SIGNED: 10 May 52
Spain RATIFIED: 8 Dec 53 FORCE: 14 Sep 55
UK Great Britain SIGNED: 10 May 52 RATIFIED: 18 Mar 59 FORCE: 18 Sep 59
Vatican/Holy See SIGNED: 4 Feb 54 RATIFIED: 10 Aug 56 FORCE: 10 Feb 57
Yugoslavia SIGNED: 10 May 52 RATIFIED: 14 May 55 FORCE: 14 Sep 55
ANNEX
552 UNTS 414. UK Great Britain. Sarawak. Force 28 Feb 63.
552 UNTS 414. UK Great Britain. British Guiana. Force 29 Sep 63.
552 UNTS 414. UK Great Britain. Fiji Islands. Force 29 Sep 63.
552 UNTS 414. UK Great Britain. Bermuda. Force 30 Nov 63.
552 UNTS 414. UK Great Britain. Gibralter. Force 29 Sep 63.
552 UNTS 414. UK Great Britain. Mauritius. Force 29 Sep 63.
552 UNTS 414. UK Great Britain. North Borneo. Force 29 Sep 63.
552 UNTS 414. UK Great Britain. Seychelles. Force 29 Sep 63.
552 UNTS 414. UK Great Britain. Brit Virgin Islands. Force 29 Nov 63.
552 UNTS 414. UK Great Britain. Hong Kong. Force 29 Sep 63.
560 UNTS 284. UK Great Britain. Bahamas. Force 12 Nov 65.
560 UNTS 284. UK Great Britain. Anguilla. Force 12 Nov 65.
560 UNTS 284. UK Great Britain. St. Lucia. Force 12 Nov 65.
560 UNTS 284. UK Great Britain. Grenada. Force 12 Nov 65.
560 UNTS 284. UK Great Britain. British Honduras. Force 21 Mar 66.
560 UNTS 284. Greece. Ratification 15 Mar 65. Force 15 Sep 65.
560 UNTS 284. UK Great Britain. Cayman Island. Force 12 Nov 65.
560 UNTS 284. UK Great Britain. Montserrat. Force 12 Nov 65.
560 UNTS 284. UK Great Britain. St. Christopher. Force 12 Nov 65.
560 UNTS 284. UK Great Britain. Brit Solomon Is. Force 21 Mar 66.
560 UNTS 284. UK Great Britain. St. Vincent. Force 12 Nov 65.
560 UNTS 284. UK Great Britain. Gilbert Islands. Force 21 Mar 66.

560 UNTS 284. Nigeria. Accession 7 Nov 63. Force 7 May 64.
560 UNTS 284. UK Great Britain. Turk-Caicose Is. Force 21 Mar 66.
560 UNTS 284. UK Great Britain. Antigua. Force 12 Nov 65.
560 UNTS 284. UK Great Britain. Dominican Republic. Force 12 Nov 65.
560 UNTS 284. Algeria. Accession 18 Aug 64. Force 18 Feb 65.
560 UNTS 284. UK Great Britain. St. Helena. Force 12 Nov 65.
560 UNTS 284. UK Great Britain. Nevis. Force 12 Nov 65.

106332 Multilateral Agreement **439 UNTS 233**
SIGNED: 10 May 52 FORCE: 20 Nov 55
REGISTERED: 2 Oct 62 Belgium
ARTICLES: 15 LANGUAGE: French. English.
HEADNOTE: PENAL JURISDICTION MATTERS NAVIGATION
TOPIC: Taxation
CONCEPTS: Territorial application. Juridical personality. Arbitration. Inland and territorial waters. Shipwreck and salvage.
INTL ORGS: Diplomatic Conference of International Maritime Law. International Court of Justice.
PROCEDURE: Amendment. Accession. Denunciation. Ratification.
PARTIES:
Argentina RATIFIED: 19 Apr 61 FORCE: 19 Oct 61
Belgium SIGNED: 10 May 52 RATIFIED: 10 Apr 61 FORCE: 10 Oct 61
Brazil SIGNED: 10 May 52
Burma RATIFIED: 8 Jul 53 FORCE: 20 Nov 55
Cambodia RATIFIED: 12 Nov 56 FORCE: 12 May 57
Costa Rica RATIFIED: 13 Jul 55 FORCE: 13 Jan 56
Denmark SIGNED: 10 May 52
United Arab Rep SIGNED: 6 Jan 55 RATIFIED: 24 Aug 55 FORCE: 24 Feb 56
France All Territories RATIFIED: 23 Apr 58 FORCE: 23 Oct 58
France French Cameroon RATIFIED: 23 Apr 58 FORCE: 23 Oct 58
France French Togoland RATIFIED: 23 Apr 58 FORCE: 23 Oct 58
France SIGNED: 10 May 52 RATIFIED: 20 May 55 FORCE: 20 Nov 55
Germany, West SIGNED: 10 May 52
Greece SIGNED: 10 May 52
Haiti RATIFIED: 17 Sep 54 FORCE: 20 Nov 55
Italy SIGNED: 10 May 52
Lebanon SIGNED: 25 May 54
Monaco SIGNED: 10 May 52
Nicaragua SIGNED: 10 May 52
Portugal SIGNED: 16 Oct 56 RATIFIED: 4 May 57 FORCE: 4 Nov 57
Spain SIGNED: 10 May 52 RATIFIED: 8 Dec 53 FORCE: 20 Nov 55
UK Great Britain SIGNED: 10 May 52 RATIFIED: 18 Mar 59 FORCE: 18 Sep 59
Vatican/Holy See SIGNED: 4 Feb 54 RATIFIED: 10 Aug 56 FORCE: 10 Feb 57
Vietnam, North RATIFIED: 26 Nov 55 FORCE: 26 May 56
Yugoslavia SIGNED: 10 May 52 RATIFIED: 21 Apr 56 FORCE: 21 Oct 56
ANNEX
552 UNTS 414. UK Great Britain. Bermuda. Force 30 Nov 63.
552 UNTS 414. UK Great Britain. Gibralter. Force 29 Sep 63.
552 UNTS 414. UK Great Britain. Mauritius. Force 29 Sep 63.
552 UNTS 414. UK Great Britain. North Borneo. Force 29 Sep 63.
552 UNTS 414. UK Great Britain. Seychelles. Force 29 Sep 63.
552 UNTS 414. UK Great Britain. Brit Virgin Islands. Force 29 Sep 63.
552 UNTS 414. UK Great Britain. Hong Kong. Force 29 Sep 63.
552 UNTS 414. UK Great Britain. Fiji Islands. Force 29 Sep 63.
560 UNTS 286. UK Great Britain. Dominican Republic. Force 21 Mar 66.
560 UNTS 286. UK Great Britain. Grenada. Force 21 Mar 66.

560 UNTS 286. UK Great Britain. Montserrat. Force 21 Mar 66.
560 UNTS 286. UK Great Britain. Antigua. Force 21 Mar 66.
560 UNTS 286. UK Great Britain. St. Christopher. Force 21 Mar 66.
560 UNTS 286. UK Great Britain. Nevis. Force 21 Mar 66.
560 UNTS 286. UK Great Britain. Anguilla. Force 21 Mar 66.
560 UNTS 286. UK Great Britain. St. Helena. Force 21 Mar 66.
560 UNTS 286. UK Great Britain. St. Lucia. Force 21 Mar 66.
560 UNTS 286. UK Great Britain. St. Vincent. Force 21 Mar 66.
560 UNTS 286. Nigeria. Qualified Accession 7 Nov 63. Force 7 May 64.
560 UNTS 286. UK Great Britain. British Honduras. Force 21 Mar 66.
560 UNTS 286. Greece. Ratification 15 Mar 65. Force 15 Sep 65.
560 UNTS 286. UK Great Britain. Brit Solomon Is. Force 21 Mar 66.
560 UNTS 286. UK Great Britain. Gilbert Islands. Force 21 Mar 66.
560 UNTS 286. UK Great Britain. Turk-Caicose Is. Force 21 Mar 66.
560 UNTS 286. UK Great Britain. Cayman Island. Force 21 Mar 66.
560 UNTS 286. UK Great Britain. Bahamas. Force 21 Mar 66.

106333 Multilateral Instrument **439 UNTS 249**
SIGNED: 26 Jan 60 FORCE: 24 Sep 60
REGISTERED: 4 Oct 62 IBRD (World Bank)
ARTICLES: 11 LANGUAGE: English.
HEADNOTE: INTERNATIONAL DEVELOPMENT ASSOCIATION
TOPIC: IGO Establishment
CONCEPTS: Default remedies. Treaty interpretation. Annex or appendix reference. Treaty violation. Diplomatic privileges. Privileges and immunities. Exchange of information and documents. Juridical personality. Arbitration. Currency. Monetary and gold transfers. Exchange rates and regulations. Fees and exemptions. Funding procedures. Garnishment of funds. Customs exemptions. Plans and standards. Admission. Establishment. Liaison with other IGO's. Internal structure. Freedom of meeting. IGO obligations. UN administrative tribunal. Inter-agency agreements.
INTL ORGS: International Bank for Reconstruction and Development. International Development Association. International Monetary Fund. United Nations.
PROCEDURE: Amendment. Accession. Denunciation. Registration.
PARTIES:
Afghanistan SIGNED: 2 Feb 61 RATIFIED: 2 Feb 61 FORCE: 2 Feb 61
Argentina SIGNED: 19 Jan 62 RATIFIED: 3 Aug 62 FORCE: 3 Aug 62
Australia SIGNED: 11 Jul 60 RATIFIED: 11 Jul 60 FORCE: 24 Sep 60
Austria SIGNED: 31 Dec 60 RATIFIED: 28 Jun 61 FORCE: 28 Jun 61
Bolivia SIGNED: 21 Jun 61 RATIFIED: 21 Jun 61 FORCE: 21 Jun 61
Brazil SIGNED: 29 Jun 61
Canada SIGNED: 9 Aug 60 RATIFIED: 9 Aug 60 FORCE: 24 Sep 60
Ceylon (Sri Lanka) SIGNED: 27 Jun 61 RATIFIED: 27 Jun 61 FORCE: 27 Jun 61
Chile SIGNED: 30 Dec 60 RATIFIED: 30 Dec 60 FORCE: 30 Dec 60
Taiwan SIGNED: 1 Aug 60 RATIFIED: 1 Aug 60 FORCE: 24 Sep 60
Colombia SIGNED: 4 Nov 60 RATIFIED: 16 Jun 61 FORCE: 16 Jun 61
Costa Rica SIGNED: 30 Jun 61 RATIFIED: 30 Jun 61 FORCE: 30 Jun 61
Cyprus SIGNED: 2 Mar 62 RATIFIED: 2 Mar 62 FORCE: 2 Mar 62
Denmark SIGNED: 30 Nov 60 RATIFIED: 30 Nov 60 FORCE: 30 Nov 60
Ecuador SIGNED: 21 Mar 60 RATIFIED: 7 Nov 61 FORCE: 7 Nov 61
El Salvador SIGNED: 23 Apr 62 RATIFIED: 23 Apr 62 FORCE: 23 Apr 62
Ethiopia SIGNED: 29 Aug 60 RATIFIED: 10 Apr 61 FORCE: 11 Apr 61

Finland SIGNED: 29 Dec 60 RATIFIED: 29 Dec 60 FORCE: 29 Dec 60

Fed of Malaya SIGNED: 2 Sep 60 RATIFIED: 2 Sep 60 FORCE: 24 Sep 60

France SIGNED: 30 Dec 60 RATIFIED: 30 Dec 60 FORCE: 30 Dec 60

Germany, West SIGNED: 21 Sep 60 RATIFIED: 24 Sep 60 FORCE: 24 Sep 60

Ghana SIGNED: 29 Dec 60 RATIFIED: 29 Dec 60 FORCE: 29 Dec 60

Greece SIGNED: 31 Oct 61 RATIFIED: 9 Jan 62 FORCE: 9 Jan 62

Guatemala SIGNED: 2 Dec 60 RATIFIED: 27 Apr 61 FORCE: 27 Apr 61

Haiti SIGNED: 13 Jun 61 RATIFIED: 13 Jun 61 FORCE: 13 Jun 61

Honduras SIGNED: 9 Aug 60 RATIFIED: 23 Dec 60 FORCE: 23 Dec 60

India SIGNED: 14 Sep 60 RATIFIED: 20 Sep 60 FORCE: 24 Sep 60

Iran SIGNED: 10 Oct 60 RATIFIED: 10 Oct 60 FORCE: 10 Oct 60

Iraq SIGNED: 7 Nov 60 RATIFIED: 29 Nov 60 FORCE: 29 Nov 60

Ireland SIGNED: 22 Dec 60 RATIFIED: 22 Dec 60 FORCE: 22 Dec 60

Israel SIGNED: 22 Dec 60 RATIFIED: 22 Dec 60 FORCE: 22 Dec 60

Italy SIGNED: 19 Sep 60 RATIFIED: 19 Sep 60 FORCE: 24 Sep 60

Japan SIGNED: 27 Dec 60 RATIFIED: 27 Dec 60 FORCE: 27 Dec 60

Jordan SIGNED: 4 Oct 60 RATIFIED: 4 Oct 60 FORCE: 4 Oct 60

Korea, South SIGNED: 18 May 61 RATIFIED: 18 May 61 FORCE: 18 May 61

Lebanon SIGNED: 10 Apr 62 RATIFIED: 10 Apr 62 FORCE: 10 Apr 62

Liberia SIGNED: 28 Mar 62 RATIFIED: 28 Mar 62 FORCE: 28 Mar 62

Libya SIGNED: 26 Jan 60 RATIFIED: 1 Aug 61 FORCE: 1 Aug 61

Mexico SIGNED: 31 Dec 60 RATIFIED: 24 Apr 61 FORCE: 24 Apr 61

Morocco SIGNED: 29 Dec 60 RATIFIED: 29 Dec 60 FORCE: 29 Dec 60

Netherlands SIGNED: 21 Sep 60 RATIFIED: 30 Jun 61 FORCE: 30 Jun 61

Nicaragua SIGNED: 30 Dec 60 RATIFIED: 30 Dec 60 FORCE: 30 Dec 60

Nigeria SIGNED: 14 Nov 61 RATIFIED: 14 Nov 61 FORCE: 14 Nov 61

Norway SIGNED: 12 Jun 60 RATIFIED: 16 Aug 60 FORCE: 24 Sep 60

Pakistan SIGNED: 9 Jun 60 RATIFIED: 9 Jun 60 FORCE: 24 Sep 60

Panama SIGNED: 1 Sep 61 RATIFIED: 1 Sep 61 FORCE: 1 Sep 61

Paraguay SIGNED: 25 Oct 60 RATIFIED: 10 Feb 61 FORCE: 10 Feb 61

Peru SIGNED: 30 Aug 61 RATIFIED: 30 Aug 61 FORCE: 30 Aug 61

Philippines SIGNED: 28 Oct 60 RATIFIED: 28 Oct 60 FORCE: 28 Oct 60

Saudi Arabia SIGNED: 30 Dec 60 RATIFIED: 30 Dec 60 FORCE: 30 Dec 60

Senegal SIGNED: 31 Aug 62 RATIFIED: 31 Aug 62 FORCE: 31 Aug 62

South Africa SIGNED: 12 Oct 60 RATIFIED: 12 Oct 60 FORCE: 12 Oct 60

Somalia SIGNED: 31 Aug 62 RATIFIED: 31 Aug 62 FORCE: 31 Aug 62

Spain SIGNED: 18 Oct 60 RATIFIED: 18 Oct 60 FORCE: 18 Oct 60

Sudan SIGNED: 25 Aug 60 RATIFIED: 25 Aug 60 FORCE: 24 Sep 60

Sweden SIGNED: 21 Jun 60 RATIFIED: 21 Jun 60 FORCE: 24 Sep 60

Syria SIGNED: 28 Jun 62 RATIFIED: 28 Jun 62 FORCE: 28 Jun 62

Thailand SIGNED: 24 Sep 60 RATIFIED: 24 Sep 60 FORCE: 24 Sep 60

Togo SIGNED: 21 Aug 62 RATIFIED: 21 Aug 62 FORCE: 21 Aug 62

Tunisia SIGNED: 30 Dec 60 RATIFIED: 30 Dec 60 FORCE: 30 Dec 60

Turkey SIGNED: 22 Dec 60 RATIFIED: 22 Dec 60 FORCE: 22 Dec 60

United Arab Rep SIGNED: 26 Oct 60 RATIFIED: 26 Oct 60 FORCE: 26 Oct 60

UK Great Britain SIGNED: 10 Sep 60 RATIFIED: 14 Sep 60 FORCE: 24 Sep 60

USA (United States) SIGNED: 9 Aug 60 RATIFIED: 9 Aug 60 FORCE: 24 Sep 60

Vietnam, South SIGNED: 27 Jul 60 RATIFIED: 27 Jul 60 FORCE: 24 Sep 60

Yugoslavia SIGNED: 26 Oct 60 RATIFIED: 26 Oct 60 FORCE: 26 Oct 60

ANNEX

480 UNTS 438. Niger. Signature 24 Apr 63. Acceptance 24 Apr 63.

480 UNTS 438. Central Afri Rep. Signature 27 Aug 63. Acceptance 27 Aug 63.

480 UNTS 438. Mauritania. Signature 10 Sep 63. Acceptance 10 Sep 63.

480 UNTS 438. Dahomey. Signature 16 Sep 63. Acceptance 16 Sep 63.

480 UNTS 438. Madagascar. Signature 25 Sep 63. Acceptance 25 Sep 63.

480 UNTS 438. Algeria. Signature 26 Sep 63. Acceptance 26 Sep 63.

480 UNTS 438. Uganda. Signature 27 Sep 63. Acceptance 27 Sep 63.

480 UNTS 438. Mali. Signature 27 Sep 63. Acceptance 27 Sep 63.

480 UNTS 438. Congo (Zaire). Signature 28 Sep 63. Acceptance 28 Sep 63.

480 UNTS 438. Burundi. Signature 28 Sep 63. Acceptance 28 Sep 63.

480 UNTS 438. Rwanda. Signature 30 Sep 63. Acceptance 30 Sep 63.

480 UNTS 438. Tanganyika. Signature 10 Sep 62. Acceptance 6 Nov 62.

480 UNTS 438. Sierra Leone. Signature 10 Sep 62. Acceptance 13 Nov 62.

480 UNTS 438. Kuwait. Signature 13 Sep 62. Acceptance 13 Sep 62.

480 UNTS 438. Burma. Signature 5 Nov 62. Acceptance 5 Nov 62.

480 UNTS 438. Dominican Republic. Signature 16 Nov 62. Acceptance 16 Nov 62.

480 UNTS 438. Upper Volta. Signature 2 May 63. Acceptance 2 May 63.

480 UNTS 438. Nepal. Signature 6 Mar 63. Acceptance 6 Mar 63.

480 UNTS 438. Laos. Signature 28 Oct 63. Acceptance 28 Oct 63.

480 UNTS 438. Ivory Coast. Signature 11 Mar 63. Acceptance 11 Mar 63.

528 UNTS 310. Belgium. Signature 2 Jul 64. Acceptance 2 Jul 64.

528 UNTS 310. Brazil. Signature 29 Jun 61. Acceptance 15 Mar 63.

528 UNTS 310. Chad. Signature 7 Nov 63. Acceptance 7 Nov 63.

528 UNTS 310. Congo (Brazzaville). Signature 8 Nov 63. Acceptance 10 Nov 63.

528 UNTS 310. Gabon. Signature 4 Nov 63. Acceptance 4 Nov 63.

528 UNTS 310. Cameroon. Signature 10 Apr 64. Acceptance 10 Apr 64.

642 UNTS 377. Zambia. Acceptance 23 Sep 65.

642 UNTS 377. Gambia. Acceptance 18 Oct 67.

642 UNTS 377. Guyana. Acceptance 4 Jan 67.

642 UNTS 377. Botswana. Acceptance 24 Jul 68.

642 UNTS 377. Malawi. Acceptance 19 Jul 65.

106334 Bilateral Agreement **442 UNTS 3**
SIGNED: 29 Aug 62 FORCE: 29 Aug 62
REGISTERED: 9 Oct 62 United Nations
ARTICLES: 6 LANGUAGE: French.
HEADNOTE: OPERATIONAL EXECUTIVE PERSONNEL
TOPIC: Tech Assistance
CONCEPTS: Treaty implementation. Annex or appendix reference. Privileges and immunities. Personnel. Responsibility and liability. Arbitration. Procedure. Negotiation. Vocational training. Compensation. Expense sharing formulae. Tax exemptions. Customs exemptions. Domestic obligation. Special projects. Status of experts. Conformity with IGO decisions.
INTL ORGS: Permanent Court of Arbitration. Arbitration Commission.
PROCEDURE: Amendment. Termination.
PARTIES:
Cameroon
United Nations

106335 Bilateral Agreement **442 UNTS 15**
SIGNED: 29 May 61 FORCE: 17 Aug 62
REGISTERED: 10 Oct 62 South Africa
ARTICLES: 15 LANGUAGE: English. Afrikaans. Swedish.
HEADNOTE: DOUBLE TAXATION DEATH DUTIES
TOPIC: Taxation

CONCEPTS: Definition of terms. Privileges and immunities. Nationality and citizenship. Exchange of official publications. Claims and settlements. Debts. Taxation. Death duties.
PROCEDURE: Ratification. Termination.
PARTIES:
South Africa
Sweden

106336 Unilateral Instrument **442 UNTS 37**
SIGNED: 30 Sep 62 FORCE: 8 Oct 62
REGISTERED: 11 Oct 62 United Nations
ARTICLES: 1 LANGUAGE: French.
HEADNOTE: ACCEPTANCE OBLIGATIONS UN CHARTER
TOPIC: UN Charter
CONCEPTS: Acceptance of UN obligations. Adherence to UN charter.
INTL ORGS: United Nations.
PARTIES:
Algeria

106337 Bilateral Exchange **442 UNTS 41**
SIGNED: 5 Apr 62 FORCE: 5 May 62
REGISTERED: 15 Oct 62 USA (United States)
ARTICLES: 2 LANGUAGE: English. Spanish.
HEADNOTE: RADIO COMMUNICATIONS AMATEUR STATIONS BEHALF THIRD PARTIES
TOPIC: Telecommunications
CONCEPTS: Amateur radio. Amateur third party message. Radio-telephone-telegraphic communications.
PROCEDURE: Termination.
PARTIES:
El Salvador
USA (United States)

106338 Bilateral Agreement **442 UNTS 49**
SIGNED: 30 Mar 62 FORCE: 1 Jun 62
REGISTERED: 15 Oct 62 USA (United States)
ARTICLES: 9 LANGUAGE: English.
HEADNOTE: UNITED STATES REACTOR FACILITIES
TOPIC: Specific Property
CONCEPTS: Definition of terms. Annex or appendix reference. Inspection and observation. Domestic legislation. Responsibility and liability. Arbitration. Special tribunals. Negotiation. Indemnities and reimbursements. General. Nuclear materials.
INTL ORGS: International Court of Justice. Arbitration Commission.
TREATY REF: 276UNTS3.
PROCEDURE: Duration.
PARTIES:
IAEA (Atom Energy)
USA (United States)

106339 Bilateral Agreement **442 UNTS 69**
SIGNED: 17 Apr 62 FORCE: 17 Apr 62
REGISTERED: 15 Oct 62 USA (United States)
ARTICLES: 6 LANGUAGE: English. Spanish.
HEADNOTE: ECONOMIC TECHNICAL RELATED ASSISTANCE
TOPIC: General Aid
CONCEPTS: Change of circumstances. Exceptions and exemptions. Diplomatic privileges. Privileges and immunities. Conformity with municipal law. General cooperation. Personnel. Funding procedures. Tax exemptions. Customs exemptions. Domestic obligation. General technical assistance. Economic assistance. Materials, equipment and services. Aid missions.
TREATY REF: DEPT. OF STATE BULLETIN 3OCT1960 P.537.
PROCEDURE: Termination.
PARTIES:
Ecuador
USA (United States)

106340 Bilateral Agreement **442 UNTS 83**
SIGNED: 3 May 62 FORCE: 3 May 62
REGISTERED: 15 Oct 62 USA (United States)
ARTICLES: 6 LANGUAGE: English.
HEADNOTE: AGRI COMMOD TITLE I
TOPIC: US Agri Commod Aid
CONCEPTS: General provisions. Annex or appendix reference. Exchange of information and documents. Reexport of goods, etc.. Exchange rates

and regulations. Transportation costs. Local currency. Commodities schedule. Purchase authorization. Surplus commodities. Mutual consultation.
PARTIES:
Israel
USA (United States)
ANNEX
460 UNTS 348. Israel. Amendment 16 Oct 62. Force 16 Oct 62.
460 UNTS 348. USA (United States). Amendment 12 Oct 62. Force 16 Oct 62.
473 UNTS 368. USA (United States). Amendment 26 Jan 63. Force 1 Feb 63.
473 UNTS 368. Israel. Amendment 1 Feb 63. Force 1 Feb 63.

106341 Bilateral Agreement **442 UNTS 99**
SIGNED: 2 May 62   FORCE: 2 May 62
REGISTERED: 15 Oct 62 USA (United States)
ARTICLES: 7 LANGUAGE: English. Spanish.
HEADNOTE: INVESTMENT GUARANTIES
TOPIC: Claims and Debts
CONCEPTS: General cooperation. Arbitration. Special tribunals. Negotiation. Reciprocity in financial treatment. Currency. Currency deposits. Payment schedules. Private investment guarantee. Most favored nation clause.
PARTIES:
Dominican Republic
USA (United States)

106342 Bilateral Agreement **442 UNTS 107**
SIGNED: 2 May 62   FORCE: 2 May 62
REGISTERED: 15 Oct 62 USA (United States)
ARTICLES: 7 LANGUAGE: English. Spanish.
HEADNOTE: PEACE CORPS
TOPIC: Direct Aid
CONCEPTS: Treaty implementation. Diplomatic privileges. Conformity with municipal law. General cooperation. Legal protection and assistance. Exchange rates and regulations. Funding procedures. Tax exemptions. Customs exemptions. Domestic obligation. Materials, equipment and services. Volunteer programs.
PROCEDURE: Termination.
PARTIES:
Dominican Republic
USA (United States)

106343 Bilateral Agreement **442 UNTS 117**
SIGNED: 3 May 62   FORCE: 3 May 62
REGISTERED: 15 Oct 62 USA (United States)
ARTICLES: 4 LANGUAGE: English.
HEADNOTE: EXPANDING TRADE AGRICULTURE
TOPIC: General Trade
CONCEPTS: Detailed regulations. General cooperation. Import quotas. Delivery schedules. Quotas. Customs duties.
PARTIES:
Ireland
USA (United States)

106344 Bilateral Agreement **442 UNTS 123**
SIGNED: 21 Apr 62   FORCE: 21 Apr 62
REGISTERED: 15 Oct 62 USA (United States)
ARTICLES: 5 LANGUAGE: English.
HEADNOTE: STATUS PERSONNEL
TOPIC: US Agri Commod Aid
CONCEPTS: Exceptions and exemptions. Status of military forces. Jurisdiction.
PARTIES:
USA (United States)
Yugoslavia
ANNEX
451 UNTS 350. Yugoslavia. Amendment 18 May 62. Force 18 May 62.
451 UNTS 350. USA (United States). Amendment 18 May 62. Force 18 May 62.
460 UNTS 352. Yugoslavia. Amendment 28 Nov 62. Force 28 Nov 62.
460 UNTS 352. USA (United States). Amendment 28 Nov 62. Force 28 Nov 62.

106345 Bilateral Exchange **442 UNTS 135**
SIGNED: 9 Feb 62   FORCE: 9 Feb 62
REGISTERED: 16 Oct 62 USA (United States)
ARTICLES: 6 LANGUAGE: English. French.
HEADNOTE: AGRI COMMOD TITLE I

TOPIC: Direct Aid
CONCEPTS: General cooperation. Exchange of information and documents. Reexport of goods, etc.. Currency deposits. Exchange rates and regulations. Purchase authorizations. Transportation costs. Local currency. Commodities schedule. Surplus commodities.
PARTIES:
Morocco
USA (United States)

106346 Bilateral Exchange **442 UNTS 155**
SIGNED: 13 Feb 62   FORCE: 13 Feb 62
REGISTERED: 16 Oct 62 USA (United States)
ARTICLES: 2 LANGUAGE: English. French.
HEADNOTE: PEACE CORPS PROGRAM
TOPIC: Direct Aid
PROCEDURE: Termination.
PARTIES:
Tunisia
USA (United States)

106347 Bilateral Agreement **442 UNTS 161**
SIGNED: 16 Feb 62   FORCE: 16 Feb 62
REGISTERED: 16 Oct 62 USA (United States)
ARTICLES: 6 LANGUAGE: English. French.
HEADNOTE: AGRI COMMOD TITLE I
TOPIC: US Agri Commod Aid
CONCEPTS: General provisions. Annex or appendix reference. Exchange of information and documents. Reexport of goods, etc.. Exchange rates and regulations. Transportation costs. Local currency. Commodities schedule. Purchase authorization. Surplus commodities. Mutual consultation.
PARTIES:
Tunisia
USA (United States)

106348 Bilateral Exchange **442 UNTS 175**
SIGNED: 12 Feb 58   FORCE: 12 Feb 58
REGISTERED: 16 Oct 62 USA (United States)
ARTICLES: 3 LANGUAGE: English.
HEADNOTE: CONTINUED APPLICATION TO GHANA
TOPIC: Admin Cooperation
CONCEPTS: Previous treaty extension.
INTL ORGS: United Nations.
TREATY REF: 162LTS59; 3UNTS253; 2'7DM476;.
PARTIES:
Ghana
USA (United States)

106349 Bilateral Agreement **442 UNTS 185**
SIGNED: 2 Mar 62   FORCE: 2 Mar 62
REGISTERED: 16 Oct 62 USA (United States)
ARTICLES: 6 LANGUAGE: English.
HEADNOTE: AGRI COMMOD TITLE I
TOPIC: US Agri Commod Aid
CONCEPTS: General provisions. Annex or appendix reference. Exchange of information and documents. Reexport of goods, etc.. Exchange rates and regulations. Transportation costs. Local currency. Commodities schedule. Purchase authorization. Surplus commodities. Mutual consultation.
PARTIES:
Korea, South
USA (United States)
ANNEX
459 UNTS 342. Korea, South. Amendment 12 Jun 62. Force 12 Jun 62.
459 UNTS 342. USA (United States). Amendment 12 Jun 62. Force 12 Jun 62.

106350 Bilateral Agreement **442 UNTS 201**
SIGNED: 5 Apr 61   FORCE: 11 Sep 61
REGISTERED: 18 Oct 62 Cuba
ARTICLES: 11 LANGUAGE: Czechoslovakian. Spanish.
HEADNOTE: HEALTH COOPERATION
TOPIC: Sanitation
CONCEPTS: Non-diplomatic delegations. General cooperation. Exchange of information and documents. Programs. Disease control. Public health. Teacher and student exchange. Vocational training. Research results. Scientific exchange. Accounting procedures. Indemnities and reim-

bursements. General technical assistance. Materials, equipment and services. Publications exchange.
PROCEDURE: Duration. Ratification. Renewal or Revival. Termination.
PARTIES:
Cuba
Czechoslovakia

106351 Multilateral Agreement **442 UNTS 215**
SIGNED: 18 Sep 62   FORCE: 18 Oct 62
REGISTERED: 18 Oct 62 Finland
ARTICLES: 6 LANGUAGE: Finnish. Danish. Swedish. Norwegian.
HEADNOTE: UNIFORM RULES MARKING NAVIGABLE WATERS
TOPIC: Water Transport
CONCEPTS: Definition of terms. Detailed regulations. Navigational conditions. Water transport. Inland and territorial waters.
PROCEDURE: Denunciation.
PARTIES:
Denmark SIGNED: 18 Sep 62 FORCE: 18 Oct 62
Finland SIGNED: 18 Sep 62 FORCE: 18 Oct 62
Norway SIGNED: 18 Sep 62 FORCE: 18 Oct 62
Sweden SIGNED: 18 Sep 62 FORCE: 18 Oct 62

106352 Multilateral Convention **442 UNTS 235**
SIGNED: 28 Jun 46   FORCE: 10 Oct 62
REGISTERED: 18 Oct 62 ILO (Labor Org)
ARTICLES: 12 LANGUAGE: English. French.
HEADNOTE: SEAFARERS PENSION
TOPIC: ILO Labor
CONCEPTS: Definition of terms. Detailed regulations. Previous treaty extension. ILO conventions. Old age and invalidity insurance. Wages and salaries.
INTL ORGS: United Nations.
TREATY REF: 423UNTS11.
PARTIES:
Multilateral
ANNEX
444 UNTS 356. Algeria. Succession 19 Oct 62.

106353 Bilateral Agreement **442 UNTS 249**
SIGNED: 5 Sep 62   FORCE: 5 Sep 62
REGISTERED: 18 Oct 62 United Nations
ARTICLES: 5 LANGUAGE: English. Persian.
HEADNOTE: DEVELOPMENT PETROLEUM RESOURCES
TOPIC: Specific Resources
CONCEPTS: Research and development. Funding procedures. IGO status. Status of experts. Conferences. Raw materials.
INTL ORGS: Economic Commission for Asia and the Far East.
PROCEDURE: Amendment.
PARTIES:
Iran
United Nations

106354 Bilateral Agreement **442 UNTS 261**
SIGNED: 22 Apr 60   FORCE: 20 Jul 61
REGISTERED: 19 Oct 62 Cuba
ARTICLES: 10 LANGUAGE: Spanish. English. Japanese.
HEADNOTE: TRADE
TOPIC: General Trade
CONCEPTS: Detailed regulations. Exceptions and exemptions. Privileges and immunities. General cooperation. Juridical personality. Expropriation. Legal protection and assistance. General property. Export quotas. Import quotas. Trade procedures. Most favored nation clause. General. Customs duties. Passenger transport. Transport of goods. Merchant vessels. Ports and pilotage.
INTL ORGS: General Agreement on Tariffs and Trade. International Monetary Fund.
TREATY REF: GATT;2UNTS40.
PROCEDURE: Duration. Ratification. Termination.
PARTIES:
Cuba
Japan
ANNEX
450 UNTS 475. Japan. Supplementation 22 Apr 60.
450 UNTS 475. Cuba. Supplementation 22 Apr 60.

106355 Bilateral Agreement **443 UNTS 3**
SIGNED: 7 Jul 62 FORCE: 30 Aug 62
REGISTERED: 22 Oct 62 United Nations
ARTICLES: 10 LANGUAGE: English. Arabic.
HEADNOTE: ASSISTANCE
TOPIC: Direct Aid
CONCEPTS: Detailed regulations. Treaty implementation. Annex or appendix reference. Visas. Privileges and immunities. Exchange of information and documents. Informational records. Inspection and observation. Operating agencies. Personnel. Public information. Responsibility and liability. Title and deeds. Use of facilities. Arbitration. Procedure. Negotiation. Import quotas. Attachment of funds. Exchange rates and regulations. Expense sharing formulae. Financial programs. Domestic obligation. General technical assistance. Economic assistance. Materials, equipment and services. IGO status.
INTL ORGS: International Atomic Energy Agency. International Court of Justice. United Nations. Arbitration Commission.
TREATY REF: 1UNTS15; 33UNTS261; 374UNTS147; 345UNTS125.
PROCEDURE: Amendment. Termination.
PARTIES:
UN Special Fund
Syria

106356 Bilateral Convention **443 UNTS 35**
SIGNED: 29 Apr 59 FORCE: 15 Oct 62
REGISTERED: 23 Oct 62 Belgium
ARTICLES: 14 LANGUAGE: French.
HEADNOTE: RECOGNITION ENFORCEMENT JUDICIAL DECISIONS ARBITRAL AWARDS
TOPIC: Admin Cooperation
CONCEPTS: Territorial application. Recognition and enforcement of legal decisions. Prizes and arbitral awards.
PROCEDURE: Denunciation. Ratification.
PARTIES:
Belgium
Switzerland

106357 Unilateral Instrument **443 UNTS 47**
SIGNED: 9 Oct 62 FORCE: 15 Oct 62
REGISTERED: 25 Oct 62 United Nations
ARTICLES: 1 LANGUAGE: English.
HEADNOTE: ACCEPTANCE OBLIGATIONS UN
TOPIC: UN Charter
CONCEPTS: Acceptance of UN obligations. Adherence to UN charter.
INTL ORGS: United Nations.
PARTIES:
Uganda

106358 Bilateral Agreement **443 UNTS 51**
SIGNED: 30 Jun 61 FORCE: 17 Apr 62
REGISTERED: 29 Oct 62 Austria
ARTICLES: 8 LANGUAGE: German. Serbo-Croat.
HEADNOTE: ESTABLISHMENT ACTIVITIES AUSTRIAN INFORMATION CENTERS
TOPIC: Admin Cooperation
CONCEPTS: Personnel. Public information. Most favored nation clause. Publications exchange. Information agency.
PARTIES:
Austria
Yugoslavia

106359 Bilateral Exchange **443 UNTS 65**
SIGNED: 31 Aug 62 FORCE: 1 Oct 62
REGISTERED: 31 Oct 62 South Africa
ARTICLES: 2 LANGUAGE: English. German.
HEADNOTE: VISA
TOPIC: Visas
CONCEPTS: Time limit. Previous treaty replacement. Visa abolition. Denial of admission. Conformity with municipal law.
TREATY REF: 272UNTS129.
PROCEDURE: Termination.
PARTIES:
Austria
South Africa

106360 Multilateral Exchange **443 UNTS 73**
SIGNED: 14 Sep 62 FORCE: 14 Oct 62
REGISTERED: 31 Oct 62 South Africa
ARTICLES: 2 LANGUAGE: English. French.

HEADNOTE: VISA AGREEMENT
TOPIC: Visas
CONCEPTS: Time limit. Visa abolition. Conformity with municipal law. Fees and exemptions.
TREATY REF: 303UNTS131.
PROCEDURE: Termination.
PARTIES:
Cameroon SIGNED: 29 Aug 62 FORCE: 29 Aug 62
FAO (Food Agri) SIGNED: 29 Aug 62 FORCE: 29 Aug 62
IAEA (Atom Energy) SIGNED: 29 Aug 62 FORCE: 29 Aug 62
ICAO (Civil Aviat) SIGNED: 29 Aug 62 FORCE: 29 Aug 62
ILO (Labor Org) SIGNED: 29 Aug 62 FORCE: 29 Aug 62
ITU (Telecommun) SIGNED: 29 Aug 62 FORCE: 29 Aug 62
UNESCO (Educ/Cult) SIGNED: 29 Aug 62 FORCE: 29 Aug 62
United Nations SIGNED: 29 Aug 62 FORCE: 29 Aug 62
UPU (Postal Union) SIGNED: 29 Aug 62 FORCE: 29 Aug 62
WHO (World Health) SIGNED: 29 Aug 62 FORCE: 29 Aug 62
WMO (Meteorology) SIGNED: 29 Aug 62 FORCE: 29 Aug 62

106361 Bilateral Convention **443 UNTS 79**
SIGNED: 28 May 62 FORCE: 27 Sep 62
REGISTERED: 31 Oct 62 South Africa
ARTICLES: 26 LANGUAGE: English. Afrikaans.
HEADNOTE: DOUBLE TAXATION FISCAL EVASION TAXES INCOME
TOPIC: Taxation
CONCEPTS: Definition of terms. Previous treaty renunciation. Exchange of official publications. Teacher and student exchange. Taxation. Tax credits. Equitable taxes. General. Tax exemptions. Air transport. Merchant vessels.
TREATY REF: 86UNTS277; 412UNTS296.
PROCEDURE: Duration. Ratification. Termination.
PARTIES:
South Africa
UK Great Britain
ANNEX
471 UNTS 338. UK Great Britain. Southwest Africa. Force 19 Dec 62.
471 UNTS 338. South Africa. Acknowledgement 8 Aug 62. Force 19 Dec 62.
645 UNTS 362. South Africa. Amendment 14 Jun 67. Force 7 Sep 68.
645 UNTS 362. UK Great Britain. Amendment 14 Jun 67. Force 7 Sep 67.

106362 Multilateral Instrument **443 UNTS 128**
SIGNED: 12 Apr 57 FORCE: 22 Feb 60
REGISTERED: 1 Nov 62 Luxembourg
ARTICLES: 32 LANGUAGE: French. German. Italian. Dutch.
HEADNOTE: EUROPEAN SCHOOL
TOPIC: Education
CONCEPTS: Definition of terms. Detailed regulations. Inspection and observation. Recognition of degrees. Exchange. Funding procedures. Subsidiary organ. Headquarters and facilities. Status of experts.
INTL ORGS: European Schools Committee. European Coal and Steel Community.
PROCEDURE: Accession. Denunciation. Ratification.
PARTIES:
Belgium SIGNED: 12 Apr 57 RATIFIED: 11 Mar 59 FORCE: 22 Feb 60
France SIGNED: 12 Apr 57 RATIFIED: 10 May 59 FORCE: 22 Feb 60
Germany, West SIGNED: 12 Apr 57
Italy SIGNED: 12 Apr 57 RATIFIED: 22 Feb 60 FORCE: 22 Feb 60
Luxembourg SIGNED: 12 Apr 57 RATIFIED: 20 Nov 59 FORCE: 22 Feb 60
Netherlands SIGNED: 12 Apr 57 RATIFIED: 19 May 60 FORCE: 19 May 60

106363 Multilateral Agreement **443 UNTS 247**
SIGNED: 14 Sep 60 FORCE: 1 Oct 60
REGISTERED: 6 Nov 62 Iran
ARTICLES: 1 LANGUAGE: English.
HEADNOTE: ESTABLISH OPEC

TOPIC: IGO Establishment
CONCEPTS: Exchange of information and documents. Admission. Establishment.
INTL ORGS: Organization of Petroleum Exporting Countries.
PARTIES:
Indonesia RATIFIED: 7 Jul 62 FORCE: 7 Jul 62
Iran SIGNED: 14 Sep 60 RATIFIED: 2 Oct 60 FORCE: 1 Oct 60
Iraq SIGNED: 14 Sep 60 RATIFIED: 27 Sep 60 FORCE: 1 Oct 60
Kuwait SIGNED: 14 Sep 60 RATIFIED: 19 Sep 60 FORCE: 1 Oct 60
Libya RATIFIED: 7 Jul 62 FORCE: 7 Jul 62
Qatar RATIFIED: 15 Jan 61 FORCE: 15 Jan 61
Saudi Arabia SIGNED: 14 Sep 60 RATIFIED: 6 Oct 60 FORCE: 1 Oct 60
Venezuela SIGNED: 14 Sep 60 RATIFIED: 30 Sep 60 FORCE: 1 Oct 60

106364 Bilateral Instrument **443 UNTS 255**
SIGNED: 29 Jun 61 FORCE: 29 Jun 61
REGISTERED: 12 Nov 62 UK Great Britain
ARTICLES: 12 LANGUAGE: English. Indonesian.
HEADNOTE: BASIC ARRANGEMENTS TRADE ECONOMIC RELATIONS
TOPIC: General Economic
CONCEPTS: Treaty implementation. General property. Establishment of commission. General economics. General trade. Currency. Economic assistance. Water transport. Merchant vessels.
INTL ORGS: Special Commission.
PROCEDURE: Termination.
PARTIES:
Indonesia
UK Great Britain

106365 Multilateral Agreement **443 UNTS 266**
SIGNED: 12 Aug 62 FORCE: 12 Aug 62
REGISTERED: 15 Nov 62 United Nations
ARTICLES: 6 LANGUAGE: French.
HEADNOTE: TECHNICAL ASSISTANCE
TOPIC: Tech Assistance
CONCEPTS: Definition of terms. Privileges and immunities. General cooperation. Exchange of information and documents. Personnel. Responsibility and liability. Title and deeds. Use of facilities. Exchange. Scholarships and grants. Vocational training. Research and development. Exchange rates and regulations. Expense sharing formulae. Local currency. Domestic obligation. General technical assistance. Materials, equipment and services. IGO status. Conformity with IGO decisions.
INTL ORGS: United Nations Technical Assistance Board.
TREATY REF: 76UNTS132; 1UNTS15; 33UNTS261; 374UNTS147.
PARTIES:
Niger SIGNED: 12 Aug 62 FORCE: 12 Aug 62
FAO (Food Agri) SIGNED: 12 Aug 62 FORCE: 12 Aug 62
IAEA (Atom Energy) SIGNED: 12 Aug 62 FORCE: 12 Aug 62
ICAO (Civil Aviat) SIGNED: 12 Aug 62 FORCE: 12 Aug 62
ILO (Labor Org) SIGNED: 12 Aug 62 FORCE: 12 Aug 62
ITU (Telecommun) SIGNED: 12 Aug 62 FORCE: 12 Aug 62
UNESCO (Educ/Cult) SIGNED: 12 Aug 62 FORCE: 12 Aug 62
United Nations SIGNED: 12 Aug 62 FORCE: 12 Aug 62
WHO (World Health) SIGNED: 12 Aug 62 FORCE: 12 Aug 62
WMO (Meteorology) SIGNED: 12 Aug 62 FORCE: 12 Aug 62
ANNEX
651 UNTS 396. IMCO (Maritime Org). Accession 13 Nov 68. Force 13 Nov 68.
651 UNTS 396. UNIDO (Industrial). Accession 13 Nov 68. Force 13 Nov 68.
651 UNTS 396. UPU (Postal Union). Accession 13 Nov 68. Force 13 Nov 68.

106366 Multilateral Agreement **443 UNTS 280**
SIGNED: 29 Aug 62 FORCE: 29 Aug 62
REGISTERED: 15 Nov 62 United Nations
ARTICLES: 6 LANGUAGE: French.
HEADNOTE: TECHNICAL ASSISTANCE

TOPIC: Tech Assistance

CONCEPTS: Definition of terms. Alien status. Privileges and immunities. Exchange of information and documents. Personnel. Responsibility and liability. Title and deeds. Exchange. Scholarships and grants. Vocational training. Research and development. Exchange rates and regulations. Expense sharing formulae. Local currency. Domestic obligation. General technical assistance. Materials, equipment and services. IGO status. Conformity with IGO decisions.

INTL ORGS: United Nations Technical Assistance Board.

TREATY REF: 76UNTS132; 1UNTS15; 33UNTS261.

PARTIES:
Cameroon SIGNED: 29 Aug 62 FORCE: 29 Aug 62
FAO (Food Agri) SIGNED: 29 Aug 62 FORCE: 29 Aug 62
IAEA (Atom Energy) SIGNED: 29 Aug 62 FORCE: 29 Aug 62
ICAO (Civil Aviat) SIGNED: 29 Aug 62 FORCE: 29 Aug 62
ILO (Labor Org) SIGNED: 29 Aug 62 FORCE: 29 Aug 62
ITU (Telecommun) SIGNED: 29 Aug 62 FORCE: 29 Aug 62
UNESCO (Educ/Cult) SIGNED: 29 Aug 62 FORCE: 29 Aug 62
United Nations SIGNED: 29 Aug 62 FORCE: 29 Aug 62
UPU (Postal Union) SIGNED: 29 Aug 62 FORCE: 29 Aug 62
WHO (World Health) SIGNED: 29 Aug 62 FORCE: 29 Aug 62
WMO (Meteorology) SIGNED: 29 Aug 62 FORCE: 29 Aug 62

106367 Multilateral Agreement **444 UNTS 3**
SIGNED: 15 May 62 FORCE: 1 Aug 62
REGISTERED: 16 Nov 62 UK Great Britain
ARTICLES: 37 LANGUAGE: English. French. Spanish. Russian.
HEADNOTE: INTERNATIONAL WHEAT AGREEMENT
TOPIC: Commodity Trade
CONCEPTS: Definition of terms. Territorial application. General provisions. General cooperation. Inspection and observation. Procedure. General trade. Export quotas. Import quotas. Balance of payments. Non-interest rates and fees. Commodity trade. Domestic obligation. Subsidiary organ. Liaison with other IGO's. Internal structure.
INTL ORGS: Food and Agricultural Organization of the United Nations. International Monetary Fund. United Nations. International Wheat Council.
TREATY REF: 203UNTS179; 270UNTS103; 349UNTS167.
PROCEDURE: Amendment. Accession. Duration. Ratification.
PARTIES:
Argentina SIGNED: 15 May 62 RATIFIED: 11 Jul 62 FORCE: 16 Jul 62
Australia SIGNED: 14 May 62 RATIFIED: 6 Jul 62 FORCE: 16 Jul 62
Austria SIGNED: 14 May 62 RATIFIED: 12 Jul 62 FORCE: 16 Jul 62
Brazil SIGNED: 11 May 62 RATIFIED: 16 Jul 62 FORCE: 16 Jul 62
Canada SIGNED: 11 May 62 RATIFIED: 16 May 62 FORCE: 16 Jul 62
Cuba SIGNED: 15 May 62 RATIFIED: 31 Oct 62 FORCE: 31 Oct 62
Dominican Republic SIGNED: 15 May 62
Fed Rhod/Nyasaland SIGNED: 14 May 62 RATIFIED: 18 Jul 62 FORCE: 18 Jul 62
France SIGNED: 14 May 62
Germany, West SIGNED: 11 May 62 FORCE: 16 Jul 62
India SIGNED: 14 May 62 RATIFIED: 29 Jun 62 FORCE: 16 Jul 62
Indonesia SIGNED: 15 May 62 RATIFIED: 29 Aug 62 FORCE: 29 Aug 62
Ireland SIGNED: 14 May 62 RATIFIED: 16 Jul 62 FORCE: 16 Jul 62
Israel SIGNED: 14 May 62 RATIFIED: 16 Jul 62 FORCE: 16 Jul 62
Italy SIGNED: 14 May 62 RATIFIED: 16 Jul 62 FORCE: 16 Jul 62
Japan SIGNED: 11 May 62 RATIFIED: 16 May 62

Korea, South SIGNED: 14 May 62 RATIFIED: 30 Jul 62 FORCE: 30 Jul 62
Liberia SIGNED: 15 May 62
Mexico SIGNED: 11 May 62
Netherlands SIGNED: 14 May 62 RATIFIED: 10 Jul 62 FORCE: 16 Jul 62
New Zealand SIGNED: 15 May 62 RATIFIED: 18 Jul 62 FORCE: 18 Jul 62
Nigeria SIGNED: 10 May 62 RATIFIED: 16 Jul 62 FORCE: 16 Jul 62
Norway SIGNED: 8 May 62 RATIFIED: 10 Jul 62 FORCE: 16 Jul 62
Philippines SIGNED: 11 May 62 RATIFIED: 10 Jul 62 FORCE: 16 Jul 62
Portugal SIGNED: 14 May 62
South Africa SIGNED: 15 May 62 RATIFIED: 10 Jul 62 FORCE: 16 Jul 62
Spain SIGNED: 14 May 62 RATIFIED: 16 Jul 62 FORCE: 16 Jul 62
Sweden SIGNED: 11 May 62 RATIFIED: 6 Jun 62 FORCE: 16 Jul 62
Switzerland SIGNED: 15 May 62 RATIFIED: 16 Jul 62 FORCE: 16 Jul 62
United Arab Rep SIGNED: 15 May 62 RATIFIED: 30 Oct 62 FORCE: 30 Oct 62
UK Great Britain SIGNED: 10 May 62 RATIFIED: 13 Jul 62 FORCE: 16 Jul 62
USA (United States) SIGNED: 11 May 62 RATIFIED: 13 Jul 62 FORCE: 16 Jul 62
USSR (Soviet Union) SIGNED: 14 May 62 RATIFIED: 19 Jul 62 FORCE: 19 Jul 62
Vatican/Holy See SIGNED: 11 May 62 RATIFIED: 10 Jul 62 FORCE: 16 Jul 62
Venezuela SIGNED: 14 May 62
ANNEX
480 UNTS 440.
480 UNTS 442.
544 UNTS 350.
546 UNTS 392.
602 UNTS 348.
602 UNTS 348.
604 UNTS 378.

106368 Bilateral Agreement **444 UNTS 171**
SIGNED: 31 Oct 62 FORCE: 31 Oct 62
REGISTERED: 16 Nov 62 United Nations
ARTICLES: 10 LANGUAGE: English.
HEADNOTE: INTERNATIONAL INSTITUTE SEISMOLOGY EARTHQUAKE ENGINEERING
TOPIC: Tech Assistance
CONCEPTS: Detailed regulations. Treaty implementation. Annex or appendix reference. Privileges and immunities. Exchange of information and documents. Inspection and observation. Operating agencies. Public information. Responsibility and liability. Title and deeds. Use of facilities. Arbitration. Procedure. Negotiation. Import quotas. Reexport of goods, etc.. Exchange rates and regulations. Expense sharing formulae. Fees and exemptions. Domestic obligation. Assistance. Materials, equipment and services. IGO status. Conformity with IGO decisions.
INTL ORGS: International Court of Justice. United Nations Educational, Scientific and Cultural Organization. United Nations. Arbitration Commission.
TREATY REF: 1UNTS15; 33UNTS261; 33UNTS295.
PROCEDURE: Amendment. Future Procedures Contemplated. Termination.
PARTIES:
Japan
UN Special Fund
ANNEX
460 UNTS 358. Japan. Acceptance 18 Apr 63. Force 18 Apr 63.

106369 Multilateral Convention **444 UNTS 193**
SIGNED: 14 Dec 59 FORCE: 27 Nov 61
REGISTERED: 21 Nov 62 Council of Europe
ARTICLES: 12 LANGUAGE: English. French.
HEADNOTE: ACADEMIC RECOGNITION UNIVERSITY QUALIFICATIONS
TOPIC: Admin Cooperation
CONCEPTS: Definition of terms. Detailed regulations. Recognition of degrees.
INTL ORGS: Council of Europe.
PROCEDURE: Accession. Denunciation. Duration. Ratification.
PARTIES:
Austria SIGNED: 25 Jul 60 RATIFIED: 6 Dec 60 FORCE: 27 Nov 61

Belgium SIGNED: 14 Dec 59
Denmark SIGNED: 16 Mar 61 RATIFIED: 26 Oct 61 FORCE: 27 Nov 61
France SIGNED: 14 Dec 59
Greece SIGNED: 14 Dec 59
Iceland SIGNED: 14 Dec 59
Italy SIGNED: 14 Dec 59
Luxembourg SIGNED: 14 Dec 59
Netherlands SIGNED: 14 Dec 59 RATIFIED: 26 Apr 62 FORCE: 27 May 62
Norway SIGNED: 14 Dec 59
Turkey SIGNED: 14 Dec 59
UK Great Britain Fed Rhod/Nyasaland RATIFIED: 30 Aug 61
UK Great Britain SIGNED: 14 Dec 59 RATIFIED: 13 Feb 61 FORCE: 27 Nov 61
ANNEX
476 UNTS 353. Norway. Ratification 5 Apr 63. Force 6 May 68.
476 UNTS 353. Italy. Ratification 6 Aug 63. Force 7 Sep 63.
476 UNTS 353. Iceland. Ratification 5 Apr 63. Force 6 May 68.
562 UNTS 334. Ireland. Force 18 May 64.
562 UNTS 334. Ireland. Signature 13 Jan 64. Ratification 17 Apr 64.
635 UNTS 356. Sweden. Ratification 11 Dec 67. Force 12 Jan 68.

106370 Bilateral Agreement **444 UNTS 207**
SIGNED: 19 Sep 60 FORCE: 17 Jan 61
REGISTERED: 23 Nov 62 IBRD (World Bank)
ARTICLES: 9 LANGUAGE: English.
HEADNOTE: LOAN INDUS BASIN PROJECT
TOPIC: IBRD Project
CONCEPTS: Default remedies. Definition of terms. Annex or appendix reference. Exchange of information and documents. Informational records. Inspection and observation. Arbitration. Procedure. Accounting procedures. Bonds. Fees and exemptions. Interest rates. Tax exemptions. Domestic obligation. Terms of loan. Loan regulations. Loan guarantee. Guarantor non-interference.
INTL ORGS: International Court of Justice. International Monetary Fund. United Nations. Special Commission.
TREATY REF: 419UNTS125.
PROCEDURE: Termination.
PARTIES:
Pakistan
IBRD (World Bank)

106371 Multilateral Agreement **444 UNTS 259**
SIGNED: 19 Sep 60 FORCE: 12 Jan 61
REGISTERED: 23 Nov 62 IBRD (World Bank)
ARTICLES: 14 LANGUAGE: English.
HEADNOTE: INDUS BASIN DEVELOPMENT FUND
TOPIC: IBRD Project
CONCEPTS: Change of circumstances. Annex or appendix reference. Exchange of information and documents. Informational records. Inspection and observation. Arbitration. Procedure. Negotiation. Accounting procedures. Indemnities and reimbursements. Currency. Investments. Exchange rates and regulations. Payment schedules. Domestic obligation. Assistance. Materials, equipment and services. Loan regulations. Plans and standards. Irrigation. Hydro-electric power.
INTL ORGS: United Nations. Special Commission.
TREATY REF: 419UNTS125.
PROCEDURE: Accession. Termination.
PARTIES:
Australia SIGNED: 19 Sep 60 FORCE: 1 Apr 60
Canada SIGNED: 19 Sep 60 FORCE: 1 Apr 60
Germany, West SIGNED: 19 Sep 60 FORCE: 1 Apr 60
New Zealand SIGNED: 19 Sep 60 FORCE: 1 Apr 60
Pakistan SIGNED: 19 Sep 60 FORCE: 1 Apr 60
IBRD (World Bank) SIGNED: 19 Sep 60 FORCE: 1 Apr 60
UK Great Britain SIGNED: 19 Sep 60 FORCE: 1 Apr 60
USA (United States) SIGNED: 19 Sep 60 FORCE: 1 Apr 60
ANNEX
503 UNTS 388. Canada. Implementation 6 Apr 64. Force 6 Apr 64.
503 UNTS 388. Pakistan. Implementation 6 Apr 64. Force 6 Apr 64.

503 UNTS 388.   Australia.   Implementation
6 Apr 64. Force 6 Apr 64.
503 UNTS 388.   New Zealand.   Implementation
6 Apr 64. Force 6 Apr 64.
503 UNTS 388. UK Great Britain. Implementation
6 Apr 64. Force 6 Apr 64.
503 UNTS 388. IBRD (World Bank). Implementation 6 Apr 64. Force 6 Apr 64.
503 UNTS 388. Germany, West. Implementation
6 Apr 64. Force 6 Apr 64.
503 UNTS 388. USA (United States). Implementation 6 Apr 64. Force 6 Apr 64.

106372   Bilateral Agreement   **445 UNTS 3**
SIGNED: 26 Nov 62   FORCE: 26 Nov 62
REGISTERED: 26 Nov 62 United Nations
ARTICLES: 6 LANGUAGE: Spanish.
HEADNOTE: PROVISION OPERATIONAL EXECU-
TIVE PERSONNEL
TOPIC: Tech Assistance
CONCEPTS: Treaty implementation. Annex or ap-
pendix reference. Privileges and immunities.
Personnel. Responsibility and liability. Arbitra-
tion. Procedure. Negotiation. Vocational train-
ing. Compensation. Expense sharing formulae.
Tax exemptions. Customs exemptions. Domestic
obligation. Special projects. Status of experts.
Conformity with IGO decisions.
INTL ORGS: Permanent Court of Arbitration. Arbi-
tration Commission.
TREATY REF: 228UNTSU67.
PROCEDURE: Amendment. Termination.
PARTIES:
Ecuador
United Nations

106373   Bilateral Exchange   **445 UNTS 23**
SIGNED: 27 May 61   FORCE: 27 May 61
REGISTERED: 27 Nov 62 USA (United States)
ARTICLES: 2 LANGUAGE: English. French.
HEADNOTE: ECONOMIC TECHNICAL RELATED
ASSISTANCE
TOPIC: General Aid
CONCEPTS: Change of circumstances. Exceptions
and exemptions. Guarantees and safeguards.
Diplomatic privileges. Privileges and immunities.
Conformity with municipal law. Personnel. Ac-
counting procedures. Attachment of funds.
Banking. Exchange rates and regulations. Fund-
ing procedures. Garnishment of funds. Seizure
funds. Tax exemptions. Customs exemptions.
Commodities and services. Domestic obligation.
General technical assistance. Economic assis-
tance. Materials, equipment and services. Aid
missions. Grants.
PROCEDURE: Termination.
PARTIES:
Dahomey
USA (United States)

106374   Bilateral Exchange   **445 UNTS 33**
SIGNED: 21 Jul 61   FORCE: 21 Jul 61
REGISTERED: 27 Nov 62 USA (United States)
ARTICLES: 2 LANGUAGE: English.
HEADNOTE: PEACE CORPS PROGRAM
TOPIC: Direct Aid
CONCEPTS: Treaty implementation. Diplomatic
privileges. Personnel. Tax exemptions. Customs
exemptions. Materials, equipment and services.
Volunteer programs.
TREATY REF: 105UNTS71.
PROCEDURE: Termination.
PARTIES:
Tanganyika
USA (United States)

106375   Bilateral Exchange   **445 UNTS 41**
SIGNED: 8 Mar 62   FORCE: 12 Mar 62
REGISTERED: 27 Nov 62 USA (United States)
ARTICLES: 2 LANGUAGE: English.
HEADNOTE: PEACE CORPS PROGRAM
TOPIC: Direct Aid
CONCEPTS: Treaty implementation. Diplomatic
privileges. Conformity with municipal law. Gen-
eral cooperation. Personnel. Tax exemptions.
Customs exemptions. Materials, equipment and
services. Volunteer programs.
PROCEDURE: Termination.

PARTIES:
Liberia
USA (United States)

106376   Bilateral Agreement   **445 UNTS 49**
SIGNED: 16 Mar 62   FORCE: 16 Mar 62
REGISTERED: 27 Nov 62 USA (United States)
ARTICLES: 6 LANGUAGE: English.
HEADNOTE: AGRI COMMOD TITLE I
TOPIC: US Agri Commod Aid
CONCEPTS: General provisions. Annex or appen-
dix reference. Exchange of information and doc-
uments. Reexport of goods, etc.. Exchange rates
and regulations. Transportation costs. Local cur-
rency. Commodities schedule. Purchase authori-
zation. Surplus commodities. Mutual consulta-
tion.
PARTIES:
Iceland
USA (United States)

106377   Bilateral Agreement   **445 UNTS 61**
SIGNED: 20 Mar 62   FORCE: 20 Mar 62
REGISTERED: 27 Nov 62 USA (United States)
ARTICLES: 6 LANGUAGE: English. Spanish.
HEADNOTE: AGRI COMMOD TITLE I
TOPIC: US Agri Commod Aid
CONCEPTS: General provisions. Annex or appen-
dix reference. Exchange of information and doc-
uments. Reexport of goods, etc.. Exchange rates
and regulations. Transportation costs. Local cur-
rency. Commodities schedule. Purchase authori-
zation. Surplus commodities. Mutual consulta-
tion.
PARTIES:
Peru
USA (United States)

106378   Bilateral Agreement   **445 UNTS 79**
SIGNED: 20 Mar 62   FORCE: 20 Mar 62
REGISTERED: 27 Nov 62 USA (United States)
ARTICLES: 3 LANGUAGE: English. French.
HEADNOTE: INVESTMENT GUARANTEES
TOPIC: Admin Cooperation
CONCEPTS: Guarantees and safeguards. Arbitra-
tion. Currency. Investments. Claims and settle-
ments.
PARTIES:
Togo
USA (United States)

106379   Bilateral Agreement   **445 UNTS 85**
SIGNED: 30 Jun 61   FORCE: 16 Jan 62
REGISTERED: 28 Nov 62 IBRD (World Bank)
ARTICLES: 8 LANGUAGE: English.
HEADNOTE: LOAN ROAD
TOPIC: IBRD Project
CONCEPTS: Default remedies. Definition of terms.
Annex or appendix reference. Exchange of infor-
mation and documents. Informational records.
Inspection and observation. Accounting proce-
dures. Bonds. Fees and exemptions. Interest
rates. Tax exemptions. Domestic obligation.
Terms of loan. Loan regulations. Loan guarantee.
Guarantor non-interference. Roads and high-
ways.
PARTIES:
Argentina
IBRD (World Bank)

106380   Bilateral Agreement   **445 UNTS 105**
SIGNED: 11 May 59   FORCE: 21 Sep 62
REGISTERED: 28 Nov 62 Denmark
ARTICLES: 13 LANGUAGE: English.
HEADNOTE: AIR SERVICES BETWEEN BEYOND
RESPECTIVE TERRITORIES
TOPIC: Air Transport
CONCEPTS: Definition of terms. Detailed regulations. Exceptions and exemptions. Treaty interpretation. Annex or appendix reference. General
cooperation. Exchange of information and documents. Arbitration. Procedure. Special tribunals.
Negotiation. Non-interest rates and fees. Most
favored nation clause. National treatment. Customs exemptions. Routes and logistics. Permit
designation. Conditions of airlines operating
permission. Overflights and technical stops. Operating authorizations and regulations.
INTL ORGS: Permanent Court of Arbitration. Inter-

national Civil Aviation Organization. United Na-
tions. Arbitration Commission.
TREATY REF: 15UNTSI95.
PROCEDURE: Amendment. Future Procedures
Contemplated. Ratification. Registration. Termi-
nation.
PARTIES:
Denmark
Sudan

106381   Bilateral Exchange   **445 UNTS 125**
SIGNED: 11 Dec 60   FORCE: 11 Dec 60
REGISTERED: 28 Nov 62 USA (United States)
ARTICLES: 2 LANGUAGE: English. Arabic.
HEADNOTE: TERMINATING JOINT SERVICES PRO-
GRAM
TOPIC: Health/Educ/Welfare
CONCEPTS: Conditions. Treaty implementation.
Annex or appendix reference. Exchange of infor-
mation and documents. Sanitation. Education.
Assets transfer. Tax exemptions. Agriculture. Ag-
ricultural commodities. Conservation of specific
resources.
TREATY   REF: 270UNTS245,269,293,317;
264UNTS247; 283UNTS181.
PARTIES:
Libya
USA (United States)

106382   Bilateral Exchange   **445 UNTS 135**
SIGNED: 23 Jan 61   FORCE: 8 Mar 62
REGISTERED: 28 Nov 62 USA (United States)
ARTICLES: 2 LANGUAGE: English.
HEADNOTE: GUARANTIES PRIVATE INVEST-
MENTS
TOPIC: Admin Cooperation
CONCEPTS: Guarantees and safeguards. Arbitra-
tion. Currency. Investments. Claims and settle-
ments.
PARTIES:
Panama
USA (United States)

106383   Bilateral Convention   **445 UNTS 143**
SIGNED: 17 Feb 61   FORCE: 9 Apr 62
REGISTERED: 28 Nov 62 USA (United States)
ARTICLES: 15 LANGUAGE: English.
HEADNOTE: DOUBLE TAXATION FISCAL EVA-
SION ESTATES
TOPIC: Taxation
CONCEPTS: Definition of terms. Previous treaty re-
placement. Nationality and citizenship. Confor-
mity with municipal law. Exchange of official
publications. Negotiation. Claims and settle-
ments. Taxation. Death duties. Tax credits. Gen-
eral.
TREATY REF: 124UNTS297; 127UNTS57.
PROCEDURE: Duration. Ratification. Termination.
PARTIES:
Canada
USA (United States)

106384   Bilateral Agreement   **445 UNTS 161**
SIGNED: 11 Dec 61   FORCE: 5 Mar 62
REGISTERED: 28 Nov 62 USA (United States)
ARTICLES: 6 LANGUAGE: English. Spanish.
HEADNOTE: TECHNICAL ECONOMIC COOPER-
ATION
TOPIC: General Aid
CONCEPTS: Definition of terms. Exceptions and
exemptions. Previous treaty replacement. Diplo-
matic privileges. Privileges and immunities. Con-
formity with municipal law. General cooperation.
Personnel. Accounting procedures. Banking.
Funding procedures. Tax exemptions. Customs
exemptions. Commodities and services. Domes-
tic obligation. General technical assistance.
Technical cooperation. Economic assistance.
Materials, equipment and services. Aid missions.
Grants.
TREATY REF: 92UNTS167; 180UNTS318.
PROCEDURE: Amendment. Termination.
PARTIES:
Panama
USA (United States)

106385   Bilateral Agreement   **445 UNTS 175**
SIGNED: 19 Dec 61   FORCE: 16 Jan 62
REGISTERED: 28 Nov 62 USA (United States)

ARTICLES: 6 LANGUAGE: English. Spanish.
HEADNOTE: ECONOMIC TECHNICAL RELATED
 ASSISTANCE
TOPIC: General Aid
CONCEPTS: Change of circumstances. Exceptions
 and exemptions. Previous treaty replacement.
 Diplomatic privileges. Privileges and immunities.
 Conformity with municipal law. General cooper-
 ation. Personnel. Exchange rates and regula-
 tions. Funding procedures. Tax exemptions. Cus-
 toms exemptions. Domestic obligation. General
 technical assistance. Economic assistance. Ma-
 terials, equipment and services. Aid missions.
TREATY REF: 198UNTS231; US ST.DEPT.BULL-
 .3OCT60,P537; ETC..
PROCEDURE: Amendment. Termination.
PARTIES:
 El Salvador
 USA (United States)

106386   Bilateral Instrument   **445 UNTS 189**
SIGNED: 2 Mar 62   FORCE: 2 Mar 62
REGISTERED: 28 Nov 62 USA (United States)
ARTICLES: 8 LANGUAGE: English.
HEADNOTE: GRANT AGRI COMMOD SCHOOL
 LUNCH PROGRAM
TOPIC: Direct Aid
CONCEPTS: Treaty implementation. Title and
 deeds. Indemnities and reimbursements. Cus-
 toms exemptions. Commodities and services.
 Domestic obligation. Assistance. Grants.
PROCEDURE: Amendment. Termination.
PARTIES:
 Cyprus
 USA (United States)

106387   Bilateral Instrument   **445 UNTS 195**
SIGNED: 7 Mar 62   FORCE: 7 Mar 62
REGISTERED: 28 Nov 62 USA (United States)
ARTICLES: 1 LANGUAGE: English. French.
HEADNOTE: ECONOMIC RELATIONS
TOPIC: General Trade
CONCEPTS: General trade.
INTL ORGS: General Agreement on Tariffs and
 Trade.
TREATY REF: GATT.
PARTIES:
 EEC (Econ Commnty)
 USA (United States)

106388   Multilateral Agreement   **445 UNTS 199**
SIGNED: 7 Mar 62   FORCE: 7 Mar 62
REGISTERED: 28 Nov 62 USA (United States)
ARTICLES: 1 LANGUAGE: English. French.
HEADNOTE: CORN SORGHUM WHEAT RICE
 POULTRY
TOPIC: Commodity Trade
CONCEPTS: Trade procedures. Commodity trade.
INTL ORGS: General Agreement on Tariffs and
 Trade.
TREATY   REF: 176UNTS3;   429UNTS268;
 435UNTS438 AND MANY MORE.
PARTIES:
 Belgium SIGNED: 7 Mar 62 FORCE: 7 Mar 62
 France SIGNED: 7 Mar 62 FORCE: 7 Mar 62
 Germany, West SIGNED: 7 Mar 62
 Italy SIGNED: 7 Mar 62 FORCE: 7 Mar 62
 Luxembourg   SIGNED: 7 Mar 62   FORCE:
 7 Mar 62
 Netherlands   SIGNED: 18 Jul 66   FORCE:
 18 Jul 66
 EEC (Econ Commnty) SIGNED: 7 Mar 62 FORCE:
 7 Mar 62
 USA (United States) SIGNED: 7 Mar 62 FORCE:
 7 Mar 62

106389   Multilateral Agreement   **445 UNTS 205**
SIGNED: 7 Mar 62   FORCE: 7 Mar 62
REGISTERED: 28 Nov 62 USA (United States)
ARTICLES: 1 LANGUAGE: English. French.
HEADNOTE: WHEAT
TOPIC: Commodity Trade
CONCEPTS: General cooperation. Negotiation. Ta-
 riffs. Trade procedures. Commodity trade.
 Quotas.
INTL ORGS: General Agreement on Tariffs and
 Trade.
PARTIES:
 Belgium SIGNED: 7 Mar 62 FORCE: 7 Mar 62
 France SIGNED: 7 Mar 62 FORCE: 7 Mar 62

Germany, West SIGNED: 7 Mar 62
Italy SIGNED: 7 Mar 62 FORCE: 7 Mar 62
Luxembourg   SIGNED: 7 Mar 62   FORCE:
 7 Mar 62
Netherlands   SIGNED: 18 Jul 62   FORCE:
 18 Jul 62
EEC (Econ Commnty) SIGNED: 7 Mar 62 FORCE:
 7 Mar 62
USA (United States) SIGNED: 7 Mar 62 FORCE:
 7 Mar 62
            ANNEX
533 UNTS 353. USA (United States). Amendment
 28 Jun 63. Force 21 Aug 63.
533 UNTS 353. EEC (Econ Commnty). Amendment 21 Aug 63. Force 21 Aug 63.
533 UNTS 356. USA (United States). Amendment
 11 Jun 64. Force 20 Jul 64.
533 UNTS 356. EEC (Econ Commnty). Amendment 12 Jul 64. Force 20 Jul 64.

106390   Bilateral Agreement   **445 UNTS 213**
SIGNED: 12 Apr 62   FORCE: 12 Apr 62
REGISTERED: 28 Nov 62 USA (United States)
ARTICLES: 5 LANGUAGE: English.
HEADNOTE: AGRI COMMOD TITLE I
TOPIC: US Agri Commod Aid
CONCEPTS: Annex or appendix reference. Ex-
 change of information and documents. Reexport
 of goods, etc.. Payment schedules. Purchase au-
 thorization. Commodities schedule. Purchase au-
 thorization. Mutual consultation.
PARTIES:
 Liberia
 USA (United States)

106391   Bilateral Agreement   **445 UNTS 227**
SIGNED. 13 Apr 62   FORCE: 13 Apr 62
REGISTERED: 28 Nov 62 USA (United States)
ARTICLES: 6 LANGUAGE: English. Portuguese.
HEADNOTE: ECONOMIC SOCIAL DEVELOPMENT
TOPIC: Non-IBRD Project
CONCEPTS: Previous treaties adherence. Operat-
 ing agencies. Financial programs. Funding proce-
 dures. Assistance. Economic assistance.
INTL ORGS: Organization for Economic Co-opera-
 tion and Development.
TREATY REF: 141UNTS003; 200UNTS306.
PROCEDURE: Duration. Termination.
PARTIES:
 Brazil
 USA (United States)

106392   Bilateral Agreement   **445 UNTS 249**
SIGNED: 16 Apr 62   FORCE: 16 Apr 62
REGISTERED: 28 Nov 62 USA (United States)
ARTICLES: 5 LANGUAGE: English.
HEADNOTE: AGRICULTURE TRADE
TOPIC: General Trade
CONCEPTS: Detailed regulations. General cooper-
 ation. Exchange of information and documents.
 Reexport of goods, etc.. Trade procedures. Com-
 modity trade. Quotas. Agricultural commodities.
PARTIES:
 Taiwan
 USA (United States)

106393   Bilateral Agreement   **445 UNTS 257**
SIGNED: 16 Apr 62   FORCE: 16 Apr 62
REGISTERED: 28 Nov 62 USA (United States)
ARTICLES: 5 LANGUAGE: English.
HEADNOTE: TRADE AGRICULTURAL COMMODI-
 TIES
TOPIC: General Trade
CONCEPTS: General cooperation. Exchange of in-
 formation and documents. Export quotas. Import
 quotas. Commodity trade. Delivery schedules.
 Quotas. Agricultural commodities. Credit provi-
 sions. Purchase authorization.
PARTIES:
 India
 USA (United States)

106394   Bilateral Exchange   **445 UNTS 265**
SIGNED: 19 Apr 62   FORCE: 19 Apr 62
REGISTERED: 28 Nov 62 USA (United States)
ARTICLES: 2 LANGUAGE: English.
HEADNOTE: ADDITIONAL PUMPING STATIONS
TOPIC: Specific Property

CONCEPTS: Previous treaties adherence. Facilities
 and property.
TREATY REF: 206UNTS93; 400UNTS315.
PARTIES:
 Canada
 USA (United States)

106395   Bilateral Agreement   **445 UNTS 273**
SIGNED: 26 Apr 62   · FORCE: 26 Apr 62
REGISTERED: 28 Nov 62 USA (United States)
ARTICLES: 3 LANGUAGE: English.
HEADNOTE: TRADE
TOPIC: General Trade
CONCEPTS: Proxy diplomacy. General cooper-
 ation. Exchange of information and documents.
 Reexport of goods, etc.. Trade procedures. Com-
 modity trade. Delivery schedules. Quotas. Pur-
 chase authorization.
PARTIES:
 UK Great Britain
 USA (United States)

106396   Bilateral Agreement   **445 UNTS 279**
SIGNED: 15 May 62   FORCE: 15 May 62
REGISTERED: 28 Nov 62 USA (United States)
ARTICLES: 4 LANGUAGE: English.
HEADNOTE: AGRICULTURAL TRADE
TOPIC: General Trade
CONCEPTS: General cooperation. Informational
 records. Reexport of goods, etc.. Trade proce-
 dures. Commodity trade. Delivery schedules.
 Quotas. Agricultural commodities.
PARTIES:
 Colombia
 USA (United States)

106397   Bilateral Exchange   **446 UNTS 3**
SIGNED: 23 Sep 61   FORCE: 23 Sep 61
REGISTERED: 29 Nov 62 Denmark
ARTICLES: 2 LANGUAGE: English.
HEADNOTE: EXEMPTION TAXATION EDUCA-
 TIONAL PURPOSES
TOPIC: Taxation
CONCEPTS: Teacher and student exchange. Tax
 exemptions.
PROCEDURE: Denunciation.
PARTIES:
 China People's Rep
 Denmark

106398   Bilateral Agreement   **446 UNTS 9**
SIGNED: 5 Mar 62   FORCE: 5 Mar 62
REGISTERED: 29 Nov 62 USA (United States)
ARTICLES: 4 LANGUAGE: English.
HEADNOTE: INTERIM   AGREEMENT   TARIFFS
 TRADE
TOPIC: General Economic
CONCEPTS: Change of circumstances. Treaty im-
 plementation. Annex or appendix reference.
 Customs duties.
INTL ORGS: General Agreement on Tariffs and
 Trade.
TREATY REF: GATT.
PROCEDURE: Termination.
PARTIES:
 Denmark
 USA (United States)

106399   Bilateral Agreement   **446 UNTS 19**
SIGNED: 5 Mar 62   FORCE: 5 Mar 62
REGISTERED: 29 Nov 62 USA (United States)
ARTICLES: 4 LANGUAGE: English.
HEADNOTE: INTERIM   AGREEMENT   TARIFFS
 TRADE
TOPIC: General Economic
CONCEPTS: Change of circumstances. Treaty im-
 plementation. Annex or appendix reference.
 Customs duties.
INTL ORGS: General Agreement on Tariffs and
 Trade.
TREATY REF: GATT.
PROCEDURE: Termination.
PARTIES:
 Finland
 USA (United States)

106400   Bilateral Agreement   **446 UNTS 29**
SIGNED: 5 Mar 62   FORCE: 5 Mar 62

REGISTERED: 29 Nov 62 USA (United States)
ARTICLES: 4 LANGUAGE: English.
HEADNOTE: INTERIM AGREEMENT TARIFFS TRADE
TOPIC: General Economic
CONCEPTS: Change of circumstances. Treaty implementation. Annex or appendix reference. Customs duties.
INTL ORGS: General Agreement on Tariffs and Trade.
TREATY REF: GATT.
PROCEDURE: Termination.
PARTIES:
 Israel
 USA (United States)

106401 Bilateral Agreement **446 UNTS 39**
SIGNED: 5 Mar 62 FORCE: 5 Mar 62
REGISTERED: 29 Nov 62 USA (United States)
ARTICLES: 4 LANGUAGE: English.
HEADNOTE: INTERIM AGREEMENT TARIFFS TRADE
TOPIC: General Economic
CONCEPTS: Change of circumstances. Treaty implementation. Annex or appendix reference. Customs duties.
INTL ORGS: General Agreement on Tariffs and Trade.
TREATY REF: GATT.
PROCEDURE: Termination.
PARTIES:
 New Zealand
 USA (United States)

106402 Bilateral Agreement **446 UNTS 47**
SIGNED: 5 Mar 62 FORCE: 5 Mar 62
REGISTERED: 29 Nov 62 USA (United States)
ARTICLES: 4 LANGUAGE: English.
HEADNOTE: INTERIM AGREEMENT TARIFFS TRADE
TOPIC: General Economic
CONCEPTS: Change of circumstances. Treaty implementation. Annex or appendix reference. Customs duties.
INTL ORGS: General Agreement on Tariffs and Trade.
TREATY REF: GATT.
PROCEDURE: Termination.
PARTIES:
 Norway
 USA (United States)

106403 Bilateral Agreement **446 UNTS 57**
SIGNED: 5 Mar 62 FORCE: 5 Mar 62
REGISTERED: 29 Nov 62 USA (United States)
ARTICLES: 4 LANGUAGE: English.
HEADNOTE: INTERIM AGREEMENT TARIFFS TRADE
TOPIC: General Trade
CONCEPTS: Change of circumstances. Treaty implementation. Annex or appendix reference. Customs duties.
INTL ORGS: General Agreement on Tariffs and Trade.
TREATY REF: GATT.
PROCEDURE: Termination.
PARTIES:
 Pakistan
 USA (United States)

106404 Bilateral Agreement **446 UNTS 65**
SIGNED: 5 Mar 62 FORCE: 5 Mar 62
REGISTERED: 29 Nov 62 USA (United States)
ARTICLES: 4 LANGUAGE: English.
HEADNOTE: INTERIM AGREEMENT TARIFFS TRADE
TOPIC: General Economic
CONCEPTS: Change of circumstances. Treaty implementation. Annex or appendix reference. Customs duties.
INTL ORGS: General Agreement on Tariffs and Trade.
TREATY REF: GATT.
PROCEDURE: Termination.
PARTIES:
 Peru
 USA (United States)

106405 Bilateral Agreement **446 UNTS 81**
SIGNED: 7 Mar 62 FORCE: 7 Mar 62
REGISTERED: 29 Nov 62 USA (United States)
ARTICLES: 4 LANGUAGE: English. French.
HEADNOTE: INTERIM AGREEMENT TARIFFS TRADE
TOPIC: General Economic
CONCEPTS: Change of circumstances. Treaty implementation. Annex or appendix reference. Customs duties.
INTL ORGS: General Agreement on Tariffs and Trade.
TREATY REF: GATT.
PROCEDURE: Termination.
PARTIES:
 EEC (Econ Commnty)
 USA (United States)

106406 Bilateral Agreement **446 UNTS 231**
SIGNED: 7 Mar 62 FORCE: 7 Mar 62
REGISTERED: 29 Nov 62 USA (United States)
ARTICLES: 4 LANGUAGE: English.
HEADNOTE: INTERIM AGREEMENT TARIFFS TRADE
TOPIC: General Economic
CONCEPTS: Change of circumstances. Treaty implementation. Annex or appendix reference. Customs duties.
INTL ORGS: General Agreement on Tariffs and Trade.
TREATY REF: GATT.
PROCEDURE: Termination.
PARTIES:
 UK Great Britain
 USA (United States)

106407 Bilateral Agreement **446 UNTS 305**
SIGNED: 19 Jan 62 FORCE: 19 Apr 62
REGISTERED: 30 Nov 62 IBRD (World Bank)
ARTICLES: 5 LANGUAGE: English.
HEADNOTE: GUARANTEE AGREEMENT
TOPIC: IBRD Project
CONCEPTS: Definition of terms. Annex or appendix reference. Exchange of information and documents. Inspection and observation. Bonds. Fees and exemptions. Tax exemptions. Domestic obligation. Terms of loan. Loan regulations. Loan guarantee. Guarantor non-interference.
PARTIES:
 Argentina
 IBRD (World Bank)

106408 Bilateral Agreement **446 UNTS 345**
SIGNED: 6 Sep 61 FORCE: 27 Dec 61
REGISTERED: 4 Dec 62 IBRD (World Bank)
ARTICLES: 5 LANGUAGE: English.
HEADNOTE: GUARANTEE INDUSTRIAL EQUIPMENT
TOPIC: IBRD Project
CONCEPTS: Definition of terms. Exchange of information and documents. Inspection and observation. Bonds. Fees and exemptions. Tax exemptions. Domestic obligation. Terms of loan. Loan regulations. Loan guarantee. Guarantor non-interference. Industry.
PARTIES:
 Costa Rica
 IBRD (World Bank)

106409 Bilateral Agreement **446 UNTS 371**
SIGNED: 13 Dec 61 FORCE: 4 May 62
REGISTERED: 4 Dec 62 IBRD (World Bank)
ARTICLES: 7 LANGUAGE: English. Spanish.
HEADNOTE: LOAN EXPRESSWAY
TOPIC: IBRD Project
CONCEPTS: Default remedies. Definition of terms. Exchange of information and documents. Informational records. Inspection and observation. Accounting procedures. Bonds. Fees and exemptions. Interest rates. Tax exemptions. Domestic obligation. Terms of loan. Loan regulations. Loan guarantee. Guarantor non-interference. Roads and highways.
PARTIES:
 IBRD (World Bank)
 Venezuela

106410 Bilateral Agreement **447 UNTS 3**
SIGNED: 28 Feb 62 FORCE: 21 May 62

REGISTERED: 4 Dec 62 IBRD (World Bank)
ARTICLES: 5 LANGUAGE: English.
HEADNOTE: GUARANTEE INDUSTRIAL CREDIT
TOPIC: IBRD Project
CONCEPTS: Definition of terms. Exchange of information and documents. Inspection and observation. Bonds. Fees and exemptions. Tax exemptions. Domestic obligation. Terms of loan. Loan regulations. Loan guarantee. Guarantor non-interference. Industry.
PARTIES:
 India
 IBRD (World Bank)

106411 Bilateral Agreement **447 UNTS 39**
SIGNED: 23 May 62 FORCE: 22 Aug 62
REGISTERED: 4 Dec 62 IBRD (World Bank)
ARTICLES: 5 LANGUAGE: English.
HEADNOTE: GUARANTEE AGREEMENT
TOPIC: IBRD Project
CONCEPTS: Definition of terms. Annex or appendix reference. Exchange of information and documents. Inspection and observation. Bonds. Fees and exemptions. Tax exemptions. Domestic obligation. Terms of loan. Loan regulations. Loan guarantee. Guarantor non-interference.
PARTIES:
 Colombia
 IBRD (World Bank)

106412 Bilateral Agreement **447 UNTS 75**
SIGNED: 10 Jun 60 FORCE: 29 Dec 60
REGISTERED: 4 Dec 62 Cuba
ARTICLES: 15 LANGUAGE: Spanish.
HEADNOTE: TRADE
TOPIC: General Trade
CONCEPTS: Detailed regulations. Exceptions and exemptions. Annex or appendix reference. Conformity with municipal law. Licenses and permits. Establishment of commission. Import quotas. Reexport of goods, etc.. Trade agencies. Financial programs. Payment schedules. Non-interest rates and fees. Most favored nation clause. Tax exemptions. Temporary importation. General transportation. Navigational conditions. Merchant vessels. Inland and territorial waters. Ports and pilotage.
INTL ORGS: Special Commission.
PROCEDURE: Duration.
PARTIES:
 Cuba
 Czechoslovakia

106413 Bilateral Agreement **447 UNTS 95**
SIGNED: 14 Feb 62 FORCE: 20 Jun 62
REGISTERED: 5 Dec 62 IBRD (World Bank)
ARTICLES: 8 LANGUAGE: English.
HEADNOTE: LOAN HOT WATER SUPPLY
TOPIC: IBRD Project
CONCEPTS: Default remedies. Definition of terms. Annex or appendix reference. Exchange of information and documents. Informational records. Inspection and observation. Accounting procedures. Bonds. Fees and exemptions. Interest rates. Tax exemptions. Domestic obligation. Terms of loan. Loan regulations. Loan guarantee. Guarantor non-interference.
PARTIES:
 Iceland
 IBRD (World Bank)

106414 Bilateral Agreement **447 UNTS 127**
SIGNED: 15 Jun 62 FORCE: 14 Sep 61
REGISTERED: 5 Dec 62 IBRD (World Bank)
ARTICLES: 5 LANGUAGE: English.
HEADNOTE: GUARANTEE INDUSTRIAL CREDIT
TOPIC: IBRD Project
CONCEPTS: Private investment guarantee. Tax exemptions. Credit provisions. Terms of loan.
PARTIES:
 Austria
 IBRD (World Bank)

106415 Bilateral Agreement **447 UNTS 161**
SIGNED: 19 Oct 61 FORCE: 21 Aug 62
REGISTERED: 5 Dec 62 IDA (Devel Assoc)
ARTICLES: 7 LANGUAGE: English.
HEADNOTE: DEVELOPMENT CREDIT IRRIGATION
TOPIC: Non-IBRD Project

CONCEPTS: Definition of terms. Detailed regulations. Previous treaty amendment. Exchange of information and documents. Informational records. Accounting procedures. Interest rates. Tax exemptions. Loan and credit. Credit provisions. Loan repayment. Terms of loan. Loan regulations. IDA development project. Irrigation.
PARTIES:
Pakistan
IDA (Devel Assoc)

106416 Bilateral Agreement **447 UNTS 191**
SIGNED: 18 Jul 62 FORCE: 23 Oct 62
REGISTERED: 5 Dec 62 IDA (Devel Assoc)
ARTICLES: 7 LANGUAGE: English.
HEADNOTE: DEVELOPMENT CREDIT PURNA IRRIGATION
TOPIC: Non-IBRD Project
CONCEPTS: Definition of terms. Detailed regulations. Previous treaty amendment. Exchange of information and documents. Informational records. Accounting procedures. Interest rates. Tax exemptions. Credit provisions. Loan repayment. Terms of loan. Loan regulations. IDA development project. Irrigation.
PARTIES:
India
IDA (Devel Assoc)

106417 Bilateral Agreement **447 UNTS 221**
SIGNED: 29 Jun 62 FORCE: 23 Oct 62
REGISTERED: 6 Dec 62 IDA (Devel Assoc)
ARTICLES: 7 LANGUAGE: English.
HEADNOTE: DEVELOPMENT CREDIT SONE IRRIGATION
TOPIC: Non-IBRD Project
CONCEPTS: Definition of terms. Detailed regulations. Previous treaty amendment. Exchange of information and documents. Informational records. Interest rates. Accounting procedures. Tax exemptions. Credit provisions. Loan repayment. Terms of loan. Loan regulations. Irrigation.
PARTIES:
India
IDA (Devel Assoc)

106418 Bilateral Agreement **447 UNTS 251**
SIGNED: 3 Feb 61 FORCE: 8 Jun 61
REGISTERED: 11 Dec 62 New Zealand
ARTICLES: 15 LANGUAGE: English. Malay.
HEADNOTE: NEW TRADING RELATIONSHIP ESTABLISHMENT
TOPIC: General Trade
CONCEPTS: Definition of terms. Detailed regulations. Territorial application. Treaty implementation. Annex or appendix reference. Previous treaty replacement. General cooperation. Tariffs. Trade procedures. Balance of payments. Most favored nation clause. Customs duties.
TREATY REF: 55UNTS187.
PROCEDURE: Duration. Ratification. Termination.
PARTIES:
Malaysia
New Zealand

106419 Bilateral Agreement **447 UNTS 277**
SIGNED: 26 Oct 61 FORCE: 10 Jul 62
REGISTERED: 12 Dec 62 IDA (Devel Assoc)
ARTICLES: 6 LANGUAGE: English.
HEADNOTE: DEVELOPMENT CREDIT ROAD CONSTRUCTION MAINTENANCE
TOPIC: Non-IBRD Project
CONCEPTS: Detailed regulations. Previous treaty amendment. Exchange of information and documents. Informational records. Accounting procedures. Interest rates. Tax exemptions. Credit provisions. Loan repayment. Terms of loan. Loan regulations. Non-bank projects. IDA development project. Roads and highways.
PARTIES:
Paraguay
IDA (Devel Assoc)

106420 Bilateral Agreement **447 UNTS 295**
SIGNED: 22 Nov 61 FORCE: 21 Aug 62
REGISTERED: 12 Dec 62 IDA (Devel Assoc)
ARTICLES: 7 LANGUAGE: English.
HEADNOTE: DEVELOPMENT CREDIT INLAND PORTS

TOPIC: Non-IBRD Project
CONCEPTS: Definition of terms. Detailed regulations. Previous treaty amendment. Exchange of information and documents. Informational records. Accounting procedures. Interest rates. Tax exemptions. Credit provisions. Loan repayment. Terms of loan. Loan regulations. Non-bank projects. IDA development project. Ports and pilotage.
PARTIES:
Pakistan
IDA (Devel Assoc)

106421 Bilateral Agreement **447 UNTS 325**
SIGNED: 29 Jun 62 FORCE: 28 Nov 62
REGISTERED: 12 Dec 62 IDA (Devel Assoc)
ARTICLES: 7 LANGUAGE: English.
HEADNOTE: DEVELOPMENT CREDIT WATER SALINITY CONTROL
TOPIC: Non-IBRD Project
CONCEPTS: Definition of terms. Detailed regulations. Previous treaty amendment. Exchange of information and documents. Informational records. Accounting procedures. Interest rates. Tax exemptions. Credit provisions. Loan repayment. Terms of loan. Loan regulations. Natural resources.
PARTIES:
Pakistan
IDA (Devel Assoc)

106422 Bilateral Agreement **448 UNTS 3**
SIGNED: 14 Sep 62 FORCE: 1 Nov 62
REGISTERED: 12 Dec 62 IDA (Devel Assoc)
ARTICLES: 6 LANGUAGE: English.
HEADNOTE: DEVELOPMENT CREDIT TELECOMMUNICATIONS
TOPIC: Non-IBRD Project
CONCEPTS: Definition of terms. Detailed regulations. Previous treaty amendment. Exchange of information and documents. Informational records. Accounting procedures. Interest rates. Tax exemptions. Credit provisions. Loan repayment. Terms of loan. Loan regulations. IDA development project. Services.
PARTIES:
India
IDA (Devel Assoc)

106423 Bilateral Agreement **448 UNTS 21**
SIGNED: 22 Dec 61 FORCE: 25 Apr 62
REGISTERED: 13 Dec 62 IDA (Devel Assoc)
ARTICLES: 7 LANGUAGE: English.
HEADNOTE: DEVELOPMENT CREDIT AMMAN WATER SUPPLY
TOPIC: Non-IBRD Project
CONCEPTS: Definition of terms. Detailed regulations. Previous treaty amendment. Exchange of information and documents. Informational records. Accounting procedures. Interest rates. Tax exemptions. Credit provisions. Loan repayment. Terms of loan. Loan regulations. IDA development project. Natural resources.
PARTIES:
Jordan
IDA (Devel Assoc)

106424 Multilateral Agreement **448 UNTS 50**
SIGNED: 15 Nov 62 FORCE: 15 Nov 62
REGISTERED: 13 Dec 62 United Nations
ARTICLES: 6 LANGUAGE: French.
HEADNOTE: TECHNICAL ASSISTANCE
TOPIC: Tech Assistance
CONCEPTS: Definition of terms. Privileges and immunities. General cooperation. Exchange of information and documents. Personnel. Responsibility and liability. Title and deeds. Use of facilities. Exchange. Scholarships and grants. Vocational training. Research and development. Exchange rates and regulations. Expense sharing formulae. Local currency. Domestic obligation. General technical assistance. Materials, equipment and services. IGO status. Conformity with IGO decisions.
INTL ORGS: United Nations Technical Assistance Board.
TREATY REF: 76UNTS132; 1UNTS15; 33UNTS261; 374UNTS147.
PROCEDURE: Amendment. Termination.

PARTIES:
Algeria SIGNED: 15 Nov 62 FORCE: 15 Nov 62
FAO (Food Agri) SIGNED: 15 Nov 62 FORCE: 15 Nov 62
IAEA (Atom Energy) SIGNED: 15 Nov 62 FORCE: 15 Nov 62
ICAO (Civil Aviat) SIGNED: 15 Nov 62 FORCE: 15 Nov 62
ILO (Labor Org) SIGNED: 15 Nov 62 FORCE: 15 Nov 62
ITU (Telecommun) SIGNED: 15 Nov 62 FORCE: 15 Nov 62
UNESCO (Educ/Cult) SIGNED: 15 Nov 62 FORCE: 15 Nov 62
United Nations SIGNED: 15 Nov 62 FORCE: 15 Nov 62
UPU (Postal Union) SIGNED: 15 Nov 62 FORCE: 15 Nov 62
WHO (World Health) SIGNED: 15 Nov 62 FORCE: 15 Nov 62
WMO (Meteorology) SIGNED: 15 Nov 62 FORCE: 15 Nov 62

106425 Bilateral Agreement **448 UNTS 67**
SIGNED: 16 Jan 61 FORCE: 16 Jan 61
REGISTERED: 17 Dec 62 Cuba
ARTICLES: 9 LANGUAGE: Spanish. Albanian.
HEADNOTE: TRADE
TOPIC: General Trade
CONCEPTS: Annex or appendix reference. Conformity with municipal law. Licenses and permits. Reexport of goods, etc.. Trade agencies. Payment schedules. Non-interest rates and fees. Most favored nation clause. Merchant vessels. Inland and territorial waters. Ports and pilotage.
PROCEDURE: Denunciation. Duration.
PARTIES:
Albania
Cuba

106426 Bilateral Agreement **448 UNTS 81**
SIGNED: 29 Mar 61 FORCE: 29 Mar 61
REGISTERED: 17 Dec 62 Cuba
ARTICLES: 13 LANGUAGE: Spanish. German.
HEADNOTE: CULTURAL SCIENTIFIC COOPERATION
TOPIC: Culture
CONCEPTS: Friendship and amity. Non-diplomatic delegations. Conformity with municipal law. Exchange of information and documents. Specialists exchange. Exchange. Teacher and student exchange. Institute establishment. Vocational training. General cultural cooperation. Artists. Athletes. Scientific exchange. Finances and payments. Mass media exchange. Press and wire services.
PROCEDURE: Amendment. Denunciation. Duration. Future Procedures Contemplated. Ratification. Renewal or Revival.
PARTIES:
Cuba
Germany, East

106427 Bilateral Treaty **448 UNTS 95**
SIGNED: 9 Apr 59 FORCE: 31 Oct 61
REGISTERED: 18 Dec 62 Israel
ARTICLES: 7 LANGUAGE: Hebrew. English.
HEADNOTE: FRIENDSHIP
TOPIC: General Amity
CONCEPTS: Friendship and amity. Alien status. Consular relations establishment. Diplomatic relations establishment. Privileges and immunities. Procedure.
PROCEDURE: Duration. Future Procedures Contemplated. Ratification. Termination.
PARTIES:
Israel
Liberia

106428 Bilateral Convention **448 UNTS 107**
SIGNED: 30 Jun 59 FORCE: 7 May 62
REGISTERED: 18 Dec 62 Israel
ARTICLES: 13 LANGUAGE: Hebrew. French.
HEADNOTE: MILITARY SERVICE PERSONS DUAL NATIONALITY
TOPIC: Milit Servic/Citiz
CONCEPTS: Definition of terms. Emergencies. Treaty interpretation. Annex or appendix reference. Procedure. Dual nationality. Certificates of service. Service in foreign army.

PROCEDURE: Denunciation. Ratification.
PARTIES:
  France
  Israel

106429 Bilateral Agreement **448 UNTS 151**
SIGNED: 28 Sep 61   FORCE: 28 Sep 61
REGISTERED: 18 Dec 62 Israel
ARTICLES: 3 LANGUAGE: Hebrew. French.
HEADNOTE: TECHNICAL COOPERATION
TOPIC: Tech Assistance
CONCEPTS: Time limit. Personnel. Scholarships
  and grants. Research and development. Expense
  sharing formulae. General technical assistance.
PARTIES:
  Dahomey
  Israel

106430 Bilateral Convention **448 UNTS 161**
SIGNED: 10 Oct 61   FORCE: 1 Dec 62
REGISTERED: 18 Dec 62 Israel
ARTICLES: 21 LANGUAGE: Hebrew. German.
  French.
HEADNOTE: EXTRADITION
TOPIC: Extradition
CONCEPTS: Time limit. Extradition, deportation
  and repatriation. Extradition requests. Extradita-
  ble offenses. Location of crime. Refusal of extra-
  dition. Provisional detainment. Material evi-
  dence. Conformity with municipal law. Indemni-
  ties and reimbursements.
PROCEDURE: Denunciation. Ratification.
PARTIES:
  Austria
  Israel

106431 Bilateral Convention **448 UNTS 191**
SIGNED: 27 Nov 61   FORCE: 28 May 62
REGISTERED: 18 Dec 62 Israel
ARTICLES: 8 LANGUAGE: Hebrew. Spanish.
HEADNOTE: CULTURAL CONVENTION
TOPIC: Culture
CONCEPTS: Friendship and amity. Tourism. Con-
  formity with municipal law. General cooperation.
  Exchange of information and documents. Public
  information. Exchange. General cultural cooper-
  ation. Artists. Scientific exchange. Research and
  development. Publications exchange. Mass me-
  dia exchange.
PROCEDURE: Denunciation. Duration. Ratification.
PARTIES:
  Guatemala
  Israel

106432 Bilateral Exchange **448 UNTS 205**
SIGNED: 11 Apr 62   FORCE: 11 Apr 62
REGISTERED: 18 Dec 62 Israel
ARTICLES: 2 LANGUAGE: French.
HEADNOTE: MOST FAVORED NATION TREAT-
  MENT
TOPIC: Mostfavored Nation
CONCEPTS: Reciprocity in trade. Most favored na-
  tion clause. Customs duties.
PROCEDURE: Duration. Renewal or Revival. Termi-
  nation.
PARTIES:
  Israel
  Vietnam, South

106433 Bilateral Agreement **448 UNTS 211**
SIGNED: 15 May 62   FORCE: 15 May 62
REGISTERED: 18 Dec 62 Israel
ARTICLES: 4 LANGUAGE: Hebrew. French.
HEADNOTE: TECHNICAL COOPERATION
TOPIC: Tech Assistance
CONCEPTS: Detailed regulations. Time limit. Con-
  formity with municipal law. General cooperation.
  Personnel. Scholarships and grants. Research
  and development. General technical assistance.
PROCEDURE: Future Procedures Contemplated.
PARTIES:
  Gabon
  Israel

106434 Bilateral Agreement **448 UNTS 219**
SIGNED: 28 May 62   FORCE: 1 Jun 62
REGISTERED: 18 Dec 62 Israel
ARTICLES: 11 LANGUAGE: French.

HEADNOTE: EXCHANGE POSTAL PARCELS
TOPIC: Postal Service
CONCEPTS: Responsibility and liability. Account-
  ing procedures. Postal services. Parcel post.
  Rates and charges.
INTL ORGS: Universal Postal Union.
TREATY REF: 365UNTS3;   291UNTS327;
  404UNTS381; 412UNTS352.
PROCEDURE: Termination.
PARTIES:
  Israel
  Netherlands

106435 Bilateral Agreement **448 UNTS 227**
SIGNED: 1 Jun 62   FORCE: 13 Aug 62
REGISTERED: 18 Dec 62 Israel
ARTICLES: 7 LANGUAGE: English.
HEADNOTE: GERMAN SECULAR PROPERTY
TOPIC: Specific Property
CONCEPTS: Currency. Payment schedules. Claims
  and settlements. Post-war claims settlement. Fa-
  cilities and property.
TREATY REF: 345UNTS91.
PARTIES:
  Germany, West
  Israel

106436 Bilateral Exchange **448 UNTS 247**
SIGNED: 1 Sep 61   FORCE: 1 Dec 61
REGISTERED: 18 Dec 62 Israel
ARTICLES: 2 LANGUAGE: Spanish.
HEADNOTE: ABOLITION VISAS HOLDERS DIPLO-
  MATIC SERVICE PASSPORTS
TOPIC: Visas
CONCEPTS: Time limit. Visa abolition. Resident
  permits.
PARTIES:
  Costa Rica
  Israel

106437 Bilateral Exchange **448 UNTS 253**
SIGNED: 4 Oct 61   FORCE: 2 Jan 62
REGISTERED: 18 Dec 62 Israel
ARTICLES: 2 LANGUAGE: Spanish.
HEADNOTE: ABOLITION VISAS HOLDERS DIPLO-
  MATIC SERVICE PASSPORTS
TOPIC: Visas
CONCEPTS: Time limit. Visa abolition. Resident
  permits.
PARTIES:
  El Salvador
  Israel

106438 Bilateral Exchange **448 UNTS 259**
SIGNED: 18 Dec 61   FORCE: 18 Mar 62
REGISTERED: 18 Dec 62 Israel
ARTICLES: 2 LANGUAGE: French.
HEADNOTE: ABOLITION VISAS HOLDERS DIPLO-
  MATIC SERVICE PASSPORTS
TOPIC: Visas
CONCEPTS: Time limit. Visa abolition. Resident
  permits.
PROCEDURE: Termination.
PARTIES:
  Dahomey
  Israel

106439 Bilateral Agreement **448 UNTS 265**
SIGNED: 13 Jun 62   FORCE: 13 Jun 62
REGISTERED: 18 Dec 62 Israel
ARTICLES: 2 LANGUAGE: Hebrew. French.
HEADNOTE: TECHNICAL COOPERATION
TOPIC: Tech Assistance
CONCEPTS: Treaty implementation. Personnel.
  Scholarships and grants. Research and develop-
  ment. General technical assistance.
PARTIES:
  Central Afri Rep
  Israel

106440 Bilateral Exchange **448 UNTS 273**
SIGNED: 22 Jun 62   FORCE: 22 Jun 62
REGISTERED: 18 Dec 62 Israel
ARTICLES: 2 LANGUAGE: English.
HEADNOTE: EDUCATION EXCHANGE FINANCING
TOPIC: Education
CONCEPTS: Annex or appendix reference. Previ-
  ous treaty replacement. Standardization. Operat-

ing agencies. General property. Education. Ex-
  change. Commissions and foundations. Teacher
  and student exchange. Scholarships and grants.
  Research and development. Accounting proce-
  dures. Funding procedures. Tax exemptions.
TREATY REF: 257UNTS55; 407UNTS256.
PARTIES:
  Israel
  USA (United States)

106441 Bilateral Agreement **448 UNTS 287**
SIGNED: 25 Jun 62   FORCE: 25 Jun 62
REGISTERED: 18 Dec 62 Israel
ARTICLES: 2 LANGUAGE: Hebrew. English.
HEADNOTE: TECHNICAL COOPERATION
TOPIC: Tech Assistance
CONCEPTS: General cooperation. Personnel.
  Scholarships and grants. Research and develop-
  ment. General technical assistance.
PARTIES:
  Israel
  Liberia

106442 Bilateral Agreement **448 UNTS 295**
SIGNED: 25 Jun 62   FORCE: 25 Jun 62
REGISTERED: 18 Dec 62 Israel
ARTICLES: 6 LANGUAGE: Hebrew. English.
HEADNOTE: CULTURAL AGREEMENT
TOPIC: Culture
CONCEPTS: Friendship and amity. Tourism. Con-
  formity with municipal law. Specialists ex-
  change. Teacher and student exchange. Ex-
  change. General cultural cooperation. Athletes.
  Scientific exchange. Research and develop-
  ment. Publications exchange. Mass media ex-
  change.
PARTIES:
  Israel
  Liberia

106443 Bilateral Exchange **448 UNTS 303**
SIGNED: 29 Jun 62   FORCE: 29 Jun 62
REGISTERED: 18 Dec 62 Israel
ARTICLES: 2 LANGUAGE: French.
HEADNOTE: ABOLITION VISAS HOLDERS DIPLO-
  MATIC SERVICE PASSPORTS
TOPIC: Visas
CONCEPTS: Visas. Accounting procedures.
PARTIES:
  Israel
  Switzerland
                ANNEX
630 UNTS 404. Israel. Amendment 23 Mar 67.
  Force 23 Mar 67.
630 UNTS 404. USA (United States). Amendment
  23 Mar 67. Force 23 Mar 67.

106444 Bilateral Exchange **448 UNTS 309**
SIGNED: 30 Aug 62   FORCE: 28 Nov 62
REGISTERED: 18 Dec 62 Israel
ARTICLES: 2 LANGUAGE: English.
HEADNOTE: ABOLITION VISAS HOLDERS DIPLO-
  MATIC SERVICE PASSPORTS
TOPIC: Visas
CONCEPTS: Time limit. Visa abolition. Resident
  permits. Visas. Fees and exemptions.
PARTIES:
  Israel
  Sierra Leone

106445 Bilateral Exchange **448 UNTS 317**
SIGNED: 28 Aug 62   FORCE: 28 Aug 62
REGISTERED: 18 Dec 62 Israel
ARTICLES: 2 LANGUAGE: English.
HEADNOTE: AGRI COMMOD
TOPIC: US Agri Commod Aid
CONCEPTS: Payment schedules. Purchase autho-
  rization. Surplus commodities. Merchant ves-
  sels.
TREATY   REF: 240UNTS3;   261UNTS331;
  314UNTS348,362; ETC..
PARTIES:
  Israel
  USA (United States)

106446 Bilateral Agreement **449 UNTS 3**
SIGNED: 24 Oct 62   FORCE: 24 Oct 62
REGISTERED: 18 Dec 62 Israel

ARTICLES: 7 LANGUAGE: Hebrew. French.
HEADNOTE: ECONOMIC TECHNICAL COOPERATION
TOPIC: General Aid
CONCEPTS: Privileges and immunities. Non-diplomatic delegations. Conformity with municipal law. Exchange of information and documents. Personnel. Public health. Exchange. Scholarships and grants. Vocational training. Expense sharing formulae. Agriculture. Technical cooperation. Economic assistance.
PROCEDURE: Denunciation. Future Procedures Contemplated. Renewal or Revival.
PARTIES:
Cameroon
Israel

106447 Bilateral Agreement **449 UNTS 15**
SIGNED: 24 Oct 62   FORCE: 24 Oct 62
REGISTERED: 18 Dec 62 Israel
ARTICLES: 5 LANGUAGE: Hebrew. French.
HEADNOTE: CULTURAL AGREEMENT
TOPIC: Culture
CONCEPTS: Friendship and amity. Tourism. Conformity with municipal law. Specialists exchange. Teacher and student exchange. Scholarships and grants. Exchange. General cultural cooperation. Artists. Scientific exchange. Research and development. Publications exchange. Mass media exchange.
PROCEDURE: Denunciation. Duration. Renewal or Revival.
PARTIES:
Cameroon
Israel

106448 Bilateral Exchange **449 UNTS 23**
SIGNED: 14 Dec 60   FORCE: 1 Jan 61
REGISTERED: 18 Dec 62 Philippines
ARTICLES: 2 LANGUAGE: English.
HEADNOTE: ABOLITION VISAS
TOPIC: Visas
CONCEPTS: Visa abolition.
PROCEDURE: Termination.
PARTIES:
Israel
Philippines

106449 Bilateral Exchange **449 UNTS 29**
SIGNED: 6 Dec 61   FORCE: 1 Feb 62
REGISTERED: 18 Dec 62 Philippines
ARTICLES: 2 LANGUAGE: English.
HEADNOTE: RECIPROCAL ABOLITION VISAS
TOPIC: Visas
CONCEPTS: Time limit. Visa abolition.
PROCEDURE: Amendment. Termination.
PARTIES:
Japan
Philippines

106450 Bilateral Exchange **449 UNTS 35**
SIGNED: 9 Mar 62   FORCE: 1 Feb 62
REGISTERED: 18 Dec 62 Philippines
ARTICLES: 2 LANGUAGE: English.
HEADNOTE: ABOLITION VISA REQUIREMENTS
TOPIC: Visas
CONCEPTS: Visa abolition.
PROCEDURE: Denunciation.
PARTIES:
Germany, West
Philippines

106451 Bilateral Exchange **449 UNTS 41**
SIGNED: 19 Dec 62   FORCE: 19 Dec 62
REGISTERED: 19 Dec 62 United Nations
ARTICLES: 2 LANGUAGE: English.
HEADNOTE: ASSUMPTION UGANDA RIGHTS OBLIGATIONS
TOPIC: Admin Cooperation
CONCEPTS: Previous treaty extension.
TREATY REF: 348UNTS177; 362UNTS340.
PARTIES:
UN Special Fund
Uganda

106452 Bilateral Agreement **449 UNTS 47**
SIGNED: 30 Jan 54   FORCE: 8 Dec 55
REGISTERED: 20 Dec 62 UK Great Britain

ARTICLES: 15 LANGUAGE: English. Arabic.
HEADNOTE: SCHEDULED AIR SERVICES BETWEEN BEYOND RESPECTIVE TERRITORIES
TOPIC: Air Transport
CONCEPTS: Definition of terms. Annex or appendix reference. Conformity with municipal law. General cooperation. Exchange of information and documents. Licenses and permits. Recognition of legal documents. Use of facilities. Arbitration. Procedure. Existing tribunals. Negotiation. Fees and exemptions. Most favored nation clause. National treatment. Customs exemptions. Competency certificate. Routes and logistics. Navigational conditions. Permit designation. Air transport. Airport facilities. Airworthiness certificates. Conditions of airlines operating permission. Operating authorizations and regulations.
INTL ORGS: International Civil Aviation Organization. Arbitration Commission.
PROCEDURE: Amendment. Future Procedures Contemplated. Ratification. Registration. Termination. Application to Non-self-governing Territories.
PARTIES:
Syria
UK Great Britain

106453 Bilateral Convention **449 UNTS 77**
SIGNED: 20 Apr 60   FORCE: 1 Sep 61
REGISTERED: 20 Dec 62 UK Great Britain
ARTICLES: 25 LANGUAGE: English. German.
HEADNOTE: UNEMPLOYMENT INSURANCE
TOPIC: Non-ILO Labor
CONCEPTS: Conditions. Definition of terms. Detailed regulations. Conformity with municipal law. Exchange of information and documents. Domestic legislation. Dispute settlement. Wages and salaries. Non-ILO labor relations. Administrative cooperation. Unemployment. Payment schedules. Claims and settlements. National treatment.
INTL ORGS: European Economic Community. International Court of Justice. Arbitration Commission.
PROCEDURE: Denunciation. Duration. Ratification. Renewal or Revival.
PARTIES:
Germany, West
UK Great Britain

106454 Bilateral Agreement **449 UNTS 119**
SIGNED: 31 Jul 61   FORCE: 10 Jul 62
REGISTERED: 20 Dec 62 UK Great Britain
ARTICLES: 5 LANGUAGE: English. Portuguese.
HEADNOTE: DOUBLE TAXATION SEA AIR TRANSPORT
TOPIC: Taxation
CONCEPTS: Definition of terms. Territorial application. Taxation. Air transport. Merchant vessels.
PROCEDURE: Duration. Ratification. Termination.
PARTIES:
Portugal
UK Great Britain

106455 Bilateral Exchange **449 UNTS 129**
SIGNED: 14 Nov 61   FORCE: 14 Nov 61
REGISTERED: 20 Dec 62 UK Great Britain
ARTICLES: 2 LANGUAGE: English. Arabic.
HEADNOTE: EXCHANGE PROFESSORS STUDENTS
TOPIC: Education
CONCEPTS: Annex type material. Personnel. Specialists exchange. Exchange. Teacher and student exchange. Professorships. Scholarships and grants. Research and development. Indemnities and reimbursements. Funding procedures. Publications exchange.
PROCEDURE: Future Procedures Contemplated.
PARTIES:
United Arab Rep
UK Great Britain
ANNEX
541 UNTS 344. UK Great Britain. Prolongation 22 Oct 64. Force 22 Oct 64.
541 UNTS 344. United Arab Rep. Prolongation 22 Oct 64. Force 22 Oct 64.
551 UNTS 321. United Arab Rep. Prolongation 5 Jul 65. Force 5 Jul 65.
551 UNTS 321. UK Great Britain. Prolongation 3 Jul 65. Force 5 Jul 65.

106456 Bilateral Agreement **449 UNTS 147**
SIGNED: 14 Mar 62   FORCE: 14 Mar 62
REGISTERED: 20 Dec 62 UK Great Britain
ARTICLES: 9 LANGUAGE: English.
HEADNOTE: PUBLIC OFFICERS AGREEMENT
TOPIC: Admin Cooperation
CONCEPTS: Definition of terms. Post-colonial administration.
PARTIES:
Tanganyika
UK Great Britain

106457 Bilateral Exchange **449 UNTS 159**
SIGNED: 30 Apr 62   FORCE: 30 May 62
REGISTERED: 20 Dec 62 UK Great Britain
ARTICLES: 2 LANGUAGE: English. Spanish.
HEADNOTE: ABOLITION VISAS
TOPIC: Visas
CONCEPTS: Emergencies. Territorial application. Time limit. Visa abolition. Denial of admission. Visas. Conformity with municipal law.
PROCEDURE: Termination.
PARTIES:
Honduras
UK Great Britain

106458 Bilateral Exchange **449 UNTS 167**
SIGNED: 30 May 62   FORCE: 30 May 62
REGISTERED: 20 Dec 62 UK Great Britain
ARTICLES: 2 LANGUAGE: English. Arabic.
HEADNOTE: LOAN
TOPIC: Loans and Credits
CONCEPTS: Interest rates. Payment schedules. Agriculture. Loan and credit. Loan repayment. Terms of loan. Natural resources. Roads and highways.
PARTIES:
Jordan
UK Great Britain
ANNEX
470 UNTS 426.   Jordan.   Supplementation 15 Sep 62. Force 15 Sep 62.
470 UNTS 426. UK Great Britain. Supplementation 11 Sep 62. Force 15 Sep 62.
474 UNTS 361. UK Great Britain. Supplementation 7 Mar 63. Force 14 Mar 63.
474 UNTS 361.   Jordan.   Supplementation 14 Mar 63. Force 14 Mar 63.

106459 Bilateral Exchange **449 UNTS 177**
SIGNED: 29 Aug 62   FORCE: 29 Aug 62
REGISTERED: 20 Dec 62 UK Great Britain
ARTICLES: 2 LANGUAGE: English.
HEADNOTE: USE AIRFIELD
TOPIC: Milit Installation
CONCEPTS: General cooperation. Use of facilities. Indemnities and reimbursements. Overflights and technical stops. Bases and facilities.
TREATY REF: 249UNTS91.
PROCEDURE: Duration.
PARTIES:
UK Great Britain
USA (United States)

106460 Bilateral Agreement **449 UNTS 183**
SIGNED: 9 Mar 56   FORCE: 11 Nov 58
REGISTERED: 26 Dec 62 Pakistan
ARTICLES: 16 LANGUAGE: English. Persian.
HEADNOTE: CULTURAL AGREEMENT
TOPIC: Culture
CONCEPTS: Definition of terms. Treaty interpretation. Friendship and amity. Conformity with municipal law. Establishment of commission. Recognition of degrees. Exchange. Teacher and student exchange. Professorships. Institute establishment. Scholarships and grants. Vocational training. General cultural cooperation. Artists. Anthropology and archeology. Publications exchange. Mass media exchange.
INTL ORGS: Special Commission.
PROCEDURE: Denunciation. Duration. Ratification.
PARTIES:
Iran
Pakistan

106461 Bilateral Exchange **449 UNTS 199**
SIGNED: 27 Aug 62   FORCE: 27 Sep 62
REGISTERED: 27 Dec 62 Belgium
ARTICLES: 2 LANGUAGE: French. Spanish.

HEADNOTE: ABOLITION PASSPORT VISA RE-
QUIREMENT
TOPIC: Visas
CONCEPTS: Emergencies. Territorial application.
Time limit. Visa abolition. Resident permits.
PROCEDURE: Denunciation.
PARTIES:
Belgium
Colombia

106462   Bilateral Agreement   **449 UNTS 207**
SIGNED: 8 Feb 62   FORCE: 8 Feb 62
REGISTERED: 27 Dec 62 IBRD (World Bank)
ARTICLES: 5 LANGUAGE: English.
HEADNOTE: GUARANTEE VOLTA PROJECT
TOPIC: IBRD Project
CONCEPTS: Definition of terms. Exchange of infor-
mation and documents. Inspection and observa-
tion. Bonds. Fees and exemptions. Tax exemp-
tions. Domestic obligation. Terms of loan. Loan
regulations. Loan guarantee. Guarantor non-
interference. Hydro-electric power.
PARTIES:
Ghana
IBRD (World Bank)

106463   Bilateral Agreement   **449 UNTS 263**
SIGNED: 21 Nov 62   FORCE: 21 Nov 62
REGISTERED: 27 Dec 62 ILO (Labor Org)
ARTICLES: 6 LANGUAGE: English.
HEADNOTE: ESTABLISH ASIAN FIELD OFFICE
TOPIC: IGO Operations
CONCEPTS: Non-visa travel documents. Privileges
and immunities. Exchange of information and
documents. Regional offices. Special status.
Status of experts.
INTL ORGS: United Nations. United Nations Spe-
cial Fund.
TREATY REF: 33UNTS261.
PROCEDURE: Amendment. Duration.
PARTIES:
Ceylon (Sri Lanka)
ILO (Labor Org)

106464   Bilateral Agreement   **450 UNTS 3**
SIGNED: 27 Dec 62   FORCE: 1 Jan 63
REGISTERED: 1 Jan 63 United Nations
ARTICLES: 7 LANGUAGE: English.
HEADNOTE: DEMOGRAPHIC TRAINING RE-
SEARCH CENTER
TOPIC: Scientific Project
CONCEPTS: Definition of terms. Previous treaty re-
placement. Conformity with municipal law. Per-
sonnel. Responsibility and liability. Use of facili-
ties. Establishment of commission. Scholarships
and grants. Vocational training. Research and
scientific projects. Research cooperation. Re-
search and development. Domestic obligation.
IGO obligations.
PROCEDURE: Duration. Renewal or Revival. Termi-
nation.
PARTIES:
India
United Nations

106465   Multilateral Instrument   **450 UNTS 11**
SIGNED: 29 Apr 58   FORCE: 30 Sep 62
REGISTERED: 3 Jan 63 United Nations
ARTICLES: 12 LANGUAGE: English. French. Chi-
nese. Russian. Spanish.
HEADNOTE: HIGH SEAS
TOPIC: Water Transport
CONCEPTS: Detailed regulations. Non-prejudice
to third party. Nationality and citizenship. Conformity with municipal law. General cooperation.
Free passage and transit. Licenses and permits.
Responsibility and liability. Investigation of violations. Humanitarian matters. Compensation. National treatment. Competency certificate. Navigational conditions. Operating authorizations
and regulations. Merchant vessels. Inland and
territorial waters. Ports and pilotage. Ocean resources.
INTL ORGS: Food and Agricultural Organization of
the United Nations. International Labour Organization. United Nations Educational, Scientific
and Cultural Organization. United Nations.
PROCEDURE: Amendment. Accession. Ratification.

PARTIES:
Afghanistan SIGNED: 30 Oct 58 RATIFIED:
28 Apr 59 FORCE: 30 Sep 62
Argentina SIGNED: 29 Apr 58
Australia SIGNED: 30 Oct 58
Austria SIGNED: 27 Oct 58
Bolivia SIGNED: 17 Oct 58
Bulgaria   SIGNED: 31 Oct 58   RATIFIED:
31 Aug 62 FORCE: 30 Sep 62
Byelorussia SIGNED: 30 Oct 58 RATIFIED:
27 Feb 61 FORCE: 30 Sep 62
Canada SIGNED: 29 Apr 58
Ceylon (Sri Lanka) SIGNED: 30 Oct 58
Taiwan SIGNED: 29 Apr 58
Central Afri Rep RATIFIED: 15 Oct 62 FORCE:
28 Oct 62
Colombia SIGNED: 29 Apr 58
Costa Rica SIGNED: 29 Apr 58
Cuba SIGNED: 29 Apr 58
Czechoslovakia SIGNED: 30 Oct 58 RATIFIED:
31 Aug 61 FORCE: 30 Sep 62
Denmark SIGNED: 29 Apr 58
Dominican Republic SIGNED: 29 Apr 58
Finland SIGNED: 27 Oct 58
France SIGNED: 30 Oct 58
Germany, West SIGNED: 30 Oct 58
Ghana SIGNED: 29 Apr 58
Guatemala   SIGNED: 29 Apr 58   RATIFIED:
27 Nov 61 FORCE: 30 Sep 62
Haiti SIGNED: 29 Apr 58 RATIFIED: 29 Mar 60
FORCE: 30 Sep 62
Hungary SIGNED: 31 Oct 58 RATIFIED: 6 Dec 61
FORCE: 30 Sep 62
Iceland SIGNED: 29 Apr 58
Indonesia   SIGNED: 8 May 58   RATIFIED:
10 Aug 61 FORCE: 30 Sep 62
Iran SIGNED: 28 May 58
Ireland SIGNED: 2 Oct 58
Israel SIGNED: 29 Apr 58 RATIFIED: 6 Sep 61
FORCE: 30 Sep 62
Lebanon SIGNED: 29 May 58
Liberia SIGNED: 27 May 58
Madagascar   RATIFIED: 31 Jul 62   FORCE:
30 Sep 62
Nepal SIGNED: 29 Apr 58 RATIFIED: 28 Dec 62
FORCE: 11 Jan 63
Netherlands SIGNED: 30 Oct 58
New Zealand SIGNED: 29 Oct 58
Nigeria RATIFIED: 26 Jun 61 FORCE: 30 Sep 62
Pakistan SIGNED: 31 Oct 58
Panama SIGNED: 2 May 58
Poland SIGNED: 31 Oct 58 RATIFIED: 29 Jun 62
FORCE: 30 Sep 62
Portugal SIGNED: 28 Oct 58 RATIFIED: 8 Jan 63
FORCE: 21 Jan 63
Romania   SIGNED: 31 Oct 58   RATIFIED:
12 Dec 61 FORCE: 30 Sep 62
Senegal   RATIFIED: 21 Dec 60   FORCE:
30 Sep 62
Sierra Leone RATIFIED: 13 Mar 62 FORCE:
30 Sep 62
Switzerland SIGNED: 24 May 58
Thailand SIGNED: 29 Apr 58
Tunisia SIGNED: 30 Oct 58
UK Great Britain SIGNED: 9 Sep 58 RATIFIED:
14 Mar 60 FORCE: 30 Sep 62
USA (United States) SIGNED: 15 Sep 58 RATI-
FIED: 12 Apr 61 FORCE: 30 Sep 62
Ukrainian SSR SIGNED: 30 Oct 58 RATIFIED:
12 Jan 61 FORCE: 30 Sep 62
Uruguay SIGNED: 29 Apr 58
USSR (Soviet Union) SIGNED: 30 Oct 58 RATI-
FIED: 22 Nov 60 FORCE: 30 Sep 62
Vatican/Holy See SIGNED: 30 Apr 58
Venezuela SIGNED: 30 Oct 58
Yugoslavia SIGNED: 29 Apr 58
ANNEX
458 UNTS 367.   South   Africa.   Accession
9 Apr 63. Force 9 May 63.
463 UNTS 366. Australia. Qualified Ratification
14 May 63. Force 13 Jun 63.
505 UNTS 328. Dominican Republic. Ratification
11 Aug 64. Force 10 Sep 64.
510 UNTS 335. Uganda. Accession 24 Sep 64.
Force 14 Oct 64.
520 UNTS 430. Albania. Qualified Accession
7 Dec 64.
521 UNTS 400. Italy. Accession 17 Dec 64. Force
17 Dec 65.
523 UNTS 340. Australia. Objection 1 Feb 65.
525 UNTS 320. Australia. Objection 1 Feb 65.
525 UNTS 320. Finland. Ratification 16 Feb 65.
Force 18 Mar 65.

539 UNTS 367.   UK Great Britain.   Objection
17 Jun 65.
543 UNTS 373. USA (United States). Objection
19 Aug 65.
547 UNTS 331. Upper Volta. Accession 4 Oct 65.
547 UNTS 331. Jamaica. Succession 8 Oct 65.
547 UNTS 331. Malawi. Accession 3 Dec 65.
552 UNTS 418.   Yugoslavia.   Ratification
28 Jan 66. Force 27 Feb 66.
555 UNTS 256. Netherlands. Qualified Ratification 18 Feb 66. Force 20 Mar 66.
560 UNTS 288.   Trinidad/Tobago.   Succession
11 Apr 66.
562 UNTS 335.   Switzerland.   Ratification
18 May 66. Force 17 Jun 66.
573 UNTS 335. USA (United States). Objection
27 Sep 66.
620 UNTS 322. Australia. Objection 31 Jan 68.
638 UNTS 292. Japan. Accession 10 Jun 68.
Force 10 Jul 68.
638 UNTS 292. Japan. Declaration 10 Jun 68.
639 UNTS 332. Thailand. Ratification 2 Jul 68.
Force 1 Aug 68.
639 UNTS 332. Thailand. Reservation 2 Jul 68.
Declaration 2 Jul 68.
646 UNTS 402. Denmark. Signature Subject to
Ratification 26 Sep 68. Force 26 Oct 68.

106466   Multilateral Protocol   **450 UNTS 169**
SIGNED: 29 Apr 58   FORCE: 30 Sep 62
REGISTERED: 3 Jan 63 United Nations
ARTICLES: 7 LANGUAGE: English. French. Chi-
nese. Russian. Spanish.
HEADNOTE: OPTIONAL PROTOCOL COMPUL-
SORY SETTLEMENT DISPUTES
TOPIC: Dispute Settlement
CONCEPTS: Time limit. Existing tribunals. Concilia-
tion. Ocean resources.
INTL ORGS: International Court of Justice. United
Nations. Arbitration Commission. Conciliation
Commission.
PROCEDURE: Ratification.
PARTIES:
Australia SIGNED: 14 May 63
Austria SIGNED: 27 Oct 58
Bolivia SIGNED: 17 Oct 58
Canada SIGNED: 29 Apr 58
Ceylon (Sri Lanka) SIGNED: 30 Oct 58
Taiwan SIGNED: 29 Apr 58
Colombia SIGNED: 29 Apr 58
Costa Rica SIGNED: 29 Apr 58
Cuba SIGNED: 29 Apr 58
Denmark SIGNED: 29 Apr 58
Dominican Republic SIGNED: 29 Apr 58
Finland SIGNED: 27 Oct 58
Fed of Malaya SIGNED: 1 May 61 FORCE:
30 Sep 62
France SIGNED: 30 Oct 58
Germany, West SIGNED: 30 Oct 58
Ghana SIGNED: 29 Apr 58
Haiti SIGNED: 29 Apr 58 RATIFIED: 29 Mar 60
FORCE: 30 Sep 62
Indonesia SIGNED: 8 May 58
Israel SIGNED: 28 Apr 58
Liberia SIGNED: 27 May 68
Luxembourg SIGNED: 10 Aug 62
Madagascar   SIGNED: 10 Aug 62   FORCE:
30 Sep 62
Nepal SIGNED: 29 Apr 58 FORCE: 27 Jan 63
Netherlands SIGNED: 31 Oct 58
New Zealand SIGNED: 29 Oct 58
Pakistan SIGNED: 6 Nov 58
Panama SIGNED: 2 May 58
Portugal SIGNED: 28 Oct 58 RATIFIED: 8 Jan 63
FORCE: 7 Feb 63
Sierra Leone SIGNED: 14 Feb 63
Switzerland SIGNED: 24 May 58
UK Great Britain SIGNED: 9 Sep 58 FORCE:
30 Sep 62
USA (United States) SIGNED: 15 Sep 58
Uruguay SIGNED: 29 Apr 58
Vatican/Holy See SIGNED: 30 Apr 58
Yugoslavia SIGNED: 29 Apr 58
ANNEX
453 UNTS 448.   Sierra   Leone.   Signature
14 Feb 63.
463 UNTS 368. Australia. Signature 14 May 63.
510 UNTS 335. Uganda. Signature 15 Sep 64.
525 UNTS 321. Finland. Ratification 16 Feb 65.
550 UNTS 409. Malawi. Signature 17 Dec 65.
552 UNTS 418.   Yugoslavia.   Ratification
28 Jan 66. Force 27 Feb 66.

555 UNTS 256. Netherlands. Qualified Ratification 18 Feb 66. Force 20 Mar 66.
562 UNTS 336. Switzerland. Ratification 18 May 66. Force 17 Jun 66.
562 UNTS 336. Malta. Succession 19 May 66. Force 21 Sep 64.
565 UNTS 319. Sweden. Signature Subject to Ratification 1 Jun 66. Ratification 28 Jun 66.
646 UNTS 404. Denmark. Ratification 26 Oct 68. Force 26 Sep 68.

106467 Bilateral Exchange **450 UNTS 201**
SIGNED: 21 Nov 60 FORCE: 22 Nov 60
REGISTERED: 3 Jan 63 Netherlands
ARTICLES: 2 LANGUAGE: English. French. Chinese. Russian. Spanish.
HEADNOTE: ABOLITION VISA REQUIREMENT
TOPIC: Visas
CONCEPTS: Emergencies. Visa abolition.
PROCEDURE: Denunciation. Duration. Renewal or Revival.
PARTIES:
Netherlands
Paraguay

106468 Bilateral Convention **450 UNTS 207**
SIGNED: 24 Jan 61 FORCE: 18 Oct 62
REGISTERED: 4 Jan 63 Netherlands
ARTICLES: 13 LANGUAGE: Spanish.
HEADNOTE: MILITARY SERVICE
TOPIC: Milit Servic/Citiz
CONCEPTS: Military service and citizenship. Dual nationality. Foreign nationals. Service in foreign army.
PROCEDURE: Denunciation. Ratification.
PARTIES:
Italy
Netherlands

106469 Bilateral Exchange **450 UNTS 215**
SIGNED: 28 May 62 FORCE: 28 May 62
REGISTERED: 4 Jan 63 Denmark
ARTICLES: 2 LANGUAGE: French.
HEADNOTE: EDUCATIONAL PROGRAM
TOPIC: Education
CONCEPTS: Definition of terms. Friendship and amity. Standardization. Conformity with municipal law. General cooperation. Exchange of information and documents. Inspection and observation. Personnel. General property. Exchange. Commissions and foundations. Scholarships and grants. Accounting procedures. Currency. Expense sharing formulae. Financial programs. Funding procedures. Special status.
TREATY REF: 147UNTS49.
PARTIES:
Denmark
USA (United States)
ANNEX
542 UNTS 386. USA (United States). Amendment 18 Feb 65. Force 25 Feb 65.
542 UNTS 386. Denmark. Amendment 25 Feb 65. Force 25 Feb 65.

106470 Bilateral Agreement **450 UNTS 229**
SIGNED: 7 Jan 63 FORCE: 7 Jan 63
REGISTERED: 4 Jan 63 United Nations
ARTICLES: 6 LANGUAGE: English.
HEADNOTE: OPERATIONAL EXECUTIVE ADMINISTRATIVE PERSONNEL
TOPIC: Tech Assistance
CONCEPTS: Treaty implementation. Annex or appendix reference. Privileges and immunities. Personnel. Responsibility and liability. Arbitration. Procedure. Negotiation. Vocational training. Compensation. Expense sharing formulae. Tax exemptions. Customs exemptions. Domestic obligation. Special projects. Status of experts. Conformity with IGO decisions.
INTL ORGS: Permanent Court of Arbitration. Arbitration Commission.
PROCEDURE: Amendment. Termination.
PARTIES:
Israel
United Nations

106471 Multilateral Agreement **450 UNTS 240**
SIGNED: 6 Dec 62 FORCE: 6 Dec 62
REGISTERED: 7 Jan 63 United Nations

ARTICLES: 6 LANGUAGE: English.
HEADNOTE: TECHNICAL ASSISTANCE
TOPIC: Tech Assistance
CONCEPTS: Detailed regulations. Privileges and immunities. General cooperation. Exchange of information and documents. Personnel. Responsibility and liability. Title and deeds. Use of facilities. Exchange. Scholarships and grants. Vocational training. Research and development. Exchange rates and regulations. Expense sharing formulae. Local currency. Domestic obligation. General technical assistance. Materials, equipment and services. IGO status. Conformity with IGO decisions.
INTL ORGS: United Nations Technical Assistance Board.
TREATY REF: 76UNTS132; 1UNTS15; 33UNTS261; 374UNTS147.
PROCEDURE: Amendment. Termination.
PARTIES:
Chad SIGNED: 6 Dec 62 FORCE: 6 Dec 62
FAO (Food Agri) SIGNED: 6 Dec 62 FORCE: 6 Dec 62
IAEA (Atom Energy) SIGNED: 6 Dec 62 FORCE: 6 Dec 62
ICAO (Civil Aviat) SIGNED: 6 Dec 62 FORCE: 6 Dec 62
ILO (Labor Org) SIGNED: 6 Dec 62 FORCE: 6 Dec 62
ITU (Telecommun) SIGNED: 6 Dec 62 FORCE: 6 Dec 62
UNESCO (Educ/Cult) SIGNED: 6 Dec 62 FORCE: 6 Dec 62
United Nations SIGNED: 6 Dec 62 FORCE: 6 Dec 62
UPU (Postal Union) SIGNED: 6 Dec 62 FORCE: 6 Dec 62
WHO (World Health) SIGNED: 6 Dec 62 FORCE: 6 Dec 62
WMO (Meteorology) SIGNED: 6 Dec 62 FORCE: 6 Dec 62

106472 Bilateral Agreement **450 UNTS 257**
SIGNED: 11 Jan 63 FORCE: 11 Jan 63
REGISTERED: 10 Jan 63 United Nations
ARTICLES: 6 LANGUAGE: French.
HEADNOTE: ARRANGEMENTS COMMISSION
TOPIC: IGO Operations
CONCEPTS: Establishment of commission. Procedure.
PARTIES:
Gabon
United Nations

106473 Bilateral Agreement **450 UNTS 267**
SIGNED: 28 Nov 62 FORCE: 28 Nov 62
REGISTERED: 11 Jan 63 United Nations
ARTICLES: 6 LANGUAGE: French.
HEADNOTE: OPERATIONAL EXECUTIVE ADMINISTRATIVE PERSONNEL
TOPIC: Tech Assistance
CONCEPTS: Treaty implementation. Annex or appendix reference. Privileges and immunities. Personnel. Responsibility and liability. Arbitration. Procedure. Negotiation. Vocational training. Expense sharing formulae. Fees and exemptions. Tax exemptions. Customs exemptions. Domestic obligation. Special projects. Status of experts. Conformity with IGO decisions.
INTL ORGS: Permanent Court of Arbitration. Arbitration Commission.
PROCEDURE: Amendment. Termination.
PARTIES:
Rwanda
United Nations

106474 Bilateral Agreement **450 UNTS 279**
SIGNED: 29 Dec 62 FORCE: 29 Dec 62
REGISTERED: 14 Jan 63 United Nations
ARTICLES: 6 LANGUAGE: French.
HEADNOTE: PROVISION ADMINISTRATIVE PERSONNEL
TOPIC: Tech Assistance
CONCEPTS: Administrative cooperation. Arbitration. Assistance.
INTL ORGS: Permanent Court of Arbitration. Arbitration Commission.
PROCEDURE: Termination.
PARTIES:
Burundi
United Nations

106475 Bilateral Agreement **450 UNTS 291**
SIGNED: 3 Oct 62 FORCE: 3 Oct 62
REGISTERED: 14 Jan 63 Denmark
ARTICLES: 13 LANGUAGE: French.
HEADNOTE: WAR GRAVES
TOPIC: Other Military
CONCEPTS: Indemnities and reimbursements. Burial arrangements. Responsibility for war dead. Upkeep of war graves. Establishment of war cemeteries.
PARTIES:
Denmark
Germany, West

106476 Multilateral Protocol **450 UNTS 309**
SIGNED: 8 Oct 60 FORCE: 10 Apr 62
REGISTERED: 17 Jan 63 Japan
ARTICLES: 7 LANGUAGE: Danish. German.
HEADNOTE: TRADE
TOPIC: General Trade
CONCEPTS: Territorial application. General cooperation. Tariffs. Trade procedures. Most favored nation clause. General transportation.
INTL ORGS: General Agreement on Tariffs and Trade.
TREATY REF: 249UNTS197; 2UNTS40; 55UNTS187.
PROCEDURE: Duration. Ratification. Termination.
PARTIES:
Bel-Lux Econ Union SIGNED: 8 Oct 60 FORCE: 10 Apr 62
Japan SIGNED: 8 Oct 60 FORCE: 10 Apr 62
Netherlands SIGNED: 8 Oct 60 FORCE: 10 Apr 62
ANNEX
647 UNTS 342. Benelux Econ Union. Interpretation 9 Feb 61.
647 UNTS 342. Japan. Interpretation 6 Mar 61.

106477 Bilateral Exchange **450 UNTS 337**
SIGNED: 1 Dec 60 FORCE: 1 Jan 61
REGISTERED: 17 Jan 63 Japan
ARTICLES: 2 LANGUAGE: English.
HEADNOTE: EXEMPTION VISA REQUIREMENTS
TOPIC: Visas
CONCEPTS: Emergencies. Time limit. Visa abolition. Denial of admission. Conformity with municipal law.
PROCEDURE: Denunciation.
PARTIES:
Japan
Pakistan

106478 Bilateral Agreement **450 UNTS 343**
SIGNED: 7 Feb 61 FORCE: 1 Aug 61
REGISTERED: 17 Jan 63 Japan
ARTICLES: 13 LANGUAGE: English.
HEADNOTE: EXCHANGE INTERNATIONAL MONEY ORDERS
TOPIC: Postal Service
CONCEPTS: Conformity with municipal law. Accounting procedures. Currency. Exchange rates and regulations. Payment schedules. Regulations. Money orders and postal checks. Rates and charges.
PROCEDURE: Duration. Termination.
PARTIES:
Australia
Japan

106479 Bilateral Agreement **450 UNTS 359**
SIGNED: 7 Mar 61 FORCE: 1 Aug 61
REGISTERED: 17 Jan 63 Japan
ARTICLES: 23 LANGUAGE: English. Japanese.
HEADNOTE: EXCHANGE INTERNATIONAL MONEY ORDERS
TOPIC: Postal Service
CONCEPTS: Conformity with municipal law. Currency. Exchange rates and regulations. Payment schedules. Postal services. Regulations. Money orders and postal checks. Rates and charges. Advice lists and orders. Telegrams.
PROCEDURE: Duration. Termination.
PARTIES:
Japan
Pakistan

106480 Bilateral Agreement **450 UNTS 373**
SIGNED: 15 Mar 61 FORCE: 15 Mar 61

REGISTERED: 17 Jan 63 Japan
ARTICLES: 8 LANGUAGE: English.
HEADNOTE: TRAINING CENTER
TOPIC: Education
CONCEPTS: Definition of terms. Annex or appendix reference. Friendship and amity. Alien status. Conformity with municipal law. General cooperation. Personnel. General property. Responsibility and liability. Institute establishment. Vocational training. Research and development. Expense sharing formulae. Tax exemptions. Customs exemptions. General technical assistance. Materials, equipment and services.
PROCEDURE: Duration. Termination.
PARTIES:
 Afghanistan
 Japan

106481 Bilateral Agreement **450 UNTS 385**
SIGNED: 20 Mar 61   FORCE: 20 Mar 61
REGISTERED: 17 Jan 63 Japan
ARTICLES: 8 LANGUAGE: English.
HEADNOTE: FISHERIES TRAINING CENTER
TOPIC: Education
CONCEPTS: Definition of terms. Annex or appendix reference. Friendship and amity. Alien status. Conformity with municipal law. General property. Responsibility and liability. Institute establishment. Vocational training. Research and development. Expense sharing formulae. General technical assistance. Materials, equipment and services.

PARTIES:
 Ceylon (Sri Lanka)
 Japan

106482 Bilateral Agreement **451 UNTS 3**
SIGNED: 15 May 61   FORCE: 18 Dec 61
REGISTERED: 17 Jan 63 Japan
ARTICLES: 9 LANGUAGE: Spanish. Japanese.
HEADNOTE: COMMERCE
TOPIC: General Trade
CONCEPTS: Detailed regulations. Exceptions and exemptions. Privileges and immunities. General cooperation. Recognition and enforcement of legal decisions. General property. Investigation of violations. Arbitration. Procedure. Export quotas. Import quotas. Reciprocity in trade. Trade procedures. Most favored nation clause. National treatment. Taxation. Recognition.
INTL ORGS: General Agreement on Tariffs and Trade. World Health Organization.
PROCEDURE: Duration. Ratification. Renewal or Revival. Termination.
PARTIES:
 Japan
 Peru

106483 Bilateral Instrument **451 UNTS 47**
SIGNED: 5 Sep 61   FORCE: 5 Sep 61
REGISTERED: 17 Jan 63 Japan
ARTICLES: 5 LANGUAGE: English. Japanese.
HEADNOTE: SETTLEMENT CLAIMS

TOPIC: Reparations
CONCEPTS: Time limit. Lump sum settlements. Loss and/or damage. Reparations and restrictions. Post-war claims settlement.
TREATY REF: 136UNTS45.
PARTIES:
 Canada
 Japan

106484 Bilateral Agreement **451 UNTS 55**
SIGNED: 25 Nov 61   FORCE: 25 Nov 61
REGISTERED: 17 Jan 63 Japan
ARTICLES: 9 LANGUAGE: English.
HEADNOTE: ESTABLISHMENT, RESEARCH INSTITUTE
TOPIC: Sanitation
CONCEPTS: Research cooperation. Research results.
PROCEDURE: Duration. Termination.
PARTIES:
 Japan
 Thailand

106485 Bilateral Exchange **451 UNTS 71**
SIGNED: 20 Dec 61   FORCE: 1 Jan 62
REGISTERED: 17 Jan 63 Japan
ARTICLES: 2 LANGUAGE: English.
HEADNOTE: WAIVER PASSPORT VISAS
TOPIC: Visas
CONCEPTS: Frontier formalities. Visa abolition. Passports non-diplomatic.
PARTIES:
 Argentina
 Japan